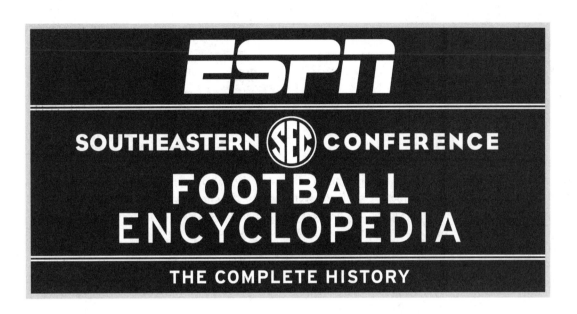

ESPN

SOUTHEASTERN SEC CONFERENCE
FOOTBALL ENCYCLOPEDIA

THE COMPLETE HISTORY

EDITED BY

Michael MacCambridge

BALLANTINE BOOKS · NEW YORK

ESPN Southeastern Conference Football Encyclopedia is an editorial work created independently by ESPN Books, an imprint of ESPN, Inc., New York. It was not published or produced with the Southeastern Conference or any school in the conference. The conference name, team names, conference logo and team logos on the helmet illustrations appearing on the book cover and throughout the book are registered trademarks of the individual institutions and cannot be reproduced without permission from the respective institutions.

Published in the United States by ESPN Books, an imprint of ESPN, Inc., New York, and Ballantine Books, an imprint of The Random House Publishing Group, a division of Random House, Inc., New York.

BALLANTINE and colophon are registered trademarks of Random House, Inc.
The ESPN Books name and logo are registered trademarks of ESPN, Inc.

ISBN: 978-0-345-51386-1

Printed in the United States of America on acid-free paper

www.ballantinebooks.com
www.espnbooks.com

9 8 7 6 5 4 3 2 1

First Edition

Helmet illustrations by Carey Chiselbrook
Helmet renderings by Mike Johnson of Chapel Design & Marketing Ltd.
Cover design by Henry Lee Studio
Page design by Paul Perlow
Editorial production services provided by Manipal Digital Systems

CONTENTS

EDITOR'S NOTE

BY MICHAEL MACCAMBRIDGE

In places like Nebraska and Oklahoma, football rivals religion. At Notre Dame, football becomes inextricably bound up with religion. But it's only in the South that, in a very real sense, football *is* a religion.

This is not necessarily a bad thing. People who think deeply about a topic often have revealing insights. This occurred to me one September night in 1998, as I was sitting in the west bleachers at Tiger Stadium in Baton Rouge, La., and overheard one keenly observant fan talking to his companion about LSU's stud nose tackle, Anthony "Booger" McFarland.

"Booger's 290 and he can run," said the man. "You 290 and can't run, you just fat. You 290 and can run, hell—you gonna be a millionaire."

And that is just what Mr. McFarland became.

At the same game, I was seated in front of a group of friends that included a comely, thirtyish blond woman who looked as if she should have been at a cocktail party. She was wearing crisp khaki slacks with a bone-colored cashmere sweater and was sporting a diamond the approximate size of a kicking tee on her ring finger. But she was there to see, not merely to be seen, and, as she raptly watched LSU's 42-6 blowout of Arkansas State, she effortlessly displayed her knowledge of Tigers football. During her animated play-by-play byplay with her friends, I was impressed to learn that she had committed to memory LSU's schedule *for the following season*. In the fourth quarter, she cursed out the p.a. announcer for misidentifying the second-string punter.

Just another typical football fan in the Southeastern Conference.

It is for people like that—for all of us who take pride in our mania—that we created the *ESPN Southeastern Conference Football Encyclopedia*. It's a condensed and updated version of our bestselling 2005 tome, the *ESPN College Football Encyclopedia*, focusing on the schools of the SEC.

Inside this book, you'll find much of the same material you found in the *College Football Encyclopedia*, expanded and updated for this edition, including:

- A pair of new essays by Chuck Culpepper, on the divine history of the SEC, and by Ivan Maisel, who has taken on the thankless and irresistible task of selecting an all-time SEC team.
- Expanded histories of every school in the SEC, as well as former conference powerhouses Georgia Tech and

Tulane, along with a complete list of players from each school who were selected in the first round of pro football drafts dating back to 1936. We've added entries for the Best Backfield and the Best Defense in each school's history.

- A new set of essays, commissioned just for this book, on the traditions and lore of each school.
- A new feature, called Record Book, provides a long list of single-game, single-season and career leaders for each SEC school, as well as an updated version of the list of annual rushing, passing and receiving leaders that first appeared in the *ESPN College Football Encyclopedia*.
- Our crowd-pleasing all-time scores section, including the date, site, opponent and final score of every game in SEC history.
- A complete bowl history for each SEC school.
- An overview of every season since 1922, highlighting SEC players and teams worthy of national attention. This provides a good snapshot of how SEC schools fared on the larger stage.

One of the things that makes college football so absorbing is the myriad local and regional variations in the game. Those very same qualities have made the sport resistant to systematic documentation, especially during its first century. The *ESPN College Football Encyclopedia* was a landmark because it provided us with a vast database from which to begin our work on future editions. As with that book, we value your input. In a project this ambitious, there are bound to be mistakes. If you spot one, tell us (by e-mail at maccambridge@mac.com) and we'll correct it in future editions of this book and the upcoming second edition of the *ESPN College Football Encyclopedia*, which should be coming to you within a couple of seasons.

In the meantime, if you're a football fan from the South and you're trying to figure out the duration of Auburn's longest winning streak, or how many times Herschel Walker won all-conference honors, or what Joe Namath's completion percentage was his senior season, or any of a million other indispensable pieces of information, chances are excellent that you'll find the answers right here within the pages of the *ESPN Southeastern Conference Football Encyclopedia*.

How to Use This Book

Each team is profiled in a quick-read format, featuring entries on Tradition, Best Player, Best Team, Best Coach, Best Backfield, etc.

Key data about the university and its football history

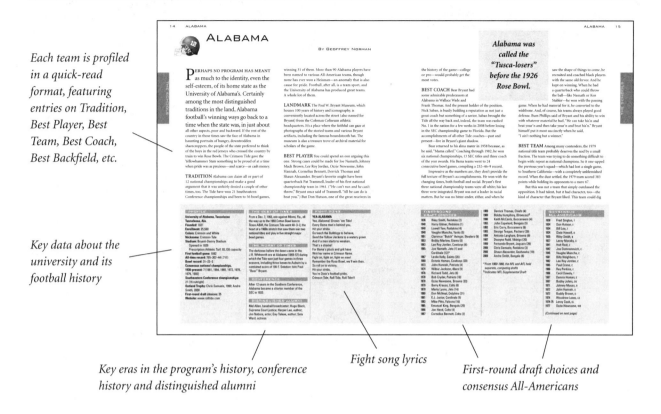

Key eras in the program's history, conference history and distinguished alumni

Fight song lyrics

First-round draft choices and consensus All-Americans

Annual rushing, passing and receiving leaders for each school

Single-game, single-season and career records for each school

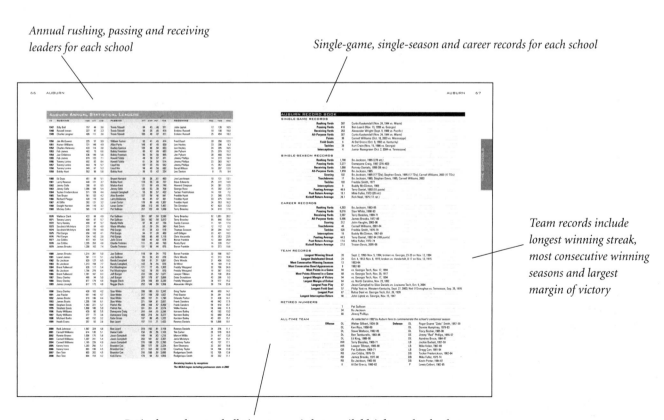

Team records include longest winning streak, most consecutive winning seasons and largest margin of victory

Retired numbers and all-time teams (when available) for each school

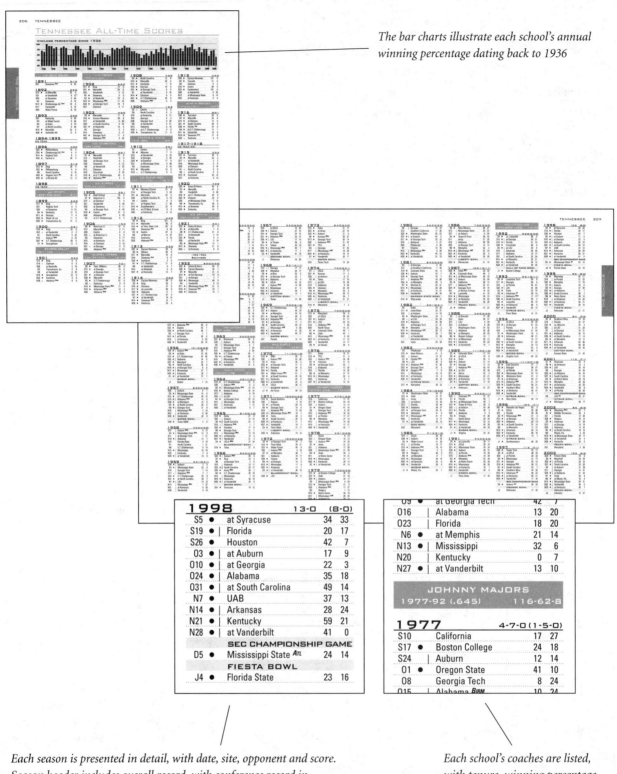

The bar charts illustrate each school's annual winning percentage dating back to 1936

Each season is presented in detail, with date, site, opponent and score. Season header includes overall record, with conference record in parentheses. Vertical bars denote conference games. At-a-glance results key shows bullets (•) for games won, equal signs (=) for ties and blanks ( ) for losses. Shaded bars denote postseason games.

Each school's coaches are listed, with tenure, winning percentage and overall win-loss record

*Complete bowl histories for
every school*

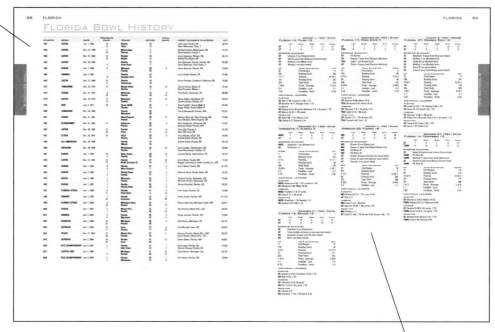

*Scoring summaries, along with
individual and team statistical
breakdown, for each bowl game*

*SEC players and teams among
NCAA statistical leaders*

*Where conference teams
finished in final polls*

*Conference players among the
top 10 in Heisman Trophy voting*

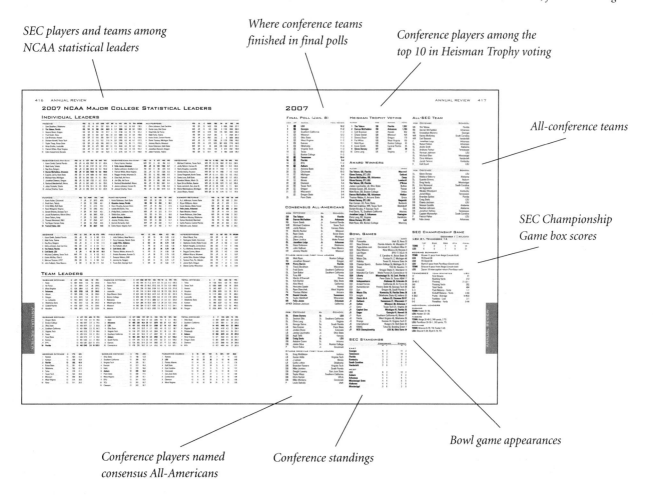

All-conference teams

*SEC Championship
Game box scores*

*Conference players named
consensus All-Americans*

Conference standings

Bowl game appearances

SEC HISTORY

The Promised Land

Rebellious. Pugnacious. Dominant. Ever since the Southeastern Conference was born back in the Edenic days of the college game, its teams have been raising Cain and delivering some righteous football.

BY CHUCK CULPEPPER

AND LO, THE 13 WISE MEN DIDST TURN UP NEAR THE banks of the River Tennessee at a "Southern Conference" banquet on the second Friday night of December in 1932. And they didst behold this 23-university "Southern Conference" to which they belonged, and they didst find it so bloated with teams that it didst threaten to float off into the cosmos forever immune to nimble management. And yea, they didst resign from the conglomerate without spite and with a kind of cordiality that typified their region, like dew or sweet tea or contemptuous humidity.

And on that Friday night in Knoxville, the president from Gainesville, the Dr. John J. Tigert, didst stand at the banquet table and confirm the rumors of the coming secession that had flowered through the region even during the prehistoric, pre-Google times. And these wise men, presidents of universities from south and west of the great green Appalachians, in search of a "more compact organization" (the prophet Tigert's phrase) didst begin anew with their 13 members—before it became 12 in 1940 and 11 in 1964 and 10 in 1966 and 12 again in 1992.

And they didst call themselves a "Southeastern Conference."

And holy mercy, they didst loose upon the gigantic continent the loudest eight-decade sporting rapture it had ever seen.

For not only had they sowed a cultural colossus that would make icons even of inanimate objects like a houndstooth hat in Alabama and a simple visor in Florida. Not only had they sowed something so destined to become familiar that quick references such as "Bo" and "Herschel" and "Emmitt" and "the Mannings" would suffice. Not only had they founded a virtual religion with singular icons such as "Hedges" and "Swamp" and that dreamy thing called a "Sugar Bowl" and the grandmother of all "tailgate parties" in a grove of trees in Mississippi with hard meats sizzling and soft chatter swirling and clear ice clinking in glasses filled with tomato juice and other products.

No, they'd birthed a long-running blare of stadium din that would trump the decibels of even the National Football League and Major League Baseball and the National Basketball Association and the Big Ten and the Pac-10 and the Atlantic Coast and the Big Eight and/or 12. With their genteel and quiet announcement, they'd spun a noise that seemed to derive from an aching need that helped it climb to some rarefied perch of clamor with peer only in the soccer theaters of Europe and South America.

And each August, as the sadistic humidity would make its final goal-line stands of the year, this always-simmering football noise would start to amplify from Louisiana to Florida to Kentucky and back to Louisiana. And it would resonate with quibbles about quarterbacks and the most intricate knowledge about which incoming 18-year-olds might prosper and which 17-year-old prospects might go where. And in the state of Alabama, the sermonic discourse would undergo an upsurge from its mere 23 hours per day in the preceding months.

And by late September's relief from summer's chokehold, and on Saturdays through November, the padded, helmeted athletes of the Southeast would try to establish the running game—or the pass in Florida, sometimes—while the defenses would try to halt this sinfulness, and this peerless American noise would start to shake and sway the map-dot towns and small cities of America's bottom right quadrant. And this noise would cause the Richter scale over at the Louisiana State geology department to wiggle during a fourth quarter one night in 1988 in Baton Rouge. And it would run hot and deafening through the dark Auburn nights on the tranquil plains of the eastern edge of Alabama. And it would help make prey of hapless visitors in the glorious meanness of Gainesville. And some nights over in Tuscaloosa, at a stadium named partly for an ursine deity who coached football especially well, it would sear into the ear canals and push goose bumps upward from the neck.

And even over in tranquil Starkville, one could cup one's ear and hear defiant cowbells.

And the racket would originate long before game time in all the various places, seeming to come right out of the hills and fog in Knoxville in a streaming flood of baby-aspirin orange. And from an Oxford, Miss., grove that became The Grove. And up in Lexington as a diversion before basketball season. And mildly in Nashville as a diversion during academic season. And even in Jacksonville,

which lacked a Southeastern Conference university but held a raucous annual October Saturday featuring animated Georgians and animated Floridians and animated blood-alcohol levels.

And as the league didst shed Sewanee in 1940 and Tulane in 1964 and Georgia Tech in 1966, and didst gain Arkansas and South Carolina in 1992. Its towns that relished tranquil lives on Sundays through Fridays would hold great Saturday gatherings: a regularly staggering 104,000 in Knoxville, 92,000 in Athens, 92,000 in Baton Rouge, 88,000 in Gainesville, 87,000 in Auburn, 80,000 in Columbia. And the 39,000 Vanderbilt-minded in Nashville would come to seem somehow quaint and measured. And the towns with the middling sounds of crickets and birds and railroads and marching bands rehearsing through incinerating Augusts would rampage with the sound of the craven need to have one's own recruits beat the pure living guts out of those bast …

… Well, out of those people from just across the state or just over the line.

And the Georgia did loathe the Florida, and the Florida the Georgia, which did also loathe the Tennessee. And the Tennessee did loathe utterly the Alabama, which loathed the Tennessee, which loathed the Auburn, which also loathed the Tennessee, which pretty much loathed the Georgia, which also loathed the Auburn in the Deep South's Oldest Rivalry (since 1892) as well as loathing somewhat the South Carolina, which came along in 1992 to add fresh loathing in case anybody needed any extra. And the Mississippi did loathe the Alabama but also the Mississippi State, which loathed the Alabama for sure but loathed with all might the Mississippi, which also loathed the LSU, which loathed the Alabama *and* the Auburn *and* then, because it did not have enough to loathe, it could loathe somewhat the Arkansas, which also came along in 1992 to add fresh loathing in case anybody needed any extra.

The Arkansas loathed mostly the Texas and would need to engender fresh loathing.

And yet, even given all that accrued loathing, all that hotness of contempt, no loathing didst tower so loathingly as the Auburn loathing for the Alabama and the Alabama loathing for the Auburn. And this particular mutual loathing didst reach full boil preceding each November as the game approached, raging as an ultimate example of

> *On Saturdays, the padded, helmeted athletes of the Southeast would try to establish the running game—or the pass in Florida, sometimes—while the defenses would try to halt this sinfulness.*

white-hot loathing: grammar-school loathing, workplace loathing, church-pew loathing, even New York Yankees-Boston Red Sox loathing.

And this fine and curiously non-violent loathing, vented so exhaustively in the stadiums, did help stir such bottomless want and need for sweet victory that not only did the noise mushroom but so also did the competition, until would come days 50, 60, 75 years on from that birthing moment in Knoxville when the general populace would often regard this "Southeastern Conference" as having generally the strongest, swiftest and scariest of American footballers. And national championships, so common from the mid-century to Alabama and occasionally to Georgia or Auburn or Tennessee or Louisiana State, would diversify to Louisiana State in 2003 and very nearly Auburn in 2004 and Florida in 2006 and Louisiana State in 2007 and Florida in 2008.

And the noise swelled.

It ricocheted through the towns in the form of scrutiny and lionization of head coaches, whose status rested well above that of mayor, often above that of governor and the relatively piddling office of United States President.

It consumed a heaping chunk of Alabama, where people didst extend something beyond reverence toward a Paul "Bear" Bryant and his gravel-for-breakfast articulation and even his houndstooth, such that his death at 69 years in 1983 sent flags to half-mast and newscasters to tears and Alabamians to telling reporters things such as, "You almost had the feeling that it might not ever happen to him."

The sound took unto itself chatter about coaches who stood in each place like topographical formations, their familiarity more fixed for fans because they stayed around longer than did players. One Ralph "Shug" Jordan, a former sugar-loving child of Selma later wounded at Normandy, manned the sideline prudently at Auburn. An ardent Mississippi cattle farmer, John Vaught, served in the Navy in World War II and seldom showed a facial twitch on the sideline at Ole Miss. Paul Dietzel and Charlie McClendon—Cholly Mac—kept Louisiana State vibrant. A clever man named Red (Sanders) coaxed even Vanderbilt to 36–22–2 during six years in the 1940s. A squat man, Wally Butts, found mid-century glory at Georgia even while advocating throwing the football more than

irregularly. And commanding Tennessee from 1926 through 1940 and then from 1946 through 1952 stood an actual brigadier general and MIT engineering degree-holder and former boxing national champion, Robert Neyland, who refused to see himself as a celebrity or to write books or to appear on television.

And the noise swelled.

The living rooms of Saturday afternoons and evenings didst resound with games carried on the air through burgeoning television contracts that grew unstoppably toward $2 billion and familiarized the nation with Vince Dooley's gentility and red sweater vest at Georgia, Pat Dye's pugnacity and blue sweater vest at Auburn and a Bear still synonymous with Alabama into the early 1980s.

The living rooms of Sunday mornings would hum with the drawls and explanations of football coaches starring in their own television shows. The radio dials of Mondays through Fridays would crackle with the exaltation and the resentment of the coach personas, especially in the case of a Steve Spurrier who had defined Florida as a 1960s quarterback who won the Heisman Trophy, and would do so again as a 1990s head coach designing zig-zagging pass routes that caused havoc to defenses and madness in a Swamp and seething through the region.

And the noise swelled.

Along came Fulmer at Tennessee, Nutt at Arkansas and Mississippi, Holtz—Holtz!—at South Carolina, Richt at Georgia, Tuberville at Auburn, a papal Urban at Florida, Miles at Louisiana State and Saban at both Louisiana State and Alabama. Along came a multiplication of bowl bids, up to eight per year, that helped heave pressure onto these increasingly wealthy people.

Along came the message boards where the fanatics bellowed for the firing of the coach, not necessarily after certain seasons or certain games or even certain quarters but verily, after certain *plays*. And where the fanatics did gossip toward the firing of *somebody else's* coach, as the Auburnites did to stoke an Alabama scandal in 2003.

And the noise swelled.

So the coaches didst call up the children, begging them to come running all grown up from the twangy towns and hoping to they could cause the roars.

So from Bessemer in Alabama to Auburn in Alabama would emerge an inconceivable phenomenon called a Vincent Edward "Bo" Jackson to average—*average!*—6.6 yards per carry over a career against the fastest, meanest defenders known to creation. So from Wrightsville in Georgia to Athens in Georgia would come a Herschel Walker to haul Georgia to a whiplash 1980 national crown as a freshman. So from Pensacola in Florida to Gainesville in Florida would bolt an Emmitt Smith to run with a football for longer and better than anybody ever had.

So from wee Drew in Mississippi would come a quarterback Archie Manning, who would follow his star to

Oxford in Mississippi to illuminate Ole Miss in the 1960s, and to marry an Olivia Williams from Philadelphia in Mississippi. And they moved to New Orleans. And New Orleans to Knoxville would come their son, a quarterback Peyton Manning, to star at Tennessee. And from New Orleans to Oxford would come another son, a quarterback Eli Manning, to star at Ole Miss.

And the noise swelled.

The fanatics of the nine states, leading their nation in attention to pigskin detail and knowledge of pigskin nuance, would hail also those who could serve society's craven need for blocking and tackling. So the food of the region did yield behemoths from towns like Canton, Ga. (John Hannah, Alabama), and Chattanooga, Tenn. (Reggie White, Tennessee), and Titusville, Fla. (Wilber Marshall, Florida) and Gonzales, La. (Glenn Dorsey, LSU), and Atlanta (Tracy Rocker, Auburn), and Excel, Ala. (Lee Roy Jordan, Alabama), and Jackson, Tenn. (Al Wilson, Tennessee), and Nashville (John Henderson, Tennessee) and heck, Miami (Derrick Thomas, Alabama).

The intellectuals of football did realize aloud the importance of the fact that Pelahatchie, Miss., produced a Frank "Bruiser" Kinard, who could play both Ole Miss lines for 708 of a possible 720 minutes in the great season of 1936, long before he reached the Pro Football Hall of Fame.

The most studious of them all, the Alabamians, did know the importance of giants, and the Crimson Tide regained its national summit in 1992 largely because Lanett, Ala., and Thomasville, Ga., had raised up John Copeland and Eric Curry, and those two had become defensive ends whose speed and ferocity seemed almost an offense itself and didst traumatize Miami's quarterback in the Sugar Bowl.

And the noise swelled.

It swelled especially at the daring bolts across the Southeast of Jackson and Walker and Smith and Alabama's Hutson and LSU's Kavanaugh and LSU's Cannon and Florida's Chandler and Florida's Hilliard and Georgia's Bailey and Tennessee's Lewis and Tennessee's Henry and Auburn's Williams-Brown-Campbell and Arkansas' McFadden and Florida's Harvin, among the hundreds.

It rose especially with the quarterbacks who held the towns' moods in their hands: Georgia's Sinkwich and LSU's Tittle and Kentucky's Parilli and Georgia's Tarkenton and Florida's Spurrier and Alabama's Namath and Alabama's Stabler and Mississippi's Manning and Auburn's Sullivan and Tennessee's Holloway and LSU's Jones and Florida's Wuerffel and Kentucky's Couch and LSU's Russell and Florida's Tebow, among the hundreds.

It exploded, this noise, at the extremely momentous, from Billy Cannon's 89-yard punt return with seven broken tackles in Baton Rouge against Ole Miss on Halloween 1959, to Alabama's 33-32 win over Ole Miss that showcased the great duel of Archie Manning and Scott Hunter and

unveiled the league on national television in 1969, to Buck Belue's 93-yard pass to Lindsay Scott in the last 90 seconds for Georgia against Florida in 1980, to Alabama's inaugural visit to Auburn in 1989, to the Florida-Tennessee feasts of contempt of the 1990s and 2000s.

It coalesced around the improbable, unthinkable and inexplicable, from Auburn's two bizarre fourth-quarter blocked punts to beat unbeaten Alabama, 17-16, in 1972, to unbeaten Tennessee's sudden and shocking fumble recovery against unbeaten Arkansas in Knoxville in November 1998, to LSU's inconceivable, multi-deflected, 74-yard touchdown pass as time expired in Kentucky in 2002.

It filled the Louisiana Superdome at the first blush of the new year in Sugar Bowls, as during the Alabama line withstanding of the Penn State assault from the 1-yard line in 1979, and the Alabama defensive back George Teague somehow running down Miami receiver Lamar Thomas along a lonely sideline in 1993, and LSU controlling Oklahoma and Ohio State before masses wearing purple and gold in 2004 and 2008.

Then, because there had not been enough noise, the addition of overtime enabled the porcine-minded of Arkansas to behold *seven*-overtime wins at Ole Miss and Kentucky in both 2001 and 2003. And, because there had not been enough noise, the capitalistic honchos of the SEC decided that the clamorous citizens of the Southeast needed more about which to vociferate.

So still more noise rang through Birmingham and then Atlanta in the early parts of Decembers, with a newfangled championship game beginning in 1992, where Antonio Langham's sudden 27-yard interception return for Alabama against Florida decided the inaugural. And a mad-scientist Spurrier could dominate the first decade, as with Florida's imaginative drive to beat Alabama in 1994. And Tennessee and Georgia and LSU and Auburn could have their heydays eventually.

And the noise swelled.

Yet amongst these idols and their deathless plays, heroes of a greater nature and a greater anonymity would emerge long about the late 1960s and the 1970s. And these men didst possess a profound bravery but did often seem

> *And the Tennessee did loathe utterly the Alabama, which loathed the Tennessee, which loathed the Auburn, which also loathed the Tennessee, which pretty much loathed the Georgia, which also loathed the Auburn.*

unaware they possessed it. And their names didst come to ring through the minds of the historians and the painfully aware as the first African-Americans to grace the last major conference to embrace them.

And they didst take on the untold burdens of pioneers, plus the unintelligent harassment from strangers and teammates, these acutely aware men with names like Nat Northington and Greg Page, who signed at Kentucky in 1966. And Lester McClain at Tennessee in 1968, and then Willie Jackson at Florida, Frank Dowsing Jr. at Mississippi State, James Owens and Thom Gossom at Auburn, Taylor Stokes, Doug Nettles and Walter Overton at Vanderbilt, Robert "Chuck" Kinnebrew, Clarence Pope, Horace King, Richard Appleby and Larry West at Georgia, Ben Williams at Ole Miss, Lora Hinton at Louisiana State.

And then came John Mitchell and Wilbur Jackson, whose eventual roles at Alabama became inevitable upon the epochal night of September 12, 1970, in Birmingham, when the University of Southern California brought its Sam "Bam" Cunningham and did overrun Alabama by 42-21 and thus, did enable the Bear to convince his devotees of the need for the inclusion of all human beings.

From that realization there did ever so slowly develop another great leap, for finally, after three more painfully slow decades, didst a Southeastern Conference university entrust its entire future to an African-American man. And when Mississippi State did choose a head coach in 2004, it chose Sylvester Croom, Alabama linebacker 1972-74, Tuscaloosan from among Bryant's first wave of pioneers.

And from Northington to Croom and all therein, this "Southeastern Conference" did then fully represent Southeastern humanity, and thereby did ratchet its caliber upward until all the people routinely rated it peerless.

And the compulsion toward victory in the towns increased even from rampant. And the business owners and the coaches and the boosters repeatedly did sin against the commandments of the National Collegiate Athletic Association, and this "Southeastern Conference" did pay for its fervor and did reveal an unusually vivid streak of depravity. And as the decades passed with the complimentary entertainment—and for some, pain—of probation upon

scandal upon malfeasance upon indiscretion upon nuisance, soon every school but one had visited some level of hoosegow.

And the Vanderbilt did lead not the football standings but the honor standings.

And lo, all through these pains of human idiocy and frailty, a singular and peculiar reverence would glow undiminished. And as telltale details, the most unusual of behaviors would persist and even deepen. And Georgians with zero botanical background and zero interest in common pruning in the yard did express a deep fondness for some fine privet hedges. And the Mississippian Staters did revere an English bulldog called Bully, and in 1939 did undergo days of mourning as Bully I lay in state in a glass coffin after a tragic meeting with a campus bus. And the Tennesseans did opt for a bluetick coonhound they called Smokey, whose name did turn up in an injury report after some unfortunate but non-fatal heat exhaustion one day in 1991.

And the Auburn parishioners did acclaim a fierce-eyed War Eagle whose VIIth incarnation, like his predecessor VI, did soar majestically and precisely to the 50-yard line each home game as a bird who clearly knoweth him some football. And the fully grown Floridians did impersonate the outsized mastication of reptiles. And the Arkansans did show the finest of humor by donning the finest of plastic pig snouts.

And the Alabamians did repeateth a beloved word: "Roll." And the South Carolinians did show an unusual durability of spirit during perennial difficulty on the scoreboards—as arguably the nation's most faithful fan base—once sending 19,200 to a spring game in between a 1–10 year and an 0–11 year, all because of the newfound presence of a Holtz. And the Louisianans, well, the Louisianans did strike from classes in 1935 and line the streets to welcome a tiger named Mike, who ultimately did reside not in student housing but in a designed habitat with a large live oak tree, a waterfall, a stream stemming from a rocky backdrop and an Italianate tower.

And the Georgians did hail as the pinnacle of their tribe one gorgeous-faced English bulldog named Uga, always suffixed by a venerable Roman numeral. And when the throne did pass from one Uga to another, the passage of the official collar did wring ceremony. And when the most somber of times did come, the people did accord these emperors burial in marble beneath the stadium end zone.

And all the people did agree, this qualified as the most esteemed ground conceivable. For long after that Friday night in 1932 in Knoxville, the stadiums of the breakaway concoction the "Southeastern Conference" had grown entrenched as sacrosanct places of loud sanctuary, places that on seven or so Saturdays per year would fill and serve as poignant outlet, plus maketh a commotion so singular that Dr. Tigert and those 12 other wise men from 1932 might look down and see that it was good.

The All-Time All-SEC Team

By Ivan Maisel

I**F YOU LOOK CLOSELY AT THE NAMES AND SCHOOL** affiliations of the 24 players on this all-time all-SEC team, what you begin to see is a short history of Southeastern Conference football.

Alabama supplied three-fifths of the starting offensive line, which makes sense when you consider that the Tide is the most successful football program never to suit up a Heisman Trophy winner. Three of the four defensive backs, and four defenders overall, played at Georgia, where Hall of Fame coach Vince Dooley made defense synonymous with the (Junkyard) Dawgs. Two linemen from Tennessee played for Gen. Robert Neyland, who applied military precision on the field as well as he did in the U.S. Army. Two of the three offensive backs are named Herschel and Bo. Nothing else need be said. Three Florida quarterbacks have won the Heisman, a tribute to the passing revolution fomented when the first of them, Steve Spurrier, returned to his alma mater in 1990 as head coach. The other two won national championships. Danny Wuerffel gets this starting position over Tim Tebow because Wuerffel took the Gators to two national championship games.

Neither Mississippi State nor South Carolina are represented. The Bulldogs last won an SEC title in 1941 and the Gamecocks didn't join the league until 1992. There is history both in who you see and in who you don't.

OFFENSE

OT FRANK "BRUISER" KINARD, MISSISSIPPI (1935-37)
He led the Rebels to the Orange Bowl in his sophomore season. Kinard so dominated the opposition that he became a two-time All-American and was voted into the inaugural class of the College Football Hall of Fame in 1951. He went on to become John Vaught's top assistant on the great Ole Miss teams of the early 1960s.

OG BOB SUFFRIDGE, TENNESSEE (1938-40)
Few linemen combined speed and smarts the way Suffridge did. The Volunteers went 31–0 in his three regular seasons, losing only two bowl games. Legendary coach Gen. Robert Neyland once said he would begin to put together his all-time offensive line by selecting Suffridge.

C DWIGHT STEPHENSON, ALABAMA (1977-79)
If Bear Bryant calls you "the best center I ever coached," you really don't need any other qualifications. When Stephenson anchored the O-line, the Crimson Tide went 34–2 and won two national championships.

OG JOHN HANNAH, ALABAMA (1970-72)
Sports Illustrated declared Hannah the best offensive lineman of all time when he played pro tackle for New England. Hannah dominated as an All-American guard on the 1971 and '72 Bama teams that won 21 consecutive regular-season games and restored the Crimson Tide to the ranks of the college football elite.

OT CHRIS SAMUELS, ALABAMA (1996-99)
This may be hard to believe, but Samuels is the only SEC offensive lineman to win the Outland Trophy since the advent of two-platoon football. His play and leadership in 1999, when he did not allow a sack or even a quarterback pressure, helped lead tailback Shaun Alexander to a school-record 1,383 yards and the Crimson Tide to its most recent SEC title.

QB DANNY WUERFFEL, FLORIDA (1993-96)
Gators coach Steve Spurrier revolutionized the SEC by opening up the passing game and his mouth—both to devastating effect. Ironic that his greatest quarterback was the soft-spoken, deeply religious Wuerffel. The total: four league titles, two national championship games, winning it all in 1996. Wuerffel won the Heisman and the Draddy, given to the sport's outstanding scholar-athlete; no one else has won both.

RB HERSCHEL WALKER, GEORGIA (1980-82)
Saying that *Hush-ul* won the 1982 Heisman and made three All-American teams is both true and inadequate. The facts miss the meaning. He came from small-town Georgia (Wrightsville), and led the Dawgs to the 1980 national title and to the brink of two more. He rushed for 5,259 yards and paved the way for underclassmen to leave early for the pros. He remains an icon.

RB **Bo Jackson, Auburn** (1982-85)
The greatest athlete since Jim Thorpe? Worth a debate. One of the greatest backs in SEC history? No debate at all. The two-time All-American and 1985 Heisman winner rushed for 4,303 yards and 43 touchdowns. More important, Jackson led the Tigers to in-state dominance after Bear Bryant retired from archrival Alabama.

RB **Darren McFadden, Arkansas** (2005-07)
Not only did he become only the second player to finish second in the Heisman Trophy voting in two seasons, but McFadden instigated a revolution in offense. The Razorbacks plugged the former high school quarterback into a Hog Wild formation, a riff on the old single-wing offense, and defenses haven't caught up yet. McFadden finished with 4,590 rushing yards in three seasons.

WR **Don Hutson, Alabama** (1931-34)
As a senior in 1934, Hutson averaged 17.2 yards a catch, astounding production for the era. In the 29-13 defeat of Stanford in the 1935 Rose Bowl, the All-American caught six passes for 165 yards, including touchdowns of 59 and 54 yards. He joined Kinard as the only SEC representatives in the inaugural class at the College Football Hall of Fame in 1951.

WR **Josh Reed, LSU** (1999-2001)
In 1999, the Tigers suffered a string of injuries at wide receiver, so the 5-11, 200-pound freshman tailback moved outside. Reed quickly became a master at running routes, and the rest became history—All-American history. In 2001, Reed caught 94 passes for 1,740 yards and won the Biletnikoff Award.

PK **Kevin Butler, Georgia** (1981-84)
We could explain how Butler was automatic inside the 40-yard line (50 of 56, .893) and nearly so from longer range (27 of 42, .643). We could explain how Georgia won seven games by three points or fewer in his career. There's the 1984 All-American team. Or we could just list all the kickers in the College Football Hall of Fame: Butler, Kevin.

DEFENSE
DE **Doug Atkins, Tennessee** (1950-52)
Atkins arrived in Knoxville a 6-8 basketball recruit. Once

Saying that Hush-ul won the 1982 Heisman and made three All-American teams is both true and inadequate. The facts miss the meaning.

Neyland got a hold of him, however, Atkins became a football player. By 1952, his senior season, he was an All-American. In 1974, Atkins was the only unanimous pick for the All-SEC Quarter Century Team selected by the conference in 1957. In 1985, he was inducted into the College Football Hall of Fame.

DT **Bill Stanfill, Georgia** (1966-68)
Stanfill combined size (6-5, 245 pounds), toughness and a motor jammed in high gear to become a three-time all-conference player (1966-68). In those seasons, Georgia won or shared two league titles. Hall of Fame coach Vince Dooley called Stanfill the best defensive lineman in his 25 seasons between the hedges.

DT **Bob Gain, Kentucky** (1947-50)
Simply put, Gain was the best player under Bear Bryant during Kentucky's most successful era. In his senior season, the two-time All-American and three-time All-SEC star helped lead Kentucky to a 13-7 upset of No. 1 Oklahoma in the Sugar Bowl.

DE **Jack Youngblood, Florida** (1968-70)
Doug Dickey, hired as the Gators coach in 1970, installed a 4-3 defense. Youngblood made it work. The senior and newly minted defensive end not only became an All-American, he set a standard in defensive play and leadership that lives in Gainesville to this day.

LB **Lee Roy Jordan, Alabama** (1960-62)
As a junior, Jordan was the best player on a 1961 national championship defense that allowed a total of 25 points in 11 games. The 1962 All-American finished his career with 31 tackles in the Orange Bowl against Oklahoma. No wonder, then, that Jordan hailed from—we kid you not—Excel, Ala.

LB **Wilber Marshall, Florida** (1980-83)
He was a three-time All-SEC and twice an All-American. Marshall finished his career in 1983 with 343 tackles, 58 of them behind the line. The latter remains a Gator record. Marshall entered the College Football Hall of Fame in 2008.

LB **Patrick Willis, Mississippi** (2003-06)
The 6-2, 240-pound Willis combined size and speed as few have. An All-American and Butkus Award winner in 2006,

Willis made 355 tackles in four seasons. In his three years as a starter, Willis made 335 stops, 231 of them on his own. That's right—he averaged 77 solo tackles a season as a starter.

CB CHAMP BAILEY, GEORGIA (1996-98)

Had Bailey been merely a defensive back, his Dawg career still would be worth recalling. The 1998 Nagurski Award winner as the nation's best defensive player made 52 tackles and intercepted three passes. But he also caught 47 passes for 744 yards and five touchdowns. Bailey, one of the first stars in a new wave of two-way players, played about 1,000 snaps that season.

CB TOMMY CASANOVA, LSU (1969-71)

The only three-time All-American in school history played both ways, but will be best remembered as a corner and a punt returner. Casanova's returns of 61 and 73 yards for touchdowns keyed a 61-17 rout of Ole Miss in his junior season of 1970. The College Football Hall of Fame elected him as a member in 1995.

S TERRY HOAGE, GEORGIA (1980-83)

He was the last player Vince Dooley signed before the 1980 season, the son of a Texas college professor. Hoage became a two-time All-American ballhawk and a two-time Academic All-American as well, with a 3.85 GPA in genetics. Oh, by the way, the Dawgs went 43–4–1 in Hoage's four seasons. In 1982, Hoage intercepted 12 passes, which remains an SEC record.

S JAKE SCOTT, GEORGIA (1966-69)

Forty years after playing his final snap between the hedges, Scott remains the Dawgs' career leader in interceptions with 16 and interception return yards with 315. In 1968, he not only became an All-American but also the only safety ever to be named the conference's Most Valuable Player.

P JIM ARNOLD, VANDERBILT (1979-82)

He made All-American as a senior, when he averaged 45.8 yards in 74 attempts for the Commodores' only eight-win team since 1950. Arnold finished his career with an average of 43.9 yards per punt. He punted 277 times in four years. Punting for Vanderbilt is one way to keep busy.

THE SCHOOLS

THE SCHOOLS

This section, the book's largest, contains historical essays and statistical data on each of the Southeastern Conference's 12 universities, plus former SEC teams Georgia Tech and Tulane.

Here's what you should know about information that appears in these pages:

- **Enrollment.** Undergraduate enrollment only.
- **National championships.** According to the NCAA's recognized list of consensus national champions since 1936 (the first year of the Associated Press poll).
- **Conference championships.** Overall and outright titles in the conference.
- **First-round draft choices.** Updated through the 2009 NFL draft.
- **Consensus All-Americans.** As designated by the NCAA. Because the NCAA recognizes multiple lists, it's quite common for a player to receive first-team All-American honors from one or more selectors and not be acknowledged as a consensus All-American.
- **All-time scores.** Compiled by BCS pollster Richard Billingsley, this section offers a bar chart for each school showing yearly winning percentage since 1936. (In calculating this percentage for this chart, as well as for every coach's career record at a school, a tie is treated as a half-win and a half-loss.) In the year-by-year summaries, the vertical lines beside opponents indicate a conference game. A bullet indicates a win, a blank indicates a loss, an equal sign indicates a tie. Conference affiliations are noted throughout.

In the early years, forfeits were not uncommon, frequently because of difficult travel arrangements. There were, however, instances where opponents did not agree on which team had forfeited. Since it's impossible to judge who did what 100 years after the fact, only the instances where *both* schools agreed are included.

American football evolved from rugby, and for over a decade it shared many of its predecessor's characteristics. Not until Walter Camp, the father of American football, established a point value system and rules of play (1878-82) did the sport assume the basic form we love today. Only games that were played

by American football rules resulting in American point values are listed in this encyclopedia.

Billingsley and the ESPN research staff went to heroic lengths to determine, once and for all, the definitive final score for every disputed game. All games with disputed scores are footnoted, but we had to decide which outcome to record. If there was overwhelming evidence one way or another, through multiple reports or consensus, we selected the majority decision. Otherwise we granted the losing team the smallest margin of defeat.

- **Team record books.** Among the new features in the *ESPN Southeastern Conference Football Encyclopedia* is this two-page section that includes significant single-game, single-season and career records for each school. This section also incorporates all-time teams (whenever a team selected by a respected authority was available) and the school's annual leaders in rushing, passing and receiving, which now appear in an easier-to-read format. Due to recent changes in official record-keeping methodology, there is a great deal of disparity. In 2002, the NCAA began including bowl game performances in school's rushing, passing and receiving statistics. Until all schools revise their historical stats according to the new NCAA standard, records will skew to more recent performances, because today's players will be credited with stats from an extra game or two (in the case of conference championship games).

Another complication: Some schools identify as their receiving leader the player who gained the most yards while others prefer the player who caught the most passes. When two players caught the same number of passes, we've listed the player who gained the most yards.

- **Team bowl histories.** Each of these new team sections begin with a chart that includes the date, opponent, pre- and post-bowl rankings of each team, plus attendance and the game's outstanding players. That's followed by a complete scoring and statistical summary of every bowl game in that school's history.

ALABAMA

BY GEOFFREY NORMAN

PERHAPS NO PROGRAM HAS MEANT as much to the identity, even the self-esteem, of its home state as the University of Alabama's. Certainly among the most distinguished traditions in the land, Alabama football's winning ways go back to a time when the state was, in just about all other aspects, poor and backward. If the rest of the country in those times saw the face of Alabama in haunting portraits of hungry, downtrodden sharecroppers, the people of the state preferred to think of the boys in the red jerseys who crossed the country by train to win Rose Bowls. The Crimson Tide gave the Yellowhammer State something to be proud of at a time when pride was as precious—and scarce—as cash money.

TRADITION Alabama can claim all or part of 12 national championships and make a good argument that it was unfairly denied a couple of other times, too. The Tide have won 21 Southeastern Conference championships and been to 56 bowl games,

winning 31 of them. More than 90 Alabama players have been named to various All-American teams, though none has ever won a Heisman—an anomaly that is also cause for pride. Football, after all, is a team sport, and the University of Alabama has produced great teams. A whole lot of them.

LANDMARK The Paul W. Bryant Museum, which houses 100 years of history and iconography, is conveniently located across the street (also named for Bryant) from the Coleman Coliseum athletic headquarters. It's a place where the faithful can gaze at photographs of the storied teams and various Bryant artifacts, including the famous houndstooth hat. The museum is also a treasure trove of archival material for scholars of the game.

BEST PLAYER You could spend an eon arguing this one. Strong cases could be made for Joe Namath, Johnny Mack Brown, Lee Roy Jordan, Ozzie Newsome, John Hannah, Cornelius Bennett, Derrick Thomas and Shaun Alexander. Bryant's favorite might have been quarterback Pat Trammell, leader of his first national championship team in 1961. ("He can't run and he can't throw," Bryant once said of Trammell. "All he can do is beat you.") But Don Hutson, one of the great receivers in

PROFILE

University of Alabama, Tuscaloosa
Tuscaloosa, Ala.
Founded: 1831
Enrollment: 25,580
Colors: Crimson and White
Nickname: Crimson Tide
Stadium: Bryant-Denny Stadium
    Opened in 1929
    Prescription Athletic Turf; 92,138 capacity
First football game: 1892
All-time record: 755–307–44 (.711)
Bowl record: 31–22–3
Consensus national championships,
1936–present: 7 (1961, 1964, 1965, 1973, 1978, 1979, 1992)
Southeastern Conference championships:
21 (16 outright)
Outland Trophy: Chris Samuels, 1999; Andre Smith, 2008
First-round draft choices: 35
Website: www.rolltide.com

THE BEST OF TIMES

From a Dec. 7, 1963, win against Miami, Fla., all the way up to the 1968 Cotton Bowl loss to Texas A&M, the Crimson Tide went 40–3–2, the heart of a 1960s stretch that saw them win two national titles and play in five straight major bowl games.

THE WORST OF TIMES

The darkness before the dawn came in the J.B. Whitworth era at Alabama (1955-57) during which the Tide won just four games in three seasons, including three losses to Auburn by a combined score of 100-7. Solution: hire Paul "Bear" Bryant.

CONFERENCE

After 12 years in the Southern Conference, Alabama became a charter member of the SEC in 1933.

DISTINGUISHED ALUMNI

Mel Allen, baseball broadcaster; Hugo Black, Supreme Court justice; Harper Lee, author; Jim Nabors, actor; Gay Talese, author; Sela Ward, actress

FIGHT SONG

YEA ALABAMA
Yea, Alabama! Drown 'em Tide!
Every Bama man's behind you,
Hit your stride.
Go teach the Bulldogs to behave,
Send the Yellow Jackets to a watery grave.
And if a man starts to weaken,
That's a shame!
For Bama's pluck and grit have
Writ her name in Crimson flame.
Fight on, fight on, fight on men!
Remember the Rose Bowl, we'll win then.
So roll on to victory,
Hit your stride,
You're Dixie's football pride,
Crimson Tide, Roll Tide, Roll Tide!!

the history of the game—college or pro—would probably get the most votes.

BEST COACH Bear Bryant had some admirable predecessors at Alabama in Wallace Wade and Frank Thomas. And the present holder of the position, Nick Saban, is busily building a reputation as not just a great coach but something of a savior. Saban brought the Tide all the way back and, indeed, the team was ranked No. 1 in the nation for a few weeks in 2008 before losing in the SEC championship game to Florida. But the accomplishments of all other Tide coaches—past and present—live in Bryant's giant shadow.

Bear returned to his alma mater in 1958 because, as he said, "Mama called." Coaching through 1982, he won six national championships, 13 SEC titles and three coach of the year awards. His Bama teams went to 24 consecutive bowl games, compiling a 232–46–9 record.

Impressive as the numbers are, they don't provide the full texture of Bryant's accomplishments. He won with the changing times, both football and social. Bryant's first three national championship teams were all white; his last three were integrated. Bryant was not a leader in racial matters. But he was no bitter-ender, either, and when he

> *Alabama was called the "Tusca-losers" before the 1926 Rose Bowl.*

saw the shape of things to come, he recruited and coached black players with the same old fervor. And he kept on winning. When he had a quarterback who could throw the ball—like Namath or Ken Stabler—he won with the passing game. When he had material for it, he converted to the wishbone. And, of course, his teams always played good defense. Bum Phillips said of Bryant and his ability to win with whatever material he had, "He can take his'n and beat your'n and then take your'n and beat his'n." Bryant himself put it most succinctly when he said, "I ain't nothing but a winner."

BEST TEAM Among many contenders, the 1979 national title team probably deserves the nod by a small fraction. The team was trying to do something difficult to begin with: repeat as national champions. So it one-upped the previous year's squad—which had lost a single game, to Southern California—with a completely unblemished record. When the dust settled, the 1979 team scored 383 points while holding its opponents to a mere 67.

But this was not a team that simply outclassed the opposition. It had talent, but it had character, too—the kind of character that Bryant liked. This team could dig

FIRST-ROUND DRAFT CHOICES	
1936	Riley Smith, Redskins (2)
1948	Harry Gilmer, Redskins (1)
1948	Lowell Tew, Redskins (4)
1948	Vaughn Mancha, Yanks (5)
1951	Clarence "Butch" Avinger, Steelers (9)
1953	Bobby Marlow, Giants (8)
1963	Lee Roy Jordan, Cowboys (6)
1965	Joe Namath, Jets (1) and Cardinals (12)*
1967	Leslie Kelly, Saints (26)
1968	Dennis Homan, Cowboys (20)
1973	John Hannah, Patriots (4)
1974	Wilbur Jackson, 49ers (9)
1976	Richard Todd, Jets (6)
1978	Bob Cryder, Patriots (18)
1978	Ozzie Newsome, Browns (23)
1979	Barry Krauss, Colts (6)
1979	Marty Lyons, Jets (14)
1980	Don McNeal, Dolphins (21)
1981	E.J. Junior, Cardinals (5)
1983	Mike Pitts, Falcons (16)
1985	Emanuel King, Bengals (25)
1986	Jon Hand, Colts (4)
1987	Cornelius Bennett, Colts (2)

1989	Derrick Thomas, Chiefs (4)
1989	Bobby Humphrey, (Broncos)S
1990	Keith McCants, Buccaneers (4)
1993	John Copeland, Bengals (5)
1993	Eric Curry, Buccaneers (6)
1993	George Teague, Packers (29)
1994	Antonio Langham, Browns (9)
1997	Dwayne Rudd, Vikings (20)
1999	Fernando Bryant, Jaguars (26)
2000	Chris Samuels, Redskins (3)
2000	Shaun Alexander, Seahawks (19)
2009	Andre Smith, Bengals (6)

*From 1960-1966, the NFL and AFL held separate, competing drafts
SIndicates NFL Supplemental Draft

CONSENSUS ALL-AMERICANS	
1930	Fred Sington, T
1934	Don Hutson, E
1934	Bill Lee, T
1934	Dixie Howell, B
1935	Riley Smith, B
1937	Leroy Monsky, G
1941	Holt Rast, E
1942	Joe Domnanovich, C
1945	Vaughn Mancha, C
1961	Billy Neighbors, T
1962	Lee Roy Jordan, C
1965	Paul Crane, C
1966	Ray Perkins, E
1966	Cecil Dowdy, T
1967	Dennis Homan, E
1967	Bobby Johns, DB
1971	Johnny Musso, B
1972	John Hannah, G
1973	Buddy Brown, G
1974	Woodrow Lowe, LB
1974-75	Leroy Cook, DL
1977	Ozzie Newsome, WR

(Continued on next page)

deep when it had to, and in the tenderloin of the season, against the team that Bryant had always considered Alabama's true archrival, Tennessee, the Tide fell behind 17-7 at the half. Bryant used an old strategy in the locker room, patting players on the back and telling them that everything was okay and insisting, "We got 'em right where we want 'em." Then he replaced starting quarterback Steadman Shealy with Don Jacobs and the Tide dominated on the way to a 27-17 win.

The Tide went on to win two other gut-check games against perennial rivals, first beating LSU, 3-0, then Auburn, 25-18. So now it was on to the Sugar Bowl as SEC champions, needing to beat Arkansas to finish the season on top of the mountain. And by now, it was almost easy. The Tide won 24-9 and, as they say, it wasn't that close. Bryant put in a signature play in order to put his stamp on the game, the team and the season: Alabama quick kicked on one series. This was the last Bryant team to win a national championship.

BEST BACKFIELD Not only has there never been a Heisman Trophy winner from Alabama, the Tide has never really fielded one of those immortal backfields that all the school's followers and fans remember and mythologize down through the seasons. No Four Horsemen or Mr. Inside and Mr. Outside. Plenty of great runners, of course—think Brown, Alexander, Johnny Musso—but no legendary band of brothers. The closest might be the 1973 backfield that scored a school-record 454 points. The unit consisted of quarterback Richard Todd with a supporting cast of Wilbur Jackson, Randy Billingsley and Willie Shelby.

That team was special for several reasons, not least of which is that it went undefeated in the regular season and lost the Sugar Bowl game to Notre Dame by one heartbreaking point. And then there was this large historical fact: Jackson—certainly the star of the backfield and perhaps of the entire team—was the first African-American scholarship player to attend Alabama. Bryant's teams had been running the wishbone successfully for a couple of seasons. So as good as this backfield was with the formation, it wasn't breaking new ground. But when Jackson (and teammate Shelby) ran over people, it was a statement not merely about Bryant and the future of Alabama football but about much larger things and how much those things had changed. And finally, it was the new, integrated

CONSENSUS ALL-AMERICANS (CONT.)	
1978	Marty Lyons, DL
1979	Jim Bunch, T
1980	E.J. Junior, DL
1981	Tommy Wilcox, DB
1982	Mike Pitts, DL
1986	Cornelius Bennett, LB
1988	Derrick Thomas, LB
1989	Keith McCants, LB
1990	Philip Doyle, PK
1992	John Copeland, DL
1992	Eric Curry, DL
1993	David Palmer, KR
1993	Antonio Langham, DB
1996	Kevin Jackson, DB
1999	Chris Samuels, OL
2005	DeMeco Ryans, LB
2008	Andre Smith, OL
2008	Antoine Caldwell, C
2008	Terrence Cody, DL

Tide. The stigma of segregation was gone and Bama was well and truly back.

BEST DEFENSE Bear Bryant loved defense. In 1961, his first national championship team at Alabama allowed an astonishingly low 25 points in 11 games. Good as that defense was, the one the following year may have been better. That 1962 team did lose one game—to Georgia Tech—by a score of 7-6. Two other teams scored seven on the Tide that season. None scored more than that, and four didn't manage to score at all. Two of those shutouts were especially satisfying. One, it should go without saying, was against Auburn, and the other against Oklahoma in the Orange Bowl. Linebacker Lee Roy Jordan made 31 tackles in that game. "I don't worry about my defense," the Bear once said of Jordan. "As long as they stay between the sidelines, Lee Roy will get 'em."

STORYBOOK SEASON Sweet as winning is, it's even sweeter beating those who consider themselves your betters, especially when nobody else believes in you. Alabama was fourth choice for the 1926 Rose Bowl after Dartmouth, Yale and Colgate had turned down the chance to play Washington. One Rose Bowl executive supposedly remarked, "I've never heard of Alabama as a football team and can't take a chance on mixing a lemon with a rose." Will Rogers referred to the Tide as "Tusca-losers," and a Los Angeles sportswriter called them "Swamp Students." Alabama fell behind 12-0 and it looked like all the disparaging remarks were true, until the Tide came back on a touchdown reception by Johnny Mack Brown—who later returned to California for a long career as a movie cowboy—and won the game, 20-19. For Alabama fans, it was more than a victory. It was validation.

BIGGEST GAME Of the many big games the Tide have been involved in, perhaps the one with the most durable and resonant consequences was played Nov. 4, 1922, on the road against the University of Pennsylvania, a national power at that time. Grantland Rice wrote that the game would be a "breather" for Penn. The Tide won 9-7, the first time Alabama had gone up north and beaten a football giant. After the game, a small white sign reading "Bama 9, Penn 7" appeared in the window of a drugstore in downtown Tuscaloosa and remained there for more than 20 years.

BIGGEST UPSET The one that Alabama fans may cherish most came at the end of the 1965 season, in the 1966 Orange Bowl, in which the Tide beat Nebraska, 39-28, to win the most improbable of Bryant's national championships. Going in, Alabama was ranked fourth in the nation behind three undefeated and untied teams. Alabama was 8–1–1, having lost to Georgia, 18-17, on a play that is disputed to this day and tied Tennessee when Ken Stabler mistakenly threw the ball out of bounds to stop the clock on fourth down deep in Vols territory with seconds remaining.

On New Year's Day, No. 2 Arkansas lost to LSU in the Cotton Bowl and No. 1 Michigan State was knocked off by UCLA in the Rose. So at kickoff, there remained only one undefeated and untied team in the nation: No. 3 Nebraska. To win at least one of the recognized national championships, the Tide merely had to go out and vanquish an unbeaten team that outweighed Bryant's "little bitty boys" by about 20 pounds per man.

On the first series, Alabama ran a tackle eligible. After scoring just before halftime, the Tide tried an onside kick, recovered the ball and went into the locker room ahead 24-7. At some point that night, while Ray Perkins was running wild with one of his many pass receptions, Bryant said to one of his assistants, "Isn't this just the damnedest football game you've ever seen?" Two days later, Alabama won its Associated Press national championship.

BEST GOAL-LINE STAND In the 1979 Sugar Bowl, second-ranked Alabama played No. 1 Penn State. Tough defense characterized the tight game, and late in the fourth quarter, with Alabama ahead 14-7, PSU recovered a fumble on the Tide's 19. The Nittany Lions had their chance and mounted a drive. Then, on third and goal at the 1, Alabama held—barely. Penn State called for time and quarterback Chuck Fusina checked the distance. He looked toward the bench and spread his hands about 10 inches apart. "You got a foot to go," defensive tackle Marty Lyons told him. "You'd better pass." Fullback Mike Guman took a handoff and went up but not over. The impact popped the rivets in linebacker Barry Krauss' helmet. A stand for the ages.

COLLEGE FOOTBALL HALL OF FAME INDUCTEES		
NAME	YEARS	INDUCTED
Frank Thomas, COACH	1931-46	1951
Don Hutson, E	1932-34	1951
Wallace Wade, COACH	1923-30	1955
Fred Sington, T	1928-30	1955
Don Whitmire, T	1941-44	1956
Johnny Mack Brown, HB	1923-25	1957
Pooley Hubert, FB	1922-25	1964
Dixie Howell, HB	1932-34	1970
John Cain, QB/FB	1930-32	1973
Lee Roy Jordan, C	1960-62	1983
Riley Smith, QB	1933-35	1985
Paul "Bear" Bryant, COACH	1958-82	1986
Vaughn Mancha, C	1944-47	1990
Harry Gilmer, HB	1944-47	1993
Ozzie Newsome, WR	1974-77	1994
John Hannah, G/T	1970-72	1999
Johnny Musso, HB	1969-71	2000
Billy Neighbors, T	1959-61	2003
Cornelius Bennett, LB	1983-86	2005
Woodrow Love, LB	1972-75	2009

PRO FOOTBALL HALL OF FAME INDUCTEES		
NAME	YEARS	INDUCTED
Don Hutson, E	1935-45	1963
Bart Starr, QB	1956-71	1977
Joe Namath, QB	1965-77	1985
John Hannah, G	1973-85	1991
Dwight Stephenson, C	1980-87	1998
Ozzie Newsome, TE	1978-90	1999
Derrick Thomas, LB	1989-99	2009

BEST COMEBACK In 1960, Alabama was working its way back to glory. It had been tied by Tulane and beaten by Tennessee when it traveled to Atlanta to play Georgia Tech, and the Tide fell behind 15-0 at the half. Bama won on defense in those days, and this looked like too big a mountain to climb. Bryant came into the dressing room and, instead of breathing fire, slapped backs and grinned and said, "We've got 'em right where we want 'em." With Trammell injured, backup Bobby Skelton took Alabama on a touchdown drive that included four fourth-down plays. Still, the Tide were down by two with time running out. Skelton took the offense downfield again and every play was a white-knuckler, the last a pass to the Tech 6. With three seconds left, the backup kicker put up a duck that hit the crossbar and limped over for a 16-15 win.

STADIUM Alabama plays in a venue that opened as Denny Stadium in 1929 with a capacity of 12,000. The namesake, school president George Hutcheson "Mike" Denny, a man who believed in football and its value to the university, took an active interest—and might even be said to have meddled—in the football program. But none can deny his place in its success. With that success came stadium improvements and expansions. By 1966 it seated 60,000, and today holds almost 84,000. In 1975, something else was added—another name. This would be one Paul William Bryant, who played end on the team that beat Stanford in the 1935 Rose Bowl. He came back to Tuscaloosa a little more than a quarter of a century later, stayed another 25 years and became … well, immortal.

RIVAL Are you kidding? Auburn, man—the school Bryant once referred to as "that cow college on the other side of the state." Back in Bryant's playing days, Alabama did not play Auburn. The schools went some 41 years between games. The series was suspended in a dispute over the per diem for the visiting team, among other things. After some pressure from legislators and other powers in the state, the schools agreed to schedule each other, and the respective student body presidents met to bury a symbolic hatchet.

For years, the game was played at Legion Field in Birmingham and was called the Iron Bowl—a fitting moniker for the spirit and the hitting. The intensity of the play is matched by the passion of the fans, who include just about every living soul in the state of Alabama, not one of whom is neutral. Weddings and birthday parties are not scheduled in Alabama on the day of this game; you couldn't get anyone to come. Old friends, even family members, tend to stop speaking to one another if their loyalties clash. "I thought I understood something about rivalries," Bill Curry said after he became the former head coach of Alabama. "But until I'd experienced Alabama-Auburn, I didn't understand anything at all." Curry never beat Auburn, helping lead to his departure.

NICKNAME What exactly, the uninitiated might wonder, is a Crimson Tide and what does it have to do with football? The "Crimson" part is easy enough. The first Alabama team wore crimson stockings and this became the school's color. Around the turn of the

20th century, some sportswriter started using a line from one of Rudyard Kipling's poems—"The thin red line of 'eroes"—when referring to the Alabama team. Then, in a very wet game, another sportswriter turned the line of red moving inexorably down the field into a tide. Thus, the Crimson Tide and one of the more haunting cheers in all of football: Rooooooooooll, Tide!

MASCOT The improbable elephant is the result of the 1930 team, which was, by the standards of the day, impressively large. According to one writer, when the Alabama team took the field for the second quarter against Mississippi, a fan shouted, "Hold your horses, the elephants are coming." That team went undefeated and stampeded Washington State in the Rose Bowl, 24-0, to win the national championship.

QUOTE "As long as they kick it off, there will be something of Coach Bryant in the game." —**Eddie Robinson**, head coach, Grambling

Turning the Tide

BY WINSTON GROOM

When people think of Alabama football, they usually think of Bear Bryant's fabulous teams from the 1960s, '70s and '80s. During his quarter-century at the university, Bryant simply dominated the sport of college football, winning 13 SEC championships, six national titles and going to a bowl game every single year. I was in Tuscaloosa during the first four seasons of that amazing run, and if you were a fan of the game, nothing was finer.

But the Alabama tradition of football excellence actually began four decades earlier, in 1923, when coach Wallace Wade guided Bama to the first of eight consecutive winning seasons. Back then, the SEC was known as the Southern Conference and Alabama won its championship, on average, every other year. Not that that impressed a lot of people. College football was dominated by teams from the East, Midwest and West Coast. The South, still reconstructing and recovering economically from the Civil War, was considered a poor relation by the rest of the country—in football as in everything else. So when the Tide played Washington in the 1926 Rose Bowl, nobody gave them a snowball's chance in hell.

But they pulled off the upset, 20-19, thanks to the great Tide quarterback Allison "Pooley" Hubert and his halfback-sidekick Johnny Mack Brown—about whom it is not any kind of exaggeration to say that he was movie-star handsome, since he actually went on to become a leading man in Hollywood Westerns. (Incidentally, Brown dated my mother when she was at Tuscaloosa studying theater at the university.)

The national shock at the outcome was eclipsed only by the tidal wave of pride that swept through the South. At every whistle-stop the victorious Bama team made on the way home from Pasadena, Southerners would shower their train with flowers and offer up cookies, cakes and pies. When the players arrived in Tuscaloosa, they were paraded triumphantly to campus in drays pulled by freshmen,

In cities and in towns as well as on the farms without towns, any citizen with access to a radio could tune in to cheer the Tide to victory. The school's success created a brand new class of fan, and today their descendants still bleed Alabama Crimson.

prompting one writer to compare it to "the return of a Roman legion after a war of conquest." The editor of the Birmingham newspaper summed it up this way, "The South had come by way of football to think in terms of causes won, not causes lost."

He was on to something.

Perceived by the rest of the country as something on the order of a public menace or a disgrace—a land of unreconstructed yahoos— Southerners considered themselves a kind of national whipping boy, and thus the victory by Alabama was

doubly sweet. The Tide did it again the following season, going to another Rose Bowl and tying Stanford, 7-7. It was then that the legend of the Crimson Tide truly began—blood-red jerseys swarming to Saturday afternoon glory on green playing fields across the country. And it wasn't just the players and students who lived that legend; in cities and in towns as well as on the farms without towns, any citizen with access to a radio could tune in to cheer the Tide to victory. The school's success created a brand new class of fan, and today their descendants still bleed Alabama Crimson.

In 1931, Coach Wade cut out for Duke, but an even more beloved mentor arrived on the Alabama football scene, Frank Thomas— Knute Rockne's star QB at Notre Dame, who had been the roommate of George Gipp. Over the next 15 years, Thomas' teams didn't have a losing season; they won five SEC and two national championships and kept the legend going. After Thomas resigned in 1947, the Tide's fortunes declined, culminating a decade later in a humiliating no-win season, which prompted the hiring of one Paul "Bear" Bryant and a return to glory.

Since Bryant's retirement in 1983, the program has had its ups and downs. There have been a few SEC championships in the post-Bear era, but only one national title: a delicious victory over trash-talking Miami in the 1992 Sugar Bowl under coach Gene Stallings, a Bryant protégé. These days the fans are restless; they want another national title. Thanks to Nick Saban, the electric thrill is back in the air.

We wait. We hope. We'll see.

Winston Groom graduated from the University of Alabama in 1965. He is the author of 15 books, including the bestselling novel Forrest Gump *and the Civil War history* Vicksburg: 1863.

ALABAMA ALL-TIME SCORES

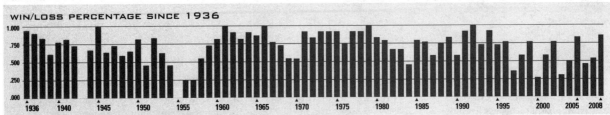

WIN/LOSS PERCENTAGE SINCE 1936

E.B. BEAUMONT
1892 (.500)   2-2

1892   2-2-0

N11	●	B'ham HS *Birm*	56	0
N12	●	B'ham HS *Birm*	4	5
D10	●	B'ham HS *Birm*	14	0
F22		Auburn *Birm*	22	32

ELI ABBOTT
1893-95, 1902 (.350)   7-13

1893   0-4-0

O14		B'ham HS	0	4
N4		B'ham HS	8	10
N11		Sewanee *Birm*	0	20
N30		Auburn *Mont*	16	40

1894   3-1-0

O27		at Mississippi	0	6
N3	●	at Tulane	18	6
N15	●	Sewanee *Birm*	24	4
N29	●	Auburn *Mont*	18	0

1895   0-4-0

N2		Georgia *ColGa*	6	30
N16		at Tulane	0	22
N18		at LSU	6	12
N23		Auburn	0	48

OTTO WAGONHURST
1896 (.667)   2-1

1896   2-1-0

O24	●	Birmingham HS	30	0
O31		Sewanee	6	10
N14	●	Mississippi State	20	0

ALLEN McCANTS
1897 (.000)   1-0

1897   1-0-0

N13	●	Tuscaloosa AC	6	0

1898
NO TEAM

W.A. MARTIN
1899 (.750)   3-1

1899   3-1-0

O21	●	Tuscaloosa AC	16	5
N11	●	Montgomery AC	16	0
N24	●	at Mississippi	7	5
N25		at New Orleans AC	0	21

M. GRIFFIN
1900 (.400)   2-3

1900   2-3-0

O21	●	Taylor School	35	0
O26	●	Mississippi	12	5
N3		Tulane	0	6
N17		Auburn *Mont*	5	53
N29		Clemson *Birm*	0	35

M.H. HARVEY
1901 (.600)   2-1-2

1901   2-1-2

O26	●	Mississippi	41	0
N9	=	Georgia *Mont*	0	0
N15		Auburn	0	17
N26	●	Mississippi State	45	0
N28	=	Tennessee *Birm*	6	6

ELI ABBOTT

1902   4-4-0

O10	●	Birmingham HS	57	0
O13	●	Marion Inst.	81	0
O18		Auburn *Birm*	0	23
N1		Georgia *Birm*	0	5
N8	●	Mississippi State	27	0
N19		Texas	0	10
N27		Georgia Tech *Birm*	26	0
N29		LSU	0	11

W.B. BLOUNT
1903-04 (.588)   10-7

1903   3-4-0

O10		at Vanderbilt	0	30
O16		Mississippi State *ColMs*	0	11
O23	●	Auburn *Mont*	18	6
N2		Sewanee *Birm*	0	23
N9	●	LSU	18	0
N14		Cumberland	0	44
N26	●	Tennessee *Birm*	24	0

1904   7-3-0

O3	●	Florida U. Club	29	0
O8	●	Clemson *Birm*	0	18
O15	●	Mississippi State *ColMs*	6	0
O24	●	Nashville	17	0
N5	●	Georgia	16	5
N12	●	Auburn *Birm*	5	29
N24		Tennessee *Birm*	0	5
D2	●	at LSU	11	0
D3	●	at Tulane	6	0
D4	●	at Pensacola AC	10	5

JACK LEAVENWORTH
1905 (.600)   6-4

1905   6-4-0

O3	●	Maryville	17	0
O7		at Vanderbilt	0	34
O14	●	Mississippi State	34	0
O21		at Georgia Tech	5	12
O25		Clemson *Colu*	0	25
N4	●	Georgia *Birm*	36	0
N9	●	Centre	21	0
N18	●	Auburn *Birm*	30	0
N23		Sewanee *Birm*	6	42
N30	●	Tennessee *Birm*	29	0

J.W.H. POLLARD
1906-09 (.783)   21-4-5

1906   5-1-0

O6	●	Maryville	6	0
O13	●	Samford	14	0
O20		at Vanderbilt	0	78
N3	●	at Mississippi State	16	4
N17	●	Auburn *Birm*	10	0
N29	●	Tennessee *Birm*	51	0

1907   5-1-2

O5	●	Maryville	17	0
O12	●	Mississippi *ColMs*	20	0
O21		Sewanee	4	54
O25	=	Georgia *Mont*	0	0
N2	●	Centre *Birm*	12	0
N16	=	Auburn *Birm*	6	6
N23	●	LSU *Mbl*	6	4
N28	●	Tennessee *Birm*	5	0

1908   6-1-1

O3	●	Wetumpka	27	0
O10	●	at Samford	17	0
O17	●	Cincinnati *Birm*	16	0
O24		at Georgia Tech	6	11
O31	●	U.T. Chattanooga	23	6
N14	=	Georgia *Birm*	6	6
N20	●	Haskell	9	8
N26	●	Tennessee *Birm*	4	0

1909   5-1-2

O2	●	Union	16	0
O9	●	Samford	14	0
O16	●	Clemson *Birm*	3	0
O23	=	Mississippi *JaM*	0	0
O30	●	Georgia *Atl*	14	0
N13	●	at Tennessee	10	0
N20	=	at Tulane	5	5
N25		LSU *Birm*	6	12

GUY LOWMAN
1910 (.500)   4-4

1910   4-4-0

O1	●	B'Ham South	25	0
O8	●	Marion Inst.	26	0
O15		Georgia *Birm*	0	22
O22		Georgia Tech	0	36
N5		Mississippi. *GrvMS*	0	16
N12		Sewanee *Birm*	0	30
N19	●	at Tulane	5	3
N24	●	Wash. & Lee *Birm*	9	0

D.V. GRAVES
1911-14 (.625)   21-12-3

1911   5-2-2

S30	●	Samford	24	0
O7	●	at B'Ham South	47	5
O14		Georgia *Birm*	3	11
O21	=	Mississippi State *ColMs*	6	6
O29	=	at Georgia Tech	0	0
N4	●	at Marion Inst.	35	0
N18	●	Tulane *Birm*	22	0
N25		Sewanee *Birm*	0	3
N30	●	Davidson *Birm*	16	6

1912   5-3-1

S28	●	Marion Inst.	52	0
O5	●	B'ham Southern	62	0
O12		at Georgia Tech	3	20
O18	●	Mississippi State *Abe*	3	11
O26		Georgia *ColGa*	9	13
N2	●	at Tulane	7	0
N9	●	Mississippi	10	9
N16	=	Sewanee *Birm*	6	6
N28	●	Tennessee *Birm*	7	0

1913   6-3-0

S27	●	Samford	27	0
O4	●	B'ham Southern	81	0
O11	●	Clemson	20	0
O18		Georgia *Birm*	0	20
O25	●	at Tulane	26	0
N1	●	Mississippi Coll. *JaM*	21	3
N9		Sewanee *Birm*	7	10
N14	●	Tennessee	6	0
N27		Mississippi State *Birm*	0	7

1914   5-4-0

O3	●	Samford	13	0
O10	●	B'Ham Southern	54	0
O17	●	Georgia Tech *Birm*	13	0
O24		at Tennessee	7	17
O31	●	Tulane	58	0
N7		Sewanee *Birm*	0	18
N13	●	U.T. Chattanooga	63	0
N26		Mississippi State *Birm*	0	9
D2		Carlisle *Birm*	3	20

THOMAS KELLY
1915-17 (.700)   17-7-1

1915   6-2-0

O2	●	Samford	44	0
O9	●	B'ham Southern	67	0
O16	●	Mississippi Coll.	40	0
O23	●	Tulane	16	0
O30	●	Sewanee *Birm*	23	10
N6		at Georgia Tech	7	21
N13		at Texas	0	20
N25	●	Mississippi *Birm*	53	0

1916   6-3-0

S30	●	B'ham Southern	13	0
O7	●	Southern	80	0
O14	●	Mississippi Coll.	13	7
O21	●	Florida *JacF*	16	0
O28	●	Mississippi	27	0
N4	●	Sewanee *Birm*	7	6
N11		at Georgia Tech	0	13
N18		at Tulane	0	33
N30		Georgia *Birm*	0	3

1917   5-2-1

O3	●	Ohio Am. Corp *Mont*	7	0
O12	●	Marion Inst.	13	0
O20	●	Mississippi Coll.	46	0
O27	●	Mississippi	64	0
N3	=	Sewanee *Birm*	3	3
N10	●	Vanderbilt *Birm*	2	7
N17	●	at Kentucky	27	0
N29		Camp Gordon *Birm*	6	19

1918
NO TEAM WWI

XEN SCOTT
1919-22 (.744)   29-9-3

1919   8-1-0

O4	●	B'ham Southern	27	0
O11	●	Mississippi	49	0
O18	●	Samford	48	0
O24	●	Marion Inst.	61	0
N1	●	Sewanee *Birm*	40	0
N8		at Vanderbilt	12	16
N15	●	at LSU	23	0
N22	●	Georgia *Atl*	6	0
N27	●	Mississippi State *Birm*	14	6

1920   10-1-0

S25	●	So. Military Acd.	59	0
O2	●	Marion Inst.	49	0
O9	●	B'ham Southern	45	0
O16	●	Mississippi Coll.	57	0
O23	●	Samford	33	0
O30	●	Sewanee *Birm*	21	0
N6	●	Vanderbilt *Birm*	14	7
N13	●	LSU	21	0
N20		Georgia *Atl*	14	21
N25	●	Mississippi State *Birm*	24	7
N27	●	at Case Coll.	40	0

1921   5-4-2

S24	●	Samford	34	14
O1	●	Spring Hill	27	7
O8	●	Marion Inst.	55	0
O15	●	Bryson Tenn.	95	0
O22		Sewanee *Birm*	0	17
O29	=	LSU *NO*	7	7
N5		Vanderbilt *Birm*	0	14
N11		Florida	2	9
N19		Georgia *Atl*	0	22
N24	=	Mississippi State *Birm*	7	7
D3		at Tulane	14	7

1922-1932
SOUTHERN

1922   6-3-1 (3-2-1)

S30	●	Marion Inst.	110	0
O7	●	Oglethorpe	41	0
O14	|	at Georgia Tech	7	33
O21	=	Sewanee *Birm*	7	7
O28	|	at Texas	10	19
N4	|	at Pennsylvania	9	7
N10	|	LSU	47	3
N18	|	at Kentucky	0	6
N25	|	Georgia *Mont*	10	6
N30	|	Mississippi State *Birm*	59	0

WALLACE WADE
1923-30 (.812) 61-13-3

1923 7-2-1 (5-1-1)
S29 ● Union 12 0
O6 ● | Mississippi 56 0
O13 at Syracuse 0 23
O20 ● | Sewanee Birm 7 0
O27 ● at Spring Hill 59 0
N3 = | at Georgia Tech 0 0
N10 ● | Kentucky 16 8
N16 ● | LSU Mont 30 3
N24 ● | Georgia Mont 36 0
N29 | Florida Birm 6 16

1924 8-1-0 (5-0-0)
S27 ● Union 55 0
O4 ● at Furman 20 0
O11 ● Mississippi Coll. 55 0
O18 ● | Sewanee Birm 14 0
O25 ● | at Georgia Tech 14 0
N1 ● | Mississippi Mont 61 0
N8 ● | Kentucky 42 7
N15 Centre Birm 0 17
N27 ● | Georgia Birm 33 0

1925 10-0-0 (7-0-0)
S26 ● Union 53 0
O2 ● B'ham Southern 50 7
O10 ● | at LSU 42 0
O17 ● | Sewanee Birm 27 0
O24 ● | at Georgia Tech 7 0
O31 ● | Mississippi State 6 0
N7 ● | Kentucky Birm 31 0
N14 ● | Florida Mont 34 0
N26 ● | Georgia Birm 27 0
ROSE BOWL
J1 ● Washington 20 19

1926 9-0-1 (8-0-0)
S24 ● Millsaps 54 0
O2 ● | at Vanderbilt 19 7
O9 ● | Mississippi State Mer 26 7
O16 ● | at Georgia Tech 21 0
O23 ● | Sewanee Birm 2 0
O30 ● | LSU 24 0
N6 ● | Kentucky Birm 14 0
N13 ● | Florida Mont 49 0
N25 ● | Georgia Birm 33 6
ROSE BOWL
J1 = Stanford 7 7

1927 5-4-1 (3-4-1)
S24 ● Millsaps 46 0
S30 ● So. Presb. U. 31 0
O8 = | LSU Birm 0 0
O15 | at Georgia Tech 0 13
O22 ● | Sewanee Birm 24 0
O29 ● | Mississippi State 13 7
N5 ● | Kentucky Birm 21 6
N12 | Florida Mont 6 13
N27 | Georgia Birm 6 20
D3 | Vanderbilt Birm 7 14

1928 6-3-0 (6-2-0)
O6 ● | Mississippi 27 0
O13 ● | at Mississippi State 46 0
O20 | Tennessee 13 15
O27 ● | Sewanee Birm 42 12
N3 at Wisconsin 0 15
N10 ● | Kentucky Mont 14 0
N17 | at Georgia Tech 13 33
N29 ● | Georgia Birm 19 0
D8 ● | LSU Birm 13 0

1929 6-3-0 (4-3-0)
S28 ● Mississippi Coll. 55 0
O5 ● | Mississippi 22 7
O12 ● U.T. Chattanooga 46 0
O19 | at Tennessee 0 6
O26 ● | Sewanee Birm 35 7
N2 | at Vanderbilt 0 13
N9 ● | Kentucky Mont 24 13
N16 ● | at Georgia Tech 14 0
N28 | Georgia Birm 0 12

1930 10-0-0 (8-0-0)
S27 ● Samford 43 0
O4 ● | Mississippi 64 0
O11 ● | Sewanee Birm 25 0
O18 ● | Tennessee 18 6
O25 ● | Vanderbilt Birm 12 7
N1 ● | at Kentucky 19 0
N8 ● | at Florida 20 0
N15 ● | LSU Mont 33 0
N27 ● | Georgia Birm 13 0
ROSE BOWL
J1 ● Washington State 24 0

FRANK THOMAS
1931-46 (.812) 115-24-7

1931 9-1-0 (7-1-0)
S26 ● Samford 42 0
O3 ● | Mississippi 55 6
O10 ● | Mississippi State Mer 53 0
O17 | at Tennessee 0 25
O24 ● | Sewanee Birm 33 0
O31 ● | Kentucky 9 7
N7 ● | Florida Birm 41 0
N14 ● | Clemson Mont 74 7
N26 ● | at Vanderbilt 14 6
D2 ● at U.T. Chattanooga 39 0

1932 8-2-0 (5-2-0)
S24 ● Southwestern 45 6
O1 ● | Mississippi State Mont 53 0
O8 ● at George Washington 28 6
O15 | Tennessee Birm 3 7
O22 ● | Mississippi 24 13
O29 ● | at Kentucky 12 7
N5 ● | Virginia Tech 9 6
N12 | at Georgia Tech 0 6
N24 ● | Vanderbilt Birm 20 0
D5 ● Saint Mary's-Cal SF 6 0

1933-PRESENT
SEC

1933 7-1-1 (5-0-1)
S30 ● Oglethorpe 34 0
O7 = | Mississippi Birm 0 0
O14 ● | Mississippi State 18 0
O21 ● | at Tennessee 12 6
O28 Fordham NYC 0 2
N4 ● | Kentucky Birm 20 0
N11 ● Virginia Tech 27 0
N18 ● | at Georgia Tech 12 9
N30 ● | at Vanderbilt 7 0

1934 10-0-0 (7-0-0)
S29 ● Samford 24 0
O5 ● | Sewanee Mont 35 6
O13 ● | Mississippi State 41 0
O20 ● | Tennessee Birm 13 6
O27 ● | Georgia Birm 26 6
N3 ● | at Kentucky 34 14
N10 ● Clemson 40 0
N17 ● | at Georgia Tech 40 0
N29 ● | Vanderbilt Birm 34 0
ROSE BOWL
J1 ● Stanford 29 13

1935 6-2-1 (4-2-0)
S28 = Samford 7 7
O5 ● at George Washington 39 0
O12 | Mississippi State 7 20
O19 ● | at Tennessee 25 0
O26 ● | at Georgia 17 7
N2 ● | Kentucky Birm 13 0
N9 ● Clemson 33 0
N16 ● | Georgia Tech Birm 38 7
N28 | at Vanderbilt 6 14

1936 8-0-1 (5-0-1)
S26 ● Samford 34 0
O3 ● Clemson 32 0
O10 ● | Mississippi State 7 0
O17 = | Tennessee Birm 0 0
O24 ● at Loyola-New Orleans 13 6
O31 ● | at Kentucky 14 0
N7 ● | Tulane Birm 34 7
N14 ● | at Georgia Tech 20 16
N25 ● | Vanderbilt Birm 14 6

1937 9-1-0 (6-0-0)
S25 ● Samford 41 0
O2 ● | Sewanee Birm 65 0
O9 ● South Carolina 20 0
O16 ● | at Tennessee 14 7
O23 ● at George Washington 19 0
O30 ● | Kentucky 41 0
N6 ● | at Tulane 9 6
N13 ● | Georgia Tech Birm 7 0
N25 ● | at Vanderbilt 9 7
ROSE BOWL
J1 California 0 13

1938 7-1-1 (4-1-1)
S24 ● at Southern California 19 7
O1 ● Samford 34 0
O8 ● North Carolina St. 14 0
O15 | Tennessee Birm 0 13
O22 ● | Sewanee 32 0
O29 ● | at Kentucky 26 6
N5 ● | Tulane Birm 3 0
N12 = | at Georgia Tech 14 14
N24 ● | Vanderbilt. Birm 7 0

1939 5-3-1 (2-3-1)
S30 ● Samford 21 0
O7 ● Fordham NYC 7 6
O14 ● Mercer 20 0
O21 | at Tennessee 0 21
O28 ● | Mississippi State 7 0
N4 = | Kentucky Birm 7 7
N11 | at Tulane 0 13
N18 | Georgia Tech Birm 0 6
N30 ● | at Vanderbilt 39 0

1940 7-2-0 (4-2-0)
S27 ● at Spring Hill 26 0
O5 ● Mercer 20 0
O12 ● Samford 31 0
O19 | Tennessee Birm 12 27
N2 ● | at Kentucky 25 0
N9 ● | Tulane Birm 13 6
N16 ● | at Georgia Tech 14 13
N23 ● | Vanderbilt Birm 25 21
N30 | Mississippi State 0 13

1941 9-2-0 (5-2-0)
S27 ● La. Lafayette 47 6
O4 | Mississippi State 0 14
O11 ● at Samford 61 0
O18 ● | at Tennessee 9 2
O25 ● | Georgia Birm 27 14
N1 ● | Kentucky 30 0
N8 ● | at Tulane 19 14
N15 ● | Georgia Tech Birm 20 0
N22 | at Vanderbilt 0 7
N29 ● at Miami, Fla. 21 7
COTTON BOWL
J1 ● Texas A&M 29 21

1942 8-3-0 (4-2-0)
S25 ● La. Lafayette Mont 54 0
O3 ● | Mississippi State 21 6
O10 ● Pensacola NAS Mbl 27 0
O17 ● | Tennessee Birm 8 0
O24 ● | at Kentucky 14 0
O31 | Georgia Atl 10 21
N7 ● South Carolina 29 0
N14 | at Georgia Tech 0 7
N21 ● | Vanderbilt Birm 27 7
N28 Georgia Pre-Flight 19 35
ORANGE BOWL
J1 ● Boston College 37 21

1943
NO TEAM WWII

1944 5-2-2 (3-1-2)
S30 = | at LSU 27 27
O7 ● at Samford 63 7
O14 ● Millsaps 55 0
O21 = | at Tennessee 0 0
O27 ● | Kentucky Mont 41 0
N4 | Georgia Birm 7 14
N11 ● | Mississippi Mbl 34 6
N18 ● | Mississippi State 19 0
SUGAR BOWL
J1 Duke 26 29

1945 10-0-0 (6-0-0)
S29 ● at Keesler AFB 21 0
O6 ● | at LSU 26 7
O13 ● South Carolina ColGa 55 0
O20 ● | Tennessee Birm 25 7
O27 ● | Georgia Birm 28 14
N3 ● | Kentucky Lou 60 19
N17 ● | at Vanderbilt 71 0
N24 ● Pensacola NAS 55 6
D1 ● | Mississippi State 55 13
ROSE BOWL
J1 ● Southern California 34 14

1946 7-4-0 (4-3-0)
S20 ● Furman Birm 26 7
S28 ● | at Tulane 7 6
O5 ● at South Carolina 14 6
O12 ● La. Lafayette 54 0
O19 | at Tennessee 0 12
O26 ● | Kentucky Mont 21 7
N2 | at Georgia 0 14
N9 | at LSU 21 31
N16 ● | Vanderbilt Birm 12 7
N23 at Boston College 7 13
N30 ● | Mississippi State 24 7

HAROLD "RED" DREW
1947-54 (.646) 54-28-7

1947 8-3-0 (5-2-0)
S20 ● Southern Miss Birm 34 7
S27 | at Tulane 20 21
O4 | at Vanderbilt 7 14
O11 ● Duquesne 26 0
O18 ● | Tennessee Birm 10 0
O25 ● | at Georgia 17 7
N1 ● | at Kentucky 13 0
N15 ● | Georgia Tech Birm 14 7
N22 ● | LSU 41 12
N29 ● at Miami, Fla. 21 6
SUGAR BOWL
J1 Texas 7 27

1948 6-4-1 (4-4-1)
S25 | at Tulane 14 21
O2 = | Vanderbilt Mbl 14 14
O8 ● Duquesne 48 6
O16 | at Tennessee 6 21
O23 ● | at Mississippi State 10 7
O30 | Georgia Birm 0 35
N6 ● Southern Miss 27 0
N13 ● | at Georgia Tech 14 12
N20 | at LSU 6 26
N27 ● | Florida 34 28
D4 ● | Auburn Birm 55 0

1949 6-3-1 (4-3-1)
S24 | Tulane Mbl 14 28
O1 | at Vanderbilt 7 14
O7 ● Duquesne 48 8
O15 = | Tennessee Birm 7 7
O22 ● | Mississippi State 35 6
O29 ● | at Georgia 14 7
N12 ● | Georgia Tech Birm 20 7
N19 ● Southern Miss 34 26
N26 ● | at Florida 35 13
D3 | Auburn Birm 13 14

1950 9-2-0 (6-2-0)
S23 ● U.T. Chattanooga Birm 27 0
S30 ● | at Tulane 26 14
O7 | Vanderbilt Mbl 22 27
O13 ● Furman 34 6
O21 | at Tennessee 9 14
O28 ● | Mississippi 14 7
N4 ● | Georgia Birm 14 7
N11 ● Southern Miss 53 0
N18 ● | at Georgia Tech 54 19
N25 ● | Florida JacF 41 13
D2 ● | Auburn Birm 34 0

1951 5-6-0 (3-5-0)
S21 ● Delta St. Mont 89 0
S29 | LSU Mbl 7 13
O6 | at Vanderbilt 20 22
O12 Villanova 18 41
O20 | Tennessee Birm 13 27
O27 ● | at Mississippi State 7 0
N3 ● | at Georgia 16 14
N10 ● Southern Miss 40 7
N17 | Georgia Tech Birm 7 27
N24 | Florida 21 30
D2 ● | Auburn Birm 25 7

1952 10-2-0 (4-2-0)
S19 ● Southern Miss Mont 20 6
S27 ● | at LSU 21 20
O3 ● at Miami, Fla. 21 7
O11 ● Virginia Tech 33 0
O18 | at Tennessee 0 20
O25 ● | Mississippi State 42 19
N1 ● | Georgia Birm 34 19
N8 ● U.T. Chattanooga 42 28
N15 | at Georgia Tech 3 7
N22 ● Maryland Mbl 27 7
N29 ● | Auburn Birm 21 0
ORANGE BOWL
J1 ● Syracuse 61 6

1953 6-3-3 (4-0-3)
S18 Southern Miss Mont 19 25
S26 = | LSU Mbl 7 7
O3 ● | at Vanderbilt 21 12
O10 ● Tulsa 41 13
O17 = | Tennessee Birm 0 0
O24 = | Mississippi State 7 7
O31 ● | at Georgia 33 12
N7 ● U.T. Chattanooga 21 14
N14 ● | Georgia Tech Birm 13 6
N21 at Maryland 0 21
N28 ● | Auburn Birm 10 7
COTTON BOWL
J1 Rice 6 28

THE SCHOOLS

1954 — 4-5-2 (3-3-2)
S17		Southern Miss Mont	2	7
S25	•	at LSU	12	0
O2	•	Vanderbilt Mbl	28	14
O9	•	Tulsa	40	0
O16	•	at Tennessee	27	0
O23		Mississippi State	7	12
O30	=	Georgia Birm	0	0
N6	•	at Tulane	0	0
N13		at Georgia Tech	0	20
N19		at Miami, Fla.	7	23
N27		Auburn Birm	0	28

J.B. WHITWORTH
1955-57 (.167)   4-24-2

1955 — 0-10-0 (0-7-0)
S24		at Rice	0	20
O1		at Vanderbilt	6	21
O8		TCU	0	21
O15		Tennessee Birm	0	20
O22		Mississippi State	7	26
O29	•	at Georgia	14	35
N5	•	Tulane Mbl	7	27
N12		Georgia Tech Birm	2	26
N18	•	at Miami, Fla.	12	34
N26		Auburn Birm	0	26

1956 — 2-7-1 (2-5-0)
S22		at Rice	13	20
O6		Vanderbilt Mbl	7	32
O13		TCU	6	23
O20		at Tennessee	0	24
O27	•	Mississippi State	13	12
N3		Georgia Birm	13	16
N10	•	at Tulane	13	7
N17		at Georgia Tech	0	27
N24	=	Southern Miss	13	13
D1		Auburn Birm	7	34

1957 — 2-7-1 (1-6-1)
S28		at LSU	0	28
O5	=	at Vanderbilt	6	6
O12		at TCU	0	28
O19		Tennessee Birm	0	14
O26		Mississippi State	13	25
N2	•	at Georgia	14	13
N9		Tulane Mbl	0	7
N16		Georgia Tech Birm	7	10
N23	•	Southern Miss	29	2
N30		Auburn Birm	0	40

PAUL "BEAR" BRYANT
1958-82 (.824)   232-46-9

1958 — 5-4-1 (3-4-1)
S27		LSU Mbl	3	13
O4	=	Vanderbilt Birm	0	0
O11	•	Furman	29	6
O18		at Tennessee	7	14
O25	•	at Mississippi State	9	7
N1	•	Georgia	12	0
N7		at Tulane	7	13
N15	•	at Georgia Tech	17	8
N22	•	Memphis	14	0
N29		Auburn Birm	8	14

1959 — 7-2-2 (4-1-2)
S19		at Georgia	3	17
S26	•	at Houston	3	0
O3	=	at Vanderbilt	7	7
O10	•	U.T. Chattanooga	13	0
O17	=	Tennessee Birm	7	7
O31	•	Mississippi State	10	0
N7	•	Tulane Mbl	19	7
N14	•	Georgia Tech Birm	9	7
N21	•	Memphis	14	7
N28	•	Auburn Birm	10	0

LIBERTY BOWL
| D19 | | Penn State | 0 | 7 |

1960 — 8-1-2 (5-1-1)
S17	•	Georgia Birm	21	6
S24	•	at Tulane	6	6
O1	•	Vanderbilt Birm	21	0
O15	•	at Tennessee	7	20
O22	•	Houston	14	0
O29	•	at Mississippi State	7	0
N5	•	Furman	51	0
N12	•	at Georgia Tech	16	15
N19	•	Tampa	34	6
N26	•	Auburn Birm	3	0

BLUEBONNET BOWL
| D17 | = | Texas | 3 | 3 |

1961 — 11-0-0 (7-0-0)
S23	•	at Georgia	32	6
S30	•	Tulane Mbl	9	0
O7	•	at Vanderbilt	35	6
O14		North Carolina St.	26	7
O21	•	Tennessee Birm	34	3
O28	•	at Houston	17	0
N4		Mississippi State	24	0
N11		Richmond	66	0
N18		Georgia Tech Birm	10	0
D2	•	Auburn Birm	34	0

SUGAR BOWL
| J1 | • | Arkansas | 10 | 3 |

1962 — 10-1-0 (6-1-0)
S22	•	Georgia Birm	35	0
S28	•	at Tulane	44	6
O6	•	Vanderbilt Birm	17	7
O13	•	Houston	14	3
O20	•	at Tennessee	27	7
O27	•	Tulsa	35	6
N3		at Mississippi State	20	0
N10		Miami, Fla.	36	3
N17		at Georgia Tech	6	7
D1	•	Auburn Birm	38	0

ORANGE BOWL
| J1 | • | Oklahoma | 17 | 0 |

1963 — 9-2-0 (6-2-0)
S21	•	at Georgia	32	7
S28	•	Tulane Mbl	28	0
O5	•	at Vanderbilt	21	6
O12	•	Florida	6	10
O19	•	Tennessee Birm	35	0
O26	•	Houston	21	13
N2	•	Mississippi State	20	19
N16	•	Georgia Tech Birm	27	11
N30		Auburn Birm	8	10
D7	•	at Miami, Fla.	17	12

SUGAR BOWL
| J1 | • | Mississippi | 12 | 7 |

1964 — 10-1-0 (8-0-0)
S19	•	Georgia	31	3
S26	•	Tulane Mbl	36	6
O3	•	Vanderbilt Birm	24	0
O10	•	North Carolina St.	21	0
O17	•	at Tennessee	19	8
O24	•	Florida	17	14
O31	•	Mississippi State Jam	23	6
N7	•	LSU Birm	17	9
N14	•	at Georgia Tech	24	7
N26	•	Auburn Birm	21	14

ORANGE BOWL
| J1 | • | Texas | 17 | 21 |

1965 — 9-1-1 (6-1-1)
S18	•	at Georgia	17	18
S25	•	Tulane Mbl	27	0
O2	•	Mississippi Birm	17	16
O9	•	at Vanderbilt	22	7
O16	=	Tennessee Birm	7	7
O23	•	Florida State	21	0
O30	•	Mississippi State Jam	10	7
N6	•	at LSU	31	7
N13	•	South Carolina	35	14
N27	•	Auburn Birm	30	3

ORANGE BOWL
| J1 | • | Nebraska | 39 | 28 |

1966 — 11-0-0 (6-0-0)
S24	•	Louisiana Tech Birm	34	0
O1	•	Mississippi Jam	17	7
O8	•	Clemson	26	0
O15	•	at Tennessee	11	10
O22	•	Vanderbilt Birm	42	6
O29	•	Mississippi State	27	14
N5	•	LSU Birm	21	0
N12	•	South Carolina	24	0
N26	•	Southern Miss Mbl	34	0
D3	•	Auburn Birm	31	0

SUGAR BOWL
| J2 | • | Nebraska | 34 | 7 |

1967 — 8-2-1 (5-1-0)
S23	=	Florida State Birm	37	37
S30	•	Southern Miss Mbl	25	3
O7	•	Mississippi Birm	21	7
O14	•	at Vanderbilt	35	21
O21		Tennessee Birm	13	24
O28	•	at Clemson	13	10
N4	•	Mississippi State	13	0
N11	•	at LSU	7	6
N18	•	South Carolina	17	0
D2	•	Auburn Birm	7	3

COTTON BOWL
| J1 | • | Texas A&M | 16 | 20 |

1968 — 8-3-0 (4-2-0)
S21	•	Virginia Tech Birm	14	7
S28	•	Southern Miss Mbl	17	14
O5		Mississippi Jam	8	10
O12	•	Vanderbilt	31	7
O19	•	at Tennessee	9	10
O26	•	Clemson	21	14
N2	•	Mississippi State	20	13
N9	•	LSU Birm	16	7
N16	•	at Miami, Fla.	14	6
N30	•	Auburn Birm	24	16

GATOR BOWL
| D28 | • | Missouri | 10 | 35 |

1969 — 6-5-0 (2-4-0)
S20	•	at Virginia Tech	17	13
S27	•	Southern Miss	63	14
O4	•	Mississippi	33	32
O11	•	at Vanderbilt	10	14
O18	•	Tennessee Birm	14	41
O25	•	at Clemson	38	13
N1	•	Mississippi State Jam	23	19
N8	•	at LSU	15	20
N15	•	Miami, Fla.	42	6
N29	•	Auburn Birm	26	49

LIBERTY BOWL
| D13 | • | Colorado | 33 | 47 |

1970 — 6-5-1 (3-4-0)
S12	•	Southern California Birm	21	42
S19	•	Virginia Tech Birm	51	18
S26	•	Florida	46	15
O3	•	Mississippi Jam	23	48
O10	•	Vanderbilt	35	11
O17	•	at Tennessee	0	24
O24	•	at Houston	30	21
O31	•	Mississippi State	35	6
N7	•	LSU Birm	9	14
N14	•	at Miami, Fla.	32	8
N28	•	Auburn Birm	28	33

BLUEBONNET BOWL
| D31 | = | Oklahoma | 24 | 24 |

1971 — 11-1-0 (7-0-0)
S10	•	at Southern California	17	10
S18	•	Southern Miss	42	6
S25	•	at Florida	38	0
O2	•	Mississippi Birm	40	6
O9	•	at Vanderbilt	42	0
O16	•	Tennessee Birm	32	15
O23	•	Houston	34	20
O30	•	Mississippi State Jam	41	10
N6	•	at LSU	14	7
N13	•	Miami, Fla.	31	3
N27	•	Auburn Birm	31	7

ORANGE BOWL
| J1 | • | Nebraska | 6 | 38 |

1972 — 10-2-0 (7-1-0)
S9	•	Duke Birm	35	12
S23	•	Kentucky Birm	35	0
S30	•	Vanderbilt	48	21
O7	•	at Georgia	25	7
O14	•	Florida	24	7
O21	•	at Tennessee	17	10
O28	•	Southern Miss Birm	48	11
N4	•	Mississippi State	58	14
N11	•	LSU Birm	35	21
N18	•	Virginia Tech	52	13
D2	•	Auburn Birm	16	17

COTTON BOWL
| J1 | • | Texas | 13 | 17 |

1973 — 11-1-0 (8-0-0)
S15	•	California Birm	66	0
S22	•	at Kentucky	28	14
S29	•	at Vanderbilt	44	0
O6	•	Georgia	28	14
O13	•	at Florida	35	14
O20	•	Tennessee Birm	42	21
O27	•	Virginia Tech	77	6
N3	•	Mississippi State Jam	35	0
N17	•	Miami, Fla.	43	13
N22	•	at LSU	21	7
D1	•	Auburn Birm	35	0

SUGAR BOWL
| D31 | • | Notre Dame | 23 | 24 |

1974 — 11-1-0 (6-0-0)
S14	•	at Maryland	21	16
S21	•	Southern Miss Birm	52	0
S28	•	Vanderbilt	23	10
O5	•	Mississippi Jam	35	21
O12	•	Florida State	8	7
O19	•	at Tennessee	28	6
O26	•	TCU Birm	41	3
N2	•	Mississippi State	35	0
N9	•	LSU Birm	30	0
N16	•	at Miami, Fla.	28	7
N29	•	Auburn Birm	17	13

ORANGE BOWL
| J1 | • | Notre Dame | 11 | 13 |

1975 — 11-1-0 (6-0-0)
S8	•	Missouri Birm	7	20
S20	•	Clemson	56	0
S27	•	at Vanderbilt	40	7
O4	•	Mississippi Birm	32	6
O11	•	Washington	52	0
O18	•	Tennessee Birm	30	7
O25	•	TCU Birm	45	0
N1	•	Mississippi State Jam	21	10
N8	•	at LSU	23	10
N15	•	Southern Miss	27	6
N29	•	Auburn Birm	28	0

SUGAR BOWL
| D31 | • | Penn State | 13 | 6 |

1976 — 9-3-0 (5-2-0)
S11	•	Mississippi Jam	7	10
S18	•	SMU Birm	56	3
S25	•	Vanderbilt	42	14
O2	•	at Georgia	0	21
O9	•	Southern Miss Birm	24	8
O16	•	at Tennessee	20	13
O23	•	Louisville	24	3
O30	•	Mississippi State	34	17
N6	•	LSU Birm	28	17
N13	•	at Notre Dame	18	21
N27	•	Auburn Birm	38	7

LIBERTY BOWL
| D20 | • | UCLA | 36 | 6 |

1977 — 11-1-0 (7-0-0)
S10	•	Mississippi Birm	34	13
S17	•	at Nebraska	24	31
S24	•	at Vanderbilt	24	12
O1	•	Georgia	18	10
O8	•	at Southern California	21	20
O15	•	Tennessee Birm	24	10
O22	•	Louisville	55	6
O29	•	Mississippi State Jam	37	7
N5	•	at LSU	24	3
N12	•	Miami, Fla.	36	0
N26	•	Auburn Birm	48	21

SUGAR BOWL
| J2 | • | Ohio State | 35 | 6 |

1978 — 11-1-0 (6-0-0)
S2	•	Nebraska Birm	20	3
S16	•	at Missouri	38	20
S23	•	Southern California Birm	14	24
S30	•	Vanderbilt	51	28
O7	•	at Washington	20	17
O14	•	Florida	23	12
O21	•	at Tennessee	30	17
O28	•	Virginia Tech	35	0
N4	•	Mississippi State Birm	35	14
N11	•	LSU	31	10
D2	•	Auburn Birm	34	16

SUGAR BOWL
| J1 | • | Penn State | 14 | 7 |

1979 — 12-0-0 (6-0-0)
S8	•	at Georgia Tech	30	6
S22	•	Baylor	45	0
S29	•	at Vanderbilt	66	3
O6	•	Wichita St.	38	0
O13	•	at Florida	40	0
O20	•	Tennessee Birm	27	17
O27	•	Virginia Tech	31	7
N3	•	Mississippi State	24	7
N10	•	at LSU	3	0
N17	•	Miami, Fla.	30	0
D1	•	Auburn Birm	25	18

SUGAR BOWL
| J1 | • | Arkansas | 24 | 9 |

1980 10-2-0 (5-1-0)

S6	●		Georgia Tech [Birm]	26	3
S20	●		Mississippi [JaM]	59	35
S27	●	|	Vanderbilt	41	0
O3	●	|	Kentucky [Birm]	45	0
O11	●		Rutgers [ERut]	17	13
O18	●	|	at Tennessee	27	0
O25	●		Southern Miss	42	7
N1		|	Mississippi State [JaM]	3	6
N8	●	|	LSU	28	7
N15			Notre Dame [Birm]	0	7
N29	●	|	Auburn [Birm]	34	18
			COTTON BOWL		
J1	●		Baylor	30	2

1981 9-2-1 (6-0-0)

S5	●	|	LSU	24	7
S12			Georgia Tech [Birm]	21	24
S19	●	|	at Kentucky	19	10
S26	●	|	at Vanderbilt	28	7
O3	●		Mississippi	38	7
O10	=		Southern Miss [Birm]	13	13
O17	●	|	Tennessee [Birm]	38	19
O24	●		Rutgers	31	7
O31	●	|	Mississippi State	13	10
N14	●		at Penn State	31	16
N28	●	|	Auburn [Birm]	28	17
			COTTON BOWL		
J1			Texas	12	14

1982 8-4-0 (3-3-0)

S11	●		at Georgia Tech	45	7
S18	●	|	Mississippi [JaM]	42	14
S25	●	|	Vanderbilt	24	21
O2	●		Arkansas State [Birm]	34	7
O9	●		Penn State [Birm]	42	21
O16		|	at Tennessee	28	35
O23	●		Cincinnati	21	3
O30	●	|	Mississippi State [JaM]	20	12
N6		|	LSU [Birm]	10	20
N13			Southern Miss	29	38
N27		|	Auburn [Birm]	22	23
			LIBERTY BOWL		
D29	●		Illinois	21	15

RAY PERKINS
1983-86 (.677) 32-15-1

1983 8-4-0 (4-2-0)

S10	●		Georgia Tech [Birm]	20	7
S17	●	|	Mississippi	40	0
S24	●	|	at Vanderbilt	44	24
O1	●		Memphis	44	13
O8			at Penn State	28	34
O15		|	Tennessee [Birm]	34	41
O29	●	|	Mississippi State	35	18
N5	●	|	at LSU	32	26
N12	●		Southern Miss [Birm]	28	16
N25			Boston College [Fox]	13	20
D3		|	Auburn [Birm]	20	23
			SUN BOWL		
D24	●		SMU	28	7

1984 5-6-0 (2-4-0)

S8			Boston College [Birm]	31	38
S15			at Georgia Tech	6	16
S22	●		La. Lafayette	37	14
S29		|	Vanderbilt	21	30
O6		|	Georgia [Birm]	14	24
O13	●		Penn State	6	0
O20		|	at Tennessee	27	28
N3	●	|	Mississippi State [JaM]	24	20
N10		|	LSU [Birm]	14	16
N17	●		at Cincinnati	29	7
D1	●	|	Auburn [Birm]	17	15

1985 9-2-1 (4-1-1)

S2	●	|	at Georgia	20	16
S14	●		Texas A&M [Birm]	23	10
S21	●		Cincinnati	45	10
S28	●	|	at Vanderbilt	40	20
O12			at Penn State	17	19
O19		|	Tennessee [Birm]	14	16
O26	●		at Memphis	28	9
N2	●	|	Mississippi State	44	28
N9	=	|	at LSU	14	14
N16	●		Southern Miss	24	13
N30	●	|	Auburn [Birm]	25	23
			ALOHA BOWL		
D28	●		Southern California	24	3

1986 10-3-0 (4-2-0)

A27	●		Ohio State [ERut]	16	10
S6	●	|	Vanderbilt	42	10
S13	●		Southern Miss [Birm]	31	17
S20	●	|	at Florida	21	7
O4	●		Notre Dame [Birm]	28	10
O11	●		Memphis	37	0
O18	●	|	at Tennessee	56	28
O25			Penn State	3	23
N1	●	|	at Mississippi State	38	3
N8		|	LSU [Birm]	10	14
N15	●		Temple	24	14
N29		|	Auburn [Birm]	17	21
			SUN BOWL		
D25	●		Washington	28	6

BILL CURRY
1987-89 (.722) 26-10

1987 7-5-0 (4-2-0)

S5	●		Southern Miss [Birm]	38	6
S12	●		at Penn State	24	13
S19		|	Florida [Birm]	14	23
S26	●	|	at Vanderbilt	30	23
O3	●		La. Lafayette [Birm]	38	10
O10			at Memphis	10	13
O17	●	|	Tennessee [Birm]	41	22
O31	●	|	Mississippi State [Birm]	21	18
N7	●	|	at LSU	22	10
N14			at Notre Dame	6	37
N27		|	Auburn [Birm]	0	10
			HALL OF FAME BOWL		
J2			Michigan	24	28

1988 9-3-0 (4-3-0)

S10	●		at Temple	37	0
S24	●	|	Vanderbilt	44	10
O1	●	|	at Kentucky	31	27
O8		|	Mississippi	12	22
O15	●	|	at Tennessee	28	20
O22	●		Penn State [Birm]	8	3
O29	●	|	at Mississippi State	53	34
N5		|	LSU	18	19
N12	●		La. Lafayette [Birm]	17	0
N25		|	Auburn [Birm]	10	15
D1	●		at Texas A&M	30	10
			SUN BOWL		
D24	●		Army	29	28

1989 10-2-0 (6-1-0)

S16	●		Memphis [Birm]	35	7
S23	●	|	Kentucky	15	3
S30	●	|	at Vanderbilt	20	14
O7	●	|	Mississippi [JaM]	62	27
O14	●		La. Lafayette	24	17
O21	●	|	Tennessee [Birm]	47	30
O28	●		at Penn State	17	16
N4	●	|	Mississippi State [Birm]	23	10
N11	●	|	at LSU	32	16
N18	●		Southern Miss	37	14
D2		|	at Auburn	20	30
			SUGAR BOWL		
J1			Miami, Fla.	25	33

GENE STALLINGS
1990-96 (.810) 70-16-1

1990 7-5-0 (5-2-0)

S8			Southern Miss [Birm]	24	27
S15		|	Florida	13	17
S22		|	at Georgia	16	17
S29	●	|	Vanderbilt	59	28
O6	●		at La. Lafayette	25	6
O20	●	|	at Tennessee	9	6
O27			Penn State	0	9
N3	●	|	at Mississippi State	22	0
N10	●	|	LSU	24	3
N17	●		Cincinnati [Birm]	45	7
D1	●	|	Auburn [Birm]	16	7
			FIESTA BOWL		
J1			Louisville	7	34

1991 11-1-0 (6-1-0)

S7	●		Temple [Birm]	41	3
S14		|	at Florida	0	35
S21	●	|	Georgia	10	0
S28	●	|	at Vanderbilt	48	17
O5	●		U.T. Chattanooga [Birm]	53	7
O12	●		Tulane	62	0
O19	●	|	Tennessee [Birm]	24	19
N2	●	|	Mississippi State	13	7
N9	●	|	at LSU	20	17
N16	●		at Memphis	10	7
N30	●	|	Auburn [Birm]	13	6
			BLOCKBUSTER BOWL		
D28	●		Colorado	30	25

1992 13-0-0 (8-0-0)

S5	●	|	Vanderbilt	25	8
S12	●		Southern Miss [Birm]	17	10
S19	●	|	Arkansas [LR]	38	11
S26	●		Louisiana Tech [Birm]	13	0
O3	●	|	South Carolina	48	7
O10	●		at Tulane	37	0
O17	●	|	at Tennessee	17	10
O24	●	|	Mississippi	31	10
N7	●	|	at LSU	31	11
N14	●	|	at Mississippi State	30	21
N26	●	|	Auburn [Birm]	17	0
			SEC CHAMPIONSHIP GAME		
D5	●		Florida [Birm]	28	21
			SUGAR BOWL		
J1	●		Miami, Fla.	34	13

1993 9-3-1 (5-2-1)

S4	●		Tulane [Birm]	31	17 †
S11	●	|	at Vanderbilt	17	6 †
S18	●	|	Arkansas	43	3 †
S25	●		Louisiana Tech [Birm]	56	3 †
O2	●	|	at South Carolina	17	6 †
O16	=	|	Tennessee [Birm]	17	17 †
O23	●	|	at Mississippi	19	14 †
O30	●		Southern Miss	40	0 †
N6		|	LSU	13	17
N13	●	|	Mississippi State	36	25 †
N20		|	at Auburn	14	22
			SEC CHAMPIONSHIP GAME		
D4			Florida [Birm]	13	28
			GATOR BOWL		
D31	●		North Carolina	24	10

1994 12-1-0 (8-0-0)

S3	●		U.T. Chattanooga [Birm]	42	13
S10	●	|	Vanderbilt	17	7
S17	●	|	at Arkansas	13	6
S24	●		Tulane [Birm]	20	10
O1	●	|	Georgia [Birm]	29	28
O8	●		Southern Miss	14	6
O15	●	|	at Tennessee	17	13
O22	●	|	Mississippi	21	10
N5	●	|	at LSU	35	17
N12	●	|	at Mississippi State	29	25
N19	●	|	Auburn [Birm]	21	14
			SEC CHAMPIONSHIP GAME		
D3			Florida [Atl]	23	24
			CITRUS BOWL		
J2	●		Ohio State	24	17

1995 8-3-0 (5-3-0)

S2	●	|	at Vanderbilt	33	25
S9	●		Southern Miss [Birm]	24	20
S16		|	Arkansas	19	20
S30	●	|	at Georgia	31	0
O7	●		North Carolina St.	27	11
O14		|	Tennessee [Birm]	14	41
O21	●	|	at Mississippi	23	9
O28	●		North Texas	38	19
N4	●	|	LSU	10	3
N11	●	|	Mississippi State	14	9
N18		|	at Auburn	27	31

1996 10-3 (6-2)

A31	●		Bowling Green [Birm]	21	7
S7	●		Southern Miss [Birm]	20	10
S14	●	|	Vanderbilt	36	26
S21	●	|	Arkansas [LR]	17	7
O5	●	|	Kentucky	35	7
O12	●		at North Carolina St.	24	19
O19	●	|	Mississippi	37	0
O26		|	at Tennessee	13	20
N9	●	|	at LSU	26	0
N16		|	at Mississippi State	16	17
N23	●	|	Auburn [Birm]	24	23
			SEC CHAMPIONSHIP GAME		
D7			Florida [Atl]	30	45
			OUTBACK BOWL		
J1	●		Michigan	17	14

MIKE DuBOSE
1997-2000 (.511) 24-23

1997 4-7 (2-6)

A30	●		Houston [Birm]	42	17
S11	●	|	at Vanderbilt	20	0
S20		|	Arkansas	16	17
S27	●		Southern Miss [Birm]	27	13
O4		|	at Kentucky	34	40
O18		|	Tennessee [Birm]	21	38
O25	●	|	at Mississippi	29	20
N1			Louisiana Tech	20	26
N8		|	LSU	0	27
N15		|	Mississippi State	20	32
N22		|	at Auburn	17	18

1998 7-5 (4-4)

S5	●		Brigham Young	38	31
S12	●	|	Vanderbilt [Birm]	32	7
S26		|	at Arkansas	6	42
O3		|	Florida	10	16
O10	●	|	Mississippi	20	17
O17	●		East Carolina	23	22
O24		|	at Tennessee	18	35
O31	●		Southern Miss	30	20
N7	●	|	at LSU	22	16
N14		|	at Mississippi State	14	26
N21	●	|	Auburn [Birm]	31	17
			MUSIC CITY BOWL		
D29			Virginia Tech	7	38

1999 10-3 (7-1)

S4	●	|	at Vanderbilt	28	17
S11	●		Houston [Birm]	37	10
S18			Louisiana Tech [Birm]	28	29
S25	●	|	Arkansas	35	28
O2	●	|	at Florida	40	39
O16	●	|	at Mississippi	30	24
O23		|	Tennessee	7	21
O30	●		Southern Miss	35	14
N6	●	|	LSU	23	17
N13	●	|	Mississippi State	19	7
N20	●	|	at Auburn	28	17
			SEC CHAMPIONSHIP GAME		
D4	●		Florida [Atl]	34	7
			ORANGE BOWL		
J1			Michigan	34	35

2000 3-8 (3-5)

S2			at UCLA	24	35
S9	●	|	Vanderbilt [Birm]	28	10
S16			Southern Miss [Birm]	0	21
S23		|	at Arkansas	21	28
S30	●	|	South Carolina	27	17
O14	●	|	Mississippi	45	7
O21		|	at Tennessee	10	20
O28			Central Florida	38	40
N4		|	at LSU	28	30
N11		|	at Mississippi State	7	29
N18		|	Auburn	0	9

DENNIS FRANCHIONE
2001-02 (.680) 17-8

2001 7-5 (4-4)

S1			UCLA	17	20
S8	●	|	at Vanderbilt	12	9
S22	●	|	Arkansas	31	10
S29		|	at South Carolina	36	37
O6	●		Texas-El Paso [Birm]	56	7
O13		|	at Mississippi	24	27
O20		|	Tennessee	24	35
N3		|	LSU	21	35
N10	●	|	Mississippi State	24	17
N17	●	|	at Auburn	31	7
N29	●		Southern Miss [Birm]	28	15
			INDEPENDENCE BOWL		
D27	●		Iowa State	14	13

2002 10-3 (6-2)

A31	●		Middle Tennessee [Birm]	39	34
S7			at Oklahoma	27	37
S14	●		North Texas	33	7
S21	●		Southern Miss	20	7
S28	●	|	at Arkansas	30	12
O5		|	Georgia	25	27
O19	●	|	Mississippi	42	7
O26	●	|	at Tennessee	34	14
N2	●	|	at Vanderbilt	30	8
N9	●	|	Mississippi State	28	14
N16	●	|	at LSU	31	0
N23		|	Auburn	7	17
N30	●		at Hawaii	21	16

MIKE SHULA
2003-06 (.531) 26-23

2003 4-9 (2-6)

A30	●		South Florida [Birm]	40	17
S6			Oklahoma	13	20
S13	●	|	Kentucky	27	17
S20			Northern Illinois	16	19
S27		|	Arkansas	31	34
O4		|	at Georgia	23	37
O11	●		Southern Miss	17	3
O18		|	at Mississippi	28	43
O25		|	Tennessee	43	51
N8	●	|	at Mississippi State	38	0
N15		|	LSU	3	27
N22		|	at Auburn	23	28
N29			at Hawaii	29	37

THE SCHOOLS

2004　　6-6　(3-5)

S4	●	Utah State	48	17
S11	● |	Mississippi	28	7
S18	●	Western Carolina	52	0
S25	|	at Arkansas	10	27
O2	|	South Carolina	3	20
O9	● |	at Kentucky	45	17
O16	●	Southern Miss	27	3
O23	|	at Tennessee	13	17
N6	● |	Mississippi State	30	14
N13	|	at LSU	10	26
N20	|	Auburn	13	21
MUSIC CITY BOWL				
D31		Minnesota	16	20

2005　　10-2　(6-2)

S3	●	Middle Tennessee	26	7
S10	●	Southern Miss	30	21
S17	●	at South Carolina	37	14
S24	|	Arkansas	24	13
O1	● |	Florida	31	3
O15	● |	at Mississippi	13	10
O22	|	Tennessee	6	3
O29	●	Utah State	35	3
N05	|	at Mississippi State	17	0
N12	|	LSU	13	16
N19	|	at Auburn	18	28
COTTON BOWL				
J2	●	Texas Tech	13	10

2006　　6-7　(2-6)

S2	●	Hawaii	25	17
S9	● |	Vanderbilt	13	10
S16	●	La. Monroe	41	7
S23	|	at Arkansas	23	24
S30	|	at Florida	13	28
O7	●	Duke	30	14
O14	● |	Mississippi	26	23
O21	|	at Tennessee	13	16
O28	●	Florida Intl	38	3
N4	|	Mississippi State	16	24
N11	|	at LSU	14	28
N18	|	Auburn	15	22
INDEPENDENCE BOWL				
D28		Oklahoma State	31	34

NICK SABAN
2007-Present (.704)　　19-8

2007　　7-6　(4-4)

S1	●	Western Carolina	52	6
S8	● |	at Vanderbilt	24	10
S15	|	Arkansas	41	38
S22	|	Georgia	23	26
S29		Florida State ᴶᵃᶜᶠ	14	21
O6	●	Houston	30	24
O13	● |	at Mississippi	27	24
O20	● |	Tennessee	41	17
N3	|	LSU	34	41
N10		at Mississippi State	12	17
N17		La. Monroe	14	21
N24	|	at Auburn	10	17
INDEPENDENCE BOWL				
D30	●	Colorado	30	24

2008　　12-2　(8-0)

A30	●	Clemson ᴬᵗˡ	34	10
S6	●	Tulane	20	6
S13	●	Western Kentucky	41	7
S20	● |	at Arkansas	49	14
S27	● |	at Georgia	41	30
O4	● |	Kentucky	17	14
O18	● |	Mississippi	24	20
O25	● |	at Tennessee	29	9
N1	●	Arkansas State	35	0
N8	● |	at Louisiana State	27	21
N15	● |	Mississippi State	32	7
N29	● |	Auburn	36	0
SEC CHAMPIONSHIP GAME				
D6		Florida ᴬᵗˡ	20	31
SUGAR BOWL				
J2		Utah	17	31

Neutral Site key: *Abe* Aberdeen, MS / *Atl* Atlanta, GA / *Birm* Birmingham, AL / *ColGa* Columbus, GA / *ColMs* Columbus, MS / *Colu* Columbia, SC / *ERut* East Rutherford, NJ / *Fox* Foxboro, MA / *GrnMS* Greenville, MS / *JacF* Jacksonville, FL / *JaM* Jackson, MS / *Lou* Louisville, KY / *LR* Little Rock, AR / *Mbl* Mobile, AL / *Mer* Meridian, MS / *Mont* Montgomery, AL / *NO* New Orleans, LA / *NYC* New York, NY / *SF* San Francisco, CA
ƒ Forfeit　† Game Later Forfieted　# Disputed Victor　* Disputed Score　‖ Designated Conference Game　|2 Counted Twice in Conference Standings

ALABAMA ANNUAL STATISTICAL LEADERS

YR	RUSHING	YDS	ATT	AVG	PASSING	ATT	CMP	PCT	YDS	RECEIVING	REC	YDS	AVG
1944	Harry Gilmer	405	72	5.6	Harry Gilmer	66	32	.49	418	Hugh Morrow	10	107	10.7
1945	Lowell Tew	715	88	8.1	Harry Gilmer	88	57	.65	905	Rebel Steiner	18	315	17.5
1946	Harry Gilmer	497	133	3.7	Harry Gilmer	160	69	.43	930	Ted Cook	24	377	15.7
1947	Lowell Tew	571	107	5.3	Harry Gilmer	93	57	.61	610	Rebel Steiner	23	295	12.8
1948	Ed Salem	288	77	3.7	Ed Salem	110	52	.47	597	Bob Hood	7	150	21.4
1949	Tom Calvin	339	88	3.9	Ed Salem	75	40	.53	558	Al Lary	17	315	18.5
1950	Bobby Marlow	882	118	7.5	Ed Salem	86	44	.51	879	Al Lary	35	756	21.6
1951	Bobby Marlow	728	114	6.4	Clell Hobson	114	66	.58	847	Ken MacAfee	14	287	20.5
1952	Bobby Marlow	950	176	5.4	Clell Hobson	63	33	.52	336	Corky Tharp	10	115	11.5
1953	Corky Tharp	607	111	5.5	Bart Starr	119	59	.50	870	Bud Willis	11	191	17.4
1954	Corky Tharp	641	139	4.6	Albert Elmore	74	39	.53	499	Bobby Luna	16	304	19.0
1955	Clay Walls	164	49	3.3	Bart Starr	96	55	.57	587	Noojin Walker	14	154	11.0
1956	Don Comstock	316	76	4.2	Bobby Smith	40	16	.40	356	Charlie Gray	7	108	15.4
1957	Jim Loftin	477	106	4.5	Bobby Smith	83	32	.39	377	Willie Beck	9	126	14.0
1958	Bobby Jackson	472	143	3.3	Bobby Jackson	58	29	.50	408	Marlin Dyess	12	204	17.0
1959	Pat Trammell	525	156	3.4	Pat Trammell	49	21	.43	293	Marlin Dyess	10	149	14.9
1960	Pat Trammell	315	76	4.1	Robert Skelton	94	43	.46	575	Butch Wilson	13	204	15.7
1961	Mike Fracchia	652	130	5.0	Pat Trammell	133	75	.56	1,035	Richard Williamson	11	206	18.7
1962	Eddie Versprille	373	76	4.9	Joe Namath	146	76	.52	1,192	Richard Williamson	24	492	20.5
1963	Benny Nelson	612	97	6.3	Joe Namath	128	63	.49	765	Jimmy Dill	19	316	16.6
1964	Steve Bowman	536	106	5.1	Joe Namath	100	64	.64	757	David Ray	19	271	14.3
1965	Steve Bowman	770	153	5.0	Steve Sloan	160	97	.61	1,453	Tommy Tolleson	32	374	11.7
1966	Kenny Stabler	397	93	4.3	Kenny Stabler	114	74	.65	956	Ray Perkins	33	490	14.8
1967	Ed Morgan	388	103	3.8	Kenny Stabler	178	103	.58	1,214	Dennis Homan	54	820	15.2
1968	Ed Morgan	450	134	3.4	Scott Hunter	227	122	.54	1,471	George Ranager	31	499	16.1
1969	Johnny Musso	516	157	3.3	Scott Hunter	266	157	.59	2,188	David Bailey	56	781	13.9
1970	Johnny Musso	1,137	226	5.0	Scott Hunter	179	103	.58	1,240	David Bailey	55	790	14.4
1971	Johnny Musso	1,088	191	5.7	Terry Davis	66	42	.64	452	David Bailey	21	286	13.6
1972	Steve Bisceglia	603	125	4.8	Terry Davis	94	50	.53	777	Wayne Wheeler	30	573	19.1
1973	Wilbur Jackson	752	95	7.9	Gary Rutledge	57	33	.58	897	Wayne Wheeler	19	530	27.9
1974	Calvin Culliver	708	116	6.1	Richard Todd	67	36	.54	656	Ozzie Newsome	20	374	18.7
1975	Johnny Davis	820	123	6.7	Richard Todd	89	47	.53	661	Ozzie Newsome	21	363	17.3
1976	Johnny Davis	668	119	5.6	Jeff Rutledge	109	62	.57	979	Ozzie Newsome	25	529	21.2
1977	Johnny Davis	931	182	5.1	Jeff Rutledge	107	64	.60	1,207	Ozzie Newsome	36	804	22.3
1978	Tony Nathan	770	111	6.9	Jeff Rutledge	140	73	.52	1,078	Keith Pugh	20	446	22.3
1979	Steadman Shealy	791	152	5.2	Steadman Shealy	81	45	.56	717	Keith Pugh	25	433	17.3
1980	Billy Jackson	606	111	5.5	Don Jacobs	76	32	.42	531	Bart Kraut	16	218	13.6
1981	Ricky Moore	347	79	4.4	Walter Lewis	66	30	.46	633	Joey Jones	12	373	31.1
1982	Ricky Moore	600	111	5.4	Walter Lewis	164	102	.62	1,515	Joey Jones	25	502	20.1
1983	Ricky Moore	947	166	5.7	Walter Lewis	256	144	.56	1,991	Joey Jones	31	468	15.1
1984	Paul Carruth	782	163	4.8	Vince Sutton	135	60	.44	662	Greg Richardson	22	357	16.2
1985	Gene Jelks	588	93	6.3	Mike Shula	229	138	.60	2,009	Albert Bell	37	648	17.5
1986	Bobby Humphrey	1,471	236	6.2	Mike Shula	235	127	.54	1,486	Albert Bell	26	315	12.1
1987	Bobby Humphrey	1,255	238	5.3	Jeff Dunn	87	36	.41	484	Clay Whitehurst	18	278	15.4
1988	Murry Hill	778	136	5.7	David Smith	223	135	.61	1,592	Greg Payne	33	442	13.4
1989	Siran Stacy	1,079	216	5.0	Gary Hollingsworth	339	205	.61	2,379	Lamonde Russell	51	622	12.2
1990	Chris Anderson	492	106	4.6	Gary Hollingsworth	282	140	.50	1,463	Lamonde Russell	28	306	10.9
1991	Siran Stacy	966	200	4.8	Danny Woodson	101	64	.63	882	David Palmer	17	314	18.5
1992	Derrick Lassic	905	178	5.1	Jay Barker	243	132	.54	1,614	David Palmer	24	297	12.4
1993	Sherman Williams	738	168	4.4	Jay Barker	171	98	.57	1,524	David Palmer	61	1,000	16.4
1994	Sherman Williams	1,341	291	4.6	Jay Barker	226	139	.62	1,996	Curtis Brown	39	639	16.4
1995	Dennis Riddle	969	236	4.1	Brian Burgdorf	162	96	.59	1,200	Curtis Brown	43	557	13.0
1996	Dennis Riddle	1,079	242	4.5	Freddie Kitchens	302	152	.50	2,124	Michael Vaughn	39	702	18.0
1997	Curtis Alexander	729	155	4.7	Freddie Kitchens	237	121	.51	1,545	Quincy Jackson	28	472	16.9
1998	Shaun Alexander	1,178	258	4.6	Andrew Zow	256	143	.56	1,169	Quincy Jackson	48	621	12.9
1999	Shaun Alexander	1,383	302	4.6	Andrew Zow	264	148	.56	1,799	Freddie Milons	65	733	11.3
2000	Ahmaad Galloway	659	137	4.8	Andrew Zow	249	120	.48	1,561	Antonio Carter	45	586	13.0
2001	Ahmaad Galloway	881	174	5.1	Tyler Watts	172	94	.55	1,325	Freddie Milons	36	626	17.4
2002	Shaud Williams	921	130	7.1	Tyler Watts	181	112	.62	1,414	Triandos Luke	41	482	11.8
2003	Shaud Williams	1,367	280	4.9	Brodie Croyle	341	182	.53	2,303	Zach Fletcher	21	498	23.7
2004	Kenneth Darby	1,062	219	4.8	Spencer Pennington	152	82	.54	974	Tyrone Prothro	25	347	13.9
2005	Ken Darby	1,242	239	5.2	Brodie Croyle	339	202	.60	2,499	DJ Hall	48	676	14.1
2006	Ken Darby	835	210	4.0	John Parker Wilson	379	216	.57	2,707	DJ Hall	62	1,056	17.0
2007	Terry Grant	891	180	5.0	John Parker Wilson	462	255	.55	2,846	DJ Hall	67	1,005	15.0
2008	Glen Coffee	1,383	233	5.9	John Parker Wilson	323	187	.58	2,273	Julio Jones	58	924	15.9

The NCAA began including postseason stats in 2002

THE SCHOOLS

THE SCHOOLS

ALABAMA RECORD BOOK

SINGLE-GAME RECORDS

Rushing Yards	291	Shaun Alexander (Nov. 9, 1996 vs. LSU)
Passing Yards	484	Scott Hunter (Nov. 29, 1969 vs. Auburn)
Receiving Yards	217	David Palmer (Sept. 11, 1993 vs. Vanderbilt)
All-Purpose Yards	317	Siran Stacy (Oct. 21, 1989 vs. Tennessee)
Points	30	Santonio Beard (Oct. 19, 2002 vs. Mississippi); Shaun Alexander (Sept. 5, 1998 vs. Brigham Young)
Field Goals	6	Philip Doyle (Oct. 6, 1990 vs. Southwestern Louisiana)
Tackles	25	DeMeco Ryans (Sept. 27, 2003 vs. Arkansas)
Interceptions	3	Five players tied

SINGLE-SEASON RECORDS

Rushing Yards	1,471	Bobby Humphrey, 1996 (236 att.)
Passing Yards	2,846	John Parker Wilson, 2007 (255-372)
Receiving Yards	1,056	DJ Hall, 2006 (62 rec.)
All-Purpose Yards	2,016	Bobby Humphrey, 1986 (1,471 rushing, 201 receiving, 344 kick returning)
Scoring	144	Shaun Alexander, 1999 (24 TDs)
Touchdowns	24	Shaun Alexander, 1999
Tackles	134	Woodrow Lowe, 1973
Interceptions	10	Hootie Ingram, 1952
Punting Average	48.7	Greg Gantt, 1973 (25 punts)
Punt Return Average	18.1	Harry Gilmer, 1947 (21 ret.)
Kickoff Return Average	33.4	Ray Ogden, 1964 (10 ret.)

CAREER RECORDS

Rushing Yards	3,565	Shaun Alexander, 1996-99
Passing Yards	7,924	John Parker Wilson, 2005-08
Receiving Yards	2,923	DJ Hall, 2004-07
All-Purpose Yards	4,958	Bobby Humphrey, 1985-88
Scoring	345	Philip Doyle, 1987-90
Touchdowns	58	John Parker Wilson, 2005-08
Tackles	327	Wayne Davis, 1983-86
Interceptions	19	Antonio Langham, 1990-93
Punting Average	43.6	Greg Gantt, 1971-73 (116 punts)
Punt Return Average	13.5	Javier Arenas, 2006-present (93 ret.)
Kickoff Return Average	28.7	Harry Gilmer, 1944-47 (20 ret.)

TEAM RECORDS

Longest Winning Streak	28	Sept. 21, 1991-Oct. 2, 1993; broken vs. Tennessee, 17-17 on Oct. 16, 1993; Sept. 30, 1978-Oct. 25, 1980; broken vs. Mississippi State, 6-3 on Nov. 1, 1980
Longest Undefeated Streak	31	Sept. 21, 1991-Oct. 30, 1993; broken vs. LSU, 13-17 on Nov. 6, 1993
Most Consecutive Winning Seasons	38	1911-50 (no team, 1943)
Most Consecutive Bowl Appearances	25	1959-83
Most Points in a Game	110	vs. Marion Institute, Sept. 30, 1922
Most Points Allowed in a Game	78	vs. Vanderbilt, Oct. 20, 1906
Largest Margin of Victory	110	vs. Marion Institute, Sept. 30, 1922
Largest Margin of Defeat	78	vs. Vanderbilt, Oct. 20, 1906
Longest Pass Play	94	Freddie Kitchens to Michael Vaughn vs. Florida, Dec. 7, 1996
Longest Field Goal	57	Van Tiffin vs. Texas A & M, Sept. 14, 1985
Longest Punt	89	Dixie Howell vs. Tennessee, Oct. 21, 1933
Longest Interception Return	98	Mark McMillian vs. Tennessee-Chattanooga, Oct. 5, 1991

RETIRED NUMBERS

NO RETIRED JERSEYS

ALL-TIME TEAM

Fans selected the players prior to the 1992 season to commemorate the school's centennial season.

Offense			**Defense**		
	OL	Fred Sington, 1928-30		DL	Bob Baumhower, 1973-76
	OL	Vaughn Mancha, 1944-47		DL	Marty Lyons, 1975-78
	OL	Billy Neighbors, 1959-61		DL	Jon Hand, 1982-85
	OL	John Hannah, 1970-72		LB	Lee Roy Jordan, 1960-62
	C	Dwight Stephenson, 1977-79		LB	Barry Krauss, 1976-78
	TE	Ozzie Newsome, 1974-77		LB	Cornelius Bennett, 1983-86
	WR	Don Hutson, 1932-34		LB	Derrick Thomas, 1985-88
	QB	Kenny Stabler, 1965-67		DB	Harry Gilmer, 1944-47
	RB	Bobby Marlow, 1950-52		DB	Don McNeal, 1977-79
	RB	Johnny Musso, 1969-71		DB	Jeremiah Castille, 1979-82
	RB	Bobby Humphrey, 1985-88		DB	Tommy Wilcox, 1979-82
	K	Van Tiffen, 1983-85		P	Johnny Cain, 1930-32

ALABAMA BOWL HISTORY

SEASON	BOWL	DATE	PRE-GAME RANK	TEAMS	SCORE	FINAL RANK	MOST VALUABLE PLAYER(S)	ATT.
1925	ROSE	Jan. 1, 1926		Alabama Washington	20 19		Johnny Mack Brown, Alabama, HB George Wilson, Washington, HB	50,000
1926	ROSE	Jan. 1, 1927		Alabama Stanford	7 7		Fred Pickhard, Alabama, T	57,417
1930	ROSE	Jan. 1, 1931		Alabama Washington State	24 0		John "Monk" Campbell, Alabama, QB	60,000
1934	ROSE	Jan. 1, 1935		Alabama Stanford	29 13		Milliard "Dixie" Howell, Alabama, HB	84,474
1937	ROSE	Jan. 1, 1938		California Alabama	13 0		Victor Bottari, California, HB	90,000
1941	COTTON	Jan. 1, 1942		Alabama Texas A&M	29 21		Jimmy Nelson, HB, Holt Rast, E, Don Whitmire, T, Alabama Martin Ruby, Texas A&M, T	38,000
1942	ORANGE	Jan. 1, 1943	10 8	Alabama Boston College	37 21			25,166
1944	SUGAR	Jan. 1, 1945	11	Duke Alabama	29 26			66,822
1945	ROSE	Jan. 1, 1946		Alabama Southern California	34 14		Harry Gilmer, Alabama, HB	93,000
1947	SUGAR	Jan. 1, 1948		Texas Alabama	27 7		Bobby Layne, Texas, QB	31,535
1952	ORANGE	Jan. 1, 1953		Alabama Syracuse	61 6			66,280
1953	COTTON	Jan. 1, 1954		Rice Alabama	28 6		R. Chapman, T; D. Hart, E; D. Meagle, HB, Rice	75,504
1959	LIBERTY	Dec. 19, 1959	12 10	Penn State Alabama	7 0		Jay Huffman, Penn State, C	36,211
1960	BLUEBONNET	Dec. 17, 1960		Alabama Texas	3 3		Lee Roy Jordan, Alabama, LB James Saxton, Texas, QB	68,000
1961	SUGAR	Jan. 1, 1962	1 9	Alabama Arkansas	10 3		Mike Fracchia, Alabama, FB	81,141
1962	ORANGE	Jan. 1, 1963	5 8	Alabama Oklahoma	17 0			72,880
1963	SUGAR	Jan. 1, 1964	8 7	Alabama Mississippi	12 7		Tim Davis, Alabama, K	82,910
1964	ORANGE	Jan. 1, 1965	5 1	Texas Alabama	21 17		Joe Namath, Alabama, QB	72,647
1965	ORANGE	Jan. 1, 1966	4 3	Alabama Nebraska	39 28	1 5	Steve Sloan, Alabama, QB	72,214
1966	SUGAR	Jan. 2, 1967	3 6	Alabama Nebraska	34 7		Kenny Stabler, Alabama, QB	60,322
1967	COTTON	Jan. 1, 1968	 9	Texas A&M Alabama	20 16		Grady Allen, DE, Edd Hargett, QB Bill Hobbs, LB, Texas A&M	75,504
1968	GATOR	Dec. 28, 1968	16 12	Missouri Alabama	35 10	9 17	Terry McMillian, Missouri, QB Mike Hall, Alabama, LB	68,011
1969	LIBERTY	Dec. 13, 1969		Colorado Alabama	47 33	16	Bob Anderson, Colorado, TB	50,042
1970	BLUEBONNET	Dec. 31, 1970	 20	Alabama Oklahoma	24 24	 20	Jeff Rouzie, Alabama, LB Greg Pruitt, Oklahoma, HB	53, 829
1971	ORANGE	Jan. 1, 1972	1 2	Nebraska Alabama	38 6	1 4	Jerry Tagge, Nebraska, QB Rich Glover, Nebraska, DG	78,151
1972	COTTON	Jan. 1, 1973	7 4	Texas Alabama	17 13	3 7	Randy Braband, Texas, LB Alan Lowry, Texas, QB	72,000
1973	SUGAR	Dec. 31, 1973	3 1	Notre Dame Alabama	24 23	1 4	Tom Clements, Notre Dame, QB	85,161
1974	ORANGE	Jan. 1, 1975	9 2	Notre Dame Alabama	13 11	6 5	Wayne Bullock, Notre Dame, FB Leroy Cook, Alabama, DE	71,801
1975	SUGAR	Dec. 31, 1975	4 8	Alabama Penn State	13 6	3 10	Richard Todd, Alabama, QB	74,331
1976	LIBERTY	Dec. 20, 1976	16 7	Alabama UCLA	36 6	11 15	Barry Krauss, Alabama, LB	52,736
1977	SUGAR	Jan. 2, 1978	3 9	Alabama Ohio State	35 6	2 11	Jeff Rutledge, Alabama, QB	76,811
1978	SUGAR	Jan. 1, 1979	2 1	Alabama Penn State	14 7	1 4	Barry Krauss, Alabama, LB	76,824
1979	SUGAR	Jan. 1, 1980	2 6	Alabama Arkansas	24 9	1 8	Major Ogilvie, Alabama, RB	77,484
1980	COTTON	Jan. 1, 1981	9 6	Alabama Baylor	30 2	6 14	Warren Lyles, Alabama, NG Major Ogilvie, Alabama, RB	74,281
1981	COTTON	Jan. 1, 1982	6 3	Texas Alabama	14 12	2 7	Robert Brewer, Texas, QB Robbie Jones, Alabama, LB	73,243
1982	LIBERTY	Dec. 29, 1982		Alabama Illinois	21 15		Jeremiah Castille, Alabama, DB	54,123
1983	SUN	Dec. 24, 1983	 6	Alabama SMU	28 7	15 12	Walter Lewis, Alabama, QB Wes Neighbors, Alabama, C	41,412
1985	ALOHA	Dec. 28, 1985	15	Alabama Southern California	24 3	13	Gene Jelks, Alabama, RB Cornelius Bennett, Alabama, LB	35,183
1986	SUN	Dec. 25, 1986	13 12	Alabama Washington	28 6	9 18	Cornelius Bennett, Alabama, LB Steve Alvord, Washington, MG	48,722
1987	HALL OF FAME	Jan. 2, 1988		Michigan Alabama	28 24	19	Jamie Morris, Michigan, TB Bobby Humphrey, Alabama, TB	60,156
1988	SUN	Dec. 30, 1988	20	Alabama Army	29 28	17	David Smith, Alabama, QB Derrick Thomas, Alabama, LB	48,719
1989	SUGAR	Jan. 1, 1990	2 7	Miami (Fla.) Alabama	33 25	1 9	Craig Erickson, Miami (Fla.), QB	77,452
1990	FIESTA	Jan. 1, 1991	18 25	Louisville Alabama	34 7	14	Browning Nagle, Louisville, QB Ray Buchanan, Louisville, FS	69,098
1991	BLOCKBUSTER	Dec. 28, 1991	8 15	Alabama Colorado	30 25	5 20	David Palmer, Alabama, WR	46,123

SEASON	BOWL	DATE	PRE-GAME RANK	TEAMS	SCORE	FINAL RANK	MOST VALUABLE PLAYER(S)	ATT.
1992	SUGAR	Jan. 1, 1993	2 1	Alabama Miami (Fla.)	34 13	1 3	Derrick Lassic, Alabama, RB	76,789
1993	GATOR	Dec. 31, 1993	18 12	Alabama North Carolina	24 10	14 19	Brian Burgdorf, Alabama, QB Corey Holliday, North Carolina, WR	67,205
1994	CITRUS	Jan. 2, 1995	6 13	Alabama Ohio State	24 17	5 14	Sherman Williams, Alabama, RB	71,195
1996	OUTBACK	Jan. 1, 1997	16 15	Alabama Michigan	17 14	11 20	Dwayne Ruud, Alabama, LB	53,161
1998	MUSIC CITY	Dec. 29, 1998		Virginia Tech Alabama	38 7	23	Corey Moore, Virginia Tech, DE	41,248
1999	ORANGE	Jan. 1, 2000	8 5	Michigan Alabama	35 34	5 8	David Terrell, Michigan, WR	70,461
2001	INDEPENDENCE	Dec. 27, 2001		Alabama Iowa State	14 13		Waine Bacon, Alabama, S Seneca Wallace, QB, Matt Word, LB, Iowa St.	45,627
2004	MUSIC CITY	Dec. 31, 2004		Minnesota Alabama	20 16		Marion Barber, Minnesota, RB	66,089
2005	COTTON	Jan. 2, 2006	13 18	Alabama Texas Tech	13 10	8 20	Brodie Croyle, Alabama, QB DeMeco Ryans, Alabama, LB	74222
2006	INDEPENDENCE	Dec. 28, 2006		Oklahoma State Alabama	34 31		Dantrell Savage, Oklahoma St., TB Jeremy Nethon, Oklahoma St., LB	45054
2007	INDEPENDENCE	Dec. 28, 2007		Alabama Colorado	30 24		John Parker Wilson, Alabama, QB Wallace Gilberry, Alabama , DE	47043
2008	SUGAR	Jan. 2, 2009	4 7	Alabama Utah	17 31	6 2	Brian Johnson, Utah, QB	71872

JANUARY 1, 1926 | ROSE
ALABAMA 20, WASHINGTON 19

	1ST	2ND	3RD	4TH	FINAL
ALA	0	0	20	0	20
WASH	6	6	0	7	19

SCORING SUMMARY
WASH   Paton 1 run (kick failed)
WASH   Cole 20 pass from Wilson (kick failed)
ALA   Hubert 8 run (Buckler kick)
ALA   Brown 61 pass from Hubert (Buckler kick)
ALA   Brown 5 run (kick failed)
WASH   Guttormsen 27 pass from Wilson (Cook kick)

ALA	TEAM STATISTICS	WASH
15	First Downs	13
220	Rushing Yards	220
4-14-3	Passing	7-16-2
141	Passing Yards	94
361	Total Yards	314
5-40.8	Punts - Average	6-37.5
0-0	Fumbles - Lost	1-1
0-0	Penalties - Yards	1-15

INDIVIDUAL LEADERS
RUSHING
ALA: Hubert 15-97, 1 TD; Brown 12-76, 1 TD.
WASH: Wilson 15-139; Paton 11-43, 1 TD.

JANUARY 1, 1927 | ROSE
ALABAMA 7, STANFORD 7

	1ST	2ND	3RD	4TH	FINAL
ALA	0	0	0	7	7
STAN	7	0	0	0	7

SCORING SUMMARY
STAN   Walker 20 pass from Bogue (Bogue kick)
ALA   Johnson 1 run (Caldwell kick)

ALA	TEAM STATISTICS	STAN
6	First Downs	12
83	Rushing Yards	134
6-14-2	Passing	13-17-1
9	Passing Yards	177
92	Total Yards	311
8-32.6	Punts - Average	6-32.2
2	Fumbles Lost	3
5	Penalty Yards	55

JANUARY 1, 1931 | ROSE
ALABAMA 24, WASHINGTON STATE 0

	1ST	2ND	3RD	4TH	FINAL
ALA	0	21	3	0	24
WSU	0	0	0	0	0

SCORING SUMMARY
ALA   Suther 62 pass from Moore (Campbell kick)
ALA   Campbell 1 run (Campbell kick)
ALA   Campbell 43 run (Campbell kick)
ALA   FG Whitworth 40

ALA	TEAM STATISTICS	WSU
9	First Downs	11
261	Rushing Yards	145
2-7-0	Passing	7-17-3
98	Passing Yards	71
359	Total Yards	216
11-40.1	Punts - Average	12-37.0
2-1	Fumbles - Lost	3-2

INDIVIDUAL LEADERS
RUSHING
ALA: Campbell 12-109, 2 TD; Holley 6-45.
WSU: Lainhart 7-70; Schwartz 12-42.

JANUARY 1, 1935 | ROSE
ALABAMA 29, STANFORD 13

	1ST	2ND	3RD	4TH	FINAL
STAN	7	0	6	0	13
ALA	0	22	0	7	29

SCORING SUMMARY
STAN   Grayson 1 run (Moscrip kick)
ALA   Howell 5 run (kick failed)
ALA   FG Smith 27
ALA   Howell 67 run (Smith kick)
ALA   Huston 46 pass from Riley (kick failed)
STAN   VanDellen 12 run
ALA   Huston 59 pass from Howell (Smith good)

STAN	TEAM STATISTICS	ALA
14	First Downs	12
204	Rushing Yards	167
5-23-4	Passing	10-13-1
86	Passing Yards	216
290	Total Yards	383
6-38.0	Punts - Average	6-44.0
0	Fumbles Lost	4
4-40	Penalties - Yards	4-40

JANUARY 1, 1938 | ROSE
CALIFORNIA 13, ALABAMA 0

	1ST	2ND	3RD	4TH	FINAL
CAL	0	7	6	0	13
ALA	0	0	0	0	0

SCORING SUMMARY
CAL   Bottari 3 run (Chapman kick)
CAL   Bottari 4 run (kick failed)

CAL	TEAM STATISTICS	ALA
10	First Downs	11
192	Rushing Yards	140
2-9-2	Passing	3-12-4
16	Passing Yards	40
208	Total Yards	180

INDIVIDUAL LEADERS
RUSHING
CAL: Bottari 32-146, 2 TD; Chapman 12-65.
ALA: Holm 14-60; Kilgrow 16-50.

JANUARY 1, 1942 | COTTON
ALABAMA 29, TEXAS A&M 21

	1ST	2ND	3RD	4TH	FINAL
ALA	0	7	13	9	29
A&M	0	7	0	14	21

SCORING SUMMARY
A&M   Cowley 12 pass from Daniels (Webster kick)
ALA   Craft 8 run (Hecht kick)
ALA   Nelson 72 punt return (kick blocked)
ALA   Nelson 21 run (Hecht kick)
ALA   FG Hecht 31
ALA   Rast 10 interception return (kick failed)
A&M   Webster 1 run (Webster kick)
A&M   Sterling 35 pass from Moser (Webster kick)

ALA	TEAM STATISTICS	A&M
1	First Downs	13
59	Rushing Yards	115
1-7-0	Passing	14-41-7
16	Passing Yards	194
75	Total Yards	309
16-36.3	Punts - Average	7-36.4
2-1	Fumbles - Lost	6-5
8-81	Penalties - Yards	1-5

INDIVIDUAL LEADERS
RUSHING
ALA: Nelson 9-38, 1 TD; Hughes 3-6.
A&M: Webster 12-52, 1 TD; Moser 16-31.
PASSING
ALA: Nelson 1-7-0, 16 yards.
A&M: Daniels 6-19-2, 87 yards, 1 TD; Moser 5-23-4, 107 yards, 1 TD.
RECEIVING
ALA: Rast 1-16.
A&M: Sterling 5-112, 1 TD; Cowley 4-39, 1 TD.

JANUARY 1, 1943 | ORANGE
ALABAMA 37, BOSTON COLLEGE 21

	1ST	2ND	3RD	4TH	FINAL
ALA	0	22	6	9	37
BC	14	7	0	0	21

SCORING SUMMARY

BC	Holovak 65 run (Connolly kick)
BC	Holovak 35 run (Connolly kick)
ALA	Leeth 14 pass from Mosley (Hecht kick)
ALA	Cook 18 pass from August (kick failed)
ALA	Jenkins 40 run (kick failed)
BC	Holovak 2 run (Connolly kick)
ALA	FG Hecht 25
ALA	August 15 run (kick failed)
ALA	Jenkins 1 run (Hecht kick)
ALA	Safety

ALA	TEAM STATISTICS	BC
13	First Downs	13
244	Rushing Yards	202
9-15-2	Passing	11-20-1
97	Passing Yards	170
341	Total Yards	372
5-39.0	Punts - Average	4-33.7
1-0	Fumbles - Lost	5-2
4-20	Penalties - Yards	3-11

JANUARY 1, 1945 | SUGAR
DUKE 29, ALABAMA 26

	1ST	2ND	3RD	4TH	FINAL
DUKE	7	6	7	9	29
ALA	12	7	0	7	26

SCORING SUMMARY

DUKE	Clark 15 run (Raether kick)
ALA	Hodges 1 run (kick failed)
ALA	Hodges 2 run (kick failed)
ALA	Jones 13 pass from Gilmer (Morrow kick)
DUKE	Davis 1 run (kick failed)
DUKE	Davis 1 run (Raether kick)
ALA	Morrow 80 interception (Morrow kick)
DUKE	Safety
DUKE	Clark 20 run (Raether kick)

DUKE	TEAM STATISTICS	ALA
19	First Downs	8
336	Rushing Yards	102
5-8-1	Passing	8-8-0
47	Passing Yards	142
383	Total Yards	244
4-34.0	Punts - Average	5-35.0
6-1	Fumbles - Lost	1-1
1-5	Penalties - Yards	2-6

INDIVIDUAL LEADERS

RUSHING
DUKE : Clark 14-123, 2 TD; Davis 27-101, 2 TD.
ALA: Gilmer 14-63; Hodges 8-29, 2 TD.

PASSING
DUKE: Lewis 4-7-1, 40 yards.
ALA: Gilmer 8-8-0, 142 yards, 1 TD.

RECEIVING
DUKE: Carver 4-35.
ALA: Jones 4-136, 1 TD.

JANUARY 1, 1946 | ROSE
ALABAMA 34, SOUTHERN CALIFORNIA 14

	1ST	2ND	3RD	4TH	FINAL
ALA	7	13	7	7	34
USC	0	0	0	14	14

ALA	TEAM STATISTICS	USC
18	First Downs	3
292	Rushing Yards	6
4-12-1	Passing	2-11-2
59	Passing Yards	35
351	Total Yards	41
4-19.5	Punts - Average	6-48.0
3-1	Fumbles - Lost	6-3
5-35	Penalties - Yards	3-15

INDIVIDUAL LEADERS

RUSHING
ALA: Gilmer 16-116, 1 TD; Corbitt 8-48.
USC: Tannehill 7-15; Morris 5-8.

PASSING
ALA: Gilmer 4-12-1, 59 yards.
USC: Lillywhite 1-6-1, 20 yards, 1 TD.

JANUARY 1, 1948 | SUGAR
TEXAS 27, ALABAMA 7

	1ST	2ND	3RD	4TH	FINAL
TEX	7	0	7	13	27
ALA	0	7	0	0	7

SCORING SUMMARY

TEX	Blount 5 pass from Layne (Guess kick)
ALA	White 8 pass from Gilmer (Morrow kick)
TEX	Vasicek fumble recovery (Guess kick)
TEX	Holder 18 interception return (Guess kick)
TEX	Layne 1 run (kick failed)

JANUARY 1, 1953 | ORANGE
ALABAMA 61, SYRACUSE 6

	1ST	2ND	3RD	4TH	FINAL
ALA	7	14	20	20	61
SYR	6	0	0	0	6

SCORING SUMMARY

ALA	Luna 28 pass from Hobson (Luna kick)
SYR	Szombathy 15 pass from Stark (kick failed)
ALA	Marlow 2 run (Luna kick)
ALA	Tharp 50 pass from Hobson (Luna kick)
ALA	Luna 38 run (Luna kick)
ALA	Lewis 4 run (Luna kick)
ALA	Lewis 30 run (kick failed)
ALA	Cummings 22 pass from Starr (kick failed)
ALA	Ingram 80 punt return (Luna kick)
ALA	Hill 60 interception return (Luna kick)

ALA	TEAM STATISTICS	SYR
25	First Downs	15
286	Rushing Yards	75
22-34-2	Passing	17-34-5
300	Passing Yards	157
586	Total Yards	232
3-30.0	Punts - Average	8-35.0
3-2	Fumbles - Lost	0-0
5-45	Penalties - Yards	5-42

INDIVIDUAL LEADERS

RUSHING
ALA: Lewis 11-77, 2 TD; Tharp 11-62, 1 TD; Luna 4-51, 1 TD.
SYR: Leberman 14-36.

PASSING
ALA: Hobson 14-22-2, 207 yards, 2 TD; Starr 8-12-0, 93 yards, 1 TD.
SYR: Stark 17-33-4, 157 yards, 1 TD.

RECEIVING
ALA: Curtis 8-65; Cummings 2-61, 1 TD.
SYR: Szombathy 5-45, 1 TD; Hoffman 5-43.

JANUARY 1, 1954 | COTTON
RICE 28, ALABAMA 6

	1ST	2ND	3RD	4TH	FINAL
ALA	6	0	0	0	6
RICE	0	14	7	7	28

SCORING SUMMARY

ALA	Lewis 1 run (kick blocked)
RICE	Maegle 79 run (Fenstemaker kick)
RICE	Maegle awarded 95 run after bench tackle by Lewis
RICE	Maegle 34 run (Fenstemaker kick)
RICE	Grantham 7 run (Burk kick)

ALA	TEAM STATISTICS	RICE
11	First Downs	14
188	Rushing Yards	379
7-16-0	Passing	4-10-2
67	Passing Yards	59
255	Total Yards	438
7-42.7	Punts - Average	8-25.1
4-4	Fumbles - Lost	1-0
6-65	Penalties - Yards	8-89

INDIVIDUAL LEADERS

RUSHING
ALA: Oliver 2-56; Starr 11-54.
RICE: Maegle 11-265, 3 TD; Kellogg 14-32.

PASSING
ALA: Starr 7-16-0, 67 yards.
RICE: Grantham 3-5-0, 43 yards.

RECEIVING
ALA: Cummings 2-37; Stone 2-20.
RICE: Holland-2-28; Bridges 1-16.

DECEMBER 19, 1959 | LIBERTY
PENN STATE 7, ALABAMA 0

	1ST	2ND	3RD	4TH	FINAL
PSU	0	7	0	0	7
ALA	0	0	0	0	0

SCORING SUMMARY

PSU	Kochman 18 pass from Hall (Stellatella kick)

PSU	TEAM STATISTICS	ALA
18	First Downs	8
278	Rushing Yards	104
2-10-0	Passing	2-8-0
41	Passing Yards	27
319	Total Yards	131
6-29.0	Punts - Average	8-34.4
4-4	Fumbles - Lost	7-4
4-45	Penalties - Yards	3-45

INDIVIDUAL LEADERS

RUSHING
PSU: Lucas 9-54.
ALA: Trammell 13-37.

PASSING
PSU: Lucas 1-4-0, 23 yards; Hall 1-6-0, 18 yards, 1 TD.
ALA: Trammell 1-4-0, 20 yards.

DECEMBER 17, 1960 | BLUEBONNET
ALABAMA 3, TEXAS 3

	1ST	2ND	3RD	4TH	FINAL
ALA	0	0	3	0	3
TEX	0	0	0	3	3

SCORING SUMMARY

ALA	FG Brooker 30
TEX	FG Petty 20

ALA	TEAM STATISTICS	TEX
4	First Downs	11
65	Rushing Yards	124
8-14-0	Passing	7-17-1
90	Passing Yards	108
155	Total Yards	232
7-40.4	Punts - Average	8-39.8
1-1	Fumbles - Lost	1-0
2-49	Penalties - Yards	2-20

INDIVIDUAL LEADERS

RUSHING
ALA: Trammell 9-29; Fracchia 6-20.
TEX: Poage 14-56; Saxton 13-48.

PASSING
ALA: Skelton 8-12-0, 90 yards.
TEX: Cotten 5-11-1, 79 yards; Collins 2-4-0, 39 yards.

RECEIVING
ALA: Rice 1-49; Abruzzese 3-15.
TEX: Collins 4-41; Saxton 1-38.

JANUARY 1, 1962 | SUGAR
ALABAMA 10, ARKANSAS 3

	1ST	2ND	3RD	4TH	FINAL
ALA	7	3	0	0	10
ARK	0	0	3	0	3

SCORING SUMMARY

ALA	Trammell 12 run (Davis kick)
ALA	FG Davis 32
ARK	FG Cissell 23

JANUARY 1, 1963 | ORANGE
ALABAMA 17, OKLAHOMA 0

	1ST	2ND	3RD	4TH	FINAL
ALA	7	7	3	0	17
OKLA	0	0	0	0	0

SCORING SUMMARY

ALA	Williamson 25 pass from Namath (Davis kick)
ALA	Clark 15 run (Davis kick)
ALA	FG Davis 19

ALA	TEAM STATISTICS	OKLA
15	First Downs	10
174	Rushing Yards	154
9-17-1	Passing	4-8-0
86	Passing Yards	106
260	Total Yards	260
8-40.5	Punts - Average	10-34.0
1-1	Fumbles - Lost	2-2
1-12	Penalties - Yards	1-5

INDIVIDUAL LEADERS

RUSHING
ALA: Versprille 14-52.
OKLA: Grisham 28-107.

PASSING
ALA: Namath 9-17-1, 86 yards, 1 TD.
OKLA: Fletcher 1-1-0, 56 yards.

RECEIVING
ALA: Williamson 4-58, 1 TD.
OKLA: Bumgardner 1-56.

JANUARY 1, 1964 | Sugar
ALABAMA 12, MISSISSIPPI 7

	1ST	2ND	3RD	4TH	FINAL
ALA	3	6	3	0	12
MISS	0	0	0	7	7

SCORING SUMMARY
ALA   FG Davis 46
ALA   FG Davis 31
ALA   FG Davis 34
ALA   FG Davis 48
MISS   Smith 5 pass from Dunn (Irwin kick)

ALA	TEAM STATISTICS	MISS
14	First Downs	9
165	Rushing Yards	77
3-11-1	Passing	11-21-3
29	Passing Yards	171
194	Total Yards	248
5-36.8	Punts - Average	4-44.0
6-3	Fumbles - Lost	11-6
3-15	Penalties - Yards	5-45

INDIVIDUAL LEADERS
RUSHING
ALA: Sloan 16-51; Nelson 16-47.
MISS: Dennis 7-37; Dunn 6-24.
PASSING
ALA: Sloan 3-10-1, 29 yards.
MISS: Dunn 8-10-0, 125 yards, 1 TD.
RECEIVING
ALA: Stephens 1-15.
MISS: Wells 4-76.

JANUARY 1, 1965 | Orange
TEXAS 21, ALABAMA 17

	1ST	2ND	3RD	4TH	FINAL
TEX	7	14	0	0	21
ALA	0	7	7	3	17

SCORING SUMMARY
TEX   Koy 79 run (Conway kick)
TEX   Sauer 69 pass from Hudson (Conway kick)
ALA   Trimble 7 pass from Namath (Ray kick)
TEX   Koy 1 run (Conway kick)
ALA   Perkins 20 pass from Namath (Ray kick)
ALA   FG Ray 24

TEX	TEAM STATISTICS	ALA
15	First Downs	18
212	Rushing Yards	49
4-17-1	Passing	20-44-2
101	Passing Yards	298
313	Total Yards	347
9-36.8	Punts - Average	5-43.4
2-1	Fumbles - Lost	3-1
3-25	Penalties - Yards	4-46

INDIVIDUAL LEADERS
RUSHING
TEX: Koy 24-133, 2 TD; Philipp 10-44.
ALA: Bowman 10-23.
PASSING
TEX: Hudson 4-13-0, 101 yards, 1 TD.
ALA: Namath 18-37-2, 255 yards, 2 TD.
RECEIVING
TEX: Sauer 3-96, 1 TD.
ALA: Perkins 5-85, 1 TD; Ogden 3-69; Trimble 4-44, 1 TD.

JANUARY 1, 1966 | Orange
ALABAMA 39, NEBRASKA 28

	1ST	2ND	3RD	4TH	FINAL
ALA	7	17	8	7	39
NEB	0	7	6	15	28

SCORING SUMMARY
ALA   Perkins 32 pass from Sloan (Ray kick)
NEB   Jeter 33 pass from Churchich (Wachholtz kick)
ALA   Kelley 4 run (Ray kick)
ALA   Perkins 11 pass from Sloan (Ray kick)
ALA   FG Ray 18
NEB   Gregory 49 pass from Churchich (pass failed)
ALA   Bowman 1 run (Perkins pass from Sloan)
NEB   Churchich 1 run (Wachholtz kick)
ALA   Bowman 3 run (Ray kick)
NEB   Jeter 14 pass from Churchich (Gregory pass from Churchich)

ALA	TEAM STATISTICS	NEB
29	First Downs	17
222	Rushing Yards	145
20-29-2	Passing	12-19-1
296	Passing Yards	232
518	Total Yards	377
5-31.2	Punts - Average	3-41.7
0-0	Fumbles - Lost	4-4
8-62	Penalties - Yards	8-86

INDIVIDUAL LEADERS
RUSHING
ALA: Kelley 26-118, 1 TD; Bowman 21-85, 2 TD.
NEB: Kirkland 7-67.
PASSING
ALA: Sloan 20-28-1, 296 yards, 2 TD.
NEB: Churchich 12-17, 232 yards, 3 TD.
RECEIVING
ALA: Perkins 9-159, 2 TD.
NEB: Jeter 3-73, 2 TD.

JANUARY 2, 1967 | Sugar
ALABAMA 34, NEBRASKA 7

	1ST	2ND	3RD	4TH	FINAL
ALA	17	7	3	7	34
NEB	0	0	0	7	7

SCORING SUMMARY
ALA   Kelley 1 run (Davis kick)
ALA   Stabler 14 run (Davis kick)
ALA   FG Davis 30
ALA   Trimble 6 run (Davis kick)
ALA   FG Davis 40
NEB   Davis 15 pass from Churchich (Wachholtz kick)
ALA   Perkins 45 pass from Stabler (Davis kick)

ALA	TEAM STATISTICS	NEB
19	First Downs	16
157	Rushing Yards	84
15-26-1	Passing	22-38-5
279	Passing Yards	213
436	Total Yards	297

JANUARY 1, 1968 | Cotton
TEXAS A&M 20, ALABAMA 16

	1ST	2ND	3RD	4TH	FINAL
ALA	7	3	6	0	16
A&M	7	6	7	0	20

SCORING SUMMARY
ALA   Stabler 3 run (Davis kick)
A&M   Stegent 13 pass from Hargett (Riggs kick)
ALA   FG Davis 36
A&M   Maxwell 7 pass from Hargett (kick failed)
A&M   Housley 20 run (Riggs kick)
ALA   Stabler 2 run (run failed)

ALA	TEAM STATISTICS	A&M
14	First Downs	13
135	Rushing Yards	114
16-26-3	Passing	11-22-0
179	Passing Yards	143
314	Total Yards	257
6-37.5	Punts - Average	10-41.0
5-2	Fumbles - Lost	3-1
4-37	Penalties - Yards	7-83

INDIVIDUAL LEADERS
RUSHING
ALA: Chatwood 12-62; Martin 5-36.
A&M: Housley 10-59, 1 TD; Stegent 18-56.
PASSING
ALA: Stabler 16-26-3, 179 yards.
A&M: Hargett 11-22-0, 143 yards, 2 TD.
RECEIVING
ALA: Homan 6-90; Willis 4-39.
A&M: Stegent 4-51, 1 TD; Harris 2-38.

DECEMBER 28, 1968 | Gator
MISSOURI 35, ALABAMA 10

	1ST	2ND	3RD	4TH	FINAL
MO	7	7	0	21	35
ALA	0	7	0	3	10

SCORING SUMMARY
MO   McMillian 4 run (Sangster kick)
ALA   Sutton 38 interception return (Dean kick)
MO   McMillian 5 run (Sangster kick)
ALA   FG Dean 25
MO   McMillian 2 run (Sangster kick)
MO   Cook 37 run (Sangster kick)
MO   Poppe 47 interception return (Sangster kick)

MO	TEAM STATISTICS	ALA
21	First Downs	6
402	Rushing Yards	-45
0-6-2	Passing	7-27-2
0	Passing Yards	77
402	Total Yards	32
5-36.0	Punts - Average	10-42.0
4-2	Fumbles - Lost	1-0
5-29	Penalties - Yards	2-14

INDIVIDUAL LEADERS
RUSHING
MO: Cook 27-179, 1 TD; McMillian 18-76, 3 TD.
ALA: Jilleba 5-20; Moore 5-10.
PASSING
MO: McMillian 0-6-2, 0 yards.
ALA: Hunter 7-25-1, 68 yards.

DECEMBER 13, 1969 | Liberty
COLORADO 47, ALABAMA 33

	1ST	2ND	3RD	4TH	FINAL
COLO	10	21	7	9	47
ALA	0	19	14	0	33

SCORING SUMMARY
COLO   Walsh 13 run (Haney kick)
COLO   FG Haney 30
COLO   Anderson 3 run (Haney kick)
ALA   Hunter 31 run (Buck kick)
ALA   Ranager 6 run (pass failed)
COLO   Walsh 15 run (Haney kick)
ALA   Musso 2 run (pass failed)
COLO   Engel 91 kickoff return (Haney kick)
ALA   Langston 55 pass from Hayden (Buck kick)
ALA   Musso 10 pass from Hayden (Buck kick)
COLO   Anderson 2 run (Haney kick)
COLO   Safety (Hayden tackled in end zone)
COLO   Anderson 3 run (Haney kick)

COLO	TEAM STATISTICS	ALA
29	First Downs	24
473	Rushing Yards	155
6-16-3	Passing	14-34-0
212	Passing Yards	90
685	Total Yards	245
2-37.5	Punts - Average	7-41
18	Return Yards	5
3-2	Fumbles - Lost	2-0
8-94	Penalties - Yards	2-24
30:57	Possession Time	29:03

INDIVIDUAL LEADERS
RUSHING
COLO: Anderson 13-254, 3 TD; Bratten 19-111.
ALA: Musso 23-107, 1 TD.
PASSING
COLO: Bratten 3-11-3, 49 yards; Anderson 3-4-0, 41 yards.
ALA: Hayden 8-21-0, 164 yards, 2 TD; Hunter 6-13-0, 48 yards.
RECEIVING
COLO: Masten 2-35; Dal Porto 2-29.
ALA: Bailey 3-43; Musso 3-22, 1 TD.

December 31, 1970 | Bluebonnet
Alabama 24, Oklahoma 24

	1st	2nd	3rd	4th	Final
ALA	7	7	3	7	24
OKLA	7	14	0	3	24

SCORING SUMMARY

OKLA	Pruitt 58 run (Derr kick)
ALA	Moore 4 pass from Hunter (Clemmy kick)
OKLA	Pruitt 25 run (Derr kick)
ALA	Bailey 5 pass from Hunter (Clemmy kick)
OKLA	Wylie 2 run (Derr kick)
ALA	FG Clemmy 21
ALA	Hunter 25 pass from Musso (Clemmy kick)
OKLA	FG Derr 42

ALA	TEAM STATISTICS	OKLA
21	First Downs	19
229	Rushing Yards	349
14-27-0	Passing	5-7-0
199	Passing Yards	66
428	Total Yards	415
4-37.0	Punts - Average	5-37.0
2-1	Fumbles - Lost	3-2
7-50	Penalties - Yards	3-42

INDIVIDUAL LEADERS

RUSHING
ALA: Musso 27-138.
OKLA: Crosswhite 20-111.

PASSING
ALA: Hunter 13-26-1, 174 yards, 2 TD.
OKLA: Mildren 5-7-0, 66 yards.

RECEIVING
ALA: Bailey 4-86, 1 TD.
OKLA: Harrison 2-45.

January 1, 1972 | Orange
Nebraska 38, Alabama 6

	1st	2nd	3rd	4th	Final
NEB	14	14	3	7	38
ALA	0	0	6	0	6

SCORING SUMMARY

NEB	Kinney 2 run (kick failed)
NEB	Rodgers 77 punt return (Damkroger pass from Tagge)
NEB	Tagge 1 run (Sanger kick)
NEB	Dixon 2 run (Sanger kick)
ALA	Davis 3 run (run failed)
NEB	FG Sanger 21
NEB	Van Brownson 1 run (Sanger kick)

NEB	TEAM STATISTICS	ALA
15	First Downs	16
183	Rushing Yards	241
11-20-0	Passing	3-13-2
159	Passing Yards	47
342	Total Yards	288
5-42.2	Punts - Average	7-43.3
3-2	Fumbles - Lost	5-2
4-50	Penalties - Yards	4-58

INDIVIDUAL LEADERS

RUSHING
NEB: Kinney 20-99, 1 TD.
ALA: Musso 15-79.

PASSING
NEB: Tagge 11-19-0, 159 yards.
ALA: Davis 3-9, 47 yards.

RECEIVING
NEB: Rodgers 4-84.
ALA: Wheeler 2-22.

January 1, 1973 | Cotton
Texas 17, Alabama 13

	1st	2nd	3rd	4th	Final
ALA	10	3	0	0	13
TEX	0	3	7	7	17

SCORING SUMMARY

ALA	FG Gantt 50
ALA	Jackson 31 run (Davis kick)
TEX	FG Schott 24
ALA	FG Davis 30
TEX	Lowry 3 run (Schott kick)
TEX	Lowry 34 run (Schott kick)

ALA	TEAM STATISTICS	TEX
15	First Downs	20
138	Rushing Yards	317
11-18-2	Passing	5-11-2
186	Passing Yards	61
324	Total Yards	378
5-29.4	Punts - Average	2-44.0
1-0	Fumbles - Lost	0-0
4-30	Penalties - Yards	0-0

INDIVIDUAL LEADERS

RUSHING
ALA: Jackson 10-64, 1 TD; Bisceglia 11-30.
TEX: Leaks 15-120; Lowry 16-117, 2 TD.

PASSING
ALA: Davis 10-17-2, 174 yards.
TEX: Lowry 5-11-2, 61 yards.

RECEIVING
ALA: Wood 5-81; Wheeler 2-57.
TEX: Moore 2-24; Kelly 1-20.

December 31, 1973 | Sugar
Notre Dame 24, Alabama 23

	1st	2nd	3rd	4th	Final
ND	6	8	7	3	24
ALA	0	10	7	6	23

SCORING SUMMARY

ND	Bullock 6 run (kick failed)
ALA	Billingsley 6 run (Davis kick)
ND	Hunter 93 kickoff return (Demmerle pass from Clements)
ALA	FG Davis 39
ALA	Jackson 5 run (Davis kick)
ND	Penick 12 run (Thomas kick)
ALA	Todd 25 pass from Stock (kick failed)
ND	FG Thomas 19

ND	TEAM STATISTICS	ALA
20	First Downs	23
252	Rushing Yards	190
7-12-0	Passing	10-15-1
169	Passing Yards	127
421	Total Yards	317
7-35.8	Punts - Average	6-46.3
4-3	Fumbles - Lost	5-2
5-45	Penalties - Yards	3-32

INDIVIDUAL LEADERS

RUSHING
ND: Bullock 19-79, 1 TD; Clements 15-74.
ALA: Jackson 11-62, 1 TD; Billingsley 7-54, 1 TD.

PASSING
ND: Clements 7-12-0, 169 yards.
ALA: Rutledge 7-12-1, 88 yards.

RECEIVING
ND: Casper 3-75; Demmerle 3-59.
ALA: Pugh 2-28; Jackson 2-22.

January 1, 1975 | Orange
Notre Dame 13, Alabama 11

	1st	2nd	3rd	4th	Final
ND	7	6	0	0	13
ALA	0	0	3	8	11

SCORING SUMMARY

ND	Bullock 4 run (Reeve kick)
ND	McLane 9 run (kick failed)
ALA	FG Ridgeway 21
ALA	Schamun 48 pass from Todd (Pugh pass from Todd)

ND	TEAM STATISTICS	ALA
15	First Downs	14
185	Rushing Yards	62
4-8-2	Passing	15-29-2
19	Passing Yards	223
204	Total Yards	285
0-0	Punt Returns - Yards	5-34
3-54	Kickoff Returns - Yards	2-32
6-38.0	Punts - Average	7-40.0
1-1	Fumbles - Lost	5-2
1-15	Penalties - Yards	1-5

INDIVIDUAL LEADERS

RUSHING
ND: Bullock 24-83, 1 TD; McLane 8-30, 1 TD.
ALA: Culliver 11-60.

PASSING
ND: Clements 4-7-1, 19 yards.
ALA: Todd 13-24-2, 194 yards, 1 TD.

RECEIVING
ND: Demmerle 2-12.
ALA: Schamun 5-126, 1 TD; Newsome 6-68.

December 31, 1975 | Sugar
Alabama 13, Penn State 6

	1st	2nd	3rd	4th	Final
ALA	3	0	7	3	13
PSU	0	0	3	3	6

SCORING SUMMARY

ALA	FG Ridgeway 25
PSU	FG Bahr 42
ALA	Stock 14 run (Ridgeway kick)
PSU	FG Bahr 37
ALA	FG Ridgeway 28

ALA	TEAM STATISTICS	PSU
14	First Downs	12
106	Rushing Yards	157
10-12-0	Passing	8-14-1
210	Passing Yards	57
316	Total Yards	214
5-40.8	Punts - Average	4-48.5
1-0	Fumbles - Lost	1-0
3-22	Penalties - Yards	0

INDIVIDUAL LEADERS

RUSHING
ALA: Shelby 8-45; Davis 12-32.
PSU: Geise 8-46; Taylor 12-36.

PASSING
ALA: Todd 10-12-0, 210 yards.
PSU: Andress 8-14-1, 57 yards.

RECEIVING
ALA: Newsome 4-97; Harris 2-69.
PSU: Cefalo 2-18; Petchel 2-13.

December 20, 1976 | Liberty
Alabama 36, UCLA 6

	1st	2nd	3rd	4th	Final
ALA	17	7	3	9	36
UCLA	0	0	0	6	6

SCORING SUMMARY
ALA FG Berrey 37
ALA Krauss 44 interception return (Berrey kick)
ALA Davis 2 run (Berrey kick)
ALA O'Rear 20 pass from Nathan (Berrey kick)
ALA FG Berrey 25
ALA FG Berrey 28
UCLA Brown 61 run (kick failed)
ALA Watson 1 run (pass failed)

ALA	TEAM STATISTICS	UCLA
23	First Downs	17
268	Rushing Yards	233
8-11-0	Passing	10-18-3
104	Passing Yards	147
372	Total Yards	380

INDIVIDUAL LEADERS
RUSHING
ALA: Nathan 9-67; Davis 11-59, 1 TD.
UCLA: Brown 16-102, 1 TD; Tyler 17-59.
PASSING
ALA: Rutledge 6-7-0, 53 yards.
UCLA: Dankworth 10-17-3, 147 yards.
RECEIVING
ALA: Neal 2-45.
UCLA: Walker 2-44; Brown 3-24.

January 2, 1978 | Sugar
Alabama 35, Ohio State 6

	1st	2nd	3rd	4th	Final
ALA	0	13	8	14	35
OSU	0	0	0	6	6

SCORING SUMMARY
ALA Nathan 1 run (Chapman kick)
ALA Bolton 27 pass from Rutledge (kick failed)
ALA Neal 3 pass from Rutledge
     (Nathan pass from Rutledge)
OSU Harrell 38 pass from Gerald (run failed)
ALA Ogilvie 1 run (Chapman kick)
ALA Davis 5 run (Chapman kick)

ALA	TEAM STATISTICS	OSU
25	First Downs	13
286	Rushing Yards	179
8-11-0	Passing	7-17-3
109	Passing Yards	103
395	Total Yards	282
1-33.0	Punts - Average	4-37.5
1-5	Penalties - Yards	4-40

INDIVIDUAL LEADERS
RUSHING
ALA: Davis 24-95, 1 TD; Crow 5-46.
OSU: Springs 10-74; Logan 13-57.
PASSING
ALA: Rutledge 8-11-0, 109 yards, 2 TD.
OSU: Gerald 7-17-3, 103 yards, 1 TD.
RECEIVING
ALA: Newsom 2-45; Ferguson 2-28.
OSU: Hunter 2-25; Springs 2-6.

January 1, 1979 | Sugar
Alabama 14, Penn State 7

	1st	2nd	3rd	4th	Final
ALA	0	7	7	0	14
PSU	0	0	7	0	7

SCORING SUMMARY
ALA Bolton 30 pass from Rutledge (McElroy kick)
PSU Fitzkee 17 pass from Fusina (Bahr kick)
ALA Ogilvie 8 run (McElroy kick)

ALA	TEAM STATISTICS	PSU
12	First Downs	12
208	Rushing Yards	19
8-15-2	Passing	15-30-4
91	Passing Yards	163
299	Total Yards	182
10-38.8	Punts - Average	10-38.7
2-1	Fumbles - Lost	2-0
11-75	Penalties - Yards	8-51

INDIVIDUAL LEADERS
RUSHING
ALA: Nathan 21-127; Whitman 11-51.
PSU: Suhey 10-48; Guman 9-22.
PASSING
ALA: Rutledge 8-15-2, 91 yards, 1 TD.
PSU: Fusina 15-30-4, 163 yards, 1 TD.
RECEIVING
ALA: Bolton 2-46, 1 TD; Whitman 2-27.
PSU: Guman 5-59; Fitzkee 3-38, 1 TD.

January 1, 1980 | Sugar
Alabama 24, Arkansas 9

	1st	2nd	3rd	4th	Final
ALA	14	3	0	7	24
ARK	3	0	6	0	9

SCORING SUMMARY
ARK FG Ordonez 34
ALA Ogilvie 22 run (McElroy kick)
ALA Ogilvie 1 run (McElroy kick)
ALA FG McElroy 25
ARK Farrell 3 pass from Scanlon (run failed)
ALA Whitman 12 run (McElroy kick)

ALA	TEAM STATISTICS	ARK
18	First Downs	21
284	Rushing Yards	97
4-7-2	Passing	22-40-2
70	Passing Yards	245
354	Total Yards	342
8-36.2	Punts - Average	7-36.2
7-61	Penalties - Yards	1-15

INDIVIDUAL LEADERS
RUSHING
ALA: Jackson 13-120; Ogilvie 14-67, 2 TD; Whitman 6-37, 1 TD.
ARK: Bowles 15-46; Anderson 6-28.
PASSING
ALA: Shealy 4-7-0, 70 yards.
ARK: Scanlon 22-39-1, 245 yards, 1 TD.
RECEIVING
ALA: Jackson 3-62.
ARK: Anderson 7-53; Farrell 3-51, 1 TD.

January 1, 1981 | Cotton
Alabama 30, Baylor 2

	1st	2nd	3rd	4th	Final
ALA	6	7	3	14	30
BU	2	0	0	0	2

SCORING SUMMARY
ALA FG Kim 29
ALA FG Kim 28
BU   Safety (Lewis tackled by Tabor in end zone)
ALA Ogilvie 1 run (Kim kick)
ALA FG Kim 42
ALA Jacobs 1 run (Kim kick)
ALA Nix 3 run (Mardini kick)

ALA	TEAM STATISTICS	BU
17	First Downs	13
241	Rushing Yards	54
5-12-0	Passing	12-27-3
98	Passing Yards	104
339	Total Yards	158
6-37.2	Punts - Average	7-35.9
5-1	Fumbles - Lost	5-4
5-89	Penalties - Yards	6-59
36:22	Possession Time	23:38

INDIVIDUAL LEADERS
RUSHING
ALA: Ogilvie 15-74, 1 TD; Carter 4-71.
BU: Jeffrey 8-18; Gentry 11-17.
PASSING
ALA: Jacobs 5-12-0, 98 yards.
BU: Jeffrey 8-19-2, 55 yards; Mangrum 4-8-1, 49 yards.
RECEIVING
ALA: Bendross 1-49; Jackson 1-20; Brown 1-20.
BU: Hold 3-41; Gentry 5-26.

January 1, 1982 | Cotton
Texas 14, Alabama 12

	1st	2nd	3rd	4th	Final
ALA	0	7	0	5	12
TEX	0	0	0	14	14

SCORING SUMMARY
ALA Bendross 6 pass from Lewis (Kim kick)
ALA FG Kim 24
TEX Brewer 30 run (Allegre kick)
TEX Orr 8 run (Allegre kick)
ALA Safety (Goodson steps out of end zone)

ALA	TEAM STATISTICS	TEX
15	First Downs	21
163	Rushing Yards	158
8-13-1	Passing	12-22-0
144	Passing Yards	201
307	Total Yards	359
5-45.2	Punts - Average	6-36.8
1-1	Fumbles - Lost	0-0
1-5	Penalties - Yards	4-17
27:58	Possession Time	32:02

INDIVIDUAL LEADERS
RUSHING
ALA: Lewis 24-79; Carter 6-44.
TEX: Clark 7-58; Jones 16-57.
PASSING
ALA: Lewis 7-12-1, 122 yards, 1 TD.
TEX: Brewer 12-21-0, 201 yards.
RECEIVING
ALA: Bendross 5-78, 1 TD; Krout 3-66.
TEX: Little 7-92; Sampleton 2-56.

December 29, 1982 | Liberty
Alabama 21, Illinois 15

	1st	2nd	3rd	4th	Final
ALA	7	0	7	7	21
ILL	0	6	0	9	15

SCORING SUMMARY
ALA Moore 4 run (Kim kick)
ILL Curtis 1 run (kick failed)
ALA Bendross 8 run (Kim kick)
ILL Williams 2 pass from Eason (pass failed)
ILL FG Bass 23
ALA Turner 1 run (Kim kick)

ALA	TEAM STATISTICS	ILL
19	First Downs	21
217	Rushing Yards	21
7-13-2	Passing	35-58-4
130	Passing Yards	423
347	Total Yards	444

INDIVIDUAL LEADERS
RUSHING
ALA: Moore 13-65, 1 TD; Turner 11-36, 1 TD.
ILL: Curtis 7-13, 1 TD.
PASSING
ALA: Lewis 7-13-2, 130 yards.
ILL: Eason 35-55-4, 423 yards, 1 TD.
RECEIVING
ALA: Jones 2-60; Bendross 3-51.
ILL: Martin 8-127; Williams 7-84, 1 TD.

December 24, 1983 | Sun
Alabama 28, SMU 7

	1st	2nd	3rd	4th	Final
ALA	14	14	0	0	28
SMU	0	0	7	0	7

SCORING SUMMARY
ALA Moore 1 run (Tiffin kick)
ALA Moore 11 run (Tiffin kick)
ALA Lewis 1 run (Tiffin kick)
ALA Jones 19 pass from Lewis (Tiffin kick)
SMU Pleasant 15 pass from McIlhenny (Herrell kick)

ALA	TEAM STATISTICS	SMU
23	First Downs	13
251	Rushing Yards	194
9-14-0	Passing	14-27-2
148	Passing Yards	148
399	Total Yards	342
2-21	Punt Returns - Yards	1-6
1-34	Kickoff Returns - Yards	3-43
6-40.0	Punts - Average	4-41.0
1-1	Fumbles - Lost	3-3
3-25	Penalties - Yards	0-0

INDIVIDUAL LEADERS
RUSHING
ALA: Moore 28-113, 2 TD; Goode 7-59.
SMU: Atkins 9-116; Dupard 13-51.
PASSING
ALA: Lewis 9-14-0, 148 yards, 1 TD.
SMU: McIlhenny 14-27-2, 148 yards, 1 TD.
RECEIVING
ALA: Jones 2-36 yards, 1 TD; Richardson 1-32.
SMU: Pleasant 3-67, 1 TD; Morris 5-63.

December 28, 1985 | Aloha
Alabama 24, Southern California 3

	1st	2nd	3rd	4th	Final
ALA	3	0	7	14	24
USC	0	3	0	0	3

SCORING SUMMARY
ALA   FG Tiffin 48
USC   FG Shafer 24
ALA   Turner 1 run (Tiffin kick)
ALA   Whitehurst 24 pass from Shula (Tiffin kick)
ALA   Bell 14 run (Tiffin kick)

December 25, 1986 | Sun
Alabama 28, Washington 6

	1st	2nd	3rd	4th	Final
ALA	0	7	14	7	28
WASH	0	6	0	0	6

SCORING SUMMARY
ALA   Humphrey 64 run (Tiffin kick)
WASH FG Jaeger 31
WASH FG Jaeger 34
ALA   Richardson 32 pass from Shula (Tiffin kick)
ALA   Humphrey 18 pass from Shula (Tiffin kick)
ALA   Humphrey 3 run (Tiffin kick)

ALA	TEAM STATISTICS	WASH
13	First Downs	16
215	Rushing Yards	102
15-26-0	Passing	20-43-2
176	Passing Yards	189
391	Total Yards	291
3-24	Punt Returns - Yards	5-68
9-45.0	Punts - Average	8-35.0
0-0	Fumbles - Lost	4-1

INDIVIDUAL LEADERS
RUSHING
ALA: Humphrey 28-159, 2 TD; Wright 4 -32.
WASH: Weathersby 9-28 yards; Fenney 11-19.
PASSING
ALA: Shula 15-26-0, 176 yards, 2 TD.
WASH: Chandler 20-43-2, 189 yards.
RECEIVING
ALA: Richardson 2-59, 1 TD; Humphrey 5-43, 1 TD.
WASH: Hill 5-77; Weathersby 5-45.

January 2, 1988 | Hall of Fame
Michigan 28, Alabama 24

	1st	2nd	3rd	4th	Final
MICH	0	14	7	7	28
ALA	3	0	6	15	24

SCORING SUMMARY
ALA   FG Doyle 51
MICH Morris 25 run (Gillette kick)
MICH Morris 14 run (Gillette kick)
MICH Morris 77 run (Gillette kick)
ALA   Cross 16 pass from Dunn (run failed)
ALA   Humphrey 1 run (Doyle kick)
ALA   Humphrey 17 run (Whitehurst pass from Dunn)
MICH Kolesar 20 pass from Brown (Gillette kick)

MICH	TEAM STATISTICS	ALA
12	First Downs	28
278	Rushing Yards	191
6-17-0	Passing	23-40-1
68	Passing Yards	269
346	Total Yards	460
6-42.5	Punts - Average	4-42.5
0-0	Fumbles - Lost	1-1
4-30	Penalties - Yards	1-5
21:42	Possession Time	38:18

INDIVIDUAL LEADERS
RUSHING
MICH: Morris 23-234, 3 TD; Bunch 3-16.
ALA: Humphrey 27-149, 2 TD; Goode 6-14.
PASSING
MICH: Brown 4-13-0, 72 yards, 1 TD.
ALA: Dunn 23-40-1, 269 yards, 1 TD.
RECEIVING
MICH: McMurtry 1-31; Kolesar 1-20, 1 TD.
ALA: Whitehurst 6-85; Cross 6-81, 1 TD.

December 24, 1988 | Sun
Alabama 29, Army 28

	1st	2nd	3rd	4th	Final
ALA	3	10	7	9	29
ARMY	7	7	14	0	28

SCORING SUMMARY
ARMY Mayweather 1 run (Walker kick)
ALA   FG Doyle 37
ARMY McWilliams 30 run (Walker kick)
ALA   FG Doyle 22
ALA   Battle 7 pass from Smith (Doyle kick)
ALA   Payne 23 pass from Smith (Doyle kick)
ARMY Mayweather 3 run (Walker kick)
ARMY Miller 57 interception return (Walker kick)
ALA   FG Doyle 32
ALA   Casteal 2 run (run failed)

ALA	TEAM STATISTICS	ARMY
29	First Downs	19
95	Rushing Yards	350
33-52-1	Passing	0-6-1
412	Passing Yards	0
507	Total Yards	350
3-32	Punt Returns - Yards	1-14
4-45.0	Punts - Average	5-39.0
1-0	Fumbles - Lost	1-0

INDIVIDUAL LEADERS
RUSHING
ALA: Hall 12-57; Shaw 7-38.
ARMY: Barnett 14-177; Mayweather 19-80, 2 TD.
PASSING
ALA: Smith 33-52-1, 412 yards, 2 TD.
ARMY: Mayweather 0-6-1, 0 yards.

January 1, 1990 | Sugar
Miami (Fla.) 33, Alabama 25

	1st	2nd	3rd	4th	Final
MIA	7	13	6	7	33
ALA	0	17	0	8	25

SCORING SUMMARY
MIA   McGuire 3 run (Huerta kick)
ALA   Battle 4 pass from Hollingsworth (Doyle kick)
MIA   Carroll 19 pass from Erickson (kick blocked)
MIA   Johnson 3 run (Huerta kick)
ALA   FG Doyle 45
ALA   Russell 7 pass from Hollingsworth (Doyle kick)
MIA   Chudzinski 11 pass from Erickson (pass failed)
MIA   Bethel 12 pass from Erickson (Huerta kick)
ALA   Wembley 9 pass from Hollingsworth
      (Russell pass from Hollingsworth)

January 1, 1991 | Fiesta
Louisville 34, Alabama 7

	1st	2nd	3rd	4th	Final
LOU	25	0	7	2	34
ALA	0	7	0	0	7

SCORING SUMMARY
LOU   Ware 70 pass from Nagle (Wilmsmeyer kick)
LOU   Dawkins 5 run (kick failed)
LOU   Cummings 37 pass from Nagle (pass failed)
LOU   Buchanan recovered blocked punt in end zone
      (pass failed)
ALA   Gardner 49 interception return (Doyle kick)
LOU   Cummings 19 pass from Nagle (Bell kick)
LOU   Safety (Woodson intentional grounding)

LOU	TEAM STATISTICS	ALA
25	First Downs	10
113	Rushing Yards	95
21-39-3	Passing	12-35-2
458	Passing Yards	94
571	Total Yards	189
3-41.0	Punts - Average	8-40.2
3-1	Fumbles - Lost	3-1
10-87	Penalties - Yards	7-40

INDIVIDUAL LEADERS
RUSHING
LOU: Bynm 8-48; Dawkins 5-38, 1 TD.
ALA: Turner 6-49; Anderson 7-26.
PASSING
LOU: Nagle 20-33-1, 451 yards, 3 TD.
ALA: Hollingsworth 10-23-1, 59 yards.
RECEIVING
LOU: McKay 5-110; Jones 2-89; Cummings 3-69, 2 TD.
ALA: Turner 4-35; Lassic 2-35.

December 28, 1991 | Blockbuster
Alabama 30, Colorado 25

	1st	2nd	3rd	4th	Final
ALA	7	3	13	7	30
COLO	7	5	7	6	25

SCORING SUMMARY
ALA   Palmer 52 punt return (Wethington kick)
COLO Phillips 1 run (Harper kick)
COLO Safety (Houston tackled in end zone)
ALA   FG Wethington 25
COLO FG Harper 33
ALA   Stacy 13 pass from Barker (pass failed)
COLO Westbrook 62 pass from Hagan (Harper kick)
ALA   Lee 12 pass from Barker (Wethington kick)
ALA   Palmer 5 run (Barker (Wethington kick)
COLO Johnson 13 pass from Hagan (pass failed)

ALA	TEAM STATISTICS	COLO
19	First Downs	8
153	Rushing Yards	-11
12-17-1	Passing	11-30-1
154	Passing Yards	210
307	Total Yards	199
7-39.8	Punts - Average	12-41.0
4-1	Fumbles - Lost	2-0
6-33	Penalties - Yards	6-60
38:10	Possession Time	21:50

INDIVIDUAL LEADERS
RUSHING
ALA: Turner 9-43; Stacy 26-11.
COLO: Hagan 14-12.
PASSING
ALA: Barker 12-16-1, 154 yards, 3 TD.
COLO: Hagan 11-30-1, 210 yards, 2 TD.
RECEIVING
ALA: Stacy 4-59, 1 TD; Lee 2-39, 1 TD.
COLO: Westbrook 3-87, 1 TD; Johnson 2-38, 1 TD.

January 1, 1993 | Sugar
Alabama 34, Miami (Fla.) 13

	1st	2nd	3rd	4th	Final
ALA	3	10	14	7	34
MIA	3	3	0	7	13

SCORING SUMMARY
ALA   FG Proctor 19
MIA   FG Prewitt 49
ALA   FG Proctor 23
ALA   Williams 2 run (Proctor kick)
MIA   FG Prewitt 42
ALA   Lassic 1 run (Proctor kick)
ALA   Teague 31 interception return (Proctor kick)
MIA   Williams 78 punt return (Prewitt kick)
ALA   Lassic 4 run (Proctor kick)

ALA	TEAM STATISTICS	MIA
15	First Downs	16
290	Rushing Yards	75
4-13-2	Passing	24-56-3
18	Passing Yards	278
308	Total Yards	353
6-44.5	Punts - Average	5-41.6
0-0	Fumbles - Lost	4-1
7-46	Penalties - Yards	6-37
36:04	Possession Time	23:56

INDIVIDUAL LEADERS
RUSHING
ALA: Lassic 28-135, 2 TD; Lynch 5-39; Williams 7-23, 1 TD.
MIA: Jones 5-28; Bennett 3-26.
PASSING
ALA: Barker 4-13-2, 18 yards.
MIA: Torretta 24-56-3, 278 yards.
RECEIVING
ALA: Wimbley 2-11.
MIA: Jones 3-64; Thomas 6-52; Williams 3-49.

DECEMBER 31, 1993 | GATOR
ALABAMA 24, NORTH CAROLINA 10

	1ST	2ND	3RD	4TH	FINAL
ALA	3	7	7	7	24
UNC	0	10	0	0	10

SCORING SUMMARY
ALA	FG Proctor 22
UNC	Henderson 1 run (Pignetti kick)
ALA	Burgdorf 33 run (Proctor kick)
UNC	FG Pignetti 23
ALA	Lynch 8 pass from Burgdorf (Proctor kick)
ALA	Key 10 pass from Burgdorf (Proctor kick)

ALA	TEAM STATISTICS	UNC
21	First Downs	14
164	Rushing Yards	42
15-23-0	Passing	19-35-0
166	Passing Yards	225
330	Total Yards	267
6-40.0	Punts - Average	7-30.1
3-0	Fumbles - Lost	1-1
4-34	Penalties - Yards	1-15

INDIVIDUAL LEADERS
RUSHING
ALA: Williams 18-94; Burgdorf 6-48, 1 TD.
UNC: C. Johnson 6-27; L. Johnson 2-24.

PASSING
ALA: Burgdorf 15-23-0, 166 yards, 2 TD.
UNC: Stanicek 19-35-0, 225 yards.

RECEIVING
ALA: Palmer 5-62; T. Johnson 2-40.
UNC: Holliday 9-125; F. Jones 2-55.

JANUARY 2, 1995 | CITRUS
ALABAMA 24, OHIO STATE 17

	1ST	2ND	3RD	4TH	FINAL
ALA	0	14	0	10	24
OSU	0	14	0	3	17

SCORING SUMMARY
ALA	Lynch 9 run (Proctor kick)
OSU	Galloway 69 pass from Hoying (Jackson kick)
OSU	Galloway 11 pass from Hoying (Jackson kick)
ALA	Williams 7 run (Proctor kick)
OSU	FG Jackson 34
ALA	FG Proctor 27
ALA	Williams 50 pass from Barker (Proctor kick)

ALA	TEAM STATISTICS	OSU
28	First Downs	15
204	Rushing Yards	96
18-37-0	Passing	11-27-1
317	Passing Yards	180
521	Total Yards	276
4-24.0	Punts - Average	7-36.1
3-3	Fumbles - Lost	4-1
4-45	Penalties - Yards	6-43

INDIVIDUAL LEADERS
RUSHING
ALA: Williams 27-166, 1 TD; Lynch 13-35.
OSU: George 15-89; Sualua 6-44.

PASSING
ALA: Barker 18-37-0, 317 yards, 1 TD.
OSU: Hoying 11-27-1, 180 yards, 2 TD.

RECEIVING
ALA: Williams 8-155, 1 TD; Malone 3-70.
OSU: Galloway 8-146, 2 TD; Dudley 2-26.

JANUARY 1, 1997 | OUTBACK
ALABAMA 17, MICHIGAN 14

	1ST	2ND	3RD	4TH	FINAL
ALA	3	0	7	7	17
MICH	0	6	0	8	14

SCORING SUMMARY
ALA	FG Brock 43
MICH	FG Hamilton 44
MICH	FG Hamilton 22
ALA	Rudd 88 interception return (Brock kick)
ALA	Alexander 46 run (Brock kick)
MICH	Shaw 9 pass from Griese (Floyd run)

ALA	TEAM STATISTICS	MICH
13	First Downs	22
182	Rushing Yards	124
9-18-1	Passing	22-38-1
65	Passing Yards	291
247	Total Yards	415
0-0	Punt Returns - Yards	4-17
1-9	Kickoff Returns - Yards	1-22
6-46.5	Punts - Average	7-26.1
2-1	Fumbles - Lost	3-0
8-42	Penalties - Yards	6-47
25:28	Possession Time	34:32

INDIVIDUAL LEADERS
RUSHING
ALA: Alexander 9-99, 1 TD; Riddle 13-58.
MICH: Williams 12-58; Floyd 6-35.

PASSING
ALA: Kitchens 9-18-1, 65 yards.
MICH: Griese 21-37-1, 287 yards, 1 TD.

RECEIVING
ALA: Vaughn 2-27; Rutledge 1-13.
MICH: Williams 5-113; Shaw 6-84, 1 TD.

DECEMBER 29, 1998 | MUSIC CITY
VIRGINIA TECH 38, ALABAMA 7

	1ST	2ND	3RD	4TH	FINAL
VT	7	3	14	14	38
ALA	0	7	0	0	7

SCORING SUMMARY
VT	Clark 43 run (Graham kick)
ALA	Vaughn 5 pass from Zow (Pflugner kick)
VT	FG Graham 44
VT	Pegues 1 run (Graham kick)
VT	Stith 4 run (Graham kick)
VT	Pegues 1 run (Graham kick)
VT	Midget 27 interception return (Graham kick)

VT	TEAM STATISTICS	ALA
15	First Downs	15
207	Rushing Yards	50
7-14-1	Passing	19-35-3
71	Passing Yards	224
278	Total Yards	274
4-30	Punt Returns - Yards	1-(-3)
1-44	Kickoff Returns - Yards	6-67
3-46.7	Punts - Average	6-29.0
0-0	Fumbles - Lost	2-1
5-31	Penalties - Yards	10-94
23:43	Possession Time	36:17

INDIVIDUAL LEADERS
RUSHING
VT: Stith 10-71, 1 TD; Clark 9-55, 1 TD; Pegues 15-41, 2 TD.
ALA: Alexander 21-55.

PASSING
VT: Clark 7-14-1, 71 yards.
ALA: Zow 19-35-3, 224 yards, 1 TD.

RECEIVING
VT: Hall 1-20; Harrison 2-11.
ALA: Alexander 8-87; Vaughn 3-55, 1 TD.

JANUARY 1, 2000 | ORANGE
MICHIGAN 35, ALABAMA 34

	1ST	2ND	3RD	4TH	OT	FINAL
MICH	0	7	21	0	7	35
ALA	0	14	14	0	6	34

SCORING SUMMARY
ALA	Alexander 5 run (Pflugner kick)
ALA	Alexander 6 run (Pflugner kick)
MICH	Terrell 27 pass from Brady (Epstein kick)
MICH	Terrell 57 pass from Brady (Epstein kick)
ALA	Alexander 50 run (Pflugner kick)
ALA	Milons 62 punt return (Pflugner kick)
MICH	Terrell 20 pass from Brady (Epstein kick)
MICH	A.Thomas 3 run (Epstein kick)
MICH	Thompson 25 pass from Brady (Epstein kick)
ALA	Carter 21 pass from Zow (kick failed)

MICH	TEAM STATISTICS	ALA
18	First Downs	12
37	Rushing Yards	184
35-47-0	Passing	13-20-1
369	Passing Yards	111
406	Total Yards	295
8-43.4	Punts - Average	9-34.4
2-1	Fumbles - Lost	1-0
10-115	Penalties - Yards	18-132
32:08	Possession Time	27:52

INDIVIDUAL LEADERS
RUSHING
MICH: A. Thomas 18-40, 1 TD.
ALA: Alexander 25-161, 3 TD, Watts 4-15.

PASSING
MICH: Brady 34-46-0, 369 yards, 4 TD.
ALA: Zow 7-14-0, 86 yards, 1 TD.

RECEIVING
MICH: Terrell 10-150, 3 TD; Shea 7-50; Thompson 3-47, 1 TD.
ALA: Carter 4-38, 1 TD; Alexander 2-21.

DECEMBER 27, 2001 | INDEPENDENCE
ALABAMA 14, IOWA STATE 13

	1ST	2ND	3RD	4TH	FINAL
ALA	0	7	0	7	14
ISU	3	7	3	0	13

SCORING SUMMARY
ISU	FG Yelk 36
ISU	Woodley 1 run (Yelk kick)
ALA	Zow 8 run (Thomas kick)
ISU	FG Yelk 41
ALA	Jones 27 pass from Zow (Thomas kick)

ALA	TEAM STATISTICS	ISU
15	First Downs	23
188	Rushing Yards	199
11-19-1	Passing	25-42-0
119	Passing Yards	284
307	Total Yards	483
2-14	Punt Returns - Yards	3-22
1-16	Kickoff Returns - Yards	3-48
7-39.9	Punts - Average	4-35.5
0-0	Fumbles - Lost	1-0
2-20	Penalties - Yards	4-32
29:22	Possession Time	30:38

INDIVIDUAL LEADERS
RUSHING
ALA: Galloway 16-90.
ISU: Haywood 20-125.

PASSING
ALA: Zow 11-19-1, 119 yards, 1 TD.
ISU: Wallace 25-42-0, 284 yards.

RECEIVING
ALA: Jones Jr. 2-44, 1 TD; Milons 3-32.
ISU: Campbell 7-109; Danielsen 5-57.

DECEMBER 31, 2004 | MUSIC CITY
MINNESOTA 20, ALABAMA 16

	1ST	2ND	3RD	4TH	FINAL
MINN	7	10	3	0	20
ALA	7	7	0	2	16

SCORING SUMMARY
ALA	McClain 2 pass from Pennington (Bostick kick)
MINN	Lipka 1 fumble return (Lloyd kick)
MINN	Barber 5 run (Lloyd kick)
MINN	FG Lloyd 27
ALA	McClain 1 run (Bostick kick)
MINN	FG Lloyd 24
ALA	Saftey

MINN	TEAM STATISTICS	ALA
23	First Downs	13
276	Rushing Yards	21
5-13-2	Passing	22-36-0
75	Passing Yards	243
351	Total Yards	264
4-10	Punt Returns - Yards	2-10
1-18	Kickoff Returns - Yards	5-76
4-37.8	Punts - Average	7-37.1
2-1	Fumbles - Lost	2-2
11-84	Penalties - Yards	4-35
37:54	Possession Time	22:06

INDIVIDUAL LEADERS
RUSHING
MINN: Barber 37-187, 1 TD; Maroney 29-105.
ALA: Brown 1-17.
PASSING
MINN: Cupito 5-12-1, 75 yards.
ALA: Pennington 22-36-0, 243 yards, 1 TD.
RECEIVING
MINN: Ellerson 3-51.
ALA: Prothro 4-82; Brown 3-56.

JANUARY 2, 2006 | COTTON
ALABAMA 13, TEXAS TECH 10

	1ST	2ND	3RD	4TH	FINAL
TT	3	0	0	7	10
ALA	7	0	3	3	13

SCORING SUMMARY
BAMA	Brown 76 pass from Croyle (Christensen kick)
TT	FG Trlica 34
BAMA	FG Christensen 31
TT	Hicks 12 pass from Hodges (Trlica kick)
BAMA	FG Christensen 45

TT	TEAM STATISTICS	ALA
18	First Downs	21
103	Rushing Yards	145
16-36-0	Passing	19-31-0
226	Passing Yards	275
329	Total Yards	420
3-25	Punt Returns-Yards	3-8
2-22	Kickoff Returns-Yards	2-32
6-41.3	Punts-Average	5-37.8
1-0	Fumbles-Lost	0-0
10-65	Penalties-Yards	4-35

INDIVIDUAL LEADERS
RUSHING
TT: Hodges 17-66.
ALA: Darby 29-81.
PASSING
TT: Hodges 15-32-0, 196 yards, 1 TD.
ALA: Croyle 19-31-0, 275 yards, 1 TD.
RECEIVING
TT: Henderson 5-46; Filani 4-67.
ALA: Brown 5-141, 1 TD; Caddell 3-63.

DECEMBER 28, 2006 | INDEPENDENCE
OKLAHOMA STATE 34, ALABAMA 31

	1ST	2ND	3RD	4TH	FINAL
OSU	7	17	0	10	34
ALA	7	7	3	14	31

SCORING SUMMARY
OSU	Savage 1 run (Ricks kick)
ALA	Caddell 18 pass from Wilson (Christensen kick)
OSU	Toston 4 run (Ricks kick)
OSU	FG Ricks 28
ALA	Castille 1 run (Christensen kick)
OSU	Toston 7 run (Ricks kick)
ALA	FG Christensen 24
OSU	Bowman 10 pass from Reid (Ricks kick)
ALA	Arenas 86 punt return (Christensen kick)
ALA	Smith 2 run (Christensen kick)
OSU	FG Ricks 27

OSU	TEAM STATISTICS	ALA
23	First Downs	18
207	Rushing Yards	108
15-30-1	Passing	18-33-1
212	Passing Yards	168
419	Total Yards	276
3-0	Punt Returns - Yards	1-86
6-116	Kickoff Returns - Yards	2-5
5-35	Punts - Average	5-36.6
3-1	Fumbles - Lost	3-2
9-77	Penalties - Yards	8-45

INDIVIDUAL LEADERS
RUSHING
OSU: Savage 19-112, 1 TD.
ALA: Johns 7-39.
PASSING
OSU: Reid 15-29-1, 212 yards, 1 TD.
ALA: Wilson 18-33-1, 168 yards, 1 TD.
RECEIVING
OSU: Pettigre 4-65; Bowman 3-50, 1 TD.
ALA: Hall 5-42; Darby 4-30.

DECEMBER 30, 2007 | INDEPENDENCE
ALABAMA 30, COLORADO 24

	1ST	2ND	3RD	4TH	FINAL
ALA	20	7	0	3	30
COLO	0	14	3	7	24

SCORING SUMMARY
ALA	FG Tiffin 41
ALA	FG Tiffin 24
ALA	Brown 15 pass from Wilson (Tiffin kick)
ALA	Caddell 34 pass from Wilson (Tiffin kick)
ALA	Stover 31 pass from Wilson (Tiffin kick)
COLO	DeVree 4 pass from Hawkins (Eberhart kick)
COLO	Sprague 25 pass from Hawkins (Eberhart kick)
COLO	FG Eberhart 39
ALA	FG Tiffin 26
COLO	DeVree 14 pass from Hawkins (Eberhart kick)

ALA	TEAM STATISTICS	COLO
22	First Downs	19
132	Rushing Yards	75
19-32-1	Passing	24-40-2
256	Passing Yards	322
388	Total Yards	397
0-0	Punt Returns - Yards	0-0
5-94	Kickoff Returns - Yards	6-126
4-45.0	Punts - Average	4-31.8
2-1	Fumbles - Lost	1-0
4-21	Penalties - Yards	4-30

INDIVIDUAL LEADERS
RUSHING
ALA: Coffee 19-72.
COLO: Charles 14-69.
PASSING
ALA: Wilson 19-32-1, 256 yards, 3 TD.
COLO: Hawkins 24-39-2, 322 yards, 3 TD.
RECEIVING
ALA: Caddell 4-76, 1 TD; D. Hall 4-58.
COLO: DeVree 9-94, 2 TD.

JANUARY 2, 2009 | SUGAR
UTAH 31, ALABAMA 17

	1ST	2ND	3RD	4TH	FINAL
UT	21	0	7	3	31
ALA	0	10	7	0	17

SCORING SUMMARY
UT	Casteel 7 pass from Johnson (Sakoda kick)
UT	Asiata 2 run (Sakoda kick)
UT	Godfrey 18 pass from Johnson (Sakoda kick)
ALA	FG Tiffin 52
ALA	Arenas 73 punt return (Tiffin kick)
ALA	Coffee 4 pass from Wilson (Tiffin kick)
UT	Reed 28 pass from Johnson (Sakoda kick)
UT	FG Sakoda 28

UT	TEAM STATISTICS	ALA
22	First Downs	15
13	Rushing Yards	31
27-41-0	Passing	18-30-2
336	Passing Yards	177
349	Total Yards	208
1-2	Punt Returns-Yards	1-73
4-93	Kickoff Returns-Yards	6-149
6-45.2	Punts-Average	4-41.5
3-1	Fumbles-Lost	1-1
10-91	Penalties-Yards	7-67

INDIVIDUAL LEADERS
RUSHING
UT: Asiata 13-29, 1 TD.
ALA: Coffee 13-36.
PASSING
UT: Johnson 27-41-0, 336 yards, 3 TD.
ALA: Wilson 18-30-2, 177 yards, 1 TD.
RECEIVING
UT: Brown 12-125; Godfrey 6-75 1 TD.
ALA: Jones 7-77; Coffee 4-40, 1 TD.

THE SCHOOLS

ARKANSAS

BY GEOFFREY NORMAN

ARKANSAS IS A RELATIVE NEWCOMER to the SEC. But when the Razorbacks joined the conference in 1992, they brought plenty to the party. This was a team that had been playing football since 1894, had won a national championship and many conference titles and had been part of some of the classic games in college football history. That includes the 1969 showdown that capped the sport's centennial season and lived up to its Game of the Century billing. Fans all over the country—including presidents of the United States—took an interest in those old Red River Shootouts. And when Lou Holtz came to Fayetteville and took the Razorbacks to the big bowl games, Arkansas fans were relieved to find that the good times hadn't ended when legendary coach Frank Broyles became full-time athletic director. Some people miss the old Texas-Arkansas rivalry, but the cross-border wars with new conference foe LSU fill the void nicely. And Arkansas has found it feels at home in the new neighborhood, going to the SEC championship game three times so far. The conference may be different, but the football—and the state's passion for it—remains the same.

TRADITION Nobody's sure exactly when it started; the 1920s is the best guess. Whenever the seeds were planted, they took root after a group of Arkansas fans got an improbable cheer going that has carried down through the years and become one of the classic war cries in all of college football. Right up there with Alabama's "Roll Tide" is the "Hog Call," and it is simplicity itself, guaranteed to raise the hair on the back of the neck of any Arkansas fan.

> *Woooooo, Pig! Sooie!*
> *Woooooo, Pig! Sooie!*
> *Woooooo, Pig! Sooie! Razorbacks!*

There is, of course, a correct way to call the Hogs. Novices are advised to practice. You begin with both arms raised high and wave your fingers as the volume rises on the word "woooooo." The arms come down in a pumping motion on the word "pig," then are extended again, vigorously, on the word "sooie."

Done right, it is a thing of beauty.

BEST PLAYER Among the most graceful players ever to stride onto a field, the six-foot, 180-pound Lance

---

PROFILE

University of Arkansas
Fayetteville, Ark.
Founded: 1871
Enrollment: 19,191
Colors: Cardinal and White
Nickname: Razorbacks
Stadium: Donald W. Reynolds Razorback Stadium
   Opened in 1938
   Grass; 72,000 capacity
First football game: 1894
All-time record: 648–445–40 (.593)
Bowl record: 11–22–3
Consensus national championships, 1936-present: 1 (1964)
Outland Trophy: Bill Brooks, 1954; Loyd Phillips, 1966
First-round draft choices: 23
Website: www.arkansasrazorbacks.com

THE BEST OF TIMES

Frank Broyles' Razorbacks ran wild in 1964 and 1965. A season-ending win over Texas Tech in 1963 launched Arkansas on a 22-game winning streak that ended with a 10-7 Cotton Bowl loss to hated LSU on New Year's Day 1966. In between, the Hogs won back-to-back Southwest Conference titles and the 1964 national championship. The 1964 Hogs racked up an astounding five consecutive shutout victories.

THE WORST OF TIMES

From 1948 to 1953, Arkansas stumbled to a 22–38 record and went just 10–26 in the SWC. The lone highlight of the period: a 16-14 win over Texas in 1951 that was the Razorbacks' first victory over the Longhorns in Fayetteville.

CONFERENCE

A charter member of the Southwest Conference in 1915, the Razorbacks remained in the SWC through 1991, before joining the SEC, one of the moves that marked a new era of conference fluidity in the college ranks.

DISTINGUISHED ALUMNI

J. William Fulbright, U.S. senator; Jerry Jones, Dallas Cowboys owner; Pat Summerall, announcer; S. Robson Walton, Wal-Mart chairman; Lucinda Williams, singer

Alworth led the 1961 Razorbacks in rushing (110 carries for 516 yards), receiving (18 catches for 320 yards), punt returns (28 for 336 yards) and kickoff returns (13 for 300 yards). He was, in short, the offense. Alworth had an 11-year career as a professional with the San Diego Chargers (where he picked up his immortal nickname, Bambi) and the Dallas Cowboys, and later became the first American Football League player inducted into the Pro Football Hall of Fame.

> *Hugo Bezdek said they played "like a wild band of razorback hogs." The name stuck.*

BEST COACH When Bowden Wyatt left the Razorbacks after the 1954 season for Tennessee, a young assistant from Baylor lobbied for the job. Arkansas turned him down in favor of a more experienced in-house man, Jack Mitchell. Three years later, Mitchell was out and Arkansas called on the man it had spurned before and who now had a year of head coaching experience at Missouri. Frank Broyles lost his first six games at the Razorbacks helm in 1958, and many fans wished the school had taken a second pass on him. Then a win over Texas A&M turned things around as the Razorbacks won out the season. The next year, they went 9–2, tied for the Southwest Conference championship and ended Georgia Tech's eight-game

winning streak in a 14-7 victory in the Gator Bowl.

Broyles kept winning and kept taking Arkansas to bowl games—10 of them altogether, nine on New Year's Day—compiling a 144–58–5 record before retiring after the 1976 season to devote himself exclusively to his duties as AD. In 1964, his 11–0 team won Arkansas' only national title, awarded by both the Football Writers Association and the Helms Foundation, whose votes came after the bowls. Good thing he got a second chance to make a first impression.

BEST TEAM The 1964 team is notable, of course, for its unblemished record. When all the bowl games had been played and all the dust had settled, the Razorbacks were the only undefeated team in the land. The AP and UPI had named Alabama national champions before the bowls, but then the Tide lost in the Orange Bowl to Texas, a team Arkansas had downed by a point in October. The Razorbacks came from behind in the Cotton Bowl to beat Nebraska 10-7 and distinguish themselves.

That 1964 squad had more than its spotless record to boast about. Four men associated with the team went on to coach college national championship teams: Broyles, of

---

FIGHT SONG

ARKANSAS FIGHT SONG
Hit that line, Hit that line, Keep on going,
Move that ball right down the field.
Give a cheer, Rah! Rah!
Never fear, Rah! Rah!
Arkansas will never yield.
On your toes Razorbacks to the finish.
Carry on with all your might.
For it's A-R-K-A-N-S-A-S for Arkansas,
Fight, Fight, Fi-i-ight.

FIRST-ROUND DRAFT CHOICES

1938	Jack Robbins, Cardinals (5)
1940	Kay Eakin, Pirates (3)
1948	Clyde Scott, Eagles (8)
1954	Lamar McHan, Cardinals (2)
1956	Preston Carpenter, Browns (13)
1962	Lance Alworth, 49ers (8)
1963	Danny Brabham, Oilers (6)*
1967	Loyd Phillips, Bears (10)
1967	Harry Jones, Eagles (19)
1978	Steve Little, Cardinals (15)
1979	Dan Hampton, Bears (4)
1983	Billy Ray Smith, Chargers (5)
1983	Gary Anderson, Chargers (20)
1984	Ray Faurot, Jets (15)
1989	Wayne Martin, Saints (19)
1989	Steve Atwater, Broncos (20)
1994	Henry Ford, Oilers (26)
2004	Shawn Andrews, Eagles (16)
2004	Ahmad Carroll, Packers (25)
2005	Matt Jones, Jaguars (21)
2007	Jamaal Anderson, Atlanta (8)
2008	Darren McFadden, Raiders (4)
2008	Felix Jones, Cowboys (22)

*From 1960-1966, the NFL and AFL held separate, competing drafts

CONSENSUS ALL-AMERICANS

1948	Clyde Scott, B
1954	Bud Brooks, G
1965	Glen Ray Hines, T
1965-66	Loyd Phillips, DT
1968	Jim Barnes, G
1969	Rodney Brand, C
1970	Dick Bumpas, DT
1977	Leotis Harris, G
1977	Steve Little, K/P
1979	Greg Kolenda, T
1981-82	Billy Ray Smith Jr., DL
1982	Steve Korte, OL
1988	Kendall Trainor, PK
1988	Wayne Martin, DL
1989	Jim Mabry, OL
2002-03	Shawn Andrews, OL
2006-07	Darren McFadden, RB
2007	Jonathan Luigs, C
2007	Felix Jones, KR

course; his assistant and former Arkansas player and team captain Barry Switzer; assistant Johnny Majors; and one of the players, Jimmy Johnson. Johnson and Switzer are the only coaches in history to have won a college national championship and a Super Bowl. They both won the NFL's big prize with the Dallas Cowboys, whose owner, Jerry Jones, also played for the 1964 Razorbacks. This, clearly, was a team with some football magic.

BEST DEFENSE Hard to argue against the 1964 team that rang up five consecutive shutouts and gave up only 57 points in the regular season. But that was in a time of field position football and low scores, so the 1977 team that gave up only 95 regular—season points has to get some consideration too. That unit was led by Dan Hampton, then a junior, who went on to glory in the NFL. The team had only one, especially agonizing, regular-season loss—to Texas by a score of 13-9—and then went down to Miami to face Oklahoma in the Orange Bowl without three of its offensive starters, who had been suspended by coach Lou Holtz. Nobody—not even Holtz himself—gave the Razorbacks much of a chance. But the Arkansas defense stepped up and stuffed Oklahoma, whose wishbone attack had led the nation in rushing. Final score: 31-6.

BEST BACKFIELD The 2006 Razorbacks team rolled up 5,292 yards of total offense on its way to the SEC championship game—which it lost to Florida. The team averaged an astonishing 6.29 yards per play. One has to wonder how they ever managed to lose. The attack was balanced enough, with 2,093 passing yards and 3,199 rushing yards. But it was the running back tandem of Darren McFadden and Felix Jones that gave defensive coordinators heartburn. Jones rushed for 1,168 yards in 154 carries. McFadden carried 284 times for 1,647 yards, and just when you least expected it, he would throw the ball. Nine times, in all, with seven completions—three of them for touchdowns. It almost wasn't fair.

BIGGEST GAME On the way to that undefeated season in 1964, Arkansas had to get past the defending national champion Texas Longhorns, who had not lost a regular-season game in four years. The game was a battle for the SWC title, possibly the national championship, and that intangible thing that goes with any great rivalry—let's call it pride.

COLLEGE FOOTBALL HALL OF FAME INDUCTEES		
NAME	YEARS	INDUCTED
Hugo Bezdek, COACH	1908-12	1954
Wear Schoonover, E	1927-29	1967
Francis Schmidt, COACH	1922-28	1971
Clyde Scott, HB	1944-48	1971
Frank Broyles, COACH	1958-76	1983
Lance Alworth, HB	1959-61	1984
Loyd Phillips, DT	1964-66	1992
Bowden Wyatt, COACH	1953-54	1997
Chuck Dicus, WR	1968-70	1999
Billy Ray Smith, DE	1979-82	2000
Wayne Harris, C	1958-60	2004
Lou Holtz, COACH	1977-83	2008

PRO FOOTBALL HALL OF FAME INDUCTEES		
NAME	YEARS	INDUCTED
Lance Alworth, F	1962-72	1978
Dan Hampton, DT/DE	1979-90	2002

The Longhorns missed an early field goal, and then the game became one of defense and punting. Midway through the second quarter, Texas punter Ernie Koy kicked one 47 yards to the Arkansas 19, where Ken Hatfield took the ball and started up the sideline. A wall of Razorbacks cleared the way until only Koy was left to stop him. Two Arkansas blockers made sure he didn't, and the Razorbacks went on to a 14-13 victory and a perfect season.

BIGGEST UPSET Even before Holtz suspended his two top running backs and best receiver just before the 1978 Orange Bowl, the Razorbacks were decided underdogs to the Oklahoma Sooners. Holtz was in his first year as head coach at Arkansas and it was his burden to follow a legend—Frank Broyles. Before the season, experts picked his team to finish fifth in the Southwest Conference. The Razorbacks surprised everyone—except, perhaps, themselves and their coach—by losing only one game. Even so, Arkansas appeared overmatched by Oklahoma, especially after the suspensions.

Texas, which was responsible for Arkansas' lone defeat, lost its bowl game earlier on New Year's Day. If Oklahoma could beat the Razorbacks, it would be No. 1. But the Sooners couldn't stop reserve tailback Roland Sales, who ran for 205 yards and picked up another 52 yards receiving.

The Razorbacks won—no, *dominated*—31-6.

HEARTBREAKER It was called the Big Shootout, and president Richard Nixon and evangelist Billy Graham were among the sellout crowd in Fayetteville on Dec. 6, 1969. Millions of others were glued to their televisions as No. 1 Texas and No. 2 Arkansas played a game that didn't disappoint. Going into the fourth quarter, the Razorbacks held a 14-0 lead. But James Street ran for a 42-yard touchdown and Texas scored its first two-point conversion of the season. Then, with four minutes left on fourth and three, Texas did something it never did—pass the ball. The 44-yard completion set up the winning score and broke many Razorbacks' hearts.

BEST GOAL-LINE STAND The 1947 Cotton Bowl was an entire season's worth of goal-line stands. The Razorbacks faced LSU in the snow on a 20-degree day and held back the Tigers and their illustrious quarterback, Y.A. Tittle, five times inside the 10—*in the first half*. With time

running out in the third quarter and the game still scoreless, Arkansas stopped LSU on the 1 and the Tigers missed a field goal attempt. As the game ended, LSU once more knocked on the door. But the Razorbacks held on their own 1 yet again, freezing the scoreless tie into the history books.

BEST COMEBACK The Razorbacks were down 17-7 to 18th-ranked LSU in the fourth quarter of a contest that would settle the 2002 SEC Western Division title. With 34 seconds left, Arkansas trailed by six with the ball on its 19 and no time-outs. It took just three plays for the Razorbacks to travel all the way down the field and into the end zone to tie the game. Understandably ebullient, the Arkansas players celebrated excessively and were penalized 15 yards on the extra point. Still, this was the Razorbacks' day. The kick was true and Arkansas made the SEC championship game for the second time since joining the conference.

STADIUM The first game at Donald W. Reynolds Razorback Stadium (on the campus in Fayetteville) saw Arkansas defeat Oklahoma A&M, 27-7, on Sept. 24, 1938. The stadium was a vast improvement over the old 300-seat facility built on a piece of land known as the Hill, and it's seen a number of improvements over the years. Its most recent and thorough renovation and expansion came before the 2001 season. The $110 million project raised the capacity from 51,000 to 72,000 and also added a number of suites.

The Razorbacks still play some of their games (two are scheduled for 2009) in Little Rock at War Memorial Stadium, which seats 53,727.

RIVAL Texas and Arkansas first played one another in 1894. The always-fierce rivalry became incandescent during the 1960s, when the schools routinely played for conference and even national championships. This was the era of the one-point heartbreaker: Texas going down 14-13 in 1964; Arkansas losing what some called the Game of the Century, 15-14, in 1969. The schools stopped playing every year, though, when Arkansas left the Southwest Conference for the SEC in 1992.

Since there is no in-state foe, another school from a bordering state assumed archrival status. LSU and Arkansas first played one another in 1901 and have met in six different cities and four different states. As is typical of rivals, they like to spoil each others' seasons. The Razorbacks upset the Tigers in a scoreless tie in the 1947 Cotton Bowl and LSU ended a 22-game Razorbacks winning streak in the same bowl in 1966. In 2007, the Razorbacks beat LSU in Baton Rouge by two points. The Tigers were ranked No. 1 at the time and, after all the bowl games had been played, they were No. 1 again.

In 1996, with the LSU-Arkansas game having attained full rivalry status, the Golden Boot trophy was introduced as spoils for the victors. The Boot is in the shape of the two states, is molded from 24-karat gold and is valued at $10,000. It stands four feet tall and weighs almost 200 pounds.

NICKNAME In 1909, the Arkansas Cardinals—as they were then known—went 7–0, scoring 186 points while allowing only 18. After a particularly satisfying win over LSU, Arkansas coach Hugo Bezdek told fans that his boys had played "like a wild band of razorback hogs." In Arkansas, everyone knew exactly what he meant. And the name stuck.

MASCOT There are both costumed and live razorbacks at Arkansas games. The live animals are not true razorbacks, which exist today only in remote parts of Australia. But the Russian boar comes close enough, and a specimen whose name is Tusk II currently has the honor. He lives on a farm near Fayetteville when he isn't attending games.

In the past, some of his predecessors have lived up to the razorback legend for orneriness. In 1977, one of them, named Big Red III, escaped during an exhibition and ran wild until he was gunned down by a farmer whose property he had ravaged. Another, named Ragnar, was known to have killed a coyote, a 450-pound domestic pig, and seven rattlesnakes. Ragnar died in 1978, and since he appeared to be indestructible, it was recorded as due to "unknown causes."

UNIFORMS The school colors have been cardinal red and white for as long as Arkansas has been playing football. In fact, before they became the Razorbacks, Arkansas football teams were called the Cardinals. The distinctive helmets with the fierce and elegant Razorbacks logos date to 1964 and that season's famous undefeated and untied team.

WEIRDNESS Arkansas has played in two games that went into seven overtimes … and won both of them, on the road. The first was in 2001, when the Razorbacks beat Mississippi, 58-56, in Oxford. Then, in 2003, the Razorbacks beat Kentucky in Lexington by a score that seems more likely to have come in a basketball game: 71-63.

LORE It is known as the Powder River Play and it led to an upset of fifth-ranked Ole Miss on Oct. 23, 1954. Bowden Wyatt's squad, known affectionately as the 25 Little Pigs, was locked in a scoreless tie with the Rebels with some six minutes left when running quarterback Buddy Benson took the snap and began what looked like a sweep. Preston Carpenter slipped past the Ole Miss

secondary, took a 33-yard pass from Benson and ran another 33 for a 66-yard touchdown that was the only score of the day. Wyatt had brought the play with him from Wyoming, where the deceptive Powder River runs a mile wide but in many places is only six inches deep.

QUOTE "After all, he's on a four-year scholarship and I'm sitting here with a one-year contract."
—**Frank Broyles**, explaining his reluctance to send in plays to his quarterback

Hog-Tied

By E. Lynn Harris

The Razorbacks rank right behind God and my family as my top passions. I've missed only one game in the last eight years, and that was because the 2008 match against Texas was rescheduled due to weather. And keep in mind that I stopped flying about three years ago (it's a writer's thing). But it doesn't matter how long it takes to drive there, I won't miss a chance to see the Hogs play.

I've been rooting for the Razorbacks since I arrived on campus in the late 1970s and became the first African-American male on the cheerleading squad. Today, my son Brandon is a second-generation Razorbacks cheerleader. It thrills me to think that my son and I are connected in this way: We have both stood on the field at Reynolds Razorback Stadium, leading the crowd in one of the most unique and original cheers known to college football, the Hog Call.

When it comes to traditions, though, the Hog Call is just the beginning. Few things rival the excitement of the Marching Razorback Band forming a huge A before the team races onto the field. Or Friday night pep rallies at the Chi Omega Greek Theatre. Or when throngs of Razorbacks fans crowd around their heroes before the players enter the stadium.

After Arkansas jolted college football in 1992 by leaving the Southwest Conference for the SEC, Razorbacks fans felt a little like foster children in a blended family. We might be cute but it was as if we needed braces or better clothes in order to fit in alongside the beautiful conference programs such as Alabama and Florida. But coach Frank Broyles was a visionary

and he knew the SEC was the best home for Arkansas football.

Any Razorbacks fan will admit that in the first couple of years in our new conference we took our bumps and bruises. This was not Arkansas football of the '60s when we were behind only Alabama and tied with Texas in victories during the decade. Soon enough, though, we established ourselves with wins at every

> *After Arkansas jolted college football in 1992 by leaving the Southwest Conference for the SEC, Razorbacks fans felt a little like foster children in a blended family. We might be cute but it was as if we needed braces or better clothes in order to fit in.*

SEC stadium except the Swamp and four Western Division championships.

We are now firmly entrenched in SEC football and I was there the night the adoption became final, when there was no more possibility of denying that we belong among the elite in the premiere conference. It was during the 2006 season when ESPN came to Fayetteville for the first time to host *College GameDay*. Fall was visible in the colorful foliage and the whistling of the wind sounded like muffled Hog calls. The Razorbacks, in the middle of an eight-game winning streak, were taking on Tennessee.

Some say we don't have any natural rivals in the SEC, but for Arkansas fans it has become easy to hate the Volunteers. First of all, their school colors (orange and white) bring back memories of still-hated former SWC rival Texas. And no Razorbacks fan born before the '90s can forget 1998's Knockdown in Knoxville, when an 8–0 Razorbacks team took on an 8–0 Volunteers squad. With victory less than two minutes away, it must have been a ghost of Neyland Stadium past that slapped the ball out of quarterback Clint Stoerner's hands. A newspaper headline the next day captured the feelings of Hogs fans, "Entire State Under Suicide Watch." How my heart ached for the Hogs, how my tears fell for Clint and his teammates. After that game I didn't read the sports pages for weeks and I still refuse to watch a replay.

And even though the 2006 edition was not one of the best Tennessee teams, they were still wearing orange and white and included a few blue-chippers from the state of Arkansas who had spurned the Razorbacks, always cause for animus. I walked onto the field right before kickoff. The stadium was packed and rocked like it was the BCS championship game. The entire student section and most of the east side of the stadium was a breathtaking burst of cardinal pom-poms. It was a beautiful sight. Adrenaline coursed through my body and my heart raced in rhythm with the band playing "Arkansas Fight." And although the night was cold and misty, it was only Tennessee and their fans who felt the chill. The Razorbacks brought the wood and beat the Vols 31-14 for their ninth straight win.

This was college football at its finest. This was *SEC* football.

E. Lynn Harris is the author of Basketball Jones *and 10 other novels, as well as one memoir. His last 10 books have all been* New York Times *bestsellers. He divides his time between Fayetteville and Atlanta.*

ARKANSAS ALL-TIME SCORES

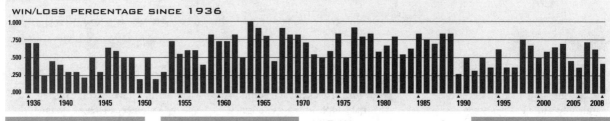

WIN/LOSS PERCENTAGE SINCE 1936

JOHN C. FUTRALL 1894-96 (.714) 5-2

1894 2-1-0
O13	•	Fort Smith HS	42	0
O27	•	at Fort Smith HS	38	0
N29		at Texas	0	54

1895 1-0-0
O12	•	Fort Smith HS	30	0

1896 2-1-0
O3	•	Fort Smith HS	10	0
O10	•	at Fort Smith HS	6	2
O24		at Drury Coll.	0	34

B.N. WILSON 1897-98 (.750) 4-1-1

1897 2-0-1
N6	•	Fort Smith HS	12	0
N20	=	at Drury Coll.	6	6
N25	•	at Ouachita College	24	0

1898 2-1-0
O22	•	Drury Coll.	17	0
N5	•	at Drury Coll.	12	6
N19		at Fort Scott HS	8	36

COLBERT SEARLES 1899-1900 (.667) 5-2-2

1899 3-1-1
O14	•	Drury Coll.	10	0
O28	•	Tulsa	11	0
N3	=	Tulsa *Mus*	0	0
N4	•	Oklahoma *Sha*	5	11
N18	•	Joplin HS	11	10

1900 2-1-1
O27	•	Webb City HS	15	0
N3	=	at Joplin HS	6	6
N10	•	Pierce C.C.	10	0
N24		at Drury Coll.	5	17

CHARLES THOMAS 1901-02 (.529) 9-8

1901 3-5-0
O12	•	Pierce C.C.	0	5
O19	•	Drury Coll.	22	0
O26	•	Fort Scott HS	6	17
N2		at Little Rock HS	0	5
N9	•	Tulsa	48	0
N16	•	K.C. Medics	6	10
N22		at LSU	0	15
N23		at Louisiana Tech	16	0

1902 6-3-0
O4	•	at Neosho HS	6	0
O11	•	at Kingfisher Coll.	15	6
O22	•	at Oklahoma	0	28
O28	•	Tulsa *Mus*	33	0
N1	•	Tahlequah S.	50	0
N8		at S.W. Missouri	5	15
N10		at Pierce C.C.	2	24
N17	•	Fort Scott HS	16	0
N27	•	Missouri Rolla	11	0

D.A. McDANIEL 1903 (.429) 3-4

1903 3-4-0
O10	•	S.W. Missouri	5	10
O16		at Missouri M.	6	17
O17	•	at Drury Coll.	10	6
O30		at Texas	0	15
O31		at Texas A&M	0	6
N7	•	Fort Smith HS	17	9
N21	•	Oklahoma	12	0

A.D. BROWN 1904-05 (.400) 6-9

1904 4-3-0
O15	•	Drury Coll.	0	12
O22	•	Fort Scott HS	22	0
N4	•	at Dallas Med.	0	5
N5	•	at Baylor	6	17
N12	•	Wichita St.	12	6
N19	•	at Fort Smith	11	5
N26	•	Missouri Rolla	11	10

1905 2-6-0
O7		Kansas	0	6
O14		at Washington, Mo.	0	6
O16		at Drury Coll.	0	12
O26	•	Chilocco	6	0
O31		Texas	0	4
N12		Transylvania, Ky.	0	5
N17		at Missouri Rolla	0	16
N30	•	KC Medics	26	0

F.C. LONGMAN 1906-07 (.406) 5-8-3

1906 2-4-2
S29	•	Chilocco	0	6
O8	=	Drury Coll.	0	0
O13	•	at Kansas	5	37
O30		at Texas	0	11
N6	•	S.E. Missouri St. *Hot*	12	0
N10		at Missouri	0	11
N24	•	at Tulane	22	0
N29	=	at LSU	6	6

1907 3-4-1
O5	•	Haskell	0	0
O12	•	Drury Coll.	23	0
O19	•	at Drury Coll.	17	6
O26	•	at St. Louis	6	42
O30	•	Texas	6	26
N6	•	at LSU	12	17
N18	•	Tennessee *Mem*	2	14
N23	•	Missouri Rolla	7	5

HUGO BEZDEK 1908-12 (.686) 29-13-1

1908 5-4-0
O3	•	Haskell	6	0
O10	•	Mississippi	33	0
O17	•	at St. Louis	0	24
O24	•	Henderson St.	51	0
O31	•	at Oklahoma	5	27
N7	•	at Texas	0	21
N14	•	Pittsburg St.	42	12
N21	•	Ouachita	73	0
N26	•	LSU *LR*	4	36

1909 7-0-0
O2	•	Henderson St.	24	0
O9	•	at Drury Coll.	12	6
O16	•	Wichita St.	23	6
O23	•	Oklahoma	21	6*
O30	•	at Ouachita	56	0
N13	•	LSU *Mem*	16	0
N25	•	Washington, Mo. *LR*	34	0

1910 7-1-0
O1	•	Drury Coll.	33	0
O9	•	Henderson St.	63	0
O15	•	Kansas State	0	5
O22	•	Texas SW	13	12
O29	•	Texas A&M	5	0
N5	•	at Washington, Mo.	50	0
N15	•	Missouri Rolla	6	2
N24	•	LSU *LR*	51	0

1911 6-2-1
S30	•	S.W. Missouri St.	100	0
O7	•	Drury Coll.	65	0
O14	•	Hendrix College	45	0
O28	•	at Texas	0	12
N4	=	at Southwestern	0	0
N11	•	Missouri Rolla *Jop*	44	3
N18	•	Kansas State *KC*	0	3
N25	•	at Washington, Mo.	3	0
N30	•	LSU *LR*	11	0

1912 4-6-0
S28	•	Henderson St.	39	6
O5	•	Hendrix College	52	0
O12	•	Oklahoma State	7	13
O18	•	Texas A&M *Dal*	0	27
O26	•	at Baylor	0	6 *
N2	•	Southwestern	25	0
N9	•	at Wisconsin	7	64
N16	•	LSU *LR*	6	7
N23	•	at Washington, Mo.	13	7
N28	•	at Texas	0	48

E.T. PICKERING 1913-14 (.556) 10-8

1913 7-2-0
O3	•	Henderson St.	3	0
O11	•	Hendrix	26	0
O18	•	Oklahoma State	3	0
O25	•	Baylor	34	0
N1	•	Austin Coll. *FrS*	26	7
N8	•	LSU *Shre*	7	12
N15	•	Mississippi *LR*	10	21
N17	•	at Ouachita	14	3
N27	•	at Tulane	14	0

1914 3-6-0
O3	•	Hendrix	13	7
O10	•	Ouachita	9	15
O17	•	St. Louis	26	0
O24	•	Missouri Rolla	0	44
O31	•	at Oklahoma State	0	46
N7	•	LSU *Shre*	20	12
N14	•	Mississippi *LR*	7	13
N21	•	Oklahoma *OkC*	7	35
N28	•	at Drury Coll.	7	28

1915-1991 SWC

T.T. McCONNELL 1915-16 (.567) 8-6-1

1915 4-2-1 (1-1-0)
O2	•	Hendrix	41	0
O9	•	Ouachita	13	9
O23	•	Oklahoma State *FrS*	14	9
O30	=	at St. Louis	0	0
N5	•	LSU *Shre*	7	13
N14	•	Oklahoma	0	24
N20	•	Missouri Rolla	46	0

1916 4-4-0 (0-2-0)
S30	•	Pittsburg St.	34	20
O7	•	Hendrix	58	0
O14	•	Oklahoma Mines	82	0
O21	•	Missouri Rolla	60	0
N5	•	LSU *Shre*	7	17
N14		at Texas	0	52
N23		Oklahoma *FrS*	13	14
N30	•	Mississippi State *Mem*	7	20

NORMAN PAINE 1917-18 (.708) 8-3-1

1917 5-1-1 (0-1-1)
O6	•	Central Mo. St.	34	0
O13	•	Hendrix	19	0
O20	•	Missouri Rolla	32	0
O27	•	Tulsa	19	7
N3	•	LSU *Shre*	14	0
N17	=	Oklahoma *FrS*	0	0
N29		at Texas	0	20

1918 3-2-0 (0-1-0)
S28	•	Camp Pike	0	6
O5	•	Missouri Rolla	6	0
O19	•	at Oklahoma	0	103
O26	•	Tulsa	23	6
N2	•	at S.W. Missouri St.	12	6

J.B. CRAIG 1919 (.429) 3-4

1919 3-4-0 (1-2-0)
O11	•	Hendrix	7	0
O18	•	Missouri Rolla	20	0
O25	•	LSU *Shre*	0	20
N1	•	Tulsa	7	63
N8	•	at Texas	7	35
N15	•	Oklahoma	7	6
N27		at Rice	7	40

G.W. McLAREN 1920-21 (.594) 8-5-3

1920 3-2-2 (2-0-1)
O9	=	Hendrix	0	0
O16	•	TCU	2	19
O22		at SMU	6	0
O30	•	Missouri Rolla	14	0
N6	•	LSU *Shre*	0	3
N13	•	at Phillips	20	0
N25		at Rice	0	0

1921 5-3-1 (2-1-0)
O1	•	Hendrix	28	0
O8	•	Drury Coll.	40	0
O15	•	Ouachita *LR*	28	0
O22		Oklahoma State	0	7
O29	•	SMU *FrS*	14	0
N5	•	LSU *Shre*	7	10
N12	•	at Phillips	0	0
N19	•	Baylor	13	12
N24	•	at TCU	14	19

FRANCIS SCHMIDT 1922-28 (.654) 41-21-3

1922 4-5-0 (1-3-0)
S30	•	Hendrix	39	0
O7	•	Drury Coll.	22	0
O14	•	Ouachita *LR*	7	13
O21	•	at Baylor	13	60
O28	•	LSU *Shre*	40	6
N4	•	Tulsa	6	13
N11		at Rice	7	31
N18		SMU	9	0
N30		Oklahoma State *FrS*	0	13

1923 6-2-1 (2-2-0)
S29	•	Central Ark.	32	0
O6	•	Drury Coll.	26	0
O13	•	Rice *LR*	23	0
O20		Baylor	0	14
O27	•	LSU *Shre*	26	13
N3	=	Ouachita	0	0
N10		at SMU	6	13
N24	•	Phillips *Mus*	32	0
D1	•	Oklahoma State *FrS*	13	0

1924 — 7-2-1 (1-2-1)

S27	●	N.E. Oklahoma	54	6
O4	●	S.W. Missouri St.	47	0
O11	●	Hendrix	34	3
O18	|	at Baylor	0	13
O25	●	Mississippi [LR]	20	0
N1	● |	LSU [SHRE]	10	7
N8	= |	SMU	14	14
N15	●	Phillips [FtS]	28	6
N21	|	at Oklahoma State	0	20
N27	● |	TCU	20	0

1925 — 4-4-1 (2-2-1)

O3		at Iowa	0	25*
O10		Oklahoma Baptist	0	6
O17	|	at Rice	9	13
O24	●	Phillips	45	0
O31	● ||	LSU [SHRE]	12	0
N7	= |	at SMU	0	0
N14	|	at TCU	0	3
N21	● ||	Oklahoma State	9	7
N28	●	at Tulsa	20	7

1926 — 5-5-0 (2-2-0)

S26	●	Central Ark.	60	0
O2	● ||	Mississippi	21	6
O9		at Oklahoma	6	13
O16	●	Hendrix [LR]	14	7
O23	● ||	Centenary	33	6
O30		at Kansas State	7	16
N6	||	LSU [SHRE]	0	14
N12	|	TCU	7	10
N19	●	at Oklahoma State	24	2
N25		at Tulsa	7	14

1927 — 8-1-0 (3-1-0)

O1	●	Ozark Coll.	32	0
O8	● |	Baylor	13	6
O15	|	at Texas A&M	6	40
O22	●	Missouri Rolla	34	0
O29	● ||	LSU [SHRE]	28	0
N5	● |	at TCU	10	3
N12	●	Oklahoma State	33	20
N19	●	Austin Coll.	42	0
N26	●	Hendrix [LR]	20	7

1928 — 7-2-0 (3-1-0)

S29		at Mississippi	0	25
O6	●	Coll. Of Ozarks	21	0
O13	● |	Baylor [TEX]	14	0
O20	|	at Texas	7	20
O29	● |	Texas A&M	27	12
N3	● ||	LSU [SHRE]	7	0
N17	●	Missouri Rolla	45	6
N24	●	Oklahoma Baptist	57	0
N29	●	Southwestern [MEM]	73	0

FRED THOMSEN
1929-41 (.480) 56-61-10

1929 — 7-2-0 (3-2-0)

S28	●	Ozark Coll.	37	0
O5	●	Henderson St.	30	7
O12	|	Texas	0	27
O19	|	at Baylor	20	31
O26	● |	at Texas A&M	14	13
N2	● ||	LSU [SHRE]	32	0
N9	●	E. Central Oklahoma	52	7
N16	●	Centenary	13	2
N28	● ||	at Oklahoma State	32	6

1930 — 3-6-0 (2-2-0)

S27	●	Ozark Coll.	27	0
O4		at Tulsa	6	26
O11	|	at TCU	0	40
O18	● |	Rice	7	6
O25	● |	Texas A&M [LR]	13	0
N1		LSU [SHRE]	12	27
N8		Oklahoma State	0	26
N15	|	Baylor	7	22
N27		at Centenary	6	7

1931 — 3-5-1 (0-4-0)

S26	●	Ozark Coll.	13	6
O3	●	Hendrix	19	0
O10	|	SMU	6	42
O17	|	at Baylor	7	19
O24		LSU [SHRE]	6	13
O31	|	TCU	0	7
N7	=	at Chicago	13	13
N21	|	at Rice	12	26
N26	●	at Centenary	6	0

1932 — 1-6-2 (1-4-0)

S24	=	Hendrix	0	0
O1		Missouri Rolla	19	20
O8	|	at TCU	12	34
O15	● |	Baylor [LR]	20	6
O22		LSU [SHRE]	0	14
N5	|	Rice	7	12
N12	|	at SMU	7	13
N18	|	Texas	0	34
N26	=	at Centenary	0	0

1933 — 7-3-1 (4-1-0)

S23	●	Ozark Coll.	40	0
S30	●	Oklahoma Baptist	42	7
O7	● |	TCU	13	0
O14	● |	Baylor [LR]	19	7
O21		LSU [SHRE]	0	20
O28	● |	SMU	3	0
N11	|	at Rice	6	7
N18	●	Hendrix	63	0
N24	● |	at Texas	20	6
N30		at Tulsa	0	7
		DIXIE CLASSIC		
J1	=	Centenary	7	7

1934 — 4-4-2 (2-3-1)

S29	●	Ozark Coll.	13	0
O6	● |	at TCU	24	10
O13	● |	Baylor [LR]	6	0
O20		LSU [SHRE]	0	16
O27	●	Missouri Rolla	20	0
N3	= |	at Texas A&M	7	7
N10	|	Rice	0	7
N17	|	at SMU	6	10
N23	|	Texas	12	19
N29	=	at Tulsa	7	7

1935 — 5-5-0 (2-4-0)

S28	●	Pittsburgh St.	12	0
O5	|	TCU	7	13
O12	|	at Baylor	6	13
O19		LSU [SHRE]	7	13
O26	●	Ozark Coll.	51	6
N2	● |	Texas A&M [LR]	14	7
N9	|	at Rice	7	20
N16	|	SMU	6	17
N22	● |	at Texas	28	13
N28	●	at Tulsa	14	7

1936 — 7-3-0 (5-1-0)

S26	●	Pittsburg St.	53	0
O3	|	at TCU	14	18
O10	● |	Baylor	14	10
O16		at George Washington	6	13
O24		LSU [SHRE]	7	19
O31	● |	at Texas A&M	18	0
N7	● |	Rice	20	14
N14	● |	at SMU	17	0
N26	●	at Tulsa	23	13
D3	● |	Texas [LR]	6	0

1937 — 6-2-2 (3-2-1)

S25	●	Central Oklahoma	25	0
O2	= |	TCU	7	7
O9	|	at Baylor	14	20
O16	● |	at Texas	21	10
O23	● |	SMU [FtS]	13	0
O30	● |	Texas A&M	26	13
N6	|	at Rice	20	26
N13	●	Mississippi [MEM]	32	6
N20	=	George Washington [LR]	0	0
N25	●	at Tulsa	28	7

1938 — 2-7-1 (1-5-0)

S24	●	Oklahoma State	27	7
O1	|	at TCU	14	21
O8	|	Baylor	6	9
O15	● |	Texas [LR]	42	6
O22		Santa Clara [SF]	6	21
O29	|	at Texas A&M	7	13
N5	|	Rice	0	3
N12	|	at SMU	6	19
N16		Mississippi [MEM]	14	20
N24	=	at Tulsa	6	6

1939 — 4-5-1 (2-3-1)

S23	●	East Central Oklahoma	32	6
S30		Mississippi State [MEM]	0	19
O7	● |	TCU	14	13
O14	|	at Baylor	7	19
O21	|	at Texas	13	14
O28		Villanova [PHIL]	0	7
N4	|	Texas A&M	0	27
N11	= |	at Rice	12	12
N17	● |	SMU [LR]	14	0
N30	●	at Tulsa	23	0

1940 — 4-6-0 (1-5-0)

S28	●	East Central Oklahoma	38	0
O5	|	at TCU	0	20
O12	● |	Baylor	12	6
O19	|	Texas [LR]	0	21
O26	●	Mississippi [MEM]	21	20
N2	|	at Texas A&M	0	17
N9	|	Rice	7	14
N16	|	at SMU	0	28
N21		Fordham [NYC]	7	27
N28	●	at Tulsa	27	21

1941 — 3-7-0 (0-6-0)

S27	●	E. Cent. Okla.	56	0
O4	|	TCU	0	9
O11	|	at Baylor	7	20
O18	|	at Texas	14	48
O25	●	at Detroit	9	6
N1	|	Texas A&M [LR]	0	7
N8	|	at Rice	12	21
N15	|	SMU	7	14
N22		Mississippi [MEM]	0	18
N27	●	at Tulsa	13	6

GEORGE COLE
1942 (.300) 3-7

1942 — 3-7-0 (0-6-0)

S26	●	Wichita St.	27	0
O3	|	at TCU	6	13
O10	|	Baylor	7	20
O17	|	Texas [LR]	6	47
O24	●	Mississippi [MEM]	7	6
O31	|	at Texas A&M	0	41
N7	|	Rice	9	40
N14	|	at SMU	6	14
N21	●	at Detroit	14	7
N26		at Tulsa	7	40

JOHN TOMLIN
1943 (.222) 2-7

1943 — 2-7-0 (1-4-0)

S25	●	Missouri Rolla	59	0
O2	|	TCU [LR]	0	13
O9		Mont Navy	12	20
O16	|	at Texas	0	34
O30	|	Texas A&M	0	13
N6	|	at Rice	7	20
N13	● |	SMU [SA]	14	12
N19		Oklahoma State [FtS]	13	19
N25		at Tulsa	0	61

GLEN ROSE
1944-45 (.405) 8-12-1

1944 — 5-5-1 (2-2-1)

S23	●	Missouri [StL]	7	6
S29		Oklahoma State [OkC]	0	19
O7	= |	at TCU	6	6
O14		Norman NAS	7	27
O21	|	Texas [LR]	0	19
O28	●	Mississippi [MEM]	26	18
N4	● |	at Texas A&M	7	6
N11	● |	Rice	12	7
N18	|	at SMU	12	20
N23		at Tulsa	2	33
D2	●	Arkansas State	41	0

1945 — 3-7-0 (1-5-0)

S22	●	at Barksdale Field	12	6
S29		Oklahoma State	14	19
O6	● |	TCU	27	14
O13	|	at Baylor	13	23
O20	|	Texas [LR]	7	34
O27	●	Mississippi [MEM]	19	0
N3	|	Texas A&M	0	34
N10	|	at Rice	7	26
N17	|	at SMU	0	21
N23		at Tulsa	13	45

JOHN BARNHILL
1946-49 (.560) 22-17-3

1946 — 6-3-2 (5-1-0)

S21	●	N.W. Louisiana St.	21	14
S28	=	at Oklahoma State	21	21
O5	● |	at TCU	34	14
O12	● |	Baylor	13	0
O19	|	at Texas	0	20
O26		Mississippi [MEM]	7	9
N2	● |	at Texas A&M	7	0
N9	● |	Rice [LR]	7	0
N16	● |	SMU	13	0
N28		at Tulsa	13	14
		COTTON BOWL		
J1	=	LSU	0	0

1947 — 6-4-1 (1-4-1)

S20	●	N.W. Louisiana St.	64	0
S27	●	North Texas [LR]	12	0
O4	● |	TCU	6	0
O11	|	at Baylor	9	17
O18	|	Texas [MEM]	6	21
O25	●	Mississippi [MEM]	19	14
N1	= |	Texas A&M	21	21
N8	|	at Rice	0	26
N15	|	at SMU	6	14
N27	●	at Tulsa	27	13
		DIXIE BOWL		
J1	●	William & Mary	21	19

1948 — 5-5-0 (2-4-0)

S18	●	Abilene Christian [LR]	40	6
S25	●	East Texas St.	46	7
O2	● |	at TCU	27	14
O9	|	Baylor	7	23
O16	|	at Texas	6	14
O30	● |	at Texas A&M	28	6
N6	|	Rice [LR]	6	25
N13	|	SMU	12	14
N20	●	Tulsa [LR]	55	18
N27		William & Mary [LR]	0	19

1949 — 5-5-0 (2-4-0)

S24	●	North Texas [LR]	33	19
O1	● |	TCU	27	7
O8	|	at Baylor	13	35
O15	|	Texas [LR]	14	27
O22	●	at Vanderbilt	7	6
O29	● |	Texas A&M	27	6
N5	|	at Rice	0	14
N12	|	at SMU	6	34
N19		William & Mary [LR]	0	20
N26	●	Tulsa	40	7

OTIS DOUGLAS
1950-52 (.300) 9-21

1950 — 2-8-0 (1-5-0)

S23		Oklahoma State [LR]	7	12
S30	●	North Texas	50	6
O7	|	at TCU	6	13
O14	● |	Baylor	27	6
O21	|	at Texas	14	19
O28		Vanderbilt [LR]	13	14
N4	|	at Texas A&M	13	42
N11	|	Rice	6	9
N18	|	SMU [LR]	7	14
N23		at Tulsa	13	28

1951 — 5-5-0 (2-4-0)

S22	●	at Oklahoma State	42	7
S29	●	Arizona State	30	13
O6	|	TCU [LR]	7	17
O13	|	at Baylor	7	9
O20	● |	Texas	16	14
O27		Santa Clara [LR]	12	21
N3	● |	Texas A&M	33	21
N10	|	at Rice	0	6
N17	|	at SMU	7	47
N24	●	Tulsa [LR]	24	7

1952 — 2-8-0 (1-5-0)

S20	●	Oklahoma State [LR]	22	20
S27		Houston	7	17
O4	|	at TCU	7	13
O11	● |	Baylor [LR]	20	17
O18	|	at Texas	7	44
O25		Mississippi [LR]	7	34
N1	|	at Texas A&M	12	31
N8	|	Rice	33	35
N15	|	SMU	17	27
N22		at Tulsa	34	44

BOWDEN WYATT
1953-54 (.524) 11-10

1953 — 3-7-0 (2-4-0)

S26		Oklahoma State [LR]	6	7
O3	● |	TCU	13	6
O10	|	at Baylor	7	14
O17	|	Texas	7	16
O24		Mississippi [MEM]	0	28
O31	● |	Texas A&M [LR]	41	14
N7	|	at Rice	0	47
N14	|	at SMU	7	13
N21		LSU [LR]	8	9
N28	●	Tulsa	27	7

1954 — 8-3-0 (5-1-0)

Date	Result	Opponent	Ark	Opp
S25	●	Tulsa	41	0
O2	● |	at TCU	20	13
O9	● |	Baylor	21	20
O16	● |	at Texas	20	7
O23	●	Mississippi LR	6	0
O30	● |	at Texas A&M	14	7
N6	● |	Rice LR	28	15
N13	|	SMU	14	21
N20		LSU Shre	6	7
N27	●	at Houston	19	0
		COTTON BOWL		
J1		Georgia Tech	6	14

JACK MITCHELL
1955-57 (.583) 17-12-1

1955 — 5-4-1 (3-2-1)

Date	Result	Opponent	Ark	Opp
S17	●	Tulsa	21	6
S24	●	Oklahoma State LR	21	0
O1	|	TCU	0	26
O8	|	at Baylor	20	25
O15	● |	Texas LR	27	20
O22		at Mississippi	7	17
O29	= |	Texas A&M	7	7
N5	● |	at Rice	10	0
N12	● |	at SMU	6	0
N19		LSU LR	7	13

1956 — 6-4-0 (3-3-0)

Date	Result	Opponent	Ark	Opp
S22	●	Hardin-Simmons	21	6
S29	●	Oklahoma State LR	19	7
O6	|	at TCU	6	41
O13	|	Baylor	7	14
O20	● |	at Texas	32	14
O27	●	Mississippi LR	14	0
N3	|	at Texas A&M	0	27
N10	● |	Rice	27	12
N17	● |	SMU LR	27	13
N24		LSU Shre	7	21

1957 — 6-4-0 (2-4-0)

Date	Result	Opponent	Ark	Opp
S21	●	Oklahoma State LR	12	0
S28	●	Tulsa	41	14
O5	● |	TCU LR	20	7
O12	● |	at Baylor	20	17
O19	|	Texas	0	17
O26	●	Mississippi Mem	12	6
N2	|	Texas A&M	6	7
N9	|	at Rice	7	13
N16	|	at SMU	22	27
N23	●	Texas Tech LR	47	26

FRANK BROYLES
1958-76 (.708) 144-58-5

1958 — 4-6-0 (2-4-0)

Date	Result	Opponent	Ark	Opp
S20	|	Baylor LR	0	12
S27		Tulsa	14	27
O4	|	at TCU	7	12
O11	|	Rice	0	24
O18	|	at Texas	6	24
O25		Mississippi LR	12	14
N1	● |	at Texas A&M	21	8
N8	●	Hardin-Simmons LR	60	15
N15	● |	SMU	13	6
N22	●	at Texas Tech	14	8

1959 — 9-2-0 (5-1-0)

Date	Result	Opponent	Ark	Opp
S19	●	Tulsa	28	0
S26	●	Oklahoma State LR	13	7
O3	● |	TCU	3	0
O10	● |	at Baylor	23	7
O17	|	Texas LR	12	13
O24		Mississippi Mem	0	28
O31	● |	Texas A&M	12	7
N7	● |	at Rice	14	10
N14	● |	at SMU	17	14
N21	●	Texas Tech LR	27	8
		GATOR BOWL		
J2	●	Georgia Tech	14	7

1960 — 8-3-0 (6-1-0)

Date	Result	Opponent	Ark	Opp
S17	●	Oklahoma State LR	9	0
S24	●	Tulsa	48	7
O1	● |	at TCU	7	0
O8	|	Baylor	14	28
O15	● |	at Texas	24	23
O22		Mississippi LR	7	10
O29	● |	at Texas A&M	7	3
N5	● |	Rice LR	3	0
N12	● |	SMU	26	3
N19	● |	at Texas Tech	34	6
		COTTON BOWL		
J2		Duke	6	7

1961 — 8-3-0 (6-1-0)

Date	Result	Opponent	Ark	Opp
S23		Mississippi JaM	0	16
S30	●	Tulsa	6	0
O7	● |	TCU LR	28	3
O14	● |	at Baylor	23	13
O21	|	Texas	7	33
O28	●	Northwestern St. LR	42	7
N4	● |	Texas A&M	15	8
N11	● |	at Rice	10	0
N18	● |	at SMU	21	7
N25	● |	Texas Tech LR	28	0
		SUGAR BOWL		
J1		Alabama	3	10

1962 — 9-2-0 (6-1-0)

Date	Result	Opponent	Ark	Opp
S22	●	Oklahoma State LR	34	7
S29	●	Tulsa	42	14
O6	● |	at TCU	42	14
O13	● |	Baylor	28	21
O20	|	at Texas	3	7
O27	●	Hardin-Simmons LR	49	7
N3	● |	at Texas A&M	17	7
N10	● |	Rice	28	14
N17	● |	SMU LR	9	7
N24	● |	at Texas Tech	34	0
		SUGAR BOWL		
J1		Mississippi	13	17

1963 — 5-5-0 (3-4-0)

Date	Result	Opponent	Ark	Opp
S21	●	Oklahoma State LR	21	0
S28		Missouri LR	6	7
O5	● |	TCU	18	3
O12	|	at Baylor	10	14
O19	|	Texas LR	13	17
O26	●	Tulsa	56	7
N2	● |	Texas A&M LR	21	7
N9	|	at Rice	0	7
N16	|	at SMU	7	14
N23	● |	Texas Tech	27	20

1964 — 11-0-0 (7-0-0)

Date	Result	Opponent	Ark	Opp
S19	●	Oklahoma State LR	14	10
S26	●	Tulsa	31	22
O3	● |	at TCU	29	6
O10	● |	Baylor LR	17	6
O17	● |	at Texas	14	13
O24	●	Wichita St. LR	17	0
O31	● |	at Texas A&M	17	0
N7	● |	Rice	21	0
N14	● |	SMU	44	0
N21	● |	at Texas Tech	17	0
		COTTON BOWL		
J1	●	Nebraska	10	7

1965 — 10-1-0 (7-0-0)

Date	Result	Opponent	Ark	Opp
S18	●	Oklahoma State LR	28	14
S25	●	Tulsa	20	12
O2	● |	TCU LR	28	0
O9	● |	at Baylor	38	7
O16	● |	Texas	27	24
O23	●	North Texas LR	55	20
O30	● |	Texas A&M LR	31	0
N6	● |	at Rice	31	0
N13	● |	at SMU	24	3
N20	● |	Texas Tech	42	24
		COTTON BOWL		
J1		LSU	7	14

1966 — 8-2-0 (5-2-0)

Date	Result	Opponent	Ark	Opp
S17	●	Oklahoma State LR	14	10
S24	●	Tulsa	27	8
O1	● |	at TCU	21	0
O8	|	Baylor	0	7
O15	● |	at Texas	12	7
O22	●	Wichita St. LR	41	0
O29	● |	at Texas A&M	34	0
N5	● |	Rice LR	31	20
N12	● |	SMU	22	0
N19	|	at Texas Tech	16	21

1967 — 4-5-1 (3-3-1)

Date	Result	Opponent	Ark	Opp
S23		Oklahoma State LR	6	7
S30		Tulsa	12	14
O7	● |	TCU	26	0
O14	= |	at Baylor	10	10
O21	|	Texas LR	12	21
O28	●	Kansas State LR	28	7
N4	|	Texas A&M	21	33
N11	● |	at Rice	23	9
N18	● |	at SMU	35	17
N25	|	Texas Tech LR	27	31

1968 — 10-1-0 (6-1-0)

Date	Result	Opponent	Ark	Opp
S21	●	Oklahoma State LR	32	15
S28	●	Tulsa	56	13
O5	● |	at TCU	17	7
O12	● |	Baylor	35	19
O19	|	at Texas	29	39
O26	●	North Texas LR	17	15
N2	● |	at Texas A&M	25	22
N9	● |	Rice	46	21
N16	● |	SMU LR	35	29
N23	● |	at Texas Tech	42	7
		SUGAR BOWL		
J1	●	Georgia	16	2

1969 — 9-2-0 (6-1-0)

Date	Result	Opponent	Ark	Opp
S20	●	Oklahoma State LR	39	0
S27	●	Tulsa	55	0
O4	● |	TCU LR	24	6
O11	● |	at Baylor	21	7
O25	●	Wichita St. LR	52	14
N1	● |	Texas A&M	35	13
N8	● |	at Rice	30	6
N15	● |	at SMU	28	15
N27	● |	Texas Tech LR	33	0
D6	|	Texas	14	15
		SUGAR BOWL		
J1		Mississippi	22	27

1970 — 9-2-0 (6-1-0)

Date	Result	Opponent	Ark	Opp
S12		Stanford LR	28	34
S19	●	Oklahoma State LR	23	7
S26	●	Tulsa	49	7
O3	● |	at TCU	49	14
O10	● |	Baylor LR	41	7
O24	●	Wichita St. LR	62	0
O31	● |	at Texas A&M	45	6
N7	● |	Rice	38	14
N14	● |	SMU	36	3
N21	● |	at Texas Tech	24	10
D5	|	at Texas	7	42

1971 — 8-3-1 (5-1-1)

Date	Result	Opponent	Ark	Opp
S11	●	California LR	51	20
S18	●	Oklahoma State LR	31	10
S25		Tulsa	20	21
O2	● |	TCU	49	15
O9	● |	at Baylor	35	7
O16	● |	Texas LR	31	7
O23	●	North Texas	60	21
O30	|	Texas A&M LR	9	17
N6	= |	at Rice	24	24
N13	● |	at SMU	18	13
N20	● |	Texas Tech	15	0
		LIBERTY BOWL		
D20		Tennessee	13	14

1972 — 6-5-0 (3-4-0)

Date	Result	Opponent	Ark	Opp
S9		Southern California LR	10	31
S23	●	Oklahoma State LR	24	23
S30	●	Tulsa	21	20
O7	● |	at TCU	27	13
O14	● |	Baylor	31	20
O21	|	at Texas	15	35
O28	●	North Texas LR	42	16
N4	|	at Texas A&M	7	10
N11	|	Rice LR	20	23
N18	|	SMU	7	22
N25	● |	at Texas Tech	24	14

1973 — 5-5-1 (3-3-1)

Date	Result	Opponent	Ark	Opp
S15		at Southern California	0	17
S22		Oklahoma State LR	6	38
S29	●	Iowa State	21	19
O6	● |	TCU LR	13	5
O13	● |	at Baylor	13	7
O20	|	Texas	6	34
O27	●	Tulsa LR	20	6
N3	● |	Texas A&M	14	10
N10	|	at Rice	7	17
N17	= |	at SMU	7	7
N24	|	Texas Tech LR	17	24

1974 — 6-4-1 (3-3-1)

Date	Result	Opponent	Ark	Opp
S14	●	Southern California LR	22	7
S21		Oklahoma State LR	7	26
S28	●	Tulsa	60	0
O5	● |	TCU	49	0
O12	|	Baylor	17	21
O19	|	at Texas	7	38
O26	●	Colorado State LR	43	9
N2	|	at Texas A&M	10	20
N9	● |	Rice	25	6
N16	= |	SMU LR	24	24
N23	● |	at Texas Tech	21	13

1975 — 10-2-0 (6-1-0)

Date	Result	Opponent	Ark	Opp
S13	●	Air Force LR	35	0
S20		at Oklahoma State	13	20
S27	●	Tulsa	31	15
O4	● |	TCU LR	19	8
O11	● |	at Baylor	41	3
O18	|	Texas	18	24
O25	●	Utah State LR	31	0
N8	● |	at Rice	20	16
N15	● |	at SMU	35	7
N22	● |	Texas Tech	31	14
D6	● |	Texas A&M LR	31	6
		COTTON BOWL		
J1	●	Georgia	31	10

1976 — 5-5-1 (3-4-1)

Date	Result	Opponent	Ark	Opp
S11	●	Utah State LR	33	16
S18	●	Oklahoma State LR	16	10
S25		Tulsa	3	9
O2	● |	TCU	46	14
O23	● |	at Houston	14	7
O30	● |	Rice	41	16
N6	= |	at Baylor	7	7
N13	|	Texas A&M LR	10	31
N20	|	SMU Shre	31	35
N27	|	Texas Tech LR	7	30
D4	|	at Texas	12	29

LOU HOLTZ
1977-83 (.735) 60-21-2

1977 — 11-1-0 (7-1-0)

Date	Result	Opponent	Ark	Opp
S10	●	New Mexico St. LR	53	10
S17	●	Oklahoma State LR	28	6
S24	●	Tulsa	37	3
O1	● |	at TCU	42	6
O15	|	Texas	9	13
O22	● |	Houston LR	34	0
O29	● |	at Rice	30	7
N5	● |	Baylor LR	35	9
N12	● |	at Texas A&M	26	20
N19	● |	SMU	47	7
N26	● |	at Texas Tech	17	14
		ORANGE BOWL		
J2	●	Oklahoma	31	6

1978 — 9-2-1 (6-2-0)

Date	Result	Opponent	Ark	Opp
S16	●	Vanderbilt LR	48	17
S23	●	at Oklahoma State	19	7
S30	●	Tulsa	21	13
O7	● |	TCU LR	42	3
O21	|	at Texas	21	28
O28	|	at Houston	9	20
N4	● |	Rice	37	7
N11	● |	at Baylor	27	14
N18	● |	Texas A&M LR	26	7
N25	● |	at SMU	27	14
D2	● |	Texas Tech	49	7
		FIESTA BOWL		
D25	=	UCLA	10	10

1979 — 10-2-0 (7-1-0)

Date	Result	Opponent	Ark	Opp
S15	●	Colorado State LR	36	3
S22	●	Oklahoma State LR	27	7
S29	●	Tulsa	33	8
O6	● |	at TCU	16	13
O13	● |	at Texas Tech	20	6
O20	● |	Texas LR	17	14
O27	|	Houston	10	13
N3	● |	at Rice	34	7
N10	● |	Baylor	29	20
N17	● |	at Texas A&M	22	10
N24	● |	SMU LR	31	7
		SUGAR BOWL		
J1		Alabama	9	24

1980 — 7-5-0 (3-5-0)

Date	Result	Opponent	Ark	Opp
S1	|	at Texas	17	23
S20	●	Oklahoma State LR	33	20
S27	●	Tulsa	13	10
O4	● |	TCU	44	7
O11	●	Wichita St. LR	27	7
O25	|	at Houston	17	24
N1	|	Rice LR	16	17
N8	|	at Baylor	15	42
N15	● |	Texas A&M	27	24
N22	|	at SMU	7	31
N29	● |	Texas Tech LR	22	16
		HALL OF FAME CLASSIC		
D27	●	Tulane	34	15

THE SCHOOLS

1981   8-4-0 (5-3-0)

S12	●	Tulsa	14	10
S19	●	Northwestern *LR*	38	7
S26	●	Mississippi *JAM*	27	13
O3		at TCU	24	28
O10	●	at Texas Tech	26	14
O17	●	Texas	42	11
O24	●	Houston *LR*	17	20
O31	●	at Rice	41	7
N7	●	Baylor *LR*	41	39
N14	●	at Texas A&M	10	7
N21		SMU	18	32
		GATOR BOWL		
D28		North Carolina	27	31

1982   9-2-1 (5-2-1)

S11	●	Tulsa	38	0
S18	●	Navy *LR*	29	17
S25	●	Mississippi *LR*	14	12
O2	●	TCU *LR*	35	0
O9	●	Texas Tech	21	3
O23	●	at Houston	38	3
O30	●	Rice	24	6
N6		at Baylor	17	24
N13	●	Texas A&M *LR*	35	0
N20	=	at SMU	17	17
D4		at Texas	7	33
		BLUEBONNET BOWL		
D31	●	Florida	28	24

1983   6-5-0 (4-4-0)

S10	●	Tulsa	17	14
S17	●	New Mexico *LR*	17	0
S24	●	Mississippi *JAM*	10	13
O1	●	at TCU	38	21
O15		Texas *LR*	3	31
O22	●	Houston	24	3
O29	●	Rice *LR*	35	0
N5		Baylor	21	24
N12	●	at Texas A&M	23	36
N19		SMU	0	17
N26	●	at Texas Tech	16	13

1984   7-4-1 (5-3-0)

S15	=	Mississippi *LR*	14	14
S22	●	Tulsa	18	9
S29	●	Navy *LR*	33	10
O6		TCU	31	32
O13	●	Texas Tech *LR*	24	0
O20	●	at Texas	18	24
O27	●	at Houston	17	3
N3	●	Rice *LR*	28	6
N10	●	at Baylor	14	9
N17	●	Texas A&M	28	0
N24		at SMU	28	31
		LIBERTY BOWL		
D27	●	Auburn	15	21

1985   10-2-0 (6-2-0)

S14	●	Mississippi *JAM*	24	19
S21	●	Tulsa *LR*	24	0
S28	●	New Mexico St. *LR*	45	13
O5	●	at TCU	41	0
O12	●	at Texas Tech	30	7
O19		Texas	13	15
O26	●	Houston *LR*	57	27
N2	●	at Rice	30	15
N9	●	Baylor *LR*	20	14
N16	●	at Texas A&M	6	10
N23	●	SMU	15	9
		HOLIDAY BOWL		
D22	●	Arizona State	18	17

1986   9-3-0 (6-2-0)

S13	●	Mississippi *LR*	21	0
S20	●	Tulsa	34	17
S27	●	New Mexico St. *LR*	42	11
O4	●	TCU	34	17
O11		Texas Tech	7	17
O18	●	at Texas	21	14
O25	●	at Houston	30	13
N1	●	Rice	45	14
N8		at Baylor	14	29
N15	●	Texas A&M *LR*	14	10
N22	●	at SMU	41	0
		ORANGE BOWL		
J1		Oklahoma	8	42

1987   9-4-0 (5-2-0)

S12	●	Mississippi *JAM*	31	10
S19	●	Tulsa	30	15
S26		Miami, Fla. *LR*	7	51
O3	●	at TCU	20	10
O10	●	at Texas Tech	31	0
O17		Texas *LR*	14	16
O24	●	Houston	21	17
O31	●	at Rice	38	14
N7	●	Baylor	10	7
N14		at Texas A&M	0	14
N28	●	New Mexico *LR*	43	25
D5	●	at Hawaii	38	20
		LIBERTY BOWL		
D29		Georgia	17	20

1988   10-2-0 (7-0-0)

S3	●	Pacific *LR*	63	14
S10	●	Tulsa	30	26
S17	●	Mississippi *LR*	21	13
O1	●	TCU	53	10
O8	●	Texas Tech *LR*	31	10
O15	●	at Texas	27	24
O22	●	at Houston	26	21
O29	●	Rice *LR*	21	14
N5	●	at Baylor	33	3
N12	●	Texas A&M	25	20
N26		at Miami, Fla.	16	18
		COTTON BOWL		
J2		UCLA	3	17

1989   10-2-0 (7-1-0)

S16	●	Tulsa	26	7
S23	●	Mississippi *JAM*	24	17
S30	●	Texas-El Paso *LR*	39	7
O7	●	at TCU *LR*	41	19
O14	●	at Texas Tech	45	13
O21		Texas	20	24
O28	●	Houston *LR*	45	39
N4	●	at Rice	38	17
N11	●	Baylor	19	10
N24	●	at Texas A&M	23	22
D2	●	SMU *LR*	38	24
		COTTON BOWL		
J1		Tennessee	27	31

1990   3-8-0 (1-7-0)

S15	●	Tulsa	28	3
S22		Mississippi *LR*	17	21
S29	●	Colorado State	31	20
O6		TCU *LR*	26	54
O13		Texas Tech	44	49
O20		at Texas	17	49
O27		at Houston	28	62
N3		Rice *LR*	11	19
N10		at Baylor	3	34
N17		Texas A&M	16	20
N24	●	at SMU	42	29

1991   6-6-0 (5-3-0)

A31		Miami, Fla. *LR*	3	31
S7	●	SMU *LR*	17	6
S21	●	La. Lafayette	9	7
S28	●	Mississippi *JAM*	17	24
O5	●	at TCU	22	21
O12	●	Houston	29	17
O19	●	Texas *LR*	14	13
N2		Baylor	5	9
N9	●	at Texas Tech	21	38
N16	●	at Texas A&M	3	13
N23	●	Rice *LR*	20	0
		INDEPENDENCE BOWL		
D29		Georgia	15	24

1992-PRESENT SEC

1992   3-7-1 (3-4-1)

S5		Citadel	3	10
S12	●	at South Carolina	45	7
S19		Alabama *LR*	11	38
S26		at Memphis	6	22
O3		Georgia	3	27
O10	●	at Tennessee	25	24
O17		Mississippi *LR*	3	17
O31	=	at Auburn	24	24
N7		at Mississippi State	3	10
N21		SMU *LR*	19	24
N27	●	LSU	30	6

1993   5-5-1 (3-4-1)

S4	●	at SMU	10	6
S11		South Carolina	18	17
S18		at Alabama	3	43 †
S25		Memphis	0	6
O2		at Georgia	20	10
O9		Tennessee *LR*	14	28
O16		Mississippi *JAM*	0	19
O30		Auburn	21	31
N6	=	Mississippi State *LR*	13	13
N13	●	Tulsa	24	11
N27		at LSU	42	24

1994   4-7-0 (2-6-0)

S3	●	SMU *LR*	34	14
S10		at South Carolina	0	14
S17		Alabama	6	13
S24		at Memphis	15	16
O1	●	Vanderbilt *LR*	42	6
O8		at Tennessee	21	38
O15		Mississippi	31	7
O29		at Auburn	14	31
N5		at Mississippi State	17	17
N12		Northern Illinois	30	27
N26		LSU *LR*	12	30

1995   8-5-0 (6-2-0)

S2		at SMU	14	17
S9	●	South Carolina	51	21
S16		at Alabama	20	19
S23	●	Memphis *LR*	27	20
S30		at Vanderbilt	35	7
O7		Tennessee	31	49
O14	●	Mississippi *MEM*	13	6
O28	●	Auburn	30	28
N4	●	Mississippi State *LR*	26	21
N11	●	La. Lafayette	24	13
N18	●	at LSU	0	28
		SEC CHAMPIONSHIP GAME		
D2		Florida *ATL*	3	34
		CARQUEST BOWL		
D30		North Carolina	10	20

1996   4-7 (2-6)

S7		SMU	10	23
S21		Alabama *LR*	7	17
S28	●	La. Monroe *LR*	38	21
O5		Florida	7	42
O12	●	Louisiana Tech *LR*	38	21
O19		at South Carolina	17	23
N2		at Auburn	7	28
N9	●	Mississippi	13	7
N16		at Tennessee	14	55
N23	●	at Mississippi State	16	13
N29		LSU *LR*	7	17

1997   4-7 (2-6)

S6	●	La. Monroe	28	16
S13		SMU *SHRE*	9	31
S20	●	at Alabama	17	16
S27	●	Louisiana Tech *LR*	17	13
O4		at Florida	7	56
O18	●	South Carolina *LR*	13	39
O25		Auburn	21	26
N6		at Mississippi	19	19
N15		Tennessee *LR*	22	30
N22	●	Mississippi State	17	7
N28		at LSU	21	31

1998   9-3 (6-2)

S5	●	La. Lafayette	38	17
S19	●	SMU *LR*	44	17
S26	●	Alabama	42	6
O3	●	Kentucky *LR*	27	20
O10	●	at Memphis	23	9
O17	●	at South Carolina	41	28
O31	●	at Auburn	24	21
N7	●	Mississippi	34	0
N14		at Tennessee	24	28
N21	●	at Mississippi State	21	22
N27	●	LSU *LR*	41	14
		CITRUS BOWL		
J1		Michigan	31	45

1999   8-4 (4-4)

S4	●	at SMU	26	0
S18	●	La. Monroe *LR*	44	6
S25		at Alabama	28	35
O2		at Kentucky	20	31
O9	●	Middle Tennessee	58	6
O16	●	South Carolina *LR*	48	14
O30	●	Auburn	34	10
N6	●	at Mississippi	16	39
N13	●	Tennessee	28	24
N20	●	Mississippi State *LR*	14	9
N26		at LSU	10	35
		COTTON BOWL		
J1	●	Texas	27	6

2000   6-6 (3-5)

S2	●	S.W. Missouri St. *LR*	38	0
S16	●	Boise State *LR*	38	31
S23	●	Alabama	28	21
S30		Georgia	7	38
O7	●	La. Monroe	52	6
O14		at South Carolina	7	27
O28		at Auburn	19	21
N4		Mississippi	24	38
N11		at Tennessee	20	63
N18	●	Mississippi State	17	10
N24	●	LSU *LR*	14	3
		LAS VEGAS BOWL		
D21		Nevada-Las Vegas	14	31

2001   7-5 (4-4)

A30	●	Nevada-Las Vegas *LR*	14	10
S8		Tennessee	3	13
S22		at Alabama	10	31
S29		at Georgia	23	34
O6		Weber St.	42	19
O13		South Carolina *LR*	10	7
O27		Auburn	42	17
N3	●	at Mississippi	58	56
N10	●	Central Florida	27	20
N17	●	Mississippi State	24	21
N23	●	at LSU	38	41
		COTTON BOWL		
J1		Oklahoma	3	10

2002   9-5 (5-3)

S7	●	Boise State	41	14
S14	●	South Florida *LR*	42	3
S28	●	Alabama	12	30
O5		at Tennessee	38	41
O12	●	at Auburn	38	17
O19	●	Kentucky	17	29
O26	●	Mississippi	48	28
N2	●	Troy State *LR*	23	0
N9	●	at South Carolina	23	0
N16	●	La. Lafayette	24	17
N23	●	at Mississippi State	26	19
N29	●	LSU *LR*	21	20
		SEC CHAMPIONSHIP GAME		
D7		Georgia *ATL*	3	30
		MUSIC CITY BOWL		
D30		Minnesota	14	29

2003   9-4 (4-4)

S6	●	Tulsa	45	13
S13	●	at Texas	38	28
S20	●	North Texas *LR*	31	7
S27	●	at Alabama	34	31
O11	●	Auburn	3	10
O18	●	Florida	28	33
O25		at Mississippi	7	19
N1	●	at Kentucky	71	63
N6	●	South Carolina *LR*	28	6
N15	●	New Mexico State	48	20
N22	●	Mississippi State	52	6
N29		at LSU	24	55
		INDEPENDENCE BOWL		
D31	●	Missouri	27	14

2004   5-6 (3-5)

S4	●	New Mexico State	63	13
S11		Texas	20	22
S18	●	La. Monroe *LR*	49	20
S25	●	Alabama	27	10
O2		at Florida	30	45
O16		at Auburn	20	38
O23		Georgia	14	20
N6		at South Carolina	32	35
N13	●	Mississippi	35	3
N20	●	at Mississippi State	24	21
N26		LSU *LR*	14	43

2005   4-7 (2-6)

S3	●	Missouri State	49	17
S10	|	Vanderbilt	24	28
S17	|	at Southern Cal	17	70
S24	|	at Alabama	13	24
O8	●	La. Monroe *LR*	44	15
O15	|	Auburn	17	34
O22	|	at Georgia	20	23
N5	|	South Carolina	10	14
N12	●	at Mississippi	28	17
N19	|	Mississippi State *LR*	44	10
N25	|	at LSU	17	19

2006   10-4 (7-1)

S2	|	Southern Cal	14	50
S9	●	Utah State	20	0
S16	●	at Vanderbilt	21	19
S23	●	Alabama	24	23
O7	●	at Auburn	27	10
O14	●	SE Missouri	63	7
O21	●	Mississippi	38	3
O28	●	La. Monroe *LR*	44	10
N04	●	at South Carolina	26	20
N11	●	Tennessee	31	14
N18	●	at Mississippi State	28	14
N24	|	LSU *LR*	26	31
		SEC CHAMPIONSHIP GAME		
D2		Florida *Atl*	28	38
		CAPITAL ONE BOWL		
J1		Wisconsin	14	17

REGGIE HERRING
2007 (.000)   0-1

2007   8-5 (4-4)

S1	●	Troy State	46	26
S15	|	at Alabama	38	41
S22	|	Kentucky	29	42
S29	|	North Texas	66	7
O6	●	Chattanooga *LR*	34	15
O13	|	Auburn	7	9
O20	●	at Mississippi	44	8
O27	●	Florida Intn'l	58	10
N03	●	South Carolina	48	36
N10	|	at Tennessee	13	34
N17	●	Mississippi State	45	31
N23	●	at LSU	50	48
		COTTON BOWL		
J1		Missouri	7	38

BOBBY PETRINO
2008-PRESENT (.417)   5-7

2008   5-7 (2-6)

A30	●	Western Illinois	28	24
S6	●	at La.-Monroe *LR*	28	27
S20	|	Alabama	14	49
S27	|	at Texas	10	52
O4	|	Florida	7	38
O11	●	at Auburn	25	22
O18	|	at Kentucky	20	21
O25	|	Mississippi	21	23
N1	●	Tulsa	30	23
N8	|	at South Carolina	21	34
N22	|	at Mississippi State	28	31
N28	●	Louisiana State *Lit*	31	30

Neutral Site key: *Atl* Atlanta, GA / *Dal* Dallas, TX / *FrS* Fort Smith, AR / *Hot* Hot Springs, AR / *JaM* Jackson, MS / *Jop* Joplin, MO / *KC* Kansas City, MO / *LR* Little Rock, AR / *Mem* Memphis, TN / *Mus* Muskogee, OK / *NYC* New York, NY / *OxC* Oklahoma City, OK / *Phil* Philadelphia, PA / *SA* San Antonio, TX / *SF* San Francisco, CA / *Sha* Shawnee, OK / *Shre* Shreveport, LA / *StL* St. Louis, MO / *Tex* Texarkana, TX
ƒ **Forfeit** † **Game Later Forfieted** # **Disputed Victor** * **Disputed Score** || **Designated Conference Game** |2 **Counted Twice in Conference Standings**

ARKANSAS ANNUAL STATISTICAL LEADERS

YR	RUSHING	YDS	ATT	AVG	PASSING	ATT	CMP	PCT	YDS	RECEIVING	REC	YDS	AVG
1945	John Hoffman	587	139	4.2	Bud Canada	69	24	.35	272	John Hoffman	11	196	17.8
1946	Ken Holland	397	112	3.5	Aubrey Fowler	40	18	.45	320	Clyde Scott	11	183	16.6
1947	Clyde Scott	659	152	4.3	Ken Holland	46	25	.54	360	Ross Pritchard	15	266	17.7
1948	Clyde Scott	670	95	7.1	Gordon Long	56	32	.57	449	Ross Pritchard	17	311	18.3
1949	Geno Mazzanti	757	123	6.2	Don Logue	79	31	.39	374	Pat Summerall	17	298	17.5
1950	Buddy Rogers	476	118	4.0	Jim Rinehart	139	59	.42	756	Bill Jurney	22	335	15.2
1951	Lamar McHan	433	127	3.4	Lamar McHan	135	53	.39	724	Pat Summerall	24	358	14.9
1952	Buddy Sutton	448	100	4.5	Lamar McHan	136	55	.40	743	Lewis Carpenter	19	335	17.6
1953	Lamar McHan	409	143	2.9	Lamar McHan	150	78	.52	1,107	Floyd Sagely	30	542	18.1
1954	Henry Moore	670	153	4.4	George Walker	85	45	.53	603	Preston Carpenter	21	234	11.1
1955	Henry Moore	701	134	5.2	George Walker	47	22	.47	347	Preston Carpenter	11	155	14.1
1956	Gerald Nesbitt	663	129	5.1	Don Christian	53	18	.34	260	Ronnie Underwood	7	154	22.0
1957	Gerald Nesbitt	624	145	4.3	George Walker	63	35	.56	587	Billy Kyser	10	179	17.9
1958	Jim Mooty	395	71	5.6	James Monroe	96	41	.43	512	Charlie Barnes	15	175	11.7
1959	Jim Mooty	519	93	5.6	James Monroe	30	19	.63	202	Steve Butler	9	107	11.9
1960	Lance Alworth	375	106	3.5	George McKinney	90	39	.43	728	Jimmy Collier	17	356	20.9
1961	Lance Alworth	516	110	4.7	George McKinney	68	32	.47	426	Lance Alworth	18	320	17.8
1962	Billy Moore	585	131	4.5	Billy Moore	91	51	.56	673	Jerry Lamb	23	378	16.4
1963	Jim Lindsey	444	130	3.4	Bill Gray	79	34	.43	483	Jerry Lamb	16	240	15.0
1964	Jack Brasuell	542	173	3.1	Fred Marshall	94	50	.53	656	Jim Lindsey	24	331	13.8
1965	Bobby Burnett	947	232	4.1	Jon Brittenum	149	75	.50	1,103	Bobby Crockett	30	487	16.2
1966	David Dickey	447	115	3.9	Jon Brittenum	143	76	.53	1,103	Tommy Burnett	29	401	13.8
1967	Russell Cody	383	95	4.0	Ronny South	142	84	.59	1,159	Max Peacock	30	468	15.6
1968	Bill Burnett	859	207	4.1	Bill Montgomery	234	134	.57	1,595	Max Peacock	39	497	12.7
1969	Bill Burnett	900	209	4.3	Bill Montgomery	173	93	.54	1,333	Chuck Dicus	42	688	16.4
1970	Bill Burnett	445	110	4.0	Bill Montgomery	195	110	.56	1,662	Chuck Dicus	38	577	15.2
1971	Dickey Morton	831	127	6.5	Joe Ferguson	271	160	.59	2,203	Mike Reppond	56	986	17.6
1972	Dickey Morton	1,188	242	4.9	Joe Ferguson	254	119	.47	1,484	Mike Reppond	36	475	13.2
1973	Dickey Morton	1,298	226	5.7	Mike Kirkland	151	75	.50	990	Jack Ettinger	28	411	14.7
1974	Ike Forte	974	187	5.2	Scott Bull	32	14	.44	238	Freddie Douglas	15	332	22.1
1975	Ike Forte	983	174	5.6	Scott Bull	71	33	.46	570	Freddie Douglas	13	232	17.8
1976	Ben Cowins	1,162	183	6.3	Ron Calcagni	57	17	.30	366	Charles Clay	7	174	24.9
1977	Ben Cowins	1,192	220	5.4	Ron Calcagni	137	73	.53	1,147	Donnie Bobo	22	454	20.6
1978	Ben Cowins	1,006	188	5.4	Ron Calcagni	103	62	.60	807	Robert Farrell	13	229	17.6
1979	Roland Sales	625	138	4.5	Kevin Scanlon	139	92	.66	1,212	Gary Stiggers	23	221	9.6
1980	James Tolbert	571	140	4.1	Tom Jones	166	93	.56	1,161	Gary Anderson	23	153	6.7
1981	Gary Anderson	616	121	5.1	Brad Taylor	99	53	.54	726	Gary Anderson	26	263	10.1
1982	Daryl Bowles	619	155	4.0	Brad Taylor	141	59	.42	1,073	Gary Anderson	26	486	18.7
1983	Derek Thomas	432	117	3.7	Brad Taylor	257	139	.54	1,837	Mark Mistler	33	401	12.2
1984	Marshall Foreman	804	183	4.4	Brad Taylor	147	82	.56	1,166	James Shibest	51	907	17.8
1985	James Rouse	550	99	5.6	Mark Calcagni	47	27	.57	561	James Shibest	20	446	22.3
1986	Greg Thomas	461	141	3.3	Greg Thomas	109	67	.61	1,032	James Shibest	22	473	21.5
1987	James Rouse	1,004	182	5.5	Quinn Grovey	62	38	.61	495	Derek Russell	16	297	18.6
1988	Barry Foster	660	132	5.0	Quinn Grovey	98	62	.63	966	Tim Horton	16	319	19.9
1989	James Rouse	895	163	5.5	Quinn Grovey	132	72	.55	1,149	Tim Horton	23	454	19.7
1990	E.D. Jackson	596	155	3.8	Quinn Grovey	235	120	.51	1,886	Derek Russell	43	897	20.9
1991	E.D. Jackson	641	143	4.5	Jason Allen	102	48	.47	603	Ron Dickerson	25	372	14.9
1992	E.D. Jackson	466	118	3.9	Barry Lunney Jr.	189	91	.48	1,015	Kirk Botkin	33	257	7.8
1993	Oscar Malone	555	89	6.2	Barry Lunney Jr.	202	104	.51	1,241	J.J. Meadors	28	429	15.3
1994	Oscar Malone	597	99	6.0	Barry Lunney Jr.	183	101	.55	1,345	J.J. Meadors	43	613	14.3
1995	Madre Hill	1,387	307	4.5	Barry Lunney Jr.	292	180	.62	2,181	Anthony Eubanks	43	596	13.9
1996	Oscar Malone	814	197	4.1	Pete Burks	224	115	.51	1,390	Anthony Eubanks	51	809	15.9
1997	Rod Stinson	413	111	3.7	Clint Stoerner	357	173	.48	2,347	Anthony Eubanks	51	870	17.1
1998	Chrys Chukwuma	870	149	5.8	Clint Stoerner	312	167	.54	2,629	Michael Williams	44	560	12.7
1999	Cedric Cobbs	668	116	5.8	Clint Stoerner	317	177	.56	2,293	Anthony Lucas	37	822	22.2
2000	Fred Talley	768	137	5.6	Robby Hampton	261	145	.56	1,548	Boo Williams	52	739	14.2
2001	Fred Talley	774	164	4.7	Zak Clark	179	88	.49	1,000	George Wilson	40	568	14.2
2002	Fred Talley	1,119	197	5.7	Matt Jones	234	122	.52	1,592	George Wilson	49	626	12.8
2003	Cedric Cobbs	1,320	227	5.8	Matt Jones	230	132	.57	1,917	George Wilson	50	900	18.0
2004	Matt Jones	622	83	7.5	Matt Jones	264	151	.57	2,073	Steven Harris	37	617	16.7
2005	Darren McFadden	1,113	176	6.3	Robert Johnson	158	89	.56	876	Peyton Hillis	38	402	10.6
2006	Darren McFadden	1,647	284	5.8	Casey Dick	132	65	.49	991	Marcus Monk	50	962	19.2
2007	Darren McFadden	1,830	325	5.6	Casey Dick	262	150	.57	1,695	Peyton Hills	49	537	11.0
2008	Michael Smith	1,072	207	5.2	Casey Dick	357	205	.57	2,586	D.J. Williams	61	723	11.9

Receiving leaders by receptions
The NCAA began including postseason stats in 2002

ARKANSAS RECORD BOOK

SINGLE-GAME RECORDS

Rushing Yards	321	Darren McFadden (Nov. 3, 2007 vs. South Carolina)
Passing Yards	387	Clint Stoerner (Nov. 28, 1997 vs. LSU)
Receiving Yards	204	Mike Reppond (Nov. 6, 1971 vs. Rice)
All-Purpose Yards	355	Darren McFadden (Nov. 3, 2007 vs. South Carolina)
Points	36	Madre Hill (Sept. 9, 1995 vs. South Carolina)
Field Goals	5	Kendall Trainor (Oct. 1, 1988 vs. TCU; Nov. 12, 1988 vs. Texas A&M)
Tackles	29	Ronnie Caveness (Oct. 19, 1963 vs. Texas)
Interceptions	5	Wear Schoonover (Oct. 26, 1929 vs. Texas A&M)

SINGLE-SEASON RECORDS

Rushing Yards	1,830	Darren McFadden, 2007 (325 att.)
Passing Yards	2,629	Clint Stoerner, 1998 (167-312)
Receiving Yards	1,004	Anthony Lucas, 1998 (43 rec.)
Scoring	120	Bill Burnett, 1969 (20 TDs)
Touchdowns	20	Bill Burnett, 1969
Tackles	174	Wayne Harris, 1960
Interceptions	10	Jim Rinehart, 1949
Punting Average	47.2	Greg Horne, 1986 (49 punts)
Punt Return Average	18.3	Johnny Cole, 1950 (16 ret.)
Kickoff Return Average	31.9	Felix Jones, 2005 (17 ret.)

CAREER RECORDS

Rushing Yards	4,590	Darren McFadden, 2005-07
Passing Yards	7,422	Clint Stoerner, 1996-99
Receiving Yards	2,879	Anthony Lucas, 1995-99
Scoring	294	Bill Burnett, 1968-70
Touchdowns	49	Bill Burnett, 1968-70
Tackles	408	Tony Bua, 2000-03
Interceptions	14	Steve Atwater, 1985-88
Punting Average	45.2	Steve Cox, 1979-80 (89 punts)
Punt Return Average	16.0	Ken Hatfield, 1962-64 (72 ret.)
Kickoff Return Average	28.2	Felix Jones, 2005-07 (62 ret.)

TEAM RECORDS

Longest Winning Streak	22	Nov. 23, 1963-Nov. 20, 1965; broken vs. LSU, 7-14 on Jan. 1, 1966
Longest Undefeated Streak	22	Nov. 23, 1963-Nov. 20, 1965; broken vs. LSU, 7-14 on Jan. 1, 1966
Most Consecutive Winning Seasons	13	1977-89
Most Consecutive Bowl Appearances	6	Twice, 1977-82; 1984-89
Most Points in a Game	100	vs. Southwest Missouri State, Sep. 30, 1911
Most Points Allowed in a Game	103	vs. Oklahoma, Oct. 19, 1918
Largest Margin of Victory	100	vs. Southwest Missouri State, Sep. 30, 1911
Largest Margin of Defeat	103	vs. Oklahoma, Oct. 19, 1918
Longest Pass Play	92	Matt Jones to Richard Smith vs. Tennessee, Oct. 5, 2002
Longest Field Goal	67	Steve Little vs. Texas, Oct. 15, 1977
Longest Punt	86	Steve Cox vs. Texas, Oct. 18, 1986
Longest Interception Return	100	Jerell Norton vs. North Texas, Sep. 29, 2007

RETIRED NUMBERS

12	Clyde "Smackover" Scott
77	Brandon Burlsworth

ALL-TIME TEAM

As selected in 1994 by committee of former players, sportswriters and sports information directors as well as fans

Offense			Defense		
	OL	Bud Brooks, 1952-54		DL	Dave Hanner 1949-51
	OL	Glen Ray Hines 1963-65		DL	Fred Williams 1949-51
	OL	R.C. Thielemann 1973-76		DL	Billy Ray Smith, Sr. 1979-82
	OL	Leotis Harris 1974-77		DL	Loyd Phillips 1964-66
	OL	Steve Korte 1981-82		DL	Dan Hampton 1975-78
	OL	Freddie Childress 1985-88		DL	Billy Ray Smith, Jr. 1979-82
	WR	Wear Schoonover 1927-29		DL	Wayne Martin 1985-88
	WR	Bobby Crockett 1963-65		LB	Wayne Harris 1958-60
	WR	Chuck Dicus 1968-70		LB	Ronnie Caveness 1962-64
	WR	Jim Benton 1970-72		LB	Cliff Powell 1967-69
	QB	Lamar McHan 1951-53		LB	Dennis Winston 1973-76
	QB	Bill Montgomery 1968-70		DB	Alton Baldwin 1943-46
	QB	Joe Ferguson 1970-72		DB	Billy Moore 1960-62
	QB	Quinn Grovey 1987-90		DB	Ken Hatfield 1962-64
	RB	Leon Campbell 1946-49		DB	Martine Bercher 1964-66
	RB	Clyde Scott 1946-48		DB	Steve Atwater 1985-88
	RB	Jim Mooty 1957-59		P	Steve Cox 1976-80
	RB	Lance Alworth 1959-61			
	RB	Barry Foster 1987-89			
	K/P	Pat Summerall 1949-51			
	K/P	Steve Little 1974-77			

ARKANSAS BOWL HISTORY

SEASON	BOWL	DATE	PRE-GAME RANK	TEAMS	SCORE	FINAL RANK	MOST VALUABLE PLAYER(S)	ATT.
1933	DIXIE CLASSIC	Jan. 1, 1934		Arkansas Centenary	7 7			12,000
1946	COTTON	Jan. 1, 1947	16 8	Arkansas LSU	0 0		Alton Baldwin, Arkansas, E, HB Y.A. Title, LSU, QB	38,000
1947	DIXIE	Jan. 1, 1948	 14	Arkansas William & Mary	21 19			22,000
1954	COTTON	Jan. 1, 1955	 10	Georgia Tech Arkansas	14 6		George Humphreys, Georgia Tech, FB Bud Brooks, Arkansas, G	75,504
1959	GATOR	Jan. 2, 1960	9	Arkansas Georgia Tech	14 7		Jim Mooty, Arkansas, HB Maxie Baughan, Georgia Tech, LB	45,104
1960	COTTON	Jan. 2, 1961	10 7	Duke Arkansas	7 6		Dwight Bumgarner, Duke, T Lance Alworth, Arkansas, HB	74,000
1961	SUGAR	Jan. 1, 1962	1 9	Alabama Arkansas	10 3		Mike Fracchia, Alabama, FB	81,141
1962	SUGAR	Jan. 1, 1963	3 6	Mississippi Arkansas	17 13		Glynn Griffin, Mississippi, QB	79,707
1964	COTTON	Jan. 1, 1965	2 6	Arkansas Nebraska	10 7		Ronnie Caveness, Arkansas, LB Fred Marshall, Arkansas, QB	75,504
1965	COTTON	Jan. 1, 1966	 2	LSU Arkansas	14 7	8 3	Joe Labruzzo, LSU, TB David McCormick, LSU, T	76,200
1968	SUGAR	Jan. 1, 1969	9 4	Arkansas Georgia	16 2	6 8	Chuck Dicus, Arkansas, FL	82,000
1969	SUGAR	Jan. 1, 1970	13 3	Mississippi Arkansas	27 22	8 7	Archie Manning, Mississippi, QB	72,858
1971	LIBERTY	Dec. 20, 1971	9 18	Tennessee Arkansas	14 13	9 16	Joe Ferguson, Arkansas, QB	51,410
1975	COTTON	Jan. 1, 1976	18 12	Arkansas Georgia	31 10	7 19	Ike Forte, Arkansas, RB Hal McAfee, Arkansas, LB	74,500
1977	ORANGE	Jan. 2, 1978	6 2	Arkansas Oklahoma	31 6	3 7	Roland Sales, Arkansas, RB Reggie Freemanm Arkansas, NG	60,987
1978	FIESTA	Dec. 25, 1978	8 15	Arkansas UCLA	10 10	11 14	James Owens, UCLA, RB Jimmy Walker, Arkansas, DT	55,227
1979	SUGAR	Jan. 1, 1980	2 6	Alabama Arkansas	24 9	1 8	Major Ogilvie, Alabama, RB	77,484
1980	HALL OF FAME CLASSIC	Dec. 27, 1980		Arkansas Temple	34 15		Gary Anderson, Arkansas, RB Billy Ray Smith, Arkansas, LB	30,000
1981	GATOR	Dec. 28, 1981	11	North Carolina Arkansas	31 27	9	Gary Anderson, Arkansas, RB Kelvin Bryant, TB, Ethan Horton, TB, UNC	71,009
1982	BLUEBONNET	Dec. 31, 1982	14	Arkansas Florida	28 24	9	Gary Anderson, Arkansas, RB Dwayne Dixon, Florida, WR	31,557
1984	LIBERTY	Dec. 27, 1984	16	Auburn Arkansas	21 15	14	Bo Jackson, Auburn, RB	50,108
1985	HOLIDAY	Dec. 22, 1985	14	Arkansas Arizona State	18 17	12	Bobby Joe Edmonds, Arkansas, RB Greg Battle, Arizona State, LB	42,324
1986	ORANGE	Jan. 1, 1987	3 9	Oklahoma Arkansas	42 8	3 15	Spencer Tillman, Oklahoma, HB Dante Jones, Oklahoma, LB	52,717
1987	LIBERTY	Dec. 29, 1987	15	Georgia Arkansas	20 17	13	Greg Thomas, Arkansas, QB	53,249
1988	COTTON	Jan. 2, 1989	9 8	UCLA Arkansas	17 3	6 12	Troy Aikman, UCLA, QB LaSalle Harper, Arkansas, LB	74,304
1989	COTTON	Jan. 1, 1990	8 10	Tennessee Arkansas	31 27	5 13	Carl Pickens, Tennessee, FS Chuck Webb, Tennessee, TB	74,358
1991	INDEPENDENCE	Dec. 29, 1991	24	Georgia Arkansas	24 15	17	Andre Hastings, Georgia, FL Torrey Evans, Georgia, LB	46,932
1995	CARQUEST	Dec. 30, 1995	 24	North Carolina Arkansas	20 10		Leon Johnson, North Carolina, RB	34,428
1998	CITRUS	Jan. 1, 1999	15 11	Michigan Arkansas	45 31	12 16	Anthony Thomas, Michigan, RB	63,584
1999	COTTON	Jan. 1, 2000	24 14	Arkansas Texas	27 6	17 21	Cedric Cobbs, Arkansas, RB D.J. Cooper, Arkansas, LB	72,723
2000	LAS VEGAS	Dec. 21, 2000		UNLV Arkansas	31 14		Jason Thomas, UNLV, QB	29,113
2001	COTTON	Jan. 1, 2002	10	Oklahoma Arkansas	10 3	6	Quentin Griffin, Oklahoma, RB Roy Williams, Oklahoma, DB	72,995
2002	MUSIC CITY	Dec. 30, 2002	 25	Minnesota Arkansas	29 14		Dan Nystrom, Minnesota, K	39,183
2003	INDEPENDENCE	Dec. 31, 2003		Arkansas Missouri	27 14		Cedric Cobbs, Arkansas, RB Caleb Miller, Arkansas, LB	49,625
2006	CAPITAL ONE	Jan. 1, 2007	6 12	Wisconsin Arkansas	17 14	7 15	John Stocco, Wisconsin, QB	60,774
2007	COTTON	Jan. 1, 2008	7	Missouri Arkansas	38 7	4	Tony Temple, Missouri, RB William Moore, Missouri, S	73,114

JANUARY 1, 1934 | DIXIE CLASSIC
ARKANSAS 7, CENTENARY 7

	1ST	2ND	3RD	4TH	FINAL
ARK	0	7	0	0	7
CEN	0	7	0	0	7

SCORING SUMMARY
ARK　Geiser 27 pass from Murphy (Geiser kick)
CEN　Oslin 20 pass from Smith (Weidman kick)

JANUARY 1, 1947 | COTTON
LSU 0, ARKANSAS 0

	1ST	2ND	3RD	4TH	FINAL
LSU	0	0	0	0	0
ARK	0	0	0	0	0

LSU	TEAM STATISTICS	ARK
15	First Downs	1
255	Rushing Yards	54
5-17-0	Passing	0-4-1
16	Passing Yards	0
271	Total Yards	54
9-30.4	Punts - Average	11-36.0
2	Fumbles Lost	3
8-50	Penalties - Yards	1-5

JANUARY 1, 1948 | DIXIE
ARKANSAS 21, WILLIAM & MARY 19

	1ST	2ND	3RD	4TH	FINAL
ARK	0	14	0	7	21
W&M	7	6	6	0	19

SCORING SUMMARY
W&M　Cloud 1 run (Magdziak kick)
W&M　Cloud 2 run (kick failed)
ARK　Pritchard 59 pass from Holland (Fowler kick)
ARK　McGaha 70 interception return (Fowler kick)
W&M　Bland 6 pass from Magdziak (kick failed)
ARK　Campbell 7 run (Fowler kick)

ARK	TEAM STATISTICS	W&M
9	First Downs	14
103	Rushing Yards	243
5-14-1	Passing	3-12-3
134	Passing Yards	47
237	Total Yards	290

JANUARY 1, 1955 | COTTON
GEORGIA TECH 14, ARKANSAS 6

	1ST	2ND	3RD	4TH	FINAL
GT	0	0	7	7	14
ARK	0	6	0	0	6

SCORING SUMMARY
ARK　Walker 3 run (kick failed)
GT　Rotenberry 3 run (Mitchell kick)
GT　Mitchell 1 run (Mitchell kick)

GT	TEAM STATISTICS	ARK
19	First Downs	10
285	Rushing Yards	141
4-15-0	Passing	7-10-1
31	Passing Yards	86
316	Total Yards	227
4-30.0	Punts - Average	4-28.0
1-0	Fumbles - Lost	0-0
4-30	Penalties - Yards	4-30

INDIVIDUAL LEADERS
RUSHING
GT: Humphreys 19-99; Thompson 12-63.
ARK: Moore 16-86; Walker 11-34, 1 TD.
PASSING
GT: Mitchell 4-10-0, 31 yards.
ARK: Walker 3-5-1, 51 yards.
RECEIVING
GT: Durham 2-20; Hair 2-11.
ARK: Lyons 2-34; Thomason 1-22.

JANUARY 2, 1960 | GATOR
ARKANSAS 14, GEORGIA TECH 7

	1ST	2ND	3RD	4TH	FINAL
ARK	0	7	7	0	14
GT	7	0	0	0	7

SCORING SUMMARY
GT　Tibbetts 51 run (Faucette kick)
ARK　Alberty 1 run (Akers kick)
ARK　Mooty 19 run (Akers kick)

ARK	TEAM STATISTICS	GT
15	First Downs	13
218	Rushing Yards	172
2-6-1	Passing	8-18-1
21	Passing Yards	64
239	Total Yards	236
4-36.5	Punts - Average	4-40.7
1-1	Fumbles - Lost	0-0
5-56	Penalties - Yards	3-15

INDIVIDUAL LEADERS
RUSHING
ARK: Mooty 18-99, 1 TD; Alworth 9-40; Alberty 12-38, 1 TD.
GT: Tibbetts 3-59, 1 TD; Anderson 12-38.
PASSING
ARK: Monroe 2-4-0, 21 yards.
GT: Braselton 8-18-1, 64 yards.
RECEIVING
ARK: Mooty 1-12
GT: Graning 3-19.

JANUARY 2, 1961 | COTTON
DUKE 7, ARKANSAS 6

	1ST	2ND	3RD	4TH	FINAL
DUKE	0	0	0	7	7
ARK	0	0	6	0	6

SCORING SUMMARY
ARK　Alworth 49 punt return (kick blocked)
DUKE　Moorman 9 pass from Altman (Browning kick)

DUKE	TEAM STATISTICS	ARK
10	First Downs	12
96	Rushing Yards	148
13-17-1	Passing	5-13-1
93	Passing Yards	71
189	Total Yards	219
8-36.9	Punts - Average	6-30.8
2-2	Fumbles - Lost	1-1
3-15	Penalties - Yards	4-40

INDIVIDUAL LEADERS
RUSHING
DUKE: Wilson 12-32; Wright 9-26.
ARK: Alberty 13-44; Alworth 11-33.
PASSING
DUKE: Altman 12-15-0, 83 yards, 1 TD.
ARK: McKinney 4-10-1, 58 yards.
RECEIVING
DUKE: Moorman 8-45, 1 TD; Wilson 3-30.
ARK: Alworth 3-41; Collier 2-30.

JANUARY 1, 1962 | SUGAR
ALABAMA 10, ARKANSAS 3

	1ST	2ND	3RD	4TH	FINAL
ALA	7	3	0	0	10
ARK	0	0	3	0	3

SCORING SUMMARY
ALA　Trammell 12 run (Davis kick)
ALA　FG Davis 32
ARK　FG Cissell 23

JANUARY 1, 1963 | SUGAR
MISSISSIPPI 17, ARKANSAS 13

	1ST	2ND	3RD	4TH	FINAL
MISS	0	10	7	0	17
ARK	0	3	10	0	13

SCORING SUMMARY
MISS　FG Irwin 30
ARK　FG McKnelly 30
MISS　Guy 33 pass from Griffin (Irwin kick)
ARK　Branch 5 pass from Moore (McKnelly kick)
MISS　Griffin 1 run (Irwin kick)
ARK　FG McKnelly 22

MISS	TEAM STATISTICS	ARK
22	First Downs	7
160	Rushing Yards	47
18-28-1	Passing	6-18-2
269	Passing Yards	123
429	Total Yards	170
2-36.0	Punts - Average	4-38.3
2-1	Fumbles - Lost	2-0
4-40	Penalties - Yards	2-13

INDIVIDUAL LEADERS
RUSHING
MISS: Jennings 9-39; Weatherly 9-36.
ARK: Branch 7-21.
PASSING
MISS: Griffin 14-23-1, 242 yards, 1 TD.
ARK: Moore 5-10-0, 55 yards, 1 TD.
RECEIVING
MISS: Guy 5-107, 1 TD; Morris 5-62.
ARK: Lamb 3-107; Branch 3-16, 1 TD.

JANUARY 1, 1965 | COTTON
ARKANSAS 10, NEBRASKA 7

	1ST	2ND	3RD	4TH	FINAL
NEB	0	7	0	0	7
ARK	3	0	0	7	10

SCORING SUMMARY
ARK　FG McKnelly 31
NEB　Wilson 1 run (Drum kick)
ARK　Burnett 3 run (McKnelly kick)

NEB	TEAM STATISTICS	ARK
11	First Downs	11
100	Rushing Yards	45
8-16-2	Passing	11-19-1
68	Passing Yards	131
168	Total Yards	176
6-33.3	Punts - Average	6-40.2
0-0	Fumbles - Lost	2-2
5-25	Penalties - Yards	6-50

INDIVIDUAL LEADERS
RUSHING
NEB: Wilson 12-84, 1 TD; Solich 11-34.
ARK: Burnett 11-23, 1 TD; Lindsey 3-14.
PASSING
NEB: Churchich 8-15-2, 68 yards.
ARK: Marshall 11-19-1, 131 yards.
RECEIVING
NEB: Wilson 1-36; White 2-18.
ARK: Lindsey 3-54; Burnett 5-44.

JANUARY 1, 1966 | COTTON
LSU 14, ARKANSAS 7

	1ST	2ND	3RD	4TH	FINAL
LSU	0	14	0	0	14
ARK	7	0	0	0	7

SCORING SUMMARY
ARK　Crockett 19 pass from Brittenum (South kick)
LSU　Labruzzo 3 run (Moreau kick)
LSU　Labruzzo 1 run (Moreau kick)

LSU	TEAM STATISTICS	ARK
15	First Downs	22
166	Rushing Yards	129
8-11-0	Passing	15-24-1
100	Passing Yards	177
266	Total Yards	306
6-42.2	Punts - Average	3-34.0
0-0	Fumbles - Lost	2-1
4-62	Penalties - Yards	2-10

INDIVIDUAL LEADERS
RUSHING
LSU: Labruzzo 21-69, 2 TD; Dousay 14-38.
ARK: Jones 10-79; Burnett 12-44.
PASSING
LSU: Screen 7-10-0, 82 yards.
ARK: Brittenum 15-24-1, 177 yards, 1 TD.
RECEIVING
LSU: Masters 4-45; Labruzzo 1-19.
ARK: Crockett 10-129, 1 TD; Jones 2-26.

JANUARY 1, 1969 | SUGAR
ARKANSAS 16, GEORGIA 2

	1ST	2ND	3RD	4TH	FINAL
ARK	0	10	0	6	16
UGA	0	2	0	0	2

SCORING SUMMARY

ARK	Dicus 27 pass from Montgomery (White kick)
UGA	Safety
ARK	FG White 34
ARK	FG White 24
ARK	FG White 31

ARK	TEAM STATISTICS	UGA
13	First Downs	13
40	Rushing Yards	75
17-39-3	Passing	11-31-1
185	Passing Yards	117
225	Total Yards	192
10-33.6	Punts - Average	10-38.6
2-2	Fumbles - Lost	5-5
4-31	Penalties - Yards	4-25

INDIVIDUAL LEADERS

RUSHING
ARK: Burnett 2-31.
UGA: Johnson 12-45.

PASSING
ARK: Montgomery 17-39-1, 185 yards, 1 TD.
UGA: Cavan 9-22-1, 103 yards.

RECEIVING
ARK: Dicus 12-169, 1 TD; Peacock 3-15.
UGA: Whittemore 5-56; Lawrence 3-54.

JANUARY 1, 1970 | SUGAR
MISSISSIPPI 27, ARKANSAS 22

	1ST	2ND	3RD	4TH	FINAL
MISS	14	10	3	0	27
ARK	0	12	3	7	22

SCORING SUMMARY

MISS	Bowen 69 run (King kick)
MISS	Manning 18 run (King kick)
ARK	Burnett 12 run (kick failed)
MISS	FG Hinton 52
MISS	Studdard 30 pass from Manning (King kick)
ARK	Dicus 47 pass from Montgomery (pass failed)
MISS	FG Hinton 36
ARK	FG McClard 35
ARK	Maxwell 6 pass from Montgomery (McClard kick)

MISS	TEAM STATISTICS	ARK
24	First Downs	21
154	Rushing Yards	189
21-35-2	Passing	17-35-2
273	Passing Yards	338
427	Total Yards	527
2-30.5	Punts - Average	6-37.6
1-1	Fumbles - Lost	0
3-22	Penalties - Yards	11-101

INDIVIDUAL LEADERS

RUSHING
MISS: Bowen 12-94, 1 TD; Manning 13-39, 1 TD.
ARK: Maxwell 8-108; Burnett 17-59, 1 TD.

PASSING
MISS: Manning 21-35-2, 273 yards, 1 TD.
ARK: Montgomery 17-34-1, 338 yards, 2 TD.

RECEIVING
MISS: Studdard 5-109, 1 TD; Reed 2-22.
ARK: Dicus 6-171, 1 TD; Maxwell 9-137, 1 TD.

DECEMBER 20, 1971 | LIBERTY
TENNESSEE 14, ARKANSAS 13

	1ST	2ND	3RD	4TH	FINAL
TENN	7	0	0	7	14
ARK	0	7	0	6	13

SCORING SUMMARY

TENN	Rudder 2 run (Hunt kick)
ARK	Hodge 36 pass from Ferguson (McClard kick)
ARK	FG McClard 19
ARK	FG McClard 30
TENN	Watson 17 run (Hunt kick)

TENN	TEAM STATISTICS	ARK
15	First Downs	22
97	Rushing Yards	167
11-21-3	Passing	18-28-3
142	Passing Yards	200
239	Total Yards	367
5-43.8	Punts - Average	3-43.6
1-1	Fumbles - Lost	2-2
7-73	Penalties - Yards	6-85

INDIVIDUAL LEADERS

RUSHING
TENN: Watson 11-39, 1 TD; Chauncey 12-34.
ARK: Saint 17-71.

PASSING
TENN: Maxwell 20-30-3, 120 yards.
ARK: Ferguson 18-28-3, 200 yards, 1 TD.

RECEIVING
TENN: Theiler 3-53.
ARK: Hodge 6-75, 1 TD.

JANUARY 1, 1976 | COTTON
ARKANSAS 31, GEORGIA 10

	1ST	2ND	3RD	4TH	FINAL
UGA	3	7	0	0	10
ARK	0	10	0	21	31

SCORING SUMMARY

UGA	FG Leavitt 35
UGA	Washington 21 pass from Robinson (Leavitt kick)
ARK	FG Little 39
ARK	Forte 1 run (Little kick)
ARK	Fuchs 5 run (Little kick)
ARK	Forrest 1 run (Little kick)
ARK	Forte 6 run (Little kick)

UGA	TEAM STATISTICS	ARK
13	First Downs	20
102	Rushing Yards	235
8-18-2	Passing	5-14-0
91	Passing Yards	89
193	Total Yards	324
6-38.7	Punts - Average	4-43.0
3-2	Fumbles - Lost	6-1
3-15	Penalties - Yards	5-35

INDIVIDUAL LEADERS

RUSHING
UGA: Harrison 14-44; Goff 16-32.
ARK: Forte 24-119, 2 TD; Fuchs 16-71, 1 TD.

PASSING
UGA: Robinson 7-15-2, 85 yards, 1 TD.
ARK: Bull 5-13-0, 89 yards.

RECEIVING
UGA: Wilson 1-29; Washington 1-21.
ARK: Douglas 2-54; Daily 1-13.

JANUARY 2, 1978 | ORANGE
ARKANSAS 31, OKLAHOMA 6

	1ST	2ND	3RD	4TH	FINAL
ARK	14	0	10	7	31
OKLA	0	0	0	6	6

SCORING SUMMARY

ARK	Sales 1 run (Little kick)
ARK	Calcagni 1 run (Little kick)
ARK	FG Little 32
ARK	Sales 4 run (Little kick)
OKLA	Hicks 8 pass from Blevins (run failed)
ARK	White 20 run (Little kick)

ARK	TEAM STATISTICS	OKLA
15	First Downs	14
317	Rushing Yards	230
7-12-1	Passing	7-14-0
90	Passing Yards	80
407	Total Yards	310
4-40.5	Punts - Average	5-44.4
2-1	Fumbles - Lost	4-3
7-50	Penalties - Yards	5-25

INDIVIDUAL LEADERS

RUSHING
ARK: Sales 22-205, 2 TD.
OKLA: Peacock 15-117; King 5-49.

PASSING
ARK: Calcagni 7-11-1, 90 yards.
OKLA: Lott 4-7-0, 42 yards.

RECEIVING
ARK: Sales 4-52.
OKLA: Rhodes 3-46.

DECEMBER 25, 1978 | FIESTA
ARKANSAS 10, UCLA 10

	1ST	2ND	3RD	4TH	FINAL
ARK	0	10	0	0	10
UCLA	0	0	3	7	10

SCORING SUMMARY

ARK	Sales 4 run (Ordonez kick)
ARK	FG Ordonez 37
UCLA	FG Boermeester 41
UCLA	Bukich 15 run (Boermeester kick)

ARK	TEAM STATISTICS	UCLA
19	First Downs	14
200	Rushing Yards	255
13-24-2	Passing	4-11-2
78	Passing Yards	61
278	Total Yards	316
8-37.3	Punts - Average	6-41.3
2-0	Fumbles - Lost	2-1
4-50	Penalties - Yards	7-67

INDIVIDUAL LEADERS

RUSHING
ARK: Cowins 24-89; Eckwood 8-44.
UCLA: Owens 17-121; Brown 11-84.

PASSING
ARK: Calcagni 11-16-0, 49 yards.
UCLA: Bukich 4-11-2, 61 yards.

RECEIVING
ARK: Farrell 2-25; Stiggers 2-33.
UCLA: Reece 2-56; McNeil 1-3.

JANUARY 1, 1980 | SUGAR
ALABAMA 24, ARKANSAS 9

	1ST	2ND	3RD	4TH	FINAL
ALA	14	3	0	7	24
ARK	3	0	6	0	9

SCORING SUMMARY
ARK FG Ordonez 34
ALA Ogilvie 22 run (McElroy kick)
ALA Ogilvie 1 run (McElroy kick)
ALA FG McElroy 25
ARK Farrell 3 pass from Scanlon (run failed)
ALA Whitman 12 run (McElroy kick)

ALA	TEAM STATISTICS	ARK
18	First Downs	21
284	Rushing Yards	97
4-7-2	Passing	22-40-2
70	Passing Yards	245
354	Total Yards	342
8-36.2	Punts - Average	7-36.2
7-61	Penalties - Yards	1-15

INDIVIDUAL LEADERS
RUSHING
ALA: Jackson 13-120; Ogilvie 14-67, 2 TD; Whitman 6-37, 1 TD.
ARK: Bowles 15-46; Anderson 6-28.
PASSING
ALA: Shealy 4-7-0, 70 yards.
ARK: Scanlon 22-39-1, 245 yards, 1 TD.
RECEIVING
ALA: Jackson 3-62.
ARK: Anderson 7-53; Farrell 3-51, 1 TD.

DECEMBER 27, 1980 | HALL OF FAME CLASSIC
ARKANSAS 34, TULANE 15

	1ST	2ND	3RD	4TH	FINAL
ARK	14	14	3	3	34
TUL	0	0	0	15	15

SCORING SUMMARY
ARK Tolbert 1 run (Ordonez kick)
ARK Anderson 80 punt return (Ordonez kick)
ARK Clyde 9 pass from Jones (Ordonez kick)
ARK Anderson 46 run (Ordonez kick)
ARK FG Ordonez 40
TUL Anderson 62 pass from Hall (Manalla kick)
ARK FG Ordonez 27
TUL Robinson 1 run (Hall run)

ARK	TEAM STATISTICS	TUL
22	First Downs	18
383	Rushing Yards	157
5-13-1	Passing	16-37-2
83	Passing Yards	241
466	Total Yards	398
2-80	Punt Returns - Yards	1-10
1-21	Kickoff Returns - Yards	5-122
4-42.5	Punts - Average	7-34.6
0-0	Fumbles Lost	3-2
1-19	Penalties - Yards	3-15

INDIVIDUAL LEADERS
RUSHING
ARK: Anderson 11-156, 1 TD; Douglas 10-83.
TUL: Lewis 5-45; Robinson 6-44, 1 TD.
PASSING
ARK: Jones 5-13-1, 83 yards, 1 TD.
TUL: Hall 16-37-2, 241 yards, 1 TD.
RECEIVING
ARK: Walters 1-36; Holloway 1-23.
TUL: Anderson 2-88, 1 TD; Griffin 2-59.

DECEMBER 28, 1981 | GATOR
NORTH CAROLINA 31, ARKANSAS 27

	1ST	2ND	3RD	4TH	FINAL
UNC	3	7	14	7	31
ARK	7	3	0	17	27

SCORING SUMMARY
UNC FG Barwick 31
ARK Holloway 66 pass from Taylor (Lahay kick)
UNC Bryant 1 run (Hayes kick)
ARK FG Lahay 28
UNC Horton 1 run (Hayes kick)
UNC Elkins 1 run (Hayes kick)
UNC Horton 4 run (Hayes kick)
ARK Clark 3 run (Clark pass from Taylor)
ARK Mason 7 pass from Taylor (Lahay kick)
ARK Safety (Hayes ran out of end zone)

UNC	TEAM STATISTICS	ARK
21	First Downs	16
283	Rushing Yards	89
7-17-0	Passing	14-21-1
53	Passing Yards	307
336	Total Yards	396
6-41.9	Punts - Average	6-36.5
3-1	Fumbles - Lost	2-1
8-55	Penalties - Yards	3-44

INDIVIDUAL LEADERS
RUSHING
UNC: Bryant 27-148, 1 TD; Horton 27-144, 2 TD.
ARK: Clark 10-40, 1 TD; Tolbert 5-27.
PASSING
UNC: Elkins 7-17-0, 53 yards.
ARK: Taylor 14-21-1, 307 yards, 2 TD.
RECEIVING
UNC: Bryant 3-24; Richardson 2-15.
ARK: Holloway 4-171, 1 TD; Anderson 5-85.

DECEMBER 31, 1982 | BLUEBONNET
ARKANSAS 28, FLORIDA 24

	1ST	2ND	3RD	4TH	FINAL
ARK	7	0	7	14	28
FLA	7	10	7	0	24

SCORING SUMMARY
ARK Anderson 16 run (Smith kick)
FLA Dixon 3 pass from Hewko (Raymond kick)
FLA FG Raymond 34
FLA Dixon 13 pass from Hewko (Raymond kick)
ARK Anderson 1 run (Smith kick)
FLA Dixon 17 pass from Hewko (Raymond kick)
ARK Clark 5 pass from Jones (Smith kick)
ARK Jones 1 run (Smith kick)

ARK	TEAM STATISTICS	FLA
28	First Downs	23
356	Rushing Yards	171
7-12-1	Passing	19-29-1
122	Passing Yards	234
478	Total Yards	405
3-43.3	Punts - Average	4-45.8
5-36	Penalties - Yards	6-50

INDIVIDUAL LEADERS
RUSHING
ARK: Anderson 26-161, 2 TD; Clark 17-77.
FLA: Jones 12-89; Hampton 21-61.
PASSING
ARK: Taylor 5-7-1, 123 yards; Jones 2-5-0, minus-1 yards, 1 TD.
FLA: Hewko 19-28-0, 234 yards, 3 TD; Jones 0-1-1, 0 yards.
RECEIVING
ARK: White 1-40; Anderson 3-37.
FLA: Dixon 8-106, 3 TD; Hampton 2-37.

DECEMBER 27, 1984 | LIBERTY
AUBURN 21, ARKANSAS 15

	1ST	2ND	3RD	4TH	FINAL
AUB	14	0	0	7	21
ARK	3	0	0	12	15

SCORING SUMMARY
ARK FG Horne 31
AUB Jackson 2 run (kick failed)
AUB Porter 35 interception return (Washington kick)
ARK Foreman 2 run (pass failed)
AUB Jackson 39 run (Knapp kick)
ARK Shibest 25 pass from Taylor (kick failed)

AUB	TEAM STATISTICS	ARK
13	First Downs	20
168	Rushing Yards	130
5-15-0	Passing	19-40-4
84	Passing Yards	226
252	Total Yards	356
9-37.9	Punts - Average	4-38.3
1	Fumbles Lost	0
8-56	Penalties - Yards	8-60

INDIVIDUAL LEADERS
RUSHING
AUB: Jackson 18-88, 2 TD.
ARK: Foreman 15-62, 1 TD; Thomas 9-56.
PASSING
AUB: Washington 5-12-0, 84 yards.
ARK: Taylor 18-34-2, 201 yards, 1 TD.
RECEIVING
AUB: Jackson 1-25.
ARK: Shibest 5-84, 1 TD; Edmonds 10-68.

DECEMBER 22, 1985 | HOLIDAY
ARKANSAS 18, ARIZONA STATE 17

	1ST	2ND	3RD	4TH	FINAL
ARK	7	0	0	11	18
ASU	3	11	0	3	17

SCORING SUMMARY
ASU FG Bostrom 47
ARK D. Thomas 9 run (Trainor kick)
ASU FG Bostrom 22
ASU Cox 16 pass from Van Raaphorst (Amoia pass from Van Raaphorst)
ARK Edmonds 17 run (Calcagni run)
ASU FG Bostrom 28
ARK FG Trainor 37

ARK	TEAM STATISTICS	ASU
21	First Downs	20
260	Rushing Yards	195
10-18-0	Passing	14-27-1
117	Passing Yards	167
377	Total Yards	362
1-10	Punt Returns - Yards	0-0
4-67	Kickoff Returns - Yards	3-81
5-37.0	Punts - Average	5-32.8
1-1	Fumbles - Lost	0-0
2-10	Penalties - Yards	2-21
32:44	Possession Time	27:16

INDIVIDUAL LEADERS
RUSHING
ARK: Rouse 15-76; Calcagni 16-45; Edmonds 7-43, 1 TD.
ASU: Crawford 18-103; Amoia 13-56.
PASSING
ARK: Calcagni 10-17-0, 117 yards.
ASU: Van Raaphorst 14-27-1, 167 yards, 1 TD.
RECEIVING
ARK: Edmonds 7-93; Centers 1-17.
ASU: Cox 3-67, 1 TD; Gallimore 4-36.

JANUARY 1, 1987 | ORANGE
OKLAHOMA 42, ARKANSAS 8

	1ST	2ND	3RD	4TH	FINAL
OKLA	0	14	14	14	42
ARK	0	0	0	8	8

SCORING SUMMARY
OKLA Tillman 77 run (Lashar kick)
OKLA Tillman 21 run (Lashar kick)
OKLA Holieway 2 run (Lashar kick)
OKLA Holieway 4 run (Lashar kick)
OKLA Stafford 13 run (Lashar kick)
OKLA Parham 49 run (Lashar kick)
ARK   Thomas 2 run (Shibest pass from Bland)

OKLA	TEAM STATISTICS	ARK
11	First Downs	17
366	Rushing Yards	48
2-5-0	Passing	16-33-5
47	Passing Yards	192
413	Total Yards	240
5-47.6	Punts - Average	9-41.1
3-2	Fumbles - Lost	2-0
4-40	Penalties - Yards	3-25
24:31	Possession Time	35:29

INDIVIDUAL LEADERS
RUSHING
OKLA: Tillman 7-109, 1 TD.
ARK: Thomas 22-59, 1 TD.
PASSING
OKLA: Holieway 2-3-0, 47 yards.
ARK: Thomas 13-26-4, 129 yards.
RECEIVING
OKLA: Shepard 1-36.
ARK: Shibest 4-83.

DECEMBER 29, 1987 | LIBERTY
GEORGIA 20, ARKANSAS 17

	1ST	2ND	3RD	4TH	FINAL
UGA	0	7	0	13	20
ARK	3	7	7	0	17

SCORING SUMMARY
ARK   FG Trainor 43
UGA   Tate 1 run (Kasay kick)
ARK   Thomas 10 run (Trainor kick)
ARK   Thomas 1 run (Trainor kick)
UGA   FG Kasay 24
UGA   Jackson 5 run (Kasay kick)
UGA   FG Kasay 39

UGA	TEAM STATISTICS	ARK
20	First Downs	19
202	Rushing Yards	258
15-25-2	Passing	7-17-2
148	Passing Yards	86
350	Total Yards	344
3-32.7	Punts - Average	3-32.7
68	Return Yards	95
2-1	Fumbles - Lost	0-0
4-45	Penalties - Yards	5-50

INDIVIDUAL LEADERS
RUSHING
UGA: Jackson 10-72, 1 TD.
ARK: Thomas 13-79, 2 TD.
PASSING
UGA: Jackson 15-25-2, 148 yards.
ARK: Thomas 7-17-2, 86 yards.
RECEIVING
UGA: Thomas 7-76.
ARK: Winston 2-36.

JANUARY 2, 1989 | COTTON
UCLA 17, ARKANSAS 3

	1ST	2ND	3RD	4TH	FINAL
UCLA	0	14	0	3	17
ARK	0	0	3	0	3

SCORING SUMMARY
UCLA Estwick 1 run (Velasco kick)
UCLA Anthony 1 pass from Aikman (Velasco kick)
ARK   FG Trainor 49
UCLA FG Velasco 32

UCLA	TEAM STATISTICS	ARK
22	First Downs	4
199	Rushing Yards	21
19-27-1	Passing	4-14-1
172	Passing Yards	21
371	Total Yards	42
3-36.0	Punts - Average	6-49.2
3-2	Fumbles - Lost	0-0
7-74	Penalties - Yards	7-61
42:43	Possession Time	17:17

INDIVIDUAL LEADERS
RUSHING
UCLA: Willis 18-120; Brown 16-56.
ARK: Grovey 7-19; Foster 6-16.
PASSING
UCLA: Aikman 19-27-1, 172 yards, 1 TD.
ARK: Grovey 2-7-0, 10 yards.
RECEIVING
UCLA: Farr 4-48; Arbuckle 1-35.
ARK: Jackson 1-8; Harshaw 1-7.

JANUARY 1, 1990 | COTTON
TENNESSEE 31, ARKANSAS 27

	1ST	2ND	3RD	4TH	FINAL
TENN	3	14	14	0	31
ARK	6	0	7	14	27

SCORING SUMMARY
TENN FG Burke 23
ARK   Foster 1 run (run failed)
TENN Morgan 84 pass from Kelly (Burke kick)
TENN Webb 1 run (Burke kick)
TENN Amsler 1 pass from Kelly (Burke kick)
ARK   Rouse 1 run (Wright kick)
TENN Webb 78 run (Burke kick)
ARK   Foster 1 run (Foster run)
ARK   Winston 67 pass from Grovey (pass failed)

TENN	TEAM STATISTICS	ARK
16	First Downs	31
320	Rushing Yards	361
9-23-2	Passing	12-22-1
150	Passing Yards	207
470	Total Yards	568
5-39.0	Punts - Average	3-44.3
0-0	Fumbles - Lost	3-2
4-36	Penalties - Yards	3-20
22:17	Possession Time	37:43

INDIVIDUAL LEADERS
RUSHING
TENN: Webb 26-250, 2 TD; Moore 1-36.
ARK: Rouse 22-134, 1 TD; Foster 22-103, 2 TD.
PASSING
TENN: Kelly 9-23-2, 150 yards, 2 TD.
ARK: Grovey 12-22-1, 207 yards, 1 TD.
RECEIVING
TENN: Morgan 2-96, 1 TD; Harper 2-28.
ARK: Russell 7-105; Winston 4-94, 1 TD.

DECEMBER 29, 1991 | INDEPENDENCE
GEORGIA 24, ARKANSAS 15

	1ST	2ND	3RD	4TH	FINAL
UGA	14	3	7	0	24
ARK	0	7	0	8	15

SCORING SUMMARY
UGA   Marshall 7 pass from Zeier (Peterson kick)
UGA   Hastings 27 pass from Zeier (Peterson kick)
UGA   FG Parkman 39
ARK   Jackson 7 run (Wright kick)
UGA   Hastings 53 run (Peterson kick)
ARK   Jackson 1 run (Jackson run)

UGA	TEAM STATISTICS	ARK
15	First Downs	22
125	Rushing Yards	188
20-31-0	Passing	12-31-5
237	Passing Yards	122
362	Total Yards	310
6-32.5	Punts - Average	4-45.3
1-0	Fumbles - Lost	1-1
10-75	Penalties - Yards	7-43

INDIVIDUAL LEADERS
RUSHING
UGA: Hastings 1-53, 1 TD; Strong 8-36.
ARK: Jackson 28-112, 2 TD; Jeffrey 9-44.
PASSING
UGA: Zeier 18-28-0, 228 yards, 2 TD.
ARK: Hill 12-31-5, 122 yards.
RECEIVING
UGA: Hastings 4-94, 1 TD.
ARK: Keith 3-38.

DECEMBER 30, 1995 | CARQUEST
NORTH CAROLINA 20, ARKANSAS 10

	1ST	2ND	3RD	4TH	FINAL
UNC	7	0	13	0	20
ARK	7	0	3	0	10

SCORING SUMMARY
ARK   Lucas 25 pass from Lunney (Latourette kick)
UNC   Ashford 18 pass from Thomas (Welch kick)
ARK   FG Latourette 26
UNC   L. Johnson 28 run (Welch kick)
UNC   Stevens 87 pass from Thomas (conversion failed)

UNC	TEAM STATISTICS	ARK
20	First Downs	26
242	Rushing Yards	162
10-23-0	Passing	16-35-2
177	Passing Yards	227
419	Total Yards	389
4-32.5	Punts - Average	4-38.8
0-0	Fumbles - Lost	1-1
4-31	Penalties - Yards	3-36
29:07	Possession Time	30:03

INDIVIDUAL LEADERS
RUSHING
UNC: L. Johnson 29-195, 1 TD.
ARK: M. Johnson 19-136.
PASSING
UNC: Thomas 10-23-0, 177 yards, 2 TD.
ARK: Lunney 16-35-2, 227 yards, 1 TD.
RECEIVING
UNC: Stevens 1-87, 1 TD; Ashford 3-38, 1 TD.
ARK: Meadors 7-101; Eubanks 3-45.

JANUARY 1, 1999 | FLORIDA CITRUS
MICHIGAN 45, ARKANSAS 31

	1ST	2ND	3RD	4TH	FINAL
MICH	3	21	0	21	45
ARK	0	10	14	7	31

SCORING SUMMARY
MICH FG Feely 43
ARK   Williams 35 pass from Stoerner (Latourette kick)
MICH Thomas 2 run (Feely kick)
MICH Gold 46 interception return (Feely kick)
ARK   FG Latourette 42
MICH Thomas 5 run (Feely kick)
ARK   Chukwuma 2 run (Latourette kick)
ARK   Chukwuma 1 run (Latourette kick)
ARK   Davenport 9 pass from Stoerner (Latourette kick)
MICH Thomas 1 run (Feely kick)
MICH Johnson 21 pass from Brady (Feely kick)
MICH Whitley 26 interception return (Feely kick)

MICH	TEAM STATISTICS	ARK
21	First Downs	20
204	Rushing Yards	116
16-30-2	Passing	17-42-2
230	Passing Yards	232
434	Total Yards	348
5-40.0	Punts - Average	7-33.9
78	Return Yards	81
1-1	Fumbles - Lost	0-0
12-104	Penalties - Yards	4-31
31:17	Possession Time	28:43

INDIVIDUAL LEADERS
RUSHING
MICH: Thomas 21-132, 3 TD; Williams 19-72.
ARK: Chukwuma 17-56, 2 TD; Hill 13-35.
PASSING
MICH: Brady 14-27-2, 209 yards, 1 TD.
ARK: Stoerner 17-42-2, 232 yards, 2 TD.
RECEIVING
MICH: Streets 7-129; Williams 2-15.
ARK: Williams 7-90, 1 TD; Lucas 3-63.

JANUARY 1, 2000 | COTTON
ARKANSAS 27, TEXAS 6

	1ST	2ND	3RD	4TH	FINAL
TEX	0	3	3	0	6
ARK	3	0	7	17	27

SCORING SUMMARY
ARK   FG Dodson 25
TEX   FG Stockton 35
ARK   Cobbs 30 pass from Stoerner (Dodson kick)
TEX   FG Stockton 22
ARK   Jenkins 42 run (Dodson kick)
ARK   Cobbs 37 run (Dodson kick)
ARK   FG Dodson 27

TEX	TEAM STATISTICS	ARK
14	First Downs	17
-27	Rushing Yards	191
24-39-0	Passing	12-23-0
212	Passing Yards	194
185	Total Yards	385
9-39.7	Punts - Average	4-39.0
0-0	Fumbles - Lost	0-0
7-40	Penalties - Yards	4-36
31:30	Possession Time	28:30

INDIVIDUAL LEADERS
RUSHING
TEX: Mitchell 13-36.
ARK: Cobbs 15-98, 1 TD; Jenkins 16-82, 1 TD.
PASSING
TEX: Applewhite 15-21-0, 121 yards; Simms 9-18-0, 91 yards.
ARK: Stoerner 12-23-2, 194 yards, 1 TD.
RECEIVING
TEX: Flowers 5-62; Nunez 6-48.
ARK: Williams 2-47; Davenport 2-25.

DECEMBER 21, 2000 | LAS VEGAS
UNLV 31, ARKANSAS 14

	1ST	2ND	3RD	4TH	FINAL
UNLV	0	14	7	10	31
ARK	7	7	0	0	14

SCORING SUMMARY
ARK   Stinson 7 pass from Hampton (O'Donohoe kick)
UNLV   Turner 19 pass from Thomas (Pieffer kick)
ARK   Williams 25 pass from Hampton (O'Donohoe kick)
UNLV* Turner 5 pass from Thomas (Pieffer kick)
UNLV   Mason 54 pass from Thomas (Pieffer kick)
UNLV   FG Pieffer 26
UNLV   Brown 18 run (Pieffer kick)

UNLV	TEAM STATISTICS	ARK
19	First Downs	15
314	Rushing Yards	127
12-17-0	Passing	18-40-0
217	Passing Yards	183
531	Total Yards	310
5-51	Punt Returns - Yards	0-0
2-33	Kickoff Returns - Yards	5-79
4-40.3	Punts - Average	7-46.1
6-1	Fumbles - Lost	0-0
12-119	Penalties - Yards	6-76
30:25	Possession Time	29:35

INDIVIDUAL LEADERS
RUSHING
UNLV: Rudolf 14-110; Brown 13-80, 1 TD.
ARK: Holmes 26-104; Howard 1-12.
PASSING
UNLV: Thomas 12-17-0, 217 yards, 3 TD.
ARK: Hampton 18-40-0, 183 yards, 2 TD.
RECEIVING
UNLV: Turner 8-126, 2 TD; Mason 3-89, 1 TD.
ARK: Williams 7-97, 1 TD; Hamilton 2-33.

JANUARY 1, 2002 | COTTON
OKLAHOMA 10, ARKANSAS 3

	1ST	2ND	3RD	4TH	FINAL
OKLA	7	0	3	0	10
ARK	0	0	0	3	3

SCORING SUMMARY
OKLA   Hybl 1 run (Duncan kick)
OKLA   FG Duncan 32
ARK   FG O'Donohoe 32

OKLA	TEAM STATISTICS	ARK
11	First Downs	6
56	Rushing Yards	37
24-32-0	Passing	2-13-1
175	Passing Yards	13
231	Total Yards	50
9-34.9	Punts - Average	8-40.5
2-1	Fumbles - Lost	1-1
9-76	Penalties - Yards	6-54
33:34	Possession Time	26:26

INDIVIDUAL LEADERS
RUSHING
OKLA: Griffin 19-56; Works 2-4.
ARK: Holmes 8-27; Jones 15-23.
PASSING
OKLA: Hybl 24-32-0, 175 yards.
ARK: Clark 2-12-1, 13 yards.
RECEIVING
OKLA: Norman 7-74; Smith 5-39.
ARK: Wilson 1-7; Pierce 1-6.

DECEMBER 30, 2002 | MUSIC CITY
MINNESOTA 29, ARKANSAS 14

	1ST	2ND	3RD	4TH	FINAL
ARK	7	0	0	7	14
MINN	6	6	7	10	29

SCORING SUMMARY
ARK   Wilson 2 pass from Jones (Carlton kick)
MINN   FG Nystrom 24
MINN   FG Nystrom 45
MINN   FG Nystrom 21
MINN   FG Nystrom 22
MINN   Utecht 19 pass from Abdul-Khaliq (Nystrom kick)
MINN   FG Nystrom 29
MINN   Tapeh 33 run (Nystrom kick)
ARK   Smith 10 pass from Sorahan (Carlton kick)

ARK	TEAM STATISTICS	MINN
19	First Downs	21
80	Rushing Yards	168
18-40-3	Passing	17-32-0
208	Passing Yards	266
288	Total Yards	434
2-15	Punt Returns - Yards	4-3
8-128	Kickoff Returns - Yards	2-42
5-34.2	Punts - Average	2-32.5
2-1	Fumbles - Lost	0-0
6-44	Penalties - Yards	9-71
21:45	Possession Time	38:15

INDIVIDUAL LEADERS
RUSHING
ARK: Talley 14-33; Jones 7-14.
MINN: Tapeh 19-99, 1 TD; Jackson II 16-37.
PASSING
ARK: Jones 12-24-2, 119 yards, 1 TD; Sorahan 6-15-1, 89 yards, 1 TD.
MINN: Abdul-Khaliq 16-31-0, 216 yards, 1 TD.
RECEIVING
ARK: Wilson 8-111, 1 TD; Smith 5-65, 1 TD.
MINN: Burns 4-88; Utecht 5-77, 1 TD.

DECEMBER 31, 2003 | INDEPENDENCE
ARKANSAS 27, MISSOURI 14

	1ST	2ND	3RD	4TH	FINAL
ARK	3	18	3	3	27
MO	7	0	7	0	14

SCORING SUMMARY
ARK   FG Balseiro 33
MO   Abron 1 run (Matheny kick)
ARK   FG Balseiro 28
ARK   Jones 1 run (Wilson pass from Jones)
ARK   Cobbs 41 run (Balseiro kick)
ARK   FG Balseiro 25
MO   Smith 5 run (Matheny kick)
ARK   FG Balseiro 24

ARK	TEAM STATISTICS	MO
19	First Downs	25
300	Rushing Yards	252
9-18-0	Passing	17-31-2
85	Passing Yards	155
385	Total Yards	407
1-14	Punt Returns - Yards	1--2
3-87	Kickoff Returns - Yards	6-120
4-30.0	Punts - Average	3-25.0
0-0	Fumbles - Lost	2-1
3-26	Penalties - Yards	5-35
30:24	Possession Time	29:36

INDIVIDUAL LEADERS
RUSHING
ARK: Cobbs 27-141, 1 TD; Birmingham 10-85; Jones 7-74, 1 TD.
MO: Abron 19-137, 1 TD; Smith 20-96, 1 TD.
PASSING
ARK: Jones 6-14-0, 49 yards.
MO: Smith 17-30-1, 155 yards.
RECEIVING
ARK: Smith 3-29; Wilson 3-25.
MO: Coffey 4-68; Omboga 8-63.

THE SCHOOLS

JANUARY 1, 2007 | CAPITAL ONE
ARKANSAS 14, WISCONSIN 17

	1ST	2ND	3RD	4TH	FINAL
ARK	7	0	0	7	14
WISC	10	7	0	0	17

SCORING SUMMARY
WISC FG Mehlhaff 52
ARK Jones 76 run (Davis kick)
WISC Hubbard 22 pass from Stocco (Mehlhaff kick)
WISC Beckum 13 pass from Stocco (Mehlhaff kick)
ARK Jones 12 run (Davis kick)

ARK	TEAM STATISTICS	WISC
18	First Downs	15
232	Rushing Yards	-5
15-32-2	Passing	14-34-2
136	Passing Yards	206
368	Total Yards	201
5-15	Punt Returns - Yards	2-19
3-54	Kickoff Returns - Yards	2-27
8-33.6	Punts - Average	7-42.7
1-0	Fumbles - Lost	1-1
12-123	Penalties - Yards	4-35

INDIVIDUAL LEADERS
RUSHING
ARK: Jones 14-150, 2 TD.
WISC: Hill 19-36.
PASSING
ARK: Dick 9-21-1, 98 yards.
WISC: Stocco 14-34-2, 206 yards, 2 TD.
RECEIVING
ARK: Johnson 4-46; Washington 3-46.
WISC: Beckum 5-82, 1 TD; Hubbard 4-73, 1 TD.

JANUARY 1, 2008 | COTTON
MISSOURI 38, ARKANSAS 7

	1ST	2ND	3RD	4TH	FINAL
MO	7	7	14	10	38
ARK	0	0	7	0	7

SCORING SUMMARY
MO Temple 22 run (Wolfert kick)
MO Temple 4 run (Wolfert kick)
MO Temple 4 run (Wolfert kick)
MO Moore 26 interception return (Wolfert kick)
ARK McFadden 3 run (Tejada kick)
MO FG Wolfert 32
MO Temple 40 run (Wolfert kick)

MO	TEAM STATISTICS	ARK
23	First Downs	19
323	Rushing Yards	164
12-29-1	Passing	19-33-1
136	Passing Yards	197
459	Total Yards	361
2-5	Punt Returns - Yards	3-2
0-0	Kickoff Returns - Yards	7-168
6-36.7	Punts - Average	5-38.8
2-2	Fumbles - Lost	5-4
6-53	Penalties - Yards	6-50

INDIVIDUAL LEADERS
RUSHING
MO: Temple 24-281, 4 TD.
ARK: McFadden 21-105, 1 TD.
PASSING
MO: Daniel 12-29-1. 136 yards.
ARK: Dick 19-32-1, 197 yards.
RECEIVING
MO: Franklin 5-77.
ARK: F. Jones 3-65; Hillis 5-52.

AUBURN

BY GEOFFREY NORMAN

To OUTSIDERS, AUBURN LONG seemed the redheaded stepchild of football in Alabama. There was the colossus up in Tuscaloosa and then there was that other school, over in "the loveliest village on the Plains." Auburn had plenty of good years and great teams and All-Americans, and when the two schools started playing each other in 1948 after a long hiatus, Auburn beat Alabama in the first game of what became perhaps college football's most bitter rivalry. But even the most devout Auburn fan and believer still felt resentment over being considered a second-class citizen when it came to football. This all changed on Dec. 2, 1989, when Auburn played Alabama at home for the first time. The days of no respect were in the rearview mirror and steadily growing smaller.

In truth, Auburn has been one of the elite teams in the nation since 1957. That was the year the 10–0 Tigers were AP national champions but could not go to a bowl because of recruiting violations. Since then they have been, arguably, the best program in the nation not to have won a national championship. They've finished in the Top 10–14 times since that year, with a record of 398–185–11, gone to 29 bowl games, produced two Heisman Trophy winners and enjoyed a pair of undefeated seasons. But the grand prize has remained out of reach; even when the 2004 Tigers ran the table, they were shut out of the national title game.

TRADITION At the intersection of College Street and Magnolia Avenue in the town of Auburn is a drugstore—Toomer's—that serves what some say is the best lemonade in the land. John Heisman supposedly stopped in for a glass now and then, which is an interesting historical bit of trivia. But to the Auburn faithful, what resonates about Toomer's Corner is the image of the trees, parking meters, signs and everything else in the vicinity draped in garlands of toilet paper. This occurs after any big win, and if the victory is big enough, the place looks like a blizzard has passed through this small section of Alabama. Rolling Toomer's Corner, then, is the peculiarly Auburn tradition.

Another tradition, which is less proprietary, dates to the 1960s. This is the Tiger Walk, which began modestly enough with a few fans lining up on Donahue Drive (named for "Iron" Mike Donahue, a former head coach) and applauding the players on their way to the stadium. The gathering grew in size and enthusiasm, and achieved a

PROFILE

Auburn University
Auburn, Ala.
Founded: 1856
Enrollment: 24,137
Colors: Navy Blue and Burnt Orange
Nickname: Tigers
Stadium: Jordan-Hare Stadium
    Opened in 1939
    Grass; 87,451 capacity
First football game: 1892
All-time record: 678–397–48 (.631)
Bowl record: 19–13–2
Consensus national championships,
1936-present: 1 (1957)
Southeastern Conference championships:
6 (4 outright)
Heisman Trophy: Pat Sullivan, 1971;
Bo Jackson, 1985
Outland Trophy: Zeke Smith, 1958;
Tracy Rocker, 1988
First-round draft choices: 25
Website: www.auburntigers.com/football

THE BEST OF TIMES

Early in the Shug Jordan era, from 1954 to 1958, Auburn went 42–8–2 and beat archrival Alabama five straight times.

THE WORST OF TIMES

The team floundered coming out of World War II, winning just five games from 1947 to 1950. Help was on the way; Jordan was hired in 1951.

CONFERENCE

After 12 years in the Southern Conference, Auburn became a charter member of the SEC in 1933.

DISTINGUISHED ALUMNI

Charles Barkley, NBA player/announcer; Rowdy Gaines, Olympic swimmer/commentator; Fob James, Alabama governor; Anne Rivers Siddons, author; Frank Thomas, baseball player

FIGHT SONG

WAR EAGLE!
War … Eagle, fly down the field.
Ever to conquer, never to yield.
War … Eagle, fearless and true.
Fight on, you orange and blue.
Go! Go! Go!
On to vict'ry, strike up the band.
Give 'em hell, give 'em hell;
Stand up and yell, Hey!
War … Eagle win for Auburn,
Power of Dixie Land!

> *"War Eagle" is the Auburn battle cry. It does not refer to the players but to a legend about a Confederate soldier and an injured baby eagle.*

permanent boost on the day of Auburn's first home game against Alabama in 1989. Hyperbole aside, the Tiger Walk has become a key ritual in any Auburn football weekend. Thousands now participate two hours before kickoff.

BEST PLAYER Auburn has produced two Heisman winners: quarterback Pat Sullivan and running back Bo Jackson. The final voting would probably come down to a contest between these two, though there might be a few nostalgic holdouts for Red Phillips, who played end on and captained the 1957 national title team.

Both Sullivan and Jackson are remembered with profound fondness at Auburn. Sullivan to Terry Beasley was a magical passing combination, and Jackson ran over an Alabama team—among others—like nobody before or since. If you had to pick one, it would probably be Jackson, based on what he did after he left Auburn. On the gridiron, the baseball diamond and in a dozen television ad campaigns, Bo knew how to get it done.

BEST COACH Though Heisman once coached at Auburn, he is not even in the running. On heart, the vote would undeniably go to Ralph "Shug" Jordan, who was both a great coach and a gentleman. The affable and unpretentious Jordan labored for 25 years in the shadow cast by Bear Bryant across the state. Still, Jordan's teams won 176 games along with the 1957 national championship. Impressive as that record is, Auburn people loved the man for his character more than the victories. To them, he was—and is—the soul of Auburn football.

However, a few unsentimental votes would undoubtedly be cast for Pat Dye, the guy who followed the guy who followed Jordan. Dye was a hardnosed, fundamentals football coach who won 99 games and four SEC championships in 12 years at Auburn.

BEST TEAM Jordan's undefeated 1957 team is special in the hearts of Auburn fans—a No. 1 ranking will do that—but there are many who believe the 2004 team *would have* finished on top if the thing had been settled on the field, the way it should have been. But the Tigers were shut out of the big game—the Orange Bowl—which turned into a beatdown of Oklahoma at the hands of USC. Auburn fans wondered what more their boys could

FIRST-ROUND DRAFT CHOICES

1950	Travis Tidwell, Giants (7)
1955	Dave Middleton, Lions (12)
1956	Joe Childress, Cardinals (7)
1958	Jim (Red) Phillips, Rams (5)
1959	Jackie Burkett, Colts (12)
1961	Ken Rice, Cardinals (8) and Bills (3)*
1965	Tucker Frederickson, Giants (1)
1968	Forrest Blue, 49ers (15)
1972	Terry Beasley, 49ers (19)
1978	Reese McCall, Colts (25)
1981	James Brooks, Chargers (24)
1986	Gerald Robinson, Vikings (14)
1986	Bo Jackson, Buccaneers (1)
1987	Brent Fullwood, Packers (4)
1988	Aundray Bruce, Falcons (1)
1994	Wayne Gandy, Rams (15)
1996	Willie Anderson, Bengals (10)
1998	Takeo Spikes, Bengals (13)
1998	Victor Riley, Chiefs (27)
2002	Kendall Simmons, Steelers (30)
2005	Ronnie Brown, Dolphins (2)
2005	Carnell Williams, Buccaneers (5)
2005	Carlos Rogers, Redskins (9)
2005	Jason Campbell, Redskins (25)
2007	Ben Grubbs, Baltimore (29)

From 1960-1966, the NFL and AFL held separate, competing drafts

CONSENSUS ALL-AMERICANS

1932	Jimmy Hitchcock, B
1957	Jimmy Phillips, E
1958	Zeke Smith, G
1960	Ken Rice, T
1964	Tucker Frederickson, B
1969	Buddy McClinton, DB
1970	Larry Willingham, DB
1971	Pat Sullivan, QB
1971	Terry Beasley, WR
1974	Ken Bernich, LB
1983, '85	Bo Jackson, RB
1984	Gregg Carr, LB
1986	Ben Tamburello, C
1986	Brent Fullwood, RB
1987-88	Tracy Rocker, DL
1987	Aundray Bruce, LB
1990	Ed King, OL
1990	David Rocker, DL
1993	Wayne Gandy, OL
1993	Terry Daniel, P
1994	Brian Robinson, DB
2001	Damon Duval, PK
2004	Carlos Rogers, DB
2005	Marcus McNeill, OL

have done than go undefeated in the regular season, winning tough games against LSU, Tennessee, Georgia (ranked No. 8 at the time) and Alabama, before knocking off Tennessee again to win the SEC championship. Still, they won their Sugar Bowl match against Virginia Tech and finished second in both polls.

There was an extra measure of sweetness to that season because it came after an ugly episode involving furtive attempts to hire a replacement for head coach Tommy Tuberville. To survive the coup and go undefeated seemed to have secured Tuberville a position for life—but it was not to be. He was gone after the 2008 season. But that 2004 team, that season and that injustice all still burn in the hearts of Auburn fans.

BEST BACKFIELD
The backfield on the 2004 team wasn't too shabby, with Jason Campbell at quarterback with Carnell "Cadillac" Williams and Ronnie Brown alongside. That combination was almost good enough to make people forget the 1983 backfield. *Almost*. But a unit made up of Jackson, Tommie Agee and Lionel "Little Train" James—with Randy Campbell at quarterback—would be hard for any fan to forget. That team went 11–1, the only loss coming to Texas in the second game of the season. Had Miami not upset Nebraska in the Orange Bowl, the Tigers likely would have finished No. 1.

BEST DEFENSE
The 1957 team, anchored by Jackie Burkett and Zeke Smith in the middle, "Red" Phillips and Jerry Wilson on the flanks, allowed four touchdowns and zero field goals in 10 games. No team scored more than one TD against Auburn that year. The closest anyone came was archrival Georgia, in a 6-0 game highlighted by back-to-back goal-line stands. The Alabama game was the last of the season for this team, since recruiting violations prevented the Tigers from going to a bowl. This made the season's sixth shutout—a 40-0 victory over the Tide— even sweeter than the No. 1 ranking in the AP poll.

STORYBOOK SEASON
The 1993 team was on probation for violations of NCAA rules. No television. No bowl game. The college football equivalent of exile to Siberia. Still, Terry Bowden's team went 11–0. This incredible run included a victory over No. 4 Florida and an especially satisfying win against defending national champion Alabama.

COLLEGE FOOTBALL HALL OF FAME INDUCTEES		
NAME	YEARS	INDUCTED
Michael Donahue, COACH	1904-06, '08-22	1951
John Heisman, COACH	1895-99	1954
Jimmy Hitchcock, HB	1930-32	1954
Walter Gilbert, C	1934-36	1956
Shug Jordan, COACH	1951-75	1982
Pat Sullivan, QB	1969-71	1991
Tucker Frederickson, HB	1962-64	1994
Bo Jackson, HB	1982-85	1998
Terry Beasley, WR	1969-71	2002
Tracy Rocker, DT	1985-88	2004
Pat Dye, COACH	1981-92	2005
Ed Dyas, FB	1958-60	2009

PRO FOOTBALL HALL OF FAME INDUCTEES		
NAME	YEARS	INDUCTED
Frank Gatski, C	1946-57	1985

BIGGEST GAME
Dec. 2, 1989, Alabama at Auburn. According to former Auburn AD David Housel, "The single most emotional day in Auburn history [was] when Alabama came to town to play on our turf." The Tiger Walk drew perhaps 10 times its usual crowd to greet the players coming into the stadium. "Donahue Drive was so crowded that the players had to walk single file, pushing their way through the people," said Housel. "There were at least 20,000 people out there. It was as though the children of Israel had been freed from pharaoh. Or the Berlin Wall had come down."

Alabama came in 10–0 and ranked No. 2 nationally, but Auburn won the game, 30-20. It provided plenty of redemption for Dye, whose success following the Jordan legend helped increase the pressure on Alabama to agree to a home-and-home series. When Dye was hired in 1981, Auburn was in the midst of a bad streak against the Tide that would run to nine losses. Asked how long he thought it would take for Auburn to beat Alabama, Dye answered, "Sixty minutes."

BIGGEST UPSET
In 1942, Georgia had Charley Trippi and Frank Sinkwich and Auburn didn't seem to have a chance. But an Auburn assistant named Jordan discovered something: Trippi tipped off plays in the way he lined up before the snaps. Auburn used the knowledge to win, 27-13—Georgia's only loss of the season.

WILDEST FINISH
On Sept. 17, 1994, Auburn was down 23-9 to LSU going into the fourth quarter and things looked bleak. Then safety Ken Alvis intercepted a pass and returned it 42 yards for a touchdown. This was the first of five Auburn interceptions that quarter, with two more of them taken to the end zone. Final score: 30-26, Auburn.

BEST COMEBACK
Oh, there have been many stirring comebacks in the history of Auburn football. But none of them is a patch on what happened at Legion Field in Birmingham on Dec. 2, 1972. Alabama was undefeated, ranked second in the nation and thinking national championship. Auburn had lost only one game but was a decided underdog, which looked valid with less than six minutes left and Alabama leading 16-3.

Then Bill Newton broke through and blocked an Alabama punt. The ball bounced into the hands of David Langner, who ran it in for a touchdown to make it 16-10.

Alabama took the kickoff but couldn't move and was forced to punt again. And again, Newton came clean and blocked it. Again, the ball bounced into Langner's hands and again, he ran it in. The score was now 17-16 and will remain that forever. People who do not remember the score, however, do remember the words they heard and saw on bumper stickers for years afterward: "Punt, Bama, Punt."

STADIUM Jordan-Hare Stadium has the ninth-largest seating capacity, at 87,000-plus, among on-campus college football stadiums. In 2005, the field in Jordan-Hare was named after Pat Dye, the coach Tigers fans remember most fondly after Shug.

Their stadium is a point of particular pride with Auburn people, who for years could not get notable opponents to come to town because the village and the stadium were both too small to accommodate opposing fans and their pride. So Auburn played many of its home games in Mobile, Montgomery and Birmingham. No more. The stadium has grown through a series of additions that began in 1949. The name was then changed from Auburn Stadium to Cliff Hare Stadium, after Clifford Leroy Hare, a member of the first Auburn football team, head of the old Southern Conference and chairman of Auburn's Faculty Athletic Committee. The bifurcated name dates to 1973, when the stadium became the first anywhere to be named for an active head coach, in this case, Ralph "Shug" Jordan, perhaps the most beloved figure in all of Auburn football. During Jordan's tenure, another 40,000 seats were added.

The playing surface is, and always has been, natural. As David Housel says, "This is an ag school. If we couldn't grow grass, we'd be out of business."

RIVAL There are rivalries, and there are rivalries. The feud between Auburn and Alabama is, perhaps, more intense than any in the country. The joke about it that made the rounds in the 1970s had Shug Jordan and Bear Bryant fishing together. Bryant wondered aloud if he could walk on water like all the Bama fans said. He stepped out onto the water and sank instantly. As he swam to the side of the boat and reached up to Jordan for assistance, Bryant said, "Shug, promise me you won't tell the Alabama fans I can't walk on water." Jordan said, "All right, Bear. Just as long as you promise not to tell the Auburn fans I helped you back in the boat."

Auburn's oldest rivalry, however, is not with Alabama, but Georgia. The Auburn-Georgia game brought football to the deep South in 1892, and the game has been played continuously—except for three war years—since 1898. It's the nation's seventh-oldest football rivalry.

DISPUTE Legion Field, 1967, and the opponent was— surprise—Alabama. The game was played in the mud and Auburn was ahead late, 3-0. Since nobody could move, the lead looked reasonably secure until Alabama QB Ken Stabler went on a long, twisting run that left players from both teams sprawled on the ground all over the field. At least two of them—both from Auburn—were there because of illegal blocks. In fact, one of the Tigers wasn't blocked at all, according to Auburn eyewitnesses. He was tackled.

Still, no flags. The touchdown counted. Alabama won the game 7-3.

It was one of those episodes on the "neutral" Legion Field site that fired Auburn's determination to play the game at home when they were the home team. So perhaps some good came of it after all.

NICKNAME This gets complicated. Auburn's nickname is the Tigers. It is the only official nickname, though Auburn has often been called the War Eagles and the Plainsmen.

The Plainsmen moniker is derived from Oliver Goldsmith's poem "The Deserted Village." The line goes: "Sweet Auburn! loveliest village of the plain, … " People appropriated the line to describe the town in Alabama that was the home of what was officially Alabama Polytechnic Institute and later became Auburn University. One thing led to another and some sportswriters, looking for a little elegant variation, took to calling the Tigers the Plainsmen.

"War Eagle" is the Auburn battle cry, equivalent to "Roll Tide" at Alabama. There are no "war eagles." The cry is singular and it does not refer to the players but to a legend involving a wounded Confederate soldier who found himself left for dead with nothing for company but an injured baby eagle. The soldier lived and recovered with the eagle. The man went on to teach at Auburn. At the first Georgia-Auburn game, in 1892, the eagle was among the spectators and, when Auburn scored, it took off and soared over the field. The Auburn fans saw this and began to shout "War Eagle!"

MASCOT It can be verified that Auburn won that War Eagle game 10-0. Other parts of the story are, no doubt, apocryphal. But the war cry has endured, and there is a golden eagle that appears at every Auburn game. That the bird, War Eagle VI, is also called Tiger accounts for some of the confusion.

UNIFORMS The overlapping AU, on Auburn helmets since 1966, gives the team one of the most instantly recognizable emblems in college football. The rest of the uniform has remained simple and largely unchanged through the years: blue jerseys at home, white on the road. Three jersey numbers have been retired: Bo Jackson's 34, Pat Sullivan's 7 and the 88 of Terry Beasley, Sullivan's favorite target.

QUOTE "College football is meant to be played on campus and on grass." —**Ralph "Shug" Jordan**

Sweet Home Auburn

BY TIM DORSEY

I was raised in south Florida, which, with all the transplants there at the time, was like growing up in the Northeast. When I got an ROTC scholarship and found myself in the fall of '79 in "The Loveliest Village on the Plains," it was my first exposure to the Deep South. Definite culture shock. Never was the difference between my surroundings and my upbringing more distilled than in the context of the thing I soon discovered called SEC football—a.k.a., sanctioned madness.

Rabid pep rallies, ubiquitous parties spilling into the streets till dawn, alumni naming their children Jordan and Hare, RVs arriving on *Tuesday* to begin tailgating—they all wound up at Jordan-Hare Stadium, along with frat boys in suits and orange-and-blue ties, sorority sisters dressed for a prom and … me in my T-shirt and flip-flops.

When I entered the stadium for that first game, I dove into a surreal sea of religious hysteria and had to recalibrate my neurons. But the full gravity of this feverish mindset didn't quite sink in until a few weeks later. I wrote a humor column for the student newspaper my first semester, and I thought it would be a hoot to use my outsider's perspective to poke a little fun at AU football.

Whoops.

You know that photo of Mussolini and his wife hanging upside-down as if they were piñatas? It was something like that. My phone rang nonstop; I was warned to stay away from the newspaper office; I slept under my bed in case hot lead came through the window.

That last measure was *probably* an overreaction. The Auburn community prides itself on its sophistication. Had I been attending, say, the University of Alabama, I would have had to transfer. With police protection.

Fast forward to my senior year. I am the editor of the student newspaper. I never miss a game. I dress in orange and blue. My throat is hoarse every Saturday after games. I have long since become one of the very people I'd joked about my freshman year. So what happened?

It has to do with something particularly Auburn. And I don't just mean football. There's something about that bucolic paradise in the middle of the east Alabama farmland. You can't

> *My senior year, we hadn't beaten the Crimson Tide in a decade, ever since the miraculous "Punt, Bama, Punt" game in '72, and we were still celebrating that.*

live there for four years and not fall in love with the place, the people, the landmark clock tower, the bitchin' landscaping. Football was simply the common bond of loyalty to a place that nurtured us through our coming of age. And Auburn football was all ours. Because back then, there were three types of people who lived in the state: 1) those who went to Alabama and rooted for the Crimson Tide; 2) those who went to Auburn and rooted for the Tigers; and 3) everyone else, who went to neither … and rooted for Bama. From Mobile to Montgomery to Huntsville, all the *Roll Tide* bumper stickers and elephant banners and photos on restaurant walls of an unmistakable profile in a houndstooth hat offered ample proof.

But that just made it better. What we had wasn't diluted. And I'm not just making lemonade. You saw someone in an Auburn jersey, you knew it was real.

And we weren't spoiled. Many years had passed since the legendary reign of coach Ralph "Shug" Jordan. Many tough losing seasons. Some schools (no need to name names here) border on open revolt if they don't make the title game every year, let alone win their conference. Not us. Nothing taken for granted. Ours was a rarefied appreciation for anything we got. My senior year, we hadn't beaten the Tide in a decade, ever since the miraculous "Punt, Bama, Punt" game in '72, and we were *still* celebrating that.

So, by 1982, I had come full circle. The Iron Bowl season finale against Alabama approached, and I wrote an editorial exhorting students to support the team that was so passionate, it was cited by a journalism professor at another school as "an invitation to riot." He obviously didn't know that Auburn people don't like to riot; instead we go across campus and throw a lot of toilet paper around Toomer's Corner.

We beat Alabama, thanks to a freshman with the name Vincent Edward Jackson, although folks knew him as Bo. He did such a number on Bear Bryant's defensive line that the old man lost his last Iron Bowl, 23-22. Pandemonium. Down came the goal posts. And I somehow found myself in the middle of Legion Field, out on the 50-yard line, jumping up and down like an idiot.

Suddenly I saw a bunch of TV cameramen stampeding toward me from the Alabama sideline like the Four Horsemen. I spun around to get away from them and slammed into a wave of giant Auburn linemen charging from the other sideline. As I dove sideways for daylight, I looked straight up at coach Pat Dye riding on the players' shoulders—laughing, maybe even weeping with joy.

And you knew it was real.

Tim Dorsey graduated from Auburn in 1983 with a B.S. in transportation. He is the author of 10 novels, including Nuclear Jellyfish *and* Florida Roadkill.

AUBURN ALL-TIME SCORES

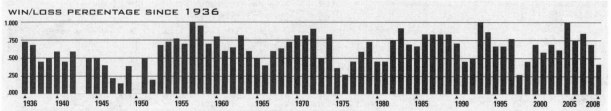

WIN/LOSS PERCENTAGE SINCE 1936

1.000	
.750	
.500	
.250	
.000	
1936 1940 1945 1950 1955 1960 1965 1970 1975 1980 1985 1990 1995 2000 2008	

DR. GEORGE PETRIE
1892 (.500) — 2-2

D.M. BALLIET
1892 (1.000) — 1-0

1892 — 3-2-0
F20	●	Georgia *Atl*	10	0
N22		Duke *Atl*	6	34
N23		North Carolina *Atl*	0	64
N25		Georgia Tech *Atl*	26	0
F22	●	Alabama *Birm*	32	22

G.H. HARVEY
1893 (.750) — 2-0-2

1893 — 2-0-2
N6	●	Vanderbilt *Mont*	30	10
N18	=	Sewanee *Atl*	14	14
N30	●	Alabama *Mont*	40	16
D7	=	Georgia Tech *Atl*	0	0

F.M. HALL
1894 (.250) — 1-3

1894 — 1-3-0
N4		Vanderbilt *Mont*	4	20
N17	●	Georgia Tech *Atl*	94	0
N24		Georgia *Atl*	8	10
N29		Alabama *Mont*	0	18

JOHN HEISMAN
1895-99 (.722) — 12-4-2

1895 — 2-1-0
N9		at Vanderbilt	6	9
N23	●	at Alabama	48	0
N28	●	Georgia *Atl*	16	6

1896 — 3-1-0
O6	●	at Mercer	46	0
N7	●	Georgia Tech	45	0
N8	●	Sewanee *Mont*	38	6
N26		Georgia *Atl*	6	12

1897 — 2-0-1
O23	●	at Mercer	26	0
O29	●	at Nashville	14	4
O30	=	at Sewanee	0	0

1898 — 2-1-0
N5	●	Georgia Tech	29	6
N15		North Carolina	0	24*
N24	●	Georgia *Atl*	18	17

1899 — 3-1-1
O14	●	Georgia Tech	63	0
O21	●	Montgomery	41	0
O28	●	Clemson	34	0
N18	=	Georgia *Atl*	0	0
N30		Sewanee *Mont*	10	11

BILLY WATKINS
1900-01 (.650) — 6-3-1

1900 — 4-0-0
O22	●	Nashville	28	0
N10	●	Tennessee *Birm*	23	0
N17	●	Alabama *Mont*	53	5
N29	●	Georgia *Atl*	44	0

1901 — 2-3-1
O19	●	Nashville *Birm*	5	23
N4		North Carolina	0	10
N8		Vanderbilt *Mont*	0	41*
N15	●	at Alabama	17	0
N20	●	at LSU	28	0
N28	=	Georgia *Atl*	0	0

R.S. KENT
1902 (.500) — 2-1-1

MIKE HARVEY
1902 (.000) — 0-2

1902 — 2-4-1
O11	●	at Georgia Tech	18	6
O18	●	Alabama *Birm*	23	0
O25	=	at Tulane	0	0
O27		at LSU	0	5
N6		Sewanee *Birm*	0	6
N15		Clemson	0	16
N27		Georgia *Atl*	5	12

BILLY BATES
1903 (.571) — 4-3

1903 — 4-3-0
O3	●	Montgomery AC	26	0
O17	●	Samford	58	0
O23	●	Alabama *Mont*	6	18
O31	●	Sewanee *Mont*	0	47
N11	●	LSU	12	0
N14	●	at Georgia Tech	10	5
N26		Georgia *Atl*	13	22

MIKE DONAHUE
1904-06, '08-22 (.730) — 99-35-5

1904 — 5-0-0
O15	●	at Clemson	5	0
O22	●	Nashville *Birm*	10	0
O29	●	Georgia Tech	12	0
N12	●	Alabama *Birm*	29	5
N24	●	Georgia *Mac*	17	6

1905 — 2-4-0
O20	●	Davidson *Birm*	0	6
O27	●	Mississippi State *ColMs*	18	0
N4		at Vanderbilt	0	54
N11		Clemson	0	6*
N18		Alabama *Birm*	0	30
N30		Georgia *Mac*	20	0*

1906 — 1-5-1
O8	=	Maryville	0	0
O13	●	Gordon	15	0
O26	●	Sewanee *Birm*	5	10
N3		at Georgia Tech	0	11
N10		at Clemson	4	6
N17		Alabama *Birm*	0	10
N29		Georgia *Mac*	0	4

W.S. KIENHOLZ
1907 (.722) — 6-2-1

1907 — 6-2-1
O5	●	Samford	23	0
O7	●	Maryville	29	0
O12	●	Gordon	34	0
O19	●	Sewanee *Birm*	6	12
O26	●	at Georgia Tech	12	6
N2	●	Clemson	12	0
N9	●	Mercer	63	0
N16	=	Alabama *Birm*	6	6
N28		Georgia *Mac*	0	6

MIKE DONAHUE

1908 — 6-1-0
O3	●	at Samford	18	0
O10	●	Gordon	42	0
O17	●	at Mercer	23	0
O24	●	Sewanee *Birm*	6	0
O31		LSU	2	10
N7	●	at Georgia Tech	44	0
N26	●	Georgia *Mont*	23	0

1909 — 5-2-0
O2	●	Samford *Mont*	11	0
O9	●	Gordon	46	0
O16	●	at Mercer	23	5
O23		at Vanderbilt	0	17
N6	●	at Georgia Tech	9	0*
N13		Sewanee *Birm*	11	12
N25	●	Georgia *Mont*	17	5*

1910 — 6-1-0
O8	●	Mississippi State	6	0
O15	●	at Samford	78	0
O22	●	Clemson	17	0
O29		at Texas	0	9
N5	●	at Georgia Tech	16	0
N12	●	Tulane *Gul*	33	0
N24	●	Georgia *Sav*	26	0

1911 — 4-2-1
O7	●	Mercer	29	0
O14	●	at Clemson	20	0*
O21		Texas A&M *Dal*	0	16
O28	●	Mississippi State *Birm*	11	5
N4	●	at Georgia Tech	11	6
N17		at Texas	5	18
N29	=	Georgia *Sav*	0	0

1912 — 6-1-1
O5	●	Mercer *ColGa*	56	0
O12	●	Florida	27	13
O19	●	Clemson	27	6
O26	●	Mississippi State *Birm*	7	0
N2	●	at Georgia Tech	27	7
N9	●	LSU *Mbl*	7	0
N23	=	Vanderbilt *Birm*	7	7
N28		at Georgia	6	12

1913 — 8-0-0
O4	●	Mercer	53	0
O11	●	Florida	55	0
O18	●	at Clemson	20	0
O25	●	Mississippi State *Birm*	34	0
N1	●	LSU *Mbl*	7	0
N8	●	at Georgia Tech	20	0
N15	●	Vanderbilt *Birm*	14	6
N22	●	Georgia *Atl*	21	7

1914 — 8-0-1
S26	●	Marion	39	0
O3	●	N. Ala. AC	60	0
O10	●	Florida *JacF*	20	0
O17	●	Clemson	28	0
O24	●	Mississippi State *Birm*	19	0
N7	●	at Georgia Tech	14	0
N14	●	Vanderbilt *Birm*	6	0
N21	=	Georgia *Atl*	0	0
D5	●	Carlisle *Atl*	7	0

1915 — 6-2-0
O1	●	Marion *Sel*	78	0
O9	●	Florida	7	0
O16	●	Clemson *And*	14	0
O23	●	Mississippi State *Birm*	26	0
O30	●	at Georgia	12	0
N6	●	Mercer	45	0
N13		Vanderbilt *Birm*	0	17
N25		at Georgia Tech	0	7

1916 — 6-2-0
O7	●	at Samford	35	0
O14	●	Mercer	92	0
O20	●	Clemson	28	0
O28	●	Mississippi State *Birm*	7	3
N4	●	Georgia *ColGa*	3	0
N11	●	Florida *JacF*	20	0
N18		Vanderbilt *Birm*	9	20
N30		at Georgia Tech	7	33

1917 — 6-2-1
O6	●	Samford	53	0
O13	●	Camp Sheridan *Mont*	13	0
O19	●	at Clemson	7	0
O27	●	Mississippi State *Birm*	13	6
N3	●	Florida	68	0
N10		Davidson *Atl*	7	21
N17	●	at Vanderbilt	31	7
N24	=	Ohio State *Mont*	0	0
N29		at Georgia Tech	7	68

1918 — 2-5-0
O19	●	Oglethorpe	58	0
O26		Camp Griffin	0	26
N3	●	at Marion	20	7
N9		Camp Gordon *ColGa*	6	14
N16		Vanderbilt *Birm*	0	21
N28		at Georgia Tech	0	41
D7		Camp Sheridan *Mont*	0	7

1919 — 8-1-0
S27	●	Marion	37	0
O4	●	at Samford	19	6
O12	●	Camp Gordon	25	13
O17	●	Clemson	7	0
O25	●	at Vanderbilt	6	7
N1	●	Georgia *ColGa*	7	0
N8	●	at Spring Hill	10	0
N15	●	Mississippi State *Birm*	7	0
N27	●	at Georgia Tech	14	7

1920 — 7-2-0
S23	●	Marion	27	0
O2	●	Samford	88	0
O9	●	Fort Benning	14	2
O15	●	at Clemson	21	0
O23	●	Vanderbilt *Birm*	56	6
O30		Georgia *ColGa*	0	7
N6	●	B'ham Southern *Mont*	49	0
N13	●	Wash. & Lee *Birm*	77	0
N25		at Georgia Tech	0	34

1921 — 5-3-0
O1	●	at Samford	35	3
O8	●	Spring Hill *Mont*	44	0
O14	●	Clemson	56	0
O22	●	Fort Benning	14	7
O29		Georgia *ColGa*	0	7
N5	●	at Tulane	14	0
N12		Centre *Birm*	0	21
N24		at Georgia Tech	0	14

1922-1932
SOUTHERN

1922 — 8-2-0 (2-1-0)
S23	●	Marion	61	0
S30	●	at Samford	72	0
O7	●	Spring Hill *Mont*	19	6
O14		at Army	6	19
O21	●	Mercer	50	6
O28	●	Fort Benning	30	0
N4	●	Georgia *ColGa*	7	3
N11	●	Tulane *Mont*	19	0
N18	●	Centre *Birm*	6	0
N30		at Georgia Tech	6	14

BOOZER PITTS
1923-24, '27 (.417) — 7-11-6

1923 — 3-3-3 (0-1-3)
S29	=	at Clemson	0	0
O6	●	B'ham Southern *Mont*	20	0
O13	●	Samford	30	0
O20		at Army	6	28
O27	●	Fort Benning	34	0
N3		Georgia *ColGa*	0	7
N10		Tulane *Mont*	6	6
N17		Centre *Birm*	0	17
N29	=	at Georgia Tech	0	0

THE SCHOOLS

1924 — 4-4-1 (2-4-1)

S27	●	at B'ham Southern	7 0
O4	●	Clemson	13 0
O11	=	Virginia Tech RICH	0 0
O18	●	Samford	17 0
O25	●	LSU BIRM	3 0
N1		at Vanderbilt	0 13
N8		Tulane MONT	6 14
N15		Georgia COLGA	0 6
N27		at Georgia Tech	0 7

DAVE MOREY
1925-27 (.500)   10-10-1

1925 — 5-3-1 (3-2-1)

S26	●	at B'ham Southern	25 6
O3	●	at Clemson	13 6
O10	●	Virginia Tech	19 0
O17		Texas DAL	0 33
O24	●	Samford	7 6
O31		Tulane MONT	0 13
N7		Georgia COLGA	0 34
N14		Vanderbilt BIRM	10 9
N26	=	at Georgia Tech	7 7

1926 — 5-4-0 (3-3-0)

S25	●	U.T. Chattanooga	15 6
O2	●	Clemson	47 0
O9		at Samford	33 14
O16		LSU MONT	0 10
O23	●	at Tulane	2 0
O30	●	Sewanee MONT	9 0
N6		Georgia COLGA	6 16*
N13		Marquette BIRM	3 19
N25		at Georgia Tech	7 20

BOOZER PITTS

1927 — 0-7-2 (0-6-1)

S24		Stetson	0 6
O1		at Clemson	0 3
O8		Florida	6 33
O15		LSU MONT	0 9
O22		Georgia COLGA	3 33*
O29	=	at Samford	9 9
N5	=	at Tulane	6 6
N12		Mississippi State BIRM	6 7
N24		at Georgia Tech	0 18

GEORGE BOHLER
1928-29 (.214)   3-11

1928 — 1-8-0 (0-7-0)

S28		B'ham Southern MONT	0 6
O6		Clemson	0 6
O13		at Florida	0 27
O20		Mississippi BIRM	0 19
O27	●	Samford	25 6
N3		Georgia COLGA	0 13
N10		at Tulane	12 13
N17		Mississippi State BIRM	0 13
N29		at Georgia Tech	0 51

JOHN FLOYD
1929 (.000)   0-4

1929 — 2-7-0 (0-7-0)

S27	●	B'ham Southern MONT	7 0
O5		at Clemson	7 26
O11		Florida MONT	0 19
O19		Vanderbilt BIRM	2 41
O26	●	Samford	6 0
N2		at Tennessee	0 27
N9		at Tulane	0 52
N16		at Georgia	0 24
N28		at Georgia Tech	6 19

CHET WYNNE
1930-33 (.590)   22-15-2

1930 — 3-7-0 (1-6-0)

S26		B'ham Southern MONT	0 7
O4	●	Spring Hill	13 0
O11		Florida JACF	0 7
O18		at Georgia Tech	12 14
O25		Georgia COLGA	7 39
N1	●	Wofford	38 6
N8		at Tulane	0 21
N15		Mississippi State BIRM	6 7
N22		at Vanderbilt	0 27
N27	●	South Carolina COLGA	25 7

1931 — 5-3-1 (3-3-0)

S25	●	B'ham Southern MONT	24 6
O10	=	at Wisconsin	7 7
O17	●	at Georgia Tech	13 0
O24		Florida JACF	12 13
O31	●	Spring Hill	27 7
N7		Tulane MONT	0 27
N14	●	Sewanee BIRM	12 0
N21		Georgia COLGA	6 12
N26	●	South Carolina MONT	13 6

1932 — 9-0-1 (6-0-1)

S23	●	B'ham Southern MONT	61 0
O1	●	Erskine	77 0
O8	●	Duke BIRM	18 7
O15	●	at Georgia Tech	6 0
O22	●	at Tulane	19 7
O29	●	Mississippi MONT	14 7
N5	●	Samford MONT	25 0
N12	●	Florida MONT	21 6
N19	●	Georgia COLGA	14 7
D3	=	South Carolina BIRM	20 20

1933- PRESENT
SEC

1933 — 5-5-0 (2-2-0)

S22	●	B'ham Southern MONT	20 7
S29	●	at Samford	19 0
O14		at Georgia Tech	6 16
O21		George Washington	6 19
O28	●	at Tulane	13 7
N4		at Duke	7 13
N11	●	Oglethorpe	27 6
N18	●	Georgia COLGA	14 6
N25		at Florida	7 14
D2		South Carolina BIRM	14 16

JACK MEAGHER
1934-42 (.558)   48-37-10

1934 — 2-8-0 (1-6-0)

S21		B'ham Southern MONT	0 7
S29	●	Oglethorpe	15 0
O6		at Tulane	0 13
O13		at LSU	6 20
O20		at Vanderbilt	6 7
O27		at Kentucky	0 9
N3		Duke BIRM	6 13
N10	●	at Georgia Tech	18 6
N17		Florida MONT	7 14
N24		Georgia COLGA	0 18

1935 — 8-2-0 (5-2-0)

S27	●	B'ham Southern MONT	25 7
O5	●	at Tulane	10 0
O12		Tennessee BIRM	6 13
O19	●	Kentucky MONT	23 0
O25		at Duke	7 0
N2		at LSU	0 6
N9	●	at Georgia Tech	33 7
N16	●	Oglethorpe	51 0
N23	●	Georgia COLGA	19 7
N30	●	Florida MIA	27 6

1936 — 7-2-2 (4-1-1)

S25	●	B'ham Southern MONT	45 0
O3	●	at Tulane	0 0
O10	●	at Tennessee	6 0
O17	●	at Detroit	6 0
O24	●	Georgia COLGA	20 13
O30		Santa Clara SF	0 12
N7	●	at Georgia Tech	13 12
N14		LSU BIRM	6 19
N21	●	Loyola-New Orleans	44 0
N28	●	Florida MONT	13 0

BACARDI BOWL
| J1 | = | Villanova | 7 7 |

1937 — 6-2-3 (4-1-2)

S24	●	B'ham Southern MONT	19 0
O2	=	at Tulane	0 0
O9	●	Villanova PHIL	0 0
O16	●	Mississippi State BIRM	33 7
O23	●	at Georgia Tech	21 0
O30		at Rice	7 13
N6	●	Tennessee BIRM	20 7
N13		at LSU	7 9
N20	●	Georgia COLGA	0 0
N27	●	Florida JACF	14 0

ORANGE BOWL
| J1 | ● | Michigan State | 6 0 |

1938 — 4-5-1 (3-3-1)

S23	●	B'ham Southern MONT	14 0
O1	=	at Tulane	0 0
O8		at Tennessee	0 7
O14	●	Mississippi State MONT	20 6
O22		at Georgia Tech	6 7
O29		at Rice	0 14
N5		Villanova PHIL	12 25
N12	●	LSU BIRM	28 6
N19	●	Georgia COLGA	23 14
N26		Florida JACF	7 9

1939 — 5-5-1 (3-3-1)

S29	●	B'ham Southern MONT	6 0
O7		at Tulane	0 12
O14	●	Mississippi State BIRM	7 0
O21		Manhattan NYC	0 7
O28		at Georgia Tech	6 7
N4		at Boston College	7 13
N11	●	Villanova BIRM	10 9
N18		at LSU	21 7
N25	●	Georgia COLGA	7 0
N30		Florida	7 7
D9		at Tennessee	0 7

1940 — 6-4-1 (3-2-1)

S27	●	Samford MONT	27 13
O5		at Tulane	20 14
O12		Mississippi State BIRM	7 7
O19		at SMU	13 20
O26	●	at Georgia Tech	16 7
N2		Georgia COLGA	13 14
N9	●	Clemson	21 7
N16		LSU BIRM	13 21
N23		at Boston College	7 33
N30	●	Florida COLGA	20 7
D7		Villanova MONT	13 10

1941 — 4-5-1 (0-4-1)

S26	●	Samford MONT	13 0
O4		at Tulane	0 32
O11	●	Louisiana Tech	34 0
O18		SMU BIRM	7 20
O25		at Georgia Tech	14 28
N1		Georgia COLGA	0 7
N8	●	Mississippi State BIRM	7 14
N15	=	LSU	7 7
N22	●	Villanova PHIL	13 0
N29	●	Clemson	28 7

1942 — 6-4-1 (3-3-0)

S18	●	U.T. Chattanooga	20 7
S26		Georgia Tech MONT	0 15
O3	●	at Tulane	27 13
O10		at Florida	0 6
O17	=	at Georgetown	6 6
O23	●	Villanova MONT	14 6
O31		Mississippi State BIRM	0 6
N7		Georgia Pre-Flight COLGA	14 41
N14	●	LSU BIRM	25 7
N21	●	Georgia COLGA	27 13
N28	●	Clemson	41 13

1943

NO TEAM WWII

CARL VOYLES
1944-47 (.405)   15-22

1944 — 4-4-0 (0-4-0)

S29	●	Samford MONT	32 0
O7	●	Fort Benning	7 0
O14	●	Georgia Tech	0 27
O21	●	Tulane	13 16
N4	●	Presbyterian	57 0
N11	●	Mississippi State BIRM	21 26
N18	●	Georgia COLGA	13 49
N24	●	Miami, Fla.	38 19

1945 — 5-5-0 (2-3-0)

S21	●	Samford MONT	38 0
S28		at Maxwell Field	0 7
O6	●	Mississippi State BIRM	0 20
O20	●	at Tulane	20 14
O27	●	at Georgia Tech	7 20
N3	●	Florida	19 0
N10	●	La. Lafayette	52 0
N17	●	Georgia COLGA	0 35
N24	●	Louisiana Tech	29 0
N30		at Miami, Fla.	7 33

1946 — 4-6-0 (1-5-0)

S27	●	Southern Miss MONT	13 12
O5	●	Furman	26 6
O12	●	St. Louis BIRM	27 7
O19		at Tulane	0 32
O26		at Georgia Tech	6 27
N2	●	Vanderbilt MONT	0 19
N9	●	Mississippi State BIRM	0 33
N16	●	Georgia COLGA	0 41
N23	●	Clemson MONT	13 21
N30	●	at Florida	47 12

1947 — 2-7-0 (1-5-0)

S27	●	Southern Miss	13 19
O4	●	Louisiana Tech	14 0
O11	●	Florida MONT	20 14
O18	●	at Georgia Tech	7 27
O25		at Tulane	0 40
N1		at Vanderbilt	0 28
N8	●	Mississippi State BIRM	0 14
N15		Georgia COLGA	6 28
N22		at Clemson	18 34

EARL BROWN
1948-50 (.172)   3-22-4

1948 — 1-8-1 (0-7-0)

S24	●	Southern Miss MONT	20 14
O2	=	Louisiana Tech	13 13
O9	●	Florida TAM	9 16
O16	●	at Georgia Tech	0 27
O23		at Tulane	6 21
O29	●	Vanderbilt MONT	0 47
N6	●	Mississippi State BIRM	0 20
N13		Georgia COLGA	14 42
N27	●	Clemson MBL	6 7
D4		Alabama BIRM	0 55

1949 — 2-4-3 (2-4-2)

S23	●	Mississippi MONT	7 40
O8	=	Florida MBL	14 14
O15		at Georgia Tech	21 35
O22		at Tulane	6 14
O29		at Vanderbilt	7 26
N5	●	Mississippi State	25 6
N19	=	Georgia COLGA	20 20
N26	=	Clemson MBL	20 20
D3	●	Alabama BIRM	14 13

1950 — 0-10-0 (0-7-0)

S22	●	Wofford MONT	14 19
S30		at Vanderbilt	0 41
O7		S.E. Louisana	0 6
O14		at Florida	7 27
O21		at Georgia Tech	0 20
O28		Tulane	0 28
N4		at Mississippi State	0 27
N18		Georgia COLGA	10 12
N25		Clemson	0 41
D2		Alabama BIRM	0 34

RALPH "SHUG" JORDAN
1951-75 (.674)   175-83-7

1951 — 5-5-0 (3-4-0)

S29	●	Vanderbilt	24 14
O5	●	Wofford MONT	30 14
O13		Florida	13 14
O20		at Georgia Tech	7 27
O27	●	at Tulane	21 0
N3		Louisiana Coll.	49 0
N10		Mississippi MBL	14 39
N17		Georgia COLGA	14 46
N24		at Clemson	0 34
D2		Alabama BIRM	7 25

1952 — 2-8-0 (0-7-0)

S27		Maryland BIRM	7 13
O4		Mississippi MEM	7 20
O11	●	Wofford	54 7
O18		at Georgia Tech	0 33
O25		Tulane MBL	6 21
N1		at Florida	21 31
N8		Mississippi State	34 49
N15		Georgia COLGA	7 13
N22	●	Clemson	3 0
N29		Alabama BIRM	0 21

1953 7-3-1 (4-2-1)

S25	●		Stetson *Mont*	47	0
O3	●	│	Mississippi	13	0
O10	=	│	at Mississippi State	21	21
O17		│	at Georgia Tech	6	36
O24	●	│	Tulane *Mbl*	34	7
O31	●	│	Florida	16	7
N6	●		at Miami, Fla.	29	20
N14	●	│	Georgia *ColGa*	39	18
N21	●		at Clemson	45	19
N28		│	Alabama *Birm*	7	10
			GATOR BOWL		
J1			Texas Tech	13	35

1954 8-3-0 (3-3-0)

S25	●		U.T. Chattanooga	45	0
O2		│	at Florida	13	19
O9		│	at Kentucky	14	21
O16		│	at Georgia Tech	7	14
O23	●		Florida State	33	0
O30	●	│	Tulane *Mbl*	27	0
N6	●		Miami, Fla. *Birm*	14	13
N13	●	│	Georgia *ColGa*	35	0
N20	●		Clemson	27	6
N27	●	│	Alabama *Birm*	28	0
			GATOR BOWL		
D31	●		Baylor	33	13

1955 8-2-1 (5-1-1)

S24	●		U.T. Chattanooga	15	6
O1	●	│	Florida	13	0
O8	=	│	Kentucky *Birm*	14	14
O15	●	│	at Georgia Tech	14	12
O22	●		Furman	52	0
O29		│	at Tulane	13	27
N5	●	│	Mississippi State	27	26
N12	●	│	Georgia *ColGa*	16	13
N19	●		Clemson *Mbl*	21	0
N26	●	│	Alabama *Birm*	26	0
			GATOR BOWL		
D31			Vanderbilt	13	25

1956 7-3-0 (4-3-0)

S29		│	Tennessee *Birm*	7	35
O6	●		Furman	41	0
O13	●	│	at Kentucky	13	0
O20		│	at Georgia Tech	7	28
O27	●		Houston	12	0
N3		│	at Florida	0	20
N10	●	│	Mississippi State	27	20
N17	●	│	Georgia *ColGa*	20	0
N24	●		Florida State	13	7
D1	●	│	Alabama *Birm*	34	7

1957 10-0-0 (7-0-0)

S28	●	│	at Tennessee	7	0
O5	●		U.T. Chattanooga	40	7
O12	●	│	Kentucky	6	0
O19	●	│	at Georgia Tech	3	0
O26	●		at Houston	48	7
N2	●	│	Florida	13	0
N9	●	│	Mississippi State *Birm*	15	7
N16	●	│	Georgia *ColGa*	6	0
N23	●		at Florida State	29	7
N30	●	│	Alabama *Birm*	40	0

1958 9-0-1 (6-0-1)

S27	●	│	Tennessee *Birm*	13	0
O4	●		U.T. Chattanooga	30	8
O11	●	│	at Kentucky	8	0
O18	=	│	at Georgia Tech	7	7
O25	●		Maryland	20	7
N1	●	│	at Florida	6	5
N8	●	│	Mississippi State	33	14
N15	●	│	Georgia *ColGa*	21	6
N22	●		Wake Forest	21	7
N29	●	│	Alabama *Birm*	14	8

1959 7-3-0 (4-3-0)

S26		│	at Tennessee	0	3
O3	●		Hardin-Simmons	35	12
O10	●	│	Kentucky	33	0
O17	●	│	at Georgia Tech	7	6
O23	●		at Miami, Fla.	21	6
O31	●	│	Florida	6	0
N7	●	│	Mississippi State *Birm*	31	0
N14		│	at Georgia	13	14
N21	●		Southern Miss	28	7
N28		│	Alabama *Birm*	0	10

1960 8-2-0 (5-2-0)

S24		│	Tennessee *Birm*	3	10
O1	●	│	at Kentucky	10	7
O8	●		U.T. Chattanooga	10	0
O15	●	│	Georgia Tech *Birm*	9	7
O22	●		Miami, Fla.	20	7
O29	●	│	at Florida	10	7
N5	●	│	Mississippi State	27	12
N12	●	│	Georgia	9	6
N19	●		Florida State	57	21
N26		│	Alabama *Birm*	0	3

1961 6-4-0 (3-4-0)

S30	●	│	at Tennessee	24	21
O7		│	Kentucky	12	14
O14	●		U.T. Chattanooga	35	7
O21		│	at Georgia Tech	6	7
O28	●		Clemson	24	14
N4	●		Wake Forest	21	7
N11		│	Mississippi State *Birm*	10	11
N18	●	│	at Georgia	10	7
N25	●	│	Florida	32	15
D2		│	Alabama *Birm*	0	34

1962 6-3-1 (4-3-0)

S29	●	│	Tennessee *Birm*	22	21
O6	●	│	at Kentucky	16	6
O13	●		U.T. Chattanooga	54	6
O20	●	│	Georgia Tech *Birm*	17	14
O27	●		at Clemson	17	14
N3		│	at Florida	3	22
N10	●	│	Mississippi State	9	3
N17		│	Georgia	21	30
N24	=		Florida State	14	14
D1		│	Alabama *Birm*	0	38

1963 9-2-0 (6-1-0)

S21	●		at Houston	21	14
S28	●	│	at Tennessee	23	19
O5	●	│	Kentucky	14	13
O12	●		U.T. Chattanooga	28	0
O19	●	│	at Georgia Tech	29	21
N2	●	│	Florida	19	0
N9		│	Mississippi State *JaM*	10	13
N16	●	│	at Georgia	14	0
N23	●		Florida State	21	15
N30	●	│	Alabama *Birm*	10	8
			ORANGE BOWL		
J1			Nebraska	7	13

1964 6-4-0 (3-3-0)

S19	●		Houston	30	0
S26	●	│	Tennessee *Birm*	3	0
O3		│	Kentucky *Birm*	0	20
O10	●		U.T. Chattanooga	33	12
O17			Georgia Tech *Birm*	3	7
O24	●		Southern Miss	14	7
O31		│	at Florida	0	14
N7	●	│	Mississippi State	12	3
N14	●	│	Georgia	14	7
N26		│	Alabama *Birm*	14	21

1965 5-5-1 (4-1-1)

S18			Baylor	8	14
S25	=	│	at Tennessee	13	13
O2	●	│	Kentucky	23	18
O9	●		U.T. Chattanooga	30	7
O16			at Georgia Tech	14	23
O23			Southern Miss	0	3
O30	●	│	Florida	28	17
N6	●	│	Mississippi State *Birm*	25	18
N13	●	│	at Georgia	21	19
N27		│	Alabama *Birm*	3	30
			LIBERTY BOWL		
D18			Mississippi	7	13

1966 4-6-0 (1-5-0)

S17	●		U.T. Chattanooga	20	6
S24		│	Tennessee *Birm*	0	28
O1		│	at Kentucky	7	17
O8	●		Wake Forest	14	6
O15			Georgia Tech *Birm*	3	17
O22	●		TCU	7	6
O29		│	at Florida	27	30
N5	●	│	Mississippi State *JaM*	13	0
N12		│	Georgia	13	21
D3		│	Alabama *Birm*	0	31

1967 6-4-0 (3-3-0)

S23	●		U.T. Chattanooga	40	6
S30		│	at Tennessee	13	27
O7	●	│	Kentucky	48	7
O14	●		Clemson	43	21
O21	●		at Georgia Tech	28	10
O27			at Miami, Fla.	0	7
N4	●	│	Florida	26	21
N11	●	│	Mississippi State	36	0
N18		│	at Georgia	0	17
D2		│	Alabama *Birm*	3	7

1968 7-4-0 (4-2-0)

S21			SMU	28	37
S28	●	│	Mississippi State *JaM*	26	0
O5	●	│	at Kentucky	26	7
O12	●		at Clemson	21	10
O19			Georgia Tech *Birm*	20	21
O26	●		Miami, Fla.	31	6
N2	●	│	at Florida	24	13
N9	●	│	Tennessee *Birm*	28	14
N16		│	Georgia	3	17
N30		│	Alabama *Birm*	16	24
			SUN BOWL		
D28	●		Arizona	34	10

1969 8-3-0 (5-2-0)

S20	●		Wake Forest	57	0
S27		│	at Tennessee	19	45
O4	●	│	Kentucky	44	3
O11	●		Clemson	51	0
O18	●		at Georgia Tech	17	14
O25		│	at LSU	20	21
N1	●	│	Florida	38	12
N8	●	│	Mississippi State	52	13
N15	●	│	at Georgia	16	3
N29	●	│	Alabama *Birm*	49	26
			BLUEBONNET BOWL		
D31			Houston	7	36

1970 9-2-0 (5-2-0)

S19	●		Southern Miss	33	14
S26	●	│	Tennessee *Birm*	36	23
O3	●	│	at Kentucky	33	15
O10	●		at Clemson	44	0
O17	●		Georgia Tech	31	7
O24		│	LSU	9	17
O31	●	│	at Florida	63	14
N7	●	│	Mississippi State *Birm*	56	0
N14		│	Georgia	17	31
N28	●	│	Alabama *Birm*	33	28
			GATOR BOWL		
J2	●		Mississippi	35	28

1971 9-2-0 (5-1-0)

S18	●		U.T. Chattanooga	60	7
S25	●	│	at Tennessee	10	9
O2	●	│	Kentucky	38	6
O9	●		Southern Miss	27	14
O16	●		at Georgia Tech	31	14
O23	●		Clemson	35	13
O30	●	│	Florida	40	7
N6	●	│	Mississippi State	30	21
N13	●	│	at Georgia	35	20
N27		│	Alabama *Birm*	7	31
			SUGAR BOWL		
J1			Oklahoma	22	40

1972 10-1-0 (6-1-0)

S9	●	│	Mississippi State *JaM*	14	3
S23	●		U.T. Chattanooga	14	7
S30	●	│	Tennessee *Birm*	10	6
O7	●	│	Mississippi *JaM*	19	13
O14		│	at LSU	7	35
O21	●		Georgia Tech	24	14
O28	●		Florida State	27	14
N4	●	│	at Florida	26	20
N18	●	│	Georgia	27	10
D2	●	│	Alabama *Birm*	17	16
			GATOR BOWL		
D30	●		Colorado	24	3

1973 6-6-0 (2-5-0)

S15	●		Oregon State *Birm*	18	9
S22	●		U.T. Chattanooga	31	0
S29		│	at Tennessee	0	21
O6	●	│	Mississippi	14	7
O13		│	LSU	6	20
O20	●		at Georgia Tech	24	10
O27	●		Houston	7	0
N3		│	Florida	8	12
N10	●	│	Mississippi State	31	17
N17		│	at Georgia	14	28
D1		│	Alabama *Birm*	0	35
			SUN BOWL		
D29			Missouri	17	34

1974 10-2-0 (4-2-0)

S14	●		Louisville *Birm*	16	3
S21	●		U.T. Chattanooga	52	0
S28	●	│	Tennessee	21	0
O4	●		at Miami, Fla.	3	0
O12	●	│	Kentucky	31	13
O19	●		Georgia Tech	31	22
O26	●		Florida State	38	6
N2		│	at Florida	14	25
N9	●	│	Mississippi State *JaM*	24	20
N16	●	│	Georgia	17	13
N29		│	Alabama *Birm*	13	17
			GATOR BOWL		
D30	●		Texas	27	3

1975 3-6-2 (1-4-1)

S13			Memphis	20	31
S20	=		at Baylor	10	10
S27		│	at Tennessee	17	21
O4			Virginia Tech	16	23
O11	●	│	at Kentucky	15	9
O18	●		at Georgia Tech	31	27
O25	●		at Florida State	17	14
N1		│	Florida	14	31†
N8	=	│	Mississippi State	21	21
N15		│	at Georgia	13	28
N29		│	Alabama *Birm*	0	28

DOUG BARFIELD
1976-80 (.500) 27-27-1

1976 3-8-0 (2-4-0)

S11			at Arizona	19	31
S18			Baylor	14	15
S25	●	│	Tennessee *Birm*	38	28
O2	●	│	Mississippi *JaM*	10	0
O9			at Memphis	27	28
O16			Georgia Tech	10	28
O23	●		Florida State	31	19
O30		│	at Florida	19	24†
N6		│	Mississippi State *JaM*	19	28
N13		│	Georgia	0	28
N27		│	Alabama *Birm*	7	38

1977 5-6-0 (4-2-0)

S10	●		Arizona	21	10
S17			Southern Miss	13	24
S24	●	│	at Tennessee	14	12
O1	●	│	Mississippi	21	15
O8			North Carolina St.	15	17
O15			at Georgia Tech	21	38
O22			at Florida State	3	24
O29	●	│	Florida	29	14†
N5		│	Mississippi State	13	27
N12	●	│	at Georgia	33	14
N26		│	Alabama *Birm*	21	48

1978 6-4-1 (3-2-1)

S16	●		at Kansas State	45	32
S23	●		at Virginia Tech	18	7
S30	●	│	Tennessee *Birm*	29	10
O7			Miami, Fla.	15	17
O14	●	│	at Vanderbilt	49	7
O21			Georgia Tech	10	24
O28	●		Wake Forest	21	7
N4		│	at Florida	7	31
N11	●	│	at Mississippi State	6	0
N18	=	│	Georgia	22	22
D2		│	Alabama *Birm*	16	34

1979 8-3-0 (4-2-0)

S15	●		Kansas State	26	18
S22	●		Southern Miss	31	9
S29		│	at Tennessee	17	35
O6	●		North Carolina St.	44	31
O13	●	│	Vanderbilt	52	35
O20	●		at Georgia Tech	38	14
O27			at Wake Forest	38	42
N3	●	│	Florida	19	13
N10	●	│	Mississippi State	14	3
N17	●	│	at Georgia	33	13
D1		│	Alabama *Birm*	18	25

1980 5-6-0 (0-6-0)

S13	●		at TCU	10	7
S20	●		Duke	35	28
S27		│	Tennessee	0	42
O4	●		Richmond	55	16
O11		│	at LSU	17	21
O18	●		Georgia Tech	17	14
O25		│	Mississippi State *JaM*	21	24
N1		│	at Florida	10	21
N8	●		Southern Miss	31	0
N15		│	Georgia	21	31
N29		│	Alabama *Birm*	18	34

PAT DYE
1981-92 (.711) 99-39-4

1981 5-6-0 (2-4-0)

S5	●		TCU	24	16
S19			Wake Forest	21	24
S26		│	at Tennessee	7	10
O3			at Nebraska	3	17
O10	●	│	LSU	19	7
O17	●		at Georgia Tech	31	7
O24		│	Mississippi State	17	21
O31	●	│	Florida	14	12
N7	●		North Texas	20	0
N14		│	at Georgia	13	24
N28		│	Alabama *Birm*	17	28

64 AUBURN

THE SCHOOLS

1982 9-3-0 (4-2-0)

S11	•		Wake Forest	28	10
S18	•		Southern Miss	21	19
S25	•	|	Tennessee	24	14
O2			Nebraska	7	41
O9	•	|	Kentucky	18	3
O16	•		Georgia Tech	24	0
O23	•	|	at Mississippi State	35	17
O30		|	at Florida	17	19
N6	•		Rutgers	30	7
N13		|	Georgia	14	19
N27	•	|	Alabama [Birm]	23	22
			TANGERINE BOWL		
D18	•		Boston College	33	26

1983 11-1-0 (6-0-0)

S10	•		Southern Miss	24	3
S17			Texas	7	20
S24	•	|	at Tennessee	37	14
O1	•		Florida State	27	24
O8	•	|	at Kentucky	49	21
O15	•		at Georgia Tech	31	13
O22	•	|	Mississippi State	28	13
O29	•	|	Florida	28	21
N5	•		Maryland	35	23
N12	•	|	at Georgia	13	7
D3	•	|	Alabama [Birm]	23	20
			SUGAR BOWL		
J2	•		Michigan	9	7

1984 9-4-0 (4-2-0)

A27			Miami, Fla. [ERut]	18	20
S15			Texas	27	35
S22	•		Southern Miss	35	12
S29	•	|	Tennessee	29	10
O6	•	|	at Mississippi	17	13
O13	•		at Florida State	42	41
O20	•		Georgia Tech	48	34
O27	•	|	at Mississippi State	24	21
N3		|	at Florida	3	24
N10	•		Cincinnati	60	0
N17	•	|	Georgia	21	12
D1		|	Alabama [Birm]	15	17
			LIBERTY BOWL		
D27	•		Arkansas	21	15

1985 8-4-0 (3-3-0)

S7	•		La. Lafayette	49	7
S14	•		Southern Miss	29	18
S28		|	at Tennessee	20	38
O5	•	|	Mississippi	41	0
O12	•		Florida State	59	27
O19	•		at Georgia Tech	17	14
O26	•	|	Mississippi State	21	9
N2		|	Florida	10	14
N9	•		East Carolina	35	10
N16	•	|	at Georgia	24	10
N30		|	Alabama [Birm]	23	25
			COTTON BOWL		
J1			Texas A&M	16	36

1986 10-2-0 (4-2-0)

S6	•		U.T. Chattanooga	42	14
S20	•		East Carolina	45	0
S27	•	|	Tennessee	34	8
O4	•		Western Carolina	55	6
O11	•	|	at Vanderbilt	31	9
O18	•		Georgia Tech	31	10
O25	•	|	at Mississippi State	35	6
N1		|	at Florida	17	18
N8	•		Cincinnati	52	7
N15		|	Georgia	16	20
N29	•	|	Alabama [Birm]	21	17
			CITRUS BOWL		
J1	•		Southern California	16	7

1987 9-1-2 (5-0-1)

S5	•		Texas	31	3
S12	•		Kansas	49	0
S26	=	|	at Tennessee	20	20
O3	•		at North Carolina	20	10
O10	•	|	Vanderbilt	48	15
O17	•		at Georgia Tech	20	10
O24	•	|	Mississippi State	38	7
O31	•	|	Florida	29	6
N7			Florida State	6	34
N14	•	|	at Georgia	27	11
N27	•	|	Alabama [Birm]	10	0
			SUGAR BOWL		
J1	=		Syracuse	16	16

1988 10-2-0 (6-1-0)

S10	•	|	Kentucky	20	10
S17	•		Kansas	56	7
S24	•	|	Tennessee	38	6
O1	•		North Carolina	47	21
O8		|	at LSU	6	7
O15	•		Akron	42	0
O22	•	|	Mississippi State	33	0
O29	•	|	at Florida	16	0
N5	•		Southern Miss	38	8
N12	•	|	Georgia	20	10
N25	•	|	Alabama [Birm]	15	10
			SUGAR BOWL		
J2			Florida State	7	13

1989 10-2-0 (6-1-0)

S9	•		Pacific	55	0
S16	•		Southern Miss	24	3
S30		|	at Tennessee	14	21
O7	•	|	at Kentucky	24	12
O14	•	|	LSU	10	6
O21			at Florida State	14	22
O28	•	|	Mississippi State	14	0
N4	•	|	Florida	10	7
N11	•		Louisiana Tech	38	23
N18	•	|	at Georgia	20	3
D2	•	|	Alabama	30	20
			HALL OF FAME BOWL		
J1	•		Ohio State	31	14

1990 8-3-1 (4-2-1)

S8	•		Fullerton St.	38	17
S15	•	|	Mississippi [JaM]	24	10
S29	=	|	Tennessee	26	26
O6	•		Louisiana Tech	16	14
O13	•	|	Vanderbilt	56	6
O20	•		Florida State	20	17
O27	•	|	at Mississippi State	17	16
N3		|	at Florida	7	48
N10			Southern Miss	12	13
N17	•	|	Georgia	33	10
D1		|	Alabama [Birm]	7	16
			PEACH BOWL		
D29	•		Indiana	27	23

1991 5-6-0 (2-5-0)

A31	•		Georgia Southern	32	17
S14	•	|	Mississippi	23	13
S21	•		Texas	14	10
S28		|	Tennessee	21	30
O5			Southern Miss	9	10
O12	•	|	Vanderbilt	24	22
O26		|	Mississippi State	17	24
N2		|	Florida	10	31
N9	•		La. Lafayette	50	7
N16		|	Georgia	27	37
N30		|	Alabama [Birm]	6	13

1992 5-5-1 (2-5-1)

S5		|	at Mississippi	21	45
S12	•		Samford	55	0
S19	•	|	LSU	30	28
S26	•		Southern Miss	16	8
O3	•	|	Vanderbilt	31	7
O10		|	at Mississippi State	7	14
O17		|	at Florida	9	24
O24	•		La. Lafayette	25	24
O31	=	|	Arkansas	24	24
N14		|	Georgia	10	14
N26		|	Alabama [Birm]	0	17

TERRY BOWDEN
1993-98 (.731) 47-17-1

1993 11-0-0 (8-0-0)

S2	•	|	Mississippi	16	12
S11	•		Samford	35	7
S18	•	|	at LSU	34	10
S25	•		Southern Miss	35	24
O2	•	|	at Vanderbilt	14	10
O9	•	|	Mississippi State	31	17
O16	•	|	Florida	38	35
O30	•	|	at Arkansas	31	21
N6	•		New Mexico St.	55	14
N13	•	|	at Georgia	42	28
N20	•	|	Alabama	22	14

1994 9-1-1 (6-1-1)

S3	•	|	at Mississippi	22	17
S10	•		La. Monroe	44	12
S17	•	|	LSU	30	26
S24	•		E. Tennessee St.	38	0
S29	•	|	Kentucky	41	14
O8	•	|	at Mississippi State	42	18
O15	•	|	at Florida	36	33
O29	•	|	Arkansas	31	14
N5	•		East Carolina	38	21
N12	=	|	Georgia	23	23
N19		|	Alabama [Birm]	14	21

1995 8-4-0 (5-3-0)

S2	•	|	Mississippi	46	13
S9	•		U.T. Chattanooga	76	10
S16		|	at LSU	6	12
S30	•	|	at Kentucky	42	21
O7	•	|	Mississippi State	48	20
O14		|	Florida	38	49
O21	•		Western Michigan	34	13
O28		|	Arkansas [LR]	28	30
N4	•		La. Monroe	38	14
N11	•	|	at Georgia	37	31
N18	•	|	Alabama	31	27
			HALL OF FAME BOWL		
J1			Penn State	14	43

1996 8-4 (4-4)

A31	•		UAB	29	0
S7	•		Fresno State	62	0
S14	•	|	at Mississippi	45	28
S21		|	LSU	15	19
O5	•	|	South Carolina	28	24
O12	•	|	at Mississippi State	49	15
O19		|	at Florida	10	51
N2	•	|	Arkansas	28	7
N9	•		La. Monroe	28	24
N16		|	Georgia	49	56
N23		|	Alabama [Birm]	23	24
			INDEPENDENCE BOWL		
D31	•		Army	32	29

1997 10-3 (6-2)

S4	•		at Virginia	28	17
S13	•	|	Mississippi	19	9
S20	•	|	at LSU	31	28
S27	•		Central Florida	41	14
O4	•	|	at South Carolina	23	6
O11	•		Louisiana Tech	49	13
O18		|	Florida	10	24
O25	•	|	at Arkansas	26	21
N1		|	Mississippi State	0	0
N15	•	|	at Georgia	45	34
N22	•	|	Alabama	18	17
			SEC CHAMPIONSHIP GAME		
D6			Tennessee [Atl]	29	30
			PEACH BOWL		
J2	•		Clemson	21	17

BILL OLIVER
1998 (.400) 2-3

1998 3-8 (1-7)

S3			Virginia	0	19
S12	•	|	at Mississippi	17	0
S19		|	LSU	19	31
O3		|	Tennessee	9	17
O10		|	at Mississippi State	21	38
O17		|	at Florida	3	24
O24	•		Louisiana Tech	32	17
O31		|	Arkansas	21	24
N7	•		Central Florida	10	6
N14		|	Georgia	17	28
N21		|	Alabama [Birm]	17	31

TOMMY TUBERVILLE
1999-08 (.680) 85-40

1999 5-6 (2-6)

S4	•		Appalachian St.	22	15
S11	•		Idaho	30	23
S18	•	|	at LSU	41	7
S25		|	Mississippi	17	24
O2		|	at Tennessee	0	24
O9		|	Mississippi State	16	18
O16		|	Florida	14	32
O30		|	at Arkansas	10	34
N6	•		Central Florida	28	10
N13	•	|	at Georgia	38	21
N20		|	Alabama	17	28

2000 9-4 (6-2)

A31	•		Wyoming	35	21
S9	•	|	at Mississippi	35	27
S16	•	|	LSU	34	17
S23	•		Northern Illinois	31	14
S30	•	|	Vanderbilt	33	0
O7		|	at Mississippi State	10	17
O14		|	at Florida	7	38
O21	•		Louisiana Tech	38	28
O28	•	|	Arkansas	21	19
N11	•	|	Georgia	29	26
N18	•	|	at Alabama	9	0
			SEC CHAMPIONSHIP GAME		
D2			Florida [Atl]	6	28
			CITRUS BOWL		
J1			Michigan	28	31

2001 7-5 (5-3)

S1	•		Ball State	30	0
S8	•	|	Mississippi	27	21
S22			at Syracuse	14	31
S29	•	|	at Vanderbilt	24	21
O6	•	|	Mississippi State	16	14
O13	•	|	Florida	23	20
O20	•		Louisiana Tech	48	41
O27		|	at Arkansas	17	42
N10	•	|	at Georgia	24	17
N17		|	Alabama	7	31
D1		|	at LSU	14	27
			PEACH BOWL		
D31			North Carolina	10	16

2002 9-4 (5-3)

S2			at Southern California	17	24
S7	•		Western Carolina	56	0
S14	•	|	Vanderbilt	31	6
S19	•	|	at Mississippi State	42	14
S28	•		Syracuse	37	34
O12		|	Arkansas	17	38
O19		|	at Florida	23	30
O26	•	|	LSU	31	7
N2	•	|	at Mississippi	31	24
N9	•		La. Monroe	52	14
N16		|	Georgia	21	24
N23	•	|	at Alabama	17	7
			CAPITAL ONE BOWL		
J1	•		Penn State	13	9

2003 8-5 (5-3)

A30			Southern California	0	23
S6			at Georgia Tech	3	17
S13	•	|	at Vanderbilt	45	7
S27	•		Western Kentucky	48	3
O4	•	|	Tennessee	28	21
O11	•	|	at Arkansas	10	3
O18	•	|	Mississippi State	45	13
O25		|	at LSU	7	31
N1	•		La. Monroe	73	7
N8		|	Mississippi	20	24
N15		|	at Georgia	7	26
N22	•	|	Alabama	28	23
			MUSIC CITY BOWL		
D31	•		Wisconsin	28	14

2004 13-0 (8-0)

S4	•		La. Monroe	31	0
S11	•	|	at Mississippi State	43	14
S18	•	|	LSU	10	9
S25	•		Citadel	33	3
O2	•	|	at Tennessee	34	10
O9	•		Louisiana Tech	52	7
O16	•	|	Arkansas	38	20
O23	•	|	Kentucky	42	10
O30	•	|	at Mississippi	35	14
N13	•	|	Georgia	24	6
N20	•	|	at Alabama	21	13
			SEC CHAMPIONSHIP GAME		
D4	•		Tennessee [Atl]	38	28
			SUGAR BOWL		
J3	•		Virginia Tech	16	13

2005 9-3 (7-1)

S3			Georgia Tech	14	23
S10	•	|	Mississippi State	28	0
S17	•		Ball State	63	3
S24	•		Western Kentucky	37	14
O1	•	|	South Carolina	48	7
O15	•	|	at Arkansas	34	17
O22		|	at LSU	17	20
O29	•	|	Mississippi	27	3
N5	•	|	at Kentucky	49	27
N12	•	|	at Georgia	31	30
N19	•	|	Alabama	28	18
			CAPITAL ONE BOWL		
J2			Wisconsin	10	24

2006 11-2 (6-2)

S	•		Washington State	40	14
S9	•	|	at Mississippi State	34	0
S16	•	|	LSU	7	3
S23	•		Buffalo	38	7
S28	•	|	at South Carolina	24	17
O7		|	Arkansas	10	27
O14	•	|	Florida	27	17
O21	•		Tulane	38	13
O28	•	|	at Mississippi	23	17
N4	•		Arkansas State	27	0
N11		|	Georgia	15	37
N18	•	|	at Alabama	22	15
			COTTON BOWL		
J1	•		Nebraska	17	14

2007   9-4   (5-3)

S1	●	Kansas State	23	13
S8		South Florlida	23	26
S15	│	Mississippi State	14	19
S22	●	New Mexico State	55	20
S29	● │	at Florida	20	17
O6	● │	Vanderbilt	35	7
O13	● │	at Arkansas	9	7
O20	│	at LSU	24	30
O27	● │	Mississippi	17	3
N3	●	Tennessee Tech	35	3
N10	│	at Georgia	20	45
N24	● │	Alabama	17	10
		CHICK-FIL-A BOWL		
D31	●	Clemson	23	20

2008   5-7   (2-6)

A30	●	La.-Monroe	34	0
S6	●	Southern Mississippi	27	13
S13	● │	at Mississippi State	3	2
S20	│	Louisiana State	21	26
S27	● │	Tennessee	14	12
O4	│	at Vanderbilt	13	14
O11	│	Arkansas	22	25
O23		at West Virginia	17	34
N1	│	at Mississippi	7	17
N8	●	Tenn.-Martin	37	20
N15	│	Georgia	13	17
N29	│	at Alabama	0	36

THE SCHOOLS

Neutral Site key: *And* Anderson, SC / *Atl* Atlanta, GA / *Birm* Birmingham, AL / *ColGa* Columbus, GA / *ColMs* Columbus, MS / *Dal* Dallas, TX / *ERut* East Rutherford, NJ / *Gulf* Gulfport, MS / *JacF* Jacksonville, FL / *JaM* Jackson, MS / *LR* Little Rock, AR / *Mac* Macon, GA / *Mbl* Mobile, AL / *Mia* Miami, FL / *Mem* Memphis, TN / *Mont* Montgomery, AL / *NYC* New York, NY / *Phil* Philadelphia, PA / *Rich* Richmond, VA / *Sav* Savannah, GA / *Sel* Selma, AL / *SF* San Francisco, CA / *Tam* Tampa, FL / *Unk* Unknown
f **Forfeit** † **Game Later Forfieted** # **Disputed Victor** * **Disputed Score** ‖ **Designated Conference Game** │2 **Counted Twice in Conference Standings**

THE SCHOOLS

AUBURN ANNUAL STATISTICAL LEADERS

YR	RUSHING	YDS	ATT	AVG	PASSING	ATT	CMP	PCT	YDS	RECEIVING	REC	YDS	AVG
1947	Billy Ball	157	44	3.6	Travis Tidwell	94	43	.46	571	John Liptak	12	126	10.5
1948	Russell Inman	227	97	2.3	Travis Tidwell	56	25	.45	476	Erskinc Russell	10	198	19.8
1949	Charlie Langner	405	111	3.6	Travis Tidwell	105	49	.47	811	Erskinc Russell	25	454	18.2
1950	Jim McGowen	225	57	3.9	William Tucker	92	41	.45	414	Fred Duart	20	250	12.5
1951	Homer Williams	721	148	4.9	Allan Parks	149	67	.45	839	Lee Hayley	33	306	9.3
1952	Charles Hataway	433	114	3.8	Dudley Spence	135	68	.50	833	Lee Hayley	24	395	16.5
1953	Fob James	482	73	6.6	Bobby Freeman	85	42	.49	603	Jim Pyburn	25	379	15.2
1954	Joe Childress	836	148	5.6	Bobby Freeman	96	54	.56	865	Jim Pyburn	28	460	16.4
1955	Fob James	879	123	7.1	Howell Tubbs	49	28	.57	471	Jimmy Phillips	14	272	19.4
1956	Tommy Lorino	692	82	8.4	Howell Tubbs	61	34	.56	514	Jimmy Phillips	23	383	16.7
1957	Tommy Lorino	443	78	5.7	Lloyd Nix	60	33	.55	542	Jimmy Phillips	15	357	23.8
1958	Tommy Lorino	349	67	5.2	Lloyd Nix	98	49	.50	682	Geral Wilson	16	207	12.9
1959	Bobby Hunt	552	98	5.6	Bobby Hunt	36	15	.42	234	Leo Sexton	8	75	9.4
1960	Ed Dyas	451	89	5.1	Bryant Harvard	59	36	.61	493	Joe Leichtnam	10	131	13.1
1961	Larry Rawson	448	121	3.7	Bobby Hunt	119	55	.46	737	Dave Edwards	25	372	14.9
1962	Jimmy Sidle	398	61	6.5	Mailon Kent	121	59	.49	748	Howard Simpson	24	301	12.5
1963	Jimmy Sidle	1,006	185	5.4	Jimmy Sidle	136	53	.39	706	George Rose	15	202	13.5
1964	Tucker Frederickson	571	129	4.4	Joseph Campbell	53	30	.57	422	Tucker Fredrickson	14	101	7.2
1965	Tom Bryan	561	133	4.2	Alex Bowden	127	59	.46	941	Freddie Hyatt	21	368	17.5
1966	Richard Plagge	420	110	3.8	Larry Blakeney	95	45	.47	491	Freddie Hyatt	33	475	14.4
1967	Al Giffin	392	121	3.2	Loran Carter	178	86	.48	1,307	Freddie Hyatt	34	553	16.3
1968	Dwight Hurston	349	110	3.2	Loran Carter	248	112	.45	1,487	Tim Christian	47	623	13.3
1969	Mickey Zofko	565	119	4.7	Pat Sullivan	257	123	.48	1,686	Terry Beasley	34	610	17.9
1970	Wallace Clark	422	86	4.9	Pat Sullivan	281	167	.59	2,586	Terry Beasley	52	1,051	20.2
1971	Tommy Lowry	499	87	5.7	Pat Sullivan	281	162	.58	2,012	Terry Beasley	55	846	15.4
1972	Terry Henley	499	87	5.7	Randy Walls	97	46	.47	736	Sandy Cannon	11	191	17.4
1973	Secdrick McIntyre	315	64	4.9	Wade Whatley	53	29	.55	340	Rett Davis	12	112	9.3
1974	Secdrick McIntyre	839	170	4.9	Phil Gargis	81	35	.43	518	Thomas Gossom	20	294	14.7
1975	Phil Gargis	658	162	4.1	Phil Gargis	94	37	.39	400	Jeff Gilligan	23	421	18.3
1976	Phil Gargis	534	142	3.8	Phil Gargis	166	80	.48	1,118	Chris Vacarella	15	353	23.5
1977	Joe Cribbs	872	161	5.4	John Crane	108	43	.40	679	Byron Franklin	13	389	29.9
1978	Joe Cribbs	1,205	253	4.8	Charlie Trotman	111	53	.48	760	Rusty Byrd	14	220	15.7
1979	James Brooks	1,208	163	7.4	Charlie Trotman	131	58	.44	875	Byron Franklin	19	373	19.6
1980	James Brooks	1,314	261	5.0	Joe Sullivan	118	64	.54	772	Byron Franklin	32	598	18.7
1981	Lionel James	561	111	5.1	Joe Sullivan	65	28	.43	370	Chris Woods	13	213	16.4
1982	Bo Jackson	829	127	6.5	Randy Campbell	158	81	.51	1,061	Chris Woods	21	406	19.3
1983	Bo Jackson	1,213	158	7.7	Randy Campbell	142	78	.55	873	Ed West	16	189	11.8
1984	Brent Fullwood	628	117	5.4	Pat Washington	171	77	.45	1,202	Freddy Weygand	32	796	24.9
1985	Bo Jackson	1,786	278	6.4	Pat Washington	142	78	.55	873	Freddy Weygand	19	367	19.3
1986	Brent Fullwood	1,391	167	8.3	Jeff Burger	222	126	.57	1,671	Lawyer Tillman	35	730	20.9
1987	Stacy Danley	468	94	5.0	Jeff Burger	267	178	.67	2,066	Duke Donaldson	43	398	9.3
1988	Stacy Danley	877	179	4.9	Reggie Slack	279	168	.60	2,230	Freddy Weygand	38	577	15.2
1989	James Joseph	817	172	4.8	Reggie Slack	252	148	.59	1,996	Alexander Wright	30	714	23.8
1990	Stacy Danley	430	103	4.2	Stan White	338	180	.53	2,242	Greg Taylor	46	650	14.1
1991	Joe Frazier	651	140	4.7	Stan White	317	158	.50	1,927	Fred Baxter	28	391	14.0
1992	James Bostic	819	186	4.4	Stan White	305	157	.51	1,790	Orlando Parker	31	438	14.1
1993	James Bostic	1,205	199	6.1	Stan White	271	164	.61	2,057	Frank Sanders	48	842	17.5
1994	Stephen Davis	1,263	221	5.7	Patrick Nix	299	169	.57	2,206	Frank Sanders	58	910	15.7
1995	Stephen Davis	1,068	180	5.9	Patrick Nix	331	201	.61	2,574	Willie Gosha	58	668	11.5
1996	Rusty Williams	439	80	5.5	Dameyune Craig	310	169	.55	2,296	Karsten Bailey	45	592	13.2
1997	Rusty Williams	277	77	4.9	Dameyune Craig	403	216	.54	3,277	Karsten Bailey	53	840	15.8
1998	Michael Burks	483	152	3.2	Gabe Gross	197	88	.45	1,222	Karsten Bailey	43	651	15.1
1999	Heath Evans	357	93	3.8	Ben Leard	157	111	.71	1,423	Ronney Daniels	56	1,068	19.1
2000	Rudi Johnson	1,567	324	4.8	Ben Leard	319	193	.61	2,158	Ronney Daniels	34	378	11.1
2001	Carnell Williams	614	120	5.1	Daniel Cobb	158	89	.56	1,165	Tim Carter	35	570	16.3
2002	Ronnie Brown	1,008	175	5.8	Jason Campbell	149	94	.63	1,215	Marcel Willis	31	417	13.5
2003	Carnell Williams	1,307	241	5.4	Jason Campbell	293	181	.62	2,267	Jeris McIntyre	41	621	15.1
2004	Carnell Williams	1,165	239	4.9	Jason Campbell	270	188	.70	2,700	Courtney Taylor	43	737	17.1
2005	Kenny Irons	1,293	256	5.1	Brandon Cox	306	177	.58	2,324	Ben Obomanu	33	357	10.8
2006	Kenny Irons	893	198	4.5	Brandon Cox	271	163	.60	2,198	Courtney Taylor	54	704	13.0
2007	Ben Tate	903	202	4.5	Brandon Cox	316	188	.59	2,080	Rodgeriqus Smith	52	705	13.6
2008	Ben Tate	664	159	4.2	Kodi Burns	179	94	.53	1,050	Rodgeriqus Smith	30	332	11.1

Receiving leaders by receptions
The NCAA began including postseason stats in 2002

AUBURN RECORD BOOK

SINGLE-GAME RECORDS

Rushing Yards	307	Curtis Kuykendall (Nov. 24, 1944 vs. Miami)
Passing Yards	416	Ben Leard (Nov. 13, 1999 vs. Georgia)
Receiving Yards	263	Alexander Wright (Sept. 9, 1989 vs. Pacific)
All-Purpose Yards	307	Curtis Kuykendall (Nov. 24, 1944 vs. Miami)
Points	36	Carnell Williams (Oct. 18, 2003 vs. Mississippi)
Field Goals	6	Al Del Greco (Oct. 9, 1982 vs. Kentucky)
Tackles	26	Kurt Crain (Nov. 15, 1986 vs. Georgia)
Interceptions	4	Junior Rosegreen (Oct. 2, 2004 vs. Tennessee)

SINGLE-SEASON RECORDS

Rushing Yards	1,786	Bo Jackson, 1985 (278 att.)
Passing Yards	3,277	Dameyune Craig, 1997 (216-403)
Receiving Yards	1,068	Ronney Daniels, 1999 (56 rec.)
All-Purpose Yards	1,859	Bo Jackson, 1985
Scoring	102	Bo Jackson, 1985 (17 TDs); Stephen Davis, 1995 (17 TDs); Carnell Williams, 2003 (17 TDs)
Touchdowns	17	Bo Jackson, 1985; Stephen Davis, 1995; Carnell Williams, 2003
Tackles	193	Freddie Smith, 1977
Interceptions	9	Buddy McClinton, 1969
Punting Average	46.9	Terry Daniel, 1993 (51 punts)
Punt Return Average	19.1	Mike Fuller, 1973 (20 ret.)
Kickoff Return Average	28.1	Rick Neel, 1975 (17 ret.)

CAREER RECORDS

Rushing Yards	4,303	Bo Jackson, 1983-85
Passing Yards	8,016	Stan White, 1990-93
Receiving Yards	2,507	Terry Beasley, 1969-71
All-Purpose Yards	5,596	James Brooks, 1977-80
Scoring	312	John Vaughn, 2003-06
Touchdowns	46	Carnell Williams, 2001-04
Tackles	528	Freddie Smith, 1976-79
Interceptions	18	Buddy McClinton, 1967-69
Punting Average	44.5	Terry Daniel, 1992-94 (169 punts)
Punt Return Average	17.6	Mike Fuller, 1972-74
Kickoff Return Average	27.0	Tristan Davis, 2005-06

TEAM RECORDS

Longest Winning Streak	20	Sept. 2, 1993-Nov. 5, 1994; broken vs. Georgia, 23-23 on Nov. 12, 1994
Longest Undefeated Streak	24	Oct. 4, 1913-Nov. 6, 1915; broken vs. Vanderbilt, 0-17 on Nov. 13, 1915
Most Consecutive Winning Seasons	12	1953-64
Most Consecutive Bowl Appearances	9	1982-90
Most Points in a Game	94	vs. Georgia Tech, Nov. 17, 1894
Most Points Allowed in a Game	68	vs. Georgia Tech, Nov. 29, 1917
Largest Margin of Victory	94	vs. Georgia Tech, Nov. 17, 1894
Largest Margin of Defeat	64	vs. North Carolina, Nov. 23, 1892
Longest Pass Play	87	Jason Campbell to Silas Daniels vs. Louisana Tech, Oct. 9, 2004
Longest Field Goal	57	Philip Yost vs. Western Kentucky, Sept. 27, 2003; Neil O'Donoghue vs. Tennessee, Sep. 25, 1976
Longest Punt	87	Rufus Deal vs. Georgia Tech, Oct. 28, 1939
Longest Interception Return	98	John Liptak vs. Georgia, Nov. 15, 1947

RETIRED NUMBERS

7	Pat Sullivan
34	Bo Jackson
88	Jimmy Phillips

ALL-TIME TEAM

As selected in 1992 by Auburn fans to commemorate the school's centennial season

Offense			Defense		
	OL	Walter Gilbert, 1934-36		DL	Roger Duane "Zeke" Smith, 1957-59
	OL	Ken Rice, 1958-60		DL	Donnie Humphrey, 1979-83
	OL	Steve Wallace, 1982-85		DL	Tracy Rocker, 1985-88
	OL	Ben Tamburello, 1983-86		DE	Jimmy "Red" Phillips, 1955-57
	OL	Ed King, 1988-90		DE	Aundray Bruce, 1984-87
	WR	Terry Beasley, 1969-71		LB	Jackie Burkett, 1957-59
	WR	Lawyer Tillman, 1985-88		LB	Mike Kolen, 1967-69
	QB	Pat Sullivan, 1969-71		LB	Gregg Carr, 1981-84
	RB	Joe Cribbs, 1976-79		DB	Tucker Frederickson, 1962-64
	RB	James Brooks, 1977-80		DB	Mike Fuller, 1972-74
	RB	Bo Jackson, 1982-85		DB	Kevin Porter, 1984-87
	K	Al Del Greco, 1980-83		P	Lewis Colbert, 1982-85

THE SCHOOLS

AUBURN BOWL HISTORY

SEASON	BOWL	DATE	PRE-GAME RANK	TEAMS	SCORE	FINAL RANK	MOST VALUABLE PLAYER(S)	ATT.
1936	BACARDI	Jan. 1, 1937		Auburn Villanova	7 7			12,000
1937	ORANGE	Jan. 1, 1938		Auburn Michigan State	6 0			18,972
1953	GATOR	Jan. 1, 1954	12 17	Texas Tech Auburn	35 13		Bobby Covazos, Texas Tech, RB Vince Dooley, Auburn, QB	28,641
1954	GATOR	Dec. 31, 1954	13 18	Auburn Baylor	33 13		Joe Childress, Auburn, FB Billy Hooper, Baylor, QB	28,426
1955	GATOR	Dec. 31, 1955	 8	Vanderbilt Auburn	25 13		Don Orr, Vanderbilt, QB Joe Childress, Auburn, FB	32,174
1963	ORANGE	Jan. 1, 1964	5 6	Nebraska Auburn	13 7			72,647
1965	LIBERTY	Dec. 18, 1965		Mississippi Auburn	13 7		Tom Bryan, Auburn, FB	38,607
1968	SUN	Dec. 28, 1968		Auburn Arizona	34 10	16	Buddy McClinton, Auburn, DB David Campbell, Auburn, T	32,307
1969	BLUEBONNET	Dec. 31, 1969	17 12	Houston Auburn	36 7	12 20	Jim Strong, Houston, HB Jerry Drones, Houston, DE	55,203
1970	GATOR	Jan. 2, 1971	10	Auburn Mississippi	35 28	10 20	Pat Sullivan, Auburn, QB Archie Manning, Mississippi, QB	71,136
1971	SUGAR	Jan. 1, 1972	3 5	Oklahoma Auburn	40 22	2 12	Jack Mildren, Oklahoma, QB	80,096
1972	GATOR	Dec. 30, 1972	6 13	Auburn Colorado	24 3	5 16	Wade Whatley, Auburn, QB Mark Cooney, Colorado, LB	71,114
1973	SUN	Dec. 29, 1973		Missouri Auburn	34 17	17	Ray Bybee, Missouri, FB John Kelsey, Missouri, TE	30,127
1974	GATOR	Dec. 30, 1974	6 11	Auburn Texas	27 3	8 17	Phil Gargis, Auburn, QB Earl Campbell, Texas, RB	63,811
1982	TANGERINE	Dec. 18, 1982	18	Auburn Boston College	33 26	14	Randy Campbell, Auburn, QB	51,296
1983	SUGAR	Jan. 2, 1984	3 8	Auburn Michigan	9 7	3 8	Bo Jackson, Auburn, RB	77,893
1984	LIBERTY	Dec. 27, 1984	16	Auburn Arkansas	21 15	14	Bo Jackson, Auburn, RB	50,108
1985	COTTON	Jan. 1, 1986	11 16	Texas A&M Auburn	36 16	6	Domingo Bryant, Texas A&M, SS Bo Jackson, Auburn, TB	73,137
1986	CITRUS	Jan. 1, 1987	10	Auburn Southern California	16 7	6	Aundray Brace, Auburn, LB	51,113
1987	SUGAR	Jan. 1, 1988	6 4	Auburn Syracuse	16 16	7 4	Don McPherson, Syracuse, QB	75,495
1988	SUGAR	Jan. 2, 1989	4 7	Florida State Auburn	13 7	3 8	Sammie Smith, Florida State, RB	75,098
1989	HALL OF FAME	Jan. 1, 1990	9 21	Auburn Ohio State	31 14	6 24	Reggie Slack, Auburn, QB	52,535
1990	PEACH	Dec. 29, 1990		Auburn Indiana	27 23	19	Stan White, QB, Darrel Crawford, LB, Auburn Vaughn Dunbar, RB, Mike Dumas, FS, Indiana	38,962
1995	OUTBACK	Jan. 1, 1996	15 16	Penn State Auburn	43 14	13 22	Bobby Engram, Penn State, WR	65,313
1996	INDEPENDENCE	Dec. 31, 1996	 24	Auburn Army	32 29	24 25	Dameyune Craig, Auburn, QB Takeo Spikes, LB, Rickey Neal, LB, Auburn	41,366
1997	PEACH	Jan. 2, 1998	13	Auburn Clemson	21 17	11	D. Craig, QB, T. Spikes, LB, Auburn R. Priester, DE, R. Abdullah, LB, Clemson	75,562
2000	CITRUS	Jan. 1, 2001	17 20	Michigan Auburn	31 28	11 18	Anthony Thomas, Michigan, RB	66,928
2001	PEACH	Dec. 31, 2001		North Carolina Auburn	16 10		Ronald Curry, North Carolina, QB Ryan Sims, North Carolina, DL	71,827
2002	CAPITAL ONE	Jan. 1, 2003	19 10	Auburn Penn State	13 9	14 16	Ronnie Brown, Auburn, TB	66,334
2003	MUSIC CITY	Dec. 31, 2003		Auburn Wisconsin	28 14		Jason Campbell, Auburn, QB	55,109
2004	SUGAR	Jan. 3, 2005	3 9	Auburn Virginia Tech	16 13	2 10	Jason Campbell, Auburn, QB	77,349
2005	CAPITAL ONE	Jan. 2, 2006		Wisconsin Auburn	24 10	15 14	Brian Calhoun, Wisconsin, RB	57,221
2006	COTTON	Jan. 1, 2006		Auburn Nebraska	17 14	9	Courtney Taylor, Auburn, WR Will Herring, Auburn, LB	66,777
2007	CHICK-FIL-A	Dec. 31, 2007		Auburn Clemson	23 20	15 21	C.J. Spiller, Clemson, RB Pat Sims, Auburn, LB	74,413

JANUARY 1, 1937 | Bacardi
Auburn 7, Villanova 7

	1ST	2ND	3RD	4TH	FINAL
AUB	7	0	0	0	7
NOVA	0	0	0	7	7

AUB	TEAM STATISTICS	NOVA
9	First Downs	7
152	Rushing Yards	129
2-12-2	Passing	2-6-1
29	Passing Yards	24
181	Total Yards	153

JANUARY 1, 1938 | Orange
Auburn 6, Michigan State 0

	1ST	2ND	3RD	4TH	FINAL
AUB	0	6	0	0	6
MSU	0	0	0	0	0

SCORING SUMMARY
AUB O'Gwynne 2 run (kick failed)

AUB	TEAM STATISTICS	MSU
12	First Downs	2
197	Rushing Yards	40
4-12-2	Passing	2-9-3
81	Passing Yards	25
278	Total Yards	65
10-33.7	Punts - Average	12-35.2
0-0	Fumbles - Lost	0-0
50	Penalty Yards	35

JANUARY 1, 1954 | Gator
Texas Tech 35, Auburn 13

	1ST	2ND	3RD	4TH	FINAL
TT	0	7	14	14	35
AUB	7	6	0	0	13

SCORING SUMMARY
AUB Duke 1 run (Davis kick)
TT Cavazos 6 run (Kirkpatrick kick)
AUB Dooley 10 run (kick failed)
TT Erwin 52 pass from Kirkpatrick (Kirkpatrick kick)
TT Lewis fumble recovery in end zone (Kirkpatrick kick)
TT Cavazos 59 run (Kirkpatrick kick)
TT Cavazos 2 run (Kirkpatrick kick)

TT	TEAM STATISTICS	AUB
11	First Downs	12
226	Rushing Yards	195
6-12-1	Passing	6-16-2
145	Passing Yards	72
371	Total Yards	267
6-33.1	Punts - Average	6-30.5
2-0	Fumbles - Lost	2-2
6-83	Penalties - Yards	5-66

INDIVIDUAL LEADERS
RUSHING
TT: Cavazos 13-141, 3 TD; Jones 2-44.
AUB: Dooley 14-56, 1 TD; Duke 4-37, 1 TD.
PASSING
TT: Kirkpatrick 3-4-0, 95 yards, 1 TD.
AUB: Dooley 4-8-0, 49 yards.

DECEMBER 31, 1954 | Gator
Auburn 33, Baylor 13

	1ST	2ND	3RD	4TH	FINAL
AUB	7	14	12	0	33
BU	7	0	6	0	13

SCORING SUMMARY
AUB Childress 7 run (Childress kick)
BU Saage 1 run (Smith kick)
AUB James 43 run (Childress kick)
AUB Long 4 pass from Freeman (Childress kick)
AUB Childress 3 run (kick failed)
BU Dupre 38 run (kick blocked)
AUB Freeman 5 run (kick failed)

AUB	TEAM STATISTICS	BU
25	First Downs	16
423	Rushing Yards	105
3-7-0	Passing	10-18-1
53	Passing Yards	134
476	Total Yards	239
2-41.0	Punts - Average	3-42.0
2-2	Fumbles - Lost	3-2
5-52	Penalties - Yards	3-25

INDIVIDUAL LEADERS
RUSHING
AUB: Childress 20-134, 2 TD; Freeman 12-80, 1 TD.
BU: Dupre 8-69, 1 TD; Jones 8-27.
PASSING
AUB: Freeman 3-7-0, 53 yards, 1 TD.
BU: Hooper 9-15-0, 112 yards.
RECEIVING
AUB: Hall 1-33; Pyburn 1-16.
BU: J.R. Smith 2-49; C. Smith 4-48.

DECEMBER 31, 1955 | Gator
Vanderbilt 25, Auburn 13

	1ST	2ND	3RD	4TH	FINAL
VAN	7	6	6	6	25
AUB	0	7	0	6	13

SCORING SUMMARY
VAN Stephenson 8 pass from Orr (Jalufka kick)
AUB James 38 pass from Tubbs (Tubbs kick)
VAN Orr 3 run (kick failed)
VAN King 1 run (kick failed)
VAN Horton 1 run (kick blocked)
AUB Phillips 4 pass from Cook (kick failed)

VAN	TEAM STATISTICS	AUB
15	First Downs	15
177	Rushing Yards	159
5-8-1	Passing	7-13-0
94	Passing Yards	142
271	Total Yards	301
4-31.7	Punts - Average	3-29.0
1-1	Fumbles - Lost	5-5
5-54	Penalties - Yards	6-59

INDIVIDUAL LEADERS
RUSHING
VAN: Horton 13-57, 1 TD; Orr 10-43, 1 TD.
AUB: Childress 15-58; James 9-42.
PASSING
VAN: Orr 4-6-1, 67 yards, 1 TD.
AUB: Tubbs 4-9-0, 101 yards, 1 TD.
RECEIVING
VAN: Scalen 2-44; Stephenson 2-23, 1 TD.
AUB: James 2-51, 1 TD; Elliott 2-41.

JANUARY 1, 1964 | Orange
Nebraska 13, Auburn 7

	1ST	2ND	3RD	4TH	FINAL
NEB	10	3	0	0	13
AUB	0	0	7	0	7

SCORING SUMMARY
NEB Claridge 68 run (Theisen kick)
NEB FG Theisen 31
NEB FG Theisen 26
AUB Sidle 13 run (Woodall kick)

NEB	TEAM STATISTICS	AUB
11	First Downs	17
204	Rushing Yards	126
4-9-0	Passing	14-27-1
30	Passing Yards	157
234	Total Yards	283
7-38.3	Punts - Average	6-35.2
2-1	Fumbles - Lost	3-1
6-65	Penalties - Yards	5-39

INDIVIDUAL LEADERS
RUSHING
NEB: Claridge 14-108, 1 TD.
AUB: Sidle 25-96, 1 TD.
PASSING
NEB: Claridge 4-9-0, 30 yards.
AUB: Sidle 12-25-0, 141 yards.
RECEIVING
NEB: Duepke 1-13.
AUB: Simpson 4-39.

DECEMBER 18, 1965 | Liberty
Mississippi 13, Auburn 7

	1ST	2ND	3RD	4TH	FINAL
MISS	0	3	7	3	13
AU	0	7	0	0	7

SCORING SUMMARY
MISS FG Keyes 42
AU Bryan 44 run (Lewis kick)
MISS Cunningham 6 pass from Graves (Keyes kick)
MISS FG Keyes 30

MISS	TEAM STATISTICS	AU
12	First Downs	15
189	Rushing Yards	156
4-12-0	Passing	11-24-1
24	Passing Yards	112
213	Total Yards	268
8-39.0	Punts - Average	9-34.8
0-0	Fumbles - Lost	0-0
5-25	Penalties - Yards	4-29

INDIVIDUAL LEADERS
RUSHING
AU: Bryan 19-111, 1 TD.
MISS: Dennis 15-75; Heidel 16-72.
PASSING
AU: Bowden 11-24-1, 112 yards.
MISS: Graves 2-10-0, 15 yards, 1 TD.
RECEIVING
AU: Hardy 4-46.
MISS: Matthews 2-9.

THE SCHOOLS

THE SCHOOLS

DECEMBER 28, 1968 | SUN
AUBURN 34, ARIZONA 10

	1ST	2ND	3RD	4TH	FINAL
AUB	10	0	14	10	34
ARIZ	0	10	0	0	10

SCORING SUMMARY
AUB FG Riley 52
AUB Zofko 6 pass from Carter (Riley kick)
ARIZ FG Hurley 37
ARIZ Arnason 11 pass from Lee (Hurley kick)
AUB Taylor 9 run (Riley kick)
AUB McClinton 32 interception return (Riley kick)
AUB Christian 43 pass from Carter (Riley kick)
AUB FG Riley 41

AUB	TEAM STATISTICS	ARIZ
12	First Downs	16
147	Rushing Yards	70
7-28-4	Passing	13-44-8
156	Passing Yards	164
303	Total Yards	234
5-35	Punt Returns - Yards	11-34
0-0	Kickoff Returns - Yards	3-51
7-26.0	Punts - Average	11-34.0
3-2	Fumbles - Lost	2-1
4-36	Penalties - Yards	4-38

INDIVIDUAL LEADERS
RUSHING
AUB: Hurston 14-49; Currier 11-29.
ARIZ: Fuimaono 18-48; Hustead 16-35.
PASSING
AUB: Carter 7-28-3, 156 yards, 2 TD.
ARIZ: Lee 6-24-6 89 yards, 1 TD; Driscoll 7-20-2, 75 yards.
RECEIVING
AUB: Zofko 1-65, 1 TD; Christian 3-62, 1 TD.
ARIZ: Gardin 5-74; Sherwood 2-40.

DECEMBER 31, 1969 | BLUEBONNET
HOUSTON 36, AUBURN 7

	1ST	2ND	3RD	4TH	FINAL
HOU	7	9	6	14	36
AUB	0	7	0	0	7

SCORING SUMMARY
HOU Mullins 1 run (Lopez kick)
HOU FG Lopez 27
HOU Strong 1 run (kick failed)
AUB Frederick 36 pass from Zofko (Riley kick)
HOU Heiskell 1 run (pass failed)
HOU Srong 12 run (Lopez kick)
HOU Mozisek 20 pass from Clark (Lopez kick)

HOU	TEAM STATISTICS	AUB
25	First Downs	14
376	Rushing Yards	1
10-19-2	Passing	13-37-2
140	Passing Yards	188
516	Total Yards	189
2-42.5	Punts - Average	6-39.8
2-1	Fumbles - Lost	1-1
6-63	Penalties - Yards	4-26

INDIVIDUAL LEADERS
RUSHING
HOU: Strong 32-184, 2 TD; Heiskell 10-70, 1 TD.
AUB: Zofko 12-31, Clark 7-32.
PASSING
HOU: Mullins 9-17-2, 120 yards.
AUB: Sullivan 10-30-1, 132 yards.
RECEIVING
HOU: Wright 4-62; Thomas 2-35.
AUB: Beasley 6-76; Fredericks 3-59, 1 TD.

JANUARY 2, 1971 | GATOR
AUBURN 35, MISSISSIPPI 28

	1ST	2ND	3RD	4TH	FINAL
AUB	14	7	14	0	35
MISS	0	14	7	7	28

SCORING SUMMARY
AUB Beasley 12 pass from Sullivan (Jett kick)
AUB Bresler 7 pass from Sullivan (Jett kick)
AUB Sullivan 37 run (Jett kick)
MISS Manning 1 run (Poole kick)
MISS Franks 34 pass from Manning (Poole kick)
AUB Zofko 6 run (Jett kick)
MISS Poole 23 pass from Chumbler (Poole kick)
AUB Willingham 55 punt return (Jett kick)
MISS Chumbler 1 run (Poole kick)

AUB	TEAM STATISTICS	MISS
23	First Downs	21
208	Rushing Yards	209
27-44-1	Passing	23-39-1
351	Passing Yards	256
559	Total Yards	465
4-40.5	Punts - Average	6-47.3
5-3	Fumbles - Lost	3-2
6-63	Penalties - Yards	2-13

INDIVIDUAL LEADERS
RUSHING
AUB: Clark 14-108; Sullivan 10-35, 1 TD.
MISS: Manning 11-95, 1 TD; Ainsworth 11-68.
PASSING
AUB: Sullivan 27-43-1, 351 yards, 2 TD.
MISS: Manning 19-28-1, 180 yards, 1 TD; Chumbler 4-11-0, 76 yards, 1 TD.
RECEIVING
AUB: Beasley 8-143, 1 TD; Bresler 4-102, 1 TD.
MISS: Poole 9-111, 1 TD; Franks 7-78, 1 TD.

JANUARY 1, 1972 | SUGAR
OKLAHOMA 40, AUBURN 22

	1ST	2ND	3RD	4TH	FINAL
OKLA	19	12	3	6	40
AUB	0	0	7	15	22

SCORING SUMMARY
OKLA Crosswhite 4 run (kick failed)
OKLA Mildren 5 run (Carroll kick)
OKLA Wylie 71 punt return (pass failed)
OKLA Mildren 4 run (run failed)
OKLA Mildren 7 run (pass failed)
OKLA FG Carroll 53
AUB Unger 1 run (Jett kick)
OKLA Pruitt 2 run (kick failed)
AUB Cannon 11 pass from Sullivan (Jett kick)
AUB Unger 1 run (Beck run)

OKLA	TEAM STATISTICS	AUB
28	First Downs	15
439	Rushing Yards	40
1-4-0	Passing	20-45-2
11	Passing Yards	250
450	Total Yards	290
5-35.4	Punts - Average	5-45.2
5-2	Fumbles - Lost	4-1
3-12	Penalties - Yards	0-0

INDIVIDUAL LEADERS
RUSHING
OKLA: Mildren 30-149, 3 TD; Pruitt 18-95, 1 TD; Crosswhite 17-78, 1 TD.
AUB: Unger 6-38, 2 TD; Lowry 5-12.
PASSING
OKLA: Mildren 1-4-0, 11 yards.
AUB: Sullivan 20-44-1, 250 yards, 1 TD.
RECEIVING
OKLA: Chandler 1-11.
AUB: Beasley 6-117; Unger 5-36.

DECEMBER 30, 1972 | GATOR
AUBURN 24, COLORADO 3

	1ST	2ND	3RD	4TH	FINAL
AUB	0	10	7	7	24
COL	0	0	0	3	3

SCORING SUMMARY
AUB FG Jett 27
AUB Whatley 1 run (Jett kick)
AUB Spivey 22 pass from Fuller (Jett kick)
COL FG Lima 33
AUB Nugent 16 pass from Beck (Jett kick)

AUB	TEAM STATISTICS	COL
13	First Downs	14
153	Rushing Yards	63
5-8-0	Passing	20-33-2
80	Passing Yards	204
233	Total Yards	267
7-40.7	Punts - Average	5-39.8
3-1	Fumbles - Lost	3-2
4-30	Penalties - Yards	5-47

INDIVIDUAL LEADERS
RUSHING
AUB: Fuller 12-72; Linderman 15-37.
COL: Matthews 8-34; Davis 14-12.
PASSING
AUB: Whatley 3-6-0, 42 yards.
COL: Johnson 17-29-2, 169 yards.
RECEIVING
AUB: Spivey 1-22, 1 TD; Cannon 1-17; Nugent 1-16, 1 TD.
COL: Keyworth 3-55; Elwood 3-49.

DECEMBER 29, 1973 | SUN
MISSOURI 34, AUBURN 17

	1ST	2ND	3RD	4TH	FINAL
MO	0	28	6	0	34
AUB	0	10	7	0	17

SCORING SUMMARY
AUB FG Pruett 35
MO Kelsey 35 pass from Link (Hill kick)
MO Bybee 2 run (Hill kick)
MO Kelsey 2 pass from Smith (Hill kick)
AUB Gossom 17 pass from Gargis (Pruett kick)
MO Mosley 84 kickoff return (Hill kick)
MO Sharp 15 pass from Smith (kick failed)
AUB Gossom 32 pass from Gargis (Pruett kick)

MO	TEAM STATISTICS	AUB
20	First Downs	11
295	Rushing Yards	113
8-14-1	Passing	7-15-1
95	Passing Yards	120
390	Total Yards	233
6-37.0	Punts - Average	6-46.0
4-1	Fumbles - Lost	5-4
2-29	Penalties - Yards	1-5

INDIVIDUAL LEADERS
RUSHING
MO: Bybee 27-127, 1 TD; Reamon 23-110.
AUB: McIntyre 10-46; Neel 7-26.
PASSING
MO: Smith 7-12-0, 60 yards, 2 TD; Link 1-2-1 35 yards, 1 TD.
AUB: Gargis 7-15-1, 120 yards, 2 TD.
RECEIVING
MO: Kelsey 2-37, 2 TD; Sharp 2-26, 1 TD.
AUB: Stivey 3-56; Gossom 2-49, 2 TD.

DECEMBER 30, 1974 | GATOR
AUBURN 27, TEXAS 3

	1ST	2ND	3RD	4TH	FINAL
AUB	14	2	0	11	27
TEX	3	0	0	0	3

SCORING SUMMARY
AUB Butler 7 pass from Gargis (Wilson kick)
AUB Jackson 2 run (Wilson kick)
TEX FG Schott 35
AUB Safety (McKinney blocked punt out of end zone)
AUB Butler 14 pass from Gargis (Nugent pass from Gargis)
AUB FG Wilson 28

AUB	TEAM STATISTICS	TEX
19	First Downs	14
256	Rushing Yards	203
7-13-2	Passing	10-21-3
70	Passing Yards	98
326	Total Yards	301
2-45.5	Punts - Average	4-28.8
7-5	Fumbles - Lost	5-4
6-70	Penalties - Yards	5-37

INDIVIDUAL LEADERS
RUSHING
AUB: McIntyre 19-89; Jackson 10-64, 1 TD.
TEX: Campbell 23-91; Atkins 11-40.
PASSING
AUB: Gargis 6-11-2, 60 yards, 2 TD.
TEX: Atkins 9-16-1, 70 yards.
RECEIVING
AUB: Nugent 2-22; Butler 2-21, 2 TD.
TEX: Thompson 1-28; Ingram 2-17.

DECEMBER 18, 1982 | TANGERINE
AUBURN 33, BOSTON COLLEGE 26

	1ST	2ND	3RD	4TH	FINAL
AU	3	20	10	0	33
BC	7	3	0	16	26

SCORING SUMMARY
BC Flutie 5 run (Snow kick)
AU FG Del Greco 19
AU Jackson 1 run (Del Greco kick)
AU Howell 2 run (Del Greco kick)
BC FG Snow 34
AU Jackson 6 run (pass failed)
AU FG Del Greco 23
AU Pratt 15 run (Del Greco kick)
BC Nizolek 2 pass from Flutie (Nizolek pass from Flutie)
BC Brennan 16 pass from Flutie (Flutie run)

AU	TEAM STATISTICS	BC
27	First Downs	24
313	Rushing Yards	115
10-16-1	Passing	22-38-2
177	Passing Yards	299
490	Total Yards	414
2-32.0	Punts - Average	3-34.3
4-1	Fumbles - Lost	3-3
3-30	Penalties - Yards	2-38

INDIVIDUAL LEADERS
RUSHING
AU: James 17-101; Jackson 14-64, 2 TD.
BC: Stradford 15-67; Krystoforski 3-19.
PASSING
AU: Campbell 10-16-1, 177 yards.
BC: Flutie 22-38-2, 299 yards, 2 TD.
RECEIVING
AU: Woods 3-67; Edwards 3-55.
BC: Brennan 7-149, 1 TD; Phelan 4-69.

JANUARY 2, 1984 | SUGAR
AUBURN 9, MICHIGAN 7

	1ST	2ND	3RD	4TH	FINAL
AUB	0	0	3	6	9
MICH	7	0	0	0	7

SCORING SUMMARY
MICH Smith 4 run (Bergeron kick)
AUB FG Del Greco 31
AUB FG Del Greco 32
AUB FG Del Greco 19

AUB	TEAM STATISTICS	MICH
21	First Downs	12
301	Rushing Yards	118
2-6-1	Passing	9-25-1
21	Passing Yards	125
322	Total Yards	243
4-42.0	Punts - Average	8-38.3
4-3	Fumbles - Lost	2-1
3-15	Penalties - Yards	6-49

INDIVIDUAL LEADERS
RUSHING
AUB: Jackson 22-130; Agee 16-93.
MICH: Rogers 17-86; Garrett 5-18.
PASSING
AUB: Campbell 2-6-1, 21 yards.
MICH: Smith 9-25-1, 125 yards.
RECEIVING
AUB: James 1-15.
MICH: Markray 3-68; Bean 3-37.

DECEMBER 27, 1984 | LIBERTY
AUBURN 21, ARKANSAS 15

	1ST	2ND	3RD	4TH	FINAL
AUB	14	0	0	7	21
ARK	3	0	0	12	15

SCORING SUMMARY
ARK FG Horne 31
AUB Jackson 2 run (kick failed)
AUB Porter 35 interception return (Washington kick)
ARK Foreman 2 run (pass failed)
AUB Jackson 39 run (Knapp kick)
ARK Shibest 25 pass from Taylor (kick failed)

AUB	TEAM STATISTICS	ARK
13	First Downs	20
168	Rushing Yards	130
5-15-0	Passing	19-40-4
84	Passing Yards	226
252	Total Yards	356
9-37.9	Punts - Average	4-38.3
1	Fumbles Lost	0
8-56	Penalties - Yards	8-60

INDIVIDUAL LEADERS
RUSHING
AUB: Jackson 18-88, 2 TD.
ARK: Foreman 15-62, 1 TD; Thomas 9-56.
PASSING
AUB: Washington 5-12-0, 84 yards.
ARK: Taylor 18-34-2, 201 yards, 1 TD.
RECEIVING
AUB: Jackson 1-25.
ARK: Shibest 5-84, 1 TD; Edmonds 10-68.

JANUARY 1, 1986 | COTTON
TEXAS A&M 36, AUBURN 16

	1ST	2ND	3RD	4TH	FINAL
AU	7	6	3	0	16
A&M	12	3	6	15	36

SCORING SUMMARY
AU Jackson 5 run (Johnson kick)
A&M Johnson 11 run (kick failed)
A&M Woodside 22 run (pass failed)
AU Jackson 73 pass from Washington (run failed)
A&M FG Slater 26
A&M Toney 21 run (pass failed)
AU FG Johnson 26
A&M Woodside 9 pass from Murray (Bernstine run)
A&M Toney 1 run (Slater kick)

AU	TEAM STATISTICS	A&M
16	First Downs	21
198	Rushing Yards	186
7-17-2	Passing	16-26-1
154	Passing Yards	292
352	Total Yards	478
5-43.8	Punts - Average	5-45.0
2-1	Fumbles - Lost	1-1
1-5	Penalties - Yards	5-45

INDIVIDUAL LEADERS
RUSHING
AU: Jackson 31-129, 1 TD; Agee 5-36.
A&M: Vick 15-67; Woodside 3-32, 1 TD.
PASSING
AU: Washington 2-7-0, 82 yards, 1 TD; Burger 5-10-2, 72 yards.
A&M: Murray 16-26-1, 292 yards, 1 TD.
RECEIVING
AU: Jackson 2-73, 1 TD; Parks 2-32.
A&M: Bernstine 6-108; Woodside 3-88, 1 TD.

JANUARY 1, 1987 | CITRUS
AUBURN 16, SOUTHERN CALIFORNIA 7

	1ST	2ND	3RD	4TH	FINAL
AU	0	14	0	2	16
USC	7	0	0	0	7

SCORING SUMMARY
USC Cotton 24 interception return (Shafer kick)
AU Reeves 3 pass from Burger (Knapp kick)
AU Fullwood 4 run (Knapp kick)
AU Safety (Peete tackled by Rocker in end zone)

AU	TEAM STATISTICS	USC
19	First Downs	10
200	Rushing Yards	44
8-18-2	Passing	12-31-4
90	Passing Yards	113
290	Total Yards	157
8-37.9	Punts - Average	4-41.5
2-2	Fumbles - Lost	1-1
9-84	Penalties - Yards	6-40

INDIVIDUAL LEADERS
RUSHING
AU: Fullwood 28-152, 1 TD; Harris 12-31.
USC: Holt 9-34; Knight 8-9.
PASSING
AU: Burger 8-18-2, 90 yards, 1 TD.
USC: Peete 12-30-4, 113 yards.
RECEIVING
AU: Gainous 2-40; Reeves 3-23, 1 TD.
USC: Affholter 6-66; White 1-17.

THE SCHOOLS

JANUARY 1, 1988 | Sugar
AUBURN 16, SYRACUSE 16

	1ST	2ND	3RD	4TH	FINAL
AUB	7	3	0	6	16
SYR	0	7	3	6	16

SCORING SUMMARY
AUB   Tillman 17 pass from Burger (Lyle kick)
SYR   Glover 12 pass from McPherson (Vesling kick)
AUB   FG Lyle 40
SYR   FG Vesling 27
AUB   FG Lyle 41
SYR   FG Vesling 32
SYR   FG Vesling 38
AUB   FG Lyle 30

AUB	TEAM STATISTICS	SYR
14	First Downs	23
41	Rushing Yards	174
25-34-1	Passing	11-21-0
229	Passing Yards	140
270	Total Yards	314
6-44.8	Punts - Average	5-35.6
1-0	Fumbles - Lost	2-0
5-43	Penalties - Yards	2-20
22:25	Possession Time	37:35

INDIVIDUAL LEADERS
RUSHING
AUB: Danley 13-42.
SYR: Orummon 17-82; Johnston 14-50.
PASSING
AUB: Burger 24-33-1, 171 yards, 1 TD.
SYR: McPherson 11-21-0, 140 yards, 1 TD.
RECEIVING
AUB: Tillman 6-125, 1 TD; Danley 7-34.
SYR: Glover 6-91, 1 TD; Kane 2-30.

JANUARY 2, 1989 | Sugar
FLORIDA STATE 13, AUBURN 7

	1ST	2ND	3RD	4TH	FINAL
FSU	10	3	0	0	13
AUB	0	7	0	0	7

SCORING SUMMARY
FSU   Williams 2 run (Andrews kick)
FSU   FG Mason 35
FSU   FG Mason 31
AUB   Reeves 20 pass from Slack (Lyle kick)

FSU	TEAM STATISTICS	AUB
21	First Downs	18
148	Rushing Yards	108
14-27-1	Passing	19-33-3
157	Passing Yards	162
305	Total Yards	270
4-35.0	Punts - Average	4-35.8
2-1	Fumbles - Lost	3-2
6-45	Penalties - Yards	5-65
33:35	Possession Time	26:25

INDIVIDUAL LEADERS
RUSHING
FSU: Smith 24-115; Carter 7-25.
AUB: Danley 19-68; Joseph 8-47.
PASSING
FSU: Ferguson 14-26-1, 157 yards.
AUB: Slack 19-33-3, 162 yards, 1 TD.
RECEIVING
FSU: Anthony 3-47; O'Malley 2-31.
AUB: Tillman 4-48; Taylor 5-35.

JANUARY 1, 1990 | Hall of Fame
AUBURN 31, OHIO STATE 14

	1ST	2ND	3RD	4TH	FINAL
AU	3	7	7	14	31
OSU	7	7	0	0	14

SCORING SUMMARY
OSU   Snow 1 run (O'Morrow kick)
AU   FG Lyle 19
OSU   Stablein 9 pass from Frey (O'Morrow kick)
AU   Taylor 11 pass from Slack (Lyle kick)
AU   Taylor 4 pass from Slack (Lyle kick)
AU   Slack 5 run (Lyle kick)
AU   Casey 2 pass from Slack (Lyle kick)

AU	TEAM STATISTICS	OSU
21	First Downs	18
171	Rushing Yards	66
16-23-2	Passing	16-31-1
141	Passing Yards	232
312	Total Yards	298
3-72	Punt Returns - Yards	4-25
2-57	Kickoff Returns - Yards	6-121
5-40.8	Punts - Average	7-41.1
1-0	Fumbles - Lost	1-0
2-15	Penalties - Yards	5-33
31:47	Possession Time	28:13

INDIVIDUAL LEADERS
RUSHING
AU: Danley 20-85; Williams 10-46.
OSU: S. Graham 12-53; Snow 13-42, 1 TD.
PASSING
AU: Slack 16-22-2, 141 yards, 3 TD.
OSU: Frey 16-31-1, 232 yards, 1 TD.
RECEIVING
AU: Wright 4-59; Taylor 4-33, 2 TD.
OSU: J. Graham 5-103; Snow 3-30.

DECEMBER 29, 1990 | Peach
AUBURN 27, INDIANA 23

	1ST	2ND	3RD	4TH	FINAL
AUB	7	10	3	7	27
IND	7	3	0	13	23

SCORING SUMMARY
AUB   White 6 run (Von Wyl kick)
IND   Green 3 run (Bonnell kick)
AUB   Smith 11 pass from White (Von Wyl kick)
IND   FG Bonnell 42
AUB   FG Von Wyl 26
AUB   FG Von Wyl 43
IND   Green 2 run (run failed)
IND   Green 11 run (Bonnell kick)
AUB   White 1 run (Von Wyl kick)

AUB	TEAM STATISTICS	IND
24	First Downs	15
89	Rushing Yards	121
31-48-0	Passing	10-19-0
351	Passing Yards	99
440	Total Yards	220
3-23.0	Punts - Average	5-41.4
2-2	Fumbles - Lost	1-1
12-75	Penalties - Yards	6-55
28:09	Possession Time	31:51

INDIVIDUAL LEADERS
RUSHING
AUB: Williams 12-52; Smith 5-24.
IND: Dunbar 21-81.
PASSING
AUB: White 31-48-0, 351 yards, 1 TD.
IND: Green 10-19-0, 99 yards.
RECEIVING
AUB: Casey 7-159; Hall 9-74.
IND: Thomas 3-43; Turner 3-26.

JANUARY 1, 1996 | Outback
PENN STATE 43, AUBURN 14

	1ST	2ND	3RD	4TH	FINAL
PSU	3	13	27	0	43
AU	0	7	0	7	14

SCORING SUMMARY
PSU   FG Conway 19
AU   Baker 25 pass from Nix (Hawkins kick)
PSU   FG Conway 22
PSU   FG Conway 38
PSU   Archie 8 pass from Richardson (Conway kick)
PSU   Engram 9 pass from Richardson (Conway kick)
PSU   Pitts 4 pass from Richardson (pass failed)
PSU   Enis 1 run (Conway kick)
PSU   Engram 20 pass from Richardson (Conway kick)
AU   McLeod 12 run (Hawkins kick)

PSU	TEAM STATISTICS	AU
22	First Downs	19
266	Rushing Yards	220
14-29-2	Passing	8-33-2
221	Passing Yards	94
487	Total Yards	314
4-33	Punt Returns - Yards	2-10
1-37	Kickoff Returns - Yards	5-101
4-35.7	Punts - Average	8-39.1
2-1	Fumbles - Lost	5-2
6-35	Penalties - Yards	5-59
32:11	Possession Time	27:49

INDIVIDUAL LEADERS
RUSHING
PSU: Pitts 15-115; Milne 12-82.
AU: Davis 12-119; Morrow 10-39.
PASSING
PSU: Richardson 13-24-1, 217 yards, 4 TD.
AU: Nix 5-25-2, 48 yards, 1 TD.
RECEIVING
PSU: Engram 4-113, 2 TD; Jurevicius 1-43.
AU: Bailey 1-32; Baker 1-25, 1 TD.

DECEMBER 31, 1996 | Independence
AUBURN 32, ARMY 29

	1ST	2ND	3RD	4TH	FINAL
AU	10	10	12	0	32
ARMY	0	7	0	22	29

SCORING SUMMARY
AU   FG Holmes 31
AU   Goodson 30 pass from Craig (Holmes kick)
AU   Gosha 7 pass from Craig (Holmes kick)
AU   FG Holmes 49
ARMY   B. Williams 3 run (Parker kick)
AU   Craig 33 run (pass failed)
AU   R. Williams 18 run (pass failed)
ARMY   Perry 12 run (Parker kick)
ARMY   B. Williams 1 run (Parker kick)
ARMY   Richardson 30 pass from McAda (B. Williams run)

AU	TEAM STATISTICS	ARMY
27	First Downs	18
195	Rushing Yards	264
24-40-1	Passing	10-16-0
372	Passing Yards	148
567	Total Yards	412
2-41.5	Punts - Average	6-43.0
3-3	Fumbles - Lost	1-1
5-47	Penalties - Yards	3-20
29:53	Possession Time	30:07

INDIVIDUAL LEADERS
RUSHING
AU: Craig 13-75, 1 TD; R. Williams 12-72, 1 TD.
ARMY: B. Williams 12-82, 2 TD; Perry 19-81, 1 TD.
PASSING
AU: Craig 24-40-1, 372 yards, 2 TD.
ARMY: McAda 10-16-0, 148 yards, 1 TD.
RECEIVING
AU: Gosha 10-132, 1 TD; Baker 5-104.
ARMY: Williams 3-74; Richardson 2-59, 1 TD.

JANUARY 2, 1998 | PEACH
AUBURN 21, CLEMSON 17

	1ST	2ND	3RD	4TH	FINAL
AUB	3	3	0	15	21
CLEM	0	7	10	0	17

SCORING SUMMARY
AUB FG Holmes 52
CLEM Speck 18 block punt return (Richardson kick)
AUB FG Holmes 24
CLEM Witherspoon 2 run (Richardson kick)
CLEM FG Richardson 48
AUB Craig 22 run (pass failed)
AUB Williams 7 run (pass failed)
AUB FG Holmes 22

AUB	TEAM STATISTICS	CLEM
18	First Downs	4
108	Rushing Yards	60
15-45-0	Passing	11-25-1
258	Passing Yards	86
366	Total Yards	146
6-25.8	Punts - Average	9-43.7
1-1	Fumbles - Lost	1-0
7-63	Penalties - Yards	5-59
32:01	Possession Time	27:59

INDIVIDUAL LEADERS
RUSHING
AUB: Willliams 18-71, 1 TD; Craig 9-26, 1 TD.
CLEM: Priester 19-62.
PASSING
AUB: Craig 15-45-0, 258 yards.
CLEM: Greene 11-25-1, 86 yards.
RECEIVING
AUB: Bailey 4-119; Goodson 4-64.
CLEM: Austin 3-32; Gardner 1-27.

JANUARY 1, 2001 | CITRUS
MICHIGAN 31, AUBURN 28

	1ST	2ND	3RD	4TH	FINAL
MICH	7	14	10	0	31
AU	0	14	7	7	28

SCORING SUMMARY
MICH Terrell 31 pass from Henson (Epstein kick)
AU Daniels 19 pass from Leard (Duval kick)
AU Robinson 20 pass from Leard (Duval kick)
MICH Askew 4 pass from Henson (Epstein kick)
MICH Thomas 11 run (Epstein kick)
MICH Thomas 25 run (Epstein kick)
AU Johnson 12 run (Duval kick)
MICH FG Epstein 41
AU Green 21 pass from Leard (Duval kick)

MICH	TEAM STATISTICS	AU
21	First Downs	23
159	Rushing Yards	92
15-21-0	Passing	28-37-2
294	Passing Yards	394
453	Total Yards	486
4-43.5	Punts - Average	3-42.7
2-1	Fumbles - Lost	2-1
2-20	Penalties - Yards	7-60
29:57	Possession Time	30:03

INDIVIDUAL LEADERS
RUSHING
MICH: Thomas 32-182, 2 TD; Bellamy 3-13.
AU: Johnson 25-85, 1 TD; Evans 3-16.
PASSING
MICH: Henson 15-20-0, 294 yards, 2 TD.
AU: Leard 28-37-2, 394 yards, 3 TD.
RECEIVING
MICH: Terrell 4-136, 1 TD; Walker 4-100.
AU: Daniels 7-98, 1 TD; Willis 5-69.

DECEMBER 31, 2001 | PEACH
NORTH CAROLINA 16, AUBURN 10

	1ST	2ND	3RD	4TH	FINAL
UNC	7	3	6	0	16
AUB	0	0	0	10	10

SCORING SUMMARY
UNC Parker 10 run (Reed kick)
UNC FG Reed 22
UNC Curry 62 run (kick failed)
AUB FG Duval 34
AUB Diamond 12 pass from Cobb (Duval kick)

UNC	TEAM STATISTICS	AUB
12	First Downs	12
174	Rushing Yards	31
13-21-1	Passing	18-28-2
114	Passing Yards	145
288	Total Yards	176
8-39.8	Punts - Average	9-49.3
2-1	Fumbles - Lost	5-1
9-73	Penalties - Yards	4-26
32:02	Possession Time	27:58

INDIVIDUAL LEADERS
RUSHING
UNC: Parker 19-131, 1 TD; Curry 10-67, 1 TD.
AUB: Brown 6-28; Butler 8-22.
PASSING
UNC: Durant 7-14-1-76 yards; Curry 5-6-0-25 yards.
AUB: Campbell 12-18-1-74 yards; Cobb 6-10-1, 71 yards, 1 TD.
RECEIVING
UNC: Aiken 7-73; Parker 3-24.
AUB: Daniels 3-21; Carter 1-21.

JANUARY 1, 2003 | CAPITAL ONE
AUBURN 13, PENN STATE 9

	1ST	2ND	3RD	4TH	FINAL
AU	0	0	7	6	13
PSU	3	3	0	3	9

SCORING SUMMARY
PSU FG Gould 21
PSU FG Gould 27
AU Brown 1 run (Duval kick)
PSU FG Gould 31
AU Brown 17 run (pass failed)

AU	TEAM STATISTICS	PSU
15	First Downs	15
200	Rushing Yards	170
10-17-1	Passing	10-27-1
78	Passing Yards	98
278	Total Yards	268
4-48.2	Punts - Average	5-38.2
1-1	Fumbles - Lost	3-0
9-84	Penalties - Yards	7-68

INDIVIDUAL LEADERS
RUSHING
AU: Brown 37-184, 2 TD; Smith 5-10.
PSU: L. Johnson 20-72; Mills 9-56.
PASSING
AU: Campbell 10-17-1, 78 yards.
PSU: Mills 8-24-1, 67 yards.
RECEIVING
AU: Aromashodu 2-18; Johnson 2-17.
PSU: T. Johnson 2-54; Kranchick 2-15.

DECEMBER 31, 2003 | MUSIC CITY
AUBURN 28, WISCONSIN 14

	1ST	2ND	3RD	4TH	FINAL
AUB	0	7	7	14	28
WIS	0	6	0	8	14

SCORING SUMMARY
WIS FG Allen 20
AUB Brown 1 run (Vaughn kick)
WIS FG Allen 35
AUB Williams 1 run (Vaughn kick)
WIS Evans 12 pass from Sorgi (Daniels pass from Sorgi)
AUB Brown 2 run (Vaughn kick)
AUB Williams 1 run (Vaughn kick)

AUB	TEAM STATISTICS	WIS
15	First Downs	18
197	Rushing Yards	58
11-23-1	Passing	17-29-1
157	Passing Yards	203
354	Total Yards	261
5-99	Punt Returns - Yards	3-35
4-64	Kickoff Returns - Yards	2-6
5-45.2	Punts - Average	4-38.5
0-0	Fumbles - Lost	2-1
8-66	Penalties - Yards	4-25
29:00	Possession Time	31:00

INDIVIDUAL LEADERS
RUSHING
AUB: Williams 18-68, 2 TD; Campbell 9-67; Brown 13-62, 2 TD.
WIS: Davis 17-77; Evans 3-19.
PASSING
AUB: Campbell 10-22-1, 138 yards.
WIS: Sorgi 13-22-1, 169 yards, 1 TD.
RECEIVING
AUB: McIntyre 3-74; Daniels 3-40.
WIS: Williams 6-57; Evans 4-51, 1 TD.

JANUARY 3, 2005 | SUGAR
AUBURN 16, VIRGINIA TECH 13

	1ST	2ND	3RD	4TH	FINAL
AU	6	3	7	0	16
VT	0	0	0	13	13

SCORING SUMMARY
AU FG Vaughn 23
AU FG Vaughn 19
AU FG Vaughn 24
AU Aromashodu 5 pass from Campbell (Vaughn kick)
VT Morgan 29 pass from Randall (conversion failed)
VT Morgan 80 pass from Randall (Pace kick)

AU	TEAM STATISTICS	VT
14	First Downs	19
110	Rushing Yards	76
11-16-1	Passing	21-38-2
189	Passing Yards	299
299	Total Yards	375
2-17	Punt Returns - Yards	1-(-5)
1-22	Kickoff Returns - Yards	2-76
4-42.0	Punts - Average	5-35.2
1-1	Fumbles - Lost	0-0
4-35	Penalties - Yards	7-57
33:34	Possession Time	26:26

INDIVIDUAL LEADERS
RUSHING
AU: Brown 15-68; Williams 19-61.
VT: Randall 9-45; Imoh 6-16.
PASSING
AU: Campbell 11-16-1, 189 yards, 1 TD.
VT: Randall 21-38-2, 299 yards, 2 TD.
RECEIVING
AU: Taylor 5-87; Mix 2-68.
VT: Morgan 3-126, 2 TD; Hyman 5-71.

JANUARY 2, 2006 | CAPITAL ONE
AUBURN 10, WISCONSIN 24

	1ST	2ND	3RD	4TH	FINAL
WISC	10	7	0	7	24
AU	0	0	3	7	10

SCORING SUMMARY
WISC Williams 30 pass from Stocco (Mehlhaff kick)
WISC FG Mehlhaff 19
WISC Daniels 13 pass from Stocco (Mehlhaff kick)
AU FG Vaughn 19
AU Taylor 9 pass from Cox (Vaughn kick)
WISC Calhoun 33 run (Mehlhaff kick)

WISC	TEAM STATISTICS	AU
24	First Downs	19
247	Rushing Yards	99
15-27-0	Passing	15-33-1
301	Passing Yards	137
548	Total Yards	236
2-5	Punt Returns - Yards	1-10
0-0	Kickoff Returns - Yards	3-58
3-45.3	Punts - Average	6-45.7
2-1	Fumbles - Lost	1-1
7-56	Penalties - Yards	5-35

INDIVIDUAL LEADERS
RUSHING
WISC: Calhoun 30-213, 1 TD.
AU: Irons 22-88.
PASSING
WISC: Stocco 15-27-0, 301 yards, 2 TD.
AU: Cox 15-33-1, 137 yards, 1 TD.
RECEIVING
WISC: Williams 6-173, 1 TD; Orr 4-74.
AU: Obomanu 5-62; Aromashodu 2-16.

JANUARY 1, 2007 | COTTON
AUBURN 17, NEBRASKA 14

	1ST	2ND	3RD	4TH	FINAL
AU	7	7	3	0	17
NEB	7	7	0	10	14

SCORING SUMMARY
NEB Swift 13 pass from Taylor (Congdon kick)
AU Stewart 9 pass from Cox (Vaughn kick)
AU Stewart 1 run (Vaughn kick)
NEB Jackson 20 run (Congdon kick)
AU FG Vaughn 42

AU	TEAM STATISTICS	NEB
12	First Downs	17
67	Rushing Yards	104
10-21-0	Passing	14-27-1
111	Passing Yards	126
178	Total Yards	230
3-3	Punt Returns - Yards	1-23
2-58	Kickoff Returns - Yards	2-40
6-43	Punts - Average	6-40.2
2-2	Fumbles - Lost	1-1
6-45	Penalties -Yards	4-45

INDIVIDUAL LEADERS
RUSHING
AU: Irons 24-72.
NEB: Lucky 25-88.
PASSING
AU: Cox 10-21-0, 111 yards, 1 TD.
NEB: Taylor 14-26-1, 126 yards, 1 TD.
RECEIVING
AU: Taylor 6-70; Rodriguez 1-18.
NEB: Lucky 6-67; Swift 3-44, 1 TD.

DECEMBER 31, 2007 | CHICK-FIL-A
AUBURN 23, CLEMSON 20

	1ST	2ND	3RD	4TH	OT	FINAL
CLEM	0	7	0	10	3	20
AU	3	0	7	7	6	23

SCORING SUMMARY
AU FG Byrum 36
CLEM Spiller 83 run (Buchholz kick)
AU Fannin 22 pass from Burns (Byrum kick)
CLEM FG Buchholz 22
CLEM Davis 1 run (Buchholz kick)
AU Tate 1 run (Byrum kick)
CLEM FG Buchholz 25
AU Burns 7 run

CLEM	TEAM STATISTICS	AU
12	First Downs	24
189	Rushing Yards	190
14-33-0	Passing	26-43-1
104	Passing Yards	233
293	Total Yards	423
1-8	Punt Returns - Yards	3-25
4-103	Kickoff Returns - Yards	3-92
8-43.1	Punts - Average	8-38.6
1-0	Fumbles - Lost	0-0
1-5	Penalties - Yards	6-40

INDIVIDUAL LEADERS
RUSHING
CLEM: Spiller 8-112, 1 TD.
AU: Burns 13-69, 1 TD; Lester 14-57.
PASSING
CLEM: Harper 14-33-0, 104 yards.
AU: Cox 25-39-1, 211 yards.
RECEIVING
CLEM: Kelly 4-36; Taylor 3-32.
AU: Fannin 5-53, 1 TD; Smith 4-45.

FLORIDA

BY GEOFFREY NORMAN

THE STORY OF FOOTBALL AT FLORIDA for most of the 20th century was one of almost Sisyphean frustration. For 80-plus years, the Gators were the Great Big Team That Couldn't—couldn't win the big game, couldn't win the conference championship, couldn't put up an undefeated season, couldn't win a national title.

Until the 1990s, Florida routinely raised the hopes of its faithful fans, only to dash them, often in some cruel or unusual way. In 1928, 1966, 1969 and 1985, the Gators went deep into the season with a shot at the national championship, but came up short each time.

Oh, sure, Florida always won a lot of games—enough to convince Gators fans that it was possible to win more. Citizens of GatorsWorld came to accept as an article of faith what Bear Bryant supposedly said about their football program, that all Florida needed was the right head man. When the Gators found him, the Bear warned, everybody else had better watch out.

And lo, in 1990 the right head man finally arrived in Gainesville, where he had also won the 1966 Heisman Trophy. Very soon, Steve Spurrier started proving Bryant right. The Gators played for the 1995 national championship, and in 1996 won it for the first time in school history. Florida became accustomed to top-10 finishes and to being a member of the college football elite.

Going into the 21st century, the Gators had become one of those football teams that—as the saying goes—"doesn't recruit; it reloads." The program has the most fertile ground in the nation to recruit from and facilities that would seduce any prospect who comes to visit. There was a brief and agonizing interlude after Spurrier's departure in 2002 when the Gators began slipping back to their old ways. Then a new savior, Urban Meyer, arrived and, in his second year (2006), won a national championship and two years later won another. In between (2007), a Florida player, Tim Tebow, won the Heisman. Florida had gone from being an also-ran to being a colossus of college football.

TRADITION Between the third and fourth quarters of every game, Gators fans stand and sway and sing "We Are the Boys of Old Florida." The Gator Chomp—made by extending both arms at about a 45-degree angle and then bringing them together sharply—is another Florida

---

PROFILE

University of Florida
Gainesville, Fla.
Founded: 1853
Enrollment: 51,725
Colors: Blue and Orange
Nickname: Gators
Stadium: Ben Hill Griffin Stadium at
Florida Field
    Opened in 1930
    Grass; 88,548 capacity
First football game: 1906
All-time record: 641–373–40 (.632)
Bowl record: 17–19
Consensus national championships,
1936-present: 3 (1996, 2006, 2008)
Southeastern Conference championships:
8 (outright)
Heisman Trophy: Steve Spurrier, 1966;
Danny Wuerffel, 1996; Tim Tebow, 2007
First-round draft choices: 39
Website: www.gatorzone.com/football/

THE BEST OF TIMES

Urban Meyer won national championships in 2006 and 2008. The Gators won 35 times in that three-year span, tied with Boise State for the most in college football.

THE WORST OF TIMES

From 1935 to 1951, the Gators posted only one season with a winning record.

CONFERENCE

After 11 years in the Southern Conference, Florida became a charter member of the SEC in 1933.

DISTINGUISHED ALUMNI

John Atanasoff, inventor of digital electronic computer; Faye Dunaway, actress; Buddy Ebsen, actor; Bob Graham, U.S. senator; Carl Hiaasen, author; Dara Torres, Olympic swimmer; Bob Vila, host of *This Old House*

FIGHT SONG

THE ORANGE & BLUE
On, brave old Florida, just keep on marching
    on your way!
On, brave old Florida, and we will cheer you
    on your play!
Rah! Rah! Rah!
And as you march along, we'll sing our victory
    song anew
With all your might go on and fight Gators
Fight for Dixie's rightly proud of you
So give a cheer for the Orange and Blue,
    Waving forever, forever
Pride of old Florida, may she droop never
We'll sing a song for the flag today, cheer for
    the team at play!
On to the goal we'll fight our way for Florida.

trademark. And then there was Mr. Two-Bit, who led fans at the Swamp in that standard football cheer from 1949 until 2008, when he retired from first-fandom. His given name is George Edmondson Jr., and he will be missed.

> *The Swamp was named by Steve Spurrier who explained, "A swamp is hot and sticky and can be dangerous."*

BEST PLAYER Well, for a long time this was an interesting argument, with many fans insisting that Florida's best player and best coach are one and the same. But according to that man, Steve Spurrier, the best Gators player ever was actually someone he coached—Danny Wuerffel, the 1996 Heisman Trophy winner and quarterback of Florida's national championship team that same season.

That debate is now academic. The undeniable best player in Florida history is QB Tim Tebow who, among other things, won a Heisman in 2007, making him the equal of both Spurrier and Wuerffel in that department. But Tebow's trophy came after his sophomore year and he nearly repeated it the following season. As prestigious as that honor is, it doesn't adequately reflect the accomplishments of this singular athlete. Tebow runs and passes and dominates opponents with his arm and his legs and his will to win. In 2007, he accounted for an astonishing 55 touchdowns. That includes seven in one game, against the South Carolina Gamecocks, coached by Spurrier—who may very well have reassessed his thinking about who, exactly, is the greatest Gator of them all. In Gainesville they tell Tebow jokes. They go like this: "Tim Tebow counted to infinity. Twice." And, "You can lead a horse to water. Tim Tebow can make him drink."

BEST COACH When Spurrier arrived in Gainesville in 1990, the Gators were in the football doghouse, ineligible for television, bowl games and the conference championship. Florida had seen two head coaches— Charley Pell and Galen Hall—leave under a cloud. So hiring Spurrier was something like the return of the prodigal son, since his years as a player were among the happiest memories of many Gators fans. By the eighth game of his 10th season as Florida's head coach, he had won 100 games at the school (faster than any other major-college coach has accomplished the feat). In all, his teams won at least nine games in every one of his 12 seasons.

Spurrier's wide-open, creative offensive schemes, which he called the Fun 'n Gun, changed the culture not only at Florida but throughout the SEC. Gators fans

---

FIRST-ROUND DRAFT CHOICES

1945	Paul Duhart, Steelers (2)
1950	Chuck Hunsinger, Bears (3)
1967	Steve Spurrier, 49ers (3)
1969	Larry Smith, Rams (8)
1970	Steve Tannen, Jets (20)
1971	Jack Youngblood, Rams (20)
1972	John Reaves, Eagles (14)
1975	Glen Cameron, Bengals (14)
1978	Wes Chandler, Saints (3)
1983	James Jones, Lions (13)
1984	Wilbur Marshall, Bears (11)
1985	Lomas Brown, Lions (6)
1985	Lorenzo Hampton, Dolphins (27)
1986	John L. Williams, Seahawks (15)
1986	Neal Anderson, Bears (27)
1987	Ricky Nattiel, Broncos (27)
1988	Clifford Charlton, Browns (21)
1989	Trace Armstrong, Bears (12)
1989	David Williams, Oilers (23)
1989	Louis Oliver, Dolphins (25)
1990	Emmitt Smith, Cowboys (17)
1991	Huey Richardson, Steelers (15)
1995	Kevin Carter, Rams (6)
1995	Ellis Johnson, Colts (15)
1997	Ike Hilliard, Giants (7)
1997	Reidel Anthony, Buccaneers (16)
1998	Fred Taylor, Jaguars (9)
1998	Mo Collins, Raiders (23)
1999	Jevon Kearse, Titans (16)
1999	Reggie McGrew, 49ers (24)
2000	Travis Taylor, Ravens (10)
2001	Gerard Warren, Browns (3)
2001	Kenyatta Walker, Buccaneers (14)
2002	Lito Sheppard, Eagles (26)
2003	Rex Grossman, Bears (22)
2007	Jarvis Moss, Broncos (17)
2007	Reggie Nelson, Jaguars (21)
2008	Derrick Harvey, Jaguars (8)
2009	Percy Harvin, Vikings (22)

CONSENSUS ALL-AMERICANS

1966	Steve Spurrier, B	
1969	Carlos Alvarez, E	
1975	Sammy Green, LB	
1980	David Little, LB	
1982-83	Wilber Marshall, DL/LB	
1984	Lomas Brown, OT	

1988	Louis Oliver, DB
1989	Emmitt Smith, RB
1991	Brad Culpepper, DL
1994	Jack Jackson, WR
1994	Kevin Carter, DL
1995	Jason Odom, OL
1996	Danny Wuerffel, QB
1996	Ike Hilliard, WR
1996	Reidel Anthony, WR
1997	Jacquez Green, WR
1997	Fred Weary, DB
2001	Jabar Gaffney, WR
2001	Mike Pearson, OL
2001	Rex Grossman, QB
2001	Alex Brown, DL
2003	Keiwan Ratliff, DB
2006	Reggie Nelson, DB
2007	Tim Tebow, QB
2008	Brandon James, KR
2008	Brandon Spikes, LB

loved him for the same qualities that rivals found infuriating: brashness, confidence and arrogance. He was, in a word, cocky. He was routinely accused of running up the score, a complaint he never denied with much conviction. Other schools and coaches lusted to beat Spurrier and Florida.

After the 2002 Orange Bowl, Spurrier resigned and left for an unhappy two-year stint in the NFL with the Washington Redskins. Things weren't much happier in Gainesville for Spurrier's successor, Ron Zook, who was fired during the 2004 season. Then, Urban Meyer, who'd brought BCS-crashing Utah into the top 10 in just two years, passed on an offer from Notre Dame to take the Florida job. Before the books are closed, Meyer may well eclipse Spurrier in all statistical categories, if not the affections of longtime Florida fans who believe it was Steve who led them to the promised land. Now that they are there, Meyer enjoys the milk and honey. In addition to those two national championships, Meyer is 25–2 at the Swamp and a glittering 11–1 against the three teams Gators fans most like to beat: Georgia, Tennessee and Florida State.

BEST TEAM The 1996 Gators, Florida's first national championship team, announced they were something special in the third game of the season, against Tennessee in Knoxville. The game was billed as a shootout between two top college quarterbacks—Wuerffel and Peyton Manning—and there was plenty of offense, with Florida winning 35-29. The Gators went to the top of the rankings and stayed there until the last weekend of November, when they went to Tallahassee to play No. 2 Florida State. The high stakes made the cross-state rivalry—one of football's fiercest—even more intense. Florida lost, 24-21, and after the game Spurrier complained that FSU had gotten away with a number of late hits on Wuerffel. He put together a video to back up the charge and continued to make his case, adding to the already bitter feelings between the two schools. That made it all the sweeter when—after beating Alabama 45-30 in the SEC championship game—Florida avenged its loss by routing Florida State, 52-20, in the Sugar Bowl.

BEST BACKFIELD The job he did as quarterback of the 1996 Florida team earned Danny Wuerffel a Heisman. But he had plenty of help in the backfield from Ike Hilliard, Fred Taylor and Reidel Anthony. That unit put up the kind of numbers that seemed almost otherworldly

COLLEGE FOOTBALL HALL OF FAME INDUCTEES		
NAME	YEARS	INDUCTED
Dale Van Sickel, E	1927-29	1975
Charles Bachman, COACH	1928-32	1978
Steve Spurrier, QB	1964-66	1986
Ray Graves, COACH	1960-69	1990
Jack Youngblood, DE	1968-70	1992
Doug Dickey, COACH	1970-78	2003
Emmitt Smith, RB	1987-89	2006
Wilber Marshall, LB	1980-83	2008

PRO FOOTBALL HALL OF FAME INDUCTEES		
NAME	YEARS	INDUCTED
Jack Youngblood	1971-84	2001

back in those pre-spread offense days. With Taylor running and Wuerffel throwing to Hilliard and Anthony, the Gators beat their SEC opponents by an average of 31 points. Florida scored 76 touchdowns and led the nation in scoring with 46.6 points per game. The Gators *averaged* 7.1 yards per play and scored 42 touchdowns through the air. The unit was an almost perfect instrument of Spurrier's vision of offense taken to the limit. In the off-seasons following, Spurrier made the circuit of coaches' clinics armed with a tape of all of Florida's TD passes from the previous two seasons, spicing up the highlights show with bits of trenchant commentary like, "Danny put that ball right where it needed to be" or, after Anthony had outleaped another overmatched defensive back, "It sure was good having Reidel there."

BEST DEFENSE Going into the 2009 national championship game, the question many, many people were asking of Florida was not could they score, but could they score *enough*. The Gators were ranked No. 2 and their opponent, No. 1 Oklahoma, was an offensive juggernaut. OU had scored more than 60 points in its previous five games, all victories, needless to say—one of them against the reigning No. 1 Texas Tech. The lowest score the Sooners had been kept to was 35.

The Gators held the Sooners to a mere 14 points—less than what Oklahoma had been averaging *a quarter*. Florida blocked a kick and intercepted the Sooners' Heisman-winning quarterback, Sam Bradford, twice. One of those came on their own 3-yard line. So one could say, on the basis of holding one of the best offenses in history to its lowest scoring total and least yardage gained in any game of the season, that the 2008 Gators defense was the best in Florida's history. Except that of the 24 defensive players who took the field for that championship game, all but one returned for the 2009 season, along with another blue-chip recruiting class. So the best may very well be yet to come.

BIGGEST GAME Consider what the Gators faced in the 1997 Sugar Bowl with the national title on the line. Florida needed to beat its fiercest rival, a team that was not only ranked No. 1 but that had defeated the Gators a month earlier. Their previous bowl game, with the national title also on the line, had been a monumental disaster. Nebraska's 62-24 blowout of Florida in the 1996 Fiesta Bowl was taken as evidence that while Florida was

fast and flashy, when it came to football fundamentals, the Gators were also soft.

A year later, in New Orleans, they had a chance to correct that reputation, avenge the loss in Tallahassee and, finally, win it all. Wuerffel had a good night and so did all the Gators. Florida whipped the No. 1 team in the nation, 52-20, slaying a history filled with demons.

BIGGEST UPSET In 1963, Florida opened with a loss to Georgia Tech and a tie against Mississippi State before barely beating Richmond in Gainesville, 35-28. The next week, the unranked Gators traveled to Tuscaloosa to play No. 3 Alabama. These were the early years of the age of Bryant and Bama wasn't losing much anywhere, and never at home. So what did the struggling Gators do? They went out and held Joe Namath's team to a mere six points, scored late in the fourth quarter and won 10-6. Florida, in fact, dominated the Tide. The triumph was exceedingly special to Florida fans, with some 10,000 greeting the Gators at the airport when they arrived home.

The magnitude of the accomplishment grew over the years and decades. It wasn't until 1982 that another Bryant-coached Alabama team lost in Tuscaloosa.

HEARTBREAKER An agonizing 31-31 "loss" to FSU at Doak Campbell Stadium in Tallahassee in 1994 tops the list. "Bitter" doesn't even begin to describe what gleeful Florida State fans still call the Choke at the Doak. It's bad enough to finish tied with anyone when you've been up 28-3 late in the third quarter. But against Florida State? Wormwood and gall would taste sweeter. The game seemed to cast a spell over Spurrier and the Gators. They lost a Sugar Bowl rematch with the Seminoles, who went on to dominate Florida for the remainder of Spurrier's tenure. He has never won in Tallahassee.

BEST COMEBACK In 1986, Auburn came to Gainesville ranked fifth in the nation and smelling blood. Kerwin Bell, the Gators quarterback, hadn't played in a month, and when he limped onto the field in the third quarter, Florida was down 17-0. Throwing to Ricky Nattiel, who was playing with a separated shoulder, Bell brought Florida to within a point, 17-16, with 30 seconds left and the PAT still to come. Florida went for two, and when Bell dropped back to pass, Auburn covered everyone except the gimpy quarterback. Bell limped in for the win.

STADIUM The official—and rather prosaic—name of Florida's facility is Ben Hill Griffin Stadium at Florida Field. But it is better and more aptly known as the Swamp. It was so named by Spurrier, who explained, "The swamp is where gators live. We feel comfortable there, but we hope our opponents feel tentative. A swamp is hot and

sticky and can be dangerous." Not to mention loud. Florida home games routinely draw more than 85,000 fans, and there is something about the low-lying terrain and the bowl-like structure that captures their cheers and amplifies them in such a way that you can actually feel the sound.

RIVAL As with many programs, there is the traditional rivalry and there is the modern one. No question, Georgia is the traditional rival. The game is played in Jacksonville, on neutral turf. (Exceptions being the 1994 and 1995 seasons, when, due to stadium construction, the games were in Athens and Gainesville.) There is an epic, carnival quality to the event, which spans the week leading up to the game and is universally known as the World's Largest Outdoor Cocktail Party, despite the schools' recent attempts to put the kibosh on the nickname. Spirits flow fiercely, in drinks and in fanaticism, with some serious bragging rights at stake.

The modern rivalry is with Florida State. The upstart from Tallahassee was a girls' school until after World War II, when the veterans came home with G.I. Bill money to spend. It was years before the Gators agreed—grudgingly— to play FSU, and more years before parity was achieved on the field. In the 1990s, both schools achieved status as national championship contenders, and the game was played for high stakes and with almost dangerously fierce emotion. There were ugly pregame incidents between players and fan behavior had become such a concern that the respective head coaches made public service announcements urging fans "check your hate at the gate." Lots of luck.

DISPUTE The 1966 FSU game in Tallahassee will be forever remembered for the Lane Fenner catch that was ruled incomplete by an SEC official. A famous photograph makes a pretty convincing case that Fenner was inbounds. The official claimed Fenner did not have control and waved off the apparent touchdown. The Gators held onto their 22-19 lead and FSU fans never got over it. One Gators loyalist, who later became a U.S. senator and governor of the state, is supposed to have told one opposing fan, "You're damn right we stole it, and that just makes it sweeter."

NICKNAME According to the legend, the first Gator appeared on a little pennant in 1908, when there were probably more alligators than people in Florida. Others ascribe the name's origins to the nickname given to Neal "Bo Gator" Storter, who began his career as a backup center and wound up the varsity team captain in 1911. *Florida Times-Union* columnist Laurence "Kiddo" Woltz first referred to the school as the Gators in print in the fall of 1911.

MASCOT A 12-foot alligator named Albert served as the official mascot throughout the 1960s, before dying in 1970. Not long after, the school switched to the cartoonish Albert Gator, a student in a costume with an orange letter sweater who roams the sideline leading cheers. Albert was soon joined by Alberta Gator, and the couple became such a hit that in 2003 a $75,000 bronze statue of the mascots was unveiled just across the street from the Swamp.

UNIFORMS After years with a distinctively interlocked U and F on their orange helmets, Florida switched to a script Gators in 1979, and that look remains today. The Gators wear blue jerseys and (usually) white pants at home, white jerseys and (usually) orange or blue pants on the road.

LORE In 1923, coached by a man named James Van Fleet, Florida traveled to Tuscaloosa to play Wallace Wade's Alabama powerhouse. A storm had turned the field into a lake. At halftime, down 6-0, Van Fleet had his starters change uniforms with the reserves and kept his players in the locker room until the last possible moment before returning for the kickoff. This little piece of psychological warfare worked and the Gators came back to score 16 unanswered points for the win. Van Fleet was then a temporary coach, moonlighting from his job as commander of the Florida ROTC unit. He was a major in the Army and later became a hero as a general in the Korean War.

In 1965, at the request of an assistant coach, Florida kidney specialist Dr. Robert Cade invented an electrolyte beverage for the football team. It was called Gatorade. The university still receives 20% of the drink's profits, to the tune of $80 million to date.

QUOTE "Running it out to keep the shutout? No, I didn't think about that. We felt having 35 points at the half, we only needed 17 more to break 50."
—**Steve Spurrier**, on whether he considered running the ball instead of passing for the end zone with less than two minutes left in Florida's 52-0 rout of Mississippi State in 2001.

Changes in Latitude, Changes in Attitude

BY TOM FARREY

A few months after graduating from the University of Florida in 1986, I took a job with *The Seattle Times*, where I worked for the better part of a decade, covering the NBA and NFL and, for a year, investigating a Washington Huskies football program that ran afoul of NCAA rules. Then I went to work for ESPN and moved to the Hartford area, where UConn basketball dominates. If there is a local chapter of Gator Nation, it's more like a sleeper cell, with an alum here or there planted on his couch watching games alone or with a neighbor who's pulling for the other team.

I was okay with the deal. You gotta understand that I've been programmed to be a reporter since way back in high school, when I did grunt work on weekends in *The Miami Herald* newsroom. I learned early on that journalists should aspire to objectivity, even when traipsing into the bias-rich zone of college sports. So while my fraternity brothers were in the stands at Florida Field marinating in equal parts Jim Beam and orange-and-blue fandom, I was in the press box training myself to think and not cheer, even when the home team did something spectacular. I was *working*.

Plus, Charley Pell made it was easy to withhold applause. The Gators coach spied on opponents' practices and his boosters paid athletes — breaking enough rules to warrant an NCAA ban on playing in bowl games. And ol' Chollie wasn't too accommodating of those who questioned his methods. I approached him after practice one day as a reporter for *The Alligator*, the student paper, and asked him about allegations of rules violations that we helped dig up. Pell wore his hat low on his forehead so I could barely see his eyes, but his words I'll never forget. In his syrup-thick Alabama tongue, he said, "Boy, what're you tryin' to do, git-a-job wi' da *Boston Globe* or da *New York Tii-iimes*?"

My professional detachment nearly melted a few months later, in 1984. Pell had been forced out midseason and the Gators wrapped up their first SEC title by beating Kentucky in Lexington, 25-17. I was in the Florida locker room after the game interviewing some of the key players—the great fullback John L.

> *One woman looked me in the eyes and thanked me for the deliverance I had bestowed upon her tortured soul. I thought, "Wow, it is great to be a Florida Gator."*

Williams, walk-on quarterback Kerwin Bell, jet-like wideout Ricky Nattiel, the formidable offensive tackle Lomas Brown. When I stepped out, Florida fans massed at the end of the tunnel mistook me for a player. (A kicker, surely.) One woman looked me in the eyes and thanked me for the deliverance I had bestowed upon her tortured soul. I thought, "Wow, it *is* great to be a Florida Gator." That night, in the press box of a darkened stadium, I wrote a column about how the victory belonged to the Boys of Old Florida—the alums who had waited patiently (and not so patiently) for this moment to arrive.

Of course, that championship was taken away for rules violations and I returned to dispassionate newsman mode, which is pretty much where I stayed into the 2000s. The first time I ever returned to Gainesville for a game, I didn't have any tribal garb apart from a faded orange pullover without a logo. So my buddy Paul dragged me to the store just outside the gates of the Swamp and I bought a blue baseball cap that said Gators on the front … in Japanese.

I thought it was funny, but Paulie just shook his head. "Only you, Farrey," he said. He knew this was my way of being a different kind of fan—the kind that couldn't be accused of violating his professional training and principles because who knew what those letters on the front of the cap were, anyway?

The thing is, I really enjoyed that game, sitting in the stands without a notepad. And since then, it's only gotten harder to keep my journalistic game face. Not only have the Gators won two national championships in three years, they've done it with class. The face of the program? Heisman Trophy-winning humanitarian Tim Tebow, who might not solve world hunger but sure breathes life into the balky ideal of the student-athlete. Urban Meyer runs his team with the cool efficiency of a top corporate manager, with no evidence to suggest he cuts the corners Pell once did. He shouldn't have to; longtime athletic director Jeremy Foley has assembled what's become recognized as a model department, with the resources to compete for the top recruits, check their behavior once on campus and get most of them out the door with degrees.

The Gators have become an easy program to pull for, at least in my living room. When they yet again compete for a conference or national title, my 12-year-old son, Cole, roots for them unabashedly. I join him in my way, with an appreciation of what this program has gone through, of how the scrutiny of the 1980s laid the foundation for its current success. To the Boys of Old Florida, that might not seem like an enthusiastic hip-hip-hooray. But for a guy with my wiring, it's the equivalent of dying my hair blue and painting my face orange.

It's a good look, I must say.

Tom Farrey is an Emmy award-winning ESPN television correspondent and author of Game On: How the Pressure to Win at All Costs Endangers Youth Sports and What Parents Can Do About It.

FLORIDA ALL-TIME SCORES

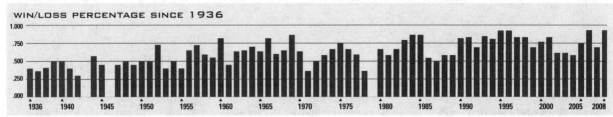

WIN/LOSS PERCENTAGE SINCE 1936

JACK FORSYTHE
1906-08 (.682)   14-6-2

1906   5-3-0
U	•	Gainesville UNK	16	6
U	•	Mercer UNK	3	27
U	•	Rollins UNK	6	0
U	•	Jacksonville AC UNK	19	0
U	•	Savannah AC UNK	2	27
U	•	Athens AC UNK	10	0
U	•	Rollins UNK	0	6
U	•	Jacksonville AC UNK	39	0

1907   4-1-1
U	•	Columbia AC UNK	6	0
U	•	Mercer UNK	0	6
U	•	Jacksonville AC UNK	21	0
U	•	Rollins UNK	9	4
U	•	Jacksonville AC UNK	17	0
U	=	Rollins UNK	0	0

1908   5-2-1
U		at Mercer	0	24
U	•	at Jacksonville AC	4	0
U	•	Gainesville	37	5
U	•	at Rollins	0	6
U	•	at Portland	6	0
U	•	Stetson	6	5
U	•	Jacksonville AC	37	0
U	=	at Stetson	0	0

G.E. PYLE
1909-13 (.764)   26-7-3

1909   6-1-1
U	•	Gainesville	5	0
U	•	Rollins	14	0
U		at Stetson	0	26
U	•	Rollins ORL	28	3
U	•	Olympics JacF	11	0
U	=	Stetson	5	5
U	•	Olympics	28	0
U	•	Tallahassee	26	0

1910   6-1-0
U	•	G'ville Guards	23	0
O22		at Mercer	0	13
U	•	Georgia Coll.	52	0
N5	•	Citadel JacF	6	2
U	•	at Rollins	38	0
U	•	Coll. Charleston	34	0
U	•	Portland	33	0

1911   5-0-1
O7	•	Citadel	15	3
O21	=	at South Carolina	6	6
O25	•	at Clemson	9	5
N3	•	Portland	9	0
N11	•	at Stetson	27	0
N30	•	Coll. Charleston JacF	21	0

1912   5-2-1
O12		at Auburn	13	27
O19	•	South Carolina	10	6
O26		Georgia Tech JacF	7	14
N4	•	Coll. of Charleston	78	0
N15	•	Stetson	23	7
N28	=	Mercer JacF	0	0
D21	•	at Tampa AC	44	0
S25	•	at Vedado Club	28	0

1913   4-3-0
O6	•	Florida Southern	144	0
O11		at Auburn	0	55
O18	•	Maryville	39	0
O25		Georgia Tech JacF	3	13
N8		at South Carolina	0	13
N15	•	Citadel	18	13
N27	•	Mercer	24	0

CHARLES McCOY
1914-16 (.474)   9-10

1914   5-2-0
O10		Auburn JacF	0	20
O17	•	King	36	0
O24	•	Sewanee JacF	0	26
O31	•	Florida Southern TAM	59	0
N7	•	Wofford	36	0
N14	•	at Citadel	7	0
N26	•	Mercer	14	0

1915   4-3-0
O9		at Auburn	0	7
O16	•	Sewanee JacF	0	7
O30	•	Florida Southern	45	0
N6		Georgia JacF	0	37
N13	•	Citadel	6	0
N18	•	Tulane	14	7
N25	•	at Mercer	34	7

1916   0-5-0
O14		at Georgia	0	21
O21	•	Alabama JacF	0	16
O28	•	Tennessee TAM	0	24
N11	•	Auburn JacF	0	20
N18	•	at Indiana	3	14

A.L. BUSSER
1917-19 (.467)   7-8

1917   2-4-0
O13	•	South Carolina	21	13
O20	•	Tulane	0	52
O27	•	Florida Southern	19	7
N3		at Auburn	0	68
N17	•	Clemson JacF	7	55
N29	•	at Kentucky	0	52

1918   0-1-0
| U | | Camp Johnson | 2 | 14 |

1919   5-3-0
O4	•	No. Georgia	33	2
O18	•	Mercer	48	0
O25	•	Georgia TAM	0	16
N1	•	Florida Southern STP	0	7
N8	•	at Tulane	2	14
N15	•	Stetson	64	0
N22	•	at South Carolina	13	0
N27	•	Oglethorpe	14	7

WILLIAM KLINE
1920-22 (.690)   19-8-2

1920   6-3-0
O9	•	Newberry	21	0
O16	•	Rollins	1	0f
O23	•	Florida Southern	13	0
O29	•	Mercer VAL	30	0
N6		Tulane TAM	0	14
N11	•	Stetson PAL	26	0
N13		at Georgia	0	56
N20	•	Stetson	21	0
N25		Oglethorpe COLGA	0	21

1921   6-3-2
O1	•	at Fort Benning	6	0
O8	•	Rollins ORL	33	0
O10		Carlestom F.	0	19
O15	•	Mercer	7	0
O22	•	at Tennessee	0	9
O29	•	Samford MONT	34	0
N5	=	South Carolina TAM	7	7
N11	•	at Alabama	9	2
N18	=	Mississippi Coll.	7	7
N24	•	Oglethorpe	21	3
D3		North Carolina JacF	10	14

1922-1932
SOUTHERN

1922   7-2-0 (2-0-0)
O7		Furman	6	7
O14	•	at Rollins	19	0
O21	•	at American Legion	14	0
O28	•	Samford	57	0
N4		at Harvard	0	24
N11	•	Mississippi Coll. TAM	58	0
N18	•	at Tulane	27	6
N25	•	at Oglethorpe	12	0
D2	•	Clemson JacF	47	14

GEN. J.A. VAN FLEET
1923-24 (.737)   12-3-4

1923   6-1-2 (1-0-2)
O6		at Army	0	20
O13	=	at Georgia Tech	7	7
O20	•	Rollins	28	0
O27	•	Wake Forest TAM	16	7
N3	•	Mercer	19	7
N10	•	at Stetson	27	0
N17	•	at Florida Southern	53	0
N24	•	Mississippi State JacF	13	13
N29	•	Alabama BIRM	16	6

1924   6-2-2 (2-0-1)
O4	•	Rollins	77	0
O11	=	at Georgia Tech	7	7
O18	•	Wake Forest TAM	34	0
O25		at Texas	7	7
N1	•	Florida Southern	27	0
N8		at Army	7	14
N14	•	at Mercer	0	10
N22	•	Mississippi State MONT	27	0
N27	•	Drake	10	0
D6	•	Wash. & Lee JacF	16	6

H.L. SEBRING
1925-27 (.600)   17-11-2

1925   8-2-0 (3-2-0)
O3	•	Mercer	24	0
O10	•	Florida Southern	9	0
O10	•	Hampden-Sydney	22	6
O17		at Georgia Tech	7	23
O24	•	Wake Forest	24	3
O31	•	Rollins	65	0
N7	•	at Clemson	42	0
N14		Alabama MONT	0	34
N21	•	Mississippi State TAM	12	0
N26	•	Wash. & Lee JacF	17	14

1926   2-6-2 (1-4-1)
S25	•	Florida Southern	16	0
O2		at Chicago	6	12
O9		Mississippi	7	12
O16	•	at Mercer	3	7
O23		Kentucky JacF	13	18
O30		at Georgia	9	32
N6	•	Clemson	33	0
N13		Alabama MONT	0	49
N20	=	Hampden-Sydney TAM	0	0
N25	=	Wash. & Lee JacF	7	7

1927   7-3-0 (5-2-0)
S24	•	Florida Southern	26	7
O1		Davidson	0	12
O8	•	at Auburn	33	6
O15		Kentucky JacF	27	6
O22		North Carolina St. TAM	6	12
O29	•	Mercer	32	6
N5		Georgia JacF	0	28
N12	•	Alabama MONT	13	6
N24	•	Wash. & Lee JacF	20	7
D3	•	Maryland JacF	7	6

CHARLES BACHMAN
1928-32 (.594)   27-18-3

1928   8-1-0 (6-1-0)
O6	•	Florida Southern	26	0
O13	•	Auburn	27	0
O20	•	Mercer	73	0
O27	•	North Carolina St. JacF	14	7
N3	•	Sewanee JacF	71	6
N10	•	Georgia SAV	26	6
N17	•	Clemson JacF	27	6
N29	•	Wash. & Lee JacF	60	6
D8	•	at Tennessee	12	13

1929   8-2-0 (6-1-0)
S28	•	Florida Southern	54	0
O5	•	VMI TAM	18	7
O11	•	Auburn MONT	19	0
O19	•	at Georgia Tech	6	19
O26	•	Georgia JacF	18	6
N2		at Harvard	0	14
N16		Clemson	13	7
N23	•	at South Carolina	20	7
N28	•	Wash. & Lee JacF	25	7
D7	•	Oregon MIA	20	6

1930   6-3-1 (4-2-1)
S27	•	Florida Southern	45	7
O4	•	North Carolina St. TAM	27	0
O11	•	Auburn JacF	7	0
O18	•	at Chicago	19	0
O25		Furman	13	14
N1	=	Georgia SAV	0	0
N8		Alabama	0	20
N15	•	Clemson JacF	27	0
N27	•	at Georgia Tech	55	7
D6	•	Tennessee JacF	6	13

1931   2-6-2 (2-4-2)
O3	•	at North Carolina St.	34	0
O10	•	North Carolina	0	0
O17		at Syracuse	12	33
O24	•	Auburn JacF	13	12
O31	•	Georgia	6	33
N7		Alabama BIRM	0	41
N14		South Carolina	6	6
N21		at Georgia Tech	0	23
N26		at UCLA	0	13
D5		Kentucky JacF	2	7

1932   3-6-0 (1-6-0)
O8	•	Sewanee JacF	19	0
O15	•	Citadel	27	7
O22	•	North Carolina St. TAM	6	17
O29		at Georgia	12	33
N4		at North Carolina	13	18
N12		Auburn MONT	6	21
N19		Georgia Tech	0	6
D3		Tennessee JacF	13	32
D17	•	UCLA	12	2

1933-PRESENT
SEC

D.K. STANLEY
1933-35 (.517)   14-13-2

1933   5-3-1 (2-3-0)
S30	•	Stetson	28	0
O7	•	Sewanee JacF	31	0
O14	=	at North Carolina St.	0	0
O21	•	North Carolina	9	0
O28		at Tennessee	6	13
N4		Georgia JacF	0	14
N11		at Georgia Tech	7	19
N25	•	Auburn	14	7
D2	•	Maryland TAM	19	0

1934 — 6-3-1 (2-2-1)

S29	●	Rollins JacF	13	2
O6	●	at Virginia Tech	20	13
O13	|	Tulane	12	28
O20	●	North Carolina St. Tam	14	0
O27		Maryland Balt	0	21
N3	|	Georgia JacF	0	14
N10	= |	Mississippi	13	13
N17	● |	Auburn Mont	14	7
N24	● |	Georgia Tech	13	12
D1	●	Stetson	14	0

1935 — 3-7-0 (1-6-0)

S28	●	Stetson	34	0
O12	|	at Tulane	7	19
O19	|	at Mississippi	6	27
O26		Maryland	6	20
N2	|	Georgia JacF	0	7
N9	|	at Kentucky	6	15
N16	● |	Sewanee	20	0
N23	|	at Georgia Tech	6	39
N30	|	Auburn Mia	6	27
D7	●	South Carolina Tam	22	0

JOSH CODY
1936-39 (.419) 17-24-2

1936 — 4-6-0 (1-5-0)

O3	●	Citadel	20	14
O10		at South Carolina	0	7
O17	●	Stetson	32	0
O24	|	at Kentucky	0	7
O31	●	Maryland	7	6
N7	|	Georgia JacF	8	26
N14	● |	Sewanee	18	7
N21	|	at Georgia Tech	14	38
N28	|	Auburn Mont	0	13
D5	|	Mississippi State	0	7

1937 — 4-7-0 (3-4-0)

S25	|	at LSU	0	19
O2	●	Stetson	18	0
O8		at Temple	6	7
O16	● |	Sewanee	21	0
O23	|	at Mississippi State	13	14
O30		at Maryland	7	13
N6	● |	Georgia JacF	6	0
N13		Clemson	9	10
N20	|	Georgia Tech	0	12
N27	|	Auburn JacF	0	14
D4	● |	Kentucky	6	0

1938 — 4-6-1 (2-2-1)

S24		Stetson	14	16
O1	|	at Mississippi State	0	22
O8	● |	Sewanee	10	6
O15		Miami, Fla.	7	19
O22	●	at Tampa	33	0
O29		at Boston College	0	33
N5	|	Georgia JacF	6	19
N12	●	Maryland	21	7
N19	= |	at Georgia Tech	0	0
N26	● |	Auburn JacF	9	7
D3		Temple	12	20

1939 — 5-5-1 (0-3-1)

S23	●	Stetson	21	0
S30		at Texas	0	12
O7	|	Mississippi State	0	14
O12	●	at Boston College	7	0
O21	●	Tampa	7	0
O28	●	at Maryland	14	0
N4		at South Carolina	0	6*
N11	|	Georgia JacF	2	6
N18	●	at Miami, Fla.	13	0
N25	|	Georgia Tech	7	21
N30	= |	at Auburn	7	7

TOM LIEB
1940-45 (.436) 20-26-1

1940 — 5-5-0 (2-3-0)

S28	|	Mississippi State	7	27
O5	●	at Tampa	23	0
O11		Villanova Phil	0	28
O19	●	Maryland	19	0
O26	|	at Tennessee	0	14
N9	● |	Georgia JacF	18	13
N16	●	at Miami, Fla.	46	6
N23	● |	at Georgia Tech	16	7
N30	|	Auburn ColGa	7	20
D7		Texas	0	26

1941 — 4-6-0 (1-3-0)

S20	●	Randolph-Macon	26	0
S27	|	at Mississippi State	0	6
O4	●	Tampa	46	6
O11		Villanova	0	6
O18		at Maryland	12	13
O25	|	at LSU	7	10
N8	|	Georgia JacF	3	19
N15	●	at Miami, Fla.	14	0
N22	● |	Georgia Tech	14	7
D20		UCLA JacF	27	30

1942 — 3-7-0 (1-3-0)

S19		at Jacksonville NAS	7	20
S26	●	Randolph-Macon	45	0
O3	●	at Tampa	26	6
O10	● |	Auburn	6	0
O17		Villanova Phil	3	13
O24	|	Mississippi State	12	26
O31		Maryland DC	0	13
N7	|	Georgia JacF	0	75
N14		at Miami, Fla.	0	12
N21	|	at Georgia Tech	7	20

1943

NO TEAM WWII

1944 — 4-3-0 (0-3-0)

S23	●	Mayport NAS	36	6
S30	|	Mississippi JacF	6	26
O7	●	Jacksonville NAS	26	20
O14	|	at Tennessee	0	40
O28	●	Maryland	14	6
N3	●	at Miami, Fla.	13	0
N11	|	Georgia JacF	12	38

1945 — 4-5-1 (1-3-1)

S22	●	Camp Blanding	31	2
S29	● |	Mississippi JacF	26	13
O6	= |	at Tulane	6	6
O13	|	Vanderbilt	0	7
O19		at Miami, Fla.	6	7
O27	●	La. Lafayette	45	0
N3	|	at Auburn	0	19
N10	|	Georgia JacF	0	34
N17	●	Presbyterian	41	0
N24		at U.S. Amphibians	0	12

RAYMOND WOLF
1946-49 (.359) 13-24-2

1946 — 0-9-0 (0-5-0)

S28	|	Mississippi JacF	7	13
O5	|	at Tulane	13	27
O12	|	at Vanderbilt	0	20
O19		Miami, Fla.	13	20
O26		at North Carolina	19	40
N9	|	Georgia JacF	14	33
N16		Villanova	20	27
N23		North Carolina St. Tam	6	37
N30	|	Auburn	12	47

1947 — 4-5-1 (0-3-1)

S27	|	Mississippi JacF	6	14
O4		North Texas	12	20
O11	|	Auburn Mont	14	20
O18	●	at North Carolina St.	7	6
O25		North Carolina	7	35
N1	●	Furman Tam	34	7
N8	|	Georgia JacF	6	34
N15	= |	at Tulane	7	7
N22	●	at Miami, Fla.	7	6
N29	●	Kansas State	25	7

1948 — 5-5-0 (1-5-0)

S25	|	Mississippi	0	14
O2	●	Tulsa	28	14
O9	● |	Auburn Tam	16	9
O16	●	Rollins	41	12
O23	|	at Georgia Tech	7	42
O30	●	at Furman	39	14
N6	|	Georgia JacF	12	20
N13	|	at Kentucky	15	34
N20	●	Miami, Fla.	27	13
N27	|	at Alabama	28	34

1949 — 4-5-1 (1-4-1)

S24	●	Citadel	13	0
O1	●	at Tulsa	40	7
O8	= |	Auburn Mbl	14	14
O15	|	Vanderbilt JacF	17	22
O22	|	Georgia Tech	14	43
O29	●	Furman	28	27
N5	● |	Georgia JacF	28	7
N12	|	Kentucky Tam	0	35
N18		at Miami, Fla.	13	28
N26	|	Alabama	13	35

BOB WOODRUFF
1950-59 (.554) 53-42-6

1950 — 5-5-0 (2-4-0)

S23	●	Citadel	7	3
S30	●	Duquesne	27	14
O7	|	at Georgia Tech	13	16
O14	● |	Auburn	27	7
O21	● |	at Vanderbilt	31	27
O28	●	Furman	19	7
N4	|	at Kentucky	6	40
N11	|	Georgia JacF	0	6
N18		Miami, Fla.	14	20
N25	|	Alabama JacF	0	34

1951 — 5-5-0 (2-4-0)

S15	●	Wyoming JacF	13	0
S22	●	Citadel	27	7
S29	|	Georgia Tech	0	27
O6	●	at Loyola-Marymount	40	7
O13	|	at Auburn	13	14
O20	● |	Vanderbilt	33	13
O27	|	Kentucky	6	14
N10	|	Georgia JacF	6	7
N17		at Miami, Fla.	6	21
N24	● |	at Alabama	30	21

1952 — 8-3-0 (3-3-0)

S20	●	Stetson	33	6
S27	|	at Georgia Tech	14	17
O4	●	Citadel JacF	33	0
O11	●	Clemson	54	13
O18	|	at Vanderbilt	13	20
O25	● |	Georgia JacF	30	0
N1	● |	Auburn	31	21
N15	|	at Tennessee	12	26
N22	●	Miami, Fla.	43	6
D6	● |	Kentucky	27	0
		GATOR BOWL		
J1	●	Tulsa	14	13

1953 — 3-5-2 (1-3-2)

S19		at Rice	16	20
S26	= |	Georgia Tech	0	0
O3	|	at Kentucky	13	26
O10	●	Stetson	45	0
O17	●	Citadel JacF	60	0
O24	= |	LSU	21	21
O31	|	at Auburn	7	16
N7	● |	Georgia JacF	21	7
N14	|	Tennessee	7	9
N28		at Miami, Fla.	10	14

1954 — 5-5-0 (5-2-0)

S18		at Rice	14	34
S25	● |	at Georgia Tech	13	12
O2	● |	Auburn	19	13
O9		Clemson JacF	7	14
O16	● |	Kentucky	21	7
O23	|	at LSU	7	20
O30	● |	Mississippi State	7	0
N6	|	Georgia JacF	13	14
N13	● |	at Tennessee	14	0
N27		Miami, Fla.	0	14

1955 — 4-6-0 (3-5-0)

S17	● |	Mississippi State	20	14
S24	|	Georgia Tech	7	14
O1	|	at Auburn	0	13
O8	●	George Washington JacF	28	0
O15	● |	LSU	18	14
O22	|	at Kentucky	7	10
N5	● |	Georgia JacF	19	13
N12	|	Tennessee	0	20
N19	|	at Vanderbilt	6	21
N26		at Miami, Fla.	6	7

1956 — 6-3-1 (5-2-0)

S22	● |	at Mississippi State	26	0
S29	=	Clemson	20	20
O6	|	Kentucky	8	17
O13	●	Rice	7	0
O20	● |	at Vanderbilt	21	7
O27	● |	at LSU	21	6
N3	● |	Auburn	20	0
N10	● |	Georgia JacF	28	0
N24	|	Georgia Tech JacF	0	28
D1		Miami, Fla.	7	20

1957 — 6-2-1 (4-2-1)

S28	●	Wake Forest	27	0
O5	● |	at Kentucky	14	7
O19	|	Mississippi State	20	29
O26	● |	LSU	22	14
N2	|	at Auburn	0	13
N9	● |	Georgia JacF	22	0
N16	● |	Vanderbilt	14	7
N23	= |	at Georgia Tech	0	0
N30	●	at Miami, Fla.	14	0

1958 — 6-4-1 (2-3-1)

S20	● |	Tulane	34	14
S27	|	Mississippi State	7	14
O10	●	at UCLA	21	14
O18	= |	Vanderbilt	6	6
O25	|	at LSU	7	10
N1	|	Auburn	5	6
N8	● |	Georgia JacF	7	6
N15	●	Arkansas State	51	7
N22	●	Florida State	21	7
N29	●	Miami, Fla. JacF	12	9
		GATOR BOWL		
D27		Mississippi	3	7

1959 — 5-4-1 (2-4-0)

S18	● |	at Tulane	30	0
S26	● |	Mississippi State	14	13
O3	●	Virginia	55	10
O10	=	at Rice	13	13
O17	|	at Vanderbilt	6	13
O24	|	LSU	0	9
O31	|	at Auburn	0	6
N7	|	Georgia JacF	10	21
N21	●	Florida State	18	8
N28	●	Miami, Fla. JacF	23	14

RAY GRAVES
1960-69 (.686) 70-31-4

1960 — 9-2-0 (5-1-0)

S17	●	George Washington JacF	30	7
S24	●	Florida State	3	0
O1	● |	Georgia Tech	18	17
O8		Rice JacF	0	10
O15	● |	Vanderbilt	12	0
O22	● |	at LSU	13	10
O29	|	Auburn	7	10
N5	● |	Georgia JacF	22	14
N12	● |	Tulane	21	6
N26	●	at Miami, Fla.	18	0
		GATOR BOWL		
D31	●	Baylor	13	12

1961 — 4-5-1 (3-3-0)

S23	●	Clemson	21	17
S30	=	Florida State	3	3
O6	● |	at Tulane	14	3
O14		at Rice	10	19
O21	● |	at Vanderbilt	7	0
O28	|	LSU	0	23
N4	|	at Georgia Tech	0	20
N11	● |	Georgia JacF	21	14
N25	|	at Auburn	15	32
D2		Miami, Fla.	6	15

1962 — 7-4-0 (4-2-0)

S22	● |	Mississippi State JaM	19	9
S29	|	Georgia Tech	0	17
O6		Duke JacF	21	28
O13	●	Texas A&M	42	6
O20	● |	Vanderbilt	42	7
O27	|	at LSU	0	23
N3	● |	Auburn	22	3
N10	● |	Georgia JacF	23	15
N17	●	Florida State	20	7
D1		at Miami, Fla.	15	17
		GATOR BOWL		
D29	●	Penn State	17	7

1963 — 6-3-1 (3-3-1)

S14	|	at Georgia Tech	0	9
S28	= |	Mississippi State	9	9
O5	●	Richmond	35	28
O12	● |	at Alabama	10	6
O19	● |	at Vanderbilt	21	0
O26	|	LSU	0	14
N2	|	at Auburn	0	19
N9	● |	Georgia JacF	21	14
N23	●	at Miami, Fla.	27	21
N30	●	Florida State	7	0

1964 — 7-3-0 (4-2-0)

S19	●	SMU	24	8
S26	● |	Mississippi State JaM	16	13
O10	● |	Mississippi	30	14
O17	●	South Carolina	37	0
O24	|	at Alabama	14	17
O31	● |	Auburn	14	0
N7	|	Georgia JacF	7	14
N21		at Florida State	7	16
N28	●	Miami, Fla.	12	10
D5	● |	at LSU	20	6

1965 7-4-0 (4-2-0)
S18 ● at Northwestern 24 14
S25 | Mississippi State 13 18
O2 ● | LSU 14 7
O9 ● | at Mississippi 17 0
O16 ● North Carolina St. 28 6
O30 | at Auburn 17 28
N6 ● | Georgia JacF 14 10
N13 ● | Tulane 51 13
N20 at Miami, Fla. 13 16
N27 ● Florida State 30 17
SUGAR BOWL
J1 Missouri 18 20

1966 9-2-0 (5-1-0)
S17 ● Northwestern 43 7
S24 ● | Mississippi State 28 7
O1 ● | at Vanderbilt 13 0
O8 ● at Florida State 22 19
O15 ● at North Carolina St. 17 10
O22 ● | at LSU 28 7
O29 ● | Auburn 30 27
N5 | Georgia JacF 10 27
N12 ● || Tulane 31 10
N26 Miami, Fla. 16 21
ORANGE BOWL
J2 ● Georgia Tech 27 12

1967 6-4-0 (4-2-0)
S23 ● Illinois 14 0
S30 ● | Mississippi State JaM 24 7
O7 | LSU 6 37
O14 ● at Tulane 35 0
O28 ● | Vanderbilt 27 22
N4 | at Auburn 21 26
N11 ● | Georgia JacF 17 16
N18 ● | Kentucky 28 12
N25 Florida State 16 21
D9 at Miami, Fla. 13 20

1968 6-3-1 (3-2-1)
S21 ● Air Force TAM 23 20
S28 ● at Florida State 9 3
O5 ● | Mississippi State 31 14
O12 ● || Tulane 24 3
O19 at North Carolina 7 22
O26 = | at Vanderbilt 14 14
N2 | Auburn 13 24
N9 | Georgia JacF 0 51
N16 ● | at Kentucky 16 14
N30 ● Miami, Fla. 14 10

1969 9-1-1 (3-1-1)
S20 ● Houston 59 34
S27 ● | Mississippi State JaM 47 35
O4 ● Florida State 21 6
O11 ● Tulane TAM 18 17
O18 ● North Carolina 52 2
O25 ● | Vanderbilt 41 20
N1 | at Auburn 12 38
N8 = | Georgia JacF 13 13
N15 ● | Kentucky 31 6
N29 ● at Miami, Fla. 35 16
GATOR BOWL
D27 ● Tennessee 14 13

DOUG DICKEY
1970-78 (.573) 58-43-2

1970 7-4-0 (3-3-0)
S12 ● Duke JacF 21 19
S19 ● | Mississippi State 34 13
S26 | at Alabama 15 46
O3 ● North Carolina St. 14 6
O10 ● at Florida State 38 27
O17 ● Richmond 20 0
O24 | at Tennessee 7 38
O31 | Auburn 14 63
N7 ● | Georgia JacF 24 17
N14 ● | Kentucky TAM 24 13
N28 Miami, Fla. 13 14

1971 4-7-0 (1-6-0)
S11 Duke TAM 6 12
S18 | Mississippi State JaM 10 13
S25 | Alabama 0 38
O2 | Tennessee 13 20
O9 | at LSU 7 48
O16 ● Florida State 17 15
O23 ● Maryland 27 23
O30 | at Auburn 7 40
N6 | Georgia JacF 7 49
N13 ● | Kentucky 35 24
N27 ● at Miami, Fla. 45 16

1972 5-5-1 (3-3-1)
S23 SMU TAM 14 21
S30 ● | Mississippi State 28 13
O7 ● at Florida State 42 13
O14 | at Alabama 7 24
O21 ● | at Mississippi 16 0
N4 | Auburn 20 26
N11 | Georgia JacF 7 10
N18 ● | Kentucky 40 0
N25 = | LSU 3 3
D2 ● Miami, Fla. 17 6
D9 North Carolina JacF 24 28

1973 7-5-0 (3-4-0)
S15 ● Kansas State 21 10
S22 ● Southern Miss TAM 14 13
S29 | Mississippi State JaM 12 33
O6 | at LSU 3 24
O13 | Alabama 14 35
O20 | Mississippi 10 13
N3 ● | at Auburn 12 8
N10 ● | Georgia JacF 11 10
N17 ● | Kentucky 20 18
N24 ● at Miami, Fla. 14 7
D1 ● Florida State 49 0
TANGERINE BOWL
D22 Miami, Ohio 7 16

1974 8-4-0 (3-3-0)
S14 ● California 21 17
S21 ● Maryland TAM 17 10
S28 ● | Mississippi State 29 13
O5 ● | LSU 24 14
O12 | at Vanderbilt 10 24
O19 ● at Florida State 24 14
O26 ● Duke 30 13
N2 ● | Auburn 25 14
N9 | Georgia 16 17
N16 | at Kentucky 24 41
N30 ● Miami, Fla. 31 7
SUGAR BOWL
D31 Nebraska 10 13

1975 9-3-0 (5-1-0)
S13 ● SMU 40 14
S20 at North Carolina St. 7 8
S27 ● | Mississippi State JaM 27 10
O4 ● | at LSU 34 6
O11 ● | Vanderbilt 35 0
O18 ● Florida State 34 8
O25 ● Duke 24 16
N1 ● | at Auburn 31 14
N8 | Georgia JacF 7 10
N15 ● | Kentucky 48 7
N29 ● at Miami, Fla. 15 11
GATOR BOWL
D29 Maryland 0 13

1976 8-4-0 (4-2-0)
S11 North Carolina TAM 21 24
S18 ● Houston 49 14
S25 ● | Mississippi State 34 30
O2 ● | LSU 28 23
O16 ● at Florida State 33 26
O23 ● | at Tennessee 20 18
O30 ● | Auburn 24 19
N6 | Georgia JacF 27 41
N13 | at Kentucky 9 28
N20 ● Rice 50 22
N27 ● Miami, Fla. Orl 19 10
SUN BOWL
J2 Texas A&M 14 37

1977 6-4-1 (3-3-0)
S17 ● at Rice 48 3
S24 ● | Mississippi State JaM 24 22
O1 | at LSU 14 36
O8 = Pittsburgh 17 17
O22 ● | Tennessee 27 17
O29 | at Auburn 14 29
N5 ● | Georgia JacF 22 17
N12 | Kentucky 7 14
N19 ● Utah 38 29
N26 ● at Miami, Fla. 31 14
D3 Florida State 9 37

1978 4-7-0 (3-3-0)
S16 SMU Orl 25 35
S30 ● | Mississippi State 34 0
O7 | LSU 21 34
O14 | at Alabama 12 23
O21 ● Army 31 7
O28 at Georgia Tech 13 17
N4 ● | Auburn 31 7
N11 | Georgia JacF 22 24
N18 ● | at Kentucky 18 16
N25 at Florida State 21 38
D2 Miami, Fla. 21 22

CHARLEY PELL
1979-84 (.556) 33-26-3

1979 0-10-1 (0-6-0)
S15 at Houston 10 14
S22 = Georgia Tech 7 7
S29 | Mississippi State JaM 10 24
O6 | at LSU 3 20
O13 | Alabama 0 40
O27 Tulsa 10 20
N3 | at Auburn 13 19
N10 | Georgia JacF 10 33
N17 | Kentucky 3 31
N24 Florida State 16 27
D1 at Miami, Fla. 24 30

1980 8-4-0 (4-2-0)
S13 ● California TAM 41 13
S20 ● at Georgia Tech 45 12
S27 ● | Mississippi State 21 15
O4 | LSU 7 24
O18 ● | at Mississippi 15 3
O25 ● Louisville 13 0
N1 ● | Auburn 21 10
N8 | Georgia JacF 21 26
N15 ● | at Kentucky 17 15
N29 Miami, Fla. 7 31
D6 at Florida State 13 17
TANGERINE BOWL
D20 ● Maryland 35 20

1981 7-5-0 (3-3-0)
S5 at Miami, Fla. 20 21
S12 ● Furman 35 7
S19 ● Georgia Tech 27 6
S26 | Mississippi State JaM 7 28
O3 ● | at LSU 24 10
O10 ● Maryland 15 10
O17 ● | Mississippi 49 3
O31 | at Auburn 12 14
N7 | Georgia JacF 21 26
N14 ● | Kentucky 33 12
N28 ● Florida State 35 3
PEACH BOWL
D31 West Virginia 6 26

1982 8-4-0 (3-3-0)
S4 ● Miami, Fla. 17 14
S11 ● Southern California 17 9
S25 ● | Mississippi State 27 17
O2 | LSU 13 24
O9 | at Vanderbilt 29 31
O16 ● West Texas St. 77 14
O30 ● | Auburn 19 17
N6 | Georgia JacF 0 44
N13 ● | at Kentucky 39 13
N20 ● at Tulane 21 7
D4 ● at Florida State 13 10
BLUEBONNET BOWL
D31 Arkansas 24 28

1983 9-2-1 (4-2-0)
S3 ● Miami, Fla. 28 3
S10 = at Southern California 19 19
S17 ● Indiana St. 17 13
S24 ● | at Mississippi State 35 12
O1 ● | at LSU 31 17
O8 ● | Vanderbilt 29 10
O22 ● East Carolina 24 17
O29 | at Auburn 21 28
N5 | Georgia JacF 9 10
N12 ● | Kentucky 24 7
D3 ● Florida State 53 14
GATOR BOWL
D30 ● Iowa 14 6

GALEN HALL
1984-89 (.686) 40-18-1

1984 9-1-1 (5-0-1)
S1 Miami, Fla. TAM 20 32
S8 = | LSU 21 21
S15 ● Tulane 63 21
S29 ● | Mississippi State 27 12
O6 ● Syracuse 16 0
O13 ● | at Tennessee 43 30
O20 ● Cincinnati 48 17
N3 ● | Auburn 24 3
N10 ● | Georgia JacF 27 0
N17 ● | at Kentucky 25 17
D1 ● at Florida State 27 17

1985 9-1-1 (5-1-0)
S7 ● at Miami, Fla. 35 23
S14 = Rutgers 28 28
S28 ● | at Mississippi State 36 22
O5 ● | at LSU 20 0
O12 ● | Tennessee 17 10
O19 ● La. Lafayette 45 0
O26 ● Virginia Tech 35 18
N2 ● | at Auburn 14 10
N9 | Georgia JacF 3 24
N16 ● | Kentucky 15 13
N30 ● Florida State 38 14

1986 6-5-0 (2-4-0)
A30 ● Georgia Southern 38 14
S6 Miami, Fla. 15 23
S20 | Alabama 7 21
S27 | at Mississippi State 10 16
O4 | LSU 17 28
O11 ● Kent State 52 9
O18 ● Rutgers ERut 15 3
N1 ● | Auburn 18 17
N8 ● | Georgia JacF 31 19
N15 | at Kentucky 3 10
N29 ● at Florida State 17 13

1987 6-6-0 (3-3-0)
S5 at Miami, Fla. 4 31
S12 ● Tulsa 52 0
S19 ● Alabama Birm 23 14
S26 ● | Mississippi State 38 3
O3 | at LSU 10 13
O10 ● Fullerton St. 65 0
O17 ● Temple 34 3
O31 | at Auburn 6 29
N7 | Georgia JacF 10 23
N14 ● | Kentucky 27 14
N28 Florida State 14 28
ALOHA BOWL
D25 UCLA 16 20

1988 7-5-0 (4-3-0)
S3 ● Montana St. 69 0
S10 ● | Mississippi JaM 27 15
S17 ● Indiana St. 58 0
S24 ● | Mississippi State 17 0
O1 ● | LSU 19 6
O8 Memphis 11 17
O15 | at Vanderbilt 9 24
O29 | Auburn 0 16
N5 | Georgia JacF 3 26
N12 ● | at Kentucky 24 19
N26 at Florida State 17 52
ALL-AMERICAN BOWL
D29 ● Illinois 14 10

GARY DARNELL
1989 (.429) 3-4

1989 7-5-0 (4-3-0)
S9 | Mississippi 19 24
S16 ● Louisiana Tech 34 7
S23 ● at Memphis 38 13
S30 ● | Mississippi State TAM 21 0
O7 ● | at LSU 16 13
O14 ● | Vanderbilt 34 11
O21 ● New Mexico 27 21
N4 | at Auburn 7 10
N11 | Georgia JacF 10 17
N18 ● | Kentucky 38 28
D2 Florida State 17 24
FREEDOM BOWL
D30 Washington 7 34

STEVE SPURRIER
1990-01 (.817) 122-27-1

1990 9-2-0 (6-1-0)
S8 ● Oklahoma State 50 7
S15 ● | at Alabama 17 13
S22 ● Furman 27 3
S29 ● | Mississippi State 34 21
O6 ● | LSU 34 8
O13 | at Tennessee 3 45
O20 ● Akron 59 0
N3 ● | Auburn 48 7
N10 ● | Georgia JacF 38 7
N17 ● | at Kentucky 47 15
D1 at Florida State 30 45

1991 10-2-0 (7-0-0)

Date		Opponent		Pts	Opp
S7	●	San Jose State		59	21
S14	●	Alabama		35	0
S21		at Syracuse		21	38
S28	●	Mississippi State	Orl	29	7
O5	●	at LSU		16	0
O12		Tennessee		35	18
O19		Northern Illinois		41	10
N2		at Auburn		31	10
N9		Georgia	JacF	45	13
N16	●	Kentucky		35	26
N30	●	Florida State		14	9
		SUGAR BOWL			
J1		Notre Dame		28	39

1992 9-4-0 (6-2-0)

Date		Opponent		Pts	Opp
S12	●	Kentucky		35	19
S19		at Tennessee		14	31
O1		at Mississippi State		6	30
O10		LSU		28	21
O17		Auburn		24	9
O24		Louisville		31	17
O31	●	Georgia	JacF	26	24
N7	●	Southern Miss		24	20
N14	●	South Carolina		14	9
N21	●	at Vanderbilt		41	21
N28	●	at Florida State		24	45
		SEC CHAMPIONSHIP GAME			
D5		Alabama	Birm	21	28
		GATOR BOWL			
D31	●	North Carolina St.		27	10

1993 11-2-0 (7-1-0)

Date		Opponent		Pts	Opp
S4	●	Arkansas State		44	6
S11	●	at Kentucky		24	20
S18	●	Tennessee		41	34
O2	●	Mississippi State		38	24
O9	●	at LSU		58	3
O16		at Auburn		35	38
O30	●	Georgia	JacF	33	26
N6		La. Lafayette		61	14
N13	●	at South Carolina		37	26
N20	●	Vanderbilt		52	0
N27		Florida State		21	33
		SEC CHAMPIONSHIP GAME			
D4	●	Alabama	Birm	28	13
		SUGAR BOWL			
J1	●	West Virginia		41	7

1994 10-2-1 (7-1-0)

Date		Opponent		Pts	Opp
S3	●	New Mexico St.		70	21
S10	●	Kentucky		73	7
S17	●	at Tennessee		31	0
O1	●	at Mississippi		38	14
O8	●	LSU		42	18
O15		Auburn		33	36
O29	●	Georgia		52	14
N5	●	Southern Miss		55	17
N12	●	South Carolina		48	17
N19	●	at Vanderbilt		24	7
N26	=	at Florida State		31	31
		SEC CHAMPIONSHIP GAME			
D3	●	Alabama	Atl	24	23
		SUGAR BOWL			
J2		Florida State		17	23

1995 12-1-0 (8-0-0)

Date		Opponent		Pts	Opp
S2	●	Houston		45	21
S9	●	at Kentucky		42	7
S16	●	Tennessee		62	37
S30	●	Mississippi		28	10
O7	●	at LSU		28	10
O14	●	at Auburn		49	38
O28	●	at Georgia		52	17
N4	●	Northern Illinois		58	20
N11	●	at South Carolina		63	7
N18	●	Vanderbilt		38	7
N25	●	Florida State		35	24
		SEC CHAMPIONSHIP GAME			
D2	●	Arkansas	Atl	34	3
		FIESTA BOWL			
J2		Nebraska		24	62

1996 12-1 (8-0)

Date		Opponent		Pts	Opp
A30	●	La. Lafayette		55	21
S7	●	Georgia So.		62	14
S21	●	at Tennessee		35	29
S28	●	Kentucky		65	0
O5	●	at Arkansas		42	7
O12	●	LSU		56	13
O19	●	Auburn		51	10
N2	●	Georgia	JacF	47	7
N9	●	at Vanderbilt		28	21
N16	●	South Carolina		52	25
N30		at Florida State		21	24
		SEC CHAMPIONSHIP GAME			
D7	●	Alabama	Atl	45	30
		SUGAR BOWL			
J2	●	Florida State		52	20

1997 10-2 (6-2)

Date		Opponent		Pts	Opp
A30	●	Southern Miss		21	6
S6	●	Central Michigan		82	6
S20	●	Tennessee		33	20
S27	●	at Kentucky		55	28
O4	●	Arkansas		56	7
O11		at LSU		21	28
O18	●	at Auburn		24	10
N1		Georgia	JacF	17	37
N8	●	Vanderbilt		20	7
N15	●	at South Carolina		48	21
N22	●	Florida State		32	29
		FLORIDA CITRUS BOWL			
J1	●	Penn State		21	6

1998 10-2 (7-1)

Date		Opponent		Pts	Opp
S5	●	Citadel		49	10
S12	●	La. Monroe		42	10
S19		at Tennessee		17	20
S26	●	Kentucky		51	35
O3	●	at Alabama		16	10
O10	●	LSU		22	10
O17	●	Auburn		24	3
O31	●	Georgia	JacF	38	7
N7	●	at Vanderbilt		45	13
N14	●	South Carolina		33	14
N21		at Florida State		12	23
		ORANGE BOWL			
J2	●	Syracuse		31	10

1999 9-4 (7-1)

Date		Opponent		Pts	Opp
S4	●	Western Michigan		55	26
S11	●	Central Florida		58	27
S18	●	Tennessee		23	21
S25	●	at Kentucky		38	10
O2	●	Alabama		39	40
O9	●	at LSU		31	10
O16	●	at Auburn		32	14
O30	●	Georgia	JacF	30	14
N6	●	Vanderbilt		13	6
N13	●	at South Carolina		20	3
N20		Florida State		23	30
		SEC CHAMPIONSHIP GAME			
D4		Alabama	Atl	7	34
		FLORIDA CITRUS BOWL			
J1		Michigan State		34	37

2000 10-3 (7-1)

Date		Opponent		Pts	Opp
S2	●	Ball State		40	19
S9	●	Middle Tennessee		55	0
S16	●	at Tennessee		27	23
S23	●	Kentucky		59	31
S30		at Mississippi State		35	47
O7	●	LSU		41	9
O14	●	Auburn		38	7
O28	●	Georgia	JacF	34	23
N4	●	at Vanderbilt		43	20
N11	●	South Carolina		41	21
N18		at Florida State		7	30
		SEC CHAMPIONSHIP GAME			
D2	●	Auburn	Atl	28	6
		SUGAR BOWL			
J2		Miami, Fla.		20	37

2001 10-2 (6-2)

Date		Opponent		Pts	Opp
S1	●	Marshall		49	14
S8	●	La. Monroe		55	6
S22	●	at Kentucky		44	10
S29	●	Mississippi State		52	0
O6	●	at LSU		44	15
O13		at Auburn		20	23
O27	●	Georgia	JacF	24	10
N3	●	Vanderbilt		71	13
N10	●	at South Carolina		54	17
N17	●	Florida State		37	13
D1		Tennessee		32	34
		ORANGE BOWL			
J1	●	Maryland		56	23

2002 8-5 (6-2)

Date		Opponent		Pts	Opp
A31	●	UAB		51	3
S7		Miami, Fla.		16	41
S14	●	Ohio U.		34	6
S21		at Tennessee		30	13
S28	●	Kentucky		41	34
O5		at Mississippi		14	17
O12		LSU		7	36
O19	●	Auburn		30	23
N2	●	Georgia	JacF	20	13
N9	●	at Vanderbilt		21	17
N16	●	South Carolina		28	7
N30		at Florida State		14	31
		OUTBACK BOWL			
J1		Michigan		30	38

2003 8-5 (6-2)

Date		Opponent		Pts	Opp
A30	●	San Jose State		65	3
S6	●	at Miami, Fla.		33	38
S13	●	Florida A&M		63	3
S20		Tennessee		10	24
S27	●	at Kentucky		24	21
O4	●	Mississippi		17	20
O11	●	at LSU		19	7
O18	●	at Arkansas		33	28
N1	●	Georgia	JacF	16	13
N8	●	Vanderbilt		35	17
N15	●	at South Carolina		24	22
N29		Florida State		34	38
		OUTBACK BOWL			
J1	●	Iowa		17	37

2004 7-5 (4-4)

Date		Opponent		Pts	Opp
S11	●	Eastern Michigan		49	10
S18	●	at Tennessee		28	30
S25	●	Kentucky		20	3
O2	●	Arkansas		45	30
O9		LSU		21	24
O16	●	Middle Tennessee		52	16
O23		at Mississippi State		31	38
O30		Georgia	JacF	24	31
N6	●	at Vanderbilt		34	17
N13	●	South Carolina		48	14
N20		at Florida State		20	13
		PEACH BOWL			
D31		Miami, Fla.		10	27

2005 9-3 (5-3)

Date		Opponent		Pts	Opp
S3	●	Wyoming		32	14
S10	●	Louisiana Tech		41	3
S17	●	Tennessee		16	7
S24	●	at Kentucky		49	28
O1		at Alabama		3	31
O8	●	Mississippi State		35	9
O15		at LSU		17	21
O29	●	Georgia	JacF	14	10
N5	●	Vanderbilt		49	42
N12		at South Carolina		22	30
N26	●	Florida State		34	7
		OUTBACK BOWL			
J2	●	Iowa		31	24

2006 13-1 (7-1)

Date		Opponent		Pts	Opp
S2	●	Southern Mississippi		34	7
S9	●	Central Florida		42	0
S16	●	at Tennessee		21	20
S23	●	Kentucky		26	7
S30	●	Alabama		28	13
O7	●	LSU		23	10
O14		at Auburn		17	27
O28	●	Georgia	JacF	21	14
N4	●	at Vanderbilt		25	19
N11	●	South Carolina		17	16
N18	●	Western Carolina		62	0
N25	●	at Florida State		21	14
		SEC CHAMPIONSHIP GAME			
D2	●	Arkansas	Atl	38	28
		BCS CHAMPIONSHIP GAME			
J8	●	Ohio State	GlAz	41	14

2007 9-4 (5-3)

Date		Opponent		Pts	Opp
S1	●	Western Kentucky		49	3
S8	●	Troy State		59	31
S15	●	Tennessee		59	20
S22	●	at Mississippi		30	24
S29		Auburn		17	20
O6		at LSU		24	28
O20	●	at Kentucky		45	37
O27		Georgia	JacF	30	42
N3	●	Vanderbilt		49	22
N10	●	at South Carolina		51	31
N17	●	Florida Atlantic		59	20
N24	●	Florida State		45	12
		CAPITAL ONE BOWL			
J1	●	Michigan		35	41

2008 13-1 (7-1)

Date		Opponent		Pts	Opp
A30	●	Hawaii		56	10
S6	●	Miami FL		26	3
S20	●	at Tennessee		30	6
S27		Mississippi		30	31
O4	●	at Arkansas		38	7
O11	●	Louisiana State		51	21
O25	●	Kentucky		63	5
N1		Georgia	Jax	49	10
N8	●	at Vanderbilt		42	14
N15	●	South Carolina		56	6
N22	●	The Citadel		70	19
N29	●	at Florida State		45	15
		SEC CHAMPIONSHIP GAME			
D6	●	Alabama	Atl	31	20
		BCS CHAMPIONSHIP GAME			
J8	●	Oklahoma	Mia	24	14

THE SCHOOLS

Neutral Site key: Atl Atlanta, GA / Balt Baltimore, MD / Birm Birmingham, AL / ColGa Columbus, GA / DC Washington, DC / ERut East Rutherford, NJ / GlAz Glendale, AZ / JacF Jacksonville, FL / JaM Jackson, MS / MBL Mobile, AL / Ori Orlando, FL / Pal Palatka, FL / Phil Philadelphia, PA / Sav Savannah, GA / StP St. Petersburg, FL / Tam Tampa, FL / Unk Unknown Unknown / Val Valdosta, GA
ƒ Forfeit † Game Later Forfeited # Disputed Victor * Disputed Score ‖ Designated Conference Game |2 Counted Twice in Conference Standings

THE SCHOOLS

FLORIDA ANNUAL STATISTICAL LEADERS

YR	RUSHING	YDS	ATT	AVG	PASSING	ATT	CMP	PCT	YDS	RECEIVING	REC	YDS	AVG
1955	Jackie Simpson	422	65	6.5	Richard Allen	56	17	.30	273	Jim Roundtree	8	110	13.8
1956	Ed Sears	370	84	4.4	Jimmy Dunn	34	15	.44	268	Jim Roundtree	9	176	19.6
1957		NA	NA	NA		NA	NA	NA	NA	Jim Roundtree	8	171	21.4
1958	Bob Milby	288	53	5.4	Mickey Ellenburg	36	15	.42	238	Don Hudson	8	118	14.8
1959	John MacBeth	257	59	4.4	Richard Allen	80	31	.39	613	Perry McGriff	14	360	25.7
1960	Don Goodman	454	95	4.8	Bobby Dodd	55	30	.55	448	Bob Hoover	10	108	10.8
1961	Don Goodman	413	111	3.7	Tom Batten	67	30	.45	460	Russ Brown	13	239	18.4
1962	Larry Dupree	604	113	5.3	Tom Shannon	100	56	.56	551	Russ Brown	15	227	15.1
1963	Larry Dupree	745	189	3.9	Tom Shannon	158	84	.53	956	Russ Brown	12	113	9.4
1964	Larry Dupree	376	101	3.7	Steve Spurrier	114	65	.57	943	Charles Casey	47	673	14.3
1965	Alan Poe	366	83	4.4	Steve Spurrier	287	148	.52	1,893	Charles Casey	58	809	13.9
1966	Larry Smith	742	162	4.6	Steve Spurrier	291	179	.62	2,012	Richard Trapp	63	872	13.8
1967	Larry Smith	754	205	3.7	Larry Rentz	140	80	.57	1,031	Richard Trapp	58	708	12.2
1968	Larry Smith	690	152	4.5	Jackie Eckdahl	125	56	.45	572	Guy McTheny	34	347	10.2
1969	Tommy Durrance	731	189	3.9	John Reaves	396	222	.56	2,896	Carlos Alvarez	88	1,329	15.1
1970	Tommy Durrance	584	167	3.5	John Reaves	376	188	.50	2,549	Carlos Alvarez	44	717	16.3
1971	Mike Rich	481	106	4.5	John Reaves	356	193	.54	2,104	Carlos Alvarez	40	517	12.9
1972	Nat Moore	845	145	5.8	David Bowden	229	198	.86	1,480	Nat Moore	25	351	14.0
1973	Vince Kendrick	516	127	4.1	David Bowden	113	62	.55	711	Lee McGriff	38	703	18.5
1974	Tony Green	856	133	6.4	Don Gaffney	87	37	.43	621	Lee McGriff	36	698	19.4
1975	Jimmy DuBose	1,307	191	6.8	Don Gaffney	90	42	.47	755	Wes Chandler	20	457	22.9
1976	Willie Wilder	654	101	6.5	Jimmy Fisher	146	83	.57	1,511	Wes Chandler	44	967	22.0
1977	Tony Green	696	119	5.8	Terry LeCount	134	62	.46	848	Wes Chandler	25	490	19.6
1978	Calvin Davis	497	126	3.9	John Brantley	170	85	.50	1,334	Cris Collinsworth	39	745	19.1
1979	Johnell Brown	306	104	2.9	Larry Ochab	185	98	.53	1,169	Cris Collinsworth	41	593	14.5
1980	James Jones	657	150	4.4	Wayne Peace	180	91	.51	1,271	Cris Collinsworth	40	599	15.0
1981	James Jones	617	166	3.7	Wayne Peace	273	159	.58	1,803	Spencer Jackson	39	449	11.5
1982	James Jones	752	150	5.0	Wayne Peace	246	174	.71	2,053	Dwayne Dixon	45	589	13.1
1983	Neal Anderson	835	162	5.2	Wayne Peace	292	186	.64	2,079	Dwayne Dixon	47	596	12.7
1984	Neal Anderson	916	157	5.8	Kerwin Bell	184	98	.53	1,614	John L. Williams	21	276	13.1
1985	Neal Anderson	1,034	238	4.3	Kerwin Bell	288	180	.63	2,687	John L. Williams	44	369	8.4
1986	Octavius Gould	562	156	3.6	Kerwin Bell	242	131	.54	1,515	Ricky Nattiel	44	679	15.4
1987	Emmitt Smith	1,341	229	5.9	Kerwin Bell	239	140	.59	1,769	Stacey Simmons	25	392	15.7
1988	Emmitt Smith	988	187	5.3	Kyle Morris	167	84	.50	1,217	Tony Lomack	22	276	12.5
1989	Emmitt Smith	1,599	284	5.6	Kyle Morris	131	65	.50	1,098	Emmitt Smith	21	207	9.9
1990	Errict Rhett	845	148	5.7	Shane Matthews	378	229	.61	2,952	Kirk Kirkpatrick	55	770	14.0
1991	Errict Rhett	1,109	224	5.0	Shane Matthews	361	218	.60	3,130	Willie Jackson	51	725	14.2
1992	Errict Rhett	903	250	3.6	Shane Matthews	463	275	.59	3,205	Willie Jackson	62	772	12.5
1993	Errict Rhett	1,289	247	5.2	Danny Wuerffel	273	159	.58	2,230	Jack Jackson	51	949	18.6
1994	Fred Taylor	873	171	5.1	Danny Wuerffel	212	132	.62	1,754	Jack Jackson	57	855	15.0
1995	Elijah Williams	858	114	7.5	Danny Wuerffel	325	210	.65	3,266	Chris Doering	70	1,045	14.9
1996	Elijah Williams	671	106	6.3	Danny Wuerffel	360	207	.58	3,625	Reidel Anthony	72	1,293	18.0
1997	Fred Taylor	1,292	214	6.0	Doug Johnson	269	148	.55	2,023	Jacquez Green	61	1,024	16.8
1998	Terry Jackson	587	105	5.6	Doug Johnson	274	154	.56	2,346	Travis McGriff	70	1,357	19.4
1999	Earnest Graham	654	117	5.6	Doug Johnson	337	190	.56	2,574	Darrell Jackson	67	1,156	17.3
2000	Robert Gillespie	678	125	5.4	Rex Grossman	223	116	.52	1,866	Jabar Gaffney	71	1,184	16.7
2001	Earnest Graham	650	125	5.2	Rex Grossman	395	259	.66	3,896	Jabar Gaffney	67	1,191	17.8
2002	Earnest Graham	1,085	240	4.5	Rex Grossman	503	287	.57	3,402	Taylor Jacobs	71	1,088	15.3
2003	Ron Carthon	595	119	5.0	Chris Leak	320	190	.59	2,435	Ben Troupe	39	638	16.4
2004	Ciatrick Fason	1,267	222	5.7	Chris Leak	399	238	.60	3,197	O.J. Small	63	719	11.4
2005	DeShawn Wynn	621	130	4.8	Chris Leak	374	235	.63	2,639	Chad Jackson	88	900	10.2
2006	DeShawn Wynn	699	143	4.9	Chris Leak	365	232	.64	2,942	Dallas Baker	60	920	15.3
2007	Tim Tebow	895	210	4.3	Tim Tebow	350	234	.67	3,286	Percy Harvin	59	858	14.5
2008	Tim Tebow	673	176	3.8	Tim Tebow	298	192	.64	2,746	Percy Harvin	40	644	16.1

Receiving leaders by receptions
The NCAA began including postseason stats in 2002

FLORIDA RECORD BOOK

SINGLE-GAME RECORDS

Rushing Yards	316	Emmitt Smith (Oct. 21, 1989 vs. New Mexico)
Passing Yards	464	Rex Grossman (Oct. 6, 2001 vs. LSU)
Receiving Yards	246	Taylor Jacobs (Aug. 31, 2002 vs. UAB)
All-Purpose Yards	316	Emmitt Smith, (Oct. 21, 1989)
Points	30	Tim Tebow (Nov. 10, 2007, vs. South Carolina)
Field Goals	6	Bobby Raymond (Nov. 17, 1984 vs. Kentucky)
Tackles	NA	
Interceptions	3	Five players tied

SINGLE-SEASON RECORDS

Rushing Yards	1,599	Emmitt Smith, 1989 (284 att.)
Passing Yards	3,896	Rex Grossman, 2001 (287-503)
Receiving Yards	1,357	Travis McGriff, 1998 (NA)
All-Purpose Yards	1,086	Emmitt Smith, 1989
Scoring	138	Tim Tebow, 2007 (23 TDs)
Touchdowns	23	Tim Tebow, 2007
Tackles	202	Sammy Green, 1977-80
Interceptions	9	Keiwan Ratliff, 2003
Punting Average	44.9	Bobby Joe Green, 1959 (54 punts)
Punt Return Average	26.7	Hal Griffin, 1947 (min. 10 ret.)
Kickoff Return Average	28.2	Jack Jackson, 1993 (17 ret.)

CAREER RECORDS

Rushing Yards	4,163	Errict Rhett, 1990-1993
Passing Yards	11,213	Chris Leak, 2003-2006
Receiving Yards	2,563	Carlos Alvarez, 1969-1971
All-Purpose Yards	5,393	Errict Rhett 1990-1993
Scoring	368	Jeff Chandler 1997-2001
Touchdowns	43	Tim Tebow, 2006-present
Tackles	475	David Little 1977-1980
Interceptions	15	Fred Weary, 1994-1997
Punting Average	44.4	Ray Criswell, 1982-1985 (161 punts)
Punt Return Average	18.6	Hal Griffin, 1946-1949 (min. 25 ret.)
Kickoff Return Average	26.1	Jack Johnson, 1992-94 (min. 30 ret.)

TEAM RECORDS

Longest Winning Streak	12	Sept. 12, 1995-Dec. 2 1995; broken vs. Nebraska, 24-62 on Jan. 2, 1996
Longest Undefeated Streak	18	Sept. 8, 1984-Nov. 2, 1985; broken vs. Georgia, 3-24 on Nov. 9, 1985
Most Consecutive Winning Seasons	21	1988-present
Most Consecutive Bowl Appearances	18	1991-present
Most Points in a Game	144	vs. Florida Southern, Oct. 6, 1913
Most Points Allowed in a Game	75	vs. Georgia, Nov. 7, 1942
Largest Margin of Victory	144	vs. Florida Southern, Oct. 6, 1913
Largest Margin of Defeat	75	vs. Georgia, Nov. 7, 1942
Longest Pass Play	99	Derrick Gaffney from Cris Collinsworth vs. Rice, Sept. 17, 1977 (tied NCAA record)
Longest Field Goal	60	Chris Perkins vs. Tulane, Sept. 15, 1984
Longest Punt	99	Bobby Joe Green vs. Georgia, Nov. 8, 1958
Longest Interception Return	60	Jackie Simpson vs. Mississipi State, Sept. 17, 1955

RETIRED NUMBERS

NO RETIRED JERSEYS

ALL-TIME TEAM

Chosen by The Gainesville Sun *in 1999*

Offense			Defense		
	G	Burton Lawless, 1972-74		DE	Jack Youngblood, 1968-70
	G	Donnie Young, 1993-96		DE	Kevin Carter, 1991-94
	T	Lomas Brown, 1981-84		DT	Brad Culpepper, 1988-91
	T	David Williams, 1985-88		DT	Ellis Johnson, 1991-94
	C	Jeff Mitchell, 1993-96		LB	Scot Brantley, 1976-79
	TE	Jim Yarbrough, 1966-68		LB	David Little, 1977-79
	WR	Carlos Alvarez, 1969-71		LB	Wilber Marshall, 1980-83
	WR	Wes Chandler, 1974-77		CB	Steve Tannen, 1967-69
	QB	Danny Wuerffel, 1993-96		CB	Jarvis Wiliams, 1984-87
	RB	Neal Anderson, 1982-85		S	Bruce Bennett, 1963-65
	RB	Emmitt Smith, 1987-89		S	Louis Oliver, 1985-88
	PK	Judd Davis, 1992-94		P	Bobby Joe Green, 1985-88
	KR	Jacquez Green, 1995-97			

FLORIDA BOWL HISTORY

SEASON	BOWL	DATE	PRE-GAME RANK	TEAMS	SCORE	FINAL RANK	MOST VALUABLE PLAYER(S)	ATT.
1952	GATOR	Jan. 1, 1953	15 12	Florida Tulsa	14 13		John Hall, Florida, RB Marv Matuszak, Tulsa, T	30,015
1958	GATOR	Dec. 27, 1958	11 14	Mississippi Florida	7 3		Bobby Franklin, Mississippi, QB Dave Hudson, Florida, E	41,312
1960	GATOR	Dec. 31, 1960	12 18	Florida Baylor	13 12		Larry Libertore, Florida, QB Bobby Ply, Baylor, QB	50,112
1962	GATOR	Dec. 29, 1962	9	Florida Penn State	17 7		Tom Shannon, Florida, Florida, QB Dave Robinson, Penn State, E	50,026
1965	SUGAR	Jan. 1, 1966	6	Missouri Florida	20 18	6	Steve Spurrier, Florida, QB	73,024
1966	ORANGE	Jan. 2, 1967	8	Florida Georgia Tech	27 12		Larry Smith, Florida, TB	75,562
1969	GATOR	Dec. 27, 1969	15 11	Florida Tennessee	14 13		Ernie Pinckert, Southern California, HB	75,562
1973	TANGERINE	Dec. 22, 1973	15	Miami (Ohio) Florida	16 7	15	Chuck Varner, Miami, B Brad Cousino, Miami, L	37,234
1974	SUGAR	Dec. 31, 1974	8 18	Nebraska Florida	13 10	9 15	Tony Davis, Nebraska, FB	68,890
1975	GATOR	Dec. 29, 1975	17 13	Maryland Florida	13 0	13	Steve Atkins, Maryland, TB Sammy Green, Florida, LB	64,012
1976	SUN	Jan. 2, 1977	10	Texas A&M Florida	37 14	7	Tony Franklin, Texas A&M, K Edgar Fields, Texas A&M, DT	33,252
1980	TANGERINE	Dec. 20, 1980		Florida Maryland	35 20		Cris Collinsworth, Florida, WR	52,541
1981	PEACH	Dec. 31, 1981		West Virginia Florida	26 6	17	Mickey Walczak, West Virginia, RB Don Stemple, West Virginia, DB	37,582
1982	BLUEBONNET	Dec. 31, 1982	14	Arkansas Florida	28 24	9	Gary Anderson, Arkansas, RB Dwayne Dixon, Florida, WR	31,557
1983	GATOR	Dec. 30, 1983	11 10	Florida Iowa	14 6	6 14	Tony Lilly, Florida, S Own Gill, Iowa, FB	81,293
1987	ALOHA	Dec. 25, 1987	10	UCLA Florida	20 16	9	Troy Aikman, UCLA, QB Emmitt Smith, Florida, RB	24,839
1988	ALL-AMERICAN	Dec. 29, 1988		Florida Illinois	14 10		Emmitt Smith, Florida, RB	48,218
1989	FREEDOM	Dec. 30, 1989		Washington Florida	34 7	23	Cary Conklin, Washington, QB Huey Richardson, Florida, LB	33,858
1991	SUGAR	Jan. 1, 1992	18 3	Notre Dame Florida	39 28	13 7	Jerome Bettis, Notre Dame, FB	76,447
1992	GATOR	Dec. 31, 1992	14 12	Florida North Carolina St.	27 10	10 17	Errict Rhett, Florida, RB Reggie Lawerence, North Carolina St., WR	71,233
1993	SUGAR	Jan. 1, 1994	8 3	Florida West Virginia	41 7	5 7	Errict Rhett, Florida, RB	75, 437
1994	SUGAR	Jan. 2, 1995	7 5	Florida State Florida	23 17	4 7	Warrick Dunn, Florida State, RB	76,224
1995	FIESTA	Jan. 2, 1996	1 2	Nebraska Florida	62 24	1 2	Tommie Frazier, Nebraska, QB Michael Booker, Nebraska, CB	75,562
1996	SUGAR	Jan. 1, 1997	3 1	Florida Florida State	52 20	1 3	Danny Wuerffel, Florida, QB	78,347
1997	FLORIDA CITRUS	Jan. 1, 1998	6 11	Florida Penn State	21 6	4 16	Fred Taylor, Florida, TB	72,940
1998	ORANGE	Jan. 2, 1999	7 18	Florida Syracuse	31 10	5 25	Travis Taylor, Florida, WR	67, 919
1999	FLORIDA CITRUS	Jan. 1, 2000	9 10	Michigan State Florida	37 34	7 12	Plaxico Burress, Michigan State, WR	62,011
2000	SUGAR	Jan. 1, 2001	2 7	Miami (Fla.) Florida	37 20	2 10	Ken Dorsey, Miami (Fla.), QB	64,407
2001	ORANGE	Jan. 2, 2002	5 6	Florida Maryland	56 23	3 11	Taylor Jacobs, Florida, WR	75,562
2002	OUTBACK	Jan. 1, 2003	12 22	Michigan Florida	38 30	9	Chris Perry, Michigan, TB	65,101
2003	OUTBACK	Jan. 1, 2004	13 17	Iowa Florida	37 17	8 24	Fred Russell, Iowa, RB	65,657
2004	PEACH	Dec. 31, 2004	14 20	Miami (Fla.) Florida	27 10	11	Roscoe Parrish, Miami (Fla.), WR Devin Hester, Miami (Fla.), CB	69,322
2005	OUTBACK	Jan. 2, 2006	16 25	Florida Iowa	31 24	12	Dallas Baker, Florida, WR	65,881
2006	BCS CHAMPIONSHIP	Jan. 8, 2007	2 1	Florida Ohio State	41 14	1 2	Chris Leak, Florida, QB Derrick Harvey, Florida, DE	74,628
2007	CAPITAL ONE	Jan. 1, 2008	9	Michigan Florida	41 35	18 13	Chad Henne, Michigan, QB	69,748
2008	BCS CHAMPIONSHIP	Jan. 8, 2009	2 1	Florida Oklahoma	24 14	1 5	Tim Tebow, Florida, QB	78,468

JANUARY 1, 1953 | GATOR
FLORIDA 14, TULSA 13

	1ST	2ND	3RD	4TH	FINAL
UF	7	7	0	0	14
UT	0	0	7	6	13

SCORING SUMMARY

UF	Casares 2 run (Casares kick)
UF	Hall 37 pass from Robinson (Casares kick)
UT	Roberts 3 run (Miner kick)
UT	Waugh 2 run (kick failed)

UF	TEAM STATISTICS	UT
20	First Downs	17
233	Rushing Yards	182
7-11-1	Passing	10-16-1
101	Passing Yards	132
334	Total Yards	314
1-38.0	Punts - Average	4-31.0
5-4	Fumbles - Lost	3-1
4-34	Penalties - Yards	11-84

INDIVIDUAL LEADERS

RUSHING
UF: Hall 17-94; Casares 21-86, 1 TD.
UT: Kercher 16-71; Waugh 15-64, 1 TD.

PASSING
UF: Dickey 4-5-0, 65 yards; Robinson 3-6-1, 35 yards, 1 TD.
UT: Morris 10-16-1, 132 yards.

RECEIVING
UF: Hall 2-66, 1 TD; O'Brien 2-22.
TUL: Miner 6-77; Roberts 3-41.

DECEMBER 27, 1958 | GATOR
MISSISSIPPI 7, FLORIDA 3

	1ST	2ND	3RD	4TH	FINAL
MISS	7	0	0	0	7
UF	3	0	0	0	3

SCORING SUMMARY

MISS	Anderson 1 run (Khayat kick)
UF	FG Booker 17

MISS	TEAM STATISTICS	UF
9	First Downs	12
157	Rushing Yards	157
2-7-0	Passing	5-11-1
27	Passing Yards	58
184	Total Yards	215
10-34.4	Punts - Average	7-44.1
5-2	Fumbles - Lost	5-3
2-10	Penalties - Yards	3-35

INDIVIDUAL LEADERS

RUSHING
MISS: Anderson 9-62, 1 TD; Lovelace 7-28.
UF: Newbern 5-59; Milby 10-35.

PASSING
MISS: Franklin 2-7-0, 27 yards.
UF: Dunn 5-11-1, 58 yards.

RECEIVING
MISS: Grantham 1-15; Daniels 1-12.
UF: Hudson 3-22; Dilts 1-13.

DECEMBER 31, 1960 | GATOR
FLORIDA 13, BAYLOR 12

	1ST	2ND	3RD	4TH	FINAL
UF	0	13	0	0	13
UT	0	0	0	12	12

SCORING SUMMARY

UF	Goodman 3 run (Cash kick)
UF	Travis fumble recovery in end zone (kick failed)
BU	Goodwin 12 pass from Ply (kick failed)
BU	Bull 3 run (pass failed)

UF	TEAM STATISTICS	BU
11	First Downs	15
176	Rushing Yards	40
5-8-0	Passing	13-27-0
57	Passing Yards	211
233	Total Yards	251
7-37.0	Punts - Average	5-33.0
3-1	Fumbles - Lost	4-3
6-70	Penalties - Yards	1-5

INDIVIDUAL LEADERS

RUSHING
UF: Libertore 14-61; Goodman 10-28, 1 TD.
BU: Bull 14-53, 1 TD.

PASSING
UF: Libertore 2-3-0, 36 yards.
BU: Ply 12-24-0, 161 yards, 1 TD.

RECEIVING
UF: Infante 3-47.
BU: Goodwin 7-129, 1 TD; Davis 3-33.

DECEMBER 29, 1962 | GATOR
FLORIDA 17, PENN STATE 7

	1ST	2ND	3RD	4TH	FINAL
UF	3	7	0	7	17
PSU	0	7	0	0	7

SCORING SUMMARY

UF	FG Hall 43
UF	Dupree 7 pass from Shannon (Hall kick)
PSU	Liske 1 run (Coates kick)
UF	Clarke 19 pass from Shannon (Hall kick)

UF	TEAM STATISTICS	PSU
14	First Downs	8
162	Rushing Yards	89
8-13-1	Passing	5-21-2
86	Passing Yards	58
248	Total Yards	147
6-23.8	Punts - Average	6-40.8
4-1	Fumbles - Lost	4-3
5-42	Penalties - Yards	2-10

INDIVIDUAL LEADERS

RUSHING
UF: Dupree 25-66; Mack 10-33.
PSU: Kochman 6-51; Hayes 10-25.

PASSING
UF: Shannon 7-9-1, 79 yards, 2 TD.
PSU: Liske 5-18-1, 58 yards.

RECEIVING
UF: Clarke 2-27, 1 TD; Brown 3-25.
PSU: Powell 4-40; Yost 1-18.

JANUARY 1, 1966 | SUGAR
MISSOURI 20, FLORIDA 18

	1ST	2ND	3RD	4TH	FINAL
MO	0	17	3	0	20
UF	0	0	0	18	18

SCORING SUMMARY

MO	Brown 16 run (Bates kick)
MO	Denny 11 pass from Roland (Bates kick)
MO	FG Bates 27
MO	FG Bates 34
UF	Harper 22 pass from Spurrier (pass failed)
UF	Casey 21 pass from Spurrier (pass failed)
UF	Spurrier 2 run (pass failed)

MO	TEAM STATISTICS	UF
18	First Downs	18
257	Rushing Yards	-2
5-14-1	Passing	22-45-1
50	Passing Yards	352
307	Total Yards	350
6-32.0	Punts - Average	8-44.0
2-2	Fumbles - Lost	1-1

INDIVIDUAL LEADERS

RUSHING
MO: Brown 23-121, 1 TD; Lane 19-76.
UF: Poe 2-11.

PASSING
MO: Lane 4-13-1, 39 yards.
UF: Spurrier 22-45-1, 352 yards, 2 TD.

RECEIVING
MO: Phelps 2-11.
UF: Casey 5-108, 1 TD; Brown 9-88; Harper 4-66, 1 TD.

JANUARY 2, 1967 | ORANGE
FLORIDA 27, GEORGIA TECH 12

	1ST	2ND	3RD	4TH	FINAL
UF	0	7	7	13	27
GT	6	0	0	6	12

SCORING SUMMARY

GT	Baynham 10 pass from King (run failed)
UF	McKeel 1 run (Barfield kick)
UF	Smith 94 run (Barfield kick)
UF	McKeel 1 run (Barfield kick)
GT	Good 25 run (pass failed)
UF	Coons 5 pass from Wages (pass failed)

UF	TEAM STATISTICS	GT
22	First Downs	17
289	Rushing Yards	197
15-32-1	Passing	16-22-4
165	Passing Yards	128
454	Total Yards	325
7-36.1	Punts - Average	6-42.3
1-1	Fumbles - Lost	2-1
4-32	Penalties - Yards	5-42

INDIVIDUAL LEADERS

RUSHING
UF: Smith 23-187, 1 TD; McKeel 3-50, 2 TD.
GT: Snow 24-110; Good 3-24, 1 TD.

PASSING
UF: Spurrier 14-30-1, 160 yards.
GT: Good 3-6-1, 86 yards; King 3-16-3, 42 yards, 1 TD.

RECEIVING
UF: Trapp 5-43; Coons 3-35, 1 TD.
GT: Snow 1-52; Smith 2-32.

DECEMBER 27, 1969 | GATOR
FLORIDA 14, TENNESSEE 13

	1ST	2ND	3RD	4TH	FINAL
UF	7	0	7	0	14
TENN	0	10	0	3	13

SCORING SUMMARY

UF	Kelley 8 blocked punt return (Franco kick)
TENN	FG Hunt 20
TENN	McClain 12 pass from Scott (Hunt kick)
UF	Alvarez 9 pass from Reaves (Franco kick)
TENN	FG Hunt 26

UF	TEAM STATISTICS	TENN
15	First Downs	23
90	Rushing Yards	214
15-27-0	Passing	12-34-2
161	Passing Yards	174
251	Total Yards	388
7-31.3	Punts - Average	2-15.0
1-1	Fumbles - Lost	1-1
2-58	Penalties - Yards	3-24

INDIVIDUAL LEADERS

RUSHING
UF: Murrance 22-62; Walker 10-33.
TENN: Watson 25-121; Patterson 8-40.

PASSING
UF: Reaves 15-26-0, 161 yards, 1 TD.
TENN: Scott 12-34-2, 174 yards, 1 TD.

RECEIVING
UF: Maliska 6-54; Alvarez 4-51, 1 TD.
TENN: Kreis 4-82; DeLong 5-50.

December 22, 1973 | Tangerine
Miami (Ohio) 16, Florida 7

	1ST	2ND	3RD	4TH	FINAL
MIA	3	0	10	3	16
UF	0	0	0	7	7

SCORING SUMMARY

MIA	FG Draudt 26
MIA	FG Draudt 45
MIA	Varner 3 run (Draudt kick)
UF	Moore 1 run (Williams kick)
MIA	FG Draudt 27

MIA	TEAM STATISTICS	UF
14	First Downs	12
239	Rushing Yards	90
1-8-0	Passing	9-21-4
6	Passing Yards	99
245	Total Yards	189
10-33.3	Punts - Average	6-34.3
2-1	Fumbles - Lost	4-3
3-39	Penalties - Yards	3-27

INDIVIDUAL LEADERS

RUSHING
MIA: Varner 28-157, 1 TD; Hitchens 20-62.
UF: Moore 16-101, 1 TD; Richards 7-49.

PASSING
MIA: Sanna 1-8-0, 6 yards.
UF: Bowden 5-9-1, 66 yards.

RECEIVING
MIA: Williams 1-6.
UF: Moore 3-30; Foldberg 2-25.

December 31, 1974 | Sugar
Nebraska 13, Florida 10

	1ST	2ND	3RD	4TH	FINAL
NEB	0	0	0	13	13
UF	7	3	0	0	10

SCORING SUMMARY

UF	Green 21 run (Posey kick)
UF	FG Posey 40
NEB	Anthony 2 run (Coyle kick)
NEB	FG Coyle 37
NEB	FG Coyle 39

NEB	TEAM STATISTICS	UF
18	First Downs	13
304	Rushing Yards	178
2-14-4	Passing	5-10-1
16	Passing Yards	97
320	Total Yards	275
3-1	Fumbles - Lost	3-1
2-17	Penalties - Yards	5-41

INDIVIDUAL LEADERS

RUSHING
NEB: Davis 17-126; Anthony 15-64, 1 TD.
UF: Dubose 17-84; Green 14-73, 1 TD.

PASSING
NEB: Humm 2-12-4, 16 yards.
UF: Gaffney 5-10-1, 97 yards.

RECEIVING
NEB: Westbrook 2-16.
UF: McGriff 2-52, Darby 1-32.

December 29, 1975 | Gator
Maryland 13, Florida 0

	1ST	2ND	3RD	4TH	FINAL
MD	7	3	0	3	13
UF	0	0	0	0	0

SCORING SUMMARY

MD	Hoover 19 pass from Dick (Sochko kick)
MD	FG Sochko 20
MD	FG Sochko 27

MD	TEAM STATISTICS	UF
15	First Downs	14
209	Rushing Yards	182
7-16-0	Passing	3-19-3
82	Passing Yards	28
291	Total Yards	210
7-39.8	Punts - Average	7-38.5
0-0	Fumbles - Lost	1-1
5-47	Penalties - Yards	6-48

INDIVIDUAL LEADERS

RUSHING
MD: Atkins 20-127; Jennings 9-53.
UF: DuBose 18-95; Green 13-31.

PASSING
MD: Dick 5-13-0, 67 yards, 1 TD.
UF: Fisher 2-12-1, 33 yards.

RECEIVING
MD: Hoover 2-24, 1 TD; Wilson 2-21.
UF: LeCount 1-25; Enclade 1-8.

January 2, 1977 | Sun
Texas A&M 37, Florida 14

	1ST	2ND	3RD	4TH	FINAL
A&M	3	13	8	13	37
FLA	0	0	7	7	14

SCORING SUMMARY

A&M	FG Franklin 39
A&M	Walker 9 run (Franklin kick)
A&M	FG Franklin 62
A&M	FG Franklin
A&M	Woodard 1 run (Woodard run)
FLA	Chandler 29 run (Posey kick)
A&M	Woodard 4 run (Franklin kick)
FLA	LeCount 1 run (Posey kick)
A&M	Woodard 15 pass from Walker (kick failed)

A&M	TEAM STATISTICS	FLA
20	First Downs	14
243	Rushing Yards	172
11-19-1	Passing	7-24-1
122	Passing Yards	50
365	Total Yards	222
5-34.0	Punts - Average	9-39.0
4-3	Fumbles - Lost	4-4
6-33	Penalties - Yards	4-26

INDIVIDUAL LEADERS

RUSHING
A&M: Woodard 25-125, 2 TD; Dickey 15-54.
FLA: Brinson 10-64; Chandler 2-38, 1 TD.

PASSING
A&M: Walker 11-18-1, 122 yards, 1 TD.
FLA: Fisher 5-13-1, 42 yards.

RECEIVING
A&M: Haack 3-42; Woodard 4 -24, 1 TD.
FLA: Chandler 2-29; Green 1-8.

December 20, 1980 | Tangerine
Florida 35, Maryland 20

	1ST	2ND	3RD	4TH	FINAL
UF	0	14	14	7	35
MD	3	6	11	0	20

SCORING SUMMARY

MD	FG Castro 35
UF	Collinsworth 24 pass from Peace (Clark kick)
MD	FG Castro 27
MD	FG Castro 27
UF	Jones 2 run (Clark kick)
MD	Wysocki 1 run (Tice run)
MD	FG Castro 43
UF	Peace 1 run (Clark kick)
UF	Collinsworth 21 pass from Peace (Clark kick)
UF	Brown 2 run (Clark kick)

UF	TEAM STATISTICS	MD
16	First Downs	9
108	Rushing Yards	177
20-34-1	Passing	12-26-3
271	Passing Yards	155
379	Total Yards	332
6-33.7	Punts - Average	4-39.0
1-0	Fumbles - Lost	4-2
11-108	Penalties - Yards	6-44

INDIVIDUAL LEADERS

RUSHING
UF: Brown 6-71, 1 TD; Peace 6-12, 1 TD.
MD: Wysocki 39-159, 1 TD; Fasano 3-13.

PASSING
UF: Peace 20-34-1, 271 yards, 2 TD.
MD: Tice 11-23-3, 129 yards.

RECEIVING
UF: Collinsworth 8-166, 2 TD; Young 8-66.
MD: Havener 4-83; Sievers 3-24.

December 31, 1981 | Peach
West Virginia 26, Florida 6

	1ST	2ND	3RD	4TH	FINAL
WVU	7	9	3	7	26
FLA	0	0	0	6	6

SCORING SUMMARY

WVU	Walczak 7 pass from Luck (Woodside kick)
WVU	FG Woodside 36
WVU	FG Woodside 42
WVU	FG Woodside 49
WVU	FG Woodside 24
WVU	Walczak 1 run (Woodside kick)
FLA	Faulkner 22 pass from Hewko (pass failed)

WVU	TEAM STATISTICS	FLA
19	First Downs	10
194	Rushing Yards	-30
14-23-1	Passing	11-20-2
107	Passing Yards	135
301	Total Yards	105
5-33.0	Punts - Average	6-40.0
1-0	Fumbles - Lost	6-4
4-17	Penalties - Yards	4-39

INDIVIDUAL LEADERS

RUSHING
WVU: Cornwell 26-97; Beck 8-37.
FLA: Jones 9-25.

PASSING
WVU: Luck 14-23-1, 107 yards, 1 TD.
FLA: Hewko 5-7-0, 88 yards, 1 TD.

RECEIVING
WVU: Walczak 8-75, 1 TD.
FLA: Mularkey 2-36.

December 31, 1982 | Bluebonnet
Arkansas 28, Florida 24

	1ST	2ND	3RD	4TH	FINAL
ARK	7	0	7	14	28
FLA	7	10	7	0	24

SCORING SUMMARY

ARK	Anderson 16 run (Smith kick)
FLA	Dixon 3 pass from Hewko (Raymond kick)
FLA	FG Raymond 34
FLA	Dixon 13 pass from Hewko (Raymond kick)
ARK	Anderson 1 run (Smith kick)
FLA	Dixon 17 pass from Hewko (Raymond kick)
ARK	Clark 5 pass from Jones (Smith kick)
ARK	Jones 1 run (Smith kick)

ARK	TEAM STATISTICS	FLA
28	First Downs	23
356	Rushing Yards	171
7-12-1	Passing	19-29-1
122	Passing Yards	234
478	Total Yards	405
3-43.3	Punts - Average	4-45.8
5-36	Penalties - Yards	6-50

INDIVIDUAL LEADERS

RUSHING
ARK: Anderson 26-161, 2 TD; Clark 17-77.
FLA: Jones 12-89; Hampton 21-61.

PASSING
ARK: Taylor 5-7-1, 123 yards; Jones 2-5-0, minus-1 yards, 1 TD.
FLA: Hewko 19-28-0, 234 yards, 3 TD; Jones 0-1-1, 0 yards.

RECEIVING
ARK: White 1-40; Anderson 3-37.
FLA: Dixon 8-106, 3 TD; Hampton 2-37.

DECEMBER 30, 1983 | GATOR
FLORIDA 14, IOWA 6

	1ST	2ND	3RD	4TH	FINAL
UF	7	7	0	0	14
IA	0	3	3	0	6

SCORING SUMMARY

UF	Anderson 1 run (Raymond kick)
IA	FG Nichol 32
UF	Drew fumble recovery in end zone (Raymond kick)
IA	FG Nichol 31

UF	TEAM STATISTICS	IA
14	First Downs	16
168	Rushing Yards	114
9-23-2	Passing	13-30-4
92	Passing Yards	167
260	Total Yards	281
7-37.5	Punts - Average	2-40.0
0-0	Fumbles - Lost	2-1
12-105	Penalties - Yards	7-44

INDIVIDUAL LEADERS

RUSHING
UF: Anderson 17-84, 1 TD; Williams 10-68.
IA: Gill 10-83; Granger 9-37.

PASSING
UF: Peace 9-22-2, 92 yards.
IA: Long 13-29-4, 167 yards.

RECEIVING
UF: Dixon 5-55.
IA: Harmon 6-90.

DECEMBER 25, 1987 | ALOHA
UCLA 20, FLORIDA 16

	1ST	2ND	3RD	4TH	FINAL
UCLA	3	7	7	3	20
UF	7	3	0	6	16

SCORING SUMMARY

UCLA	FG Velasco 34
UF	Simmons 7 pass from Bell (McGinty kick)
UF	FG McGinty 32
UCLA	Brown 1 run (Velasco kick)
UCLA	Thompson 5 pass from Aikman (Velasco kick)
UCLA	FG Velasco 32
UF	Williams 14 pass from Bell (kick failed)

UCLA	TEAM STATISTICS	UF
15	First Downs	24
48	Rushing Yards	185
19-30-2	Passing	19-38-0
173	Passing Yards	188
221	Total Yards	373

INDIVIDUAL LEADERS

RUSHING
UCLA: Ball 23-49; Brown 10-29, 1 TD.
UF: Smith 17-128; Williams 8-43.

PASSING
UCLA: Aikman 19-30-0, 173 yards, 1 TD.
UF: Bell 19-38-0, 188 yards, 2 TD.

RECEIVING
UCLA: Anderson 4-52; Pickert 3-37.
UF: Snead 3-62; Smith 4-19.

DECEMBER 29, 1988 | ALL-AMERICAN
FLORIDA 14, ILLINOIS 10

	1ST	2ND	3RD	4TH	FINAL
FLA	7	0	0	7	14
ILL	0	7	0	3	10

SCORING SUMMARY

FLA	Smith 55 run (Francis kick)
ILL	Jones 30 run (Higgins kick)
ILL	FG Higgins 44
FLA	Smith 2 run (Francis kick)

FLA	TEAM STATISTICS	ILL
12	First Downs	17
187	Rushing Yards	55
8-16-2	Passing	20-38-2
69	Passing Yards	194
256	Total Yards	249
3-10	Punt Returns - Yards	0-0
3-90	Kickoff Returns - Yards	3-60
4-29.8	Punts - Average	7-35.3
1-1	Fumbles - Lost	1-1
5-36	Penalties - Yards	8-59
26:38	Possession Time	33:22

INDIVIDUAL LEADERS

RUSHING
FLA: Smith 28-159, 2 TD; McClendon 9-34.
ILL: Jones 18-88, 1 TD; Griffith 5-8.

PASSING
FLA: Morris 6-12-2, 50 yards.
ILL: George 20-37-2, 194 yards.

RECEIVING
FLA: Barber 4-29; Smith 2-19.
ILL: Bellamy 5-49; Williams 5-49.

DECEMBER 30, 1989 | FREEDOM
WASHINGTON 34, FLORIDA 7

	1ST	2ND	3RD	4TH	FINAL
WASH	17	10	0	7	34
UF	7	0	0	0	7

SCORING SUMMARY

WASH	Bailey 21 pass from Conklin (McCallum kick)
UF	Douglas 67 run (Francis kick)
WASH	FG McCallum 21
WASH	Riley 10 pass from Conklin (McCallum kick)
WASH	Fields recovered blocked punt in end zone (McCallum kick)
WASH	FG McCallum 32
WASH	Brunell 20 run (Jolley kick)

WASH	TEAM STATISTICS	UF
28	First Downs	10
191	Rushing Yards	83
24-44-0	Passing	11-28-1
242	Passing Yards	148
433	Total Yards	231
7-37.0	Punts - Average	8-32.9
0-0	Fumbles - Lost	7-3
9-86	Penalties - Yards	9-85

INDIVIDUAL LEADERS

RUSHING
WASH: Lewis 27-97; Turner 7-38.
UF: Douglas 9-65, 1 TD; Smith 7-17.

PASSING
WASH: Conklin 21-39-0, 217 yards, 2 TD.
UF: Douglas 8-18-1, 91 yards.

RECEIVING
WASH: McKay 5-83; Lewis 6-44.
UF: Barber 2-41.

JANUARY 1, 1992 | SUGAR
NOTRE DAME 39, FLORIDA 28

	1ST	2ND	3RD	4TH	FINAL
ND	0	7	10	22	39
UF	10	6	0	12	28

SCORING SUMMARY

UF	Jackson 15 pass from Matthews (Czyzewski kick)
UF	FG Czyzewski 26
UF	FG Czyzewski 24
ND	Dawson 40 pass from Mirer (Hentrich kick)
UF	FG Czyzewski 36
ND	FG Pendergast 23
ND	Smith 4 pass from Mirer (Hentrich kick)
UF	FG Czyzewski 37
UF	FG Czyzewski 24
ND	Bettis 3 run (Brooks pass from Mirer)
ND	Bettis 49 run (Pendergast kick)
UF	Houston 36 pass from Matthews (pass failed)
ND	Bettis 39 run (Pendergast kick)

ND	TEAM STATISTICS	UF
23	First Downs	29
279	Rushing Yards	141
14-19-1	Passing	28-58-2
154	Passing Yards	370
433	Total Yards	511
4-3	Fumbles - Lost	0-0
3-15	Penalties - Yards	4-40
29:00	Possession Time	31:00

INDIVIDUAL LEADERS

RUSHING
ND: Bettis 16-150, 3 TD; Culver 13-93; Brooks 13-68.
UF: Rhett 15-63; McClendon 7-34.

PASSING
ND: Mirer 14-19-1, 154 yards, 2 TD.
UF: Matthews 28-58-2, 370 yards, 2 TD.

RECEIVING
ND: Smith 7-75; Dawson 2-49, 1 TD.
UF: Jackson 8-148, 1 TD; Houston 3-52, 1 TD; Sullivan 4-47.

DECEMBER 31, 1992 | GATOR
FLORIDA 27, NC STATE 10

	1ST	2ND	3RD	4TH	FINAL
UF	0	10	10	7	27
NCST	0	0	3	7	10

SCORING SUMMARY

UF	FG Davis 26
UF	Matthews 1 run (Davis kick)
UF	Jackson 17 pass from Matthews (Davis kick)
NCST	FG Videtich 23
UF	FG Davis 42
NCST	Shaw 11 pass from Jordan (Videtich kick)
UF	Houston 34 pass from Matthews (Davis kick)

UF	TEAM STATISTICS	NCST
26	First Downs	13
221	Rushing Yards	82
19-38-0	Passing	22-42-2
247	Passing Yards	213
468	Total Yards	295
5-41.0	Punts - Average	11-39.3
3-2	Fumbles - Lost	2-1
6-44	Penalties - Yards	1-10

INDIVIDUAL LEADERS

RUSHING
UF: Rhett 30-182; Matthews 8-8, 1 TD.
NCST Barbour 11-50.

PASSING
UF: Matthews 19-38-0, 247 yards, 2 TD.
NCST: Jordan 22-42-2, 213 yards, 1 TD.

RECEIVING
UF: Rhett 7-60; Jackson 3-42, 1 TD; Houston 2-40, 1 TD.
NCST: Lawrence 5-77; Auer 5-48; Shaw 5-33, 1 TD.

THE SCHOOLS

JANUARY 1, 1994 | SUGAR
FLORIDA 41, WEST VIRGINIA 7

	1ST	2ND	3RD	4TH	FINAL
UF	7	14	14	6	41
WVU	7	0	0	0	7

SCORING SUMMARY
WVU   Kearney 32 pass from Kelchner (Mazzone kick)
UF   Rhett 3 run (Davis kick)
UF   Wright 52 interception return (Davis kick)
UF   Jackson 39 pass from Dean (Davis kick)
UF   Rhett 2 run (Davis kick)
UF   Rhett 1 run (Davis kick)
UF   FG Davis 43
UF   FG Davis 26

UF	TEAM STATISTICS	WVU
30	First Downs	16
201	Rushing Yards	122
24-39-1	Passing	16-40-1
280	Passing Yards	143
481	Total Yards	265
2-1	Fumbles - Lost	2-1
5-43	Penalties - Yards	8-71
33:22	Possession Time	26:38

INDIVIDUAL LEADERS
RUSHING
UF: Rhett 25-105, 3 TD; Foy 10-53.
WVU: Walker 13-59; Woodard 2-18.

PASSING
UF: Dean 22-37-1, 244 yards, 1 TD.
WVU: Kelchner 13-27-0, 123 yards, 1 TD.

RECEIVING
UF: W. Jackson 9-131; J. Jackson 3-32.
WVU: Kearney 4-59, 1 TD; Baker 4-46.

JANUARY 2, 1995 | SUGAR
FLORIDA STATE 23, FLORIDA 17

	1ST	2ND	3RD	4TH	FINAL
FSU	3	17	3	0	23
UF	3	7	0	7	17

SCORING SUMMARY
FSU   FG Mowrey 21
UF   FG Davis 22
FSU   Ellison 73 pass from Dunn (Mowrey kick)
FSU   McCorvey 16 pass from Kanell (Mowrey kick)
UF   Hilliard 82 pass from Wuerffel (Davis kick)
FSU   FG Mowrey 24
FSU   FG Mowrey 45
UF   Wuerffel 1 run (Davis kick)

FSU	TEAM STATISTICS	UF
21	First Downs	23
76	Rushing Yards	5
24-41-0	Passing	30-43-1
325	Passing Yards	449
401	Total Yards	454
4-39.0	Punts - Average	3-45.7
0-0	Fumbles - Lost	2-2
0-0	Penalties - Yards	2-2
27:56	Possession Time	32:04

INDIVIDUAL LEADERS
RUSHING
FSU: Dunn 14-58; Crockett 5-19.
UF: Williams 10-27; Taylor 8-18.

PASSING
FSU: Kanell 23-40-0, 252 yards, 1 TD.
UF: Wuerffel 28-39-1, 394 yards, 1 TD.

RECEIVING
FSU: Ellison 4-102, 1 TD; McCorvey 4-84, 1 TD.
UF: Jackson 6-128; Hilliard 3-119, 1 TD.

JANUARY 2, 1996 | FIESTA
NEBRASKA 62, FLORIDA 24

	1ST	2ND	3RD	4TH	FINAL
NEB	6	29	14	13	62
UF	10	0	8	6	24

SCORING SUMMARY
UF   FG Edmiston 23
NEB   Phillips 16 pass from Frazier (kick blocked)
UF   Wuerffel 1 run (Edmiston kick)
NEB   Phillips 42 run (Brown kick)
NEB   Safety (Wuerffel sacked in end zone)
NEB   Green 1 run (Brown kick)
NEB   FG Brown 26
NEB   Booker 42 interception return (Brown kick)
NEB   FG Brown 24
NEB   Frazier 35 run (Brown kick)
UF   Hilliard 35 pass from Wuerffel (Anthony pass from Wuerffel)
NEB   Frazier 75 run (Brown kick)
NEB   Phillips 15 run (kick blocked)
NEB   Berringer 1 run (Retzlaff kick)
UF   Anthony 93 kickoff return (run failed)

NEB	TEAM STATISTICS	UF
27	First Downs	15
524	Rushing Yards	-28
6-15-2	Passing	20-38-3
105	Passing Yards	297
629	Total Yards	269
1-36.0	Punts - Average	4-41.3
1-0	Fumbles - Lost	1-1
4-30	Penalties - Yards	9-78

INDIVIDUAL LEADERS
RUSHING
NEB: Frazier 16-199, 2 TD; Phillips 25-165, 3 TD; Green 9-68, 1 TD.
UF: Williams 6-6.

PASSING
NEB: Frazier 6-14-2, 105 yards, 1 TD.
UF: Wuerffel 17-31-3, 255 yards, 1 TD.

RECEIVING
NEB: Johnson 2-43; Holbein 1-33.
UF: Doering 8-123; Hilliard 6-100, 1 TD.

JANUARY 2, 1997 | SUGAR
FLORIDA 52, FLORIDA STATE 20

	1ST	2ND	3RD	4TH	FINAL
UF	10	14	14	14	52
FSU	3	14	3	0	20

SCORING SUMMARY
UF   Hilliard 5 pass from Wuerffel (Edmiston kick)
FSU   FG Bentley 43
UF   FG Edmiston 32
UF   Taylor 2 run (Edmiston kick)
FSU   Green 29 pass from Busby (Bentley kick)
UF   Hilliard 31 pass from Wuerffel (Edmiston kick)
FSU   Dunn 12 run (Bentley kick)
FSU   FG Bentley 45
UF   Hilliard 8 pass from Wuerffel (Edmiston kick)
UF   Wuerffel 16 run (Edmiston kick)
UF   Jackson 42 run (Edmiston kick)
UF   Jackson 1 run (Edmiston kick)

UF	TEAM STATISTICS	FSU
26	First Downs	13
203	Rushing Yards	70
18-34-1	Passing	17-42-2
306	Passing Yards	271
509	Total Yards	341
7-48.1	Punts - Average	8-46.4
1-0	Fumbles - Lost	0-0
15-102	Penalties - Yards	14-115
36:27	Possession Time	23:33

INDIVIDUAL LEADERS
RUSHING
UF: Jackson 12-118, 2 TD; Taylor 18-60, 1 TD.
FSU: Dunn 9-29, 1 TD.

PASSING
UF: Wuerffel 18-34-1, 306 yards, 3 TD.
FSU: Busby 17-41-1, 271 yards, 1 TD.

RECEIVING
UF: Hilliard 7-150, 3 TD; Green 5-79; Anthony 4-50.
FSU: Green 3-86, 1 TD; Cooper 4-82.

JANUARY 1, 1998 | FLORIDA CITRUS
FLORIDA 21, PENN STATE 6

	1ST	2ND	3RD	4TH	FINAL
UF	14	0	0	7	21
PSU	0	3	3	0	6

SCORING SUMMARY
UF   Brindise 1 run (Cooper kick)
UF   Green 35 pass from Johnson (Cooper kick)
PSU   FG Forney 42
PSU   FG Jackson 30
UF   Green 37 pass from Palmer (Cooper kick)

UF	TEAM STATISTICS	PSU
23	First Downs	9
254	Rushing Yards	47
9-19-2	Passing	10-32-3
143	Passing Yards	92
397	Total Yards	139
5-36.4	Punts - Average	7-42.1
2-1	Fumbles - Lost	0-0
5-46	Penalties - Yards	1-5

INDIVIDUAL LEADERS
RUSHING
UF: Taylor 43-234; Carroll 9-28.
PSU: Eberly 14-53; Watson 4-5.

PASSING
UF: Johnson 5-12-1, 77 yards, 1 TD; Brindise 3-6-1, 29 yards.
PSU: McQuery 10-32-3, 92 yards.

RECEIVING
UF: Green 2-72, 2 TD; Taylor 1-19.
PSU: Brown 3-25; Natasi 2-26.

JANUARY 2, 1999 | ORANGE
FLORIDA 31, SYRACUSE 10

	1ST	2ND	3RD	4TH	FINAL
FLA	14	14	0	3	31
SYR	0	3	0	7	10

SCORING SUMMARY
FLA   Taylor 51 pass from Johnson (Chandler kick)
FLA   Taylor 26 pass from Johnson (Chandler kick)
SYR   FG Trout 36
FLA   Kinney 4 pass from Palmer (Chandler kick)
FLA   Palmer 2 run (Chandler kick)
FLA   FG Chandler 32
SYR   M. Jackson 62 pass from McNabb (Trout kick)

FLA	TEAM STATISTICS	SYR
18	First Downs	18
133	Rushing Yards	129
22-31-0	Passing	14-30-1
308	Passing Yards	192
441	Total Yards	321
7-36.9	Punts - Average	5-43.0
0-0	Fumbles - Lost	3-3
11-76	Penalties - Yards	2-20
31:48	Possession Time	28:12

INDIVIDUAL LEADERS
RUSHING
FLA: Jackson 21-108; Taylor 2-16.
SYR: McNabb 20-72; Brown 5-31.

PASSING
FLA: Johnson 12-17-0, 195 yards, 2 TD; Palmer 10-14-0, 113 yards, 1 TD.
SYR: McNabb 14-30-1, 192 yards, 1 TD.

RECEIVING
FLA: Taylor 7-159, 2 TD; Karim 4-79.
SYR: M.Jackson 1-62, 1 TD; K. Johnson 4-49.

January 1, 2000 | Florida Citrus
Michigan State 37, Florida 34

	1ST	2ND	3RD	4TH	FINAL
MSU	3	17	6	11	37
UF	7	14	6	7	34

SCORING SUMMARY
MSU FG Edinger 46
UF Taylor 12 pass from Johnson (Chandler kick)
MSU Burress 37 pass from Burke (Edinger kick)
MSU Turner 24 fumble return (Edinger kick)
UF Taylor 8 pass from Johnson (Chandler kick)
MSU FG Edinger 20
UF Johnson 1 run (Chandler kick)
MSU Burress 21 pass from Burke (pass failed)
UF Taylor 39 pass from Johnson (pass failed)
UF Gillespie 2 run (Chandler kick)
MSU Burress 30 pass from Burke (Scott pass from Burke)
MSU FG Edinger 39

MSU	TEAM STATISTICS	UF
25	First Downs	27
143	Rushing Yards	67
21-35-2	Passing	25-51-0
257	Passing Yards	300
400	Total Yards	367
3-43.3	Punts - Average	6-35.5
3-1	Fumbles - Lost	4-2
7-80	Penalties - Yards	10-100
32:49	Possession Time	27:11

INDIVIDUAL LEADERS
RUSHING
MSU: Clemons 20-105; Duckett 14-77.
UF: Gilespie 15-74, 1 TD; Carroll 5-14.
PASSING
MSU: Burke 21-35-2, 257 yards, 3 TD.
UF: Johnson 24-50-0, 288 yards, 3 TD.
RECEIVING
MSU: Burress 13-185, 3 TD; Baker 2-21.
UF: Taylor 11-156, 3 TD; Jackson 5-61.

January 2, 2001 | Sugar
Miami (Fla.) 37, Florida 20

	1ST	2ND	3RD	4TH	FINAL
MIA	10	3	14	10	37
UF	7	3	7	3	20

SCORING SUMMARY
UF Wells 23 pass from Grossman (Chandler kick)
MIA FG Sievers 44
MIA Shockey 8 pass from Dorsey (Sievers kick)
MIA FG Sievers 29
UF FG Chandler 51
UF Graham 36 run (Chandler kick)
MIA Williams 19 pass from Dorsey (Sievers kick)
MIA Davenport 2 pass from Dorsey (Sievers kick)
UF FG Chandler 26
MIA FG Sievers 29
MIA Davenport 3 run (Sievers kick)

MIA	TEAM STATISTICS	UF
28	First Downs	25
184	Rushing Yards	140
22-40-2	Passing	24-51-3
270	Passing Yards	312
454	Total Yards	452
2-44.0	Punts - Average	5-46.8
157	Return Yards	120
0	Fumbles Lost	0
11-109	Penalties - Yards	9-79
35:19	Possession Time	24:41

INDIVIDUAL LEADERS
RUSHING
MIA: Portis 18-97; Jackson 12-62.
UF: Graham 15-136, 1 TD.
PASSING
MIA: Dorsey 22-40-2, 270 yards, 3 TD.
UF: Grossman 18-41-3, 312 yards, 1 TD.
RECEIVING
MIA: Moss 6-89; Shockey 4-47, 1 TD.
UF: Caldwell 6-100; Gaffney 7-75.

January 2, 2002 | Orange
Florida 56, Maryland 23

	1ST	2ND	3RD	4TH	FINAL
FLA	14	14	21	7	56
MD	7	3	0	13	23

SCORING SUMMARY
FLA Graham 1 run (Chandler kick)
FLA Jacobs 46 pass from Berlin (Chandler kick)
MD J. Williams 64 pass from Hill (Novak kick)
MD FG Novak 20
FLA Jacobs 15 pass from Grossman (Chandler kick)
FLA Gaffney 4 pass from Grossman (Chandler kick)
FLA Graham 6 run (Chandler kick)
FLA Gillespie 11 run (Chandler kick)
FLA Gaffney 33 pass from Grossman (Chandler kick)
MD Riley 1 run (pass failed)
FLA Perez 10 pass from Grossman (Chandler kick)
MD Riley 10 run (Novak kick)

FLA	TEAM STATISTICS	MD
30	First Downs	19
203	Rushing Yards	103
33-49-2	Passing	23-39-1
456	Passing Yards	257
659	Total Yards	360
2-1	Fumbles - Lost	0-0
6-43	Penalties - Yards	4-20
28:26	Possession Time	31:34

INDIVIDUAL LEADERS
RUSHING
FLA: Graham 16-149, 2 TD; Gillespie 4-63, 1 TD.
MD: Hill 11-31; Riley 9-23, 2 TD.
PASSING
FLA: Grossman 20-28-0, 248 yards, 4 TD; Berlin 11-19-2, 196 yards, 1 TD.
MD: Hill 23-39-1, 257 yards, 1 TD.
RECEIVING
FLA: Jacobs 10-170, 2 TD; Gaffney 7-118, 2 TD; Caldwell 4-47.
MD: J. Williams 4-91, 1 TD; Murphy 5-42.

January 1, 2003 | Outback
Michigan 38, Florida 30

	1ST	2ND	3RD	4TH	FINAL
MICH	7	14	14	3	38
UF	0	16	7	7	30

SCORING SUMMARY
MICH Perry 4 run (Finley kick)
UF Graham 2 run (Leach kick)
UF Graham 1 run (run failed)
MICH Perry 1 run (Finley kick)
UF FG Leach 29
MICH Bellamy 8 pass from Navarre (Finley kick)
UF Ratliff 33 pass from Grossman (Leach kick)
MICH Perry 7 run (Finley kick)
MICH Perry 12 run (Finley kick)
UF Walker 3 pass from Grossman (Leach kick)
MICH FG Finley 33

MICH	TEAM STATISTICS	UF
17	First Downs	28
104	Rushing Yards	183
21-37-0	Passing	21-42-1
319	Passing Yards	323
423	Total Yards	506
3-29	Punt Returns - Yards	3-10
2-45	Kickoff Returns - Yards	5-101
9-38.6	Punts - Average	8-32.1
1-0	Fumbles - Lost	2-2
3-23	Penalties - Yards	6-38
32:39	Possession Time	27:21

INDIVIDUAL LEADERS
RUSHING
MICH: Perry 28-85, 4 TD; Bellamy 2-20.
UF: Graham 22-120, 2 TD; Carthon 6-56.
PASSING
MICH: Navarre 21-36-0, 319 yards, 1 TD.
UF: Grossman 21-41-0, 323 yards, 2 TD.
RECEIVING
MICH: Perry 6-108; Edwards 4-110.
UF: Jacobs 7-88; Carthon 3-65.

January 1, 2004 | Outback
Iowa 37, Florida 17

	1ST	2ND	3RD	4TH	FINAL
UI	7	13	14	3	37
UF	7	0	3	7	17

SCORING SUMMARY
UF Kight 70 pass from Leak (Leach kick)
UI Brown 3 run from Chandler (Kaeding kick)
UI FG Kaeding 47
UI Chandler 5 run (Kaeding kick)
UI Melloy recovered blocked punt (Kaeding kick)
UF FG Leach 48
UI Russell 34 run (Kaeding kick)
UI FG Kaeding 38
UF Baker 25 pass from Leak (Leach kick)

UI	TEAM STATISTICS	UF
22	First Downs	16
238	Rushing Yards	57
13-26-0	Passing	22-41-1
170	Passing Yards	268
408	Total Yards	325
5-71	Punt Returns - Yards	3-26
3-54	Kickoff Returns - Yards	5-66
7-42.6	Punts - Average	10-40.1
1-0	Fumbles - Lost	1-0
3-15	Penalties - Yards	4-43
34:10	Possession Time	25:50

INDIVIDUAL LEADERS
RUSHING
UI: Russell 21-150, 1 TD; Lewis 12-45.
UF: Carthon 10-44; Fason 4-23.
PASSING
UI: Chandler 13-25-0, 170 yards, 1 TD.
UF: Leak 22-41-1, 268 yards, 1 TD.
RECEIVING
UI: Brown 6-96, 1 TD; Hinkel 3-44.
UF: Kight 2-75, 1 TD; Perez 7-70.

December 31, 2004 | Peach
Miami (Fla.) 27, Florida 10

	1ST	2ND	3RD	4TH	FINAL
MIA	7	10	7	3	27
UF	0	3	7	0	10

SCORING SUMMARY
MIA Hester 78 blocked field goal (Peattie kick)
UF FG Leach 34
MIA FG Peattie 47
MIA Parrish 72 punt return (Peattie kick)
MIA Moore 20 pass from Berlin (Peattie kick)
UF Cornelius 45 pass from Leak (Leach kick)
MIA FG Peattie 32

MIA	TEAM STATISTICS	UF
16	First Downs	22
106	Rushing Yards	144
13-24-1	Passing	19-39-2
171	Passing Yards	262
277	Total Yards	406
4-81	Punt Returns - Yards	2-17
2-31	Kickoff Returns - Yards	2-34
6-33.3	Punts - Average	7-40.9
2-1	Fumbles - Lost	1-0
4-30	Penalties - Yards	8-74
28:51	Possession Time	31:09

INDIVIDUAL LEADERS
RUSHING
MIA: Gore 25-80; Moss 4-18.
UF: Fason 17-94; Leak 14-38.
PASSING
MIA: Berlin 13-24-1, 171 yards, 1 TD.
UF: Leak 19-39-2, 262 yards, 1 TD.
RECEIVING
MIA: Parrish 4-63; Leggett 2-41.
UF: Small 8-92; Cornelius 1-45, 1 TD.

THE SCHOOLS

JANUARY 2, 2006 | OUTBACK
FLORIDA 31, IOWA 24

	1ST	2ND	3RD	4TH	FINAL
UI	0	7	0	17	24
UF	7	17	7	0	31

SCORING SUMMARY
UF   McCollum 6 return of blocked punt (Hetland kick)
UF   FG Hetland 21
UF   Brown 60 interception return (Hetland kick)
UI   Solomon 20 pass from Tate (Schlicher kick)
UF   Baker 24 pass from Leak (Hetland kick)
UF   Baker 38 pass from Leak (Hetland kick)
UI   Hinkel 4 pass from Tate (Schlicher kick)
UI   Hinkel 14 pass from Tate (Schlicher kick)
UI   FG Schlicher 45

UI	TEAM STATISTICS	UF
23	First Downs	26
64	Rushing Yards	169
32-55-1	Passing	25-40-0
346	Passing Yards	278
410	Total Yards	447
1-2	Punt Returns - Yards	3-32
6-113	Kickoff Returns - Yards	4-35
6-30.7	Punts - Average	3-46.3
0-0	Fumbles - Lost	1-1
8-60	Penalties - Yards	5-30

INDIVIDUAL LEADERS
RUSHING:
UI: Young 13-34.
UF: Moore 13-88.
PASSING
UI: Tate 32-55-1, 346 yards, 3 TD.
UF: Leak 25-40-0, 278 yards, 2 TD.
RECEIVING
UI: Hinkel 9-87, 2 TD; Solomon 7-96, 1 TD.
UF: Baker 10-147, 2 TD; Jackson 7-76.

JANUARY 8, 2007 | BCS CHAMPIONSHIP
FLORIDA 41, OHIO STATE 14

	1ST	2ND	3RD	4TH	FINAL
UF	14	20	0	7	41
OSU	7	7	0	0	14

SCORING SUMMARY
OSU   Ginn Jr. 93 kickoff return (Pettrey kick)
UF   Baker 14 pass from Leak (Hetland kick)
UF   Harvin 4 run (Hetland kick)
UF   Wynn 2 run (Hetland kick)
OSU   Pittman 18 run (Pettrey kick)
UF   FG Hetland 42
UF   FG Hetland 40
UF   Caldwell 1 pass from Tebow (Hetland kick)
UF   Tebow 1 run (Hetland kick)

UF	TEAM STATISTICS	OSU
21	First Downs	8
156	Rushing Yards	47
26-37-0	Passing	4-14-1
214	Passing Yards	35
370	Total Yards	82
4-28	Punt Returns - Yards	1-13
1-33	Kickoff Returns - Yards	6-193
4-44.3	Punts - Average	6-37.8
0-0	Fumbles - Lost	1-1
6-50	Penalties - Yards	5-50

TEAM STATISTICS
RUSHING
UF: Wynn 19-69, 1 TD.
OSU: Pittman 10-62, 1 TD.
PASSING
UF: Leak 25-36-0, 213 yards, 1 TD.
OSU: Smith 4-14-1, 35 yards.
RECEIVING
UF: Harvin 9-60; Cornelius 5-50.
OSU: Gonzalez 2-11; Hartline 1-13.

JANUARY 1, 2008 | CAPITAL ONE
MICHIGAN 41, FLORIDA 35

	1ST	2ND	3RD	4TH	FINAL
MICH	7	14	7	13	41
FLA	7	7	14	7	35

SCORING SUMMARY
MICH   Manningham 21 pass from Henne (Lopata kick)
UF   Harvin 10 pass from Tebow (Ijjas kick)
UF   Caldwell 18 pass from Tebow (Ijjas kick)
MICH   Hart 3 run (Lopata kick)
MICH   Arrington 1 pass from Henne (Lopata kick)
MICH   Hart 1 run (Lopata kick)
UF   Tebow 1 run (Ijjas kick)
UF   Caldwell 14 pass from Tebow (Ijjas kick)
MICH   FG Lopata 37
UF   Harvin 10 run (Ijjas kick)
MICH   Arrington 18 pass from Henne (Lopata kick)
MICH   FG Lopata 41

MICH	TEAM STATISTICS	FLA
28	First Downs	18
151	Rushing Yards	230
25-39-2	Passing	18-34-0
373	Passing Yards	169
524	Total Yards	399
0-0	Punt Returns - Yards	2-41
6-118	Kickoff Returns - Yards	5-52
2-44.5	Punts - Average	3-39.3
4-2	Fumbles - Lost	1-0
8-65	Penalties - Yards	9-49

TEAM STATISTICS
RUSHING
MICH: Hart 32-129, 2 TD.
FLA: Harvin 13-165, 1 TD.
PASSING
MICH: Henne 25-39-2, 373 yards, 3 TD.
FLA: Tebow 17-33-0, 154 yards, 3 TD.
RECEIVING
MICH: Arrington 9-153, 2 TD.
FLA: Harvin 9-77, 1 TD.

JANUARY 8, 2009 | BCS CHAMPIONSHIP
FLORIDA 24, OKLAHOMA 14

	1ST	2ND	3RD	4TH	FINAL
UF	0	7	7	10	24
OKLA	0	7	0	7	14

SCORING SUMMARY
UF   Murphy 20 pass from Tebow (Phillips kick)
OKLA   Gresham 6 pass from Bradford (Stevens kick)
UF   Harvin 2 run (Phillips kick)
OKLA   Gresham 11 pass from Bradford (Stevens kick)
UF   FG Phillips 27
UF   Nelson 4 pass from Tebow (Phillips kick)

UF	TEAM STATISTICS	OKLA
24	First Downs	25
249	Rushing Yards	107
18-30-2	Passing	26-41-2
231	Passing Yards	256
480	Total Yards	363
1-1	Punt Returns - Yards	1-15
3-51	Kickoff Returns - Yards	5-118
3-51.7	Punts - Average	3-38.7
0-0	Fumbles - Lost	0-0
8-81	Penalties - Yards	4-31

TEAM STATISTICS
RUSHING
UF: Harvin 9-122, 1 TD.
OK: Brown 22-110.
PASSING
UF: Tebow 18-30-2, 231 yards, 2 TD.
OK: Bradford 26-41-2, 256 yards 2 TD.
RECEIVING
UF: Hernandez 5-57; Harvin 5-49.
OK: Gresham 8-62, 2 TD; Iglesias 5-58.

GEORGIA

BY GEOFFREY NORMAN

Several schools have won national championships and fielded Heisman winners. And these accomplishments go a long way toward making a program eligible for "elite" status in the universe of college football. But a few teams have gone even further and become iconic.

To get to this level, you need to have been coached, at some time, by a man whose name is mythic—like, oh, Pop Warner. You need a stadium that doesn't even have to go by its proper name, so when the team is at home, you could say it plays "between the hedges." You need a mascot that everyone in the world recognizes—an English bulldog would do nicely. And you need a war cry that has been appropriated all over the football world but resonates best in the original, "How 'bout them Dawgs!"

One team, of course, has all these things and, thus, an undeniable place in the pantheon of college football programs. It is impossible, in short, to imagine college football without the University of Georgia.

TRADITION Back in the late 1800s, when the Georgia football field was located not far from the university chapel, students began the custom of ringing the chapel bell until midnight following every Georgia win. The tradition originally mandated that only Bulldogs freshmen ring the bell. Now, everyone is welcome to ring in another night of celebration following a victory.

BEST PLAYER Georgia has produced a number of All-Americans and two Heisman winners. The first to capture both honors was Frank Sinkwich, a single-wing tailback, who won the Heisman in 1942, when he set an SEC record of 2,187 yards of total offense. Sinkwich was small—only 5-10, 185 pounds—but he was shifty, and any defense that played him to run made itself vulnerable to the pass. In his career, Sinkwich ran for 30 touchdowns, passed for 30 more and accounted for more than 4,600 yards of total offense. Losing only one game in his senior year, he became the first Heisman winner from a Southern school and the greatest back in Georgia history. That is, until the 1980s and the arrival of one Herschel Walker, who immediately lit up the college football world like a comet.

Walker was a freshman listed as the third-string tailback on the depth chart when the 1980 season started. In the first game, with Tennessee keeping the Georgia

---

PROFILE

University of Georgia
Athens, Ga.
Founded: 1785
Enrollment: 34,180
Colors: Red and Black
Nickname: Bulldogs
Stadium: Sanford Stadium
    Opened in 1929
    Grass; 92,746 capacity
First football game: 1892
All-time record: 723–384–54 (.653)
Bowl record: 25–16–3
Consensus national championships, 1936-present: 2 (1942, 1980)
Southeastern Conference championships: 12 (8 outright)
Heisman Trophy: Frank Sinkwich, 1942; Herschel Walker, 1982
Outland Trophy: Bill Stanfill, 1968
First-round draft choices: 26
Website: www.georgiadogs.com

THE BEST OF TIMES

Vince Dooley's Dawgs won a national title and 23 straight conference games, and went 43–4–1 in the four seasons from 1980 to 1983.

THE WORST OF TIMES

From 1949 through 1956, Georgia lost to archrival Georgia Tech eight straight times.

CONFERENCE

After 12 seasons in the Southern Conference (1922-32), Georgia became a charter member of the Southeastern Conference in 1933.

DISTINGUISHED ALUMNI

Kim Basinger, actress; Pete Correll, chairman of Georgia-Pacific Corp.; Phil Gramm, U.S. senator; Pat Mitchell, president of PBS; Hala Moddelmog, president of Church's Chicken; Deborah Norville, TV journalist

FIGHT SONG

GLORY
Glory, glory to old Georgia!
Glory, glory to old Georgia!
Glory, glory to old Georgia!
G-E-O-R-G-I-A.
Glory, glory to old Georgia!
Glory, glory to old Georgia!
Glory, glory to old Georgia!
G-E-O-R-G-I-A.

Dooley preached the old-time religion of football fundamentals: defense, the running game, kicking. It was never flashy but it worked.

offense bottled up and leading 15-0, he got his chance and scored twice. Walker flattened future pro Bill Bates on one touchdown run to bring the Bulldogs back for a 16-15 victory. He never looked back.

Walker had four 200-yard rushing games that season—and the Bulldogs finished the year undefeated, untied and as consensus national champs. He rushed for 1,616 yards and finished third in the Heisman balloting. The next season, he finished second. As a junior, he finally won the award, then left school for the United States Football League. There has never been another three years in Bulldogs history to compare with the Walker era, when the Bulldogs swept to three straight SEC titles and lost just three games in three seasons.

BEST COACH The legendary Pop Warner did briefly coach the Bulldogs (then known as the Red and Black). Wally Butts won a share of the national championship in 1942, and also had the face of a Georgia Bulldog. But Georgia's best coach was, without a doubt, Vince Dooley.

A former Auburn quarterback (there is a remarkable amount of cross-fertilization between these longtime

rivals), Dooley was hired in 1964 at the young age of 31 to bring Georgia back to respectability. Butts had resigned in 1960 and his successor, Johnny Griffith, had his troubles, especially against the teams he needed to beat, going 1–8 against Auburn, Florida and Georgia Tech.

Twenty-five years later, when Dooley left the sideline to become full-time athletic director, his record was 201–77–10. His teams had won one national championship and finished on top of the SEC six times. Under Dooley, the Bulldogs went to 20 bowl games.

Dooley was not an innovator. He preached the old-time religion of football fundamentals: defense, the running game, kicking. It was never flashy but it worked, and it made believers out of Bulldogs fans, who were also attracted to Dooley's homespun wisdom. After spurning an offer to coach at his alma mater in 1980, Dooley rightly said, "The overriding factor was I had too much invested here. I wouldn't leave. This has been my home for 17 years. I'm a Bulldog and proud to be one."

Dooley also earned a reputation as a player's coach. In 1976, after Georgia won its first SEC title in eight years,

FIRST-ROUND DRAFT CHOICES

1943	Frank Sinkwich, Lions (1)
1945	Charley Trippi, Cardinals (1)
1948	Dan Edwards, Steelers (9)
1949	Johnny Rauch, Lions (2)
1953	Harry Babcock, 49ers (1)
1969	Bill Stanfill, Dolphins (11)
1972	Royce Smith, Saints (8)
1982	Lindsay Scott, Saints (13)
1989	Tim Worley, Steelers (7)
1990	Ben Smith, Eagles (22)
1990	Rodney Hampton, Giants (24)
1993	Garrison Hearst, Cardinals (3)
1994	Bernard Williams, Eagles (14)
1998	Robert Edwards, Patriots (18)
1999	Champ Bailey, Redskins (7)
1999	Matt Stinchcomb, Raiders (18)
2001	Richard Seymour, Patriots (6)
2001	Marcus Stroud, Jaguars (13)
2002	Charles Grant, Saints (25)
2003	Johnathan Sullivan, Saints (6)
2003	George Foster, Broncos (20)
2004	Ben Watson, Patriots (32)
2005	Thomas Davis, Panthers (14)
2005	David Pollack, Bengals (17)
2009	Matthew Stafford, Lions (1)
2009	Knowshon Moreno, Broncos (12)

CONSENSUS ALL-AMERICANS

1927	Tom Nash, E
1931	Vernon Smith, E
1941-42	Frank Sinkwich, B
1946	Charley Trippi, B
1967	Ed Chandler, T
1968	Bill Stanfill, DT
1968	Jake Scott, DB
1971	Royce Smith, G
1975	Randy Johnson, G
1976	Joel Parrish, G
1980-82	Herschel Walker, RB
1982-83	Terry Hoage, DB
1984	Kevin Butler, PK
1984	Jeff Sanchez, DB
1985	Pete Anderson, C
1988	Tim Worley, RB
1992	Garrison Hearst, RB
1998	Champ Bailey, DB
1998	Matt Stinchcomb, OL
2002, '04	David Pollack, DE
2004	Thomas Davis, FS
2005	Max Jean-Gilles, OL
2005	Greg Blue, DB

he fulfilled a vow to his team that he'd shave his head—mimicking chrome-domed defensive coordinator Erk Russell—to mark the accomplishment.

BEST TEAM The 1942 team lost one game—an upset by Auburn—but won the Rose Bowl and a national championship. The 1946 squad was undefeated and untied but was not a consensus national champion. So the choice is the 1980 team, which also went undefeated and untied, and was consensus national champ as well.
The Bulldogs came from behind to beat Tennessee in the season opener. They beat South Carolina—in a battle of ranked teams—in the eighth game of the season to move up to No. 2. The next week, Georgia trailed rival Florida 21-20 with 63 seconds to play and the ball on the Bulldogs' 7-yard line. A 93-yard TD pass from Buck Belue to Lindsay Scott—a play that will live forever in Bulldogs hearts—saved the day and the season. Georgia went to the Sugar Bowl to play Notre Dame. Herschel Walker ran for two touchdowns and the Bulldogs won, 17-10, to take their throne as undisputed champions.

BEST BACKFIELD In the hot glow of the present, the 2008 pairing of Matthew Stafford throwing and Knowshon Moreno running looks so good that you can't fathom how there could be any competition. No Georgia team ever rolled up more yards in a season (more than 5,500), and it would be hard to imagine any looking more unstoppable while doing it. But that backfield was broken up before its time by the temptations of the NFL—so call it the best of the 21st century.
Then, go back to 1942 when tailback Frank Sinkwich scored 27 touchdowns on his way to the Heisman and his backfield mate, Charley Trippi, amassed more than 1,000 yards in total offense. Georgia lost only one game that year, a heartbreaker to Auburn. The Bulldogs went to the Rose Bowl and beat UCLA 9-0. With Sinkwich nursing injuries, Trippi ran for 130 yards and was named outstanding player of the game. All in all, it was a dream season, and that backfield tandem is what people remember about it.

BEST DEFENSE Defensive football at Georgia isn't defined so much by any one squad as it is by an entire era

COLLEGE FOOTBALL HALL OF FAME INDUCTEES		
NAME	YEARS	INDUCTED
Pop Warner, COACH	1895-96	1951
Bob McWhorter, HB	1910-13	1954
Frank Sinkwich, HB	1940-42	1954
Charley Trippi, HB	1942, '45-46	1959
Vernon Smith, E	1929-31	1979
Bill Hartman, FB	1935-37	1984
Fran Tarkenton, QB	1958-60	1987
Vince Dooley, COACH	1964-88	1994
Wallace Butts, COACH	1939-60	1997
Bill Stanfill, DT	1966-68	1998
Herschel Walker, RB	1980-82	1999
Terry Hoage, S	1980-83	2000
Kevin Butler, PK	1981-84	2001
John Rauch, QB	1945-48	2003

PRO FOOTBALL HALL OF FAME INDUCTEES		
NAME	YEARS	INDUCTED
Charley Trippi, HB/QB	1947-55	1968
Fran Tarkenton, QB	1961-78	1986

and an iconic defensive coordinator who just looked like Georgia football. And talked like it, too.
The legend of Erk Russell was solidified after a poor 1974 season, when the coach with the famously shaved head (a rarity in those days) christened his boys the Junkyard Dogs and encouraged the school band to play a few bars from Jim Croce's popular tune, "Bad, Bad Leroy Brown," whenever the defense made a big play.
The unit was pure Russell. No stars, just heart. He described a Junkyard Dog this way: "the runt of the litter. Nobody wants him, and he is hungry. We had three walk-ons, four QBs, and three running backs in our original Junkyard Dog starting cast, which averaged 208 pounds across the front. In short, a Junkyard Dog is one who must stretch and strain all of his potential just to survive. Then, he can think about being good."
Russell's defenses were pretty good. He was the Bulldogs' defensive coordinator for 17 seasons. In 192 games, his units held the opposition to 17 points or fewer 135 times. In 73 of those games, the opposition scored in the single digits and in 26 it was completely shut out. "If we score," he liked to say, "we may win. If they *never* score, we'll never lose."

STORYBOOK SEASON After Walker left to join the USFL, little was expected of the 1983 Bulldogs. The team began the campaign with gaping holes at tailback and at quarterback, where John Lastinger's main gift was for leadership. With grit and defense, the Bulldogs scrapped their way to a 9–1–1 regular season and went to the Cotton Bowl to play undefeated, untied, No. 2 Texas. The Bulldogs leaned on their defense to keep the score close and waited for their chance. That came when Texas fumbled a punt late in the game. Georgia turned opportunity into a touchdown and won 10-9 to finish No. 4 in the nation.

BIGGEST GAME A 15-0 win on Oct. 12, 1929, over Yale—reigning football power from the East—at the dedication of Sanford Stadium still resonates down the years. There were so many satisfying elements to that victory, not least that nobody expected the Bulldogs to win and that they did it in front of a crowd (30,000) that exceeded the capacity of the new stadium. The other

Bulldogs from New Haven were whipped so convincingly that they never came south again.

BIGGEST UPSET Defending national champion Alabama was ahead 17-10 in Athens on Sept. 18, 1965, and had Georgia pinned inside its own 30-yard line with 2:08 to play. On second and eight, quarterback Kirby Moore passed to Pat Hodgson, who then lateraled to Bob Taylor, who ran the ball in for a touchdown. The play covered 73 yards. Georgia went for two against a frustrated Crimson Tide and Moore again hit Hodgson—no lateral necessary. Georgia 18, Alabama 17. To this day, Tide fans insist that Hodgson's knees were on the ground before he lateraled to Taylor for the decisive touchdown. The film was pretty clearly on Alabama's side, but as Bear Bryant said, "You don't win games in the movies on Monday."

TRAGEDY The University of Virginia and the University of Georgia met in Atlanta in 1897 to play football, a sport still in its infancy. Virginia owned a decisive lead when Richard Vonalbade Gammon, one of Georgia's best players, was injured badly enough to be taken from the field and delivered by horse-drawn ambulance to a nearby hospital. He died there the next morning.

Gammon's death ignited a campaign to abolish football in the state of Georgia. A bill had made it through the legislature and was on the governor's desk for his signature when he received a letter from Gammon's mother. "It would be inexpressibly sad," she pleaded, "to have the cause he held so dear injured by his sacrifice. Grant me the right to request that the boy's death should not be used to defeat the most cherished object of his life." The governor refused to sign the bill. Football in Georgia survived.

BEST COMEBACK Down 20-0 to Georgia Tech on Dec. 2, 1978, a true freshman named Buck Belue (could there be a better name for a Georgia quarterback?) entered the game for the Bulldogs and provided the spark they needed. But a 21-20 Georgia lead vanished when Drew Hill returned a kick 101 yards and Tech converted a two-point attempt. Belue was undaunted, which may have been his greatest asset as a football player. He drove the Bulldogs 84 yards, including a 43-yard touchdown pass to Amp Arnold, who also took a pitch from Belue and ran it in for the extra points and a 29-28 victory.

STADIUM Sanford is now more than 75 years old and, with a capacity of 92,700, seats more than three times the number of fans (30,000) who attended the first game played there. English privet hedges surround the field and the playing surface is natural grass. Other football teams play in stadiums with shrubbery surrounding the field, but the Georgia Bulldogs' landscaping became immortal when a sportswriter of the 1930s (some insist it was Grantland Rice) observed that the Bulldogs had their opponents "between the hedges."

RIVAL A poll of the house would probably divide the Bulldogs faithful in thirds on this issue. One-third would say Auburn and have a good case, since it is the South's oldest continuous football rivalry. Georgia's greatest coach, Vince Dooley, played at Auburn. And Auburn's sainted Shug Jordan was the basketball coach at Georgia from 1947 to 1950, before becoming head football coach at Auburn (1951 to 1975). The game is played late in the season and there is generally a lot riding on it.

But another game—often the next one on Georgia's schedule—would get the votes of another third of the Bulldogs faithful: in-state and one-time SEC rival Georgia Tech. Lose to Tech and you'll hear about it all year long. This game means only marginally less today than it did in the era of Bobby Dodd's powerhouse Tech teams in the two decades following World War II.

And then … there is what for ages has been referred to as "the world's largest outdoor cocktail party." Ordinarily, Georgia vs. Florida is played in Jacksonville on what is supposed to be neutral turf. The faithful come from both states for the obligatory tailgating and a game that has been increasingly decisive in the SEC and national championship picture. The intensity has always been there, but when Steve Spurrier arrived at Florida he managed to jack it up several notches. Then came Urban Meyer who made Florida into … well, customary contenders for the national championship and the one team any other team would most love to beat. Which just made the Bulldogs that much hungrier.

NICKNAME The origin of the Bulldogs moniker is obscure and is typically linked to the strong ties between the University of Georgia and Yale. Georgia's first president, Abraham Baldwin, was a Yale man, and some of the early structures on campus were copied from Yale buildings. In 1920, a writer for the *Atlanta Journal* suggested the name, arguing that there was "a certain dignity about a bulldog, as well as ferocity." Later that year, another writer used "Bulldogs" five times in an account of a game with Virginia that ended in a scoreless tie. The name stuck.

MASCOT The latest in a long line of English bulldogs wearing the spiked collar and red jersey made its debut in the first game of the 2008 season. This was Uga VII, and there is no more recognizable mascot in all of college football. *Sports Illustrated* acknowledged this obvious fact when it put Uga V on its April 28, 1997, cover. Uga V also appeared in the Clint Eastwood film *Midnight in the Garden of Good and Evil*. Uga IV joined Herschel Walker

at the Downtown Athletic Club in New York for the presentation of the Heisman Trophy. All six former Ugas are buried near the main gate in the embankment of the south stands at Sanford. Before each game, flowers are placed on their graves.

And if you're looking to win a bar bet, here's a nugget of trivia. The first Georgia mascot wasn't a bulldog—it was a goat.

UNIFORMS Red jerseys and the famous "silver britches." Coach Wally Butts introduced them in 1939.

When Dooley redesigned the uniform in 1964, he went for more subdued white pants. Then, before the 1980 season, he went back to the silver britches and the Bulldogs wore them on their march to the national title.

QUOTE "Win in football. That's the bottom line. It doesn't really matter what you do in the other stuff as long as you're winning in football." —**Vince Dooley**, asked to give advice to his successor as athletic director before stepping down in 2004 after four decades with the Georgia program

True Colors

BY FURMAN BISHER

Once upon a time they came by carriage or train, and in time, by motorcar, to see the town of Athens, Georgia, swath itself in Red and Black, the autumn splendor of football. There is nothing like a day of football in an American college town, leaves dressed out in their changing hues, streets aclamor with milling fans all headed for one eventual destination. In Athens, it's Sanford Stadium.

On other campuses, stadiums have taken on names of men who led football squads—as in Neyland at Tennessee, Bryant at Alabama, Jordan at Auburn—but the University of Georgia stubbornly holds to a tradition dating to 1929, when the name of a career college administrator, S.V. Sanford, was stamped onto the school's new stadium on the day the Bulldogs of Georgia beat the *other* Bulldogs from someplace up North.

It isn't original to Athens, but the Bulldog Walk has become a central part of the gameday experience. The ceremonial march, led by the Redcoat Marching Band, begins with the athletes alighting from buses on Lumpkin Street. They walk through the Stegeman Hall parking lot and a sea of ebullient worshippers clad in Red and Black to that field surrounded by those famous hedges. Once, as a member of the visiting Tar Heels, I fell into the hedges and narrowly escaped spending the rest of the afternoon thus trapped. But in another way—in the sense that I moved to the Athens area and came to love the Bulldogs and put away the Carolina blue and replaced it with Red and Black—I have been trapped in those hedges for decades now.

Tailgating, as on other campuses across the land, is as much a part of a football Saturday in Athens as breathing. There was a time when the festivities concentrated around Stegeman Hall, but as open spaces got gobbled up, creative tailgaters were

> *Once, as a member of the visiting Tar Heels, I fell into the hedges and narrowly escaped spending the rest of the afternoon thus trapped. But in another sense I have been trapped in those hedges for decades now.*

forced into scattered colonies. Parking has become as precious as victory— well, almost. Behind Sanford Stadium, on half-moon-shaped Field Street, are the choice spaces, available only through a whopping contribution to the athletics department. Way back in 1929, Sanford seated just 30,000. Now, after numerous additions, it has become a city unto itself, accommodating more than 92,000 on the day of a game; a fortress of Bulldogs, armed and in full fury.

The university considers itself the first such public institution in the nation, and true, it exercised its grant in 1785, before the University of North Carolina. But the Tar Heels became an active institution first. Athens town grew itself around the university. In neighboring Atlanta, football may be a matter of some importance, but the city is able to absorb the crush of people produced by a football game at Georgia Tech with barely a bulge. Not Athens. Football is essential to the economy here and a gameday loss brings a cloak of doom down on the town. There are times when the citizens are considerably more concerned about who the coach is than about who the president is. (The President of the United States, that is, not of the university. Little is of less importance to genuine Bulldogs fans than who the president of the university might be.)

What really cements the relationship between the town and football is that so many old-time Bulldogs eventually came back to Georgia and made it their home. Frank Sinkwich, Georgia's first Heisman Trophy winner, settled here. And Charley Trippi. Zippy Morocco, too. And Bill Hartman from a much earlier age. Looking around Athens on a fall Saturday, you can see a lot of Red and Black festooning the old town and you realize that those colors are forever. Only the names inside the colors change.

Furman Bisher has written 12 books and over a thousand magazine articles in 69 years as a sports journalist. He lives in Fayetteville, Ga., and still columnizes for the Atlanta Journal-Constitution.

Georgia All-Time Scores

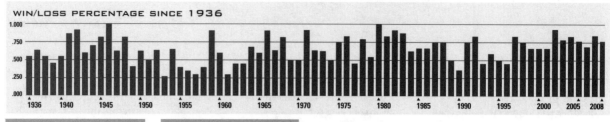

WIN/LOSS PERCENTAGE SINCE 1936

1.000 / .750 / .500 / .250 / .000

1936 · 1940 · 1945 · 1950 · 1955 · 1960 · 1965 · 1970 · 1975 · 1980 · 1985 · 1990 · 1995 · 2000 · 2005 · 2008

DR. CHARLES HERTY
1892 (.500)   1-1

1892   1-1-0
| J30 | ● | Mercer | 50 | 0 |
| F20 | | Auburn *Atl* | 0 | 10 |

ERNEST BROWN
1893 (.500)   2-2-1

1893   2-2-1
N4		Georgia Tech	6	28
N7		at Vanderbilt	10	35	*
N30	=	at Savannah AC	0	0
D1	●	Augusta AC *Aug*	24	0
D9	●	Furman *Aug*	22	8

ROBERT WINSTON
1894 (.833)   5-1

1894   5-1-0
O29		Sewanee	8	12
N3	●	at So. Carolina St.	40	0
N10	●	at Wofford	10	0
N17	●	at Augusta AC	66	0
N24		Auburn *Atl*	10	8
N29	●	at Savannah AC	22	0

GLENN "POP" WARNER
1895-96 (.636)   7-4

1895   3-4-0
O19	●	Wofford	34	0
O26		North Carolina *Atl*	0	6
O31		North Carolina *Atl*	6	10
N2		Alabama *ColGa*	30	6
N9		Sewanee *Atl*	22	0
N23		at Vanderbilt	0	6
N28		Auburn *Atl*	6	16

1896   4-0-0
O24		at Wofford	26	0
O31		North Carolina *Atl*	24	16
N9	●	Sewanee	26	0
N26		Auburn *Atl*	12	6

CHARLES McCARTHY
1897-98 (.667)   6-3

1897   2-1-0
O9	●	Clemson	24	0
O23	●	Georgia Tech	28	0
N20		Virginia *Atl*	4	17

1898   4-2-0
O8	●	Clemson	20	8
O15	●	Atlanta AC	14	0
O22	●	Georgia Tech	15	0
O29		Vanderbilt *Atl*	4	0
N12		North Carolina *Mac*	0	44	*
N24		Auburn *Atl*	17	18

GORDON SAUSSY
1899 (.417)   2-3-1

1899   2-3-1
O7	●	Clemson	11	0
O21		Sewanee *Atl*	0	12
O28	●	Georgia Tech	33	0	*
N11		at Tennessee	0	5
N18	=	Auburn *Atl*	0	0
N30		North Carolina *Atl*	0	5

E.E. JONES
1900 (.333)   2-4

1900   2-4-0
O13	●	Georgia Tech *Atl*	12	0
O20	●	South Carolina	5	0
O27		Sewanee *Atl*	6	21
N10		Clemson	5	39
N17		North Carolina *Ral*	0	55
N29		Auburn *Atl*	0	44

BILLY REYNOLDS
1901-02 (.433)   5-7-3

1901   1-5-2
O12	●	South Carolina *Aug*	10	5
O19		at Vanderbilt	0	47
O21		at Sewanee	0	47
O26		Clemson	5	29
N2		North Carolina *Atl*	0	27
N9	=	Alabama *Mont*	0	0
N16		Davidson	6	16
N28	=	Auburn *Atl*	0	0

1902   4-2-1
O18	●	Furman	11	0
O25	=	at Georgia Tech	0	0
N1	●	Alabama *Birm*	5	0
N7	●	Davidson	20	0
N8		at Clemson	0	36
N11	●	Sewanee *Atl*	0	11
N27	●	Auburn *Atl*	12	5

M.M. DICKINSON
1903, '05 (.308)   4-9

1903   3-4-0
O10		Clemson	0	29
O17		South Carolina	0	17
O24	●	at Georgia Tech	38	0
O31	●	Vanderbilt	0	33
N7	●	at Tennessee	5	0
N14		at Savannah	0	6
N26	●	Auburn *Atl*	22	13

CHARLES A. BARNARD
1904 (.167)   1-5

1904   1-5-0
O8	●	Florida U. Club *Mac*	52	0
O22		at Clemson	0	10
O26		at South Carolina	0	2
N5		at Alabama	5	16
N12		at Georgia Tech	6	23
N24		Auburn *Mac*	6	17	*

M.M. DICKINSON

1905   1-5-0
O3		Cumberland	10	39
O21		Clemson	0	35
N4		Alabama *Birm*	0	36
N11	●	North Georgia	16	12
N18		at Georgia Tech	0	46
N30		Auburn *Mac*	0	20	*

W.S. WHITNEY
1906-07 (.417)   4-6-2

1906   2-4-1
O13	●	Davidson	0	15
O20		at Clemson	0	6
N3		at Mercer	55	0
N10		Georgia Tech	0	17
N21	=	Tennessee	0	0
N29	●	Auburn *Mac*	4	0
D2		at Savannah AC	0	12

1907   4-3-1
O5	●	North Georgia	57	0
O12		Tennessee	0	15
O19		at Mercer	26	6
O25	=	Alabama *Mont*	0	0
N2		at Georgia Tech	6	10
N7	●	Clemson *Aug*	8	0
N11		Sewanee	0	16
N28	●	Auburn *Mac*	6	0

BRANCH BOCOCK
1907-08 (.682)   7-3-1

1908   5-2-1
O3	●	North Georgia	16	0
O17	●	South Carolina	29	6
O24		at Tennessee	0	10
O31	●	Mercer	10	0
N5	●	Clemson *Aug*	8	0
N14	=	Alabama *Birm*	6	6
N21	●	Davidson	2	0
N26		Auburn *Mont*	0	23

J. COULTER/FRANK DOBSON
1909 (.286)   1-4-2

1909   1-4-2
O9	=	at Citadel	0	0
O16	=	Davidson	0	0
O23	●	at Tennessee	3	0
O30		Alabama *Atl*	0	14
N10		Clemson *Aug*	0	5
N20		at Georgia Tech	6	12
N25		Auburn *Mont*	5	17	*

W.A. CUNNINGHAM
1910-19 (.679)   43-18-9

1910   6-2-1
O1	●	Locust Grove	101	0
O8	●	Gordon	79	0
O15	●	Alabama *Birm*	22	0
O22	●	Tennessee	35	5
O29	●	Mercer	21	0
N5		at Sewanee	12	15
N10	=	Clemson *Aug*	0	0
N19	●	at Georgia Tech	11	6
N24		Auburn *Sav*	0	26

1911   7-1-1
S30	●	Alabama Presbyterian	51	0
O7	●	South Carolina	38	0
O14	●	Alabama *Birm*	11	3
O21	●	Sewanee	12	3
O28	●	Mercer	8	5
N4		at Vanderbilt	0	17
N9	●	Clemson *Aug*	22	0
N18	●	at Georgia Tech	5	0
N29	=	Auburn *Sav*	0	0

1912   6-1-1
O5	●	U.T. Chattanooga	33	0
O12	●	Citadel	33	0
O19		Vanderbilt *Atl*	0	46
O26	●	Alabama *ColGa*	13	9
N2	●	Sewanee	13	13
N9	●	Clemson *Aug*	27	6
N16	●	at Georgia Tech	20	0
N28	●	Auburn	12	6

1913   6-2-0
O4	●	Alabama Presbyterian	108	0
O11	●	North Georgia	51	0
O18	●	Alabama *Birm*	20	0
O25	●	Virginia *Atl*	6	13
N1	●	North Carolina	19	6
N6	●	Clemson *Aug*	18	15
N15	●	at Georgia Tech	14	0
N22	●	Auburn *Atl*	7	21

1914   3-5-1
S26	●	North Georgia	81	0
O3	●	Citadel	13	0
O10	●	at Sewanee	7	6
O17	●	North Carolina *Atl*	6	41
O24	●	at Virginia	0	28
O31	●	Mississippi State	0	9
N7	●	Clemson	13	35
N14		at Georgia Tech	0	7
N21	=	Auburn *Atl*	0	0

1915   5-2-2
S28	●	Newberry	79	0
O1	●	North Georgia	64	0
O9	=	at U.T. Chattanooga	6	6
O16	●	at Citadel	39	0
O23		Virginia	7	9
O30		Auburn	0	12
N6	●	Florida *JacF*	37	0
N13	=	at Georgia Tech	0	0
N25	●	Clemson	13	0

1916   6-3-0
S30	●	Citadel	6	0
O7	●	Clemson *And*	26	0
O14	●	Florida	21	0
O21	●	at Virginia	13	7
O28		at Navy	3	27
N4	●	Auburn *ColGa*	0	3
N11	●	Furman	49	0
N18		Georgia Tech	0	21
N30	●	Alabama *Birm*	3	0

1917-1918
NO TEAM WWI

1919   4-2-3
O4	●	Citadel	28	0
O11	●	South Carolina	14	0
O18	●	Sewanee	13	0
O25	●	Florida *Tam*	16	0
N1	●	Auburn *ColGa*	0	7
N7	●	Virginia	7	7
N15	=	Tulane *Aug*	7	7
N22	●	Alabama *Atl*	0	6
N27	=	Clemson	0	0

H.J. STEGEMAN
1920-22 (.741)   20-6-3

1920   8-0-1
O2	●	Citadel	40	0
O9	●	at South Carolina	37	0
O13	●	at Furman	7	0
O23	●	at Oglethorpe	27	3
O30	●	Auburn *ColGa*	7	0
N6	=	at Virginia	0	0
N13	●	Florida	56	0
N20	●	Alabama *Atl*	21	14
N25	●	Clemson	55	0

1921   7-2-1
O1	●	Mercer	28	0
O8	●	Furman	27	7
O15		at Harvard	7	10
O22	●	Oglethorpe	14	0
O29	●	Auburn *ColGa*	7	0
N6	●	Virginia	21	0
N13	=	at Vanderbilt	7	7
N19	●	Alabama *Atl*	22	0
N25	●	Clemson	28	0
N27		Dartmouth *Atl*	0	7

1922-1932 SOUTHERN

1922 — 5-4-1 (1-3-1)
S23	●	Newberry	82 13
S30	●	Mercer	41 0
O7		at Chicago	0 20
O14	●	at Furman	7 0
O21		Tennessee	7 3
O28	●	Oglethorpe	26 6
N4		Auburn *ColGa*	3 7
N11	=	at Virginia	6 6
N18		Vanderbilt	0 12
N25		Alabama *Mont*	6 10

GEORGE WOODRUFF 1923-27 (.649)   30-16-1

1923 — 5-3-1 (3-2-0)
S29	●	Mercer	7 0
O6	●	Oglethorpe	20 6
O13		at Yale	0 40
O20	●	at Tennessee	17 0
N3	●	Auburn *ColGa*	7 0
N10	●	Virginia	13 0
N17		at Vanderbilt	7 35
N24		Alabama *Mont*	0 36
D1	=	Centre	3 3

1924 — 7-3-0 (5-1-0)
S27	●	Mercer	26 7
O4		South Carolina	18 0
O11		at Yale	6 7
O18	●	Furman *Aug*	22 0
O25	●	at Vanderbilt	3 0
N1	●	Tennessee	33 0
N8	●	at Virginia	7 0
N15	●	Auburn *ColGa*	6 0
N27		Alabama *Birm*	0 33
N29		at Centre	7 14

1925 — 4-5-0 (2-4-0)
S26	●	at Mercer	32 0
O3		Virginia	6 7
O10		at Yale	7 35
O17	●	Furman *Aug*	21 0
O24		Vanderbilt	26 7
O31		at Tennessee	7 12
N7	●	Auburn *ColGa*	34 0
N14		at Georgia Tech	0 3
N26		Alabama *Birm*	0 27

1926 — 5-4-0 (4-2-0)
S25	●	Mercer	20 0
O2	●	at Virginia	27 7*
O9	●	at Yale	0 10
O16		Furman	7 14
O23		at Vanderbilt	13 14
O30	●	Florida	32 9
N6	●	Auburn *ColGa*	16 6*
N13	●	at Georgia Tech	14 13
N25		Alabama *Birm*	6 33

1927 — 9-1-0 (6-1-0)
O1		Virginia	32 0
O8		at Yale	14 10
O15	●	Furman	32 0
O22	●	Auburn *ColGa*	33 3*
O29	●	at Tulane	31 0
N5	●	Florida *JacF*	28 0
N12		Clemson	32 0
N19		Mercer	26 7
N27		Alabama *Birm*	20 6
D3		at Georgia Tech	0 12

HARRY MEHRE 1928-37 (.626)   59-34-6

1928 — 4-5-0 (2-4-0)
O6	●	Mercer	52 0
O13		at Yale	6 21
O20	●	Furman	7 0
O27		Tulane	20 14
N3	●	Auburn *ColGa*	13 0
N10		Florida *Sav*	6 26
N17		LSU	12 13
N29		Alabama *Birm*	0 19
D8		Georgia Tech	6 20

1929 — 6-4-0 (4-2-0)
S28		Oglethorpe	6 13
O5	●	Furman	27 0
O12		Yale	15 0
O19	●	at North Carolina	19 12
O26		Florida *JacF*	6 18
N2		Tulane *ColGa*	15 21
N9		NYU *Brnx*	19 27
N16	●	Auburn	24 0
N28	●	Alabama *Birm*	12 0
D7	●	Georgia Tech	12 6

1930 — 7-2-1 (3-2-1)
S27	●	Oglethorpe	31 6
O4	●	Mercer	51 0
O11	●	at Yale	18 14
O18	●	North Carolina	26 0
O25	●	Auburn *ColGa*	39 7
N1	=	Florida *Sav*	0 0
N8	●	NYU *NYC*	7 6
N15		at Tulane	0 25
N27		Alabama *Birm*	0 13
D6	●	at Georgia Tech	13 0

1931 — 8-2-0 (6-1-0)
O3	●	Virginia Tech	40 0
O10	●	at Yale	26 7
O17	●	at North Carolina	32 7*
O24	●	Vanderbilt	9 0
O31	●	at Florida	33 6
N7		NYU *Brnx*	7 6
N14		Tulane	7 20
N21	●	Auburn *ColGa*	12 6
N28	●	Georgia Tech	35 6
D12		at Southern California	0 60

1932 — 2-5-2 (2-4-2)
O1		Virginia Tech	6 7
O8		at Tulane	25 34
O15	=	North Carolina	6 6
O22		at Vanderbilt	6 12
O29		Florida	33 12
N5		NYU *Brnx*	7 13
N11	●	at Clemson	32 18
N19	●	Auburn *ColGa*	7 14
N26	=	at Georgia Tech	0 0

1933-Present SEC

1933 — 8-2-0 (3-1-0)
S30	●	North Carolina St.	20 10
O7	●	Tulane	26 13
O14	●	at North Carolina	30 0
O20	●	at Mercer	13 12
O28	●	NYU	25 0
N4		Florida *JacF*	14 0
N11	●	at Yale	7 0
N18		Auburn *ColGa*	6 14
N25		at Georgia Tech	7 6
D2		at Southern California	0 31

1934 — 7-3-0 (3-2-0)
S29	●	Stetson	42 0
O6	●	at Furman	7 2
O13		North Carolina	0 14
O20		at Tulane	6 7
O27		Alabama *Birm*	6 26
N3	●	Florida *JacF*	14 0
N10	●	at Yale	14 7
N17	●	North Carolina St.	27 0
N24	●	Auburn *ColGa*	18 0
D1		Georgia Tech	7 0

1935 — 6-4-0 (2-4-0)
S28	●	Mercer	31 0
O5	●	at U.T. Chattanooga	40 0
O12	●	Furman	31 7
O19	●	at North Carolina St.	13 0
O26		Alabama	7 17
N2		Florida *JacF*	7 0
N9	●	at Tulane	26 13
N16		LSU	0 13
N23		Auburn *ColGa*	7 19
N30		at Georgia Tech	7 19

1936 — 5-4-1 (3-3-0)
S26	●	Mercer	15 6
O3	●	Furman	13 0
O10		at LSU	7 47
O17		Rice	6 13
O24		Auburn *ColGa*	13 20
O31		Tennessee	0 46
N7	●	Florida *JacF*	26 8
N14	●	at Tulane	12 6
N21	=	Fordham *NYC*	7 7
N28	●	Georgia Tech	16 6

1937 — 6-3-2 (1-2-2)
S25	●	Oglethorpe	60 0
O2	●	at South Carolina	13 7
O9	●	Clemson	14 0
O16	●	at Holy Cross	6 7
O23	●	Mercer	19 0
O30		at Tennessee	0 32
N6		Florida *JacF*	0 6
N13	●	Tulane	7 6
N20	=	Auburn *ColGa*	0 0
N27	=	at Georgia Tech	6 6
D10		at Miami, Fla.	26 8*

JOEL HUNT 1938 (.550)   5-4-1

1938 — 5-4-1 (1-2-1)
S27	●	Citadel	20 0
O1	●	at South Carolina	7 6
O9	●	Furman	38 7
O17	●	Mercer	28 19
O26		at Holy Cross	6 29
N5	●	Florida *JacF*	19 6
N12		at Tulane	6 28
N19		Auburn *ColGa*	14 23
N27	=	Georgia Tech	0 0
D2		at Miami, Fla.	7 13

WALLACE BUTTS 1939-60 (.615)   140-86-9

1939 — 5-6-0 (1-3-0)
S30	●	Citadel	26 0
O7		at Furman	0 20
O14		Holy Cross	0 13
O21		Kentucky *Lou*	6 13
O28		NYU *Brnx*	13 14
N4	●	Mercer	16 9
N11	●	Florida *JacF*	6 2
N18	●	South Carolina	33 7
N25		Auburn *ColGa*	0 7
D2		at Georgia Tech	0 13
D8	●	at Miami, Fla.	13 0

1940 — 5-4-1 (2-3-1)
S27	●	at Oglethorpe	53 0
O5	●	at South Carolina	33 2
O12		Mississippi	14 28
O19		at Columbia	13 19
O25	=	Kentucky	7 7
N2	●	Auburn *ColGa*	14 13
N9		Florida *JacF*	13 18
N16		at Tulane	13 21
N30		Georgia Tech	21 19
D6	●	at Miami, Fla.	28 7

1941 — 9-1-1 (3-1-1)
S27	●	at Mercer	81 0
O4	●	South Carolina	34 6
O10	=	Mississippi	14 14
O18	●	at Columbia	7 3
O25		Alabama *Birm*	14 27
N1	●	Auburn *ColGa*	7 0
N8	●	Florida *JacF*	19 3
N15	●	Centre	47 6
N22	●	Dartmouth	35 0
N29	●	at Georgia Tech	21 0
ORANGE BOWL			
J1	●	TCU	40 26

1942 — 11-1-0 (6-1-0)
S19	●	Kentucky *Lou*	7 6
S25	●	Jacksonville NAS *Mac*	14 0
O3	●	Furman	40 7
O10	●	Mississippi *Mem*	48 13
O17	●	Tulane	40 0
O24	●	at Cincinnati	35 13
O31	●	Alabama *Atl*	21 10
N7	●	Florida *JacF*	75 0
N14	●	at U.T. Chattanooga	40 0
N21		Auburn *ColGa*	13 27
N28	●	Georgia Tech	34 0
ROSE BOWL			
J1	●	UCLA	9 0

1943 — 6-4-0 (0-3-0)
S17	●	Presbyterian	25 7
S25		at LSU	27 34
O1	●	Tennessee Tech	67 0
O8	●	Wake Forest	7 0
O10		at Daniel Field	7 18
O23		LSU *ColGa*	6 27
O29		Samford	39 0
N5	●	Presbyterian	40 12
N13		VMI *Atl*	46 7
N27		at Georgia Tech	0 48

1944 — 7-3-0 (4-2-0)
S29	●	Wake Forest	7 14
O6	●	Presbyterian	67 0
O13	●	Kentucky	13 12
O20	●	Daniel Field	57 6
O28		LSU *Atl*	7 15
N4	●	Alabama *Birm*	14 7
N11	●	Florida *JacF*	38 12
N18	●	Auburn *ColGa*	49 13
N24		Clemson	21 7
D2		Georgia Tech	0 44

1945 — 9-2-0 (4-2-0)
S22	●	Murray St.	49 0
S29	●	Clemson	20 0
O5	●	at Miami, Fla.	27 21
O13	●	at Kentucky	48 6
O20		LSU	0 32
O27		Alabama *Birm*	14 28
N3	●	at U.T. Chattanooga	34 7
N10	●	Florida *JacF*	34 0
N17	●	Auburn *ColGa*	35 0
	●	at Georgia Tech	33 0
OIL BOWL			
J1	●	Tulsa	20 6

1946 — 11-0-0 (5-0-0)
S27	●	Clemson	35 12
O5	●	at Temple	35 7
O11	●	Kentucky	28 13
O19	●	Oklahoma State	33 13
O26	●	at Furman	70 7
N2	●	Alabama	14 0
N9	●	Florida *JacF*	33 14
N16	●	Auburn *ColGa*	41 0
N23	●	at U.T. Chattanooga	48 27
N30	●	Georgia Tech	35 7
SUGAR BOWL			
J1	●	North Carolina	20 10

1947 — 7-4-1 (3-3-0)
S19	●	Furman	13 7
S27		at North Carolina	7 14
O4	●	LSU	35 19
O11		at Kentucky	0 26
O18	●	at Oklahoma State	20 7
O25		Alabama	7 17
O31	●	Clemson	21 6
N8	●	Florida *JacF*	34 6
N15	●	Auburn *ColGa*	28 6
N22	●	at U.T. Chattanooga	27 0
N29		at Georgia Tech	0 7
GATOR BOWL			
J1	=	Maryland	20 20

1948 — 9-2-0 (6-0-0)
S25	●	U.T. Chattanooga	14 7
O2		North Carolina	14 21
O9	●	Kentucky	35 12
O16		at LSU	22 0
O22	●	at Miami, Fla.	42 21
O30	●	Alabama *Birm*	35 0
N6	●	Florida *JacF*	20 12
N13	●	Auburn *ColGa*	42 14
N20	●	Furman	33 0
N27		Georgia Tech	21 13
ORANGE BOWL			
J1		Texas	28 41

1949 — 4-6-1 (1-4-1)
S16	●	Furman	25 0
S23	●	U.T. Chattanooga	42 6
O1		at North Carolina	14 21
O8		at Kentucky	0 25
O14	●	LSU	7 0
O21		at Miami, Fla.	9 13
O29		Alabama	7 14
N5		Florida *JacF*	7 28
N12	●	Duquesne *ColGa*	40 0
N19	=	Auburn	20 20
N26		at Georgia Tech	6 7

1950 — 6-3-3 (3-2-1)
S23		Maryland	27 7
S29	=	St. Mary's Cal. *SF*	7 7
O7	=	North Carolina	0 0
O14	●	Mississippi State	27 0
O21	=	at LSU	13 13
O27	●	at Boston College	19 7
N4	●	Alabama *Birm*	7 14
N11	●	Florida *JacF*	6 0
N18	●	Auburn *ColGa*	12 10
N25	●	Furman	40 0
D2		Georgia Tech	0 7
PRESIDENTIAL CUP			
D9		Texas A&M *CP*	20 40

104 GEORGIA

THE SCHOOLS

1951 5-5-0 (2-4-0)

S22	●	George Washington	33	0
S29	●	at North Carolina	28	16
O6	|	at Mississippi State	0	6
O13		Maryland	7	43
O20	|	LSU	0	7
O27	●	Boston College	35	28
N3	|	Alabama	14	16
N10	● |	Florida JacF	7	6
N17	● |	Auburn ColGa	46	14
D1	|	at Georgia Tech	6	48

1952 7-4-0 (4-3-0)

S20	● |	at Vanderbilt	19	7
S27	● |	at Tulane	21	16
O4	●	North Carolina	49	0
O11		Maryland	0	37
O18	● |	at LSU	27	14
O25	|	Florida JacF	0	30
N1	|	Alabama Birm	19	34
N8	●	at Pennsylvania	34	27
N15	● |	Auburn ColGa	13	7
N29	|	Georgia Tech	9	23
D5	●	at Miami, Fla.	35	13

1953 3-8-0 (1-5-0)

S19	●	Villanova Phil	32	19
S26	● |	Tulane	16	14
O3		Texas A&M Dal	12	14
O10		at Maryland	13	40
O17	|	LSU	6	14
O24	●	North Carolina	27	14
O31	|	Alabama	12	33
N7	|	Florida JacF	7	21
N14	|	Auburn ColGa	18	39
N21		Southern Miss JaM	0	14
N28	|	at Georgia Tech	12	28

1954 6-3-1 (3-2-1)

S18	●	at Florida State	14	0
S25	●	Clemson	14	7
O2		Texas A&M	0	6
O9	●	at North Carolina	21	7
O16	● |	Vanderbilt	16	14
O23	● |	at Tulane	7	0
O30	= |	Alabama Birm	0	0
N6	● |	Florida JacF	14	13
N13	|	Auburn ColGa	0	35
N27	|	Georgia Tech	3	7

1955 4-6-0 (2-5-0)

S17	|	Mississippi Atl	13	26
S24	● |	Vanderbilt	14	13
O1		at Clemson	7	26
O8	●	North Carolina	28	7
O15	●	at Florida State	47	14
O22	|	Tulane	0	14
O29	● |	Alabama	35	14
N5	|	Florida JacF	13	19
N12	|	Auburn ColGa	13	16
N26	|	at Georgia Tech	3	21

1956 3-6-1 (1-6-0)

S22	|	at Vanderbilt	0	14
S29	●	Florida State	3	0
O6	|	Mississippi State	7	19
O13	●	at North Carolina	26	12
O19	=	at Miami, Fla.	7	7
O27	|	Kentucky	7	14
N3	● |	Alabama Birm	16	13
N10	|	Florida JacF	0	28
N17	|	Auburn ColGa	0	20
D1	|	Georgia Tech	0	35

1957 3-7-0 (3-4-0)

S21		Texas Atl	7	26
S28	|	Vanderbilt	6	9
O5		at Michigan	0	26
O11	● |	at Tulane	13	6
O19		Navy Nor	14	27
O26	● |	at Kentucky	33	14
N2	|	Alabama	13	14
N9	|	Florida JacF	0	22
N16	|	Auburn ColGa	0	6
N30	● |	at Georgia Tech	7	0

1958 4-6-0 (2-4-0)

S20		at Texas	8	13
S27	|	at Vanderbilt	14	21
O4		South Carolina	14	24
O11	●	Florida State JacF	28	13
O25	● |	Kentucky	28	0
N1	|	at Alabama	0	12
N8	|	Florida JacF	6	7
N15	|	Auburn ColGa	6	21
N22	●	Citadel	76	0
N29	● |	Georgia Tech	16	3

1959 10-1-0 (7-0-0)

S19	● |	Alabama	17	3
S26	● |	Vanderbilt	21	6
O3		at South Carolina	14	30
O10	●	Hardin-Simmons	35	6
O17	● |	Mississippi State Atl	15	0
O24	● |	at Kentucky	14	7
O31	●	Florida State	42	0
N7	● |	Florida JacF	21	10
N14	● |	Auburn	14	13
N28	● |	at Georgia Tech	21	14
		ORANGE BOWL		
J1	●	Missouri	14	0

1960 6-4-0 (4-3-0)

S17	|	Alabama Birm	6	21
S24	● |	at Vanderbilt	18	7
O1	●	South Carolina	38	6
O7		at Southern California	3	10
O15	● |	Mississippi State	20	17
O22	● |	at Kentucky	17	13
O29	●	Tulsa	45	7
N5	|	Florida JacF	14	22
N12	|	at Auburn	6	9
N26	● |	Georgia Tech	7	6

JOHNNY GRIFFITH
1961-63 (.400) 10-16-4

1961 3-7-0 (2-5-0)

S23	|	Alabama	6	32
S30	|	Vanderbilt	0	21
O7	●	South Carolina	17	14
O14		at Florida State	0	3
O21	● |	Mississippi State Atl	10	7
O28	● |	Kentucky	16	15
N3		at Miami, Fla.	7	32
N11	|	Florida JacF	14	21
N18	|	Auburn	7	10
D2	|	at Georgia Tech	7	22

1962 3-4-3 (2-3-1)

S22	|	Alabama Birm	0	35
S29	● |	at Vanderbilt	10	0
O6	=	at South Carolina	7	7
O13	●	at Clemson	24	16
O20		Florida State	0	18
O27	= |	Kentucky	7	7
N3	=	North Carolina St.	10	10
N10	|	Florida JacF	15	23
N17	● |	at Auburn	30	21
D1	|	Georgia Tech	6	37

1963 4-5-1 (2-4-0)

S21	|	Alabama	7	32
S28	● |	Vanderbilt	20	0
O5	●	South Carolina	27	7
O12	=	at Clemson	7	7
O18	●	at Miami, Fla.	31	14
O26	● |	at Kentucky	17	14
N2		at North Carolina	7	28
N9	|	Florida JacF	14	21
N16	|	Auburn	0	14
N30	|	at Georgia Tech	3	14

VINCE DOOLEY
1964-88 (.715) 201-77-10

1964 7-3-1 (3-2-0)

S19	|	at Alabama	3	31
S26	● |	at Vanderbilt	7	0
O3	=	at South Carolina	7	7
O10	●	Clemson	19	7
O17		Florida State	14	17
O24	● |	Kentucky	21	7
O31	●	North Carolina	24	8
N7	● |	Florida JacF	14	7
N14	|	at Auburn	7	14
N28	●	Georgia Tech	7	0
		SUN BOWL		
D26	●	Texas Tech	7	0

1965 6-4-0 (3-3-0)

S18	● |	Alabama	18	17
S25	● |	Vanderbilt	24	10
O2	●	at Michigan	15	7
O9	● ||	Clemson	23	9
O16		at Florida State	3	10
O23	|	at Kentucky	10	28
O30	●	at North Carolina	47	35
N6	|	Florida JacF	10	14
N13	|	Auburn	19	21
N27	●	at Georgia Tech	17	7

1966 10-1-0 (6-0-0)

S17	● |	Mississippi State JaM	20	17
S24	●	VMI Roa	43	7
O1	●	at South Carolina	7	0
O8	● |	Mississippi	9	3
O14		at Miami, Fla.	6	7
O22	● |	Kentucky	27	15
O29	● ||	North Carolina	28	3
N5	● |	Florida JacF	27	10
N12	● |	at Auburn	21	13
N26	●	Georgia Tech	23	14
		COTTON BOWL		
D31	●	SM	24	9

1967 7-4-0 (4-2-0)

S23	● |	Mississippi State	30	0
S30	● ||	at Clemson	24	17
O7	●	South Carolina	21	0
O14	|	Mississippi JaM	20	29
O21	●	VMI	56	6
O28	● |	at Kentucky	31	7
N4		at Houston	14	15
N11	|	Florida JacF	16	17
N18	● |	Auburn	17	0
N25	●	at Georgia Tech	21	14
		LIBERTY BOWL		
D16		North Carolina St.	7	14

1968 8-1-2 (5-0-1)

S14	= |	at Tennessee	17	17
S28	●	Clemson	31	13
O5	●	at South Carolina	21	20
O12	● |	Mississippi	21	7
O19	● |	Vanderbilt	32	6
O26	● |	at Kentucky	35	14
N2	=	Houston	10	10
N9	● |	Florida JacF	51	0
N16	● |	at Auburn	17	3
N30	●	Georgia Tech	47	8
		SUGAR BOWL		
J1		Arkansas	2	16

1969 5-5-1 (2-3-1)

S20	●	Tulane	35	0
S27	●	at Clemson	30	0
O4	●	South Carolina	41	16
O11	|	Mississippi JaM	17	25
O18	● |	at Vanderbilt	40	8
O25	● |	Kentucky	30	0
N1	|	Tennessee	3	17
N8	= |	Florida JacF	13	13
N15	|	Auburn	3	16
N29		at Georgia Tech	0	6
		SUN BOWL		
D20		Nebraska	6	45

1970 5-5-0 (3-3-0)

S19		at Tulane	14	17
S26	●	Clemson	38	0
O3	|	Mississippi State JaM	6	7
O10	|	Mississippi	21	31
O17	● |	Vanderbilt	37	3
O24	● |	at Kentucky	19	3
O31	●	South Carolina	52	34
N7	|	Florida JacF	17	24
N14	● |	at Auburn	31	17
N28		Georgia Tech	7	17

1971 11-1-0 (5-1-0)

S11	●	Oregon State	56	25
S18	●	Tulane	17	7
S25	●	at Clemson	28	0
O2	● |	Mississippi State	35	7
O9	● |	Mississippi JaM	38	7
O16	● |	at Vanderbilt	24	0
O23	● |	Kentucky	34	0
O30	●	at South Carolina	24	0
N6	● |	Florida JacF	49	7
N13	|	Auburn	20	35
N25	●	at Georgia Tech	28	24
		GATOR BOWL		
D31	●	North Carolina	7	3

1972 7-4-0 (4-3-0)

S16	●	Baylor	24	14
S23		at Tulane	13	24
S30	●	North Carolina St.	28	22
O7	|	Alabama	7	25
O14	● |	Mississippi JaM	14	13
O21	● |	Vanderbilt	28	3
O28	● |	at Kentucky	13	7
N4	|	Tennessee	0	14
N11	● |	Florida JacF	10	7
N18	|	at Auburn	10	27
D2	●	Georgia Tech	27	7

1973 7-4-1 (3-4-0)

S15	=	Pittsburgh	7	7
S22	●	Clemson	31	14
S29	●	North Carolina St.	31	12
O6	|	at Alabama	14	28
O13	● |	Mississippi	20	0
O20	|	at Vanderbilt	14	18
O27	|	Kentucky	7	12
N3	● |	at Tennessee	35	31
N10	|	Florida JacF	10	11
N17	● |	Auburn	28	14
D1	●	at Georgia Tech	10	3
		PEACH BOWL		
D28	●	Maryland	17	16

1974 6-6-0 (4-2-0)

S14	●	Oregon State	48	35
S21	|	Mississippi State JaM	14	38
S28	●	South Carolina	52	14
O5		at Clemson	24	28
O12	● |	Mississippi	49	0
O19	● |	Vanderbilt	38	31
O26	● |	at Kentucky	24	20
N2		Houston	24	31
N9	● |	Florida JacF	17	16
N16	|	at Auburn	13	17
N30		Georgia Tech	14	34
		TANGERINE BOWL		
D21		Miami, Ohio	10	21

1975 9-3-0 (5-1-0)

S13		Pittsburgh	9	19
S20	● |	Mississippi State	28	6
S27	●	at South Carolina	28	20
O4	●	Clemson	35	7
O11	|	at Mississippi	13	28
O18	● |	at Vanderbilt	47	3
O25	● |	Kentucky	21	13
N1	●	Richmond	28	24
N8	● |	Florida JacF	10	7
N15	● |	Auburn	28	13
N27	●	at Georgia Tech	42	26
		COTTON BOWL		
J1		Arkansas	10	31

1976 10-2-0 (5-1-0)

S11	●	California	36	24
S18	●	at Clemson	41	0
S25	●	South Carolina	20	12
O2	● |	Alabama	21	0
O9	|	at Mississippi	17	21
O16	● |	Vanderbilt	45	0
O23	● |	at Kentucky	31	7
O30	●	Cincinnati	31	17
N6	● |	Florida JacF	41	27
N13	● |	at Auburn	28	0
N27	●	Georgia Tech	13	10
		SUGAR BOWL		
J1		Pittsburgh	3	27

1977 5-6-0 (2-4-0)

S10	●	Oregon	27	16
S17		Clemson	6	7
S24	●	at South Carolina	15	13
O1	|	at Alabama	10	18
O8	● |	Mississippi	14	13
O15	● |	at Vanderbilt	24	13
O22	|	Kentucky	0	33
O29	●	Richmond	23	7
N5	|	Florida JacF	17	22
N12	|	Auburn	14	33
N26		at Georgia Tech	7	16

1978 9-2-1 (5-0-1)

S16	●	Baylor	16	14
S23	●	Clemson	12	0
S30		at South Carolina	10	27
O7	● |	Mississippi	42	3
O14	● |	at LSU	24	17
O21	● |	Vanderbilt	31	10
O28	● |	at Kentucky	17	16
N4	●	VMI	41	3
N11	● |	Florida JacF	24	22
N18	= |	at Auburn	22	22
D2	●	Georgia Tech	29	28
		BLUEBONNET BOWL		
D31		Stanford	22	25

1979 6-5-0 (5-1-0)

S15		Wake Forest	21	22
S22		at Clemson	7	12
S29		South Carolina	20	27
O6	● |	at Mississippi	24	21
O13	● |	LSU	21	14
O20	● |	at Vanderbilt	31	10
O27	● |	Kentucky	20	6
N3		Virginia	0	31
N10	● |	Florida JacF	33	10
N17	|	Auburn	13	33
D1	●	at Georgia Tech	16	3

GEORGIA 105

1980 12-0-0 (6-0-0)
S6 ● | at Tennessee 16 15
S13 ● Texas A&M 42 0
S20 ● Clemson 20 16
S27 ● TCU 34 3
O11 ● | Mississippi 28 21
O18 ● | Vanderbilt 41 0
O25 ● | at Kentucky 27 0
N1 ● South Carolina 13 10
N8 ● | Florida JacF 26 21
N15 ● | at Auburn 31 21
N29 ● Georgia Tech 38 20
SUGAR BOWL
J1 ● Notre Dame 17 10

1981 10-2-0 (6-0-0)
S5 ● | Tennessee 44 0
S12 ● California 27 13
S19 at Clemson 3 13
S26 ● South Carolina 24 0
O10 ● | at Mississippi 37 7
O17 ● | at Vanderbilt 53 21
O24 ● | Kentucky 21 0
O31 ● Temple 49 3
N7 ● | Florida JacF 26 21
N14 ● | Auburn 24 13
N28 ● at Georgia Tech 44 7
SUGAR BOWL
J1 Pittsburgh 20 24

1982 11-1-0 (6-0-0)
S6 ● Clemson 13 7
S11 ● Brigham Young 17 14
S25 ● at South Carolina 34 18
O2 ● | at Mississippi State 29 22
O9 ● | Mississippi 33 10
O16 ● | Vanderbilt 27 13
O23 ● | at Kentucky 27 14
O30 ● Memphis 34 3
N6 ● | Florida JacF 44 0
N13 ● | at Auburn 19 14
N27 ● Georgia Tech 38 18
SUGAR BOWL
J1 Penn State 23 27

1983 10-1-1 (5-1-0)
S3 ● UCLA 19 8
S17 = at Clemson 16 16
S24 ● South Carolina 31 13
O1 ● | Mississippi State 20 7
O8 ● | at Mississippi 36 11
O15 ● | at Vanderbilt 20 13
O22 ● | Kentucky 47 21
O29 ● Temple 31 14
N5 ● | Florida JacF 10 9
N12 | Auburn 7 13
N26 ● at Georgia Tech 27 24
COTTON BOWL
J2 ● Texas 10 9

1984 7-4-1 (4-2-0)
S8 ● Southern Miss 26 19
S22 ● Clemson 26 23
S29 at South Carolina 10 17
O6 ● | Alabama Birm 24 14
O13 ● | Mississippi 18 12
O20 ● | Vanderbilt 62 35
O27 ● | at Kentucky 37 7
N3 ● Memphis 13 3
N10 | Florida JacF 0 27
N17 | at Auburn 12 21
D1 Georgia Tech 18 35
CITRUS BOWL
D22 = Florida State 17 17

1985 7-3-2 (3-2-1)
S2 | Alabama 16 20
S14 ● Baylor 17 14
S21 ● at Clemson 20 13
S28 ● South Carolina 35 21
O12 ● | Mississippi JaM 49 21
O19 = | at Vanderbilt 13 13
O26 ● | Kentucky 26 6
N2 ● Tulane 58 3
N9 ● | Florida JacF 24 3
N16 | Auburn 10 24
N30 at Georgia Tech 16 20
SUN BOWL
D28 = Arizona 13 13

1986 8-4-0 (4-2-0)
S13 ● Duke 31 7
S20 Clemson 28 31
S27 ● at South Carolina 31 26
O4 ● | Mississippi 14 10
O11 | at LSU 14 23
O18 ● | Vanderbilt 38 16
O25 ● | at Kentucky 31 9
N1 ● Richmond 28 13
N8 | Florida JacF 19 31
N15 ● | at Auburn 20 16
N29 ● Georgia Tech 31 24
HALL OF FAME BOWL
D23 Boston College 24 27

1987 9-3-0 (4-2-0)
S5 ● Virginia 30 22
S12 ● Oregon State 41 7
S19 at Clemson 20 21
S26 ● South Carolina 13 6
O3 ● | at Mississippi 31 14
O10 | LSU 23 26
O17 ● | at Vanderbilt 52 24
O24 ● | Kentucky 17 14
N7 ● | Florida JacF 23 10
N14 | Auburn 11 27
N28 ● at Georgia Tech 30 16
LIBERTY BOWL
D29 ● Arkansas 20 17

1988 9-3-0 (5-2-0)
S3 ● | Tennessee 28 17
S10 ● TCU 38 10
S17 ● | at Mississippi State 42 35
S24 at South Carolina 10 23
O1 ● | Mississippi 36 12
O8 ● | Vanderbilt 41 22
O22 | at Kentucky 10 16
O29 ● William & Mary 59 24
N5 ● | Florida JacF 26 3
N12 | at Auburn 10 20
N26 ● Georgia Tech 24 3
GATOR BOWL
J1 ● Michigan State 34 27

RAY GOFF
1989-95 (.574) 46-34-1

1989 6-6-0 (4-3-0)
S16 ● Baylor 15 3
S23 ● | Mississippi State 23 6
S30 South Carolina 20 24
O7 | at Tennessee 14 17
O14 | at Mississippi 13 17
O21 ● | at Vanderbilt 35 16
O28 ● | Kentucky 34 23
N4 ● Temple 37 10
N11 ● | Florida JacF 17 10
N18 | Auburn 3 20
D2 at Georgia Tech 22 33
PEACH BOWL
D30 Syracuse 18 19

1990 4-7-0 (2-5-0)
S8 | at LSU 13 18
S15 ● Southern Miss 18 17
S22 ● | Alabama 17 16
S29 ● East Carolina 19 15
O6 at Clemson 3 34
O13 | Mississippi 12 28
O20 ● | Vanderbilt 39 28
O27 | at Kentucky 24 26
N10 | Florida JacF 7 38
N17 | at Auburn 10 33
D1 Georgia Tech 23 40

1991 9-3-0 (4-3-0)
A31 ● Western Carolina 48 0
S7 ● | LSU 31 10
S21 | at Alabama 0 10
S28 ● Fullerton St. 27 14
O5 ● Clemson 27 12
O12 ● | at Mississippi 37 17
O19 | at Vanderbilt 25 27
O26 ● | Kentucky 49 27
N9 | Florida JacF 13 45
N16 ● | Auburn 37 27
N30 ● at Georgia Tech 18 15
INDEPENDENCE BOWL
D29 ● Arkansas 24 15

1992 10-2-0 (6-2-0)
S5 ● | at South Carolina 28 6
S12 | Tennessee 31 34
S19 ● Fullerton St. 56 0
S26 ● | Mississippi 37 11
O3 ● | at Arkansas 27 3
O10 ● Georgia So. 34 7
O17 ● | Vanderbilt 30 20
O24 ● | at Kentucky 40 7
O31 | Florida JacF 24 26
N14 ● | at Auburn 14 10
N28 ● Georgia Tech 31 17
FLORIDA CITRUS BOWL
J1 ● Ohio State 21 14

1993 5-6-0 (2-6-0)
S4 | South Carolina 21 23
S11 | at Tennessee 6 38
S18 ● Texas Tech 52 37
S25 | at Mississippi 14 31
O2 | Arkansas 10 20
O9 ● Southern Miss 54 24
O16 ● | at Vanderbilt 41 3
O23 ● | Kentucky 33 28
O30 | Florida JacF 26 33
N13 | Auburn 28 42
N25 ● at Georgia Tech 43 10

1994 6-4-1 (3-4-1)
S3 ● | at South Carolina 24 21
S10 | Tennessee 23 41
S17 ● La. Monroe 70 6
S24 ● | Mississippi 17 14
O1 | Alabama Birm 28 29
O8 ● Clemson 40 14
O15 | Vanderbilt 30 43
O22 ● | at Kentucky 34 30
O29 | at Florida 14 52
N12 = | at Auburn 23 23
N25 ● Georgia Tech 48 10

1995 6-6-0 (3-5-0)
S2 ● | South Carolina 42 23
S9 | at Tennessee 27 30
S16 ● New Mexico St. 40 13
S23 | at Mississippi 10 18
S30 | Alabama 0 31
O7 ● at Clemson 19 17
O14 ● | at Vanderbilt 17 6
O21 ● | Kentucky 12 3
O28 | Florida 17 52
N11 | Auburn 31 37
N23 ● at Georgia Tech 18 17
PEACH BOWL
D30 Virginia 27 34

JIM DONNAN
1996-2000 (.678) 40-19

1996 5-6 (3-5)
A31 Southern Miss 7 11
S14 | at South Carolina 14 23
S21 ● Texas Tech 15 12
O5 ● | at Mississippi State 38 19
O12 | Tennessee 17 29
O19 ● | Vanderbilt 13 2
O26 | at Kentucky 17 24
N2 | Florida JacF 7 47
N16 ● | at Auburn 56 49
N23 | Mississippi 27 31
N30 ● Georgia Tech 19 10

1997 10-2 (6-2)
A30 ● Arkansas State 38 7
S13 ● | South Carolina 31 15
S20 ● La. Monroe 42 3
O4 ● | Mississippi State 47 0
O11 | at Tennessee 13 38
O18 ● | at Vanderbilt 34 13
O25 ● | Kentucky 23 13
N1 ● | Florida JacF 37 17
N15 | Auburn 34 45
N22 ● | at Mississippi 21 14
N29 ● at Georgia Tech 27 24
OUTBACK BOWL
J1 ● Wisconsin 33 6

1998 9-3 (6-2)
S5 ● Kent 56 3
S12 ● | at South Carolina 17 3
S19 ● Wyoming 16 9
O3 ● | at LSU 28 27
O10 | Tennessee 3 22
O17 ● | Vanderbilt 31 6
O24 ● | at Kentucky 28 26
O31 | Florida JacF 7 38
N14 ● | at Auburn 28 17
N21 ● | Mississippi 24 17
N28 Georgia Tech 19 21
PEACH BOWL
D31 ● Virginia 35 33

1999 8-4 (5-3)
S4 ● Utah State 38 7
S11 ● | South Carolina 24 9
S25 ● Central Florida 24 23
O2 ● | LSU 23 22
O9 | at Tennessee 20 37
O16 ● | at Vanderbilt 27 17
O23 ● | Kentucky 49 34
O30 | Florida JacF 14 30
N13 | Auburn 21 38
N20 ● | at Mississippi 20 17
N27 at Georgia Tech 48 51
OUTBACK BOWL
J1 ● Purdue 28 25

2000 8-4 (5-3)
S2 ● Geo. Southern 29 7
S9 | at South Carolina 10 21
S23 ● New Mexico St. 37 0
S30 ● | at Arkansas 38 7
O7 ● | Tennessee 21 10
O14 ● | Vanderbilt 29 19
O21 ● | at Kentucky 34 30
O28 | Florida JacF 23 34
N11 | at Auburn 26 29
N18 ● | Mississippi 32 14
N25 Georgia Tech 15 27
OAHU BOWL
D24 ● Virginia 37 14

MARK RICHT
2001-Present (.786) 81-22

2001 8-4 (5-3)
S1 ● Arkansas State 45 17
S8 | South Carolina 9 14
S29 ● | Arkansas 34 23
O6 ● | at Tennessee 26 24
O13 ● | at Vanderbilt 30 14
O20 ● | Kentucky 43 29
O27 | Florida JacF 10 24
N10 | Auburn 17 24
N17 ● | at Mississippi 35 15
N24 ● at Georgia Tech 31 17
D1 ● Houston 35 7
MUSIC CITY BOWL
D28 Boston College 16 20

2002 13-1 (7-1)
A31 ● Clemson 31 28
S14 ● | at South Carolina 13 7
S21 ● Northwestern St. 45 7
S28 ● New Mexico State 41 10
O5 ● | at Alabama 27 25
O12 ● | Tennessee 18 13
O19 ● | Vanderbilt 48 17
O26 ● | at Kentucky 52 24
N2 | Florida JacF 13 20
N9 ● | Mississippi 31 17
N16 ● | at Auburn 24 21
N30 ● Georgia Tech 51 7
SEC CHAMPIONSHIP GAME
D7 ● Arkansas Atl 30 3
SUGAR BOWL
J1 ● Florida State 26 13

2003 11-3 (6-2)
A30 ● at Clemson 30 0
S6 ● Middle Tennessee 29 10
S13 ● | South Carolina 31 7
S20 | at LSU 10 17
O4 ● | Alabama 37 23
O11 ● | at Tennessee 41 14
O18 ● | at Vanderbilt 27 8
O25 ● UAB 16 13
N1 | Florida JacF 13 16
N15 ● | Auburn 26 7
N22 ● | Kentucky 30 10
N29 ● at Georgia Tech 34 17
SEC CHAMPIONSHIP GAME
D6 LSU Atl 13 34
CAPITAL ONE BOWL
J1 ● Purdue 34 27

THE SCHOOLS

2004   10-2   (6-2)

S4	●	Ga. Southern	48	28
S11	● |	at South Carolina	20	16
S18	●	Marshall	13	3
O2	● |	LSU	45	16
O9	|	Tennessee	14	19
O16	● |	Vanderbilt	33	3
O23	● |	at Arkansas	20	14
O30	● |	Florida *JacF*	31	24
N6	● |	at Kentucky	62	17
N13	|	at Auburn	6	24
N27	●	Georgia Tech	19	13
		OUTBACK BOWL		
J1	●	Wisconsin	24	21

2005   10-3   (6-2)

S3	●	Boise State	48	13
S10	● |	South Carolina	17	15
S17	●	La. Monroe	44	7
S24	● |	at Mississippi State	23	10
O8	● |	at Tennessee	27	14
O15	● |	at Vanderbilt	34	17
O22	● |	Arkansas	23	20
O29	|	Florida *JacF*	10	14
N12	|	Auburn	30	31
N19	● |	Kentucky	45	13
N26	●	at Georgia Tech	14	7
		SEC CHAMPIONSHIP GAME		
D3	●	LSU *Atl*	34	14
		SUGAR BOWL		
J2		West Virginia	35	38

2006   9-4   (4-4)

S2	●	Western Kentucky	48	12
S9	● |	at South Carolina	18	0
S16	● |	Ala.-Birmingham	34	0
S23	●	Colorado	14	13
S30	● |	at Mississippi	14	9
O7	|	Tennessee	33	51
O14	|	Vanderbilt	22	24
O21	● |	Mississippi State	27	24
O28	|	Florida *JacF*	14	21
N4	|	at Kentucky	20	24
N11	● |	at Auburn	37	15
N25	●	Georgia Tech	15	12
		CHICK-FIL-A BOWL		
D30	●	Virginia Tech	31	24

2007   11-2   (6-2)

S1	●	Oklahoma State	35	14
S8	|	South Carolina	12	16
S15	●	Western Carolina	45	16
S22	● |	at Alabama	26	23
S29	● |	Mississippi	45	17
O6	|	at Tennessee	14	35
O13	● |	at Vanderbilt	20	17
O27	● |	Florida *JacF*	42	30
N3	●	Troy State	44	34
N10	● |	Auburn	45	20
N17	● |	Kentucky	24	13
N24	●	at Georgia Tech	31	17
		SUGAR BOWL		
J1	●	Hawaii	41	10

2008   10-3   (6-2)

A30	●	Georgia Southern	45	21
S6	●	Central Michigan	56	17
S13	● |	at South Carolina	14	7
S20	●	at Arizona State	27	10
S27	|	Alabama	30	41
O11	● |	Tennessee	26	14
O18	● |	Vanderbilt	24	14
O25	● |	at Louisiana State	52	38
N1	|	Florida *JacF*	10	49
N08	● |	at Kentucky	42	38
N15	● |	at Auburn	17	13
N29		Georgia Tech	42	45
		CAPITAL ONE BOWL		
J1	●	Michigan State	24	12

GEORGIA ANNUAL STATISTICAL LEADERS

YR	RUSHING	YDS	ATT	AVG	PASSING	ATT	CMP	PCT	YDS	RECEIVING	REC	YDS	AVG
1950	Billy Mixon	705	134	5.3	Mal Cook	68	35	.51	535	Zippy Morocco	13	206	15.8
1951	Lauren Hargrove	422	89	4.7	Zeke Bratkowski	248	116	.47	1,578	Harry Babcock	41	666	16.2
1952	Bob Clemens	460	106	4.3	Zeke Bratkowski	262	131	.50	1,824	Johnny Carson	32	467	14.6
1953	Bob Clemens	586	120	4.9	Zeke Bratkowski	224	113	.50	1,461	Johnny Carson	45	663	14.7
1954	Bobby Garrard	442	93	4.8	Jimmy Harper	71	29	.40	407	Roy Wilkins	6	70	11.7
1955	Bobby Garrard	533	107	5.0	Dick Young	97	48	.50	875	James Orr	24	443	18.5
1956	Carl Manning	348	83	4.2	William Hearn	61	26	.43	294	Roy Wilkins	9	116	12.9
1957	Theron Sapp	599	137	4.4	Charley Britt	77	31	.40	415	James Orr	16	237	14.8
1958	Theron Sapp	635	114	5.6	Charley Britt	75	31	.41	535	Norman King	8	138	17.3
1959	Bill Godfrey	319	79	4.0	Fran Tarkenton	102	62	.61	736	Bobby Towns	18	263	14.6
1960	Fred Brown	355	78	4.6	Fran Tarkenton	185	108	.58	1,189	Fred Brown	31	275	8.9
1961	Bill McKenny	328	81	4.0	Larry Rakestraw	136	88	.65	710	Bill McKenny	23	202	8.8
1962	Leon Armbrester	266	64	4.2	Larry Rakestraw	196	78	.40	1,135	Mickey Babb	20	354	17.7
1963	Larry Rakestraw	170	102	1.7	Larry Rakestraw	209	103	.50	1,297	Pat Hodgson	24	375	15.6
1964	Preston Ridlehuber	368	110	3.3	Lynn Hughes	54	17	.31	408	Leon Armbrester	7	104	14.9
1965	Preston Ridlehuber	401	142	2.8	Kirby Moore	60	32	.53	487	Pat Hodgson	26	312	12.0
1966	Ronnie Jenkins	669	171	3.9	Kirby Moore	80	36	.45	524	Billy Payne	12	144	12.0
1967	Ronnie Jenkins	646	170	3.8	Kirby Moore	116	46	.40	699	Dennis Hughes	18	356	20.0
1968	Bruce Kemp	553	140	4.0	Mike Cavan	207	116	.56	1,619	Charley Whittemore	40	608	15.2
1969	Julian Smiley	494	124	4.0	Mike Cavan	162	71	.44	946	Charley Whittemore	28	452	16.1
1970	Ricky Lake	570	135	4.2	Mike Cavan	79	42	.53	651	Charley Whittemore	46	620	13.5
1971	Andy Johnson	870	174	5.0	Andy Johnson	77	33	.43	341	Lynn Hunnicutt	14	141	10.1
1972	Jimmy Poulos	556	150	3.7	James Ray	121	55	.45	756	Bob Burns	23	389	16.9
1973	Jimmy Poulos	702	167	4.2	Andy Johnson	120	43	.36	506	Richard Appleby	12	171	14.3
1974	Glynn Harrison	959	149	6.4	Matt Robinson	121	60	.50	1,317	Richard Appleby	23	510	22.2
1975	Glynn Harrison	894	131	6.8	Matt Robinson	72	29	.40	369	Richard Appleby	13	221	17.0
1976	Kevin McLee	1,058	218	4.9	Matt Robinson	81	36	.44	609	Gene Washington	20	469	23.5
1977	Kevin McLee	717	178	4.0	Jeff Pyburn	55	25	.45	312	Jesse Murray	13	216	16.7
1978	Willie McClendon	1,312	287	4.6	Jeff Pyburn	133	72	.54	878	Lindsay Scott	36	484	13.4
1979	Matt Simon	589	152	3.9	Buck Belue	112	59	.53	719	Lindsay Scott	34	512	15.0
1980	Herschel Walker	1,616	274	5.9	Buck Belue	156	77	.49	1,314	Amp Arnold	20	357	17.9
1981	Herschel Walker	1,891	385	4.9	Buck Belue	188	114	.61	1,603	Lindsay Scott	42	728	17.3
1982	Herschel Walker	1,752	335	4.9	John Lastinger	148	62	.42	907	Clarence Kay	12	175	14.6
1983	Keith Montgomery	519	120	4.3	John Lastinger	137	68	.50	796	Herman Archie	31	355	11.5
1984	Andre Smith	665	110	6.0	Todd Williams	130	64	.49	620	Scott Williams	19	204	10.7
1985	Keith Henderson	731	108	6.8	James Jackson	112	51	.46	759	Herman Archie	10	116	11.6
1986	Lars Tate	954	188	5.1	James Jackson	181	100	.55	1,475	Lars Tate	22	214	9.7
1987	Lars Tate	1,016	208	4.9	James Jackson	132	67	.51	1,026	John Thomas	25	391	15.6
1988	Tim Worley	1,216	191	6.4	Wayne Johnson	122	66	.54	945	John Thomas	23	354	15.4
1989	Rodney Hampton	1,059	218	4.9	Greg Talley	174	92	.53	1,330	Kirk Warner	30	404	13.5
1990	Garrison Hearst	717	162	4.4	Greg Talley	123	72	.59	871	Sean Hummings	25	376	15.0
1991	Garrison Hearst	968	153	6.3	Eric Zeier	286	159	.56	1,984	Andre Hastings	48	683	14.2
1992	Garrison Hearst	1,594	228	7.0	Eric Zeier	258	151	.59	2,248	Andre Hastings	52	860	16.5
1993	Terrell Davis	824	167	4.9	Eric Zeier	425	269	.63	3,525	Brice Hunter	76	970	12.8
1994	Terrell Davis	445	97	4.6	Eric Zeier	433	259	.60	3,396	Brice Hunter	59	799	13.5
1995	Torin Kirtsey	603	134	4.5	Hines Ward	112	69	.62	872	Juan Daniels	46	726	15.8
1996	Robert Edwards	800	184	4.3	Mike Bobo	344	175	.51	2,440	Hines Ward	52	900	17.3
1997	Robert Edwards	908	165	5.5	Mike Bobo	306	199	.65	2,751	Hines Ward	55	715	13.0
1998	Olandis Gary	698	143	4.9	Quincy Carter	290	176	.61	2,484	Tony Small	48	675	14.1
1999	Jasper Sanks	896	177	5.1	Quincy Carter	380	216	.57	2,713	Terrence Edwards	53	772	14.6
2000	Brett Millican	375	67	5.6	Quincy Carter	183	91	.50	1,250	Terrence Edwards	53	704	13.3
2001	Verron Haynes	691	126	5.5	David Greene	324	192	.59	2,789	Terrence Edwards	39	613	15.7
2002	Musa Smith	1,324	260	5.1	David Greene	379	218	.58	2,924	Terrence Edwards	59	1,004	17.0
2003	Michael Cooper	673	156	4.3	David Greene	438	264	.60	3,307	Reggie Brown	49	662	13.5
2004	Thomas Brown	875	172	5.1	David Greene	299	175	.59	2,508	Reggie Brown	53	860	16.2
2005	Thomas Brown	736	147	5.0	D.J. Shockley	310	173	.56	2,588	Leonard Pope	39	541	13.9
2006	Kregg Lumpkin	798	162	4.9	Matthew Stafford	256	135	.53	1,749	Martrez Milner	30	425	14.2
2007	Knowshon Moreno	1,334	248	5.4	Matthew Stafford	348	194	.56	2,523	Sean Bailey	39	615	15.8
2008	Knowshon Moreno	1,400	250	5.6	Matthew Stafford	383	235	.61	3,459	Mohamed Massaquoi	58	920	15.9

Receiving leaders by receptions
The NCAA began including postseason stats in 2002

THE SCHOOLS

GEORGIA RECORD BOOK

SINGLE-GAME RECORDS

Rushing Yards	283	Herschel Walker (Oct. 18, 1980 vs. Vanderbilt)
Passing Yards	544	Eric Zeier (Oct. 9, 1993 vs. Southern Mississipi)
Receiving Yards	201	Fred Gibson (Oct. 20, 2001 vs. Kentucky)
All-Purpose Yards	290	Rodney Hampton (Oct. 3, 1987 vs. Ole Miss)
Scoring	30	Robert Edwards (Sept. 2, 1995 vs. South Carolina)
Field Goals	6	Billy Bennett (Nov. 24, 2001 vs. Georgia Tech)
Tackles	26	Knox Culpepper (Nov. 26, 1983 vs. Georgia Tech)
Interceptions	3	Four players tied

SINGLE-SEASON RECORDS

Rushing Yards	1,891	Herschel Walker, 1981 (385 att.)
Passing Yards	3,525	Eric Zeier, 1993 (269-425)
Receiving Yards	1,004	Terrence Edwards, 2002 (59 rec.)
All-Purpose Yards	2,067	Herschel Walker, 1981 (1,891 rush, 84 rec., 92 KO ret.)
Scoring	131	Billy Bennett, 2003 (31 FG, 38 PAT)
Touchdowns	21	Garrison Hearst, 1992
Tackles	170	Knox Culpepper, 1984
Interceptions	12	Terry Hoage, 1982
Punting Average	63.0	Bobby Walden, 1958 (3 punts)
Punt Return Average	15.7	Scott Woerner, 1980 (31 ret.)
Kickoff Return Average	36.0	Gene Washington, 1973 (8 ret.)

CAREER RECORDS

Rushing Yards	5,259	Herschel Walker, 1980-82
Passing Yards	11,528	David Greene, 2001-04
Receiving Yards	3,093	Terrence Edwards, 1999-2002
All-Purpose Yards	5,749	Herschel Walker, 1980-82
Scoring	409	Billy Bennett, 2000-03
Touchdowns	52	Herschel Walker, 1980-82
Tackles	467	Ben Zambiasi, 1974-77
Interceptions	16	Jake Scott, 1967-68
Punting Average	43.2	Chip Andrews, 1983-84 (109 punts)
Punt Return Average	14.9	Thomas Flowers, 2004-07 (55 ret.)
Kickoff Return Average	25.6	Ramarcus Brown, 2005-08 (32 ret.)

TEAM RECORDS

Longest Winning Streak	17	Nov. 4, 1945-Sept. 19, 1947, broken vs. North Carolina, 7-14 on Sep. 27, 1947
Longest Undefeated Streak	17	Nov. 4, 1945-Sept. 19, 1947, broken vs. North Carolina, 7-14 on Sep. 27, 1947
Most Consecutive Winning Seasons	13	1964-76
Most Consecutive Bowl Appearances	12	1997-present
Most Points in a Game	108	vs. Alabama Presbyterian, Oct. 4, 1913
Most Points Allowed in a Game	60	vs. Southern California, Dec. 12, 1931
Largest Margin of Victory	108	vs. Alabama Presbyterian, Oct. 4, 1913
Largest Margin of Defeat	60	vs. Southern California, Dec. 12, 1931
Longest Pass Play	93	David Greene to Tyson Browning vs. LSU, Sep. 20, 2003
Longest Field Goal	60	Kevin Butler vs. Clemson, Sep. 22, 1984
Longest Punt	87	Spike Jones vs. Auburn, Nov. 18, 1967
Longest Interception Return	100	Charlie Britt vs. Florida, Nov. 7, 1959

RETIRED NUMBERS

	21	Frank Sinkwich
	34	Herschel Walker
	40	Theron Sapp
	62	Charley Trippi

ALL-TIME TEAM

No all-time or all-century team available

GEORGIA BOWL HISTORY

SEASON	BOWL	DATE	PRE-GAME RANK	TEAMS	SCORE	FINAL RANK	MOST VALUABLE PLAYER(S)	ATT.
1941	ORANGE	Jan. 1, 1942	14	Georgia TCU	40 26			35,786
1942	ROSE	Jan. 1, 1943	2 13	Georgia UCLA	9 0		Charles Trippi, Georgia, HB	93,000
1945	OIL	Jan. 1, 1946		Georgia Tulsa	20 6			27,000
1946	SUGAR	Jan. 1, 1947	3 9	Georgia North Carolina	20 10			68,936
1947	GATOR	Jan. 1, 1948		Georgia Maryland	20 20		Lu Gambino, Maryland, HB	16,666
1948	ORANGE	Jan. 1, 1949	8	Texas Georgia	41 28			60,523
1950	PRESIDENTIAL CUP	Dec. 9, 1950		Texas A&M Georgia	40 20		Bob Smith, Texas A&M, RB Zippy Morocco, Georgia, HB	12,245
1959	ORANGE	Jan. 1, 1960	5 18	Georgia Missouri	14 0			72,186
1964	SUN	Dec. 26, 1964		Georgia Texas Tech	7 0		Preston Ridlehuber, Georgia, QB Jim Wilson, Georgia, T	28,500
1966	COTTON	Dec. 31, 1966	4 10	Georgia SMU	24 9		Kent Lawrence, Georgia, TB George Patton, Georgia, T	75,400
1967	LIBERTY	Dec. 16, 1967		North Carolina St. Georgia	14 7		Jim Donnan, North Carolina St., QB	35,045
1968	SUGAR	Jan. 1, 1969	9 4	Arkansas Georgia	16 2	6 8	Chuck Dicus, Arkansas, FL	82,000
1969	SUN	Dec. 20, 1969	14	Nebraska Georgia	45 6	11	Paul Rogers, Nebraska, HB Jerry Murtaugh, Nebraska, LB	29,723
1971	GATOR	Dec. 31, 1971	6	Georgia North Carolina	7 3	7	Jimmy Poulos, Georgia, TB James Webster, North Carolina, LB	71,208
1973	PEACH	Dec. 28, 1973	18	Georgia Maryland	17 16	20	Louis Carter, Maryland, TB Sylvester Boler, Georgia, LB	38,107
1974	TANGERINE	Dec. 21, 1974	15	Miami (Ohio) Georgia	21 10	10	Sherman Smith, Miami, B Brad Cousino, Miami, L	37,234
1975	COTTON	Jan. 1, 1976	18 12	Arkansas Georgia	31 10	7 19	Ike Forte, Arkansas, RB Hal McAfee, Arkansas, LB	74,500
1976	SUGAR	Jan. 1, 1977	1 5	Pittsburgh Georgia	27 3	1 10	Matt Cavanaugh, Pittsburgh, QB	75,212
1978	BLUEBONNET	Dec. 31, 1978	11	Stanford Georgia	25 22	17 16	Steve Dils, Stanford, QB Gordy Ceresino, Stanford, LB	34,084
1980	SUGAR	Jan. 1, 1981	1 7	Georgia Notre Dame	17 10	1 9	Herschel Walker, Georgia, RB	77,895
1981	SUGAR	Jan. 1, 1982	10 2	Pittsburgh Georgia	24 20	4 6	Dan Marino, Pittsburgh, QB	77,224
1982	SUGAR	Jan. 1, 1983	2 1	Penn State Georgia	27 23	1 4	Todd Blackledge, Penn State, QB	78,124
1983	COTTON	Jan. 2, 1984	7 2	Georgia Texas	10 9	4 5	John Lastinger, Georgia, QB Jeff Leiding, Texas, LB	67,891
1984	CITRUS	Dec. 22, 1984	15	Georgia Florida State	17 17	17	James Jackson, Georgia, QB	51,821
1985	SUN	Dec. 28, 1985		Georgia Arizona	13 13		Peter Anderson, Georgia, C Max Zendejas, Arizona, K	52,203
1986	HALL OF FAME	Dec. 23, 1986	17	Boston College Georgia	27 24	19	James Jackson, Georgia, QB	25,368
1987	LIBERTY	Dec. 29, 1987	15	Georgia Arkansas	20 17	13	Greg Thomas, Arkansas, QB	53,249
1988	GATOR	Jan. 1, 1989	19	Georgia Michigan State	34 27	15	Wayne Johnson, Georgia, QB Andre Rison, Michigan State, WR	76,236
1989	PEACH	Dec. 30, 1989		Syracuse Georgia	19 18		M. Owens, RB, T. Wooden, LB, Syracuse R. Hampton, RB, M. Lewis, LB, Georgia	44,991
1991	INDEPENDENCE	Dec. 29, 1991	24	Georgia Arkansas	24 15	17	Andre Hastings, Georgia, FL Torrey Evans, Georgia, LB	46,932
1992	FLORIDA CITRUS	Jan. 1, 1993	8 15	Georgia Ohio State	21 14	8 18	Garrison Hearst, Georgia, RB	65,861
1995	PEACH	Dec. 30, 1995	18	Virginia Georgia	34 27	16	Tiki Barber, RB, Skeet Jones, LB, Virginia Hines Ward, QB, Whit Marshall, LB, Georgia	70,284
1997	OUTBACK	Jan. 1, 1998	12	Georgia Wisconsin	33 6	10	Mike Bobo, Georgia, QB	56,186
1998	PEACH	Dec. 31, 1998	19 13	Georgia Virginia	35 33	14 18	Olandis Gary, RB, Champ Bailey, DB, Georgia Aaron Brooks, QB, Wally Rainer, LB, Virginia	72,876
1999	OUTBACK	Jan. 1, 2000	21 19	Georgia Purdue	28 25	16 25	Drew Brees, Purdue, QB	54,059
2000	JEEP O'AHU	Dec. 24, 2000		Georgia Virginia	37 14		Terrence Edwards, Georgia, WR	24,187
2001	MUSIC CITY	Dec. 28, 2001	16	Boston College Georgia	20 16	21 22	William Green, Boston College, RB	46,125
2002	SUGAR	Jan. 1, 2003	4 16	Georgia Florida State	26 13	3 21	Musa Smith, Georgia, TB	74,269
2003	CAPITAL ONE	Jan. 1, 2004	11 12	Georgia Purdue	34 27	7 18	David Greene, Georgia, QB	64,565
2004	OUTBACK	Jan. 1, 2005	8 16	Georgia Wisconsin	24 21	7 17	David Pollack, Georgia, DE	62,414
2005	SUGAR	Jan. 2, 2006	11 8	West Virginia Georgia	38 35	5 10	Steve Slaton, West Virginia, RB	74,458
2006	CHICK-FIL-A	Dec. 30, 2006	14	Georgia Virginia Tech	31 24	23 19	Matthew Stafford, Georgia, QB Tony Taylor, Georgia, LB	75,406
2007	SUGAR	Jan. 1, 2008	4 10	Georgia Hawaii	41 10	2 19	Marcus Howard, Georgia, DE	74,383
2008	CAPITAL ONE	Jan. 1, 2009	16 19	Georgia Michigan State	24 12	13 24	Matthew Stafford, Georgia, QB	59,681

THE SCHOOLS

JANUARY 1, 1942 | Orange
GEORGIA 40, TCU 26

	1ST	2ND	3RD	4TH	FINAL
UGA	19	14	7	0	40
TCU	7	0	7	12	26

SCORING SUMMARY
UGA Keuper 2 run (Costa kick)
UGA Conger 61 pass from Sinkwich (kick failed)
UGA Kimsey 60 run from Sinkwich (kick failed)
TCU Gillespie 4 run (Medanich kick)
UGA Davis 15 pass from Sinkwich (Costa kick)
UGA Davis 23 pass from Todd (Costa kick)
UGA Sinkwich 43 run (Costa kick)
TCU Alford 20 pass from Nix (Roach kick)
TCU Alford 15 run from Nix (run failed)
TCU Kring 53 pass from Gillespie (run failed)

UGA	TEAM STATISTICS	TCU
12	First Downs	8
218	Rushing Yards	71
12-24-4	Passing	9-24-6
281	Passing Yards	137
499	Total Yards	208
4-22.2	Punts - Average	7-37.0
3-3	Fumbles - Lost	1-0
7-54	Penalties - Yards	2-24

JANUARY 1, 1943 | Rose
GEORGIA 9, UCLA 0

	1ST	2ND	3RD	4TH	FINAL
UGA	0	0	0	9	9
UCLA	0	0	0	0	0

SCORING SUMMARY
UGA Saftey blocked punt
UGA Sinkwich 1 run (Costa kick)

UGA	TEAM STATISTICS	UCLA
24	First Downs	5
212	Rushing Yards	97
12-30-2	Passing	4-15-4
161	Passing Yards	62
373	Total Yards	159

INDIVIDUAL LEADERS
RUSHING
UGA: Trippi 27-115; Sinkwich 11-33, 1 TD.
UCLA: Snelling 5-41.

JANUARY 1, 1946 | Oil
GEORGIA 20, Tulsa 6

	1ST	2ND	3RD	4TH	FINAL
UGA	7	0	0	13	20
TUL	0	6	0	0	6

SCORING SUMMARY
UGA Smith 3 run (Jernigan kick)
TUL Wilson 1 run (kick failed)
UGA Donaldson 54 pass from Trippi (Jernigan kick)
UGA Trippi 69 punt return (kick failed)

UGA	TEAM STATISTICS	TUL
14	First Downs	7
178	Rushing Yards	69
5-15-1	Passing	6-21-0
110	Passing Yards	79
288	Total Yards	148

JANUARY 1, 1947 | Sugar
GEORGIA 20, North Carolina 10

	1ST	2ND	3RD	4TH	FINAL
UGA	0	0	13	7	20
UNC	0	7	3	0	10

SCORING SUMMARY
UNC Pupa 4 run (Cox kick)
UGA Rauch 4 run (Jernigan kick)
UNC FG Cox 27
UGA Edwards 67 pass from Trippi (kick blocked)
UGA Rauch 13 run (Jernigan kick)

UGA	TEAM STATISTICS	UNC
12	First Downs	17
175	Rushing Yards	166
3-14-1	Passing	8-14-1
81	Passing Yards	99
256	Total Yards	265
7-32.7	Punts - Average	6-38.0
0-0	Fumbles - Lost	1-1

INDIVIDUAL LEADERS
RUSHING
UGA: Trippi 15-77.
UNC: Justice 18-37.

JANUARY 1, 1948 | Gator
MARYLAND 20, GEORGIA 20

	1ST	2ND	3RD	4TH	FINAL
MD	0	7	13	0	20
UGA	0	0	7	13	20

SCORING SUMMARY
MD Gambino 35 run (McHugh kick)
UGA Rauch 1 run (Geri kick)
MD Gambino 1 run (kick failed)
MD Gambino 24 pass from Baroni (McHugh kick)
UGA Geri 4 run (kick failed)
UGA Donaldson 9 pass from Rauch (Geri kick)

MD	TEAM STATISTICS	UGA
16	First Downs	19
247	Rushing Yards	219
7-14-1	Passing	12-20-1
127	Passing Yards	187
374	Total Yards	406
5-44.2	Punts - Average	4-40.0
0-0	Fumbles - Lost	2-1
5-66	Penalties - Yards	4-80

INDIVIDUAL LEADERS
RUSHING
MD: Gambino 22-165, 2 TD; Idzik 2-32.
UGA: Donaldson 10-69; Geri 7-56, 1 TD.
PASSING
MD: Tucker 4-5-0; Baroni 2-3-0, 1 TD.
UGA: Rauch 12-20-1, 187 yards, 1 TD.
RECEIVING
MD: Gambino 2-69, 1 TD; Evans 4-45.
UGA: Henderson 1-62; Edwards 3-44.

JANUARY 1, 1949 | Orange
TEXAS 41, Georgia 28

	1ST	2ND	3RD	4TH	FINAL
TEX	13	7	7	14	41
UGA	7	7	7	7	28

SCORING SUMMARY
UGA Bodine 71 interception return (Geri kick)
TEX Borneman 4 run (Clay kick)
TEX Landry 14 run (kick failed)
UGA Geri 1 run (Geri kick)
TEX Samuels 21 run (Clay kick)
TEX Proctor 24 pass from Campbell (Clay kick)
UGA Geri 6 run (Geri kick)
UGA Walston 37 pass from Rauch (Geri kick)
TEX Clay 2 run (Clay kick)
TEX Clay 4 run (Clay kick)

TEX	TEAM STATISTICS	UGA
19	First Downs	9
332	Rushing Yards	56
5-10-0	Passing	11-17-2
70	Passing Yards	161
402	Total Yards	217
5-40.0	Punts - Average	5-41.0
2-1	Fumbles - Lost	1-1
5-55	Penalties - Yards	6-50

INDIVIDUAL LEADERS
RUSHING
TEX: Landry 17-117, 1 TD; Pyle 11-76; Clay 13-70, 2 TD.
UGA: Geri 15-45, 2 TD.
PASSING
TEX: Campbell 5-10-0, 70 yards, 1 TD.
UGA: Rauch 11-17-2, 161 yards, 1 TD.

DECEMBER 9, 1950 | Presidential Cup
TEXAS A&M 40, GEORGIA 20

	1ST	2ND	3RD	4TH	FINAL
A&M	20	13	7	0	40
UGA	0	0	7	13	20

SCORING SUMMARY
A&M Smith 100 kickoff return (Hooper kick)
A&M Lippman 2 run (kick failed)
A&M Smith 81 run (Hooper kick)
A&M Tidwell 6 run (Hooper kick)
A&M Tidwell 6 run (Hooper kick)
A&M Tidwell 36 run (kick failed)
UGA Morocco 30 run (Durand kick)
UGA Morocco 65 punt return (Durand kick)
UGA Hargrove 1 run (kick failed)

JANUARY 1, 1960 | Orange
GEORGIA 14, Missouri 0

	1ST	2ND	3RD	4TH	FINAL
UGA	7	0	7	0	14
MO	0	0	0	0	0

SCORING SUMMARY
UGA McKenny 29 pass from Tarkenton (Pennington kick)
UGA Box 33 pass from Tarkenton (Pennington kick)

14	TEAM STATISTICS	MO
14	First Downs	17
88	Rushing Yards	80
9-21-2	Passing	14-24-3
128	Passing Yards	180
216	Total Yards	260
7-46.9	Punts - Average	6-38.7
1-0	Fumbles - Lost	3-0
7-44	Penalties - Yards	7-72

INDIVIDUAL LEADERS
RUSHING
UGA: Brown 10-39.
MO: West 9-37; Smith 14-21.
PASSING
UGA: Tarkenton 9-16-1, 128 yards, 2 TD.
MO: Snowden 11-17-1, 152 yards.
RECEIVING
UGA: Box 1-33, 1 TD; Brown 3-29.
MO: Sloan 6-73; Smith 3-35.

DECEMBER 26, 1964 | Sun
GEORGIA 7, Texas Tech 0

	1ST	2ND	3RD	4TH	FINAL
UGA	0	7	0	0	7
TT	0	0	0	0	0

SCORING SUMMARY
UGA Lankewicz 2 run (Etter kick)

UGA	TEAM STATISTICS	TT
17	First Downs	7
245	Rushing Yards	32
5-9-0	Passing	11-24-1
84	Passing Yards	96
329	Total Yards	128
2-6	Punt Returns - Yards	3-26
2-33	Kickoff Returns - Yards	2-50
4-38.0	Punts - Average	8-37.0
3-3	Fumbles - Lost	1-0
7-45	Penalties - Yards	8-37

INDIVIDUAL LEADERS
RUSHING
UGA: Ridlehuber 19-87.
TT: Agan 5-20.
PASSING
UGA: Ridlehuber 4-5-0, 77 yards.
TT: Wilson 11-24-1, 96 yards.
RECEIVING
UGA: Barber 1-52; Brown 3-29.
TT: Agan 3-11.

DECEMBER 31, 1966 | Cotton
GEORGIA 24, SMU 9

	1ST	2ND	3RD	4TH	FINAL
UGA	10	7	0	7	24
SMU	3	6	0	0	9

SCORING SUMMARY
UGA Lawrence 74 run (Etter kick)
SMU FG Partee 22
UGA FG Etter 28
UGA Payne 20 pass from Moore (Etter kick)
SMU Richardson 1 run (kick failed)
UGA Jenkins 4 run (Etter kick)

UGA	TEAM STATISTICS	SMU
17	First Downs	11
284	Rushing Yards	40
6-14-1	Passing	10-20-3
79	Passing Yards	165
363	Total Yards	205
4-28.5	Punts - Average	4-36.5
2-1	Fumbles - Lost	1-1
3-37	Penalties - Yards	7-45

INDIVIDUAL LEADERS
RUSHING
UGA: Lawrence 16-149, 1 TD; Jenkins 23-88, 1 TD.
SMU: Jernigan 9-28; Richardson 11-24, 1 TD.
PASSING
UGA: Moore 6-11-1, 79 yards, 1 TD.
SMU: White 9-17-1, 160 yards.
RECEIVING
UGA: Payne 3-49, 1 TD; Johnson 2-27.
SMU: Levias 3-62; Richardson 3-45.

DECEMBER 16, 1967 | LIBERTY
NC STATE 14, GEORGIA 7

	1ST	2ND	3RD	4TH	FINAL
NCST	0	7	0	7	14
UGA	0	7	0	0	7

SCORING SUMMARY
NCST Martell 6 pass from Donnan (Warren kick)
UGA Jenkins 1 run (McCullough kick)
NCST Barchuk 1 run (Warren kick)

NCST	TEAM STATISTICS	UGA
14	First Downs	14
79	Rushing Yards	140
17-25-1	Passing	11-23-1
128	Passing Yards	136
207	Total Yards	276
6-41.6	Punts - Average	5-35.6
2-1	Fumbles - Lost	2-0
3-45	Penalties - Yards	6-67

INDIVIDUAL LEADERS
RUSHING
NCST: Bowers 10-35; Barchuk 13-20, 1 TD.
UGA: Jenkins 16-33, 1 TD.
PASSING
NCST: Donnan 15-24-1, 121 yards, 1 TD.
UGA: Moore 10-22-0, 124 yards.
RECEIVING
NCST: Martell 7-69, 1 TD.
UGA: Hughes 6-86.

JANUARY 1, 1969 | SUGAR
ARKANSAS 16, GEORGIA 2

	1ST	2ND	3RD	4TH	FINAL
ARK	0	10	0	6	16
UGA	0	2	0	0	2

SCORING SUMMARY
ARK Dicus 27 pass from Montgomery (White kick)
UGA Safety
ARK FG White 34
ARK FG White 24
ARK FG White 31

ARK	TEAM STATISTICS	UGA
13	First Downs	13
40	Rushing Yards	75
17-39-3	Passing	11-31-1
185	Passing Yards	117
225	Total Yards	192
10-33.6	Punts - Average	10-38.6
2-2	Fumbles - Lost	5-5
4-31	Penalties - Yards	4-25

INDIVIDUAL LEADERS
RUSHING
ARK: Burnett 2-31.
UGA: Johnson 12-45.
PASSING
ARK: Montgomery 17-39-1, 185 yards, 1 TD.
UGA: Cavan 9-22-1, 103 yards.
RECEIVING
ARK: Dicus 12-169, 1 TD; Peacock 3-15.
UGA: Whittemore 5-56; Lawrence 3-54.

DECEMBER 20, 1969 | SUN
NEBRASKA 45, GEORGIA 6

	1ST	2ND	3RD	4TH	FINAL
NEB	18	0	14	13	45
UGA	0	0	0	6	6

SCORING SUMMARY
NEB FG Rogers 50
NEB FG Rogers 32
NEB Kinney 10 run (pass failed)
NEB FG Rogers 42
NEB FG Rogers 37
NEB Green 7 pass from Brownson (Rogers kick)
NEB Brownson 1 run (Rogers kick)
NEB Schneiss 1 run (kick failed)
UGA Gilbert 6 run (kick failed)
NEB Tagge 2 run (Rogers kick)

NEB	TEAM STATISTICS	UGA
17	First Downs	11
190	Rushing Yards	55
18-35-2	Passing	11-35-6
165	Passing Yards	130
355	Total Yards	185
3-38	Punt Returns - Yards	2-11
7-35.0	Punts - Average	10-42.0
1-0	Fumbles - Lost	2-2
6-50	Penalties - Yards	3-31

INDIVIDUAL LEADERS
RUSHING
NEB: Green 13-46.
UGA Paine 13-41.
PASSING
NEB: Brownson 11-18, 109 yards, 1 TD.
UGA: Gilbert 10-30, 116 yards.
RECEIVING
NEB: Ingles 4-55.
UGA: Whittemore 5-86.

DECEMBER 31, 1971 | GATOR
GEORGIA 7, NORTH CAROLINA 3

	1ST	2ND	3RD	4TH	FINAL
UGA	0	0	7	0	7
UNC	0	0	3	0	3

SCORING SUMMARY
UNC FG Craven 35
UGA Poulos 25 run (Braswell kick)

UGA	TEAM STATISTICS	UNC
13	First Downs	9
238	Rushing Yards	115
6-17-0	Passing	6-14-1
84	Passing Yards	66
322	Total Yards	181
10-34.8	Punts - Average	10-46.6
2-1	Fumbles - Lost	2-1
5-29	Penalties - Yards	3-15

INDIVIDUAL LEADERS
RUSHING
UGA: Poulos 20-161, 1 TD; Johnson 19-50.
UNC: Jolley 20-77, Hamlin 5-17.
PASSING
UGA: Johnson 6-13-0, 84 yards.
UNC: Miller 6-14-1, 66 yards.
RECEIVING
UGA: Hunnicut 4-58; Greene 1-26.
UNC: Sigler 2-32; Cowell 1-19.

DECEMBER 28, 1973 | PEACH
GEORGIA 17, MARYLAND 16

	1ST	2ND	3RD	4TH	FINAL
UGA	0	10	7	0	17
MARY	0	10	0	6	16

SCORING SUMMARY
UGA Poulos 62 pass from Johnson (Leavitt kick)
MARY White 68 pass from Carter (Mayer kick)
MARY FG Mayer 36
UGA FG Leavitt 26
UGA Johnson 1 run (Leavitt kick)
MARY FG Mayer 25
MARY FG Mayer 28

UGA	TEAM STATISTICS	MARY
11	First Downs	15
170	Rushing Yards	219
5-16-1	Passing	8-18-1
114	Passing Yards	242
284	Total Yards	461
8-41.3	Punts - Average	6-31.8
2-2	Fumbles - Lost	4-3
1-5	Penalties - Yards	5-63

INDIVIDUAL LEADERS
RUSHING
UGA: King 16-57.
MARY: Carter 29-126.
PASSING
UGA: Johnson 5-16-1, 114 yards, 1 TD.
MARY: Kinard 4-8-1, 113 yards.
RECEIVING
UGA: Poulos 2-62, 1 TD.
MARY: White 1-106, 1 TD.

DECEMBER 21, 1974 | TANGERINE
MIAMI (OHIO) 21, GEORGIA 10

	1ST	2ND	3RD	4TH	FINAL
MIA	14	7	0	0	21
UGA	3	0	7	0	10

SCORING SUMMARY
MIA Carpenter 1 run (Draudt kick)
UGA FG Leavitt 20
MIA Taylor 7 pass from Smith (Draudt kick)
MIA Smith 8 run (Draudt kick)
UGA Goff 1 run (Leavitt kick)

MIA	TEAM STATISTICS	UGA
18	First Downs	17
228	Rushing Yards	74
3-8-0	Passing	11-24-0
39	Passing Yards	200
267	Total Yards	274
5-36.0	Punts - Average	4-30.0
3-3	Fumbles - Lost	5-2
3-25	Penalties - Yards	20-24

INDIVIDUAL LEADERS
RUSHING
MIA: Carpenter 30-114, 1 TD; Smith 22-90, 1 TD.
UGA: Harrison 17-69.
PASSING
MIA: Smith 1-2-0, 7 yards; Sanna 2-24-0, 22 yards.
UGA: Robinson 11-24-0, 190 yards.
RECEIVING
MIA: Schulte 1-15; Taylor 1-7, 1 TD.
UGA: Appleby 6-102; Wilson 3-45.

THE SCHOOLS

JANUARY 1, 1976 | COTTON
ARKANSAS 31, GEORGIA 10

	1ST	2ND	3RD	4TH	FINAL
UGA	3	7	0	0	10
ARK	0	10	0	21	31

SCORING SUMMARY
UGA   FG Leavitt 35
UGA   Washington 21 pass from Robinson (Leavitt kick)
ARK   FG Little 39
ARK   Forte 1 run (Little kick)
ARK   Fuchs 5 run (Little kick)
ARK   Forrest 1 run (Little kick)
ARK   Forte 6 run (Little kick)

UGA	TEAM STATISTICS	ARK
13	First Downs	20
102	Rushing Yards	235
8-18-2	Passing	5-14-0
91	Passing Yards	89
193	Total Yards	324
6-38.7	Punts - Average	4-43.0
3-2	Fumbles - Lost	6-1
3-15	Penalties - Yards	5-35

INDIVIDUAL LEADERS
RUSHING
UGA: Harrison 14-44; Goff 16-32.
ARK: Forte 24-119, 2 TD; Fuchs 16-71, 1 TD.
PASSING
UGA: Robinson 7-15-2, 85 yards, 1 TD.
ARK: Bull 5-13-0, 89 yards.
RECEIVING
UGA: Wilson 1-29; Washington 1-21.
ARK: Douglas 2-54; Daily 1-13.

JANUARY 1, 1977 | SUGAR
PITTSBURGH 27, GEORGIA 3

	1ST	2ND	3RD	4TH	FINAL
PITT	7	14	3	3	27
UGA	0	0	3	0	3

SCORING SUMMARY
PITT   Cavanaugh 6 run (Long kick)
PITT   Jones 59 pass from Cavanaugh (Long kick)
PITT   Dorsett 11 run (Long kick)
UGA   FG Leavitt 25
PITT   FG Long 42
PITT   FG Long 31

PITT	TEAM STATISTICS	UGA
24	First Downs	14
288	Rushing Yards	135
10-18-0	Passing	3-22-4
192	Passing Yards	46
480	Total Yards	181
5-36.8	Punts - Average	8-47.1
2-1	Fumbles - Lost	4-2
6-66	Penalties - Yards	4-30

INDIVIDUAL LEADERS
RUSHING
PITT: Dorsett 32-202, 1 TD.
UGA: Goff 17-76.
PASSING
PITT: Cavanaugh 10-18-0, 192 yards, 1 TD.
UGA: Robinson 2-15-2, 33 yards.

DECEMBER 31, 1978 | BLUEBONNET
STANFORD 25, GEORGIA 22

	1ST	2ND	3RD	4TH	FINAL
STAN	0	0	22	3	25
UGA	3	12	7	0	22

SCORING SUMMARY
UGA   FG Robinson 31
UGA   Prince 22 pass from Belue (kick failed)
UGA   Prince 8 pass from Pyburn (kick failed)
UGA   Pyburn 1 run (Robinson kick)
STAN   Margerum 32 pass from Dils (pass failed)
STAN   Nelson 20 pass from Dils (Naber run)
STAN   Margerum 14 pass from Dils (Nelson pass from Dils)
STAN   FG Naber 24

STAN	TEAM STATISTICS	UGA
20	First Downs	27
128	Rushing Yards	315
17-28-0	Passing	11-18-1
210	Passing Yards	189
338	Total Yards	504
1-6	Punt Returns - Yards	4-38
2-45	Kickoff Returns - Yards	4-81
8-41.6	Punts - Average	1-35.0
2-1	Fumbles - Lost	6-5
2-34	Penalties - Yards	5-43

INDIVIDUAL LEADERS
RUSHING
STAN: Nelson 16-100; Francis 11-67.
UGA: McClendon 30-115; Womack 13-60.
PASSING
STAN: Dils 17-28-0, 210 yards, 3 TD.
UGA: Pyburn 6-12-1, 87 yards, 1 TD; Belue 4-4-0, 59 yards, 1 TD.
RECEIVING
STAN: Margerum 5-87, 2 TD; Francis 5-48.
UGA: Scott 5-67; Prince 2-30, 1 TD.

JANUARY 1, 1981 | SUGAR
GEORGIA 17, NOTRE DAME 10

	1ST	2ND	3RD	4TH	FINAL
UGA	10	7	0	0	17
ND	3	0	7	0	10

SCORING SUMMARY
ND   FG Oliver 50
UGA   FG Robinson 46
UGA   Walker 1 run (Robinson kick)
UGA   Walker 3 run (Robinson kick)
ND   Carter 1 run (Oliver kick)

UGA	TEAM STATISTICS	ND
10	First Downs	17
120	Rushing Yards	190
1-13-0	Passing	14-28-3
7	Passing Yards	138
127	Total Yards	328
11-38.5	Punts - Average	5-42.0
0	Fumbles Lost	1-1
6-32	Penalties - Yards	8-69

INDIVIDUAL LEADERS
RUSHING
UGA: Walker 36-150, 2 TD.
ND: Carter 27-109, 1 TD.
PASSING
UGA: Belue 1-12-0, 7 yards.
ND: Kiel 14-27-3, 138 yards.
RECEIVING
UGA: Arnold 1-7.
ND: Holohan 4-44.

JANUARY 1, 1982 | SUGAR
PITTSBURGH 24, GEORGIA 20

	1ST	2ND	3RD	4TH	FINAL
PITT	0	3	7	14	24
UGA	0	7	6	7	20

SCORING SUMMARY
UGA   Walker 8 run (Butler kick)
PITT   FG Everett 41
PITT   Dawkins 30 pass from Marino (Everett kick)
UGA   Walker 10 run (kick failed)
PITT   Brown 6 pass from Marino (Everett kick)
UGA   Kay 6 pass from Belue (Butler kick)
PITT   Brown 33 pass from Marino (Everett kick)

PITT	TEAM STATISTICS	UGA
27	First Downs	11
208	Rushing Yards	141
26-41-2	Passing	8-15-2
261	Passing Yards	83
469	Total Yards	224
2-44.5	Punts - Average	6-39.5
5-3	Fumbles - Lost	2-2
14-96	Penalties - Yards	5-35

INDIVIDUAL LEADERS
RUSHING
PITT: Thomas 26-129; DiBartola 13-68.
UGA: Walker 25-84, 2 TD.
PASSING
PITT: Marino 26-41-2, 261 yards, 3 TD.
UGA: Belue 8-15-2, 83 yards.
RECEIVING
PITT: Dawkins 6-77, 1 TD; DiBartola 8-64; Brown 6-62, 2 TD.
UGA: Walker 3-53.

JANUARY 1, 1983 | SUGAR
PENN STATE 27, GEORGIA 23

	1ST	2ND	3RD	4TH	FINAL
PSU	7	13	0	7	27
UGA	3	7	7	6	23

SCORING SUMMARY
PSU   Warner 2 run (Gancitano kick)
UGA   FG Butler 27
PSU   FG Gancitano 38
PSU   Warner 9 run (Gancitano kick)
PSU   FG Grancitano 45
UGA   Archie 10 pass from Lastinger (Butler kick)
UGA   Walker 1 run (Butler kick)
PSU   Garrity 47 pass from Blackledge (Gancitano kick)
UGA   Kay 9 pass from Lastinger (run failed)

PSU	TEAM STATISTICS	UGA
19	First Downs	19
139	Rushing Yards	160
13-23-0	Passing	12-28-2
228	Passing Yards	166
367	Total Yards	326
7-42.5	Punts - Average	8-41.7
2-1	Fumbles - Lost	3-0
7-39	Penalties - Yards	7-42

INDIVIDUAL LEADERS
RUSHING
PSU: Warner 18-117, 2 TD.
UGA: Walker 28-103, 1 TD.
PASSING
PSU: Blackledge 13-23-0, 228 yards, 1 TD.
UGA: Lastinger 12-27-2, 166 yards, 2 TD.
RECEIVING
PSU: Garrity 4-116, 1 TD.
UGA: Kay 5-61, 1 TD.

JANUARY 2, 1984 | COTTON
GEORGIA 10, TEXAS 9

	1ST	2ND	3RD	4TH	FINAL
UGA	3	0	0	7	10
TEX	3	0	6	0	9

SCORING SUMMARY
TEX FG Ward 22
UGA FG Butler 43
TEX FG Ward 40
TEX FG Ward 27
UGA Lastinger 17 run (Butler kick)

UGA	TEAM STATISTICS	TEX
13	First Downs	14
149	Rushing Yards	110
6-20-1	Passing	8-26-2
66	Passing Yards	168
215	Total Yards	278
9-41.2	Punts - Average	7-46.7
2-1	Fumbles - Lost	4-2
3-25	Penalties - Yards	6-52

INDIVIDUAL LEADERS
RUSHING
UGA: Montgomery 11-40; Lane 1-35.
TEX: Robinson 28-88; Orr 7-19.
PASSING
UGA: Lastinger 6-19-1, 66 yards.
TEX: McIvor 8-26-2, 168 yards.
RECEIVING
UGA: Harris 2-33; Wisham 1-14.
TEX: Micho 2-59; Epps 1-44.

DECEMBER 22, 1984 | CITRUS
GEORGIA 17, FLORIDA STATE 17

	1ST	2ND	3RD	4TH	FINAL
FSU	0	0	3	14	17
UGA	0	14	0	3	17

SCORING SUMMARY
UGA Tate 4 run (Butler kick)
UGA Tate 2 run (Butler kick)
FSU FG Schmidt 32
FSU Smith 1 run (run failed)
UGA FG Butler 36
FSU Wessel 14 blocked punt return (Holloman run)

FSU	TEAM STATISTICS	UGA
18	First Downs	15
161	Rushing Yards	189
10-26-2	Passing	9-18-1
85	Passing Yards	178
246	Total Yards	367
8-38.6	Punts - Average	8-37.1
3-1	Fumbles - Lost	5-1
8-65	Penalties - Yards	6-42

INDIVIDUAL LEADERS
RUSHING
FSU: Smith 10-65, 1 TD; Snipes 8-60.
UGA: Tate 11-75, 2 TD; T. Jackson 12-46.
PASSING
FSU: Thomas 10-26-2, 85 yards.
UGA: J. Jackson 7-16-1, 159 yards.
RECEIVING
FSU: Hester 3-26; Carter 2-15.
UGA: Lane 2-64; S. Williams 2-45.

DECEMBER 28, 1985 | SUN
GEORGIA 13, ARIZONA 13

	1ST	2ND	3RD	4TH	FINAL
UGA	0	3	0	10	13
ARIZ	0	3	10	0	13

SCORING SUMMARY
UGA   FG Crumley 37
ARIZ FG Zendejas 22
ARIZ FG Zendejas 52
ARIZ Rudolph 35 interception return (Zendejas kick)
UGA   FG Jacobs 44
UGA   Tate 2 run (Jacobs kick)

UGA	TEAM STATISTICS	ARIZ
18	First Downs	11
211	Rushing Yards	99
5-8-2	Passing	13-22-0
51	Passing Yards	133
262	Total Yards	232
1-3	Punt Returns - Yards	0-0
2-31	Kickoff Returns - Yards	3-63
2-27.0	Punts - Average	4-40.0
1-1	Fumbles - Lost	2-2
4-20	Penalties - Yards	4-40

INDIVIDUAL LEADERS
RUSHING
UGA : Tate 22-71, 1 TD; Henderson 12-59.
ARIZ: Adams 13-51; Jenkins 6-22.
PASSING
UGA : Jackson 4 -7-2, 42 yards.
ARIZ: Jenkins 13-22-0, 133 yards.
RECEIVING
UGA : Tate 2-16; Sadowski 1-15.
ARIZ: Fairholm 4-40; Adams 3-33.

DECEMBER 23, 1986 | HALL OF FAME
BOSTON COLLEGE 27, GEORGIA 24

	1ST	2ND	3RD	4TH	FINAL
BC	3	17	0	7	27
UGA	7	0	10	7	24

SCORING SUMMARY
UGA Jackson 7 run (Crumley kick)
BC   FG Lowe 23
BC   Casparriello 4 pass from Halloran (Lowe kick)
BC   Stradford 1 run (Lowe kick)
BC   FG Lowe 37
UGA FG Jacobs 28
UGA Moss 81 interception return (Crumley kick)
UGA Jackson 5 run (Crumley kick)
BC   Martin 5 pass from Halloran (Lowe kick)

BC	TEAM STATISTICS	UGA
26	First Downs	18
111	Rushing Yards	94
31-52-2	Passing	21-13-0
316	Passing Yards	178
427	Total Yards	272
4-63	Punt Returns - Yards	1-2
5-51	Kickoff Returns - Yards	6-112
8-33.8	Punts - Average	7-44.9
3-0	Fumbles - Lost	4-2
6-45	Penalties - Yards	3-30
31:00	Possession Time	29:00

INDIVIDUAL LEADERS
RUSHING
BC: Stradford 20-122, 1 TD; Halloran 9-22.
UGA: Tate 17-63; Jackson 13-6, 2 TD.
PASSING
BC: Halloran 31-52-2, 316 yards, 2 TD.
UGA: Jackson 13-21-0, 178 yards.
RECEIVING
BC: Martin 9-98, 1 TD; Casparriello 7-75, 1 TD.
UGA: Thomas 7-75; Tate 2-52.

DECEMBER 29, 1987 | LIBERTY
GEORGIA 20, ARKANSAS 17

	1ST	2ND	3RD	4TH	FINAL
UGA	0	7	0	13	20
ARK	3	7	7	0	17

SCORING SUMMARY
ARK FG Trainor 43
UGA Tate 1 run (Kasay kick)
ARK Thomas 10 run (Trainor kick)
ARK Thomas 1 run (Trainor kick)
UGA FG Kasay 24
UGA Jackson 5 run (Kasay kick)
UGA FG Kasay 39

UGA	TEAM STATISTICS	ARK
20	First Downs	19
202	Rushing Yards	258
15-25-2	Passing	7-17-2
148	Passing Yards	86
350	Total Yards	344
3-32.7	Punts - Average	3-32.7
68	Return Yards	95
2-1	Fumbles - Lost	0-0
4-45	Penalties - Yards	5-50

INDIVIDUAL LEADERS
RUSHING
UGA: Jackson 10-72, 1 TD.
ARK: Thomas 13-79, 2 TD.
PASSING
UGA: Jackson 15-25-2, 148 yards.
ARK: Thomas 7-17-2, 86 yards.
RECEIVING
UGA: Thomas 7-76.
ARK: Winston 2-36.

JANUARY 1, 1989 | GATOR
GEORGIA 34, MICHIGAN STATE 27

	1ST	2ND	3RD	4TH	FINAL
UGA	7	10	10	7	34
MSU	0	7	6	14	27

SCORING SUMMARY
UGA Hampton 6 pass from Johnson (Kasay kick)
UGA FG Crumley 39
UGA Hampton 30 pass from Johnson (Kasay kick)
MSU Rison 4 pass from McAllister (Langeloh kick)
UGA Warner 18 pass from Johnson (Kasay kick)
MSU Rison 55 pass from McAllister (kick failed)
UGA FG Crumley 36
MSU Ezor 3 run (Langeloh kick)
UGA Hampton 32 run (Kasay kick)
MSU Rison 50 pass from McAllister (Langeloh kick)

UGA	TEAM STATISTICS	MSU
22	First Downs	22
182	Rushing Yards	158
15-27-0	Passing	14-24-0
227	Passing Yards	288
409	Total Yards	446
4-34.0	Punts - Average	6-42.8
0-0	Fumbles - Lost	1-0
5-25	Penalties - Yards	8-102

INDIVIDUAL LEADERS
RUSHING
UGA: Hampton 10-109, 1 TD; Johnson 14-30.
MSU: Ezor 33-146, 1 TD; Selzer 5-13.
PASSING
UGA: Johnson 15-27-0, 227 yards, 3 TD.
MSU: McAllister 14-24-0, 228, 3 TD.
RECEIVING
UGA: Hampton 4-71, 2 TD; Worley 3-36.
MSU: Rison 9-252, 3 TD; Montgomery 4-21.

DECEMBER 30, 1989 | Peach
SYRACUSE 19, GEORGIA 18

	1ST	2ND	3RD	4TH	FINAL
SYR	7	0	3	9	19
UGA	7	3	8	0	18

SCORING SUMMARY
UGA	Warner 5 pass from Talley (Kasay kick)
SYR	Owens 1 run (Biskup kick)
UGA	FG Kasay 20
UGA	Safety
UGA	Hampton 4 pass from Talley (pass failed)
SYR	FG Biskup 32
SYR	Moore 19 pass from McDonald (pass failed)

SYR	TEAM STATISTICS	UGA
27	First Downs	12
245	Rushing Yards	113
22-34-3	Passing	10-19-1
224	Passing Yards	88
469	Total Yards	201
3-41.0	Punts - Average	7-41.0
3-1	Fumbles - Lost	1-0
2-10	Penalties - Yards	3-30

INDIVIDUAL LEADERS
RUSHING
SYR: Owens 14-112, 1 TD.
UGA: Hampton 14-32.
PASSING
SYR: Scharr 12-21-3, 100 yards; McDonald 10-13-0, 135 yards, 1 TD.
UGA: Talley 8-14-1, 93 yards, 2 TD.
RECEIVING
SYR: Hampton 7-62, 1 TD.
UGA: Owens 5-62; Moore 4-60, 1 TD.

DECEMBER 29, 1991 | Independence
GEORGIA 24, ARKANSAS 15

	1ST	2ND	3RD	4TH	FINAL
UGA	14	3	7	0	24
ARK	0	7	0	8	15

SCORING SUMMARY
UGA	Marshall 7 pass from Zeier (Peterson kick)
UGA	Hastings 27 pass from Zeier (Peterson kick)
UGA	FG Parkman 39
ARK	Jackson 7 run (Wright kick)
UGA	Hastings 53 run (Peterson kick)
ARK	Jackson 1 run (Jackson run)

UGA	TEAM STATISTICS	ARK
15	First Downs	22
125	Rushing Yards	188
20-31-0	Passing	12-31-5
237	Passing Yards	122
362	Total Yards	310
6-32.5	Punts - Average	4-45.3
1-0	Fumbles - Lost	1-1
10-75	Penalties - Yards	7-43

INDIVIDUAL LEADERS
RUSHING
UGA: Hastings 1-53, 1 TD; Strong 8-36.
ARK: Jackson 28-112, 2 TD; Jeffrey 9-44.
PASSING
UGA : Zeier 18-28-0, 228 yards, 2 TD.
ARK: Hill 12-31-5, 122 yards.
RECEIVING
UGA : Hastings 4-94, 1 TD.
ARK: Keith 3-38.

JANUARY 1, 1993 | Florida Citrus
GEORGIA 21, OHIO STATE 14

	1ST	2ND	3RD	4TH	FINAL
UGA	7	0	7	7	21
OSU	0	7	7	0	14

SCORING SUMMARY
UGA	Hearst 1 run (Peterson kick)
OSU	Smith 1 run (Williams kick)
UGA	Hearst 5 run (Peterson kick)
OSU	Smith 5 run (Williams kick)
UGA	Harvey 1 run (Peterson kick)

UGA	TEAM STATISTICS	OSU
26	First Downs	18
202	Rushing Yards	179
21-31-0	Passing	8-24-1
242	Passing Yards	110
444	Total Yards	289
6-39.0	Punts - Average	8-37.1
2-2	Fumbles - Lost	1-1
3-30	Penalties - Yards	5-35

INDIVIDUAL LEADERS
RUSHING
UGA: Hearst 28-163, 2 TD; Davis 7-42.
OSU: Smith 25-112, 2 TD; Harris 7-38.
PASSING
UGA: Zeier 21-31-0, 242 yards.
OSU: Herbstreit 8-24-1, 110 yards.
RECEIVING
UGA: Hastings 8-113; Mitchell 2-39.
OSU: Smith 2-49; Stablein 2-31.

DECEMBER 30, 1995 | Peach
VIRGINIA 34, GEORGIA 27

	1ST	2ND	3RD	4TH	FINAL
UVA	14	10	3	7	34
UGA	3	11	3	10	27

SCORING SUMMARY
UVA	Barber 1 run (Garcia kick)
UVA	Brooks 5 run (Garcia kick)
UGA	FG 36 Parkman
UGA	FG 37 Parkman
UVA	FG 36 Garcia
UVA	Allen 82 pass from Groh (Garcia kick)
UGA	Ward 1 run (Hunter run)
UGA	FG 20 Parkman
UVA	FG 36 Parkman
UGA	FG 42 Parkman
UGA	Fergerson 10 fumble return (Parkman kick)
UVA	Allen 83 kickoff return (Garcia kick)

UVA	TEAM STATISTICS	UGA
10	First Downs	20
100	Rushing Yards	112
10-20-1	Passing	31-59-2
156	Passing Yards	413
256	Total Yards	525
8-42.4	Punts - Average	5-33.0
4-2	Fumbles - Lost	1-1
3-30	Penalties - Yards	6-40
25:35	Possession Time	34:25

INDIVIDUAL LEADERS
RUSHING
UVA: Barber 20-103, 1 TD; Brooks 7-23, 1 TD.
UGA: Ward 9-56, 1 TD; Kirtsey 16-43.
PASSING
UVA: Groh 10-20-1, 156 yards, 1 TD.
UGA: Ward 31-59-2, 413 yards.
RECEIVING
UVA: Allen 5-111, 1 TD; Jeffers 4-47.
UGA: Bowie 10-156; Hunter 7-67; Allen 4-48.

JANUARY 1, 1998 | Outback
GEORGIA 33, WISCONSIN 6

	1ST	2ND	3RD	4TH	FINAL
UGA	12	7	7	7	33
WISC	0	0	0	6	6

SCORING SUMMARY
UGA	Edwards 2 run (kick blocked)
UGA	Edwards 40 run (pass failed)
UGA	Gary 3 run (Hines kick)
UGA	Edwards 13 run (Hines kick)
UGA	Allen 7 pass from Bobo (Hines kick)
WISC	Retzlaff 12 pass from Kavanagh (kick failed)

UGA	TEAM STATISTICS	WISC
25	First Downs	18
207	Rushing Yards	74
26-29-0	Passing	14-36-2
235	Passing Yards	160
442	Total Yards	234
1-0	Punt Returns - Yards	2-0
1-16	Kickoff Returns - Yards	5-104
3-35.7	Punts - Average	5-43.6
2-1	Fumbles - Lost	0-0
5-59	Penalties - Yards	7-71
34:05	Possession Time	25:55

INDIVIDUAL LEADERS
RUSHING
UGA: Edwards 22-110, 3 TD; Gary 4-61, 1 TD.
WISC: McCullough 4-37; Dayne 14-36.
PASSING
UGA: Bobo 26-28-0, 235 yards, 1 TD.
WISC: Samuel 8-27-2, 84 yards; Kavanagh 6-9-0, 76 yards, 1 TD.
RECEIVING
UGA: Ward 12-122; Allen 3-22, 1 TD.
WISC: Chambers 4-46; Hayes 5-44.

DECEMBER 31, 1998 | Peach
GEORGIA 35, VIRGINIA 33

	1ST	2ND	3RD	4TH	FINAL
UGA	0	7	14	14	35
UVA	0	21	6	6	33

SCORING SUMMARY
UVA	Southern 2 run (Braverman kick)
UVA	Wilkins 43 pass from Brooks (Braverman kick)
UVA	Jones 24 pass from Brooks (Braverman kick)
UGA	Small 11 pass from Carter (Hines kick)
UGA	Bailey 14 pass from Carter (Hines kick)
UGA	Gary 15 run (Hines kick)
UVA	Wilkins 67 pass from Brooks (kick failed)
UGA	Gary 2 run (Hines kick)
UGA	Carter 1 run (Hines kick)
UVA	Brooks 30 run (pass failed)

UGA	TEAM STATISTICS	UVA
19	First Downs	21
159	Rushing Yards	198
18-33-3	Passing	13-35-1
222	Passing Yards	236
381	Total Yards	434
0-0	Fumbles - Lost	3-1
8-74	Penalties - Yards	9-71
28:01	Possession Time	31:59

INDIVIDUAL LEADERS
RUSHING
UGA: Gary 19-110, 2 TD; Carter 14-41, 1 TD.
UVA: Jones 23-96; Brooks 14-88, 1 TD.
PASSING
UGA: Carter 18-33-3, 222 yards, 2 TD.
UVA: Brooks 12-32-1, 226 yards, 3 TD.
RECEIVING
UGA: Bailey 3-73, 1 TD; Greer 2-60.
UVA: Wilkins 6-161, 2 TD; Jones 4-46, 1 TD.

JANUARY 1, 2000 | OUTBACK
GEORGIA 28, PURDUE 25

	1ST	2ND	3RD	4TH	OT	FINAL
UGA	0	10	8	7	3	28
PU	19	6	0	0	0	25

SCORING SUMMARY
PU	Daniels 3 pass from Brees (Dorsch kick)
PU	Daniels 11 pass from Brees (kick failed)
PU	Sutherland 21 pass from Brees (pass failed)
PU	James 32 pass from Brees (pass failed)
UGA	Edwards 74 run (Hines kick)
UGA	FG Hines 32
UGA	Carter 8 run (Pass run)
UGA	McMichael 8 pass from Carter (Hines kick)
UGA	FG Hines 21

UGA	TEAM STATISTICS	PU
21	First Downs	30
154	Rushing Yards	150
20-33-0	Passing	36-60-1
243	Passing Yards	378
397	Total Yards	528
2-24	Punt Returns - Yards	1-1
3-63	Kickoff Returns - Yards	2-31
3-48.0	Punts - Average	3-45.3
2-2	Fumbles - Lost	2-1
10-55	Penalties - Yards	14-153
25:11	Possession Time	34:49

INDIVIDUAL LEADERS
RUSHING
UGA: Edwards 2-70, 1 TD; Carter 16-41, 1 TD.
PU: Lowe 15-87; Sutherland 2-65.
PASSING
UGA: Carter 20-33-0, 243 yards, 1 TD.
PU: Brees 36-60-1, 378 yards, 4 TD.
RECEIVING
UGA: Edwards 8-97; Greer 5-86.
PU: Daniels 12-103, 2 TD; James 4-65, 1 TD.

DECEMBER 24, 2000 | JEEP O'AHU
GEORGIA 37, VIRGINIA 14

	1ST	2ND	3RD	4TH	FINAL
GA	17	7	0	13	37
UVA	0	7	7	0	14

SCORING SUMMARY
GA	FG Bennett 35
GA	Edwards 40 run (Bennett kick)
GA	Curry fumble recovery (Bennett kick)
UVA	Dotson 14 run (Greene kick)
GA	Haynes 3 run (Bennett good)
UVA	Thweatt 58 fumble return (Greene kick)
GA	Gary 21 pass from Phillips (Bennett kick)
GA	Burnett 4 fumble return (kick failed)

GA	TEAM STATISTICS	UVA
21	First Downs	20
157	Rushing Yards	144
25-39-1	Passing	22-36-2
241	Passing Yards	226
398	Total Yards	370
5-42.6	Punts - Average	5-44.8
1-1	Fumbles - Lost	4-2
4-20	Penalties - Yards	4-29
29:57	Possession Time	30:03

INDIVIDUAL LEADERS
RUSHING
GA: Edwards 5-97, 1 TD.
UVA: Womack 15-48.
PASSING
GA: Phillips 22-35-1, 213 yards, 1 TD.
UVA: Spinner 14-22-2, 153 yards.
RECEIVING
GA: Edwards 8-79.
UVA: McGrew 4-40.

DECEMBER 28, 2001 | MUSIC CITY
BOSTON COLLEGE 20, GEORGIA 16

	1ST	2ND	3RD	4TH	FINAL
BC	3	10	0	7	20
UGA	7	3	6	0	16

SCORING SUMMARY
UGA	Gibson 15 pass from Greene (Bennett kick)
BC	FG Sciortino 25
BC	Dewalt 10 pass from St. Pierre (Sciortino kick)
BC	FG Sciortino 26
UGA	FG Bennett 24
UGA	Haynes 1 run (kick failed)
BC	Green 7 run (Sciortino kick)

BC	TEAM STATISTICS	UGA
16	First Downs	23
197	Rushing Yards	122
9-25-0	Passing	22-39-2
109	Passing Yards	288
306	Total Yards	410
0-0	Punt Returns - Yards	3-7
3-28	Kickoff Returns - Yards	5-177
6-37.5	Punts - Average	3-43.7
2-0	Fumbles - Lost	2-2
4-20	Penalties - Yards	9-74
35:02	Possession Time	24:58

INDIVIDUAL LEADERS
RUSHING
BC: Green 35-149, 1 TD; St. Pierre 8-44.
UGA: Haynes 27-132, 1 TD.
PASSING
BC: St. Pierre 9-25-0, 109 yards, 1 TD.
UGA: Greene 22-38-2, 288 yards, 1 TD.
RECEIVING
BC: Dewalt 3-62, 1 TD.
UGA: Gibson 6-109, 1 TD; Mitchell 4-54; McMichael 4-47.

JANUARY 1, 2003 | SUGAR
GEORGIA 26, FLORIDA STATE 13

	1ST	2ND	3RD	4TH	FINAL
UGA	3	14	6	3	26
FSU	0	7	6	0	13

SCORING SUMMARY
UGA	FG Bennett 23
FSU	Boldin 5 pass from Walker (Beitia kick)
UGA	Thornton 71 interception return (Bennett kick)
UGA	Edwards 37 pass from Shockley (Bennett kick)
UGA	FG Bennett 42
UGA	FG Bennett 25
FSU	Thorpe 40 pass from Boldin (run failed)
UGA	FG Bennett 35

UGA	TEAM STATISTICS	FSU
11	First Downs	18
151	Rushing Yards	115
10-15-0	Passing	13-26-2
125	Passing Yards	147
276	Total Yards	262
4-48.2	Punts - Average	5-40.4
1-1	Fumbles - Lost	2-1
6-59	Penalties - Yards	5-37
26:09	Possession Time	33:51

INDIVIDUAL LEADERS
RUSHING
GEO: Smith 23-145; Milton 5-13.
FSU: Washington 10-48; Boldin 13-34.
PASSING
GEO: Greene 9-14-0, 88 yards.
FSU: Boldin 6-14-0, 78 yards, 1 TD.
RECEIVING
GEO: Edwards 3-60, 1 TD; Johnson 1-34.
FSU: Thorpe 1-40, 1 TD; Boldin 3-34, 1 TD.

JANUARY 1, 2004 | CAPITAL ONE
GEORGIA 34, PURDUE 27

	1ST	2ND	3RD	4TH	OT	FINAL
GEO	14	10	0	3	7	34
PUR	0	10	0	17	0	27

SCORING SUMMARY
GEO	Gibson 6 pass from Greene (Bennett kick)
GEO	Gibson 4 pass from Greene (Bennett kick)
GEO	FG Bennett 28
GEO	Brown 11 pass from Greene (Bennett kick)
PUR	Orton 17 run (Jones kick)
PUR	FG Jones 27
PUR	Orton 2 run (Jones kick)
GEO	FG Bennett 40
PUR	Chambers 3 pass from Orton (Jones kick)
PUR	FG Jones 44
GEO	Lumpkin 1 run (Bennett kick)

GEO	TEAM STATISTICS	PUR
23	First Downs	15
113	Rushing Yards	59
27-37-0	Passing	20-35-1
327	Passing Yards	230
440	Total Yards	289
4-34	Punt Returns - Yards	5-53
2-48	Kickoff Returns - Yards	6-163
6-44.7	Punts - Average	9-44.4
34	Return Yards	53
2-2	Fumbles - Lost	1-0
10-90	Penalties - Yards	10-69
35:29	Possession Time	24:31

INDIVIDUAL LEADERS
RUSHING
GEO: Lumpkin 27-90, 1 TD.
PUR: Void 15-63.
PASSING
GEO: Greene 27-37-0, 327 yards, 3 TD.
PUR: Orton 20-34-1, 230 yards, 1 TD.
RECEIVING
GEO: Brown 5-99, 1 TD; Gary 2-53; Browning 2-48.
PUR: Standeford 7-102; Stubblefield 8-99.

JANUARY 1, 2005 | OUTBACK
GEORGIA 24, WISCONSIN 21

	1ST	2ND	3RD	4TH	FINAL
UGA	3	7	14	0	24
WISC	3	3	7	8	21

SCORING SUMMARY
UGA	FG Coutu 20
WISC	FG Allen 46
WISC	FG Allen 44
UGA	Gibson 19 pass from Greene (Coutu kick)
UGA	Thomas 24 pass from Greene (Coutu kick)
UGA	Brown 29 run (Coutu kick)
WISC	Charles 19 pass from Stocco (Allen kick)
WISC	Crooks 11 Interception return (Orr pass from Stocco)

UGA	TEAM STATISTICS	WISC
21	First Downs	14
196	Rushing Yards	60
19-41-2	Passing	12-27-0
264	Passing Yards	170
460	Total Yards	230
5-45	Punt Returns - Yards	3-34
4-49	Kickoff Returns - Yards	5-49
6-33.2	Punts - Average	7-44.3
1-1	Fumbles - Lost	2-2
8-85	Penalties - Yards	7-45
29:05	Possession Time	30:55

INDIVIDUAL LEADERS
RUSHING
UGA: Brown 16-111, 1 TD; Ware 12-61.
WISC: Davis 21-79; Donovan 2-15.
PASSING
UGA: Greene 19-38-2, 264 yards, 2 TD.
WISC: Stocco 12-27-0, 170 yards, 1 TD.
RECEIVING
UGA: Pope 3-65; Brown 4-44.
WISC: Williams 3-56; Charles 3-52, 1 TD.

JANUARY 2, 2006 | SUGAR
GEORGIA 35, WEST VIRGINIA 38

	1ST	2ND	3RD	4TH	FINAL
WVU	21	10	0	7	38
UGA	0	21	7	7	35

SCORING SUMMARY

WVU	Slaton 52 run (McAfee kick)
WVU	Reynaud 3 pass from P White (McAfee kick)
WVU	Reynaud 13 run (McAfee kick)
WVU	Slaton 18 run (McAfee kick)
UGA	Lumpkin 34 run (Coutu kick)
UGA	Brown 52 run (Coutu kick)
WVU	FG Mcafee 27
UGA	Pope 4 pass from Shockley (Coutu kick)
UGA	Bryant 34 run (Coutu kick)
WVU	Slaton 52 run (McAfee kick)
UGA	McClendon 43 pass from Shockley (Coutu kick)

WVU	TEAM STATISTICS	UGA
27	First Downs	27
382	Rushing Yards	224
11-14-0	Passing	20-33-0
120	Passing Yards	277
502	Total Yards	501
1-19	Punt Returns – Yards	2-31
5-111	Kickoff Returns - Yards	2-28
4-36.0	Punts – Average	3-45.7
1-0	Fumbles – Lost	4-3
9-74	Penalties – Yards	4-50

INDIVIDUAL LEADERS

RUSHING
WVU: Slaton 26-204, 3 TD.
UGA: Brown 9-78, 1 TD.

PASSING
WVU: P White 11-14-0, 120 yards, 1 TD.
UGA: Shockley 20-33-0, 277 yards, 3 TD.

RECEIVING
WVU: Reynaud 6-48, 1 TD; Myles 4-64.
UGA: Pope 6-50, 1 TD; Massaquoi 4-43.

DECEMBER 30, 2006 | CHICK-FIL-A
GEORGIA 31, VIRGINIA TECH 24

	1ST	2ND	3RD	4TH	FINAL
UGA	3	0	10	18	31
VT	0	21	0	3	24

SCORING SUMMARY

UGA	FG Coutu 39 yd
VT	Ore 1 run (Pace kick)
VT	Ore 1 run (Pace kick)
VT	Wheeler 53 pass from Royal (Pace kick)
UGA	FG Coutu 51
UGA	Milner 6 pass from Stafford (Coutu kick)
UGA	Lumpkin 3 run (Milner pass from Stafford)
UGA	FG Coutu 28
UGA	Southerland 1 run (Coutu kick)
VT	FG Pace 28

UGA	TEAM STATISTICS	VT
9	First Downs	9
71	Rushing Yards	42
9-21-1	Passing	14-27-3
129	Passing Yards	147
200	Total Yards	189
3-24	Punt Returns - Yards	2-53
4-81	Kickoff Returns - Yards	6-105
7-37.7	Punts - Average	4-48.8
1-0	Fumbles - Lost	1-1
4-31	Penalties - Yards	8-78

INDIVIDUAL LEADERS

RUSHING
UGA: Lumpkin 12-39, 1 TD.
VT: Ore 20-42, 2 TD.

PASSING
UGA: Stafford 9-21-1, 129 yards, 1 TD.
VT: Glennon 13-26-3, 94 yards.

RECEIVING
UGA: Milner 3-49, 1 TD; Massaquoi 2-18.
VT: Royal 4-45; Ore 4-11.

JANUARY 1, 2008 | SUGAR
GEORGIA 41, HAWAII 10

	1ST	2ND	3RD	4TH	FINAL
HAW	3	0	0	7	10
UGA	14	10	14	3	41

SCORING SUMMARY

UGA	Moreno 17 run (Coutu kick)
HAW	FG Kelly 41
UGA	Moreno 11 run (Coutu kick)
UGA	FG Coutu 52
UGA	Bailey 11 pass from Stafford (Coutu kick)
UGA	Howard fumble recovery in end zone (Coutu kick)
UGA	Brown 1 run (Coutu kick)
UGA	FG Coutu 45
HAW	Grice-Mullen 16 pass from Graunke (Kelly kick)

HAW	TEAM STATISTICS	UGA
20	First Downs	19
-5	Rushing Yards	160
35-57-4	Passing	14-27-1
311	Passing Yards	175
306	Total Yards	335
3-8	Punt Returns - Yards	0-0
7-175	Kickoff Returns - Yards	3-128
3-34.0	Punts - Average	3-48.3
2-2	Fumbles - Lost	1-0
11-90	Penalties - Yards	11-100

INDIVIDUAL LEADERS

RUSHING
HAW: Pilares 7-26.
UGA: T. Brown 19-73, 1 TD; Moreno 9-61, 2 TD.

PASSING
HAW: Brennan 22-38-3, 169 yards; Graunke 13-19-1, 142 yards, 1 TD.
UGA: Stafford 14-23-1, 175 yards, 1 TD.

RECEIVING
HAW: Rivers 10-105.
UGA: Massaquoi 5-54; Durham 3-48.

JANUARY 1, 2009 | CAPITAL ONE
GEORGIA 24, MICHIGAN STATE 12

	1ST	2ND	3RD	4TH	FINAL
UGA	3	0	14	7	24
MSU	3	3	0	6	12

SCORING SUMMARY

UGA	FG Walsh 32
MSU	FG Swenson 20
MSU	FG Swenson 32
UGA	Moore 35 pass from Stafford (Walsh kick)
UGA	White 21 pass from Stafford (Walsh kick)
MSU	Ringer 1 run (pass failed).
UGA	Moreno 21 pass from Stafford (Walsh kick).

UGA	TEAM STATISTICS	MSU
19	First Downs	16
81	Rushing Yards	31
20-31-1	Passing	22-39-1
250	Passing Yards	205
331	Total Yards	236
1-38	Punt Returns - Yards	1-15
4-78	Kickoff Returns - Yards	4-88
5-47.4	Punts - Average	5-38
1-1	Fumbles - Lost	1-0
7-53	Penalties - Yards	5-50

INDIVIDUAL LEADERS

RUSHING
UGA: Moreno 23-62.
MSU: Ringer 20-47, 1 TD.

PASSING
UGA: Stafford 20-31-1, 250 yards. 4 TD.
MSU: Hoyer 18-34-1, 169 yards.

RECEIVING
UGA: Moore 6-97, 1 TD; Moreno 6-63, 1 TD.
MSU: Cunningham 6-52; Dell 5-61.

KENTUCKY

BY GEOFFREY NORMAN

CASUAL SPORTS FANS KNOW Kentucky as a school that has had a bit of success in basketball. The large shadow cast by Wildcats hoops has obscured the school's football accomplishments and even chased away a coach who decided there simply was not enough oxygen in Lexington for both him and Adolph Rupp to breathe. In 1953, Bear Bryant left Kentucky for Texas A&M, then moved on to Alabama and immortality.

Kentucky may have lost an opportunity to become a permanent first-class football power, but it has made tantalizing moves in the half-century since Bryant's departure—including a 10–1 season and a No. 6 ranking in 1977. And, with the arrival of coach Rich Brooks in 2003, Kentucky may have found the man to lead the program to something more than a reputation as the SEC also-ran you should never overlook. Brooks took the Wildcats to three consecutive bowl games from 2006 to '08, winning them all. Kentucky had back-to-back eight-win seasons in '06 and '07—a first since 1976-77

(and more fun this time around, because the Wildcats weren't on probation). The 2007 team even defeated eventual national champion LSU. Under Brooks, the Wildcats may have, at last, arrived.

TRADITION Kentucky plays its October home games at night, under the lights, so fans can enjoy an unusual "daily double." This consists of the racing card at the Keeneland Race Course in the afternoon and the football game later at Commonwealth Stadium. With the exception of 1944, when he was a member of the Burma Bridge Bombers in World War II, 90-year-old Wildcat alum Jim Brown has been in attendance at every home football game since he was a UK freshman in 1938. That's a streak of 409 consecutive games, and counting.

BEST PLAYER Kentucky fans would doubtless vote for Tim Couch, the Wildcats' All-American quarterback who finished fourth in the 1998 Heisman balloting. Couch is, hands down, the most popular player in UK history.

As a sophomore, he led the nation in pass attempts, completions, yardage and completion percentage. Wildcats fans can only wonder what he might have accomplished had he not given up his senior year of eligibility to enter the NFL draft, where he was the No. 1 pick of the Cleveland Browns. In his slightly abbreviated career, Couch set seven NCAA

PROFILE

University of Kentucky
Lexington, Ky.
Founded: 1865
Enrollment: 27,000
Colors: Blue and White
Nickname: Wildcats
Stadium: Commonwealth Stadium
    Opened in 1973
    Grass; 67,942 capacity
First football game: 1881
All-time record: 559–553–44 (.503)
Bowl record: 8–5
Southeastern Conference championships:
2 (1 outright)
Outland Trophy: Bob Gain, 1950
First-round draft choices: 15
Website: www.ukathletics.com

THE BEST OF TIMES

Eight straight winning seasons and three major bowl bids during the eight-year tenure of Paul "Bear" Bryant, from 1946 to 1953.

THE WORST OF TIMES

Kentucky went without a conference win in five of its first 12 SEC seasons, beginning in 1933. The Wildcats mustered six wins only twice during that span.

CONFERENCE

After 11 years in the Southern Conference, Kentucky became a charter member of the SEC in 1933.

DISTINGUISHED ALUMNI

Pat Riley, NBA coach and executive; Ashley Judd, actress; Mitch McConnell, U.S. senator; Story Musgrave, astronaut

records, 14 SEC records and 26 school records.

The runners-up would be quarterback Babe Parilli, lineman Bob Gain—winner of the 1950 Outland Trophy—and Art Still, the outstanding defensive player on the great Kentucky teams of the mid-1970s. Still was the first pick of the Kansas City Chiefs in 1978 and went on to a distinguished 12-year NFL career.

BEST COACH Bear Bryant coached the Wildcats from 1946 to 1953. His teams had winning seasons in all of those years and his 60 wins are the best of any Kentucky coach. His 1950 squad finished on top in the SEC, the first of two conference championships won by the Wildcats. Bryant's Kentucky teams went to four bowl games, including successive Orange, Sugar and Cotton Bowls from 1949 to '51.

BEST TEAM The 1950 team went 11–1 during the regular season and was rewarded with an invitation to the Sugar Bowl, where it faced Bud Wilkinson's Oklahoma team, the colossus of college football and winner of 31 straight. The Wildcats won, 13-7, and might have been named national champions except that the final rankings

> *Kentucky was the first team in NCAA history to go from a winless record to a bowl in one year.*

were determined before the bowl games in those days. (Jeff Sagarin's retrospective computer ratings rank the Wildcats No. 1 for that season.) As it was, Kentucky finished No. 7 in the AP poll. The 1950-51 school year was especially sweet at Kentucky, since Rupp's basketball team took the national title, beating Kansas State 68-58 and finishing 32–2. The only other Kentucky team with a legitimate claim as best Wildcats squad would be coach Fran Curci's 1977 bunch that defeated Penn State, LSU, Georgia, Florida and Tennessee—all on the road. The Wildcats' final record was 11–1 and they were ranked No. 6 in the nation. However, since the team was on probation, it did not play in a bowl game.

BEST DEFENSE There are three contenders from three different eras. The "immortals of [18]98" gave up exactly no points—not a one—in the an entire season and outscored their opponents 180-0. Then there was that 1950 Bryant team that opened its 11–1 season with four shutouts and allowed an average of 5.8 points per game. And finally, the 1977 team had a defense that held very tough opposition (see *Best Team*) to a mere 10.1 points per game.

FIGHT SONG
ON, ON U OF K
On, on, U of K, we are right for the fight today,
Hold that ball and hit that line;
Ev'ry Wildcat star will shine;
We'll fight, fight, fight
For the blue and white
As we roll to that goal, varsity,
And we'll kick, pass and run
'til the battle is won,
And we'll bring home the victory.

FIRST-ROUND DRAFT CHOICES	
1951	Bob Gain, Packers (5)
1952	Vito (Babe) Parilli, Packers (4)
1954	Steve Meilinger, Redskins (8)
1958	Lou Michaels, Rams (4)
1962	Irv Goode, Cardinals (12)
1963	Tom Hutchinson, Browns (9)
1966	Rick Norton, Dolphins (2)*
1966	Sam Ball, Colts (15)
1966	Rodger Bird, Raiders*
1977	Warren Bryant, Falcons (6)
1977	Randy Burke, Colts (26)
1978	Art Still, Chiefs (2)
1985	George Adams, Giants (19)
1999	Tim Couch, Browns (1)
2003	Dewayne Robertson, Jets (4)

*From 1960-1966, the NFL and AFL held separate, competing drafts

CONSENSUS ALL-AMERICANS	
1950	Bob Gain, T
1950-51	Babe Parilli, B
1956-57	Lou Michaels, T
1965	Sam Ball, T
1977	Art Still, DL
1998	Tim Couch, QB
1999	James Whalen, TE
2002	Derek Abney, AP/KR

BEST BACKFIELD The 1984 Wildcats team that went 9–3 did it on some very strong legs. Senior running back George Adams rolled up 1,085 yards and 13 touchdowns on the ground and caught 33 balls for 330 yards and one TD. Freshman Mark Higgs ran for 476 yards, averaging more than six yards per carry. Sophomore Marc Logan ran for 400 yards. When they were done, Higgs, Adams and Logan were ranked second, third and fourth, respectively, in career rushing at Kentucky. They still rank in the top seven in school history. The quarterback on that unit, Bill Ransdell, threw for 1,748 yards and 11 touchdowns.

BIGGEST GAME On Oct. 4, 1997, Kentucky trailed Alabama late in the fourth quarter. The Wildcats returned a blocked field goal for a touchdown to take the lead—only to see Alabama send it into overtime with a field goal. On Kentucky's first possession in overtime, Couch hit Craig Yeast for the game-winning touchdown to give the Wildcats a 40-34 victory. It was the first time Kentucky had beaten Alabama in 75 years, inspiring the fans to storm the field and tear down the goalposts for the first, and only, time in school history.

BIGGEST UPSET In 1964, on the road against top-ranked Mississippi, the Wildcats had to come from behind twice in the second half to pull out a 27-21 victory. Rick Kestner caught nine balls, three of them for touchdowns—two from quarterback Rick Norton, the other a halfback pass from Rodger Bird—and a team under the whip of coach Charlie Bradshaw tasted glory.

HEARTBREAKER In 1965, after turning down a Gator Bowl bid in hopes of an invitation to the more prestigious Cotton Bowl, Kentucky lost to 3–5 Houston in the next-to-last game of the season and then lost to Tennessee in the finale. The Wildcats stayed home for the holidays.

BEST COMEBACK In Kentucky's case, the most memorable reversal of fortune was from one season to the next. Coach Jerry Claiborne, a Wildcat during the Bryant years, had taken over a demoralized program. In his first year, 1982, the team went 0–10–1. The following year, the Wildcats were 6–5–1 and played in the Hall of Fame Classic, making them the first team in NCAA history to go from a winless record to a bowl game in one year.

COLLEGE FOOTBALL HALL OF FAME INDUCTEES		
NAME	YEARS	INDUCTED
Bob Gain, T/G	1947-50	1980
Babe Parilli, QB	1949-51	1982
Paul Bryant, COACH	1946-53	1986
Lou Michaels, T	1955-57	1992
Jerry Claiborne, COACH	1982-89	1999

PRO FOOTBALL HALL OF FAME INDUCTEES		
NAME	YEARS	INDUCTED
George Blanda, QB/PK	1949-75	1981

STADIUM Commonwealth Stadium was built in 1973 with a seating capacity of 57,800, some 20,000 more than that of Stoll Field, which had been the Wildcats' home for 56 years. Commonwealth was expanded in 1999 and now accommodates 67,942 fans. On sellout days, it is the third-largest "city" in the entire state. The Bermuda grass surface of C.M. Newton Field (named after the longtime Kentucky AD) was laid down in 2001.

RIVAL Tennessee would garner the most votes among the SEC candidates, but the game against Louisville—resurrected in 1994 after 70 dormant years—generates more passion. Unlike most fierce in-state rivalries, this game is not the last of the season but often the first, which means one team's season will be tarnished right out of the box. The winner gets the Governor's Cup and its fans have the right to gloat insufferably all season long.

NICKNAME The Wildcats nickname was coined after a 6-2 win over Illinois in 1909. In a chapel service that followed the game, Commandant Carbusier, head of the school's military department, said the team had "fought like wildcats."

MASCOT The first costumed mascot, Wildcat, appeared in 1976. The second, Scratch, made his debut in 1996. There is a live mascot who lives with the Kentucky Department of Fish and Wildlife. His name is Blue. His predecessors have included TNT, Whiskers, Hot Tamale, Colonel and the first of the line, a cat named Tom.

UNIFORMS Kentucky's uniforms have changed several times over the years, but the colors date to 1892. They were originally blue and yellow. When a student asked what shade of blue, a player pulled off his necktie and held it up, so the blue in his necktie it was. The yellow was dropped in favor of white one year later. An odd addendum to the uniform came under Bryant, who gave the Jones twins, Harry and Larry, the numbers 1A and 1B. Harry, 1A, led the Wildcats in all-purpose yards in 1951 and Larry, 1B, was tops in kickoff returns the following season.

QUOTE "If I weren't so old, I'd have torn them down myself." —Athletic director **C.M. Newton**, after celebrating fans tore down the goalposts in the wake of Kentucky's 1997 win over Alabama, its first victory over the Tide in 75 years

The Kentucky Blues

BY BILLY REED

The truth be told, being a Kentucky football fan actually is more fun than the team's history book might indicate—especially on those October Saturdays when the thoroughbreds are running at Keeneland Race Course in the afternoon and the Wildcats are playing at night in Commonwealth Stadium, the team's 67,000-seat home on the edge of campus. Any visitor from Athens or Baton Rouge or Gainesville can tell you that it's a long day's night of fun that requires the endurance of a marathon runner. Post time for the first race is 1 p.m., and the final down hasn't usually been played until around 10. So that's nine hours of betting, partying, tailgating, screaming, chicken-wing scarfing and Kentucky-bourbon swilling.

Like Keeneland, Wildcats football has had its share of photo finishes. And in any close football game, the Cats almost always find a way to snatch defeat from the jaws of victory. That's why their detractors like to call the Big Blue the Big Blew. Losing the close ones has gotten to be such a UK tradition that Commonwealth Stadium has become a sort of Wrigley Field South. Kentucky fans love to play what former coach Jerry Claiborne called "that old iffin' game."

For example, if the Cats had only played a little pass defense against LSU on the last play of the 2002 game, then the Tigers wouldn't have been able to complete a Hail Mary for the win even as then-Wildcat coach Guy Morriss was being doused with Gatorade on national TV. Or take the final game of the 1987 season, with Kentucky sitting first-and-goal on the Tennessee 5-yard line and trailing 24-20 with less than four minutes left. If coach Jerry Claiborne hadn't called Mark Higgs's number four straight times only to have the man who earlier in the game had become UK's all-time leading rusher

wind up 18 inches short of a TD, then the Wildcats wouldn't have finished 5–6 and out of bowl consideration, nor would Kentucky's record against the Volunteers since 1984 now stand at 0–24. At most schools, that kind of bad mojo would be regarded as cruel and unusual punishment. At Kentucky, it's just another reason to bring up the Curse of the Bear.

It says a lot about the football program that the tenure of Paul "Bear"

It says a lot about the football program that the tenure of Paul "Bear" Bryant, who coached the Cats from 1946 through 1953, is still regarded as UK's golden era.

Bryant, who coached the Cats from 1946 through 1953, is still regarded as UK's golden era. Kentucky's signature win under Bryant was a 13-7 upset of top-ranked, unbeaten Oklahoma in the Sugar Bowl on Jan. 1, 1951. That should have given UK the national title, but, in those days, the bowls didn't count in the final polls. So when Adolph Rupp's basketball squad won the NCAA title later that year, Kentucky didn't get recognized as the first program to win football and basketball titles in the same academic year.

Bryant bolted Lexington in the winter of 1953, ostensibly because the university's president reneged on a promise to force Rupp to retire because of Kentucky's involvement in the big point-shaving scandal. But the real reason was that Lexington was too small to contain two coaches of their magnitude. Since Rupp was a living legend while Bryant was just beginning

to establish his reputation, the Bear found himself exiled to Texas A&M. Bryant's wife, Mary Harmon, went into shock. Instead of hobnobbing with the Bluegrass bluebloods, poor Mrs. Bryant was stuck with a bunch of Texas Aggies with oil 'neath their fingernails.

Folklore has it that, on his way out of town, Bear placed a curse on the program. Maybe he did, maybe he didn't. But it's a fact that since his departure, Kentucky 1) has never returned to any of the three major bowls— Sugar, Orange, Cotton—to which he took them; 2) was twice caught violating NCAA rules and slapped with probations that derailed the coaching careers of Fran Curci and Hal Mumme; and 3) has suffered more gut-wrenching losses that any program and its fans should have to endure.

Wildcats football supporters, however, have come to accept their fate with a stoicism that is foreign to their basketball counterparts. If anything, all the heartbreaking losses have bonded fans into what former coach Bill Curry called "the fellowship of the miserable." All it takes to make them happy is a seven- or eight-win season and a trip to a minor bowl. Every fall, bowl honchos pray for UK to be "bowl eligible," because they know the team's large, loyal fan base can always be counted on to show in numbers upwards of 25,000 to any bowl that's played east of the Mississippi.

In recent years, Kentucky has shown enough improvement under coach Rich Brooks—three straight bowl-game wins for the first time, even if they were at mid-level bowls—so there's hope that Bryant's curse might be losing potency. But down at Keeneland you'll get some pretty long odds on that. The horse players around Lexington have seen the Cats come out on the short end of too many photo finishes to believe that any good news will last for long.

*In 50 years as a professional sportswriter, **Billy Reed** has known and covered every Kentucky football coach since Bear Bryant. He was sports editor of the* Louisville Courier-Journal *from 1977 to '87 and had a 29-year association with* Sports Illustrated.

KENTUCKY ALL-TIME SCORES

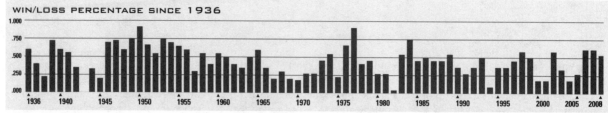

WIN/LOSS PERCENTAGE SINCE 1936

1.000 .750 .500 .250 .000
1936 1940 1945 1950 1955 1960 1965 1970 1975 1980 1985 1990 1995 2000 2005 2008

NO HEAD COACH

1881   1-2-0
N12		Transylvania, Ky.	7	1
N19		Transylvania, Ky.	1	2
D3		Transylvania, Ky.	2	3

1882-1890
NO TEAM

S.M. POTTINGER/J.P. SELBY
1891 (.500)   1-1

1891   1-1-0
P10	•	Georgetown	8	2
D19		Centre	0	10

A.M. MILLER/JOHN A. THOMPSON
1892 (.357)   2-4-1

1892   2-4-1
O29	=	Transylvania, Ky.	0	0
N5		Central U.	6	8
N12		at Central U.	4	8
N19	•	at Louisville	14	10
N26		at VMI	0	34
D3		Central U.	6	10
D10	•	Transylvania, Ky.	10	4

JOHN A. THOMPSON
1893 (.688)   5-2-1

1893   5-2-1
O14	•	Georgetown	80	0
O21	•	at Tennessee	56	0
O28	•	at Centre Coll.	4	6
N4	•	Transylvania, Ky.	28	0
N11		Central U.	36	48
N18	•	Cincinnati YMCA	14	4
N25	•	Transylvania, Ky.	38	28
N30	=	Indiana	24	24

W.P. FINNEY
1894 (.714)   5-2

1894   5-2-0
S22		at Cincinnati	4	32
O6	•	Georgetown	40	6
O13	•	Miami (Ohio)	28	6
O20	•	Jefferson AC	64	0
N10	•	Kentucky U.	44	0
N17		Centre Coll.	0	67
N29	•	Central University	38	10

CHARLES MASON
1895 (.444)   4-5

1895   4-5-0
O5	•	at Frankfort AC	10	0
O12		at Purdue	0	32
O14		at DePauw	0	18
O19	•	at Centre Coll.	6	0
O26		at Georgetown	0	10
N3	•	Kentucky U.	26	0
N15		Ohio State	6	8
N23	•	Louisville AC	16	10
N28		Centre Coll.	0	16

DUDLEY SHORT
1896 (.333)   3-6

1896   3-6-0
O3		Lexington AC	0	10
O10		at Vanderbilt	0	6
O17		at Cateletts AC	4	6
O24	•	Transylvania, Ky.	36	6
O31		at Centre Coll.	0	32
N7		Central Univ.	62	0
N14		Centre Coll.	0	44
N21	•	at Georgetown	16	0
N27		at Louisville	4	30

LYMAN B. EATON
1897 (.333)   2-4

1897   2-4-0
O2	•	Transylvania, Ky.	8	6
O11		at Ky. Wesleyan	0	4
O23	•	Georgetown	20	4
O30		at Vanderbilt	0	50
N6		Central U.	0	18
N25		Centre Coll.	0	36

W.R. BASS
1898-99 (.813)   12-2-2

1898   7-0-0
O1	•	Transylvania, Ky.	18	0
O8	•	at Georgetown	28	0
O15	•	Co.H of 8th	59	0
O29	•	at Louisville AC	16	0
N5	•	Centre Coll.	6	0
N12	•	160th Indiana	17	0
N19	•	New Castle AC	36	0

1899   5-2-2
O7	•	Transylvania, Ky.	23	6
O18	•	Miami (Ohio)	18	5
O21	=	at Centre Coll.	11	11
N4		at Tennessee	0	12
N11		Central U.	0	5
N18	•	Georgetown	34	0
N21	=	Wash. & Lee	0	0
N22	•	Wash. & Lee	6	0
N30	•	Alumni	6	5

W.H. KILER
1900-01 (.342)   6-12-1

1900   4-6-0
S29		at Cincinnati	6	20
O6	•	Louisville YMCA	12	6
O13		at Centre Coll.	0	5
O20		All-Kentucky	0	5
O27		Central U.	0	6
N3	•	at Louisville YMCA	12	0
N10		Avondale	5	11
N17	•	Georgetown	12	0
N24		at Central U.	0	11
N29	•	Transylvania, Ky.	12	0

1901   2-6-1
O5		at Vanderbilt	0	22
O12	=	Cincinnati	0	0
O19	•	at Georgetown	17	0
O26		Transylvania, Ky.	0	27
N2		at Avondale AC	6	17
N9		at Louisville YMCA	0	11
N16		Central U.	0	5
N23		at Tennessee	0	5
N28		Cincinnati AC	16	0

E.W. McLEOD
1902 (.389)   3-5-1

1902   3-5-1
S27	•	Q&C RR	22	0
O4	•	Miami (Ohio)	11	5
O18	•	Georgetown	28	0
O25		at Nashville	0	11
O27		at Mooney School	0	23
N1		at Central U.	0	15
N8		at Louisville YMCA	0	17
N15	=	Cincinnati	6	6
N27		Transylvania, Ky.	5	6

C.A. WRIGHT
1903 (.875)   7-1

1903   7-1-0
S25	•	Cynthiana	39	0
O3	•	Xavier	21	0
O10	•	Berea Coll.	17	0
O17	•	KMI	18	0
O24	•	Miami (Ohio)	47	0
N2	•	Georgetown	51	0
N7	•	Marietta	11	5
N26		Transylvania, Ky.	0	17

F.E. SCHACT
1904-05 (.775)   15-4-1

1904   9-1-0
S30	•	Paris AC	28	0
O8	•	at Indiana	12	0
O12	•	at Central U.	40	0
O15	•	Berea Coll.	42	0
O18	•	Bethany W. Va.	6	0
O22		at Cincinnati	0	11
N5	•	KMI	11	0
N12	•	at Georgetown	35	0
N19	•	Central U.	81	0
N24	•	Transylvania, Ky.	21	4

1905   6-3-1
S27	•	Cynthiana	52	0
S30	•	Cattleburg A	23	0
O7		at Indiana	0	29
O14	•	KMI	12	4
O28	•	Berea Coll.	46	0
N2	•	at Marshall	53	0
N4		at West Virginia	0	45
N11	•	Cumberland	12	0
N18		at St. Louis	0	82
N25	=	Central U.	11	11

J. WHITE GUYN
1906-08 (.700)   17-7-1

1906   4-3-0
O6		at Vanderbilt	0	28
O13	•	Eminence AC	48	0
O27	•	KMI	16	11
N2		Marietta	0	16
N10	•	Tennessee	21	0
N24	•	at Georgetown	19	0
N29	•	Centre Coll.	6	12

1907   9-1-1
S21	•	at Ky. Wesleyan	17	0
S28	•	Winchester AC	6	0
S28	•	Louisville Manual	30	0
O5		at Vanderbilt	0	40
O12	•	Morris-Harvey	29	0
O21	•	Hanover	40	0
N9	=	at Tennessee	0	0
N11	•	at Maryville	5	2
N16	•	Georgetown	38	0
N28	•	Centre	11	0
D5	•	Transylvania, Ky.	5	0

1908   4-3-0
O10	•	Berea Coll.	17	0
O17		at Tennessee	0	7
O19	•	at Maryville	18	0
O31		Sewanee	0	12
N7		at Michigan	0	62
N14	•	Rose Poly	12	0
N26	•	Centre Coll.	40	0

E.R. SWEETLAND
1909-10, '12 (.821)   23-5

1909   9-1-0
S25	•	Ky Wesleyan	18	0
O2	•	Berea Coll.	28	0
O9		at Illinois	6	2
O16	•	Tennessee	17	0
O22		at North Carolina St.	6	15
O28	•	Rose Poly	43	0
N3	•	at Georgetown	22	6
N6	•	St. Mary's Coll.	29	0
N13	•	Transylvania, Ky.	77	0
N25	•	Centre Coll.	15	6

1910   7-2-0
S24	•	Ohio U.	12	0
O1	•	Maryville	12	5
O8	•	North Carolina	11	0
O15	•	at Ky. Wesleyan	42	0
O22	•	Georgetown	37	0
O29		Tulane	10	3
N5	•	at Tennessee	10	0
N12		at St. Louis	0	9
N24		Centre Coll.	6	12

P.P. DOUGLASS
1911 (.700)   7-3

1911   7-3-0
S30	•	Maryville	13	0
O7	•	Morris-Harvey	12	0
O14	•	at Miami (Ohio)	12	0
O21	•	Lexington HS	17	0
O28		Cincinnati	0	6
N4	•	at Georgetown	18	0
N11		at Vanderbilt	0	18
N18	•	Transylvania, Ky.	5	12
N23	•	Centre Coll.	8	5
N30	•	Tennessee	12	0

E.R. SWEETLAND

1912   7-2-0
S28	•	Maryville	34	0
O5	•	Marshall	13	6
O12		Miami (Ohio)	8	13
O19		at Cincinnati	19	13
O26	•	Louisville	41	0
N2		VMI	2	3
N9	•	Hanover	64	0
N16		at Tennessee	13	6
N28	•	at YMI of Cincy	56	0

ALPHA BRUMAGE
1913-14 (.688)   11-5

1913   6-2-0
S27	•	Butler	21	7
O4		at Illinois	0	21
O18	•	Ohio Northern	21	0
O25	•	Cincinnati	27	7
N1	•	Earlham	28	10
N8	•	Willington	33	0
N22	•	at Louisville	20	0
N27		Tennessee	7	13

1914   5-3-0
S26	•	Wilmington	87	0
O3	•	Maryville	80	0
O17	•	Mississippi State	19	13
O24	•	Earlham	81	3
O31		at Cincinnati	7	14
N7		at Purdue	6	40
N14	•	Louisville	42	0
N26		at Tennessee	6	23

J.J. TIGERT
1915-16 (.767)   10-2-3

1915   6-1-1
O2	●	Butler	33 0
O9	●	Earlham	54 13
O16		at Mississippi State	0 12
O23	=	Sewanee	7 7
O30	●	Cincinnati	27 6
N6		at Louisville	15 0
N13	●	Purdue	7 0
N25		Tennessee	6 0

1916   4-1-2
S30	●	Butler	39 3
O7	●	Centre	68 0
O14		Vanderbilt	0 45
O21	●	Sewanee	0 0
O28	●	at Cincinnati	32 0*
N18		Mississippi State	13 3
N30	=	at Tennessee	0 0

S.A. BOLES
1917 (.389)   3-5-1

1917   3-5-1
S29	●	Butler	33 0
O6		Maryville	19 0
O13	=	Miami (Ohio)	0 0
O20		Vanderbilt	0 5
O27		Sewanee *CHAT*	0 7
N3		at Centre	0 3
N10		at Mississippi State	0 14
N17		Alabama	0 27
N29	●	Florida	52 0

ANDY GILL
1918-19 (.500)   5-5-1

1918   2-1-0
O5	●	at Indiana	24 7
N2		at Vanderbilt	0 33
N9		at Georgetown	21 3

1919   3-4-1
O4		Georgetown	12 0
O11		Indiana	0 24
O18		at Ohio State	0 49
O25	●	at Sewanee	6 0
N1	=	Vanderbilt	0 0
N8		at Cincinnati	0 7
N15		at Centre	0 56
N27	●	Tennessee	13 0

W.J. JUNEAU
1920-22 (.560)   13-10-2

1920   3-4-1
O2	●	Southwestern	62 0
O9	●	Maryville	31 0
O16		at Miami (Ohio)	0 14
O23	=	Sewanee	6 6
O30	●	at Vanderbilt	0 20
N6	●	Cincinnati	7 6
N13		Centre	0 49
N25		at Tennessee	7 14

1921   4-3-1
O1	●	Ky. Wesleyan	68 0
O8	●	Marshall	28 0
O15		Vanderbilt	14 21
O22	●	Georgetown	33 0
O29		Sewanee *Lou*	0 6
N5		at Centre	0 55
N12	●	VMI *Lou*	14 7
N24	=	Tennessee	0 0

1922-1932
SOUTHERN

1922   6-3-0 (2-2-0)
S30	●	Marshall	16 0
O7	●	Cincinnati	15 0
O14	●	Louisville	73 0*
O21	●	at Georgetown	40 6
O28	●	Sewanee	7 0
N4		Centre	3 27
N11		at Vanderbilt	0 9
N18	●	Alabama	6 0
N30		at Tennessee	7 14

J. WINN
1923 (.556)   4-3-2

1923   4-3-2 (0-2-2)
S29	●	Marshall	41 0
O6		at Cincinnati	14 0
O13	=	Wash. & Lee	6 6
O20	●	Maryville	28 0
O27		Georgetown	35 0
N3		at Centre	0 10
N10		at Alabama	8 16
N17	=	Georgia Tech *UNK*	3 3
N29		Tennessee	0 18

FRED J. MURPHY
1924-26 (.463)   12-14-1

1924   4-5-0 (2-3-0)
O4	●	Louisville	29 0
O11	●	Georgetown	42 0
O18		Wash. & Lee	7 10
O25		Sewanee	7 0
N1		Centre	0 7
N8		at Alabama	7 42
N15		VMI	3 10
N27	●	at Tennessee	27 6
D6		W. V. Wesleyan *ChWV*	7 24

1925   6-3-0 (4-2-0)
S26	●	Maryville	13 6
O3		at Chicago	0 9
O10	●	Clemson	19 6
O17		Wash. & Lee	0 25
O24	●	Sewanee	14 0
O31	●	at Centre	16 0
N7		Alabama *BIRM*	0 31
N14	●	VMI *ChWV*	7 0
N26		Tennessee	23 20

1926   2-6-1 (1-4-1)
O2	●	Maryville	25 0
O9		at Indiana	6 14
O16		Wash. & Lee	13 14
O23	●	Florida *JacF*	18 13
O30	●	Virginia Tech	13 13
N6		Alabama *BIRM*	0 14
N13		VMI *ChWV*	9 10
N20		Centre	0 7
N25		at Tennessee	0 6

HARRY GAMAGE
1927-33 (.556)   32-25-5

1927   3-6-1 (1-5-0)
S24	=	Maryville	6 6
O1		Indiana	0 21
O8	●	Ky. Wesleyan	13 7
O15		Florida *JacF*	6 27
O22		Wash. & Lee	0 25
O29		at Vanderbilt	6 34
N5		Alabama *BIRM*	6 21
N12	●	VMI *ChWV*	25 0
N19	●	at Centre	53 0
N24		Tennessee	0 20

1928   4-3-1 (2-2-1)
O6	●	Carson-Newman	61 0
O13	●	Wash. & Lee	6 0
O20		at Northwestern	0 7
O27	●	Centre	8 0
N3		at Vanderbilt	7 14
N10		Alabama *MONT*	0 14
N17	●	VMI	18 6
N29	=	at Tennessee	0 0

1929   6-1-1 (3-1-1)
O5	●	Maryville	40 0
O12	●	Wash. & Lee	20 6
O19	●	Carson-Newman	58 0
O26	●	at Centre	33 0
N2	●	Clemson	44 6
N9		Alabama *MONT*	13 24
N16	=	at VMI	23 12
N28		at Tennessee	6 6

1930   5-3-0 (4-3-0)
O4	●	Sewanee	37 0
O11	●	Maryville	57 0
O18	●	Wash. & Lee	33 14
O25	●	Virginia	47 0
N1		Alabama	0 19
N8		at Duke	7 14
N15	●	VMI	26 0
N27		at Tennessee	0 8

1931   5-2-2 (4-2-2)
O3	●	Maryville	19 0
O10	●	Wash. & Lee	45 0
O17	=	at Maryland	6 6
O24	●	Virginia Tech	20 6
O31		at Alabama	7 9
N7		Duke	0 7
N14		at VMI	20 12
N26		Tennessee	6 6
D5		Florida *JacF*	7 2

1932   4-5-0 (4-5-0)
S24	●	VMI	23 0
O1	●	Sewanee	18 0
O8		at Georgia Tech	12 6
O15	●	Wash. & Lee	53 7
O22		at Virginia Tech	0 7
O29		Alabama	7 12
N5		at Duke	0 13
N12		Tulane	3 6
N24		at Tennessee	0 26

1933-PRESENT
SEC

1933   5-5-0 (2-3-0)
S23	●	Maryville	46 2
S30	●	Sewanee	7 0
O7	●	Georgia Tech	7 6
O14		at Cincinnati	3 0
O21		Wash. & Lee *ROA*	0 7
O28		Duke	7 14
N4		Alabama *BIRM*	0 20
N11	●	VMI	21 6
N18		at Tulane	0 34
N30		Tennessee	0 27

C.A. WYNNE
1934-37 (.513)   20-19

1934   5-5-0 (1-3-0)
S22	●	Maryville	26 0
S29	●	Wash. & Lee	0 7
O6	●	at Cincinnati	27 0
O13		Clemson	7 0
O20		at North Carolina	0 6
O27	●	Auburn	9 0
N3		Alabama	14 34
N10	●	at Southwestern	33 0
N17		Tulane	7 20
N29		at Tennessee	0 19

1935   5-4-0 (3-3-0)
S21	●	Maryville	60 0
S27	●	at Xavier	21 7
O5		at Ohio State	6 19
O12	●	Georgia Tech	25 6
O19		Auburn *MONT*	0 23
N2		Alabama *BIRM*	0 13
N9	●	Florida	15 6
N16		at Tulane	13 20
N28	●	Tennessee	27 0

1936   6-4-0 (1-3-0)
S19	●	Maryville	54 3
S25	●	at Xavier	21 0
O3	●	VMI	38 0
O10		at Georgia Tech	0 34
O17	●	at Wash. & Lee	39 7
O24		Florida	7 0
O31		Alabama	0 14
N7		Manhattan *BKLN*	7 13
N14	●	Clemson	7 6
N26		at Tennessee	6 7

1937   4-6-0 (0-5-0)
S25		at Vanderbilt	0 12
O2	●	at Xavier	6 0
O9		Georgia Tech	0 32
O16	●	Wash. & Lee	41 6
O23	●	Manhattan	19 0
O30		Alabama	0 41
N6	●	South Carolina	27 7
N13		at Boston College	0 13
N25		Tennessee	0 13
D4		at Florida	0 6

A.D. KIRWAN
1938-44 (.464)   24-28-4

1938   2-7-0 (0-4-0)
S24	●	Maryville	46 7
O1	●	Oglethorpe	66 0
O8		Vanderbilt	7 14
O15		Wash. & Lee	0 8
O22		at Xavier	7 26
O29		Alabama	6 26
N5		at Georgia Tech	18 19
N12		Clemson	0 14
N24		at Tennessee	0 46

1939   6-2-1 (2-2-1)
S30	●	VMI	21 0
O7	●	at Vanderbilt	21 13
O14	●	Oglethorpe	59 0
O21	●	Georgia *Lou*	13 6
O28	●	at Xavier	21 0
N4	=	Alabama *Birm*	7 7
N11		at Georgia Tech	6 13
N18	●	West Virginia	13 6
N30		Tennessee	0 19

1940   5-3-2 (1-2-2)
S21	●	Baldwin Wallace	59 7
S27	●	at Xavier	13 0
O5	●	Wash. & Lee	47 12
O12	=	at Vanderbilt	7 7
O19	●	George Washington	24 0
O25	=	at Georgia	7 7
N2		Alabama	0 25
N9	●	Georgia Tech *Lou*	26 7
N16		at West Virginia	7 9
N23		at Tennessee	0 33

1941   5-4-0 (0-4-0)
S27	●	Virginia Tech *Lou*	37 14
O4	●	at Wash. & Lee	7 0
O11		Vanderbilt	15 39
O18	●	at Xavier	21 6
O25	●	West Virginia	18 6
N1		at Alabama	0 30
N8		at Georgia Tech	13 20
N15	●	Southwestern	33 19
N22		Tennessee	7 20

1942   3-6-1 (0-5-0)
S19		Georgia *Lou*	6 7
S25	●	at Xavier	35 19
O3	●	Wash. & Lee	53 0
O10		Vanderbilt	6 7
O17	=	Virginia Tech *ROA*	21 21
O24		Alabama	0 14
O30	●	at George Washington	27 6
N7		at Georgia Tech	7 47
N14		West Virginia	0 7
N21		at Tennessee	0 26

1943
NO TEAM WWII

1944   3-6-0 (1-5-0)
S23	●	Mississippi	27 7
S30		at Tennessee	13 26
O7		Michigan State	0 2
O13		at Georgia	12 13
O20	●	VMI	262
O27		Alabama *MONT*	0 41
N4		Mississippi State *MEM*	0 26
N18	●	West Virginia	40 9
N25		Tennessee	7 21

BERNIE SHIVELY
1945 (.200)   2-8

1945   2-8-0 (0-5-0)
S21	●	Mississippi *MEM*	7 21
S29	●	Cincinnati	13 7
O6		at Michigan State	6 7
O13		Georgia	6 48
O20		at Vanderbilt	6 19
O27		at Cincinnati	7 16
N3		Alabama *Lou*	19 60
N10	●	at West Virginia	19 6
N17		Marquette	13 19
N24		Tennessee	0 14

PAUL "BEAR" BRYANT
1946-53 (.710)   60-23-5

1946   7-3-0 (2-3-0)
S21	●	Mississippi	20 7*
S28	●	at Cincinnati	26 7
O5	●	Xavier	70 0
O11		at Georgia	13 28
O19	●	Vanderbilt	10 7
O26	●	Alabama *MONT*	7 21
N2	●	Michigan State	39 14
N9	●	at Marquette	35 0
N16	●	West Virginia	13 0
N23		at Tennessee	0 7

124 KENTUCKY

THE SCHOOLS

1947 8-3-0 (2-3-0)

S20	|	at Mississippi	7	14
S27	●	Cincinnati	20	0
O4	●	at Xavier	20	7
O11	● |	Georgia	26	0
O18	● |	at Vanderbilt	14	0
O25	●	at Michigan State	7	6
N1	|	Alabama	0	13
N8	●	at West Virginia	15	6
N15	●	Evansville	36	0
N22	|	Tennessee	6	13
		GREAT LAKES BOWL		
D6	●	Villanova	24	14

1948 5-3-2 (1-3-1)

S25	●	Xavier	48	7
O2	|	Mississippi	7	20
O9	|	at Georgia	12	35
O16	|	Vanderbilt	7	26
O23	●	at Marquette	25	0
O30	●	at Cincinnati	28	7
N6	=	Villanova	13	13
N13	● |	Florida	34	15
N20	= |	at Tennessee	0	0
N26	●	at Miami, Fla.	25	5

1949 9-3-0 (4-1-0)

S17	●	Southern Miss	71	7
S24	● |	at LSU	19	0
O1	● |	at Mississippi	47	0
O8	● |	Georgia	25	0
O15	●	Citadel	44	0
O22		at SMU	7	20
O29	●	Cincinnati	14	7
N5	●	at Xavier	21	7
N12	● |	Florida TAM	35	0
N19	|	Tennessee	0	6
N25	●	at Miami, Fla.	21	6
		ORANGE BOWL		
J2		Santa Clara	13	21

1950 11-1-0 (5-1-0)

S16	●	North Texas	25	0
S23	● |	LSU	14	0
S30	● |	Mississippi	27	0
O7	●	Dayton	40	0
O14	●	Cincinnati	41	7
O21	●	Villanova PHIL	34	7
O28	● |	at Georgia Tech	28	14
N4	● |	Florida	40	6
N11	● |	at Mississippi State	48	21
N18	●	North Dakota	83	0
N25	|	at Tennessee	0	7
		SUGAR BOWL		
J1	●	Oklahoma	13	7

1951 8-4-0 (3-3-0)

S15	●	Tennessee Tech	72	13
S22		at Texas	6	7
S29	|	at Mississippi	17	21
O6	|	Georgia Tech	7	13
O13	● |	Mississippi State	27	0
O20	●	Villanova	35	13
O27	● |	at Florida	14	6
N3	●	Miami, Fla.	32	0
N10	● |	at Tulane	37	0
N17	●	George Washington	47	13
N24	|	Tennessee	0	28
		COTTON BOWL		
J1	●	TCU	20	7

1952 5-4-2 (1-3-2)

S20		Villanova	6	25
S27	= |	Mississippi	13	13
O4	●	at Texas A&M	10	7
O11	|	LSU	7	34
O18	|	at Mississippi State	14	27
O25	●	at Cincinnati	14	6
O31	●	at Miami, Fla.	29	0
N8	● |	Tulane	27	6
N15	●	Clemson	27	14
N22	= |	at Tennessee	14	14
D6	|	at Florida	0	27

1953 7-2-1 (4-1-1)

S19		Texas A&M	6	7
S26	|	at Mississippi	6	22
O3	● |	Florida	26	13
O10	= |	at LSU	6	6
O17	● |	Mississippi State	32	13
O24	●	Villanova	19	0
O31	●	at Rice	19	13
N7	● |	at Vanderbilt	40	14
N14	●	Memphis	20	7
N21	● |	Tennessee	27	21

BLANTON COLLIER
1954-61 (.531) 41-36-3

1954 7-3-0 (5-2-0)

S18		Maryland	0	20
S25	|	Mississippi MEM	9	28
O2	● |	LSU	7	6
O9	● |	Auburn	21	14
O16	|	at Florida	7	21
O23	● |	at Georgia Tech	13	6
O30	●	Villanova	28	3
N6	● |	Vanderbilt	19	7
N13	●	Memphis	33	7
N20	● |	at Tennessee	14	13

1955 6-3-1 (3-3-1)

S17	|	at LSU	7	19
S24	● |	Mississippi	21	14
O1	●	Villanova	28	0
O8	= |	Auburn BIRM	14	14
O15	|	Mississippi State	14	20
O22	● |	Florida	10	7
O29	●	Rice	20	16
N5	|	at Vanderbilt	0	34
N12	●	Memphis	41	7
N19	● |	Tennessee	23	0

1956 6-4-0 (4-4-0)

S22	|	Georgia Tech	6	14
S29	|	Mississippi MEM	7	37
O6	● |	at Florida	17	8
O13	|	Auburn	0	13
O20	● |	LSU	14	0
O27	● |	at Georgia	14	7
N3	●	at Maryland	14	0
N10	● |	Vanderbilt	7	6
N17	●	Xavier	33	0
N24	|	at Tennessee	7	20

1957 3-7-0 (1-7-0)

S21	|	at Georgia Tech	0	13
S28	|	Mississippi	0	15
O5	|	Florida	7	14
O12	|	at Auburn	0	6
O19	|	at LSU	0	21
O26	|	Georgia	14	33
N2	●	Memphis	53	7
N9	|	at Vanderbilt	7	12
N16	●	Xavier	27	0
N23	● |	Tennessee	20	6

1958 5-4-1 (3-4-1)

S13	●	Hawaii LOU	51	0
S20	● |	Georgia Tech	13	0
S27	|	Mississippi MEM	6	27
O11	|	Auburn	0	8
O18	|	at LSU	7	32
O25	|	at Georgia	0	28
N1	● |	Mississippi State	33	12
N8	= |	Vanderbilt	0	0
N15	●	Xavier	20	6
N22	● |	at Tennessee	6	2

1959 4-6-0 (1-6-0)

S19	|	Georgia Tech	12	14
S26	|	Mississippi	0	16
A2	●	Detroit	32	7
A10	|	Auburn	0	33
O17	|	LSU	0	9
O24	|	Georgia	7	14
O30	●	at Miami, Fla.	22	3
N7	|	at Vanderbilt	6	11
N14	●	Xavier	41	0
N21	● |	Tennessee	20	0

1960 5-4-1 (2-4-1)

S17	|	at Georgia Tech	13	23
S24	|	Mississippi MEM	6	21
O1	|	Auburn	7	10
O8	●	Marshall	55	0
O15	● |	LSU	3	0
O22	|	Georgia	13	17
O29	●	at Florida State	23	0
N5	● |	Vanderbilt	27	0
N12	●	Xavier	49	0
19	= |	at Tennessee	10	10

1961 5-5-0 (2-4-0)

S23		Miami, Fla.	7	14
S30	|	Mississippi	6	20
O7	● |	at Auburn	14	12
O14	●	Kansas State	21	8
O21	|	at LSU	14	24
O28	|	at Georgia	15	16
N4	●	Florida State	20	0
N11	● |	at Vanderbilt	16	3
N18	●	Xavier	9	0
N25	|	Tennessee	16	26

CHARLIE BRADSHAW
1962-68 (.386) 25-41-4

1962 3-5-2 (2-3-1)

S22	=	Florida State	0	0
S29	|	Mississippi JAM	0	14
O6	|	Auburn	6	16
O12	●	at Detroit	27	8
O20	|	LSU	0	7
O27	= |	at Georgia	7	7
N2		at Miami, Fla.	17	25
N10	● |	Vanderbilt	7	0
N17		Xavier	9	14
N24	● |	at Tennessee	12	10

1963 3-6-1 (0-5-1)

S21	●	Virginia Tech	33	14
S28	|	Mississippi	7	31
O5	|	at Auburn	13	14
O12	●	Detroit	35	18
O19	|	at LSU	7	28
O26	|	Georgia	14	17
N2		Miami, Fla.	14	20
N9	= |	at Vanderbilt	0	0
N16	●	at Baylor	19	7
N23	|	Tennessee	0	19

1964 5-5-0 (4-2-0)

S19	●	Detroit	13	6
S26	● |	Mississippi JAM	27	21
O3	● |	Auburn BIRM	20	0
O10		at Florida State	6	48
O17	|	LSU	7	27
O24	|	at Georgia	7	21
O31		at West Virginia	21	26
N7	● |	Vanderbilt	22	21
N14		Baylor	15	17
N21	● |	at Tennessee	12	7

1965 6-4-0 (3-3-0)

S18	●	at Missouri	7	0
S25	● |	Mississippi	16	7
O2	|	at Auburn	18	23
O9	●	Florida State	26	24
O16	|	at LSU	21	31
O23	● |	Georgia	28	10
O30	●	West Virginia	28	8
N6	● |	at Vanderbilt	34	0
N13		at Houston	21	38
N20	|	Tennessee	3	19

1966 3-6-1 (2-4-0)

S17	●	North Carolina	10	0
S24	|	Mississippi JAM	0	17
O1	● |	Auburn	17	7
O8		Virginia Tech	0	7
O15	|	LSU	0	30
O22	|	at Georgia	15	27
O29	=	at West Virginia	14	14
N5	● |	Vanderbilt	14	10
N12		Houston	18	56
N19	|	at Tennessee	19	28

1967 2-8-0 (1-6-0)

S23		at Indiana	10	12
S30	|	Mississippi	13	26
O7	|	at Auburn	7	48
O14		Virginia Tech	14	24
O21	|	at LSU	7	30
O28	|	Georgia	7	31
N4	●	West Virginia	22	7
N11	● |	at Vanderbilt	12	7
N18	|	at Florida	12	28
N25	|	Tennessee	7	17

1968 3-7-0 (0-7-0)

S21	●	Missouri	12	6
S28	|	Mississippi JAM	14	30
O5	|	Auburn	7	26
O12	●	Oregon State	35	34
O19	|	at LSU	3	13
O26	|	Georgia	14	35
N2	●	at West Virginia	35	16
N9	|	Vanderbilt	0	6
N16	|	Florida	14	16
N23	|	at Tennessee	7	24

JOHN RAY
1969-72 (.233) 10-33

1969 2-8-0 (1-6-0)

S20		Indiana	30	58
S27	● |	Mississippi	10	9
O4	|	at Auburn	3	44
O11	●	at Virginia Tech	7	6
O18	|	LSU	10	37
O25	|	at Georgia	0	30
N1		West Virginia	6	7
N8	|	at Vanderbilt	6	42
N15	|	at Florida	6	31
N22	|	Tennessee	26	31

1970 2-9-0 (0-7-0)

S12		at North Carolina	10	20
S19	●	Kansas State	16	3
S26	|	Mississippi JAM	17	20
O3	|	Auburn	15	33
O10		Utah State	6	35
O17	|	at LSU	7	14
O24	|	Georgia	3	19
O31	●	North Carolina St.	27	2
N7	|	Vanderbilt	17	18
N14	|	Florida TAM	13	24
N21	|	at Tennessee	0	45

1971 3-8-0 (1-6-0)

S11	●	at Clemson	13	10
S18		at Indiana	8	26
S25	|	Mississippi	20	34
O2	|	at Auburn	6	38
O9		Ohio U.	6	35
O16	|	LSU	13	17
O23	|	at Georgia	0	34
O30	●	Virginia Tech	33	27
N6	● |	at Vanderbilt	14	7
N13	|	at Florida	24	35
N20	|	Tennessee	7	21

1972 3-8-0 (2-5-0)

S16	●	Villanova	25	7
S23	|	Alabama BIRM	0	35
S30		Indiana	34	35
O7	● |	Mississippi State	17	13
O14		at North Carolina	20	31
O21	|	at LSU	0	10
O28	|	Georgia	7	13
N4		at Tulane	7	18
N11	● |	Vanderbilt	14	13
N18	|	at Florida	0	40
N25	|	at Tennessee	7	17

FRAN CURCI
1973-81 (.470) 46-52-2

1973 5-6-0 (3-4-0)

S15	●	Virginia Tech	31	26
S22	|	Alabama	14	28
S29		at Indiana	3	17
O6	● |	Mississippi State JAM	42	14
O13		North Carolina	10	16
O20	|	at LSU	21	28
O27	● |	at Georgia	12	7
N3	●	Tulane	34	7
N10	● |	at Vanderbilt	27	17
N17	|	at Florida	18	20
N24	|	Tennessee	14	16

1974 6-5-0 (3-3-0)

S14	●	at Virginia Tech	38	7
S21		at West Virginia	3	16
S28	●	Indiana	28	22
O5		Miami (Ohio)	10	14
O12	|	at Auburn	13	31
O19	● |	LSU	20	13
O26	|	Georgia	20	24
N2	●	at Tulane	30	7
N9	● |	Vanderbilt	38	12
N16	● |	Florida	41	24
N23	|	at Tennessee	7	24

1975 2-8-1 (0-6-0)

S13	●	Virginia Tech	27	8
S20		Kansas	10	14
S27	=	Maryland	10	10
O4		at Penn State	3	10
O11	|	Auburn	9	15
O18	|	at LSU	14	17
O25	|	at Georgia	13	21
N1	●	Tulane	23	10
N8	|	at Vanderbilt	3	13
N15	|	at Florida	7	48
N22	|	Tennessee	13	17

1976 8-4-0 (4-2-0)

S11	●	Oregon State	38	13
S18		at Kansas	16	37
S25	●	West Virginia	14	10
O2	●	Penn State	22	6
O9	|	Mississippi State JAM	7	14†
O16	● |	LSU	21	7
O23	|	Georgia	7	31
O30		at Maryland	14	24
N6	● |	Vanderbilt	14	0
N13	● |	Florida	28	9
N20	● |	at Tennessee	7	0
		PEACH BOWL		
D31	●	North Carolina	21	0

KENTUCKY 125

THE SCHOOLS

1977 10-1-0 (6-0-0)

S10	●	North Carolina	10	7
S17		at Baylor	6	21
S24	●	West Virginia	28	13
O1	●	at Penn State	24	20
O8	● |	Mississippi State	23	7
O15	● |	at LSU	33	13
O22	● |	at Georgia	33	0
O29	●	Virginia Tech	32	0
N5	● |	at Vanderbilt	28	6
N12	● |	at Florida	14	7
N19	● |	Tennessee	21	17

1978 4-6-1 (2-4-0)

S16	=	at South Carolina	14	14
S23	●	Baylor	25	21
S30		at Maryland	3	20
O7		Penn State	0	30
O14	● |	at Mississippi	24	17
O21	|	LSU	0	21
O28	|	Georgia	16	17
N4	●	at Virginia Tech	28	0
N11	● |	Vanderbilt	53	2
N18	|	Florida	16	18
N25	|	at Tennessee	14	29

1979 5-6-0 (3-3-0)

S15		Miami (Ohio)	14	15
S22		at Indiana	10	18
S29	●	Maryland	14	7
O6		at West Virginia	6	10
O13	● |	Mississippi	14	3
O20	|	at LSU	19	23
O27	|	at Georgia	6	20
N3	●	Bowling Green	20	14
N10	● |	at Vanderbilt	29	10
N17	● |	at Florida	31	3
N24	|	Tennessee	17	20

1980 3-8-0 (1-5-0)

S6	●	Utah State	17	10
S13		at Oklahoma	7	29
S20		Indiana	30	36
S27	●	Bowling Green	21	20
O3	|	Alabama [Birm]	0	45
O18	|	LSU	10	17
O25	|	Georgia	0	27
N1		at Tulane	22	24
N8	● |	Vanderbilt	31	10
N15	|	Florida	15	17
N22	|	at Tennessee	14	45

1981 3-8-0 (2-4-0)

S5	●	North Texas	28	6
S19	|	Alabama	10	19
S26		at Kansas	16	21
O3		Clemson	3	21
O10		South Carolina	14	28
O17	|	at LSU	10	24
O24	|	at Georgia	0	21
O31		Virginia Tech	3	29
N7	● |	at Vanderbilt	17	10
N14	|	at Florida	12	33
N21	● |	Tennessee	21	10

JERRY CLAIBORNE
1982-89 (.472) 41-46-3

1982 0-10-1 (0-6-0)

S11		at Kansas State	9	23
S18		Oklahoma	8	29
S25	=	Kansas	13	13
O2		at Clemson	6	24
O9	|	at Auburn	3	18
O16	|	LSU	10	34
O23	|	Georgia	14	27
O30		at Virginia Tech	3	29
N6	|	Vanderbilt	10	23
N13	|	Florida	13	39
N20	|	at Tennessee	7	28

1983 6-5-1 (2-4-0)

S3	●	Central Michigan	31	14
S10	●	Kansas State	31	12
S17	●	Indiana	24	13
S24	●	Tulane	26	14
O8	|	Auburn	21	49
O15	● |	at LSU	21	13
O22	|	at Georgia	21	47
O29	=	Cincinnati	13	13
N5	● |	at Vanderbilt	17	8
N12	|	at Florida	7	24
N19	|	Tennessee	0	10
		HALL OF FAME CLASSIC		
D22		West Virginia	16	20

1984 9-3-0 (3-3-0)

S8	●	Kent State	42	0
S15	●	at Indiana	48	14
S22	●	at Tulane	30	26
O6	●	Rutgers	27	14
O13	● |	at Mississippi State	17	13
O20	|	LSU	10	36
O27	|	Georgia	7	37
N3	●	North Texas	31	7
N10	● |	Vanderbilt	27	18
N17	|	Florida	17	25
N24	● |	at Tennessee	17	12
		HALL OF FAME CLASSIC		
D29	●	Wisconsin	20	19

1985 5-6-0 (1-5-0)

S14		Bowling Green	26	30
S21	●	Tulane	16	11
S28	●	Cincinnati	27	7
O5	●	Clemson	26	7
O12	● |	Mississippi State	33	19
O19	|	at LSU	0	10
O26	|	at Georgia	6	26
N2	●	East Tenn. St.	23	13
N9	|	at Vanderbilt	24	31
N16	|	at Florida	13	15
N23	|	Tennessee	0	42

1986 5-5-1 (2-4-0)

S13	=	Rutgers	16	16
S20	●	Kent State	37	12
S27	●	at Cincinnati	37	20
O4	●	Southern Miss	32	0
O11	|	Mississippi [Jam]	13	33
O18	|	LSU	16	25
O25	|	Georgia	9	31
N1		at Virginia Tech	15	17
N8	● |	Vanderbilt	34	22
N15	● |	Florida	10	3
N22	|	at Tennessee	9	28

1987 5-6-0 (1-5-0)

S12	●	Utah State	41	0
S19	●	Indiana	34	15
S26		Rutgers [ERut]	18	19
O3	●	Ohio U.	28	0
O10	● |	Mississippi	35	6
O17	|	at LSU	9	34
O24	|	at Georgia	14	17
O31	●	Virginia Tech	14	7
N7	|	at Vanderbilt	29	38
N14	|	at Florida	14	27
N21	|	Tennessee	22	24

1988 5-6-0 (2-5-0)

S3	●	Central Michigan	18	7
S10	|	at Auburn	10	20
S17		at Indiana	15	36
S24	●	Kent State	38	14
O1	|	Alabama	27	31
O15	|	at LSU	12	15
O22	● |	Georgia	16	10
O29	●	So. Illinois	24	10
N5	● |	Vanderbilt	14	13
N12	|	Florida	19	24
N19	|	at Tennessee	24	28

1989 6-5-0 (2-5-0)

S9	●	Indiana	17	14
S16	●	North Carolina	13	6
S23	|	at Alabama	3	15
O7	|	Auburn	12	24
O14	●	Rutgers	33	26
O21	● |	LSU	27	21
O28	|	at Georgia	23	34
N4	●	Cincinnati	31	0
N11	● |	at Vanderbilt	15	11
N18	|	at Florida	28	38
N25	|	Tennessee	10	31

BILL CURRY
1990-96 (.333) 26-52

1990 4-7-0 (3-4-0)

S1	●	Central Michigan	20	17
S8		Rutgers [ERut]	8	24
S15		Indiana	24	45
S22		at North Carolina	13	16
O6	|	at Mississippi	29	35
O13	● |	Mississippi State	17	15
O20	|	at LSU	20	30
O27	● |	Georgia	26	24
N10	● |	Vanderbilt	28	21
N17	|	Florida	15	47
N24	|	at Tennessee	28	42

1991 3-8-0 (0-7-0)

S7	●	Miami (Ohio)	23	20
S21		at Indiana	10	13
S28	●	Kent State	24	6
O5	|	Mississippi	14	35
O12	|	at Mississippi State	6	31
O19	|	LSU	26	29
O26	|	at Georgia	27	49
N2	●	Cincinnati	20	17
N9	|	at Vanderbilt	7	17
N16	|	at Florida	26	35
N23	|	Tennessee	7	16

1992 4-7-0 (2-6-0)

S5	●	Central Michigan	21	14
S12	|	at Florida	19	35
S19	●	Indiana	37	25
S26	● |	South Carolina	13	9
O3	|	at Mississippi	14	24
O17	● |	at LSU	27	25
O24	|	Georgia	7	40
O31	|	Mississippi State	36	37
N7	|	Vanderbilt	7	20
N14		at Cincinnati	13	17
N21	|	at Tennessee	13	34

1993 6-6-0 (4-4-0)

S4	●	Kent State	35	0
S11	|	Florida	20	24
S18		at Indiana	8	24
S23	● |	at South Carolina	21	17
O2	● |	Mississippi	21	0
O16	● |	LSU	35	17
O23	|	at Georgia	28	33
O30	● |	at Mississippi State	26	17
N6	|	at Vanderbilt	7	12
N13	●	East Carolina	6	3
N20	|	Tennessee	0	48
		PEACH BOWL		
D31		Clemson	13	14

1994 1-10-0 (0-8-0)

S3	●	Louisville	20	14
S10	|	at Florida	7	73
S17		Indiana	29	59
S24	|	South Carolina	9	23
S29	|	at Auburn	14	41
O15	|	at LSU	13	17
O22	|	Georgia	30	34
O29	|	Mississippi State	7	47
N5	|	Vanderbilt	6	24
N12		La. Monroe	14	21
N19	|	at Tennessee	0	52

1995 4-7-0 (2-6-0)

S2		Louisville	10	13
S9	|	Florida	7	42
S16	●	at Indiana	17	10
S23	● |	at South Carolina	35	30
S30	|	Auburn	21	42
O14	● |	LSU	24	16
O21	|	at Georgia	3	12
O28	|	at Mississippi State	32	42
N4	|	at Vanderbilt	10	14
N11	●	Cincinnati	33	14
N18	|	Tennessee	31	34

1996 4-7 (3-5)

A31		Louisville	14	38
S7		at Cincinnati	3	24
S21	●	Indiana	3	0
S28	|	at Florida	0	65
O5	|	at Alabama	7	35
O12	|	South Carolina	14	25
O19	|	at LSU	14	41
O26	● |	Georgia	24	17
N9	● |	Mississippi State	24	21
N16	● |	Vanderbilt	25	0
N23	|	at Tennessee	10	56

HAL MUMME
1997-2000 (.435) 20-26

1997 5-6 (2-6)

A30	●	Louisville	38	24
S6	|	at Mississippi State	27	35
S20	●	at Indiana	49	7
S27	|	Florida	28	55
O4	● |	Alabama	40	34
O11	|	at South Carolina	24	38
O18	●	La. Monroe	49	14
O25	|	at Georgia	13	23
N1	|	LSU	28	63
N15	● |	at Vanderbilt	21	10
N22	|	Tennessee	31	59

1998 7-5 (4-4)

S5	●	at Louisville	68	34
S12	●	Ea. Kentucky	52	7
S19	●	Indiana	31	27
S26	|	at Florida	35	51
O3	|	Arkansas [LR]	20	27
O10	● |	South Carolina	33	28
O17	● |	at LSU	39	36
O24	|	Georgia	26	28
N7	● |	Mississippi State	37	35
N14	● |	Vanderbilt	55	17
N21	|	at Tennessee	21	59
		OUTBACK BOWL		
J1		Penn State	14	26

1999 6-6 (4-4)

S4		Louisville	28	56
S11	●	Connecticut	45	14
S18	●	at Indiana	44	35
S25	|	Florida	10	38
O2	● |	Arkansas	31	20
O9	● |	at South Carolina	30	10
O16	● |	LSU	31	5
O23	|	at Georgia	34	49
N4	|	at Mississippi State	22	23
N13	● |	at Vanderbilt	19	17
N20	|	Tennessee	21	56
		MUSIC CITY BOWL		
D29		Syracuse	13	20

2000 2-9 (0-8)

S2		at Louisville	34	40
S9	●	South Florida	27	9
S16	●	Indiana	41	34
S23	|	at Florida	31	59
S30	|	at Mississippi	17	35
O7	|	South Carolina	17	20
O14	|	at LSU	0	34
O21	|	Georgia	30	34
N4	|	Mississippi State	17	35
N11	|	Vanderbilt	20	24
N18	|	at Tennessee	20	59

GUY MORRISS
2001-02 (.391) 9-14

2001 2-9 (1-7)

S1		Louisville	10	36
S8	●	Ball State	28	20
S22	|	Florida	10	44
S29	|	Mississippi	31	42
O6	|	at South Carolina	6	42
O13	|	LSU	25	29
O20	|	at Georgia	29	43
N3	|	at Mississippi State	14	17
N10	● |	at Vanderbilt	56	30
N17	|	Tennessee	35	38
D1		at Indiana	15	26

2002 7-5 (3-5)

S1	●	at Louisville	22	17
S7	●	Texas-El Paso	77	17
S14	●	Indiana	27	17
S21	●	Middle Tennessee	44	22
S28	|	at Florida	34	41
O12	|	South Carolina	12	16
O19	● |	at Arkansas	29	17
O26	|	Georgia	24	52
N2	● |	at Mississippi State	45	24
N9	|	LSU	30	33
N16	● |	Vanderbilt	41	21
N30	|	at Tennessee	0	24

RICH BROOKS
2003-Present (.432) 32-42

2003 4-8 (1-7)

A31		Louisville	24	40
S6	●	Murray St.	37	6
S13	|	at Alabama	17	27
S20	●	at Indiana	34	17
S27	|	Florida	21	24
O9	|	at South Carolina	21	27
O18	●	Ohio U.	35	14
O25	● |	Mississippi State	42	17
N1	|	Arkansas	63	71
N15	|	at Vanderbilt	17	28
N22	|	at Georgia	10	30
N29	|	Tennessee	7	20

2004   2-9   (1-7)

S5		at Louisville	0	28
S18	●	Indiana	51	32
S25		at Florida	3	20
O2		Ohio U.	16	28
O9		Alabama	17	45
O16		South Carolina	7	12
O23		at Auburn	10	42
O30		at Mississippi State	7	22
N6		Georgia	17	62
N13	●	Vanderbilt	14	13
N27		at Tennessee	31	37

2005   3-8   (2-6)

S4		Louisville	24	31
S10	●	Idaho State	41	29
S17		at Indiana	14	38
S24		Florida	28	49
O8		at South Carolina	16	44
O22		at Mississippi	7	13
O29	●	Mississippi State	13	7
N5		Auburn	27	49
N12	●	at Vanderbilt	48	43
N19		at Georgia	13	45
N26		Tennessee	8	27

2006   8-5   (4-4)

S3		at Louisville	28	59
S9	●	Texas State	41	7
S16	●	Mississippi	31	14
S23		at Florida	7	26
S30	●	Central Michigan	45	36
O7		South Carolina	17	24
O14		at LSU	0	49
O28	●	at Mississippi State	34	31
N4		Georgia	24	20
N11	●	Vanderbilt	38	26
N18	●	La. Monroe	42	40
N25		at Tennessee	12	17
MUSIC CITY BOWL				
D29	●	Clemson	28	20

2007   8-5   (3-5)

S1	●	Eastern Kentucky	50	10
S8	●	Kent State	56	20
S15	●	Louisville	40	34
S22	●	at Arkansas	42	29
S29	●	Florida Atlantic	45	17
O4		at South Carolina	23	38
O13	●	LSU	43	37
O20		Florida	37	45
O27		Mississippi State	14	31
N10	●	at Vanderbilt	27	20
N17		at Georgia	13	24
N24		Tennessee	50	52
MUSIC CITY BOWL				
D31	●	Florida State	35	28

2008   7-6   (2-6)

A31	●	at Louisville	27	2
S6	●	Norfolk State	38	3
S13	●	Middle Tennessee State	20	14
S27	●	Western Kentucky	41	3
O4		at Alabama	14	17
O11		South Carolina	17	24
O18	●	at Arkansas	21	20
O25		at Florida	5	63
N1	●	at Mississippi State	14	13
N8		Georgia	38	42
N15		Vanderbilt	24	31
N29		at Tennessee	10	28
LIBERTY BOWL				
J2	●	East Carolina	25	19

Neutral Site key: *Birm* Birmingham, AL / *Bkln* Brooklyn, NY / *Chat* Chattanooga, TN / *ChWV* Charleston, WV / *ERut* East Rutherford, NJ / *JacF* Jacksonville, FL / *JaM* Jackson, MS / *Lou* Louisville, KY / *LR* Little Rock, AR / *Mem* Memphis, TN / *Mont* Montgomery, AL / *Phil* Philadelphia, PA / *Roa* Roanoke, VA / *Tam* Tampa, FL / *Unk* Unknown

f Forfeit † Game Later Forfieted # Disputed Victor * Disputed Score || Designated Conference Game |2 Counted Twice in Conference Standings

KENTUCKY ANNUAL STATISTICAL LEADERS

YR	RUSHING	YDS	ATT	AVG	PASSING	ATT	CMP	PCT	YDS	RECEIVING	REC	YDS	AVG
1946	Don Phelps	271	57	4.8	Phil Cutchin	56	26	.46	399		NA	NA	NA
1947	Don Phelps	416	80	5.2	George Blanda	114	53	.46	484	Wallace Jones	9	93	10.3
1948	Ralph Genito	327	54	6.1	George Blanda	128	67	.52	967	Wallace Jones	19	243	12.8
1949	Bill Leskovar	722	152	4.8	Babe Parilli	150	81	.54	1,081	Al Bruno	12	224	18.7
1950	Bill Leskovar	673	118	5.7	Babe Parilli	203	114	.56	1,627	Al Bruno	38	589	15.5
1951	Tom Fillion	671	117	5.7	Babe Parilli	239	136	.57	1,643	Steve Meilinger	41	576	14.0
1952	Allen Felch	623	130	4.8	Dick Shatto	54	19	.35	221	Steve Meilinger	16	326	20.4
1953	Ralph Paolone	620	108	5.7	Bob Hardy	47	24	.51	418	Steve Meilinger	18	308	17.1
1954	Dick Rushing	369	75	4.9	Bob Hardy	108	57	.53	887	H. Schnellenberger	19	254	13.4
1955	Bob Dougherty	401	94	4.3	Bob Hardy	106	58	.55	777	H. Schnellenberger	20	287	14.4
1956	Bobby Cravens	338	78	4.3	Delmar Hughes	42	14	.33	206	Doug Shively	7	107	15.3
1957	Bobby Cravens	669	141	4.7	Lowell Hughes	83	40	.48	447	Jim Urbaniak	13	194	14.9
1958	Bobby Cravens	441	104	4.2	Lowell Hughes	72	36	.50	437	Calvin Bird	21	373	17.8
1959	Charles Sturgeon	417	101	4.1	Lowell Hughes	67	30	.45	375	Calvin Bird	16	151	9.4
1960	Charles Sturgeon	291	58	5.0	Jerry Woolum	125	63	.50	767	Tom Hutchinson	30	455	15.2
1961	Gary Steward	285	79	3.6	Jerry Woolum	125	70	.56	892	Tom Hutchinson	32	543	17.0
1962	Darrell Cox	363	81	4.5	Jerry Woolum	157	83	.53	1,100	Tom Hutchinson	32	485	15.2
1963	Rodger Bird	382	85	4.5	Rick Norton	182	79	.43	1,177	Darrell Cox	20	333	16.7
1964	Rodger Bird	671	133	5.0	Rick Norton	202	106	.52	1,514	Rick Kestner	42	639	15.2
1965	Rodger Bird	646	179	3.6	Rick Norton	214	113	.53	1,823	Bob Windsor	30	426	14.2
1966	Bob Windsor	356	101	3.5	Terry Beadles	113	47	.42	725	Larry Seiple	28	499	17.8
1967	Dicky Lyons	473	138	3.4	Dave Bair	164	66	.40	634	Phil Thompson	36	377	10.5
1968	Dicky Lyons	392	134	2.9	Stan Forston	129	48	.37	643	Phil Thompson	29	397	13.7
1969	Roger Gann	646	180	3.6	Bernie Scruggs	183	80	.44	969	Jim Grant	33	344	10.4
1970	Lee Clymer	441	118	3.7	Bernie Scruggs	209	115	.55	1,181	Jim Grant	24	251	10.5
1971	Lee Clymer	455	96	4.7	Bernie Scruggs	102	44	.43	554	Jim Grant	10	205	20.5
1972	Sonny Collins	502	128	3.9	Dinky McKay	185	80	.43	879	Jack Alvarez	41	487	11.9
1973	Sonny Collins	1,213	224	5.4	Mike Fanuzzi	84	33	.39	572	Elmore Stephens	16	282	17.6
1974	Sonny Collins	970	177	5.5	Mike Fanuzzi	83	32	.39	438	Randy Burke	12	127	10.6
1975	Sonny Collins	1,150	248	4.6	Cliff Hite	101	35	.35	430	Vin Hoover	18	198	11.0
1976	Derrick Ramsey	771	187	4.1	Derrick Ramsey	103	51	.50	659	Randy Burke	15	152	10.1
1977	Derrick Ramsey	618	159	3.9	Derrick Ramsey	156	74	.47	892	Dave Trosper	25	340	13.6
1978	Freddie Williams	313	89	3.5	Larry McCrimmon	106	35	.33	752	Felix Wilson	43	727	16.9
1979	Shawn Donigan	847	187	4.5	Terry Henry	76	30	.39	408	Felix Wilson	33	534	16.2
1980	Randy Brooks	578	166	3.5	Larry McCrimmon	137	69	.50	1,060	Jim Campbell	33	394	11.9
1981	Lawrence Lee	275	78	3.5	Randy Jenkins	170	84	.49	1,079	Rick Massie	29	448	15.4
1982	George Adams	720	185	3.9	Randy Jenkins	187	92	.49	933	Robert Mangas	22	293	13.3
1983	George Adams	763	166	4.6	Randy Jenkins	203	118	.58	1,272	Oliver White	26	252	9.7
1984	George Adams	1,085	253	4.3	Bill Ransdell	266	148	.56	1,748	George Adams	33	330	10.0
1985	Marc Logan	715	175	4.1	Bill Ransdell	231	133	.58	1,744	Marc Logan	32	314	9.8
1986	Ivy Joe Hunter	621	103	6.0	Bill Ransdell	256	151	.59	1,610	Cornell Burbage	24	331	13.8
1987	Mark Higgs	1,278	193	6.6	Glenn Fohr	163	74	.45	973	Charlie Darrington	26	365	14.0
1988	Alfred Rawls	477	101	4.7	Glenn Fohr	201	91	.45	1,260	Ivy Joe Hunter	17	160	9.4
1989	Alfred Rawls	893	185	4.8	Freddie Maggard	231	130	.56	1,515	Phil Logan	28	337	12.0
1990	Al Baker	780	170	4.6	Freddie Maggard	188	109	.58	1,051	Phil Logan	37	565	15.3
1991	Terry Samuels	307	77	4.0	Pookie Jones	138	81	.59	954	Neal Clark	47	647	13.8
1992	Terry Samuels	380	98	3.9	Pookie Jones	203	97	.48	1,434	Kurt Johnson	20	318	15.9
1993	Moe Williams	928	164	5.7	Pookie Jones	163	85	.52	1,071	Alfonzo Browning	20	335	16.8
1994	Moe Williams	805	160	5.0	Antonio O'Ferral	107	48	.45	642	Leon Smith	27	375	13.9
1995	Moe Williams	1,600	294	5.4	Billy Jack Haskins	154	93	.60	1,176	Craig Yeast	24	337	14.0
1996	Derick Logan	700	190	3.7	Billy Jack Haskins	175	93	.53	967	Craig Yeast	26	378	14.5
1997	Anthony White	723	129	5.6	Tim Couch	547	363	.66	3,884	Craig Yeast	73	873	12.0
1998	Derek Homer	716	137	5.2	Tim Couch	553	400	.72	4,275	Craig Yeast	85	1,311	15.4
1999	Anthony White	562	121	4.6	Dusty Bonner	465	303	.65	3,266	James Whalen	90	1,019	11.3
2000	Chad Scott	611	130	4.7	Jared Lorenzen	559	321	.57	3,687	Derek Smith	50	716	14.3
2001	Artose Pinner	441	100	4.4	Jared Lorenzen	292	167	.57	2,179	Derek Abney	66	741	11.2
2002	Artose Pinner	1,414	283	5.0	Jared Lorenzen	327	183	.56	2,267	Aaron Boone	41	706	17.2
2003	Arliss Beach	366	103	3.6	Jared Lorenzen	336	191	.57	2,221	Derek Abney	51	616	12.1
2004	Shane Boyd	297	102	2.9	Shane Boyd	263	138	.52	1,328	Glenn Holt	49	415	8.5
2005	Rafael Little	1,045	197	5.3	Andre' Woodson	253	146	.58	1,644	Rafael Little	46	449	9.8
2006	Rafael Little	673	140	4.8	Andre' Woodson	419	264	.63	3,515	Keenan Burton	77	1,036	13.5
2007	Rafael Little	1,013	190	5.3	Andre' Woodson	518	327	.63	3,709	Keenan Burton	66	741	11.2
2008	Tony Dixon	430	132	3.3	Mike Hartline	311	172	.55	1,666	Dicky Lyons	33	264	8.0

Receiving leaders by receptions
The NCAA began including postseason stats in 2002

THE SCHOOLS

KENTUCKY RECORD BOOK

SINGLE-GAME RECORDS

Rushing Yards	299	Moe Williams (Sept. 23, 1995 vs. South Carolina)
Passing Yards	528	Jared Lorenzen (Oct. 21, 2000 vs. Georgia)
Receiving Yards	269	Craig Yeast (Nov. 14, 1998 vs. Vanderbilt)
All-Purpose Yards	429	Moe Williams (Sept. 23, 1995 vs. South Carolina)
Points	25	Calvin Bird (Sept. 13, 1958 vs. Hawaii)
Field Goals	5	Doug Pelfrey (Oct. 31, 1992 vs. Miss. State)
Tackles	29	Randy Holleran (Oct. 20, 1990 vs. LSU)
Interceptions	3	Five players tied

SINGLE-SEASON RECORDS

Rushing Yards	1,600	Moe Williams, 1995 (294 att.)
Passing Yards	4,275	Tim Couch, 1998 (553 att.)
Receiving Yards	1,311	Craig Yeast, 1998 (85 rec.)
All-Purpose Yards	1,982	Rafael Little, 2005
Scoring	102	Moe Williams, 1995 (17 TDs)
Touchdowns	17	Moe Williams, 1995
Tackles	183	Marty Moore, 1991
Interceptions	9	Jerry Claiborne, 1949
Punting Average	45.6	Glenn Pakulak, 2002 (66 punts)
Punt Return Average	22.6	Rafael Little, 2006 (14 ret.)
Kickoff Return Average	30.4	Calvin Bird, 1959 (14 ret.)

CAREER RECORDS

Rushing Yards	3,835	Sonny Collins, 1972-75
Passing Yards	10,354	Jared Lorenzen 2000-03
Receiving Yards	2,899	Craig Yeast 1995-98
All-Purpose Yards	5,856	Derek Abney, 2000-03
Scoring	246	Joey Worley, 1984-87
Touchdowns	32	Craig Yeast 1995-98
Tackles	521	Jim Kovach, 1974-76, 1978
Interceptions	14	Darryl Bishop 1971-73
Punting Average	44.4	Glenn Pakulak, 2000-02 (134 punts)
Punt Return Average	15.4	Dicky Lyons Sr. 1966-68 (69 ret.)
Kickoff Return Average	27.1	Calvin Bird, 1958-60 (37 ret.)

TEAM RECORDS

Longest Winning Streak	12	Oct. 28, 1909-Nov. 5, 1910; broken vs. St. Louis, 0-9 on Nov. 12, 1910
Longest Undefeated Streak	12	Oct. 28, 1909-Nov. 5, 1910; broken vs. St. Louis, 0-9 on Nov. 12, 1910
Most Consecutive Winning Seasons	14	1903-16
Most Consecutive Bowl Appearances	3	1949-51, 2006-08
Most Points in a Game	87	vs. Wilmington, Sept. 26, 1914
Most Points Allowed in a Game	82	vs. St. Louis, Nov. 18, 1905
Largest Margin of Victory	87	vs. Wilmington, Sept. 26, 1914
Largest Margin of Defeat	82	vs. St. Louis, Nov. 18, 1905
Longest Pass Play	97	Tim Couch to Craig Yeast vs. Florida, Sept. 26, 1998
Longest Field Goal	53	Doug Pelfrey vs. Indiana, Sept. 21, 1991; vs. Cincinnati, Nov. 2, 1991
Longest Punt	80	Paul Calhoun vs. Indiana, Sept. 27, 1983
Longest Interception Return	100	David Hunter vs. West Virginia, Nov. 2, 1968

RETIRED NUMBERS

NO RETIRED JERSEYS

ALL-TIME TEAM

Chosen by the Lexington Herald-Leader *in 1990 for the 100th season of Kentucky football*

Offense			Defense		
	OL	Doug Moseley, 1949-51		DL	Bob Gain, 1947-50
	OL	Ray Correll, 1951-53		DL	Lou Michaels, 1955-57
	OL	Irv Goode, 1959-61		DL	Jeff Van Note, 1966-68
	OL	Sam Ball, 1963-65		DL	Dave Roller, 1968-70
	OL	Warren Bryant, 1973-76		DL	Art Still, 1974-77
	E	Steve Meilinger, 1951-53		LB	Jay Rhodemyre, 1942, 1946-47
	E	Tom Hutchinson, 1960-62		LB	Joe Federspiel, 1969-71
	QB	Babe Parilli, 1949-51		DB	Jerry Claiborne, 1946, 1948-49
	B	Shipwreck Kelly, 1929-31		DB	Darryl Bishop, 1971-73
	B	Rodger Bird, 1963-65		DB	Mike Siganos, 1974-77
	B	Sonny Collins, 1972-75		DB	Paul Calhoun, 1982-84
	PK	Joey Worley, 1984-87		RET	Dicky Lyons, 1966-68

KENTUCKY BOWL HISTORY

SEASON	BOWL	DATE	PRE-GAME RANK	TEAMS	SCORE	FINAL RANK	MOST VALUABLE PLAYER(S)	ATT.
1947	**GREAT LAKES**	Dec. 6, 1947		**Kentucky** Villanova	24 14			14,908
1949	**ORANGE**	Jan. 2, 1950	15 11	Santa Clara Kentucky	21 13			64,816
1950	**SUGAR**	Jan. 1, 1951	7 1	**Kentucky** Oklahoma	13 7		Walt Yowarsky, Kentucky, T	80,206
1951	**COTTON**	Jan. 1, 1952	15 11	**Kentucky** TCU	20 7		E. Clark, HB, R. Correll, G, V. Parilli, QB, Kent. Keith Flowers, TCU, FB	75,562
1976	**PEACH**	Dec. 31, 1976	19	**Kentucky** North Carolina	21 0	18	Rod Stewart, Kentucky, TB Mike Martin, Kentucky, LB	54,123
1983	**HALL OF FAME CLASSIC**	Dec. 22, 1983	18	**West Virginia** Kentucky	20 16	16	Jeff Hostetler, West Virginia QB	42,000
1984	**HALL OF FAME CLASSIC**	Dec. 29, 1984	20	**Kentucky** Wisconsin	20 19	19	Mark Logan, Kentucky, RB Todd Gregoire, Wisconsin, K	47,300
1993	**PEACH**	Dec. 31, 1993	24	**Clemson** Kentucky	14 13	23	Pookie Jones, QB, Zane Beehn, LB, Kentucky Emory Smith, RB, Brentson Buckner, DE, Clemson	75,562
1998	**OUTBACK**	Jan. 1, 1999	22	**Penn State** Kentucky	26 14	17	Courtney Brown, Penn State, DE	66,005
1999	**MUSIC CITY**	Dec. 29, 1999		**Syracuse** Kentucky	20 13		James Mungro, Syracuse, RB	59,221
2006	**MUSIC CITY**	Dec. 29, 2006		**Kentucky** Clemson	28 20		Andre' Woodson, Kentucky, QB	68,024
2007	**MUSIC CITY**	Dec. 31, 2007		**Kentucky** Florida State	35 28		Andre' Woodson, Kentucky, QB	68,661
2008	**LIBERTY**	Jan. 2, 2009		**Kentucky** East Carolina	25 19		Ventrell Jenkins, Kentucky, DE	56,125

DECEMBER 6, 1947 | GREAT LAKES
KENTUCKY 24, VILLANOVA 14

	1ST	2ND	3RD	4TH	FINAL
UK	3	0	7	14	24
NOVA	0	0	0	14	14

SCORING SUMMARY
UK FG Blanda 27
UK Howe 29 run (Blanda kick)
UK Boller 15 run (Blanda kick)
UK Boller 49 interception return (Blanda kick)
NOVA Pasquariello 10 run (Siano kick)
NOVA Sheahan 9 pass from Gordon (Siano kick)

UK	TEAM STATISTICS	NOVA
14	First Downs	10
177	Rushing Yards	90
14-25-1	Passing	12-18-1
107	Passing Yards	138
284	Total Yards	228
7-38.0	Punts - Average	9-33.0
1-0	Fumbles - Lost	2-0
2-10	Penalties - Yards	2-30

JANUARY 2, 1950 | ORANGE
SANTA CLARA 21, KENTUCKY 13

	1ST	2ND	3RD	4TH	FINAL
SC	0	0	14	7	21
UK	0	7	0	6	13

SCORING SUMMARY
UK Jamerson 2 run (Brooks kick)
SC Pasco 2 run (Vargas kick)
SC Haynes 2 run (Vargas kick)
UK Clark 52 pass from Parilli (kick failed)
SC Vogel 17 run (Vargas kick)

SC	TEAM STATISTICS	UK
8	First Downs	18
144	Rushing Yards	184
3-12-1	Passing	6-11-2
79	Passing Yards	122
223	Total Yards	306
7-41.2	Punts - Average	9-38.9
2-2	Fumbles - Lost	1-1
4-30	Penalties - Yards	4-22.5

JANUARY 1, 1951 | SUGAR
KENTUCKY 13, OKLAHOMA 7

	1ST	2ND	3RD	4TH	FINAL
UK	7	6	0	0	13
OKLA	0	0	0	7	7

SCORING SUMMARY
UK Jamerson 22 pass from Parilli (Gain kick)
UK Jamerson 1 run (kick failed)
OKLA Green 17 pass from Vessels (Weatherall kick)

INDIVIDUAL LEADERS
RUSHING
UK: Jamerson 15-58, 1 TD.
OKLA: Heath 20-121.
PASSING
UK: Parilli 9-12-0, 105 yards, 1 TD.
OKLA: Arnold 2-5-0, 21 yards.
RECEIVING
UK: Bruno 3-57.
OKLA: Vessels 2-21.

JANUARY 1, 1952 | COTTON
KENTUCKY 20, TCU 7

	1ST	2ND	3RD	4TH	FINAL
UK	7	6	0	7	20
TCU	0	0	7	0	7

SCORING SUMMARY
UK Clark 5 pass from Parilli (Jones kick)
UK Clark 12 pass from Parilli (kick failed)
TCU Floyd 43 run (Flowers kick)
UK Hamilton 4 run (Jones kick)

UK	TEAM STATISTICS	TCU
13	First Downs	15
213	Rushing Yards	201
8-20-1	Passing	5-17-1
85	Passing Yards	99
298	Total Yards	300
6-34.7	Punts - Average	5-40.8
0-0	Fumbles - Lost	2-1
6-40	Penalties - Yards	7-32

INDIVIDUAL LEADERS
RUSHING
UK: Fillion 10-73; Jones 11-42.
TCU: Floyd 14-115, 1 TD; McKown 16-42.
PASSING
UK: Parilli 8-20-1, 85 yards, 2 TD.
TCU: McKown 1-8-0, 51 yards.
RECEIVING
UK: Meilinger 3-61; Clark 2-17, 2 TD.
TCU: Vaught 1-51; Medanich 3-43.

DECEMBER 31, 1976 | PEACH
KENTUCKY 21, NORTH CAROLINA 0

	1ST	2ND	3RD	4TH	FINAL
UK	0	0	7	14	21
UNC	0	0	0	0	0

SCORING SUMMARY
UK Stewart 1 run (Pierce kick)
UK Stewart 13 run (Pierce kick)
UK Stewart 3 run (Pierce kick)

UK	TEAM STATISTICS	UNC
19	First Downs	5
318	Rushing Yards	84
2-9-1	Passing	3-15-3
16	Passing Yards	24
334	Total Yards	108
8-34.6	Punts - Average	7-33.7
4-2	Fumbles - Lost	3-2
7-55	Penalties - Yards	2-10

INDIVIDUAL LEADERS
RUSHING
UK: Stewart 19-104, 3 TD; Brooks 8-66.
UNC: Paschal 11-41.
PASSING
UK: Ramsey 2-8-0, 16 yards.
UNC: Kupec 3-15-3, 24 yards.
RECEIVING
UK: Hill 1-13.
UNC: Mabry 1-11.

DECEMBER 22, 1983 | HALL OF FAME CLASSIC
WEST VIRGINIA 20, KENTUCKY 16

	1ST	2ND	3RD	4TH	FINAL
WVU	3	0	7	10	20
UK	0	10	0	6	16

SCORING SUMMARY
WVU FG Woodside 39
UK Jenkins 26 pass from Mayes (Hutcherson kick)
UK FG Hutcherson 32
WVU Hollins 16 pass from Hostetler (Woodside kick)
WVU Bennett 2 pass from Hostetler (Woodside kick)
WVU FG Woodside 23
UK Phillips 13 pass from Ransdell (kick failed)

WVU	TEAM STATISTICS	UK
18	First Downs	19
231	Rushing Yards	123
10-23-1	Passing	19-34-1
88	Passing Yards	216
319	Total Yards	339
1-15	Punt Returns - Yards	3-63
4-29	Kickoff Returns - Yards	3-62
6-39.7	Punts - Average	4-34.5
1-0	Fumbles - Lost	2-1
1-5	Penalties - Yards	1-15
30:48	Possession Time	29:12

INDIVIDUAL LEADERS
RUSHING
WVU: Gray 32-149; Hostetler 6-30.
UK: Adams 19-69; Lee 6-25.
PASSING
WVU: Hostetler 10-23-1, 88 yards, 2 TD.
UK: Jenkins 9-17-1, 73 yards; Ransdell 9-15-0, 117 yards, 1 TD.
RECEIVING
WVU: Hollins 3-22, 1 TD; Bennett 3-28, 1 TD.
UK: Phillips 6-78, 1 TD; Pitts 3-37.

THE SCHOOLS

DECEMBER 29, 1984 | HALL OF FAME CLASSIC
KENTUCKY 20, WISCONSIN 19

	1ST	2ND	3RD	4TH	FINAL
UK	0	7	10	3	20
WISC	10	6	3	0	19

SCORING SUMMARY
WISC FG Gregoire 40
WISC McFadden 3 pass from Howard (Gregoire kick)
WISC FG Gregoire 27
UK   Logan 9 run (Worley kick)
WISC FG Gregoire 20
UK   FG Worley 22
WISC FG Gregoire 40
UK   Logan 27 pass from Ransdell (Worley kick)
UK   FG Worley 52

UK	TEAM STATISTICS	WISC
19	First Downs	17
124	Rushing Yards	181
18-34-0	Passing	19-30-2
188	Passing Yards	203
312	Total Yards	384
3-(-1)	Punt Returns - Yards	3-78
4-133	Kickoff Returns - Yards	5-100
6-37.5	Punts - Average	5-41.4
1-0	Fumbles - Lost	0-0
6-49	Penalties - Yards	13-133
28:57	Possession Time	31:03

INDIVIDUAL LEADERS
RUSHING
UK: Adams 18-62; Higgs 9-39.
WISC: Armentrout 15-105; Harrison 14-52.

PASSING
UK: Ransdell 18-34-0, 188 yards, 1 TD.
WISC: Howard 19-29-1, 203 yards, 1 TD.

RECEIVING
UK: Phillips 6-55; Adams 5-34.
WISC: Pearson 5-55; Toon 4-48.

DECEMBER 31, 1993 | PEACH
CLEMSON 14, KENTUCKY 13

	1ST	2ND	3RD	4TH	FINAL
CLEM	7	0	0	7	14
UK	0	3	0	10	13

SCORING SUMMARY
CLEM Smith 1 run (Welch kick)
UK   FG Nickles 34
UK   Chatman 5 pass from Jones (Nickles kick)
UK   FG Nickles 26
CLEM T. Smith 21 pass from Sapp (Welch kick)

CLEM	TEAM STATISTICS	UK
14	First Downs	20
119	Rushing Yards	139
8-16-3	Passing	16-32-0
129	Passing Yards	154
248	Total Yards	293
6-38.8	Punts - Average	5-40.6
1-0	Fumbles - Lost	2-2
10-75	Penalties - Yards	4-35
31:09	Possession Time	28:51

INDIVIDUAL LEADERS
RUSHING
CLEM: Blunt 15-59; Smith 8-45, 1 TD.
UK: Williams 13-58; Hood 8-36.

PASSING
CLEM: Sapp 5-9-1, 109 yards, 1 TD.
UK: Jones 16-32-0, 154 yards, 1 TD.

RECEIVING
CLEM: E. Smith 1-57; T. Smith 4-56, 1 TD.
UK: Calvert 2-32; Wyatt 4-28.

JANUARY 1, 1999 | OUTBACK
PENN STATE 26, KENTUCKY 14

	1ST	2ND	3RD	4TH	FINAL
PSU	3	10	6	7	26
UK	14	0	0	0	14

SCORING SUMMARY
UK   Mickelsen 36 pass from Couch (Hanson kick)
PSU   FG Forney 43
UK   White 16 pass from Couch (Hanson kick)
PSU   Nastasi 56 pass from Thompson (Forney kick)
PSU   FG Forney 26
PSU   FG Forney 21
PSU   FG Forney 25
PSU   Fields 19 run (Forney kick)

PSU	TEAM STATISTICS	UK
24	First Downs	24
233	Rushing Yards	105
14-27-0	Passing	30-48-2
187	Passing Yards	336
420	Total Yards	441
2-25	Punt Returns - Yards	0-0
3-64	Kickoff Returns - Yards	4-126
3-30.3	Punts - Average	3-17.0
1-1	Fumbles - Lost	1-1
8-58	Penalties - Yards	14-103
27:07	Possession Time	32:53

INDIVIDUAL LEADERS
RUSHING
PSU: McCoo 21-105; Harris 13-54.
UK: White 8-61; Homer 12-26.

PASSING
PSU: Thompson 14-27-0, 187 yards, 1 TD.
UK: Couch 30-48-2, 336 yards, 2 TD.

RECEIVING
PSU: Stewart 7-71; Nastasi 2-70, 1 TD.
UK: Mickelsen 3-65, 1 TD; Homer 7-64.

DECEMBER 29, 1999 | MUSIC CITY
SYRACUSE 20, KENTUCKY 13

	1ST	2ND	3RD	4TH	FINAL
SYR	0	7	0	13	20
UK	10	0	0	3	13

SCORING SUMMARY
UK   Shanklin 3 run (Samuel kick)
UK   FG Samuel 22
SYR   Johnson 2 run (Trout kick)
UK   FG Samuel 35
SYR   Mungro 32 run (Trout kick)
SYR   Mungro 20 run (run failed)

SYR	TEAM STATISTICS	UK
19	First Downs	18
276	Rushing Yards	57
11-15-0	Passing	30-45-1
128	Passing Yards	308
404	Total Yards	365
2-29	Punt Returns - Yards	0-0
4-78	Kickoff Returns - Yards	4-54
3-33.0	Punts - Average	4-45.0
3-2	Fumbles - Lost	3-1
3-20	Penalties - Yards	4-20
31:24	Possession Time	28:36

INDIVIDUAL LEADERS
RUSHING
SYR: Mungro 12-162, 2 TD; Brown 22-87.
UK: Homer 1-24; Bonner 9-16.

PASSING
SYR: Nunes 11-15-0, 128 yards.
UK: Bonner 30-45-1, 308 yards.

RECEIVING
SYR: Spotwood 5-77; Woodcock 2-37.
UK: White 8-85; Smith 5-56; Shanklin 5-34.

DECEMBER 29, 2006 | MUSIC CITY
KENTUCKY 28, CLEMSON 20

	1ST	2ND	3RD	4TH	FINAL
CLEM	0	6	0	14	20
UK	7	7	7	7	28

SCORING SUMMARY
UK   Johnson 1 run (Seiber kick)
CLEM Barry 32 pass from Proctor (kick failed)
UK   Ford 70 pass from Woodson (Seiber kick)
UK   Lyons Jr. 24 pass from Woodson (Seiber kick)
UK   Tamme 13 pass from Woodson (Seiber kick)
CLEM Grisham 17 pass from Proctor (run failed)
CLEM Kelly 17 pass from Proctor (Palmer pass from Proctor)

CLEM	TEAM STATISTICS	UK
19	First Downs	21
130	Rushing Yards	100
23-39-1	Passing	21-29-0
272	Passing Yards	309
402	Total Yards	409
1-1	Punt Returns - Yards	3-59
4-77	Kickoff Returns - Yards	2-41
3-43.7	Punts – Average	4-25
3-3	Fumbles – Lost	2-2
5-50	Penalties – Yards	8-84

INDIVIDUAL LEADERS
RUSHING
CLEM: Davis 8-53.
KENT: Little 17-54.

PASSING
CLEM: Proctor 23-39-1, 272 yards, 3 TD.
KENT: Woodson 20-28-0, 299 yards, 3 TD.

RECEIVING
CLEM: Kelly 6-66, 1 TD; Stuckey 5-93.
KENT: Burton 5-30; Tamme 4-59, 1 TD.

DECEMBER 31, 2007 | MUSIC CITY
KENTUCKY 35, FLORIDA STATE 28

	1ST	2ND	3RD	4TH	FINAL
UK	7	7	14	7	35
FSU	7	7	0	14	28

SCORING SUMMARY
UK   Tamme 14 pass from Woodson (Seiber kick)
FSU   Weatherford 6 run (Cismesia kick)
UK   S. Johnson 13 pass from Woodson (Seiber kick)
FSU   Carter 24 interception return (Cismesia kick)
UK   Little 2 pass from Woodson (Seiber kick)
UK   Dixon 4 run (Seiber kick)
FSU   Weatherford 1 run (Cismesia kick)
UK   S. Johnson 38 pass from Woodson (Seiber kick)
FSU   Carr 7 pass from Weatherford (Cismesia kick)

UK	TEAM STATISTICS	FSU
29	First Downs	22
143	Rushing Yards	204
32-50-1	Passing	22-50-2
358	Passing Yards	276
501	Total Yards	480
2-36	Punt Returns - Yards	1-16
3-57	Kickoff Returns - Yards	3-44
5-39.8	Punts - Average	6-41.7
5-3	Fumbles - Lost	1-0
7-45	Penalties - Yards	10-102

INDIVIDUAL LEADERS
RUSHING
UK: Little 28-152.
FSU: A. Smith 17-156.

PASSING
UK: Woodson 32-50-1, 358 yards, 4 TD.
FSU: Weatherford 22-48-2, 276 yards, 1 TD.

RECEIVING
UK: S. Johnson 7-124, 2 TD; Little 8-50, 1 TD.
FSU: Parker 8-105; Carr 6-99, 1 TD.

KENTUCKY 25, EAST CAROLINA 19

	1ST	2ND	3RD	4TH	FINAL
UK	0	3	13	9	25
ECU	3	13	3	0	19

SCORING SUMMARY

ECU	FG Hartman 22
ECU	Simmons 28 run (Hartman kick)
UK	FG Seiber 21
ECU	Freeney 80 pass from Pinkney (kick failed)
UK	Jones 99 kickoff return (PAT blocked)
UK	Lanxter 19 pass from Hartline (Seiber kick)
ECU	FG Hartman 43
UK	FG Seiber 34
UK	Jenkins 56 fumble return (PAT blocked)

UK	TEAM STATISTICS	ECU
16	First Downs	17
106	Rushing Yards	101
19-31-1	Passing	18-36-0
204	Passing Yards	296
310	Total Yards	397
3-19	Punt Returns - Yards	1-16
5-153	Kickoff Returns - Yards	2-30
6-41.8	Punts - Average	8-47.8
1-0	Fumbles - Lost	2-1
4-35	Penalties - Yards	4-17

INDIVIDUAL LEADERS

RUSHING
UK: Dixon 28-89.
ECU: Simmons 10-44, 1 TD.

PASSING
UK: Hartline 19-31-1, 204 yards, 1 TD.
ECU: Pickney 18-36-0, 296 yards, 1 TD.

RECEIVING
UK: Lanxter 5-46, 1 TD; McCaskill 3-64.
ECU: Drew 5-120, Freeney 5-112, 1 TD.

THE SCHOOLS

LSU

By Geoffrey Norman

THERE IS SOMETHING ABOUT LSU football that is special and, well, different—just like the spelling on the "Geaux Tigers" bumper stickers you see all over the state. Tigers football is as much a part of Louisiana's unique culture and history as jambalaya and Bourbon Street.

The state's mythic political figure, governor Huey P. Long, was a devout fan and often used his considerable political muscle to help the team. The Kingfish once informed the Ringling Brothers circus that if it brought its show to town on the same night that LSU was playing, he would have no choice but to enforce an obscure "animal-dipping" law. The circus canceled. On another occasion, Long leaned on the railroads to discount tickets for students traveling to an LSU away game. His argument about reassessing the value of railroad bridges was especially persuasive, and the kids rode cheap.

The fervor for LSU football has not diminished since those days. You can sense a little something different in the air, an undeniable electricity that makes your skin tingle, when you are in Baton Rouge on game day. People come from all over the state to see the game. And since the Tigers famously play at night, these fans have all day to, well, prepare. Tailgaters eat and drink like they are in the French Quarter, and the fragrances of crawfish étouffé and *cochon du lait* fill the air around Tiger Stadium. By the time the Tigers come onto the field, emotions are at a roaring boil.

TRADITION Louisiana is a passionate place—part French and part antebellum South—and football is an emotional sport. Nowhere is the evidence greater than at a Tiger Stadium night game in Baton Rouge. The Tigers began playing most of their home games under the lights in 1931, which seems appropriate, Louisiana being a nocturnal sort of place. With the entire day to get pumped, at kickoff the fans are so loud that the stadium—indeed, the whole city—fairly throbs with noise. After one crucial LSU score against Auburn in 1988, the celebration was loud enough to move the seismograph at the university's geology department.

BEST PLAYER Billy Cannon was an unusual blend of size and speed during the days of two-way football. Cannon had no problem playing defense, but it was as a running back that he made his reputation. And his

PROFILE

Louisiana State University
Baton Rouge, La.
Founded: 1860
Enrollment: 31,234
Colors: Purple and Gold
Nickname: Tigers
Stadium: Tiger Stadium
    Opened in 1924
    Grass; 92,400 capacity
First football game: 1893
All-time record: 698–385–47 (.645)
Bowl record: 21–18–1
Consensus national championships, 1936–present: 3 (1958, 2003, 2007)
Southeastern Conference championships: 10 (8 outright)
Heisman Trophy: Billy Cannon, 1959
Outland Trophy: Glenn Dorsey, 2007
First-round draft choices: 30
Website: www.lsusports.net

THE BEST OF TIMES

Billy Cannon's last two years at LSU, featuring a national title (1958) and Cannon's Heisman Trophy (1959), were definitely a high point, as were titles under coaches Nick Saban (2003) and Les Miles (2007).

THE WORST OF TIMES

From 1989 to 1994, the Tigers had six straight losing seasons and never won more than three conference games in any single season.

CONFERENCE

After 11 years in the Southern Conference, LSU became a charter member of the SEC in 1993.

DISTINGUISHED ALUMNI

Shaquille O'Neal, NBA player; James Carville, campaign manager/commentator; Elizabeth Ashley, actress; John Breaux, U.S. senator; Bill Conti, composer; Carlos Roberto Flores, president of Honduras; Rex Reed, drama critic

FIGHT SONG

FIGHT FOR LSU
Like knights of old, let's fight to hold
The glory of the Purple and Gold
Let's carry through, let's die or do
To win this game for LSU
Keep trying for the high score
Come on and fight
We want some more, some more
Come on you Tigers, fight, fight, fight
For dear old LSU.
Rah!

HEY FIGHTING TIGER
Hey! Fightin' Tigers, fight all the way!
Hey! Fightin' Tigers, win the game today!
You've got the know how, you're doing fine,
Hang on to the ball, as you hit the wall,
And smash right through the line!
You've got to go for the touchdown, run up the
    score,
Make Mike the Tiger stand right up and roar!
ROAR!
Give it all of your might as you fight tonight
And keep the goal in view!
Victory for LSU!

The mascot's cage is left near the visitors' locker room, where opponents are sure to walk by.

versatility didn't stop there. In the 1959 Sugar Bowl he helped LSU cap an undefeated, untied national championship season by throwing a touchdown pass and kicking the extra point in a 7-0 victory over Clemson. He also punted and returned kicks, as everyone in Louisiana and Mississippi can still tell you. Cannon won the 1959 Heisman Trophy and was drafted by both the NFL and the AFL. He went with the AFL's Houston franchise and had a long, distinguished career with the Oilers, Raiders and Chiefs. Cannon ran into difficulties after football, serving a term in prison for his role in a counterfeiting scheme. Still, the Tigers faithful never abandoned him. No LSU fan would ever turn his back on Billy Cannon, and he remains, easily, the most beloved player in LSU history.

BEST COACH Great way to start a fight in Baton Rouge. Some still argue for Paul Dietzel and the national title of 1958. Others swear by the lengthy reign of Charlie McClendon, the beloved Cholly Mac, who presided over Tigers football from 1962 to 1979. But for pure, unadorned accomplishment, you have to start the argument with Nick Saban. When he arrived in Baton Rouge from Michigan State in 2000, it had been more than a decade since LSU's

last SEC championship. The team had gone 3–8 the previous season and the 1958 team was a fading, sepia-toned memory.

With stout defense and a recruiting effort that kept the best players in state, Saban promptly got the Tigers winning again. They were 8–4 in his first year, and in 2001, LSU won the SEC and then beat Illinois in the Sugar Bowl. It was the first Top 10 finish for the Tigers since 1987. In 2003, Saban's team topped that, losing just one game early in the season before toppling Oklahoma 21-14 in the Sugar Bowl, the BCS championship game. In four years, he'd taken the Tigers all the way to the summit. At the end of the 2004 season, Saban accepted an NFL job, leaving with a record of 48–16. Tigers fans loved him—and their second consensus national championship—too much to be angry.

Until he returned to the college ranks, that is, taking the head job at … *Alabama*. Words like "betrayal" and "traitor" were among the nicer terms that were used in Louisiana to describe Saban. Meanwhile, his successor at LSU, Les Miles, took the Tigers to the top in 2007, three years into his tour. Miles had always been a Michigan man and there were rumors he would be going to Ann Arbor after winning the championship. But he stayed.

FIRST-ROUND DRAFT CHOICES

1944	Steve Van Buren, Eagles (5)
1948	Y.A. Tittle, Lions (6)
1951	Ebert Van Buren, Eagles (7)
1951	Kenny Konz, Browns (14)
1957	Earl Leggett, Bears (13)
1960	Billy Cannon, Rams (1)* and Oilers**
1960	Johnny Robinson, Lions (3)
1962	Wendell Harris, Colts (9)
1962	Earl Gros, Packers (14)
1963	Jerry Stovall, Cardinals (2) and Jets (3)*
1966	George Rice, Bears (12)
1973	Bert Jones, Colts (2)
1975	Mike Williams, Chargers (22)
1977	A.J. Duhe, Dolphins (13)
1979	Charles Alexander, Bengals (12)
1988	Wendell Davis, Bears (27)
1989	Eric Hill, Cardinals (10)
1991	Harvey Williams, Chiefs (21)
1996	Eddie Kennison, Rams (18)
1997	David LaFleur, Cowboys (22)
1998	Alan Faneca, Steelers (26)
1999	Anthony McFarland, Buccaneers (15)
2004	Michael Clayton, Buccaneers (15)
2005	Marcus Spears, Cowboys (20)
2006	Joseph Addai, Colts (30)
2007	JaMarcus Russell, Raiders (1)
2007	LaRon Landry, Redskins (6)
2007	Dwayne Bowe, Chiefs (23)
2007	Craig Davis, Chargers (30)
2008	Glenn Dorsey, Chiefs (5)
2009	Tyson Jackson, Chiefs (3)

*From 1960-1966, the NFL and AFL held separate, competing drafts
**First "territorial selection" by Houston in the inaugural AFL draft held Nov. 22, 1959

CONSENSUS ALL-AMERICANS

1935-36	Gaynell Tinsley, E
1939	Ken Kavanaugh, E
1954	Sid Fournet, T
1958-59	Billy Cannon, B
1961	Roy Winston, G
1962	Jerry Stovall, B
1970	Mike Anderson, LB
1970-71	Tommy Casanova, DB
1972	Bert Jones, QB
1977-78	Charles Alexander, RB
1987	Wendell Davis, SE
1987	Nacho Albergamo, C
1997	Alan Faneca, OG
1997	Chad Kessler, P
2001	Josh Reed, WR
2003	Chad Lavalais, DL
2004	Ben Wilkerson, OL
2004	Marcus Spears, DL
2006	LaRon Landry, DB
2007	Glenn Dorsey, DL
2007	Craig Steltz, DB

The Tigers did not repeat in 2008 and one of their losses—a heartbreaker—was to Alabama … and Saban.

BEST TEAM The 1958 champs were young—mostly juniors and sophomores—with low expectations. Add the fact that Dietzel hadn't exactly set fire to the world in his three previous seasons (going 11–17–2 over the span), and what they accomplished becomes all the more remarkable. Dietzel had a kind of gimmick in those days before unlimited substitution. He played three units: The White Team went both ways, the Go Team specialized in offense and the defense was a unit called the Chinese Bandits.

The three-platoon system worked, and it didn't hurt that Cannon was in the White Team's backfield. The Tigers won every game and were named national champions in both major polls at the end of the regular season, which was customary in those days. The Tigers crowned their perfect season by shutting out Clemson, 7-0, in the Sugar Bowl.

BEST BACKFIELD The 2006 team went 11–2 (the losses were to Auburn and to eventual national champ Florida), beat Notre Dame soundly in the Sugar Bowl and ran up some gaudy offensive statistics. The Tigers averaged over 400 yards a game and did it in a balanced fashion, passing for 252 and rushing for 166. The interesting aspect of those statistics is that while strong-armed quarterback JaMarcus Russell was responsible for the passing numbers, the rushing yards were run up by a platoon of running backs: Jacob Hester, Alley Broussard, Keiland Williams, Charles Scott and others. So many that none of them had 100 carries for the season. It was running back by committee, and it worked.

BEST DEFENSE Sentimentalists would vote for the Chinese Bandits of 1958. This was one of the units Dietzel played on his way to the national championship, and arguably the least talented of his three if you measured by sheer athleticism. But if you were looking for grit, the Chinese Bandits were the place to find it. Apart from talents such as Mel Branch, who played almost 10 years in the pros, the unit was mostly composed of kids who made up in aggression what they lacked in skill. You had to be aggressive to play noseguard at 185 pounds, even in those days.

The more realistic choice would be between the 1970 and the 2003 squads. The 1970 defense was anchored by Tommy Casanova, and they barely lost to Nebraska in the

COLLEGE FOOTBALL HALL OF FAME INDUCTEES		
NAME	YEARS	INDUCTED
Dana X. Bible, COACH	1916	1951
Mike Donahue, COACH	1923-27	1951
Biff Jones, COACH	1932-34	1954
Bernie Moore, COACH	1935-47	1954
Gaynell Tinsley, E	1934-36	1956
Ken Kavanaugh, E	1937-39	1963
Doc Fenton, E/QB	1904-09	1971
Charles McClendon, COACH	1962-79	1986
Tommy Casanova, CB	1969-71	1995
Billy Cannon, HB	1957-59	2008

Orange Bowl, 17-12, with the Cornhuskers winning the national championship. The 2003 unit helped LSU win the national title by allowing, in 14 games, only 19 touchdowns and 252 yards a game—of which a mere 67 came on the ground.

STORYBOOK SEASON
Before the 2001 season (Saban's second), the Tigers were considered strong contenders for the SEC West and a first-time appearance in the conference title game. After two warmup wins against non-conference opponents, the Tigers were ready to begin their run. But the Auburn game was postponed until December in the wake of the Sept. 11 terrorist attacks. So LSU played its first conference game in Knoxville, losing to the Vols, 26-18, then losing the home opener to Florida, 44-15. Another conference loss, this one to Mississippi, looked like the last nail in the coffin. Somehow the Tigers hung on, beating Alabama and Arkansas. The rescheduled game against Auburn was now for the Western Division title.

LSU won easily and went on to a rematch with Tennessee in the SEC championship game. With a win, the Vols would go to the Rose Bowl and play Miami for the national championship. During the game, LSU starting quarterback Rohan Davey went down with an injury, as did running back LaBrandon Toefield. No matter. Backup QB Matt Mauck stood strong and the defense made crucial stops. With a remarkable 31-20 upset, the Tigers won the conference title, as so many LSU fans originally thought they would. The Tigers just took the long way to get there.

BIGGEST GAME The 1959 Tigers were defending national champions and riding an 18-game winning streak on Halloween night against a very tough Mississippi team. Both the Rebels and the Tigers played field position and defense, sometimes punting the ball on first down. LSU trailed 3-0 in the fourth quarter and the Tiger Stadium crowd could feel the glory slipping away. Facing third and 17 on their own 42, the Rebels' Jake Gibbs punted. Cannon took the ball on the 11 and started down the sideline against what looked like solid coverage. Fans still listen to J.C. Politz's frantic radio call of Cannon's storied run, 45 years later. According to legend, seven Mississippi players had a shot at Cannon, but none were able to bring him down. Cannon's return lifted LSU to a 7-3 win, and though the Tigers didn't repeat as national champions, the game and the run have attained something close to immortality.

BIGGEST UPSET The 1965 Arkansas Razorbacks were the nation's No. 2-ranked team, winners of 22 straight leading up to the 1966 Cotton Bowl. LSU, with a record of 7–3, seemed overmatched, especially when Arkansas went 87 yards for a touchdown on its second possession. But with little Joe Labruzzo scooting through holes, LSU mounted two touchdown drives in the second quarter and held on for a 14-7 win, denying Arkansas the national title.

PRO FOOTBALL HALL OF FAME INDUCTEES		
NAME	YEARS	INDUCTED
Steve Van Buren, HB	1944-51	1965
Y.A. Tittle, QB	1948-64	1971
Jim Taylor, FB	1958-67	1976

WILDEST FINISH With time running out—or perhaps, having run out—against Mississippi on Nov. 4, 1972, Bert Jones completed a game-winning touchdown pass to Brad Davis in the south end zone of Tiger Stadium. Rebels fans swear that time did not merely stand still that night, but actually moved backward. According to game accounts, four seconds remained when Jones dropped back 10 yards, pump-faked and threw incomplete. Incredibly, the clock still showed one second. Jones then threw the fabled score for a 17-16 LSU victory. The finish prompted Ole Miss fans to erect a sign at the Mississippi-Louisiana state line: "You are now entering Louisiana. Set your clocks back four seconds."

BEST GOAL-LINE STAND For sheer Homeric drama, it would be hard to beat Billy Cannon and Warren Rabb stopping a Mississippi runner on the 1 in the 1959 Halloween epic. For sheer nocturnal madness, it would be the time in 1988 when LSU stopped Texas A&M on the 2. A bank of stadium lights went out after that series, giving birth to the Lights Out Defense.

BEST COMEBACK The Bluegrass Miracle. Down 30-27 at Kentucky on Nov. 9, 2002, LSU had 11 seconds to go 87 yards. The Tigers got 12 yards on one play. Then, with fireworks going off, Kentucky players dumping Gatorade on their coach's head and students streaming onto the field to tear down the goalposts, quarterback Marcus Randall completed a 75-yard touchdown pass to Devery Henderson for the improbable win.

STADIUM Tiger Stadium is among the legendary venues of college football. The structure is one of those places that leaves an imprint on visiting players, fans, coaches and broadcasters. Famously known as Death Valley, it is routinely cited as one of the toughest places for visitors to play. In *Sports Illustrated*, Rick Reilly put it plainly: "College football is LSU's Tiger Stadium at night." The official capacity is 91,600, but more than 92,000 fans regularly pile in for games of special importance. As the sixth-largest on-campus stadium, Tiger Stadium ranks in the top 10 every year for average attendance.

The original 12,000-seat stadium opened Thanksgiving 1924 with a game against then-archrival Tulane. By 1936, it held 46,000 and one end had been closed to give the stadium a horseshoe shape. The other end was closed in 1953 to form a bowl of 68,000 seats. Additional expansions and renovations further raised capacity, made seating more comfortable and added skyboxes. A new press facility and club seats were added for the 2005 season.

RIVAL There was a time, certainly, when in-state rival Tulane was the team that LSU fans most wanted to beat. LSU's first football game was against Tulane, a 34-0 loss in 1893. The game was played for state bragging rights and something called the Rag. The Rag was a flag splitting the two teams' colors: purple and gold, green and white. The original Rag was lost, but a new one was awarded to the Tigers after their 48-17 win over Tulane in 2001.

With time, Tulane's football fortunes ebbed and LSU has now won three times more often in the series. Meanwhile, the rivalry with Mississippi has gained intensity. They are neighboring states and SEC West rivals. And then there is the Halloween tradition. Five years after the 1959 game, on another Halloween, LSU won an 11-10 thriller on a late touchdown and two-point conversion. An overtime game at Oxford on Halloween 1998 ended in a Mississippi win. The Halloween series stands at 3–3–1 and surely qualifies as a rivalry.

NICKNAME After a 6–0 season in 1896, the LSU football team adopted the nickname Tigers, a typical choice at a time when football teams commonly used ferocious animals as monikers. The LSU Tigers, however, had a less zoological pedigree that went back to the Civil War and a battalion from New Orleans who had dressed gaudily (as Zouaves) and fought fiercely in Virginia. These soldiers, known as the Louisiana Tigers, were the ancestors of the football Fighting Tigers.

MASCOT There have been five Mike the Tigers. The first served for 20 years and died during a six-game losing streak in 1956. His death was kept secret until the streak was broken. Mike V's quarters, just north of the stadium, are equipped with a pool, scratching post and climbing platform. Before home games, Mike rides in a cage to a spot near the visitors' locker room where opposing players are sure to walk past him. Just in case they forget where they are.

UNIFORMS Old Gold and Royal Purple made their first official appearance in 1893 on the uniforms of LSU's baseball team. Later that year, the football coach and some

THE SCHOOLS

players wanted some ribbon to decorate their jerseys for the program's first game. The stores were stocking ribbons in Mardi Gras colors—purple, gold and green. The green, however, was in short supply, so the players and their coach bought up all the purple and gold. The rest, as they say, is history.

LORE The championship seasons of 1958, 2003 and 2007 are fresher and more vivid in the memory of LSU fans, but there was another one of those mythic teams way back in 1908. The Tigers went 10–0 that season and were known as the "point-a-minute team" for scoring 442 points in 450 minutes of play. Their star, G. Ellwood "Doc" Fenton, scored a remarkable 125 of those himself.

QUOTE There is an LSU cheer that is brilliantly alliterative and culturally perfect, somehow working in both Cajun cuisine and football:

Hot boudin
Cold coosh-coosh
Come on, Tigers
Poosh, poosh, poosh

What a Good Friend He Was

By John Ed Bradley

He called late one night. We hadn't seen each other in 29 years, not since I left LSU and put football behind me. "When I die," he said, "I want you to spread my ashes out on the field. Will you promise to do that for me?"

I'd never fully recovered from the experience of playing in Tiger Stadium and I figured he was suffering from the same psychic hangover, haunted by those nights long ago when we wore the purple and gold and played side by side on the offensive line. I'd loved him like a brother, so turning him down wasn't easy. "It's hard for me to go back there," I said. "I get emotional when I do, remembering how it was. I'm not right for days afterward. You should ask somebody else."

"No," he said. "Spread them out on the Ponderosa, will you? That's where my best memories are. It's what I remember when I remember LSU."

He was talking about the practice fields, the place down by the river where we'd sacrificed the bulk of our college years to exhausting, often violent tasks meant to improve our chances come Saturday night. The Ponderosa had four regular-size fields, complete with goalposts and yard markings. A tall hurricane fence draped with Army-green tarpaulin surrounded the area.

"Okay," I told him, "I'll do it. But you aren't dying, are you?"

He took too long to answer. "I'm not sure," he said. And then he hung up.

For days I gave a start every time the phone rang. I said "Hello" and waited for his wife to tell me he was down at the crematorium in a shiny brass urn with his name and a Tiger emblem engraved on the side. It messed with my head, what he'd asked me to do.

> *In my quiet moments, I wondered if I'd ever kicked up somebody's ashes back when I was playing. Fell down in ashes. Ate ashes. When I beat my fist against the ground after getting whipped or screwing up an assignment, was I beating ashes?*

In my quiet moments, I wondered if I'd ever kicked up somebody's ashes back when I was playing. Fell down in ashes. *Ate* ashes. When I beat my fist against the ground after getting whipped or screwing up an assignment, was I beating ashes?

I'm sorry if I was. I'm sorry to all the LSU dead I must've rolled around in when I was young and played for the team.

I realized, of course, that I would have to go at night to keep from being noticed. I flashed to a picture of my creaky, 50-year-old form scaling the fence with my teammate tucked under my arm. I saw the Louisiana moon and the Louisiana stars. I could even hear the words I would pray as I removed the lid and let the wind blow his remains out over the grass: "Dear Lord, you probably wouldn't remember him as a player— he never started—but what a good friend he was."

Weeks went by. At last I got tired of the burden of his love and called him back. "Are you dying?" I asked.

"We're all dying," he answered.

"*I'm* not dying," I said, raising my voice more than I should have.

Once again, he was a long time before answering. "Yeah, that might be true, John Ed, but we were teammates and *you promised*."

And so I went back to waiting, resigned to my role in a drama that won't end until I fertilize the Ponderosa with all that's left of him. The call might come tonight; it might be another 30 years before someone tells me it's time. In any case, I keep the gas tank of my pickup full. There's a flashlight in the glove compartment and a change of clothes on the back seat. "Lord," I'll say, standing out there in the night as the wind blows, "forgive us, please, for loving anything of this world so much."

John Ed Bradley is a magazine writer and the author of seven books, including It Never Rains in Tiger Stadium, *a memoir about his years as an LSU football player.*

LSU All-Time Scores

WIN/LOSS PERCENTAGE SINCE 1936

DR. CHARLES E. COATES
1893 (.000)   0-1

1893   0-1-0
N25		at Tulane	0	34

ALBERT P. SIMMONS
1894-95 (.833)   5-1

1894   2-1-0
N30	●	at Natchez AC	26	0
D3		Mississippi	6	26
D21	●	Centenary	30	0

1895   3-0-0
O26	●	Tulane	8	4
N2	●	Centenary *JAL*	16	6
N18	●	Alabama	12	6

ALLEN W. JEARDEAU
1896-97 (.875)   7-1

1896   6-0-0
O10	●	Centenary	46	0
O24	●	at Tulane	1	0f
N13	●	Mississippi *VIC*	12	4
N16	●	Texas	14	0
N20	●	Mississippi State	52	0
N28	●	at Southern AC	6	0

1897   1-1-0
D20	●	Montgomery AC	28	6
J8		Cincinnati	0	26*

EDMOND A. CHAVANNE
1898, 1900 (.600)   3-2

1898   1-0-0
D14	●	Tulane	37	0

JOHN P. GREGG
1899 (.200)   1-4

1899   1-4-0
N1		Mississippi *MER*	0	11
N12		Sewanee	0	34
N30		at Texas	0	29
D2		at Texas A&M	0	52
D8	●	Tulane	38	0

EDMOND A. CHAVANNE

1900   2-2-0
N11	●	Millsaps	70	0
N17		at Tulane	0	29
N30	●	Millsaps *JAL*	5	6
D5	●	LSU Alumni	10	0

W.S. BORELAND
1901-03 (.681)   15-7

1901   5-1-0
O28	●	at Louisiana Tech	57	0
N7	●	Mississippi	46	0
N16	●	at Tulane	11	0#
N20	●	Auburn	0	28
N22	●	Arkansas	15	0
N28	●	New Orleans YMCA	38	0

1902   6-1-0
O16	●	at La. Lafayette	42	0
O18	●	Texas *SA*	5	0
O27	●	Auburn	5	0
N8	●	Mississippi *NO*	6	0
N17		Vanderbilt	5	27
N27	●	at Mississippi State	6	0
N29	●	at Alabama	11	0

1903   4-5-0
O14	●	LSU Alumni	16	0
O24	●	Eagles - New Orleans	33	0
O30	●	at Louisiana Tech	16	0
O31	●	at Shreveport AC	5	0
N7		at Mississippi State	0	11
N9		at Alabama	0	18
N11		at Auburn	0	12
N16		Cumberland	0	41
N21		Mississippi *NO*	0	11

D.A. KILLIAN
1904-06 (.563)   8-6-2

1904   3-4-0
O16	●	Louisiana Tech	17	0
O22		at Shreveport AC	0	16
O29		at Louisiana Tech	0	6
N5	●	Mississippi	5	0
N10	●	Nashville Med.	16	0
N19		at Tulane	0	5
D2		Alabama	0	11

1905   3-0-0
N18	●	Louisiana Tech	16	0
N25	●	at Tulane	5	0
D2	●	Mississippi State	15	0

1906   2-2-2
O10	●	Monroe AC	5	0
O20		Mississippi	0	9
O27	=	Mississippi State *COLMS*	0	0
N9	●	Louisiana Tech	17	0
N19		Texas A&M	12	21
N29	=	Arkansas	6	6

EDGAR R. WINGARD
1907-08 (.850)   17-3

1907   7-3-0
O11	●	Louisiana Tech	28	0
O19		at Texas	5	12
O21		at Texas A&M	5	11
O28	●	Samford	57	0
N6		Arkansas	17	12
N9	●	Mississippi State	23	11
N16	●	Mississippi *JAM*	23	0
N23		Alabama *MBL*	4	6
N30	●	Baylor	48	0
D25	●	at Havana U.	56	0

1908   10-0-0
O3	●	N.O. Gym Club	41	0
O11	●	Jackson Br.- N.O.	81	5
O17	●	Texas A&M *NO*	26	0
O26	●	Southwestern	55	0
O31	●	at Auburn	10	2
N7	●	Mississippi State	50	0
N10	●	Baylor	89	0
N16	●	Haskell *NO*	32	0
N23	●	at Louisiana Tech	22	0
N26	●	Arkansas *LR*	36	4

JOE G. PRITCHARD
1909 (.800)   4-1

JOHN W. MAYHEW
1909-10 (.333)   3-6

1909   6-2-0
O2	●	Jackson Br.-N.O.	70	0
O9	●	Mississippi	10	0
O16	●	Mississippi State	15	0
O30		Sewanee *NO*	6	15
N4	●	Louisiana Tech *ALEXL*	23	0
N13		Arkansas *MEM*	0	16
N18	●	Transylvania, Ky.	52	0
N25	●	Alabama *BIRM*	12	6

1910   1-5-0
O15	●	Mississippi Coll.	40	0
O21		Mississippi State *COLMS*	0	3
O29		Sewanee *NO*	5	31
N5		at Vanderbilt	0	22
N19		at Texas	0	12
N24		Arkansas *LR*	0	51

JAMES K. (PAT) DWYER
1911-13 (.680)   16-7-2

1911   6-3-0
O7	●	La. Lafayette	42	0
O14	●	Northwestern St.	46	0
O20	●	Mississippi Coll.	40	0
O28	●	Meteor AC	40	0
N4		at Baylor	6	0
N12		Mississippi State *GUL*	0	6
N18		Southwestern Texas *HOU*	6	17
N30		Arkansas *LR*	0	11
D9	●	Tulane	6	0

1912   4-3-0
O5	●	La-Lafayette	85	3
O11	●	Mississippi Coll.	45	0
O19		Mississippi	7	10
N2		Mississippi State	0	7
N9		Auburn *MBL*	0	7
N16	●	Arkansas *LR*	7	6
N28	●	at Tulane	21	3

1913   6-1-2
O4	●	at Louisiana Tech	20	2
O11	●	at La. Lafayette	26	0
O18	●	Jefferson Coll.	45	6
O23	●	Baylor	50	0
N1		Auburn *MBL*	0	7
N8	●	Arkansas *SHRE*	12	7
N15	=	at Mississippi State	0	0
N22	●	Tulane	40	0
N27	=	Texas A&M *HOU*	7	7

E.T. McDONALD
1914-16 (.659)   14-7-1

1914   4-4-1
S27	●	La. Lafayette	54	0
O3	●	Louisiana Tech	60	0
O10	●	Mississippi Coll.	14	0
O17		Mississippi	0	21
O24	●	Jefferson Coll.	14	13
O31		Texas A&M *DAL*	9	63
N7		Arkansas *SHRE*	12	20
N14		Haskell *NO*	0	31
N26	=	at Tulane	0	0

1915   6-2-0
O1	●	Jefferson Coll.	42	0
O8	●	Mississippi Coll.	14	0
O15	●	at Mississippi	28	0
O22		Georgia Tech *NO*	7	36
O30	●	Mississippi State	10	0
N5	●	Arkansas *SHRE*	13	7
N17		at Rice	0	6
N25	●	Tulane	12	0

IRVING R. PRAY
1916, '19, '22 (.550)   11-9

D.X. BIBLE
1916 (.667)   1-0-2

1916   7-1-2
S30	●	at La. Lafayette	24	0
O7	●	Jefferson Coll.	59	0
O14	●	Texas A&M *GAL*	13	0
O21	●	Mississippi Coll.	50	7
O28	●	Sewanee *NO*	7	0
N5	●	Arkansas *SHRE*	17	7
N11	●	at Mississippi State	13	3
N18	●	Mississippi	41	0
N24	=	Rice	7	7
N30	=	at Tulane	14	14

WAYNE SUTTON
1917 (.375)   3-5

1917   3-5-0
O6	●	La. Lafayette	20	6
O13	●	at Mississippi	52	7
O20		Sewanee *NO*	0	3
O27		Texas A&M *SA*	0	27
N3		Arkansas *SHRE*	0	14
N10	●	Mississippi Coll.	34	0
N17		Mississippi State	0	9
N29		Tulane	6	28

1918
NO TEAM WWI

IRVING R. PRAY

1919   6-2-0
O4	●	La. Lafayette	39	0
O11	●	Jefferson Coll.	38	0
O18	●	Mississippi	12	0*
O25	●	Arkansas *SHRE*	20	0
N1		at Mississippi State	0	6
N8	●	Mississippi Coll.	24	0
N15		Alabama	0	23
N22	●	at Tulane	27	6

BRANCH BOCOCK
1920-21 (.706)   11-4-2

1920   5-3-1
O2	●	Jefferson Coll.	81	0
O2	●	Northwestern St.	34	0
O9	●	Spring Hill	40	0
O16	=	at Texas A&M	0	0
O23		Mississippi State	7	12
O30	●	Mississippi Coll.	41	9
N6		Arkansas *SHRE*	3	0
N13		at Alabama	0	21
N25		Tulane	0	21

1921   6-1-1
O8	●	Northwestern St.	78	0
O15	●	Texas A&M	6	0
O22	●	Spring Hill	41	7
O29	=	Alabama *NO*	7	7
N5	●	Arkansas *SHRE*	10	7
N12	●	Mississippi	21	0
N19		at Tulane	0	21
D3	●	at Mississippi State	17	14

1922-1932
SOUTHERN

IRVING R. PRAY

1922   3-7-0 (1-2-0)
S30	●	Northwestern St.	13	0
O7		Loyola-New Orleans	0	7
O14		at SMU	0	51
O20		at Texas A&M	0	47
O28		Arkansas *SHRE*	6	40
N2	●	Spring Hill	25	7
N7		Rutgers *NYC*	0	25
N10	I	at Alabama	3	47
N18	I	Mississippi State	0	7
N30	● I	Tulane	25	14

MIKE DONAHUE
1923-27 (.544)   23-19-3

1923   3-5-1 (0-3-0)
S29	●	Northwestern St.	40	0
O6	●	La. Lafayette	7	3
O13	●	Spring Hill	33	0
O20		Texas A&M	0	28
O27		Arkansas *SHRE*	13	26
N2		Mississippi Coll. *VIC*	0	0
N16	I	Alabama *MONT*	3	30
N24	I	at Tulane	0	20
D1	I	at Mississippi State	7	14

1924 5-4-0 (0-3-0)

S27	●	Spring Hill	7	6
O4	●	La. Lafayette	31	7
O11	●	Indiana Ind	20	14
O18	●	at Rice	12	0
O25	|	Auburn Birm	0	3
N1		Arkansas Shre	7	10
N8	|	at Georgia Tech	7	28
N15	●	Northwestern St.	40	0
N27	|	Tulane	0	13

1925 5-3-1 (0-2-1)

S26	●	Northwestern St.	27	0
O3	●	La. Lafayette	38	0
O10	|	Alabama	0	42
O17	●	LSU JV	6	0
O24	= |	at Tennessee	0	0
O31		Arkansas Shre	0	12
N7	●	Rice	6	0
N14	●	at Loyola-New Orleans	13	0
N21	|	Tulane	0	16

1926 6-3-0 (3-3-0)

S25	●	Northwestern St.	47	0
O2	●	La. Lafayette	34	0
O9	|	Tennessee	7	14
O16	● |	Auburn Mont	10	0
O23	|	Mississippi State JaL	6	7
O30	|	at Alabama	0	24
N6	●	Arkansas Shre	14	0
N13	● |	Mississippi	3	0
N25	● |	at Tulane	7	0

1927 4-4-1 (2-3-1)

S24	●	Louisiana Tech	45	0
O1	●	La. Lafayette	52	0
O8	= |	Alabama Birm	0	0
O15	● |	Auburn Mont	9	0
O22	● |	Mississippi State JaL	9	7
O29		Arkansas Shre	0	28
N5	|	at Mississippi	7	12
N12	|	at Georgia Tech	0	23
N24	|	Tulane	6	13

RUSS COHEN
1928-31 (.635) 23-13-1

1928 6-2-1 (3-1-1)

O6	●	La. Lafayette	46	0
O13	●	Louisiana Coll.	41	0
O20	● |	Mississippi State JaL	31	0
O27	●	Spring Hill	30	7
N3		Arkansas Shre	0	7
N10	● |	Mississippi	19	6
N17	● |	at Georgia	13	12
N29	= |	at Tulane	0	0
D8	|	Alabama Birm	0	13

1929 6-3-0 (3-2-0)

S28	●	Louisiana Coll.	58	0
O5	●	La. Lafayette	58	0
O12	● |	Sewanee	27	14
O19	● |	Mississippi State JaL	31	6
O26	●	Louisiana Tech	53	7
N2		Arkansas Shre	0	32
N9	|	at Duke	6	32
N16	● |	Mississippi	13	6
N28	|	Tulane	0	21

1930 6-4-0 (2-4-0)

S20	●	S.D. Wesleyan	76	0
S27	●	Louisiana Tech	71	0
O4	●	La. Lafayette	85	0
O11	|	at South Carolina	6	7
O18	|	Mississippi State JaL	6	8
O25	● |	Sewanee	12	0
N1	●	Arkansas Shre	27	12
N8	● |	Mississippi	6	0
N15	|	Alabama Mont	0	33
N27	|	at Tulane	7	12

1931 5-4-0 (3-2-0)

S26		at TCU	0	3
O3	●	Spring Hill	35	0
O10	● |	South Carolina	19	12
O17	● |	Mississippi State	31	0
O24	●	Arkansas Shre	13	6
O31	|	Sewanee	6	12
N7		at Army	0	20
N14	● |	Mississippi JaL	26	3
N28	|	at Tulane	7	34

BIFF JONES
1932-34 (.742) 20-5-6

1932 6-3-1 (4-0-0)

S24	=	TCU	3	3
O1		at Rice	8	10
O8	●	Spring Hill	80	0
O15	● |	Mississippi State Mor	24	0
O22	●	Arkansas Shre	14	0
O29	● |	Sewanee	38	0
N5	● |	at South Carolina	6	0
N12		at Centenary	0	6
N26	● |	Tulane	14	0
D17		Oregon	0	12

1933-Present
SEC

1933 7-0-3 (3-0-2)

S30	●	Rice	13	0
O7	●	Millsaps	40	0
O14	=	Centenary	0	0
O21	●	Arkansas Shre	20	0
O28	= |	Vanderbilt	7	7
N4	●	South Carolina	30	7
N18	● |	Mississippi	31	0
N25	● |	Mississippi State Mor	21	6
D2	= |	at Tulane	7	7
D9	● |	Tennessee	7	0

1934 7-2-2 (4-2-0)

S29	=	at Rice	9	9
O6	=	SMU	14	14
O13	● |	Auburn	20	6
O20	●	Arkansas Shre	16	0
O27	● |	at Vanderbilt	29	0
N3	● |	Mississippi State	25	3
N10	●	at George Washington	6	0
N17	● |	Mississippi JaL	14	0
D1	|	Tulane	12	13
D8	|	at Tennessee	13	19
D15	●	Oregon	14	13

BERNIE MOORE
1935-47 (.672) 83-39-6

1935 9-2-0 (5-0-0)

S28		Rice	7	10
O5	●	Texas	18	6
O12	●	Manhattan Bkln	32	0
O19	●	Arkansas Shre	13	7
O26	● |	at Vanderbilt	7	2
N2	● |	Auburn	6	0
N9	● |	Mississippi State	28	13
N16	● |	at Georgia	13	0
N23	●	La. Lafayette	56	0
N30	● |	at Tulane	41	0
		SUGAR BOWL		
J1		TCU	2	3

1936 9-1-1 (6-0-0)

S26	●	Rice	20	7
O3	=	at Texas	6	6
O10	● |	Georgia	47	7
O17	● |	Mississippi	13	0
O24	●	Arkansas Shre	19	7
O31	● |	at Vanderbilt	19	0
N7	● |	Mississippi State	12	0
N14	● |	Auburn Birm	19	6
N21	●	La. Lafayette	93	0
N28	● |	Tulane	33	0
		SUGAR BOWL		
J1		Santa Clara	14	21

1937 9-2-0 (5-1-0)

S25	● |	Florida	19	0
O2	●	Texas	9	0
O9	●	at Rice	13	0
O16	● |	Mississippi	13	0
O23	|	at Vanderbilt	6	7
O30	●	Loyola-New Orleans	52	6
N6	● |	Mississippi State	41	0
N13	● |	Auburn	9	7
N20	●	Northwestern St.	52	0
N27	● |	at Tulane	20	7
		SUGAR BOWL		
J1		Santa Clara	0	6

1938 6-4-0 (2-4-0)

S24	|	Mississippi	7	20
O1	●	at Texas	20	0
O8	●	Rice	3	0
O15	●	Loyola-New Orleans	47	0
O22	● |	Vanderbilt	7	0
O29	|	at Tennessee	6	14
N5	● |	Mississippi State	32	7
N12	|	Auburn Birm	6	28
N19	●	La. Lafayette	32	0
N26	|	Tulane	0	14

1939 4-5-0 (1-5-0)

S30	|	Mississippi	7	14
O7	●	at Holy Cross	26	7
O14	●	Rice	7	0
O21	●	Loyola-New Orleans	20	0
O28	● |	at Vanderbilt	12	6
N4	|	Tennessee	0	20
N11	|	Mississippi State	12	15
N18	|	Auburn	7	21
D2	|	at Tulane	20	33

1940 6-4-0 (3-3-0)

S21	●	Louisiana Tech	39	7
S28	|	Mississippi	6	19
O5	●	Holy Cross	25	0
O12		at Rice	0	23
O19	●	Mercer	20	0
O26	● |	Vanderbilt	7	0
N2	|	at Tennessee	0	28
N9	|	Mississippi State	7	22
N16	● |	Auburn Birm	21	13
N30	● |	Tulane	14	0

1941 4-4-2 (2-2-2)

S20	●	Louisiana Tech	25	0
S27		Holy Cross	13	19
O4		at Texas	0	34
O11	= |	Mississippi State	0	0
O18	●	Rice	27	0
O25	● |	Florida	10	7
N1	|	Tennessee	6	13
N8	|	Mississippi	12	13
N15	= |	Auburn	7	7
N29	● |	at Tulane	19	0

1942 7-3-0 (3-2-0)

S19	●	Northwestern St.	40	0
S26	●	Texas A&M	16	7
O3		at Rice	14	27
O10	● |	Mississippi State	16	6
O17	● |	Mississippi	21	7
O24	●	Georgia Pre-Flight	34	0
O31	|	at Tennessee	0	26
N7	●	Fordham NYC	26	13
N14	|	Auburn Birm	7	25
N26	● |	Tulane	18	6

1943 6-3-0 (2-2-0)

S25	● |	Georgia	34	27
O2	●	Rice	20	7
O9		Texas A&M	13	28
O16	●	Louisiana Army	28	7
O23	● |	Georgia ColGa	27	6
O30	●	TCU	14	0
N6	|	at Georgia Tech	7	42
N20	|	at Tulane	0	27
		ORANGE BOWL		
J1	●	Texas A&M	19	14

1944 2-5-1 (2-3-1)

S30	= |	Alabama	27	27
O7		at Rice	13	14
O14		Texas A&M	0	7
O21	|	Mississippi State	6	13
O28	● |	Georgia Atl	15	7
N4	|	Tennessee	0	13
N18	|	Georgia Tech	6	14
N25	● |	Tulane	25	6

1945 7-2-0 (5-2-0)

S29	●	Rice	42	0
O6	|	Alabama	7	26
O13	●	Texas A&M	31	12
O20	● |	at Georgia	32	0
O27	● |	Vanderbilt	39	7
N3	● |	Mississippi	32	13
N10	|	Mississippi State	20	27
N17	● |	at Georgia Tech	9	7
D1	● |	at Tulane	33	0

1946 9-1-1 (5-1-0)

S28	●	at Rice	7	6
O5	● |	Mississippi State	13	6
O12	●	Texas A&M	33	9
O19	|	Georgia Tech	7	26
O26	● |	at Vanderbilt	14	0
N2	● |	Mississippi	34	21
N9	● |	Alabama	31	21
N15	●	at Miami, Fla.	20	7
N22	●	Fordham	40	0
N30	● |	Tulane	41	27
		COTTON BOWL		
J1	=	Arkansas	0	0

1947 5-3-1 (2-3-1)

S27	●	Rice	21	14
O4	|	at Georgia	19	35
O11	●	Texas A&M	19	13
O17	●	at Boston College	14	13
O25	● |	Vanderbilt	19	13
N1	|	Mississippi	18	20
N15	● |	Mississippi State	21	6
N22	|	at Alabama	12	41
D6	= |	at Tulane	6	6

GAYNELL (GUS) TINSLEY
1948-54 (.507) 35-34-6

1948 3-7-0 (1-5-0)

S18		at Texas	0	33
O2	●	at Rice	26	13
O9	●	Texas A&M	14	13
O16	|	Georgia	0	22
O23		at North Carolina	7	34
O30	|	Mississippi	19	49
N6	|	at Vanderbilt	7	48
N13	|	Mississippi State	0	7
N20	● |	Alabama	26	6
N27	|	Tulane	0	46

1949 8-3-0 (4-2-0)

S24	|	Kentucky	0	19
O1	●	Rice	14	7
O8	●	Texas A&M	34	0
O14	|	at Georgia	0	7
O22	●	North Carolina	13	7
O29	● |	Mississippi	34	7
N5	● |	Vanderbilt	33	13
N12	● |	Mississippi State	34	7
N19	●	S.E. Louisiana	48	7
N26	● |	at Tulane	21	0
		SUGAR BOWL		
J2		Oklahoma	0	35

1950 4-5-2 (2-3-2)

S23	|	at Kentucky	0	14
S30	●	Pacific	19	0
O7		at Rice	20	35
O14	|	Georgia Tech	0	13
O21	= |	Georgia	13	13
N4	● |	Mississippi	40	14
N11	● |	at Vanderbilt	33	7
N18	|	Mississippi State	7	13
N24	●	Villanova	13	7
D2	= |	at Tulane	14	14
D9		at Texas	6	21

1951 7-3-1 (4-2-1)

S22	●	Southern Miss	13	0
S29	● |	Alabama Mbl	13	7
O6	●	Rice	7	6*
O13	|	at Georgia Tech	7	25
O20	● |	at Georgia	7	0
O27		Maryland	0	27
N3	= |	Mississippi	6	6
N10	|	Vanderbilt	13	20
N17	● |	Mississippi State	3	0
N24	●	Villanova Shre	45	7
D1	● |	Tulane	14	13

1952 3-7-0 (2-5-0)

S20		Texas	14	35
S27	|	Alabama	20	21
O4	●	at Rice	27	7
O11	● |	at Kentucky	34	7
O18	|	Georgia	14	27
O25		at Maryland	6	34
N1	|	at Mississippi	0	28
N8	|	Tennessee	3	22
N15	|	Mississippi State	14	33
N29	● |	at Tulane	16	0

1953 5-3-3 (2-3-3)

S19	●	Texas	20	7
S26	= I	Alabama MBL	7	7
O3	●	Boston College	42	6
O10	= I	Kentucky	6	6
O17	● I	at Georgia	14	6
O24	= I	at Florida	21	21
O31	I	Mississippi	16	27
N7	I	at Tennessee	14	32
N14	I	Mississippi State	13	26
N21	●	Arkansas LR	9	8
N28	● I	Tulane	32	13

1954 5-6-0 (2-5-0)

S18		at Texas	6	20
S25	I	Alabama	0	12
O2	I	at Kentucky	6	7
O9	I	at Georgia Tech	20	30
O16	●	Texas Tech	20	13
O23	● I	Florida	20	7
O30	I	Mississippi	6	21
N6	●	U.T. Chattanooga	26	19
N13	I	Mississippi State	0	25
N20	●	Arkansas SHRE	7	6
N27	● I	at Tulane	14	13

PAUL DIETZEL
1955-61 (.651) 46-24-3

1955 3-5-2 (2-3-1)

S17	● I	Kentucky	19	7
S24		Texas A&M DAL	0	28
O1	=	at Rice	20	20
O8	I	Georgia Tech	0	7
O15	I	at Florida	14	18
O29	I	Mississippi	26	29
N5		at Maryland	0	13
N12	● I	Mississippi State	34	7
N19	●	Arkansas LR	13	7
N26	= I	Tulane	13	13

1956 3-7-0 (1-5-0)

S29		Texas A&M	6	9
O6		at Rice	14	23
O13	I	at Georgia Tech	7	39
O20	I	at Kentucky	0	14
O27	I	Florida	6	21
N3	I	Mississippi	17	46
N10	●	Oklahoma State	13	0
N17	I	Mississippi State	13	32
N24	●	Arkansas SHRE	21	7
D1	● I	at Tulane	7	6

1957 5-5-0 (4-4-0)

S21		Rice	14	20
S28	● I	Alabama	28	0
O5	●	at Texas Tech	19	14
O12	● I	Georgia Tech	20	13
O19	● I	Kentucky	21	0
O26	I	at Florida	14	22
N2	I	at Vanderbilt	0	7
N9	I	at Mississippi	12	14
N16	I	Mississippi State	6	14
N30	● I	Tulane	25	6

1958 11-0-0 (6-0-0)

S20	●	at Rice	26	6
S27	● I	Alabama MBL	13	3
O4	●	Hardin-Simmons	20	6
O10	●	at Miami, Fla.	41	0
O18	● I	Kentucky	32	7
O25	● I	Florida	10	7
N1	● I	Mississippi	14	0
N8	●	Duke	50	18
N15	● I	Mississippi State JAM	7	6
N22	● I	at Tulane	62	0
		SUGAR BOWL		
J1	●	Clemson	7	0

1959 9-2-0 (5-1-0)

S19	●	Rice	26	3
S26	●	TCU	10	0
O3	●	Baylor SHRE	22	0
O10	●	Miami, Fla.	27	3
O17	● I	at Kentucky	9	0
O24	● I	at Florida	9	0
O31	● I	Mississippi	7	3
N7	I	at Tennessee	13	14
N14	● I	Mississippi State	27	0
N21	● I	Tulane	14	6
		SUGAR BOWL		
J1		Mississippi	0	21

1960 5-4-1 (2-3-1)

S17	●	Texas A&M	9	0
O1		Baylor	3	7
O8	I	at Georgia Tech	2	6
O15	I	at Kentucky	0	3
O22	I	Florida	10	13
O29	= I	at Mississippi	6	6
N5	●	South Carolina	35	6
N12	● I	Mississippi State	7	3
N19	●	Wake Forest	16	0
N26	● I	at Tulane	17	6

1961 10-1-0 (6-0-0)

S23		at Rice	3	16
S30	●	Texas A&M	16	7
O7	● I	Georgia Tech	10	0
O14	●	at South Carolina	42	0
O21	● I	Kentucky	24	14
O28	● I	at Florida	23	0
N4	● I	Mississippi	10	7
N11	●	at North Carolina	30	0
N18	● I	Mississippi State	14	6
N25	● I	Tulane	62	0
		ORANGE BOWL		
J1	●	Colorado	25	7

CHARLES McCLENDON
1962-79 (.682) 135-61-7

1962 9-1-1 (5-1-0)

S22	●	Texas A&M	21	0
S29	=	Rice	6	6
O6	● I	at Georgia Tech	10	7
O13	●	Miami, Fla.	17	3
O20	● I	at Kentucky	7	0
O27	● I	Florida	23	0
N3	I	Mississippi	7	15
N10	●	TCU	5	0
N17	● I	Mississippi State JAM	28	0
N24	● I	at Tulane	38	3
		COTTON BOWL		
J1	●	Texas	13	0

1963 7-4-0 (4-2-0)

S21	●	Texas A&M	14	6
S28		at Rice	12	21
O5	● I	Georgia Tech	7	6
O11	●	at Miami, Fla.	3	0
O19	● I	Kentucky	28	7
O26	● I	at Florida	14	0
N2	I	Mississippi	3	37
N9	●	TCU	28	14
N16	I	Mississippi State JAM	6	7
N23	● I	Tulane	20	0
		BLUEBONNET BOWL		
D21		Baylor	7	14

1964 8-2-1 (4-2-1)

S19	●	Texas A&M	9	6
S26	●	at Rice	3	0
O10	●	North Carolina	20	3
O17	● I	at Kentucky	27	7
O24	= I	Tennessee	3	3
O31	● I	Mississippi	11	10
N7	I	Alabama BIRM	9	17
N14	● I	Mississippi State	14	10
N21	● I	at Tulane	13	3
D5	I	Florida	6	20
		SUGAR BOWL		
J1	●	Syracuse	13	10

1965 8-3-0 (3-3-0)

S18	●	Texas A&M	10	0
S25	●	Rice	42	14
O2	I	at Florida	7	14
O9	●	at Miami, Fla.	34	27
O16	● I	Kentucky	31	21
O23	●	South Carolina	21	7
O30	I	Mississippi JAM	0	23
N6	I	Alabama	7	31
N13	● I	Mississippi State	37	20
N20	● I	Tulane	62	0
		COTTON BOWL		
J1	●	Arkansas	14	7

1966 5-4-1 (3-3-0)

S17	●	South Carolina	28	12
S24		at Rice	15	17
O1	●	Miami, Fla.	10	8
O8	=	Texas A&M	7	7
O15	● I	at Kentucky	30	0
O22	I	Florida	7	28
O29	I	Mississippi	0	17
N5	I	Alabama BIRM	0	21
N12	● I	Mississippi State	17	7
N19	● II	at Tulane	21	7

1967 7-3-1 (3-2-1)

S23	●	Rice	20	14
S30	●	Texas A&M	17	6
O7	● I	at Florida	37	6
O14		Miami, Fla.	15	17
O21	● I	Kentucky	30	7
O28	I	at Tennessee	14	17
N4	= I	Mississippi JAM	13	13
N11	I	Alabama	6	7
N18	● I	Mississippi State	55	0
N25	●	Tulane	41	27
		SUGAR BOWL		
J1	●	Wyoming	20	13

1968 8-3-0 (4-2-0)

S21	●	Texas A&M	13	12
S28	●	at Rice	21	7
O5	●	Baylor	48	16
O11		at Miami, Fla.	0	30
O19	● I	Kentucky	13	3
O26	● II	TCU	10	7
N2	I	Mississippi	24	27
N9	I	Alabama BIRM	7	16
N16	● I	Mississippi State	20	16
N23	● II	Tulane	34	10
		PEACH BOWL		
D30	●	Florida State	31	27

1969 9-1-0 (4-1-0)

S20	●	Texas A&M	35	6
S27	●	at Rice	42	0
O4	●	Baylor	63	8
O10	●	at Miami, Fla.	20	0
O18	● I	at Kentucky	37	10
O25	● I	Auburn	21	20
N1	I	Mississippi JAM	23	26
N8	● I	Alabama	20	15
N15	● I	Mississippi State	61	6
N22	●	Tulane	27	0

1970 9-3-0 (5-0-0)

S19		Texas A&M	18	20
S26	●	Rice	24	0
O3	●	Baylor	31	10
O10	●	Pacific	34	0
O17	● I	Kentucky	14	7
O24	● I	at Auburn	17	9
N7	● I	Alabama BIRM	14	9
N14	● I	Mississippi State	38	7
N21		at Notre Dame	0	3
N28	●	at Tulane	26	14
D5	● I	Mississippi	61	17
		ORANGE BOWL		
J1		Nebraska	12	17

1971 9-3-0 (3-2-0)

S11		Colorado	21	31
S18	●	Texas A&M	37	0
S25	●	at Wisconsin	38	28
O2	●	Rice	38	3
O9	● I	Florida	48	7
O16	● I	at Kentucky	17	13
O30	I	Mississippi JAM	22	24
N6	I	Alabama	7	14
N13	● I	Mississippi State JAM	28	3
N20	●	Notre Dame	28	8
N27	●	Tulane	36	7
		SUN BOWL		
D18	●	Iowa State	33	15

1972 9-2-1 (4-1-1)

S16	●	Pacific	31	13
S23	●	Texas A&M	42	17
S30	●	Wisconsin	27	7
O7	●	at Rice	12	6
O14	● I	Auburn	35	7
O21	● I	Kentucky	10	0
N4	● I	Mississippi	17	16
N11	I	Alabama BIRM	21	35
N18	● I	Mississippi State	28	14
N25	= I	at Florida	3	3
D2	●	at Tulane	9	3
		BLUEBONNET BOWL		
D30		Tennessee	17	24

1973 9-3-0 (5-1-0)

S15	●	Colorado	17	6
S22	●	Texas A&M	28	23
S29	●	Rice	24	9
O6	● I	Florida	24	3
O13	● I	at Auburn	20	6
O20	● I	Kentucky	28	21
O27	●	at South Carolina	33	29
N3	● I	Mississippi JAM	51	14
N17	● I	Mississippi State	26	7
N22	I	Alabama	7	21
D1		at Tulane	0	14
		ORANGE BOWL		
J1		Penn State	9	16

1974 5-5-1 (2-4-0)

S14	●	Colorado	42	14
S21		Texas A&M	14	21
S28	=	at Rice	10	10
O5	I	at Florida	14	24
O12	● I	Tennessee	20	10
O19	I	at Kentucky	13	20
N2	● I	Mississippi	24	0
N9	I	Alabama BIRM	0	30
N16	I	Mississippi State JAM	6	7
N23	●	Tulane	24	22
N30	●	Utah	35	10

1975 4-7-0 (1-5-0)

S13		at Nebraska	7	10
S20		Texas A&M	8	39
S27	●	Rice SHRE	16	13
O4	I	Florida	6	34
O11	I	at Tennessee	10	24
O18	● I	Kentucky	17	14
O25	●	South Carolina	24	6
N1	I	Mississippi JAM	13	17
N8	I	Alabama	10	23
N15	I	Mississippi State	6	16†
N22	●	at Tulane	42	6

1976 6-4-1 (2-4-0)

S11	=	Nebraska	6	6
S18	●	Oregon State	28	11
S25	●	Rice	31	0
O2	I	at Florida	23	28
O9	● I	Vanderbilt	33	20
O16	I	at Kentucky	7	21
O30	● I	Mississippi	45	0
N6	I	Alabama BIRM	17	28
N13	I	Mississippi State JAM	13	21†
N20	●	Tulane	17	7
N27	●	Utah	35	7

1977 8-4-0 (4-2-0)

S17		at Indiana	21	24
S24	●	Rice	77	0
O1	● I	Florida	36	14
O8	● I	at Vanderbilt	28	15
O15	I	Kentucky	13	33
O22	●	Oregon	56	17
O29	● I	Mississippi JAM	28	21
N5	I	Alabama	3	24
N12	● I	Mississippi State	27	24
N19	●	at Tulane	20	17
N26	●	Wyoming	66	7
		SUN BOWL		
D31		Stanford	14	24

1978 8-4-0 (3-3-0)

S16	●	Indiana	24	17
S23	●	Wake Forest	13	11
S30	●	at Rice	37	7
O7	● I	at Florida	34	21
O14	I	Georgia	17	24
O21	● I	at Kentucky	21	0
N4	● I	Mississippi	30	8
N11	I	Alabama BIRM	10	31
N18	I	Mississippi State JAM	14	16
N25	●	Tulane	40	21
D2	●	Wyoming	24	17
		LIBERTY BOWL		
D23		Missouri	15	20

1979 7-5-0 (4-2-0)

S15	●	at Colorado	44	0
S22	●	Rice	47	3
S29		Southern California	12	17
O6	● I	Florida	20	3
O13	I	at Georgia	14	21
O20	● I	Kentucky	23	19
O27		Florida State	19	24
N3	● I	Mississippi JAM	28	24
N10	I	Alabama	0	3
N17	● I	Mississippi State	21	3
N24		at Tulane	13	24
		TANGERINE BOWL		
D22	●	Wake Forest	34	10

JERRY STOVALL
1980-83 (.511) 22-21-2

1980 7-4-0 (4-2-0)

S6		Florida State	0	16
S13	●	Kansas State	21	0
S20	●	Colorado	23	20
S27		at Rice	7	17
O4	● I	at Florida	24	7
O11	● I	Auburn	21	17
O18	● I	at Kentucky	17	10
N1	● I	Mississippi	38	16
N8	I	at Alabama	7	28
N15	I	Mississippi State JAM	31	55
N22	●	Tulane	24	7

1981 3-7-1 (1-4-1)

S5		ǀ	Alabama	7	24
S12			at Notre Dame	9	27
S19	●		Oregon State	27	24
S26	●		Rice	28	14
O3		ǀ	Florida	10	24
O10		ǀ	at Auburn	7	19
O17	●	ǀ	Kentucky	24	10
O24			Florida State	14	38
O31	=	ǀ	Mississippi [JaM]	27	27
N14		ǀ	Mississippi State	9	17
N28			at Tulane	7	48

1982 8-3-1 (4-1-1)

S18	●		Oregon State	45	7
S25	●		Rice	52	13
O2	●	ǀ	at Florida	24	13
O9	=	ǀ	Tennessee	24	24
O16	●	ǀ	at Kentucky	34	10
O23	●		South Carolina	14	6
O30	●	ǀ	Mississippi	45	8
N6	●	ǀ	Alabama [Birm]	20	10
N13		ǀ	at Mississippi State	24	27
N20	●		Florida State	55	21
N27			Tulane	28	31
			ORANGE BOWL		
J1			Nebraska	20	21

1983 4-7-0 (0-6-0)

S10			Florida State	35	40
S17	●		at Rice	24	10
S24	●		Washington	40	14
O1		ǀ	Florida	17	31
O8		ǀ	at Tennessee	6	20
O15		ǀ	Kentucky	13	21
O22	●		South Carolina	20	6
O29		ǀ	Mississippi [JaM]	24	27
N5		ǀ	Alabama	26	32
N12		ǀ	Mississippi State	26	45
N19	●		at Tulane	20	7

BILL ARNSPARGER
1984-86 (.750) 26-8-2

1984 8-3-1 (4-1-1)

S8	=	ǀ	at Florida	21	21
S15	●		Wichita St.	47	7
S22	●		Arizona	27	26
S29	●		at Southern California	23	3
O13	●	ǀ	Vanderbilt	34	27
O20	●	ǀ	at Kentucky	36	10
O27			Notre Dame	22	30
N3	●	ǀ	Mississippi	32	29
N10	●	ǀ	Alabama [Birm]	16	14
N17		ǀ	at Mississippi State	14	16
N24	●		Tulane	33	15
			SUGAR BOWL		
J1			Nebraska	10	28

1985 9-2-1 (4-1-1)

S14	●		at North Carolina	23	13
S21	●		Colorado State	17	3
O5		ǀ	Florida	0	20
O12	●	ǀ	at Vanderbilt	49	7
O19	●	ǀ	Kentucky	10	0
N2	●	ǀ	Mississippi [JaM]	14	0
N9	=	ǀ	Alabama	14	14
N16	●	ǀ	Mississippi State	17	15
N23	●		at Notre Dame	10	7
N30	●		at Tulane	31	19
D7	●		East Carolina	35	15
			LIBERTY BOWL		
D27			Baylor	7	21

1986 9-3-0 (5-1-0)

S13	●		Texas A&M	35	17
S20			Miami, Ohio	12	21
O4	●	ǀ	at Florida	28	17
O11	●	ǀ	Georgia	23	14
O18	●	ǀ	at Kentucky	25	16
O25	●		North Carolina	30	3
N1		ǀ	Mississippi	19	21
N8	●	ǀ	Alabama [Birm]	14	10
N15	●	ǀ	Mississippi State [JaM]	47	0
N22	●		Notre Dame	21	19
N29	●		Tulane	37	17
			SUGAR BOWL		
J1			Nebraska	15	30

MIKE ARCHER
1987-90 (.598) 27-18-1

1987 10-1-1 (5-1-0)

S5	●		at Texas A&M	17	3
S12	●		Fullerton St.	56	12
S19	●		Rice	49	16
S26	=		Ohio State	13	13
O3	●	ǀ	Florida	13	10
O10	●	ǀ	at Georgia	26	23
O17	●	ǀ	Kentucky	34	9
O31	●	ǀ	Mississippi [JaM]	42	13
N7		ǀ	Alabama	10	22
N14	●	ǀ	Mississippi State	34	14
N21	●		at Tulane	41	36
			GATOR BOWL		
D31	●		South Carolina	30	13

1988 8-4-0 (6-1-0)

S3	●		Texas A&M	27	0
S17	●	ǀ	at Tennessee	34	9
S24			at Ohio State	33	36
O1		ǀ	at Florida	6	19
O8	●	ǀ	Auburn	7	6
O15	●	ǀ	Kentucky	15	12
O29	●	ǀ	Mississippi	31	20
N5	●	ǀ	at Alabama	19	18
N12	●	ǀ	at Mississippi State	20	3
N19			Miami, Fla.	3	44
N26	●		Tulane	44	14
			HALL OF FAME BOWL		
J2			Syracuse	10	23

1989 4-7-0 (2-5-0)

S2			at Texas A&M	16	28
S16			Florida State	21	31
S30	●		Ohio U.	57	6
O7		ǀ	Florida	13	16
O14		ǀ	at Auburn	6	10
O21		ǀ	at Kentucky	21	27
O28		ǀ	Tennessee	39	45
N4	●	ǀ	at Mississippi	35	30
N11		ǀ	Alabama	16	32
N18	●	ǀ	Mississippi State	44	20
N25	●		at Tulane	27	7

1990 5-6-0 (2-5-0)

S8	●	ǀ	Georgia	18	13
S15	●		Miami, Ohio	35	7
S22		ǀ	at Vanderbilt	21	24
S29	●		Texas A&M	17	8
O6		ǀ	at Florida	8	34
O20	●	ǀ	Kentucky	30	20
O27			at Florida State	3	42
N3		ǀ	Mississippi	10	19
N10		ǀ	at Alabama	3	24
N17		ǀ	Mississippi State [JaM]	22	34
N24	●		Tulane	16	13

CURLEY HALLMAN
1991-94 (.364) 16-28

1991 5-6-0 (3-4-0)

S7		ǀ	at Georgia	10	31
S14			at Texas A&M	7	45
S21	●	ǀ	Vanderbilt	16	14
O5		ǀ	Florida	0	16
O12	●		Arkansas State	70	14
O19	●	ǀ	at Kentucky	29	26
O26			Florida State	16	27
N2	●	ǀ	Mississippi [JaM]	25	22
N9		ǀ	Alabama	17	20
N16		ǀ	Mississippi State	19	28
N23	●		at Tulane	39	20

1992 2-9-0 (1-7-0)

S5			Texas A&M	22	31
S12	●	ǀ	Mississippi State	24	3
S19		ǀ	at Auburn	28	30
S26			Colorado State	14	17
O3		ǀ	Tennessee	0	20
O10		ǀ	at Florida	21	28
O17		ǀ	Kentucky	25	27
O31		ǀ	Mississippi [JaM]	0	32
N7		ǀ	Alabama	11	31
N21	●		Tulane	24	12
N27		ǀ	at Arkansas	6	30

1993 5-6-0 (3-5-0)

S4			at Texas A&M	0	24
S11	●	ǀ	at Mississippi State	18	16
S18		ǀ	Auburn	10	34
S25		ǀ	at Tennessee	20	42
O2	●		Utah State	38	17
O9		ǀ	Florida	3	58
O16		ǀ	at Kentucky	17	35
O30	●	ǀ	Mississippi	19	17
N6	●	ǀ	at Alabama	17	13
N20	●		Tulane	24	10
N27		ǀ	Arkansas	24	42

1994 4-7-0 (3-5-0)

S3			Texas A&M	13	18
S10	●	ǀ	Mississippi State	44	24
S17		ǀ	at Auburn	26	30
O1		ǀ	South Carolina	17	18
O8		ǀ	at Florida	18	42
O15	●	ǀ	Kentucky	17	13
O29		ǀ	at Mississippi	21	34
N5		ǀ	Alabama	17	35
N12			Southern Miss	18	20
N19	●		at Tulane	49	25
N26	●	ǀ	Arkansas [LR]	30	12

GERRY DiNARDO
1995-99 (.570) 32-24-1

1995 7-4-1 (4-3-1)

S2			at Texas A&M	17	33
S9	●	ǀ	at Mississippi State	34	16
S16	●	ǀ	Auburn	12	6
S23	●		Rice	52	7
S30	=	ǀ	at South Carolina	20	20
O7		ǀ	Florida	10	28
O14		ǀ	at Kentucky	16	24
O21	●		North Texas	49	7
N4		ǀ	at Alabama	3	10
N11	●	ǀ	Mississippi	38	9
N18	●	ǀ	Arkansas	28	0
			INDEPENDENCE BOWL		
D29	●		Michigan State	45	26

1996 10-2 (6-2)

S7	●		Houston	35	34
S21	●	ǀ	at Auburn	19	15
S28	●		New Mexico St.	63	7
O5	●	ǀ	Vanderbilt	35	0
O12		ǀ	at Florida	13	56
O19	●	ǀ	Kentucky	41	14
O26	●	ǀ	Mississippi State	28	20
N9		ǀ	Alabama	0	26
N16	●	ǀ	at Mississippi	39	7
N23	●		Tulane	35	17
N29	●	ǀ	Arkansas [LR]	17	7
			PEACH BOWL		
D28	●		Clemson	10	7

1997 9-3 (6-2)

S6	●		Texas El Paso	55	3
S13	●	ǀ	at Mississippi State	24	9
S20		ǀ	Auburn	28	31
S27	●		Akron	56	0
O4	●	ǀ	at Vanderbilt	7	6
O11	●	ǀ	Florida	28	21
O18		ǀ	Mississippi	21	36
N1	●	ǀ	at Kentucky	63	28
N8	●	ǀ	at Alabama	27	0
N15			Notre Dame	6	24
N28	●	ǀ	Arkansas	31	21
			INDEPENDENCE BOWL		
D28	●		Notre Dame	27	9

1998 4-7 (2-6)

S12	●		Arkansas State	42	6
S19	●	ǀ	at Auburn	31	19
S26	●		Idaho	53	20
O3		ǀ	Georgia	27	28
O10		ǀ	at Florida	10	22
O17		ǀ	Kentucky	36	39
O24	●	ǀ	Mississippi State	41	6
O31		ǀ	at Mississippi	31	37
N7		ǀ	Alabama	16	22
N21			at Notre Dame	36	39
N27		ǀ	Arkansas [LR]	14	41

HAL HUNTER
1999 (1.000) 1-0

1999 3-8 (1-7)

S4	●		San Jose State	29	21
S11	●		North Texas	52	0
S18		ǀ	Auburn	7	41
O2		ǀ	at Georgia	22	23
O9		ǀ	Florida	10	31
O16		ǀ	at Kentucky	5	31
O23		ǀ	at Mississippi State	16	17
O30		ǀ	Mississippi	23	42
N6		ǀ	at Alabama	17	23
N13			Houston	7	20
N26	●	ǀ	Arkansas	35	10

NICK SABAN
2000-04 (.750) 48-16

2000 8-4 (5-3)

S2	●		Western Carolina	58	0
S9	●		Houston	28	13
S16		ǀ	at Auburn	17	34
S23			UAB	10	13
S30	●	ǀ	Tennessee	38	31
O7		ǀ	at Florida	9	41
O14	●	ǀ	Kentucky	34	0
O21	●	ǀ	Mississippi State	45	38
N4	●	ǀ	Alabama	30	28
N11	●	ǀ	at Mississippi	20	9
N25		ǀ	Arkansas [LR]	3	14
			PEACH BOWL		
D29	●		Georgia Tech	28	14

2001 10-3 (5-3)

S1	●		Tulane	48	17
S8	●		Utah State	31	14
S29		ǀ	at Tennessee	18	26
O6		ǀ	Florida	15	44
O13	●	ǀ	at Kentucky	29	25
O20	●	ǀ	at Mississippi State	42	0
O27		ǀ	Mississippi	24	35
N3	●	ǀ	at Alabama	35	21
N10	●		Middle Tennessee	30	14
N23	●	ǀ	Arkansas	41	38
D1	●	ǀ	Auburn	27	14
			SEC CHAMPIONSHIP GAME		
D8	●		Tennessee [Atl]	31	20
			SUGAR BOWL		
J1	●		Illinois	47	34

2002 8-5 (5-3)

S1			at Virginia Tech	8	26
S7	●		Citadel	35	10
S14	●		Miami, Ohio	33	7
S28	●	ǀ	Mississippi State	31	13
O5	●		La. Lafayette	48	0
O12	●	ǀ	at Florida	36	7
O19	●	ǀ	South Carolina	38	14
O26		ǀ	at Auburn	7	31
N9	●	ǀ	at Kentucky	33	30
N16		ǀ	Alabama	0	31
N23	●	ǀ	Mississippi	14	13
N29		ǀ	at Arkansas	20	21
			COTTON BOWL		
J1			Texas	20	35

2003 13-1 (7-1)

A30	●		La. Monroe	49	7
S6	●		at Arizona	59	13
S13	●		Western Illinois	35	7
S20	●	ǀ	Georgia	17	10
S27	●	ǀ	at Mississippi State	41	6
O11		ǀ	Florida	7	19
O18	●	ǀ	at South Carolina	33	7
O25	●	ǀ	Auburn	31	7
N1	●		Louisiana Tech	49	10
N15	●	ǀ	at Alabama	27	3
N22	●	ǀ	at Mississippi	17	14
N29	●	ǀ	Arkansas	55	24
			SEC CHAMPIONSHIP GAME		
D6	●		Georgia [Atl]	34	13
			SUGAR BOWL		
J4	●		Oklahoma	21	14

2004 9-3 (6-2)

S4	●		Oregon State	22	21
S11	●		Arkansas State	53	3
S18		ǀ	at Auburn	9	10
S25	●	ǀ	Mississippi State	51	0
O2		ǀ	at Georgia	16	45
O9	●	ǀ	at Florida	24	21
O23	●		Troy State	24	20
O30	●	ǀ	Vanderbilt	24	7
N13	●	ǀ	Alabama	26	10
N20	●	ǀ	Mississippi	27	24
N26	●	ǀ	Arkansas [LR]	43	14
			CAPITAL ONE BOWL		
J1			Iowa	25	30

THE SCHOOLS

THE SCHOOLS

LES MILES
2005-PRESENT (.792)   42-11

2005   11-2 (7-1)
S10	●	at Arizona State	35	31
S26		Tennessee	27	30
O1	●	at Mississippi State	37	7
O8	●	at Vanderbilt	34	6
O15	●	Florida	21	17
O22	●	Auburn	20	17
O29	●	North Texas	56	3
N05	●	Appalachian State	24	0
N12	●	at Alabama	16	13
N19	●	at Missisippi	40	7
N25	●	Arkansas	19	17
		SEC CHAMPIONSHIP GAME		
D3		Georgia Atl	14	34
		PEACH BOWL		
D30	●	Miami, Fla.	40	3

2006   11-2 (6-2)
S2	●	La.-Lafayette	45	3
S9	●	Arizona	45	3
S16		at Auburn	3	7
S23	●	Tulane	49	7
S30	●	Mississippi State	48	17
O7		at Florida	10	23
O14	●	Kentucky	49	0
O21	●	Fresno State	38	6
N4	●	at Tennessee	28	24
N11	●	Alabama	28	14
N18	●	Mississippi	23	20
N24	●	at Arkansas	31	26
		SUGAR BOWL		
J3	●	Notre Dame	41	14

2007   12-2 (6-2)
A30	●	at Mississippi State	45	0
S8	●	Virginia Tech	48	7
S15	●	Middle Tennessee State	44	0
S22	●	South Carolina	28	16
S29	●	at Tulane	34	9
O6	●	Florida	28	24
O13		at Kentucky	37	43
O20	●	Auburn	30	24
N3	●	at Alabama	41	34
N10	●	Louisiana Tech	58	10
N17	●	at Mississippi	41	24
N23		Arkansas	48	50
		SEC CHAMPIONSHIP GAME		
D1	●	Tennessee Atl	21	14
		BCS CHAMPIONSHIP GAME		
J7	●	Ohio State NO	38	24

2008   8-5 (3-5)
A30	●	Appalachian State	41	13
S13	●	North Texas	41	3
S20	●	at Auburn	26	21
S27	●	Mississippi State	34	24
O11		at Florida	21	51
O18	●	at South Carolina	24	17
O25		Georgia	38	52
N01	●	Tulane	35	10
N08		Alabama	21	27
N15	●	Troy State	40	31
N22		Mississippi	13	31
N28		at Arkansas	30	31
		CHICK-FIL-A BOWL		
D31	●	Georgia Tech	38	3

LSU ANNUAL STATISTICAL LEADERS

YR	RUSHING	YDS	ATT	AVG	PASSING	ATT	CMP	PCT	YDS	RECEIVING	REC	YDS	AVG
1945	Gene Knight	667	85	7.8	Y.A. Tittle	77	35	.45	404	Clyde Lindsey	11	147	13.4
1946	Gene Knight	473	95	5.0	Y.A. Tittle	92	45	.49	780	Sam Lyle	7	162	23.1
1947	Rip Collins	315	73	4.3	Y.A. Tittle	96	49	.51	489	Ray Bullock	12	188	15.7
1948	Rip Collins	277	58	4.8	Charlie Pevey	99	37	.37	607	Abner Wimberly	10	197	19.7
1949	Billy Baggett	481	87	5.5	Charlie Pevey	86	36	.42	521	Sam Lyle	20	268	13.4
1950	Billy Baggett	778	119	6.5	Norm Stevens	108	42	.39	551	Warren Virgets	25	455	18.2
1951	Leroy Labat	574	152	3.8	Jim Barton	75	29	.39	417	Warren Virgets	17	263	15.5
1952	Al Doggett	382	71	5.4	Norm Stevens	97	52	.54	583	Jim Mitchell	17	209	12.3
1953	Jerry Marchand	696	137	5.1	Al Doggett	142	68	.48	822	Jerry Marchand	13	192	14.8
1954	Chuck Jons	408	88	4.6	Al Doggett	104	34	.33	459	Joe Tuminello	13	181	13.9
1955	O.K. Ferugson	465	117	4.0	M.C. Reynolds	115	51	.44	660	Chuck Johns	14	217	15.5
1956	Jimmy Taylor	552	117	4.7	M.C. Reynolds	70	30	.43	385	J.W. Brodnax	13	123	9.5
1957	Jimmy Taylor	762	162	4.7	Win Turner	41	16	.39	231	Billy Cannon	11	199	18.1
1958	Billy Cannon	686	115	6.0	Warren Rabb	90	45	.50	591	Johnny Robinson	16	235	14.7
1959	Billy Cannon	598	139	4.3	Warren Rabb	65	33	.51	422	Johnny Robinson	16	181	11.3
1960	Jerry Stovall	298	65	4.6	Lynn Amedee	67	31	.46	438	Jerry Stovall	12	114	9.5
1961	Earl Gros	406	90	4.5	Lynn Amedee	94	40	.43	485	Wendell Harris	10	177	17.7
1962	Jerry Stovall	368	89	4.1	Lynn Amedee	63	24	.38	457	Jerry Stovall	9	213	23.7
1963	Don Schwab	553	108	5.1	Pat Screen	38	22	.58	194	Billy Truax	10	112	11.2
1964	Don Schwab	583	160	3.6	Pat Screen	99	55	.56	561	Doug Moreau	33	391	11.8
1965	Joe Labruzzo	509	103	4.9	Nelson Stokley	50	32	.64	468	Doug Moreau	29	468	16.1
1966	Jimmy Dousay	441	104	4.2	Fred Haynes	91	39	.43	424	Billy Masters	24	241	10.0
1967	Tommy Allen	535	106	5.0	Nelson Stokley	130	71	.55	939	Tommy Morel	28	404	14.4
1968	Kenny Newfield	441	85	5.2	Mike Hillman	118	64	.54	787	Tommy Morel	42	564	13.4
1969	Eddie Ray	591	115	5.1	Mike Hillman	167	93	.56	1,180	Lonny Myles	43	559	13.0
1970	Art Cantrelle	892	247	3.6	Buddy Lee	138	73	.53	1,162	Andy Hamilton	39	870	22.3
1971	Art Cantrelle	649	133	4.9	Bert Jones	119	66	.55	945	Andy Hamilton	45	854	19.0
1972	Chris Dantin	707	165	4.3	Bert Jones	199	103	.52	1,446	Gerald Keigley	27	433	16.0
1973	Brad Davis	904	173	5.2	Mike Miley	107	60	.56	978	Brad Boyd	16	259	16.2
1974	Brad Davis	701	169	4.1	Billy Broussard	103	41	.40	700	Brad Boyd	18	275	15.3
1975	Terry Robiskie	765	214	3.6	Pat Lyons	168	72	.43	457	Carl Otis Trimble	16	177	11.1
1976	Terry Robiskie	1,117	224	5.0	Pat Lyons	133	54	.41	685	Carl Otis Trimble	14	211	15.1
1977	Charles Alexander	1,686	311	5.4	Steve Ensminger	159	71	.45	952	Carlos Carson	23	552	24.0
1978	Charles Alexander	1,172	281	4.2	David Woodley	153	79	.52	995	Mike Quintela	30	352	11.7
1979	Hokie Gajan	568	134	4.2	Steve Ensminger	174	80	.46	1,168	Carlos Carson	39	608	15.6
1980	Jesse Myles	403	76	5.3	Alan Risher	143	82	.57	971	Greg LaFleur	18	243	13.5
1981	Jesse Myles	202	72	2.8	Alan Risher	238	150	.63	1,780	Orlando McDaniel	41	719	17.5
1982	Dalton Hilliard	901	193	4.7	Alan Risher	234	149	.64	1,834	Eric Martin	45	817	18.2
1983	Dalton Hilliard	747	177	4.2	Jeff Wickersham	337	193	.57	2,542	Eric Martin	52	1,064	20.5
1984	Dalton Hilliard	1,268	254	5.0	Jeff Wickersham	312	178	.57	2,165	Eric Martin	47	668	14.2
1985	Dalton Hilliard	1,134	258	4.4	Jeff Wickersham	346	209	.60	2,145	Garry James	50	414	8.3
1986	Harvey Williams	700	178	3.9	Tommy Hodson	288	175	.61	2,261	Wendell Davis	80	1,244	15.6
1987	Harvey Williams	1,001	154	6.5	Tommy Hodson	265	162	.61	2,125	Wendell Davis	72	993	13.8
1988	Eddie Fuller	647	153	4.2	Tommy Hodson	293	154	.53	2,074	Tony Moss	55	957	17.4
1989	Eddie Fuller	649	140	4.6	Tommy Hodson	317	183	.58	2,655	Tony Moss	59	934	15.8
1990	Harvey Williams	953	205	4.6	Chad Loup	141	75	.53	975	Todd Kinchen	34	660	19.4
1991	Odell Beckham	397	81	4.9	Chad Loup	174	102	.59	1,181	Todd Kinchen	53	855	16.1
1992	Robert Davis	527	123	4.3	Jamie Howard	200	101	.51	1,349	Scott Ray	38	534	14.1
1993	Jay Johnson	558	106	5.3	Jamie Howard	248	106	.43	1,319	Brett Bech	30	429	14.3
1994	Jermaine Sharp	750	135	5.6	Jamie Howard	274	140	.51	1,997	Brett Bech	45	772	17.2
1995	Kevin Faulk	852	174	4.9	Jamie Howard	212	112	.53	1,493	Sheddrick Wilson	60	845	14.1
1996	Kevin Faulk	1,282	248	5.2	Herb Tyler	187	109	.58	1,688	David LaFleur	30	439	14.6
1997	Kevin Faulk	1,144	205	5.6	Herb Tyler	209	127	.61	1,581	Larry Foster	43	579	13.5
1998	Kevin Faulk	1,279	229	5.6	Herb Tyler	250	153	.61	2,018	Larry Foster	56	722	12.9
1999	Rondell Mealey	637	170	3.7	Josh Booty	333	162	.49	1,830	Jerel Myers	64	854	13.3
2000	LaBrandon Toefield	682	165	4.1	Josh Booty	290	145	.50	2,121	Josh Reed	65	1,127	17.3
2001	LaBrandon Toefield	992	230	4.3	Rohan Davey	367	217	.59	3,347	Josh Reed	94	1,740	18.5
2002	Domanick Davis	931	193	4.8	Marcus Randall	181	87	.48	1,173	Michael Clayton	57	749	13.1
2003	Justin Vincent	1,001	154	6.5	Matt Mauck	358	229	.64	2,825	Michael Clayton	78	1,079	13.8
2004	Alley Broussard	867	142	6.1	Marcus Randall	162	102	.63	1,269	Craig Davis	43	659	15.3
2005	Joseph Addai	911	187	4.9	JaMarcus Russell	310	187	.60	2,434	Dwayne Bowe	41	710	17.3
2006	Jacob Hester	440	94	4.7	JaMarcus Russell	342	232	.68	3,129	Dwayne Bowe	65	990	15.2
2007	Jacob Hester	1,103	225	4.9	Matt Flynn	359	202	.56	2,407	Brandon LaFell	50	656	13.1
2008	Charles Scott	1,174	217	5.4	Jarrett Lee	269	143	.53	1,873	Brandon LaFell	63	929	14.7

The NCAA began including postseason stats in 2002

LSU RECORD BOOK

SINGLE-GAME RECORDS

Rushing Yards	250	Alley Broussard (Nov. 20, 2004 vs. Mississippi)
Passing Yards	528	Rohan Davey (Nov. 3, 2001 vs. Alabama)
Receiving Yards	293	Josh Reed (Nov. 3, 2001 vs. Alabama)
All-Purpose Yards	376	Kevin Faulk (Sept. 7, 1996 vs. Houston)
Points	30	Kevin Faulk (Nov. 1, 1997 vs. Kentucky); Carlos Carson (Sept. 24, 1977 vs. Rice)
Field Goals	4	7 players tied
Tackles	21	Al Richardson (Oct. 23, 1982 vs. South Carolina)
Interceptions	3	7 players tied

SINGLE-SEASON RECORDS

Rushing Yards	1,686	Charles Alexander, 1977 (311 att.)
Passing Yards	3,347	Rohan Davey, 2001 (217-367)
Receiving Yards	1,740	Josh Reed, 2001 (94 rec.)
All-Purpose Yards	2,120	Domanick Davis, 2002 (31 rush., 130 rec., 499 punt ret., 500 kickoff ret.)
Scoring	147	Colt David, 2007 (2 TDs, 26 FGs, 63 PAT)
Touchdowns	19	LaBrandon Toefield, 2001 (19 rushing)
Tackles	154	Bradie James, 2002
Interceptions	8	Chris Williams, 1978
Punting Average	50.3	Chad Kessler, 1997 (39 punts)
Punt Return Average	15.4	Pinky Rohm (35 ret.)
Kickoff Return Average	24.7	Domanick Davis, 1999 (25 ret.)

CAREER RECORDS

Rushing Yards	4,557	Kevin Faulk, 1995-98
Passing Yards	9,115	Tommy Hodson, 1986-89
Receiving Yards	3,001	Josh Reed, 1999-2001
All Purpose Yards	6,883	Kevin Faulk, 1995-1998
Scoring	369	Colt David, 2005-08
Touchdowns	53	Kevin Faulk, 1995-98
Tackles	452	Al Richardson, 1979-82
Interceptions	20	Chris Williams, 1977-80
Punting Average	44.1	Patrick Fisher, 2004-07 (85 punts)
Punt Return Average	12.0	Domanick Davis, 1999-2002 (94 ret.)
Kickoff Return Average	22.8	Domanick Davis, 1999-2002 (95 ret.)

TEAM RECORDS

Longest Winning Streak	19	Nov. 30, 1957-Oct. 31, 1959; broken vs. Tennessee, 13-14 on Nov. 7, 1959
Longest Undefeated Streak	19	Nov. 30, 1957-Oct. 31, 1959; broken vs. Tennessee, 13-14 on Nov. 7, 1959
Most Consecutive Winning Seasons	16	1958-73
Most Consecutive Bowl Appearances	9	2000-present
Most Points in a Game	93	vs. Louisana-Lafayette, Nov. 21, 1936
Most Points Allowed in a Game	93	vs. Texas A&M, Oct. 31, 1914
Largest Margin of Victory	93	vs. Louisana-Lafayette, Nov. 21, 1936
Largest Margin of Defeat	55	vs. Florida, Oct. 9, 1993
Longest Pass Play	82	Steve Ensmiger to Carlos Carson vs. Georgia, Oct. 14, 1978
Longest Field Goal	54	Wade Richey vs. Kentucky, Oct. 19, 1996; Ron Lewis vs. North Carolina, Sep. 14, 1985
Longest Punt	86	Donnie Jones vs. Kentucky, Nov. 9, 2002
Longest Interception Return	100	Greg Jackson vs. Mississippi State, Nov. 12, 1988

RETIRED JERSEYS

	20	Billy Cannon

ALL-TIME TEAM

Fans statewide selected the players from the 1893-1993 teams

Offense			Defense		
	OG	Tyler LaFauci, 1971-73		DT	Fred Miller, 1960-62
	OG	Eric Andolsek, 1984-87		DT	Ronnie Estay, 1969-71
	OT	Charles "Bo" Strange, 1958-60		DT	A.J. Duhe, 1973-76
	OT	Lance Smith, 1981-84		DT	Henry Thomas, 1983-86
	C	Nacho Albergamo, 1984-87		LB	Roy "Moonie" Winston, 1959-61
	WR	Eric Martin, 1981-84		LB	Mike Anderson, 1968-70
	WR	Wendell Davis, 1984-87		LB	Warren Capone, 1971-73
	QB	Bert Jones, 1970-72		LB	Liffort Hobley, 1980-84
	RB	Jimmy Taylor, 1956-57		LB	Michael Brooks, 1983-86
	RB	Billy Cannon, 1957-59		DB	Johnny Robinson, 1957-59
	RB	Charles Alexander, 1975-78		DB	Jerry Stovell, 1960-62
	RB	Dalton Hilliard, 1982-85		DB	Tommy Casanova, 1969-71
	PK	David Browndyke, 1986-89		P	Tommy Davis, 1953-58

LSU Bowl History

SEASON	BOWL	DATE	PRE-GAME RANK	TEAMS	SCORE	FINAL RANK	MOST VALUABLE PLAYER(S)	ATT.
1935	SUGAR	Jan. 1, 1936		TCU LSU	3 2			35,000
1936	SUGAR	Jan. 1, 1937	6 2	Santa Clara LSU	21 14			38,483
1937	SUGAR	Jan. 1, 1938	9 8	Santa Clara LSU	6 0			40,000
1943	ORANGE	Jan. 1, 1944		LSU Texas A&M	19 14			25,203
1946	COTTON	Jan. 1, 1947	8 16	LSU Arkansas	0 0		Y.A. Tittle, LSU, QB Alton Baldwin, Arkansas, E	38,000
1949	SUGAR	Jan. 2, 1950	2 9	Oklahoma LSU	35 0		Leon Heath, Oklahoma, FB	82,000
1958	SUGAR	Jan. 1, 1959	1 12	LSU Clemson	7 0		Billy Cannon, LSU, HB	78,084
1959	SUGAR	Jan. 1, 1960	2 3	Mississippi LSU	21 0		Bobby Franklin, Mississippi, QB	77,484
1961	ORANGE	Jan. 1, 1962	4 7	LSU Colorado	25 7			68,150
1962	COTTON	Jan. 1, 1963	7 4	LSU Texas	13 0		Lynn Amedee, LSU, QB Johnny Treadwell, Texas, G	75,504
1963	BLUEBONNET	Dec. 21, 1963		Baylor LSU	14 7		Don Trull, Baylor, QB James Ingram, Baylor, E	50,000
1964	SUGAR	Jan. 1, 1965	7	LSU Syracuse	13 10		Doug Moreau, LSU, FL	80,096
1965	COTTON	Jan. 1, 1966	 2	LSU Arkansas	14 7	8 3	Joe Labruzzo, LSU, TB David McCormick, LSU, T	76,200
1967	SUGAR	Jan. 1, 1968	 6	LSU Wyoming	20 13		Glenn Smith, LSU, HB	61,346
1968	PEACH	Dec. 30, 1968	 19	LSU Florida State	31 27	19	Mike Hillman, LSU, QB Buddy Millican, LSU, DE	35,545
1970	ORANGE	Jan. 1, 1971	3 5	Nebraska LSU	17 12	1 7	Jerry Tagge, Nebraska, QB Willie Harper, Nebraska, DE	80,699
1971	SUN	Dec. 18, 1971	11	LSU Iowa State	33 15	11	Bert Jones, LSU, QB Matt Blair, Iowa State, LB	33,503
1972	BLUEBONNET	Dec. 30, 1972	11 10	Tennessee LSU	24 17	8 11	Condredge Holloway, Tennessee, QB Carl Johnson, Tennessee, DE	52,961
1973	ORANGE	Jan. 1, 1974	6 13	Penn State LSU	16 9	5 13	Tom Shuman, Penn State, QB Randy Crowder, Penn State, DT	60,477
1977	SUN	Dec. 31, 1977		Stanford LSU	24 14	15	Gordy Ceresino, Stanford, LB Charles Alexander, LSU, TB	31,318
1978	LIBERTY	Dec. 23, 1978	18	Missouri LSU	20 15	15	James Wilder, Missouri, RB	53,064
1979	TANGERINE	Dec. 22, 1979		LSU Wake Forest	34 10		David Woodley, LSU, QB	38,142
1982	ORANGE	Jan. 1, 1983	3 13	Nebraska LSU	21 20	3 11	Turner Gill, Nebraska, QB Dave Rimington, Nebraska, C	68,713
1984	SUGAR	Jan. 1, 1985	5 11	Nebraska LSU	28 10	4 15	Craig Sundberg, Nebraska, QB	75,608
1985	LIBERTY	Dec. 27, 1985	 12	Baylor LSU	21 7	17 20	Cody Carlson, Baylor, QB	40,186
1986	SUGAR	Jan. 1, 1987	6 5	Nebraska LSU	30 15	5 10	Steve Taylor, Nebraska, QB	76,234
1987	GATOR	Dec. 31, 1987	7 9	LSU South Carolina	30 13	5 15	Wendell Davis, LSU, SE Harold Green, South Carolina RB	82,119
1988	HALL OF FAME	Jan. 2, 1989	17 16	Syracuse LSU	23 10	13 19	Robert Drummond, Syracuse, RB	51,112
1995	INDEPENDENCE	Dec. 29, 1995		LSU Michigan State	45 26		Kevin Faulk, LSU, RB Gabe Northern, LSU, DE	48,835
1996	PEACH	Dec. 28, 1996	17	LSU Clemson	10 7	12	Herb Tyler, QB, Anthony McFarland, DL, LSU Raymond Priester, DE, Trevor Pryce, LB, Clemson	75,562
1997	INDEPENDENCE	Dec. 28, 1997	15	LSU Notre Dame	27 9	13	Rondell Mealey, LSU, RB Arnold Miller, LSU, DE	50,459
2000	PEACH	Dec. 29, 2000	 15	LSU Georgia Tech	28 14	22 17	Rohan Davey, LSU, QB Bradie James, LSU, LB	73,614
2001	SUGAR	Jan. 1, 2002	12 7	LSU Illinois	47 34	7 12	Rohan Davey, LSU, QB	75,562
2002	COTTON	Jan. 1, 2003	9	Texas LSU	35 20	6	Roy Williams, Texas, WR Cory Redding, Texas, DE	70,817
2003	SUGAR	Jan. 4, 2004	2 3	LSU Oklahoma	21 14	2 3	Justin Vincent, RB, LSU	79,342
2004	CAPITAL ONE	Jan. 1, 2005	11 12	Iowa LSU	30 25	8 16	Drew Tate, Iowa, QB	70,227
2005	PEACH	Dec. 30, 2005	10 9	LSU Miami (Fla.)	40 3	6 17	Matt Flynn, QB, LSU Melvin Oliver, DE, LSU	65,620
2006	SUGAR	Jan. 3, 2007	4 11	LSU Notre Dame	41 14	3 17	JaMarcus Russell, QB, LSU	77,781
2007	BCS CHAMPIONSHIP	Jan. 7, 2008	2 1	LSU Ohio State	38 24	1 5	Matt Flynn, QB, LSU Ricky Jean-Francois, DE, LSU	79,651
2008	CHICK-FIL-A	Dec. 31, 2008	 14	LSU Georgia Tech	38 3	 22	Jordan Jefferson, QB, LSU Perry Riley, LB, LSU	71,423

THE SCHOOLS

JANUARY 1, 1936 | Sugar
TCU 3, LSU 2

	1ST	2ND	3RD	4TH	FINAL
TCU	0	3	0	0	3
LSU	0	2	0	0	2

SCORING SUMMARY
LSU   Safety (Baugh fumbles in end zone)
TCU   FG Manton 26

TCU	TEAM STATISTICS	LSU
6	First Downs	9
121	Rushing Yards	120
3-8-1	Passing	3-21-3
54	Passing Yards	59
175	Total Yards	179
14-46.0	Punts - Average	13-44.7
2-1	Fumbles - Lost	3-2
4-20	Penalties - Yards	3-33

INDIVIDUAL LEADERS
RUSHING
TCU: Lawrence 6-54; Baugh 22-45.
LSU: Crass 15-34; Reed 6-29.
PASSING
TCU: Baugh 2-7-1, 29 yards.
LSU: Mickal 2-14-3, 36 yards.
RECEIVING
TCU: Walls 1-25, Meyer 1-18.
LSU: Barrett 3-59.

JANUARY 1, 1937 | Sugar
Santa Clara 21, LSU 14

	1ST	2ND	3RD	4TH	FINAL
SCL	14	0	0	7	21
LSU	0	7	0	7	14

SCORING SUMMARY
SCL   Gomez 26 pass from Falaschi (Pellegrini kick)
SCL   Finney 30 pass from Pellegrini (Pellegrini kick)
LSU   Tinsley 50 pass from Crass (Crass kick)
SCL   Falaschi 1 run (Smith from Gomez)
LSU   Reed 10 pass from Crass (Milner kick)

SCL	TEAM STATISTICS	LSU
10	First Downs	7
108	Rushing Yards	44
6-12-4	Passing	7-21-2
74	Passing Yards	125
182	Total Yards	169

JANUARY 1, 1938 | Sugar
Santa Clara 6, LSU 0

	1ST	2ND	3RD	4TH	FINAL
SCL	0	6	0	0	6
LSU	0	0	0	0	0

SCORING SUMMARY
SCL   Coughlan 1 pass from Pellegrini (kick failed)

SCL	TEAM STATISTICS	LSU
5	First Downs	10
34	Rushing Yards	106
5-13-3	Passing	8-21-0
67	Passing Yards	95
101	Total Yards	201

JANUARY 1, 1944 | Orange
LSU 19, Texas A&M 14

	1ST	2ND	3RD	4TH	FINAL
LSU	12	0	7	0	19
A&M	7	0	7	0	14

SCORING SUMMARY
LSU   Van Buren 11 run (kick failed)
LSU   Goode 24 pass from Van Buren (kick failed)
A&M   Burditt 21 pass from Hallmark (Burditt kick)
LSU   Van Buren 63 run (Van Buren kick)
A&M   Settegast 18 pass from Hallmark (Burditt kick)

LSU	TEAM STATISTICS	A&M
7	First Downs	7
207	Rushing Yards	4
4-12-0	Passing	14-32-5
172	Passing Yards	199
379	Total Yards	203
10-40.3	Punts - Average	9-41.8
3-3	Fumbles - Lost	5-2
7-81	Penalties - Yards	4-35

JANUARY 1, 1947
LSU 0, Arkansas 0

	1ST	2ND	3RD	4TH	FINAL
LSU	0	0	0	0	0
ARK	0	0	0	0	0

LSU	TEAM STATISTICS	ARK
15	First Downs	1
255	Rushing Yards	54
5-17-0	Passing	0-4-1
16	Passing Yards	0
271	Total Yards	54
9-30.4	Punts - Average	11-36.0
2	Fumbles Lost	3
8-50	Penalties - Yards	1-5

JANUARY 2, 1950 | Sugar
Oklahoma 35, LSU 0

	1ST	2ND	3RD	4TH	FINAL
OKLA	0	14	7	14	35
LSU	0	0	0	0	0

SCORING SUMMARY
OKLA   Heath 86 run (Tipps kick)
OKLA   Heath 34 run (Tipps kick)
OKLA   Thomas 34 pass from Pearson (Tipps kick)
OKLA   Thomas 5 run (Tipps kick)
OKLA   Royal 5 run (Tipps kick)

OKLA	TEAM STATISTICS	LSU
10	First Downs	8
286	Rushing Yards	38
2-11-4	Passing	9-20-2
74	Passing Yards	121
360	Total Yards	159
7-37.4	Punts - Average	8-33.6
4-4	Fumbles - Lost	4-4
8-40	Penalties - Yards	6-40

INDIVIDUAL LEADERS
RUSHING
OKLA: Heath 15-170, 2 TD.
LSU: West 5-26.
PASSING
OKLA: Pearson 2-7-0, 74 yards, 1 TD.
LSU: Pevy 5-11-0, 82 yards.
RECEIVING
OKLA: Goad 1-40.
LSU: Baggett 4-50.

JANUARY 1, 1959 | Sugar
LSU 7, Clemson 0

	1ST	2ND	3RD	4TH	FINAL
LSU	0	0	7	0	7
CLEM	0	0	0	0	0

SCORING SUMMARY
LSU   Mangham 9 pass from Cannon (Cannon kick)

LSU	TEAM STATISTICS	CLEM
9	First Downs	12
114	Rushing Yards	168
4-11-0	Passing	2-4-0
68	Passing Yards	23
182	Total Yards	191
6-41.7	Punts - Average	6-32.8
4-2	Fumbles - Lost	3-2
5-35	Penalties - Yards	2-20

INDIVIDUAL LEADERS
RUSHING
LSU: Cannon 13-51; Davis 2-17.
CLEM: Hayes 17-55; Usry 10-29.

JANUARY 1, 1960 | Sugar
Mississippi 21, LSU 0

	1ST	2ND	3RD	4TH	FINAL
MISS	0	7	7	7	21
LSU	0	0	0	0	0

SCORING SUMMARY
MISS   Woodruff 43 pass from Gibbs (Franklin kick)
MISS   Granthan 18 pass from Franklin (Khayat kick)
MISS   Blair 9 pass from Franklin (Khayat kick)

MISS	TEAM STATISTICS	LSU
19	First Downs	6
140	Rushing Yards	-15
15-27-2	Passing	9-25-2
223	Passing Yards	89
363	Total Yards	74
6-37.5	Punts - Average	12-34.3
4-2	Fumbles - Lost	2-0
7-65	Penalties - Yards	4-30

INDIVIDUAL LEADERS
RUSHING
MISS: Flowers 19-60; Blair 8-26.
LSU: Cannon 6-8.
PASSING
MISS: Franklin 10-15-1, 148 yards, 2 TD; Gibbs 4-10-1,
    65 yards, 1 TD.
LSU: Rabb 4-15-0, 36 yards.
RECEIVING
MISS: Flowers 4-64.
LSU: Cannon 3-39; McClain 3-31.

JANUARY 1, 1962 | Orange
LSU 25, Colorado 7

	1ST	2ND	3RD	4TH	FINAL
LSU	5	6	14	0	25
COLO	0	7	0	0	7

SCORING SUMMARY
LSU   FG Harris 30
LSU   Safety (blocked punt)
COLO   Schweninger 59 interception return
    (Hillebrand kick)
LSU   Crawford 1 run (run failed)
LSU   Field 9 run (Harris kick)
LSU   Sykes recovered blocked punt in end zone
    (Harris kick)

LSU	TEAM STATISTICS	COLO
19	First Downs	7
206	Rushing Yards	24
8-18-3	Passing	12-39-0
109	Passing Yards	105
315	Total Yards	129
4-33.8	Punts - Average	8-22.1
2-1	Fumbles - Lost	2-1
65	Penalty Yards	35

INDIVIDUAL LEADERS
RUSHING
LSU: Gros 10-55; Field 8-36, 1 TD.
COLO: Schweninger 5-9.
PASSING
LSU: Amedee 6-12-2, 88 yards.
COLO: Weidner 11-36-0, 98 yards.
RECEIVING
LSU: Wilkins 3-58; Campbell 3-30.
COLO: Hillebrand 4-52; Meadows 3-24.

JANUARY 1, 1963 | Cotton
LSU 13, Texas 0

	1ST	2ND	3RD	4TH	FINAL
LSU	0	3	7	3	13
TEX	0	0	0	0	0

SCORING SUMMARY
LSU   FG Amedee 23
LSU   Field 22 run (Amedee kick)
LSU   FG Amedee 37

LSU	TEAM STATISTICS	TEX
17	First Downs	9
126	Rushing Yards	80
13-21-0	Passing	8-22-3
133	Passing Yards	92
259	Total Yards	172
9-41.8	Punts - Average	8-46.8
0-0	Fumbles - Lost	2-2
1-15	Penalties - Yards	4-44

INDIVIDUAL LEADERS
RUSHING
LSU: Stovall 12-36; LeBlanc 6-23.
TEX: Cook 10-39; Wade 3-17.
PASSING
LSU: Amedee 9-13-0, 94 yards.
TEX: Genung 5-9-0, 59 yards; Wade 3-13-3, 33 yards.
RECEIVING
LSU: Truax 3-49; Cranford 2-16.
TEX: Green 1-18; Dixon 1-17.

December 21, 1963 | Bluebonnet
Baylor 14, LSU 7

	1st	2nd	3rd	4th	Final
BU	0	0	0	14	14
LSU	7	0	0	0	7

SCORING SUMMARY
LSU   Soefker 8 run (Moreau kick)
BU   Ingram 7 pass from Trull (Davies kick)
BU   Ingram 13 pass from Trull (Davies kick)

BU	TEAM STATISTICS	LSU
27	First Downs	4
130	Rushing Yards	95
26-37-1	Passing	1-5-0
255	Passing Yards	13
385	Total Yards	108
4-34.0	Punts - Average	7-37.3
1-1	Fumbles - Lost	1-0
2-30	Penalties - Yards	2-10

INDIVIDUAL LEADERS
RUSHING
BU: Hoffman 15-70; Mitchell 10-32.
LSU: Ezell 9-30; Schwab 7-25.
PASSING
BU: Trull 26-37-1, 255 yards, 2 TD.
LSU: Ezell 1-5-0, 13 yards.
RECEIVING
BU: Ingram 11-163, 2 TD; Elkins 7-66.
LSU: Truax 1-13.

January 1, 1965 | Sugar
LSU 13, Syracuse 10

	1st	2nd	3rd	4th	Final
LSU	2	0	8	3	13
SYR	10	0	0	0	10

SCORING SUMMARY
SYR   FG Smith 23
LSU   Safety
SYR   Clarke 28 blocked punt return (Smith kick)
LSU   Moreau 57 pass from Ezell
       (Labruzzo pass from Ezell)
LSU   FG Moreau 28

LSU	TEAM STATISTICS	SYR
11	First Downs	10
161	Rushing Yards	151
6-15-1	Passing	8-20-1
114	Passing Yards	52
275	Total Yards	203
9-36.2	Punts - Average	6-37.5
4-0	Fumbles - Lost	3-1
4-46	Penalties - Yards	5-55

INDIVIDUAL LEADERS
RUSHING
LSU: Schwab 17-81.
SYR: Nance 15-70; Little 8-46.
PASSING
LSU: Ezell 2-5-0, 67 yards, 1 TD.
SYR: King 6-15-0, 41 yards.
RECEIVING
LSU: Moreau 2-54, 1 TD; Labruzzo 2-45.
SYR: Cripps 2-18; Mahle 3-15.

January 1, 1966 | Cotton
LSU 14, Arkansas 7

	1st	2nd	3rd	4th	Final
LSU	0	14	0	0	14
ARK	7	0	0	0	7

SCORING SUMMARY
ARK   Crockett 19 pass from Brittenum (South kick)
LSU   Labruzzo 3 run (Moreau kick)
LSU   Labruzzo 1 run (Moreau kick)

LSU	TEAM STATISTICS	ARK
15	First Downs	22
166	Rushing Yards	129
8-11-0	Passing	15-24-1
100	Passing Yards	177
266	Total Yards	306
6-42.2	Punts - Average	3-34.0
0-0	Fumbles - Lost	2-1
4-62	Penalties - Yards	2-10

INDIVIDUAL LEADERS
RUSHING
LSU: Labruzzo 21-69, 2 TD; Dousay 14-38.
ARK: Jones 10-79; Burnett 12-44.
PASSING
LSU: Screen 7-10-0, 82 yards.
ARK: Brittenum 15-24-1, 177 yards, 1 TD.
RECEIVING
LSU: Masters 4-45; Labruzzo 1-19.
ARK: Crockett 10-129, 1 TD; Jones 2-26.

January 1, 1968 | Sugar
LSU 20, Wyoming 13

	1st	2nd	3rd	4th	Final
LSU	0	0	7	13	20
WYO	0	13	0	0	13

SCORING SUMMARY
WYO   Kiick 1 run (DePoyster kick)
WYO   FG DePoyster 24
WYO   FG DePoyster 49
LSU   Smith 1 run (Hurd kick)
LSU   Morel 8 pass from Stokely (kick failed)
LSU   Morel 14 pass from Stokely (Hurd kick)

LSU	TEAM STATISTICS	WYO
12	First Downs	20
151	Rushing Yards	167
6-20-0	Passing	14-24-4
91	Passing Yards	239
242	Total Yards	406
9-31.1	Punts - Average	4-49.0
0	Fumbles - Lost	1-1
3-25	Penalties - Yards	5-65

INDIVIDUAL LEADERS
RUSHING
LSU: Smith 16-74, 1 TD; Allen 16-41.
WYO: Kiick 19-75, 1 TD; Williams 16-64.

December 30, 1968 | Peach
LSU 31, Florida State 27

	1st	2nd	3rd	4th	Final
LSU	0	10	14	7	31
FSU	7	6	0	14	27

SCORING SUMMARY
FSU   Bailey 36 run (Guthrie kick)
FSU   Gunter 75 pass from Cappleman (kick failed)
LSU   Burns 39 punt return (Lumpkin kick)
LSU   FG Lumpkin 32
LSU   Hamlett 11 pass from Hillman (Lumpkin kick)
LSU   Stobler 11 pass from Hillman (Lumpkin kick)
FSU   Sellers 7 pass from Cappleman (pass failed)
FSU   Sellers 4 pass from Cappleman (Glass pass from Cappleman)
LSU   LeBlanc 3 run (Lumpkin kick)

LSU	TEAM STATISTICS	FSU
22	First Downs	19
151	Rushing Yards	92
17-30-1	Passing	21-41-1
233	Passing Yards	221
384	Total Yards	313
4-41.5	Punts - Average	9-34.6
5-4	Fumbles - Lost	1-0
7-70	Penalties - Yards	8-90

INDIVIDUAL LEADERS
RUSHING
LSU: LeBlanc 14-97, 1 TD; Matte 5-20.
FSU: Bailey 11-75, 1 TD; Gunter 8-30.
PASSING
LSU: Hillman 16-29-1, 229 yards, 2 TD.
FSU: Cappleman 21-41-1, 221 yards, 3 TD.
RECEIVING
LSU: West 2-144; Morel 6-103.
FSU: Sellers 8-75, 2 TD; Tyson 1-31.

January 1, 1971 | Orange
Nebraska 17, LSU 12

	1st	2nd	3rd	4th	Final
NEB	10	0	0	7	17
LSU	0	3	9	0	12

SCORING SUMMARY
NEB   FG Rogers 26
NEB   Orduna 3 run (Rogers kick)
LSU   FG Lumpkin 36
LSU   FG Lumpkin 25
LSU   Coffee 31 pass from Lee (kick failed)
NEB   Tagge 1 run (Rogers kick)

NEB	TEAM STATISTICS	LSU
18	First Downs	20
132	Rushing Yards	54
14-28-2	Passing	17-32-1
161	Passing Yards	227
293	Total Yards	281
6-37.7	Punts - Average	8-32.5
4-3	Fumbles - Lost	4-3
8-67	Penalties - Yards	4-27

INDIVIDUAL LEADERS
RUSHING
NEB: Orduna 63, 1 TD.
LSU: Jones 8-54.
PASSING
NEB: Tagge 12-25, 153 yards.
LSU: Lee 17-32-1, 182 yards, 1 TD.
RECEIVING
NEB: List 4-63.
LSU: Hamilton 9-146.

December 18, 1971 | Sun
LSU 33, Iowa State 15

	1st	2nd	3rd	4th	Final
LSU	6	0	13	14	33
ISU	0	3	6	6	15

SCORING SUMMARY
LSU   FG Michaelson 39
LSU   FG Michaelson 39
ISU   FG Shoemaker 32
LSU   Hamilton 37 pass from Jones (Michaelson kick)
LSU   Kelgley 21 pass from Jones (kick failed)
ISU   Marquardt 30 pass from Carlson (pass failed)
ISU   Krepfle 1 pass from Carlson (pass failed)
LSU   Michaelson 6 pass from Jones (Michaelson kick)
LSU   Jones 6 run (Michaelson kick)

LSU	TEAM STATISTICS	ISU
13	First Downs	16
187	Rushing Yards	83
12-23-1	Passing	19-35-1
227	Passing Yards	249
414	Total Yards	332
5-29.0	Punts - Average	9-34.0
60	Penalty Yards	61

INDIVIDUAL LEADERS
RUSHING
LSU: Shoreu 12-68; Walker 9-37.
ISU: Amundson 15-56.
PASSING
LSU: Jones 12-18-0, 227 yards, 3 TD.
ISU: Carlson 18-32-2, 230 yards, 2 TD.
RECEIVING
LSU: Hamilton 6-165, 1 TD.
ISU: Krepfle 6-88, 1 TD; Amundson 4-46.

December 30, 1972 | Bluebonnet
Tennessee 24, LSU 17

	1st	2nd	3rd	4th	Final
TENN	14	10	0	0	24
LSU	3	0	7	7	17

SCORING SUMMARY
LSU   FG Jackson 29
TENN   Young 6 pass from Holloway (Townsend kick)
TENN   Holloway 15 run (Townsend kick)
TENN   FG Townsend 33
TENN   Holloway 10 run (Townsend kick)
LSU   Jones 2 run (Jackson kick)
LSU   Davis 1 run (Jackson kick)

TENN	TEAM STATISTICS	LSU
17	First Downs	18
179	Rushing Yards	187
11-19-1	Passing	7-20-1
94	Passing Yards	90
273	Total Yards	277
6-41.2	Punts - Average	5-37.0
0-0	Fumbles - Lost	1-0
4-35	Penalties - Yards	3-35

INDIVIDUAL LEADERS
RUSHING
TENN: Holloway 19-74, 2 TD; Chancey 13-73.
LSU: Davis 16-88, 1 TD.
PASSING
TENN: Holloway 11-19-1, 94 yards, 1 TD.
LSU: Jones 7-19-0, 90 yards.
RECEIVING
TENN: Stanback 4-41.
LSU: Boyd 2-33.

JANUARY 1, 1974 | ORANGE
PENN STATE 16, LSU 9

	1ST	2ND	3RD	4TH	FINAL
PSU	3	13	0	0	16
LSU	7	0	2	0	9

SCORING SUMMARY
LSU	Rogers 3 run (Jackson kick)
PSU	FG Bahr 44
PSU	Herd 72 pass from Shuman (Bahr kick)
PSU	Cappelletti 1 run (kick failed)
LSU	Safety (Shuman fumbled snap in end zone)

PSU	TEAM STATISTICS	LSU
9	First Downs	19
28	Rushing Yards	205
6-17-1	Passing	8-20-1
157	Passing Yards	69
185	Total Yards	274
7-34.7	Punts - Average	8-46.8
1-0	Fumbles - Lost	3-1
3-37	Penalties - Yards	3-30

INDIVIDUAL LEADERS
RUSHING
PSU: Cappelletti 26-50, 1 TD.
LSU: Davis 19-70; Robiskie 10-58.
PASSING
PSU: Shuman 6-17-1, 157 yards, 1 TD.
LSU: Miley 8-18-1, 69 yards.
RECEIVING
PSU: Herd 1-72, 1 TD; Hayman 3-35.
LSU: Davis 6-20.

DECEMBER 31, 1977 | SUN
STANFORD 24, LSU 14

	1ST	2ND	3RD	4TH	FINAL
STAN	0	10	7	7	24
LSU	7	7	0	0	14

SCORING SUMMARY
LSU	Quintela 3 pass from Ensminger (Conway kick)
STAN	Lofton 49 pass from Benjamin (Nabor kick)
STAN	FG Nabor 36
LSU	Alexander 7 run (Conway kick)
STAN	Lofton 2 pass from Benjamin (Nabor kick)
STAN	Nelson 35 pass from Benjamin (Nabor kick)

STAN	TEAM STATISTICS	LSU
21	First Downs	21
103	Rushing Yards	307
23-36-0	Passing	7-23-3
269	Passing Yards	68
372	Total Yards	375
2-(-2)	Punt Returns - Yards	1-0
2-39	Kickoff Returns - Yards	2-25
6-36.0	Punts - Average	4-35.0
0-0	Fumbles - Lost	2-1
7-65	Penalties - Yards	5-45

INDIVIDUAL LEADERS
RUSHING
STAN: Nelson 11-36; Finley 7-30.
LSU: Alexander 31-197, 1 TD; Simmons 11-47.
PASSING
STAN: Benjamin 23-36, 269 yards, 3 TD.
LSU: Ensminger 7-21, 55 yards, 1 TD.
RECEIVING
STAN: Lofton 4 -79, 2 TD; Nelson 6-77, 1 TD.
LSU: Simmons 2-26; Quintela 2-11, 1 TD.

DECEMBER 23, 1978 | LIBERTY
MISSOURI 20, LSU 15

	1ST	2ND	3RD	4TH	FINAL
MO	7	13	0	0	20
LSU	3	0	6	6	15

SCORING SUMMARY
MO	Grant 13 run (Brockhaus kick)
LSU	FG Conway 37
MO	Winslow 16 pass from Bradley (Brockhaus kick)
MO	Wilder 3 run (kick failed)
LSU	Alexander 1 run (kick failed)
LSU	Woodley 1 run (pass failed)

MO	TEAM STATISTICS	LSU
18	First Downs	12
200	Rushing Yards	194
11-21-1	Passing	14-31-4
117	Passing Yards	170
317	Total Yards	364
6-38.3	Punts - Average	4-36.5
0-0	Fumbles - Lost	2-1
8-75	Penalties - Yards	6-49

INDIVIDUAL LEADERS
RUSHING
MO: Wilder 28-115, 1 TD; Gant 6.-46.
LSU: Alexander 24-133, 1 TD.
PASSING
MO: Bradley 11-21-1, 117 yards, 1 TD.
LSU: Woodley 9-22-2, 123 yards.
RECEIVING
MO: Wilder 4-20.
LSU: Quintella 6-81; Carson 6-77.

DECEMBER 22, 1979 | TANGERINE
LSU 34, WAKE FOREST 10

	1ST	2ND	3RD	4TH	FINAL
LSU	14	10	0	10	34
WFU	0	3	7	0	10

SCORING SUMMARY
LSU	Woodley 13 run (Barthel kick)
LSU	Woodley 3 run (Barthel kick)
LSU	Murphree 19 pass from Woodley (Barthel kick)
LSU	FG Barthel 31
WFU	FG Denfeld 43
WFU	Baumgardner 34 pass from Venuto (Harnish kick)
LSU	FG Barthel 41
LSU	Ensminger 4 run (Barthel kick)

LSU	TEAM STATISTICS	WFU
24	First Downs	16
258	Rushing Yards	30
16-26-1	Passing	15-30-4
273	Passing Yards	233
531	Total Yards	263
2-38.5	Punts - Average	7-36.9
2-2	Fumbles - Lost	4-1
6-44	Penalties - Yards	4-30

INDIVIDUAL LEADERS
RUSHING
LSU: Woodley 10-68, 2 TD; Hernandez 14-58.
WFU: McDougald 15-54; Ventresca 2-19.
PASSING
LSU: Woodley 11-19-1, 199 yards, 1 TD.
WFU: Venuto 10-20-3, 165 yards, 1 TD.
RECEIVING
LSU: Carson 3-76; Porter 3-73.
WFU: Baumgardner 6-128, 1 TD; McDougald 2-30.

JANUARY 1, 1983 | ORANGE
NEBRASKA 21, LSU 20

	1ST	2ND	3RD	4TH	FINAL
NEB	7	0	7	7	21
LSU	7	7	3	3	20

SCORING SUMMARY
NEB	Schellen 5 run (Seibel kick)
LSU	Hilliard 1 run (Betanzos kick)
LSU	Hilliard 1 run (Betanzos kick)
LSU	FG Betanzos 28
NEB	Rozier 11 pass from Gill (Seibel kick)
NEB	Gill 1 run (Seibel kick)
LSU	FG Betanzos 49

NEB	TEAM STATISTICS	LSU
22	First Downs	12
219	Rushing Yards	38
13-22-2	Passing	14-30-2
184	Passing Yards	173
403	Total Yards	211
1-31.0	Punts - Average	6-39.2
4-4	Fumbles - Lost	1-0
4-25	Penalties - Yards	8-54
34:32	Possession Time	25:28

INDIVIDUAL LEADERS
RUSHING
NEB: Rozier 26-118.
LSU: Hilliard 18-29, 2 TD.
PASSING
NEB: Gill 13-22-2, 184 yards, 1 TD.
LSU: Risher 14-30-2, 173 yards.
RECEIVING
NEB: Fryar 5-84.
LSU: Hilliard 5-82.

JANUARY 1, 1985 | SUGAR
NEBRASKA 28, LSU 10

	1ST	2ND	3RD	4TH	FINAL
NEB	0	7	7	14	28
LSU	3	7	0	0	10

SCORING SUMMARY
LSU	FG Lewis 37
LSU	Hilliard 2 run (Lewis kick)
NEB	DuBose 31 pass from Sundberg (Klein kick)
NEB	Sundberg 9 run (Klein kick)
NEB	Frain 24 pass from Sundberg (Klein kick)
NEB	Frain 17 pass from Sundberg (Klein kick)

NEB	TEAM STATISTICS	LSU
23	First Downs	21
280	Rushing Yards	183
10-18-3	Passing	20-38-5
143	Passing Yards	221
423	Total Yards	404

INDIVIDUAL LEADERS
RUSHING
NEB: DuBose 102 yards.
LSU: Hilliard 16-86, 1 TD.
PASSING
NEB: Sundberg 10-15-3, 143 yards, 3 TD.
LSU: Wickersham 20-37-5, 221 yards.
RECEIVING
NEB: Frain 4-53, 2 TD.
LSU: James 4-25.

DECEMBER 27, 1985 | LIBERTY
BAYLOR 21, LSU 7

	1ST	2ND	3RD	4TH	FINAL
BU	7	3	3	8	21
LSU	7	0	0	0	7

SCORING SUMMARY
LSU	Jefferson 79 punt return (Lewis kick)
BU	Clark 5 pass from Carlson (Syler kick)
BU	FG Syler 23
BU	FG Syler 35
BU	Simpson 15 pass from Carlson (Clark pass from Carlson)

BU	TEAM STATISTICS	LSU
26	First Downs	9
215	Rushing Yards	91
18-30-0	Passing	13-27-1
274	Passing Yards	101
489	Total Yards	192
6-31.5	Punts - Average	8-40.6
6-40	Penalties - Yards	5-41
37:14	Possession Time	22:46

INDIVIDUAL LEADERS
RUSHING
BU: Perry 7-45, Rutledge 10-36.
LSU: Hilliard 20-66.

PASSING
BU: Carlson 9-12-0, 161 yards, 2 TD.
LSU: Wickersham 11-24-1, 95 yards.

RECEIVING
BU: Simpson 3-117, 1 TD; Clark 3-31, 1 TD.
LSU: James 4-25.

JANUARY 1, 1987 | SUGAR
NEBRASKA 30, LSU 15

	1ST	2ND	3RD	4TH	FINAL
NU	0	10	7	13	30
LSU	7	0	0	8	15

SCORING SUMMARY
LSU	Williams 1 run (Browndyke kick)
NU	FG Klein 42
NU	Taylor 2 run (Klein kick)
NU	Knox 1 run (Klein kick)
NU	Millikan 3 pass from Taylor (Klein kick)
NU	Knox 1 run (kick failed)
LSU	Moss 24 pass from Hodson (Lee pass from Hodson)

NU	TEAM STATISTICS	LSU
22	First Downs	10
242	Rushing Yards	32
11-20-0	Passing	14-30-1
110	Passing Yards	159
352	Total Yards	191

INDIVIDUAL LEADERS
RUSHING
NU: Knox 16-84 yards, 2 TD.
LSU: Williams 12-48, 1 TD.

PASSING
NU: Taylor 11-19-0, 110 yards, 1 TD.
LSU: Hodson 14-30-1, 159 yards, 1 TD.

RECEIVING
NU: Banderas 4-42.
LSU: Davis 3-63.

DECEMBER 31, 1987 | GATOR
LSU 30, SOUTH CAROLINA 13

	1ST	2ND	3RD	4TH	FINAL
LSU	14	6	7	3	30
SC	3	3	0	7	13

SCORING SUMMARY
LSU	Davis 39 pass from Hodson (Browndyke kick)
LSU	Davis 12 pass from Hodson (Browndyke kick)
SC	FG Mackie 44
LSU	FG Browndyke 27
SC	FG Mackie 39
LSU	FG Browndyke 18
LSU	Davis 25 pass from Hodson (Browndyke kick)
SC	Green 10 run (Mackie kick)
LSU	FG Browndyke 23

LSU	TEAM STATISTICS	SC
17	First Downs	21
122	Rushing Yards	25
20-32-0	Passing	28-47-4
224	Passing Yards	304
346	Total Yards	329
3-37.6	Punts - Average	2-40.5
5-3	Fumbles - Lost	2-1
10-107	Penalties - Yards	6-49

INDIVIDUAL LEADERS
RUSHING
LSU: Fuller 14-48; Martin 8-38.
SC: Green 15-72, 1 TD; Bethea 1-9.

PASSING
LSU: Hodson 20-32-0, 224 yards, 3 TD.
SC: Ellis 28-47-4, 304 yards.

RECEIVING
LSU: Davis 9-132, 3 TD; Martin 3-43.
SC: Smith 4-79; Bethea 4-69; Sharpe 6-53.

JANUARY 2, 1989 | HALL OF FAME
SYRACUSE 23, LSU 10

	1ST	2ND	3RD	4TH	FINAL
SYR	7	3	7	6	23
LSU	0	0	3	0	10

SCORING SUMMARY
SYR	Drummond 2 run (Greene kick)
SYR	FG Greene 38
LSU	Windom 19 run (Browndyke kick)
LSU	FG Browndyke 35
SYR	Drummond 1 run (Greene kick)
SYR	Glover 4 pass from Philcox (kick failed)

SYR	TEAM STATISTICS	LSU
24	First Downs	14
208	Rushing Yards	76
16-23-0	Passing	18-35-3
130	Passing Yards	221
338	Total Yards	297
0-0	Punt Returns - Yards	2-6
3-47	Kickoff Returns - Yards	4-69
5-39.6	Punts - Average	3-32.0
1-0	Fumbles - Lost	0-0
4-37	Penalties - Yards	5-48
34:08	Possession Time	25:52

INDIVIDUAL LEADERS
RUSHING
SYR: Drummond 23-122, 2 TD; Johnston 19-74.
LSU: Windom 7-32, 1 TD; Jones 4-25.

PASSING
SYR: Philcox 16-23-0, 130 yards, 1 TD.
LSU: Hodson 16-33-3, 192 yards.

RECEIVING
SYR: Moore 6-56; Glover 4-41, 1 TD.
LSU: Moss 5-96; Fuller 5-53.

DECEMBER 29, 1995 | INDEPENDENCE
LSU 45, MICHIGAN STATE 26

	1ST	2ND	3RD	4TH	FINAL
LSU	7	14	21	3	45
MSU	7	17	0	2	26

SCORING SUMMARY
MSU	Muhammed 78 pass from Banks (Gardner kick)
LSU	Cleveland 6 run (LaFleur kick)
MSU	Greene 3 run (kick blocked)
MSU	Mason 100 kick return (Greene run)
MSU	FG Gardner 37
LSU	Kennison 92 kick return (LaFleur kick)
LSU	Faulk 51 run (LaFleur kick)
LSU	Faulk 5 run (LaFleur kick)
LSU	Northern 37 fumble return (LaFleur kick)
LSU	Kennison 27 pass from Tyler (LaFleur kick)
LSU	FG Richey 48
MSU	Safety

LSU	TEAM STATISTICS	MSU
17	First Downs	23
272	Rushing Yards	100
10-20-1	Passing	22-44-3
164	Passing Yards	348
436	Total Yards	448
4-150	Kickoff Returns - Yards	7-158
4-44.5	Punts - Average	6-37.5
2-1	Fumbles - Lost	4-3
5-42	Penalties - Yards	9-80

INDIVIDUAL LEADERS
RUSHING
LSU: Faulk 25-234, 2 TD.
MSU: Renaud 16-79.

PASSING
LSU: Tyler 10-20-1, 164 yards, 1 TD.
MSU: Banks 22-44-3, 348 yards, 1 TD.

RECEIVING
LSU: Kennison 5-124, 1 TD.
MSU: Muhammed 9-171, 1 TD.

DECEMBER 28, 1996 | PEACH
LSU 10, CLEMSON 7

	1ST	2ND	3RD	4TH	FINAL
LSU	0	10	0	0	10
CLEM	7	0	0	0	7

SCORING SUMMARY
CLEM	Greene 5 run (Padgett kick)
LSU	Faulk 3 run (Richey kick)
LSU	FG Richey 22

LSU	TEAM STATISTICS	CLEM
17	First Downs	12
124	Rushing Yards	192
14-21-0	Passing	6-20-0
163	Passing Yards	66
287	Total Yards	258
7-42.3	Punts - Average	10-38.2
3-1	Fumbles - Lost	3-2
7-43	Penalties - Yards	7-69
30:15	Possession Time	29:45

INDIVIDUAL LEADERS
RUSHING
LSU: Faulk 23-64, 1 TD; Tyler 12-38.
CLEM: Priester 25-151; Smith 9-40.

PASSING
LSU: Tyler 14-21-0, 163 yards.
CLEM: Greene 6-20-0, 66 yards.

RECEIVING
LSU: LaFleur 4-63; Savoie 2-40.
CLEM: Smith 2-25; Woods 1-22.

DECEMBER 28, 1997 | INDEPENDENCE
LSU 27, NOTRE DAME 9

	1ST	2ND	3RD	4TH	FINAL
LSU	0	3	10	14	27
ND	3	3	0	3	9

SCORING SUMMARY
ND	FG Cengia 33
LSU	FG Richey 37
ND	FG Cengia 21
LSU	FG Richey 42
LSU	Booty 12 pass from Tyler (Richey kick)
ND	FG Cengia 33
LSU	Mealey 2 run (Richey kick)
LSU	Mealey 1 run (Richey kick)

LSU	TEAM STATISTICS	ND
19	First Downs	19
265	Rushing Yards	128
5-12-0	Passing	13-25-0
61	Passing Yards	115
326	Total Yards	243
3-38	Punt Returns - Yards	2-23
2-34	Kickoff Returns - Yards	4-61
4-35.8	Punts - Average	5-45.0
0-0	Fumbles - Lost	1-1
5-55	Penalties - Yards	5-30

INDIVIDUAL LEADERS
RUSHING
LSU: Mealey 34-222, 2 TD.
ND: Denson 20-101.
PASSING
LSU: Tyler 5-12-0, 61 yards, 1 TD.
ND: Powlus 8-18-0, 66 yards.
RECEIVING
LSU: Booty 5-61, 1 TD.
ND: Johnson 5-49.

DECEMBER 29, 2000 | PEACH
LSU 28, GEORGIA TECH 14

	1ST	2ND	3RD	4TH	FINAL
LSU	3	0	6	19	28
GT	7	7	0	0	14

SCORING SUMMARY
LSU	FG Corbello 32
GT	Burns 32 run (Manget kick)
GT	Hatch 9 run (Manget kick)
LSU	Banks 3 pass from Davey (Corbello kick)
LSU	Reed 9 pass from Davey (Reed pass from Davey)
LSU	FG Corbello 49
LSU	Banks 3 pass from Davey (Robinson pass from Davey)

LSU	TEAM STATISTICS	GT
21	First Downs	19
90	Rushing Yards	140
25-44-0	Passing	19-38-2
284	Passing Yards	177
374	Total Yards	317
8-40.8	Punts - Average	5-48.2
3-1	Fumbles - Lost	7-4
7-59	Penalties - Yards	6-45
37:10	Possession Time	22:50

INDIVIDUAL LEADERS
RUSHING
LSU: Toefield 22-78; Davis 8-25.
GT: Burns 17-96, 1 TD; Hatch 6-45, 1 TD.
PASSING
LSU: Davey 17-25-0, 174 yards, 3 TD; Booty 8-19-0, 110 yards.
GT: Godsey 19-36-2, 177 yards.
RECEIVING
LSU: Reed 9-96, 1 TD; Banks 7-71, 2 TD.
GT: Watkins 3-45; Campbell 5-31.

JANUARY 1, 2002 | SUGAR
LSU 47, ILLINOIS 34

	1ST	2ND	3RD	4TH	FINAL
LSU	7	27	7	6	47
ILL	0	7	14	13	34

SCORING SUMMARY
LSU	Davis 4 run (Corbello kick)
LSU	Davis 25 run (Corbello kick)
LSU	Davis 16 run (Corbello kick)
LSU	Reed 5 pass from Davey (Corbello kick)
ILL	Hodges 2 pas from Kittner (Christofilakos kick)
LSU	Royal 7 pass from Davey (Corbello kick)
ILL	Lloyd 17 pass from Kittner (Christofilakos kick)
LSU	Reed 32 pass from Davey (Corbello kick)
ILL	Lloyd 10 pass from Kittner (Christofilakos kick)
ILL	Young 17 pass from Kittner (Christofilakos kick)
LSU	Davis 4 run (pass failed)
ILL	Young 40 pass from Lloyd (pass failed)

LSU	TEAM STATISTICS	ILL
32	First Downs	14
151	Rushing Yards	61
31-53-0	Passing	15-36-1
444	Passing Yards	302
595	Total Yards	363
3-36	Punt Returns - Yards	2-9
6-147	Kickoff Returns - Yards	5-89
8-39.4	Punts - Average	9-40.4
2-1	Fumbles - Lost	1-1
13-113	Penalties - Yards	4-39
39:16	Possession Time	20:44

INDIVIDUAL LEADERS
RUSHING
LSU: Davis 28-129, 4 TD; Henderson 13-55.
ILL: Harvey 9-42.
PASSING
LSU: Davey 31-53-0, 444 yards, 3 TD.
ILL: Kittner 14-35-1, 262 yards, 4 TD.
RECEIVING
LSU: Reed 14-239, 2 TD; Clayton 8-120.
ILL: Young 6-178, 2 TD; Lloyd 5-56, 2 TD.

JANUARY 1, 2003 | COTTON
TEXAS 35, LSU 20

	1ST	2ND	3RD	4TH	FINAL
TEX	7	14	7	7	35
LSU	10	7	0	3	20

SCORING SUMMARY
LSU	FG Corbello 26
TEX	Jackson 46 fumble recovery for TD (Mangum kick)
LSU	Toefield 20 pass from Randall (Corbello kick)
LSU	Davis 10 run (Corbello kick)
TEX	R. Williams 51 pass from Simms (Mangum kick)
TEX	Benson 1 run (Mangum kick)
TEX	R. Williams 39 run (Mangum kick)
TEX	I. Williams 8 pass from Simms (Mangum kick)
LSU	FG Corbello 39

TEX	TEAM STATISTICS	LSU
15	First Downs	25
113	Rushing Yards	248
15-28-1	Passing	19-46-1
269	Passing Yards	193
382	Total Yards	441
1-14	Punt Returns - Yards	1-0
4-77	Kickoff Returns - Yards	5-109
7-37.3	Punts - Average	4-48.8
0-0	Fumbles - Lost	3-2
6-60	Penalties - Yards	4-28
23:09	Possession Time	36:51

INDIVIDUAL LEADERS
RUSHING
TEX: Young 11-49; Benson 12-46, 1 TD.
LSU: Davis 13-85, 1 TD; Randall 11-78.
PASSING
TEX: Simms 15-28-1, 269 yards 2 TD.
LSU: Randall 19-45-1, 193 yards, 1 TD.
RECEIVING
TEX: R. Williams 4-142, 1 TD; Thomas 4-59.
LSU: Clayton 6-88; Davis 3-31.

JANUARY 4, 2004 | SUGAR
LSU 21, OKLAHOMA 14

	1ST	2ND	3RD	4TH	FINAL
LSU	7	7	7	0	21
OU	0	7	0	7	14

SCORING SUMMARY
LSU	Green 24 run (Gaudet kick)
OU	Jones 1 run (DiCarlo kick)
LSU	Vincent 18 run (Gaudet kick)
LSU	Spears 20 interception return (Gaudet kick)
OU	Jones 1 run (DiCarlo kick)

LSU	TEAM STATISTICS	OU
13	First Downs	12
159	Rushing Yards	52
14-24-2	Passing	13-37-2
153	Passing Yards	102
312	Total Yards	154
3-26	Punt Returns - Yards	5-36
0-0	Kickoff Returns - Yards	2-24
8-34.0	Punts - Average	8-45.9
1-1	Fumbles - Lost	2-0
8-65	Penalties - Yards	11-70
31:19	Possession Time	28:41

INDIVIDUAL LEADERS
RUSHING
LSU: Vincent 16-117, 1 TD; Mauck 14-27.
OU: Jones 20-59, 2 TD; Clayton 4-38.
PASSING
LSU: Mauck 13-22-2, 124 yards.
OU: White 13-37-2, 102 yards.
RECEIVING
LSU: Jones 3-54; Clayton 4-38.
OU: Clayton 4-32; Wilson 3-31.

JANUARY 1, 2005 | CAPITAL ONE
IOWA 30, LSU 25

	1ST	2ND	3RD	4TH	FINAL
IA	7	7	3	13	30
LSU	0	12	0	13	25

SCORING SUMMARY
IA	Solomon 57 pass from Tate (Schlicher kick)
LSU	FG Jackson 29
LSU	FG Jackson 47
IA	Considine 7 blocked punt return (Schlicher kick)
LSU	Broussard 74 run (kick failed)
IA	FG Schlicher 19
IA	Simmons 4 run (Schlicher kick)
LSU	Green 22 pass from Russell (Jackson kick)
LSU	Green 3 pass from Russell (kick failed)
IA	Holloway 56 pass from Tate

IA	TEAM STATISTICS	LSU
16	First Downs	19
47	Rushing Yards	118
20-32-2	Passing	23-35-1
287	Passing Yards	228
334	Total Yards	346
5-45	Punt Returns - Yards	4-42
5-76	Kickoff Returns - Yards	5-134
6-49.2	Punts - Average	6-30.2
1-0	Fumbles - Lost	1-0
9-50	Penalties - Yards	5-42
25:48	Possession Time	34:12

INDIVIDUAL LEADERS
RUSHING
IA: Simmons 13-35, 1 TD.
LSU: Broussard 13-109, 1 TD.
PASSING
IA: Tate 20-32-2, 287 yards, 2 TD.
LSU: Russell 12-15-0, 128 yards, 2 TD.
RECEIVING
IA: Hinkel 10-93; Solomon 4-81, 1 TD.
LSU: Bowe 8-122; Green 6-59, 2 TD.

DECEMBER 30, 2005 | PEACH
LOUISIANA STATE 40, MIAMI (FLA.) 3

	1ST	2ND	3RD	4TH	FINAL
MIA	3	0	0	0	3
LSU	3	17	14	6	40

SCORING SUMMARY
MIA   FG Peattie 21
LSU   FG Jackson 37
LSU   Davis 51 pass from Flynn (David kick)
LSU   FG Jackson 47
LSU   Addai 4 pass from Flynn (David kick)
LSU   Addai 6 run (David kick)
LSU   Hester 1 run (David kick)
LSU   FG David 35
LSU   FG Jackson 50

MIA	TEAM STATISTICS	LSU
6	First Downs	26
53	Rushing Yards	272
10-23-1	Passing	13-22-0
100	Passing Yards	196
153	Total Yards	468
0-0	Punt Returns - Yards	4-46
3-39	Kickoff Returns - Yards	0-0
8-43.0	Punts - Average	1-41.0
0-0	Fumbles - Lost	1-0
6-40	Penalties - Yards	8-50

INDIVIDUAL LEADERS
RUSHING
MIA: Jones 8-50.
LSU: Addai 24-130, 1 TD.

PASSING
MIA: Wright 10-21-0, 100 yards.
LSU: Flynn 13-22-0, 196 yards, 2 TD.

RECEIVING
MIA: Hill 4-36; Hester 2-40.
LSU: Davis 5-99, 1 TD; Bowe 3-51.

JANUARY 3, 2007 | SUGAR
LOUISIANA STATE 41, NOTRE DAME 14

	1ST	2ND	3RD	4TH	FINAL
ND	7	7	0	0	14
LSU	14	7	13	7	41

SCORING SUMMARY
LSU   Williams 3 run (David kick)
LSU   Bowe 11 pass from Russell (David kick)
ND   Grimes 24 pass from Quinn (Gioia kick)
ND   Samardzija 10 pass from Quinn (Gioia kick)
LSU   Russell 5 run (David kick)
LSU   FG David 25
LSU   FG David 37
LSU   LaFell 58 pass from Russell (David kick)
LSU   Williams 20 run (Gaudet kick)

ND	TEAM STATISTICS	LSU
17	First Downs	31
143	Rushing Yards	245
15-35-2	Passing	21-34-1
148	Passing Yards	332
291	Total Yards	577
0-0	Punt Returns - Yards	1-0
6-128	Kickoff Returns - Yards	3-48
5-47.4	Punts - Average	2-43.5
0-0	Fumbles - Lost	2-1
4-40	Penalties - Yards	9-95

INDIVIDUAL LEADERS
RUSHING
ND: Walker 22-128.
LSU: Williams 14-107, 2 TD.

PASSING
ND: Quinn 15-35-2, 148 yards, 2 TD.
LSU: Russell 21-34-1, 332 yards, 2 TD.

RECEIVING
ND: Samardzija 8-59, 1 TD; McKnight 3-22.
LSU: Doucet 8-115; Bowe 5-78, 1 TD.

JANUARY 7, 2008 | BCS CHAMPIONSHIP
LSU 38, OHIO STATE 24

	1ST	2ND	3RD	4TH	FINAL
LSU	3	21	7	7	38
OSU	10	0	7	7	24

SCORING SUMMARY
OSU   C. Wells 65 run (Pretorius kick)
OSU   FG Pretorius 25
LSU   FG David 32
LSU   Dickson 13 pass from Flynn (David kick)
LSU   LaFell 10 pass from Flynn (David kick)
LSU   Hester 1 run (David kick)
LSU   Doucet 4 pass from Flynn (David kick)
OSU   Robiskie 5 pass from Boeckman (Pretorius kick)
LSU   Dickson 5 pass from Flynn (David kick)
OSU   Hartline 15 pass from Boeckman (Pretorius kick)

LSU	TEAM STATISTICS	OSU
25	First Downs	17
152	Rushing Yards	145
19-27-1	Passing	15-26-2
174	Passing Yards	208
326	Total Yards	353
1-8	Punt Returns - Yards	1-9
2-22	Kickoff Returns - Yards	7-124
3-56.7	Punts - Average	3-50.0
2-0	Fumbles - Lost	3-1
4-36	Penalties - Yards	7-83

INDIVIDUAL LEADERS
RUSHING
LSU: Hester 21-86, 1 TD.
OSU: C. Wells 20-146, 1 TD.

PASSING
LSU: Flynn 19-27-1, 174 yards, 4 TD.
OSU: Boeckman 15-26-2, 208 yards, 2 TD.

RECEIVING
LSU: Doucet 7-51, 1 TD; Dickson 4-44, 2 TD.
OSU: Hartline 6-75, 1 TD; Saine 3-69.

DECEMBER 31, 2008 | CHICK-FIL-A
LOUISIANA STATE 38, GEORGIA TECH 3

	1ST	2ND	3RD	4TH	FINAL
LSU	7	28	3	0	38
GT	3	0	0	0	3

SCORING SUMMARY
LSU   Scott 2 run (David kick)
GT   FG Blair 24
LSU   Scott 4 run (David kick)
LSU   Scott 1 run (David kick)
LSU   Dickson 25 pass from Jefferson (David kick)
LSU   Williams 17 run (David kick)
LSU   FG David 53

LSU	TEAM STATISTICS	GT
19	First Downs	15
161	Rushing Yards	164
17-27-0	Passing	8-25-1
163	Passing Yards	150
324	Total Yards	314
2-36	Punt Returns - Yards	2-11
1-23	Kickoff Returns - Yards	4-87
4-41.5	Punts - Average	3-33.3
1-0	Fumbles - Lost	3-2
6-60	Penalties - Yards	4-40

INDIVIDUAL LEADERS
RUSHING
LSU: Scott 15-65, 3 TD.
GT: Dwyer 10-67.

PASSING
LSU: Jefferson 16-25-0, 142 yards, 1 TD.
GT: Nesbitt 8-24-1, 150 yards.

RECEIVING
LSU: Dickson 4-50, 1 TD; Byrd 3-10.
GT: Dwyer 3-66; Thomas 3-32.

MISSISSIPPI

BY GEOFFREY NORMAN

NO PLACE IS MORE QUINTESSENTIALLY Southern than Oxford, Miss., where William Faulkner wrote his novels and the Ole Miss Rebels play their home games. As Faulkner famously said, "The past is never dead. It's not even past." Mississippi football, which is drenched in nostalgia, might be one of the best arguments for this proposition. The team's nickname, of course, speaks volumes, as does the fact that on gameday, the stadium was, until recently, filled with Confederate flags. (Since the school couldn't legally ban flags without getting into First Amendment difficulties, it did the next best thing and banned sticks.) Mississippi was, needless to say, one of the last of the all-white football teams. Mercifully, those days are largely unmourned.

Leaving the troubling questions of race aside, there is something about Mississippi football that seems to long for the past and its glories, both real and imagined. As the 21st century approached, it appeared the Rebels' best seasons were behind them. The 1950s—when Ole Miss ruled the SEC—was the golden epoch. Time, it seemed, had passed Ole Miss by. SEC powers such as Florida, Tennessee and Georgia were too big, too powerful, too New South. Mississippi was still a small, rural, largely agrarian state and couldn't hope to compete.

Ole Miss football experienced a renaissance, however, in the late 1990s and into the opening years of the 21st century under coaches Tommy Tuberville and David Cutliffe. And then came something of an apotheosis (to use a good, Faulknerian word) when a quarterback with a storied name out of the Ole Miss past—Manning—took the Rebels to a 10–3 record in 2003, the co-championship of the SEC West and a victory in the Cotton Bowl. After Eli departed for the NFL, football fortunes at Ole Miss began to decline again. In 2007, the team lost all their conference games. But that, too, changed with the arrival of a new coach, Houston Nutt, who took the Rebels on a remarkable run that included beating eventual national champ Florida on the road and a Cotton Bowl victory over Texas Tech, a team that had been ranked No. 2 through mid-November. The Rebels were relevant again.

TRADITION Near the center of the Ole Miss campus, there's a 10-acre plot shaded by oak trees and carpeted in lush grass. This is the Grove, and it is where

PROFILE

University of Mississippi
Oxford, Miss.
Founded: 1844
Enrollment: 17,325
Colors: Cardinal Red and Navy Blue
Nickname: Rebels
Stadium: Vaught-Hemingway
Stadium/Hollingsworth Field
    Opened in 1915
    AstroPlay; 60,580 capacity
First football game: 1893
All-time record: 602–468–35 (.563)
Bowl record: 20–12
Consensus national championships:
1936-present: 1 (1960)
Southeastern Conference championships:
6 (outright)
First-round draft choices: 17
Website: www.olemisssports.collegesports.com

THE BEST OF TIMES

At the height of John Vaught's reign, from 1954 to 1963, the Rebels went 90–13–4 and played in eight major bowl games.

THE WORST OF TIMES

From 1972 to 1985, the Rebels were ineffectual, never able to win more than six games in any single season.

CONFERENCE

In 1933, after 11 years in the Southern Conference, Ole Miss became a charter member of the SEC.

DISTINGUISHED ALUMNI

Haley Barbour, Mississippi governor; Kate Jackson, actress; Trent Lott, U.S. senator; Gerald McRaney, actor; Jeanne Shaheen, New Hampshire governor; Roosevelt Skerrit, prime minister of Dominica; Shepard Smith, news anchor

> *Archie Manning never won a national or an SEC title, but he is a legend in the state.*

fans gather on gameday to tailgate in a fashion that is redolent of the Old South. The women are drop-dead gorgeous, wearing dresses and sometimes even hats, as if it's still 1959. The men wear ties … well, many of them, anyway. There are cocktails—plenty of them. And of course, there is mouthwatering food, some served on china with linen napkins to dab that spot of mayonnaise from your cheek. It is, easily, the most gracious, civilized tailgating scene in all of football and is so seductive that at kickoff, many seats remain empty. Some people just can't quit the party.

In 1983, coach Billy Brewer was looking for a way to let his players in on the Grove experience. So two hours before kickoff, he walked the team from the athletic dormitory, across the campus, to the stadium. The walk took them through the Grove, down a gauntlet of adoring fans. In 1998, the 1962 team, whose 10–0 record remains the Rebels' only perfect season, made a gift to Ole Miss of an arch, erected at the east end of the Grove. Now the players enter the Grove under the Walk of Champions Arch.

STADIUM Naturally, a program so in love with the past plays in a stadium born way back when. In 1915, students helped lay the foundation and erect the first

grandstand of what is now Vaught-Hemingway Stadium at Hollingsworth Field. In 1950, an 80-yard press box was added, and by 1980 capacity was 41,000. Renovations completed in 2002 brought capacity to 60,580, making it the state's largest facility. Judge William Hemingway, professor of law and longtime chairman of the Committee on Athletics, is the namesake. John Howard Vaught, legendary Ole Miss coach, was added in 1982. In 1998, the field was named for Dr. Jerry Hollingsworth for "his continuing generous support to the entire Ole Miss athletic department."

BEST PLAYER Archie Manning never won a national championship or an SEC title. His most memorable performance was in a nationally televised, primetime loss. He is, nevertheless, a legend in Mississippi, where his gutsiness is considered the ideal to which all Rebels players should aspire. Manning lost games, but somehow he was never defeated. In his career, Manning threw for 4,753 yards and ran—mostly in wonderfully improvised and daring scrambles—for another 823. The second player selected in the 1971 NFL draft, Manning played brilliantly for the hapless New Orleans Saints. Manning and Chucky Mullins

FIGHT SONG

FORWARD REBELS

Forward, Rebels, march to fame,
Hit that line and win this game
We know that you'll fight it through,
For your colors red and blue.
Rah, rah, rah!
Rebels you are the Southland's pride,
Take that ball and hit your stride,
Don't stop till the victory's won
for your Ole Miss.
Fight, fight for your Ole Miss!

FIRST-ROUND DRAFT CHOICES

1939	Parker Hall, Rams (3)
1942	Merle Hapes, Giants (8)
1954	Ed Beatty, Rams (10)
1961	Bobby Crespino, Browns (10)
1963	Jim Dunaway, Vikings (3)
1966	Stan Hindman, 49ers (11)
1966	Mike Dennis, Bills (8)*
1971	Archie Manning, Saints (2)
1985	Freddie Joe Nunn, Cardinals (18)
1990	Tony Bennett, Packers (18)
1991	Kelvin Pritchett, Cowboys (20)
1994	Tim Bowens, Dolphins (20)
1998	John Avery, Dolphins (29)
2001	Deuce McAllister, Saints (23)
2004	Eli Manning, Chargers (1)
2005	Chris Spencer, Seahawks (26)
2007	Patrick Willis, 49ers (11)
2009	Michael Oher, Ravens (23)
2009	Peria Jerry, Falcons (24)

*From 1960-1966, the NFL and AFL held separate, competing drafts

CONSENSUS ALL-AMERICANS

1947	Charlie Conerly, B
1953	Crawford Mims, G
1959	Charlie Flowers, B
1960	Jake Gibbs, B
1962	Jim Dunaway, T
1979	Jim Miller, P
1992	Everett Lindsay, OL
1998	Rufus French, TE
2001	Terrence Metcalf, OL
2006	Patrick Willis, LB
2008	Michael Oher, OL

(who, tragically, was paralyzed in a homecoming game) are the only Ole Miss players whose jerseys have been retired.

There was talk of retiring the number worn by another Manning—Eli—but that has died down. In tribute to the legendary Ole Miss family, the road leading to the new $18 million indoor practice facility was named Manning Way.

BEST COACH In 1946, Harold "Red" Drew was head coach at Mississippi and the fans were expecting big things. Then, after just one season, Drew left for Alabama to replace Frank Thomas, and John Vaught, his line coach, took over. Vaught's team won the SEC in his first year as head coach, going 9–2. Quarterback Charlie Conerly finished fourth in the Heisman voting and life was good at Ole Miss. Vaught won another five SEC titles before he stepped down for health reasons in 1970. He returned to the sideline three games into the 1973 season and then retired for good. Three of Vaught's teams were named national champions by various ratings services. From 1950 to 1959, Ole Miss was 80–21–5. Only Oklahoma had a better record during that decade. Vaught's teams put up just one losing record in his near quarter century at Ole Miss, giving him a final mark of 190–61–12. His record at home was 57–6–2, including one string of 34 games without a defeat.

Still, Vaught was about more than numbers. On the one hand, the man was an innovator who brought the split-T to Southern football and won games on the arms of passing quarterbacks such as Conerly, Jake Gibbs and Manning. But defense is what fans remember Vaught's teams for (and, this being Mississippi, they do remember). In 1959, Ole Miss gave up exactly three touchdowns on the way to a 10–1 record. This team routinely punted the ball on first or second down, because for them the best offense truly was a good— make that *phenomenal*—defense.

BEST TEAM The 1959 group was named SEC Team of the Decade in an AP poll. Rightfully so. The Rebels were named national champions by four different ratings services. Had it not been for their one loss, they would doubtless have been consensus champs. That loss came on Halloween on a mythic punt return by LSU's Billy Cannon. Mississippi got a chance for atonement in the Sugar Bowl, when they handled LSU, 21-0. Fittingly, the Rebels allowed the Tigers just six first downs and 74 yards total offense in the shutout. Case closed.

COLLEGE FOOTBALL HALL OF FAME INDUCTEES		
NAME	YEARS	INDUCTED
Bruiser Kinard, T	1935-37	1951
Edwin Hale, QB	1915-16, '20-21	1963
Charlie Conerly, HB	1942, '46-47	1966
Barney Poole, E	1942-48	1974
John H. Vaught, COACH	1947-70, '73	1979
Archie Manning, QB	1968-70	1989
Parker Hall, HB	1936-38	1991
Jake Gibbs, QB	1958-60	1995
Charlie Flowers, FB	1957-59	1997

PRO FOOTBALL HALL OF FAME INDUCTEES		
NAME	YEARS	INDUCTED
Gene Hickerson, G	1958-73	2007
Bruiser Kinard, T	1938-47	1971

BEST DEFENSE Among many great defensive teams of the Vaught era, none is remembered as well nor as fondly as the 1959 unit that led the nation in scoring defense, allowing a Scrooge-like 1.9 points per game and shutting out eight opponents. The Rebels gave up just three touchdowns that year: one by rushing, one by passing and one by (Billy Cannon) magic. They were, otherwise, just about perfect and have remained so in memory.

BEST BACKFIELD The best backfield in Rebels football history does not, interestingly, include a starter named Manning. Perhaps that's because when they were at Oxford, Archie and Eli tended to take over the show and leave their supporting cast in the shadows. That was not the case with quarterback Romaro Miller during the 2000 season. He passed for 2,012 yards and his backfield mates, Deuce McAllister and Joe Gunn, ran for 1,205. McAllister is the No. 1 rusher in Rebels history. Gunn is No. 2. In career passing yardage, among Ole Miss quarterbacks Miller is ranked second behind his 2000 backup, Eli.

STORYBOOK SEASON Things started off on the wrong foot in 2003. The Rebels were 2–2, staring mediocrity in the face after high preseason hopes. Then quarterback Eli Manning, son of the sainted Archie, took control. Mississippi finished with a 10–3 record and tied for the lead in the SEC West (with eventual co-national champion LSU). The Rebels beat Oklahoma State in the Cotton Bowl and Eli outdid his father, getting picked one spot higher—first overall—in the 2004 NFL draft.

The 2008 season would come in a close second. In Nutt's first season at the helm, Ole Miss opened 3–4, then ran the table. A Cotton Bowl win over Texas Tech gave the Rebels a record of 9–4 and a No. 14 ranking in the AP poll.

BIGGEST GAME Ole Miss was unranked on Oct. 5, 2002, when mighty Florida came to town ranked sixth in the country. The Gators had a national championship on their minds and quarterback Rex Grossman was a leading Heisman contender. Ole Miss and Eli Manning were 13-point underdogs. The crowd of 61,000—the second-highest ever to attend a game on the Mississippi campus—saw Manning complete 18 of 33 attempts for 254 yards and Mississippi come back from a 14-2 halftime deficit to surprise the Gators, 17-14. The next season, Manning and the confident Rebels did it to the No. 24

Gators again, 20-17, this time at the Swamp. In 2008, Ole Miss made it seem routine. The Rebels toppled the Gators yet again at the Swamp, the only pothole in Florida's march to a national championship.

BIGGEST UPSET One of many powerful Notre Dame squads came to Jackson on Sept. 17, 1977. An Irish backup quarterback named Joe Montana watched helplessly from the bench as Rebels fullback James Storey caught two touchdown passes in the 20-13 Ole Miss victory. The Irish went on to run the table, finishing with a win over Texas in the Cotton Bowl that earned them a national championship.

HEARTBREAKER On Oct. 4, 1969, Mississippi played Alabama at Legion Field in Birmingham in the first regular-season college football game televised in prime time. The halftime score, with the Tide up 14-7, was ordinary enough. But in the second half, a shootout erupted between Archie Manning and Alabama's Scott Hunter, each matching the other touchdown for touchdown. Two coaches raised on the old SEC religion of defense and running had, it appeared, lost their minds. In the final minutes, Alabama trailed by five facing fourth and 18. Bear Bryant told his quarterback, "Run the best thing you've got." It was good enough for a touchdown and Ole Miss lost, 33-32, in what ABC's Chris Schenkel said was "the greatest duel two quarterbacks ever had. You had to be there to believe it." Manning was 33 of 52 for 436 yards. He ran for 104 and was responsible for five touchdowns, all told. When Bryant greeted Vaught, an old friend, in the middle of the field after the game, he said, "Wasn't that the worst college football game you've ever seen?" Vaught, also a disciple of defense, agreed.

WILDEST FINISH Another loss, this time to Arkansas on Nov. 3, 2001, after seven overtimes and by a mountain-high 58-56 score. Ole Miss was going for the two-point conversion that would have sent the marathon into an eighth overtime when Jermaine Petty stopped tight end Doug Zeigler just shy of the goal line. The media had been invited to come down to the sideline from the press box with five minutes to go in regulation. An hour and 10 minutes later, the game finally ended, lasting a total of 4:14; the contest would be the longest game in Division I-A that season.

BEST GOAL-LINE STAND On Nov. 28, 1992, Ole Miss defeated rival Mississippi State, 17-10. Not overly impressive until you consider that the Bulldogs ran 11 plays inside the Rebels' 10-yard line in the final 2:30 but failed to even the score.

BEST COMEBACK At one point during a Sept. 26, 1998, game, the Rebels found themselves trailing

Southern Methodist by a 41-19 margin. Then Ole Miss scored 22 unanswered points in the final 10 minutes of regulation. They finished the job in overtime, claiming an improbable 48-41 victory.

RIVAL LSU gets the nod, with Mississippi State finishing a close second. The Tigers and the Rebels battled for SEC and national championships in the late 1950s, adding heat to the rivalry. In 1959, Mississippi might have gone undefeated had it not been for a sensational punt return by LSU's Cannon that led to a 7-3 loss. The in-state rivalry with the Bulldogs is known as the Battle for the Golden Egg. The "egg" is actually a trophy shaped like an old-time football, which Ole Miss has won consistently over the decades.

NICKNAME The team became the Rebels in 1936. A student newspaper–sponsored contest yielded 200 entries and this one, from a Vicksburg judge, was the clear winner among the newsmen asked to choose from five finalists. Although flying the Confederate battle flag rubbed emotions in the state exceedingly raw in the 1980s and hurt Ole Miss' efforts to recruit black players, the nickname has not seemed to inspire the same kind of bad feelings.

UNIFORMS In 1893, when Ole Miss was about to field its first football team, a discussion about school colors took place. The team manager suggested that a union of the crimson of Harvard and navy blue of Yale would be "very harmonious and that it was well to have the spirit of both of these good colleges." There has long been gray in the color scheme, which for better or worse evokes the South and the Civil War. Another remnant of that time was the Colonel Rebel logo on the team's helmets, which was discontinued after the 1982 season, less than a decade after the football team was integrated. Colonel Rebel was ousted as a sideline mascot in 2003—although the logo is still licensed by Ole Miss and appears on stationery, coffee cups and other souvenirs.

TRAGEDY Defensive back Chucky Mullins, paralyzed during the 1989 homecoming game, became a national hero for his courage and good cheer. During Mullins' rehab, President George H. W. Bush, among other notables, visited him. Shortly after returning to the university to resume work on his degree, he stopped breathing, lost consciousness and died on May 1, 1991. An award in his name is given to the Rebels' outstanding defensive player and an annual banquet in his honor raises funds to assist Ole Miss students who have been the victims of serious accidents.

QUOTE "I may give out but I'll never give up."
—Chucky Mullins

From Dixie With Love

By Wright Thompson

I close my eyes.

The air smells like sweat and fresh grass. I am standing on the sideline of the Ole Miss practice field in the shadow of Vaught-Hemingway. I glance over and watch for a moment as they paint the word "Rebels" on the outside of the stadium. Today they are also cleaning the inside, then stocking it as if for a long voyage. Big dragonflies buzz around like fighter jets. The sky is Ole Miss blue. For a moment, I stand there, just letting the sounds of football cover me. The thump of a foot on a ball, toe to leather. A sudden shriek of a whistle. The screams of a linebacker: "Tall right! Raider! Raider!" The coach screaming even louder: "Tempo! Tempo!" The calm, measured words of the quarterback: "Blue 43 ... Blue 43 ... Hut ... Hut."

The coach claps and the entire team claps with him, the sun shining off the blue helmets of young men from all over the country, from California to the Mississippi Delta, young men who can never truly appreciate how many hopes and dreams hang on their actions every Saturday afternoon. The coach understands. "Nowhere to hide!" he yells. "Nowhere to hide today. We're watching everything you do. Everything counts. Let's rock and roll."

I leave practice for a moment, wandering inside the cool belly of the stadium, then out into the bowl, working row by row, section by section, over to my family's seats. Section O, row 61, seats 1 to 4. There are about a dozen folks in the entire stadium when I sit down, relaxing in the shadow of the upper deck, picturing this place full, imagining what that holy noise will be like. Chill bumps run up and down my arm. The only sound today comes from the gas-powered pressure washers, pushing 3,700 pounds of

water per square inch, making sure this place is spotless.

I love these seats. I love that my late father picked them out, carefully measuring the distance to car and restroom and elevator and concession stands. I love that Stephen Wiley Vaught sits just a few rows over from us. He was my daddy's college roommate, maybe his best friend in the world, and not long ago he

> *Practice comes to a close—just a few weeks before the first game. The town is alive. Courthouse Square in the center of Oxford is jumping. The Grove is ready for action. Classes started last week. Football season's not coming any longer. It's here.*

summed up attending the installation of a new Episcopal bishop thusly, without irony: "I haven't seen anything this impressive since Archie Manning's junior year."

I love seeing former Ole Miss coach Billy Brewer jog past the practice field with his shirt off. Once, he was king of this town. Then scandal, a firing and a lawsuit against the school tore down his throne. But I love that he still comes. I wonder whether he hears the echoes. I imagine we all do. I think he does for sure. Once, he asked a stranger to sit in the cab of his pickup truck and listen to Elvis Presley sing "Dixie." Yes, he remembers. And there he is now, stopped on a concourse, peering

down into the heat, watching another coach scream at the Ole Miss Rebels, "No free lunches out here!"

Practice comes to a close—just a few weeks before the first game. The town is alive. Courthouse Square in the center of Oxford is jumping. The Grove is ready for action. Classes started last week. Football season's not *coming* any longer. It's *here*. A few hours later, I stick my head into the first band practice of the year. "Pride of the South," it reads on the side of the building. They're in a semicircle, flutes and piccolos in front, working up to the shining sousaphones in the back.

Finally, after months of waiting, it happens. The first slow "Dixie." The title on the sheet music says, "From Dixie With Love." The drums start first. Then an A-flat, an F, a D-flat and we're off. The trumpets and mellophones come in. Then the bass drums boom heavily. The snares rattle, the drummers jump up and down. Rising tidal waves of brass, each reaching higher than the one before, carry everyone along for the ride. The band is going full speed, gameday speed, low to the ground and accelerating, a trombone player tapping his foot. Cymbals crash, the notes bouncing around the room, playing a song for our fathers and for our children.

I close my eyes once more and I see an ocean of red and blue, grandmothers in Chanel and frat boys in Widespread Panic hats. I see Stephen Wiley Vaught in seersucker and white bucks. I see the green grass of the Grove and the young boys wearing replica jerseys. I see my mama unloading a tailgate and I see my daddy smiling outside the stadium with a piece of fried chicken in his hand.

I see home.

Wright Thompson *is a senior writer for ESPN.com and* ESPN The Magazine. *He lives with his wife, Sonia, in Oxford, Miss. His Vaught-Hemingway season tickets are in Section O.*

MISSISSIPPI ALL-TIME SCORES

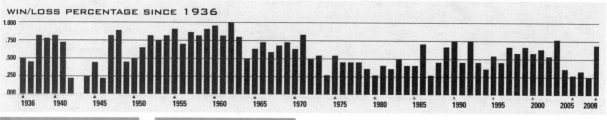

WIN/LOSS PERCENTAGE SINCE 1936

DR. A.L. BONDURANT
1893 (.800) 4-1

1893 4-1-0
N11	●	SWBU	56	0
N18	●	Memphis *Mem*	16	0
N25	●	SWBU *JaTn*	36	0
N30		at So. AC	0	24
D2		at Tulane	12	4

C.D. CLARK
1894 (.857) 6-1

1894 6-1-0
O20	●	St. Thomas HS	62	0
O27	●	Alabama *JaM*	6	0
N10		at Vanderbilt	0	40
N17	●	at Memphis AC	12	0
N29		at Tulane	8	2
D1		at So. AC	6	0
D3		at LSU	26	6

H.L. FAIRBANKS
1895 (.667) 2-1

1895 2-1-0
O12	●	St. Thomas Hall	18	0
N23	●	at Memphis AC	2	0
N28		Tulane	4	28

J.W. HOLLISTER
1896 (.333) 1-2

1896 1-2-0
N6	●	St.Thomas HS	20	0
N13		LSU *Vic*	4	12
N26		at Tulane	0	10

1897
NO TEAM

T.G. SCARBROUGH
1898 (.500) 1-1

1898 1-1-0
D12		at Tulane	9	14
D17		St.Thomas HS	9	2

W.H. LYON
1899 (.429) 3-4

1899 3-4-0
O27	●	at Central U.	13	6
O28		U. of Nashville	0	11
N1	●	LSU *Mer*	11	0
N4		Vanderbilt *Mem*	0	11
N12		Sewanee *Mem*	0	12
N24		Alabama *JaM*	5	7
N30	●	at Tulane	15	0

Z.N. ESTES, JR.
1900 (.000) 0-3

1900 0-3-0
O6		at Vanderbilt	0	6
O26		at Alabama	5	12
N29		at Tulane	0	12

WILLIAM SHIBLEY / DANIEL S. MARTIN
1901 (.333) 2-4

1901 2-4-0
O19	●	Memphis U. Sch.	6	0
O26		at Alabama	0	41
O28		at Mississippi State	0	17
N2	●	SWBU	17	0
N7		at LSU	0	46
N28		at Tulane	11	25

DANIEL S. MARTIN
1902 (.571) 4-3

1902 4-3-0
O11		at Vanderbilt	0	29
O18	●	Cumberland	38	0
O25		at Mississippi State	21	0
N1	●	Memphis U. Sch.	42	0
N8		LSU *NO*	0	6
N15		Tennessee *Mem*	10	11
N27	●	at Tulane	10	0

MIKE HARVEY
1903-04 (.591) 6-4-1

1903 2-1-1
O24		at Vanderbilt	0	33
N7	●	at Memphis Med. Coll.	17	0
N14	=	Mississippi State	6	6
N21	●	LSU *NO*	11	0

1904 4-3-0
O15		at Vanderbilt	0	69
O22	●	Mississippi State *CoLMs*	17	5
O29	●	SWBU	114	0
N5		at LSU	0	5
N12	●	Memphis Med. Coll. *JaM*	42	0
N19	●	Nashville *Mem*	12	5
N24		at Tulane	0	22

NO HEAD COACH

1905 0-2-0
N20		Cumberland	0	18
N30		Mississippi State *JaM*	0	11

T.S. HAMMOND
1906 (.667) 4-2

1906 4-2-0
O4	●	Maryville	16	6
O13		at Vanderbilt	0	29
O20	●	at LSU	9	0
N3	●	at Tulane	17	0
N12		Sewanee *Mem*	0	24
N29	●	Mississippi State *JaM*	29	5

FRANK MASON
1907 (.000) 0-6

1907 0-6-0
O12		Alabama *CoLMs*	0	20
O19		S.E. Missouri. St.	6	12
O26		Sewanee *Mem*	0	65
N9		Vanderbilt *Mem*	0	60
N16		LSU *JaM*	0	23
N28		Mississippi State *JaM*	0	15

FRANK KYLE
1908 (.375) 3-5

1908 3-5-0
O3	●	Memphis U. Sch.	30	0
O10		at Arkansas	0	33
O17	●	S.E. Missouri. St. *Mem*	17	0
O24		at Vanderbilt	0	29
O29	●	Mississippi Coll. *JaM*	41	0
O31		at Tulane	0	10
N10		Southwestern	5	9
N26		Mississippi State *JaM*	6	44

DR. N.P. STAUFFER
1909-11 (.692) 17-7-2

1909 4-3-2
O2	●	Memphis U. Sch.	18	0
O5	●	Memphis Med. Coll.	15	0
O9		at LSU	0	10
O16		at Tulane	0	5
O23	=	Alabama *JaM*	0	0
O30		at Vanderbilt	0	17
N13	=	at Henderson-Brown	12	12
N18	●	Union	45	0
N25	●	Mississippi State *JaM*	9	5

1910 7-1-0
O1	●	Memphis HS	10	0
O5	●	Memphis Med. Coll..	2	0
O13	●	at Tulane	16	0
O21	●	at Mississippi Coll.	24	0
O29	●	at Vanderbilt	2	9
N5	●	Alabama *GrnMS*	16	0
N12	●	at Memphis Med. Coll..	44	0
N24	●	Mississippi State *JaM*	30	0

1911 6-3-0
S30	●	Memphis HS	42	0
O5	●	Southwestern	41	0
O13	●	Louisiana Tech	15	0
O24	●	at Henderson St.	24	11
O27		at Texas A&M	0	17
O30	●	Mississippi Coll. *JaM*	28	0
N4	●	Mercer	34	0
N18		at Vanderbilt	0	21
N30	●	Mississippi State *JaM*	0	6

LEO DeTRAY
1912 (.625) 5-3

1912 5-3-0
O5	●	Memphis HS	34	0
O12	●	Castle Heights	1	0 *f*
O19	●	at LSU	10	7
O26		at Vanderbilt	0	24
N1	●	Mississippi Coll.	12	0
N9		at Alabama	9	10
N13		Texas *Hou*	14	53
N16	●	at Memphis Med. Coll..	47	6

WILLIAM DRIVER
1913-14 (.600) 11-7-2

1913 6-3-1
O8		at VMI	0	14
O11		at Virginia Tech	14	35 *
O15	●	at Virginia Med.	7	6
O23	●	Union	46	0
N1	●	Louisiana Tech	26	0
N7		at Hendrix	6	8
N15	●	Arkansas *LR*	21	10
N22	●	Cumberland *Mem*	7	0
N27		at Southern Miss	13	7
N29	=	at Ouachita	0	0

1914 5-4-1
O3	●	Arkansas State	20	0
O10	●	Southwestern	14	0
O17	●	at LSU	21	0
O28	●	Mississippi Coll. *JaM*	7	7
O31	●	Ouachita *Mem*	0	7
N7	●	at Tulane	21	6
N14	●	Arkansas *LR*	13	7
N17		at Texas	7	66
N20		Southwestern *Geo*	0	18
N26		Texas A&M *Beau*	7	14

FRED ROBBINS
1915-16 (.294) 5-12

1915 2-6-0
O1		Arkansas State	0	10
O8	●	Southwestern	13	6
O15		LSU	0	28
O23		Vanderbilt *Mem*	0	91
O30		Hendrix	32	7
N6		Mississippi State *Tup*	0	65
N13		Mississippi Coll. *JaM*	6	74
N25		Alabama *Birm*	0	53

1916 3-6-0
S30	●	Union	30	0
O7	●	Arkansas State	20	0
O14	●	Hendrix	61	0
O21		at Vanderbilt	0	35
O28		at Alabama	0	27
N3		Mississippi State *Tup*	0	36
N11		at Transylvania, Ky.	3	13
N18		at LSU	0	41
N30		Mississippi Coll. *JaM*	14	36

C.R. "DUDY" NOBLE
1917-18 (.250) 2-7-1

1917 1-4-1
O6	=	Arkansas State	0	0
O13		LSU	7	52
O27		at Alabama	0	64
N3		Mississippi State *Tup*	14	41
N10		at Sewanee	7	69
N29	●	Mississippi Coll. *JaM*	21	0

1918 1-3-0
N9		Payne Field *WPt*	0	6
N16	●	Union	39	0
N28		at Mississippi State	0	34
D7		Mississippi State	0	13

R.L. SULLIVAN
1919-21 (.458) 11-13

1919 4-4-0
O4	●	Arkansas State	32	0
O11		at Alabama	0	49
O18		at LSU	0	12 *
O25		at Tulane	12	27
O31	●	Union	25	6
N8		Mississippi State *Clar*	0	33
N15	●	Southwestern	30	0
N27	●	Mississippi Coll. *JaM*	6	0

1920 4-3-0
O2	●	Arkansas State	33	0
O9	●	at Southern Miss	54	0
O16		at B'ham Southern	6	27
O23		at Tulane	0	32
O29	●	Union	86	0
N6		Mississippi State *Grn*	0	20
N12	●	Southwestern	38	6

1921 3-6-0
O1	●	Memphis	82	0
O8		at Tulane	0	26
O15	●	Millsaps	49	0
O22	●	Southwestern	35	0
O29		Mississippi State *Grn*	0	21
N5		Mississippi Coll. *Vic*	7	27
N12		at LSU	0	21
N19		at Tenn. Doctors	6	24
D31		at Havanna U.	0	14

1922-1932 SOUTHERN

R.A. COWELL
1922-23 (.425) 8-11-1

1922 4-5-1 (0-2-0)
S30	=	Union	0	0
O7		at Centre	0	55
O14	●	Southwestern	23	0
O21		Mississippi State *JaM*	13	19
O28		at Tennessee	0	49
N4	●	B'ham Southern	6	0
N11	●	Hendrix	13	7
N18		at Tenn. Doctors	0	32
N25		Fort Benning *ColGa*	13	14
N30	●	at Millsaps	19	7

1923 — 4-6-0 (0-4-0)

S29	●	Bethel Coll.	14	6
O6	|	at Alabama	0	56
O13	●	Southwestern	33	0
O20	|	Mississippi State JaM	6	13
O27		at St. Louis	3	28
N3	●	B'ham Southern	6	0
N10		Mississippi Coll. MER	0	6
N17	|	at Tulane	0	19
N24	|	at Tennessee	0	10
D1	●	Fort Benning ColGa	19	7

CHESTER BARNARD
1924 (.444) 4-5

1924 — 4-5-0 (0-3-0)

O4	●	Arkansas State	10	7
O11	●	Southwestern	7	0
O18	|	Mississippi State JaM	0	20
O25		Arkansas LR	0	20
N1	|	Alabama Mont	0	61
N8	|	Sewanee Mem	0	21
N15		at Furman	2	7
N22	●	Mississippi Coll.	10	6
N27	●	at Millsaps	7	0

HOMER HAZEL
1925-29 (.489) 21-22-3

1925 — 5-5-0 (0-4-0)

S26	●	Arkansas State	53	0
O3		at Texas	0	25
O10	|	at Tulane	7	26
O17	●	Union	7	6
O24	|	Mississippi State JaM	0	6
O31	|	at Vanderbilt	0	7
N7	|	Sewanee Chat	9	10
N14	●	at Mississippi Coll.	19	7
N21	●	Southwestern	31	0
N26	●	at Millsaps	21	0

1926 — 5-4-0 (2-2-0)

S25	●	Arkansas State	28	0
O2		at Arkansas	6	21
O9	● |	at Florida	12	7
O16	●	Loyola-Chicago	13	7
O23		at Drake	15	33
O30	|	at Tulane	0	6
N6	●	at Southwestern	32	27
N13	|	at LSU	0	3
N25	● |	at Mississippi State	7	6

1927 — 5-3-1 (3-2-0)

S24	●	Coll. Of Ozarks	58	0
O1	|	at Tulane	7	19
O7	=	Hendrix	0	0
O15	|	at Tennessee	7	21
O22	●	at Southwestern	39	0
O29	● |	at Sewanee	28	14
N5	● |	LSU	12	7
N11		Loyola-Chicago JaM	6	7
N24	● |	Mississippi State	20	12

1928 — 5-4-0 (3-3-0)

S29	●	Arkansas	25	0
O6	|	at Alabama	0	27
O13	|	at Tennessee	12	13
O20	● |	Auburn Birm	19	0
O27		at Loyola-New Orleans	14	34
N3	● |	Clemson	26	7
N10	|	at LSU	6	19
N17	●	at Southwestern	34	2
N29	● |	at Mississippi State	20	19

1929 — 1-6-2 (0-4-2)

S28	|	at Vanderbilt	7	19
O5	|	at Alabama	7	22
O12	|	at Tennessee	7	52
O18	●	at Loyola-New Orleans	26	24
O26		at SMU	0	52
N2	= |	Sewanee	6	6
N9		at Purdue	7	27
N16	|	at LSU	6	13
N28	= |	Mississippi State	7	7

ED WALKER
1930-37 (.500) 38-38-8

1930 — 3-5-1 (1-5-0)

S26	●	Union	64	0
O4	|	at Alabama	0	64
O11	|	at Tennessee	0	27
O18	|	Sewanee	7	13
O25	=	at Chicago	0	0
N1	|	at Vanderbilt	0	24
N8	|	at LSU	0	6
N14	●	Southwestern	37	6
N27	● |	at Mississippi State	20	0

1931 — 2-6-1 (1-5-0)

S19	●	Western Kentucky	13	6
S26	|	at Tulane	0	31
O3	|	at Alabama	6	55
O10	|	at Tennessee	0	38
O24	=	at Southwestern	20	20
O30		at Marquette	6	13
N7	|	Sewanee	0	7
N14	|	LSU JaM	3	26
N26	● |	Mississippi State	25	14

1932 — 5-6-0 (2-3-0)

S24	●	Southern Miss	49	0
O1	|	at Tennessee	0	33
O8	●	Samford	26	6
O15		at Centenary	6	13
O22	|	at Alabama	13	24
O29	|	Auburn Mont	7	14
N5		at Minnesota	0	26
N12	● |	Sewanee	27	6
N19	●	at Southwestern	7	0
N24	● |	at Mississippi State	13	0
D3		at Tulsa	0	26

1933-PRESENT
SEC

1933 — 6-3-2 (2-2-1)

S23	=	at Southwestern	6	6
S30	●	Southern Miss	45	0
O7	= |	Alabama Birm	0	0
O14	●	at Marquette	7	0
O21	● |	Sewanee	41	0
O28	●	Clemson Mer	13	0
N4	●	B'Ham Southern	12	0
N11	|	at Tennessee	6	35
N18	|	at LSU	0	31
N25		Centenary JaM	6	7
D2	● |	Mississippi State	31	0

1934 — 4-5-1 (2-3-1)

S29	●	Memphis	44	0
O5	●	Southwestern Clar	19	0
O13	|	at Tennessee	0	27
O20		Samford	6	7
O27	● |	Sewanee	19	6
N3	|	at Tulane	0	15
N10	= |	at Florida	13	13
N17	|	LSU JaM	0	14
N24		at Centenary	6	13
D1	● |	Mississippi State JaM	7	3

1935 — 9-3-0 (3-1-0)

S20	●	at Millsaps	20	0
S28	●	Memphis	92	0
O5	●	Southwestern	33	0
O11	● |	Sewanee Clar	33	0
O19	● |	Florida	27	6
O26		at Marquette	7	33
N1	●	at St. Louis	21	7
N9	|	Tennessee Mem	13	14
N16	●	at Centre	26	0
N23	●	Centenary JaM	6	0
N30	● |	Mississippi State	14	6
ORANGE BOWL				
J1		Catholic U.	19	20

1936 — 5-5-2 (0-3-1)

S19	●	Union	45	0
S26	|	at Tulane	6	7
O2		at Temple	7	12
O9	=	at George Washington	0	0
O17	|	at LSU	0	13
O24	●	Catholic U.	14	0
O31	●	at Centenary	24	7
N7	●	Loyola-New Orleans	34	0
N14		at Marquette	0	33
N21	|	at Mississippi State	6	26
N27	●	at Miami, Fla.	14	0
D5	= |	Tennessee Mem	0	0

1937 — 4-5-1 (0-4-0)

S25	●	Louisiana Tech	13	0
O1	=	at Temple	0	0
O9	●	St. Louis	21	0
O16	|	at LSU	0	13
O23	●	Ouachita	46	0
O30	|	at Tulane	7	14
N5	● |	at George Washington	27	6
N13		Arkansas Mem	6	32
N25	|	Mississippi State	7	9
D4	|	Tennessee Mem	0	32

HARRY J. MEHRE
1938-45 (.598) 39-26-1

1938 — 9-2-0 (3-2-0)

S24	● |	at LSU	20	7
O1	●	Louisiana Tech	27	7
O8	●	Southern Miss	14	0
O15	|	at Vanderbilt	7	13
O22	●	Centenary	47	14
O29	●	at George Washington	25	0
N5	●	at St. Louis	14	12
N12	● |	Sewanee	39	0
N16	●	Arkansas Mem	20	14
N26	● |	at Mississippi State	19	6
D3	|	Tennessee Mem	0	47

1939 — 7-2-0 (2-2-0)

S30	● |	at LSU	14	7
O7	●	at Southwestern	41	0
O14	●	at Centenary	34	0
O21	●	St. Louis	42	0
O28	|	at Tulane	6	18
N4	● |	Vanderbilt Mem	14	7
N11	●	at Southern Miss	27	7
N18	●	Memphis	46	7
N25	|	Mississippi State	6	18

1940 — 9-2-0 (3-1-0)

S21	●	Union	37	0
S28	● |	at LSU	19	6
O5	●	at Southwestern	27	6
O12	● |	at Georgia	28	14
O19	●	Duquesne	14	6
O26		Arkansas Mem	20	21
N2	● |	at Vanderbilt	13	7
N9	●	at Holy Cross	34	7
N16	●	Memphis	38	7
N23	|	at Mississippi State	0	19
N29	●	at Miami, Fla.	21	7

1941 — 6-2-1 (2-1-1)

S26		at Georgetown	6	16
O4	●	Southwestern	27	0
O10	= |	at Georgia	14	14
O18	●	at Holy Cross	21	0
O25	● |	at Tulane	20	13
N1	●	at Marquette	12	6
N8	● |	at LSU	13	12
N22	●	Arkansas Mem	18	0
N29	|	Mississippi State	0	6

1942 — 2-7-0 (0-5-0)

S26	●	Kentucky Teachers	39	6
O2		at Georgetown	6	14
O10	|	Georgia Mem	13	48
O17	|	at LSU	7	21
O24		Arkansas Mem	6	7
O31	●	Memphis	48	0
N7	|	Vanderbilt Mem	0	19
N14	|	Tennessee Mem	0	14
N28	|	at Mississippi State	13	34

1943

NO TEAM WWII

1944 — 2-6-0 (2-3-0)

S23	|	at Kentucky	7	27
S30	● |	Florida JacF	26	6
O7	|	Tennessee Mem	7	20
O21		Tulsa Mem	0	47
O28		Arkansas Mem	18	26
N4		Jackson AAB	0	10
N11	|	Alabama Mbl	6	34
N25	● |	Mississippi State	13	8

1945 — 4-5-0 (3-3-0)

S21	● |	Kentucky Mem	21	7
S29	|	Florida JacF	13	26
O6	● |	at Vanderbilt	14	7
O13	●	Louisiana Tech	26	21
O27		Arkansas Mem	0	19
N3	|	at LSU	13	32
N10	|	Tennessee Mem	0	34
N24	● |	at Mississippi State	7	6
N29		at U.T. Chattanooga	6	31

HAROLD "RED" DREW
1946 (.222) 2-7

1946 — 2-7-0 (1-6-0)

S21	|	at Kentucky	7	20*
S28	● |	Florida JacF	13	7
O5	|	Vanderbilt Mem	0	7
O12	|	at Georgia Tech	7	24
O19		Louisiana Tech	6	7
O26	●	Arkansas Mem	9	7
N2	|	at LSU	21	34
N9	|	Tennessee Mem	14	18
N23	|	Mississippi State	0	20

JOHN H. VAUGHT
1947-70, '73 (.745) 190-61-12

1947 — 9-2-0 (6-1-0)

S20	● |	Kentucky	14	7
S27	● |	Florida JacF	14	6
O4	●	South Carolina Mem	33	0
O11	|	at Vanderbilt	6	10
O18	● |	at Tulane	27	14
O25		Arkansas Mem	14	19
N1	● |	at LSU	20	18
N8	● |	Tennessee Mem	43	13
N15	●	U.T. Chattanooga	52	0
N29	● |	at Mississippi State	33	14
DELTA BOWL				
J1	●	TCU	13	9

1948 — 8-1-0 (6-1-0)

S25	● |	at Florida	14	0
O2	● |	at Kentucky	20	7
O9	● |	Vanderbilt	20	7
O16	|	at Tulane	7	20
O23	●	Boston College Mem	32	13
O30	● |	at LSU	49	19
N6	●	at U.T. Chattanooga	34	7
N13	● |	Tennessee Mem	16	13
N27	● |	Mississippi State	34	7

1949 — 4-5-1 (2-4-0)

S16	●	at Memphis	40	7
S23	● |	Auburn Mont	40	7
O1	|	Kentucky	0	47
O8	|	at Vanderbilt	27	28
O14	=	at Boston College	25	25
O22		at TCU	27	33
O29	|	at LSU	7	34
N5	●	U.T. Chattanooga	47	27
N12	|	Tennessee Mem	7	35
N26	● |	at Mississippi State	26	0

1950 — 5-5-0 (1-5-0)

S22	●	at Memphis	39	7
S30	|	at Kentucky	0	27
O7	●	Boston College	54	0
O14	|	at Vanderbilt	14	20
O21	|	at Tulane	20	27
O28	●	TCU Mem	19	7
N4	|	at LSU	14	40
N11	●	U.T. Chattanooga	20	0
N18	|	at Tennessee	0	35
D2	● |	Mississippi State	27	20

1951 — 6-3-1 (4-2-1)

S21	●	at Memphis	32	0
S29	● |	Kentucky	21	17
O5	●	Boston College Mem	34	7
O13	|	Vanderbilt Mem	20	34
O20	● |	Tulane	25	6
O26		at Miami, Fla.	7	20
N3	= |	at LSU	6	6
N10	● |	Auburn Mbl	39	14
N17	|	Tennessee	21	46
D1	● |	at Mississippi State	49	7

1952 — 8-1-2 (4-0-2)

S19	●	at Memphis	54	6
S27	= |	at Kentucky	13	13
O4	● |	Auburn Mem	20	7
O11	= |	at Vanderbilt	21	21
O18	● |	at Tulane	20	14
O25	●	Arkansas LR	34	7
N1	● |	LSU	28	0
N8	●	at Houston	6	0
N15	●	Maryland	21	14
N29	● |	Mississippi State	20	14
SUGAR BOWL				
J1		Georgia Tech	7	24

1953 — 7-2-1 (4-1-1)

S19	●	U.T. Chattanooga JaM	39	6
S26	● |	Kentucky	22	6
O3	|	at Auburn	0	13
O10	● |	Vanderbilt	28	6
O17	● |	at Tulane	45	14
O24	●	Arkansas Mem	28	0
O31	● |	at LSU	27	16
N7	●	North Texas	40	7
N14		at Maryland	0	38
N28	= |	at Mississippi State	7	7

1954 9-2-0 (5-1-0)

S17 ●	North Texas MEM	35	12
S25 ●	│ Kentucky MEM	28	9
O2 ●	Villanova PHIL	52	0
O9 ●	│ at Vanderbilt	22	7
O16 ●	│ Tulane	34	7
O23	‖ Arkansas LR	0	6
O30 ●	│ at LSU	21	6
N6 ●	at Memphis	51	0
N13 ●	at Houston	26	0
N27 ●	│ Mississippi State	14	0
	SUGAR BOWL		
J1	Navy	0	21

1955 10-1-0 (5-1-0)

S17 ●	│ Georgia ATL	26	13
S24	│ at Kentucky	14	21
O1 ●	North Texas	33	0
O8 ●	│ Vanderbilt MEM	13	0
O15 ●	│ at Tulane	27	13
O22 ●	Arkansas	17	7
O29 ●	│ at LSU	29	26
N5 ●	at Memphis	39	6
N12 ●	Houston JAM	27	11
N26 ●	│ at Mississippi State	26	0
	COTTON BOWL		
J2 ●	TCU	14	13

1956 7-3-0 (4-2-0)

S22 ●	North Texas	45	0
S29 ●	│ Kentucky MEM	37	7
O6 ●	Houston JAM	14	0
O13 ●	│ Vanderbilt	16	0
O20	│ Tulane JAM	3	10
O27	Arkansas LR	0	14
N3 ●	│ at LSU	46	17
N10 ●	at Memphis	26	0
N17	│ at Tennessee	7	27
D1 ●	│ Mississippi State	13	7

1957 9-1-1 (5-0-1)

S21 ●	at Trinity	44	0
S28 ●	│ at Kentucky	15	0
O5 ●	Hardin-Simmons	34	7
O12 ●	│ at Vanderbilt	28	0
O18 ●	│ at Tulane	50	0
O26	Arkansas MEM	6	12
N2 ●	Houston JAM	20	7
N9 ●	│ LSU	14	12
N16 ●	│ Tennessee MEM	14	7
N30 =	│ at Mississippi State	7	7
	SUGAR BOWL		
J1 ●	Texas	39	7

1958 9-2-0 (4-2-0)

S20 ●	at Memphis	17	0
S27 ●	│ Kentucky MEM	27	6
O4 ●	at Trinity	21	0
O11 ●	│ at Tulane	19	8
O18 ●	Hardin-Simmons	24	0
O25 ●	Arkansas LR	14	12
N1	│ at LSU	0	14
N8 ●	‖ Houston	56	7
N15	│ at Tennessee	16	18
N29 ●	│ Mississippi State	21	0
	GATOR BOWL		
D27 ●	Florida	7	3

1959 10-1-0 (5-1-0)

S19 ●	at Houston	16	0
S26 ●	│ at Kentucky	16	0
O3 ●	Memphis	43	0
O10 ●	│ at Vanderbilt	33	0
O17 ●	│ Tulane	53	7
O24 ●	Arkansas MEM	28	0
O31	│ at LSU	3	7
N7 ●	U.T. Chattanooga	58	0
N14 ●	│ Tennessee MEM	37	7
N28 ●	│ at Mississippi State	42	0
	SUGAR BOWL		
J1 ●	LSU	21	0

1960 10-0-1 (5-0-1)

S17 ●	at Houston	42	0
S24 ●	│ Kentucky MEM	21	6
O1 ●	at Memphis	31	20
O8 ●	│ at Vanderbilt	26	0
O15 ●	│ at Tulane	26	13
O22 ●	Arkansas LR	10	7
O29 =	│ LSU	6	6
N5 ●	U.T. Chattanooga	45	0
N12 ●	│ at Tennessee	24	3
N26 ●	│ Mississippi State	35	9
	SUGAR BOWL		
J2 ●	Rice	14	6

1961 9-2-0 (5-1-0)

S23 ●	Arkansas JAM	16	0
S30 ●	│ at Kentucky	20	6
O7 ●	Florida State	33	0
O14 ●	Houston MEM	47	7
O21 ●	│ Tulane JAM	41	0
O28 ●	│ Vanderbilt	47	0
N4	│ at LSU	7	10
N11 ●	U.T. Chattanooga	54	0
N18 ●	│ Tennessee MEM	24	10
D2 ●	│ at Mississippi State	37	7
	COTTON BOWL		
J1	Texas	7	12

1962 10-0-0 (6-0-0)

S22 ●	at Memphis	21	7
S29 ●	│ Kentucky JAM	14	0
O6 ●	Houston JAM	40	7
O20 ●	│ Tulane JAM	21	0
O27 ●	│ Vanderbilt MEM	35	0
N3 ●	│ at LSU	15	7
N10 ●	U.T. Chattanooga	52	7
N17 ●	│ at Tennessee	19	6
D1 ●	│ Mississippi State	13	6
	SUGAR BOWL		
J1 ●	Arkansas	17	13

1963 7-1-2 (5-0-1)

S21 =	at Memphis	0	0
S28 ●	│ at Kentucky	31	7
O5 ●	at Houston	20	6
O19 ●	│ at Tulane	21	0
O26 ●	│ Vanderbilt	27	7
N2 ●	│ at LSU	37	3
N9 ●	Tampa	41	0
N16 ●	│ Tennessee MEM	20	0
N30 =	│ at Mississippi State	10	10
	SUGAR BOWL		
J1	Alabama	7	12

1964 5-5-1 (2-4-1)

S19 ●	Memphis	30	0
S26	│ Kentucky JAM	21	27
O3 ●	Houston	31	9
O10	│ at Florida	14	30
O17 ●	│ at Tulane	14	9
O24 =	│ at Vanderbilt	7	7
O31	│ at LSU	10	11
N7 ●	Tampa	36	0
N14 ●	│ at Tennessee	30	0
D5	│ Mississippi State	17	20
	BLUEBONNET BOWL		
D19	Tulsa	7	14

1965 7-4-0 (5-3-0)

S18 ●	at Memphis	34	14
S25	│ at Kentucky	7	16
O2	│ Alabama BIRM	16	17
O9	│ Florida	0	17
O16 ●	│ Tulane JAM	24	7
O23 ●	│ Vanderbilt	24	7
O30 ●	│ LSU JAM	23	0
N6	at Houston	3	17
N13 ●	│ Tennessee MEM	14	13
N27 ●	│ at Mississippi State	21	0
	LIBERTY BOWL		
D18 ●	Auburn	13	7

1966 8-3-0 (5-2-0)

S17 ●	at Memphis	13	0
S24 ●	│ Kentucky JAM	17	0
O1	│ Alabama JAM	7	17
O8	│ at Georgia	3	9
O15 ●	Southern Miss	14	7
O22 ●	Houston MEM	27	6
O29 ●	│ at LSU	17	0
N12 ●	│ at Tennessee	14	7
N19 ●	│ Vanderbilt JAM	34	0
N26 ●	│ Mississippi State	24	0
	BLUEBONNET BOWL		
D17	Texas	0	19

1967 6-4-1 (4-2-1)

S23	at Memphis	17	27
S30 ●	│ at Kentucky	26	13
O7	│ Alabama BIRM	7	21
O14 ●	│ Georgia JAM	29	20
O21 ●	Southern Miss MEM	23	14
O28 ●	Houston	14	13
N4 =	│ LSU JAM	13	13
N18	│ Tennessee MEM	7	20
N25 ●	│ at Vanderbilt	28	7
D2 ●	│ at Mississippi State	10	3
	SUN BOWL		
D30	Texas El Paso	7	14

1968 7-3-1 (3-2-1)

S21 ●	at Memphis	21	7
S28 ●	│ Kentucky JAM	30	14
O5 ●	│ Alabama JAM	10	8
O12	│ at Georgia	7	21
O19 ●	Southern Miss	21	13
O26	Houston JAM	7	29
N2 ●	│ at LSU	27	24
N9 ●	U.T. Chattanooga	38	16
N16	│ at Tennessee	0	31
N30 =	│ Mississippi State	17	17
	LIBERTY BOWL		
D14 ●	Virginia Tech	34	17

1969 8-3-0 (4-2-0)

S20 ●	Memphis	28	3
S27	│ at Kentucky	9	10
O4	│ Alabama BIRM	32	33
O11 ●	│ Georgia JAM	25	17
O18 ●	Southern Miss	69	7
O25	at Houston	11	25
N1 ●	│ LSU JAM	26	23
N8 ●	U.T. Chattanooga	21	0
N15 ●	│ Tennessee JAM	38	0
N27 ●	│ at Mississippi State	48	22
	SUGAR BOWL		
J1 ●	Arkansas	27	22

1970 7-4-0 (4-2-0)

S19 ●	at Memphis	47	13
S26 ●	│ Kentucky JAM	20	17
O3 ●	│ Alabama JAM	48	23
O10 ●	│ at Georgia	31	21
O17	Southern Miss	14	30
O24 ●	│ at Vanderbilt	26	16
N7 ●	Houston	24	13
N14 ●	U.T. Chattanooga	44	7
N26	│ Mississippi State	14	19
D5	│ at LSU	17	61
	GATOR BOWL		
J2	Auburn	28	35

BILLY R. KINARD
1971-73 (.640) 16-9

1971 10-2-0 (4-2-0)

S11 ●	Long Beach St. JAM	29	13
S18 ●	at Memphis	49	21
S25 ●	│ at Kentucky	34	20
O2	│ Alabama BIRM	6	40
O9	│ Georgia JAM	7	38
O16 ●	Southern Miss	20	6
O23 ●	│ Vanderbilt	28	7
O30 ●	│ LSU JAM	24	22
N6 ●	at Tampa	28	27
N13 ●	U.T. Chattanooga	49	10
N25 ●	│ at Mississippi State	48	0
	PEACH BOWL		
D30 ●	Georgia Tech	41	18

1972 5-5-0 (2-5-0)

S16 ●	at Memphis	34	29
S23 ●	at South Carolina	21	0
S30 ●	Southern Miss	13	9
O7	│ Auburn JAM	13	19
O14	│ Georgia JAM	13	14
O21	│ Florida	0	16
O28 ●	│ at Vanderbilt	31	7
N4	│ at LSU	16	17
N18	│ at Tennessee	0	17
N25 ●	│ Mississippi State	51	14

JOHN H. VAUGHT

1973 6-5-0 (4-3-0)

S8 ●	Villanova JAM	24	6
S15	at Missouri	0	17
S22	Memphis JAM	13	17
S29 ●	Southern Miss	41	0
O6	│ at Auburn	7	14
O13	│ at Georgia	0	20
O20 ●	│ at Florida	13	10
O27 ●	│ Vanderbilt	24	14
N3	│ LSU JAM	14	51
N17 ●	│ Tennessee JAM	28	18
N24 ●	│ Mississippi State JAM	38	10

KEN COOPER
1974-77 (.432) 19-25

1974 3-8-0 (0-6-0)

S14 ●	Missouri JAM	10	0
S21	at Memphis	7	15
S28 ●	Southern Miss	20	14
O5	│ Alabama JAM	21	35
O12	│ at Georgia	0	49
O19	South Carolina	7	10
O26	│ at Vanderbilt	14	24
N2	│ at LSU	0	24
N16	│ Tennessee MEM	17	29
N23	│ Mississippi State JAM	13	31
N30 ●	at Tulane	26	10

1975 6-5-0 (5-1-0)

S6	at Baylor	10	20
S13	at Texas A&M	0	7
S20	at Tulane	3	14
S27 ●	Southern Miss	24	8
O4	│ Alabama BIRM	6	32
O11 ●	│ Georgia	28	13
O18	South Carolina JAM	29	35
O25 ●	│ Vanderbilt	17	7
N1 ●	│ LSU JAM	17	13
N15 ●	│ Tennessee MEM	23	6
N22 ●	│ Mississippi State JAM	13	7

1976 5-6-0 (3-4-0)

S4	at Memphis	16	21
S11 ●	│ Alabama JAM	10	7
S18 ●	Tulane	34	7
S25 ●	at Southern Miss	28	0
O2	│ Auburn JAM	0	10
O9 ●	│ Georgia	21	17
O16	at South Carolina	7	10
O23 ●	│ at Vanderbilt	20	3
O30	│ at LSU	0	45
N13	│ at Tennessee	6	32
N20	│ Mississippi State JAM	11	28†

1977 5-6-0 (2-5-0)

S3 ●	Memphis JAM	7	3
S10	│ Alabama BIRM	13	34
S17 ●	Notre Dame JAM	20	13
S24	Southern Miss	19	27
O1	│ at Auburn	15	21
O8	│ at Georgia	13	14
O15 ●	South Carolina	17	10
O22 ●	│ Vanderbilt	26	14
O29	│ LSU JAM	21	28
N12 ●	│ Tennessee MEM	43	14
N19	│ Mississippi State JAM	14	18†

STEVE SLOAN
1978-82 (.373) 20-34-1

1978 5-6-0 (2-4-0)

S9 ●	Memphis JAM	14	7
S23	at Missouri	14	45
S30 ●	Southern Miss JAM	16	13
O7	│ at Georgia	3	42
O14	│ Kentucky	17	24
O21	at South Carolina	17	18
O28 ●	│ at Vanderbilt	35	10
N4	│ at LSU	8	30
N11 ●	Tulane	13	3
N18	│ at Tennessee	17	41
N25 ●	│ Mississippi State JAM	27	7

1979 4-7-0 (3-3-0)

S15 ●	at Memphis	38	34
S22	Missouri JAM	7	33
S29	Southern Miss JAM	8	38
O6	│ Georgia	21	24
O13	│ at Kentucky	3	14
O20	at South Carolina	14	21
O27 ●	│ Vanderbilt	63	28
N3	│ LSU JAM	24	28
N10	at Tulane	15	49
N17 ●	│ Tennessee JAM	44	20
N24 ●	│ Mississippi State JAM	14	9

1980 3-8-0 (2-4-0)

S6	Texas A&M JAM	20	23
S13 ●	Memphis	61	7
S20	Alabama JAM	35	59
S27	Tulane	24	26
O4	Southern Miss JAM	22	28
O11	│ at Georgia	21	28
O18	│ Florida	3	15
O25 ●	│ at Vanderbilt	27	14
N1	│ at LSU	16	38
N15 ●	│ Tennessee MEM	20	9
N22	│ Mississippi State JAM	14	19

1981 4-6-1 (1-4-1)

S5	●	at Tulane	19	18
S12	●	at South Carolina	20	13
S19	●	at Memphis	7	3
S26		Arkansas [JaM]	13	27
O3		at Alabama	7	38
O10	|	Georgia	7	37
O17	|	at Florida	3	49
O24	|	Vanderbilt	23	27
O31	= |	LSU [JaM]	27	27
N14	|	at Tennessee	20	28
N21	● |	Mississippi State [JaM]	21	17

1982 4-7-0 (0-6-0)

S4	●	Memphis	27	10
S11	●	Southern Miss	28	19
S18	|	Alabama [JaM]	14	42
S25		Arkansas [LR]	12	14
O9	|	at Georgia	10	33
O16	●	TCU	27	9
O23	|	at Vanderbilt	10	19
O30	|	at LSU	8	45
N6	●	Tulane [JaM]	45	14
N13	|	Tennessee [JaM]	17	30
N20	|	Mississippi State [JaM]	10	27

BILLY BREWER
1983-93 (.536) 66-57-3

1983 6-6-0 (4-2-0)

S3		at Memphis	17	37
S10		at Tulane	23	27†
S17	|	at Alabama	0	40
S24	●	Arkansas [JaM]	13	10
O1		Southern Miss	7	27
O8	|	Georgia	11	36
O15	●	at TCU	20	7
O22	● |	Vanderbilt	21	14
O29	● |	LSU [JaM]	27	24
N12	● |	at Tennessee	13	10
N19	● |	Mississippi State [JaM]	24	23
		INDEPENDENCE BOWL		
D10		Air Force	3	9

1984 4-6-1 (1-5-0)

S8	●	Memphis	22	6
S15	=	Arkansas [LR]	14	14
S22	●	Louisiana Tech	14	8
S29	●	Tulane	19	14
O6	|	Auburn	13	17
O13	|	at Georgia	12	18
O20		Southern Miss [JaM]	10	13
O27	|	at Vanderbilt	20	37
N3	|	at LSU	29	32
N17	|	Tennessee [JaM]	17	41
N24	● |	Mississippi State [JaM]	24	3

1985 4-6-1 (2-4-0)

S7	=	at Memphis	17	17
S14		Arkansas [JaM]	19	24
S21	●	Arkansas State	18	16
S28	●	at Tulane	27	10
O5	|	at Auburn	0	41
O12	|	Georgia [JaM]	21	49
O26	● |	Vanderbilt	35	7
N2	|	LSU [JaM]	0	14
N9		at Notre Dame	14	37
N16	|	at Tennessee	14	34
N23	● |	Mississippi State [JaM]	45	27

1986 8-3-1 (4-2-0)

S6	●	Memphis [JaM]	28	6
S13		Arkansas [LR]	0	21
S20	=	Arkansas State	10	10
S27	●	Tulane	35	10
O4	|	at Georgia	10	14
O11	● |	Kentucky [JaM]	33	13
O18	●	La. Lafayette	21	20
O25	● |	at Vanderbilt	28	12
N1	● |	at LSU	21	19
N15	|	Tennessee [JaM]	10	22
N22	● |	Mississippi State [JaM]	24	3
		INDEPENDENCE BOWL		
D20	●	Texas Tech	20	17

1987 3-8-0 (1-5-0)

S5		at Memphis	10	16
S12		Arkansas [JaM]	10	31
S19	●	Arkansas State	47	10
S26		at Tulane	24	31
O3	|	Georgia	14	31
O10	|	at Kentucky	6	35
O17	●	La. Lafayette	24	14
O24	● |	Vanderbilt	42	14
O31	|	LSU [JaM]	13	42
N14	|	at Tennessee	13	55
N21	|	Mississippi State [JaM]	20	30

1988 5-6-0 (3-4-0)

S3	●	Memphis [JaM]	24	6
S10	|	Florida [JaM]	15	27
S17		Arkansas [LR]	13	21
O1	|	at Georgia	12	36
O8	● |	at Alabama	22	12
O15	●	Arkansas State	25	22
O22	● |	at Vanderbilt	36	28
O29	|	at LSU	20	31
N5		Tulane	9	14
N12	|	Tennessee	12	20
N26	● |	Mississippi State [JaM]	33	6

1989 8-4-0 (4-3-0)

S2	●	at Memphis	20	13
S9	● |	at Florida	24	19
S16	●	Arkansas State	34	31
S23		Arkansas [JaM]	17	24
O7	|	Alabama [JaM]	27	62
O14	● |	Georgia	17	13
O21	●	at Tulane	32	28
O28	● |	Vanderbilt	24	16
N4	|	LSU	30	35
N18	|	at Tennessee	21	33
N25	● |	Mississippi State [JaM]	21	11
		LIBERTY BOWL		
D28	●	Air Force	42	29

1990 9-3-0 (5-2-0)

S8	●	Memphis	23	21
S15	|	Auburn [JaM]	10	24
S22	●	Arkansas [LR]	21	17
S29	●	Tulane	31	21
O6	● |	Kentucky	35	29
O13	● |	at Georgia	28	12
O20	●	Arkansas State	42	13
O27	● |	at Vanderbilt	14	13
N3	● |	at LSU	19	10
N17		Tennessee [MEM]	13	22
N24	● |	Mississippi State [JaM]	21	9
		GATOR BOWL		
J1		Michigan	3	35

1991 5-6-0 (1-6-0)

A31	●	at Tulane	22	3
S7	●	at Memphis	10	0
S14	|	at Auburn	13	23
S21	●	Ohio U.	38	14
S28	●	Arkansas [JaM]	24	17
O5	● |	at Kentucky	35	14
O12	|	Georgia	17	37
O26	|	Vanderbilt	27	30
N2	|	LSU [JaM]	22	25
N16	|	at Tennessee	25	36
N23	|	at Mississippi State	9	24

1992 9-3-0 (5-3-0)

S5	● |	Auburn	45	21
S12	●	Tulane	35	9
S19	|	at Vanderbilt	9	31
S26	|	at Georgia	11	37
O3	● |	Kentucky	24	14
O17	● |	Arkansas [LR]	17	3
O24	|	at Alabama	10	31
O31	● |	LSU [JaM]	32	0
N7	●	Memphis	17	12
N14	●	Louisiana Tech	13	6
N28	● |	Mississippi State	17	10
		LIBERTY BOWL		
D31	●	Air Force	13	0

1993 5-6-0 (3-5-0)

S2	|	at Auburn	12	16
S11	●	U.T. Chattanooga	40	7
S18	● |	Vanderbilt	49	7
S25	● |	Georgia	31	14
O2	|	at Kentucky	0	21
O16	● |	Arkansas [JaM]	19	0
O23	|	Alabama	14	19†
O30	|	at LSU	17	19
N6		at Memphis	3	19
N13	●	Northern Illinois	44	0
N27	|	at Mississippi State	13	20

JOE LEE DUNN
1994 (.364) 4-7

1994 4-7-0 (2-6-0)

S3	|	Auburn	17	22
S10	●	So. Illinois	59	3
S17	● |	at Vanderbilt	20	14
S24	|	at Georgia	14	17
O1	|	Florida	14	38
O15	|	at Arkansas	7	31
O22	|	at Alabama	10	21
O29	● |	LSU	34	21
N5		Memphis	16	17
N12	●	at Tulane	38	0
N26	|	Mississippi State	17	21

TOMMY TUBERVILLE
1995-98 (.556) 25-20

1995 6-5-0 (3-5-0)

S2	|	at Auburn	13	46
S9	●	Indiana St.	56	10
S23	● |	Georgia	18	10
S30	|	at Florida	10	28
O7	●	Tulane	20	17
O14	|	Arkansas [MEM]	6	13
O21	|	Alabama	9	23
O28	● |	Vanderbilt	21	10
N4	●	at Memphis	34	3
N11	|	at LSU	9	38
N25	● |	at Mississippi State	13	10

1996 5-6 (2-6)

A31	●	Idaho St.	38	14
S7	●	VMI [JaM]	31	7
S14	|	Auburn	28	45
S21	● |	at Vanderbilt	20	9
O3	|	Tennessee [MEM]	3	41
O19	|	at Alabama	0	37
O26	●	Arkansas State	38	21
N9	|	at Arkansas	7	13
N16	|	LSU	7	39
N23	● |	at Georgia	31	27
N30	|	Mississippi State	0	17

1997 8-4 (4-4)

A30	●	Central Florida	24	23
S6	●	SMU	23	15
S13	|	at Auburn	9	19
S27	● |	Vanderbilt	15	3
O4	|	at Tennessee	17	31
O18	● |	at LSU	36	21
O25	|	Alabama	20	29
N6	● |	Arkansas	19	9
N15	●	at Tulane	41	24
N22	|	Georgia	14	21
N29	● |	at Mississippi State	15	14
		MOTOR CITY BOWL		
D26	●	Marshall	34	31

1998 7-5 (3-5)

S5	●	Memphis	30	10
S12	|	Auburn	0	17
S19	● |	at Vanderbilt	30	6
S26	●	at SMU	48	41
O3	● |	South Carolina	30	28
O10	|	at Alabama	17	20
O24	●	Arkansas State	30	17
O31	● |	LSU	37	31
N7	|	at Arkansas	0	34
N21	|	at Georgia	17	24
N26	|	Mississippi State	6	28
		INDEPENDENCE BOWL		
D31	●	Texas Tech	35	18

DAVID CUTCLIFFE
1998-2004 (.603) 44-29

1999 8-4 (4-4)

S4	●	at Memphis	3	0
S11	●	Arkansas State	38	14
S18	|	Vanderbilt	34	37
S25	● |	at Auburn	24	17
O2	● |	at South Carolina	36	10
O9	●	Tulane	20	13
O16	|	Alabama	24	30
O30	● |	at LSU	42	23
N6	● |	Arkansas	38	16
N20	|	Georgia	17	20
N25	|	at Mississippi State	20	23
		INDEPENDENCE BOWL		
D31	●	Oklahoma	27	25

2000 7-5 (4-4)

S2	●	Tulane	49	20
S9	|	Auburn	27	35
S16	● |	at Vanderbilt	12	7
S30	● |	Kentucky	35	17
O7	●	Arkansas State	35	10
O14	|	at Alabama	7	45
O28	●	Nevada-Las Vegas	43	40
N4	● |	at Arkansas	38	24
N11	|	LSU	9	20
N18	|	at Georgia	14	32
N23	● |	Mississippi State	45	30
		MUSIC CITY BOWL		
D28		West Virginia	38	49

2001 7-4 (4-4)

S1	●	Murray St.	49	14
S8	|	at Auburn	21	27
S29	● |	at Kentucky	42	31
O6	●	at Arkansas State	35	17
O13	● |	Alabama	27	24
O20	●	Middle Tennessee	45	17
O27	● |	at LSU	35	24
N3	|	Arkansas	56	58
N17	|	Georgia	15	35
N22	|	at Mississippi State	28	36
D1	● |	Vanderbilt	38	27

2002 7-6 (3-5)

A31	●	La. Monroe	31	3
S7	●	Memphis	38	16
S14		at Texas Tech	28	42
S21	● |	Vanderbilt	45	38
O5	● |	Florida	17	14
O12	●	Arkansas State	52	17
O19	|	at Alabama	7	42
O26	|	at Arkansas	28	48
N2	|	Auburn	24	31
N9	|	at Georgia	17	31
N23	|	at LSU	13	14
N28	● |	Mississippi State	24	12
		INDEPENDENCE BOWL		
D27	●	Nebraska	27	23

2003 10-3 (7-1)

A30	● |	at Vanderbilt	24	21
S6		at Memphis	34	44
S13	●	La. Monroe	59	14
S27		Texas Tech	45	49
O4	● |	at Florida	20	17
O11	●	Arkansas State	55	0
O18	● |	Alabama	43	28
O25	● |	Arkansas	19	7
N1	● |	South Carolina	43	40
N8	● |	at Auburn	24	20
N22	|	LSU	14	17
N27	● |	at Mississippi State	31	0
		COTTON BOWL		
J2	●	Oklahoma State	31	28

2004 4-7 (3-5)

S4		Memphis	13	20
S11	|	at Alabama	7	28
S18	● |	Vanderbilt	26	23
S25		at Wyoming	32	37
O2	●	Arkansas State	28	21
O9	● |	at South Carolina	31	28
O16	|	Tennessee	17	21
O30	|	Auburn	14	35
N13	|	at Arkansas	3	35
N20	|	at LSU	24	27
N27	● |	Mississippi State	20	3

ED ORGERON
2005-07 (.286) 10-25

2005 3-8 (1-7)

S5	●	at Memphis	10	6
S17	|	at Vanderbilt	23	31
S24		Wyoming	14	24
O1	|	at Tennessee	10	27
O8	●	Citadel	27	7
O15	|	Alabama	10	13
O22	● |	Kentucky	13	7
O29	|	at Auburn	3	27
N12	|	Arkansas	17	28
N19	|	LSU	7	40
N26	|	at Mississippi State	14	35

2006 4-8 (2-6)

S3	●	Memphis	28	25
S9		at Missouri	7	34
S16	|	at Kentucky	14	31
S23		Wake Forest	3	27
S30	|	Georgia	9	14
O7	● |	Vanderbilt	17	10
O14	|	at Alabama	23	26
O21	|	at Arkansas	3	38
O28	|	Auburn	17	23
N4	●	Northwestern State	27	7
N18	|	at LSU	20	23
N25	● |	Mississippi State	20	17

2007   3-9   (0-8)

S1	●	at Memphis	23	21
S8		Missouri	25	38
S15	|	at Vanderbilt	17	31
S22	|	Florida	24	30
S29	|	at Georgia	17	45
O6	●	Louisiana Tech	24	0
O13	|	Alabama	24	27
O20	|	Arkansas	8	44
O27	|	at Auburn	3	17
N3	●	Northwestern State	38	31
N17	|	LSU	24	41
N23	|	at Mississippi State	14	17

HOUSTON NUTT
2008-PRESENT (.692)   9-4

2008   9-4   (5-3)

A30	●	Memphis	41	24
S6		at Wake Forest	28	30
S13	●	Samford	34	10
S20	|	Vanderbilt	17	23
S27	● |	at Florida	31	30
O4	|	South Carolina	24	31
O18	|	at Alabama	20	24
O25	● |	at Arkansas	23	21
N1	● |	Auburn	17	7
N15	● |	La.-Monroe	59	0
N22	● |	at Louisiana State	31	13
N28	● |	Mississippi State	45	0
		COTTON BOWL		
J2	●	Texas Tech	47	34

Neutral Site key: *ATL* Atlanta, GA / *BEAU* Beaumont, TX / *BIRM* Birmingham, AL / *CHAT* Chattanooga, TN / *CLAR* Clarksdale, MS / *COLGA* Columbus, GA / *COLMS* Columbus, MS / *JACF* Jacksonville, FL / *JATN* Jackson, TN / *GEO* Georgetown, TX / *GRN* Greenwood, MS / *GRVMS* Greenville, MS / *HOU* Houston, TX / *JAM* Jackson, MS / *LR* Little Rock, AR / *MBL* Mobile, AL / *MEM* Memphis, TN / *MER* Meridian, MS / *MONT* Montgomery, AL / *NO* New Orleans, LA / *PHIL* Philadelphia, PA / *TUP* Tupelo, MS / *VIC* Vicksburg, MS / *WPT* West Point, MS
ƒ **Forfeit** † **Game Later Forfieted** # **Disputed Victor** * **Disputed Score** || **Designated Conference Game** |2 **Counted Twice in Conference Standings**

THE SCHOOLS

MISSISSIPPI ANNUAL STATISTICAL LEADERS

YR	RUSHING	YDS	ATT	AVG	PASSING	ATT	CMP	PCT	YDS	RECEIVING	REC	YDS	AVG
1946	Clayton Blount	280	49	5.7	Charlie Conerly	124	65	.52	609	Ray Poole	29	282	9.7
1947	Charlie Conerly	435	114	3.8	Charlie Conerly	232	133	.57	1,366	Barney Poole	52	511	9.8
1948	Jerry Tiblier	379	70	5.4	Farley Salmon	79	36	.46	415	Barney Poole	18	253	14.1
1949	Kayo Dottley	1,312	208	6.3	Rocky Byrd	85	42	.49	918	Jack Stribling	22	598	27.2
1950	Kayo Dottley	1,007	191	5.3	Rocky Byrd	83	42	.51	771	Jack Stribling	22	457	20.8
1951	Allen Murihead	501	105	4.8	Jimmy Lear	91	34	.37	727	James Slay	7	179	25.6
1952	Harol Lofton	698	137	5.1	Jimmy Lear	118	55	.47	975	James Slay	14	274	19.6
1953	Slick McCool	564	127	4.4	Lea Pasley	66	32	.48	713	Earl Blair	10	213	21.3
1954	Allen Murihead	443	63	7.0	Eagle Day	85	40	.47	879	Earl Blair	18	472	26.2
1955	Paige Cothren	520	93	5.6	Eagle Day	95	47	.49	724	Billy Kinard	23	371	16.1
1956	Paige Cothren	560	115	4.9	Raymond Brown	85	40	.47	653	Leroy Reed	14	278	19.9
1957	Allen Brown	530	99	5.4	Raymond Brown	53	24	.45	308	Billy Lott	5	71	14.2
1958	Charlie Flowers	559	107	5.2	Bobby Ray Franklin	121	56	.46	710	Kent Lovelace	14	178	12.7
1959	Charlie Flowers	733	141	5.2	Jake Gibbs	94	46	.49	755	Dewey Partridge	13	142	10.9
1960	Jim Anderson	505	104	4.9	Jake Gibbs	109	66	.61	970	Bobby Crespino	30	408	13.6
1961	Billy Ray Adams	575	91	6.3	Doug Elmore	84	50	.60	741	Ralph Smith	14	254	18.1
1962	Glynn Griffing	278	74	3.8	Glynn Griffing	122	72	.59	882	Louis Guy	24	295	12.3
1963	Fred Roberts	273	70	3.9	Perry Lee Dunn	89	51	.57	820	Allen Brown	16	221	13.8
1964	Mike Dennis	571	134	4.3	Jimmy Weatherly	170	91	.54	1,034	Mike Dennis	29	276	9.5
1965	Mike Dennis	525	152	3.5	Jimmy Heidel	95	52	.55	586	Mike Dennis	23	246	10.7
1966	Doug Cunningham	653	139	4.7	Bruce Newell	101	54	.53	702	Mac Hiak	20	267	13.4
1967	Stephen Hindman	829	215	3.9	Bruce Newell	121	53	.44	663	Mac Hiak	33	475	14.4
1968	Stephen Hindman	475	129	3.7	Archie Manning	263	127	.48	1,510	Hank Shows	27	276	10.2
1969	Archie Manning	502	124	4.0	Archie Manning	265	154	.58	1,762	Floyd Franks	54	720	13.3
1970	Randy Reed	668	157	4.3	Archie Manning	233	121	.52	1,481	Floyd Franks	46	668	14.5
1971	Stephen Ainsworth	629	134	4.7	Norris Weese	102	56	.55	650	Riley Myers	27	390	14.4
1972	Stephen Ainsworth	634	161	3.9	Norris Weese	163	77	.47	917	Burney Veazey	29	374	12.9
1973	Paul Hofer	642	123	5.2	Norris Weese	55	32	.58	401	Rick Kimbrough	29	459	15.8
1974	James Reed	461	110	4.2	Kenny Lyons	132	51	.39	583	Rick Kimbrough	23	271	11.8
1975	Michael Sweet	653	146	4.5	Tim Ellis	92	49	.53	621	Rick Kimbrough	31	407	13.1
1976	Michael Sweet	513	118	4.3	Tim Ellis	132	59	.45	740	Robert Frabis	20	220	11.0
1977	James Storey	564	143	3.9	Tim Ellis	78	35	.45	551	Curtis Weathers	23	395	17.2
1978	Leon Perry	673	148	4.5	John Fourcade	86	36	.42	461	Freddie Williams	30	232	7.7
1979	Leon Perry	678	160	4.2	John Fourcade	196	115	.59	1,521	Ken Toler	23	441	19.2
1980	William Hooper	619	155	4.0	John Fourcade	286	157	.55	1,897	Breck Tyler	33	535	16.2
1981	Andre Thomas	548	128	4.3	John Fourcade	251	137	.55	1,533	Michael Harmon	46	750	16.3
1982	Andre Thomas	686	173	4.0	Kent Austin	307	186	.61	2,026	Buford McGee	42	365	8.7
1983	Buford McGee	580	141	4.1	Kent Austin	211	107	.51	1,077	Buford McGee	39	272	7.0
1984	Nathan Wonsley	479	116	4.1	Kent Austin	302	177	.59	1,889	Nathan Wonsley	36	248	6.9
1985	Nathan Wonsley	462	116	4.0	Kent Austin	147	89	.61	1,116	J.R. Ambrose	38	708	18.6
1986	Willie Goodloe	526	119	4.4	Mark Young	178	87	.49	1,154	J.R. Ambrose	32	578	18.1
1987	Shawn Sykes	379	88	4.3	Mark Young	261	140	.54	1,490	J.R. Ambrose	42	515	12.3
1988	Joe Mickles	528	115	4.6	Mark Young	312	156	.50	1,969	Willie Green	38	648	17.1
1989	Randy Baldwin	642	107	6.0	John Darnell	301	167	.55	2,326	Willie Green	41	816	19.9
1990	Randy Baldwin	970	163	6.0	Russ Shows	126	57	.45	953	Darrick Owens	18	305	16.9
1991	Tyrone Ashley	503	82	6.1	Russ Shows	198	99	.50	1,369	Darrick Owens	23	329	14.3
1992	Cory Philpot	994	190	5.2	Russ Shows	224	118	.53	1,400	Eddie Small	39	558	14.3
1993	Marvin Courtney	343	71	4.8	Lawrence Adams	195	110	.56	1,415	Roell Preston	35	455	13.0
1994	Dou Innocent	910	182	5.0	Josh Nelson	308	168	.55	2,028	Ta'Boris Fisher	41	483	11.8
1995	Dou Innocent	868	192	4.5	Josh Nelson	250	143	.57	1,675	LeMay Thomas	56	801	14.3
1996	John Avery	788	181	4.4	Paul Head	172	104	.60	1,014	Ta'Boris Fisher	40	417	10.4
1997	John Avery	862	166	5.2	Stewart Patridge	352	228	.65	2,667	Rufus French	43	345	8.0
1998	Deuce McAllister	1,082	212	5.1	Romaro Miller	326	184	.56	2,273	Cory Peterson	41	601	14.7
1999	Joe Gunn	951	182	5.2	Romaro Miller	270	147	.54	1,999	Cory Peterson	46	610	13.3
2000	Deuce McAllister	767	159	4.8	Romaro Miller	295	161	.55	2,012	Grant Heard	44	655	14.9
2001	Joe Gunn	870	200	4.4	Eli Manning	408	259	.63	2,948	Chris Collins	54	692	12.8
2002	Ronald McClendon	378	96	3.9	Eli Manning	481	279	.58	3,401	Chris Collins	55	812	14.8
2003	Tremaine Turner	809	173	4.7	Eli Manning	441	275	.62	3,600	Chris Collins	77	949	12.3
2004	Vashon Pearson	807	158	5.1	Ethan Flatt	220	123	.56	1,530	Mario Hill	36	426	11.8
2005	Mico McSwain	612	124	4.9	Michael Spurlock	267	142	.53	1,703	Mike Espy	52	543	10.4
2006	BenJarvus Green-Ellis	1,000	234	4.3	Brent Schaeffer	244	115	.47	1,442	Mike Wallace	24	410	17.1
2007	BenJarvus Green-Ellis	1,137	230	4.9	Seth Adams	297	163	.55	1,979	Mike Wallace	38	716	18.8
2008	Dexter McCluster	655	109	6.0	Jevan Snead	327	184	.56	2,762	Shay Hodge	44	725	16.5

Receiving leaders by receptions
The NCAA began including postseason stats in 2002

MISSISSIPPI RECORD BOOK

SINGLE-GAME RECORDS

Rushing Yards	242	Dou Innocent (Nov. 25, 1995 vs. Mississippi State)
Passing Yards	436	Archie Manning (Oct. 26, 1969 vs. Alabama)
Receiving Yards	210	Eddie Small (Sept. 18, 1993 vs. Vanderbilt)
All-Purpose Yards	317	Deuce McAllister (Nov. 6, 1999 vs. Arkansas)
Points	42	Showboat Boykin (Dec. 1, 1951 vs. Mississippi State)
Field Goals	6	Jonathan Nichols (Sept. 27, 2003 vs. Texas Tech)
Tackles	NA	
Interceptions	3	Gary Hall (Nov. 30, 1974 vs. Tulane)

SINGLE-SEASON RECORDS

Rushing Yards	1,312	Kayo Dottley, 1949 (208 att)
Passing Yards	3,600	Eli Manning, 2003 (275-441)
Receiving Yards	949	Chris Collins, 2003 (77 rec.)
All-Purpose Yards	1,692	Deuce McAllister, 1999
Scoring	124	Jonathan Nichols, 2003 (25 FGs, 49 PATs)
Touchdowns	17	Deuce McAllister, 2000
Tackles	168	Jeff Herrod, 1986
Interceptions	10	Bobby Wilson, 1949
Punting Average	48.7	Merle Hapes, 1940 (23 punts)
Punt Return Average	15.1	Junie Hovious, 1940 (33 ret.)
Kickoff Return Average	26.1	Deuce McAllister, 1999 (25 ret.)

CAREER RECORDS

Rushing Yards	3,060	Deuce McAllister, 1997-2000
Passing Yards	10,119	Eli Manning, 2000-03
Receiving Yards	2,621	Chris Collins, 2000-03 (198 rec.)
All-Purpose Yards	4,889	Deuce McAllister, 1997-2000
Scoring	344	Jonathan Nichols, 2001-04
Touchdowns	41	Deuce McAllister, 1997-2000
Tackles	528	Jeff Herrod, 1984-87
Interceptions	20	Bobby Wilson, 1946-49
Punting Average	46	Merle Hapes, 1939-41 (69 punts)
Punt Return Average	13.6	Junie Hovious, 1938-41 (84 ret.)
Kickoff Return Average	22.2	Paul Hofer, 1972-75 (51 ret.)

TEAM RECORDS

Longest Winning Streak	13	Oct.1, 1955-Oct. 13, 1956; broken vs. Tulane, 3-10 on Oct. 20, 1956
Longest Undefeated Streak	21	Nov. 7, 1959-Oct. 28, 1961; broken vs. LSU, 7-10 on Nov. 4, 1961
Most Consecutive Winning Seasons	13	1951-63
Most Consecutive Bowl Appearances	15	1957-71
Most Points in a Game	114	vs. Southwest Baptist, Oct. 29, 1904
Most Points Allowed in a Game	91	vs. Vanderbilt, Oct. 23, 1915
Largest Margin of Victory	114	vs. Southwest Baptist, Oct. 29, 1904
Largest Margin of Defeat	91	vs. Vanderbilt, Oct. 23, 1915
Longest Pass Play	83	Josh Nelson to Lemay Thomas vs Mississippi State, Nov. 26, 1994
Longest Field Goal	59	Cloyce Hinton vs. Georgia, Oct. 11, 1969
Longest Punt	92	Bill Smith vs. Southern Miss, Oct. 20, 1984
Longest Interception Return	103	Louis Guy vs. Tennessee (Nov. 17, 1962); Ray Hapes vs. Ouachita (Oct. 23, 1937)

RETIRED NUMBERS

18	Archie Manning
28	Chucky Mullins

ALL-TIME TEAM

As selected in 1992 by fans to commemorate the school's centennial season

Offense			Defense		
	E	Floyd Franks, 1968-70		DL	Bruiser Kinnard, 1935-37
	E	Barney Poole, 1942, 1947-48		DL	Kelvin Pritchett, 1988-90
	OL	Jim Dunaway, 1960-62		DL	Ben Williams, 1972-75
	OL	Gene Hickerson, 1955-57		LB	Tony Bennett, 1986-89
	OL	Stan Hindman, 1963-65		LB	Kenny Dill, 1961-63
	OL	Everett Lindsay, 1989-92		LB	Larry Grantham, 1957-59
	OL	Marvin Terrell, 1957-57		LB	Jeff Herrod, 1984-87
	C	Dawson Pruett, 1987-90		LB	Freddie Joe Nunn, 1981-84
	QB	Archie Manning, 1968-70		DB	Billy Brewer, 1957-59
	RB	Charlie Conerly, 1942, 1946-47		DB	Glenn Cannon, 1967-69
	RB	John (Kayo) Dottley, 1947-50		DB	Chris Mitchell, 1987-90
	RB	Charlie Flowers, 1957-59		DB	Jimmy Patton, 1952-54
	PK	Robert Khayat, 1957-59		DB	Todd Sandroni, 1987-90
				P	Jim Miller, 1976-79

MISSISSIPPI BOWL HISTORY

SEASON	BOWL	DATE	PRE-GAME RANK	TEAMS	SCORE	FINAL RANK	MOST VALUABLE PLAYER(S)	ATT.
1935	ORANGE	Jan. 1, 1936		Catholic Mississippi	20 19			6,568
1947	DELTA	Jan. 1, 1948	13	Mississippi TCU	13 9		Charlie Conerly, Mississippi, QB	28,120
1952	SUGAR	Jan. 1, 1953	2 7	Georgia Tech Mississippi	24 7		Leon Hardemann, Georgia Tech, HB	80,205
1954	SUGAR	Jan. 1, 1955	5 6	Navy Mississippi	21 0		Joe Gattuso, Navy, FB	80,205
1955	COTTON	Jan. 2, 1956	10 6	Mississippi TCU	14 13		Buddy Alliston, Mississippi, G Eagle Day, Mississippi, QB	75,504
1957	SUGAR	Jan. 1, 1958	7 11	Mississippi Texas	39 7		Raymond Brown, Mississippi, QB	76,535
1958	GATOR	Dec. 27, 1958	11 14	Mississippi Florida	7 3		Bobby Franklin, Mississippi, QB Dave Hudson, Florida, E	41,312
1959	SUGAR	Jan. 1, 1960	2 3	Mississippi LSU	21 0		Bobby Franklin, Mississippi, QB	44,683
1960	SUGAR	Jan. 2, 1961	2	Mississippi Rice	14 6		Jake Gibbs, Mississippi, QB	80,331
1961	COTTON	Jan. 1, 1962	3 5	Texas Mississippi	12 7		Mike Cotten, Texas, QB Bob Moses, Texas, E	75,504
1962	SUGAR	Jan. 1, 1963	3 6	Mississippi Arkansas	17 13		Glynn Griffin, Mississippi, QB	79,707
1963	SUGAR	Jan. 1, 1964	8 7	Alabama Mississippi	12 7		Tim Davis, Alabama, K	82,910
1964	BLUEBONNET	Dec. 19, 1964		Tulsa Mississippi	14 7		Jerry Rhome, Tulsa, QB Willy Townes, Tulsa, DT	50,000
1965	LIBERTY	Dec. 18, 1965		Mississippi Auburn	13 7		Tom Bryan, Auburn, FB	38,607
1966	BLUEBONNET	Dec. 17, 1966		Texas Mississippi	19 0		Chris Gilbert, Texas, RB Fred Edwards, Texas, LB	67,000
1967	SUN	Dec. 30, 1967		UTEP Mississippi	14 7		Bill Stevens, UTEP, QB Fred Carr, UTEP, LB	34,685
1968	LIBERTY	Dec. 14, 1968		Mississippi Virginia Tech	34 17		Steve Hindman, Mississippi, TB	46,206
1969	SUGAR	Jan. 1, 1970	13 3	Mississippi Arkansas	27 22	8 7	Archie Manning, Mississippi, QB	72,858
1970	GATOR	Jan. 2, 1971	10	Auburn Mississippi	35 28	10 20	Pat Sullivan, Auburn, QB Archie Manning, Mississippi, QB	71,136
1971	PEACH	Dec. 30, 1971	17	Mississippi Georgia Tech	41 18	15	Norris Weese, Mississippi, QB Crowell Armstrong, Mississippi, LB	36,771
1983	INDEPENDENCE	Dec. 10, 1983	16	Air Force Mississippi	9 3	13	Marty Louthan, Air Force, QB Andre Townsend, Mississippi, DT	41,274
1986	INDEPENDENCE	Dec. 20, 1986		Mississippi Texas Tech	20 17		Mark Young, Mississippi, QB James Mosley, Texas Tech, DE	46,369
1989	LIBERTY	Dec. 28, 1989		Mississippi Air Force	42 29		Randy Baldwin, Mississippi, RB	60,128
1990	GATOR	Jan. 1, 1991	12 15	Michigan Mississippi	35 3	7 21	Michigan offensive line	68,927
1992	LIBERTY	Dec. 31, 1992	20	Mississippi Air Force	13 0	16	Cassius Ware, Mississippi, LB	32,107
1997	MOTOR CITY	Dec. 26, 1997		Mississippi Marshall	34 31	22	Stewart Patridge, Mississippi, QB	43,340
1998	INDEPENDENCE	Dec. 31, 1998		Mississippi Texas Tech	35 18		Romaro Miller, Mississippi, QB Kendrick Clancy, Mississippi, DL	46,862
1999	INDEPENDENCE	Dec. 31, 1999		Mississippi Oklahoma	27 25	22	Tim Strickland, Mississippi, CB Josh Heupel, Oklahoma, QB	49,873
2000	MUSIC CITY	Dec. 28, 2000		West Virginia Mississippi	49 38		Brad Lewis, West Virginia, QB	22,026
2002	INDEPENDENCE	Dec. 27, 2002		Mississippi Nebraska	27 23		Eli Manning, Mississippi, QB Chris Kelsay, Nebraska, DE	46,096
2003	COTTON	Jan. 2, 2004	16 21	Mississippi Oklahoma State	31 28	13	Eli Manning, Mississippi, QB Josh Cooper, Mississippi, DE	73,928
2008	COTTON	Jan. 2, 2009		Mississippi Texas Tech	47 34	14 12	Dexter McCluster, Mississippi, WR Marshay Green, Mississippi, CB	88,175

JANUARY 1, 1936 | Orange
CATHOLIC 20, MISSISSIPPI 19

	1ST	2ND	3RD	4TH	FINAL
CA	7	6	7	0	20
MISS	0	6	0	13	19

SCORING SUMMARY
CA   Adamaitis 2 yard run (Milligan kick)
CA   Foley 48 pass from Adamaitis (kick failed)
MISS Peters 67 run (kick failed)
CA   Rydewski 24 blocked punt return (Makofske kick)
MISS Bernard 3 run (kick failed)
MISS Poole 24 pass from Baumsten (Richardson kick)

CA	TEAM STATISTICS	MISS
7	First Downs	15
124	Rushing Yards	212
1-3-2	Passing	3-12-4
48	Passing Yards	53
172	Total Yards	265
13-41.0	Punts - Average	11-38.0
1-1	Fumbles - Lost	3-2
1-10	Penalties - Yards	3-30

INDIVIDUAL LEADERS
RUSHING
CA: Makofske 12-46; Carroll 12-45.
MISS: Peters 11-89, 1 TD; Rogers 16-50.
PASSING
CA: Adamaitis 1-3-2, 48 yards, 1 TD.
MISS: Baumsten 3-12-4, 53 yards, 1 TD.
RECEIVING
CA: Foley 1-48, 1 TD.
MISS: Poole 1-24, 1 TD.

JANUARY 1, 1948 | Delta
MISSISSIPPI 13, TCU 9

	1ST	2ND	3RD	4TH	FINAL
MISS	0	0	0	13	13
TCU	0	9	0	0	9

SCORING SUMMARY
TCU   Berry 30 interception return (Pitcock kick)
TCU   Safety (Conerly blocked punt out of end zone)
MISS Johnson 30 pass from Conerly (kick failed)
MISS Howell 13 pass from Conerly (Oswalt kick)

MISS	TEAM STATISTICS	TCU
15	First Downs	15
111	Rushing Yards	141
12-30-4	Passing	6-11-2
186	Passing Yards	55
297	Total Yards	196
3-40.6	Punts - Average	5-42.8
1-1	Fumbles - Lost	2-2
7-35	Penalties - Yards	5-45

INDIVIDUAL LEADERS
RUSHING
MISS: Salmon 6-48; Harrell 6-18.
TCU: Stout 15-73; McKelvey 7-26.
PASSING
MISS: Conerly 12-28-3, 186 yards, 2 TD.
TCU: Berry 3-5-1, 32 yards.
RECEIVING
MISS: Johnson 1-79, 1 TD; Howell 2-25, 1 TD.
TCU: Bailey 3-23; Stout 1-13.

JANUARY 1, 1953 | Sugar
GEORGIA TECH 24, MISSISSIPPI 7

	1ST	2ND	3RD	4TH	FINAL
GT	0	10	7	7	24
MISS	7	0	0	0	7

SCORING SUMMARY
MISS Dillard 4 run (Lear kick)
GT   Brigman 1 run (Rodgers kick)
GT   FG Rodgers 25
GT   Hardemann 6 run (Rodgers kick)
GT   Knox 26 pass from Rodgers (Rodgers kick)

GT	TEAM STATISTICS	MISS
16	First Downs	15
194	Rushing Yards	137
10-18-1	Passing	11-23-3
101	Passing Yards	150
295	Total Yards	287
6-41.8	Punts - Average	7-35.4
5-2	Fumbles - Lost	5-3
5-42	Penalties - Yards	6-60

INDIVIDUAL LEADERS
RUSHING
GT: Hardemann 14-76, 1 TD; Turner 20-56.
MISS: Dillard 17-39, 1 TD; Westerman 7-36.
PASSING
GT: Brigman 5-7-1, 39 yards; Rodgers 4-9-0, 55 yards, 1 TD.
MISS: Lear 8-19-3, 122 yards.
RECEIVING
GT: Hardemann 2-24; Marks 2-14.
MISS: Slay 1-45; Bridges 2-25.

JANUARY 1, 1955 | Sugar
NAVY 21, MISSISSIPPI 0

	1ST	2ND	3RD	4TH	FINAL
MISS	0	0	0	0	0
NAVY	7	0	14	0	21

SCORING SUMMARY
NAVY Gattuso 3 run (Weaver kick)
NAVY Weaver 16 pass from Welsh (Weaver kick)
NAVY Gattuso 1 run (Weaver kick)

MISS	TEAM STATISTICS	NAVY
5	First Downs	20
78	Rushing Yards	295
5-18-0	Passing	12-28-4
43	Passing Yards	147
121	Total Yards	442
9-36.1	Punts - Average	4-33.8
2-1	Fumbles - Lost	1-0
6-50	Penalties - Yards	1-15

INDIVIDUAL LEADERS
RUSHING
MISS: Cothren 7-24.
NAVY: Weaver 16-106; Gattuso 16-11, 2 TD.
PASSING
MISS: Day 2-9-0, 16 yards; Patton 3-6-0, 27 yards.
NAVY: Welsh 8-14-0, 76 yards, 1 TD.
RECEIVING
MISS: Muirhead 2-16.
NAVY: Weaver 3-39, 1 TD; Beagle 3-19.

JANUARY 2, 1956 | Cotton
MISSISSIPPI 14, TCU 13

	1ST	2ND	3RD	4TH	FINAL
MISS	0	7	0	7	14
TCU	7	6	0	0	13

SCORING SUMMARY
TCU   Swink 1 run (Pollard kick)
TCU   Swink 39 run (kick failed)
MISS Cothren 3 run (Cothren kick)
MISS Lott 5 run (Cothren kick)

MISS	TEAM STATISTICS	TCU
12	First Downs	11
92	Rushing Yards	233
10-21-0	Passing	2-5-2
137	Passing Yards	20
229	Total Yards	253
6-42.7	Punts - Average	5-28.8
1-1	Fumbles - Lost	2-1
6-80	Penalties - Yards	8-80

INDIVIDUAL LEADERS
RUSHING
MISS: Cothren 12-79, 1 TD; Kinard 3-7.
TCU: Swink 19-107, 2 TD; Taylor 10-76.
PASSING
MISS: Day 10-21-0, 137 yards.
TCU: Finney 1-3-2, 13 yards.
RECEIVING
MISS: Kinard 6-83; Blair 1-28.
TCU: Williams 1-13; Nikkel 1-7.

JANUARY 1, 1958 | Sugar
MISSISSIPPI 39, TEXAS 7

	1ST	2ND	3RD	4TH	FINAL
MISS	6	13	7	13	39
TEX	0	0	0	7	7

SCORING SUMMARY
MISS Brown 1 run (kick failed)
MISS Williams 3 pass from Brown (Khayat kick)
MISS Lovelace 9 run (Khayat kick)
MISS Franklin 3 run (Khayat kick)
TEX   Blanch 1 run (Lackey kick)
MISS Brown 92 run (Khayat kick)
MISS Taylor 12 pass from Brewer (kick failed)

MISS	TEAM STATISTICS	TEX
18	First Downs	13
304	Rushing Yards	192
7-16-0	Passing	2-11-4
71	Passing Yards	14
375	Total Yards	206
7-34.7	Punts - Average	5-38.2
5-2	Fumbles - Lost	7-4
9-95	Penalties - Yards	6-30

INDIVIDUAL LEADERS
RUSHING
MISS: Brown 15-157 yards, 2 TD; Franklin 9-64, 1 TD.
TEX: Blanch 11-58, 1 TD; Allen 8-43; Fondren 8-39.
PASSING
MISS: Brown 3-8-0, 24 yards, 1 TD.
TEX: Lackey 2-5-2, 14 yards.
RECEIVING
MISS: Taylor 2-20, 1 TD; Willaims 2-15, 1 TD.
TEX: Ramirez 1-3.

DECEMBER 27, 1958 | Gator
MISSISSIPPI 7, FLORIDA 3

	1ST	2ND	3RD	4TH	FINAL
MISS	7	0	0	0	7
UF	3	0	0	0	3

SCORING SUMMARY
MISS Anderson 1 run (Khayat kick)
UF   FG Booker 17

MISS	TEAM STATISTICS	UF
9	First Downs	12
157	Rushing Yards	157
2-7-0	Passing	5-11-1
27	Passing Yards	58
184	Total Yards	215
10-34.4	Punts - Average	7-44.1
5-2	Fumbles - Lost	5-3
2-10	Penalties - Yards	3-35

INDIVIDUAL LEADERS
RUSHING
MISS: Anderson 9-62, 1 TD; Lovelace 7-28.
UF: Newbern 5-59; Milby 10-35.
PASSING
MISS: Franklin 2-7-0, 27 yards.
UF: Dunn 5-11-1, 58 yards.
RECEIVING
MISS: Grantham 1-15; Daniels 1-12.
UF: Hudson 3-22; Dilts 1-13.

JANUARY 1, 1960 | Sugar
MISSISSIPPI 21, LSU 0

	1ST	2ND	3RD	4TH	FINAL
MISS	0	7	7	7	21
LSU	0	0	0	0	0

SCORING SUMMARY
MISS Woodruff 43 pass from Gibbs (Franklin kick)
MISS Granthan 18 pass from Franklin (Khayat kick)
MISS Blair 9 pass from Franklin (Khayat kick)

MISS	TEAM STATISTICS	LSU
19	First Downs	6
140	Rushing Yards	-15
15-27-2	Passing	9-25-2
223	Passing Yards	89
363	Total Yards	74
6-37.5	Punts - Average	12-34.3
4-2	Fumbles - Lost	2-0
7-65	Penalties - Yards	4-30

INDIVIDUAL LEADERS
RUSHING
MISS: Flowers 19-60; Blair 8-26.
LSU: Cannon 6-8.
PASSING
MISS: Franklin 10-15-1, 148 yards, 2 TD; Gibbs 4-10-1, 65 yards, 1 TD.
LSU: Rabb 4-15-0, 36 yards.
RECEIVING
MISS: Flowers 4-64.
LSU: Cannon 3-39; McClain 3-31.

JANUARY 2, 1961 | Sugar
MISSISSIPPI 14, RICE 6

	1ST	2ND	3RD	4TH	FINAL
MISS	7	0	0	7	14
RICE	0	0	6	0	6

SCORING SUMMARY
MISS Gibbs 8 run (Green kick)
RICE Blume 2 run (kick failed)
MISS Gibbs 3 run (Green kick)

MISS	TEAM STATISTICS	RICE
13	First Downs	19
143	Rushing Yards	103
5-15-0	Passing	14-28-4
43	Passing Yards	178
186	Total Yards	281
5-42.4	Punts - Average	3-34.0
1-1	Fumbles - Lost	2-0
2-10	Penalties - Yards	6-30

INDIVIDUAL LEADERS
RUSHING
MISS: Anderson 15-59; Doty 4-25.
RICE: Blume 7-54, 1 TD.
PASSING
MISS: Gibbs 5-15-0, 43 yards.
RICE: Cox 11-20-1, 143 yards.
RECEIVING
MISS: Crespini 2-21; Blair 2-18.
RICE: Webb 3-31.

JANUARY 1, 1962 | COTTON
TEXAS 12, MISSISSIPPI 7

	1ST	2ND	3RD	4TH	FINAL
MISS	0	0	7	0	7
TEX	6	6	0	0	12

SCORING SUMMARY
TEX   Saxton 1 run (kick blocked)
TEX   Collins 24 pass from Cotten (run failed)
MISS   Davis 20 pass from Griffing (Sullivan kick)

MISS	TEAM STATISTICS	TEX
17	First Downs	12
127	Rushing Yards	123
15-37-5	Passing	6-13-3
192	Passing Yards	60
319	Total Yards	183
4-32.5	Punts - Average	5-40.2
1-1	Fumbles - Lost	2-1
4-30	Penalties - Yards	3-35

INDIVIDUAL LEADERS
RUSHING
MISS: Griffing 10-45; Doty 5-29.
TEX: Poage 11-54; Cotten 11-25.
PASSING
MISS: Griffing 12-29-3, 163 yards, 1 TD.
TEX: Cotten 6-13-3, 60 yards, 1 TD.
RECEIVING
MISS: Guy 4-43; Doty 4-41.
TEX: Collins 2-30, 1 TD; Saxton 3-18.

JANUARY 1, 1963 | SUGAR
MISSISSIPPI 17, ARKANSAS 13

	1ST	2ND	3RD	4TH	FINAL
MISS	0	10	7	0	17
ARK	0	3	10	0	13

SCORING SUMMARY
MISS   FG Irwin 30
ARK   FG McKnelly 30
MISS   Guy 33 pass from Griffin (Irwin kick)
ARK   Branch 5 pass from Moore (McKnelly kick)
MISS   Griffin 1 run (Irwin kick)
ARK   FG McKnelly 22

MISS	TEAM STATISTICS	ARK
22	First Downs	7
160	Rushing Yards	47
18-28-1	Passing	6-18-2
269	Passing Yards	123
429	Total Yards	170
2-36.0	Punts - Average	4-38.3
2-1	Fumbles - Lost	2-0
4-40	Penalties - Yards	2-13

INDIVIDUAL LEADERS
RUSHING
MISS: Jennings 9-39; Weatherly 9-36.
ARK: Branch 7-21.
PASSING
MISS: Griffin 14-23-1, 242 yards, 1 TD.
ARK: Moore 5-10-0, 55 yards, 1 TD.
RECEIVING
MISS: Guy 5-107, 1 TD; Morris 5-62.
ARK: Lamb 3-107; Branch 3-16, 1 TD.

JANUARY 1, 1964 | SUGAR
ALABAMA 12, MISSISSIPPI 7

	1ST	2ND	3RD	4TH	FINAL
ALA	3	6	3	0	12
MISS	0	0	0	7	7

SCORING SUMMARY
ALA   FG Davis 46
ALA   FG Davis 31
ALA   FG Davis 34
ALA   FG Davis 48
MISS   Smith 5 pass from Dunn (Irwin kick)

ALA	TEAM STATISTICS	MISS
14	First Downs	9
165	Rushing Yards	77
3-11-1	Passing	11-21-3
29	Passing Yards	171
194	Total Yards	248
5-36.8	Punts - Average	4-44.0
6-3	Fumbles - Lost	11-6
3-15	Penalties - Yards	5-45

INDIVIDUAL LEADERS
RUSHING
ALA: Sloan 16-51; Nelson 16-47.
MISS: Dennis 7-37; Dunn 6-24.
PASSING
ALA: Sloan 3-10-1, 29 yards.
MISS: Dunn 8-10-0, 125 yards, 1 TD.
RECEIVING
ALA: Stephens 1-15.
MISS: Wells 4-76.

DECEMBER 19, 1964 | BLUEBONNET
TULSA 14, MISSISSIPPI 7

	1ST	2ND	3RD	4TH	FINAL
TUL	0	7	7	0	14
MISS	0	7	0	0	7

SCORING SUMMARY
MISS   Weatherly 1 run (Irwin kick)
TUL   Rhome 1 run (Twilley kick)
TUL   Fletcher 35 pass from Rhome (Twilley kick)

TUL	TEAM STATISTICS	MISS
19	First Downs	10
71	Rushing Yards	104
22-36-1	Passing	16-24-2
252	Passing Yards	113
323	Total Yards	217
7-31.6	Punts - Average	8-31.1
1-0	Fumbles - Lost	2-0
4-30	Penalties - Yards	4-50

INDIVIDUAL LEADERS
RUSHING
TUL: Daugherty 6-32; Rhome 22-29, 1 TD.
MISS: Dennis 17-73.
PASSING
TUL: Rhome 22-36-1, 252 yards, 1 TD.
MISS: Weatherly 16-24-2, 113 yards.
RECEIVING
TUL: Roberts 8-108; Daugherty 9-80.
MISS: Dennis 9-114.

DECEMBER 18, 1965 | LIBERTY
MISSISSIPPI 13, AUBURN 7

	1ST	2ND	3RD	4TH	FINAL
MISS	0	3	7	3	13
AU	0	7	0	0	7

SCORING SUMMARY
MISS   FG Keyes 42
AU   Bryan 44 run (Lewis kick)
MISS   Cunningham 6 pass from Graves (Keyes kick)
MISS   FG Keyes 30

MISS	TEAM STATISTICS	AU
12	First Downs	15
189	Rushing Yards	156
4-12-0	Passing	11-24-1
24	Passing Yards	112
213	Total Yards	268
8-39.0	Punts - Average	9-34.8
0-0	Fumbles - Lost	0-0
5-25	Penalties - Yards	4-29

INDIVIDUAL LEADERS
RUSHING
AU: Bryan 19-111, 1 TD.
MISS: Dennis 15-75; Heidel 16-72.
PASSING
AU: Bowden 11-24-1, 112 yards.
MISS: Graves 2-10-0, 15 yards, 1 TD.
RECEIVING
AU: Hardy 4-46.
MISS: Matthews 2-9.

DECEMBER 17, 1966 | BLUEBONNET
TEXAS 19, MISSISSIPPI 0

	1ST	2ND	3RD	4TH	FINAL
TEX	6	0	6	7	19
MISS	0	0	0	0	0

SCORING SUMMARY
TEX   Bradley 25 run (kick failed)
TEX   Gilbert 1 run (pass failed)
TEX   Bradley 4 run (Conway kick)

TEX	TEAM STATISTICS	MISS
19	First Downs	7
285	Rushing Yards	143
5-17-4	Passing	10-26-4
95	Passing Yards	65
380	Total Yards	208
3-42.0	Punts - Average	7-28.4
3-3	Fumbles - Lost	0-0
4-34	Penalties - Yards	8-84

INDIVIDUAL LEADERS
RUSHING
TEX: Gilbert 26-156, 1 TD; Bradley 20-105, 2 TD.
MISS: Cunningham 12-60; Street 6-39.
PASSING
TEX: Bradley 4-12-2, 49 yards; White 1-5-2, 46 yards.
MISS: Newell 9-20-2, 54 yards.
RECEIVING
TEX: Higgins 1-46; Gennusa 2-30.
MISS: Matthews 3-24; Cunningham 3-17.

DECEMBER 30, 1967 | SUN
UTEP 14, MISSISSIPPI 7

	1ST	2ND	3RD	4TH	FINAL
UTEP	0	0	0	14	14
MISS	0	7	0	0	7

SCORING SUMMARY
MISS   Newell 1 run (Brown kick)
UTEP   Karns 5 pass from Stevens (Waddles kick)
UTEP   McHenry 4 run (Waddles kick)

UTEP	TEAM STATISTICS	MISS
16	First Downs	6
75	Rushing Yards	38
16-35-1	Passing	12-23-1
201	Passing Yards	71
276	Total Yards	109
6-25	Punt Returns - Yards	8-75
1-7	Kickoff Returns - Yards	4-98
12-39.0	Punts - Average	11-42.0
0-0	Fumbles - Lost	4-3
9-92	Penalties - Yards	5-33

INDIVIDUAL LEADERS
RUSHING
UTEP: McHenry 13-73, 1 TD; White 17-72.
MISS: Hindman 15-53.
PASSING
UTEP: Stevens 13-26-1, 155 yards, 1 TD.
MISS: Newell 12-23-1, 71 yards.
RECEIVING
UTEP: Wallace 6-83; Karns 5-56, 1 TD.
MISS: Matthews 4-25; Haik 3-24.

DECEMBER 14, 1968 | LIBERTY
MISSISSIPPI 34, VIRGINIA TECH 17

	1ST	2ND	3RD	4TH	FINAL
MISS	0	14	7	13	34
VT	17	0	0	0	17

SCORING SUMMARY
VT   Edwards 58 run (Simsack kick)
VT   Smoot 7 run (Simsack kick)
VT   FG Simsack 29
MISS   Shows 21 pass from Manning (Brown kick)
MISS   Felts 23 pass from Manning (Brown kick)
MISS   Hindman 79 run (Brown kick)
MISS   Bailey 70 interception return (Brown kick)
MISS   FG Brown 46
MISS   FG Brown 26

MISS	TEAM STATISTICS	VT
7	First Downs	14
185	Rushing Yards	330
12-28-1	Passing	1-7-0
141	Passing Yards	2
326	Total Yards	332
5-37.4	Punts - Average	7-40.7
3-2	Fumbles - Lost	5-3
4-30	Penalties - Yards	12-120

INDIVIDUAL LEADERS
RUSHING
MISS: Hindman 15-121, 1 TD; Bowen 19-65.
VT: Edwards 12-119, 1 TD, Smoot 21-91, 1 TD.
PASSING
MISS: Manning 12-28-0, 141 yards, 2 TD.
VT: Humphries 1-3-0, 2 yards.

JANUARY 1, 1970 | SUGAR
MISSISSIPPI 27, ARKANSAS 22

	1ST	2ND	3RD	4TH	FINAL
MISS	14	10	3	0	27
ARK	0	12	3	7	22

SCORING SUMMARY
MISS   Bowen 69 run (King kick)
MISS   Manning 18 run (King kick)
ARK   Burnett 12 run (kick failed)
MISS   FG Hinton 52
MISS   Studdard 30 pass from Manning (King kick)
ARK   Dicus 47 pass from Montgomery (pass failed)
MISS   FG Hinton 36
ARK   FG McClard 35
ARK   Maxwell 6 pass from Montgomery (McClard kick)

MISS	TEAM STATISTICS	ARK
24	First Downs	21
154	Rushing Yards	189
21-35-2	Passing	17-35-2
273	Passing Yards	338
427	Total Yards	527
2-30.5	Punts - Average	6-37.6
1-1	Fumbles - Lost	0
3-22	Penalties - Yards	11-101

INDIVIDUAL LEADERS
RUSHING
MISS: Bowen 12-94, 1 TD; Manning 13-39, 1 TD.
ARK: Maxwell 8-108; Burnett 17-59, 1 TD.
PASSING
MISS: Manning 21-35-2, 273 yards, 1 TD.
ARK: Montgomery 17-34-1, 338 yards, 2 TD.
RECEIVING
MISS: Studdard 5-109, 1 TD; Reed 2-22.
ARK: Dicus 6-171, 1 TD; Maxwell 9-137, 1 TD.

JANUARY 2, 1971 | GATOR
AUBURN 35, MISSISSIPPI 28

	1ST	2ND	3RD	4TH	FINAL
AUB	14	7	14	0	35
MISS	0	14	7	7	28

SCORING SUMMARY
AUB   Beasley 12 pass from Sullivan (Jett kick)
AUB   Bresler 7 pass from Sullivan (Jett kick)
AUB   Sullivan 37 run (Jett kick)
MISS   Manning 1 run (Poole kick)
MISS   Franks 34 pass from Manning (Poole kick)
AUB   Zofko 6 run (Jett kick)
MISS   Poole 23 pass from Chumbler (Poole kick)
AUB   Willingham 55 punt return (Jett kick)
MISS   Chumbler 1 run (Poole kick)

AUB	TEAM STATISTICS	MISS
23	First Downs	21
208	Rushing Yards	209
27-44-1	Passing	23-39-1
351	Passing Yards	256
559	Total Yards	465
4-40.5	Punts - Average	6-47.3
5-3	Fumbles - Lost	3-2
6-63	Penalties - Yards	2-13

INDIVIDUAL LEADERS
RUSHING
AUB: Clark 14-108; Sullivan 10-35, 1 TD.
MISS: Manning 11-95, 1 TD; Ainsworth 11-68.
PASSING
AUB: Sullivan 27-43-1, 351 yards, 2 TD.
MISS: Manning 19-28-1, 180 yards, 1 TD; Chumbler 4-11-0, 76 yards, 1 TD.
RECEIVING
AUB: Beasley 8-143, 1 TD; Bresler 4-102, 1 TD.
MISS: Poole 9-111, 1 TD; Franks 7-78, 1 TD.

DECEMBER 30, 1971 | PEACH
MISSISSIPPI 41, GEORGIA TECH 18

	1ST	2ND	3RD	4TH	FINAL
MISS	10	28	0	3	41
GT	0	6	6	6	18

SCORING SUMMARY
MISS   Weese 1 run (Hinton kick)
MISS   FG Hinton 25
MISS   Porter 2 run (Hinton kick)
MISS   Porter 10 run (Hinton kick)
MISS   Felts 15 pass from Lyons (Hinton kick)
MISS   Myers 11 pass from Weese (Hinton kick)
GT   Healy 2 run (run failed)
GT   Healy 1 run (pass failed)
GT   Healy 1 run (run failed)
MISS   FG Hinton 30

MISS	TEAM STATISTICS	GT
17	First Downs	16
179	Rushing Yards	166
9-18-1	Passing	13-26-2
139	Passing Yards	151
318	Total Yards	317
5-37.4	Punts - Average	5-31.2
2-1	Fumbles - Lost	3-3
5-25	Penalties - Yards	8-38

INDIVIDUAL LEADERS
RUSHING
MISS: Ainsworth 28-119; Porter 8-26, 2 TD.
GT: Hennessey 6-57; Cunningham 5-30.
PASSING
MISS: Weese 7-14-0, 23 yards, 1 TD.
GT: McAshan 13-26-2, 151 yards.
RECEIVING
MISS: Myers 2-49, 1 TD; Barry 3-39.
GT: Owings 5-87; Oven 3-26.

DECEMBER 10, 1983 | INDEPENDENCE
AIR FORCE 9, MISSISSIPPI 3

	1ST	2ND	3RD	4TH	FINAL
AFA	3	3	3	0	9
MISS	0	3	0	0	3

SCORING SUMMARY
AFA   FG Pavlich 44
AFA   FG Pavlich 39
MISS   FG Teevan 39
AFA   FG Pavlich 27

AFA	TEAM STATISTICS	MISS
18	First Downs	11
277	Rushing Yards	106
6-7-1	Passing	11-27-2
71	Passing Yards	138
348	Total Yards	244
3-30.3	Punts - Average	5-43.6
3-3	Fumbles - Lost	1-0
4-19	Penalties - Yards	4-20

INDIVIDUAL LEADERS
RUSHING
AFA: Brown 12-91; Louthan 25-67.
MISS: McGee 22-111; Humphrey 6-15.
PASSING
AFA: Louthan 6-7-0, 71 yards.
MISS: Powell 11-27-2, 138 yards.
RECEIVING
AFA: Kirby 3-49.
MISS: Moffett 6-96.

DECEMBER 20, 1986 | INDEPENDENCE
MISSISSIPPI 20, TEXAS TECH 17

	1ST	2ND	3RD	4TH	FINAL
MISS	7	10	0	3	20
TT	0	7	7	3	17

SCORING SUMMARY
MISS   Goodloe 1 run (Owen kick)
MISS   Mickles 9 run (Owen kick)
MISS   FG Owen 21
TT   Gray 1 run (Segrist kick)
TT   Scurlark 33 interception return (Segrist kick)
TT   FG Segrist 19
MISS   FG Owen 48

MISS	TEAM STATISTICS	TT
26	First Downs	18
60	Rushing Yards	175
31-50-1	Passing	17-40-1
343	Passing Yards	181
403	Total Yards	356
6-45.5	Punts - Average	8-41.5
1-1	Fumbles - Lost	2-0
5-33	Penalties - Yards	5-60

INDIVIDUAL LEADERS
RUSHING
MISS: Myers 4-69; Mickles 10-53, 1 TD.
TT: Farris 17-99.
PASSING
MISS: Young 31-50-1, 343 yards.
TT: Tolliver 17-40-1, 181 yards.
RECEIVING
MISS: Ambrose 8-102.
TT: Price 9-74; Walker 3-71.

DECEMBER 28, 1989 | LIBERTY
MISSISSIPPI 42, AIR FORCE 29

	1ST	2ND	3RD	4TH	FINAL
MISS	14	14	7	7	42
AFA	9	0	6	14	29

SCORING SUMMARY
MISS   Hines 23 pass from Darnell (Hogue kick)
AFA   FG Woods 37
MISS   Baldwin 23 run (Hogue kick)
AFA   Dowis 2 run (pass failed)
MISS   Baldwin 21 run (Hogue kick)
MISS   Coleman 58 punt return (Hogue kick)
AFA   Johnson 3 run (run failed)
MISS   Coleman 11 run (Hogue kick)
MISS   Thigpen 8 pass from Shows (Hogue kick)
AFA   Senn 35 pass from McDowell (pass failed)
AFA   Senn 21 pass from McDowell (Durham run)

MISS	TEAM STATISTICS	AFA
30	First Downs	25
225	Rushing Yards	259
21-37-0	Passing	14-24-2
285	Passing Yards	233
510	Total Yards	492
5-38.2	Punts - Average	4-43.3
2-2	Fumbles - Lost	3-2
7-45	Penalties - Yards	2-12
27:15	Possession Time	32:45

INDIVIDUAL LEADERS
RUSHING
MISS: Baldwin 15-177, 2 TD.
AFA: Dowis 18-92, 1 TD; Johnson 10-48, 1 TD.
PASSING
MISS: Darnell 19-33-0, 261 yards, 1 TD.
AFA: McDowell 7-8-2, 147 yards, 2 TD.
RECEIVING
MISS: Green 5-72; Hines 3-69, 1 TD.
AFA: Senn 7-150, 2 TD; Van Hulzen 5-57.

JANUARY 1, 1991 | GATOR
MICHIGAN 35, MISSISSIPPI 3

	1ST	2ND	3RD	4TH	FINAL
MICH	7	7	21	0	35
MISS	0	3	0	0	3

SCORING SUMMARY
MICH Howard 63 pass from Grbac (Carlson kick)
MISS FG Lee 51
MICH Bunch 7 pass from Grbac (Carlson kick)
MICH Howard 50 pass from Grbac (Carlson kick)
MICH Bunch 5 run (Carlson kick)
MICH Alexander 33 pass from Grbac (Carlson kick)

MICH	TEAM STATISTICS	MISS
35	First Downs	20
391	Rushing Yards	93
20-32-1	Passing	18-32-4
324	Passing Yards	240
715	Total Yards	333
2-24.5	Punts - Average	5-38.0
2-1	Fumbles - Lost	4-2
6-69	Penalties - Yards	4-49

INDIVIDUAL LEADERS
RUSHING
MICH: Vaughn 15-128; Powers 14-112; Bunch 11-54, 1 TD.
MISS: Baldwin 8-53; Thigpen 6-32.
PASSING
MICH: Grbac 16-25-1, 296 yards, 4 TD.
MISS: Shows 13-21-3, 175 yards.
RECEIVING
MICH: Howard 6-167, 2 TD; Alexander 2-50, 1 TD.
MISS: Brownlee 5-71; Roberts 4-67.

DECEMBER 31, 1992 | LIBERTY
MISSISSIPPI 13, AIR FORCE 0

	1ST	2ND	3RD	4TH	FINAL
MISS	7	3	0	3	13
AFA	0	0	0	0	0

SCORING SUMMARY
MISS Innocent 2 run (Lee kick)
MISS FG Lee 24
MISS FG Lee 29

MISS	TEAM STATISTICS	AFA
13	First Downs	14
168	Rushing Yards	104
9-19-0	Passing	10-17-2
163	Passing Yards	81
331	Total Yards	185
5-33	Punts - Average	5-20.2
2-1	Fumbles - Lost	2-1
7-57	Penalties - Yards	6-53

INDIVIDUAL LEADERS
RUSHING
MISS: Innocent 16-62, 1 TD.
AFA: Pastorello 13-49.
PASSING
MISS: Shows 9-19-0, 163 yards.
AFA: Teigen 5-8-1, 55 yards.
RECEIVING
MISS: Courtney 4-63.
AFA: Hufford 2-18.

DECEMBER 26, 1997 | MOTOR CITY
MISSISSIPPI 34, MARSHALL 31

	1ST	2ND	3RD	4TH	FINAL
MISS	7	0	14	13	34
MAR	10	7	0	14	31

SCORING SUMMARY
MISS Avery 1 run (Lindsey kick)
MAR Moss 80 pass from Pennington (Malashevich kick)
MAR FG Malashevich 36
MAR Colclough 19 pass from Pennington (Malashevich kick)
MISS Rone 13 pass from Patridge (Lindsey kick)
MISS McAllister 20 pass from Patridge (Lindsey kick)
MAR Chapman 6 pass from Pennington (Malashevich kick)
MISS Heard 19 pass from Patridge (kick failed)
MAR Chapman 9 run (Malashevich kick)
MISS McAllister 1 run (Lindsey kick)

MISS	TEAM STATISTICS	MAR
29	First Downs	23
179	Rushing Yards	170
29-48-1	Passing	23-45-0
332	Passing Yards	337
511	Total Yards	507
4-41.8	Punts - Average	7-39.7
0-0	Fumbles - Lost	3-2
7-71	Penalties - Yards	10-93
34:21	Possession Time	25:39

INDIVIDUAL LEADERS
RUSHING
MISS: Avery 27-110, 1 TD; McAllister 8-71, 1 TD.
MAR: Chapman 19-152, 1 TD.
PASSING
MISS: Patridge 29-47-1, 332 yards, 3 TD.
MAR: Pennington 23-45-0, 337 yards, 3 TD.
RECEIVING
MISS: Heard 3-81, 1 TD; Peterson 7-66.
MAR: Moss 6-173, 1 TD; Colclough 8-84, 1 TD.

DECEMBER 31, 1998 | INDEPENDENCE
MISSISSIPPI 35, TEXAS TECH 18

	1ST	2ND	3RD	4TH	FINAL
MISS	7	7	0	21	35
TT	7	3	0	8	18

SCORING SUMMARY
TT Dorris 22 pass from Peters (Birkholz kick)
MISS Lucas 33 pass from Miller (McGee kick)
MISS McAllister 32 pass from Miller (McGee kick)
TT FG Birkholz 49
MISS Peterson 26 pass from Miller (McGee kick)
MISS McAllister 4 run (McGee kick)
TT McCullar 14 fumble return (Winn pass from Tittle)
MISS McAllister 43 kickoff return (McGee kick)

MISS	TEAM STATISTICS	TT
19	First Downs	18
139	Rushing Yards	82
14-23-1	Passing	16-30-2
216	Passing Yards	203
355	Total Yards	285
5-32.4	Punts - Average	6-30.8
3-2	Fumbles - Lost	2-1
7-86	Penalties - Yards	5-55
34:47	Possession Time	25:13

INDIVIDUAL LEADERS
RUSHING
MISS: McAllister 27-83, 1 TD.
TT: Williams 23-95.
PASSING
MISS: Miller 14-23-1, 216, 3 TD.
TT: Tittle 11-19-2, 134 yards; Peters 5-11-0, 69 yards, 1 TD.
RECEIVING
MISS: McAllister 2-55, 1 TD; Peterson 3-54.
TT: Dorris 5-66, 1 TD; Hart 4-50.

DECEMBER 31, 1999 | INDEPENDENCE
MISSISSIPPI 27, OKLAHOMA 25

	1ST	2ND	3RD	4TH	FINAL
MISS	7	14	0	6	27
OKLA	3	0	15	7	25

SCORING SUMMARY
MISS McAllister 25 pass from Miller (Binkley kick)
OKLA FG Duncan 34
MISS Bettis 9 pass from Miller (Binkley kick)
MISS McAllister 80 run (Binkley kick)
OKLA Jackson 3 pass from Heupel (Duncan kick)
OKLA Daniels 41 pass from Heupel (Hammons pass from Heupel)
MISS FG Binkley 29
OKLA Griffin 17 pass from Heupel (Duncan kick)
MISS FG Binkley 39

MISS	TEAM STATISTICS	OKLA
19	First Downs	27
159	Rushing Yards	91
18-29-2	Passing	39-54-1
202	Passing Yards	390
361	Total Yards	481
5-39.4	Punts - Average	1-10.0
1-0	Fumbles - Lost	3-3
3-13	Penalties - Yards	4-35
29:24	Possession Time	30:36

INDIVIDUAL LEADERS
RUSHING
MISS: McAllister 17-121, 1 TD.
OKLA: Griffin 12-86.
PASSING
MISS: Miller 18-28-2, 202 yards, 2 TD.
OKLA: Heupel 39-53-1, 390 yards, 3 TD.
RECEIVING
MISS: McAllister 3-55, 1 TD; Peterson 5-51.
OKLA: Daniels 6-109, 1 TD; Jackson 10-76, 1 TD.

DECEMBER 28, 2000 | MUSIC CITY
WEST VIRGINIA 49, MISSISSIPPI 38

	1ST	2ND	3RD	4TH	FINAL
MISS	3	6	7	22	38
WVU	7	28	14	0	49

SCORING SUMMARY
WVU Ours 40 pass from Lewis (Rauh kick)
MISS FG Binkley 23
WVU Ivy 11 pass from Lewis (Rauh kick)
MISS FG Binkley 47
WVU Brown 35 pass from Lewis (Rauh kick)
MISS FG Binkley 26
WVU Brown 60 pass from Lewis (Rauh kick)
WVU Ours 1 run (Rauh kick)
WVU Terry 99 kickoff return (Rauh kick)
WVU Ivy 10 pass from Lewis (Rauh Kick)
MISS Miller 7 run (Binkley kick)
MISS Armstrong 23 pass from Manning (Binkley kick)
MISS Rayford 18 pass from Manning (Binkley kick)
MISS Sanford 16 pass from Manning (Taylor pass from Miller)

MISS	TEAM STATISTICS	WVU
28	First Downs	19
96	Rushing Yards	114
28-51-3	Passing	15-21-1
388	Passing Yards	318
484	Total Yards	432
2-18	Punt Returns - Yards	0-0
4-83	Kickoff Returns - Yards	5-171
3-29.3	Punts - Average	2-39.0
1-0	Fumbles - Lost	0-0
12-93	Penalties - Yards	8-77
35:16	Possession Time	24:44

INDIVIDUAL LEADERS
RUSHING
MISS: Gunn 8-34; Miller 7-32, 1 TD.
WVU: Cobourne 27-125.
PASSING
MISS: Miller 16-31-2, 221 yards; Manning 12-20-1, 167 yards, 3 TD.
WVU: Lewis 15-21-1, 318 yards, 5 TD.
RECEIVING
MISS: Collins 5-65; Rayford 2-61, 1 TD; Armstrong 3-59, 1 TD.
WVU: Brown 6-156, 2 TD; Ivy 6-99, 2 TD.

December 27, 2002 | Independence
Mississippi 27, Nebraska 23

	1ST	2ND	3RD	4TH	FINAL
MISS	0	14	10	3	27
NEB	3	14	3	3	23

SCORING SUMMARY
NEB   FG Brown 29
NEB   Herian 41 pass from Lord (Brown kick)
MISS   Johnson 11 pass from Manning (Nichols kick)
NEB   Groce 60 punt return (Brown kick)
MISS   Sanford 1 run (Nichols kick)
MISS   FG Nichols 37
NEB   FG Brown 23
MISS   Sanford 1 run (Nichols kick)
NEB   FG Brown 29
MISS   FG Nichols 43

MISS	TEAM STATISTICS	NEB
20	First Downs	17
52	Rushing Yards	266
25-44-0	Passing	7-17-2
313	Passing Yards	93
365	Total Yards	359
3-23	Punt Returns - Yards	8-102
5-80	Kickoff Returns - Yards	5-105
8-43.8	Punts - Average	6-43.8
1-0	Fumbles - Lost	0-0
6-41	Penalties - Yards	6-70
30:31	Possession Time	29:29

INDIVIDUAL LEADERS
RUSHING
MISS: McClendon 12-36.
NEB: Diedrick 13-92; Lord 17-83.
PASSING
MISS: Manning 25-44-1, 313 yards, 1 TD.
NEB: Lord 7-16-2, 93 yards, 1 TD.
RECEIVING
MISS: Flowers 6-76.
NEB: Herian 1-41, 1 TD.

January 2, 2004 | Cotton
Mississippi 31, Oklahoma State 28

	1ST	2ND	3RD	4TH	FINAL
MISS	7	10	7	7	31
OSU	7	7	0	14	28

SCORING SUMMARY
MISS   Turner 16 pass from Manning (Nichols kick)
OSU   Morency 4 run (Phillips kick)
OSU   Bell 3 run (Phillips kick)
MISS   Espy 25 pass from Manning (Nichols kick)
MISS   FG Nichols 33
MISS   Turner 2 run (Nichols kick)
MISS   Manning 1 run (Nichols kick)
OSU   Morency 1 run (Phillips kick)
OSU   R. Woods 17 pass from Fields (Phillips kick)

MISS	TEAM STATISTICS	OSU
24	First Downs	22
190	Rushing Yards	110
22-31-1	Passing	21-33-0
259	Passing Yards	307
449	Total Yards	417
3-57	Punt Returns - Yards	1-15
0-0	Kickoff Returns - Yards	3-57
3-38.0	Punts - Average	3-37.7
1-0	Fumbles - Lost	1-0
2-20	Penalties - Yards	6-49
31:29	Possession Time	28:31

INDIVIDUAL LEADERS
RUSHING
MISS: Turner 20-133, 1 TD; Pearson 12-42.
OSU: Morency 15-59, 2 TD; Bell 14-46, 1 TD.
PASSING
MISS: Manning 22-31-1, 259 yards, 2 TD.
OSU: Fields 21-33-0, 307 yards, 1 TD.
RECEIVING
MISS: Collins 8-75; Johnson 3-53; Espy 2-47, 1 TD.
OSU: R. Woods 11-223, 1 TD; D. Woods 4-51.

January 2, 2009 | Cotton
Mississippi 47, Texas Tech 34

	1ST	2ND	3RD	4TH	FINAL
MISS	7	17	14	9	47
TT	14	7	0	13	34

SCORING SUMMARY
TT   Britton 35 pass from Harrell (Williams kick)
TT   McBath 45 interception return (Williams kick)
MISS   Harris 8 pass from Snead (Shene kick)
MISS   Wallace 41 pass from Snead (Shene kick)
TT   Crabtree 2 pass from Harrell (Williams kick)
MISS   Harris 21 pass from Snead (Shene kick)
MISS   FG Shene 27
MISS   Green 65 interception return (Shene kick)
MISS   Bolden 17 run (Shene kick)
TT   Britton 12 pass from Harrell (Williams kick)
MISS   Safety Harrell tackled in end zone
MISS   McCluster 4 run (Shene kick)
TT   Morris 17 pass from Harrell (two-point conversion failed)

MISS	TEAM STATISTICS	TT
26	First Downs	24
223	Rushing Yards	105
18-29-1	Passing	36-58-2
292	Passing Yards	364
515	Total Yards	469
4-79	Punt Returns - Yards	1-0
4-91	Kickoff Returns - Yards	7-158
2-37.6	Punts - Average	4-41
2-2	Fumbles - Lost	1-0
2-15	Penalties - Yards	8-62

INDIVIDUAL LEADERS
RUSHING
MISS: Bolden 11-101, 1 TD.
TT: Woods 6-46.
PASSING
MISS: Snead 18-29-1, 292 yards, 3 TD.
TT: Harrell 36-58-2, 364 yards, 4 TD.
RECEIVING
MISS: McCluster 6-83; Wallace 4-80, 1 TD.
TT: Morris 10-89, 1 TD; Britton 5-87, 2 TD.

MISSISSIPPI STATE

BY GEOFFREY NORMAN

THE HISTORY OF MISSISSIPPI STATE football might best be characterized by the word "struggle." No program in the SEC has had to reinvent and rebuild itself more often than the Bulldogs. This, perhaps, accounts for an abiding toughness and a reputation as the school that other, more successful SEC programs, overlook at their peril. MSU keeps picking itself up, coming back and searching for new ways to break through. That includes hiring Sylvester Croom in 2003—the SEC's first African-American head coach. Croom resigned after a disappointing 2008 season, but that does not diminish the magnitude of his breakthrough or of MSU's boldness.

The first football game played at what was then Mississippi A&M College took place on Thanksgiving Day 1892. A team made up of faculty members defeated one composed of students, 4-0. On Nov. 16, 1895, the school played and lost its first intercollegiate game, 21-0, at Southwestern Baptist (now Union University) in Jackson, Tenn. The Aggies, as they were then called, lost

their first home game the next season. There was no football in 1897, when an epidemic of yellow fever swept the state. And the next year the cadets of A&M were involved in the Spanish-American War. Football would have to wait. In 1901, though, A&M fielded a team that, in its first game, fought to a scoreless tie against Christian Brothers College in Memphis. The first victory in school history, 17-0, came at home two days later, on Oct. 28, 1901, against the best of all possible opponents—the University of Mississippi.

This was the first of many highs that have sustained the program and kept the cowbells ringing in Starkville.

TRADITION Nobody quite knows how MSU's famed cowbell tradition originated. The consensus is that ringing cowbells to support Mississippi State's fortunes began in the late 1930s and early 1940s, a period still considered the golden age of Bulldogs football. According to legend, during a home game against Mississippi, a Jersey cow wandered onto the playing field. MSU won the game convincingly and some fans viewed this as an omen, bringing the cow to every game from then on. After awhile, they dropped the cow and settled on the cowbell as the talisman. MSU fans adopted the cowbell with relish, and, because the folks from Oxford disparaged State as the "aggie school," there was something defiant in

> **Life magazine and 2,500 mourners attended Bully I's funeral in 1939 after he was hit by a bus.**

the choice. The cowbell flourished during the 1950s and '60s—through long droughts in Bulldogs fortunes. The addition of a handle enabled fans to really ring that thing and make some noise. But the practice proved too distracting for the SEC, which imposed a ban on artificial noisemakers at conference football and basketball games in 1974. The rule, however, does not apply to nonconference games. Ring away.

BEST PLAYER Linebacker Johnie Cooks led MSU to its first back-to-back bowl appearances and was SEC Defensive Player of the Year in 1981. He also earned the defensive MVP in that year's Hall of Fame Bowl. In his 45 games at MSU, Cooks made 392 tackles and went on to a 10-year NFL career with the Colts, Giants and Browns. Cooks was inducted into the Mississippi Sports Hall of Fame in 2004.

BEST COACH On the advice of Tennessee's Robert Neyland, in 1939 MSU hired a young UT assistant coach named Allyn McKeen to take over the top spot. In 1940, McKeen's squad went 10–0–1, MSU's only undefeated season since a 3–0–2 campaign in 1903. McKeen's 1941 Bulldogs won the SEC title with an 8–1–1 overall record and a 4–0–1 conference mark. That 1941 team played the kind of tough defense one would expect from a Neyland protégé, shutting out Florida, Alabama, LSU and Mississippi—the last three on the road. McKeen coached the Bulldogs until 1948, when he was fired after losing to Mississippi in consecutive seasons. Even so, his winning percentage of .764 (65–19–3) is the best of any MSU coach—a group that includes, among others, Murray Warmath, Darrell Royal and Jackie Sherrill.

BEST TEAM McKeen picked the 1940 squad, which featured a defense anchored by All-American end Buddy Elrod. The only blemish—if it could be called that—was an early-season tie in Birmingham with Auburn, after which the Bulldogs ran the table in such dominant fashion that the AP crowned MSU the "undisputed king of football in the Deep South." The team finished the season ranked No. 9 by the AP and beat Georgetown, 14-7, in the Orange Bowl on New Year's Day 1941—the first bowl victory in school history.

BEST DEFENSE The 1981 squad held opponents to fewer than 12 points a game. It was good enough to

FIGHT SONG

HAIL STATE!
Hail dear 'ole State!
Fight for that victory today.
Hit that line and tote that ball,
Cross the goal before you fall!
And then we'll yell, yell, yell, yell!
For dear 'ole State we'll yell like H-E-L-L!
Fight for Mis-sis-sip-pi State,
Win that game today.

FIRST-ROUND DRAFT CHOICES

1956	Art Davis, Steelers (5)
1959	Billy Stacy, Cardinals, (3)
1975	Jimmy Webb, 49ers (10)
1982	Johnie Cooks, Colts (2)
1982	Glen Collins, Bengals (26)
1983	Michael Haddix, Eagles (8)
1996	Walt Harris, Bears (13)
1996	Eric Moulds, Bills (24)

CONSENSUS ALL-AMERICANS

| 1974 | Jimmy Webb, DL |
| 2000 | Fred Smoot, DB |

earn the team an invitation to the Hall of Fame Bowl, where the Bulldogs defense peaked. Led by Johnie Cooks and All-SEC defensive back Rob Fesmire, MSU held Kansas to 35 yards in 40 rushing attempts en route to a 10-0 shutout.

BEST BACKFIELD

The 1974 Mississippi State team is remembered, arguably, with more affection than just about any squad in MSU history. And the character of that team was shaped by the dominant personality of quarterback Rockey Felker, who returned to Starkville in 1986 for a five-year stint as head coach and now serves as the recruiting coordinator and running backs coach.

As a player, Felker was feisty, creative and competitive, and he was the spark that made the team's veer offense work. But he was not the dominant force. That was Walter Packer, who averaged almost six yards per carry in his MSU career.

That 1974 team went 9–3 and finished No. 18 in the AP poll. The backfield had perhaps its finest day at the Sun Bowl, with Packer running for 183 yards and fellow running back Terry Vitrano gaining another 164. MSU beat North Carolina 26-24, and its 455 yards of total rushing still stands as a Sun Bowl record.

STORYBOOK SEASON

The 1998 Bulldogs, recovering from the effects of NCAA penalties for recruiting violations, went on a late-season run that included wins over Alabama, Arkansas and Mississippi to win the SEC Western Division—their first SEC championship of any kind since 1941. In the conference title game, the Bulldogs led Tennessee 14-10 in the fourth quarter, before the eventual national champion Vols pulled it out, 24-14. Mississippi State then played Texas in the Cotton Bowl—the first time in nearly 60 years that the Bulldogs had gone to a New Year's Day bowl.

BIGGEST GAME

Rebuilding and recovering from a scandal that resulted in forfeits of all but two Bulldogs victories from 1975 to '77, MSU hired Emory Bellard in 1979 to turn things around. Bellard brought the wishbone formation—which he was credited with inventing—from Texas A&M, and after a rough first season things began to look up. The Bulldogs stood at 6–2 on Nov. 1, 1980, when defending national champion Alabama came to Jackson riding a 28-game winning streak. Defenders Johnie Cooks and Glen Collins shut down the Bama offense, and quarterback John Bond did enough with the modified formation Bellard called the wingbone to give MSU a 6-3 lead well into the fourth quarter. A Bulldogs goal-line

stand in the final minute preserved the score. Billy Jackson, a freshman defensive end, recovered a fumble by Alabama's Don Jacobs with six seconds left and the Tide at the Bulldogs' 3-yard line. The victory was MSU's first over Alabama since 1957.

COLLEGE FOOTBALL HALL OF FAME INDUCTEES		
NAME	YEARS	INDUCTED
Bernie Bierman, COACH	1925-26	1955
Jackie Parker, QB	1952-53	1976
Darrell Royal, COACH	1954-55	1983
Allyn McKeen, COACH	1939-48	1991
D.D. Lewis, LB	1965-67	2001

BIGGEST UPSET

MSU was not considered a first-class football power in the South, much less the nation, on the last day of October in 1935, when the Maroons (as they were then known) faced powerful Army at West Point, where MSU coach Major Ralph Sasse had previously served as head coach. Those were the days when eastern schools like Army dominated college football. But the Maroons hung on and hung around, and in the final minute of the game they trailed Army, 7-6. Then quarterback Pee Wee Armstrong threw a 65-yard touchdown pass to Fred Waters to shock the sporting world and put MSU on the football map with a 13-7 win over the mighty Cadets.

HEARTBREAKER

The Nov. 29, 1997, game against Ole Miss would determine which of the schools would make it to a bowl game. MSU held a 14-7 lead with time winding down. The Rebels drove the field to score a touchdown, then converted a two-point attempt for a one-point win. For many Bulldogs fans, the bitter taste from that loss still lingers.

STADIUM

Davis Wade Stadium at Scott Field is the second oldest on-campus stadium in Division I-A, dating back to 1914 when it was called simply New Athletic Field. In 1920, the name was changed to Scott Field in honor of Don Magruder Scott, an Olympic sprinter and one of Mississippi State's first football stars. Improvements in 1928, '36 and '48 raised capacity to 35,000. The most recent expansion, begun in 2000, increased seating to 55,082, including 50 skyboxes and 1,700 club-level seats. The bill for this project came in at more than $30 million and was made possible, in large part, by the generosity of the late Floyd Davis Wade Sr. of Meridian, an alumnus and booster for whom the stadium is named.

RIVAL

Ole Miss, of course. Passions ran so high in the early days of the rivalry that, after a brawl in 1927, the student bodies got together and came up with a trophy for the winner. This was done, of course, in the name of sportsmanship.

The trophy is shaped like an old-time football and looks remarkably like an egg. So the Golden Egg was hatched. At 92 games, the rivalry ranks among the top

10 longest uninterrupted active series in college football. The game has been played on 10 different fields in seven cities, but since 1991 it has been strictly a home-and-home affair. Since then, the series stands at 9–9.

NICKNAME MSU's teams were known as the Aggies until 1932, when the school's name changed from Mississippi A&M to Mississippi State College. Then the nickname became the Maroons, a reference to the school's maroon and white uniforms. The official nickname changed to Bulldogs in 1961 when the school attained university status.

MASCOT Bully XX (a registered English bulldog) represents Mississippi State at football games. Many of his predecessors roamed the Starkville campus at will or bedded down in frat houses but, like XIX, Bully XX is housed at the School of Veterinary Medicine. The original Bully debuted shortly after MSU's 1935 upset of Army.

His tenure came to a sad end on Nov. 19, 1939, when he was killed by a campus school bus. Three days later, 2,500 mourners paid their final respects to Bully I, who was buried under the bench at the 50-yard line of Scott Field. *Life* magazine covered the funeral.

UNIFORMS Before Mississippi A&M's 1895 game at Southwestern Baptist, W.M. Mathews, the Aggie coach/captain/QB, chose maroon and white as the team's colors. Since then, nobody has seen any reason for change, though from time to time some gray has been added to the scheme. In 1938, coach Spike Nelson decked out the team in gold uniforms, but neither the gold nor Nelson returned for 1939—the first year, ironically, of the golden age of MSU football.

QUOTE "There ain't but one color that matters here, and that color is maroon." —**Sylvester Croom**, first African-American head coach in the SEC

On the Significance of the Cowbell

BY KYLE VEAZEY

The cowbell does not produce a particularly warm sound. It's best described as a clank, a rattle, a clack. Put together the sound of 40,000 or so cowbells in a stadium and it sounds like millions of Tic Tacs being shaken about in a hundred-yard tin.

But it's the sweetest sound to the ears of fans of Mississippi State football, who gather on the fall Saturdays at Davis Wade Stadium at Scott Field in Starkville, many with cowbell in fist, in an eternal hope that *this* is the year. They've rung them through huge wins—the school's only outright Southeastern Conference title, a week before the attack on Pearl Harbor, and the Western Division title in 1998—but they've seen a lot more losses. Mississippi State has lost the third-most SEC games in history, and—with all due respect to Nashville's West End Avenue—no SEC school has more frustrated its faithful.

So they hold tight to tradition, to hope and, yes, to the cowbell. You wouldn't dare blame them, not to their face. It's hardly a prop to be shaken at games and thrown in the backseat on the drive home. (Call it a prop, as I once did in an article, and prepare for the e-mails.) No, a Mississippi State fan's cowbell is his rock, his badge, his prized possession, a symbol of his dedication to a team that all too often robs his hopes with little or no return on the emotional investment. Cowbells are given as graduation gifts, both high school and college; as wedding presents; as birthday gifts. Sterling silver versions with wooden handles sit on the mantles of well-to-do Bulldogs boosters.

The last time the university named a new president, he rang one. When a distinguished visitor comes to campus—such as, in September 2008, former secretary of state Colin Powell—he or she is given one. (Powell rang his; the crowd gave its loudest approval of the night.) If you're a new-to-campus Mississippi State freshman and don't have a cowbell, a trip to the campus bookstore in the suffocating late-August

It didn't take long for State's opponents to take notice of the cowbells, which led to a 9-to-1 vote banning artificial noisemakers at SEC games. Which points to another of the cowbell's connotations: It's a symbol of defiance.

humidity is a necessity. Has been for as long as most can remember.

No one can speak with authority about the origin of the cowbell, but there is a generally accepted story. With MSU facing archrival Ole Miss in a spirited battle (is there any other kind of game between the two schools?) in the 1930s, a Jersey cow wandered onto the field. Mississippi State won. The cow was captured as a good-luck charm.

Faced with the difficulty of parading a bovine to Scott Field on fall Saturdays, over time a useful bit of metonymy took place and the cowbell itself became the

charm. In the 1960s, a couple of MSU professors started welding handles to the cowbells, making them much easier to give a vigorous shake—and produce a more resonant ring.

It didn't take long for State's opponents to take notice, which led to a 9-to-1 vote banning artificial noisemakers at SEC games. (Guess which school was the solo dissenter?) Which points to another of the cowbell's connotations: It's a symbol of defiance, and Mississippi State folks are just fine with that, thank you very much.

Signs at entrances to Scott Field remind fans about the ban. No problem: Just stick the cowbell somewhere a guard can't see it (purse? back pocket?). The man with the badge isn't going to waste much time searching for the contraband, since the man with the badge probably has a cowbell in his back pocket, too. And when the school re-visited its secondary logos last year, one of the new arrivals included a cowbell.

Mississippi is a fiercely divided two-school state, and the cowbell also serves as a symbol of the school's heritage as—to use the derogatory term—a "cow college," the one with the Extension Service and the farm on campus and all the dairy products from on-campus cattle being sold on campus. What better item to convey that identity than a cowbell?

The symbols at other SEC schools are unique but natural: a bluetick coonhound in Knoxville, houndstooth in Tuscaloosa, hedges in Athens.

Here, it's four inches of bicycle handle, seven inches of metal and decades of meaning. And the good people of Starkville are just fine with that, thank you very much.

*Though he lives in Starkville, **Kyle Veazey** does not own a cowbell. But he does cover Mississippi State sports for* The Clarion-Ledger, *Mississippi's statewide newspaper.*

MISSISSIPPI STATE ALL-TIME SCORES

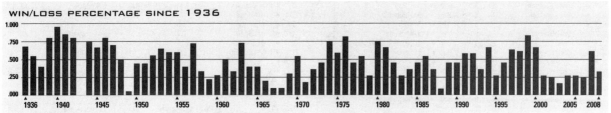

WIN/LOSS PERCENTAGE SINCE 1936

W.M. MATTHEWS		
1895 (.000)		0-2

1895
0-2-0
N16	at Union	0	21
D7	at Memphis AC	0	16

J.B. HILDEBRAND		
1896 (.000)		0-4

1896
0-4-0
O10	Union	0	8
N14	at Alabama	0	20
N20	at LSU	0	52
N21	at New Orleans AC	0	55

1897-1900
NO TEAM

L.B. HARVEY		
1901 (.500)		2-2-1

1901
2-2-1
O26	=	at Christian Brothers	0	0
O28	●	Mississippi	17	0
N2	●	at Meridian AC	11	5
N9		at Tulane	6	24
N26		at Alabama	0	45

L. GWINN		
1902 (.250)		1-4-1

1902
1-4-1
O17		Cumberland	6	15
O25		Mississippi	0	21
N1	=	at Tulane	11	11
N8		at Alabama	0	27
N15	●	at Samford	26	0
N27		LSU	0	6

DAN MARTIN		
1903-06 (.479)		10-11-3

1903
3-0-2
O16	●	Alabama *CoLMs*	11	0
O24	●	at Meridian AC	43	0
N7	●	LSU	11	0
N14	=	at Mississippi	6	6
D5	=	at Tulane	0	0

1904
2-5-0
O1		Vanderbilt *CoLMs*	0	61
O15		Alabama *CoLMs*	0	6
O22		Mississippi *CoLMs*	5	17
O29		at Tulane	0	10
N11	●	Tenn. Med. Coll.	59	0
N18	●	Cumberland	5	27
N25	●	Louisiana Tech	32	5

1905
3-4-0
O14		at Alabama	0	34
O20	●	at Marion Inst.	38	0
O27	●	Auburn *JAM*	0	18
N11	●	Samford	44	0
N18	●	Cumberland	5	27
N30	●	Mississippi *JAM*	11	0
D2		at LSU	0	15

1906
2-2-1
S29	●	Samford	30	0
O13	●	Marion Inst.	62	0
O27	=	LSU *CoLMs*	0	0
N3		Alabama	4	16
N29		Mississippi *JAM*	5	29

FRED FURMAN		
1907-08 (.563)		9-7

1907
6-3-0
O2	●	Southwestern	7	0
O10	●	at Sewanee	0	38
O12	●	at Samford	12	5
O19	●	Union	80	0
O24	●	Mercer *CoLMs*	75	0
O30	●	Drury Coll.	6	0
N9		at LSU	11	23
N16		Tennessee *MEM*	4	11
N28	●	Mississippi *JAM*	15	0

1908
3-4-0
O10	●	Louisiana Tech	47	0
O17		at Georgia Tech	0	23
O23		La. Lafayette *CoLMs*	5	6
O31	●	Transylvania, Ky.	12	5
N7		at LSU	0	50
N14		at Tulane	0	23
N26	●	Mississippi *JAM*	44	6

W.D. CHADWICK		
1909-13 (.698)		29-12-2

1909
5-4-0
O2	●	B'ham Southern	21	0
O9	●	Cumberland	34	6
O16		at LSU	0	15
O22	●	Southwestern *CoLMs*	31	0
O30		at Tulane	0	2
N2	●	Union *CoLMs*	25	0
N8		at Samford	0	6
N13	●	U.T. Chattanooga	37	6
N25	●	Mississippi *JAM*	5	9

1910
7-2-0
O1	●	Mississippi Coll.	24	0
O8		at Auburn	0	6
O15	●	Memphis U. Sch.	6	0
O21	●	LSU *CoLMs*	3	0
O31	●	Tennessee	48	0
N5		at Tulane	10	0
N12	●	B'ham Southern	46	0
N18	●	Samford	82	0
N24		Mississippi *JAM*	0	30

1911
7-2-1
S29	●	Mississippi Coll.	27	6
O7	●	Southwestern	30	0
O14	●	Samford	48	0
O21	=	Alabama *CoLMs*	6	6
O28	●	Auburn *BIRM*	5	11
N3	●	B'ham Southern	62	0
N12	●	LSU *GUL*	6	0
N20		Tulane	4	5
N30	●	Mississippi *JAM*	6	0
J1	●	Havana AC *HAV*	12	0

1912
4-3-0
O4	●	Mississippi Coll.	19	0
O12	●	Tenn. Med. Coll.	32	0
O18	●	Alabama *ABE*	7	0
O26	●	Auburn *BIRM*	0	7
N2	●	at LSU	7	0
N9		at Tulane	24	27
N16	●	Texas A&M *HOU*	7	41

1913
6-1-1
O4	●	Samford	66	0
O10	●	Mississippi Coll.	1	0	*f*
O17	●	Transylvania, Ky. *CoLMs*	31	0
O25	●	Auburn *BIRM*	0	34
N1	●	at Texas A&M	6	0
N8	●	Tulane	32	0
N15	=	LSU	0	0
N27	●	Alabama *BIRM*	7	0

E.C. HAYES		
1914-16 (.640)		15-8-2

1914
6-2-0
O3	●	Marion Inst.	54	0
O10	●	Cumberland	77	0
O17	●	at Kentucky	13	19
O24	●	Auburn *BIRM*	0	19
O31	●	at Georgia	9	0
N7	●	Mercer	66	0
N14	●	Tulane *JAM*	61	0
N26	●	Alabama *BIRM*	9	0

1915
5-2-1
O2	●	Mississippi Coll. *JAM*	12	0
O9	=	Transylvania, Ky.	0	0
O16	●	Kentucky	12	0
O23	●	Auburn *BIRM*	0	26
O30	●	at LSU	0	10
N6	●	Mississippi *TUP*	65	0
N13	●	Tennessee	14	0
N25	●	Texas A&M *DAL*	7	0

1916
4-4-1
O6	●	Mississippi Coll. *ABE*	6	13
O14	●	at U.T. Chattanooga	33	0
O21	●	Transylvania, Ky.	13	0
O28	●	Auburn *BIRM*	3	7
N3	●	Mississippi *TUP*	36	0
N11		LSU	3	13
N18	●	at Kentucky	3	13
N20	=	at Maryville	7	7
N30	●	Arkansas *MEM*	20	7

SID ROBINSON		
1917-19 (.750)		15-5

1917
6-1-0
O5	●	Marion Inst.	18	6
O13	●	Mississippi Coll.	68	0
O27	●	Auburn *BIRM*	6	13
N3	●	Mississippi *TUP*	41	14
N10	●	Kentucky	14	0
N17	●	at LSU	9	0
N29	●	Haskell *MEM*	7	6

1918
3-2-0
N2		Payne Field	6	7
N9	●	Camp Shelby	12	0
N16		Park Field	0	6
N28	●	Mississippi	34	0
D7	●	at Mississippi	13	0

1919
6-2-0
O4	●	Spring Hill	12	6
O11	●	Mississippi Coll.	56	7
O18	●	at Tennessee	6	0
O25	●	Samford	39	0
N1	●	LSU	6	0
N8	●	Mississippi *CLAR*	33	0
N15	●	Auburn *BIRM*	0	7
N27	●	Alabama *BIRM*	6	14

FRED HOLTKAMP		
1920-21 (.559)		9-7-1

1920
5-3-0
O2	●	Mississippi Coll.	27	0
O9		at Indiana	0	24
O16	●	So. Military Acad.	33	0
O23	●	at LSU	12	7
O30	●	Tennessee	13	7
N6	●	Mississippi *GRN*	20	0
N13	●	at Tulane	0	6
N25	●	Alabama *BIRM*	7	24

1921
4-4-1
O1	●	B'ham Southern	20	7
O8	●	Ouachita	21	6
O15	●	Mississippi Coll. *JAM*	14	13
O22		at Tulane	0	7
O29	●	Mississippi *GRN*	21	0
N5		Tennessee *MEM*	7	14
N11		at Texas	7	54
N24	=	Alabama *BIRM*	7	7
D3		LSU	14	17

1922-1932 SOUTHERN

C.R. "DUDY" NOBLE		
1922 (.444)		3-4-2

1922
3-4-2 (2-3-0)
O7	●	B'ham Southern	14	0
O14	=	Samford	0	0
O21	●	Mississippi *JAM*	19	13
O28		at Tulane	0	26
N4	=	Ouachita	7	7
N11		Tennessee *MEM*	3	31
N18	●	at LSU	7	0
N25		Drake	6	48
N30		Alabama *BIRM*	0	59

EARL ABLE		
1923-24 (.611)		10-6-2

1923
5-2-2 (2-1-2)
O6	●	Millsaps	28	6
O13	●	Ouachita	6	0
O20	●	Mississippi *JAM*	13	6
O27		Tennessee *MEM*	3	7
N3	=	at Vanderbilt	0	0
N10	●	Union	6	0
N17		at Illinois	0	27
N24	=	Florida *JacF*	13	13
D1	●	LSU	14	7

1924
5-4-0 (3-2-0)
O4	●	Millsaps	28	6
O11		Ouachita	0	12
O18	●	Mississippi *JAM*	20	0
O25	●	Tennessee *MEM*	7	2
N1	●	at Tulane	14	6
N8		at Vanderbilt	0	18
N15	●	Mississippi Coll.	7	6
N22		Florida *MONT*	0	27
N27		at Washington, Mo.	6	12

BERNIE BIERMAN		
1925-26 (.500)		8-8-1

1925
3-4-1 (1-4-0)
O3	●	Millsaps	34	0
O10	=	Ouachita	3	3
O17		at Tulane	3	25
O24	●	Mississippi *JAM*	6	0
O31		at Alabama	0	6
N7	●	Mississippi Coll.	46	0
N14		at Tennessee	9	14
N21		Florida *TAM*	0	12

1926
5-4-0 (2-3-0)
S25	●	at B'ham Southern	19	7
O2	●	Mississippi Coll.	41	0
O9		Alabama *MER*	7	26
O16	●	Millsaps	34	0
O23		LSU *JAM*	7	6
O30		Tennessee	0	33
N6	●	at Tulane	14	0
N13		at Indiana	6	19
N25		Mississippi	6	7

J.W. HANCOCK
1927-29 (.417) 8-12-4

1927 5-3-0 (2-3-0)
O1 • B'ham Southern 27 0
O8 • Louisiana Tech 14 0
O15 • | at Tulane 13 6
O22 | LSU [JaM] 7 9
O29 | at Alabama 7 13
N12 • | Auburn [Birm] 7 0
N18 • Millsaps 6 0
N24 | at Mississippi 12 20

1928 2-4-2 (1-4-0)
S29 • Ouachita 20 6
O6 | Tulane [JaM] 6 51
O13 | Alabama 0 46
O20 | LSU [JaM] 0 31
N3 = at Michigan State 6 6
N10 = Centenary 6 6
N17 • | Auburn [Birm] 13 0
N29 | Mississippi 19 20

1929 1-5-2 (0-3-1)
S27 Henderson-Brown 0 7
O5 | at Georgia Tech 13 27
O12 | at Tulane 0 34
O19 | LSU [JaM] 6 31
N2 • Mississippi Coll. 6 0
N9 Michigan State [JaM] 19 33
N16 = Millsaps 0 0
N28 = | at Mississippi 7 7

CHRIS CAGLE
1930 (.222) 2-7

1930 2-7-0 (2-3-0)
S27 Southwestern 0 14
O4 Mississippi Coll. [JaM] 12 13
O11 Millsaps 13 19
O18 • | LSU [JaM] 8 6
O25 | at North Carolina St. 0 14
N1 | at Tulane 0 53
N8 Henderson St. 7 25
N15 • | Auburn [Birm] 7 6
N27 | Mississippi 0 20

RAY DAUBER
1931-32 (.313) 5-11

1931 2-6-0 (0-5-0)
S26 • at Millsaps 10 7
O3 Mississippi Coll. 2 6
O10 | Alabama [Mer] 0 53
O17 | at LSU 0 31
O31 | at Tulane 7 59
N7 | North Carolina St. 0 6
N14 • Southwestern 14 0
N26 | at Mississippi 14 25

1932 3-5-0 (0-4-0)
O1 | Alabama [Mont] 0 53
O8 • Mississippi Coll. [JaM] 18 7
O15 | LSU [Mor] 0 24
O22 • Millsaps 9 8
O27 at Indiana 0 19
N5 | at Tennessee 0 31
N12 • Southwestern 6 0
N24 | Mississippi 0 13

1933-PRESENT
SEC

ROSS McKECHNIE
1933-34 (.375) 7-12-1

1933 3-6-1 (1-5-1)
S30 • Millsaps 12 0
O7 | at Tennessee 0 20
O14 | at Alabama 0 18
O21 = | at Vanderbilt 7 7
O27 at Southwestern 0 6
N4 • Mississippi Coll. 18 0
N11 | at Tulane 0 33
N18 • | Sewanee 26 13
N25 | LSU [Mor] 6 21
D2 | at Mississippi 0 31

1934 4-6-0 (0-5-0)
S21 • at Samford 13 7
S29 | at Vanderbilt 0 7
O5 Millsaps 6 7
O13 | at Alabama 0 41
O20 • at Southwestern 21 6
O26 • Mississippi Coll. 13 6
N3 | at LSU 3 25
N10 | at Tennessee 0 14
N17 • at Loyola-New Orleans 20 6
D1 | Mississippi [JaM] 3 7

RALPH SASSE
1935-37 (.656) 20-10-2

1935 8-3-0 (2-3-0)
S20 • Samford 19 6
S28 | at Vanderbilt 9 14
O4 • Millsaps 45 0
O12 • | at Alabama 20 7
O18 • at Loyola-New Orleans 6 0
O26 • at Xavier 7 0
N2 • at Army 13 7
N9 | at LSU 13 28
N15 • at Southern Miss 27 0
N23 • | Sewanee 25 0
N30 | at Mississippi 6 14

1936 7-3-1 (3-2-0)
S26 • Millsaps 20 0
O3 • Samford 35 0
O10 | at Alabama 0 7
O17 • Loyola-New Orleans [Mer] 32 0
O24 = TCU [Dal] 0 0
O31 • | Sewanee [JaM] 68 0
N7 | at LSU 0 12
N21 • | Mississippi 26 6
N28 • Mercer 32 0
D5 • | at Florida 7 0

ORANGE BOWL
J1 Duquesne 12 13

1937 5-4-1 (3-2-0)
S25 • Delta St. 39 0
O2 • Samford 38 0
O9 Texas A&M [Tyl] 0 14
O16 | Auburn [Birm] 7 33
O23 • | Florida 14 13
O30 = at Centenary 0 0
N6 | at LSU 0 41
N12 • | Sewanee 12 0
N25 • | at Mississippi 9 7
D4 Duquesne 0 9

SPIKE NELSON
1938 (.400) 4-6

1938 4-6-0 (1-4-0)
S25 • Samford 19 0
O1 • | Florida 22 0
O8 • Louisiana Tech 48 0
O14 | Auburn [Mont] 6 20
O21 • at Duquesne 12 7
O29 | at Tulane 0 27
N5 | at LSU 7 32
N12 Centenary [Mer] 0 19
N19 at Southwestern 3 7
N26 | Mississippi 6 19

ALLYN McKEEN
1939-48 (.764) 65-19-3

1939 8-2-0 (3-2-0)
S23 • Samford 45 0
S30 • Arkansas [Mem] 19 0
O7 • | at Florida 14 0
O14 | Auburn [Birm] 0 7
O21 • Southwestern 37 0
O28 | at Alabama 0 7
N4 • B'ham Southern 28 0
N11 • | at LSU 15 12
N18 • Millsaps 40 0
N25 • | at Mississippi 18 6

1940 10-0-1 (4-0-1)
S28 • | at Florida 27 7
O5 • La. Lafayette 20 0
O12 = | Auburn [Birm] 7 7
O19 • Samford 40 7
O26 • at North Carolina St. 26 10
N2 • at Southwestern 13 0
N9 • | at LSU 22 7
N16 • Millsaps 46 13
N23 • | Mississippi 19 0
N30 • | at Alabama 13 0

ORANGE BOWL
J1 • Georgetown 14 7

1941 8-1-1 (4-0-1)
S27 • | Florida 6 0
O4 • | at Alabama 14 0
O11 = | at LSU 0 0
O25 • Union 56 7
N1 • at Southwestern 20 6
N8 • | Auburn [Birm] 14 7
N15 at Duquesne 0 16
N22 • Millsaps 49 6
N29 • | at Mississippi 6 0
D6 • at San Francisco 26 13

1942 8-2-0 (5-2-0)
S26 • Union 35 2
O3 | at Alabama 6 21
O10 | at LSU 6 16
O17 • | at Vanderbilt 33 0
O24 • | at Florida 26 12
O31 • | Auburn [Birm] 6 0
N7 • | at Tulane 7 0
N14 • Duquesne 28 6
N28 • | Mississippi 34 13
D5 • San Francisco [Mem] 19 7

1943
NO TEAM WWII

1944 6-2-0 (3-2-0)
S30 • Jackson AAB 41 0
O7 • Millsaps 56 0
O14 • Arkansas State 49 20
O21 • | at LSU 13 6
N4 • | Kentucky [Mem] 26 0
N11 • | Auburn [Birm] 26 21
N18 | at Alabama 0 19
N25 | at Mississippi 8 13

1945 6-3-0 (2-3-0)
S29 • La. Lafayette 31 0
O6 • | Auburn [Birm] 20 0
O13 • Detroit [Mem] 41 6
O20 • Maxwell 16 6
N3 | at Tulane 13 14
N10 • | at LSU 27 20
N17 • Northwestern St. 54 0
N24 | Mississippi 6 7
D1 | at Alabama 13 55

1946 8-2-0 (3-2-0)
S28 • U.T. Chattanooga 41 7
O5 | at LSU 6 13
O12 • at Michigan State 6 0
O19 • San Francisco [Mem] 48 20
O26 • | at Tulane 14 7
N2 • Murray St. 69 0
N9 • | Auburn [Birm] 33 0
N16 • Northwestern St. 27 0
N23 • | at Mississippi 20 0
N30 | at Alabama 7 24

1947 7-3-0 (2-2-0)
S26 • U.T. Chattanooga 19 0
O4 at Michigan State 0 7
O11 • at San Francisco 21 14
O18 • Duquesne 34 0
O25 • Hardin-Simmons 27 7
N1 • | at Tulane 20 0
N8 • | Auburn [Birm] 14 0
N15 | at LSU 6 21
N22 • Southern Miss 14 7
N29 | Mississippi 14 33

1948 4-4-1 (3-3-0)
S25 • | at Tennessee 21 6
O2 = Baylor [Mem] 7 7
O9 Clemson 7 21
O16 • Cincinnati 27 0
O23 | Alabama 7 10
O30 | at Tulane 0 9
N6 • | Auburn [Birm] 20 0
N13 • | at LSU 7 0
N27 | at Mississippi 7 34

SLICK MORTON
1949-51 (.315) 8-18-1

1949 0-8-1 (0-6-0)
S24 | at Tennessee 0 10
O1 Baylor 6 14
O8 = at Clemson 7 7
O15 at Cincinnati 0 19
O22 | at Alabama 6 35
O29 | at Tulane 6 54
N5 | at Auburn 6 25
N12 | at LSU 7 34
N26 | Mississippi 0 26

1950 4-5-0 (3-4-0)
S23 • Arkansas State 67 0
S30 • | Tennessee 7 0
O7 Baylor [Shre] 7 14
O14 | at Georgia 0 27
O28 | at Alabama 7 14
N4 • | Auburn 27 0
N11 | Kentucky 21 48
N18 • | at LSU 13 7
D2 | at Mississippi 20 27

1951 4-5-0 (2-5-0)
S22 • Arkansas State 32 0
S29 | at Tennessee 0 14
O6 • | Georgia 6 0
O13 | at Kentucky 0 27
O27 | Alabama 0 7
N3 • | at Tulane 10 7
N10 • at Memphis 27 20
N17 | at LSU 0 3
D1 | Mississippi 7 49

MURRAY WARMATH
1952-53 (.605) 10-6-3

1952 5-4-0 (3-4-0)
S27 | Tennessee [Mem] 7 14
O4 • Arkansas State 41 14
O11 • North Texas 14 0
O18 • | Kentucky 27 14
O25 | at Alabama 19 42
N1 | at Tulane 21 34
N8 • | at Auburn 49 4
N15 • | at LSU 33 14
N29 | at Mississippi 14 20

1953 5-2-3 (3-1-3)
S19 • at Memphis 34 6
S26 • | at Tennessee 26 0
O3 • North Texas 21 6
O10 = | Auburn 21 21
O17 | at Kentucky 13 32
O24 = | at Alabama 7 7
O31 Texas Tech [JaM] 20 27
N7 • | at Tulane 21 0
N14 • | at LSU 26 13
N28 = | Mississippi 7 7

DARRELL ROYAL
1954-55 (.600) 12-8

1954 6-4-0 (3-3-0)
S18 • Memphis 27 7
S25 | Tennessee [Mem] 7 19
O2 • Arkansas State 46 13
O9 • | at Tulane 14 0
O15 at Miami, Fla. 13 27
O23 • | at Alabama 12 7
O30 | at Florida 0 7
N6 • North Texas 48 26
N13 • | at LSU 25 0
N27 | at Mississippi 0 14

1955 6-4-0 (4-4-0)
S17 | at Florida 14 20
S24 • | at Tennessee 13 7
O1 • Memphis 33 0
O8 • | Tulane 14 0
O15 • | at Kentucky 20 14
O22 • | at Alabama 26 7
O29 • North Texas 20 7
N5 | at Auburn 26 27
N12 | at LSU 7 34
N26 | Mississippi 0 26

WADE WALKER
1956-61 (.411) 22-32-2

1956 4-6-0 (2-5-0)
S22 | Florida 0 26
S29 at Houston 7 18
O6 • | at Georgia 19 7
O13 • Trinity 18 6
O20 • Arkansas State 19 9
O27 | at Alabama 12 13
N3 | at Tulane 14 20
N10 | at Auburn 20 27
N17 • | at LSU 32 13
D1 | at Mississippi 7 13

1957 6-2-1 (4-2-1)
S28 • Memphis 10 6
O5 | at Tennessee 9 14
O12 • Arkansas State 47 13
O19 • | at Florida 29 20
O26 • | at Alabama 25 13
N2 • | Tulane [JaM] 27 6
N9 | Auburn [Birm] 7 15
N16 • | at LSU 14 6
N30 = | Mississippi 7 7

1958 3-6-0 (1-6-0)
S27 • | at Florida 14 7
O4 | Tennessee [Mem] 8 13
O11 • Memphis 28 6
O18 • Arkansas State 38 0
O25 | Alabama 7 9
N1 | at Kentucky 12 33
N8 | at Auburn 14 33
N15 | LSU [JaM] 6 7
N29 | at Mississippi 0 21

1959 — 2-7-0 (0-7-0)

S26	|	at Florida	13	14
O3	|	at Tennessee	6	22
O10	•	Arkansas State	49	14
O17	|	Georgia [ATL]	0	15
O24	•	Memphis	28	23
O31	|	at Alabama	0	10
N7	|	Auburn [BIRM]	0	31
N14	|	at LSU	0	27
N28	|	Mississippi	0	42

1960 — 2-6-1 (0-5-1)

S24		Houston	10	14
O1	= |	Tennessee [MEM]	0	0
O8	•	Arkansas State	29	9
O15	|	at Georgia	17	20
O22	•	Memphis	21	0
O29	|	Alabama	0	7
N5	|	at Auburn	12	27
N12	|	at LSU	3	7
N26	|	at Mississippi	9	35

1961 — 5-5-0 (1-5-0)

S23	•	Texas Tech [JAM]	6	0
S30	•	at Houston	10	7
O7	|	at Tennessee	3	17
O14	•	Arkansas State	38	0
O21	|	Georgia [ATL]	7	10
O28	•	at Memphis	23	16
N4	|	at Alabama	0	24
N11	• |	Auburn [BIRM]	11	10
N18	|	at LSU	6	14
D2	|	Mississippi	7	37

PAUL DAVIS
1962-66 (.420) 20-28-2

1962 — 3-6-0 (2-5-0)

S22	|	Florida [JAM]	9	19
O6	• |	Tennessee [MEM]	7	6
O12	• |	at Tulane	35	6
O20	•	at Houston	9	3
O27		Memphis	7	28
N3	|	Alabama	0	20
N10	|	at Auburn	3	9
N17	|	LSU [JAM]	0	28
D1	|	at Mississippi	6	13

1963 — 7-2-2 (4-1-2)

S21	•	Samford	43	0
S28	= |	at Florida	9	9
O5	• |	at Tennessee	7	0
O12	• |	Tulane [JAM]	31	10
O19	•	Houston	20	0
O26		at Memphis	10	17
N2	|	at Alabama	19	20
N9	• |	Auburn [JAM]	13	10
N16	• |	LSU [JAM]	7	6
N30	= |	Mississippi	10	10
		LIBERTY BOWL		
D21	•	North Carolina St.	16	12

1964 — 4-6-0 (2-5-0)

S19		at Texas Tech	7	21
S26	|	Florida [JAM]	13	16
O3	|	Tennessee [MEM]	13	14
O10	• |	Tulane	17	6
O17	•	Southern Miss	48	7
O24	•	Houston	18	13
O31	|	Alabama [JAM]	6	23
N7	|	at Auburn	3	12
N14	|	at LSU	10	14
D5	• |	at Mississippi	20	17

1965 — 4-6-0 (1-5-0)

S18	•	at Houston	36	0
S25	• |	at Florida	18	13
O2	•	Tampa	48	7
O9	•	Southern Miss	27	9
O16		at Memphis	13	33
O22	|	at Tulane	15	17
O30	|	Alabama [JAM]	7	10
N6	|	Auburn [BIRM]	18	25
N13	|	at LSU	20	37
N27	|	Mississippi	0	21

1966 — 2-8-0 (0-6-0)

S17	|	Georgia [JAM]	17	20
S24	|	at Florida	7	28
O1	•	Richmond	20	0
O8	•	Southern Miss	10	9
O15		at Houston	0	28
O22		at Florida State	0	10
O29	|	at Alabama	14	27
N5	|	Auburn [JAM]	0	13
N12	|	at LSU	7	17
N26	|	at Mississippi	0	24

CHARLEY SHIRA
1967-72 (.270) 16-45-2

1967 — 1-9-0 (0-6-0)

S23	|	at Georgia	0	30
S30	|	Florida [JAM]	7	24
O7	•	at Texas Tech	7	3
O14		Southern Miss	14	21
O21		Houston	6	43
O28		at Florida State	12	24
N4	|	at Alabama	0	13
N11	|	at Auburn	0	36
N18	|	at LSU	0	55
D2	|	Mississippi	3	10

1968 — 0-8-2 (0-4-2)

S21		Louisiana Tech	13	20
S28	|	Auburn [JAM]	0	26
O5	|	at Florida	14	31
O12		Southern Miss	14	47
O19	= ||	Texas Tech [JAM]	28	28
O26		at Tampa	17	24
N2	|	at Alabama	13	20
N9		Florida State	14	27
N16	|	at LSU	16	20
N30	= |	at Mississippi	17	17

1969 — 3-7-0 (0-5-0)

S20	•	Richmond	17	14
S27	|	Florida [JAM]	35	47
O4		at Houston	0	74
O11	•	Southern Miss	34	20
O18	•	at Texas Tech	30	26
O25		at Florida State	17	20
N1	|	Alabama [JAM]	19	23
N8	|	at Auburn	13	52
N15	|	at LSU	6	61
N27	|	Mississippi	22	48

1970 — 6-5-0 (3-4-0)

S12	•	Oklahoma State [JAM]	14	13
S19	|	at Florida	13	34
S26	• |	Vanderbilt [MEM]	20	6
O3	• |	Georgia [JAM]	7	6
O10		Houston	14	31
O17	•	Texas Tech [JAM]	20	16
O24	•	Southern Miss	51	15
O31	|	at Alabama	6	35
N7	|	Auburn [BIRM]	0	56
N14	|	at LSU	7	38
N26	• |	at Mississippi	19	14

1971 — 2-9-0 (1-7-0)

S11		at Oklahoma State	7	26
S18	• |	Florida [JAM]	13	10
S25	|	Vanderbilt	19	49
O2	|	at Georgia	7	35
O9		at Florida State	9	27
O16	•	Lamar	24	7
O23	|	Tennessee [MEM]	7	10
O30	|	Alabama [JAM]	10	41
N6	|	at Auburn	21	30
N13	|	LSU [JAM]	3	28
N25	|	Mississippi	0	48

1972 — 4-7-0 (1-6-0)

S9	|	Auburn [JAM]	3	14
S16	•	La. Monroe	42	7
S23	• |	at Vanderbilt	10	6
S30	|	at Florida	13	28
O7	|	at Kentucky	13	17
O14		Florida State [JAM]	21	25
O21	•	Southern Miss	26	7
O28	•	Houston	27	13
N4	|	at Alabama	14	58
N18	|	at LSU	14	28
N25	|	at Mississippi	14	51

BOB TYLER
1973-78 (.604) 39-25-3

1973 — 4-5-2 (2-5-0)

S15	=	La. Monroe	21	21
S22	• |	Vanderbilt	52	21
S29	• |	Florida [JAM]	33	12
O6	|	Kentucky [JAM]	14	42
O13	•	at Florida State	37	12
O20	•	at Louisville	18	7
O27	=	Southern Miss	10	10
N3	|	Alabama [JAM]	0	35
N10	|	at Auburn	17	31
N17	|	at LSU	7	26
N24	|	Mississippi [JAM]	10	38

1974 — 9-3-0 (3-3-0)

S7	•	William & Mary [JAM]	49	7
S21	• |	Georgia [JAM]	38	14
S28	|	at Florida	13	29
O5	•	Kansas State	21	16
O12	•	at Lamar	37	21
O19	•	at Memphis	29	28
O26	•	Louisville	56	7
N2	|	at Alabama	0	35
N9	|	Auburn [JAM]	20	24
N16	• |	LSU [JAM]	7	6
N23	• |	Mississippi [JAM]	31	13
		SUN BOWL		
D28	•	North Carolina	26	24

1975 — 6-4-1 (1-4-1)

S6	•	at Memphis	17	7
S20	|	at Georgia	6	28
S27	|	Florida [JAM]	10	27
O4	•	Southern Miss	7	3†
O11	•	at Rice	28	14†
O18	•	North Texas	15	12
O25	•	at Louisville	28	14†
N1	|	Alabama [JAM]	10	21
N8	= |	at Auburn	21	21†
N15	• |	at LSU	16	6†
N22	|	Mississippi [JAM]	7	13

1976 — 9-2-0 (4-2-0)

S4	•	North Texas	7	0†
S18	•	Louisville	30	21†
S25	|	at Florida	30	34
O2	•	Cal Poly Pomona	38	0†
O9	• |	Kentucky [JAM]	14	7†
O16	•	at Memphis	42	33†
O23	•	at Southern Miss	14	6†
O30	|	at Alabama	17	34
N6	• |	Auburn [JAM]	28	19†
N13	• |	LSU [JAM]	21	13†
N20	• |	Mississippi [JAM]	28	11†

1977 — 5-6-0 (2-4-0)

S3	•	North Texas	17	15†
S10	•	at Washington	27	18†
S24	|	Florida [JAM]	22	24
O1	•	at Kansas State	24	21†
O8	|	at Kentucky	7	23
O15		at Memphis	13	21
O22		Southern Miss	7	14
O29	|	Alabama [JAM]	7	37
N5	• |	at Auburn	27	13†
N12	|	at LSU	24	27
N19	• |	Mississippi [JAM]	18	14†

1978 — 6-5-0 (2-4-0)

S2	•	West Texas St. [JAM]	28	0
S9	•	North Texas [IRV]	17	5
S23	•	at Memphis	44	14
S30	|	at Florida	0	34
O7		at Southern Miss	17	22
O14	•	Florida State	55	27
O28	• |	Tennessee [MEM]	34	21
N4	|	Alabama [BIRM]	14	35
N11	|	Auburn	0	6
N18	• |	LSU [JAM]	16	14
N25	|	Mississippi [JAM]	7	27

EMORY BELLARD
1979-85 (.468) 37-42

1979 — 3-8-0 (2-4-0)

S8		Memphis [JAM]	13	14
S22		at Maryland	14	35
S29	• |	Florida [JAM]	24	10
O6	• |	Tennessee [MEM]	28	9
O13		at Florida State	6	17
O20	•	Marshall	48	0
O27		Southern Miss	7	21
N3	|	at Alabama	7	24
N10	|	at Auburn	3	14
N17	|	at LSU	3	21
N24	|	Mississippi [JAM]	9	14

1980 — 9-3-0 (5-1-0)

S6	•	at Memphis	34	7
S13	•	Louisiana Tech	31	11
S20	• |	at Vanderbilt	24	14
S27	|	at Florida	15	21
O4	•	at Illinois	28	21
O11		Southern Miss	14	42
O18	•	at Miami, Fla.	34	31
O25	• |	Auburn [JAM]	24	21
N1	• |	Alabama [JAM]	6	3
N15	• |	LSU [JAM]	55	31
N22	• |	Mississippi [JAM]	19	14
		SUN BOWL		
D27		Nebraska	17	31

1981 — 8-4-0 (4-2-0)

S5	•	Memphis [JAM]	20	3
S19	• |	Vanderbilt	29	9
S26	• |	Florida [JAM]	28	7
O3		Missouri [JAM]	3	14
O10	•	at Colorado State	37	27
O17	•	Miami, Fla.	14	10
O24	• |	at Auburn	21	17
O31	|	at Alabama	10	13
N7		Southern Miss [JAM]	6	7
N14	• |	at LSU	17	9
N21	|	Mississippi [JAM]	17	21
		HALL OF FAME CLASSIC		
D31	•	Kansas	10	0

1982 — 5-6-0 (2-4-0)

S4	•	at Tulane	30	21
S11	•	Arkansas State	31	10
S18	•	at Memphis	41	17
S25	|	at Florida	17	27
O2	|	Georgia	22	29
O9		Southern Miss [JAM]	14	20
O16		at Miami, Fla.	14	31
O23	|	Auburn	17	35
O30	|	Alabama [JAM]	12	20
N13	• |	LSU	27	24
N20	• |	Mississippi [JAM]	27	10

1983 — 3-8-0 (1-5-0)

S3	•	Tulane	14	9
S17	•	Navy [JAM]	38	10
S24	|	Florida	12	35
O1	|	at Georgia	7	20
O8		Southern Miss [JAM]	6	31
O15		Miami, Fla.	7	31
O22	|	at Auburn	13	28
O29	|	at Alabama	18	35
N5		Memphis	13	30
N12	• |	at LSU	45	26
N19	|	Mississippi [JAM]	23	24

1984 — 4-7-0 (1-5-0)

S1	•	at Tulane	30	3
S8	•	Colorado State	14	9
S22		at Missouri	30	47
S29	|	at Florida	12	27
O6	•	Southern Miss [JAM]	27	18
O13	|	Kentucky	13	17
O20		at Memphis	12	23
O27	|	Auburn	21	24
N3	|	Alabama [JAM]	20	24
N17	• |	LSU	16	14
N24	|	Mississippi [JAM]	3	24

1985 — 5-6-0 (0-6-0)

S7	•	Arkansas State	22	14
S14	•	Syracuse	30	3
S21	•	Southern Miss [JAM]	23	20
S28	|	Florida	22	36
O5	•	Memphis	31	28
O12	|	at Kentucky	19	33
O19	•	Tulane	31	27
O26	|	at Auburn	9	21
N2	|	at Alabama	28	44
N16	|	at LSU	15	17
N23	|	Mississippi [JAM]	27	45

ROCKEY FELKER
1986-90 (.382) 21-34

1986 — 6-5-0 (2-4-0)

S6	•	at Syracuse	24	17
S13	• |	at Tennessee	27	23
S20		Southern Miss [JAM]	24	28
S27	• |	Florida	16	10
O4	•	at Memphis	34	17
O11	•	Arkansas State	24	9
O18	•	at Tulane	34	27
O25	|	Auburn	6	35
N1	|	Alabama	3	38
N15	|	LSU [JAM]	0	47
N22	|	Mississippi [JAM]	3	24

1987 — 4-7-0 (1-5-0)

S5	•	La. Lafayette	31	3
S12	|	Tennessee	10	38
S19	•	Louisiana Tech	14	13
S26	|	at Florida	3	38
O3	•	Memphis	9	6
O17		Southern Miss [JAM]	14	18
O24	|	at Auburn	7	38
O31	|	Alabama [BIRM]	18	21
N7		Tulane	19	30
N14	|	at LSU	14	34
N21	• |	Mississippi [JAM]	30	20

THE SCHOOLS

1988   1-10-0 (0-7-0)

S3	●	Louisiana Tech	21	14
S10		at Vanderbilt	20	24
S17		Georgia	35	42
S24		at Florida	0	17
O1		at Memphis	10	31
O15		Southern Miss *JAM*	21	38
O22		at Auburn	0	33
O29		Alabama	34	53
N12		LSU	3	20
N19		at Tulane	22	27
N26		Mississippi *JAM*	6	33

1989   5-6-0 (1-6-0)

S2	●	Vanderbilt	42	7
S9	●	at Southern Miss	26	23
S23		at Georgia	6	23
S30		Florida *TAM*	0	21
O7	●	La. Monroe	28	14
O21	●	Memphis	35	10
O28		at Auburn	0	14
N4		Alabama *BIRM*	10	23
N11	●	Tulane	27	7
N18		at LSU	20	44
N25		Mississippi *JAM*	11	21

1990   5-6-0 (1-6-0)

S8		Tennessee	7	40
S15	●	Fullerton St.	27	13
S22	●	Southern Miss	13	10
S29		at Florida	21	34
O13		at Kentucky	15	17
O20	●	at Tulane	38	17
O27		Auburn	16	17
N3		Alabama	0	22
N10	●	at Memphis	27	23
N17	●	LSU *JAM*	34	22
N24		Mississippi *JAM*	9	21

JACKIE SHERRILL
1991-03 (.493)   74-76-2

1991   7-5-0 (4-3-0)

A31	●	Fullerton St.	47	3
S7	●	Texas	13	6
S14	●	Tulane	48	0
S21	●	at Tennessee	24	26
S28		Florida *ORL*	7	29
O12	●	Kentucky	31	6
O19		Memphis	23	28
O26		at Auburn	24	17
N2		at Alabama	7	13
N16	●	at LSU	28	19
N23		Mississippi	24	9
		LIBERTY BOWL		
D29		Air Force	15	38

1992   7-5-0 (4-4-0)

S5	●	at Texas	28	10
S12	●	at LSU	3	24
S19	●	at Memphis	20	16
O1	●	Florida	30	6
O10	●	Auburn	14	7
O17		at South Carolina	6	21
O24		Arkansas State	56	6
O31	●	at Kentucky	37	36
N7	●	Arkansas	10	3
N14		Alabama	21	30
N28	●	at Mississippi	10	17
		PEACH BOWL		
J2		North Carolina	17	21

1993   3-6-2 (2-5-1)

S4	●	Memphis	35	45
S11		LSU	16	18
S25	●	at Tulane	36	10
O2		at Florida	24	38
O9		at Auburn	17	31
O16	●	South Carolina	23	0
O23	=	Arkansas State	15	15
O30		Kentucky	17	26
N6	=	Arkansas *LR*	13	13
N13		at Alabama	25	36 †
N27		Mississippi	20	13

1994   8-4-0 (5-3-0)

S3	●	at Memphis	17	6
S10		at LSU	24	44
S24	●	Tennessee	24	21
O1	●	Arkansas State	49	3
O8		Auburn	18	42
O15	●	at South Carolina	41	36
O22	●	Tulane	66	22
O29	●	at Kentucky	47	7
N5	●	Arkansas	17	7
N12		Alabama	25	29
N26	●	at Mississippi	21	17
		PEACH BOWL		
J1		North Carolina St.	24	28

1995   3-8-0 (1-7-0)

S2	●	Memphis	28	18
S9		LSU	16	34
S16	●	at Baylor	30	21
S23		at Tennessee	14	52
S30		La. Monroe	32	34
O7		at Auburn	20	48
O14		South Carolina	39	65
O28	●	Kentucky	42	32
N4		Arkansas *LR*	21	26
N11		at Alabama	9	14
N25		Mississippi	10	13

1996   5-6 (3-5)

S7		at Memphis	31	10
S21		Louisiana Tech	23	38
S28	●	at South Carolina	14	10
O5		Georgia	19	38
O12		Auburn	15	49
O26		at LSU	20	28
N2	●	La. Monroe	59	0
N9		at Kentucky	21	24
N16	●	Alabama	17	16
N23		Arkansas	13	16
N30	●	at Mississippi	17	0

1997   7-4 (4-4)

A30	●	Memphis	13	10
S6	●	Kentucky	35	27
S13		LSU	9	24
S27	●	South Carolina	37	17
O4		at Georgia	0	47
O11	●	La. Monroe	24	10
O25	●	Central Florida	35	28
N1	●	at Auburn	20	0
N15	●	at Alabama	32	20
N22		at Arkansas	7	17
N29		Mississippi	14	15

1998   8-5 (6-2)

S5	●	Vanderbilt	42	0
S12	●	at Memphis	14	6
S19		at Oklahoma State	23	42
S26	●	at South Carolina	38	0
O10	●	Auburn	38	21
O17	●	East Tenn. St.	53	6
O24		at LSU	6	41
N7		at Kentucky	35	37
N14	●	Alabama	26	14
N21	●	Arkansas	22	21
N26	●	at Mississippi	28	6
		SEC CHAMPIONSHIP GAME		
D5		Tennessee *ATL*	14	24
		COTTON BOWL		
J1		Texas	11	38

1999   10-2 (6-2)

S4	●	Middle Tennessee	40	7
S11	●	Memphis	13	10
S18	●	Oklahoma State	29	11
S25		South Carolina	17	0
O2	●	at Vanderbilt	42	14
O9	●	at Auburn	18	16
O23	●	LSU	17	16
N4	●	Kentucky	23	22
N13		at Alabama	7	19
N20	●	Arkansas *LR*	9	14
N25		Mississippi	23	20
		PEACH BOWL		
D30	●	Clemson	17	7

2000   8-4 (4-4)

S2	●	at Memphis	17	3
S14	●	at Brigham Young	44	28
S23		at South Carolina	19	23
S30	●	Florida	47	35
O7	●	Auburn	17	10
O21		at LSU	38	45
O28	●	Middle Tennessee	61	35
N4	●	at Kentucky	35	17
N11	●	Alabama	29	7
N18		Arkansas	10	17
N23		at Mississippi	30	45
		INDEPENDENCE BOWL		
D31	●	Texas A&M	43	41

2001   3-8 (2-6)

S3	●	Memphis	30	10
S20		South Carolina	14	16
S29		at Florida	0	52
O6		at Auburn	14	16
O13		Troy State	9	21
O20		LSU	0	42
N3		Kentucky	17	14
N10		at Alabama	17	24
N17		at Arkansas	21	24
N22	●	Mississippi	36	28
D1		Brigham Young	38	41

2002   3-9 (0-8)

A31		at Oregon	13	36
S14	●	Jacksonville St.	51	13
S19		Auburn	14	42
S28		at LSU	13	31
O5		at South Carolina	10	34
O12	●	Troy State	11	8
O19	●	at Memphis	29	17
N2		Kentucky	24	45
N9		at Alabama	14	28
N16		Tennessee	17	35
N23		Arkansas	19	26
N28		at Mississippi	12	24

2003   2-10 (1-7)

A30		Oregon	34	42
S13		at Tulane	28	31
S20		at Houston	35	42
S27		LSU	6	41
O4	●	Vanderbilt	30	21
O11	●	Memphis	35	27
O18		at Auburn	13	45
O25		at Kentucky	17	42
N8		Alabama	0	38
N15		at Tennessee	21	59
N22		at Arkansas	6	52
N27		Mississippi	0	31

SYLVESTER CROOM
2004-08 (.356)   21-38

2004   3-8 (2-6)

S4	●	Tulane	28	7
S11		Auburn	14	43
S18	●	Maine	7	9
S25		at LSU	0	51
O2		at Vanderbilt	13	31
O9		UAB	13	27
O23	●	Florida	38	31
O30		Kentucky	22	7
N6		at Alabama	14	30
N20		Arkansas	21	24
N27		at Mississippi	3	20

2005   3-8 (1-7)

S3	●	Murray State	38	6
S10		at Auburn	0	28
S17	●	Tulane *SHRE*	21	14
S24		Georgia	10	23
O1		LSU	7	37
O8		at Florida	9	35
O22		Houston	16	28
O29		at Kentucky	7	13
N5		Alabama	0	17
N19		at Arkansas	10	44
N26	●	Mississippi	35	14

2006   3-9 (1-7)

A31		South Carolina	0	15
S9		Auburn	0	34
S16		Tulane	29	32
S23	●	at Ala.-Birmingham	16	10
S30		at LSU	17	48
O7		West Virginia	14	42
O14	●	Jacksonville State	35	3
O21		at Georgia	24	27
O28		Kentucky	31	34
N4	●	at Alabama	24	16
N18		Arkansas	14	28
N25		at Mississippi	17	20

2007   8-5 (4-4)

A30		LSU	0	45
S8	●	at Tulane	38	17
S15	●	at Auburn	19	14
S22		Gardner-Webb	31	15
S29		at South Carolina	21	38
O6		Ala.-Birmingham	30	13
O13		Tennessee	21	33
O20		at West Virginia	13	38
O27	●	at Kentucky	31	14
N10	●	Alabama	17	12
N17		at Arkansas	31	45
N23		Mississippi	17	14
		LIBERTY BOWL		
D29	●	Central Florida	10	3

2008   4-8 (2-6)

A30		at Louisiana Tech	14	22
S6	●	Southeastern Louisiana	34	10
S13		Auburn	2	3
S20		at Georgia Tech	7	38
S27		at Louisiana State	24	34
O11	●	Vanderbilt	17	14
O18		at Tennessee	3	34
O25		Middle Tennessee State	31	22
N1		Kentucky	13	14
N15		at Alabama	7	32
N22	●	Arkansas	31	28
N28		at Mississippi	0	45

Neutral Site key: *ABE* Aberdeen, MS / *ATL* Atlanta, GA / *BIRM* Birmingham, AL / *CLAR* Clarksdale, MS / *COLMS* Columbus, MS / *DAL* Dallas, TX / *GRN* Greenwood, MS / *GUL* Gulfport, MS / *HAV* Havana, Cuba / *HOU* Houston, TX / *INV* Irving, TX / *JACF* Jacksonville ,FL / *JAM* Jackson, MS / *LR* Little Rock, AR / *MEM* Memphis, TN / *MER* Meridian, MS / *MONT* Montgomery, AL / *MON* Monroe, LA / *ORL* Orlando, FL / *SHRE* Shreveport, LA / *TAM* Tampa, FL / *TUP* Tupelo, MS / *TYL* Tyler, TX /
ƒ Forfeit / † Game Later Forfieted / # Disputed Victor / * Disputed Score / || Designated Conference Game / 2 Counted Twice in Conference Standings

MISSISSIPPI STATE ANNUAL STATISTICAL LEADERS

YR	RUSHING	YDS	ATT	AVG	PASSING	ATT	CMP	PCT	YDS	RECEIVING	REC	YDS	AVG
1946	Tom McWilliams	347	77	4.5	Billy Murphy	60	21	.35	279	Kermit Davis	11	158	14.4
1947	Tom McWilliams	625	137	4.6	Tom McWilliams	61	30	.49	360	Harper Davis	15	229	15.3
1948	Tom McWilliams	436	121	3.6	Tom McWilliams	74	41	.55	412	Harper Davis	12	94	7.8
1949	Wally Beech	403	90	4.5	Don Robinson	105	29	.28	303	Murray Alexander	14	131	9.4
1950	Wally Beech	529	111	4.8	Frank Branch	40	24	.60	313	Steve Clark	14	150	10.7
1951	Wally Beech	421	98	4.3	Frank Branch	44	20	.45	198	John Katusa	10	73	7.3
1952	Joe Fortunato	779	128	6.1	Jackie Parker	97	45	.46	811	Norm Duplain	14	265	18.9
1953	Charles Evans	549	109	5.0	Jackie Parker	69	41	.59	603	Art Davis	11	150	13.6
1954	Art Davis	670	132	5.1	Bobby Collins	45	20	.44	337	Levaine Hollingshead	11	180	16.4
1955	Jim Harness	497	90	5.5	Bill Stanton	57	27	.47	554	Ron Bennett	12	248	20.7
1956	Billy Stacy	613	138	4.4	Bill Stacy	71	32	.45	464	Ron Bennett	15	227	15.1
1957	Molly Halbert	386	76	5.1	Bill Stacy	41	13	.32	248	Gil Peterson	7	95	13.6
1958	Jack Batte	292	62	4.7	Bill Stacy	70	32	.46	388	P.L. Blake	6	85	14.2
1959	Billy Hill	257	63	4.1	John Correro	44	21	.48	251	Lee Welch	14	127	9.1
1960	Mackie Weaver	354	88	4.0	Charlie Furlow	114	63	.55	599	Lee Welch	12	98	8.2
1961	Billy Hill	337	85	4.0	Charlie Furlow	65	36	.55	389	Johnny Baker	22	323	14.7
1962	Ode Burrell	310	71	4.4	Charlie Furlow	111	62	.56	744	Ode Burrell	24	204	8.5
1963	Hoyle Granger	481	113	4.3	Sonny Fisher	74	36	.49	353	Tommy Inman	12	179	14.9
1964	Hoyle Granger	604	129	4.7	Ashby Cook	61	35	.57	426	Tommy Inman	21	338	16.1
1965	Hoyle Granger	449	108	4.2	Ashby Cook	162	78	.48	1,032	Don Saget	24	373	15.5
1966	Andy Rhoades	295	75	3.9	Don Saget	166	69	.42	753	Marcus Rhoden	31	365	11.8
1967	Tommy Pharr	326	136	2.4	Tommy Pharr	71	26	.37	279	Johnny Woitt	8	82	10.3
1968	Tommy Pharr	239	141	1.7	Tommy Pharr	319	173	.54	1,838	Sammy Milner	64	909	14.2
1969	Steve Whaley	275	89	3.1	Tommy Pharr	258	140	.54	1,603	Sammy Milner	64	745	11.6
1970	Lewis Grubbs	644	155	4.2	Joe Reed	294	138	.47	1,616	David Smith	74	987	13.3
1971	Lewis Grubbs	419	134	3.1	Hal Chealander	155	66	.43	937	Eric Hoggatt	28	365	13.0
1972	Melvin Barkum	522	132	4.0	Rockey Felker	161	74	.46	992	Bill Buckley	47	776	16.5
1973	Wayne Jones	1,193	212	5.6	Rockey Felker	106	60	.57	782	Bill Buckley	41	661	16.1
1974	Walter Packer	994	157	6.3	Rockey Felker	155	73	.47	1,147	Howard Lewis	21	330	15.7
1975	Walter Packer	1,012	180	5.6	Bruce Threadgill	123	43	.35	575	Gavin Rees	18	292	16.2
1976	Dennis Johnson	859	152	5.7	Bruce Threadgill	89	45	.51	807	Robert Chatman	15	277	18.5
1977	Dennis Johnson	529	114	4.6	Bruce Threadgill	219	91	.42	1,317	Mardye McDole	29	510	17.6
1978	James Jones	687	130	5.3	Dave Marler	287	163	.57	2,422	Mardye McDole	48	1,035	21.6
1979	Fred Collins	591	128	4.6	Tony Black	62	23	.37	363	Mardye McDole	20	380	19.0
1980	Michael Haddix	724	133	5.4	John Bond	133	59	.44	849	Mardye McDole	19	289	15.2
1981	Michael Haddix	622	110	5.7	John Bond	144	65	.45	875	Glen Young	19	263	13.8
1982	Michael Haddix	813	122	6.7	John Bond	183	91	.50	1,591	Danny Knight	37	924	25.0
1983	John Bond	612	164	3.7	John Bond	205	92	.45	1,306	Danny Knight	34	671	19.7
1984	Don Smith	545	128	4.3	Don Smith	176	75	.43	1,236	Mikel Williams	23	177	7.7
1985	Don Smith	554	190	2.9	Don Smith	312	143	.46	2,332	Jeff Patton	34	416	12.2
1986	Don Smith	740	159	4.7	Don Smith	244	120	.49	1,609	Fred Hadley	28	529	18.9
1987	Hank Phillips	848	184	4.6	Mike Davis	129	60	.47	779	Fred Hadley	28	499	17.8
1988	Jesse Anderson	468	102	4.6	Tony Shell	335	153	.46	1,884	Fred Hadley	29	477	16.4
1989	Kenny Roberts	511	108	4.7	Tony Shell	87	45	.52	499	Jesse Anderson	21	230	11.0
1990	Kenny Roberts	523	93	5.6	Tony Shell	293	151	.52	1,909	Jerry Bouldin	32	447	14.0
1991	Sleepy Robinson	543	154	3.5	Sleepy Robinson	141	77	.55	1,167	Willie Harris	24	529	22.0
1992	Kenny Roberts	597	106	5.6	Greg Plump	129	54	.42	863	Willie Harris	35	574	16.4
1993	Michael Davis	883	205	4.3	Todd Jordan	294	131	.45	1,935	Chris Jones	24	541	22.5
1994	Michael Davis	929	196	4.7	Derrick Taite	220	110	.50	1,806	Eric Moulds	39	845	21.7
1995	Keffer McGee	1,072	235	4.6	Derrick Taite	309	165	.53	2,241	Eric Moulds	62	779	12.6
1996	Robert Isaac	527	117	4.5	Derrick Taite	171	75	.44	1,009	Lamont Woodberry	27	305	11.3
1997	James Johnson	1,069	217	4.9	Matt Wyatt	201	92	.46	1,369	Lamont Woodberry	24	342	14.3
1998	James Johnson	1,383	236	5.9	Wayne Madkin	199	96	.48	1,532	Kevin Prentiss	38	681	17.9
1999	Dontae Walker	384	76	5.1	Wayne Madkin	257	135	.53	1,884	Kelvin Lowe	43	834	19.4
2000	Dicenzo Miller	1,005	160	6.3	Wayne Madkin	246	138	.56	1,908	Terrell Grindle	31	436	14.1
2001	Dicenzo Miller	676	132	5.1	Kevin Fant	170	94	.55	1,352	Justin Jenkins	42	661	15.7
2002	Justin Griffith	471	91	5.2	Kevin Fant	311	163	.52	1,918	Ray Ray Bivines	40	511	12.8
2003	Nick Turner	696	123	5.7	Kevin Fant	351	186	.53	2,151	Justin Jenkins	62	880	14.2
2004	Jerious Norwood	1,050	195	5.4	Omarr Conner	206	107	.52	1,224	Will Prosser	24	328	13.7
2005	Jerious Norwood	1,136	191	5.9	Omarr Conner	167	86	.51	903	Will Prosser	28	286	10.2
2006	Anthony Dixon	668	169	4.0	Mike Henig	169	74	.44	1,201	Tony Burks	35	850	24.3
2007	Anthony Dixon	1,066	287	3.7	Wesley Carroll	255	134	.53	1,392	Jamayel Smith	33	510	15.5
2008	Anthony Dixon	869	197	4.4	Tyson Lee	260	153	.59	1,519	Brandon McRae	51	518	10.2

Receiving leaders by receptions
The NCAA began including postseason stats in 2002

THE SCHOOLS

MISSISSIPI STATE RECORD BOOK

SINGLE-GAME RECORDS

Rushing Yards	247	Jerious Norwood (Oct. 22, 2005 vs. Houston)
Passing Yards	466	Derrick Taite (Oct. 22, 1994 vs. Tulane)
Receiving Yards	215	David Smith (Oct. 17, 1970 vs. Texas Tech)
All-Purpose Yards	344	Nick Turner (Nov. 15, 2003 vs. Tennessee)
Points	42	Harry McArthur (Oct. 10, 1914 vs. Cumberland)
Field Goals	5	Tim Rogers (Jan. 2, 1995 vs. North Carolina St.); Brian Hazelwood (Nov. 21, 1998 vs. Arkansas)
Tackles	29	Ray Costict (Oct. 9, 1976 vs. Kentucky)
Interceptions	4	Jack Nix (Sept. 30, 1939 vs. Arkansas)

SINGLE-SEASON RECORDS

Rushing Yards	1,383	James Johnson, 1998 (236 att.)
Passing Yards	2,422	Dave Marler, 1978 (163-287)
Receiving Yards	1,035	Mardye McDole, 1978 (48 rec.)
All-Purpose Yards	1,664	Nick Turner, 2003
Scoring	120	Jackie Parker, 1952 (16 TDs, 24 PATs)
Touchdowns	16	Anthony Dixon, 2007; Jackie Parker, 1952
Tackles	186	Calvin Zanders, 1983
Interceptions	6	Five players tied
Punting Average	46.5	Andy Russ, 1996
Punt Return Average	21.7	Marcus Rhoden, 1965 (19 ret.)
Kickoff Return Average	32.8	Eric Moulds, 1994 (13 ret.)

CAREER RECORDS

Rushing Yards	3,212	Jerious Norwood, 2002-05
Passing Yards	6,336	Wayne Madkin, 1998-2001
Receiving Yards	2,214	Mardye McDole, 1977-80 (116 rec.)
All-Purpose Yards	4,169	Walter Packer, 1973-76
Scoring	218	Brian Hazelwood, 1995-98
Touchdowns	34	Anthony Dixon, 2006-present
Tackles	467	Ray Costict, 1973-76
Interceptions	16	Walt Harris, 1992-95
Punting Average	43.4	Jeff Walker, 1996-99 (141 punts)
Punt Return Average	15.2	Frank Dowsing, 1970-72 (26 ret.)
Kickoff Return Average	26.6	Dan Bland, 1963-65 (42 ret.)

TEAM RECORDS

Longest Winning Streak	13	Oct. 17, 1942-Nov. 11, 1944; broken vs. Alabama, 0-19 on Nov. 18, 1944
Longest Undefeated Streak	21	Nov. 4, 1939-Nov. 8, 1941; broken vs. Duquesne, 0-16 on Nov. 15, 1941
Most Consecutive Winning Seasons	8	1939-47
Most Consecutive Bowl Appearances	3	1999-2000
Most Points in a Game	82	vs. Howard College, Nov. 18, 1910
Most Points Allowed in a Game	74	vs. Houston, Oct. 4, 1969
Largest Margin of Victory	82	vs. Howard College, Nov. 18, 1910, 82-0
Largest Margin of Defeat	74	vs. Houston, Oct. 4, 1969
Longest Pass Play	91	Kevin Fant to Terrell Grindle vs. Kentucky, Nov. 2, 2002
Longest Field Goal	54	Artie Cosby vs. Memphis State, Oct. 5, 1985
Longest Punt	84	Mike Patrick vs. Alabama, Nov. 2, 1974
Longest Interception Return	100	Anthony Johnson vs. Alabama, Nov. 10, 2007

RETIRED NUMBERS

NO RETIRED JERSEYS

ALL-TIME TEAM

No all-time or all-century team available

MISSISSIPPI STATE BOWL HISTORY

SEASON	BOWL	DATE	PRE-GAME RANK	TEAMS	SCORE	FINAL RANK	MOST VALUABLE PLAYER(S)	ATT.
1936	ORANGE	Jan. 1, 1937	14	Duquesne Mississippi State	13 12			9,210
1940	ORANGE	Jan. 1, 1941	9 13	Mississippi State Georgetown	14 7			29,554
1963	LIBERTY	Dec. 21, 1963		Mississippi State North Carolina State	16 12		Ode Burrell, Mississippi State, HB	8,309
1974	SUN	Dec. 28, 1974		Mississippi State North Carolina	26 24	17	Terry Vitrano, Mississippi State, FB Jimmy Webb, Mississippi State, DT	30,131
1980	SUN	Dec. 27, 1980	8 17	Nebraska Mississippi State	31 17	7 19	Jeff Quinn, Nebraska, QB Jimmy Williams, Nebraska, DE	34,723
1981	HALL OF FAME CLASSIC	Dec. 31, 1981		Mississippi State Kansas	10 0		John Bond, Mississippi St., QB Johnie Cooks, Mississippi St., LB	41,672
1991	LIBERTY	Dec. 29, 1991		Air Force Mississippi State	38 15	25	Rob Perez, Air Force, QB	61,497
1992	PEACH	Jan. 2, 1993	19 24	North Carolina Mississippi State	21 17	19 23	Natrone Means, RB, Bracey Walker, DB, UNC Greg Plump, QB, Marc Woodard, LB, MSU	69,125
1994	PEACH	Jan. 1, 1995		North Carolina State Mississippi State	28 24	17 24	T. Stephens, RB, D. Covington, LB, C. Reeves, DT, T. Rogers, K, L. Williams, DL, Mississippi St.	75,562
1998	COTTON	Jan. 1, 1999	20 25	Texas Mississippi State	38 11	15	Ricky Williams, Texas, RB Aaron Babino, Texas, LB	72,611
1999	PEACH	Dec. 30, 1999	15	Mississippi State Clemson	17 7	13	Wayne Madkin, Mississippi State, QB Keith Adams, Clemson, LB	73,315
2000	INDEPENDENCE	Dec. 31, 2000		Mississippi State Texas A&M	43 OT 41		Ja'Mar Toombs, Texas A&M, RB Willie Blade, Mississippi State, DT	36,974
2007	LIBERTY	Dec. 29, 2007		Mississippi State Central Florida	10 3		Derek Pegues, Mississippi State, FS	63,816

JANUARY 1, 1937 | ORANGE
Duquesne 13, Mississippi State 12

	1ST	2ND	3RD	4TH	FINAL
DUQ	0	7	0	6	13
MSU	6	6	0	0	12

SCORING SUMMARY
MSU Pickle 10 run (kick failed)
DUQ Brumbaugh 1 run (Brumbaugh kick)
MSU Walters 40 pass from Armstrong (kick failed)
DUQ Hefferle 72 pass from Brumbaugh (kick failed)

DUQ	TEAM STATISTICS	MSU
14	First Downs	12
184	Rushing Yards	133
3-13-0	Passing	5-18-4
98	Passing Yards	150
282	Total Yards	283
9-24.7	Punts - Average	6-43.0
0-0	Fumbles - Lost	0-0
1-5	Penalties - Yards	1-5

JANUARY 1, 1941 | ORANGE
Mississippi State 14, Georgetown 7

	1ST	2ND	3RD	4TH	FINAL
MSU	7	7	0	0	14
GEO	0	0	7	0	7

SCORING SUMMARY
MSU Tripson blocked punt recovery (Dees kick)
MSU Jefferson 2 run (Bruce kick)
GEO Castiglia 2 run (Lio kick)

MSU	TEAM STATISTICS	GEO
8	First Downs	14
69	Rushing Yards	117
5-11-3	Passing	9-22-0
50	Passing Yards	104
119	Total Yards	221
11-36.8	Punts - Average	8-28.2
2-2	Fumbles - Lost	1-1
11-71	Penalties - Yards	9-90

DECEMBER 21, 1963 | LIBERTY
Mississippi State 16, NC State 12

	1ST	2ND	3RD	4TH	FINAL
MSU	13	3	0	0	16
NCSU	0	6	0	6	12

SCORING SUMMARY
MSU Inman 11 blocked kick return (Canale kick)
MSU Fisher 3 run (kick failed)
MSU FG Canale 43
NCSU Rossi 1 run (pass failed)
NCSU Barlow 5 pass from Rossi (pass failed)

MSU	TEAM STATISTICS	NCSU
16	First Downs	15
275	Rushing Yards	176
3-6-1	Passing	5-12-0
28	Passing Yards	58
303	Total Yards	234
2-1	Fumbles - Lost	2-2
11-122	Penalties - Yards	3-25

INDIVIDUAL LEADERS
RUSHING
MSU: Grainger 13-94.
NCSU: Rossi 18-67, 1 TD.
PASSING
MSU: Ficher 2-5-1, 10 yards.
NCSU: Rossi 5-12-0, 58 yards.

DECEMBER 28, 1974 | SUN
Mississippi State 26, North Carolina 24

	1ST	2ND	3RD	4TH	FINAL
MSU	7	3	10	6	26
UNC	7	0	14	3	24

SCORING SUMMARY
MSU Packer 1 run (Nichels kick)
UNC Betterson 1 run (Alexander kick)
MSU FG Nichels 24
UNC Betterson 6 run (Alexander kick)
MSU Packer 16 run (Nichels kick)
UNC Jerome 28 pass from Kupec (Alexander kick)
MSU FG Nichels 32
UNC FG Alexander 26
MSU Vitrano 2 run (kick failed)

MSU	TEAM STATISTICS	UNC
25	First Downs	22
455	Rushing Yards	277
3-8-0	Passing	5-15-1
44	Passing Yards	125
499	Total Yards	402
3-35.0	Punts - Average	4-38.0
1-1	Fumbles - Lost	3-0
5-45	Penalties - Yards	2-30

INDIVIDUAL LEADERS
RUSHING
MSU: Packer 24-183, 2 TD; Vitrano 20-164, 1 TD.
UNC: Voight 17-90; Betterson 19-84, 2 TD.
PASSING
MSU: Felker 2-7-0, 33 yards.
UNC: Kupec 5-15-1, 125 yards, 1 TD.
RECEIVING
MSU: Lewis 2-27; Barkum 1-17.
UNC: Norton 2-61; Jerome 2-42, 1 TD.

DECEMBER 27, 1980 | SUN
Nebraska 31, Mississippi State 17

	1ST	2ND	3RD	4TH	FINAL
NEB	7	10	7	7	31
MSU	0	0	3	14	17

SCORING SUMMARY
NEB Brown 23 run (Seibel kick)
NEB FG Seibel 22
NEB Finn 8 pass from Quinn (Seibel kick)
MSU FG Moore 47
NEB Franklin 2 run (Seibel kick)
MSU Bond 1 run (Morgan kick)
NEB McCrady 52 pass from Quinn (Seibel kick)
MSU Haddix 3 pass from Bond (Morgan kick)

NEB	TEAM STATISTICS	MSU
16	First Downs	15
159	Rushing Yards	93
9-19-1	Passing	7-19-2
159	Passing Yards	102
318	Total Yards	195
3-32	Punt Returns - Yards	1-(-3)
2-39	Kickoff Returns - Yards	4-116
8-42.0	Punts - Average	5-50.0
1-1	Fumbles - Lost	5-4
4-37	Penalties - Yards	4-30

INDIVIDUAL LEADERS
RUSHING
NEB: Franklin 17-67, 1 TD; Redwine 13-42.
MSU: King 23-96; Haddix 4-14.
PASSING
NEB: Quinn 9-19-2, 159 yards, 2 TD.
MSU: Bond 7-19-1, 102 yards, 1 TD.
RECEIVING
NEB: McCrady 2-107, 1 TD; Brown 2-16.
MSU: McDole 4-69; Price 1-25.

DECEMBER 31, 1981 | HALL OF FAME CLASSIC
MISSISSIPPI STATE 10, KANSAS 0

	1ST	2ND	3RD	4TH	FINAL
MSU	7	3	0	0	10
KU	0	0	0	0	0

SCORING SUMMARY
MSU   Bond 17 run (Morgan kick)
MSU   FG Moore 14

MSU	TEAM STATISTICS	KU
12	First Downs	14
236	Rushing Yards	35
5-16-0	Passing	15-31-2
51	Passing Yards	171
287	Total Yards	206
4-38	Punt Returns - Yards	4-19
1-15	Kickoff Returns - Yards	3-68
9-49.1	Punts - Average	9-45.2
5-1	Fumbles - Lost	1-1
10-65	Penalties - Yards	7-82

INDIVIDUAL LEADERS
RUSHING
MSU: Bond 17-79, 1 TD; King 14-38.
KU: Taylor 20-61; Jones 7-20.
PASSING
MSU: Bond 5-16-0, 51 yards.
KU: Smith 8-22-2, 61 yards; Frederick 7-9-0, 110 yards.
RECEIVING
MSU: Haddix 2-16; Price 1-15.
KU: Capers 2-57; Taylor 7-41.

DECEMBER 29, 1991 | LIBERTY
AIR FORCE 38, MISSISSIPPI STATE 15

	1ST	2ND	3RD	4TH	FINAL
AFA	14	7	3	14	38
MSU	0	7	0	8	15

SCORING SUMMARY
AFA   Jones 1 run (Wood kick)
AFA   Perez 1 run (Wood kick)
AFA   Yates 35 fumble return (Wood kick)
MSU   Edwards 4 pass from Robinson (Garnderk kick)
AFA   FG Wood 20
AFA   Hufford 31 run (Wood kick)
MSU   Davis 7 run (Jordan pass from Robinson)
AFA   Simpson fumble recovery in end zone (Wood kick)

AFA	TEAM STATISTICS	MSU
19	First Downs	18
318	Rushing Yards	163
1-2-1	Passing	13-24-1
10	Passing Yards	121
328	Total Yards	284
4-48.3	Punts - Average	4-37.8
2-0	Fumbles - Lost	3-2
4-31	Penalties - Yards	5-35

INDIVIDUAL LEADERS
RUSHING
AFA: Perez 26-114, 1 TD.
MSU: Roberts 8-66.
PASSING
AFA: Perez 1-2-1, 10 yards.
MSU: Robinson 6-12-0, 49 yards, 1 TD.
RECEIVING
AFA: Wilkie 1-10.
MSU: Roberts 4-28.

JANUARY 2, 1993 | PEACH
NORTH CAROLINA 21, MISSISSIPPI STATE 17

	1ST	2ND	3RD	4TH	FINAL
UNC	0	0	14	7	21
MSU	14	0	0	3	17

SCORING SUMMARY
MSU   Truitt 2 pass from Plump (Gardner kick)
MSU   Roberts 22 run (Gardner kick)
UNC   Means 1 run (Pignetti kick)
UNC   Walker 24 blocked punt return (Pignetti kick)
UNC   Baskerville 44 interception return (Pignetti kick)
MSU   FG Gardner 46

UNC	TEAM STATISTICS	MSU
13	First Downs	24
149	Rushing Yards	144
7-17-2	Passing	25-45-2
106	Passing Yards	296
255	Total Yards	440
6-38.2	Punts - Average	3-36.7
1-1	Fumbles - Lost	1-0
4-36	Penalties - Yards	9-87
25:27	Possession Time	34:33

INDIVIDUAL LEADERS
RUSHING
UNC: Means 21-128, 1 TD.
MSU: Roberts 9-64, 1 TD; Davis 10-32.
PASSING
UNC: Thomas 7-16-2, 106 yards.
MSU: Plump 24-40-2, 287 yards, 1 TD.
RECEIVING
UNC: Brooks 2-60; Jerry 2-20.
MSU: Harris 8-127; Roberts 5-49.

JANUARY 1, 1995 | PEACH
NC STATE 28, MISSISSIPPI STATE 24

	1ST	2ND	3RD	4TH	FINAL
NCST	7	6	8	7	28
MSU	6	7	8	3	24

SCORING SUMMARY
MSU   FG Rogers 37
NCST   Stephens 2 run (Videtich kick)
MSU   FG Rogers 21
MSU   FG Videtich 45
MSU   Davis 11 run (Rogers kick)
NCST   FG Videtich 36
MSU   Safety
MSU   FG Rogers 29
MSU   FG Rogers 36
NCST   Dickerson 3 pass from Harvey (Harvey run)
NCST   King 11 run (Videtich kick)
MSU   FG Rogers 30

NCST	TEAM STATISTICS	MSU
20	First Downs	16
172	Rushing Yards	117
14-25-1	Passing	14-29-0
164	Passing Yards	185
336	Total Yards	302
3-48.0	Punts - Average	3-53.0
2-1	Fumbles - Lost	0-0
2-15	Penalties - Yards	6-53
33:11	Possession Time	26:49

INDIVIDUAL LEADERS
RUSHING
NCST: Stephens 21-105, 1 TD; King 6-38, 1 TD.
MSU: Davis 13-51, 1 TD; Bouie 12-51.
PASSING
NCST: Harvey 11-18-0, 139 yards, 1 TD.
MSU: Taite 13-28-0, 141 yards.
RECEIVING
NCST: Grissett 2-68; Dickerson 3-31, 1 TD.
MSU: McGee 2-62; Jones 3-39.

JANUARY 1, 1999 | COTTON
TEXAS 38, MISSISSIPPI STATE 11

	1ST	2ND	3RD	4TH	FINAL
MSU	0	3	0	8	11
TEX	7	7	24	0	38

SCORING SUMMARY
TEX   McGarity 59 pass from Applewhite (Stockton kick)
TEX   McGarity 52 pass from Applewhite (Stockton kick)
MSU   FG Hazelwood 39
TEX   Williams 37 run (Stockton kick)
TEX   FG Stockton 47
TEX   Williams 2 run (Stockton kick)
TEX   Cavil 18 pass from Applewhite (Stockton kick)
MSU   Grant 5 pass from Wyatt (Johnson run)

MSU	TEAM STATISTICS	TEX
18	First Downs	27
87	Rushing Yards	238
16-40-1	Passing	15-26-0
205	Passing Yards	225
292	Total Yards	463
7-41.0	Punts - Average	6-37.2
2-1	Fumbles - Lost	1-0
9-89	Penalties - Yards	5-55
27:59	Possession Time	32:01

INDIVIDUAL LEADERS
RUSHING
MSU: Johnson 22-112; McKinley 2-7.
TEX: Williams 30-203, 2 TD; Mitchell 7-26.
PASSING
MSU: Wyatt 12-24-0, 156 yards, 1 TD; Madkin 4-16-1, 49 yards.
TEX: Applewhite 15-26-0, 225 yards 3 TD.
RECEIVING
MSU: Grant 4-62, 1 TD; Cooper 4-38.
TEX: McGarity 4-132, 2 TD; Williams 5-45.

DECEMBER 30, 1999 | PEACH
MISSISSIPPI STATE 17, CLEMSON 7

	1ST	2ND	3RD	4TH	FINAL
MSU	0	0	3	14	17
CLEM	0	0	0	7	7

SCORING SUMMARY
MSU   FG Westerfield 39
MSU   Madkin 2 run (Westerfield kick)
CLEM   Streeter 1 run (Lazzara kick)
MSU   Walker 15 pass from Madkin (Westerfield kick)

MSU	TEAM STATISTICS	CLEM
16	First Downs	24
89	Rushing Yards	85
17-38-0	Passing	25-56-5
176	Passing Yards	306
265	Total Yards	391
2-1	Fumbles - Lost	1-1
21-188	Penalties - Yards	8-82
30:41	Possession Time	29:19

INDIVIDUAL LEADERS
RUSHING
MSU: Madkin 5-37, 1 TD; Miller 10-24.
CLEM: Rambert 18-70.
PASSING
MSU: Madkin 17-38-0, 176 yards, 1 TD.
CLEM: Streeter 24-50-4, 301 yards.
RECEIVING
MSU: Miller 3-54, Sirmones 2-21.
CLEM: Wofford 6-147; Gardner 7-75.

DECEMBER 31, 2000 | INDEPENDENCE
MISSISSIPPI STATE 43, TEXAS A&M 41

	1ST	2ND	3RD	4TH	OT	FINAL
MSU	0	14	7	14	8	43
A&M	14	6	0	15	6	41

SCORING SUMMARY
A&M	Whitaker 9 run (Kitchens kick)
A&M	Toombs 4 run (Kitchens kick)
MSU	Walker 40 run (Westerfield kick)
MSU	Miller 4 pass from Madkin (Westerfield kick)
A&M	Ferguson 42 pass from Farris (kick blocked)
MSU	Walker 1 run (Westerfield kick)
A&M	Johnson 35 pass from Farris (Whitaker run)
A&M	Toombs 13 run (Kitchens kick)
MSU	Walker 32 run (Westerfield kick)
MSU	Lee 3 pass from Madkin (Westerfield kick)
A&M	Toombs 25 run (kick blocked)
MSU	Griffith blocked PAT return
MSU	Madkin 6 run

MSU	TEAM STATISTICS	A&M
16	First Downs	14
246	Rushing Yards	209
9-19-0	Passing	9-11-1
71	Passing Yards	133
317	Total Yards	342
7-37.1	Punts - Average	7-34.3
4-1	Fumbles - Lost	1-1
6-45	Penalties - Yards	7-71

INDIVIDUAL LEADERS
RUSHING
MSU: Walker 16-143, 3 TD.
A&M: Toombs 35-193, 3 TD.
PASSING
MSU: Madkin 9-19-0, 71 yards, 2 TD.
A&M: Farris 9-11-1, 133 yards, 2 TD.
RECEIVING
MSU: Miller 4-30, 1 TD.
A&M: Ferguson 3-54, 1 TD.

DECEMBER 29, 2007 | LIBERTY
MISSISSIPPI STATE 10, CENTRAL FLORIDA 3

	1ST	2ND	3RD	4TH	FINAL
UCF	0	3	0	0	3
MSU	0	3	0	7	10

SCORING SUMMARY
UCF	FG Torres 45
MSU	FG Carlson 22
MSU	Dixon 1 run (Carlson kick)

UCF	TEAM STATISTICS	MSU
13	First Downs	10
131	Rushing Yards	160
10-24-3	Passing	8-20-1
88	Passing Yards	39
219	Total Yards	199
6-54	Punt Returns - Yards	2-5
1-6	Kickoff Returns - Yards	2-29
6-42.8	Punts - Average	11-34.9
2-1	Fumbles - Lost	0-0
3-25	Penalties - Yards	5-45

INDIVIDUAL LEADERS
RUSHING
UCF: Kevin Smith 35-119.
MSU: Dixon 24-86, 1 TD.
PASSING
UCF: Israel 10-24-3, 88 yards.
MSU: Carroll 8-18-1, 39 yards.
RECEIVING
UCF: Ross 2-27; Kevin Smith 3-12.
MSU: Ducre 3-10; Dixon 1-10.

SOUTH CAROLINA

BY GEOFFREY NORMAN

LOYALTY IN THE FACE OF ADVERSITY is plainly the virtue that best characterizes the University of South Carolina's football program. There is nothing exceptional about a school that routinely wins or contends for national and conference championships, packing its stadium on Saturdays with fervent fans even when the team is struggling. Fans of the perennial powers understand—sort of—that you can't win them all and you can't be on top every year.

But the South Carolina Gamecocks have never won a national championship. They've never been ranked No. 1. Nor have they finished on top of the SEC since joining in 1992. Before that year, the Gamecocks had been to just eight bowl games and lost them all.

And yet, at every home game, Williams-Brice Stadium in Columbia is packed with more than 80,000 of the most loyal, long-suffering fans in all of college football. South Carolina, like its neighboring states, is passionate about football. But it is also a small state; thus, homegrown talent is in short supply.

The Gamecocks must compete with in-state archrival Clemson and with out-of-state recruiting vultures from Tennessee, Georgia and Alabama.

The Gamecocks have brought in head coaches who won national titles elsewhere—Paul Dietzel, who did it at LSU, and Lou Holtz, who'd been No. 1 at Notre Dame. And in 2005, South Carolina reloaded with Steve Spurrier, who won nearly 82 percent of his games at Florida and took the team to a national championship in 1996.

One thing for sure that Spurrier does not have to worry about in Columbia are the fans. Their loyalty is solid.

TRADITION The sense of gravity is palpable before home games. The Gamecocks take the field flanked by the school's marching band, which plays Richard Strauss' "Thus Spake Zarathustra" (a.k.a., the theme to *2001: A Space Odyssey*) as the players pour onto the field. The band, the Mighty Sound of the Southeast, travels to all away games.

BEST PLAYER George Rogers was the nation's second-leading rusher in 1979 and topped that in 1980 when he finished first with 1,894 yards and won the Heisman Trophy. Rogers conclusively established his bona fides by gaining more than 140 yards in back-to-back

---

PROFILE

University of South Carolina
Columbia, S.C.
Founded: 1801
Enrollment: 27,390
Colors: Garnet and Black
Nickname: Gamecocks
Stadium: Williams-Brice Stadium
    Opened in 1934
    Grass; 80,250 capacity
First football game: 1892
All-time record: 527-530-44 (.499)
Bowl record: 4-10
Heisman Trophy: George Rogers, 1980
First-round draft choices: 9
Website: www.gamecocksonline.com

THE BEST OF TIMES

It's hard to argue with the second and third seasons of the Lou Holtz era. After an 0–11 season extended their losing streak to 21 games, South Carolina went 8-4 and 9-3, landing two New Year's bowl berths and establishing the Gamecocks for the first time as a force to be reckoned with in the SEC.

THE WORST OF TIMES

During one span over the 1963 and 1964 seasons, the Gamecocks went winless in 15 straight games.

CONFERENCE

Few schools are as well traveled as the Gamecocks, who played in the Southern Conference from 1922 to 1952, then spent nearly two decades in the ACC (1953-71), before spending the next 20 years as an independent. In 1992, they joined the SEC.

DISTINGUISHED ALUMNI

Alex English, NBA player; Leeza Gibbons, TV personality; Ernest "Fritz" Hollings, U.S. senator; Robert McNair, owner, Houston Texans; Darius Rucker, Dean Felber, Jim "Soni" Sonefeld and Mark Bryan, musicians, Hootie & the Blowfish

> *At every home game, Williams-Brice is packed with more than 80,000 of the most loyal, long-suffering fans in all of college football.*

performances on the road against national powers Southern California and Michigan. He carried the Gamecocks to a rare national television appearance in that year's Gator Bowl against Pittsburgh and fellow Heisman candidate Hugh Green. Rogers rushed for over 100 yards in 22 consecutive games, and the New Orleans Saints made him the first player selected in the 1981 NFL draft.

BEST COACH A tough call. Glory has eluded South Carolina coaches and, in fact, none has ever gone on to another Bowl Subdivision (or Division I-A) head coaching job. Five years ago, the nod would have gone to Lou Holtz, who has the gaudiest lifetime résumé. Gamecocks fans expected big things from Holtz when he arrived in 1999, inheriting a program that had gone 1–10 the previous season. The turnaround did not occur immediately; Holtz's first team lost every game. Then things got decidedly better and the Gamecocks accomplished the following firsts under Holtz's leadership: 17 wins over two seasons, back-to-back

New Year's Day bowl victories and Top 20 finishes in 2000 and 2001, and Holtz winning SEC Coach of the Year honors in 2000.

But, like most USC coaches, Holtz wound up with a mediocre overall record (33–37) and earned only one win in six tries over archrival Clemson.

Longtime Gamecocks fans would also express a fondness for Rex Enright, who also finished his career with a losing record (64–69–7). Enright took over as head coach in 1938 and stayed until 1955, with three years off to serve in the Navy during World War II. He made his legend where Holtz struggled, against Clemson, beating the Tigers seven times in his last 10 seasons—at a time when Clemson was a national power.

But the answer to the question, "Who is the best head coach in South Carolina football history?" would almost certainly have to be, "The guy they got."

In four seasons, Spurrier has done the following: put together a winning record (28–22), taken the Gamecocks to three bowl games, defeated Florida for the first time since the '30s and won at Tennessee for the first time ever. Fans are expecting even better things to come.

BEST TEAM Expectations were not especially high before the 1984 season. Then Joe Morrison's team won nine straight, including a victory over Notre Dame in South Bend. The Gamecocks also beat Georgia, Pitt, Kansas State and Florida State, and were ranked No. 2 in the nation, behind Washington, with Navy coming up. The game had been scheduled for Columbia but was switched to Annapolis so South Carolina could get an additional home game the following year. Perhaps because they were on the road, or maybe because the high national ranking made them dizzy, the Gamecocks were upset by the Midshipmen. Hard as the defeat was to accept, it was made even worse when Washington also lost that weekend. If the Gamecocks had beaten Navy, they would have been No. 1. The team bounced back against Clemson, rallying from a 21-3 deficit to win 22-21, but went on to lose to Oklahoma State in the Gator Bowl and finish No. 11 in the AP rankings.

BEST BACKFIELD Some longtime Gamecocks fans might cast a sentimental vote for the Alex Hawkins–King Dixon unit of 1958 that went 7–3 (including a 26-6 win over a highly ranked Clemson team) and just missed a shot at the Orange Bowl. Hawkins was one of the game's legendary hellraisers who went on to a distinguished NFL career, while Dixon, his opposite in temperament, served in the Marines and eventually as South Carolina's athletic director. And then there are those who would say that any backfield with George Rogers in it would probably be in the running for the title. But the vote has to go to the 1975 backfield led by Clarence Williams, who rushed for 2,311 career yards, including eight 100-yard games, while at South Carolina. Both he and Kevin Long gained more than 1,000 yards that year, and quarterback Jeff Grantz kept defenses honest. The team went 7–5, routed Clemson, 56-20, and earned a berth in the Tangerine Bowl, where they fell to Miami of Ohio.

BEST DEFENSE A case could be made for the 1953 team that beat highly ranked West Virginia in a huge upset that moved the Gamecocks into the top 15 for the first time in their history. But the honors go to the 1956 team that held opponents to a total of 67 points while finishing fourth in the nation in total defense and third in passing defense. That Gamecocks squad, the first for head coach Warren Giese, shut out four opponents, closing out a 7–3 campaign with 13-0 wins over Maryland and Wake Forest.

BIGGEST GAME The Gamecocks were an unranked and much-overlooked independent when they played

COLLEGE FOOTBALL HALL OF FAME INDUCTEES		
NAME	YEARS	INDUCTED
George Rogers, HB	1977-80	1997
Lou Holtz, COACH	1999-2004	2008

mighty Michigan in Ann Arbor on Sept. 27, 1980. Michigan was aware of Rogers and stacked its defense to stop him. Even so, Rogers ran the ball 36 times for 142 yards. Ahead 14-3, Michigan opened the second half by marching to the Gamecocks 8, then fumbled into the end zone. South Carolina recovered and drove 80 yards to score on a two-yard run by Rogers. Later, the Gamecocks sniffed out a fake punt by Michigan and scored on a short drive for a win that put South Carolina on the map and made Rogers the front-runner for the Heisman.

BIGGEST UPSET North Carolina was ranked No. 3 in the nation on Oct. 24, 1981, when South Carolina QB Gordon Beckham completed 16 of 17 passes and led the Gamecocks to a 31-13 blowout. USC's loss two weeks later to the University of the Pacific made the win even more remarkable. Pacific couldn't afford a charter flight to South Carolina and stayed in one of the cheapest motels in Columbia. The Gamecocks had improved to 5–3 after upsetting the Tar Heels, but finished their first season after Rogers' departure with a 6–6 mark.

TRAGEDY Steve "The Cadillac" Wadiak did not play football in high school. He learned the game in the Navy during World War II and was playing sandlot ball in Chicago when a Gamecocks loyalist saw that he had talent and alerted coach Rex Enright. Wadiak's 2,878 yards rushing made him the Gamecocks' all-time leading rusher for 28 years, until Rogers came along and broke his record. After graduating in 1951, Wadiak was drafted by the Pittsburgh Steelers and also had an offer from Montreal in the Canadian Football League. He was working his way toward a decision when he was killed in an automobile accident on March 9, 1952. Wadiak was much loved by Gamecocks fans for his enthusiasm and for the spark he provided, especially against Clemson, and the team's MVP award is named after him.

WILDEST FINISH In a 1952 game in Norfolk, Va., that was sponsored by the Shriners and called the Oyster Bowl, South Carolina was trailing a heavily favored Virginia team, 14-0, midway through the fourth quarter. Dick Balka, a Notre Dame transfer, came in as quarterback and with three quick completions moved the Gamecocks more than 70 yards. With the score 14-7, Virginia fumbled away the kickoff inside its own 5-yard line. The Gamecocks quickly scored and tied the game. A clip on the next kickoff put Virginia deep in the hole. South Carolina recovered a fumble in the end zone to make it three touchdowns in less than two minutes and a 21-14 final.

BEST GOAL-LINE STAND South Carolina was leading Tennessee, 24-17, late in the fourth quarter in 1992 when the Volunteers scored a touchdown. Rather than kick for the tie, UT went for two points and the win. The Vols' quarterback, Heath Shuler, faked a pass and had what looked like clear sailing to the end zone—except for Hank Campbell. The walk-on linebacker made the stop, saved the game and was named SEC defensive player of the week for his effort.

BEST COMEBACK The Gamecocks were struggling at Clemson in 1964. Quarterback Dan Reeves was hobbled by a badly injured foot, and the game turned into a long defensive battle after Clemson kicked a field goal on its first possession. Down 3-0 late in the fourth quarter, the Gamecocks replaced Reeves with backup Jim Rogers. A 45-yard completion to J.R. Wilburn put the ball on the Clemson 15. On third down, Rogers rolled out to pass but couldn't find an open receiver. So he scrambled for the crucial first down, then kept going, all the way to the end zone. South Carolina won, 7-3, in Death Valley.

STADIUM Williams-Brice Stadium was built in 1934 under the New Deal's Works Progress Administration. The original structure was called Carolina Stadium and seated some 17,600 fans. There have been several improvements and additions over the years, including one in 1972 that enlarged capacity to more than 53,000. This project was financed by a bequest from the estate of Martha Williams Brice, whose husband was a Gamecocks letterman from 1922 to 1924. The facility was dedicated as Williams-Brice Stadium at the season opener in 1972. The most recent improvements, completed before the 1996 season, raised capacity to the current 80,250. Those seats are routinely filled, consistently making the Gamecocks among the top 20 in the nation in home attendance.

RIVAL Clemson and South Carolina played in 100 straight seasons (and a total of 106 times) through 2008, making theirs the third-longest uninterrupted series in all of college football. And that's only the beginning of the story. College football fans were appalled when players from both squads fought on the field at the 2004 game—behavior that cost both schools bowl trips for which they were otherwise eligible. Unfortunate as this was, it was not without precedent. In 1902, when the game was still played on the fairgrounds of Columbia on what was called Big Thursday, South Carolina won 12-6. The Clemson cadets, who had bivouacked on the fairgrounds, were so unhappy with the result that they marched, with fixed bayonets, on the South Carolina campus and a riot ensued. The series was suspended

until 1909, when Clemson—then known as Clemson Agricultural College—got its revenge, 6-0. Unlike many other states, in South Carolina, the "aggie school" receives favorable political treatment and thus has a decided advantage in football.

DISPUTE When Thomas Hill fell on Derek Watson's fumble in the end zone with less than a minute to go, the Gamecocks went ahead of Clemson, 14-13, on Nov. 18, 2000. It looked like the end of a three-game losing streak to the Tigers until, with just 10 seconds left, Woody Dantzler completed a 50-yard pass to Rod Gardner, whom Gamecocks fans swear to this day pushed a South Carolina defender out of the way. Gardner wasn't called for a penalty and Clemson won on a 25-yard field goal.

NICKNAME The South Carolina football players were described in a 1902 newspaper story as having "fought like gamecocks." The simile stuck. But modern non-Carolinians might ask, "What does that mean?"

The gamecock is a pugnacious rooster, bred for fighting. The fights go on until one bird dies, and they bring in lots of passionate wagering. Though it has long been outlawed in the United States, cockfighting is still hugely popular in some parts of the world. Cockfighting was commonplace and accepted in the American Colonies, however, and one able Revolutionary War figure from South Carolina, General Thomas Sumter, was nicknamed the Gamecock. Another American general—one considerably less esteemed in South Carolina—went on to the White House and kept fighting cocks there. He was Ulysses S. Grant.

UNIFORMS Garnet and black have been South Carolina's colors for a century, and coach Joe Morrison famously dressed entirely in black during his tenure. Since 1975, the team's helmet has featured a fierce gamecock set inside a big block-letter C, though the helmet itself has changed colors—first white, then red through much of the '80s, then black for a season in 2004, and back to the classic white ever since.

LORE During the early 1980s, the Gamecocks came to be known as Fire Ants and Black Magic, after defensive coordinator Tom Gadd described the defense as looking like "a bunch of fire ants getting after the football." The Black Magic nickname was the result of Morrison's trademark black coaching attire.

QUOTE "The chicken curse is on South Carolina and they'll never win big." —**Doug Nye**, sports editor of *The Columbia Record*, remarking in 1963 on South Carolina's football misfortunes

All the Way

BY LOU HOLTZ

The University of South Carolina has the most loyal and patient fans. I nicknamed them Job. The state motto is *Dum spiro spero*, Latin for "While I breathe, I hope." South Carolina fans live their motto. Williams-Brice Stadium seats 80,000 people and they pack it for each and every home game. This is understandable at powerhouse programs like Oklahoma, Florida, Ohio State—but before 2000, South Carolina had won all of one bowl game in its 107-year history and had never won a New Year's Day bowl. The Gamecocks have won exactly one conference championship in the history of the school and that was in the ACC in 1971, when they ended the season with a 6–5 record.

When I went to coach the Gamecocks in 1999, they had lost nine games in a row, and in my first year we went 0 for 11. Now, won-loss records can be deceiving, so let me assure you: That year we really weren't as good as our record would indicate. But we *still* sold out every home game.

Not only do the fans show up, they bring their game faces. The Gamecocks take the field in the most electric atmosphere in college football. The band plays the theme music from *2001*, the fans scream at the top of their lungs and, after this has built up to a crescendo, smoke billows and the Gamecocks emerge to a thunderous ovation. I still get chills thinking about it.

Even the tailgating at Williams-Brice is unique because of the Cockaboose Railroad. Thirty or so

real cabooses sit on a train track some 50 yards away from the stadium. The right to use the train cars sells for hundreds of thousands of dollars and there's an eternal waiting list. All the other tailgaters—and they number in the tens of thousands—set up in the fairground parking lot, and let me tell you, they wrote the book on how to party before, and after, the game.

But the best thing about South

> *In our first game of 2000, we beat New Mexico State, 31-0, and broke the country's longest active losing streak. The students tore down the goalposts. In our second game, we upset Georgia, 21-10, and the fans again tore them down. I thought, "They must do this after every win."*

Carolina football is that it brings together old, young, rich, poor, white, black, conservative and liberal to cheer for the Gamecocks. When we beat Ohio State in the Outback Bowl on January 1, 2001, some 40,000 fans traveled to Tampa for the game. I wasn't sure we would have enough people back home to keep the supermarkets open. The next year

we beat OSU, again on January 1, and we received the same fan support.

That level of involvement on the part of students and community has a deep impact. The football players develop an abiding love for the school and for the city of Columbia. I cannot remember one athlete who didn't enjoy going to school there or who wanted to transfer. The students are so appreciative. In our first game of 2000, we beat New Mexico State, 31-0, and broke the country's longest active losing streak. The students tore down the goalposts. In our second game, we upset Georgia, 21-10, and the fans again tore them down. I thought, "They must do this after every win."

The University of South Carolina is the only Football Bowl Subdivision school with the nickname Gamecocks. The term refers to a type of rooster that in ancient Greece was considered sacred because of its magnanimity, courage, skill and constancy. Over the centuries, other noble attributes that have been associated with the gamecock include alertness, diligence, energy, defiance and vigilance. Those terms don't always describe South Carolina's football team, but they sure fit its fans. Every August we had a football clinic for women only, and as many as 2,500 would show up.

No one is rooting harder than I am for Steve Spurrier to win an SEC championship. Nobody deserves it more than Gamecocks fans.

It *will* happen.

Lou Holtz is the only head coach in NCAA history to take six different schools to bowl games. Inducted into the College Football Hall of Fame in 2008, he's now a football analyst on ESPN.

SOUTH CAROLINA ALL-TIME SCORES

WIN/LOSS PERCENTAGE SINCE 1936

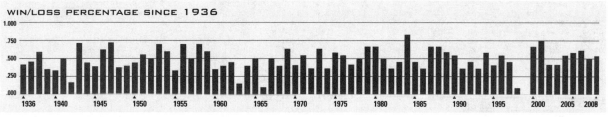

NO HEAD COACH

1892 0-1-0
D24	Furman ChSC	0	44

1893
NO TEAM

1894 0-2-0
N3	Georgia	0	40
N11	Augusta YMCA	4	16

1895 2-1-0
N2	●	Columbia AA	20	0
N8	●	Furman	14	10
N14	●	Wofford	0	10

W.H. WHALEY
1896 (.250)   1-3

1896 1-3-0
O31	at Charleston YMCA	4	6
N12 ●	Clemson	12	6
N19 ●	Wofford	4	6
N26	at Furman	0	12

W.P. MURPHY
1897 (.000)   0-3

1897 0-3-0
O23	at Charleston YMCA	0	4
N10	Clemson	6	18*
N26	Charleston YMCA	0	6

W. WERTENBAKER
1898 (.333)   1-2

1898 1-2-0
O18	●	Bingham	16	5
N17		Clemson	0	24
N24		at Davidson	0	6

I.O. HUNT
1899-1900 (.500)   6-6

1899 2-3-0
O15	●	Columbia YMCA	5	0
N9		Clemson	0	34
N15	●	Bingham	11	5
N22		at Bingham	6	18
N30		at Davidson	0	5

1900 4-3-0
O20		at Georgia	0	5
O25	●	Guilford	10	0
N1		Clemson	0	51
N10	●	North Carolina St.	12	0
N17		at Furman	27	0
N22		at Davidson	0	5
N29	●	at North Carolina St.	17	5

B.W. DICKSON
1901 (.429)   3-4

1901 3-4-0
O12		Georgia Aug	5	10
O22		Furman	12	0
O24	●	at Bingham	11	6
O30		Davidson	5	12
N9		at Georgia Tech	0	13
N12	●	N.C.M.A.	47	0
N18		at Wofford	5	11

C.R. WILLIAMS
1902-03 (.824)   14-3

1902 6-1-0
O15	●	Guilford	10	0
O21	●	N.C.M.A.	60	0
O25	●	Bingham	28	0
O30	●	Clemson	12	6
N6	●	St. Albans	5	0
N14		at Furman	0	10
N28	●	Charleston M.C.	80	0

1903 8-2-0
O2	●	Columbia YMCA	24	0
O6	●	Welsh Neck	89	0
O10	●	North Carolina	0	17
O17	●	at Georgia	17	0
O23	●	Guilford	29	0
O29	●	Tennessee	24	0
N8	●	at Davidson	29	12
N14	●	at North Carolina St.	5	6
N21	●	at Charleston	6	0
N26	●	at Georgia Tech	16	0

CHRISTIE BENET
1904-05, '08-09 (.453)   13-16-3

1904 4-3-1
O7	●	Welsh Neck	14	0
O15	●	at North Carolina	0	27
O20	●	Guilford	21	4
O26	●	Georgia	2	0
N5	=	at North Carolina St.	0	0
N12	●	Davidson	0	6
N19	●	at Charleston AC	0	6
N24	●	at Wash. & Lee	25	0

1905 4-2-1
O13	●	Welsh Neck	14	0
O20	●	Bingham	19	6
O26	●	North Carolina St.	0	29
N4	=	at Davidson	6	4
N11	=	at Bingham	5	5
N18	●	Virginia Tech Roa	0	34
N30	●	at Citadel	47	0

1906
NO TEAM

DOUGLAS McKAY
1907 (1.000)   3-0

1907 3-0-0
N16	●	Charleston	14	4
N21	●	Georgia Coll.	4	0
N28	●	at Citadel	12	0

CHRISTIE BENET

1908 3-5-1
O3	=	Ridgewood	0	0
O10	●	Charleston	17	0
O17	●	at Georgia	6	29
O22	●	Charleston AA	4	15
O29	●	Davidson	0	22
N4	●	at Georgia MS	19	5
N7		Bingham	6	10
N14	●	at North Carolina	0	22
N26	●	at Citadel	12	0

1909 2-6-0
O9		N.C. Medical Coll.	0	5
O16		at Georgia Tech	0	59
O23		Wake Forest	0	8
O28	●	Charleston	17	11
N4		Clemson	0	6
N13		Davidson Char	5	29
N20		at Mercer	3	5
N25	●	at Citadel	11	5

JOHN H. NEFF
1910-11 (.400)   5-8-2

1910 4-4-0
O8	●	Charleston	8	0
O15	●	Georgia MS Aug	14	0
O22	●	Lenoir	33	0
O27	●	Wake Forest	6	0
N3		Clemson	0	24
N12		at Davidson	0	53
N19	●	North Carolina Dur	6	23*
N24		at Citadel	0	5

1911 1-4-2
O7		at Georgia	0	38
O14	●	at Charleston	16	0
O21	=	Florida	6	6
N2		Clemson	0	27
N11		at North Carolina	0	21
N18		Davidson	0	10
N30	=	at Citadel	0	0

N.B. EDGERTON
1912-15 (.586)   19-13-3

1912 5-2-1
O5	●	Wake Forest	10	3
O14		at Virginia	0	19
O19		at Florida	6	10
O26	●	at Charleston	68	0
O31		Clemson	22	7
N9	=	at North Carolina	6	6
N16	●	Porter	66	0
N28	●	Citadel	26	2

1913 4-3-0
O4		at Virginia	0	54
O11	●	Wake Forest	27	10
O18		North Carolina	3	13
O30		Clemson	0	32
N8	●	Florida	13	0
N15		at Davidson	10	0
N26	●	Citadel	42	13

1914 5-5-1
S30	●	Mach. Mates	30	7
O3		at Georgia Tech	0	20
O12		at North Carolina	0	48
O17		at Virginia	7	49
O24	=	Newberry	13	13
O29		Clemson	6	29
N4	●	at Wofford	25	0
N7	●	Wake Forest	26	0
N14		Davidson	7	13
N19	●	at Newberry	47	6
N26	●	Citadel	7	6

1915 5-3-1
O2	●	Newberry	29	0
O9	●	Presbyterian	41	0
O21	●	at North Carolina St.	19	10
O28	=	Clemson	0	0
N4	●	at Wofford	33	6
N6	●	Cumberland	68	0
N13		Virginia	0	13
N20		at Georgetown	0	61
N25		Citadel	0	3

RICE WARREN
1916 (.222)   2-7

1916 2-7-0
O7		Newberry	0	10
O14	●	Wofford	23	3
O21		at Tennessee	0	26
O26		Clemson	0	27
N4		Wake Forest	7	33
N11		at Virginia	6	35
N18	●	Mercer	47	0
N23		at Furman	0	14
N30		Citadel	2	20

DIXON FOSTER
1917, '19 (.265)   4-12-1

1917 3-5-0
O6	●	Newberry	38	0
O13		at Florida	13	21
O25		Clemson	13	21
N3		Erskine	13	14
N8	●	Furman Flo	26	0
N17		at Wofford	0	20
N24		Presbyterian	14	20
N29		Citadel	20	0

FRANK DOBSON
1918 (.625)   2-1-1

1918 2-1-1
N2	●	Clemson	0	39
N16	●	at Furman	20	12
N23	●	Wofford	13	0
N28	=	Citadel Ora	0	0

DIXON FOSTER

1919 1-7-1
S27	●	Presbyterian	0	6
O4	●	Erskine	6	0
O11		at Georgia	0	14
O18		Davidson	0	7
O30		Clemson	6	19
N8		Tennessee	6	6
N15		at Wash. & Lee	0	26
N22		Florida	0	13
N27		Citadel	7	14

SOL METZGER
1920-24 (.587)   26-18-2

1920 5-4-0
O2	●	Wofford	10	0
O9		Georgia	0	37
O16		at North Carolina	0	7
O21	●	Presbyterian Aug	14	0
O28	●	Clemson	3	0
N6		at Davidson	0	27
N13		at Navy	0	63
N20	●	Newberry	48	0
N25		at Citadel	7	6

1921 5-1-2
O1	●	Erskine	13	7
O8	●	Newberry	7	0
O15	=	North Carolina	7	7
O22	●	Presbyterian	48	0
O27	●	Clemson	21	0
N5	=	Florida Tam	7	7
N12		at Furman	0	7
N19	●	Citadel	13	0

1922-1952
SOUTHERN

1922 5-4-0 (0-3-0)
S29	●	Erskine	13	0
O7	●	Presbyterian	7	0
O14	l	at North Carolina	7	10
O20	●	Wofford	20	0
O26	l	Clemson	0	3
N4	l	Sewanee	6	7
N11	●	Furman	27	7
N16	●	Citadel Ora	13	0
N30	l	at Centre	0	42

1923 4-6-0 (0-4-0)
S29	●	Erskine	35	0
O6	●	Presbyterian	3	7
O13	l	at North Carolina St.	0	7
O19	●	Newberry	24	0
O25	l	Clemson	6	7
N3	l	North Carolina	0	13
N10	●	at Furman	3	23
N15	l	Citadel Ora	12	0
N17	l	Wash. & Lee	7	13
N29	l	Wake Forest	14	7

1924 7-3-0 (3-2-0)
S27	●	Erskine	47	0
O4	l	at Georgia	0	18
O11	● l	North Carolina St.	10	0
O17	●	Presbyterian	29	0
O23	● l	Clemson	3	0
O29	●	Citadel Ora	14	3
N1	● l	at North Carolina	10	7
N8		Furman	0	10
N15	l	Sewanee	0	10
N27	l	Wake Forest	7	0

THE SCHOOLS

BRANCH BOCOCK
1925-26 (.650) — 13-7

1925 — 7-3-0 (2-2-0)
S26	●	Erskine	33 0
O3		North Carolina	0 7
O11	●	at North Carolina St.	7 6
O16	●	Wofford	6 0
O22	●	Clemson	33 0
O28		Citadel ORA	30 6
O31		Virginia Tech RICH	0 6
N14		at Furman	0 2
N20	●	Presbyterian	21 0
N28	●	Centre	20 0

1926 — 6-4-0 (4-2-0)
S25	●	Erskine	41 0
O2	●	Maryland	12 0
O9		at North Carolina	0 7
O15	●	Wofford	27 13
O21	●	Clemson	24 0
O28		Citadel ORA	9 12
O30		Virginia	0 6
N6	●	Virginia Tech RICH	19 0
N13		Furman	7 10
N20	●	North Carolina St.	20 14

HARRY LIGHTSEY
1927 (.444) — 4-5

1927 — 4-5-0 (2-4-0)
S24	●	Erskine	13 6
O1		at Maryland	0 26
O8	●	at Virginia	13 12
O15	●	North Carolina	14 6
O20		Clemson	0 20
O27		Citadel ORA	6 0
N5		Virginia Tech RICH	0 35
N12		at Furman	0 33
N24		North Carolina St.	0 34

BILLY LAVAL
1928-34 (.592) — 39-26-6

1928 — 6-2-2 (2-2-1)
S22	●	Erskine	19 0
S29	●	at Chicago	6 0
O6	●	at Virginia	24 13
O13	●	Maryland	21 7
O19	●	Presbyterian	13 0
O25		Clemson	0 32
N1	=	Citadel ORA	0 0
N10		at North Carolina	0 0
N17	●	Furman	6 0
N29		at North Carolina St.	7 18

1929 — 6-5-0 (2-5-0)
S28	●	Erskine	26 7
O5		Virginia	0 6
O12	●	at Maryland	26 6
O18	●	Presbyterian	41 0
O24		Clemson	14 21
O31	●	Citadel ORA	27 14
N9		North Carolina	0 40
N16	●	at Furman	2 0
N23		Florida	7 20
N30	●	at North Carolina St.	20 6
D7		at Tennessee	0 54

1930 — 6-4-0 (4-3-0)
S20	●	Erskine	19 0
S27	●	at Duke	22 0
O4		at Georgia Tech	0 45
O11	●	LSU	7 6
O23		Clemson	7 20
O30	●	Citadel ORA	13 0
N8		at Furman	0 14
N15	●	Sewanee	14 13
N22	●	North Carolina St.	19 0
N27		Auburn ColGa	7 25

1931 — 5-4-1 (3-3-1)
S26	●	Duke	7 0
O3		at Georgia Tech	13 25
O10		at LSU	12 19
O22	●	Clemson	21 0
O29	●	Citadel ORA	26 7
N7	●	Furman	27 0
N14	=	Florida JacF	6 6
N21	●	North Carolina St.	21 0
N26		Auburn MonT	6 13
D5		Centre	7 9

1932 — 5-4-2 (2-2-2)
S24	●	Sewanee	7 3
O1	●	at Villanova	7 6
O8		Wake Forest CHAR	0 6
O14	●	Wofford	19 0
O20	●	Clemson	14 0
O29		at Tulane	0 6
N5		LSU	0 6
N12		at Furman	0 14
N19		Citadel	19 0
N24	=	at North Carolina St.	7 7
D3	=	Auburn BIRM	20 20

1933 — 6-3-1 (3-0-0)
S23	●	Wofford	31 0
S29		at Temple	6 26
O7		Villanova	6 15
O19	●	Clemson	7 0
O26	●	Citadel ORA	12 6
O28	●	at Virginia Tech	12 0
N4		at LSU	7 30
N11	●	North Carolina St.	14 0
N19	=	Furman	0 0
D2		Auburn BIRM	16 14

1934 — 5-4-0 (2-3-0)
S29	●	Erskine	25 0
O6	●	VMI	22 6
O13		at North Carolina St.	0 6
O18	●	Citadel ORA	20 6
O25		Clemson	0 19
N3		Virginia Tech	20 0
N10		at Villanova	0 20
N17	●	at Furman	2 0
N29		Wash. & Lee	7 14

DON McCALLISTER
1935-37 (.397) — 13-20-1

1935 — 3-7-0 (1-4-0)
S21	●	Erskine	33 0
S28		at Duke	0 47
O5		North Carolina St.	0 14
O12		at Davidson	6 13
O17	●	Citadel ORA	25 0
O24		Clemson	0 44
N2		at Virginia Tech	0 27
N16		Furman	7 20
N23	●	Wash. & Lee	2 0
D7		Florida TAM	0 22

1936 — 5-7-0 (2-5-0)
S19	●	Erskine	38 0
S26		at VMI	7 24
O3		Duke	0 21
O10		Florida	7 0
O17		Virginia Tech	14 0
O22		Clemson	0 19
O30	●	Citadel ORA	9 0
N7		Villanova	0 14
N14		at Furman	6 23
N21		North Carolina	0 14
N26		at Xavier	13 21
D11		at Miami, Fla.	6 3

1937 — 5-6-1 (2-2-1)
S18	●	Emory & Henry	45 7
S25	=	at North Carolina	13 13
O2		Georgia	7 13
O9		at Alabama	0 20
O16	●	Davidson	12 7
O21		Clemson	6 34
O29	●	Citadel ORA	21 6
N6		at Kentucky	7 27
N13		Furman	0 12
N20	●	Presbyterian	64 0
D3	●	at Miami, Fla.	3 0
D25		at Catholic U.	14 27

REX ENRIGHT
1938-42, '46-55 (.482) — 64-69-7

1938 — 6-4-1 (2-2-0)
S19	●	Erskine	53 0
S24	●	at Xavier	6 0
O1		Georgia	6 7
O8		Wake Forest	19 20
O14	●	Davidson SUM	25 0
O20		Clemson	12 34
O28	=	Villanova ORA	6 6
N5	●	Duquesne	7 0
N12	●	at Furman	27 6
N19		Fordham NYC	0 13
N28		at Catholic U.	7 0

1939 — 3-6-1 (1-3-0)
S23		at Wake Forest	7 19
S29		Catholic U.	0 12
O6		Villanova PHIL	0 40
O13	●	Davidson SUM	7 0
O19		Clemson	0 27
O27	=	West Virginia ORA	6 6
N4		Florida	6 0*
N11		Furman	7 33
N18		at Georgia	7 33
N25		Miami, Fla.	7 6

1940 — 3-6-0 (1-3-0)
O5		Georgia	2 33
O11		at Duquesne	21 27
O24		Clemson	13 21
N2		at Penn State	0 12
N9		Kansas State	20 13
N16		at Furman	7 25
N22	●	Miami, Fla.	7 2
N28	●	Wake Forest CHAR	6 7
D7	●	at Citadel	31 6

1941 — 4-4-1 (4-0-1)
S27	●	at North Carolina	13 7
O4		at Georgia	6 34
O11	●	Wake Forest	6 6
O23	●	Clemson	18 14
O31	●	Citadel ORA	13 6
N8		at Kansas State	0 3
N15	●	Furman	26 7
N21	●	at Miami, Fla.	6 7
N29		Penn State	12 19

1942 — 1-7-1 (1-4-0)
S26	=	Tennessee	0 0
O3		at North Carolina	6 18
O10		at West Virginia	0 13
O22		Clemson	6 18
O30	●	Citadel ORA	14 0
N7		at Alabama	0 29
N14		Furman	0 6
N21		at Miami, Fla.	6 13
D5		Wake Forest CHAR	14 33

J.P. MORAN
1943 (.714) — 5-2

1943 — 5-2-0 (2-1-0)
S25	●	Newberry	19 7
O2		176th Infantry	7 13
O9	●	Presbyterian	20 7
O21	●	Clemson	33 6
O30	●	Charleston CG ORA	20 0
N6		North Carolina	6 21
N25	●	Wake Forest CHAR	13 2

WILLIAM NEWTON
1944 (.444) — 3-4-2

1944 — 3-4-2 (1-3-0)
S23	●	Newberry	48 0
S30		Georgia Pre-Flight	14 20
O7	=	at Miami, Fla.	0 0
O19		Clemson	13 20
O27	=	Charleston CG ORA	6 6
N4	●	at North Carolina	6 0
N11	●	Presbyterian	28 7
N18		Duke	7 34
N23		Wake Forest CHAR	13 19

JOHNNIE McMILLAN
1945 (.389) — 2-4-3

1945 — 2-4-3 (0-2-2)
S22		at Duke	0 60
S29	●	Presbyterian	40 0
O6		Camp Blanding	20 6
O13		Alabama MonT	0 55
O25	=	Clemson	0 0
N9	=	at Miami, Fla.	13 13
N22	=	Wake Forest CHAR	13 13
D1		Maryland	13 19

GATOR BOWL
J1		Wake Forest	14 26

REX ENRIGHT

1946 — 5-3-0 (4-2-0)
S29	●	Newberry	21 0
O5		Alabama	6 14
O11	●	at Furman	14 7
O24		Clemson	26 14
N1	●	Citadel ORA	19 7
N9	●	at Maryland	21 17
N16		Duke	0 39
N28		Wake Forest CHAR	0 35

1947 — 6-2-1 (4-1-1)
S20	●	Newberry	27 6
S27		Maryland	13 19
O4		Mississippi MEM	0 33
O11	●	Furman	26 8
O23	●	Clemson	21 19
O31		at Miami, Fla.	8 0
N7	●	Citadel ORA	12 0
N15	=	at Duke	0 0
N27	●	Wake Forest CHAR	6 0

1948 — 3-5-0 (1-3-0)
S24	●	Newberry	46 0
O1	●	at Furman	7 0
O9		at Tulane	0 14
O21		Clemson	7 13
O30		at West Virginia	12 35
N6		Maryland	7 19
N13	●	at Tulsa	27 7
N25		Wake Forest	0 38

1949 — 4-6-0 (3-3-0)
S24		at Baylor	6 20
S30		Furman	7 14
O8		North Carolina	13 28
O2o	●	Clemson	27 13
O29		at Maryland	7 44
N5	●	at Marquette	6 3
N11		Miami, Fla.	7 13
N19		at Georgia Tech	3 13
N26	●	Wake Forest	27 20
D3	●	Citadel	42 0

1950 — 3-4-2 (2-4-1)
S23		Duke	0 14
S30		at Georgia Tech	7 0
O6	●	at Furman	21 6
O19	=	Clemson	14 14
O27	●	at George Washington	34 20
N3	=	Marquette	13 13
N11	●	at Citadel	7 19
N18	●	North Carolina	7 14
N25		Wake Forest	7 14

1951 — 5-4-0 (5-3-0)
S22		Duke	6 34
S29	●	Citadel	26 7
O6	●	Furman	21 6
O13		at North Carolina	6 21
O25	●	Clemson	20 0
N3		George Washington	14 20
N10	●	at West Virginia	34 13
N17	●	at Virginia	27 28
N24	●	Wake Forest	21 6*

1952 — 5-5-0 (3-4-0)
S20	●	Wofford	33 0
S27		at Army	7 28
O4	●	at Furman	27 7
O11		Duke	7 33
O23	●	Clemson	6 0
N1	●	Virginia Nor	21 14
N8	●	at Citadel	35 0
N15		North Carolina	19 27
N22		West Virginia	6 13
N29		Wake Forest W-S	14 39

1953-1971 ACC

1953 — 7-3-0 (2-3-0)
S19		Duke	7 20
S26	●	Citadel	25 0
O3		at Virginia	19 0
O10		Furman	27 13
O22	●	Clemson	14 7
O31		at Maryland	6 24
N7	●	North Carolina	18 0
N14	●	at West Virginia	20 14
N21	●	Wofford	49 0
N26		Wake Forest CHAR	13 19

1954 — 6-4-0 (3-3-0)
S25	●	at Army	34 20
O2		West Virginia	6 26
O9	●	at Furman	27 7
O21	●	Clemson	13 8
O30		Maryland	0 20
N6		at North Carolina	19 21
N13	●	Virginia	27 0
N20	●	at Duke	7 26
N27	●	Wake Forest	20 19
D4	●	at Citadel	19 6

1955 — 3-6-0 (1-5-0)

S17	●		Wofford	26	7
S24		I	Wake Forest W-S	19	34
O1			Navy	0	26
O8	●		Furman	19	0
O20		I	Clemson	14	28
O29		I	at Maryland	0	27
N5		I	North Carolina NOR	14	32
N12		I	Duke	7	41
N26	●	I	at Virginia	21	14

WARREN GIESE
1956-60 (.570) 28-21-1

1956 — 7-3-0 (5-2-0)

S15	●		Wofford	26	13
S22	●	I	Duke	7	0
S28			at Miami, Fla.	6	14
O6	●	I	North Carolina	14	0
O13	●	I	Virginia RICH	27	13
O25		I	Clemson	0	7
N3	●		at Furman	13	6
N10		I	at North Carolina St.	7	14
N17	●	I	Maryland	13	0
N22	●	I	Wake Forest CHAR	13	0

1957 — 5-5-0 (2-5-0)

S21		I	Duke	14	26
S28	●		Wofford	26	0
O5	●		at Texas	27	21
O12	●		Furman	58	13
O24		I	Clemson	0	13
N2		I	Maryland	6	10
N9		I	at North Carolina	6	28
N16	●	I	at Virginia	13	0
N23		I	North Carolina	26	29
N30	●	I	at Wake Forest	26	7

1958 — 7-3-0 (5-2-0)

S20	●	I	Duke	8	0
S27			at Army	8	45
O4	●		at Georgia	24	14
O11		I	at North Carolina	0	6
O23	●	I	Clemson	26	6
N1		I	at Maryland	6	10
N8	●		at Furman	32	7
N15	●	I	Virginia	28	14
N22	●	I	North Carolina St.	12	7
N27	●	I	Wake Forest	24	7

1959 — 6-4-0 (4-3-0)

S19	●	I	Duke	12	7
S26	●		Furman	30	0
O3	●		Georgia	30	14
O10		I	at North Carolina	6	19
O22		I	Clemson	0	27
O31	●	I	Maryland	22	6
N7	●	I	at Virginia	32	20
N13			at Miami, Fla.	6	26
N21	●	I	North Carolina St.	12	7
N28		I	Wake Forest CHAR	20	43

1960 — 3-6-1 (3-3-1)

S24		I	Duke	0	31
O1			at Georgia	6	38
O14			at Miami, Fla.	6	21
O22	●	I	North Carolina	22	6
O29		I	at Maryland	0	15
N5			at LSU	6	35
N12		I	at Clemson	2	12
N19	=	I	North Carolina St.	8	8
N26	●	I	Wake Forest	41	20
D3	●	I	Virginia	26	0

MARVIN BASS
1961-65 (.380) 17-29-4

1961 — 4-6-0 (3-4-0)

S23		I	Duke	6	7
S30	●	I	at Wake Forest	10	7
O7			at Georgia	14	17
O14			LSU	0	42
O21		I	North Carolina	0	17
O28	●	I	Maryland	20	10
N4		I	at Virginia	20	28
N11	●	I	Clemson	21	14
N18		I	at North Carolina St.	14	38
N25	●		at Vanderbilt	23	7

1962 — 4-5-1 (3-4-0)

S22			at Northwestern	20	37
S29		I	at Duke	8	21
O6	=		Georgia	7	7
O13	●	I	Wake Forest	27	6
O20		I	at North Carolina	14	19
O27		I	at Maryland	11	13
N3	●	I	Virginia	40	6
N10	●	I	North Carolina St.	17	6
N17	●		at Detroit	26	13
N24		I	at Clemson	17	20

1963 — 1-8-1 (1-5-1)

S21		I	at Duke	14	22
S28	●	I	Maryland	21	13
O5			at Georgia	7	27
O12		I	North Carolina St.	6	18
O19	=	I	at Virginia	10	10
O26		I	North Carolina	0	7
N2			Tulane	7	20
N9			at Memphis	0	9
N16		I	at Wake Forest	19	20
N28		I	Clemson	20	24

1964 — 3-5-2 (2-3-1)

S19	=	I	Duke	9	9
S26		I	at Maryland	6	24
O3	=		Georgia	7	7
O10			at Nebraska	6	28
O17			at Florida	0	37
O24		I	at North Carolina	6	24
O31		I	at North Carolina St.	14	17
N7	●		Citadel	17	14
N14	●	I	Wake Forest	23	13
N28	●	I	at Clemson	7	3

1965 — 5-5-0 (4-2-0)

S18	●		at Citadel	13	3
S25		I	Duke	15	20
O2	●	I	North Carolina St.	13	7
O9			at Tennessee	3	24
O16	●	I	Wake Forest	38	7
O23			at LSU	7	21
O30		I	Maryland	14	27
N6	●	I	at Virginia	17	7†
N13			at Alabama	14	35
N20	●	I	Clemson	17	16

PAUL DIETZEL
1966-74 (.443) 42-53-1

1966 — 1-9-0 (1-3-0)

S17			at LSU	12	28
S24			Memphis	7	16
O1			Georgia	0	7
O8	●	I	at North Carolina St.	31	21
O15		I	Wake Forest	6	10
O22			at Tennessee	17	29
O29		I	at Maryland	2	14
N5			Florida State	10	32
N12			at Alabama	0	24
N26		I	at Clemson	10	35

1967 — 5-5-0 (4-2-0)

S16	●		Iowa State	34	3
S23	●	I	North Carolina	16	10
S30	●	I	at Duke	21	17
O7			at Georgia	0	21
O14			at Florida State	0	17
O21	●	I	Virginia	24	23
O28	●	I	Maryland	31	0
N4		I	at Wake Forest	21	35
N18			at Alabama	0	17
N25		I	Clemson	12	23

1968 — 4-6-0 (4-3-0)

S21		I	Duke	7	14
S28	●	I	at North Carolina	32	27
O5			Georgia	20	21
O12		I	at North Carolina St.	12	36
O19		I	at Maryland	19	21
O26			Florida State	28	35
N2	●	I	at Virginia	49	28
N9	●	I	at Wake Forest	34	21
N16			Virginia Tech	6	17
N23	●	I	at Clemson	7	3

1969 — 7-4-0 (6-0-0)

S20	●	I	Duke	27	20
S27	●	I	North Carolina	14	6
O4			at Georgia	16	41
O11	●	I	North Carolina St.	21	16
O18	●		at Virginia Tech	17	16
O25	●	I	Maryland	17	0
N1			at Florida State	9	34
N8			at Tennessee	14	29
N15	●	I	at Wake Forest	24	6
N22	●	I	Clemson	27	13
			PEACH BOWL		
D30			West Virginia	3	14

1970 — 4-6-1 (3-2-1)

S12			at Georgia Tech	20	23
S19	●	I	Wake Forest	43	7
S26	=	I	at North Carolina St.	7	7
O3	●		Virginia Tech	24	7
O10	●	I	at North Carolina	35	21
O17		I	at Maryland	15	21
O24			Florida State	13	21
O31			at Georgia	34	52
N7			Tennessee	18	20
N14		I	Duke	38	42
N21	●	I	at Clemson	38	32

1971 — 6-5-0 (4-2-0)

S11	●		Georgia Tech	24	7
S18		I	at Duke	12	28
S25	●	I	North Carolina St.	24	6
O2	●		at Memphis	7	3
O9	●	I	Virginia	34	14
O16	●	I	Maryland	35	6
O23			at Florida State	18	49
O30			Georgia	0	24
N6			at Tennessee	6	35
N20	●	I	Wake Forest	24	7
N27		I	Clemson	7	17

1972-1991
INDEPENDENT

1972 — 4-7-0

S9		Virginia	16	24
S16		at Georgia Tech	6	34
S23		Mississippi	0	21
S30	●	Memphis	34	7
O14	●	Appalachian St.	41	7
O21		Miami, Ohio	8	21
O28		at North Carolina St.	24	42
N4	●	Wake Forest	35	3
N11		at Virginia Tech	20	45
N18	●	Florida State	24	21
N25		at Clemson	6	7

1973 — 7-4-0

S15	●	Georgia Tech	41	28
S21		at Houston	19	27
S29		Miami, Ohio	11	13
O6	●	at Virginia Tech	27	24
O13	●	at Wake Forest	28	12
O20	●	Ohio U.	38	22
O27		LSU	29	33
N3		North Carolina St.	35	56
N10	●	Appalachian St.	35	14
N17	●	at Florida State	52	12
N24	●	Clemson	32	20

1974 — 4-7-0

S14		at Georgia Tech	20	35
S21		Duke	14	20
S28		at Georgia	14	52
O5		Houston	14	24
O12		Virginia Tech	17	31
O19	●	at Mississippi	10	7
O26	●	North Carolina	31	23
N2		at North Carolina St.	27	42
N9	●	Appalachian St.	21	18
N16	●	Wake Forest	34	21
N23		at Clemson	21	39

JIM CARLEN
1975-81 (.555) 45-36-1

1975 — 7-5-0

S13	●	Georgia Tech	23	17
S20	●	at Duke	24	16
S27		Georgia	20	28
O4	●	Baylor	24	13
O11	●	Virginia	41	14
O18	●	Mississippi JAM	35	29
O25		at LSU	6	24
N1		at North Carolina St.	21	28
N8		Appalachian St.	34	39
N15	●	Wake Forest	37	26
N22	●	Clemson	56	20
		TANGERINE BOWL		
D20		Miami, Ohio	7	20

1976 — 6-5-0

S4	●	Appalachian St.	21	10
S11	●	at Georgia Tech	27	17
S18	●	Duke	24	6
S25		at Georgia	12	20
O2		at Baylor	17	18
O9	●	Virginia	35	7
O16	●	Mississippi	10	7
O23		Notre Dame	6	13
O30	●	North Carolina St.	27	7
N13		Wake Forest	7	10
N20		at Clemson	9	28

1977 — 5-7-0

S3	●	Appalachian St.	32	17
S10	●	Georgia Tech	17	0
S17	●	Miami, Ohio	42	19
S24		Georgia	13	15
O1	●	East Carolina	19	16
O8		Duke	21	25
O15		at Mississippi	10	17
O22		at North Carolina	0	17
O29		at North Carolina St.	3	7
N12	●	at Wake Forest	24	14
N19		Clemson	27	31
N26		at Hawaii	7	24

1978 — 5-5-1

S9	●	Furman	45	10
S16	=	Kentucky	14	14
S23		at Duke	12	16
S30	●	Georgia	27	10
O7		at Georgia Tech	3	6
O14	●	Ohio U.	24	7
O21	●	Mississippi	18	17
O28		North Carolina	22	24
N4		at North Carolina St.	13	22
N18	●	Wake Forest	37	14
N25		at Clemson	23	41

1979 — 8-4-0

S8		at North Carolina	0	28
S15	●	Western Michigan	24	7
S22	●	Duke	35	0
S29	●	at Georgia	27	20
O6	●	Oklahoma State	23	16
O20	●	Mississippi	21	14
O27		at Notre Dame	17	18
N3	●	North Carolina St.	30	28
N10		at Florida State	7	27
N17	●	Wake Forest	35	14
N24	●	Clemson	13	9
		HALL OF FAME CLASSIC		
D29		Missouri	14	24

1980 — 8-4-0

S6	●	Pacific	37	0
S13	●	Wichita St.	73	0
S20		at Southern California	13	23
S27	●	at Michigan	17	14
O4	●	North Carolina St.	30	10
O11	●	Duke	20	7
O18	●	Cincinnati	49	7
N1		at Georgia	10	13
N8	●	Citadel	45	24
N15	●	Wake Forest	39	38
N22		at Clemson	6	27
		GATOR BOWL		
D29		Pittsburgh	9	37

1981 — 6-6-0

S5	●	at Wake Forest	23	6
S12		Mississippi	13	20
S19	●	Duke	17	3
S26		at Georgia	0	24
O3		Pittsburgh	28	42
O10	●	at Kentucky	28	14
O17	●	Virginia	21	3
O24	●	at North Carolina	31	13
O31	●	North Carolina St.	20	12
N7		Pacific	21	23
N21		Clemson	13	29
D5		at Hawaii	10	33

RICHARD BELL
1982 (.364) 4-7

1982 — 4-7-0

S4	●	Pacific	41	6
S11	●	Richmond	30	10
S18		Duke	17	30
S25		Georgia	18	34
O2	●	Cincinnati	37	10
O16		Furman	23	28
O23		at LSU	6	14
O30		at North Carolina St.	3	33
N6		Florida State	26	56
N13	●	Navy	17	14
N20		at Clemson	6	24

THE SCHOOLS

JOE MORRISON
1983-88 (.580)   39-28-2

1983   5-6-0
S3		North Carolina	8	24
S10	●	Miami, Ohio	24	3
S17	●	at Duke	31	24
S24		at Georgia	13	31
O1		Southern California	38	14
O8		Notre Dame	6	30
O22		at LSU	6	20
O29	●	North Carolina St.	31	17
N5		at Florida State	30	45
N12	●	Navy	31	7
N19		Clemson	13	22

1984   10-2-0
S8	●	Citadel	31	24
S22	●	Duke	21	0
S29	●	Georgia	17	10
O6	●	Kansas State	49	17
O13	●	Pittsburgh	45	21
O20	●	at Notre Dame	36	32
O27	●	East Carolina	42	20
N3	●	at North Carolina St.	35	28
N10	●	Florida State	38	26
N17	●	at Navy	21	38
N24	●	at Clemson	22	21
		GATOR BOWL		
D28		Oklahoma State	14	21

1985   5-6-0
A31	●	Citadel	56	17
S7	●	Appalachian St.	20	13
S21		Michigan	3	34
S28		at Georgia	21	35
O5		at Pittsburgh	7	42
O12	●	Duke	28	7
O26	●	at East Carolina	52	10
N2		North Carolina St.	17	21
N9		at Florida State	14	56
N16	●	Navy	34	31
N23		Clemson	17	24

1986   3-6-2
A30		Miami, Fla.	14	34
S6		at Virginia	20	30
S13	●	Western Carolina	45	24
S27		Georgia	26	31
O4		Nebraska	24	27
O11	=	at Virginia Tech	27	27
O25	●	East Carolina	38	3
N1		at North Carolina St.	22	23
N8		Florida State	28	45
N15	●	Wake Forest	48	21
N22	=	at Clemson	21	21

1987   8-4-0
S5	●	Appalachian St.	24	3
S12	●	Western Carolina	31	6
S26		at Georgia	6	13
O3		at Nebraska	21	30
O10	●	Virginia Tech	40	10
O17	●	Virginia	58	10
O24	●	East Carolina	34	12
O31	●	North Carolina St.	48	0
N14	●	at Wake Forest	30	0
N21	●	Clemson	20	7
D5		at Miami, Fla.	16	20
		GATOR BOWL		
D31		LSU	13	30

1988   8-4-0
S3	●	North Carolina	31	10
S10	●	Western Carolina	38	0
S17	●	East Carolina	17	0
S24	●	Georgia	23	10
O1	●	Appalachian St.	35	9
O8	●	at Virginia Tech	26	24
O15		at Georgia Tech	0	34
O29	●	at North Carolina St.	23	7
N5		Florida State	0	59
N12	●	Maryland	19	8
N19		at Clemson	10	29
		LIBERTY BOWL		
D28		Indiana	10	34

SPARKY WOODS
1989-93 (.464)   24-28-3

1989   6-4-1
S2	●	Duke	27	21
S9	=	Virginia Tech	17	17
S16		at West Virginia	21	45
S23	●	Georgia Tech	21	10
S30	●	at Georgia	24	20
O7	●	East Carolina	47	14
O21	●	Western Carolina	24	3
O28	●	North Carolina St.	10	20
N4		at Florida State	10	35
N11	●	at North Carolina	27	20
N18		Clemson	0	45

1990   6-5-0
S1	●	Duke	21	10
S8	●	North Carolina	27	5
S22	●	at Virginia Tech	35	24
S29		at Georgia Tech	6	27
O13	●	East Carolina	37	7
O20		Citadel	35	38
O27		at North Carolina St.	29	38
N3		Florida State	10	41
N10	●	So. Illinois	38	13
N17	●	at Clemson	15	24
N22	●	West Virginia	29	10

1991   3-6-2
S7	=	Duke	24	24
S14	●	at West Virginia	16	21
S21	●	Virginia Tech	28	21
S28		at East Carolina	20	31
O5		East Tenn. St.	55	7
O12		Louisiana Tech	12	12
O19	●	Georgia Tech	23	14
N2		North Carolina St.	21	38
N9		at Florida State	10	38
N16		at North Carolina	17	21
N23		Clemson	24	41

1992-Present   SEC

1992   5-6-0 (3-5-0)
S5		Georgia	6	28
S12		Arkansas	7	45
S19		East Carolina	18	20
S26		at Kentucky	9	13
O3		at Alabama	7	48
O17	●	Mississippi State	21	6
O24	●	at Vanderbilt	21	17
O31	●	Tennessee	24	23
N7	●	Louisiana Tech	14	13
N14		at Florida	9	14
N21	●	at Clemson	24	13

1993   4-7-0 (2-6-0)
S4	●	at Georgia	23	21
S11		at Arkansas	17	18
S18	●	Louisiana Tech	34	3
S23		Kentucky	17	21
O2		Alabama	6	17†
O9	●	East Carolina	27	3
O16		at Mississippi State	0	23
O23	●	Vanderbilt	22	0
O30		at Tennessee	3	55
N13		Florida	26	37
N20		Clemson	13	16

BRAD SCOTT
1994-98 (.420)   23-32-1

1994   7-5-0 (4-4-0)
S3		Georgia	21	24
S10	●	Arkansas	14	0
S17	●	Louisiana Tech	31	6
S24	●	at Kentucky	23	9
O1	●	at LSU	18	17
O8		East Carolina	42	56
O15		Mississippi State	36	41
O22	●	at Vanderbilt	19	16
O29		Tennessee	22	31
N12		at Florida	17	48
N19	●	at Clemson	33	7
		CARQUEST BOWL		
J2	●	West Virginia	24	21

1995   4-6-1 (2-5-1)
S2		at Georgia	23	42
S9		at Arkansas	21	51
S16	●	Louisiana Tech	68	21
S23		Kentucky	30	35
S30	=	LSU	20	20
O7	●	Kent State	77	14
O14	●	at Mississippi State	65	39
O21	●	Vanderbilt	52	14
O28		at Tennessee	21	56
N11		Florida	7	63
N18		Clemson	17	38

1996   6-5 (4-4)
S7	●	Central Florida	33	14
S14	●	Georgia	23	14
S21		East Carolina	7	23
S28		Mississippi State	10	14
O5		at Auburn	24	28
O12	●	at Kentucky	25	14
O19	●	Arkansas	23	17
O26	●	at Vanderbilt	27	0
N2		Tennessee	14	31
N16	●	at Florida	25	52
N23	●	at Clemson	34	31

1997   5-6 (3-5)
S6	●	Central Florida	33	31
S13		at Georgia	15	31
S20	●	at East Carolina	26	0
S27		at Mississippi State	17	37
O4		Auburn	6	23
O11	●	Kentucky	38	24
O18	●	Arkansas LR	39	13
O25	●	Vanderbilt	35	3
N1		at Tennessee	7	22
N15		Florida	21	48
N22		Clemson	21	47

1998   1-10 (0-8)
S5		Ball State	38	20
S12		Georgia	3	17
S19		Marshall	21	24
S26		Mississippi State	0	38
O3		at Mississippi	28	30
O10		at Kentucky	28	33
O17		Arkansas	28	41
O24		at Vanderbilt	14	17
O31		Tennessee	14	49
N14		at Florida	14	33
N21		at Clemson	19	28

LOU HOLTZ
1999-2004 (.471)   33-37

1999   0-11 (0-8)
S4		at North Carolina St.	0	10
S11		at Georgia	9	24
S18		East Carolina	3	21
S25		at Mississippi State	0	17
O2		Mississippi	10	36
O9		Kentucky	10	30
O16		Arkansas LR	14	48
O23		Vanderbilt	10	11
O30		at Tennessee	7	30
N13		Florida	3	20
N20		Clemson	21	31

2000   8-4 (5-3)
S2	●	New Mexico St.	31	0
S9	●	Georgia	21	10
S16	●	Eastern Michigan	41	6
S23	●	Mississippi State	23	19
S30		at Alabama	17	27
O7	●	at Kentucky	20	17
O14	●	Arkansas	27	7
O21	●	at Vanderbilt	30	14
O28		Tennessee	14	17
N11		at Florida	21	41
N18	●	at Clemson	14	16
		OUTBACK BOWL		
J1	●	Ohio State	24	7

2001   9-3 (5-3)
S1	●	Boise State	32	13
S8	●	at Georgia	14	9
S20	●	at Mississippi State	16	14
S29	●	Alabama	37	36
O6	●	Kentucky	42	6
O13	●	Arkansas LR	7	10
O20	●	Vanderbilt	46	14
O27		at Tennessee	10	17
N3	●	Wofford	38	14
N10		Florida	17	54
N17	●	Clemson	20	15
		OUTBACK BOWL		
J1	●	Ohio State	31	28

2002   5-7 (3-5)
A31	●	New Mexico State	34	24
S7		at Virginia	21	34
S14		Georgia	7	13
S21	●	Temple	42	21
S28	●	at Vanderbilt	20	14
O5	●	Mississippi State	34	10
O12	●	at Kentucky	16	12
O19	●	at LSU	14	38
N2	●	Tennessee	10	18
N9	●	Arkansas	0	23
N16	●	at Florida	7	28
N23	●	at Clemson	20	27

2003   5-7 (2-6)
A30	●	La. Lafayette	14	7
S6	●	Virginia	31	7
S13	●	at Georgia	7	31
S20	●	UAB	42	10
S27	●	at Tennessee	20	23
O9	●	Kentucky	27	21
O18	●	LSU	7	33
O25	●	Vanderbilt	35	24
N1	●	at Mississippi	40	43
N6	●	Arkansas LR	6	28
N15	●	Florida	22	24
N22	●	Clemson	17	63

2004   6-5 (4-4)
S4	●	at Vanderbilt	31	6
S11	●	Georgia	16	20
S18	●	South Florida	34	3
S25	●	Troy	17	7
O2	●	at Alabama	20	3
O9	●	Mississippi	28	31
O16	●	at Kentucky	12	7
O30	●	Tennessee	29	43
N6	●	Arkansas	35	32
N13	●	at Florida	14	48
N20	●	at Clemson	7	29

STEVE SPURRIER
2005-present (.560)   28-22

2005   7-5 (5-3)
S1	●	Central Florida	24	15
S10	●	at Georgia	15	17
S17	●	Alabama	14	37
S24	●	Troy State	45	20
O01	●	at Auburn	7	48
O08	●	Kentucky	44	16
O22	●	Vanderbilt	35	28
O29	●	at Tennessee	16	15
N05	●	at Arkansas	14	10
N12	●	Florida	30	22
N19	●	Clemson	9	13
		INDEPENDENCE BOWL		
D30	●	Missouri	31	38

2006   8-5 (3-5)
A31	●	at Mississippi State	15	0
S9	●	Georgia	0	18
S16	●	Wofford	27	20
S23	●	Florida Atlantic	45	6
S28	●	Auburn	17	24
O7	●	at Kentucky	24	17
O21	●	at Vanderbilt	31	13
O28	●	Tennessee	24	31
N4	●	Arkansas	20	26
N11	●	at Florida	16	17
N18	●	Middle Tennessee State	52	7
N25	●	at Clemson	31	28
		LIBERTY BOWL		
D29	●	Houston	44	36

2007   6-6 (3-5)
S1	●	La.-Lafayette	28	14
S8	●	at Georgia	16	12
S15	●	South Carolina State	38	3
S22	●	at LSU	16	28
S29	●	Mississippi State	38	21
O4	●	Kentucky	38	23
O13	●	at North Carolina	21	15
O20	●	Vanderbilt	6	17
O27	●	at Tennessee	24	27
N3	●	at Arkansas	36	48
N10	●	Florida	31	51
N24	●	Clemson	21	23

2008   7-6   (4-4)

A28	●		North Carolina State	34	0
S04		‖	at Vanderbilt	17	24
S13		‖	Georgia	7	14
S20	●		Wofford	23	13
S27	●		Ala.-Birmingham	26	13
O4	●	‖	at Mississippi	31	24
O11	●	‖	at Kentucky	24	17
O18		‖	Louisiana State	17	24
N1	●	‖	Tennessee	27	6
N8	●	‖	Arkansas	34	21
N15		‖	at Florida	6	56
N29			at Clemson	14	31
OUTBACK BOWL					
J1			Iowa	10	31

Neutral Site key: *Aug* Augusta, GA / *Birm* Birmingham, AL / *Char* Charlotte, NC / *ChSC* Charleston, SC / *ColGa* Columbus, GA / *Dur* Durham, NC / *Flo* Florence, SC / *JacF* Jacksonville, FL / *JaM* Jackson, MS / *LR* Little Rock, AR / *Mem* Memphis, TN / *Mont* Montgomery, AL / *Nor* Norfolk, VA / *NYC* New York, NY / *Ora* Orangeburg, SC / *Phil* Philadelphia, PA / *Rich* Richmond, VA / *Roa* Roanoke, VA / *Sum* Sumter, SC / *Tam* Tampa, FL / *W-S* Winston-Salem, NC
ƒ **Forfeit** † **Game Later Forfieted** # **Disputed Victor** * **Disputed Score** ‖ **Designated Conference Game** ‖2 **Counted Twice in Conference Standings**

SOUTH CAROLINA ANNUAL STATISTICAL LEADERS

YR	RUSHING	YDS	ATT	AVG	PASSING	ATT	CMP	PCT	YDS	RECEIVING	REC	YDS	AVG
1947	Bishop Strickland	510	94	5.4		NA	NA	NA	NA		NA	NA	NA
1948	Steve Wadiak	420	51	8.2		NA	NA	NA	NA		NA	NA	NA
1949	Steve Wadiak	775	152	5.1	John Boyle	84	29	.35	383	Jim Pinkerton	18	333	18.5
1950	Steve Wadiak	998	164	6.1	Ed Pasky	52	21	.40	196	Steve Wadiak	12	83	6.9
1951	Steve Wadiak	685	176	3.9	Dick Balka	57	26	.46	401	W.A. Skelton	13	204	15.7
1952	Gene Wilson	403	130	3.1	Johnny Gramling	144	61	.42	709	Clyde Bennett	34	502	14.8
1953	Gene Wilson	502	77	6.5	Johnny Gramling	132	68	.52	1,045	Clyde Bennett	23	413	18.0
1954	Mike Caskey	556	83	6.7	Mackie Prickett	116	68	.59	682	Carl Brazell	29	241	8.3
1955	Carl Brazell	305	46	6.6	Mackie Prickett	73	35	.48	513	Carl Brazell	11	162	14.7
1956	King Dixon	655	136	4.8	Mackie Prickett	44	15	.34	193	Alex Hawkins	10	91	9.1
1957	Alex Hawkins	450	110	4.1	Alex Hawkins	12	9	.75	153	Julius Derrick	6	126	21.0
1958	John Saunders	653	128	5.1	Bobby Bunch	23	13	.57	177	King Dixon	10	189	18.9
1959	Phil Lavoie	522	121	4.3	Steve Satterfield	44	17	.39	180	Jimmy Hunter	9	60	6.7
1960	Buddy Bennett	401	79	5.1	Dave Sowell	38	17	.45	190	Billy Gambrell	12	106	8.8
1961	Dick Day	400	100	4.0	Jim Costen	146	61	.42	764	Billy Gambrell	24	243	10.1
1962	Billy Gambrell	582	106	5.5	Dan Reeves	131	66	.50	930	Billy Gambrell	21	226	10.8
1963	Marty Rosen	382	87	4.4	Dan Reeves	146	62	.42	657	Larry Gill	14	188	13.4
1964	Phil Branson	276	86	3.2	Dan Reeves	164	83	.51	974	J.R. Wilburn	21	236	11.2
1965	Ben Garnto	437	89	4.9	Mike Fair	175	89	.51	1,049	J.R. Wilburn	38	562	14.8
1966	Benny Galloway	580	129	4.5	Mike Fair	82	31	.38	467	Ben Garnto	19	243	12.8
1967	Warren Muir	805	187	4.3	Mike Fair	165	79	.48	970	Fred Zeigler	35	370	10.6
1968	Rudy Holloman	530	110	4.8	Tommy Suggs	207	110	.53	1,544	Fred Zeigler	59	848	14.4
1969	Warren Muir	969	225	4.3	Tommy Suggs	196	109	.56	1,342	Fred Zeigler	52	658	12.7
1970	Tommy Simmons	572	163	3.5	Tommy Suggs	269	136	.51	2,030	Jim Mitchell	41	842	20.5
1971	Tommy Simmons	430	126	3.4	Glenn Morris	229	104	.45	1,313	Jim Mitchell	47	618	13.1
1972	Jay Lynn Hodgin	675	188	3.6	Dobby Grossman	117	61	.52	874	Mike Haggard	46	639	13.9
1973	Jay Lynn Hodgin	862	172	5.0	Jeff Grantz	121	62	.51	864	Marty Woolbright	23	347	15.1
1974	Jay Lynn Hodgin	941	154	6.1	Jeff Grantz	95	39	.41	642	Mike Farrell	18	258	14.3
1975	Kevin Long	1,133	189	6.0	Jeff Grantz	216	120	.56	1,815	Philip Logan	39	716	18.4
1976	Clarence Williams	873	175	5.0	Ron Bass	199	110	.55	1,320	Philip Logan	41	678	16.5
1977	Spencer Clark	777	134	5.8	Ron Bass	176	82	.47	1,140	Philip Logan	21	415	19.8
1978	George Rogers	1,006	176	5.7	Garry Harper	135	62	.46	776	Zion McKinney	19	281	14.8
1979	George Rogers	1,681	311	5.4	Garry Harper	143	73	.51	929	Zion McKinney	23	387	16.8
1980	George Rogers	1,894	324	5.8	Garry Harper	177	90	.51	1,266	Willie Scott	34	469	13.8
1981	Johnnie Wright	834	214	3.9	Gordon Beckham	180	92	.51	1,221	Horace Smith	27	451	16.7
1982	Thomas Dendy	848	139	6.1	Gordon Beckham	146	63	.43	725	Chris Corley	24	163	6.8
1983	Thomas Dendy	725	132	5.5	Allen Mitchell	172	80	.47	1,142	Ira Hillary	30	422	14.1
1984	Thomas Dendy	634	102	6.2	Mike Hold	137	64	.47	1,385	Ira Hillary	27	564	20.9
1985	Thomas Dendy	560	119	4.7	Mike Hold	208	107	.51	1,596	Sterling Sharpe	32	471	14.7
1986	Anthony Smith	469	96	4.9	Todd Ellis	340	205	.60	3,020	Sterling Sharpe	74	1,106	14.9
1987	Harold Green	1,022	227	4.5	Todd Ellis	432	241	.56	3,206	Sterling Sharpe	62	915	14.8
1988	Harold Green	606	164	3.7	Todd Ellis	391	198	.51	2,353	Harold Green	36	315	8.8
1989	Harold Green	989	202	4.9	Todd Ellis	187	103	.55	1,374	Robert Brooks	34	471	13.9
1990	Mike Dingle	746	187	4.0	Bobby Fuller	294	171	.58	2,372	Robert Brooks	33	548	16.6
1991	Brandon Bennett	702	153	4.6	Bobby Fuller	340	202	.59	2,524	Robert Brooks	55	684	12.4
1992	Brandon Bennett	646	150	4.3	Steve Taneyhill	162	86	.53	1,272	Brandon Bennett	22	194	8.8
1993	Brandon Bennett	853	194	4.4	Steve Taneyhill	291	149	.51	1,930	Toby Cates	27	541	20.0
1994	Brandon Bennett	854	190	4.5	Steve Taneyhill	403	257	.64	2,486	Brandon Bennett	47	340	7.2
1995	Duce Staley	736	127	5.8	Steve Taneyhill	389	261	.67	3,094	Stanley Pritchett	62	664	10.7
1996	Duce Staley	1,116	219	5.1	Anthony Wright	244	131	.54	1,850	Corey Bridges	28	399	14.3
1997	Troy Hambrick	604	114	5.3	Anthony Wright	252	139	.55	1,685	Jermale Kelly	43	618	14.4
1998	Troy Hambrick	701	143	4.9	Anthony Wright	273	145	.53	1,899	Zola Davis	48	733	15.3
1999	Derek Watson	394	113	3.5	Phil Petty	146	65	.45	803	Jermale Kelly	24	366	15.3
2000	Derek Watson	1,066	187	5.7	Phil Petty	315	170	.54	2,285	Jermale Kelly	42	640	15.2
2001	Andrew Pinnock	622	115	5.4	Phil Petty	288	164	.57	1,926	Brian Scott	47	730	15.5
2002	Corey Jenkins	655	160	4.1	Corey Jenkins	180	100	.56	1,334	Ryan Brewer	28	299	10.7
2003	Daccus Turman	646	132	4.9	Dondrial Pinkins	322	162	.50	2,127	Troy Williamson	31	428	13.8
2004	Demetris Summers	487	88	5.5	Syvelle Newton	131	70	.53	1,093	Troy Williamson	43	835	19.4
2005	Mike Davis	666	146	4.6	Blake Mitchell	315	186	.59	2,370	Sidney Rice	70	1,143	16.3
2006	Cory Boyd	823	164	5.0	Blake Mitchell	202	135	.67	1,789	Sidney Rice	72	1,090	15.1
2007	Cory Boyd	903	180	5.0	Blake Mitchell	255	152	.60	1,747	Kenny McKinley	77	968	12.6
2008	Mike Davis	573	163	3.5	Chris Smelley	302	169	.56	1,922	Kenny McKinley	54	642	11.9

Receiving leaders by receptions
All statistics include postseason

SOUTH CAROLINA RECORD BOOK

SINGLE-GAME RECORDS

Rushing Yards	278	Brandon Bennett (Oct. 5, 1991 vs. East Tennesse State)
Passing Yards	473	Steve Taneyhill (Oct. 14, 1995 vs Mississippi State)
Receiving Yards	210	Troy Williamson (Sept. 18, 2004 vs. South Florida)
All-Purpose Yards	NA	
Points	30	Sidney Rice (Sept. 23, 2006 vs. Florida Atlantic)
Field Goals	5	Collin Mackie (Nov. 22, 1990 vs. West Virginia)
Tackles	29	James Seawright (Nov. 3, 1984 vs. North Carolina St.)
Interceptions	4	Pat Watson (Nov. 9, 1968 vs. Wake Forest); Bryant Gilliard (Nov. 10, 1984 vs. Florida State)

SINGLE-SEASON RECORDS

Rushing Yards	1,894	George Rogers, 1980 (324 att.)
Passing Yards	3,206	Todd Ellis, 1987 (241-432)
Receiving Yards	1,143	Sidney Rice, 2005 (70 rec.)
All-Purpose Yards	1,917	George Rogers, 1980
Scoring	113	Collin Mackie, 1987
Touchdowns	16	Harold Green, 1987
Tackles	179	Mike Durrah, 1983
Interceptions	9	Bryant Gilliard, 1984
Punting Average	44.3	Daren Parker, 1989 (49 punts)
Punt Return Average	17.1	Billy Stephens, 1951 (18 ret.)
Kickoff Return Average	31.2	Raynard Brown, 1984 (11 ret.)

CAREER RECORDS

Rushing Yards	5,204	George Rogers, 1977-80
Passing Yards	9,953	Todd Ellis, 1986-89
Receiving Yards	2,781	Kenny McKinley, 2005-08
All-Purpose Yards	5,932	George Rogers, 1977-80
Scoring	330	Collin Mackie, 1987-90
Touchdowns	33	George Rogers, 1977-80
Tackles	405	J.D. Fuller, 1979, 1981-83
Interceptions	14	Bo Davies, 1969-71
Punting Average	42.3	Ryan Succop, 2005-07
Punt Return Average	17.1	Billy Stephens, 1949-51
Kickoff Return Average	24.7	Kent Hagood 1981, 1983-85

TEAM RECORDS

Longest Winning Streak	9	Sept. 8, 1984-Nov. 10, 1984; broken by Navy, 21-38 on Nov. 17, 1984
Longest Undefeated Streak	9	Sept. 8, 1984-Nov. 10, 1984; broken by Navy, 21-38 on Nov. 17, 1984
Most Consecutive Winning Seasons	7	1928-34
Most Consecutive Bowl Appearances	2	Four times
Most Points in a Game	89	vs. Welsh Neck, Oct. 6, 1903
Most Points Allowed in a Game	63	vs. Navy, Nov. 13, 1920; vs. Florida, Nov. 11, 1995; vs. Clemson, Nov. 22, 2003
Largest Margin of Victory	89	vs. Welsh Neck, Oct 6, 1903
Largest Margin of Defeat	63	vs. Navy, Nov. 13, 1920
Longest Pass Play	99	Dondrial Pinkins to Troy Williamson, vs. Virginia, Sept. 7, 2003
Longest Field Goal	58	Mark Fleetwood vs. Georgia, Sept. 25, 1982
Longest Punt	90	Bill Jeffords vs. North Carolina, Nov. 4, 1924
Longest Interception Return	102	Mel Baxley vs. Georgia Tech, Sept. 15, 1973

RETIRED NUMBERS

2	Sterling Sharpe
37	Steve Wadiak
38	George Rogers
56	Mike Johnson

ALL-TIME TEAM

In 1992, South Carolina celebrated its football centennial by selecting two all-time teams: 12 players from the pre-World War II era (when players went boths ways) and 29 from the modern (postwar) era.

1892-1945		Post-1945 Offense		Post-1945 Defense	
B	Tatum Gressette, 1920-21	G	Steve Courson, 1973-76	L	John LeHeup, 1970-72
B	Ed "Bru" Boineau, 1928-30	G	Del Wilkes, 1980-81, 1983-84	L	Emanuel Weaver, 1980-81
B	Earl Clay, 1931-33	T	Dave DeCamilla, 1968-70	L	Andrew Provence, 1980-82
B	Fred Hambright, 1931-33	T	Chuck Slaughter, 1978, 1981	L	Roy Hart, 1983-84, 1986-87
L	Luke Hill, 1911-15	C	Bryant Meeks, 1945-46	L	Kevin Hendrix, 1985-88
L	Joe Wheeler, 1920-23	C	Mike McCabe, 1973-75	LB	Ed Baxley, 1979-80
L	Julian Beall, 1927-29	TE	Jay Saldi, 1973, 1975	LB	James Seawright, 1981-84
L	Lou Sossamon, 1940-42	TE	Willie Scott, 1977-80	LB	Corey Miller, 1988-90
L	Larry Craig, 1935-38	WR	Fred Ziegler, 1967-69	DB	Bobby Bryant, 1964-66
L	Alex Urban, 1938, 1940	WR	Sterling Sharpe, 1983, 1985-87	DB	Dick Harris, 1969-71
L	Dominic Fusci, 1942-43, 1946	QB	Jeff Grantz, 1973-75	DB	Rick Sanford, 1975-78
L	James "Skimp" Harrison, 1942-44	RB	Steve Wadiak, 1948-51	DB	Brad Edwards, 1984-87
		RB	George Rogers, 1977-80	P	Max Runager, 1974, 1976-78
		RB	Harold Green, 1986-89		
		PK	Collin Mackie, 1987-90		
		KR	Robert Brooks, 1988-91		

THE SCHOOLS

SOUTH CAROLINA BOWL HISTORY

SEASON	BOWL	DATE	PRE-GAME RANK	TEAMS	SCORE	FINAL RANK	MOST VALUABLE PLAYER(S)	ATT.
1945	GATOR	Jan. 1, 1946		Wake Forest / South Carolina	26 / 14		Nick Sacrinty, Wake Forest, QB	7,362
1969	PEACH	Dec. 30, 1969		West Virginia / South Carolina	14 / 3		Ed Williams, West Virginia, FB / Carl Crennel, West Virginia, MG	48,452
1975	TANGERINE	Dec. 20, 1975	16	Miami (Ohio) / South Carolina	20 / 7	12	Robert Carpenter, Miami, B / Jeff Kelly, Miami, L	20,247
1979	HALL OF FAME CLASSIC	Dec. 28, 1979	16	Missouri / South Carolina	24 / 14		Phil Bradley, Missouri, QB	62,785
1980	GATOR	Dec. 29, 1980	3 / 18	Pittsburgh / South Carolina	37 / 9	2	Rick Trocano, Pittsburgh, QB / George Rogers, South Carolina, RB	72,297
1984	GATOR	Dec. 28, 1984	9 / 7	Oklahoma State / South Carolina	21 / 14	7 / 11	Thurman Thomas, Oklahoma State, RB	82,138
1987	GATOR	Dec. 31, 1987	7 / 9	LSU / South Carolina	30 / 13	5 / 15	Wendell Davis, LSU, SE / Harold Green, South Carolina, RB	82,119
1988	LIBERTY	Dec. 28, 1988		Indiana / South Carolina	34 / 10	20	Dave Schnell, Indiana, QB	39,210
1994	CARQUEST	Jan. 2, 1995		South Carolina / West Virginia	24 / 21		Steve Taneyhill, South Carolina, QB	50,833
2000	OUTBACK	Jan. 1, 2001	19	South Carolina / Ohio State	24 / 7	19	Ryan Brewer, South Carolina, WR	65,229
2001	OUTBACK	Jan. 1, 2002	14 / 22	South Carolina / Ohio State	31 / 28	13	Phil Petty, South Carolina, QB	66,249
2005	INDEPENDENCE	Dec. 30, 2005		Missouri / South Carolina	38 / 31		Brad Smith, Missouri, QB / Marcus King, Missouri, CB	75,562
2006	LIBERTY	Dec. 29, 2006		South Carolina / Houston	44 / 36		Blake Mitchell, South Carolina, QB	56,103
2008	OUTBACK	Jan. 1, 2009		Iowa / South Carolina	31 / 10	20	Shonn Greene, Iowa, RB	55,117

JANUARY 1, 1946 | Gator
WAKE FOREST 26, SOUTH CAROLINA 14

	1ST	2ND	3RD	4TH	FINAL
WFU	6	0	6	14	26
SC	0	7	0	7	14

SCORING SUMMARY
WFU Sacrinty 3 run (kick failed)
SC Giles 1 run (Brembs kick)
WFU Brinkley 3 run (kick blocked)
WFU Brinkley 1 run (Sacrinty kick)
WFU Smathers 25 run (Sacrinty kick)
SC Brembs 90 interception return (Brembs kick)

WFU	TEAM STATISTICS	SC
24	First Downs	7
378	Rushing Yards	88
1-6-2	Passing	4-11-1
18	Passing Yards	69
396	Total Yards	157
3-24	Kickoff Returns - Yards	5-63
3-27.0	Punts - Average	7-37.0
3-1	Fumbles - Lost	3-1
8-70	Penalties - Yards	1-5

DECEMBER 30, 1969 | Peach
WEST VIRGINIA 14, SOUTH CAROLINA 3

	1ST	2ND	3RD	4TH	FINAL
WVU	7	0	0	7	14
SC	0	3	0	0	3

SCORING SUMMARY
WVU Gresham 10 run (Braxton kick)
SC FG DuPre 37
WVU Braxton 1 run (Braxton kick)

WVU	TEAM STATISTICS	SC
21	First Downs	11
356	Rushing Yards	64
1-2-0	Passing	11-23-2
3	Passing Yards	126
359	Total Yards	190
9-28.8	Punts - Average	6-39.3

INDIVIDUAL LEADERS
RUSHING
WVU: Williams 35-208; Gresham 16-98, 1 TD.
SC: Muir 18-52; Holloman 7-18.
PASSING
WVU: Sherwood 1-2-0, 3 yards.
SC: Suggs 9-17-1, 98 yards.
RECEIVING
WVU: Braxton 1-3.
SC: Hamrick 4-64; Holloman 5-33.

DECEMBER 20, 1975 | Tangerine
MIAMI (OHIO) 20, SOUTH CAROLINA 7

	1ST	2ND	3RD	4TH	FINAL
MIA	7	7	3	3	20
SC	0	0	7	0	7

SCORING SUMMARY
MIA Carpenter 5 run (Johnson kick)
MIA Carpenter 1 run (Johnson kick)
MIA FG Johnson 47
SC Amrein 3 run (Marino kick)
MIA FG Johnson 33

MIA	TEAM STATISTICS	USC
19	First Downs	17
238	Rushing Yards	56
10-13-1	Passing	18-29-1
137	Passing Yards	228
375	Total Yards	284
4-35.8	Punts - Average	6-44.8
0-0	Fumbles - Lost	1-0
5-35	Penalties - Yards	3-24

INDIVIDUAL LEADERS
RUSHING
MIA: Carpenter 29-120, 2 TD; Smith 17-64.
SC: Williams 9-57; Long 11-19.
PASSING
MIA: Smith 10-13-1, 137 yards.
SC: Grantz 18-29-1, 228 yards.
RECEIVING
MIA: Joecken 3-68; Walker 4-44.
SC: Logan 9-109; Stephens 4-51.

DECEMBER 29, 1979 | Hall of Fame Classic
MISSOURI 24, SOUTH CAROLINA 14

	1ST	2ND	3RD	4TH	FINAL
MO	0	17	7	0	24
SC	6	0	8	0	14

SCORING SUMMARY
SC McKinney 20 pass from Harper (run failed)
MO FG Verrilli 22
MO Newman 28 pass from Bradley (Verrilli kick)
MO Bradley 1 run (Verrilli kick)
SC Harper 11 run (McKinney pass from Harper)
MO Ellis 12 run (Verrilli kick)

MO	TEAM STATISTICS	SC
17	First Downs	20
209	Rushing Yards	142
7-11-0	Passing	13-20-1
72	Passing Yards	121
281	Total Yards	263
2-(-2)	Punt Returns - Yards	1-(-1)
2-41	Kickoff Returns - Yards	4-79
6-44.3	Punts - Average	6-35.0
2-1	Fumbles - Lost	1-1
5-50	Penalties - Yards	2-16

INDIVIDUAL LEADERS
RUSHING
MO: Wilder 24-95; Ellis 12-81, 1 TD.
SC: Rogers 25-133; Clark 10-48.
PASSING
MO: Bradley 7-11-0, 72 yards, 1 TD.
SC: Harper 13-19-1, 121 yards, 1 TD.
RECEIVING
MO: Newman 1-28, 1 TD; Blair 2-22.
SC: McKinney 6-87, 1 TD; Rogers 3-18.

THE SCHOOLS

DECEMBER 29, 1980 | GATOR
PITTSBURGH 37, SOUTH CAROLINA 9

	1ST	2ND	3RD	4TH	FINAL
PITT	10	7	17	3	37
SC	0	3	0	6	9

SCORING SUMMARY
PITT Trocano 1 run (Trout kick)
PITT FG Trout 35
SC FG Leopard 39
PITT Collier 3 pass from Marino (Trout kick)
PITT FG Trout 25
PITT McMillan 3 run (Trout kick)
PITT McMillan 42 pass from Trocano (Trout kick)
PITT FG Trout 29
SC Gillespie 14 pass from Beckham (kick failed)

PITT	TEAM STATISTICS	SC
22	First Downs	17
165	Rushing Yards	116
17-35-3	Passing	11-27-3
233	Passing Yards	168
398	Total Yards	284
3-30.3	Punts - Average	7-30.0
1-1	Fumbles - Lost	3-2
11-73	Penalties - Yards	3-12

INDIVIDUAL LEADERS
RUSHING
PITT: McMillan 13-59, 1 TD; Hawkins 9-50; Trocano 8-41, 1 TD.
SC: Rogers 27-113; Wright 4-23.
PASSING
PITT: Trocano 10-21-2, 155 yards, 1 TD; Marino 7-13-0, 78 yards, 1 TD.
SC: Harper 7-16-1, 116 yards; Beckham 4-10-1, 52 yards, 1 TD.
RECEIVING
PITT: Collier 5-57, 1 TD; Collins 3-50; McMillan 2-46, 1 TD.
SC: Scott 7-109; Gillespie 2-32, 1 TD.

DECEMBER 28, 1984 | GATOR
OKLAHOMA STATE 21, SOUTH CAROLINA 14

	1ST	2ND	3RD	4TH	FINAL
OKST	7	6	0	8	21
SC	0	0	14	0	14

SCORING SUMMARY
OKST Thomas 1 run (Roach kick)
OKST Hilger 6 pass from Thomas (kick failed)
SC Wade 24 pass from Lewis (Hagler kick)
SC Hillary 57 pass from Hold (Hagler kick)
OKST Hanna 25 pass from Hilger (Harris pass from Hilger)

OKST	TEAM STATISTICS	SC
21	First Downs	15
165	Rushing Yards	104
25-42-1	Passing	8-21-1
211	Passing Yards	194
376	Total Yards	298
5-35.4	Punts - Average	7-41.7
2-0	Fumbles - Lost	6-3
3-21	Penalties - Yards	5-38

INDIVIDUAL LEADERS
RUSHING
OKST: Thomas 32-155, 1 TD.
SC: Lewis 6-36; Hold 18-33.
PASSING
OKST: Hilger 21-41-1, 205 yards, 1 TD.
SC: Hold 7-20-1, 170 yards, 1 TD; Lewis 1-1-0, 24 yards, 1 TD.
RECEIVING
OKST: Hanna 8-92, 1 TD; Lewis 3-33.
SC: Hillary 2-75, 1 TD; Poole 1-45; Wade 1-24, 1 TD.

DECEMBER 31, 1987 | GATOR
LSU 30, SOUTH CAROLINA 13

	1ST	2ND	3RD	4TH	FINAL
LSU	14	6	7	3	30
SC	3	3	0	7	13

SCORING SUMMARY
LSU Davis 39 pass from Hodson (Browndyke kick)
LSU Davis 12 pass from Hodson (Browndyke kick)
SC FG Mackie 44
LSU FG Browndyke 27
SC FG Mackie 39
LSU FG Browndyke 18
LSU Davis 25 pass from Hodson (Browndyke kick)
SC Green 10 run (Mackie kick)
LSU FG Browndyke 23

LSU	TEAM STATISTICS	SC
17	First Downs	21
122	Rushing Yards	25
20-32-0	Passing	28-47-4
224	Passing Yards	304
346	Total Yards	329
3-37.6	Punts - Average	2-40.5
5-3	Fumbles - Lost	2-1
10-107	Penalties - Yards	6-49

INDIVIDUAL LEADERS
RUSHING
LSU: Fuller 14-48; Martin 8-38.
SC: Green 15-72, 1 TD; Bethea 1-9.
PASSING
LSU: Hodson 20-32-0, 224 yards, 3 TD.
SC: Ellis 28-47-4, 304 yards.
RECEIVING
LSU: Davis 9-132, 3 TD; Martin 3-43.
SC: Smith 4-79; Bethea 4-69; Sharpe 6-53.

DECEMBER 28, 1988 | LIBERTY
INDIANA 34, SOUTH CAROLINA 10

	1ST	2ND	3RD	4TH	FINAL
IND	7	10	3	14	34
SC	0	0	10	0	10

SCORING SUMMARY
IND Thompson 7 run (Stoyanovich kick)
IND Miller 10 pass from Schnell (Stoyanovich kick)
IND FG Stoyanovich 28
SC Tolbert 34 block punt return (Mackie kick)
IND FG Stoyanovich 19
SC FG Mackie 43
IND Turner 88 pass from Schnell (Stoyanovich kick)
IND Thompson 8 run (Stoyanovich kick)

IND	TEAM STATISTICS	SC
23	First Downs	12
185	Rushing Yards	23
17-32-1	Passing	15-37-3
390	Passing Yards	130
575	Total Yards	153
6-26.0	Punts - Average	9-38.0
1-0	Fumbles - Lost	1-1
6-40	Penalties - Yards	2-15

INDIVIDUAL LEADERS
RUSHING
IND: Thompson 26-140, 2 TD.
SC: Green 11-41.
PASSING
IND: Schnell 16-31-1, 378 yards, 2 TD.
SC: Ellis 15-37-3, 130 yards.
RECEIVING
IND: Turner 5-182, 1 TD; Thompson 2-14, 2 TD.
SC: Brooks 2-35.

JANUARY 2, 1995 | CARQUEST
SOUTH CAROLINA 24, WEST VIRGINIA 21

	1ST	2ND	3RD	4TH	FINAL
SC	7	10	7	0	24
WVU	0	7	14	0	21

SCORING SUMMARY
SC Foster 2 pass from Taneyhill (Morton kick)
SC FG 47 Morton
WVU Walker 24 run (Baumann kick)
SC Taneyhill 4 run (Morton kick)
WVU Purnell 6 pass from Johnston (Baumann kick)
SC Pritchett 1 run (Morton kick)
WVU Purnell 7 pass from Johnston (Baumann kick)

SC	TEAM STATISTICS	WVU
21	First Downs	16
148	Rushing Yards	150
26-36-0	Passing	19-32-1
227	Passing Yards	240
375	Total Yards	390
4-35.2	Punts - Average	2-54.0
6-2	Fumbles - Lost	3-2
6-38	Penalties - Yards	7-55

JANUARY 1, 2001 | OUTBACK
SOUTH CAROLINA 24, OHIO STATE 7

	1ST	2ND	3RD	4TH	FINAL
SC	0	3	7	14	24
OSU	0	0	7	0	7

SCORING SUMMARY
SC FG Corse 23
SC Brewer 7 run (Corse kick)
OSU Gurr fumble recovery in end zone (Stultz kick)
SC Brewer 28 pass from Petty (Corse kick)
SC Brewer 2 run (Corse kick)

SC	TEAM STATISTICS	OSU
18	First Downs	16
218	Rushing Yards	85
9-19-1	Passing	16-28-2
175	Passing Yards	173
393	Total Yards	258
2-18	Punt Returns - Yards	3-43
2-33	Kickoff Returns - Yards	5-100
4-46.8	Punts - Average	6-37.5
1-0	Fumbles - Lost	3-1
7-50	Penalties - Yards	9-65
33:33	Possession Time	26:27

INDIVIDUAL LEADERS
RUSHING
SC: Brewer 19-109, 2 TD; Pinnock 11-33.
OSU: Wells 14-52; Combs 8-25.
PASSING
SC: Petty 9-19-1, 175 yards, 1 TD.
OSU: Bellisari 14-25-1, 157 yards.
RECEIVING
SC: Brewer 3-92, 1 TD; Kelly 3-43.
OSU: Rambo 2-65; Sanders 5-47.

THE SCHOOLS

JANUARY 1, 2002 | OUTBACK
SOUTH CAROLINA 31, OHIO STATE 28

	1ST	2ND	3RD	4TH	FINAL
SC	0	14	14	3	31
OSU	0	0	7	21	28

SCORING SUMMARY
SC	Pinnock 1 run (Weaver kick)
SC	Scott 7 pass from Petty (Weaver kick)
SC	Gause 50 pass from Petty (kick failed)
SC	Pinnock 10 run (Watson pass from Petty)
OSU	Bellisari 2 run (Nugent kick)
OSU	Sanders 16 pass from Bellisari (Nugent kick)
OSU	Wells 1 run (Nugent kick)
OSU	Sanders 9 pass from Bellisari (Nugent kick)
SC	FG Weaver 42

SC	TEAM STATISTICS	OSU
17	First Downs	21
120	Rushing Yards	64
19-37-1	Passing	22-37-1
227	Passing Yards	324
347	Total Yards	388
2-16	Punt Returns - Yards	4-20
4-66	Kickoff Returns - Yards	4-101
6-47.7	Punts - Average	5-44.6
2-1	Fumbles - Lost	2-2
8-43	Penalties - Yards	6-40
31:23	Possession Time	28:37

INDIVIDUAL LEADERS
RUSHING
SC: Brewer 5-61; Pinnock 12-49, 2 TD.
OSU: Wells 19-37, 1 TD; Ross 1-13.
PASSING
SC: Petty 19-37-1, 227 yards, 2 TD.
OSU: Bellisari 21-35-1, 320 yards, 2 TD.
RECEIVING
SC: Scott 7-83, 1 TD; Gause 3-72, 1 TD.
OSU: Jenkins 8-152; Vance 5-61; Sanders 5-56, 2 TD.

DECEMBER 30, 2005 | INDEPENDENCE
MISSOURI 38, SOUTH CAROLINA 31

	1ST	2ND	3RD	4TH	FINAL
SC	21	7	0	3	31
MO	0	14	7	17	38

SCORING SUMMARY
SC	Rice 23 pass from Mitchell (Brown kick)
SC	Davis 5 run (Brown kick)
SC	Askins 20 pass from Mitchell (Brown kick)
MO	King 99 interception return (Crossett kick)
SC	Davis 2 run (Brown kick)
MO	Coffman 5 pass from Smith (Crossett kick)
MO	Smith 31 run (Crossett kick)
MO	Smith 4 run (Crossett kick)
MO	FG Crossett 50
SC	FG Brown 30
MO	Smith 1 run (Crossett kick)

SC	TEAM STATISTICS	MO
21	First Downs	21
142	Rushing Yards	203
20-38-3	Passing	23-43-1
266	Passing Yards	301
408	Total Yards	504
3-29	Punt Returns - Yards	1-0
6-177	Kickoff Returns - Yards	2-38
6-40.0	Punts - Average	5-45.8
1-0	Fumbles - Lost	1-1
5-52	Penalties - Yards	8-87

INDIVIDUAL LEADERS
RUSHING
SC: Davis 18-125, 2 TD.
MO: Smith 21-150, 3 TD.
PASSING
SC: Mitchell 20-38-3, 266 yards, 2 TD.
MO: Smith 21-37-1, 282 yards, 1 TD.
RECEIVING
SC: Rice 12-191, 1 TD; Davis 3-11.
MO: Coffman 8-99, 1 TD; Rucker 5-83.

DECEMBER 29, 2006 | LIBERTY
SOUTH CAROLINA 44, HOUSTON 36

	1ST	2ND	3RD	4TH	FINAL
SC	7	20	3	14	44
HOU	7	21	0	8	36

SCORING SUMMARY
HOU	Marshall 32 pass from Kolb (Bell kick)
SC	Boyd 2 run (Succop kick)
SC	Pavlovic 1 pass from Mitchell (kick failed)
HOU	Hafner 4 pass from Kolb (Bell kick)
SC	Rice 19 pass from Mitchell (Succop kick)
HOU	Battle 42 run (Bell kick)
SC	Boyd 9 run (Succop kick)
HOU	Marshall 77 pass from Kolb (Bell kick)
SC	FG Succop 45
SC	McKinley 43 pass from Mitchell (Succop kick)
SC	McKinley 43 pass from Mitchell (Succop kick)
HOU	Battle 3 run (Alridge run)

SC	TEAM STATISTICS	HOU
25	First Downs	27
189	Rushing Yards	135
19-29-1	Passing	27-40-1
323	Passing Yards	392
512	Total Yards	527
1-11	Punt Returns - Yards	1-11
4-67	Kickoff Returns - Yards	3-86
2-45	Punts - Average	3-42.3
1-0	Fumbles - Lost	2-1
9-93	Penalties - Yards	4-40

INDIVIDUAL LEADERS
RUSHING
SC: Boyd 18-94, 2 TD.
HOU: Battle 11-85, 2 TD.
PASSING
SC: Mitchell 19-29-1, 323 yards, 4 TD.
HOU: Kole 26-39-1, 386 yards, 3 TD.
RECEIVING
SC: Rice 8-139, 1 TD; Boyd 4-45.
HOU: Marshall 9-201, 2 TD; Avery 7-72.

JANUARY 1, 2009 | OUTBACK
IOWA 31, SOUTH CAROLINA 10

	1ST	2ND	3RD	4TH	FINAL
SC	0	0	0	10	10
IA	14	7	10	0	31

SCORING SUMMARY
IA	Stross 6 pass from Stanzi (Murray kick)
IA	Greene 1 run (Murray kick)
IA	Greene 1 run (Murray kick)
IA	FG Murray 18
IA	Greene 11 run (Murray kick)
SC	Cook 10 pass from Smelley (Succop kick)
SC	FG Succop 48

SC	TEAM STATISTICS	UI
17	First Downs	22
43	Rushing Yards	181
26-50-3	Passing	13-19-2
270	Passing Yards	147
313	Total Yards	328
1-5	Punt Returns - Yards	0-0
6-125	Kickoff Returns - Yards	3-44
2-42.5	Punts - Average	2-44
2-2	Fumbles - Lost	2-1
10-100	Penalties - Yards	6-50

INDIVIDUAL LEADERS
RUSHING
SC: Garcia 5-25.
IA: Greene 29-121, 3 TD.
PASSING
SC: Smelley 16-31-0, 179 yards, 1 TD.
IA: Stanzi 13-19-2, 147 yards, 1 TD.
RECEIVING
SC: McKinley 6-86; Barnes 5-40.
IA: Myers 4-49; Moeaki 3-43.

TENNESSEE

BY GEOFFREY NORMAN

THE SCHOOLS

THE IDENTITY AND PERSONALITY OF the Tennessee Volunteers resonate instantly with any fan of the game. Just try to imagine college football without orange jerseys, bluetick coonhounds, that Promethean stadium on the river, checkered end zones and Saturday crowds the size of a small city.

This is, in short, one of the major brands. Tennessee has won 774 football games and three national championships, the most recent coming in 1998 (the very first BCS title). Four Vols have been runners-up in the Heisman voting and no history of college football would be complete without the legendary Tennessee coach who actually managed to dominate Bear Bryant. The Vols are, without doubt, among college football's elite.

TRADITION Tennessee plays its home games in a stadium that sits on the banks of the Tennessee River, so it was probably inevitable that some fan would decide to beat the traffic by getting to the game by boat. Former Volunteers broadcaster George Mooney is credited as the first to try it, in 1962. Others followed his example, and soon there was a fairly substantial flotilla of all manner of vessels out on the river on game day. This became the Volunteer Navy, and today the crews of more than 200 boats join up for a floating tailgate party whenever Tennessee plays at home.

"Rocky Top" is not the official Vols fight song, though it might as well be. The song was first played at a 1972 game as part of a county music show and has been part of the Tennessee football personality ever since.

BEST PLAYER Archie Manning, patriarch of the famous quarterback clan, is still known by his first name in Mississippi. His son Peyton could have gone to Ole Miss and been welcomed as the prince of destiny. But football fortunes were on the wane in Oxford, so Peyton chose Tennessee and became a legend himself among Volunteers faithful. He came in for injured starting quarterback Jerry Colquitt in the first game of his freshman year and went on a mythic (and ultimately, fruitless) four-year quest for a national championship. But he did just about everything else a quarterback could do. In his Tennessee career, Manning set 33 school, seven SEC and two NCAA records. He threw 89 touchdown passes and passed for a total of more than 11,000 yards.

PROFILE

University of Tennessee
Knoxville, Tenn.
Founded: 1794
Enrollment: 20,400
Colors: Orange and White
Nickname: Volunteers
Stadium: Neyland Stadium
    Opened in 1921
    Grass; 102,038 capacity
First football game: 1891
All-time record: 774–327–54 (.703)
Bowl record: 25–22
Consensus national championships,
1936-present: 3 (1938, 1951, 1998)
Southeastern Conference championships:
13 (9 outright)
Outland Trophy: Steve DeLong, 1964;
John Henderson, 2000
First-round draft choices: 39
Website: utsports.com

THE BEST OF TIMES

It's got to be Phillip Fulmer and the Vols' run from 1995 to 1998. They posted a 45–5 mark, culminating in the 1998 national title.

THE WORST OF TIMES

From 1958 to 1964, Tennessee was unable to win more than six games in any season and didn't make a single bowl appearance.

CONFERENCE

After 12 years in the Southern Conference, Tennessee became a charter member of the SEC in 1933.

DISTINGUISHED ALUMNI

Deanna Carter, singer; Cormac McCarthy, author; Todd Helton, baseball player; Chamique Holdsclaw, WNBA player; Chad Holliday, CEO of DuPont; Allan Houston, NBA player; Ali Hussein Abu Ragheb, prime minister of Jordan; Chris Moneymaker, World Series of Poker winner; Kevin Nash, pro wrestler; Ron Rice, CEO of Hawaiian Tropic

FIGHT SONG

DOWN THE FIELD
(Here's to Old Tennessee)
Here's to old Tennessee
Never we'll sever
We pledge our loyalty
Forever and ever
Backing our football team
Faltering never
Cheer and fight with all of your might
For Tennessee.

In Neyland's first tour as coach, the Volunteers ran off unbeaten streaks of 33 and 28 games.

In 1,381 attempts, he was intercepted 33 times. That's why today there's a road leading to Neyland Stadium called Peyton Manning Pass.

Manning could have gone pro after his third year of eligibility—he had already graduated—but he came back for one more shot at a national title and a Heisman. Neither was meant to be. The Vols came up short and Manning was second to Michigan's Charles Woodson in the 1997 balloting. When he did leave for the NFL, Manning's record with the Vols was 39–6 as a starter, with four of those losses coming against nemesis Florida.

Close runners-up to Manning would be a couple of defensive giants: Doug Atkins, who helped Tennessee to a 29–4–1 record during his three varsity years (1950-52); and Reggie White (1980-83), who holds all the Tennessee sack records—single game (4), season (15) and career (32).

BEST COACH Three Tennessee football coaches are in the College Football Hall of Fame and Phillip Fulmer, who resigned in 2008, has better numbers (152–52) than two of them—Doug Dickey and Bowden Wyatt. But the best Tennessee coach occupies a space that is separate and almost alone, where he keeps company with a few other

titans of the game. If Alabama has a Bear, then Tennessee has a General. And in this case, he happens to have been a real one.

When he first took the job in 1926, Robert Neyland—a West Point graduate who served in France during World War I—was an ROTC instructor and Tennessee had to share him with the Army, first for a peacetime tour in Panama and then for duty in the China-Burma-India theater, where he served as a brigadier general during World War II. In his tours as head football coach at Tennessee, the Vols were a national power, running up undefeated streaks of 33 and 28 games and appearing in the Orange, Rose and Sugar Bowls. Neyland's 1939 team shut out 10 consecutive opponents. When he returned from WWII in 1946, he guided Tennessee to the Orange Bowl. But the following two seasons produced mediocre records (5–5 and 4–4–2) and predictable murmurings that the game had passed the General by. He was a single-wing man and this was the age of the T-formation.

Neyland proved the whisperers wrong, going 7–2–1 in 1949 and 11–1 in 1950 with, according to two rating services, a national title. He followed that up with an undefeated regular season and a consensus national

FIRST-ROUND DRAFT CHOICES		CONSENSUS ALL-AMERICANS	
1940	George Cafego, Cardinals (1)	1929	Gene McEver, B
1952	Bert Rechichar, Browns (10)	1933	Beattie Feathers, B
1953	Doug Atkins, Browns (11)	1938	Bowden Wyatt, E
1964	Dick Evey, Bears (14)	1939	Ed Molinski, G
1965	Steve DeLong, Bears (6) and Chargers (6)*	1939	George Cafego, B
		1940	Bob Suffridge, G
1968	Bob Johnson, Bengals (2)	1946	Dick Huffman, T
1970	Jack Reynolds, Rams (22)	1951	Hank Lauricella, B
1977	Stanley Morgan, Patriots (25)	1952	John Michels, G
1979	Robert Shaw, Cowboys (27)	1956	John Majors, B
1980	Roland James, Patriots (14)	1965	Frank Emanuel, LB
1982	Anthony Hancock, Chiefs (11)	1966	Paul Naumoff, LB
1983	Willie Gault, Bears (18)	1967	Bob Johnson, C
1984	Clyde Duncan, Cardinals (17)	1968	Charles Rosenfelder, G
1985	Alvin Toles, Saints (24)	1968-69	Steve Kiner, LB
1986	Tim McGee, Bengals (21)	1969-70	Chip Kell, G
1988	Terry McDaniel, Raiders (9)	1971	Bobby Majors, DB
1988	Anthony Miller, Chargers (15)	1975-76	Larry Seivers, E/SE
1989	Keith DeLong, 49ers (28)	1979	Roland James, DB
1991	Charles McRae, Buccaneers (7)	1983	Reggie White, DL
1991	Antone Davis, Eagles (8)	1984	Bill Mayo, OG
1991	Alvin Harper, Cowboys (12)	1985	Tim McGee, WR
1992	Dale Carter, Chiefs (20)	1989	Eric Still, OL
1992	Chris Mims, Chargers (23)	1990	Antone Davis, OL
1993	Todd Kelly, 49ers (27)		
1994	Heath Shuler, Redskins (3)		
1995	James Stewart, Jaguars (19)		
1998	Peyton Manning, Colts (1)		
1998	Terry Fair, Lions (20)		
1998	Marcus Nash, Broncos (30)		
1999	Al Wilson, Broncos (31)		
2000	Jamal Lewis, Ravens (5)		
2000	Shaun Ellis, Jets (12)		
2002	John Henderson, Jaguars (9)		
2002	Donte' Stallworth, Saints (13)		
2002	Albert Haynesworth, Titans (15)		
2006	Jason Allen, Dolphins (16)		
2007	Justin Harrell, Packers (16)		
2007	Robert Meachem, Saints (27)		
2008	Jerod Mayo, Patriots (10)		
2009	Robert Ayers, Broncos (18)		

From 1960-1966, the NFL and AFL held separate, competing drafts

(Continued on next page)

championship. In Neyland's last season, 1952, the Vols were 8–2–1, making his record in his third stint as head coach 54–17–4. Overall, the General went 173–31–12.

The record doesn't tell the story of the man, though. Neyland's approach to the game reflected his military roots. He preached organization, discipline and teamwork. He stressed, above all, defense and the kicking game. In his 216 games as head coach, an astonishing 112 of Tennessee's opponents failed to score. The 71 consecutive scoreless quarters against Tennessee during his tenure still stands as an NCAA record.

CONSENSUS ALL-AMERICANS (CONT.)	
1991	Dale Carter, DB
1997	Peyton Manning, QB
1998	Al Wilson, LB
1999	Cosey Coleman, OL
1999	Deon Grant, DB
2000-01	John Henderson, DL
2003	Dustin Colquitt, P
2004	Michael Munoz, OL
2008	Eric Berry, DB

BEST TEAM The 1939 Vols were 10–0 during the regular season but lost to Southern California, 14-0, in the Rose Bowl. Because of that single loss, the choice for best Vols team ever is the 1998 national championship squad that went 13–0, defeating Florida State 23-16 in the Fiesta Bowl. What made that season especially sweet for Vols fans is that it came on the heels of the Peyton Manning era. Besides winning it all, this Tennessee team did something no Manning-led UT team had ever done—beat Florida. The Vols did it in overtime in Knoxville in front of more than 107,000 fans. It doesn't get any better than that.

BEST BACKFIELD The 1951 unit that carried the Vols to a national championship ran out of the single wing and its 3,068 yards of total rushing remains a single-season record at Tennessee. The tailback was the essential element in the formation, and in Hank Lauricella, the Vols had one of the best ever. That season, Lauricella ran for 881 yards—averaging 7.9 yards per carry—and finished second in the Heisman voting to Dick Kazmaier from Princeton. Lauricella led the team in passing, total offense and punting his junior and senior years, and rushing his senior year. Wingback Bert Rechichar, fullback Andy Kozar and blocking back Jimmy Hahn rounded out what must rank as one of the most explosive single-wing units ever.

BEST DEFENSE Hard to argue with a crew that pitched nothing but shutouts, which is what the 1939 Vols did during the regular season. Anchored by two All-Americans—guard Ed Molinski and back George Cafego—the Vols blanked all 10 of their opponents, allowing just 2.2 yards per play. Tennessee's offense, meanwhile, ran up 212 points. The wonder is that the team somehow managed to lose, 14-0, to USC in the Rose Bowl. Still, that regular season of perfect defense is

the last time any unit has accomplished the feat in college football.

BIGGEST GAME 1998 was the first year of the Bowl Championship Series (BCS), which had been devised to preserve the existing bowl games in college football while arranging for an official national title match. It was a new—and controversial, to say the very least—alternative to a playoff system. In its first season, the BCS ranking matched Tennessee and Florida State in the Fiesta Bowl for the crown on Jan. 4, 1999. Tennessee was undefeated and ranked No. 1 going in. The Seminoles had lost once during the regular season. The Vols jumped ahead on an interception returned for a touchdown by Dwayne Goodrich. And though Florida State stayed close through three quarters, the Vols regained a decisive edge when Tee Martin hit Peerless Price on a 79-yard touchdown pass with just 9:17 remaining, making the score 20-9. Florida State battled back to within a touchdown, then recovered a late Tennessee fumble to give itself a chance to tie. UT would have none of that. The Vols' defense forced another turnover, sealing a 23-16 win and the national championship.

BIGGEST UPSET On Oct. 20, 1928, the Vols played Alabama in Tuscaloosa. So heavily favored was Alabama that before the game, Neyland asked Bama coach Wallace Wade if they could end it early if the score got out of hand. This was pure gamesmanship—before the word had even been invented. It was a statement game for Neyland's team, and the Vols made their statement early. Halfback Gene McEver returned the opening kickoff 98 yards for a touchdown, whereupon Tennessee settled in and played Neyland football. Final score: Tennessee 15, Alabama 13. This game, more than any other, established the Neyland dynasty and secured Tennessee's place at the head table of college football.

HEARTBREAKER Tennessee entered the SEC championship game on Dec. 8, 2001, with a No. 2 ranking and a trip to the national title game on the line. But the uninspired Vols fell 31-20 to No. 21-ranked LSU and had to settle for the Citrus Bowl—which turned out to be Michigan's misfortune as well. The Vols took their frustrations out on the Wolverines in a 45-17 beating.

BEST COMEBACK Down 31-7 to Notre Dame in the second quarter, the Vols' chances looked bad enough.

But this game, on Nov. 9, 1991, was in South Bend, making Tennessee's situation dire—until an unexpected boost just before the half as the Irish lined up for a field goal. The Vols blocked the kick and ran the ball back 85 yards for a touchdown. Tennessee headed to the locker room inspired and with new life. The Vols rode that momentum all the way to an improbable, nail-biting 35-34 victory sealed by a missed 27-yard Notre Dame field goal attempt as time expired.

STADIUM Officially, it is Neyland Stadium at Shields-Watkins Field. The seating capacity is 102,038 and change—though 108,768 fans packed Neyland for the 2004 game with rival Florida. The stadium is the fourth largest in all of college football and one of only two in the country that can be accessed by water (the other is Washington's Husky Stadium). The Vols play their home games on natural grass—Tifway 419 hybrid-Bermuda, to be precise—that features one of the most recognizable end zone paint jobs. The orange-and-white checkerboard pattern first appeared on Oct. 10, 1964, when Boston College came to town, and lasted until an artificial surface was installed in 1968. The memory lingered, however, and the checkerboarding—along with the grass—returned in 1989.

RIVAL The Vols' traditional rival is Alabama, the only SEC team with a better overall record. Bear Bryant is said to have relished a victory over Tennessee even more than he did beating Auburn, though he couldn't say so out loud. But he remembered the Tennessee rivalry from his own playing days at Alabama and added to it during the eight years he was head coach at Kentucky, during which he went 0–5–2 against General Neyland's teams.

The game was traditionally played on the third Saturday in October, but recently the vicissitudes of modern scheduling have changed that. Still, the winning team lights up cigars to celebrate—a tradition established by Bryant and picked up by Tennessee in the 1990s. As close and intense as the series has been, it is characterized by streaks. Alabama won seven straight from 1986 to 1992. Tennessee turned the Tide, so to

COLLEGE FOOTBALL HALL OF FAME INDUCTEES

NAME	YEARS	INDUCTED
Gene McEver, HB	1928-29, 1931	1954
Beattie Feathers, HB	1931-33	1955
Bob Neyland, COACH	1926-52	1956
Bobby Dodd, QB	1928-30	1959
Herman Hickman, G	1929-31	1959
Bob Suffridge, G	1938-40	1961
Nathan Dougherty, G	1906-09	1967
George Cafego, HB	1937-39	1969
Bowden Wyatt, E/COACH	1936-38; 1955-62	1972
Hank Lauricella, HB	1949-51	1981
Doug Atkins, T	1950-52	1985
Johnny Majors, HB	1954-56	1987
Joe Steffy, G	1944-47	1987
Bob Johnson, C	1965-67	1989
Ed Molinski, G	1938-40	1990
Steve DeLong, MG	1962-64	1993
John Michels, G	1950-52	1996
Steve Kiner, LB	1967-69	1999
Reggie White, DT	1980-83	2002
Doug Dickey, COACH	1964-69	2003
Frank Emanuel, LB	1963-65	2004
Chip Kell, G/C	1968-70	2006

PRO FOOTBALL HALL OF FAME INDUCTEES

NAME	YEARS	INDUCTED
Doug Atkins, DE	1953-69	1982
Reggie White, DE/DT	1985-2000	2006

speak, and took nine of 10 from 1995 to 2004. Then the momentum seemed to shift again, as Alabama has won three of four since.

The more contemporary, but equally intense rivalry between Tennessee and Florida is a product of Steve Spurrier's rise to SEC glory. Since the conference expanded to 12 teams and two divisions in 1992, Florida and Tennessee have combined to represent the Eastern Division in 14 of 17 SEC championship games, winning nine of them. The Gators and the Vols, then, are two alpha wolves fighting over the same turf. The game is played in September and usually is both teams' first major test of the season.

NICKNAME Tennessee began officially calling itself the Volunteer State in 1905. The name is a reflection of the way Tennesseans have historically responded when they heard the call to arms. It started during the American Revolution, when virtually all 1,000 of the men living in the settlements that eventually became the state of Tennessee volunteered to fight the British. In the War of 1812, when 3,500 troops from Tennessee were needed, 25,000 men volunteered. During the Mexican War, the War Department established a quota of 2,800 from the state and 30,000 stepped forward. The name was first attached to the football team in 1902 in a story that appeared in *The Atlanta Constitution*. Three years later, the *Knoxville Journal* reported that the school teams had officially taken the name Volunteers. "The name sounds good," the story concluded, "and it is likely that it will stick." Right they were.

MASCOT During halftime of the 1953 Mississippi State game, a competition was held to determine which of several coonhounds would serve as the official mascot of the Tennessee football team. As each dog was introduced, fans "voted" with their cheers. The last dog introduced was a bluetick named Blue Smokey who, when he heard the cheers, let out a distinctive, musical bark. The fans cheered again, the dog sang once more and soon there was a chorus of cheering followed by Blue Smokey's barking. He got the job. The current Smokey is the ninth (or IXth, to be technical) in this distinguished line, and

his predecessors have led interesting lives. One was dognapped by some Kentucky students and also got into it with the Baylor Bear. Smokey VI suffered heat exhaustion in a 1991 game with UCLA and was carried on the Vols' injury report until he made it back to the sideline later in the season.

UNIFORMS Tennessee's famous orange was copied from the common American daisy, a flower that grew abundantly on a little elevated piece of ground known as the Hill near the stadium. The color became official in 1891, but the team didn't appear in the distinctive burnt-orange jerseys until the first game of the 1922 season, when the Vols beat Emory & Henry, 50-0. That was good enough reason to keep them. The distinctive capital T with the clipped serifs has been a staple of Tennessee helmets since 1967, replacing a block-letter T after three years of use.

QUOTE "If Neyland could score a touchdown against you, he had you beat. If he could score two, he had you in a rout." —**Herman Hickman**, one of Robert Neyland's stars and later part of *Sports Illustrated*'s original staff, on the General's passion for defensive football

Reckon They Never Will

BY GENE WOJCIECHOWSKI

I must have heard the song 52,000 times, but I still don't know the words to "Rocky Top." In fact, there's a free power-steamed corned beef on rye at Gus's Good Times Deli off The Strip if you can recite the whole thing. The song is the college football equivalent of R.E.M.'s "It's the End of the World As We Know It (And I Feel Fine)." You mumble away like Tommy Boy until you hit the chorus and then—boom—you're belting out, "Rocky Top, you'll always be … home sweet home to me … Good ol' Rocky Top—whoo! Rocky Top, Tennessee."

Next verse, same mumbling.

I'm Class of 1979, otherwise known as the semi-oblivion years (a Bluebonnet Bowl appearance, and loss, the lone highlight of sorts). We were three seasons into the reign of Johnny Majors. It would get better, but not until after my diploma was already on the wall.

Doug's Rug, which is what they first called the Doug Dickey-approved artificial turf at Neyland Stadium, was still the football surface of choice. Why, I have no idea. The stuff was like a green Brillo pad. Playing on it left killer rug burns, and the mere thought of soap and water touching your freshly sandpapered knees and elbows was enough to make walk-on scrubs (me) and actual scholarship players (them) weep in the corner of the shower.

The turf was replaced in 1994 by soft, soothing Bermuda grass, thus making the place the most perfect gameday setting in the land. On this there is no debate. (Sorry, U-Dub.)

And while we're at it with the superlatives, Tennessee also has the best helmet logo (the Power T), the best end zones (orange and white checkerboard) and the best mascot (Smokey the Bluetick Coonhound). It has the best water view (close enough to toss goalposts into the Tennessee River—it's happened), the best nickname (the one-of-a-kind Volunteers), and the best play-by-play man (John "Give … Him … Six!" Ward, now retired). It has the best Hand of God play (Arkansas QB Clint Stoerner, without being touched by a

> *Tennessee has the best helmet logo (the Power T), the best end zones (orange and white checkerboard), the best water view (close enough to toss goalposts into the Tennessee River— it's happened) and the best and most wonderfully abrasive fight song.*

Tennessee player, fumbles late in a 1998 game, which allows UT to score in the waning seconds, preserve its perfect record and go on to win its first national title in 47 years) and, yeah, the best and most wonderfully abrasive fight song. You know your fight song has arrived when opposing coaches blare it on their practice fields.

Between the last game I saw as an undergrad in '79 (UT 31, Vandy 10) and the most recent Vols game I covered for ESPN (Phillip Fulmer's 2008 finale—UT 28, Kentucky 10), only a handful of things have changed. The stadium now needs Weight Watchers—it's up to 102,038 seats,

but that doesn't include SROs. In the area immediately surrounding Neyland, there's a Peyton Manning Pass, a Johnny Majors Drive, a Phillip Fulmer Way, a Neyland Drive and a Tee Martin Drive. And the inflatable "bubble" practice facility I remember so well because players used to ralph in trash cans there during winter workouts has been replaced by a massive permanent structure.

But the important stuff stays the same. Nobody has messed with that T logo. Gen. Robert Neyland's Seven Game Maxims are still posted in the UT locker room—home and away. Bama vs. Tennessee is still the only rivalry that matters, though Florida vs. Tennessee has grown a full set of teeth. The huge rock on Frat Row (close to Sigma Chi, Johnny Majors' house) gets painted with a new slogan every football week. The Vol Navy still has pre-kickoff fleet exercises at dock's edge. Pee Wee King and Redd Stewart's "The Tennessee Waltz" never sounds prettier than when it's played by the Pride of the Southland Band after a game.

This is the place where George Cafego, Bobby Dodd, Bob Suffridge, Doug Atkins, Hank Lauricella, Bobby and Johnny Majors, Condredge Holloway, Jack Reynolds, Stanley Morgan, Reggie White, Al Wilson, Peyton Manning, Jamal Lewis, the punting Colquitts, Jason Witten and Albert Haynesworth, among others, earned their college football chops. In East Tennessee on a Saturday fall afternoon or evening, it is the only place.

Football was first played at Tennessee in 1891. It will be played here in 2091. And even then, not a single soul will know all the words to "Rocky Top."

Gene Wojciechowski is a senior national columnist for ESPN.com and ESPN The Magazine. *Much to the dismay of his wife, he has been known to fly his large orange Tennessee flag in front of the house after UT victories.*

TENNESSEE ALL-TIME SCORES

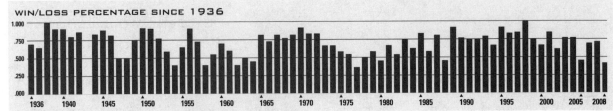

WIN/LOSS PERCENTAGE SINCE 1936

NO HEAD COACH

1891 0-1-0
| N21 | Sewanee *Chat* | 0 | 24 |

1892 2-5-0
O15 ●	at Maryville	25	0
O21 ●	at Vanderbilt	0	12*
O24	at Sewanee	0	54
N2	Sewanee	0	10
N12 ●	Chattanooga AC *Chat*	16	6
N17	Vanderbilt	0	10
N24	Wake Forest	6	10

1893 2-4-0
O21	Kentucky	0	56
N3	at Wake Forest	0	64
N4	at Duke	0	70
N7	at North Carolina	0	60
N18 ●	Maryville	32	0
N30 ●	Asheville AA	12	6

1894-1895
NO TEAM

1896 4-0-0
O22 ●	Williamsburg	10	6
O24 ●	Chattanooga AC *Chat*	4	0
N14 ●	Virginia Tech	6	4
N26 ●	Central U.	30	0

1897 4-1-0
O15 ●	King	28	0
O23 ●	Williamsburg	6	0
N8	North Carolina	0	16
N25 ●	Virginia Tech *Roa*	18	0
N26	at Bristol AC	12	0

1898
NO TEAM

J.A. PIERCE
1899-1900 (.654)   8-4-1

1899 5-2-0
O11 ●	King	11	5
O21	Virginia Tech	0	5
O28	at Sewanee	0	51
N4 ●	Kentucky	12	0
N11 ●	Georgia	5	0
N23 ●	Wash. & Lee	11	0
N30 ●	Transylvania, Ky.	41	0

1900 3-2-1
O10 ●	King	22	0
O22 =	at Vanderbilt	0	0
N1 ●	North Carolina	5	22
N10 ●	Auburn *Birm*	0	23
N27 ●	U.T. Chattanooga	28	0
D1 ●	Georgetown	12	6

GEORGE KELLEY
1901 (.500)   3-3-2

1901 3-3-2
O12 ●	King	8	0
O19 =	Clemson	6	6
O26	at Nashville	5	16
N2	Transylvania, Ky.	0	6
N9	at Vanderbilt	0	22
N16 ●	Georgetown	12	0
N23 ●	Kentucky	5	0
N28 =	Alabama *Birm*	6	6

H.F. FISHER
1902-03 (.588)   10-7

1902 6-2-0
O11 ●	King	12	0
O21 ●	Maryville	34	0
O25	Vanderbilt	5	12
N1 ●	Sewanee	6	0
N7 ●	at Nashville	10	0
N15 ●	Mississippi *Mem*	11	10
N22 ●	at Georgia Tech	10	6
N27	Clemson	0	11

1903 4-5-0
O3 ●	Maryville	17	0
O10 ●	Carson-Newman	38	0
O17 ●	at Vanderbilt	0	40
O29 ●	at South Carolina	0	24
O31 ●	at Nashville	10	0
N7	Georgia	0	5
N14	Sewanee	0	17
N21 ●	Georgia Tech	11	0
N26	Alabama *Birm*	0	24

S.D. CRAWFORD
1904 (.389)   3-5-1

1904 3-5-1
O1 ●	Maryville	17	0
O15 =	Nashville	0	0
O22	at Georgia Tech	0	2
O29	Sewanee	0	12
N5	at Vanderbilt	0	22
N12	Clemson	0	6
N16	Cincinnati	0	35
N19 ●	at U.T. Chattanooga	23	0
N24 ●	Alabama *Birm*	5	0

J.D. DePREE
1905-06 (.306)   4-11-3

1905 3-5-1
S30 ●	Deaf School	16	6
O7 ●	American U.	104	0
O14 =	at Clemson	5	5
O21	Vanderbilt	0	45
O28 ●	at Sewanee	6	11
N4	at Georgia Tech	0	45
N18 ●	Centre	31	5
N30 ●	Alabama *Birm*	0	29
D3	at U.T. Chattanooga	0	5

1906 1-6-2
O6 ●	American U.	10	0
O13 ●	Maryville	0	11
O20	Centre	0	6
O25 =	at American U.	5	5
N3	Sewanee	0	17
N10	at Kentucky	0	21
N19	at Clemson	0	16
N21 =	at Georgia	0	0
N29	Alabama *Birm*	0	51

GEORGE LEVENE
1907-09 (.589)   15-10-3

1907 7-2-1
O5 ●	Tenn. Military	30	0
O12 ●	at Georgia	15	0
O19 ●	at Georgia Tech	4	6
O21 ●	at Clemson	4	0
O26 ●	Maryville	34	0
N2 ●	U.T. Chattanooga	57	0
N9 ●	Kentucky	0	0
N16 ●	Mississippi State *Mem*	11	4
N18 ●	Arkansas *Mem*	14	2
N28 ●	Alabama *Birm*	0	5

1908 7-2-0
O3 ●	North Carolina	12	0
O10 ●	Maryville	39	5
O17 ●	Kentucky	7	0
O24 ●	Georgia	10	0
O31 ●	at Georgia Tech	6	5
N7 ●	at Vanderbilt	9	16
N14 ●	Clemson	6	5
N21 ●	U.T. Chattanooga	35	6
N26 ●	Alabama *Birm*	0	4

1909 1-6-2
O2 =	Centre	0	0
O9	North Carolina	0	3
O16	at Kentucky	0	17
O23	Georgia	0	3
O30	Georgia Tech	0	29
N6	at Vanderbilt	0	51
N13	Alabama	0	10
N20 =	at U.T. Chattanooga	0	0
N25 ●	Transylvania, Ky.	11	0

ANDREW A. STONE
1910 (.389)   3-5-1

1910 3-5-1
O1 ●	Centre	2	17
O8 ●	Mooney	7	0
O15 ●	at Vanderbilt	0	18
O22	at Georgia	5	35
O29	at Samford	17	0
O31	at Mississippi State	0	48
N5	Kentucky	0	10
N12 ●	Maryville	13	0
N19 =	U.T. Chattanooga	6	6

Z.G. CLEVENGER
1911-15 (.628)   26-15-2

1911 3-4-2
O7 ●	Mooney School	27	0
O14 ●	at Georgia Tech	0	24
O21 ●	Maryville	22	5
O28 ●	at North Carolina St.	0	16
N4 =	Centre	0	0
N11 ●	at Virginia Tech	11	36
N18 ●	Southwestern	22	0
N25 =	at UT Med. School	0	0
N30 ●	at Kentucky	0	12

1912 4-4-0
O5 ●	King	101	0
O12 ●	Maryville	38	0
O19 ●	at Tenn. Med. Coll.	62	0
O26 ●	Sewanee *Chat*	6	33
N2 ●	Centre	67	0
N9 ●	at Mercer	14	27
N16 ●	Kentucky	6	13
N28 ●	Alabama *Birm*	0	7

1913 6-3-0
S27 ●	Carson-Newman	58	0
O4 ●	Athens	95	0
O11 ●	Maryville	75	0
O18 ●	Sewanee *Chat*	6	17
O26 ●	Davidson	9	0
N1 ●	U.T. Chattanooga	21	0
N8 ●	at Vanderbilt	6	7
N14 ●	at Alabama	0	6
N27 ●	at Kentucky	13	7

1914 9-0-0
S26 ●	Carson-Newman	89	0
O3 ●	King	55	3
O10 ●	Clemson	27	0
O17 ●	at Louisville	66	0
O24 ●	Alabama	17	7
O31 ●	U.T. Chattanooga	67	0
N7 ●	at Vanderbilt	16	14
N14 ●	Sewanee *Chat*	14	7
N26 ●	Kentucky	23	6

1915 4-4-0
S25 ●	Carson-Newman	101	0
O2 ●	Tusculm	21	0
O9 ●	Clemson	0	3
O16 ●	Centre	80	0
O23 ●	Cumberland	101	0
O30 ●	at Vanderbilt	0	35
N13 ●	at Mississippi State	0	14
N25 ●	at Kentucky	0	6

JOHN R. BENDER
1916-20 (.741)   18-5-4

1916 8-0-1
S30 ●	Tusculum	33	0
O7 ●	Maryville	32	6
O14 ●	at Clemson	14	0
O21 ●	South Carolina	26	0
O28 ●	Florida *Tam*	24	0
N4 ●	at U.T. Chattanooga	12	7
N11 ●	Vanderbilt	10	6
N18 ●	Sewanee *Chat*	17	0
N30 ●	Kentucky	0	0

1917-1918
NO TEAM WWI

1919 3-3-3
S27 ●	Tusculum	29	6
O3 ●	Maryville	32	2
O11 =	at Vanderbilt	3	3
O18 ●	Mississippi State	0	6
O25 ●	at Clemson	0	14
N1 ●	North Carolina	0	0
N8 =	at South Carolina	6	6
N15 ●	Cincinnati	33	12
N27 ●	at Kentucky	0	13

1920 7-2-0
S25 ●	Emory & Henry	45	0
O2 ●	Maryville	47	0
O9 ●	Vanderbilt	0	20
O16 ●	at U.T. Chattanooga	35	0
O23 ●	Clemson	26	0
O30 ●	at Mississippi State	7	13
N6 ●	Transylvania, Ky.	49	0
N13 ●	at Sewanee	20	0
N25 ●	Kentucky	14	7

M.B. BANKS
1921-25 (.633)   27-15-3

1921 6-2-1
S24 ●	Emory & Henry	27	0
O1 ●	at Maryville	7	0
O8 ●	U.T. Chattanooga	21	0
O15 ●	at Dartmouth	3	14
O22 ●	Florida	9	0
O29 ●	at Vanderbilt	0	14
N5 ●	Mississippi State *Mem*	14	7
N12 ●	Sewanee	21	0
N24 ●	at Kentucky	0	0

1922-1932
SOUTHERN

1922 8-2-0 (4-2-0)
S23 ●	Emory & Henry	50	0
S30 ●	Carson-Newman	32	7
O7 ●	Maryville	21	0
O14 ●	at Fort Benning	15	0
O21 │	at Georgia	3	7
O28 │	Mississippi	49	0
N4 │	Vanderbilt	6	14
N11 │	Mississippi State *Mem*	31	3
N18 ●	Sewanee *Chat*	18	7
N30 ●	Kentucky	14	7

THE SCHOOLS

1923   5-4-1 (4-2-0)
S29		at Army	0	41
O6	=	Maryville	14	14
O13	●	Georgetown	13	6
O20		Georgia	0	17
O27		Mississippi State *Mem*	7	3
N3		Tulane	13	2
N10		at Vanderbilt	7	51
N17		VMI	0	33
N24		Mississippi	10	0
N29		at Kentucky	18	0

1924   3-5-0 (0-4-0)
O04	●	Emory & Henry	27	0
O11	●	Maryville	28	10
O18	●	Carson-Newman	13	0
O25		Mississippi State *Mem*	2	7
N1		at Georgia	0	33
N8		Centre	0	32
N15		at Tulane	7	26
N27		Kentucky	6	27

1925   5-2-1 (2-2-1)
O3	●	Emory & Henry	51	0
O10	●	Maryville	13	0
O17		at Vanderbilt	7	34
O24	=	LSU	0	0
O31	●	Georgia	12	7
N7		at Centre	12	0
N14		Mississippi State	14	9
N26		at Kentucky	20	23

ROBERT R. NEYLAND
1926-34, '36-40, '46-52 (.829) 173-31-12

1926   8-1-0 (5-1-0)
S25	●	Carson-Newman	13	0
O2	●	North Carolina	34	0
O9	●	at LSU	14	7
O15	●	Maryville	6	0
O23	●	Centre	30	7
O30	●	at Mississippi State	33	0
N6	●	Sewanee	12	0
N13	●	at Vanderbilt	3	20
N25	●	Kentucky	6	0

1927   8-0-1 (5-0-1)
S24	●	Carson-Newman	33	0
O1	●	at North Carolina	26	0
O8	●	Maryville	7	0
O15	●	Mississippi	21	7
O22	●	Transylvania, Ky.	57	0
O29	●	Virginia	42	0
N5	●	Sewanee	32	12
N12	●	Vanderbilt	7	7
N24	●	at Kentucky	20	0

1928   9-0-1 (6-0-1)
S29	●	Maryville	41	0
O6	●	Centre	41	7
O13	●	Mississippi	13	12
O20	●	at Alabama	15	13
O27	●	Wash. & Lee	26	7
N3	●	Carson-Newman	57	0
N10	●	Sewanee	37	0
N17	●	at Vanderbilt	6	0
N29	=	Kentucky	0	0
D8	●	Florida	13	12

1929   9-0-1 (6-0-1)
S28	●	Centre	40	6
O5	●	at U.T. Chattanooga	20	0
O12	●	Mississippi	52	7
O19	●	Alabama	6	0
O26	●	Wash. & Lee *Roa*	30	0
N2	●	Auburn	27	0
N9	●	Carson-Newman	73	0
N16	●	Vanderbilt	13	0
N28	=	at Kentucky	6	6
D7	●	South Carolina	54	0

1930   9-1-0 (6-1-0)
S27	●	Maryville	54	0
O4	●	at Centre	18	0
O11	●	Mississippi	27	0
O18	●	at Alabama	6	18
O25	●	North Carolina	9	7
N1	●	Clemson	27	0
N8	●	Carson-Newman	34	0
N15	●	at Vanderbilt	13	0
N27	●	Kentucky	8	0
D6	●	Florida *JacF*	13	6

1931   9-0-1 (6-0-1)
S26	●	Maryville	33	0
O3	●	Clemson	44	0
O10	●	Mississippi	38	0
O17	●	Alabama	25	0
O24	●	at North Carolina	7	0
O31	●	Duke	25	2
N7	●	Carson-Newman	31	0
N14	●	Vanderbilt	21	7
N26	=	at Kentucky	6	6
D6	●	NYU *Brnx*	13	0

1932   9-0-1 (7-0-1)
S24	●	at U.T. Chattanooga	13	0
O1	●	Mississippi	33	0
O8	●	North Carolina	20	7
O15	●	Alabama *Birm*	7	3
O22	●	Maryville	60	0
O29	●	Duke	16	13
N5	●	Mississippi State	31	0
N12	=	at Vanderbilt	0	0
N24	●	Kentucky	26	0
D3	●	Florida *JacF*	32	13

1933-Present
SOUTHEASTERN

1933   7-3-0
S30	●	Virginia Tech	27	0
O7	●	Mississippi State	20	0
O14		at Duke	2	10
O21		Alabama	6	12
O28		Florida	13	6
N4		at George Washington	13	0
N11		Mississippi	35	6
N18		Vanderbilt	33	6
N30		at Kentucky	27	0
D9		at LSU	0	7

1934   8-2-0 (5-1-0)
S29	●	Centre	32	0
O6	●	at North Carolina	19	7
O13	●	Mississippi	27	0
O20	●	Alabama *Birm*	6	13
O27	●	Duke	14	6
N3		Fordham *NYC*	12	13
N10	●	Mississippi State	14	0
N17	●	at Vanderbilt	13	6
N29	●	Kentucky	19	0
D8	●	LSU	19	13

W.H. BRITTON
1935 (.444)   4-5

1935   4-5-0 (2-3-0)
S28	●	Southwestern	20	0
O5		North Carolina	13	38
O12	●	Auburn *Birm*	13	6
O19		Alabama	0	25
O26	●	Centre	25	14
N2		at Duke	6	19
N9	●	Mississippi *Mem*	14	13
N16		Vanderbilt	7	13
N28		at Kentucky	0	27

ROBERT R. NEYLAND

1936   6-2-2 (3-1-2)
S26	●	U.T. Chattanooga	13	0
O3		at North Carolina	6	14
O10		Auburn	0	6
O17		Alabama *Birm*	0	0
O24	●	Duke	15	13
O31		at Georgia	46	0
N7		Maryville	34	0
N14	●	at Vanderbilt	26	13
N26		Kentucky	7	6
D5	=	Mississippi *Mem*	0	0

1937   6-3-1 (4-3-0)
S25	●	Wake Forest	32	0
O2	●	Virginia Tech	27	0
O9		at Duke	0	0
O16		Alabama	7	14
O23	●	Sewanee	32	0
O30		Georgia	32	0
N6		Auburn *Birm*	7	20
N13		Vanderbilt	7	13
N25		at Kentucky	13	0
D4	●	Mississippi *Mem*	32	0

1938   11-0-0 (7-0-0)
S24	●	Sewanee	26	3
O1	●	Clemson	20	7
O8	●	Auburn	7	0
O15	●	Alabama *Birm*	13	0
O22	●	Citadel	44	0
O29	●	LSU	14	6
N5	●	U.T. Chattanooga	45	0
N12	●	at Vanderbilt	14	0
N24	●	Kentucky	46	0
D3	●	Mississippi *Mem*	47	0
		ORANGE BOWL		
J2	●	Oklahoma	17	0

1939   10-1-0 (6-0-0)
S29	●	at North Carolina St.	13	0
O7	●	Sewanee	40	0
O14	●	at U.T. Chattanooga	28	0
O21	●	Alabama	21	0
O28	●	Mercer	17	0
N4	●	at LSU	20	0
N11	●	Citadel	34	0
N18	●	Vanderbilt	13	0
N30	●	at Kentucky	19	0
D9	●	Auburn	7	0
		ROSE BOWL		
J1		Southern California	0	14

1940   10-1-0 (5-0-0)
S28	●	Mercer	49	0
O5	●	Duke	13	0
O12	●	U.T. Chattanooga	53	0
O19	●	Alabama *Birm*	27	12
O26	●	Florida	14	0
N2	●	LSU	28	0
N9	●	at Southwestern	41	0
N16	●	Virginia	41	14
N23	●	Kentucky	33	0
N30	●	at Vanderbilt	20	0
		SUGAR BOWL		
J1		Boston College	13	19

JOHN BARNHILL
1941-45 (.846)   32-5-2

1941   8-2-0 (3-1-0)
S20	●	Furman	32	6
O4		at Duke	0	19
O11	●	Dayton	26	0
O18	●	Alabama	2	9
O25	●	Cincinnati	21	6
N1	●	at LSU	13	6
N8	●	Samford	28	6
N15		at Boston College	14	7
N22	●	at Kentucky	20	7
N29	●	Vanderbilt	26	7

1942   9-1-1 (4-1-0)
S26	=	at South Carolina	0	0
O3	●	Fordham	0	14
O10	●	Dayton	34	6
O17	●	Alabama *Birm*	0	8
O24	●	Furman	52	7
O31	●	LSU	26	0
N7	●	Cincinnati	34	12
N14	●	Mississippi *Mem*	14	0
N21	●	Kentucky	26	0
N28	●	at Vanderbilt	19	7
		SUGAR BOWL		
J1	●	Tulsa	14	7

1943
NO TEAM WWII

1944   7-1-1 (5-0-1)
S30	●	Kentucky	26	13
O7	●	Mississippi *Mem*	20	7
O14	●	Florida	40	0
O21	=	Alabama	0	0
O28	●	Clemson	26	7
N4	●	at LSU	13	0
N18	●	Temple	27	14
N25	●	at Kentucky	21	7
		ROSE BOWL		
J1		Southern California	0	25

1945   8-1-0 (3-1-0)
S29	●	Wake Forest	7	6
O6	●	William & Mary	48	13
O13	●	U.T. Chattanooga	30	0
O20	●	Alabama *Birm*	7	25
O27	●	Villanova	33	2
N3	●	North Carolina	20	6
N10	●	Mississippi *Mem*	34	0
N24	●	at Kentucky	14	0
D1	●	Vanderbilt	45	0

ROBERT R. NEYLAND

1946   9-2-0 (5-0-0)
S28	●	Georgia Tech	13	9
O5	●	at Duke	12	7
O12	●	U.T. Chattanooga	47	7
O19	●	Alabama	12	0
O26	●	Wake Forest	6	19
N2	●	North Carolina	20	14
N9	●	Mississippi *Mem*	18	14
N16	●	at Boston College	33	13
N23	●	Kentucky	7	0
N30	●	at Vanderbilt	7	6
		ORANGE BOWL		
J1		Rice	0	8

1947   5-5-0 (2-3-0)
S27		at Georgia Tech	0	27
O4		Duke	7	19
O11	●	U.T. Chattanooga	26	7
O18		Alabama *Birm*	0	10
O25	●	Tennessee Tech	49	0
N1		at North Carolina	6	20
N8		Mississippi *Mem*	13	43
N15		Boston College	38	13
N22	●	at Kentucky	13	6
N29	●	Vanderbilt	12	7

1948   4-4-2 (2-3-1)
S25		Mississippi State	6	21
O2	=	at Duke	7	7
O9	●	U.T. Chattanooga	26	0
O16	●	Alabama	21	6
O23	●	Tennessee Tech	41	0
O30	●	North Carolina	7	14
N6	●	at Georgia Tech	13	6
N13		Mississippi *Mem*	13	16
N20	=	Kentucky	0	0
N27	●	at Vanderbilt	6	28

1949   7-2-1 (4-1-1)
S24	●	Mississippi State	10	0
O1		Duke	7	21
O8	●	U.T. Chattanooga	39	7
O15	=	Alabama *Birm*	7	7
O22	●	Tennessee Tech	36	6
O29	●	at North Carolina	35	6
N5		Georgia Tech	13	30
N12	●	Mississippi *Mem*	35	7
N19	●	at Kentucky	6	0
N26	●	Vanderbilt	26	20

1950   11-1-0 (4-1-0)
S23	●	Southern Miss	56	0
S30	●	at Mississippi State	0	7
O7	●	at Duke	28	7
O14	●	U.T. Chattanooga	41	0
O21	●	Alabama	14	9
O28	●	Wash. & Lee	27	20
N4	●	North Carolina	16	0
N11	●	Tennessee Tech	48	14
N18	●	Mississippi	35	0
N25	●	Kentucky	7	0
D2	●	at Vanderbilt	43	0
		COTTON BOWL		
J1	●	Texas	20	14

1951   10-1-0 (5-0-0)
S29	●	Mississippi State	14	0
O6	●	Duke	26	0
O13	●	U.T. Chattanooga	42	13
O20	●	Alabama *Birm*	27	13
O27	●	Tennessee Tech	68	0
N3	●	at North Carolina	27	0
N10	●	Wash. & Lee	60	14
N17	●	at Mississippi	46	21
N24	●	at Kentucky	28	0
D1	●	Vanderbilt	35	27
		SUGAR BOWL		
J1		Maryland	13	28

1952   8-2-1 (5-0-1)
S27	●	Mississippi State *Mem*	14	7
O4		at Duke	0	7
O11	●	U.T. Chattanooga	26	6
O18	●	Alabama	20	0
O25	●	Wofford	50	0
N1	●	North Carolina	41	14
N8	●	at LSU	22	3
N15	●	Florida	26	12
N22	=	Kentucky	14	14
N29	●	at Vanderbilt	46	0
		COTTON BOWL		
J1		Texas	0	16

HARVEY ROBINSON
1953-54 (.500)   10-10-1

1953   6-4-1 (3-2-1)

S26		Mississippi State	0	26
O3		Duke	7	21
O10	•	U.T. Chattanooga	40	7
O17	=	Alabama *Birm*	0	0
O24	•	Louisville	59	6
O31	•	at North Carolina	20	6
N7	•	LSU	32	14
N14		at Florida	9	7
N21		at Kentucky	21	27
N28		Vanderbilt	33	6
D5		at Houston	19	33

1954   4-6-0 (1-5-0)

S25	•	Mississippi State *Mem*	19	7
O2		at Duke	6	7
O9	•	U.T. Chattanooga	20	14
O16		Alabama	0	27
O23	•	Dayton	14	7
O30	•	North Carolina	26	20
N6		at Georgia Tech	7	28
N13		Florida	0	14
N20		Kentucky	13	14
N27		at Vanderbilt	0	26

BOWDEN WYATT
1955-62 (.622)   49-29-4

1955   6-3-1 (3-2-1)

S24		Mississippi State	7	13
O1		Duke	0	21
O8	•	U.T. Chattanooga	13	0
O15	•	Alabama *Birm*	20	0
O22	•	Dayton	53	7
O29	•	at North Carolina	48	7
N5	=	Georgia Tech	7	7
N12		at Florida	20	0
N19		at Kentucky	0	23
N26		Vanderbilt	20	14

1956   10-1-0 (6-0-0)

S29	•	Auburn *Birm*	35	7
O6	•	at Duke	33	20
O13	•	U.T. Chattanooga	42	20
O20	•	Alabama	24	0
O27	•	Maryland	34	7
N3	•	North Carolina	20	0
N10	•	at Georgia Tech	6	0
N17	•	Mississippi	27	7
N24	•	Kentucky	20	7
D1	•	at Vanderbilt	27	7
SUGAR BOWL				
J1	•	Baylor	7	13

1957   8-3-0 (4-3-0)

S28		Auburn	0	7
O5	•	Mississippi State	14	9
O12	•	U.T. Chattanooga	28	13
O19	•	Alabama *Birm*	14	0
O26	•	at Maryland	16	0
N2	•	at North Carolina	35	0
N9	•	Georgia Tech	21	6
N16		Mississippi *Mem*	7	14
N23		at Kentucky	6	20
N30		Vanderbilt	20	6
GATOR BOWL				
D28	•	Texas A&M	3	0

1958   4-6-0 (4-3-0)

S27	•	Auburn *Birm*	0	13
O4	•	Mississippi State *Mem*	13	8
O11	•	at Georgia Tech	7	21
O18	•	Alabama	14	7
O25	•	Florida State	0	10
N1	•	North Carolina	7	21
N8	•	U.T. Chattanooga	6	14
N15	•	Mississippi	18	16
N22		Kentucky	2	6
N29		at Vanderbilt	10	6

1959   5-4-1 (3-4-1)

S26	•	Auburn	3	0
O3	•	Mississippi State	22	6
O10		Georgia Tech	7	14
O17	=	Alabama *Birm*	7	7
O24	•	U.T. Chattanooga	23	0
O31	•	at North Carolina	29	7
N7	•	LSU	14	13
N14	•	Mississippi *Mem*	7	37
N21		at Kentucky	0	20
N28		Vanderbilt	0	14

1960   6-2-2 (3-2-2)

S24	•	Auburn *Birm*	10	3
O1	=	Mississippi State *Mem*	0	0
O8	•	Tampa	62	7
O15	•	Alabama	20	7
O22	•	U.T. Chattanooga	35	0
O29	•	North Carolina	27	14
N5		at Georgia Tech	7	14
N12		Mississippi	3	24
N19	•	Kentucky	10	10
N26		at Vanderbilt	35	0

1961   6-4-0 (4-3-0)

S30		Auburn	21	24
O7	•	Mississippi State	17	3
O14	•	Tulsa	52	6
O21	•	Alabama *Birm*	3	34
O28	•	U.T. Chattanooga	20	7
N4	•	at North Carolina	21	22
N11	•	Georgia Tech	10	6
N18	•	Mississippi *Mem*	10	24
N25		at Kentucky	26	16
D2	•	Vanderbilt	41	7

1962   4-6-0 (2-6-0)

S29	•	Auburn *Birm*	21	22
O6	•	Mississippi State *Mem*	6	7
O13	•	at Georgia Tech	0	17
O20	•	Alabama	7	27
O27	•	U.T. Chattanooga	48	14
N3	•	Wake Forest	23	0
N10	•	Tulane	28	16
N17	•	Mississippi	6	19
N24	•	Kentucky	10	12
D1	•	at Vanderbilt	30	0

JIM McDONALD
1963 (.500)   5-5

1963   5-5-0 (3-5-0)

S21	•	Richmond	34	6
S28	•	Auburn	19	23
O5		Mississippi State	0	7
O12	•	Georgia Tech	7	23
O19	•	Alabama *Birm*	0	35
O26	•	U.T. Chattanooga	49	7
N9	•	at Tulane	26	0
N16	•	Mississippi *Mem*	0	20
N23	•	at Kentucky	19	0
N30		Vanderbilt	14	0

DOUG DICKEY
1964-69 (.738)   46-15-4

1964   4-5-1 (1-5-1)

S19	•	U.T. Chattanooga	10	6
S26	•	Auburn *Birm*	0	3
O3	•	Mississippi State *Mem*	14	13
O10	•	Boston College	16	14
O17	•	Alabama	8	19
O24	=	at LSU	3	3
N7	•	at Georgia Tech	22	14
N14	•	Mississippi	0	30
N21	•	Kentucky	7	12
N28		at Vanderbilt	0	7

1965   8-1-2 (3-1-2)

S18	•	Army	21	0
S25	=	Auburn	13	13
O9	=	South Carolina	24	3
O16	=	Alabama *Birm*	7	7
O23	•	Houston	17	8
N6	•	Georgia Tech	21	7
N13	•	Mississippi *Mem*	13	14
N20	•	at Kentucky	19	3
N27	•	Vanderbilt	21	3
D4	•	UCLA *Mem*	37	34
BLUEBONNET BOWL				
D18	•	Tulsa	27	6

1966   8-3-0 (4-2-0)

S24	•	Auburn *Birm*	28	0
O1	•	Rice	23	3
O8	•	at Georgia Tech	3	6
O15	•	Alabama	10	11
O22	||	South Carolina	29	17
O29	•	Army *Mem*	38	7
N5	•	U.T. Chattanooga	28	10
N12	•	Mississippi	7	14
N19	•	Kentucky	28	19
N26	•	at Vanderbilt	28	0
GATOR BOWL				
D31	•	Syracuse	18	12

1967   9-2-0 (6-0-0)

S16	•	at UCLA	16	20
S30	•	Auburn	27	13
O14	•	Georgia Tech	24	13
O21	•	Alabama *Birm*	24	13
O28	•	LSU	17	14
N4	•	at Tampa	38	0
N11	•	Tulane	35	14
N18	•	Mississippi *Mem*	20	7
N25	•	at Kentucky	17	7
D2	•	Vanderbilt	41	14
ORANGE BOWL				
J1		Oklahoma	24	26

1968   8-2-1 (4-1-1)

S14	=	Georgia	17	17
S28	•	Memphis	24	17
O5	•	at Rice	52	0
O12	•	at Georgia Tech	24	7
O19	•	Alabama	10	9
N2	•	UCLA	42	18
N9	•	Auburn *Birm*	14	28
N16	•	Mississippi	31	0
N23	•	Kentucky	24	7
N30	•	at Vanderbilt	10	7
COTTON BOWL				
J1	•	Texas	13	36

1969   9-2-0 (5-1-0)

S20	•	U.T. Chattanooga	31	0
S27	•	Auburn	45	19
O4	•	at Memphis	55	16
O11	•	Georgia Tech	26	8
O18	•	Alabama *Birm*	41	14
N1	•	at Georgia	17	3
N8	•	South Carolina	29	14
N15	•	Mississippi *JAM*	0	38
N22	•	at Kentucky	31	26
N29	•	Vanderbilt	40	27
GATOR BOWL				
D27	•	Florida	13	14

BILL BATTLE
1970-76 (.723)   59-22-2

1970   11-1-0 (4-1-0)

S19	•	SMU	28	3
S26	•	Auburn *Birm*	23	36
O3	•	Army	48	3
O10	•	at Georgia Tech	17	6
O17	•	Alabama	24	0
O24	•	Florida	38	7
O31	•	Wake Forest *Mem*	41	7
N7	•	at South Carolina	20	18
N21	•	Kentucky	45	0
N28	•	at Vanderbilt	24	6
D5	•	UCLA	28	17
SUGAR BOWL				
J1	•	Air Force	34	13

1971   10-2-0 (4-2-0)

S18	•	Santa Barbara	48	6
S25	•	Auburn	9	10
O2	•	at Florida	20	13
O9	•	Georgia Tech	10	6
O16	•	Alabama *Birm*	15	32
O23	•	Mississippi State *Mem*	10	7
O30	•	Tulsa	38	3
N6	•	South Carolina	35	6
N20	•	at Kentucky	21	7
N27	•	Vanderbilt	19	7
D4	•	Penn State	31	11
LIBERTY BOWL				
D20	•	Arkansas	14	13

1972   10-2-0 (4-2-0)

S9	•	at Georgia Tech	34	3
S16	•	Penn State	28	21
S23	•	Wake Forest	45	6
S30	•	Auburn *Birm*	6	10
O7	•	at Memphis	38	7
O21	•	Alabama	10	17
O28	•	Hawaii	34	2
N4	•	at Georgia	14	0
N18	•	Mississippi	17	0
N25	•	Kentucky	17	7
D2	•	at Vanderbilt	30	10
BLUEBONNET BOWL				
D30	•	LSU	24	17

1973   8-4-0 (3-3-0)

S15	•	Duke	21	17
S22	•	at Army	37	18
S29	•	Auburn	21	0
O6	•	Kansas *Mem*	28	27
O13	•	Georgia Tech	20	14
O20	•	Alabama *Birm*	21	42
O27	•	TCU	39	7
N3		Georgia	31	35
N17	•	Mississippi *JAM*	18	28
N24	•	at Kentucky	16	14
D1	•	Vanderbilt	20	17
GATOR BOWL				
D29	•	Texas Tech	19	28

1974   7-3-2 (2-3-1)

S7	=	UCLA	17	17
S21	•	Kansas	17	3
S28	•	at Auburn	0	21
O5	•	Tulsa	17	10
O12	•	at LSU	10	20
O19	•	Alabama	6	28
O26	•	Clemson	29	28
N9	•	Memphis	34	6
N16	•	Mississippi *Mem*	29	17
N23	•	Kentucky	24	7
N30	•	at Vanderbilt	21	21
LIBERTY BOWL				
D16	•	Maryland	7	3

1975   7-5-0 (3-3-0)

S13	•	Maryland	26	8
S20	•	at UCLA	28	34
S27	•	Auburn	21	17
O11	•	LSU	24	10
O18	•	Alabama *Birm*	7	30
O25	•	North Texas	14	21
N1	•	Colorado State	28	7
N8	•	Utah	40	7
N15	•	Mississippi *Mem*	6	23
N22	•	at Kentucky	17	13
N29	•	Vanderbilt	14	17
D6	•	at Hawaii	28	6

1976   6-5-0 (2-4-0)

S11	•	Duke	18	21
S18	•	TCU	31	0
S25	•	Auburn *Birm*	28	38
O2	•	Clemson	21	19
O9	•	at Georgia Tech	42	7
O16	•	Alabama	13	20
O23	•	Florida	18	20
N6	•	at Memphis	21	14
N13	•	Mississippi	32	6
N20	•	Kentucky	0	7
N27	•	at Vanderbilt	13	10

JOHNNY MAJORS
1977-92 (.645)   116-62-8

1977   4-7-0 (1-5-0)

S10	•	California	17	27
S17	•	Boston College	24	18
S24	•	Auburn	12	14
O1	•	Oregon State	41	10
O8	•	Georgia Tech	8	24
O15	•	Alabama *Birm*	10	24
O22	•	at Florida	17	27
N5	•	Memphis	27	14
N12	•	Mississippi *Mem*	14	43
N19	•	at Kentucky	17	21
N26	•	Vanderbilt	42	7

1978   5-5-1 (3-3-0)

S16	•	UCLA	0	13
S23	=	Oregon State	13	13
S30	•	Auburn *Birm*	10	29
O7	•	Army	31	13
O21	•	Alabama	17	30
O28	•	Mississippi State *Mem*	21	34
N4	•	Duke	34	0
N11	•	at Notre Dame	14	31
N18	•	Mississippi	41	17
N25	•	Kentucky	29	14
D2	•	at Vanderbilt	41	15

1979   7-5-0 (3-3-0)

S15	•	at Boston College	28	16
S22	•	Utah	51	18
S29	•	Auburn	35	17
O6	•	Mississippi State *Mem*	9	28
O13	•	Georgia Tech	31	0
O20	•	Alabama *Birm*	17	27
N3	•	Rutgers	7	13
N10	•	Notre Dame	40	18
N17	•	Mississippi *JAM*	20	44
N24	•	at Kentucky	20	17
D1	•	Vanderbilt	31	10
BLUEBONNET BOWL				
D31	•	Purdue	22	27

TENNESSEE 209

1980 — 5-6-0 (3-3-0)

S6		|	Georgia	15	16
S13			Southern California	17	20
S20	●		Washington State	35	23
S27	●	|	at Auburn	42	0
O11	●		at Georgia Tech	23	10
O18		|	Alabama	0	27
O25			Pittsburgh	6	30
N1			Virginia	13	16
N15		|	Mississippi MEM	9	20
N22	●	|	Kentucky	45	14
N29	●	|	at Vanderbilt	51	13

1981 — 8-4-0 (3-3-0)

S5		|	at Georgia	0	44
S12			at Southern California	7	43
S19	●		Colorado State	42	0
S26	●	|	Auburn	10	7
O10	●		Georgia Tech	10	7
O17		|	Alabama BIRM	19	38
O24	●		at Memphis	28	9
N7	●		Wichita St.	24	21
N14	●	|	Mississippi	28	20
N21		|	at Kentucky	10	21
N28	●	|	Vanderbilt	38	34
			GARDEN STATE BOWL		
D13	●		Wisconsin	28	21

1982 — 6-5-1 (3-2-1)

S4			Duke	24	25
S11	●		Iowa State	23	21
S25		|	at Auburn	14	24
O2	●		Washington State	10	3
O9	=	|	at LSU	24	24
O16	●	|	Alabama	35	28
O23			at Georgia Tech	21	31
N6	●		Memphis	29	3
N13	●	|	Mississippi JAM	30	17
N20	●	|	Kentucky	28	7
N27		|	at Vanderbilt	21	28
			PEACH BOWL		
D31			Iowa	22	28

1983 — 9-3-0 (4-2-0)

S3			Pittsburgh	3	13
S10	●		New Mexico	31	6
S24		|	Auburn	14	37
O1	●		Citadel MEM	45	6
O8	●	|	LSU	20	6
O15	●	|	Alabama BIRM	41	34
O22	●		Georgia Tech	37	3
O29	●		Rutgers ERUT	7	0
N12		|	Mississippi	10	13
N19	●	|	at Kentucky	10	0
N26	●	|	Vanderbilt	34	24
			CITRUS BOWL		
D17	●		Maryland	30	23

1984 — 7-4-1 (3-3-0)

S1	●		Washington State	34	27
S15	●		Utah	27	21
S22	=		Army	24	24
S29		|	at Auburn	10	29
O13		|	Florida	30	43
O20	●	|	Alabama	28	27
O27	●		at Georgia Tech	24	21
N10	●		Memphis	41	9
N17	●	|	Mississippi JAM	41	17
N24		|	Kentucky	12	17
D1	●	|	at Vanderbilt	29	13
			SUN BOWL		
D22			Maryland	27	28

1985 — 9-1-2 (5-1-0)

S14	=		UCLA	26	26
S28	●	|	Auburn	38	20
O5	●		Wake Forest	31	29
O12		|	at Florida	10	17
O19	●	|	Alabama BIRM	16	14
O26	=		Georgia Tech	6	6
N2	●		Rutgers	40	0
N9	●		at Memphis	17	7
N16	●	|	Mississippi	34	14
N23	●	|	at Kentucky	42	0
N30	●	|	Vanderbilt	30	0
			SUGAR BOWL		
J1	●		Miami, Fla.	35	7

1986 — 7-5-0 (3-3-0)

S6	●		New Mexico	35	21
S13		|	Mississippi State	23	27
S27		|	at Auburn	8	34
O4	●		Texas-El Paso	26	16
O11			Army	21	25
O18		|	Alabama	28	56
O25			at Georgia Tech	13	14
N8	●		Memphis	33	3
N15	●	|	Mississippi JAM	22	10
N22	●	|	Kentucky	28	9
N29	●	|	at Vanderbilt	35	20
			LIBERTY BOWL		
D29	●		Minnesota	21	14

1987 — 10-2-1 (4-1-1)

A30	●		Iowa ERUT	23	22
S5	●		Colorado State	49	3
S12	●	|	at Mississippi State	38	10
S26	=	|	Auburn	20	20
O3	●		California	38	12
O17		|	Alabama BIRM	22	41
O24	●		Georgia Tech	29	15
O31			at Boston College	18	20
N7	●		Louisville	41	10
N14	●	|	Mississippi	55	13
N21	●	|	at Kentucky	24	22
N28	●	|	Vanderbilt	38	36
			PEACH BOWL		
J2	●		Indiana	27	22

1988 — 5-6-0 (3-4-0)

S3		|	at Georgia	17	28
S10			Duke	26	31
S17		|	LSU	9	34
S24		|	at Auburn	6	38
O1			Washington State	24	52
O15		|	Alabama	20	28
O22	●		at Memphis	38	25
N5	●		Boston College	10	7
N12	●	|	at Mississippi	20	12
N19	●	|	Kentucky	28	24
N26	●	|	at Vanderbilt	14	7

1989 — 11-1-0 (6-1-0)

S2	●		Colorado State	17	14
S9	●		at UCLA	24	6
S16	●		Duke	28	6
S30	●	|	Auburn	21	14
O7	●	|	Georgia	17	14
O21		|	Alabama BIRM	30	47
O28	●	|	at LSU	45	39
N11	●		Akron	52	9
N18	●	|	Mississippi	33	21
N25	●	|	at Kentucky	31	10
D2	●	|	Vanderbilt	17	10
			COTTON BOWL		
J1	●		Arkansas	31	27

1990 — 9-2-2 (5-1-1)

A26	=		Colorado ANA	31	31
S1	●		Pacific	55	7
S8	●	|	at Mississippi State	40	7
S15	●		Texas-El Paso	56	0
S29	=	|	at Auburn	26	26
O13	●	|	Florida	45	3
O20		|	Alabama	6	9
N3	●		Temple	41	20
N10			Notre Dame	29	34
N17	●	|	Mississippi	22	13
N24	●	|	Kentucky	42	28
D1	●	|	at Vanderbilt	49	20
			SUGAR BOWL		
J1	●		Virginia	23	22

1991 — 9-3-0 (5-2-0)

S5	●		at Louisville	28	11
S14	●		UCLA	30	16
S21	●	|	Mississippi State	26	24
S28	●	|	Auburn	30	21
O12		|	at Florida	18	35
O19		|	Alabama BIRM	19	24
N2	●		Memphis	52	24
N9	●		at Notre Dame	35	34
N16	●	|	Mississippi	36	25
N23	●	|	at Kentucky	16	7
N30	●	|	Vanderbilt	45	0
			FIESTA BOWL		
J1			Penn State	17	42

PHILLIP FULMER
1992-2008 (.745) 152-52

1992 — 9-3-0 (5-3-0)

S5	●		La. Lafayette	38	3
S12	●	|	at Georgia	34	31
S19	●	|	Florida	31	14
S26	●		Cincinnati	40	0
O3	●	|	at LSU	20	0
O10		|	Arkansas	24	25
O17		|	Alabama	10	17
O31		|	at South Carolina	23	24
N14	●		at Memphis	26	21
N21	●	|	Kentucky	34	13
N28	●	|	at Vanderbilt	29	25
			HALL OF FAME BOWL		
J1	●		Boston College	38	23

1993 — 9-2-1 (6-1-1)

S4	●		Louisiana Tech	50	0
S11	●	|	Georgia	38	6
S18		|	at Florida	34	41
S25	●	|	LSU	42	20
O2	●		Duke	52	19
O9	●	|	Arkansas LR	28	14
O16	=	|	Alabama BIRM	17	17†
O30	●	|	South Carolina	55	3
N6	●		Louisville	45	10
N20	●	|	at Kentucky	48	0
N27	●	|	Vanderbilt	62	14
			CITRUS BOWL		
J1			Penn State	13	31

1994 — 8-4-0 (5-3-0)

S3			at UCLA	23	25
S10	●	|	at Georgia	41	23
S17		|	Florida	0	31
S24		|	at Mississippi State	21	24
O1	●		Washington State	10	9
O8	●	|	Arkansas	38	21
O15		|	Alabama	13	17
O29	●	|	at South Carolina	31	22
N12	●		Memphis	24	13
N19	●	|	Kentucky	52	0
N26	●	|	at Vanderbilt	65	0
			GATOR BOWL		
D30	●		Virginia Tech	45	23

1995 — 11-1-0 (7-1-0)

S2	●		East Carolina	27	7
S9	●	|	Georgia	30	27
S16		|	at Florida	37	62
S23	●	|	Mississippi State	52	14
S30	●		Oklahoma State	31	0
O7	●	|	at Arkansas	49	31
O14	●	|	Alabama BIRM	41	14
O28	●	|	South Carolina	56	21
N4	●		Southern Miss	42	0
N18	●	|	at Kentucky	34	31
N25	●	|	Vanderbilt	12	7
			CITRUS BOWL		
J1	●		Ohio State	20	14

1996 — 10-2 (7-1)

A31	●		Nevada-Las Vegas	62	3
S7	●		UCLA	35	20
S21		|	Florida	29	35
O3	●	|	Mississippi MEM	41	3
O12	●	|	at Georgia	29	17
O26	●	|	Alabama	20	13
N2	●	|	at South Carolina	31	14
N9			at Memphis	17	21
N16	●	|	Arkansas	55	14
N23	●	|	Kentucky	56	10
N30	●	|	at Vanderbilt	14	7
			CITRUS BOWL		
J1	●		Northwestern	48	28

1997 — 11-2 (7-1)

A30	●		Texas Tech	52	17
S6	●		at UCLA	30	24
S20		|	at Florida	20	33
O4	●	|	Mississippi	31	17
O11	●	|	Georgia	38	13
O18	●	|	Alabama BIRM	38	21
N1	●	|	South Carolina	22	7
N8	●		Southern Miss	44	20
N15	●	|	Arkansas LR	30	22
N22	●	|	at Kentucky	59	31
N29	●	|	Vanderbilt	17	10
			SEC CHAMPIONSHIP GAME		
D6	●		Auburn ATL	30	29
			ORANGE BOWL		
J2			Nebraska	17	42

1998 — 13-0 (8-0)

S5	●		at Syracuse	34	33
S19	●	|	Florida	20	17
S26	●		Houston	42	7
O3	●	|	at Auburn	17	9
O10	●	|	at Georgia	22	3
O24	●	|	Alabama	35	18
O31	●	|	at South Carolina	49	14
N7	●		UAB	37	13
N14	●	|	Arkansas	28	24
N21	●	|	Kentucky	59	21
N28	●	|	at Vanderbilt	41	0
			SEC CHAMPIONSHIP GAME		
D5	●		Mississippi State ATL	24	14
			FIESTA BOWL		
J4	●		Florida State	23	16

1999 — 9-3 (6-2)

S4	●		Wyoming	42	17
S18		|	at Florida	21	23
S25	●		Memphis	17	16
O2	●	|	Auburn	24	0
O9	●	|	Georgia	37	20
O23	●	|	at Alabama	21	7
O30	●	|	South Carolina	30	7
N6	●		Notre Dame	38	14
N13		|	at Arkansas	24	28
N20	●	|	at Kentucky	56	21
N27	●	|	Vanderbilt	38	10
			FIESTA BOWL		
J2			Nebraska	21	31

2000 — 8-4 (5-3)

S2	●		Southern Miss	19	16
S16		|	Florida	23	27
S23	●		La. Monroe	70	3
S30		|	at LSU	31	38
O7		|	at Georgia	10	21
O21	●	|	Alabama	20	10
O28	●	|	at South Carolina	17	14
N4	●		at Memphis	19	17
N11	●	|	Arkansas	63	20
N18	●	|	Kentucky	59	20
N25	●	|	at Vanderbilt	28	26
			COTTON BOWL		
J1			Kansas State	21	35

2001 — 11-2 (7-1)

S1	●		Syracuse	33	9
S8	●	|	at Arkansas	13	3
S29	●	|	LSU	26	18
O6		|	Georgia	24	26
O20	●	|	at Alabama	35	24
O27	●	|	South Carolina	17	10
N3	●		at Notre Dame	28	18
N10	●		Memphis	49	28
N17	●	|	at Kentucky	38	35
N24	●	|	Vanderbilt	38	0
D1	●	|	at Florida	34	32
			SEC CHAMPIONSHIP GAME		
D8			LSU ATL	20	31
			CITRUS BOWL		
J1	●		Michigan	45	17

2002 — 8-5 (5-3)

A31	●		Wyoming NASH	47	7
S7	●		Middle Tennessee	26	3
S21		|	Florida	13	30
S28	●		Rutgers	35	14
O5	●	|	Arkansas	41	38
O12		|	at Georgia	13	18
O26		|	Alabama	14	34
N2	●	|	at South Carolina	18	10
N9			Miami, Fla.	3	26
N16	●	|	at Mississippi State	35	17
N23	●	|	at Vanderbilt	24	0
N30	●	|	Kentucky	24	0
			PEACH BOWL		
D31			Maryland	3	30

2003 — 10-3 (6-2)

A30	●		Fresno State	24	6
S6	●		Marshall	34	24
S20	●	|	at Florida	24	10
S27	●	|	South Carolina	23	20
O4		|	at Auburn	21	28
O11		|	Georgia	14	41
O25	●	|	at Alabama	51	43
N1	●		Duke	23	6
N8	●		at Miami, Fla.	10	6
N15	●	|	Mississippi State	59	21
N22	●	|	Vanderbilt	48	0
N29	●	|	at Kentucky	20	7
			PEACH BOWL		
J2			Clemson	14	27

THE SCHOOLS

2004   10-3   (7-1)

S5	●	Nevada-Las Vegas	42	17
S18		Florida	30	28
S25	●	Louisiana Tech	42	17
O2		Auburn	10	34
O9	●	at Georgia	19	14
O16	●	at Mississippi	21	17
O23	●	Alabama	17	13
O30	●	at South Carolina	43	29
N6		Notre Dame	13	17
N20	●	at Vanderbilt	38	33
N27	●	Kentucky	37	31

SEC CHAMPIONSHIP GAME

D4		Auburn *Atl*	28	38

COTTON BOWL

J1	●	Texas A&M	38	7

2005   5-6   (3-5)

S3	●	Ala.-Birmingham	17	10
S17		at Florida	7	16
S26	●	at LSU	30	27
O1		Mississippi	27	10
O8		Georgia	14	27
O22		at Alabama	3	6
O29		South Carolina	15	16
N5		at Notre Dame	21	41
N12	●	Memphis	20	16
N19		Vanderbilt	24	28
N26	●	at Kentucky	27	8

2006   9-4   (5-3)

S2	●	California	35	18
S9	●	Air Force	31	30
S16		Florida	20	21
S23	●	Marshall	33	7
S30	●	at Memphis	41	7
O7	●	at Georgia	51	33
O21	●	Alabama	16	13
O28	●	at South Carolina	31	24
N4		LSU	24	28
N11		at Arkansas	14	31
N18	●	at Vanderbilt	39	10
N25	●	Kentucky	17	12

OUTBACK BOWL

J1		Penn State	10	20

2007   10-4   (6-2)

S1		at California	31	45
S8	●	Southern Mississippi	39	19
S15		at Florida	20	59
S22	●	Arkansas State	48	27
O6	●	Georgia	35	14
O13	●	at Mississippi State	33	21
O20		at Alabama	17	41
O27	●	South Carolina	27	24
N3		La.-Lafayette	59	7
N10	●	Arkansas	34	13
N17	●	Vanderbilt	25	24
N24	●	at Kentucky	52	50

SEC CHAMPIONSHIP GAME

D1		LSU *Atl*	14	21

OUTBACK BOWL

J1	●	Wisconsin	21	17

2008   5-7   (3-5)

S1		at UCLA	24	27
S13	●	Ala.-Birmingham	35	3
S20		Florida	6	30
S27		at Auburn	12	14
O4	●	Northern Illinois	13	9
O11		at Georgia	14	26
O18	●	Mississippi State	34	3
O25		Alabama	9	29
N1		at South Carolina	6	27
N8		Wyoming	7	13
N22	●	at Vanderbilt	20	10
N29	●	Kentucky	28	10

TENNESSEE ANNUAL STATISTICAL LEADERS

YR	RUSHING	YDS	ATT	AVG	PASSING	ATT	CMP	PCT	YDS	RECEIVING	REC	YDS	AVG
1950	Andy Kozar	648	126	5.1	Hank Lauricella	72	23	.32	364	Bert Rechichar	9	205	22.8
1951	Hank Lauricella	881	111	7.9	Hank Lauricella	51	24	.47	352	John Davis	8	160	20.0
1952	Andy Kozar	660	122	5.4	Pat Shires	38	15	.39	252	John Davis	14	297	21.2
1953	Jimmy Wade	675	158	4.3	Jimmy Wade	63	25	.40	451	Jerry Hyde	8	173	21.6
1954	Tom Tracy	794	116	6.8	Johnny Majors	24	8	.33	107	Hugh Garner	5	57	11.4
1955	Johnny Majors	657	183	3.6	Johnny Majors	65	36	.55	476	Buddy Cruze	12	232	19.3
1956	Tommy Bronson	562	105	5.4	Johnny Majors	59	36	.61	552	Buddy Cruze	20	357	17.9
1957	Bobby Gordon	526	167	3.2	Bobby Gordon	40	20	.50	260	Tommy Potts	10	123	12.3
1958	Bill Majors	294	148	1.9	Bill Majors	25	17	.68	215	Murray Armstrong	14	195	13.9
1959	Glenn Glass	261	75	3.5	Gene Etter	36	22	.61	298	Cotton Letner	8	92	11.5
1960	Glenn Glass	478	90	5.3	Glenn Glass	26	11	.42	167	Ken Waddell	8	60	7.5
1961	Mallon Faircloth	475	123	3.9	Mallon Faircloth	52	31	.60	460	Hubert McClain	11	149	13.5
1962	George Canale	455	79	5.8	Bobby Morton	40	20	.50	305	John Bill Hudson	15	259	17.3
1963	Mallon Faircloth	652	137	4.8	Mallon Faircloth	75	31	.41	509	Buddy Fisher	12	242	20.2
1964	Stan Mitchell	325	94	3.5	Art Galiffa	59	29	.49	338	Hal Wantland	21	284	13.5
1965	Walter Chadwick	470	101	4.7	Dewey Warren	79	44	.56	588	Johnny Mills	23	328	14.3
1966	Charlie Fulton	463	109	4.2	Dewey Warren	229	136	.59	1,716	Johnny Mills	48	725	15.1
1967	Walter Chadwick	645	144	4.5	Dewey Warren	132	78	.59	1,053	Richmond Flowers	41	585	14.3
1968	Richard Pickens	736	133	5.5	Bubba Wyche	237	134	.57	1,539	Ken DeLong	34	393	11.6
1969	Curt Watson	807	146	5.5	Bobby Scott	191	92	.48	1,352	Gary Kreis	38	609	16.0
1970	Curt Watson	791	190	4.3	Bobby Scott	252	118	.47	1,697	Joe Thompson	37	502	13.6
1971	Curt Watson	766	193	4.0	Jim Maxwell	102	46	.45	544	Joe Thompson	15	247	16.5
1972	Haskel Stanback	890	183	4.9	Condredge Holloway	120	73	.61	807	Emmon Love	20	280	14.0
1973	Haskel Stanback	682	165	4.1	Condredge Holloway	154	89	.58	1,149	Stanley Morgan	22	511	23.2
1974	Stanley Morgan	723	128	5.6	Condredge Holloway	133	76	.57	1,146	Larry Seivers	25	347	13.9
1975	Stanley Morgan	809	133	6.1	Randy Wallace	145	72	.50	1,318	Larry Seivers	41	840	20.5
1976	Bobby Emmons	462	75	6.2	Randy Wallace	130	68	.52	1,046	Larry Seivers	51	737	14.5
1977	Kelsey Finch	770	154	5.0	Jimmy Streater	105	59	.56	742	Reggie Harper	30	331	11.0
1978	Jimmy Streater	593	146	4.1	Jimmy Streater	198	101	.51	1,418	Reggie Harper	31	356	11.5
1979	Hubert Simpson	792	157	5.0	Jimmy Streater	161	80	.50	1,256	Anthony Hancock	34	687	20.2
1980	James Berry	543	131	4.1	Steve Alatorre	119	58	.49	747	Anthony Hancock	33	580	17.6
1981	James Berry	500	129	3.9	Steve Alatorre	154	81	.53	1,171	Anthony Hancock	32	437	13.7
1982	Chuck Coleman	600	113	5.3	Alan Cockrell	294	174	.59	2,021	Willie Gault	50	668	13.4
1983	Johnnie Jones	1,116	191	5.8	Alan Cockrell	243	128	.53	1,683	Clyde Duncan	33	640	19.4
1984	Johnnie Jones	1,290	229	5.6	Tony Robinson	253	156	.62	1,963	Tim McGee	54	809	15.0
1985	Keith Davis	684	141	4.9	Tony Robinson	143	91	.64	1,246	Tim McGee	50	947	18.9
1986	William Howard	787	177	4.4	Jeff Francis	233	150	.64	1,946	Joey Clinkscales	37	511	13.8
1987	Reggie Cobb	1,197	237	5.1	Jeff Francis	201	121	.60	1,512	Thomas Woods	26	335	12.9
1988	Reggie Cobb	547	118	4.6	Jeff Francis	314	191	.61	2,237	Thomas Woods	58	689	11.9
1989	Chuck Webb	1,236	209	5.9	Andy Kelly	156	92	.59	1,299	Thomas Woods	34	511	15.0
1990	Tony Thompson	1,261	219	5.8	Andy Kelly	304	179	.59	2,241	Carl Pickens	53	917	17.3
1991	James Stewart	939	190	4.9	Andy Kelly	361	228	.63	2,759	Carl Pickens	49	877	17.9
1992	Charlie Garner	928	154	6.0	Heath Shuler	224	130	.58	1,712	Cory Fleming	40	490	12.3
1993	Charlie Garner	1,161	159	7.3	Heath Shuler	285	184	.65	2,353	Craig Faulkner	40	680	17.0
1994	James Stewart	1,028	170	6.1	Peyton Manning	144	89	.62	1,141	Joey Kent	36	470	13.1
1995	Jay Graham	1,438	272	5.3	Peyton Manning	380	244	.64	2,954	Joey Kent	69	1,055	15.3
1996	Jay Graham	797	179	4.6	Peyton Manning	380	243	.64	3,287	Joey Kent	68	1,080	15.9
1997	Jamal Lewis	1,364	232	5.9	Peyton Manning	477	287	.60	3,819	Marcus Nash	76	1,170	15.4
1998	Travis Henry	970	176	5.5	Tee Martin	267	153	.57	2,164	Peerless Price	61	920	15.1
1999	Jamal Lewis	816	182	4.5	Tee Martin	305	165	.54	2,317	Cedrick Wilson	57	827	14.5
2000	Travis Henry	1,314	253	5.2	Casey Clausen	194	121	.62	1,473	Cedrick Wilson	62	681	11.0
2001	Travis Stephens	1,464	291	5.0	Casey Clausen	354	227	.64	2,969	Kelley Washington	64	1,010	15.8
2002	Cedric Houston	779	153	5.1	Casey Clausen	310	194	.63	2,297	Jason Witten	39	493	12.6
2003	Cedric Houston	744	149	5.0	Casey Clausen	412	233	.57	2,968	James Banks	42	621	14.8
2004	Gerald Riggs	1,107	193	5.7	Erik Ainge	198	109	.55	1,452	Tony Brown	31	388	12.5
2005	Arian Foster	879	183	4.8	Rick Clausen	209	120	.57	1,441	Robert Meachem	29	383	13.2
2006	LaMarcus Coker	696	108	6.4	Erik Ainge	348	233	.67	2,989	Robert Meachem	71	1,298	18.3
2007	Arian Foster	1,193	245	4.9	Erik Ainge	519	325	.63	3,522	Lucas Taylor	73	1,000	13.7
2008	Arian Foster	570	131	4.4	Jonathan Crompton	167	86	.52	889	Gerald Jones	30	323	10.8

Receiving leaders by receptions
NCAA began including postseason stats in 2002

TENNESSEE RECORD BOOK

SINGLE-GAME RECORDS

Rushing Yards	294	Chuck Webb (Nov. 18, 1989 vs. Mississippi)
Passing Yards	523	Peyton Manning (Nov. 22, 1997 vs. Kentucky)
Receiving Yards	256	Kelley Washington (Sept. 29, 2001 vs. LSU)
All-Purpose Yards	294	Chuck Webb (Nov. 18, 1989 vs. Mississippi)
Points	30	Gene McEver (Dec. 7, 1929 vs. South Carolina)
Field Goals	5	Three players tied
Tackles	28	Tom Fisher (Sept. 26, 1964 vs. Auburn)
Interceptions	3	Eight players tied

SINGLE-SEASON RECORDS

Rushing Yards	1,464	Travis Stephens, 2001
Passing Yards	3,819	Peyton Manning, 1997
Receiving Yards	1,298	Robert Meachem, 2006
All-Purpose Yards	1,721	Reggie Cobb, 1987
Scoring	130	Gene McEver, 1929
Touchdowns	21	Gene McEver, 1929
Tackles	194	Andy Spiva, 1976
Interceptions	10	Bobby Majors, 1970
Punting Average	46.9	Jimmy Colquitt, (45 punts)
Punt Return Average	25.9	Bill Blackstock, (12 ret.)
Kickoff Return Average	29.8	Dale Carter, 1990 (17 ret.)

CAREER RECORDS

Rushing Yards	3,078	Travis Henry, 1997-2000
Passing Yards	11,201	Peyton Manning, 1994-97
Receiving Yards	2,814	Joey Kent, 1993-96
All-Purpose Yards	4,624	Stanley Morgan, 1973-76
Scoring	371	Jeff Hall, 1995-98
Touchdowns	44	Gene McEver, 1928-31
Tackles	547	Andy Spiva, 1973-76
Interceptions	18	Tim Priest, 1968-70
Punting Average	43.9	Jimmy Colquitt, 1981-84 (201 punts)
Punt Return Average	14.7	Bert Rechichar, 1949-51 (55 ret.)
Kickoff Return Average	32.6	George Cafego, 1937-39 (12 ret.)

TEAM RECORDS

Longest Winning Streak	23	Nov. 25, 1937-Dec. 9, 1939; broken by Southern California, 0-14 on Jan. 1, 1939
Longest Undefeated Streak	33	Nov. 25, 1926-Oct. 11, 1930; broken by Alabama, 6-18 on Oct. 18, 1930
Most Consecutive Winning Seasons	17	1936-53
Most Consecutive Bowl Appearances	16	1989-2004
Most Points in a Game	104	vs. American U., Oct. 7, 1905
Most Points Allowed in a Game	70	vs. Duke, Nov. 4, 1893
Largest Margin of Victory	104	vs. American U., Oct. 7, 1905
Largest Margin of Defeat	70	vs. Duke, Nov. 4, 1893
Longest Pass Play	90	Casey Clausen to Mark Jones, vs. Georgia, Oct. 11, 2003
Longest Field Goal	60	Fuad Reveiz vs. Georgia Tech, Oct. 23, 1982
Longest Punt	100	A.H. Douglas vs. Clemson, Nov. 27, 1902
Longest Interception Return	100	Ray Martin vs. Louisville, Oct. 24, 1953

RETIRED NUMBERS

16	Peyton Manning		62	Clyde Fuson
32	Bill Nowling		91	Doug Atkins
49	Rudy Klarer		92	Reggie White
61	Willis Tucker			

ALL-TIME TEAM

Players from 1891 to 1990 were selected by a fan vote and a panel of school officials

Offense			Defense		
	OG	Harry Galbreath, 1984-87		DE	Doug Atkins, 1950-52
	OG	Eric Still, 1986-89		DE	Dale Jones, 1983-86
	OT	Tim Irwin, 1978-80		DT	Reggie White, 1980-83
	OT	Bruce Wilkerson, 1983-86		DT	Marion Hobby, 1986-89
	C	Bob Johnson, 1965-67		MG	Steve DeLong, 1962-64
	WR	Stanley Morgan, 1973-76		LB	Steve Kiner, 1967-69
	WR	Larry Seivers, 1974-76		LB	Jack Reynolds, 1967-69
	WR	Willie Gault, 1979-82		LB	Keith DeLong, 1985-88
	QB	Condredge Holloway, 1972-74		DB	Bobby Majors, 1969-71
	B	Hank Lauricella, 1949-51		DB	Eddie Brown, 1971-73
	B	Johnny Majors, 1954-56		DB	Roland James, 1976-79
	RB	Curt Watson, 1969-71		DB	Bill Bates, 1979-82
	RB	Reggie Cobb, 1987-88		P	Craig Colquitt, 1975-77
	PK	Fuad Reveiz, 1981-84			

TENNESSEE BOWL HISTORY

SEASON	BOWL	DATE	PRE-GAME RANK	TEAMS	SCORE	FINAL RANK	MOST VALUABLE PLAYER(S)	ATT.
1938	**ORANGE**	Jan. 2, 1939	2 4	**Tennessee** Oklahoma	17 0			32,191
1939	**ROSE**	Jan. 1, 1940	3 2	**Southern California** Tennessee	14 0		Ambrose Schindler, Southern California, QB	92,200
1940	**SUGAR**	Jan. 1, 1941	5 4	**Boston College** Tennessee	19 13			68,486
1942	**SUGAR**	Jan. 1, 1943	7 4	**Tennessee** Tulsa	14 7			58,361
1944	**ROSE**	Jan. 1, 1945	7 12	**Southern California** Tennessee	25 0		James Hardy, Southern California, QB	91,000
1946	**ORANGE**	Jan. 1, 1947	10 7	**Rice** Tennessee	8 0			36,152
1950	**COTTON**	Jan. 1, 1951	4 3	**Tennessee** Texas	20 14		A. Kozar, FB, H. Lauricella, HB, Tennessee H. Sherrod, DE, Tenn.; B. McFadin, Texas, G	75,349
1951	**SUGAR**	Jan. 1, 1952	3 1	**Maryland** Tennessee	28 13		Ed Modzelewski, Maryland, FB	80,187
1952	**COTTON**	Jan. 1, 1953	10 8	**Texas** Tennessee	16 0		Richard Ochoa, FB, Harley Sewell, G, Texas Bob Griesbach, Tennessee, LB	75,504
1956	**SUGAR**	Jan. 1, 1957	11 2	**Baylor** Tennessee	13 7		Del Shofner, Baylor, HB	81,000
1957	**GATOR**	Dec. 28, 1957	13 9	**Tennessee** Texas A&M	3 0		Bobby Gordon, Tennessee, TB John David Crow, Texas A&M, HB	41,160
1965	**BLUEBONNET**	Dec. 18, 1965	7	**Tennessee** Tulsa	27 6	7	Dewey Warren, Tennessee, QB Frank Emanuel, Tennessee, LB	40,000
1966	**GATOR**	Dec 31, 1966		**Tennessee** Syracuse	18 12		Dewey Warren, Tennessee, QB Floyd Little, Syracuse, HB	60,312
1967	**ORANGE**	Jan. 1, 1968	3 2	**Oklahoma** Tennessee	26 24		Bob Warmack, Oklahoma, QB	77,993
1968	**COTTON**	Jan. 1, 1969	5 8	**Texas** Tennessee	36 13	3 13	Tom Campbell, LB, Charles Speyrer, WR, James Street, QB, Texas	75,562
1969	**GATOR**	Dec. 27, 1969	15 11	**Florida** Tennessee	14 13	14 15	Mike Kelley, Florida, LB Curt Watson, Tennessee, FB	72,248
1970	**SUGAR**	Jan. 1, 1971	4 11	**Tennessee** Air Force	34 13	4 16	Bobby Scott, Tennessee, QB	82,113
1971	**LIBERTY**	Dec. 20, 1971	9 18	**Tennessee** Arkansas	14 13	9 16	Joe Ferguson, Arkansas, QB	51,140
1972	**BLUEBONNET**	Dec. 30, 1972	11 10	**Tennessee** LSU	24 17	8 11	Condredge Holloway, Tennessee, QB Carl Johnson, Tennessee, DE	52,961
1973	**GATOR**	Dec. 29, 1973	11 20	**Texas Tech** Tennessee	28 19	11 19	Joe Barnes, Texas Tech, QB Haskell Stanback, Tennessee, TB	62,109
1974	**LIBERTY**	Dec. 16, 1974	10	**Tennessee** Maryland	7 3	20 13	Randy White, Maryland, DT	51,284
1979	**BLUEBONNET**	Dec. 31, 1979	12	**Purdue** Tennessee	27 22	10	Mark Herrmann, Purdue, QB Roland James, Tennessee, DB	40,542
1981	**GARDEN STATE**	Dec. 13, 1981		**Tennessee** Wisconsin	28 21		S. Alatorre, QB, A. Hancock, WR, Tennessee Randy Wright, Wisconsin, QB	38,782
1982	**PEACH**	Dec. 31, 1982		**Iowa** Tennessee	28 22		Chuck Long, Iowa, QB Clay Uhlenhake, Iowa, DT	50,134
1983	**CITRUS**	Dec. 17, 1983	16	**Tennessee** Maryland	30 23		Johnnie Jones, Tennessee, RB	50,183
1984	**SUN**	Dec. 22, 1984	12	**Maryland** Tennessee	28 27	12	Rick Badanjek, Maryland, FB Carl Zander, Tennessee, LB	50,126
1985	**SUGAR**	Jan. 1, 1986	8 2	**Tennessee** Miami (Fla.)	35 7	4 9	Daryl Dickey, Tennessee, QB	77,432
1986	**LIBERTY**	Dec. 29, 1986		**Tennessee** Minnesota	21 14		Jeff Francis, Tennessee, QB	51,327
1987	**PEACH**	Jan. 2, 1988	17	**Tennessee** Indiana	27 12	14	Reggie Cobb, Tennessee, TB Van Waiters, Indiana, LB	58,737
1989	**COTTON**	Jan. 1, 1990	8 10	**Tennessee** Arkansas	31 27	5 13	Carl Pickens, Tennessee, FS Chuck Webb, Tennessee, TB	74,358
1990	**SUGAR**	Jan. 1, 1991	10	**Tennessee** Virginia	23 22	8 23	Andy Kelly, Tennessee, QB	75,132
1991	**FIESTA**	Jan. 1, 1992	6 10	**Penn State** Tennessee	42 17	3 14	O.J. McDuffie, Penn State, WR Reggie Givens, Penn State, OLB	71,133
1992	**HALL OF FAME**	Jan. 1, 1993	17 16	**Tennessee** Boston College	38 23	12 21	Heath Shuler, Tennessee, QB	52,056
1993	**CITRUS**	Jan. 1, 1994	13 6	**Penn State** Tennessee	31 13	8 12	Bobby Engram, Penn State, WR	72,456
1994	**GATOR**	Dec. 30, 1994	17	**Tennessee** Virginia Tech	45 23	22	James Stewart, Tennessee, TB Maurice DeShazo, Virginia Tech, QB	62,200
1995	**CITRUS**	Jan. 1, 1996	4T 4T	**Tennessee** Ohio State	20 14	3 6	Jay Graham, Tennessee, RB	70,797
1996	**CITRUS**	Jan. 1, 1997	9 11	**Tennessee** Northwestern	48 28	9 15	Peyton Manning, Tennessee, QB	63,467
1997	**ORANGE**	Jan. 2, 1998	2 3	**Nebraska** Tennessee	42 17	2 7	Ahman Green, Nebraska, RB	74,002
1998	**FIESTA**	Jan. 4, 1999	1 2	**Tennessee** Florida State	23 16	1 3	Peerless Price, Tennessee, WR Dwayne Goodrich, Tennessee, CB	80,470
1999	**FIESTA**	Jan. 2, 2000	3 6	**Nebraska** Tennessee	31 21	3 9	Eric Crouch, Nebraska, QB Mike Brown, Nebraska, DB	71,526
2000	**COTTON**	Jan. 1, 2001	11 21	**Kansas State** Tennessee	35 21	9	Jonathan Beasley, Kansas State, QB Chris Johnson, Kansas State, DE	63,465
2001	**CITRUS**	Jan. 1, 2002	8 17	**Tennessee** Michigan	45 17	4 20	Casey Clausen, Tennessee, QB	59,693
2002	**PEACH**	Dec. 31, 2002	20	**Maryland** Tennessee	30 3	13	Scott McBrien, Maryland, QB E.J. Henderson, Maryland, LB	68,330
2003	**PEACH**	Jan. 2, 2004		**Clemson** Tennessee	27 14	15 22	Chad Jasmin, Clemson, RB LeRoy Hill, Clemson, LB	75,125

THE SCHOOLS

SEASON	BOWL	DATE	PRE-GAME RANK	TEAMS	SCORE	FINAL RANK	MOST VALUABLE PLAYER(S)	ATT.
2004	**COTTON**	Jan. 1, 2005	15	**Tennessee**	**38**	13	Rick Clausen, Tennessee, QB	75,562
			22	Texas A&M	7		Justin Harrell, Tennessee, DT	
2006	**OUTBACK**	Jan. 1, 2007		**Penn State**	**20**	24	Tony Hunt, Penn State, RB	65,601
			17	Tennessee	10	25		
2007	**OUTBACK**	Jan. 1, 2008	16	**Tennessee**	**21**	12	Erik Ainge, Tennessee, QB	60,121
			18	Wisconsin	17	24		

JANUARY 2, 1939 | ORANGE
TENNESSEE 17, OKLAHOMA 0

	1ST	2ND	3RD	4TH	FINAL
TENN	7	3	0	7	17
OKLA	0	0	0	0	0

SCORING SUMMARY
TENN   Foxx 8 run (Wyatt kick)
TENN   FG Wyatt 22
TENN   Wood 19 run (Foxx Kick)

TENN	TEAM STATISTICS	OKLA
16	First Downs	5
217	Rushing Yards	25
5-16-0	Passing	9-26-1
51	Passing Yards	56
268	Total Yards	81
12-37.1	Punts - Average	13-40.6
2-2	Fumbles - Lost	2-2
17-157	Penalties - Yards	9-85

INDIVIDUAL LEADERS
RUSHING
TENN: Coffman 12-56; Cafego 13-45.
OKLA: McCullough 9-9.
PASSING
TENN: Wood 2-5-0, 40 yards.
OKLA: McCullough 7-19-1, 37 yards.
RECEIVING
TENN: Cifers 1-23.
OKLA: Clark 3-30.

JANUARY 1, 1940 | ROSE
USC 14, TENNESSEE 0

	1ST	2ND	3RD	4TH	FINAL
USC	0	7	0	7	14
TENN	0	0	0	0	0

SCORING SUMMARY
USC   Schindler 1 run (Jones kick)
USC   Krueger 1 pass from Schindler (Gaspar kick)

USC	TEAM STATISTICS	TENN
18	First Downs	9
229	Rushing Yards	71
7-14-1	Passing	6-14-2
43	Passing Yards	70
272	Total Yards	141
8-40.1	Punts - Average	11-39.2
1-0	Fumbles - Lost	1-1

INDIVIDUAL LEADERS
RUSHING
USC: Schindler 19-75, 1 TD; Lansdell 18-68.
TENN: Butler 5-40; Coffman 3-15.

JANUARY 1, 1941 | SUGAR
BOSTON COLLEGE 19, TENNESSEE 13

	1ST	2ND	3RD	4TH	FINAL
BC	0	0	13	6	19
TENN	7	0	6	0	13

SCORING SUMMARY
TENN   Thompson 4 run (Foxx kick)
BC   Connally 13 run (Maznicki kick)
TENN   Warren 2 run (kick failed)
BC   Holovak 1 run (kick failed)
BC   O'Rourke 24 run (kick failed)

BC	TEAM STATISTICS	TENN
11	First Downs	13
142	Rushing Yards	124
6-14-3	Passing	9-22-2
106	Passing Yards	121
248	Total Yards	245
6-35.0	Punts - Average	7-36.0
1-1	Fumbles - Lost	1-1
3-25	Penalties - Yards	4-36

INDIVIDUAL LEADERS
RUSHING
BC: O'Rourke 7-52, 1 TD.
TENN: Fozz 7-41; Thompson 11-40, 1 TD.
PASSING
BC: O'Rourke 5-11-2, 85 yards.
TENN: Thompson 4-9-1, 42 yards.
RECEIVING
BC: Zabilski 2-39.
TENN: Coleman 3-49.

JANUARY 1, 1943 | SUGAR
TENNESSEE 14, TULSA 7

	1ST	2ND	3RD	4TH	FINAL
TENN	0	6	2	6	14
TUL	0	7	0	0	7

SCORING SUMMARY
TUL   Purdin 9 pass from Dobbs (LaForce kick)
TENN   Gold 3 run (kick failed)
TENN   Safey (Crawford blocked punt out of end zone)
TENN   Fuson 1 run (kick failed)

TENN	TEAM STATISTICS	TUL
14	First Downs	10
208	Rushing Yards	-39
7-17-0	Passing	17-27-2
88	Passing Yards	168
296	Total Yards	129
2-2	Fumbles - Lost	0-0

JANUARY 1, 1945 | ROSE
USC 25, TENNESSEE 0

	1ST	2ND	3RD	4TH	FINAL
TENN	0	0	0	0	0
USC	6	6	0	13	25

SCORING SUMMARY
USC   Callahan 11 blocked punt (kick failed)
USC   Salata 19 pass from Hardy (kick failed)
USC   Hardy 9 run (West kick)
USC   MacLachan 7 run (kick failed)

TENN	TEAM STATISTICS	USC
8	First Downs	15
152	Rushing Yards	262
3-14-1	Passing	5-15-0
17	Passing Yards	43
169	Total Yards	305
13-32.2	Punts - Average	11-32.6
2-1	Fumbles - Lost	1-1
5-35	Penalties - Yards	4-25

INDIVIDUAL LEADERS
RUSHING
TENN: Stephens 15-89; Manning 5-28.
USC: Burnside 13-114.

JANUARY 1, 1947 | ORANGE
RICE 8, TENNESSEE 0

	1ST	2ND	3RD	4TH	FINAL
RICE	8	0	0	0	8
TENN	0	0	0	0	0

SCORING SUMMARY
RICE   Safety (Murphy blocks punt out of endzone)
RICE   Kenney 50 run (kick failed)

RICE	TEAM STATISTICS	TENN
9	First Downs	5
208	Rushing Yards	105
0-4-2	Passing	4-19-4
0	Passing Yards	32
208	Total Yards	137
13-44.0	Punts - Average	15-38.8
4-3	Fumbles - Lost	2-0
4-40	Penalties - Yards	6-67

JANUARY 1, 1951 | COTTON
TENNESSEE 20, TEXAS 14

	1ST	2ND	3RD	4TH	FINAL
TENN	7	0	0	13	20
TEX	0	14	0	0	14

SCORING SUMMARY
TENN   Gruble 5 pass from Payne (Shires kick)
TEX   Townsend 5 run (Tompkins kick)
TEX   Dawson 35 pass from Tompkins (Tompkins kick)
TENN   Kozar 5 run (kick failed)
TENN   Kozar 1 run (Shires kick)

TENN	TEAM STATISTICS	TEX
18	First Downs	12
295	Rushing Yards	146
3-8-2	Passing	5-14-1
45	Passing Yards	97
340	Total Yards	243
6-32.8	Punts - Average	7-29.3
4-1	Fumbles - Lost	1-1
4-35	Penalties - Yards	5-55

INDIVIDUAL LEADERS
RUSHING
TENN: Lauricella 16-131; Kozar 20-92, 2 TD.
TEX: Townsend 23-105, 1 TD; Dawson 8-42.
PASSING
TENN: Lauricella 1-6-2, 23 yards; Rechichar 1-1-0, 18 yards.
TEX: Tompkins 5-14-1, 97 yards, 1 TD.
RECEIVING
TENN: Rechichar 1-23; Lauricella 1-18.
TEX: Dawson 2-65, 1 TD; Stolhandske 3-32.

JANUARY 1, 1952 | SUGAR
MARYLAND 28, TENNESSEE 13

	1ST	2ND	3RD	4TH	FINAL
MARY	7	14	7	0	28
TENN	0	6	0	7	13

SCORING SUMMARY
MARY   Fullerton 2 run (Decker kick)
MARY   Shemonski 6 pass from Fullerton (Decker kick)
MARY   Scarbath 1 run (Decker kick)
TENN   Rechichar 4 pass from Payne (kick failed)
MARY   Fullerton 46 interception (Decker kick)
TENN   Payne 2 run (Rechichar kick)

MARY	TEAM STATISTICS	TENN
18	First Downs	12
289	Rushing Yards	81
7-13-1	Passing	9-19-4
62	Passing Yards	75
351	Total Yards	156
8-38.8	Punts - Average	7-43.0
7-3	Fumbles-Lost	2-2
12-120	Penalty Yards	2-20

INDIVIDUAL LEADERS
RUSHING
MARY: Modzelewski 28-153.
TENN: Payne 11-54, 1 TD; Kozar 9-29.
PASSING
MARY: Scarbath 6-9-0, 57 yards.
TENN: Payne 7-14-1, 61 yards, 1 TD.
RECEIVING
MARY: Shemonski 3-19, 1 TD.
TENN: Rechichar 3-27, 1 TD.

JANUARY 1, 1953 | COTTON
TEXAS 16, TENNESSEE 0

	1ST	2ND	3RD	4TH	FINAL
TENN	0	0	0	0	0
TEX	2	7	0	7	16

SCORING SUMMARY
TEX Safety (Griffith tackled by Massey in end zone)
TEX Dawson 4 run (Dawson kick)
TEX Quinn 1 run (Dawson kick)

TENN	TEAM STATISTICS	TEX
6	First Downs	20
-14	Rushing Yards	269
3-6-0	Passing	2-8-1
46	Passing Yards	32
32	Total Yards	301
7-40.9	Punts - Average	5-35.4
5-3	Fumbles - Lost	5-3
3-30	Penalties - Yards	5-55

INDIVIDUAL LEADERS
RUSHING
TENN: Schwanger 5-22; Wade 7-4.
TEX: Ochoa 26-108; Quinn 19-67, 1 TD.
PASSING
TENN: Shires 2-4-0, 23 yards.
TEX: Jones 2-5-1, 32 yards.
RECEIVING
TENN: Morgan 2-23; Kolenik 1-23.
TEX: Quinn 1-23; Spring 1-9.

JANUARY 1, 1957 | SUGAR
BAYLOR 13, TENNESSEE 7

	1ST	2ND	3RD	4TH	FINAL
BU	0	6	0	7	13
TENN	0	0	7	0	7

SCORING SUMMARY
BU Marcontell 12 pass from Jones (kick failed)
TENN Majors 1 run (Burklow kick)
BU Humphrey 1 run (Berry kick)

BU	TEAM STATISTICS	TENN
13	First Downs	10
275	Rushing Yards	146
3-11-0	Passing	1-10-4
24	Passing Yards	16
299	Total Yards	162
8-32.6	Punts - Average	5-41.6
60	Penalty Yards	55

INDIVIDUAL LEADERS
RUSHING
BU: Shofner 14-88.
TENN: Majors 15-59, 1 TD; Bronson 8-56.
PASSING
BU: Jones 2-4-0, 19 yards, 1 TD.
TENN: Majors 1-7-2, 16 yards.
RECEIVING
BU: Marcontell 3-24, 1 TD.
TENN: Urbano 1-16.

DECEMBER 28, 1957 | GATOR
TENNESSEE 3, TEXAS A&M 0

	1ST	2ND	3RD	4TH	FINAL
TENN	0	0	0	3	3
A&M	0	0	0	0	0

SCORING SUMMARY
TENN FG Burklow 17

TENN	TEAM STATISTICS	A&M
14	First Downs	8
135	Rushing Yards	142
4-6-0	Passing	3-8-0
56	Passing Yards	27
191	Total Yards	169
8-36.0	Punts - Average	7-38.0
2-1	Fumbles - Lost	2-2
3-30	Penalties - Yards	3-35

INDIVIDUAL LEADERS
RUSHING
TENN: Gordon 32-60; Bronson 11-31.
A&M: Crow 14-46; Osborne 12-31.
PASSING
TENN: Gordon 4-6-0, 56 yards.
A&M: Milstead 2-5-0, 16 yards.
RECEIVING
TENN: Darty 2-26; Anderson 1-20.
A&M: Smith 1-11; Marks 1-11.

DECEMBER 18, 1965 | BLUEBONNET
TENNESSEE 27, TULSA 6

	1ST	2ND	3RD	4TH	FINAL
TENN	6	14	7	0	27
TUL	6	0	0	0	6

SCORING SUMMARY
TENN Wantland 4 pass from Warren (kick failed)
TUL McDermott 1 run (kick failed)
TENN Warren 1 run (Leake kick)
TENN Warren 1 run (Leake kick)
TENN Mitchell 11 run (Leake kick)

TENN	TEAM STATISTICS	TUL
11	First Downs	16
181	Rushing Yards	73
3-7-1	Passing	23-47-4
37	Passing Yards	250
218	Total Yards	323
6-42.8	Punts - Average	5-35.0
4-2	Fumbles - Lost	3-3
8-80	Penalties - Yards	1-15

INDIVIDUAL LEADERS
RUSHING
TENN: Warren 18-39, 2 TD; Mitchell 7-49, 1 TD.
TUL: McDermott 7-37, 1 TD; Lakusiak 9-18.
PASSING
TENN: Warren 3-7-1, 37 yards, 1 TD.
TUL: Anderson 23-47-4, 250 yards.
RECEIVING
TENN: Wantland 2-24, 1 TD.
TUL: Twilley 8-78; McDermott 7-74.

DECEMBER 31, 1966 | GATOR
TENNESSEE 18, SYRACUSE 12

	1ST	2ND	3RD	4TH	FINAL
TENN	3	15	0	0	18
SYR	0	0	6	6	12

SCORING SUMMARY
TENN FG Wright 36
TENN FG Wright 38
TENN Denney 24 pass from Warren (pass failed)
TENN Flowers 2 pass from Warren (kick failed)
SYR Csonka 8 run (run failed)
SYR Little 3 run (run failed)

TENN	TEAM STATISTICS	SYR
14	First Downs	20
85	Rushing Yards	348
17-29-1	Passing	2-7-3
244	Passing Yards	16
329	Total Yards	364
3-43.0	Punts - Average	2-39.5
2-2	Fumbles - Lost	3-1
4-44	Penalties - Yards	7-79

INDIVIDUAL LEADERS
RUSHING
TENN: Chadwick 12-47; Pickens 6-36.
SYR: Little 29-216, 1 TD; Csonka 18-114, 1 TD.
PASSING
TENN: Warren 17-29-1, 244 yards, 2 TD.
SYR: Cassata 2-7-3, 16 yards.
RECEIVING
TENN: Mills 8-86; Flowers 5-80, 1 TD.
SYR: Little 2-16.

JANUARY 1, 1968 | ORANGE
OKLAHOMA 26, TENNESSEE 24

	1ST	2ND	3RD	4TH	FINAL
OKLA	7	12	0	7	26
TENN	0	0	14	10	24

SCORING SUMMARY
OKLA Warmack 7 run (Vachon kick)
OKLA Hinton 20 pass from Warmack (kick failed)
OKLA Owens 1 run (run failed)
TENN Glover 36 interception return (Kremser kick)
TENN Fulton 5 run (Kremser kick)
OKLA Stephenson 25 interception return (Vachon kick)
TENN FG Kremser 26
TENN Warren 1 run (Kremser kick)

OKLA	TEAM STATISTICS	TENN
18	First Downs	18
203	Rushing Yards	172
9-18-2	Passing	12-24-3
107	Passing Yards	160
310	Total Yards	332
5-47.0	Punts - Average	2-32.0
0-0	Fumbles - Lost	1-1
2-10	Penalties - Yards	4-27

INDIVIDUAL LEADERS
RUSHING
OKLA: Warmack 17-81, 1 TD; Owens 17-61, 1 TD.
TENN: Chadwick 12-72.
PASSING
OKLA: Warmack, 9-18-2, 107 yards, 1 TD.
TENN: Warren 12-23-2. 160 yards.
RECEIVING
OKLA: Hinton 5-87, 1 TD.
TENN: Flowers 4-59; DeLong 4-53.

JANUARY 1, 1969 | COTTON
TEXAS 36, TENNESSEE 13

	1ST	2ND	3RD	4TH	FINAL
TENN	0	0	7	6	13
TEX	13	15	8	0	36

SCORING SUMMARY
TEX Worster 14 run (Feller kick)
TEX Speyrer 78 pass from Street (kick failed)
TEX Koy 9 run (Feller kick)
TEX Gilbert 5 run (Speyrer pass from Street)
TENN Kreis 17 pass from Scott (Kremser kick)
TEX Speyrer 79 pass from Street (Bradley run)
TENN Price 3 pass from Scott (pass failed)

TENN	TEAM STATISTICS	TEX
16	First Downs	22
83	Rushing Yards	279
16-41-3	Passing	8-14-1
192	Passing Yards	234
275	Total Yards	513
8-42.1	Punts - Average	7-40.7
5-0	Fumbles - Lost	3-2
4-17	Penalties - Yards	5-60

INDIVIDUAL LEADERS
RUSHING
TENN: Pearce 2-26; Pickens 8-20.
TEX: Worster 10-85, 1 TD; Gilbert 13-82, 1 TD.
PASSING
TENN: Scott 11-30-3, 159 yards, 2 TD.
TEX: Street 7-13-1, 200 yards, 2 TD.
RECEIVING
TENN: Kreis 3-77, 1 TD; McClain 3-57.
TEX: Speyrer 5-161, 2 TD; Bradley 1-34.

THE SCHOOLS

DECEMBER 27, 1969 | GATOR
FLORIDA 14, TENNESSEE 13

	1ST	2ND	3RD	4TH	FINAL
UF	7	0	7	0	14
TENN	0	10	0	3	13

SCORING SUMMARY
UF Kelley 8 blocked punt return (Franco kick)
TENN FG Hunt 20
TENN McClain 12 pass from Scott (Hunt kick)
UF Alvarez 9 pass from Reaves (Franco kick)
TENN FG Hunt 26

UF	TEAM STATISTICS	TENN
15	First Downs	23
90	Rushing Yards	214
15-27-0	Passing	12-34-2
161	Passing Yards	174
251	Total Yards	388
7-31.3	Punts - Average	2-15.0
1-1	Fumbles - Lost	1-1
2-58	Penalties - Yards	3-24

INDIVIDUAL LEADERS
RUSHING
UF: Murrance 22-62; Walker 10-33.
TENN: Watson 25-121; Patterson 8-40.
PASSING
UF: Reaves 15-26-0, 161 yards, 1 TD.
TENN: Scott 12-34-2, 174 yards, 1 TD.
RECEIVING
UF: Maliska 6-54; Alvarez 4-51, 1 TD.
TENN: Kreis 4-82; DeLong 5-50.

JANUARY 1, 1971 | SUGAR
TENNESSEE 34, AIR FORCE 13

	1ST	2ND	3RD	4TH	FINAL
TENN	24	0	7	3	34
AFA	7	0	6	0	13

SCORING SUMMARY
TENN McLeary 5 run (Hunt kick)
TENN FG Hunt 30
TENN McLeary 20 run (Hunt kick)
TENN Theiler 10 pass from Scott (Hunt kick)
AFA Haas fumble recovery (Barry kick)
TENN Majors 57 punt return (Hunt kick)
AFA Bassa 27 pass from Parker (kick failed)
TENN FG Hunt 33

TENN	TEAM STATISTICS	AFA
24	First Downs	15
86	Rushing Yards	-12
24-46-2	Passing	23-46-4
306	Passing Yards	239
392	Total Yards	227
5-31.4	Punts - Average	8-34.5
7-3	Fumbles - Lost	7-4
8-74	Penalties - Yards	0

INDIVIDUAL LEADERS
RUSHING
TENN: Watson 14-57; McLeary 14-39, 2 TD.
AFA: Bream 16-16.
PASSING
TENN: Scott 22-40-2, 288 yards, 1 TD.
AFA: Parker 23-46-4, 239 yards, 1 TD.
RECEIVING
TENN: Thompson 9-125.
AFA: Bassa 10-114, 1 TD; Bolen 6-60.

DECEMBER 20, 1971 | LIBERTY
TENNESSEE 14, ARKANSAS 13

	1ST	2ND	3RD	4TH	FINAL
TENN	7	0	0	7	14
ARK	0	7	0	6	13

SCORING SUMMARY
TENN Rudder 2 run (Hunt kick)
ARK Hodge 36 pass from Ferguson (McClard kick)
ARK FG McClard 19
ARK FG McClard 30
TENN Watson 17 run (Hunt kick)

TENN	TEAM STATISTICS	ARK
15	First Downs	22
97	Rushing Yards	167
11-21-3	Passing	18-28-3
142	Passing Yards	200
239	Total Yards	367
5-43.8	Punts - Average	3-43.6
1-1	Fumbles - Lost	2-2
7-73	Penalties - Yards	6-85

INDIVIDUAL LEADERS
RUSHING
TENN: Watson 11-39, 1 TD; Chauncey 12-34.
ARK: Saint 17-71.
PASSING
TENN: Maxwell 20-30-3, 120 yards.
ARK: Ferguson 18-28-3, 200 yards, 1 TD.
RECEIVING
TENN: Theiler 3-53.
ARK: Hodge 6-75, 1 TD.

DECEMBER 30, 1972 | BLUEBONNET
TENNESSEE 24, LSU 17

	1ST	2ND	3RD	4TH	FINAL
TENN	14	10	0	0	24
LSU	3	0	7	7	17

SCORING SUMMARY
LSU FG Jackson 29
TENN Young 6 pass from Holloway (Townsend kick)
TENN Holloway 15 run (Townsend kick)
TENN FG Townsend 33
TENN Holloway 10 run (Townsend kick)
LSU Jones 2 run (Jackson kick)
LSU Davis 1 run (Jackson kick)

TENN	TEAM STATISTICS	LSU
17	First Downs	18
179	Rushing Yards	187
11-19-1	Passing	7-20-1
94	Passing Yards	90
273	Total Yards	277
6-41.2	Punts - Average	5-37.0
0-0	Fumbles - Lost	1-0
4-35	Penalties - Yards	3-35

INDIVIDUAL LEADERS
RUSHING
TENN: Holloway 19-74, 2 TD; Chancey 13-73.
LSU: Davis 16-88, 1 TD.
PASSING
TENN: Holloway 11-19-1, 94 yards, 1 TD.
LSU: Jones 7-19-0, 90 yards.
RECEIVING
TENN: Stanback 4-41.
LSU: Boyd 2-33.

DECEMBER 29, 1973 | GATOR
TEXAS TECH 28, TENNESSEE 19

	1ST	2ND	3RD	4TH	FINAL
TT	7	7	7	7	28
TENN	0	3	10	6	19

SCORING SUMMARY
TT Barnes 7 run (Grimes kick)
TT Williams 79 pass from Barnes (Grimes kick)
TENN FG Townsend 30
TENN Stanback 5 run (Townsend kick)
TT Tillman 7 pass from Barnes (Grimes kick)
TENN FG Townsend 37
TENN Stanback 7 pass from Holloway (pass failed)
TT Isaac 3 run (Grimes kick)

TT	TEAM STATISTICS	TENN
19	First Downs	18
276	Rushing Yards	153
8-11-0	Passing	17-28-1
154	Passing Yards	190
430	Total Yards	343
6-40.9	Punts - Average	4-40.5
3-1	Fumbles - Lost	1-1
5-55	Penalties - Yards	1-3

INDIVIDUAL LEADERS
RUSHING
TT: Mosley 8-85; Barnes 16-73, 1 TD.
TENN: Stanback 19-95, 1 TD; Chancey 11-53.
PASSING
TT: Barnes 8-11-0, 154 yards, 2 TD.
TENN: Holloway 17-27-1, 190 yards, 1 TD.
RECEIVING
TT: Williams 3-94, 1 TD; Tillman 2-30, 1 TD.
TENN: Yarbrough 4-28; Howard 3-18.

DECEMBER 16, 1974 | LIBERTY
TENNESSEE 7, MARYLAND 3

	1ST	2ND	3RD	4TH	FINAL
TENN	0	0	0	7	7
MARY	0	3	0	0	3

SCORING SUMMARY
MARY FG Mayer 28
TENN Seivers 11 pass from Wallace (Townsend kick)

TENN	TEAM STATISTICS	MARY
15	First Downs	16
173	Rushing Yards	108
7-16-0	Passing	15-24-2
65	Passing Yards	158
238	Total Yards	266
7-39.1	Punts - Average	6-41.0
4-2	Fumbles - Lost	3-3
8-69	Penalties - Yards	4-63

INDIVIDUAL LEADERS
RUSHING
TENN: Gayles 17-106.
MARY: Carter 22-65.
PASSING
TENN: Holloway 6-15-0, 54 yards.
MARY: Avellini 15-22-2, 158 yards.
RECEIVING
TENN: Seivers 4-38, 1 TD.
MARY: Carter 6-68.

DECEMBER 31, 1979 | BLUEBONNET
PURDUE 27, TENNESSEE 22

	1ST	2ND	3RD	4TH	FINAL
PUR	0	14	7	6	27
TENN	0	0	6	16	22

SCORING SUMMARY
PUR   McCall 6 run (Seibel kick)
PUR   Burrell 12 pass from Herrmann (Seibel kick)
PUR   Young 12 pass from Herrmann (Seibel kick)
TENN Ford 8 pass from Streater (pass failed)
TENN Berry 15 pass from Ingram (Simpson run)
TENN Simpson 1 run (Simpson pass from Streater)
PUR   Young 17 pass from Herrmann (pass failed)

PUR	TEAM STATISTICS	TENN
31	First Downs	19
180	Rushing Yards	146
21-39-0	Passing	17-36-3
303	Passing Yards	234
483	Total Yards	380
7-43.6	Punts - Average	6-38.0
2-1	Fumbles - Lost	3-2
3-25	Penalties - Yards	7-56

INDIVIDUAL LEADERS
RUSHING
PUR: McCall 18-91, 1 TD.
TENN: Simpson 16-47, 1 TD.
PASSING
PUR: Herrmann 21-39-0, 303 yards, 3 TD.
TENN: Streater 16-34-3, 219 yards, 1 TD.
RECEIVING
PUR: Burrell 8-144, 1 TD.
TENN: Gault 4-22.

DECEMBER 13, 1981 | GARDEN STATE
TENNESSEE 28, WISCONSIN 21

	1ST	2ND	3RD	4TH	FINAL
TENN	13	8	0	7	28
WISC	7	0	0	14	21

SCORING SUMMARY
TENN FG Reveiz 22
WISC Cole 3 run (Doran kick)
TENN Gault 87 kickoff return (Reveiz kick)
TENN FG Reveiz 48
TENN Hancock 43 pass from Alatorre (Cofer pass from Alatorre)
WISC Nault 6 pass from Wright (Doran kick)
TENN Alatorre 6 run (Reveiz kick)
WISC McFadden 11 pass from Wright (Doran kick)

TENN	TEAM STATISTICS	WISC
27	First Downs	22
89	Rushing Yards	177
24-42-0	Passing	14-37-3
315	Passing Yards	212
404	Total Yards	389
6-45.2	Punts - Average	6-36.7
4-0	Fumbles - Lost	1-1
8-84	Penalties - Yards	6-73

INDIVIDUAL LEADERS
RUSHING
TENN: Berry 10-44; Morris 10-39.
WISC: Davis 6-44; Cole 9-39, 1 TD.
PASSING
TENN: Alatorre 24-42-0, 315 yards, 1 TD.
WISC: Wright 9-21-1, 123 yards, 2 TD.
RECEIVING
TENN: Hancock 11-196, 1 TD; Miller 4-42.
WISC: Nault 5-85, 1 TD; McFadden 3-74, 1 TD.

DECEMBER 31, 1982 | PEACH
IOWA 28, TENNESSEE 22

	1ST	2ND	3RD	4TH	FINAL
IA	0	21	7	0	28
TENN	7	0	12	3	22

SCORING SUMMARY
TENN Cockrell 6 run (Reveiz kick)
IA   Moritz 57 pass from Long (Nichol kick)
IA   Harmon 18 pass from Long (Nichol kick)
IA   Harmon 8 pass from Long (Nichol kick)
TENN Coleman 10 run (kick failed)
IA   Phillips 2 run (Nichol kick)
TENN Gault 19 pass from Cockrell (pass failed)
TENN FG Reveiz 27

IA	TEAM STATISTICS	TENN
24	First Downs	23
110	Rushing Yards	154
19-26-1	Passing	22-41-0
304	Passing Yards	221
414	Total Yards	375
5-35.0	Punts - Average	5-45.0
1-1	Fumbles - Lost	2-1
3-30	Penalties - Yards	7-47

INDIVIDUAL LEADERS
RUSHING
IA: Gill 16-70; Phillips 10-34, 1 TD.
TENN: Coleman 11-103, 1 TD; Fumas 12-52.
PASSING
IA: Long 19-26-1, 304 yards, 3 TD.
TENN: Cockrell 22-41-0, 221 yards, 1 TD.
RECEIVING
IA: Moritz 8-168, 1 TD; Harmon 3-44, 2 TD.
TENN: Wilson 7-62; Duncan 3-52.

DECEMBER 17, 1983 | CITRUS
TENNESSEE 30, MARYLAND 23

	1ST	2ND	3RD	4TH	FINAL
TENN	7	3	6	14	30
MD	3	6	11	3	23

SCORING SUMMARY
MD   FG Atkinson 18
TENN Taylor 12 pass from Cockrell (Reveiz kick)
MD   FG Atkinson 36
MD   FG Atkinson 31
TENN FG Reveiz 25
MD   FG Atkinson 22
TENN Henderson 19 run (pass failed)
MD   Badanjek 3 run (Badanjek run)
TENN Jones 1 run (Reveiz kick)
TENN Jones 2 run (Reveiz kick)
MD   FG Atkinson 26

TENN	TEAM STATISTICS	MD
25	First Downs	17
201	Rushing Yards	95
16-23-1	Passing	18-28-1
185	Passing Yards	253
386	Total Yards	348
1-47.0	Punts - Average	0-0.0
1-1	Fumbles - Lost	3-1
1-5	Penalties - Yards	6-32

INDIVIDUAL LEADERS
RUSHING
TENN: Jones 29-154, 2 TD; Henderson 11-57, 1 TD.
MD: Joyner 17-58; Badanjek 14-44, 1 TD.
PASSING
TENN: Cockrell 16-23-1, 185 yards, 1 TD.
MD: Reich 14-22-1, 192 yards; Esiason 4-6-0, 61 yards.
RECEIVING
TENN: Duncan 6-59; Taylor 4-68, 1 TD.
MD: Davis 4-66; Joyner 4-65.

DECEMBER 22, 1984 | SUN
MARYLAND 28, TENNESSEE 27

	1ST	2ND	3RD	4TH	FINAL
MD	0	0	22	6	28
TENN	10	11	6	0	27

SCORING SUMMARY
TENN Jones 2 run (Reveiz kick)
TENN FG Reveiz 24
TENN FG Reveiz 52
TENN McGee 6 pass from Robinson (McGee pass from Robinson)
MD   Neal 57 run (pass failed)
MD   FG Atkinson 23
MD   Badanjek 1 run (run failed)
MD   Edmunds 40 pass from Reich (Atkinson kick)
TENN Panuska 100 kickoff return (pass failed)
MD   Badanjek 1 run (pass failed)

MD	TEAM STATISTICS	TENN
22	First Downs	13
229	Rushing Yards	148
17-28-1	Passing	15-24-0
201	Passing Yards	132
430	Total Yards	280
4-56	Punt Returns - Yards	3-24
4-47.0	Punts - Average	5-42.0
2-2	Fumbles - Lost	1-0
8-63	Penalties - Yards	6-49
35:57	Possession Time	24:03

INDIVIDUAL LEADERS
RUSHING
MD: Neal 12-107, 1 TD; Badanjek 21-90, 2 TD.
TENN: Jones 16-69, 1 TD; Robinson 8-43.
PASSING
MD: Reich 17-28-1, 201 yards, 1 TD.
TENN: Robinson 15-24 -0, 132 yards, 1 TD.
RECEIVING
MD: Hill 4-69; Edmunds 3-53, 1 TD.
TENN: McGee 6-66, 1 TD; Howard 3-22.

JANUARY 1, 1986 | SUGAR
TENNESSEE 35, MIAMI (FLA.) 7

	1ST	2ND	3RD	4TH	FINAL
TENN	0	14	14	7	35
MIA	7	0	0	0	7

SCORING SUMMARY
MIA   Irvin 18 pass from Testaverde (Cox kick)
TENN Smith 6 pass from Dickey (Reveiz kick)
TENN McGee fumble recovery (Reveiz kick)
TENN Henderson 1 run (Reveiz kick)
TENN Powell 60 run (Reveiz kick)
TENN Wilson 6 run (Reveiz kick)

TENN	TEAM STATISTICS	MIA
16	First Downs	22
211	Rushing Yards	95
15-25-1	Passing	23-44-4
131	Passing Yards	237
342	Total Yards	332
6-39.1	Punts - Average	6-37.6
2-1	Fumbles - Lost	5-2
11-125	Penalties - Yards	15-120
31:01	Possession Time	28:59

INDIVIDUAL LEADERS
RUSHING
TENN: Powell 11-104, 1 TD.
MIA: Williams 8-45.
PASSING
TENN: Dickey 15-25-1, 131 yards, 1 TD.
MIA: Testaverde 20-36-3, 217 yards, 1 TD.
RECEIVING
TENN: McGee 7-94.
MIA: Irvin 5-91, TD; Perriman 5-43.

THE SCHOOLS

THE SCHOOLS

December 29, 1986 | Liberty
Tennessee 21, Minnesota 14

	1ST	2ND	3RD	4TH	FINAL
TENN	7	7	0	7	21
MINN	0	3	8	3	14

SCORING SUMMARY

TENN	Clinkscales 18 pass from Francis (Reveiz kick)
TENN	Howard 23 pass from Francis (Reveiz kick)
MINN	FG Lohmiller 27
MINN	Foggie 11 run (Thompson run)
MINN	FG Lohmiller 25
TENN	Clinkscales 15 pass from Francis (Reveiz kick)

TENN	TEAM STATISTICS	MINN
17	First Downs	20
81	Rushing Yards	238
22-31-0	Passing	10-25-0
243	Passing Yards	136
324	Total Yards	374
5-38.4	Punts - Average	3-39.7
4-1	Fumbles - Lost	2-2
5-49	Penalties - Yards	5-30
28:40	Possession Time	31:20

INDIVIDUAL LEADERS

RUSHING
TENN: Howard 16-63.
MINN: Thompson 25-136.

PASSING
TENN: Francis 22-31-0, 243 yards, 3 TD.
MINN: Foggie 10-25-0, 136 yards.

RECEIVING
TENN: Clinkscales 7-72, 2 TD; Miller 6-72.
MINN: Anderson 3-31.

January 2, 1988 | Peach
Tennessee 27, Indiana 22

	1ST	2ND	3RD	4TH	FINAL
TENN	14	7	0	6	27
IU	3	7	6	6	22

SCORING SUMMARY

TENN	Cobb 6 run (Reich kick)
IU	FG Stoyanovich 52
TENN	Miller 45 pass from Francis (Reich kick)
TENN	Cleveland 15 pass from Francis (Reich kick)
IU	Jones 43 pass from Schnell (Stoyanovich kick)
IU	Thompson 12 run (pass failed)
IU	Jorden 12 run (pass failed)
TENN	Cobb 9 run (pass failed)

TENN	TEAM STATISTICS	IU
26	First Downs	16
244	Rushing Yards	96
21-27-0	Passing	18-33-2
230	Passing Yards	218
474	Total Yards	314
2-36.0	Punts - Average	6-30.0
2-2	Fumbles - Lost	0-0
5-35	Penalties - Yards	4-37
33:19	Possession Time	26:41

INDIVIDUAL LEADERS

RUSHING
TENN: Cobb 21-146, 2 TD; Davis 9-51.
IU: Thompson 18-67, 1 TD.

PASSING
TENN: Francis 20-26-0, 225 yards, 2 TD.
IU: Schnell 18-33-2, 218 yards, 1 TD.

RECEIVING
TENN: Miller 5-78, 1 TD; Woods 4-43.
IU: Jones 7-150, 1 TD; Thompson 6-28.

January 1, 1990 | Cotton
Tennessee 31, Arkansas 27

	1ST	2ND	3RD	4TH	FINAL
TENN	3	14	14	0	31
ARK	6	0	7	14	27

SCORING SUMMARY

TENN	FG Burke 23
ARK	Foster 1 run (run failed)
TENN	Morgan 84 pass from Kelly (Burke kick)
TENN	Webb 1 run (Burke kick)
TENN	Amsler 1 pass from Kelly (Burke kick)
ARK	Rouse 1 run (Wright kick)
TENN	Webb 78 run (Burke kick)
ARK	Foster 1 run (Foster run)
ARK	Winston 67 pass from Grovey (pass failed)

TENN	TEAM STATISTICS	ARK
16	First Downs	31
320	Rushing Yards	361
9-23-2	Passing	12-22-1
150	Passing Yards	207
470	Total Yards	568
5-39.0	Punts - Average	3-44.3
0-0	Fumbles - Lost	3-2
4-36	Penalties - Yards	3-20
22:17	Possession Time	37:43

INDIVIDUAL LEADERS

RUSHING
TENN: Webb 26-250, 2 TD; Moore 1-36.
ARK: Rouse 22-134, 1 TD; Foster 22-103, 2 TD.

PASSING
TENN: Kelly 9-23-2, 150 yards, 2 TD.
ARK: Grovey 12-22-1, 207 yards, 1 TD.

RECEIVING
TENN: Morgan 2-96, 1 TD; Harper 2-28.
ARK: Russell 7-105; Winston 4-94, 1 TD.

January 1, 1991 | Sugar
Tennessee 23, Virginia 22

	1ST	2ND	3RD	4TH	FINAL
TENN	0	0	3	20	23
UVA	9	7	0	6	22

SCORING SUMMARY

UVA	Steele 10 run (kick blocked)
UVA	FG McInerney 22
UVA	Kirby 1 run (McInerney kick)
TENN	FG Burke 27
TENN	Thompson 7 run (Burke kick)
UVA	FG McInerney 43
TENN	Pickens 15 pass from Kelly (Burke kick)
UVA	FG McInerney 44
TENN	Thompson 1 run (pass failed)

TENN	TEAM STATISTICS	UVA
28	First Downs	25
191	Rushing Yards	287
24-35-2	Passing	9-24-3
273	Passing Yards	62
464	Total Yards	349
2-20.0	Punts - Average	1-48.0
1-1	Fumbles - Lost	1-0
5-65	Penalties - Yards	5-30
23:32	Possession Time	36:28

INDIVIDUAL LEADERS

RUSHING
TENN: Thompson 25-154, 2 TD.
UVA: Fisher 15-90; Moore 11-76; Kirby 21-75, 1 TD.

PASSING
TENN: Kelly 24-35-2, 273 yards, 1 TD.
UVA: Moore 9-22-2, 62 yards.

RECEIVING
TENN: Moore 7-97; Pickens 6-87, 1 TD.
UVA: Kirby 4-27.

January 1, 1992 | Fiesta
Penn State 42, Tennessee 17

	1ST	2ND	3RD	4TH	FINAL
PSU	7	0	14	21	42
TENN	10	0	7	0	17

SCORING SUMMARY

PSU	Gash 10 pass from Sacca (Fayak kick)
TENN	Stewart 1 run (Becksvoort kick)
TENN	FG Becksvoort 24
TENN	Fleming 44 pass from Kelly (Becksvoort kick)
PSU	LaBarca 3 pass from Sacca (Fayak kick)
PSU	Brady 13 pass from Sacca (Fayak kick)
PSU	Anderson 2 run (Fayak kick)
PSU	Givens 23 fumble return (Fayak kick)
PSU	McDuffie 37 pass from Sacca (Fayak kick)

PSU	TEAM STATISTICS	TENN
12	First Downs	25
76	Rushing Yards	171
11-28-0	Passing	21-43-1
150	Passing Yards	270
226	Total Yards	441
9-47.9	Punts - Average	6-36.3
0-0	Fumbles - Lost	5-3
3-36	Penalties - Yards	3-34

INDIVIDUAL LEADERS

RUSHING
PSU: Anderson 17-57, 1 TD; Gash 7-15.
TENN: Stewart 15-84, 1 TD; Hayden 13-56.

PASSING
PSU: Sacca 11-28-0, 150 yards, 4 TD.
TENN: Kelly 20-40-1, 273 yards, 1 TD.

RECEIVING
PSU: McDuffie 4-78, 1 TD; Drayton 3-35.
TENN: Pickens 8-100; Fleming 2- 68, 1 TD.

January 1, 1993 | Hall of Fame
Tennessee 38, Boston College 23

	1ST	2ND	3RD	4TH	FINAL
TENN	14	0	17	7	38
BC	0	7	0	16	23

SCORING SUMMARY

TENN	Shuler 1 run (Becksvoort kick)
TENN	Fleming 27 pass from Shuler (Becksvoort kick)
BC	Mitchell 12 from Foley (Gordon kick)
TENN	Shuler 14 run (Becksvoort kick)
TENN	FG Becksvoort 25
TENN	Phillips 69 pass from Shuler (Becksvoort kick)
TENN	Fleming 48 pass from Colquitt (Becksvoort kick)
BC	Mitchell 17 pass from Foley (Mitchell pass from Foley)
BC	Campbell 7 run (Boyd pass from Foley)

TENN	TEAM STATISTICS	BC
20	First Downs	22
157	Rushing Yards	103
19-26-0	Passing	23-47-1
293	Passing Yards	268
450	Total Yards	371
2-18	Punt Returns - Yards	2-2
2-48	Kickoff Returns - Yards	3-52
4-41.3	Punts - Average	5-37.0
1-1	Fumbles - Lost	1-0
5-40	Penalties - Yards	5-25
29:31	Possession Time	30:29

INDIVIDUAL LEADERS

RUSHING
TENN: Garner 10-45; Hayden 7-33; Shuler 6-31, 2 TD.
BC: Dukes 15-83; Campbell 11-42, 1 TD.

PASSING
TENN: Shuler 18-23-0, 245 yards, 2 TD.
BC: Foley 23-46-1, 268 yards, 2 TD.

RECEIVING
TENN: Fleming 5-102, 2 TD; Phillips 3-88, 1 TD.
BC: Mitchell 9-100, 2 TD; Cannon 3-63.

JANUARY 1, 1994 | CITRUS
PENN STATE 31, TENNESSEE 13

	1ST	2ND	3RD	4TH	FINAL
PSU	7	10	7	7	31
TENN	10	3	0	0	13

SCORING SUMMARY
TENN	FG Becksvoort 46
TENN	Fleming 19 pass from Shuler (Becksvoort kick)
PSU	Carter 3 run (Fayak kick)
PSU	FG Fayak 19
TENN	FG Becksvoort 50
PSU	Carter 14 run (Fayak kick)
PSU	Brady 7 pass from Collins (Fayak kick)
PSU	Engram 15 pass from Collins (Fayak kick)

PSU	TEAM STATISTICS	TENN
20	First Downs	16
209	Rushing Yards	135
15-24-1	Passing	23-44-1
162	Passing Yards	213
371	Total Yards	348
6-32.0	Punts - Average	6-44.2
0-0	Fumbles - Lost	0-0
4-30	Penalties - Yards	10-79

INDIVIDUAL LEADERS
RUSHING
PSU: Carter 19-93, 2 TD; Archie 13-69.
TENN: Garner 16-89; Williams 1-38.
PASSING
PSU: Collins 15-24-1, 162 yards, 2 TD.
TENN: Shuler 22-42-1, 205 yards, 1 TD.
RECEIVING
PSU: Engram 7-107, 1 TD; O'Neal 2-19.
TENN: Fleming 7-101, 1 TD; Phillips 3-23.

DECEMBER 30, 1994 | GATOR
TENNESSEE 45, VIRGINIA TECH 23

	1ST	2ND	3RD	4TH	FINAL
TENN	14	21	0	10	45
VT	0	10	6	7	23

SCORING SUMMARY
TENN	Stewart 1 run (Becksvoort kick)
TENN	Nash 36 pass from Manning (Becksvoort kick)
TENN	Graham 1 run (Becksvoort kick)
VT	Thomas 1 run (Williams kick)
TENN	Stewart 1 run (Becksvoort kick)
TENN	Jones 19 pass from Stewart (Becksvoort kick)
VT	FG Williams 28
VT	DeShazo 7 run (kick failed)
TENN	Stewart 5 run (Becksvoort kick)
TENN	FG Becksvoort 19
VT	Still 9 pass from Druckenmiller (Williams kick)

TENN	TEAM STATISTICS	VT
18	First Downs	22
245	Rushing Yards	189
16-23-0	Passing	23-38-2
250	Passing Yards	237
495	Total Yards	426
5-43.6	Punts - Average	5-43.4
0-0	Fumbles - Lost	5-1
7-58	Penalties - Yards	3-25

INDIVIDUAL LEADERS
RUSHING
TENN: Stewart 22-85, 3 TD; Jones 1-76.
VT: Thomas 19-102, 1 TD; DeShazo 11-39, 1 TD.
PASSING
TENN: Manning 12-19-0, 189 yards, 1 TD.
VT: DeShazo 17-30-2, 140 yards.
RECEIVING
TENN: Kent 6-119; Nash 3-54, 1 TD.
VT: Still 5-79, 1 TD; Holmes 5-45.

JANUARY 1, 1996 | CITRUS
TENNESSEE 20, OHIO STATE 14

	1ST	2ND	3RD	4TH	FINAL
TENN	0	7	7	6	20
OSU	7	0	0	7	14

SCORING SUMMARY
OSU	George 2 run (Jackson kick)
TENN	Graham 69 run (Hall kick)
TENN	Kent 47 pass from Manning (Hall kick)
OSU	Dudley 32 pass from Hoying (Jackson kick)
TENN	FG Hall 29
TENN	FG Hall 25

TENN	TEAM STATISTICS	OSU
15	First Downs	17
145	Rushing Yards	89
20-35-0	Passing	19-38-1
182	Passing Yards	246
327	Total Yards	335
9-34.2	Punts-Average	7-48.1
1-1	Fumbles-Lost	5-3
8-43	Penalties-Yards	6-57
30:39	Possession Time	29:21

INDIVIDUAL LEADERS
RUSHING
TENN: Graham 26-168, 1 TD.
OSU: George 25-107, 1 TD.
PASSING
TENN: Manning 20-35-0, 182 yards, 1 TD.
OSU: Hoying 19-38-1, 246 yards, 1 TD.
RECEIVING
TENN: Kent 7-109, 1 TD.
OSU: Glenn 7-95; Dudley 5-106, 1 TD.

JANUARY 1, 1997 | CITRUS
TENNESSEE 48, NORTHWESTERN 28

	1ST	2ND	3RD	4TH	FINAL
TENN	21	10	7	10	48
NU	0	21	0	7	28

SCORING SUMMARY
TENN	Price 43 pass from Manning (Hall kick)
TENN	Manning 10 run (Hall kick)
TENN	Kent 11 pass from Manning (Hall kick)
NU	D. Autry 2 run (Gowins kick)
NU	Musso 20 pass from Schnur (Gowins kick)
NU	D. Autry 28 run (Gowins kick)
TENN	Kent 67 pass from Manning (Hall kick)
TENN	FG Hall 19
TENN	Hines 30 interception return (Hall kick)
TENN	FG Hall 28
NU	Bates 22 pass from Schnur (Gowins kick)
TENN	Moore 6 pass from Manning (Hall kick)

TENN	TEAM STATISTICS	NU
29	First Downs	22
115	Rushing Yards	43
27-39-0	Passing	27-51-4
408	Passing Yards	242
523	Total Yards	285
4-35.8	Punts - Average	6-37.3
4-2	Fumbles - Lost	1-1
13-112	Penalties - Yards	5-40

INDIVIDUAL LEADERS
RUSHING
TENN: Graham 14-79; Levine 7-33.
NU: D. Autry 17-66, 2 TD; Gooch 2-10.
PASSING
TENN: Manning 27-39-0, 408 yards, 4 TD.
NU: Schnur 25-45-3, 228 yards, 2 TD.
RECEIVING
TENN: Kent 5-122, 2 TD; Price 6-110, 1 TD.
NU: Bates 10-97, 1 TD; Musso 10-91, 1 TD.

JANUARY 2, 1998 | ORANGE
NEBRASKA 42, TENNESSEE 17

	1ST	2ND	3RD	4TH	FINAL
NEB	7	7	21	7	42
TENN	0	3	6	8	17

SCORING SUMMARY
NEB	Green 1 run (Brown kick)
NEB	Wiggins 10 run (Brown kick)
TENN	FG Hall 44
NEB	Frost 1 run (Brown kick)
NEB	Frost 11 run (Brown kick)
TENN	Price 5 pass from Manning (pass failed)
NEB	Green 22 run (Brown kick)
NEB	Frost 9 run (Brown kick)
TENN	McCullough 3 pass from Martin (Stephens pass from Martin)

NEB	TEAM STATISTICS	TENN
30	First Downs	16
409	Rushing Yards	128
9-12-0	Passing	25-35-1
125	Passing Yards	187
534	Total Yards	315
4-39.0	Punts - Average	6-52.3
3-2	Fumbles - Lost	2-2
8-63	Penalties - Yards	5-37
36:03	Possession Time	23:57

INDIVIDUAL LEADERS
RUSHING
NEB: Green 29-206, 2 TD; Makovicka 9-61; Frost 17-60, 3 TD.
TENN: Lewis 14-90; Levine 2-30.
PASSING
NEB: Frost 9-12-0, 125 yards.
TENN: Manning 21-31-1, 134 yards, 1 TD.
RECEIVING
NEB: K. Jackson 4-56; Green 3-31.
TENN: Nash 5-53; McCullough 3-50, 1 TD.

JANUARY 4, 1999 | FIESTA
TENNESSEE 23, FLORIDA STATE 16

	1ST	2ND	3RD	4TH	FINAL
TENN	0	14	0	9	23
FSU	0	9	0	7	16

SCORING SUMMARY
TENN	Bryson 4 pass from Martin (Hall kick)
TENN	Goodrich 54 interception return (Hall kick)
FSU	McCray 1 run (kick failed)
FSU	FG Janikowski 34
TENN	Price 79 pass from Martin (kick failed)
TENN	FG Hall 23
FSU	Outzen 7 run (Janikowksi kick)

TENN	TEAM STATISTICS	FSU
16	First Downs	13
114	Rushing Yards	108
11-19-2	Passing	9-22-2
278	Passing Yards	145
392	Total Yards	253
5-38.0	Punts - Average	9-39.8
3-2	Fumbles - Lost	4-1
9-55	Penalties - Yards	12-110

INDIVIDUAL LEADERS
RUSHING
TENN: Stephens 13-60; Henry 19-28.
FSU: Minor 15-83; Warrick 1-11.
PASSING
TENN: Martin 11-18-2, 278 yards, 2 TD.
FSU: Outzen 9-22-2, 145 yards.
RECEIVING
TENN: Price 4-199, 1 TD; Bryson 3-34, 1 TD.
FSU: Dugans 6-135; McCray 1-11.

THE SCHOOLS

JANUARY 2, 2000 | FIESTA
NEBRASKA 31, TENNESSEE 21

	1ST	2ND	3RD	4TH	FINAL
NEB	14	3	7	7	31
TENN	0	7	7	7	21

SCORING SUMMARY
NEB	Alexander 7 run (Brown kick)
NEB	Newcombe 60 punt return (Brown kick)
NEB	FG Brown 31
TENN	Stallworth 9 pass from Martin (Walls kick)
TENN	Henry 4 run (Walls kick)
NEB	Golliday 13 pass from Crouch (Brown kick)
NEB	Buckhalter 2 run (Brown kick)
TENN	Stallworth 44 pass from Wilson (Walls kick)

NEB	TEAM STATISTICS	TENN
23	First Downs	17
321	Rushing Yards	44
9-15-0	Passing	20-35-2
148	Passing Yards	267
469	Total Yards	311
6-39.5	Punts - Average	7-43.1
1-1	Fumbles - Lost	1-0
8-59	Penalties - Yards	5-41

INDIVIDUAL LEADERS
RUSHING
NEB: Alexander 21-108, 1 TD; Miller 8-87.
TENN: Henry 10-31, 1 TD; Lewis 8-19.

PASSING
NEB: Crouch 9-15-0, 148 yards, 1 TD.
TENN: Martin 19-34-2, 223 yards, 1 TD.

RECEIVING
NEB: Davison 2-68; Bowling 2-45.
TENN: Stallworth 8-108, 2 TD; Wilson 7-75.

JANUARY 1, 2001 | COTTON
KANSAS STATE 35, TENNESSEE 21

	1ST	2ND	3RD	4TH	FINAL
TENN	0	14	0	7	21
KSU	7	14	14	0	35

SCORING SUMMARY
KSU	Beasley 14 run (Rheem kick)
TENN	Martin 17 pass from Clausen (Walls kick)
KSU	Morgan 56 pass from Beasley (Rheem kick)
KSU	Morgan 10 pass from Beasley (Rheem kick)
TENN	Greer 78 interception return (Walls kick)
KSU	Scobey 12 run (Rheem kick)
KSU	Scobey 6 run (Rheem kick)
TENN	Henry 81 run (Walls kick)

TENN	TEAM STATISTICS	KSU
12	First Downs	25
178	Rushing Yards	297
7-25-3	Passing	13-27-1
120	Passing Yards	210
298	Total Yards	507
8-29.2	Punts - Average	5-34.0
1-0	Fumbles - Lost	1-1
5-40	Penalties - Yards	7-44
21:34	Possession Time	38:26

INDIVIDUAL LEADERS
RUSHING
TENN: Henry 17-180, 1 TD.
KSU: Scobey 28-147, 2 TD; Beasley 17-98, 1 TD.

PASSING
TENN: Clausen 7-25-3, 120 yards, 1 TD.
KSU: Beasley 13-27-1, 210 yards, 2 TD.

RECEIVING
TENN: Wilson 3-54; Parker 1-27.
KSU: Morgan 7-145, 2 TD; Lockett 3-22.

JANUARY 1, 2002 | CITRUS
TENNESSEE 45, MICHIGAN 17

	1ST	2ND	3RD	4TH	FINAL
TENN	10	14	7	14	45
MICH	0	10	0	7	17

SCORING SUMMARY
TENN	FG Walls 32
TENN	Washington 3 pass from Clausen (Walls kick)
TENN	Clausen 1 run (Walls kick)
MICH	Askew 14 pass from Navarre (Epstein kick)
TENN	Clausen 1 run (Walls kick)
MICH	FG Epstein 28
TENN	Witten 64 pass from Clausen (Walls kick)
TENN	Washington 37 pass from Clausen (Walls kick)
TENN	Stephens 3 run (Walls kick)
MICH	Bell 24 pass from Navarre (Epstein kick)

TENN	TEAM STATISTICS	MICH
22	First Downs	20
97	Rushing Yards	103
27-35-0	Passing	21-39-1
406	Passing Yards	240
503	Total Yards	343
4-36	Punt Returns - Yards	3-14
3-67	Kickoff Returns - Yards	8-125
5-31.8	Punts - Average	7-39.6
3-32	Penalties - Yards	6-42
34:13	Possession Time	25:47

INDIVIDUAL LEADERS
RUSHING
TENN: Stallworth 2-44; Stephens 16-38, 1 TD.
MICH: Askew 9-76; Perry 17-41.

PASSING
TENN: Clausen 26-34-0, 393 yards, 3 TD.
MICH: Navarre 21-39-1, 240 yards, 2 TD.

RECEIVING
TENN: Witten 6-125, 1 TD; Stallworth 8-119; Washington 6-70, 2 TD.
MICH: Walker 5-100; Joppru 5-45.

DECEMBER 31, 2002 | PEACH
MARYLAND 30, TENNESSEE 3

	1ST	2ND	3RD	4TH	FINAL
MARY	7	10	3	10	30
TENN	0	3	0	0	3

SCORING SUMMARY
MARY	McBrien 1 run (Novak kick)
MARY	Cox 54 interception return (Novak kick)
TENN	FG Walls 38
MARY	FG Novak 48
MARY	FG Novak 44
MARY	McBrien 6 run (Novak kick)
MARY	FG Novak 25

MARY	TEAM STATISTICS	TENN
17	First Downs	18
154	Rushing Yards	45
11-19-0	Passing	23-37-1
120	Passing Yards	242
274	Total Yards	287
3-50.3	Punts - Average	6-47.7
2-1	Fumbles - Lost	1-1
2-10	Penalties - Yards	8-68

INDIVIDUAL LEADERS
RUSHING
MARY: Perry 15-50.
TENN: Houston 9-34.

PASSING
MARY: McBrien 11-19-0, 120 yards.
TENN: Clausen 23-37-1, 242 yards.

RECEIVING
MARY: Harrison 4-74.
TENN: Brown 5-75.

JANUARY 2, 2004 | PEACH
CLEMSON 27, TENNESSEE 14

	1ST	2ND	3RD	4TH	FINAL
CLEM	10	14	0	3	27
TENN	7	7	0	0	14

SCORING SUMMARY
CLEM	Coleman 8 run (Hunt kick)
CLEM	FG Hunt 23
TENN	Hannon 19 pass from Clausen (Wilhoit kick)
CLEM	Jasmin 15 run (Hunt kick)
TENN	Jones 30 pass from Clausen (Wilhoit kick)
CLEM	Browning 8 run (Hunt kick)
CLEM	FG Hunt 28

CLEM	TEAM STATISTICS	TENN
25	First Downs	28
153	Rushing Yards	38
22-40-1	Passing	31-56-0
246	Passing Yards	384
399	Total Yards	422
4-67	Punt Returns - Yards	1-5
0-0	Kickoff Returns - Yards	2-46
5-42.0	Punts - Average	8-38.5
1-0	Fumbles - Lost	1-1
6-45	Penalties - Yards	10-119
27:51	Possession Time	32:09

INDIVIDUAL LEADERS
RUSHING
CLEM: Jasmin 15-130, 1 TD; Hamilton 4-23.
TENN: Houston 6-24; Riggs 2-10.

PASSING
CLEM: Whitehurst 22-40-1, 246 yards.
TENN: Clausen 31-55-0, 384 yards, 2 TD.

RECEIVING
CLEM: Hamilton 5-69; Youngblood 3-64.
TENN: Jones 5-66, 1 TD; Hannon 4-57, 1 TD.

JANUARY 1, 2005 | COTTON
TENNESSEE 38, TEXAS A&M 7

	1ST	2ND	3RD	4TH	FINAL
TENN	14	14	10	0	38
A&M	0	0	0	7	7

SCORING SUMMARY
TENN	Fayton 57 pass from Clausen (Wilhoit kick)
TENN	Anderson 12 pass from Clausen (Wilhoit kick)
TENN	Houston 8 run (Wilhoit kick)
TENN	Brown 13 pass from Clausen (Wilhoit kick)
TENN	Riggs 9 run (Wilhoit kick)
TENN	FG Wilhoit 37
A&M	Taylor 5 pass from McNeal (Pegram kick)

TENN	TEAM STATISTICS	A&M
32	First Downs	17
241	Rushing Yards	77
19-31-0	Passing	23-38-1
233	Passing Yards	241
474	Total Yards	318
3-20	Punt Returns - Yards	1-(-6)
0-0	Kickoff Returns - Yards	3-47
4-34.0	Punts - Average	5-43.2
1-0	Fumbles - Lost	4-4
9-100	Penalties - Yards	7-65
40:22	Possession Time	19:38

INDIVIDUAL LEADERS
RUSHING
TENN: Riggs 18-102, 1 TD; Houston 13-62, 1 TD.
A&M: Thomas 1-54.

PASSING
TENN: Clausen 18-27-0, 222 yards, 3 TD.
A&M: McNeal 23-38-1, 241 yards, 1 TD.

RECEIVING
TENN: Fayton 3-94, 1 TD.
A&M: Mobley 5-70; Taylor 5-39, 1 TD.

JANUARY 1, 2007 | OUTBACK
TENNESSEE 10, PENN STATE 20

	1ST	2ND	3RD	4TH	FINAL
TENN	3	7	0	0	10
PSU	0	10	0	10	20

SCORING SUMMARY
TENN FG Wilhoit 44
PSU FG Kelly 34
PSU Quarless 2 pass from Morelli (Kelly kick)
TENN Coker 42 run (Wilhoit kick)
PSU Davis 86 fumble return (Kelly kick)
PSU FG Kelly 24

TENN	TEAM STATISTICS	PSU
17	First Downs	19
83	Rushing Yards	183
25-37-1	Passing	14-25-0
267	Passing Yards	197
350	Total Yards	380
1-2	Punt Returns - Yards	2-29
1-21	Kickoff Returns - Yards	2-34
5-44	Punts - Average	4-37.5
2-2	Fumbles - Lost	0-0
7-55	Penalties - Yards	6-45

INDIVIDUAL LEADERS
RUSHING
TENN: Foster 12-65.
PSU: Hunt 31-158.
PASSING
TENN: Ainge 25-37-1, 267 yards.
PSU: Morelli 14-25-0, 197 yards, 1 TD.
RECEIVING
TENN: Swain 7-84; Brown 7-66.
PSU: Norwood 4-35; Butler 3-73.

JANUARY 1, 2008 | OUTBACK
TENNESSEE 21, WISCONSIN 17

	1ST	2ND	3RD	4TH	FINAL
WISC	7	7	3	0	17
TENN	7	14	0	0	21

SCORING SUMMARY
TENN Jones 3 run (Lincoln kick)
WISC Donovan 6 run (Mehlhaff kick)
TENN Briscoe 29 pass from Ainge (Lincoln kick)
TENN Cottam 31 pass from Ainge (Lincoln kick)
WISC Crooks 4 pass from Donovan (Mehlhaff kick)
WISC FG Mehlhaff 27

WISC	TEAM STATISTICS	TENN
16	First Downs	18
192	Rushing Yards	66
14-25-1	Passing	25-43-0
155	Passing Yards	365
347	Total Yards	431
3-21	Punt Returns - Yards	4-26
4-103	Kickoff Returns - Yards	2-50
6-44.7	Punts - Average	7-42.1
1-1	Fumbles - Lost	2-1
2-10	Penalties - Yards	5-60

INDIVIDUAL LEADERS
RUSHING
WISC: Hill 16-132.
TENN: Hardesty 7-35; A. Foster 16-31.
PASSING
WISC: Donovan 14-24-1, 155 yards, 1 TD.
TENN: Ainge 25-43-0, 365 yards, 2 TD.
RECEIVING
WISC: Graham 7-75.
TENN: Briscoe 7-101, 1 TD; Moore 4-86.

THE SCHOOLS

VANDERBILT

BY GEOFFREY NORMAN

VANDERBILT HAS HAD TO TRAVEL A hard football road. The university is exceedingly proud of its high academic standards and will not tolerate them being compromised. Yet it plays in the SEC, perhaps the toughest football neighborhood of all. Vanderbilt, then, is the nerd at a party full of jocks. The best comparison might be to Northwestern in the Big Ten—although Vandy's football renaissance has been more recent and, without a major bowl trip to its credit, not quite as remarkable.

Vanderbilt fans believe in their university and are exceedingly proud of it. They are sympathetic to the challenges of the football team and still believe that the right combination of motivated recruits will, one day, give them what has become the grail of Vanderbilt football: a winning season. Fans can dream of a national championship, or even just an SEC championship. At one point during the 2008 season, those dreams seemed on the verge of coming true. The Commodores were 5–0, having beaten three SEC teams—Auburn, Ole Miss and South Carolina. Then the team fell back to earth and finished 6–6. Still, that was good enough to get the Commodores their first bowl game in 26 years and, following a stirring 16-14 win over Boston College in the Music City Bowl, their first winning season in just as long.

The spirit of another era in Vanderbilt football, one long since past, lives on. In those early days of the 20th century, the Commodores ran off winning seasons as effortlessly as the university now produces Rhodes scholars. There once was a time when they beat archrival Tennessee so routinely that when the Vols hired their legendary coach, Robert Neyland, his first order was to beat Vandy. Now Vanderbilt boosters have to settle for the occasional victory over one conference behemoth or another, and under coach Bobby Johnson there have been a few such upsets. Since 2005, the Commodores have beaten Tennessee, Arkansas, South Carolina and Georgia on the road. For Alabama or LSU, those would be gratifying wins. For Vanderbilt, they are treasures to be savored and remembered.

TRADITION It's not an old tradition but it is certainly unique. In sync with the program's squeaky-clean image, the team instituted a no-cursing policy on the football field in 2002, policing its own language as a step toward discipline. That's one helluva commitment.

PROFILE
Vanderbilt University
Nashville, Tenn.
Founded: 1873
Enrollment: 6,530
Colors: Black and Gold
Nickname: Commodores
Stadium: Vanderbilt Stadium
Opened in 1981
Grass; 39,773 capacity
First football game: 1890
All-time record: 553–548–50 (.502)
Bowl record: 2–1–1
First-round draft choices: 9
Website: www.vucommodores.com

THE BEST OF TIMES
From 1915 to 1935, Vanderbilt enjoyed 21 consecutive winning seasons.

THE WORST OF TIMES
The Commodores averaged fewer than two wins per year, going 15–60–5 in the eight seasons from 1960 to 1967.

CONFERENCE
After 11 seasons in the Southern Conference, Vanderbilt became a charter member of the SEC in 1933.

DISTINGUISHED ALUMNI
Lamar Alexander, U.S. senator; Dierks Bentley, singer; Roy Blount Jr., author; Grantland Rice, sportswriter; Fred Thompson, actor, U.S. senator; Robert Penn Warren, author, poet

In the early 20th Century, Vandy delivered winning seasons as effortlessly as the school now produces Rhodes scholars.

BEST PLAYER Quarterback Bill Wade was SEC Player of the Year in 1951, when he led Vandy to a 6–5 record that included wins over both Alabama and LSU. He completed 111 of 223 passes for 1,609 yards that season, with 13 touchdown passes. Wade was the first-round pick of the Los Angeles Rams, who traded him to Chicago. In 1963, he scored two touchdowns in the Bears' 14-10 win over the New York Giants in the NFL championship game.

BEST COACH Dan McGugin guided the Commodores for three decades—1904 to 1934—with one year off, 1918, for military duty. His first squad outscored opponents 474-4 and finished 9–0. McGugin finished his career 197–55–19 and has more than four times as many wins as any other coach in Vanderbilt history. He's also a member of the College Football Hall of Fame.

BEST TEAM McGugin's 1904 team would probably get the nod, though some Commodores fans hold a special affection for his 1922 team that outscored opponents 177-16 and ran up a record of 8–0–1. There were three Hall of Famers associated with that team:

McGugin; assistant coach Wallace Wade, who went on to glory at Alabama; and team captain Jess Neely, whose career at Rice was equally impressive.

In the modern era, the distinction of best team belongs to the 1955 squad. Under coach Art Guepe (1953-62), the Commodores finished 8–3 and received an invitation to the Gator Bowl, a first in team history. There, Vandy beat No. 8 Auburn, 25-13.

BEST DEFENSE In 1974, the Commodores' defense was coached by someone named Bill Parcells and it was, unsurprisingly, a pretty tough bunch. The unit was led by nose tackle Tom Galbierz, an All-SEC selection, and defensive back Jay Chesley, who intercepted five passes and ran two back for touchdowns. But the player fans remember best is freshman Dennis Harrison, who had 40 total tackles during the season and was named defensive player of the game in the Peach Bowl. Like his coach, Harrison went on to a successful NFL career.

BEST BACKFIELD Jay Cutler had an All-SEC season in 2005, completing 273 of 462 passes for 3,073 yards.

FIGHT SONG

DYNAMITE

Dynamite, Dynamite
When VANDY starts to fight.
Down the field with blood to yield,
If need be, save the shield.
If vict'ry's won, when battle's done,
Then Vandy's name will rise in fame.
But, Win or lose,
The Fates will choose,
And Vandy's game will be the same.
Dynamite, Dynamite
When Vandy starts to fight!
Fight!

FIRST-ROUND DRAFT CHOICES

1943	Jack Jenkins, Redskins (10)
1952	Bill Wade, Rams (1)
1956	Charlie Horton, Rams (11)
1958	Phil King, Giants (12)
1960	Tom Moore, Packers (5)
1984	Leonard Coleman, Colts (8)
1986	Will Wolford, Bills (20)
2006	Jay Cutler, Broncos (11)
2008	Chris Williams, Bears (14)

CONSENSUS ALL-AMERICANS

Year	Player	Pos
1923	Lynn Bomar	E
1924	Henry Wakefield	E
1932	Pete Gracey	C
1958	George Deiderich	G
1982	Jim Arnold	P
1984	Ricky Anderson	P

Against Kentucky, he threw five touchdowns to receiver Earl Bennett. Cutler was the story, but not the whole story. Defenses couldn't ignore running back Cassen Jackson-Garrison, who averaged more than 5.5 yards per carry, gained almost 600 yards on the season and scored eight touchdowns.

STORYBOOK SEASON

The Commodores started the 1982 season 1–2. But coach George MacIntyre got things turned around and Vandy took seven of its next eight, including wins over powerhouse Florida and archrival Tennessee. Vandy received an invitation to the Hall of Fame Bowl and lost a 36-28 shootout to Air Force.

COLLEGE FOOTBALL HALL OF FAME INDUCTEES		
NAME	YEARS	INDUCTED
Dan McGugin, COACH	1904-17, '19-34	1951
Ray Morrison, COACH	1918-39	1954
Lynn Bomar, E	1921-24	1956
Carl Hinkle, C	1935-37	1959
Bill Spears, QB	1925-27	1962
Josh Cody, T	1914-16, '19	1970
John Tigert, HB	1901-03	1970
Bill Edwards, COACH	1949-62	1986
Red Sanders, COACH	1940-42, '46-48	1996

BIGGEST GAME

The inaugural game in the new Dudley Field, on Oct. 14, 1922, was played against Michigan in a coaching battle of wits that matched McGugin with his brother-in-law, Michigan's Fielding "Hurry-Up" Yost. McGugin had played at Michigan in the early 1900s under Yost, adding to the drama. The crucial moment came on a fourth-and-goal play at the 1, when a Vandy defender got an extra burst by pushing off the goalpost to stop a Michigan runner, preserving the 0-0 tie. Though not a win, it was a statement game. As one impressed Detroit reporter wrote, "Michigan was lucky to escape with their lives."

BIGGEST UPSET

Playing No. 12 Alabama in Mobile on Oct. 7, 1950, the Commodores spoiled the Tide's season with a 27-22 win that no one saw coming. Another victory over Alabama also merits mention. On Nov. 22, 1941, Vandy topped the Tide 7-0 in Nashville. Bama finished that season 9–2 and, with a victory over Texas A&M in the Cotton Bowl, was named national champion by Deke Houlgate's popular mathematical system syndicated in newspapers at the time. The Commodores wound up 8–2 but did not play in a bowl game.

HEARTBREAKER

A 25-23 loss to No. 1 Oklahoma on Sept. 10, 1977, was particularly stinging, and not just because of the close margin. An official ruled—incorrectly, according to the faithful—that the Commodores had not recovered a fumble in the end zone that would've made the difference. At Vandy, you live for upsets like this, especially in a season that ran to a doleful 2–9 conclusion.

WILDEST FINISH

The Sept. 18, 1999, 37-34 overtime win against Mississippi was Vandy's first SEC road victory in five seasons. The Commodores came back and tied the game on a Greg Zolman-to-Todd Yoder touchdown pass with 49 seconds left in regulation. On Mississippi's first overtime possession, the Commodores held and forced a field goal. Then, on a third and goal, Zolman hit his tight end, Elliott Carson, for the touchdown and the win.

BEST COMEBACK

Nov. 19, 2005, will live in the memory of Vanderbilt fans. It's a day on which the Commodores did something they had not done in 30 years: beat Tennessee in Knoxville. (In fact, it had been 23 years since they had beaten the Vols *anywhere*.) It was Cutler's final game and for most of the way, the Commodores held the lead. Then, with less than nine minutes remaining, Tennessee scored and took a 24-21 lead.

Vanderbilt stalled on two possessions and got the ball back for a last chance with 1:40 left. Three Cutler passes to Earl Bennett made it 28-24. Then, Tennessee's Rick Clausen moved the ball to the Commodores' 11-yard line and had time for three more plays. The first two were incomplete. Jared Fagen intercepted the third with :01 left on the clock. It could not have been any better.

STADIUM

Old Dudley Field—so named in honor of Dr. William Dudley, dean of the Vanderbilt Medical College—was the Commodores' home from 1892 until 1922, when it was replaced by the new Dudley Field. That stood until 1980, when a booster-financed rebuilding effort called for a serious change. With the exception of a section of metal bleachers seating 12,088, the whole place was demolished and replaced by Vanderbilt Stadium in 1981, at a cost of $10.1 million. The entire project was completed in just nine months. When the NFL's Tennessee Oilers moved to Nashville in 1998, they played their home games at Vanderbilt Stadium. Seating capacity is now 39,773, with improvements under way that won't add to that figure.

RIVAL

Before Tennessee hired General Robert R. Neyland in 1925, Vandy had the Vols' number, regularly beating UT since 1892. But that soon changed, and Tennessee has dominated the rivalry ever since. One notable exception came in Nov. 27, 1982, when the Commodores were playing for a rare bowl bid and quarterback Whit Taylor rose to the occasion, completing 24 of 41 passes for 391 yards. With the score tied 21-21 late in the fourth quarter, Taylor took the Commodores on an 84-yard drive, finishing it with a one-yard touchdown run with 2:53 remaining. Any win against Tennessee is sweet; this one was pure nectar. Almost as good as the one that came 23 years later (see *Best Comeback*). Almost.

TRAGEDY Irby Rice "Rabbit" Curry was the Commodores' team captain, starring at both running back and quarterback from 1914 to '16. He went to war after graduation and was killed while flying a combat mission over France. When the Commodores began playing at the new Dudley Field in 1922, the old facility, now used for practices, was renamed in his honor. More recently, running back Kwane Doster was shot and killed not far from his home in Ybor City, Fla., over the 2004 Christmas holiday.

NICKNAME The university's founder, Cornelius Vanderbilt, was nicknamed Commodore to honor his business acumen and success. *Nashville Banner* writer William Beard first applied the term to the school's athletes in an 1897 story. Beard himself had played quarterback for Vandy five years earlier.

MASCOT First there was George, the basset hound that belonged to halfback Toby Wilt. During the 1964 Tennessee game, George chased a Tennessee walking horse—a sort of unofficial Vols mascot—out of the stadium, to the delight of Vanderbilt fans. The Commodores defeated Tennessee that day, 7-0. George was crowned mascot for life, which,

unfortunately didn't last very long. He died two years later and was succeeded by a female basset named Samantha, who remained on campus until 1970. Since then the school has been content with a costumed Commodore as its mascot.

UNIFORMS Opinions vary on the origins of the black and gold. Some say the original colors were orange and black, a present from a judge famous in the Nashville area, W.L. Granbery, who was a graduate of Princeton. Others credit various Princeton alums with the choice. When members of the 1890 team were asked in the 1930s how the colors came to be black and gold, they said they couldn't remember. Vanderbilt first put a star on its helmet in 1969, with the initial V set inside. It remained there through most of the school's many helmet designs over the following two decades, before being removed in favor of a larger V in 1991. When Bobby Johnson arrived in 2002, he returned the star to the side of the helmet, where it has remained since.

QUOTE "There is no way you can be Harvard Monday through Friday and try to be Alabama on Saturday." —**Art Guepe**, Vanderbilt head coach from 1953 to '62

One Small Kick

BY BUSTER OLNEY

Bryant Hahnfeldt waited for Vanderbilt coach Bobby Johnson to make eye contact with him, and when it came, it seemed so routine, so casual. "Okay, let's go," Johnson said, and Hahnfeldt, the Commodores' kicker, jogged onto the field.

So routine, so casual. Or maybe not. Johnson had effectively charged Hahnfeldt with the responsibility of kicking a 45-yard field goal that would give Vanderbilt the lead in the waning minutes of the 2008 Music City Bowl—a field goal that could end 25 consecutive years of losing seasons and a field goal that could give the Commodores their first bowl win in 53 years. Vanderbilt trailed Boston College, 14-13, with less than four minutes remaining, and Hahnfeldt's kick would either add another layer of misery for alumni or provide relief.

Art Demmas had been a lineman with the 1955 Vanderbilt team that beat Auburn in the Gator Bowl, and as Hahnfeldt lined up for the field goal, Demmas stood among friends in the stands, freezing, fretting about the kick. "It was a nervous time," he said later.

Hahnfeldt understood better than most of his teammates what a bowl victory would mean to the university, to alumni like Demmas. He had grown up in Nashville, just minutes away from the Vanderbilt campus, and knew the history. There was a time in the early 20th century when Vanderbilt had been a dominant program, including one season, 1904, when the Commodores outscored their opponents 474-4. There were

times when Vanderbilt had an assistant coach named Bear Bryant and a defensive coordinator named Bill Parcells, years when it handily beat Tennessee.

But over the decades, Vanderbilt's rigid academic standards made it extremely difficult to build a roster deep enough to compete in the Southeastern Conference. After

> *The ball was snapped and held and coming off Hahnfeldt's foot it felt low. For an instant, he wondered if he would hear a dreaded double-thump—the sound of the ball being blocked immediately after the kick.*

quarterback Whit Taylor led the Commodores to the Hall of Fame Bowl in 1982, the losing streak began … and continued year after year, amid constant debate about whether or not Vanderbilt should drop out of the SEC.

Johnson took over the program in 2002 and, slowly, there was improvement—more and more near-misses, the hopes for a winning season climbing. Vanderbilt won the first five games of the 2008 season, breaking into the Top 25—before losing six of their next seven. So this was the weight Hahnfeldt bore on his shoulders; this was what Hahnfeldt

had in his mind, what he knew out of habit he had to block out. He also blocked out what happened at halftime, when he practiced a field goal and missed it badly, hooking the ball. He told himself, "Okay, I'm glad you got that out of your system."

The alumni watched from the stands and Demmas, a longtime referee in the National Football League, found himself thinking about the snap, the hold, the possibility of a block—all the things that might go right or wrong on a kick. Hahnfeldt didn't think about any of that. The ball was snapped and held and coming off his foot it felt low. For an instant, he wondered if he would hear a dreaded double-thump—the sound of the ball being blocked immediately after the kick.

But the ball rose beyond the outstretched arms of the Boston College defenders, sailed toward the end zone and finally fell—over the crossbar and between the uprights. Demmas and his friends yelled and teammates pounded on Hahnfeldt's pads and helmet in celebration. The Commodores hung on, the streak of losing seasons was over and Demmas announced that they were all going out to dinner.

At the restaurant, somebody ordered champagne and Demmas raised a glass. "Here's to the Commodores," he said.

In the days that followed, Hahnfeldt was approached by many alums, each of them offering the same two words: "Thank you."

*The Commodores went 8–4 in **Buster Olney**'s freshman year at Vanderbilt, and for years after he graduated, he wondered if he somehow jinxed the school. He now covers baseball for* ESPN The Magazine.

VANDERBILT ALL-TIME SCORES

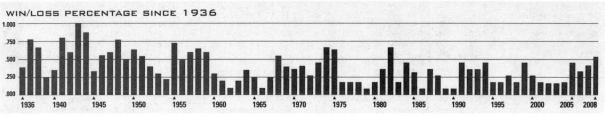

WIN/LOSS PERCENTAGE SINCE 1936
1936 1940 1945 1950 1955 1960 1965 1970 1975 1980 1985 1990 1995 2000 2005 2008

THE SCHOOLS

ELLIOTT H. JONES
1890-92 (.615)   8-5

1890   1-0-0
| N27 | ● | Nashville | 40 | 0 |

1891   3-1-0
N7		at Sewanee	22	0
N14		Washington, Mo.	6	24
N26	●	Sewanee	26	4
D4		at Washington, Mo.	4	0

1892   4-4-0
O15	●	at Sewanee	4	22
O21	●	Tennessee	12	0*
O28	●	Nashville	40	0
N5	●	Washington, Mo.	4	14
N12	●	Sewanee	14	28
N17	●	at Tennessee	10	0
N19	●	at Georgia Tech	20	10
N24	●	North Carolina	0	24

W.J. KELLER
1893 (.857)   6-1

1893   6-1-0
U	●	Memphis AC	68	0
U	●	at Sewanee	10	8
N6	●	Auburn *Mont*	10	30
N7	●	Georgia	35	10*
N19	●	at Louisville AC	36	12
N23	●	Sewanee	10	0
D1	●	Central Kentucky	12	0

HENRY THORNTON
1894 (.875)   7-1

1894   7-1-0
O6	●	at Memphis AC	64	0
O20	●	Centre	6	0
O27	●	at Louisville AC	8	10
N4	●	Auburn *Mont*	20	4
N10	●	Mississippi	40	0
N21	●	Central Kentucky	34	6
N24	●	at Cumberland	62	0
N29	●	Sewanee	12	0

C.L. UPTON
1895 (.611)   5-3-1

1895   5-3-1
O12	●	at Missouri	0	16
O19	●	at Central Kentucky	10	0
O28	●	North Carolina	0	12
N2	=	Centre	0	0
N7	●	at Nashville AC	20	4
N9	●	Auburn	9	6
N16	●	Virginia *Atl*	4	6
N23	●	Georgia	6	0
N28	●	at Sewanee	18	6

R.G. ACTON
1896-98 (.575)   10-7-3

1896   3-2-2
O10	●	Kentucky	6	0
O17	●	at Centre	0	46
N7		Missouri *StL*	6	26
U	●	at Central Kentucky	0	0
U	●	at Southwestern	36	0
U	●	Nashville	0	0
N27	●	at Sewanee	10	4

1897   6-0-1
U	●	at Kentucky St. Coll.	24	0
U	●	Central Kentucky	14	0
O19	●	VMI	12	0
O30	●	at Kentucky	50	0
N6	●	at North Carolina	31	0
N26	●	Sewanee	10	0
D6	=	Virginia	0	0

1898   1-5-0
O22		Cincinnati	0	10*
O29		at Georgia	0	4
N5	●	Nashville	5	0
N12		at Virginia	0	18
N19		Central Kentucky	0	10
N25		Sewanee	4	19

J.L. CRANE
1899-1900 (.639)   11-6-1

1899   7-2-0
O6	●	at Cumberland	32	0
O13	●	Miami, Ohio	12	0
O20		Cincinnati	0	6
O28		Indiana	0	20
N4	●	at Mississippi	11	0
N11	●	Bethel	22	0
N18	●	Texas	6	0
N25	●	Central Kentucky	21	16
U	●	at Nashville	5	0

1900   4-4-1
O6	●	Mississippi	6	0
O13		at Texas	0	22
O22	=	Tennessee	0	0
U		Central Kentucky	0	11
N3		North Carolina	0	48
U	●	Central Ky.	27	0
U		Sewanee	10	11
U	●	Bethel	29	0
U	●	Nashville	18	0

W.H. WATKINS
1901-02 (.853)   14-2-1

1901   6-1-1
O5	●	Kentucky	22	0
O12	●	Central Kentucky	25	0
O19	●	Georgia	47	0
N2		at Washington, Mo.	11	12
N8	●	Auburn *Mont*	41	0*
N9	●	Tennessee	22	0
N16	=	Sewanee	0	0
N28	●	at Nashville	10	0

1902   8-1-0
S27	●	at Cumberland	45	0
O11	●	Mississippi	29	0
O18	●	at Centre	24	17
O25	●	at Tennessee	12	5
N1	●	Washington, Mo.	33	12
N8	●	Transylvania, Ky.	16	5
N15	●	at Tulane	23	5
N17	●	at LSU	27	5
N27	●	Sewanee	5	11

J.H. HENRY
1903 (.813)   6-1-1

1903   6-1-1
O3		Cumberland	0	6
O10	●	Alabama	30	0
O17	●	Tennessee	40	0
O24	●	Mississippi	33	0
O31	●	at Georgia	33	0
N6	=	at Texas	5	5
N14	●	Washington, Mo.	41	0
N21	●	Sewanee	10	5

DAN McGUGIN
1904-17, '19-34 (.762)   197-55-19

1904   9-0-0
O1	●	Mississippi State *ColMs*	61	0
O8	●	Georgetown, Ky.	66	0
O15	●	Mississippi	69	0
O22	●	Missouri Mines	29	4
O29	●	at Centre	97	0
N5	●	Tennessee	22	0
N12	●	Nashville	81	0
N19	●	at Centre	22	0
N24	●	Sewanee	27	0

1905   7-1-0
S30	●	Maryville	97	0
O7	●	Alabama	34	0
O14	●	at Michigan	0	18
O21	●	at Tennessee	45	0
O28	●	Texas	33	0
N4	●	Auburn	54	0
N18	●	Clemson	41	0
N30	●	Sewanee	68	4

1906   8-1-0
O6	●	Kentucky	28	0
O13	●	Mississippi	29	0
O20	●	Alabama	78	0
O27	●	Texas	45	0
N3	●	at Michigan	4	10
N10	●	Rose Poly	33	0
N17	●	at Georgia Tech	37	6
N24	●	Carlisle	4	0
N29	●	Sewanee	20	0

1907   5-1-1
O5	●	Kentucky	40	0
O12	=	at Navy	6	6
O19	●	Rose Poly	65	10
N2	●	Michigan	0	8
N9	●	Mississippi *Mem*	60	0
N16	●	Georgia Tech	54	0
N23	●	Sewanee	17	12

1908   7-2-1
S26	●	Southwestern	11	5
O3	●	Maryville	32	0
O10	●	Rose Poly	32	0
O17	●	Clemson	41	0
O24	●	Mississippi	29	0
O31	●	at Michigan	6	24
N7	●	Tennessee	16	9
N14	●	Ohio State	6	17
N21	●	at Washington, Mo.	28	0
N26	=	Sewanee	6	6

1909   7-3-0
S25	●	Southwestern	52	0
O2	●	Mercer	28	5
O9	●	Rose Poly	28	3
O16	●	Alumni	0	3
O23	●	Auburn	17	0
O30	●	Mississippi	17	0
N6	●	Tennessee	51	0
N13	●	at Ohio State	0	5
N20	●	at Washington, Mo.	12	0
N25	●	Sewanee	5	16

1910   8-0-1
S24	●	Mooney	34	0
O1	●	Rose Poly	23	0
O8	●	Castle Heights	14	0
O15	●	Tennessee	18	0
O22	=	at Yale	0	0
O29	●	Mississippi	9	2
N5	●	LSU	22	0
N12	●	at Georgia Tech	23	0
N24	●	Sewanee	23	6

1911   8-1-0
S30	●	B'Ham Southern	40	0
O7	●	Maryville	46	0
O14	●	Rose Poly	33	0
O21	●	Centre	45	0
O28	●	at Michigan	8	9
N4	●	Georgia	17	0
N11	●	Kentucky	18	0
N18	●	Mississippi	21	0
N30	●	Sewanee	31	0

1912   8-1-1
S28	●	Bethel	105	0
O5	●	Maryville	100	3
O12	●	Rose Poly	54	0
O19	●	Georgia *Atl*	46	0
O26	●	Mississippi	24	0
N2	●	Virginia	13	0
N9	●	at Harvard	3	9
N16	●	Centre	23	0
N23	=	Auburn *Mont*	7	7
N28	●	Sewanee	16	0

1913   5-3-0
O4	●	Maryville	59	0
O11	●	Centre	48	0
O18	●	Henderson-Brown	33	0
O25	●	Michigan	2	33
N1	●	at Virginia	0	34
N8	●	Tennessee	7	6
N15	●	Auburn *Mont*	6	14
N22	●	Sewanee	63	13

1914   2-6-0
O3	●	Henderson-Brown	42	6
O10	●	at Michigan	3	23
O17	●	Centre	59	0
O24	●	North Carolina	9	10
O31	●	Virginia	7	20
N7	●	Tennessee	14	16
N14	●	Auburn *Mont*	0	6
N21	●	Sewanee	13	14

1915   9-1-0
S25	●	Middle Tennessee	51	0
O2	●	Southwestern	47	0
O9	●	Georgetown, Ky.	75	0
O13	●	Cumberland	60	0
O16	●	Henderson-Brown	100	0
O23	●	Mississippi *Mem*	91	0
O30	●	Tennessee	35	0
N6	●	at Virginia	10	35
N13	●	Auburn *Mont*	17	0
N20	●	Sewanee	27	3

1916   7-1-1
S30	●	Southwestern	86	0
O7	●	Transylvania, Ky.	42	0
O14	●	at Kentucky	45	0
O21	●	Mississippi	35	0
O28	●	Virginia	27	6
N4	●	Rose Poly	67	0
N11	●	at Tennessee	6	10
N18	●	Auburn *Mont*	20	9
N25	=	Sewanee	0	0

1917   5-3-0
O6	●	Transylvania, Ky.	41	0
O13	●	at Chicago	0	48
O20	●	at Kentucky	5	0
O27	●	Samford	69	0
N3	●	at Georgia Tech	0	83
N10	●	Alabama *Mont*	7	2
N17	●	Auburn	7	31
N29	●	Sewanee	13	6

RAY MORRISON
1918, '35-39 (.566)   29-22-2

1918   4-2-0
O19	●	Camp Greenleaf	0	6
O26	●	Camp Hancock	6	25
N2	●	Kentucky	33	0
N9	●	Tennessee JV	76	0
N16	●	Auburn *Mont*	21	0
N28	●	Sewanee	40	0

THE SCHOOLS

DAN McGUGIN

1919　5-1-2
O4	●	Union	41 0
O11	=	Tennessee	3 3
O18		at Georgia Tech	0 20
O25	●	Auburn	7 6
N1	●	at Kentucky	0 0
N8	●	Alabama	16 12
N15	●	at Virginia	10 6
N27	●	Sewanee	33 21

1920　5-3-1
O2	●	B'ham Southern	54 0
O9	●	at Tennessee	20 0
O16	●	Georgia Tech	0 44
O23	●	Auburn *Mont*	6 56
O30	●	Kentucky	20 0
N6	●	Alabama *Mont*	7 14
N13	●	at Middle Tennessee	34 0
N20	●	Virginia	7 7
N27	●	Sewanee	21 3

1921　7-0-1
O1	●	Middle Tennessee	34 0
O8	●	Mercer	42 0
O15	●	at Kentucky	21 14
O21	●	Texas *Dal*	20 0
O29	●	Tennessee	14 0
N5	●	Alabama *Mont*	14 0
N13	●	Georgia	7 7
N19	●	Sewanee	9 0

1922-1932 SOUTHERN

1922　8-0-1 (4-0-0)
S30	●	Middle Tennessee	38 0
O7	●	Henderson-Brown	33 0
O14	=	Michigan	0 0
O21	●	Texas *Dal*	20 10
O28	●	Mercer	25 0
N4	●	at Tennessee	14 6
N11	●	Kentucky	9 0
N18	●	at Georgia	12 0
N25		Sewanee	26 0

1923　5-2-1 (4-0-1)
O6	●	Samford	27 0
O13	●	at Michigan	0 3
O20	●	Texas *Dal*	0 16
O27	●	Tulane	17 0
N3	=	Mississippi State	0 0
N10	●	Tennessee	51 7
N17	●	Georgia	35 7
N24	●	Sewanee	77 0

1924　6-3-1 (3-3-0)
S27	●	Henderson-Brown	13 0
O4	●	B'ham Southern	61 0
O11	=	at Quantico Marines	13 13
O18	●	at Tulane	13 21
O25	●	Georgia	0 3
N1	●	Auburn	13 0
N8	●	Mississippi State	18 0
N15	●	at Georgia Tech	3 0
N22	●	at Minnesota	16 0
N29		Sewanee	0 16

1925　6-3-0 (3-3-0)
S26	●	Middle Tennessee	27 0
O3	●	Henderson-Brown	41 0
O10	●	Texas	14 6
O17	●	Tennessee	34 7
O24	●	at Georgia	7 26
O31	●	Mississippi	7 0
N7	●	Georgia Tech	0 7
N14	●	Auburn *Mont*	9 10
N21	●	Sewanee	19 7

1926　8-1-0 (4-1-0)
S25	●	Middle Tennessee	69 0
O2	●	Alabama	7 19
O9	●	Bryson	48 0
O16	●	Texas *Dal*	7 0
O23	●	Georgia	14 13
O30	●	Southwestern	50 0
N6	●	at Georgia Tech	13 7
N13	●	Tennessee	20 3
N20	●	Sewanee	13 0

1927　8-1-2 (5-0-2)
S24	●	at U.T. Chattanooga	45 18
O1	●	Ouachita	39 10
O8	●	at Centre	53 6
O15	●	Texas *Dal*	6 13
O22	●	Tulane	32 0
O29	●	Kentucky	34 6
N6	=	Georgia Tech	0 0
N12	●	at Tennessee	7 7
N19	●	Maryland	39 20
N26	●	Sewanee	26 6
D3	●	Alabama *Mont*	14 7

1928　8-2-0 (4-2-0)
S29	●	at U.T. Chattanooga	20 0
O6	●	Colgate	12 7
O13	●	Texas *AL*	13 12
O20	●	at Tulane	13 6
O27	●	Virginia	34 0
N3	●	Kentucky	14 7
N10	●	at Georgia Tech	7 19
N17		Tennessee	0 6
N24	●	Centre	26 0
D1	●	Sewanee	13 0

1929　7-2-0 (5-1-0)
S28	●	Mississippi	19 7
O5	●	Ouachita	26 6
O12	●	at Minnesota	6 15
O19	●	Auburn *Mont*	41 2
O26	●	Maryville	33 0
N2	●	Alabama	13 0
N9	●	Georgia Tech	23 7
N16	●	at Tennessee	0 13
N23	●	Sewanee	26 6

1930　8-2-0 (5-2-0)
S27	●	U.T. Chattanooga	39 0
O4	●	at Minnesota	33 7
O11	●	Virginia Tech	40 0
O18	●	Spring Hill	27 6
O25	●	Alabama *Mont*	7 12
N1	●	Mississippi	24 0
N8	●	at Georgia Tech	6 0
N15	●	Tennessee	0 13
N22	●	Auburn	27 0
D1	●	Maryland	22 7

1931　5-4-0 (3-4-0)
S26	●	Western Kentucky	52 0
O3	●	North Carolina	13 0
O10	●	at Ohio State	26 21
O17	●	Tulane	0 19
O24	●	at Georgia	0 9
O31	●	at Georgia Tech	49 7
N7	●	Maryland	39 12
N14	●	at Tennessee	7 21
N26	●	Alabama	6 14

1932　6-1-2 (4-1-2)
S24	●	Mercer	20 7
O1	●	at North Carolina	39 7
O8	●	Western Kentucky	26 0
O15	=	at Tulane	6 6
O22	●	Georgia	12 6
O29	●	Georgia Tech	12 0
N5	●	Maryland *DC*	13 0
N12	=	Tennessee	0 0
N24	●	Alabama *Mont*	0 20

1933-PRESENT SEC

1933　4-3-3 (2-2-2)
S23	●	Cumberland	50 0
S30	●	at Oklahoma	0 0
O7	●	North Carolina	20 13
O14	●	at Ohio State	0 20
O21	=	Mississippi State	7 7
O28	=	at LSU	7 7
N4	●	at Georgia Tech	9 6
N11	●	Sewanee	27 14
N18	●	at Tennessee	6 33
N30		Alabama	0 7

1934　6-3-0 (4-3-0)
S29		Mississippi State	7 0
O6	●	at Georgia Tech	27 12
O13	●	Cincinnati	32 0
O20	●	Auburn	7 6
O27	●	LSU	0 29
N3	●	at George Washington	7 6
N10	●	Sewanee	19 0
N17	●	Tennessee	6 13
N29		Alabama *Mont*	0 34

RAY MORRISON

1935　7-3-0 (5-1-0)
S21	●	Union	34 0
S28	●	Mississippi State	14 9
O5	●	Cumberland	32 7
O12	●	at Temple	3 6
O19	●	Fordham *NYC*	7 13
O26	●	LSU	2 7
N2	●	at Georgia Tech	14 13
N9	●	Sewanee	46 0
N16	●	at Tennessee	13 7
N28	●	Alabama	14 6

1936　3-5-1 (1-3-1)
S26	●	Middle Tennessee	45 0
O3	●	at Chicago	37 0
O10	●	Southwestern	0 12
O17	●	at SMU	0 16
O24	=	Georgia Tech	0 0
O31	●	LSU	0 19
N7	●	Sewanee	14 0
N14	●	Tennessee	13 26
N25	●	Alabama *Mont*	6 14

1937　7-2-0 (4-2-0)
S25		Kentucky	12 0
O2	●	Chicago	18 0
O8	●	at Southwestern	17 6
O13	●	at SMU	6 0
O23	●	LSU	7 6
O30	●	at Georgia Tech	0 14
N6	●	Sewanee	41 0
N13	●	at Tennessee	13 7
N25	●	Alabama	7 9

1938　6-3-0 (4-3-0)
S24	●	at Washington, Mo.	20 0
O1	●	Western Kentucky	12 0
O8	●	at Kentucky	14 7
O15	●	Mississippi	13 7
O22	●	at LSU	0 7
O29	●	Georgia Tech	13 7
N5	●	Sewanee	14 0
N12	●	Tennessee	0 14
N24	●	Alabama *Mont*	0 7

1939　2-7-1 (1-6-0)
S23	=	Tennessee Tech	13 13
S30	●	at Rice	13 12
O7	●	Kentucky	13 21
O14	●	VMI	13 20
O21	●	at Georgia Tech	6 14
O28	●	LSU	6 12
N4	●	Mississippi *Mem*	7 14
N11	●	Sewanee	25 7
N18	●	at Tennessee	0 13
N30		Alabama	0 39

RED SANDERS
1940-42, '46-48 (.617) 36-22-2

1940　3-6-1 (0-5-1)
S28	●	Wash. & Lee	19 0
O5		at Princeton	6 7
O12	=	Kentucky	7 7
O19	●	at Georgia Tech	0 19
O26	●	at LSU	0 7
N2	●	Mississippi	7 13
N9	●	Sewanee	20 0
N16	●	Tennessee Tech	21 0
N23	●	Alabama *Mont*	21 25
N30		Tennessee	0 20

1941　8-2-0 (3-2-0)
S27	●	at Purdue	3 0
O4	●	Tennessee Tech	42 0
O11	●	at Kentucky	39 15
O18	●	Georgia Tech	14 7
O25	●	Princeton	46 7
N1	●	Tulane	14 34
N8	●	Sewanee	20 0
N15	●	at Louisville	68 0
N22	●	Alabama	7 0
N29	●	at Tennessee	7 26

1942　6-4-0 (2-4-0)
S26	●	Tennessee Tech	52 0
O3	●	Purdue	26 0
O10	●	at Kentucky	7 6
O17	●	Mississippi State	0 33
O24	●	Centre	66 0
O31	●	at Tulane	21 28
N7	●	Mississippi *Mem*	19 0
N14	●	at Union	27 0
N21	●	Alabama *Mont*	7 27
N28		Tennessee	7 19

E.H. ALLEY
1943 (1.000)　5-0

1943　5-0-0 (0-0-0)
S25	●	at Tennessee Tech	30 0
O9	●	at Camp Campbell	40 14
O16	●	Milligan	26 6
O30	●	Carson-Newman	12 6
N13	●	Tennessee Tech	47 7

DOBY BARTLING
1944-45 (.500)　6-6-1

1944　3-0-1 (0-0-0)
O7	=	at Sewanee	0 0
O14	●	Tennessee Tech	19 7
O21	●	at Tennessee Tech	20 9
O28	●	Sewanee	28 7

1945　3-6-0 (2-4-0)
S29	●	Tennessee Tech	12 0
O6		Mississippi	7 14
O13	●	at Florida	7 0
O20	●	Kentucky	19 6
O27	●	at LSU	7 39
N3	●	VMI	13 27
N10	●	U.T. Chattanooga	6 13
N17	●	Alabama	0 71
D1	●	at Tennessee	0 45

RED SANDERS

1946　5-4-0 (3-4-0)
S28	●	Tennessee Tech	35 0
O5	●	Mississippi *Mem*	7 0
O12	●	Florida	20 0
O19	●	at Kentucky	7 10
O26	●	LSU	0 14
N2	●	Auburn	19 0
N9	●	North Carolina St. *Mont*	7 0
N16	●	Alabama *Mont*	7 12
N30	●	Tennessee	6 7

1947　6-4-0 (3-3-0)
S27	●	at Northwestern	3 0
O4	●	Alabama	14 7
O11	●	Mississippi	10 6
O18	●	Kentucky	0 14
O25	●	at LSU	13 19
N1	●	Auburn	28 0
N8	●	Tennessee Tech	68 0
N14	●	at Miami, Fla.	33 7
N22	●	Maryland	6 20
N29	●	at Tennessee	7 12

1948　8-2-1 (4-2-1)
S25		Georgia Tech	0 13
O2	=	Alabama *Mbl*	14 14
O9	●	at Mississippi	7 20
O16	●	at Kentucky	26 7
O23	●	at Yale	35 0
O29	●	Auburn *Mont*	47 0
N6	●	LSU	48 7
N13	●	Marshall	56 0
N20	●	Maryland *DC*	34 0
N27	●	Tennessee	28 6
D3	●	at Miami, Fla.	33 6

BILL EDWARDS
1949-52 (.524)　21-19-2

1949　5-5-0 (4-4-0)
S24	●	at Georgia Tech	7 12
O1	●	Alabama	14 7
O8	●	Mississippi	28 27
O15	●	Florida *JacF*	22 17
O22	●	Arkansas	6 7
O29	●	Auburn	26 7
N5	●	at LSU	13 33
N12	●	Tulane	14 41
N19	●	Marshall	27 0
N26	●	at Tennessee	20 26

1950　7-4-0 (3-4-0)
S23	●	Middle Tennessee	47 0
S30	●	Auburn	41 0
O7	●	Alabama *Mbl*	27 22
O14	●	Mississippi	20 14
O21	●	Florida	27 31
O28	●	Arkansas *LR*	14 13
N3	●	at U.T. Chattanooga	34 12
N11	●	LSU	7 33
N18	●	at Memphis	29 13
N25	●	at Tulane	6 35
D2		Tennessee	0 43

VANDERBILT 229

1951 6-5-0 (3-5-0)

S22	●	Middle Tennessee	22	7
S29		at Auburn	14	24
O6	●	Alabama	22	20
O13	●	Mississippi MEM	34	20
O20		at Florida	13	33
O27		Georgia Tech	7	8
N3	●	U.T. Chattanooga	19	14
N10	●	at LSU	20	13
N17		Tulane	10	14
N24	●	Memphis	13	7
D1		at Tennessee	27	35

1952 3-5-2 (1-4-1)

S20		Georgia	7	19
S27		at Virginia	0	27
O4	=	at Northwestern	20	20
O11	=	Mississippi	21	21
O18	●	Florida	20	13
O25		at Georgia Tech	0	30
N1	●	Wash. & Lee	67	7
N7	●	at Miami, Fla.	9	0
N15		at Tulane	7	16
N29		Tennessee	0	46

ART GUEPE
1953-62 (.425) 39-54-7

1953 3-7-0 (1-5-0)

S26		at Pennsylvania	7	13
O3		Alabama	12	21
O10		at Mississippi	6	28
O17		at Baylor	6	47
O24	●	Virginia	28	13
O31		Georgia Tech	0	43
N7		Kentucky	14	40
N14	●	at Tulane	21	7
N21	●	Middle Tennessee	31	13
N28		at Tennessee	6	33

1954 2-7-0 (1-5-0)

S25		Baylor	19	25
O2		Alabama MBL	14	28
O9		Mississippi	7	22
O16		at Georgia	14	16
O30		at Rice	13	34
N6		at Kentucky	7	19
N13		Tulane	0	6
N20	●	Villanova	34	19
N27	●	Tennessee	26	0

1955 8-3-0 (4-3-0)

S24		at Georgia	13	14
O1	●	Alabama	21	6
O8		Mississippi MEM	0	13
O14	●	at U.T. Chattanooga	12	0
O22	●	Middle Tennessee	46	0
O29	●	Virginia	34	7
N5	●	Kentucky	34	0
N12	●	at Tulane	20	7
N19	●	Florida	21	6
N26		at Tennessee	14	20
		GATOR BOWL		
D31	●	Auburn	25	13

1956 5-5-0 (2-5-0)

S22	●	Georgia	14	0
S29	●	U.T. Chattanooga	46	7
O6	●	Alabama MBL	32	7
O13		at Mississippi	0	16
O20		Florida	7	21
O27	●	at Middle Tennessee	23	13
N3	●	at Virginia	6	2
N10		at Kentucky	6	7
N17		Tulane	6	13
D1		Tennessee	7	27

1957 5-3-2 (3-3-1)

S21	=	Missouri	7	7
S28	●	at Georgia	9	6
O5	=	Alabama	6	6
O12		Mississippi	0	28
O19	●	at Penn State	32	20
N2	●	LSU	7	0
N9	●	Kentucky	12	7
N16		at Florida	7	14
N23	●	Citadel	27	0
N30		at Tennessee	6	20

1958 5-2-3 (2-1-3)

S20	●	at Missouri	12	8
S27	●	Georgia	21	14
O4	=	Alabama MONT	0	0
O11		Clemson	7	12
O18	=	at Florida	6	6
O25	●	Virginia	39	6
O31	●	at Miami, Fla.	28	15
N8	=	at Kentucky	0	0
N15	●	Tulane	12	0
N29		Tennessee	6	10

1959 5-3-2 (3-2-2)

S26		at Georgia	6	21
O3	=	Alabama	7	7
O10		Mississippi	0	33
O17	●	Florida	13	6
O24	●	at Virginia	33	0
O31		at Minnesota	6	20
N7	●	Kentucky	11	6
N14	=	at Tulane	6	6
N21	●	Florence St.	42	7
N28	●	at Tennessee	14	0

1960 3-7-0 (0-7-0)

S24		Georgia	7	18
O1		Alabama MONT	0	21
O8		Mississippi	0	26
O15		at Florida	0	12
O22	●	at Marquette	23	6
O29	●	Clemson	22	20
N5		at Kentucky	0	27
N12	●	William & Mary	22	8
N19		Tulane	0	20
N26		Tennessee	0	35

1961 2-8-0 (1-6-0)

S23	●	West Virginia	16	6
S30	●	at Georgia	21	0
O7		Alabama	6	35
O14		at UCLA	21	28
O21		Florida	0	7
O28		at Mississippi	0	47
N11		Kentucky	3	16
N17		at Tulane	14	17
N25		South Carolina	7	23
D2		at Tennessee	7	41

1962 1-9-0 (1-6-0)

S22		at West Virginia	0	26
S29		Georgia	0	10
O6		Alabama MONT	7	17
O13		Citadel	6	21
O20		at Florida	7	42
O27		Mississippi MEM	0	35
N3		Boston College	22	27
N10		at Kentucky	0	7
N17	●	Tulane	20	0
D1		Tennessee	0	30

JACK GREEN
1963-66 (.225) 7-29-4

1963 1-7-2 (0-5-2)

S21		Furman	13	14
S28		at Georgia	0	20
O5		Alabama	6	21
O19		Florida	0	21
O26		at Mississippi	7	27
N2		at Boston College	6	19
N9	=	Kentucky	0	0
N16	=	at Tulane	10	10
N23	●	George Washington	31	0
N30		at Tennessee	0	14

1964 3-6-1 (1-4-1)

S19		at Georgia Tech	2	14
S26		Georgia	0	7
O3		Alabama MONT	0	24
O10	●	Wake Forest	9	6
O17	●	at George Washington	14	0
O24	=	Mississippi	7	7
N7		at Kentucky	21	22
N14		Tulane	2	7
N20		at Miami, Fla.	17	35
N28	●	Tennessee	7	0

1965 2-7-1 (1-5-0)

S18	=	Georgia Tech	10	10
S25		at Georgia	10	24
O2		at Wake Forest	0	7
O9		Alabama	7	22
O16	●	Virginia Tech	21	10
O23		at Mississippi	7	24
O30	●	at Tulane	13	0
N6		Kentucky	0	34
N13		Miami, Fla.	14	28
N27		at Tennessee	3	21

1966 1-9-0 (0-6-0)

S17	●	Citadel	24	0
S24		at Georgia Tech	0	42
O1		Florida	0	13
O15		Virginia Tech RICH	6	21
O22		Alabama MONT	6	42
O29		Tulane	12	13
N5		at Kentucky	10	14
N12		Navy	14	30
N19		Mississippi JAM	0	34
N26		Tennessee	0	28

BILL PACE
1967-72 (.373) 22-38-3

1967 2-7-1 (0-6-0)

S23		Georgia Tech	10	17
S30	●	William & Mary	14	12
O7	●	at North Carolina	21	7
O14		Alabama	21	35
O28		at Florida	22	27
N4		at Tulane	14	27
N11		Kentucky	7	12
N18	=	at Navy	35	35
N25		Mississippi	7	28
D2		at Tennessee	14	41

1968 5-4-1 (2-3-1)

S21	●	VMI	25	12
S28	●	at Army	17	13
O5		North Carolina	7	8
O12		at Alabama	7	31
O19		at Georgia	6	32
O26	=	Florida	14	14
N2	●	Tulane	21	7
N9	●	at Kentucky	6	0
N23	●	at Davidson	53	20
N30		Tennessee	7	10

1969 4-6-0 (2-3-0)

S20		at Michigan	14	42
S27		Army	6	16
O4		at North Carolina	22	38
O11	●	Alabama	14	10
O18		Georgia	8	40
O25		at Florida	20	41
N1	●	at Tulane	26	23
N8	●	Kentucky	42	6
N22	●	Davidson	63	8
N29		at Tennessee	27	40

1970 4-7-0 (1-5-0)

S12	●	U.T. Chattanooga	39	6
S19	●	Citadel	52	0
S26		Mississippi State MEM	6	20
O3		North Carolina	7	10
O10		at Alabama	11	35
O17		at Georgia	3	7
O24		Mississippi	16	26
O31		Tulane	7	10
N7	●	at Kentucky	18	17
N21	●	at Tampa	36	28
N28		Tennessee	6	24

1971 4-6-1 (1-5-0)

S11	●	U.T. Chattanooga	20	19
S18	=	Louisville	0	0
S25	●	at Mississippi State	49	19
O2		at Virginia	23	27
O9		Alabama	0	42
O16		Georgia	0	24
O23		at Mississippi	7	28
O30	●	at Tulane	13	9
N6		Kentucky	7	14
N20	●	Tampa	10	7
N27		at Tennessee	7	19

1972 3-8-0 (0-6-0)

S9	●	U.T. Chattanooga	24	7
S23		Mississippi State	6	10
S30		at Alabama	21	48
O7	●	Virginia	10	7
O14	●	at William & Mary	21	17
O21		at Georgia	3	28
O28		Mississippi	7	31
N11		at Kentucky	13	14
N18		Tulane	7	21
N25		at Tampa	7	30
D2		Tennessee	10	30

STEVE SLOAN
1973-74 (.565) 12-9-2

1973 5-6-0 (1-5-0)

S15	●	U.T. Chattanooga	14	12
S22		at Mississippi State	21	52
S29		Alabama	0	44
O6	●	at Virginia	39	22
O13	●	William & Mary	20	7
O20	●	Georgia	18	14
O27		at Mississippi	14	24
N10		Kentucky	17	27
N17		at Tulane	3	24
N24	●	Tampa	18	16
D1		at Tennessee	17	20

1974 7-3-2 (2-3-1)

S14	●	U.T. Chattanooga	28	6
S21	●	VMI	45	7
S28		at Alabama	10	23
O12	●	Florida	24	10
O19		at Georgia	31	38
O26	●	Mississippi	24	14
N2	●	at Army	38	14
N9		at Kentucky	12	38
N16	●	Tulane	30	22
N23	●	at Louisville	44	0
N30	=	Tennessee	21	21
		PEACH BOWL		
D28	=	Texas Tech	6	6

FRED PANCOAST
1975-78 (.295) 13-31

1975 7-4-0 (2-4-0)

S13	●	U.T. Chattanooga	17	7
S20	●	at Rice	9	6
S27		Alabama	7	40
O4	●	at Tulane	6	3
O11		at Florida	0	35
O18		Georgia	3	47
O25		at Mississippi	7	17
N1	●	Virginia	17	14
N8	●	Kentucky	13	3
N15	●	Army	23	14
N29	●	at Tennessee	17	14

1976 2-9-0 (0-6-0)

S11		Oklahoma	3	24
S18	●	Wake Forest	27	24
S25		at Alabama	14	42
O2		Tulane	13	24
O9		at LSU	20	33
O16		at Georgia	0	45
O23		Mississippi	3	20
N6		at Kentucky	0	14
N13	●	Air Force	34	10
N20		at Cincinnati	7	33
N27		Tennessee	10	13

1977 2-9-0 (0-6-0)

S10		at Oklahoma	23	25
S17	●	at Wake Forest	3	0
S24		Alabama	12	24
O1		at Tulane	7	36
O8		LSU	15	28
O15		Georgia	13	24
O22		at Mississippi	14	26
N5		Kentucky	6	28
N12		at Air Force	28	34
N19	●	Cincinnati	13	9
N26		at Tennessee	7	42

1978 2-9-0 (0-6-0)

S16		Arkansas LR	17	48
S23	●	Furman	17	10
S30		at Alabama	28	51
O7		Tulane	3	38
O14		Auburn	7	49
O21		at Georgia	10	31
O28		Mississippi	10	35
N4		at Memphis	14	35
N11		at Kentucky	2	53
N18	●	Air Force	41	27
D2		Tennessee	15	41

GEORGE MacINTYRE
1979-85 (.327) 25-52-1

1979 1-10-0 (0-6-0)

S15		at Indiana	13	44
S22		Citadel	14	27
S29		Alabama	3	66
O6		at Tulane	14	42
O13		at Auburn	35	52
O20		Georgia	10	31
O27		at Mississippi	28	63
N3	●	Memphis	13	3
N10		Kentucky	10	29
N17		at Air Force	29	30
D1		at Tennessee	10	31

1980 2-9-0 (0-6-0)

S13		at Maryland	6	31
S20		Mississippi State	14	24
S27		at Alabama	0	41
O11		Tulane	21	43
O18		at Georgia	0	41
O25		Mississippi	14	27
N1	●	at Memphis	14	10
N8		at Kentucky	10	31
N15		Miami, Fla.	17	24
N22	●	U.T. Chattanooga	31	29
N29		Tennessee	13	51

THE SCHOOLS

1981   4-7-0 (1-5-0)

S12 ●	Maryland	23	17
S19	at Mississippi State	9	29
S26	Alabama	7	28
O3	at Miami, Fla.	16	48
O10	at Tulane	10	14
O17	Georgia	21	53
O24 ●	at Mississippi	27	23
O31 ●	Memphis	26	0
N7	Kentucky	10	17
N21 ●	U.T. Chattanooga	28	14
N28	at Tennessee	34	38

1982   8-4-0 (4-2-0)

S11 ●	at Memphis	24	14
S18 ●	at North Carolina	10	34
S25 ●	at Alabama	21	24
O2 ●	Tulane	24	21
O9 ●	Florida	31	29
O16 ●	at Georgia	13	27
O23 ●	Mississippi	19	10
N6 ●	at Kentucky	23	10
N13	Virginia Tech	45	0
N20 ●	U.T. Chattanooga	27	16
N27 ●	Tennessee	28	21
	HALL OF FAME CLASSIC		
D31	Air Force	28	36

1983   2-9-0 (0-6-0)

S10	Maryland	14	21
S17 ●	Iowa State	29	26
S24	Alabama	24	44
O1 ●	at Tulane	30	17
O8	at Florida	10	29
O15	Georgia	13	20
O22	at Mississippi	14	21
O29	Memphis	7	24
N5	Kentucky	8	17
N12	at Virginia Tech	10	21
N26	at Tennessee	24	34

1984   5-6-0 (2-4-0)

S8	Kansas State	26	14
S15 ●	at Maryland	23	14
S22 ●	Kansas	41	6
S29 ●	at Alabama	30	21
O6	Tulane	23	27
O13	at LSU	27	34
O20	at Georgia	35	62
O27 ●	Mississippi	37	20
N10 ●	at Kentucky	18	27
N17	Virginia Tech	3	23
D1	Tennessee	13	29

1985   3-7-1 (1-4-1)

S7 ●	U.T. Chattanooga	7	0
S14	at Kansas	16	42
S21	at Iowa State	17	20
S28	Alabama	20	40
O5 ●	at Tulane	24	17
O12	LSU	7	49
O19 =	Georgia	13	13
O26	at Mississippi	7	35
N9 ●	Kentucky	31	24
N16	Virginia Tech	24	38
N30	at Tennessee	0	30

	WATSON BROWN		
	1986-90 (.182)	10-45	

1986   1-10-0 (0-6-0)

S6	at Alabama	10	42
S13	at Maryland	21	35
S20	Tulane	17	35
O4 ●	Duke	24	18
O11	Auburn	9	31
O18	at Georgia	16	38
O25	Mississippi	12	28
N1	Memphis	21	22
N8	at Kentucky	22	34
N15	at Virginia Tech	21	29
N29	Tennessee	20	35

1987   4-7-0 (1-5-0)

S12 ●	Memphis	27	17
S19	at Duke	31	35
S26	Alabama	23	30
O3	at Tulane	17	27
O10	at Auburn	15	48
O17	Georgia	24	52
O24	at Mississippi	14	42
O31 ●	Rutgers	27	13
N7 ●	Kentucky	38	29
N21 ●	Maryland	34	24
N28	at Tennessee	36	38

1988   3-8-0 (2-5-0)

S10 ●	Mississippi State	24	20
S17 ●	Rutgers ᴱᴿᵁᵀ	31	30
S24	at Alabama	10	44
O1	Duke	15	17
O8	at Georgia	22	41
O15 ●	Florida	24	9
O22	Mississippi	28	36
N5	at Kentucky	13	14
N12	at Army	19	24
N19	at Memphis	9	28
N26	Tennessee	7	14

1989   1-10-0 (0-7-0)

S2	at Mississippi State	7	42
S23 ●	Ohio U.	54	10
S30	Alabama	14	20
O7	at Memphis	10	13
O14	at Florida	11	34
O21	Georgia	16	35
O28	at Mississippi	16	21
N4	at Virginia Tech	0	18
N11	Kentucky	11	15
N18	Tulane	13	37
D2	at Tennessee	10	17

1990   1-10-0 (1-6-0)

S8	at SMU	7	44
S22 ●	LSU	24	21
S29	at Alabama	28	59
O6	Syracuse	14	49
O13	at Auburn	6	56
O20	at Georgia	28	39
O27	Mississippi	13	14
N10	at Kentucky	21	28
N17	Army	38	42
N24	Wake Forest	28	56
D1	Tennessee	20	49

	GERRY DiNARDO		
	1991-94 (.409)	18-26	

1991   5-6-0 (3-4-0)

S7	at Syracuse	10	37
S14 ●	SMU	14	11
S21	at LSU	14	16
S28	Alabama	17	48
O5	at Duke	13	17
O12	Auburn	22	24
O19 ●	Georgia	27	25
O26 ●	at Mississippi	30	27
N2 ●	at Army	41	10
N9 ●	Kentucky	17	7
N30	at Tennessee	0	45

1992   4-7-0 (2-6-0)

S5 ●	at Alabama	8	25
S12 ●	Duke	42	37
S19 ●	Mississippi	31	9
O3	at Auburn	7	31
O10	Wake Forest	6	40
O17	at Georgia	20	30
O24	South Carolina	17	21
N7 ●	at Kentucky	20	7
N14 ●	at Navy	27	7
N21 ●	Florida	21	41
N28	Tennessee	25	29

1993   4-7-0 (1-7-0)

S4 ●	at Wake Forest	27	12
S11	Alabama	6	17 †
S18	at Mississippi	7	49
O2	Auburn	10	14
O9 ●	Cincinnati	17	7
O16	Georgia	3	41
O23	at South Carolina	0	22
N6 ●	Kentucky	12	7
N13 ●	Navy	41	7
N20	at Florida	0	52
N27	at Tennessee	14	62

1994   5-6-0 (2-6-0)

S3 ●	Wake Forest	35	14
S10	at Alabama	7	17
S17	Mississippi	14	20
O1	Arkansas ᴸᴿ	6	42
O8	at Cincinnati	34	24
O15 ●	at Georgia	43	30
O22	South Carolina	16	19
O29 ●	Northern Illinois	17	16
N5 ●	at Kentucky	24	6
N19	Florida	7	24
N26	Tennessee	0	65

	ROD DOWHOWER		
	1995-96 (.182)	4-18	

1995   2-9-0 (1-7-0)

S2 ●	Alabama	25	33
S16	at Notre Dame	0	41
S23	TCU	3	16
S30	Arkansas	7	35
O14	Georgia	6	17
O21	at South Carolina	14	52
O28	at Mississippi	10	21
N4 ●	Kentucky	14	10
N11	Louisiana Tech	29	6
N18	at Florida	7	38
N25	at Tennessee	7	12

1996   2-9 (0-8)

S5	Notre Dame	7	14
S14	at Alabama	26	36
S21	Mississippi	9	20
O5	at LSU	0	35
O12 ●	at North Texas	19	7
O19	at Georgia	2	13
O26	South Carolina	0	27
N2 ●	UAB	31	15
N9	Florida	21	28
N16	at Kentucky	0	25
N30	Tennessee	7	14

	WOODY WIDENHOFER		
	1997-2001 (.273)	15-40	

1997   3-8 (0-8)

A30	North Texas	29	12
S11	Alabama	0	20
S20 ●	TCU	40	16
S27	at Mississippi	3	15
O4	LSU	6	7
O11 ●	at Northern Illinois	17	7
O18	Georgia	13	34
O25	at South Carolina	3	35
N8	at Florida	7	20
N15	Kentucky	10	21
N29	at Tennessee	10	17

1998   2-9 (1-7)

S5	at Mississippi State	0	42
S12	Alabama ᴹᴼᴺᵀ	7	32
S19	Mississippi	6	30
O3	at TCU	16	19
O10	Western Michigan	24	27
O17	at Georgia	6	31
O24 ●	South Carolina	17	14
O31 ●	Duke	36	33
N7	Florida	13	45
N14	at Kentucky	17	55
N28	Tennessee	0	41

1999   5-6 (2-6)

S4	Alabama	17	28
S11 ●	Northern Illinois	34	31
S18 ●	at Mississippi	37	34
S25 ●	at Duke	31	14
O2	Mississippi State	14	42
O9 ●	Citadel	58	0
O16	Georgia	17	27
O23 ●	at South Carolina	11	10
N6	at Florida	6	13
N13	Kentucky	17	19
N27	at Tennessee	10	38

2000   3-8 (1-7)

S2	Miami, Ohio	30	33
S9	Alabama ᴹᴼᴺᵀ	10	28
S16	Mississippi	7	12
S23 ●	Duke	26	7
S30	at Auburn	0	33
O7	at Wake Forest	17	10
O14	at Georgia	19	29
O21	South Carolina	14	30
N4	Florida	20	43
N11 ●	at Kentucky	24	20
N25	Tennessee	26	28

2001   2-9 (0-8)

A30	Middle Tennessee	28	37
S8	Alabama	9	12
S22 ●	Richmond	28	22
S29	Auburn	21	24
O13	Georgia	14	30
O20	at South Carolina	14	46
O27 ●	at Duke	42	28
N3	at Florida	13	71
N10	Kentucky	30	56
N24	at Tennessee	0	38
D1	at Mississippi	27	38

	BOBBY JOHNSON		
	2002-Present (.325)	27-56	

2002   2-10 (0-8)

A31	at Georgia Tech	3	45
S7 ●	Furman	49	18
S14	at Auburn	6	31
S21	at Mississippi	38	45
S28	South Carolina	14	20
O12	Middle Tennessee	20	21
O19	at Georgia	17	48
O26 ●	Connecticut	28	24
N2	Alabama	8	30
N9	Florida	17	21
N16	at Kentucky	21	41
N23	Tennessee	0	24

2003   2-10 (1-7)

A30	Mississippi	21	24
S6 ●	U.T. Chattanooga	51	6
S13	Auburn	7	45
S20	at TCU	14	30
S27	Georgia Tech	17	24
O4	at Mississippi State	21	30
O11	Navy	27	37
O18	Georgia	8	27
O25	at South Carolina	24	35
N8	at Florida	17	35
N15 ●	Kentucky	28	17
N22	at Tennessee	0	48

2004   2-9 (1-7)

S4	South Carolina	6	31
S18	at Mississippi	23	26
S25	at Navy	26	29
O2 ●	Mississippi State	31	13
O9	Rutgers	34	37
O16	at Georgia	3	33
O23 ●	Eastern Kentucky	19	7
O30	at LSU	7	24
N6	Florida	17	34
N13	at Kentucky	13	14
N20	Tennessee	33	38

2005   5-6 (3-5)

S1 ●	at Wake Forest	24	20
S10 ●	at Arkansas	28	24
S17 ●	Mississippi	31	13
S24 ●	Richmond	37	13
O1	Middle Tennessee State	15	17
O8	LSU	6	34
O15	Georgia	17	34
O22	at South Carolina	28	35
N5 ●	at Florida	42	49
N12 ●	Kentucky	43	48
N19 ●	at Tennessee	28	24

2006   4-8 (1-7)

S2	at Michigan	7	27
S9	at Alabama	10	13
S16	Arkansas	19	21
S23 ●	Tennessee State	38	9
S30 ●	Temple	43	14
O7	at Mississippi	10	17
O14 ●	at Georgia	24	22
O21	South Carolina	13	31
O28 ●	at Duke	45	28
N4	Florida	19	25
N11 ●	at Kentucky	26	39
N18	Tennessee	10	39

2007   5-7 (2-6)

S1 ●	Richmond	41	17
S8	Alabama	10	24
S15 ●	Mississippi	31	17
S29 ●	Eastern Michigan	30	7
O6	at Auburn	7	35
O13	Georgia	17	20
O20 ●	at South Carolina	17	6
O27 ●	Miami (Ohio)	24	13
N3	at Florida	22	49
N10	Kentucky	20	27
N17	at Tennessee	24	25
N24	Wake Forest	17	31

2008   7-6 (4-4)

A28 ●	at Miami (Ohio)	34	13
S4 ●	South Carolina	24	17
S13 ●	Rice	38	21
S20 ●	at Mississippi	23	17
O4 ●	Auburn	14	13
O11	at Mississippi State	14	17
O18	at Georgia	14	24
O25	Duke	7	10
N8	Florida	14	42
N15 ●	at Kentucky	31	24
N22	Tennessee	10	20
N29	at Wake Forest	10	23
	MUSIC CITY BOWL		
D31 ●	Boston College	16	14

VANDERBILT ANNUAL STATISTICAL LEADERS

YR	RUSHING	YDS	ATT	AVG	PASSING	ATT	CMP	PCT	YDS	RECEIVING	REC	YDS	AVG
1946	J.P. Moore	263	73	3.6	Jamie Wade	44	12	.27	222	John North	11	100	9.1
1947	Dean Davidson	461	90	5.1	Jamie Wade	70	27	.39	506	John North	11	197	17.9
1948	Herb Rich	514	95	5.4	Bob Berry	27	15	.56	360	Bucky Curtis	12	259	21.6
1949	Herb Rich	668	177	3.8	Jamie Wade	143	62	.43	1,021	Bucky Curtis	22	446	20.3
1950	Jim Tabor	654	111	5.9	Bill Wade	177	76	.43	1,596	Bucky Curtis	27	791	29.3
1951	R.C. Allen	321	74	4.3	Bill Wade	223	110	.49	1,609	Ben Roderick	40	627	15.7
1952	R.C. Allen	397	106	3.7	Bill Krietemeyer	153	69	.45	999	Ben Roderick	29	384	13.2
1953	Charles Horton	461	75	6.1	Jim Looney	82	61	.74	362	Charles Hawkins	19	269	14.2
1954	Don Hunt	474	95	5.0	Jim Looney	132	54	.41	813	Joe Stephenson	16	352	22.0
1955	Phil King	628	98	6.4	Don Orr	80	30	.38	486	Joe Stephenson	11	204	18.5
1956	Phil King	651	129	5.0	Boyce Smith	57	27	.47	361	Bob Taylor	12	187	15.6
1957	Phil King	438	115	3.8	Boyce Smith	98	49	.50	664	Phil King	14	172	12.3
1958	Tom Moore	584	145	4.0	Boyce Smith	105	49	.47	638	Tom Moore	12	135	11.3
1959	Tom Moore	676	125	5.4	Russ Morris	92	44	.48	579	Tom Moore	14	170	12.1
1960	Jim Johnson	312	77	4.1	Hank Lesesne	130	54	.42	620	Jeff Starling	14	127	9.1
1961	Hank Lesesne	325	112	2.9	Hank Lesesne	126	50	.40	607	Jeff Starling	25	273	10.9
1962	Hank Lesesne	214	105	2.0	Hank Lesesne	157	65	.41	741	Jeff Starling	34	494	14.5
1963	Bill Waldrup	244	67	3.6	Jon Cleveland	94	39	.41	512	Bennett Baldwin	15	176	11.7
1964	Bob Sullins	512	133	3.8	David Waller	141	61	.43	646	Bennett Baldwin	20	261	13.1
1965	Jim Whiteside	297	103	2.9	Bob Kerr	82	33	.40	346	Toby Wilt	13	171	13.2
1966	Jim Whiteside	267	94	2.8	Gary Davis	153	62	.41	777	Rusty Cantwell	17	157	9.2
1967	Jim Whiteside	255	105	2.4	Roger May	149	82	.55	929	Bob Goodridge	79	1,114	14.1
1968	Allan Spear	438	142	3.1	John Miller	201	99	.49	1,164	Curt Chesley	48	543	11.3
1969	Doug Mathews	849	167	5.1	Watson Brown	111	69	.62	696	Curt Chesley	44	516	11.7
1970	Steve Burger	552	162	3.4	Denny Painter	106	43	.41	563	Curt Chesley	33	393	11.9
1971	Jamie O'Rourke	677	165	4.1	Steve Burger	134	57	.43	671	Gary Chesley	19	253	13.3
1972	Lonnie Sadler	423	122	3.5	Steve Lainhart	89	34	.38	524	Walter Overton	20	317	15.9
1973	Jamie O'Rourke	592	132	4.5	Fred Fisher	234	128	.55	1,450	Jesse Mathers	34	423	12.4
1974	Jamie O'Rourke	933	201	4.6	David Lee	159	85	.53	1,173	Jesse Mathers	23	369	16.0
1975	Lonnie Sadler	536	175	3.1	Fred Fisher	106	51	.48	552	Barry Burton	31	306	9.9
1976	Adolph Groves	347	96	3.6	Randy Hampton	107	53	.50	805	Martin Cox	38	738	19.4
1977	Frank Mordica	449	133	3.4	Mike Wright	211	106	.50	1,383	Martin Cox	48	783	16.3
1978	Frank Mordica	1,065	173	6.2	Van Heflin	155	76	.49	984	Martin Cox	40	674	16.9
1979	Frank Mordica	830	162	5.1	Van Heflin	124	64	.52	748	Preston Brown	52	786	15.1
1980	Terry Potter	579	149	3.9	Whit Taylor	173	72	.42	899	Wamon Buggs	37	448	12.1
1981	Van Heflin	374	105	3.6	Whit Taylor	357	209	.59	2,318	Wamon Buggs	54	778	14.4
1982	Keith Edwards	340	88	3.9	Whit Taylor	406	228	.56	2,481	Allama Matthews	61	797	13.1
1983	Carl Woods	644	160	4.0	Kurt Page	493	286	.58	3,178	Keith Edwards	97	909	9.4
1984	Carl Woods	688	192	3.6	Kurt Page	350	203	.58	2,405	Keith Edwards	60	576	9.6
1985	Carl Woods	615	160	3.8	John Gromos	224	124	.55	1,483	Everett Crawford	50	533	10.7
1986	Carl Woods	552	107	5.2	Mark Wracher	134	75	.56	827	Everett Crawford	40	517	12.9
1987	Eric Jones	665	179	3.7	Eric Jones	229	139	.61	1,954	Carl Parker	42	806	19.2
1988	Eric Jones	305	144	2.1	Eric Jones	360	196	.54	2,548	Boo Mitchell	78	1,213	15.6
1989	Carlos Thomas	254	61	4.2	John Gromos	320	154	.48	1,744	Brad Gaines	67	634	9.5
1990	Carlos Thomas	680	113	6.0	Mike Healy	130	75	.58	1,041	Clarence Sevillian	29	536	18.5
1991	Corey Harris	1,103	229	4.8	Marcus Wilson	63	32	.51	491	Corey Harris	23	283	12.3
1992	Tony Jackson	652	114	5.7	Marcus Wilson	164	75	.46	1,030	Clarence Sevillian	33	701	21.2
1993	Tony Jackson	607	120	5.1	Ronnie Gordon	98	40	.41	400	Kenny Simon	15	166	11.1
1994	Jermaine Johnson	877	167	5.3	Ronnie Gordon	203	86	.42	991	Kenny Simon	20	271	13.6
1995	Jermaine Johnson	1,072	267	4.0	Damian Allen	136	62	.46	728	Sanford Ware	34	402	11.8
1996	Jason Dunnavant	374	131	2.9	Damian Allen	279	118	.42	1,472	Todd Yoder	21	471	22.4
1997	Jimmy Williams	527	98	5.4	Damian Allen	283	128	.45	1,544	Jimmy Williams	24	183	7.6
1998	Rodney Williams	608	126	4.8	Greg Zolman	145	69	.48	969	Tavarus Hogans	28	366	13.1
1999	Rodney Williams	644	148	4.4	Greg Zolman	300	154	.51	2,059	Tavarus Hogans	53	837	15.8
2000	Jared McGrath	527	133	4.0	Greg Zolman	354	187	.53	2,441	Dan Stricker	61	994	16.3
2001	Lew Thomas	675	105	6.4	Greg Zolman	357	186	.52	2,512	Dan Stricker	65	1,079	16.6
2002	Kwane Doster	798	160	5.0	Jay Cutler	212	103	.49	1,433	Dan Stricker	44	620	14.1
2003	Norval McKenzie	639	162	3.9	Jay Cutler	327	187	.57	1,347	Erik Davis	41	638	15.6
2004	Norval McKenzie	446	102	4.4	Jay Cutler	241	147	.61	1,544	Brandon Smith	41	553	13.5
2005	Cassen Jackson-Garrison	539	97	5.6	Jay Cutler	462	273	.59	3,073	Earl Bennett	79	876	11.1
2006	Chris Nickson	694	146	4.8	Chris Nickson	292	160	.55	2,085	Earl Bennett	82	1,146	14.0
2007	Cassen Jackson-Garrison	594	148	4.0	Mackenzi Adams	183	101	.55	1,043	Earl Bennett	75	830	11.1
2008	Jared Hawkins	593	139	4.3	Mackenzi Adams	156	77	.49	882	Sean Walker	36	520	14.4

Receiving leaders by receptions
The NCAA began including postseason stats in 2002

VANDERBILT RECORD BOOK

SINGLE-GAME RECORDS

Rushing Yards	321	Frank Mordica (Nov. 18, 1978 vs. Air Force)
Passing Yards	464	Whit Taylor (Nov. 28, 1981 vs. Tennessee)
Receiving Yards	223	Earl Bennett (Sept. 1, 2007 vs. Richmond); Frank Mordica (Nov. 18, 1978 vs. Air Force)
All-Purpose Yards	521	Whit Taylor (Nov. 28, 1981 vs. Tennessee)
Points	30	Earl Bennett (Nov. 12, 2005 vs. Kentucky)
Field Goals	4	John Markham (Sept. 23, 2000 vs. Duke)
Tackles	37	Chris Gaines (Oct. 3, 1987 vs. Tulane)
Interceptions	3	Ryan Hamilton (Sept. 23, 2008 vs. Ole Miss)

SINGLE-SEASON RECORDS

Rushing Yards	1,103	Corey Harris, 1991 (229 att.)
Passing Yards	3,178	Kurt Page, 1983 (286-493)
Receiving Yards	1,213	Boo Mitchell, 1988 (78 rec.)
All-Purpose Yards	3,288	Jay Cutler, 2005
Scoring	90	Jack Jenkins, 1941
Touchdowns	14	Allama Matthews, 1982
Tackles	214	Chris Gaines, 1987
Interceptions	8	Leonard Coleman, 1982; Scott Wingfield, 1973
Punting Average	48.2	Ricky Anderson, 1984 (58 punts)
Punt Return Average	18.4	Lee Nalley, 1948 (43 ret.)
Kickoff Return Average	25.7	D.J. Moore, 2007 (32 ret.)

CAREER RECORDS

Rushing Yards	2,632	Frank Mordica, 1976-79
Passing Yards	8,697	Jay Cutler, 2002-05
Receiving Yards	2,964	Boo Mitchell, 1985-88
All-Purpose Yards	9,953	Jay Cutler, 2002-05
Scoring	255	Bryant Hahnfeldt, 2005-08
Touchdowns	26	Dean Davidson, 1947-50
Tackles	458	Andrew Coleman, 1978-81
Interceptions	15	Leonard Coleman, 1980-83
Punting Average	45.5	Ricky Anderson, 1981-84 (111 punts)
Punt Return Average	15.3	Lee Nalley, 1947-49 (112 ret.)
Kickoff Return Average	21.1	Mark Johnson, 1986-90 (107 ret.)

TEAM RECORDS

Longest Winning Streak	13	Nov. 14, 1903-Oct. 7, 1905; broken by Michigan, 0-18 on Oct. 14, 1905
Longest Undefeated Streak	21	Nov. 27, 1920-Oct. 6, 1923; broken by Michigan, 0-3 on Oct. 13, 1923
Most Consecutive Winning Seasons	21	1915-36
Most Consecutive Bowl Appearances	1	Vanderbilt has appeared in four bowl games, none in consecutive seasons
Most Points in a Game	105	vs. Bethel College, Sept. 28, 1912
Most Points Allowed in a Game	83	vs. Georgia Tech, Nov. 3, 1917
Largest Margin of Victory	105	vs. Bethel College, Sept. 28, 1912
Largest Margin of Defeat	83	vs. Georgia Tech, Nov. 3, 1917
Longest Pass Play	88	Marcus Wilson to Clarence Sevillian vs. Tennessee, Nov. 28, 1992
Longest Field Goal	55	Steve Yenner vs. Louisana Tech, Nov. 11, 1995
Longest Punt	82	Ricky Anderson vs. Georgia, Oct. 20, 1984
Longest Interception Return	98	John Gamble vs. Citadel, Sep. 17, 1966

RETIRED NUMBERS

NO RETIRED JERSEYS

ALL-TIME TEAM

No all-time or all-century team available

VANDERBILT BOWL HISTORY

SEASON	BOWL	DATE	PRE-GAME RANK	TEAMS	SCORE	FINAL RANK	MOST VALUABLE PLAYER(S)	ATT.
1955	**GATOR**	Dec. 31, 1955	8	**Vanderbilt** **Auburn**	25 13		Don Orr, Vanderbilt, QB Joe Childress, Auburn, FB	32,174
1974	**PEACH**	Dec. 28, 1974		**Vanderbilt** **Texas Tech**	6 6		Dennis Harrison, Vanderbilt, DT Larry Isaac, Texas Tech, TB	31,695
1982	**HALL OF FAME CLASSIC**	Dec. 31, 1982		**Air Force** **Vanderbilt**	36 28		Carl Dieudonne, Air Force, DE Whit Taylor, Vanderbilt, QB	75,000
2008	**MUSIC CITY**	Dec. 31, 2008		**Vanderbilt** **Boston College**	16 14		Brett Upson, Vanderbilt, P	54,520

DECEMBER 31, 1955 | GATOR
VANDERBILT 25, AUBURN 13

	1ST	2ND	3RD	4TH	FINAL
VAN	7	6	6	6	25
AUB	0	7	0	6	13

SCORING SUMMARY
VAN Stephenson 8 pass from Orr (Jalufka kick)
AUB James 38 pass from Tubbs (Tubbs kick)
VAN Orr 3 run (kick failed)
VAN King 1 run (kick failed)
VAN Horton 1 run (kick blocked)
AUB Phillips 4 pass from Cook (kick failed)

VAN	TEAM STATISTICS	AUB
15	First Downs	15
177	Rushing Yards	159
5-8-1	Passing	7-13-0
94	Passing Yards	142
271	Total Yards	301
4-31.7	Punts - Average	3-29.0
1-1	Fumbles - Lost	5-5
5-54	Penalties - Yards	6-59

INDIVIDUAL LEADERS
RUSHING
VAN: Horton 13-57, 1 TD; Orr 10-43, 1 TD.
AUB: Childress 15-58; James 9-42.
PASSING
VAN: Orr 4-6-1, 67 yards, 1 TD.
AUB: Tubbs 4-9-0, 101 yards, 1 TD.
RECEIVING
VAN: Scalen 2-44; Stephenson 2-23, 1 TD.
AUB: James 2-51, 1 TD; Elliott 2-41.

DECEMBER 28, 1974 | PEACH
VANDERBILT 6, TEXAS TECH 6

	1ST	2ND	3RD	4TH	FINAL
TT	0	0	3	3	6
VANDY	0	3	0	3	6

SCORING SUMMARY
VANDY FG Adams 31
TT FG Hall 26
VANDY FG Adams 26
TT FG Hall 35

TT	TEAM STATISTICS	VANDY
19	First Downs	10
306	Rushing Yards	140
3-10-1	Passing	5-17-1
35	Passing Yards	60
341	Total Yards	200
6-36.0	Punts - Average	8-40.0
3-2	Fumbles - Lost	1-1
1-14	Penalties - Yards	1-5

INDIVIDUAL LEADERS
RUSHING
TT: Hoskins 13-116; Isaac 20-101.
VANDY: O'Rourke 17-76; Sadler 8-31.
PASSING
TT: Dunevin 3-8-0, 35 yards.
VANDY: Lee 5-14-1, 60 yards.
RECEIVING
TT: Felux 2-21; Williams 1-14.
VANDY: Burton 2-36; O'Rourke 2-15.

DECEMBER 31, 1982 | HALL OF FAME CLASSIC
AIR FORCE 36, VANDERBILT 28

	1ST	2ND	3RD	4TH	FINAL
AFA	7	7	3	19	36
VAN	7	14	7	0	28

SCORING SUMMARY
VAN Jordan 28 pass from Taylor (Anderson kick)
AFA Louthan 1 run (Pavlich kick)
AFA Brown 19 run (Pavlich kick)
VAN Roach 15 pass from Taylor (Anderson kick)
VAN Jordan 4 pass from Taylor (Anderson kick)
AFA FG Pavlich 21
VAN Jordan 4 pass from Taylor (Anderson kick)
AFA Sundquist 3 run (pass failed)
AFA Kershner 3 run (pass failed)
AFA Louthan 46 run (Pavlich kick)

AFA	TEAM STATISTICS	VAN
23	First Downs	26
331	Rushing Yards	35
11-17-0	Passing	38-51-3
136	Passing Yards	456
467	Total Yards	491
0-0	Punt Returns - Yards	2-7
4-84	Kickoff Returns - Yards	6-102
5-36.0	Punts - Average	2-32.5
1-0	Fumbles - Lost	2-2
8-75	Penalties - Yards	4-39
39:18	Possession Time	20:42

INDIVIDUAL LEADERS
RUSHING
AFA: Kershner 32-132, 1 TD; Louthan 16-74, 2 TD.
VAN: Edwards 5-21; Matthews 1-13.
PASSING
AFA: Louthan 11-17-0, 136 yards.
VAN: Taylor 38-51-3, 452 yards, 4 TD.
RECEIVING
AFA: Greenwood 6-77; Kirby 2-30.
VAN: Jordan 20-173, 3 TD; Scott 5-93.

DECEMBER 31, 2008 | MUSIC CITY
VANDERBILT 16, BOSTON COLLEGE 14

	1ST	2ND	3RD	4TH	FINAL
BC	0	7	0	7	14
VAN	6	0	7	3	16

SCORING SUMMARY
VAN FG Hahnfeldt 42
VAN FG Hahnfeldt 26
BC Harris 4 pass from Davis (Aponavicius kick)
VAN Richardson fumble recovery in end zone (Hahnfeldt kick)
BC Larmond 55 pass from Davis (Aponavicius kick)
BC FG Hahnfeldt 45

BC	TEAM STATISTICS	VAN
17	First Downs	8
141	Rushing Yards	79
15-36-2	Passing	10-20-0
190	Passing Yards	121
331	Total Yards	200
5-(-14)	Punt Returns - Yards	3-14
4-76	Kickoff Returns - Yards	2-35
8-39.8	Punts - Average	9-42.6
3-1	Fumbles - Lost	1-0
3-34	Penalties - Yards	0-0

INDIVIDUAL LEADERS
RUSHING
BC: Harris 15-68.
VAN: Nickson 8-57.
PASSING
BC: Davis 15-36-2, 190 yards, 2 TD.
VAN: Smith 10-17-0, 121.
RECEIVING
BC: Harris 5-25, 1 TD; Purvis 4-29.
VAN: Umoh 3-29; Walker 2-68.

GEORGIA TECH

BY BOB HARIG

MUCH OF COLLEGE FOOTBALL'S history has unfolded at Georgia Tech. The Atlanta engineering institution was the first school to win all four traditional major bowls: Rose, Orange, Sugar and Cotton. The Yellow Jackets have played in 37 bowl games altogether, winning 22 of them, Tech's first full-time coach, John Heisman, is the inspiration behind college football's most prestigious award. Its stadium, more than 90 years old, is named for another legendary coach, Bobby Dodd, who once had a 31-game unbeaten streak. Georgia Tech has had only 12 coaches since 1904—and they've guided the Yellow Jackets to 15 conference titles and four national championships.

TRADITION Before each home game, the team runs onto Grant Field behind the Rambling Wreck, a 1930 Model A. Ford Sport Coupe. After a victory, the players sing the school's fight song, "Ramblin' Wreck," to the student section. At away games, Tech band members ask the stadium's public-address announcer to page

George P. Burdell, a mythical character in college lore. (In 1927, the fictional Burdell's name appeared on class rosters, registration forms and grade reports.)

Off the field, first-year students are instructed to decorate their "rat caps" (distinctive Tech symbols of freshman status) by writing the school's winning football scores rightside up on the sides of the cap—and writing the losing scores upside down. Tech's traditions aren't solely for students, either; on the way to games, Tech supporters stop by The Varsity, an Atlanta landmark, to order a chili dog, onion rings and a Frosted Orange.

BEST PLAYER Quarterback Joe Hamilton was the Heisman runner-up in 1999, matching the highest previous finish by a Tech player (quarterback Billy Lothridge finished second in the 1963 voting). An equally dangerous runner and passer, Hamilton helped the Yellow Jackets lead the nation in total offense and rank second in scoring in 1999. His 734 rushing yards were the most ever by a Division I-A quarterback who also had 3,000 yards passing. Hamilton was a consensus first-team All-American selection and ACC Player of the Year that season, as well as winner of the Davey O'Brien National Quarterback Award. He owns a number of Tech passing records and finished his career as the ACC's all-time leader in total offense and touchdown passes. For his

---

PROFILE

Georgia Institute of Technology
Atlanta, Ga.
Founded: 1885
Enrollment: 16,793
Colors: Old Gold, White
Nickname: Yellow Jackets
Stadium: Bobby Dodd Stadium/Grant Field
   Opened in 1913
   Grass; 55,000 capacity
First football game: 1892
All-time record: 662–446–43 (.597)
Bowl record: 22–15
Consensus national championships,
1936-present: 1 (1990)
Southeastern Conference championships:
5 (3 outright)
Atlantic Coast Conference championships:
2 (1 outright)
First-round draft choices: 9
Website: www.ramblinwreck.com

THE BEST OF TIMES

From 1951 to 1956, Tech went 59–7–3 and won six straight major bowl games.

THE WORST OF TIMES

From 1892 to 1903, Tech had just two winning seasons, compiling a record of 9–32–5.

CONFERENCE

Georgia Tech joined the Atlantic Coast Conference in 1979 (but didn't start competing in football until 1983) after three times being a charter member of other conferences: Southwest Intercollegiate Athletic Association (1894), Southern Conference (1922) and SEC (1933).

DISTINGUISHED ALUMNI

Jimmy Carter, U.S. president; Nomar Garciaparra, MLB player; David Duval, PGA golfer; Jeff Foxworthy, comedian; Sam Nunn, U.S. senator; Dick Truly, astronaut and administrator of NASA

career, Hamilton threw for 8,882 yards and 65 touchdowns on his way to piling up 10,640 yards of total offense.

BEST COACH The chalkheads' pick is John Heisman, who coached at eight schools but carved much of his reputation at Tech, where he had a 102–29–7 record from 1904 to 1919 and brought the school its first national title in 1917. He was the first paid college coach in the country, with a salary of $2,250 plus 30 percent of the gate receipts. (He also coached baseball and basketball at the school.) He left after the 1919 season—not because of the 7–3 record, but because he was divorcing his wife and agreed to leave Atlanta.

The sentimental choice, however, is Bobby Dodd, who may be a less significant figure in football history but is peerless in Tech annals. From 1945 to 1966, Dodd went 165–64–8 (.713) and guided Tech to a 31-game unbeaten streak from 1950 to 1953. He was 9–4 in bowl games and won eight straight, including six in consecutive seasons: 1952 Orange, 1953 Sugar, 1954 Sugar, 1955 Cotton, 1956 Sugar and 1956 Gator. He also beat Georgia eight straight times. Dodd was known as an excellent sideline coach, and he emphasized finesse and well-rehearsed

> *Bobby Dodd was known as an excellent sideline coach, and he emphasized finesse and well-rehearsed execution.*

execution. So as not to wear out the players before Saturdays, practices were laid-back, with little hitting but great attention to detail. "There's no point in rough scrimmages before a bowl game," he once said. "Your top players learn nothing playing against the third team, and you risk injury."

And finally, the name Bobby Ross should be included here for engineering (pardon the pun) one of the great turnarounds in school history, if not in all of college football history. In the first two years of Ross' short regime, the Yellow Jackets won five games. They improved in his third season, winning seven. And in his fourth, they were undefeated (with one tie) and won a share of the national championship.

BEST TEAM Though Georgia Tech boasts four national champion squads, the 1952 team was the only one to complete a 12–0 season. Those 12 victories, which included four shutouts, were part of an 18-game winning streak from 1951 to 1953 and a 31-game unbeaten streak from 1950 to 1953. The 1952 team had six players who were first-team on at least one All-American lineup. The Yellow Jackets completed their perfect season by defeating

FIGHT SONG

RAMBLIN' WRECK

I'm a Ramblin' Wreck from Georgia
  Tech and a hell of an engineer,
A helluva, helluva, helluva, helluva, hell
  of an engineer,
Like all the jolly good fellows, I drink
  my whiskey clear,
I'm a Ramblin' Wreck from Georgia
  Tech and a hell of an engineer.
Oh, if I had a daughter, sir, I'd dress her
  in White and Gold,
And put her on the campus, to cheer the
  brave and bold.
But if I had a son, sir, I'll tell you what
  he'd do.
He would yell, "To Hell with Georgia,"
  like his daddy used to do.
Oh, I wish I had a barrel of rum and
  sugar three thousand pounds,
A college bell to put it in and a clapper
  to stir it around.
I'd drink to all good fellows who come
  from far and near.
I'm a ramblin' gamblin' hell of an
  engineer.

FIRST-ROUND DRAFT CHOICES

1945	Eddie Prokop, Yanks (4)
1955	Larry Morris, Rams (7)
1963	Rufus Guthrie, Rams (10)
1964	Ted Davis, Chargers (8)*
1979	Kent Hill, Rams (26)
1979	Eddie Lee Ivery, Packers (15)
1992	Marco Coleman, Dolphins (12)
1998	Keith Brooking, Falcons (12)
2007	Calvin Johnson, Lions (2)

*From 1960-1966, the NFL and AFL held
separate, competing drafts

CONSENSUS ALL-AMERICANS

1917	Everett Strupper, B
1918	Ashel Day, C
1918	Joe Guyon, T
1918, '20	Bill Fincher, E
1928	Peter Pund, C
1942	Harvey Hardy, G
1944	Phil Tinsley, E
1946	Paul Duke, C
1947	Bob Davis, T
1952	Hal Miller, T
1953	Larry Morris, C
1959	Maxie Baughan, C
1966	Jim Breland, C
1970	Rock Perdoni, DT
1973	Randy Rhino, DB
1990	Ken Swilling, FS
1998	Craig Page, C
1999	Joe Hamilton, QB
2000	Chris Brown, OT
2006	Calvin Johnson, WR

Mississippi, 24-7, in the Sugar Bowl. "The best football team that I coached," Dodd once said. After Duke fell to Tech, 28-7, Blue Devils head coach Bill Murray called Tech "the greatest team in the country." A week later, Army went down 45-6; Cadets coach Red Blaik said, "I never compare teams, but I repeat, this team could play in any league."

BEST DEFENSE The 1990 team that won a share of the national championship was—as one might expect—strong on both sides of the ball. But the defense was especially starchy, with Marco Coleman putting pressure on quarterbacks from the outside and All-American defensive back Ken Swilling patrolling the secondary. The defense that they anchored did not allow a touchdown for 19 consecutive quarters and came up huge in a crucial game, a 6-3 slugfest win over Virginia Tech, which came a week after their frantic, 41-38 upset of No. 1 Virginia.

BEST BACKFIELD The 1999 unit with Hamilton pulling the trigger at quarterback averaged 509 yards of offense per game—slightly more than 283 by passing and just over 225 rushing. Balanced, yes, though Heisman runner-up Hamilton accounted for the majority of the fireworks. But he had help from running back Sean Gregory, who ran for more than 800 yards and scored 13 touchdowns. Ralph Friedgen was in his second-to-last year as Tech's offensive coordinator, before moving on to become the head guy at Maryland. On the way out, he it played fast and loose with imaginative play-calling and multiple formations, sometimes putting receiver Dez White into the backfield as part of a wishbone package. It was an explosive, unpredictable unit, exciting for everyone except the opposing defensive coordinator.

BIGGEST GAME This is no misprint: Georgia Tech 222, Cumberland 0. It happened on Oct. 7, 1916, an act of revenge for a 22-0 whipping Cumberland handed the Tech baseball team the previous spring. Tech scored nine touchdowns in the first quarter. Futile on offense, Cumberland began to kick the ball back to the Jackets after receiving it and never recorded a first down. Tech coach Heisman agreed to shorten the periods from 15 to 12.5 minutes, but Tech still scored 180 points by the end of the third quarter—beating the record of 153 set by

Michigan four years earlier. Tech scored 32 touchdowns, averaged 3.8 points per minute and carried the ball for 978 yards. Running up the score? The Jackets never threw a pass, nor did they make a single first down—because they scored within four downs on every possession. Cumberland provided so little opposition that Heisman put his team through a hard half-hour scrimmage after the game.

COLLEGE FOOTBALL HALL OF FAME INDUCTEES		
NAME	YEARS	INDUCTED
William Alexander, COACH	1920-44	1951
John Heisman, COACH	1904-19	1954
Buck Flowers, HB	1916-20	1955
Peter Pund, C	1926-28	1963
Joe Guyon, HB/T	1912-13,'17-18	1971
Everett Strupper, HB	1915-17	1972
Bill Fincher, E/T	1916-20	1974
Bobby Davis, T	1944-47	1978
George Morris, C	1950-52	1981
Maxie Baughan, C	1957-59	1988
Larry Morris, C	1951-54	1992
Bobby Dodd, COACH	1945-66	1993
Ray Beck, G	1948-51	1997
Randy Rhino, S	1972-74	2002
Pat Swilling, DE	1982-85	2009

PRO FOOTBALL HALL OF FAME INDUCTEES		
NAME	YEARS	INDUCTED
Joe Guyon, HB	1919-27	1966
Billy Shaw, G	1961-69	1999

BIGGEST UPSET Tech's 7-6 victory over top-ranked Alabama on Nov. 17, 1962, ended the Crimson Tide's 26-game unbeaten streak. Dodd called it his greatest victory, as Tech thwarted Alabama comeback efforts by preventing a two-point conversion attempt and intercepting a Joe Namath pass in the end zone with just 1:05 left. It was Tech's second victory over a Bear Bryant-coached team. And probably one that lingered in the memory for Dodd, who engaged in a well-publicized feud with Bryant that contributed to Tech leaving the SEC and dropping Alabama from its schedule.

STADIUM Heisman insisted on a stadium and actually got convicts to perform some of the initial labor on what became the oldest on-campus stadium in Division I-A. Grant Field (now Bobby Dodd Stadium at Historic Grant Field) opened in 1913. A year later, the first permanent concrete stands were built—by GT students themselves—on the west side of the field, thanks to a gift from Atlanta merchant and Tech trustee John W. Grant. The stadium has grown tremendously since its original 5,600-seat configuration. Nestled within Atlanta's skyline, it now has a capacity of 55,000. After the 1985 season, the stadium's south stands were razed and replaced with the William C. Wardlaw Center, a multipurpose facility for athletic and academic departments. The name Bobby Dodd Stadium was added in 1988 after the death of the legendary Tech coach and athletic director.

RIVAL Tech has played Georgia 103 times (through the 2008 season), including every year since 1925. The series began in 1893, when the Yellow Jackets traveled to Athens and won 28-6 to post the first football victory in school history. Tech is 39–56–5 overall against Georgia. Tech's 51-48 overtime win in 1999 was the highest-scoring game in the series and featured 1,104 yards of

total offense. At one point under Dodd, the Yellow Jackets won eight in a row over the Bulldogs. "Old Georgia Bulldogs hated him because he made it look so easy," wrote *The Atlanta Journal-Constitution*'s Furman Bisher. "It seemed that Georgia might never beat Georgia Tech again."

Then, in this century, it began to seem as if Tech might never beat Georgia again—until the 2008 season that ended a long seven-game drought.

STORYBOOK SEASON In 1990, the Yellow Jackets were just two seasons removed from a 3–8 campaign. While the 1989 team had posted a 7–4 record, the first winning season under Coach Ross, there was little to portend what was to happen the next year. That 1990 Tech squad began the season unranked and finished as the only unbeaten team in major college football. Among the highlights of Tech's season was a dramatic 41-38 victory over No. 1 Virginia in what many consider to be the best game in ACC history. Tech rallied from 13-0 and 28-14 deficits, then scored the winning points with just seven seconds remaining on a 37-yard field goal by Scott Sisson. The Jackets defeated Nebraska, 45-21, in the Florida Citrus Bowl to cap the 11–0–1 campaign and win the national title in the United Press International coaches' poll. (Colorado, which went 11–1–1 with the help of a controversial clipping penalty to beat Notre Dame in the Orange Bowl, was named champion in the Associated Press poll.)

NICKNAME The school has two official nicknames: Yellow Jackets and Rambling Wreck. Tech opened its doors in 1888, and the fight song "Ramblin' Wreck" dates back to the school's earliest years, when a large portion of the student body traveled to Athens to watch Tech play

Georgia in baseball. The legendary song was adapted from an old folk ballad, "The Sons of the Gamboliers," and was so renowned worldwide that Richard Nixon and Nikita Khrushchev sang it together during their meeting in Moscow in 1959. The Yellow Jackets nickname, which first appeared in *The Atlanta Constitution* in 1905, originally referred to Tech supporters, many of whom came to games sporting yellow coats and jackets.

MASCOT The official Rambling Wreck car made its first appearance on Grant Field before the Sept. 30, 1961, home opener against Rice, and has led the team onto the field at every home game since. The bumblebee mascot, Buzz, debuted in 1980.

UNIFORMS The Yellow Jackets are among the few teams that wear white jerseys at home. They returned to this traditional uniform in 1995, when NCAA rules permitted such a change. The uniform consists of a white jersey (with unusually thick numerals), gold pants and a gold helmet with an interlocking GT logo. During the late 1960s and early 1970s, Tech experimented with various combinations of gold jerseys, white pants and white helmets. In the mid-1970s, NCAA rules required a "dark" home jersey, so the Yellow Jackets went to a black jersey with gold or white pants and a gold helmet. When Ross became the head coach in 1987, the black was replaced with a dark blue.

QUOTE "Toe meets leather!"
—**Al Ciraldo**, Tech's longtime radio announcer, on every kickoff

With additional reporting by Geoffrey Norman

Class on Saturday

BY BILL CURRY

The *Southeastern Conference*'s Georgia Tech is not an oxymoron. Our most ancient lettermen, 66 years of age and beyond, remember the swagger and the passion of our halcyon days prior to 1964, when we were in the SEC. As a league, we were the envy of the nation … in Atlanta, Tech was the only show in town … and we knew, in our overheated young minds, that we were the Greatest Show on Earth.

Our coach was the Legend, our running backs sleek and fast, our kicking game always solid, our defense loaded and our offense … well, functional. Our academics were uppermost, our stands were full, our fans sophisticated if quiet, our press unrivaled, our schedule brutal and our reputations excessive.

The Legend, Robert Lee Dodd, himself a product of the Tennessee Volunteers' Legend, Gen. Robert Reese Neyland, was present for every minute of Tech's membership in the SEC. He came to Atlanta as an assistant in 1931, became head coach in 1945 and dominated the scene until his retirement in 1966, two years after Tech's withdrawal from the conference.

When we scored, which was just enough most of the time, one of us would invariably wonder aloud, "Is there anyone in the west stands?" Our well-heeled backers thought it crude to wear anything other than Sunday Go to Meeting clothes and rude to make alarming noises, regardless of the circumstances on the field. Our wives and girlfriends were invited to sit on our sideline, prompting scary moments like the time I hit a Vanderbilt fullback out of bounds, knocking him up close and personal just inches short of Lynda Gresham, wife of my co-captain, Johnny Gresham. Has anyone other than coach Robert Lee Dodd ever invited women onto their sideline in the *Southeastern Conference*?!

The Legend, more affectionately known as the Whistle or the Gray Fox, depending on the day of the week (gamedays were the Fox days), had a very short introductory speech for us each year. "If you are not a good football player, it's not your fault. It's mine for inviting you here. Regardless of that, I will love you and take good care of you here. Football should be fun. I will not run you off like other SEC

> *From his brown fedora to the perfect gray suit, sparkling gold tie and polished wingtips, Coach Dodd bespoke poise and confidence before even opening his mouth.*

schools do every year. But understand this one thing: If you cut class, you will regret it the rest of your life."

"Nobody else could coach like Dodd and get away with it," Paul "Bear" Bryant of Alabama once lamented. "I'd rather look across the field and see anybody other than Dodd on Saturdays. He can beat you with his brain."

Coach Dodd's well-documented insistence on class attendance, a consequence of his having never graduated, resulted in a very un-SEC-like 90%-plus graduation rate, made possible by a large tutoring bill and— you're not going to believe this— *Saturday morning* classes. No kidding. A full academic load at Tech included Saturday classes, and as Coach Dodd made absolutely clear, we were students first, football players second. So Saturdays in the fall, we dutifully trudged up the hill at 8 a.m., looked engaged in our accounting and statistics classes, bounded down to the

pre-game meal where we choked down steak, dry toast and honey, got taped and showed up for the team meeting roughly an hour before kickoff at 2 p.m.

Coach Dodd would wait until our 65 sweaty bodies (no air conditioning back then, of course) were packed into the small meeting room under the east stands before making his patented calm entrance. Had he been a singer, he would have been Bing Crosby. From his brown fedora to the perfect gray suit, sparkling gold tie and polished wingtips, he bespoke poise and confidence before even opening his mouth.

We waited, mesmerized, hushed in the sure knowledge we were about to be encouraged and inspired one more time, no matter the opponent or the mood, the odds on the game or the weather. Once Frank Sexton, a distinguished defensive end back in the early 1960s, leaned over to me with tears in his eyes and said, "I don't know why we wouldn't just die for that guy."

The Gray Fox hadn't said a word yet.

When Bobby Dodd did speak, he was brief. "Men, *Georgie* …" He refused to pronounce correctly the name of our cross-state rival, but he had no trouble with the "Georgia" in Georgia Tech. "*Georgie* is a fine football team, rough, tough and big. They will be emotional. They will be screaming and yelling. We will not. We will conserve our energy, because we are smarter than they are. The game will begin and, while they may take the lead, we will be in control.

"You will do as I have taught you: no turnovers, great defense, great kicking game and perfect field position. Then, sometime in the fourth quarter, because we are smarter than they are, they will make a mistake, we will get the ball, I will think of something and we will win."

He did, and we did.

It was magic.

Bill Curry *played for Bobby Dodd from 1960 to '64 and literally owes his education to the legendary Gray Fox. The success Curry enjoyed playing in the NFL and coaching college ball are a direct result of his time with Dodd.*

Georgia Tech All-Time Scores

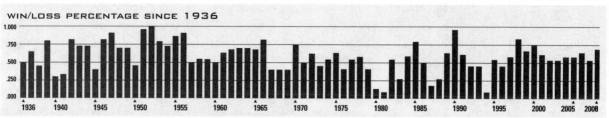

WIN/LOSS PERCENTAGE SINCE 1936

1936 1940 1945 1950 1955 1960 1965 1970 1975 1980 1985 1990 1995 2000 2005 2008

NO HEAD COACH

1892 — 0-3-0
N5	●	at Mercer	6 12
N19		Vanderbilt	10 20
N25		Auburn	0 26

1893 — 2-1-1
N4	●	at Georgia	28 6
N11	●	Mercer	10 6
N30		St. Albans	0 6
D7	=	Auburn	0 0

1894 — 0-3-0
O27		Savannah AA	0 8
N17		Auburn	0 94
N29		Fort McPhersons	0 34

1895
NO TEAM

1896 — 1-1-1
O31	●	at Mercer	6 4
N7		at Auburn	0 45
N21	=	Mercer	12 12

1897 — 0-1-0
O23		at Georgia	0 28

1898 — 0-3-0
O22		at Georgia	0 15
N5		at Auburn	6 29
N24		Clemson *Aug*	0 23

1899 — 0-5-0
O14		at Auburn	0 63
O23		Sewanee	0 30
O28		at Georgia	0 33*
N11		Nashville *GrvSC*	0 15
N30		Clemson *GrvSC*	5 41

1900 — 0-4-0
O13		Georgia	0 12
O20		Nashville	0 23
O29		Sewanee	0 34
D7		Davidson	6 38

1901 — 4-0-1
O12	●	Gordon	29 0
O15	●	Furman	17 0
O18	●	Wofford *Aug*	33 0
O26	=	at Furman	5 5
N9	●	South Carolina	13 0

1902 — 0-6-2
O11		Auburn	6 18
O18		Clemson	5 44
O25	=	Georgia	0 0
N1	=	at Furman	0 0
N8		St. Albans	0 17
N13		Davidson	6 7
N22		Tennessee	6 10
N27		Alabama *Birm*	0 26

1903 — 2-5-0
O17		Clemson	0 73
O24		Georgia	0 38
O31	●	at Howard Coll.	37 0
N7	●	Florida Coll.	17 0
N14		Auburn	5 10
N21		at Tennessee	0 11
N26		South Carolina	0 16

JOHN HEISMAN
1904-19 (.764)   102-29-7

1904 — 8-1-1
O1	●	Fort Mc Phersons	11 5
O8	●	Florida State Coll.	35 0
O15	●	Mooney Sch.	51 0
O17	●	Florida U. Club	77 0
O22	●	Tennessee	2 0
O29		at Auburn	0 12
N5	=	Clemson	11 11
N12	●	Georgia	23 6
N16	●	Tenn. Med.	59 0
N24	●	Cumberland	18 0

1905 — 6-0-1
O7	●	North Georgia	54 0
O21	●	Alabama	12 5
O28	●	Cumberland	18 0
N4	●	Tennessee	45 0
N11	=	Sewanee	18 18
N18	●	Georgia	46 0
N30	●	Clemson	17 10

1906 — 5-3-1
S29	=	Maryville	6 6
O6	●	North Georgia	11 0
O13	●	U.T. Chattanooga	18 0
O20		Sewanee	0 16
O27	●	Davidson	4 0
N3	●	Auburn	11 0
N10	●	at Georgia	17 0
N17		Vanderbilt	6 37
N29	●	Clemson	0 10

1907 — 4-4-0
O5	●	Gordon	51 0
O12	●	North Georgia	70 0
O19	●	Tennessee	6 4
O26	●	Auburn	6 12
N2	●	Georgia	10 6
N9	●	Sewanee	0 18
N16	●	at Vanderbilt	0 54
N28	●	Clemson	5 6

1908 — 6-3-0
O3	●	Gordon	32 0
O10	●	Mooney	30 0
O17	●	Mississippi State	23 0
O24	●	Alabama	11 6
O31		Tennessee	5 6
N7		Auburn	0 44
N14		Sewanee	0 6
N19	●	Mercer	16 6
N26	●	Clemson	30 6

1909 — 7-2-0
O2	●	Gordon	18 6
O9	●	Mooney Sch.	35 6
O16	●	South Carolina	59 0
O23		Sewanee	0 15
O30	●	at Tennessee	29 0
N6		Auburn	0 9*
N13	●	at Mercer	35 0
N20	●	Georgia	12 6
N25	●	Clemson	29 3

1910 — 5-3-0
O1	●	Gordon	57 0
O8	●	U.T. Chattanooga	18 0
O15	●	Mercer	46 0
O22	●	at Alabama	36 0
N5		Auburn	0 16
N12		Vanderbilt	0 23
N19		Georgia	6 11
N24	●	Clemson	34 0

1911 — 6-2-1
S30	●	11th Cavalry	22 5
O7	●	at Samford	28 0
O14	●	Tennessee	24 0
O21	●	Mercer	17 0
O29	=	Alabama	0 0
N4		Auburn	6 11
N11	●	Sewanee	23 0
N18		Georgia	0 5
N30	●	Clemson	31 0

1912 — 5-3-1
S28	=	11th Cavalry	0 0
O5	●	at Citadel	20 16
O12	●	Alabama	20 3
O19	●	at Mercer	16 6
O26	●	Florida *JacF*	14 7
N2		Auburn	7 27
N9		Sewanee	0 7
N16		Georgia	0 20
N28	●	Clemson	20 0*

1913 — 7-2-0
S27	●	Fort McPhersons	19 0
O4	●	at Citadel	47 0
O11	●	at U.T. Chattanooga	71 6
O18	●	Mercer	33 0
O25	●	Florida *JacF*	13 3
N1	●	Sewanee	33 0
N8		Auburn	0 20
N15		Georgia	0 14
N27	●	Clemson	34 0*

1914 — 6-2-0
O3	●	South Carolina	20 0
O10	●	Mercer	105 0
O17		Alabama *Birm*	0 13
O24	●	VMI	28 7
O31	●	Sewanee	20 0
N7		Auburn	0 14
N14		Georgia	7 0
N26	●	Clemson	26 6

1915 — 7-0-1
O2	●	Mercer	52 0
O9	●	Davidson	27 7
O16	●	Transylvania, Ky.	67 0
O22	●	LSU *NO*	36 7
O30	●	North Carolina	23 3
N6	●	Alabama	21 7
N13	=	Georgia	0 0
N25	●	Auburn	7 0

1916 — 8-0-1
S30	●	Mercer	61 0
O7	●	Cumberland	222 0
O14	●	Davidson	9 0
O21	●	North Carolina	10 6
O28	=	Wash. & Lee	7 7
N4	●	Tulane	45 0
N11	●	Alabama	13 0
N18	●	at Georgia	21 0
N30	●	Auburn	33 7

1917 — 9-0-0
S29	●	Furman	25 0
S29	●	Wake Forest	33 0
O6	●	Pennsylvania	41 0
O13	●	Davidson	32 10
O20	●	Wash. & Lee	63 0
N3	●	Vanderbilt	83 0
N10	●	at Tulane	48 0
N17	●	Carlisle	98 0
N29	●	Auburn	68 7

1918 — 6-1-0
O5	●	Clemson	28 0
O12	●	Furman	118 0
O19	●	11th Cavalry	123 0
O26	●	Camp Gordon	28 0
N10	●	North Carolina St.	128 0
N23		at Pittsburgh	0 32
N28	●	Auburn	41 0

1919 — 7-3-0
S20	●	5th Division	48 0
S27	●	Furman	74 0
O4	●	Wake Forest	14 0
O11	●	Clemson	28 0
O18	●	Vanderbilt	20 0
O25		at Pittsburgh	6 16
N1	●	Davidson	33 0
N8		Wash. & Lee	0 3
N15	●	Georgetown	27 0
N27	●	Auburn	7 14

WILLIAM ALEXANDER
1920-44 (.580)   134-95-15

1920 — 8-1-0
S25	●	Wake Forest	44 0
O2	●	Oglethorpe	55 0
O9	●	Davidson	66 0
O16	●	at Vanderbilt	44 0
O23		at Pittsburgh	3 10
O30	●	Centre	24 0
N6	●	Clemson	7 0
N13	●	Georgetown	35 6
N25	●	Auburn	34 0

1921 — 8-1-0
S24	●	Wake Forest	42 0
O1	●	Oglethorpe	41 0
O8	●	Davidson	70 0
O15	●	Furman	69 0
O22	●	Rutgers	48 14
O29		Penn State *NYC*	7 28
N5	●	Clemson	48 7
N12	●	Georgetown	21 7
N24	●	Auburn	14 0

1922-1932
SOUTHERN

1922 — 7-2-0(4-0-0)
S30	●	Oglethorpe	31 6
O7	●	Davidson	19 0
O14	|	Alabama	33 7
O21		at Navy	0 13
O28		Notre Dame	3 13
N4	● |	Clemson	21 7
N11	●	Georgetown	19 7
N18	|	North Carolina St.	17 0
N30	|	Auburn	14 6

1923 — 3-2-4(0-0-4)
S29	●	Oglethorpe	28 13
O6	●	VMI	10 7
O13	= |	Florida	7 7
O20	|	Georgetown	20 10
O27		at Notre Dame	7 35
N3	= |	Alabama	0 0
N10		at Penn State	0 7
N17	= |	Kentucky *Unk*	3 3
N29	|	Auburn	0 0

1924 — 5-3-1(3-2-1)
S27	●	Oglethorpe	19 0
O4	● |	VMI	3 0
O11	= |	Florida	7 7
O18	|	Penn State	15 13
O25	|	Alabama	0 14
N1		at Notre Dame	3 34
N8	● |	LSU	28 7
N15	|	Vanderbilt	0 3
N27	● |	Auburn	7 0

THE SCHOOLS

1925 6-2-1 (4-1-1)
S26	•	Oglethorpe	13 7
U3	|	VMI	33 0
O10	•	Penn State *Bnx*	16 7
O17	|	Florida	23 7
O24	|	Alabama	0 7
O31	•	Notre Dame	0 13
N7	•	at Vanderbilt	7 0
N14	|	Georgia	3 0
N26 =	•	Auburn	7 7

1926 4-5-0 (4-3-0)
S25	•	Oglethorpe	6 7
O2	•	VMI	13 0
O9	•	Tulane	9 6
O16	|	Alabama	0 21
O23	|	Wash. & Lee	19 7
O30	|	at Notre Dame	0 12
N6	|	Vanderbilt	7 13
N13	|	Georgia	13 14
N25	•	Auburn	20 7

1927 8-1-1 (7-0-1)
O1	•	VMI	7 0
O8	|	Tulane	13 6
O15	|	Alabama	13 0
O22	•	North Carolina	13 0
O29	|	at Notre Dame	7 26
N6 =	•	at Vanderbilt	0 0
N12	•	LSU	23 0
N19	•	Oglethorpe	19 7
N24	•	Auburn	18 0
D3	•	Georgia	12 0

1928 10-0-0 (7-0-0)
O6	•	VMI	13 0
O13	|	at Tulane	12 0
O20	•	Notre Dame	13 0
O27	|	at North Carolina	20 7
N3	•	Oglethorpe	32 7
N10	|	Vanderbilt	19 7
N17	|	Alabama	33 13
N29	•	Auburn	51 0
D8	•	Georgia	20 6
ROSE BOWL			
J1	•	California	8 7

1929 3-6-0 (3-5-0)
O5	•	Mississippi State	27 13
O12	|	North Carolina	7 18
O19	•	Florida	19 6
O26	|	at Tulane	14 20
N2	|	Notre Dame	6 26
N9	|	at Vanderbilt	7 23
N16	|	Alabama	0 14
N28	•	Auburn	19 6
D7	|	at Georgia	6 12

1930 2-6-1 (2-4-1)
O4	•	South Carolina	45 0
O11	|	at Carnegie Tech	0 31
O18	•	Auburn	14 12
O25	|	Tulane	0 28
N1 =	|	at North Carolina	6 6
N8	|	Vanderbilt	0 6
N15	|	at Pennsylvania	7 34
N27	|	Florida	7 55
D6	|	Georgia	0 13

1931 2-7-1 (2-4-1)
O3	•	South Carolina	25 13
O10	|	Carnegie Tech	0 13
O17	|	Auburn	0 13
O24	|	at Tulane	0 33
O31	|	Vanderbilt	7 49
N7 =	|	North Carolina	19 19
N14	|	at Pennsylvania	12 13
N21	•	Florida	23 0
N28	|	at Georgia	6 35
D26	|	California	6 19*

1932 4-5-1 (4-4-1)
O1	•	Clemson	32 14
O8	|	Kentucky	6 12
O15	|	Auburn	0 6
O22	•	at North Carolina	43 14
O29	|	at Vanderbilt	0 12
N5	|	Tulane	14 20
N12	•	Alabama	6 0
N19	•	at Florida	6 0
N26 =	|	Georgia	0 0
D17	|	at California	7 27

1933-1963 SEC

1933 5-5-0 (2-5-0)
S30	•	Clemson	39 2
O7	|	at Kentucky	6 7
O14	•	Auburn	16 6
O21	|	Tulane	0 7
O28	|	at North Carolina	10 6
N4	|	Vanderbilt	6 9
N11	•	Florida	19 7
N18	|	Alabama	9 12
N25	|	Georgia	6 7
D2	•	Duke	6 0

1934 1-9-0 (0-6-0)
S29	•	Clemson	12 7
O6	|	Vanderbilt	12 27
O13	|	at Duke	0 20
O20	|	at Michigan	2 9
O27	|	at Tulane	12 20
N3	|	North Carolina	0 26
N10	|	Auburn	6 18
N17	|	Alabama	0 40
N24	|	at Florida	12 13
D1	|	at Georgia	0 7

1935 5-5-0 (3-4-0)
S28	•	Presbyterian	33 0
O5	•	Sewanee	32 0
O12	|	at Kentucky	6 25
O19	•	Duke	6 0
O26	|	at North Carolina	0 19
N2	|	Vanderbilt	13 14
N9	|	Auburn	7 33
N16	|	Alabama *Birm*	7 38
N23	•	Florida	39 6
N30	•	Georgia	19 7

1936 5-5-1 (3-3-1)
S26	•	Presbyterian	55 0
O3	•	Sewanee	58 0
O10	|	Kentucky	34 0
O17	|	at Duke	6 19
O24 =	|	at Vanderbilt	0 0
O31	|	Clemson	13 14
N7	|	Auburn	12 13
N14	|	Alabama	16 20
N21	•	Florida	38 14
N28	|	at Georgia	6 16
D26	•	California	13 7

1937 6-3-1 (3-2-1)
S24	•	Presbyterian	59 0
O2	•	Mercer	28 0
O9	|	at Kentucky	32 0
O16	|	Duke	19 20
O23	|	Auburn	0 21
O30	•	Vanderbilt	14 0
N6	•	Clemson	7 0
N13	|	Alabama *Birm*	0 7
N20	•	at Florida	12 0
N27 =	|	Georgia	6 6

1938 3-4-3 (2-1-3)
O1	•	Mercer	19 0
O8	|	Notre Dame	6 14
O15	|	at Duke	0 6
O22 =	|	Vanderbilt	7 6
O29	|	at Vanderbilt	7 13
N5	|	Kentucky	19 18
N12 =	|	Alabama	14 14
N19 =	|	Florida	0 0
N27 =	|	at Georgia	0 0
D26	|	at California	0 13

1939 8-2-0 (6-0-0)
O7	|	at Notre Dame	14 17
O14	•	Samford	35 0
O21	|	Vanderbilt	14 6
O28	•	Auburn	7 6
N4	|	Duke	6 7
N11	•	Kentucky	13 6
N18	•	Alabama *Birm*	6 0
N25	•	at Florida	21 7
D2	|	Georgia	13 0
ORANGE BOWL			
J1	•	Missouri	21 7

1940 3-7-0 (1-5-0)
O5	•	Samford	27 0
O12	|	at Notre Dame	20 26
O19	•	Vanderbilt	19 0
O26	|	Auburn	7 16
N2	|	at Duke	7 41
N9	|	Kentucky *Lou*	7 26
N16	|	Alabama	13 14
N23	|	Florida	7 16
N30	|	at Georgia	19 21
D28	•	California	13 0

1941 3-6-0 (2-4-0)
O4	•	U.T. Chattanooga	20 0
O11	|	Notre Dame	0 20
O18	|	at Vanderbilt	7 14
O25	•	Auburn	28 14
N1	|	Duke	0 14
N8	•	Kentucky	20 13
N15	|	Alabama *Birm*	0 20
N22	|	at Florida	7 14
N29	|	Georgia	0 21

1942 9-2-0 (4-1-0)
S26	•	Auburn	15 0
O3	|	at Notre Dame	13 6
O10	•	U.T. Chattanooga	30 6
O17	•	Davidson	33 0
O24	•	at Navy	21 0
O31	•	at Duke	26 7
N7	•	Kentucky	47 7
N14	•	Alabama	7 0
N21	•	Florida	20 7
N28	|	at Georgia	0 34
COTTON BOWL			
J1	|	Texas	7 14

1943 8-3-0 (3-0-0)
S25	•	North Carolina	20 7
O2	|	at Notre Dame	13 55
O9	|	Georgia Pre-Flight	35 7
O16	•	Fort Benning	27 0
O23	|	Navy *Balt*	14 28
O30	|	Duke	7 14
N6	|	LSU	42 7
N13	|	at Tulane	33 0
N20	•	Clemson	41 6
N27	•	Georgia	48 0
SUGAR BOWL			
J1	•	Tulsa	20 18

1944 8-3-0 (4-0-0)
S30	•	Clemson	51 0
O7	|	North Carolina	28 0
O14	•	Auburn	27 0
O21	|	Navy	17 15
O27	•	Georgia Pre-Flight	13 7
N4	|	at Duke	13 19
N11	•	Tulane	34 7
N18	•	at LSU	14 6
N25	|	Notre Dame	0 21
D2 •	|	at Georgia	44 0
ORANGE BOWL			
J1	|	Tulsa	12 26

BOBBY DODD
1945-66 (.713)   165-64-8

1945 4-6-0 (2-2-0)
S29	•	at North Carolina	20 14
O6	|	Notre Dame	7 40
O13	•	Samford	43 0
O20	|	Navy *Balt*	6 20
O27	•	Auburn	20 7
N3	|	Duke	6 14
N10	•	at Tulane	41 7
N17	|	LSU	7 9
N24	•	Clemson	7 21
D1	|	Georgia	0 33

1946 9-2-0 (4-2-0)
S28	|	at Tennessee	9 13
O5	•	VMI	32 6
O12	|	Mississippi	24 7
O19	|	at LSU	26 7
O26	|	Auburn	27 6
N2	|	at Duke	14 0
N9	|	Navy	28 20
N16	|	Tulane	35 7
N23	|	Furman	41 7
N30	|	at Georgia	7 35
OIL BOWL			
J1	•	St. Mary's	41 19

1947 10-1-0 (4-1-0)
S27	|	Tennessee	27 0
O4 •	|	at Tulane	20 6*
O11	•	VMI	20 0
O18	•	Auburn	27 7
O25	•	Citadel	38 0
N1	|	Duke	7 0
N8	•	Navy *Balt*	16 14
N15	•	Alabama *Birm*	7 14
N22	|	Furman	51 0
N29	|	Georgia	7 0
ORANGE BOWL			
J1	•	Kansas	20 14

1948 7-3-0 (4-3-0)
S25 •	|	at Vanderbilt	13 0
O2 •	|	Tulane	13 7
O9	|	Wash. & Lee	27 0
O16 •	|	Auburn	27 0
O23	|	Florida	42 7
O30 •	|	at Duke	19 7
N6	|	Tennessee	6 13
N13	|	Alabama	12 14
N20 •	|	Citadel	54 0
N27	|	at Georgia	13 21

1949 7-3-0 (5-2-0)
S24 •	|	Vanderbilt	12 7
O1	|	at Tulane	0 18
O8	|	Wash. & Lee	36 0
O15 •	|	Auburn	35 21
O22 •	|	at Florida	43 14
O29	|	Duke	14 27
N5 •	|	at Tennessee	30 13
N12	|	Alabama *Birm*	7 20
N19 •	|	South Carolina	13 3
N26 •	|	Georgia	7 6

1950 5-6-0 (4-2-0)
S23	|	at SMU	13 33
S30	|	South Carolina	0 7
O7 •	|	Florida	16 13
O14 •	|	at LSU	13 0
O21	|	Auburn	20 0
O28	|	Kentucky	14 28
N4	|	at Duke	21 30
N11	|	VMI	13 14
N18	|	Alabama	19 54
N25 •	|	Davidson	46 14
D2	|	at Georgia	7 0

1951 11-0-1 (7-0-0)
S22 •	|	SMU	21 7
S29 •	|	at Florida	27 0
O6 •	|	at Kentucky	13 7
O13 •	|	LSU	25 7
O20 •	|	Auburn	27 7
O27 •	|	at Vanderbilt	8 7
N3 •	|	Duke	14 14
N10 •	|	VMI	34 7
N17 •	|	Alabama *Birm*	27 7
N24 •	|	Davidson	34 7
D1 •	|	Georgia	48 6
ORANGE BOWL			
J1 •	|	Baylor	17 14

1952 12-0-0 (6-0-0)
S20 •	|	Citadel	54 6
S27 •	|	Florida	17 14
O4 •	|	at SMU	20 7
O11 •	|	Tulane	14 0
O18 •	|	Auburn	33 0
O25 •	|	Vanderbilt	30 0
N1 •	|	at Duke	28 7
N8 •	|	Army	45 6
N15 •	|	Alabama	7 3
N22 •	|	Florida State	30 0
N29 •	|	at Georgia	23 9
SUGAR BOWL			
J1 •	|	Mississippi	24 7

1953 9-2-1 (4-1-1)
S19 •	|	Davidson	53 0
S26 =	|	at Florida	0 0
O3 •	|	SMU	6 4
O10 •	|	at Tulane	27 13
O17 •	|	Auburn	36 6
O24	|	at Notre Dame	14 27
O31 •	|	at Vanderbilt	43 0
N7	|	Clemson	20 7
N14 •	|	Alabama *Birm*	6 13
N21 •	|	Duke	13 10
N28 •	|	Georgia	28 12
SUGAR BOWL			
J1 •	|	West Virginia	42 19

1954 8-3-0 (6-2-0)
S18	|	Tulane	28 0
S25	|	Florida	12 13
O2 •	|	at SMU	10 7
O9	|	LSU	30 20
O16 •	|	Auburn	14 7
O23	|	Kentucky	6 13
O30	|	at Duke	20 21
N6 •	|	Tennessee	28 7
N13 •	|	Alabama	20 0
N27 •	|	at Georgia	7 3
COTTON BOWL			
J1 •	|	Arkansas	14 6

1955   9-1-1 (4-1-1)
S17	●	Miami, Fla.	14	6
S24	●	at Florida	14	7
O1		SMU	20	7
O8	●	at LSU	7	0
O15		Auburn	12	14
O22	●	Florida State	34	0
O29	●	Duke	27	0
N5	=	at Tennessee	7	7
N12	●	Alabama *Birm*	26	2
N26		Georgia	21	3

SUGAR BOWL
J2	●	Pittsburgh	7	0

1956   10-1-0 (7-1-0)
S22	●	at Kentucky	14	6
S29	●	at SMU	9	7
O13	●	LSU	39	7
O20	●	Auburn	28	7
O27	●	Tulane	40	0
N3	●	at Duke	7	0
N10		Tennessee	0	6
N17	●	Alabama	27	0
N24	●	Florida *JacF*	28	0
D1	●	at Georgia	35	0

GATOR BOWL
D29	●	Pittsburgh	21	14

1957   4-4-2 (3-4-1)
S21	●	Kentucky	13	0
S28	=	SMU	0	0
O12		at LSU	13	20
O19		Auburn	0	3
O26	●	at Tulane	20	13
N2		Duke	13	0
N9		at Tennessee	6	21
N16	●	Alabama *Birm*	10	7
N23	=	Florida	0	0
N30		Georgia	0	7

1958   5-4-1 (2-3-1)
S20		at Kentucky	0	13
S26	●	Florida State	17	3
O4	●	Tulane	14	0
O11		Tennessee	21	7
O18	=	Auburn	7	7
O25		at SMU	0	20
N1	●	at Duke	10	8
N8	●	Clemson	13	0
N15		Alabama	8	17
N29		at Georgia	3	16

1959   6-5-0 (3-3-0)
S19	●	at Kentucky	14	12
S26	●	SMU	16	12
O3	●	Clemson	16	6
O10	●	at Tennessee	14	7
O17		Auburn	6	7
O24	●	at Tulane	21	13
O31		Duke	7	10
N7	●	at Notre Dame	14	10
N14	●	Alabama *Birm*	7	9
N28		Georgia	14	21

GATOR BOWL
J2		Arkansas	7	14

1960   5-5-0 (4-4-0)
S17		Kentucky	23	13
S24	●	at Rice	16	13
O1		at Florida	17	18
O8	●	LSU	6	2
O15		Auburn *Birm*	7	9
O22	●	Tulane	14	6
O29		at Duke	0	6
N5	●	Tennessee	14	7
N12		Alabama	15	16
N26		at Georgia	6	7

1961   7-4-0 (4-3-0)
S22	●	at Southern California	27	7
S30	●	Rice	24	0
O7		at LSU	0	10
O14	●	Duke	21	0
O21	●	Auburn	7	6
O28	●	at Tulane	35	0
N4	●	Florida	20	0
N11		at Tennessee	6	10
N18		Alabama *Birm*	0	10
D2	●	Georgia	22	7

GATOR BOWL
D30		Penn State	15	30

1962   7-3-1 (5-2-0)
S22	●	Clemson	26	9
S29	●	at Florida	17	0
O6		LSU	7	10
O13	●	Tennessee	17	0
O20	●	Auburn *Birm*	14	17
O27	●	Tulane	42	12
N3	●	at Duke	20	9
N10	=	Florida State	14	14
N17	●	Alabama	7	6
D1	●	at Georgia	37	6

BLUEBONNET BOWL
D22		Missouri	10	14

1963   7-3-0 (4-3-0)
S14	●	Florida	9	0
S28	●	Clemson	27	0
O5		at LSU	6	7
O12	●	at Tennessee	23	7
O19		Auburn	21	29
O26	●	at Tulane	17	3
N2	●	Duke	30	6
N9	●	Florida State	15	7
N16		Alabama *Birm*	11	27
N30	●	Georgia	14	3

**1964-1982
INDEPENDENT**

1964   7-3-0 (0-0-0)
S19	●	Vanderbilt	14	2
S26	●	Miami, Fla.	20	0
O3	●	Clemson	14	7
O10	●	Navy *JacF*	17	0
O17	●	Auburn *Birm*	7	3
O24	●	Tulane	7	6
O31	●	at Duke	21	8
N7		Tennessee	14	22
N14		Alabama	7	24
N28		at Georgia	0	7

1965   7-3-1 (0-0-0)
S18	=	at Vanderbilt	10	10
S25		Texas A&M	10	14
O2	●	Clemson	38	6
O9	●	at Tulane	13	10
O16	●	Auburn	23	14
O23	●	Navy	37	16
O30	●	Duke	35	23
N6		at Tennessee	7	21
N13	●	Virginia	42	19
N27		Georgia	7	17

GATOR BOWL
D31	●	Texas Tech	31	21

1966   9-2-0 (0-0-0)
S17	●	Texas A&M	38	3
S24	●	Vanderbilt	42	0
O1	●	Clemson	13	12
O8	●	Tennessee	6	3
O15	●	Auburn *Birm*	17	3
O22	●	Tulane	35	17
O29	●	at Duke	48	7
N5	●	Virginia	14	13
N12	●	Penn State	21	0
N26		at Georgia	14	23

ORANGE BOWL
J2		Florida	12	27

**BUD CARSON
1967-71 (.500)   27-27**

1967   4-6-0 (0-0-0)
S23	●	at Vanderbilt	17	10
S30	●	TCU	24	7
O7	●	Clemson	10	0
O14		at Tennessee	13	24
O21		Auburn	10	28
O28	●	at Tulane	12	23
N4	●	Duke	19	7
N10		at Miami, Fla.	7	49
N18		Notre Dame	3	36
N25		Georgia	14	21

1968   4-6-0 (0-0-0)
S21	●	TCU	17	7
S28	●	Miami, Fla.	7	10
O5	●	Clemson	24	21
O12		Tennessee	7	24
O19	●	Auburn *Birm*	21	20
O26	●	Tulane	23	19
N2		at Duke	30	46
N9		Navy	15	35
N16		at Notre Dame	6	34
N30		at Georgia	8	47

1969   4-6-0 (0-0-0)
S20	●	SMU	24	21
S27	●	Baylor	17	10
O4		Clemson	10	21
O11		at Tennessee	8	26
O18		Auburn	14	17
O25		at Southern California	18	29
N1	●	Duke	20	7
N8		at Tulane	7	14
N15	●	Notre Dame	20	38
N29	●	Georgia	6	0

1970   9-3-0 (0-0-0)
S12	●	South Carolina	23	20
S19	●	Florida State	23	13
S26	●	Miami, Fla.	31	21
O3	●	Clemson	28	7
O10		Tennessee	6	17
O17		at Auburn	7	31
O24	●	Tulane	20	6
O31	●	at Duke	24	16
N7	●	Navy	30	8
N14		at Notre Dame	7	10
N28	●	at Georgia	17	7

SUN BOWL
D19		Texas Tech	17	9

1971   6-6-0 (0-0-0)
S11		at South Carolina	7	24
S18	●	Michigan State	10	0
S25	●	Army	13	16
O2	●	Clemson	24	14
O9		at Tennessee	6	10
O16	●	Auburn	14	31
O23	●	at Tulane	24	16
O30	●	Duke	21	0
N6	●	Navy	34	21
N13	●	Florida State	12	6
N27		Georgia	24	28

PEACH BOWL
D30		Mississippi	18	41

**BILL FULCHER
1972-73 (.543)   12-10-1**

1972   7-4-1 (0-0-0)
S9		Tennessee	3	34
S16	●	South Carolina	34	6
S23	●	at Michigan State	21	16
S30	=	Rice	36	36
O7		Clemson	31	9
O21		at Auburn	14	24
O28	●	Tulane	21	7
N4		at Duke	14	20
N11	●	Boston College	42	10
N18	●	Navy	30	7
D2		at Georgia	7	27

LIBERTY BOWL
D18	●	Iowa State	31	30

1973   5-6-0 (0-0-0)
S15	●	at South Carolina	28	41
S22		Southern California	6	23
S29	●	Clemson	29	21
O6	●	Army	14	10
O13		at Tennessee	14	20
O20		Auburn	10	24
O27	●	at Tulane	14	23
N3		Duke	12	10
N10	●	VMI	36	7
N17	●	Navy *JacF*	26	22
D1		Georgia	3	10

**FRANKLIN "PEPPER" RODGERS
1974-79 (.522)   34-31-2**

1974   6-5-0 (0-0-0)
S9		Notre Dame	7	31
S14	●	South Carolina	35	20
S21		Pittsburgh	17	27
S28		at Clemson	17	21
O5	●	Virginia	28	24
O12	●	North Carolina	29	28
O19		at Auburn	22	31
O26	●	Tulane	27	7
N2		at Duke	0	9
N16	●	Navy	22	0
N30	●	at Georgia	34	14

1975   7-4-0 (0-0-0)
S13		at South Carolina	17	23
S20	●	Miami, Fla.	38	23
S27	●	Clemson	33	28
O4	●	Florida State	30	0
O11	●	VMI	38	10
O18	●	Auburn	27	31
O25	●	at Tulane	23	0
N1	●	Duke	21	6
N8	●	at Notre Dame	3	24
N15	●	Navy	14	13
N27		Georgia	26	42

1976   4-6-1 (0-0-0)
S11		South Carolina	17	27
S18	●	Pittsburgh	14	42
S25	=	Clemson	24	24
O2	●	Virginia	35	14
O9		Tennessee	7	42
O16	●	at Auburn	28	10
O23	●	Tulane	28	16
O30		at Duke	7	31
N6	●	Notre Dame	23	14
N13	●	at Navy	28	34
N27	●	at Georgia	10	13

1977   6-5-0 (0-0-0)
S10		at South Carolina	0	17
S17	●	Miami, Fla.	10	6
S24		at Clemson	14	31
O1	●	Air Force	30	3
O8	●	at Tennessee	24	8
O15	●	Auburn	38	21
O22	●	at Tulane	38	14
O29	●	Duke	24	25
N5		at Notre Dame	14	69
N12		at Navy	16	20
N26	●	Georgia	16	7

1978   7-5-0 (0-0-0)
S9	●	at Duke	10	28
S16		California	22	34
S23	●	Tulane	27	17
S30	●	Citadel	28	0
O7	●	South Carolina	6	3
O14	●	Miami, Fla.	24	19
O21	●	at Auburn	24	10
O28	●	Florida	17	13
N11	●	at Air Force	42	21
N18	●	Notre Dame	21	38
D2		at Georgia	28	29

PEACH BOWL
D25		Purdue	21	41

1979   4-6-1 (0-0-0)
S8		Alabama	6	30
S22	=	at Florida	7	7
S29	●	William & Mary	33	7
O6		at Notre Dame	13	21
O13		at Tennessee	0	31
O20		Auburn	14	38
O27		at Tulane	7	12
N3	●	Duke	24	14
N10	●	Air Force	21	0
N17	●	Navy	24	14
D1		Georgia	3	16

**BILL CURRY
1980-86 (.423)   31-43-4**

1980   1-9-1 (0-0-0)
S6		Alabama *Birm*	3	26
S20		Florida	12	45
S27	●	Memphis	17	8
O4		at North Carolina	0	33
O11		Tennessee	10	23
O18		at Auburn	14	17
O25		Tulane	14	31
N1		at Duke	12	17
N8	=	Notre Dame	3	3
N15		Navy	8	19
N29		at Georgia	20	38

1981   1-10-0 (0-0-0)
S12	●	Alabama *Birm*	24	21
S19		at Florida	6	27
S26		Memphis	15	28
O3		North Carolina	7	28
O10		at Tennessee	7	10
O17		Auburn	7	31
O24		at Tulane	10	27
O31		Duke	24	38
N7		at Notre Dame	3	35
N14		Navy	14	20
N28		Georgia	7	44

1982 6-5-0 (0-0-0)

S11		Alabama	7 45
S18	●	Citadel	36 7
S25		at Memphis	24 20
O2		at North Carolina	0 41
U9		at Iulane	19 13
O16		at Auburn	0 24
O23		Tennessee	31 21
O30		Duke	21 38
N6		Virginia	38 32
N13		at Wake Forest	45 7
N27		at Georgia	18 38

1983-PRESENT ACC

1983 3-8-0 (3-3-0)

S10		Alabama *BIRM*	7 20
S17		Furman	14 17
S24		at Clemson	14 41
O1		North Carolina	21 38
O8	●	at North Carolina St.	20 10
O15		Auburn	13 31
O22		at Tennessee	3 37
O29		at Duke	26 32
N3	●	Virginia	31 27
N12	●	Wake Forest	49 33
N26		Georgia	24 27

1984 6-4-1 (3-2-1)

S15	●	Alabama	16 6
S22	●	Citadel	48 3
S29	●	Clemson	28 21
O6		North Carolina St.	22 27
O13	=	at Virginia	20 20
O20		at Auburn	34 48
O27		Tennessee	21 24
N3	●	Duke	31 3
N10	●	at North Carolina	17 24
N17	●	at Wake Forest	24 7
D1	●	at Georgia	35 18

1985 9-2-1 (5-1-0)

S14	●	at North Carolina St.	28 18
S21		Virginia	13 24
S28	●	at Clemson	14 3
O5		North Carolina	31 0
O12	●	Western Carolina	24 17
O19		Auburn	14 17
O26	=	at Tennessee	6 6
N2	●	at Duke	9 0
N9	●	U.T. Chattanooga	35 7
N16	●	Wake Forest	41 10
N30		Georgia	20 16
		HALL OF FAME CLASSIC	
D31	●	Michigan State	17 14

1986 5-5-1 (3-3-0)

S13	=	Furman	17 17
S20	●	at Virginia	28 14
S27		Clemson	3 27
O4		at North Carolina	20 21
O11	●	North Carolina St.	59 21
O18		at Auburn	10 31
O25	●	Tennessee	14 13
N1	●	Duke	34 6
N8	●	VMI	52 6
N22		at Wake Forest	21 24
N29		at Georgia	24 31

BOBBY ROSS 1987-91 (.543) 31-26-1

1987 2-9-0 (0-6-0)

S12	●	Citadel	51 12
S19		North Carolina	23 30
S26		at Clemson	12 33
O3		at North Carolina St.	0 17
O10	●	Indiana St.	38 0
O17		Auburn	10 20
O24		at Tennessee	15 29
O31		at Duke	14 48
N7		Virginia	14 23
N21		Wake Forest	6 33
N28		Georgia	16 30

1988 3-8-0 (0-7-0)

S10	●	U.T. Chattanooga	24 10
S17		at Virginia	16 17
S24		Clemson	13 30
O1		North Carolina St.	6 14
O8		at Maryland	8 13
O15	●	South Carolina	34 0
O22		at North Carolina	17 20
O29		Duke	21 31
N5	●	VMI	34 7
N12	●	at Wake Forest	24 28
N26		at Georgia	3 24

1989 7-4-0 (4-3-0)

S9		at North Carolina St.	28 38
S16		Virginia	10 17
S23		at South Carolina	10 21
O7	●	Maryland	28 24
O14	●	at Clemson	30 14
O21	●	North Carolina	17 14
O28		at Duke	19 30
N4	●	Western Carolina	34 7
N18	●	Wake Forest	43 14
N25	●	Boston College	13 12
D2	●	Georgia	33 22

1990 11-0-1 (6-0-1)

S8	●	North Carolina St.	21 13
S22	●	U.T. Chattanooga	44 9
S29	●	South Carolina	27 6
O6	●	at Maryland	31 3
O13	●	Clemson	21 19
O20	=	at North Carolina	13 13
O27	●	Duke	48 31
N3	●	at Virginia	41 38
N10	●	Virginia Tech	6 3
N17	●	at Wake Forest	42 7
D1	●	at Georgia	40 23
		CITRUS BOWL	
J1	●	Nebraska	45 21

1991 8-5-0 (5-2-0)

A28		Penn State *ERUT*	22 34
S14	●	at Boston College	30 14
S19	●	Virginia	24 21
S28		at Clemson	7 9
O5		at North Carolina St.	21 28
O12	●	Maryland	34 10
O19		at South Carolina	14 23
O26	●	North Carolina	35 14
N2	●	at Duke	17 6
N9	●	Furman	19 17
N16	●	Wake Forest	27 3
N30		Georgia	15 18
		ALOHA BOWL	
D25	●	Stanford	18 17

BILL LEWIS 1992-94 (.367) 11-19

1992 5-6-0 (4-4-0)

S12	●	Western Carolina	37 19
S19		at Virginia	24 55
S26		Clemson	20 16
O3		North Carolina St.	16 13
O10		at Maryland	28 26
O17		Florida State	24 29
O24		at North Carolina	14 26
O31		Duke	20 17
N7		at Baylor	27 31
N14		Wake Forest	10 23
N28		at Georgia	17 31

1993 5-6-0 (3-5-0)

S11	●	Furman	37 3
S16		Virginia	14 35
S25		at Clemson	13 16
O2		at Florida State	0 51
O9	●	Maryland	38 0
O16		North Carolina	3 41
O23		at North Carolina St.	23 28
O30	●	at Duke	47 14
N6	●	Baylor	37 27
N13	●	at Wake Forest	38 28
N25		Georgia	10 43

GEORGE O'LEARY 1994-2001 (.612) 52-33

1994 1-10-0 (0-8-0)

S1		Arizona	14 19
S10	●	Western Carolina	45 26
S24		Duke	12 27
O1		at North Carolina St.	13 21
O8		at North Carolina	24 31
O15		Virginia	7 24
O22		at Maryland	27 42
N5		Florida State	10 41
N12		at Clemson	10 20
N19		Wake Forest	13 20
N25		at Georgia	10 48

1995 6-5-0 (5-3-0)

S2	●	Furman	51 7
S7		at Arizona	19 20
S16		at Virginia	14 41
S28	●	Maryland	31 3
O7	●	at Duke	37 21
O14	●	North Carolina	27 25
O21	●	at Florida State	10 42
O28		Clemson	3 24
N4	●	at Wake Forest	24 23
N11	●	North Carolina St.	27 19
N23		Georgia	17 18

1996 5-6 (4-4)

S7	●	at North Carolina St.	28 16
S14	●	Wake Forest	30 10
S21		at North Carolina	0 16
S26	●	Duke	48 22
O5		Virginia	13 7
O19		at Clemson	25 28
O26	●	Central Florida	27 20
N2		Florida State	3 49
N14		at Maryland	10 13
N23		Navy	26 36
N30		at Georgia	10 19

1997 7-5 (5-3)

S6		at Notre Dame	13 17
S20	●	at Wake Forest	28 26
S27	●	Clemson	23 20
O4		at Boston College	42 14
O11	●	North Carolina St.	27 17
O18		at Florida State	0 38
O30		North Carolina	13 16
N8		at Virginia	31 35
N15	●	at Duke	41 38
N22	●	Maryland	37 18
N29		Georgia	24 27
		CARQUEST BOWL	
D29	●	West Virginia	35 30

1998 10-2 (7-1)

S5		Boston College	31 41
S12	●	New Mexico St.	42 7
S26	●	at North Carolina	43 21
O3		Duke	41 13
O10	●	at North Carolina St.	47 24
O17	●	Virginia	41 38
O24		Florida State	7 34
O31	●	Maryland *BALT*	31 14
N12	●	at Clemson	24 21
N21	●	Wake Forest	63 35
N28	●	at Georgia	21 19
		GATOR BOWL	
J1		Notre Dame	35 28

1999 8-4 (5-3)

S4	●	at Navy	49 14
S11		at Florida State	35 41
S18	●	Central Florida	41 10
S30	●	Maryland	49 31
O9	●	North Carolina	31 24
O16	●	at Duke	38 31
O30	●	North Carolina St.	48 21
N6		at Virginia	38 45
N13	●	Clemson	45 42
N20	●	at Wake Forest	23 26
N27	●	Georgia	51 48
		GATOR BOWL	
J1	●	Miami, Fla.	13 28

2000 9-3 (6-2)

S2	●	Central Florida	21 17
S9	●	Florida State	21 26
S16	●	Navy	40 13
S21		at North Carolina St.	23 30
S30	●	at North Carolina	42 28
O14	●	Wake Forest	52 20
O21	●	Duke	45 10
O28	●	at Clemson	31 28
N9	●	Virginia	35 0
N18	●	at Maryland	35 22
N25	●	at Georgia	27 15
		PEACH BOWL	
D29	●	LSU	14 28

MAC McWHORTER 2001 (1.000) 1-0

2001 8-5 (4-4)

A26	●	Syracuse *ERUT*	13 7
S1	●	Citadel	35 7
S8	●	at Navy	70 7
S29		Clemson	44 47
O6	●	at Duke	37 10
O11		Maryland	17 20
O20	●	North Carolina St.	27 17
N1	●	North Carolina	28 21
N10		at Virginia	38 39
N17	●	at Wake Forest	38 33
N24		Georgia	17 31
D1		at Florida State	17 28
		SEATTLE BOWL	
D27	●	Stanford	24 14

CHAN GAILEY 2002-07 (.571) 44-33

2002 7-6 (4-4)

A31	●	Vanderbilt	45 3
S7	●	at Connecticut	31 14
S14		at Clemson	19 24
S21	●	Brigham Young	28 19
S28	●	at North Carolina	21 13
O5		Wake Forest	21 24
O17		at Maryland	10 34
O26	●	Virginia	23 15
N2	●	at North Carolina St.	24 17
N9		Florida State	13 21
N16	●	Duke	17 2
N30		at Georgia	7 51
		SILICON VALLEY BOWL	
D31		Fresno State	21 30

2003 7-6 (4-4)

A30		at Brigham Young	13 24
S6	●	Auburn	17 3
S13		at Florida State	13 14
S20		Clemson	3 39
S27	●	at Vanderbilt	24 17
O4		North Carolina St.	29 21
O11	●	at Wake Forest	24 7
O23	●	Maryland	7 3
N8	●	at Duke	17 41
N15	●	North Carolina	41 24
N22	●	at Virginia	17 29
N29	●	Georgia	17 34
		HUMANITARIAN BOWL	
J3	●	Tulsa	52 10

2004 7-5 (4-4)

S4	●	Samford	28 7
S11	●	at Clemson	28 24
S18		at North Carolina	13 34
O2		Miami, Fla.	3 27
O9	●	at Maryland	20 7
O16	●	Duke	24 7
O28		Virginia Tech	20 34
N6	●	at North Carolina St.	24 14
N13	●	Connecticut	30 10
N20	●	Virginia	10 30
N27	●	at Georgia	13 19
		CHAMPS SPORTS BOWL	
D21	●	Syracuse	51 14

2005 7-5 (5-3)

S3	●	at Auburn	23 14
S10	●	North Carolina	27 21
S17	●	Connecticut	28 13
S24		at Virginia Tech	7 51
O6		North Carolina State	14 17
O15	●	at Duke	35 10
O29		Clemson	10 9
N5	●	Wake Forest	30 17
N12		at Virginia	17 27
N19	●	at Miami, Fla.	14 10
N26		Georgia	7 14
		EMERALD BOWL	
D29	●	Utah	10 38

2006   9-5   (7-1)

S2		Notre Dame	10	14
S9	●	Samford	38	6
S16	●	Troy State	35	20
S21	● |	Virginia	24	7
S30	● |	at Virginia Tech	38	27
O7	● |	Maryland	27	23
O21	|	at Clemson	7	31
O28	● |	Miami, Fla.	30	23
N4	● |	North Carolina State	31	23
N11	● |	at North Carolina	7	0
N18	● |	Duke	49	21
N25		at Georgia	12	15

ACC CHAMPIONSHIP GAME

D2		Wake Forest *JacF*	6	9

GATOR BOWL

J1		West Virginia	35	38

2007   7-6   (4-4)

S1	●	at Notre Dame	33	3
S8	●	Samford	69	14
S15	|	Boston College	10	24
S22	|	at Virginia	23	28
S29	● |	Clemson	13	3
O6	|	at Maryland	26	28
O13	● |	at Miami, Fla.	17	14
O20	● |	Army	34	10
N1	|	Virginia Tech	3	27
N10	● |	at Duke	41	24
N17	● |	North Carolina	27	25
N24		Georgia	17	31

HUMANITARIAN BOWL

D31		Fresno State	28	40

PAUL JOHNSON
2008-PRESENT (.692)   9-4

2008   9-4   (5-3)

A28	●	Jacksonville State	41	14
S6	● |	at Boston College	19	16
S13	|	at Virginia Tech	17	20
S20	●	Mississippi State	38	7
O4	● |	Duke	27	0
O11	●	Gardner-Webb	10	7
O18	● |	at Clemson	21	17
O25	|	Virginia	17	24
N1	● |	Florida State	31	28
N8	|	at North Carolina	7	28
N20	● |	Miami FL	41	23
N29	●	at Georgia	45	42

CHICK-FIL-A BOWL

D31		LSU	3	38

THE SCHOOLS

GEORGIA TECH ANNUAL STATISTICAL LEADERS

YR	RUSHING	YDS	ATT	AVG	PASSING	ATT	CMP	PCT	YDS	RECEIVING	REC	YDS	AVG
1950	Bobby North	663	145	4.6	Darrell Crawford	96	54	.56	546	John Weigle	23	368	16.0
1951	Leon Hardeman	647	126	5.1	Darrell Crawford	150	83	.55	1,237	Buck Martin	37	506	13.7
1952	Bill Teas	825	151	5.5	Bill Brigman	125	64	.51	794	Buck Martin	28	398	14.2
1953	Bill Teas	610	111	5.5	Pepper Rodgers	85	51	.60	643	Henry Hair	16	187	11.7
1954	Jimmy Thompson	442	47	9.4	Bill Brigman	77	39	.51	573	Henry Hair	24	270	11.3
1955	George Volkert	583	81	7.2	Toppy Vann	36	31	.86	270	George Volkert	8	171	21.4
1956	Ken Owen	497	107	4.6	Toppy Vann	65	34	.52	446	Stan Flowers	10	141	14.1
1957	Lester Simerville	275	86	3.2	Fred Braselton	107	56	.52	486	Jerome Green	9	86	9.6
1958	Floyd Faucette	473	83	5.7	Fred Braselton	78	35	.45	319	Fred Murphy	12	143	11.9
1959	Floyd Faucette	330	69	4.8	Fred Braselton	64	32	.50	368	Taz Anderson	10	89	8.9
1960	Chick Graning	315	82	3.8	Stan Gann	96	43	.45	523	Chick Graning	16	158	9.9
1961	Mike McNames	350	94	3.7	Stan Gann	79	43	.54	450	Billy Williamson	21	221	10.5
1962	Billy Lothridge	478	128	3.7	Billy Lothridge	156	83	.53	1,006	Billy Martin	21	323	15.4
1963	Ray Mendheim	427	93	4.6	Billy Lothridge	153	76	.50	1,017	Billy Martin	19	221	11.6
1964	Johnny Gresham	437	99	4.4	Jerry Priestley	77	37	.48	441	Johnny Gresham	22	290	13.2
1965	Lenny Snow	597	125	4.8	Kim King	191	112	.59	1,331	Craig Baynham	30	368	12.3
1966	Lenny Snow	761	202	3.8	Kim King	124	64	.52	690	Steve Almond	24	265	11.0
1967	Lenny Snow	385	118	3.3	Kim King	145	67	.46	742	John Sias	42	671	16.0
1968	Kenny Bounds	188	56	3.4	Larry Good	191	97	.51	1,337	John Sias	61	902	14.8
1969	Brent Cunningham	459	118	3.9	Jack Williams	59	30	.51	358	Steve Foster	19	200	10.5
1970	Brent Cunningham	740	144	5.1	Eddie McAshan	223	110	.49	1,138	Larry Studdard	29	355	12.2
1971	Greg Horne	500	123	4.1	Eddie McAshan	234	125	.53	1,186	Mike Oven	33	361	10.9
1972	Greg Horne	558	139	4.0	Eddie McAshan	241	125	.52	1,756	Jimmy Robinson	48	812	16.9
1973	Cleo Johnson	451	92	4.9	Jim Stevens	217	119	.55	1,481	Jimmy Robinson	34	597	17.6
1974	David Sims	881	144	3.8	Rudy Allen	52	28	.54	357	Jimmy Robinson	19	224	11.8
1975	David Sims	590	72	8.2	Danny Myers	27	16	.59	272	Steve Raible	13	277	21.3
1976	David Sims	803	163	4.9	Gary Lanier	33	16	.48	290	John Steele	14	233	16.6
1977	Eddie Lee Ivery	900	153	5.9	Gary Lanier	26	10	.38	182	Drew Hill	7	102	14.6
1978	Eddie Lee Ivery	1,562	267	5.9	Mike Kelley	197	96	.49	1,479	Drew Hill	36	708	19.7
1979	Ronny Cone	617	126	4.9	Mike Kelley	300	149	.50	2,051	Kris Kentera	25	526	21.0
1980	David Allen	466	134	3.5	Mike Kelley	137	68	.50	832	Marlon Heggs	29	483	16.7
1981	Robert Lavette	866	188	4.6	Mike Kelley	151	78	.52	887	Robert Lavette	45	307	6.8
1982	Robert Lavette	1,208	280	4.3	Jim Bob Taylor	232	135	.58	1,839	Robert Lavette	25	286	11.4
1983	Robert Lavette	803	186	4.3	John Dewberry	134	74	.55	790	Robert Lavette	21	123	18.5
1984	Robert Lavette	1,189	260	4.6	John Dewberry	206	126	.61	1,846	Ken Whisenhunt	27	517	19.1
1985	Cory Collier	606	139	4.4	John Dewberry	193	110	.57	1,557	Gary Lee	29	645	22.2
1986	Jerry Mays	842	148	5.7	Rick Strom	167	87	.52	1,011	Gary Lee	24	386	16.1
1987	Malcolm King	383	89	4.3	Darrell Gast	179	80	.45	1,104	Greg Lester	33	593	18.0
1988	Jerry Mays	942	194	4.9	Todd Rampley	275	154	.56	1,579	Jerry Mays	46	338	7.3
1989	Jerry Mays	1,349	249	5.4	Shawn Jones	271	142	.52	1,748	Jerry Mays	37	275	7.4
1990	William Bell	891	161	5.5	Shawn Jones	245	142	.58	2,008	Emmett Merchant	29	489	16.9
1991	Jimy Lincoln	913	199	4.6	Shawn Jones	339	178	.53	2,288	Greg Lester	35	676	19.3
1992	Michael Smith	336	74	4.5	Shawn Jones	362	190	.52	2,397	Bobby Rodriguez	51	621	12.2
1993	Dorsey Levens	823	114	7.2	Donnie Davis	237	137	.58	1,739	Omar Cassidy	26	395	15.2
1994	C.J. Williams	564	120	4.7	Tommy Luginbill	327	182	.56	2,128	Charlie Simmons	40	587	14.7
1995	C.J. Williams	1,138	245	4.6	Donnie Davis	223	124	.56	1,462	Harvey Middleton	31	444	14.3
1996	C.J. Williams	663	174	3.8	Joe Hamilton	188	108	.57	1,342	Harvey Middleton	64	804	12.6
1997	Charles Wiley	567	150	3.8	Joe Hamilton	268	173	.65	2,314	Harvey Middleton	52	839	16.1
1998	Joe Burns	474	98	4.8	Joe Hamilton	259	145	.56	2,166	Dez White	46	973	18.0
1999	Sean Gregory	837	172	4.9	Joe Hamilton	305	203	.67	3,060	Kelly Campbell	69	1,105	16.0
2000	Joe Burns	908	220	4.1	George Godsey	349	222	.64	2,906	Kelly Campbell	59	963	16.3
2001	Joe Burns	1,165	282	4.1	George Godsey	384	249	.65	3,085	Kelly Campbell	56	708	12.6
2002	Tony Hollings	633	92	6.9	A.J. Suggs	363	208	.57	2,242	Kerry Watkins	71	1,050	14.8
2003	P.J. Daniels	1,447	283	5.1	Reggie Ball	350	181	.52	1,996	Jonathan Smith	78	1,138	14.6
2004	P.J. Daniels	714	154	4.6	Reggie Ball	330	164	.50	2,147	Calvin Johnson	48	837	17.4
2005	P.J. Daniels	930	198	4.7	Reggie Ball	379	182	.48	2,165	Calvin Johnson	54	888	16.4
2006	Tashard Choice	1,473	297	5.0	Reggie Ball	304	135	.44	1,820	Calvin Johnson	76	1,202	15.8
2007	Tashard Choice	1,379	261	4.9	Taylor Bennett	327	162	.50	2,136	Greg Smith	37	588	15.9
2008	Jonathan Dwyer	1,328	190	7.0	Josh Nesbitt	99	46	.47	658	Demaryius Thomas	36	595	16.5

Receiving leaders by receptions
All statistics include postseason

GEORGIA TECH RECORD BOOK

SINGLE-GAME RECORDS

Rushing Yards	356	Eddie Lee Ivery (Nov. 11, 1978 vs. Air Force)
Passing Yards	486	George Godsey (Nov. 10, 2001 vs. Virginia)
Receiving Yards	243	Dez White (Oct. 17, 1998 vs. Virginia)
All-Purpose Yards	367	Eddie Lee Ivery (Nov. 11, 1978 vs. Air Force)
Points	24	Seven players tied
Field Goals	5	Ron Rice (Sept. 18, 1982 vs. The Citadel)
Tackles	28	Eric Wilcox (Nov. 25, 1967 vs. Georgia)
Interceptions	3	Six players tied

SINGLE-SEASON RECORDS

Rushing Yards	1,562	Eddie Lee Ivery, 1978 (267 att.)
Passing Yards	3,085	George Godsey, 2001 (249-384)
Receiving Yards	1,202	Calvin Johnson, 2006 (76 rec.)
All-Purpose Yards	1,879	Eddie Lee Ivery, 1978
Scoring	114	Robert Lavette, 1982
Touchdowns	19	Robert Lavette, 1982
Tackles	188	Joe Harris, 1974
Interceptions	9	Jeff Ford, 1969 and Willie Clay, 1991
Punting Average	45.6	Rodney Williams, 1997 (47 punts)
Punt Return Average	22.6	Jimmy Brown, 1965 (10 ret.)
Kickoff Return Average	30.0	Drew Hill, 1978 (19 ret.)

CAREER RECORDS

Rushing Yards	4,066	Robert Lavette, 1981-84
Passing Yards	8,882	Joe Hamilton, 1996-99
Receiving Yards	2,927	Calvin Johnson, 2004-06
All-Purpose Yards	5,393	Robert Lavette, 1981-84
Scoring	322	Luke Manget, 1999-02
Touchdowns	46	Robert Lavette, 1981-84
Tackles	467	Keith Brooking, 1994-97
Interceptions	16	Willie Clay, 1988-91
Punting Average	45.3	Durant Brooks, 2006-07 (144 punts)
Punt Return Average	15.2	Charlie Rogers, 1995-99 (32 ret.)
Kickoff Return Average	25.4	Drew Hill, 1975-78 (94 ret.)

TEAM RECORDS

Longest Winning Streak	18	Nov. 10, 1951-Sep. 19, 1953; broken vs. Florida, 0-0 on Sep. 26, 1953
Longest Undefeated Streak	33	Nov. 14, 1914-Nov. 10, 1918; broken vs. Pittsburgh, 0-32 on Nov. 23, 1918
Most Consecutive Winning Seasons	18	1908-25
Most Consecutive Bowl Appearances	12	1997-present
Most Points in a Game	222	vs. Cumberland, Oct. 7, 1916
Most Points Allowed in a Game	94	vs. Auburn, Nov. 17, 1894
Largest Margin of Victory	222	vs. Cumberland, Oct, 7, 1916
Largest Margin of Defeat	94	vs. Auburn, Nov. 17, 1894
Longest Pass Play	96	Brandon Shaw to Charlie Rogers vs. Central Florida, Oct. 26, 1996
Longest Field Goal	55	Three players tied
Longest Punt	85	Buck Flowers vs. Davidson, Oct. 9, 1920
Longest Interception Return	100	Jeff Ford vs. Notre Dame, Nov. 15, 1969

RETIRED JERSEYS

	19	Clint Castleberry

ALL-TIME TEAM

As selected in 1991 by fans to commemorate the school's centennial season

Offense			Defense		
	RB	Eddie Lee Ivery, 1978		DL	Rock Perdoni, 1970
	RB	Robert Lavette, 1984		DL	Larry Stallings, 1962
	QB	Billy Lothridge, 1963		DL	Pat Swilling, 1985
	C	Billy Curry, 1964		LB	Maxie Baughan, 1959
	G	Rufus Guthrie, 1962		LB	George Morris, 1952
	G	Billy Shaw, 1960		LB	Larry Morris, 1952
	T	John Davis, 1986		LB	Lucius Sanford, 1977
	T	Kent Hill, 1978		CB	Randy Rhino, 1974
	TE	Billy Martin, 1963		CB	Reginald Rutland, 1986
	WR	Drew Hill, 1978		S	Don Bessillieu, 1978
	WR	Jimmy Robinson, 1974		S	Ken Swilling, 1991
	K	Scott Sisson, 1992		P	Billy Lothridge, 1963

THE SCHOOLS

GEORGIA TECH BOWL HISTORY

SEASON	BOWL	DATE	PRE-GAME RANK	TEAMS	SCORE	FINAL RANK	MOST VALUABLE PLAYER(S)	ATT.
1928	ROSE	Jan. 1, 1929		Georgia Tech California	8 7		Benjamin Lom, California, HB	66,604
1939	ORANGE	Jan. 1, 1940	16 6	Georgia Tech Missouri	21 7			29,278
1942	COTTON	Jan. 1, 1943	11 5	Texas Georgia Tech	14 7		Jack Freeman, G, Roy McKay, B, Mauldin, T, TX Harvey Hardy, G, Jack Marshall, E, Georgia Tech	36,000
1943	SUGAR	Jan. 1, 1944	13 15	Georgia Tech Tulsa	20 18			69,134
1944	ORANGE	Jan. 1, 1945	 13	Tulsa Georgia Tech	26 12		Victor Bottari, California, HB	90,000
1946	OIL	Jan. 1, 1947	11	Georgia Tech St. Mary's	41 19			23,000
1947	ORANGE	Jan. 1, 1948	10 12	Georgia Tech Kansas	20 14			59,578
1951	ORANGE	Jan. 1, 1952	5 9	Georgia Tech Baylor	17 14			65,839
1952	SUGAR	Jan. 1, 1953	2 7	Georgia Tech Mississippi	24 7		Leon Hardemann, Georgia Tech, HB	80,205
1953	SUGAR	Jan. 1, 1954	8 10	Georgia Tech West Virginia	42 19		"Pepper" Rodgers, Georgia Tech, QB	80,187
1954	COTTON	Jan. 1, 1955	 10	Georgia Tech Arkansas	14 6		George Humphreys, Georgia Tech, FB Bud Brooks, Arkansas, G	75,504
1955	SUGAR	Jan. 2, 1956	7 11	Georgia Tech Pittsburgh	7 0		Franklin Brooks, Georgia Tech, G	71,666
1956	GATOR	Dec. 29, 1956	4 13	Georgia Tech Pittsburgh	21 14		Wade Mitchell, Georgia Tech, QB Corny Salvaterra, Pittsburgh, QB	36,256
1959	GATOR	Jan. 2, 1960	9	Arkansas Georgia Tech	14 7		Jim Mooty, Arkansas, HB Maxie Baughan, Georgia Tech, LB	45,104
1961	GATOR	Dec. 30, 1961	17 13	Penn State Georgia Tech	30 15		Galen Hall, Penn State, QB Joe Auer, Georgia Tech, HB	50,202
1962	BLUEBONNET	Dec. 22, 1962		Missouri Georgia Tech	14 10		Bill Tobin, Missouri, B Conrad Hitchler, Missouri, E	55,000
1965	GATOR	Dec. 31, 1965	 10	Georgia Tech Texas Tech	31 21		Lenny Snow, Georgia Tech, TB Donny Anderson, Texas Tech, RB	60,127
1966	ORANGE	Jan. 2, 1967	 8	Florida Georgia Tech	27 12		Larry Smith, Florida, TB	72,426
1970	SUN	Dec. 19, 1970	13 19	Georgia Tech Texas Tech	17 9	13	Rock Perdoni, Georgia Tech, DT Bill Flowers, Georgia Tech, LB	30,512
1971	PEACH	Dec. 30, 1971	17	Mississippi Georgia Tech	41 18	15	Norris Weese, Mississippi, QB Crowell Armstrong, Mississippi	36,771
1972	LIBERTY	Dec. 18, 1972		Georgia Tech Iowa State	31 30	20	Jim Stevens, Georgia Tech, QB	50,021
1978	PEACH	Dec. 25, 1978	17	Purdue Georgia Tech	41 21	13	Mark Herrmann, Purdue Calvin Clark, Purdue, DT	20,277
1985	HALL OF FAME CLASSIC	Dec. 31, 1985		Georgia Tech Michigan State	17 14	19	Mark Ingram, Michigan State, WR	45,000
1990	CITRUS	Jan. 1, 1991	2 19	Georgia Tech Nebraska	45 21	2 24	Shawn Jones, Georgia Tech, QB	72,328
1991	ALOHA	Dec. 25, 1991	 17	Georgia Tech Stanford	18 17	 22	Shawn Jones, Georgia Tech, QB Tommy Vardell, Stanford, RB	34,433
1997	CARQUEST	Dec. 29, 1997		Georgia Tech West Virginia	35 30	25	Joe Hamilton, Georgia Tech, QB	28,262
1998	GATOR	Jan. 1, 1999	12 17	Georgia Tech Notre Dame	35 28	9 22	Dez White, WR, Joe Hamilton, QB, Ga. Tech Autry Denson, Notre Dame, RB	70,791
1999	GATOR	Jan. 1, 2000	23 17	Miami (Fla.) Georgia Tech	28 13	15 20	Nate Webster, Miami (Fla.), LB Joe Hamilton, Georgia Tech, QB	43,416
2000	PEACH	Dec. 29, 2000	 15	LSU Georgia Tech	28 14	22 17	Rohan Davey, LSU, QB Bradie James, LSU, LB	73,614
2001	SEATTLE	Dec. 27, 2001	 11	Georgia Tech Stanford	24 14	24 16	George Godsey, Georgia Tech, QB	30,144
2002	SILICON VALLEY	Dec. 31, 2002		Fresno State Georgia Tech	30 21		Rodney Davis, Jason Stewart, Fresno State Asen Asparuhov, Fresno State	10,142
2003	HUMANITARIAN	Jan. 3, 2004		Georgia Tech Tulsa	52 10		P.J. Daniels, Georgia Tech, RB Cort Moffitt, Tulsa, P	23,118
2004	CHAMPS SPORTS	Dec. 21, 2004		Georgia Tech Syracuse	51 14		Reggie Ball, Georgia Tech, QB	28,237
2005	EMERALD	Dec. 29, 2005	 24	Utah Georgia Tech	38 10		Travis LaTendresse, Utah, WR; Eric Weddle, Utah, DB	25,742
2006	GATOR	Jan. 1, 2007	13	West Virginia Georgia Tech	38 35	10	Pat White, West Virginia, QB; Calvin Johnson, Georgia Tech, WR	67,714
2007	HUMANITARIAN	Dec. 31, 2007		Georgia Tech Fresno State	28 40		Jonathan Dwyer, Georgia Tech, RB; Tom Brandstater, Fresno State, QB	27,062
2008	CHICK-FIL-A	Dec. 31, 2008	 14	LSU Georgia Tech	38 3	 22	Jordan Jefferson, LSU, QB; Perry Riley, LSU, LB	35,183

JANUARY 1, 1929 | Rose
GEORGIA TECH 8, CALIFORNIA 7

	1ST	2ND	3RD	4TH	FINAL
GT	0	2	6	0	8
CAL	0	0	0	7	7

SCORING SUMMARY
GT   Saftey
GT   R. Thomason 14 run (kick failed)
CAL   Phillips 10 pass from Lom (Barr kick)

GT	TEAM STATISTICS	CAL
5	First Downs	11
166	Rushing Yards	204
1-3-0	Passing	4-12-1
23	Passing Yards	67
189	Total Yards	271
12-31.1	Punts - Average	12-35.7
2	Fumbles Lost	2
35	Penalty Yards	10

JANUARY 1, 1940 | Orange
GEORGIA TECH 21, MISSOURI 7

	1ST	2ND	3RD	4TH	FINAL
GT	7	7	7	0	21
MO	7	0	0	0	7

SCORING SUMMARY
MO   Christman 1 run (Cunningham kick)
GT   Ector 1 run (Goree kick)
GT   Ison 31 run (Goree kick)
GT   Wheby 59 run (Goree kick)

GT	TEAM STATISTICS	MO
12	First Downs	14
210	Rushing Yards	151
8-14-1	Passing	8-26-1
91	Passing Yards	76
301	Total Yards	227
7-33.0	Punts - Average	7-33.0
6-3	Fumbles - Lost	2-1
6-36	Penalties - Yards	3-15

JANUARY 1, 1943 | Cotton
TEXAS 14, GEORGIA TECH 7

	1ST	2ND	3RD	4TH	FINAL
GT	0	0	0	7	7
TEX	7	0	7	0	14

SCORING SUMMARY
TEX   Minor 4 pass from McKay (Field kick)
TEX   Field 60 punt return (McKay kick)
GT   Eldredge 4 run (Jordan kick)

GT	TEAM STATISTICS	TEX
10	First Downs	15
57	Rushing Yards	201
8-20-1	Passing	5-9-1
138	Passing Yards	23
195	Total Yards	224
8-31.4	Punts - Average	7-30.6
2	Fumbles Lost	2
4-20	Penalties - Yards	2-20

JANUARY 1, 1944 | Sugar
GEORGIA TECH 20, TULSA 18

	1ST	2ND	3RD	4TH	FINAL
GT	0	7	6	7	20
TUL	6	12	0	0	18

JANUARY 1, 1945 | Orange
TULSA 26, GEORGIA TECH 12

	1ST	2ND	3RD	4TH	FINAL
UT	14	0	12	0	26
GT	0	0	6	6	12

SCORING SUMMARY
UT   Shedlosky 14 pass from Moss (Moss kick)
UT   Shedlosky 3 run (Moss kick)
UT   White 35 run (kick failed)
GT   McIntosh 51 pass from Broyles (kick failed)
UT   Wilson 90 kickoff return (kick failed)
GT   Taylor 2 run (kick failed)

GT	TEAM STATISTICS	TEX
4	First Downs	17
180	Rushing Yards	36
6-16-0	Passing	19-34-2
137	Passing Yards	304
317	Total Yards	340
6-38.8	Punts - Average	4-25.7
2-1	Fumbles - Lost	6-3
4-41	Penalties - Yards	1-15

JANUARY 1, 1947 | Oil
GEORGIA TECH 41, ST. MARY'S 19

	1ST	2ND	3RD	4TH	FINAL
GT	7	20	7	7	41
STM	0	7	6	6	19

JANUARY 1, 1948 | Orange
GEORGIA TECH 20, KANSAS 14

	1ST	2ND	3RD	4TH	FINAL
GT	0	7	13	0	20
KU	0	7	0	7	14

SCORING SUMMARY
GT   Patton 26 pass from Still (Bowen kick)
KU   Evans 12 run (Fambrough kick)
GT   Queen 15 pass from Still (kick failed)
GT   Patton 5 pass from Still (Bowen kick)
KU   Evans 13 pass from Hogan (Fambrough kick)

GT	TEAM STATISTICS	KU
9	First Downs	14
99	Rushing Yards	93
11-19-1	Passing	10-19-1
109	Passing Yards	148
208	Total Yards	241
9-39.7	Punts - Average	7-34.3
1-1	Fumbles - Lost	4-1
10-67.5	Penalties - Yards	5-37.5

JANUARY 1, 1952 | Orange
GEORGIA TECH 17, BAYLOR 14

	1ST	2ND	3RD	4TH	FINAL
GT	7	0	0	10	17
BU	7	7	0	0	14

SCORING SUMMARY
BU   Parma 1 run (Brocato kick)
GT   Hardeman 3 run (Rodgers kick)
BU   Coody 4 run (Brocato kick)
GT   Martin 22 pass from Crawford (Rodgers kick)
GT   FG Rodgers 16

GT	TEAM STATISTICS	BU
9	First Downs	17
107	Rushing Yards	206
6-14-1	Passing	7-18-3
84	Passing Yards	93
191	Total Yards	299
7-35.3	Punts - Average	6-34.3
1-1	Fumbles - Lost	3-0
6-60	Penalties - Yards	7-85

INDIVIDUAL LEADERS
RUSHING
GT: Hardeman 17-44, 1 TD; Crawford 9-36.
BU: Parma 19-107, 1 TD; Carpenter 15-65.
PASSING
GT: Crawford 6-14-1, 84 yards, 1 TD.
BU: Isbell 8-18-3, 93 yards.
RECEIVING
GT: Martin 4-49, 1 TD.
BU: Riley 3-35; Williams 3-32.

JANUARY 1, 1953 | Sugar
GEORGIA TECH 24, MISSISSIPPI 7

	1ST	2ND	3RD	4TH	FINAL
GT	0	10	7	7	24
MISS	7	0	0	0	7

SCORING SUMMARY
MISS   Dillard 4 run (Lear kick)
GT   Brigman 1 run (Rodgers kick)
GT   FG Rodgers 25
GT   Hardemann 6 run (Rodgers kick)
GT   Knox 26 pass from Rodgers (Rodgers kick)

GT	TEAM STATISTICS	MISS
16	First Downs	15
194	Rushing Yards	137
10-18-1	Passing	11-23-3
101	Passing Yards	150
295	Total Yards	287
6-41.8	Punts - Average	7-35.4
5-2	Fumbles - Lost	5-3
5-42	Penalties - Yards	6-60

INDIVIDUAL LEADERS
RUSHING
GT: Hardemann 14-76, 1 TD; Turner 20-56.
MISS: Dillard 17-39, 1 TD; Westerman 7-36.
PASSING
GT: Brigman 5-7-1, 39 yards; Rodgers 4-9-0, 55 yards, 1 TD.
MISS: Lear 8-19-3, 122 yards.
RECEIVING
GT: Hardemann 2-24; Marks 2-14.
MISS: Slay 1-45; Bridges 2-25.

JANUARY 1, 1954 | Sugar
GEORGIA TECH 42, WEST VIRGINIA 19

	1ST	2ND	3RD	4TH	FINAL
GT	14	6	9	13	42
WVU	0	6	0	13	19

SCORING SUMMARY
GT   Hensley 24 pass from Rodgers (Rodgers kick)
GT   Durham 2 pass from Rodgers (Rodgers kick)
WVU   Williams 5 run (kick failed)
GT   Hair 5 pass from Rodgers (kick failed)
GT   FG Rodgers 18
GT   Hardeman 23 run (kick failed)
WVU   Marconi 1 run (Allman kick)
GT   Ruffin 43 run (kick blocked)
WVU   Allman 1 run (kick failed)
GU   Teas 9 run (Turner kick)

GT	TEAM STATISTICS	WVU
19	First Downs	19
170	Rushing Yards	223
20-35-2	Passing	7-18-2
268	Passing Yards	78
438	Total Yards	301
1-36.0	Punts - Average	2-28.5
3-1	Fumbles - Lost	5-4
7-45	Penalties - Yards	5-35

INDIVIDUAL LEADERS
RUSHING
GT: Ruffin 3-58, 1 TD; Teas 9-32, 1 TD.
WVU: Anderson 13-57; Moss 5-36.
PASSING
GT: Rodgers 16-26-2, 195 yards, 3 TD.
WVU: Wyant 4-15-2, 29 yards; Anderson 3-3-0, 49 yards.

JANUARY 1, 1955 | Cotton
GEORGIA TECH 14, ARKANSAS 6

	1ST	2ND	3RD	4TH	FINAL
GT	0	0	7	7	14
ARK	0	6	0	0	6

SCORING SUMMARY
ARK   Walker 3 run (kick failed)
GT   Rotenberry 3 run (Mitchell kick)
GT   Mitchell 1 run (Mitchell kick)

GT	TEAM STATISTICS	ARK
19	First Downs	10
285	Rushing Yards	141
4-15-0	Passing	7-10-1
31	Passing Yards	86
316	Total Yards	227
4-30.0	Punts - Average	4-28.0
1-0	Fumbles - Lost	0-0
4-30	Penalties - Yards	4-30

INDIVIDUAL LEADERS
RUSHING
GT: Humphreys 19-99; Thompson 12-63.
ARK: Moore 16-86; Walker 11-34, 1 TD.
PASSING
GT: Mitchell 4-10-0, 31 yards.
ARK: Walker 3-5-1, 51 yards.
RECEIVING
GT: Durham 2-20; Hair 2-11.
ARK: Lyons 2-34; Thomason 1-22.

JANUARY 2, 1956 | Sugar
GEORGIA TECH 7, PITTSBURGH 0

	1ST	2ND	3RD	4TH	FINAL
GT	7	0	0	0	7
PITT	0	0	0	0	0

SCORING SUMMARY
GT   Mitchell 1 run (Mitchell kick)

GT	TEAM STATISTICS	PITT
10	First Downs	19
142	Rushing Yards	217
0-3-1	Passing	8-18-1
0	Passing Yards	94
142	Total Yards	311
6-33.8	Punts - Average	4-38.7
2-0	Fumbles - Lost	4-2
1-15	Penalties - Yards	8-72

INDIVIDUAL LEADERS
RUSHING
GT: Owen 7-29; Mattison 7-27.
PITT: Grier 6-51; Cimarolli 11-37.

THE SCHOOLS

THE SCHOOLS

December 29, 1956 | Gator
Georgia Tech 21, Pittsburgh 14

	1ST	2ND	3RD	4TH	FINAL
GT	7	7	7	0	21
PITT	0	7	7	0	14

SCORING SUMMARY
GT Owen 2 run (Mitchell kick)
GT Nabors 6 pass from Volkert (Mitchell kick)
PITT Bowan 42 pass from Salvaterra (Walton pass from Salvaterra)
GT Rotenberry 5 run (Mitchell kick)
PITT Salvaterra 1 run (Bagamery kick)

GT	TEAM STATISTICS	PITT
10	First Downs	16
162	Rushing Yards	246
3-3-0	Passing	3-11-2
45	Passing Yards	67
207	Total Yards	313
5-41.2	Punts - Average	3-36.0
1-1	Fumbles - Lost	2-2
1-13	Penalties - Yards	0-0

INDIVIDUAL LEADERS
RUSHING
GT: Flowers 4-63; Mattison 11-43.
PITT: Jelic 10-66; Passodelis 10-38.
PASSING
GT: Mitchell 2-2-0, 39 yards; Volkert 1-1-0, 6 yards, 1 TD.
PITT: Salvaterra 3-10-2, 67 yards, 1 TD.
RECEIVING
GT: Nabors 2-32, 1 TD; Rotenberry 1-13.
PITT: Bowan 1-42, 1 TD; Walton 1-21.

January 2, 1960 | Gator
Arkansas 14, Georgia Tech 7

	1ST	2ND	3RD	4TH	FINAL
ARK	0	7	7	0	14
GT	7	0	0	0	7

SCORING SUMMARY
GT Tibbetts 51 run (Faucette kick)
ARK Alberty 1 run (Akers kick)
ARK Mooty 19 run (Akers kick)

ARK	TEAM STATISTICS	GT
15	First Downs	13
218	Rushing Yards	172
2-6-1	Passing	8-18-1
21	Passing Yards	64
239	Total Yards	236
4-36.5	Punts - Average	4-40.7
1-1	Fumbles - Lost	0-0
5-56	Penalties - Yards	3-15

INDIVIDUAL LEADERS
RUSHING
ARK: Mooty 18-99, 1 TD; Alworth 9-40; Alberty 12-38, 1 TD.
GT: Tibbetts 3-59, 1 TD; Anderson 12-38.
PASSING
ARK: Monroe 2-4-0, 21 yards.
GT: Braselton 8-18-1, 64 yards.
RECEIVING
ARK: Mooty 1-12.
GT: Graning 3-19.

December 31, 1961 | Gator
Penn State 30, Georgia Tech 15

	1ST	2ND	3RD	4TH	FINAL
PSU	0	14	6	10	30
GT	2	7	0	6	15

SCORING SUMMARY
GT Safety (Hall intentional grounding in end zone)
GT Auer 68 run (Lothridge kick)
PSU Gursky 13 pass from Hall (Jonas kick)
PSU Kochman 27 pass from Hall (Jonas kick)
PSU Powell 35 pass from Hall (kick failed)
GT Auer 14 run (run failed)
PSU FG Jonas 23
PSU Torris 1 run (Jonas kick)

PSU	TEAM STATISTICS	GT
13	First Downs	19
138	Rushing Yards	211
12-22-0	Passing	12-24-2
175	Passing Yards	201
313	Total Yards	412
8-41.0	Punts - Average	5-27.6
1-1	Fumbles - Lost	6-3
6-63	Penalties - Yards	2-14

INDIVIDUAL LEADERS
RUSHING
PSU: Kochman 13-76; Torris 12-27, 1 TD.
GT: Auer 10-98, 2 TD; Williamson 11-44.
RECEIVING
PSU: Robinson 4-40; Anderson 3-40.
GT: Williamson 4-102; Martin 3-36.

December 22, 1962 | Bluebonnet
Missouri 14, Georgia Tech 10

	1ST	2ND	3RD	4TH	FINAL
MO	7	0	7	0	14
GT	0	7	3	0	10

SCORING SUMMARY
MO Johnson 21 run (Leistritz kick)
GT Auer 6 run (Lothridge kick)
MO Tobin 77 run (Leistritz kick)
GT FG Lothridge 26

MO	TEAM STATISTICS	GT
10	First Downs	13
258	Rushing Yards	169
0-7-2	Passing	5-15-4
0	Passing Yards	68
258	Total Yards	237
5-39.6	Punts - Average	6-38.5
2-2	Fumbles - Lost	0-0
4-35	Penalties - Yards	1-5

INDIVIDUAL LEADERS
RUSHING
MO: Tobin 11-114, 1 TD; Johnson 8-66, 1 TD.
GT: Auer 10-67, 1 TD; McNames 13-57.
PASSING
MO: Johnson 0-5-1, 0 yards.
GT: Lothridge 5-15-4, 68 yards.

December 31, 1965 | Gator
Georgia Tech 31, Texas Tech 21

	1ST	2ND	3RD	4TH	FINAL
GT	0	9	7	15	31
TT	7	0	14	0	21

SCORING SUMMARY
TT Agan 4 pass from Wilson (Gill kick)
GT Smith 2 run (Henry kick)
GT Safety
GT Snow 1 run (Henry kick)
TT Anderson 1 run (Gill kick)
TT Shipley 15 pass from Wilson (Gill kick)
GT Priestley 1 run (Priestley run)
GT Varner 13 run (Henry kick)

GT	TEAM STATISTICS	TT
27	First Downs	17
364	Rushing Yards	113
5-10-1	Passing	22-40-2
77	Passing Yards	283
441	Total Yards	396
4-32.5	Punts - Average	3-41.6
2-1	Fumbles - Lost	3-3
5-57	Penalties - Yards	2-25

INDIVIDUAL LEADERS
RUSHING
GT: Snow 35-136, 1 TD; Smith 15-73, 1 TD.
TT: Anderson 13-85, 1 TD, Agan 4-21.
PASSING
GT: King 4-7-1, 58 yards.
TT: Wilson 22-40-2, 283 yards, 2 TD.
RECEIVING
GT: Baynham 2-52; Gautier 1-19.
TT: Anderson 9-138; Shipley 5-64, 1 TD.

January 2, 1967 | Orange
Florida 27, Georgia Tech 12

	1ST	2ND	3RD	4TH	FINAL
UF	0	7	7	13	27
GT	6	0	0	6	12

SCORING SUMMARY
GT Baynham 10 pass from King (run failed)
UF McKeel 1 run (Barfield kick)
UF Smith 94 run (Barfield kick)
UF McKeel 1 run (Barfield kick)
GT Good 25 run (pass failed)
UF Coons 5 pass from Wages (pass failed)

UF	TEAM STATISTICS	GT
22	First Downs	17
289	Rushing Yards	197
15-32-1	Passing	16-22-4
165	Passing Yards	128
454	Total Yards	325
7-36.1	Punts - Average	6-42.3
1-1	Fumbles - Lost	2-1
4-32	Penalties - Yards	5-42

INDIVIDUAL LEADERS
RUSHING
UF: Smith 23-187, 1 TD; McKeel 3-50, 2 TD.
GT: Snow 24-110; Good 3-24, 1 TD.
PASSING
UF: Spurrier 14-30-1, 160 yards.
GT: Good 3-6-1, 86 yards; King 3-16-3, 42 yards, 1 TD.
RECEIVING
UF: Trapp 5-43; Coons 3-35, 1 TD.
GT: Snow 1-52; Smith 2-32.

December 19, 1970 | Sun
Georgia Tech 17, Texas Tech 9

	1ST	2ND	3RD	4TH	FINAL
GT	7	3	0	7	17
TT	0	0	9	0	9

SCORING SUMMARY
GT Healy 2 run (Thigpen kick)
GT FG Moore 21
TT McCutchen 7 run (Ingram kick)
TT Safety (blocked punt out of end zone)
GT McNamara 2 run (Thigpen kick)

GT	TEAM STATISTICS	TT
18	First Downs	13
186	Rushing Yards	215
13-19-1	Passing	3-11-3
138	Passing Yards	28
324	Total Yards	243
2-36	Punt Returns - Yards	1-1
2-15	Kickoff Returns - Yards	4-62
7-34.0	Punts - Average	4-41.0
0-0	Fumbles - Lost	6-3
7-66	Penalties - Yards	4-40

INDIVIDUAL LEADERS
RUSHING
GT: Healy 20-59, 1 TD; Cunningham 14-42.
TT: Hargrave 8-83; McCutchen 22-81, 1 TD.
PASSING
GT: Williams 11-14-1, 123 yards.
TT: Napper 3-11-3, 28 yards.
RECEIVING
GT: Pallman 3-42; Macy 3-37.
TT: Odom 2-23.

December 30, 1971 | Peach
Mississippi 41, Georgia Tech 18

	1ST	2ND	3RD	4TH	FINAL
MISS	10	28	0	3	41
GT	0	6	6	6	18

SCORING SUMMARY
MISS Weese 1 run (Hinton kick)
MISS FG Hinton 25
MISS Porter 2 run (Hinton kick)
MISS Porter 10 run (Hinton kick)
MISS Felts 15 pass from Lyons (Hinton kick)
MISS Myers 11 pass from Weese (Hinton kick)
GT Healy 2 run (run failed)
GT Healy 1 run (pass failed)
GT Healy 1 run (run failed)
MISS FG Hinton 30

MISS	TEAM STATISTICS	GT
17	First Downs	16
179	Rushing Yards	166
9-18-1	Passing	13-26-2
139	Passing Yards	151
318	Total Yards	317
5-37.4	Punts - Average	5-31.2
2-1	Fumbles - Lost	3-3
5-25	Penalties - Yards	8-38

INDIVIDUAL LEADERS
RUSHING
MISS: Ainsworth 28-119; Porter 8-26, 2 TD.
GT: Hennessey 6-57; Cunningham 5-30.
PASSING
MISS: Weese 7-14-0, 23 yards, 1 TD.
GT: McAshan 13-26-2, 151 yards.
RECEIVING
MISS: Myers 2-49, 1 TD; Barry 3-39.
GT: Owings 5-87; Oven 3-26.

DECEMBER 18, 1972 | LIBERTY
GEORGIA TECH 31, IOWA STATE 30

	1ST	2ND	3RD	4TH	FINAL
GT	3	14	7	7	31
ISU	14	7	3	6	30

SCORING SUMMARY
GT   FG Bonifay 32
ISU   Harris 13 pass from Amundson (Goedjen kick)
ISU   Moore 1 run (Goedjen kick)
GT   Robinson 9 pass from Stevens (kick failed)
GT   Faulkner 19 interception return (Thigpen kick)
ISU   Jones 93 kickoff return (Goedjen kick)
GT   Healy 22 pass from Stevens (Thigpen kick)
ISU   FG Goedjen 30
GT   McNamara 3 pass from Stevens (Thigpen kick)
ISU   Harris pass from Amundson (pass failed)

GT	TEAM STATISTICS	ISU
18	First Downs	18
123	Rushing Yards	185
12-15-1	Passing	10-19-2
157	Passing Yards	153
278	Total Yards	338
5-2	Fumbles - Lost	3-2
1-5	Penalties - Yards	4-39

INDIVIDUAL LEADERS
RUSHING
GT: Southall 22-48; Healy 11-46.
ISU: Amundson 13-78; Moore 19-50, 1 TD.
PASSING
GT: Stevens 12-15-1, 157 yards, 3 TD.
ISU: Amundson 10-19-2, 153 yards, 2 TD.
RECEIVING
GT: Oven 3-38; Robinson 3-29, 1 TD.
ISU: Harris 4-46, 2 TD; Jones 2-65.

DECEMBER 25, 1978 | PEACH
PURDUE 41, GEORGIA TECH 21

	1ST	2ND	3RD	4TH	FINAL
PUR	21	13	0	7	41
GT	0	7	0	14	21

SCORING SUMMARY
PUR   Jones 3 run (Savereen kick)
PUR   Jones 8 run (Savereen kick)
PUR   Smith 10 pass from Herrmann (Savereen kick)
PUR   Herrmann 2 run (Savereen kick)
GT   Lee 1 run (Smith kick)
PUR   Macon 1 run (kick failed)
GT   Moore 3 pass from Kelley (Hill run)
GT   Hill 31 pass from Kelley (pass failed)

PUR	TEAM STATISTICS	GT
24	First Downs	14
157	Rushing Yards	12
12-27-2	Passing	17-38-2
166	Passing Yards	168
323	Total Yards	180
5-36.6	Punts - Average	7-36.7
3-1	Fumbles - Lost	2-2
9-78	Penalties - Yards	5-48

INDIVIDUAL LEADERS
RUSHING
PUR: Macon 19-66, 1 TD; Jones 13-50, 2 TD.
GT: Lee 6-24, 1 TD.
PASSING
PUR: Herrmann 12-24-2, 166 yards, 2 TD.
GT: Kelley 17-38-2, 168 yards, 2 TD.
RECEIVING
PUR: Burrell 4-55, 1 TD; Harris 2-38.
GT: Hill 5-77, 1 TD; Hardie 4-40.

DECEMBER 31, 1985 | HALL OF FAME CLASSIC
GEORGIA TECH 17, MICHIGAN STATE 14

	1ST	2ND	3RD	4TH	FINAL
GT	0	0	7	10	17
MSU	0	7	7	0	14

SCORING SUMMARY
MSU   Ingram 6 pass from Yarema (Caudell kick)
GT   Rampley 1 run (Bell kick)
MSU   Ingram 27 pass from Yarema (Caudell kick)
GT   FG Bell 40
GT   King 5 run (Bell kick)

GT	TEAM STATISTICS	MSU
16	First Downs	14
182	Rushing Yards	148
12-23-1	Passing	6-15-1
99	Passing Yards	85
281	Total Yards	233
1-11	Punt Returns - Yards	2-14
2-30	Kickoff Returns - Yards	4-47
6-37.8	Punts - Average	6-36.7
2-0	Fumbles - Lost	2-1
5-47	Penalties - Yards	3-28
35:03	Possession Time	24:57

INDIVIDUAL LEADERS
RUSHING
GT: King 16-122, 1 TD; Kelsey 8-30.
MSU: White 33-158; Morse 2-8.
PASSING
GT: Rampley 12-23-1, 99 yards.
MSU: Yarema 6-15-1, 85 yards, 2 TD.
RECEIVING
GT: Massey 2-23; Mayes 3-22.
MSU: Ingram 3-70, 2 TD; Rison 1-18.

JANUARY 1, 1991 | CITRUS
GEORGIA TECH 45, NEBRASKA 21

	1ST	2ND	3RD	4TH	FINAL
GT	7	17	7	14	45
NEB	0	14	7	0	21

SCORING SUMMARY
GT   Scotten 2 run (Sisson kick)
GT   Merchant 22 pass from Jones (Sisson kick)
GT   Bell 2 pass from Jones (Sisson kick)
NEB   Mitchell 30 pass from Haase (Barrios kick)
NEB   Brown 50 run (Barrios kick)
GT   FG Sisson 37
GT   Jones 1 run (Sisson kick)
NEB   Washington 21 pass from Haase (Barrios kick)
GT   Bell 6 run (Sisson kick)
GT   Bell 57 run (Sisson kick)

GT	TEAM STATISTICS	NEB
19	First Downs	14
190	Rushing Yards	126
16-23-1	Passing	14-25-0
277	Passing Yards	209
467	Total Yards	335
6-40.2	Punts - Average	8-39.2
2-1	Fumbles - Lost	3-2
5-50	Penalties - Yards	6-69

INDIVIDUAL LEADERS
RUSHING
GT: Bell 16-127, 2 TD; Jones 11-41, 1 TD.
NEB: Brown 11-99, 1 TD; Turner 2-21.
PASSING
GT: Jones 16-23-1, 277 yards, 2 TD.
NEB: Haase 14-21-0, 209 yards.
RECEIVING
GT: Bell 4-53, 1 TD; Rodriguez 3-66.
NEB: Mitchell 5-138, 1 TD; Turner 3-24.

DECEMBER 25, 1991 | ALOHA
GEORGIA TECH 18, STANFORD 17

	1ST	2ND	3RD	4TH	FINAL
GT	10	0	0	8	18
STAN	7	10	0	0	17

SCORING SUMMARY
STAN   Vardell 6 run (Mills kick)
GT   Smith 2 pass from Jones (Sisson kick)
GT   FG Sisson 24
STAN   FG Mills 38
STAN   Vardell 2 run (Mills kick)
GT   Jones 1 run (Lincoln run)

GT	TEAM STATISTICS	STAN
14	First Downs	19
198	Rushing Yards	159
14-30-1	Passing	16-32-1
61	Passing Yards	170
259	Total Yards	329
7-47.4	Punts - Average	6-42.3
3-2	Fumbles - Lost	2-1
6-50	Penalties - Yards	6-49

INDIVIDUAL LEADERS
RUSHING
GT: Jones 10-48, 1 TD; Smith 7-47.
STAN: Vardell 21-104, 2 TD; Milburn 12-56.
PASSING
GT: Jones 14-29-1, 61 yards, 1 TD.
STAN: Stenstrom 16-32-1, 170 yards.
RECEIVING
GT: Wilkerson 3-25; Lester 3-20; Smith 3-17, 1 TD.
STAN: Walsh 5-61; Lasley 5-33.

DECEMBER 29, 1997 | CARQUEST
GEORGIA TECH 35, WEST VIRGINIA 30

	1ST	2ND	3RD	4TH	FINAL
GT	14	14	0	7	35
WVU	7	7	10	6	30

SCORING SUMMARY
GT   Wilder 1 run (Chambers kick)
WVU   Zereoue 14 run (Taylor kick)
GT   Hamilton 30 run (Chambers kick)
GT   Lillie 3 pass from Hamilton (Chambers kick)
WVU   Porter 21 pass from Bulger (Taylor kick)
GT   Hamilton 9 run (Chambers kick)
WVU   Zereoue 19 run (Taylor kick)
WVU   FG Taylor 21
GT   Wiley 5 run (Chambers kick)
WVU   Porter 74 pass from Bulger (pass failed)

GT	TEAM STATISTICS	WVU
28	First Downs	24
210	Rushing Yards	56
19-36-0	Passing	25-40-1
274	Passing Yards	353
484	Total Yards	409
4-42.0	Punts - Average	3-43.3
1-1	Fumbles - Lost	1-1
10-86	Penalties - Yards	9-75
35:02	Possession Time	24:58

INDIVIDUAL LEADERS
RUSHING
GT: Hamilton 14-82, 2 TD; Rogers 16-75.
WVU: Zereoue 17-84, 2 TD.
PASSING
GT: Hamilton 19-36-0, 274 yards, 1 TD.
WVU: Bulger 25-40-1, 353 yards, 2 TD.
RECEIVING
GT: Steagall 7-112, Middleton 4-45.
WVU: Porter 4-124, 2 TD; Foreman 12-110.

JANUARY 1, 1999 | GATOR
GEORGIA TECH 35, NOTRE DAME 28

	1ST	2ND	3RD	4TH	FINAL
GT	7	14	7	7	35
ND	7	0	13	8	28

SCORING SUMMARY
GT	Hamilton 5 pass from Burns (Chambers kick)
ND	Denson 9 run (Sanson kick)
GT	Rogers 2 run (Chambers kick)
GT	Sheridan 9 pass from Hamilton (Chambers kick)
ND	Denson 1 run (Sanson kick)
ND	Jackson 2 run (kick blocked)
GT	White 44 pass from Hamilton (Chambers kick)
ND	Denson 1 run (Brown pass from Jackson)
GT	White 55 pass from Hamilton (Chambers kick)

GT	TEAM STATISTICS	ND
23	First Downs	20
194	Rushing Yards	150
14-21-0	Passing	13-24-0
242	Passing Yards	159
436	Total Yards	309
3-34.7	Punts - Average	5-36.6
2-1	Fumbles - Lost	2-1
7-53	Penalties - Yards	6-30
30:47	Possession Time	29:13

INDIVIDUAL LEADERS
RUSHING
GT: C. Rogers 13-82, 1 TD; P. Rogers 10-28.
ND: Denson 26-130, 3 TD; Jackson 12-12, 1 TD.

PASSING
GT: Hamilton 13-20-0, 237 yards, 3 TD.
ND: Jackson 13-24-0, 150 yards.

RECEIVING
GT: White 4-129, 2 TD; Rogers 4-52.
ND: Johnson 5-43; Brown 2-42.

JANUARY 1, 2000 | GATOR
MIAMI (FLA.) 28, GEORGIA TECH 13

	1ST	2ND	3RD	4TH	FINAL
MIA	7	14	0	7	28
GT	0	7	6	0	13

SCORING SUMMARY
MIA	Jackson 8 run (Crosland kick)
MIA	King 15 pass from Kelly (Crosland kick)
GT	Hamilton 17 run (Manget kick)
MIA	Portis 73 run (Crosland kick)
GT	FG Manget 25
GT	FG Manget 36
MIA	Wayne 17 pass from Dorsey (Crosland kick)

MIA	TEAM STATISTICS	GT
22	First Downs	29
220	Rushing Yards	176
16-32-1	Passing	20-40-2
208	Passing Yards	245
428	Total Yards	421
5-42.6	Punts - Average	6-26.2
1-1	Fumbles - Lost	1-0
9-90	Penalties - Yards	7-65
27:40	Possession Time	32:20

INDIVIDUAL LEADERS
RUSHING
MIA: Portis 12-117, 1 TD; Jackson 21-107, 1 TD.
GT: Gregory 16-64; Hamilton 22-49, 1 TD.

PASSING
MIA: Kelly 9-17-1, 127 yards, 1 TD; Dorsey 7-15-0, 81 yards, 1 TD.
GT: Hamilton 20-40-2, 245 yards.

RECEIVING
MIA: Franks 3-72; Moss 3-53; Wayne 4-44, 1 TD.
GT: White 8-100; Campbell 3-39.

DECEMBER 29, 2000 | PEACH
LSU 28, GEORGIA TECH 14

	1ST	2ND	3RD	4TH	FINAL
LSU	3	0	6	19	28
GT	7	7	0	0	14

SCORING SUMMARY
LSU	FG Corbello 32
GT	Burns 32 run (Manget kick)
GT	Hatch 9 run (Manget kick)
LSU	Banks 3 pass from Davey (Corbello kick)
LSU	Reed 9 pass from Davey (Reed pass from Davey)
LSU	FG Corbello 49
LSU	Banks 3 pass from Davey (Robinson pass from Davey)

LSU	TEAM STATISTICS	GT
21	First Downs	19
90	Rushing Yards	140
25-44-0	Passing	19-38-2
284	Passing Yards	177
374	Total Yards	317
8-40.8	Punts - Average	5-48.2
3-1	Fumbles - Lost	7-4
7-59	Penalties - Yards	6-45
37:10	Possession Time	22:50

INDIVIDUAL LEADERS
RUSHING
LSU: Toefield 22-78; Davis 8-25.
GT: Burns 17-96, 1 TD; Hatch 6-45, 1 TD.

PASSING
LSU: Davey 17-25-0, 174 yards, 3 TD; Booty 8-19-0, 110 yards.
GT: Godsey 19-36-2, 177 yards.

RECEIVING
LSU: Reed 9-96, 1 TD; Banks 7-71, 2 TD.
GT: Watkins 3-45; Campbell 5-31.

DECEMBER 27, 2001 | SEATTLE
GEORGIA TECH 24, STANFORD 14

	1ST	2ND	3RD	4TH	FINAL
GT	7	10	0	7	24
STAN	0	3	3	8	14

SCORING SUMMARY
GT	Glover 5 run (Manget kick)
STAN	FG Biselli 35
GT	Campbell 34 pass from Godsey (Manget kick)
GT	FG Manget 20
STAN	FG Biselli 26
STAN	Johnson 4 pass from Lewis (Wells pass from Lewis)
GT	Campbell 2 run (Manget kick)

GT	TEAM STATISTICS	STAN
20	First Downs	20
137	Rushing Yards	125
23-38-0	Passing	17-34-0
266	Passing Yards	225
403	Total Yards	350
4-44.3	Punts - Average	4-35.0
0-0	Fumbles - Lost	0-0
3-35	Penalties - Yards	4-20
29:37	Possession Time	30:23

INDIVIDUAL LEADERS
RUSHING
GT: Gregory 19-91; Hall 7-32.
STAN: Allen 10-41; Carter 11-37.

PASSING
GT: Godsey 23-37-0, 266 yards, 1 TD.
STAN: Fasani 11-21-0, 115 yards.

RECEIVING
GT: Campbell 10-106, 1 TD; Smith 4-58.
STAN: Johnson 6-45, 1 TD; Powell 5-94.

DECEMBER 31, 2002 | SILICON VALLEY
FRESNO STATE 30, GEORGIA TECH 21

	1ST	2ND	3RD	4TH	FINAL
GT	7	0	14	0	21
FRES	3	10	7	10	30

SCORING SUMMARY
FRES	FG Asparuhov 22
GT	Watkins 35 pass from Suggs (Manget kick)
FRES	FG Asparuhov 42
FRES	Meza 48 interception return (Asparuhov kick)
GT	Bilbo 1 run (Manget kick)
FRES	Davis 3 run (Asparuhov kick)
GT	Smith 42 pass from Bilbo (Manget kick)
FRES	FG Asparuhov 33
FRES	Davis 28 run (Asparuhov kick)

GT	TEAM STATISTICS	FRES
16	First Downs	20
130	Rushing Yards	186
9-27-6	Passing	16-31-0
218	Passing Yards	188
348	Total Yards	374
4-59	Punt Returns - Yards	3-7
3-54	Kickoff Returns - Yards	2-72
5-38.6	Punts - Average	7-37.3
2-1	Fumbles - Lost	3-2
5-53	Penalties - Yards	10-94
21:54	Possession Time	38:06

INDIVIDUAL LEADERS
RUSHING
GT: Eziemefe 3-38; Smith 7-35.
FRES: Davis 37-153, 2 TD; Pinegar 9-20.

PASSING
GT: Bilbo 7-20-4, 178 yards, 1 TD.
FRES: Pinegar 16-31-0, 188 yards.

RECEIVING
GT: Bridges 3-94; Watkins 5-82, 1 TD.
FRES: Gilbert 4-84; Jamison 5-50.

JANUARY 3, 2004 | HUMANITARIAN
GEORGIA TECH 52, TULSA 10

	1ST	2ND	3RD	4TH	FINAL
GT	7	3	21	21	52
TUL	0	3	0	7	10

SCORING SUMMARY
GT	Daniels 9 run (Burnett kick)
TUL	FG DeVault 22
GT	FG Burnett 29
GT	Daniels 1 run (Burnett kick)
GT	Woods 2 run (Burnett kick)
GT	Daniels 33 run (Burnett kick)
GT	Daniels 38 run (Schroeder kick)
GT	Hatch 1 run (Schroeder kick)
TUL	Mills 18 pass from Smith (DeVault kick)
GT	Hatch 7 run (Schroeder kick)

GT	TEAM STATISTICS	TUL
15	First Downs	10
371	Rushing Yards	-56
7-13-0	Passing	17-27-0
19	Passing Yards	200
390	Total Yards	144
4-20	Punt Returns - Yards	2-13
2-57	Kickoff Returns - Yards	6-91
5-42.8	Punts - Average	7-45.0
1-1	Fumbles - Lost	7-6
5-45	Penalties - Yards	6-35
35:07	Possession Time	24:53

INDIVIDUAL LEADERS
RUSHING
GT: Daniels 31-307, 4 TD; Woods 10-40, 1 TD; Hatch 8-33, 2 TD.
TUL: Richardson 7-13.

PASSING
GT: Ball 4-10-0, 16 yards.
TUL: Kilian 11-21-0, 97 yards; Smith 6-6-0, 103 yards, 1 TD.

RECEIVING
GT: Smith 3-14.
TUL: Blankenship 3-76; Landrum 3-55; Mills 3-27, 1 TD.

DECEMBER 21, 2004 | CHAMPS SPORTS
GEORGIA TECH 51, SYRACUSE 14

	1ST	2ND	3RD	4TH	FINAL
GT	7	3	21	21	52
TUL	0	3	0	7	10

SCORING SUMMARY
GT	Reis 20 interception return (Bell kick)
SYR	Patterson 21 run (kick failed)
GT	Johnson 10 pass from Ball (Bell kick)
GT	Curry 80 pass from Ball (Bell kick)
GT	Daniels 2 run (Bell kick)
GT	Johnson 5 run (Bell kick)
GT	Ball 11 run (Bell kick)
GT	Daniels 1 run (Bell kick)
SYR	Gregory 25 pass from Patterson (Rhodes pass to Darlington)
GT	Safety

GT	TEAM STATISTICS	SYR
28	First Downs	20
286	Rushing Yards	51
13-20-1	Passing	22-39-2
228	Passing Yards	230
514	Total Yards	281
2-7	Punt Returns - Yards	2-8
3-75	Kickoff Returns - Yards	4-100
2-35.5	Punts - Average	7-34.4
3-2	Fumbles - Lost	1-1
5-38	Penalties - Yards	7-45
35:50	Possession Time	24:10

INDIVIDUAL LEADERS
RUSHING
GT: Daniels 17-119, 2 TD; Ball 9-38, 1 TD.
SYR: Gregory 1-16; Rhodes 9-14.
PASSING
GT: Ball 12-19-1, 207 yards 2 TD.
SYR: Patterson 21-34-1, 219 yards, 1 TD.
RECEIVING
GT: Curry 3-105, 1 TD; Johnson 2-61, 1 TD.
SYR: Gregory 5-66, 1 TD; Jones 6-61.

DECEMBER 29, 2005 | EMERALD
GEORGIA TECH 10, UTAH 38

	1ST	2ND	3RD	4TH	FINAL
GT	0	7	3	0	10
UT	13	7	3	15	38

SCORING SUMMARY
UT	Latendresse 14 pass from Ratliff (kick failed)
UT	Latendresse 24 pass from Ratliff (Beardall kick)
UT	Latendresse 25 pass from Ratliff (Beardall kick)
GT	Cooper 32 pass from Ball (Bell kick)
GT	FG Bell 29
UT	FG Beardall 23
UT	Latendresse 16 pass from Ratliff (Latendresse pass from Ratliff)
UT	Ganther 41 run (Beardall kick)

GT	TEAM STATISTICS	UT
20	First Downs	31
127	Rushing Yards	169
18-38-2	Passing	30-42-2
258	Passing Yards	381
385	Total Yards	550
2-(-2)	Punt Returns – Yards	1-5
6-115	Kickoff Returns - Yards	3-61
8-33.3	Punts – Average	5-40.6
0-0	Fumbles – Lost	1-0
4-39	Penalties – Yards	7-64

INDIVIDUAL LEADERS
RUSHING
GT: Daniels 20-109.
UT: Ganther 22-120, 1 TD.
PASSING
GT: Ball 18-38-2, 258 yards, 1 TD.
UT: Ratliff 30-41-1, 381 yards, 4 TD.
RECEIVING
GT: Bilbo 4-103; Cooper 3-45, 1 TD.
UTAH: Latendresse 16-214, 4 TD; Hernandez 8-75.

JANUARY 1, 2007 | GATOR
GEORGIA TECH 35, WEST VIRGINIA 38

	1ST	2ND	3RD	4TH	FINAL
GT	14	14	7	0	35
WVU	7	10	21	0	38

SCORING SUMMARY
WVU	Schmitt 1 run (McAfee kick)
GT	Johnson 31 pass from Bennett (Bell kick)
GT	Choice 3 run (Bell kick)
G	Johnson 48 pass from Bennett (Bell kick)
WVU	FG Mcafee 25
GT	Johnson 27 pass from Bennett (Bell kick)
WVU	Schmitt 11 run (McAfee kick)
GT	Choice 5 run (Bell kick)
WVU	Gonzales 57 pass from White (McAfee kick)
WVU	Myles 14 pass from White (McAfee kick)
WVU	White 15 run (McAfee kick)

GT	TEAM STATISTICS	WVU
20	First Downs	20
160	Rushing Yards	311
19-29-1	Passing	9-15-0
326	Passing Yards	131
486	Total Yards	442
3-25	Punt Returns - Yards	1-4
6-72	Kickoff Returns - Yards	4-120
4-46	Punts - Average	5-40.8
2-1	Fumbles - Lost	0-0
5-37	Penalties - Yards	3-30

INDIVIDUAL LEADERS
RUSHING
GT: Choice 27-169, 2 TD.
WVU: White 22-145, 1 TD.
PASSING
GT: Bennett 19-29-1, 326 yards, 3 TD.
WVU: White 9-15-0, 131 yards, 2 TD.
RECEIVING
GT: Johnson 9-186, 2 TD; Choice 4-28.
WVU: Myles 6-54, 1 TD; Slaton 2-20.

DECEMBER 31, 2007 | HUMANITARIAN
FRESNO STATE 40, GEORGIA TECH 28

	1ST	2ND	3RD	4TH	FINAL
GT	7	0	14	7	28
FRES	3	17	14	6	40

SCORING SUMMARY
GT	Thomas 35 pass from Bennett (Bell kick)
FRES	FG Stitser 21
FRES	Moore 6 run (Stitser kick)
FRES	Lubinsky 3 pass from Brandstater (Stitser kick)
FRES	FG Stitser 39
FRES	Smith 43 run (Stitser kick)
GT	Dwyer 36 run (Bell kick)
FRES	Brandstater 24 run (Stitser kick)
GT	Dwyer 2 run (Bell kick)
GT	Donley 20 pass from Booker (Bell kick)
FRES	Smith 32 run (pass failed)

GT	TEAM STATISTICS	FRES
23	First Downs	29
161	Rushing Yards	286
17-32-1	Passing	23-31-0
218	Passing Yards	285
379	Total Yards	571
1-10	Punt Returns - Yards	0-0
7-60	Kickoff Returns - Yards	5-125
4-37.8	Punts - Average	2-12.0
1-0	Fumbles - Lost	2-1
8-62	Penalties - Yards	10-80

INDIVIDUAL LEADERS
RUSHING
GT: Choice 12-69; Dwyer 12-62, 2 TD.
FRES: Smith 18-152, 2 TD.
PASSING
GT: Booker 7-15-1, 116 yards, 1 TD; Bennett 9-15-0, 91 yards, 1 TD.
FRES: Brandstater 23-30-0, 285 yards, 1 TD.
RECEIVING
GT: Thomas 4-69, 1 TD; J. Johnson 4-61.
FRES: Moore 7-80; Pascoe 6-72.

DECEMBER 31, 2008 | CHICK-FIL-A
LOUISIANA STATE 38, GEORGIA TECH 3

	1ST	2ND	3RD	4TH	FINAL
LSU	7	28	3	0	38
GT	3	0	0	0	3

SCORING SUMMARY
LSU	Scott 2 run (David kick)
GT	FG Blair 24
LSU	Scott 4 run (David kick)
LSU	Scott 1 run (David kick)
LSU	Dickson 25 pass from Jefferson (David kick)
LSU	Williams 17 run (David kick)
LSU	FG David 53

LSU	TEAM STATISTICS	GT
19	First Downs	15
161	Rushing Yards	164
17-27-0	Passing	8-25-1
163	Passing Yards	150
324	Total Yards	314
2-36	Punt Returns - Yards	2-11
1-23	Kickoff Returns - Yards	4-87
4-41.5	Punts - Average	3-33.3
1-0	Fumbles - Lost	3-2
6-60	Penalties - Yards	4-40

INDIVIDUAL LEADERS
RUSHING
LSU: Scott 15-65, 3 TD.
GT: Dwyer 10-67.
PASSING
LSU: Jefferson 16-25-0, 142 yards, 1 TD.
GT: Nesbitt 8-24-1, 150 yards.
RECEIVING
LSU: Dickson 4-50, 1 TD; Byrd 3-10.
GT: Dwyer 3-66; Thomas 3-32.

THE SCHOOLS

TULANE

By Kevin Gleason

JUST SIX MONTHS AFTER AN 8–5 season and a win in the 2002 Hawaii Bowl, the Tulane football team was jolted by news that budget-pinching school administrators were considering moving the program to Division II status or shutting it down completely. Weeks of discussion and a "Save the Wave" drive ensued, and Tulane board chairman John Koernor finally announced the school would keep its D1-A status.

Though the program's fortunes underscored the plight of many mid-major conference schools locked out of BCS riches, over the years Tulane certainly hasn't performed as if it deserved that fate. The Green Wave went 12–0 and finished ranked No. 7 in 1998, and has sent three quarterbacks—Shaun King, Patrick Ramsey and J.P. Losman—to the NFL since that season.

The school's proud football heritage dates all the way back to 1893 and includes an epic early era when football mastermind Clark Shaughnessy was head coach, along with a 33-year stint (from 1933 to 1965) as

a member of the Southeastern Conference. Competing in the modern SEC proved a tough task for the private school, and Tulane left after nine straight losing seasons, including an 0–10 mark in 1962. The Green Wave played as an independent from 1966 to 1995, before joining Conference USA as a charter member in 1996.

TRADITION In addition to the fight song played before and after every Tulane athletic event, Tulane has one of the most distinctive cheers in college athletics, "The Hullabaloo." With its origins going back to the 1800s, it can be heard after every Tulane score:

A one, a two
A helluva hullabaloo
A hu-la-ba-loo ray ray!
A hu-la-ba-loo ray ray!
Hoo-ray! Hoo-ray!
Vars-uh, vars-uh, tee-ay!
Tee-ay! Tee-ay!
Vars-uh, vars-uh, tee-ay!
Tulane!!

BEST PLAYER Some would point to two-time All-American end Gerald "Jerry" Dalrymple, the cornerstone of the 1931 squad that went to the Rose Bowl. But it's hard to argue with the prolific running

---

PROFILE

Tulane University
New Orleans, La.
Founded: 1834
Enrollment: 11,157
Colors: Olive Green and Sky Blue
Nickname: Green Wave
Stadium: Louisiana Superdome
 Opened in 1975
 Momentum Turf; 69,703 capacity
First football game: 1893
All-time record: 485–563–38 (.463)
Bowl record: 4–6
Southeastern Conference Championships:
3 (2 outright)
Conference USA championships: 1 (outright)
First-round draft choices: 5
Website: www.tulanegreenwave.com

THE BEST OF TIMES

From 1929 to 1931, Tulane went 28–2 over three seasons under coach Bernie Bierman.

THE WORST OF TIMES

In 1962, Tulane went 0–10, scoring just 76 points.

CONFERENCE

Tulane was a charter member of Conference USA in 1996. From 1966 to 1995, the Green Wave were an independent. They competed in the SEC from 1933 to 1965 and in the Southern Conference from 1922 to 1932.

DISTINGUISHED ALUMNI

Newt Gingrich, U.S. representative and Speaker of the House; Huey Long, U.S. senator; Bruce Paltrow, television and movie producer; Jerry Springer, talkshow host; D.B. Sweeney, actor; David Filo, co-founder of Yahoo!

The "Hullabaloo" cheer—heard after every Tulane score—is one of the most unique in college football.

back Mewelde Moore, who gained 6,505 yards from 2000 to '03 to become Tulane's career all-purpose yardage leader. The total was almost 2,000 yards more than the previous record holder, Michael Pierce (4,627 from 1987 to '89), and 1,300 yards more than the current No. 2, Matt Forté (5,261 from 2004 to '07). The Baton Rouge native wasn't heavily recruited out of high school (Nick Saban later admitted that LSU went after him too late) and was never a burner, but from early in his freshman year, he showed himself to be a scrappy runner and an agile receiver. The two-sport star (he played in the San Diego Padres organization from 2001 to '03) eventually gave up baseball and was chosen by the Minnesota Vikings in the 2004 NFL draft.

BEST COACH Clark Shaughnessy was just 23 years old when he took his first head-coaching job, at Tulane in 1915. Over the next 12 seasons (with a year off in 1921), he developed a regional powerhouse, compiling a 59–28–7 record. Although he would become the father of the T-formation, Shaughnessy was still running a single-wing offense in the 1910s and 1920s at Tulane. It was his missionary zeal that helped transform both the

program and the school's image. After compiling a 17–1–1 record over the 1924 and 1925 seasons, Tulane earned an invitation to the Rose Bowl (school president Dr. A. B. Dinwiddie didn't approve the trip). Because of the 1925 football team's success, it took Shaughnessy just five days to raise $300,000 to help pay for Tulane Stadium, which served as the home of Tulane football for the next half-century and was the site of the first Sugar Bowl as well as three Super Bowls. After the 1926 season, Shaughnessy left for crosstown rival Loyola University—where he convinced that institution's leaders to change the school's name to the more grandiose Loyola of the South. He was succeeded at Tulane by two more University of Minnesota alums, Bernie Bierman (who coached the Green Wave to the Rose Bowl in the 1931 season) and Ted Cox (who in 1934 coached them to the Sugar Bowl).

BEST TEAM The 1998 squad was the first Tulane team to win 12 games in a season and the third unbeaten, untied squad in school history (5–0 in 1900 and 9–0 in 1929). Only one opponent, Louisville, came within a touchdown of Tulane. Still, the question will always

FIGHT SONG

TULANE FIGHT SONG
Green wave green wave
Hats off to thee.
We're out to
Fight fight fight
For our victory.
Shout to the skies
Our Green Wave war cries.
The bravest we'll defy.
Hold that line for
Olive and blue.
We will cheer for you.
So fight, fight, fight, old Tulane
Fight on to victory.

FIRST-ROUND DRAFT CHOICES

1945	Joe Renfroe, Tigers (3)
1946	Dub Jones, Cardinals (2)
1961	Tommy Mason, Vikings (1) and Patriots (2)*
2002	Patrick Ramsey, Redskins (32)
2004	J.P. Losman, Bills (22)

From 1960-1966, the NFL and AFL held separate, competing drafts

CONSENSUS ALL-AMERICANS

1931	Jerry Dalrymple, E
1932	Don Zimmerman, B
1939	Harley McCollum, T
1941	Ernie Blandin, T

remain: Just how good was that team? Thanks to the Bowl Alliance, now called the BCS, the Green Wave didn't play in a major bowl game against one of the big boys of college football. Tulane was loaded with talent. King threw 38 touchdowns on the season, including three in a 49-35 win over Army. He became the first Tulane player to run for 100 yards and throw for 300 in the same game.

The only blemish on the season came when Tommy Bowden accepted the coaching job at Clemson and departed before the Liberty Bowl. Bowden was succeeded by Chris Scelfo, who was on the sideline when Tulane completed its perfect season with a win over Brigham Young.

COLLEGE FOOTBALL HALL OF FAME INDUCTEES		
NAME	YEARS	INDUCTED
Jerry Dalrymple, E	1929-31	1954
Bernie Bierman, COACH	1927-31	1955
Monk Simons, HB	1932-34	1963
Clark Shaughnessy, COACH	1915-20, '22-26	1968
Lester Lautenschlaeger, QB	1922-25	1975
Bill Banker, HB	1927-29	1977
Eddie Price, FB	1946-49	1982
John Green, G	1942-45	1989

BEST DEFENSE The 1931 defense—anchored by Tulane Hall of Famers Wop Glover, Nollie Felts and Dalrymple, the unanimous All-American—shut out eight of its regular-season opponents and allowed a total of 35 points. Only one team scored as many as 14 against the Green Wave until the Rose Bowl, when Southern California spoiled what would have been a perfect season, winning 21-12.

BEST BACKFIELD With Patrick Ramsey at quarterback and Mewelde Moore the featured running back, the 2001 Tulane backfield was potent enough that one wonders how the team managed only a 3–9 record. (A quick look at their defense answers the question.) Moore ran for 1,421 yards, making him the first Tulane 1,000-yard rusher in more than 50 years. In a game against Cincinnati, he gained a school record 249 yards. Ramsey, meanwhile, set school career records for touchdown passes, completions, attempts and passing yards. The only thing that backfield came up short on was …wins.

BIGGEST GAME The Green Wave and its green head coach faced a stern challenge in the 1998 Liberty Bowl. BYU, which went 9–4 that season, was the nation's fifth-ranked defensive team and another member of the "don't get no respect" fraternity of schools that were playing to make a statement. But King ran for a game-high 109 yards and passed for 276 yards and two scores to lead Tulane's team of destiny to a 41-27 rout of the Cougars, the Green Wave's first bowl victory in 28 years.

"We had something to prove today," King said after the game. "Hopefully, we answered some of our doubters. We've always been confident in our ability and our character. We've got a great group of guys who work hard and know what it takes to be successful."

BIGGEST UPSET Go back to the season-ender in an otherwise uninspired 1982 season. Tulane came in with a 3–7 record. LSU came in ranked No. 12 in the nation and bound for the Orange Bowl. None of it kept Tulane from recording a 31-28 upset on Nov. 27—in Baton Rouge, to boot. Tulane won it when Mike McKay tossed a 31-yard touchdown pass to Reggie Reginelli on fourth down with 5:15 left.

DISPUTE Tulane lost to Miami on Oct. 14, 1972, after the Hurricanes were mistakenly awarded a *fifth*-down play on the Tulane 32-yard line with 1:03 left. Miami promptly scored the winning touchdown to beat the Green Wave 24-21.

ADVERSITY The 2005 Tulane team returned 44 letter winners and 17 starters and felt good about the upcoming season. Then, before the team played its first game, Hurricane Katrina hit New Orleans. Tulane cancelled the fall semester. The Superdome, where the Green Wave played their home games, was badly damaged. Amid the greater suffering caused by the storm, these were not tragedies but inconveniences, and the Tulane team treated them that way. The Green Wave did not cancel a single game, playing 11 games in 11 different stadiums, including "home" games in Baton Rouge, Lafayette, and Ruston, La., as well as one in Mobile, Ala. The team played hard and finished with perhaps the most admirable 2–9 record in the history of the game.

HEARTBREAKER Tulane took an 18-game win streak into the 1932 Rose Bowl, with a team that had shut out eight of its 11 opponents in the 1931 regular season. Southern California jumped out to a 21-0 lead before Tulane's two second-half scores narrowed the gap to 21-12. But there would be no more scoring. The loss was particularly frustrating, since Tulane's offense outgained USC's, 341 yards to 218. Not only was Tulane's perfect season ruined, but the game probably cost Tulane the mythical national title, as the Dickinson System declared the Trojans the champions.

STADIUM For years, Tulane played its home games on campus at Tulane Stadium, home of Super Bowls IV, VI and IX. The stadium was demolished in 1980 and is now the site of an athletics and recreation center. Tulane had already vacated it, moving into the Louisiana Superdome in 1975, the year it opened. The Superdome is also renowned, having hosted six Super Bowls, four men's Final Fours and 33 Sugar Bowls. What's been lost in the

transition, of course, is the sense of intimacy and homefield advantage offered by Tulane Stadium.

RIVAL Tulane's biggest rival has always been LSU. The series began in 1893. From 1893 to 1938, passion between the schools increased, going from harmless pranks to a riot in Tiger Stadium when raging fans from both teams took to the field kicking and swinging after the Wave won on Nov. 26, 1938. LSU leads the series 67–23–7. The Tigers have won 17 straight meetings against the Green Wave, dating back to that memorable Tulane upset of 1982.

NICKNAME From 1893 to 1919, Tulane teams were known as the Olive and Blue, the school's official colors. One of the student newspapers, *The Tulane Weekly*, began calling the football team the Greenbacks in 1919. Tulane has been called the Green Wave for nearly nine decades now, thanks to a journalist named Earl Sparling. Sparling was editor of the *Tulane Hullabaloo* when he wrote a football song and had it printed in the paper. That was 1920. The title was "The Rolling Green Wave." The paper began using the nickname to describe Tulane athletic teams.

MASCOT Mascots come in all shapes and sizes, but a pelican riding shotgun on a surfboard is clearly of the unique variety. Such was Tulane's mascot for more than 50 years. The pelican was turned into a mischievous little boy in 1945—the product of John Chase, a local cartoonist who drew the covers of Tulane game programs. The boy was called Greenie.

In the 1960s, athletic director Dr. Rix Yard wanted a more masculine symbol for the teams. Yard called upon Art Evans, who had created the Purdue Boilermaker and Southern California's Trojan. Evans designed an ominous Green Wave that was adopted in 1964 and became an athletic department staple for more than 20 years. In 1998, Tulane introduced a new set of icons featuring the return of the pelican, dubbed Riptide after a student vote.

UNIFORMS Tulane's uniforms bear a resemblance to Michigan State's. The jerseys and pants are green with solid white numbers. The helmets have changed dramatically over the years. White helmets were worn until 1997. Today's design has a dark green background with a white T outlined in blue and a green-blue wave wrapped around the T. Current coach Bob Toledo added the school name to the jerseys when he took over in 2007.

LORE Tulane played its first football game on Nov. 18, 1893, losing to the Southern Athletic Club, 12-0. Curiously, Tulane coach T.L. Bayne played for the opponents.

QUOTE "Spring practice is necessary for perfection." —**Jerry Dalrymple**, Tulane's two-time All-American end and leader of the team that played in the 1932 Rose Bowl

With additional reporting by Geoffrey Norman

Fight or Flight

BY RICH COHEN

I lived with a football player my freshman year at Tulane. He was there when I arrived in my dorm, asleep on the narrow twin bed across from my narrow twin bed, having arrived in the middle of August for the two-a-day practices by which freshman recruits were bled of their dignity and any extra fat. He was huge, the bed sagged beneath him, and the sheets, tangled around his body, were yellowed with dry sweat.

My roommate, Andrew McQuaid (who asked to be called Lone Wolf though he was always surrounded by a chattering pack), was a Bon Jovi fan, air drummed wearing headphones but no shirt, and drove a red van with a surfer painted on its starboard side. In those first weeks, because I had no friends of my own, I was friends with his friends— linemen from Louisiana, Florida, Texas. I moved among them like an amulet, an ornament, a charm. Whereas I consider myself a regular size American male, these guys were supersized. Like Mike Millich, who put a shot of Jack Daniels in my drink, destroying my daiquiri, and said, "You've been snake bit." And Perry Perkoski, who, when I complained about the snake bite, said, "Then don't order a girl drink, son." Through them I was able to glimpse the life of the Tulane football player—which, like the life of football players in every college, existed in a parallel universe.

These players, who you might see crossing campus in fleshy herds, lived in their own dorms—except for Andrew, since he was a walk-on— attended their own parties, were obsessed by their own thoughts. This was not like high school, where a football player was you with a bigger body or you with a weird intensity or you with a different kind of father. This was something else, even at

Tulane—which, despite having been a member of the SEC for 30-odd years, was known as a school for, well, if not smart kids, then for kids who were going to be spending their time with smart kids later on. The football program was Spartan both in its single-mindedness and cultlike secrecy.

I was obsessed by the legends of the football players' dining room.

> *This was not like high school, where a football player was you with a bigger body or you with a weird intensity or you with a different kind of father. This was something else.*

I used to sit with Lone Wolf in bars uptown, drinking Monsoons and asking, "Tell me again Andrew, what's it like in the football players' dining hall?"

"Well, friend," he would say, "there are steaks as big as manhole covers and they toss them out like Mardi Gras doubloons, spiked with tongs into the open mouths of linebackers, and the blood runs into the corners of the room, where it's lapped up by nose tackles and other madmen."

Once the season began, we drifted apart—Andrew into his world of squats and road games and me into the mezzanine world of the Superdome, where Tulane plays home games. The scene around Tulane football when I was at school (I wonder if it's still this way after the hurricane, when the Dome became a place in which we tore open our chests and showed each other our

diseased hearts) was mannered and strange. A few hours before a game, you would pick up your date in a dorm under the leafy trees across campus. You would walk along St. Charles Avenue, the sun shining through the trees and making a pattern on the ground. You would say, "A crazy man in the Quarter told me the future can be read in these shadows." You would look at your girl in her surprisingly short dress and think, "Lucky me" or "I wonder if we will marry"—though now you cannot remember her name. You would walk along fraternity row, where the lawns were crowded with boys and their dates and kegs and tubs of crawfish, everyone getting a quick buzz on before the ride to the game, in which Tulane played Rice or Vanderbilt or whomever—it didn't really matter unless it was LSU. And then it mattered a lot.

The Superdome holds 73,000 people. Back then Tulane games would draw perhaps 20,000. You put 20,000 people in a space made for nearly four times that number and the result is a special kind of melancholy. The students were there but not watching, or were watching but not caring, or were caring but not about this moment and not about this game.

Now and then, however, something would happen on the field. A great player who previously had been invisible to us—QB Shaun King, say— would blaze forth like a Roman candle, wildly alive, running from the huge men trying to kill him, looking down field for a receiver, for anyone, then deciding (or seeming to), "To hell with it, it's just me," tucking the ball beneath his arm and taking off. We were all on our feet by then, our jackets thrown across our seat backs, our ties untied, screaming for this one man in flight for his life.

Rich Cohen is the author of six books, including Sweet and Low *and* Israel Is Real. *He lives in an incredibly beautiful house, with an incredibly beautiful woman, in a part of Connecticut the real estate people describe as "rolling country."*

TULANE ALL-TIME SCORES

WIN/LOSS PERCENTAGE SINCE 1936

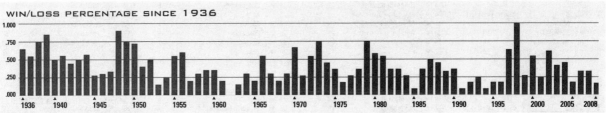

T.L. BAYNE
1893, '95 (.500)   4-4

1893   1-2-0
N18		Southern AC	0	12
N25	●	LSU	34	0
D2		Mississippi	4	12

FRED SWEET
1894 (.000)   0-4

1894   0-4-0
O27		at Texas	0	12
N3		Alabama	6	18
N17		Sewanee	6	12
N29		Mississippi	2	8

T.L. BAYNE

1895   3-2-0
O26		at LSU	4	8
N9	●	Southern AC	12	0
N16	●	Alabama	22	0
N23		at Texas	0	16
N28	●	Mississippi	28	4

HARRY BAUM
1896 (.600)   3-2

1896   3-2-0
O17	●	Alumni	12	0
O24		LSU	0	1*f*
N9		at Vicksburg AC	48	0
N14		Texas	4	12
N26	●	Mississippi	10	0

1897
NO TEAM

JOHN LOMBARD
1898 (.500)   1-1

1898   1-1-0
| D12 | ● | Mississippi | 14 | 9 |
| D14 | | at LSU | 0 | 37 |

H.H. COLLIER
1899 (.071)   0-6-1

1899   0-6-1
N11		Sewanee	0	23
N18	=	Southern AC	0	0
N20		Texas	0	11
N25		at Texas	0	32
N27		Texas A&M *Hou*	0	22
N30		Mississippi	0	15
D8		at LSU	0	38

H.T. SUMMERSGILL
1900-01 (.818)   9-2

1900   5-0-0
O27	●	Southern AC	23	0
N3	●	at Alabama	6	0
N10	●	Milsaps	35	0
N17	●	LSU	29	0
N29	●	Mississippi	12	0

1901   4-2-0
O16	●	at Meridian	15	0
O26		at Mobile YMCA	0	2
N2	●	YMCA	23	0
N9	●	Mississippi State	24	6
N16		LSU	0	11#
N28	●	Mississippi	25	11

VIRGINIUS DABNEY
1902 (.286)   1-4-2

1902   1-4-2
O18	●	Alumni	26	0
O25	=	Auburn	0	0
N1	●	Mississippi State	11	11
N8		at Texas A&M	5	17
N15		Vanderbilt	5	23
N24		Texas	0	6
N27		Mississippi	0	10

CHARLES ESHELMAN
1903 (.500)   2-2-1

1903   2-2-1
O31	●	Meridian AA	46	0
N7		Shreveport AA	0	23
N18	●	Cumberland	0	28
N26	●	Richmond	8	5
D5	=	Mississippi State	0	0

T. BARRY/J. JANVIER
1904 (.714)   5-2

1904   5-2-0
23	●	Louisiana Tech	11	0
O29	●	Mississippi State	10	0
N5	●	at Marion	10	0
N12		Sewanee	0	18
N19	●	LSU	5	0
N24	●	Mississippi	22	0
D3		Alabama	0	6

J. TOBIN/H. LUDLOW
1905 (.000)   0-1

1905   0-1-0
| N25 | | LSU | 5 | 0 |

JOHN RUSS
1906 (.100)   0-4-1

1906   0-4-1
O27	=	Samford	0	0
N3		Mississippi	0	17
N10		Sewanee	0	35
N17		Texas A&M	0	18
N24		Arkansas	0	22

JOE CURTIS
1907-08 (.769)   10-3

1907   3-2-0
O26	●	Samford	13	0
N2	●	Drury	12	0
N5	●	Centre	28	9
N9		Arkansas Coll.	12	17
N16		Texas A&M	6	18

1908   7-1-0
O10	●	N.O. Gym Club	11	0
O24	●	Centre	10	0
O31	●	Mississippi	10	0
N7	●	Baylor	10	2
N14	●	Mississippi State	23	0
N18	●	at Texas	28	15
N21		at Baylor	0	6
N26	●	Washington, Mo.	11	0

BUSTER BROWN
1909 (.556)   4-3-2

1909   4-3-2
O9	●	N.O. Gym Club	12	0
O16	●	Mississippi	5	0
O23		Centre	0	6
O30	●	Mississippi State	2	0
N6	●	Cincinnati	6	0
N13	=	Texas	10	10
N20	=	Alabama	5	5
N25		Southwestern, Tex.	0	18
J1		at Havana AC	0	11

A.A. MASON
1910-12 (.438)   10-13-1

1910   0-7-0
O13		Mississippi	0	16
O26		at Centre	0	35
O29		at Kentucky	3	10
N5		Mississippi State	0	10
N12		Auburn *Gul*	0	33
N19		Alabama	3	5
N24		Texas A&M *Hou*	0	17

1911   5-3-1
O12	●	Mississippi Coll.	10	0
O18	●	La. Lafayette	27	0
O21	●	Louisiana Tech	45	0
O28	●	Samford	10	0
N4		Sewanee	3	9
N18		at Alabama	0	22
N20	=	at Mississippi State	5	4
N30	=	Wash. & Lee	5	5
D9		at LSU	0	6

1912   5-3-0
O8	●	Jefferson	37	0
O12	●	La. Lafayette	95	0*
O19	●	Mississippi Coll.	19	6
O26	●	Samford	35	0
N2		Alabama	0	7
N9	●	Mississippi State	27	24
N19		at Texas A&M	0	41
N28		LSU	3	21

A.C. HOFFMAN
1913 (.375)   3-5

1913   3-5-0
O11	●	Jefferson	13	0
O18		Mississippi Coll.	3	32
O25		Alabama	0	26
N1	=	at St. Louis	12	6
N8		at Mississippi State	0	32
N15	●	Southwestern	31	9
N22		at LSU	0	40
N27		Arkansas	0	14

E.R. SWEETLAND
1914 (.500)   3-3-1

1914   3-3-1
O17	●	La. Lafayette	33	0
O24	●	Centenary	82	0
O27	●	Jefferson	24	7
O31		at Alabama	0	58
N7		Mississippi	6	20
N14		Mississippi State *JaM*	0	61
N26	=	LSU	0	0

CLARK SHAUGHNESSY
1915-20, '22-26 (.665) 59-28-7

1915   4-4-0
S25	●	at St. Paul	24	0
O9	●	La. Lafayette	13	0
O16	●	Spring Hill	36	13
O23		at Alabama	0	16
O30		Mississippi Coll.	6	20
N13	●	Samford	32	3
N18		at Florida	7	14
N25		at LSU	0	12

1916   4-3-1
O14	●	Spring Hill	14	0
O21	●	Jefferson	39	3
O27	●	Mississippi Coll. *JaM*	13	3
N4		at Georgia Tech	0	45
N11	●	at Rice	13	23
N18	●	Alabama	33	0
N30	=	LSU	14	14
D9		Georgetown	0	61

1917   5-3-0
O6	●	Jefferson	32	0
O13	●	Spring Hill	28	0
O20	●	at Florida	52	0
O27	●	Wash. Aty.	19	0
N2		at Texas A&M	0	35
N10		Georgia Tech	0	48
N17		Rice	0	16
N29	●	at LSU	28	6

1918   4-1-1
N2	●	Camp Shelby	7	0
N9	●	Camp Beauregard	13	6
N13	●	Spring Hill	32	0
N16		Camp Pike	7	10
N23	=	Pensacola NAS	0	0
N28	●	La. Lafayette	74	0

1919   6-2-1
O4	●	Jefferson	27	0
O11	●	La. Lafayette	73	0
O18	●	at Spring Hill	21	0
O25	●	Mississippi	27	12
N1	●	Mississippi Coll.	49	0
N8	●	Florida	14	2
N15	=	Georgia *Aug*	7	7
N22		LSU	6	27
N27		Wash. & Lee	0	7

1920   6-2-1
O2	●	La. Lafayette	79	0*
O9	●	Mississippi Coll.	29	0
O16	●	Rice	0	0
O23	●	at Mississippi	32	0
O30		at Michigan	0	21
N6	●	Florida *TaM*	14	0
N13	●	Mississippi State	6	0
N25	●	at LSU	21	0
D4		Detroit	0	7

MYRON FULLER
1921 (.400)   4-6

1921   4-6-0
O1		Mississippi Coll.	0	14
O8	●	Mississippi	26	0
O15		at Rice	7	6
O22	●	Mississippi State	7	0
O29		at Detroit	10	14
N5		Auburn	0	14
N12		at Washington, Mo.	6	14
N19	●	LSU	21	0
N24		Centre	0	21
D3		Alabama	7	14

258 TULANE

THE SCHOOLS

1922-1932 SOUTHERN

CLARK SHAUGHNESSY

1922 4-4-0 (1-4-0)

O7	●		Mississippi Coll.	30	0
O14	●		Spring Hill	30	10
O21	●		Fort Benning	18	0
O28	●	|	Mississippi State	26	0
N4		|	North Carolina	12	19
N11		|	Auburn MONT	0	19
N18		|	Florida	6	27
N30		|	at LSU	14	25

1923 6-3-1 (2-2-1)

S29	●		La. Lafayette	20	2
O6	●		Mississippi Coll.	18	3
O13			Texas BEAU	0	33
O20	●		Louisiana Tech	13	7
O27		|	at Vanderbilt	0	17
N3		|	at Tennessee	2	13
N10	=	|	Auburn MONT	6	6
N17	●	|	Mississippi	19	0
N24	●	|	LSU	20	0
N29	●		Washington, Mo.	19	8

1924 8-1-0 (4-1-0)

S27	●		La. Lafayette	14	0
O4	●		Mississippi Coll.	32	7
O11	●		Louisiana Tech	42	12
O18	●	|	Vanderbilt	21	13
O25	●		Spring Hill	33	0
N1		|	Mississippi State	6	14
N8	●	|	Auburn MONT	14	6
N15	●	|	Tennessee	26	7
N27	●	|	at LSU	13	0

1925 9-0-1 (5-0-0)

S26	●		Louisiana Coll.	77	0
O3	=		Missouri	6	6
O10	●	|	Mississippi	26	7
O17	●	|	Mississippi State	25	3
O24	●		Northwestern CHI	18	7
O31	●	|	Auburn MONT	13	0
N7	●		Louisiana Tech	37	9*
N14	●	|	Sewanee	14	0
N21	●	|	at LSU	16	0
N26	●		at Centenary	14	0

1926 3-5-1 (2-4-0)

S25	●		Louisiana Tech	40	0
O2	=		at Missouri	0	0
O9		|	at Georgia Tech	6	9
O16			at NYU	0	21
O23		|	Auburn	0	2
O30	●	|	Mississippi	6	0
N6		|	Mississippi State	0	14
N13	●	|	Sewanee	19	7
N25		|	LSU	0	7

BERNIE BIERMAN
1927-31 (.771) 36-10-2

1927 2-5-1 (2-5-1)

O1	●	|	Mississippi	19	7
O8		|	at Georgia Tech	6	13
O15		|	Mississippi State	6	13
O22		|	at Vanderbilt	0	32
O29		|	Georgia	0	31
N5	=	|	Auburn	6	6
N12		|	Sewanee	6	12
N24	●	|	at LSU	13	6

1928 6-3-1 (3-3-1)

S29	●		at Northwestern St.	65	0
O6	●	|	Mississippi State JAM	51	6
O13		|	Georgia Tech	0	12
O20		|	Vanderbilt	6	13
O27		|	at Georgia	14	20
N3	●		Milsaps	27	0
N10	●	|	Auburn	13	12
N17	●	|	Sewanee	41	6
N24	●		Louisiana Coll.	47	7
N29	=	|	LSU	0	0

1929 9-0-0 (6-0-0)

S28	●		Northwestern St.	40	6
O5	●		Texas A&M	13	10
O12	●	|	Mississippi State	34	0
O19	●		La. Lafayette	60	0
O26	●	|	Georgia Tech	20	14
N2	●	|	Georgia COLGA	21	15
N9	●	|	Auburn	52	0
N16	●	|	Sewanee	18	0
N28	●	|	at LSU	21	0

1930 8-1-0 (5-0-0)

S27	●		La. Lafayette	84	0
O4			at Northwestern	0	14
O11	●		Texas A&M DAL	19	9
O18	●		B'ham Southern	21	0
O25	●	|	at Georgia Tech	28	0
N1	●	|	Mississippi State	53	0
N8	●	|	Auburn	21	0
N15	●	|	Georgia	25	0
N27	●	|	LSU	12	7

1931 11-1-0 (8-0-0)

S26	●	|	Mississippi	31	0
O3	●		Texas A&M	7	0
O10	●		Spring Hill	40	0
O17	●	|	at Vanderbilt	19	0
O24	●	|	Georgia Tech	33	0
O31	●	|	Mississippi State	59	7
N7	●	|	Auburn MONT	27	0
N14	●	|	at Georgia	20	0
N21	●	|	Sewanee	40	0
N28	●	|	LSU	34	7
D5	●		Washington State	28	14
			ROSE BOWL		
J1			Southern California	12	21

TED COX
1932-35 (.725) 28-10-2

1932 6-2-1 (5-2-1)

O1	●		Texas A&M	26	14
O8	●	|	Georgia	34	25
O15	=	|	Vanderbilt	6	6
O22		|	Auburn	7	19
O29	●	|	South Carolina	6	0
N5	●	|	at Georgia Tech	20	14
N12	●	|	at Kentucky	6	3
N19	●	|	Sewanee	26	0
N26		|	at LSU	0	14

1933-1965 SEC

1933 6-3-1 (4-2-1)

S30			Texas A&M	6	13
O7		|	at Georgia	13	26
O14	●		Maryland	20	0
O21	●	|	at Georgia Tech	7	0
O28		|	Auburn	7	13
N4	●		Colgate BNX	7	0
N11	●	|	Mississippi	33	0
N18	●	|	Kentucky	34	0
N25	●	|	Sewanee	26	9
D2	=	|	LSU	7	7

1934 10-1-0 (8-0-0)

S29	●	|	U.T. Chattanooga	41	0
O6	●	|	Auburn	13	0
O13	●	|	at Florida	28	12
O20	●	|	Georgia	7	6
O27	●	|	Georgia Tech	20	12
N3	●	|	Mississippi	15	0
N10			Colgate	6	20
N17	●	|	at Kentucky	20	7
N24	●	|	Sewanee	32	0
D1	●	|	at LSU	13	12
			SUGAR BOWL		
J1	●		Temple	20	14

1935 6-4-0 (3-3-0)

S28	●		VMI	44	0
O5		|	Auburn	0	10
O12	●	|	Florida	19	7
O19			at Minnesota	0	20
O26	●	|	Sewanee	33	0
N2	●		Colgate	14	6
N9		|	Georgia	13	26
N16	●	|	Kentucky	20	13
N23	●		Northwestern St.	13	0
N30		|	LSU	0	41

LOWELL "RED" DAWSON
1936-41 (.644) 36-19-4

1936 6-3-1 (2-3-1)

S26	●	|	Mississippi	7	6
O3	=	|	Auburn	0	0
O10	●		Centenary	19	0
O17	●		Colgate NYC	28	6
O24	●		North Carolina	21	7
O31	●		Louisiana Tech	22	13
N7		|	Alabama BIRM	7	34
N14		|	Georgia	6	12
N21	●	|	Sewanee	53	6
N28		|	at LSU	0	33

1937 5-4-1 (2-3-1)

S25	●		Clemson	7	0
O2	=	|	Auburn	0	0
O9	●		Mississippi Coll.	84	0
O16	●		Colgate BUF	7	6
O23			at North Carolina	0	13
O30	●	|	Mississippi	14	7
N6		|	Alabama	6	9
N13		|	at Georgia	6	7
N20	●	|	Sewanee	13	7
N27		|	LSU	7	20

1938 7-2-1 (4-1-1)

S24			Clemson	10	13
O1	=	|	Auburn	0	0
O8	●		at North Carolina	17	14
O15	●		Rice	26	17
O22	●		Mercer	51	0
O29	●	|	Mississippi State	27	0
N5		|	Alabama BIRM	0	3
N12	●	|	Georgia	28	6
N19	●	|	Sewanee	38	0
N26	●	|	at LSU	14	0

1939 8-1-1 (5-0-0)

S30	●		Clemson	7	6
O7	●	|	Auburn	12	0
O14	●		Fordham	7	0
O21	=		North Carolina	14	14
O28	●	|	Mississippi	18	6
N11	●	|	Alabama	13	0
N18	●		at Columbia	25	0
N25	●	|	Sewanee	52	0
D2	●	|	LSU	33	20
			SUGAR BOWL		
J1			Texas A&M	13	14

1940 5-5-0 (1-3-0)

S28			Boston College	7	27
O5		|	Auburn	14	20
O12			Fordham NYC	7	20
O19	●		Rice	15	6
O26	●		at North Carolina	14	13
N2	●		Clemson	13	0
N9		|	Alabama BIRM	6	13
N16	●	|	Georgia	21	13
N23	●		Northwestern St.	47	0
N30		|	at LSU	0	14

1941 5-4-0 (2-3-0)

S27	●		Boston College	21	7
O4	●	|	Auburn	32	0
O11			at Rice	9	10
O18	●		North Carolina	52	6
O25		|	Mississippi	13	20
N1	●	|	at Vanderbilt	34	14
N8		|	Alabama	14	19
N15	●		NYU BNX	45	0
N29		|	LSU	0	19

CLAUDE SIMONS, JR.
1942-45 (.435) 13-17-1

1942 4-5-0 (1-4-0)

S26	●		at Southern California	27	13
O3		|	Auburn	13	27
O10	●		Rice	18	7
O17		|	at Georgia	0	40
O24	●		North Carolina	29	14
O31	●	|	Vanderbilt	28	21
N7		|	Mississippi State	0	7
N14			Georgia Pre-Flight	0	7
N26		|	at LSU	6	18

1943 3-3-0 (1-1-0)

O2			Memphis Navy	7	41
O9	●		at Rice	33	0
O23	●		SMU	12	6
O30			Georgia Pre-Flight	13	14
N13		|	Georgia Tech	0	33
N20	●	|	LSU	27	0

1944 4-3-0 (1-2-0)

O7			at Notre Dame	0	26
O14	●		Rice	21	0
O21	●	|	Auburn	16	13
O28	●		SMU	27	7
N11		|	at Georgia Tech	7	34
N18	●		Clemson	36	20
N25		|	at LSU	6	25

1945 2-6-1 (1-3-1)

O6	=	|	Florida	6	6
O13			at Rice	7	13
O20		|	Auburn	14	20
O27	●		SMU	19	7
N3	●	|	Mississippi State	14	13
N10		|	Georgia Tech	7	41
N17			Clemson	20	47
N24			Notre Dame	6	32
D1		|	LSU	0	33

HENRY E. FRNKA
1946-51 (.569) 31-23-4

1946 3-7-0 (2-4-0)

S28		|	Alabama	6	7
O5	●	|	Florida	27	13
O12			Rice	6	25
O19	●	|	Auburn	32	0
O26		|	Mississippi State	7	14
N9	●		Clemson	54	13
N16		|	at Georgia Tech	7	35
N23			Notre Dame	0	41
N30		|	at LSU	27	41
D21			Southern California	13	20

1947 2-5-2 (2-3-2)

S27	●	|	Alabama	21	20
O4		|	Georgia Tech	6	20*
O11			at Rice	0	33
O18		|	Mississippi	14	27
O25	●	|	Auburn	40	0
N1		|	Mississippi State	0	20
N15	=	|	Florida	7	7
N22			at Notre Dame	6	59
D6	=	|	LSU	6	6

1948 9-1-0 (5-1-0)

S25	●	|	Alabama	21	14
O2		|	at Georgia Tech	7	13
O9	●		South Carolina	14	0
O16	●	|	Mississippi	20	7
O23	●	|	Auburn	21	6
O30	●	|	Mississippi State	9	0
N6	●		VMI	28	7
N13	●		Baylor	35	13
N20	●		at Cincinnati	6	0
N27	●	|	at LSU	46	0

1949 7-2-1 (5-1-0)

S24	●	|	Alabama MBL	28	14
O1	●	|	Georgia Tech	18	0
O8	●		SE. Louisiana	40	0
O15			at Notre Dame	7	46
O22	●	|	Auburn	14	6
O29	●	|	Mississippi State	54	6
N5	=		Navy	21	21
N12	●	|	at Vanderbilt	41	14
N19	●		at Virginia	28	14
N26		|	LSU	0	21

1950 6-2-1 (3-1-1)

S30		|	Alabama	14	26
O7	●		Louisiana Coll.	64	0
O14			Notre Dame	9	13
O21	●	|	Mississippi	27	20
O28	●	|	at Auburn	28	0
N11	●		Navy BALT	27	0
N18	●		Virginia	42	18
N25	●	|	Vanderbilt	35	6
D2	=	|	LSU	14	14

1951 4-6-0 (1-5-0)

S29	●		Miami, Fla.	21	7
O6			Baylor	14	27
O13	●		Holy Cross	20	14
O20		|	at Mississippi	6	25
O27		|	Auburn	0	21
N3		|	Mississippi State	7	10
N10		|	Kentucky	0	37
N17	●	|	at Vanderbilt	14	10
N24	●		S.E. Louisiana	48	7
D1		|	at LSU	13	14

RAYMOND WOLF
1952-53 (.325) 6-13-1

1952 5-5-0 (3-5-0)

S27		|	Georgia	16	21
O4	●		Santa Clara	35	0
O11		|	at Georgia Tech	0	14
O18		|	Mississippi	14	20
O25	●	|	Auburn MBL	21	6
N1	●	|	Mississippi State	34	21
N8		|	at Kentucky	6	27
N15	●	|	Vanderbilt	16	7
N22	●		Louisiana Coll.	46	14
N29		|	LSU	0	16

THE SCHOOLS

1953   1-8-1 (0-7-0)

S19 •	Citadel	54	6
S26	at Georgia	14	16
O3	at Michigan	7	26
O10	Georgia Tech	13	27
O17	Mississippi	14	45
O24	Auburn *Mbl*	7	34
O31 =	Army	0	0
N7	Mississippi State	0	21
N14	Vanderbilt	7	21
N28	at LSU	13	32

ANDY PILNEY
1954-61 (.350)   25-49-6

1954   1-6-3 (1-6-1)

S18 •	at Georgia Tech	0	28
S25 =	Memphis	13	13
O2 =	North Carolina	7	7
O9	Mississippi State	0	14
O16	at Mississippi	7	34
O23	Georgia	0	7
O30	Auburn *Mbl*	0	27
N6 =	Alabama	0	0
N13 •	at Vanderbilt	6	0
N27	LSU	13	14

1955   5-4-1 (3-3-1)

S17 •	VMI	20	7
S24	at Texas	21	35
O1	Northwestern	21	0
O8	at Mississippi State	0	14
O15	Mississippi	13	27
O22 •	at Georgia	14	0
O29 •	Auburn	27	13
N5 •	Alabama *Mbl*	27	7
N12	Vanderbilt	7	20
N26 =	at LSU	13	13

1956   6-4-0 (3-3-0)

S22 •	Virginia Tech	21	14
S29	Texas	6	7
O6 •	at Northwestern	20	13
O13 •	Navy	21	6
O20	Mississippi *JaM*	10	3
O27	at Georgia Tech	0	40
N3 •	Mississippi State	20	14
N10	Alabama	7	13
N17 •	at Vanderbilt	13	6
D1	LSU	6	7

1957   2-8-0 (1-5-0)

S20	Virginia Tech	13	14
S28	at Texas	6	20
O5 •	at Marquette	20	6
O11	Georgia	6	13
O18	Mississippi	0	50
O26	Georgia Tech	13	20
N2	Mississippi State *JaM*	6	27
N9 •	Alabama *Mbl*	7	0
N16	at Army	14	20
N30	at LSU	6	25

1958   3-7-0 (1-5-0)

S20	at Florida	14	34
S26	Texas	20	21
O4	at Georgia Tech	0	14
O11	Mississippi	8	19
O18 •	Navy *Nor*	14	6
O25	at Kansas	9	14
O31 •	Texas Tech	27	0
N7	Alabama	13	7
N15	at Vanderbilt	0	12
N22	LSU	0	62

1959   3-6-1 (0-5-1)

S18	Florida	0	30
S25	at Miami, Fla.	7	26
O3 •	Wake Forest	6	0
O9 •	Detroit	25	0
O17	at Mississippi	7	53
O24	Georgia Tech	13	21
O30 •	Texas Tech	17	7
N7	Alabama *Mbl*	7	19
N14 =	Vanderbilt	6	6
N21	at LSU	6	14

1960   3-6-1 (1-4-1)

S17 •	at California	7	3
S24 =	Alabama	6	6
O1	at Rice	7	10
O15	Mississippi	13	26
O22	at Georgia Tech	6	14
O28 •	William & Mary	40	8
N5	at Texas Tech	21	35
N12	at Florida	6	21
N19 •	at Vanderbilt	20	0
N26	LSU	6	17

1961   2-8-0 (1-5-0)

S23	at Stanford	7	9
S30	Alabama *Mbl*	0	9
O6	Florida	3	14
O14 •	Virginia Tech	27	14
O21	Mississippi *JaM*	0	41
O28	Georgia Tech	0	35
N4	at Clemson	6	21
N11	Miami, Fla.	0	6
N17 •	Vanderbilt	17	14
N25	at LSU	0	62

TOMMY O'BOYLE
1962-65 (.163)   6-33-1

1962   0-10-0 (0-7-0)

S21	Stanford	3	6
S28	Alabama	6	44
O6	at Texas	8	35
O12	Mississippi State	6	35
O20	Mississippi *JaM*	0	21
O27	at Georgia Tech	12	42
N3	Virginia Tech	22	24
N10	at Tennessee	16	28
N17	at Vanderbilt	0	20
N24	LSU	3	38

1963   1-8-1 (0-6-1)

S20	Texas	0	21
S28	Alabama *Mbl*	0	28
O4	Miami, Fla.	0	28
O12	Mississippi State *JaM*	10	31
O19	Mississippi	0	21
O26	Georgia Tech	3	17
N2 •	at South Carolina	20	7
N9	Tennessee	0	26
N16 =	Vanderbilt	10	10
N23	at LSU	0	20

1964   3-7-0 (1-5-0)

S19	at Texas	0	31
S26	Alabama *Mbl*	6	36
O10	at Mississippi State	6	17
O17	Mississippi	9	14
O24	at Georgia Tech	6	7
O31 •	VMI	25	6
N6 ||	at Miami, Fla.	0	21
N14 •	at Vanderbilt	7	2
N21	LSU	3	13
N28 •	Duke	17	0

1965   2-8-0 (1-5-0)

S18	at Texas	0	31
S25	Alabama *Mbl*	0	27
O2 •	Miami, Fla.	24	16
O9	Georgia Tech	10	13
O16 •	Mississippi *JaM*	7	24
O22 •	Mississippi State	17	15
O30	Vanderbilt	0	13
N6	Stanford	0	16
N13 •	at Florida	13	51
N20	at LSU	0	62

1966-1995
INDEPENDENT

JIM PITTMAN
1966-70 (.413)   21-30-1

1966   5-4-1

S17 •	Virginia Tech	13	0
S24 •	Texas A&M	21	13
O1	at Stanford	14	33
O8 •	at Virginia	20	6
O15 •	Cincinnati	28	21
O22	at Georgia Tech	17	35
O29 •	at Vanderbilt	13	12
N5 =	Miami, Fla.	10	10
N12	at Florida	10	31
N19	LSU	7	21

1967   3-7-0

S23	Miami, Ohio	3	14
S30 •	at North Carolina	36	11
O6 •	at Miami, Fla.	14	34
O14	Florida	0	35
O21	Air Force	10	13
O28 •	Georgia Tech	23	12
N4 •	Vanderbilt	27	14
N11	at Tennessee	14	35
N18	Virginia	10	14
N25	at LSU	27	41

1968   2-8-0

S14	at Houston	7	54
S28	Texas A&M	3	35
O5	Tampa	14	17
O12	at Florida	3	24
O19 •	Boston College	28	14
O26 •	at Georgia Tech	19	23
N2	at Vanderbilt	7	21
N9 •	Tulsa	25	15
N16	at Virginia	47	63
N23	at LSU	10	34

1969   3-7-0

S20	at Georgia	0	35
S27	West Virginia	17	35
O4	at Boston College	24	28
O11	Florida *TAM*	17	18
O18 •	at Pittsburgh	26	22
O25	Notre Dame	0	37
N1	Vanderbilt	23	26
N8 •	Georgia Tech	14	7
N15 •	Virginia	31	0
N22	at LSU	0	27

1970   8-4-0

S12	at Texas Tech	14	21
S19 •	Georgia	17	14
S26 •	at Illinois	23	9
O3	at Cincinnati	6	3
O10	at Air Force	3	24
O17 •	North Carolina	24	17
O24 •	at Georgia Tech	6	20
O31 •	at Vanderbilt	10	7
N7 •	Miami, Fla.	31	16
N21 •	North Carolina St.	31	0
N28	LSU	14	26

LIBERTY BOWL
D12 •	Colorado	17	3

BENNIE ELLENDER
1971-75 (.482)   27-29

1971   3-8-0

S11 •	Texas Tech	15	9
S18 •	at Georgia	7	17
S25 •	at Rice	11	14
O2	William & Mary	3	14
O9 •	at North Carolina	37	29
O16 •	Pittsburgh	33	8
O23	Georgia Tech	16	24
O30	Vanderbilt	9	13
N6	Ohio U.	7	30
N13	at Notre Dame	7	21
N27	at LSU	7	36

1972   6-5-0

S16 •	at Boston College	10	0
S23 •	Georgia	24	13
S30	at Michigan	7	41
O7 •	Pittsburgh	38	6
O14	at Miami, Fla.	21	24
O21 •	at West Virginia	19	31
O28	at Georgia Tech	7	21
N4 •	Kentucky	18	7
N11 •	Ohio U.	44	6
N18 •	at Vanderbilt	21	7
D2	LSU	3	9

1973   9-3-0

S22 •	Boston College	21	16
S29 •	VMI	42	0
O6 •	at Pittsburgh	24	6
O13 •	at Duke	24	17
O20 •	North Carolina	16	0
O27 •	Georgia Tech	23	14
N3	at Kentucky	7	34
N10 •	Navy	17	15
N17 •	Vanderbilt	24	3
N24	at Maryland	9	42
D1 •	LSU	14	0

BLUEBONNET BOWL
D29	Houston	7	47

1974   5-6-0

S14 •	La. Lafayette	17	16
S21 •	at Army	31	14
S28 •	West Virginia	17	14
O12 •	at Air Force	10	3
O19 •	Citadel	30	3
O26 •	at Georgia Tech	7	27
N2	Kentucky	7	30
N9 •	at Boston College	3	27
N16 •	at Vanderbilt	22	30
N23	at LSU	22	24
N30	Mississippi	10	26

1975   4-7-0

S13 •	at Clemson	17	13
S20 •	Mississippi	14	3
S27 •	Syracuse	13	31
O4	Vanderbilt	3	6
O11 •	at Boston College	17	7
O18 •	at West Virginia	16	14
O25	Georgia Tech	0	23
N1	at Kentucky	10	23
N8	Air Force	12	13
N15	North Carolina	15	17
N22	LSU	6	42

LARRY SMITH
1976-79 (.400)   18-27

1976   2-9-0

S11	Cincinnati	14	21
S18 •	at Mississippi	7	34
S25	Boston College	3	27
O2 •	at Vanderbilt	24	13
O9	at Syracuse	0	3
O16 •	Army	23	10
O23	at Georgia Tech	16	28
O30 •	Memphis	7	14
N6 •	West Virginia	28	32
N13 •	Rutgers	20	29
N20	at LSU	7	17

1977   3-8-0

S10	at Memphis	9	27
S17	Stanford	17	21
S24	at SMU	23	28
O1 •	Vanderbilt	36	7
O8 •	at Boston College	28	30
O15 •	Cincinnati	16	13
O22 •	Georgia Tech	14	38
O29 •	at Pittsburgh	0	48
N5 •	at Miami, Fla.	13	10
N12 •	at Rutgers	8	47
N19	LSU	17	20

1978   4-7-0

S9	at Maryland	7	31
S16	Pittsburgh	6	24
S23 •	at Georgia Tech	17	27
S30	at Stanford	14	17
O7 •	at Vanderbilt	38	3
O14 •	Boston College	9	3
O21	TCU	7	13
O28 •	Memphis	41	24
N4 •	Miami, Fla.	20	16
N11 •	at Mississippi	3	13
N25	at LSU	21	40

1979   9-3-0

S8 •	Stanford	33	10
S15 •	at Rice	17	21
S22 •	at TCU	33	19
S29 •	SMU	24	17
O6 •	Vanderbilt	42	14
O13 •	at Southern Miss	20	19
O20	at West Virginia	17	27
O27 •	Georgia Tech	12	7
N3 •	at Boston College	43	8
N10 •	Mississippi	49	15
N24 •	LSU	24	13

LIBERTY BOWL
D22	Penn State	6	9

VINCE GIBSON
1980-82 (.500)   17-17

1980   7-5-0

S6	Southern Miss	14	17
S13	at Stanford	14	19
S20 •	Rice	35	14
S27 •	at Mississippi	26	24
O4	SMU	21	31
O11 •	at Vanderbilt	43	21
O18 •	Air Force	28	7
O25 •	at Georgia Tech	31	14
N1 •	Kentucky	24	22
N15 •	Memphis	21	16
N22	at LSU	7	24

HALL OF FAME CLASSIC
D27	Arkansas	15	34

1981   6-5-0

S5	Mississippi	18	19
S12	Clemson	5	13
S19	at Southern Miss	3	21
O3	at Rice	16	20
O10 •	Vanderbilt	14	10
O17 •	at Air Force	31	13
O24 •	Georgia Tech	27	10
O31	at Cincinnati	13	17
N7 •	Maryland	14	7
N14 •	at Memphis	24	7
N28 •	LSU	48	7

THE SCHOOLS

1982 — 4-7-0

S4	Mississippi State	21	30
S11	at SMU	7	51
S18 ●	Rice	30	6
O2	at Vanderbilt	21	24
O9	Georgia Tech	13	19
O16	Southern Miss	10	22
O23 ●	Memphis	17	10
O30 ●	Baylor	30	15
N6	Mississippi	14	45
N20	Florida	7	21
N27 ●	at LSU	31	28

WALLY ENGLISH
1983-84 (.318)   7-15

1983 — 4-7-0

S3	at Mississippi State	9	14
S10 ●	Mississippi *JAM*	27	23 †
S17 ●	Florida State	34	28 †
S24	at Kentucky	14	26
O1	Vanderbilt	17	30
O8	at Memphis	25	28
O15 ●	La. Lafayette	17	15
O22 ●	at Southern Miss	14	7
O29	at Baylor	18	24
N5	Virginia Tech	10	26
N19	LSU	7	20

1984 — 3-8-0

S1	Mississippi State	3	30
S15	at Florida	21	63
S22	Kentucky	26	30
S29	at Mississippi	14	19
O6 ●	at Vanderbilt	27	23
O13 ●	Southern Miss	35	7
O20	at Florida State	6	27
N3	at Virginia Tech	6	13
N10	at Pittsburgh	10	21
N17 ●	Memphis	14	9
N24	at LSU	15	33

MACK BROWN
1985-87 (.324)   11-23

1985 — 1-10-0

A31	Florida State	12	38
S14	at TCU	13	30
S21	at Kentucky	11	16
S28	Mississippi	10	27
O5	Vanderbilt	17	24
O12	at Memphis	21	38
O19	at Mississippi State	27	31
N2	at Georgia	3	58
N9 ●	La. Lafayette	27	17
N23	at Southern Miss	6	24
N30	LSU	19	31

1986 — 4-7-0

S13	TCU	31	48
S20 ●	at Vanderbilt	35	17
S27	at Mississippi	10	35
O4	Wichita St.	20	21
O11	at Florida State	21	54
O18	Mississippi State	27	34
O25 ●	Southern Miss	35	20
N1 ●	La. Lafayette	42	39
N8	Louisville	12	23
N15 ●	Memphis	15	6
N29	at LSU	17	37

1987 — 6-6-0

S5 ●	at Louisville	40	42
S12 ●	Iowa State	25	12
S19	at Southern Miss	24	31
S26 ●	Mississippi	31	24
O3 ●	Vanderbilt	27	17
O17	at Memphis	36	45
O24 ●	Virginia Tech	57	30
O31	at Florida State	14	73
N7 ●	at Mississippi State	30	19
N14 ●	La. Lafayette	38	10
N21	LSU	36	41

INDEPENDENCE BOWL

D19	Washington	12	24

GREG DAVIS
1988-91 (.311)   14-31

1988 — 5-6-0

S3 ●	U.T. Chattanooga	33	19
S10	at Iowa State	13	30
S17 ●	Kansas State	20	16
S24 ●	Memphis	20	19
O1	Florida State	28	48
O8	Southern Miss	13	38
O22	Louisville	35	38
O29	La. Lafayette	34	51
N5 ●	at Mississippi	14	9
N19 ●	Mississippi State	27	22
N26	at LSU	14	44

1989 — 4-8-0

S2	at Hawaii	26	31
S9 ●	Rice	20	19
S16 ●	La. Lafayette	17	10
S23	at Florida State	9	59
S30	Iowa State	24	25
O7	at Southern Miss	21	30
O21	Mississippi	28	32
O28	at Virginia Tech	13	30
N4 ●	Memphis	38	34
N11	at Mississippi State	7	27
N18 ●	at Vanderbilt	37	13
N25	LSU	7	27

1990 — 4-7-0

S1	La. Lafayette	6	48
S8 ●	at Rice	21	10
S15 ●	SMU	43	7
S22	Florida State	13	31
S29	at Mississippi	21	31
O6 ●	at Memphis	14	21
O13	Southern Miss	14	20
O20	Mississippi State	17	38
O27 ●	Cincinnati	49	7
N10 ●	at Syracuse	26	24
N24	at LSU	13	16

1991 — 1-10-0

A31	Mississippi	3	22
S7	at Florida State	11	38
S14	at Mississippi State	0	48
S21	Rice	19	28
S28	Syracuse	0	24
O5	SMU	17	31
O12	at Alabama	0	62
O19	at Southern Miss	14	47
N2	at East Carolina	28	38
N9 ●	Navy	34	7
N23	LSU	20	39

BUDDY TEEVENS
1992-96 (.179)   10-46

1992 — 2-9-0

S5 ●	at SMU	13	12
S12	at Mississippi	9	35
S19	at Iowa State	14	38
S26 ●	Nevada	34	17
O10	Alabama	0	37
O15	Southern Miss	7	17
O24	Boston College	3	17
O31	Memphis	20	62
N7	at Navy	17	20
N14	at Florida State	7	70
N21	at LSU	12	24

1993 — 3-9-0

S4	Alabama *BIRM*	17	31
S11	at Rice	0	34 †
S18 ●	William & Mary	10	0
S25	Mississippi State	10	36
O2 ●	Navy	27	25
O9	La. Lafayette	15	36
O16	at TCU	7	14
O30	at Boston College	14	42
N6 ●	at Southern Miss	17	15
N13	North Carolina	10	42
N20	at LSU	10	24
D4	at Hawaii	17	56

1994 — 1-10-0

S3	Southern Miss	10	25
S10 ●	at Rice	15	13
S17	at North Carolina	0	49
S24	Alabama *BIRM*	10	20
O8	at Memphis	0	13
O15	TCU	28	30
O22	at Mississippi State	22	66
O29	at Maryland	10	38
N5	Navy	15	17
N12	Mississippi	0	38
N19	LSU	25	49

1995 — 2-9-0

S2	Maryland	10	29
S9 ●	Wake Forest	35	9
S16 ●	at Rice	17	15
S30	at Southern Miss	0	45
O7	at Mississippi	17	20
O14	Memphis	8	23
O21	at TCU	11	16
O28	La. Lafayette	28	32
N4	at Louisville	14	34
N11	Rutgers	40	45
N18	at Navy	7	35

1996-Present
CONFERENCE USA

1996 — 2-9   (1-4)

A30 ●	at Cincinnati	34	14
S14	Rice	14	21
S21	at Memphis	10	17
O5 ●	TCU	35	7
O12	Louisville	20	23
O19	at Army	10	34
O26	Southern Miss	28	31
N2	Houston	17	20
N9	Syracuse	7	31
N16	at Navy	21	35
N23	at LSU	17	35

TOMMY BOWDEN
1997-98 (.818)   18-4

1997 — 7-4   (5-1)

S6 ●	Cincinnati	31	17
S13	Rice	24	30
S20	at Syracuse	19	30
O4 ●	Army	41	0
O11 ●	at Louisville	64	33
O18 ●	East Carolina	33	16
O25	at Southern Miss	13	34
N1 ●	at La. Lafayette	56	0
N8 ●	Memphis	26	14
N15	Mississippi	24	41
N22 ●	at Houston	44	10

1998 — 12-0   (6-0)

S5 ●	at Cincinnati	52	34
S12 ●	at SMU	31	21
S26 ●	Navy	42	24
O3 ●	Southern Miss	21	7
O17 ●	Louisville	28	22
O24 ●	at Rutgers	52	24
O31 ●	La. Lafayette	72	20
N7 ●	at Memphis	41	31
N14 ●	at Army	49	35
N21 ●	Houston	48	20
N26 ●	Louisiana Tech	63	30

LIBERTY BOWL

D31 ●	Brigham Young	41	27

CHRIS SCELFO
1999-2006 (.394)   37-57

1999 — 3-8   (1-5)

S6	at Southern Miss	14	48
S11 ●	SMU	53	19
S18	Army	48	28
O2	at Syracuse	17	47
O9	at Mississippi	13	20
O16 ●	La. Lafayette	48	32
O23	at East Carolina	7	52
O30	Memphis	7	49
N6	at Houston	31	36
N13	at Navy	21	45
N20	UAB	20	23

2000 — 6-5   (3-4)

S2	at Mississippi	20	49
S16	at East Carolina	17	37
S23 ●	at SMU	29	17
S30 ●	Cincinnati	24	19
O7 ●	at La. Lafayette	38	37
O14	Southern Miss	24	56
O21	at Army	17	21
O28	at Louisville	32	35
N4 ●	Houston	41	23
N11 ●	Navy	50	38
N18 ●	Memphis	37	14

2001 — 3-9   (1-6)

A25	at Brigham Young	35	70
S1	at LSU	17	48
S8	East Carolina	24	51
S22	Central Florida	29	36
S29	Southern U.	41	7
O6	at Cincinnati	33	46
O13 ●	TCU	48	22
O20	at UAB	27	34
O27	at Army	35	42
N3	Louisville	7	52
N10 ●	at Navy	42	39
N17	at Southern Miss	6	59

2002 — 8-5   (4-4)

A31 ●	Southern U.	37	19
S7 ●	at Houston	34	13
S14	at East Carolina	20	24
S21	at Memphis	10	38
S28	Texas	0	49
O5	at La. Monroe	52	9
O12 ●	Cincinnati	35	17
O19 ●	UAB	35	14
O26 ●	Navy	51	30
N9	at TCU	10	17
N16	Army	10	14
N23	Southern Miss	31	10

HAWAII BOWL

D25 ●	Hawaii	36	28

2003 — 5-7   (3-5)

S1	TCU	35	38
S6 ●	Northwestern St.	27	24
S13 ●	Mississippi State	31	28
S20 ●	at Army	50	33
S27	at Texas	18	63
O11	Houston	42	45
O17	at Louisville	28	47
O25	Memphis	9	41
N1	at Navy	17	35
N8 ●	at UAB	38	24
N15	at Southern Miss	14	28
N22 ●	East Carolina	28	18

2004 — 5-6   (3-5)

S4	at Mississippi State	7	28
S11 ●	Florida A&M	39	19
S25	Southern Miss	14	32
O9	at East Carolina	25	27
O16	at Memphis	24	49
O23 ●	UAB	59	55
O30	at Houston	3	24
N6 ●	Navy	42	10
N13 ●	Army	45	31
N27 ●	at TCU	35	31
D4	Louisville	7	55

2005 — 2-9   (1-7)

S17	Mississippi State *SHRE*	14	21
S24 ●	at SMU	31	10
O1 ●	Southeastern Louisiana *BAR*	28	21
O8	Houston *LAF*	14	35
O14	Texas-El Paso *RUS*	21	45
O21	at Central Florida	24	34
O29	Marshall *MBL*	26	27
N5	at Navy	21	49
N12	at Rice	34	42
N19	Tulsa *MOR*	14	38
N26	at Southern Mississippi	7	26

2006 — 4-8   (2-6)

S9	at Houston	7	45
S16 ●	at Mississippi State	32	29
S23	at LSU	7	49
S30	SMU	28	33
O7 ●	Rice	38	24
O14	at Texas-El Paso	20	34
O21	at Auburn	13	38
O28 ●	Army	42	28
N4	at Marshall	21	42
N11	Southern Mississippi	3	31
N18 ●	Central Florida	10	9
N24	at Tulsa	3	38

BOB TOLEDO
2007-PRESENT (.250)   6-18

2007   4-8 (3-5)
S8		Mississippi State	17	38
S15		Houston	10	34
S22	●	Southeastern Louisiana	35	27
S29		LSU	9	34
O6		at Army	17	20
O13		at Ala.-Birmingham	21	26
O20	●	at SMU	41	34
O27		Memphis	27	28
N3		Tulsa	25	49
N10	●	Texas-El Paso	34	19
N17	●	at Rice	45	31
N24		at East Carolina	12	35

2008   2-10 (1-7)
S6		at Alabama	6	20
S13		at East Carolina	24	28
S20	●	La.-Monroe	24	10
S25	●	SMU	34	27
O4		Army	13	44
O11		at Texas-El Paso	21	24
O25		Rice	17	42
N1		at LSU	10	35
N8		at Houston	14	42
N15		Ala.-Birmingham	24	41
N22		at Tulsa	7	56
N29		at Memphis	6	45

THE SCHOOLS

Neutral Site Key: *Aug* Augusta, GA / *Balt* Baltimore, MD / *BaR* Baton Rouge, LA / *Beau* Beaumont, TX / *Birm* Birmingham, AL / *Bnx* Bronx, NY / *Buf* Buffalo, NY / *Chi* Chicago, IL / *ColGa* Columbus, GA / *Dal* Dallas, TX / *Gul* Gulfport, MS / *Hou* Houston, TX / *JaM* Jackson, MS / *Laf* Lafayette, LA / *Mbl* Mobile, AL / *Mont* Montgomery, AL / *Mor* Monroe, LA / *Nor* Norfolk, VA / *NYC* New York, NY / *Tam* Tampa, FL / *Rus* Ruston, LA / *Shre* Shreveport, LA
ƒ Forfeit † Game Later Forfieted # Disputed Victor * Disputed Score || Designated Conference Game ¦2 Counted Twice in Conference Standings

THE SCHOOLS

TULANE ANNUAL STATISTICAL LEADERS

YR	RUSHING	YDS	ATT	AVG	PASSING	ATT	CMP	PCT	YDS	RECEIVING	REC	YDS	AVG
1945	Richard Hoot	238	48	5.0	Ernest Crouch	78	31	.40	487	Richard Hoot	11	195	17.7
1946	Eddie Price	309	49	6.3	Jim Keeton	51	21	.41	282	Ed Heider	16	193	12.1
1947	Eddie Price	471	106	4.4	Bennie Ellender	62	29	.47	286	Kenneth Tarzetti	8	89	11.1
1948	Eddie Price	1,178	188	6.3	Joe Ernst	123	57	.46	809	Dick Sheffield	17	316	18.6
1949	Eddie Price	1,137	171	6.6	Joe Ernst	88	49	.56	575	Dick Sheffield	24	376	15.7
1950	Harold Waggoner	663	98	6.8	Joe Ernst	128	69	.54	990	Joe Shinn	24	358	14.9
1951	Max McGee	537	123	4.4	Fred Dempsey	101	48	.48	575	W.C. McElhannon	33	484	14.7
1952	Max McGee	428	109	3.9	Peter Clement	129	59	.46	664	W.C. McElhannon	27	387	14.3
1953	Max McGee	430	82	5.2	Peter Clement	93	46	.49	472	Eddie Bravo	14	137	9.8
1954	Bobby Saia	422	99	4.3	Fred Wilcox	41	19	.46	193	Harry Duvigneaud	11	103	9.4
1955	Ronny Quillian	685	150	4.6	Gene Newton	49	21	.43	312	Otis Gilmore	9	124	13.8
1956	Ronny Quillian	625	156	4.0	Gene Newton	48	21	.44	280	Will Billon	10	143	14.3
1957	Claude Mason	338	61	5.5	Carleton Sweeney	48	22	.46	306	Claude Mason	9	132	14.7
1958	Percy Colon	288	64	4.5	Ritchie Petitbon	125	66	.53	728	Pete Abadie	21	266	12.7
1959	Terry Terrebonne	407	103	4.0	Phil Nugent	102	41	.40	411	Pete Abadie	14	188	13.4
1960	Tommy Mason	663	120	5.5	Phil Nugent	139	67	.48	880	Tommy Mason	28	376	13.4
1961	Gordon Rush	191	42	4.5	Jack Domingue	97	41	.42	338	Thomas Emerson	11	116	10.5
1962	Jerry Graves	200	48	4.2	Ted Miller	103	54	.52	548	Clem Dellenger	39	375	9.6
1963	George Smith	217	60	3.6	Al Burguieres	147	58	.39	664	Ron Chapoton	14	130	9.3
1964	George Smith	307	77	4.0	David East	192	85	.44	846	Lanis O'Steen	24	232	9.7
1965	Carl Crowder	301	90	3.3	Bobby Duhon	151	64	.42	807	Jerry Colquette	36	466	12.9
1966	Bobby Duhon	748	151	5.0	Bobby Duhon	126	56	.44	577	Lanis O'Steen	21	240	11.4
1967	Warren Bankston	473	121	3.9	Bobby Duhon	144	67	.47	753	Nick Pizzolatto	22	282	12.8
1968	Warren Bankston	473	102	4.6	Wayne Francingues	162	66	.41	938	Sonny Pisarich	18	279	15.5
1969	Jimmy Batey	320	59	5.4	Rusty Lachaussee	199	90	.45	1,291	Steve Barrios	23	353	15.3
1970	David Abercrombie	993	219	4.5	Mike Walker	133	56	.42	1,038	Steve Barrios	20	505	25.3
1971	Ricky Hebert	819	210	3.9	Mike Walker	162	64	.40	995	Maxie LeBlanc	25	423	16.9
1972	Doug Bynum	507	108	4.7	Steve Foley	147	74	.50	914	Frank Anderson	17	186	10.9
1973	Steve Foley	601	124	4.8	Steve Foley	112	58	.52	824	Jaime Garza	21	261	12.4
1974	Steve Treuting	523	136	3.8	Terry Looney	128	57	.45	829	Jaime Garza	24	457	19.0
1975	Don Lemon	420	102	4.1	Buddy Gilbert	264	108	.41	1,559	Jaime Garza	27	539	20.0
1976	Bill Kramer	467	121	3.9	Roch Hontas	114	61	.54	697	Zack Mitchell	18	212	11.8
1977	Marvin Christian	691	170	4.1	Roch Hontas	186	118	.63	1,277	Alton Alexis	30	357	11.9
1978	Marvin Christian	879	185	4.8	Roch Hontas	190	108	.57	1,350	Alton Alexis	28	384	13.7
1979	Marvin Christian	582	120	4.9	Roch Hontas	367	215	.59	2,345	Alton Alexis	47	557	11.9
1980	Marvin Lewis	424	80	5.3	Nickie Hall	322	159	.49	2,039	Robert Griffin	45	801	17.8
1981	Marvin Lewis	860	198	4.3	Mike McKay	124	78	.63	927	Nolan Franz	35	611	17.5
1982	Kelvin Robinson	334	70	4.8	Mike McKay	260	152	.58	1,903	Robert Griffin	56	784	14.0
1983	Elton Veals	471	99	4.8	Jon English	184	97	.53	1,258	Larry Route	38	421	11.1
1984	Mike Jones	573	129	4.4	Ken Karcher	230	112	.49	1,341	Larry Route	46	478	10.4
1985	Terrence Jones	377	118	3.2	Ken Karcher	306	175	.57	1,991	Marc Zeno	73	1,137	15.6
1986	Rodney Hunter	657	153	4.3	Terrence Jones	284	159	.56	2,124	Marc Zeno	68	1,033	15.2
1987	Melvin Adams	421	83	5.1	Terrence Jones	319	192	.60	2,551	Marc Zeno	77	1,206	15.7
1988	Terrence Jones	454	164	2.8	Terrence Jones	329	162	.49	2,305	Jerome McIntosh	52	908	17.5
1989	Stanley Barre	418	118	3.5	Deron Smith	423	237	.56	2,613	Jerome McIntosh	55	899	16.3
1990	Chance Miller	805	190	4.2	Deron Smith	361	193	.53	2,282	Melvin Ferdinand	57	757	13.3
1991	Chance Miller	580	163	3.6	Jerome Woods	192	115	.60	1,238	Wil Ursin	70	969	13.8
1992	Joey Perry	429	98	4.4	Shawn Meadows	146	66	.45	752	Wil Ursin	55	755	13.7
1993	Jerald Sowell	403	79	5.1	Craig Randall	305	151	.50	1,565	Wil Ursin	50	565	11.3
1994	Jerald Sowell	609	156	3.9	Tracey Watts	204	91	.45	916	Derrick Franklin	45	450	10.0
1995	Jamaican Dartez	544	150	3.6	Shaun King	199	92	.46	1,046	Derrick Franklin	29	462	15.9
1996	Jerald Sowell	595	154	3.9	Shaun King	273	132	.48	1,574	Jeff Liggon	26	348	13.4
1997	Toney Converse	777	137	5.7	Shaun King	363	199	.55	2,567	P.J. Franklin	58	703	12.1
1998	Toney Converse	871	156	5.6	Shaun King	328	223	.68	3,232	P.J. Franklin	74	1,174	15.9
1999	Toney Converse	366	89	4.1	Patrick Ramsey	513	310	.60	3,410	JaJuan Dawson	96	1,051	10.9
2000	Mewelde Moore	890	174	5.1	Patrick Ramsey	389	229	.59	2,833	Adrian Burnette	74	1,075	14.5
2001	Mewelde Moore	1,421	262	5.4	Patrick Ramsey	448	256	.57	2,935	Mewelde Moore	65	756	11.6
2002	Mewelde Moore	1,138	288	4.0	J.P. Losman	401	230	.57	2,468	Mewelde Moore	52	545	10.5
2003	Mewelde Moore	915	185	5.0	J.P. Losman	422	251	.60	3,077	Roydell Williams	66	1,006	15.2
2004	Matt Forté	624	110	4.5	Lester Ricard	231	143	.62	1,881	Roydell Williams	52	826	15.9
2005	Matt Forté	655	169	3.8	Lester Ricard	323	166	.51	1,932	Preston Brown	47	720	15.3
2006	Matt Forté	859	163	5.3	Lester Ricard	400	229	.57	2,795	Preston Brown	51	607	11.9
2007	Matt Forté	2,127	361	5.9	Anthony Scelfo	205	111	.54	1,396	Jeremy Williams	46	773	16.8
2008	Andre Anderson	864	174	5.0	Kevin Moore	334	187	.56	2,194	Brian King	41	544	13.3

Receiving leaders by receptions
The NCAA began including postseason stats in 2002

TULANE RECORD BOOK

SINGLE-GAME RECORDS

Rushing Yards	342	Matt Forté (Oct. 20, 2007 vs. SMU)
Passing Yards	447	Patrick Ramsey (Sept. 18, 1999 vs. Army)
Receiving Yards	271	Jerome McIntosh (Nov. 18, 1989 vs. Vanderbilt)
All-Purpose Yards	342	Matt Forté (Oct. 20, 2007 vs. SMU)
Points	31	Charles Flournoy (Nov. 7, 1925 vs. Louisiana Tech)
Field Goals	5	Brad Palazzo (Oct. 11, 1997 vs. Louisville); Bart Baldwin (Sept. 10, 1994 vs. Rice)
Tackles	NA	
Interceptions	4	Jimmy Glisson (Nov. 19, 1949 vs. Virginia)

SINGLE-SEASON RECORDS

Rushing Yards	2,127	Matt Forté, 2007 (361 att.)
Passing Yards	3,410	Patrick Ramsey, 1999 (310-513)
Receiving Yards	1,206	Marc Zeno, 1987 (77 rec.)
All-Purpose Yards	2,420	Matt Forté, 2007 (2,127 rush, 282 rec., 11 return)
Scoring	140	Matt Forté, 2007 (23 TDs, 1 2-point conv.)
Touchdowns	23	Matt Forté, 2007 (23 rush)
Tackles	172	Burnell Dent, 1983
Interceptions	9	Jimmy Glisson, 1949; Paul Ellis, 1970
Punting Average	46.2	Brad Hill, 1997 (42 punts)
Punt Return Average	20.8	Joe Bullard, 1969 (19 ret.)
Kickoff Return Average	38.2	Bobby Kellogg, 1939 (6 ret.)

CAREER RECORDS

Rushing Yards	4,364	Mewelde Moore, 2000-03
Passing Yards	9,205	Patrick Ramsey, 1998-2001
Receiving Yards	3,725	Marc Zeno, 1984-87
All-Purpose Yards	6,505	Mewelde Moore, 2000-03
Scoring	333	Seth Marler, 1999-2002
Touchdowns	44	Matt Forté, 2004-07
Tackles	492	Burnell Dent, 1982-85
Interceptions	18	Paul Ellis, 1969-71
Punting Average	43.8	Casey Roussel, 1997-2001 (178 punts)
Punt Return Average	14.2	Joe Bullard, 1969-71 (74 ret.)
Kickoff Return Average	24.9	Jerry Graves, 1962-64 (40 ret.)

TEAM RECORDS

Longest Winning Streak	18	Oct. 11, 1930-Dec. 5, 1931; broken by Southern California, 12-21 on Jan. 1, 1931
Longest Undefeated Streak	18	Oct. 11, 1930-Dec. 5, 1931; broken by Southern California, 12-21 on Jan. 1, 1931
Most Consecutive Winning Seasons	12	1928-39
Most Consecutive Bowl Appearances	2	1979-80
Most Points in a Game	95	vs. Louisiana-Lafayette, Oct. 12, 1912
Most Points Allowed in a Game	73	vs. Florida State, Oct. 31, 1987
Largest Margin of Victory	95	vs. Louisiana-Lafayette, Oct. 12, 1912
Largest Margin of Defeat	63	vs. Florida State, Nov. 14, 1992
Longest Pass Play	94	Shaun King to JaJaun Dawson vs. SMU, Sep. 12, 1998
Longest Field Goal	54	Ed Murray vs. Memphis, Oct. 28, 1978; Mark Olivari vs. Air Force, Nov. 8, 1975
Longest Punt	87	O.J. Key vs. Florida, Oct. 5, 1946
Longest Interception Return	100	David Herbert vs. Rice, Sep. 25, 1971

RETIRED NUMBERS

NO RETIRED JERSEYS

ALL-TIME TEAM

No all-time or all-century team available

TULANE BOWL HISTORY

SEASON	BOWL	DATE	PRE-GAME RANK	TEAMS	SCORE	FINAL RANK	MOST VALUABLE PLAYER(S)	ATT.
1931	ROSE	Jan. 1, 1932		Southern California Tulane	21 12		Ernie Pinckert, Southern California, HB	75,562
1934	SUGAR	Jan. 1, 1935		Tulane Temple	20 14			22,026
1939	SUGAR	Jan. 1, 1940	1 5	Texas A&M Tulane	14 13			73,000
1970	LIBERTY	Dec. 12, 1970		Tulane Colorado	17 3	17	Dave Abercrombie, Tulane, TB	44,640
1973	BLUEBONNET	Dec. 29, 1973	14 17	Houston Tulane	47 7	9 20	D.C. Nobles, Houston, QB Deryl McGallion, Houston, LB	44,358
1979	LIBERTY	Dec. 22, 1979	 15	Penn State Tulane	9 6		Roch Hontas, Tulane, QB	50,021
1980	HALL OF FAME CLASSIC	Dec. 27, 1980		Arkansas Tulane	34 15		Gary Anderson, Arkansas, RB Billy Ray Smith, Arkansas, LB	30,000
1987	INDEPENDENCE	Dec. 19, 1987		Washington Tulane	24 12		Chris Chandler, Washington, QB David Rill, Washington, LB	44,683
1998	LIBERTY	Dec. 31, 1998	10	Tulane BYU	41 27	7	Shaun King, Tulane, QB	52,192
2002	HAWAII	Dec. 25, 2002		Tulane Hawaii	36 28		Lynaris Elpheage, Tulane, CB	31,535

JANUARY 1, 1932 | ROSE
USC 21, TULANE 12

	1ST	2ND	3RD	4TH	FINAL
USC	0	7	14	0	21
TUL	0	0	6	6	12

SCORING SUMMARY
USC	Sparling 6 run (Baker kick)
USC	Pinckert 28 run (Baker kick)
USC	Pinckert 23 run (Baker kick)
TUL	Haynes 7 pass from Zimmerman (kick blocked)
TUL	Glover 3 run (pass failed)

USC	TEAM STATISTICS	TUL
9	First Downs	18
183	Rushing Yards	280
1-6-2	Passing	5-19-2
23	Passing Yards	61
206	Total Yards	341
2-1	Fumbles - Lost	3-2
4-20	Penalties - Yards	6-30

INDIVIDUAL LEADERS
RUSHING
USC: Shaver 14-73; Pinckert 5-63, 2 TD.
TUL: Glover 13-123, 1TD; Zimmerman 21-92.

JANUARY 1, 1935 | SUGAR
TULANE 20, TEMPLE 14

	1ST	2ND	3RD	4TH	FINAL
TUL	0	7	7	6	20
TEM	7	7	0	0	14

SCORING SUMMARY
TEM	Tester 7 pass from Smukler (Smukler kick)
TEM	Smukler 3 run (Smukler kick)
TUL	Simons 85 kickoff return (Mintz kick)
TUL	Hardy 11 pass from Bryan (Mintz kick)
TUL	Hardy 25 pass from Mintz (kick failed)

TUL	TEAM STATISTICS	TEM
10	First Downs	13
140	Rushing Yards	182
8-16-1	Passing	3-13-1
88	Passing Yards	19
228	Total Yards	201
3-2	Fumbles - Lost	2-1
2-20	Penalties - Yards	2-7

JANUARY 1, 1940 | SUGAR
TEXAS A&M 14, TULANE 13

	1ST	2ND	3RD	4TH	FINAL
A&M	7	0	0	7	14
TUL	0	0	7	6	13

SCORING SUMMARY
A&M	Kimbrough 1 run (Price kick)
TUL	Kellogg 75 punt return (Thibaut kick)
TUL	Butler 2 run (kick blocked)
A&M	Kimbrough 18 pass from Smith (Price kick)

A&M	TEAM STATISTICS	TUL
18	First Downs	8
244	Rushing Yards	193
8-15-1	Passing	0-4-0
62	Passing Yards	0
306	Total Yards	193
2-2	Fumbles - Lost	1-0
2-30	Penalties - Yards	2-20

INDIVIDUAL LEADERS
RUSHING
A&M: Kimbrough 25-159, 1 TD; Connatser 9-31.
TUL: Butler 10-55, 1 TD; Cassibry 11-42.
PASSING
A&M: Price 8-15-1, 62 yards.
TUL: Kellogg 0-2-0, 0 yards.

DECEMBER 12, 1970 | LIBERTY
TULANE 17, COLORADO 3

	1ST	2ND	3RD	4TH	FINAL
TUL	3	0	7	7	17
COLO	0	3	0	0	3

SCORING SUMMARY
TUL	FG Gibson 19
COLO	FG Haney 33
TUL	Abercrombie 2 run (Gibson kick)
TUL	Abercrombie 4 run (Gibson kick)

TUL	TEAM STATISTICS	COLO
15	First Downs	13
213	Rushing Yards	155
3-9-1	Passing	3-7-1
28	Passing Yards	20
241	Total Yards	175
6-38.5	Punts - Average	7-42.9
56	Return Yards	28
4-0	Fumbles - Lost	4-1
5-39	Penalties - Yards	5-52
27:52	Possession Time	32:08

INDIVIDUAL LEADERS
RUSHING
TUL: Abercrombie 25-128, 2 TD; Marshall 13-87.
COLO: Tarver 29-65.
PASSING
TUL: Walker 3-8-1, 28 yards.
COLO: Arendt 3-7-1, 20 yards.
RECEIVING
TUL: Barrios 2-34.
COLO: Dal Porto 2-17.

DECEMBER 29, 1973 | BLUEBONNET
HOUSTON 47, TULANE 7

	1ST	2ND	3RD	4TH	FINAL
HOU	7	14	14	12	47
TUL	0	7	0	0	7

SCORING SUMMARY
HOU	Johnson 75 run (Terrell kick)
HOU	Parker 1 run (Terrell kick)
HOU	Parker 3 run (Terrell kick)
TUL	Forner 32 pass from Gilbert (Falgoust kick)
HOU	Nobles 3 run (Terrell kick)
HOU	McGraw 1 run (Terrell kick)
HOU	McGraw 32 run (kick failed)
HOU	Husmann 7 run (kick failed)

HOU	TEAM STATISTICS	TUL
26	First Downs	10
402	Rushing Yards	102
12-29-1	Passing	6-24-4
253	Passing Yards	71
655	Total Yards	173
3-43.3	Punts - Average	9-39.2
6-4	Fumbles - Lost	2-1
5-55	Penalties - Yards	4-26

INDIVIDUAL LEADERS
RUSHING
HOU: Johnson 5-114, 1 TD; McGraw 13-108, 2 TD; Parker 12-47, 2 TD.
TUL: Bynum 12-40; Treuting 2-27.
PASSING
HOU: Nobles 8-13-0, 201 yards; Husman 4-6-1, 52 yards.
TUL: Foley 4-16-4, 32 yards; Gilbert 2-5-0, 39 yards, 1 TD.
RECEIVING
HOU: Willingham 3-105; Bassler 1-60.
TUL: Forner 1-32, 1 TD; Thibodeaux 2-19.

DECEMBER 22, 1979 | LIBERTY
PENN STATE 9, TULANE 6

	1ST	2ND	3RD	4TH	FINAL
PSU	0	6	0	3	9
TUL	0	0	0	6	6

SCORING SUMMARY
PSU	FG Menhardt 33
PSU	FG Menhardt 27
TUL	FG Murray 26
TUL	FG Murray 26
PSU	FG Menhardt 20

PSU	TEAM STATISTICS	TUL
27	First Downs	10
242	Rushing Yards	-8
6-11-2	Passing	21-39-0
95	Passing Yards	210
337	Total Yards	202
2-2	Fumbles - Lost	1-0
1-5	Penalties - Yards	5-40

INDIVIDUAL LEADERS
RUSHING
PSU: Suhey 19-112; Warner 14-57.
TUL: Christian 6-12.
PASSING
PSU: Rocco 5-10-2, 56 yards.
TUL: Hontas 21-39-0, 210 yards.
RECEIVING
PSU: Donovan 2-53.
TUL: Alexis 7-77; Griffin 3-50.

December 27, 1980 | Hall of Fame Classic
Arkansas 34, Tulane 15

	1ST	2ND	3RD	4TH	FINAL
ARK	14	14	3	3	34
TUL	0	0	0	15	15

SCORING SUMMARY
ARK	Tolbert 1 run (Ordonez kick)
ARK	Anderson 80 punt return (Ordonez kick)
ARK	Clyde 9 pass from Jones (Ordonez kick)
ARK	Anderson 46 run (Ordonez kick)
ARK	FG Ordonez 40
TUL	Anderson 62 pass from Hall (Manalla kick)
ARK	FG Ordonez 27
TUL	Robinson 1 run (Hall run)

ARK	TEAM STATISTICS	TUL
22	First Downs	18
383	Rushing Yards	157
5-13-1	Passing	16-37-2
83	Passing Yards	241
466	Total Yards	398
2-80	Punt Returns - Yards	1-10
1-21	Kickoff Returns - Yards	5-122
4-42.5	Punts - Average	7-34.6
0-0	Fumbles - Lost	3-2
1-19	Penalties - Yards	3-15

INDIVIDUAL LEADERS
RUSHING
ARK: Anderson 11-156, 1 TD; Douglas 10-83.
TUL: Lewis 5-45; Robinson 6-44, 1 TD.
PASSING
ARK: Jones 5-13-1, 83 yards, 1 TD.
TUL: Hall 16-37-2, 241 yards, 1 TD.
RECEIVING
ARK: Walters 1-36; Holloway 1-23.
TUL: Anderson 2-88, 1 TD; Griffin 2-59.

December 19, 1987 | Independece
Washington 24, Tulane 12

	1ST	2ND	3RD	4TH	FINAL
WASH	7	14	0	3	24
TUL	0	10	0	2	12

SCORING SUMMARY
WASH	Covington 3 run (Brownlee kick)
TUL	Price 44 punt return (Wiggins kick)
TUL	FG Wiggins 21
WASH	Ames 5 pass from Chandler (Brownlee kick)
WASH	Franklin 5 pass from Chandler (Brownlee kick)
WASH	FG Wyles 41
TUL	Safety (Chandler kneeled in end zone)

WASH	TEAM STATISTICS	TUL
22	First Downs	21
147	Rushing Yards	131
16-32-3	Passing	17-40-1
249	Passing Yards	248
396	Total Yards	379
4-32.8	Punts - Average	6-43.7
1-0	Fumbles - Lost	2-1
10-67	Penalties - Yards	7-73

INDIVIDUAL LEADERS
RUSHING
WASH: Weathersby 14-84.
TUL: Jones 18-91.
PASSING
WASH: Chandler 15-30-3, 234 yards, 2 TD.
TUL: Jones 17-40-1, 248 yards.
RECEIVING
WASH: Weathersby 5-64; Franklin 4-61, 1 TD.
TUL: Zeno 7-116; Pierce 2-56.

December 31, 1998 | Liberty
Tulane 41, BYU 27

	1ST	2ND	3RD	4TH	FINAL
TUL	10	10	14	7	41
BYU	6	0	0	21	27

SCORING SUMMARY
BYU	Horton 11 pass from Feterik (kick failed)
TUL	FG Palazzo 31
TUL	Jordan 79 interception return (Palazzo kick)
TUL	King 3 run (Palazzo kick)
TUL	FG Palazzo 23
TUL	Cook 60 pass from King (Palazzo kick)
TUL	Dartez 13 pass from King (Palazzo kick)
BYU	Cupp 3 run (Pochman kick)
TUL	Converse 5 run (Palazzo kick)
BYU	Cupp 18 pass from Feterik (Pochman kick)
BYU	Mahe 3 run (Pochman kick)

TUL	TEAM STATISTICS	BYU
28	First Downs	20
252	Rushing Yards	54
23-38-0	Passing	27-44-1
276	Passing Yards	267
528	Total Yards	321
4-41.5	Punts - Average	7-33.6
2-0	Fumbles - Lost	3-0
8-59	Penalties - Yards	10-110
31:15	Possession Time	28:45

INDIVIDUAL LEADERS
RUSHING
TUL: King 16-109, 1 TD; Converse 18-103, 1 TD.
BYU: Mahe 16-70, 1 TD.
PASSING
TUL: King 23-38-0, 276 yards, 2 TD.
BYU: Feterik 27-44-1, 267 yards, 2 TD.
RECEIVING
TUL: Dawson 6-83.
BYU: Horton 6-67, 1 TD; Sitake 5-77.

December 25, 2002 | Hawaii
Tulane 36, Hawaii 28

	1ST	2ND	3RD	4TH	FINAL
TUL	0	6	20	10	36
HAW	7	7	0	14	28

SCORING SUMMARY
HAW	Mitchell 1 run (Ayat kick)
HAW	Galeai 2 run (Ayat kick)
TUL	FG Marler 23
TUL	FG Marler 37
TUL	Elpheage 60 punt return (pass failed)
TUL	Losman 1 run (Losman run)
TUL	Moore 25 run (pass failed)
HAW	Colbert 57 pass from Withy-Allen (Ayat kick)
TUL	Losman 3 run (Davis pass from Losman)
HAW	Colbert 31 pass from Withy-Allen (Ayat kick)
TUL	Safety

TUL	TEAM STATISTICS	HAW
25	First Downs	23
144	Rushing Yards	66
20-39-0	Passing	32-52-1
240	Passing Yards	363
384	Total Yards	429
4-143	Punt Returns - Yards	1-13
2-57	Kickoff Returns - Yards	4-75
4-47.0	Punts - Average	5-53.8
3-1	Fumbles - Lost	5-2
6-64	Penalties - Yards	12-88
31:49	Possession Time	28:11

INDIVIDUAL LEADERS
RUSHING
TUL: Moore 30-116, 1 TD; Losman 12-21, 2 TD.
HAW: Mitchell 5-38, 1 TD; Withy-Allen 9-21.
PASSING
TUL: Losman 20-39-0, 240 yards.
HAW: Withy-Allen 18-31-1, 239 yards, 2 TD; Chang 14-21-0, 124 yards.
RECEIVING
TUL: Moore 6-80; Narcisse 5-64.
HAW: Colbert 9-158, 2 TD; Cockheran 9-87.

THE SCHOOLS

ANNUAL
REVIEW

ANNUAL REVIEW

What follows is a year-by-year rundown of the history of Southeastern Conference football, incorporating final poll rankings, consensus All-Americans, bowl game results, all-SEC teams, Heisman Trophy balloting, other award winners and instances in which conference schools and players ranked among the NCAA team and individual statistical leaders.

Final Polls. From 1936 on, each season's review begins with the final writers' and, eventually, coaches' poll of the season, with SEC teams in bold.

The writers' poll, conducted by the Associated Press, held a final poll after the bowls in the 1965 season, went back to a final poll before the bowls in the 1966 and 1967 seasons, and then returned to a post-bowl final poll from 1968 onward. The coaches' poll, which from 1950-1992 was conducted by United Press and United Press International, started running a final poll after the bowls with the 1974 season.

Consensus All-Americans. We start with 1922, when the Southern Conference—from which the SEC split off in 1933—began play. We have included a full list of each year's consensus All-Americans, with the names of all SEC players in bold, as well as players who received first-team All-American mentions.

Conference Standings. We run an annual review of the SEC standings—as well as the first 11 seasons of the Southern Conference—throughout the years, assembled from NCAA records and Richard Billingsley's all-time scores database.

All-SEC Teams. Starting in 1984, we have included the official all-conference squads as voted by the SEC coaches.

SEC Championship Game. You will find box scores for every SEC championship game since the inception of the conference's two-division format in 1992.

NCAA Statistical Leaders. Reliable statistics to determine top 10 category leaders in college football before 1937 simply don't exist. It wasn't until Homer Cooke, founder of the NCAA's statistical service, began contacting every school in the country in 1937 that the NCAA began to tabulate national statistical rankings. Even in Cooke's early years, leaders were often determined with one or more games for a team going unreported. Those discrepancies, as well as missing data for part of the 1950s, makes the first few decades of the NCAA's record-keeping a somewhat rough guide to the era. Progress began in earnest in 1970, when the NCAA began to determine most category champions on a per-game basis rather than by accumulated totals. In any case, we've isolated SEC performers who landed on the NCAA lists throughout. We've also included information on former SEC schools Georgia Tech and Tulane, whose exploits are highlighted before they left the conference in 1964 and 1966, respectively.

1922

CONSENSUS ALL-AMERICANS

POS	NAME	SCHOOL
B	Harry Kipke	Michigan
B	Gordon Locke	Iowa
B	John Thomas	Chicago
B	Edgar Kaw	Cornell
E	Brick Muller	California
E	Wendell Taylor	Navy
T	C. Herbert Treat	Princeton
T	John Thurman	Pennsylvania
G	Frank Schwab	Lafayette
G	Charles Hubbard	Harvard
C	Ed Garbisch	Army

BOWL GAMES

DATE	GAME	SCORE
D25	San Diego East-West Christmas Classic	West Virginia 21, Gonzaga 13
J1	Rose	Southern California 14, Penn State 3

STANDINGS

Southern

	CONFERENCE			OVERALL		
	W	L	T	W	L	T
Florida State	7	1	0	10	2	0
North Carolina	5	0	0	9	1	0
Vanderbilt	4	0	0	8	0	1
Georgia Tech	4	0	0	7	2	0
Virginia Tech	3	0	0	8	1	1
Florida	2	0	0	7	2	0
Tennessee	4	2	0	8	2	0
Auburn	2	1	0	8	2	0
Alabama	3	2	1	6	3	1
Kentucky	2	2	0	6	3	0
Virginia	1	1	1	4	4	1
Mississippi State	2	3	0	3	4	2
Wash. & Jeff.	1	2	0	5	3	1
Clemson	1	2	0	5	4	0
Maryland	1	2	0	4	5	1
LSU	1	2	0	3	7	0
Georgia	1	3	1	5	4	1
Tulane	1	4	0	4	4	0
South Carolina	0	3	0	5	4	0
Mississippi	0	2	0	4	5	1
North Carolina St.	0	5	0	4	6	0
Sewanee	1	3	1	3	4	1

1923

CONSENSUS ALL-AMERICANS

POS	NAME	SCHOOL
B	George Pfann	Cornell
B	Red Grange	Illinois
B	William Mallory	Yale
B	Harry Wilson	Penn State
E	Pete McRae	Syracuse
E	Ray Ecklund	Minnesota
E	**Lynn Bomar**	**Vanderbilt**
T	Century Milstead	Yale
T	Marty Below	Wisconsin
G	Charles Hubbard	Harvard
G	James McMillen	Illinois
C	Jack Blott	Michigan

OTHERS RECEIVING FIRST-TEAM HONORS

B	John Levi	Haskell
B	Earl Martineau	Minnesota
E	Homer Hazel	Rutgers
T	Frank Sundstrom	Cornell
G	Joe Bedenk	Penn State

BOWL GAMES

DATE	GAME	SCORE
J1	Rose	Navy 14, Washington 14

STANDINGS

Southern

	CONFERENCE			OVERALL		
	W	L	T	W	L	T
Vanderbilt	4	0	1	5	2	1
Wash. & Lee	4	0	1	6	3	1
VMI	5	1	0	9	1	0
Virginia Tech	4	1	0	6	3	0
Alabama	5	1	1	7	2	1
Tennessee	4	2	0	5	4	1
Maryland	2	1	0	7	2	1
Florida	1	0	2	6	1	2
North Carolina	2	1	1	5	3	1
Georgia	3	2	0	5	3	1
Mississippi State	2	1	2	5	2	2
Tulane	2	2	1	6	3	1
Clemson	1	1	1	5	2	1
Georgia Tech	0	0	4	3	2	4
Auburn	0	1	3	3	3	3
Kentucky	0	2	2	4	3	2
North Carolina St.	1	4	0	3	7	0
Virginia	0	3	1	3	5	1
Sewanee	0	2	0	5	4	1
Mississippi	0	4	0	4	6	0
South Carolina	0	4	0	4	6	0
LSU	0	3	0	3	5	1

1924

CONSENSUS ALL-AMERICANS

POS	NAME	SCHOOL
B	Red Grange	Illinois
B	Harry Stuhldreher	Notre Dame
B	Jimmy Crowley	Notre Dame
B	Elmer Layden	Notre Dame
E	Jim Lawson	Stanford
E	Dick Luman	Yale
E	**Henry Wakefield**	**Vanderbilt**
T	Ed McGinley	Pennsylvania
T	Ed Weir	Nebraska
G	Joe Pondelik	Chicago
G	Carl Diehl	Dartmouth
C	Edwin Horrell	California

OTHERS RECEIVING FIRST-TEAM HONORS

B	Homer Hazel	Rutgers
B	Eddie Dooley	Dartmouth
B	Charles Darling	Boston College
B	Raymond Pond	Yale
B	Walter Koppisch	Columbia
E	Edmond Stout	Princeton
E	Henry Bjorkman	Dartmouth
E	Hilary Mahaney	Holy Cross
E	Charley Berry	Lafayette
T	Frank Gowdy	Chicago
T	Bob Beattie	Princeton
G	Gus Farwick	Army
G	Alton Papworth	Pennsylvania
G	Edgar Garbisch	Army
G	Edliff Slaughter	Michigan
C	Winslow Lovejoy	Yale

BOWL GAMES

DATE	GAME	SCORE
D25	Los Angeles Christmas Festival	Southern California 20, Missouri 7
J1	Rose	Notre Dame 27, Stanford 10
J1	Dixie Classic	West Virginia Wesleyan 9, SMU 7

STANDINGS

Southern

	CONFERENCE			OVERALL		
	W	L	T	W	L	T
Alabama	5	0	0	8	1	0
Georgia	5	1	0	7	3	0
Florida	2	0	1	6	2	2
Tulane	4	1	0	8	1	0
Wash. & Lee	4	1	1	6	3	1
South Carolina	3	2	0	7	3	0
Sewanee	3	2	0	6	4	0
Virginia	3	2	0	5	4	0
Mississippi State	3	2	0	5	4	0
Georgia Tech	3	2	1	5	3	1
Vanderbilt	3	3	0	6	3	1
Virginia Tech	2	2	3	4	2	3
VMI	2	3	1	6	3	1
Kentucky	2	3	0	4	5	0
North Carolina	2	3	0	4	5	0
Maryland	1	2	1	3	3	3
Auburn	2	4	1	4	4	1
North Carolina St.	1	4	1	2	6	2
LSU	0	3	0	5	4	0
Mississippi	0	3	0	4	5	0
Tennessee	0	4	0	3	5	0
Clemson	0	3	0	2	6	0

1925

CONSENSUS ALL-AMERICANS

POS	NAME	SCHOOL
B	Andy Oberlander	Dartmouth
B	Red Grange	Illinois
B	Ernie Nevers	Stanford
B	Benny Friedman	Michigan
B	George Wilson	Washington
E	Bennie Oosterbaan	Michigan
E	George Tully	Dartmouth
T	Ed Weir	Nebraska
T	Ralph Chase	Pittsburgh
G	Carl Diehl	Dartmouth
G	Ed Hess	Ohio State
C	Ed McMillan	Princeton

OTHERS RECEIVING FIRST-TEAM HONORS

B	J. Edward Tryon	Colgate
B	Charles Flourney	Tulane
B	Jacob Slagle	Princeton
E	Charles Born	Army
E	George Thayer	Pennsylvania
E	Ted Sloan	Drake
E	Dick Romney	Iowa
T	Edgar Lindenmeyer	Missouri
T	John Joss	Yale
T	Nate Parker	Dartmouth
G	Herbert Sturhahn	Yale
G	Harry Hawkins	Michigan
G	Brice Taylor	Southern California
G	Dana Carey	California
C	Tim Lowry	Northwestern
C	Robert Brown	Michigan

BOWL GAMES

DATE	GAME	SCORE
J1	Rose	Alabama 20, Washington 19

STANDINGS

Southern

	CONFERENCE			OVERALL		
	W	L	T	W	L	T
Alabama	7	0	0	10	0	0
Tulane	5	0	0	9	0	1
North Carolina	4	0	1	7	1	1
Washington & Lee	5	1	0	5	5	0
Virginia	4	1	1	7	1	1
Georgia Tech	4	1	1	6	2	1
Kentucky	4	2	0	6	3	0
Florida	3	2	0	8	2	0
Auburn	3	2	1	5	3	1
Vanderbilt	3	3	0	6	3	0
Virginia Tech	3	3	1	5	3	2
South Carolina	2	2	0	7	3	0
Tennessee	2	2	1	5	2	1
VMI	2	4	0	6	4	0
Georgia	2	4	0	4	5	0
Sewanee	1	4	0	4	4	1
Mississippi State	1	4	0	3	4	1
LSU	0	2	1	5	3	1
North Carolina St.	0	4	1	3	5	1
Mississippi	0	4	0	5	5	0
Maryland	0	4	0	2	5	1
Clemson	0	4	0	1	7	0

1926

CONSENSUS ALL-AMERICANS

POS	NAME	SCHOOL
B	Benny Friedman	Michigan
B	Mort Kaer	Southern California
B	Ralph Baker	Northwestern
B	Herb Joesting	Minnesota
E	Bennie Oosterbaan	Michigan
E	Vic Hanson	Syracuse
I	Frank Wickhorst	Navy
T	Bud Sprague	Army
G	Harry Connaughton	Georgetown
G	Bernie Shively	Illinois
C	Bud Boeringer	Notre Dame

OTHERS RECEIVING FIRST-TEAM HONORS

B	Roy Randall	Brown
B	George Wilson	Army
B	George Wilson	Lafayette
B	Tom Hamilton	Navy
B	Charles Rogers	Pennsylvania
B	Marty Karow	Ohio State
E	Ted Shipkey	Stanford
E	Hoyt Winslett	Alabama
E	Hal Broda	Brown
T	Lloyd Yoder	Carnegie Tech
T	Orland Smith	Brown
T	Lonnie Stiner	Nebraska
T	Bob Johnson	Northwestern
T	Al Lassman	NYU
G	Herbert Sturhahn	Yale
G	Edwin Hayes	Ohio State
C	John Butler	Pennsylvania

BOWL GAMES

DATE	GAME	SCORE
J1	Rose	Alabama 7, Stanford 7

STANDINGS

Southern

	CONFERENCE			OVERALL		
	W	L	T	W	L	T
Alabama	8	0	0	9	0	1
Tennessee	5	1	0	8	1	0
Vanderbilt	4	1	0	8	1	0
South Carolina	4	2	0	6	4	0
Georgia	4	2	0	5	4	0
Virginia	4	2	1	6	2	2
Virginia Tech	3	2	1	5	3	1
Wash. & Lee	3	2	1	4	3	2
Georgia Tech	4	3	0	4	5	0
LSU	3	3	0	6	3	0
Auburn	3	3	0	5	4	0
North Carolina	3	3	0	4	5	0
Mississippi	2	2	0	5	4	0
Mississippi State	2	3	0	5	4	0
VMI	2	4	0	5	5	0
Tulane	2	4	0	3	5	1
Maryland	1	3	1	5	4	1
Florida	1	4	1	2	6	2
Kentucky	1	4	1	2	6	1
Clemson	1	3	0	2	7	0
North Carolina St.	0	4	0	4	5	0
Sewanee	0	5	0	2	6	0

1927

CONSENSUS ALL-AMERICANS

POS	NAME	SCHOOL
B	Gibby Welch	Pittsburgh
B	Morley Drury	Southern California
B	Red Cagle	Army
B	Herb Joesting	Minnesota
E	Bennie Oosterbaan	Michigan
E	**Tom Nash**	**Georgia**
T	Jesse Hibbs	Southern California
T	Ed Hake	Pennsylvania
G	Bill Webster	Yale
G	John P. Smith	Notre Dame
C	Larry Bettencourt	St. Mary's (Cal.)
C	John Charlesworth	Yale

OTHERS RECEIVING FIRST-TEAM HONORS

B	**Bill Spears**	**Vanderbilt**
B	Mike Miles	Princeton
B	Christy Flanagan	Notre Dame
E	**Ivey Shiver**	**Georgia**
T	Sidney Quarrier	Yale
T	Bud Sprague	Army
T	Leo Raskowski	Ohio State
T	John H. Smith	Pennsylvania
T	Bill Kern	Pittsburgh
G	Russ Crane	Illinois
G	Harold Hanson	Minnesota
C	Bill Reitsch	Illinois

BOWL GAMES

DATE	GAME	SCORE
J2	Rose	Stanford 7, Pittsburgh 6

STANDINGS

Southern

	CONFERENCE			OVERALL		
	W	L	T	W	L	T
North Carolina St.	4	0	0	9	1	0
Georgia Tech	7	0	1	8	1	1
Tennessee	5	0	1	8	0	1
Georgia	6	1	0	9	1	0
Vanderbilt	5	0	2	8	1	2
Florida	5	2	0	7	3	0
Mississippi	3	2	0	5	3	1
Virginia	4	4	0	5	4	0
Clemson	2	2	0	5	3	1
Alabama	3	4	1	5	4	1
LSU	2	3	1	4	4	1
Mississippi State	2	3	0	5	3	0
Virginia Tech	2	3	0	5	4	0
Wash. & Lee	2	3	0	4	4	1
Maryland	3	5	0	4	7	0
VMI	2	4	0	6	4	0
South Carolina	2	4	0	4	5	0
Tulane	2	5	1	2	5	1
North Carolina	2	5	0	4	6	0
Sewanee	1	4	0	2	6	0
Kentucky	1	5	0	3	6	1
Auburn	0	6	1	0	7	2

1928

CONSENSUS ALL-AMERICANS

POS	NAME	SCHOOL
B	Red Cagle	Army
B	Paul Scull	Pennsylvania
B	Ken Strong	NYU
B	Howard Harpster	Carnegie Mellon
B	Charles Carroll	Washington
E	Irv Phillips	California
E	Wes Fesler	Ohio State
T	Otto Pommerening	Michigan
T	Mike Getto	Pittsburgh
G	Seraphim Post	Stanford
G	Don Robesky	Stanford
G	Edward Burke	Navy
C	Pete Pund	Georgia Tech

OTHERS RECEIVING FIRST-TEAM HONORS

B	Earl Clark	Colorado College
B	Warner Mizell	Georgia Tech
B	Don Williams	Southern California
B	Lloyd Brazil	Detroit
E	Ike Frankian	St. Mary's (Cal.)
E	**Dale Van Sickel**	**Florida**
E	Kenneth Haycraft	Minnesota
E	Theodore Rosenzweig	Carnegie Mellon
T	Albert Nowack	Illinois
T	Frank Speer	Georgia Tech
T	Fred Miller	Notre Dame
T	Jesse Hibbs	Southern California
T	Forrest Douds	Wash. & Jeff.
G	George Gibson	Minnesota
G	Dan McMullen	Nebraska
G	Leroy Wietz	Illinois
G	Peter Westra	Iowa
C	Charles Howe	Princeton

BOWL GAMES

DATE	GAME	SCORE
J1	Rose	Georgia Tech 8, California 7

STANDINGS

Southern	CONFERENCE			OVERALL		
	W	L	T	W	L	T
Georgia Tech	7	0	0	10	0	0
Tennessee	6	0	1	9	0	1
Florida	6	1	0	8	1	0
Virginia Tech	4	1	0	7	2	0
Alabama	6	2	0	6	3	0
LSU	3	1	1	6	2	1
Vanderbilt	4	2	0	8	2	0
Clemson	4	2	0	8	3	0
Tulane	3	3	1	6	3	1
Mississippi	3	3	0	5	4	0
South Carolina	2	2	1	6	2	2
North Carolina	2	2	2	5	3	2
Kentucky	2	2	1	4	3	1
Maryland	2	3	1	6	3	1
VMI	2	3	1	5	3	2
Georgia	2	4	0	4	5	0
North Carolina St.	1	3	1	4	5	1
Mississippi State	1	4	0	2	4	2
Virginia	1	6	0	2	6	1
Wash. & Lee	1	6	0	2	8	0
Sewanee	0	5	0	2	7	0
Auburn	0	7	0	1	8	0

1929

CONSENSUS ALL-AMERICANS

POS	NAME	SCHOOL
B	Frank Carideo	Notre Dame
B	Ralph Welch	Purdue
B	Red Cagle	Army
B	**Gene McEver**	**Tennessee**
E	Joe Donchess	Pittsburgh
E	Wes Fesler	Ohio State
T	Bronko Nagurski	Minnesota
T	Elmer Sleight	Purdue
G	Jack Cannon	Notre Dame
G	Ray Montgomery	Pittsburgh
C	Ben Ticknor	Harvard

OTHERS RECEIVING FIRST-TEAM HONORS

B	Bill Banker	Tulane
B	Toby Uansa	Pittsburgh
B	**Tony Holm**	**Alabama**
B	Willis Glassgow	Iowa
B	Earl Pomeroy	Utah
B	Alton Marsters	Dartmouth
B	Merle Hufford	Washington
E	Francis Tappaan	Southern California
E	Wear Schoonover	Arkansas
E	Robert Tanner	Minnesota
T	George Ackerman	St. Mary's (Cal.)
T	Lou Gordon	Illinois
T	Ray Richards	Nebraska
T	Marion Hammon	SMU
G	Bert Schwarz	California
G	Harry Anderson	Northwestern
G	**John Brown**	**Vanderbilt**
C	Roy Riegels	California

BOWL GAMES

DATE	GAME	SCORE
J1	Rose	Southern California 47, Pittsburgh 14

STANDINGS

Southern	CONFERENCE			OVERALL		
	W	L	T	W	L	T
Tulane	6	0	0	9	0	0
Tennessee	6	0	1	9	0	1
North Carolina	7	1	0	9	1	0
Florida	6	1	0	8	2	0
Vanderbilt	5	1	0	7	2	0
Kentucky	3	1	1	6	1	1
VMI	4	2	0	8	2	0
Georgia	4	2	0	6	4	0
Duke	2	1	0	4	6	0
LSU	3	2	0	6	3	0
Alabama	4	3	0	6	3	0
Clemson	3	3	0	8	3	0
Virginia Tech	2	3	0	5	4	0
Georgia Tech	3	5	0	3	6	0
Virginia	1	3	2	4	3	2
Maryland	1	3	1	4	4	2
South Carolina	2	5	0	6	5	0
Wash. & Lee	1	4	1	3	5	1
Mississippi	0	4	2	1	6	2
Mississippi State	0	3	1	1	5	2
Sewanee	0	4	1	2	5	2
Auburn	0	7	0	2	7	0
North Carolina St.	0	5	0	1	8	0

1930

CONSENSUS ALL-AMERICANS

POS	NAME	SCHOOL
B	Frank Carideo	Notre Dame
B	Marchy Schwartz	Notre Dame
B	Erny Pinckert	Southern California
B	Leonard Macaluso	Colgate
E	Wes Fesler	Ohio State
E	Frank Baker	Northwestern
T	**Fred Sington**	**Alabama**
T	Milo Lubratovich	Wisconsin
G	Ted Beckett	California
G	Barton Koch	Baylor
C	Ben Ticknor	Harvard

OTHERS RECEIVING FIRST-TEAM HONORS

B	Marty Brill	Notre Dame
B	Fayette Russell	Northwestern
B	**Bobby Dodd**	**Tennessee**
B	Orv Mohler	Southern California
B	Jim Murphy	Fordham
B	Phil Moffatt	Stanford
E	Jerry Dalrymple	Tulane
E	Garrett Arbelbide	Southern California
T	Mel Hein	Washington State
T	Glen Edwards	Washington State
T	Hugh Rhea	Nebraska
T	Jack Price	Army
G	Frederick Linehan	Yale
G	Bert Metzger	Notre Dame
G	Wade Woodworth	Northwestern
G	**Ralph Maddox**	**Georgia**
G	Henry Wisniewski	Fordham

BOWL GAMES

DATE	GAME	SCORE
J1	Rose	Alabama 24, Washington State 0

STANDINGS

Southern	CONFERENCE			OVERALL		
	W	L	T	W	L	T
Alabama	8	0	0	10	0	0
Tulane	5	0	0	8	1	0
Tennessee	6	1	0	9	1	0
Duke	4	1	1	8	1	2
Vanderbilt	5	2	0	8	2	0
Maryland	4	2	0	7	5	0
Florida	4	2	1	6	3	1
North Carolina	4	2	2	5	3	2
Clemson	3	2	0	8	2	0
Georgia	3	2	1	7	2	1
Kentucky	4	3	0	5	3	0
South Carolina	4	3	0	6	4	0
Virginia Tech	2	3	1	5	3	1
Mississippi State	2	3	0	2	7	0
Georgia Tech	2	4	1	2	6	1
LSU	2	4	0	6	4	0
Virginia	2	5	0	4	6	0
Sewanee	1	4	0	3	6	1
Mississippi	1	5	0	3	5	1
North Carolina St.	1	5	0	2	8	0
Auburn	1	6	0	3	7	0
Wash. & Lee	0	4	1	3	6	1
VMI	0	5	0	3	6	0

1931

CONSENSUS ALL-AMERICANS

POS	NAME	SCHOOL
B	Gus Shaver	Southern California
B	Marchy Schwartz	Notre Dame
B	Pug Rentner	Northwestern
B	Barry Wood	Harvard
E	Jerry Dalrymple	Tulane
E	**Vernon Smith**	**Georgia**
T	Jesse Quatse	Pittsburgh
T	Jack Riley	Northwestern
T	Dallas Marvil	Northwestern
G	Biggie Munn	Minnesota
G	John Baker	Southern California
C	Tommy Yarr	Notre Dame

OTHERS RECEIVING FIRST-TEAM HONORS

B	**Johnny Cain**	**Alabama**
B	Erny Pinckert	Southern California
B	Don Zimmerman	Tulane
B	Rusty Gill	California
E	John Orsi	Colgate
E	Paul Moss	Purdue
E	Henry Cronkite	Kansas State
T	Paul Schwegler	Washington
T	Jack Price	Army
T	Joe Kurth	Notre Dame
T	Nordy Hoffman	Notre Dame
G	**Herman Hickman**	**Tennessee**
C	Maynard Morrison	Michigan
C	Stan Williamson	Southern California
C	Charles Miller	Purdue

BOWL GAMES

DATE	GAME	SCORE
J1	Rose	Southern California 21, Tulane 12

STANDINGS

Southern

	CONFERENCE			OVERALL		
	W	L	T	W	L	T
Tulane	8	0	0	11	1	0
Tennessee	6	0	1	9	0	1
Alabama	7	1	0	9	1	0
Georgia	6	1	0	8	2	0
Maryland	4	1	1	8	1	1
Kentucky	4	2	2	5	2	2
LSU	3	2	0	5	4	0
Sewanee	3	3	0	6	3	1
Auburn	3	3	0	5	3	1
Duke	3	3	1	5	3	2
South Carolina	3	3	1	5	4	1
North Carolina	2	3	3	4	3	3
Vanderbilt	3	4	0	5	4	0
Wash. & Lee	2	3	0	4	5	1
Florida	2	4	2	2	6	2
Georgia Tech	2	4	1	2	7	1
VMI	2	4	0	3	6	1
North Carolina St.	2	4	0	3	6	0
Virginia Tech	1	4	1	3	4	2
Clemson	1	4	0	1	6	2
Mississippi	1	5	0	2	6	1
Virginia	0	5	1	1	7	2
Mississippi State	0	5	0	2	6	0

1932

CONSENSUS ALL-AMERICANS

POS	NAME	SCHOOL
B	Harry Newman	Michigan
B	Warren Heller	Pittsburgh
B	Don Zimmerman	Tulane
B	**Jimmy Hitchcock**	**Auburn**
E	Paul Moss	Purdue
E	Joe Skladany	Pittsburgh
T	Joe Kurth	Notre Dame
T	Ernie Smith	Southern California
G	Milt Summerfelt	Army
G	Bill Corbus	Stanford
C	**Pete Gracey**	**Vanderbilt**

OTHERS RECEIVING FIRST-TEAM HONORS

B	Roy Horstmann	Purdue
B	Angel Brovelli	St. Mary's (Cal.)
B	Frank Christensen	Utah
B	George Melinkovich	Notre Dame
E	Ted Petoskey	Michigan
E	Jose Martinez-Zorrilla	Cornell
E	Dave Nisbet	Washington
G	Robert Smith	Colgate
G	John Vaught	TCU
G	Aaron Rosenberg	Southern California
G	Joe Gailus	Ohio State
C	Art Krueger	Marquette
C	Lawrence Ely	Nebraska
C	Chuck Bernard	Michigan

BOWL GAMES

DATE	GAME	SCORE
J2	Rose	Southern California 35, Pittsburgh 0

STANDINGS

Southern

	CONFERENCE			OVERALL		
	W	L	T	W	L	T
LSU	4	0	0	6	3	1
Tennessee	7	0	1	9	0	1
Auburn	6	0	1	9	0	1
Virginia Tech	6	1	0	8	1	0
Alabama	5	2	0	8	2	0
Vanderbilt	4	1	2	6	1	2
North Carolina St.	3	1	1	6	1	2
Tulane	5	2	1	6	2	1
Duke	5	3	0	7	3	0
Georgia Tech	4	4	1	4	5	1
South Carolina	2	2	2	5	4	2
Kentucky	4	5	0	4	5	0
Virginia	2	3	0	5	4	0
Mississippi	2	3	0	5	6	0
Georgia	2	4	2	2	5	2
Maryland	2	4	0	5	6	0
North Carolina	2	5	1	3	5	2
VMI	1	4	0	2	8	0
Wash. & Lee	1	4	0	1	9	0
Florida	1	6	0	3	6	0
Clemson	0	4	0	3	5	1
Mississippi State	0	4	0	3	5	0
Sewanee	0	6	0	2	7	1

1933

CONSENSUS ALL-AMERICANS

POS	NAME	SCHOOL
B	Cotton Warburton	Southern California
B	George Sauer	Nebraska
B	**Beattie Feathers**	**Tennessee**
B	Duane Purvis	Purdue
E	Joe Skladany	Pittsburgh
E	Paul Geisler	Centenary
T	Fred Crawford	Duke
T	Francis Wistert	Michigan
G	Bill Corbus	Stanford
G	Aaron Rosenberg	Southern California
C	Chuck Bernard	Michigan

OTHERS RECEIVING FIRST-TEAM HONORS

B	Pug Lund	Minnesota
B	Jack Buckler	Army
B	Norman Franklin	Oregon State
E	Bill Smith	Washington
E	Frank Larson	Minnesota
E	Tony Matal	Columbia
E	Edgar Manske	Northwestern
T	Charles Ceppi	Princeton
T	Ade Schwammel	Oregon State
T	John Dempsey	Bucknell
T	John Yezerski	St. Mary's (Cal.)
G	Francis Schammel	Iowa
G	Larry Stevens	Southern California

BOWL GAMES

DATE	GAME	SCORE
J1	Dixie Classic	Arkansas 7, Centenary 7
J1	Rose	Columbia 7, Stanford 0

SEC STANDINGS

	CONFERENCE			OVERALL		
	W	L	T	W	L	T
Alabama	5	0	1	7	1	1
LSU	3	0	2	7	0	3
Georgia	3	1	0	8	2	0
Tennessee	5	2	0	7	3	0
Tulane	4	2	1	6	3	1
Mississippi	2	2	1	6	3	2
Vanderbilt	2	2	2	4	3	3
Auburn	2	2	0	5	5	0
Florida	2	3	0	5	3	1
Kentucky	2	3	0	5	5	0
Georgia Tech	2	5	0	5	5	0
Mississippi State	1	5	1	3	6	1
Sewanee	0	6	0	3	6	0

1934

CONSENSUS ALL-AMERICANS

POS	NAME	SCHOOL
B	Bobby Grayson	Stanford
B	Pug Lund	Minnesota
B	**Dixie Howell**	**Alabama**
B	Fred Borries	Navy
E	**Don Hutson**	**Alabama**
E	Frank Larson	Minnesota
T	**Bill Lee**	**Alabama**
T	Bob Reynolds	Stanford
G	Chuck Hartwig	Pittsburgh
G	Bill Bevan	Minnesota
C	Darrell Lester	TCU
C	George Shotwell	Pittsburgh
C	Jack Robinson	Notre Dame

OTHERS RECEIVING FIRST-TEAM HONORS

POS	NAME	SCHOOL
B	Jay Berwanger	Chicago
B	Bill Wallace	Rice
B	Arleigh Williams	California
B	Ed Goddard	Washington State
B	Bones Hamilton	Stanford
B	Isadore Weinstock	Pittsburgh
B	Bobby Wilson	SMU
B	Duane Purvis	Purdue
E	Monk Moscrip	Stanford
E	Merle Wendt	Ohio State
E	Joe Bogdanski	Colgate
T	George Maddox	Kansas State
T	Ed Widseth	Minnesota
T	James Steen	Syracuse
T	Slade Cutter	Navy
T	Cash Gentry	Oklahoma
T	Clyde Carter	SMU
G	George Barclay	North Carolina
G	Regis Monahan	Ohio State
G	Ken Ormiston	Pittsburgh
C	Ellmore Patterson	Chicago
C	Elmer Ward	Utah State
C	Elwood Kalbaugh	Princeton

BOWL GAMES

DATE	GAME	SCORE
J1	Rose	Alabama 29, Stanford 13
J1	Sugar	Tulane 20, Temple 14
J1	Orange	Bucknell 26, Miami (Fla.) 0

SEC STANDINGS

	CONFERENCE			OVERALL		
	W	L	T	W	L	T
Tulane	8	0	0	10	1	0
Alabama	7	0	0	10	0	0
Tennessee	5	1	0	8	2	0
LSU	4	2	0	7	2	2
Georgia	3	2	0	7	3	0
Vanderbilt	4	3	0	6	3	0
Florida	2	2	1	6	3	1
Mississippi	2	3	1	4	5	1
Kentucky	1	3	0	5	5	0
Auburn	1	6	0	2	8	0
Mississippi State	0	5	0	4	6	0
Sewanee	0	4	0	2	7	0
Georgia Tech	0	6	0	1	9	0

1935

CONSENSUS ALL-AMERICANS

POS	NAME	SCHOOL
B	Jay Berwanger	Chicago
B	Bobby Grayson	Stanford
B	Bobby Wilson	SMU
B	**Riley Smith**	**Alabama**
E	Wayne Millner	Notre Dame
E	James Moscrip	Stanford
E	**Gaynell Tinsley**	**LSU**
T	Ed Widseth	Minnesota
T	Larry Lutz	California
G	John Weller	Princeton
G	Sidney Wagner	Michigan State
G	J.C. Wetsel	SMU
C	Gomer Jones	Ohio State
C	Darrell Lester	TCU

OTHERS RECEIVING FIRST-TEAM HONORS

POS	NAME	SCHOOL
B	Bill Shakespeare	Notre Dame
B	Ed Goddard	Washington State
B	Sheldon Beise	Minnesota
B	Ozzie Simmons	Iowa
B	Sammy Baugh	TCU
E	Bill Shuler	Army
E	Merle Wendt	Ohio State
T	Dick Smith	Minnesota
T	Truman Spain	SMU
T	Charles Wasicek	Colgate
T	Art Detzel	Pittsburgh
G	Paul Tangora	Northwestern
G	Inwood Smith	Ohio State
G	Ed Michaels	Villanova
G	Dub Wheeler	Oklahoma

HEISMAN TROPHY VOTING

	PLAYER	POS	SCHOOL	TOTAL
1	Jay Berwanger	RB	Chicago	84
2	Monk Meyer	HB	Army	29
3	Bill Shakespeare	HB	Notre Dame	23
4	Pepper Constable	FB	Princeton	20

BOWL GAMES

DATE	GAME	SCORE
J1	Rose	Stanford 7, SMU 0
J1	Sugar	TCU 3, LSU 2
J1	Orange	Catholic 20, Mississippi 19
J1	Sun	Hardin-Simmons 14, New Mexico St. 14

SEC STANDINGS

	CONFERENCE			OVERALL		
	W	L	T	W	L	T
LSU	5	0	0	9	2	0
Vanderbilt	5	1	0	7	3	0
Mississippi	3	1	0	9	3	0
Auburn	5	2	0	8	2	0
Alabama	4	2	0	6	2	1
Tulane	3	3	0	6	4	0
Kentucky	3	3	0	5	4	0
Georgia Tech	3	4	0	5	5	0
Mississippi State	2	3	0	8	3	0
Tennessee	2	3	0	4	5	0
Georgia	2	4	0	6	4	0
Florida	1	6	0	3	7	0
Sewanee	0	6	0	2	7	0

1936

FINAL POLL (NOV. 30)

AP	SCHOOL	FINAL RECORD
1	Minnesota	7-1-0
2	LSU	9-1-1
3	Pittsburgh	8-1-1
4	Alabama	8-0-1
5	Washington	7-2-1
6	Santa Clara	8-1-0
7	Northwestern	7-1-0
8	Notre Dame	6-2-1
9	Nebraska	7-2-0
10	Pennsylvania	7-1-0
11	Duke	9-1-0
12	Yale	7-1-0
13	Dartmouth	7-1-1
14	Duquesne	8-2-0
15	Fordham	5-1-2
16	TCU	9-2-2
17	Tennessee	6-2-2
18	Arkansas	7-3-0
19	Navy	6-3-0
20	Marquette	7-2-0

CONSENSUS ALL-AMERICANS

POS	NAME	SCHOOL
B	Sammy Baugh	TCU
B	Ace Parker	Duke
B	Ray Buivid	Marquette
B	Sam Francis	Nebraska
E	Larry Kelley	Yale
E	Gaynell Tinsley	LSU
T	Ed Widseth	Minnesota
T	Averell Daniell	Pittsburgh
G	Steve Reid	Northwestern
G	Max Starcevich	Washington
C	Alex Wojciechowicz	Fordham
C	Mike Basrak	Duquesne

OTHERS RECEIVING FIRST-TEAM HONORS

POS	NAME	SCHOOL
B	Nello Falaschi	Santa Clara
B	Kent Ryan	Utah State
B	Clint Frank	Yale
B	Jim Cain	Washington
B	Ed Goddard	Washington State
B	Andy Uram	Minnesota
T	Frank Kinard	Mississippi
T	Marcel Chesbro	Colgate
T	Ed Franco	Fordham
G	Joe Routt	Texas A&M
G	Bill Glassford	Pittsburgh
G	Alex Drobnitch	Denver
G	Arthur White	Alabama
G	John Lautar	Notre Dame
C	Bob Herwig	California

HEISMAN TROPHY VOTING

	PLAYER	POS	SCHOOL	TOTAL
1	Larry Kelley	E	Yale	213
2	Sam Francis	FB	Nebraska	47
3	Ray Buivid	HB	Marquette	46
4	Sammy Baugh	QB	TCU	40
5	Clint Frank	QB	Yale	33
6	Ace Parker	HB	Duke	28
7	Ed Widseth	T	Minnesota	25

BOWL GAMES

DATE	GAME	SCORE
J1	Bacardi	Auburn 7, Villanova 7
J1	Rose	Pittsburgh 21, Washington 0
J1	Sugar	Santa Clara 21, LSU 14
J1	Cotton	TCU 16, Marquette 6
J1	Orange	Duquesne 13, Mississippi State 12
J1	Sun	Hardin-Simmons 34, Texas-El Paso 6

SEC STANDINGS

	CONFERENCE			OVERALL		
	W	L	T	W	L	T
LSU	6	0	0	9	1	1
Alabama	5	0	1	8	0	1
Auburn	4	1	1	7	2	2
Tennessee	3	1	2	6	2	2
Mississippi State	3	2	0	7	3	1
Georgia	3	3	0	5	4	1
Georgia Tech	3	3	1	5	5	1
Tulane	2	3	1	6	3	1
Vanderbilt	1	3	1	3	5	1
Kentucky	1	3	0	6	4	0
Florida	1	5	0	4	6	0
Mississippi	0	3	1	5	5	2
Sewanee	0	5	0	0	6	1

1937 NCAA MAJOR COLLEGE STATISTICAL LEADERS

INDIVIDUAL LEADERS

PASSING/COMPLETIONS	G	ATT	COM	PCT	INT	I%	YDS	YDA	COM.PG
1 Davey O'Brien, TCU	10	234	94	40.2	18	7.7	969	4.1	9.4
2 Dwight Sloan, Arkansas	9	164	78	47.6	9	5.5	1074	6.5	8.7
3 Billy Patterson, Baylor	9	196	72	36.7	15	7.7	1109	5.7	8.0
4 Tommy Thompson, Tulsa	10	128	53	41.4	5	3.9	956	7.5	5.3
5 Jack Robbins, Arkansas	8	113	49	43.3	13	11.5	780	6.9	6.1
6 Joseph Gray, Oregon State	7	109	48	44.0	13	11.9	477	4.4	6.9
7 Edward Boell, NYU	8	81	47	58.0	9	11.1	507	6.3	5.9
7 Gene Barnett, Texas Tech	11	120	47	39.2	4	3.3	510	4.3	4.3
9 Frank Filchock, Indiana	8	92	45	48.9	10	10.9	585	6.4	5.6
10 Kenny Washington, UCLA	9	85	41	48.2	6	7.1	390	4.6	4.6

ALL-PURPOSE YARDS	G	RUSH	REC	INT	PR	KR	YDS	TPG
1 Byron "Whizzer" White, Colorado	8	1121	0	103	587	159	1970	246.3

RUSHING/YARDS	G	ATT	YDS	AVG	YPG
1 Byron "Whizzer" White, Colorado	8	181	1121	6.2	140.1
2 Walter Mayberry, Florida	11	164	818	5.0	74.4
3 Bob Holmes, Texas Tech	11	142	760	5.4	69.1
4 Elmer Tarbox, Texas Tech	11	126	737	5.8	67.0
5 Marshall Goldberg, Pittsburgh	10	115	701	6.1	70.1
6 Clint Frank, Yale	8	157	667	4.2	83.4
7 Dick Cassiano, Pittsburgh	10	69	620	9.0	62.0
8 Charlie Holm, Alabama	9	117	607	5.2	67.4
9 Ambrose Schindler, Southern California	10	134	599	4.5	59.9
10 Eric Tipton, Duke	10	125	594	4.8	59.4
10 Joe Kilgrow, Alabama	9	128	594	4.6	66.0

RUSHING/YARDS PER CARRY	G	ATT	YDS	YPC
1 Dick Cassiano, Pittsburgh	10	69	620	9.0
2 George Cafego, Tennessee	10	72	501	7.0
3 Byron "Whizzer" White, Colorado	8	181	1121	6.2
4 Marshall Goldberg, Pittsburgh	10	115	701	6.1
5 Harold Van Every, Minnesota	8	88	526	6.0
6 Elmer Tarbox, Texas Tech	11	126	737	5.8
7 Elmore Hackney, Duke	10	85	490	5.8
8 Bob Holmes, Texas Tech	11	142	760	5.4
9 Charlie Holm, Alabama	9	117	607	5.2
10 Johnny Pingel, Michigan State	9	116	590	5.1

Based on top 30 rushers

RECEIVING/RECEPTIONS	G	REC	YDS	YPR	YPG	RPG
1 Jim Benton, Arkansas	10	48	814	17.0	81.4	4.8
2 Ray Hamilton, Arkansas	10	29	306	10.6	30.6	2.9
3 Herschel Ramsey, Texas Tech	11	27	337	12.5	30.6	2.5
4 Sam Boyd, Baylor	9	23	365	15.9	40.6	2.6
5 Harry Shorten, NYU	9	23	323	14.0	35.9	2.6
6 Johnny Hall, TCU	9	21	203	9.7	22.6	2.3
7 Jack Robbins, Arkansas	8	20	361	18.1	45.1	2.5
8 Walter Nelson, Michigan State	9	18	388	21.6	43.1	2.0
8 Frank Steen, Rice	10	18	263	14.6	26.3	1.8
8 Don Looney, TCU	10	18	181	10.1	18.1	1.8

PUNTING	PUNT	YDS	AVG
1 Johnny Pingel, Michigan State	49	2101	42.9
2 Byron "Whizzer" White, Colorado	63	2679	42.5
3 Jerry Dowd, St. Mary's (Cal.)	91	3851	42.3
4 Joe Woitkowski, Fordham	36	1521	42.3
5 Ray King, Minnesota	21	883	42.1
6 George Cafego, Tennessee	59	2480	42.0
7 Eric Tipton, Duke	90	3656	40.6
8 Larry Atwell, Brown	30	1213	40.4
9 Bob Bailey, Clemson	53	2120	40.0
10 James Fenton, Auburn	60	2400	40.0

SCORING	TDS	XPT	FG	PTS
1 Byron "Whizzer" White, Colorado	16	23	1	122
2 Andy Farkas, Detroit	19	0	1	117
3 William Tranavitch, Rutgers	13	12	0	90
4 Victor Bottari, California	12	0	0	72
5 Clint Frank, Yale	11	0	0	66
6 Paul Shu, VMI	9	11	0	65
7 Elmore Hackney, Duke	9	10	0	64
8 Walter Nielsen, Arizona	8	9	2	63
9 Harry Clark, West Virginia	10	0	0	60
9 William Osmanski, Holy Cross	10	0	0	60

TEAM LEADERS

RUSHING OFFENSE	G	YDS	YPG
1 Colorado	8	2480	310.0
2 North Carolina	9	2285	253.9
3 Pittsburgh	10	2530	253.0
4 Tulane	10	2401	240.1
5 Minnesota	8	1887	235.9
5 Harvard	8	1887	235.9
7 Texas Tech	11	2538	230.7
8 Alabama	9	1992	221.3
9 California	10	2210	221.0
10 Navy	9	1973	219.2

PASSING OFFENSE	G	ATT	COM	INT	PCT	YDS	YPA	YPG	I%	YPC
1 Arkansas	10	310	136	30	43.9	1850	6.0	185.0	9.7	13.6
2 TCU	10	244	99	20	40.6	1005	4.1	100.5	8.2	10.2
3 NYU	9	171	85	18	49.7	1097	6.4	121.9	10.5	12.9
4 Columbia	9	181	83	14	45.9	1070	5.9	118.9	7.7	12.9
5 Baylor	9	201	79	20	39.3	1223	6.1	135.9	10.0	15.5
6 SMU	11	203	74	30	36.9	1053	5.2	95.7	14.8	14.2
7 Southern California	10	143	64	14	44.8	751	5.3	75.1	9.8	11.7
8 Tulsa	10	163	63	14	38.7	1149	7.0	114.9	8.6	18.2
9 Oklahoma	9	125	61	10	48.8	528	4.2	58.7	8.0	8.7
9 Texas Tech	11	170	61	14	35.9	643	3.8	58.5	8.2	10.5

Ranking based on number of completions

TOTAL OFFENSE	G	YDS	YPG
1 Colorado	8	3003	375.4
2 North Carolina	9	2933	325.9
3 Minnesota	8	2428	303.5
4 Harvard	8	2427	303.4
5 NYU	9	2699	299.9
6 Fordham	8	2355	294.4
7 Navy	9	2642	293.6
8 Texas Tech	11	3181	289.2
9 Pittsburgh	10	2864	286.4
10 Arkansas	10	2823	282.3

RUSHING DEFENSE	G	YDS	YPG
1 Santa Clara	8	202	25.3
2 Pittsburgh	10	405	40.5
3 Washington	9	445	49.4
4 Oklahoma	9	536	59.6
5 Dartmouth	6	367	61.2
6 Illinois	8	520	65.0
6 Ohio State	8	520	65.0
8 Michigan State	9	588	65.3
9 Alabama	9	589	65.4
10 Tulane	10	667	66.7

PASSING DEFENSE	G	ATT	COM	PCT	YPC	INT	I%	YDS	YPA	YPG
1 Harvard	8	81	16	19.8	15.5	11	13.6	248	3.1	31.0
2 Chicago	5	49	13	26.5	13.2	11	22.4	171	3.5	34.2
3 Michigan State	9	85	24	28.2	12.9	13	15.3	310	3.6	34.4
4 Iowa State	5	57	12	21.1	15.8	14	24.6	190	3.3	38.0
5 Oklahoma	9	95	31	32.6	11.3	15	15.8	349	3.7	38.8
6 Clemson	9	83	27	32.5	13.2	13	15.7	356	4.3	39.6
7 Princeton	8	94	26	27.7	12.2	13	13.8	318	3.4	39.8
8 California	10	134	39	29.1	10.5	24	17.9	410	3.1	41.0
9 Florida	11	124	39	31.5	12.1	16	12.9	472	3.8	42.9
10 Marquette	9	94	27	28.7	14.7	15	16.0	396	4.2	44.0

Based on 37 teams whose opponents had the lowest pass completion percentage

TOTAL DEFENSE	G	YDS	YPG
1 Santa Clara	8	559	69.9
2 Pittsburgh	10	928	92.8
3 Oklahoma	9	885	98.3
4 Michigan State	9	898	99.8
5 Washington	9	947	105.2
6 Dartmouth	6	672	112.0
7 California	10	1126	112.6
8 Ohio State	8	924	115.5
9 Alabama	9	1042	115.8
10 Tulane	10	1167	116.7

SCORING OFFENSE	G	PTS	AVG
1 Colorado	8	248	31.0

SCORING DEFENSE	G	PTS	AVG
1 Santa Clara	8	9	1.1

1937

FINAL POLL (NOV. 29)

AP	SCHOOL	FINAL RECORD
1	Pittsburgh	9-0-1
2	California	10-0-1
3	Fordham	7-0-1
4	**Alabama**	**9-1-0**
5	Minnesota	6-2-0
6	Villanova	8-0-1
7	Dartmouth	7-0-2
8	**LSU**	**9-2-0**
9	Notre Dame	6-2-1
9	Santa Clara	9-0-0
11	Nebraska	6-1-2
12	Yale	6-1-1
13	Ohio State	6-2-0
14	Arkansas	6-2-2
14	Holy Cross	8-0-2
15	TCU	4-4-2
17	Colorado	8-1-0
18	Rice	6-3-2
19	North Carolina	7-1-1
20	Duke	7-2-1

SEC STANDINGS

	Conference			Overall		
	W	L	T	W	L	T
Alabama	6	0	0	9	1	0
LSU	5	1	0	9	2	0
Auburn	4	1	2	6	2	3
Vanderbilt	4	2	0	7	2	0
Mississippi State	3	2	0	5	4	1
Georgia Tech	3	2	1	6	3	1
Tennessee	4	3	0	6	3	1
Florida	3	4	0	4	7	0
Tulane	2	3	1	5	4	1
Georgia	1	2	2	6	3	2
Mississippi	0	4	0	4	5	1
Kentucky	0	5	0	4	6	0
Sewanee	0	6	0	2	7	0

CONSENSUS ALL-AMERICANS

POS	NAME	SCHOOL
B	Clint Frank	Yale
B	Marshall Goldberg	Pittsburgh
B	Byron "Whizzer" White	Colorado
B	Sam Chapman	California
E	Chuck Sweeney	Notre Dame
E	Andy Bershak	North Carolina
T	Ed Franco	Fordham
T	Tony Matisi	Pittsburgh
G	Joe Routt	Texas A&M
G	**Leroy Monsky**	**Alabama**
C	Alex Wojciechowicz	Fordham

OTHERS RECEIVING FIRST-TEAM HONORS

B	Corby Davis	Indiana
B	**Joe Kilgrow**	**Alabama**
B	George Karamatic	Gonzaga
E	Perry Schwartz	California
E	Ray King	Minnesota
E	Brud Holland	Cornell
E	John Wysocki	Villanova
E	Frank Souchak	Pittsburgh
E	Jim Benton	Arkansas
E	Bill Daddio	Pittsburgh
T	Ed Beinor	Notre Dame
T	Vic Markov	Washington
T	**Frank Kinard**	**Mississippi**
T	J.B. Hale	TCU
T	Al Babartsky	Fordham
T	Fred Shirey	Nebraska
G	Gus Zarnas	Ohio State
G	Phil Dougherty	Santa Clara
G	Vard Stockton	California
C	**Carl Hinkle**	**Vanderbilt**
C	Charles Brock	Nebraska
C	Bob Herwig	California

HEISMAN TROPHY VOTING

	PLAYER	POS	SCHOOL	TOTAL
1	Clint Frank	QB	Yale	524
2	Byron "Whizzer" White	HB	Colorado	264
3	Marshall Goldberg	RB	Pittsburgh	211
4	Alex Wojciechowicz	C/LB	Fordham	85

AWARD WINNERS

PLAYER	AWARD
Clint Frank, HB, Yale	Maxwell

BOWL GAMES

DATE	GAME	SCORE
J1	**Orange**	**Auburn 6, Michigan State 0**
J1	**Rose**	**California 13, Alabama 0**
J1	Cotton	Rice 28, Colorado 14
J1	**Sugar**	**Santa Clara 6, LSU 0**
J1	Sun	West Virginia 7, Texas Tech 6

1938 NCAA Major College Statistical Leaders

Individual Leaders

PASSING/COMPLETIONS

		G	ATT	COM	PCT	INT	I%	YDS	YDA	COM.PG
1	Davey O'Brien, TCU	10	167	93	55.7	4	2.4	1457	8.7	9.3
2	Billy Patterson, Baylor	10	206	84	40.8	17	8.3	1334	6.5	8.4
3	Hugh McCullough, Oklahoma	10	111	70	63.1	6	5.4	647	5.8	7.0
4	Sid Luckman, Columbia	9	132	66	50.0	8	6.1	856	6.5	7.3
5	Lemuel Cooke, Navy	9	122	63	51.6	7	5.7	815	6.7	7.0
5	Paul Christman, Missouri	9	145	63	43.4	19	13.1	1087	7.5	7.0
7	Johnny Pingel, Michigan State	9	101	54	53.5	NA	NA	571	5.7	6.0
7	Everett Kischer, Iowa State	9	107	54	50.5	8	7.5	653	6.1	6.0
9	**Parker Hall, Mississippi**	11	99	51	51.5	6	6.1	860	8.7	4.6
10	Gilbert Humphrey, Yale	8	104	49	47.1	8	7.7	603	5.8	6.1

ALL-PURPOSE YARDS

		G	RUSH	REC	INT	PR	KR	YDS	YPG
1	**Parker Hall, Mississippi**	11	698	0	128	0	594	1420	129.1

RUSHING/YARDS

		G	ATT	YDS	AVG	YPG
1	Len Eshmont, Fordham	9	132	831	6.3	92.3
2	Dick Cassiano, Pittsburgh	10	141	742	5.3	74.2
3	**Parker Hall, Mississippi**	11	108	698	6.5	63.5
4	Dominic Principe, Fordham	9	121	692	5.7	76.9
5	Bob O'Mara, Duke	9	156	685	4.4	76.1
6	**Warren Brunner, Tulane**	10	136	662	4.9	66.2
7	Elmer Tarbox, Texas Tech	10	127	637	5.0	63.7
8	Harold Stebbins, Pittsburgh	10	136	616	4.5	61.6
9	Victor Bottari, California	11	159	578	3.6	52.5
10	Kenny Washington, UCLA	10	147	573	3.9	57.3

RUSHING/YARDS PER CARRY

		G	ATT	YDS	YPC
1	**Parker Hall, Mississippi**	11	108	698	6.5
2	George Muha, Carnegie Tech	7	81	514	6.3
3	Len Eshmont, Fordham	9	132	831	6.3
4	Dominic Principe, Fordham	9	121	692	5.7
5	Dick Cassiano, Pittsburgh	10	141	742	5.3
6	Henry Wilder, Iowa State	9	105	545	5.2
7	Johnny Pingel, Michigan State	9	110	556	5.0
7	Elmer Tarbox, Texas Tech	10	127	637	5.0
9	Dick Todd, Texas A&M	9	99	493	5.0
10	**Warren Brunner, Tulane**	10	136	662	4.9

Based on top 20 rushers

RECEIVING/RECEPTIONS

		G	REC	YDS	YPR	YPG	RPG
1	Sam Boyd, Baylor	10	32	537	16.8	53.7	3.2
2	Charles Heileman, Iowa State	9	29	320	11.0	35.6	3.2
3	Bill Dewell, SMU	10	26	437	16.8	43.7	2.6
4	James Starmer, Missouri	9	25	437	17.5	48.6	2.8
5	Michael Lukac, Temple	10	23	350	15.2	35.0	2.3
5	Bill Jennings, Oklahoma	10	23	217	9.4	21.7	2.3
7	Earle Clark, TCU	10	22	411	18.7	41.1	2.2
8	Eugene Corrotto, Oklahoma	10	21	188	9.0	18.8	2.1
9	Bud Orf, Missouri	9	18	218	12.1	24.2	2.0
10	Elmer Tarbox, Texas Tech*	10	17	364	21.4	36.4	1.7

* Six players tied for number of receptions, but Tarbox had the most yardage

PUNTING

		PUNT	YDS	AVG
1	Jerry Dowd, St. Mary's (Cal.)	62	2711	43.7
2	Johnny Pingel, Michigan State	99	4138	41.8
3	**Neil Cavette, Georgia Tech**	46	1909	41.5
4	Nile Kinnick, Iowa	41	1686	41.1
5	Kay Eakin, Arkansas	41	1683	41.1
6	George Stirnweiss, North Carolina	60	2455	40.9
7	Carl Nery, Duquesne	49	1985	40.5
8	Eric Tipton, Duke	59	2378	40.3
9	Michael Kabealo, Ohio State	42	1692	40.3
10	**Dick McGowen, Auburn**	55	2214	40.3

PUNT AND KICKOFF RETURNS/YARDS

		RET	YDS	AVG
1	**Parker Hall, Mississippi**	32	594	18.6
2	Spec Kelly, Auburn	31	559	18.0
3	Dick Todd, Texas A&M	32	506	15.8
4	Billy Patterson, Baylor	37	488	13.2
5	Shad Bryant, Clemson	27	487	18.0
6	Davey O'Brien, TCU	37	458	12.4
7	Grenny Lansdell, Southern California	27	438	16.2
8	Tony Canadeo, Gonzaga	25	432	17.3
9	**Warren Brunner, Tulane**	28	416	14.9
10	Mike Klotovich, St. Mary's (Cal.)	28	393	14.0

SCORING

		TDS	XPT	FG	PTS
1	**Parker Hall, Mississippi**	11	7	0	73
2	Irving Hall, Brown	10	9	0	69
3	Dick Cassiano, Pittsburgh	11	0	0	66
4	Victor Bottari, California	8	13	0	61
5	William Osmanski, Holy Cross	10	0	0	60
5	Connie Sparks, TCU	10	0	0	60
5	Elmer Tarbox, Texas Tech	10	0	0	60
8	Bill Hutchinson, Dartmouth	7	12	1	57
9	Charles Long, Army	6	14	0	50
10	Seven tied	–	–	–	48

INTERCEPTIONS

		INT	YDS
1	Elmer Tarbox, Texas Tech	11	89
2	**Parker Hall, Mississippi**	7	128
3	Russell Busk, Iowa	6	98
3	Davey O'Brien, TCU	6	86
3	Otis Rogers, Oklahoma	6	47
3	Nile Kinnick, Iowa	6	39
3	George Watson, North Carolina	6	36
3	Dudley Akins, Texas Tech*	5	117
8	**Bill Schneller, Mississippi***	5	110
8	Val Boehm, Xavier*	5	67

* Six tied with five; these three players had the most yards

Team Leaders

RUSHING OFFENSE

		G	ATT	YDS	AVG	YPG
1	Fordham	9	567	2674	4.7	297.1
2	**Tulane**	10	547	2541	4.6	254.1
3	Penn State	8	397	2012	5.1	251.5
4	Carnegie Tech	7	341	1751	5.1	250.1
5	Texas Tech	10	470	2501	5.3	250.1
6	Dartmouth	7	323	1663	5.1	237.6
7	Pittsburgh	10	543	2280	4.2	228.0
8	Army	10	422	2196	5.2	219.6
9	Minnesota	8	452	1717	3.8	214.6
10	Brown	8	383	1705	4.5	213.1

PASSING OFFENSE/YPG

		G	ATT	COM	INT	PCT	YDS	YPA	YPG	I%	YPC
1	TCU	10	201	108	7	53.7	1641	8.2	164.1	3.5	15.2
2	Yale	8	196	92	15	46.9	1080	5.5	135.0	7.7	11.7
3	Missouri	9	172	79	23	45.9	1215	7.1	135.0	13.4	15.4
4	Baylor	10	216	86	18	39.8	1349	6.2	134.9	8.3	15.7
5	Arkansas	9	250	78	34	31.2	1169	4.7	129.9	13.6	15.0
6	SMU	10	203	71	26	36.9	1282	6.3	128.2	10.3	17.1
7	Navy	9	202	87	16	43.1	1132	5.6	125.8	7.9	13.0
8	Chicago	7	161	60	17	37.3	841	5.2	120.1	10.6	14.0
9	NYU	8	183	78	17	42.6	921	5.0	115.1	9.3	11.8
10	Oklahoma	10	213	108	16	50.7	1082	5.1	108.2	7.5	10.0

TOTAL OFFENSE

		G	P	YDS	AVG	YPG
1	Fordham	9	649	3074	4.7	341.6
2	TCU	10	677	3332	4.9	333.2
3	Texas Tech	10	570	3266	5.7	326.6
4	Army	10	579	3243	5.6	324.3
5	Dartmouth	7	405	2133	5.3	304.7
6	Missouri	9	563	2716	4.8	301.8
7	NYU	8	515	2404	4.7	300.5
8	Navy	9	599	2635	4.4	292.8
9	Carnegie Tech	7	384	2046	5.3	292.3
10	**Tulane**	10	606	2898	4.8	289.8

RUSHING DEFENSE

		G	ATT	YDS	AVG	YPG
1	Oklahoma	10	285	433	1.5	43.3
2	**Alabama**	7	219	319	1.5	45.6
3	Duke	9	253	508	2.0	56.4
4	Georgetown	6	234	353	1.5	58.8
5	Santa Clara	8	272	485	1.8	60.6
6	Southern California	10	340	640	1.9	64.0
7	Fordham	9	303	597	2.0	66.3
8	Carnegie Tech	6	208	485	2.3	80.8
9	Cornell	7	241	586	2.4	83.7
10	Xavier	8	281	678	2.4	84.8

PASSING DEFENSE

		G	ATT	COM	PCT	YPC	INT	I%	YDS	YPA	YPG
1	Penn State	8	59	10	16.9	10.5	14	23.7	105	1.8	13.1
2	Colgate	7	62	14	22.6	13.1	4	6.5	184	3.0	26.3
3	Lafayette	8	67	24	35.8	9.8	14	20.9	236	3.5	29.5
4	**Alabama**	7	61	18	29.5	12.6	13	21.3	226	3.7	32.3
5	**Georgia Tech**	6	51	16	31.4	13.3	5	9.8	212	4.2	35.3
6	Fordham	9	120	31	25.8	11.2	17	14.2	348	2.9	38.7
7	Idaho	6	69	13	18.8	18.8	13	18.8	244	3.5	40.7
8	Bucknell	8	68	25	36.8	13.4	9	13.2	334	4.9	41.8
9	Carnegie Tech	6	53	15	28.3	17.3	14	26.4	260	4.9	43.3
10	**Vanderbilt**	9	77	32	41.6	12.3	7	9.1	395	5.1	43.9

TOTAL DEFENSE

		G	P	YDS	AVG	YPG
1	**Alabama**	7	280	545	1.9	77.9
2	Oklahoma	10	457	966	2.1	96.6
3	Fordham	9	423	945	2.2	105.0
4	Duke	9	336	961	2.9	106.8
5	Georgetown	6	321	652	2.0	108.7
6	Southern California	10	481	1113	2.3	111.3
7	Santa Clara	8	412	962	2.3	120.3
8	Carnegie Tech	6	261	745	2.9	124.2
9	Xavier	8	388	1129	2.9	141.1
10	Lafayette	8	373	1130	3.0	141.3

SCORING OFFENSE

		G	PTS	AVG
1	Dartmouth	9	254	28.2
2	**Tennessee**	10	276	27.6
3	Texas Tech	10	274	27.4

Based on top 15 teams in winning percentage

SCORING DEFENSE

		G	PTS	AVG
1	Duke	9	0	0.0
2	Oklahoma	10	12	1.2
3	**Tennessee**	10	16	1.6

Based on top 15 teams in winning percentage

1938

Final Poll (Dec. 5)

AP	SCHOOL	FINAL RECORD
1	TCU	11-0-0
2	**Tennessee**	**11-0-0**
3	Duke	9-1-0
4	Oklahoma	10-1-0
5	Notre Dame	8-1-0
6	Carnegie Tech	7-2-0
7	Southern California	9-2-0
8	Pittsburgh	8-2-0
9	Holy Cross	8-1-0
10	Minnesota	6-2-0
11	Texas Tech	10-1-0
12	Cornell	5-1-1
13	**Alabama**	**7-1-1**
14	California	10-1-0
15	Fordham	6-1-2
16	Michigan	6-1-1
17	Northwestern	4-2-2
18	Villanova	8-0-1
19	**Tulane**	**7-2-1**
20	Dartmouth	7-2-0

Consensus All-Americans

POS	NAME	SCHOOL
B	Davey O'Brien	TCU
B	Marshall Goldberg	Pittsburgh
B	Bob MacLeod	Dartmouth
B	Vic Bottari	California
E	Waddy Young	Oklahoma
E	Brud Holland	Cornell
E	**Bowden Wyatt**	**Tennessee**
T	Ed Beinor	Notre Dame
T	Alvord Wolff	Santa Clara
G	Ralph Heikkinen	Michigan
G	Ed Bock	Iowa State
C	Ki Aldrich	TCU

Others receiving first-team honors

POS	NAME	SCHOOL
B	**Parker Hall**	**Mississippi**
B	Johnny Pingel	Michigan State
B	Howard Weiss	Wisconsin
B	**George Cafego**	**Tennessee**
B	Sid Luckman	Columbia
B	Eric Tipton	Duke
E	Earl Brown	Notre Dame
E	John Wysocki	Villanova
E	Bill Daddio	Pittsburgh
T	Bob Voigts	Northwestern
T	Bill McKeever	Cornell
T	I.B. Hale	TCU
G	Harry Smith	Southern California
G	Sid Roth	Cornell
G	Francis Twedell	Minnesota
G	**Bob Suffridge**	**Tennessee**
C	Dan Hill	Duke

Heisman Trophy Voting

	PLAYER	POS	SCHOOL	TOTAL
1	Davey O'Brien	QB	TCU	519
2	Marshall Goldberg	RB	Pittsburgh	294
3	Sid Luckman	QB	Columbia	154
4	Bob MacLeod	HB	Dartmouth	78
5	Vic Bottari	RB	California	67
6	Howard Weiss	FB	Wisconsin	60
7	**Geroge Cafego**	**TB**	**Tennessee**	**55**
8	Ki Aldrich	C	TCU	48
9	Whitey Beinor	TB	Notre Dame	47
10	Dan Hill	C	Duke	38

Award Winners

PLAYER	AWARD
Davey O'Brien, QB, TCU	Maxwell

Bowl Games

DATE	GAME	SCORE
J2	Rose	Southern California 7, Duke 3
J2	**Orange**	**Tennessee 17, Oklahoma 0**
J2	Sugar	TCU 15, Carnegie Mellon 7
J2	Sun	Utah 26, New Mexico 0
J2	Cotton	St. Mary's (Cal.) 20, Texas Tech 13

SEC Standings

	CONFERENCE			OVERALL		
	W	L	T	W	L	T
Tennessee	7	0	0	11	0	0
Alabama	4	1	1	7	1	1
Tulane	4	1	1	7	2	1
Mississippi	3	2	0	9	2	0
Georgia Tech	2	1	3	3	4	3
Vanderbilt	4	3	0	6	3	0
Auburn	3	3	1	4	5	1
Florida	2	2	1	4	6	1
Georgia	1	2	1	5	4	1
LSU	2	4	0	6	4	0
Mississippi State	1	4	0	4	6	0
Kentucky	0	4	0	2	7	0
Sewanee	0	6	0	1	8	0

1939 NCAA MAJOR COLLEGE STATISTICAL LEADERS

INDIVIDUAL LEADERS

PASSING/COMPLETIONS	G	ATT	COM	PCT	INT	I%	YDS	YPA	COM.PG
1 Kay Eakin, Arkansas	10	193	78	40.4	18	9.3	962	5.0	7.8
2 Paul Christman, Missouri	9	136	63	46.3	12	8.8	677	5.0	7.0
3 Doc Plunkett, Vanderbilt	10	163	61	37.4	19	11.7	867	5.3	6.1
4 Harold Hursh, Indiana	8	125	59	47.2	11	8.8	913	7.3	7.4
5 Charles Edwards, Citadel	11	108	53	49.1	10	9.3	602	5.6	4.8
6 Glenn Cowart, TCU	10	110	51	46.4	5	4.6	639	5.8	5.1
7 Jim Lalanne, North Carolina	10	96	50	52.1	11	11.5	602	6.3	5.0
7 Ernie Lain, Rice	11	122	50	41.0	8	6.6	580	4.8	4.5
9 Edward Boell, NYU	8	87	45	51.7	12	13.8	431	5.0	5.6
10 Marion Pugh, Texas A&M	10	84	43	51.2	10	11.9	458	5.5	4.3

ALL-PURPOSE YARDS	G	RUSH	REC	INT	PR	KR	YDS	YPG
Tom Harmon, Michigan	8	868	110	98	0	132	1208	151.0

RUSHING/YARDS	G	ATT	YDS	AVG	YPG
1 John Polanski, Wake Forest	10	137	882	6.4	88.2
2 Tom Harmon, Michigan	8	129	868	6.7	108.5
3 Kenny Washington, UCLA	10	168	811	4.8	81.1
4 Red Mayberry, Wake Forest	10	148	784	5.3	78.4
5 Johnny Knolla, Creighton	9	106	720	6.8	80.0
6 Harold Van Every, Minnesota	8	132	676	5.1	84.5
7 Grenny Lansdell, Southern California	9	136	675	5.0	75.0
8 John Black, Arizona	10	173	630	3.6	63.0
9 Tony Gallovich, Wake Forest	10	100	622	6.2	62.2
10 Jack Crain, Texas	9	92	610	6.6	67.8

RUSHING/YARDS PER CARRY	G	ATT	YDS	YPC
1 Jackie Robinson, UCLA	10	42	514	12.2
2 Jim Strausbaugh, Ohio State	8	71	526	7.4
3 Harvey Johnson, Mississippi State	10	87	592	6.8
3 Johnny Knolla, Creighton	9	106	720	6.8
5 Tom Harmon, Michigan	8	129	868	6.7
6 Jack Crain, Texas	9	92	610	6.6
7 John Polanski, Wake Forest	10	137	882	6.4
8 Tony Gallovich, Wake Forest	10	100	622	6.2
9 George McAfee, Duke	9	96	596	6.2
10 Red Mayberry, Wake Forest	10	148	784	5.3

Based on top 20 rushers

RECEIVING/RECEPTIONS	G	REC	YDS	YPR	YPG	RPG
1 Ken Kavanaugh, LSU	9	30	467	15.6	51.9	3.3
2 Don Looney, TCU	10	29	405	14.0	40.5	2.9
3 Robert David, Citadel	11	28	360	12.9	32.7	2.5
4 George Radman, North Carolina	10	25	247	9.9	24.7	2.5
5 Joe Anderson, Vanderbilt	10	23	181	7.9	18.1	2.3
6 Bill Jennings, Oklahoma	9	21	244	11.6	27.1	2.3
7 Earle Clark, TCU	10	19	328	17.3	32.8	1.9
7 Ed Hiestand, Vanderbilt	10	19	289	15.2	28.9	1.9
7 Durwood Horner, TCU	10	19	224	11.8	22.4	1.9
10 Ralph Atwood, Arkansas	10	18	183	10.2	18.3	1.8

PUNTING	PUNT	YDS	AVG
1 Harry Dunkle, North Carolina	37	1725	46.6
2 Stanley Nyhan, Tulane	38	1692	44.5
3 Charley Boswell, Alabama	38	1643	43.2
4 Neil Cavette, Georgia Tech	31	1336	43.1
5 Dick McGowen, Auburn	92	3959	43.0
6 Banks McFadden, Clemson	56	2393	42.7
7 Bill Sewell, Washington State	38	1620	42.6
8 Nelson Catlett, VMI	47	1992	42.4
9 Herschel Mosley, Alabama	51	2143	42.0
10 Charles O'Rourke, Boston College	47	1950	41.5

PUNT RETURNS/YARDS	PR	YDS	AVG
1 Bosh Pritchard, VMI	42	583	13.9
2 Derace Moser, Texas A&M	24	404	16.8
3 Dick McGowen, Auburn	37	379	10.2
4 George McAfee, Duke	37	365	9.9
5 Olie Cordill, Rice	26	351	13.5
6 William Conatser, Texas A&M	24	339	14.1
7 George Kiick, Bucknell	36	334	9.3
8 Ernie Steele, Washington	26	318	12.2
9 Jack Crain, Texas	17	317	18.6
10 Red Mayberry, Wake Forest	34	300	8.8

KICKOFF RETURNS/YARDS	KR	YDS	AVG
1 Nile Kinnick, Iowa	15	377	25.1
2 Red Mayberry, Wake Forest	8	328	41.0
3 Winfred Bynum, Centenary	9	287	31.9
4 George Clay, Tulane	6	229	38.2
5 Johnny Knolla, Creighton	10	216	21.6
6 R. H. Miller, Chicago	12	212	17.7
7 Melvin Seelye, Kansas State	10	210	21.0
8 Harold Van Every, Minnesota	8	198	24.8
9 Bob Olson, Oregon State	5	186	37.2
10 Jim Groves, Stanford	7	181	25.9

SCORING	TDS	XPT	FG	PTS
1 Tom Harmon, Michigan	14	15	1	102
2 John Polanski, Wake Forest	13	6	0	84
3 Vito Ananis, Boston College	12	1	0	73
4 Harvey Johnson, Mississippi State	10	2	0	62
5 John Kimbrough, Texas A&M	10	0	0	60
6 Jack Crain, Texas	8	8	0	56
7 Bobby Kellogg, Tulane	8	7	0	55
8 Ray Hare, Gonzaga	8	6	0	54
8 Ken Kavanaugh, LSU	9	0	0	54
8 Grenny Lansdell, Southern California	9	0	0	54
8 Red Mayberry, Wake Forest	9	0	0	54

INTERCEPTIONS	INT	YDS
1 Harold Van Every, Minnesota	8	59
1 Nile Kinnick, Iowa	8	52
3 Bosh Pritchard, VMI	7	199
3 John Black, Arizona	7	69
5 Dick McGowen, Auburn	6	134
5 Thomas Harrison, Florida	6	68
5 Pete Cignetti, Boston College	6	41
5 Kay Eakin, Arkansas	6	40
5 Hal McCullough, Cornell	6	3
10 Ray Portillo, Oklahoma State*	5	114

* Nine tied with five; Portillo had the most yards

TEAM LEADERS

RUSHING OFFENSE	G	ATT	YDS	AVG	YPG
1 Wake Forest	10	516	2903	5.6	290.3
2 Tulane	9	573	2348	4.1	260.9
3 Tennessee	10	510	2553	5.0	255.3
4 Minnesota	8	470	1891	4.0	236.4
5 Boston College	10	460	2236	4.9	223.6
6 Clemson	9	436	1972	4.5	219.1
7 Cornell	8	391	1726	4.4	215.8
8 Ohio State	8	380	1711	4.5	213.9
9 Mississippi	9	399	1890	4.7	210.0
10 Brown	9	414	1861	4.5	206.8

PASSING OFFENSE/YPG	G	ATT	COM	INT	PCT	YDS	YPA	YPG	I%	YPC
1 TCU	10	245	120	16	49.0	1485	6.1	148.5	6.5	12.4
2 Princeton	8	153	67	12	43.8	1055	6.9	131.9	7.8	15.7
3 Indiana	8	142	69	14	48.6	1032	7.3	129.0	9.9	15.0
4 Vanderbilt	10	214	84	22	39.3	1146	5.4	114.6	10.3	13.6
5 Southern California	9	183	84	12	45.9	1008	5.5	112.0	6.6	12.0
6 Lehigh	9	176	65	17	36.9	989	5.6	109.9	9.7	15.2
7 Arkansas	10	242	91	25	37.6	1091	4.5	109.1	10.3	12.0
8 Oregon	8	137	58	11	42.3	866	6.3	108.3	8.0	14.9
9 LSU	9	159	67	16	42.1	918	5.8	102.0	10.1	13.7
10 Kansas	7	121	51	12	42.1	708	5.9	101.1	9.9	13.9

TOTAL OFFENSE	G	P	YDS	AVG	YPG
1 Ohio State	8	514	2474	4.8	309.3
2 Tennessee	10	590	3083	5.2	308.3
3 Mississippi	9	519	2770	5.3	307.8
4 Southern California	9	606	2763	4.6	307.0
5 Wake Forest	10	563	3062	5.4	306.2
6 Creighton	9	583	2692	4.6	299.1
7 Boston College	10	565	2990	5.3	299.0
8 Brown	9	549	2663	4.9	295.9
9 Cornell	8	481	2354	4.9	294.3
10 Minnesota	8	544	2296	4.2	287.0

RUSHING DEFENSE	G	ATT	YDS	AVG	YPG
1 San Jose State	13	387	444	1.2	34.2
2 Texas A&M	10	272	415	1.5	41.5
3 Boston College	10	294	583	2.0	58.3
4 Tulane	9	287	547	1.9	60.8
5 Tennessee	10	331	631	1.9	63.1
6 Georgetown	5	190	327	1.7	65.4
7 Southern California	9	291	649	2.2	72.1
8 Mississippi	9	302	675	2.2	75.0
9 Santa Clara	9	328	703	2.1	78.1
10 Baylor	10	306	804	2.6	80.4

PASSING DEFENSE	G	ATT	COM	PCT	YPC	INT	I%	YDS	YPA	YPG
1 Kansas	7	77	25	32.5	9.6	6	7.8	239	3.1	34.1
2 Texas A&M	10	175	48	27.4	7.3	28	16.0	348	2.0	34.8
3 Xavier	9	83	19	22.9	16.5	12	14.5	314	3.8	34.9
4 Clemson	9	86	28	32.6	11.9	13	15.1	333	3.9	37.0
5 San Jose State	13	195	45	23.1	10.7	29	14.9	483	2.5	37.2
6 Tennessee	10	128	49	38.3	8.0	22	17.2	392	3.1	39.2
7 VMI	10	143	42	29.4	9.6	16	11.2	402	2.8	40.2
8 Pittsburgh	9	96	31	32.3	12.2	15	15.6	379	3.9	42.1
9 Princeton	8	86	28	32.6	12.3	15	15.1	345	4.0	43.1
10 Georgia	7	68	24	35.3	12.7	10	14.7	304	4.5	43.4

TOTAL DEFENSE	G	P	YDS	AVG	YPG
1 San Jose State	13	582	927	1.6	71.3
2 Texas A&M	10	447	763	1.7	76.3
3 Tennessee	10	459	1023	2.2	102.3
4 Boston College	10	454	1029	2.3	102.9
5 Georgetown	5	258	591	2.3	118.2
6 Arizona	10	537	1333	2.5	133.3
7 Southern California	9	439	1228	2.8	136.4
8 Florida	11	529	1505	2.8	136.8
9 Xavier	9	419	1245	3.0	138.3
10 Manhattan	5	262	698	2.7	139.6

SCORING OFFENSE	G	PTS	AVG
1 Utah	9	256	28.4

SCORING DEFENSE	G	PTS	AVG
1 Tennessee	10	0	0.0

ANNUAL REVIEW

1939

FINAL POLL (DEC. 11)

AP	SCHOOL	FINAL RECORD
1	Texas A&M	11-0-0
2	Tennessee	10-1-0
3	Southern California	8-0-2
4	Cornell	8-0-0
5	Tulane	8-1-1
6	Missouri	8-2-0
7	UCLA	6-0-4
8	Duke	8-1-0
9	Iowa	6-1-1
10	Duquesne	8-0-1
11	Boston College	9-2-0
12	Clemson	9-1-0
13	Notre Dame	7-2-0
14	Santa Clara	5-1-3
15	Ohio State	6-2-0
16	Georgia Tech	8-2-0
17	Fordham	6-2-0
18	Nebraska	7-1-1
19	Oklahoma	6-2-1
20	Michigan	6-2-0

SEC STANDINGS

	CONFERENCE			OVERALL		
	W	L	T	W	L	T
Tennessee	6	0	0	10	1	0
Georgia Tech	6	0	0	8	2	0
Tulane	5	0	0	8	1	1
Mississippi State	3	2	0	8	2	0
Auburn	3	3	1	5	5	1
Mississippi	2	2	0	7	2	0
Kentucky	2	2	1	6	2	1
Alabama	2	3	1	5	3	1
Georgia	1	3	0	5	6	0
LSU	1	5	0	4	5	0
Vanderbilt	1	6	0	2	7	1
Florida	0	3	1	5	5	1
Sewanee	0	3	0	3	5	0

CONSENSUS ALL-AMERICANS

POS	NAME	SCHOOL
B	Nile Kinnick	Iowa
B	Tom Harmon	Michigan
B	John Kimbrough	Texas A&M
B	George Cafego	Tennessee
E	Esco Sarkkinen	Ohio State
E	Ken Kavanaugh	LSU
T	Nick Drahos	Cornell
T	Harley McCollum	Tulane
G	Harry Smith	Southern California
G	Ed Molinski	Tennessee
C	John Schiechl	Santa Clara

OTHERS RECEIVING FIRST-TEAM HONORS

B	Paul Christman	Missouri
B	Banks McFadden	Clemson
B	Donald Scott	Ohio State
B	Kenny Washington	UCLA
E	Bud Kerr	Notre Dame
E	Paul Severin	North Carolina
E	Frank Ivy	Oklahoma
E	Harlan Gustafson	Pennsylvania
E	Dave Rankin	Purdue
T	Jim Reeder	Illinois
T	Joe Boyd	Texas A&M
T	Harry Stella	Army
G	Bob Suffridge	Tennessee
C	John Haman	Northwestern
C	Carey Cox	Alabama

HEISMAN TROPHY VOTING

PLAYER	POS	SCHOOL	TOTAL
1 Nile Kinnick	HB	Iowa	651
2 Tom Harmon	HB	Michigan	405
3 Paul Christman	QB	Missouri	391
4 George Cafego	TB	Tennessee	296

AWARD WINNERS

PLAYER	AWARD
Nile Kinnick, HB, Iowa	Maxwell

BOWL GAMES

DATE	GAME	SCORE
J1	Sun	Arizona State 0, Catholic 0
J1	Cotton	Clemson 6, Boston College 3
J1	Orange	Georgia Tech 21, Missouri 7
J1	Rose	Southern California 14, Tennessee 0
J1	Sugar	Texas A&M 14, Tulane 13

1940 NCAA Major College Statistical Leaders

Individual Leaders

PASSING/COMPLETIONS

		G	ATT	COM	PCT	INT	I%	YDS	YPA	COM.PG
1	Billy Sewell, Washington State	10	174	86	49.4	17	9.8	1023	5.9	8.6
2	David Allerdice, Princeton	8	144	76	52.8	17	11.8	989	6.9	9.5
2	Johnny Supulski, Manhattan	9	148	76	51.4	17	11.5	1190	8.0	8.4
4	Paul Christman, Missouri	9	154	69	44.8	14	9.1	1131	7.3	7.7
5	Bill Dudley, Virginia	9	140	67	47.9	9	6.4	722	5.2	7.4
6	Andy Tomasic, Temple	9	115	56	48.7	11	9.6	646	5.6	6.2
7	Ray Mallouf, SMU	10	107	54	50.5	9	8.4	692	6.5	5.4
8	Harold Hursh, Indiana	8	111	53	47.7	10	9.0	699	6.3	6.6
9	Jack Jacobs, Oklahoma	9	99	49	49.5	12	12.1	584	5.9	5.4
10	Marion Pugh, Texas A&M	9	86	48	55.8	5	5.8	653	7.6	5.3

ALL-PURPOSE YARDS

		G	RUSH	REC	INT	PR	KR	YDS	YPG
1	Tom Harmon, Michigan	8	844	0	20	244	204	1312	164.0

RUSHING/YARDS

		G	ATT	YDS	AVG	YPG
1	Al Ghesquiere, Detroit	9	146	957	6.6	106.3
2	Tom Harmon, Michigan	8	186	844	4.5	105.5
3	Johnny Knolla, Creighton	10	181	813	4.5	81.3
4	Merle Hapes, Mississippi	11	120	807	6.7	73.4
4	Bob Westfall, Michigan	8	190	807	4.2	100.9
6	Harvey Johnson, Mississippi State	10	117	721	6.2	72.1
7	Tony Gallovich, Wake Forest	10	124	709	5.7	70.9
8	Bobby Robertson, Southern California	9	147	694	4.7	77.1
9	Jim Reynolds, Oklahoma State	10	202	685	3.4	68.5
10	John Polanski, Wake Forest	10	147	655	4.5	65.5

RUSHING/YARDS PER CARRY

		G	ATT	YDS	YPC
1	James Farrell, Lafayette	9	81	585	7.2
2	Merle Hapes, Mississippi	11	120	807	6.7
3	Al Ghesquiere, Detroit	9	146	957	6.6
4	Bud Nygren, San Jose State	12	100	624	6.2
5	Harvey Johnson, Mississippi State	10	117	721	6.2
6	Walter Zirinski, Lafayette	9	108	638	5.9
7	Tony Gallovich, Wake Forest	10	124	709	5.7
8	Hugh Gallarneau, Stanford	9	106	597	5.6
9	Francis Reagan, Pennsylvania	8	124	652	5.3
10	Len Eshmont, Fordham	8	118	620	5.3

Based on top 20 rushers

RECEIVING/RECEPTIONS

		G	REC	YDS	YPR	YPG	RPG
1	Eddie Bryant, Virginia	9	30	222	7.4	24.7	3.3
2	Steve Lach, Duke	9	26	333	12.8	37.0	2.9
3	Bill Jennings, Oklahoma	9	26	292	11.2	32.4	2.9
4	Lenny Krouse, Penn State	8	25	420	16.8	52.5	3.1
4	Dick Humbert, Richmond	9	25	390	15.6	43.3	2.8
6	Don Vosberg, Marquette	9	24	526	21.9	58.4	2.7
7	Johnny Allen, San Jose State	12	21	373	17.8	31.1	1.8
7	Nick Gianakos, Virginia	9	21	296	14.1	32.9	2.3
9	Felix Fletcher, Washington State	10	20	274	13.7	27.4	2.0
9	Don Greeley, Washington State	10	20	188	9.4	18.8	2.0
9	Phil Roach, TCU	10	20	179	9.0	17.9	2.0

PUNTING

		PUNT	YDS	AVG
1	Owen Price, Texas-El Paso	30	1440	48.0
2	Jack Jacobs, Oklahoma	33	1483	44.9
3	Dick McGowen, Auburn	43	1879	43.7
4	Sherwood Fries, Colorado State	60	2553	42.6
5	Paul McClung, Colorado	41	1722	42.0
6	Norm Standlee, Stanford	28	1171	41.8
7	Don Scott, Ohio State	39	1630	41.8
8	Art Jones, Richmond	65	2713	41.7
9	Steve Lach, Duke	31	1280	41.3
10	Leonard Isberg, Oregon	36	1484	41.2

PUNT RETURNS/YARDS

		PR	YDS	AVG
1	Junie Hovious, Mississippi	33	498	15.1
2	Art Jones, Richmond	33	481	14.6
3	Tony Gallovich, Wake Forest	35	429	12.3
4	Ernie Steele, Washington	30	425	14.2
5	Eddie Bryant, Virginia	28	421	15.0
6	Marvin Bell, Utah State	35	408	11.7
7	Jackie Robinson, UCLA	19	399	21.0
8	Bill Geyer, Colgate	34	392	11.5
9	George Moyer, Lafayette	28	388	13.9
10	Johnny Knolla, Creighton	36	378	10.5

KICKOFF RETURNS/YARDS

		KR	YDS	AVG
1	Jack Emigh, Montana	18	395	21.9
2	Noah Mullins, Kentucky	11	394	35.8
3	Bill Dudley, Virginia	14	356	25.4
4	Bill Geyer, Colgate	13	351	27.0
5	George Franck, Minnesota	6	305	50.8
6	George Nixon, Idaho	11	286	26.0
7	Leo Stasica, Colorado	8	269	33.6
8	Chuck Peters, Penn State	5	261	52.2
9	Johnny Knolla, Creighton	11	257	23.4
10	Leland Morris, Syracuse	6	246	41.0

SCORING

		TDS	XPT	FG	PTS
1	Tom Harmon, Michigan	16	18	1	117
2	Francis Reagan, Pennsylvania	17	1	0	103
3	Walter Zirinski, Lafayette	14	14	3	83
4	Frank Maznicki, Boston College	10	19	0	79
5	Merle Hapes, Mississippi	12	0	0	72
6	Mike Holovak, Boston College	11	1	0	67
7	Junie Hovious, Mississippi	9	11	0	65
8	Tony Gallovich, Wake Forest	9	9	0	63
9	John Martin, Oklahoma	10	0	0	60
9	Owen Price, Texas-El Paso	10	0	0	60

INTERCEPTIONS

		INT	YDS
1	Dick Morgan, Tulsa	7	210
1	Jack Crain, Texas	7	160
1	Junie Hovious, Mississippi	7	146
1	Joe Muha, VMI	7	108
1	John Hanna, Santa Clara	7	92
1	Walter Williams, Boston U.	7	72
1	Noble Doss, Texas	7	33
8	E.H. Wheeler, Virginia Tech*	6	84
8	Bill Dudley, Virginia*	6	83
8	T.A. Weems, Rice*	6	79

* Eight tied with six; these three players had the most yards

Team Leaders

RUSHING OFFENSE

		G	ATT	YDS	AVG	YPG
1	Lafayette	9	492	2758	5.6	306.4
2	Texas Tech	10	580	2637	4.5	263.7
3	Detroit	9	495	2183	4.4	242.6
4	Michigan	8	471	1921	4.1	240.1
5	Tennessee	10	476	2394	5.0	239.4
6	Navy	9	525	2019	3.8	224.3
7	Penn State	8	423	1785	4.2	223.1
8	Minnesota	8	407	1782	4.4	222.8
9	Boston College	10	489	2227	4.6	222.7
10	Colgate	8	425	1767	4.2	220.9

PASSING OFFENSE/YPG

		G	ATT	COM	INT	PCT	YDS	YPA	YPG	I%	YPC
1	Cornell	8	152	83	14	54.6	1490	9.8	186.3	9.2	18.0
2	Georgia	8	175	74	17	42.3	1164	6.7	145.5	9.7	15.7
3	Manhattan	9	179	87	20	48.6	1292	7.2	143.6	11.2	14.9
4	Texas-El Paso	9	201	89	15	44.3	1280	6.4	142.2	7.5	14.4
5	Missouri	9	174	75	15	43.1	1248	7.2	138.7	8.6	16.6
6	Marquette	9	185	72	21	38.9	1227	6.6	136.3	11.4	17.0
7	Princeton	8	169	80	20	47.3	1066	6.3	133.3	11.8	13.3
8	Georgia Tech	7	164	67	15	40.9	905	5.5	129.3	9.2	13.5
9	Washington, Mo.	9	168	77	15	45.8	1144	6.8	127.1	8.9	14.9
10	Washington State	10	210	99	22	47.1	1206	5.7	120.6	10.5	12.2

TOTAL OFFENSE

		G	P	YDS	AVG	YPG
1	Lafayette	9	577	3314	5.7	368.2
2	Cornell	8	496	2945	5.9	368.1
3	Texas Tech	10	701	3376	4.8	337.6
4	Detroit	9	661	2901	4.4	322.3
5	Boston College	10	623	3177	5.1	317.7
6	Navy	9	690	2850	4.1	316.7
7	Missouri	9	550	2799	5.1	311.0
8	Texas-El Paso	9	614	2790	4.5	310.0
9	Mississippi	11	611	3406	5.6	309.6
10	Duke	9	518	2783	5.4	309.2

RUSHING DEFENSE

		G	ATT	YDS	AVG	YPG
1	Texas A&M	9	305	399	1.3	44.3
2	Navy	9	249	443	1.8	49.2
3	Mississippi State	10	350	505	1.4	50.5
4	Santa Clara	8	241	429	1.8	53.6
5	Arizona	9	320	488	1.5	54.2
6	Boston College	10	334	600	1.8	60.0
7	Detroit	9	300	572	1.9	63.6
8	San Jose State	12	383	834	2.2	69.5
9	Lafayette	9	307	634	2.1	70.4
10	Duquesne	7	218	498	2.3	71.1

PASSING DEFENSE

		G	ATT	COM	PCT	YPC	INT	I%	YDS	YPA	YPG
1	Harvard	8	101	27	26.7	9.9	20	19.8	266	2.6	33.3
2	Utah State	7	71	24	33.8	11.3	6	8.5	272	3.8	38.9
3	Indiana	8	67	22	32.8	15.8	11	16.4	347	5.2	43.4
4	West Virginia	9	81	34	42.0	11.9	10	12.4	403	5.0	44.8
5	Montana	7	62	22	35.5	14.4	12	19.4	316	5.1	45.1
6	Richmond	8	108	38	35.2	9.6	12	11.1	363	3.4	45.4
7	Michigan	8	86	24	27.9	15.6	16	18.6	374	4.3	46.8
8	Navy	9	94	35	37.2	12.0	13	13.8	421	4.5	46.8
9	Wake Forest	10	111	34	30.6	13.9	11	9.9	471	4.2	47.1
10	Cornell	8	113	42	37.2	9.0	24	21.2	380	3.4	47.5

TOTAL DEFENSE

		G	P	YDS	AVG	YPG
1	Navy	9	343	864	2.5	96.0
2	Santa Clara	8	360	876	2.4	109.5
3	Boston College	10	468	1117	2.4	111.7
4	San Jose State	12	546	1517	2.8	126.4
5	Mississippi State	10	533	1270	2.4	127.0
6	Penn State	8	324	1073	3.3	134.1
7	Tennessee	10	499	1365	2.7	136.5
8	Alabama	9	454	1246	2.7	138.4
9	Detroit	9	436	1260	2.9	140.0
10	Nebraska	9	409	1299	3.2	144.3

SCORING OFFENSE

		G	PTS	AVG
1	Boston College	10	320	32.0
2	Tennessee	10	318	31.8
3	Georgetown	9	273	30.3
4	Lafayette	9	238	26.4
5	Michigan	8	196	24.5

Based on top 15 teams in winning percentage

SCORING DEFENSE

		G	PTS	AVG
1	Tennessee	10	26	2.6
2	Lafayette	9	33	3.7
3	Texas A&M	9	34	3.8
4	Georgetown	9	37	4.1
5	Michigan	8	34	4.3

Based on top 15 teams in winning percentage

1940

FINAL POLL (DEC. 2)

AP	SCHOOL	FINAL RECORD
1	Minnesota	8-0-0
2	Stanford	10-0-0
3	Michigan	7-1-0
4	**Tennessee**	**10-1-0**
5	Boston College	11-0-0
6	Texas A&M	9-1-0
7	Nebraska	8-2-0
8	Northwestern	6-2-0
9	**Mississippi State**	**10-0-1**
10	Washington	7-2-0
11	Santa Clara	6-1-1
12	Fordham	7-2-0
13	Georgetown	8-2-0
14	Pennsylvania	6-1-1
15	Cornell	6-2-0
16	SMU	8-1-1
17	Hardin-Simmons	9-0-0
18	Duke	7-2-0
19	Lafayette	9-0-0

CONSENSUS ALL-AMERICANS

POS	NAME	SCHOOL
B	Tom Harmon	Michigan
B	John Kimbrough	Texas A&M
B	Frank Albert	Stanford
B	George Franck	Minnesota
E	Gene Goodreault	Boston College
E	Dave Rankin	Purdue
T	Nick Drahos	Cornell
T	Alf Bauman	Northwestern
T	Urban Odson	Minnesota
G	**Bob Suffridge**	**Tennessee**
G	Marshall Robnett	Texas A&M
C	Rudy Mucha	Washington

OTHERS RECEIVING FIRST-TEAM HONORS

B	Francis Reagan	Pennsylvania
B	Charles O'Rourke	Boston College
B	Hugh Gallarneau	Stanford
E	Paul Severin	North Carolina
E	**Buddy Elrod**	**Mississippi State**
E	Ed Frutig	Michigan
E	Jay MacDowell	Washington
T	Bob Reinhard	California
T	Forrest Behm	Nebraska
T	Mike Enich	Iowa
G	Warren Alfson	Nebraska
G	Augie Lio	Georgetown
G	Ray Frankowski	Washington
G	Helge Pukema	Minnesota
G	**Ed Molinski**	**Tennessee**
C	Chet Gladchuk	Boston College
C	Ray Frick	Pennsylvania
C	Leon Gajecki	Penn State

HEISMAN TROPHY VOTING

	PLAYER	POS	SCHOOL	TOTAL
1	Tom Harmon	HB	Michigan	1303
2	John Kimbrough	RB	Texas A&M	841
3	George Franck	HB	Minnesota	102
4	Frankie Albert	QB	Stanford	90
5	Paul Christman	QB	Missouri	66

AWARD WINNERS

PLAYER	AWARD
Tom Harmon, HB, Michigan	Maxwell

BOWL GAMES

DATE	GAME	SCORE
J1	**Orange**	**Mississippi State 14, Georgetown 7**
J1	Rose	Stanford 21, Nebraska 13
J1	**Sugar**	**Boston College 19, Tennessee 13**
J1	Cotton	Texas A&M 13, Fordham 12
J1	Sun	Case Western Reserve 26, Arizona State 13

SEC STANDINGS

	CONFERENCE			OVERALL		
	W	L	T	W	L	T
Tennessee	5	0	0	10	1	0
Mississippi State	4	0	1	10	0	1
Mississippi	3	1	0	9	2	0
Alabama	4	2	0	7	2	0
Auburn	3	2	1	6	4	1
LSU	3	3	0	6	4	0
Georgia	2	3	1	5	4	1
Florida	2	3	0	5	5	0
Kentucky	1	2	2	5	3	2
Tulane	1	3	0	5	5	0
Georgia Tech	1	5	0	3	7	0
Vanderbilt	0	5	1	3	6	1
Sewanee	0	1	0	3	5	0

1941 NCAA MAJOR COLLEGE STATISTICAL LEADERS

INDIVIDUAL LEADERS

PASSING/COMPLETIONS	G	ATT	COM	PCT	INT	I%	YDS	YPA	COM.PG
1 Bud Schwenk, Washington, Mo.	9	234	114	48.7	19	8.1	1457	6.2	12.7
2 Owen Price, Texas-El Paso	9	208	94	45.2	19	9.1	997	4.8	10.4
3 Angelo Bertelli, Notre Dame	9	124	70	56.5	11	8.9	1037	8.4	7.8
3 Paul Governali, Columbia	8	167	70	41.9	10	6.0	810	4.9	8.8
5 Derace Moser, Texas A&M	10	166	67	40.4	19	11.5	912	5.5	6.7
6 Elmer Madarik, Detroit	9	128	64	50.0	7	5.5	874	6.8	7.1
7 Johnny Podesto, St. Mary's (Cal.)	9	142	61	43.0	20	14.1	1000	7.0	6.8
8 John Cochran, Wake Forest	10	139	59	42.4	20	14.4	1125	8.1	5.9
9 Jimmy Richardson, Marquette	9	91	58	63.7	7	7.7	536	5.9	6.4
10 Bill Dudley, Virginia	9	107	57	53.3	8	7.5	856	8.0	6.3

ALL-PURPOSE YARDS	G	RUSH	REC	INT	PR	KR	YDS	YPG
1 Bill Dudley, Virginia	9	968	60	76	481	89	1674	186.0

RUSHING/YARDS	G	ATT	YDS	AVG	YPG
1 Frank Sinkwich, Georgia	10	209	1103	5.3	110.3
2 Bill Dudley, Virginia	9	155	968	6.2	107.6
3 Bob Steuber, Missouri	9	113	855	7.6	95.0
4 John Grigas, Holy Cross	10	179	826	4.6	82.6
5 Pat Harder, Wisconsin	8	142	731	5.1	91.4
6 Bob Westfall, Michigan	8	156	688	4.4	86.0
7 Bill Daley, Minnesota	8	158	685	4.3	85.6
8 Maurice Wade, Missouri	9	105	681	6.5	75.7
9 Andy Tomasic, Temple	9	173	677	3.9	75.2
10 Dick Fisher, Ohio State	8	134	674	5.0	84.3

RUSHING/YARDS PER CARRY	G	ATT	YDS	YPC
1 Bob Steuber, Missouri	9	113	855	7.6
2 Isadore Spector, Utah	8	78	559	7.2
3 Maurice Wade, Missouri	9	105	681	6.5
4 Bill Dudley, Virginia	9	155	968	6.2
5 Harry Ice, Missouri	9	98	603	6.2
6 Frank Sinkwich, Georgia	10	209	1103	5.3
7 George Sutch, Temple	9	107	561	5.2
8 Pat Harder, Wisconsin	8	142	731	5.1
9 Dick Fisher, Ohio State	8	134	674	5.0
10 Bill Busik, Navy	9	124	609	4.9

Based on top 20 rushers

RECEIVING/RECEPTIONS	G	REC	YDS	YPR	YPG	RPG
1 Hank Stanton, Arizona	10	50	820	16.4	82.0	5.0
2 Allen Lindow, Washington, Mo.	9	39	472	12.1	52.4	4.3
3 Lenny Krouse, Penn State	9	32	536	16.8	59.6	3.6
4 Bill Pufalt, Washington, Mo.	9	29	405	14.0	45.0	3.2
5 Walter McDonald, Tulane	9	27	437	16.2	48.6	3.0
6 Milton Crain, Baylor	10	26	152	5.8	15.2	2.6
7 Marshall Spivey, Texas A&M	10	25	363	14.5	36.3	2.5
7 Clarence Turley, Washington, Mo.	9	25	262	10.5	29.1	2.5
7 Robert Henderson, Texas A&M	10	25	229	9.2	22.9	2.5
10 Howard Keating, Detroit	9	24	277	11.5	30.8	2.7

PUNTING	PUNT	YDS	AVG
1 Owen Price, Texas-El Paso	40	1813	45.3
2 Merle Hapes, Mississippi	32	1425	44.5
3 Bill Busik, Navy	41	1797	43.8
4 Preston Johnston, SMU	67	2857	42.6
5 Robert Riddell, Denver	35	1465	41.9
6 Booty Payne, Clemson	47	1960	41.7
7 Harry Dunkle, North Carolina	71	2954	41.6
8 Jim Blumenstock, Fordham	62	2571	41.5
9 J.E. Dickson, Rice	63	2603	41.3
10 Emil Banjavcic, Arizona	41	1662	40.5

PUNT RETURNS/YARDS	PR	YDS	AVG
1 Bill Geyer, Colgate	33	616	18.7
2 Bob Margarita, Brown	40	549	13.7
3 Bill Hillenbrand, Indiana	41	524	12.8
4 Bill Dudley, Virginia	28	481	17.2
5 Van Davis, Georgia	36	464	12.9
6 Junie Hovious, Mississippi	36	457	12.7
7 Thomas Roblin, Oregon	30	428	14.3
8 Andy Tomasic, Temple	31	420	13.5
9 Don Austin, Texas Tech	29	397	13.7
10 Henry Mazur, Army	36	387	10.8

KICKOFF RETURNS/YARDS	KR	YDS	AVG
1 Earl Ray, Wyoming	23	496	21.6
2 Bill Geyer, Colgate	15	350	23.3
3 Owen Price, Texas-El Paso	10	282	28.2
4 Monk Gafford, Auburn	13	271	20.8
5 Royal Lohry, Iowa State	9	270	30.0
6 Vern Lockard, Colorado	11	268	24.4
7 Charles McNulty, Manhattan	10	261	26.1
8 John Polanski, Wake Forest	8	257	32.1
9 Harold Stockbridge, Rice	10	253	25.3
10 Stanley Szymakowski, Lehigh	10	245	24.5

SCORING	TDS	XPT	FG	PTS
1 Bill Dudley, Virginia	18	23	1	134
2 Jack Crain, Texas	11	23	1	92
3 Jack Jenkins, Vanderbilt	12	15	1	90
4 Winston Siegfried, Duke	13	2	0	80
5 Charlie Timmons, Clemson	9	23	0	77
6 Van Davis, Georgia	12	1	0	73
7 Pat Harder, Wisconsin	10	9	1	72
7 John Petrella, Penn State	12	0	0	72
9 Bob Steuber, Missouri	9	14	0	68
10 Fred Evans, Notre Dame	11	1	0	67

INTERCEPTIONS	INT	YDS
1 Bobby Robertson, Southern California	9	126
1 Bill Sibley, Texas A&M	9	57
3 Clyde Ehrhardt, Georgia	8	162
3 Owen Price, Texas-El Paso	8	124
3 Dale Bradley, Nebraska	8	115
6 Edgar Jones, Pittsburgh*	6	215
6 Bob Dethman, Oregon State*	6	119
6 Andy Tomasic, Temple*	6	83
6 Noble Doss, Texas*	6	82
6 Jack Jacobs, Oklahoma*	6	77

* Eight players tied with six; these had the most yards

TEAM LEADERS

RUSHING OFFENSE	G	ATT	YDS	AVG	YPG
1 Missouri	9	488	2769	5.7	307.7
2 Duke	9	498	2392	4.8	265.8
3 Minnesota	8	476	2062	4.3	257.8
4 Utah	8	398	2054	5.2	256.8
5 Syracuse	8	395	2007	5.1	250.9
6 Navy	9	494	2249	4.6	249.9
7 Georgia	10	511	2397	4.7	239.7
8 Texas	10	460	2372	5.2	237.2
9 Clemson	9	437	2132	4.9	236.9
10 Michigan	8	420	1871	4.5	233.9

PASSING OFFENSE/YPG	G	ATT	COM	INT	PCT	YDS	YPA	YPG	I%	YPC
1 Arizona	10	231	106	18	45.9	1777	7.7	177.7	7.8	16.8
2 Texas A&M	10	294	126	30	42.9	1657	5.6	165.7	10.2	13.2
3 Washington, Mo.	9	238	116	20	48.7	1472	6.2	163.6	8.4	12.7
4 Detroit	9	185	94	11	50.8	1307	7.1	145.2	6.0	13.9
5 Notre Dame	9	148	81	14	54.7	1223	8.3	135.9	9.5	15.1
6 Texas-El Paso	9	261	112	27	42.9	1219	4.7	135.4	10.3	10.9
7 Wake Forest	10	197	88	24	44.7	1335	6.8	133.5	12.2	15.2
8 San Francisco	6	102	41	10	40.2	756	7.4	126.0	9.8	18.4
9 St. Mary's (Cal.)	9	165	69	23	41.8	1116	6.8	124.0	13.9	16.2
10 SMU	10	200	68	17	34.0	1201	6.0	120.1	8.5	17.7

TOTAL OFFENSE	G	P	YDS	AVG	YPG
1 Duke	9	619	3350	5.4	372.2
2 Arizona	10	668	3573	5.3	357.3
3 Georgia	10	695	3504	5.0	350.4
4 Utah	8	496	2803	5.7	350.4
5 Texas	10	621	3500	5.6	350.0
6 Missouri	9	557	3102	5.6	344.7
7 Tulane	9	640	2951	4.6	327.9
8 Fordham	8	515	2616	5.1	327.0
9 Detroit	9	631	2881	4.6	320.1
10 Clemson	9	559	2879	5.2	319.9

RUSHING DEFENSE	G	ATT	YDS	AVG	YPG
1 Duquesne	8	235	448	1.9	56.0
2 Georgia	10	323	596	1.8	59.6
3 Texas Tech	10	328	617	1.9	61.7
4 Navy	9	311	560	1.8	62.2
5 Texas	10	323	659	2.0	65.9
6 Tulane	9	311	597	1.9	66.3
7 Santa Clara	9	302	598	2.0	66.4
8 Notre Dame	9	340	611	1.8	67.9
9 Utah	8	268	602	2.2	75.3
10 Rice	10	357	812	2.3	81.2

PASSING DEFENSE	G	ATT	COM	PCT	YPC	INT	I%	YDS	YPA	YPG
1 Purdue	8	74	21	28.4	10.3	11	14.9	217	2.9	27.1
2 Boston U.	8	85	23	27.1	12.2	15	17.7	280	3.3	35.0
3 Denver	9	98	34	34.7	10.5	17	17.4	357	3.6	39.7
4 Idaho	9	105	30	28.6	12.4	17	16.2	371	3.5	41.2
5 Lafayette	9	105	39	37.1	10.7	24	22.9	418	4.0	46.4
6 Harvard	8	97	27	27.8	13.9	9	9.3	376	3.9	47.0
7 Florida	8	98	23	23.5	16.6	16	16.3	381	3.9	47.6
8 Mississippi State	7	95	28	29.5	12.0	16	16.8	336	3.5	48.0
9 San Jose State	10	122	40	32.8	12.3	20	16.4	490	4.0	49.0
9 Villanova	7	89	30	33.7	11.4	15	16.9	343	3.9	49.0

TOTAL DEFENSE	G	P	YDS	AVG	YPG
1 Duquesne	8	363	885	2.4	110.6
2 Navy	9	449	1258	2.8	139.8
3 Detroit	9	453	1282	2.8	142.4
4 Notre Dame	9	481	1283	2.7	142.6
5 Georgia	10	499	1429	2.9	142.9
6 Texas Tech	10	512	1432	2.8	143.2
7 Duke	9	433	1311	3.0	145.7
8 San Jose State	10	467	1465	3.1	146.5
9 Virginia	9	496	1362	2.7	151.3
10 Rutgers	8	390	1211	3.1	151.4

SCORING OFFENSE	G	PTS	AVG
1 Duke	9	311	34.6
2 Texas	10	338	33.8
3 Virginia	9	279	31.0
4 Georgia	10	279	27.9
5 Texas A&M	10	266	26.6
6 Utah	8	209	26.1
7 Vanderbilt	10	260	26.0
8 Clemson	9	233	25.9
9 Arizona	10	253	25.3
9 William & Mary	10	253	25.3

SCORING DEFENSE	G	PTS	AVG
1 Duquesne	8	23	2.9
2 Texas Tech	10	30	3.0
3 Oregon State	9	33	3.7
4 Navy	9	34	3.8
5 Missouri	9	37	4.1
6 Duke	9	41	4.6
7 Texas A&M	10	46	4.6
8 Virginia	9	42	4.7
9 Minnesota	8	38	4.8
10 Detroit	9	43	4.8

1941

Final Poll (Dec. 1)

AP	SCHOOL	FINAL RECORD
1	Minnesota	8-0-0
2	Duke	9-1-0
3	Notre Dame	8-0-1
4	Texas	8-1-1
5	Michigan	6-1-1
6	Fordham	8-1-0
7	Missouri	8-2-0
8	Duquesne	8-0-0
9	Texas A&M	9-2-0
10	Navy	7-1-1
11	Northwestern	5-3-0
12	Oregon State	8-2-0
13	Ohio State	6-1-1
14	**Georgia**	**9-1-1**
15	Pennsylvania	7-1-0
16	**Mississippi State**	**8-1-1**
17	**Mississippi**	**6-2-1**
18	**Tennessee**	**8-2-0**
19	Washington State	6-4-0
20	**Alabama**	**9-2-0**

SEC Standings

	Conference			Overall		
	W	L	T	W	L	T
Mississippi State	4	0	1	8	1	1
Tennessee	3	1	0	8	2	0
Alabama	5	2	0	9	2	0
Georgia	3	1	1	9	1	1
Mississippi	2	1	1	6	2	1
Vanderbilt	3	2	0	8	2	0
LSU	2	2	2	4	4	2
Tulane	2	3	0	5	4	0
Georgia Tech	2	4	0	3	6	0
Florida	1	3	0	4	6	0
Auburn	0	4	1	4	5	1
Kentucky	0	4	0	5	4	0

Consensus All-Americans

POS	NAME	SCHOOL
B	Bob Westfall	Michigan
B	Bruce Smith	Minnesota
B	Frank Albert	Stanford
B	Bill Dudley	Virginia
B	**Frank Sinkwich**	**Georgia**
E	**Holt Rast**	**Alabama**
E	Bob Dove	Notre Dame
T	Dick Wildung	Minnesota
T	Ernie Blandin	Tulane
G	Endicott Peabody	Harvard
G	Ray Frankowski	Washington
C	Darold Jenkins	Missouri

Others receiving first-team honors

B	Steve Lach	Duke
B	Derace Moser	Texas A&M
E	Dave Schreiner	Wisconsin
E	Malcolm Kutner	Texas
E	John Rokisky	Duquesne
E	Jim Lansing	Fordham
E	Joe Blalock	Clemson
T	Alf Bauman	Northwestern
T	Bob Reinhard	California
G	Ralph Fife	Pittsburgh
G	Bernie Crimmins	Notre Dame
G	Chal Daniel	Texas
C	Vince Banonis	Detroit

Heisman Trophy Voting

	PLAYER	POS	SCHOOL	TOTAL
1	Bruce Smith	HB	Minnesota	554
2	Angelo Bertelli	QB	Notre Dame	345
3	Frank Albert	QB	Stanford	336
4	**Frank Sinkwich**	**HB**	**Georgia**	**249**
5	Bill Dudley	HB	Virginia	237
6	Endicott Peabody	G	Harvard	153
7	Edgar Jones	RB	Pittsburgh	151
8	Bob Westfall	FB	Michigan	147
9	Steve Lach	HB	Duke	126
10	Jack Crain	RB	Texas	102

Award Winners

PLAYER	AWARD
Bill Dudley, HB, Virginia	Maxwell

Bowl Games

DATE	GAME	SCORE
J1	**Cotton**	**Alabama 29, Texas A&M 21**
J1	**Orange**	**Georgia 40, TCU 26**
J1	Rose	Oregon State 20, Duke 16
J1	Sugar	Fordham 2, Missouri 0
J1	Sun	Tulsa 6, Texas Tech 0

1942 NCAA Major College Statistical Leaders

Individual Leaders

PASSING/COMPLETIONS	G	ATT	COM	PCT	INT	I%	YDS	YPA	COM.PG
1 Ray Evans, Kansas	10	200	101	50.5	9	4.5	1117	5.6	10.1
2 Otto Graham, Northwestern	10	182	89	48.9	18	9.9	1092	6.0	8.9
3 Paul Governali, Columbia	9	165	87	52.7	18	10.9	1442	8.7	9.7
4 Frank Sinkwich, Georgia	**11**	**166**	**84**	**50.6**	**7**	**4.2**	**1392**	**8.4**	**7.6**
5 Tabb Gillette, Virginia	9	144	82	56.9	14	9.7	920	6.4	9.1
6 Angelo Bertelli, Notre Dame	11	162	72	44.4	16	9.9	1039	6.4	6.5
7 Vic Clark, Texas-El Paso	9	136	71	52.2	12	8.8	846	6.2	7.9
8 Glenn Dobbs, Tulsa	10	107	67	62.6	4	3.7	1066	10.0	6.7
9 Tom Mont, Maryland	9	127	66	52.0	12	9.5	1076	8.5	7.3
9 Emery Nix, TCU	10	154	66	42.9	9	5.8	672	4.4	6.6

ALL-PURPOSE YARDS	G	RUSH	REC	INT	PR	KR	YDS	YPG
NA								

RUSHING/YARDS	G	ATT	YDS	AVG	YPG
1 Rudy Mobley, Hardin-Simmons	9	187	1281	6.9	142.3
2 Bob Steuber, Missouri	12	149	1098	7.4	91.5
3 Camp Wilson, Hardin-Simmons	9	196	981	5.0	109.0
4 Mike Holovak, Boston College	9	174	965	5.5	107.2
5 Gene Fekete, Ohio State	10	185	910	4.9	91.0
6 Bruce Smith, Great Lakes NAS	12	144	849	5.9	70.8
7 Bob Kennedy, Washington State	10	226	813	3.6	81.3
8 Frank Sinkwich, Georgia	**11**	**175**	**795**	**4.5**	**72.3**
9 Elroy Hirsch, Wisconsin	10	141	767	5.4	76.7
10 Roy Dale McKay, Texas	10	132	701	5.3	70.1

RUSHING/YARDS PER CARRY	G	ATT	YDS	YPC
1 Bob Steuber, Missouri	12	149	1098	7.4
2 Charlie Trippi, Georgia	**11**	**98**	**673**	**6.9**
3 Rudy Mobley, Hardin-Simmons	9	187	1281	6.9
4 Bruce Smith, Great Lakes NAS	12	144	849	5.9
5 Mike Holovak, Boston College	9	174	965	5.5
6 Elroy Hirsch, Wisconsin	10	141	767	5.4
7 Roy Dale McKay, Texas	10	132	701	5.3
8 Jackie Field, Texas	10	122	646	5.3
9 Joe Day, Oregon State	10	123	630	5.1
10 Camp Wilson, Hardin-Simmons	9	196	981	5.0

Based on top 15 rushers

RECEIVING/RECEPTIONS	G	REC	YDS	YPR	YPG	RPG
1 Bill Rogers, Texas A&M	10	39	432	11.1	43.2	3.9
2 Albert Salem, Texas-El Paso	9	36	401	11.1	44.6	4.0
3 Sax Judd, Tulsa	10	35	509	14.5	50.9	3.5
4 Van Davis, Georgia	**11**	**33**	**455**	**13.8**	**41.4**	**3.0**
5 Harding Miller, SMU	11	32	531	16.6	48.3	2.9
6 Van Hall, TCU	10	27	231	8.6	23.1	2.7
7 John Ferguson, California	10	26	338	13.0	33.8	2.6
8 Otto Schnellbacher, Kansas	10	25	366	14.6	36.6	2.5
9 George Poschner, Georgia*	**10**	**24**	**493**	**20.5**	**49.3**	**2.4**
9 John Kelleher, Columbia*	9	24	412	17.2	45.8	2.7

*Six players tied with 24; these had the most yards

PUNTING	PUNT	YDS	AVG
1 Bobby Cifers, Tennessee	**37**	**1586**	**42.9**
2 Art Faircloth, North Carolina St.	54	2279	42.2
3 John Strzykalski, Marquette	42	1760	41.9
4 Tom Douglas, Dartmouth	60	2485	41.4
5 Mike Cooke, North Carolina	45	1860	41.3
6 Barney Welch, Texas A&M	39	1609	41.3
7 Joe Muha, VMI	44	1804	41.0
8 Jerry Moore, Vanderbilt	**40**	**1608**	**40.2**
9 Joe Colone, Penn State	46	1845	40.1
10 Earl Dolaway, Indiana	30	1202	40.1

PUNT RETURNS/YARDS	PR	YDS	AVG
1 Bill Hillenbrand, Indiana	23	481	20.9

KICKOFF RETURNS/YARDS	KR	YDS	AVG
1 Frank Porto, California	17	483	28.4

SCORING	TDS	XPT	FG	PTS
1 Bob Steuber, Missouri	18	13	0	121
2 Frank Sinkwich, Georgia	**16**	**0**	**0**	**96**
2 Rudy Mobley, Hardin-Simmons	16	0	0	96
4 Gene Fekete, Ohio State	10	29	1	92
5 Paul Sarringhaus, Ohio State	13	0	0	78
6 Ralph Tate, Oklahoma State	10	12	0	72
7 Robert Kennedy, Washington State	11	3	0	69
8 John Bezemes, Holy Cross	11	0	0	66

INTERCEPTIONS	INT	YDS
1 Ray Evans, Kansas	10	76

Team Leaders

RUSHING OFFENSE	G	ATT	YDS	AVG	YPG
1 Hardin-Simmons	9	508	2767	5.4	307.4
2 Boston College	9	538	2635	4.9	292.8
3 Ohio State	10	571	2833	5.0	283.3
4 Missouri	12	597	3230	5.4	269.2
5 Texas	10	532	2496	4.7	249.6
6 Iowa Pre-Flight	10	515	2493	4.8	249.3
7 Auburn	**9**	**500**	**2223**	**4.4**	**247.0**
8 Great Lakes NAS	12	619	2906	4.7	242.2
9 Pennsylvania	9	518	2162	4.2	240.2
10 Georgia	**11**	**491**	**2624**	**5.3**	**238.5**

PASSING OFFENSE/YPG	G	ATT	COM	INT	PCT	YDS	YPA	YPG	I%	YPC
1 Tulsa	10	245	138	9	56.3	2339	9.5	233.9	3.7	16.9
2 Georgia	**11**	**245**	**122**	**18**	**49.8**	**2101**	**8.6**	**191.0**	**7.4**	**17.2**
3 Columbia	9	199	96	21	48.2	1661	8.3	184.6	10.6	17.3
4 Creighton	9	157	78	13	49.7	1393	8.9	154.8	8.3	17.9
5 Maryland	9	170	90	15	52.9	1364	8.0	151.6	8.8	15.2
6 Virginia	9	222	110	22	49.5	1307	5.9	145.2	9.9	11.9
7 SMU	11	271	111	30	41.0	1535	5.7	139.5	11.1	13.8
8 Texas-El Paso	9	199	89	19	44.7	1195	6.0	132.8	9.6	13.4
9 St. Mary's (Cal.)	10	184	79	16	42.9	1246	6.8	124.6	8.7	15.8
10 Georgia Tech	**10**	**178**	**68**	**18**	**38.2**	**1208**	**6.8**	**120.8**	**10.1**	**17.8**

TOTAL OFFENSE	G	P	YDS	AVG	YPG
1 Georgia	**11**	**736**	**4725**	**6.4**	**429.5**
2 Tulsa	10	627	4261	6.8	426.1
3 Boston College	9	672	3697	5.5	410.8
4 Ohio State	10	680	3975	5.8	397.5
5 Missouri	12	NA	4272	NA	356.0
6 Hardin-Simmons	9	574	3130	5.5	347.8
7 Iowa Pre-Flight	10	NA	3356	NA	335.6
8 Georgia Tech	**10**	**NA**	**3304**	**NA**	**330.4**
9 Indiana	10	620	3301	5.3	330.1
10 Texas	10	679	3205	4.7	320.5

RUSHING DEFENSE	G	ATT	YDS	AVG	YPG
1 Boston College	9	294	440	1.5	48.9
2 Texas	10	306	575	1.9	57.5
3 William & Mary	11	329	734	2.2	66.7
4 Alabama	**10**	**329**	**743**	**2.3**	**74.3**
5 Tennessee	**10**	**347**	**760**	**2.2**	**76.0**
6 Miami (Fla.)	9	341	717	2.1	79.7
7 Tulsa	10	345	839	2.4	83.9
8 North Carolina Navy	9	358	842	2.4	84.2
9 Minnesota	9	320	762	2.4	84.7
10 St. Mary's (Cal.)	10	337	852	2.5	85.2

PASSING DEFENSE	G	ATT	COM	PCT	YPC	INT	I%	YDS	YPA	YPG
1 Harvard	9	81	29	35.8	14.1	6	7.4	409	5.0	45.4
2 Texas-El Paso	8	105	40	38.1	9.1	5	4.8	363	3.5	45.4
3 Miami (Fla.)	9	115	46	40.0	9.5	19	16.5	437	3.8	48.6
4 Penn State	8	93	32	34.4	12.2	11	11.8	389	4.2	48.6
5 South Carolina	9	99	32	32.3	14.2	15	15.2	453	4.6	50.3
6 Lafayette	9	105	35	33.3	13.0	17	16.2	455	4.3	50.6
7 Manhattan	8	75	32	42.7	13.0	8	10.7	415	5.5	51.9
8 Richmond	10	130	33	25.4	15.8	14	10.8	520	4.0	52.0
9 Washington	10	129	41	31.8	13.6	22	10.1	556	4.3	55.6
10 Detroit	9	156	42	26.9	11.9	18	11.5	501	3.2	55.7

TOTAL DEFENSE	G	P	YDS	AVG	YPG
1 Texas	10	483	1173	2.4	117.3
2 Miami (Fla.)	9	456	1154	2.5	128.2
3 Boston College	9	501	1186	2.4	131.8
4 William & Mary	11	NA	1516	NA	137.8
5 North Carolina Navy	9	NA	1428	NA	142.8
6 Tennessee	**10**	**484**	**1435**	**3.0**	**143.5**
7 Minnesota	9	437	1314	3.0	146.0
8 Tulsa	10	489	1487	3.0	148.7
9 Holy Cross	10	483	1494	3.1	149.4
10 Great Lakes NAS	12	NA	1917	NA	159.8

SCORING OFFENSE	G	PTS	AVG
1 Tulsa	10	427	42.7

SCORING DEFENSE	G	PTS	AVG
1 Tulsa	10	32	3.2

1942

FINAL POLL (NOV. 30)

AP	SCHOOL	FINAL RECORD
1	Ohio State	9-1-0
2	**Georgia**	**11-1-0**
3	Wisconsin	8-1-1
4	Tulsa	10-1-0
5	**Georgia Tech**	**9-2-0**
6	Notre Dame	7-2-2
7	**Tennessee**	**9-1-1**
8	Boston College	8-2-0
9	Michigan	7-3-0
10	**Alabama**	**8-3-0**
11	Texas	9-2-0
12	Stanford	6-4-0
13	UCLA	7-4-0
14	William & Mary	9-1-1
15	Santa Clara	7-2-0
16	**Auburn**	**6-4-1**
17	Washington State	6-2-2
18	**Mississippi State**	**8-2-0**
19	Holy Cross	5-4-1
19	Minnesota	5-4-0
19	Penn State	6-1-1

CONSENSUS ALL-AMERICANS

POS	NAME	SCHOOL
B	**Frank Sinkwich**	**Georgia**
B	Paul Governali	Columbia
B	Mike Holovak	Boston College
B	Bill Hillenbrand	Indiana
E	Dave Schreiner	Wisconsin
E	Bob Dove	Notre Dame
T	Dick Wildung	Minnesota
T	Albert Wistert	Michigan
G	Chuck Taylor	Stanford
G	**Harvey Hardy**	**Georgia Tech**
G	Julie Franks	Michigan
C	**Joe Domnanovich**	**Alabama**

OTHERS RECEIVING FIRST-TEAM HONORS

B	Pat Harder	Wisconsin
B	Glenn Dobbs	Tulsa
B	**Roy Gafford**	**Auburn**
B	Bob Kennedy	Washington State
B	Angelo Bertelli	Notre Dame
B	Jackie Fellows	Fresno State
B	Bob Steuber	Missouri
E	Bob Shaw	Ohio State
E	Don Currivan	Boston College
E	Bernard Kuczynski	Pennsylvania
T	**Clyde Johnson**	**Kentucky**
T	Robin Olds	Army
T	Charles Csuri	Ohio State
T	Derrell Palmer	TCU
T	**Don Whitmire**	**Alabama**
T	Gil Bouley	Boston College
G	Lindell Houston	Ohio State
G	Garrard Ramsey	William and Mary
G	Alex Agase	Illinois
G	Merv Pregulman	Michigan
C	Fred Naumetz	Boston College
C	Spencer Moseley	Yale

HEISMAN TROPHY VOTING

PLAYER		POS	SCHOOL	TOTAL
1	**Frank Sinkwich**	**HB**	**Georgia**	**1059**
2	Paul Governali	QB	Columbia	218
3	**Clint Castleberry**	**RB**	**Georgia Tech**	**99**
4	Mike Holovak	RB	Boston College	90
5	Bill Hillenbrand	HB	Indiana	86
6	Angelo Bertelli	QB	Notre Dame	75
7	Dick Wildung	T	Minnesota	71
8	Gene Fekete	FB	Ohio State	65
9	Glenn Dobbs	RB	Tulsa	63
10	Dave Schreiner	E	Wisconsin	60

AWARD WINNERS

PLAYER	AWARD
Paul Governali, QB, Columbia	Maxwell

BOWL GAMES

DATE	GAME	SCORE
J1	Orange	Alabama 37, Boston College 21
J1	Rose	Georgia 9, UCLA 0
J1	Sugar	Tennessee 14, Tulsa 7
J1	Cotton	Texas 14, Georgia Tech 7
J1	Sun	Second Air Force 13, Hardin-Simmons 7

SEC STANDINGS

	CONFERENCE			OVERALL		
	W	L	T	W	L	T
Georgia	6	1	0	11	1	0
Tennessee	4	1	0	9	1	1
Georgia Tech	4	1	0	9	2	0
Mississippi State	5	2	0	8	2	0
Alabama	4	2	0	8	3	0
LSU	3	2	0	7	3	0
Auburn	3	3	0	6	4	1
Vanderbilt	2	4	0	6	4	0
Florida	1	3	0	3	7	0
Tulane	1	4	0	4	5	0
Kentucky	0	5	0	3	6	1
Mississippi	0	5	0	2	7	0

1943 NCAA MAJOR COLLEGE STATISTICAL LEADERS

INDIVIDUAL LEADERS

PASSING/COMPLETIONS	G	ATT	COM	PCT	INT	I%	YDS	YPA	COM.PG
1 Johnny Cook, Georgia	10	157	73	46.5	20	12.7	1007	6.4	7.3
2 Bob Hoernschemeyer, Indiana	10	154	69	44.8	15	9.7	1133	7.4	6.9
3 Eddie Prokop, Georgia Tech	10	133	66	49.6	17	12.8	806	6.1	6.6
4 Tony Hubka, Temple	8	109	59	54.1	10	9.2	549	5.0	7.4
5 Howard Tippee, Iowa State	8	122	56	45.9	13	10.7	637	5.2	7.0
6 David Marshall, Princeton	7	120	52	43.3	17	14.2	588	4.9	7.4
7 James Hallmark, Texas A&M	9	120	48	40.0	14	11.7	719	6.0	5.3
8 Don Kasprzak, Dartmouth	7	92	46	50.0	8	8.7	644	7.0	6.6
8 Jim Lucas, TCU	8	132	46	34.8	15	11.4	622	4.7	5.8
10 Clyde LeForce, Tulsa	7	90	43	47.8	5	5.6	557	6.2	6.1

ALL-PURPOSE YARDS	G	RUSH	REC	INT	PR	KR	YDS	YPG
1 Stan Koslowski, Holy Cross	8	784	63	50	438	76	1411	176.4

RUSHING/YARDS	G	ATT	YDS	AVG	YPG
1 Creighton Miller, Notre Dame	10	151	911	6.0	91.1
2 Steve Van Buren, LSU	8	150	847	5.6	105.9
3 Tony Butkovich, Purdue	9	142	833	5.9	92.6
4 Bill Daley, Michigan	9	120	817	6.8	90.8
5 Stan Koslowski, Holy Cross	8	161	784	4.9	98.0
6 Eddie Bray, Illinois	10	117	739	6.3	73.9
7 Jim Mello, Notre Dame	10	137	704	5.1	70.4
8 Ernie Parks, Ohio State	9	161	693	4.3	77.0
9 Dean Sensanbaugher, Ohio State	9	150	677	4.5	75.2
10 Joseph Kane, Pennsylvania	9	104	671	6.5	74.6

RUSHING/YARDS PER CARRY	G	ATT	YDS	YPC
1 Bill Daley, Michigan	9	120	817	6.8
2 Joseph Kane, Pennsylvania	9	104	671	6.5
3 Eddie Bray, Illinois	10	117	739	6.3
4 Creighton Miller, Notre Dame	10	151	911	6.0
5 Tony Butkovich, Purdue	9	142	833	5.9
6 Steve Van Buren, LSU	8	150	847	5.6
7 Jim Mello, Notre Dame	10	137	704	5.1
8 Stan Koslowski, Holy Cross	8	161	784	4.9
9 Dean Sensanbaugher, Ohio State	9	150	677	4.5
10 Ernie Parks, Ohio State	9	161	693	4.3

Based on top 10 rushers

RECEIVING/RECEPTIONS	G	REC	YDS	YPR	YPG	RPG
1 Neill Armstrong, Oklahoma State	7	39	317	8.1	45.3	5.6
2 Marion Flanagan, Texas A&M	9	23	403	17.5	44.8	2.6
3 James Dorough, Georgia Tech	10	20	290	14.5	29.0	2.0
3 Pete Pihos, Indiana	10	20	241	12.1	24.1	2.0
5 Billy Collins, VMI	8	19	333	17.5	41.6	2.4
5 Ben Jones, Arkansas	9	19	279	14.7	31.0	2.1
5 Tom Rock, Columbia	8	19	250	13.2	31.3	2.4

PUNTING	PUNT	YDS	AVG
1 Harold Cox, Arkansas	37	1518	41.0
2 Frank Meuhlheuser, Colgate	32	1258	39.3
3 Stan Koslowski, Holy Cross	40	1570	39.3
4 John Monahan, Dartmouth	37	1448	39.1
5 Stanley Turner, Texas A&M	72	2742	38.1
6 George Maxon, Army	35	1321	37.7

PUNT RETURNS/YARDS	PR	YDS	AVG
1 Marion Flanagan, Texas A&M	49	475	9.7

KICKOFF RETURNS/YARDS	KR	YDS	AVG
1 Paul Copoulos, Marquette	11	384	34.9

SCORING	TDS	XPT	FG	PTS
1 Steve Van Buren, LSU	14	14	0	98
2 Tony Butkovich, Purdue	16	0	0	96
3 Bob Brumley, Oklahoma	10	16	1	79
4 Johnny Cook, Georgia	13	0	0	78
4 Creighton Miller, Notre Dame	13	0	0	78
6 Stan Koslowski, Holy Cross	11	9	0	75
7 Charles Avery, Minnesota	12	0	0	72
7 Howard Blose, Cornell	12	0	0	72
9 Elroy Hirsch, Michigan	11	2	0	68
10 Eddie Prokop, Georgia Tech	7	24	0	66

INTERCEPTIONS	INT	YDS
1 Jay Stoves, Washington	7	139

TEAM LEADERS

RUSHING OFFENSE	G	ATT	YDS	AVG	YPG
1 Iowa Pre-Flight	10	481	3244	6.7	324.4
2 Notre Dame	10	625	3137	5.0	313.7
3 Duke	9	487	2660	5.5	295.6
4 Michigan	9	508	2648	5.2	294.2
5 Washington	4	197	1170	5.9	292.5
6 Army	10	499	2568	5.1	256.8
7 Texas	8	362	2016	5.6	252.0
8 Minnesota	9	410	2202	5.4	244.7
9 Navy	9	444	2165	4.9	240.6
10 Holy Cross	8	449	1876	4.2	234.5

PASSING OFFENSE/YPG	G	ATT	COM	INT	PCT	YDS	YPA	YPG	I%	YPC
1 Brown	8	142	67	13	47.2	1065	7.5	133.1	9.2	15.9
2 Tulsa	7	141	69	7	48.9	931	6.6	133.0	5.0	13.5
3 Texas A&M	9	197	78	24	39.6	1186	6.0	131.8	12.2	15.2
4 Georgia	9	164	75	21	45.7	1146	7.0	127.3	12.8	15.3
5 Arkansas	8	212	80	28	37.7	1015	4.8	126.9	13.2	12.7
6 Indiana	10	168	76	16	45.2	1241	7.4	124.1	9.5	16.3
7 Dartmouth	7	123	62	13	50.4	849	6.9	121.3	10.6	13.7
8 Georgia Tech	9	159	79	20	49.7	1011	6.4	112.3	12.6	12.8
9 Notre Dame	10	106	60	12	56.6	1043	9.8	104.3	11.3	17.4
10 Princeton	7	144	62	18	43.1	721	5.0	103.0	12.5	11.6

TOTAL OFFENSE	G	P	YDS	AVG	YPG
1 Notre Dame	10	734	4180	5.7	418.0
2 Iowa Pre-Flight	10	583	3929	6.7	392.9
3 Washington	4	250	1499	6.0	374.8
4 Duke	9	566	3299	5.8	366.6
5 Michigan	9	582	3269	5.6	363.2
6 Army	10	639	3545	5.5	354.5
7 Texas	8	499	2814	5.7	351.8
8 Tulsa	7	425	2379	5.6	339.9
9 Georgia	9	593	2969	5.0	329.9
10 Holy Cross	8	587	2628	4.5	328.5

RUSHING DEFENSE	G	ATT	YDS	AVG	YPG
1 Duke	9	235	355	1.5	39.4
2 Tulsa	7	229	327	1.4	46.7
3 Penn State	9	312	505	1.6	56.1
4 Washington	4	112	245	2.2	61.3
5 Holy Cross	8	254	517	2.0	64.6
6 Texas	8	223	556	2.5	69.5
7 Navy	9	347	667	1.9	74.1
8 Army	10	347	765	2.2	76.5
9 Texas A&M	9	361	773	2.1	85.9
10 Southern California	8	311	715	2.3	89.4

PASSING DEFENSE	G	ATT	COM	PCT	YPC	YDS	YPA	YPG
1 North Carolina	8	92	29	31.5	10.1	292	3.2	36.5
2 Texas A&M	9	138	33	23.9	12.3	407	2.9	45.2
3 Iowa State	8	86	29	33.7	13.8	400	4.7	50.0
4 Columbia	8	78	33	42.3	12.3	406	5.2	50.8
5 Northwestern	8	67	28	41.8	14.8	415	6.2	51.9
6 Indiana	10	103	39	37.9	14.2	555	5.4	55.5
7 Purdue	9	113	38	33.6	13.5	514	4.5	57.1
8 Wisconsin	9	72	29	40.3	18.0	523	7.3	58.1

TOTAL DEFENSE	G	P	YDS	AVG	YPG
1 Duke	9	405	1095	2.7	121.7
2 Tulsa	7	383	881	2.3	125.9
3 Penn State	9	439	1176	2.7	130.7
4 Texas A&M	9	488	1178	2.4	130.9
5 Holy Cross	8	371	1104	3.0	138.0
6 Texas	8	357	1110	3.1	138.8
7 Army	10	521	1525	2.9	152.5
8 Navy	9	499	1451	2.9	161.2
9 Southern California	8	413	1299	3.1	162.4
10 Michigan	8	460	1313	2.9	164.1

SCORING OFFENSE	G	PTS	AVG
1 Duke	9	335	37.2

SCORING DEFENSE	G	PTS	AVG
1 Duke	9	34	3.8

1943

FINAL POLL (NOV. 29)

AP	SCHOOL	FINAL RECORD
1	Notre Dame	9-1-0
2	Iowa Pre-Flight	9-1-0
3	Michigan	8-1-0
4	Navy	8-1-0
5	Purdue	9-0-0
6	Great Lakes NAS	10-2-0
7	Duke	8-1-0
8	Del Monte Pre-Flight	7-1-0
9	Northwestern	6-2-0
10	March Field	9-1-0
11	Army	7-2-1
12	Washington	4-1-0
13	**Georgia Tech**	**8-3-0**
14	Texas	7-1-1
15	Tulsa	6-1-1
16	Dartmouth	6-1-0
17	Bainbridge NTS	7-0-0
18	Colorado College	7-0-0
19	Pacific	7-2-0
20	Pennsylvania	6-2-1

CONSENSUS ALL-AMERICANS

POS	NAME	SCHOOL
B	Angelo Bertelli	Notre Dame
B	Creighton Miller	Notre Dame
B	Bill Daley	Michigan
B	Bob Odell	Pennsylvania
E	Ralph Heywood	Southern California
E	John Yonakor	Notre Dame
T	Jim White	Notre Dame
T	Don Whitmire	Navy
G	Alex Agase	Purdue
G	Pat Filley	Notre Dame
C	Casimir Myslinski	Army

OTHERS RECEIVING FIRST-TEAM HONORS		
B	Otto Graham	Northwestern
B	John Podesto	Pacific
B	Tony Butkovich	Purdue
E	Pete Pihos	Indiana
E	Joe Parker	Texas
E	Herb Hein	Northwestern
E	Albert Channell	Navy
E	Bob Gantt	Duke
T	Pat Preston	Duke
T	Art McCaffray	Pacific
T	Frank Merritt	Army
T	Merv Pregulman	Michigan
G	**John Steber**	**Georgia Tech**
G	George Brown	Navy
G	Harold Fisher	Southwestern

HEISMAN TROPHY VOTING

PLAYER		POS	SCHOOL	TOTAL
1	Angelo Bertelli	QB	Notre Dame	648
2	Bob Odell	HB	Pennsylvania	177
3	Otto Graham	QB	Northwestern	140
4	Creighton Miller	HB	Notre Dame	134
5	**Eddie Prokop**	**RB**	**Georgia Tech**	**85**
6	Hal Hamburg	HB	Navy	73
7	Bill Dailey	FB	Michigan	71
8	Tony Butkovich	FB	Purdue	65
9	Jim White	T	Notre Dame	52

AWARD WINNERS

PLAYER	AWARD
Bob Odell, HB, Pennsylvania	Maxwell

BOWL GAMES

DATE	GAME	SCORE
J1	**Orange**	**LSU 19, Texas A&M 14**
J1	**Sugar**	**Georgia Tech 20, Tulsa 18**
J1	Rose	Southern California 29, Washington 0
J1	Cotton	Randolph Field 7, Texas 7
J1	Sun	Southwestern Texas 7, New Mexico 0

SEC STANDINGS
CONFERENCE PLAYED AN ABBREVIATED
SCHEDULE DUE TO WORLD WAR II

	CONFERENCE			OVERALL		
	W	L	T	W	L	T
Georgia Tech	3	0	0	8	3	0
LSU	2	2	0	6	3	0
Tulane	1	1	0	3	3	0
Georgia	0	3	0	6	4	0

1944 NCAA Major College Statistical Leaders

Individual Leaders

PASSING/COMPLETIONS	G	ATT	COM	PCT	INT	I%	YDS	YPA	COM.PG
1 Paul Rickards, Pittsburgh	9	178	84	47.2	20	11.2	997	5.6	9.3
2 Frank Dancewicz, Notre Dame	10	153	68	44.4	12	7.8	989	6.5	6.8
3 James Cashion, Texas A&M	11	113	59	52.2	12	10.6	852	7.5	5.4
4 Bob Waterfield, UCLA	10	136	55	40.4	19	14.0	901	6.6	5.5
5 Allan Dekdebrun, Cornell	9	121	53	43.8	13	10.7	648	5.4	5.9
6 Gordon Long, Arkansas	11	155	51	32.9	19	12.3	823	5.3	4.6
7 Bobby Layne, Texas	9	91	50	54.9	5	5.5	662	7.3	5.6
8 Bob Fenimore, Oklahoma State	8	79	49	62.0	5	6.3	861	10.9	6.1
9 John Yungwirth, Northwestern	9	99	48	48.5	11	11.1	613	6.2	5.3
9 James Youel, Great Lakes NAS	12	113	48	42.5	6	5.3	818	7.2	4.0

ALL-PURPOSE YARDS	G	RUSH	REC	INT	PR	KR	YDS	YPG
1 Wayne "Red" Williams, Minnesota	9	911	0	0	242	314	1467	163.0

RUSHING/YARDS	G	ATT	YDS	AVG	YPG
1 Wayne "Red" Williams, Minnesota	9	136	911	6.7	101.2
2 Les Horvath, Ohio State	9	163	905	5.6	100.6
3 Bob Fenimore, Oklahoma State	8	162	897	5.5	112.1
4 Curtis Kuykendall, Auburn	8	127	841	6.6	105.1
5 Buddy Young, Illinois	10	94	840	8.9	84.0
6 Boris Dimancheff, Purdue	10	175	830	4.7	83.0
7 Paul Patterson, Illinois	10	131	790	6.0	79.0
8 John Duda, Virginia	9	125	716	5.7	79.6
9 Dub Jones, Tulane	7	140	700	5.0	100.0
10 Bob Kelly, Notre Dame	10	136	681	5.0	68.1

RUSHING/YARDS PER CARRY	G	ATT	YDS	YPC
1 Glenn Davis, Army	9	58	667	11.5
2 Buddy Young, Illinois	10	94	840	8.9
3 Anthony Minisi, Pennsylvania	8	78	551	7.1
4 Wayne "Red" Williams, Minnesota	9	136	911	6.7
5 Curtis Kuykendall, Auburn	8	127	841	6.6
6 Buster Stephens, Tennessee	8	101	631	6.2
7 Paul Patterson	10	131	790	6.0
8 Billy Rutland, Georgia	9	100	599	6.0
9 Camp Wilson, Tulsa	9	98	573	5.8
10 John Duda, Virginia	9	125	716	5.7

Based on top 20 rushers

RECEIVING/RECEPTIONS	G	REC	YDS	YPR	YPG	RPG
1 Reid Moseley, Georgia	9	32	506	15.8	56.2	3.6
2 Neill Armstrong, Oklahoma State	8	27	325	12.0	40.6	3.4
3 Barney White, Tulsa	9	25	450	18.0	50.0	2.8
4 John Howell, Texas A&M	11	24	394	16.4	35.8	2.2
5 Robert Folsom, SMU	10	21	246	11.7	24.6	2.1
6 Abe Addams, Indiana	9	21	332	15.8	36.9	2.3
7 Pat Thrash, South Carolina	9	20	298	14.9	33.1	2.2
7 Lamar Dingler, Arkansas	11	20	291	14.6	26.5	1.8
7 George Gilbert, Columbia	8	20	218	10.9	27.3	2.5
10 Cecil Hankins, Oklahoma State	8	19	474	24.9	59.3	2.4
10 Merle Gibson, TCU	10	19	371	19.5	37.1	1.9

PUNTING	PUNT	YDS	AVG
1 Bob Waterfield, UCLA	60	2575	42.9
2 Bob Wiese, Michigan	24	988	41.2
3 Jack Breslin, Michigan State	20	816	40.8
4 Walter Sheridan, Holy Cross	37	1503	40.6
5 Bobby Goff, Texas A&M	50	2014	40.3
6 Sid Tinsley, Clemson	52	2066	39.7
7 Louis Yacopec, Pittsburgh	24	951	39.6
8 Tom Davis, Duke	32	1226	38.3
9 Wayne Morgan, Columbia	24	915	38.1
10 Bob Kelly, Notre Dame	26	983	37.8

PUNT RETURNS/YARDS	PR	YDS	AVG
1 Joe Stuart, California	39	372	9.5
2 Elwood Petchel, Penn State	22	328	14.9
3 Glenn Davis, Army	16	294	18.4

KICKOFF RETURNS/YARDS	KR	YDS	AVG
1 Paul Copoulos, Marquette	14	337	24.1
2 Joe Stuart, California	15	317	21.1

SCORING	TDS	XPT	FG	PTS
1 Glenn Davis, Army	20	0	0	120
2 Bob Kelley, Notre Dame	13	6	0	84
2 Tom McWilliams, Mississippi State	14	0	0	84
4 Richard Brinkley, Wake Forest	13	0	0	78
4 Buddy Young, Illinois	13	0	0	78
6 Bob Fenimore, Oklahoma State	12	5	0	77
7 Keith DeCourcey, Washington	12	0	0	72
7 Boris Dimancheff, Purdue	12	0	0	72
7 Les Horvath, Ohio State	12	0	0	72
7 Fred Robbins, Lafayette	12	0	0	72

INTERCEPTIONS	INT	YDS
1 Jim Hardy, Southern California	8	73
2 Joe Stuart, California	7	NA

Team Leaders

RUSHING OFFENSE	G	ATT	YDS	AVG	YPG
1 Army	9	381	2687	7.1	298.6
2 Tulane	7	385	2074	5.4	296.3
3 Illinois	10	449	2940	6.5	294.0
4 Auburn	6	319	1752	5.5	292.0
5 Ohio State	9	542	2506	4.6	278.4
6 Virginia	9	481	2468	5.1	274.2
7 Minnesota	9	452	2381	5.3	264.6
8 Randolph Field	10	424	2574	6.1	257.4
9 Michigan	10	528	2541	4.8	254.1
10 Navy	9	470	2166	4.6	240.7

PASSING OFFENSE	G	ATT	COM	INT	PCT	YDS	YPA	YPG	I%	YPC
1 Tulsa	9	178	102	11	57.3	1857	10.4	206.3	6.2	18.2
2 Georgia Tech	6	125	53	10	42.4	852	6.8	142.0	8.0	16.1
3 Georgia	9	153	73	13	47.7	1244	8.1	138.2	8.5	17.0
4 Army	9	120	64	8	53.3	1190	9.9	132.2	6.7	18.6
5 Oklahoma State	8	110	63	8	57.3	1008	9.2	126.0	7.3	16.0
6 Pittsburgh	9	212	97	28	45.8	1117	5.3	124.1	13.2	11.5
7 Notre Dame	10	181	81	16	44.8	1229	6.8	122.9	8.8	15.2
8 Texas	9	166	88	12	53.0	1092	6.6	121.3	7.2	12.4
9 Randolph Field	10	160	66	12	41.3	1196	7.5	119.6	7.5	18.1
10 Texas A&M	11	177	88	18	49.7	1300	7.3	118.2	10.2	14.8

TOTAL OFFENSE	G	P	YDS	AVG	YPG
1 Tulsa	9	576	3912	6.8	434.7
2 Army	9	501	3877	7.7	430.8
3 Randolph Field	10	584	3770	6.5	377.0
4 Auburn	6	399	2191	5.5	365.2
5 Ohio State	9	635	3264	5.1	362.7
6 Illinois	10	521	3559	6.8	355.9
7 Notre Dame	10	690	3552	5.1	355.2
8 Georgia	9	680	3193	4.7	354.8
9 Navy	9	620	3159	5.1	351.0
10 Tulane	7	463	2381	5.1	340.1

RUSHING DEFENSE	G	ATT	YDS	AVG	YPG
1 Randolph Field	10	289	296	1.0	29.6
2 Navy	9	282	484	1.7	53.8
3 Virginia	9	276	499	1.8	55.4
4 Army	9	298	518	1.7	57.6
5 Texas A&M	11	390	845	2.2	76.8
6 Wake Forest	7	207	573	2.8	81.9
7 Tulsa	9	249	737	3.0	81.9
8 Yale	5	181	414	2.3	82.8
9 Southern California	9	277	759	2.7	84.3
10 Michigan State	6	220	532	2.4	88.7

PASSING DEFENSE	G	ATT	COM	PCT	YPC	INT	I%	YDS	YPA	YPG
1 Michigan State	6	66	14	21.2	11.4	12	18.2	160	2.4	26.7
2 Colgate	6	66	15	22.7	15.9	10	15.2	238	3.6	39.7
3 Virginia	9	120	33	27.5	11.3	17	14.2	373	3.1	41.4
4 Alabama	7	97	30	30.9	10.7	14	14.4	320	3.3	45.7
5 Wake Forest	7	96	28	29.2	11.9	12	12.5	334	3.5	47.7
6 Northwestern	9	90	32	35.6	14.4	9	10.0	462	5.1	51.3
7 South Carolina	9	108	36	33.3	13.4	17	15.7	483	4.5	53.7
8 Great Lakes NAS	12	197	65	33.0	10.0	24	12.2	648	3.3	54.0
9 Florida	7	83	25	30.1	15.6	14	16.9	389	4.7	55.6
10 TCU	10	128	48	37.5	11.8	16	12.5	567	4.4	56.7

TOTAL DEFENSE	G	P	YDS	AVG	YPG
1 Virginia	9	394	872	2.2	96.9
2 Randolph Field	10	516	1108	2.1	110.8
3 Michigan State	6	286	692	2.4	115.3
4 Army	9	499	1162	2.3	129.1
5 Wake Forest	7	303	907	3.0	129.6
6 Navy	9	447	1227	2.7	136.3
7 Yale	5	260	707	2.7	141.4
8 Alabama	7	365	1008	2.8	144.0
9 Southern California	9	434	1385	3.2	153.9
10 Texas A&M	11	607	1754	2.9	159.5

SCORING OFFENSE	G	PTS	AVG
1 Army	9	504	56.0

SCORING DEFENSE	G	PTS	AVG
1 Army	9	35	3.9

1944

Final Poll (Dec. 4)

AP	SCHOOL	FINAL RECORD
1	Army	9-0-0
2	Ohio State	9-0-0
3	Randolph Field	12-0-0
4	Navy	6-3-0
5	Bainbridge NTS	9-0-0
6	Iowa Pre-Flight	10-1-0
7	Southern California	8-0-2
8	Michigan	8-2-0
9	Notre Dame	8-2-0
10	4th Air Force	7-0-2
11	Duke	6-4-0
12	**Tennessee**	**7-1-1**
13	**Georgia Tech**	**8-3-0**
14	Norman NAS	6-0-0
15	Illinois	5-4-1
16	El Toro, CA, Marines	7-1-0
17	Great Lakes NAS	9-2-1
18	Fort Pierce	9-0-0
19	St. Mary's Pre-Flight	4-4-0
20	2nd Air Force	10-4-1

Consensus All-Americans

POS	NAME	SCHOOL
B	Les Horvath	Ohio State
B	Glenn Davis	Army
B	Doc Blanchard	Army
B	Bob Jenkins	Navy
E	**Phil Tinsley**	**Georgia Tech**
E	Paul Walker	Yale
E	Jack Dugger	Ohio State
T	Don Whitmire	Navy
T	John Ferraro	Southern California
G	Bill Hackett	Ohio State
G	Ben Chase	Navy
C	John Tavener	Indiana

Others receiving first-team honors

B	Bob Fenimore	Oklahoma State
B	Doug Kenna	Army
B	Boris Dimancheff	Purdue
B	Buddy Young	Illinois
B	Earl Girard	Wisconsin
E	Hubert Bechtol	Texas
E	Barney Poole	Army
T	Bill Willis	Ohio State
T	George Savitsky	Pennsylvania
G	Hamilton Nichols	Rice
G	John Green	Army
G	Joe Stanowicz	Army
G	Bill Hachten	California
G	Ellis Jones	Tulsa
G	Clyde Flowers	TCU
G	Ralph Serpico	Illinois
C	**Tex Warrington**	**Auburn**
C	Felto Prewitt	Tulsa

Heisman Trophy Voting

	PLAYER	POS	SCHOOL	TOTAL
1	Les Horvath	QB	Ohio State	412
2	Glenn Davis	HB	Army	287
3	Doc Blanchard	FB	Army	237
4	Don Whitmire	T	Navy	115
5	Buddy Young	HB	Illinois	105
6	Bob Kelly	HB	Notre Dame	76
7	Bob Jenkins	HB	Navy	60
8	Doug Kenna	QB	Army	56
9	Bob Fenimore	HB	Oklahoma State	54
10	**Thomas McWilliams**	**TB**	**Mississippi State**	**37**

Award Winners

PLAYER	AWARD
Glenn Davis, HB, Army	Maxwell

Bowl Games

DATE	GAME	SCORE
J1	Cotton	Oklahoma State 34, TCU 0
J1	**Sugar**	**Duke 29, Alabama 26**
J1	Rose	Southern California 25, Tennessee 0
J1	**Orange**	**Tulsa 26, Georgia Tech 12**
J1	Sun	Southwestern 35, U. of Mexico 0

SEC Standings

Conference played an abbreviated schedule due to World War II

	CONFERENCE			OVERALL		
	W	L	T	W	L	T
Vanderbilt	0	0	0	3	0	1
Georgia Tech	4	0	0	8	3	0
Tennessee	5	0	1	7	1	1
Georgia	4	2	0	7	3	0
Alabama	3	1	2	5	2	2
Mississippi State	3	2	0	6	2	0
LSU	2	3	1	2	5	1
Mississippi	2	3	0	2	6	0
Tulane	1	2	0	4	3	0
Kentucky	1	5	0	3	6	0
Florida	0	3	0	4	3	0
Auburn	0	4	0	4	4	0

1945 NCAA MAJOR COLLEGE STATISTICAL LEADERS

INDIVIDUAL LEADERS

PASSING/COMPLETIONS	G	ATT	COM	PCT	INT	I%	YDS	YPA	COM.PG
1 Al Dekdebrun, Cornell	9	194	90	46.4	15	7.7	1227	6.3	10.0
2 Leon Joslin, TCU	10	142	69	48.6	11	7.7	955	6.7	6.9
3 Jerry Niles, Iowa	9	179	63	35.2	15	8.4	872	4.9	7.0
4 Herman Wedemeyer, St. Mary's (Cal.)	8	103	59	57.3	5	4.9	1040	10.1	7.4
4 Jack Price, Baylor	11	125	59	47.2	16	12.8	708	5.7	5.4
6 **Harry Gilmer, Alabama**	9	88	57	64.8	3	3.4	905	10.3	6.3
7 Art Dakos, Yale	9	109	56	51.4	10	9.2	723	6.6	6.2
8 Bob DeMoss, Purdue	10	117	55	47.0	12	10.3	742	6.3	5.5
9 Russell Reader, Michigan State	9	90	53	58.9	5	5.6	613	6.8	5.9
10 **Ed Holtsinger, Georgia Tech**	9	116	49	42.4	9	7.8	682	5.9	5.4

ALL-PURPOSE YARDS	G	RUSH	REC	INT	PR	KR	YDS	YPG
1 Bob Fenimore, Oklahoma State	8	1048	12	129	157	231	1577	197.1

RUSHING/YARDS	G	ATT	YDS	AVG	YPG
1 Bob Fenimore, Oklahoma State	8	142	1048	7.4	131.0
2 Glenn Davis, Army	9	82	944	11.5	104.9
3 Ollie Cline, Ohio State	9	171	931	5.4	103.4
4 Walter Schlinkman, Texas Tech	10	145	871	6.0	87.1
5 Ed Cody, Purdue	10	157	847	5.4	84.7
6 Stan Koslowski, Holy Cross	9	186	841	4.5	93.4
7 George Taliaferro, Indiana	10	156	728	4.7	72.8
8 Doc Blanchard, Army	9	101	718	7.1	79.8
9 **Lowell Tew, Alabama**	9	88	715	8.1	79.4
10 Linwood Sexton, Wichita State	8	120	707	5.9	88.4

RUSHING/YARDS PER CARRY	G	ATT	YDS	YPC
1 Glenn Davis, Army	9	82	944	11.5
2 **Lowell Tew, Alabama**	9	88	715	8.1
3 **Gene Knight, LSU**	9	85	679	8.0
4 Guy Brown, Detroit	9	82	610	7.4
5 Bob Fenimore, Oklahoma State	8	142	1048	7.4
6 Cal Rossi, UCLA	6	95	679	7.1
7 Doc Blanchard, Army	9	101	718	7.1
8 Walter Schlinkman, Texas Tech	10	145	871	6.0
9 Linwood Sexton, Wichita State	8	120	707	5.9
10 Dick Conners, Northwestern	9	116	671	5.8
Based on top 20 rushers				

RECEIVING/RECEPTIONS	G	REC	YDS	YPR	YPG	RPG
1 **Reid Moseley, Georgia**	10	31	662	21.4	66.2	3.1
1 Gene Wilson, SMU	11	31	311	10.0	28.3	2.8
3 Steve Contos, Michigan State	9	31	285	9.2	31.7	3.4
4 Hub Bechtol, Texas	10	25	389	15.6	38.9	2.5
5 Denny O'Connor, St. Mary's (Cal.)	8	23	373	16.2	46.6	2.9
6 Bill Canfield, Purdue	10	23	314	13.7	31.4	2.3
7 Joe Joiner, Baylor	11	21	319	15.2	29.0	1.9
7 Paul Walker, Yale	9	21	277	13.2	30.8	2.3
9 **Wallace Jones, Kentucky**	6	19	369	19.4	61.5	3.2
9 Jesse Mason, TCU	10	19	218	11.5	21.8	1.9

PUNTING	PUNT	YDS	AVG
1 Howard Maley, SMU	59	2458	41.7
2 Harry Ghaul, Miami (Fla.)	63	2584	41.0
3 Floyd Lang, Penn State	22	893	40.6
4 Herman Wedemeyer, St. Mary's (Cal.)	24	963	40.1
5 Stan Koslowski, Holy Cross	37	1471	39.8
6 Robert Evans, Pennsylvania	40	1570	39.3
7 Bob Fenimore, Oklahoma State	23	897	39.0
8 Hardy Brown, Tulsa	40	1552	38.8
9 Jimmy Plyler, Texas	49	1897	38.7
10 **George Blanda, Kentucky**	32	1232	38.5

PUNT RETURNS/YARDS	PR	YDS	AVG
1 Jake Leicht, Oregon	28	395	14.1
2 Jimmy Jo Robinson, Pittsburgh	17	307	18.1
3 Jack Burns, Temple	NA	301	NA

KICKOFF RETURNS/YARDS	KR	YDS	AVG
1 Allen Dekdebrun, Cornell	14	321	22.9

SCORING	TDS	XPT	FG	PTS
1 Doc Blanchard, Army	19	1	0	115
2 Glenn Davis, Army	18	0	0	108
3 Harry Ghaul, Miami (Fla.)	13	22	0	100
4 Lou Kusserow, Columbia	15	0	0	90
5 Stan Koslowski, Holy Cross	12	15	0	87
6 Bob Fenimore, Oklahoma State	12	0	0	72
6 Ed Cody, Purdue	12	0	0	72
8 Herman Wedemeyer, St. Mary's (Cal.)	9	17	0	71
8 William Cromer, Colorado State	10	11	0	71
10 Five tied	11	0	0	66

INTERCEPTIONS	INT	YDS
1 Jake Leicht, Oregon	9	195
1 Herman Wedemeyer, St. Mary's (Cal.)	9	120

TEAM LEADERS

RUSHING OFFENSE	G	ATT	YDS	AVG	YPG
1 Army	9	424	3238	7.6	359.8
2 **LSU**	9	443	2705	6.1	300.6
3 **Alabama**	9	440	2679	6.1	297.7
4 Oklahoma State	8	383	2293	6.0	286.6
5 Notre Dame	9	451	2395	5.3	266.1
6 Maryland	7	345	1846	5.4	263.7
7 **Mississippi State**	8	443	2028	4.6	253.5
8 Ohio State	9	505	2133	4.2	237.0
9 Colorado College	8	366	1882	5.1	235.3
10 Indiana	10	484	2331	4.8	233.1

PASSING OFFENSE/YPG	G	ATT	COM	INT	PCT	YDS	YPA	YPG	I%	YPC
1 St. Mary's (Cal.)	8	150	74	16	49.3	1290	8.6	161.3	10.7	17.4
2 Cornell	9	207	95	17	45.9	1351	6.5	150.1	8.2	14.2
3 **Georgia**	9	159	71	17	44.7	1335	8.4	148.3	10.7	18.8
4 Oklahoma State	8	113	54	11	47.8	1070	9.5	133.8	9.7	19.8
5 Wake Forest	5	93	44	8	47.3	634	6.8	126.8	8.6	14.4
6 **Alabama**	9	117	71	4	60.7	1116	9.5	124.0	3.4	15.7
7 SMU	11	263	123	26	46.8	1310	5.0	119.1	9.9	10.7
8 TCU	10	190	87	19	45.8	1183	6.2	118.3	10.0	13.6
9 Colgate	6	94	46	8	48.9	694	7.4	115.7	8.5	15.1
10 South Carolina	7	103	44	14	42.7	808	7.8	115.4	13.6	18.4

TOTAL OFFENSE	G	P	YDS	AVG	YPG
1 Army	9	526	4164	7.9	462.7
2 **Alabama**	9	557	3795	6.8	421.7
3 Oklahoma State	8	496	3363	6.8	420.4
4 St. Mary's (Cal.)	8	502	2995	6.0	374.4
5 **Georgia**	9	575	3291	5.7	365.7
6 LSU	9	539	3269	6.1	363.2
7 Notre Dame	9	626	3180	5.1	353.3
8 Maryland	7	427	2433	5.7	347.6
9 Indiana	10	619	3254	5.3	325.4
10 Yale	9	648	2911	4.5	323.4

RUSHING DEFENSE	G	ATT	YDS	AVG	YPG
1 **Alabama**	9	320	305	1.0	33.9
2 **Tennessee**	7	231	385	1.7	55.0
3 Temple	8	296	520	1.8	65.0
4 St. Mary's (Cal.)	8	240	591	2.5	73.9
5 Penn State	8	295	634	2.1	79.3
6 Yale	9	300	721	2.4	80.1
7 Army	9	357	728	2.0	80.9
8 Texas	10	353	813	2.3	81.3
9 **Mississippi State**	8	256	670	2.6	83.8
10 Tulsa	10	353	850	2.4	85.0

PASSING DEFENSE	G	ATT	COM	PCT	YPC	YDS	YPA	YPG
1 Holy Cross	8	104	27	26.0	11.1	301	2.9	37.6
2 Virginia	6	63	18	28.6	14.8	267	4.2	44.5
3 Texas A&M	10	119	37	31.1	12.1	446	3.7	44.6
4 Iowa	9	83	32	38.6	13.5	433	5.2	48.1
5 **Georgia**	6	72	25	34.7	11.6	289	4.0	48.2
6 Pittsburgh	10	103	39	37.9	12.8	501	4.9	50.1
7 Michigan State	9	99	34	34.3	14.6	497	5.0	55.2
8 Virginia Tech	6	85	27	31.8	12.4	334	3.9	55.7
9 Illinois	9	118	34	28.8	15.2	518	4.4	57.6
10 **Florida**	9	104	40	38.5	13.4	536	5.2	59.6

TOTAL DEFENSE	G	P	YDS	AVG	YPG
1 **Alabama**	9	452	989	2.2	109.9
2 Temple	8	403	1005	2.5	125.6
3 Holy Cross	8	371	1131	3.0	141.4
4 **Mississippi State**	8	365	1191	3.3	148.9
5 St. Mary's (Cal.)	8	397	1236	3.1	154.5
6 Tulsa	10	491	1550	3.2	155.0
7 Yale	9	427	1441	3.4	160.1
8 **Tennessee**	7	368	1142	3.1	163.1
9 Indiana	10	536	1641	3.1	164.1
10 Army	9	515	1528	3.0	169.8

SCORING OFFENSE	G	PTS	AVG
1 Army	9	412	45.8

SCORING DEFENSE	G	PTS	AVG
1 St. Mary's (Cal.)	8	32	4.0

1945

Final Poll (Dec. 3)

AP	SCHOOL	FINAL RECORD
1	Army	9-0-0
2	Navy	7-1-1
3	**Alabama**	**10-0-0**
4	Indiana	9-0-1
5	Oklahoma State	9-0-0
6	Michigan	7-3-0
7	St. Mary's (Cal.)	6-2-0
8	Pennsylvania	6-2-0
9	Notre Dame	7-2-1
10	Texas	10-1-0
11	Southern California	7-4-0
12	Ohio State	7-2-0
13	Duke	6-2-0
14	**Tennessee**	**8-1-0**
15	**LSU**	**7-2-0**
16	Holy Cross	8-2-0
17	Tulsa	8-3-0
18	**Georgia**	**9-2-0**
19	Wake Forest	5-3-1
20	Columbia	8-1-0

Consensus All-Americans

POS	NAME	SCHOOL
B	Glenn Davis	Army
B	Doc Blanchard	Army
B	Herman Wedemeyer	St. Mary's (Cal.)
B	Bob Fenimore	Oklahoma State
E	Dick Duden	Navy
E	Hubert Bechtol	Texas
E	Bob Ravensberg	Indiana
E	Max Morris	Northwestern
T	Tex Coulter	Army
T	George Savitsky	Pennsylvania
G	Warren Amling	Ohio State
G	John Green	Army
C	**Vaughn Mancha**	**Alabama**

Others receiving first-team honors

B	**Harry Gilmer**	**Alabama**
B	Arnold Tucker	Army
B	Tom McWilliams	Army
E	Hank Foldberg	Army
E	Dick Pitzer	Army
T	Albert Nemetz	Army
T	**Mike Castronis**	**Georgia**
T	Tom Hughes	Purdue
G	John Mastrangelo	Notre Dame
G	Al Sparlis	UCLA
G	Art Gerometta	Army
C	Dick Scott	Navy
C	Herschel Fuson	Army

Heisman Trophy Voting

PLAYER	POS	SCHOOL	TOTAL
1 Doc Blanchard	FB	Army	860
2 Glenn Davis	HB	Army	638
3 Bob Fenimore	HB	Oklahoma State	187
4 Herman Wedemeyer	HB	St. Mary's (Cal.)	152
5 **Harry Gilmer**	**HB**	**Alabama**	**132**
6 Frank Dancewicz	QB	Notre Dame	56
7 Warren Amling	G	Ohio State	42
8 Pete Pihos	FB	Indiana	38

Award Winners

PLAYER	AWARD
Doc Blanchard, FB, Army	Maxwell

Bowl Games

DATE	GAME	SCORE
J1	**Rose**	**Alabama 34, Southern California 14**
J1	**Oil**	**Georgia 20, Tulsa 6**
J1	Orange	Miami (Fla.) 13, Holy Cross 6
J1	Sun	New Mexico 34, Denver 24
J1	Sugar	Oklahoma State 33, St. Mary's (Cal.) 13
J1	Cotton	Texas 40, Missouri 27
J1	Gator	Wake Forest 26, South Carolina 14
J1	Raisin	Drake 13, Fresno State 12

SEC Standings
Conference played an abbreviated schedule due to World War II

	Conference W	L	T	Overall W	L	T
Alabama	6	0	0	10	0	0
Tennessee	3	1	0	8	1	0
LSU	5	2	0	7	2	0
Georgia	4	2	0	9	2	0
Mississippi	3	3	0	4	5	0
Georgia Tech	2	2	0	4	6	0
Mississippi State	2	3	0	6	3	0
Auburn	2	3	0	5	5	0
Vanderbilt	2	4	0	3	6	0
Florida	1	3	1	4	5	1
Tulane	1	3	1	2	6	1
Kentucky	0	5	0	2	8	0

1946 NCAA Major College Statistical Leaders

Individual Leaders

PASSING/COMPLETIONS	G	ATT	COM	PCT	INT	I%	YDS	YPA	TD	TD%	COM.PG
1 Travis Tidwell, Auburn	10	158	79	50.0	10	6.3	943	6.0	5	3.2	7.9
2 Bobby Layne, Texas	10	140	77	55.0	14	10.0	1122	8.0	6	4.3	7.7
3 Ben Raimondi, Indiana	9	138	74	53.6	8	5.8	956	6.9	7	5.1	8.2
4 Harry Gilmer, Alabama	11	160	69	43.1	10	6.3	930	5.8	5	3.1	6.3
5 Bob Thomason, VMI	10	126	66	52.4	4	3.2	833	6.6	10	7.9	6.6
6 Charlie Conerly, Mississippi	9	124	64	51.6	13	10.5	641	5.2	3	2.4	7.1
7 Vic Clark, Texas-El Paso	8	107	61	57.0	8	7.5	604	5.6	6	5.6	7.6
7 Clyde LeForce, Tulsa	12	125	61	48.8	7	5.6	807	6.5	7	5.6	6.1
9 Bob DeMoss, Purdue	8	122	59	48.4	9	7.4	814	6.7	6	4.9	7.4
10 Dick Working, Washington & Lee	7	108	56	51.9	14	13.0	741	6.9	8	7.4	8.0
10 Bill Mackrides, Nevada	8	115	56	48.7	6	6.1	1254	10.9	17	14.8	7.0

ALL-PURPOSE YARDS	G	RUSH	REC	INT	PR	KR	YDS	YPG
1 Rudy Mobley, Hardin-Simmons	10	1262	13		79	273	138	1765	176.5

RUSHING/YARDS	G	ATT	YDS	AVG	YPG
1 Rudy Mobley, Hardin-Simmons	10	227	1262	5.6	126.2
2 Gene Roberts, U.T. Chattanooga	10	167	1113	6.7	111.3
3 Charlie Justice, North Carolina	10	131	943	7.2	94.3
4 Joe Golding, Oklahoma	10	126	902	7.2	90.2
5 Levi Jackson, Yale	9	134	806	6.0	89.6
6 Roger Stephens, Cincinnati	10	101	774	7.7	77.4
7 Travis Tidwell, Auburn	10	181	772	4.3	77.2
8 Charley Trippi, Georgia	10	115	744	6.5	74.4
9 Art Hodges, Wichita State	10	152	733	4.8	73.3
10 Glenn Davis, Army	10	123	712	5.8	71.2

RUSHING/YARDS PER CARRY	G	ATT	YDS	YPC
1 Roger Stephens, Cincinnati	10	101	774	7.7
2 Charlie Justice, North Carolina	10	131	943	7.2
3 Joe Golding, Oklahoma	10	126	902	7.2
4 George Guerre, Michigan State	10	90	633	7.0
5 Joseph Rogers, Villanova	10	90	620	6.9
6 Wally Kretz, Cornell	9	89	602	6.8
7 Gene Roberts, U.T. Chattanooga	10	167	1113	6.7
8 Forrest Hall, San Francisco	9	89	579	6.5
9 Charley Trippi, Georgia	10	115	744	6.5
10 Levi Jackson, Yale	9	134	806	6.0

Based on top 20 rushers

RECEIVING/RECEPTIONS	G	REC	YDS	YPR	YPG	RPG
1 Neill Armstrong, Oklahoma State	10	32	479	15.0	47.9	3.2
2 James Montgomery, Arizona State	11	32	399	12.5	36.3	2.9
3 Broughton Williams, Florida	8	29	490	16.9	61.3	3.6
3 Red O'Quinn, Wake Forest	9	29	441	15.2	49.0	3.2
5 Barney Poole, Mississippi	9	28	277	9.9	30.8	3.1
6 John Roderick, Yale	9	27	403	14.9	44.8	3.0
7 George Blomquist, North Carolina St.	10	26	403	15.5	40.3	2.6
7 Sam Marusich, Texas-El Paso	9	26	382	14.7	42.4	2.9
9 Lou Mihajlovich, Indiana	9	25	300	12.0	33.3	2.8
10 Ted Cook, Alabama	11	24	377	15.7	34.3	2.2

PUNTING	PUNT	YDS	AVG
1 John Galvin, Purdue	30	1286	42.9
2 Fred Wendt, Texas-El Paso	46	1969	42.8
3 Charley Loiacano, Lafayette	43	1832	42.6
4 Leslie Palmer, North Carolina St.	31	1296	41.8
5 Harry Ghaul, Miami (Fla.)	59	2449	41.5
6 Jerry Moore, Vanderbilt	53	2178	41.1
7 Charlie Conerly, Mississippi	57	2331	40.9
8 Don Rezzer, Denver	30	1221	40.7
9 Bill Long, Oklahoma State	38	1543	40.6
10 Billy Richards, SMU	63	2552	40.5

PUNT RETURNS/YARDS	PR	YDS	AVG
1 Harry Gilmer, Alabama	37	436	11.8
2 Herman Wedemeyer, St. Mary's (Cal.)	26	397	15.3
3 Clyde LeForce, Tulsa	25	382	15.3
4 Walt Slater, Tennessee	26	347	13.3
5 George Clark, Duke	21	344	16.4
6 Travis Tidwell, Auburn	29	341	11.8
7 Lindy Berry, TCU	23	315	13.7
8 Shorty McWilliams, Mississippi State	19	306	16.1
9 Joe Wright, Detroit	19	305	16.1
10 Harold Griffin, Florida	15	302	20.1

KICKOFF RETURNS/YARDS	KR	YDS	AVG
1 Forrest Hall, San Francisco	15	573	38.2
2 Bob Longacre, William & Mary	9	375	41.7
3 Charlie Justice, North Carolina	10	344	34.4
4 Louie Viau, Kings Point	10	343	34.3
5 Harold Griffin, Florida	13	311	23.9
6 Art Hodges, Wichita State	14	296	21.1
7 Howard Turner, North Carolina St.	7	275	39.3
8 Wally Kretz, Cornell	11	273	24.8
9 Don Phelps, Kentucky	6	270	45.0
10 Charley Loiacano, Lafayette	15	265	17.7

SCORING	TDS	XPT	FG	PTS
1 Gene Roberts, U.T. Chattanooga	18	9	0	117
2 Rudy Mobley, Hardin-Simmons	16	0	0	96
3 Forrest Hall, San Francisco	13	9	0	87
4 Charley Trippi, Georgia	14	0	0	84
5 Herman Hering, Rutgers	12	8	0	80
6 Glenn Davis, Army	13	0	0	78
7 Charlie Justice, North Carolina	12	0	0	72
8 Clyde LeForce, Tulsa	5	34	1	67
9 Jack Cloud, William & Mary	11	0	0	66
10 Doc Blanchard, Army	10	2	0	62

INTERCEPTIONS	INT	YDS
1 Larry Hatch, Washington	8	114
1 Harry Gilmer, Alabama	8	79
3 Arnold Tucker, Army	8	57
4 Phil O'Donnell, Harvard	7	176

Team Leaders

RUSHING OFFENSE	G	ATT	YDS	AVG	YPG
1 Notre Dame	9	567	3061	5.4	340.1
2 Hardin-Simmons	10	540	2906	5.4	290.6
3 Utah	8	418	2108	5.0	263.5
4 Detroit	10	510	2632	5.2	263.2
5 UCLA	10	508	2598	5.1	259.8
6 Oklahoma	10	499	2354	4.7	235.4
7 North Carolina	10	452	2341	5.2	234.1
8 Yale	9	452	2100	4.6	233.3
9 Pennsylvania	8	378	1865	4.9	233.1
10 Army	10	454	2242	4.9	224.2

PASSING OFFENSE/YPG	G	ATT	COM	INT	PCT	YDS	YPA	TD	YPG	I%	YPC
1 Nevada	8	156	68	14	43.6	1569	10.1	20	198.1	9.0	23.1
2 Georgia	10	206	112	9	54.4	1737	8.4	23	173.7	4.4	15.5
3 Texas	10	186	99	19	53.2	1569	8.4	12	156.9	10.2	15.8
4 Oklahoma State	11	252	107	25	42.5	1652	6.6	13	150.2	9.9	15.4
5 Michigan	9	162	73	22	45.1	1322	8.2	10	146.9	13.6	18.1
6 Boston College	9	175	82	14	46.9	1266	7.2	14	140.7	8.0	15.4
7 Indiana	9	185	95	15	51.4	1264	6.8	8	140.4	8.1	13.3
8 Marquette	9	189	90	19	47.6	1243	6.6	13	138.1	10.1	13.8
9 Princeton	8	167	68	14	40.7	1096	6.6	4	137.0	8.4	16.1
10 Washington & Lee	8	165	87	20	52.7	1085	6.6	12	135.6	12.1	12.5

TOTAL OFFENSE	G	P	YDS	AVG	YPG
1 Notre Dame	9	690	3972	5.8	441.3
2 Georgia	10	622	3946	6.3	394.6
3 Nevada	8	484	3114	6.4	389.3
4 UCLA	10	646	3779	5.8	377.9
5 Hardin-Simmons	10	642	3594	5.6	359.4
6 Michigan	9	579	3166	5.5	351.8
7 Boston College	9	598	3159	5.3	351.0
8 Yale	9	598	3095	5.2	343.9
9 Utah	8	531	2747	5.2	343.4
10 Pennsylvania	8	503	2720	5.4	340.0

RUSHING DEFENSE	G	ATT	YDS	AVG	YPG
1 Oklahoma	10	359	580	1.6	58.0
2 Mississippi State	10	334	664	2.0	66.4
3 Harvard	9	330	679	2.1	75.4
4 South Carolina	8	292	637	2.2	79.6
5 Notre Dame	9	321	753	2.3	83.7
6 North Carolina St.	10	360	850	2.4	85.0
7 Yale	9	310	769	2.5	85.4
8 William & Mary	10	349	895	2.6	89.5
9 Tulsa	10	360	930	2.6	93.0
10 Texas	10	374	934	2.5	93.4

PASSING DEFENSE	G	ATT	COM	PCT	YPC	YDS	YPA	YPG
1 Holy Cross	9	107	35	32.7	13.8	483	4.5	53.7
2 West Texas St.	10	124	43	34.7	13.3	570	4.6	57.0
3 Notre Dame	9	144	54	37.5	9.7	522	3.6	58.0
4 Indiana	9	127	39	30.7	13.8	538	4.2	59.8
5 Florida	9	84	39	46.4	14.3	557	6.6	61.9
6 Rice	10	168	62	36.9	10.2	630	3.8	63.0
7 Detroit	10	160	55	34.4	11.5	634	4.0	63.4
8 Penn State	8	133	46	34.6	11.1	509	3.8	63.6
9 West Virginia	10	131	47	35.9	13.7	642	4.9	64.2
10 Navy	9	115	43	37.4	13.4	578	5.0	64.2

TOTAL DEFENSE	G	P	YDS	AVG	YPG
1 Notre Dame	9	465	1275	2.7	141.7
2 Oklahoma	10	539	1550	2.9	155.0
3 Penn State	8	454	1271	2.8	158.9
4 North Carolina St.	10	501	1621	3.2	162.1
5 Rice	10	547	1663	3.0	166.3
6 Davidson	9	432	1498	3.5	166.4
7 Hardin-Simmons	10	537	1673	3.1	167.3
8 Mississippi State	10	502	1695	3.4	169.5
9 Harvard	9	501	1536	3.1	170.7
10 Texas	10	562	1760	3.1	176.0

SCORING OFFENSE	G	PTS	AVG
1 Georgia	10	372	37.2

SCORING DEFENSE	G	PTS	AVG
1 Notre Dame	9	24	2.7

1946

FINAL POLL (DEC. 2)

AP	SCHOOL	FINAL RECORD
1	Notre Dame	8-0-1
2	Army	9-0-1
3	**Georgia**	**11-0-0**
4	UCLA	10-1-0
5	Illinois	8-2-0
6	Michigan	6-2-1
7	**Tennessee**	**9-2-0**
8	**LSU**	**9-1-1**
9	North Carolina	8-2-1
10	Rice	9-2-0
11	**Georgia Tech**	**9-2-0**
12	Yale	7-1-1
13	Pennsylvania	6-2-0
14	Oklahoma	8-3-0
15	Texas	8-2-0
16	Arkansas	6-3-2
17	Tulsa	9-1-0
18	North Carolina St.	8-3-0
19	Delaware	10-0-0
20	Indiana	6-3-0

CONSENSUS ALL-AMERICANS

POS	NAME	SCHOOL
B	John Lujack	Notre Dame
B	**Charley Trippi**	**Georgia**
B	Glenn Davis	Army
B	Doc Blanchard	Army
E	Burr Baldwin	UCLA
E	Hubert Bechtol	Texas
E	Hank Foldberg	Army
T	George Connor	Notre Dame
T	Warren Amling	Ohio State
T	**Dick Huffman**	**Tennessee**
G	Alex Agase	Illinois
G	Weldon Humble	Rice
C	**Paul Duke**	**Georgia Tech**

OTHERS RECEIVING FIRST-TEAM HONORS

E	Elmer Madar	Michigan
T	George Savitsky	Pennsylvania
G	John Mastrangelo	Notre Dame
C	George Strohmeyer	Notre Dame

HEISMAN TROPHY VOTING

PLAYER	POS	SCHOOL	TOTAL
1 Glenn Davis	HB	Army	792
2 **Charley Trippi**	**HB**	**Georgia**	**435**
3 John Lujack	QB	Notre Dame	379
4 Doc Blanchard	FB	Army	267
5 Arnie Tucker	QB	Army	257
6 Herman Wedemeyer	HB	St. Mary's (Cal.)	101
7 Burr Baldwin	E	UCLA	49
8 Bobby Layne	QB	Texas	45

AWARD WINNERS

PLAYER	AWARD
Charley Trippi, HB, Georgia	**Maxwell**
George Connor, T, Notre Dame	Outland

BOWL GAMES

DATE	GAME	SCORE
J1	Tangerine	Catawba 31, Maryville 6
J1	**Cotton**	**LSU 0, Arkansas 0**
J1	Sun	Cincinnati 18, Virginia Tech 6
J1	**Oil**	**Georgia Tech 41, St. Mary's (Cal.) 19**
J1	Rose	Illinois 45, UCLA 14
J1	Gator	Oklahoma 34, North Carolina St. 13
J1	**Sugar**	**Georgia 20, North Carolina 10**
J1	**Orange**	**Rice 8, Tennessee 0**
J1	Raisin	San Jose State 20, Utah State 0
J1	Harbor	Montana State 13, New Mexico 13
J4	Alamo	Hardin-Simmons 20, Denver 0

SEC STANDINGS

	CONFERENCE			OVERALL		
	W	L	T	W	L	T
Georgia	5	0	0	11	0	0
Tennessee	5	0	0	9	2	0
LSU	5	1	0	9	1	1
Georgia Tech	4	2	0	9	2	0
Mississippi State	3	2	0	8	2	0
Alabama	4	3	0	7	4	0
Vanderbilt	3	4	0	5	4	0
Kentucky	2	3	0	7	3	0
Tulane	2	4	0	3	6	0
Auburn	1	5	0	4	6	0
Mississippi	1	6	0	2	7	0
Florida	0	5	0	0	9	0

1947 NCAA Major College Statistical Leaders

Individual Leaders

PASSING/COMPLETIONS	G	ATT	COM	PCT	INT	I%	YDS	YPA	TD	TD%	COM.PG
1 Charlie Conerly, Mississippi	10	233	133	57.1	7	3.0	1367	5.9	18	7.7	13.3
2 Johnny Rauch, Georgia	11	181	98	54.1	10	5.5	1352	7.5	10	5.5	8.9
3 Fred Enke Jr., Arizona	10	184	88	47.8	10	5.4	1406	7.6	11	6.0	8.8
4 Rex Olsen, Brigham Young	10	158	79	50.0	13	8.2	982	6.2	7	4.4	7.9
5 Dick Working, Washington & Lee	10	143	78	54.5	9	6.3	895	6.3	6	4.2	7.8
6 Norm Van Brocklin, Oregon	10	168	76	45.2	12	7.1	939	5.6	9	5.4	7.6
7 Perry Moss, Illinois	9	127	71	59.9	7	5.5	719	5.7	5	3.9	7.9
8 Frank Downing, Lafayette	9	126	67	53.2	11	8.7	731	5.8	4	3.2	7.4
9 Bobby Layne, Texas	10	115	63	54.9	7	6.1	965	8.4	9	7.8	6.3
10 Tex Furse, Yale *	9	99	61	61.6	5	5.1	722	7.3	1	1.0	6.8

* Two others tied with 61 completions, but they had a lower completion percentage

ALL-PURPOSE YARDS	G	RUSH	REC	INT	PR	KR	YDS	YPG
1 Wilton Davis, Hardin-Simmons	10	1173	79	0	295	251	1798	179.8

RUSHING/YARDS	G	ATT	YDS	AVG	YPG
1 Wilton Davis, Hardin-Simmons	10	193	1173	6.1	117.3
2 Lou Gambino, Maryland	10	125	904	7.2	90.4
3 Frank Neilson, Utah	10	152	885	5.8	88.5
4 Harry Szulborski, Purdue	9	136	851	6.3	94.6
5 Bobby Forbes, Florida	10	118	766	6.5	76.6
6 Elwyn Rowan, Army	9	123	750	6.1	83.3
7 Ed Smith, Texas-El Paso	9	135	742	5.5	82.4
8 Charles Hall, Arizona	10	124	686	5.5	68.6
9 Linwood Sexton, Wichita State	10	92	685	7.4	68.5
10 Mike Kaysserian, Detroit	10	87	684	7.9	68.4

RUSHING/YARDS PER CARRY	G	ATT	YDS	YPC
1 Jack Kurkowski, Detroit	10	61	614	10.1
2 Mike Kaysserian, Detroit	10	87	684	7.9
3 Linwood Sexton, Wichita State	10	92	685	7.4
4 Lou Gambino, Maryland	10	125	904	7.2
5 Jack Weisenburger, Michigan	9	101	682	6.8
6 Bobby Forbes, Florida	10	118	766	6.5
7 Harry Szulborski, Purdue	9	136	851	6.3
8 Elwyn Rowan, Army	9	123	750	6.1
9 Wilton Davis, Hardin-Simmons	10	193	1173	6.1
10 Art Hodges, Wichita State	10	108	630	5.8

Based on top 20 rushers

RECEIVING/RECEPTIONS	G	REC	YDS	TD	YPR	YPG	RPG
1 Barney Poole, Mississippi	10	52	513	8	9.9	51.3	5.2
2 Dan Edwards, Georgia	11	38	540	4	14.2	49.1	3.5
3 Vince Cisterna, Northern Arizona	9	33	441	2	13.4	49.0	3.7
4 John Smith, Arizona	10	31	568	6	18.3	56.8	3.1
5 Bill Swiacki, Columbia	9	31	517	4	16.7	57.4	3.4
6 George Brodnax, Georgia Tech	10	31	400	5	12.9	40.0	3.1
7 Tom Bienemann, Drake	9	30	345	4	11.5	38.3	3.3
8 John Setear, Yale	9	28	290	1	10.4	32.2	3.1
9 Jim Powell, Tennessee	10	27	407	3	15.1	40.7	2.7
10 Lou Mihajlovich, Indiana	9	26	349	2	13.4	38.8	2.9

PUNTING	PUNT	YDS	AVG
1 Leslie Palmer, North Carolina St.	65	2816	43.3
2 Forrest Bast, Lehigh	56	2419	43.2
3 Fred Folger, Duke	68	2910	42.8
4 Jack Pesek, Nebraska	42	1793	42.7
5 Charlie Justice, North Carolina	61	2538	41.6
6 George Grimes, Virginia	50	2040	40.8
7 Zack Clinard, Vanderbilt	50	2030	40.6
8 Harry Ghaul, Miami (Fla.)	63	2539	40.3
9 Bob Dean, Cornell	41	1648	40.2
10 Norm Van Brocklin, Oregon	66	2647	40.1

PUNT RETURNS/YARDS	PR	YDS	AVG
1 Lindy Berry, TCU	42	493	11.7
2 Jake Leicht, Oregon	35	480	13.7

KICKOFF RETURNS/YARDS	KR	YDS	AVG
1 Doak Walker, SMU	10	387	38.7
2 Garner Barnett, Arizona State	15	373	24.9
3 Herman Wedemeyer, St. Mary's (Cal.)	20	361	18.1

SCORING	TDS	XPT	FG	PTS
1 Lou Gambino, Maryland	16	0	0	96
2 Jack Cloud, William & Mary	15	0	0	90
2 Wilton Davis, Hardin-Simmons	15	0	0	90
4 Doak Walker, SMU	11	18	1	87
5 Terry Brennan, Notre Dame	11	0	0	66
5 Mike Kaysserian, Detroit	11	0	0	66
7 J.R. Boone, Tulsa	10	1	0	61
8 Elwyn Rowan, Army *	10	0	0	60

* Tied with seven others

INTERCEPTIONS	INT	YDS
1 John Bruce, William & Mary	9	78
2 George Sims, Baylor	8	208
2 Phil O'Donnell, Harvard	8	171
2 Ed Stec, Bucknell	8	NA
5 Jackie Jensen, California	7	114
5 Allen Davis, Utah	7	NA
5 Van Heuitt, St. Mary's (Cal.)	7	NA
5 Billy Vigh, Rutgers	7	NA
5 Darrell Royal, Oklahoma	7	38
5 Paul Page, SMU	7	37

Team Leaders

RUSHING OFFENSE	G	ATT	YDS	AVG	YPG
1 Detroit	10	504	3197	6.3	319.7
2 Penn State	9	527	2713	5.1	301.4
3 Wichita State	10	457	2904	6.4	290.4
4 Notre Dame	9	514	2464	4.8	273.8
5 Hardin-Simmons	10	511	2693	5.3	269.3
6 Missouri	10	566	2581	4.6	258.1
7 Oklahoma	10	535	2484	4.6	248.4
8 California	10	463	2470	5.3	247.0
9 Army	9	443	2223	5.0	247.0
10 Michigan	9	429	2149	5.0	238.8

PASSING OFFENSE/YPG	G	ATT	COM	INT	PCT	YDS	YPA	TD	YPG	I%	YPC
1 Michigan	9	153	77	16	50.3	1565	10.2	15	173.9	10.5	20.3
2 Arizona	10	226	107	14	47.3	1680	7.4	13	168.0	6.2	15.7
3 Indiana	9	164	83	17	50.6	1393	8.5	10	154.8	10.4	16.8
4 Mississippi	10	256	147	8	57.4	1496	5.8	19	149.6	3.1	10.2
5 Clemson	9	153	67	19	43.8	1331	8.7	12	147.9	12.4	19.9
6 Brigham Young	10	215	100	18	46.5	1433	6.7	11	143.3	8.4	14.3
7 San Francisco	10	175	79	11	45.1	1407	8.0	8	140.7	6.3	17.8
8 Texas A&M	10	251	117	28	46.6	1389	5.5	10	138.9	11.2	11.9
9 Notre Dame	9	154	86	9	55.8	1213	7.9	12	134.8	5.8	14.1
10 Wake Forest	10	207	86	19	41.5	1327	6.4	9	132.7	9.2	15.4

TOTAL OFFENSE	G	P	YDS	AVG	YPG
1 Michigan	9	582	3714	6.4	412.7
2 Notre Dame	9	668	3677	5.5	408.6
3 Detroit	10	652	4002	6.1	400.2
4 Penn State	9	606	3275	5.4	363.9
5 California	10	627	3625	5.8	362.5
6 Hardin-Simmons	10	634	3573	5.6	357.3
7 Wichita State	10	550	3478	6.3	347.8
8 Missouri	10	707	3428	4.8	342.8
9 San Francisco	10	617	3385	5.5	338.5
9 Nevada	10	684	3385	4.9	338.5

RUSHING DEFENSE	G	ATT	YDS	AVG	YPG
1 Penn State	9	240	153	0.6	17.0
2 William & Mary	10	307	615	2.0	61.5
3 Georgia Tech	10	380	743	2.0	74.3
4 North Carolina	10	347	881	2.5	88.1
5 Boston College	9	295	805	2.7	89.4
6 Holy Cross	10	371	899	2.4	89.9
7 South Carolina	9	329	820	2.5	91.1
8 Alabama	10	342	912	2.7	91.2
9 Utah	9	319	831	2.6	92.3
10 UCLA	9	338	838	2.5	93.1

PASSING DEFENSE	G	ATT	COM	INT	YPC	PCT	I%	YDS	YPA	TD	YPG
1 North Carolina St.	9	86	31	36.0	11.4	15	17.4	354	4.1	1	39.3
2 Colorado College	9	85	24	28.2	15.9	9	10.6	382	4.5	5	42.4
3 Maryland	10	132	40	30.3	11.2	20	15.2	446	3.4	3	44.6
4 Davidson	10	130	40	30.8	12.2	13	10.0	486	3.7	2	48.6
5 Iowa State	9	91	33	36.3	14.7	11	12.1	486	5.3	5	54.0
6 Notre Dame	9	155	53	34.2	9.5	11	7.1	504	3.3	2	56.0
7 Penn State	9	147	40	27.2	13.5	22	15.0	538	3.7	2	59.8
8 Lehigh	9	128	41	32.0	13.1	19	14.8	539	4.2	4	59.9
9 Georgia	11	116	45	38.8	15.1	16	13.8	678	5.8	6	61.6
10 San Francisco	10	148	45	30.4	13.8	17	11.5	620	4.2	4	62.0

TOTAL DEFENSE	G	P	YDS	AVG	YPG
1 Penn State	9	387	691	1.8	76.8
2 William & Mary	10	466	1345	2.9	134.5
3 Georgia Tech	10	535	1418	2.7	141.8
4 Davidson	10	502	1487	3.0	148.7
5 Georgia	11	531	1763	3.3	160.3
6 Holy Cross	10	528	1658	3.1	165.8
7 South Carolina	9	469	1509	3.2	167.7
8 Notre Dame	9	535	1514	2.8	168.2
9 North Carolina St.	9	413	1518	3.7	168.7
10 Pennsylvania	8	417	1401	3.4	175.1

SCORING OFFENSE	G	PTS	AVG
1 Michigan	9	345	38.3
2 Penn State	9	319	35.4
3 Notre Dame	9	291	32.3
4 Nevada	10	308	30.8
5 William & Mary	10	301	30.1
6 Rutgers	9	262	29.1
7 Kansas	10	290	29.0
8 Detroit	10	276	27.6
9 California	10	275	27.5
10 Pennsylvania	8	219	27.4

SCORING DEFENSE	G	PTS	AVG
1 Penn State	9	27	3.0
2 Georgia Tech	10	35	3.5
3 Pennsylvania	8	35	4.4
4 Notre Dame	9	52	5.8
5 Michigan	9	53	5.9
6 Kentucky	10	59	5.9
7 North Carolina St.	9	57	6.3
8 William & Mary	10	66	6.6
9 Texas	10	67	6.7
10 Southern California	9	65	7.2

1947

Final Poll (Dec. 8)

AP	SCHOOL	FINAL RECORD
1	Notre Dame	9-0-0
2	Michigan	10-0-0
3	SMU	9-0-2
4	Penn State	9-0-1
5	Texas	10-1-0
6	**Alabama**	**8-3-0**
7	Pennsylvania	7-0-1
8	Southern California	7-2-1
9	North Carolina	8-2-0
10	Georgia Tech	10-1-0
11	Army	5-2-2
12	Kansas	8-1-2
13	**Mississippi**	**9-2-0**
14	William & Mary	9-2-0
15	California	9-1-0
16	Oklahoma	7-2-1
17	North Carolina St.	5-3-1
18	Rice	6-3-1
19	Duke	4-3-2
20	Columbia	7-2-0

Consensus All-Americans

POS	NAME	SCHOOL
B	John Lujack	Notre Dame
B	Bob Chappuis	Michigan
B	Doak Walker	SMU
B	**Charley Conerly**	**Mississippi**
B	Bobby Layne	Texas
E	Paul Cleary	Southern California
E	Bill Swiacki	Columbia
T	**Bob Davis**	**Georgia Tech**
T	George Connor	Notre Dame
G	Joe Steffy	Army
G	Bill Fischer	Notre Dame
C	Chuck Bednarik	Pennsylvania

Others receiving first-team honors

B	Bump Elliott	Michigan
B	Ray Evans	Kansas
B	Tony Minisi	Pennsylvania
E	Leon Hart	Notre Dame
E	**Barney Poole**	**Mississippi**
T	George Savitsky	Pennsylvania
T	John Ferraro	Southern California
T	Dick Harris	Texas
T	Ziggy Czarobski	Notre Dame
G	Rod Franz	California
G	Steve Suhey	Penn State
C	Dick Scott	Navy

Heisman Trophy Voting

	PLAYER	POS	SCHOOL	TOTAL
1	John Lujack	QB	Notre Dame	742
2	Bob Chappuis	HB	Michigan	555
3	Doak Walker	RB	SMU	196
4	**Charley Conerly**	**HB**	**Mississippi**	**186**
5	**Harry Gilmer**	**HB**	**Alabama**	**115**
6	Bobby Layne	QB	Texas	75
7	Chuck Bednarik	C	Pennsylvania	65
8	Bill Swiacki	E	Columbia	61

Award Winners

PLAYER	AWARD
Doak Walker, HB, SMU	Maxwell
Joe Steffy, G, Army	Outland

Bowl Games

DATE	GAME	SCORE
D6	**Great Lakes**	**Kentucky 24, Villanova 14**
J1	Tangerine	Catawba 7, Marshall 0
J1	Dixie	Arkansas 21, William & Mary 19
J1	**Gator**	**Georgia 20, Maryland 20**
J1	**Orange**	**Georgia Tech 20, Kansas 14**
J1	Sun	Miami (Ohio) 13, Texas Tech 12
J1	Rose	Michigan 49, Southern California 0
J1	**Delta**	**Mississippi 13, TCU 9**
J1	Salad	Nevada 13, North Texas 6
J1	**Sugar**	**Texas 27, Alabama 7**
J1	Cotton	Penn State 13, SMU 13
J1	Raisin	Pacific 26, Wichita State 14
J1	Harbor	Hardin-Simmons 53, San Diego State 0

SEC Standings

	CONFERENCE			OVERALL		
	W	L	T	W	L	T
Mississippi	6	1	0	9	2	0
Georgia Tech	4	1	0	10	1	0
Alabama	5	2	0	8	3	0
Georgia	3	3	0	7	4	1
Vanderbilt	3	3	0	6	4	0
Mississippi State	2	2	0	7	3	0
Tulane	2	3	2	2	5	2
LSU	2	3	1	5	3	1
Kentucky	2	3	0	8	3	0
Tennessee	2	3	0	5	5	0
Auburn	1	5	0	2	7	0
Florida	0	3	1	4	5	1

1948 NCAA MAJOR COLLEGE STATISTICAL LEADERS

INDIVIDUAL LEADERS

PASSING/COMPLETIONS	G	ATT	COM	PCT	INT	I%	YDS	YPA	TD	TD%	COM.PG
1 Stan Heath, Nevada	9	222	126	56.8	9	4.1	2005	9.0	22	9.9	14.0
2 Jim Finks, Tulsa	10	214	115	53.7	16	7.5	1376	6.4	7	3.3	11.5
3 Bobby Thomason, VMI	9	177	95	53.7	NA	NA	1252	7.1	14	7.9	10.6
4 Jimmy Walthall, West Virginia	11	164	83	50.6	16	9.8	1136	6.9	12	7.3	7.5
5 Eddie Songin, Boston College	9	169	83	49.1	15	8.9	1172	6.9	13	7.7	9.2
6 Gil Johnson, SMU	10	125	76	60.8	13	10.4	1022	8.2	9	7.2	7.6
7 Michael Boyda, Washington & Lee	10	157	75	47.8	14	8.9	1000	6.4	5	3.2	7.5
8 John Ford, Hardin-Simmons	8	121	72	59.5	NA	NA	1114	9.2	9	7.4	9.0
9 Jimmy Southard, Georgia Tech	10	121	71	58.7	NA	NA	1130	9.3	7	5.8	7.1
9 Johnny Rauch, Georgia	10	141	71	50.4	13	9.2	1307	9.3	5	3.6	7.1*

ALL-PURPOSE YARDS	G	RUSH	REC	INT	PR	KR	YDS	YPG
1 Lou Kusserow, Columbia	9	766	463	19	130	359	1737	193.0

RUSHING/YARDS	G	ATT	YDS	AVG	YPG
1 Fred Wendt, Texas-El Paso	10	184	1570	8.5	157.0
2 Ed Price, Tulane	10	188	1178	6.3	117.8
3 Jackie Jensen, California	10	137	1010	7.4	101.0
4 Harry Szulborski, Purdue	9	183	989	5.4	109.9
5 Wilton Davis, Hardin-Simmons	8	135	889	6.6	111.1
6 Gil Stephenson, Army	9	153	887	5.8	98.6
7 Johnny Papit, Virginia	9	135	884	6.5	98.2
8 Charles Hunsinger, Florida	10	116	842	7.3	84.2
9 George Thomas, Oklahoma	10	126	835	6.6	83.5
10 Jay Van Noy, Utah State	10	145	825	5.7	82.5

RUSHING/YARDS PER CARRY	G	ATT	YDS	YPC
1 Fred Wendt, Texas-El Paso	10	184	1570	8.5
2 John Panelli, Notre Dame	10	92	692	7.5
3 Pug Gabrel, Texas-El Paso	10	110	820	7.5
4 Jackie Jensen, California	10	137	1010	7.4
5 Charles Hunsinger, Florida	10	116	842	7.3
6 Bob Stuart, Army	9	114	801	7.0
7 George Thomas, Oklahoma	10	126	835	6.6
8 Wilton Davis, Hardin-Simmons	8	135	889	6.6
9 Johnny Papit, Virginia	9	135	884	6.5
10 Ray Borneman, Texas	10	110	700	6.4

Based on top 22 rushers

RECEIVING/RECEPTIONS	G	REC	YDS	TD	YPR	YPG	RPG
1 Johnny "Red" O'Quinn, Wake Forest	9	39	605	7	15.5	67.2	4.3
2 Jim Powell, Tennessee	10	36	462	2	12.8	46.2	3.6
3 Bob McChesney, Hardin-Simmons	8	36	445	5	12.4	55.6	4.5
4 Robert Larsen, Arizona	10	35	408	0	11.7	40.8	3.5
4 Jimmy Ford, Tulsa	10	35	403	2	11.5	40.3	3.5
6 James Lukens, Washington & Lee	10	33	439	1	13.3	43.9	3.3
7 Art Weiner, North Carolina	10	31	481	6	15.5	48.1	3.1
8 Morris Bailey, TCU	10	29	346	1	11.9	34.6	2.9
9 Dick Wilkins, Oregon	10	27	520	5	19.3	52.0	2.7
9 Brian Bell, Washington & Lee	10	27	409	4	15.1	40.9	2.7

PUNTING	PUNT	YDS	AVG
1 Charlie Justice, North Carolina	62	2728	44.0
2 Hall Haynes, Santa Clara	47	2045	43.5
3 Dike Eddleman, Illinois	59	2531	42.9
4 Paul Stombaugh, Furman	72	3031	42.1
5 Doak Walker, SMU	35	1474	42.1
6 Albin Collins, LSU	65	2691	41.4
7 George Taliaferro, Indiana	55	2233	40.6
8 Levi Jackson, Yale	49	1989	40.6
9 Michael Boyda, Washington & Lee	47	1908	40.6
10 Harry Ghaul, Miami (Fla.)	69	2781	40.3

PUNT RETURNS/YARDS	PR	YDS	AVG
1 Lee Nalley, Vanderbilt	43	791	18.4
2 Jack Mitchell, Oklahoma	22	515	23.4
3 Hal Littleford, Tennessee	36	448	12.4
4 Henry Pryor, Rutgers	24	444	18.5
5 George Sims, Baylor	15	375	25.0
6 William Doherty, Villanova	25	365	14.6
7 Wilford White, Arizona State	16	354	22.1
8 Charlie Justice, North Carolina	19	332	17.5
9 Bud French, Kansas	25	302	12.1
10 Bobby Vinson, Army	25	295	11.8

KICKOFF RETURNS/YARDS	KR	YDS	AVG
1 Billy Gregus, Wake Forest	19	503	26.5
1 John Freeman, Portland	21	503	24.0
3 Jerry Williams, Washington State	16	478	29.9
4 Jerry Hiller, Marquette	20	462	23.1
5 Bob Goode, Texas A&M	16	407	25.4
6 Ray Malcolm, Montana	17	406	23.9
7 Brooks Biddle, Washington	18	385	21.4
8 Andy Davis, George Washington	19	382	20.1
9 Leonard Corbin, Case Western Reserve	15	378	25.2
10 Lou Kusserow, Columbia	13	359	27.6

SCORING	TDS	XPT	FG	PTS
1 Fred Wendt, Texas-El Paso	20	32	0	152
2 Lou Kusserow, Columbia	18	0	0	108
3 Wilford White, Arizona State	11	20	3	95
4 Dick Talboom, Wyoming	11	28	0	94
5 Joe Geri, Georgia	9	36	0	90
6 Doak Walker, SMU	11	22	0	88
7 Ray Mathews, Clemson	13	0	0	78
8 Jay Van Noy, Utah State	11	7	0	73
9 Six tied	12	0	0	72

INTERCEPTIONS	INT	YDS
1 Jay Van Noy, Utah State	8	228
1 Eli Maricich, Georgia	8	189
1 Bill Olson, Columbia	8	124

TEAM LEADERS

RUSHING OFFENSE	G	ATT	YDS	AVG	YPG
1 Texas-El Paso	10	614	3783	6.2	378.3
2 Army	9	509	2955	5.8	328.3
3 Notre Dame	10	600	3194	5.3	319.4
4 Michigan State	10	498	3041	6.1	304.1
5 Oklahoma	10	555	2964	5.3	296.4
6 California	10	536	2788	5.2	278.8
7 Missouri	10	512	2665	5.2	266.5
8 Detroit	9	431	2285	5.3	253.9
9 Cornell	9	497	2283	4.6	253.7
10 Hardin-Simmons	8	377	2025	5.4	253.1

PASSING OFFENSE	G	ATT	COM	YPC	PCT	YDS	YPA	TD	YPG
1 Nevada	9	245	140	16.4	57.1	2295	9.4	27	255.0
2 Georgia Tech	10	206	112	15.6	54.4	1746	8.5	14	174.6
3 Tulsa	10	265	130	12.1	49.1	1576	5.9	7	157.6
4 San Francisco	10	216	95	14.4	44.0	1364	6.3	11	151.6
5 Georgia	10	162	83	18.1	51.2	1506	9.3	7	150.6
6 Michigan	9	168	77	17.6	45.8	1355	8.1	16	150.6
7 SMU	10	183	109	13.5	59.6	1471	8.0	17	147.1
8 Boston College	9	202	97	13.6	48.0	1318	6.5	14	146.4
9 Minnesota	9	168	79	16.2	47.0	1283	7.6	9	142.6
10 VMI	9	192	98	13.1	51.0	1281	6.7	15	142.3

TOTAL OFFENSE	G	P	YDS	AVG	YPG
1 Nevada	9	630	4383	7.0	487.0
2 Texas-El Paso	10	664	4249	6.4	424.9
3 Army	9	622	3711	6.0	412.3
4 Michigan State	10	627	4027	6.4	402.7
5 Notre Dame	10	708	3964	5.6	396.4
6 Hardin-Simmons	8	498	3139	6.3	392.4
7 Oklahoma	10	654	3802	5.8	380.2
8 Miami (Ohio)	9	546	3412	6.2	379.1
9 California	10	692	3726	5.4	372.6
10 Missouri	10	679	3695	5.4	369.5

RUSHING DEFENSE	G	ATT	YDS	AVG	YPG
1 Georgia Tech	10	374	749	2.0	74.9
2 Penn State	9	311	750	2.4	83.3
3 Minnesota	9	312	786	2.5	87.3
4 Michigan	9	373	789	2.1	87.7
5 North Carolina	10	363	885	2.4	88.5
6 Pennsylvania	8	299	714	2.4	89.3
7 Vanderbilt	11	428	993	2.3	90.3
8 Georgia	10	371	946	2.5	94.6
9 California	10	379	957	2.5	95.7
10 Clemson	10	376	1001	2.7	100.1

PASSING DEFENSE	G	ATT	COM	PCT	YPC	YDS	YPA	TD	YPG
1 Northwestern	9	129	42	32.6	11.6	487	3.8	2	54.1
2 Brigham Young	11	144	55	38.2	10.9	599	4.2	1	54.5
3 Maryland	10	130	45	34.6	12.2	550	4.2	5	55.0
4 Brown	9	128	43	33.6	11.7	504	3.9	6	56.0
5 Richmond	10	151	50	33.1	11.8	590	3.9	5	59.0
6 Rice	10	134	54	40.3	11.9	645	4.8	6	64.5
7 Utah	10	152	52	34.2	12.6	655	4.3	3	65.5
8 Montana St.	9	93	41	44.1	14.8	608	6.5	7	67.6
9 Hardin-Simmons	8	89	44	49.4	12.3	542	6.1	2	67.8
10 South Carolina	8	125	47	37.6	11.8	555	4.4	7	69.4

TOTAL DEFENSE	G	P	YDS	AVG	YPG
1 Georgia Tech	10	524	1513	2.9	151.3
2 Penn State	9	454	1424	3.1	158.2
3 Clemson	10	529	1760	3.3	176.0
4 North Carolina	10	558	1767	3.2	176.7
5 Villanova	10	544	1840	3.4	184.0
6 Vanderbilt	11	634	2044	3.2	185.8
7 Minnesota	9	481	1674	3.5	186.0
8 Maryland	10	550	1862	3.4	186.2
9 Army	9	583	1676	2.9	186.2
10 Tennessee	10	590	1875	3.2	187.5

SCORING OFFENSE	G	PTS	AVG
1 Nevada	9	400	44.4
2 Michigan State	10	359	35.9
3 Texas-El Paso	10	349	34.9
4 Lafayette	9	277	34.6
5 Oklahoma	10	336	33.6
6 Army	9	294	32.7
7 Notre Dame	10	320	32.0
8 Missouri	10	308	30.8
9 Vanderbilt	11	328	29.8
10 Arizona State	9	264	29.3

SCORING DEFENSE	G	PTS	AVG
1 Michigan	9	44	4.9
2 Clemson	10	53	5.3
3 Tulane	10	60	6.0
4 Penn State	9	55	6.1
5 Vanderbilt	11	73	6.6
6 William & Mary	10	67	6.7
7 Georgia Tech	10	69	6.9
8 California	10	80	8.0
8 North Carolina	10	80	8.0
10 Oregon	10	82	8.2

1948

Final Poll (Nov. 29)

AP	SCHOOL	FINAL RECORD
1	Michigan	9-0-0
2	Notre Dame	9-0-1
3	North Carolina	9-1-1
4	California	10-1-0
5	Oklahoma	10-1-0
6	Army	8-0-1
7	Northwestern	8-2-0
8	**Georgia**	**9-2-0**
9	Oregon	9-2-0
10	SMU	9-1-1
11	Clemson	11-0-0
12	**Vanderbilt**	**8-2-1**
13	**Tulane**	**9-1-0**
14	Michigan State	6-2-2
15	**Mississippi**	**8-1-0**
16	Minnesota	7-2-0
17	William & Mary	7-2-2
18	Penn State	7-1-1
19	Cornell	8-1-0
20	Wake Forest	6-4-0

Consensus All-Americans

POS	NAME	SCHOOL
B	Doak Walker	SMU
B	Charlie Justice	North Carolina
B	Jackie Jensen	California
B	Emil Sitko	Notre Dame
B	Clyde Scott	Arkansas
E	Dick Rifenburg	Michigan
E	Leon Hart	Notre Dame
T	Leo Nomellini	Minnesota
T	Alvin Wistert	Michigan
G	Buddy Burris	Oklahoma
G	Bill Fischer	Notre Dame
C	Chuck Bednarik	Pennsylvania

Others receiving first-team honors

B	**John Rauch**	**Georgia**
B	Stan Heath	Nevada
B	Bobby Stuart	Army
B	Art Murakowski	Northwestern
B	Bobby Gage	Clemson
B	Pete Elliott	Michigan
B	George Taliaferro	Indiana
B	Jack Cloud	William & Mary
E	Art Weiner	North Carolina
E	**George Brodnax**	**Georgia Tech**
E	Sam Tamburo	Penn State
E	**Barney Poole**	**Mississippi**
E	Dale Armstrong	Dartmouth
T	Laurie Niemi	Washington State
T	**Paul Lea**	**Tulane**
T	Jim Turner	California
G	**William Healy**	**Georgia Tech**
G	Joe Henry	Army
G	Marty Wendell	Notre Dame
G	Rod Franz	California
C	Alex Sarkisian	Northwestern

Heisman Trophy Voting

	PLAYER	POS	SCHOOL	TOTAL
1	Doak Walker	RB	SMU	778
2	Charlie Justice	RB	North Carolina	443
3	Chuck Bednarik	C	Pennsylvania	336
4	Jackie Jensen	RB	California	143
5	Stan Heath	QB	Nevada	113
6	Norm Van Brocklin	QB	Oregon	83
7	Emil Sitko	HB	Notre Dame	73
8	Jack Mitchell	QB	Oklahoma	68

Award Winners

PLAYER	AWARD
Chuck Bednarik, C, Pennsylvania	Maxwell
Bill Fischer, G, Notre Dame	Outland

Bowl Games

DATE	GAME	SCORE
D18	Shrine	Hardin-Simmons 40, Ouachita 12
D30	Camellia	Hardin-Simmons 49, Wichita State 12
J1	Tangerine	Murray St. 21, Sul Ross St. 21
J1	Dixie	Baylor 20, Wake Forest 7
J1	Gator	Clemson 24, Missouri 23
J1	Rose	Northwestern 20, California 14
J1	Sugar	Oklahoma 14, North Carolina 6
J1	Cotton	SMU 21, Oregon 13
J1	**Orange**	**Texas 41, Georgia 28**
J1	Harbor	Villanova 27, Nevada 7
J1	Sun	West Virginia 21, Texas-El Paso 12
J1	Delta	William & Mary 20, Oklahoma State 0
J1	Salad	Drake 14, Arizona 13
J1	Raisin	Occidental 21, Colorado State 20

SEC Standings

	CONFERENCE			OVERALL		
	W	L	T	W	L	T
Georgia	6	0	0	9	2	0
Mississippi	6	1	0	8	1	0
Tulane	5	1	0	9	1	0
Vanderbilt	4	2	1	8	2	1
Georgia Tech	4	3	0	7	3	0
Alabama	4	4	1	6	4	1
Mississippi State	3	3	0	4	4	1
Tennessee	2	3	1	4	4	2
Kentucky	1	3	1	5	3	2
Florida	1	5	0	5	5	0
LSU	1	5	0	3	7	0
Auburn	0	7	0	1	8	1

1949 NCAA MAJOR COLLEGE STATISTICAL LEADERS

INDIVIDUAL LEADERS

PASSING/COMPLETIONS	G	ATT	COM	PCT	INT	I%	YDS	YPA	TD	TD%	COM.PG
1 Adrian Burk, Baylor	10	191	110	57.6	6	3.1	1428	7.5	14	7.3	11.0
2 Tom O'Malley, Cincinnati	10	225	108	48.0	15	6.7	1617	7.2	16	7.1	10.8
3 Eddie Songin, Boston College	9	210	106	50.5	15	7.1	1318	6.3	8	3.8	11.8
4 Lindy Berry, TCU	10	220	106	48.2	23	10.5	1445	6.6	11	5.0	10.6
5 Paul Campbell, Texas	10	182	91	50.0	12	6.6	1372	7.5	7	3.9	9.1
6 Buddy Lex, William & Mary	10	168	90	53.6	13	7.7	1325	7.9	18	10.7	9.0
7 Ed Jesse, Nevada	9	185	89	48.1	13	7.0	1159	6.3	5	2.7	9.9
8 Eddie Kriwiel, Wichita State	10	184	88	47.8	22	12.0	1253	6.8	10	5.4	8.8
9 Dick Doheny, Fordham	8	140	87	62.1	5	3.6	1127	8.1	13	9.3	10.9
9 Jim Powers, Southern California	9	148	87	58.8	11	7.4	1215	8.2	12	8.1	9.7

ALL-PURPOSE YARDS	G	RUSH	REC	INT	PR	KR	YPG
1 Johnny Papit, Virginia	9	1214	0	0	0	397	179.0

RUSHING/YARDS	G	ATT	YDS	AVG	YPG
1 John Dottley, Mississippi	10	208	1312	6.3	131.2
2 Johnny Papit, Virginia	9	197	1214	6.2	134.9
3 Ed Price, Tulane	10	171	1137	6.6	113.7
4 John Pont, Miami (Ohio)	9	128	977	7.6	108.6
5 Johnny Bright, Drake	9	170	975	5.7	108.3
6 Al Egler, Colgate	9	142	933	6.6	103.7
7 Lynn Chandnois, Michigan State	9	129	885	6.9	98.3
8 Pug Gabrel, Texas-El Paso	10	145	881	6.1	88.1
9 George Thomas, Oklahoma	10	133	859	6.5	85.9
10 Ollie Matson, San Francisco	10	156	853	5.5	85.3

RUSHING/YARDS PER CARRY	G	ATT	YDS	YPC
1 John Pont, Miami (Ohio)	9	128	977	7.6
2 Lynn Chandnois, Michigan State	9	129	885	6.9
3 Ed Price, Tulane	10	171	1137	6.6
4 Al Egler, Colgate	9	142	933	6.6
5 Walker Jones, Wyoming	10	119	777	6.5
6 John Karras, Illinois	9	127	826	6.5
7 George Thomas, Oklahoma	10	133	859	6.5
8 Charles Hunsinger, Florida	10	122	774	6.3
9 Lindell Pearson, Oklahoma	10	119	753	6.3
10 John Dottley, Mississippi	10	208	1312	6.3

Based on top 20 rushers

RECEIVING/RECEPTIONS	G	REC	YDS	TD	YPR	RPG	YPG
1 Art Weiner, North Carolina	10	52	762	7	14.7	5.2	76.2
2 Alex Loyd, Oklahoma State	10	47	669	2	14.2	4.7	66.9
3 Vito Ragazzo, William & Mary	10	44	793	15	18.0	4.4	79.3
4 Ben Procter, Texas	10	43	724	5	16.8	4.3	72.4
4 Pete Brown, Davidson	10	43	509	2	11.8	4.3	50.9
6 Jim Kelly, Cincinnati	10	42	478	2	11.4	4.2	47.8
6 J.D. Ison, Baylor	10	42	457	6	10.9	4.2	45.7
8 Gene Ackerman, Missouri	10	40	576	2	14.4	4.0	57.6
9 Al Pfeifer, Fordham	8	38	477	8	12.6	4.8	59.6
10 Mott Price, Davidson	10	37	538	1	14.5	3.7	53.8
10 Morris Bailey, TCU	10	37	501	3	13.5	3.7	50.1

PUNTING	PUNT	YDS	AVG
1 Paul Stombaugh, Furman	57	2550	44.7
2 Charlie Justice, North Carolina	63	2777	44.1
3 Hall Haynes, Santa Clara	58	2558	44.1
4 Ed Brown, San Francisco	51	2178	42.7
5 John Caputo, Utah State	65	2730	42.0
6 Harold Chaffee, Colorado State	33	1386	42.0
7 Jackie Calvert, Clemson	25	1045	41.8
8 Bob Manire, Colorado	35	1463	41.8
9 Fred Montsdeoca, Florida	62	2579	41.6
10 William Hardisty, Pittsburgh	39	1607	41.2

PUNT RETURNS/YARDS	PR	YDS	AVG
1 Lee Nalley, Vanderbilt	35	498	14.2
2 Gene Gibson, Cincinnati	21	438	20.9
3 Jimmy Nutter, Wichita State	23	426	18.5
4 Selmer Pederson, Wyoming	24	386	16.1
5 Frank Neilson, Utah	27	356	13.2
6 Lindy Berry, TCU	18	334	18.6
6 Mitford Johnson, Baylor	21	334	15.9
8 Jimmy Jordan, Georgia Tech	20	306	15.3
9 Jack Christiansen, Colorado State	20	301	15.1
10 Ollie Matson, San Francisco	17	298	17.5

KICKOFF RETURNS/YARDS	KR	YDS	AVG
1 Johnny Subda, Nevada	18	444	24.7
2 Jay Van Noy, Utah State	19	441	23.2
3 Bennie Aldridge, Oklahoma State	19	404	21.3
4 Vernon Wynott, Columbia	18	399	22.2
5 Johnny Papit, Virginia	17	397	23.4
6 Woodley Lewis, Oregon	9	387	43.0
7 John Pont, Miami (Ohio)	13	385	29.6
8 Hi Faubion, Kansas State	17	383	22.5
8 Ernie Johnson, UCLA	17	383	22.5
10 Jack O'Loughlin, Montana	16	368	23.0

SCORING	TDS	XPT	FG	PTS
1 George Thomas, Oklahoma	19	3	0	117
2 Vito Ragazzo, William & Mary	15	0	0	90
3 John Dottley, Mississippi	14	0	0	84
4 Doak Walker, SMU	11	17	0	83
5 Eddie Talboom, Wyoming	8	31	0	79
6 James Cain, Army	13	0	0	78
6 James Monachino, California	13	0	0	78
6 Gil Stephenson, Army	13	0	0	78
9 Randy Clay, Texas	8	28	0	76
9 John Glorioso, Missouri	8	28	0	76

INTERCEPTIONS	INT	YDS
1 Bobby Wilson, Mississippi	10	70
2 Jimmy Glisson, Tulane	9	141
2 Bill Sheffold, Oregon State	9	138
2 Jim Rinehart, Arkansas	9	NA
2 Charles Lentz, Michigan	9	NA
2 George Skipworth, Duke	9	88
2 J.W. Sherrill, Tennessee	9	NA

TEAM LEADERS

RUSHING OFFENSE	G	ATT	YDS	AVG	YPG
1 Texas-El Paso	10	626	3332	5.3	333.2
2 Oklahoma	10	564	3203	5.7	320.3
3 Villanova	9	461	2642	5.7	293.6
4 Notre Dame	10	568	2914	5.1	291.4
5 Wyoming	10	501	2841	5.7	284.1
6 Army	9	523	2485	4.8	276.1
7 Illinois	9	484	2460	5.1	273.3
8 Boston U.	8	423	2162	5.1	270.3
9 Cornell	9	471	2420	5.1	268.9
10 Idaho	8	379	2042	5.4	255.3

PASSING OFFENSE/YPG	G	ATT	COM	INT	PCT	YDS	YPA	TD	YPG	I%	YPC
1 Fordham	8	185	108	12	58.4	1467	7.9	16	183.4	6.5	13.6
2 Southern California	9	225	128	12	56.9	1582	7.0	14	175.8	5.3	12.4
3 Oklahoma State	10	254	114	18	44.9	1755	6.9	13	175.5	7.1	15.4
4 William & Mary	10	218	112	16	51.4	1730	7.9	23	173.0	7.3	15.4
5 TCU	10	264	121	28	45.8	1693	6.4	15	169.3	10.6	14.0
6 Cincinnati	10	234	111	18	47.4	1664	7.1	16	166.4	7.7	15.0
7 Texas	10	209	105	13	50.2	1659	7.9	10	165.9	6.2	15.8
8 SMU	10	195	99	19	50.8	1621	8.3	11	162.1	9.7	16.4
9 Denver	10	208	99	25	47.6	1612	7.8	9	161.2	12.0	16.3
10 Davidson	10	267	127	24	47.6	1578	5.9	7	157.8	9.0	12.4

TOTAL OFFENSE	G	P	YDS	AVG	YPG
1 Notre Dame	10	722	4348	6.0	434.8
2 Villanova	9	624	3896	6.2	432.9
3 Oklahoma	10	676	4093	6.1	409.3
4 Texas-El Paso	10	715	3997	5.6	399.7
5 Army	9	650	3542	5.4	393.6
6 Boston U.	8	555	3094	5.6	386.8
7 Mississippi	10	680	3864	5.7	386.4
8 Missouri	10	746	3859	5.2	385.9
9 Cornell	9	601	3429	5.7	381.0
10 Miami (Ohio)	9	592	3421	5.8	380.1

RUSHING DEFENSE	G	ATT	YDS	AVG	YPG
1 Oklahoma	10	343	556	1.6	55.6
2 Kentucky	11	455	788	1.7	71.6
3 Minnesota	9	349	742	2.1	82.4
4 Notre Dame	10	417	864	2.1	86.4
5 Maryland	9	356	844	2.4	93.8
6 Army	9	393	906	2.3	100.7
7 Villanova	9	362	924	2.6	102.7
8 Virginia	9	373	931	2.5	103.4
9 LSU	10	447	1074	2.4	107.4
10 Duke	9	355	980	2.8	108.9

PASSING DEFENSE	G	ATT	COM	PCT	YPC	INT	I%	YDS	YPA	TD	YPG
1 Miami (Fla.)	9	122	40	32.8	12.3	10	8.2	492	4.0	4	54.7
2 Miami (Ohio)	9	127	39	30.7	12.7	20	15.8	495	3.9	5	55.0
3 Wyoming	10	161	48	29.8	12.0	18	11.2	576	3.6	1	57.6
4 Purdue	9	106	41	38.7	13.5	5	4.7	553	5.2	7	61.4
5 Iowa State	9	112	16	14.3	34.8	15.2	15	1730	7.3	3	65.9
6 Nebraska	9	125	52	41.6	11.4	18	14.4	595	4.8	6	66.1
7 Texas	10	194	71	36.6	9.9	13	6.7	706	3.6	4	70.6
8 Wichita State	10	130	50	38.5	14.2	16	12.3	708	5.4	7	70.8
9 Tennessee	10	161	64	39.8	11.8	26	16.2	752	4.7	4	75.2
10 Alabama	10	172	61	35.5	12.5	15	8.7	761	4.4	1	76.1

TOTAL DEFENSE	G	P	YDS	AVG	YPG
1 Kentucky	11	653	1692	2.6	153.8
2 Army	9	594	1670	2.8	185.6
3 Maryland	9	549	1686	3.1	187.3
4 Wyoming	10	604	1895	3.1	189.5
5 Villanova	9	526	1815	3.5	201.7
6 Oklahoma	10	633	2027	3.2	202.7
7 Texas	10	627	2060	3.3	206.0
8 Minnesota	9	570	1940	3.4	215.6
9 LSU	10	620	2158	3.5	215.8
10 Drake	9	574	1952	3.4	216.9

SCORING OFFENSE	G	PTS	AVG
1 Army	9	354	39.3
2 Wyoming	10	375	37.5
3 Oklahoma	10	364	36.4
4 Notre Dame	10	360	36.0
5 Arizona State	9	321	35.7
6 Michigan State	9	309	34.3
7 Cornell	9	284	31.6
8 California	10	305	30.5
9 Rutgers	9	266	29.6
10 Villanova	9	265	29.4

SCORING DEFENSE	G	PTS	AVG
1 Kentucky	11	53	4.8
2 Wyoming	10	65	6.5
3 LSU	10	74	7.4
4 Army	9	68	7.6
5 Maryland	9	75	8.3
6 Rice	10	84	8.4
7 Colorado State	10	86	8.6
7 Notre Dame	10	86	8.6
9 Oklahoma	10	88	8.8
10 Minnesota	9	80	8.9

1949

Final Poll (Nov. 28)

AP	SCHOOL	FINAL RECORD
1	Notre Dame	10-0-0
2	Oklahoma	11-0-0
3	California	10-1-0
4	Army	9-0-0
5	Rice	10-1-0
6	Ohio State	7-1-2
7	Michigan	6-2-1
8	Minnesota	7-2-0
9	**LSU**	**8-3-0**
10	Pacific	10-0-0
11	**Kentucky**	**9-3-0**
12	Cornell	8-1-0
13	Villanova	8-1-0
14	Maryland	9-1-0
15	Santa Clara	8-2-1
16	North Carolina	7-4-0
17	**Tennessee**	**7-2-1**
18	Princeton	6-3-0
19	Michigan State	6-3-0
20	Baylor	8-2-0
20	Missouri	7-4-0

Consensus All-Americans

POS	NAME	SCHOOL
B	Emil Sitko	Notre Dame
B	Doak Walker	SMU
B	Arnold Galiffa	Army
B	Bob Williams	Notre Dame
E	Leon Hart	Notre Dame
E	James Williams	Rice
T	Leo Nomellini	Minnesota
T	Alvin Wistert	Michigan
G	Rod Franz	California
G	Ed Bagdon	Michigan State
C	Clayton Tonnemaker	Minnesota

Others Receiving First-Team Honors

B	Lynn Chandnois	Michigan State
B	Charlie Justice	North Carolina
B	**Eddie Price**	**Tulane**
B	Darrell Royal	Oklahoma
B	Eddie LeBaron	Pacific
B	John Papit	Virginia
B	George Thomas	Oklahoma
B	Randall Clay	Texas
B	George Sella	Princeton
E	Art Weiner	North Carolina
E	Jim Owens	Oklahoma
E	Dan Foldberg	Army
E	Ken Rose	Stanford
E	Ken Powell	North Carolina
T	Allen Wahl	Michigan
T	Wade Walker	Oklahoma
T	Jim Martin	Notre Dame
T	Jim Turner	California
T	Thurman McGraw	Colorado State
G	John Schweder	Pennsylvania
G	Stan West	Oklahoma
G	Bernie Barkouskie	Pittsburgh
G	Bud McFadin	Texas
G	**Bob Gain**	**Kentucky**
G	Forrest Klein	California
C	Tom Novak	Nebraska
C	Joe Watson	Rice

Heisman Trophy Voting

	PLAYER	POS	SCHOOL	TOTAL
1	Leon Hart	E	Notre Dame	995
2	Charlie Justice	RB	North Carolina	272
3	Doak Walker	RB	SMU	229
4	Arnold Galiffa	QB	Army	196
5	Bob Williams	QB	Notre Dame	189
6	Eddie LeBaron	QB	Pacific	122
7	Clayton Tonnemaker	C	Minnesota	81
8	Emil Sitko	HB	Notre Dame	79

Award Winners

PLAYER	AWARD
Leon Hart, E, Notre Dame	Maxwell
Ed Bagdon, G, Michigan State	Outland

Bowl Games

DATE	GAME	SCORE
D31	Raisin	San Jose State 20, Texas Tech 13
J1	Salad	Xavier 33, Arizona State 21
J2	Tangerine	St. Vincent 7, Emory & Henry 6
J2	Gator	Maryland 20, Missouri 7
J2	Rose	Ohio State 17, California 14
J2	**Sugar**	**Oklahoma 35, LSU 0**
J2	Cotton	Rice 27, North Carolina 13
J2	Sun	Texas-El Paso 33, Georgetown 20
J2	**Orange**	**Santa Clara 21, Kentucky 13**

SEC Standings

	CONFERENCE			OVERALL		
	W	L	T	W	L	T
Tulane	5	1	0	7	2	1
Kentucky	4	1	0	9	3	0
Tennessee	4	1	1	7	2	1
Georgia Tech	5	2	0	7	3	0
LSU	4	2	0	8	3	0
Alabama	4	3	1	6	3	1
Vanderbilt	4	4	0	5	5	0
Auburn	2	4	2	2	4	3
Mississippi	2	4	0	4	5	1
Florida	1	4	1	4	5	1
Georgia	1	4	1	4	6	1
Mississippi State	0	6	0	0	8	1

1950 NCAA MAJOR COLLEGE STATISTICAL LEADERS

INDIVIDUAL LEADERS

PASSING/COMPLETIONS	G	ATT	COM	PCT	INT	I%	YDS	YPA	TD	TD%	COM.PG
1 Don Heinrich, Washington	10	221	134	60.6	9	4.1	1846	8.4	14	6.3	13.4
2 Dave Cunningham, Utah	9	217	119	54.8	12	5.5	1146	5.3	13	6.0	13.2
3 Bill Weeks, Iowa State	10	220	116	52.7	16	7.3	1552	7.1	9	4.1	11.6
4 **Babe Parilli, Kentucky**	11	203	114	56.2	12	5.9	1627	8.0	23	11.3	10.4
5 Don Klosterman, Loyola-Marymount	9	207	113	54.6	11	5.3	1582	7.6	19	9.2	12.6
6 Ed Ford, Hardin-Simmons	10	199	111	55.8	7	3.5	1777	8.9	12	6.0	11.1
7 Fred Benners, SMU	10	192	109	56.8	12	6.3	1361	7.1	9	4.7	10.9
8 Billy Cox, Duke	10	206	108	52.4	15	7.3	1428	6.9	8	3.9	10.8
9 Chuck Maloy, Holy Cross	10	242	104	43.0	19	7.9	1572	6.5	14	5.8	10.4
10 Bob Williams, Notre Dame	9	210	99	47.1	15	7.1	1035	4.9	10	4.8	11.0

ALL-PURPOSE YARDS	G	RUSH	REC	INT	PR	KR	YDS	YPG
1 Wilford White, Arizona State	10	1502	225	0	64	274	2065	206.5

RUSHING/YARDS	G	ATT	YDS	AVG	YPG
1 Wilford White, Arizona State	10	199	1502	7.5	150.2
2 Bobby Reynolds, Nebraska	9	193	1342	7.0	149.1
3 Bob Smith, Texas A&M	10	199	1302	6.5	130.2
4 Johnny Bright, Drake	9	183	1232	6.7	136.9
5 Wade Stinson, Kansas	10	167	1129	6.8	112.9
6 Hugh McElhenny, Washington	10	179	1107	6.2	110.7
7 Everett Grandelius, Michigan State	9	163	1023	6.3	113.7
8 **John Dottley, Mississippi**	10	191	1007	5.3	100.7
9 Steve Wadiak, South Carolina	10	162	998	6.2	99.8
10 Jake Roberts, Tulsa	11	138	954	6.9	86.7

RUSHING/YARDS PER CARRY	G	ATT	YDS	YPC
1 Wilford White, Arizona State	10	199	1502	7.5
2 **Bobby Marlow, Alabama**	11	118	882	7.5
3 Bobby Reynolds, Nebraska	9	193	1342	7.0
4 Jake Roberts, Tulsa	11	138	954	6.9
5 Wade Stinson, Kansas	10	167	1129	6.8
6 Johnny Bright, Drake	9	183	1232	6.7
7 Max Clark, Houston	10	129	860	6.7
8 Bob Smith, Texas A&M	10	199	1302	6.5
9 Billy Vessels, Oklahoma	10	135	870	6.4
10 John Olszewski, California	10	151	950	6.3

Based on top 20 rushers

RECEIVING/RECEPTIONS	G	REC	YDS	TD	YPR	YPG	RPG
1 Gordon Cooper, Denver	10	46	569	8	12.4	56.9	4.6
2 Tom Bienemann, Drake	9	45	615	2	13.7	68.3	5.0
3 Jim Doran, Iowa State	10	42	652	6	15.5	65.2	4.2
4 Don Stonesifer, Northwestern	9	42	560	5	13.3	62.2	4.7
5 Ceep Youmans, Duke	10	40	446	1	11.2	44.6	4.0
6 Bill McColl, Stanford	10	39	671	4	17.2	67.1	3.9
7 Sy Wilhelmi, Iowa State	10	38	442	2	11.6	44.2	3.8
7 Herman Fisher, Nevada	9	38	434	1	11.4	48.2	4.2
9 Fred Snyder, Loyola-Marymount	9	36	596	9	16.6	66.2	4.0
9 John Thomas, Oregon State	9	36	350	1	9.7	38.9	4.0

PUNTING	PUNT	YDS	AVG
1 Zack Jordan, Colorado	38	1830	48.2
2 Pat Brady, Nevada	35	1642	46.9
3 Milt Smith, Utah	47	2030	43.2
4 Bud Wallace, North Carolina	27	1150	42.6
5 Rex Berry, Brigham Young	28	1187	42.4
6 James Hammond, Wisconsin	26	1079	41.5
7 Dolph Simons, Kansas	32	1318	41.2
8 Larry Isbell, Baylor	56	2307	41.2
9 Bob Moore, UCLA	63	2583	41.0
10 Glenn Drahn, Iowa	56	2296	41.0

PUNT RETURNS/YARDS	PR	YDS	AVG
1 Dave Waters, Washington & Lee	30	445	14.8
2 Jesse Thomas, Michigan State	18	358	19.9
3 **Bert Rechichar, Tennessee**	20	349	17.5
4 Bobby Dan Dillon, Texas	15	334	22.3
5 Bob Shemonski, Maryland	28	334	11.9
6 Duane Rice, Colorado State	16	328	20.5
7 Gene Gibson, Cincinnati	16	322	20.1
8 **Johnny Cole, Arkansas**	16	293	18.3
9 **George Kinek, Tulane**	20	277	13.9
10 Alex Webster, North Carolina St.	14	276	19.7

KICKOFF RETURNS/YARDS	KR	YDS	AVG
1 Chuck Hill, New Mexico	27	729	27.0
2 Sterling Wingo, Virginia Tech	20	462	23.1
3 John Henry Johnson, St. Mary's (Cal.)	16	423	26.4
4 Ralph Longmore, Duquesne	19	402	21.2
5 Sammy Hurt, U.T. Chattanooga	22	368	16.7
6 George Bean, Utah	21	366	17.4
7 William Lohr, West Virginia	19	362	19.1
8 William Farris, Richmond	18	355	19.7
9 Ted Narleski, UCLA	14	348	24.9
10 Norm Rohter, Marquette	15	342	22.8

SCORING	TDS	XPT	FG	PTS
1 Bobby Reynolds, Nebraska	22	25	0	157
2 Wilford White, Arizona State	22	1	1	136
3 Eddie Talboom, Wyoming	15	40	0	130
4 Johnny Bright, Drake	18	0	0	108
5 Johnny Turco, Holy Cross	17	0	0	102
6 Bob Shemonski, Maryland	16	1	0	97
7 Max Clark, Houston	11	24	0	90
7 Merwin Hodel, Colorado	15	0	0	90
7 Billy Vessels, Oklahoma	15	0	0	90
10 Fred Cone, Clemson	14	2	0	86

INTERCEPTIONS	INT	YDS
1 Hank Rich, Arizona State	12	135
2 Al Brosky, Illinois	11	96
3 Tom Hardiman, Georgetown	9	155

TEAM LEADERS

RUSHING OFFENSE	G	ATT	YDS	AVG	YPG
1 Arizona State	10	620	3470	5.6	347.0
2 Princeton	9	503	2929	5.8	325.4
3 Nebraska	9	510	2894	5.7	321.6
4 Kansas	10	524	3116	5.9	311.6
5 Tulsa	11	619	3384	5.5	307.6
6 Washington & Lee	10	578	2995	5.2	299.5
7 Pacific	11	619	3278	5.3	298.0
8 Clemson	9	504	2648	5.3	294.2
9 Oklahoma	10	562	2931	5.2	293.1
10 Army	9	477	2568	5.4	285.3

PASSING OFFENSE/YPG	G	ATT	COM	INT	PCT	YDS	YPA	TD	YPG	I%	YPC
1 SMU	10	296	156	24	52.7	2146	7.3	14	214.6	8.1	13.8
2 Hardin-Simmons	10	228	130	8	57.0	2061	9.0	15	206.1	3.5	15.9
3 Washington	10	260	149	12	57.3	2041	7.9	14	204.1	4.6	13.7
4 Loyola-Marymount	9	228	122	12	53.5	1674	7.3	20	186.0	5.3	13.7
5 Duke	10	236	121	21	51.3	1639	6.9	10	163.9	8.9	13.5
6 George Washington	9	228	113	17	49.6	1475	6.5	7	163.9	7.5	13.1
7 Holy Cross	10	247	105	20	42.5	1585	6.4	14	158.5	8.1	15.1
8 Drake	9	182	101	11	55.5	1420	7.8	12	157.8	6.0	14.1
9 Iowa State	10	226	117	18	51.8	1574	7.0	9	157.4	8.0	13.5
10 **Kentucky**	11	230	125	14	54.3	1714	7.5	27	155.8	6.1	13.7

TOTAL OFFENSE	G	P	YDS	AVG	YPG
1 Arizona State	10	792	4704	5.9	470.4
2 Princeton	9	617	3903	6.3	433.7
3 Tulsa	11	783	4747	6.1	431.5
4 SMU	10	630	3881	6.2	431.2
5 Loyola-Marymount	9	775	3781	4.9	420.1
6 **Alabama**	11	773	4576	5.9	416.0
7 Oklahoma	10	706	4154	5.9	415.4
8 Washington	10	694	4116	5.9	411.6
9 Nebraska	9	618	3666	5.9	407.3
10 Pacific	11	800	4399	5.5	399.9

RUSHING DEFENSE	G	ATT	YDS	AVG	YPG
1 Ohio State	9	341	576	1.7	64.0
2 Princeton	9	326	611	1.9	67.9
3 Wake Forest	9	330	626	1.9	69.6
4 San Francisco	11	435	820	1.9	74.5
5 Wyoming	9	343	788	2.3	87.6
6 **Tulane**	9	373	824	2.2	91.6
7 **Kentucky**	11	482	1021	2.1	92.8
8 Michigan State	9	344	874	2.5	97.1
9 Maryland	10	421	1016	2.4	101.6
10 Loyola-Marymount	9	348	960	2.8	106.7

PASSING DEFENSE	G	ATT	COM	PCT	YPC	INT	I%	YDS	YPA	TD	YPG
1 **Tennessee**	11	149	65	43.6	11.4	23	15.4	743	5.0	2	67.5
2 Indiana	9	127	51	40.2	12.3	12	9.5	629	5.0	3	69.9
3 Tulsa	11	181	59	32.6	13.1	12	6.6	770	4.3	3	70.0
4 Duke	10	147	67	45.6	10.6	17	11.6	707	4.8	3	70.7
5 Montana	9	127	48	37.8	13.8	19	15.0	661	5.2	4	73.4
6 Iowa State	10	113	42	37.2	17.6	9	8.0	741	6.6	4	74.1
7 Penn State	9	141	52	36.9	12.9	18	12.8	671	4.8	8	74.6
8 Harvard	8	101	35	34.7	17.1	2	2.0	599	5.9	6	74.9
9 Army	9	155	59	38.1	11.5	18	11.6	679	4.4	1	75.4
10 **Mississippi State**	9	102	49	48.0	14.3	7	6.9	703	6.9	7	78.1

TOTAL DEFENSE	G	P	YDS	AVG	YPG
1 Wake Forest	9	491	1469	3.0	163.2
2 **Kentucky**	11	671	1895	2.8	172.3
3 Wyoming	9	493	1559	3.2	173.2
4 Army	9	637	1705	2.7	189.4
5 Miami (Fla.)	10	653	1968	3.0	196.8
6 Cornell	9	547	1788	3.3	198.7
7 Tennessee	11	673	2208	3.3	200.7
8 Tulane	9	557	1807	3.2	200.8
9 **Mississippi State**	9	470	1828	3.9	203.1
10 San Francisco	11	693	2240	3.2	203.6

SCORING OFFENSE	G	PTS	AVG
1 Princeton	9	349	38.8

SCORING DEFENSE	G	PTS	AVG
1 Army	9	40	4.4

1950

FINAL POLL (NOV. 27)

UP	AP	SCHOOL	FINAL RECORD
1	1	Oklahoma	10-1-0
2	2	Army	8-1-0
4	3	Texas	9-2-0
5	4	Tennessee	11-1-0
3	5	California	9-1-1
6	6	Princeton	9-0-0
7	7	Kentucky	11-1-0
8	8	Michigan State	8-1-0
9	9	Michigan	6-3-1
10	10	Clemson	9-0-1
13	11	Washington	8-2-0
14	12	Wyoming	10-0-0
12	13	Illinois	7-2-0
11	14	Ohio State	6-3-0
16	15	Miami (Fla.)	9-1-1
16	16	Alabama	9-2-0
18	17	Nebraska	6-2-1
	18	Tulsa	9-1-1
	18	Washington & Lee	8-3-0
20	20	Tulane	6-2-1
15		SMU	6-4-0
19		Stanford	5-3-2

CONSENSUS ALL-AMERICANS

POS	NAME	SCHOOL
B	Vic Janowicz	Ohio State
B	Kyle Rote	SMU
B	**Babe Parilli**	**Kentucky**
B	Leon Heath	Oklahoma
E	Dan Foldberg	Army
E	Bill McColl	Stanford
T	**Bob Gain**	**Kentucky**
T	Jim Weatherall	Oklahoma
G	Bud McFadin	Texas
G	Les Richter	California
C	Jerry Groom	Notre Dame

OTHERS RECEIVING FIRST-TEAM HONORS

B	Bob Williams	Notre Dame
B	Bob Reynolds	Nebraska
B	Don Heinrich	Washington
B	Everett Grandelius	Michigan St.
B	Dick Kazmaier	Princeton
B	Eddie Talboom	Wyoming
B	Johnny Bright	Drake
B	Ed Withers	Wisconsin
B	Francis Bagnell	Pennsylvania
B	Bob Smith	Texas A&M
B	Jackie Calvert	Clemson
E	**Bucky Curtis**	**Vanderbilt**
E	Don Stonesifer	Northwestern
E	Jim Doran	Iowa State
T	Holland Donan	Princeton
T	Allen Wahl	Michigan
T	Charles Shira	Army
T	J.D. Kimmel	Army
G	Bob Ward	Maryland
G	**Ted Daffer**	**Tennessee**
G	Bill Ciarvino	Lehigh
G	Bernard Lemonick	Pennsylvania
G	**Jerome Helluin**	**Tulane**
C	Redmond Finney	Princeton
C	Bob McCullough	Ohio State
C	Bill Vohaska	Illinois
C	Irvin Holdash	North Carolina
C	Donn Moomaw	UCLA

HEISMAN TROPHY VOTING

PLAYER		POS	SCHOOL	TOTAL
1	Vic Janowicz	HB	Ohio State	633
2	Kyle Rote	HB	SMU	280
3	Francis Bagnell	B	Pennsylvania	231
4	**Babe Parilli**	**QB**	**Kentucky**	**214**
5	Bob Reynolds	HB	Nebraska	174
6	Bob Williams	QB	Notre Dame	159
7	Leon Heath	FB	Oklahoma	125
8	Dan Foldberg	E	Army	103

AWARD WINNERS

PLAYER	AWARD
Francis Bagnell, HB, Pennsylvania	Maxwell
Bob Gain, T, Kentucky	**Outland**

BOWL GAMES

DATE	GAME	SCORE
D9	**Presidential Cup**	**Texas A&M 40, Georgia 20**
J1	Tangerine	Morris Harvey 35, Emory & Henry 6
J1	Orange	Clemson 15, Miami (Fla.) 14
J1	Salad	Miami (Ohio) 34, Arizona State 21
J1	Rose	Michigan 14, California 6
J1	**Sugar**	**Kentucky 13, Oklahoma 7**
J1	**Cotton**	**Tennessee 20, Texas 14**
J1	Gator	Wyoming 20, Wash. & Lee 7
J1	Sun	West Texas State 14, Cincinnati 13

SEC STANDINGS

	CONFERENCE			OVERALL		
	W	L	T	W	L	T
Kentucky	5	1	0	11	1	0
Tennessee	4	1	0	11	1	0
Alabama	6	2	0	9	2	0
Tulane	3	1	1	6	2	1
Georgia Tech	4	2	0	5	6	0
Georgia	3	2	1	6	3	3
Vanderbilt	3	4	0	7	4	0
Mississippi State	3	4	0	4	5	0
LSU	2	3	2	4	5	2
Florida	2	4	0	5	5	0
Mississippi	1	5	0	5	5	0
Auburn	0	7	0	0	10	0

1951 NCAA Major College Statistical Leaders

Individual Leaders

PASSING/COMPLETIONS

		G	ATT	COM	PCT	INT	I%	YDS	YPA	TD	TD%	COM.PG
1	Don Klosterman, Loyola-Marymount	9	315	159	50.5	21	6.7	1843	5.9	9	2.9	17.7
2	Babe Parilli, Kentucky	11	239	136	56.9	12	5.0	1643	6.9	19	8.0	12.4
3	Don Leahy, Marquette	11	232	127	54.7	15	6.5	1543	6.7	12	5.2	11.5
4	Tom Dublinski, Utah	11	239	124	51.9	11	4.6	1418	5.9	14	5.9	11.3
5	Don Babers, Oklahoma State	10	247	121	49.0	13	5.3	1352	5.5	10	4.1	12.1
6	Bob Hart, Hardin-Simmons	12	229	117	51.1	14	6.1	1380	6.0	8	3.5	9.8
7	Zeke Bratkowski, Georgia	10	248	116	46.8	29	11.7	1578	6.4	6	2.4	11.6
8	Bill Wade, Vanderbilt	11	223	111	49.8	10	4.5	1609	7.2	13	5.8	10.1
9	Fred Benners, SMU	10	204	108	52.9	12	5.9	1306	6.4	9	4.4	10.8
10	Larry Isbell, Baylor	10	214	105	49.1	18	8.4	1430	6.7	10	4.7	10.5

ALL-PURPOSE YARDS

		G	RUSH	REC	INT	PR	KR	YDS	YPG
1	Ollie Matson, San Francisco	9	1566	58	18	115	280	2037	226.3

RUSHING/YARDS

		G	ATT	YDS	AVG	YPG
1	Ollie Matson, San Francisco	9	245	1566	6.4	174.0
2	Frank Goode, Hardin-Simmons	12	270	1399	5.2	116.6
3	Howard Waugh, Tulsa	11	165	1118	6.8	101.6
4	Gene Shannon, Houston	10	144	1059	7.4	105.9
5	Tommy McCormick, Pacific	10	191	1001	5.2	100.1
6	Hugh McElhenny, Washington	10	169	936	5.5	93.6
7	Johnny Bright, Drake	9	160	927	5.8	103.0
8	John Kastan, Boston U.	10	133	886	6.7	88.6
9	Hank Lauricella, Tennessee	10	111	881	7.9	88.1
10	Buck McPhail, Oklahoma	10	101	865	8.6	86.5

RUSHING/YARDS PER CARRY

		G	ATT	YDS	YPC
1	Buck McPhail, Oklahoma	10	101	865	8.6
2	Hank Lauricella, Tennessee	10	111	881	7.9
3	Dick Modzelewski, Maryland	9	113	834	7.4
4	Gene Shannon, Houston	10	144	1059	7.4
5	Glenn Lippman, Texas A&M	10	118	801	6.8
6	Howard Waugh, Tulsa	11	165	1118	6.8
7	John Kastan, Boston U.	10	133	886	6.7
8	Ollie Matson, San Francisco	9	245	1566	6.4
9	Ray Oliverson, Brigham Young	10	129	822	6.4
10	Jack Crocker, Tulsa	11	133	817	6.1

Based on top 20 rushers

RECEIVING/RECEPTIONS

		G	REC	YDS	TD	YPR	YPG	RPG
1	Dewey McConnell, Wyoming	10	47	725	8	15.4	72.5	4.7
2	Ed Barker, Washington State	10	46	864	9	18.8	86.4	4.6
2	Jim David, Colorado State	10	46	551	5	12.0	55.1	4.6
4	Karl Kluckhohn, Colgate	9	45	616	5	13.7	68.4	5.0
4	Fred Snyder, Loyola-Marymount	9	45	539	2	12.0	59.9	5.0
6	Bill McColl, Stanford	10	42	607	7	14.5	60.7	4.2
7	Harry Babcock, Georgia	10	41	666	2	16.2	66.6	4.1
8	Ben Roderick, Vanderbilt	11	40	627	5	15.7	57.0	3.6
8	George Wooden, Oklahoma State	10	40	502	2	12.6	50.2	4.0
8	Wesley Bomm, Columbia	8	40	444	1	11.1	55.5	5.0
8	Jimmy Walker, Texas-El Paso	10	40	440	3	11.0	44.0	4.0

PUNTING

		PUNT	YDS	AVG
1	Chuck Spaulding, Wyoming	37	1610	43.5
2	Des Koch, Southern California	33	1429	43.3
3	Bobby Wilson, Alabama	65	2724	41.9
4	Jerry Norton, SMU	32	1338	41.8
5	Joe Bevere, Drake	47	1941	41.3
6	Red Smith, Duke	47	1913	40.7
7	Dave Mann, Oregon State	45	1827	40.6
8	Bob Moore, UCLA	52	2096	40.3
9	Bud Wallace, North Carolina	65	2613	40.2
10	Avatus Stone, Syracuse	52	2090	40.2

PUNT RETURNS/YARDS

		PR	YDS	AVG
1	Tom Murphy, Holy Cross	25	533	21.3
2	Johnny Williams, Southern California	39	438	11.2
3	Selmer Pederson, Wyoming	39	420	10.8
4	Robert Lary, Texas A&M	24	388	16.2
5	James Lesane, Virginia	35	387	11.1
6	John Hall, Florida	24	369	15.4
7	Billy Stephens, South Carolina	19	355	18.7
8	Bud Carson, North Carolina	25	318	12.7
9	Bill Blackstock, Tennessee	12	311	25.9
10	Lindy Hanson, Boston U.	21	306	14.6

KICKOFF RETURNS/YARDS

		KR	YDS	AVG
1	Chuck Hill, New Mexico	17	504	29.6
2	Robert Byrne, Montana	21	446	21.2
3	Johnny Williams, Southern California	15	408	27.2
3	Alex Webster, North Carolina St.	15	408	27.2
5	Robert Mischak, Army	12	376	31.3
6	Larry Parker, North Carolina	17	372	21.9
7	Harry Jones, Kentucky	15	371	24.7
8	Steve Wadiak, South Carolina	13	350	26.9
9	Gilbert Gonzales, Arizona	13	348	26.8
10	Bino Barreira, George Washington	19	341	17.9

SCORING

		TDS	XPT	FG	PTS
1	Ollie Matson, San Francisco	21	0	0	126
2	Hugh McElhenny, Washington	17	23	0	125
3	Bill Parsons, Tulsa	16	0	0	96
4	Ray Oliverson, Brigham Young	15	0	0	90
4	John Kastan, Boston U.	15	0	0	90
6	Frank Goode, Hardin-Simmons	14	0	0	84
6	Harold Payne, Tennessee	14	0	0	84
6	Johnny Bright, Drake	14	0	0	84
6	Eddie Macon, Pacific	14	0	0	84
10	Four tied				78

INTERCEPTIONS

		INT	YDS
1	George Shaw, Oregon	13	136
2	Bill Albrecht, Washington	12	140
3	Alfred Brosky, Illinois	10	183
3	Robert Reid, Baylor	10	130
5	Eddie Macon, Pacific	9	245
6	Pete Konek, Kansas	8	180
6	Lester Kennedy, Tulane	8	103
6	Chester Lyssy, Hardin-Simmons	8	96
6	John Thompson, Texas Tech	8	74
6	Mike Zinkiewicz, Holy Cross	8	72

Team Leaders

RUSHING OFFENSE

		G	ATT	YDS	AVG	YPG
1	Arizona State	10	559	3348	6.0	334.8
2	Tulsa	11	647	3622	5.6	329.3
3	Maryland	9	496	2906	5.9	322.9
4	Oklahoma	10	589	3160	5.4	316.0
5	Pacific	10	678	3153	4.7	315.3
6	Tennessee	10	532	3068	5.8	306.8
7	California	10	551	3044	5.5	304.4
8	Michigan State	9	530	2630	5.0	292.2
9	Princeton	9	522	2604	5.0	289.3
10	San Francisco	9	520	2544	4.9	282.7

PASSING OFFENSE/YPG

		G	ATT	COM	INT	PCT	YDS	YPA	TD	YPG	I%	YPC
1	Loyola-Marymount	9	324	164	22	50.6	1895	5.8	10	210.6	6.8	11.6
2	Missouri	10	284	124	30	43.7	1762	6.2	12	176.2	10.6	14.2
3	SMU	10	286	144	23	50.4	1734	6.1	11	173.4	8.0	12.0
4	Colgate	9	235	110	20	46.8	1560	6.6	13	173.3	8.5	14.2
5	Boston U.	10	212	117	17	55.2	1680	7.9	16	168.0	8.0	14.4
6	Washington	10	257	123	21	47.9	1622	6.3	12	162.2	8.2	13.2
7	Oregon	10	314	134	26	42.7	1620	5.2	24	162.0	8.3	12.1
8	Georgia	10	263	121	32	46.0	1618	6.2	7	161.8	12.2	13.4
9	Oklahoma State	10	291	143	19	49.1	1603	5.5	11	160.3	6.5	11.2
10	Iowa State	9	218	109	18	50.0	1425	6.5	16	158.3	8.3	13.1

TOTAL OFFENSE

		G	P	YDS	AVG	YPG
1	Tulsa	11	836	5282	6.3	480.2
2	Maryland	9	616	3810	6.2	423.3
3	Princeton	9	671	3753	5.6	417.0
4	Arizona State	10	689	4162	6.0	416.2
5	Cincinnati	11	796	4491	5.6	408.3
6	Oklahoma	10	693	4062	5.9	406.2
7	Holy Cross	10	810	4055	5.0	405.5
8	Michigan State	9	667	3627	5.4	403.0
9	Pacific	10	844	4016	4.8	401.6
10	California	10	685	3980	5.8	398.0

RUSHING DEFENSE

		G	ATT	YDS	AVG	YPG
1	San Francisco	9	288	464	1.6	51.6
2	Wisconsin	9	344	599	1.7	66.6
3	Princeton	9	359	669	1.9	74.3
4	Maryland	9	321	680	2.1	75.6
5	Holy Cross	10	415	973	2.3	97.3
6	Oklahoma	10	418	1049	2.5	104.9
7	Georgia Tech	11	477	1164	2.4	105.8
8	Tennessee	10	460	1071	2.3	107.1
9	Southern California	11	466	1179	2.5	107.2
10	Illinois	9	422	1020	2.4	113.3

PASSING DEFENSE

		G	ATT	COM	PCT	YPC	INT	I%	YDS	YPA	TD	YPG
1	Washington & Lee	10	151	53	35.1	12.8	24	15.9	679	4.5	5	67.9
2	Miami (Fla.)	10	174	65	37.4	10.8	11	6.3	700	4.0	6	70.0
3	Columbia	8	141	50	35.5	12.5	7	5.0	624	4.4	2	78.0
4	Indiana	9	128	53	41.4	13.2	14	10.9	702	5.5	8	78.0
5	Vanderbilt	11	125	53	42.4	16.2	18	14.4	861	6.9	3	78.3
6	Purdue	9	128	48	37.5	15.4	10	7.8	737	5.8	8	81.9
7	Colorado State	10	167	71	42.5	11.8	10	6.0	838	5.0	7	83.8
8	Furman	10	151	68	45.0	12.4	14	9.3	841	5.6	7	84.1
9	Boston U.	10	178	60	33.7	14.2	18	10.1	853	4.8	5	85.3
10	Denver	10	165	70	42.4	12.3	21	12.7	863	5.2	4	86.3

TOTAL DEFENSE

		G	P	YDS	AVG	YPG
1	Wisconsin	9	539	1393	2.6	154.8
2	Princeton	9	513	1592	3.1	176.9
3	Georgia Tech	11	708	2190	3.1	199.1
4	Kentucky	11	630	2265	3.6	205.9
5	San Francisco	9	561	1885	3.4	209.4
6	Illinois	9	552	1954	3.5	217.1
7	Holy Cross	10	647	2212	3.4	221.2
8	Oklahoma	10	655	2215	3.4	221.5
9	Virginia	9	553	1995	3.6	221.7
10	Denver	10	617	2230	3.6	223.0

SCORING OFFENSE

		G	PTS	AVG
1	Maryland	9	353	39.2

SCORING DEFENSE

		G	PTS	AVG
1	Wisconsin	9	53	5.9

1951

FINAL POLL (DEC. 3)

UP	AP	SCHOOL	FINAL RECORD
1	1	**Tennessee**	**10-1-0**
2	2	Michigan State	9-0-0
4	3	Maryland	10-0-0
3	4	Illinois	9-0-1
5	5	**Georgia Tech**	**11-0-1**
6	6	Princeton	9-0-0
7	7	Stanford	9-2-0
8	8	Wisconsin	7-1-1
9	9	Baylor	8-2-1
11	10	Oklahoma	8-2-0
10	11	TCU	6-5-0
12	12	California	8-2-0
	13	Virginia	8-1-0
14	14	San Francisco	9-0-0
17	15	**Kentucky**	**8-4-0**
	16	Boston U.	6-4-0
17	17	UCLA	5-3-1
14	18	Washington State	7-3-0
	19	Clemson	7-3-0
17	19	Holy Cross	8-2-0
13		Notre Dame	7-2-1
14		Purdue	5-4-0
20		Kansas	8-2-0

CONSENSUS ALL-AMERICANS

POS	NAME	SCHOOL
B	Dick Kazmaier	Princeton
B	**Hank Lauricella**	**Tennessee**
B	**Babe Parilli**	**Kentucky**
B	Johnny Karras	Illinois
E	Bill McColl	Stanford
E	Bob Carey	Michigan St.
T	Don Coleman	Michigan St.
T	Jim Weatherall	Oklahoma
G	Bob Ward	Maryland
G	Les Richter	California
C	Dick Hightower	SMU

OTHERS RECEIVING FIRST-TEAM HONORS

B	Larry Isbell	Baylor
B	Frank Gifford	Southern California
B	Ollie Matson	San Francisco
B	Gary Kerkorian	Stanford
B	Ed Modzelewski	Maryland
B	Al Dorow	Michigan St.
B	Hugh McElhenny	Washington
B	Bobby Dillon	Texas
B	Harry Agganis	Boston U.
E	Stan Williams	Baylor
E	Bill Howton	Rice
E	Hal Faverty	Wisconsin
E	Ed Bell	Pennsylvania
E	Frank McPhee	Princeton
E	Pat O'Donahue	Wisconsin
E	Dewey McConnell	Wyoming
T	Jack Little	Texas A&M
T	Bob Toneff	Notre Dame
T	Charles Ulrich	Illinois
T	**Lamar Wheat**	**Georgia Tech**
T	**Bill Pearman**	**Tennessee**
T	Doug Conway	TCU
G	**Ray Beck**	**Georgia Tech**
G	Nick Liotta	Villanova
G	Marv Matuszak	Tulsa
G	**Ted Daffer**	**Tennessee**
G	George Mrkonic	Kansas
G	Joe Palumbo	Virginia
C	**Doug Moseley**	**Kentucky**
C	Pat Cannamela	Southern California
C	**George Tarasovic**	**LSU**
C	Charles Boerio	Illinois

AP named Weatherall, Richter and Beck to its first-team All-American defense, but not offense

HEISMAN TROPHY VOTING

	PLAYER	POS	SCHOOL	TOTAL
1	Dick Kazmaier	HB	Princeton	1777
2	**Hank Lauricella**	**RB**	**Tennessee**	**424**
3	**Babe Parilli**	**QB**	**Kentucky**	**344**
4	Bill McColl	E	Stanford	313
5	John Bright	RB	Drake	230
6	John Karras	HB	Illinois	223
7	Larry Isbell	QB	Baylor	163
8	Hugh McElhenny	FB	Washington	103
9	Ollie Matson	FB	San Francisco	95
10	Don Coleman	T	Michigan State	93

AWARD WINNERS

PLAYER	AWARD
Dick Kazmaier, HB, Princeton	Maxwell
Jim Weatherall, T, Oklahoma	Outland

BOWL GAMES

DATE	GAME	SCORE
J1	Tangerine	Stetson 35, Arkansas State 20
J1	**Orange**	**Georgia Tech 17, Baylor 14**
J1	Salad	Houston 26, Dayton 21
J1	Rose	Illinois 40, Stanford 7
J1	**Cotton**	**Kentucky 20, TCU 7**
J1	Gator	Miami (Fla.) 14, Clemson 0
J1	**Sugar**	**Maryland 28, Tennessee 13**
J1	Sun	Texas Tech 25, Pacific 14

SEC STANDINGS

	CONFERENCE			OVERALL		
	W	L	T	W	L	T
Georgia Tech	7	0	0	11	0	1
Tennessee	5	0	0	10	1	0
LSU	4	2	1	7	3	1
Mississippi	4	2	1	6	3	1
Kentucky	3	3	0	8	4	0
Auburn	3	4	0	5	5	0
Vanderbilt	3	5	0	6	5	0
Alabama	3	5	0	5	6	0
Florida	2	4	0	5	5	0
Georgia	2	4	0	5	5	0
Mississippi State	2	5	0	4	5	0
Tulane	1	5	0	4	6	0

1952 NCAA Major College Statistical Leaders

Individual Leaders

PASSING/COMPLETIONS

		G	ATT	COM	PCT	INT	I%	YDS	YPA	TD	TD%	COM.PG
1	Don Heinrich, Washington	10	270	137	50.7	17	6.3	1647	6.1	13	4.8	13.7
2	Tommy O'Connell, Illinois	9	224	133	59.4	17	7.6	1761	7.9	12	5.4	14.8
3	Zeke Bratkowski, Georgia	11	262	131	50.0	16	6.1	1824	7.0	12	4.6	11.9
4	Chuck Maloy, Holy Cross	10	288	126	43.8	16	5.6	1514	5.3	13	4.5	12.6
5	Johnny Borton, Ohio State	9	196	115	58.7	6	3.1	1555	7.9	15	7.7	12.8
6	Jim Haluska, Wisconsin	9	199	112	56.3	18	9.0	1410	7.1	12	6.0	12.4
7	Roger Franz, Fordham	8	216	105	48.6	12	5.6	1392	6.4	6	2.8	13.1
8	Dale Samuels, Purdue	9	185	104	56.2	6	3.2	1131	6.1	10	5.4	11.6
9	Ted Marchibroda, Detroit	9	240	103	42.9	13	5.4	1637	6.8	9	3.8	11.4
10	Dick Shinaut, Texas-El Paso	11	208	102	49.0	15	7.2	1520	7.3	13	6.3	9.3

ALL-PURPOSE YARDS

		G	RUSH	REC	INT	PR	KR	YDS	YPG
1	Billy Vessels, Oklahoma	10	1072	165	10	120	145	1512	151.2

RUSHING/YARDS

		G	ATT	YDS	AVG	YPG
1	Howie Waugh, Tulsa	10	164	1372	8.4	137.2
2	Billy Vessels, Oklahoma	10	161	1072	6.7	107.2
3	Buck McPhail, Oklahoma	10	161	1018	6.3	101.8
4	Bobby Marlow, Alabama	11	176	950	5.4	86.4
5	Dick Clasby, Harvard	9	205	950	4.6	105.6
6	Alan Ameche, Wisconsin	9	205	946	4.6	105.1
7	Rod Williams, Hardin-Simmons	10	180	898	5.0	89.8
8	Gene Filipski, Villanova	9	138	889	6.4	98.8
9	Dick Curran, Arizona State	9	114	870	7.6	96.7
10	John Olszewski, California	10	160	845	5.3	84.5

RUSHING/YARDS PER CARRY

		G	ATT	YDS	YPC
1	Howie Waugh, Tulsa	10	164	1372	8.4
2	Dick Curran, Arizona State	9	114	870	7.6
3	Dick Stults, San Jose State	9	118	801	6.8
4	Billy Vessels, Oklahoma	10	161	1072	6.7
5	Gene Filipski, Villanova	9	138	889	6.4
6	Buck McPhail, Oklahoma	10	161	1018	6.3
7	Homer Smith, Princeton	9	133	821	6.2
8	Joe Fortunato, Mississippi State	9	128	779	6.1
9	Tom McCormick, Pacific	9	142	782	5.5
10	Billy Reynolds, Pittsburgh	9	135	748	5.5

Based on top 20 rushers

RECEIVING/RECEPTIONS

		G	REC	YDS	TD	YPR	YPG	RPG
1	Ed Brown, Fordham	8	57	774	6	13.6	96.8	7.1
2	Joe McClaran, Drake	9	47	666	6	14.2	74.0	5.2
3	John Carroll, Holy Cross	10	46	609	4	13.2	60.9	4.6
4	Rocky Ryan, Illinois	9	45	714	5	15.9	79.3	5.0
5	Rex Smith, Illinois	9	45	642	4	14.3	71.3	5.0
6	Al Ward, Columbia	9	43	615	3	14.3	68.3	4.8
6	Bernie Flowers, Purdue	9	43	603	7	14.0	67.0	4.8
8	George Black, Washington	10	42	637	7	15.2	63.7	4.2
9	Monte Brethauer, Oregon	10	41	486	2	11.9	48.6	4.1
10	Jimmy Byron, VMI*	10	40	755	8	18.9	75.5	4.0

*Four tied with 40; Byron had the most yards

PUNTING

		PUNT	YDS	AVG
1	Des Koch, Southern California	47	2043	43.5
2	Zack Jordan, Colorado	57	2474	43.4
3	Paul Chapman, Citadel	61	2519	41.3
4	Jerry Norton, SMU	44	1813	41.2
5	Bud Wallace, North Carolina	70	2877	41.1
6	Jerry Jeffries, Hardin-Simmons	46	1877	40.8
7	Roger Franz, Fordham	36	1469	40.8
8	Jack Williams, Virginia Tech	66	2686	40.7
9	Buddy Bellis, Montana	61	2483	40.7
10	Udell Westover, Brigham Young	40	1620	40.5

PUNT RETURNS/YARDS

		PR	YDS	AVG
1	Horton Nesrsta, Rice	44	536	12.2
2	Jim Sears, Southern California	30	478	15.9
3	Eddie Knowles, Virginia	32	365	11.4
4	Billy Anderson, Virginia Tech	20	334	16.7
5	Cecil Ingram, Alabama	30	329	11.0
6	Gil Reich, Kansas	19	327	17.2
7	Harold Farmer, Wyoming	24	264	11.0
8	Paul Larson, California	24	261	10.9
9	Billy Polson, Houston	22	260	11.8
10	John Zibnack, Denver	18	258	14.3

KICKOFF RETURNS/YARDS

		KR	YDS	AVG
1	Curly Powell, VMI	27	517	19.1
2	Larry Spencer, Wake Forest	11	464	42.2
3	Fob James, Auburn	17	414	24.4
4	Don Ellis, Texas A&M	17	413	24.3
5	Don Booth, Virginia Tech	18	413	22.9
6	Jerry Blitz, Harvard	13	392	30.2
7	Carroll Hardy, Colorado	12	386	32.2
8	Ken Kessaris, Brown	13	379	29.2
9	Richard Towers, Kansas State	18	378	21.0
10	Robert Mercier, Columbia	16	361	22.6

SCORING

		TDS	XPT	FG	PTS
1	Jackie Parker, Mississippi State	16	24	0	120
2	Billy Vessels, Oklahoma	18	0	0	108
3	Robert Haner, Villanova	13	21	0	99
4	Buford Long, Florida	14	0	0	84
5	Billy Quinn, Texas	13	0	0	78
5	Tom McCormick, Pacific	13	0	0	78
7	Tom Miner, Tulsa	5	41	1	74
8	Five tied				72

INTERCEPTIONS

		INT	YDS
1	Cecil Ingram, Alabama	10	163
2	Bobby Renn, Davidson	9	121
2	Jim Psaltis, Southern California	9	113
4	Bill Stits, UCLA	8	235
4	Joe McNicholas, Villanova	8	102
4	Jack Sherry, Penn State	8	101
4	Al Brosky, Illinois	8	77
4	Don Eyer, Penn State	8	67
4	Joe Boring, Texas A&M	8	67
4	Ron Fraley, TCU	8	36

Team Leaders

RUSHING OFFENSE

		G	ATT	YDS	AVG	YPG
1	Tulsa	10	540	3215	6.0	321.5
2	Oklahoma	10	609	3036	5.0	303.6
3	California	10	553	2814	5.1	281.4
4	San Jose State	9	439	2478	5.6	275.3
5	Michigan State	9	508	2452	4.8	272.4
6	Texas	10	610	2695	4.4	269.5
7	Princeton	9	474	2410	5.1	267.8
8	West Virginia	9	487	2375	4.9	263.9
9	Arizona	10	479	2548	5.3	254.8
10	Virginia	10	559	2525	4.5	252.5

PASSING OFFENSE/YPG

		G	ATT	COM	INT	PCT	YDS	YPA	TD	YPG	I%	YPC
1	Fordham	8	277	136	15	49.1	1806	6.5	13	225.8	5.4	13.3
2	Illinois	9	245	141	20	57.6	1929	7.9	13	214.3	8.2	13.7
3	Detroit	9	264	112	18	42.4	1769	6.7	11	196.6	6.8	15.8
4	Ohio State	9	217	124	9	57.1	1709	7.9	16	189.9	4.1	13.8
5	Cincinnati	10	194	116	9	59.8	1864	9.6	15	186.4	4.6	16.1
6	Oregon	9	285	126	32	44.2	1720	6.0	9	172.0	11.2	13.7
7	Pennsylvania	9	192	98	13	51.0	1547	8.1	10	171.9	6.8	15.8
8	Washington	10	285	142	21	49.8	1708	6.0	13	170.8	7.4	12.0
9	Georgia	11	266	134	16	50.4	1878	7.1	13	170.7	6.0	14.0
10	Wisconsin	9	211	117	19	55.5	1476	7.0	13	164.0	9.0	12.6

TOTAL OFFENSE

		G	P	YDS	AVG	YPG
1	Tulsa	10	685	4666	6.8	466.6
2	San Jose State	9	612	3871	6.3	430.1
3	Michigan State	9	667	3858	5.8	428.7
4	Princeton	9	643	3852	6.0	428.0
5	Oklahoma	10	721	4255	5.9	425.5
6	Wisconsin	9	678	3497	5.2	388.6
7	Cincinnati	10	658	3882	5.9	388.2
8	Texas	10	767	3865	5.0	386.5
9	Mississippi	10	749	3831	5.1	383.1
10	West Virginia	9	633	3395	5.4	377.2
10	Maryland	9	648	3395	5.2	377.2

RUSHING DEFENSE

		G	ATT	YDS	AVG	YPG
1	Michigan State	9	342	755	2.2	83.9
2	Navy	9	421	843	2.0	93.7
3	UCLA	9	360	847	2.4	94.1
4	Princeton	9	373	865	2.3	96.1
5	Wake Forest	10	418	997	2.4	99.7
6	Holy Cross	10	449	1039	2.3	103.9
7	Yale	9	378	950	2.5	105.6
8	Georgia Tech	11	473	1175	2.5	106.8
9	Syracuse	9	357	964	2.7	107.1
10	Fordham	8	357	885	2.5	110.6

PASSING DEFENSE

		G	ATT	COM	PCT	YPC	INT	I%	YDS	YPA	TD	YPG
1	Virginia	10	161	50	31.1	10.1	16	10.0	503	3.1	3	50.3
2	Duke	10	125	44	35.2	11.7	14	11.2	516	4.1	1	51.6
3	Tennessee	10	116	44	37.9	12.1	10	8.6	531	4.6	3	53.1
4	Brigham Young	10	105	43	41.0	14.1	13	12.4	605	5.8	5	60.5
5	Georgia Tech	11	191	71	37.2	10.3	NA	NA	730	3.8	0	66.4
6	Southern California	10	184	62	33.7	10.8	31	16.8	668	3.6	1	66.8
7	Alabama	11	160	68	42.5	11.1	24	15.0	755	4.7	6	68.6
8	Vanderbilt	10	152	58	38.2	12.1	20	13.2	703	4.6	4	70.3
9	Mississippi State	9	133	50	37.6	12.7	9	6.8	636	4.8	4	70.7
10	Colgate	9	187	61	32.6	10.7	20	10.7	652	3.5	7	72.4

TOTAL DEFENSE

		G	P	YDS	AVG	YPG
1	Tennessee	10	578	1667	2.9	166.7
2	Georgia Tech	11	664	1905	2.9	173.2
3	Southern California	10	642	1775	2.8	177.5
4	Virginia	10	657	1963	3.0	196.3
5	Maryland	9	516	1808	3.5	200.9
6	Navy	9	604	1884	3.1	209.3
7	West Virginia	9	612	1901	3.1	211.2
8	Duke	10	623	2121	3.4	212.1
9	Wake Forest	10	586	2142	3.7	214.2
10	Houston	10	637	2150	3.4	215.0

SCORING OFFENSE

		G	PTS	AVG
1	Oklahoma	10	407	40.7

SCORING DEFENSE

		G	PTS	AVG
1	Southern California	10	47	4.7

1952

FINAL POLL (DEC. 1)

UP	AP	SCHOOL	FINAL RECORD
1	1	Michigan State	9-0-0
2	2	Georgia Tech	12-0-0
3	3	Notre Dame	7-2-1
4	4	Oklahoma	8-1-1
5	5	Southern California	10-1-0
6	6	UCLA	8-1-0
7	7	Mississippi	8-1-2
8	8	Tennessee	8-2-1
9	9	Alabama	10-2-0
11	10	Texas	9-2-0
10	11	Wisconsin	6-3-1
	12	Tulsa	8-2-1
13	11	Maryland	7-2-0
	14	Syracuse	7-3-0
	15	Florida	8-3-0
18	16	Duke	8-2-0
15	17	Ohio State	6-3-0
12	18	Purdue	4-3-2
14	19	Princeton	8-1-0
19	20	Kentucky	5-4-2
15		Pittsburgh	6-3-0
17		Navy	6-2-1
19		Houston	8-2-0

CONSENSUS ALL-AMERICANS

POS	NAME	SCHOOL
B	Jack Scarbath	Maryland
B	Johnny Lattner	Notre Dame
B	Billy Vessels	Oklahoma
B	Jim Sears	Southern California
E	Frank McPhee	Princeton
E	Bernie Flowers	Purdue
T	Dick Modzelewski	Maryland
T	Hal Miller	Georgia Tech
G	John Michels	Tennessee
G	Elmer Willhoite	Southern California
C	Donn Moomaw	UCLA

OTHERS RECEIVING FIRST-TEAM HONORS

B	Gene Filipski	Villanova
B	Paul Giel	Minnesota
B	Don McAuliffe	Michigan St.
B	Buck McPhail	Oklahoma
B	Don Heinrich	Washington
B	Leon Hardeman	Georgia Tech
B	Bobby Moorhead	Georgia Tech
B	John Olszewski	California
B	Paul Cameron	UCLA
B	Lowell Perry	Michigan
E	Tom Stolhandske	Texas
E	Ed Bell	Pennsylvania
E	Buck Martin	Georgia Tech
E	Joe Collier	Northwestern
E	Steve Meilinger	Kentucky
E	Tom Scott	Virginia
T	Kline Gilbert	Mississippi
T	Ed Meadows	Duke
T	David Suminski	Wisconsin
T	Doug Atkins	Tennessee
T	Harvey Achziger	Colorado State
T	Bob Fleck	Syracuse
T	Jerry Minnick	Nebraska
T	Oliver Spencer	Kansas
G	Harley Sewell	Texas
G	Marv Matuszak	Tulsa
G	Steve Eisenhauer	Navy
G	Mike Takacs	Ohio State
C	Tom Catlin	Oklahoma
C	Pete Brown	Georgia Tech
C	Dick Tamburo	Michigan St.
C	Joe Schmidt	Pittsburgh
C	George Morris	Georgia Tech

HEISMAN TROPHY VOTING

	PLAYER	POS	SCHOOL	TOTAL
1	Billy Vessels	HB	Oklahoma	525
2	Jack Scarbath	QB	Maryland	367
3	Paul Giel	TB	Minnesota	329
4	Donn Moomaw	LB	UCLA	257
5	Johnny Lattner	HB	Notre Dame	253
6	Paul Cameron	HB	UCLA	218
7	Jim Sears	HB	Southern Cal	173
8	Don McAuliffe	HB	Michigan State	164
9	Don Heinrich	QB	Washington	153
10	Tom Catlin	C	Oklahoma	150

AWARD WINNERS

PLAYER	AWARD
Johnny Lattner, HB, Notre Dame	Maxwell
Dick Modzelewski, T, Maryland	Outland

BOWL GAMES

DATE	GAME	SCORE
J1	Tangerine	Texas A&M-Comm. 33, Tennessee Tech 0
J1	Orange	Alabama 61, Syracuse 6
J1	Gator	Florida 14, Tulsa 13
J1	Sugar	Georgia Tech 24, Mississippi 7
J1	Rose	Southern California 7, Wisconsin 0
J1	Cotton	Texas 16, Tennessee 0
J1	Sun	Pacific 26, Southern Miss 7

SEC STANDINGS

	CONFERENCE			OVERALL		
	W	L	T	W	L	T
Georgia Tech	6	0	0	12	0	0
Tennessee	5	0	1	8	2	1
Mississippi	4	0	2	8	1	2
Alabama	4	2	0	10	2	0
Georgia	4	3	0	7	4	0
Florida	3	3	0	8	3	0
Mississippi State	3	4	0	5	4	0
Tulane	3	5	0	5	5	0
Kentucky	1	3	2	5	4	2
LSU	2	5	0	3	7	0
Vanderbilt	1	4	1	3	5	2
Auburn	0	7	0	2	8	0

1953 NCAA MAJOR COLLEGE STATISTICAL LEADERS

INDIVIDUAL LEADERS

PASSING/COMPLETIONS

		G	ATT	COM	PCT	INT	I%	YDS	YPA	TD	TD%	COM.PG
1	Bob Garrett, Stanford	10	205	118	57.6	10	4.9	1637	8.0	17	8.3	11.8
2	Zeke Bratkowski, Georgia	11	224	113	50.4	23	10.3	1461	6.5	6	2.7	10.3
3	Sandy Lederman, Washington	10	189	92	48.7	14	7.4	1157	6.1	8	4.2	9.2
4	Paul Larson, California	10	171	85	49.7	16	9.4	1431	8.4	6	3.5	8.5
5	Tony Rados, Penn State	9	171	81	47.4	12	7.0	1025	6.0	8	4.7	9.0
6	Don Rydalch, Utah	10	128	78	60.9	8	6.3	980	7.7	7	5.5	7.8
6	Lamar McHan, Arkansas	10	150	78	52.0	11	7.3	1107	7.4	8	5.3	7.8
8	Richard Carr, Columbia	9	191	77	40.3	18	9.4	1367	7.2	13	6.8	8.6
9	Don Ellis, Texas A&M	10	171	76	44.4	14	8.2	950	5.6	4	2.3	7.6
10	Dick Thomas, Northwestern	9	145	74	51.0	7	4.8	933	6.4	5	3.5	8.2
10	Cotton Davidson, Baylor	10	156	74	47.4	16	10.3	1092	7.0	9	5.8	7.4

ALL-PURPOSE YARDS

		G	RUSH	REC	INT	PR	KR	YDS	YPG
1	J.C. Caroline, Illinois	9	1256	52	0	129	33	1470	163.3

RUSHING/YARDS

		G	ATT	YDS	AVG	YPG
1	J.C. Caroline, Illinois	9	194	1256	6.5	139.6
2	Kosse Johnson, Rice	10	187	944	5.0	94.4
3	Ken Cardella, Arizona	10	148	915	6.2	91.5
4	Bob Watkins, Ohio State	9	153	875	5.7	97.2
5	Neil Worden, Notre Dame	10	145	859	5.9	85.9
6	Dicky Maegle, Rice	10	114	833	7.3	83.3
7	Alan Ameche, Wisconsin	9	165	801	4.9	89.0
8	Larry Grigg, Oklahoma	10	130	792	6.1	79.2
9	Bobby Cavazos, Texas Tech	11	97	757	7.8	68.8
10	Chet Hanulak, Maryland	10	77	753	9.8	75.3

RUSHING/YARDS PER CARRY

		G	ATT	YDS	YPC
1	Chet Hanulak, Maryland	10	77	753	9.8
2	Dick Imer, Montana	8	86	703	8.2
3	Bobby Cavazos, Texas Tech	11	97	757	7.8
4	Dicky Maegle, Rice	10	114	833	7.3
5	J.C. Caroline, Illinois	9	194	1256	6.5
6	Ken Cardella, Arizona	10	148	915	6.2
7	Larry Grigg, Oklahoma	10	130	792	6.1
8	Neil Worden, Notre Dame	10	145	859	5.9
9	Bob Watkins, Ohio State	9	153	875	5.7
10	Bill Bowman, William & Mary	10	132	722	5.5

Based on top 20 rushers

RECEIVING/RECEPTIONS

		G	REC	YDS	TD	YPR	YPG	RPG
1	John Carson, Georgia	11	45	663	4	14.7	60.3	4.1
1	Ken Buck, Pacific	10	45	660	5	14.7	66.0	4.5
1	Sam Morley, Stanford	10	45	594	6	13.2	59.4	4.5
4	John Steinberg, Stanford	10	32	425	3	13.3	42.5	3.2
5	Dave McLaughlin, Dartmouth	9	31	592	6	19.1	65.8	3.4
6	Floyd Sagely, Arkansas	10	30	542	3	18.1	54.2	3.0
6	John Allen, Arizona State	10	30	505	8	16.8	50.5	3.0
6	Chester Lyssy, Hardin-Simmons	11	30	389	5	13.0	35.4	2.7
6	Jim Garrity, Penn State	9	30	349	3	11.6	38.8	3.3
10	Dale Hopp, Columbia	9	29	437	4	15.1	48.6	3.2
10	Andy Nacrelli, Fordham	9	29	428	3	14.8	47.6	3.2

PUNTING

		PUNT	YDS	AVG
1	Zeke Bratkowski, Georgia	50	2130	42.6
2	Bart Starr, Alabama	30	1242	41.4
3	Paul Cameron, UCLA	31	1280	41.3
4	Dick Clasby, Harvard	30	1230	41.0
5	Jack Williams, Virginia Tech	30	1227	40.9
6	Lamar McHan, Arkansas	46	1849	40.2
7	Homer Smith, Princeton	30	1200	40.0
8	Tom Yewcic, Michigan State	31	1234	39.8
9	Walt Hynoski, Pennsylvania	37	1469	39.7
10	George Broeder, Iowa	34	1350	39.7

PUNT RETURNS/YARDS

		PR	YDS	AVG
1	Paul Giel, Minnesota	17	288	16.9
2	Paul Cameron, UCLA	21	284	13.5
3	Bobby Lee, New Mexico	13	252	19.4
3	Eddie West, North Carolina St.	23	239	10.4
5	Jimmy Wade, Tennessee	18	235	13.1
6	Jack Stone, West Virginia	13	233	17.9
6	Lamar McHan, Arkansas	21	233	11.1
8	Ron Drzewiecki, Marquette	10	232	23.2
9	Lenny Moore, Penn State	13	228	17.5
10	Merrill Green, Oklahoma	5	225	45.0

KICKOFF RETURNS/YARDS

		KR	YDS	AVG
1	Max McGee, Tulane	17	371	21.8
2	Howard Cassady, Ohio State	15	343	22.9
3	L.G. Dupre, Baylor	14	340	24.3
4	Johnny Lattner, Notre Dame	8	331	41.4
5	Carl Bolt, Washington & Lee	12	325	27.1
6	Jim Thacker, Davidson	12	311	25.9
7	Ken Keller, North Carolina	13	299	23.0
8	Bill Teer, North Carolina St.	12	289	24.1
9	Charles Horton, Vanderbilt	15	284	18.9
10	Jim Bradley, New Mexico State	15	281	18.7

SCORING

		TDS	XPT	FG	PTS
1	Earl Lindley, Utah State	13	3	0	81
2	Bobby Cavazos, Texas Tech	13	2	0	80
3	Larry Grigg, Oklahoma	13	0	0	78
3	Fred Mahaffey, Denver	13	0	0	78
3	Johnny Mapp, VMI	13	0	0	78
6	Robert Burgmeier, Detroit	12	0	0	72
6	Paul Cameron, UCLA	12	0	0	72
6	Jimmy Wade, Tennessee	12	0	0	72
9	Don Lewis, Texas Tech	11	1	0	67
9	Joe Mastrogiovanni, Wyoming	9	13	0	67

INTERCEPTIONS

		INT	YDS
1	Bob Garrett, Stanford	9	80
2	Bobby Luna, Alabama	6	158
2	Paul Larson, California	6	102
2	Ralph Carr, Oregon State	6	86
2	Levi Johns, LSU	6	80
2	Charlie Sumner, William & Mary	6	70
2	Jerry Barger, Duke	6	55

TEAM LEADERS

RUSHING OFFENSE

		G	ATT	YDS	AVG	YPG
1	Oklahoma	10	591	3069	5.2	306.9
2	Cincinnati	10	463	2947	6.4	294.7
3	Texas Tech	11	567	3172	5.6	288.4
4	Notre Dame	10	616	2881	4.7	288.1
5	West Virginia	9	477	2536	5.3	281.8
6	Illinois	9	478	2481	5.2	275.7
7	Rice	10	547	2735	5.0	273.5
8	Arizona	10	505	2689	5.3	268.9
9	Maryland	10	483	2578	5.3	257.8
10	Furman	9	459	2242	4.9	249.1

PASSING OFFENSE/YPG

		G	ATT	COM	INT	PCT	YDS	YPA	TD	YPG	I%	YPC
1	Stanford	10	230	130	13	56.5	1795	7.8	19	179.5	5.7	13.8
2	Pacific	10	235	113	16	48.1	1716	7.3	15	171.6	6.8	15.2
3	Dartmouth	9	177	90	18	50.9	1493	8.4	15	165.9	10.2	16.6
4	California	10	195	94	19	48.2	1612	8.3	7	161.2	9.7	17.1
5	Columbia	9	192	77	18	40.1	1367	7.1	13	151.9	9.4	17.8
6	Syracuse	9	175	92	11	52.6	1320	7.5	11	146.7	6.3	14.3
7	Georgia	11	247	118	25	47.8	1575	6.4	8	143.2	10.1	13.3
8	Mississippi	10	169	75	17	44.4	1411	8.3	6	141.1	10.1	18.8
9	Baylor	10	199	98	18	49.3	1394	7.0	10	139.4	9.1	14.2
10	Washington	10	224	106	19	47.3	1369	6.1	8	136.9	8.5	12.9

TOTAL OFFENSE

		G	P	YDS	AVG	YPG
1	Cincinnati	10	577	4095	7.1	409.5
2	Notre Dame	10	753	3839	5.1	383.9
3	West Virginia	9	593	3398	5.7	377.6
4	Texas Tech	11	694	4141	6.0	376.5
5	Utah	10	722	3751	5.2	375.1
6	Maryland	10	593	3595	6.1	359.5
7	Rice	10	682	3586	5.3	358.6
8	Illinois	9	575	3205	5.6	356.1
9	Oklahoma	10	652	3521	5.4	352.1
10	Army	9	622	3136	5.0	348.4

RUSHING DEFENSE

		G	ATT	YDS	AVG	YPG
1	Maryland	10	362	839	2.3	83.9
2	Syracuse	9	328	920	2.8	102.2
3	Holy Cross	10	403	1069	2.7	106.9
4	West Virginia	9	351	975	2.8	108.3
5	UCLA	9	375	1021	2.7	113.4
6	Army	9	392	1031	2.6	114.6
7	Iowa	9	367	1051	2.9	116.8
8	Navy	9	412	1084	2.6	120.4
9	Notre Dame	10	394	1207	3.1	120.7
10	Texas-El Paso	9	384	1107	2.9	123.0

PASSING DEFENSE

		G	ATT	COM	PCT	YPC	INT	I%	YDS	YPA	TD	YPG
1	Richmond	9	104	34	32.7	10.7	14	13.5	363	3.5	0	40.3
2	Cincinnati	10	135	43	31.9	9.7	13	9.6	417	3.1	2	41.7
3	Marquette	10	115	41	35.7	10.9	13	11.3	448	3.9	2	44.8
4	Tennessee	11	148	59	39.9	10.1	16	10.8	594	4.0	2	54.0
5	Brown	9	112	43	38.4	11.9	11	9.8	512	4.6	4	56.9
6	Oregon	10	104	41	39.4	14.1	8	7.7	578	5.6	2	57.8
7	Kansas State	10	111	52	46.8	11.5	14	12.6	597	5.4	2	59.7
8	Kansas	10	105	44	41.9	13.9	14	13.3	610	5.8	3	61.0
9	Arizona State	10	138	52	37.7	11.8	8	5.8	613	4.4	5	61.3
10	Mississippi State	10	119	50	42.0	12.8	8	6.7	639	5.4	2	63.9

TOTAL DEFENSE

		G	P	YDS	AVG	YPG
1	Cincinnati	10	527	1843	3.5	184.3
2	UCLA	9	520	1696	3.3	188.4
3	Maryland	10	577	1932	3.3	193.2
4	Yale	9	494	1754	3.6	194.9
5	Syracuse	9	489	1769	3.6	196.6
6	Oklahoma	10	583	1969	3.4	196.9
7	Texas-El Paso	9	515	1787	3.5	198.6
8	Wichita State	9	490	1789	3.7	198.8
9	Detroit	10	586	1996	3.4	199.6
10	West Virginia	9	516	1835	3.6	203.9

SCORING OFFENSE

		G	PTS	AVG
1	Texas Tech	11	428	38.9

SCORING DEFENSE

		G	PTS	AVG
1	Maryland	10	31	3.1

1953

FINAL POLL (NOV. 30)

UP	AP	SCHOOL	FINAL RECORD
1	1	Maryland	10-1-0
2	2	Notre Dame	9-0-1
3	3	Michigan State	9-1-0
5	4	Oklahoma	9-1-1
4	5	UCLA	8-2-0
6	6	Rice	9-2-0
7	7	Illinois	7-1-1
9	8	**Georgia Tech**	**9-2-1**
10	9	Iowa	5-3-1
13	10	West Virginia	8-2-0
8	11	Texas	7-3-0
12	12	Texas Tech	11-1-0
11	13	**Alabama**	**6-3-3**
16	14	Army	7-1-1
14	15	Wisconsin	6-2-1
15	16	Kentucky	7-2-1
	17	**Auburn**	**7-3-1**
18	18	Duke	7-2-1
17	19	Stanford	6-3-1
19	20	Michigan	6-3-0
20		Ohio State	6-3-0

CONSENSUS ALL-AMERICANS

POS	NAME	SCHOOL
B	Johnny Lattner	Notre Dame
B	Paul Giel	Minnesota
B	Paul Cameron	UCLA
B	J.C. Caroline	Illinois
E	Don Dohoney	Michigan St.
E	Carlton Massey	Texas
T	Stan Jones	Maryland
T	Art Hunter	Notre Dame
G	J.D. Roberts	Oklahoma
G	**Crawford Mims**	**Mississippi**
C	**Larry Morris**	**Georgia Tech**

OTHERS RECEIVING FIRST-TEAM HONORS

B	Alan Ameche	Wisconsin
B	Bob Garrett	Stanford
B	Kosse Johnson	Rice
B	**Jackie Parker**	**Mississippi St.**
B	Bernie Faloney	Maryland
E	Ken Buck	Pacific
E	**John Carson**	**Georgia**
E	**Steve Meilinger**	**Kentucky**
E	Sam Morley	Stanford
E	Joe Collier	Northwestern
T	Ed Meadows	Duke
T	Jack Shanafelt	Pennsylvania
T	Jim Ray Smith	Baylor
T	John Hudson	Rice
G	Milt Bohart	Washington
G	**Ray Correll**	**Kentucky**
G	Bob Fleck	Syracuse
G	Steve Eisenhauer	Navy
C	Matt Hazeltine	California
C	Jerry Hilgenberg	Iowa
C	Bob Orders	West Virginia

HEISMAN TROPHY VOTING

	PLAYER	POS	SCHOOL	TOTAL
1	Johnny Lattner	HB	Notre Dame	1850
2	Paul Giel	TB	Minnesota	1794
3	Paul Cameron	HB	UCLA	444
4	Bernie Faloney	QB	Maryland	258
5	Bob Garrett	QB	Stanford	231
6	Alan Ameche	FB	Wisconsin	211
7	J.C. Caroline	HB	Illinois	193
8	J.D. Roberts	G	Oklahoma	108
9	Lamar McHan	QB	Arkansas	78
10	**Steve Meilinger**	**E**	**Kentucky**	**65**

AWARD WINNERS

PLAYER	POS	SCHOOL	AWARD NAME
Johnny Lattner, HB, Notre Dame			Maxwell
J.D. Roberts, G, Oklahoma			Outland

BOWL GAMES

DATE	GAME	SCORE
J1	Tangerine	Arkansas State 7, Texas A&M-Commerce 7
J1	Rose	Michigan State 28, UCLA 20
J1	**Sugar**	**Georgia Tech 42, West Virginia 19**
J1	Orange	Oklahoma 7, Maryland 0
J1	**Cotton**	**Rice 28, Alabama 6**
J1	**Gator**	**Texas Tech 35, Auburn 13**
J1	Sun	Texas-El Paso 37, Southern Miss 14

SEC STANDINGS

	CONFERENCE			OVERALL		
	W	L	T	W	L	T
Alabama	4	0	3	6	3	3
Georgia Tech	4	1	1	9	2	1
Kentucky	4	1	1	7	2	1
Mississippi	4	1	1	7	2	1
Auburn	4	2	1	7	3	1
Mississippi State	3	1	3	5	2	3
Tennessee	3	2	1	6	4	1
LSU	2	3	3	5	3	3
Florida	1	3	2	3	5	2
Vanderbilt	1	5	0	3	7	0
Georgia	1	5	0	3	8	0
Tulane	0	7	0	1	8	1

1954 NCAA MAJOR COLLEGE STATISTICAL LEADERS

INDIVIDUAL LEADERS

PASSING/COMPLETIONS	G	ATT	COM	PCT	INT	I%	YDS	YPA	TD	TD%	COM.PG
1 Paul Larson, California	10	195	125	64.1	8	4.1	1537	7.9	10	5.1	12.5
2 George Shaw, Oregon	10	196	91	46.4	11	5.6	1358	6.9	10	5.1	9.1
3 Len Dawson, Purdue	9	167	87	52.1	8	4.8	1464	8.8	15	9.0	9.7
4 John Brodie, Stanford	10	163	81	49.7	16	9.8	937	5.7	2	1.2	8.1
5 Ken Ford, Hardin-Simmons	10	146	78	53.4	9	6.2	948	6.5	7	4.8	7.8
6 Bill Beagle, Dartmouth	9	145	76	52.4	10	6.9	867	6.0	5	3.5	8.4
7 Dave Dungan, Utah	11	128	74	57.8	4	3.1	862	6.7	5	3.9	6.7
8 John Stephans, Holy Cross	10	149	73	49.0	11	7.4	800	5.4	8	5.4	7.3
9 Mackie Prickett, South Carolina	10	116	68	58.6	9	7.8	682	5.9	1	0.9	6.8
9 Ralph Guglielmi, Notre Dame	10	127	68	53.4	7	5.5	1162	9.1	6	4.7	6.8

ALL-PURPOSE YARDS	G	RUSH	REC	INT	PR	KR	YDS	YPG
1 Art Luppino, Arizona	10	1359	50	84	68	632	2193	219.3

RUSHING/YARDS	G	ATT	YDS	AVG	YPG
1 Art Luppino, Arizona	10	179	1359	7.6	135.9
2 Lenny Moore, Penn State	9	136	1082	8.0	120.2
3 Tommy Bell, Army	9	96	1020	10.6	113.3
4 Sam Pino, Boston U.	9	154	933	6.1	103.7
5 Dicky Maegle, Rice	10	144	905	6.3	90.5
6 Dick Imer, Montana	9	111	889	8.0	98.8
7 Joe Childress, Auburn	10	148	836	5.7	83.6
8 John Bayuk, Colorado	10	145	824	5.7	82.4
9 Fred Mahaffey, Denver	10	143	813	5.7	81.3
10 Tom Tracy, Tennessee	10	116	794	6.8	79.4

RUSHING/YARDS PER CARRY	G	ATT	YDS	YPC
1 Tommy Bell, Army	9	96	1020	10.6
2 Dick Imer, Montana	9	111	889	8.0
3 Lenny Moore, Penn State	9	136	1082	8.0
4 Art Luppino, Arizona	10	179	1359	7.6
5 Tom Tracy, Tennessee	10	116	794	6.8
6 Dicky Maegle, Rice	10	144	905	6.3
7 Sam Pino, Boston U.	9	154	933	6.1
8 Fred Mahaffey, Denver	10	143	813	5.7
9 John Bayuk, Colorado	10	145	824	5.7
10 Joe Childress, Auburn	10	148	836	5.7

Based on top 10 rushers

RECEIVING/RECEPTIONS	G	REC	YDS	TD	YPR	YPG	RPG
1 Jim Hanifan, California	10	44	569	7	12.9	56.9	4.4
2 John Stewart, Stanford	10	36	577	2	16.0	57.7	3.6
3 Jim Carmichael, California	10	33	420	2	12.7	42.0	3.3
4 Carl Brazell, South Carolina	10	29	241	1	8.3	24.1	2.9
5 Jerry Mertens, Drake	9	28	495	4	17.7	55.0	3.1
5 Jim Pyburn, Auburn	10	28	460	4	16.4	46.0	2.8
7 Andrew Nacrelli, Fordham	9	25	493	2	19.7	54.8	2.8
7 Max Pierce, Utah	11	25	457	3	18.3	41.5	2.3
7 Larry Ross, Denver	10	25	378	4	15.1	37.8	2.5
7 Robert Dee, Holy Cross	10	25	236	2	9.4	23.6	2.5

PUNTING	PUNT	YDS	AVG
1 A.L. Terpening, New Mexico	41	1869	45.6
2 Ted Rohde, Kansas	29	1270	43.8
3 Bobby Brengle, Tennessee	30	1275	42.5
4 Ray Taylor, TCU	44	1844	41.9
5 Carroll Hardy, Colorado	26	1082	41.6
6 Walt Hynoski, Pennsylvania	47	1941	41.3
7 James Withrow, Oregon State	30	1215	40.5
8 Bobby Collins, Mississippi State	33	1330	40.3
8 John Caruso, Tulane	33	1330	40.3
10 Bob Heydenfeldt, UCLA	26	1037	39.9

PUNT RETURNS/YARDS	PR	YDS	AVG
1 Dicky Maegle, Rice	15	293	19.5
2 Jack Yohe, William & Mary	13	277	21.3
3 Earl Smith, Iowa	15	267	17.8
4 Sam Brown, UCLA	10	262	26.2
5 Bob McNamara, Minnesota	14	252	18.0
6 Lee Riley, Detroit	13	240	18.5
7 Fred Tesone, Denver	13	230	17.7
8 Gordon Malloy, Miami (Fla.)	9	223	24.8
9 Ron Waller, Maryland	13	199	15.3
10 Ron Younker, Penn State	12	193	16.1

KICKOFF RETURNS/YARDS	KR	YDS	AVG
1 Art Luppino, Arizona	20	632	31.6
2 George Marinkov, North Carolina St.	13	465	35.8
3 Lon Turner, Dartmouth	17	407	23.9
4 Jackie Simpson, Florida	13	324	24.9
5 Dick Mackey, Arizona State	17	323	19.0
6 Gene Hendrix, Drake	17	317	18.6
7 Ron Drzewiecki, Marquette	12	315	26.3
8 Frank Eidom, SMU	13	292	22.5
9 Paul Larson, California	10	285	28.5
9 Dick Imer, Montana	11	285	25.9

SCORING	TDS	XPT	FG	PTS
1 Art Luppino, Arizona	24	22	0	166
2 Buddy Leake, Oklahoma	9	25	0	79
3 Tommy Bell, Army	13	0	0	78
3 Lenny Moore, Penn State	13	0	0	78
5 Fred Mahaffey, Denver	12	1	0	73
6 Dicky Maegle, Rice	12	0	0	72
7 Rusty Fairly, Denver	9	16	0	70
8 Carroll Hardy, Colorado	9	14	0	68
9 Six tied				66

INTERCEPTIONS	INT	YDS
1 Gary Glick, Colorado State	8	168
2 Rusty Fairly, Denver	7	62
2 Jerry Barger, Duke	7	50
2 Whitey Rouviere, Miami (Fla.)	7	18
2 Dick Jackson, Cornell	7	NA
2 James Miller, Wisconsin	6	117
6 Pat Oleksiak, Tennessee	6	99
6 Lenny Moore, Penn State	6	96
6 George Walker, Arkansas	6	90
6 Dick Mackey, Arizona State	6	83
6 Mackie Prickett, South Carolina	6	63

TEAM LEADERS

RUSHING OFFENSE	G	ATT	YDS	AVG	YPG
1 Army	9	468	2898	6.2	322.0
2 Texas Tech	10	562	3164	5.6	316.4
3 Colorado	10	492	3160	6.4	316.0
4 Oklahoma	10	591	2962	5.0	296.2
5 UCLA	9	454	2578	5.7	286.4
6 Miami (Fla.)	9	497	2558	5.1	284.2
7 Arizona	10	502	2765	5.5	276.5
8 Penn State	9	421	2415	5.7	268.3
9 Navy	10	507	2677	5.3	267.2
10 Nebraska	10	467	2657	5.7	265.7

PASSING OFFENSE/YPG	G	ATT	COM	INT	PCT	YDS	YPA	TD	YPG	I%	YPC
1 Purdue	9	195	99	11	50.8	1596	8.2	15	177.3	5.6	16.1
2 California	10	228	139	13	61.0	1724	7.6	11	172.4	5.7	12.4
3 Oregon	10	229	107	13	46.7	1601	7.0	13	160.1	5.7	15.0
4 Mississippi	10	175	81	9	46.3	1554	8.9	10	155.4	5.1	19.2
5 Notre Dame	10	178	89	9	50.0	1460	8.2	11	146.0	5.1	16.4
6 Dartmouth	9	220	112	20	51.0	1301	5.9	8	144.6	9.1	11.6
7 Missouri	10	188	92	11	49.0	1399	7.4	14	139.9	5.9	15.2
8 Holy Cross	10	247	118	20	47.8	1391	5.6	15	139.1	8.1	11.8
9 Washington	10	237	109	16	46.0	1360	5.7	6	136.0	6.8	12.5
10 Hardin-Simmons	10	228	111	17	48.7	1352	5.9	11	135.2	7.5	12.2

TOTAL OFFENSE	G	P	YDS	AVG	YPG
1 Army	9	575	4038	7.0	448.7
2 Texas Tech	10	677	4223	6.2	422.3
3 Arizona	10	643	4020	6.3	402.0
4 Navy	9	620	3544	5.7	393.8
5 Mississippi	10	663	3868	5.8	386.8
6 Notre Dame	10	729	3853	5.3	385.3
7 Oklahoma	10	679	3827	5.6	382.7
8 Denver	10	637	3718	5.8	371.8
9 Boston U.	9	557	3304	5.9	367.1
10 UCLA	9	561	3299	5.9	366.6

RUSHING DEFENSE	G	ATT	YDS	AVG	YPG
1 UCLA	9	314	659	2.1	73.2
2 Oklahoma	10	378	870	2.3	87.0
3 Mississippi	10	375	901	2.4	90.1
4 Clemson	10	388	969	2.5	96.9
5 Navy	9	353	923	2.6	102.6
6 Notre Dame	10	354	1094	3.1	109.4
7 West Virginia	9	361	990	2.7	110.0
8 Wisconsin	9	359	1045	2.9	116.1
9 Wichita State	10	393	1170	3.0	117.0
10 Cincinnati	10	368	1184	3.2	118.4

PASSING DEFENSE	G	ATT	COM	PCT	YPC	INT	I%	YDS	YPA	TD	YPG
1 Alabama	11	122	43	35.2	11.7	10	8.2	504	4.1	0	45.8
2 Richmond	9	97	33	34.0	12.8	12	12.4	424	4.4	1	47.1
3 Detroit	9	98	39	39.8	11.1	11	11.2	432	4.4	2	48.0
4 Kansas State	10	111	45	40.5	11.4	6	5.4	515	4.6	6	51.5
5 Arkansas	10	122	48	39.3	11.2	17	13.9	538	4.4	1	53.8
6 Boston College	9	130	42	32.3	12.5	11	8.5	524	4.0	3	58.2
7 Georgia Tech	10	118	51	43.2	11.5	15	12.7	587	5.0	3	58.7
8 Auburn	10	105	44	41.9	13.7	12	11.4	601	5.7	5	60.1
9 Florida	10	104	47	45.2	13.2	7	6.7	619	6.0	0	61.9
9 Texas A&M	10	98	45	45.9	13.8	8	8.2	619	6.3	11	61.9

TOTAL DEFENSE	G	P	YDS	AVG	YPG
1 Mississippi	10	537	1723	3.2	172.3
2 Richmond	9	505	1570	3.1	174.4
3 Clemson	10	528	1761	3.3	176.1
4 Boston College	9	511	1661	3.3	184.6
5 Oklahoma	10	561	1863	3.3	186.3
6 West Virginia	9	521	1680	3.2	186.7
7 Denver	10	559	1886	3.4	188.6
8 UCLA	9	530	1708	3.2	189.8
9 Navy	9	495	1714	3.5	190.4
10 Cincinnati	10	521	1984	3.8	198.4

SCORING OFFENSE	G	PTS	AVG
1 UCLA	9	367	40.8

SCORING DEFENSE	G	PTS	AVG
1 UCLA	9	40	4.4

1954

FINAL POLL (NOV. 29)

UP	AP	SCHOOL	FINAL RECORD
2	1	Ohio State	10-0-0
1	2	UCLA	9-0-0
3	3	Oklahoma	10-0-0
4	4	Notre Dame	9-1-0
5	5	Navy	8-2-0
6	6	**Mississippi**	**9-2-0**
7	7	Army	7-2-0
12	8	Maryland	7-2-1
10	9	Wisconsin	7-2-0
8	10	Arkansas	8-3-0
9	11	Miami (Fla.)	8-1-0
	12	West Virginia	8-1-0
	13	**Auburn**	**8-3-0**
14	14	Duke	8-2-1
15	15	Michigan	6-3-0
	16	Virginia Tech	8-0-1
11	17	Southern California	8-4-0
	18	Baylor	7-4-0
18	19	Rice	7-3-0
15	20	Penn State	7-2-0
13		**Georgia Tech**	**8-3-0**
17		SMU	6-3-1
18		Denver	9-1-0
20		Minnesota	7-2-0

SEC STANDINGS

	CONFERENCE			OVERALL		
	W	L	T	W	L	T
Mississippi	6	0	0	9	2	0
Georgia Tech	6	2	0	8	3	0
Kentucky	5	2	0	7	3	0
Florida	5	2	0	5	5	0
Georgia	3	2	1	6	3	1
Auburn	3	3	0	8	3	0
Mississippi State	3	3	0	6	4	0
Alabama	3	3	2	4	5	2
LSU	2	5	0	5	6	0
Tulane	1	6	1	1	6	3
Tennessee	1	5	0	4	6	0
Vanderbilt	1	5	0	2	7	0

CONSENSUS ALL-AMERICANS

POS	NAME	SCHOOL
B	Ralph Guglielmi	Notre Dame
B	Howard Cassady	Ohio State
B	Alan Ameche	Wisconsin
B	Dicky Maegle	Rice
E	Max Boydston	Oklahoma
E	Ron Beagle	Navy
T	Jack Ellena	UCLA
T	**Sid Fournet**	**LSU**
G	Bud Brooks	Arkansas
G	Calvin Jones	Iowa
C	Kurt Burris	Oklahoma

OTHERS RECEIVING FIRST-TEAM HONORS

B	Tommy Bell	Army
B	Bob Davenport	UCLA
B	Paul Larson	California
B	Bob McNamara	Minnesota
E	Dean Dugger	Ohio State
E	Frank McDonald	Miami
E	Don Holleder	Army
T	**Darris McCord**	**Tennessee**
T	Art Walker	Michigan
T	**Rex Boggan**	**Mississippi**
T	Frank Varrichione	Notre Dame
G	Tom Bettis	Purdue
G	Frank Mincevich	South Carolina
G	Jim Salsbury	UCLA
G	Ralph Chesnauskas	Army
C	**Hal Easterwood**	**Mississippi St.**
C	Matt Hazeltine	California

HEISMAN TROPHY VOTING

	PLAYER	POS	SCHOOL	TOTAL
1	Alan Ameche	FB	Wisconsin	1068
2	Kurt Burris	LB	Oklahoma	838
3	Howard Cassady	HB	Ohio State	810
4	Ralph Guglielmi	QB	Notre Dame	691
5	Paul Larson	QB	California	271
6	Dicky Maegle	RB	Rice	258
7	Jack Ellena	T	UCLA	193
8	George Shaw	QB	Oregon	182
9	Pete Vann	QB	Army	134
10	Bob McNamara	FB	Minnesota	104

AWARD WINNERS

PLAYER	AWARD
Ron Beagle, E, Navy	Maxwell
Bill Brooks, G, Arkansas	Outland

BOWL GAMES

DATE	GAME	SCORE
D 31	**Gator**	**Auburn 33, Baylor 13**
J1	Tangerine	Nebraska-Omaha 7, Eastern Kentucky 6
J1	Orange	Duke 34, Nebraska 7
J1	**Cotton**	**Georgia Tech 14, Arkansas 6**
J1	**Sugar**	**Navy 21, Mississippi 0**
J1	Rose	Ohio State 20, Southern California 7
J1	Sun	Texas-El Paso 47, Florida State 20

1955 NCAA MAJOR COLLEGE STATISTICAL LEADERS

INDIVIDUAL LEADERS

PASSING/COMPLETIONS	G	ATT	COM	PCT	INT	I%	YDS	YPA	TD	TD%	COM.PG
1 George Welsh, Navy	9	150	94	62.7	6	4.0	1319	8.8	8	5.3	10.4
2 Claude Benham, Columbia	9	188	89	47.3	15	8.0	999	5.3	7	3.7	9.9
3 Len Dawson, Purdue	9	155	87	56.1	14	9.0	1005	6.5	7	4.5	9.7
4 John Brodie, Stanford	10	133	76	57.1	7	5.3	1024	7.7	5	3.8	7.6
5 Bill Beagle, Dartmouth	9	155	75	48.4	12	7.7	812	5.2	6	3.9	8.3
6 Ken Ford, Hardin-Simmons	10	135	73	54.1	10	7.4	854	6.3	8	5.9	7.3
7 James Haluska, Wisconsin	9	132	71	53.8	10	7.6	1036	7.8	6	4.6	7.9
8 Nick Consoles, Wake Forest	10	123	66	53.7	8	6.5	787	6.4	6	4.9	6.6
9 Joe Clements, Texas	10	128	65	50.8	13	10.2	818	6.4	6	4.7	6.5
10 John Roach, SMU	10	141	64	45.4	14	9.9	907	6.4	6	4.3	6.4

ALL-PURPOSE YARDS	G	RUSH	REC	INT	PR	KR	YDS	YPG
1 Jim Swink, TCU	10	1283	111	46	64	198	1702	170.2

RUSHING/Yards	G	ATT	YDS	AVG	YPG
1 Art Luppino, Arizona	10	209	1313	6.3	131.3
2 Jim Swink, TCU	10	157	1283	8.2	128.3
3 Howard Cassady, Ohio State	9	161	958	6.0	106.4
4 Fob James, Auburn	10	123	879	7.1	87.9
5 Sam Brown, UCLA	10	130	829	6.4	82.9
6 Bob Moss, West Virginia	10	98	807	8.2	80.7
7 Joel Wells, Clemson	10	135	782	5.8	78.2
8 Bob Pascal, Duke	10	156	750	4.8	75.0
9 James Bakhtiar, Virginia	10	158	733	4.6	73.3
10 Jim Shanley, Oregon	10	100	711	7.1	71.1

RUSHING/Yards Per Carry	G	ATT	YDS	YPC
1 Bob Moss, West Virginia	10	98	807	8.2
2 Jim Swink, TCU	10	157	1283	8.2
3 Fob James, Auburn	10	123	879	7.1
4 Jim Shanley, Oregon	10	100	711	7.1
5 Tommy McDonald, Oklahoma	10	103	702	6.8
6 Sam Brown, UCLA	10	130	829	6.4
7 Art Luppino, Arizona	10	209	1313	6.3
8 Credell Green, Washington	10	108	652	6.0
9 Howard Cassady, Ohio State	9	161	958	6.0
10 Joel Wells, Clemson	10	135	782	5.8

Based on top 20 rushers

RECEIVING/Receptions	G	REC	YDS	TD	YPR	YPG	RPG
1 Harold Burnine, Missouri	10	44	594	2	13.5	59.4	4.4
2 John Bredice, Boston U.	8	35	468	4	13.4	58.5	4.4
3 Bill Barnes, Wake Forest	10	31	349	0	11.3	34.9	3.1
4 Ron Beagle, Navy	9	30	451	4	15.0	50.1	3.3
5 Terry Hurley, Montana	10	25	431	2	17.2	43.1	2.5
6 Jim Orr, Georgia	10	24	443	3	18.5	44.3	2.4
6 Gary Sanders, Colorado State	10	24	351	3	14.6	35.1	2.4
6 Monte Pascoe, Dartmouth	9	24	331	3	13.8	36.8	2.7
6 Charles Massegee, Hardin-Simmons	10	24	321	4	13.4	32.1	2.4
6 George Seitz, Columbia	9	24	286	1	11.9	31.8	2.7

PUNTING	PUNT	YDS	AVG
1 Don Chandler, Florida	22	975	44.3
2 Earl Morrall, Michigan State	22	944	42.9
3 Ted Rohde, Kansas	20	846	42.3
4 William Schmitt, Pittsburgh	22	931	42.3
5 Kelvin Kleber, Minnesota	32	1347	42.1
6 Ray Westfall, Oregon State	30	1254	41.8
7 Homer Jenkins, Colorado	32	1306	40.8
8 Clarence McCluskey, Arizona	33	1340	40.6
9 Lou Mele, Utah	31	1259	40.6
10 Bobby Wolfenden, Virginia Tech	29	1157	39.9

PUNT RETURNS/Yards	PR	YDS	AVG
1 Mike Sommer, George Washington	24	330	13.8
2 Jon Arnett, Southern California	16	282	17.6
3 Jackie Simpson, Florida	17	267	15.7
4 Ron Lind, Drake	12	253	21.1
5 John Majors, Tennessee	21	234	11.1
6 Terry Barr, Michigan	15	222	14.8
7 Charles Horton, Vanderbilt	21	220	10.5
8 Dewey Tompkins, Pacific	14	210	15.0
9 Howard Cassady, Ohio State	17	205	12.1
10 Tommy McDonald, Oklahoma	10	199	19.9

KICKOFF RETURNS/Yards	KR	YDS	AVG
1 Sam Woolwine, VMI	22	471	21.4
2 Jon Arnett, Southern California	15	417	27.8
3 Ron Lind, Drake	19	392	20.6
4 Carl Brazell, South Carolina	12	378	31.5
5 Lee Hermsen, Marquette	16	372	23.3
6 Billy Odom, Florida State	13	358	27.5
7 Walter Fondren, Texas	15	341	22.7
8 Jim Brown, Syracuse	10	320	32.0
9 Rex Fischer, Nebraska	16	316	19.8
10 Howard Cassady, Ohio State	10	313	31.3

SCORING	TDS	XPT	FG	PTS
1 Jim Swink, TCU	20	5	0	125
2 Jon Arnett, Southern California	15	18	0	108
3 Tommy McDonald, Oklahoma	16	0	0	96
3 Ed Vereb, Maryland	16	0	0	96
3 Art Luppino, Arizona	13	18	0	96
6 Howard Cassady, Ohio State	15	0	0	90
7 Paige Cothren, Mississippi	6	20	6	74
8 Charles Horton, Vanderbilt	12	1	0	73
9 Sam Brown, UCLA	9	15	0	69
10 Jack Morris, Oregon	8	19	0	67

INTERCEPTIONS	INT	YDS
1 Sam Wesley, Oregon State	7	61
2 Milton Campbell, Indiana	6	111
2 Dale Boyd, Duke	6	88
2 Dick James, Oregon	6	68
5 Tony Teresa, San Jose State	5	112
5 Bill Barnes, Wake Forest	5	99
5 Lou Mele, Utah	5	95
5 Claude Benham, Columbia	5	71
5 Paul Hornung, Notre Dame	5	59
5 Jerry Curtright, Missouri	5	47

TEAM LEADERS

RUSHING OFFENSE	G	ATT	YDS	AVG	YPG
1 Oklahoma	10	661	3289	5.0	328.9
2 TCU	10	555	2857	5.1	285.7
3 Army	9	461	2555	5.5	283.9
4 Ohio State	9	508	2504	4.9	278.2
5 Notre Dame	10	601	2727	4.5	272.7
6 West Virginia	10	489	2639	5.4	263.9
7 Oregon	10	513	2527	4.9	252.7
8 Wichita State	10	505	2484	4.9	248.4
9 Miami (Fla.)	9	467	2201	4.7	244.6
10 Auburn	10	468	2413	5.2	241.3

PASSING OFFENSE/YPG	G	ATT	COM	INT	PCT	YDS	YPA	TD	YPG	I%	YPC
1 Navy	9	195	116	8	59.5	1666	8.5	13	185.1	4.1	14.4
2 Stanford	10	244	130	15	53.3	1605	6.6	11	160.5	6.1	12.3
3 Hardin-Simmons	10	244	132	15	54.1	1517	6.2	15	151.7	6.1	11.5
4 Denver	10	160	80	11	50.0	1465	9.2	19	146.5	6.9	18.3
5 Wisconsin	9	171	84	13	49.1	1309	7.7	11	145.4	7.6	15.6
6 Drake	8	135	68	9	50.4	1093	8.1	11	136.6	6.7	16.1
7 Purdue	9	191	104	18	54.5	1213	6.4	8	134.8	9.4	11.7
8 Texas	10	209	96	20	45.9	1291	6.2	11	129.1	9.6	13.4
8 Wake Forest	10	180	92	15	51.1	1291	7.2	9	129.1	8.3	14.0
10 Michigan State	9	98	52	9	53.1	1124	11.5	7	124.9	9.2	21.6

TOTAL OFFENSE	G	P	YDS	AVG	YPG
1 Oklahoma	10	756	4107	5.4	410.7
2 West Virginia	10	642	3845	6.0	384.5
3 Denver	10	606	3689	6.1	368.9
4 Michigan State	9	521	3280	6.3	364.4
5 Navy	9	625	3227	5.2	358.6
6 Notre Dame	10	722	3573	4.9	357.3
7 Stanford	10	737	3551	4.8	355.1
8 TCU	10	637	3531	5.5	353.1
9 Miami (Fla.)	9	562	3104	5.5	344.9
10 Mississippi	10	609	3396	5.6	339.6

RUSHING DEFENSE	G	ATT	YDS	AVG	YPG
1 Maryland	10	342	759	2.2	75.9
2 Army	9	340	732	2.2	81.3
3 Holy Cross	10	374	951	2.5	95.1
4 Auburn	10	405	1078	2.7	107.8
5 Wichita State	10	428	1131	2.6	113.1
6 Oklahoma	10	426	1136	2.7	113.6
7 Boston College	8	268	940	3.5	117.5
8 West Virginia	10	406	1267	3.1	126.7
9 Colgate	9	358	1154	3.2	128.2
10 Vanderbilt	10	466	1298	2.8	129.8

PASSING DEFENSE	G	ATT	COM	PCT	YPC	INT	I%	YDS	YPA	TD	YPG
1 Florida	10	92	37	40.2	11.4	3	3.3	420	4.6	2	42.0
2 Navy	9	101	36	35.6	10.8	8	7.9	387	3.8	0	43.0
3 Michigan	9	86	28	32.6	14.4	10	11.6	402	4.7	4	44.7
4 Nebraska	10	103	28	27.2	16.0	10	9.7	449	4.4	3	44.9
5 George Washington	9	107	36	33.6	11.6	18	16.8	417	3.9	2	46.3
6 Kentucky	10	96	36	37.5	13.3	13	13.5	479	5.0	6	47.9
7 Detroit	9	93	34	36.6	13.9	5	5.4	474	5.1	3	52.7
8 Harvard	8	89	37	41.6	12.4	6	6.7	460	5.2	4	57.5
9 Indiana	9	93	37	39.8	14.4	13	14.0	533	5.7	6	59.2
10 Washington	10	119	55	46.2	10.9	14	11.8	600	5.0	3	60.0

TOTAL DEFENSE	G	P	YDS	AVG	YPG
1 Army	9	499	1446	2.9	160.7
2 Maryland	10	537	1691	3.1	169.1
3 Navy	9	481	1635	3.4	181.7
4 Auburn	10	531	1832	3.5	183.2
5 Holy Cross	10	539	1835	3.4	183.5
6 Oklahoma	10	578	1864	3.2	186.4
7 Detroit	9	484	1747	3.6	194.1
8 West Virginia	10	560	1948	3.5	194.8
9 George Washington	9	527	1779	3.4	197.7
10 Georgia Tech	10	516	1999	3.9	199.9

SCORING OFFENSE	G	PTS	AVG
1 Oklahoma	10	365	36.5

SCORING DEFENSE	G	PTS	AVG
1 Georgia Tech	10	46	4.6
2 Oklahoma	10	54	5.4

1955

FINAL POLL (NOV. 28)

UP	AP	SCHOOL	FINAL RECORD
1	1	Oklahoma	11-0-0
2	2	Michigan State	9-1-0
3	3	Maryland	10-1-0
4	4	UCLA	9-2-0
6	5	Ohio State	7-2-0
5	6	TCU	9-2-0
7	7	Georgia Tech	9-1-1
10	8	Auburn	8-2-1
8	9	Notre Dame	8-2-0
9	10	Mississippi	10-1-0
11	11	Pittsburgh	7-4-0
13	12	Michigan	7-2-0
12	13	Southern California	6-4-0
18	14	Miami (Fla.)	6-3-0
20	15	Miami (Ohio)	9-0-0
20	16	Stanford	6-3-1
14	17	Texas A&M	7-2-0
20	18	Navy	6-2-1
17	19	West Virginia	8-2-0
15	20	Army	6-3-0
15		Duke	7-2-1
19		Iowa	3-5-1

CONSENSUS ALL-AMERICANS

POS	NAME	SCHOOL
B	Howard Cassady	Ohio State
B	Jim Swink	TCU
B	Earl Morrall	Michigan St.
B	Paul Hornung	Notre Dame
E	Ron Beagle	Navy
E	Ron Kramer	Michigan
T	Norman Masters	Michigan St.
T	Bruce Bosley	West Virginia
G	Bo Bolinger	Oklahoma
G	Calvin Jones	Iowa
G	Hardiman Cureton	UCLA
C	Bob Pellegrini	Maryland

OTHERS RECEIVING FIRST-TEAM HONORS

POS	NAME	SCHOOL
B	Jon Arnett	Southern California
B	**Joe Childress**	**Auburn**
B	**Art Davis**	**Mississippi State**
B	Don Schaefer	Notre Dame
B	Tommy McDonald	Oklahoma
B	Bob Davenport	UCLA
E	Harold Burnine	Missouri
E	Rommie Loudd	UCLA
E	**Howard Schnellenberger**	**Kentucky**
T	Herb Gray	Texas
T	Sam Huff	West Virginia
T	**Frank D'Agostino**	**Auburn**
T	Paul Wiggin	Stanford
T	John Witte	Oregon State
T	Mike Sandusky	Maryland
G	Jim Parker	Ohio State
G	**Tony Sardisco**	**Tulane**
G	James D. Brown	UCLA
G	Pat Bisceglia	Notre Dame
G	**Scott Suber**	**Mississippi State**
C	Hugh Pitts	TCU

HEISMAN TROPHY VOTING

	PLAYER	POS	SCHOOL	TOTAL
1	Howard Cassady	HB	Ohio State	2219
2	Jim Swink	RB	TCU	742
3	George Welsh	QB	Navy	383
4	Earl Morrall	QB	Michigan State	323
5	Paul Hornung	QB	Notre Dame	321
6	Bob Pellegrini	C	Maryland	294
7	Ron Beagle	E	Navy	212
8	Ron Kramer	E	Michigan	192
9	Bo Bolinger	G	Oklahoma	148
10	Calvin Jones	G	Iowa	138

AWARD WINNERS

PLAYER	AWARD
Howard Cassady, HB, Ohio State	Maxwell
Calvin Jones, G, Iowa	Outland

BOWL GAMES

DATE	GAME	SCORE
D31	**Gator**	**Vanderbilt 25, Auburn 13**
J2	Tangerine	Juniata 6, Missouri Valley 6
J2	Rose	Michigan State 17, UCLA 14
J2	**Cotton**	**Mississippi 14, TCU 13**
J2	**Sugar**	**Georgia Tech 7, Pittsburgh 0**
J2	Orange	Oklahoma 20, Maryland 6
J2	Sun	Wyoming 21, Texas Tech 14

SEC STANDINGS

	CONFERENCE			OVERALL		
	W	L	T	W	L	T
Mississippi	5	1	0	10	1	0
Auburn	5	1	1	8	2	1
Georgia Tech	4	1	1	9	1	1
Tennessee	3	2	1	6	3	1
Vanderbilt	4	3	0	8	3	0
Mississippi State	4	4	0	6	4	0
Kentucky	3	3	1	6	3	1
Tulane	3	3	1	5	4	1
LSU	2	3	1	3	5	2
Florida	3	5	0	4	6	0
Georgia	2	5	0	4	6	0
Alabama	0	7	0	0	10	0

1956 NCAA MAJOR COLLEGE STATISTICAL LEADERS

INDIVIDUAL LEADERS

PASSING/COMPLETIONS	G	ATT	COM	PCT	INT	I%	YDS	YPA	TD	TD%	COM.PG
1 John Brodie, Stanford	10	240	139	57.9	14	5.8	1633	6.8	12	5.0	13.9
2 Bob Newman, Washington State	10	170	91	53.5	8	4.7	1240	7.3	8	4.7	9.1
3 Bob Reinhart, San Jose State	10	172	90	52.3	5	2.9	1138	6.6	10	5.8	9.0
4 Guy Martin, Colgate	9	170	88	51.8	15	8.8	1100	6.5	9	5.3	9.8
5 Gene Saur, Hardin-Simmons	10	133	78	58.6	10	7.5	968	7.3	8	6.0	7.8
6 Ralph Hunsaker, Arizona	10	148	75	50.7	12	8.1	823	5.6	4	2.7	7.5
7 Joe Clements, Texas	10	151	74	49.0	16	10.6	793	5.3	7	4.6	7.4
8 Tom Flores, Pacific	10	127	73	57.5	8	6.3	1119	8.8	11	8.7	7.3
9 Charlie Arnold, SMU	10	157	71	45.2	14	8.9	964	6.1	8	5.1	7.1
9 Carroll Johnston, Brigham Young	10	167	71	42.5	15	9.0	945	5.7	8	4.8	7.1

ALL-PURPOSE YARDS	G	RUSH	REC	INT	PR	KR	YDS	YPG
1 Jack Hill, Utah State	10	920	215	132	21	403	1691	169.1

RUSHING/YARDS	G	ATT	YDS	AVG	YPG
1 Jim Crawford, Wyoming	10	200	1104	5.5	110.4
2 Bill Barnes, Wake Forest	10	168	1010	6.0	101.0
3 Jim Brown, Syracuse	8	158	986	6.2	123.3
4 Jack Hill, Utah State	10	140	920	6.6	92.0
5 Jim Bakhtiar, Virginia	10	203	879	4.3	87.9
6 Mel Dillard, Purdue	9	193	873	4.5	97.0
7 Tommy McDonald, Oklahoma	10	119	853	7.2	85.3
8 Clendon Thomas, Oklahoma	10	104	817	7.9	81.7
9 Don Clark, Ohio State	9	139	797	5.7	88.6
10 C.R. Roberts, Southern California	10	120	775	6.5	77.5

RUSHING/YARDS PER CARRY	G	ATT	YDS	YPC
1 **Tommy Lorino, Auburn**	**10**	**82**	**692**	**8.4**
2 Clendon Thomas, Oklahoma	10	104	817	7.9
3 Tommy McDonald, Oklahoma	10	119	853	7.2
4 Bob Mulgado, Arizona State	10	107	721	6.7
5 Jack Hill, Utah State	10	140	920	6.6
6 C.R. Roberts, Southern California	10	120	775	6.5
7 Jim Brown, Syracuse	8	158	986	6.2
8 Ed Sutton, North Carolina	10	120	748	6.2
9 Bill Barnes, Wake Forest	10	168	1010	6.0
10 Don Clark, Ohio State	9	139	797	5.7

Based on top 20 rushers

RECEIVING/RECEPTIONS	G	REC	YDS	TD	YPR	YPG	RPG
1 Art Powell, San Jose State	10	40	583	5	14.6	58.3	4.0
2 Bill Steiger, Washington State	10	39	607	5	15.6	60.7	3.9
3 Connie Baird, Hardin-Simmons	10	37	455	1	12.3	45.5	3.7
4 Brad Bomba, Indiana	9	31	407	1	13.1	45.2	3.4
5 Larry Aldrich, Idaho	9	30	409	1	13.6	45.4	3.3
5 Charles James, Missouri	10	30	362	3	12.1	36.2	3.0
7 Al Jamison, Colgate	9	29	289	6	10.0	32.1	3.2
8 Paul Camera, Stanford	10	28	350	2	12.5	35.0	2.8
9 Farrell Funston, Pacific	10	27	563	5	20.9	56.3	2.7
9 Don Ellingsen, Washington State	10	27	455	1	16.9	45.5	2.7
9 Johnny Wilson, Denver	10	27	383	4	14.2	38.3	2.7

PUNTING	PUNT	YDS	AVG
1 Kirk Wilson, UCLA	30	1479	49.3
2 Larry Barnes, Colorado State	27	1212	44.9
3 **John Barnes, Tennessee**	**26**	**1118**	**43.0**
4 Boyd Dowler, Colorado	41	1726	42.1
5 Jim Wood, Oklahoma State	34	1421	41.8
6 Ted Rohde, Kansas	26	1082	41.6
7 Ernie Zampese, Southern California	27	1112	41.2
8 Jack Hill, Utah State	29	1195	41.2
9 Wally Vale, North Carolina	31	1274	41.1
10 Jerry Lott, New Mexico	33	1346	40.8

PUNT RETURNS/YARDS	PR	YDS	AVG
1 **Billy Stacy, Mississippi State**	**24**	**290**	**12.1**
2 Ron Lind, Drake	14	268	19.1
3 **Phil King, Vanderbilt**	**20**	**247**	**12.4**
4 Charlie Sidwell, William & Mary	8	205	25.6
5 Leroy Phelps, Oregon	12	204	17.0
6 Joe Morrison, Cincinnati	6	198	33.0
7 Luther Carr, Washington	12	179	14.9
7 Victor Rabbits, West Virginia	12	177	14.8
9 **Jefferson Davis, Georgia**	**6**	**176**	**29.3**
9 Jim Shanley, Oregon	10	176	17.6

KICKOFF RETURNS/YARDS	KR	YDS	AVG
1 Sam Woolwine, VMI	18	503	27.9
2 Paul Hornung, Notre Dame	16	496	31.0
3 Charlie Sidwell, William & Mary	20	467	23.4
4 Jack Hill, Utah State	14	403	28.8
5 Lynn White, New Mexico	14	368	26.3
6 Weldon Jackson, Brigham Young	15	358	23.9
7 Art Powell, San Jose State	15	352	23.5
8 Robert Fee, Indiana	15	326	21.7
8 Ron Lind, Drake	15	326	21.7
10 Walter Fondren, Texas	17	325	19.1

SCORING	TDS	XPT	FG	PTS
1 Clendon Thomas, Oklahoma	18	0	0	108
2 Jim Brown, Syracuse	14	22	0	106
3 Jack Hill, Utah State	15	15	0	105
4 Tommy McDonald, Oklahoma	17	0	0	102
5 Jim Crawford, Wyoming	14	12	0	96
6 Bob Kyasky, Army	14	1	0	85
7 John Bayuk, Colorado	11	0	0	66
7 John Call, Colgate	11	0	0	66
9 Dean Derby, Washington	7	18	1	63
10 Hewes Agnew, Princeton	10	1	0	61

INTERCEPTIONS	INT	YDS
1 Jack Hill, Utah State	7	132
1 Milt Plum, Penn State	7	72
3 John Bookman, Miami (Fla.)	6	137
3 Tommy McDonald, Oklahoma	6	136
3 Ernie Zampese, Southern California	6	98
3 James Ridlon, Syracuse	6	70
7 **Joe Brodsky, Florida**	**5**	**244**
7 Darrell Roberts, California	5	81
7 Ronnie Morris, Tulsa	5	0

TEAM LEADERS

RUSHING OFFENSE	G	ATT	YDS	AVG	YPG
1 Oklahoma	10	675	3910	5.8	391.0
2 Virginia Tech	10	621	2835	4.6	283.5
3 **Auburn**	**10**	**515**	**2760**	**5.4**	**276.0**
3 Army	9	481	2484	5.2	276.0
5 Ohio State	9	524	2468	4.7	274.2
6 Southern California	10	560	2695	4.8	269.5
7 Washington	10	583	2688	4.6	268.8
8 Yale	9	463	2385	5.2	265.0
9 Texas A&M	10	564	2638	4.7	263.8
10 Michigan State	9	486	2312	4.8	256.9

PASSING OFFENSE	G	ATT	COM	INT	PCT	YDS	YPA	TD	I%	YPC	YPG
1 Washington State	10	281	150	15	53.4	2068	7.4	13	5.3	13.8	206.8
2 Stanford	10	305	170	18	55.7	2044	6.7	16	5.9	12.0	204.4
3 Pacific	10	231	124	11	53.7	1889	8.2	13	4.8	15.2	188.9
4 San Jose State	10	294	147	15	50.0	1881	6.4	15	5.1	12.8	188.1
5 Hardin-Simmons	10	249	131	23	52.6	1569	6.3	9	9.2	12.0	156.9
6 Rice	10	194	107	15	55.2	1373	7.1	7	7.7	12.8	137.3
7 Navy	9	172	89	13	51.7	1197	7.0	10	7.6	13.4	133.0
7 Texas	10	228	108	22	47.4	1303	5.7	9	9.6	12.1	130.3
9 Colgate	9	184	92	16	50.0	1161	6.3	11	8.7	12.6	129.0
10 Brigham Young	10	264	105	23	39.8	1286	4.9	12	8.7	12.2	128.6

TOTAL OFFENSE	G	P	YDS	AVG	YPG
1 Oklahoma	10	775	4817	6.2	481.7
2 Hardin-Simmons	10	786	3912	5.0	391.2
3 **Auburn**	**10**	**670**	**3749**	**5.6**	**374.9**
4 Pacific	10	684	3645	5.3	364.5
5 Arizona State	10	625	3609	5.8	360.9
6 Michigan State	9	585	3231	5.5	359.0
7 TCU	10	718	3563	5.0	356.3
8 Virginia Tech	10	726	3559	4.9	355.9
9 Yale	9	574	3199	5.6	355.4
10 Denver	10	676	3505	5.2	350.5

RUSHING DEFENSE	G	ATT	YDS	AVG	YPG
1 Miami (Fla.)	10	425	1069	2.5	106.9
2 Navy	9	400	1018	2.5	113.1
3 Holy Cross	9	372	1110	3.0	123.3
4 **Georgia Tech**	**10**	**405**	**1284**	**3.2**	**128.4**
5 Boston College	9	402	1171	2.9	130.1
6 Texas A&M	10	437	1302	3.0	130.2
7 West Virginia	10	467	1369	2.9	136.9
8 Oklahoma	10	487	1383	2.8	138.3
9 Iowa	9	430	1285	3.0	142.8
10 **Mississippi**	**10**	**454**	**1449**	**3.2**	**144.9**

PASSING DEFENSE	G	ATT	COM	PCT	YPC	INT	I%	YDS	YPA	TD	YPG
1 Villanova	9	113	35	31.0	11.3	10	8.9	394	3.5	4	43.8
2 Dartmouth	9	108	38	35.2	10.7	15	13.9	408	3.8	4	45.3
3 South Carolina	10	107	43	40.2	11.1	7	6.5	476	4.4	3	47.6
4 Penn State	9	121	30	24.8	14.5	18	14.9	436	3.6	2	48.2
5 TCU	10	114	34	29.8	14.6	19	16.7	497	4.4	4	49.7
5 Wake Forest	10	143	47	32.9	10.6	13	9.1	497	3.5	1	49.7
7 **Mississippi**	**10**	**118**	**48**	**40.7**	**10.5**	**21**	**17.8**	**506**	**4.3**	**1**	**50.6**
8 Clemson	10	128	50	39.1	10.5	12	9.4	526	4.1	0	52.6
8 **Auburn**	**10**	**109**	**45**	**41.3**	**11.7**	**4**	**3.7**	**528**	**4.8**	**4**	**52.8**
10 North Carolina St.	10	95	44	46.3	12.1	9	9.5	530	5.6	5	53.0

TOTAL DEFENSE	G	P	YDS	AVG	YPG
1 Miami (Fla.)	10	590	1894	3.2	189.4
2 Oklahoma	10	634	1938	3.1	193.8
3 **Mississippi**	**10**	**572**	**1955**	**3.4**	**195.5**
4 South Carolina	10	558	1998	3.6	199.8
5 **Georgia Tech**	**10**	**537**	**2003**	**3.7**	**200.3**
6 Navy	9	543	1840	3.4	204.4
7 **Auburn**	**10**	**540**	**2083**	**3.9**	**208.3**
8 Texas A&M	10	601	2088	3.5	208.8
9 Penn State	9	534	1903	3.6	211.4
10 Pittsburgh	10	591	2154	3.6	215.4

SCORING OFFENSE	G	PTS	AVG
1 Oklahoma	10	466	46.6

SCORING DEFENSE	G	PTS	AVG
1 **Georgia Tech**	**10**	**33**	**3.3**

1956

FINAL POLL (DEC. 3)

UP	AP	SCHOOL	FINAL RECORD
1	1	Oklahoma	10-0-0
2	2	Tennessee	**10-1-0**
3	3	Iowa	9-1-0
4	4	Georgia Tech	**10-1-0**
5	5	Texas A&M	9-0-1
6	6	Miami (Fla.)	8-1-1
7	7	Michigan	7-2-0
8	8	Syracuse	7-2-0
10	9	Michigan State	7-2-0
13	10	Oregon State	7-3-1
11	11	Baylor	9-2-0
9	12	Minnesota	6-1-2
12	13	Pittsburgh	7-3-1
14	14	TCU	8-3-0
	15	Ohio State	6-3-0
19	16	Navy	6-1-2
	17	George Washington	8-1-1
15	18	Southern California	8-2-0
	19	Clemson	7-2-2
18	20	Colorado	8-2-1
16		Wyoming	10-0-0
17		Yale	8-1-0
20		Duke	5-4-1

CONSENSUS ALL-AMERICANS

POS	NAME	SCHOOL
B	Jim Brown	Syracuse
B	**John Majors**	**Tennessee**
B	Tommy McDonald	Oklahoma
B	John Brodie	Stanford
E	Joe Walton	Pittsburgh
E	Ron Kramer	Michigan
T	John Witte	Oregon State
T	**Lou Michaels**	**Kentucky**
G	Jim Parker	Ohio State
G	Bill Glass	Baylor
C	Jerry Tubbs	Oklahoma

OTHERS RECEIVING FIRST-TEAM HONORS

POS	NAME	SCHOOL
B	Bill Barnes	Wake Forest
B	Jim Crawford	Wyoming
B	Paul Hornung	Notre Dame
B	Jack Pardee	Texas A&M
B	Don Bosseler	Miami (Fla.)
E	**Buddy Cruze**	**Tennessee**
E	Bill Steiger	Washington State
T	Norman Hamilton	TCU
T	Bob Hobert	Minnesota
T	Alex Karras	Iowa
T	Charles Krueger	Texas A&M
T	Paul Wiggin	Stanford
T	Ed Gray	Oklahoma
G	**John Barrow**	**Florida**
G	Sam Valentine	Penn State
C	**Don Stephenson**	**Georgia Tech**

HEISMAN TROPHY VOTING

	PLAYER	POS	SCHOOL	TOTAL
1	Paul Hornung	QB	Notre Dame	1066
2	**John Majors**	**RB**	**Tennessee**	**994**
3	Tommy McDonald	HB	Oklahoma	973
4	Jerry Tubbs	C	Oklahoma	724
5	Jim Brown	HB	Syracuse	561
6	Ron Kramer	E	Michigan	518
7	John Brodie	QB	Stanford	281
8	Jim Parker	G	Ohio State	248
9	Kenny Ploen	QB	Iowa	150
10	Jim Arnett	HB	Southern Cal	128

AWARD WINNERS

PLAYER	AWARD
Tommy McDonald, HB, Oklahoma	Maxwell
Jim Parker, G, Ohio State	Outland

BOWL GAMES

DATE	GAME	SCORE
D29	**Gator**	**Georgia Tech 21, Pittsburgh 14**
J1	Tangerine	West Texas State 20, Southern Miss 13
J1	Orange	Colorado 27, Clemson 21
J1	Rose	Iowa 35, Oregon State 19
J1	**Sugar**	**Baylor 13, Tennessee 7**
J1	Cotton	TCU 28, Syracuse 27
J1	Sun	George Washington 13, Texas-El Paso 0

SEC STANDINGS

	CONFERENCE			OVERALL		
	W	L	T	W	L	T
Tennessee	6	0	0	10	1	0
Georgia Tech	7	1	0	10	1	0
Florida	5	2	0	6	3	1
Mississippi	4	2	0	7	3	0
Auburn	4	3	0	7	3	0
Kentucky	4	4	0	6	4	0
Tulane	3	3	0	6	4	0
Vanderbilt	2	5	0	5	5	0
Mississippi State	2	5	0	4	6	0
Alabama	2	5	0	2	7	1
LSU	1	5	0	3	7	0
Georgia	1	6	0	3	6	1

ANNUAL REVIEW

1957 NCAA Major College Statistical Leaders

Individual Leaders

PASSING/COMPLETIONS	G	ATT	COM	PCT	INT	I%	YDS	YPA	TD	TD%	COM.PG
1 Ken Ford, Hardin-Simmons	10	205	115	56.1	11	5.4	1254	6.1	14	6.8	11.5
2 Bob Newman, Washington State	10	188	104	55.3	13	6.9	1391	7.4	13	6.9	10.4
3 Lee Grosscup, Utah	10	137	94	68.6	2	1.5	1398	10.2	10	7.3	9.4
4 Bob Winters, Utah State	10	179	92	51.4	9	5.0	1139	6.4	7	3.9	9.2
5 Billy Baker, Furman	10	150	88	58.7	5	3.3	846	5.6	6	4.0	8.8
6 Tom Flores, Pacific	10	184	82	44.6	10	5.4	980	5.3	5	2.7	8.2
7 Tom Forrestal, Navy	10	159	80	50.3	17	10.7	1117	7.0	8	5.0	8.0
8 Jack Douglas, Stanford	10	146	78	53.4	6	4.1	957	6.6	10	6.9	7.8
9 Roger LaBrasca, Drake	8	145	74	51.0	10	6.9	1054	7.3	12	8.3	9.3
9 Tommy Greene, Holy Cross	9	159	74	46.5	12	7.6	1297	8.2	11	6.9	8.2

ALL-PURPOSE YARDS	G	RUSH	REC	INT	PR	KR	YDS	YPG
1 Overton Curtis, Utah State	10	616	193	60	44	695	1608	160.8

RUSHING/YARDS	G	ATT	YDS	AVG	YPG
1 Leon Burton, Arizona State	10	117	1126	9.6	112.6
2 Bob Stransky, Colorado	10	183	1097	6.0	109.7
3 Bob Anderson, Army	9	153	983	6.4	109.2
4 Bill Austin, Rutgers	9	193	946	4.9	105.1
5 Chuck Shea, Stanford	10	163	840	5.2	84.0
6 Jim Bakhtiar, Virginia	10	194	822	4.2	82.2
7 Clendon Thomas, Oklahoma	10	130	816	6.3	81.6
8 Jimmy Taylor, LSU	10	162	762	4.7	76.2
9 Nub Beamer, Oregon State	10	173	760	4.4	76.0
10 Wray Carlton, Duke	10	143	749	5.2	74.9

RUSHING/YARDS PER CARRY	G	ATT	YDS	YPC
1 Leon Burton, Arizona State	10	117	1126	9.6
2 Don Perkins, New Mexico	10	112	744	6.6
3 Bob Anderson, Army	9	153	983	6.3
4 Clendon Thomas, Oklahoma	10	130	816	6.3
5 Bob Stransky, Colorado	10	183	1097	6.0
6 Bobby Mulgado, Arizona State	10	121	681	5.6
7 Pete Hart, Hardin-Simmons	10	120	669	5.6
8 Jim Pace, Michigan	9	123	664	5.4
9 Pete Dawkins, Army	9	124	665	5.4
10 Wray Carlton, Duke	10	143	749	5.2

Based on top 20 rushers

RECEIVING/RECEPTIONS	G	REC	YDS	TD	YPR	YPG	RPG
1 Stuart Vaughan, Utah	10	53	756	5	14.3	75.6	5.3
2 Gary Kapp, Utah State	10	45	633	4	14.1	63.3	4.5
3 Don Ellingsen, Washington State	10	45	559	3	12.4	55.9	4.5
4 Fred Dugan, Dayton	10	37	546	3	14.8	54.6	3.7
5 Jim Gibbons, Iowa	9	36	587	4	16.3	65.2	4.0
6 Al Jamison, Colgate	9	33	420	6	12.7	46.7	3.7
7 Jerry Mertens, Drake	8	29	509	6	17.6	63.6	3.6
7 Gene Leek, Arizona	10	29	310	1	10.7	31.0	2.9
9 Chuck Chatfield, Pacific	10	28	404	1	14.4	40.4	2.8
9 Pete Jokanovich, Navy	10	28	339	0	12.1	33.9	2.8

PUNTING	PUNT	YDS	AVG
1 Dave Sherer, SMU	36	1620	45.0
2 Bobby Gordon, Tennessee	40	1708	42.7
3 Bobby Jordan, VMI	39	1642	42.1
4 Gerald Nesbit, Arkansas	32	1344	42.0
5 Kirk Wilson, UCLA	31	1302	42.0
6 Robert Haas, Missouri	27	1126	41.7
7 Bill Gundy, Dartmouth	23	934	40.6
8 Walter Fondren, Texas	37	1502	40.6
9 Larry DeVincentis, Cincinnati	39	1583	40.6
10 Lou Michaels, Kentucky	47	1908	40.6

PUNT RETURNS/YARDS	PR	YDS	AVG
1 Bobby Mulgado, Arizona State	14	267	19.1
2 Sterling Hammack, Oregon State	22	253	11.5
3 Jakie Sandefer, Oklahoma	17	249	14.6
4 Corbin Bailey, Virginia Tech	15	242	16.1
5 Bobby Gordon, Tennessee	22	231	10.5
6 Dave Parr, Villanova	9	208	23.1
7 Howard Cook, Colorado	14	186	13.3
8 Clendon Thomas, Oklahoma	7	178	25.4
9 Jim Shofner, TCU	11	168	15.3
10 John Maio, Boston U.	10	167	16.7

KICKOFF RETURNS/YARDS	KR	YDS	AVG
1 Overton Curtis, Utah State	23	695	30.2
2 Stan Dobosz, Florida State	19	390	20.5
3 Billy Cannon, LSU	11	343	31.2
4 Jim Jones, Washington	12	342	28.5
5 Dewey Bohling, Hardin-Simmons	18	337	18.7
6 Wilmer Fowler, Northwestern	14	336	24.0
7 Dick Haley, Pittsburgh	14	329	23.5
8 Dick Christy, North Carolina St.	7	318	45.4
9 Clarence Bruton, Marquette	12	310	25.8
10 Jim Shanley, Oregon	10	309	30.9

SCORING	TDS	XPT	FG	PTS
1 Leon Burton, Arizona State	16	0	0	96
2 Bobby Mulgado, Arizona State	9	36	1	93
3 Jimmy Taylor, LSU	12	14	0	86
4 Bob Anderson, Army	14	0	0	84
5 Dick Christy, North Carolina St.	13	2	1	83
6 William Atkins, Auburn	11	13	1	82
7 Joe Belland, Arizona State	13	0	0	78
8 Bob Stransky, Colorado	12	5	0	77
9 Bill Austin, Rutgers	12	2	0	74
10 Wray Carlton, Duke	10	11	0	71

INTERCEPTIONS	INT	YDS
1 Ray Toole, North Texas	7	133
1 Carroll Johnston, Brigham Young	7	89
3 Bobby Mulgado, Arizona State	6	113
3 James Dunn, Florida	6	71
5 Frank Finney, Brown	5	155
5 Bob Winters, Utah State	5	87
5 Reece Whitley, Virginia	5	81
5 John David Crow, Texas A&M	5	39
5 Barry Maroney, Cincinnati	5	27
5 Bobby Lackey, Texas	5	15

Team Leaders

RUSHING OFFENSE	G	ATT	YDS	AVG	YPG
1 Colorado	10	616	3224	5.2	322.4
2 Mississippi	10	582	3057	5.3	305.7
3 Ohio State	9	555	2681	4.8	297.9
4 Army	9	535	2674	5.0	297.1
5 Oklahoma	10	679	2970	4.4	297.0
6 Arizona State	10	520	2922	5.6	292.2
7 Wisconsin	9	503	2437	4.8	270.8
8 Michigan State	9	533	2367	4.4	263.0
9 Princeton	9	474	2323	4.9	258.1
10 Miami (Fla.)	10	567	2540	4.5	254.0

PASSING OFFENSE	G	ATT	COM	INT	PCT	YDS	YPA	TD	I%	YPC	YPG
1 Utah	10	218	133	14	61.0	1952	9.0	5	6.4	14.7	195.2
2 Washington State	10	253	136	19	53.8	1808	7.1	17	7.5	13.3	180.8
3 Holy Cross	9	189	84	16	44.4	1508	8.0	12	8.5	18.0	167.6
4 Arizona	10	294	155	19	52.7	1540	5.2	4	6.5	9.9	154.0
5 Drake	8	174	86	12	49.4	1231	7.1	12	6.9	14.3	153.9
6 Arizona State	10	152	81	7	53.3	1527	10.0	19	4.6	18.9	152.7
7 Hardin-Simmons	10	242	135	15	55.8	1510	6.2	15	5.4	11.2	151.0
8 Navy	10	230	113	14	49.1	1469	6.4	15	6.1	13.0	146.9
9 Iowa	9	146	77	17	52.7	1289	8.8	11	11.6	16.7	143.2
10 Penn State	9	185	90	8	48.6	1187	6.4	11	4.3	13.2	131.9

TOTAL OFFENSE	G	P	YDS	AVG	YPG
1 Arizona State	10	672	4449	6.6	444.9
2 Colorado	10	743	4152	5.6	415.2
3 Navy	10	719	3844	5.3	384.4
4 Iowa	9	599	3459	5.8	384.3
5 Michigan State	9	669	3455	5.2	383.9
6 Army	9	648	3376	5.2	375.1
7 Oklahoma	10	776	3600	4.6	360.0
8 Mississippi	10	673	3556	5.3	355.6
9 Utah	10	628	3476	5.5	347.6
9 Rice	10	672	3476	5.2	347.6

RUSHING DEFENSE	G	ATT	YDS	AVG	YPG
1 Auburn	10	390	674	1.7	67.4
2 Miami (Fla.)	10	418	998	2.4	99.8
3 Arizona State	10	381	1035	2.7	103.5
4 Princeton	9	338	974	2.9	108.2
5 Navy	10	427	1096	2.6	109.6
6 Iowa	9	372	1014	2.7	112.7
7 Boston College	9	381	1032	2.7	114.7
8 Michigan State	9	422	1055	2.5	117.2
9 Cincinnati	10	402	1220	3.0	122.0
10 Syracuse	9	368	1107	3.0	123.0

PASSING DEFENSE	G	ATT	COM	PCT	YPC	INT	I%	YDS	YPA	TD	YPG
1 Georgia Tech	10	73	31	42.5	10.8	7	9.6	334	4.6	1	33.4
2 Missouri	10	96	41	42.7	9.9	10	10.3	404	4.2	3	40.4
3 Tulane	10	94	33	35.1	12.5	10	10.6	413	4.4	5	41.3
4 Virginia Tech	10	108	38	35.2	12.8	9	8.3	485	4.5	3	48.5
5 Mississippi	10	133	45	33.8	11.1	19	14.3	500	3.8	1	50.0
6 Tennessee	10	109	49	45.0	10.2	6	5.5	501	4.6	3	50.1
7 Navy	10	127	39	30.7	13.6	20	15.8	530	4.2	1	53.0
7 Florida	9	107	39	36.4	12.2	15	14.0	477	4.5	1	53.0
9 Kentucky	10	115	37	32.2	14.4	12	10.4	531	4.6	1	53.1
10 Texas A&M	10	140	54	38.6	9.9	16	11.4	534	3.8	16	53.4

TOTAL DEFENSE	G	P	YDS	AVG	YPG
1 Auburn	10	529	1330	2.5	133.0
2 Navy	10	554	1626	2.9	162.6
3 Georgia Tech	10	546	1778	3.3	177.8
4 Tennessee	10	574	1847	3.2	184.7
5 Michigan State	9	556	1724	3.1	191.6
6 Miami (Fla.)	10	579	2002	3.5	200.2
7 TCU	10	570	2022	3.5	202.2
8 Florida	9	494	1822	3.7	202.4
9 Cincinnati	10	556	2065	3.7	206.5
10 Mississippi	10	561	2074	3.7	207.4

SCORING OFFENSE	G	PTS	AVG
1 Arizona State	10	397	39.7

SCORING DEFENSE	G	PTS	AVG
1 Auburn	10	28	2.8

1957

FINAL POLL (DEC. 2)

UP	AP	SCHOOL	FINAL RECORD
2	1	**Auburn**	**10-0-0**
1	2	Ohio State	9-1-0
3	3	Michigan State	8-1-0
4	4	Oklahoma	10-1-0
6	5	Navy	9-1-1
5	6	Iowa	7-1-1
8	7	**Mississippi**	**9-1-1**
7	8	Rice	7-4-0
10	9	Texas A&M	8-3-0
9	10	Notre Dame	7-3-0
11	11	Texas	6-4-1
12	12	Arizona State	10-0-0
16	13	**Tennessee**	**8-3-0**
	14	**Mississippi State**	**6-2-1**
20	15	North Carolina St.	7-1-2
14	16	Duke	6-3-2
	17	**Florida**	**6-2-1**
13	18	Army	7-2-0
14	19	Wisconsin	6-3-0
	20	VMI	9-0-1
17		Oregon	7-4-0
18		Clemson	7-3-0
18		UCLA	8-2-0

CONSENSUS ALL-AMERICANS

POS	NAME	SCHOOL
B	John David Crow	Texas A&M
B	Walt Kowalczyk	Michigan State
B	Bob Anderson	Army
B	Clendon Thomas	Oklahoma
E	**Jimmy Phillips**	**Auburn**
E	Dick Wallen	UCLA
T	**Lou Michaels**	**Kentucky**
T	Alex Karras	Iowa
G	Bill Krisher	Oklahoma
G	Al Ecuyer	Notre Dame
C	Dan Currie	Michigan State

OTHERS RECEIVING FIRST-TEAM HONORS

B	Jim Bakhtiar	Virginia
B	Lee Grosscup	Utah
B	King Hill	Rice
B	Bob Stransky	Colorado
B	**Jimmy Taylor**	**LSU**
B	Dick Christy	North Carolina St.
B	Jim Pace	Michigan
B	Tom Forrestal	Navy
E	Fred Dugan	Dayton
E	Jim Gibbons	Iowa
T	Charlie Krueger	Texas A&M
T	Tom Topping	Duke
G	**Bill Johnson**	**Tennessee**
G	**Jack Simpson**	**Mississippi**
G	Aurelius Thomas	Ohio State
C	Bob Reifsnyder	Navy
C	**Don Stephenson**	**Georgia Tech**

HEISMAN TROPHY VOTING

	PLAYER	POS	SCHOOL	TOTAL
1	John David Crow	RB	Texas A&M	1183
2	Alex Karras	DT	Iowa	693
3	Walt Kowalczyk	HB	Michigan State	630
4	**Lou Michaels**	**T**	**Kentucky**	**330**
5	Tom Forrestal	QB	Navy	232
6	**Jim Phillips**	**E**	**Auburn**	**216**
7	Bob Anderson	HB	Army	204
8	Dan Currie	C	Michigan State	197
9	Clendon Thomas	HB	Oklahoma	185
10	Lee Grosscup	QB	Utah	147

AWARD WINNERS

PLAYER	AWARD
Bob Reifsnyder, T, Navy	Maxwell
Alex Karras, T, Iowa	Outland

BOWL GAMES

DATE	GAME	SCORE
D28	**Gator**	**Tennessee 3, Texas A&M 0**
J1	Tangerine	Texas A&M-Commerce 10, Southern Miss 9
J1	Sun	Louisville 34, Drake 20
J1	**Sugar**	**Mississippi 39, Texas 7**
J1	Cotton	Navy 20, Rice 7
J1	Rose	Ohio State 10, Oregon 7
J1	Orange	Oklahoma 48, Duke 21

SEC STANDINGS

	CONFERENCE			OVERALL		
	W	L	T	W	L	T
Auburn	7	0	0	10	0	0
Mississippi	5	0	1	9	1	1
Florida	4	2	1	6	2	1
Mississippi State	4	2	1	6	2	1
Tennessee	4	3	0	8	3	0
LSU	4	4	0	5	5	0
Vanderbilt	3	3	1	5	3	2
Georgia Tech	3	4	1	4	4	2
Georgia	3	4	0	3	7	0
Alabama	1	6	1	2	7	1
Tulane	1	5	0	2	8	0
Kentucky	1	7	0	3	7	0

1958 NCAA Major College Statistical Leaders

Individual Leaders

PASSING/COMPLETIONS	G	ATT	COM	PCT	INT	I%	YDS	YPA	TD	TD%	COM.PG
1 Buddy Humphrey, Baylor	10	195	112	57.4	8	4.1	1316	6.7	7	3.6	11.2
2 Ralph Hunsaker, Arizona	10	191	106	55.5	13	6.8	1129	5.9	5	2.6	10.6
3 Randy Duncan, Iowa	9	172	101	58.7	9	5.2	1347	7.8	11	6.4	11.2
4 Rich Mayo, Air Force	10	174	98	56.3	6	3.5	1019	5.9	11	6.3	9.8
5 Charles Milstead, Texas A&M	10	167	88	52.7	11	6.6	1135	6.8	5	3.0	8.8
6 Dick Longfellow, West Virginia	10	156	79	50.6	12	7.7	948	6.1	6	3.9	7.9
7 Bob Nicolet, Stanford	10	146	77	52.7	5	3.4	724	5.0	3	2.1	7.7
8 Dick Norman, Stanford	10	133	76	57.1	7	5.3	717	5.4	3	2.3	7.6
9 Arnold Dempsey, Virginia	10	152	74	48.7	11	7.2	697	4.6	2	1.3	7.4
10 Jack Lee, Cincinnati	10	130	71	54.6	11	8.5	951	7.3	5	3.9	7.1
10 Frank Finney, Brown	9	142	71	50.0	10	7.0	982	6.9	8	5.6	7.9

ALL-PURPOSE YARDS	G	RUSH	REC	INT	PR	KR	YDS	YPG
1 Dick Bass, Pacific	10	1361	121	5	164	227	1878	187.8

RUSHING/YARDS	G	ATT	YDS	AVG	YPG
1 Dick Bass, Pacific	10	205	1361	6.6	136.1
2 Bob White, Ohio State	9	218	859	3.9	95.4
3 Dwight Nichols, Iowa State	10	220	815	3.7	81.5
4 Pete Hart, Hardin-Simmons	10	163	785	4.8	78.5
5 Billy Austin, Rutgers	10	145	747	5.2	83.0
6 Jake Crouthamel, Dartmouth	9	123	722	5.9	80.2
7 Weldon Jackson, Brigham Young	10	101	698	6.9	69.8
8 Billy Cannon, LSU	10	115	686	6.0	68.6
9 Larry Hickman, Baylor	10	151	670	4.4	67.0
10 John Saunders, South Carolina	10	128	653	5.1	65.3

RUSHING/YARDS PER CARRY	G	ATT	YDS	YPC
1 Ray Jauch, Iowa	9	72	506	7.0
2 Weldon Jackson, Brigham Young	10	101	698	6.9
3 Wayne Schneider, Colorado State	10	84	580	6.9
4 Dick Bass, Pacific	10	205	1361	6.6
5 Sam Horner, VMI	10	102	612	6.0
6 Prentice Gautt, Oklahoma	10	105	627	6.0
7 Billy Cannon, LSU	10	115	686	6.0
8 Leon Burton, Arizona State	10	108	642	5.9
9 Duane Wood, Oklahoma State	10	83	492	5.9
10 Jake Crouthamel, Dartmouth	9	123	722	5.9

Based on top 60 rushers

RECEIVING/RECEPTIONS	G	REC	YDS	TD	YPR	YPG	RPG
1 Dave Hibbert, Arizona	10	61	606	4	9.9	60.6	6.1
2 Sonny Randle, Virginia	10	47	642	5	13.7	64.2	4.7
3 Chris Burford, Stanford	10	45	493	2	11.0	49.3	4.5
4 John Tracey, Texas A&M	10	37	466	2	12.6	46.6	3.7
5 Ray Siminski, Furman	9	35	568	5	16.2	63.1	3.9
6 Bob Simms, Rutgers	9	33	468	9	14.2	52.0	3.7
7 Irvin Nikolai, Stanford	10	32	343	0	10.7	34.3	3.2
8 Sonny Oates, Hardin-Simmons	10	31	402	0	13.0	40.2	3.1
8 Gerry Moore, Baylor	10	31	357	2	11.5	35.7	3.1
8 Mel Reight, West Virginia	10	31	329	2	10.6	32.9	3.1

PUNTING	PUNT	YDS	AVG
1 Bobby Walden, Georgia	44	1993	45.3
2 Boyd Dowler, Colorado	33	1429	43.3
3 Don Coker, North Carolina	31	1339	43.2
4 Tommy Davis, LSU	38	1623	42.7
5 Sam Horner, VMI	28	1193	42.6
5 Joe Delany, Georgia Tech	28	1193	42.6
7 Doug Hatcher, South Carolina	20	834	41.7
8 Dainard Paulson, Oregon State	35	1449	41.4
9 Brad Myers, Michigan	24	989	41.2
10 John Lands, Montana	23	943	41.0

PUNT RETURNS/YARDS	PR	YDS	AVG
1 Howard Cook, Colorado	24	242	10.1
2 John Horrillo, Oregon State	20	227	11.4
3 David Ray, Vanderbilt	10	199	19.9
4 Dwight Nichols, Iowa State	18	195	10.8
5 Dale Hackbart, Wisconsin	7	193	27.6
6 Jake Crouthamel, Dartmouth	11	188	17.1
7 Ronnie Morris, Tulsa	12	183	15.3
8 Dean Look, Michigan State	5	179	35.8
9 Jim Colclough, Boston College	19	177	9.3
10 Mike Quinlan, Air Force	11	172	15.6

KICKOFF RETURNS/YARDS	KR	YDS	AVG
1 Sonny Randle, Virginia	21	506	24.1
2 Wray Carlton, Duke	13	332	25.5
3 Billy Stacy, Mississippi State	12	309	25.8
4 Ronnie Morris, Tulsa	11	305	27.7
5 Warren Livingston, Arizona	12	302	25.2
6 Frank Reginelli, Marquette	14	301	21.5
7 Tom Newell, Drake	14	300	21.4
8 Jim Crotty, Notre Dame	12	297	24.8
9 Overton Curtis, Utah State	9	296	32.9
10 Claude King, Houston	10	291	29.1

SCORING	TDS	XPT	FG	PTS
1 Dick Bass, Pacific	18	8	0	116
2 Billy Austin, Rutgers	16	10	0	106
3 Ron Burton, Northwestern	12	4	0	76
4 Billy Cannon, LSU	11	8	0	74
4 Frank Finney, Brown	10	14	0	74
4 Pete Dawkins, Army	12	2	0	74
7 Bob White, Ohio State	12	0	0	72
8 Leon Burton, Arizona State	11	4	0	70
9 Calvin Bird, Kentucky	10	5	0	65
10 Bob Simms, Rutgers	9	10	0	64

KICK SCORING	XPA	XP	FG	PTS
1 Bobby Khayat, Mississippi	24	22	4	34
2 John Sheppard, Florida State	21	19	3	28
3 George Pupich, Air Force	16	12	5	27
4 Bill Bucek, Rice	14	12	4	24
5 Ben Grosse, Kansas State	8	8	5	23
6 Bob Prescott, Iowa	24	18	1	21
7 Tommy Wells, Georgia Tech	10	7	4	19
8 David Kilgore, Ohio State	17	15	1	18
8 Monty Stickles, Notre Dame	19	15	1	18
10 Charles Rash, Missouri	16	14	1	17

INTERCEPTIONS	INT	YDS
1 Jim Norton, Idaho	9	222
2 Dale Hackbart, Wisconsin	7	77
2 James Grazione, Villanova	7	76
4 Billy Austin, Rutgers	6	128
4 Dick Young, Wichita State	6	107
4 Ted Colna, George Washington	6	65
4 Ken Hohl, Holy Cross	6	22
8 Abner Haynes, North Texas	5	122
8 Jim Kerr, Penn State	5	122
8 Bill Bucek, Rice	5	84

Team Leaders

RUSHING OFFENSE	G	ATT	YDS	AVG	YPG
1 Pacific	10	502	2596	5.2	259.6
2 Oklahoma	10	633	2574	4.1	257.4
3 Arizona State	10	548	2539	4.6	253.9
4 Brigham Young	10	538	2497	4.6	249.7
5 Colorado	10	523	2495	4.8	249.5
6 Penn State	10	597	2429	4.1	242.9
7 California	10	603	2380	3.9	238.0
8 Tulsa	10	582	2364	4.1	236.4
9 Iowa	9	444	2123	4.8	235.9
10 Purdue	9	550	2094	3.8	232.7

PASSING OFFENSE	G	ATT	COM	INT	PCT	YDS	YPA	TD	I%	YPC	YPG
1 Army	9	187	87	13	46.5	1550	8.3	13	7.0	17.8	172.2
2 Iowa	9	205	115	11	56.1	1530	7.5	11	5.4	13.3	170.0
3 San Jose State	9	253	131	14	51.8	1528	6.0	11	5.5	11.7	169.8
4 Baylor	10	253	140	11	55.3	1687	6.7	9	4.4	12.1	168.7
5 SMU	10	208	113	16	54.3	1661	8.0	15	7.7	14.7	166.1
6 Navy	9	194	106	14	54.6	1445	7.4	15	7.2	13.6	160.6
7 Stanford	10	305	164	14	53.8	1581	5.2	7	4.6	9.6	158.1
8 Notre Dame	10	198	94	22	47.5	1561	7.9	13	11.1	16.6	156.1
9 Texas A&M	10	233	119	16	51.1	1541	6.6	6	6.9	12.9	154.1
10 Washington State	10	188	115	10	61.2	1463	7.8	18	5.3	12.7	146.3

TOTAL OFFENSE	G	P	YDS	AVG	YPG
1 Iowa	9	649	3653	5.6	405.9
2 Pacific	10	657	3804	5.8	380.4
3 Arizona State	10	694	3795	5.5	379.5
4 Army	9	630	3380	5.4	375.6
5 Notre Dame	10	710	3697	5.2	369.7
6 Air Force	10	732	3605	4.9	360.5
7 Oklahoma	10	762	3517	4.6	351.7
8 Baylor	10	715	3356	4.7	335.6
9 Brown	9	622	3019	4.9	335.4
10 West Virginia	10	720	3319	4.6	331.9

RUSHING DEFENSE	G	ATT	YDS	AVG	YPG
1 Auburn	10	370	796	2.2	79.6
2 Tulsa	10	398	825	2.1	82.5
3 Pittsburgh	10	407	913	2.2	91.3
4 Army	9	346	837	2.4	93.0
5 Syracuse	9	382	849	2.2	94.3
5 Purdue	9	372	849	2.3	94.3
7 Florida	10	395	948	2.4	94.8
8 Boston College	10	404	1060	2.6	106.0
9 TCU	10	401	1104	2.8	110.4
10 LSU	10	461	1151	2.5	115.1

PASSING DEFENSE	G	ATT	COM	INT	PCT	YDS	YPA	TD	I%	YPC	YPG
1 Iowa State	10	109	41	15	37.6	390	3.6	2	13.8	9.5	39.0
2 Brown	9	108	36	NA	33.3	403	3.7	6	NA	11.2	44.8
3 Georgia Tech	10	129	55	12	42.6	571	4.4	3	9.3	10.4	57.1
4 Harvard	9	105	47	NA	44.8	526	5.0	2	NA	11.2	58.4
4 Colorado	10	129	50	9	38.8	590	4.6	6	7.0	11.8	59.0
6 Alabama	10	133	55	19	41.4	600	4.5	2	14.3	10.9	60.0
7 Washington State	10	140	55	NA	39.3	607	4.3	2	NA	11.0	60.7
8 Oregon	10	122	56	7	45.9	656	5.4	2	5.7	11.7	65.6
9 Georgia	10	141	58	NA	41.1	673	4.8	8	NA	11.6	67.3
10 Florida State	10	126	51	14	40.5	675	5.4	2	11.1	13.2	67.5

TOTAL DEFENSE	G	P	YDS	AVG	YPG
1 Auburn	10	521	1575	3.0	157.5
2 Purdue	9	485	1590	3.3	176.7
3 Army	9	561	1643	2.9	182.6
4 Harvard	9	512	1720	3.4	191.1
5 LSU	10	624	1934	3.1	193.4
6 Boston College	10	558	1942	3.5	194.2
7 Pittsburgh	10	569	1961	3.4	196.1
8 North Texas	10	542	2017	3.7	201.7
9 Georgia Tech	10	552	2018	3.7	201.8
10 Tulsa	10	595	2030	3.4	203.0

SCORING OFFENSE	G	PTS	AVG
1 Rutgers	9	301	33.4
2 Army	9	264	29.3
2 Syracuse	9	264	29.3
4 Oklahoma	10	279	27.9
5 LSU	10	275	27.5
6 Arizona State	10	271	27.1
7 West Virginia	10	268	26.8
8 Pacific	10	266	26.6
9 Iowa	9	234	26.0
10 Air Force	10	247	24.7

SCORING DEFENSE	G	PTS	AVG
1 Oklahoma	10	49	4.9
2 Oregon	10	50	5.0
3 LSU	10	53	5.3
4 Army	9	49	5.4
5 Auburn	10	62	6.2
6 Mississippi	10	65	6.5
7 Syracuse	9	59	6.6
8 Vanderbilt	10	71	7.1
9 Alabama	10	75	7.5
10 TCU	10	78	7.8

1958

FINAL POLL (DEC. 1)

UP	AP	SCHOOL	FINAL RECORD
1	1	**LSU**	**11-0-0**
2	2	Iowa	8-1-1
3	3	Army	8-0-1
4	4	**Auburn**	**9-0-1**
5	5	Oklahoma	10-1-0
8	6	Air Force	9-0-2
6	7	Wisconsin	7-1-1
7	8	Ohio State	6-1-2
10	9	Syracuse	8-2-0
9	10	TCU	8-2-1
12	11	**Mississippi**	**9-2-0**
13	12	Clemson	8-3-0
11	13	Purdue	6-1-2
15	14	**Florida**	**6-4-1**
	15	South Carolina	7-3-0
16	16	California	7-4-0
14	17	Notre Dame	6-4-0
18	18	SMU	6-4-0
	19	Oklahoma State	8-3-0
	20	Rutgers	8-1-0
17		Northwestern	5-4-0

CONSENSUS ALL-AMERICANS

POS	NAME	SCHOOL
B	Randy Duncan	Iowa
B	Pete Dawkins	Army
B	**Billy Cannon**	**LSU**
B	Bob White	Ohio State
E	Buddy Dial	Rice
E	Sam Williams	Michigan State
T	Ted Bates	Oregon State
T	Brock Strom	Air Force
G	John Guzik	Pittsburgh
G	**Zeke Smith**	**Auburn**
G	**George Deiderich**	**Vanderbilt**
C	Bob Harrison	Oklahoma

OTHERS RECEIVING FIRST-TEAM HONORS

POS	NAME	SCHOOL
B	Bob Anderson	Army
B	Joe Kapp	California
B	Don Meredith	SMU
B	Nick Pietrosante	Notre Dame
B	Billy Austin	Rutgers
E	Al Goldstein	North Carolina
E	Jim Houston	Ohio State
E	Curtis Merz	Iowa
E	Jim Wood	Oklahoma State
E	Monty Stickles	Notre Dame
T	Andrew Cvercko	Northwestern
T	Don Floyd	TCU
T	**Vel Heckman**	**Florida**
T	Gene Selawski	Purdue
T	Hogan Wharton	Houston
T	Ron Luciano	Syracuse
T	Jim Marshall	Ohio State
G	Bob Novogratz	Army
G	John Wooten	Colorado
G	Al Ecuyer	Notre Dame
C	**Max Fugler**	**LSU**
C	**Jackie Burkett**	**Auburn**

HEISMAN TROPHY VOTING

	PLAYER	POS	SCHOOL	TOTAL
1	Pete Dawkins	HB	Army	1394
2	Randy Duncan	QB	Iowa	1021
3	**Billy Cannon**	HB	**LSU**	975
4	Bob White	RB	Ohio State	365
5	Joe Kapp	QB	California	227
6	Billy Austin	TB	Rutgers	197
7	Bob Harrison	C	Oklahoma	187
8	Dick Bass	RB	Pacific	96
9	Don Meredith	QB	SMU	75
10	Nick Pietrosante	FB	Notre Dame	70

AWARD WINNERS

PLAYER	AWARD
Pete Dawkins, HB, Army	Maxwell
Zeke Smith, G, Auburn	**Outland**

BOWL GAMES

DATE	GAME	SCORE
D13	Bluegrass	Oklahoma State 15, Florida State 6
D27	**Gator**	**Mississippi 7, Florida 3**
D27	Tangerine	Texas A&M-Commerce 26, Missouri Valley 7
D31	Sun	Wyoming 14, Hardin-Simmons 6
J1	Cotton	Air Force 0, TCU 0
J1	Rose	Iowa 38, California 12
J1	**Sugar**	**LSU 7, Clemson 0**
J1	Orange	Oklahoma 21, Syracuse 6

SEC STANDINGS

	CONFERENCE			OVERALL		
	W	L	T	W	L	T
LSU	6	0	0	11	0	0
Auburn	6	0	1	9	0	1
Mississippi	4	2	0	9	2	0
Vanderbilt	2	1	3	5	2	3
Tennessee	4	3	0	4	6	0
Kentucky	3	4	1	5	4	1
Alabama	3	4	1	5	4	1
Florida	2	3	1	6	4	1
Georgia Tech	2	3	1	5	4	1
Georgia	2	4	0	4	6	0
Tulane	1	5	0	3	7	0
Mississippi State	1	6	0	3	6	0

1959 NCAA MAJOR COLLEGE STATISTICAL LEADERS

INDIVIDUAL LEADERS

PASSING/COMPLETIONS	G	ATT	COM	PCT	INT	I%	YDS	YPA	TD	TD%	COM.PG
1 Dick Norman, Stanford	10	263	152	57.8	12	4.6	1963	7.5	11	4.2	15.2
2 Jack Lee, Cincinnati	10	232	132	56.9	6	2.6	1535	6.6	7	3.0	13.2
3 Pete Hall, Marquette	10	237	120	50.6	14	5.9	1589	6.7	7	3.0	12.0
4 Rich Mayo, Air Force	10	211	110	52.1	10	4.7	1212	5.7	6	2.8	11.0
5 Don Meredith, SMU	10	181	105	58.0	10	5.5	1266	7.0	11	6.1	10.5
5 Joe Caldwell, Army	9	188	105	55.9	7	3.7	1343	7.1	9	4.8	11.7
5 Charley Johnson, New Mexico State	10	199	105	52.8	8	4.0	1449	7.3	18	9.1	10.5
8 Fran Curci, Miami (Fla.)	10	195	100	51.3	14	7.2	1068	5.5	5	2.6	10.0
8 Gale Weidner, Colorado	10	207	100	48.3	13	6.3	1200	5.8	7	3.4	10.0
10 Dick Soergel, Oklahoma State	10	155	93	60.0	4	2.6	1102	7.1	8	5.2	9.3

ALL-PURPOSE YARDS	G	RUSH	REC	INT	PR	KR	YDS	YPG
1 Pervis Atkins, New Mexico State	10	971	301	23	241	264	1800	180.0

RUSHING/YARDS	G	ATT	YDS	AVG	YPG
1 Pervis Atkins, New Mexico State	10	130	971	7.5	97.1
2 Tom Watkins, Iowa State	10	158	843	5.3	84.3
3 Dwight Nichols, Iowa State	10	207	746	3.6	74.6
4 Dick Bass, Pacific	9	139	742	5.3	82.4
5 Billy Brown, New Mexico	10	95	740	7.8	74.0
6 Charlie Flowers, Mississippi	10	141	733	5.2	73.3
7 Abner Haynes, North Texas	10	116	730	6.3	73.0
8 Bob Crandall, New Mexico	10	116	729	6.3	72.9
9 Fred Doelling, Pennsylvania	9	133	707	5.3	78.6
10 Nolan Jones, Arizona State	11	143	689	4.8	62.6

RUSHING/YARDS PER CARRY	G	ATT	YDS	YPC
1 Billy Brown, New Mexico	10	95	740	7.8
2 Pervis Atkins, New Mexico State	10	130	971	7.5
3 Charles Bowers, Hardin-Simmons	10	86	619	7.2
4 Ernie Davis, Syracuse	10	98	686	7.0
5 Ger Schwedes, Syracuse	10	90	567	6.3
6 Abner Haynes, North Texas	10	116	730	6.3
7 Bob Crandall, New Mexico	10	116	729	6.3
8 Jerry Hill, Wyoming	10	97	579	6.0
9 Larry Wilson, Utah	10	98	559	5.7
10 Joe Bellino, Navy	10	99	564	5.7
Based on top 42 rushers				

RECEIVING/RECEPTIONS	G	REC	YDS	TD	YPR	YPG	RPG
1 Chris Burford, Stanford	10	61	756	6	12.4	75.6	6.1
2 Bill Carpenter, Army	9	43	591	3	13.7	65.7	4.8
3 Dick Evans, VMI	10	35	698	9	19.9	69.8	3.5
4 Ben Robinson, Stanford	10	34	595	2	17.5	59.5	3.4
5 Bill Miller, Miami (Fla.)	10	33	395	1	12.0	39.5	3.3
6 Paul Maguire, Citadel	10	32	549	10	17.2	54.9	3.2
7 Ed Kovac, Cincinnati	10	31	332	5	10.7	33.2	3.1
7 Bud Whitehead, Florida State	10	31	320	2	10.3	32.0	3.1
9 Don Norton, Iowa	9	30	428	4	14.3	47.6	3.3
9 Glynn Gregory, SMU	10	30	369	2	12.3	36.9	3.0
9 Bill Voss, Hardin-Simmons	10	30	319	4	10.6	31.9	3.0

PUNTING	PUNT	YDS	AVG
1 John Hadl, Kansas	43	1961	45.6
2 Dainard Paulson, Oregon State	32	1459	45.6
3 Bobby Joe Green, Florida	54	2425	44.9
4 Joe Zuger, Arizona State	42	1882	44.8
5 Gary Dunn, Brigham Young	39	1747	44.8
6 Lamont Miller, Utah State	26	1157	44.5
7 Willie Vasquez, Texas-El Paso	23	1021	44.4
8 Paul Gustafson, Montana	26	1131	43.5
9 Keith Lincoln, Washington State	41	1779	43.4
10 Paul Maguire, Citadel	32	1370	42.8

PUNT RETURNS/YARDS	PR	YDS	AVG
1 Pervis Atkins, New Mexico State	16	241	15.1
2 George Fleming, Washington	23	231	10.0
3 Billy Cannon, LSU	15	221	14.7
4 Charley Brown, Arizona State	18	213	11.8
5 Jacque MacKinnon, Colgate	12	210	17.5
6 Gerald Mauren, Iowa	10	181	18.1
7 George Usry, Clemson	16	175	10.9
7 John Majors, Tennessee	22	175	8.0
9 David Ames, Richmond	7	174	24.9
10 Gordon Speer, Rice	12	172	14.3

KICKOFF RETURNS/YARDS	KR	YDS	AVG
1 Don Perkins, New Mexico	15	520	34.7
2 Ronald Miller, Oregon State	15	453	30.2
3 Calvin Bird, Kentucky	14	426	30.4
4 Paul Choquette, Brown	15	354	23.6
5 Tom Gravins, Virginia	17	346	20.4
6 Terry Terrebone, Tulane	13	335	25.8
7 Walter Mince, Arizona	14	329	23.5
8 Joe Allen, Hardin-Simmons	16	325	20.3
9 Alger Pugh, Virginia Tech	12	305	25.4
10 Sandy Stephens, Minnesota	11	299	27.2

SCORING	TDS	XPT	FG	PTS
1 Pervis Atkins, New Mexico State	17	5	0	107
2 Skip Face, Stanford	11	25	3	100
2 Nolan Jones, Arizona State	11	25	3	100
2 Ger Schwedes, Syracuse	16	4	0	100
5 Abner Haynes, North Texas	14	6	0	90
5 Ed Kovac, Cincinnati	15	0	0	90
7 Larry Wilson, Utah	13	6	0	84
8 Bruce Maher, Detroit	11	8	0	74
8 Don Perkins, New Mexico	12	2	0	74
10 Bill Mathis, Clemson	11	4	0	70

KICK SCORING	XPA	XP	FG	PTS
1 Bobby Khayat, Mississippi	29	25	5	40
2 Danny Villanueva, New Mexico State	35	28	3	37
3 Edgar Beach, New Mexico	32	28	2	34
4 Durward Pennington, Georgia	28	26	2	32
5 Karl Holzwarth, Wisconsin	10	10	7	31
6 Nolan Jones, Arizona State	25	21	3	30
7 Skip Face, Stanford	20	19	3	28
7 George Fleming, Washington	21	16	4	28
9 Sam Stellatella, Penn State	23	20	2	26
9 Ed Dyas, Auburn	17	14	4	26

INTERCEPTIONS	INT	YDS
1 Bud Whitehead, Florida State	6	111
1 Bob Cyphers, Dayton	6	62
1 Bob Schloredt, Washington	6	53
1 George Fleming, Washington	6	27
1 Tony Banfield, Oklahoma State	6	12
6 Rich Lucas, Penn State	5	114
6 Alger Pugh, Virginia Tech	5	103
6 Willie Wood, Southern California	5	83
6 Terry Parks, North Texas	5	80
6 Don Johnston, Washington State	5	51
6 Russ Morris, Vanderbilt	5	40
6 Chuck Roberts, New Mexico	5	37
6 Nick Pannes, Brown	5	24
6 Ed Hino, George Washington	5	14

TEAM LEADERS

RUSHING OFFENSE	G	ATT	YDS	AVG	YPG
1 Syracuse	10	578	3136	5.4	313.6
2 North Texas	10	534	2908	5.4	290.8
3 New Mexico	10	535	2898	5.4	289.8
4 Oklahoma	10	620	2735	4.4	273.5
5 Utah	10	551	2570	4.7	257.0
6 Wyoming	10	550	2520	4.6	252.0
7 Southern California	10	583	2493	4.3	249.3
8 Mississippi	10	528	2391	4.5	239.1
9 Iowa	9	440	2151	4.9	239.0
10 Iowa State	10	502	2287	4.6	228.7

PASSING OFFENSE/YPG	G	ATT	COM	INT	PCT	YPA	TD	YPG	I%	YPC	YDS
1 Stanford	10	307	176	18	57.3	7.4	11	227.8	5.9	12.9	2278
2 Marquette	10	281	139	18	49.5	6.7	10	187.0	6.4	13.5	1870
3 San Jose State	10	268	149	19	55.6	6.9	12	185.2	7.1	12.4	1852
4 Army	9	260	133	15	51.2	6.3	10	182.3	5.8	12.3	1641
5 Boston College	9	222	111	11	50.0	7.1	10	175.3	5.0	14.2	1578
6 Cincinnati	10	241	135	6	56.0	6.6	9	158.5	2.5	11.7	1585
7 New Mexico State	10	216	114	9	52.8	7.3	18	157.3	4.2	13.8	1573
8 Hardin-Simmons	10	275	134	23	48.7	5.6	8	154.2	8.4	11.5	1542
9 Pacific	9	196	88	10	44.9	7.0	5	152.3	5.1	15.6	1371
10 Wake Forest	10	218	90	18	41.3	6.9	13	149.8	8.3	16.6	1498

TOTAL OFFENSE	G	P	YDS	AVG	YPG
1 Syracuse	10	738	4515	6.1	451.5
2 Iowa	9	632	3399	5.4	377.7
3 New Mexico State	10	618	3756	6.1	375.6
4 North Texas	10	655	3713	5.7	371.3
5 Mississippi	10	698	3686	5.3	368.6
6 Utah	10	712	3651	5.1	365.1
7 Wyoming	10	686	3577	5.2	357.7
8 New Mexico	10	639	3562	5.6	356.2
9 Stanford	10	665	3467	5.2	346.7
10 Oklahoma	10	731	3405	4.7	340.5

RUSHING DEFENSE	G	ATT	YDS	AVG	YPG
1 Syracuse	10	302	193	0.6	19.3
2 LSU	10	390	908	2.3	90.8
3 Mississippi	10	384	939	2.4	93.9
4 Southern California	10	408	981	2.4	98.1
5 TCU	10	404	1017	2.5	101.7
6 Clemson	10	391	1085	2.8	108.5
7 Pennsylvania	9	401	988	2.5	109.8
8 Wyoming	10	433	1098	2.5	109.8
9 South Carolina	10	376	1115	3.0	111.5
10 Detroit	10	383	1129	2.9	112.9

PASSING DEFENSE	G	ATT	COM	PCT	YPC	INT	I%	YDS	YPA	TD	YPG
1 Alabama	10	116	46	39.7	9.9	20	17.2	457	3.9	1	45.7
2 Montana	9	96	35	36.5	11.9	9	9.4	415	4.3	5	46.1
3 LSU	10	169	56	33.1	9.4	13	7.7	524	3.1	0	52.4
4 Mississippi	10	132	61	46.2	8.7	17	12.9	533	4.0	1	53.3
5 Iowa State	10	141	50	35.5	11.1	22	15.6	553	3.9	1	55.3
6 North Texas	10	138	49	35.5	11.9	18	13.0	581	4.2	0	58.1
7 Wake Forest	10	128	57	44.5	10.9	15	11.7	621	4.9	7	62.1
8 Kentucky	10	146	58	39.7	10.8	12	8.2	626	4.3	2	62.6
9 Auburn	10	173	62	35.8	10.3	14	8.1	636	3.7	3	63.6
10 Tennessee	10	133	62	46.6	10.8	13	9.8	668	5.0	4	66.8

TOTAL DEFENSE	G	P	YDS	AVG	YPG
1 Syracuse	10	486	962	2.0	96.2
2 LSU	10	559	1432	2.6	143.2
3 Mississippi	10	516	1472	2.9	147.2
4 Alabama	10	549	1799	3.3	179.9
5 Wyoming	10	572	1805	3.2	180.5
6 Auburn	10	565	1825	3.2	182.5
7 Southern California	10	603	1844	3.1	184.4
8 Illinois	9	533	1713	3.2	190.3
9 TCU	10	578	1945	3.4	194.5
10 North Texas	10	553	1965	3.6	196.5

SCORING OFFENSE	G	PTS	AVG
1 Syracuse	10	390	39.0
2 New Mexico State	10	332	33.2
3 Mississippi	10	329	32.9
4 North Texas	10	295	29.5
5 Wyoming	10	287	28.7
6 Clemson	10	262	26.2
7 New Mexico	10	260	26.0
8 Iowa	9	233	25.9
9 Penn State	10	255	25.5
10 Iowa State	10	248	24.8

SCORING DEFENSE	G	PTS	AVG
1 Mississippi	10	21	2.1
2 LSU	10	29	2.9
3 Alabama	10	52	5.2
3 TCU	10	52	5.2
5 Auburn	10	58	5.8
6 Syracuse	10	59	5.9
7 Wyoming	10	62	6.2
8 Washington	10	65	6.5
9 Texas	10	73	7.3
10 North Texas	10	75	7.5

1959

FINAL POLL (DEC. 7)

UP	AP	SCHOOL	FINAL RECORD
1	1	Syracuse	11-0-0
2	2	Mississippi	10-1-0
3	3	LSU	9-2-0
4	4	Texas	9-2-0
5	5	Georgia	10-1-0
6	6	Wisconsin	7-3-0
8	7	TCU	8-3-0
7	8	Washington	10-1-0
9	9	Arkansas	9-2-0
13	10	Alabama	7-2-2
11	11	Clemson	9-2-0
10	12	Penn State	9-2-0
12	13	Illinois	5-3-1
13	14	Southern California	8-2-0
17	15	Oklahoma	7-3-0
	16	Wyoming	9-1-0
18	17	Notre Dame	5-5-0
20	18	Missouri	6-5-0
20	19	Florida	5-4-1
19	20	Pittsburgh	6-4-0
15		Auburn	7-3-0
16		Michigan State	5-4-0

CONSENSUS ALL-AMERICANS

POS	NAME	SCHOOL
B	Richie Lucas	Penn State
B	Billy Cannon	LSU
B	Charlie Flowers	Mississippi
B	Ron Burton	Northwestern
E	Bill Carpenter	Army
E	Monty Stickles	Notre Dame
T	Dan Lanphear	Wisconsin
T	Don Floyd	TCU
G	Roger Davis	Syracuse
G	Bill Burrell	Illinois
C	Maxie Baughan	Georgia Tech

OTHERS RECEIVING FIRST-TEAM HONORS

B	Dean Look	Michigan State
B	Don Meredith	SMU
B	Dwight Nichols	Iowa State
B	Jack Spikes	TCU
B	Bob Schloredt	Washington
B	Jim Mooty	Arkansas
E	Carroll Dale	Virginia Tech
E	Marlin McKeever	Southern California
E	Don Norton	Iowa
E	Chris Burford	Stanford
E	Fred Mautino	Syracuse
T	Mike McGee	Duke
T	Ken Rice	Auburn
T	Robert Yates	Syracuse
G	Maurice Doke	Texas
G	Pat Dye	Georgia
G	Marvin Terrell	Mississippi
G	Zeke Smith	Auburn
C	Jim Andreotti	Northwestern
C	E.J. Holub	Texas Tech

HEISMAN TROPHY VOTING

	PLAYER	POS	SCHOOL	TOTAL
1	Billy Cannon	HB	LSU	1929
2	Richie Lucas	QB	Penn State	613
3	Don Meredith	QB	SMU	286
4	Bill Burrell	G	Illinois	196
5	Charlie Flowers	FB	Mississippi	193
6	Dean Look	HB	Michigan State	176
7	Dale Hackbart	QB	Wisconsin	134
8	Dwight Nichols	RB	Iowa State	126
9	Monty Stickles	E	Notre Dame	126
10	Ron Burton	RB	Northwestern	122

AWARD WINNERS

PLAYER	AWARD
Richie Lucas, QB, Penn State	Maxwell
Mike McGee, T, Duke	Outland

BOWL GAMES

DATE	GAME	SCORE
D19	Bluebonnet	Clemson 23, TCU 7
D19	Liberty	Penn State 7, Alabama 0
D 31	Sun	New Mexico State 28, North Texas 8
J1	Tangerine	Middle Tennessee 21, Presbyterian 12
J1	Orange	Georgia 14, Missouri 0
J1	Sugar	Mississippi 21, LSU 0
J1	Cotton	Syracuse 23, Texas 14
J1	Rose	Washington 44, Wisconsin 8
J2	Gator	Arkansas 14, Georgia Tech 7

SEC STANDINGS

	CONFERENCE			OVERALL		
	W	L	T	W	L	T
Georgia	7	0	0	10	1	0
Mississippi	5	1	0	10	1	0
LSU	5	1	0	9	2	0
Alabama	4	1	2	7	2	2
Auburn	4	3	0	7	3	0
Vanderbilt	3	2	2	5	3	2
Georgia Tech	3	3	0	6	5	0
Tennessee	3	4	1	5	4	1
Florida	2	4	0	5	4	1
Kentucky	1	6	0	4	6	0
Tulane	0	5	1	3	6	1
Mississippi State	0	7	0	2	7	0

1960 NCAA Major College Statistical Leaders

Individual Leaders

PASSING/COMPLETIONS	G	ATT	COM	PCT	INT	I%	YDS	YPA	TD	TD%	COM.PG
1 Harold Stephens, Hardin-Simmons	10	256	145	56.6	14	5.5	1254	4.9	3	1.2	14.5
2 Norm Snead, Wake Forest	10	259	123	47.4	14	5.4	1676	6.5	10	3.9	12.3
3 Melvin Melin, Washington State	10	221	119	53.8	13	5.9	1638	7.4	11	5.0	11.9
4 Charley Johnson, New Mexico State	10	199	109	54.8	6	3.0	1511	7.6	13	6.5	10.9
5 Fran Tarkenton, Georgia	**10**	**185**	**108**	**58.4**	**12**	**6.5**	**1189**	**6.4**	**7**	**3.8**	**10.8**
5 Rich Mayo, Air Force	10	238	108	45.4	18	7.6	1168	4.9	7	2.9	10.8
7 Roman Gabriel, North Carolina St.	10	186	105	56.5	7	3.8	1176	6.3	8	4.3	10.5
8 Ron Miller, Wisconsin	9	188	97	51.6	16	8.5	1351	7.2	8	4.3	10.8
9 Dick Norman, Stanford	10	201	95	47.3	13	6.5	1057	5.3	4	2.0	9.5
10 John Furman, Texas-El Paso	10	192	94	49.0	7	3.7	1094	5.7	4	2.1	9.4

ALL-PURPOSE YARDS	G	RUSH	REC	INT	PR	KR	YDS	YPG
1 Pervis Atkins, New Mexico State	10	611	468	23	218	293	1613	161.3

RUSHING/YARDS	G	ATT	YDS	AVG	YPG
1 Bob Gaiters, New Mexico State	10	197	1338	6.8	133.8
2 Tom Larscheid, Utah State	10	124	1044	8.4	104.4
3 Ernie Davis, Syracuse	9	112	877	7.8	97.4
4 Bob Ferguson, Ohio State	9	160	853	5.3	94.8
5 Dave Hoppmann, Iowa State	10	161	844	5.2	84.4
6 Joe Bellino, Navy	10	168	834	5.0	83.4
7 Bill Kilmer, UCLA	10	163	803	4.9	80.3
8 Hugh Scott, Princeton	9	140	760	5.4	84.4
9 Robert Thompson, Arizona	10	92	732	8.0	73.2
10 Al Rozycki, Dartmouth	9	169	725	4.3	80.6

RUSHING/YARDS PER CARRY	G	ATT	YDS	YPC
1 Pervis Atkins, New Mexico State	10	65	611	9.4
2 Tom Larscheid, Utah State	10	124	1044	8.4
3 Robert Thompson, Arizona	10	92	732	8.0
4 Ernie Davis, Syracuse	9	112	877	7.8
5 Larry Ferguson, Iowa	9	90	665	7.4
6 Ken Bolin, Houston	10	75	542	7.2
7 Norris Stevenson, Missouri	10	85	610	7.2
8 Bob Gaiters, New Mexico State	10	197	1338	6.8
9 Mike Quinlan, Air Force	10	93	585	6.3
10 Bobby Santiago, New Mexico	10	98	591	6.0

Based on top 40 rushers

RECEIVING/RECEPTIONS	G	REC	YDS	TD	YPR	YPG	RPG
1 Hugh Campbell, Washington State	10	66	881	10	13.3	88.1	6.6
2 Claude Moorman, Duke	10	46	431	2	9.4	43.1	4.6
3 Del Williams, Texas-El-Paso	10	36	414	2	11.5	41.4	3.6
4 Bob Coolbaugh, Richmond	10	35	380	2	10.9	38.0	3.5
5 Joe Kehoe, Virginia	10	34	378	2	11.1	37.8	3.4
6 Reg Carolan, Idaho	10	33	498	3	15.1	49.8	3.3
7 Fred Brown, Georgia	**10**	**31**	**275**	**3**	**8.9**	**27.5**	**3.1**
8 Tom Hutchinson, Kentucky	**10**	**30**	**455**	**4**	**15.2**	**45.5**	**3.0**
8 E.A. Sims, New Mexico State	10	30	415	2	13.8	41.5	3.0
8 Bobby Crespino, Mississippi	**10**	**30**	**408**	**4**	**13.6**	**40.8**	**3.0**
8 Gary Collins, Maryland	10	30	404	4	13.5	40.4	3.0

PUNTING	PUNT	YDS	AVG
1 Dick Fitzsimmons, Denver	25	1106	44.2
2 Bobby Walden, Georgia	**38**	**1657**	**43.6**
3 Kent Rockholt, San Jose State	33	1412	42.8
4 Willie Vasquez, Texas-El Paso	31	1318	42.5
5 Bill Kilmer, UCLA	35	1481	42.3
6 Jerry Stovall, LSU	**64**	**2694**	**42.1**
7 Jim Bakken, Wisconsin	36	1508	41.9
8 George Canale, Tennessee	**26**	**1084**	**41.7**
9 Tom Gilburg, Syracuse	28	1159	41.4
10 Laurien Stapp, Alabama	**42**	**1726**	**41.1**

PUNT RETURNS/YARDS	PR	YDS	AVG
1 Lance Alworth, Arkansas	18	307	17.1
2 Pat Fischer, Nebraska	13	276	21.2
3 Glen Adams, Army	16	270	16.9
4 Arny Byrd, Rutgers	14	249	17.8
5 Donnie Smith, Missouri	10	230	23.0
6 Ossie McCarty, Arizona State	16	223	13.9
6 Earl Stoudt, Richmond	18	223	12.4
8 Bake Turner, Texas Tech	25	221	8.8
9 John Sullivan, Princeton	9	219	24.3
10 Pervis Atkins, New Mexico State	10	218	21.8

KICKOFF RETURNS/YARDS	KR	YDS	AVG
1 Bruce Samples, Brigham Young	23	577	25.1
2 Tom Hennessey, Holy Cross	12	401	33.4
3 Herman Urenda, Pacific	15	389	25.9
4 Skip Face, Stanford	19	387	20.4
5 Dennis Condie, Maryland	10	352	35.2
6 Jack Richardson, Kansas State	12	345	28.8
7 Calvin Bird, Kentucky	**14**	**344**	**24.6**
8 Tom Watkins, Iowa State	14	332	23.7
9 Lance Alworth, Arkansas	14	328	23.4
9 Nicholas Russo, Villanova	15	328	21.9

SCORING	TDS	XPT	FG	PTS
1 Bob Gaiters, New Mexico State	23	7	0	145
2 Joe Bellino, Navy	18	2	0	110
3 Nolan Jones, Arizona State	8	27	6	93
4 Tom Larscheid, Utah State	15	2	0	92
5 Pervis Atkins, New Mexico State	12	8	0	80
6 Bob Ferguson, Ohio State	13	0	0	78
6 Tommy Mason, Tulane	**13**	**0**	**0**	**78**
6 Donnie Smith, Missouri	13	0	0	78
9 Hugh Campbell, Washington State	11	10	0	76
9 Joe Hernandez, Arizona	12	4	0	76

KICK SCORING	XPA	XP	FG	PTS
1 Ed Dyas, Auburn	**13**	**12**	**13**	**51**
2 Nolan Jones, Arizona State	25	25	6	43
3 Durward Pennington, Georgia	**18**	**16**	**8**	**40**
4 Edgar Beach, New Mexico	29	27	4	39
4 Bill Tobin, Missouri	33	30	3	39
6 John Suder, Kansas	30	27	3	36
7 George Fleming, Washington	25	23	4	35
7 Jack Carter, Memphis	36	29	2	35
9 Tommy Wells, Georgia Tech	**13**	**10**	**8**	**34**
10 Lon Armstrong, Clemson	25	24	3	33

INTERCEPTIONS	INT	YDS
1 Bob O'Billovich, Montana	7	71
1 Ray Timmons, Miami (Fla.)	7	46
3 Bryant Harvard, Auburn	**6**	**113**
3 Thomas O'Rourke, Villanova	6	91
3 Mickey Bruce, Oregon	6	68
3 Grimm Mason, Oregon State	6	41
3 Del Williams, Texas-El Paso	6	39
3 Bobby Bethune, Mississippi State	**6**	**30**
9 Bill Munsey, Minnesota*	5	130
9 James Boylan, Washington State*	5	82

*Six tied with five; these had the most yards

Team Leaders

RUSHING OFFENSE	G	ATT	YDS	AVG	YPG
1 Utah State	10	553	3120	5.6	312.0
2 Memphis	10	484	2782	5.7	278.2
3 New Mexico State	10	452	2639	5.8	263.9
4 Syracuse	9	451	2309	5.1	256.6
5 Wyoming	10	595	2553	4.3	255.3
6 Iowa	9	439	2284	5.2	253.8
7 Missouri	10	571	2500	4.4	250.0
8 Arizona State	10	548	2489	4.5	248.9
9 Southern Miss	10	532	2445	4.6	244.5
10 Princeton	9	464	2132	4.6	236.9

PASSING OFFENSE	G	ATT	COM	INT	PCT	YDS	YPA	TD	I%	YPC	YPG
1 Washington State	10	247	132	16	53.4	1855	7.5	14	6.5	14.1	185.5
2 Wisconsin	9	229	113	17	49.3	1526	6.7	8	7.4	13.5	169.6
3 Wake Forest	10	265	125	15	47.2	1692	6.4	10	5.7	13.5	169.2
4 Kentucky	**10**	**220**	**114**	**14**	**51.8**	**1633**	**7.4**	**13**	**6.4**	**14.3**	**163.3**
5 Baylor	10	205	109	14	53.2	1618	7.9	9	6.8	14.8	161.8
6 New Mexico State	10	218	113	8	51.8	1557	7.1	14	3.7	13.8	155.7
7 Detroit	9	201	96	10	47.8	1386	6.9	11	5.0	14.4	154.0
8 San Jose State	9	213	105	7	49.3	1382	6.5	8	3.3	13.2	153.6
9 Denver	10	230	107	18	46.5	1489	6.5	9	7.8	13.9	148.9
10 VMI	10	214	103	14	48.1	1424	6.7	8	6.5	13.8	142.4

TOTAL OFFENSE	G	P	YDS	AVG	YPG
1 New Mexico State	10	670	4196	6.3	419.6
2 Memphis	10	612	3744	6.1	374.4
2 Utah State	10	638	3744	5.9	374.4
4 Mississippi	**10**	**646**	**3624**	**5.6**	**362.4**
5 Southern Miss	10	670	3467	5.2	346.7
6 Wyoming	10	706	3333	4.7	333.3
7 Arizona State	10	683	3331	4.9	333.1
8 Oregon	10	650	3311	5.1	331.1
9 Oregon State	10	613	3306	5.4	330.6
10 Washington State	10	645	3295	5.1	329.5

RUSHING DEFENSE	G	ATT	YDS	AVG	YPG
1 Wyoming	10	345	824	2.4	82.4
2 Utah State	10	369	847	2.3	84.7
3 Alabama	**10**	**378**	**891**	**2.4**	**89.1**
4 Mississippi	**10**	**386**	**892**	**2.3**	**89.2**
5 Yale	9	369	945	2.6	105.0
6 Memphis	10	386	1080	2.8	108.0
7 Southern Miss	10	373	1082	2.9	108.2
8 Missouri	10	377	1092	2.9	109.2
9 Florida	**10**	**397**	**1105**	**2.8**	**110.5**
10 Washington	10	363	1117	3.1	111.7

PASSING DEFENSE	G	ATT	COM	PCT	YPC	INT	I%	YDS	YPA	TD	YPG
1 Iowa State	10	93	29	31.2	10.4	7	7.5	302	3.2	2	30.2
2 Dayton	10	96	32	33.3	14.2	10	10.4	454	4.7	4	45.4
3 Kansas	10	113	43	38.1	11.2	12	10.6	483	4.3	4	48.3
4 Kentucky	**10**	**124**	**47**	**37.9**	**11.1**	**17**	**13.7**	**522**	**4.2**	**3**	**52.2**
5 Tennessee	**10**	**130**	**58**	**44.6**	**9.3**	**13**	**10.0**	**538**	**4.1**	**2**	**53.8**
6 Colorado	10	119	46	38.7	12.1	11	9.2	557	4.7	1	55.7
7 Citadel	10	126	54	42.9	10.6	16	12.7	570	4.5	4	57.0
8 Syracuse	9	129	47	36.4	11.0	11	8.5	516	4.0	1	57.3
9 Auburn	**10**	**132**	**46**	**34.8**	**12.8**	**21**	**15.9**	**590**	**4.5**	**3**	**59.0**
10 Kansas State	10	105	53	50.5	11.7	7	6.7	619	5.9	1	61.9

TOTAL DEFENSE	G	P	YDS	AVG	YPG
1 Wyoming	10	477	1496	3.1	149.6
2 Alabama	**10**	**536**	**1576**	**2.9**	**157.6**
3 Mississippi	**10**	**542**	**1686**	**3.1**	**168.6**
4 Syracuse	9	520	1559	3.0	173.2
5 Auburn	**10**	**526**	**1741**	**3.3**	**174.1**
6 Kentucky	**10**	**545**	**1831**	**3.4**	**183.1**
7 Kansas	10	555	1872	3.4	187.2
8 Army	10	530	1916	3.6	191.6
9 Missouri	10	563	1493	2.7	194.3
10 Utah State	10	566	1945	3.4	194.5

SCORING OFFENSE	G	PTS	AVG
1 New Mexico State	10	374	37.4
2 Memphis	10	303	30.3
3 Yale	9	253	28.1
4 Missouri	10	274	27.4
5 Mississippi	**10**	**266**	**26.6**
6 Utah State	10	261	26.1
7 Iowa	9	234	26.0
8 Princeton	9	232	25.8
9 Washington	10	255	25.5
10 Rutgers	9	225	25.0

SCORING DEFENSE	G	PTS	AVG
1 LSU	**10**	**50**	**5.0**
2 Alabama	**10**	**53**	**5.3**
3 Rice	10	58	5.8
4 Mississippi	**10**	**64**	**6.4**
5 Utah State	10	65	6.5
6 Wyoming	10	71	7.1
7 Dartmouth	9	66	7.3
8 Florida	**10**	**74**	**7.4**
9 Texas	10	75	7.5
10 Rutgers	9	69	7.7

1960

FINAL POLL (NOV. 28)

UP	AP	SCHOOL	FINAL RECORD
1	1	Minnesota	8-2-0
3	2	**Mississippi**	**10-0-1**
2	3	Iowa	8-1-0
6	4	Navy	9-2-0
4	5	Missouri	10-1-0
5	6	Washington	10-1-0
7	7	Arkansas	8-3-0
8	8	Ohio State	7-2-0
9	9	**Alabama**	**8-1-2**
11	10	Duke	8-3-0
9	11	Kansas	7-2-1
12	12	Baylor	8-3-0
14	13	**Auburn**	**8-2-0**
18	14	Yale	9-0-0
13	15	Michigan State	6-2-1
	16	Penn State	7-3-0
18	17	New Mexico State	11-0-0
16	18	**Florida**	**9-2-0**
15	19	Purdue	4-4-1
	19	Syracuse	7-2-0
17		Texas	7-3-1
18		**Tennessee**	**6-2-2**

CONSENSUS ALL-AMERICANS

POS	NAME	SCHOOL
B	**Jake Gibbs**	**Mississippi**
B	Joe Bellino	Navy
B	Bob Ferguson	Ohio State
B	Ernie Davis	Syracuse
E	Mike Ditka	Pittsburgh
E	Danny LaRose	Missouri
T	Bob Lilly	TCU
T	**Ken Rice**	**Auburn**
G	Tom Brown	Minnesota
G	Joe Romig	Colorado
C	E.J. Holub	Texas Tech

OTHERS RECEIVING FIRST-TEAM HONORS

B	**Ed Dyas**	**Auburn**
B	Larry Ferguson	Iowa
B	Roman Gabriel	North Carolina St.
B	John Hadl	Kansas
B	Bill Kilmer	UCLA
B	Pervis Atkins	New Mexico State
E	Bill Miller	Miami
E	Claude Moorman	Duke
T	Jerry Beabout	Purdue
T	Merlin Olsen	Utah State
G	Wayne Harris	Arkansas
G	Mark Manders	Iowa
G	Ben Balme	Yale
C	Roy McKasson	Washington

NE named Holub as a G

HEISMAN TROPHY VOTING

	PLAYER	POS	SCHOOL	TOTAL
1	Joe Bellino	HB	Navy	1303
2	Tom Brown	G	Minnesota	731
3	**Jake Gibbs**	**QB**	**Mississippi**	**453**
4	**Ed Dyas**	**FB**	**Auburn**	**319**
5	Bill Kilmer	HB	UCLA	280
6	Mike Ditka	E	Pittsburgh	223
7	Tom Matte	QB	Ohio State	165
8	Danny LaRose	E	Missouri	136
9	Pervis Atkins	HB	New Mexico State	124
10	E.J. Holub	C	Texas Tech	117

AWARD WINNERS

PLAYER	AWARD
Joe Bellino, HB, Navy	Maxwell
Tom Brown, G, Minnesota	Outland

BOWL GAMES

DATE	GAME	SCORE
D17	**Bluebonnet**	**Alabama 3, Texas 3**
D17	Liberty	Penn State 41, Oregon 12
D30	Tangerine	Citadel 27, Tennessee Tech 0
D31	**Gator**	**Florida 13, Baylor 12**
D31	Sun	New Mexico State 20, Utah State 13
J2	Cotton	Duke 7, Arkansas 6
J2	**Sugar**	**Mississippi 14, Rice 6**
J2	Orange	Missouri 21, Navy 14
J2	Rose	Washington 17, Minnesota 7

SEC STANDINGS

	CONFERENCE			OVERALL		
	W	L	T	W	L	T
Mississippi	5	0	1	10	0	1
Florida	5	1	0	9	2	0
Alabama	5	1	1	8	1	2
Auburn	5	2	0	8	2	0
Georgia	4	3	0	6	4	0
Tennessee	3	2	2	6	2	2
Georgia Tech	4	4	0	5	5	0
LSU	2	3	1	5	4	1
Kentucky	2	4	1	5	4	1
Tulane	1	4	1	3	6	1
Mississippi State	0	5	1	2	6	1
Vanderbilt	0	7	0	3	7	0

1961 NCAA MAJOR COLLEGE STATISTICAL LEADERS

INDIVIDUAL LEADERS

PASSING/COMPLETIONS	G	ATT	COM	PCT	INT	I%	YDS	YPA	TD	TD%	COM.PG
1 Chon Gallegos, San Jose State	10	197	117	59.4	13	6.6	1480	7.5	14	7.1	11.7
2 Ron Miller, Wisconsin	9	198	104	52.5	11	5.6	1487	7.5	11	5.6	11.6
3 Roman Gabriel, North Carolina St.	10	186	99	53.2	6	3.2	937	5.0	8	4.3	9.9
4 Ron Klemick, Navy	10	183	86	47.0	13	7.1	1045	5.7	6	3.3	8.6
5 Billy Canty, Furman	10	168	84	50.0	12	7.1	884	5.3	8	4.8	8.4
5 John Furman, Texas-El Paso	10	180	84	46.7	10	5.6	1026	5.7	10	5.6	8.4
7 Matthew Szykowny, Iowa	9	139	79	56.8	15	10.8	1078	7.8	7	5.0	8.8
7 Eddie Wilson, Arizona	10	154	79	51.3	7	4.6	1294	8.4	10	6.5	7.9
9 Pat McCarthy, Holy Cross	10	165	76	46.1	11	6.7	1081	6.6	11	6.7	7.6
10 Pat Trammell, Alabama	10	133	75	56.4	2	1.5	1035	7.8	8	6.0	7.5

ALL-PURPOSE YARDS	G	RUSH	REC	PR	KR	YDS	YPG
1 Jim Pilot, New Mexico State	10	1278	20	161	147	1606	160.6

RUSHING/YARDS	G	ATT	YDS	AVG	YPG
1 Jim Pilot, New Mexico State	10	191	1278	6.7	127.8
2 Pete Pedro, West Texas State	10	137	976	7.1	97.6
3 Bob Ferguson, Ohio State	9	202	938	4.6	104.2
4 Dave Hoppmann, Iowa State	10	229	920	4.0	92.0
5 James Saxton, Texas	10	107	846	7.9	84.6
6 Ernie Davis, Syracuse	10	150	823	5.5	82.3
7 Tom Larscheid, Utah State	10	121	773	6.4	77.3
8 Tom Campbell, Furman	10	157	767	4.9	76.7
9 Robert Thompson, Arizona	10	103	752	7.3	75.2
10 Earl Stoudt, Richmond	10	162	704	4.4	70.4

RUSHING/YARDS PER CARRY	G	ATT	YDS	YPC
1 James Saxton, Texas	10	107	846	7.9
2 Robert Thompson, Arizona	10	103	752	7.3
3 Pete Pedro, West Texas State	10	137	976	7.1
4 Angelo Dabiero, Notre Dame	10	92	637	6.9
5 Jim Pilot, New Mexico State	10	191	1278	6.7
6 Tom Larscheid, Utah State	10	121	773	6.4
7 Billy Ray Adams, Mississippi	10	91	574	6.3
8 Alan White, Wake Forest	10	93	586	6.3
9 Mike McClellan, Oklahoma	10	82	508	6.2
10 Mike Haffner, UCLA	10	117	696	5.9
Based on top 42 rushers				

RECEIVING/RECEPTIONS	G	REC	YDS	TD	YPR	YPG	RPG
1 Hugh Campbell, Washington State	10	53	723	5	13.6	72.3	5.3
2 Pat Richter, Wisconsin	9	47	817	8	17.4	90.8	5.2
3 Bill Miller, Miami (Fla.)	10	43	640	2	14.9	64.0	4.3
4 Al Snyder, Holy Cross	10	38	558	5	14.7	55.8	3.8
5 Oscar Donahue, San Jose State	10	35	527	5	15.1	52.7	3.5
6 Larry Vargo, Detroit	9	32	601	8	18.8	66.8	3.6
7 Tom Hutchinson, Kentucky	10	32	543	4	17.0	54.3	3.2
8 Buddy Iles, TCU	10	31	479	2	15.5	47.9	3.1
9 Gary Collins, Maryland	10	30	428	4	14.3	42.8	3.0
10 Royce Cassell, New Mexico State	10	29	519	7	17.9	51.9	2.9
10 Joe Borich, Utah	10	29	486	5	16.8	48.6	2.9

PUNTING	PUNT	YDS	AVG
1 Joe Zuger, Arizona State	31	1305	42.1
2 Henry Lesesne, Vanderbilt	41	1702	41.5
3 Russ Warren, Columbia	25	1028	41.1
4 Jim Bakken, Wisconsin	39	1583	40.6
5 Clyde Marsh, Citadel	46	1863	40.5
5 Bill Wright, Brigham Young	46	1863	40.5
7 Terry Isaacson, Air Force	39	1572	40.3
8 Dick Fitzsimmons, New Mexico	39	1568	40.2
9 Eddie Werntz, Clemson	56	2251	40.2
10 Bill Ruby, Wake Forest	55	2211	40.2

PUNT RETURNS/YARDS	PR	YDS	AVG
1 Lance Alworth, Arkansas	28	336	12.0
2 Jay Wilkinson, Duke	22	328	14.9
3 Tom Larscheid, Utah State	12	281	23.4
3 Darrell Cox, Kentucky	21	281	13.4
5 Fred Colvard, West Virginia	12	196	16.3
6 Tom Brown, Maryland	8	194	24.3
7 John Hadl, Kansas	17	191	11.2
7 W.E. Richardson, Alabama	21	191	9.1
9 Larry Cox, Xavier	13	183	14.1
10 Al Snyder, Holy Cross	10	182	18.2

KICKOFF RETURNS/YARDS	KR	YDS	AVG
1 Dick Mooney, Idaho	23	494	21.5
2 Paul Allen, Brigham Young	12	481	40.1
3 Ken Bolin, Houston	19	437	23.0
4 Terry Isaacson, Air Force	20	397	19.9
5 Jack Morris, South Carolina	13	375	28.8
6 Mack Burton, San Jose State	14	368	26.3
6 Jerry Logan, West Texas State	15	368	24.5
8 Paul Costa, Notre Dame	16	359	22.4
9 Rudy Carvajal, California	20	358	17.9
10 Larry McIntire, Tulane	15	348	23.2

SCORING	TDS	XPT	FG	PTS
1 Jim Pilot, New Mexico State	21	12	0	138
2 Pete Pedro, West Texas State	22	0	0	132
3 Tom Larscheid, Utah State	15	6	0	96
4 Ernie Davis, Syracuse	15	4	0	94
4 Wendell Harris, LSU	8	28	6	94
6 Bob Smith, UCLA	10	16	3	85
7 Robert Thompson, Arizona	13	4	0	82
8 Nolan Jones, Arizona State	8	20	3	77
9 Butch Blume, Rice	6	20	6	74
10 Sam Mudie, Rutgers	10	10	0	70

KICK SCORING	XPA	XP	FG	PTS
1 Greg Mather, Navy	23	22	11	55
2 Tim Davis, Alabama	27	22	9	49
3 Wendell Harris, LSU	29	26	6	44
4 Pete Smolanovich, New Mexico State	39	38	1	41
4 Jack Carter, Memphis	43	38	1	41
6 Carl Choate, Baylor	23	23	5	38
6 Dick Heydt, Army	28	26	4	38
6 Butch Blume, Rice	22	20	6	38
9 Jim Turner, Utah State	36	30	2	36
10 Dick Van Raaphorst, Ohio State	27	23	4	35
10 Don Jonas, Penn State	22	17	6	35

INTERCEPTIONS	INT	YDS
1 Joe Zuger, Arizona State	10	121
2 Tom Brown, Maryland	8	95
3 Junior Edge, North Carolina	7	104
4 Sam Mudie, Rutgers	6	167
4 John Maisel, Oklahoma State	6	141
4 Tony Carmignani, Furman	6	123
4 Bob McDonough, Air Force	6	95
8 Stinson Jones, VMI *	5	127
8 Jackie Farland, Boston U. *	5	92
8 Angelo Dabiero, Notre Dame *	5	78
8 John Snider, Syracuse *	5	59
*Ten tied with five; these had the most yards		

TEAM LEADERS

RUSHING OFFENSE	G	ATT	YDS	AVG	YPG
1 New Mexico State	10	489	2991	6.1	299.1
2 Texas	10	552	2858	5.2	285.8
3 Utah State	10	534	2818	5.3	281.8
4 Ohio State	9	522	2447	4.7	271.9
5 West Texas State	10	461	2475	5.4	247.5
6 Wyoming	9	535	2205	4.1	245.0
7 Michigan State	9	463	2135	4.6	237.2
8 Bowling Green	9	519	2132	4.1	236.9
9 Mississippi	10	472	2360	5.0	236.0
10 Memphis	10	435	2341	5.4	234.1

PASSING OFFENSE	G	ATT	COM	INT	PCT	YDS	YPA	TD	I%	YPC	YPG
1 Wisconsin	9	226	117	12	51.8	1696	7.5	13	5.3	14.5	188.4
2 Mississippi	10	202	109	8	54.0	1827	9.0	19	4.0	16.8	182.7
3 Detroit	9	245	103	20	42.0	1639	6.7	13	8.2	15.9	182.1
4 Holy Cross	10	242	108	14	44.6	1625	6.7	13	5.8	15.0	162.5
5 Washington State	10	231	117	17	50.6	1561	6.8	10	7.4	13.3	156.1
6 San Jose State	10	223	127	15	57.0	1561	7.0	15	6.7	12.3	156.1
7 Navy	10	244	110	20	45.1	1545	6.3	8	8.2	14.0	154.5
8 Iowa	9	172	94	17	54.7	1319	7.7	9	9.9	14.0	146.6
9 Maryland	10	215	115	17	53.5	1464	6.8	12	7.9	12.7	146.4
10 Arizona	10	180	90	8	50.0	1456	8.1	12	4.4	16.2	145.6

TOTAL OFFENSE	G	P	YDS	AVG	YPG
1 Mississippi	10	674	4187	6.2	418.7
2 New Mexico State	10	631	4009	6.4	400.9
3 Utah State	10	669	3911	5.8	391.1
4 Texas	10	700	3831	5.5	383.1
5 Arizona	10	588	3722	6.3	372.2
6 Penn State	10	706	3691	5.2	369.1
7 Memphis	10	610	3690	6.0	369.0
8 Ohio State	9	612	3142	5.1	349.1
9 Arizona State	10	658	3353	5.1	335.3
10 West Texas State	10	575	3290	5.7	329.0

RUSHING DEFENSE	G	ATT	YDS	AVG	YPG
1 Utah State	10	325	508	1.6	50.8
2 Alabama	10	321	550	1.7	55.0
3 Villanova	9	290	640	2.2	71.1
4 LSU	10	386	794	2.1	79.4
5 Mississippi	10	378	804	2.1	80.4
6 Minnesota	9	364	759	2.1	84.3
7 Bowling Green	9	317	780	2.5	86.7
8 Wyoming	9	319	803	2.5	89.2
9 Texas	10	376	902	2.4	90.2
10 Georgia Tech	10	365	949	2.6	94.9

PASSING DEFENSE	G	ATT	COM	PCT	YPC	INT	I%	YDS	YPA	TD	YPG
1 Pennsylvania	9	124	44	35.5	11.6	14	11.3	512	4.1	4	56.9
2 Yale	9	111	48	43.2	10.9	11	9.9	523	4.7	5	58.1
3 Arkansas	10	121	57	47.1	11.0	10	8.3	629	5.2	5	62.9
4 Mississippi	10	149	58	38.9	11.2	13	8.7	649	4.4	1	64.9
5 Dartmouth	9	148	44	40.0	13.4	12	10.9	591	5.4	4	65.7
6 Columbia	9	124	42	33.9	14.1	14	11.3	592	4.8	6	65.8
7 Southern California	10	111	50	45.0	13.3	10	9.0	666	6.0	6	66.6
8 Brown	9	90	44	48.9	15.0	9	10.0	600	6.7	9	66.7
9 Oregon	10	112	50	44.6	13.4	8	7.1	672	6.0	1	67.2
10 Kansas State	10	109	42	38.5	16.4	10	9.2	687	6.3	6	68.7

TOTAL DEFENSE	G	P	YDS	AVG	YPG
1 Alabama	10	524	1326	2.5	132.6
2 Utah State	10	512	1393	2.7	139.3
3 Mississippi	10	527	1453	2.8	145.3
4 Bowling Green	9	460	1456	3.2	161.8
5 Wyoming	9	438	1511	3.4	167.9
6 LSU	10	564	1703	3.0	170.3
7 Villanova	9	470	1559	3.3	173.2
8 Texas	10	577	1761	3.1	176.1
9 Missouri	10	560	1769	3.2	176.9
10 Arkansas	10	548	1774	3.2	177.4

SCORING OFFENSE	G	PTS	AVG
1 Utah State	10	387	38.7
2 New Mexico State	10	341	34.1
3 Memphis	10	332	33.2
4 Mississippi	10	326	32.6
5 West Texas State	10	309	30.9
6 Texas	10	291	29.1
7 Arizona	10	288	28.8
7 Arizona State	10	287	28.7
8 Alabama	10	287	28.7
10 Rutgers	9	246	27.3

SCORING DEFENSE	G	PTS	AVG
1 Alabama	10	22	2.2
2 Mississippi	10	40	4.0
3 Bowling Green	9	42	4.7
4 LSU	10	50	5.0
4 Georgia Tech	10	50	5.0
6 Michigan State	9	50	5.6
7 Missouri	10	57	5.7
8 Texas	10	59	5.9
9 Miami (Fla.)	10	70	7.0
10 Memphis	10	75	7.5

1961

FINAL POLL (DEC. 4)

UP	AP	SCHOOL	FINAL RECORD
1	1	**Alabama**	**11-0-0**
2	2	Ohio State	8-0-1
4	3	Texas	10-1-0
3	4	**LSU**	**10-1-0**
5	5	**Mississippi**	**9-2-0**
6	6	Minnesota	8-2-0
7	7	Colorado	9-2-0
9	8	Michigan State	7-2-0
8	9	Arkansas	8-3-0
10	10	Utah State	9-1-1
11	11	Missouri	7-2-1
11	12	Purdue	6-3-0
13	13	**Georgia Tech**	**7-4-0**
16	14	Syracuse	8-3-0
	15	Rutgers	9-0-0
	16	UCLA	7-4-0
	17	Arizona	8-1-1
19	17	Penn State	8-3-0
	17	Rice	7-4-0
14	20	Duke	7-3-0
15		Kansas	7-3-1
17		Wyoming	6-1-2
18		Wisconsin	6-3-0
19		Penn State	8-3-0

CONSENSUS ALL-AMERICANS

POS	NAME	SCHOOL
B	Ernie Davis	Syracuse
B	Bob Ferguson	Ohio State
B	Jimmy Saxton	Texas
B	Sandy Stephens	Minnesota
E	Gary Collins	Maryland
E	Bill Miller	Miami (Fla.)
T	**Billy Neighbors**	**Alabama**
T	Merlin Olsen	Utah State
G	**Roy Winston**	**LSU**
G	Joe Romig	Colorado
C	Alex Kroll	Rutgers

OTHERS RECEIVING FIRST-TEAM HONORS

B	**Billy Ray Adams**	**Mississippi**
B	Lance Alworth	Arkansas
B	Roman Gabriel	North Carolina St.
B	John Hadl	Kansas
E	Jerry Hillebrand	Colorado
E	Greg Mather	Navy
E	Bob Mitinger	Penn State
E	Pat Richter	Wisconsin
T	Bobby Bell	Minnesota
T	Ed Blaine	Missouri
T	Don Talbert	Texas
G	Dave Behrman	Michigan State
C	Ron Hull	UCLA
C	Bill Van Buren	Iowa

FW named Neighbors as a G

HEISMAN TROPHY VOTING

	PLAYER	POS	SCHOOL	TOTAL
1	Ernie Davis	HB	Syracuse	824
2	Bob Ferguson	FB	Ohio State	771
3	Jimmy Saxton	RB	Texas	551
4	Sandy Stephens	QB	Minnesota	543
5	**Pat Trammel**	**QB**	**Alabama**	**362**
6	Joe Romig	G	Colorado	279
7	John Hadl	QB	Kansas	172
8	Gary Collins	TE	Maryland	167
9	Roman Gabriel	QB	North Carolina St.	155
10	Merlin Olsen	DT	Utah State	93

AWARD WINNERS

PLAYER	AWARD
Bob Ferguson, FB, Ohio State	Maxwell
Merlin Olsen, T, Utah State	Outland

BOWL GAMES

DATE	GAME	SCORE
N23	Mercy	Fresno State 36, Bowling Green 6
D9	Gotham	Baylor 24, Utah State 9
D9	Aviation	New Mexico 28, Western Michigan 12
D16	Bluebonnet	Kansas 33, Rice 7
D16	Liberty	Syracuse 15, Miami (Fla.) 14
D29	Tangerine	Lamar 21, Middle Tennessee 14
D30	Gator	**Penn State 30, Georgia Tech 15**
D30	Sun	Villanova 17, Wichita State 9
J1	Orange	**LSU 25, Colorado 7**
J1	Sugar	**Alabama 10, Arkansas 3**
J1	Rose	Minnesota 21, UCLA 3
J1	Cotton	**Texas 12, Mississippi 7**

SEC STANDINGS

	CONFERENCE			OVERALL		
	W	L	T	W	L	T
Alabama	7	0	0	11	0	0
LSU	6	0	0	10	1	0
Mississippi	5	1	0	9	2	0
Georgia Tech	4	3	0	7	4	0
Tennessee	4	3	0	6	4	0
Florida	3	3	0	4	5	1
Auburn	3	4	0	6	4	0
Kentucky	2	4	0	5	5	0
Georgia	2	5	0	3	7	0
Mississippi State	1	5	0	5	5	0
Tulane	1	5	0	2	8	0
Vanderbilt	1	6	0	2	8	0

ANNUAL REVIEW

1962 NCAA Major College Statistical Leaders

Individual Leaders

PASSING/COMPLETIONS	G	ATT	COM	PCT	INT	I%	YDS	YPA	TD	TD%	COM.PG
1 Don Trull, Baylor	10	229	125	54.6	12	5.2	1627	7.1	11	4.8	12.5
2 George Mira, Miami (Fla.)	10	260	122	46.9	16	6.2	1572	6.0	10	3.9	12.2
3 Dick Shiner, Maryland	10	203	121	59.6	16	7.9	1324	6.5	4	2.0	12.1
4 Tom Myers, Northwestern	9	195	116	59.5	14	7.2	1537	7.9	13	6.7	12.9
5 Terry Baker, Oregon State	10	203	112	55.2	5	2.5	1738	8.6	15	7.4	11.2
6 Jerry Gross, Detroit	9	212	105	49.5	13	6.1	1317	6.2	6	2.8	11.7
7 Dave Mathieson, Washington State	10	198	104	52.5	8	4.0	1472	7.4	12	6.1	10.4
8 Junior Edge, North Carolina	10	185	103	55.7	12	6.5	1234	6.7	7	3.8	10.3
9 Archie Roberts, Columbia	9	170	102	60.0	6	3.5	1076	6.3	6	3.5	11.3
10 Gary Cuozzo, Virginia	10	181	98	54.1	9	5.0	1136	6.3	6	3.3	9.8

ALL-PURPOSE YARDS	G	RUSH	REC	PR	KR	YDS	YPG
1 Gary Wood, Cornell	9	889	7	69	430	1395	155.0

RUSHING/YARDS	G	ATT	YDS	AVG	YPG
1 Jim Pilot, New Mexico State	10	208	1247	6.0	124.7
2 Eldon Fortie, Brigham Young	10	199	1149	5.8	114.9
3 Gale Sayers, Kansas	10	158	1125	7.1	112.5
4 Gary Wood, Cornell	9	173	889	5.1	98.8
5 Joe Don Looney, Oklahoma	10	137	852	6.2	85.2
6 Pete Pedro, West Texas State	10	134	831	6.2	83.1
7 Johnny Roland, Missouri	10	159	830	5.2	83.0
8 Dave Casinelli, Memphis	9	173	826	4.8	91.8
9 Bobby Santiago, New Mexico	10	151	806	5.3	80.6
10 Dave Hoppmann, Iowa State	10	198	798	4.0	79.8

RUSHING/YARDS PER CARRY	G	ATT	YDS	YPC
1 Gale Sayers, Kansas	10	158	1125	7.1
2 Willie Brown, Southern California	10	80	555	6.9
3 Tony Lorick, Arizona State	10	105	704	6.7
4 John Cook, Furman	10	99	655	6.6
5 Joe Don Looney, Oklahoma	10	137	852	6.2
6 Pete Pedro, West Texas State	10	134	831	6.2
7 Sherman Lewis, Michigan State	9	98	590	6.0
8 Jim Pilot, New Mexico State	10	208	1247	6.0
9 Mel Renfro, Oregon	10	126	753	6.0
10 Junior Coffey, Washington	10	98	581	5.9
Based on top 42 rushers				

RECEIVING/RECEPTIONS	G	REC	YDS	TD	YPR	YPG	RPG
1 Vern Burke, Oregon State	10	69	1007	10	14.6	100.7	6.9
2 John Simmons, Tulsa	10	65	860	9	13.2	86.0	6.5
3 Hugh Campbell, Washington State	10	57	849	7	14.9	84.9	5.7
4 Tom Brown, Maryland	10	47	557	4	11.9	55.7	4.7
5 James Cure, Marshall	10	46	667	3	14.5	66.7	4.6
6 Paul Flatley, Northwestern	9	45	632	5	14.0	70.2	5.0
7 Bob Lacey, North Carolina	10	44	668	5	15.2	66.8	4.4
7 Bill Turner, California	10	44	537	6	12.2	53.7	4.4
9 Art Graham, Boston College	10	41	823	7	20.1	82.3	4.1
9 Al Snyder, Holy Cross	10	41	703	6	17.1	70.3	4.1
9 Jim Kelly, Notre Dame	10	41	523	4	12.8	52.3	4.1

PUNTING	PUNT	YDS	AVG
1 Joe Don Looney, Oklahoma	34	1474	43.4
2 Dave Marion, Wyoming	36	1544	42.9
3 Cotton Clark, Alabama	21	893	42.5
4 George Canale, Tennessee	53	2221	41.9
5 Bob Paterson, San Jose State	37	1524	41.2
6 Chuck Raisig, Penn State	35	1439	41.1
7 Hagood Clarke, Florida	46	1886	41.0
8 Dick Fitzsimmons, New Mexico	41	1681	41.0
9 Jon Kilgore, Auburn	57	2320	40.7
10 Danny Thomas, SMU	69	2808	40.7

PUNT RETURNS/YARDS	PR	YDS	AVG
1 Darrell Roberts, Utah State	16	660	22.8
2 Ken Hatfield, Arkansas	18	267	14.8
3 Woody Houston, New Mexico State	22	266	12.1
4 Jay Wilkinson, Duke	28	259	9.3
4 Paul Lea, Oklahoma	17	254	14.9
6 Dave Marion, Wyoming	9	244	27.1
7 Cotton Clark, Alabama	16	243	15.2
8 Ken Waldrop, Army	18	235	13.1
9 Russell Vollmer, Memphis	11	224	20.4
10 Nat Whitmyer, Washington	17	220	12.9

KICKOFF RETURNS/YARDS	KR	YDS	AVG
1 Donnie Frederick, Wake Forest	29	660	22.8
2 Jerry Graves, Tulane	21	513	24.4
3 Jim Blakeney, California	18	456	25.3
4 Gary Wood, Cornell	20	430	21.5
5 Billy Gambrell, South Carolina	17	422	24.8
6 Marvin Woodson, Indiana	16	418	26.1
6 Ronnie Graham, Rice	20	418	20.9
8 Larry Coyer, Marshall	13	393	30.2
9 Ronnie Jackson, North Carolina	17	386	22.7
10 Eddie Taylor, Citadel	18	377	20.9

SCORING	TDS	XPT	FG	PTS
1 Jerry Logan, West Texas State	13	32	0	110
2 Cotton Clark, Alabama	15	2	0	92
2 Jim Pilot, New Mexico State	15	2	0	92
4 Billy Lothridge, Georgia Tech	9	20	5	89
5 Eldon Fortie, Brigham Young	14	2	0	86
5 Bill King, Dartmouth	14	2	0	86
7 Billy Moore, Arkansas	14	0	0	84
7 Bob Jencks, Miami (Ohio)	6	24	8	84
9 Johnny Roland, Missouri	13	0	0	78
9 Mel Renfro, Oregon	13	0	0	78
9 Pat McCarthy, Holy Cross	12	6	0	78

KICK SCORING	XPA	XP	FG	PTS
1 Bob Jencks, Miami (Ohio)	26	24	8	48
1 Bill Wellstead, Dartmouth	30	27	7	48
3 John Seedborg, Arizona State	39	37	3	46
3 Tom McKnelly, Arkansas	37	33	3	42
5 Al Woodall, Auburn	20	17	8	41
6 John Gavin, Air Force	21	18	7	39
6 Billy Reynolds, Duke	23	18	7	39
8 Jim McKee, Ohio U.	31	25	4	37
9 Gary Kroner, Wisconsin	27	27	3	36
10 Buck Corey, Oregon	31	29	2	35
10 Billy Lothridge, Georgia Tech	24	20	5	35

INTERCEPTIONS	INT	YDS
1 Byron Beaver, Houston	10	56
2 Gene Frantz, Brigham Young	9	133
2 Tom MacDonald, Notre Dame	9	81
2 Dan Espalin, Oregon State	9	67
5 Jerry Richardson, West Texas State	8	100
6 Jim McGowan, Boston College	7	182
6 Billy Ryan, North Texas	7	174
6 David Gibson, West Texas State	7	129
9 Jerry Logan, West Texas State *	6	168
9 Tom Brown, Maryland *	6	122
9 Steve Shafer, Utah State *	6	82
*Five tied with six; these had the most yards		

Team Leaders

RUSHING OFFENSE	G	ATT	YDS	AVG	YPG
1 Ohio State	9	528	2510	4.8	278.9
2 Oklahoma	10	561	2659	4.7	265.9
3 Michigan State	9	498	2383	4.8	264.8
4 Kansas	10	520	2610	5.0	261.0
5 West Texas State	10	506	2555	5.0	255.5
6 Missouri	10	585	2549	4.4	254.9
7 Washington	10	597	2514	4.2	251.4
8 Utah State	10	538	2464	4.6	246.4
9 Nebraska	10	541	2455	4.5	245.5
10 New Mexico	10	527	2428	4.6	242.8

PASSING OFFENSE	G	ATT	COM	INT	PCT	YDS	YPA	TD	I%	YPC	YPG
1 Tulsa	10	295	154	17	52.2	1993	6.8	18	5.8	12.9	199.3
2 Northwestern	9	225	130	15	57.8	1758	7.8	13	6.7	13.5	195.3
3 Oregon State	10	234	124	7	53.0	1951	8.3	19	3.0	15.7	195.1
4 California	10	272	146	20	53.7	1795	6.6	15	7.4	12.3	179.5
5 Baylor	10	254	133	14	52.4	1714	6.7	12	5.5	12.9	171.4
6 Washington State	10	234	118	11	50.4	1644	7.0	13	4.7	13.9	164.4
7 Wisconsin	9	216	112	9	51.9	1444	6.7	14	4.2	12.9	160.4
8 Florida State	10	223	118	8	52.9	1596	7.2	12	3.6	13.5	159.6
9 Miami (Fla.)	10	260	122	16	46.9	1572	6.0	10	6.2	12.9	157.2
10 Auburn	10	258	122	15	47.3	1512	5.9	6	5.8	12.4	151.2

TOTAL OFFENSE	G	P	YDS	AVG	YPG
1 Arizona State	10	629	3844	6.1	384.4
2 Oregon State	10	675	3752	5.6	375.2
3 Oklahoma	10	677	3693	5.5	369.3
4 Mississippi	9	627	3276	5.2	364.0
5 Dartmouth	9	598	3275	5.5	363.9
6 Northwestern	9	674	3267	4.8	363.0
7 Arkansas	10	717	3570	5.0	357.0
8 Utah State	10	701	3535	5.0	353.5
9 Oregon	10	654	3530	5.4	353.0
10 Wisconsin	9	600	3142	5.2	349.1

RUSHING DEFENSE	G	ATT	YDS	AVG	YPG
1 Minnesota	9	362	470	1.3	52.2
2 Alabama	10	321	601	1.9	60.1
3 Mississippi	9	300	610	2.0	67.8
4 LSU	10	349	832	2.4	83.2
5 Memphis	9	321	758	2.4	84.2
6 Bowling Green	9	316	788	2.5	87.6
7 Arkansas	10	381	907	2.4	90.7
8 Auburn	10	411	930	2.3	93.0
9 Michigan State	9	368	851	2.3	94.6
10 Villanova	9	359	857	2.4	95.2

PASSING DEFENSE	G	ATT	COM	PCT	YPC	INT	I%	YDS	YPA	TD	YPG
1 New Mexico	10	117	46	39.3	12.3	15	12.8	568	4.9	3	56.8
2 Boston U.	9	94	36	38.3	15.5	8	8.5	558	5.9	6	62.0
3 Memphis	9	115	49	42.6	11.6	18	15.7	566	4.9	1	62.9
4 Missouri	10	150	59	39.3	11.6	17	11.3	686	4.6	3	68.6
5 Yale	9	110	54	49.1	11.5	8	7.3	621	5.6	5	69.0
6 Florida State	10	148	67	45.3	10.3	13	8.8	693	4.7	3	69.3
7 Oklahoma	10	162	59	36.4	12.2	16	9.9	718	4.4	3	71.8
8 Kansas State	10	115	51	44.3	14.3	9	7.8	722	4.3	3	72.7
9 Texas-El Paso	9	121	44	36.4	15.2	11	9.1	669	5.5	7	74.3
10 Mississippi	9	146	60	41.1	11.2	7	4.8	670	4.6	2	74.4

TOTAL DEFENSE	G	P	YDS	AVG	YPG
1 Mississippi	9	446	1280	2.9	142.2
2 Memphis	9	436	1324	3.0	147.1
3 Alabama	10	542	1598	2.9	159.8
4 Minnesota	9	568	1505	2.6	167.2
5 Missouri	10	532	1811	3.4	181.1
6 Dartmouth	9	470	1664	3.5	184.9
6 Bowling Green	9	467	1664	3.6	184.9
8 Villanova	9	504	1701	3.4	189.0
9 Michigan State	9	553	1753	3.2	194.8
10 Auburn	10	599	1973	3.3	197.3

SCORING OFFENSE	G	PTS	AVG
1 Wisconsin	9	285	31.7
2 Arizona State	10	304	30.4
3 West Texas State	10	297	29.7
4 Memphis	9	261	29.0
5 Arkansas	10	286	28.6
6 Oregon State	10	273	27.3
7 Utah State	10	273	27.3
8 Alabama	10	272	27.2
9 Oklahoma	10	267	26.7
10 Northwestern	9	237	26.3

SCORING DEFENSE	G	PTS	AVG
1 LSU	10	34	3.4
2 Alabama	10	39	3.9
3 Oklahoma	10	44	4.4
4 Mississippi	9	40	4.4
5 Missouri	10	52	5.2
6 Southern California	10	55	5.5
7 Texas	10	59	5.9
8 Dartmouth	9	57	6.3
9 Minnesota	9	61	6.8
10 Florida State	10	69	6.9

1962

FINAL POLL (DEC. 3)

UP	AP	SCHOOL	FINAL RECORD
1	**1**	Southern California	11-0-0
2	**2**	Wisconsin	8-2-0
3	**3**	**Mississippi**	**10-0-0**
4	**4**	Texas	9-1-1
5	**5**	**Alabama**	**10-1-0**
6	**6**	**Arkansas**	**9-2-0**
8	**7**	**LSU**	**9-1-1**
7	**8**	Oklahoma	8-3-0
9	**9**	Penn State	9-2-0
10	**10**	Minnesota	6-2-1

CONSENSUS ALL-AMERICANS

POS	NAME	SCHOOL
B	Terry Baker	Oregon State
B	**Jerry Stovall**	**LSU**
B	Mel Renfro	Oregon
B	George Saimes	Michigan State
E	Hal Bedsole	Southern California
E	Pat Richter	Wisconsin
T	Bobby Bell	Minnesota
T	**Jim Dunaway**	**Mississippi**
G	Johnny Treadwell	Texas
G	Jack Cvercko	Northwestern
C	**Lee Roy Jordan**	**Alabama**

OTHERS RECEIVING FIRST-TEAM HONORS

B	George Mira	Miami (Fla.)
B	Tom Myers	Northwestern
B	**Glynn Griffing**	**Mississippi**
B	Dave Hoppman	Iowa State
B	Bill Moore	Arkansas
B	Roger Kochman	Penn State
B	Eldon Fortie	Brigham Young
E	Conrad Hitchler	Missouri
E	Dave Robinson	Penn State
T	Steve Barnett	Oregon
T	Don Brumm	Purdue
T	**Fred Miller**	**LSU**
G	Jean Berry	Duke
G	Leon Cross	Oklahoma
G	**Rufus Guthrie**	**Georgia Tech**
G	Damon Bame	Southern California
C	Donald McKinnon	Dartmouth

HEISMAN TROPHY VOTING

PLAYER	POS	SCHOOL	TOTAL
1 Terry Baker	QB	Oregon State	707
2 **Jerry Stovall**	**HB**	**LSU**	**618**
3 Bobby Bell	T	Minnesota	429
4 **Lee Roy Jordan**	**LB**	**Alabama**	**321**
5 George Mira	QB	Miami (Fla.)	284
6 Pat Richter	E	Wisconsin	276
7 George Saimes	HB	Michigan State	254
8 **Billy Lothridge**	**QB**	**Georgia Tech**	**162**
9 Ron Vander Kelen	QB	Wisconsin	139
10 Eldon Fortie	TB	Brigham Young	136

AWARD WINNERS

PLAYER	AWARD
Terry Baker, QB, Oregon State	Maxwell
Bobby Bell, T, Minnesota	Outland

BOWL GAMES

DATE	GAME	SCORE
D15	Gotham	Nebraska 36, Miami (Fla.) 34
D15	Liberty	Oregon State 6, Villanova 0
D22	**Bluebonnet**	**Missouri 14, Georgia Tech 10**
D22	Tangerine	Houston 49, Miami (Ohio) 21
D29	**Gator**	**Florida 17, Penn State 7**
D31	Sun	West Texas State 15, Ohio U. 14
J1	**Orange**	**Alabama 17, Oklahoma 0**
J1	**Cotton**	**LSU 13, Texas 0**
J1	**Sugar**	**Mississippi 17, Arkansas 13**
J1	Rose	Southern California 42, Wisconsin 37

SEC STANDINGS

	CONFERENCE			OVERALL		
	W	L	T	W	L	T
Mississippi	6	0	0	10	0	0
Alabama	6	1	0	10	1	0
LSU	5	1	0	9	1	1
Georgia Tech	5	2	0	7	3	1
Florida	4	2	0	7	4	0
Auburn	4	3	0	6	3	1
Georgia	2	3	1	3	4	3
Kentucky	2	3	1	3	5	2
Mississippi State	2	5	0	3	6	0
Tennessee	2	6	0	4	6	0
Vanderbilt	1	6	0	1	9	0
Tulane	0	7	0	0	10	0

1963 NCAA Major College Statistical Leaders

Individual Leaders

PASSING/COMPLETIONS	G	ATT	COM	PCT	INT	I%	YDS	YPA	TD	TD%	COM.PG
1 Don Trull, Baylor	10	308	174	56.5	12	3.9	2157	7.0	12	3.9	17.4
2 George Mira, Miami (Fla.)	10	335	172	51.3	14	4.2	2155	6.4	10	3.0	17.2
3 Jerry Rhome, Tulsa	10	258	150	58.1	13	5.0	1909	7.4	10	3.9	15.0
4 Bill Munson, Utah State	10	201	120	59.7	3	1.5	1699	8.5	12	6.0	12.0
5 Dick Shiner, Maryland	10	222	108	48.6	8	3.6	1165	5.2	10	4.5	10.8
6 Roger Staubach, Navy	10	161	107	66.5	6	3.7	1474	9.2	7	4.4	10.7
7 Tom LaFramboise, Louisville	10	204	104	51.0	12	5.9	1205	5.9	9	4.4	10.4
8 Larry Rakestraw, Georgia	**10**	**209**	**103**	**49.3**	**14**	**6.7**	**1297**	**6.2**	**7**	**3.4**	**10.3**
9 Archie Roberts, Columbia	9	164	101	61.6	10	6.1	1184	7.2	11	6.7	11.2
9 Bob Berry, Oregon	10	171	101	59.1	7	4.1	1675	9.8	16	9.4	10.1
9 Scotty Glacken, Duke	10	200	101	50.5	8	4.0	1265	6.3	12	6.0	10.1
9. Craig Morton, California	10	207	101	48.8	12	5.8	1475	7.1	14	6.8	10.1
9 Merv Holland, George Washington	9	215	101	47.0	11	5.1	1312	6.1	8	3.7	11.2

ALL-PURPOSE YARDS	G	RUSH	REC	PR	KR	YDS	YPG
1 Gary Wood, Cornell	9	818	15	57	618	1508	167.6

RUSHING/YARDS	G	ATT	YDS	AVG	YPG
1 Dave Casinelli, Memphis	10	219	1016	4.6	101.6
2 Jimmy Sidle, Auburn	**10**	**185**	**1006**	**5.4**	**100.6**
3 Gale Sayers, Kansas	10	132	917	6.9	91.7
4 Jack Mahone, Marshall	10	163	884	5.4	88.4
5 Jim Grisham, Oklahoma	10	153	861	5.6	86.1
6 Bob Schweickert, Virginia Tech	10	155	839	5.4	83.9
7 Mike Garrett, Southern California	10	128	833	6.5	83.3
8 Gary Wood, Cornell	9	166	818	4.9	90.9
9 Tony Lorick, Arizona State	9	105	805	7.7	89.4
10 Terry Isaacson, Air Force	10	162	801	4.9	80.1

RUSHING/YARDS PER CARRY	G	ATT	YDS	YPC
1 Tony Lorick, Arizona State	9	105	805	7.7
2 Larry Campbell, Utah State	10	82	585	7.1
3 Gale Sayers, Kansas	10	132	917	6.9
4 Charley Taylor, Arizona State	9	88	595	6.8
5 Mike Garrett, Southern California	10	128	833	6.5
6 Sherman Lewis, Michigan State	9	90	577	6.4
7 Benny Nelson, Alabama	**10**	**97**	**613**	**6.3**
8 Rudy Johnson, Nebraska	10	91	573	6.3
9 Walt Mainer, Xavier	10	120	744	6.2
10 Pat Donnelly, Navy	10	99	603	6.1

Based on top 42 rushers

RECEIVING/RECEPTIONS	G	REC	YDS	TD	YPR	YPG	RPG
1 Lawrence Elkins, Baylor	10	70	873	8	12.5	87.3	7.0
2 Vern Burke, Oregon State	10	48	794	9	16.5	79.4	4.8
2 Stan Crisson, Duke	10	48	559	7	11.6	55.9	4.8
2 Bob Lacey, North Carolina	10	48	533	1	11.1	53.3	4.8
5 Darryl Hill, Maryland	10	43	516	7	12.0	51.6	4.3
6 Bob Long, Wichita State	9	42	653	9	15.5	72.6	4.7
7 Nick Spinelli, Miami (Fla.)	10	41	501	4	12.2	50.1	4.1
8 James Ingram, Baylor	10	40	537	4	13.4	53.7	4.0
8 James Cure, Marshall	10	40	534	2	13.4	53.4	4.0
10 Jim Curry, Cincinnati	9	39	621	3	15.9	69.0	4.3
10 John Simmons, Tulsa	10	39	543	3	13.9	54.3	3.9
10 John Parry, Brown	8	39	457	4	11.7	57.1	4.9

PUNTING	PUNT	YDS	AVG
1 Danny Thomas, SMU	48	2110	44.0
2 Len Frketich, Oregon State	24	1013	42.2
3 Kroghie Andresen, Citadel	38	1581	41.6
4 James Keller, Texas A&M	66	2739	41.5
5 Merlin Norenberg, Northwestern	32	1325	41.4
6 Norm Limpert, Bowling Green	42	1735	41.3
7 Olie Cordill, Memphis	22	909	41.3
8 Frank Lambert, Mississippi	**37**	**1524**	**41.2**
9 Jon Kilgore, Auburn	**51**	**2101**	**41.2**
10 Billy Lothridge, Georgia Tech	**46**	**1886**	**41.0**

PUNT RETURNS/YARDS	PR	YDS	AVG
1 Ken Hatfield, Arkansas	21	350	16.7
2 Larry Elliott, Oklahoma State	11	225	20.5
3 Gene Fleming, Rice	22	224	10.2
4 Junior Powell, Penn State	18	221	12.3
5 Joe Labruzzo, LSU	**9**	**215**	**23.9**
6 Jim Gray, Toledo	13	212	16.3
7 Rickie Harris, Arizona	12	209	17.4
8 George Rose, Auburn	**23**	**205**	**8.9**
9 Tom Vaughn, Iowa State	13	204	15.7
10 Jimmy Heidel, Mississippi	**18**	**200**	**11.1**

KICKOFF RETURNS/YARDS	KR	YDS	AVG
1 Gary Wood, Cornell	19	618	32.5
2 Steve Bramwell, Washington	18	565	31.4
3 Tom Blanchfield, California	16	470	29.4
4 Donny Anderson, Texas Tech	18	448	24.9
5 Larry Elliott, Oklahoma State	20	437	21.9
6 Joe Lopasky, Houston	16	423	26.4
7 Floyd Hudlow, Arizona	13	422	32.5
8 Robert Dunn, Villanova	14	416	29.7
9 Dick Drummond, George Washington	16	403	25.2
10 Jim Blakeney, California	14	397	28.4

SCORING	TDS	XPT	FG	PTS
1 Cosmo Iacavazzi, Princeton	14	0	0	84
1 Dave Casinelli, Memphis	14	0	0	84
3 Terry Isaacson, Air Force	13	2	0	80
4 Jay Wilkinson, Duke	12	0	0	72
4 Rick Leeson, Pittsburgh	7	15	5	72
6 Billy Lothridge, Georgia Tech	**3**	**15**	**12**	**69**
7 Henry Schichtle, Wichita State	7	17	3	68
8 Benny Nelson, Alabama	**10**	**2**	**0**	**62**
9 Nine tied				60

KICK SCORING	XPA	XP	FG	PTS
1 Fred Marlin, Navy	41	37	5	52
2 Hugh Crosby, Texas	24	24	9	51
2 Billy Lothridge, Georgia Tech	**19**	**15**	**12**	**51**
4 Alva Holaday, Air Force	25	23	7	44
5 Woody Woodall, Auburn	**23**	**23**	**6**	**41**
6 H.L. Daniels, Texas Tech	18	15	8	39
7 George Jarman, Oklahoma	32	29	3	38
8 Charles Gogolak, Princeton	35	31	2	37
9 Pete Gogolak, Cornell	18	18	6	36
9 Braden Beck, Stanford	12	12	8	36
9 Justin Canale, Mississippi State	**20**	**15**	**7**	**36**

INTERCEPTIONS	INT	YDS
1 Dick Kern, William & Mary	8	116
2 Bruce Bennett, Florida	**6**	**83**
2 Mike Dundy, Illinois	6	82
2 Larry Shields, Oklahoma	6	66
2 Ollie Ross, West Texas State	6	52
6 Walter Roberts, San Jose State	5	131
6 Sonny Fisher, Mississippi State	**5**	**109**
6 Tom MacDonald, Notre Dame	5	63
6 James Hudson, Texas	5	56
6 Dick McCauley, Northwestern	5	36
6 Jimmy Heidel, Mississippi	**5**	**8**

Team Leaders

RUSHING OFFENSE	G	ATT	YDS	AVG	YPG
1 Nebraska	10	561	2626	4.7	262.6
2 Princeton	9	509	2246	4.4	249.6
3 Army	10	564	2479	4.4	247.9
4 Oklahoma	10	562	2469	4.4	246.9
5 Kansas	10	512	2431	4.7	243.1
6 Cincinnati	10	462	2320	5.0	232.0
7 Texas	10	590	2316	3.9	231.6
8 Pittsburgh	10	501	2302	4.6	230.2
9 Air Force	10	496	2297	4.6	229.7
10 Memphis	10	509	2292	4.5	229.2

PASSING OFFENSE	G	ATT	COM	INT	PCT	YDS	YPA	TD	I%	YPC	YPG
1 Tulsa	10	352	199	22	56.5	2448	7.0	14	6.3	12.3	244.8
2 Miami (Fla.)	10	338	173	14	51.2	2183	6.5	10	4.1	12.6	218.3
3 Baylor	10	320	177	13	55.3	2159	6.7	12	4.1	12.2	215.9
4 Utah State	10	241	133	7	55.2	1852	7.7	14	2.9	13.9	185.2
5 Oregon	10	212	118	10	55.7	1851	8.7	17	4.7	15.7	185.1
6 San Jose State	10	248	136	17	54.8	1834	7.4	14	6.9	13.5	183.4
7 Wichita	9	172	97	6	56.4	1571	9.1	13	3.5	16.2	174.6
8 Navy	10	186	121	8	65.1	1690	9.1	8	4.3	14.0	169.0
9 Mississippi	**9**	**191**	**104**	**12**	**54.5**	**1500**	**7.9**	**17**	**6.3**	**14.4**	**166.7**
10 Northwestern	9	192	98	16	51.0	1473	7.7	7	8.3	15.0	163.7

TOTAL OFFENSE	G	P	YDS	AVG	YPG
1 Utah State	10	669	3953	5.9	395.3
2 Wichita State	9	564	3496	6.2	388.4
3 Pittsburgh	10	706	3772	5.3	377.2
4 Oregon	10	635	3607	5.7	360.7
5 Arizona State	9	563	3235	5.7	359.4
6 Navy	10	656	3512	5.4	351.2
7 Cincinnati	10	616	3494	5.7	349.4
8 Nebraska	10	685	3476	5.1	347.6
9 Tulsa	10	652	3415	5.2	341.5
10 North Carolina	10	730	3414	4.7	341.4

RUSHING DEFENSE	G	ATT	YDS	AVG	YPG
1 Mississippi	**9**	**315**	**696**	**2.2**	**77.3**
2 Texas	10	319	802	2.5	80.2
3 Southern Miss	9	304	724	2.4	80.4
4 Michigan State	9	343	738	2.2	82.0
5 Memphis	10	342	833	2.4	83.3
6 Clemson	10	344	931	2.7	93.1
7 Utah State	10	403	932	2.3	93.2
8 Syracuse	10	358	938	2.6	93.8
9 Pittsburgh	10	352	970	2.8	97.0
10 Wichita State	9	295	876	3.0	97.3

PASSING DEFENSE	G	ATT	COM	PCT	YPC	INT	I%	YDS	YPA	TD	YPG
1 Texas-El Paso	10	104	35	33.7	12.5	7	6.7	438	4.2	5	43.8
2 Southern Miss	9	115	49	42.6	9.3	14	12.2	457	4.0	3	50.8
3 Mississippi	**9**	**123**	**47**	**38.2**	**11.1**	**13**	**10.6**	**522**	**4.2**	**3**	**58.0**
4 Ohio U.	10	125	49	39.2	12.7	6	4.8	621	5.0	5	62.1
5 Toledo	9	101	38	37.6	15.0	6	5.9	569	5.6	5	63.2
6 Boston U.	8	108	46	42.6	11.0	6	5.6	507	4.7	1	63.4
7 Harvard	9	127	50	39.4	12.7	11	8.7	634	5.0	3	70.4
8 Princeton	9	162	68	42.0	9.8	13	8.0	667	4.1	2	74.1
9 Georgia Tech	**10**	**152**	**60**	**39.5**	**12.4**	**9**	**5.9**	**743**	**4.9**	**2**	**74.3**
9 VMI	10	143	64	44.8	11.6	8	5.6	743	5.2	5	74.3

TOTAL DEFENSE	G	P	YDS	AVG	YPG
1 Southern Miss	9	419	1181	2.8	131.2
2 Mississippi	**9**	**438**	**1218**	**2.8**	**135.3**
3 Memphis	10	500	1637	3.3	163.7
4 Michigan State	9	516	1567	3.0	174.1
5 Clemson	10	544	1847	3.4	184.7
6 Princeton	9	519	1715	3.3	190.6
7 Auburn	**10**	**584**	**1910**	**3.3**	**191.0**
8 Utah State	10	599	1925	3.2	192.5
9 Florida	**10**	**555**	**1942**	**3.5**	**194.2**
9 Texas	10	530	1942	3.7	194.2

SCORING OFFENSE	G	PTS	AVG
1 Utah State	10	317	31.7
2 Navy	10	314	31.4
3 Arizona State	9	249	27.7
4 Princeton	9	247	27.4
5 Nebraska	10	260	26.0
6 Wichita State	9	233	25.9
7 Syracuse	10	255	25.5
8 Oregon	10	253	25.3
9 Air Force	10	249	24.9
10 Cincinnati	10	238	23.8

SCORING DEFENSE	G	PTS	AVG
1 Mississippi	**9**	**33**	**3.7**
2 Memphis	10	52	5.2
3 Texas	10	65	6.5
4 Michigan State	9	63	7.0
5 Southern Miss	9	64	7.1
6 Mississippi State	**10**	**82**	**8.2**
7 Harvard	9	76	8.4
8 Missouri	10	86	8.6
9 Yale	9	78	8.7
10 Alabama	**10**	**88**	**8.8**

1963

FINAL POLL (DEC. 9)

UP	AP	SCHOOL	FINAL RECORD
1	1	Texas	11-0-0
2	2	Navy	9-2-0
4	3	Illinois	8-1-1
3	4	Pittsburgh	9-1-0
6	5	**Auburn**	**9-2-0**
5	6	Nebraska	10-1-0
7	7	**Mississippi**	**7-1-2**
9	8	**Alabama**	**9-2-0**
10	9	Michigan State	6-2-1
8	10	Oklahoma	8-2-0

CONSENSUS ALL-AMERICANS

POS	NAME	SCHOOL
B	Roger Staubach	Navy
B	Sherman Lewis	Michigan State
B	Jim Grisham	Oklahoma
B	Gale Sayers	Kansas
B	Paul Martha	Pittsburgh
E	Vern Burke	Oregon State
E	Lawrence Elkins	Baylor
T	Scott Appleton	Texas
T	Carl Eller	Minnesota
G	Bob Brown	Nebraska
G	Rick Redman	Washington
C	Dick Butkus	Illinois

OTHERS RECEIVING FIRST-TEAM HONORS

POS	NAME	SCHOOL
B	Tommy Ford	Texas
B	**Billy Lothridge**	**Georgia Tech**
B	**Jimmy Sidle**	**Auburn**
B	Don Trull	Baylor
B	Tom Vaughn	Iowa State
B	Tommy Crutcher	TCU
B	Jay Wilkinson	Duke
E	Bob Lacey	North Carolina
E	Jim Kelly	Notre Dame
E	David Parks	Texas Tech
E	**Billy Martin**	**Georgia Tech**
T	Ernie Borghetti	Pittsburgh
T	Ken Kortas	Louisville
T	Harry Schuh	Memphis
G	**Steve DeLong**	**Tennessee**
G	Mike Reilly	Iowa
G	Damon Bame	Southern California
C	**Kenny Dill**	**Mississippi**

HEISMAN TROPHY VOTING

	PLAYER	POS	SCHOOL	TOTAL
1	Roger Staubach	QB	Navy	1860
2	**Billy Lothridge**	**QB**	**Georgia Tech**	**504**
3	Sherman Lewis	RB	Michigan State	369
4	Don Trull	QB	Baylor	253
5	Scott Appleton	T	Texas	194
6	Dick Butkus	C	Illinois	172
7	**Jimmy Sidle**	**QB**	**Auburn**	**123**
8	Terry Isaacson	RB	Air Force	104
9	Jay Wilkinson	RB	Duke	84
10	George Mira	QB	Miami (Fla.)	80

AWARD WINNERS

PLAYER	AWARD
Roger Staubach, QB, Navy	Maxwell
Scott Appleton, T, Texas	Outland

BOWL GAMES

DATE	GAME	SCORE
D21	**Bluebonnet**	**Baylor 14, LSU 7**
D21	**Liberty**	**Mississippi St. 16, North Carolina St. 12**
D28	Gator	North Carolina 35, Air Force 0
D28	Tangerine	Western Kentucky 27, Coast Guard 0
D31	Sun	Oregon 21, SMU 14
J1	Rose	Illinois 17, Washington 7
J1	**Sugar**	**Alabama 12, Mississippi 7**
J1	**Orange**	**Nebraska 13, Auburn 7**
J1	Cotton	Texas 28, Navy 6

SEC STANDINGS

	CONFERENCE			OVERALL		
	W	L	T	W	L	T
Mississippi	5	0	1	7	1	2
Auburn	6	1	0	9	2	0
Alabama	6	2	0	9	2	0
Mississippi State	4	1	2	7	2	2
LSU	4	2	0	7	4	0
Georgia Tech	4	3	0	7	3	0
Florida	3	3	1	6	3	1
Tennessee	3	5	0	5	5	0
Georgia	2	4	0	4	5	1
Vanderbilt	0	5	2	1	7	2
Kentucky	0	5	1	3	6	1
Tulane	0	6	1	1	8	1

1964 NCAA Major College Statistical Leaders

Individual Leaders

PASSING/COMPLETIONS	G	ATT	COM	PCT	INT	I%	YDS	YPA	TD	TD%	COM.PG
1 Jerry Rhome, Tulsa	10	326	224	68.7	4	1.2	2870	8.8	32	9.8	22.4
2 Craig Morton, California	10	308	185	60.1	9	2.9	2121	6.9	13	4.2	18.5
3 Gary Snook, Iowa	9	311	151	48.6	14	4.5	2062	6.6	11	3.5	16.8
4 John Torok, Arizona State	10	251	139	55.4	14	5.6	2356	9.4	20	8.0	13.9
5 Tom LaFramboise, Louisville	10	242	122	50.4	18	7.4	1380	5.7	4	1.7	12.2
6 Steve Tensi, Florida State	10	204	121	59.3	10	4.9	1681	8.2	14	6.9	12.1
6 Richie Badar, Indiana	9	245	121	49.4	15	6.1	1571	6.4	9	3.7	13.4
8 Roger Staubach, Navy	10	204	119	58.3	10	4.9	1131	5.5	4	2.0	11.9
9 Terry Southall, Baylor	10	225	118	52.4	20	8.9	1623	7.2	10	4.4	11.8
10 Dan Simrell, Toledo	10	215	115	53.5	13	6.1	1239	5.8	4	1.9	11.5

ALL-PURPOSE YARDS	G	RUSH	REC	PR	KR	YDS	YPG
1 Donny Anderson, Texas Tech	10	966	396	28	320	1710	171.0

RUSHING/YARDS	G	ATT	YDS	AVG	YPG
1 Brian Piccolo, Wake Forest	10	252	1044	4.1	104.4
2 Jim Grabowski, Illinois	9	186	1004	5.4	111.6
3 Al Nelson, Cincinnati	10	201	973	4.8	97.3
4 Donny Anderson, Texas Tech	10	211	966	4.6	96.6
5 Jim Nance, Syracuse	10	190	951	5.0	95.1
6 Mike Garrett, Southern California	10	217	948	4.4	94.8
7 Ray Handley, Stanford	10	197	936	4.8	93.6
8 Cosmo Iacavazzi, Princeton	9	172	909	5.3	101.0
9 Bo Hickey, Maryland	10	182	894	4.9	89.4
10 Jack Mahone, Marshall	10	190	878	4.6	87.8

RUSHING/YARDS PER CARRY	G	ATT	YDS	YPC
1 Dick Gordon, Michigan State	9	123	741	6.0
2 Stew Williams, Bowling Green	10	109	609	5.6
3 Floyd Little, Syracuse	10	149	828	5.6
4 Ron Coleman, Utah	10	108	596	5.5
5 Jack Lentz, Holy Cross	10	148	800	5.4
6 Jim Grabowski, Illinois	9	186	1004	5.4
7 Clarence Williams, Washington State	10	147	783	5.3
8 Cosmo Iacavazzi, Princeton	9	172	909	5.3
9 Chuck Mercein, Yale	9	141	737	5.2
10 Gale Sayers, Kansas	10	122	633	5.2
Based on top 42 rushers				

RECEIVING/RECEPTIONS	G	REC	YDS	TD	YPR	YPG	RPG
1 Howard Twilley, Tulsa	10	95	1178	13	12.4	117.8	9.5
2 Jack Snow, Notre Dame	10	60	1114	9	18.6	111.4	6.0
3 Karl Noonan, Iowa	9	59	933	4	15.8	103.7	6.6
4 Fred Biletnikoff, Florida State	10	57	987	11	17.3	98.7	5.7
5 Jack Schraub, California	10	52	633	2	12.2	63.3	5.2
6 Lawrence Elkins, Baylor	10	50	851	7	17.0	85.1	5.0
7 Bob Daugherty, Tulsa	10	48	498	4	10.4	49.8	4.8
8 Charles Casey, Florida	10	47	673	4	14.3	67.3	4.7
9 Henry Burch, Toledo	9	47	420	1	8.9	46.7	5.2
10 Bill Malinchak, Indiana	9	46	634	5	13.8	70.4	5.1

PUNTING	PUNT	YDS	AVG
1 Frank Lambert, Mississippi	50	2205	44.1
2 David Lewis, Stanford	34	1486	43.7
3 Doug Dusenbury, Kansas State	61	2647	43.4
4 Buddy French, Alabama	42	1802	42.9
5 Danny Thomas, SMU	58	2488	42.9
6 Larry Seiple, Kentucky	35	1474	42.1
7 Norm Limpert, Bowling Green	31	1305	42.1
8 Lou Bobich, Michigan State	37	1536	41.5
9 Mickey Rice, Idaho	55	2283	41.5
10 Ron Widby, Tennessee	74	3041	41.1

PUNT RETURNS/YARDS	PR	YDS	AVG
1 Ken Hatfield, Arkansas	31	518	16.7
2 David Ferguson, Rice	34	381	11.2
3 Wayne Swinford, Georgia	34	343	10.1
4 Steve Bramwell, Washington	29	314	10.8
5 Jeff Jordan, Tulsa	21	285	13.6
6 Kent Oborn, Brigham Young	22	278	12.6
7 Floyd Little, Syracuse	11	270	24.5
8 Curley Waters, West Texas State	18	265	14.7
9 Floyd Hudlow, Arizona	8	251	31.4
10 Joe Vargo, Penn State	19	233	12.3

KICKOFF RETURNS/YARDS	KR	YDS	AVG
1 Don Bland, Mississippi State	20	558	27.9
2 Larry Elliott, Oklahoma State	20	508	25.4
3 Ron Smith, Wisconsin	19	481	25.3
4 Roger Davis, Virginia	21	461	22.0
5 John Gutekunst, Duke	21	458	21.8
6 Chuck Hughes, Texas-El Paso	17	446	26.2
7 Barry Ellman, Pennsylvania	15	421	28.1
8 Tom Vaughn, Iowa State	17	402	23.6
9 Willie Loper, Toledo	16	399	24.9
10 Bob Hall, Brown	19	395	20.8

SCORING	TDS	XPT	FG	PTS
1 Brian Piccolo, Wake Forest	17	9	0	111
2 Howard Twilley, Tulsa	13	32	0	110
3 Al Nelson, Cincinnati	13	4	0	82
4 Bob Timberlake, Michigan	8	20	4	80
5 Jim Nance, Syracuse	13	0	0	78
6 Kent McCloughan, Nebraska	12	2	0	74
7 Tom Nowatzke, Indiana	10	10	1	73
7 Doug Moreau, LSU	4	10	13	73
9 Floyd Little, Syracuse	12	0	0	72
10 David Ray, Alabama	2	23	12	71

KICK SCORING	XPA	XP	FGA	FG	PTS
1 David Ray, Alabama	25	23	17	12	59
2 Charles Gogolak, Princeton	26	25	16	9	52
3 Les Murdock, Florida State	26	22	14	9	49
4 David Conway, Texas	24	24	12	7	45
4 Tom McKnelly, Arkansas	28	27	11	6	45
4 Doug Moreau, LSU	9	6	20	13	45
7 Bernardo Bramson, Maryland	18	17	17	9	44
8 Braden Beck, Stanford	16	15	16	9	42
8 Billy Carl Irwin, Mississippi	23	21	11	7	42
10 George Squires, Wyoming	21	20	12	7	41

INTERCEPTIONS	INT	YDS
1 Tony Carey, Notre Dame	8	121
2 George Donnelly, Illinois	8	54
3 Jeff Jordan, Tulsa	7	124
3 C.D. Lowery, Utah	7	92
3 Arnie Chonko, Ohio State	7	72
3 Jim Hunt, California	7	65
3 Teddy Roberts, Texas Tech	7	62
8 Ken Boston, Missouri *	6	166
8 Les Palm, Oregon *	6	73
8 Winfred Bailey, Florida State *	6	69
*Six tied with six; these had the most yards		

Team Leaders

RUSHING OFFENSE	G	ATT	YDS	AVG	YPG
1 Syracuse	10	544	2510	4.6	251.0
2 Bowling Green	10	491	2393	4.9	239.3
3 Cincinnati	10	493	2383	4.8	238.3
4 Michigan	10	516	2141	4.1	237.9
5 Oklahoma	10	560	2276	4.1	227.6
6 Nebraska	10	538	2265	4.2	226.5
7 Princeton	9	432	1968	4.6	218.7
8 Dartmouth	9	394	1958	5.0	217.6
9 Villanova	8	411	1715	4.2	214.4
10 New Mexico	11	550	2331	4.2	211.9

PASSING OFFENSE	G	ATT	COM	INT	PCT	YDS	YPA	TD	I%	YPC	YPG
1 Tulsa	10	377	244	12	64.7	3179	8.4	34	3.2	13.0	317.9
2 Arizona State	10	281	151	19	53.7	2559	9.1	23	6.8	16.9	255.9
3 Iowa	9	321	154	14	48.0	2125	6.6	11	4.4	13.8	236.1
4 California	10	316	192	9	60.8	2187	6.9	14	2.9	11.4	218.7
5 Notre Dame	10	222	120	13	54.1	2105	9.5	16	5.9	17.5	210.5
6 Florida State	10	249	147	10	59.0	2027	8.1	15	4.0	13.8	202.7
7 Baylor	10	282	141	21	50.0	2023	7.2	13	7.5	14.3	202.3
8 Oregon	10	259	132	13	51.0	1793	6.9	17	5.0	13.6	179.3
9 Indiana	9	250	123	15	49.2	1597	6.4	9	6.0	13.0	177.4
10 Southern California	10	221	112	11	50.7	1704	7.7	11	5.0	15.2	170.4

TOTAL OFFENSE	G	P	YDS	AVG	YPG
1 Tulsa	10	729	4618	6.3	461.8
2 Notre Dame	10	694	4014	5.8	401.4
3 Arizona State	10	646	3762	5.8	376.2
4 Dartmouth	9	573	3284	5.7	364.9
5 Southern California	10	659	3526	5.4	352.6
6 Nebraska	10	696	3485	5.0	348.5
7 Utah State	10	616	3484	5.7	348.4
8 Michigan	9	659	3074	4.7	341.6
9 Florida State	10	658	3410	5.2	341.0
10 Bowling Green	10	637	3343	5.2	334.3

RUSHING DEFENSE	G	ATT	YDS	AVG	YPG
1 Washington	10	346	613	1.8	61.3
2 Notre Dame	10	351	687	2.0	68.7
3 Florida State	10	355	750	2.1	75.0
4 Auburn	10	376	819	2.2	81.9
5 Rutgers	9	324	757	2.3	84.1
6 Texas	10	390	844	2.2	84.4
7 Villanova	8	323	683	2.1	85.4
8 Syracuse	10	368	861	2.3	86.1
9 Michigan	9	326	781	2.4	86.8
10 Illinois	9	323	786	2.4	87.3

PASSING DEFENSE	G	ATT	COM	PCT	YPC	INT	I%	YDS	YPA	TD	YPG
1 Kent State	9	118	41	34.7	11.8	7	5.9	482	4.1	4	53.6
2 Florida	10	150	57	38.0	11.2	16	10.7	640	4.3	3	64.0
3 Nebraska	10	135	60	44.4	11.1	7	5.2	665	4.9	1	66.5
4 LSU	10	142	61	43.0	11.3	9	6.3	689	4.9	2	68.9
5 Boston College	9	112	45	40.2	14.5	7	6.3	652	5.8	4	72.4
6 Xavier	10	136	61	44.9	12.3	8	5.9	750	5.5	4	75.0
7 Citadel	10	162	59	36.4	12.8	6	3.7	755	4.7	6	75.5
8 Ohio U.	10	155	64	41.3	12.3	7	4.5	789	5.1	4	78.9
9 VMI	10	132	63	47.7	12.6	4	3.0	796	6.0	8	79.6
10 SMU	10	128	61	47.7	13.1	9	7.0	797	6.2	8	79.7

TOTAL DEFENSE	G	P	YDS	AVG	YPG
1 Auburn	10	495	1647	3.3	164.7
2 Nebraska	10	517	1670	3.2	167.0
3 LSU	10	529	1757	3.3	175.7
4 Arkansas	10	567	1805	3.2	180.5
5 Florida State	10	550	1811	3.3	181.1
6 Syracuse	10	525	1859	3.5	185.9
7 Bowling Green	10	527	1883	3.6	188.3
8 Alabama	10	560	1912	3.4	191.2
9 Villanova	8	488	1555	3.2	194.4
10 Florida	10	535	1944	3.6	194.4

SCORING OFFENSE	G	PTS	AVG
1 Tulsa	10	384	38.4
2 Utah State	10	294	29.4
3 Notre Dame	10	287	28.7
4 Bowling Green	10	275	27.5
5 Dartmouth	9	235	26.1
6 Syracuse	10	254	25.4
7 Nebraska	10	249	24.9
8 Villanova	8	193	24.1
9 Princeton	9	216	24.0
10 Alabama	10	233	23.3

SCORING DEFENSE	G	PTS	AVG
1 Arkansas	10	57	5.7
2 Colgate	9	52	5.8
3 Villanova	8	47	5.9
4 Princeton	9	53	5.9
5 Utah	10	62	6.2
6 Texas	10	64	6.4
7 Florida State	10	66	6.6
8 Alabama	10	67	6.7
9 Nebraska	10	75	7.5
10 Arizona	10	76	7.6

1964

FINAL POLL (NOV. 30)

UP	AP	SCHOOL	FINAL RECORD
1	1	Alabama	10-1-0
2	2	Arkansas	11-0-0
3	3	Notre Dame	9-1-0
4	4	Michigan	9-1-0
5	5	Texas	10-1-0
6	6	Nebraska	9-2-0
7	7	LSU	8-2-1
8	8	Oregon State	8-3-0
9	9	Ohio State	7-2-0
10	10	Southern California	7-3-0

CONSENSUS ALL-AMERICANS

POS	NAME	SCHOOL
B	John Huarte	Notre Dame
B	Gale Sayers	Kansas
B	Lawrence Elkins	Baylor
B	**Tucker Frederickson**	**Auburn**
E	Jack Snow	Notre Dame
E	Fred Biletnikoff	Florida State
T	Larry Kramer	Nebraska
T	Ralph Neely	Oklahoma
G	Rick Redman	Washington
G	Glenn Ressler	Penn State
C	Dick Butkus	Illinois

OTHERS RECEIVING FIRST-TEAM HONORS

B	Floyd Little	Syracuse
B	Craig Morton	California
B	Jerry Rhome	Tulsa
B	Bob Schweickert	Virginia Tech
B	Bob Timberlake	Michigan
B	Clarence Williams	Washington State
B	Bob Berry	Oregon
B	**Larry Dupree**	**Florida**
B	Tom Nowatzke	Indiana
B	Cosmo Iacavazzi	Princeton
B	Jim Grabowski	Illinois
B	Mike Garrett	Southern California
B	Ken Willard	North Carolina
B	Arnold Chonko	Ohio State
B	Brian Piccolo	Wake Forest
E	Donny Anderson	Texas Tech
E	Karl Noonan	Iowa
E	Alphonse Dotson	Grambling
T	**Steve DeLong**	**Tennessee**
T	Stas Maliszewski	Princeton
T	**Jim Wilson**	**Georgia**
T	Bill Yearby	Michigan
T	**Remi Prudhomme**	**LSU**
T	Harry Schuh	Memphis
G	Ronnie Caveness	Arkansas
G	Tommy Nobis	Texas
G	Bill Fisk	Southern California
G	Al Atkinson	Villanova
G	**Wayne Freeman**	**Alabama**
G	Jack O'Billovich	Oregon State
C	Dwight Kelley	Ohio State
C	Pat Killorin	Syracuse
LB	Jim Carroll	Notre Dame
LB	Carl McAdams	Oklahoma

HEISMAN TROPHY VOTING

	PLAYER	POS	SCHOOL	TOTAL
1	John Huarte	QB	Notre Dame	1026
2	Jerry Rhome	QB	Tulsa	952
3	Dick Butkus	LB	Illinois	505
4	Bob Timberlake	QB	Michigan	361
5	Jack Snow	E	Notre Dame	187
6	**Tucker Frederickson**	**FB**	**Auburn**	**184**
7	Craig Morton	QB	California	181
8	**Steve DeLong**	**MG**	**Tennessee**	**176**
9	Cosmo Iacavazzi	RB	Princeton	165
10	Brian Piccolo	RB	Wake Forest	124

AWARD WINNERS

PLAYER	AWARD
Glenn Ressler, C-G, Penn State	Maxwell
Steve DeLong, T, Tennessee	**Outland**

BOWL GAMES

DATE	GAME	SCORE
D12	Tangerine	East Carolina 14, Massachusetts 13
D19	**Bluebonnet**	**Tulsa 14, Mississippi 7**
D19	Liberty	Utah 32, West Virginia 6
D26	**Sun**	**Georgia 7, Texas Tech 0**
J1	Cotton	Arkansas 10, Nebraska 7
J1	**Sugar**	**LSU 13, Syracuse 10**
J1	Rose	Michigan 34, Oregon State 7
J1	**Orange**	**Texas 21, Alabama 17**
J2	Gator	Florida State 36, Oklahoma 19

SEC STANDINGS

	CONFERENCE			OVERALL		
	W	L	T	W	L	T
Alabama	8	0	0	10	1	0
Florida	4	2	0	7	3	0
Kentucky	4	2	0	5	5	0
LSU	4	2	1	8	2	1
Georgia	3	2	0	7	3	1
Auburn	3	3	0	6	4	0
Mississippi	2	4	1	5	5	1
Mississippi State	2	5	0	4	6	0
Vanderbilt	1	4	1	3	6	1
Tennessee	1	5	1	4	5	1
Tulane	1	5	0	3	7	0

1965 NCAA Major College Statistical Leaders

Individual Leaders

PASSING/COMPLETIONS	G	ATT	COM	PCT	INT	I%	YDS	YPA	TD	TD%	COM.PG
1 Bill Anderson, Tulsa	10	509	296	58.2	14	2.8	3464	6.8	30	5.9	29.6
2 Billy Stevens, Texas El-Paso	10	432	196	45.4	29	6.7	3042	7.0	21	4.9	19.6
3 Tom Wilson, Texas Tech	10	283	172	60.8	16	5.7	2119	7.5	18	6.4	17.2
4 Vidal Carlin, North Texas	10	341	159	46.6	18	5.3	1723	5.1	12	3.5	15.9
5 Steve Spurrier, Florida	**10**	**287**	**148**	**51.6**	**13**	**4.5**	**1893**	**6.6**	**14**	**4.9**	**14.8**
6 Ken Lucas, Pittsburgh	10	268	144	53.7	15	5.6	1921	7.2	10	3.7	14.4
7 Bob Griese, Purdue	10	238	142	59.7	8	3.4	1719	7.2	11	4.6	14.2
8 Bob Hall, Brown	9	254	135	53.1	17	6.7	1340	5.3	8	3.2	15.0
9 Carroll Williams, Xavier	10	262	128	48.9	14	5.3	1847	7.0	20	7.6	12.8
10 Chuck Burt, Wisconsin	10	235	121	51.5	22	9.4	1143	4.9	5	2.1	12.1

ALL-PURPOSE YARDS	G	RUSH	REC	PR	KR	YDS	YPG
1 Floyd Little, Syracuse	10	1065	248	423	254	1990	199.0

RUSHING/YARDS	G	ATT	YDS	AVG	YPG
1 Mike Garrett, Southern California	10	267	1440	5.4	144.0
2 Jim Grabowski, Illinois	10	252	1258	5.0	125.8
3 Jim Bohl, New Mexico State	10	182	1187	6.5	118.7
4 Roy Shivers, Utah State	10	189	1138	6.0	113.8
5 Pete Pifer, Oregon State	10	234	1095	4.7	109.5
6 Floyd Little, Syracuse	10	193	1065	5.5	106.5
7 Ray McDonald, Idaho	10	213	1000	4.7	100.0
8 Bill Asbury, Kent State	10	238	998	4.2	99.8
9 Bobby Burnett, Arkansas	10	232	947	4.1	94.7
10 Charlie Brown, Missouri	10	174	937	5.4	93.7

RUSHING/YARDS PER CARRY	G	ATT	YDS	YPC
1 Mel Farr, UCLA	10	112	785	7.0
2 Jim Bohl, New Mexico State	10	182	1187	6.5
3 Garrett Ford, West Virginia	10	140	894	6.4
4 Roy Shivers, Utah State	10	189	1138	6.0
5 Larry Csonka, Syracuse	10	136	795	5.9
6 Harry Wilson, Nebraska	10	120	672	5.6
7 Floyd Little, Syracuse	10	193	1065	5.5
8 Bob Apisa, Michigan State	10	121	666	5.5
9 Mike Garrett, Southern California	10	267	1440	5.4
10 Charlie Brown, Missouri	10	174	937	5.4

Based on top 40 rushers

RECEIVING/RECEPTIONS	G	REC	YDS	TD	YPR	YPG	RPG
1 Howard Twilley, Tulsa	10	134	1779	16	13.3	177.9	13.4
2 Chuck Hughes, Texas-El Paso	10	80	1519	12	19.0	151.9	8.0
3 Neal Sweeney, Tulsa	10	78	883	8	11.3	88.3	7.8
4 John Love, North Texas	10	76	994	7	13.1	99.4	7.6
5 George Pearce, William & Mary	10	61	796	6	13.0	79.6	6.1
6 Ken McLean, Texas A&M	10	60	835	3	13.9	83.5	6.0
6 Donny Anderson, Texas Tech	10	60	797	7	13.3	79.7	6.0
8 Charles Casey, Florida	**10**	**58**	**809**	**8**	**13.9**	**80.9**	**5.8**
9 Harlan Lane, Baylor	10	56	643	3	11.5	64.3	5.6
10 Jack Clancy, Michigan	10	52	762	5	14.7	76.2	5.2

PUNTING	PUNT	YDS	AVG
1 Dave Lewis, Stanford	29	1302	44.9
2 Joe Payton, Arizona	56	2498	44.6
3 Chuck Kolb, Arizona State	65	2860	44.0
4 Phil Scoggins, Texas A&M	88	3837	43.6
5 David Conway, Texas	52	2252	43.3
6 Jerry DePoyster, Wyoming	36	1559	43.3
7 Rodney Stewart, Duke	41	1755	42.8
8 Joe Rodriguez, Idaho	36	1516	42.1
9 Dick McGraw, Mississippi State	**48**	**2021**	**42.1**
10 Mike Bragg, Richmond	67	2794	41.7

PUNT RETURNS/YARDS	PR	YDS	AVG
1 Nick Rassas, Notre Dame	24	459	19.1
2 Larry Wachholtz, Nebraska	31	452	14.6
3 Charlie Greer, Colorado	26	431	16.6
4 Johnny Roland, Missouri	32	430	13.4
5 Floyd Little, Syracuse	18	423	23.5
6 Marcus Rhoden, Mississippi State	**19**	**413**	**21.7**
7 Doug Cunningham, Mississippi	**33**	**405**	**12.3**
8 Mike Carroll, New Mexico State	28	384	13.7
9 Joe Souliere, Bowling Green	18	372	20.7
10 Eddie Willis, VMI	24	349	14.5

KICKOFF RETURNS/YARDS	KR	YDS	AVG
1 Eric Crabtree, Pittsburgh	24	636	26.5
2 Steve Bramwell, Washington	22	573	26.0
3 Donny Anderson, Texas Tech	22	541	24.6
4 Bob Grim, Oregon State	23	524	22.8
5 Dan Bland, Mississippi State	**20**	**499**	**25.0**
6 Donald Dennis, West Texas State	17	482	28.4
7 Tom Barrington, Ohio State	14	480	34.3
8 Mike Junker, Xavier	22	479	21.8
9 Preston Ridlehuber, Georgia	**20**	**468**	**23.4**
10 Benny Galloway, South Carolina	19	463	24.4

SCORING	TDS	XPT	FG	PTS
1 Howard Twilley, Tulsa	16	31	0	127
2 Floyd Little, Syracuse	19	0	0	114
3 Donny Anderson, Texas Tech	17	0	0	102
4 Mike Garrett, Southern California	16	0	0	96
4 Roy Shivers, Utah State	16	0	0	96
4 Mickey Jackson, Marshall	16	0	0	96
4 Bobby Burnett, Arkansas	16	0	0	96
8 Ray McDonald, Idaho	15	0	0	90
9 Charley Harraway, San Jose State	14	0	0	84
10 Charley Gogolak, Princeton	0	33	16	81

KICK SCORING	XPA	XP	FGA	FG	PTS
1 Charles Gogolak, Princeton	33	33	23	16	81
2 Ronny South, Arkansas	44	42	11	6	60
3 Frank Rogers, Colorado	18	16	17	13	55
4 Dick Kenney, Michigan State	23	20	18	11	53
5 Joe Cook, Texas-El Paso	41	37	10	5	52
5 Bob Wolfe, Colorado State	33	28	15	8	52
7 Ken Ivan, Notre Dame	31	27	11	7	48
8 Bob Etter, Georgia	**18**	**16**	**13**	**10**	**46**
9 Dave Conway, Texas	24	21	16	8	45
9 Jerry DePoyster, Wyoming	26	21	18	8	45
9 Larry Wachholtz, Nebraska	39	36	6	3	45

INTERCEPTIONS	INT	YDS
1 Bob Sullivan, Maryland	10	61
2 Jim Miller, New Mexico State	8	111
2 Billy Devrow, Southern Miss	8	45
4 Henry King, Utah State	7	193
4 Ron Bostwick, Texas-El Paso	7	183
4 Tony Golmont, North Carolina St.	7	86
4 Dick Gingrich, Penn State	7	66
8 Nick Rassas, Notre Dame	6	197
8 David Fronek, Wisconsin	6	115

Team Leaders

RUSHING OFFENSE	G	ATT	YDS	AVG	YPG
1 Nebraska	10	573	2900	5.1	290.0
2 Southern California	10	527	2562	4.9	256.2
3 Missouri	10	566	2473	4.4	247.3
4 Syracuse	10	536	2390	4.5	239.0
5 Cornell	9	476	2143	4.5	238.1
6 Michigan State	10	547	2375	4.3	237.5
7 Dartmouth	9	462	2107	4.6	234.1
8 Arkansas	10	516	2261	4.4	226.1
9 Penn State	10	525	2247	4.3	224.7
10 Princeton	9	461	1991	4.3	221.2

PASSING OFFENSE	G	ATT	COM	INT	PCT	YDS	YPA	TD	I%	YPC	YPG
1 Tulsa	10	510	296	14	58.0	3464	6.8	30	2.8	11.7	346.4
2 Texas-El Paso	10	446	202	30	45.3	3211	7.2	23	6.7	15.9	321.1
3 North Texas State	10	420	194	23	46.2	2172	5.2	14	5.5	11.2	217.2
4 Louisville	10	297	134	20	45.1	2149	7.2	13	6.7	16.0	214.9
5 Texas Tech	10	291	173	16	59.5	2126	7.3	18	5.5	12.3	212.6
6 Pittsburgh	10	289	155	16	53.6	2065	7.1	12	5.5	13.3	206.5
7 Florida	**10**	**309**	**158**	**13**	**51.1**	**2033**	**6.6**	**16**	**4.2**	**12.9**	**203.3**
8 Oregon	10	301	139	20	46.2	2022	6.7	16	6.6	14.5	202.2
9 Brigham Young	10	264	128	15	48.5	1920	7.3	21	5.7	15.0	192.0
10 Kentucky	**10**	**236**	**124**	**19**	**52.5**	**1902**	**8.1**	**11**	**8.1**	**15.3**	**190.2**

TOTAL OFFENSE	G	P	YDS	AVG	YPG
1 Tulsa	10	780	4278	5.5	427.8
2 Nebraska	10	760	4040	5.3	404.0
3 Southern California	10	682	3748	5.5	374.8
4 Brigham Young	10	695	3691	5.3	369.1
5 Texas-El Paso	10	707	3653	5.2	365.3
6 Princeton	9	646	3277	5.1	364.1
7 Arkansas	10	692	3602	5.2	360.2
8 Dartmouth	9	608	3239	5.3	359.9
9 Utah State	10	693	3563	5.1	356.3
10 Michigan State	10	717	3561	5.0	356.1

RUSHING DEFENSE	G	ATT	YDS	AVG	YPG
1 Michigan State	10	338	456	1.3	45.6
2 Buffalo	10	421	737	1.8	73.7
3 Southern Miss	9	335	673	2.0	74.8
4 Arkansas	10	355	749	2.1	74.9
5 Notre Dame	10	389	754	1.9	75.4
6 Utah State	10	372	839	2.3	83.9
7 Cincinnati	10	367	841	2.3	84.1
8 Florida	**10**	**408**	**884**	**2.2**	**88.4**
9 Dartmouth	9	339	801	2.4	89.0
10 Miami (Ohio)	10	373	898	2.4	89.8

PASSING DEFENSE	G	ATT	COM	PCT	YPC	INT	I%	YDS	YPA	TD	YPG
1 Toledo	10	146	57	39.0	12.2	13	8.9	698	4.8	2	69.8
2 Columbia	9	140	53	37.9	13.2	12	8.6	700	5.0	4	77.8
3 Colgate	10	189	71	37.6	11.0	21	11.1	778	4.1	6	77.8
4 Bowling Green	9	144	65	45.1	11.2	8	5.6	730	5.1	4	81.1
5 Citadel	10	132	66	50.0	12.3	9	6.8	812	6.2	7	81.2
6 Iowa State	10	150	61	40.7	13.5	8	5.3	821	5.5	4	82.1
7 Holy Cross	10	136	61	44.9	13.7	10	7.4	833	6.1	4	83.3
8 Vanderbilt	**10**	**151**	**77**	**51.0**	**11.0**	**14**	**9.3**	**847**	**5.6**	**4**	**84.7**
9 Southern Miss	9	189	67	35.4	11.6	20	10.6	777	4.1	2	86.3
10 Yale	9	166	77	46.4	10.2	14	8.4	783	4.7	4	87.0

TOTAL DEFENSE	G	P	YDS	AVG	YPG
1 Southern Miss	9	524	1450	2.8	161.1
2 Michigan State	10	572	1699	3.0	169.9
3 Toledo	10	593	1820	3.1	182.0
4 Buffalo	10	621	1831	2.9	183.1
5 Bowling Green	9	499	1680	3.4	186.7
6 Notre Dame	10	598	1944	3.3	194.4
7 Florida	**10**	**617**	**2017**	**3.3**	**201.7**
8 Nebraska	10	607	2028	3.3	202.8
9 Miami (Ohio)	10	544	2088	3.8	208.8
10 Harvard	9	557	1887	3.4	209.7

SCORING OFFENSE	G	PTS	AVG
1 Arkansas	10	324	32.4
2 Nebraska	10	321	32.1
3 Tulsa	10	315	31.5
4 Princeton	9	281	31.2
5 Texas-El Paso	10	304	30.4
6 Dartmouth	9	271	30.1
7 West Virginia	10	279	27.9
8 Utah State	10	271	27.1
9 Notre Dame	10	270	27.0
10 Colorado State	10	264	26.4

SCORING DEFENSE	G	PTS	AVG
1 Michigan State	10	62	6.2
2 Southern Miss	9	60	6.7
3 Harvard	9	62	6.9
4 Notre Dame	10	73	7.3
5 Buffalo	10	78	7.8
6 Dartmouth	9	71	7.9
7 Alabama	**10**	**79**	**7.9**
8 Missouri	10	83	8.3
9 Nebraska	10	90	9.0

1965

FINAL POLL (JAN. 3)

AP	SCHOOL	FINAL RECORD
1	**Alabama**	**9-1-1**
2	Michigan State	10-1-0
3	Arkansas	10-1-0
4	UCLA	8-2-1
5	Nebraska	10-1-0
6	Missouri	8-2-1
7	**Tennessee**	**8-1-2**
8	**LSU**	**8-3-0**
9	Notre Dame	7-2-1
10	Southern California	7-2-1

CONSENSUS ALL-AMERICANS

POS	OFFENSE	SCHOOL
B	Mike Garrett	Southern California
B	Jim Grabowski	Illinois
B	Bob Griese	Purdue
B	Donny Anderson	Texas Tech
E	Howard Twilley	Tulsa
E	Freeman White	Nebraska
T	Sam Ball	Kentucky
T	Glen Ray Hines	Arkansas
G	Dick Arrington	Notre Dame
G	Stas Maliszewski	Princeton
C	**Paul Crane**	**Alabama**

OTHERS RECEIVING FIRST-TEAM HONORS

B	Clint Jones	Michigan State
B	Floyd Little	Syracuse
B	**Steve Spurrier**	**Florida**
B	Steve Juday	Michigan State
E	Bobby Crockett	Arkansas
E	**Chuck Casey**	**Florida**
E	Gene Washington	Michigan State
T	Wayne Foster	Washington State
T	Ron Goovert	Michigan State
T	**George Patton**	**Georgia**
T	Karl Singer	Purdue
T	Francis Peay	Missouri
G	Doug Van Horn	Ohio State
G	Harold Lucas	Michigan State
K	Charlie Gogolak	Princeton

POS	DEFENSE	SCHOOL
E	Aaron Brown	Minnesota
E	Bubba Smith	Michigan State
T	Walt Barnes	Nebraska
T	Loyd Phillips	Arkansas
T	Bill Yearby	Michigan
LB	Carl McAdams	Oklahoma
LB	Tommy Nobis	Texas
LB	**Frank Emanuel**	**Tennessee**
B	George Webster	Michigan State
B	Johnny Roland	Missouri
B	Nick Rassas	Notre Dame

OTHERS RECEIVING FIRST-TEAM HONORS

DL	Tony Jeter	Nebraska
DL	Jerry Shay	Purdue
DL	Ed Weisacosky	Miami (Fla.)
DL	Joe Fratangelo	North Carolina
DL	**Jack Thornton**	**Auburn**
DL	**Lynn Matthews**	**Florida**
LB	Dwight Kelley	Ohio State
DB	**Bruce Bennett**	**Florida**

HEISMAN TROPHY VOTING

	PLAYER	POS	SCHOOL	TOTAL
1	Mike Garrett	TB	Southern Cal	926
2	Howard Twilley	E	Tulsa	528
3	Jim Grabowski	FB	Illinois	481
4	Donny Anderson	RB	Texas Tech	408
5	Floyd Little	HB	Syracuse	287
6	Steve Juday	QB	Michigan State	281
7	Tommy Nobis	LB	Texas	205
8	Bob Griese	QB	Purdue	193
9	**Steve Spurrier**	**QB**	**Florida**	**93**
10	**Steve Sloan**	**QB**	**Alabama**	**92**

AWARD WINNERS

PLAYER	AWARD
Tommy Nobis, LB, Texas	Maxwell
Tommy Nobis, LB, Texas	Outland

BOWL GAMES

DATE	GAME	SCORE
D11	Tangerine	East Carolina 31, Maine 0
D18	**Liberty**	**Mississippi 13, Auburn 7**
D18	**Bluebonnet**	**Tennessee 27, Tulsa 6**
D31	Gator	Georgia Tech 31, Texas Tech 21
D31	Sun	Texas-El Paso 13, TCU 12
J1	**Orange**	**Alabama 39, Nebraska 28**
.J1	Sugar	Missouri 20, Florida 18
J1	**Cotton**	**LSU 14, Arkansas 7**
J1	Rose	UCLA 14, Michigan State 12

SEC STANDINGS

	CONFERENCE			OVERALL		
	W	L	T	W	L	T
Alabama	6	1	1	9	1	1
Auburn	4	1	1	5	5	1
Florida	4	2	0	7	4	0
Tennessee	3	1	2	8	1	2
Mississippi	5	3	0	7	4	0
LSU	3	3	0	8	3	0
Kentucky	3	3	0	6	4	0
Georgia	3	3	0	6	4	0
Mississippi State	1	5	0	4	6	0
Vanderbilt	1	5	0	2	7	1
Tulane	1	5	0	2	8	0

1966 NCAA Major College Statistical Leaders

Individual Leaders

	Passing/Completions	G	ATT	COM	PCT	INT	I%	YDS	YPA	TD	TD%	COM.PG
1	John Eckman, Wichita State	10	458	195	42.6	34	7.4	2339	5.1	7	1.5	19.5
2	Mark Reed, Arizona	10	365	193	52.9	16	4.4	2368	6.5	20	5.5	19.3
3	**Steve Spurrier, Florida**	**10**	**291**	**179**	**61.5**	**8**	**2.8**	**2012**	**6.9**	**16**	**5.5**	**17.9**
4	Terry Southall, Baylor	10	337	173	51.3	23	6.8	1986	5.9	16	4.8	17.3
5	Hank Washington, West Texas State	10	281	163	58.0	16	5.7	2107	7.5	17	6.1	16.3
6	Danny Holman, San Jose State	10	260	160	61.5	12	4.6	1925	7.4	12	4.6	16.0
7	Benny Russell, Louisville	10	310	142	45.8	12	3.9	2016	6.5	14	4.5	14.2
8	Virgil Carter, Brigham Young	10	293	141	48.1	16	5.5	2182	7.4	21	7.2	14.1
9	Billy Stevens, Texas-El Paso	10	305	140	45.9	17	5.6	2088	6.8	19	6.2	14.0
10	**Dewey Warren, Tennessee**	**10**	**229**	**136**	**59.4**	**7**	**3.1**	**1716**	**7.5**	**18**	**7.9**	**13.6**

	All-Purpose Yards	G	RUSH	REC	PR	KR	YDS	YPG
1	Frank Quayle, Virginia	10	727	420	30	439	1616	161.6

	Rushing/Yards	G	ATT	YDS	TD	AVG	YPG
1	Ray McDonald, Idaho	10	259	1329	14	5.1	132.9
2	Don Fitzgerald, Kent State	10	296	1245	12	4.2	124.5
3	Jim Bohl, New Mexico State	10	218	1148	13	5.3	114.8
4	Pete Pifer, Oregon State	10	230	1088	12	4.7	108.8
5	Chris Gilbert, Texas	10	206	1080	6	5.2	108.0
6	Garrett Ford, West Virginia	10	236	1068	7	4.5	106.8
7	Dick Post, Houston	10	185	1061	5	5.7	106.1
8	Cornelius Davis, Kansas State	10	210	1028	6	4.9	102.8
9	Larry Csonka, Syracuse	10	197	1012	7	5.1	101.2
10	Pete Larson, Cornell	9	206	979	9	4.8	108.8

	Rushing/Yards Per Carry	G	ATT	YDS	YPC
1	Bobby Leo, Harvard	9	130	827	6.4
2	Mel Farr, UCLA	10	138	809	5.9
3	Vic Gatto, Harvard	9	121	700	5.8
4	Dick Post, Houston	10	185	1061	5.7
5	Jack Layland, Pacific	11	145	830	5.7
6	Clem Turner, Cincinnati	10	153	840	5.5
7	Jim Bohl, New Mexico State	10	218	1148	5.3
8	Chris Gilbert, Texas	10	206	1080	5.2
9	Larry Csonka, Syracuse	10	197	1012	5.1
10	Ray McDonald, Idaho	10	259	1329	5.1

Based on top 34 rushers

	Receiving/Receptions	G	REC	YDS	TD	YPR	YPG	RPG
1	Glenn Meltzer, Wichita State	10	91	1115	4	12.3	111.5	9.1
2	Jack Clancy, Michigan	10	76	1079	4	14.2	107.9	7.6
2	Jim Greth, Arizona	10	76	1003	8	13.2	100.3	7.6
4	John Love, North Texas	10	68	1130	10	16.6	113.0	6.8
5	Chuck Albertson, William & Mary	10	67	792	4	11.8	79.2	6.7
6	Jim Beirne, Purdue	10	64	768	8	12.0	76.8	6.4
7	**Dick Trapp, Florida**	**10**	**63**	**872**	**7**	**13.8**	**87.2**	**6.3**
8	John Wright, Illinois	10	60	831	4	13.9	83.1	6.0
9	Jim Zamberlan, Louisville	10	59	747	4	12.7	74.7	5.9
10	Phil Odle, Brigham Young	10	58	920	5	15.9	92.0	5.8
10	Dave Szymakowski, West Texas State	10	58	842	6	14.5	84.2	5.8

	Punting	PUNT	YDS	AVG
1	**Ron Widby, Tennessee**	**48**	**2104**	**43.8**
2	Gary Houser, Oregon State	45	1971	43.8
3	Donnie Gibbs, TCU	61	2611	42.8
4	Mike Bragg, Richmond	58	2482	42.8
5	Joe Randall, Brown	61	2605	42.7
6	Bill Bradley, Texas	45	1913	42.5
7	Dave Morgan, Kansas	46	1950	42.4
8	Steve O'Neal, Texas A&M	67	2834	42.3
9	Randy Cardin, San Jose State	66	2785	42.2
10	Bob Coble, Kansas State	70	2919	41.7
10	Brant Conley, Tulsa	68	2836	41.7
10	Dan Darragh, William & Mary	45	1877	41.7

	Punt Returns/Yards	PR	YDS	TD	AVG
1	Vic Washington, Wyoming	34	443	2	13.0
2	**Dicky Lyons, Kentucky**	**25**	**419**	**2**	**16.8**
3	Kent Oborn, Brigham Young	31	393	1	12.7
4	Don Bean, Houston	19	384	3	20.2
5	Martine Bercher, Arkansas	24	375	3	15.6
6	**Doug Cunningham, Mississippi**	**33**	**369**	**2**	**11.2**
7	Reg Matthews, Texas-El Paso	19	367	2	19.3
8	Doug James, Princeton	23	365	1	15.9
9	Billy Woods, North Texas	20	351	3	17.6
10	**Sammy Grezaffi, LSU**	**25**	**309**	**1**	**12.4**

	Kickoff Returns/Yards	KR	YDS	TD	AVG
1	**Marcus Rhoden, Mississippi State**	**26**	**572**	**1**	**22.0**
2	John Ginter, Indiana	26	532	0	20.5
3	Tom Schinke, Wisconsin	21	527	0	25.1
4	Gary Rowe, North Carolina St.	20	505	0	25.3
5	Jim Baker, Rutgers	22	495	1	22.5
6	Tom Busch, Iowa State	18	484	0	26.9
7	Dave Riggs, North Carolina	23	480	0	20.9
8	Bob Baxter, Memphis	19	449	0	23.6
9	Andy Beath, Duke	25	447	0	17.9
10	Frank Quayle, Virginia	18	439	0	24.4

	Scoring	TDS	XPT	FG	PTS
1	Ken Hebert, Houston	11	41	2	113
2	Jim Bohl, New Mexico State	15	8	0	98
3	Leeland Jones, Buffalo	16	0	0	96
4	Floyd Little, Syracuse	15	2	0	92
5	Ray McDonald, Idaho	15	0	0	90
6	Marvin Hubbard, Colgate	13	7	1	88
6	John Love, North Texas	10	26	0	88
8	Tom Francisco, Virginia Tech	14	0	0	84
9	Bob Griese, Purdue	6	33	4	81
10	Four tied				72

	Kick Scoring	XPA	XP	FGA	FG	PTS
1	Jerry DePoyster, Wyoming	39	32	38	13	71
2	**Bob Etter, Georgia**	**22**	**21**	**15**	**12**	**57**
3	**Steve Davis, Alabama**	**28**	**25**	**18**	**10**	**55**
4	Tom Fambrough, West Texas State	35	33	10	6	51
4	Kurt Zimmerman, UCLA	33	33	11	6	51
6	**Jimmy Keyes, Mississippi**	**20**	**20**	**17**	**10**	**50**
7	Harold Deters, North Carolina St.	19	19	22	10	49
8	Al Lavan, Colorado State	30	27	10	7	48
9	Bunky Henry, Georgia Tech	32	32	10	5	47
9	Joe Azzaro, Notre Dame	38	35	5	4	47
9	Ken Hebert, Houston	46	41	7	2	47

	Interceptions	INT	YDS	TD
1	Henry King, Utah State	11	180	2
1	Charlie West, Texas-El Paso	11	105	1
3	Tom Wilson, Colgate	8	125	0
3	Abelardo Alba, New Mexico State	8	112	1
3	Don Peterson, San Jose State	8	110	0
3	**Gerald Warfield, Mississippi**	**8**	**77**	**0**
7	Tom Schoen, Notre Dame*	7	112	2
7	Gus Holloman, Houston*	7	105	0
7	Gary Adams, Arkansas*	7	93	0
7	Bobby Roberts, Brigham Young*	7	87	1

*11 tied with seven; these had the most yards

Team Leaders

	Rushing Offense	G	ATT	YDS	AVG	TD	YPG
1	Harvard	9	514	2421	4.7	24	269.0
2	Dartmouth	9	453	2298	5.1	23	255.3
3	Idaho	10	539	2435	4.5	20	243.5
4	Houston	10	439	2420	5.5	21	242.0
5	Colgate	10	532	2367	4.4	28	236.7
6	UCLA	10	503	2338	4.6	28	233.8
7	Oregon State	10	530	2335	4.4	19	233.5
8	Michigan State	10	523	2305	4.4	29	230.5
9	Tulane	10	513	2297	4.5	14	229.7
10	Colorado	10	523	2224	4.3	21	222.4

	Passing Offense	G	ATT	COM	INT	PCT	YDS	YPA	TD	I%	YPC	YPG
1	Tulsa	10	387	205	19	53.0	2720	7.0	22	4.9	13.3	272.0
2	North Texas	10	415	184	31	44.3	2595	6.3	25	7.5	14.1	259.5
3	Arizona	10	407	210	19	51.6	2551	6.3	20	4.7	12.1	255.1
4	Florida State	10	351	187	14	53.3	2467	7.0	13	4.0	13.2	246.7
5	Brigham Young	10	329	161	21	48.9	2416	7.3	22	6.4	15.0	241.6
6	Texas-El Paso	10	360	165	19	45.8	2410	6.7	24	5.3	14.6	241.0
7	Wichita State	10	460	196	34	42.6	2347	5.1	7	7.4	12.0	234.7
8	West Texas State	10	309	174	19	56.3	2313	7.5	17	6.2	13.3	231.3
9	**Florida**	**10**	**328**	**199**	**11**	**60.7**	**2242**	**6.8**	**17**	**3.4**	**11.3**	**224.2**
10	Louisville	10	322	149	14	46.3	2157	6.7	14	4.4	14.5	215.7

	Total Offense	G	P	YDS	AVG	TD	YPG
1	Houston	10	678	4372	6.4	44	437.2
2	Brigham Young	10	748	4006	5.4	36	400.6
3	Notre Dame	10	703	3915	5.6	44	391.5
4	West Texas State	10	672	3898	5.8	36	389.8
5	Dartmouth	9	610	3499	5.7	37	388.8
6	Florida State	10	735	3746	5.1	34	374.6
7	UCLA	10	682	3735	5.5	35	373.5
8	Tulsa	10	704	3618	5.1	28	361.8
9	**Florida**	**10**	**714**	**3611**	**5.1**	**30**	**361.1**
10	Idaho	10	746	3590	4.8	23	359.0

	Rushing Defense	G	ATT	YDS	AVG	TD	YPG
1	Wyoming	10	357	385	1.1	2	38.5
2	North Texas	10	408	513	1.3	5	51.3
3	Michigan State	10	336	514	1.5	6	51.4
4	Southern Miss	10	376	600	1.6	6	60.0
5	Virginia Tech	10	363	723	2.0	4	72.3
6	Texas-El Paso	10	374	728	1.9	10	72.8
7	Syracuse	10	341	738	2.2	5	73.8
8	**Mississippi**	**10**	**410**	**741**	**1.8**	**3**	**74.1**
9	Notre Dame	10	384	793	2.1	2	79.3
10	**Alabama**	**10**	**336**	**797**	**2.4**	**2**	**79.7**

	Passing Defense	G	ATT	COM	PCT	YPC	INT	I%	YDS	YPA	TD	YPG
1	Toledo	10	142	56	39.4	12.6	9	6.3	704	5.0	8	70.4
2	Oklahoma	10	171	75	43.9	11.6	15	8.8	873	5.1	1	87.3
3	Xavier	10	169	74	43.8	12.4	6	3.6	915	5.4	4	91.5
4	Missouri	10	159	68	42.8	13.6	14	8.8	922	5.8	1	92.2
5	**Alabama**	**10**	**208**	**86**	**41.3**	**11.0**	**24**	**11.5**	**944**	**4.5**	**3**	**94.4**
6	**Tennessee**	**10**	**187**	**76**	**40.6**	**12.4**	**16**	**8.6**	**946**	**5.1**	**3**	**94.6**
7	Michigan	10	196	82	41.8	11.6	9	4.6	953	4.9	6	95.3
8	Harvard	9	176	70	39.8	12.3	14	8.0	863	4.9	1	95.9
9	Colgate	10	217	88	40.6	11.0	28	12.9	966	4.5	4	96.6
10	South Carolina	10	154	72	46.8	13.4	13	8.4	968	6.3	8	96.8

	Total Defense	G	P	YDS	AVG	TD	YPG
1	Southern Miss	10	602	1637	2.7	12	163.7
2	**Alabama**	**10**	**544**	**1741**	**3.2**	**5**	**174.1**
3	**Mississippi**	**10**	**621**	**1751**	**2.8**	**6**	**175.1**
4	Notre Dame	10	633	1876	3.0	3	187.6
5	Wyoming	10	668	1883	2.8	9	188.3
6	Georgia Tech	10	602	2066	3.4	8	206.6
7	Miami (Fla.)	10	646	2068	3.2	9	206.8
8	Michigan State	10	596	2093	3.5	13	209.3
9	Toledo	10	607	2097	3.5	21	209.7
10	**Tennessee**	**10**	**628**	**2099**	**3.3**	**8**	**209.9**

	Scoring Offense	G	PTS	AVG
1	Notre Dame	10	362	36.2
2	Houston	10	335	33.5
3	Wyoming	10	327	32.7
4	New Mexico State	10	321	32.1
5	Dartmouth	9	273	30.3
6	North Texas	10	298	29.8
7	Michigan State	10	293	29.3
7	Texas-El Paso	10	293	29.3
9	Purdue	10	283	28.3
10	UCLA	10	281	28.1

	Scoring Defense	G	PTS	AVG
1	**Alabama**	**10**	**37**	**3.7**
2	Notre Dame	10	38	3.8
3	**Mississippi**	**10**	**46**	**4.6**
4	Colgate	10	67	6.7
5	Harvard	9	60	6.7
6	Wyoming	10	69	6.9
7	Arkansas	10	73	7.3
8	Miami (Ohio)	10	76	7.6
9	Georgia Tech	10	81	8.1

1966

FINAL POLL (DEC. 5)

AP	SCHOOL	FINAL RECORD
1	Notre Dame	9-0-1
2	Michigan State	9-0-1
3	Alabama	11-0-0
4	Georgia	10-1-0
5	UCLA	9-1-0
6	Nebraska	9-2-0
7	Purdue	9-2-0
8	Georgia Tech	9-2-0
9	Miami (Fla.)	8-2-1
10	SMU	8-3-0

CONSENSUS ALL-AMERICANS

POS	OFFENSE	SCHOOL
B	Steve Spurrier	Florida
B	Nick Eddy	Notre Dame
B	Mel Farr	UCLA
B	Clint Jones	Michigan State
E	Jack Clancy	Michigan
E	Ray Perkins	Alabama
T	Cecil Dowdy	Alabama
T	Ron Yary	Southern California
G	Tom Regner	Notre Dame
G	LaVerne Allers	Nebraska
C	Jim Breland	Georgia Tech

OTHERS RECEIVING FIRST-TEAM HONORS

B	Lenny Snow	Georgia Tech
B	Bob Griese	Purdue
B	Floyd Little	Syracuse
B	Larry Csonka	Syracuse
E	Gene Washington	Michigan State
E	Jim Bierne	Purdue
E	Austin Denney	Tennessee
T	Maurice Moorman	Texas A&M
T	Wayne Mass	Clemson
T	Jerry West	Michigan State
G	Gary Bugenhagen	Syracuse
G	Ed Chandler	Georgia
C	Ray Pryor	Ohio State

POS	DEFENSE	SCHOOL
E	Bubba Smith	Michigan State
E	Alan Page	Notre Dame
T	Loyd Phillips	Arkansas
T	Tom Greenlee	Washington
MG	Wayne Meylan	Nebraska
MG	John LaGrone	SMU
LB	Jim Lynch	Notre Dame
LB	Paul Naumoff	Tennessee
B	George Webster	Michigan State
B	Tom Beier	Miami (Fla.)
B	Nate Shaw	Southern California

OTHERS RECEIVING FIRST-TEAM HONORS

T	Dennis Byrd	North Carolina St.
T	Pete Duranko	Notre Dame
T	George Patton	Georgia
MG	John Richardson	UCLA
LB	Bob Matheson	Duke
LB	Townsend Clarke	Army
B	Frank Loria	Virginia Tech
B	Larry Wachholtz	Michigan State
B	Bobby Johns	Alabama
B	E. Winters Mabry	Dartmouth
B	Ray Perkins	Alabama

HEISMAN TROPHY VOTING

	PLAYER	POS	SCHOOL	TOTAL
1	Steve Spurrier	QB	Florida	1659
2	Bob Griese	QB	Purdue	816
3	Nick Eddy	HB	Notre Dame	456
4	Gary Beban	QB	UCLA	318
5	Floyd Little	HB	Syracuse	296
6	Clint Jones	RB	Michigan State	204
7	Mel Farr	HB	UCLA	115
8	Terry Hanratty	QB	Notre Dame	98
9	Loyd Phillips	T	Arkansas	67
10	George Patton	DT	Georgia	62

AWARD WINNERS

PLAYER	AWARD
Jim Lynch, LB, Notre Dame	Maxwell
Loyd Phillips, T, Arkansas	Outland

BOWL GAMES

DATE	GAME	SCORE
D10	Liberty	Miami (Fla.) 14, Virginia Tech 7
D10	Tangerine	Morgan St. 14, West Chester 6
D17	Bluebonnet	Texas 19, Mississippi 0
D24	Sun	Wyoming 28, Florida State 20
D31	Cotton	Georgia 24, SMU 9
D31	Gator	Tennessee 18, Syracuse 12
J2	Orange	Florida 27, Georgia Tech 12
J2	Sugar	Alabama 34, Nebraska 7
J2	Rose	Purdue 14, Southern California 13

SEC STANDINGS

	CONFERENCE W	L	T	OVERALL W	L	T
Alabama	6	0	0	11	0	0
Georgia	6	0	0	10	1	0
Florida	5	1	0	9	2	0
Mississippi	5	2	0	8	3	0
Tennessee	4	2	0	8	3	0
LSU	3	3	0	5	4	1
Kentucky	2	4	0	3	6	1
Auburn	1	5	0	4	6	0
Mississippi State	0	6	0	2	8	0
Vanderbilt	0	6	0	1	9	0

1967 NCAA Major College Statistical Leaders

Individual Leaders

	Passing/Completions	G	ATT	COM	PCT	INT	I%	YDS	YPA	TD	TD%	COM.PG
1	Terry Stone, New Mexico	10	336	160	47.6	19	5.7	1946	5.8	9	2.7	16.0
2	Jimmy Poole, Davidson	9	264	157	59.5	12	4.6	1611	6.1	9	3.4	17.4
3	Sal Olivas, New Mexico State	10	321	156	48.6	16	5.0	2225	6.9	18	5.6	15.6
4	Mike Livingston, SMU	10	250	152	60.8	14	5.6	1750	7.0	10	4.0	15.2
5	Kim Hammond, Florida State	10	241	140	58.1	10	4.2	1991	8.3	15	6.2	14.0
6	Paul Toscano, Wyoming	10	241	134	55.6	10	4.2	1791	7.4	18	7.5	13.4
7	John Cartwright, Navy	10	241	129	53.5	9	3.7	1537	6.4	9	3.7	12.9
8	John Schneider, Toledo	10	245	127	51.8	11	4.5	1650	6.7	10	4.1	12.7
9	Marty Domres, Columbia	9	229	121	52.8	12	5.2	1378	6.0	6	2.6	13.4
10	Steve Ramsey, North Texas	9	269	119	44.2	19	7.1	1732	6.4	21	7.8	13.2

	All-Purpose Yards	G	RUSH	REC	PR	KR	YDS	YPG
1	O.J. Simpson, Southern California	9	1415	109	0	176	1700	188.9

	Rushing/Yards	G	ATT	YDS	TD	AVG	YPG
1	O.J. Simpson, Southern California	9	266	1415	11	5.3	157.2
2	Eugene Morris, West Texas State	10	191	1274	11	6.7	127.4
3	Max Anderson, Arizona State	10	191	1188	10	6.2	118.8
4	Butch Colson, East Carolina	10	252	1135	14	4.5	113.5
5	Larry Csonka, Syracuse	10	261	1127	8	4.3	112.7
6	Doug Dalton, New Mexico State	10	177	1123	10	6.3	112.3
7	Paul Gipson, Houston	10	187	1100	11	5.9	110.0
8	Buddy Gore, Clemson	10	230	1045	8	4.5	104.5
9	Chris Gilbert, Texas	10	205	1019	9	5.0	101.9
10	Ron Johnson, Michigan	10	220	1005	7	4.6	100.5

	Rushing/Yards Per Carry	G	ATT	YDS	YPC
1	Eugene Morris, West Texas State	10	191	1274	6.7
2	Leroy Keyes, Purdue	10	149	986	6.6
3	Doug Dalton, New Mexico State	10	177	1123	6.3
4	Max Anderson, Arizona State	10	191	1188	6.2
5	Bill Mayo, Dayton	10	128	771	6.0
6	Paul Gipson, Houston	10	187	1100	5.9
7	Charles Jarvis, Army	10	144	774	5.4
8	O.J. Simpson, Southern California	9	266	1415	5.3
9	Al Moore, Miami (Ohio)	10	135	717	5.3
10	Chris Gilbert, Texas	10	205	1019	5.0

Based on top 34 rushers

	Receiving/Receptions	G	REC	YDS	TD	YPR	YPG	RPG
1	**Bob Goodridge, Vanderbilt**	**10**	**79**	**1114**	**6**	**14.1**	**111.4**	**7.9**
2	Rick Eber, Tulsa	10	78	1168	12	15.0	116.8	7.8
3	Phil Odle, Brigham Young	10	77	971	9	12.6	97.1	7.7
4	Ron Sellers, Florida State	10	70	1228	8	17.5	122.8	7.0
5	Ace Hendricks, New Mexico	10	67	1094	6	16.3	109.4	6.7
6	Rob Taylor, Navy	10	61	818	6	13.4	81.8	6.1
7	**Richard Trapp, Florida**	**10**	**58**	**708**	**1**	**12.2**	**70.8**	**5.8**
7	Emilio Vallez, New Mexico	10	58	650	4	11.2	65.0	5.8
9	Jerry Levias, SMU	10	57	724	7	12.7	72.4	5.7
10	Allan Bream, Iowa	10	55	703	5	12.8	70.3	5.5

	Punting	PUNT	YDS	AVG
1	Zenon Andrusyshyn, UCLA	34	1503	44.2
2	Ken Hebert, Houston	42	1831	43.6
3	Gary Houser, Oregon State	40	1736	43.4
4	Dale Livingston, Western Michigan	49	2122	43.3
5	**Eddie Ray, LSU**	**52**	**2226**	**42.8**
6	Tom Galloway, Texas-El Paso	62	2647	42.7
7	Bob Coble, Kansas State	61	2605	42.7
8	Steve O'Neal, Texas A&M	81	3402	42.0
9	Dickie Dunaway, Southern Miss	58	2430	41.9
10	Bill Bradley, Texas	65	2717	41.8

	Punt Returns/Yards	PR	YDS	TD	AVG
1	Mike Battle, Southern California	47	570	2	12.1
2	Vic Washington, Wyoming	53	565	1	10.7
3	Don Bean, Houston	45	522	2	11.6
4	**Jimmy Carter, Auburn**	**38**	**473**	**2**	**12.4**
5	John Mallory, West Virginia	36	453	2	12.6
6	Tom Schoen, Notre Dame	42	447	1	10.6
7	Benny Goodwin, Oklahoma State	35	422	1	12.1
8	Frank Loria, Virginia Tech	30	420	1	14.0
9	Fred Combs, North Carolina St.	22	417	2	19.0
10	Charles Greer, Colorado	28	408	1	14.6

	Kickoff Returns/Yards	KR	YDS	TD	AVG
1	Joe Casas, New Mexico	23	602	1	26.2
2	**Dave Strong, Vanderbilt**	**28**	**577**	**0**	**20.6**
3	Charlie Smith, Utah	20	544	1	27.2
4	Nick Pappas, Memphis	17	527	1	31.0
5	Ron Johnson, Michigan	26	498	0	19.2
6	Jim Kirkpatrick, Purdue	20	487	0	24.4
7	Altie Taylor, Utah State	15	478	1	31.9
8	**Dicky Lyons, Kentucky**	**18**	**474**	**1**	**26.3**
9	Curley Watters, West Texas State	20	460	1	23.0
10	Kenny Dutton, Maryland	24	454	0	18.9

	Scoring	TDS	XPT	FG	PTS
1	Leroy Keyes, Purdue	19	0	0	114
2	Roland Moss, Toledo	16	0	0	96
2	David Dickey, Arkansas	16	0	0	96
4	Butch Colson, East Carolina	15	2	0	92
5	Don Abbey, Penn State	9	25	3	88
6	Ken Hebert, Houston	7	38	2	86
7	Doug Dalton, New Mexico State	14	0	0	84
8	Rick Eber, Tulsa	13	2	0	80
9	Ron Shanklin, North Texas	13	0	0	78
10	**Dicky Lyons, Kentucky**	**11**	**4**	**1**	**73**

	Kick Scoring	XPA	XP	FGA	FG	PTS
1	Gerald Warren, North Carolina St.	19	19	22	17	70
2	Jerry DePoyster, Wyoming	31	21	37	15	66
3	Zenon Andrusyshyn, UCLA	35	31	27	11	64
4	Dennis Patera, Brigham Young	35	29	22	11	62
5	Joe Azzaro, Notre Dame	40	37	10	8	61
6	**Karl Kremser, Tennessee**	**32**	**30**	**15**	**10**	**60**
7	Jerry Waddles, Texas-El Paso	38	30	18	9	57
8	Ken Juskowich, West Virginia	22	20	23	12	56
9	Al Gonzales, New Mexico State	42	37	8	6	55
10	Grant Guthrie, Florida State	27	26	14	9	53

	Interceptions	INT	YDS	TD
1	Steve Haterius, West Texas State	11	90	0
2	Ron Davidson, Virginia Tech	9	149	0
3	Wes Plummer, Arizona State	8	161	0
3	Jim Bevans, Army	8	124	0
3	Steve Bailey, Xavier	8	42	0
6	Bill Hobbs, Texas A&M *	7	162	2
6	Kerr Kump, VMI *	7	160	1
6	**Mike Jones, Tennessee ***	**7**	**150**	**0**
6	Dick Stiverson, Wichita State *	7	111	1
6	Bobby Roberts, Brigham Young *	7	96	1

*12 tied with seven; these had the most yards.

Team Leaders

	Rushing Offense	G	ATT	YDS	AVG	TD	YPG
1	Houston	10	553	2709	4.9	29	270.9
2	West Texas State	10	449	2497	5.6	22	249.7
3	Texas Tech	10	558	2444	4.4	19	244.4
4	Oregon State	10	582	2389	4.1	21	238.9
5	**LSU**	**10**	**554**	**2361**	**4.3**	**27**	**236.1**
6	East Carolina	10	569	2316	4.1	22	231.6
7	Syracuse	10	561	2298	4.1	16	229.8
8	Southern California	10	568	2285	4.0	19	228.5
9	Colorado State	10	571	2282	4.0	20	228.2
10	Yale	9	504	2053	4.1	24	228.1

	Passing Offense	G	ATT	COM	INT	PCT	YDS	YPA	TD	I%	YPC	YPG
1	Texas-El Paso	9	367	164	26	44.7	2710	7.4	28	7.1	16.5	301.1
2	Tulsa	10	389	207	24	53.2	2639	6.8	26	6.2	12.7	263.9
3	Florida State	10	352	190	21	54.0	2584	7.3	18	6.0	13.6	258.4
4	New Mexico	10	416	193	27	46.4	2491	6.0	13	6.5	12.9	249.1
5	New Mexico State	10	333	163	16	48.9	2359	7.1	18	4.8	14.5	235.9
6	Davidson	9	323	192	14	59.4	2080	6.4	14	4.3	10.8	231.1
7	Brigham Young	10	370	177	17	47.8	2264	6.1	20	4.6	12.8	226.4
8	North Texas	9	334	145	22	43.4	2012	6.0	25	6.6	13.9	223.6
9	SMU	10	330	189	23	57.3	2207	6.7	13	7.0	11.7	220.7
10	Wyoming	10	278	156	11	56.1	2077	7.5	20	4.0	13.3	207.7

	Total Offense	G	P	YDS	AVG	TD	YPG
1	Houston	10	738	4279	5.8	41	427.9
2	Purdue	10	778	4236	5.4	41	423.6
3	New Mexico State	10	734	4181	5.7	41	418.1
4	Arizona State	10	756	4148	5.5	44	414.8
5	West Texas State	10	681	4066	6.0	32	406.6
6	Brigham Young	10	816	3962	4.9	33	396.2
7	Notre Dame	10	788	3911	5.0	42	391.1
8	Texas-El Paso	9	679	3476	5.1	39	386.2
9	Tulsa	10	787	3818	4.9	40	381.8
10	Florida State	10	723	3786	5.2	29	378.6

	Rushing Defense	G	ATT	YDS	AVG	TD	YPG
1	Wyoming	10	376	423	1.1	6	42.3
2	Syracuse	10	354	548	1.5	9	54.8
3	Southern Miss	9	350	541	1.5	5	60.1
4	Nebraska	10	420	675	1.6	7	67.5
5	Virginia Tech	10	365	724	2.0	3	72.4
6	Missouri	10	438	739	1.7	3	73.9
7	Arizona State	10	401	789	2.0	13	78.9
8	North Texas	9	376	712	1.9	10	79.1
9	Utah State	10	373	808	2.2	8	80.8
10	West Virginia	10	425	821	1.9	8	82.1

	Passing Defense	G	ATT	COM	PCT	YPC	INT	I%	YDS	YPA	TD	YPG
1	Nebraska	10	207	78	37.7	11.6	11	5.3	901	4.4	1	90.1
2	Virginia	10	170	76	44.7	12.1	13	7.7	918	5.4	2	91.8
2	Oregon	10	143	65	45.5	14.1	7	4.9	918	6.4	6	91.8
4	Oklahoma State	10	175	71	40.6	13.3	11	6.3	945	5.4	4	94.5
5	**Georgia**	**10**	**214**	**77**	**36.0**	**12.3**	**18**	**8.4**	**947**	**4.4**	**5**	**94.7**
6	Kent State	10	229	92	40.2	10.7	15	6.6	986	4.3	5	98.6
7	Dayton	10	199	89	44.7	11.1	11	5.5	990	5.0	1	99.0
8	Columbia	9	119	47	39.5	19.2	10	8.4	901	7.6	9	100.1
9	Missouri	10	188	88	46.8	11.5	11	5.9	1013	5.4	5	101.3
10	Toledo	10	206	84	40.8	12.1	16	7.8	1014	4.9	4	101.4

	Total Defense	G	P	YDS	AVG	TD	YPG
1	Nebraska	10	627	1576	2.5	8	157.6
2	Missouri	10	626	1752	2.8	8	175.2
3	Wyoming	10	652	1852	2.8	13	185.2
4	Syracuse	10	588	1921	3.3	15	192.1
5	Toledo	10	618	1984	3.2	9	198.4
6	Southern Miss	9	567	1794	3.2	13	199.3
7	North Texas	9	632	1821	2.9	16	202.3
8	Southern California	10	634	2031	3.2	9	203.1
9	West Virginia	10	654	2036	3.1	13	203.6
10	Houston	10	677	2076	3.1	17	207.6

	Scoring Offense	G	PTS	AVG
1	Texas-El Paso	9	323	35.9
2	Arizona State	10	350	35.0
3	New Mexico State	10	346	34.6
4	Notre Dame	10	337	33.7
5	Houston	10	322	32.2
6	Yale	9	278	30.9
6	North Texas	9	278	30.9
8	Tulsa	10	304	30.4
9	Purdue	10	291	29.1
10	Harvard	9	256	28.4

	Scoring Defense	G	PTS	AVG
1	Oklahoma	10	68	6.8
2	Missouri	10	76	7.6
3	Toledo	10	83	8.3
3	Nebraska	10	83	8.3
5	Southern California	10	84	8.4
6	North Carolina St.	10	87	8.7
7	Colorado	10	92	9.2
8	Army	10	94	9.4
9	Wyoming	10	99	9.9

1967

Final Poll (Nov. 27)

UP	AP	SCHOOL	FINAL RECORD
1	1	Southern California	9-1-0
2	2	**Tennessee**	**8-1-0**
3	3	Oklahoma	8-1-0
6	4	Indiana	9-1-0
4	5	Notre Dame	8-2-0
5	6	Wyoming	10-0-0
8	7	Oregon State	7-2-1
7	8	**Alabama**	**7-1-1**
9	9	Purdue	8-2-0
	10	Penn State	8-2-0
10		UCLA	7-2-1

Consensus All-Americans

POS	OFFENSE	SCHOOL
B	Gary Beban	UCLA
B	Leroy Keyes	Purdue
B	O.J. Simpson	Southern California
B	Larry Csonka	Syracuse
E	**Dennis Homan**	**Alabama**
E	Ron Sellers	Florida State
T	Ron Yary	Southern California
T	**Ed Chandler**	**Georgia**
G	Harry Olszewski	Clemson
G	Rich Stotter	Houston
C	**Bob Johnson**	**Tennessee**

OTHERS RECEIVING FIRST-TEAM HONORS

E	Ken Hebert	Houston
E	Ted Kwalick	Penn State
E	Jim Seymour	Notre Dame
T	Larry Slagle	UCLA
G	Garry Cassells	Indiana
G	Bob Kalsu	Oklahoma
G	Phil Tucker	Texas Tech
PK	Jerry DePoyster	Wyoming

POS	DEFENSE	SCHOOL
E	Ted Hendricks	Miami (Fla.)
E	Tim Rossovich	Southern California
T	Dennis Byrd	NC State
MG	Granville Liggins	Oklahoma
MG	Wayne Meylan	Nebraska
LB	Adrian Young	Southern California
LB	Don Manning	UCLA
B	Tom Schoen	Notre Dame
B	Frank Loria	Virginia Tech
B	**Bobby Johns**	**Alabama**
B	Dick Anderson	Colorado

OTHERS RECEIVING FIRST-TEAM HONORS

E	Bob Stein	Minnesota
E	**John Garlington**	**LSU**
E	Kevin Hardy	Notre Dame
E	Bill Staley	Utah State
T	Mike Dirks	Wyoming
T	Greg Pipes	Baylor
T	Jess Lewis	Oregon State
MG	Jon Sandstrom	Oregon State
LB	Corby Robertson	Texas
LB	Bill Hobbs	Texas A&M
LB	Tom Beutler	Toledo
LB	**D.D. Lewis**	**Mississippi State**
LB	Fred Carr	UTEP
B	Fred Combs	North Carolina St.
B	Harry Cheatwood	Oklahoma State
B	Jim Smith	Oregon
B	**Al Dorsey**	**Tennessee**

Heisman Trophy Voting

	PLAYER	POS	SCHOOL	TOTAL
1	Gary Beban	QB	UCLA	1968
2	O.J. Simpson	TB	Southern Cal	1722
3	Leroy Keyes	HB	Purdue	1366
4	Larry Csonka	FB	Syracuse	136
5	Kim Hammond	QB	Florida State	90
6	**Bob Johnson**	**C**	**Tennessee**	**76**
7	Granville Liggins	NG	Oklahoma	61
8	**Dewey Warren**	**QB**	**Tennessee**	**56**
9	Wayne Meylan	MG	Nebraska	55
10	Terry Hanratty	QB	Notre Dame	54

Award Winners

PLAYER	AWARD
Gary Beban, QB, UCLA	Maxwell
Ron Yary, T, Southern California	Outland
O.J. Simpson, RB, Southern California	Camp

Bowl Games

DATE	GAME	SCORE
D2	Pasadena	West Texas State 35, Cal St.-Northridge 13
D16	**Liberty**	**North Carolina St. 14, Georgia 7**
D16	Tangerine	Tennessee-Martin 25, West Chester 8
D23	Bluebonnet	Colorado 31, Miami (Fla.) 21
D30	Gator	Florida State 17, Penn State 17
D30	**Sun**	**Texas-El Paso 14, Mississippi 7**
J1	Sugar	**LSU 20, Wyoming 13**
J1	**Orange**	**Oklahoma 26, Tennessee 24**
J1	Rose	Southern California 14, Indiana 3
J1	**Cotton**	**Texas A&M 20, Alabama 16**

SEC Standings

	CONFERENCE			OVERALL		
	W	L	T	W	L	T
Tennessee	6	0	0	9	2	0
Alabama	5	1	0	8	2	1
Georgia	4	2	0	7	4	0
Florida	4	2	0	6	4	0
Mississippi	4	2	1	6	4	1
LSU	3	2	1	7	3	1
Auburn	3	3	0	6	4	0
Kentucky	1	6	0	2	8	0
Vanderbilt	0	6	0	2	7	1
Mississippi State	0	6	0	1	9	0

ANNUAL REVIEW

1968 NCAA Major College Statistical Leaders

Individual Leaders

PASSING/COMPLETIONS	G	ATT	COM	PCT	INT	I%	YDS	YPA	TD	TD%	COM.PG
1 Chuck Hixson, SMU	10	468	265	56.6	23	4.9	3103	6.6	21	4.5	26.5
2 Greg Cook, Cincinnati	10	411	219	53.3	17	4.1	3272	8.0	25	6.1	21.9
3 Gordon Slade, Davidson	9	322	190	59.0	13	4.0	2109	6.5	14	4.4	21.1
4 Marty Domres, Columbia	9	344	183	53.2	15	4.4	2206	6.4	11	3.2	20.3
5 Steve Ramsey, North Texas	10	332	177	53.3	17	5.1	2516	7.6	24	7.2	17.7
6 Tommy Pharr, Mississippi State	**10**	**319**	**173**	**54.2**	**18**	**5.6**	**1838**	**5.8**	**9**	**2.8**	**17.3**
7 Edd Hargett, Texas A&M	10	348	169	48.6	14	4.0	2321	6.7	16	4.6	16.9
8 Mike Stripling, Tulsa	10	347	164	47.3	15	4.3	1968	5.7	8	2.3	16.4
9 Bill Cappleman, Florida State	10	287	162	56.4	11	3.8	2410	8.4	25	8.7	16.2
9 Leo Hart, Duke	10	301	162	53.8	11	3.7	2238	7.4	11	3.7	16.2

ALL-PURPOSE YARDS	G	RUSH	REC	PR	KR	YDS	YPG
1 O.J. Simpson, Southern California	10	1709	126	0	131	1966	196.6

RUSHING/YARDS	G	ATT	YDS	TD	AVG	YPG
1 O.J. Simpson, Southern California	10	355	1709	22	4.8	170.9
2 Eugene Morris, West Texas State	10	262	1571	17	6.0	157.1
3 Paul Gipson, Houston	10	242	1550	13	6.4	155.0
4 Steve Owens, Oklahoma	10	357	1536	21	4.3	153.6
5 Art Malone, Arizona State	10	235	1431	15	6.1	143.1
6 Ron Johnson, Michigan	10	255	1391	19	5.5	139.1
7 Bill Enyart, Oregon State	10	293	1304	17	4.5	130.4
8 Ron Poe James, New Mexico State	10	225	1291	12	5.7	129.1
9 Frank Quayle, Virginia	10	175	1213	12	6.9	121.3
10 Bryant Mitchell, Rutgers	10	238	1204	9	5.1	120.4

RUSHING/YARDS PER CARRY	G	ATT	YDS	YPC
1 Frank Quayle, Virginia	10	175	1213	6.9
2 Paul Gipson, Houston	10	242	1550	6.4
3 John Riggins, Kansas	10	140	866	6.2
4 Chris Gilbert, Texas	10	184	1132	6.2
5 Art Malone, Arizona State	10	235	1431	6.1
6 Ed Podolak, Iowa	10	154	937	6.1
7 Eugene Morris, West Texas State	10	262	1571	6.0
8 Ron Poe James, New Mexico State	10	225	1291	5.7
9 Ron Johnson, Michigan	10	255	1391	5.5
10 Charley Jarvis, Army	10	208	1110	5.3

Based on top 32 rushers

RECEIVING/RECEPTIONS	G	REC	YDS	TD	YPR	YPG	RPG
1 Ron Sellers, Florida State	10	86	1496	12	17.4	149.6	8.6
2 Jerry Levias, SMU	10	80	1131	8	14.1	113.1	8.0
2 Tom Rossley, Cincinnati	10	80	1072	4	13.4	107.2	8.0
4 Gene Washington, Stanford	10	71	1117	8	15.7	111.7	7.1
5 Barry Moore, North Texas	10	69	1053	7	15.3	105.3	6.9
6 Harry Wood, Tulsa	10	65	988	5	15.2	98.8	6.5
6 Henley Carter, Duke	10	65	892	2	13.7	89.2	6.5
8 Sammy Milner, Mississippi State	**10**	**64**	**909**	**5**	**14.2**	**90.9**	**6.4**
9 Mike Kelly, Davidson	9	63	936	11	14.9	104.0	7.0
10 John Sias, Georgia Tech	10	61	902	4	14.8	90.2	6.1

PUNTING	PUNT	YDS	AVG
1 Danny Pitcock, Wichita State	71	3067	43.2
2 Benny Rhoads, Cincinnati	45	1913	42.5
3 Bob Coble, Kansas State	77	3249	42.2
4 Zenon Andrusyshyn, UCLA	55	2316	42.1
5 Bob Jacobs, Wyoming	72	3031	42.1
6 Ken Sanders, Tulane	63	2640	41.9
7 Bill Bell, Kansas	41	1714	41.8
8 Roy Gerela, New Mexico State	57	2371	41.6
9 Julian Fagan, Mississippi	**75**	**3120**	**41.6**
10 Mike Hall, TCU	51	2117	41.5

PUNT RETURNS/YARDS	PR	YDS	TD	AVG
1 Roger Wehrli, Missouri	41	478	0	11.7
2 Jake Scott, Georgia	**35**	**440**	**1**	**12.6**
2 Lenny Randle, Arizona State	37	440	2	11.9
4 George Burrell, Pennsylvania	33	436	1	13.2
5 Larry Alford, Texas Tech	38	430	1	11.3
6 Curley Watters, West Texas State	21	368	2	17.5
7 Doug Mathews, Vanderbilt	**30**	**354**	**2**	**11.8**
8 Mark Williams, Washington State	20	333	3	16.7
9 Bob Zimpfer, Bowling Green	24	332	1	13.8
10 Kerr Kump, VMI	32	327	1	10.2

KICKOFF RETURNS/YARDS	KR	YDS	TD	AVG
1 Mike Adamle, Northwestern	34	732	0	21.5
2 Bobby Hall, North Carolina St.	29	721	0	24.9
3 J.D. Lewis, Pittsburgh	31	650	0	21.0
4 Jeff Allen, Iowa State	23	599	0	26.0
5 David Smith, Mississippi State	**27**	**590**	**0**	**21.9**
6 Mack Herron, Kansas State	21	583	2	27.8
7 Frank Slaton, San Jose State	24	578	0	24.1
8 Ed Hicklin, Duke	27	555	0	20.6
9 Don McCauley, North Carolina	25	553	0	22.1
10 Bill Carey, Columbia	27	528	0	19.6

SCORING	TDS	XPT	FG	PTS
1 Jim O'Brien, Cincinnati	12	31	13	142
2 O.J. Simpson, Southern California	22	0	0	132
3 Steve Owens, Oklahoma	21	0	0	126
4 Ron Johnson, Michigan	19	2	0	116
5 Bob Houmard, Ohio U.	19	0	0	114
5 Eugene Morris, West Texas State	19	0	0	114
7 Bill Enyart, Oregon State	17	0	0	102
8 Dave Bennett, Boston College	16	0	0	96
8 James Otis, Ohio State	16	0	0	96
8 Bill Burnett, Arkansas	16	0	0	96
8 Art Malone, Arizona State	16	0	0	96

KICK SCORING	XPA	XP	FGA	FG	PTS
1 Paul Ray Powell, Arizona State	55	47	15	10	77
2 Jim O'Brien, Cincinnati	34	31	25	13	70
3 Bob Jacobs, Wyoming	29	26	28	14	68
4 Clarence Redic, West Texas State	35	34	28	11	67
5 Ardie Jensen, Army	32	31	18	11	64
6 John Riley, Auburn	**26**	**25**	**26**	**12**	**61**
6 Terry Leiweke, Houston	57	52	11	3	61
8 Scott Hempel, Notre Dame	51	45	9	5	60
8 Bill Bell, Kansas	53	45	9	5	60
10 Kenneth Crots, Toledo	29	29	17	9	56

INTERCEPTIONS	INT	YDS	TD
1 Al Worley, Washington	14	130	1
2 Jerry Todd, Memphis	11	79	0
3 Tom Curtis, Michigan	10	182	0
3 Jake Scott, Georgia	**10**	**175**	**2**
3 Paul Shires, Houston	10	45	0
6 John Pollock, Rutgers	9	180	1
6 Bill Young, Tennessee	**9**	**53**	**0**
8 Jim McCall, Army	8	137	1
8 Rick Reed, Washington State	8	137	0
8 Jimmy Livingston, SMU	8	104	0
8 John Salmon, Boston College	8	83	0
8 Rich Moriarty, Arizona	8	75	0
8 Neal Smith, Penn State	8	74	0

Team Leaders

RUSHING OFFENSE	G	ATT	YDS	AVG	TD	YPG
1 Houston	10	633	3617	5.7	36	361.7
2 Texas	10	642	3315	5.2	37	331.5
3 Ohio State	9	589	2758	4.7	33	306.4
4 Notre Dame	10	657	3059	4.7	38	305.9
5 Kansas	10	594	2999	5.0	33	299.9
6 Princeton	9	580	2653	4.6	26	294.8
7 Arizona State	10	625	2903	4.6	37	290.3
8 West Texas State	10	570	2878	5.0	26	287.8
9 Virginia	10	573	2800	4.9	27	280.0
10 Penn State	10	614	2739	4.5	33	273.9

PASSING OFFENSE	G	ATT	COM	INT	PCT	YDS	YPA	TD	I%	YPC	YPG
1 Cincinnati	10	433	226	22	52.2	3358	7.8	25	5.1	14.9	335.8
2 SMU	10	485	270	24	55.7	3130	6.5	21	5.0	11.6	313.0
3 Texas-El Paso	10	455	199	21	43.7	2884	6.3	20	4.6	14.5	288.4
4 Florida State	10	356	195	13	54.8	2844	8.0	29	3.7	14.6	284.4
5 Duke	10	346	186	14	53.8	2653	7.7	11	4.1	14.3	265.3
6 North Texas	10	357	180	19	50.4	2546	7.1	25	5.3	14.1	254.6
7 Stanford	10	297	157	18	52.9	2516	8.5	18	6.1	16.0	251.6
8 Tulsa	10	435	213	19	49.0	2515	5.8	12	4.4	11.8	251.5
9 Columbia	9	351	186	15	53.0	2246	6.4	12	4.3	12.1	249.6
10 Davidson	9	327	192	14	58.7	2139	6.5	14	4.3	11.1	237.7

TOTAL OFFENSE	G	P	YDS	AVG	TD	YPG
1 Houston	10	846	5620	6.6	55	562.0
2 Notre Dame	10	909	5044	5.5	51	504.4
3 Boston College	9	739	4161	5.6	34	462.3
4 Yale	9	756	4107	5.4	45	456.3
5 Ohio State	9	762	4041	5.3	41	449.0
6 Texas	10	796	4476	5.6	43	447.6
7 Arizona State	10	848	4473	5.3	50	447.3
8 Cincinnati	10	801	4421	5.5	37	442.1
9 Kansas	10	777	4420	5.7	47	442.0
10 Iowa	10	759	4404	5.8	45	440.4

RUSHING DEFENSE	G	ATT	YDS	AVG	TD	YPG
1 Arizona State	10	403	570	1.4	10	57.0
2 Miami (Ohio)	10	359	775	2.2	5	77.5
3 Wyoming	10	458	782	1.7	6	78.2
4 Notre Dame	10	358	793	2.2	11	79.3
5 Southern Miss	10	347	815	2.3	12	81.5
6 Penn State	10	404	831	2.1	6	83.1
7 Alabama	**10**	**401**	**849**	**2.1**	**7**	**84.9**
8 Auburn	**10**	**410**	**878**	**2.1**	**9**	**87.8**
9 Tennessee	**10**	**371**	**933**	**2.5**	**6**	**93.3**
10 Houston	10	413	947	2.3	13	94.7

PASSING DEFENSE	G	ATT	COM	PCT	YPC	INT	I%	YDS	YPA	TD	YPG
1 Kent State	10	183	75	41.0	14.3	10	5.5	1076	5.9	9	107.6
2 Toledo	10	249	106	42.6	10.8	17	6.8	1141	4.6	8	114.1
3 Western Michigan	9	200	80	40.0	12.9	20	10.0	1034	5.2	3	114.9
4 Davidson	9	137	71	51.8	14.7	10	7.3	1045	7.6	8	116.1
5 Missouri	10	185	74	40.0	15.8	17	9.2	1169	6.3	7	116.9
6 Harvard	9	196	96	49.0	11.1	17	8.7	1064	5.4	4	118.2
7 West Virginia	10	203	91	44.8	13.4	14	6.9	1215	6.0	4	121.5
8 Nebraska	10	251	107	42.6	11.5	8	3.2	1230	4.9	2	123.0
9 Bowling Green	10	239	110	46.0	11.4	20	8.4	1250	5.2	7	125.0
10 Xavier	10	225	102	45.3	12.4	16	7.1	1269	5.6	9	126.9

TOTAL DEFENSE	G	P	YDS	AVG	TD	YPG
1 Wyoming	10	732	2068	2.8	14	206.8
2 Miami (Ohio)	10	632	2324	3.7	13	232.4
3 Georgia	**10**	**650**	**2351**	**3.6**	**9**	**235.1**
4 Syracuse	10	705	2354	3.3	18	235.4
5 Alabama	**10**	**682**	**2387**	**3.5**	**13**	**238.7**
6 Arizona State	10	734	2396	3.3	21	239.6
7 Arizona	10	749	2406	3.2	14	240.6
8 Missouri	10	683	2411	3.5	16	241.1
9 Bowling Green	10	675	2452	3.6	19	245.2
10 Notre Dame	10	644	2490	3.9	23	249.0

SCORING OFFENSE	G	PTS	AVG
1 Houston	10	425	42.5
2 Arizona State	10	414	41.4
3 Kansas	10	380	38.0
4 Notre Dame	10	376	37.6
4 Ohio U.	10	376	37.6
6 Yale	9	317	35.2
7 Texas	10	343	34.3
8 Penn State	10	339	33.9
9 Arkansas	10	334	33.4
10 Ohio State	9	296	32.9

SCORING DEFENSE	G	PTS	AVG
1 Georgia	**10**	**98**	**9.8**
2 Miami (Ohio)	10	99	9.9
3 Harvard	9	90	10.0
4 California	11	114	10.4
5 Alabama	**10**	**104**	**10.4**
6 Penn State	10	106	10.6
7 Tennessee	**10**	**110**	**11.0**
8 Arizona	10	115	11.5
9 Wyoming	10	118	11.8
10 Missouri	10	126	12.6

1968

FINAL POLL (JAN. 3)

AP	SCHOOL	FINAL RECORD
1	Ohio State	10-0-0
2	Penn State	11-0-0
3	Texas	9-1-1
4	Southern California	9-1-1
5	Notre Dame	7-2-1
6	Arkansas	10-1-0
7	Kansas	9-2-0
8	**Georgia**	**8-1-2**
9	Missouri	8-3-0
10	Purdue	8-2-0
11	Oklahoma	7-4-0
12	Michigan	8-2-0
13	**Tennessee**	**8-2-1**
14	SMU	8-3-0
15	Oregon State	7-3-0
16	**Auburn**	**7-4-0**
17	**Alabama**	**8-3-0**
18	Houston	6-2-2
19	**LSU**	**8-3-0**
20	Ohio U.	10-1-0

CONSENSUS ALL-AMERICANS

POS	OFFENSE	SCHOOL
B	O.J. Simpson	Southern California
B	Leroy Keyes	Purdue
B	Terry Hanratty	Notre Dame
B	Chris Gilbert	Texas
E	Ted Kwalick	Penn State
E	Jerry LeVias	SMU
T	Dave Foley	Ohio State
T	George Kunz	Notre Dame
G	**Charles Rosenfelder**	**Tennessee**
G	Jim Barnes	Arkansas
G	Mike Montler	Colorado
C	John Didion	Oregon State

OTHERS RECEIVING FIRST-TEAM HONORS

B	Ron Johnson	Michigan
B	Bobby Douglass	Kansas
B	Paul Gipson	Houston
B	Bill Enyart	Oregon State
E	Ron Sellers	Florida State
E	Jim Seymour	Notre Dame
T	John Shinners	Xavier
G	Joe Armstrong	Nebraska
G	**Guy Dennis**	**Florida**

POS	DEFENSE	SCHOOL
E	Ted Hendricks	Miami (Fla.)
E	John Zook	Kansas
T	**Bill Stanfill**	**Georgia**
T	Joe Greene	North Texas
MG	Ed White	California
MG	Chuck Kyle	Purdue
LB	**Steve Kiner**	**Tennessee**
LB	Dennis Onkotz	Penn State
B	**Jake Scott**	**Georgia**
B	Roger Wehrli	Missouri
B	Al Worley	Washington

OTHERS RECEIVING FIRST-TEAM HONORS

E	Ron Carpenter	North Carolina St.
T	Loyd Wainscott	Texas
T	**David Campbell**	**Auburn**
LB	Bob Babich	Miami (Ohio)
LB	Ken Johnson	Army
LB	Mike Widger	Virginia Tech
LB	**Mike Hall**	**Alabama**
LB	**Chip Healy**	**Vanderbilt**
LB	Ron Pritchard	Arizona State
LB	Dale McCullers	Florida State
LB	Bill Hobbs	Texas A&M
B	Mike Battle	Southern California
B	Al Brenner	Michigan State
B	**Jim Weatherford**	**Tennessee**

HEISMAN TROPHY VOTING

	PLAYER	POS	SCHOOL	TOTAL
1	O.J. Simpson	TB	Southern California	2853
2	Leroy Keyes	HB	Purdue	1103
3	Terry Hanratty	QB	Notre Dame	387
4	Ted Kwalick	TE	Penn State	254
5	Ted Hendricks	DE	Miami (Fla.)	174
6	Ron Johnson	HB	Michigan	158
7	Bob Douglass	QB	Kansas	132
8	Chris Gilbert	RB	Texas	124
9	Brian Dowling	QB	Yale	119
10	Ron Sellers	WR	Florida State	91

AWARD WINNERS

PLAYER	AWARD
O.J. Simpson, RB, Southern California	Maxwell
Bill Stanfill, T, Georgia	**Outland**
O.J. Simpson, RB, Southern California	Camp

BOWL GAMES

DATE	GAME	SCORE
D7	Pasadena	Grambling 34, Cal St. Sacramento 7
D14	**Liberty**	**Mississippi 34, Virginia Tech 17**
D27	Tangerine	Richmond 49, Ohio U. 42
D28	**Sun**	**Auburn 34, Arizona 10**
D28	**Gator**	**Missouri 35, Alabama 10**
D30	**Peach**	**LSU 31, Florida State 27**
D31	Bluebonnet	SMU 28, Oklahoma 27
J1	**Sugar**	**Arkansas 16, Georgia 2**
J1	Rose	Ohio State 27, Southern California 16
J1	Orange	Penn State 15, Kansas 14
J1	**Cotton**	**Texas 36, Tennessee 13**

SEC STANDINGS

	CONFERENCE			OVERALL		
	W	L	T	W	L	T
Georgia	5	0	1	8	1	2
Tennessee	4	1	1	8	2	1
Alabama	4	2	0	8	3	0
LSU	4	2	0	8	3	0
Auburn	4	2	0	7	4	0
Mississippi	3	2	1	7	3	1
Florida	3	2	1	6	3	1
Vanderbilt	2	3	1	5	4	1
Mississippi State	1	4	1	0	8	2
Kentucky	0	7	0	3	7	0

ANNUAL REVIEW

1969 NCAA Major College Statistical Leaders

Individual Leaders

PASSING/COMPLETIONS	G	ATT	COM	PCT	INT	I%	YDS	YPA	TD	TD%	COM.PG
1 John Reaves, Florida	**10**	**396**	**222**	**56.1**	**19**	**4.8**	**2896**	**7.3**	**24**	**6.1**	**22.2**
2 Chuck Hixson, SMU	10	362	217	59.9	15	4.1	2313	6.4	9	2.5	21.7
3 Dennis Shaw, San Diego State	10	335	199	59.4	26	7.8	3185	9.5	39	11.6	19.9
4 Gordon Slade, Davidson	10	321	198	61.7	12	3.7	2177	6.8	21	6.5	19.8
5 Jim Plunkett, Stanford	10	336	197	58.6	15	4.5	2673	8.0	20	6.0	19.7
6 Lynn Dickey, Kansas State	10	372	196	52.7	19	5.1	2476	6.7	14	3.8	19.6
7 Steve Ramsey, North Texas	10	414	195	47.1	31	7.5	2828	6.8	24	5.8	19.5
8 Bill Cappleman, Florida State	10	344	183	53.2	18	5.2	2467	7.2	14	4.1	18.3
9 Charlie Richards, Richmond	10	356	175	49.2	15	4.2	2556	7.2	21	5.9	17.5
10 Mike Phipps, Purdue	10	321	169	52.6	18	5.6	2527	7.9	23	7.2	16.9

ALL-PURPOSE YARDS	G	RUSH	REC	PR	KR	YDS	YPG
1 Lynn Moore, Army	10	983	44	223	545	1795	179.5

RUSHING/YARDS	G	ATT	YDS	TD	AVG	YPG
1 Steve Owens, Oklahoma	10	358	1523	23	4.3	152.3
2 Ed Marinaro, Cornell	9	277	1409	14	5.1	156.6
3 Joe Moore, Missouri	10	260	1312	5	5.0	131.2
4 Jim Strong, Houston	10	190	1293	11	6.8	129.3
5 Clarence Davis, Southern California	10	282	1275	9	4.5	127.5
6 John Isenbarger, Indiana	10	233	1217	5	5.2	121.7
7 Ron Poe James, New Mexico State	10	258	1181	8	4.6	118.1
8 Don McCauley, North Carolina	10	204	1092	8	5.4	109.2
9 Duane Thomas, West Texas State	10	199	1072	10	5.4	107.2
10 Lee Bouggess, Louisville	10	267	1064	6	4.0	106.4

RUSHING/YARDS PER CARRY	G	ATT	YDS	YPC
1 Bob Duncan, Citadel	10	136	936	6.9
2 Jim Strong, Houston	10	190	1293	6.8
3 Bill Taylor, Michigan	10	123	808	6.6
4 Dave Buchanan, Arizona State	10	143	908	6.3
5 Tony Harris, Toledo	10	146	849	5.8
6 Bob Gresham, West Virginia	10	190	1057	5.6
7 Ted Heiskell, Houston	10	158	870	5.5
8 Duane Thomas, West Texas State	10	199	1072	5.4
9 Don McCauley, North Carolina	10	204	1092	5.4
10 John Isenbarger, Indiana	10	233	1217	5.2

Based on top 32 rushers

RECEIVING/RECEPTIONS	G	REC	YDS	TD	YPR	YPG	RPG
1 Jerry Hendren, Idaho	10	95	1452	12	15.3	145.2	9.5
2 Carlos Alvarez, Florida	**10**	**88**	**1329**	**12**	**15.1**	**132.9**	**8.8**
3 Tim Delaney, San Diego Sate	10	85	1259	14	14.8	125.9	8.5
4 Barry Moore, North Texas	10	71	1130	5	15.9	113.0	7.1
5 Mike Kelly, Davidson	10	70	891	6	12.7	89.1	7.0
6 Sammy Milner, Mississippi State	**10**	**64**	**745**	**6**	**11.6**	**74.5**	**6.4**
7 Elmo Wright, Houston	10	63	1275	14	20.2	127.5	6.3
8 Todd Snyder, Ohio U.	10	62	835	8	13.5	83.5	6.2
9 George Hannen, Davidson	10	58	709	8	12.2	70.9	5.8
10 Walker Gillette, Richmond	10	57	1090	11	19.1	109.0	5.7
10 Fred Mathews, Bowling Green	10	57	528	6	9.3	52.8	5.7

PUNTING	PUNT	YDS	AVG
1 Ed Marsh, Baylor	68	2965	43.6
2 Spike Jones, Georgia	**71**	**3089**	**43.5**
3 Ken Sanders, Tulane	66	2858	43.3
4 Mike Nehl, Oregon State	56	2414	43.1
5 Pat Barrett, Miami (Fla.)	45	1940	43.1
6 Ken Duncan, Tulsa	34	1452	42.7
7 Bob Jacobs, Wyoming	79	3358	42.5
8 Stefan Schroeder, Pacific	53	2237	42.2
9 Zenon Andrusyshyn, UCLA	47	1979	42.1
10 Jess Garcia, Utah State	87	3645	41.9

PUNT RETURNS/YARDS	PR	YDS	TD	AVG
1 Chris Farasopoulos, Brigham Young	35	527	1	15.1
2 George Hannen, Davidson	21	471	3	22.4
3 Bobby Majors, Tennessee	**37**	**457**	**2**	**12.4**
4 Larry Zelina, Ohio State	23	431	2	18.7
5 Bill Cornman, Pacific	34	430	1	12.6
6 Billy Watson, Citadel	27	397	2	14.7
7 Joe Bullard, Tulane	19	395	1	20.8
8 Bernie Barbour, North Texas	36	371	0	10.3
9 Tom Deckert, San Diego State	26	346	0	13.3
10 Lenny Randle, Arizona State	22	343	3	15.6

KICKOFF RETURNS/YARDS	KR	YDS	TD	AVG
1 Stan Brown, Purdue	26	698	2	26.8
2 Gordon Utgard, Baylor	37	669	0	18.1
3 Dave Garnett, Pittsburgh	25	653	0	26.1
4 Gary Hammond, SMU	27	617	0	22.9
5 Doug Mathews, Vanderbilt	**26**	**607**	**0**	**23.3**
6 Bob Warren, Brown	26	599	0	23.0
7 Eric Allen, Michigan State	29	598	0	20.6
8 Arnold Thomas, Southern Miss	31	585	0	18.9
9 Bob Darby, California	23	556	0	24.2
10 Chris Farasopul, Brigham Young	17	548	1	32.2

SCORING	TDS	XPT	FG	PTS
1 Steve Owens, Oklahoma	23	0	0	138
2 Mack Herron, Kansas State	21	0	0	126
3 Bill Burnett, Arkansas	20	0	0	120
4 Bob Anderson, Colorado	19	0	0	114
5 Tommy Durrance, Florida	**18**	**2**	**0**	**110**
6 Stan Brown, Purdue	18	0	0	108
6 Tom Reynolds, San Diego State	18	0	0	108
8 Jim Braxton, West Virginia	12	24	3	105
9 Jim Otis, Ohio State	16	0	0	96
10 Bob Moore, Oregon	15	2	0	92

KICK SCORING	XPA	XP	FGA	FG	PTS
1 Bob Jacobs, Wyoming	23	22	27	18	76
2 Dennis Leuthauser, Air Force	32	27	25	16	75
3 Henry Brown, Missouri	39	35	20	12	71
3 Steve Horowitz, Stanford	44	41	18	10	71
3 Ed Gallardo, Arizona State	48	41	16	10	71
6 John Riley, Auburn	**46**	**39**	**21**	**10**	**69**
7 George Hunt, Tennessee	**38**	**35**	**13**	**10**	**65**
8 Mark Lumpkin, LSU	**44**	**38**	**13**	**8**	**62**
8 Al Limahelu, San Diego State	60	59	8	1	62
10 Bill McClard, Arkansas	44	40	9	7	61
10 Happy Feller, Texas	45	43	8	6	61

INTERCEPTIONS	INT	YDS	TD
1 Seth Miller, Arizona State	11	63	0
2 Neal Smith, Penn State	10	78	1
3 Jeff Ford, Georgia Tech	9	257	3
3 Jay Morrison, New Mexico	9	144	0
3 Mike Sensibaugh, Ohio State	9	125	0
3 Buddy McClinton, Auburn	**9**	**92**	**0**
7 Tom Curtis, Michigan *	8	165	0
7 David Berrong, Memphis *	8	136	0
7 John Gates, Oklahoma State *	8	113	0
7 L.D. Rowden, Houston *	8	113	1
7 Bob Wroe, Columbia *	8	92	0

*10 tied with eight; these players had the most yards

Team Leaders

RUSHING OFFENSE	G	ATT	YDS	AVG	TD	YPG
1 Texas	10	684	3630	5.3	51	363.0
2 Houston	10	583	3170	5.4	32	317.0
3 Ohio State	9	599	2774	4.6	36	308.2
4 Dartmouth	9	537	2654	4.9	22	294.9
5 West Virginia	10	625	2925	4.7	30	292.5
6 Notre Dame	10	663	2905	4.4	31	290.5
7 Michigan	10	625	2776	4.4	37	277.6
8 Oklahoma	10	639	2664	4.2	31	266.4
9 North Carolina	10	630	2615	4.2	16	261.5
10 Arizona State	10	553	2513	4.5	32	251.3

PASSING OFFENSE	G	ATT	COM	INT	PCT	YDS	YPA	TD	I%	YPC	YPG
1 San Diego State	10	417	244	28	58.5	3742	9.0	43	6.7	15.3	374.2
2 Florida	**10**	**413**	**233**	**20**	**56.4**	**3016**	**7.3**	**24**	**4.8**	**12.9**	**301.6**
3 Stanford	10	382	217	17	56.8	2985	7.8	26	4.5	13.8	298.5
4 North Texas	10	447	206	36	46.1	2944	6.6	25	8.1	14.3	294.4
5 Idaho	10	469	223	33	47.5	2741	5.8	16	7.0	12.3	274.1
6 Alabama	**10**	**328**	**195**	**11**	**59.5**	**2707**	**8.3**	**14**	**3.4**	**13.9**	**270.7**
7 Purdue	10	333	176	20	52.9	2679	8.0	23	6.0	15.2	267.9
8 Richmond	10	373	185	16	49.6	2651	7.1	23	4.3	14.3	265.1
9 Florida State	10	356	191	19	53.7	2550	7.2	16	5.3	13.4	255.0
10 Kansas State	10	379	197	19	52.0	2501	6.6	14	5.0	12.7	250.1

TOTAL OFFENSE	G	P	YDS	AVG	TD	YPG
1 San Diego State	10	840	5322	6.3	61	532.2
2 Houston	10	835	5138	6.2	53	513.8
3 Stanford	10	840	4944	5.9	43	494.4
4 Ohio State	9	829	4439	5.4	53	493.2
5 Texas	10	817	4721	5.8	56	472.1
6 Missouri	10	859	4507	5.2	44	450.7
7 Notre Dame	10	868	4489	5.2	44	448.9
8 Florida	**10**	**826**	**4348**	**5.3**	**43**	**434.8**
9 Purdue	10	794	4325	5.4	47	432.5
10 UCLA	10	762	4304	5.6	43	430.4

RUSHING DEFENSE	G	ATT	YDS	AVG	TD	YPG
1 LSU	**10**	**353**	**389**	**1.1**	**5**	**38.9**
2 Wyoming	10	395	663	1.7	10	66.3
3 Auburn	**10**	**392**	**796**	**2.0**	**6**	**79.6**
4 Pacific	10	400	834	2.1	3	83.4
5 Toledo	10	453	838	1.8	7	83.8
6 Notre Dame	10	374	851	2.3	8	85.1
7 Miami (Ohio)	10	410	858	2.1	11	85.8
8 Texas	10	420	900	2.1	6	90.0
9 Yale	9	442	819	1.9	12	91.0
10 Houston	10	406	944	2.3	10	94.4

PASSING DEFENSE	G	ATT	COM	PCT	YPC	INT	I%	YDS	YPA	TD	YPG
1 Dayton	10	156	68	43.6	13.2	11	7.1	900	5.8	5	90.0
2 Dartmouth	9	192	80	41.7	10.3	19	9.9	821	4.3	4	91.2
3 Pennsylvania	9	166	72	43.4	11.5	18	10.8	826	5.0	6	91.8
4 Penn State	10	221	86	38.9	11.3	24	10.9	972	4.4	3	97.2
5 Xavier	10	169	80	47.3	12.4	10	5.9	992	5.9	9	99.2
6 Buffalo	9	157	71	45.2	12.8	6	3.8	911	5.8	4	101.2
7 Virginia	10	173	72	41.6	14.9	11	6.4	1073	6.2	10	107.3
8 Syracuse	10	232	106	45.7	10.2	13	5.6	1082	4.7	9	108.2
9 Duke	10	159	71	44.7	15.7	10	6.3	1112	7.0	11	111.2
10 Wake Forest	10	171	93	54.4	12.5	13	7.6	1161	6.8	11	116.1

TOTAL DEFENSE	G	P	YDS	AVG	TD	YPG
1 Toledo	10	703	2091	3.0	18	209.1
2 Yale	9	646	1932	3.0	16	214.7
3 Penn State	10	681	2181	3.2	10	218.1
4 Notre Dame	10	664	2187	3.3	14	218.7
5 Syracuse	10	659	2236	3.4	16	223.6
6 Texas	10	707	2260	3.2	11	226.0
7 LSU	**10**	**714**	**2285**	**3.2**	**13**	**228.5**
8 Buffalo	9	565	2065	3.7	11	229.4
9 Dartmouth	9	611	2077	3.4	12	230.8
10 Virginia	10	643	2358	3.7	21	235.8

SCORING OFFENSE	G	PTS	AVG
1 San Diego State	10	464	46.4
2 Ohio State	9	383	42.6
3 Texas	10	414	41.4
4 Houston	10	386	38.6
5 Arizona State	10	383	38.3
6 Auburn	**10**	**363**	**36.3**
7 Missouri	10	362	36.2
8 Purdue	10	354	35.4
9 LSU	**10**	**349**	**34.9**
9 Michigan	10	349	34.9
9 Stanford	10	349	34.9

SCORING DEFENSE	G	PTS	AVG
1 Arkansas	10	76	7.6
2 Penn State	10	87	8.7
3 LSU	**10**	**91**	**9.1**
4 Buffalo	9	89	9.9
5 Georgia	**10**	**101**	**10.1**
6 Texas	10	102	10.2
7 UCLA	10	103	10.3
8 Ohio State	9	93	10.3
9 Utah	10	107	10.7

1969

Final Poll (Jan. 2)

UP	AP	SCHOOL	FINAL RECORD
1	1	Texas	11-0-0
2	2	Penn State	11-0-0
4	3	Southern California	10-0-1
5	4	Ohio State	8-1-0
9	5	Notre Dame	8-2-1
6	6	Missouri	9-2-0
3	7	Arkansas	9-2-0
13	8	**Mississippi**	**8-3-0**
8	9	Michigan	8-3-0
7	10	**LSU**	**9-1-0**
12	11	Nebraska	9-2-0
16	12	Houston	9-2-0
10	13	UCLA	8-1-1
17	14	**Florida**	**9-1-1**
11	15	**Tennessee**	**9-2-0**
	16	Colorado	8-3-0
18	17	West Virginia	10-1-0
18	18	Purdue	8-2-0
14	19	Stanford	7-2-1
15	20	**Auburn**	**8-3-0**

Consensus All-Americans

POS	OFFENSE	SCHOOL
B	Mike Phipps	Purdue
B	Steve Owens	Oklahoma
B	Jim Otis	Ohio State
B	Bob Anderson	Colorado
E	Jim Mandich	Michigan
E	Walker Gillette	Richmond
E	**Carlos Alvarez**	**Florida**
T	Bob McKay	Texas
T	John Ward	Oklahoma State
G	**Chip Kell**	**Tennessee**
G	Bill Bridges	Houston
C	Rodney Brand	Arkansas

OTHERS RECEIVING FIRST-TEAM HONORS

B	Steve Worster	Texas
B	Warren Muir	South Carolina
B	Charlie Pittman	Penn State
B	Rex Kern	Ohio State
E	Chuck Dicus	Arkansas
E	Charles Speyrer	Texas
T	Jim Reilly	Notre Dame
T	**Bob Asher**	**Vanderbilt**
T	Sid Smith	Southern California
G	Bobby Wuensch	Texas
G	Ron Saul	Michigan State
G	Mike Carroll	Missouri
G	Larry DiNardo	Notre Dame

POS	DEFENSE	SCHOOL
E	Jim Gunn	Southern California
E	Phil Olsen	Utah State
T	Mike Reid	Penn State
T	Mike McCoy	Notre Dame
MG	Jim Stillwagon	Ohio State
LB	**Steve Kiner**	**Tennessee**
LB	Dennis Onkotz	Penn State
LB	Mike Ballou	UCLA
B	Jack Tatum	Ohio State
B	**Buddy McClinton**	**Auburn**
B	Tom Curtis	Michigan

OTHERS RECEIVING FIRST-TEAM HONORS

E	Bill Brundige	Colorado
E	Floyd Reese	UCLA
E	Rick Campbell	Texas Tech
T	Al Cowlings	Southern California
LB	**George Bevan**	**LSU**
LB	Cliff Powell	Arkansas
LB	Don Parish	Stanford
LB	Glen Halsell	Texas
LB	John Small	Citadel
LB	Jim Corigall	Kent State
B	Denton Fox	Texas Tech
B	**Glenn Cannon**	**Mississippi**
B	Curtis Johnson	Toledo
B	Neal Smith	Penn State
K	Bob Jacobs	Wyoming

Heisman Trophy Voting

	PLAYER	POS	SCHOOL	TOTAL
1	Steve Owens	FB	Oklahoma	1488
2	Mike Phipps	QB	Purdue	1334
3	Rex Kern	QB	Ohio State	856
4	**Archie Manning**	**QB**	**Mississippi**	**582**
5	Mike Reid	DT	Penn State	297
6	Mike McCoy	DT	Notre Dame	290
7	Jim Otis	FB	Ohio State	121
8	Jim Plunkett	QB	Stanford	120
9	**Steve Kiner**	**LB**	**Tennessee**	**109**
10	Jack Tatum	DB	Ohio State	105

Award Winners

PLAYER	AWARD
Mike Reid, DT, Penn State	Maxwell
Mike Reid, DT, Penn State	Outland
Steve Owens, RB, Oklahoma	Camp

Bowl Games

DATE	GAME	SCORE
D6	Pasadena	San Diego State 28, Boston U. 7
D13	**Liberty**	**Colorado 47, Alabama 33**
D20	**Sun**	**Nebraska 45, Georgia 6**
D26	Tangerine	Toledo 56, Davidson 33
D27	**Gator**	**Florida 14, Tennessee 13**
D30	Peach	West Virginia 14, South Carolina 3
D31	**Bluebonnet**	**Houston 36, Auburn 7**
J1	**Sugar**	**Mississippi 27, Arkansas 22**
J1	Orange	Penn State 10, Missouri 3
J1	Rose	Southern California 10, Michigan 3
J1	Cotton	Texas 21, Notre Dame 17

SEC Standings

	CONFERENCE			OVERALL		
	W	L	T	W	L	T
Tennessee	5	1	0	9	2	0
LSU	4	1	0	9	1	0
Auburn	5	2	0	8	3	0
Florida	3	1	1	9	1	1
Mississippi	4	2	0	8	3	0
Georgia	2	3	1	5	5	1
Vanderbilt	2	3	0	4	6	0
Alabama	2	4	0	6	5	0
Kentucky	1	6	0	2	8	0
Mississippi State	0	5	0	3	7	0

1970 NCAA Major College Statistical Leaders

Individual Leaders

PASSING	G	ATT	COM	PCT	INT	I%	YDS	YPA	TD	TD%	COM.PG
1 Sonny Sixkiller, Washington	10	362	186	51.4	22	6.1	2303	6.4	15	4.1	18.6
2 Bob Parker, Air Force	11	402	199	49.5	15	3.7	2789	6.9	21	5.2	18.1
3 Mark Thompson, Davidson	10	352	179	50.9	18	5.1	2202	6.3	14	4.0	17.9
4 Chuck Hixson, SMU	9	285	160	56.1	18	6.3	1763	6.2	10	3.5	17.8
5 Brian Sipe, San Diego State	11	337	195	57.9	20	5.9	2618	7.8	23	6.8	17.7
6 Jim Plunkett, Stanford	11	358	191	53.4	18	5.0	2715	7.6	18	5.0	17.4
7 Dan Fouts, Oregon	11	361	188	52.1	24	6.7	2390	6.6	16	4.4	17.1
7 John Reaves, Florida	**11**	**376**	**188**	**50.0**	**19**	**5.1**	**2549**	**6.8**	**13**	**3.5**	**17.1**
9 Pat Sullivan, Auburn	**10**	**281**	**167**	**59.4**	**12**	**4.3**	**2586**	**9.2**	**17**	**6.1**	**16.7**
10 John Read, Pacific	9	309	149	48.2	19	6.2	1697	5.5	13	4.2	16.6

ALL-PURPOSE	G	RUSH	REC	RET	YDS	YPG
1 Don McCauley, North Carolina	11	1720	235	66	2021	183.7
2 Ed Marinaro, Cornell	9	1425	129	0	1554	172.7
3 Phil Mosser, William & Mary	11	1286	139	447	1872	170.2
4 Larry McCutcheon, Colorado State	11	1008	486	316	1810	164.5
5 Brian Bream, Air Force	10	1276	237	0	1513	151.3
6 Eric Allen, Michigan State	10	811	125	575	1511	151.1
7 Henry Hawthorne, Kansas State	11	399	501	748	1648	149.8
8 Clarence Davis, Southern California	11	972	203	444	1619	147.2
9 Gary Hammond, SMU	11	891	489	224	1604	145.8
10 Jake Green, Colorado State	11	468	459	679	1601	145.5

RUSHING/YARDS PER GAME	G	ATT	YDS	TD	AVG	YPG
1 Ed Marinaro, Cornell	9	285	1425	12	5.0	158.3
2 Don McCauley, North Carolina	11	324	1720	19	5.3	156.4
3 Hank Bjorklund, Princeton	8	179	1081	7	6.0	135.1
4 Gary Kosins, Dayton	9	344	1172	18	3.4	130.2
5 Brian Bream, Air Force	10	294	1276	19	4.3	127.6
6 Mike Adamle, Northwestern	10	304	1255	8	4.1	125.5
7 Roger Lawson, Western Michigan	10	168	1205	13	7.2	120.5
8 Bill Gary, Ohio U.	9	265	1064	11	4.0	118.2
9 Phil Mosser, William & Mary	11	212	1286	9	6.1	116.9
10 John Brockington, Ohio State	9	240	1041	15	4.3	115.7

RUSHING/YARDS PER CARRY	G	ATT	YDS	YPC
1 Roger Lawson, Western Michigan	10	168	1205	7.2
2 Bob Duncan, Citadel	9	139	881	6.3
3 Phil Mosser, William & Mary	11	212	1286	6.1
4 Hank Bjorklund, Princeton	8	179	1081	6.0
5 John Riggins, Kansas	11	209	1131	5.4
6 Don McCauley, North Carolina	11	324	1720	5.3
7 Dick Jauron, Yale	9	182	962	5.3
8 Monroe Eley, Arizona State	8	141	739	5.2
9 Sam Scarber, New Mexico	10	184	961	5.2
10 Johnny Musso, Alabama	**11**	**226**	**1137**	**5.0**

Based on top 24 rushers

RECEIVING	G	REC	YDS	TD	YPR	YPG	RPG
1 Mike Mikolayunas, Davidson	10	87	1128	8	13.0	112.8	8.7
2 Tom Gatewood, Notre Dame	10	77	1123	7	14.6	112.3	7.7
3 Don Fair, Toledo	11	76	893	4	11.8	81.2	6.9
4 Mike Siani, Villanova	11	74	1358	12	18.4	123.5	6.7
4 Ernie Jennings, Air Force	11	74	1289	17	17.4	117.2	6.7
4 Wes Chesson, Duke	11	74	1080	3	14.6	98.2	6.7
4 David Smith, Mississippi State	**11**	**74**	**987**	**6**	**13.3**	**89.7**	**6.7**
8 Tim Delaney, San Diego State	10	62	794	6	12.8	79.4	6.2
9 Bob Newland, Oregon	11	67	1123	7	16.8	102.1	6.1
10 J.D. Hill, Arizona State	10	58	908	10	15.7	90.8	5.8

PUNTING	PUNT	YDS	AVG
1 Marv Bateman, Utah	65	2971	45.7
2 Ray Guy, Southern Miss	69	3126	45.3
3 Jim McCann, Arizona State	48	2026	42.2
4 Mike Parrott, Houston	64	2656	41.5
5 Paul Staroba, Michigan	54	2241	41.5
6 Ron Davis, Idaho	88	3643	41.4
7 Scott Hamm, Air Force	53	2184	41.2
8 Bob Jacobs, Wyoming	84	3444	41.0
9 Ken Duncan, Tulsa	67	2747	41.0
10 Jack Anderson, Clemson	35	1435	41.0

PUNT RETURNS	PR	YDS	TD	AVG
1 Steve Holden, Arizona State	17	327	2	19.2
2 Bob Wicks, Utah State	16	279	2	17.4
3 Ralph McGill, Tulsa	27	460	2	17.0
4 Greg Campbell, Louisville	16	267	2	16.7
5 Raymond Brown, West Texas State	15	250	0	16.7
6 Don Kelley, Clemson	24	389	2	16.2
7 Craig Burns, LSU	**21**	**339**	**2**	**16.1**
8 Tom Myers, Syracuse	29	436	0	15.0
9 Mike Reynolds, Texas-El Paso	25	375	2	15.0
10 Gary Windy, Illinois	17	252	1	14.8

KICKOFF RETURNS	KR	YDS	TD	AVG
1 Stan Brown, Purdue	19	638	3	33.6
2 Macon Hughes, Rice	15	459	2	30.6
3 Jim Krieg, Washington	19	576	2	30.3
4 Dick Harris, South Carolina	30	880	1	29.3
5 Rod Foster, Harvard	11	307	0	27.9
6 Jon Robertson, San Diego State	20	557	1	27.9
7 Henry Hawthorne, Kansas State	23	632	0	27.5
8 Ron Po James, New Mexico State	25	680	0	27.2
9 Cliff Branch, Colorado	21	564	2	26.9
10 Dick Graham, Oklahoma State	17	449	2	26.4

SCORING	TDS	XPT	FG	PTS	PTPG
1 Brian Bream, Air Force	20	0	0	120	12.0
1 Gary Kosins, Dayton	18	0	0	108	12.0
3 Don McCauley, North Carolina	21	0	0	126	11.5
4 Fred Willis, Boston College	16	0	0	96	10.7
5 Ernie Jennings, Air Force	19	0	0	114	10.4
6 John Short, Dartmouth	15	0	0	90	10.0
6 John Brockington, Ohio State	15	0	0	90	10.0
8 Ed Marinaro, Cornell	14	2	0	86	9.6
9 Steve Worster, Texas	14	0	0	84	8.4
9 J.D. Hill, Arizona State	14	0	0	84	8.4

KICK SCORING	XPA	XP	FGA	FG	PTS	PTPG
1 Bill McClard, Arkansas	51	50	15	10	80	7.3
2 Gardner Jett, Auburn	**44**	**41**	**12**	**10**	**71**	**7.1**
3 Happy Feller, Texas	57	55	14	5	70	7.0
3 Dave Haney, Colorado	36	34	18	12	70	7.0
5 George Hunt, Tennessee	**43**	**42**	**21**	**10**	**72**	**6.5**
5 Tom Duncan, Toledo	44	36	21	12	72	6.5
7 Don Ekstrand, Arizona State	47	38	12	9	65	6.5
8 Paul Rogers, Nebraska	52	48	12	7	69	6.3
9 Matias Garza, West Texas State	32	29	21	11	62	6.2
10 Kim Braswell, Georgia	**24**	**22**	**17**	**13**	**61**	**6.1**

INTERCEPTIONS	INT	YDS	TD	INT/GM
1 Mike Sensibaugh, Ohio State	8	40	0	1.00
2 Bobby Majors, Tennessee	**10**	**177**	**0**	**0.91**
3 Neovia Greyer, Wisconsin	9	116	0	0.90
4 Jeff Varnadoe, Citadel	9	251	3	0.82
4 Tim Priest, Tennessee	**9**	**174**	**0**	**0.82**
4 Paul Ellis, Tulane	9	109	0	0.82
7 Raymond Brown, West Texas State	8	162	1	0.80
7 Tom Elias, Western Michigan	8	136	1	0.80
9 Joe Bullard, Tulane	8	167	1	0.73
9 Craig Burns, LSU	**8**	**117**	**0**	**0.73**
9 Ron Ayala, Southern California	8	113	0	0.73
9 Dan Hansen, Brigham Young	8	108	0	0.73
9 Bo Davies, South Carolina	8	41	0	0.73

Team Leaders

RUSHING OFFENSE	G	ATT	YDS	AVG	TD	YPG
1 Texas	10	715	3745	5.2	51	374.5
2 New Mexico	10	637	3501	5.5	33	350.1
3 Ohio State	9	564	2761	4.9	32	306.8
4 Colorado	10	625	2998	4.8	29	299.8
5 Arizona State	10	595	2982	5.0	22	298.2
6 North Carolina	11	732	3137	4.3	31	285.2
7 Penn State	10	617	2768	4.5	31	276.8
8 Cincinnati	11	639	3011	4.7	27	273.7
9 Dartmouth	9	510	2368	4.6	30	263.1
10 Western Michigan	10	558	2631	4.7	22	263.1

PASSING OFFENSE	G	ATT	COM	INT	PCT	YDS	YPA	TD	I%	YPC	YPG
1 Auburn	**10**	**311**	**181**	**12**	**58.2**	**2885**	**9.3**	**17**	**3.9**	**15.9**	**288.5**
2 Oregon	11	441	230	28	52.2	3100	7.0	22	6.4	13.5	281.8
3 San Diego State	11	390	215	24	55.1	3029	7.8	28	6.2	14.1	275.4
4 Washington	10	415	213	26	51.3	2723	6.6	22	6.3	12.8	272.3
5 Stanford	11	391	206	21	52.7	2950	7.5	18	5.4	14.3	268.2
6 Florida State	11	345	175	16	50.7	2837	8.2	17	4.6	16.2	257.9
7 Air Force	11	404	200	15	49.5	2801	6.9	21	3.7	14.0	254.6
8 Notre Dame	10	283	162	15	57.2	2527	8.9	16	5.3	15.6	252.7
9 Villanova	11	385	193	18	50.1	2709	7.0	23	4.7	14.0	246.3
10 Florida	**11**	**396**	**195**	**21**	**49.2**	**2622**	**6.6**	**15**	**5.3**	**13.4**	**238.4**

TOTAL OFFENSE	G	P	YDS	AVG	TD	YPG
1 Arizona State	10	870	5145	5.9	42	514.5
2 Notre Dame	10	924	5105	5.5	45	510.5
3 Auburn	**10**	**684**	**4850**	**7.1**	**43**	**485.0**
4 Texas	10	840	4681	5.6	56	468.1
5 Southern California	11	869	4956	5.7	44	450.5
6 Dartmouth	9	713	3892	5.5	39	432.4
7 Stanford	11	866	4687	5.4	39	426.1
8 West Virginia	11	823	4677	5.7	42	425.2
9 Air Force	11	902	4660	5.2	46	423.6
10 Colorado	10	840	4229	5.0	35	422.9

RUSHING DEFENSE	G	ATT	YDS	AVG	TD	YPG
1 LSU	**11**	**356**	**574**	**1.6**	**2**	**52.2**
2 Tennessee	**11**	**428**	**972**	**2.3**	**6**	**88.4**
3 Dartmouth	9	384	820	2.1	4	91.1
4 North Carolina	11	405	1048	2.6	12	95.3
5 Notre Dame	10	376	962	2.6	6	96.2
6 Penn State	10	442	1008	2.3	12	100.8
7 Miami (Ohio)	10	504	1050	2.1	8	105.0
8 Michigan	10	416	1051	2.5	5	105.1
9 Yale	9	407	958	2.4	6	106.4
10 Ohio State	9	391	965	2.5	4	107.2

PASSING DEFENSE	G	ATT	COM	PCT	YPC	INT	I%	YDS	YPA	TD	YPG
1 Toledo	11	251	88	35.1	9.7	24	9.6	856	3.4	1	77.8
2 Northwestern	10	191	61	31.9	13.0	18	9.4	793	4.2	4	79.3
3 Miami (Ohio)	10	191	84	44.0	10.5	14	7.3	881	4.6	6	88.1
4 Dayton	10	221	74	33.5	12.5	15	6.8	928	4.2	3	92.8
5 Dartmouth	9	188	76	40.4	11.3	18	9.6	857	4.6	2	95.2
6 San Diego State	11	230	85	37.0	12.5	12	5.2	1062	4.6	6	96.5
7 Bowling Green	9	164	77	47.0	12.1	12	7.3	935	5.7	5	103.9
8 Tulane	11	247	106	42.9	11.2	28	11.3	1184	4.8	1	107.6
9 Rice	10	191	86	45.0	12.6	19	10.0	1087	5.7	5	108.7
10 Harvard	9	195	82	42.1	11.9	16	8.2	979	5.0	7	108.8

TOTAL DEFENSE	G	P	YDS	AVG	TD	YPG
1 Toledo	11	727	2044	2.8	8	185.8
2 Dartmouth	9	572	1677	2.9	6	186.3
3 Miami (Ohio)	10	695	1931	2.8	14	193.1
4 San Diego State	11	742	2263	3.0	16	205.7
5 Notre Dame	10	658	2207	3.4	10	220.7
6 Tulane	11	801	2497	3.1	15	227.0
7 Arizona State	10	729	2378	3.3	15	237.8
8 Dayton	10	703	2423	3.4	18	242.3
9 LSU	**11**	**746**	**2689**	**3.6**	**10**	**244.5**
10 Ohio State	9	628	2224	3.5	11	247.1

SCORING OFFENSE	G	PTS	AVG
1 Texas	10	412	41.2
2 Nebraska	11	409	37.2
3 Arkansas	11	402	36.5
4 Arizona State	10	357	35.7
5 Auburn	**10**	**355**	**35.5**
6 Dartmouth	9	311	34.6
7 Washington	10	334	33.4
8 San Diego State	11	364	33.1
9 Notre Dame	10	330	33.0
10 Air Force	11	353	32.1

SCORING DEFENSE	G	PTS	AVG
1 Dartmouth	9	42	4.7
2 Toledo	11	76	6.9
3 LSU	**11**	**96**	**8.7**
4 Michigan	10	90	9.0
5 Tennessee	**11**	**103**	**9.4**
6 Notre Dame	10	97	9.7
7 Cincinnati	11	108	9.8
8 Ohio State	9	93	10.3
9 Yale	9	97	10.8
10 San Diego State	11	123	11.2

1970

FINAL POLL (JAN. 5)

AP	SCHOOL	FINAL RECORD
1	Nebraska	11-0-1
2	Notre Dame	10-1-0
3	Texas	10-1-0
4	**Tennessee**	**11-1-0**
5	Ohio State	9-1-0
6	Arizona State	11-0-0
7	**LSU**	**9-3-0**
8	Stanford	9-3-0
9	Michigan	9-1-0
10	**Auburn**	**9-2-0**
11	Arkansas	9-2-0
12	Toledo	12-0-0
13	Georgia Tech	9-3-0
14	Dartmouth	9-0-0
15	Southern California	6-4-1
16	Air Force	9-3-0
17	Tulane	8-4-0
18	Penn State	7-3-0
19	Houston	8-3-0
20	**Mississippi**	**7-4-0**
20	Oklahoma	7-4-1

CONSENSUS ALL-AMERICANS

POS	OFFENSE	SCHOOL
QB	Jim Plunkett	Stanford
RB	Steve Worster	Texas
RB	Don McCauley	North Carolina
E	Tom Gatewood	Notre Dame
E	Ernie Jennings	Air Force
E	Elmo Wright	Houston
T	Dan Dierdorf	Michigan
T	Bobby Wuensch	Texas
T	Bob Newton	Nebraska
G	**Chip Kell**	**Tennessee**
G	Larry DiNardo	Notre Dame
C	Don Popplewell	Colorado

OTHERS RECEIVING FIRST-TEAM HONORS

QB	Joe Theisman	Notre Dame
RB	John Brockington	Ohio State
RB	Ed Marinaro	Cornell
RB	Leon Burns	Long Beach State
E	Chuck Dicus	Arkansas
E	Jim Braxton	West Virginia
E	Jan White	Ohio State
G	Henry Allison	San Diego State
K	Marv Bateman	Utah
K	Bill McClard	Arkansas

POS	DEFENSE	SCHOOL
E	Bill Atessis	Texas
E	Charlie Weaver	Southern California
T	Rock Perdoni	Georgia Tech
T	Dick Bumpas	Arkansas
MG	Jim Stillwagon	Ohio State
LB	Jack Ham	Penn State
LB	**Mike Anderson**	**LSU**
B	Jack Tatum	Ohio State
B	**Larry Willingham**	**Auburn**
B	Dave Elmendorf	Texas A&M
B	**Tommy Casanova**	**LSU**

OTHERS RECEIVING FIRST-TEAM HONORS

E	**Jack Youngblood**	**Florida**
T	Bruce James	Arkansas
T	Marty Huff	Michigan
T	Jimmy Poston	South Carolina
T	Mel Long	Toledo
T	Win Headley	Wake Forest
T	Joe Ehrmann	Syracuse
MG	Henry Hill	Michigan
LB	Jerry Murtaugh	Nebraska
LB	**Jackie Walker**	**Tennessee**
B	Clarence Scott	Kansas State
B	Murry Bowden	Dartmouth
B	Dick Harris	South Carolina
B	Mike Sensibaugh	Ohio State
B	Clarence Ellis	Notre Dame

HEISMAN TROPHY VOTING

	PLAYER	POS	SCHOOL	TOTAL
1	Jim Plunkett	QB	Stanford	2229
2	Joe Theismann	QB	Notre Dame	1410
3	**Archie Manning**	**QB**	**Mississippi**	**849**
4	Steve Worster	FB	Texas	398
5	Rex Kern	QB	Ohio State	188
6	**Pat Sullivan**	**QB**	**Auburn**	**180**
7	Jack Tatum	DB	Ohio State	173
8	Ernie Jennings	WR	Air Force	118
9	Don McCauley	RB	North Carolina	57
10	Lynn Dickey	QB	Kansas State	49

AWARD WINNERS

PLAYER	AWARD
Jim Plunkett, QB, Stanford	Maxwell
Jim Stillwagon, MG, Ohio State	Outland
Jim Plunkett, QB, Stanford	Camp
Jim Stillwagon, MG, Ohio State	Lombardi

BOWL GAMES

DATE	GAME	SCORE
D12	Liberty	Tulane 17, Colorado 3
D19	Sun	Georgia Tech 17, Texas Tech 9
D19	Pasadena	Long Beach State 24, Louisville 24
D28	Tangerine	Toledo 40, William & Mary 12
D30	Peach	Arizona State 48, North Carolina 26
D31	**Bluebonnet**	**Alabama 24, Oklahoma 24**
J1	**Sugar**	**Tennessee 34, Air Force 13**
J1	**Orange**	**Nebraska 17, LSU 12**
J1	Cotton	Notre Dame 24, Texas 11
J1	Rose	Stanford 27, Ohio State 17
J2	**Gator**	**Auburn 35, Mississippi 28**

SEC STANDINGS

	CONFERENCE			OVERALL		
	W	L	T	W	L	T
LSU	5	0	0	9	3	0
Tennessee	4	1	0	11	1	0
Auburn	5	2	0	9	2	0
Mississippi	4	2	0	7	4	0
Florida	3	3	0	7	4	0
Georgia	3	3	0	5	5	0
Mississippi State	3	4	0	6	5	0
Alabama	3	4	0	6	5	1
Vanderbilt	1	5	0	4	7	0
Kentucky	0	7	0	2	9	0

1971 NCAA Major College Statistical Leaders

Individual Leaders

PASSING	G	ATT	COM	PCT	INT	I%	YDS	YPA	TD	TD%	COM.PG
1 Brian Sipe, San Diego State	11	369	196	53.1	21	5.7	2532	6.9	17	4.6	17.8
2 Don Strock, Virginia Tech	11	356	195	54.8	19	5.3	2577	7.2	12	3.4	17.7
3 John Reaves, Florida	**11**	**356**	**193**	**54.2**	**21**	**5.9**	**2104**	**5.9**	**17**	**4.8**	**17.5**
4 Gary Huff, Florida State	11	327	184	56.3	18	5.5	2736	8.4	23	7.0	16.7
5 Pat Sullivan, Auburn	**10**	**281**	**162**	**57.7**	**11**	**3.9**	**2012**	**7.2**	**20**	**7.1**	**16.2**
6 Gary Fox, Wyoming	11	328	171	52.1	20	6.1	2336	7.1	14	4.3	15.5
7 Don Bunce, Stanford	11	297	162	54.5	16	5.4	2265	7.6	13	4.4	14.7
8 Joe Ferguson, Arkansas	11	271	160	59.0	12	4.4	2203	8.1	11	4.1	14.5
9 Dennis Morrison, Kansas State	11	333	157	47.1	14	4.2	1800	5.4	8	2.4	14.3
10 Carlos Brown, Pacific	11	320	154	48.1	22	6.9	1607	5.0	5	1.6	14.0

ALL-PURPOSE	G	RUSH	REC	PR	KR	YDS	YPG
1 Ed Marinaro, Cornell	9	1881	51	0	0	1932	214.7
2 Bernard Jackson, Washington State	11	1189	185	0	744	2118	192.5
3 Robert Newhouse, Houston	11	1757	35	0	196	1988	180.7
4 Eric Allen, Michigan State	11	1494	275	0	193	1962	178.4
5 Greg Pruitt, Oklahoma	11	1665	108	1	172	1946	176.9
6 Howard Stevens, Louisville	10	1429	168	24	120	1741	174.1
7 Phil Mosser, William & Mary	10	885	212	0	617	1714	171.4
8 Johnny Rodgers, Nebraska	12	259	872	548	304	1983	165.3
9 Paul Loughran, Temple	9	468	198	291	502	1459	162.1
10 Woodrow Green, Arizona State	10	1209	94	165	152	1620	162.0

RUSHING/YARDS PER GAME	G	ATT	YDS	TD	AVG	YPG
1 Ed Marinaro, Cornell	9	356	1881	24	5.3	209.0
2 Robert Newhouse, Houston	11	277	1757	12	6.3	159.7
3 Greg Pruitt, Oklahoma	11	178	1665	17	9.4	151.4
4 Howard Stevens, Louisville	10	250	1429	12	5.7	142.9
5 Lydell Mitchell, Penn State	11	254	1567	26	6.2	142.5
6 Eric Allen, Michigan State	11	259	1494	18	5.8	135.8
7 Charlie Davis, Colorado	11	219	1386	10	6.3	126.0
8 Bobby Moore, Oregon	10	249	1211	7	4.9	121.1
9 Woodrow Green, Arizona State	10	208	1209	9	5.8	120.9
10 Paul Miles, Bowling Green	10	274	1185	7	4.3	118.5

RUSHING/YARDS PER CARRY	G	ATT	YDS	YPC
1 Greg Pruitt, Oklahoma	11	178	1665	9.4
2 Jon Hall, Citadel	11	169	1230	7.3
3 Bernard Jackson, Washington State	11	177	1189	6.7
4 Fred Henry, New Mexico	10	176	1129	6.4
5 Robert Newhouse, Houston	11	277	1757	6.3
6 Charlie Davis, Colorado	11	219	1386	6.3
7 Lydell Mitchell, Penn State	11	254	1567	6.2
8 Jack Mildren, Oklahoma	11	193	1140	5.9
9 Woodrow Green, Arizona State	10	208	1209	5.8
10 Eric Allen, Michigan State	11	259	1494	5.8

Based on top 24 rushers

RECEIVING	G	REC	YDS	TD	YPR	YPG	RPG
1 Tom Reynolds, San Diego State	10	67	1070	7	16.0	107.0	6.7
2 Brian Baima, Citadel	11	64	1237	13	19.3	112.5	5.8
3 Rhett Dawson, Florida State	11	62	817	7	13.2	74.3	5.6
4 Mike Reppond, Arkansas	10	56	986	3	17.6	98.6	5.6
5 Terry Beasley, Auburn	**10**	**55**	**846**	**12**	**15.4**	**84.6**	**5.5**
6 Bob Wicks, Utah State	11	58	862	5	14.9	78.4	5.3
7 Leland Glass, Oregon	9	46	584	6	12.7	64.9	5.1
8 Willie Hatter, Northern Illinois	10	50	615	1	12.3	61.5	5.0
9 Geoff DeLapp, California	10	48	464	1	9.7	46.4	4.8
10 Jim Butler, Tulsa	11	50	486	0	9.7	44.2	4.5

PUNTING	PUNT	YDS	AVG
1 Marv Bateman, Utah	68	3271	48.1
2 Jim Benien, Oklahoma State	77	3504	45.5
3 Lowell Ramsey, Wake Forest	46	2001	43.5
4 Dave Green, Ohio U.	33	1416	42.9
5 Ray Guy, Southern Miss	73	3132	42.9
6 Russell Brown, William & Mary	51	2183	42.8
7 Nick Vidnovic, North Carolina	60	2568	42.8
8 Darryl Haas, Air Force	67	2814	42.0
8 Tom Moore, Navy	67	2814	42.0
10 Steve Hunter, Idaho	73	3059	41.9

PUNT RETURNS	PR	YDS	TD	AVG
1 Golden Richards, Brigham Young	33	624	4	18.9
2 Ed Rideout, Boston College	15	271	1	18.1
3 Johnny Rodgers, Nebraska	33	548	3	16.6
4 Dean Campbell, Texas	14	232	0	16.6
5 Steven Solow, Pennsylvania	17	279	0	16.4
6 Cliff Branch, Colorado	31	505	4	16.3
7 Bill Cahill, Washington	26	421	1	16.2
8 John Sefcik, Columbia	22	310	0	14.1
9 Jeff Varnadoe, Citadel	33	455	2	13.8
10 Bobby McKinney, Alabama	**25**	**326**	**1**	**13.0**

KICKOFF RETURNS	KR	YDS	TD	AVG
1 Paul Loughran, Temple	15	502	1	33.5
2 Bob Allen, Ohio U.	14	421	0	30.1
3 Greg Johnson, Wisconsin	19	540	0	28.4
4 Ray Taroli, Oregon State	32	908	1	28.4
5 Mike Fink, Missouri	21	594	2	28.3
6 John Chatman, Pittsburgh	16	447	0	27.9
7 Bruce Miller, Rutgers	19	524	1	27.6
8 Bernard Jackson, Washington State	27	744	2	27.6
9 Eddie Woodard, Kent State	23	632	1	27.5
10 Don Gilley, Wichita State	17	454	1	26.7
10 Benny Reed, Texas-El Paso	17	454	0	26.7

SCORING	TDS	XPT	FG	PTS	PTPG
1 Ed Marinaro, Cornell	24	4	0	148	16.4
2 Lydell Mitchell, Penn State	29	0	0	174	15.8
3 Eric Allen, Michigan State	18	2	0	110	10.0
3 Johnny Musso, Alabama	**16**	**4**	**0**	**100**	**10.0**
5 Joe Schwartz, Toledo	18	0	0	108	9.8
6 Jack Mildren, Oklahoma	17	4	0	106	9.6
7 Greg Pruitt, Oklahoma	17	0	0	102	9.3
8 Bill Butler, Kansas State	16	0	0	96	8.7
9 Larry Russell, Wake Forest	15	4	0	94	8.5
10 Johnny Rodgers, Nebraska	17	0	0	102	8.5
10 Hank Bjorklund, Princeton	11	2	0	68	8.5

KICK SCORING	XPA	XP	FGA	FG	PTS	PTPG
1 John Carroll, Oklahoma	62	53	12	9	80	7.3
2 Nick Mike-Mayer, Temple	28	26	17	12	62	6.9
3 Don Ekstrand, Arizona State	53	48	10	9	75	6.8
3 Dana Coin, Michigan	54	54	12	7	75	6.8
3 Bill Davis, Alabama	**40**	**36**	**16**	**13**	**75**	**6.8**
6 Albert Vitiello, Penn State	62	59	13	5	74	6.7
7 Bill McClard, Arkansas	38	35	22	12	71	6.5
8 Frank Fontes, Florida State	31	30	24	13	69	6.3
9 Rich Sanger, Nebraska	64	60	9	5	75	6.3
10 Rodrigo Garcia, Stanford	27	24	27	14	66	6.0
10 George Hunt, Tennessee	**30**	**30**	**15**	**12**	**66**	**6.0**

INTERCEPTIONS	INT	YDS	TD	INT/GM
1 Frank Polito, Villanova	12	261	2	1.20
2 Jackie Wallace, Arizona	11	135	1	1.00
3 Tom Myers, Syracuse	8	57	0	0.89
4 Dave Atkinson, Brigham Young	9	120	0	0.82
5 Pete Carroll, Pacific	8	131	0	0.73
6 Larry Marshall, Maryland	6	131	0	0.67
6 Nick Holm, Houston	6	45	0	0.67
8 Dan Hansen, Brigham Young *	7	233	2	0.64
8 Dave Chaney, San Jose State *	7	136	2	0.64
8 Willie Osley, Illinois *	7	127	1	0.64

*Six tied with seven; these had the most yards

Team Leaders

RUSHING OFFENSE	G	ATT	YDS	AVG	TD	YPG
1 Oklahoma	11	761	5196	6.8	56	472.4
2 New Mexico	11	747	4229	5.7	43	384.5
3 Michigan	11	768	3714	4.8	46	337.6
4 Alabama	**11**	**705**	**3565**	**5.1**	**34**	**324.1**
5 Cornell	9	578	2884	5.0	28	320.4
6 Penn State	11	619	3347	5.4	42	304.3
7 Wake Forest	11	744	3344	4.5	26	304.0
8 Georgia	**11**	**691**	**3337**	**4.8**	**39**	**303.4**
9 Colgate	10	672	3008	4.5	33	300.8
10 Arizona State	11	615	3278	5.3	29	298.0

PASSING OFFENSE	G	ATT	COM	INT	PCT	YDS	YPA	TD	I%	YPC	YPG
1 San Diego State	11	409	211	27	51.6	2765	6.8	18	6.6	13.1	251.4
2 Florida State	11	338	186	20	55.0	2750	8.1	23	5.9	14.8	250.0
3 Virginia Tech	11	368	202	20	54.9	2695	7.3	12	5.4	13.3	245.0
4 Washington	11	354	152	24	42.9	2606	7.4	18	6.8	17.1	236.9
5 Auburn	**10**	**316**	**180**	**13**	**57.0**	**2277**	**7.2**	**24**	**4.1**	**12.7**	**227.7**
6 Wyoming	11	346	176	22	50.9	2416	7.0	16	6.4	13.7	219.6
7 Stanford	11	328	176	16	53.7	2414	7.4	13	4.9	13.7	219.5
8 Arkansas	11	293	170	16	58.0	2327	7.9	11	5.5	13.7	211.5
9 Florida	**11**	**381**	**205**	**23**	**53.8**	**2233**	**5.9**	**19**	**6.0**	**10.9**	**203.0**
10 Utah State	11	300	150	11	50.0	2185	7.3	15	3.7	14.6	198.6

TOTAL OFFENSE	G	P	YDS	AVG	TD	YPG
1 Oklahoma	11	839	6232	7.4	66	566.5
2 New Mexico	11	862	5149	6.0	48	468.1
3 Arizona State	11	844	5121	6.1	52	465.5
4 Citadel	11	777	5030	6.5	46	457.3
5 Penn State	11	798	4995	6.3	60	454.1
6 Houston	11	836	4993	6.0	42	453.9
7 Arkansas	11	875	4898	5.6	43	445.3
8 Nebraska	12	976	5252	5.4	56	437.7
9 Colorado	11	820	4538	5.5	43	412.5
10 Michigan	11	882	4397	5.0	51	399.7

RUSHING DEFENSE	G	ATT	YDS	AVG	TD	YPG
1 Michigan	11	418	696	1.7	3	63.3
2 Nebraska	12	500	1031	2.1	7	85.9
3 Notre Dame	10	383	864	2.3	3	86.4
4 Western Michigan	10	407	932	2.3	7	93.2
5 Miami (Ohio)	10	408	953	2.3	4	95.3
6 Georgia	**11**	**424**	**1076**	**2.5**	**6**	**97.8**
7 Toledo	11	539	1199	2.2	11	109.0
8 Alabama	**11**	**423**	**1281**	**3.0**	**4**	**116.5**
9 Stanford	11	519	1282	2.5	10	116.5
10 Penn State	11	483	1292	2.7	3	117.5

PASSING DEFENSE	G	ATT	COM	PCT	YPC	INT	I%	YDS	YPA	TD	YPG
1 Texas Tech	11	147	55	37.4	12.0	14	9.5	661	4.5	2	60.1
2 Cincinnati	11	164	66	40.2	11.3	18	11.0	748	4.6	5	68.0
3 Toledo	11	195	68	34.9	11.4	18	9.2	776	4.0	2	70.5
4 New Mexico State	11	176	63	35.8	13.7	12	6.8	865	4.9	3	78.6
5 Louisville	10	193	69	35.8	12.3	20	10.4	846	4.4	3	84.6
6 Miami (Ohio)	10	211	92	43.6	10.2	14	6.6	940	4.5	4	94.0
7 Vanderbilt	**11**	**196**	**89**	**45.4**	**11.6**	**13**	**6.6**	**1035**	**5.3**	**7**	**94.1**
8 Kent State	11	177	82	46.3	12.9	11	6.2	1054	6.0	5	95.8
9 LSU	**11**	**223**	**101**	**45.3**	**11.0**	**17**	**7.6**	**1108**	**5.0**	**4**	**100.7**
10 Texas-Arlington	11	194	85	43.8	13.3	13	7.0	1132	5.8	7	102.9

TOTAL DEFENSE	G	P	YDS	AVG	TD	YPG
1 Toledo	11	734	1975	2.7	13	179.5
2 Michigan	11	632	1977	3.1	9	179.7
3 Miami (Ohio)	10	619	1893	3.1	8	189.3
4 Notre Dame	10	598	1981	3.3	11	198.1
5 Nebraska	12	769	2435	3.2	12	202.9
6 Louisville	10	666	2082	3.1	11	208.2
7 Alabama	**11**	**663**	**2417**	**3.6**	**10**	**219.7**
8 Stanford	11	761	2424	3.2	14	220.4
9 Georgia	**11**	**690**	**2575**	**3.7**	**16**	**234.1**
10 Boston College	11	732	2654	3.6	14	241.3

SCORING OFFENSE	G	PTS	AVG
1 Oklahoma	11	494	44.9
2 Penn State	11	454	41.3
3 Nebraska	12	469	39.1
4 Arizona State	11	417	37.9
5 Michigan	11	409	37.2
6 Citadel	11	366	33.3
7 Alabama	**11**	**362**	**32.9**
8 Washington	11	357	32.5
9 Toledo	11	355	32.3
10 Georgia	**11**	**353**	**32.1**

SCORING DEFENSE	G	PTS	AVG
1 Michigan	11	70	6.4
2 Alabama	**11**	**84**	**7.6**
3 Nebraska	12	98	8.2
4 Toledo	11	91	8.3
5 Notre Dame	10	86	8.6
6 Tennessee	**11**	**108**	**9.8**
7 Georgia	**11**	**112**	**10.2**
8 Boston College	11	117	10.6
9 Louisville	10	111	11.1
10 Stanford	11	123	11.2

1971

FINAL POLL (JAN. 3)

AP	SCHOOL	FINAL RECORD
1	Nebraska	13-0-0
2	Oklahoma	11-1-0
3	Colorado	10-2-0
4	**Alabama**	**11-1-0**
5	Penn State	11-1-0
6	Michigan	11-1-0
7	**Georgia**	**11-1-0**
8	Arizona State	11-1-0
9	**Tennessee**	**10-2-0**
10	Stanford	9-3-0
11	**LSU**	**9-3-0**
12	**Auburn**	**9-2-0**
13	Notre Dame	8-2-0
14	Toledo	12-0-0
15	**Mississippi**	**10-2-0**
16	Arkansas	8-3-1
17	Houston	9-3-0
18	Texas	8-3-0
19	Washington	8-3-0
20	Southern California	6-4-1

CONSENSUS ALL-AMERICANS

POS	OFFENSE	SCHOOL
QB	**Pat Sullivan**	**Auburn**
RB	Ed Marinaro	Cornell
RB	Greg Pruitt	Oklahoma
RB	**Johnny Musso**	**Alabama**
E	**Terry Beasley**	**Auburn**
E	Johnny Rodgers	Nebraska
T	Jerry Sisemore	Texas
T	Dave Joyner	Penn State
G	**Royce Smith**	**Georgia**
G	Reggie McKenzie	Michigan
C	Tom Brahaney	Oklahoma

OTHERS RECEIVING FIRST-TEAM HONORS

RB	Eric Allen	Michigan State
RB	Lydell Mitchell	Penn State
RB	Bobby Moore	Oregon
E	Doug Kingsriter	Minnesota
T	**John Hannah**	**Alabama**
T	John Vella	Southern California
C	Tom DeLeone	Ohio State

POS	DEFENSE	SCHOOL
E	Walt Patulski	Notre Dame
E	Willie Harper	Nebraska
T	Larry Jacobson	Nebraska
T	Mel Long	Toledo
T	Sherman White	California
LB	Mike Taylor	Michigan
LB	Jeff Siemon	Stanford
B	**Bobby Majors**	**Tennessee**
B	Clarence Ellis	Notre Dame
B	Ernie Jackson	Duke
B	**Tommy Casanova**	**LSU**

OTHERS RECEIVING FIRST-TEAM HONORS

E	Herb Orvis	Colorado
E	Smylie Gebhart	Georgia Tech
T	Ron Curl	Michigan State
T	**Ronnie Estay**	**LSU**
T	Rich Glover	Nebraska
LB	**Jackie Walker**	**Tennessee**
LB	Dave Chaney	San Jose State
LB	Charlie Zapiec	Penn State
B	Eric Hutchinson	Northwestern
B	Thom Darden	Michigan
B	Tom Myers	Syracuse
B	Craig Clemons	Iowa
K	Bill McClard	Arkansas

HEISMAN TROPHY VOTING

	PLAYER	POS	SCHOOL	TOTAL
1	**Pat Sullivan**	**QB**	**Auburn**	**1597**
2	Ed Marinaro	RB	Cornell	1445
3	Greg Pruitt	RB	Oklahoma	586
4	**Johnny Musso**	**RB**	**Alabama**	**365**
5	Lydell Mitchell	RB	Penn State	251
6	Jack Mildren	QB	Oklahoma	208
7	Jerry Tagge	QB	Nebraska	168
8	Chuck Ealy	QB	Toledo	137
9	Walt Patulski	DE	Notre Dame	121
10	Eric Allen	RB	Michigan State	109

AWARD WINNERS

PLAYER	AWARD
Ed Marinaro, RB, Cornell	Maxwell
Larry Jacobson, DT, Nebraska	Outland
Pat Sullivan, QB, Auburn	**Camp**
Walt Patulski, DE, Notre Dame	Lombardi

BOWL GAMES

DATE	GAME	SCORE
D18	**Sun**	**LSU 33, Iowa State 15**
D18	Pasadena	Memphis 28, San Jose State 9
D20	**Liberty**	**Tennessee 14, Arkansas 13**
D27	Fiesta	Arizona State 45, Florida State 38
D28	Tangerine	Toledo 28, Richmond 3
D30	**Peach**	**Mississippi 41, Georgia Tech 18**
D31	Bluebonnet	Colorado 29, Houston 17
D31	**Gator**	**Georgia 7, North Carolina 3**
J1	**Sugar**	**Oklahoma 40, Auburn 22**
J1	**Orange**	**Nebraska 38, Alabama 6**
J1	Cotton	Penn State 30, Texas 6
J1	Rose	Stanford 13, Michigan 12

SEC STANDINGS

	CONFERENCE			OVERALL		
	W	L	T	W	L	T
Alabama	7	0	0	11	1	0
Georgia	5	1	0	11	1	0
Auburn	5	1	0	9	2	0
Tennessee	4	2	0	10	2	0
Mississippi	4	2	0	10	2	0
LSU	3	2	0	9	3	0
Vanderbilt	1	5	0	4	6	1
Florida	1	6	0	4	7	0
Kentucky	1	6	0	3	8	0
Mississippi State	1	7	0	2	9	0

1972 NCAA Major College Statistical Leaders

Individual Leaders

PASSING	G	ATT	COM	PCT	INT	I%	YDS	YPA	TD	TD%	COM.PG
1 Don Strock, Virginia Tech	11	427	228	53.4	27	6.3	3243	7.6	16	3.8	20.7
2 Gary Huff, Florida State	11	385	206	53.5	23	6.0	2893	7.5	25	6.5	18.7
3 Tony Adams, Utah State	11	351	204	58.1	9	2.6	2797	8.0	22	6.3	18.5
4 Mike Boryla, Stanford	11	350	183	52.3	20	5.7	2284	6.5	14	4.0	16.6
5 Joe Pisarcik, New Mexico State	11	382	182	47.6	15	3.9	2179	5.7	8	2.1	16.5
6 Gary Keithley, Texas-El Paso	9	252	144	57.1	10	4.0	1870	7.4	7	2.8	16.0
7 Dan Fouts, Oregon	11	348	171	49.1	19	5.5	2041	5.9	12	3.5	15.5
8 Bruce Gadd, Rice	11	322	170	52.8	22	6.8	2064	6.4	11	3.4	15.5
9 Scotty Shipp, Davidson	10	286	149	52.1	22	7.7	1845	6.5	9	3.2	14.9
10 Buddy Palazzo, Southern Miss	11	289	160	55.4	16	5.5	1888	6.5	8	2.8	14.5
10 Tim Dydo, Xavier	11	327	160	48.9	18	5.5	1568	4.8	5	1.5	14.5

ALL-PURPOSE	G	RUSH	REC	PR	KR	YDS	YPG
1 Howard Stevens, Louisville	10	1294	221	377	240	2132	213.2
2 Pete Van Valkenburg, Brigham Young	10	1386	98	26	328	1838	183.8
3 Johnny Rodgers, Nebraska	11	267	942	618	184	2011	182.8
4 Steve Odom, Utah	11	59	663	244	984	1950	177.3
5 Otis Armstrong, Purdue	11	1361	55	0	452	1868	169.8
6 Woody Green, Arizona State	10	1363	115	12	117	1607	160.7
7 Adolph Bellizeare, Pennsylvania	9	849	149	129	263	1390	154.4
8 Dick Jauron, Yale	9	1055	75	41	207	1378	153.1
9 Paul Loughran, Temple	9	593	196	146	438	1373	152.6
10 Anthony Davis, Southern California	11	1034	115	44	468	1661	151.0

RUSHING/Yards Per Game	G	ATT	YDS	TD	AVG	YPG
1 Pete Van Valkenburg, Brigham Young	10	232	1386	12	6.0	138.6
2 Bob Hitchens, Miami (Ohio)	10	326	1370	15	4.2	137.0
3 Woody Green, Arizona State	10	209	1363	15	6.5	136.3
4 Howard Stevens, Louisville	10	259	1294	13	5.0	129.4
5 Otis Armstrong, Purdue	11	243	1361	9	5.6	123.7
6 Mark Kellar, Northern Illinois	11	285	1314	9	4.6	119.5
7 Carl Crumpler, East Carolina	11	340	1309	17	3.9	119.0
8 Dick Jauron, Yale	9	160	1055	12	6.6	117.2
9 Jim Jennings, Rutgers	11	287	1262	9	4.4	114.7
10 Mike Strachan, Iowa State	11	267	1260	8	4.7	114.5

RUSHING/Yards Per Carry	G	ATT	YDS	YPC
1 Dick Jauron, Yale	9	160	1055	6.6
2 Woody Green, Arizona State	10	209	1363	6.5
3 Pete Van Valkenburg, Brigham Young	10	232	1386	6.0
4 Mitchell True, Pacific	11	206	1164	5.7
5 Anthony Davis, Southern California	11	184	1034	5.6
6 Otis Armstrong, Purdue	11	243	1361	5.6
7 Puddin Jones, Houston	11	222	1216	5.5
8 Cleveland Cooper, Navy	11	192	1046	5.4
9 Adolph Bellizeare, Pennsylvania	9	168	849	5.1
10 Bob McCall, Arizona	11	228	1148	5.0

Based on top 26 rushers

RECEIVING	G	REC	YDS	TD	YPR	YPG	RPG
1 Tom Forzani, Utah State	11	85	1169	8	13.8	106.3	7.7
2 Clinton Graves, Temple	9	63	707	3	11.2	78.6	7.0
3 Barry Smith, Florida State	10	69	1243	13	18.0	124.3	6.9
4 Chip Regine, Brown	9	51	681	6	13.4	75.7	5.7
5 Walt Walker, Davidson	11	62	1031	8	16.6	93.7	5.6
5 Jeff Calabrese, Toledo	11	62	886	2	14.3	80.5	5.6
7 Bert Calland, Navy	11	61	650	2	10.7	59.1	5.5
8 Greg Taylor, Texas-El Paso	10	53	878	4	16.6	87.8	5.3
9 Ken Matthews, Long Beach State	11	58	938	2	16.2	85.3	5.3
10 Gary Barnes, Louisville	10	52	655	4	12.6	65.5	5.2

PUNTING	PUNT	YDS	AVG
1 Ray Guy, Southern Miss	58	2680	46.2
2 Bruce Barnes, UCLA	48	2078	43.3
3 Chuck Ramsey, Wake Forest	72	3110	43.2
4 Dan Marrelli, Utah	57	2462	43.2
5 Danny White, Arizona State	51	2193	43.0
6 Randy Lee, Tulane	70	2996	42.8
7 Greg Gantt, Alabama	**44**	**1874**	**42.6**
8 Gary Keithley, Texas-El Paso	47	2002	42.6
9 Marty Shuford, Arizona	77	3273	42.5
10 Bill Armstrong, California	64	2675	41.8

PUNT RETURNS	PR	YDS	TD	AVG
1 Randy Rhino, Georgia Tech	25	441	1	17.6
2 George Ewing, Tulane	16	264	3	16.5
3 Johnny Rodgers, Nebraska	39	618	2	15.8
4 Carl Roaches, Texas A&M	19	287	2	15.1
5 Gerald Tinker, Kent State	19	268	1	14.1
6 Lynn Swann, Southern California	18	253	1	14.1
7 Kris Silverthorn, SMU	32	443	2	13.8
8 Bill Simpson, Michigan State	21	286	2	13.6
9 Steve Haggerty, Colorado	26	352	1	13.5
10 Robert Smith, Maryland	23	308	1	13.4

KICKOFF RETURNS	KR	YDS	TD	AVG
1 Larry Williams, Texas Tech	16	493	0	30.8
2 Byron Florence, Northern Illinois	16	456	1	28.5
3 Fran Meagher, Holy Cross	16	451	1	28.2
4 Kerry Marbury, West Virginia	20	554	1	27.7
5 Theopolis Bell, Arizona	18	449	0	24.9
6 Doug Nettles, Vanderbilt	**23**	**566**	**0**	**24.6**
7 Earl Douthitt, Iowa	22	541	0	24.6
8 Eddie Woodard, Kent State	21	516	1	24.6
9 Steve Odom, Utah	41	984	0	24.0
10 Dornell Harris, Memphis	19	453	0	23.8

SCORING	TDS	XPT	FG	PTS	PTPG
1 Harold Henson, Ohio State	20	0	0	120	12.0
2 Kerry Marbury, West Virginia	18	0	0	108	10.8
3 Howard Stevens, Louisville	17	0	0	102	10.2
4 Anthony Davis, Southern California	18	0	0	108	9.8
5 Terry Metcalf, Long Beach State	16	2	0	98	9.8
6 Stan Fritts, North Carolina St.	17	4	0	106	9.6
7 Johnny Rodgers, Nebraska	17	0	0	102	9.3
7 Carl Crumpler, East Carolina	17	0	0	102	9.3
9 Bob Hitchens, Miami (Ohio)	15	0	0	90	9.0
9 Woody Green, Arizona State	15	0	0	90	9.0

KICK SCORING	XPA	XP	FGA	FG	PTS	PTPG
1 Fred Lima, Colorado	36	35	34	15	80	7.3
2 Rich Sanger, Nebraska	62	58	14	6	76	6.9
3 Frank Nester, West Virginia	50	47	14	9	74	6.7
4 Dave Strock, Virginia Tech	30	28	29	15	73	6.6
5 Juan Cruz, Arizona State	62	53	12	6	71	6.5
6 Mike Rae, Southern California	52	43	10	8	67	6.1
6 Ricky Townsend, Tennessee	**31**	**31**	**19**	**12**	**67**	**6.1**
8 Don Grimes, Texas Tech	30	30	18	12	66	6.0
8 Ted Perry, Dartmouth	32	30	13	8	54	6.0
10 Rick Fulcher, Oklahoma	40	38	15	9	65	5.9

INTERCEPTIONS	INT	YDS	TD	INT/GM
1 Mike Townsend, Notre Dame	10	39	0	1.00
2 John Provost, Holy Cross	9	175	1	0.90
2 Harry Harrison, Mississippi	**9**	**129**	**0**	**0.90**
4 David Langner, Auburn	**8**	**156**	**0**	**0.80**
5 Peter Knight, Cornell	7	96	0	0.78
5 Denny Costello, Miami (Ohio)	7	52	0	0.78
7 Ron Karlis, Western Michigan	8	247	2	0.73
7 Randy Rhino, Georgia Tech	8	171	1	0.73
7 Ray Guy, Southern Miss	8	137	0	0.73
7 Alvin Brown, Oklahoma State	8	117	0	0.73
7 Jackie Wallace, Arizona	8	115	1	0.73
7 Dave Atkinson, Brigham Young	8	88	1	0.73

Team Leaders

RUSHING OFFENSE	G	ATT	YDS	AVG	TD	YPG
1 Oklahoma	11	803	4057	5.1	39	368.8
2 UCLA	11	673	3810	5.7	38	346.4
3 Arizona State	11	619	3681	5.9	46	334.6
4 Oklahoma State	11	707	3497	4.9	24	317.9
5 Notre Dame	10	594	3043	5.1	28	304.3
6 Alabama	**11**	**704**	**3332**	**4.7**	**42**	**302.9**
7 Yale	9	538	2636	4.9	32	292.9
8 Miami (Ohio)	10	683	2806	4.1	25	280.6
9 New Mexico	11	686	3085	4.5	25	280.5
10 Texas	10	598	2760	4.6	29	276.0

PASSING OFFENSE/YPG	G	ATT	COM	INT	PCT	YDS	YPA	TD	YPG	I%	YPC
1 Virginia Tech	11	440	233	28	53.0	3348	7.6	18	304.4	6.4	14.4
2 Utah State	11	392	222	13	56.6	3164	8.1	24	287.6	3.3	14.3
3 Florida State	11	389	209	23	53.7	2974	7.6	28	270.4	5.9	14.2
4 San Diego State	11	327	184	25	56.3	2525	7.7	18	229.5	7.7	13.7
5 Stanford	11	386	203	23	52.6	2509	6.5	16	228.1	6.0	12.4
6 West Virginia	11	334	161	18	48.2	2506	7.5	17	227.8	5.4	15.6
7 California	11	361	182	32	50.4	2444	6.8	20	222.2	8.9	13.4
8 Nebraska	11	306	161	20	52.6	2431	7.9	23	221.0	6.5	15.1
9 New Mexico State	11	412	195	16	47.3	2428	5.9	10	220.7	3.9	12.5
10 Texas-El Paso	10	323	169	12	52.3	2164	6.7	10	216.4	3.7	12.8

TOTAL OFFENSE	G	P	YDS	AVG	TD	YPG
1 Arizona State	11	856	5681	6.6	67	516.5
2 Oklahoma	11	953	5255	5.5	48	477.7
3 Nebraska	11	928	4843	5.2	60	440.3
4 Utah State	11	804	4783	5.9	40	434.8
5 North Carolina St.	11	846	4758	5.6	49	432.5
6 Southern California	11	830	4731	5.7	53	430.1
7 Notre Dame	10	766	4238	5.5	36	423.8
8 West Virginia	11	796	4531	5.7	51	411.9
9 Virginia Tech	11	857	4527	5.3	38	411.5
10 Alabama	**11**	**832**	**4501**	**5.4**	**53**	**409.2**

RUSHING DEFENSE	G	ATT	YDS	AVG	TD	YPG
1 Louisville	10	430	821	1.9	7	82.1
2 Western Michigan	11	454	980	2.2	14	89.1
3 Southern California	11	488	1036	2.1	9	94.2
4 Miami (Ohio)	10	365	961	2.6	8	96.1
5 Pacific	11	428	1112	2.6	10	101.1
6 Oklahoma	11	409	1124	2.7	6	102.2
7 East Carolina	11	443	1200	2.7	15	109.1
8 Nebraska	11	516	1240	2.4	5	112.7
9 Bowling Green	10	458	1134	2.5	8	113.4
10 Alabama	**11**	**459**	**1263**	**2.8**	**8**	**114.8**

PASSING DEFENSE	G	ATT	COM	PCT	YPC	INT	I%	YDS	YPA	TD	YPG
1 Vanderbilt	**11**	**164**	**61**	**37.2**	**14.5**	**11**	**6.7**	**883**	**5.4**	**5**	**80.3**
2 Northwestern	11	129	57	44.2	15.6	7	5.4	889	6.9	8	80.8
3 Tennessee	**11**	**213**	**85**	**39.9**	**10.6**	**20**	**9.4**	**904**	**4.2**	**4**	**82.2**
4 Michigan	11	200	82	41.0	11.4	17	8.5	932	4.7	1	84.7
5 Toledo	11	177	70	39.5	13.5	13	7.3	947	5.4	8	86.1
6 Iowa	11	172	78	45.3	12.7	11	6.4	989	5.8	6	89.9
7 Baylor	11	199	72	36.2	13.8	18	9.1	995	5.0	4	90.5
8 Wichita State	11	209	76	36.4	13.5	27	12.9	1029	4.9	8	93.5
9 Marshall	10	154	66	42.9	14.4	8	5.2	951	6.2	2	95.1
10 Alabama	**11**	**215**	**105**	**48.8**	**10.2**	**20**	**9.3**	**1071**	**5.0**	**7**	**97.4**

TOTAL DEFENSE	G	P	YDS	AVG	TD	YPG
1 Louisville	10	689	2025	2.9	8	202.5
2 Alabama	**11**	**674**	**2334**	**3.5**	**15**	**212.2**
3 Michigan	11	680	2372	3.5	7	215.6
4 Nebraska	11	764	2411	3.2	11	219.2
5 Oklahoma	11	691	2494	3.6	8	226.7
6 Miami (Ohio)	10	596	2276	3.8	15	227.6
7 Southern California	11	772	2534	3.3	14	230.4
8 Tennessee	**11**	**738**	**2539**	**3.4**	**10**	**230.8**
9 Tampa	11	730	2600	3.6	12	236.4
10 Bowling Green	10	661	2437	3.7	17	243.7

SCORING OFFENSE	G	PTS	AVG
1 Arizona State	11	513	46.6
2 Nebraska	11	461	41.9
3 Southern California	11	425	38.6
4 West Virginia	11	402	36.5
5 Alabama	**11**	**393**	**35.7**
6 Oklahoma	11	385	35.0
7 North Carolina St.	11	360	32.7
8 Penn State	11	358	32.5
9 Utah	11	354	32.2
10 UCLA	11	351	31.9

SCORING DEFENSE	G	PTS	AVG
1 Michigan	11	57	5.2
2 Oklahoma	11	74	6.7
3 Tennessee	**11**	**83**	**7.5**
4 Nebraska	11	91	8.3
5 Louisville	10	91	9.1
6 Tampa	11	114	10.4
7 Southern California	11	117	10.6
8 Texas	10	108	10.8
9 LSU	**11**	**121**	**11.0**
10 Miami (Ohio)	10	116	11.6

1972

Final Poll (Jan. 3)

AP	SCHOOL	FINAL RECORD
1	Southern California	12-0-0
2	Oklahoma	11-1-0
3	Texas	10-1-0
4	Nebraska	9-2-1
5	Auburn	10-1-0
6	Michigan	10-1-0
7	Alabama	10-2-0
8	Tennessee	10-2-0
9	Ohio State	9-2-0
10	Penn State	10-2-0
11	LSU	9-2-1
12	North Carolina	11-1-0
13	Arizona State	10-2-0
14	Notre Dame	8-3-0
15	UCLA	8-3-0
16	Colorado	8-4-0
17	North Carolina St.	8-3-1
18	Louisville	9-1-0
19	Washington State	7-4-0
20	Georgia Tech	7-4-1

Consensus All-Americans

POS	OFFENSE	SCHOOL
QB	Bert Jones	LSU
RB	Greg Pruitt	Oklahoma
RB	Otis Armstrong	Purdue
RB	Woody Green	Arizona State
WR	Johnny Rodgers	Nebraska
TE	Charles Young	Southern California
T	Jerry Sisemore	Texas
T	Paul Seymour	Michigan
G	John Hannah	Alabama
G	Ron Rusnak	North Carolina
C	Tom Brahaney	Oklahoma

Others receiving first-team honors

QB	John Hufnagel	Penn State
QB	Gary Huff	Florida State
RB	Sam Cunningham	Southern California
RB	Dick Jauron	Yale
WR	Steve Holden	Arizona State
WR	Barry Smith	Florida State
T	Daryl White	Nebraska
T	John Hicks	Ohio State
T	Pete Adams	Southern California
G	Bill Singletary	Temple
G	Jim Krapf	Alabama
K	Ricky Townsend	Tennessee

POS	DEFENSE	SCHOOL
E	Willie Harper	Nebraska
E	Bruce Bannon	Penn State
T	Greg Marx	Notre Dame
T	Dave Butz	Purdue
MG	Rich Glover	Nebraska
LB	Randy Gradishar	Ohio State
LB	John Skorupan	Penn State
B	Brad VanPelt	Michigan State
B	Cullen Bryant	Colorado
B	Robert Popelka	SMU
B	Randy Logan	Michigan

Others receiving first-team honors

DL	Roger Goree	Baylor
DL	John Grant	Southern California
DL	Bud Magrum	Colorado
DL	John LeHeup	South Carolina
DL	Derland Moore	Oklahoma
LB	Steve Brown	Oregon State
LB	Tom Jackson	Louisville
LB	Warren Capone	LSU
LB	Jamie Rotella	Tennessee
LB	John Mitchell	Alabama
LB	Richard Wood	Southern California
LB	Jim Youngblood	Tennessee Tech
DB	Ray Guy	Southern Miss
DB	Randy Rhino	Georgia Tech
DB	Calvin Jones	Washington
DB	Drane Scrivener	Tulsa
DB	Conrad Graham	Tennessee

Heisman Trophy Voting

	PLAYER	POS	SCHOOL	TOTAL
1	Johnny Rodgers	WR	Nebraska	1310
2	Greg Pruitt	HB	Oklahoma	966
3	Rich Glover	MG	Nebraska	652
4	Bert Jones	QB	LSU	351
5	Terry Davis	QB	Alabama	338
6	John Hufnagel	QB	Penn State	292
7	George Amundsen	QB	Iowa State	219
8	Otis Armstrong	HB	Purdue	208
9	Don Strock	QB	Virginia Tech	144
10	Gary Huff	QB	Florida State	138

Award Winners

PLAYER	AWARD
Brad VanPelt, DB, Michigan State	Maxwell
Rich Glover, MG, Nebraska	Outland
Johnny Rodgers, WR, Nebraska	Camp
Rich Glover, MG, Nebraska	Lombardi

Bowl Games

DATE	GAME	SCORE
D18	Liberty	Georgia Tech 31, Iowa State 30
D23	Fiesta	Arizona State 49, Missouri 35
D29	Peach	North Carolina St. 49, West Virginia 13
D29	Tangerine	Tampa 21, Kent 18
D30	Gator	Auburn 24, Colorado 3
D30	Sun	North Carolina 32, Texas Tech 28
D30	Bluebonnet	Tennessee 24, LSU 17
D31	Sugar	Oklahoma 14, Penn State 0
J1	Orange	Nebraska 40, Notre Dame 6
J1	Rose	Southern California 42, Ohio State 17
J1	Cotton	Texas 17, Alabama 13

SEC Standings

	CONFERENCE			OVERALL		
	W	L	T	W	L	T
Alabama	7	1	0	10	2	0
Auburn	6	1	0	10	1	0
LSU	4	1	1	9	2	1
Tennessee	4	2	0	10	2	0
Georgia	4	3	0	7	4	0
Florida	3	3	1	5	5	1
Mississippi	2	5	0	5	5	0
Kentucky	2	5	0	3	8	0
Mississippi State	1	6	0	4	7	0
Vanderbilt	0	6	0	3	8	0

ANNUAL REVIEW

1973 NCAA Major College Statistical Leaders

Individual Leaders

PASSING	G	ATT	COM	PCT	INT	I%	YDS	YPA	TD	TD%	COM.PG
1 Jesse Freitas, San Diego State	11	347	227	65.4	17	4.9	2993	8.6	21	6.1	20.6
2 Gary Sheide, Brigham Young	10	294	177	60.2	12	4.1	2350	8.0	22	7.5	17.7
3 David Harper, Davidson	10	329	175	53.2	19	5.8	1885	5.7	11	3.3	17.5
4 Dave Jaynes, Kansas	11	330	172	52.1	9	2.7	2131	6.5	13	3.9	15.6
4 Bill Hatty, Villanova	11	341	172	50.4	19	5.6	1947	5.7	10	2.9	15.6
6 Gene Swick, Toledo	11	301	165	54.8	17	5.7	2234	7.4	15	5.0	15.0
6 Craig Kimball, San Jose State	11	305	165	54.1	14	4.6	1940	6.4	14	4.6	15.0
8 Danny White, Arizona State	11	265	146	55.1	12	4.5	2609	9.8	23	8.7	13.3
8 Jan Stuebbe, Colorado State	11	310	146	47.1	15	4.8	1938	6.3	11	3.6	13.3
10 Mark Allen, Cornell	9	272	119	43.8	11	4.0	1590	5.8	10	3.7	13.2

ALL-PURPOSE	G	RUSH	REC	PR	KR	YDS	YPG
1 Willard Harrell, Pacific	10	1319	18	88	352	1777	177.7
2 Walt Peacock, Louisville	11	1291	139	0	467	1897	172.5
3 Adolph Bellizeare, Pennsylvania	8	746	192	173	222	1333	166.6
4 Archie Griffin, Ohio State	10	1428	32	0	182	1642	164.2
5 Woody Green, Arizona State	10	1182	328	25	54	1589	158.9
6 Mark Van Eeghen, Colgate	10	1089	177	0	322	1588	158.8
7 Joe Washington, Oklahoma	11	1173	89	260	222	1744	158.5
8 Mike Esposito, Boston College	11	1293	126	0	318	1737	157.9
9 Mark Kellar, Northern Illinois	11	1719	17	0	0	1736	157.8
10 Tony Dorsett, Pittsburgh	11	1586	84	0	22	1692	153.8

RUSHING/Yards Per Game	G	ATT	YDS	TD	AVG	YPG
1 Mark Kellar, Northern Illinois	11	291	1719	16	5.9	156.3
2 Tony Dorsett, Pittsburgh	11	288	1586	12	5.5	144.2
3 Archie Griffin, Ohio State	10	225	1428	6	6.3	142.8
4 Roosevelt Leaks, Texas	10	229	1415	14	6.2	141.5
5 John Cappelletti, Penn State	11	286	1522	17	5.3	138.4
6 Willard Harrell, Pacific	10	209	1319	14	6.3	131.9
7 Jim Jennings, Rutgers	11	303	1353	21	4.5	123.0
8 Woody Green, Arizona State	10	184	1182	9	6.4	118.2
9 Dickey Morton, Arkansas	11	226	1298	5	5.7	118.0
10 Mike Esposito, Boston College	11	254	1293	15	5.1	117.5

RUSHING/Yards Per Carry	G	ATT	YDS	YPC
1 Kermit Johnson, UCLA	11	150	1129	7.5
2 Joe Washington, Oklahoma	11	176	1173	6.7
3 Woody Green, Arizona State	10	184	1182	6.4
4 Ben Malone, Arizona State	11	176	1129	6.4
5 Archie Griffin, Ohio State	10	225	1428	6.3
6 Willard Harrell, Pacific	10	209	1319	6.3
7 Roosevelt Leaks, Texas	10	229	1415	6.2
8 Tom Sloan, Temple	10	173	1036	6.0
9 Phil Rogers, Virginia Tech	10	175	1036	5.9
10 Mark Kellar, Northern Illinois	11	291	1719	5.9

Based on top 25 rushers

RECEIVING	G	REC	YDS	TD	YPR	YPG	RPG
1 Jay Miller, Brigham Young	11	100	1181	8	11.8	107.4	9.1
2 Pat McInally, Harvard	9	56	752	7	13.4	93.6	6.2
3 Hank Cook, New Mexico State	11	65	1111	8	17.1	101.0	5.9
4 Don Clune, Pennsylvania	9	53	882	7	16.6	98.0	5.9
5 Darold Nogle, San Diego State	11	59	945	6	16.0	85.9	5.4
6 Walt Walker, Davidson	10	52	606	2	11.7	60.6	5.2
7 Greg Hudson, Arizona State	11	54	788	7	14.6	71.6	4.9
8 Charles Dancer, Baylor	11	53	927	7	17.5	84.3	4.8
8 Willie Miller, Colorado State	11	53	793	6	15.0	72.1	4.8
10 Mike Telep, Columbia	9	43	572	1	13.3	63.6	4.8

PUNTING	PUNT	YDS	AVG
1 Chuck Ramsey, Wake Forest	87	3898	44.8
2 Mike Patrick, Mississippi State	**60**	**2670**	**44.5**
3 Steve Bauer, New Mexico	61	2696	44.2
4 Neil Clabo, Tennessee	**56**	**2442**	**43.6**
5 Skip Boyd, Washington	68	2917	42.9
6 Brian Doherty, Notre Dame	39	1665	42.7
7 Bob McKenzie, Oregon State	51	2173	42.6
8 Joe Marion, Wyoming	70	2982	42.6
9 Rod Blackford, Colorado State	68	2890	42.5
10 Jeff West, Cincinnati	55	2337	42.5

PUNT RETURNS	PR	YDS	TD	AVG
1 Gary Hayman, Penn State	23	442	1	19.2
2 Mike Fuller, Auburn	**20**	**381**	**0**	**19.1**
3 Rick Kimbrough, Mississippi	**20**	**368**	**0**	**18.4**
4 Tom Fleming, Dartmouth	14	258	1	18.4
5 Neal Colzie, Ohio State	38	639	2	16.8
6 John Moseley, Missouri	19	314	2	16.5
7 Danny Colbert, Tulsa	19	292	1	15.4
8 John Betham, Brigham Young	39	553	1	14.2
9 Craig Zaltosky, Stanford	21	299	1	14.2
10 Frank Polito, Villanova	20	280	2	14.0

KICKOFF RETURNS	KR	YDS	TD	AVG
1 Steve Odom, Utah	21	618	1	29.4
2 James Sykes, Rice	21	601	1	28.6
3 W.C. Paige, Texas-El Paso	17	451	0	26.5
4 Raymond Rhodes, Tulsa	19	501	0	26.4
5 Mike Fuller, Auburn	**16**	**420**	**1**	**26.3**
6 Larry Williams, Texas Tech	19	491	1	25.8
7 Douglas Jackson, Columbia	18	463	0	25.7
8 George Heath, Virginia Tech	16	411	0	25.7
9 John Moseley, Missouri	17	434	0	25.5
10 Burrell Duvauchelle, Harvard	15	381	0	25.4

SCORING	TDS	XPT	FG	PTS	PTPG
1 Jim Jennings, Rutgers	21	2	0	128	11.6
2 Larry Poole, Kent State	18	0	0	108	9.8
2 Steve Davis, Oklahoma	18	0	0	108	9.8
4 John Cappelletti, Penn State	17	0	0	102	9.3
4 Mike Esposito, Boston College	17	0	0	102	9.3
6 Willard Harrell, Pacific	15	2	0	92	9.2
7 Mark Van Eeghen, Colgate	15	0	0	90	9.0
8 Mark Kellar, Northern Illinois	16	2	0	98	8.9
9 Kermit Johnson, UCLA	16	0	0	96	8.7
10 Roosevelt Leaks, Texas	14	0	0	84	8.4
10 Woody Green, Arizona State	14	0	0	84	8.4
10 Barty Smith, Richmond	14	0	0	84	8.4

KICK SCORING	XPA	XP	FGA	FG	PTS	PTPG
1 Efren Herrera, UCLA	64	60	11	8	84	7.6
2 Danny Kush, Arizona State	58	49	7	6	67	7.4
3 Chris Bahr, Penn State	42	37	19	11	70	7.0
3 Bob Thomas, Notre Dame	45	43	18	9	70	7.0
5 Rod Garcia, Stanford	25	22	29	18	76	6.9
6 Bill Davis, Alabama	**53**	**51**	**14**	**8**	**75**	**6.8**
7 Tom Goedjen, Iowa State	25	25	24	15	70	6.4
8 Steve Mike-Mayer, Maryland	38	33	24	12	69	6.3
9 Dave Draudt, Miami (Ohio)	21	20	27	14	62	6.2
10 Rick Fulcher, Oklahoma	53	49	11	6	67	6.1

INTERCEPTIONS	INT	YDS	TD	INT/GM
1 Mike Gow, Illinois	10	142	1	0.91
2 Tony Pawlik, Rutgers	8	137	0	0.80
3 John Provost, Holy Cross	8	138	0	0.73
3 Artimus Parker, Southern California	8	100	0	0.73
3 Barry Hill, Iowa State	8	99	0	0.73
3 Scott Wingfield, Vanderbilt	**8**	**63**	**0**	**0.73**
7 Jim Bolding, East Carolina	7	84	0	0.70
7 Joe Spicer, Miami (Ohio)	7	64	0	0.70
9 Bob Fuhriman, Utah State	7	115	1	0.64
9 Bill Howe, Xavier	7	104	0	0.64
9 Danny Reece, Southern California	7	86	1	0.64
9 Dennis Downey, Oregon State	7	83	1	0.64

Team Leaders

RUSHING OFFENSE	G	ATT	YDS	AVG	TD	YPG
1 UCLA	11	690	4403	6.4	56	400.3
2 Alabama	**11**	**664**	**4027**	**6.1**	**38**	**366.1**
3 Oklahoma	11	755	3975	5.3	36	361.4
4 Ohio State	10	669	3588	5.4	41	358.8
5 Texas	10	638	3502	5.5	43	350.2
5 Notre Dame	10	673	3502	5.2	35	350.2
7 Houston	11	720	3798	5.3	29	345.3
8 Northern Illinois	11	664	3465	5.2	39	315.0
9 Arizona State	11	586	3412	5.8	41	310.2
10 SMU	11	659	3395	5.2	23	308.6

PASSING OFFENSE	G	ATT	COM	INT	PCT	YDS	YPA	TD	I%	YPC	YPG
1 San Diego State	11	385	247	24	64.2	3355	8.7	24	6.2	13.6	305.0
2 Brigham Young	11	410	235	19	57.3	2930	7.1	24	4.6	12.5	266.4
3 Arizona State	11	298	158	13	53.0	2808	9.4	25	4.4	17.8	255.3
4 Pennsylvania	9	246	133	11	54.1	2182	8.9	17	4.5	16.4	242.4
5 Tulsa	11	356	204	22	57.3	2601	7.3	21	6.2	12.8	236.5
6 Toledo	11	303	163	17	53.8	2234	7.4	15	5.6	13.7	203.1
7 Colorado State	11	371	169	19	45.6	2200	5.9	11	5.1	13.0	200.0
8 Washington	11	320	128	31	40.0	2154	6.7	18	9.7	16.8	195.8
9 Davidson	10	343	180	21	52.5	1952	5.7	11	6.1	10.8	195.2
10 Kansas	11	337	174	11	51.6	2139	6.3	13	3.3	12.3	194.5

TOTAL OFFENSE	G	P	YDS	AVG	TD	YPG
1 Arizona State	11	884	6220	7.0	66	565.5
2 Alabama	**11**	**758**	**5288**	**7.0**	**55**	**480.7**
3 UCLA	11	783	5177	6.6	62	470.6
4 Houston	11	901	5093	5.7	42	463.0
5 Notre Dame	10	815	4614	5.7	46	461.4
6 Temple	10	786	4555	5.8	46	455.5
7 Oklahoma	11	857	4986	5.8	51	453.3
8 Brigham Young	11	932	4811	5.2	42	437.4
9 San Diego State	11	819	4777	5.8	42	434.3
10 Texas	10	741	4218	5.7	47	421.8

RUSHING DEFENSE	G	ATT	YDS	AVG	TD	YPG
1 Miami (Ohio)	10	424	770	1.8	2	77.0
2 Penn State	11	427	848	2.0	6	77.1
3 Notre Dame	10	390	824	2.1	3	82.4
4 Michigan	11	444	1075	2.4	2	97.7
5 Houston	11	431	1090	2.5	10	99.1
6 Cincinnati	11	491	1147	2.3	6	104.3
7 Oklahoma	11	475	1166	2.5	8	106.0
8 Maryland	11	467	1233	2.6	4	112.1
9 Pacific	10	407	1142	2.8	7	114.2
10 Long Beach State	11	499	1282	2.6	8	116.5

PASSING DEFENSE	G	ATT	COM	PCT	YPC	INT	I%	YDS	YPA	TD	YPG
1 Nebraska	11	142	40	28.2	11.0	15	10.6	439	3.1	1	39.9
2 Michigan State	11	139	54	38.8	11.4	14	10.1	613	4.4	4	55.7
3 Iowa	11	107	48	44.9	14.9	11	10.3	716	6.7	7	65.1
4 Ohio State	10	170	73	42.9	10.5	11	6.5	765	4.5	2	76.5
5 Texas A&M	11	146	59	40.4	14.3	7	4.8	844	5.8	11	76.7
6 Indiana	11	142	67	47.2	13.5	9	6.3	905	6.4	2	82.3
7 Illinois	11	187	71	38.0	12.8	23	12.3	912	4.9	2	82.9
8 Furman	11	184	83	45.1	11.3	17	9.2	935	5.1	4	85.0
9 Florida	**11**	**165**	**72**	**43.6**	**13.0**	**10**	**6.1**	**938**	**5.7**	**7**	**85.3**
10 Kansas	11	165	73	44.2	13.6	25	15.2	994	6.0	3	90.4

TOTAL DEFENSE	G	P	YDS	AVG	TD	YPG
1 Miami (Ohio)	10	645	1774	2.8	6	177.4
2 Notre Dame	10	615	2012	3.3	7	201.2
3 Penn State	11	689	2253	3.3	13	204.8
4 Ohio State	10	613	2056	3.4	5	205.6
5 Michigan	11	661	2396	3.6	7	217.8
6 Oklahoma	11	712	2492	3.5	15	226.5
7 Dartmouth	9	621	2172	3.5	13	241.3
8 Florida	**11**	**743**	**2656**	**3.6**	**18**	**241.5**
9 Cincinnati	11	760	2665	3.5	12	242.3
10 Houston	11	714	2690	3.8	15	244.5

SCORING OFFENSE	G	PTS	AVG
1 Arizona State	11	491	44.6
2 UCLA	11	470	42.7
3 Alabama	**11**	**454**	**41.3**
4 Penn State	11	431	39.2
5 Ohio State	10	371	37.1
6 Texas	10	364	36.4
7 Oklahoma	11	400	36.4
8 Notre Dame	10	358	35.8
9 Temple	10	353	35.3
10 North Carolina St.	11	365	33.2

SCORING DEFENSE	G	PTS	AVG
1 Ohio State	10	43	4.3
2 Michigan	11	68	6.2
3 Notre Dame	10	66	6.6
4 Miami (Ohio)	10	69	6.9
5 Alabama	**11**	**89**	**8.1**
6 Cincinnati	11	109	9.9
7 Pacific	10	109	10.9
8 Penn State	11	120	10.9
9 Richmond	10	112	11.2
10 Maryland	11	124	11.3

1973

FINAL POLL (JAN. 3)

AP	SCHOOL	FINAL RECORD
1	Notre Dame	11-0-0
2	Ohio State	10-0-1
3	Oklahoma	10-0-1
4	**Alabama**	**11-1-0**
5	Penn State	12-0-0
6	Michigan	10-0-1
7	Nebraska	9-2-1
8	Southern California	9-2-1
9	Arizona State	11-1-0
9	Houston	11-1-0
10	Texas Tech	11-1-0
12	UCLA	9-2-0
13	**LSU**	**9-3-0**
14	Texas	8-3-0
15	Miami (Ohio)	11-0-0
16	North Carolina St.	9-3-0
17	Missouri	8-4-0
18	Kansas	7-4-1
19	**Tennessee**	**8-4-0**
20	Maryland	8-4-0
20	Tulane	9-3-0

CONSENSUS ALL-AMERICANS

POS	OFFENSE	SCHOOL
QB	Dave Jaynes	Kansas
RB	John Cappelletti	Penn State
RB	Roosevelt Leaks	Texas
RB	Woody Green	Arizona State
RB	Kermit Johnson	UCLA
WR	Lynn Swann	Southern California
TE	Dave Casper	Notre Dame
T	John Hicks	Ohio State
G/T	Booker Brown	Southern California
G	**Buddy Brown**	**Alabama**
G	Bill Yoest	North Carolina St.
C	Bill Wyman	Texas

OTHERS RECEIVING FIRST-TEAM HONORS

QB	Danny White	Arizona State
RB	Tony Dorsett	Pittsburgh
RB	Archie Griffin	Ohio State
WR	**Wayne Wheeler**	**Alabama**
WR	Danny Buggs	West Virginia
TE	Andre Tillman	Texas Tech
T	Eddie Foster	Oklahoma
T	Daryl White	Nebraska
T	Al Oliver	UCLA
G	**Tyler Lafauci**	**LSU**
K	**Ricky Townsend**	**Tennessee**
KR	Steve Odom	Utah

POS	DEFENSE	SCHOOL
L	John Dutton	Nebraska
L	Dave Gallagher	Michigan
L	Lucious Selmon	Oklahoma
L	Tony Cristiani	Miami (Fla.)
LB	Randy Gradishar	Ohio State
LB	Rod Shoate	Oklahoma
LB	Richard Wood	Southern California
B	Mike Townsend	Notre Dame
B	Artimus Parker	Southern California
B	Dave Brown	Michigan
B	Randy Rhino	Georgia Tech

OTHERS RECEIVING FIRST-TEAM HONORS

L	Charlie Hall	Tulane
L	Paul Vellano	Maryland
L	Pat Donovan	Stanford
L	Randy White	Maryland
L	Bill Kollar	Montana State
L	Ed Jones	Tennessee State
L	Randy Crowder	Penn State
L	Van DeCree	Ohio State
L	Roger Stillwell	Stanford
LB	Ed O'Neill	Penn State
LB	**Warren Capone**	**LSU**
LB	**Woodrow Lowe**	**Alabama**
LB	Cleveland Vann	Oklahoma State
B	John Moseley	Missouri
B	Matt Blair	Iowa State
B	Jimmy Allen	UCLA
B	**Harry Harrison**	**Mississippi**
P	Chuck Ramsey	Wake Forest

HEISMAN TROPHY VOTING

	PLAYER	POS	SCHOOL	TOTAL
1	John Cappelletti	HB	Penn State	1057
2	John Hicks	OT	Ohio State	524
3	Roosevelt Leaks	RB	Texas	482
4	David Jaynes	QB	Kansas	394
5	Archie Griffin	TB	Ohio State	326
6	Randy Gradishar	LB	Ohio State	282
7	Lucious Selmon	NG	Uklahoma	250
8	Woody Green	HB	Arizona State	247
9	Danny White	QB	Arizona State	166
10	Kermit Johnson	RB	UCLA	122

AWARD WINNERS

PLAYER	AWARD
John Cappelletti, RB, Penn State	Maxwell
John Hicks, OT, Ohio State	Outland
John Cappelletti, RB, Penn State	Camp
John Hicks, OT, Ohio State	Lombardi

BOWL GAMES

DATE	BOWL	SCORE
D17	Liberty	North Carolina St. 31, Kansas 18
D21	Fiesta	Arizona State 28, Pittsburgh 7
D22	**Tangerine**	**Miami (Ohio) 16, Florida 7**
D28	**Peach**	**Georgia 17, Maryland 16**
D29	Bluebonnet	Houston 47, Tulane 7
D29	**Sun**	**Missouri 34, Auburn 17**
D29	**Gator**	**Texas Tech 28, Tennessee 19**
D31	**Sugar**	**Notre Dame 24, Alabama 23**
J1	Cotton	Nebraska 19, Texas 3
J1	Rose	Ohio State 42, Southern California 21
J1	**Orange**	**Penn State 16, LSU 9**

SEC STANDINGS

	CONFERENCE			OVERALL		
	W	L	T	W	L	T
Alabama	8	0	0	11	1	0
LSU	5	1	0	9	3	0
Mississippi	4	3	0	6	5	0
Tennessee	3	3	0	8	4	0
Georgia	3	4	0	7	4	1
Florida	3	4	0	7	5	0
Kentucky	3	4	0	5	6	0
Auburn	2	5	0	6	6	0
Mississippi State	2	5	0	4	5	2
Vanderbilt	1	5	0	5	6	0

1974 NCAA Major College Statistical Leaders

Individual Leaders

PASSING	G	ATT	COM	PCT	INT	I%	YDS	YPA	TD	TD%	COM.PG
1 Steve Bartkowski, California	11	325	182	56.0	7	2.2	2580	7.9	12	3.7	16.5
2 Gary Sheide, Brigham Young	11	300	181	60.3	19	6.3	2174	7.2	23	7.7	16.5
3 Gene Swick, Toledo	11	287	178	62.0	14	4.9	2235	7.8	13	4.5	16.2
4 Kevin Sigler, Cornell	9	248	143	57.7	14	5.6	1648	6.6	8	3.2	15.9
5 Craig Kimball, San Jose State	12	356	175	49.2	19	5.3	2401	6.7	23	6.5	14.6
6 Mark Driscoll, Colorado State	9	246	122	49.6	14	5.7	2016	8.2	19	7.7	13.6
7 Craig Penrose, San Diego State	10	235	132	56.2	9	3.8	1683	7.2	10	4.3	13.2
8 Jeb Blount, Tulsa	11	261	143	54.8	13	5.0	1860	7.1	15	5.7	13.0
9 Tom Vosberg, Dayton	11	305	141	46.2	18	5.9	1914	6.3	12	3.9	12.8
10 Steve Joachim, Temple	10	221	128	57.9	13	5.9	1950	8.8	20	9.0	12.8
10 Mike Cordova, Stanford	10	295	128	43.4	13	4.4	1569	5.3	10	3.4	12.8

ALL-PURPOSE	G	RUSH	REC	PR	KR	YDS	YPG
1 Louie Giammona, Utah State	10	1534	79	16	355	1984	198.4
2 Willard Harrell, Pacific	10	1308	133	65	262	1768	176.8
3 Anthony Davis, Southern California	11	1354	87	0	467	1908	173.5
4 Joe Washington, Oklahoma	11	1321	71	332	180	1904	173.1
5 Jim Pooler, Northwestern	11	949	25	21	807	1802	163.8
6 Archie Griffin, Ohio State	11	1620	52	0	71	1743	158.5
7 Rick Upchurch, Minnesota	11	942	209	125	440	1716	156.0
8 James Betterson, North Carolina	11	1082	53	0	512	1647	149.7
9 Stanley Morgan, Tennessee	**11**	**723**	**234**	**375**	**255**	**1587**	**144.3**
10 Bill Marek, Wisconsin	9	1215	76	0	0	1291	143.4

RUSHING/Yards Per Game	G	ATT	YDS	TD	AVG	YPG
1 Louie Giammona, Utah State	10	329	1534	8	4.7	153.4
2 Archie Griffin, Ohio State	11	236	1620	12	6.9	147.3
3 Bill Marek, Wisconsin	9	205	1215	18	5.9	135.0
4 Willard Harrell, Pacific	10	224	1308	12	5.8	130.8
5 Dave Preston, Bowling Green	11	324	1414	19	4.4	128.5
6 Andrew Johnson, Citadel	11	248	1373	7	5.5	124.8
7 Anthony Davis, Southern California	11	288	1354	13	4.7	123.1
8 Joe Washington, Oklahoma	11	194	1321	12	6.8	120.1
9 Fred Solomon, Tampa	11	193	1300	19	6.7	118.2
10 Walter Snickenberger, Princeton	9	214	1043	16	4.9	115.9

RUSHING/Yards Per Carry	G	ATT	YDS	YPC
1 Archie Griffin, Ohio State	11	236	1620	6.9
2 Joe Washington, Oklahoma	11	194	1321	6.8
3 Fred Solomon, Tampa	11	193	1300	6.7
4 Laverne Smith, Kansas	11	176	1181	6.7
5 Artie Owens, West Virginia	11	174	1130	6.5
6 Gordon Bell, Michigan	11	174	1048	6.0
7 Bill Marek, Wisconsin	9	205	1215	5.9
8 Willard Harrell, Pacific	10	224	1308	5.8
9 Andrew Johnson, Citadel	11	248	1373	5.5
10 Sonny Collins, Kentucky	9	177	970	5.5

Based on top 25 rushers

RECEIVING	G	REC	YDS	TD	YPR	YPG	RPG
1 Dwight McDonald, San Diego State	11	86	1157	7	13.5	105.2	7.8
2 John Ross, Toledo	11	77	866	2	11.2	78.7	7.0
3 Gary Pomeroy, Davidson	9	51	744	4	14.6	82.7	5.7
4 Dave Quehl, Holy Cross	11	62	801	6	12.9	72.8	5.6
5 Bruce Starks, Cornell	9	47	624	2	13.3	69.3	5.2
6 Pat McInally, Harvard	9	46	655	8	14.2	72.8	5.1
7 Steve Rivera, California	11	56	938	4	16.8	85.3	5.1
8 Willie Miller, Colorado State	11	53	1193	9	22.5	108.5	4.8
9 Theopolis Bell, Arizona	11	53	700	11	13.2	63.6	4.8
10 Steve Largent, Tulsa	11	52	844	14	16.2	76.7	4.7

PUNTING	PUNT	YDS	AVG
1 Joe Parker, Appalachian State	63	2791	44.3
2 Johnny Evans, North Carolina St.	38	1653	43.5
3 Neil Clabo, Tennessee	**64**	**2758**	**43.1**
4 Joe Marion, Wyoming	56	2380	42.5
5 Skip Boyd, Washington	57	2405	42.2
6 Phil Waganheim, Maryland	52	2194	42.2
7 Dan Vess, Wichita State	73	3073	42.1
8 Mark Stanley, Texas A&M	59	2478	42.0
9 Bernie Ruoff, Syracuse	57	2388	41.9
10 Mitch Hoopes, Arizona	55	2299	41.8

PUNT RETURNS	PR	YDS	TD	AVG
1 John Provost, Holy Cross	13	238	2	18.3
2 Adolph Bellizeare, Pennsylvania	14	255	2	18.2
3 Keith Wright, Memphis	13	218	1	16.8
4 Mike Fuller, Auburn	**30**	**502**	**3**	**16.7**
5 Devon Ford, Appalachian State	35	568	1	16.2
6 Martin Mitchell, Tulane	15	231	2	15.4
7 Joe Washington, Oklahoma	24	332	1	13.8
8 Wes Hankins, Oklahoma State	23	309	1	13.4
9 Tony Gillick, Missouri	12	160	1	13.3
10 Greg Johnson, Marshall	14	186	0	13.3

KICKOFF RETURNS	KR	YDS	TD	AVG
1 Anthony Davis, Southern California	11	467	3	42.5
2 Luther Blue, Iowa State	12	393	1	32.8
3 Mike Carter, Princeton	14	402	0	28.7
4 Len Willis, Ohio State	14	401	2	28.6
5 James Betterson, North Carolina	18	512	0	28.4
6 Dick Pawlewicz, William & Mary	15	426	1	28.4
7 Mike Harris, Tampa	15	420	1	28.0
8 Tom Marvaso, Cincinnati	15	416	1	27.7
9 Bobby Ward, Memphis	16	438	0	27.4
10 Robert Dow, LSU	**15**	**403**	**1**	**26.9**

SCORING	TDS	XPT	FG	PTS	PTPG
1 Bill Marek, Wisconsin	19	0	0	114	12.7
2 Keith Barnette, Boston College	22	2	0	134	12.2
3 Fred Solomon, Tampa	19	6	0	120	10.9
4 Walter Snickenberger, Princeton	16	0	0	96	10.7
5 Dave Preston, Bowling Green	19	0	0	114	10.4
6 Anthony Davis, Southern California	18	2	0	110	10.0
7 Steve Beaird, Baylor	16	0	0	96	8.7
8 Jim Germany, New Mexico State	14	2	0	86	8.6
9 Donald Fanelli, Cornell	10	0	0	60	8.6
10 Larry Poole, Kent State	15	0	0	90	8.2

KICK SCORING	XPA	XP	FGA	FG	PTS	PTPG
1 Steve Mike-Mayer, Maryland	36	34	25	15	79	7.2
2 Don Bitterlich, Temple	44	44	15	9	71	7.1
3 Tom Klaban, Ohio State	51	50	10	8	74	6.7
4 Fred Steinfort, Boston College	46	44	15	9	71	6.5
5 Dave Lawson, Air Force	15	13	31	19	70	6.4
6 Clark Kemble, Colorado State	33	30	28	13	69	6.3
7 Bob Berg, New Mexico	17	14	24	18	68	6.2
8 Mark Adams, Vanderbilt	**35**	**34**	**13**	**11**	**67**	**6.1**
8 Al Knapp, Utah State	19	19	25	16	67	6.1
10 Ron Ploger, San Jose State	38	35	21	12	71	5.9

INTERCEPTIONS	INT	YDS	TD	INT/GM
1 Mike Haynes, Arizona State	11	115	1	0.92
2 John Provost, Holy Cross	10	157	1	0.91
3 Barry Hill, Iowa State	9	90	0	0.82
4 A.J. Jacobs, Louisville	8	211	2	0.73
5 Dennis Anderson, Arizona	7	72	0	0.70
6 Tim Paul, Hawaii	6	60	0	0.67
7 Charles Phillips, Southern California	7	302	3	0.64
7 Ed Jones, Rutgers	7	94	0	0.64
7 Ken Shibata, Hawaii	7	49	0	0.64

Team Leaders

RUSHING OFFENSE	G	ATT	YDS	AVG	TD	YPG
1 Oklahoma	11	813	4827	5.9	47	438.8
2 Ohio State	11	685	4006	5.8	46	364.2
3 Texas	11	674	3487	5.2	40	317.0
4 Houston	11	720	3448	4.8	27	313.5
5 Michigan	11	686	3372	4.9	31	306.5
6 Alabama	**11**	**686**	**3288**	**4.8**	**32**	**298.9**
7 Tampa	11	553	3182	5.8	30	289.3
8 Wisconsin	11	612	3162	5.2	38	287.5
8 Georgia Tech	11	650	3162	4.9	27	287.5
10 Kentucky	**11**	**632**	**3124**	**4.9**	**24**	**284.0**

PASSING OFFENSE	G	ATT	COM	INT	PCT	YDS	YPA	TD	I%	YPC	YPG
1 Colorado State	11	367	171	24	46.6	2880	7.8	23	6.5	16.8	261.8
2 California	11	331	184	8	55.6	2599	7.9	14	2.4	14.1	236.3
3 San Diego State	11	358	174	18	48.6	2496	7.0	15	5.0	14.3	226.9
4 Tulsa	11	342	182	20	53.2	2417	7.1	20	5.8	13.3	219.7
5 San Jose State	12	394	188	22	47.7	2574	6.5	25	5.6	13.7	214.5
6 Toledo	11	309	187	14	60.5	2335	7.6	13	4.5	12.5	212.3
7 Brigham Young	11	321	192	22	59.8	2314	7.2	25	6.9	12.1	210.4
8 Temple	10	233	134	16	57.5	2027	8.7	20	6.9	15.1	202.7
9 Stanford	11	383	180	17	47.0	2195	5.7	15	4.4	12.2	199.5
10 Cornell	9	255	146	14	57.3	1735	6.8	9	5.5	11.9	192.8

TOTAL OFFENSE	G	P	YDS	AVG	TD	YPG
1 Oklahoma	11	896	5585	6.2	60	507.7
2 Ohio State	11	783	4966	6.3	55	451.5
3 Temple	10	738	4473	6.1	44	447.3
4 Notre Dame	11	919	4779	5.2	39	434.5
5 North Carolina	11	810	4691	5.8	47	426.5
6 Vanderbilt	**11**	**825**	**4570**	**5.5**	**37**	**415.5**
7 Nebraska	11	815	4532	5.6	48	412.0
8 San Diego State	11	847	4521	5.3	37	411.0
9 Maryland	11	824	4484	5.4	37	407.6
10 Colorado State	11	803	4476	5.6	36	406.9

RUSHING DEFENSE	G	ATT	YDS	AVG	TD	YPG
1 Notre Dame	11	488	1131	2.3	7	102.8
2 Michigan	11	438	1163	2.7	3	105.7
3 Brown	9	369	972	2.6	10	108.0
4 Brigham Young	11	473	1226	2.6	5	111.5
5 Miami (Ohio)	10	454	1153	2.5	6	115.3
6 San Jose State	12	527	1394	2.6	15	116.2
7 Penn State	11	499	1322	2.6	8	120.2
8 Arizona State	12	588	1522	2.6	11	126.8
9 Yale	9	395	1149	2.9	3	127.7
10 Rutgers	11	530	1434	2.7	11	130.4

PASSING DEFENSE	G	ATT	COM	PCT	YPC	INT	I%	YDS	YPA	TD	YPG
1 Iowa	11	130	50	38.5	14.5	6	4.6	723	5.6	7	65.7
2 Texas A&M	11	166	64	38.6	11.7	16	9.6	751	4.5	4	68.3
3 Furman	11	143	62	43.4	12.4	11	7.7	769	5.4	3	69.9
4 Texas Tech	11	174	63	36.2	12.6	16	9.2	796	4.6	6	72.4
5 Alabama	**11**	**201**	**82**	**40.8**	**10.0**	**15**	**7.5**	**822**	**4.1**	**1**	**74.7**
6 South Carolina	11	118	57	48.3	14.5	8	6.8	827	7.0	1	75.2
7 Tulane	11	142	62	43.7	14.5	13	9.2	902	6.4	4	82.0
8 Rice	11	154	67	43.5	13.7	11	7.1	919	6.0	3	83.5
9 Appalachian State	11	158	67	42.4	13.8	10	6.3	927	5.9	5	84.3
10 Georgia Tech	11	147	69	46.9	13.7	10	6.8	944	6.4	6	85.8

TOTAL DEFENSE	G	P	YDS	AVG	TD	YPG
1 Notre Dame	11	693	2147	3.1	14	195.2
2 Texas A&M	11	688	2272	3.3	16	206.5
3 Michigan	11	659	2353	3.6	7	213.9
4 Miami (Ohio)	10	640	2190	3.4	9	219.0
5 Alabama	**11**	**679**	**2421**	**3.6**	**9**	**220.1**
6 Oklahoma	11	745	2547	3.4	9	231.5
7 Rutgers	11	781	2643	3.4	19	240.3
8 Brown	9	576	2268	3.9	17	252.0
9 Houston	11	714	2779	3.9	17	252.6
10 Oklahoma State	11	736	2780	3.8	20	252.7

SCORING OFFENSE	G	PTS	AVG
1 Oklahoma	11	473	43.0
2 Ohio State	11	420	38.2
3 Boston College	11	375	34.1
4 Temple	10	335	33.5
5 Texas	11	364	33.1
6 Nebraska	11	360	32.7
7 Southern California	11	345	31.4
8 Wisconsin	11	341	31.0
9 North Carolina	11	340	30.9
10 Michigan	11	324	29.5

SCORING DEFENSE	G	PTS	AVG
1 Michigan	11	75	6.8
2 Yale	9	67	7.4
3 Alabama	**11**	**83**	**7.5**
4 Miami (Ohio)	10	76	7.6
5 Oklahoma	11	92	8.4
6 Maryland	11	97	8.8
7 Ohio State	11	111	10.1
8 Penn State	11	122	11.1
8 Nebraska	11	122	11.1
10 Southern California	11	125	11.4

1974

FINAL POLL (JAN. 3)

UP	AP	SCHOOL	FINAL RECORD
PB	1	Oklahoma	11-0-0
1	2	Southern California	10-1-1
5	3	Michigan	10-1-0
3	4	Ohio State	10-2-0
2	5	**Alabama**	**11-1-0**
4	6	Notre Dame	10-2-0
7	7	Penn State	10-2-0
6	8	**Auburn**	**10-2-0**
8	9	Nebraska	9-3-0
10	10	Miami (Ohio)	10-0-1
9	11	North Carolina St.	9-2-1
18	12	Michigan State	7-3-1
13	13	Maryland	8-4-0
14	14	Baylor	8-4-0
12	15	**Florida**	**8-4-0**
15	16	Texas A&M	8-3-0
17	17	**Mississippi State**	**9-3-0**
0	17	Texas	8-4-0
11	19	Houston	8-3-1
15	20	**Tennessee**	**7-3-2**
19		Tulsa	8-3-0

PB: Team on probation

CONSENSUS ALL-AMERICANS

POS	OFFENSE	SCHOOL
QB	Steve Bartkowski	California
RB	Archie Griffin	Ohio State
RB	Joe Washington	Oklahoma
RB	Anthony Davis	Southern California
WR	Pete Demmerle	Notre Dame
TE	Bennie Cunningham	Clemson
T	Kurt Schumacher	Ohio State
T	Marvin Crenshaw	Nebraska
G	Ken Huff	North Carolina
G	John Roush	Oklahoma
G	Gerry DiNardo	Notre Dame
C	Steve Myers	Ohio State

OTHERS RECEIVING FIRST-TEAM HONORS

QB	Steve Joachim	Temple
QB	Tom Clements	Notre Dame
QB	David Humm	Nebraska
WR	Pat McInally	Harvard
WR	Larry Burton	Purdue
T	Bob Simmons	Texas
T	Chris Mackie	California
T	**Craig Hertwig**	**Georgia**
T	Al Krevis	Boston College
G	John Nessel	Penn State
C	Geoff Reece	Washington State
C	Aubrey Schulz	Baylor
C	**Sylvester Croom**	**Alabama**
C	Rik Bonness	Nebraska
K	Dave Lawson	Air Force

POS	DEFENSE	SCHOOL
L	Randy White	Maryland
L	Mike Hartenstine	Penn State
L	Pat Donovan	Stanford
L	**Jimmy Webb**	**Mississippi State**
L	**Leroy Cook**	**Alabama**
MG	Louie Kelcher	SMU
MG	Rubin Carter	Miami (Fla.)
LB	Rod Shoate	Oklahoma
LB	Richard Wood	Southern California
LB	**Ken Bernich**	**Auburn**
LB	**Woodrow Lowe**	**Alabama**
B	Dave Brown	Michigan
B	Pat Thomas	Texas A&M
B	John Provost	Holy Cross

OTHERS RECEIVING FIRST-TEAM HONORS

DL	Mack Mitchell	Houston
DL	Michael Fanning	Notre Dame
DL	Doug English	Texas
DL	Van DeCree	Ohio State
LB	Greg Collins	Notre Dame
LB	Brad Cousino	Miami (Ohio)
LB	Bob Breunig	Arizona State
MG	Gary Burley	Pittsburgh
B	Randy Rhino	Georgia Tech
B	Charles Phillips	Southern California
B	Robert Giblin	Houston
B	**Mike Williams**	**LSU**
B	Neal Colzie	Ohio State
B	Randy Hughes	Oklahoma
P	Tom Skladany	Ohio State
K	Dave Lawson	Air Force

HEISMAN TROPHY VOTING

	PLAYER	POS	SCHOOL	TOTAL
1	Archie Griffin	TB	Ohio State	1920
2	Anthony Davis	TB	Southern Cal	819
3	Joe Washington	HB	Oklahoma	661
4	Tom Clements	QB	Notre Dame	244
5	David Humm	QB	Nebraska	210
6	Dennis Franklin	DE	Michigan	100
7	Rod Shoate	LB	Oklahoma	97
8	Gary Scheide	QB	Brigham Young	90
9	Randy White	DT	Maryland	85
10	Steve Bartkowski	QB	California	74

AWARD WINNERS

PLAYER	AWARD
Steve Joachim, QB, Temple	Maxwell
Randy White, DT, Maryland	Outland
Archie Griffin, RB, Ohio State	Camp
Randy White, DT, Maryland	Lombardi

BOWL GAMES

DATE	BOWL	SCORE
D16	Liberty	**Tennessee 7, Maryland 3**
D21	Tangerine	**Miami (Ohio) 21, Georgia 10**
D23	Bluebonnet	Houston 31, North Carolina St. 31
D28	Sun	**Mississippi State 26, North Carolina 24**
D28	Fiesta	Oklahoma State 16, Brigham Young 6
D28	Peach	**Texas Tech 6, Vanderbilt 6**
D30	Gator	**Auburn 27, Texas 3**
D31	Sugar	**Nebraska 13, Florida 10**
J1	Orange	**Notre Dame 13, Alabama 11**
J1	Cotton	Penn State 41, Baylor 20
J1	Rose	Southern California 18, Ohio State 17

SEC STANDINGS

	CONFERENCE			OVERALL		
	W	L	T	W	L	T
Alabama	6	0	0	11	1	0
Auburn	4	2	0	10	2	0
Georgia	4	2	0	6	6	0
Mississippi State	3	3	0	9	3	0
Florida	3	3	0	8	4	0
Kentucky	3	3	0	6	5	0
Tennessee	2	3	1	7	3	2
Vanderbilt	2	3	1	7	3	2
LSU	2	4	0	5	5	1
Mississippi	0	6	0	3	8	0

1975 NCAA Major College Statistical Leaders

Individual Leaders

PASSING	G	ATT	COM	PCT	INT	I%	YDS	YPA	TD	TD%	COM.PG
1 Craig Penrose, San Diego State	11	349	198	56.7	24	6.9	2660	7.6	15	4.3	18.0
2 Gene Swick, Toledo	11	308	190	61.7	12	3.9	2487	8.1	15	4.9	17.3
2 Steve Myer, New Mexico	11	353	190	53.8	14	4.0	2501	7.1	21	5.9	17.3
4 Joe Bruner, La.-Monroe	11	312	160	51.3	15	4.8	2025	6.5	7	2.2	14.5
5 Jack Henderson, Oregon	11	321	151	47.0	16	5.0	1492	4.6	6	1.9	13.7
6 Ron Beible, Princeton	9	244	123	50.4	10	4.1	1503	6.2	7	2.9	13.7
7 Pat Degnan, Utah	11	289	140	48.4	21	7.3	1621	5.6	7	2.4	12.7
8 Joe Roth, California	10	225	126	56.0	7	3.1	1880	8.4	14	6.2	12.6
9 Bob Bateman, Brown	9	206	112	54.4	7	3.4	1428	6.9	8	3.9	12.4
10 Gifford Nielsen, Brigham Young	9	180	110	61.1	7	3.9	1474	8.2	10	5.6	12.2

ALL-PURPOSE	G	RUSH	REC	PR	KR	YDS	YPG
1 Louie Giammona, Utah State	11	1454	33	124	434	2045	185.9
2 Ricky Bell, Southern California	11	1875	24	0	0	1899	172.6
3 Chuck Muncie, California	11	1460	392	0	19	1871	170.1
4 Tony Dorsett, Pittsburgh	11	1544	191	0	105	1840	167.3
5 John Zeglinski, Wake Forest	11	591	354	243	542	1730	157.3
6 Dan Watkins, Kent State	10	916	59	47	508	1530	153.0
7 Walter Peacock, Louisville	11	1013	0	43	612	1668	151.6
8 Herb Lusk, Long Beach State	11	1596	62	0	0	1658	150.7
9 Gordon Bell, Michigan	11	1335	67	18	207	1627	147.9
10 Archie Griffin, Ohio State	11	1357	158	0	91	1606	146.0

RUSHING/Yards Per Game	G	ATT	YDS	TD	AVG	YPG
1 Ricky Bell, Southern California	11	357	1875	13	5.3	170.5
2 Herb Lusk, Long Beach State	11	310	1596	13	5.1	145.1
3 Tony Dorsett, Pittsburgh	11	228	1544	11	6.8	140.4
4 Chuck Muncie, California	11	228	1460	13	6.4	132.7
5 Louie Giammona, Utah State	11	303	1454	11	4.8	132.2
6 Mike Voight, North Carolina	10	259	1250	11	4.8	125.0
7 Archie Griffin, Ohio State	11	245	1357	4	5.5	123.4
8 Gordon Bell, Michigan	11	255	1335	12	5.2	121.4
9 Fred Williams, Arizona State	11	248	1316	9	5.3	119.6
10 Jimmy DuBose, Florida	**11**	**191**	**1307**	**6**	**6.8**	**118.8**

RUSHING/Yards Per Carry	G	ATT	YDS	YPC
1 Jimmy DuBose, Florida	**11**	**191**	**1307**	**6.8**
2 Tony Dorsett, Pittsburgh	11	228	1544	6.8
3 Wendell Tyler, UCLA	11	187	1216	6.5
4 Chuck Muncie, California	11	228	1460	6.4
5 Dennis Bolden, Arkansas State	11	186	1191	6.4
6 Kevin Long, South Carolina	11	179	1114	6.2
7 Dan Saleet, Bowling Green	10	194	1114	5.7
8 Earl Campbell, Texas	11	198	1118	5.6
9 Cleveland Franklin, Baylor	11	200	1112	5.6
10 Archie Griffin, Ohio State	11	245	1357	5.5

Based on top 27 rushers

RECEIVING	G	REC	YDS	TD	YPR	YPG	RPG
1 Bob Farnham, Brown	9	56	701	2	12.5	77.9	6.2
2 Dave Quehl, Holy Cross	11	63	959	5	15.2	87.2	5.7
3 Steve Rivera, California	10	57	790	4	13.9	79.0	5.7
4 Preston Dennard, New Mexico	11	59	962	6	16.3	87.5	5.4
5 Pat Tilley, Louisiana Tech	10	53	926	6	17.5	92.6	5.3
6 Duke Fergerson, San Diego State	11	57	886	4	15.5	80.5	5.2
7 Tony Hill, Stanford	11	55	916	7	16.7	93.3	5.0
8 John Filliez, Marshall	11	54	657	7	12.2	59.7	4.9
9 Neil Chamberlin, Princeton	9	44	519	0	11.8	57.7	4.9
10 Greg Bauer, Oregon	11	52	616	4	11.8	56.0	4.7

PUNTING	PUNT	YDS	AVG
1 Tom Skladany, Ohio State	36	1681	46.7
2 Rick Engles, Tulsa	36	1678	46.6
3 Cliff Parsley, Oklahoma State	58	2598	44.8
4 Gavin Hedrick, Washington State	50	2235	44.7
5 Johnny Evans, North Carolina St.	42	1873	44.6
6 Jim Walton, Boston College	49	2171	44.3
7 Dennis Anderson, Arizona	53	2300	43.4
8 Bob Grupp, Duke	40	1720	43.0
9 Tommy Cheyne, Arkansas	37	1591	43.0
10 Don Fechtman, North Texas	66	2825	42.8

PUNT RETURNS	PR	YDS	TD	AVG
1 Donnie Ross, New Mexico State	21	338	1	16.1
2 Danny Reece, Southern California	26	409	1	15.7
3 Vernie Kelley, Pacific	19	294	0	15.5
4 Stanley Morgan, Tennessee	**20**	**284**	**2**	**14.2**
5 Henry Jenkins, Rutgers	20	277	1	13.8
6 Gordon Jones, Pittsburgh	28	373	0	13.3
7 Randy Rich, New Mexico	25	325	1	13.0
8 Devon Ford, Appalachian State	21	260	0	12.4
9 Ronnie Barber, LSU	**14**	**173**	**0**	**12.4**
10 Troy Slade, Duke	23	283	0	12.3

KICKOFF RETURNS	KR	YDS	TD	AVG
1 John Schultz, Maryland	13	403	1	31.0
2 Keith Jenkins, Cincinnati	15	437	1	29.1
3 Theopolis Bell, Arizona	16	453	0	28.3
4 Rick Neel, Auburn	**17**	**474**	**1**	**27.9**
5 Tim Morgan, Miami (Fla.)	14	385	1	27.5
6 Mike Tsoutsouvas, Fresno State	13	354	0	27.2
7 Terry Eurick, Notre Dame	13	347	0	26.7
8 Robert Dow, LSU	**23**	**598**	**0**	**26.0**
9 Henry White, Colgate	13	335	0	25.8
10 Dave Schick, Iowa	24	610	1	25.4

SCORING	TDS	XPT	FG	PTS	PTPG
1 Pete Johnson, Ohio State	25	0	0	150	13.6
2 Dave Preston, Bowling Green	14	0	0	84	9.3
3 David Hines, Arkansas State	17	0	0	102	9.3
4 Herb Lusk, Long Beach State	16	0	0	96	8.7
5 Don Bitterlich, Temple	0	32	21	95	8.6
6 Ted Brown, North Carolina St.	13	6	0	84	8.4
7 Chuck Muncie, California	15	0	0	90	8.2
8 Walt Hodges, Central Michigan	12	0	0	72	8.0
9 Tony Dorsett, Pittsburgh	14	0	0	84	7.6
9 Steve Largent, Tulsa	14	0	0	84	7.6
9 John Sciarra, UCLA	14	0	0	84	7.6

FIELD GOALS	FGA	FGM	PCT	FGG
1 Don Bitterlich, Temple	31	21	0.68	1.91
2 Bob Berg, New Mexico	26	18	0.69	1.64
2 Chris Bahr, Penn State	33	18	0.55	1.64
4 Lou Rodriguez, San Jose State	32	16	0.50	1.45
5 David Jacobs, Syracuse	30	14	0.47	1.40
6 Lee Pistor, Arizona	19	15	0.79	1.36
6 Gary Davis, Appalachian State	20	15	0.75	1.36
6 Dan Shepherd, Cincinnati	22	15	0.68	1.36
9 Jose Violante, Brown	19	12	0.63	1.33
10 Chris Dennis, Miami (Fla.)	21	13	0.62	1.30

INTERCEPTIONS	INT	YDS	TD	INT/GM
1 Jim Bolding, East Carolina	10	51	0	1.00
2 Cedric Brown, Kent State	8	107	1	0.89
3 Craig Cassady, Ohio State	8	78	0	0.73
4 Vernie Kelley, Pacific	8	51	0	0.67
5 Ed Oaks, Vanderbilt	**7**	**117**	**0**	**0.64**
5 Gerald Small, San Jose State	7	104	2	0.64
5 Billy Hardee, Virginia Tech	7	83	0	0.64
5 Preston Lanier, McNeese St.	7	80	0	0.64
5 Mike Lecklider, Ball State	7	61	0	0.64
5 Roy Gordon, Dayton	7	48	0	0.64
5 Mike Martinez, Arizona State	7	32	0	0.64

Team Leaders

RUSHING OFFENSE	G	ATT	YDS	AVG	TD	YPG
1 Arkansas State	11	746	3745	5.0	42	340.5
2 Michigan	11	686	3679	5.4	34	334.5
3 Georgia Tech	11	692	3627	5.2	32	329.7
4 UCLA	11	699	3619	5.2	40	329.0
5 Central Michigan	11	740	3613	4.9	32	328.5
6 Arkansas	11	659	3523	5.3	33	320.3
7 Kansas	11	670	3488	5.2	27	317.1
8 Ohio State	11	678	3480	5.1	43	316.4
9 Appalachian State	11	693	3438	5.0	32	312.5
10 Texas	11	656	3413	5.2	43	310.3

PASSING OFFENSE	G	ATT	COM	INT	PCT	YDS	YPA	TD	I%	YPC	YPG
1 San Diego State	11	411	238	27	57.9	3204	7.8	17	6.6	13.5	291.3
2 New Mexico	11	354	191	14	54.0	2529	7.1	22	4.0	13.2	229.9
3 California	11	307	170	9	55.4	2522	8.2	17	2.9	14.8	229.3
4 Toledo	11	312	190	12	60.9	2487	8.0	15	3.8	13.1	226.1
5 Louisiana Tech	10	265	143	12	54.0	2226	8.4	17	4.5	15.6	222.6
6 Stanford	11	374	189	20	50.5	2432	6.5	21	5.3	12.9	221.1
7 Tulsa	11	309	164	17	53.1	2417	7.8	19	5.5	14.7	219.7
8 Fresno State	11	330	168	30	50.9	2149	6.5	10	9.1	12.8	195.4
9 Brown	9	250	134	15	53.6	1726	6.9	9	6.0	12.9	191.8
10 La.-Monroe	11	316	161	15	50.9	2030	6.4	7	4.7	12.6	184.5

TOTAL OFFENSE	G	P	YDS	AVG	TD	YPG
1 California	11	834	5044	6.0	43	458.5
2 Tulsa	11	800	4937	6.2	45	448.8
3 UCLA	11	828	4753	5.7	46	432.1
4 South Carolina	11	781	4746	6.1	41	431.5
5 Arizona	11	832	4666	5.6	40	424.2
6 Arizona State	11	861	4634	5.4	36	421.3
7 Appalachian State	11	861	4605	5.3	42	418.6
8 San Diego State	11	806	4520	5.6	35	410.9
9 Long Beach State	11	815	4509	5.5	35	409.9
10 Ohio State	11	785	4477	5.7	49	407.0

RUSHING DEFENSE	G	ATT	YDS	AVG	TD	YPG
1 Texas A&M	11	448	883	2.0	4	80.3
2 Miami (Ohio)	11	462	947	2.0	8	86.1
3 Central Michigan	11	435	993	2.3	4	90.3
4 Alabama	**11**	**460**	**1037**	**2.3**	**5**	**94.3**
5 Arkansas State	11	475	1115	2.3	7	101.4
6 San Jose State	11	470	1133	2.4	7	103.0
7 Boston College	11	450	1269	2.8	11	115.4
8 Rutgers	11	465	1293	2.8	5	117.5
9 Michigan	11	484	1323	2.7	7	120.3
10 Navy	11	486	1341	2.8	7	121.9

PASSING DEFENSE	G	ATT	COM	PCT	YPC	INT	I%	YDS	YPA	TD	YPG
1 VMI	11	113	40	35.4	14.1	12	10.6	562	5.0	6	51.1
2 Florida State	11	116	53	45.7	13.2	11	9.5	698	6.0	4	63.5
3 Wisconsin	11	129	51	39.5	14.1	22	17.1	717	5.6	8	65.2
4 North Carolina St.	11	144	64	44.4	12.1	6	4.2	775	5.4	5	70.5
5 Navy	11	187	74	39.6	11.8	15	8.0	871	4.7	4	79.2
6 Baylor	11	154	69	44.8	13.0	12	7.8	896	5.8	5	81.5
7 Memphis	11	193	85	44.0	10.6	13	6.7	903	4.7	5	82.1
8 Bowling Green	11	196	78	39.8	11.7	17	8.7	914	4.7	5	83.1
9 Rutgers	11	212	88	41.5	10.7	19	9.0	940	4.4	2	85.5

TOTAL DEFENSE	G	P	YDS	AVG	TD	YPG
1 Texas A&M	11	645	2022	3.1	10	183.8
2 Alabama	**11**	**677**	**2046**	**3.0**	**7**	**186.0**
3 Navy	11	673	2212	3.3	11	201.1
4 Rutgers	11	677	2233	3.3	7	203.0
5 Central Michigan	11	625	2268	3.6	12	206.2
6 Miami (Ohio)	11	679	2353	3.5	18	213.9
7 Arkansas State	11	711	2372	3.3	9	215.6
8 Nebraska	11	678	2465	3.6	15	224.1
9 Boston College	11	650	2563	3.9	15	233.0
10 Southern Miss	11	616	2572	4.2	16	233.8

SCORING OFFENSE	G	PTS	AVG
1 Ohio State	11	374	34.0
2 Tulsa	11	368	33.5
3 Texas	11	363	33.0
4 Alabama	**11**	**361**	**32.8**
5 Arkansas State	11	355	32.3
6 Nebraska	11	353	32.1
7 Rutgers	11	347	31.5
8 Appalachian State	11	337	30.6
9 Oklahoma	11	330	30.0
9 California	11	330	30.0
9 Arizona	11	330	30.0
9 Arizona State	11	330	30.0

SCORING DEFENSE	G	PTS	AVG
1 Alabama	**11**	**66**	**6.0**
2 Ohio State	11	79	7.2
3 Arkansas State	11	81	7.4
4 Rutgers	11	91	8.3
5 Citadel	11	97	8.8
6 Central Michigan	11	102	9.3
7 Florida	**11**	**104**	**9.5**
7 Texas A&M	11	104	9.5
9 Penn State	11	110	10.0

1975

FINAL POLL (JAN. 3)

UP	AP	SCHOOL	FINAL RECORD
1	1	Oklahoma	11-1-0
2	2	Arizona State	12-0-0
3	3	**Alabama**	**11-1-0**
4	4	Ohio State	11-1-0
5	5	UCLA	9-2-1
7	6	Texas	10-2-0
6	7	Arkansas	10-2-0
8	8	Michigan	8-2-2
9	9	Nebraska	10-2-0
10	10	Penn State	9-3-0
12	11	Texas A&M	10-2-0
16	12	Miami (Ohio)	11-1-0
11	13	Maryland	9-2-1
15	14	California	8-3-0
13	15	Pittsburgh	8-4-0
	16	Colorado	9-3-0
19	17	Southern California	8-4-0
13	18	Arizona	9-2-0
19	19	**Georgia**	**9-3-0**
17	20	West Virginia	9-3-0
17		Notre Dame	8-3-0

CONSENSUS ALL-AMERICANS

POS	OFFENSE	SCHOOL
QB	John Sciarra	UCLA
RB	Archie Griffin	Ohio State
RB	Ricky Bell	Southern California
RB	Chuck Muncie	California
E	Steve Rivera	California
E	**Larry Seivers**	**Tennessee**
T	Bob Simmons	Texas
T	Dennis Lick	Wisconsin
G	**Randy Johnson**	**Georgia**
G	Ted Smith	Ohio State
C	Rik Bonness	Nebraska

OTHERS RECEIVING FIRST-TEAM HONORS

QB	Marty Akins	Texas
QB	Gene Swick	Toledo
RB	Tony Dorsett	Pittsburgh
RB	Earl Campbell	Texas
E	Don Buckey	North Carolina St.
E	Henry Marshall	Missouri
E	Mike Barber	Louisiana Tech
E	Ken MacAfee	Notre Dame
OL	Randy Cross	UCLA
OL	Ken Jones	Arkansas State
OL	Tom Rafferty	Penn State
OL	Marvin Powell	Southern California
OL	Mark Koncar	Colorado
OL	Terry Webb	Oklahoma
K	Bob Berg	New Mexico
KR	Joe Washington	Oklahoma

POS	DEFENSE	SCHOOL
E	**Leroy Cook**	**Alabama**
E	Jimbo Elrod	Oklahoma
T	Lee Roy Selmon	Oklahoma
T	Steve Niehaus	Notre Dame
MG	Dewey Selmon	Oklahoma
LB	Ed Simonini	Texas A&M
LB	Greg Buttle	Penn State
LB	**Sammy Green**	**Florida**
B	Chet Moeller	Navy
B	Tim Fox	Ohio State
B	Pat Thomas	Texas A&M

OTHERS RECEIVING FIRST-TEAM HONORS

DL	Ken Novak	Purdue
LB	Ray Preston	Syracuse
LB	Reggie Williams	Dartmouth
LB	**Woodrow Lowe**	**Alabama**
B	Don Dufek	Michigan
B	Wonder Monds	Nebraska
B	Mike Haynes	Arizona State
P	Tom Skladany	Ohio State

HEISMAN TROPHY VOTING

	PLAYER	POS	SCHOOL	TOTAL
1	Archie Griffin	TB	Ohio State	1800
2	Chuck Muncie	RB	California	730
3	Ricky Bell	TB	Southern Cal	708
4	Tony Dorsett	RB	Pittsburgh	616
5	Joe Washington	HB	Oklahoma	250
6	**Jimmy DuBose**	**RB**	**Florida**	**112**
7	John Sciarra	QB	UCLA	86
8	Gordon Bell	TB	Michigan	84
9	Lee Roy Selmon	DT	Oklahoma	79
10	Gene Swick	QB	Toledo	73

AWARD WINNERS

PLAYER	AWARD
Archie Griffin, RB, Ohio State	Maxwell
Lee Roy Selmon, DT, Oklahoma	Outland
Archie Griffin, RB, Ohio State	Camp
Lee Roy Selmon, DT, Oklahoma	Lombardi

BOWL GAMES

DATE	BOWL	SCORE
D20	Tangerine	Miami (Ohio) 20, South Carolina 7
D22	Liberty	Southern California 20, Texas A&M 0
D26	Fiesta	Arizona State 17, Nebraska 14
D26	Sun	Pittsburgh 33, Kansas 19
D27	Bluebonnet	Texas 38, Colorado 21
D29	**Gator**	**Maryland 13, Florida 0**
D31	**Sugar**	**Alabama 13, Penn State 6**
D31	Peach	West Virginia 13, North Carolina St. 10
J1	**Cotton**	**Arkansas 31, Georgia 10**
J1	Orange	Oklahoma 14, Michigan 6
J1	Rose	UCLA 23, Ohio State 10

SEC STANDINGS

	CONFERENCE			OVERALL		
	W	L	T	W	L	T
Alabama	6	0	0	11	1	0
Florida	5	1	0	9	3	0
Georgia	5	1	0	9	3	0
Mississippi	5	1	0	6	5	0
Tennessee	3	3	0	7	5	0
Vanderbilt	2	4	0	7	4	0
Mississippi State*	1	4	1	6	4	1
Auburn	1	4	1	3	6	2
LSU	1	5	0	4	7	0
Kentucky	0	6	0	2	8	1

*Conference record later forfeited to 0-6-0

1976 NCAA Major College Statistical Leaders

Individual Leaders

PASSING		G	ATT	COM	PCT	INT	I%	YDS	YPA	TD	TD%	COM.PG
1	Tommy Kramer, Rice	11	501	269	53.7	19	3.8	3317	6.6	21	4.2	24.5
2	Jack Thompson, Washington State	11	355	208	58.6	14	3.9	2762	7.8	20	5.6	18.9
3	Guy Benjamin, Stanford	9	295	170	57.6	17	5.8	1982	6.7	12	4.1	18.9
4	Gifford Nielsen, Brigham Young	11	372	207	55.6	19	5.1	3192	8.6	29	7.8	18.8
5	Joe Roth, California	10	295	154	52.2	18	6.1	1789	6.1	7	2.4	15.4
6	Leamon Hall, Army	11	344	162	47.1	27	7.8	2174	6.3	15	4.4	14.7
7	Jack Henderson, Oregon	11	298	157	52.7	16	5.4	1582	5.3	6	2.0	14.3
8	Bob Graustein, Pennsylvania	9	230	127	55.2	16	7.0	1429	6.2	2	0.9	14.1
9	Ed Smith, Michigan State	10	257	132	51.4	10	3.9	1749	6.8	13	5.1	13.2
10	Dan Hagemann, Utah	9	222	117	52.7	14	6.3	1585	7.1	10	4.5	13.0

ALL-PURPOSE		G	RUSH	REC	PR	KR	YDS	YPG
1	Tony Dorsett, Pittsburgh	11	1948	73	0	0	2021	183.7
2	Arthur Whittington, SMU	11	789	145	209	700	1843	167.5
3	Jerome Persell, Western Michigan	10	1505	38	0	18	1561	156.1
4	Ricky Bell, Southern California	10	1417	85	0	0	1502	150.2
5	Terry Miller, Oklahoma State	11	1541	0	0	92	1633	148.5
6	Andre Herrera, Southern Illinois	11	1588	26	-6	0	1608	146.2
7	James Sykes, Rice	11	435	653	0	464	1552	141.1
8	Rob Lytle, Michigan	11	1402	81	0	26	1509	137.2
9	Al Hunter, Notre Dame	11	1058	189	1	241	1489	135.4
10	Anthony Anderson, Temple	10	803	174	0	367	1344	134.4

RUSHING/Yards Per Game		G	ATT	YDS	TD	AVG	YPG
1	Tony Dorsett, Pittsburgh	11	338	1948	21	5.8	177.1
2	Jerome Persell, Western Michigan	10	269	1505	19	5.6	150.5
3	Andre Herrera, Southern Ilinois	11	287	1588	16	5.5	144.4
4	Ricky Bell, Southern California	10	276	1417	14	5.1	141.7
5	Terry Miller, Oklahoma State	11	268	1541	19	5.8	140.1
6	Mike Voight, North Carolina	11	315	1407	18	4.5	127.9
7	Rob Lytle, Michigan	11	203	1402	13	6.9	127.5
8	Derrick Jensen, Texas-Arlington	11	233	1266	7	5.4	115.1
9	John Pagliaro, Yale	9	179	1023	16	5.7	113.7
10	Mike Williams, New Mexico	11	258	1240	9	4.8	112.7

RUSHING/Yards Per Carry		G	ATT	YDS	YPC
1	Leroy Harris, Arkansas State	11	150	1046	7.0
2	Rob Lytle, Michigan	11	203	1402	6.9
3	Laverne Smith, Kansas	11	148	978	6.6
4	Ben Cowins, Arkansas	11	183	1162	6.3
5	Tony Dorsett, Pittsburgh	11	338	1948	5.8
6	Terry Miller, Oklahoma State	11	268	1541	5.8
7	Jeff Logan, Ohio State	11	204	1169	5.7
8	John Pagliaro, Yale	9	179	1023	5.7
9	Jerome Persell, Western Michigan	10	269	1505	5.6
10	Andre Herrera, Southern Illinois	11	287	1588	5.5

Based on top 38 rushers

RECEIVING		G	REC	YDS	TD	YPR	YPG	RPG
1	Billy Ryckman, Louisiana Tech	11	77	1382	10	17.9	125.6	7.0
2	James Sykes, Rice	11	76	653	2	8.6	59.4	6.9
3	Mike Levenseller, Washington State	11	67	1124	8	16.8	102.2	6.1
4	Doug Cunningham, Rice	10	57	770	3	13.5	77.0	5.7
5	David Oliver, La.-Lafayette	11	59	876	10	14.8	79.6	5.4
6	Keith Hartwig, Arizona	11	54	1134	10	21.0	103.1	4.9
7	Tony Hill, Stanford	9	44	696	8	15.8	77.3	4.9
8	Greg Bauer, Oregon	11	53	632	2	11.9	57.5	4.8
8	Dan Doornink, Washington State	11	53	469	3	8.8	42.6	4.8
10	Jeff Gowan, Illinois Sttate	10	48	696	1	14.5	69.6	4.8

PUNTING		PUNT	YDS	AVG
1	Russell Erxleben, Texas	61	2842	46.6
2	Johnny Evans, North Carolina St.	47	2168	46.1
3	Mike Deutsch, Colorado State	68	3134	46.1
4	Russ Henderson, Virginia	69	3168	45.9
5	Larry Swider, Pittsburgh	58	2600	44.8
6	Frank Corrall, UCLA	42	1874	44.6
7	Steve Little, Arkansas	63	2797	44.4
8	Joe Parker, Appalachian State	50	2210	44.2
9	Don Fechtman, North Texas	54	2381	44.1
10	Cliff Parsley, Oklahoma State	61	2666	43.7

PUNT RETURNS		PUNT	YDS	TD	AVG
1	Henry Jenkins, Rutgers	30	449	0	15.0
2	Keith Wright, Memphis	16	228	2	14.2
3	Will Mosley, Northwestern State	14	196	1	14.0
4	**Preston Brown, Vanderbilt**	**16**	**213**	**1**	**13.3**
5	Michael Coulter, UCLA	14	179	0	12.8
6	John Harris, Arizona State	15	188	1	12.5
7	Jim Smith, Michigan	15	313	0	12.5
8	Rick Morrison, Ball State	19	234	0	12.3
9	**Stan Black, Mississippi State**	**16**	**196**	**0**	**12.2**
10	Rich Mauti, Penn State	17	208	0	12.2

KICKOFF RETURNS		KR	YDS	TD	AVG
1	Ira Matthews, Wisconsin	14	415	2	29.6
2	Drew Hill, Georgia Tech	20	546	0	27.3
3	James Sykes, Rice	18	464	1	25.8
4	Billy Waddy, Colorado	22	566	1	25.7
5	Bruce Montagner, Indiana State	17	437	1	25.7
6	Steve Kuehl, Bowling Green	14	359	0	25.6
7	Art Gore, Duke	22	563	0	25.6
8	Robert Taylor, Idaho	16	401	1	25.1
9	**Robert Dow, LSU**	**20**	**499**	**0**	**24.9**
10	Luther Blue, Iowa State	14	349	1	24.9

SCORING		TDS	XPT	FG	PTS	PTPG
1	Tony Dorsett, Pittsburgh	22	2	0	134	12.2
2	Jerome Persell, Western Michigan	19	4	0	118	11.8
3	John Pagliaro, Yale	16	0	0	96	10.7
4	Terry Miller, Oklahoma State	19	0	0	114	10.4
5	Mike Voight, North Carolina	18	2	0	110	10.0
6	Pete Johnson, Ohio State	18	0	0	108	9.8
7	Arry Moody, Louisiana Tech	17	4	0	106	9.6
8	George Woodard, Texas A&M	17	0	0	102	9.3
9	Andre Herrera, Southern Illinois	16	2	0	98	8.9
10	Ricky Bell, Southern California	14	2	0	86	8.6

FIELD GOALS		FGA	FGM	PCT	FGG
1	Tony Franklin, Texas A&M	26	17	0.65	1.55
2	Craig Jones, VMI	18	15	0.83	1.50
3	Carson Long, Pittsburgh	23	16	0.70	1.45
3	Jim Breech, California	24	16	0.67	1.45
5	Brian Hall, Texas Tech	20	15	0.75	1.36
5	Dave Taylor, Brigham Young	29	15	0.52	1.36
7	Paul Marchese, Kent State	25	16	0.64	1.33
8	Pete Conaty, East Carolina	23	14	0.61	1.27
8	Rade Savich, Central Michigan	24	14	0.58	1.27
8	Tom Drake, Colorado State	27	14	0.52	1.27

INTERCEPTIONS		INT	YDS	TD	INT/GM
1	Anthony Francis, Houston	10	118	0	0.91
2	Bob Jury, Pittsburgh	9	105	0	0.82
3	Dennis Thurman, Southern California	8	170	1	0.73
3	Jeff Nixon, Richmond	8	132	0	0.73
3	Lester Hayes, Texas A&M	8	87	0	0.73
3	Ron Irving, La.-Lafayette	8	26	1	0.73
7	Scott Erdmann, Wisconsin	7	143	1	0.64
7	John Harris, Arizona State	7	130	1	0.64
7	Mark Wood, Drake	7	98	0	0.64
7	Mike Galpin, Navy	7	87	0	0.64

Team Leaders

RUSHING OFFENSE		G	ATT	YDS	AVG	TD	YPG
1	Michigan	11	661	3989	6.0	42	362.6
2	UCLA	11	691	3755	5.4	41	341.4
3	Oklahoma	11	657	3540	5.4	33	321.8
4	Kansas	11	701	3271	4.7	29	297.4
5	East Carolina	11	734	3263	4.4	28	296.6
6	Yale	9	564	2658	4.7	24	295.3
7	Pittsburgh	11	671	3198	4.8	32	290.7
8	Texas-Arlington	11	636	3153	5.0	26	286.6
9	Western Michigan	11	677	3136	4.6	32	285.1
10	Oklahoma State	11	672	3085	4.6	31	280.5

PASSING OFFENSE		G	ATT	COM	INT	PCT	YDS	YPA	TD	I%	YPC	YPG
1	Brigham Young	11	403	223	19	55.3	3386	8.4	31	4.7	15.2	307.8
2	Rice	11	504	270	19	53.6	3337	6.6	21	3.8	12.4	303.4
3	Washington State	11	442	250	22	56.6	3265	7.4	21	5.0	13.1	296.8
4	Louisiana Tech	11	307	159	19	51.8	2697	8.8	22	6.2	17.0	245.2
5	Stanford	11	408	223	23	54.7	2669	6.5	16	5.6	12.0	242.6
6	Utah	11	368	187	21	50.8	2603	7.1	14	5.7	13.9	236.6
7	San Jose State	11	323	178	11	55.1	2579	8.0	23	3.4	14.5	234.5
8	California	11	385	205	21	53.2	2365	6.1	10	5.5	11.5	215.0
9	Michigan State	11	337	171	13	50.7	2322	6.9	17	3.9	13.6	211.1
10	Arizona State	11	326	153	18	46.9	2304	7.1	16	5.5	15.1	209.5

TOTAL OFFENSE		G	P	YDS	AVG	TD	YPG
1	Michigan	11	760	4929	6.5	55	448.1
2	Iowa State	11	889	4836	5.4	47	439.6
3	Southern California	11	802	4757	5.9	49	432.5
4	UCLA	11	836	4690	5.6	48	426.4
5	San Jose State	11	781	4682	6.0	46	425.6
6	Brigham Young	11	857	4668	5.4	44	424.4
7	Louisiana Tech	11	818	4560	5.6	46	414.5
8	Houston	11	853	4555	5.3	41	414.1
9	Nebraska	12	913	4894	5.4	50	407.8
10	Bowling Green	11	890	4425	5.0	38	402.3

RUSHING DEFENSE		G	ATT	YDS	AVG	TD	YPG
1	Rutgers	11	407	923	2.3	4	83.9
2	Texas A&M	11	457	1064	2.3	7	96.7
3	Yale	9	362	966	2.7	6	107.3
4	Pittsburgh	11	495	1243	2.5	7	113.0
5	Michigan	11	457	1254	2.7	6	114.0
6	Maryland	11	466	1284	2.8	7	116.7
7	Notre Dame	11	483	1324	2.7	10	120.4
8	East Carolina	11	493	1353	2.7	10	123.0
9	Cincinnati	11	510	1367	2.7	10	124.3
10	Dartmouth	9	406	1138	2.8	7	126.4

PASSING DEFENSE		G	ATT	COM	PCT	YPC	INT	I%	YDS	YPA	TD	YPG
1	Western Michigan	11	175	74	42.3	11.7	10	5.7	863	4.9	6	78.5
2	Lamar	11	151	65	43.0	13.3	12	7.9	866	5.7	7	78.7
3	**Vanderbilt**	**11**	**155**	**72**	**46.5**	**12.4**	**9**	**5.8**	**892**	**5.8**	**6**	**81.1**
4	VMI	10	151	70	46.4	11.9	9	6.0	835	5.5	3	83.5
5	Ohio U.	11	196	70	35.7	13.2	15	7.7	921	4.7	9	83.7
6	William & Mary	11	177	75	42.4	12.5	14	7.9	936	5.3	5	85.1
7	Florida State	11	135	68	50.4	14.0	5	3.7	949	7.0	7	86.3
8	Furman	11	174	68	39.1	14.2	10	5.7	965	5.5	8	87.7
9	Indiana State	10	129	65	50.4	13.5	8	6.2	880	6.8	5	88.0
10	Illinois State	11	173	71	41.0	13.7	9	5.2	970	5.6	6	88.2

TOTAL DEFENSE		G	P	YDS	AVG	TD	YPG
1	Rutgers	11	629	1971	3.1	9	179.2
2	Maryland	11	666	2321	3.5	11	211.0
3	East Carolina	11	712	2355	3.3	12	214.1
4	Texas A&M	11	722	2356	3.3	16	214.2
5	Yale	9	557	2034	3.7	9	226.0
6	Pittsburgh	11	726	2519	3.5	15	229.0
7	**LSU**	**11**	**702**	**2564**	**3.7**	**19**	**233.1**
8	Colgate	10	692	2407	3.5	17	240.7
9	Long Beach State	11	715	2649	3.7	14	240.8
10	Michigan	11	721	2666	3.7	10	242.4

SCORING OFFENSE		G	PTS	AVG
1	Michigan	11	426	38.7
2	UCLA	11	385	35.0
3	Southern California	11	372	33.8
4	Iowa State	11	369	33.5
5	Nebraska	12	389	32.4
6	Pittsburgh	11	354	32.2
6	San Jose State	11	354	32.2
8	Brigham Young	11	351	31.9
9	Louisiana Tech	11	336	30.5
10	Texas A&M	11	327	29.7

SCORING DEFENSE		G	PTS	AVG
1	Rutgers	11	81	7.4
1	Michigan	11	81	7.4
3	Maryland	11	85	7.7
4	Yale	9	77	8.6
5	Cincinnati	11	114	10.4
6	East Carolina	11	116	10.5
7	**Georgia**	**11**	**118**	**10.7**
8	Ball State	11	124	11.3
9	Brown	9	102	11.3
10	San Diego State	11	125	11.4

1976

Final Poll (Jan. 4)

UP	AP	SCHOOL	FINAL RECORD
1	1	Pittsburgh	12-0-0
2	2	Southern California	11-1-0
3	3	Michigan	10-2-0
4	4	Houston	10-2-0
6	5	Oklahoma	9-2-1
5	6	Ohio State	9-2-1
8	7	Texas A&M	10-2-0
11	8	Maryland	11-1-0
7	9	Nebraska	9-3-1
10	10	**Georgia**	**10-2-0**
9	11	**Alabama**	**9-3-0**
12	12	Notre Dame	9-3-0
13	13	Texas Tech	10-2-0
14	14	Oklahoma State	9-3-0
15	15	UCLA	9-2-1
16	16	Colorado	8-4-0
17	17	Rutgers	11-0-0
19	18	**Kentucky**	**8-4-0**
18	19	Iowa State	8-3-0
	20	**Mississippi State**	**9-2-0**
19		Baylor	7-3-1

Consensus All-Americans

POS	OFFENSE	SCHOOL
QB	Tommy Kramer	Rice
RB	Tony Dorsett	Pittsburgh
RB	Ricky Bell	Southern California
RB	Rob Lytle	Michigan
SE	**Larry Seivers**	**Tennessee**
TE	Ken MacAfee	Notre Dame
T	Mike Vaughan	Oklahoma
T	Chris Ward	Ohio State
G	**Joel Parrish**	**Georgia**
G	Mark Donahue	Michigan
C	Derrel Gofourth	Oklahoma State
PK	Tony Franklin	Texas A&M

Others Receiving First-Team Honors

QB	Gifford Nielsen	Brigham Young
RB	Terry Miller	Oklahoma State
SE	Luther Blue	Iowa State
T	Steve Schindler	Boston College
T	**Warren Bryant**	**Kentucky**
T	**Mike Wilson**	**Georgia**
T	Ted Albrecht	California
T	Marvin Powell	Southern California
G	T.J. Humphreys	Arkansas State
C	Billy Bryan	Duke
C	John Yarno	Idaho
K	Steve Little	Arkansas
KR	Jim Smith	Michigan

POS	DEFENSE	SCHOOL
E	Ross Browner	Notre Dame
E	Bob Brudzinski	Ohio State
T	Wilson Whitley	Houston
T	Gary Jeter	Southern California
T	Joe Campbell	Maryland
MG	Al Romano	Pittsburgh
LB	Robert Jackson	Texas A&M
LB	Jerry Robinson	UCLA
B	Bill Armstrong	Wake Forest
B	Gary Green	Baylor
B	Dennis Thurman	Southern California
B	Dave Butterfield	Nebraska

Others Receiving First-Team Honors

DL	Eddie Edwards	Miami (Fla.)
DL	Mike Fultz	Nebraska
DL	Duncan McColl	Stanford
LB	Thomas Howard	Texas Tech
LB	Brian Ruff	Citadel
LB	Calvin O'Neal	Michigan
LB	Kurt Allerman	Penn State
B	Eric Harris	Memphis
B	Oscar Edwards	UCLA
P	Russell Erxleben	Texas

Heisman Trophy Voting

	PLAYER	POS	SCHOOL	TOTAL
1	Tony Dorsett	RB	Pittsburgh	2357
2	Ricky Bell	TB	Southern Cal	1346
3	Rob Lytle	RB	Michigan	413
4	Terry Miller	RB	Oklahoma State	197
5	Tommy Kramer	QB	Rice	63
6	Gifford Nielson	QB	Brigham Young	45
7	**Ray Goff**	**QB**	**Georgia**	**44**
8	Mike Voight	RB	North Carolina	41
9	Joe Roth	QB	California	32
10	Jeff Dankworth	QB	UCLA	31

Award Winners

PLAYER	AWARD
Tony Dorsett, RB, Pittsburgh	Maxwell
Ross Browner, DE, Notre Dame	Outland
Tony Dorsett, RB, Pittsburgh	Camp
Wilson Whitley, DT, Houston	Lombardi

Bowl Games

DATE	BOWL	SCORE
D13	Independence	McNeese St. 20, Tulsa 16
D18	Tangerine	Oklahoma State 49, Brigham Young 21
D20	**Liberty**	**Alabama 36, UCLA 6**
D25	Fiesta	Oklahoma 41, Wyoming 7
D27	Gator	Notre Dame 20, Penn State 9
D31	**Peach**	**Kentucky 21, North Carolina 0**
D31	Bluebonnet	Nebraska 27, Texas Tech 24
J1	**Sugar**	**Pittsburgh 27, Georgia 3**
J1	Cotton	Houston 30, Maryland 21
J1	Orange	Ohio State 27, Colorado 10
J1	Rose	Southern California 14, Michigan 6
J2	**Sun**	**Texas A&M 37, Florida 14**

SEC Standings

	CONFERENCE			OVERALL		
	W	L	T	W	L	T
Georgia	5	1	0	10	2	0
Alabama	5	2	0	9	3	0
Mississippi State*	4	2	0	9	2	0
Florida	4	2	0	8	4	0
Kentucky	4	2	0	8	4	0
Mississippi	3	4	0	5	6	0
LSU	2	4	0	6	4	1
Tennessee	2	4	0	6	5	0
Auburn	2	4	0	3	8	0
Vanderbilt	0	6	0	2	9	0

*Conference record later forfeited to 0-6-0

1977 NCAA Major College Statistical Leaders

Individual Leaders

PASSING	G	ATT	COM	PCT	INT	I%	YDS	YPA	TD	TD%	COM.PG
1 Guy Benjamin, Stanford	10	330	208	63.0	15	4.5	2521	7.6	19	5.8	20.8
2 Jack Thompson, Washington State	11	329	192	58.4	13	4.0	2372	7.2	13	4.0	17.5
3 Ken Smith, Boston College	9	257	149	58.0	20	7.8	2073	8.1	17	6.6	16.6
4 Doug Williams, Grambling	11	352	181	51.4	18	5.1	3286	9.3	38	10.8	16.5
5 Mark Herrmann, Purdue	11	319	175	54.9	27	8.5	2453	7.7	18	5.6	15.9
6 Joe Davis, San Diego State	11	290	174	60.0	12	4.1	2360	8.1	24	8.3	15.8
7 Jim Freitas, Long Beach State	8	264	124	47.0	16	6.1	1358	5.1	15	5.7	15.5
8 Marc Wilson, Brigham Young	11	277	164	59.2	18	6.5	2418	8.7	24	8.7	14.9
9 Randy Hertel, Rice	11	356	156	43.8	24	6.7	1620	4.6	9	2.5	14.2
10 Randy Gomez, Utah	11	315	155	49.2	16	5.1	2126	6.7	12	3.8	14.1

ALL-PURPOSE	G	RUSH	REC	PR	KR	YDS	YPG
1 Earl Campbell, Texas	11	1744	111	0	0	1855	168.6
2 Henry White, Colgate	11	1032	306	67	448	1853	168.5
3 Larry Key, Florida State	11	1117	243	0	461	1821	165.5
4 Mose Rison, Central Michigan	10	1241	59	0	330	1630	163.0
5 Terry Miller, Oklahoma State	11	1680	2	0	104	1786	162.4
6 Charles Alexander, LSU	**11**	**1686**	**80**	**0**	**0**	**1766**	**160.5**
7 Joe Gattuso, Navy	11	1292	169	0	212	1673	152.1
8 Darrin Nelson, Stanford	11	1069	524	79	0	1672	152.0
9 David Turner, San Diego State	11	1252	417	0	0	1669	151.7
10 Robert Woods, Grambling	11	210	719	279	417	1625	147.7

RUSHING/ YARDS PER GAME	G	ATT	YDS	TD	AVG	YPG
1 Earl Campbell, Texas	11	267	1744	18	6.5	158.5
2 Charles Alexander, LSU	**11**	**311**	**1686**	**17**	**5.4**	**153.3**
3 Terry Miller, Oklahoma State	11	314	1680	14	5.4	152.7
4 Jerome Persell, Western Michigan	10	264	1339	14	5.1	133.9
5 John Pagliaro, Yale	9	239	1159	14	4.8	128.8
6 Bo Robinson, West Texas State	11	201	1399	12	7.0	127.2
7 Mose Rison, Central Michigan	10	238	1241	11	5.2	124.1
8 Amos Lawrence, North Carolina	10	193	1211	6	6.3	121.1
9 Bobby Windom, Eastern Michigan	11	246	1322	9	5.4	120.2
10 Darrell Lipford, Western Carolina	11	280	1318	16	4.7	119.8

RUSHING/YARDS PER CARRY	G	ATT	YDS	YPC
1 Henry White, Colgate	11	131	1032	7.9
2 Bo Robinson, West Texas State	11	201	1399	7.0
3 I.M. Hipp, Nebraska	11	197	1301	6.6
4 Earl Campbell, Texas	11	267	1744	6.5
5 Gwain Durden, U.T. Chattanooga	11	164	1049	6.4
6 Amos Lawrence, North Carolina	10	193	1211	6.3
7 Myron Hardeman, Wyoming	11	186	1165	6.3
8 Mike Smith, U.T. Chattanooga	11	172	1062	6.2
9 Darrin Nelson, Stanford	11	183	1069	5.8
10 Ron Springs, Ohio State	11	190	1092	5.7

RECEIVING	G	REC	YDS	TD	YPR	YPG	RPG
1 Wayne Tolleson, Western Carolina	11	73	1101	7	15.1	100.1	6.6
2 Emanuel Tolbert, SMU	11	64	996	6	15.6	90.5	5.8
3 Mike Moore, Grambling	11	60	1122	12	18.7	102.0	5.5
3 Paul Proffitt, Drake	11	60	778	5	13.0	70.7	5.5
5 Rod Foppe, Louisiana Tech	11	59	1274	5	21.6	115.8	5.4
5 Rick Morrison, Ball State	11	59	908	8	15.4	82.5	5.4
7 Dave Petzke, Northern Illinois	11	57	746	5	13.1	67.8	5.2
8 Steve Young, Wake Forest	10	51	483	3	9.5	48.3	5.1
9 Mike Riley, Citadel	11	56	724	2	12.9	65.8	5.1
10 David Houser, Rice	11	55	795	5	14.5	72.3	5.0
10 Todd Christensen, Brigham Young	10	50	603	5	12.1	60.3	5.0

PUNTING	PUNT	YDS	AVG
1 Jim Miller, Mississippi	**66**	**3029**	**45.9**
2 Craig Colquitt, Tennessee	**66**	**2969**	**45.0**
3 Gavin Hedrick, Washington State	53	2368	44.7
4 Steve Little, Arkansas	48	2127	44.3
5 Ken Rosenthal, SMU	62	2741	44.2
6 Rick Partridge, Utah	68	2980	43.8
7 Luke Prestridge, Baylor	63	2755	43.7
8 David Appleby, Texas A&M	57	2466	43.3
9 Mike Deutsch, Colorado State	71	3057	43.1
10 Mike Connell, Cincinnati	60	2568	42.8

PUNT RETURNS	PUNT	YDS	TD	AVG
1 Robert Woods, Grambling	11	279	3	25.4
2 Jimmy Cefalo, Penn State	18	247	2	13.7
3 Phil McConkey, Navy	19	257	1	13.5
4 Max Hudspeth, New Mexico	22	291	1	13.2
5 Jimmy Bryant, Utah State	18	226	0	12.6
6 Tony Nathan, Alabama	**18**	**223**	**0**	**12.4**
7 Johnnie Johnson, Texas	44	538	1	12.2
7 Vondell Robertson, Central Michigan	22	269	0	12.2
9 Freddie Nixon, Oklahoma	22	266	1	12.1
10 Gordon Jones, Pittsburgh	23	275	1	12.0

KICKOFF RETURNS	KR	YDS	TD	AVG
1 Tony Ball, U.T. Chattanooga	13	473	0	36.4
2 Larry Anderson, Louisiana Tech	14	435	2	31.1
3 James Otis Doss, Mississippi State	**16**	**450**	**0**	**28.1**
4 Steve Woods, Fresno State	16	447	1	27.9
5 Gary Moore, Tennessee	**14**	**376**	**0**	**26.9**
5 Tony Felder, Texas-Arlington	14	376	0	26.9
7 Joe Jamiel, Brown	11	293	0	26.6
8 Robert Woods, Grambling	16	417	2	26.1
9 Norman Warren, Kent State	22	569	1	25.9
10 Ralph Stringer, North Carolina St.	19	488	0	25.7

SCORING	TDS	XPT	FG	PTS	PTPG
1 Earl Campbell, Texas	19	0	0	114	10.4
2 Darrell Lipford, Western Carolina	18	0	0	108	9.8
3 Charles Alexander, LSU	**17**	**2**	**0**	**104**	**9.5**
4 John Pagliaro, Yale	14	0	0	84	9.3
5 Russell Erxleben, Texas	0	39	14	81	9.0
6 Mike Jones, North Texas	16	2	0	98	8.9
7 Joel Payton, Ohio State	13	2	0	80	8.9
8 Steve Little, Arkansas	0	37	19	94	8.5
9 Jerome Persell, Western Michigan	14	0	0	84	8.4
9 Ronnie Smith, San Diego State	14	0	0	84	8.4

FIELD GOALS	FGA	FGM	PCT	FGG
1 Paul Marchese, Kent State	27	18	0.67	1.80
2 Steve Little, Arkansas	30	19	0.63	1.73
3 Paul Rogind, Minnesota	26	18	0.69	1.64
4 John Roveta, La.-Lafayette	25	19	0.76	1.58
5 Russell Erxleben, Texas	26	14	0.54	1.56
6 Hans Nielsen, Michigan State	28	17	0.61	1.55
7 Tom McNamara, Utah	23	16	0.70	1.45
7 Jim Breech, California	27	16	0.59	1.45
7 Tony Franklin, Texas A&M	28	16	0.57	1.45
7 Dave Jacobs, Syracuse	29	16	0.55	1.45

INTERCEPTIONS	INT	YDS	TD	INT/GM
1 Paul Lawler, Colgate	7	53	0	0.78
2 Leroy Paul, Texas Southern	8	113	0	0.73
2 John Sturges, Navy	8	88	0	0.73
4 Kevin White, Citadel	7	102	0	0.64
4 Zac Henderson, Oklahoma	7	89	0	0.64
4 Paul Murphy, Boston College	7	61	0	0.64
4 Bryan Ferguson, Miami (Fla.)	7	50	0	0.64
4 Dave Abrams, Indiana	7	24	0	0.64
4 Charles Johnson, Grambling	7	14	0	0.64
10 Tom Pridemore, West Virginia	6	123	1	0.60
10 Sherman Taylor, Wichita State	6	41	0	0.60

Team Leaders

RUSHING OFFENSE	G	ATT	YDS	AVG	TD	YPG
1 Oklahoma	11	709	3618	5.1	40	328.9
2 Ohio State	11	731	3534	4.8	39	321.3
3 West Texas State	11	697	3503	5.0	32	318.5
4 Texas	11	646	3369	5.2	39	306.3
5 LSU	**11**	**674**	**3352**	**5.0**	**35**	**304.7**
6 U.T. Chattanooga	11	660	3332	5.0	26	302.9
7 Nebraska	11	655	3328	5.1	31	302.5
8 Texas A&M	11	709	3304	4.7	29	300.4
9 Alabama	**11**	**697**	**3268**	**4.7**	**34**	**297.1**
10 Central Michigan	11	741	3213	4.3	31	292.1

PASSING OFFENSE	G	ATT	COM	INT	PCT	YDS	YPA	TD	I%	YPC	YPG
1 Brigham Young	11	457	277	23	60.6	3758	8.2	41	5.0	13.6	341.6
2 Grambling	11	373	187	20	50.1	3360	9.0	38	5.4	18.0	305.5
3 Stanford	11	372	235	15	63.2	2856	7.7	20	4.0	12.2	259.6
4 California	11	391	214	16	54.7	2837	7.3	18	4.1	13.3	257.9
5 San Diego State	11	331	192	16	58.0	2685	8.1	26	4.8	14.0	244.1
6 Purdue	11	350	190	30	54.3	2631	7.5	18	8.6	13.8	239.2
7 Washington State	11	346	202	13	58.4	2581	7.5	14	3.8	12.8	234.6
8 Louisiana Tech	11	300	151	18	50.3	2552	8.5	9	6.0	16.9	232.0
9 Long Beach State	10	388	186	20	47.9	2249	5.8	19	5.2	12.1	224.9
10 Florida State	11	323	176	18	54.5	2466	7.6	18	5.6	14.0	224.2

TOTAL OFFENSE	G	P	YDS	AVG	TD	YPG
1 Colgate	11	794	5347	6.7	49	486.1
2 Grambling	11	805	5329	6.7	58	484.5
3 Brigham Young	11	881	5172	5.9	55	470.2
4 Southern California	11	839	4959	5.9	37	450.8
5 Notre Dame	11	918	4840	5.3	47	440.0
6 Texas	11	792	4805	6.1	53	436.8
7 Stanford	11	846	4750	5.6	32	431.8
8 Fresno State	11	873	4695	5.4	44	426.8
9 Penn State	11	865	4646	5.4	39	422.4
10 Arizona State	11	928	4643	5.0	45	422.1

RUSHING DEFENSE	G	ATT	YDS	AVG	TD	YPG
1 Jackson State	11	446	746	1.7	6	67.8
2 Cincinnati	11	478	871	1.8	8	79.2
3 Notre Dame	11	447	981	2.2	3	89.2
4 Texas	11	471	1002	2.1	5	91.1
5 Fresno State	11	494	1165	2.4	12	105.9
6 Louisiana Tech	11	481	1167	2.4	5	106.1
7 Central Michigan	11	475	1209	2.5	13	109.9
8 San Diego State	11	512	1243	2.4	12	113.0
9 Texas Southern	11	495	1249	2.5	16	113.5
10 Michigan	11	488	1287	2.6	6	117.0

PASSING DEFENSE	G	ATT	COM	PCT	YPC	INT	I%	YDS	YPA	TD	YPG
1 Tennessee State	9	156	52	33.3	11.8	10	6.4	611	3.9	4	67.9
2 Brown	9	158	75	47.5	10.3	9	5.7	776	4.9	3	86.2
3 Northern Illinois	11	165	74	44.8	13.2	9	5.5	974	5.9	8	88.5
4 Indiana	11	178	74	41.6	13.3	13	7.3	984	5.5	5	89.5
4 Arkansas	11	227	98	43.2	10.0	17	7.5	984	4.3	1	89.5
6 Wisconsin	11	149	58	38.9	17.3	7	4.7	1002	6.7	4	91.1
7 Nebraska	11	202	89	44.1	11.7	17	8.4	1037	5.1	6	94.3
8 Western Carolina	11	172	86	50.0	12.4	12	7.0	1066	6.2	3	96.9
9 Tennessee	**11**	**179**	**78**	**43.6**	**13.7**	**10**	**5.6**	**1067**	**6.0**	**6**	**97.0**
10 Northwestern State	11	188	73	38.8	14.7	12	6.4	1072	5.7	8	97.5

TOTAL DEFENSE	G	P	YDS	AVG	TD	YPG
1 Jackson State	11	688	2277	3.3	14	207.0
2 Tennessee State	9	609	1883	3.1	11	209.2
3 Louisiana Tech	11	708	2421	3.4	16	220.1
4 Central Michigan	11	671	2422	3.6	19	220.2
5 Texas	11	737	2461	3.3	13	223.7
6 Brown	9	573	2071	3.6	12	230.1
7 Ohio State	11	694	2539	3.7	10	230.8
8 Fresno State	11	750	2548	3.4	21	231.6
9 Kentucky	**11**	**728**	**2590**	**3.6**	**12**	**235.5**
10 Texas Southern	11	705	2606	3.7	25	236.9

SCORING OFFENSE	G	PTS	AVG
1 Grambling	11	462	42.0
2 Brigham Young	11	433	39.4
3 Texas	11	431	39.2
4 Oklahoma	11	395	35.9
5 Pittsburgh	11	394	35.8
6 Notre Dame	11	382	34.7
7 Colgate	11	380	34.5
8 Ball State	11	377	34.3
9 LSU	**11**	**375**	**34.1**
10 Arizona State	11	369	33.5

SCORING DEFENSE	G	PTS	AVG
1 North Carolina	11	81	7.4
2 Ohio State	11	85	7.7
3 Arkansas	11	95	8.6
4 Michigan	11	97	8.8
5 Kentucky	**11**	**111**	**10.1**
6 Tennessee State	9	91	10.1
7 Jackson State	11	112	10.2
8 Texas	11	114	10.4
9 Brown	9	96	10.7
9 Dartmouth	9	96	10.7

1977

Final Poll (Jan. 3)

UP	AP	SCHOOL	FINAL RECORD
1	1	Notre Dame	11-1-0
2	2	Alabama	11-1-0
3	3	Arkansas	11-1-0
5	4	Texas	11-1-0
4	5	Penn State	11-1-0
PB	6	Kentucky	10-1-0
6	7	Oklahoma	10-2-1
7	8	Pittsburgh	9-2-0
8	9	Michigan	10-2-0
9	10	Washington	8-4-0
12	11	Ohio State	9-3-0
10	12	Nebraska	9-3-0
12	13	Southern California	8-4-0
11	14	Florida State	10-2-0
15	15	Stanford	9-3-0
19	16	San Diego State	10-1-0
14	17	North Carolina	8-3-1
18	18	Arizona State	9-3-0
	19	Clemson	8-3-1
16	20	Brigham Young	9-2-0
16		North Texas	9-2-0
19		North Carolina St.	8-4-0

PB: Team on probation

Consensus All-Americans

POS	OFFENSE	SCHOOL
QB	Guy Benjamin	Stanford
RB	Earl Campbell	Texas
RB	Terry Miller	Oklahoma State
RB	Charles Alexander	LSU
WR	John Jefferson	Arizona State
WR	Ozzie Newsome	Alabama
TE	Ken MacAfee	Notre Dame
T	Chris Ward	Ohio State
T	Dan Irons	Texas Tech
G	Mark Donahue	Michigan
G	Leotis Harris	Arkansas
C	Tom Brzoza	Pittsburgh
PK	Steve Little	Arkansas

Others receiving first-team honors

QB	Matt Cavanaugh	Pittsburgh
QB	Doug Williams	Grambling
WR	Wes Chandler	Florida
T	Joe Bostic	Clemson
T	Keith Dorney	Penn State
T	Dennis Baker	Wyoming
C	Tom Davis	Nebraska
C	Walt Downing	Michigan

POS	DEFENSE	SCHOOL
L	Ross Browner	Notre Dame
L	Art Still	Kentucky
L	Brad Shearer	Texas
L	Randy Holloway	Pittsburgh
L	Dee Hardison	North Carolina
LB	Jerry Robinson	UCLA
LB	Tom Cousineau	Ohio State
LB	Gary Spani	Kansas State
B	Dennis Thurman	Southern California
B	Zac Henderson	Oklahoma
B	Luther Bradley	Notre Dame
B	Bob Jury	Pittsburgh

Others receiving first-team honors

MG	Aaron Brown	Ohio State
MG	Randy Sidler	Penn State
MG	Reggie Kinlaw	Oklahoma
LB	John Anderson	Michigan
LB	Lucius Sanford	Georgia Tech
LB	George Cumby	Oklahoma
LB	Mike Woods	Cincinnati
P	Russell Erxleben	Texas

Heisman Trophy Voting

	PLAYER	POS	SCHOOL	TOTAL
1	Earl Campbell	RB	Texas	1547
2	Terry Miller	TB	Oklahoma State	812
3	Ken MacAfee	TE	Notre Dame	343
4	Doug Williams	QB	Grambling	266
5	Ross Browner	DE	Notre Dame	213
6	Guy Benjamin	QB	Stanford	111
7	Matt Cavanaugh	QB	Pittsburgh	86
8	Rick Leach	QB	Michigan	59
9	Charles Alexander	TB	LSU	54
10	Wes Chandler	WR	Florida	50

Award Winners

PLAYER	AWARD
Tony Dorsett, RB, Pittsburgh	Maxwell
Ross Browner, DE, Notre Dame	Maxwell
Brad Shearer, DT, Texas	Outland
Ken MacAfee, TE, Notre Dame	Camp
Ross Browner, DE, Notre Dame	Lombardi

Bowl Games

DATE	BOWL	SCORE
D17	Independence	Louisiana Tech 24, Louisville 14
D19	Liberty	Nebraska 21, North Carolina 17
D22	All-American	Maryland 17, Minnesota 7
D23	Tangerine	Florida State 40, Texas Tech 17
D25	Fiesta	Penn State 42, Arizona State 30
D30	Gator	Pittsburgh 34, Clemson 3
D31	Peach	North Carolina St. 24, Iowa State 14
D31	Bluebonnet	Southern California 47, Texas A&M 28
D31	Sun	Stanford 24, LSU 14
J2	Orange	Arkansas 31, Oklahoma 6
J2	Sugar	Alabama 35, Ohio State 6
J2	Cotton	Notre Dame 38, Texas 10
J2	Rose	Washington 27, Michigan 20

SEC Standings

	CONFERENCE			OVERALL		
	W	L	T	W	L	T
Alabama	7	0	0	11	1	0
Kentucky	6	0	0	10	1	0
LSU	4	2	0	8	4	0
Auburn	4	2	0	5	6	0
Florida	3	3	0	6	4	1
Mississippi State*	2	4	0	5	6	0
Georgia	2	4	0	5	6	0
Mississippi	2	5	0	5	6	0
Tennessee	1	5	0	4	7	0
Vanderbilt	0	6	0	2	9	0

*Conference record later forfeited to 0-6-0

1978 NCAA Major College Statistical Leaders

Individual Leaders

PASSING	G	ATT	COM	PCT	INT	I%	YDS	YPA	TD	TD%	COM.PG
1 Steve Dils, Stanford	11	391	247	63.2	15	3.8	2943	7.5	22	5.6	22.5
2 Mike Ford, SMU	11	389	224	57.6	23	5.9	3007	7.7	17	4.4	20.4
3 Mark Halda, San Diego State	11	358	205	57.3	14	3.9	2262	6.3	14	3.9	18.6
4 Ed Luther, San Jose State	12	386	205	53.1	23	6.0	2275	5.9	13	3.4	17.1
5 Ed Smith, Michigan State	10	292	169	57.9	8	2.7	2226	7.6	20	6.8	16.9
6 Jack Thompson, Washington State	11	348	175	50.3	20	5.7	2333	6.7	17	4.9	15.9
7 Randy Hertel, Rice	10	279	156	55.9	11	3.9	1677	6.0	12	4.3	15.6
8 Mark Hutsell, East Tennessee State	11	294	171	58.2	15	5.1	2160	7.3	14	4.8	15.5
9 Paul McGaffigan, Long Beach State	11	302	170	56.3	13	4.3	2164	7.2	9	3.0	15.5
10 David Spriggs, New Mexico State	11	317	169	53.3	25	7.9	2558	8.1	17	5.4	15.4

ALL-PURPOSE	G	RUSH	REC	PR	KR	YDS	YPG
1 Charles White, Southern California	12	1760	191	0	145	2096	174.7
2 Eddie Lee Ivery, Georgia Tech	11	1562	238	79	0	1879	170.8
3 Billy Sims, Oklahoma	11	1762	35	0	0	1797	163.4
4 Joe Holland, Cornell	9	1396	31	0	36	1463	162.6
5 Darrin Nelson, Stanford	11	1061	446	254	13	1774	161.3
6 Cormac Carney, Air Force	11	-9	870	67	807	1735	157.7
7 Obie Graves, Cal St.-Fullerton	12	1789	103	0	0	1892	157.7
8 Ottis Anderson, Miami (Fla.)	11	1268	47	0	395	1710	155.5
9 Theotis Brown, UCLA	11	1199	74	0	434	1707	155.2
10 Bernard Jackson, North Texas	11	1453	76	0	75	1604	145.8

RUSHING/Yards Per Game	G	ATT	YDS	TD	AVG	YPG
1 Billy Sims, Oklahoma	11	231	1762	20	7.6	160.2
2 Joe Holland, Cornell	9	273	1396	16	5.1	155.1
3 Obie Graves, Cal St.-Fullerton	12	275	1789	9	6.5	149.1
4 Charles White, Southern California	12	342	1760	12	5.1	146.7
5 Eddie Lee Ivery, Georgia Tech	11	267	1562	9	5.9	142.0
6 Bernard Jackson, North Texas	11	269	1453	6	5.4	132.1
7 Nathan Poole, Louisville	11	212	1394	15	6.6	126.7
8 James Hadnot, Texas Tech	11	251	1369	5	5.5	124.5
9 Ted Brown, North Carolina St.	11	302	1350	11	4.5	122.7
10 Jerome Persell, Western Michigan	11	309	1346	6	4.4	122.4

RUSHING/Yards Per Carry	G	ATT	YDS	YPC
1 Billy Sims, Oklahoma	11	231	1762	7.6
2 Nathan Poole, Louisville	11	212	1394	6.6
3 Obie Graves, Cal St.-Fullerton	12	275	1789	6.5
4 Darrin Nelson, Stanford	11	167	1061	6.4
5 Bernell Quinn, Southern Illinois	9	152	939	6.2
6 Frank Mordica, Vanderbilt	**11**	**173**	**1065**	**6.2**
7 Theotis Brown, UCLA	11	200	1199	6.0
8 Emmett King, Houston	11	183	1095	6.0
9 Joe Morris, Syracuse	10	170	1001	5.9
10 Eddie Lee Ivery, Georgia Tech	11	267	1562	5.9

Based on top 38 rushers

RECEIVING	G	REC	YDS	TD	YPR	YPG	RPG
1 Dave Petzke, Northern Illinois	11	91	1217	11	13.4	110.6	8.3
2 Gerald Harp, Western Carolina	11	62	1155	11	18.6	105.0	5.6
2 Emanuel Tolbert, SMU	11	62	1040	11	16.8	94.5	5.6
4 Vernon Henry, Long Beach State	11	60	985	6	16.4	89.5	5.5
4 Rick Beasley, Appalachian State	11	60	971	4	16.2	88.3	5.5
6 David Shula, Dartmouth	9	49	656	1	13.4	72.9	5.4
6 Phil Francis, Stanford	9	49	378	0	7.7	42.0	5.4
8 Cormac Carney, Air Force	11	57	870	8	15.3	79.1	5.2
9 Jeff Groth, Bowling Green	11	56	874	8	15.6	79.5	5.1
10 Jerry Butler, Clemson	11	54	864	3	16.0	78.5	4.9

PUNTING	PUNT	YDS	AVG
1 Maury Buford, Texas Tech	71	3131	44.1
2 Tom Orosz, Ohio State	43	2464	43.9
3 Rick Partridge, Utah	56	1889	43.9
4 Russell Erxleben, Texas	72	3128	43.4
5 Scott Schafer, Air Force	62	2679	43.2
6 Jim Miller, Mississippi	**76**	**3283**	**43.2**
7 Eddie Hare, Tulsa	66	2846	43.1
8 Ray Stachowicz, Michigan State	39	1681	43.1
9 Guy McClure, Utah State	55	2367	43.0
10 Don Clayton, Wyoming	57	2446	42.9

PUNT RETURNS	PUNT	YDS	TD	AVG
1 Ira Matthews, Wisconsin	16	270	3	16.9
2 Richard Ellender, McNeese St.	22	349	3	15.9
3 Kenny Brown, Nebraska	19	278	1	14.6
4 Willie Jordan, Clemson	20	277	0	13.8
5 Gerald Hall, East Carolina	36	478	1	13.3
6 Darrin Nelson, Stanford	20	254	0	12.7
7 Larry Carter, Kentucky	**29**	**354**	**2**	**12.2**
8 Scott Woerner, Georgia	**23**	**279**	**1**	**12.1**
9 James Johnson, Eastern Michigan	24	287	2	12.0
10 Eddie Hood, Vanderbilt	**14**	**166**	**0**	**11.9**

KICKOFF RETURNS	KR	YDS	TD	AVG
1 Drew Hill, Georgia Tech	19	570	2	30.0
2 Howard Ballage, Colorado	18	530	1	29.4
3 Ken Hill, Yale	11	322	1	29.3
4 Jimmy Bryant, Utah State	20	551	1	27.5
5 Theotis Brown, UCLA	16	434	1	27.1
6 Sean McCall, Virginia	19	511	0	26.9
7 Jesse Williams, Richmond	17	455	1	26.8
8 Lindsay Scott, Georgia	**20**	**529**	**1**	**26.4**
9 Charles Fowler, Appalachian State	21	555	0	26.4
10 Ronnie Horton, East Tennessee State	17	447	1	26.3

SCORING	TDS	XPT	FG	PTS	PTPG
1 Billy Sims, Oklahoma	20	0	0	120	10.9
2 Joe Holland, Cornell	16	0	0	96	10.7
3 Joe Cribbs, Auburn	**16**	**2**	**0**	**98**	**9.8**
4 Lester Brown, Clemson	17	0	0	102	9.3
5 Matt Bahr, Penn State	0	31	22	97	8.8
6 Charles Alexander, LSU	**16**	**0**	**0**	**96**	**8.7**
6 Nathan Poole, Louisville	16	0	0	96	8.7
8 Scott McConnell, Appalachian State	14	4	0	88	8.0
8 Willie Todd, Central Michigan	13	2	0	80	8.0
10 James Jones, Mississippi State	**13**	**6**	**0**	**84**	**7.6**

FIELD GOALS	FGA	FGM	PCT	FGG
1 Matt Bahr, Penn State	27	22	0.82	2.00
2 Steve Steinke, Utah State	24	18	0.75	1.64
3 Nathan Ritter, North Carolina St.	19	17	0.90	1.60
3 Doug Dobbs, Arkansas State	22	17	0.77	1.60
5 Berj Yepremian, Florida	**20**	**16**	**0.80**	**1.50**
5 Bill Adams, Texas Tech	20	16	0.80	1.50
5 Dave Jacobs, Syracuse	23	16	0.70	1.50
5 Ed Loncar, Maryland	26	16	0.62	1.50
5 Jim Sturch, Air Force	26	16	0.62	1.50
10 Rex Robinson, Georgia	**17**	**15**	**0.88**	**1.40**
10 Scott Sovereen, Purdue	21	15	0.71	1.40
10 Steven Duncan, San Diego State	23	15	0.65	1.40
10 Rade Savich, Central Michigan	24	15	0.63	1.40

INTERCEPTIONS	INT	YDS	TD	INT/GM
1 Pete Harris, Penn State	10	155	0	0.91
2 Chris Williams, LSU	**8**	**72**	**0**	**0.73**
3 Roland James, Tennessee	**7**	**126**	**1**	**0.70**
4 Arnie Pinkston, Yale	6	27	0	0.67
5 Jeff Nixon, Richmond	7	171	2	0.64
5 Glenn Verrette, Holy Cross	7	164	1	0.64
5 Marty Morrison, North Texas	7	111	1	0.64
5 Darrol Ray, Oklahoma	7	99	0	0.64
5 David Hill, SMU	7	88	2	0.64
5 Kim Anderson, Arizona State	7	44	0	0.64

Team Leaders

RUSHING OFFENSE	G	ATT	YDS	AVG	TD	YPG
1 Oklahoma	11	721	4703	6.5	51	427.5
2 Nebraska	11	699	3715	5.3	40	337.7
3 Texas-Arlington	11	664	3368	5.1	25	306.2
4 Cal St.-Fullerton	12	687	3632	5.3	28	302.7
5 Houston	11	663	3306	5.0	30	300.5
6 Clemson	11	681	3262	4.8	37	296.5
7 Ohio State	11	688	3160	4.6	35	287.3
8 Alabama	**11**	**638**	**3158**	**4.9**	**31**	**287.1**
9 Michigan	11	694	3152	4.5	31	286.5
10 Arkansas	11	677	3119	4.6	34	283.5

PASSING OFFENSE	G	ATT	COM	INT	PCT	YDS	YPA	TD	I%	YPC	YPG
1 SMU	11	391	225	23	57.5	3038	7.8	18	5.9	13.5	276.2
2 Stanford	11	401	251	17	62.6	2947	7.3	24	4.2	11.7	267.9
3 Florida State	11	369	206	16	55.8	2749	7.4	23	4.3	13.3	249.9
4 California	11	345	189	24	54.8	2698	7.8	17	7.0	14.3	245.3
5 New Mexico State	11	341	180	29	52.8	2667	7.8	18	8.5	14.8	242.5
6 Mississippi State	**11**	**311**	**177**	**18**	**56.9**	**2637**	**8.5**	**14**	**5.8**	**14.9**	**239.7**
7 Michigan State	11	340	194	10	57.1	2631	7.7	22	2.9	13.7	239.2
8 Brigham Young	12	416	210	22	50.5	2858	6.9	14	5.3	13.6	238.2
9 Long Beach State	11	369	202	16	54.7	2521	6.8	9	4.3	12.5	229.2
10 Tennessee State	11	305	163	18	53.4	2455	8.0	15	5.9	15.1	223.2

TOTAL OFFENSE	G	P	YDS	AVG	TD	YPG
1 Nebraska	11	897	5515	6.1	53	501.4
2 Oklahoma	11	816	5382	6.6	59	489.3
3 Michigan State	11	838	5294	6.3	54	481.3
4 Clemson	11	866	4804	5.5	44	436.7
5 Stanford	11	886	4791	5.4	38	435.5
6 Furman	11	817	4648	5.7	42	422.5
7 Cal St.-Fullerton	12	863	5053	5.9	36	421.1
8 Houston	11	852	4619	5.4	43	419.9
9 Arizona State	11	905	4566	5.0	41	415.1
10 Missouri	11	820	4557	5.6	45	414.3

RUSHING DEFENSE	G	ATT	YDS	AVG	TD	YPG
1 Penn State	11	408	599	1.5	4	54.5
2 Southern California	12	471	1096	2.3	4	91.3
3 Arizona State	11	494	1074	2.2	13	97.6
4 U.T. Chattanooga	11	463	1098	2.4	11	99.8
5 Ball State	11	472	1124	2.4	4	102.2
6 Tennessee State	11	448	1193	2.7	8	108.5
7 Texas	11	535	1222	2.3	11	111.1
8 Michigan	11	426	1240	2.9	6	112.7
9 Pittsburgh	11	535	1243	2.3	10	113.0
10 Arkansas	11	468	1250	2.7	10	113.6

PASSING DEFENSE	G	ATT	COM	PCT	YPC	INT	I%	YDS	YPA	TD	YPG
1 Boston College	11	155	73	47.1	9.8	10	6.5	716	4.6	3	65.1
2 East Carolina	11	180	70	38.9	12.0	19	10.6	837	4.7	3	76.1
3 Miami (Ohio)	11	213	85	39.9	12.2	15	7.0	1039	4.9	5	94.5
4 Arkansas State	11	172	70	40.7	15.1	13	7.6	1054	6.1	3	95.8
4 Cincinnati	11	207	81	39.1	13.0	14	6.8	1054	5.1	11	95.8
4 William & Mary	11	181	88	48.6	12.0	7	3.9	1054	5.8	7	95.8
7 Northern Illinois	11	175	80	45.7	13.8	16	9.1	1100	6.3	2	100.0
8 Clemson	11	209	96	45.9	11.5	23	11.0	1103	5.3	4	100.3
9 Central Michigan	11	215	81	37.7	13.7	22	10.2	1111	5.2	6	101.0
10 Richmond	11	188	86	45.7	13.0	17	9.0	1114	5.9	10	101.3

TOTAL DEFENSE	G	P	YDS	AVG	TD	YPG
1 Penn State	11	729	2243	3.1	10	203.9
2 East Carolina	11	720	2253	3.1	10	204.8
3 Ball State	11	719	2333	3.2	7	212.1
4 Michigan	11	665	2372	3.6	10	215.6
5 Tennessee State	11	689	2537	3.7	18	230.6
6 Texas A&M	11	716	2630	3.7	20	239.1
7 Central Michigan	11	738	2645	3.6	15	240.5
8 Texas	11	781	2646	3.4	17	240.5
9 Arkansas State	11	698	2668	3.8	15	242.5
10 Arkansas	11	706	2685	3.8	18	244.1

SCORING OFFENSE	G	PTS	AVG
1 Oklahoma	11	440	40.0
2 Nebraska	11	420	38.2
3 Michigan State	11	411	37.4
4 Michigan	11	362	32.9
5 Clemson	11	351	31.9
6 Missouri	11	348	31.6
7 Appalachian State	11	338	30.7
8 Alabama	**11**	**331**	**30.1**
8 Central Michigan	11	331	30.1
10 Houston	11	330	30.0

SCORING DEFENSE	G	PTS	AVG
1 Ball State	11	82	7.5
2 Michigan	11	88	8.0
3 Penn State	11	97	8.8
4 Purdue	11	109	9.9
5 Clemson	11	116	10.5
6 Central Michigan	11	119	10.8
7 Navy	11	120	10.9
8 East Carolina	11	123	11.2
9 Maryland	11	125	11.4
10 Rutgers	11	131	11.9

TURNOVER MARGIN	G	FR	INT	TOT	FL	INTL	TOT	MAR
1 Penn State	11	14	28	42	6	14	20	2.0
2 North Texas	11	21	28	49	22	6	28	1.9
3 McNeese St.	11	20	24	44	14	11	25	1.7
4 Rutgers	11	16	23	39	11	10	21	1.6
4 Clemson	11	15	23	38	15	5	20	1.6

1978

Final Poll (Jan. 3)

UP	AP	SCHOOL	FINAL RECORD
2	1	Alabama	11-1-0
1	2	Southern California	12-1-0
3	3	Oklahoma	11-1-0
4	4	Penn State	11-1-0
5	5	Michigan	10-2-0
6	6	Clemson	11-1-0
6	7	Notre Dame	9-3-0
8	8	Nebraska	9-3-0
9	9	Texas	9-3-0
11	10	Houston	9-3-0
10	11	Arkansas	9-2-1
PB	12	Michigan State	8-3-0
13	13	Purdue	9-2-1
	14	UCLA	8-3-1
14	15	Missouri	8-4-0
15	16	Georgia	9-2-1
16	17	Stanford	8-4-0
19	18	North Carolina St.	9-3-0
18	19	Texas A&M	8-4-0
	20	Maryland	9-3-0
17		Navy	9-3-0
19		Arizona State	9-3-0

PB: Team on probation

Consensus All-Americans

POS	OFFENSE	SCHOOL
QB	Chuck Fusina	Penn State
RB	Billy Sims	Oklahoma
RB	Charles White	Southern California
RB	Ted Brown	North Carolina St.
RB	Charles Alexander	LSU
WR	Emanuel Tolbert	SMU
TE	Kellen Winslow	Missouri
T	Keith Dorney	Penn State
T	Kelvin Clark	Nebraska
G	Pat Howell	Southern California
G	Greg Roberts	Oklahoma
C	Dave Huffman	Notre Dame
C	Jim Ritcher	North Carolina St.

Others receiving first-team honors

QB	Rick Leach	Michigan
WR	Gordon Jones	Pittsburgh
WR	Jerry Butler	Clemson
WR	Kirk Gibson	Michigan State
TE	Mark Brammer	Michigan State
T	Matt Miller	Colorado
K	Tony Franklin	Texas A&M

POS	DEFENSE	SCHOOL
L	Al Harris	Arizona State
L	Bruce Clark	Penn State
L	Hugh Green	Pittsburgh
L	Mike Bell	Colorado State
L	Marty Lyons	Alabama
LB	Bob Golic	Notre Dame
LB	Jerry Robinson	UCLA
LB	Tom Cousineau	Ohio State
B	Johnnie Johnson	Texas
B	Kenny Easley	UCLA
B	Jeff Nixon	Richmond

Others receiving first-team honors

DL	Jimmy Walker	Arkansas
DL	Dan Hampton	Arkansas
DL	Don Smith	Miami (Fla.)
DL	Reggie Kinlaw	Oklahoma
DL	Matt Millen	Penn State
LB	Ken Fantetti	Wyoming
LB	John Corker	Oklahoma State
B	Henry Williams	San Diego State
B	Pete Harris	Penn State
P	Russell Erxleben	Texas

Heisman Trophy Voting

	PLAYER	POS	SCHOOL	TOTAL
1	Billy Sims	HB	Oklahoma	827
2	Chuck Fusina	QB	Penn State	750
3	Rick Leach	QB	Michigan	435
4	Charles White	TB	Southern Cal	354
5	Charles Alexander	TB	LSU	282
6	Ted Brown	RB	North Carolina St.	82
	Steve Fuller	QB	Clemson	82
8	Eddie Lee Ivery	RB	Georgia Tech	81
9	Jack Thompson	QB	Washington State	72
10	Jerry Robinson	LB	UCLA	70

Award Winners

PLAYER	AWARD
Chuck Fusina, QB, Penn State	Maxwell
Greg Roberts, G, Oklahoma	Outland
Billy Sims, RB, Oklahoma	Camp
Bruce Clark, D, Penn State	Lombardi

Bowl Games

DATE	BOWL	SCORE
D16	Garden State	Arizona State 34, Rutgers 18
D16	Independence	East Carolina 35, Louisiana Tech 13
D20	All-American	Texas A&M 28, Iowa State 12
D22	Holiday	Navy 23, Brigham Young 16
D23	Liberty	Missouri 20, LSU 15
D23	Tangerine	North Carolina St. 30, Pittsburgh 17
D23	Sun	Texas 42, Maryland 0
D25	Fiesta	Arkansas 10, UCLA 10
D25	Peach	Purdue 41, Georgia Tech 21
D29	Gator	Clemson 17, Ohio State 15
D31	Bluebonnet	Stanford 25, Georgia 22
J1	Sugar	Alabama 14, Penn State 7
J1	Cotton	Notre Dame 35, Houston 34
J1	Orange	Oklahoma 31, Nebraska 24
J1	Rose	Southern California 17, Michigan 10

SEC Standings

	CONFERENCE			OVERALL		
	W	L	T	W	L	T
Alabama	6	0	0	11	1	0
Georgia	5	0	1	9	2	1
Auburn	3	2	1	6	4	1
LSU	3	3	0	8	4	0
Tennessee	3	3	0	5	5	1
Florida	3	3	0	4	7	0
Mississippi State	2	4	0	6	5	0
Mississippi	2	4	0	5	6	0
Kentucky	2	4	0	4	6	1
Vanderbilt	0	6	0	2	9	0

1979 NCAA Major College Statistical Leaders

Individual Leaders

PASSING	G	ATT	COM	PCT	INT	I%	YDS	YPA	TD	TD%	RATING
1 Turk Schonert, Stanford	11	221	148	67.0	6	2.7	1922	8.7	19	8.6	163.0
2 Brian Broomell, Temple	11	214	120	56.1	11	5.1	2103	9.8	22	10.3	162.3
3 Paul McDonald, Southern California	11	240	153	63.8	5	2.1	1989	8.3	17	7.1	152.6
4 Marc Wilson, Brigham Young	11	427	250	58.6	15	3.5	3720	8.7	29	6.8	147.1
5 Art Schlichter, Ohio State	11	179	94	52.5	5	2.8	1519	8.5	13	7.3	142.2
6 Eric Hipple, Utah State	10	238	144	60.5	6	2.5	1924	8.1	13	5.5	141.4
7 Rich Campbell, California	11	322	216	67.1	12	3.7	2618	8.1	13	4.0	141.2
8 Sam King, Nevada-Las Vegas	11	188	103	54.8	10	5.3	1594	8.5	12	6.4	136.4
9 Mark Hutsell, East Tennessee State	11	302	186	61.6	14	4.6	2276	7.5	17	5.6	134.2
10 Dan Marino, Pittsburgh	9	193	115	59.6	7	3.6	1508	7.8	9	4.7	133.4

ALL-PURPOSE	G	RUSH	REC	PR	KR	YDS	YPG
1 Charles White, Southern California	10	1803	138	0	0	1941	194.1
2 James Brooks, Auburn	**11**	**1208**	**15**	**0**	**577**	**1800**	**163.6**
3 Joe Morris, Syracuse	11	1372	38	0	313	1723	156.6
4 Anthony Collins, East Carolina	11	1130	92	0	473	1695	154.1
5 Freeman McNeil, UCLA	10	1396	140	0	0	1536	153.6
6 George Rogers, South Carolina	11	1548	122	0	0	1670	151.8
7 Homer Jones, Brigham Young	11	546	404	95	579	1624	147.6
8 Billy Sims, Oklahoma	11	1506	42	0	0	1548	140.7
9 Charlie Wysocki, Maryland	9	1140	26	0	96	1262	140.2
10 Rodney Smith, La.-Lafayette	11	782	156	70	506	1514	137.6

RUSHING/Yards Per Game	G	ATT	YDS	TD	AVG	YPG
1 Charles White, Southern California	10	293	1803	18	6.2	180.3
2 George Rogers, South Carolina	11	286	1548	8	5.4	140.7
3 Freeman McNeil, UCLA	10	271	1396	6	5.2	139.6
4 Billy Sims, Oklahoma	11	224	1506	22	6.7	136.9
5 Vagas Ferguson, Notre Dame	11	301	1437	17	4.8	130.6
6 Charlie Wysocki, Maryland	9	247	1140	8	4.6	126.7
7 Joe Morris, Syracuse	11	238	1372	7	5.8	124.7
8 James Hadnot, Texas Tech	11	273	1371	1	5.0	124.6
9 Dennis Mosley, Iowa	11	270	1267	12	4.7	115.2
10 Floyd Allen, VMI	11	265	1249	8	4.7	113.5

RUSHING/Yards Per Carry	G	ATT	YDS	YPC
1 Gwain Durden, U.T. Chattanooga	9	114	885	7.8
2 James Brooks, Auburn	**11**	**163**	**1208**	**7.4**
3 Anthony Collins, East Carolina	11	154	1130	7.3
4 Jarvis Redwine, Nebraska	11	148	1042	7.0
5 Billy Sims, Oklahoma	11	224	1506	6.7
6 Gary Allen, Hawaii	11	162	1032	6.4
7 Charles White, Southern California	10	293	1803	6.2
8 Joe Morris, Syracuse	11	238	1372	5.8
9 Tom Vigorito, Virginia	11	184	1044	5.7
10 Stump Mitchell, Citadel	10	165	925	5.6

Based on top 36 rushers

RECEIVING	G	REC	YDS	TD	YPR	YPG	RPG
1 Rick Beasley, Appalachian State	11	74	1205	12	16.3	109.5	6.7
2 Steve Coury, Oregon State	11	66	842	5	12.8	76.5	6.0
3 James Murphy, Utah State	11	63	1067	6	16.9	97.0	5.7
4 Gerald Harp, Western Carolina	10	57	1009	10	17.7	100.9	5.7
5 Howard Robinson, Lamar	11	59	842	12	14.3	76.5	5.4
6 Mike House, Pacific	10	52	548	2	10.5	54.8	5.2
7 Wayne Baumgardner, Wake Forest	11	55	1000	8	18.2	90.9	5.0
8 Preston Brown, Vanderbilt	**11**	**52**	**786**	**3**	**15.1**	**71.5**	**4.7**
8 Matt Bouza, California	11	52	717	4	13.8	65.2	4.7
10 Earl Cooper, Rice	10	47	463	2	9.9	46.3	4.7

PUNTING	PUNT	YDS	AVG
1 Clay Brown, Brigham Young	43	1950	45.3
2 Mike Smith, Wyoming	70	3125	44.6
3 Jim Miller, Mississippi	**53**	**2362**	**44.6**
4 David Sims, Clemson	72	3198	44.4
5 Ray Stachowicz, Michigan State	62	2749	44.3
6 Steve Cox, Arkansas	42	1840	43.8
7 Casey Murphy, Temple	40	1718	42.9
8 Greg Cater, U.T. Chattanooga	62	2638	42.5
9 Mike Hubach, Kansas	69	2934	42.5
10 Skip Johnston, Auburn	**50**	**2120**	**42.4**

PUNT RETURNS	PR	YDS	TD	AVG
1 Jeffrey Shockley, Tennessee State	27	456	1	16.9
2 Basil Banks, Oklahoma	17	260	0	15.3
3 Raymond Butler, Southern California	21	303	1	14.4
4 Anthony Carter, Michigan	20	265	1	13.2
5 Mark Lee, Washington	21	271	3	12.9
6 Roland James, Tennessee	**19**	**243**	**1**	**12.8**
7 Ken Smith, Rutgers	14	177	0	12.6
8 Kenny Easley, UCLA	27	336	0	12.4
9 Mike Guess, Ohio State	22	273	0	12.4
10 Marcellus Greene, Arizona	15	183	1	12.2

KICKOFF RETURNS	KR	YDS	TD	AVG
1 Stevie Nelson, Ball State	18	565	1	31.4
2 Derek Hughes, Michigan State	16	497	2	31.1
3 James Brooks, Auburn	**21**	**577**	**0**	**27.5**
4 Cedric Jones, Duke	20	542	1	27.1
5 Homer Jones, Brigham Young	22	579	0	26.3
6 Jim Stone, Notre Dame	19	493	0	25.9
7 Danny Miller, Citadel	15	383	1	25.5
8 Dwight Robertson, Oregon	25	632	0	25.3
9 Jeff Washington, VMI	19	477	0	25.1
10 Anthony Allen, Washington	15	376	1	25.1

SCORING	TDS	XPT	FG	PTS	PTPG
1 Billy Sims, Oklahoma	22	0	0	132	12.0
2 Mark Bornholdt, Ball State	19	0	0	114	11.4
3 Charles White, Southern California	18	0	0	108	10.8
4 Vagas Ferguson, Notre Dame	17	0	0	102	9.3
5 Dennis Mosley, Iowa	16	0	0	96	8.7
6 Joe Cribbs, Auburn	**15**	**4**	**0**	**94**	**8.5**
7 Rick Parros, Utah State	15	0	0	90	8.2
8 Vlade Janakievski, Ohio State	0	42	15	87	7.9
9 Wardell Wright, Drake	14	2	0	86	7.8
10 Butch Woolfolk, Michigan	13	0	0	78	7.8

FIELD GOALS	FGA	FGM	PCT	FGG
1 Ish Ordonez, Arkansas	22	18	0.82	1.64
2 Dale Castro, Maryland	21	17	0.81	1.55
2 Bill Adams, Texas Tech	24	17	0.71	1.55
2 John Goodson, Texas	28	17	0.61	1.55
5 Vlade Janakievski. Ohio State	18	15	0.83	1.36
5 Gary Anderson, Syracuse	21	15	0.71	1.36
5 Obed Ariri, Clemson	21	15	0.71	1.36
5 Don Stump, McNeese St.	21	15	0.71	1.36
5 Alan McElroy, Alabama	**22**	**15**	**0.68**	**1.36**
5 Rex Robinson, Georgia	**25**	**15**	**0.60**	**1.36**

INTERCEPTIONS	INT	YDS	TD	INT/GM
1 Joe Callan, Ohio U.	9	110	0	1.00
2 Sharay Fields, New Mexico	10	67	0	0.83
3 Gene Coleman, Miami (Fla.)	9	102	0	0.82
4 Monk Bonasorte, Florida State	8	100	0	0.73
5 Bill Kay, Purdue	7	15	0	0.70
6 Tim Wilbur, Indiana	7	165	2	0.64
6 Ralph Lary, Maryland	7	102	0	0.64
6 Al McCloud, U.T. Chattanooga	7	68	1	0.64
9 Mike Brown, Columbia	5	73	0	0.56
9 Barry Pizor, Dartmouth	5	45	0	0.56
9 Darryl Hemphill, West Texas State	5	35	0	0.56
9 Mike Kachmer, Brown	5	28	0	0.56
9 Chip Kelly, Yale	5	27	0	0.56
9 Dave Chandler, Princeton	5	18	0	0.56

Team Leaders

RUSHING OFFENSE	G	ATT	YDS	AVG	TD	YPG
1 East Carolina	11	692	4053	5.9	47	368.5
2 Oklahoma	11	652	3868	5.9	46	351.6
3 Nebraska	11	715	3796	5.3	35	345.1
4 Alabama	**11**	**763**	**3792**	**5.0**	**38**	**344.7**
5 Texas-Arlington	11	650	3315	5.1	33	301.4
6 Auburn	11	579	3279	5.7	31	298.1
7 Houston	11	653	3257	5.0	29	296.1
8 Central Michigan	11	741	3183	4.3	29	289.4
9 Syracuse	11	656	3071	4.7	26	279.2
10 Southern California	11	569	3043	5.3	30	276.6

PASSING OFFENSE	G	ATT	COM	INT	PCT	YDS	YPA	TD	I%	YPC	YPG
1 Brigham Young	11	464	276	16	59.5	4051	8.7	33	3.4	14.7	368.3
2 San Jose State	11	421	245	15	58.2	3135	7.4	22	3.6	12.8	285.0
3 California	11	370	245	14	66.2	2974	8.0	15	3.8	12.1	270.4
4 Utah State	11	352	197	12	56.0	2949	8.4	22	3.4	15.0	268.1
5 Tennessee St.	11	382	196	20	51.3	2741	7.2	27	5.2	14.0	249.2
6 Lamar	11	404	237	18	58.7	2729	6.8	24	4.5	11.5	248.1
7 Stanford	11	316	198	9	62.7	2466	7.8	25	2.8	12.5	224.2
8 Tulane	11	387	226	15	58.4	2464	6.4	24	3.9	10.9	224.0
9 Wake Forest	11	375	200	17	53.3	2449	6.5	16	4.5	12.2	222.6
10 Western Carolina	11	320	158	22	49.4	2448	7.7	17	6.9	15.5	222.5

TOTAL OFFENSE	G	P	YDS	AVG	TD	YPG
1 Brigham Young	11	832	5735	6.9	59	521.4
2 East Carolina	11	846	5228	6.2	51	475.3
3 Nevada-Las Vegas	12	957	5664	5.9	51	472.0
4 Southern California	11	826	5136	6.2	48	466.9
5 Nebraska	11	899	5113	5.7	46	464.8
6 Temple	11	770	4815	6.3	49	437.7
7 San Jose State	11	836	4795	5.7	42	435.9
8 Utah State	11	825	4727	5.7	45	429.7
9 Alabama	**11**	**875**	**4715**	**5.4**	**44**	**428.6**
10 Oklahoma	11	741	4712	6.4	50	428.4

RUSHING DEFENSE	G	ATT	YDS	AVG	TD	YPG
1 Yale	9	363	675	1.9	5	75.0
2 Nebraska	11	418	1024	2.4	6	93.1
3 Western Michigan	11	435	1091	2.5	7	99.2
4 Michigan	11	443	1092	2.5	8	99.3
5 Alabama	**11**	**393**	**1121**	**2.9**	**2**	**101.9**
6 Texas	11	468	1163	2.5	3	105.7
7 Pittsburgh	11	498	1172	2.4	8	106.5
8 Texas-Arlington	11	471	1213	2.6	10	110.3
9 Central Michigan	11	446	1224	2.7	11	111.3
10 Clemson	11	450	1292	2.9	5	117.5

PASSING DEFENSE	G	ATT	COM	PCT	YPC	INT	I%	YDS	YPA	TD	YPG
1 Western Carolina	11	163	74	45.4	11.5	8	4.9	852	5.2	5	77.5
2 Alabama	**11**	**218**	**78**	**35.8**	**11.0**	**25**	**11.5**	**860**	**3.9**	**5**	**78.2**
3 Texas	11	191	75	39.3	11.5	15	7.9	864	4.5	5	78.5
4 Virginia	11	191	84	44.0	11.6	16	8.4	974	5.1	6	88.5
4 Maryland	11	215	92	42.8	10.6	16	7.4	974	4.5	6	88.5
6 La.-Monroe	11	188	90	47.9	11.3	18	9.6	1014	5.4	5	92.2
7 East Tennessee State	11	191	89	46.6	11.8	10	5.2	1046	5.5	7	95.1
8 Ohio U.	11	185	76	41.1	13.9	17	9.2	1055	5.7	10	95.9
9 Colorado	11	188	76	40.4	14.1	10	5.3	1071	5.7	8	97.4
10 Houston	11	180	84	46.7	13.0	19	10.6	1089	6.1	3	99.0

TOTAL DEFENSE	G	P	YDS	AVG	TD	YPG
1 Yale	9	540	1579	2.9	10	175.4
2 Alabama	**11**	**611**	**1981**	**3.2**	**7**	**180.1**
3 Texas	11	659	2027	3.1	8	184.3
4 Pittsburgh	11	732	2315	3.2	11	210.5
5 Nebraska	11	665	2383	3.6	12	216.6
6 Western Michigan	11	651	2398	3.7	12	218.0
7 Clemson	11	696	2612	3.8	8	237.5
8 Maryland	11	748	2631	3.5	15	239.2
9 Central Michigan	11	689	2646	3.8	17	240.5
10 Florida State	11	715	2669	3.7	18	242.6

SCORING OFFENSE	G	PTS	AVG
1 Brigham Young	11	447	40.6
2 Oklahoma	11	382	34.7
3 East Carolina	11	380	34.5
4 Ohio State	11	374	34.0
5 Southern California	11	372	33.8
6 Temple	11	371	33.7
7 Nebraska	11	366	33.3
8 Alabama	11	359	32.6
9 U.T. Chattanooga	11	349	31.7
10 Utah State	11	347	31.5

SCORING DEFENSE	G	PTS	AVG
1 Alabama	**11**	**58**	**5.3**
2 Texas	11	90	8.2
3 Clemson	11	92	8.4
4 Dartmouth	9	86	9.6
5 Pittsburgh	11	106	9.6
6 Arkansas	11	108	9.8
6 McNeese St.	11	108	9.8
8 Ohio State	11	109	9.9
9 Nebraska	11	114	10.4
10 Yale	9	94	10.4

TURNOVER MARGIN	G	FR	INT	TOT	FL	INTL	TOT	MAR
1 Toledo	11	28	18	46	14	6	20	2.4
2 West Texas State	11	28	14	42	13	10	23	1.7
3 Dartmouth	9	13	14	27	6	6	12	1.7
4 Georgia	**11**	**28**	**21**	**49**	**12**	**20**	**32**	**1.5**
5 Ohio State	11	14	17	31	10	5	15	1.5
6 Drake	11	25	13	38	12	12	24	1.3
7 Alabama	**11**	**14**	**25**	**39**	**18**	**8**	**26**	**1.2**
7 Florida State	11	15	23	38	8	17	25	1.2
7 Southern Miss	11	14	23	37	14	10	24	1.2
7 Stanford	11	18	16	34	12	9	21	1.2

1979

FINAL POLL (JAN. 3)

UP	AP	SCHOOL	FINAL RECORD
1	1	Alabama	12-0-0
2	2	Southern California	11-0-1
3	3	Oklahoma	11-1-0
4	4	Ohio State	11-1-0
5	5	Houston	11-1-0
8	6	Florida State	11-1-0
6	7	Pittsburgh	11-1-0
9	8	Arkansas	10-2-0
7	9	Nebraska	10-2-0
10	10	Purdue	10-2-0
11	11	Washington	9-3-0
13	12	Texas	9-3-0
12	13	Brigham Young	11-1-0
15	14	Baylor	8-4-0
14	15	North Carolina	8-3-1
PB	16	Auburn	8-3-0
17	17	Temple	10-2-0
19	18	Michigan	8-4-0
16	19	Indiana	8-4-0
18	20	Penn State	8-4-0
20		Missouri	7-5-0

PB: Team on probation

CONSENSUS ALL-AMERICANS

POS	OFFENSE	SCHOOL
QB	Marc Wilson	Brigham Young
RB	Charles White	Southern California
RB	Billy Sims	Oklahoma
RB	Vagas Ferguson	Notre Dame
WR	Ken Margerum	Stanford
TE	Junior Miller	Nebraska
T	Greg Kolenda	Arkansas
T	Jim Bunch	Alabama
G	Brad Budde	Southern California
G	Ken Fritz	Ohio State
C	Jim Ritcher	North Carolina St.
PK	Dale Castro	Maryland

OTHERS RECEIVING FIRST-TEAM HONORS

RB	George Rogers	South Carolina
WR	Art Monk	Syracuse
T	Melvin Jones	Houston
T	Tim Foley	Notre Dame

POS	DEFENSE	SCHOOL
L	Hugh Green	Pittsburgh
L	Steve McMichael	Texas
L	Bruce Clark	Penn State
L	Jim Stuckey	Clemson
MG	Ron Simmons	Florida State
LB	George Cumby	Oklahoma
LB	Ron Simpkins	Michigan
LB	Mike Singletary	Baylor
B	Kenny Easley	UCLA
B	Johnnie Johnson	Texas
B	Roland James	Tennessee
P	Jim Miller	Mississippi

OTHERS RECEIVING FIRST-TEAM HONORS

DL	Curtis Greer	Michigan
DL	Jacob Green	Texas A&M
LB	David Hodge	Houston
LB	Dennis Johnson	Southern California
B	Mark Haynes	Colorado

FC named Simmons as a DL

HEISMAN TROPHY VOTING

	PLAYER	POS	SCHOOL	TOTAL
1	Charles White	TB	Southern Cal	1695
2	Billy Sims	HB	Oklahoma	773
3	Marc Wilson	QB	Brigham Young	589
4	Art Schlichter	QB	Ohio State	251
5	Vagas Ferguson	TB	Notre Dame	162
6	Paul McDonald	QB	Southern Cal	92
7	George Rogers	RB	South Carolina	81
8	Mark Herrmann	QB	Purdue	54
9	Ron Simmons	NG	Florida State	41
10	Steadman Shealy	QB	Alabama	31

AWARD WINNERS

PLAYER	AWARD
Charles White, RB, Southern California	Maxwell
Jim Ritcher, C, North Carolina St.	Outland
Charles White, RB, Southern California	Camp
Brad Budde, G, Southern California	Lombardi

BOWL GAMES

DATE	BOWL	SCORE
D15	Independence	Syracuse 31, McNeese St. 7
D15	Garden State	Temple 28, California 17
D21	Holiday	Indiana 38, Brigham Young 37
D22	Tangerine	LSU 34, Wake Forest 10
D22	Liberty	Penn State 9, Tulane 6
D22	Sun	Washington 14, Texas 7
D25	Fiesta	Pittsburgh 16, Arizona 10
D28	Gator	North Carolina 17, Michigan 15
D29	All-American	Missouri 24, South Carolina 14
D31	Peach	Baylor 24, Clemson 18
D31	Bluebonnet	Purdue 27, Tennessee 22
J1	Sugar	Alabama 24, Arkansas 9
J1	Cotton	Houston 17, Nebraska 14
J1	Orange	Oklahoma 24, Florida State 7
J1	Rose	Southern California 17, Ohio State 16

SEC STANDINGS

	CONFERENCE			OVERALL		
	W	L	T	W	L	T
Alabama	6	0	0	12	0	0
Georgia	5	1	0	6	5	0
Auburn	4	2	0	8	3	0
LSU	4	2	0	7	5	0
Tennessee	3	3	0	7	5	0
Kentucky	3	3	0	5	6	0
Mississippi	3	3	0	4	7	0
Mississippi State	2	4	0	3	8	0
Vanderbilt	0	6	0	1	10	0
Florida	0	6	0	0	10	1

1980 NCAA Major College Statistical Leaders

Individual Leaders

PASSING	CL	G	ATT	COM	PCT	INT	I%	YDS	YPA	TD	TD%	RATING
1 Jim McMahon, Brigham Young	JR	12	445	284	63.8	18	4.0	4571	10.3	47	10.6	176.9
2 Joe Adams, Tennessee State	SR	10	333	200	60.1	21	6.3	2848	8.6	30	9.0	149.0
3 John Elway, Stanford	SO	11	379	248	65.4	11	2.9	2889	7.6	27	7.1	147.2
4 Steve Woods, U.T. Chattanooga	JR	10	194	100	51.6	13	6.7	1827	9.4	17	8.8	146.2
5 Mark Herrmann, Purdue	SR	10	340	220	64.7	17	5.0	2923	8.6	19	5.6	145.4
6 Larry Gentry, Nevada-Las Vegas	SR	11	209	113	54.1	16	7.7	1691	8.1	22	10.5	141.5
7 Art Schlichter, Ohio State	JR	11	191	102	53.4	8	4.2	1628	8.5	12	6.3	137.4
8 Ricky Hardin, Utah	SR	11	290	179	61.7	19	6.6	2459	8.5	15	5.2	136.9
9 Tom Flick, Washington	SR	11	280	168	60.0	11	3.9	2178	7.8	15	5.4	135.2
10 Kevin Starkey, Long Beach State	SR	11	248	138	55.7	16	6.5	1955	7.9	19	7.7	134.2

ALL-PURPOSE	CL	G	RUSH	REC	PR	KR	YDS	YPG
1 Marcus Allen, Southern California	JR	10	1563	231	0	0	1794	179.4
2 Rich Diana, Yale	JR	10	1074	212	145	318	1749	174.9
3 Alvin Lewis, Colorado State	SR	11	1047	335	139	400	1921	174.6
4 Herschel Walker, Georgia	**FR**	**11**	**1616**	**70**	**0**	**119**	**1805**	**164.1**
5 George Rogers, South Carolina	SR	11	1781	23	0	0	1804	164.0
6 Gerald Willhite, San Jose State	JR	11	1210	491	0	42	1743	158.5
7 Stump Mitchell, Citadel	SR	11	1647	57	0	0	1704	154.9
8 James Brooks, Auburn	**SR**	**11**	**1314**	**63**	**56**	**226**	**1659**	**150.8**
9 Calvin Murray, Ohio State	SR	11	1192	197	0	236	1625	147.7
10 Anthony Collins, East Carolina	SR	11	503	119	0	990	1612	146.5

RUSHING/Yards Per Game	CL	G	ATT	YDS	TD	AVG	YPG
1 George Rogers, South Carolina	SR	11	297	1781	14	6.0	161.9
2 Marcus Allen, Southern California	JR	10	354	1563	14	4.4	156.3
3 Stump Mitchell, Citadel	SR	11	291	1647	14	5.7	149.7
4 Herschel Walker, Georgia	**FR**	**11**	**274**	**1616**	**15**	**5.9**	**146.9**
5 Jarvis Redwine, Nebraska	SR	9	156	1119	9	7.2	124.3
6 Charlie Wysocki, Maryland	JR	11	334	1359	11	4.1	123.5
7 Freeman McNeil, UCLA	SR	9	203	1105	10	5.4	122.8
8 Cyrus Lawrence, Virginia Tech	SO	10	271	1221	8	4.5	122.1
9 James Brooks, Auburn	**SR**	**11**	**261**	**1314**	**9**	**5.0**	**119.5**
10 Dwayne Crutchfield, Iowa State	JR	11	284	1312	11	4.6	119.3

RUSHING/Yards Per Carry	CL	G	ATT	YDS	YPC
1 Jarvis Redwine, Nebraska	SR	9	156	1119	7.2
2 Calvin Murray, Ohio State	SR	11	185	1192	6.4
3 Dennis Gentry, Baylor	JR	10	147	883	6.0
4 George Rogers, South Carolina	SR	11	297	1781	6.0
5 Herschel Walker, Georgia	**FR**	**11**	**274**	**1616**	**5.9**
6 Kelvin Bryant, North Carolina	SO	11	177	1039	5.9
7 Stump Mitchell, Citadel	SR	11	291	1647	5.7
8 Darrin Nelson, Stanford	JR	10	161	889	5.5
9 Freeman McNeil, UCLA	SR	9	203	1105	5.4
10 Garry White, Minnesota	SR	11	177	959	5.4

Based on top 38 rushers

RECEIVING	CL	G	REC	YDS	TD	YPR	YPG	RPG
1 Dave Young, Purdue	SR	11	67	917	8	13.7	83.4	6.1
2 James Murphy, Utah State	SR	11	66	966	10	14.6	87.8	6.0
3 Keith Chappelle, Iowa	SR	11	64	1037	6	16.2	94.3	5.8
4 Rainey Meszaros, Pacific	JR	12	68	1062	3	15.6	88.5	5.7
5 Mike Jones, Tennessee State	SO	10	55	934	13	17.0	93.4	5.5
5 Cris Crissy, Princeton	SR	10	55	653	3	11.9	65.3	5.5
7 Bart Burrell, Purdue	SR	11	58	888	6	15.3	80.7	5.3
8 Dave Shula, Dartmouth	SR	10	52	758	3	14.6	75.8	5.2
9 Scott Phillips, Brigham Young	SR	12	60	689	7	11.5	57.4	5.0
9 Gerald Harp, Western Carolina	SR	11	55	854	3	15.5	77.6	5.0
9 Gerald Willhite, San Jose State	JR	11	55	491	3	8.9	44.6	5.0

PUNTING	CL	PUNT	YDS	AVG
1 Steve Cox, Arkansas	SR	47	2186	46.5
2 Ray Stachowicz, Michigan State	SR	71	3278	46.2
3 Rohn Stark, Florida State	JR	57	2576	45.2
4 Eric Kaifes, SMU	JR	68	3034	44.6
5 Jim Arnold, Vanderbilt	**SO**	**72**	**3180**	**44.2**
6 Bucky Scribner, Kansas	SO	66	2909	44.1
7 Jack Weil, Wyoming	FR	43	1892	44.0
8 Rick Hanschu, Eastern Michigan	SO	57	2487	43.6
9 Steve Streater, North Carolina	SR	59	2560	43.4
10 Mike Black, Arizona State	SO	53	2299	43.4

PUNT RETURNS	CL	PR	YDS	TD	AVG
1 Scott Woerner, Georgia	**SR**	**31**	**488**	**1**	**15.7**
2 Fulton Walker, West Virginia	SR	21	307	1	14.6
3 Lonell Phea, Houston	JR	17	232	0	13.6
4 Ray Horton, Washington	SO	18	238	1	13.2
5 John Simmons, SMU	SR	27	330	2	12.2
6 John Holt, West Texas State	SR	14	160	2	11.4
7 Darnell Clash, Wyoming	FR	39	433	0	11.1
8 Dave Martin, Villanova	SR	13	144	1	11.1
9 Mardye McDole, Mississippi State	**SR**	**23**	**251**	**1**	**10.9**
10 Eugene Young, Oregon	FR	33	359	0	10.9

KICKOFF RETURNS	CL	KR	YDS	TD	AVG
1 Mike Fox, San Diego State	SO	11	361	0	32.8
2 Anthony Carter, Michigan	SO	14	411	0	29.4
3 Tony Felder, Texas-Arlington	SR	15	424	1	28.3
4 Glen Young, Mississippi State	**SO**	**19**	**525**	**1**	**27.6**
5 Willie Gault, Tennessee	**SO**	**24**	**662**	**3**	**27.6**
6 Anthony Collins, East Carolina	SR	37	990	2	26.8
7 Carlen Charleston, North Texas	FR	22	587	0	26.7
8 David Toloumu, Hawaii	JR	15	391	0	26.1
9 Peter Lavery, Dartmouth	SO	15	382	1	25.5
10 Johnny Smith, Lamar	SR	17	431	0	25.4

SCORING	CL	TDS	XPT	FG	PTS	PTPG
1 Sammy Winder, Southern Miss	JR	20	0	0	120	10.9
2 J.C. Watts, Oklahoma	SR	18	0	0	108	9.8
3 Bill Capece, Florida State	SR	0	38	22	104	9.5
4 Vlade Janakievski, Ohio State	SR	0	45	15	90	9.0
5 Marcus Allen, Southern California	JR	14	0	0	84	8.4
6 Herschel Walker, Georgia	**FR**	**15**	**0**	**0**	**90**	**8.2**
6 Amos Lawrence, North Carolina	SR	15	0	0	90	8.2
6 Roger Craig, Nebraska	SO	15	0	0	90	8.2
9 Obed Ariri, Clemson	SR	0	18	23	87	7.9
10 Stump Mitchell, Citadel	SR	14	2	0	86	7.8
10 Gerald Willhite, San Jose State	JR	14	2	0	86	7.8

FIELD GOALS	CL	FGA	FGM	PCT	FGG
1 Obed Ariri, Clemson	SR	30	23	0.77	2.10
2 Bill Capece, Florida State	SR	30	22	0.73	2.00
3 Harry Oliver, Notre Dame	JR	23	18	0.78	1.64
3 Chuck Nelson, Washington	SO	26	18	0.69	1.64
5 Steve Fehr, Navy	JR	23	17	0.74	1.55
6 Herb Menhardt, Penn State	SR	21	15	0.71	1.50
6 Vlade Janakievski, Ohio State	SR	22	15	0.68	1.50
8 John Cooper, Boston College	JR	21	16	0.76	1.45
8 Rex Robinson, Georgia	**SR**	**22**	**16**	**0.73**	**1.45**
8 Jon Poole, Colorado State	FR	22	16	0.73	1.45
8 Rick Anderson, Purdue	JR	23	16	0.70	1.45

INTERCEPTIONS	CL	INT	YDS	TD	INT/GM
1 Ronnie Lott, Southern California	SR	8	166	1	0.73
1 Steve McNamee, William & Mary	SR	8	125	0	0.73
1 Greg Benton, Drake	SR	8	119	0	0.73
1 Jeff Hipp, Georgia	**SR**	**8**	**104**	**0**	**0.73**
1 Mike Richardson, Arizona State	SO	8	89	2	0.73
1 Vann McElroy, Baylor	JR	8	73	0	0.73
7 Rocky Delgadillo, Harvard	JR	7	130	1	0.70
7 Dave Kimichik, Cornell	JR	7	19	0	0.70
9 Fred Marion, Miami (Fla.)	JR	7	85	0	0.64
9 Gill Byrd, San Jose State	SO	7	69	0	0.64
9 John Simmons, SMU	SR	7	62	2	0.64
9 David Morris, North Texas	SR	7	56	0	0.64

Team Leaders

RUSHING OFFENSE	G	ATT	YDS	AVG	TD	YPG
1 Nebraska	11	739	4161	5.6	45	378.3
2 Oklahoma	11	691	3961	5.7	48	360.1
3 Alabama	**11**	**633**	**3381**	**5.3**	**35**	**307.4**
4 South Carolina	11	620	3291	5.3	35	299.2
5 McNeese St.	11	671	3275	4.9	27	297.7
6 Baylor	11	687	3266	4.8	29	296.9
7 Mississippi State	**11**	**651**	**3135**	**4.8**	**28**	**285.0**
8 Citadel	11	641	3066	4.8	32	278.7
9 Furman	11	595	3021	5.1	24	274.6
10 North Carolina	11	633	2977	4.7	26	270.6

PASSING OFFENSE	G	ATT	COM	INT	PCT	YDS	YPA	TD	I%	YPC	YPG
1 Brigham Young	12	498	317	21	63.7	4918	9.9	49	4.2	15.5	409.8
2 Illinois	11	471	250	15	53.1	3227	6.9	20	3.2	12.9	293.4
3 Purdue	11	375	243	17	64.8	3216	8.6	20	4.5	13.2	292.4
4 Tennessee State	10	346	203	24	58.7	2896	8.4	30	6.9	14.3	289.6
5 Pittsburgh	11	378	196	28	51.9	2952	7.8	25	7.4	15.1	268.4
6 Stanford	11	383	251	12	65.5	2921	7.6	27	3.1	11.6	265.5
7 California	11	381	249	17	65.4	2862	7.5	8	4.5	11.5	260.2
8 La.-Monroe	11	408	213	25	52.2	2828	6.9	18	6.1	13.3	257.1
9 Appalachian State	11	376	190	17	50.5	2781	7.4	15	4.5	14.6	252.8
10 San Jose State	11	368	186	26	50.5	2712	7.4	18	7.1	14.6	246.5

TOTAL OFFENSE	G	P	YDS	AVG	TD	YPG
1 Brigham Young	12	847	6420	7.6	74	535.0
2 Nebraska	11	913	5576	6.1	59	506.9
3 Oklahoma	11	775	4954	6.4	50	450.4
4 Nevada-Las Vegas	11	825	4908	5.9	50	446.2
5 Purdue	11	845	4856	5.7	35	441.5
6 Baylor	11	901	4848	5.4	41	440.7
7 Stanford	11	846	4759	5.6	41	432.6
8 Ohio State	11	812	4703	5.8	45	427.5
9 Utah	11	827	4617	5.6	33	419.7
10 Drake	11	852	4603	5.4	38	418.5

RUSHING DEFENSE	G	ATT	YDS	AVG	TD	YPG
1 Pittsburgh	11	449	718	1.6	3	65.3
2 Yale	10	428	833	1.9	6	83.3
3 Nebraska	11	454	950	2.1	7	86.4
4 Florida State	11	408	984	2.4	2	89.5
5 Southern California	11	413	1064	2.6	6	96.7
6 Virginia Tech	11	473	1126	2.4	4	102.4
7 Baylor	11	460	1160	2.5	7	105.5
8 Notre Dame	11	434	1208	2.8	7	109.8
9 Ohio U.	11	481	1269	2.6	11	115.4
10 Navy	11	471	1284	2.7	9	116.7

PASSING DEFENSE	G	ATT	COM	PCT	YPC	INT	I%	YDS	YPA	TD	YPG
1 Kansas State	11	152	75	49.3	13.4	10	6.6	1005	6.6	8	91.4
2 Iowa State	11	242	86	35.5	11.7	11	4.5	1006	4.2	6	91.5
3 Southern Miss	11	196	94	48.0	11.1	11	5.6	1043	5.3	2	94.8
4 Western Michigan	11	219	92	42.0	11.6	13	5.9	1063	4.9	5	96.6
5 Alabama	**11**	**210**	**93**	**44.3**	**11.8**	**14**	**6.7**	**1093**	**5.2**	**7**	**99.4**
6 Notre Dame	11	234	108	46.2	10.5	9	3.8	1137	4.9	6	103.4
7 LSU	**11**	**226**	**91**	**40.3**	**12.5**	**15**	**6.6**	**1142**	**5.1**	**7**	**103.8**
8 Navy	11	225	109	48.4	10.8	17	7.6	1172	5.2	4	106.5
9 Toledo	11	211	96	45.5	12.4	17	8.1	1189	5.6	5	108.1
9 Northern Illinois	11	199	106	53.3	11.2	13	6.5	1189	6.0	4	108.1

TOTAL DEFENSE	G	P	YDS	AVG	TD	YPG
1 Pittsburgh	11	753	2260	3.0	13	205.5
2 Florida State	11	649	2290	3.5	8	208.2
3 Nebraska	11	713	2300	3.2	10	209.1
4 Notre Dame	11	668	2345	3.5	13	213.2
5 Virginia Tech	11	703	2401	3.4	11	218.3
6 Navy	11	696	2456	3.5	13	223.3
7 Alabama	**11**	**730**	**2487**	**3.4**	**11**	**226.1**
8 Southern California	11	651	2577	4.0	15	234.3
9 Yale	10	670	2427	3.6	14	242.7
10 Southern Miss	11	656	2801	4.3	20	254.6

SCORING OFFENSE	G	PTS	AVG
1 Brigham Young	12	560	46.7
2 Nebraska	11	439	39.9
3 Nevada-Las Vegas	11	384	34.9
4 Oklahoma	11	378	34.4
5 Ohio State	11	368	33.5
6 Florida State	11	352	32.0
7 Tennessee State	10	312	31.2
8 Pittsburgh	11	343	31.2
9 South Carolina	11	339	30.8
10 Washington	11	327	29.7

SCORING DEFENSE	G	PTS	AVG
1 Florida State	11	85	7.7
2 Nebraska	11	93	8.5
3 Alabama	**11**	**96**	**8.7**
4 Virginia Tech	11	109	9.9
5 Navy	11	111	10.1
5 Notre Dame	11	111	10.1
7 Pittsburgh	11	121	11.0
8 Michigan	11	123	11.2
8 North Carolina	11	123	11.2
10 Central Michigan	11	127	11.5
10 Georgia	**11**	**127**	**11.5**

TURNOVER MARGIN	G	FR	INT	TOT	FL	INTL	TOT	MAR
1 Georgia	**11**	**20**	**24**	**44**	**11**	**10**	**21**	**2.1**
1 Ohio State	11	16	25	41	9	9	18	2.1
3 Missouri	11	21	23	44	14	9	23	1.9
4 Florida State	11	19	18	37	6	11	17	1.8
5 Arizona State	11	21	21	42	15	9	24	1.6
6 Drake	11	16	27	43	14	13	27	1.5
7 Florida	**11**	**20**	**18**	**38**	**9**	**15**	**24**	**1.3**
8 Navy	11	14	17	31	11	7	18	1.2
8 Richmond	11	24	13	37	6	18	24	1.2
8 McNeese St.	11	22	23	45	19	13	32	1.2
8 Washington	11	24	16	40	16	11	27	1.2

1980

Final Poll (Jan. 3)

UP	AP	SCHOOL	FINAL RECORD
1	1	**Georgia**	**12-0-0**
2	2	Pittsburgh	11-1-0
3	3	Oklahoma	10-2-0
4	4	Michigan	10-2-0
5	5	Florida State	10-2-0
6	6	**Alabama**	**10-2-0**
7	7	Nebraska	10-2-0
8	8	Penn State	10-2-0
10	9	Notre Dame	9-2-1
9	10	North Carolina	11-1-0
12	11	Southern California	8-2-1
11	12	Brigham Young	12-1-0
14	13	UCLA	9-2-0
13	14	Baylor	10-2-0
15	15	Ohio State	9-3-0
17	16	Washington	9-3-0
16	17	Purdue	9-3-0
18	18	Miami (Fla.)	9-3-0
	19	**Mississippi State**	**9-3-0**
20	20	SMU	8-4-0
19		**Florida**	**8-4-0**

Consensus All-Americans

POS	OFFENSE	SCHOOL
QB	Mark Herrmann	Purdue
RB	George Rogers	South Carolina
RB	**Herschel Walker**	**Georgia**
RB	Jarvis Redwine	Nebraska
WR	Ken Margerum	Stanford
TE	Dave Young	Purdue
L	Mark May	Pittsburgh
L	Keith Van Horne	Southern California
L	Nick Eyre	Brigham Young
L	Louis Oubre	Oklahoma
L	Randy Schleusener	Nebraska
C	John Scully	Notre Dame

Others receiving first-team honors

RB	Freeman McNeil	UCLA
WR	Anthony Carter	Michigan
L	Bill Dugan	Penn State
L	Frank Ditta	Baylor
L	Roy Foster	Southern California
K	**Rex Robinson**	**Georgia**

POS	DEFENSE	SCHOOL
L	Hugh Green	Pittsburgh
L	**E.J. Junior**	**Alabama**
L	Kenneth Sims	Texas
L	Leonard Mitchell	Houston
MG	Ron Simmons	Florida State
LB	Mike Singletary	Baylor
LB	Lawrence Taylor	North Carolina
LB	**David Little**	**Florida**
LB	Bob Crable	Notre Dame
B	Kenny Easley	UCLA
B	Ronnie Lott	Southern California
B	John Simmons	SMU

Others receiving first-team honors

L	Derrie Nelson	Nebraska
L	Hosea Taylor	Houston
L	Scott Zettek	Notre Dame
B	**Scott Woerner**	**Georgia**
P	Rohn Stark	Florida State

Heisman Trophy Voting

	PLAYER	POS	SCHOOL	TOTAL
1	George Rogers	RB	South Carolina	1128
2	Hugh Green	DE	Pittsburgh	861
3	**Herschel Walker**	**TB**	**Georgia**	**683**
4	Mark Herrmann	QB	Purdue	405
5	Jim McMahon	QB	Brigham Young	189
6	Art Schlichter	QB	Ohio State	158
7	Neil Lomax	QB	Portland State	69
8	Jarvis Redwine	RB	Nebraska	64
9	Ken Easley	DB	UCLA	44
10	Anthony Carter	WR	Michigan	34

Award Winners

PLAYER	AWARD
Hugh Green, DE, Pittsburgh	Maxwell
Mark May, OT, Pittsburgh	Outland
Hugh Green, DE, Pittsburgh	Camp
Hugh Green, DE, Pittsburgh	Lombardi

Bowl Games

DATE	BOWL	SCORE
D13	Independence	Southern Miss 16, McNeese State 14
D14	Garden State	Houston 35, Navy 0
D19	Holiday	Brigham Young 46, SMU 45
D20	**Tangerine**	**Florida 35, Maryland 20**
D26	Fiesta	Penn State 31, Ohio State 19
D27	All-American	Arkansas 34, Tulane 15
D27	**Sun**	**Nebraska 31, Mississippi State 17**
D27	Liberty	Purdue 28, Missouri 25
D29	Gator	Pittsburgh 37, South Carolina 9
D31	Bluebonnet	North Carolina 16, Texas 7
J1	**Sugar**	**Georgia 17, Notre Dame 10**
J1	**Cotton**	**Alabama 30, Baylor 2**
J1	Rose	Michigan 23, Washington 6
J1	Orange	Oklahoma 18, Florida State 17
J2	Peach	Miami (Fla.) 20, Virginia Tech 10

SEC Standings

	CONFERENCE			OVERALL		
	W	L	T	W	L	T
Georgia	6	0	0	12	0	0
Alabama*	5	1	0	10	2	0
Mississippi State	2	4	0	9	3	0
Florida	4	2	0	8	4	0
LSU	4	2	0	7	4	0
Tennessee	3	3	0	5	6	0
Mississippi*	2	4	0	3	8	0
Kentucky	1	5	0	3	8	0
Auburn	0	6	0	5	6	0
Vanderbilt	0	6	0	2	9	0

* Alabama-Mississippi game did not count in standings

1981 NCAA Major College Statistical Leaders

Individual Leaders

PASSING	CL	G	ATT	COM	PCT	INT	I%	YDS	YPA	TD	TD%	RATING
1 Jim McMahon, Brigham Young	SR	10	423	272	64.3	7	1.7	3555	8.4	30	7.1	155.0
2 Dan Marino, Pittsburgh	JR	10	339	200	59.0	21	6.2	2615	7.7	34	10.0	144.5
3 Buck Belue, Georgia	**SR**	**11**	**188**	**114**	**60.6**	**9**	**4.8**	**1603**	**8.5**	**12**	**6.4**	**143.8**
4 Tony Eason, Illinois	JR	11	406	248	61.1	14	3.5	3360	8.3	20	4.9	140.0
5 Mike Pagel, Arizona State	SR	11	321	171	53.3	14	4.4	2484	7.7	29	9.0	139.4
6 Scott Campbell, Purdue	SO	11	321	185	57.6	13	4.1	2686	8.4	18	5.6	138.3
7 Sam King, Nevada-Las Vegas	SR	12	433	255	58.9	19	4.4	3778	8.7	18	4.2	137.1
8 Bob Holly, Princeton	SR	10	338	206	61.0	9	2.7	2622	7.8	16	4.7	136.4
9 Doug Flutie, Boston College	FR	9	192	105	54.7	8	4.2	1652	8.6	10	5.2	135.8
10 Jim Kelly, Miami (Fla.)	JR	11	285	168	59.0	14	4.9	2403	8.4	13	4.6	135.0

ALL-PURPOSE	CL	G	RUSH	REC	PR	KR	YDS	YPG
1 Marcus Allen, Southern California	SR	11	2342	217	0	0	2559	232.6
2 Herschel Walker, Georgia	**SO**	**11**	**1891**	**84**	**0**	**92**	**2067**	**187.9**
3 Rich Diana, Yale	SR	10	1442	147	76	205	1870	187.0
4 Darrin Nelson, Stanford	SR	11	1014	846	138	0	1998	181.6
5 Barry Redden, Richmond	SR	10	1629	107	0	0	1736	173.6
6 Larry Van Pelt, Princeton	SR	9	528	400	52	407	1387	154.1
7 Amero Ware, Drake	JR	11	1353	330	0	0	1683	153.0
8 Joe Morris, Syracuse	SR	11	1194	203	0	265	1662	151.1
9 Tim Spencer, Ohio State	JR	11	1121	205	0	307	1633	148.5
10 Buford Jordan, McNeese St.	SO	11	1267	106	0	234	1607	146.1

RUSHING/Yards Per Game	CL	G	ATT	YDS	TD	AVG	YPG
1 Marcus Allen, Southern California	SR	11	403	2342	22	5.8	212.9
2 Herschel Walker, Georgia	**SO**	**11**	**385**	**1891**	**18**	**4.9**	**171.9**
3 Barry Redden, Richmond	SR	10	335	1629	10	4.9	162.9
4 Rich Diana, Yale	SR	10	293	1442	14	4.9	144.2
5 Eddie Meyers, Navy	SR	10	277	1318	8	4.8	131.8
6 Eric Dickerson, SMU	JR	11	255	1428	19	5.6	129.8
7 Cyrus Lawrence, Virginia Tech	JR	11	325	1403	8	4.3	127.5
8 Amero Ware, Drake	JR	11	290	1353	7	4.7	123.0
9 James Bettis, Cincinnati	SR	10	246	1226	6	5.0	122.6
10 Walter Poole, Southern Illinois	SR	9	229	1092	10	4.8	121.3

RUSHING/Yards Per Carry	CL	G	ATT	YDS	YPC
1 Del Rogers, Utah	SR	11	170	1127	6.6
2 Stanley Wilson, Oklahoma	JR	10	156	1008	6.5
3 Buford Jordan, McNeese St.	SO	11	205	1267	6.2
4 Roger Craig, Nebraska	JR	11	173	1060	6.1
5 Curt Warner, Penn State	JR	9	171	1044	6.1
6 Danny Miller, Citadel	SR	11	191	1138	6.0
7 Stanford Jennings, Furman	SO	11	197	1168	5.9
8 Marcus Allen, Southern California	SR	11	403	2342	5.8
9 Butch Woolfolk, Michigan	SR	11	226	1273	5.6
10 Eric Dickerson, SMU	JR	11	255	1428	5.6

Based on top 30 rushers

RECEIVING	CL	G	REC	YDS	TD	YPR	YPG	RPG
1 Pete Harvey, North Texas	SR	9	57	743	3	13.0	82.6	6.3
2 Darrin Nelson, Stanford	SR	11	67	846	5	12.6	76.9	6.1
3 Darius Durham, San Diego State	JR	11	65	988	7	15.2	89.8	5.9
4 Jim Sandusky, Nevada-Las Vegas	JR	12	68	1346	6	19.8	112.2	5.7
5 Gordon Hudson, Brigham Young	SO	12	67	960	10	14.3	80.0	5.6
6 Herbert Harris, Lamar	JR	11	61	911	7	14.9	82.8	5.5
6 Tim Kearse, San Jose State	JR	11	61	842	7	13.8	76.5	5.5
6 Mark Raugh, West Virginia	JR	11	61	585	3	9.6	53.2	5.5
9 Jeff Champine, Colorado State	SO	12	66	882	10	13.4	73.5	5.5
10 Steve Bryant, Purdue	SR	11	60	971	11	16.2	88.3	5.5
10 Jeff Dean, Western Carolina	SR	11	60	839	2	14	76.3	5.5

PUNTING	CL	PUNT	YDS	AVG
1 Reggie Roby, Iowa	JR	44	2193	49.8
2 Rohn Stark, Florida State	SR	64	2941	46.0
3 Tom Striegel, Southern Illinois	SR	60	2752	45.9
4 Scott Vernoy, Cal St.-Fullerton	SR	72	3270	45.4
5 Maury Buford, Texas Tech	SR	78	3493	44.8
6 Mike Horan, Long Beach State	SR	63	2814	44.7
7 Larry Martin, West Texas State	SR	62	2766	44.6
8 Guy McClure, Utah State	SR	62	2758	44.5
9 James Gargus, TCU	FR	59	2608	44.2
10 Malcolm Simmons, Alabama	**SO**	**60**	**2637**	**43.9**

PUNT RETURNS	CL	PR	YDS	TD	AVG
1 Glen Young, Mississippi State	**JR**	**19**	**307**	**2**	**16.2**
2 Keith Humphries, Louisville	FR	16	239	1	14.9
3 John Thomas, TCU	SO	17	244	0	14.4
4 Irving Fryar, Nebraska	SO	24	318	2	13.2
5 Andy Molls, Kentucky	**JR**	**33**	**420**	**1**	**12.7**
6 Willie Gault, Tennessee	**JR**	**31**	**381**	**1**	**12.3**
7 Fred Fernandes, Utah State	SO	28	342	2	12.2
8 Darnell Clash, Wyoming	SO	28	339	1	12.1
9 Greg Poole, North Carolina	JR	29	349	0	12.0
10 Anthony Allen, Washington	JR	15	178	1	11.9

KICKOFF RETURNS	CL	KR	YDS	TD	AVG
1 Frank Minnifield, Louisville	JR	11	334	1	30.4
2 Eric Martin, LSU	**FR**	**18**	**526**	**1**	**29.2**
3 Anthony Carter, Michigan	JR	15	406	0	27.1
4 James Caver, Missouri	JR	14	378	0	27.0
5 Steve Brown, Oregon	JR	26	694	1	26.7
6 Peter Lavery, Dartmouth	JR	13	331	0	25.5
7 Carl Monroe, Utah	JR	21	528	0	25.1
8 Phil Smith, San Diego State	SO	22	553	0	25.1
9 Kent Hagood, South Carolina	FR	21	519	1	24.7
10 Mark Bridgman, Furman	SO	15	368	0	24.5

SCORING	CL	TDS	XPT	FG	PTS	PTPG
1 Marcus Allen, Southern California	SR	23	0	0	138	12.5
2 Herschel Walker, Georgia	**SO**	**20**	**0**	**0**	**120**	**10.9**
3 Eric Dickerson, SMU	JR	19	0	0	114	10.4
4 Buford Jordon, McNeese St.	SO	18	2	0	110	10.0
5 Dwayne Crutchfield, Iowa State	SR	17	2	0	104	9.5
6 Rich Diana, Yale	SR	15	0	0	90	9.0
7 Darrell Shepard, Oklahoma	SR	13	2	0	80	8.9
8 Darrin Nelson, Stanford	SR	16	0	0	96	8.7
9 Kevin Butler, Georgia	**FR**	**0**	**37**	**19**	**94**	**8.5**
10 Luis Zendejas, Arizona State	FR	0	45	16	93	8.5

FIELD GOALS	CL	FGA	FGM	PCT	FGG
1 Bruce Lahay, Arkansas	SR	24	19	0.79	1.73
1 Kevin Butler, Georgia	**FR**	**26**	**19**	**0.73**	**1.73**
1 Larry Roach, Oklahoma State	FR	28	19	0.68	1.73
4 Gary Anderson, Syracuse	SR	19	18	0.95	1.64
4 Eddie Garcia, SMU	SR	22	18	0.82	1.64
4 Brian Clark, Florida	**SR**	**24**	**18**	**0.75**	**1.64**
4 Steve Fehr, Navy	SR	25	18	0.72	1.64
4 Dan Miller, Miami (Fla.)	SR	27	18	0.67	1.64
9 Peter Kim, Alabama	**JR**	**20**	**15**	**0.75**	**1.50**
10 Luis Zendejas, Arizona State	FR	20	16	0.80	1.45
10 Chuck Nelson, Washington	JR	20	16	0.80	1.45

INTERCEPTIONS	CL	INT	YDS	TD	INT/GM
1 Sam Shaffer, Temple	SR	9	76	0	0.90
2 Lou King, Iowa	SR	8	62	0	0.73
3 Butch Lacroix, Houston	JR	7	52	0	0.70
4 Eric Williams, North Carolina St.	JR	7	107	0	0.64
4 Russell Carter, SMU	SO	7	102	0	0.64
4 Martin Bayless, Bowling Green	SO	7	55	1	0.64
4 George Radachowsky, Boston College	SO	7	51	0	0.64
4 Reno Hutchins, Tulsa	SR	7	47	0	0.64
4 William Graham, Texas	SR	7	15	0	0.64
10 Andy Fladung, Illinois State	SO	5	32	0	0.62

Team Leaders

RUSHING OFFENSE	G	ATT	YDS	AVG	TD	YPG
1 Oklahoma	11	656	3677	5.6	36	334.3
2 Nebraska	11	661	3635	5.5	27	330.5
3 Southern California	11	605	3293	5.4	27	299.4
4 SMU	11	659	3226	4.9	33	293.3
5 Georgia	**11**	**656**	**3102**	**4.7**	**29**	**282.0**
6 McNeese St.	11	624	3091	5.0	34	281.0
7 Alabama	**11**	**706**	**3082**	**4.4**	**18**	**280.2**
8 North Carolina	11	626	3019	4.8	32	274.5
9 Michigan	11	572	2973	5.2	28	270.3
10 Arizona State	11	581	2933	5.0	20	266.6
10 Southern Miss	11	603	2933	4.9	30	266.6

PASSING OFFENSE	G	ATT	COM	INT	PCT	YDS	YPA	TD	I%	YPC	YPG
1 Brigham Young	12	538	329	12	61.2	4283	8.0	35	2.2	13.0	356.9
2 Nevada-Las Vegas	12	492	284	22	57.7	4230	8.6	20	4.5	14.9	352.5
3 Illinois	11	409	250	14	61.1	3398	8.3	20	3.4	13.6	308.9
4 San Diego State	11	447	265	15	59.3	3366	7.5	21	3.4	12.7	306.0
5 La.-Monroe	11	495	239	17	48.3	3180	6.4	26	3.4	13.3	289.1
6 Princeton	10	371	224	11	60.4	2826	7.6	20	3.0	12.6	282.6
7 Stanford	11	410	241	14	58.8	3066	7.5	22	3.4	12.7	278.7
8 Vanderbilt	**11**	**476**	**269**	**20**	**56.5**	**3036**	**6.4**	**19**	**4.2**	**11.3**	**276.0**
9 Wake Forest	11	472	286	24	60.6	2986	6.3	20	5.1	10.4	271.5
10 San Jose State	11	407	209	20	51.4	2969	7.3	27	4.9	14.2	269.9

TOTAL OFFENSE	G	P	YDS	AVG	TD	YPG
1 Arizona State	11	908	5486	6.0	49	498.7
2 Nevada-Las Vegas	12	935	5867	6.3	44	488.9
3 Brigham Young	12	931	5764	6.2	59	480.3
4 Georgia	**11**	**865**	**4912**	**5.7**	**42**	**446.5**
5 Stanford	11	885	4880	5.5	40	443.6
6 Nebraska	11	842	4812	5.7	41	437.5
7 San Jose State	11	867	4692	5.4	45	426.5
8 Ohio State	11	865	4677	5.4	45	425.2
9 Wichita State	11	861	4674	5.4	34	424.9
10 Appalachian State	11	832	4645	5.6	29	422.3

RUSHING DEFENSE	G	ATT	YDS	AVG	TD	YPG
1 Pittsburgh	11	406	686	1.7	6	62.4
2 Georgia	**11**	**391**	**797**	**2.0**	**5**	**72.5**
3 San Jose State	11	414	880	2.1	12	80.0
4 Maryland	11	404	923	2.3	4	83.9
5 Iowa	11	421	956	2.3	7	86.9
6 Mississippi State	**11**	**429**	**968**	**2.3**	**6**	**88.0**
7 Clemson	11	421	976	2.3	4	88.7
8 Utah	11	405	995	2.5	13	90.5
9 Ohio State	11	380	1060	2.8	5	96.4
10 Texas	11	477	1062	2.2	9	96.5

PASSING DEFENSE	G	ATT	COM	PCT	YPC	INT	I%	YDS	YPA	TD	YPG
1 Nebraska	11	215	103	47.9	10.7	19	8.8	1101	5.1	3	100.1
2 Northern Illinois	11	195	91	46.7	12.4	14	7.2	1125	5.8	10	102.3
3 West Virginia	11	248	98	39.5	11.7	22	8.9	1148	4.6	5	104.4
4 Kansas	11	237	110	46.4	10.5	15	6.3	1150	4.9	6	104.5
5 Kent State	11	213	104	48.8	11.5	16	7.5	1195	5.6	4	108.6
6 Columbia	10	182	86	47.3	13.2	4	2.2	1139	6.3	6	113.9
7 Southern Miss	11	241	106	44.0	11.8	11	4.6	1254	5.2	7	114.0
8 Missouri	11	275	134	48.7	9.4	18	6.5	1255	4.6	5	114.1
9 Central Michigan	11	232	121	52.2	10.6	11	4.7	1281	5.5	6	116.5
10 Oklahoma	11	240	113	47.1	12.0	13	5.4	1355	5.6	7	123.2

TOTAL DEFENSE	G	P	YDS	AVG	TD	YPG
1 Pittsburgh	11	708	2473	3.5	14	224.8
2 Texas	11	756	2584	3.4	16	234.9
3 Houston	11	703	2592	3.7	11	235.6
4 Central Michigan	11	704	2621	3.7	14	238.3
5 Southern Miss	11	711	2629	3.7	10	239.0
6 Nebraska	11	718	2645	3.7	9	240.5
7 Missouri	11	786	2708	3.4	14	246.2
8 Clemson	11	753	2767	3.7	9	251.5
9 Oklahoma State	11	764	2781	3.6	21	252.8
10 Iowa	11	736	2790	3.8	14	253.6

SCORING OFFENSE	G	PTS	AVG
1 Brigham Young	12	465	38.7
2 Arizona State	11	394	35.8
3 SMU	11	365	33.2
4 Pittsburgh	11	361	32.8
5 Ohio State	11	356	32.4
6 San Jose State	11	355	32.3
7 Georgia	**11**	**352**	**32.0**
8 Nebraska	11	349	31.7
9 Penn State	11	345	31.4
10 North Carolina	11	344	31.3
10 Wyoming	11	344	31.3

SCORING DEFENSE	G	PTS	AVG
1 Southern Miss	11	89	8.1
2 Clemson	11	90	8.2
3 Georgia	**11**	**98**	**8.9**
4 Nebraska	11	103	9.4
5 North Carolina	11	123	11.2
6 Virginia Tech	11	128	11.6
7 Iowa	11	129	11.7
8 Hawaii	11	130	11.8
9 Central Michigan	11	131	11.9
10 Bowling Green	11	132	12.0

TURNOVER MARGIN	G	FR	INT	TOT	FL	INTL	TOT	MAR
1 Tulsa	11	23	25	48	18	6	24	2.2
2 Bowling Green	11	19	19	38	4	12	16	2.0
3 SMU	11	17	31	48	17	10	27	1.9
4 Hawaii	11	21	13	34	7	7	14	1.8
4 Wyoming	11	15	22	37	13	4	17	1.8
6 Southern Illinois	11	23	15	38	10	11	21	1.5
7 Penn State	11	22	20	42	10	16	26	1.5
7 Clemson	11	16	23	39	14	9	23	1.5
7 Texas-Arlington	11	28	14	42	16	10	26	1.5
10 Harvard	10	11	25	36	14	9	23	1.3

1981

FINAL POLL (JAN. 3)

UP	AP	SCHOOL	FINAL RECORD
1	1	Clemson	12-0-0
4	2	Texas	10-1-1
3	3	Penn State	10-2-0
2	4	Pittsburgh	11-1-0
PB	5	SMU	10-1-0
5	6	**Georgia**	**10-2-0**
6	7	**Alabama**	**9-2-1**
PB	8	Miami (Fla.)	9-2-0
8	9	North Carolina	10-2-0
7	10	Washington	10-2-0
9	11	Nebraska	9-3-0
10	12	Michigan	9-3-0
11	13	Brigham Young	11-2-0
13	14	Southern California	9-3-0
12	15	Ohio State	9-3-0
PB	16	Arizona State	9-2-0
18	17	West Virginia	9-3-0
15	18	Iowa	8-4-0
20	19	Missouri	8-4-0
14	20	Oklahoma	7-4-1
16		Arkansas	8-3-0
17		**Mississippi State**	**7-4-0**
19		Southern Miss	9-1-1

PB: Team on probation

CONSENSUS ALL-AMERICANS

POS	OFFENSE	SCHOOL
QB	Jim McMahon	Brigham Young
RB	Marcus Allen	Southern California
RB	**Herschel Walker**	**Georgia**
WR	Anthony Carter	Michigan
TE	Tim Wrightman	UCLA
L	Sean Farrell	Penn State
L	Roy Foster	Southern California
L	Terry Crouch	Oklahoma
L	Ed Muransky	Michigan
L	Terry Tausch	Texas
L	Kurt Becker	Michigan
C	Dave Rimington	Nebraska

OTHERS RECEIVING FIRST-TEAM HONORS

QB	Dan Marino	Pittsburgh
RB	Rich Diana	Yale
RB	Darrin Nelson	Stanford
RB	Curt Warner	Penn State
WR	Stanley Washington	TCU
WR	Julius Dawkins	Pittsburgh
L	David Drechsler	North Carolina
K	Bruce Lahay	Arkansas

POS	DEFENSE	SCHOOL
L	Billy Ray Smith	Arkansas
L	Kenneth Sims	Texas
L	Andre Tippett	Iowa
L	Tim Krumrie	Wisconsin
LB	Bob Crable	Notre Dame
LB	Jeff Davis	Clemson
LB	Sal Sunseri	Pittsburgh
DB	**Tommy Wilcox**	**Alabama**
DB	Mike Richardson	Arizona State
DB	Terry Kinard	Clemson
DB	Fred Marion	Miami (Fla.)
P	Reggie Roby	Iowa

OTHERS RECEIVING FIRST-TEAM HONORS

L	Steve Clark	Utah
L	**David Galloway**	**Florida**
L	Harvey Armstrong	SMU
L	**Glen Collins**	**Mississippi State**
L	Jimmy Williams	Nebraska
L	Jeff Gaylord	Missouri
L	Lester Williams	Miami (Fla.)
LB	**Johnnie Cooks**	**Mississippi State**
LB	Chip Banks	Southern California
DB	Johnny Jackson	Air Force
DB	Steve Cordle	Fresno State
DB	Matt Vanden Boom	Wisconsin
P	Rohn Stark	Florida State

HEISMAN TROPHY VOTING

	PLAYER	POS	SCHOOL	TOTAL
1	Marcus Allen	TB	Southern Cal	1797
2	**Herschel Walker**	**TB**	**Georgia**	**1199**
3	Jim McMahon	QB	Brigham Young	706
4	Dan Marino	QB	Pittsburgh	256
5	Art Schlichter	QB	Ohio State	149
6	Darrin Nelson	RB	Stanford	48
7	Anthony Carter	WR	Michigan	42
8	Kenneth Sims	DT	Texas	34
9	Reggie Collier	QB	Southern Miss	30
10	Rich Diana	RB	Yale	23

AWARD WINNERS

PLAYER	AWARD
Marcus Allen, RB, Southern California	Maxwell
Dave Rimington, C, Nebraska	Outland
Marcus Allen, RB, Southern California	Camp
Kenneth Sims, DT, Texas	Lombardi
Jim McMahon, QB, Brigham Young	O'Brien

BOWL GAMES

DATE	BOWL	SCORE
D12	Independence	Texas A&M 33, Oklahoma State 16
D13	**Garden State**	**Tennessee 28, Wisconsin 21**
D18	Holiday	Brigham Young 38, Washington St. 36
D19	Tangerine	Missouri 19, Southern Miss 17
D19	California	Toledo 27, San Jose State 25
D26	Sun	Oklahoma 40, Houston 14
D28	Gator	North Carolina 31, Arkansas 27
D30	Liberty	Ohio State 31, Navy 28
D31	Bluebonnet	Michigan 33, UCLA 14
D31	**All-American**	**Mississippi State 10, Kansas 0**
D31	**Peach**	**West Virginia 26, Florida 6**
J1	Sugar	Pittsburgh 24, Georgia 20
J1	Orange	Clemson 22, Nebraska 15
J1	Fiesta	Penn State 26, Southern California 10
J1	**Cotton**	**Texas 14, Alabama 12**
J1	Rose	Washington 28, Iowa 0

SEC STANDINGS

	CONFERENCE			OVERALL		
	W	L	T	W	L	T
Georgia	6	0	0	10	2	0
Alabama*	6	0	0	9	2	1
Mississippi State	4	2	0	8	4	0
Tennessee	3	3	0	8	4	0
Florida	3	3	0	7	5	0
Auburn	2	4	0	5	6	0
Kentucky	2	4	0	3	8	0
Mississippi*	1	4	1	4	6	1
LSU	1	4	1	3	7	1
Vanderbilt	1	5	0	4	7	0

* Alabama-Mississippi game did not count in standings

1982 NCAA Major College Statistical Leaders

Individual Leaders

PASSING	CL	G	ATT	COM	PCT	INT	I%	YDS	YPA	TD	TD%	RATING
1 Tom Ramsey, UCLA	SR	11	311	191	61.4	10	3.2	2824	9.1	21	6.8	153.5
2 Alan Risher, LSU	**SR**	**11**	**234**	**149**	**63.7**	**8**	**3.4**	**1834**	**7.8**	**17**	**7.3**	**146.6**
3 John Elway, Stanford	SR	11	405	262	64.7	12	3.0	3242	8.0	24	5.9	145.6
4 Wayne Peace, Florida	**JR**	**11**	**246**	**174**	**70.7**	**10**	**4.1**	**2053**	**8.4**	**8**	**3.3**	**143.4**
5 Ben Bennett, Duke	JR	11	374	236	63.1	12	3.2	3033	8.1	20	5.4	142.5
6 Steve Young, Brigham Young	JR	11	367	230	62.7	18	4.9	3100	8.5	18	4.9	140.0
7 Tim Riordan, Temple	JR	11	247	157	63.6	7	2.8	1840	7.5	13	5.3	137.8
8 Jeff Tedford, Fresno State	SR	11	298	153	51.3	18	6.0	2620	8.8	21	7.1	136.4
9 Ken Vierra, Utah	SO	10	166	85	51.2	6	3.6	1315	7.9	13	7.8	136.4
10 Todd Blackledge, Penn State	JR	11	292	161	55.1	14	4.8	2218	7.6	22	7.5	134.2

ALL-PURPOSE	CL	G	RUSH	REC	PR	KR	YDS	YPG
1 Carl Monroe, Utah	SR	11	1507	108	0	421	2036	185.1
2 Sam DeJarnette, Southern Miss	SO	11	1545	32	0	405	1982	180.2
3 Ernest Anderson, Oklahoma State	JR	11	1877	103	0	0	1980	180.0
4 Herschel Walker, Georgia	**JR**	**11**	**1752**	**89**	**0**	**36**	**1877**	**170.6**
5 Napoleon McCallum, Navy	SO	10	739	196	379	332	1646	164.6
6 Eric Dickerson, SMU	SR	11	1617	60	0	0	1677	152.5
7 Henry Ellard, Fresno State	SR	11	100	1510	-1	44	1653	150.3
8 Mike Rozier, Nebraska	JR	12	1689	46	0	55	1790	149.2
9 Tim Spencer, Ohio State	SR	11	1371	115	0	117	1603	145.7
10 Robert Lavette, Georgia Tech	SO	11	1208	286	0	76	1570	142.7

RUSHING/Yards Per Game	CL	G	ATT	YDS	TD	AVG	YPG
1 Ernest Anderson, Oklahoma State	JR	11	353	1877	8	5.3	170.6
2 Herschel Walker, Georgia	**JR**	**11**	**335**	**1752**	**16**	**5.2**	**159.3**
3 Eric Dickerson, SMU	SR	11	232	1617	17	7.0	147.0
4 Mike Rozier, Nebraska	JR	12	242	1689	15	7.0	140.7
5 Sam DeJarnette, Southern Miss	SO	11	311	1545	14	5.0	140.5
6 Carl Monroe, Utah	SR	11	309	1507	4	4.9	137.0
7 Michael Gunter, Tulsa	JR	11	195	1464	11	7.5	133.1
8 Tim Spencer, Ohio State	SR	11	252	1371	12	5.4	124.6
9 Lawrence Ricks, Michigan	SR	11	243	1300	8	5.3	118.2
10 Robert Lavette, Georgia Tech	SO	11	280	1208	19	4.3	109.8

RUSHING/Yards Per Carry	CL	G	ATT	YDS	YPC
1 Michael Gunter, Tulsa	JR	11	195	1464	7.5
2 Marcus Dupree, Oklahoma	FR	11	129	905	7.0
3 Mike Rozier, Nebraska	JR	12	242	1689	7.0
4 Eric Dickerson, SMU	SR	11	232	1617	7.0
5 Tony Baker, East Carolina	FR	10	126	827	6.6
6 Vincent Jackson, Auburn	**FR**	**10**	**127**	**829**	**6.5**
7 Allen Harvin, Cincinnati	SR	11	191	1161	6.1
8 Thomas Dendy, South Carolina	FR	10	140	848	6.1
9 Willie Joyner, Maryland	JR	10	177	1039	5.9
10 Ken Lacy, Tulsa	SR	11	199	1097	5.5

Based on top 30 rushers

RECEIVING	CL	G	REC	YDS	TD	YPR	YPG	RPG
1 Vincent White, Stanford	SR	10	68	677	8	10.0	67.7	6.8
2 Mike Martin, Illinois	SR	11	69	941	5	13.6	85.5	6.3
3 Darren Long, Long Beach State	SR	11	68	749	3	11.0	68.1	6.2
4 Gordon Hudson, Brigham Young	JR	11	67	928	6	13.9	84.4	6.1
5 Henry Ellard, Fresno State	SR	11	62	1510	15	24.4	137.3	5.6
6 Allama Matthews, Vanderbilt	**SR**	**11**	**61**	**797**	**14**	**13.1**	**72.5**	**5.5**
7 Darral Hambrick, Nevada-Las Vegas	SR	11	60	1060	8	17.7	96.4	5.5
8 Jeff Simmons, Southern California	SR	11	56	973	5	17.4	88.5	5.1
8 Robert Griffin, Tulane	JR	11	56	784	0	14.0	71.3	5.1
8 Norman Jordan, Vanderbilt	**SR**	**11**	**56**	**470**	**3**	**8.4**	**42.7**	**5.1**

PUNTING	CL	PUNT	YDS	AVG
1 Reggie Roby, Iowa	SR	52	2501	48.1
2 Jimmy Colquitt, Tennessee	**SO**	**46**	**2157**	**46.9**
3 Bucky Scribner, Kansas	SR	76	3481	45.8
4 Jim Arnold, Vanderbilt	**SR**	**74**	**3389**	**45.8**
5 Mike Mees, Brigham Young	SR	40	1824	45.6
6 John Kidd, Northwestern	JR	52	2371	45.6
7 Craig James, SMU	SR	66	2963	44.9
8 Ralf Mojsiejenko, Michigan State	SO	77	3434	44.6
9 Mike Black, Arizona State	SR	64	2835	44.3
10 Ron Stowe, Baylor	SR	62	2703	43.6

PUNT RETURNS	CL	PR	YDS	TD	AVG
1 Lionel James, Auburn	**JR**	**25**	**394**	**0**	**15.8**
2 Anthony Carter, Michigan	SR	17	265	1	15.6
3 Irving Fryar, Nebraska	JR	18	277	1	15.4
4 Frank Minnifield, Louisville	SR	11	165	1	15.0
5 Richie Hall, Colorado State	SR	24	320	0	13.3
6 Gerald McNeil, Baylor	JR	16	202	0	12.6
7 Fred Young, New Mexico State	JR	20	244	1	12.2
8 Louis Lipps, Southern Miss	JR	23	280	1	12.2
9 Jack Westbrook, Georgia Tech	JR	21	255	1	12.1
10 Willie Drewrey, West Virginia	SO	25	300	1	12.0

KICKOFF RETURNS	CL	KR	YDS	TD	AVG
1 Carl Monroe, Utah	SR	14	421	1	30.1
2 Vance Johnson, Arizona	SO	13	353	1	27.2
3 Elton Akins, Army	SO	26	701	2	27.0
4 Harry Roberts, Oklahoma State	FR	14	376	0	26.9
5 Dokie Williams, UCLA	SR	17	449	0	26.4
6 Clarence Verdin, La.-Lafayette	SO	12	315	1	26.2
7 Greg Allen, Florida State	SO	20	515	0	25.7
8 Sam DeJarnette, Southern Miss	SO	16	405	1	25.3
9 Allen Pinkett, Notre Dame	FR	14	354	1	25.3
10 Phil Smith, San Diego State	SR	18	450	0	25.0
10 Waymon Aldridge, Nevada-Las Vegas	SR	15	375	0	25.0

SCORING	CL	TDS	XPT	FG	PTS	PTPG
1 Greg Allen, Florida State	SO	21	0	0	126	11.5
2 Robert Lavette, Georgia Tech	SO	19	0	0	114	10.4
3 Paul Woodside, West Virginia	SO	0	26	28	110	10.0
4 Chuck Nelson, Washington	SR	0	34	25	109	9.9
5 Herschel Walker, Georgia	**JR**	**17**	**2**	**0**	**104**	**9.5**
6 Eric Dickerson, SMU	SR	17	0	0	102	9.3
7 Vincent White, Stanford	SR	15	2	0	92	9.2
8 Fuad Reveiz, Tennessee	**SO**	**0**	**20**	**27**	**101**	**9.2**
8 Mike Bass, Illinois	SR	0	32	23	101	9.2
10 Stu Crum, Tulsa	SR	0	37	21	100	9.1

FIELD GOALS	CL	FGA	FGM	PCT	FGG
1 Paul Woodside, West Virginia	SO	31	28	0.90	2.55
2 Fuad Reveiz, Tennessee	**SO**	**31**	**27**	**0.87**	**2.45**
3 Chuck Nelson, Washington	SR	26	25	0.96	2.27
4 Mike Bass, Illinois	SR	26	23	0.89	2.09
5 Luis Zendejas, Arizona State	SO	28	21	0.75	1.91
5 Stu Crum, Tulsa	SR	29	21	0.72	1.91
7 Brooks Barwick, North Carolina	JR	23	20	0.87	1.82
8 Mike Johnston, Notre Dame	JR	22	19	0.86	1.73
9 Mark Fleetwood, South Carolina	JR	18	17	0.94	1.55
9 Kevin Butler, Georgia	**SO**	**21**	**17**	**0.81**	**1.55**
9 Steve Clark, Southern Miss	JR	23	17	0.74	1.55

INTERCEPTIONS	CL	INT	YDS	TD	INT/GM
1 Terry Hoage, Georgia	**JR**	**12**	**51**	**0**	**1.20**
2 Jeff Sanchez, Georgia	**JR**	**9**	**49**	**0**	**0.82**
3 Jeremiah Castille, Alabama	**SR**	**7**	**60**	**0**	**0.78**
4 Leonard Coleman, Vanderbilt	**JR**	**8**	**101**	**0**	**0.73**
5 Dave Duerson, Notre Dame	SR	7	104	0	0.64
5 Sherman Cocroft, San Jose State	JR	7	72	0	0.64
5 Lendell Jones, Maryland	JR	7	48	0	0.64
8 Johnny Rembert, Clemson	SR	6	128	0	0.60
8 Larry Harris, Florida State	JR	6	49	0	0.60
8 Eric Fox, Fresno State	SO	6	32	0	0.60

Team Leaders

RUSHING OFFENSE	G	ATT	YDS	AVG	TD	YPG
1 Nebraska	12	762	4732	6.2	52	394.3
2 Oklahoma	11	696	3724	5.4	34	338.5
3 Tulsa	11	645	3346	5.2	32	304.2
4 Air Force	12	723	3620	5.0	37	301.7
5 Southern Miss	11	644	3131	4.9	32	284.6
6 SMU	11	619	3041	4.9	26	276.5
7 Georgia	**11**	**647**	**3023**	**4.7**	**28**	**274.8**
8 New Mexico	11	564	2998	5.3	29	272.5
9 Alabama	**11**	**636**	**2935**	**4.6**	**29**	**266.8**
10 Wichita State	11	626	2919	4.7	25	265.4

PASSING OFFENSE	G	ATT	COM	INT	PCT	YDS	YPA	TD	I%	YPC	YPG
1 Long Beach State	11	522	300	23	57.5	3595	6.9	19	4.4	12.0	326.8
2 Duke	11	414	258	16	62.3	3349	8.1	23	3.9	13.0	304.5
3 Stanford	11	422	268	13	63.5	3311	7.8	25	3.1	12.4	301.0
4 Illinois	11	453	279	15	61.6	3254	7.2	17	3.3	11.7	295.8
5 Brigham Young	11	385	240	20	62.3	3188	8.3	19	5.2	13.3	289.8
6 UCLA	11	335	205	12	61.2	3070	9.2	23	3.6	15.0	279.1
7 Nevada-Las Vegas	11	420	216	16	51.4	3008	7.2	17	3.8	13.9	273.5
8 San Diego State	12	455	250	18	54.9	3264	7.2	21	4.0	13.1	272.0
9 Pacific	11	493	244	22	49.5	2931	5.9	14	4.5	12.0	266.5
10 Boston College	11	365	173	20	47.4	2924	8.0	16	5.5	16.9	265.8

TOTAL OFFENSE	G	P	YDS	AVG	TD	YPG
1 Nebraska	12	976	6223	6.4	65	518.6
2 Brigham Young	11	797	5128	6.4	46	466.2
3 Florida State	11	825	5123	6.2	51	465.7
4 Duke	11	845	4990	5.9	38	453.6
5 New Mexico	11	801	4822	6.0	47	438.4
6 North Carolina	11	901	4768	5.3	37	433.5
7 UCLA	11	836	4757	5.7	46	432.5
8 Long Beach State	11	867	4738	5.5	30	430.7
9 Air Force	12	890	5099	5.7	43	424.9
10 Penn State	11	812	4652	5.7	43	422.9

RUSHING DEFENSE	G	ATT	YDS	AVG	TD	YPG
1 Virginia Tech	11	379	544	1.4	2	49.5
2 San Jose State	11	405	804	2.0	8	73.1
3 Maryland	11	396	959	2.4	12	87.2
4 LSU	**11**	**406**	**1004**	**2.5**	**6**	**91.3**
5 Pittsburgh	11	367	1029	2.8	6	93.5
6 Arizona State	11	488	1046	2.1	7	95.1
7 Southern California	11	410	1047	2.6	8	95.2
8 Notre Dame	11	414	1050	2.5	9	95.5
9 Arkansas	11	430	1064	2.5	8	96.7
10 Clemson	11	401	1071	2.7	7	97.4

PASSING DEFENSE	G	ATT	COM	PCT	YPC	INT	I%	YDS	YPA	TD	YPG
1 Missouri	11	277	121	43.7	11.2	14	5.1	1358	4.9	7	123.5
2 Kansas	11	201	87	43.3	16.1	7	3.5	1402	7.0	13	127.5
3 New Mexico State	11	244	111	45.5	12.8	13	5.3	1417	5.8	16	128.8
3 Iowa State	11	233	111	47.6	12.8	13	5.6	1417	6.1	8	128.8
5 Arizona State	11	257	115	44.7	12.8	11	4.3	1472	5.7	5	133.8
6 North Carolina	11	284	141	49.6	10.6	10	3.5	1490	5.2	8	135.5
7 Louisville	11	241	122	50.6	12.3	10	4.1	1498	6.2	10	136.2
8 Kansas State	11	283	137	48.4	11.0	19	6.7	1508	5.3	4	137.1
9 Texas Tech	11	227	109	48.0	14.3	15	6.6	1562	6.9	10	142.0
10 Mississippi State	**11**	**236**	**132**	**55.9**	**12.0**	**11**	**4.7**	**1578**	**6.7**	**0**	**143.5**

TOTAL DEFENSE	G	P	YDS	AVG	TD	YPG
1 Arizona State	11	745	2518	3.4	12	228.9
2 North Carolina	11	692	2602	3.8	16	236.5
3 Pittsburgh	11	683	2681	3.9	12	243.7
4 LSU	**11**	**704**	**2707**	**3.8**	**18**	**246.1**
5 Central Michigan	11	731	2731	3.7	18	248.3
6 Arkansas	11	700	2743	3.9	12	249.4
7 Southern California	11	742	2917	3.9	15	265.2
8 Virginia Tech	11	800	3060	3.8	16	278.2
9 Texas	11	767	3081	4.0	18	280.1
10 Notre Dame	11	760	3123	4.1	16	283.9

SCORING OFFENSE	G	PTS	AVG
1 Nebraska	12	493	41.1
2 Florida State	11	388	35.3
3 UCLA	11	375	34.1
4 New Mexico	11	374	34.0
5 Penn State	11	368	33.5
6 LSU	**11**	**365**	**33.2**
7 Brigham Young	11	358	32.5
8 Maryland	11	353	32.1
9 Fresno State	11	352	32.0
10 SMU	11	347	31.5
10 Texas	11	347	31.5

SCORING DEFENSE	G	PTS	AVG
1 Arkansas	11	115	10.5
2 Arizona State	11	124	11.3
3 Pittsburgh	11	132	12.0
4 Georgia	**11**	**133**	**12.1**
5 Nebraska	12	147	12.2
6 North Carolina	11	139	12.6
7 Virginia Tech	11	141	12.8
8 Southern California	11	143	13.0
9 Texas	11	144	13.1
10 Clemson	11	147	13.4

1982

Final Poll (Jan. 3)

UP	AP	SCHOOL	FINAL RECORD
1	1	Penn State	11-1-0
2	2	SMU	11-0-1
3	3	Nebraska	12-1-0
4	4	**Georgia**	**11-1-0**
5	5	UCLA	10-1-1
6	6	Arizona State	10-2-0
7	7	Washington	10-2-0
PB	8	Clemson	9-1-1
8	9	Arkansas	9-2-1
9	10	Pittsburgh	9-3-0
11	11	**LSU**	**8-3-1**
12	12	Ohio State	9-3-0
10	13	Florida State	9-3-0
14	14	**Auburn**	**9-3-0**
PB	15	Southern California	8-3-0
16	16	Oklahoma	8-4-0
18	17	Texas	9-3-0
13	18	North Carolina	8-4-0
19	19	West Virginia	9-3-0
20	20	Maryland	8-4-0
15		Michigan	8-4-0
17		**Alabama**	**8-4-0**

PB: Team on probation

Consensus All-Americans

POS	OFFENSE	SCHOOL
QB	John Elway	Stanford
RB	**Herschel Walker**	**Georgia**
RB	Eric Dickerson	SMU
RB	Mike Rozier	Nebraska
WR	Anthony Carter	Michigan
TE	Gordon Hudson	Brigham Young
L	Don Mosebar	Southern California
L	Steve Korte	Arkansas
L	Jimbo Covert	Pittsburgh
L	Bruce Matthews	Southern California
C	Dave Rimington	Nebraska
PK	Chuck Nelson	Washington

Others receiving first-team honors

WR	Kenny Jackson	Penn State
L	David Drechsler	North Carolina
L	Bill Fralic	Pittsburgh

POS	DEFENSE	SCHOOL
L	Billy Ray Smith	Arkansas
L	Vernon Maxwell	Arizona State
L	**Mike Pitts**	**Alabama**
L	**Wilber Marshall**	**Florida**
L	Gabriel Rivera	Texas Tech
L	Rick Bryan	Oklahoma
MG	George Achica	Southern California
LB	Darryl Talley	West Virginia
LB	Ricky Hunley	Arizona
LB	Marcus Marek	Ohio State
DB	Terry Kinard	Clemson
DB	Mike Richardson	Arizona State
DB	**Terry Hoage**	**Georgia**
P	**Jim Arnold**	**Vanderbilt**

Others receiving first-team honors

L	Mike Charles	Syracuse
L	William Fuller	North Carolina
L	Gary Lewis	Oklahoma State
LB	Mark Stewart	Washington
DB	Dave Duerson	Notre Dame
DB	Mark Robinson	Penn State
DB	**Jeremiah Castille**	**Alabama**

Heisman Trophy Voting

	PLAYER	POS	SCHOOL	TOTAL
1	**Herschel Walker**	**TB**	**Georgia**	**1926**
2	John Elway	QB	Stanford	1231
3	Eric Dickerson	TB	SMU	465
4	Anthony Carter	WR	Michigan	142
5	Dave Rimington	C	Nebraska	137
6	Todd Blackledge	QB	Penn State	108
7	Tom Ramsey	QB	UCLA	65
8	Tony Eason	QB	Illinois	60
9	Dan Marino	QB	Pittsburgh	47
10	Mike Rozier	RB	Nebraska	40
11	Curt Warner	TB	Penn State	40

Award Winners

PLAYER	AWARD
Herschel Walker, RB, Georgia	**Maxwell**
Dave Rimington, C, Nebraska	Outland
Herschel Walker, RB, Georgia	**Camp**
Dave Rimington, C, Nebraska	Lombardi
Todd Blackledge, QB, Penn State	O'Brien

Bowl Games

DATE	BOWL	SCORE
D11	Independence	Wisconsin 14, Kansas State 3
D17	Holiday	Ohio State 47, Brigham Young 17
D18	**Tangerine**	**Auburn 33, Boston College 26**
D18	California	Fresno State 29, Bowling Green 28
D25	Sun	North Carolina 26, Texas 10
D25	Aloha	Washington 21, Maryland 20
D29	**Liberty**	**Alabama 21, Illinois 15**
D30	Gator	Florida State 31, West Virginia 12
D31	**All-American**	**Air Force 36, Vanderbilt 28**
D31	**Bluebonnet**	**Arkansas 28, Florida 24**
D31	**Peach**	**Iowa 28, Tennessee 22**
J1	**Sugar**	**Penn State 27, Georgia 23**
J1	Fiesta	Arizona State 32, Oklahoma 21
J1	**Orange**	**Nebraska 21, LSU 20**
J1	Cotton	SMU 7, Pittsburgh 3
J1	Rose	UCLA 24, Michigan 14

SEC Standings

	CONFERENCE			OVERALL		
	W	L	T	W	L	T
Georgia	6	0	0	11	1	0
LSU	4	1	1	8	3	1
Auburn	4	2	0	9	3	0
Vanderbilt	4	2	0	8	4	0
Tennessee	3	2	1	6	5	1
Alabama	3	3	0	8	4	0
Florida	3	3	0	8	4	0
Mississippi State	2	4	0	5	6	0
Mississippi	0	6	0	4	7	0
Kentucky	0	6	0	0	10	1

1983 NCAA Major College Statistical Leaders

Individual Leaders

PASSING	CL	G	ATT	COM	PCT	INT	I%	YDS	YPA	TD	TD%	RATING
1 Steve Young, Brigham Young	SR	11	429	306	71.3	10	2.3	3902	9.1	33	7.7	168.5
2 Chuck Long, Iowa	JR	10	236	144	61.0	8	3.4	2434	10.3	14	5.9	160.4
3 Mike Eppley, Clemson	JR	11	166	99	59.6	9	5.4	1410	8.5	13	7.8	146.0
4 Cody Carlson, Baylor	FR	11	180	98	54.4	7	3.9	1617	9.0	12	6.7	144.1
5 Rick Neuheisel, UCLA	SR	11	236	163	69.1	10	4.2	1947	8.3	9	3.8	142.5
6 Randall Cunningham, Nevada-Las Vegas	JR	11	316	189	59.8	8	2.5	2545	8.1	18	5.7	141.2
7 Marlon Adler, Missouri	JR	11	175	102	58.3	13	7.4	1603	9.2	11	6.3	141.1
8 Brad Baumberger, Wyoming	SR	12	189	112	59.3	7	3.7	1551	8.2	10	5.3	138.2
9 Jack Trudeau, Illinois	SO	11	324	203	62.7	13	4.0	2446	7.6	18	5.6	136.4
10 Raphel Cherry, Hawaii	JR	11	299	170	56.9	15	5.0	2478	8.3	18	6.0	136.3

ALL-PURPOSE	CL	G	RUSH	REC	PR	KR	YDS	YPG
1 Napoleon McCallum, Navy	JR	11	1587	166	272	360	2385	216.8
2 Mike Rozier, Nebraska	SR	12	2148	106	0	232	2486	207.2
3 Shawn Faulkner, Western Michigan	SR	11	1668	221	0	0	1889	171.7
4 Curtis Adams, Central Michigan	JR	11	1431	86	0	234	1751	159.2
5 Jim Sandusky, San Diego State	SR	12	-15	1171	381	340	1877	156.4
6 Allen Pinkett, Notre Dame	SO	11	1394	288	0	0	1682	152.9
7 Ricky Edwards, Northwestern	SR	11	561	570	0	523	1654	150.4
8 Steve Bartalo, Colorado State	FR	10	1113	284	0	0	1397	139.7
9 Keith Byars, Ohio State	SO	11	1126	338	0	37	1501	136.5
10 Mike Grayson, Duke	SR	11	785	582	110	22	1499	136.3

RUSHING/Yards Per Game	CL	G	ATT	YDS	TD	AVG	YPG
1 Mike Rozier, Nebraska	SR	12	275	2148	29	7.8	179.0
2 Shawn Faulkner, Western Michigan	SR	11	394	1668	7	4.2	151.6
3 Napoleon McCallum, Navy	JR	11	331	1587	10	4.8	144.3
4 Curtis Adams, Central Michigan	JR	11	267	1431	15	5.4	130.1
5 Allen Pinkett, Notre Dame	SO	11	252	1394	16	5.5	126.7
6 Kirby Warren, Pacific	SR	12	304	1423	12	4.7	118.6
7 Reggie Dupard, SMU	SO	11	197	1249	9	6.3	113.5
8 Johnnie Jones, Tennessee	**JR**	**10**	**191**	**1116**	**5**	**5.8**	**111.6**
9 Steve Bartalo, Colorado State	FR	10	292	1113	8	3.8	111.3
10 Bo Jackson, Auburn	**SO**	**11**	**158**	**1213**	**12**	**7.7**	**110.3**

RUSHING/Yards Per Carry	CL	G	ATT	YDS	YPC
1 Mike Rozier, Nebraska	SR	12	275	2148	7.8
2 Bo Jackson, Auburn	**SO**	**11**	**158**	**1213**	**7.7**
3 Earl Johnson, Oklahoma	FR	10	148	945	6.4
4 Reggie Dupard, SMU	SO	11	197	1249	6.3
5 Eric Denson, Wichita State	SO	10	163	1017	6.2
6 Jeff Atkins, SMU	FR	11	154	937	6.1
7 Johnnie Jones, Tennessee	**JR**	**10**	**191**	**1116**	**5.8**
8 Tyrone Anthony, North Carolina	SR	11	184	1063	5.8
9 D.J. Dozier, Penn State	FR	12	174	1002	5.8
10 Ricky Moore, Alabama	**JR**	**11**	**166**	**947**	**5.7**

Based on top 30 rushers

RECEIVING	CL	G	REC	YDS	TD	YPR	YPG	RPG
1 Keith Edwards, Vanderbilt	**JR**	**11**	**97**	**909**	**0**	**9.4**	**82.6**	**8.8**
2 Ricky Edwards, Northwestern	SR	11	83	570	0	6.9	51.8	7.5
3 Tracy Henderson, Iowa State	SO	11	81	1051	8	13.0	95.5	7.4
4 Chuck Scott, Vanderbilt	**JR**	**11**	**70**	**971**	**9**	**13.9**	**88.3**	**6.4**
4 Mark Dowdell, Bowling Green	JR	11	70	679	5	9.7	61.7	6.4
6 Ed Washington, Ohio U.	SR	11	68	866	5	12.7	78.8	6.2
7 Brian Brennan, Boston College	SR	11	67	1168	8	17.4	106.2	6.1
7 Mike Leuck, Ball State	JR	11	67	667	4	10.0	60.6	6.1
9 Mike Grayson, Duke	SR	11	66	582	2	8.8	52.9	6.0
10 Dave Naumcheff, Ball State	SR	11	65	1065	6	16.4	96.8	5.9

PUNTING	CL	PUNT	YDS	AVG
1 Jack Weil, Wyoming	SR	52	2371	45.6
2 Mike Saxon, San Diego State	SR	57	2594	45.5
3 Harry Newsome, Wake Forest	JR	42	1911	45.5
4 Kip Shenefelt, Temple	SO	65	2860	44.0
5 Ralf Mojsiejenko, Michigan State	JR	74	3249	43.9
6 John Teltschik, Texas	SO	63	2753	43.7
7 Dale Hatcher, Clemson	JR	47	2049	43.6
8 Randall Cunningham, Nevada-Las Vegas	JR	56	2436	43.5
9 John Tolish, Duke	JR	53	2300	43.4
10 Paul Calhoun, Kentucky	**JR**	**69**	**2981**	**43.2**

PUNT RETURNS	CL	PR	YDS	TD	AVG
1 Jim Sandusky, San Diego State	SR	20	381	1	19.0
2 Tim Gordon, Tulsa	FR	11	171	1	15.5
3 Tim Moffett, Mississippi	**JR**	**17**	**238**	**1**	**14.0**
4 Jeff Smith, Nebraska	JR	19	264	1	13.9
5 Leonard Harris, Texas Tech	SR	26	346	1	13.3
6 Norman Jefferson, LSU	**FR**	**18**	**238**	**1**	**13.2**
7 Jerry Dunlap, South Carolina	FR	27	354	0	13.1
8 Napoleon McCallum, Navy	JR	21	272	0	13.0
9 Lew Barnes, Oregon	JR	25	323	1	12.9
10 Ed Koban, Syracuse	SR	18	224	0	12.4

KICKOFF RETURNS	CL	KR	YDS	TD	AVG
1 Henry Williams, East Carolina	JR	19	591	2	31.1
2 Cory Collier, Georgia Tech	FR	12	360	0	30.0
3 Randall Morris, Tennessee	**SR**	**15**	**447**	**0**	**29.8**
4 Tim Golden, Long Beach State	SR	15	424	1	28.3
5 Roy Lewis, Cal St.-Fullerton	JR	25	690	0	27.6
6 Tony Mayes, Kentucky	**FR**	**14**	**375**	**0**	**26.8**
7 Eddie Harris, Toledo	SO	11	290	0	26.4
8 Malcolm Pittman, Virginia	JR	20	486	0	24.3
9 Reggie Sutton, Miami (Fla.)	FR	14	332	0	23.7
10 Terrell Smith, Ball State	JR	22	519	0	23.6

SCORING	CL	TDS	XPT	FG	PTS	PTPG
1 Mike Rozier, Nebraska	SR	29	0	0	174	14.5
2 Keith Byars, Ohio State	SO	20	0	0	120	10.9
3 Luis Zendejas, Arizona State	JR	0	28	28	112	10.2
4 Allen Pinkett, Notre Dame	SO	18	2	0	110	10.0
5 Max Zendejas, Arizona	SO	0	39	20	99	9.0
6 Bruce Kallmeyer, Kansas	SR	0	26	24	98	8.9
7 Curtis Adams, Central Michigan	JR	16	0	0	96	8.7
7 Marty Louthan, Air Force	SR	16	0	0	96	8.7
9 Paul Woodside, West Virginia	JR	0	35	19	92	8.4
10 Bob Bergeron, Michigan	SR	0	30	15	75	8.3

FIELD GOALS	CL	FGA	FGM	PCT	FGG
1 Luis Zendejas, Arizona State	JR	37	28	0.76	2.55
2 Bruce Kallmeyer, Kansas	SR	29	24	0.83	2.18
3 Randy Pratt, California	SR	27	22	0.82	2.00
4 Jose Oceguera, Long Beach State	JR	29	22	0.76	1.83
5 Bobby Raymond, Florida	**JR**	**23**	**20**	**0.87**	**1.82**
5 Max Zendejas, Arizona	SO	25	20	0.80	1.82
5 Jeff Jaeger, Washington	FR	26	20	0.77	1.82
8 Paul Woodside, West Virginia	JR	23	19	0.83	1.73
9 Bob Bergeron, Michigan	SR	17	15	0.88	1.67
10 Bob Pauling, Clemson	SR	20	18	0.90	1.64
10 Rocky Costello, Fresno State	SR	22	18	0.82	1.64
10 Kevin Butler, Georgia	**JR**	**23**	**18**	**0.78**	**1.64**
10 Larry Roach, Oklahoma State	JR	26	18	0.69	1.64
10 Alan Smith, Texas A&M	JR	26	18	0.69	1.64

INTERCEPTIONS	CL	INT	YDS	TD	INT/GM
1 Martin Bayless, Bowling Green	SR	10	64	0	0.91
2 Mark Brandon, Toledo	JR	9	66	1	0.82
3 Jim Bowman, Central Michigan	JR	8	87	1	0.73
4 Les Miller, Cal St.-Fullerton	JR	7	233	2	0.70
4 Russell Carter, SMU	SR	7	40	0	0.70
6 Scott Case, Oklahoma	SR	8	110	1	0.67
7 Phil Parker, Michigan State	JR	7	203	1	0.64
7 Ricky Hunley, Arizona	SR	7	123	2	0.64
7 Sherman Cocroft, San Jose State	SR	7	76	0	0.64
7 Kevin Young, Ball State	SR	7	72	0	0.64
7 Kirk Perry, Louisville	JR	7	69	0	0.64
7 Mark Collins, Cal St.-Fullerton	SO	7	52	0	0.64
7 Adam Hinds, Oklahoma State	JR	7	37	0	0.64
7 Clarence Baldwin, Maryland	SR	7	5	0	0.64

Team Leaders

RUSHING OFFENSE	G	ATT	YDS	AVG	TD	YPG
1 Nebraska	12	724	4820	6.7	66	401.7
2 Air Force	11	650	3811	5.9	43	346.5
3 Auburn	**11**	**600**	**3231**	**5.4**	**28**	**293.7**
4 Virginia Tech	11	615	3069	5.0	27	279.0
5 Tulsa	11	598	3052	5.1	28	277.5
6 Central Michigan	11	591	3048	5.2	24	277.1
7 North Carolina	11	600	3046	5.1	24	276.9
8 Michigan	11	614	3042	5.0	28	276.5
9 Oklahoma	12	667	3251	4.9	30	270.9
10 Wyoming	12	711	3239	4.6	33	269.9

PASSING OFFENSE	G	ATT	COM	INT	PCT	YDS	YPA	TD	I%	YPC	YPG
1 Brigham Young	11	458	324	11	70.7	4193	9.2	37	2.4	12.9	381.2
2 Bowling Green	11	480	305	17	63.5	3320	6.9	16	3.5	10.9	301.8
3 Vanderbilt	**11**	**519**	**296**	**31**	**57.0**	**3299**	**6.4**	**14**	**6.0**	**11.1**	**299.9**
4 Kansas	11	407	216	24	53.1	3146	7.7	16	5.9	14.6	286.0
5 Duke	11	480	305	13	63.5	3132	6.5	17	2.7	10.3	284.7
6 Colorado State	12	444	280	20	63.1	3373	7.6	12	4.5	12.0	281.1
7 Iowa	11	315	181	10	57.5	3072	9.8	20	3.2	17.0	279.3
8 California	11	416	234	22	56.2	3057	7.3	14	5.3	13.1	277.9
9 Boston College	11	385	198	18	51.4	2942	7.6	18	4.7	14.9	267.5
10 Stanford	11	420	210	24	50.0	2802	6.7	15	5.7	13.3	254.7

TOTAL OFFENSE	G	P	YDS	AVG	TD	YPG
1 Brigham Young	11	865	6426	7.4	65	584.2
2 Nebraska	12	916	6560	7.2	84	546.7
3 Iowa	11	807	5366	6.6	48	487.8
4 Air Force	11	776	5039	6.5	46	458.1
5 Boston College	11	832	4928	5.9	44	448.0
6 Florida State	11	831	4889	5.9	47	444.5
7 North Carolina	11	865	4860	5.6	41	441.8
8 Utah	11	830	4721	5.7	40	429.2
9 Notre Dame	11	799	4713	5.9	37	428.5
10 Alabama	**11**	**823**	**4665**	**5.7**	**37**	**424.1**

RUSHING DEFENSE	G	ATT	YDS	AVG	TD	YPG
1 Virginia Tech	11	367	763	2.1	4	69.4
2 Illinois	11	422	1034	2.5	5	94.0
3 Michigan	11	360	1051	2.9	5	95.5
4 Texas	11	452	1054	2.3	5	95.8
5 Missouri	11	401	1075	2.7	6	97.7
6 Arizona	11	401	1081	2.7	8	98.3
7 West Virginia	11	401	1099	2.7	10	99.9
8 Oklahoma State	11	437	1122	2.6	5	102.0
9 SMU	11	469	1130	2.4	4	102.7
10 Toledo	11	437	1142	2.6	10	103.8

PASSING DEFENSE	G	ATT	COM	PCT	YPC	INT	I%	YDS	YPA	TD	YPG
1 Ohio U.	11	221	112	50.7	11.3	7	3.2	1268	5.7	5	115.3
2 Texas	11	259	104	40.2	12.3	13	5.0	1278	4.9	5	116.2
3 La.-Lafayette	10	205	93	45.4	12.8	11	5.4	1190	5.8	11	119.0
4 TCU	11	208	90	43.3	15.1	11	5.3	1362	6.5	11	123.8
5 Texas A&M	11	228	110	48.2	12.7	9	3.9	1402	6.1	10	127.5
6 Southern Miss	11	267	131	49.1	11.3	14	5.2	1481	5.5	7	134.6
7 Army	11	250	130	52.0	12.0	7	2.8	1566	6.3	12	142.4
8 Wake Forest	11	267	142	53.2	11.1	11	4.1	1580	5.9	7	143.6
9 Eastern Michigan	11	238	138	58.0	11.6	9	3.8	1603	6.7	10	145.7
10 Wisconsin	11	290	140	48.3	11.8	21	7.2	1656	5.7	13	150.5

TOTAL DEFENSE	G	P	YDS	AVG	TD	YPG
1 Texas	11	711	2332	3.3	10	212.0
2 SMU	11	764	2817	3.7	11	256.1
2 Virginia Tech	11	751	2817	3.8	10	256.1
4 Miami (Fla.)	11	770	2853	3.7	12	259.4
5 Michigan	11	683	2937	4.3	17	267.0
6 Southern Miss	11	768	2981	3.9	14	271.0
7 Oklahoma	12	847	3322	3.9	28	276.8
8 Pittsburgh	11	736	3067	4.2	14	278.8
9 Tennessee	**11**	**756**	**3069**	**4.1**	**13**	**279.0**
10 West Virginia	11	745	3105	4.2	18	282.3

SCORING OFFENSE	G	PTS	AVG
1 Nebraska	12	624	52.0
2 Brigham Young	11	484	44.0
3 Ohio State	11	382	34.7
4 Iowa	11	374	34.0
5 Wisconsin	11	359	32.6
6 Air Force	11	358	32.5
7 Florida State	11	353	32.1
7 Arizona	11	353	32.1
9 Michigan	11	348	31.6
10 Alabama	**11**	**338**	**30.7**
10 Clemson	11	338	30.7
10 Illinois	11	338	30.7

SCORING DEFENSE	G	PTS	AVG
1 Virginia Tech	11	91	8.3
2 Texas	11	104	9.5
3 Miami (Fla.)	11	106	9.6
4 SMU	11	109	9.9
5 Southern Miss	11	128	11.6
6 Central Michigan	11	136	12.4
7 Pittsburgh	11	137	12.5
8 Tennessee	**11**	**142**	**12.9**
9 Oklahoma State	11	148	13.5
10 Georgia	**11**	**149**	**13.5**

1983

Final Poll (Jan. 3)

UP	AP	SCHOOL	FINAL RECORD
1	1	Miami (Fla.)	11-1-0
2	2	Nebraska	12-1-0
3	3	**Auburn**	**11-1-0**
4	4	Georgia	10-1-1
5	5	Texas	11-1-0
6	6	**Florida**	**9-2-1**
7	7	Brigham Young	11-1-0
9	8	Michigan	9-3-0
8	9	Ohio State	9-3-0
10	10	Illinois	10-2-0
PB	11	Clemson	9-1-1
11	12	SMU	10-2-0
15	13	Air Force	10-2-0
14	14	Iowa	9-3-0
12	15	**Alabama**	**8-4-0**
16	16	West Virginia	9-3-0
13	17	UCLA	7-4-1
19	18	Pittsburgh	8-3-1
20	19	Boston College	9-3-0
	20	East Carolina	8-3-0
17		Penn State	8-4-1
18		Oklahoma State	8-4-0

PB: Team on probation

Consensus All-Americans

POS	OFFENSE	SCHOOL
QB	Steve Young	Brigham Young
RB	Mike Rozier	Nebraska
RB	**Bo Jackson**	**Auburn**
RB	Greg Allen	Florida State
RB	Napoleon McCallum	Navy
WR	Irving Fryar	Nebraska
TE	Gordon Hudson	Brigham Young
L	Bill Fralic	Pittsburgh
L	Terry Long	East Carolina
L	Dean Steinkuhler	Nebraska
L	Doug Dawson	Texas
C	Tony Slaton	Southern California
PK	Luis Zendejas	Arizona State

Others receiving first-team honors

WR	Gerald McNeil	Baylor
L	Stefan Humphries	Michigan
L	Brian Blados	North Carolina
L	Conrad Goode	Missouri
C	Tom Dixon	Michigan
PK	Bruce Kallmeyer	Kansas

POS	DEFENSE	SCHOOL
L	Rick Bryan	Oklahoma
L	**Reggie White**	**Tennessee**
L	William Perry	Clemson
L	William Fuller	North Carolina
LB	Ricky Hunley	Arizona
LB	**Wilber Marshall**	**Florida**
LB	Ron Rivera	California
LB	Jeff Leiding	Texas
DB	Russell Carter	SMU
DB	Jerry Gray	Texas
DB	**Terry Hoage**	**Georgia**
DB	Don Rogers	UCLA
P	Jack Weil	Wyoming

Others receiving first-team honors

L	Don Thorp	Illinois
L	Bruce Smith	Virginia Tech
L	**Freddie Gilbert**	**Georgia**
L	Ron Faurot	Arkansas
LB	Chip Banks	Southern California
DB	Mossy Cade	Texas
P	**Jim Colquitt**	**Tennessee**
P	Randall Cunningham	UNLV

Heisman Trophy Voting

	PLAYER	POS	SCHOOL	TOTAL
1	Mike Rozier	RB	Nebraska	1801
2	Steve Young	QB	Brigham Young	1172
3	Doug Flutie	QB	Boston College	253
4	Turner Gill	QB	Nebraska	190
5	**Terry Hoage**	**DB**	**Georgia**	**112**
6	Napoleon McCallum	HB	Navy	104
7	Jeff Hostetler	QB	West Virginia	71
8	Bill Fralic	OT	Pittsburgh	66
9	**Walter Lewis**	**QB**	**Alabama**	**54**
10	Boomer Esiason	QB	Maryland	51

Award Winners

PLAYER	AWARD
Mike Rozier, RB, Nebraska	Maxwell
Dean Steinkuhler, G, Nebraska	Outland
Mike Rozier, RB, Nebraska	Camp
Dean Steinkuhler, G, Nebraska	Lombardi
Steve Young, QB, Brigham Young	O'Brien

Bowl Games

DATE	BOWL	SCORE
D10	**Independence**	**Air Force 9, Mississippi 3**
D17	California	No. Illinois 20, Cal St.-Fullerton 13
D17	**Florida Citrus**	**Tennessee 30, Maryland 23**
D22	**All-American**	**West Virginia 20, Kentucky 16**
D23	Holiday	Brigham Young 21, Missouri 17
D24	**Sun**	**Alabama 28, SMU 7**
D26	Aloha	Penn State 13, Washington 10
D29	Liberty	Notre Dame 19, Boston College 18
D30	**Gator**	**Florida 14, Iowa 6**
D30	Peach	Florida State 28, North Carolina 3
D31	Bluebonnet	Oklahoma State 24, Baylor 14
J2	**Sugar**	**Auburn 9, Michigan 7**
J2	**Cotton**	**Georgia 10, Texas 9**
J2	Orange	Miami (Fla.) 31, Nebraska 30
J2	Fiesta	Ohio State 28, Pittsburgh 23
J2	Rose	UCLA 45, Illinois 9

SEC Standings

	CONFERENCE			OVERALL		
	W	L	T	W	L	T
Florida	5	0	1	9	1	1
LSU	4	1	1	8	3	1
Auburn	4	2	0	9	4	0
Georgia	4	2	0	7	4	1
Kentucky	3	3	0	9	3	0
Tennessee	3	3	0	7	4	1
Vanderbilt	2	4	0	5	6	0
Alabama	2	4	0	5	6	0
Mississippi	1	5	0	4	6	1
Mississippi State	1	5	0	4	7	0

1984 NCAA Major College Statistical Leaders

Individual Leaders

PASSING	CL	G	ATT	COM	PCT	INT	I%	YDS	YPA	TD	TD%	RATING
1 Doug Flutie, Boston College	SR	11	386	233	60.4	11	2.9	3454	9.0	27	7.0	152.9
2 Robbie Bosco, Brigham Young	JR	12	458	283	61.8	11	2.4	3875	8.5	33	7.2	151.8
3 Bernie Kosar, Miami (Fla.)	SO	12	416	262	63.0	16	3.9	3642	8.8	25	6.0	148.7
4 Kerwin Bell, Florida	**FR**	**11**	**184**	**98**	**53.3**	**7**	**3.8**	**1614**	**8.8**	**16**	**8.7**	**148.0**
5 Randall Cunningham, Nevada-Las Vegas	SR	12	332	208	62.7	9	2.7	2628	7.9	24	7.2	147.6
6 Frank Reich, Maryland	SR	9	169	108	63.9	5	3.0	1446	8.6	9	5.3	147.4
7 Chuck Long, Iowa	JR	12	283	187	66.1	13	4.6	2410	8.5	16	5.7	147.1
8 John Dewberry, Georgia Tech	JR	11	205	126	61.5	10	4.9	1846	9.0	11	5.4	145.1
9 Bob DeMarco, Central Michigan	SR	11	173	98	56.7	4	2.3	1427	8.3	12	6.9	144.2
10 Doug Gaynor, Long Beach State	JR	10	385	248	64.4	17	4.4	3230	8.4	16	4.2	139.8

ALL-PURPOSE	CL	G	RUSH	REC	PR	KR	YDS	YPG
1 Keith Byars, Ohio State	JR	11	1655	453	0	176	2284	207.6
2 Ronnie Harmon, Iowa	JR	9	907	318	0	262	1487	165.2
3 Kenneth Davis, TCU	JR	11	1611	200	0	0	1811	164.6
4 Rueben Mayes, Washington State	JR	11	1637	113	0	18	1768	160.7
5 George Adams, Kentucky	**SR**	**11**	**1085**	**330**	**0**	**274**	**1689**	**153.5**
6 George Swarn, Miami (Ohio)	SO	11	1282	187	0	147	1616	146.9
7 Dalton Hilliard, LSU	**JR**	**11**	**1268**	**204**	**0**	**143**	**1615**	**146.8**
8 Darryl Clack, Arizona State	JR	10	1052	385	0	18	1455	145.5
9 Curtis Adams, Central Michigan	SR	10	1204	55	0	168	1427	142.7
10 Ethan Horton, North Carolina	SR	11	1247	254	0	0	1501	136.5

RUSHING/Yards Per Game	CL	G	ATT	YDS	TD	AVG	YPG
1 Keith Byars, Ohio State	JR	11	313	1655	22	5.3	150.5
2 Rueben Mayes, Washington State	JR	11	258	1637	11	6.3	148.8
3 Kenneth Davis, TCU	JR	11	211	1611	15	7.6	146.5
4 Curtis Adams, Central Michigan	SR	10	222	1204	13	5.4	120.4
5 Johnnie Jones, Tennessee	**SR**	**11**	**229**	**1290**	**10**	**5.6**	**117.3**
6 George Swarn, Miami (Ohio)	SO	11	269	1282	5	4.8	116.5
7 Dalton Hilliard, LSU	**JR**	**11**	**254**	**1268**	**13**	**5.0**	**115.3**
8 Ethan Horton, North Carolina	SR	11	238	1247	6	5.2	113.4
9 Robert Lavette, Georgia Tech	SR	11	260	1189	14	4.6	108.1
10 Greg Allen, Florida State	SR	9	133	971	8	7.3	107.9

RUSHING/Yards Per Carry	CL	G	ATT	YDS	YPC
1 Kenneth Davis, TCU	JR	11	211	1611	7.6
2 Greg Allen, Florida State	SR	9	133	971	7.3
3 Doug DuBose, Nebraska	SO	11	156	1040	6.7
4 Rueben Mayes, Washington State	JR	11	258	1637	6.3
5 Reggie Dupard, SMU	JR	11	196	1157	5.9
6 Johnnie Jones, Tennessee	**SR**	**11**	**229**	**1290**	**5.6**
7 Curtis Adams, Central Michigan	SR	10	222	1204	5.4
8 Keith Byars, Ohio State	JR	11	313	1655	5.3
9 Jeff Smith, Nebraska	SR	10	177	935	5.3
10 Ethan Horton, North Carolina	SR	11	238	1247	5.2

Based on top 23 rushers

RECEIVING	CL	G	REC	YDS	TD	YPR	YPG	RPG
1 David Williams, Illinois	JR	11	101	1278	8	12.7	116.2	9.2
2 Charles Lockett, Long Beach State	SO	11	75	1112	4	14.8	101.1	6.8
3 Larry Willis, Fresno State	SR	12	79	1251	8	15.8	104.3	6.6
4 Gerard Phelan, Boston College	SR	11	64	971	3	15.2	88.3	5.8
4 Tracy Henderson, Iowa State	JR	11	64	941	6	14.7	85.5	5.8
6 Willie Smith, Miami (Fla.)	SO	12	66	852	5	12.9	71.0	5.5
7 Steve Griffin, Purdue	JR	11	60	991	4	16.5	90.1	5.5
7 Keith Edwards, Vanderbilt	**SR**	**11**	**60**	**576**	**2**	**9.6**	**52.4**	**5.5**
9 Mark Templeton, Long Beach State	SO	11	59	451	4	7.6	41.0	5.4
10 Bernard White, Bowling Green	JR	11	56	400	0	7.1	36.4	5.1

PUNTING	CL	PUNT	YDS	AVG
1 Ricky Anderson, Vanderbilt	**SR**	**58**	**2796**	**48.2**
2 Bill Smith, Mississippi	**SO**	**44**	**2099**	**47.7**
3 Randall Cunningham, Nevada-Las Vegas	SR	59	2803	47.5
4 Rick Donnelly, Wyoming	SR	63	2993	47.5
5 Tom Tupa, Ohio State	FR	41	1927	47.0
6 Adam Kelly, Minnesota	JR	59	2726	46.2
7 Lee Johnson, Brigham Young	SR	57	2594	45.5
8 Chip Andrews, Georgia	**SR**	**63**	**2860**	**45.4**
9 Buzzy Sawyer, Baylor	SR	72	3226	44.8
10 Paul Calhoun, Kentucky	**SR**	**60**	**2664**	**44.4**

PUNT RETURNS	CL	PR	YDS	TD	AVG
1 Ricky Nattiel, Florida	**SO**	**22**	**346**	**1**	**15.7**
2 Jeff Smith, Nebraska	SR	15	225	0	15.0
3 Shane Swanson, Nebraska	SR	19	275	1	14.5
4 Scott Thomas, Air Force	SO	24	304	0	12.7
5 Ron Milus, Washington	JR	17	211	1	12.4
6 Bob Morse, Michigan State	SO	17	204	1	12.0
7 Harold Young, Rutgers	SR	21	251	0	12.0
8 Erroll Tucker, Utah	JR	22	261	1	11.9
9 Bobby Edmonds, Arkansas	JR	25	294	0	11.8
10 Willie Drewrey, West Virginia	SR	30	343	1	11.4

KICKOFF RETURNS	CL	KR	YDS	TD	AVG
1 Keith Henderson, Texas Tech	FR	13	376	1	28.9
2 Joe Rowley, New Mexico State	FR	15	411	1	27.4
3 Willie Drewrey, West Virginia	SR	20	546	1	27.3
4 Curt Duncan, Northwestern	SO	17	464	1	27.3
5 Larry Jackson, Michigan State	SR	20	522	1	26.1
6 Tony Cherry, Oregon	JR	29	751	0	25.9
7 Vai Sikahema, Brigham Young	JR	15	376	0	25.1
8 Sheldon Gaines, Long Beach State	JR	24	575	1	24.0
9 Derrick McAdoo, Baylor	SO	14	335	0	23.9
10 Ronnie Harmon, Iowa	JR	11	262	0	23.8

SCORING	CL	TDS	XP	FG	PTS	PTPG
1 Keith Byars, Ohio State	JR	24	0	0	144	13.1
2 Allen Pinkett, Notre Dame	JR	18	0	0	108	9.8
3 John Lee, UCLA	JR	0	17	29	104	9.5
4 Bobby Raymond, Florida	**SR**	**0**	**34**	**23**	**103**	**9.4**
4 Chris White, Illinois	JR	0	31	24	103	9.4
6 Rick Badanjek, Maryland	JR	16	6	0	102	9.3
6 Kenneth Davis, TCU	JR	17	0	0	102	9.3
8 Reggie Dupard, SMU	JR	16	0	0	96	8.7
8 Jeff Jaeger, Washington	SO	0	30	22	96	8.7
10 Derek Schmidt, Florida State	FR	0	42	17	93	8.5

FIELD GOALS	CL	FGA	FGM	PCT	FGG
1 John Lee, UCLA	JR	33	29	0.88	2.64
2 Chris White, Illinois	JR	28	24	0.86	2.18
2 Mike Prindle, Western Michigan	SR	30	24	0.80	2.18
4 Bobby Raymond, Florida	**SR**	**26**	**23**	**0.89**	**2.09**
4 Kevin Butler, Georgia	**SR**	**28**	**23**	**0.82**	**2.09**
6 Jeff Jaeger, Washington	SO	28	22	0.79	2.00
7 Max Zendejas, Arizona	JR	27	21	0.78	1.91
7 Richard Spelman, Hawaii	SR	29	21	0.72	1.91
9 Tom Angstadt, Rutgers	SR	28	19	0.68	1.90
10 Fuad Reveiz, Tennessee	**SR**	**23**	**20**	**0.87**	**1.82**

INTERCEPTIONS	CL	INT	YDS	TD	INT/GM
1 Tony Thurman, Boston College	SR	12	99	0	1.09
2 Nate Harris, Tulsa	SR	8	131	0	0.73
2 Bryant Gilliard, South Carolina	SR	8	29	0	0.73
2 Sean Thomas, TCU	SR	8	25	0	0.73
5 Ron Cross, Fresno State	JR	8	132	0	0.67
6 Ashley Lee, Virginia Tech	SR	7	155	0	0.64
6 Paul Calhoun, Kentucky	SR	7	91	0	0.64
6 Jerry Gray, Texas	SR	7	67	0	0.64
9 Rod Brown, Oklahoma State *	SR	6	157	1	0.55
9 DeWayne Bowden, Houston *	SR	6	140	1	0.55

*Eight tied with 0.55; these had the most yards

Team Leaders

RUSHING OFFENSE	G	ATT	YDS	AVG	TD	YPG
1 Army	11	779	3798	4.9	34	345.3
2 Air Force	11	659	3591	5.4	36	326.5
3 Nebraska	11	695	3422	4.9	39	311.1
4 TCU	11	605	3126	5.2	34	284.2
5 Florida State	11	571	3021	5.3	23	274.6
6 Utah	12	674	3263	4.8	34	271.9
7 Auburn	**12**	**673**	**3086**	**4.6**	**33**	**257.2**
8 Wyoming	12	603	3043	5.0	31	253.6
9 Washington State	11	522	2775	5.3	26	252.3
10 Ohio State	11	574	2772	4.8	35	252.0

PASSING OFFENSE	G	ATT	COM	INT	PCT	YDS	YPA	TD	I%	YPC	YPG
1 Brigham Young	12	496	305	13	61.5	4154	8.4	34	2.6	13.6	346.2
2 Miami (Fla.)	12	450	279	17	62.0	3826	8.5	25	3.8	13.7	318.8
3 Boston College	11	392	236	11	60.2	3473	8.9	27	2.8	14.7	315.7
4 Long Beach State	11	431	271	20	62.9	3423	7.9	16	4.6	12.6	311.2
5 Illinois	11	423	276	10	65.2	3130	7.4	22	2.4	11.3	284.5
6 Fresno State	12	432	233	13	53.9	3380	7.8	23	3.0	14.5	281.7
7 Purdue	11	398	229	14	57.5	3019	7.6	15	3.5	13.2	274.5
8 Bowling Green	11	416	265	13	63.7	2960	7.1	21	3.1	11.2	269.1
9 Vanderbilt	**11**	**437**	**246**	**16**	**56.3**	**2920**	**6.7**	**20**	**3.7**	**11.9**	**265.5**
10 Louisville	11	428	211	39	49.3	2823	6.6	19	9.1	13.4	256.6

TOTAL OFFENSE	G	P	YDS	AVG	TD	YPG
1 Brigham Young	12	902	5838	6.5	55	486.5
2 Boston College	11	825	5317	6.4	50	483.4
3 TCU	11	835	5103	6.1	47	463.9
4 Florida State	11	807	4959	6.1	42	450.8
5 Miami (Fla.)	12	865	5367	6.2	45	447.2
6 Maryland	11	828	4910	5.9	43	446.4
7 Illinois	11	875	4860	5.6	35	441.8
8 Ohio State	11	820	4803	5.9	47	436.6
9 South Carolina	11	794	4797	6.0	46	436.1
10 Washington State	11	803	4762	5.9	40	432.9

RUSHING DEFENSE	G	ATT	YDS	AVG	TD	YPG
1 Oklahoma	11	386	757	2.0	4	68.8
2 Virginia Tech	11	437	787	1.8	7	71.5
3 Arizona	11	383	831	2.2	9	75.5
4 Nebraska	11	438	867	2.0	6	78.8
5 Cal St.-Fullerton	12	426	1183	2.8	8	98.6
6 Iowa	12	439	1193	2.7	7	99.4
7 Central Michigan	11	424	1102	2.6	5	100.2
8 Southern California	11	398	1138	2.9	6	103.5
9 Toledo	11	411	1181	2.9	6	107.4
10 Baylor	11	467	1243	2.7	15	113.0

PASSING DEFENSE	G	ATT	COM	PCT	YPC	INT	I%	YDS	YPA	TD	YPG
1 Texas Tech	11	196	89	45.4	14.2	12	6.1	1263	6.4	9	114.8
2 Wichita State	11	221	109	49.3	11.7	9	4.1	1278	5.8	9	116.2
3 Syracuse	11	220	108	49.1	12.1	10	4.5	1312	6.0	4	119.3
4 Memphis	11	227	95	41.9	14.2	11	4.8	1349	5.9	10	122.6
5 Nebraska	11	256	115	44.9	11.9	16	6.3	1369	5.3	7	124.5
6 La.-Lafayette	11	260	116	44.6	12.6	8	3.1	1456	5.6	10	132.4
7 Iowa State	11	222	102	45.9	14.7	8	3.6	1497	6.7	16	136.1
8 Colorado	11	198	114	57.6	13.3	3	1.5	1519	7.7	13	138.1
9 Arizona State	11	275	131	47.6	11.8	12	4.4	1550	5.6	10	140.9
10 California	11	206	105	51.0	14.8	7	3.4	1556	7.6	16	141.5

TOTAL DEFENSE	G	P	YDS	AVG	TD	YPG
1 Nebraska	11	694	2236	3.2	13	203.3
2 Oklahoma	11	726	2477	3.4	13	225.2
3 Virginia Tech	11	772	2574	3.3	14	234.0
4 Central Michigan	11	746	2899	3.9	14	263.5
5 Toledo	11	745	2908	3.9	12	264.4
6 Syracuse	11	698	2967	4.3	14	269.7
7 Iowa	12	790	3239	4.1	20	269.9
8 Oklahoma State	11	774	2989	3.9	14	271.7
9 Washington	11	798	3050	3.8	13	277.3
10 Memphis	11	734	3060	4.2	22	278.2

SCORING OFFENSE	G	PTS	AVG
1 Boston College	11	404	36.7
2 Brigham Young	12	432	36.0
3 Florida State	11	389	35.4
4 Ohio State	11	374	34.0
5 TCU	11	362	32.9
6 Nebraska	11	359	32.6
7 South Carolina	11	357	32.5
8 Maryland	11	352	32.0
9 Clemson	11	346	31.5
9 Air Force	11	346	31.5

SCORING DEFENSE	G	PTS	AVG
1 Nebraska	11	105	9.5
2 Virginia Tech	11	127	11.5
3 Washington	11	128	11.6
4 Toledo	11	134	12.2
4 Oklahoma State	11	134	12.2
6 Oklahoma	11	136	12.4
7 Arkansas	11	138	12.5
8 Central Michigan	11	141	12.8
9 Syracuse	11	151	13.7
10 Brigham Young	12	166	13.8

1984

FINAL POLL (JAN. 3)

UPI	AP	SCHOOL	FINAL RECORD
1	1	Brigham Young	13-0-0
2	2	Washington	11-1-0
7	3	**Florida**	**9-1-1**
3	4	Nebraska	10-2-0
4	5	Boston College	10-2-0
6	6	Oklahoma	9-2-1
5	7	Oklahoma State	10-2-0
8	8	SMU	10-2-0
10	9	UCLA	9-3-0
9	10	Southern California	9-3-0
13	11	South Carolina	10-2-0
11	12	Maryland	9-3-0
12	13	Ohio State	9-3-0
14	14	**Auburn**	**9-4-0**
16	15	**LSU**	**8-3-1**
15	16	Iowa	8-4-1
19	17	Florida State	7-3-2
	18	Miami (Fla.)	8-5-0
19	19	**Kentucky**	**9-3-0**
17	20	Virginia	8-2-2
18		West Virginia	8-4-0

CONSENSUS ALL-AMERICANS

POS	OFFENSE	SCHOOL
QB	Doug Flutie	Boston College
RB	Keith Byars	Ohio State
RB	Kenneth Davis	TCU
RB	Rueben Mayes	Washington State
WR	David Williams	Illinois
WR	Eddie Brown	Miami (Fla.)
TE	Jay Novacek	Wyoming
T	Bill Fralic	Pittsburgh
T	**Lomas Brown**	**Florida**
G	Del Wilkes	South Carolina
G	Jim Lachey	Ohio State
G	**Bill Mayo**	**Tennessee**
C	Mark Traynowicz	Nebraska
PK	**Kevin Butler**	**Georgia**

OTHERS RECEIVING FIRST-TEAM HONORS

RB	Greg Allen	Florida State
WR	Jerry Rice	Mississippi Valley State
TE	Rob Bennett	West Virginia
TE	Mark Bavaro	Notre Dame
L	Carlton Walker	Utah
L	**Lance Smith**	**LSU**
L	Dan Lynch	Washington State
PK	John Lee	UCLA

POS	DEFENSE	SCHOOL
DL	Bruce Smith	Virginia Tech
DL	Tony Degrate	Texas
DL	Ron Holmes	Washington
DL	Tony Casillas	Oklahoma
LB	**Gregg Carr**	**Auburn**
LB	Jack Del Rio	Southern California
LB	Larry Station	Iowa
DB	Jerry Gray	Texas
DB	Tony Thurman	Boston College
DB	**Jeff Sanchez**	**Georgia**
DB	David Fulcher	Arizona State
DB	Rod Brown	Oklahoma State
P	**Ricky Anderson**	**Vanderbilt**

OTHERS RECEIVING FIRST-TEAM HONORS

DL	William Perry	Clemson
DL	Leslie O'Neal	Oklahoma State
DL	Ray Childress	Texas A&M
DL	**Fred Nunn**	**Mississippi**
LB	Duane Bickett	Southern California
LB	James Seawright	South Carolina
DB	Bret Clark	Nebraska
DB	Richard Johnson	Wisconsin
DB	Kyle Morrell	Brigham Young

HEISMAN TROPHY VOTING

	PLAYER	POS	SCHOOL	TOTAL
1	Doug Flutie	QB	Boston College	2240
2	Keith Byars	TB	Ohio State	1251
3	Robbie Bosco	QB	Brigham Young	443
4	Bernie Kosar	QB	Miami (Fla.)	320
5	Kenneth Davis	RB	TCU	86
6	Bill Fralic	OT	Pittsburgh	81
7	Chuck Long	QB	Iowa	37
8	Greg Allen	RB	Florida State	37
9	Jerry Rice	WR	Mississippi Valley State	36
10	Rueben Mayes	RB	Washington State	32

AWARD WINNERS

PLAYER	AWARD
Doug Flutie, QB, Boston College	Maxwell
Bruce Smith, DT, Virginia Tech	Outland
Doug Flutie, QB, Boston College	Camp
Tony Degrate, DT, Texas	Lombardi
Doug Flutie, QB, Boston College	O'Brien

BOWL GAMES

DATE	BOWL	SCORE
D15	Independence	Air Force 23, Virginia Tech 7
D15	California	Nevada-Las Vegas 30, Toledo 13
D21	Holiday	Brigham Young 24, Michigan 17
D22	Cherry	Army 10, Michigan State 6
D22	**Florida Citrus**	**Florida State 17, Georgia 17**
D22	**Sun**	**Maryland 28, Tennessee 27**
D26	Freedom	Iowa 55, Texas 17
D27	**Liberty**	**Auburn 21, Arkansas 15**
D28	Gator	Oklahoma State 21, South Carolina 14
D29	**All-American**	**Kentucky 20, Wisconsin 19**
D29	Aloha	SMU 27, Notre Dame 20
D31	Peach	Virginia 27, Purdue 24
D31	Bluebonnet	West Virginia 31, TCU 14
J1	**Sugar**	**Nebraska 28, LSU 10**
J1	Cotton	Boston College 45, Houston 28
J1	Rose	Southern California 20, Ohio State 17
J1	Fiesta	UCLA 39, Miami (Fla.) 37
J1	Orange	Washington 28, Oklahoma 17

SEC STANDINGS

	CONFERENCE			OVERALL		
	W	L	T	W	L	T
Florida*	5	0	1	9	1	1
LSU	4	1	1	8	3	1
Auburn	4	2	0	9	4	0
Georgia	4	2	0	7	4	1
Kentucky	3	3	0	9	3	0
Tennessee	3	3	0	7	4	1
Vanderbilt	2	4	0	5	6	0
Alabama	2	4	0	5	6	0
Mississippi	1	5	0	4	6	1
Mississippi State	1	5	0	4	7	0

* Conference championship later vacated

ALL-SEC TEAM

POS	OFFENSE	SCHOOL
QB	Kurt Page	Vanderbilt
RB	Dalton Hilliard	LSU
RB	Johnnie Jones	Tennessee
WR	Chuck Scott	Vanderbilt
WR	Eric Martin	LSU
C	Phil Bromley	Florida
OL	Lomas Brown	Florida
OL	Lance Smith	LSU
OL	Bill Mayo	Tennessee
OL	Jeff Lott	Auburn
TE	Jim Popp	Vanderbilt
TE	Corwyn Aldredge	Mississippi State
K	Kevin Butler	Georgia

POS	DEFENSE	SCHOOL
L	Freddie Joe Nunn	Mississippi
L	Alonzo Johnson	Florida
L	Jon Hand	Alabama
L	Ben Thomas	Auburn
L	Tim Newton	Florida
LB	Gregg Carr	Auburn
LB	Cornelius Bennett	Alabama
LB	Knox Culpepper	Georgia
DB	Jeff Sanchez	Georgia
DB	Paul Calhoun	Kentucky
DB	Liffort Hobley	LSU
DB	Jeffery Dale	LSU
P	Ricky Anderson	Vanderbilt

1985 NCAA Major College Statistical Leaders

Individual Leaders

PASSING		CL	G	ATT	COM	PCT	INT	I%	YDS	YPA	TD	TD%	RATING
1	Jim Harbaugh, Michigan	JR	11	212	139	65.6	6	2.8	1913	9.0	18	8.5	163.7
2	**Kerwin Bell, Florida**	**SO**	**11**	**288**	**180**	**62.5**	**8**	**2.8**	**2687**	**9.3**	**21**	**7.3**	**159.4**
3	Chuck Long, Iowa	SR	11	351	231	65.8	15	4.3	2978	8.5	26	7.4	153.0
4	Jim Karsatos, Ohio State	JR	11	254	158	62.2	8	3.2	2115	8.3	19	7.5	150.5
5	**Mike Shula, Alabama**	**JR**	**11**	**229**	**138**	**60.3**	**8**	**3.5**	**2009**	**8.8**	**16**	**7.0**	**150.0**
6	Vinny Testaverde, Miami (Fla.)	JR	11	352	216	61.4	15	4.3	3238	9.2	21	6.0	149.8
7	Robbie Bosco, Brigham Young	SR	13	511	338	66.1	24	4.7	4273	8.4	30	5.9	146.4
8	Kevin Sweeney, Fresno State	JR	11	295	177	60.0	7	2.4	2604	8.8	14	4.8	145.1
9	Jim Everett, Purdue	SR	11	450	285	63.3	11	2.4	3651	8.1	23	5.1	143.5
10	Doug Gaynor, Long Beach State	SR	12	452	321	71.0	18	4.0	3563	7.9	19	4.2	143.1

ALL-PURPOSE		CL	G	RUSH	REC	PR	KR	YDS	YPG
1	Napoleon McCallum, Navy	SR	11	1327	358	157	488	2330	211.8
2	Paul Palmer, Temple	JR	9	1516	131	0	96	1743	193.7
3	George Swarn, Miami (Ohio)	JR	11	1511	424	0	17	1952	177.5
4	Lorenzo White, Michigan State	SO	11	1908	28	0	0	1936	176.0
5	**Bo Jackson, Auburn**	**SR**	**11**	**1786**	**73**	**0**	**0**	**1859**	**169.0**
6	Ronnie Harmon, Iowa	SR	11	1111	597	0	147	1855	168.6
7	Thurman Thomas, Oklahoma State	SO	11	1553	98	115	15	1781	161.9
8	Ernest Givins, Louisville	SR	11	204	577	154	801	1736	157.8
9	Tony Cherry, Oregon	SR	10	1006	245	0	286	1537	153.7
10	Webster Slaughter, San Diego State	SR	12	58	1071	264	413	1806	150.5

RUSHING/Yards Per Game		CL	G	ATT	YDS	TD	AVG	YPG
1	Lorenzo White, Michigan State	SO	11	386	1908	17	4.9	173.5
2	Paul Palmer, Temple	JR	9	279	1516	9	5.4	168.4
3	**Bo Jackson, Auburn**	**SR**	**11**	**278**	**1786**	**17**	**6.4**	**162.4**
4	Thurman Thomas, Oklahoma State	SO	11	302	1553	15	5.1	141.2
5	George Swarn, Miami (Fla.)	JR	11	309	1511	12	4.9	137.4
6	Barry Word, Virginia	SR	10	207	1224	6	5.9	122.4
7	Napoleon McCallum, Navy	SR	11	287	1327	14	4.6	120.6
8	Reggie Dupard, SMU	SR	11	235	1278	14	5.4	116.2
9	Doug DuBose, Nebraska	JR	10	203	1161	8	5.7	116.1
10	Steve Bartalo, Colorado State	JR	12	338	1368	12	4.0	114.0

RUSHING/Yards Per Carry		CL	G	ATT	YDS	YPC
1	Chris Hardy, San Diego State	JR	12	158	1150	7.3
2	Gordon Brown, Tulsa	SR	11	169	1201	7.1
3	**Bo Jackson, Auburn**	**SR**	**11**	**278**	**1786**	**6.4**
4	Barry Word, Virginia	SR	10	207	1224	5.9
5	Doug DuBose, Nebraska	JR	10	203	1161	5.7
6	Charles Gladman, Pittsburgh	SO	10	194	1085	5.6
7	Reggie Dupard, SMU	SR	11	235	1278	5.4
8	Paul Palmer, Temple	JR	9	279	1516	5.4
9	Rueben Mayes, Washington State	SR	11	228	1236	5.4
10	Jamelle Holieway, Oklahoma	FR	9	161	861	5.3

Based on top 23 rushers

RECEIVING		CL	G	REC	YDS	TD	YPR	YPG	RPG
1	Rodney Carter, Purdue	SR	11	98	1099	4	11.2	99.9	8.9
2	Brad Muster, Stanford	SO	9	78	654	4	8.4	72.7	8.7
3	David Williams, Illinois	SR	11	85	1047	8	12.3	95.2	7.7
4	Webster Slaughter, San Diego State	SR	12	82	1071	10	13.1	89.3	6.8
5	Marc Zeno, Tulane	SO	11	73	1137	3	15.6	103.4	6.6
6	Reggie Bynum, Oregon State	SR	10	61	703	7	11.5	70.3	6.1
7	Loren Richey, Utah	JR	12	73	971	7	13.3	80.9	6.1
8	Richard Estell, Kansas	SR	12	70	1109	4	15.8	92.4	5.8
9	Charles Lockett, Long Beach State	JR	12	69	949	10	13.8	79.1	5.7
10	Mark Bellini, Brigham Young	JR	11	63	1008	14	16.0	91.6	5.7

PUNTING		CL	PUNT	YDS	AVG
1	Mark Simon, Air Force	JR	53	2507	47.3
2	Barry Helton, Colorado	SO	52	2392	46.0
3	Steve Kidd, Rice	JR	55	2525	45.9
4	**Lewis Colbert, Auburn**	**SR**	**57**	**2611**	**45.8**
5	**Bill Smith, Mississippi**	**JR**	**79**	**3579**	**45.3**
6	John Teltschik, Texas	SR	58	2622	45.2
7	**Chris Mohr, Alabama**	**FR**	**44**	**1984**	**45.1**
8	Buzzy Sawyer, Baylor	SR	52	2330	44.8
9	**Ray Criswell, Florida**	**SR**	**55**	**2459**	**44.7**
10	Greg Montgomery, Michigan State	SO	69	3084	44.7

PUNT RETURNS		CL	PR	YDS	TD	AVG
1	Erroll Tucker, Utah	SR	16	389	2	24.3
2	Kelvin Martin, Boston College	JR	30	509	1	17.0
3	Scott Schwedes, Syracuse	JR	24	384	2	16.0
4	Stephen Baker, Fresno State	JR	17	243	1	14.3
5	Gilvanni Johnson, Michigan	SR	12	169	1	14.1
6	Tyrone Thurman, Texas Tech	FR	31	419	0	13.5
7	Robb Schnitzler, Nebraska	JR	16	207	0	12.9
8	Tony Brooks, TCU	FR	11	131	0	11.9
9	B.J. Edmonds, Arkansas	SR	40	466	0	11.6
10	Nate Odomes, Wisconsin	JR	14	160	0	11.4

KICKOFF RETURNS		CL	KR	YDS	TD	AVG
1	Erroll Tucker, Utah	SR	24	698	2	29.1
2	Ernest Givins, Louisville	SR	29	801	2	27.6
3	Curtis Duncan, Northwestern	JR	11	299	0	27.2
4	Reggie McKinney, East Carolina	FR	13	332	0	25.5
5	Luther Johnson, Texas-El Paso	JR	29	725	2	25.0
6	Bobby Clair, East Carolina	SR	17	423	0	24.9
7	Joe Redding, La.-Lafayette	FR	33	814	1	24.7
8	Jerry Harris, Memphis	JR	15	369	0	24.6
9	Keith Ross, Florida State	FR	17	418	0	24.6
10	Napoleon McCallum, Navy	SR	20	488	0	24.4

SCORING		CL	TDS	XP	FG	PTS	PTPG
1	Bernard White, Bowling Green	SR	19	0	0	114	10.4
2	**Bo Jackson, Auburn**	**SR**	**17**	**0**	**0**	**102**	**9.3**
2	**Carlos Reveiz, Tennessee**	**JR**	**0**	**30**	**24**	**102**	**9.3**
2	Lorenzo White, Michigan State	SO	17	0	0	102	9.3
2	Steve Gage, Tulsa	JR	17	0	0	102	9.3
6	Barry Belli, Fresno State	SO	0	46	18	100	9.1
7	Derek Schmidt, Florida State	SO	0	44	18	98	8.9
8	Rob Houghtlin, Iowa	SO	0	46	17	97	8.8
9	George Swarn, Miami (Ohio)	JR	16	0	0	96	8.7
9	Thurman Thomas, Oklahoma State	SO	16	0	0	96	8.7
9	Reggie Dupard, SMU	SR	16	0	0	96	8.7
9	John Lee, UCLA	SR	0	33	21	96	8.7

FIELD GOALS		CL	FGA	FGM	PCT	FGG
1	John Diettrich, Ball State	SR	29	25	0.86	2.27
2	**Carlos Reveiz, Tennessee**	**JR**	**28**	**24**	**0.86**	**2.18**
3	Max Zendejas, Arizona	SR	29	22	0.76	2.00
4	John Lee, UCLA	SR	24	21	0.88	1.91
4	Jeff Jaeger, Washington	JR	24	21	0.88	1.91
4	Massimo Manca, Penn State	SR	26	21	0.81	1.91
7	Jeff Ward, Texas	JR	24	19	0.79	1.73
7	**Joe Worley, Kentucky**	**SO**	**28**	**19**	**0.68**	**1.73**
9	Derek Schmidt, Florida State	SO	25	18	0.72	1.64
9	Gary Gussman, Miami (Ohio)	SO	26	18	0.69	1.64
9	Barry Belli, Fresno State	SO	26	18	0.69	1.64

INTERCEPTIONS		CL	INT	YDS	TD	INT/GM
1	**Chris White, Tennessee**	**SR**	**9**	**168**	**1**	**0.82**
1	Kevin Walker, East Carolina	SR	9	155	1	0.82
3	Mike Romero, Cal St.-Fullerton	SR	8	84	1	0.73
4	Tom Rotello, Air Force	JR	8	103	2	0.67
5	Teryl Austin, Pittsburgh	SO	7	186	0	0.64
5	Mark Moore, Oklahoma State	JR	7	176	1	0.64
5	Jay Norvell, Iowa	SR	7	93	0	0.64
5	Doug Pavek, Army	SR	7	80	0	0.64
5	Markus Paul, Syracuse	FR	7	53	0	0.64
5	Lavance Northington, Oregon State	JR	7	39	0	0.64

Team Leaders

RUSHING OFFENSE		G	ATT	YDS	AVG	TD	YPG
1	Nebraska	11	697	4117	5.9	40	374.3
2	Army	11	699	3700	5.3	43	336.4
3	Oklahoma	11	749	3694	4.9	35	335.8
4	**Auburn**	**11**	**620**	**3438**	**5.5**	**36**	**312.5**
5	Tulsa	11	627	3371	5.4	27	306.5
6	**Georgia**	**11**	**584**	**3249**	**5.6**	**30**	**295.4**
7	Air Force	12	688	3519	5.1	42	293.2
8	Arkansas	11	685	2922	4.3	29	265.6
9	Colorado	11	647	2858	4.4	23	259.8
10	SMU	11	599	2730	4.6	27	248.2

PASSING OFFENSE		G	ATT	COM	INT	PCT	YDS	YPA	TD	I%	YPC	YPG
1	Brigham Young	13	560	366	24	65.4	4608	8.2	32	4.3	12.6	354.5
2	Purdue	11	471	292	13	62.0	3760	8.0	23	2.8	12.9	341.8
3	Miami (Fla.)	11	368	227	16	61.7	3501	9.5	24	4.3	15.4	318.3
4	Iowa	11	382	247	15	64.7	3292	8.6	29	3.9	13.3	299.3
5	Long Beach State	12	456	323	18	70.8	3575	7.8	19	3.9	11.1	297.9
6	New Mexico	11	395	194	24	49.1	3245	8.2	12	6.1	16.7	295.0
7	San Diego State	12	437	269	21	61.6	3447	7.9	24	4.8	12.8	287.2
8	Illinois	11	462	290	17	62.8	2992	6.5	16	3.7	10.3	272.0
9	Boston College	12	455	249	28	54.7	3230	7.1	13	6.2	13.0	269.2
10	Utah	12	449	253	23	56.3	3199	7.1	20	5.1	12.6	266.6

TOTAL OFFENSE		G	P	YDS	AVG	TD	YPG
1	Brigham Young	13	1035	6502	6.3	57	500.2
2	Nebraska	11	841	5197	6.2	46	472.5
3	New Mexico	11	912	5165	5.7	37	469.5
4	Iowa	11	815	5106	6.3	52	464.2
5	Fresno State	11	858	5079	5.9	50	461.7
6	Miami (Fla.)	11	828	5076	6.1	46	461.5
7	Washington State	11	836	4851	5.8	41	441.0
8	San Diego State	12	827	5242	6.3	39	436.8
9	Purdue	11	822	4801	5.8	36	436.5
10	Oklahoma	11	860	4697	5.5	42	427.0

RUSHING DEFENSE		G	ATT	YDS	AVG	TD	YPG
1	UCLA	11	370	773	2.1	11	70.3
2	Oklahoma	11	405	988	2.4	4	89.8
3	**Georgia**	**11**	**440**	**1095**	**2.5**	**9**	**99.5**
4	Syracuse	11	430	1099	2.6	8	99.9
5	Iowa	11	434	1117	2.6	8	101.5
6	Michigan	11	385	1135	2.9	2	103.2
7	Pittsburgh	11	445	1136	2.6	13	103.3
8	**LSU**	**11**	**388**	**1178**	**3.0**	**6**	**107.1**
9	Arizona	11	434	1196	2.8	12	108.7
10	Air Force	12	466	1307	2.8	8	108.9

PASSING DEFENSE		G	ATT	COM	PCT	YPC	INT	I%	YDS	YPA	TD	YPG
1	Oklahoma	11	245	107	43.7	10.7	18	7.3	1140	4.7	5	103.6
2	Texas Tech	11	184	87	47.3	13.8	9	4.9	1204	6.5	6	109.5
3	Baylor	11	221	96	43.4	13.4	14	6.3	1289	5.8	7	117.2
4	Texas A&M	11	256	106	41.4	13.8	16	6.3	1461	5.7	4	132.8
5	SMU	11	242	116	47.9	12.8	11	4.5	1480	6.1	11	134.5
6	Oklahoma State	11	268	125	46.6	12.1	20	7.5	1512	5.6	7	137.5
7	Central Michigan	10	233	128	54.9	10.8	14	6.0	1377	5.9	2	137.7
8	Western Michigan	11	263	141	53.6	10.8	15	5.7	1520	5.8	7	138.2
9	Toledo	11	301	144	47.8	10.6	17	5.6	1523	5.1	6	138.5
10	Kansas State	11	227	114	50.2	13.7	13	5.7	1557	6.9	6	141.5

TOTAL DEFENSE		G	P	YDS	AVG	TD	YPG
1	Oklahoma	11	650	2128	3.3	9	193.5
2	Michigan	11	689	2790	4.0	5	253.6
3	Toledo	11	763	2880	3.8	17	261.8
4	Central Michigan	10	672	2658	4.0	16	265.8
5	Iowa	11	755	3044	4.0	16	276.7
6	Nebraska	11	765	3070	4.0	16	279.1
7	UCLA	11	733	3100	4.2	20	281.8
8	Texas A&M	11	765	3101	4.1	19	281.9
9	**Florida**	**11**	**726**	**3111**	**4.3**	**19**	**282.8**
10	Southern Miss	11	722	3169	4.4	18	288.1

SCORING OFFENSE		G	PTS	AVG
1	Fresno State	11	430	39.1
2	Iowa	11	412	37.5
3	Air Force	12	446	37.2
4	Miami (Fla.)	11	399	36.3
5	Nebraska	11	398	36.2
6	Utah	12	405	33.7
7	Brigham Young	13	435	33.5
8	Florida State	11	368	33.5
9	Army	11	365	33.2
10	Bowling Green	11	348	31.6

SCORING DEFENSE		G	PTS	AVG
1	Michigan	11	75	6.8
2	Oklahoma	11	93	8.5
3	**LSU**	**11**	**113**	**10.3**
4	Georgia Tech	11	118	10.7
5	Penn State	11	128	11.6
6	Arkansas	11	129	11.7
7	**Tennessee**	**11**	**133**	**12.1**
7	Arizona	11	133	12.1
9	Nebraska	11	136	12.4
10	Iowa	11	142	12.9

1985

FINAL POLL (JAN. 3)

UP	AP	SCHOOL	FINAL RECORD
1	1	Oklahoma	11-1-0
2	2	Michigan	10-1-1
3	3	Penn State	11-1-0
4	4	**Tennessee**	**9-1-2**
PB	5	**Florida**	**9-1-1**
7	6	Texas A&M	10-2-0
6	7	UCLA	9-2-1
5	8	Air Force	12-1-0
8	9	Miami (Fla.)	10-2-0
9	10	Iowa	10-2-0
10	11	Nebraska	9-3-0
12	12	Arkansas	10-2-0
14	13	**Alabama**	**9-2-1**
11	14	Ohio State	9-3-0
13	15	Florida State	9-3-0
17	16	Brigham Young	11-3-0
15	17	Baylor	9-3-0
19	18	Maryland	9-3-0
18	19	Georgia Tech	9-2-1
20	20	**LSU**	**9-2-1**
16		Fresno State	11-0-1

PB: Team on probation

CONSENSUS ALL-AMERICANS

POS	OFFENSE	SCHOOL
QB	Chuck Long	Iowa
RB	**Bo Jackson**	**Auburn**
RB	Lorenzo White	Michigan State
RB	Thurman Thomas	Oklahoma State
RB	Reggie Dupard	SMU
RB	Napoleon McCallum	Navy
WR	David Williams	Illinois
WR	**Tim McGee**	**Tennessee**
TE	Willie Smith	Miami (Fla.)
L	Jim Dombrowski	Virginia
L	Jeff Bregel	Southern California
L	Brian Jozwiak	West Virginia
L	John Rienstra	Temple
L	J.D. Maarleveld	Maryland
L	Jamie Dukes	Florida State
C	**Pete Anderson**	**Georgia**
PK	John Lee	UCLA

OTHERS RECEIVING FIRST-TEAM HONORS

WR	Lew Barnes	Oregon
L	**Jeff Zimmerman**	**Florida**
L	Don Smith	Army
C	Gene Chilton	Texas
C	Bill Lewis	Nebraska
KR	Erroll Tucker	Utah

POS	DEFENSE	SCHOOL
L	Tim Green	Syracuse
L	Leslie O'Neal	Oklahoma State
L	Tony Casillas	Oklahoma
L	Mike Ruth	Boston College
L	Mike Hammerstein	Michigan
LB	Brian Bosworth	Oklahoma
LB	Larry Station	Iowa
LB	Johnny Holland	Texas A&M
DB	David Fulcher	Arizona State
DB	Brad Cochran	Michigan
DB	Scott Thomas	Air Force
P	Barry Helton	Colorado

OTHERS RECEIVING FIRST-TEAM HONORS

DL	Pat Swilling	Georgia Tech
DL	Jim Skow	Nebraska
LB	**Cornelius Bennett**	**Alabama**
LB	Pepper Johnson	Ohio State
DB	Allan Durden	Arizona
DB	Michael Zordich	Penn State
DB	Thomas Everett	Baylor
DB	Mark Moore	Oklahoma State
P	**Bill Smith**	**Mississippi**
P	**Lewis Colbert**	**Auburn**

HEISMAN TROPHY VOTING

	PLAYER	POS	SCHOOL	TOTAL
1	**Bo Jackson**	**TB**	**Auburn**	**1509**
2	Chuck Long	QB	Iowa	1464
3	Robbie Bosco	QB	Brigham Young	459
4	Lorenzo White	TB	Michigan State	391
5	Vinny Testaverde	QB	Miami (Fla.)	249
6	Jim Everett	QB	Purdue	77
7	Napoleon McCallum	HB	Navy	72
8	Allen Pinkett	TB	Notre Dame	71
9	Joe Dudek	HB	Plymouth State	56
10	Brian McClure	QB	Bowling Green	54
10	Thurman Thomas	TB	Oklahoma State	54

AWARD WINNERS

PLAYER	AWARD
Herschel Walker, RB, Georgia	**Maxwell**
Chuck Long, QB, Iowa	Maxwell
Mike Ruth, NG, Boston College	Outland
Bo Jackson, RB, Auburn	**Camp**
Tony Casillas, NG, Oklahoma	Lombardi
Chuck Long, QB, Iowa	O'Brien
Brian Bosworth, LB, Oklahoma	Butkus

BOWL GAMES

DATE	BOWL	SCORE
D14	California	Fresno State 51, Bowling Green 7
D21	Cherry	Maryland 35, Syracuse 18
D21	Independence	Minnesota 20, Clemson 13
D22	Holiday	Arkansas 18, Arizona State 17
D27	**Liberty**	**Baylor 21, LSU 7**
D28	**Aloha**	**Alabama 24, Southern California 3**
D28	**Sun**	**Arizona 13, Georgia 13**
D28	Florida Citrus	Ohio State 10, Brigham Young 7
D30	Gator	Florida State 34, Oklahoma State 23
D30	Freedom	Washington 20, Colorado 17
D31	Bluebonnet	Air Force 24, Texas 16
D31	Peach	Army 31, Illinois 29
D31	All-American	Georgia Tech 17, Michigan State 14
J1	Fiesta	Michigan 27, Nebraska 23
J1	Orange	Oklahoma 25, Penn State 10
J1	**Cotton**	**Texas A&M 36, Auburn 16**
J1	Rose	UCLA 45, Iowa 28
J1	**Sugar**	**Tennessee 35, Miami (Fla.) 7**

SEC STANDINGS

	CONFERENCE			OVERALL		
	W	L	T	W	L	T
Florida*	5	1	0	9	1	1
Tennessee	5	1	0	9	1	2
LSU	4	1	1	9	2	1
Alabama	4	1	1	9	2	1
Georgia	3	2	1	7	3	2
Auburn	3	3	0	8	4	0
Mississippi	2	4	0	4	6	1
Vanderbilt	1	4	1	3	7	1
Kentucky	1	5	0	5	6	0
Mississippi State	0	6	0	5	6	0

* Not eligible for conference title

ALL-SEC TEAM

POS	OFFENSE	SCHOOL
QB	Mike Shula	Alabama
RB	Bo Jackson	Auburn
RB	Dalton Hilliard	LSU
WR	Tim McGee	Tennessee
WR	Al Bell	Alabama
C	Peter Anderson	Georgia
OL	Will Wolford	Vanderbilt
OL	Jeff Zimmerman	Florida
OL	Bruce Wilkerson	Tennessee
OL	Steve Wallace	Auburn
TE	Jim Popp	Vanderbilt
K	Carlos Reveiz	Tennessee

POS	DEFENSE	SCHOOL
L	Jon Hand	Alabama
L	Gerald Williams	Auburn
L	Roland Barbay	LSU
L	Greg Waters	Georgia
L	Harold Hallman	Auburn
LB	Michael Brooks	LSU
LB	Alonzo Johnson	Florida
LB	Cornelius Bennett	Alabama
LB	Dale Jones	Tennessee
DB	Chris White	Tennessee
DB	Tom Powell	Auburn
DB	Jon Little	Georgia
DB	Norman Jefferson	LSU
DB	Freddie Robinson	Alabama
P	Bill Smith	Mississippi

1986 NCAA Major College Statistical Leaders

Individual Leaders

PASSING	CL	G	ATT	COM	PCT	INT	I%	YDS	YPA	TD	TD%	RATING
1 Vinny Testaverde, Miami (Fla.)	SR	10	276	175	63.4	9	3.3	2557	9.3	26	9.4	165.8
2 Jim Harbaugh, Michigan	SR	12	254	167	65.8	8	3.2	2557	10.1	10	3.9	157.0
3 Dave Yarema, Michigan State	SR	11	297	200	67.3	11	3.7	2581	8.7	16	5.4	150.7
4 Shawn Halloran, Boston College	SR	10	258	159	61.6	6	2.3	2090	8.1	17	6.6	146.8
5 Mark Vlasic, Iowa	SR	9	152	93	61.2	4	2.6	1234	8.1	9	5.9	143.7
6 Tom Hodson, LSU	**FR**	**11**	**288**	**175**	**60.8**	**8**	**2.8**	**2261**	**7.9**	**19**	**6.6**	**142.9**
7 Jeff Francis, Tennessee	**SO**	**11**	**233**	**150**	**64.4**	**6**	**2.6**	**1946**	**8.4**	**9**	**3.9**	**142.1**
8 Lee Saltz, Temple	SR	11	203	117	57.6	7	3.5	1727	8.5	12	5.9	141.7
9 Jeff Van Raaphorst, Arizona State	SR	11	239	144	60.3	11	4.6	1988	8.3	15	6.3	141.6
10 Ned James, New Mexico	SR	11	215	125	58.1	8	3.7	1777	8.3	14	6.5	141.6

ALL-PURPOSE	CL	G	RUSH	REC	PR	KR	YDS	YPG
1 Paul Palmer, Temple	SR	11	1866	110	0	657	2633	239.4
2 Rick Calhoun, Cal St.-Fullerton	SR	12	1398	125	138	522	2183	181.9
3 Tim Brown, Notre Dame	JR	11	254	910	75	698	1937	176.1
4 Bobby Humphrey, Alabama	**SO**	**12**	**1471**	**201**	**0**	**344**	**2016**	**168.0**
5 Gary Patton, Eastern Michigan	JR	11	1058	371	0	384	1813	164.8
6 Troy Stradford, Boston College	SR	10	1188	445	0	0	1633	163.3
7 Sterling Sharpe, South Carolina	JR	11	104	1106	190	377	1777	161.6
8 Kelvin Farmer, Toledo	SR	11	1532	203	0	0	1735	157.7
9 Steve Bartalo, Colorado State	SR	11	1419	289	0	0	1708	155.3
10 Chuck Smith, Navy	JR	9	933	280	0	135	1348	149.8

RUSHING/Yards Per Game	CL	G	ATT	YDS	TD	AVG	YPG
1 Paul Palmer, Temple	SR	11	346	1866	15	5.4	169.6
2 Kelvin Farmer, Toledo	SR	11	299	1532	16	5.1	139.3
3 Steve Bartalo, Colorado State	SR	11	366	1419	19	3.9	129.0
4 Brent Fullwood, Auburn	**SR**	**11**	**167**	**1391**	**10**	**8.3**	**126.5**
5 Derrick Fenner, North Carolina	SO	10	200	1250	6	6.3	125.0
6 Rodney Stevenson, Central Michigan	SO	9	208	1104	14	5.3	122.7
7 Bobby Humphrey, Alabama	**SO**	**12**	**236**	**1471**	**15**	**6.2**	**122.6**
8 Reggie Taylor, Cincinnati	SR	11	256	1325	11	5.2	120.5
9 Troy Stradford, Boston College	SR	10	218	1188	10	5.4	118.8
10 Rick Calhoun, Cal St.-Fullerton	SR	12	259	1398	11	5.4	116.5

RUSHING/Yards Per Carry	CL	G	ATT	YDS	YPC
1 Brent Fullwood, Auburn	**SR**	**11**	**167**	**1391**	**8.3**
2 Tony Jeffery, TCU	JR	9	122	861	7.1
3 Terrence Flagler, Clemson	SR	11	180	1176	6.5
4 Derrick Ellison, Tulsa	SO	11	170	1064	6.3
5 Derrick Fenner, North Carolina	SO	10	200	1250	6.3
6 Bobby Humphrey, Alabama	**SO**	**12**	**236**	**1471**	**6.2**
7 Darrell Thompson, Minnesota	FR	11	217	1240	5.7
8 Troy Stradford, Boston College	SR	10	218	1188	5.4
9 Rick Calhoun, Cal St.-Fullerton	SR	12	259	1398	5.4
10 Paul Palmer, Temple	SR	11	346	1866	5.4

RECEIVING	CL	G	REC	YDS	TD	YPR	YPG	RPG
1 Mark Templeton, Long Beach State	SR	11	99	688	2	6.9	62.5	9.0
2 Loren Richey, Utah	SR	9	67	775	6	11.6	86.1	7.4
3 Wendell Davis, LSU	**JR**	**11**	**80**	**1244**	**11**	**15.6**	**113.1**	**7.3**
4 Dave Montagne, Oregon State	SR	11	78	862	2	11.1	78.4	7.1
5 Sterling Sharpe, South Carolina	JR	11	74	1106	10	14.9	100.5	6.7
6 Guy Liggins, San Jose State	JR	11	72	983	6	13.7	89.4	6.6
7 Marc Zeno, Tulane	JR	11	68	1033	7	15.2	93.9	6.2
8 James Brim, Wake Forest	SR	11	66	930	5	14.1	84.5	6.0
9 Rod Bernstine, Texas A&M	SR	11	65	710	5	10.9	64.5	5.9
10 Craig McEwen, Utah	SR	11	64	721	7	11.3	65.5	5.8

PUNTING	CL	PUNT	YDS	AVG
1 Greg Horne, Arkansas	SR	49	2313	47.2
2 Alexander Waits, Texas	FR	48	2214	46.1
3 Chris Becker, TCU	SO	59	2717	46.1
4 Barry Helton, Colorado	JR	57	2599	45.6
5 Bill Smith, Mississippi	**SR**	**57**	**2522**	**44.3**
6 Brian Shulman, Auburn	**SO**	**49**	**2161**	**44.1**
7 Cris Carpenter, Georgia	**SO**	**41**	**1808**	**44.1**
8 Mike Preacher, Oregon	SR	49	2141	43.7
9 Mark Simon, Air Force	SR	63	2754	43.7
10 Tom Tupa, Ohio State	JR	50	2180	43.6

PUNT RETURNS	CL	PR	YDS	TD	AVG
1 Rod Smith, Nebraska	JR	12	227	1	18.9
2 Kwante Hampton, Long Beach State	SR	24	363	2	15.1
3 Riccardo Ingram, Georgia Tech	JR	16	233	0	14.6
4 Jeff Joseph, Arizona State	JR	15	212	0	14.1
5 Milt Garner, Kansas	JR	14	193	2	13.8
6 Tyrone Thurman, Texas Tech	SO	33	444	2	13.5
7 Dana Brinson, Nebraska	SO	27	340	0	12.6
8 Kelvin Martin, Boston College	SR	18	222	1	12.3
9 Thomas Henley, Stanford	SR	29	353	1	12.2
10 Andrew Mott, Southern Miss	SR	36	438	1	12.2

KICKOFF RETURNS	CL	KR	YDS	TD	AVG
1 Terrance Roulhac, Clemson	SR	17	561	0	33.0
2 Blair Thomas, Penn State	SO	12	383	1	31.9
3 Tim Brown, Notre Dame	JR	25	698	2	27.9
4 Steve Jones, Washington	SO	15	407	0	27.1
5 Keith Jones, Illinois	SO	15	398	0	26.5
6 Keith Ross, Florida State	SO	22	583	1	26.5
7 Chris Thomas, Miami (Ohio)	JR	17	441	1	25.9
8 Vince Delgado, California	JR	11	285	0	25.9
9 Tom Rotello, Air Force	SR	20	518	0	25.9
10 Lonnie White, Southern California	SR	26	656	0	25.2

SCORING	CL	TDS	XP	FG	PTS	PTPG
1 Steve Bartalo, Colorado State	SR	19	0	0	114	10.4
2 Rodney Stevenson, Central Michigan	SO	14	0	0	84	9.3
3 Lars Tate, Georgia	**JR**	**17**	**0**	**0**	**102**	**9.3**
4 Scott Slater, Texas A&M	JR	0	37	21	100	9.1
5 Gary Coston, Arizona	FR	0	34	21	97	8.8
6 Tim Lashar, Oklahoma	SR	0	60	12	96	8.7
6 Barry Belli, Fresno State	JR	0	33	21	96	8.7
6 Kelvin Farmer, Toledo	SR	16	0	0	96	8.7
9 Bobby Humphrey, Alabama	**SO**	**17**	**2**	**0**	**104**	**8.7**
10 Chris Kinzer, Virginia Tech	SO	0	27	22	93	8.5
10 Jeff Jaeger, Washington	SR	0	42	17	93	8.5

FIELD GOALS	CL	FGA	FGM	PCT	FGG
1 Chris Kinzer, Virginia Tech	SO	27	22	0.82	2.00
2 Gary Coston, Arizona	FR	24	21	0.88	1.91
2 Scott Slater, Texas A&M	JR	27	21	0.78	1.91
2 John Carney, Notre Dame	SR	28	21	0.75	1.91
2 Barry Belli, Fresno State	JR	31	21	0.68	1.91
6 John Duvic, Northwestern	SR	23	19	0.83	1.73
6 Steve DeLine, Colorado State	SR	24	19	0.79	1.73
8 Jeff Jaeger, Washington	SR	21	17	0.81	1.55
8 John Diettrich, Ball State	SR	23	17	0.74	1.55
8 Joe Worley, Kentucky	**JR**	**25**	**17**	**0.68**	**1.55**
8 Bryan Lowe, Boston College	SO	25	17	0.68	1.55

INTERCEPTIONS	CL	INT	YDS	TD	INT/GM
1 Bennie Blades, Miami (Fla.)	JR	10	128	0	0.91
2 Teddy Johnson, Oregon State	SO	9	86	0	0.82
3 Toi Cook, Stanford	SR	7	115	0	0.78
4 Ron Francis, Baylor	SR	8	25	0	0.73
4 Elton Slater, La.-Lafayette	SR	8	1	0	0.73
6 Jim King, Colorado State	SR	7	83	0	0.64
6 Ed Hulbert, Oregon	SR	7	48	0	0.64
6 Chris Wagner, Western Michigan	FR	7	17	0	0.64
9 Jeff Wilcox, Brigham Young	SR	7	110	0	0.58

Team Leaders

RUSHING OFFENSE	G	ATT	YDS	AVG	TD	YPG
1 Oklahoma	11	719	4452	6.2	51	404.7
2 Nebraska	11	656	3360	5.1	40	305.5
3 Tulsa	11	652	3184	4.9	24	289.5
4 Central Michigan	10	591	2798	4.7	26	279.8
5 Army	11	689	3042	4.4	33	276.5
6 Clemson	11	648	3007	4.6	28	273.4
7 Pacific	11	677	2960	4.4	22	269.1
8 Alabama	**12**	**585**	**3167**	**5.4**	**25**	**263.9**
9 Georgia	**11**	**596**	**2802**	**4.7**	**24**	**254.7**
10 North Carolina	11	553	2777	5.0	16	252.5

PASSING OFFENSE	G	ATT	COM	INT	PCT	YDS	YPA	TD	I%	YPC	YPG
1 San Jose State	11	456	276	23	60.5	3437	7.5	21	5.0	12.5	312.5
2 Wyoming	12	564	305	22	54.1	3523	6.2	30	3.9	11.6	293.6
3 South Carolina	11	356	216	23	60.7	3187	9.0	23	6.5	14.8	289.7
4 Utah	11	451	264	14	58.5	3157	7.0	25	3.1	12.0	287.0
5 Oregon State	11	527	312	22	59.2	3149	6.0	10	4.2	10.1	286.3
6 Miami (Fla.)	11	338	209	11	61.8	3095	9.2	30	3.3	14.8	281.4
7 Long Beach State	11	449	259	21	57.7	3069	6.8	21	4.7	11.8	279.0
8 Texas-El Paso	12	437	270	21	61.8	3231	7.4	23	4.8	12.0	269.3
9 Cincinnati	11	374	237	12	63.4	2831	7.6	13	3.2	11.9	257.4
10 San Diego State	11	390	241	12	61.8	2766	7.1	14	3.1	11.5	251.5

TOTAL OFFENSE	G	P	YDS	AVG	TD	YPG
1 San Jose State	11	909	5295	5.8	43	481.4
2 Oklahoma	11	807	5210	6.5	58	473.6
3 Texas A&M	11	895	4842	5.4	39	440.2
4 New Mexico	12	897	5269	5.9	42	439.1
5 Baylor	11	889	4827	5.4	34	438.8
6 North Carolina	11	822	4796	5.8	34	436.0
7 Michigan	12	870	5175	5.9	44	431.3
8 Utah	11	823	4684	5.7	35	425.8
9 Iowa	11	772	4628	6.0	42	420.7
10 Auburn	**11**	**766**	**4580**	**6.0**	**45**	**416.4**

RUSHING DEFENSE	G	ATT	YDS	AVG	TD	YPG
1 Oklahoma	11	408	668	1.6	1	60.7
2 San Jose State	11	387	724	1.9	4	65.8
3 Penn State	11	383	767	2.0	5	69.7
4 Arizona	11	392	928	2.4	9	84.4
5 Baylor	11	396	977	2.5	11	88.8
6 Brigham Young	12	439	1066	2.4	12	88.8
7 Washington	11	400	978	2.4	10	88.9
8 Pittsburgh	11	433	1027	2.4	8	93.4
9 Nebraska	11	442	1051	2.4	7	95.5
10 Fresno State	11	462	1097	2.4	4	99.7

PASSING DEFENSE	G	ATT	COM	PCT	YPC	INT	I%	YDS	YPA	TD	YPG
1 Oklahoma	11	263	128	48.7	9.4	18	6.8	1198	4.6	7	108.9
2 Tennessee	**11**	**203**	**99**	**48.8**	**12.6**	**13**	**6.4**	**1248**	**6.1**	**7**	**113.5**
3 Bowling Green	11	221	109	49.3	11.5	20	9.0	1257	5.7	4	114.3
4 Florida	**11**	**227**	**119**	**52.4**	**10.8**	**16**	**7.0**	**1287**	**5.7**	**4**	**117.0**
5 Oklahoma State	11	193	105	54.4	12.7	12	6.2	1331	6.9	6	121.0
6 Mississippi State	**11**	**197**	**103**	**52.3**	**13.8**	**8**	**4.1**	**1423**	**7.2**	**9**	**129.4**
7 Toledo	11	263	146	55.5	10.0	16	6.1	1464	5.6	8	133.1
8 Mississippi	**11**	**268**	**127**	**47.4**	**11.7**	**14**	**5.2**	**1484**	**5.5**	**6**	**134.9**
9 Georgia Tech	11	253	129	51.0	11.7	14	5.5	1506	6.0	9	136.9
9 Miami (Fla.)	11	291	130	44.7	11.6	21	7.2	1506	5.2	7	136.9

TOTAL DEFENSE	G	P	YDS	AVG	TD	YPG
1 Oklahoma	11	671	1866	2.8	8	169.6
2 Nebraska	11	700	2590	3.7	17	235.5
3 Baylor	11	707	2727	3.9	23	247.9
4 Texas A&M	11	721	2835	3.9	22	257.7
5 Miami (Fla.)	11	777	2886	3.7	13	262.4
6 Hawaii	12	781	3223	4.1	24	268.6
7 Washington	11	728	2982	4.1	19	271.1
8 Iowa	11	717	3031	4.2	18	275.5
9 Pittsburgh	11	758	3046	4.0	23	276.9
10 Brigham Young	12	789	3334	4.2	24	277.8

SCORING OFFENSE	G	PTS	AVG
1 Oklahoma	11	466	42.4
2 Miami (Fla.)	11	420	38.2
3 Nebraska	11	416	37.8
4 Auburn	**11**	**379**	**34.5**
5 Washington	11	372	33.8
6 Florida State	11	366	33.3
7 San Jose State	11	360	32.7
7 Texas A&M	11	360	32.7
9 Arizona State	11	357	32.5
10 UCLA	11	354	32.2

SCORING DEFENSE	G	PTS	AVG
1 Oklahoma	11	73	6.6
2 Auburn	**11**	**115**	**10.5**
3 Penn State	11	123	11.2
4 Miami (Fla.)	11	136	12.4
5 Arkansas	11	142	12.9
6 Alabama	**12**	**157**	**13.1**
7 Nebraska	11	150	13.6
7 Mississippi	**11**	**150**	**13.6**
7 Fresno State	11	150	13.6
10 Arizona State	11	152	13.8

1986

Final Poll (Jan. 3)

UP	AP	SCHOOL	FINAL RECORD
1	1	Penn State	12-0-0
2	2	Miami (Fla.)	11-1-0
3	3	Oklahoma	11-1-0
5	4	Arizona State	10-1-1
4	5	Nebraska	10-2-0
8	6	Auburn	10-2-0
6	7	Ohio State	10-3-0
7	8	Michigan	11-2-0
9	9	Alabama	10-3-0
11	10	LSU	9-3-0
10	11	Arizona	9-3-0
13	12	Baylor	9-3-0
12	13	Texas A&M	9-3-0
14	14	UCLA	8-3-1
16	15	Arkansas	9-3-0
15	16	Iowa	9-3-0
19	17	Clemson	8-2-2
17	18	Washington	8-3-1
18	19	Boston College	9-3-0
	20	Virginia Tech	9-2-1
20		Florida State	7-4-1

Consensus All-Americans

POS	OFFENSE	SCHOOL
QB	Vinny Testaverde	Miami (Fla.)
RB	Brent Fullwood	Auburn
RB	Paul Palmer	Temple
RB	Terrence Flagler	Clemson
RB	Brad Muster	Stanford
RB	D.J. Dozier	Penn State
WR	Cris Carter	Ohio State
TE	Keith Jackson	Oklahoma
L	Jeff Bregel	Southern California
L	Randy Dixon	Pittsburgh
L	Danny Villa	Arizona State
L	John Clay	Missouri
C	Ben Tamburello	Auburn
PK	Jeff Jaeger	Washington

Others receiving first-team honors

WR	Wendell Davis	LSU
WR	Tim Brown	Notre Dame
L	Jeff Zimmerman	Florida
L	Chris Conlin	Penn State
L	Dave Croston	Iowa
L	Paul Kiser	Wake Forest
L	John Elliott	Michigan
L	Randall McDaniel	Arizona State
L	Mark Hutson	Oklahoma
L	Harris Barton	North Carolina
L	John Phillips	Clemson
PK	Marty Zendejas	Nevada
PK	Jeff Ward	Texas

POS	DEFENSE	SCHOOL
L	Jerome Brown	Miami (Fla.)
L	Danny Noonan	Nebraska
L	Tony Woods	Pittsburgh
L	Jason Buck	Brigham Young
L	Reggie Rogers	Washington
LB	Cornelius Bennett	Alabama
LB	Shane Conlan	Penn State
LB	Brian Bosworth	Oklahoma
LB	Chris Spielman	Ohio State
DB	Thomas Everett	Baylor
DB	Tim McDonald	Southern California
DB	Bennie Blades	Miami (Fla.)
DB	Rod Woodson	Purdue
DB	Garland Rivers	Michigan
P	Barry Helton	Colorado

Others receiving first-team honors

DL	Tim Johnson	Penn State
DL	Al Noga	Hawaii
LB	Terry Maki	Air Force
DB	John Little	Georgia
DB	Gordon Lockbaum	Holy Cross
DB	Mark Moore	Oklahoma State
P	Greg Horne	Arkansas
P	Bill Smith	Mississippi
P	Greg Montgomery	Michigan State

Heisman Trophy Voting

	PLAYER	POS	SCHOOL	TOTAL
1	Vinny Testaverde	QB	Miami (Fla.)	2213
2	Paul Palmer	TB	Temple	672
3	Jim Harbaugh	QB	Michigan	458
4	Brian Bosworth	LB	Oklahoma	395
5	Gordie Lockbaum	TB	Holy Cross	242
6	Brent Fullwood	TB	Auburn	129
7	Cornelius Bennett	LB	Alabama	96
8	D.J. Dozier	TB	Penn State	77
9	Kevin Sweeney	QB	Fresno State	73
10	Chris Spielman	LB	Ohio State	60

Award Winners

PLAYER	AWARD
Vinny Testaverde, QB, Miami (Fla.)	Maxwell
Jason Buck, DT, Brigham Young	Outland
Vinny Testaverde, QB, Miami (Fla.)	Camp
Cornelius Bennett, LB, Alabama	Lombardi
Vinny Testaverde, QB, Miami (Fla.)	O'Brien
Brian Bosworth, LB, Oklahoma	Butkus
Thomas Everett, DB, Baylor	Thorpe

Bowl Games

DATE	GAME	SCORE
D13	California	San Jose State 37, Miami (Ohio) 7
D20	Independence	Mississippi 20, Texas Tech 17
D23	Hall of Fame	Boston College 27, Georgia 24
D25	Sun	Alabama 28, Washington 6
D27	Aloha	Arizona 30, North Carolina 21
D27	Gator	Clemson 27, Stanford 21
D29	Liberty	Tennessee 21, Minnesota 14
D30	Holiday	Iowa 39, San Diego State 38
D30	Freedom	UCLA 31, Brigham Young 10
D31	Bluebonnet	Baylor 21, Colorado 9
D31	All-American	Florida State 27, Indiana 13
D31	Peach	Virginia Tech 25, North Carolina St. 24
J1	Rose	Arizona State 22, Michigan 15
J1	Florida Citrus	Auburn 16, Southern California 7
J1	Cotton	Ohio State 28, Texas A&M 12
J1	Orange	Oklahoma 42, Arkansas 8
J1	Sugar	Nebraska 30, LSU 15
J2	Fiesta	Penn State 14, Miami (Fla.) 10

SEC Standings

	CONFERENCE			OVERALL		
	W	L	T	W	L	T
LSU	5	1	0	9	3	0
Auburn	4	2	0	10	2	0
Alabama	4	2	0	10	3	0
Mississippi	4	2	0	8	3	1
Georgia	4	2	0	8	4	0
Tennessee	3	3	0	7	5	0
Florida	2	4	0	6	5	0
Mississippi State	2	4	0	6	5	0
Kentucky	2	4	0	5	5	1
Vanderbilt	0	6	0	1	10	0

All-SEC Team

POS	OFFENSE	SCHOOL
QB	Don Smith	Mississippi State
QB	Tommy Hodson	LSU
RB	Brent Fullwood	Auburn
RB	Bobby Humphrey	Alabama
WR	Wendell Davis	LSU
WR	Ricky Nattiel	Florida
C	Wes Neighbors	Alabama
C	Ben Tamburello	Auburn
OL	Eric Andolsek	LSU
OL	Jeff Zimmerman	Florida
OL	Bruce Wilkerson	Tennessee
OL	Wilbur Strozier	Georgia
TE	Brian Kinchen	LSU
K	Van Tiffin	Alabama

POS	DEFENSE	SCHOOL
L	Tracy Rocker	Auburn
L	Henry Thomas	LSU
L	Roland Barbay	LSU
LB	Jeff Herrod	Mississippi
LB	Toby Caston	LSU
LB	Cornelius Bennett	Alabama
LB	Aundray Bruce	Auburn
LB	Dale Jones	Tennessee
DB	Stevon Moore	Mississippi
DB	Freddie Robinson	Alabama
DB	Jarvis Williams	Florida
DB	Adran White	Florida
DB	Jeff Noblin	Mississippi
P	Bill Smith	Mississippi

1987 NCAA Major College Statistical Leaders

Individual Leaders

PASSING		CL	G	ATT	COM	PCT	INT	I%	YDS	YPA	TD	TD%	RATING
1	Don McPherson, Syracuse	SR	11	229	129	56.3	11	4.8	2341	10.2	22	9.6	164.3
2	Troy Aikman, UCLA	JR	11	243	159	65.4	6	2.5	2354	9.7	16	6.6	163.6
3	Chuck Hartlieb, Iowa	SR	12	299	196	65.6	8	2.7	2855	9.6	19	6.4	161.4
4	Rodney Peete, Southern California	JR	11	291	175	60.1	9	3.1	2460	8.5	19	6.5	146.5
5	**Eric Jones, Vanderbilt**	**JR**	**11**	**229**	**139**	**60.7**	**11**	**4.8**	**1954**	**8.5**	**16**	**7.0**	**145.8**
6	**Jeff Burger, Auburn**	**SR**	**11**	**267**	**178**	**66.7**	**9**	**3.4**	**2066**	**7.7**	**13**	**4.9**	**141.0**
7	Todd Santos, San Diego State	SR	12	492	306	62.2	15	3.1	3932	8.0	26	5.3	140.7
8	**Tom Hodson, LSU**	**SO**	**11**	**265**	**162**	**61.1**	**9**	**3.4**	**2125**	**8.0**	**15**	**5.7**	**140.4**
9	Terrence Jones, Tulane	JR	11	319	192	60.2	13	4.1	2551	8.0	20	6.3	139.9
10	Steve Walsh, Miami (Fla.)	SO	11	298	176	59.1	7	2.4	2249	7.6	19	6.4	138.8

ALL-PURPOSE		CL	G	RUSH	REC	PR	KR	YDS	YPG
1	Eric Wilkerson, Kent State	JR	11	1221	269	0	584	2074	188.6
2	Thurman Thomas, Oklahoma State	SR	11	1613	184	0	141	1938	176.2
3	Eric Metcalf, Texas	JR	11	1161	238	324	202	1925	175.0
4	Terance Mathis, New Mexico	JR	11	36	1132	16	677	1861	169.2
5	Craig Heyward, Pittsburgh	JR	11	1655	198	0	0	1853	168.5
6	Tim Brown, Notre Dame	SR	11	144	846	401	456	1847	167.9
7	**Bobby Humphrey, Alabama**	**JR**	**11**	**1255**	**170**	**0**	**356**	**1781**	**161.9**
8	Blair Thomas, Penn State	JR	11	1414	300	0	58	1772	161.1
9	Tony Jeffery, TCU	SR	10	1353	257	0	0	1610	161.0
10	Jamie Morris, Michigan	SR	11	1469	126	0	147	1742	158.4

RUSHING/Yards Per Game		CL	G	ATT	YDS	TD	AVG	YPG
1	Elbert Woods, Nevada-Las Vegas	SR	11	259	1658	10	6.4	150.7
2	Craig Heyward, Pittsburgh	JR	11	357	1655	11	4.6	150.5
3	Thurman Thomas, Oklahoma State	SR	11	250	1613	18	6.5	146.6
4	Tony Jeffery, TCU	SR	10	202	1353	10	6.7	135.3
5	Jamie Morris, Michigan	SR	11	259	1469	11	5.7	133.6
6	Lorenzo White, Michigan State	SR	11	322	1459	14	4.5	132.6
7	Blair Thomas, Penn State	JR	11	268	1414	11	5.3	128.6
8	Keith Jones, Nebraska	SR	10	170	1232	13	7.2	123.2
9	Sammie Smith, Florida State	SO	10	172	1230	7	7.2	123.0
10	**Emmitt Smith, Florida**	**FR**	**11**	**229**	**1341**	**13**	**5.9**	**121.9**

RUSHING/Yards Per Carry		CL	G	ATT	YDS	YPC
1	Keith Jones, Nebraska	SR	10	170	1232	7.2
2	Sammie Smith, Florida State	SO	10	172	1230	7.2
3	Michael Dowis, Air Force	SO	12	194	1315	6.8
4	Tony Jeffery, TCU	SR	10	202	1353	6.7
5	**Mark Higgs, Kentucky**	**SR**	**11**	**193**	**1278**	**6.6**
6	Thurman Thomas, Oklahoma State	SR	11	250	1613	6.5
7	Elbert Woods, Nevada-Las Vegas	SR	11	259	1658	6.4
8	**Emmitt Smith, Florida**	**FR**	**11**	**229**	**1341**	**5.9**
9	Jamie Morris, Michigan	SR	11	259	1469	5.7
10	Darrell Thompson, Minnesota	SO	11	224	1229	5.5

Based on top 23 rushers

RECEIVING		CL	G	REC	YDS	TD	YPR	YPG	RPG
1	Jason Phillips, Houston	JR	11	99	875	3	8.8	79.5	9.0
2	Guy Liggins, San Jose State	SR	11	77	1208	10	15.7	109.8	7.0
2	Marc Zeno, Tulane	SR	11	77	1206	13	15.7	109.6	7.0
4	Ron Jenkins, Fresno State	SR	11	76	985	3	13.0	89.5	6.9
5	Terance Mathis, New Mexico	JR	11	73	1132	8	15.5	102.9	6.6
6	**Wendell Davis, LSU**	**SR**	**11**	**72**	**993**	**7**	**13.8**	**90.3**	**6.6**
7	Kendal Smith, Utah State	JR	11	67	1048	7	15.6	95.3	6.1
8	Shane Hall, New Mexico	SR	11	66	415	0	6.3	37.7	6.0
9	Bill Hoffman, Wyoming	SR	12	68	786	3	11.6	65.5	5.7
10	Roger Boone, Duke	SO	11	62	587	0	9.5	53.4	5.6

PUNTING		CL	PUNT	YDS	AVG
1	Tom Tupa, Ohio State	SR	63	2963	47.0
2	Doug Robison, Stanford	SR	44	2011	45.7
3	Scott Tabor, California	SR	66	2993	45.4
4	Craig Salmon, North Carolina St.	SR	64	2877	45.0
5	Greg Montgomery, Michigan State	SR	62	2772	44.7
6	Chris Becker, TCU	JR	59	2594	44.0
7	Barry Helton, Colorado	SR	40	1758	44.0
8	Tony Rhynes, Nevada-Las Vegas	FR	56	2447	43.7
9	Monte Robbins, Michigan	SR	45	1964	43.6
10	Alex Waits, Texas	SO	43	1873	43.6

PUNT RETURNS		CL	PR	YDS	TD	AVG
1	Alan Grant, Stanford	JR	27	446	2	16.5
2	Barry Sanders, Oklahoma State	SO	15	244	2	16.3
3	Donnell Woolford, Clemson	JR	21	326	2	15.5
4	**Nate Lewis, Georgia**	**JR**	**14**	**195**	**1**	**13.9**
5	James Henry, Southern Miss	JR	41	556	4	13.6
6	Eric Metcalf, Texas	JR	24	324	1	13.5
7	Bernard Hall, Oklahoma	SO	11	145	0	13.2
8	Monty Gilbreath, San Diego State	SO	16	205	0	12.8
9	Joey Hamilton, Louisville	JR	17	209	0	12.3
10	Rodney Taylor, Northern Illinois	JR	23	282	1	12.3

KICKOFF RETURNS		CL	KR	YDS	TD	AVG
1	Barry Sanders, Oklahoma State	SO	14	442	2	31.6
2	Darryl Usher, Illinois	SR	15	445	0	29.7
3	Darrin Greer, California	SO	18	510	0	28.3
4	James Dixon, Houston	JR	33	908	1	27.5
5	**Sam Martin, LSU**	**SR**	**17**	**459**	**0**	**27.0**
6	Brock Smith, Fresno State	SR	19	512	1	27.0
7	Randal Hill, Miami (Fla.)	FR	19	497	0	26.2
8	John Hood, Central Michigan	SO	19	489	1	25.7
9	James Saxon, San Jose State	SR	19	488	0	25.7
10	Jon Jeffries, Virginia Tech	FR	22	561	1	25.5

SCORING		CL	TDS	XP	FG	PTS	PTPG
1	Paul Hewitt, San Diego State	JR	24	0	0	144	12.0
2	Derek Schmidt, Florida State	SR	0	47	23	116	10.6
3	**Reggie Cobb, Tennessee**	**FR**	**20**	**0**	**0**	**120**	**10.0**
3	Thurman Thomas, Oklahoma State	SR	18	2	0	110	10.0
5	John Harvey, Texas-El Paso	JR	18	0	0	108	9.8
6	Collin Mackie, South Carolina	FR	0	37	23	106	9.6
7	Alfredo Velasco, UCLA	SO	0	46	18	100	9.1
8	Bernie Parmalee, Ball State	FR	15	0	0	90	9.0
8	Harold Green, South Carolina	SO	15	0	0	90	9.0
10	Kenny Jackson, San Jose State	SR	16	2	0	98	8.9

FIELD GOALS		CL	FGA	FGM	PCT	FGG
1	Collin Mackie, South Carolina	FR	30	23	0.77	2.09
1	Derek Schmidt, Florida State	SR	31	23	0.74	2.09
3	Jeff Shudak, Iowa State	FR	25	20	0.80	1.82
3	Gary Gussman, Miami (Ohio)	SR	25	20	0.80	1.82
5	David Treadwell, Clemson	SR	21	18	0.86	1.80
6	Rob Houghtlin, Iowa	SR	29	21	0.72	1.75
7	Chip Browndyke, Houston	SR	24	19	0.79	1.73
8	Alfredo Velasco, UCLA	SO	22	18	0.82	1.64
8	John Ivanic, Northern Illinois	FR	24	18	0.75	1.64
10	Greg Cox, Miami (Fla.)	SR	22	17	0.77	1.55

INTERCEPTIONS		CL	INT	YDS	TD	INT/GM
1	Keith McMeans, Virginia	FR	9	35	0	0.90
2	Todd Krumm, Michigan State	SR	9	129	0	0.82
2	Chuck Cecil, Arizona	SR	9	77	0	0.82
4	Johnny Jackson, Houston	SO	8	218	3	0.73
4	Ricky Dixon, Oklahoma	SR	8	214	1	0.73
4	Eric Allen, Arizona State	SR	8	185	2	0.73
4	Brad Edwards, South Carolina	SR	8	132	2	0.73
4	Kevin Cook, Virginia	SO	8	14	0	0.73
9	Rodney Rice, Brigham Young	JR	6	51	1	0.67
10	Brett Whitley, Northwestern	SR	7	202	0	0.64
10	A.J. Greene, Wake Forest	JR	7	128	2	0.64
10	Falanda Newton, TCU	JR	7	117	0	0.64
10	**Todd Sandroni, Mississippi**	**FR**	**7**	**47**	**0**	**0.64**
10	Brad Humphreys, Stanford	SR	7	22	0	0.64

Team Leaders

RUSHING OFFENSE		G	ATT	YDS	AVG	TD	YPG
1	Oklahoma	11	730	4717	6.5	52	428.8
2	Air Force	12	784	4635	5.9	43	386.3
3	Nebraska	11	673	4108	6.1	40	373.5
4	Colorado	11	665	3370	5.1	28	306.4
5	Army	11	749	3278	4.4	28	298.0
6	Northern Illinois	11	701	3246	4.6	31	295.1
7	TCU	11	618	3241	5.2	24	294.6
8	**Georgia**	**11**	**596**	**3019**	**5.1**	**27**	**274.5**
9	Florida State	11	530	2995	5.7	34	272.3
10	Arkansas	12	753	3196	4.2	31	266.3

PASSING OFFENSE		G	ATT	COM	INT	PCT	YDS	YPA	TD	I%	YPC	YPG
1	San Jose State	11	450	271	13	60.2	3719	8.3	26	2.9	13.7	338.1
2	San Diego State	12	509	314	16	61.7	3990	7.8	26	3.1	12.7	332.5
3	Utah	12	525	306	21	58.3	3884	7.4	25	4.0	12.7	323.7
4	Duke	11	470	266	20	56.6	3443	7.3	23	4.3	12.9	313.0
5	Wyoming	12	522	282	19	54.0	3703	7.1	27	3.6	13.1	308.6
6	Houston	11	499	283	18	56.7	3265	6.5	15	3.6	11.5	296.8
7	Iowa	12	413	255	13	61.7	3559	8.6	23	3.2	14.0	296.6
8	New Mexico	11	514	284	27	55.3	3230	6.3	17	5.3	11.4	293.6
9	Brigham Young	12	477	276	23	57.9	3501	7.3	18	4.8	12.7	291.8
10	Oregon State	11	489	257	26	52.6	3152	6.4	19	5.3	12.3	286.5

TOTAL OFFENSE		G	P	YDS	AVG	TD	YPG
1	Oklahoma	11	829	5497	6.6	61	499.7
2	Nebraska	11	835	5379	6.4	56	489.0
3	Florida State	11	848	5361	6.3	52	487.4
4	Wyoming	12	951	5655	5.9	49	471.3
5	San Jose State	11	831	5119	6.2	49	465.4
6	UCLA	11	826	4886	5.9	45	444.2
7	Air Force	12	904	5320	5.9	48	443.3
8	**LSU**	**11**	**747**	**4843**	**6.5**	**42**	**440.3**
8	Syracuse	11	778	4843	6.2	45	440.3
10	San Diego State	12	924	5263	5.7	46	438.6

RUSHING DEFENSE		G	ATT	YDS	AVG	TD	YPG
1	Michigan State	11	360	676	1.9	5	61.5
2	Clemson	11	388	880	2.3	10	80.0
3	San Jose State	11	408	926	2.3	9	84.2
4	UCLA	11	373	936	2.5	7	85.1
5	South Carolina	11	419	1036	2.5	6	94.2
6	Miami (Fla.)	11	455	1064	2.3	5	96.7
7	Arkansas	12	393	1208	3.1	9	100.7
8	Oklahoma	11	456	1163	2.6	4	105.7
9	Nebraska	11	423	1177	2.8	10	107.0
10	Texas A&M	11	463	1203	2.6	9	109.4

PASSING DEFENSE		G	ATT	COM	PCT	YPC	INT	I%	YDS	YPA	TD	YPG
1	Oklahoma	11	248	108	43.5	10.4	25	10.1	1126	4.5	3	102.4
2	Illinois	11	185	83	44.9	13.9	9	4.9	1152	6.2	5	104.7
3	Kansas	11	190	95	50.0	12.8	6	3.2	1212	6.4	11	110.2
4	Pittsburgh	11	220	86	39.1	14.8	8	3.6	1273	5.8	5	115.7
5	Navy	11	184	106	57.6	13.2	11	6.0	1399	7.6	10	127.2
6	West Virginia	11	252	131	52.0	11.2	14	5.6	1465	5.8	7	133.2
6	South Carolina	11	295	132	44.7	11.1	23	7.8	1465	5.0	5	133.2
8	Memphis	11	243	124	51.0	12.0	12	4.9	1485	6.1	12	135.0
9	Texas A&M	11	265	116	43.8	12.8	12	4.5	1489	5.6	7	135.4
10	**Florida**	**11**	**269**	**128**	**47.6**	**11.8**	**12**	**4.5**	**1512**	**5.6**	**4**	**137.5**

TOTAL DEFENSE		G	P	YDS	AVG	TD	YPG
1	Oklahoma	11	704	2289	3.3	7	208.1
2	Michigan State	11	676	2482	3.7	13	225.6
3	South Carolina	11	714	2501	3.5	11	227.4
4	Pittsburgh	11	699	2563	3.7	11	233.0
5	Clemson	11	704	2640	3.8	17	240.0
6	Miami (Fla.)	11	739	2682	3.6	10	243.8
7	Texas A&M	11	728	2692	3.7	16	244.7
8	Nebraska	11	734	2912	4.0	15	264.7
9	**Florida**	**11**	**744**	**2956**	**4.0**	**13**	**268.7**
10	**Auburn**	**11**	**752**	**3012**	**4.0**	**11**	**273.8**

SCORING OFFENSE		G	PTS	AVG
1	Oklahoma	11	479	43.5
2	Florida State	11	450	40.9
3	Nebraska	11	423	38.5
4	UCLA	11	406	36.9
5	Miami (Fla.)	11	392	35.6
6	San Jose State	11	390	35.5
7	Oklahoma State	11	374	34.0
8	Wyoming	12	407	33.9
9	Syracuse	11	363	33.0
10	**Tennessee**	**12**	**395**	**32.9**

SCORING DEFENSE		G	PTS	AVG
1	Oklahoma	11	82	7.5
2	South Carolina	11	111	10.1
2	Miami (Fla.)	11	111	10.1
4	Pittsburgh	11	114	10.4
5	**Auburn**	**11**	**116**	**10.5**
6	Nebraska	11	133	12.1
7	Florida State	11	135	12.3
8	Michigan State	11	136	12.4
9	Michigan	11	148	13.5
10	Syracuse	11	153	13.9

1987

FINAL POLL (JAN. 3)

UP	AP	SCHOOL	FINAL RECORD
1	1	Miami (Fla.)	12-0-0
2	2	Florida State	11-1-0
3	3	Oklahoma	11-1-0
4	4	Syracuse	11-0-1
5	5	LSU	10-1-1
6	6	Nebraska	10-2-0
7	7	Auburn	9-1-2
8	8	Michigan State	9-2-1
11	9	UCLA	10-2-0
9	10	Texas A&M	10-2-0
12	11	Oklahoma State	10-2-0
10	12	Clemson	10-2-0
14	13	Georgia	9-3-0
13	14	Tennessee	10-2-1
15	15	South Carolina	8-4-0
15	16	Iowa	10-3-0
	17	Notre Dame	8-4-0
17	18	Southern California	8-4-0
18	19	Michigan	8-4-0
	20	Arizona State	7-4-1
19		Texas	7-5-1
20		Indiana	8-4-0

CONSENSUS ALL-AMERICANS

POS	OFFENSE	SCHOOL
QB	Don McPherson	Syracuse
RB	Lorenzo White	Michigan State
RB	Craig Heyward	Pittsburgh
WR	Tim Brown	Notre Dame
WR	Wendell Davis	LSU
TE	Keith Jackson	Oklahoma
L	Mark Hutson	Oklahoma
L	Dave Cadigan	Southern California
L	John Elliott	Michigan
L	Randall McDaniel	Arizona State
C	Nacho Albergamo	LSU
PK	David Treadwell	Clemson

OTHERS RECEIVING FIRST-TEAM HONORS

RB	Gaston Green	UCLA
RB	Bobby Humphrey	Alabama
RB	Thurman Thomas	Oklahoma State
WR	Sterling Sharpe	South Carolina
WR	Marc Zeno	Tulane
WR	Ernie Jones	Indiana
L	John McCormick	Nebraska
L	Stacy Searels	Auburn
PK	Marty Zendejas	Nevada

POS	DEFENSE	SCHOOL
L	Daniel Stubbs	Miami (Fla.)
L	Chad Hennings	Air Force
L	Tracy Rocker	Auburn
L	Ted Gregory	Syracuse
L	John Roper	Texas A&M
LB	Chris Spielman	Ohio State
LB	Aundray Bruce	Auburn
LB	Dante Jones	Oklahoma
DB	Bennie Blades	Miami (Fla.)
DB	Deion Sanders	Florida State
DB	Rickey Dixon	Oklahoma
DB	Chuck Cecil	Arizona
P	Tom Tupa	Ohio State

OTHERS RECEIVING FIRST-TEAM HONORS

DL	Broderick Thomas	Nebraska
DL	Michael Dean Perry	Clemson
DL	Tony Cherico	Arkansas
DL	Darrell Reed	Oklahoma
LB	Ken Norton	UCLA
LB	Ezekial Gadson	Pittsburgh
LB	Chris Gaines	Vanderbilt
LB	Kurt Crain	Auburn
LB	Paul McGowan	Florida State
DB	Jarvis Williams	Florida
DB	Donnell Woolford	Clemson

HEISMAN TROPHY VOTING

	PLAYER	POS	SCHOOL	TOTAL
1	Tim Brown	WR	Notre Dame	1442
2	Don McPherson	QB	Syracuse	831
3	Gordie Lockbaum	TB	Holy Cross	657
4	Lorenzo White	TB	Michigan State	632
5	Craig Heyward	RB	Pittsburgh	170
6	Chris Spielman	LB	Ohio State	110
7	Thurman Thomas	TB	Oklahoma State	99
8	Gaston Green	TB	UCLA	73
9	Emmitt Smith	RB	Florida	70
10	Bobby Humphrey	HB	Alabama	63

AWARD WINNERS

PLAYER	AWARD
Don McPherson, QB, Syracuse	Maxwell
Chad Hennings, DT, Air Force	Outland
Tim Brown, WR, Notre Dame	Camp
Chris Spielman, LB, Ohio State	Lombardi
Don McPherson, QB, Miami (Fla.)	Maxwell
Don McPherson, QB, Syracuse	O'Brien
Paul McGowan, LB, Florida State	Butkus
Bennie Blades, DB, Miami (Fla.)	Thorpe
Rickey Dixon, DB, Oklahoma	Thorpe
Don McPherson, QB, Syracuse	Unitas

BOWL GAMES

DATE	GAME	SCORE
D12	California	Eastern Michigan 30, San Jose St. 27
D19	Independence	Washington 24, Tulane 12
D22	All-American	Virginia 22, Brigham Young 16
D25	Sun	Oklahoma State 35, West Virginia 33
D25	Aloha	UCLA 20, Florida 16
D29	Liberty	Georgia 20, Arkansas 17
D30	Freedom	Arizona State 33, Air Force 28
D30	Holiday	Iowa 20, Wyoming 19
D31	Gator	LSU 30, South Carolina 13
D31	Bluebonnet	Texas 32, Pittsburgh 27
J1	Citrus	Clemson 35, Penn State 10
J1	Fiesta	Florida State 31, Nebraska 28
J1	Orange	Miami (Fla.) 20, Oklahoma 14
J1	Rose	Michigan St. 20, Southern California 17
J1	Cotton	Texas A&M 35, Notre Dame 10
J1	Sugar	Auburn 16, Syracuse 16
J2	Hall of Fame	Michigan 28, Alabama 24
J2	Peach	Tennessee 27, Indiana 22

SEC STANDINGS

	CONFERENCE			OVERALL		
	W	L	T	W	L	T
Auburn	5	0	1	9	1	2
LSU	5	1	0	10	1	1
Tennessee	4	1	1	10	2	1
Georgia	4	2	0	9	3	0
Alabama	4	2	0	7	5	0
Florida	3	3	0	6	6	0
Kentucky	1	5	0	5	6	0
Mississippi State	1	5	0	4	7	0
Vanderbilt	1	5	0	4	7	0
Mississippi	1	5	0	3	8	0

ALL-SEC TEAM

POS	OFFENSE	SCHOOL
QB	Jeff Burger	Auburn
QB	Tommy Hodson	LSU
RB	Bobby Humphrey	Alabama
RB	Emmitt Smith	Florida
WR	Wendell Davis	LSU
WR	Lawyer Tillman	Auburn
OL	Kim Stephens	Georgia
OL	Stacy Searels	Auburn
OL	Harry Galbreath	Tennessee
OL	Eric Andolsek	LSU
C	Nacho Albergamo	LSU
TE	Howard Cross	Alabama
TE	Walter Reeves	Auburn
PK	Win Lyle	Auburn

POS	DEFENSE	SCHOOL
L	Tracy Rocker	Auburn
L	Jerry Reese	Kentucky
L	Darrell Phillips	LSU
LB	Kurt Crain	Auburn
LB	John Brantley	Georgia
LB	Aundray Bruce	Auburn
LB	Derrick Thomas	Alabama
DB	Kevin Porter	Auburn
DB	Louis Oliver	Florida
DB	Jarvis Williams	Florida
DB	Chris Carrier	LSU
P	Brian Shulman	Auburn

1988 NCAA Major College Statistical Leaders

Individual Leaders

PASSING	CL	G	ATT	COM	PCT	INT	I%	YDS	YPA	TD	TD%	RATING
1 Timm Rosenbach, Washington State	JR	11	302	199	65.9	10	3.3	2791	9.2	23	7.6	162.0
2 Mike Gundy, Oklahoma State	JR	11	236	153	64.8	12	5.1	2163	9.2	19	8.1	158.2
3 Chip Ferguson, Florida State	SR	10	194	122	62.9	11	5.7	1714	8.8	16	8.3	153.0
4 Troy Aikman, UCLA	SR	11	327	209	63.9	8	2.5	2599	8.0	23	7.0	149.0
5 Todd Philcox, Syracuse	SR	11	234	141	60.3	11	4.7	2076	8.9	16	6.9	147.9
6 Steve Walsh, Miami (Fla.)	JR	11	390	233	59.7	12	3.1	3115	8.0	29	7.4	145.2
7 Warren Jones, Hawaii	SR	12	259	138	53.3	11	4.3	2268	8.8	19	7.3	142.6
8 Scott Mitchell, Utah	SO	11	533	323	60.6	15	2.8	4322	8.1	29	5.4	141.0
9 Randy Welniak, Wyoming	SR	12	324	184	56.8	9	2.8	2627	8.1	21	6.5	140.7
10 Rodney Peete, Southern California	SR	11	338	208	61.5	10	3.0	2654	7.9	18	5.3	139.2

ALL-PURPOSE	CL	G	RUSH	REC	PR	KR	YDS	YPG
1 Barry Sanders, Oklahoma State	JR	11	2628	106	95	421	3250	295.5
2 Johnny Johnson, San Jose State	JR	12	1219	668	0	315	2202	183.5
3 Eric Wilkerson, Kent State	SR	11	1325	73	0	502	1900	172.7
4 Tony Boles, Michigan	JR	10	1359	64	0	302	1725	172.5
5 Kendal Smith, Utah State	SR	11	25	1196	141	525	1887	171.6
6 Michael Pierce, Tulane	JR	10	345	534	0	765	1644	164.4
7 Andrew Greer, Ohio U.	JR	11	863	114	0	810	1787	162.5
8 Anthony Thompson, Indiana	JR	11	1546	219	0	0	1765	160.5
9 Eric Metcalf, Texas	SR	10	932	333	192	117	1574	157.4
10 Darren Lewis, Texas A&M	SO	11	1692	13	0	0	1705	155.0

RUSHING/Yards Per Game	CL	G	ATT	YDS	TD	AVG	YPG
1 Barry Sanders, Oklahoma State	JR	11	344	2628	37	7.6	238.9
2 Darren Lewis, Texas A&M	SO	11	306	1692	7	5.5	153.8
3 Anthony Thompson, Indiana	JR	11	329	1546	24	4.7	140.6
4 Tony Boles, Michigan	JR	10	248	1359	9	5.5	135.9
5 Ken Clark, Nebraska	JR	12	232	1497	12	6.5	124.8
6 Eric Bieniemy, Colorado	SO	10	219	1243	10	5.7	124.3
7 Blake Ezor, Michigan State	JR	11	290	1358	10	4.7	123.5
8 Eric Wilkerson, Kent State	SR	11	247	1325	14	5.4	120.5
9 Steve Broussard, Washington State	JR	10	189	1141	11	6.0	114.1
10 Don Riley, Central Michigan	JR	11	215	1238	7	5.8	112.6

RUSHING/Yards Per Carry	CL	G	ATT	YDS	YPC
1 Barry Sanders, Oklahoma State	JR	11	344	2628	7.6
2 Ken Clark, Nebraska	JR	12	232	1497	6.5
3 Tim Worley, Georgia	**JR**	**11**	**191**	**1216**	**6.4**
4 Steve Broussard, Washington State	JR	10	189	1141	6.0
5 Kennard Martin, North Carolina	SO	11	193	1146	5.9
6 Curvin Richards, Pittsburgh	FR	11	207	1228	5.9
7 Don Riley, Central Michigan	JR	11	215	1238	5.8
8 Terry Allen, Clemson	SO	11	199	1139	5.7
9 Eric Bieniemy, Colorado	SO	10	219	1243	5.7
10 Darren Lewis, Texas A&M	SO	11	306	1692	5.5

Based on top 23 rushers

RECEIVING	CL	G	REC	YDS	TD	YPR	YPG	RPG
1 Jason Phillips, Houston	SR	11	108	1444	15	13.4	131.3	9.8
2 James Dixon, Houston	SR	11	102	1103	11	10.8	100.3	9.3
3 Boo Mitchell, Vanderbilt	**SR**	**11**	**78**	**1213**	**5**	**15.6**	**110.3**	**7.1**
4 Hart Lee Dykes, Oklahoma State	SR	11	74	1278	14	17.3	116.2	6.7
5 Roger Boone, Duke	JR	11	73	630	2	8.6	57.3	6.6
6 Tom Waddle, Boston College	SR	11	70	902	5	12.9	82.0	6.4
7 Greg Washington, Kansas State	JR	11	69	928	9	13.4	84.4	6.3
8 Clarkston Hines, Duke	JR	11	68	1067	10	15.7	97.0	6.2
9 Marv Cook, Iowa	SR	9	55	645	3	11.7	71.7	6.1
10 Kevin Evans, San Jose State	JR	10	61	887	4	14.5	88.7	6.1

PUNTING	CL	PUNT	YDS	AVG
1 Keith English, Colorado	SR	51	2297	45.0
2 Pat Thompson, Brigham Young	SR	49	2195	44.8
3 Kent Elmore, Tennessee	**JR**	**41**	**1818**	**44.3**
4 Tony Rhynes, Nevada-Las Vegas	JR	66	2905	44.0
5 Martin Bailey, Wake Forest	SR	46	2012	43.7
6 Bill Rudison, Akron	JR	58	2511	43.3
7 Chris Mohr, Alabama	**SR**	**58**	**2475**	**42.7**
8 Tom Kilpatrick, Wyoming	SR	50	2131	42.6
9 Jim Sirois, Cal St.-Fullerton	SR	59	2513	42.6
10 Bobby Lilljedahl, Texas	JR	61	2598	42.6

PUNT RETURNS	CL	PR	YDS	TD	AVG
1 Deion Sanders, Florida State	SR	33	503	1	15.2
2 Marcus Cherry, Boston College	SR	15	206	1	13.7
3 James Henry, Southern Miss	SR	23	309	2	13.4
4 Ricky Watters, Notre Dame	SO	19	253	2	13.3
5 Darryl Henley, UCLA	SR	21	279	2	13.3
6 Carl Platt, South Carolina	SO	21	266	0	12.7
7 Chuck Carswell, Georgia	**FR**	**31**	**388**	**0**	**12.5**
8 Kimble Anders, Houston	SO	17	205	0	12.1
9 Larry Hargrove, Ohio U.	JR	21	253	1	12.1
10 John Miller, Michigan State	SR	15	179	0	11.9

KICKOFF RETURNS	CL	KR	YDS	TD	AVG
1 Raghib Ismail, Notre Dame	FR	12	433	2	36.1
2 Chris Oldham, Oregon	JR	26	764	1	29.4
3 Erik Mortensen, Brigham Young	FR	14	398	1	28.4
4 Carlos Snow, Ohio State	SO	19	513	1	27.0
5 Larry Khan-Smith, Hawaii	SO	32	852	1	26.6
6 Chris Williams, North Carolina St.	SO	18	468	0	26.0
7 Tim Frager, Boston College	SO	19	491	0	25.8
8 Patrick Rowe, San Diego State	SO	31	799	0	25.8
9 Quinton McCracken, Duke	FR	19	483	1	25.4
10 Tony Boles, Michigan	JR	12	302	0	25.2

SCORING	CL	TDS	XP	FG	PTS	PTPG
1 Barry Sanders, Oklahoma State	JR	39	0	0	234	21.3
2 Anthony Thompson, Indiana	JR	24	0	0	144	13.1
3 Chris Jacke, Texas-El Paso	SR	0	48	25	123	10.3
4 Charlie Baumann, West Virginia	SR	0	58	18	112	10.2
5 Roman Anderson, Houston	FR	0	51	19	108	9.8
5 Tim Worley, Georgia	**JR**	**18**	**0**	**0**	**108**	**9.8**
7 Carlos Huerta, Miami (Fla.)	FR	0	44	21	107	9.7
8 Johnny Johnson, San Jose State	JR	19	2	0	116	9.7
9 Kendall Trainor, Arkansas	SR	0	30	24	102	9.3
10 Cary Blanchard, Oklahoma State	SO	0	67	11	100	9.1

FIELD GOALS	CL	FGA	FGM	PCT	FGG
1 Kendall Trainor, Arkansas	SR	27	24	0.89	2.18
2 Chris Jacke, Texas-El Paso	SR	27	25	0.93	2.08
3 Rob Keen, California	SO	25	21	0.84	1.91
3 Carlos Huerta, Miami (Fla.)	FR	27	21	0.78	1.91
5 David Browndyke, LSU	**JR**	**23**	**19**	**0.83**	**1.73**
5 John Hopkins, Stanford	SO	24	19	0.79	1.73
5 Roman Anderson, Houston	FR	25	19	0.76	1.73
5 Philip Doyle, Alabama	**SO**	**31**	**19**	**0.61**	**1.73**
9 Kenny Stucker, Ball State	FR	23	18	0.78	1.64
9 Pat O'Morrow, Ohio State	JR	23	18	0.78	1.64
9 Collin Mackie, South Carolina	SO	24	18	0.75	1.64
9 Charlie Baumann, West Virginia	SR	25	18	0.72	1.64
9 John Langeloh, Michigan State	SO	26	18	0.69	1.64
9 Steve Loop, Fresno State	JR	27	18	0.67	1.64

INTERCEPTIONS	CL	INT	YDS	TD	INT/GM
1 Kurt Larson, Michigan State	SR	8	78	1	0.73
1 Andy Logan, Kent State	SR	8	54	0	0.73
3 Todd Sandroni, Mississippi	**SO**	**7**	**33**	**1**	**0.70**
4 Greg Jackson, LSU	**SR**	**7**	**221**	**2**	**0.64**
4 Eddie Moore, Memphis	JR	7	51	0	0.64
4 Tony McCorvey, Bowling Green	SR	7	33	0	0.64
7 Deion Sanders, Florida State	SR	5	116	2	0.56
8 Stanley Richards, Texas *	SO	6	92	0	0.55
8 Adrian Jones, Missouri *	JR	6	84	0	0.55
8 Lavon Edwards, Utah *	FR	6	74	0	0.55
8 Patrick Williams, Arkansas *	JR	6	57	1	0.55
8 David Johnson, Central Michigan *	SO	6	56	0	0.55

*Nine tied with 0.55; these had the most yards

Team Leaders

RUSHING OFFENSE	G	ATT	YDS	AVG	TD	YPG
1 Nebraska	12	735	4588	6.2	47	382.3
2 Air Force	12	734	4530	6.2	48	377.5
3 Army	11	786	3813	4.9	35	346.6
4 Oklahoma	11	668	3777	5.7	36	343.4
5 Oklahoma State	11	561	3492	6.2	47	317.5
6 West Virginia	11	621	3228	5.2	40	293.5
7 Colorado	11	614	3095	5.0	34	281.4
8 Kent State	11	624	3073	4.9	28	279.4
9 Clemson	11	625	3054	4.9	32	277.6
10 Texas A&M	12	653	3102	4.8	33	258.5

PASSING OFFENSE	G	ATT	COM	INT	PCT	YDS	YPA	TD	I%	YPC	YPG
1 Utah	11	543	327	20	60.2	4355	8.0	29	3.7	13.3	395.9
2 Houston	11	580	344	15	59.3	4153	7.2	38	2.6	12.1	377.5
3 Duke	11	496	292	20	58.9	3868	7.8	24	4.0	13.2	351.6
4 Brigham Young	12	475	258	20	54.3	3874	8.2	26	4.2	15.0	322.8
5 Miami (Fla.)	11	441	260	13	59.0	3503	7.9	35	3.0	13.5	318.5
6 Utah State	11	455	248	21	54.5	3278	7.2	19	4.6	13.2	298.0
7 Iowa	12	419	260	10	62.1	3324	7.9	15	2.4	12.8	277.0
8 Texas Tech	11	364	194	11	53.3	2917	8.0	20	3.0	15.0	265.2
9 Oregon State	11	445	275	9	61.8	2896	6.5	18	2.0	10.5	263.3
10 Western Michigan	11	397	221	18	55.7	2863	7.2	22	4.5	13.0	260.3

TOTAL OFFENSE	G	P	YDS	AVG	TD	YPG
1 Utah	11	901	5795	6.4	48	526.8
2 Oklahoma State	11	803	5667	7.1	66	515.2
3 Washington State	11	854	5439	6.4	49	494.5
4 Houston	11	832	5331	6.4	55	484.6
5 West Virginia	11	816	5310	6.5	56	482.7
6 Wyoming	12	922	5741	6.2	62	478.4
7 Nebraska	12	898	5735	6.4	59	477.9
8 Duke	11	868	5111	5.9	39	464.6
9 Southern California	11	911	5077	5.6	45	461.6
10 Brigham Young	12	909	5483	6.0	47	456.9

RUSHING DEFENSE	G	ATT	YDS	AVG	TD	YPG
1 Auburn	**11**	**334**	**695**	**2.1**	**3**	**63.2**
2 Southern California	11	313	843	2.7	7	76.6
3 Miami (Fla.)	11	419	908	2.2	4	82.5
4 Arkansas	11	394	1010	2.6	12	91.8
5 Alabama	**11**	**401**	**1053**	**2.6**	**8**	**95.7**
6 North Carolina St.	11	451	1140	2.5	5	103.6
7 Central Michigan	11	441	1165	2.6	10	105.9
8 UCLA	11	416	1173	2.8	10	106.6
9 Wyoming	12	437	1314	3.0	14	109.5
10 Notre Dame	11	403	1236	3.1	6	112.4

PASSING DEFENSE	G	ATT	COM	PCT	YPC	INT	I%	YDS	YPA	TD	YPG
1 Baylor	11	237	97	40.9	13.4	9	3.8	1296	5.5	11	117.8
2 Pittsburgh	11	208	87	41.8	15.0	13	6.3	1308	6.3	7	118.9
3 Florida	**11**	**254**	**121**	**47.6**	**11.2**	**16**	**6.3**	**1360**	**5.4**	**10**	**123.6**
4 Purdue	11	232	93	40.1	15.4	16	6.9	1430	6.2	10	130.0
5 Florida State	11	278	110	39.6	13.1	18	6.5	1443	5.2	10	131.2
6 Nebraska	12	282	123	43.6	13.2	16	5.7	1618	5.7	10	134.8
7 Navy	11	212	105	49.5	14.1	7	3.3	1484	7.0	8	134.9
8 Georgia Tech	11	252	129	51.2	11.8	14	5.6	1528	6.1	8	138.9
9 Eastern Michigan	10	212	124	58.5	11.3	11	5.2	1395	6.6	7	139.5
10 Kentucky	**11**	**250**	**134**	**53.6**	**11.5**	**10**	**4.0**	**1535**	**6.1**	**11**	**139.5**

TOTAL DEFENSE	G	P	YDS	AVG	TD	YPG
1 Auburn	**11**	**666**	**2399**	**3.6**	**9**	**218.1**
2 Miami (Fla.)	11	726	2662	3.7	11	242.0
3 Florida	**11**	**710**	**2726**	**3.8**	**18**	**247.8**
4 Pittsburgh	11	697	2796	4.0	20	254.2
5 Baylor	11	686	2835	4.1	24	257.7
6 Ball State	11	664	2887	4.3	18	262.5
7 Nebraska	12	743	3153	4.2	20	262.8
8 North Carolina St.	11	783	2907	3.7	11	264.3
9 Fresno State	11	738	2909	3.9	17	264.5
10 Southern California	11	655	2958	4.5	19	268.9

SCORING OFFENSE	G	PTS	AVG
1 Oklahoma State	11	522	47.5
2 West Virginia	11	472	42.9
3 Wyoming	12	497	41.4
4 Houston	11	452	41.1
5 Florida State	11	442	40.2
6 Nebraska	12	474	39.5
7 Utah	11	399	36.3
8 Miami (Fla.)	11	395	35.9
9 Texas-El Paso	12	427	35.6
10 Washington State	11	391	35.5

SCORING DEFENSE	G	PTS	AVG
1 Auburn	**11**	**79**	**7.2**
2 Miami (Fla.)	11	113	10.3
3 Notre Dame	11	135	12.3
4 Fresno State	11	139	12.6
5 North Carolina St.	11	142	12.9
6 Michigan State	11	143	13.0
7 Oklahoma	11	147	13.4
8 Clemson	11	151	13.7
9 Michigan	11	153	13.9
10 Alabama	**11**	**160**	**14.5**

1988

Final Poll (Jan. 3)

UP	AP	School	Final Record
1	1	Notre Dame	12-0-0
2	2	Miami (Fla.)	11-1-0
3	3	Florida State	11-1-0
4	4	Michigan	9-2-1
5	5	West Virginia	11-1-0
6	6	UCLA	10-2-0
9	7	Southern California	10-2-0
7	**8**	**Auburn**	**10-2-0**
8	9	Clemson	10-2-0
10	10	Nebraska	11-2-0
11	11	Oklahoma State	10-2-0
13	12	Arkansas	10-2-0
12	13	Syracuse	10-2-0
14	14	Oklahoma	9-3-0
15	**15**	**Georgia**	**9-3-0**
16	16	Washington State	9-3-0
17	**17**	**Alabama**	**9-3-0**
	18	Houston	9-3-0
	19	**LSU**	**8-4-0**
19	20	Indiana	8-3-1
17		North Carolina St.	8-3-1
20		Wyoming	11-2-0

Consensus All-Americans

Pos	Offense	School
QB	Steve Walsh	Miami (Fla.)
QB	Troy Aikman	UCLA
RB	Barry Sanders	Oklahoma State
RB	Anthony Thompson	Indiana
RB	**Tim Worley**	**Georgia**
WR	Jason Phillips	Houston
WR	Hart Lee Dykes	Oklahoma State
TE	Marv Cook	Iowa
L	Tony Mandarich	Michigan State
L	Anthony Phillips	Oklahoma
L	Mike Utley	Washington State
L	Mark Stepnoski	Pittsburgh
C	Jake Young	Nebraska
C	John Vitale	Michigan
PK	Kendall Trainor	Arkansas

Others receiving first-team honors

QB	Rodney Peete	Southern California
RB	Darren Lewis	Texas A&M
WR	Clarkston Hines	Duke
WR	Erik Affholter	Southern California
TE	**Troy Sadowski**	**Georgia**
TE	**Wesley Walls**	**Mississippi**
L	Pat Tomberlin	Florida State
L	Steve Wisniewski	Penn State
L	Andy Heck	Notre Dame
PK	Chris Jacke	Texas-El Paso
RS	Tyrone Thurman	Texas Tech

Pos	Defense	School
L	Mark Messner	Michigan
L	**Tracy Rocker**	**Auburn**
L	Wayne Martin	Arkansas
L	Frank Stams	Notre Dame
L	Bill Hawkins	Miami (Fla.)
LB	**Derrick Thomas**	**Alabama**
LB	Broderick Thomas	Nebraska
LB	Michael Stonebreaker	Notre Dame
DB	Deion Sanders	Florida State
DB	Donnell Woolford	Clemson
DB	**Louis Oliver**	**Florida**
DB	Darryl Henley	UCLA
P	Keith English	Colorado

Others receiving first-team honors

L	Dave Haight	Iowa
L	Tim Ryan	Southern California
LB	Carnell Lake	UCLA
LB	Britt Hager	Texas
LB	Jerry Olsavsky	Pittsburgh
LB	**Keith DeLong**	**Tennessee**
DB	Markus Paul	Syracuse
DB	Mark Carrier	Southern California
P	Pat Thompson	Brigham Young

Heisman Trophy Voting

Player		Pos	School	Total
1	Barry Sanders	TB	Oklahoma St.	1878
2	Rodney Peete	QB	Southern Cal	912
3	Troy Aikman	QB	UCLA	582
4	Steve Walsh	QB	Miami (Fla.)	341
5	Major Harris	QB	West Virginia	280
6	Tony Mandarich	OT	Michigan State	52
7	Timm Rosenbach	QB	Washington St.	44
8	Deion Sanders	CB	Florida State	22
9	Anthony Thompson	TB	Indiana	21
10	**Derrick Thomas**	**LB**	**Alabama**	**20**

Award Winners

Player	Award
Barry Sanders, RB, Oklahoma State	Maxwell
Tracy Rocker, DT, Auburn	**Outland**
Barry Sanders, RB, Oklahoma State	Camp
Tracy Rocker, DT, Auburn	**Lombardi**
Troy Aikman, QB, UCLA	O'Brien
Derrick Thomas, LB, Alabama	**Butkus**
Deion Sanders, DB, Florida State	Thorpe
Rodney Peete, QB, Southern California	Unitas

Bowl Games

Date	Game	Score
D10	California	Fresno State 35, Western Michigan 30
D23	Independence	Southern Miss 38, Texas-El Paso 18
D24	**Sun**	**Alabama 29, Army 28**
D25	Aloha	Washington State 24, Houston 22
D28	Liberty	Indiana 34, South Carolina 10
D29	Freedom	Brigham Young 20, Colorado 17
D29	**All-American**	**Florida 14, Illinois 10**
D30	Holiday	Oklahoma State 62, Wyoming 14
D31	Peach	North Carolina St. 28, Iowa 23
J1	**Gator**	**Georgia 34, Michigan State 27**
J2	Citrus	Clemson 13, Oklahoma 6
J2	Orange	Miami (Fla.) 23, Nebraska 3
J2	Rose	Michigan 22, Southern California 14
J2	Fiesta	Notre Dame 34, West Virginia 21
J2	**Hall of Fame**	**Syracuse 23, LSU 10**
J2	Cotton	UCLA 17, Arkansas 3
J2	**Sugar**	**Florida State 13, Auburn 7**

Conference Standings

	Conference			Overall		
	W	L	T	W	L	T
Auburn	6	1	0	10	2	0
LSU	6	1	0	8	4	0
Georgia	5	2	0	9	3	0
Alabama	4	3	0	9	3	0
Florida	4	3	0	7	5	0
Tennessee	3	4	0	5	6	0
Mississippi	3	4	0	5	6	0
Kentucky	2	5	0	5	6	0
Vanderbilt	2	5	0	3	8	0
Mississippi State	0	7	0	1	10	0

All-SEC Team

Pos	Offense	School
QB	Tommy Hodson	LSU
RB	Tim Worley	Georgia
RB	Eddie Fuller	LSU
RB	Emmitt Smith	Florida
WR	Boo Mitchell	Vanderbilt
WR	Tony Moss	LSU
C	Todd Wheeler	Georgia
OL	Ralph Norwood	LSU
OL	David Williams	Florida
OL	Larry Rose	Alabama
OL	Eric Still	Tennessee
OL	Jim Thompson	Auburn
TE	Wesley Walls	Mississippi
K	David Browndyke	LSU

Pos	Defense	School
L	Trace Armstrong	Auburn
L	Tracy Rocker	Auburn
L	Bill Goldberg	Georgia
L	Darrell Phillips	LSU
L	Jeff Roth	Florida
LB	Keith DeLong	Tennessee
LB	Quentin Riggins	Auburn
LB	Eric Hill	LSU
LB	Derrick Thomas	Alabama
DB	Carlo Cheattom	Auburn
DB	Louis Oliver	Florida
DB	Todd Sandroni	Mississippi
DB	Ben Smith	Georgia
P	Brian Shulman	Auburn

1989 NCAA Major College Statistical Leaders

Individual Leaders

PASSING		CL	G	ATT	COM	PCT	INT	I%	YDS	YPA	TD	TD%	RATING
1	Ty Detmer, Brigham Young	SO	12	412	265	64.3	15	3.6	4560	11.1	32	7.8	175.6
2	David Brown, Duke	SO	9	163	104	63.8	6	3.7	1479	9.1	14	8.6	161.0
3	Dan Speltz, Cal St.-Fullerton	SR	11	309	214	69.3	11	3.6	2671	8.6	20	6.5	156.1
4	Shawn Moore, Virginia	JR	11	221	125	56.6	7	3.2	2078	9.4	18	8.1	156.1
5	Andre Ware, Houston	JR	11	578	365	63.2	15	2.6	4699	8.1	46	8.0	152.5
6	Bill Scharr, Syracuse	JR	11	169	107	63.3	8	4.7	1625	9.6	9	5.3	152.2
7	Peter Tom Willis, Florida State	SR	11	346	211	61.0	9	2.6	3124	9.0	20	5.8	150.7
8	Major Harris, West Virginia	JR	11	224	131	58.5	10	4.5	1939	8.7	16	7.1	145.8
9	Greg Frey, Ohio State	JR	11	215	128	59.5	7	3.3	1900	8.8	12	5.6	145.7
10	Bret Oberg, Iowa State	SR	11	245	152	62.0	9	3.7	2242	9.2	9	3.7	143.7

ALL-PURPOSE		CL	G	RUSH	REC	PR	KR	YDS	YPG
1	Mike Pringle, Cal St.-Fullerton	SR	11	1727	249	0	714	2690	244.6
2	Sheldon Canley, San Jose State	JR	11	1201	353	0	959	2513	228.5
3	Chuck Weatherspoon, Houston	JR	11	1146	735	415	95	2391	217.4
4	Anthony Thompson, Indiana	SR	11	1793	201	0	394	2388	217.1
5	Terance Mathis, New Mexico	SR	12	38	1315	0	785	2138	178.2
6	**Emmitt Smith, Florida**	**JR**	**11**	**1599**	**207**	**0**	**0**	**1806**	**164.2**
7	Steve Broussard, Washington State	SR	11	1237	326	0	227	1790	162.7
8	Andrew Greer, Ohio U.	SR	11	903	227	0	598	1728	157.1
9	Blaise Bryant, Iowa State	JR	11	1516	202	0	0	1718	156.2
10	Emmanuel Hazard, Houston	JR	11	0	1689	0	0	1689	153.6

RUSHING/Yards Per Game		CL	G	ATT	YDS	TD	AVG	YPG
1	Anthony Thompson, Indiana	SR	11	358	1793	24	5.0	163.0
2	Mike Pringle, Cal St.-Fullerton	SR	11	296	1727	16	5.8	157.0
3	Emmitt Smith, Florida	JR	11	284	1599	14	5.6	145.4
4	Blaise Bryant, Iowa State	JR	11	299	1516	19	5.1	137.8
5	James Gray, Texas Tech	SR	11	263	1509	18	5.7	137.2
6	Stacey Robinson, Northern Illinois	JR	11	223	1443	19	6.5	131.2
7	Blake Ezor, Michigan State	SR	9	226	1120	16	5.0	124.4
8	Derrick Douglas, Louisiana Tech	SR	10	281	1232	11	4.4	123.2
9	Jerry Mays, Georgia Tech	SR	11	249	1349	8	5.4	122.6
10	Blair Thomas, Penn State	SR	11	264	1341	5	5.1	121.9

RUSHING/Yards Per Carry		CL	G	ATT	YDS	YPC
1	Dee Dowis, Air Force	SR	12	172	1286	7.5
2	J.J. Flannigan, Colorado	SR	11	164	1187	7.2
3	Stacey Robinson, Northern Illinois	JR	11	223	1443	6.5
4	Ken Clark, Nebraska	SR	10	198	1196	6.0
5	**Chuck Webb, Tennessee**	**FR**	**11**	**209**	**1236**	**5.9**
6	Mike Pringle, Cal St.-Fullerton	SR	11	296	1727	5.8
7	James Gray, Texas Tech	SR	11	263	1509	5.7
8	**Emmitt Smith, Florida**	**JR**	**11**	**284**	**1599**	**5.6**
9	Aaron Craver, Fresno State	JR	11	225	1248	5.5
10	Brian Mitchell, La.-Lafayette	SR	11	237	1311	5.5

Based on top 23 rushers

RECEIVING		CL	G	REC	YDS	TD	YPR	YPG	RPG
1	Emmanuel Hazard, Houston	JR	11	142	1689	22	11.9	153.5	12.9
2	Richard Buchanan, Northwestern	JR	11	94	1115	9	11.9	101.4	8.6
3	Eric Henley, Rice	SO	11	81	900	5	11.1	81.8	7.4
4	Terance Mathis, New Mexico	SR	12	88	1315	13	14.9	109.6	7.3
5	Monty Gilbreath, San Diego State	SR	12	80	903	4	11.3	75.3	6.7
6	Dan Bitson, Tulsa	JR	11	73	1425	16	19.5	129.5	6.6
7	Michael Smith, Kansas State	SO	11	70	816	2	11.7	74.2	6.4
8	Rocky Palamara, Cal St.-Fullerton	SR	11	69	1024	10	14.8	93.1	6.3
9	**Brad Gaines, Vanderbilt**	**JR**	**11**	**67**	**634**	**2**	**9.5**	**57.6**	**6.1**
10	Dennis Smith, Utah	SR	12	73	1089	18	14.9	90.8	6.1

PUNTING		CL	PUNT	YDS	AVG
1	Tom Rouen, Colorado	SO	36	1651	45.9
2	Kirk Maggio, UCLA	SR	45	2036	45.2
3	Rob Myers, Washington State	SR	52	2326	44.7
4	Shawn McCarthy, Purdue	SR	69	3075	44.6
5	Daren Parker, South Carolina	JR	49	2170	44.3
6	Pete Rutter, Baylor	SR	57	2496	43.8
7	Robbie Keen, California	JR	59	2565	43.5
8	Tim Luke, Colorado State	JR	51	2199	43.1
9	Greg Hertzog, West Virginia	JR	40	1718	43.0
10	Chris Gardocki, Clemson	SR	44	1878	42.7

PUNT RETURNS		CL	PR	YDS	TD	AVG
1	Larry Hargrove, Ohio U.	SR	17	309	2	18.2
2	Herb Jackson, Ball State	JR	16	262	0	16.4
3	Dwight Pickens, Fresno State	SR	30	470	1	15.7
4	Jeff Sydner, Hawaii	FR	19	293	1	15.4
5	Tyrone Hughes, Nebraska	FR	15	227	0	15.1
6	Dee Smith, Louisville	SR	14	207	0	14.8
7	O.J. McDuffie, Penn State	SO	19	278	1	14.6
8	Jeff Campbell, Colorado	SR	25	365	0	14.6
9	Terrell Buckley, Florida State	FR	22	313	1	14.2
10	Troy Vincent, Wisconsin	SO	17	235	1	13.8

KICKOFF RETURNS		CL	KR	YDS	TD	AVG
1	Tony Smith, Southern Miss	SO	14	455	2	32.5
2	Mike Bellamy, Illinois	SR	14	432	0	30.9
3	Chris Oldham, Oregon	SR	14	402	0	28.7
4	Kelvin Means, Fresno State	SO	18	509	0	28.3
5	**Arthur Marshall, Georgia**	**SO**	**16**	**445**	**0**	**27.8**
6	Ron Gray, Air Force	SO	21	571	0	27.2
7	Deral Boykin, Kansas	SO	14	365	0	26.1
8	Raymond Patterson, Northern Illinois	FR	15	390	0	26.0
9	Alan Grant, Stanford	SR	16	412	0	25.8
10	**Kurt Johnson, Kentucky**	**FR**	**21**	**537**	**1**	**25.6**

SCORING		CL	TDS	XP	FG	PTS	PTPG
1	Anthony Thompson, Indiana	SR	25	4	0	154	14.0
2	Emmanuel Hazard, Houston	JR	22	2	0	134	12.2
3	Roman Anderson, Houston	SO	0	65	22	131	11.9
4	James Gray, Texas Tech	SR	20	0	0	120	10.9
4	Blaise Bryant, Iowa State	JR	19	6	0	120	10.9
6	Blake Ezor, Michigan State	SR	16	0	0	96	10.7
7	Mike Pringle, Cal St.-Fullerton	SR	19	2	0	116	10.6
7	Jamal Farmer, Hawaii	FR	19	2	0	116	10.6
9	Brian Mitchell, La.-Lafayette	SR	19	0	0	114	10.4
9	Stacey Robinson, Northern Illinois	JR	19	0	0	114	10.4

FIELD GOALS		CL	FGA	FGM	PCT	FGG
1	**Philip Doyle, Alabama**	**JR**	**25**	**22**	**0.88**	**2.00**
1	Gregg McCallum, Oregon	SO	29	22	0.76	2.00
1	Roman Anderson, Houston	SO	34	22	0.65	2.00
4	Mickey Thomas, Virginia Tech	FR	25	21	0.84	1.91
4	Jason Hanson, Washington State	SO	27	21	0.78	1.91
6	David Fuess, Tulsa	SR	23	20	0.87	1.82
6	Todd Wright, Arkansas	FR	23	20	0.87	1.82
6	Kevin Nicholl, Central Michigan	SR	24	20	0.83	1.82
6	Chris Gardocki, Clemson	SR	26	20	0.77	1.82
6	Cary Blanchard, Oklahoma State	JR	26	20	0.77	1.82

INTERCEPTIONS		CL	INT	YDS	TD	INT/GM
1	Cornelius Price, Houston	JR	12	187	2	1.09
1	Bob Navarro, Eastern Michigan	JR	12	73	0	1.09
3	**Ben Smith, Georgia**	**SR**	**10**	**54**	**0**	**0.91**
4	Kevin Smith, Texas A&M	SO	9	75	1	0.82
5	Walter Briggs, Hawaii	SR	9	116	1	0.75
6	Tracy Saul, Texas Tech	FR	8	157	0	0.73
6	Robert Blackmon, Baylor	SR	8	150	2	0.73
8	Todd Lyght, Notre Dame	JR	8	42	0	0.67
8	Greg Koperek, Pacific	SR	6	50	0	0.67
10	Leroy Butler, Florida State*	SR	7	139	1	0.64
10	Robert O'Neil, Clemson*	FR	7	96	0	0.64
10	Rob Thomson, Syracuse*	JR	7	74	1	0.64

*Six tied with 0.64; these had the most yards

Team Leaders

RUSHING OFFENSE		G	ATT	YDS	AVG	TD	YPG
1	Nebraska	11	641	4128	6.4	40	375.3
2	Colorado	11	666	4090	6.1	54	371.8
3	Air Force	12	736	4272	5.8	50	356.0
4	Army	11	738	3813	5.2	37	346.6
5	Oklahoma	11	684	3679	5.4	39	334.5
6	Northern Illinois	11	680	3638	5.3	40	330.7
7	Arkansas	11	680	3456	5.1	34	314.2
8	Notre Dame	12	673	3452	5.1	42	287.7
9	Fresno State	11	581	2918	5.0	38	265.3
10	Hawaii	11	555	2760	5.0	31	250.9

PASSING OFFENSE		G	ATT	COM	INT	PCT	YDS	YPA	TD	I%	YPC	YPG
1	Houston	11	694	434	16	62.5	5624	8.1	55	2.3	13.0	511.3
2	Brigham Young	12	433	279	15	64.4	4732	10.9	33	3.5	17.0	394.3
3	Utah	12	556	298	21	53.6	4064	7.3	39	3.8	13.6	338.7
4	Duke	11	439	279	20	63.6	3553	8.1	29	4.6	12.7	323.0
5	Florida State	11	387	230	11	59.4	3448	8.9	25	2.8	15.0	313.5
6	New Mexico	12	532	290	22	54.5	3732	7.0	23	4.1	12.9	311.0
7	Miami (Fla.)	11	465	254	22	54.6	3406	7.3	24	4.7	13.4	309.6
8	San Diego State	12	449	262	20	58.4	3697	8.2	16	4.5	14.1	308.1
9	SMU	11	551	303	22	55.0	3047	5.5	14	4.0	10.1	277.0
10	Washington State	11	332	205	15	61.7	2972	9.0	20	4.5	14.5	270.2

TOTAL OFFENSE		G	P	YDS	AVG	TD	YPG
1	Houston	11	904	6874	7.6	70	624.9
2	Brigham Young	12	852	6485	7.6	61	540.4
3	Nebraska	11	809	5646	7.0	63	513.3
4	Duke	11	866	5519	6.4	46	501.7
5	Air Force	12	886	5753	6.5	59	493.3
6	Colorado	11	768	5201	6.8	59	472.8
7	San Diego State	12	951	5610	5.9	46	467.5
8	Southern California	11	864	5029	5.8	39	457.2
9	Miami (Fla.)	11	898	4995	5.6	46	454.1
10	Florida State	11	779	4965	6.4	46	451.4

RUSHING DEFENSE		G	ATT	YDS	AVG	TD	YPG
1	Southern California	11	322	676	2.1	5	61.5
2	Miami (Fla.)	11	391	760	1.9	4	69.1
3	Virginia Tech	11	401	914	2.3	9	83.1
4	**Florida**	**11**	**397**	**975**	**2.5**	**8**	**88.6**
5	Clemson	11	336	1041	3.1	7	94.6
6	Hawaii	12	428	1152	2.7	16	96.0
7	Fresno State	11	376	1081	2.9	10	98.3
8	Louisville	11	416	1098	2.6	7	99.8
9	San Jose State	11	436	1105	2.5	10	100.5
10	**Alabama**	**11**	**376**	**1107**	**2.9**	**11**	**100.6**

PASSING DEFENSE		G	ATT	COM	PCT	YPC	INT	I%	YDS	YPA	TD	YPG
1	Kansas State	11	156	95	60.9	15.0	7	4.5	1422	9.1	11	129.3
2	Illinois	11	259	127	49.0	12.2	18	7.0	1545	6.0	3	140.5
3	Navy	11	198	105	53.0	14.8	9	4.5	1554	7.8	10	141.3
4	**Mississippi State**	**11**	**288**	**148**	**51.4**	**10.8**	**12**	**4.2**	**1599**	**5.6**	**10**	**145.4**
5	Miami (Fla.)	11	318	153	48.1	10.6	21	6.6	1621	5.1	4	147.4
6	Baylor	11	273	141	51.6	11.6	22	8.1	1634	6.0	8	148.5
7	Indiana	11	217	123	56.7	13.4	9	4.2	1654	7.6	15	150.4
8	**Auburn**	**11**	**278**	**141**	**50.7**	**12.0**	**11**	**4.0**	**1686**	**6.1**	**3**	**153.3**
8	**Florida**	**11**	**286**	**154**	**53.8**	**10.9**	**17**	**5.9**	**1686**	**5.9**	**10**	**153.3**
10	Boston College	11	230	116	50.4	14.7	17	7.4	1707	7.4	9	155.2

TOTAL DEFENSE		G	P	YDS	AVG	TD	YPG
1	Miami (Fla.)	11	709	2381	3.4	8	216.5
2	Southern California	11	635	2627	4.1	14	238.8
3	**Florida**	**11**	**683**	**2661**	**3.9**	**18**	**241.9**
4	Virginia Tech	11	705	2671	3.8	19	242.8
5	Clemson	11	690	2947	4.3	14	267.9
6	**Auburn**	**11**	**686**	**2956**	**4.3**	**11**	**268.7**
7	Eastern Michigan	11	740	3014	4.1	20	274.0
8	Nebraska	11	727	3015	4.1	21	274.1
9	Baylor	11	749	3077	4.1	20	279.7
10	Illinois	11	721	3136	4.3	15	285.1

SCORING OFFENSE		G	PTS	AVG
1	Houston	11	589	53.5
2	Nebraska	11	492	44.7
3	Colorado	11	452	41.1
4	Brigham Young	12	484	40.3
5	Hawaii	12	457	38.1
6	Air Force	11	411	37.4
7	Fresno State	12	446	37.2
8	Miami (Fla.)	11	393	35.7
9	Florida State	11	383	34.8
10	Oklahoma	11	380	34.5

SCORING DEFENSE		G	PTS	AVG
1	Miami (Fla.)	11	102	9.3
2	**Auburn**	**11**	**117**	**10.6**
3	Southern California	11	122	11.1
4	Penn State	11	130	11.8
5	Clemson	11	131	11.9
6	Michigan State	11	150	13.6
6	Colorado	11	150	13.6
6	Houston	11	150	13.6
9	Texas A&M	11	161	14.6
9	Illinois	11	161	14.6

1989

FINAL POLL (JAN. 2)

UPI	AP	SCHOOL	FINAL RECORD
1	1	Miami (Fla.)	11-1-0
3	2	Notre Dame	12-1-0
2	3	Florida State	10-2-0
4	4	Colorado	11-1-0
5	5	Tennessee	11-1-0
6	6	Auburn	10-2-0
8	7	Michigan	10-2-0
9	8	Southern California	9-2-1
7	9	Alabama	10-2-0
10	10	Illinois	10-2-0
12	11	Nebraska	10-2-0
11	12	Clemson	10-2-0
13	13	Arkansas	10-2-0
PB	14	Houston	9-2-0
14	15	Penn State	8-3-1
16	16	Michigan State	8-4-0
19	17	Pittsburgh	8-3-1
15	18	Virginia	10-3-0
16	19	Texas Tech	9-3-0
	20	Texas A&M	8-4-0
	21	West Virginia	8-3-1
18	22	Brigham Young	10-3-0
20	23	Washington	8-4-0
	24	Ohio State	8-4-0
	25	Arizona	8-4-0

PB: Team on probation

CONSENSUS ALL-AMERICANS

POS	OFFENSE	SCHOOL
QB	Andre Ware	Houston
RB	Anthony Thompson	Indiana
RB	Emmitt Smith	Florida
WR	Clarkston Hines	Duke
WR	Terance Mathis	New Mexico
TE	Mike Busch	Iowa State
L	Jim Mabry	Arkansas
L	Bob Kula	Michigan State
L	Mohammed Elewonibi	Brigham Young
L	Joe Garten	Colorado
L	Eric Still	Tennessee
C	Jake Young	Nebraska
PK	Jason Hanson	Washington State

OTHERS RECEIVING FIRST-TEAM HONORS

QB	Major Harris	West Virginia
RB	Blair Thomas	Penn State
RB	Johnny Bailey	Texas A&T-Kingsville
WR	Emmanuel Hazard	Houston
L	Chris Port	Duke
L	Doug Glaser	Nebraska
L	Ed King	Auburn
C	Michael Tanks	Florida State
KR	Raghib Ismail	Notre Dame

POS	DEFENSE	SCHOOL
L	Chris Zorich	Notre Dame
L	Greg Mark	Miami (Fla.)
L	Tim Ryan	Southern California
L	Moe Gardner	Illinois
LB	Percy Snow	Michigan State
LB	Keith McCants	Alabama
LB	Alfred Williams	Colorado
DB	Todd Lyght	Notre Dame
DB	Mark Carrier	Southern California
DB	Tripp Welborne	Michigan
DB	LeRoy Butler	Florida State
P	Tom Rouen	Colorado

OTHERS RECEIVING FIRST-TEAM HONORS

L	Odell Haggins	Florida State
L	Ray Savage	Virginia
LB	Kanavis McGhee	Colorado
LB	Andre Collins	Penn State
LB	James Francis	Baylor
DB	Chris Oldham	Oregon
P	Robbie Keen	California

HEISMAN TROPHY VOTING

	PLAYER	POS	SCHOOL	TOTAL
1	Andre Ware	QB	Houston	1073
2	Anthony Thompson	TB	Indiana	1003
3	Major Harris	QB	West Virginia	709
4	Tony Rice	QB	Notre Dame	523
5	Darian Hagan	QB	Colorado	292
6	Dee Dowis	QB	Air Force	145
7	Emmitt Smith	RB	Florida	140
8	Percy Snow	LB	Michigan State	70
9	Ty Detmer	QB	Brigham Young	49
10	Raghib Ismail	WR	Notre Dame	48
10	Blair Thomas	TB	Penn State	48

AWARD WINNERS

PLAYER	AWARD
Anthony Thompson, RB, Indiana	Maxwell
Mohammed Elewonibi, G, Brigham Young	Outland
Anthony Thompson, RB, Indiana	Camp
Percy Snow, LB, Michigan State	Lombardi
Andre Ware, QB, Houston	O'Brien
Percy Snow, LB, Michigan State	Butkus
Mark Carrier, DB, Southern California	Thorpe
Tony Rice, QB, Notre Dame	Unitas

BOWL GAMES

DATE	GAME	SCORE
D9	California	Fresno State 27, Ball State 6
D16	Independence	Oregon 27, Tulsa 24
D25	Aloha	Michigan State 33, Hawaii 13
D28	Liberty	Mississippi 42, Air Force 29
D28	All-American	Texas Tech 49, Duke 21
D29	Holiday	Penn State 50, Brigham Young 39
D30	Gator	Clemson 27, West Virginia 7
D30	Sun	Pittsburgh 31, Texas A&M 28
D30	Peach	Syracuse 19, Georgia 18
D30	Freedom	Washington 34, Florida 7
D31	Copper	Arizona 17, North Carolina St. 10
J1	Hall of Fame	Auburn 31, Ohio State 14
J1	Fiesta	Florida State 41, Nebraska 17
J1	Citrus	Illinois 31, Virginia 21
J1	Orange	Notre Dame 21, Colorado 6
J1	Rose	Southern California 17, Michigan 10
J1	Cotton	Tennessee 31, Arkansas 27
J1	Sugar	Miami (Fla.) 33, Alabama 25

SEC STANDINGS

	CONFERENCE			OVERALL		
	W	L	T	W	L	T
Tennessee	6	1	0	11	1	0
Alabama	6	1	0	10	2	0
Auburn	6	1	0	10	2	0
Mississippi	4	3	0	8	4	0
Florida	4	3	0	7	5	0
Georgia	4	3	0	6	6	0
Kentucky	2	5	0	6	5	0
LSU	2	5	0	4	7	0
Mississippi State	1	6	0	5	6	0
Vanderbilt	0	7	0	1	10	0

ALL-SEC TEAM

POS	OFFENSE	SCHOOL
QB	Gary Hollingsworth	Alabama
RB	Emmitt Smith	Florida
RB	Chuck Webb	Tennessee
WR	Tony Moss	LSU
WR	Willie Green	Mississippi
C	John Hudson	Auburn
OL	John Uurden	Florida
OL	Ed King	Auburn
OL	Eric Still	Tennessee
OL	Terrill Chatman	Alabama
OL	Antone Davis	Tennessee
OL	Mike Pfeifer	Kentucky
TE	Lamonde Russell	Alabama
K	Philip Doyle	Alabama

POS	DEFENSE	SCHOOL
L	Oliver Barnett	Kentucky
L	Marion Hobby	Tennessee
L	Willie Wyatt	Alabama
LB	Keith McCants	Alabama
LB	Quentin Riggins	Auburn
LB	Huey Richardson	Florida
LB	Tony Bennett	Mississippi
LB	Craig Ogletree	Auburn
DB	Richard Fain	Florida
DB	John Mangum	Alabama
DB	Ben Smith	Georgia
DB	Efrum Thomas	Alabama
P	Kent Elmore	Tennessee

1990 NCAA Major College Statistical Leaders

Individual Leaders

PASSING	CL	G	ATT	COM	PCT	INT	I%	YDS	YPA	TD	TD%	RATING
1 Shawn Moore, Virginia	SR	10	241	144	59.8	8	3.3	2262	9.4	21	8.7	160.7
2 Ty Detmer, Brigham Young	JR	12	562	361	64.2	28	5.0	5188	9.2	41	7.3	155.9
3 Casey Weldon, Florida State	JR	11	182	112	61.5	4	2.2	1600	8.8	12	6.6	152.7
4 Dan McGwire, San Diego State	SR	11	449	270	60.1	7	1.6	3833	8.5	27	6.0	148.6
5 David Klingler, Houston	JR	11	643	374	58.2	20	3.1	5140	8.0	54	8.4	146.8
6 Craig Erickson, Miami (Fla.)	SR	11	393	225	57.3	7	1.8	3363	8.6	22	5.6	144.0
7 Shane Matthews, Florida	**SO**	**11**	**378**	**229**	**60.6**	**12**	**3.2**	**2952**	**7.8**	**23**	**6.1**	**139.9**
8 Garrett Gabriel, Hawaii	SR	12	320	165	51.6	16	5.0	2752	8.6	25	7.8	139.6
9 Troy Kopp, Pacific	SO	9	428	243	56.8	14	3.3	3311	7.7	31	7.2	139.1
10 Rick Mirer, Notre Dame	SO	11	200	110	55.0	6	3.0	1824	9.1	8	4.0	138.8

ALL-PURPOSE	CL	G	RUSH	REC	PR	KR	YDS	YPG
1 Glyn Milburn, Stanford	SO	11	729	632	267	594	2222	202.0
2 Sheldon Canley, San Jose State	SR	11	1248	386	5	574	2213	201.2
3 Chuck Weatherspoon, Houston	SR	11	1097	560	196	185	2038	185.3
4 Eric Bieniemy, Colorado	SR	11	1628	159	0	31	1818	165.3
5 Jeff Sydner, Hawaii	SO	12	390	820	483	265	1958	163.2
6 Greg Lewis, Washington	SR	10	1279	345	0	0	1624	162.4
7 Russell White, California	SO	11	1000	127	0	629	1756	159.6
8 Dwayne Owens, Oregon State	FR	9	364	49	0	1014	1427	158.6
9 Raghib Ismail, Notre Dame	JR	11	537	702	151	336	1726	156.9
10 Dion Johnson, East Carolina	JR	9	266	90	167	879	1402	155.8

RUSHING/Yards Per Game	CL	G	ATT	YDS	TD	AVG	YPG
1 Gerald Hudson, Oklahoma State	SR	11	279	1642	10	5.9	149.3
2 Eric Bieniemy, Colorado	SR	11	288	1628	17	5.7	148.0
3 Darren Lewis, Texas A&M	SR	12	291	1691	18	5.8	140.9
4 Greg Lewis, Washington	SR	10	229	1279	8	5.6	127.9
5 Tico Duckett, Michigan State	SO	11	249	1376	10	5.5	125.1
6 Roger Grant, Utah State	JR	11	266	1370	8	5.2	124.6
7 Mike Mayweather, Army	SR	11	274	1338	10	4.9	121.6
8 Trevor Cobb, Rice	SO	11	283	1325	10	4.7	120.5
9 Sheldon Canley, San Jose State	SR	11	296	1248	12	4.2	113.5
10 Stacey Robinson, Northern Illinois	SR	11	193	1238	19	6.4	112.6

RUSHING/Yards Per Carry	CL	G	ATT	YDS	YPC
1 Chuck Weatherspoon, Houston	SR	11	158	1097	6.9
2 Robert Smith, Ohio State	FR	11	164	1064	6.5
3 Stacey Robinson, No. Illinois	SR	11	193	1238	6.4
4 Leodis Flowers, Nebraska	JR	9	149	940	6.3
5 Jon Vaughn, Michigan	SO	11	201	1236	6.1
6 Gerald Hudson, Oklahoma State	SR	11	279	1642	5.9
7 Darren Lewis, Texas A&M	SR	12	291	1691	5.8
8 Tony Thompson, Tennessee	**SR**	**12**	**219**	**1261**	**5.8**
9 Howard Griffith, Illinois	SR	11	186	1056	5.7
10 Eric Bieniemy, Colorado	SR	11	288	1628	5.7

Based on top 22 rushers

RECEIVING	CL	G	REC	YDS	TD	RPG	YPR	YPG
1 Patrick Rowe, San Diego State	JR	11	71	1392	8	6.5	19.6	126.6
2 Aaron Turner, Pacific	SO	11	66	1264	11	6.0	19.2	114.9
3 Herman Moore, Virginia	JR	11	54	1190	13	4.9	22.0	108.2
4 Andy Boyce, Brigham Young	SR	12	79	1241	13	6.6	15.7	103.4
5 Dennis Arey, San Diego State	SR	11	68	1118	10	6.2	16.4	101.6
6 Chris Smith, Brigham Young	SR	12	68	1156	2	5.7	17.0	96.3
7 Keenan McCardell, Nevada-Las Vegas	SR	11	68	1046	8	6.2	15.4	95.1
8 Manny Hazard, Houston	SR	10	78	946	9	7.8	12.1	94.6
9 Ed McCaffrey, Stanford	SR	10	61	917	8	6.1	15.0	91.7
10 Lawrence Dawsey, Florida State	SR	11	65	999	7	5.9	15.4	90.8

PUNTING	CL	PUNT	YDS	AVG
1 Cris Shale, Bowling Green	SR	66	3087	46.8
2 Brian Greenfield, Pittsburgh	SR	50	2280	45.6
3 Jason Hanson, Washington State	JR	59	2679	45.4
4 Chris Gardocki, Clemson	JR	53	2350	44.3
5 Greg Hertzog, West Virginia	SR	62	2697	43.5
6 Scott McAlister, North Carolina	JR	79	3433	43.5
7 Brad Williams, Arizona State	SR	56	2422	43.3
8 Klaus Wilmsmeyer, Louisville	JR	48	2062	43.0
9 Todd Rawsthorne, Western Michigan	JR	35	1502	42.9
10 Trent Thompson, Temple	JR	42	1795	42.7

PUNT RETURNS	CL	PR	YDS	TD	AVG
1 Dave McCloughan, Colorado	SR	32	524	2	16.4
2 Beno Bryant, Washington	SO	36	560	3	15.6
3 Jeff Graham, Ohio State	SR	22	327	2	14.9
4 Tony James, Mississippi State	**SO**	**23**	**341**	**2**	**14.8**
5 Tripp Welborne, Michigan	SR	31	455	0	14.7
6 Terrell Buckley, Florida State	SO	24	350	2	14.6
7 George Coghill, Wake Forest	SO	19	275	1	14.5
8 Rob Turner, Indiana	JR	27	373	2	13.8
9 Tony Smith, Southern Miss	JR	38	507	2	13.3
10 Joey Smith, Louisville	SR	29	382	0	13.2

KICKOFF RETURNS	CL	KR	YDS	TD	AVG
1 Dale Carter, Tennessee	**JR**	**17**	**507**	**1**	**29.8**
2 Desmond Howard, Michigan	JR	16	472	1	29.5
3 Tyrone Hughes, Nebraska	SO	18	523	1	29.0
4 Ray Washington, New Mexico State	JR	22	638	1	29.0
5 Randy Jones, Duke	SR	24	678	2	28.3
6 Andre Hastings, Georgia	**FR**	**15**	**422**	**1**	**28.1**
7 Milt Stegall, Miami (Ohio)	JR	18	497	1	27.6
8 Russell White, California	SO	24	629	1	26.2
9 Dion Johnson, East Carolina	JR	34	879	1	25.9
10 Dexter Pointer, Utah State	JR	30	769	0	25.6

SCORING	CL	TDS	XP	FG	PTS	PTPG
1 Stacey Robinson, Northern Illinois	SR	19	6	0	120	10.9
2 Aaron Craver, Fresno State	SR	18	0	0	108	10.8
3 Roman Anderson, Houston	JR	0	58	19	115	10.5
4 Amp Lee, Florida State	SO	18	0	0	108	9.8
5 Andy Trakas, San Diego State	SO	0	53	18	107	9.7
6 Darren Lewis, Texas A&M	SR	19	0	0	114	9.5
7 Eric Bieniemy, Colorado	SR	17	0	0	102	9.3
8 Carlos Huerta, Miami (Fla.)	JR	0	50	17	101	9.2
9 Michale Pollak, Texas	SR	0	39	20	99	9.0
10 Greg Burke, Tennessee	**SR**	**0**	**50**	**19**	**107**	**8.9**

FIELD GOALS	CL	FGA	FGM	PCT	FGG
1 Philip Doyle, Alabama	**SR**	**29**	**24**	**0.83**	**2.18**
2 Clint Gwaltney, North Carolina	JR	27	21	0.78	1.91
3 Michale Pollak, Texas	SR	26	20	0.77	1.82
4 Chris Gardocki, Clemson	JR	24	19	0.79	1.73
4 John Kasay, Georgia	**SR**	**24**	**19**	**0.79**	**1.73**
4 Roman Anderson, Houston	JR	25	19	0.76	1.73
4 Bob Wright, Temple	SR	25	19	0.76	1.73
4 Jeff Shudak, Iowa State	SR	27	19	0.70	1.73
9 Andy Trakas, San Diego State	SO	26	18	0.69	1.64
9 Rusty Hanna, Toledo	SO	29	18	0.62	1.64

INTERCEPTIONS	CL	INT	YDS	TD	INT/GM
1 Jerry Parks, Houston	JR	8	124	1	0.73
2 Will White, Florida	**SO**	**7**	**116**	**0**	**0.70**
3 Darryl Lewis, Arizona	SR	7	192	2	0.64
3 Shawn Vincent, Akron	SR	7	191	0	0.64
3 Ron Carpenter, Miami (Ohio)	JR	7	164	1	0.64
3 Darren Perry, Penn State	SR	7	125	1	0.64
3 Mike Welch, Baylor	SR	7	80	0	0.64
3 Ozzie Jackson, Akron	SR	7	50	0	0.64
9 Jaime Mendez, Kansas State	FR	6	154	1	0.60
9 Dave Bielinski, Bowling Green	SO	6	63	0	0.60

Team Leaders

RUSHING OFFENSE	G	ATT	YDS	AVG	TD	YPG
1 Northern Illinois	11	619	3791	6.1	36	344.6
2 Nebraska	11	641	3740	5.8	36	340.0
3 Army	11	746	3647	4.9	30	331.5
4 Texas A&M	12	661	3829	5.8	37	319.1
5 Oklahoma	11	637	3182	5.0	41	289.3
6 Colorado	12	629	3254	5.2	33	271.2
7 Air Force	11	653	2942	4.5	28	267.5
8 Virginia	11	520	2831	5.4	31	257.4
9 Clemson	11	623	2808	4.5	24	255.3
10 Michigan State	11	590	2793	4.7	34	253.9

PASSING OFFENSE	G	ATT	COM	INT	PCT	YDS	YPA	TD	I%	YPC	YPG
1 Houston	11	659	386	20	58.6	5213	7.9	54	3.0	13.5	473.9
2 Brigham Young	12	580	373	29	64.3	5379	9.3	41	5.0	14.4	448.3
3 San Diego State	11	485	287	8	59.2	4086	8.4	29	1.7	14.2	371.5
4 Pacific	11	535	303	16	56.6	4051	7.6	40	3.0	13.4	368.3
5 Miami (Fla.)	11	434	246	8	56.7	3573	8.2	22	1.8	14.5	324.8
6 Missouri	11	404	246	19	60.9	3248	8.0	18	4.7	13.2	295.3
7 TCU	11	511	258	20	50.5	3237	6.3	24	3.9	12.5	294.3
8 San Jose State	11	393	219	15	55.7	3208	8.2	27	3.8	14.6	291.6
9 Florida	**11**	**415**	**246**	**16**	**59.3**	**3197**	**7.7**	**25**	**3.9**	**13.0**	**290.6**
10 New Mexico	12	510	237	23	46.5	3221	6.3	18	4.5	13.6	268.4

TOTAL OFFENSE	G	P	YDS	AVG	TD	YPG
1 Houston	11	905	6455	7.1	63	586.8
2 Brigham Young	12	968	6788	7.0	64	565.7
3 San Diego State	11	927	5798	6.3	57	527.1
4 Virginia	11	804	5516	6.9	55	501.5
5 Miami (Fla.)	11	842	5312	6.3	49	482.9
6 Texas A&M	12	875	5653	6.5	50	471.1
7 San Jose State	11	872	5116	5.9	51	465.1
8 Pacific	11	835	5080	6.1	47	461.8
9 Fresno State	11	868	5026	5.8	45	456.9
10 Florida	**11**	**855**	**4978**	**5.8**	**44**	**452.6**

RUSHING DEFENSE	G	ATT	YDS	AVG	TD	YPG
1 Washington	11	392	735	1.9	10	66.8
2 Clemson	11	369	789	2.1	5	71.7
3 Miami (Fla.)	11	387	877	2.3	7	79.7
4 San Jose State	11	410	916	2.2	9	83.3
5 Florida	**11**	**386**	**941**	**2.4**	**8**	**85.5**
6 Alabama	**11**	**402**	**1007**	**2.5**	**6**	**91.5**
7 Penn State	11	401	1040	2.6	8	94.5
8 Iowa	11	392	1095	2.8	14	99.5
9 Central Michigan	11	392	1097	2.8	2	99.7
10 Ball State	11	461	1120	2.4	8	101.8

PASSING DEFENSE	G	ATT	COM	PCT	INT	I%	YDS	YPA	TD	TD%	RAT
1 Alabama	**11**	**309**	**141**	**45.6**	**15**	**4.9**	**1516**	**4.9**	**5**	**1.6**	**82.5**
2 Central Michigan	11	289	129	44.6	15	5.2	1462	5.1	6	2.1	83.6
3 Ball State	11	247	116	47.0	17	6.9	1329	5.4	4	1.6	83.7
4 Miami (Ohio)	11	244	106	43.4	15	6.2	1327	5.4	8	3.3	87.7
5 Texas	11	314	129	41.1	13	4.1	1780	5.7	7	2.2	87.8
6 Clemson	11	309	149	48.2	14	4.5	1597	5.2	5	1.6	87.9
7 Tennessee	12	336	163	48.5	24	7.1	1737	5.2	12	3.6	89.4
8 Louisville	11	279	141	50.5	19	6.8	1641	5.9	4	1.4	91.1
9 Fresno State	11	346	144	41.6	11	3.2	2109	6.1	5	1.5	91.2
10 Penn State	11	361	178	49.3	23	6.4	2023	5.6	9	2.5	91.9

TOTAL DEFENSE	G	P	YDS	AVG	TD	YPG
1 Clemson	11	678	2386	3.5	10	216.9
2 Ball State	11	708	2449	3.5	12	222.6
3 Alabama	**11**	**711**	**2523**	**3.5**	**11**	**229.4**
4 Central Michigan	11	681	2559	3.8	8	232.6
5 Florida	**11**	**708**	**2834**	**4.0**	**17**	**257.6**
6 Louisville	11	737	2855	3.9	13	259.5
7 Nebraska	11	724	2898	4.0	16	263.5
8 Auburn	**11**	**738**	**3002**	**4.1**	**22**	**272.9**
9 Miami (Ohio)	11	765	3036	4.0	26	276.0
10 North Carolina St.	11	772	3054	4.0	17	277.6

SCORING OFFENSE	G	PTS	AVG
1 Houston	11	511	46.5
2 Brigham Young	12	510	42.5
3 San Diego State	11	459	41.7
4 Virginia	11	442	40.2
5 Florida State	11	435	39.5
6 Nebraska	11	413	37.5
7 Tennessee	**12**	**442**	**36.8**
8 Miami (Fla.)	11	401	36.5
8 Oklahoma	11	401	36.5
10 Washington	11	394	35.8

SCORING DEFENSE	G	PTS	AVG
1 Central Michigan	11	98	8.9
2 Clemson	11	109	9.9
3 Ball State	11	121	11.0
4 Alabama	**11**	**127**	**11.5**
5 Southern Miss	11	141	12.8
6 Louisville	11	142	12.9
7 Nebraska	11	147	13.4
8 Washington	11	150	13.6
9 Penn State	11	155	14.1
10 North Carolina St.	11	162	14.7

1990

FINAL POLL (JAN. 2)

UP	AP	SCHOOL	FINAL RECORD
2	1	Colorado	11-1-1
1	2	Georgia Tech	11-0-1
3	3	Miami (Fla.)	10-2-0
4	4	Florida State	10-2-0
5	5	Washington	10-2-0
6	6	Notre Dame	9-3-0
8	7	Michigan	9-3-0
7	8	**Tennessee**	**9-2-2**
9	9	Clemson	10-2-0
PB	10	Houston	10-1-0
10	11	Penn State	9-3-0
11	12	Texas	10-2-0
PB	13	**Florida**	**9-2-0**
12	14	Louisville	10-1-1
13	15	Texas A&M	9-3-1
14	16	Michigan State	8-3-1
PB	17	Oklahoma	8-3-0
16	18	Iowa	8-4-0
19	19	**Auburn**	**8-3-1**
22	20	Southern California	8-4-1
23	21	**Mississippi**	**9-3-0**
17	22	Brigham Young	10-3-0
15	23	Virginia	8-4-0
17	24	Nebraska	9-3-0
24	25	Illinois	8-4-0
20		San Jose State	9-2-1
21		Syracuse	7-4-2
25		Virginia Tech	6-5-0

PB: Team on probation

CONSENSUS ALL-AMERICANS

POS	OFFENSE	SCHOOL
QB	Ty Detmer	Brigham Young
RB	Eric Bieniemy	Colorado
RB	Darren Lewis	Texas A&M
WR	Raghib Ismail	Notre Dame
WR	Herman Moore	Virginia
TE	Chris Smith	Brigham Young
OL	**Antone Davis**	**Tennessee**
OL	Joe Garten	Colorado
OL	**Ed King**	**Auburn**
OL	Stacy Long	Clemson
C	John Flannery	Syracuse
PK	**Philip Doyle**	**Alabama**

OTHERS RECEIVING FIRST-TEAM HONORS

QB	Shawn Moore	Virginia
RB	Greg Lewis	Washington
RB	Mike Mayweather	Army
WR	Lawrence Dawsey	Florida State
WR	Ed McCaffrey	Stanford
OL	Greg Skrepenak	Michigan
OL	Dean Dingman	Michigan
C	Mike Arthur	Texas A&M

POS	DEFENSE	SCHOOL
DL	Russell Maryland	Miami (Fla.)
DL	Chris Zorich	Notre Dame
DL	Moe Gardner	Illinois
DL	**David Rocker**	**Auburn**
LB	Alfred Williams	Colorado
LB	Michael Stonebreaker	Notre Dame
LB	Maurice Crum	Miami (Fla.)
DB	Tripp Welborne	Michigan
DB	Darryll Lewis	Arizona
DB	Ken Swilling	Georgia Tech
DB	Todd Lyght	Notre Dame
P	Brian Greenfield	Pittsburgh

OTHERS RECEIVING FIRST-TEAM HONORS

DL	Mitch Donahue	Wyoming
DL	Kenny Walker	Nebraska
DL	**Huey Richardson**	**Florida**
LB	Scott Ross	Southern California
DB	**Will White**	**Florida**
DB	Stanley Richard	Texas
P	Cris Shale	Bowling Green

HEISMAN TROPHY VOTING

	PLAYER	POS	SCHOOL	TOTAL
1	Ty Detmer	QB	Brigham Young	1482
2	Raghib Ismail	WR	Notre Dame	1177
3	Eric Bieniemy	TB	Colorado	798
4	Shawn Moore	QB	Virginia	465
5	David Klingler	QB	Houston	125
6	Herman Moore	WR	Virginia	68
7	Greg Lewis	TB	Washington	41
8	Craig Erickson	QB	Miami (Fla.)	31
	Darren Lewis	RB	Texas A&M	31
10	Mike Mayweather	HB	Army	20

AWARD WINNERS

PLAYER	AWARD
Ty Detmer, QB, Brigham Young	Maxwell
Russell Maryland, DT, Miami (Fla.)	Outland
Raghib Ismail, WR, Notre Dame	Camp
Chris Zorich, NT, Notre Dame	Lombardi
Ty Detmer, QB, Brigham Young	O'Brien
Alfred Williams, LB, Colorado	Butkus
Darryll Lewis, DB, Arizona	Thorpe
Craig Erickson, QB, Miami (Fla.)	Unitas
Greg Lewis, RB, Washington	Walker

BOWL GAMES

DATE	GAME	SCORE
D8	California	San Jose St. 48, Central Michigan 24
D15	Independence	Louisiana Tech 34, Maryland 34
D25	Aloha	Syracuse 28, Arizona 0
D27	Liberty	Air Force 23, Ohio State 11
D28	Blockbuster	Florida State 24, Penn State 17
D28	All-American	NC State 31, Southern Miss 27
D29	**Peach**	**Auburn 27, Indiana 23**
D29	Freedom	Colorado State 32, Oregon 31
D29	Holiday	Texas A&M 65, Brigham Young 14
D31	Copper	California 17, Wyoming 15
J1	Hall of Fame	Clemson 30, Illinois 0
J1	Orange	Colorado 10, Notre Dame 9
J1	Citrus	Georgia Tech 45, Nebraska 21
J1	**Fiesta**	**Louisville 34, Alabama 7**
J1	Cotton	Miami (Fla.) 46, Texas 3
J1	**Gator**	**Michigan 35, Mississippi 3**
J1	Rose	Washington 46, Iowa 34
J1	**Sugar**	**Tennessee 23, Virginia 22**

SEC STANDINGS

	CONFERENCE			OVERALL		
	W	L	T	W	L	T
Florida*	6	1	0	9	2	0
Tennessee	5	1	1	9	2	2
Mississippi	5	2	0	9	3	0
Alabama	5	2	0	7	5	0
Auburn	4	2	1	8	3	1
Kentucky	3	4	0	4	7	0
LSU	2	5	0	5	6	0
Georgia	2	5	0	4	7	0
Mississippi State	1	6	0	5	6	0
Vanderbilt	1	6	0	1	10	0

* Not eligible for conference title

ALL-SEC TEAM

POS	OFFENSE	SCHOOL
QB	Shane Matthews	Florida
RB	Randy Baldwin	Mississippi
RB	Tony Thompson	Tennessee
WR	Todd Kinchen	LSU
WR	Carl Pickens	Tennessee
C	Blake Miller	LSU
C	Roger Shultz	Alabama
OL	Terrill Chatman	Alabama
OL	Antone Davis	Alabama
OL	Ed King	Auburn
OL	Charles McRae	Tennessee
OL	Rob Selby	Auburn
TE	Kirk Kirkpatrick	Florida
K	Philip Doyle	Alabama

POS	DEFENSE	SCHOOL
L	Kelvin Pritchett	Mississippi
L	David Rocker	Auburn
L	George Thornton	Alabama
LB	Randy Holleran	Kentucky
LB	John Sullins	Alabama
LB	Godfrey Miles	Florida
LB	Huey Richardson	Florida
DB	Dale Carter	Tennessee
DB	Richard Fain	Florida
DB	Efrum Thomas	Alabama
DB	Will White	Florida
P	David Lawrence	Vanderbilt
P	Kent Elmore	Tennessee

1991 NCAA Major College Statistical Leaders

Individual Leaders

PASSING	CL	G	ATT	COM	PCT	INT	I%	YDS	YPA	TD	TD%	RATING
1 Elvis Grbac, Michigan	JR	11	228	152	66.7	5	2.2	1955	8.6	24	10.5	169.0
2 Ty Detmer, Brigham Young	SR	12	403	249	61.8	12	3.0	4031	10.0	35	8.7	168.5
3 Jeff Garcia, San Jose State	SO	9	160	99	61.9	5	3.1	1519	9.5	12	7.5	160.1
4 Matt Blundin, Virginia	SR	9	224	135	60.3	0	0.0	1902	8.5	19	8.5	159.6
5 Troy Kopp, Pacific	JR	12	449	275	61.3	16	3.6	3767	8.4	37	8.2	151.8
6 Steve Stenstrom, Stanford	SO	9	197	119	60.4	7	3.6	1683	8.5	15	7.6	150.2
7 Tony Sacca, Penn State	SR	12	292	169	57.9	5	1.7	2488	8.5	21	7.2	149.8
8 Rick Mirer, Notre Dame	JR	12	234	132	56.4	10	4.3	2116	9.0	18	7.7	149.2
9 Shane Matthews, Florida	**JR**	**11**	**361**	**218**	**60.4**	**18**	**5.0**	**3130**	**8.7**	**28**	**7.8**	**148.8**
10 Keithen McCant, Nebraska	SR	11	168	97	57.7	8	4.8	1454	8.7	13	7.7	146.5

ALL-PURPOSE	CL	G	RUSH	REC	PR	KR	YDS	YPG
1 Ryan Benjamin, Pacific	JR	12	1581	612	4	798	2995	249.6
2 Vaughn Dunbar, Indiana	SR	11	1699	252	0	262	2213	201.2
3 Marshall Faulk, San Diego State	FR	9	1429	201	0	33	1663	184.8
4 Trevor Cobb, Rice	JR	11	1692	136	0	16	1844	167.6
5 Corey Harris, Vanderbilt	**SR**	**11**	**1103**	**283**	**0**	**445**	**1831**	**166.5**
6 Tony Smith, Southern Miss	SR	9	998	97	115	271	1481	164.6
7 Desmond Howard, Michigan	JR	11	165	950	261	373	1749	159.0
7 Chris Hughley, Tulsa	JR	10	1326	74	0	190	1590	159.0
9 Russell White, California	JR	11	1177	139	0	408	1724	156.7
10 Dion Johnson, East Carolina	SR	11	255	743	162	513	1673	152.1

RUSHING/Yards Per Game	CL	G	ATT	YDS	TD	AVG	YPG
1 Marshall Faulk, San Diego State	FR	9	201	1429	21	7.1	158.8
2 Vaughn Dunbar, Indiana	SR	11	336	1699	11	5.1	154.5
3 Trevor Cobb, Rice	JR	11	360	1692	14	4.7	153.8
4 Jason Davis, Louisiana Tech	JR	10	244	1351	14	5.5	135.1
5 Chris Hughley, Tulsa	JR	10	267	1326	8	5.0	132.6
6 Ryan Benjamin, Pacific	JR	12	226	1581	13	7.0	131.8
7 Tony Sands, Kansas	SR	11	273	1442	9	5.3	131.1
8 Billy Smith, Central Michigan	SR	11	374	1440	6	3.9	130.9
9 Derek Brown, Nebraska	SO	11	230	1313	14	5.7	119.4
10 Mike Gaddis, Oklahoma	SR	11	221	1240	14	5.6	112.7

RUSHING/Yards Per Carry	CL	G	ATT	YDS	YPC
1 Ron Rivers, Fresno State	SO	10	134	984	7.3
2 Marshall Faulk, San Diego State	FR	9	201	1429	7.1
3 Ryan Benjamin, Pacific	JR	12	226	1581	7.0
4 Kevin Williams, UCLA	JR	10	168	1089	6.5
5 Derek Brown, Nebraska	SO	11	230	1313	5.7
6 Mike Gaddis, Oklahoma	SR	11	221	1240	5.6
7 Jason Davis, Louisiana Tech	JR	10	244	1351	5.5
8 Brian Copeland, Colorado State	SR	10	190	1028	5.4
9 Lamont Warren, Colorado	FR	9	157	830	5.3
10 Tony Sands, Kansas	SR	11	273	1442	5.3

Based on top 30 rushers

RECEIVING	CL	G	REC	YDS	TD	RPG	YPR	YPG
1 Aaron Turner, Pacific	JR	11	92	1604	18	8.4	17.4	145.8
2 Marcus Grant, Houston	JR	11	78	1262	10	7.1	16.2	114.7
3 Greg Primus, Colorado State	JR	11	67	1081	8	6.1	16.1	98.3
3 Ryan Yarborough, Wyoming	SO	11	53	1081	13	4.8	20.4	98.3
5 Carl Winston, New Mexico	SO	12	76	1177	7	6.3	15.5	98.1
6 Mario Bailey, Washington	SR	11	62	1037	17	5.6	16.7	94.3
7 Sean LaChapelle, UCLA	JR	11	68	987	11	6.2	14.5	89.7
8 Wilbert Ursin, Tulane	SO	11	70	969	9	6.4	13.8	88.1
9 Fred Gilbert, Houston	JR	11	106	957	7	9.6	9.0	87.0
10 Desmond Howard, Michigan	JR	11	61	950	19	5.5	15.6	86.4

PUNTING	CL	PUNT	YDS	AVG
1 Mark Bounds, Texas Tech	SR	53	2481	46.8
2 Jason Christ, Air Force	SR	50	2283	45.7
3 Pete Raether, Arkansas	SO	65	2836	43.6
4 Shayne Edge, Florida	**FR**	**46**	**1991**	**43.3**
5 Charles Langston, Houston	SR	52	2246	43.2
6 Eric Bruun, Purdue	SR	59	2548	43.2
7 Garret Henson, New Mexico State	SR	54	2326	43.1
8 Rusty Carlsen, Utah State	SR	56	2410	43.0
9 Ray Magana, Long Beach State	SR	57	2446	42.9
10 David Lawrence, Vanderbilt	**JR**	**54**	**2308**	**42.7**

PUNT RETURNS	CL	PR	YDS	TD	AVG
1 Bo Campbell, Virginia Tech	JR	15	273	0	18.2
2 Desmond Howard, Michigan	JR	15	261	1	17.4
3 David Palmer, Alabama	**FR**	**24**	**386**	**3**	**16.1**
4 Kevin Williams, Miami (Fla.)	SO	36	560	3	15.6
5 James McMillion, Iowa State	SO	17	251	0	14.8
6 Kevin Smith, Texas A&M	SR	19	275	2	14.5
7 Michael James, Arkansas	SR	19	272	1	14.3
8 Darnell Stephens, Clemson	FR	25	352	1	14.1
9 Brad Clark, Brigham Young	JR	20	269	1	13.5
10 Marshall Roberts, Rutgers	SR	34	454	0	13.4

KICKOFF RETURNS	CL	KR	YDS	TD	AVG
1 Fred Montgomery, New Mexico State	JR	25	734	1	29.4
2 Ronald Rice, Eastern Michigan	FR	11	319	0	29.0
3 Jeff Sydner, Hawaii	JR	18	495	0	27.5
4 Courtney Hawkins, Michigan State	SR	20	548	0	27.4
5 Eric Blount, North Carolina	SR	25	679	1	27.2
6 Andre Hastings, Georgia	**SO**	**14**	**380**	**0**	**27.1**
7 Floyd Foreman, Utah State	SR	27	730	0	27.0
8 Gary Melton, Rutgers	SR	17	435	1	25.6
9 Charles Levy, Arizona	FR	27	682	0	25.3
10 Donovan Moore, Oregon	JR	13	327	0	25.2

SCORING	CL	TDS	XP	FG	PTS	PTPG
1 Marshall Faulk, San Diego State	FR	23	2	0	140	15.6
2 Desmond Howard, Michigan	JR	23	0	0	138	12.6
3 Tommy Vardell, Stanford	SR	20	0	0	120	10.9
4 Jerome Bettis, Notre Dame	SO	20	0	0	120	10.0
5 Aaron Turner, Pacific	JR	18	0	0	108	9.8
6 Mario Bailey, Washington	SR	17	0	0	102	9.3
7 Russell White, California	JR	16	2	0	98	8.9
7 Doug Brien, California	SO	0	41	19	98	8.9
9 Derek Mahoney, Fresno State	SO	0	63	11	96	8.7
10 Jason Davis, Louisiana Tech	JR	14	0	0	84	8.4
10 Calvin Jones, Nebraska	FR	14	0	0	84	8.4

FIELD GOALS	CL	FGA	FGM	PCT	FGG
1 Doug Brien, California	SO	28	19	0.68	1.73
2 Dan Eichloff, Kansas	SO	24	18	0.75	1.64
3 Jason Elam, Hawaii	JR	24	19	0.79	1.58
4 Carlos Huerta, Miami (Fla.)	SR	21	17	0.81	1.55
4 John Biskup, Syracuse	JR	22	17	0.77	1.55
4 Nelson Welch, Clemson	FR	26	17	0.65	1.55
4 Lin Elliott, Texas Tech	SR	26	17	0.65	1.55
8 Eric Lange, Tulsa	JR	18	16	0.89	1.45
9 Joe Wood, Air Force	SR	22	17	0.77	1.42
9 Craig Fayak, Penn State	SO	26	17	0.65	1.42

INTERCEPTIONS	CL	INT	YDS	TD	INT/GM
1 Terrell Buckley, Florida State	JR	12	238	2	1.00
2 Carlton Gray, UCLA	JR	10	119	1	0.91
3 Willie Clay, Georgia Tech	SR	9	66	1	0.75
4 Ray Buchanan, Louisville	JR	8	89	0	0.73
4 Tracy Saul, Texas Tech	JR	8	79	0	0.73
6 Richard Palmer, Eastern Michigan	SO	7	219	1	0.64
6 Ron Carpenter, Miami (Ohio)	JR	7	197	1	0.64
6 Ron Edwards, Utah State	SR	7	146	2	0.64
6 Walter Bailey, Washington	JR	7	114	2	0.64
6 Willie Lindsey, Northwestern	JR	7	52	0	0.64

Team Leaders

RUSHING OFFENSE	G	ATT	YDS	AVG	TD	YPG
1 Nebraska	11	595	3885	6.5	45	353.2
2 Air Force	12	760	4057	5.3	34	338.1
3 Fresno State	11	613	3303	5.4	42	300.3
4 Army	11	701	3222	4.6	23	292.9
5 Hawaii	12	626	3416	5.5	32	284.7
6 Notre Dame	12	584	3229	5.5	37	269.1
7 Texas A&M	11	633	2850	4.5	34	259.1
8 Clemson	11	614	2813	4.6	28	255.7
9 Alabama	**11**	**557**	**2772**	**5.0**	**24**	**252.0**
10 Oklahoma	11	606	2752	4.5	33	250.2

PASSING OFFENSE	G	ATT	COM	INT	PCT	YDS	YPA	TD	I%	YPC	YPG
1 Houston	11	591	330	24	55.8	4101	6.9	33	4.1	12.4	372.8
2 Brigham Young	12	420	257	14	61.2	4125	9.8	35	3.3	16.1	343.8
3 Pacific	12	500	300	18	60.0	4114	8.2	42	3.6	13.7	342.8
4 Florida	**11**	**390**	**235**	**19**	**60.3**	**3393**	**8.7**	**32**	**4.9**	**14.4**	**308.5**
5 East Carolina	11	414	229	10	55.3	3379	8.2	30	2.4	14.8	307.2
6 San Jose State	11	374	211	14	56.4	3338	8.9	21	3.7	15.8	303.5
7 New Mexico	12	518	246	24	47.5	3584	6.9	20	4.6	14.6	298.7
8 Wyoming	11	400	227	10	56.7	3264	8.2	24	2.5	14.4	296.7
9 Miami (Fla.)	11	396	223	11	56.3	3244	8.2	20	2.8	14.5	294.9
10 Washington State	11	395	218	16	55.2	3028	7.7	19	4.1	13.9	275.3

TOTAL OFFENSE	G	P	YDS	AVG	TD	YPG
1 Fresno State	11	922	5961	6.5	62	541.9
2 Pacific	12	871	6135	7.0	61	511.3
3 Nebraska	11	800	5571	7.0	60	506.5
4 San Jose State	11	813	5279	6.5	47	479.9
5 Brigham Young	12	837	5754	6.9	54	479.5
6 San Diego State	12	955	5739	6.0	52	478.3
7 Washington	11	861	5191	6.0	60	471.9
8 Tennessee	**11**	**878**	**5145**	**5.9**	**36**	**467.7**
9 Florida	**11**	**787**	**5028**	**6.4**	**45**	**457.1**
10 UCLA	11	831	5019	6.0	39	456.3

RUSHING DEFENSE	G	ATT	YDS	AVG	TD	YPG
1 Clemson	11	360	587	1.6	5	53.4
2 Washington	11	390	738	1.9	6	67.1
3 Florida State	12	398	994	2.5	9	82.8
4 Texas A&M	11	393	946	2.4	13	86.0
5 Penn State	12	408	1120	2.7	9	93.3
6 Florida	**11**	**399**	**1103**	**2.8**	**7**	**100.3**
7 Louisiana Tech	11	386	1105	2.9	8	100.5
8 UCLA	11	403	1110	2.8	13	100.9
9 Oklahoma	11	403	1140	2.8	5	103.6
10 Michigan	11	397	1142	2.9	7	103.8

PASSING DEFENSE	G	ATT	COM	PCT	INT	I%	YDS	YPA	TD	TD%	RAT
1 Texas	11	304	115	37.8	15	4.9	1513	5.0	7	2.3	77.4
2 Texas A&M	11	290	129	44.5	14	4.8	1500	5.2	6	2.1	85.1
3 Washington	11	340	156	45.9	21	6.2	1870	5.5	6	1.8	85.6
4 Miami (Fla.)	11	346	175	50.6	19	5.5	1724	5.0	7	2.0	88.1
5 Penn State	12	397	172	43.3	26	6.6	2246	5.7	13	3.3	88.6
6 Virginia	11	267	137	51.3	12	4.5	1512	5.7	1	0.4	91.1
7 Arizona State	11	290	143	49.3	23	7.9	1676	5.8	9	3.1	92.2
8 Tulsa	11	275	129	46.9	18	6.6	1586	5.8	10	3.6	94.3
9 Georgia Tech	12	369	178	48.2	18	4.9	1989	5.4	12	3.3	94.5
10 Oklahoma	11	328	161	49.1	25	7.6	2004	6.1	10	3.1	95.2

TOTAL DEFENSE	G	P	YDS	AVG	TD	YPG
1 Texas A&M	11	683	2446	3.6	19	222.4
2 Washington	11	730	2608	3.6	12	237.1
3 Texas	11	769	2848	3.7	15	258.9
4 Clemson	11	718	2895	4.0	17	263.2
5 Miami (Ohio)	11	747	2980	4.0	15	270.9
6 Iowa	11	712	2987	4.2	20	271.5
7 Central Michigan	11	741	3001	4.0	16	272.8
8 Georgia Tech	12	831	3333	4.0	22	277.8
9 Penn State	12	805	3366	4.2	22	280.5
10 Florida State	12	776	3375	4.3	22	281.3

SCORING OFFENSE	G	PTS	AVG
1 Fresno State	11	486	44.2
2 Washington	11	461	41.9
3 Nebraska	11	454	41.3
4 California	11	406	36.9
4 Michigan	11	406	36.9
6 Florida State	12	439	36.6
7 Texas A&M	11	402	36.5
8 Pacific	12	435	36.3
9 Penn State	12	432	36.0
10 Notre Dame	12	426	35.5

SCORING DEFENSE	G	PTS	AVG
1 Miami (Fla.)	11	100	9.1
2 Washington	11	101	9.2
3 Alabama	**11**	**118**	**10.7**
4 Virginia	11	119	10.8
5 Miami (Ohio)	11	140	12.7
6 Oklahoma	11	143	13.0
7 Texas A&M	11	144	13.1
8 Texas	11	145	13.2
9 Bowling Green	11	147	13.4
10 Clemson	11	148	13.5

1991

FINAL POLL (JAN. 2)

UP	AP	SCHOOL	FINAL RECORD
2	1	Miami (Fla.)	12-0-0
1	2	Washington	12-0-0
3	3	Penn State	11-2-0
4	4	Florida State	11-2-0
5	5	Alabama	11-1-0
6	6	Michigan	10-2-0
7	7	Florida	10-2-0
8	8	California	10-2-0
9	9	East Carolina	11-1-0
10	10	Iowa	10-1-1
11	11	Syracuse	10-2-0
13	12	Texas A&M	10-2-0
12	13	Notre Dame	10-3-0
14	14	Tennessee	9-3-0
15	15	Nebraska	9-2-1
16	16	Oklahoma	9-3-0
20	17	Georgia	9-3-0
17	18	Clemson	9-2-1
19	19	UCLA	9-3-0
18	20	Colorado	8-3-1
21	21	Tulsa	10-2-0
22	22	Stanford	8-4-0
24	23	Brigham Young	8-3-2
23	24	North Carolina St.	9-3-0
	25	Air Force	10-3-0
25		Ohio State	8-4-0

CONSENSUS ALL-AMERICANS

POS	OFFENSE	SCHOOL
QB	Ty Detmer	Brigham Young
RB	Vaughn Dunbar	Indiana
RB	Trevor Cobb	Rice
RB	Russell White	California
WR	Desmond Howard	Michigan
WR	Mario Bailey	Washington
TE	Kelly Blackwell	TCU
OL	Greg Skrepenak	Michigan
OL	Bob Whitfield	Stanford
OL	Jeb Flesch	Clemson
OL	Jerry Ostroski	Tulsa
OL	Mirko Jurkovic	Notre Dame
C	Jay Leeuwenburg	Colorado
PK	Carlos Huerta	Miami (Fla.)

OTHERS RECEIVING FIRST-TEAM HONORS

QB	Casey Weldon	Florida State
RB	Amp Lee	Florida State
RB	Marshall Faulk	San Diego State
WR	Carl Pickens	Tennessee
TE	Derek Brown	Notre Dame
TE	Mark Chmura	Boston College
OL	Eugene Chung	Virginia Tech
OL	Leon Searcy	Miami (Fla.)
OL	Troy Auzenne	California
OL	Ray Roberts	Virginia
OL	Tim Simpson	Illinois
K	Jason Hanson	Washington State
KR	Qadry Ismail	Syracuse

POS	DEFENSE	SCHOOL
DL	Steve Emtman	Washington
DL	Santana Dotson	Baylor
DL	Brad Culpepper	Florida
DL	Leroy Smith	Iowa
LB	Robert Jones	East Carolina
LB	Marvin Jones	Florida State
LB	Levan Kirkland	Clemson
DB	Terrell Buckley	Florida State
DB	Dale Carter	Tennessee
DB	Kevin Smith	Texas A&M
DB	Darryl Williams	Miami (Fla.)
P	Mark Bounds	Texas Tech

OTHERS RECEIVING FIRST-TEAM HONORS

DL	Joel Steed	Colorado
DL	Shane Dronett	Texas
DL	Rob Bodine	Clemson
DL	Robert Stewart	Alabama
LB	Marco Coleman	Georgia Tech
LB	David Hoffman	Washington
LB	Steve Tovar	Ohio State
LB	Joe Bowden	Oklahoma
LB	Darrin Smith	Miami (Fla.)
LB	Erick Anderson	Michigan
DB	Darren Perry	Penn State
DB	Troy Vincent	Wisconsin
DB	Matt Darby	UCLA
PR	Kevin Williams	Miami (Fla.)

HEISMAN TROPHY VOTING

	PLAYER	POS	SCHOOL	TOTAL
1	Desmond Howard	WR	Michigan	2077
2	Casey Weldon	QB	Florida State	503
3	Ty Detmer	QB	Brigham Young	445
4	Steve Emtman	DT	Washington	357
5	Shane Matthews	QB	Florida	246
6	Vaughn Dunbar	TB	Indiana	173
7	Jeff Blake	QB	East Carolina	114
8	Terrell Buckley	CB	Florida State	102
9	Marshall Faulk	RB	San Diego State	52
10	Bucky Richardson	QB	Texas A&M	45

AWARD WINNERS

PLAYER	AWARD
Desmond Howard, WR, Michigan	Maxwell
Steve Emtman, DT, Washington	Outland
Desmond Howard, WR, Michigan	Camp
Steve Emtman, DT, Washington	Lombardi
Ty Detmer, QB, Brigham Young	O'Brien
Erick Anderson, LB, Michigan	Butkus
Terrell Buckley, DB, Florida State	Thorpe
Casey Weldon, QB, Florida State	Unitas
Trevor Cobb, RB, Rice	Walker

BOWL GAMES

DATE	GAME	SCORE
D14	California	Bowling Green 28, Fresno State 21
D25	Aloha	Georgia Tech 18, Stanford 17
D28	Blockbuster	Alabama 30, Colorado 25
D29	Liberty	Air Force 38, Mississippi State 15
D29	Independence	Georgia 24, Arkansas 15
D29	Gator	Oklahoma 48, Virginia 14
D30	Holiday	Brigham Young 13, Iowa 13
D30	Freedom	Tulsa 28, San Diego State 17
D31	Copper	Indiana 24, Baylor 0
D31	Sun	UCLA 6, Illinois 3
J1	Citrus	California 37, Clemson 13
J1	Peach	East Carolina 37, North Carolina St. 34
J1	Cotton	Florida State 10, Texas A&M 2
J1	Orange	Miami (Fla.) 22, Nebraska 0
J1	Fiesta	Penn State 42, Tennessee 17
J1	Hall of Fame	Syracuse 24, Ohio State 17
J1	Rose	Washington 34, Michigan 14
J1	Sugar	Notre Dame 39, Florida 28

SEC STANDINGS

	CONFERENCE			OVERALL		
	W	L	T	W	L	T
Florida	7	0	0	10	2	0
Alabama	6	1	0	11	1	0
Tennessee	5	2	0	9	3	0
Georgia	4	3	0	9	3	0
Mississippi State	4	3	0	7	5	0
LSU	3	4	0	5	6	0
Vanderbilt	3	4	0	5	6	0
Auburn	2	5	0	5	6	0
Mississippi	1	6	0	5	6	0
Kentucky	0	7	0	3	8	0

ALL-SEC TEAM

POS	OFFENSE	SCHOOL
QB	Shane Matthews	Florida
RB	Corey Harris	Vanderbilt
RB	Siran Stacy	Alabama
WR	Todd Kinchen	LSU
WR	Carl Pickens	Tennessee
C	Cal Dixon	Florida
UL	Eddie Blake	Auburn
OL	Hesham Ismail	Florida
OL	Tom Myslenski	Tennessee
OL	John James	Mississippi State
OL	Kevin Mawae	LSU
TE	Victor Hall	Auburn
K	Arden Czyzewski	Florida

POS	DEFENSE	SCHOOL
L	Brad Culpepper	Florida
L	Robert Stewart	Alabama
L	Nate Williams	Mississippi State
LB	Tim Paulk	Florida
LB	Dwayne Simmons	Georgia
LB	Ephesians Bartley	Florida
LB	Darryl Hardy	Tennessee
DB	Dale Carter	Tennessee
DB	Richard Fain	Florida
DB	Efrum Thomas	Alabama
DB	Will White	Florida
P	David Lawrence	Vanderbilt
P	Kent Elmore	Tennessee

1992 NCAA Major College Statistical Leaders

Individual Leaders

	PASSING	CL	G	ATT	COM	PCT	INT	I%	YDS	YPA	TD	TD%	RATING
1	Elvis Grbac, Michigan	SR	9	169	112	66.3	12	7.1	1465	8.7	15	8.9	154.2
2	Marvin Graves, Syracuse	JR	11	242	146	60.3	12	5.0	2296	9.5	14	5.8	149.2
3	Ryan Hancock, Brigham Young	SO	9	288	165	57.3	13	4.5	2635	9.2	17	5.9	144.6
4	Bert Emanuel, Rice	JR	11	179	94	52.5	6	3.4	1558	8.7	11	6.2	139.2
5	Kordell Stewart, Colorado	SO	9	252	151	59.9	9	3.6	2109	8.4	12	4.8	138.8
6	**Eric Zeier, Georgia**	**SO**	**11**	**258**	**151**	**58.5**	**12**	**4.7**	**2248**	**8.7**	**12**	**4.7**	**137.8**
7	Jimmy Klingler, Houston	SO	11	504	303	60.1	18	3.6	3818	7.6	32	6.4	137.6
8	Bobby Goodman, Virginia	SR	11	232	130	56.0	12	5.2	1707	7.4	21	9.1	137.4
9	Joe Youngblood, Central Michigan	JR	11	278	161	57.9	13	4.7	2209	8.0	18	6.5	136.7
10	Trent Dilfer, Fresno State	SO	12	331	174	52.6	14	4.2	2828	8.5	20	6.0	135.8

	ALL-PURPOSE	CL	G	RUSH	REC	PR	KR	YDS	YPG
1	Ryan Benjamin, Pacific	SR	11	1441	434	96	626	2597	236.1
2	Glyn Milburn, Stanford	SR	12	851	405	573	292	2121	176.8
3	Marshall Faulk, San Diego State	SO	10	1630	128	0	0	1758	175.8
4	**Garrison Hearst, Georgia**	**JR**	**11**	**1547**	**324**	**0**	**39**	**1910**	**173.6**
5	Henry Bailey, Nevada-Las Vegas	SO	11	15	832	219	817	1883	171.2
6	O.J. McDuffie, Penn State	SR	11	133	977	398	323	1831	166.5
7	Chuckie Dukes, Boston College	SR	11	1387	194	0	225	1806	164.2
8	Curtis Conway, Southern California	JR	11	37	764	324	652	1777	161.6
9	Tyrone Wheatley, Michigan	SO	10	1122	141	0	260	1523	152.3
10	Trevor Cobb, Rice	SR	11	1386	283	0	0	1669	151.7
10	Darnay Scott, San Diego State	SO	11	20	1150	0	499	1669	151.7

	RUSHING/Yards Per Game	CL	G	ATT	YDS	TD	AVG	YPG
1	Marshall Faulk, San Diego State	SO	10	265	1630	15	6.2	163.0
2	**Garrison Hearst, Georgia**	**JR**	**11**	**228**	**1547**	**19**	**6.8**	**140.6**
3	Ryan Benjamin, Pacific	SR	11	231	1441	13	6.2	131.0
4	Chuckie Dukes, Boston College	SR	11	238	1387	10	5.8	126.1
5	Trevor Cobb, Rice	SR	11	279	1386	11	5.0	126.0
6	Travis Sims, Hawaii	SR	12	220	1498	9	6.8	124.8
7	Reggie Brooks, Notre Dame	SR	11	167	1343	13	8.0	122.1
8	LeShon Johnson, Northern Illinois	JR	11	265	1338	6	5.0	121.6
9	Byron Morris, Texas Tech	SO	11	242	1279	10	5.3	116.3
10	Deland McCullough, Miami (Ohio)	FR	9	227	1026	6	4.5	114.0

	RUSHING/Yards Per Carry	CL	G	ATT	YDS	YPC
1	Reggie Brooks, Notre Dame	SR	11	167	1343	8.0
2	Calvin Jones, Nebraska	SO	11	168	1210	7.2
3	Travis Sims, Hawaii	SR	12	220	1498	6.8
4	**Garrison Hearst, Georgia**	**JR**	**11**	**228**	**1547**	**6.8**
5	Tyrone Wheatley, Michigan	SO	10	170	1122	6.6
6	Napoleon Kaufman, Washington	SO	11	162	1045	6.5
7	Ryan Benjamin, Pacific	SR	11	231	1441	6.2
8	Marshall Faulk, San Diego State	SO	10	265	1630	6.2
9	Anthony Barbour, North Carolina St.	SR	12	199	1204	6.1
10	Derek Brown, Nebraska	JR	10	170	1015	6.0

Based on top 25 rushers

	RECEIVING	CL	G	REC	YDS	TD	RPG	YPR	YPG
1	Lloyd Hill, Texas Tech	JR	11	76	1261	12	6.9	16.6	114.6
2	Marcus Badgett, Maryland	SR	11	75	1240	9	6.8	16.5	112.7
3	Ryan Yarborough, Wyoming	JR	12	86	1351	12	7.2	15.7	112.6
4	Victor Bailey, Missouri	SR	11	75	1210	6	6.8	16.1	110.0
5	Aaron Turner, Pacific	SR	11	79	1171	11	7.2	14.8	106.5
6	Darnay Scott, San Diego State	SO	11	68	1150	9	6.2	16.9	104.6
7	Charles Johnson, Colorado	JR	11	57	1149	5	5.2	20.2	104.5
8	Bryan Reeves, Nevada	JR	11	81	1114	10	7.4	13.8	101.3
9	Sean Dawkins, California	JR	11	65	1070	14	5.9	16.5	97.3
10	Michael Westbrook, Colorado	SO	11	76	1060	8	6.9	13.9	96.4

	PUNTING	CL	PUNT	YDS	AVG
1	Ed Bunn, Texas-El Paso	SR	41	1955	47.7
2	Mitch Berger, Colorado	JR	53	2493	47.0
3	Brian Parvin, Nevada-Las Vegas	SR	57	2637	46.3
4	Sean Snyder, Kansas State	SR	80	3572	44.6
5	Jeff Buffaloe, Memphis	SR	52	2317	44.6
6	Jason Elam, Hawaii	SR	49	2179	44.5
7	Todd Sauerbrun, West Virginia	SO	53	2348	44.3
8	Jim DiGuilio, Indiana	SO	53	2347	44.3
9	David Davis, Texas A&M	SR	70	3067	43.8
10	**Todd Jordan, Mississippi State**	**JR**	**52**	**2267**	**43.6**

	PUNT RETURNS	CL	PR	YDS	TD	AVG
1	Lee Gissendaner, Northwestern	JR	15	327	1	21.8
2	James McMillion, Iowa State	JR	23	435	3	18.9
3	Glyn Milburn, Stanford	SR	31	573	3	18.5
4	Jamie Mouton, Houston	SR	18	278	1	15.4
5	Corey Sawyer, Florida State	SO	33	488	1	14.8
6	Henry Bailey, Nevada-Las Vegas	SO	15	219	1	14.6
7	Napoleon Kaufman, Washington	SO	19	269	0	14.2
8	Marc Baxter, Temple	FR	12	167	0	13.9
9	Derrick Alexander, Michigan	SR	25	343	2	13.7
10	O.J. McDuffie, Penn State	SR	30	398	0	13.3

	KICKOFF RETURNS	CL	KR	YDS	TD	AVG
1	Fred Montgomery, New Mexico State	SR	14	457	0	32.6
2	Leroy Gallman, Duke	SR	14	433	0	30.9
3	Lew Lawhorn, Temple	SO	20	600	2	30.0
4	Chris Singleton, Nevada	JR	17	497	0	29.2
5	Brad Breedlove, Duke	SR	15	438	0	29.2
6	Craig Thompson, Eastern Michigan	JR	18	490	1	27.2
7	Polee Banks, Cal St.-Fullerton	JR	14	370	0	26.4
8	John Lewis, Minnesota	SR	29	755	1	26.0
9	Courtney Burton, Ohio U.	JR	21	545	1	26.0
10	Eric Redmon, Louisiana Tech	SO	12	310	0	25.8

	SCORING	CL	TDS	XP	FG	PTS	PTPG
1	**Garrison Hearst, Georgia**	**JR**	**21**	**0**	**0**	**126**	**11.5**
2	Richie Anderson, Penn State	SR	19	2	0	116	10.6
3	Marshall Faulk, San Diego State	SO	15	2	0	92	9.2
4	Joe Allison, Memphis	JR	0	32	23	101	9.2
5	Greg Hill, Texas A&M	SO	17	0	0	102	8.5
6	Tyrone Wheatley, Michigan	SO	14	0	0	84	8.4
7	Trevor Cobb, Rice	SR	15	2	0	92	8.4
8	Calvin Jones, Nebraska	SO	15	0	0	90	8.2
8	Craig Thomas, Michigan State	JR	15	0	0	90	8.2
10	Rusty Hanna, Toledo	SR	0	26	21	89	8.1
10	Nelson Welch, Clemson	SO	0	23	22	89	8.1

	FIELD GOALS	CL	FGA	FGM	PCT	FGG
1	Joe Allison, Memphis	JR	25	23	0.92	2.10
2	**Scott Ethridge, Auburn**	**SO**	**28**	**22**	**0.79**	**2.00**
2	Nelson Welch, Clemson	SO	28	22	0.79	2.00
2	Rich Thompson, Wisconsin	SR	32	22	0.69	2.00
5	Rusty Hanna, Toledo	SR	29	21	0.72	1.90
6	Tommy Thompson, Oregon	JR	31	20	0.65	1.80
7	Eric Lange, Tulsa	SR	23	19	0.83	1.70
7	Scott Sisson, Georgia Tech	SR	24	19	0.79	1.70
9	Sean Jones, Utah State	SR	24	18	0.75	1.60
9	Daron Alcorn, Akron	SR	26	18	0.69	1.60

	INTERCEPTIONS	CL	INT	YDS	TD	INT/GM
1	Carlton McDonald, Air Force	SR	8	109	1	0.73
2	C.J. Masters, Kansas State	SR	7	152	2	0.64
2	Tyronne Drakeford, Virginia Tech	JR	7	121	1	0.64
2	Greg Evans, TCU	JR	7	121	0	0.64
2	Joe Bair, Bowling Green	JR	7	51	0	0.64
2	Chris Owens, Akron	SR	7	49	0	0.64
2	Corey Sawyer, Florida State	SO	7	0	0	0.64
8	Deon Figures, Colorado	SR	6	21	0	0.60
8	Herman O'Berry, Oregon	SO	6	3	0	0.60
10	Terryl Ulmer, Southern Miss *	JR	6	132	0	0.55
10	Rico Wesley, TCU *	JR	6	125	0	0.55
10	Jaime Mendez, Kansas State *	JR	6	121	0	0.55
10	Greg Grandison, East Carolina *	SR	6	104	0	0.55
10	Charlie Brennan, Boston College *	SR	6	88	0	0.55

*11 tied with 0.55; these had the most yards

Team Leaders

	RUSHING OFFENSE	G	ATT	YDS	AVG	TD	YPG
1	Nebraska	11	618	3610	5.8	40	328.2
2	Hawaii	12	630	3519	5.6	32	293.3
3	Notre Dame	11	555	3090	5.6	34	280.9
4	Army	11	667	2934	4.4	23	266.7
5	Michigan	11	531	2909	5.5	28	264.5
6	Clemson	11	580	2828	4.9	21	257.1
7	Air Force	11	610	2665	4.4	26	242.3
8	Baylor	11	570	2641	4.6	24	240.1
9	Colorado State	12	571	2881	5.0	25	240.1
10	Virginia	11	513	2589	5.0	19	235.4

	PASSING OFFENSE	G	ATT	COM	INT	PCT	YDS	YPA	TD	I%	YPC	YPG
1	Houston	11	619	368	24	59.5	4478	7.2	36	3.9	12.2	407.1
2	Maryland	11	514	304	23	59.1	3628	7.1	18	4.5	11.9	329.8
3	Miami (Fla.)	11	457	259	7	56.7	3476	7.6	23	1.5	13.4	316.0
4	Nevada	11	497	268	27	53.9	3328	6.7	23	5.4	12.4	302.5
5	Brigham Young	12	405	222	19	54.8	3575	8.8	27	4.7	16.1	297.9
6	Colorado	11	398	232	20	58.3	3271	8.2	22	5.0	14.1	297.4
7	Missouri	11	442	258	12	58.4	3223	7.3	13	2.7	12.5	293.0
8	Pittsburgh	12	455	266	20	58.5	3483	7.7	23	4.4	13.1	290.3
9	**Florida**	**12**	**503**	**290**	**18**	**57.7**	**3440**	**6.8**	**25**	**3.6**	**11.9**	**286.7**
10	East Carolina	11	497	272	27	54.7	3085	6.2	27	5.4	11.3	280.5

	TOTAL OFFENSE	G	P	YDS	AVG	TD	YPG
1	Houston	11	842	5714	6.8	48	519.5
2	Fresno State	12	881	5791	6.6	61	482.6
3	Notre Dame	11	808	5174	6.4	52	470.4
4	Maryland	11	945	5131	5.4	37	466.5
5	Michigan	11	806	5120	6.4	51	465.5
6	Florida State	11	851	5080	6.0	49	461.8
7	Brigham Young	12	879	5517	6.3	44	459.8
8	Pittsburgh	12	919	5429	5.9	35	452.4
9	**Georgia**	**11**	**732**	**4954**	**6.8**	**41**	**450.4**
10	Boston College	11	817	4822	5.9	41	438.4

	RUSHING DEFENSE	G	ATT	YDS	AVG	TD	YPG
1	**Alabama**	**12**	**395**	**660**	**1.7**	**5**	**55.0**
2	Arizona	11	384	716	1.9	4	65.1
3	**Mississippi**	**11**	**413**	**895**	**2.2**	**10**	**81.4**
4	Michigan	11	369	985	2.7	6	89.5
5	Syracuse	11	339	1007	3.0	10	91.5
6	Florida State	11	400	1103	2.8	3	100.3
7	Memphis	11	447	1107	2.5	9	100.6
8	Miami (Fla.)	11	406	1118	2.8	4	101.6
9	Notre Dame	11	399	1222	3.1	9	111.1
10	Toledo	11	466	1248	2.7	8	113.5

	PASSING DEFENSE	G	ATT	COM	PCT	INT	I%	YDS	YPA	TD	TD%	RAT
1	Western Michigan	11	283	121	42.8	15	5.3	1522	5.4	5	1.8	83.2
2	**Alabama**	**12**	**330**	**164**	**49.7**	**22**	**6.7**	**1670**	**5.1**	**6**	**1.8**	**84.9**
3	Colorado	11	257	105	40.9	18	7.0	1461	5.7	8	3.1	84.9
4	Stanford	12	354	161	45.5	18	5.1	1869	5.3	10	2.8	89.0
5	Miami (Fla.)	11	358	173	48.3	18	5.0	1861	5.2	10	2.8	91.2
6	**Auburn**	**11**	**270**	**117**	**43.3**	**16**	**5.9**	**1565**	**5.8**	**10**	**3.7**	**92.4**
7	**Mississippi**	**11**	**362**	**169**	**46.7**	**17**	**4.7**	**2014**	**5.6**	**10**	**2.8**	**93.1**
8	Southern Miss	11	297	143	48.2	19	6.4	1692	5.7	9	3.0	93.2
9	Toledo	11	325	148	45.5	13	4.0	1880	5.8	7	2.2	93.2
10	**Georgia**	**11**	**302**	**151**	**50.0**	**12**	**4.0**	**1699**	**5.6**	**5**	**1.7**	**94.8**

	TOTAL DEFENSE	G	P	YDS	AVG	TD	YPG
1	**Alabama**	**12**	**725**	**2330**	**3.2**	**11**	**194.2**
2	Arizona	11	747	2783	3.7	9	253.0
3	Memphis	11	766	2788	3.6	20	253.5
4	Louisiana Tech	11	698	2822	4.0	15	256.5
5	**Auburn**	**11**	**699**	**2837**	**4.1**	**20**	**257.9**
6	**Mississippi**	**11**	**775**	**2909**	**3.8**	**20**	**264.5**
7	Arizona State	11	734	2957	4.0	18	268.8
8	Miami (Fla.)	11	764	2979	3.9	14	270.8
9	Colorado	11	731	3058	4.2	19	278.0
10	Stanford	12	821	3369	4.1	23	280.8

	SCORING OFFENSE	G	PTS	AVG
1	Fresno State	12	486	40.5
2	Nebraska	11	427	38.8
3	Florida State	11	419	38.1
4	Notre Dame	11	409	37.2
5	Michigan	11	393	35.7
6	Penn State	11	388	35.3
7	Houston	11	378	34.4
8	Hawaii	12	394	32.8
9	Miami (Fla.)	11	356	32.4
10	**Georgia**	**11**	**352**	**32.0**

	SCORING DEFENSE	G	PTS	AVG
1	Arizona	11	98	8.9
2	**Alabama**	**12**	**109**	**9.1**
3	Miami (Fla.)	11	127	11.5
4	Ohio State	11	137	12.5
5	Michigan	11	140	12.7
6	**Georgia**	**11**	**141**	**12.8**
7	Washington	11	148	13.5
8	Toledo	11	153	13.9
9	Texas A&M	12	168	14.0
10	Louisiana Tech	11	167	15.2

	TURNOVER MARGIN	G	FR	INT	TOT	FL	INTL	TOT	MAR
1	Nebraska	11	14	16	30	5	7	12	1.6
2	Akron	11	10	24	34	7	11	18	1.5
2	Miami (Fla.)	11	11	18	29	6	7	13	1.5
4	**Alabama**	**12**	**15**	**22**	**37**	**10**	**10**	**20**	**1.4**
5	Rice	11	12	18	30	8	8	16	1.3
5	Southern Miss	11	11	19	30	6	10	16	1.3
5	**Tennessee**	**11**	**14**	**11**	**25**	**7**	**4**	**11**	**1.3**
8	Wake Forest	11	15	13	28	7	9	16	1.1
9	Stanford	12	16	18	34	12	9	21	1.1
10	Arizona	11	10	16	26	8	7	15	1.0

1992

Final Poll (Jan. 2)

UP	AP	SCHOOL	FINAL RECORD
1	1	**Alabama**	**13-0-0**
2	2	Florida State	11-1-0
3	3	Miami (Fla.)	11-1-0
4	4	Notre Dame	10-1-1
5	5	Michigan	9-0-3
7	6	Syracuse	10-2-0
6	7	Texas A&M	12-1-0
8	8	**Georgia**	**10-2-0**
9	9	Stanford	10-3-0
11	10	**Florida**	**9-4-0**
10	11	Washington	9-3-0
12	12	**Tennessee**	**9-3-0**
13	13	Colorado	9-2-1
14	14	Nebraska	9-3-0
17	15	Washington State	9-3-0
16	16	**Mississippi**	**9-3-0**
15	17	North Carolina St.	9-3-1
19	18	Ohio State	8-3-1
18	19	North Carolina	9-3-0
20	20	Hawaii	11-2-0
21	21	Boston College	8-3-1
23	22	Kansas	8-4-0
	23	**Mississippi State**	**7-5-0**
22	24	Fresno State	9-4-0
25	25	Wake Forest	8-4-0

Consensus All-Americans

POS	OFFENSE	SCHOOL
QB	Gino Toretta	Miami (Fla.)
RB	Marshall Faulk	San Diego State
RB	**Garrison Hearst**	**Georgia**
WR	O.J. McDuffie	Penn State
WR	Sean Dawkins	California
TE	Chris Gedney	Syracuse
OL	Lincoln Kennedy	Washington
OL	Will Shields	Nebraska
OL	Aaron Taylor	Notre Dame
OL	Willie Roaf	Louisiana Tech
OL	**Everett Lindsay**	**Mississippi**
C	Mike Compton	West Virginia
PK	Joe Allison	Memphis

Others Receiving First-Team Honors

WR	Ryan Yarborough	Wyoming
WR	Lloyd Hill	Texas Tech
OL	Tony Boselli	Southern California
OL	Ben Coleman	Wake Forest
C	Mike Devlin	Iowa
PK	Scott Sisson	Georgia Tech
PK	Jason Elam	Hawaii
KR	Curtis Conway	Southern California

POS	DEFENSE	SCHOOL
DL	**Eric Curry**	**Alabama**
DL	**John Copeland**	**Alabama**
DL	Chris Slade	Virginia
DL	Rob Waldrop	Arizona
LB	Marcus Buckley	Texas A&M
LB	Marvin Jones	Florida State
LB	Micheal Barrow	Miami (Fla.)
DB	Carlton McDonald	Air Force
DB	Carlton Gray	UCLA
DB	Deon Figures	Colorado
DB	Ryan McNeil	Miami (Fla.)
P	Sean Snyder	Kansas State

Others Receiving First-Team Honors

DL	Coleman Rudolph	Georgia Tech
DL	Chris Hutchinson	Michigan
DL	Travis Hill	Nebraska
LB	David Hoffman	Washington
LB	Steve Tovar	Ohio State
LB	Darrin Smith	Miami (Fla.)
DB	Patrick Bates	Texas A&M
DB	Lance Gunn	Texas
P	Ed Bunn	UTEP
P	Josh Miller	Arizona

Heisman Trophy Voting

	PLAYER	POS	SCHOOL	TOTAL
1	Gino Torretta	QB	Miami (Fla.)	1400
2	Marshall Faulk	RB	San Diego St.	1080
3	**Garrison Hearst**	**RB**	**Georgia**	**982**
4	Marvin Jones	LB	Florida State	392
5	Reggie Brooks	RB	Notre Dame	294
6	Charlie Ward	QB	Florida State	126
7	Micheal Barrow	LB	Miami (Fla.)	64
8	Drew Bledsoe	QB	Washington St.	48
9	Glyn Milburn	RB	Stanford	47
10	**Eric Curry**	**DE**	**Alabama**	**47**

Award Winners

PLAYER	AWARD
Gino Torretta, QB, Miami (Fla.)	Maxwell
Will Shields, G, Nebraska	Outland
Gino Torretta, QB, Miami (Fla.)	Camp
Marvin Jones, LB, Florida State	Lombardi
Gino Torretta, QB, Miami (Fla.)	O'Brien
Marvin Jones, LB, Florida State	Butkus
Deon Figures, DB, Colorado	Thorpe
Gino Torretta, QB, Miami (Fla.)	Unitas
Garrison Hearst, RB, Georgia	**Walker**
Joe Allison, K, Memphis	Groza

Bowl Games

DATE	GAME	SCORE
D18	Las Vegas	Bowling Green 35, Nevada 34
D25	Aloha	Kansas 23, Brigham Young 20
D29	Freedom	Fresno State 24, Southern California 7
D29	Copper	Washington State 31, Utah 28
D30	Holiday	Hawaii 27, Illinois 17
D31	Sun	Baylor 20, Arizona 15
D31	Gator	**Florida 27, North Carolina St. 10**
D31	Liberty	**Mississippi 13, Air Force 0**
D31	Independence	Wake Forest 39, Oregon 35
J1	Orange	Florida State 27, Nebraska 14
J1	Citrus	**Georgia 21, Ohio State 14**
J1	Rose	Michigan 38, Washington 31
J1	Cotton	Notre Dame 28, Texas A&M 3
J1	Blockbuster	Stanford 24, Penn State 3
J1	Fiesta	Syracuse 26, Colorado 22
J1	Hall of Fame	**Tennessee 38, Boston College 23**
J1	Sugar	**Alabama 34, Miami (Fla.) 13**
J2	Peach	**North Carolina 21, Mississippi State 17**

SEC Standings

	CONFERENCE			OVERALL		
	W	L	T	W	L	T
EAST						
Florida	6	2	0	9	4	0
Georgia	6	2	0	10	2	0
Tennessee	5	3	0	9	3	0
South Carolina	3	5	0	5	6	0
Vanderbilt	2	6	0	4	7	0
Kentucky	2	6	0	4	7	0
WEST						
Alabama	8	0	0	13	0	0
Mississippi	5	3	0	9	3	0
Mississippi State	4	4	0	7	5	0
Arkansas	3	4	1	3	7	1
Auburn	2	5	1	5	5	1
LSU	1	7	0	2	9	0

All-SEC Team

POS	OFFENSE	SCHOOL
QB	Shane Matthews	Florida
RB	Garrison Hearst	Georgia
RB	James Bostic	Alabama
WR	Andre Hastings	Georgia
WR	Willie Jackson	Florida
C	Tobie Sheils	Alabama
OL	Everett Lindsay	Mississippi
OL	Ernest Dye	South Carolina
OL	Mike Stowell	Tennessee
OL	John James	Mississippi State
TE	Kirk Botkin	Arkansas
PK	Scott Etheridge	Auburn

POS	DEFENSE	SCHOOL
L	Eric Curry	Alabama
L	John Copeland	Alabama
L	Todd Kelly	Tennessee
LB	Derrick Oden	Alabama
LB	James Willis	Auburn
LB	Mitch Davis	Georgia
LB	Lemanski Hall	Alabama
DB	Antonio Langham	Alabama
DB	George Teague	Alabama
DB	Will White	Florida
DB	Johnny Dixon	Mississippi
P	Todd Jordan	Mississippi State

SEC Championship Game

December 5 | Birmingham
Alabama 28, Florida 21

	1ST	2ND	3RD	4TH	FINAL
ALA	7	7	7	7	28
FLA	7	0	7	7	21

Scoring Summary
FLA	Rhett 5 pass from Matthews (Davis kick)
ALA	Lassic 3 run (Proctor kick)
ALA	Brown 30 pass from Barker (Proctor kick)
ALA	Lassic 15 run (Proctor kick)
FLA	W. Jackson 4 pass from Matthews (Davis kick)
ALA	Langham 27 interception return (Proctor kick)

ALABAMA	TEAM STATISTICS	FLORIDA
15	First Downs	22
132	Rushing Yards	30
10-18-0	Passing	30-49-2
154	Passing Yards	287
286	Total Yards	317
3-31	Punt Returns - Yards	4-23
3-14	Kickoff Returns - Yards	5-71
10-32.6	Punts - Average	7-40
0-0	Fumbles - Lost	0-0
11-75	Penalties - Yards	4-30

Individual Leaders
RUSHING
ALA: Lassic 21-117, 2 TD.
FLA: Rhett 22-59, TD.
PASSING
ALA: Barker 10-18-0, 154 yards, TD.
FLA: Matthews 30-49-2, 287 yards, 2 TD.
RECEIVING
ALA: Palmer 5-101; Williams 2-16.
FLA: Rhett 10-82, TD; J.Jackson 9-100, TD.

1993 NCAA Major College Statistical Leaders

Individual Leaders

PASSING	CL	G	ATT	COM	PCT	INT	I%	YDS	YPA	TD	TD%	RATING
1 Trent Dilfer, Fresno State	JR	11	333	217	65.2	4	1.2	3276	9.8	28	8.4	173.1
2 Dave Barr, California	JR	11	275	187	68.0	12	4.4	2619	9.5	21	7.6	164.5
3 Darrell Bevell, Wisconsin	SO	11	256	177	69.1	10	3.9	2294	9.0	19	7.4	161.1
4 Charlie Ward, Florida State	SR	11	380	264	69.5	4	1.1	3032	8.0	27	7.1	157.8
5 Maurice DeShazo, Virginia Tech	JR	11	230	129	56.1	7	3.0	2080	9.0	22	9.6	157.5
6 Heath Shuler, Tennessee	**JR**	**11**	**285**	**184**	**64.6**	**8**	**2.8**	**2354**	**8.3**	**25**	**8.8**	**157.3**
7 Glenn Foley, Boston College	SR	11	363	222	61.2	10	2.8	3397	9.4	25	6.9	157.0
8 Chris Vargas, Nevada	SR	11	490	331	67.6	18	3.7	4265	8.7	34	6.9	156.2
9 John Walsh, Brigham Young	SO	11	397	244	61.5	15	3.8	3727	9.4	28	7.1	156.0
10 Rob Johnson, Southern California	JR	12	405	278	68.6	5	1.2	3285	8.1	26	6.4	155.5

ALL-PURPOSE	CL	G	RUSH	REC	PR	KR	YDS	YPG
1 LeShon Johnson, Northern Illinois	SR	11	1976	106	0	0	2082	189.3
2 Terrell Willis, Rutgers	FR	11	1261	61	0	704	2026	184.2
3 Marshall Faulk, San Diego State	JR	12	1530	644	0	0	2174	181.2
4 Byron Morris, Texas Tech	JR	11	1752	150	0	0	1902	172.9
5 Mike Adams, Texas	SO	11	68	908	256	622	1854	168.6
6 Napoleon Kaufman, Washington	JR	11	1299	139	25	388	1851	168.3
7 David Palmer, Alabama	**JR**	**12**	**278**	**1000**	**244**	**439**	**1961**	**163.4**
8 Tyrone Wheatley, Michigan	JR	9	1005	152	0	246	1403	155.9
9 Chris Penn, Tulsa	SR	11	2	1578	134	0	1714	155.8
10 John Leach, Wake Forest	SR	11	1089	340	9	253	1691	153.7

RUSHING/Yards Per Game	CL	G	ATT	YDS	TD	AVG	YPG
1 LeShon Johnson, Northern Illinois	SR	11	327	1976	12	6.0	179.6
2 Byron Morris, Texas Tech	JR	11	298	1752	22	5.9	159.3
3 Brent Moss, Wisconsin	JR	11	276	1479	14	5.4	134.5
4 Ron Rivers, Fresno State	SR	11	216	1440	14	6.7	130.9
5 Marshall Faulk, San Diego State	JR	12	300	1530	21	5.1	127.5
6 Junior Smith, East Carolina	JR	11	278	1352	9	4.9	122.9
7 Napoleon Kaufman, Washington	JR	11	226	1299	14	5.7	118.1
8 David Small, Cincinnati	SR	10	223	1180	17	5.3	118.0
9 Calvin Jones, Nebraska	JR	9	185	1043	12	5.6	115.9
10 Terrell Willis, Rutgers	FR	11	195	1261	13	6.5	114.6

RUSHING/Yards Per Carry	CL	G	ATT	YDS	YPC
1 Charlie Garner, Tennessee	**SR**	**11**	**159**	**1161**	**7.3**
2 Ron Rivers, Fresno State	SR	11	216	1440	6.7
3 Ki-Jana Carter, Penn State	SO	9	155	1026	6.6
4 Terrell Willis, Rutgers	FR	11	195	1261	6.5
5 Lee Becton, Notre Dame	JR	10	164	1044	6.4
6 James Bostic, Auburn	**JR**	**11**	**199**	**1205**	**6.1**
7 LeShon Johnson, Northern Illinois	SR	11	327	1976	6.0
8 Robert Walker, West Virginia	SO	11	201	1191	5.9
9 Byron Morris, Texas Tech	JR	11	298	1752	5.9
10 Napoleon Kaufman, Washington	JR	11	226	1299	5.7

Based on top 21 rushers

RECEIVING	CL	G	REC	YDS	TD	RPG	YPR	YPG
1 Chris Penn, Tulsa	SR	11	105	1578	12	9.5	15.0	143.5
2 Ryan Yarborough, Wyoming	SR	11	67	1512	16	6.1	22.6	137.5
3 Bryan Reeves, Nevada	SR	10	91	1362	17	9.1	15.0	136.2
4 Darnay Scott, San Diego State	JR	11	75	1262	10	6.8	16.8	114.7
5 Johnnie Morton, Southern California	SR	12	78	1373	12	6.5	17.6	114.4
6 Charles Johnson, Colorado	SR	11	57	1082	9	5.2	19.0	98.4
7 Demond Thompkins, UNLV	JR	11	62	1068	8	5.6	17.2	97.1
8 Michael Stephens, Nevada	SR	11	80	1062	7	7.3	13.3	96.6
9 Isaac Bruce, Memphis	SR	11	74	1054	10	6.7	14.2	95.8
10 Brian Oliver, Ball State	JR	11	62	1010	10	5.6	16.3	91.8

PUNTING	CL	PUNT	YDS	AVG
1 Chris MacInnis, Air Force	SR	49	2303	47.0
2 Terry Daniel, Auburn	**JR**	**51**	**2393**	**46.9**
3 Mike Nesbitt, New Mexico	SR	53	2387	45.0
4 Brad Faunce, Nevada-Las Vegas	JR	61	2745	45.0
5 Pat O'Neill, Syracuse	SR	44	1950	44.3
6 Scott Milanovich, Maryland	SO	50	2189	43.8
7 Bryne Diehl, Alabama	**JR**	**56**	**2441**	**43.6**
8 Scott Tyner, Oklahoma State	SR	75	3249	43.3
9 Alan Boardman, Brigham Young	FR	56	2415	43.1
10 Stephen Wilson, Hawaii	JR	46	1976	43.0

PUNT RETURNS	CL	PR	YDS	TD	AVG
1 Aaron Glenn, Texas A&M	SR	17	339	2	19.9
2 Shawn Summers, Tennessee	**SO**	**18**	**255**	**1**	**14.2**
3 Lee Gissendaner, Northwestern	SR	16	223	0	13.9
4 Scott Gumina, Mississippi State	JR	13	180	1	13.9
5 Andre Coleman, Kansas State	SR	27	362	1	13.4
6 Eddie Kennison, LSU	**FR**	**20**	**266**	**0**	**13.3**
7 Todd Dixon, Wake Forest	SR	13	167	1	12.9
8 James Dye, Utah State	SO	21	256	1	12.2
9 Bobby Engram, Penn State	SO	33	402	0	12.2
10 Greg Myers, Colorado State	SO	27	325	0	12.0

KICKOFF RETURNS	CL	KR	YDS	TD	AVG
1 Leeland McElroy, Texas A&M	FR	15	590	3	39.3
2 Chris Hewitt, Cincinnati	FR	14	441	1	31.5
3 Tyler Anderson, Brigham Young	SR	19	568	1	29.9
4 Andre Coleman, Kansas State	SR	15	434	0	28.9
5 Jack Jackson, Florida	**SO**	**17**	**480**	**1**	**28.2**
6 Polee Banks, New Mexico State	SR	14	394	1	28.1
7 Demond Thompkins, UNLV	JR	16	442	0	27.6
8 Steve Mehl, Pacific	SR	15	410	0	27.3
9 Mike Adams, Texas	SO	23	622	0	27.0
10 Dondra Jolly, Army	JR	19	510	0	26.8

SCORING	CL	TDS	XP	FG	PTS	PTPG
1 Byron Morris, Texas Tech	JR	22	2	0	134	12.2
2 Marshall Faulk, San Diego State	JR	24	0	0	144	12.0
3 Darnell Campbell, Boston College	SR	21	0	0	126	11.5
4 Bryan Reeves, Nevada	SR	17	0	0	102	10.2
4 David Small, Cincinnati	SR	17	0	0	102	10.2
6 Lindsey Chapman, California	SR	17	0	0	102	9.3
6 J.J. Stokes, UCLA	JR	17	0	0	102	9.3
8 Ryan Yarborough, Wyoming	SR	16	2	0	98	8.9
9 Calvin Jones, Nebraska	JR	13	0	0	78	8.7
10 John Becksvoort, Tennessee	**JR**	**0**	**59**	**12**	**95**	**8.6**

FIELD GOALS	CL	FGA	FGM	PCT	FGG
1 Michael Proctor, Alabama	**SO**	**29**	**22**	**0.76**	**1.83**
2 Bjorn Merten, UCLA	FR	25	20	0.80	1.82
3 Nathan Morreale, Utah State	FR	27	19	0.70	1.73
3 Kanon Parkman, Georgia	**SO**	**27**	**19**	**0.70**	**1.73**
5 Jon Baker, Arizona State	JR	26	18	0.69	1.64
6 Tom Dallen, Cincinnati	JR	22	17	0.77	1.55
6 Tom Burke, Mississippi State	SR	23	17	0.74	1.55
6 Aaron Price, Washington State	SR	31	17	0.55	1.55
9 Tommy Thompson, Oregon	SR	21	16	0.76	1.45
9 Chris Boniol, Louisiana Tech	SR	22	16	0.73	1.45
9 Scott Szeredy, Texas	SR	22	16	0.73	1.45

INTERCEPTIONS	CL	INT	YDS	TD	INT/GM
1 Orlanda Thomas, La.-Lafayette	JR	9	84	1	0.82
2 Anthony Bridges, Louisville	JR	7	184	2	0.64
2 Alundis Brice, Mississippi	**JR**	**7**	**98**	**2**	**0.64**
2 Antonio Langham, Alabama	**SR**	**7**	**67**	**1**	**0.64**
2 Troy Jensen, San Jose State	SR	7	60	0	0.64
6 Ernest Boyd, Utah	JR	6	126	1	0.60
7 Orlando Watters, Arkansas	**SR**	**6**	**185**	**2**	**0.55**
7 Marvin Goodwin, UCLA	JR	6	136	0	0.55
7 Nathan Bennett, Rice	SR	6	123	1	0.55
7 Tony Bouie, Arizona	JR	6	100	0	0.55
7 David Thomas, Miami (Ohio)	JR	6	63	0	0.55
7 Walt Harris, Mississippi State	SO	6	59	0	0.55
7 Marcus Jenkins, Kentucky	**SR**	**6**	**45**	**0**	**0.55**
7 Jeff Messenger, Wisconsin	JR	6	41	0	0.55

Team Leaders

RUSHING OFFENSE	G	ATT	YDS	AVG	TD	YPG
1 Army	11	660	3283	5.0	35	298.5
2 Oregon State	11	675	3254	4.8	25	295.8
3 Nebraska	11	589	3167	5.4	39	287.9
4 Air Force	12	713	3419	4.8	29	284.9
5 Hawaii	12	569	3247	5.7	35	270.6
6 Notre Dame	11	561	2868	5.1	37	260.7
7 North Carolina	12	628	3036	4.8	39	253.0
8 Wisconsin	11	557	2759	5.0	26	250.8
9 West Virginia	11	542	2684	5.0	28	244.0
10 Virginia Tech	11	582	2671	4.6	28	242.8

PASSING OFFENSE	G	ATT	COM	INT	PCT	YDS	YPA	TD	I%	YPC	YPG
1 Nevada	11	516	343	19	66.5	4373	8.5	34	3.7	12.7	397.5
2 Brigham Young	11	458	278	18	60.7	4060	8.9	31	3.9	14.6	369.1
3 Maryland	11	473	302	21	63.8	3823	8.1	26	4.4	12.7	347.5
4 Florida	**12**	**488**	**284**	**21**	**58.2**	**4072**	**8.3**	**41**	**4.3**	**14.3**	**339.3**
5 Stanford	11	474	308	14	65.0	3709	7.8	27	3.0	12.0	337.2
6 Florida State	12	469	327	6	69.7	3909	8.3	37	1.3	12.0	325.8
7 Utah	12	433	278	10	64.2	3891	9.0	22	2.3	14.0	324.3
8 Georgia	**11**	**432**	**272**	**7**	**63.0**	**3552**	**8.2**	**24**	**1.6**	**13.1**	**322.9**
9 San Diego State	12	465	269	14	57.8	3836	8.2	28	3.0	14.3	319.7
10 Fresno State	11	350	225	5	64.3	3425	9.8	29	1.4	15.2	311.4

TOTAL OFFENSE	G	P	YDS	AVG	TD	YPG
1 Nevada	11	955	6260	6.6	56	569.1
2 Florida State	12	939	6576	7.0	63	548.0
3 Fresno State	11	808	5863	7.3	53	533.0
4 Boston College	11	827	5570	6.7	51	506.4
5 Utah	12	906	5815	6.4	43	484.6
6 Tennessee	**11**	**762**	**5286**	**6.9**	**58**	**480.6**
7 Florida	**12**	**888**	**5719**	**6.4**	**59**	**476.6**
8 Texas Tech	11	854	5225	6.1	51	475.0
9 Brigham Young	11	853	5222	6.1	51	474.7
10 Colorado	11	841	5175	6.2	40	470.5

RUSHING DEFENSE	G	ATT	YDS	AVG	TD	YPG
1 Arizona	11	368	331	0.9	5	30.1
2 Washington State	11	438	949	2.2	11	86.3
3 La.-Lafayette	11	378	975	2.6	12	88.6
4 Notre Dame	11	331	985	3.0	8	89.5
5 Florida State	12	397	1182	3.0	6	98.5
6 Mississippi	**11**	**463**	**1127**	**2.4**	**8**	**102.5**
7 North Carolina	12	410	1230	3.0	10	102.5
8 Michigan	11	379	1179	3.1	6	107.2
9 Florida	**12**	**417**	**1334**	**3.2**	**9**	**111.2**
10 Illinois	11	444	1265	2.8	10	115.0

PASSING DEFENSE	G	ATT	COM	PCT	INT	I%	YDS	YPA	TD	TD%	RAT
1 Texas A&M	11	292	116	39.7	13	4.5	1339	4.6	5	1.7	75.0
2 Alabama	**12**	**310**	**144**	**46.5**	**22**	**7.1**	**1539**	**5.0**	**9**	**2.9**	**83.5**
3 Mississippi	**11**	**264**	**117**	**44.3**	**15**	**5.7**	**1453**	**5.5**	**5**	**1.9**	**85.4**
4 Miami (Fla.)	11	288	138	47.9	17	5.9	1517	5.3	6	2.1	87.2
5 Tennessee	**11**	**347**	**167**	**48.1**	**18**	**5.2**	**2105**	**6.1**	**7**	**2.0**	**95.4**
6 Iowa	11	291	143	49.1	18	6.2	1798	6.2	6	2.1	95.5
7 Central Michigan	11	302	151	50.0	13	4.3	1730	5.7	6	2.0	96.1
8 Florida State	12	376	181	48.1	15	4.0	2232	5.9	9	2.4	97.9
9 Auburn	**11**	**349**	**153**	**43.8**	**15**	**4.3**	**2039**	**5.8**	**15**	**4.3**	**98.5**
10 Cincinnati	11	315	164	52.1	14	4.4	1867	5.9	7	2.2	100.3

TOTAL DEFENSE	G	P	YDS	AVG	TD	YPG
1 Mississippi	**11**	**727**	**2580**	**3.5**	**13**	**234.5**
2 Arizona	11	739	2606	3.5	14	236.9
3 Texas A&M	11	740	2724	3.7	10	247.6
4 Miami (Fla.)	11	723	2814	3.9	15	255.8
5 Alabama	**12**	**738**	**3104**	**4.2**	**19**	**258.7**
6 Florida State	12	773	3414	4.4	15	284.5
7 Bowling Green	11	715	3285	4.6	22	298.6
8 Washington State	11	773	3287	4.3	27	298.8
9 Ohio State	11	744	3293	4.4	19	299.4
10 Indiana	11	747	3336	4.5	18	303.3

SCORING OFFENSE	G	PTS	AVG
1 Florida State	12	518	43.2
2 Tennessee	**11**	**471**	**42.8**
3 Fresno State	11	437	39.7
4 Florida	**12**	**472**	**39.3**
5 Nebraska	11	421	38.3
6 Nevada	11	419	38.1
7 Texas Tech	11	409	37.2
8 Texas A&M	11	404	36.7
9 Notre Dame	11	403	36.6
10 West Virginia	11	401	36.5

SCORING DEFENSE	G	PTS	AVG
1 Florida State	12	113	9.4
2 Texas A&M	11	119	10.8
3 Miami (Fla.)	11	138	12.5
4 Mississippi	**11**	**142**	**12.9**
5 Tennessee	**11**	**144**	**13.1**
6 Alabama	**12**	**158**	**13.2**
7 Indiana	11	152	13.8
8 Michigan	11	153	13.9
9 Arizona	11	161	14.6
10 West Virginia	11	171	15.5

TURNOVER MARGIN	G	FR	INT	TOT	FL	INTL	TOT	MAR
1 UCLA	11	21	18	39	13	7	20	1.7
2 Fresno State	11	15	16	31	9	5	14	1.6
3 Cincinnati	11	13	14	27	5	7	12	1.4
4 Tennessee	**11**	**15**	**18**	**33**	**11**	**9**	**20**	**1.2**
4 Texas A&M	11	19	13	32	7	12	19	1.2
4 Mississippi	**11**	**15**	**15**	**30**	**3**	**14**	**17**	**1.2**
4 Penn State	11	11	21	32	6	13	19	1.2
4 Colorado	11	13	13	26	6	7	13	1.2
9 Notre Dame	11	10	12	22	5	5	10	1.1
9 Texas Tech	11	16	14	30	11	7	18	1.1
9 Clemson	11	11	17	28	9	7	16	1.1

1993

FINAL POLL (JAN. 3)

CNN	AP	SCHOOL	FINAL RECORD
1	1	Florida State	12-1-0
2	2	Notre Dame	11-1-0
3	3	Nebraska	11-1-0
PB	4	**Auburn**	**11-0-0**
4	5	Florida	11-2-0
5	6	Wisconsin	10-1-1
6	7	West Virginia	11-1-0
7	8	Penn State	10-2-0
8	9	Texas A&M	10-2-0
9	10	Arizona	10-2-0
10	11	Ohio State	10-1-1
11	12	Tennessee	9-2-1
12	13	Boston College	9-3-0
13	14	Alabama	9-3-1
15	15	Miami (Fla.)	9-3-0
16	16	Colorado	8-3-1
14	17	Oklahoma	9-3-0
17	18	UCLA	8-4-0
21	19	North Carolina	10-3-0
18	20	Kansas State	9-2-1
19	21	Michigan	8-4-0
20	22	Virginia Tech	9-3-0
22	23	Clemson	9-3-0
23	24	Louisville	9-3-0
24	25	California	9-4-0
25		Southern California	8-5-0

PB: Team on probation

CONSENSUS ALL-AMERICANS

POS	OFFENSE	SCHOOL
QB	Charlie Ward	Florida State
RB	Marshall Faulk	San Diego State
RB	LeShon Johnson	Northern Illinois
WR	J.J. Stokes	UCLA
WR	Johnnie Morton	Southern California
OL	Mark Dixon	Virginia
OL	Stacy Seegars	Clemson
OL	Aaron Taylor	Notre Dame
OL	**Wayne Gandy**	**Auburn**
C	Jim Pyne	Virginia Tech
PK	Bjorn Merten	UCLA
KR	**David Palmer**	**Alabama**

OTHERS RECEIVING FIRST-TEAM HONORS

RB	**Errict Rhett**	**Florida**
WR	Ryan Yarborough	Wyoming
TE	Carlester Crumpler	East Carolina
TE	Pete Mitchell	Boston College
OL	Korey Stringer	Ohio State
OL	Marcus Spears	Northwestern State
OL	Rich Braham	West Virginia
OL	Todd Steussie	California
OL	**Bernard Williams**	**Georgia**
K	**John Becksvoort**	**Tennessee**
K	John Stewart	SMU

POS	DEFENSE	SCHOOL
DL	Rob Waldrop	Arizona
DL	Dan Wilkinson	Ohio State
DL	Sam Adams	Texas A&M
LB	Trev Alberts	Nebraska
LB	Derrick Brooks	Florida State
LB	Jamir Miller	UCLA
DB	**Antonio Langham**	**Alabama**
DB	Aaron Glenn	Texas A&M
DB	Jeff Burris	Notre Dame
DB	Corey Sawyer	Florida State
P	**Terry Daniel**	**Auburn**

OTHERS RECEIVING FIRST-TEAM HONORS

DL	Lou Benfatti	Penn State
DL	Derrick Alexander	Florida State
DL	Shante Carver	Arizona State
DL	Kevin Patrick	Miami (Fla.)
DL	Bryant Young	Notre Dame
LB	Barron Wortham	Texas-El Paso
LB	Dana Howard	Illinois
DB	Bobby Taylor	Notre Dame
DB	Bracey Walker	North Carolina
DB	Jaime Mendez	Kansas State

HEISMAN TROPHY VOTING

	PLAYER	POS	SCHOOL	TOTAL
1	Charlie Ward	QB	Florida State	2310
2	**Heath Shuler**	**QB**	**Tennessee**	**688**
3	**David Palmer**	**RB**	**Alabama**	**292**
4	Marshall Faulk	RB	San Diego State	250
5	Glenn Foley	QB	Boston College	180
6	LeShon Johnson	RB	Northern Illinois	176
7	J.J. Stokes	WR	UCLA	131
8	Tyrone Wheatley	RB	Michigan	100
9	Trent Dilfer	QB	Fresno State	91
10	**Eric Zeier**	**QB**	**Georgia**	**85**

AWARD WINNERS

PLAYER	AWARD
Charlie Ward, QB, Florida State	Maxwell
Rob Waldrop, NG, Arizona	Outland
Charlie Ward, QB, Florida State	Camp
Aaron Taylor, OT, Notre Dame	Lombardi
Charlie Ward, QB, Florida State	O'Brien
Trev Alberts, LB, Nebraska	Butkus
Antonio Langham, DB, Alabama	**Thorpe**
Charlie Ward, QB, Florida State	Unitas
Byron Morris, RB, Texas Tech	Walker
Judd Davis, K, Florida	**Groza**
Rob Waldrop, NG, Arizona	Nagurski

BOWL GAMES

DATE	GAME	SCORE
D17	Las Vegas	Utah State 42, Ball State 33
D24	Sun	Oklahoma 41, Texas Tech 10
D25	Aloha	Colorado 41, Fresno State 30
D28	Liberty	Louisville 18, Michigan State 7
D29	Copper	Kansas State 52, Wyoming 17
D30	Holiday	Ohio State 28, Brigham Young 21
D30	Freedom	Southern California 28, Utah 21
D31	**Gator**	**Alabama 24, North Carolina 10**
D31	Alamo	California 37, Iowa 3
D31	**Peach**	**Clemson 14, Kentucky 13**
D31	Independence	Virginia Tech 45, Indiana 20
J1	Fiesta	Arizona 29, Miami (Fla.) 0
J1	Carquest	Boston College 31, Virginia 13
J1	Orange	Florida State 18, Nebraska 16
J1	Hall of Fame	Michigan 42, North Carolina St. 7
J1	Cotton	Notre Dame 24, Texas A&M 21
J1	**Citrus**	**Penn State 31, Tennessee 13**
J1	Rose	Wisconsin 21, UCLA 16
J1	**Sugar**	**Florida 41, West Virginia 7**

SEC STANDINGS

	CONFERENCE			OVERALL		
	W	L	T	W	L	T
EAST						
Florida	7	1	0	11	2	0
Tennessee	6	1	1	9	2	1
Kentucky	4	4	0	6	6	0
Georgia	2	6	0	5	6	0
South Carolina	2	6	0	4	7	0
Vanderbilt	1	7	0	4	7	0
WEST						
Auburn*	8	0	0	11	0	0
Alabama**	5	2	1	9	3	1
Arkansas	3	4	1	5	5	1
Mississippi	3	5	0	5	6	0
LSU	3	5	0	5	6	0

* Not eligible for SEC title **Conference record later forfeited to 0-8-0

ALL-SEC TEAM

POS	OFFENSE	SCHOOL
QB	Eric Zeier	Georgia
RB	Charlie Garner	Tennessee
RB	Brandon Bennett	South Carolina
WR	Brice Hunter	Georgia
WR	Jack Jackson	Florida
C	Kevin Mawae	LSU
UL	Jason Odom	Florida
OL	Ryan Bell	Vanderbilt
OL	Isaac Davis	Arkansas
OL	Anthony Redmon	Auburn
TE	Harold Bishop	LSU
PK	John Becksvoort	Tennessee

POS	DEFENSE	SCHOOL
L	Henry Ford	Arkansas
L	William Gaines	Florida
L	Jeremy Nunley	Florida
LB	Dwayne Dotson	Mississippi
LB	Ernest Dickson	South Carolina
LB	Lemanski Hall	Alabama
LB	Marty Moore	Kentucky
LB	Randall Godfrey	Georgia
DB	Antonio Langham	Alabama
DB	Marcus Jenkins	Kentucky
DB	Orlando Watters	Arkansas
DB	Johnny Dixon	Mississippi
P	Terry Daniel	Auburn

SEC CHAMPIONSHIP GAME

DECEMBER 4 | BIRMINGHAM
FLORIDA 28, ALABAMA 13

	1ST	2ND	3RD	4TH	FINAL
FLA	7	7	7	7	28
ALA	7	3	3	0	13

SCORING SUMMARY

ALA Lynch 1 run (Proctor kick)
FLA Houston 13 pass from Dean (Davis kick)
ALA FG Proctor 45
FLA Dean 2 run (Davis kick)
ALA FG Proctor 25
FLA Jackson 43 pass from Dean (Davis kick)
FLA Rhett 4 run (Davis kick)

FLORIDA	TEAM STATISTICS	ALABAMA
20	First Downs	17
118	Rushing Yards	103
21-38-2	Passing	17-29-2
271	Passing Yards	161
374	Total Yards	279
5-95	Punt Returns - Yards	4-32
1-17	Kickoff Returns - Yards	4-94
7-39.4	Punts - Average	7-43.6
1-0	Fumbles - Lost	3-0
13-95	Penalties - Yards	6-70

INDIVIDUAL LEADERS

RUSHING
FLA: Rhett 22-88, TD.
ALA: Palmer 16-93.

PASSING
FLA: Dean 20-37-2, 256 yards, 2 TD.
ALA: Palmer 8-16-1, 90 yards.

RECEIVING
FLA: W. Jackson 9-114; J. Jackson 4-62; TD.
ALA: Malone 3-37; Palmer 3-23.

1994 NCAA Major College Statistical Leaders

Individual Leaders

PASSING	CL	G	ATT	COM	PCT	INT	I%	YDS	YPA	TD	TD%	RATING
1 Kerry Collins, Penn State	SR	11	264	176	66.7	7	2.7	2679	10.2	21	8.0	172.9
2 Terry Dean, Florida	**JR**	**10**	**180**	**109**	**60.6**	**10**	**5.6**	**1492**	**8.3**	**20**	**11.1**	**155.7**
3 Jay Barker, Alabama	**SR**	**12**	**226**	**139**	**61.5**	**5**	**2.2**	**1996**	**8.8**	**14**	**6.2**	**151.7**
4 Danny Wuerffel, Florida	**SO**	**12**	**212**	**132**	**62.3**	**9**	**4.3**	**1754**	**8.3**	**18**	**8.5**	**151.3**
5 Rob Johnson, Southern California	SR	9	255	170	66.7	6	2.4	2210	8.7	12	4.7	150.3
6 Mike McCoy, Utah	SR	11	381	247	64.8	11	2.9	3035	8.0	28	7.4	150.2
7 Max Knake, TCU	JR	11	316	184	58.2	7	2.2	2624	8.3	24	7.6	148.6
8 Steve Stenstrom, Stanford	SR	9	333	217	65.2	6	1.8	2822	8.5	16	4.8	148.6
9 Todd Collins, Michigan	SR	11	264	172	65.2	7	2.7	2356	8.9	11	4.2	148.6
10 Ryan Henry, Bowling Green	SO	11	293	174	59.4	11	3.8	2368	8.1	25	8.5	147.9

ALL-PURPOSE	CL	G	RUSH	REC	PR	KR	YDS	YPG
1 Rashaan Salaam, Colorado	JR	11	2055	294	0	0	2349	213.6
2 Brian Pruitt, Central Michigan	SR	11	1890	69	0	330	2289	208.1
3 Andre Davis, TCU	JR	11	1494	522	0	0	2016	183.3
4 Napoleon Kaufman, Washington	SR	11	1390	199	8	229	1826	166.0
5 Ki-Jana Carter, Penn State	JR	11	1539	123	0	81	1743	158.5
6 Chris Darkins, Minnesota	JR	11	1443	299	0	0	1742	158.4
7 Lawrence Phillips, Nebraska	SO	12	1722	172	0	0	1894	157.8
8 Terrell Fletcher, Wisconsin	SR	11	1235	172	0	314	1721	156.5
9 Alex Van Dyke, Nevada	JR	11	1	1246	5	451	1703	154.8
10 Terrell Willis, Rutgers	SO	11	1080	71	0	546	1697	154.3

RUSHING/Yards Per Game	CL	G	ATT	YDS	TD	AVG	YPG
1 Rashaan Salaam, Colorado	JR	11	298	2055	24	6.9	186.8
2 Brian Pruitt, Central Michigan	SR	11	292	1890	20	6.5	171.8
3 Lawrence Phillips, Nebraska	SO	12	286	1722	16	6.0	143.5
4 Ki-Jana Carter, Penn State	JR	11	198	1539	23	7.8	139.9
5 Andre Davis, TCU	JR	11	260	1494	7	5.7	135.8
6 Alex Smith, Indiana	FR	11	265	1475	10	5.6	134.1
7 Chris Darkins, Minnesota	JR	11	277	1443	11	5.2	131.2
8 Napoleon Kaufman, Washington	SR	11	255	1390	9	5.5	126.4
9 Billy West, Pittsburgh	SO	11	252	1358	6	5.4	123.5
10 Ryan Christopherson, Wyoming	SR	12	300	1455	10	4.8	121.3

RUSHING/Yards Per Carry	CL	G	ATT	YDS	YPC
1 Ki-Jana Carter, Penn State	JR	11	198	1539	7.8
2 Rashaan Salaam, Colorado	JR	11	298	2055	6.9
3 Brian Pruitt, Central Michigan	SR	11	292	1890	6.5
4 Terrell Fletcher, Wisconsin	SR	11	205	1235	6.0
5 Lawrence Phillips, Nebraska	SO	12	286	1722	6.0
6 Mike Alstott, Purdue	JR	11	202	1188	5.9
7 Sharmon Shah, UCLA	SO	11	210	1227	5.8
8 Andre Davis, TCU	JR	11	260	1494	5.7
9 Stephen Davis, Auburn	**JR**	**11**	**221**	**1263**	**5.7**
10 Marcellus Chrishon, Nevada	SR	9	189	1076	5.7

Based on top 30 rushers

RECEIVING	CL	G	REC	YDS	TD	RPG	YPR	YPG
1 Marcus Harris, Wyoming	SO	12	71	1431	11	5.9	20.2	119.3
2 Keyshawn Johnson, Southern Cal	JR	10	58	1140	6	5.8	19.7	114.0
3 Alex Van Dyke, Nevada	JR	11	98	1246	10	8.9	12.7	113.3
4 Kevin Jordan, UCLA	JR	11	73	1228	7	6.6	16.8	111.6
5 Randy Gatewood, Nevada-Las Vegas	SR	11	88	1203	6	8.0	13.7	109.4
6 Stepfret Williams, La.-Monroe	JR	11	57	1106	10	5.2	19.4	100.6
7 Justin Armour, Stanford	SR	11	67	1092	7	6.1	16.3	99.3
8 Amani Toomer, Michigan	JR	11	49	1033	5	4.5	21.1	93.9
9 Bobby Engram, Penn State	JR	11	52	1029	7	4.7	19.8	93.6
10 Lucious Davis, New Mexico State	JR	11	54	985	11	4.9	18.2	89.6

PUNTING	CL	PUNT	YDS	AVG
1 Todd Sauerbrun, West Virginia	SR	72	3486	48.4
2 Jason Bender, Georgia Tech	SR	55	2503	45.5
3 Brad Maynard, Ball State	JR	59	2684	45.5
4 Brian Lambert, La.-Monroe	SR	55	2479	45.1
5 Gary Layton, Miami (Ohio)	SR	55	2477	45.0
6 Terry Daniel, Auburn	**SR**	**53**	**2358**	**44.5**
7 Darren Schager, UCLA	SR	53	2342	44.2
8 John Stonehouse, Southern California	JR	61	2693	44.2
9 Greg Ivy, Oklahoma State	JR	64	2818	44.0
10 Jeff Beckley, Boston College	SR	58	2545	43.9

PUNT RETURNS	CL	PR	YDS	TD	AVG
1 Steve Clay, Eastern Michigan	JR	14	278	1	19.9
2 Nilo Silvan, Tennessee	**JR**	**15**	**272**	**0**	**18.1**
3 Ray Peterson, San Diego State	JR	12	190	2	15.8
4 Kevin Alexander, Utah State	JR	14	199	1	14.2
5 Eddie Kennison, LSU	**SO**	**36**	**439**	**1**	**12.2**
6 Antonio Freeman, Virginia Tech	SR	39	467	1	12.0
7 Parrish Foster, New Mexico State	SR	14	167	0	11.9
8 Greg Myers, Colorado State	JR	25	294	0	11.8
9 Ryan Roskelly, Memphis	JR	40	468	1	11.7
10 Dane Johnson, Texas Tech	FR	27	313	1	11.6

KICKOFF RETURNS	CL	KR	YDS	TD	AVG
1 Eric Moulds, Mississippi State	**JR**	**13**	**426**	**0**	**32.8**
2 David Dunn, Fresno State	SR	35	1013	0	28.9
3 Marcus Wall, North Carolina	JR	27	743	1	27.5
4 Parrish Foster, New Mexico State	SR	14	385	0	27.5
5 Derrick Mason, Michigan State	SO	36	966	1	26.8
6 Joey Galloway, Ohio State	SR	15	401	1	26.7
7 Ashaundai Smith, Kansas	JR	17	448	1	26.4
8 Ben Bronson, Baylor	SR	18	470	1	26.1
9 Seth Smith, Michigan	FR	18	468	1	26.0
9 Brian Davis, Memphis	JR	16	416	0	26.0
9 Jack Jackson, Florida	**JR**	**15**	**390**	**0**	**26.0**

SCORING	CL	TDS	XP	FG	PTS	PTPG
1 Rashaan Salaam, Colorado	JR	24	0	0	144	13.1
2 Ki-Jana Carter, Penn State	JR	23	0	0	138	12.6
3 Brian Pruitt, Central Michigan	SR	22	0	0	132	12.0
4 Brian Leaver, Bowling Green	SR	0	42	21	105	9.6
5 Judd Davis, Florida	**SR**	**0**	**65**	**14**	**107**	**8.9**
6 Rodney Thomas, Texas A&M	SR	16	0	0	96	8.7
7 Tyrone Wheatley, Michigan	SR	13	0	0	78	8.7
8 Remy Hamilton, Michigan	SO	0	23	24	95	8.6
8 Steve McLaughlin, Arizona	SR	0	26	23	95	8.6
10 Brett Conway, Penn State	SO	0	62	10	92	8.4

FIELD GOALS	CL	FGA	FGM	PCT	FGG
1 Remy Hamilton, Michigan	SO	29	24	0.83	2.18
2 Steve McLaughlin, Arizona	SR	29	23	0.79	2.09
3 Brian Leaver, Bowling Green	SR	24	21	0.88	1.91
3 Nick Garritano, Nevada-Las Vegas	SR	26	21	0.81	1.91
5 Ryan Williams, Virginia Tech	SR	21	17	0.81	1.70
5 Mike Chalberg, Minnesota	JR	23	17	0.74	1.70
7 John Wales, Washington	SO	25	18	0.72	1.64
8 Kanon Parkman, Georgia	**JR**	**22**	**17**	**0.77**	**1.55**
8 Rafael Garcia, Virginia	SO	22	17	0.77	1.55
8 Jon Baker, Arizona State	SR	24	17	0.71	1.55
8 Marty Kent, Louisiana Tech	FR	24	17	0.71	1.55
8 Kyle Bryant, Texas A&M	FR	25	17	0.68	1.55

INTERCEPTIONS	CL	INT	YDS	TD	INT/GM
1 Aaron Beasley, West Virginia	JR	10	133	2	0.83
2 Brian Robinson, Auburn	**JR**	**8**	**140**	**1**	**0.73**
2 Ronde Barber, Virginia	FR	8	56	0	0.73
4 Demetrice Martin, Michigan State	JR	7	41	0	0.64
5 Carlos Yancy, Georgia	**SR**	**6**	**154**	**1**	**0.55**
5 Kareem Leary, Utah	SR	6	140	2	0.55
5 Bart Thomas, Texas Tech	SR	6	91	0	0.55
5 Ray Jackson, Colorado State	JR	6	71	0	0.55
5 Joe Crocker, Virginia	JR	6	54	1	0.55
5 Ernest Boyd, Utah	SR	6	41	0	0.55
5 Walt Harris, Mississippi State	**JR**	**6**	**41**	**1**	**0.55**
5 Brian Watkins, Air Force	SR	6	28	0	0.55
5 Denorse Mosley, Pittsburgh	SO	6	27	0	0.55
5 Orlanda Thomas, La.-Lafayette	SR	6	25	0	0.55

Team Leaders

RUSHING OFFENSE	G	ATT	YDS	AVG	TD	YPG
1 Nebraska	12	687	4080	5.9	44	340.0
2 Air Force	12	720	3657	5.1	36	304.8
3 Colorado	11	517	3206	6.2	40	291.5
4 Central Michigan	11	571	3132	5.5	37	284.7
5 Oregon State	11	640	3072	4.8	24	279.3
6 Penn State	11	450	2760	6.1	45	250.9
7 Army	11	619	2738	4.4	22	248.9
8 Kansas	11	558	2718	4.9	31	247.1
9 Toledo	11	509	2667	5.2	28	242.5
10 Wisconsin	11	497	2649	5.3	23	240.8

PASSING OFFENSE	G	ATT	COM	INT	PCT	YDS	YPA	TD	I%	YPC	YPG
1 Georgia	**11**	**462**	**276**	**14**	**59.7**	**3721**	**8.1**	**24**	**3.0**	**13.5**	**338.3**
2 Nevada	11	463	279	16	60.3	3625	7.8	29	3.5	13.0	329.5
3 Brigham Young	12	475	287	14	60.4	3755	7.9	29	3.0	13.1	312.9
4 Florida	**12**	**435**	**267**	**21**	**61.4**	**3740**	**8.6**	**43**	**4.8**	**14.0**	**311.7**
5 Stanford	11	422	255	12	60.4	3358	8.0	18	2.8	13.2	305.3
6 San Diego State	11	410	257	16	62.7	3244	7.9	27	3.9	12.6	294.9
7 Florida State	11	441	264	18	59.9	3234	7.3	21	4.1	12.3	294.0
8 Wyoming	12	409	225	19	55.0	3367	8.2	21	4.7	15.0	280.6
9 Utah	11	387	249	11	64.3	3061	7.9	28	2.8	12.3	278.3
10 Maryland	11	428	291	13	68.0	3037	7.1	23	3.0	10.4	276.1

TOTAL OFFENSE	G	P	YDS	AVG	TD	YPG
1 Penn State	11	749	5722	7.6	68	520.2
2 Nevada	11	901	5581	6.2	55	507.4
3 Colorado	11	773	5448	7.0	52	495.3
4 Florida State	11	853	5314	6.2	52	483.1
5 Nebraska	12	897	5734	6.4	59	477.8
6 New Mexico	12	937	5664	6.0	51	472.0
7 Georgia	**11**	**754**	**5135**	**6.8**	**41**	**466.8**
8 Florida	**12**	**851**	**5553**	**6.5**	**62**	**462.8**
9 Brigham Young	12	955	5489	5.7	45	457.4
10 Wyoming	12	929	5468	5.9	38	455.7

RUSHING DEFENSE	G	ATT	YDS	AVG	TD	YPG
1 Virginia	11	323	700	2.2	9	63.6
2 Arizona	11	369	715	1.9	6	65.0
3 Washington State	11	418	812	1.9	4	73.8
4 Nebraska	12	401	951	2.4	8	79.3
5 Florida	**12**	**387**	**1015**	**2.6**	**9**	**84.6**
6 Texas A&M	11	440	1016	2.3	11	92.4
7 Miami (Fla.)	11	409	1065	2.6	4	96.8
8 Florida State	11	378	1077	2.8	6	97.9
9 Utah	11	410	1163	2.8	11	105.7
10 Memphis	11	419	1172	2.8	8	106.5

PASSING DEFENSE	G	ATT	COM	PCT	INT	I%	YDS	YPA	TD	TD%	RAT
1 Miami (Fla.)	11	293	143	48.8	18	6.1	1365	4.7	5	1.7	81.3
2 La.-Lafayette	11	309	135	43.7	19	6.2	1626	5.3	10	3.2	86.3
3 Texas Tech	11	283	122	43.1	17	6.0	1623	5.7	8	2.8	88.6
4 Florida State	11	376	180	47.9	15	4.0	1860	5.0	13	3.5	92.9
5 Washington State	11	314	140	44.6	10	3.2	1707	5.4	9	2.9	93.3
6 Mississippi	**11**	**300**	**134**	**44.7**	**19**	**6.3**	**1708**	**5.7**	**13**	**4.3**	**94.1**
7 Kansas State	11	279	130	46.6	12	4.3	1596	5.7	7	2.5	94.3
8 Virginia Tech	11	354	168	47.5	15	4.2	1945	5.5	10	2.8	94.5
9 Memphis	11	310	162	52.3	13	4.2	1602	5.2	7	2.3	94.7
10 Nebraska	12	364	172	47.3	17	4.7	2155	5.9	10	2.8	96.7

TOTAL DEFENSE	G	P	YDS	AVG	TD	YPG
1 Miami (Fla.)	11	702	2430	3.5	9	220.9
2 Washington State	11	732	2519	3.4	13	229.0
3 Memphis	11	729	2774	3.8	15	252.2
4 Nebraska	12	765	3106	4.1	18	258.8
5 Texas A&M	11	758	2920	3.9	17	265.5
6 Boston College	11	697	2927	4.2	19	266.1
7 Florida State	11	754	2937	3.9	19	267.0
8 Western Michigan	11	726	3047	4.2	23	277.0
9 Illinois	11	700	3138	4.5	16	285.3
10 Arizona	11	688	3140	4.6	19	285.5

SCORING OFFENSE	G	PTS	AVG
1 Penn State	11	526	47.8
2 Florida	**12**	**521**	**43.4**
3 Nevada	11	414	37.6
4 Utah	11	410	37.3
5 Florida State	11	405	36.8
6 Nebraska	12	435	36.3
7 Colorado	11	398	36.2
8 Bowling Green	11	391	35.5
9 Colorado State	11	386	35.1
10 Central Michigan	11	376	34.2

SCORING DEFENSE	G	PTS	AVG
1 Miami (Fla.)	11	119	10.8
2 Nebraska	12	145	12.1
3 Washington State	11	133	12.1
4 Texas A&M	11	147	13.4
5 Kansas State	11	156	14.2
5 Illinois	11	156	14.2
7 Alabama	**12**	**173**	**14.4**
8 Memphis	11	159	14.5
9 Boston College	11	162	14.7
10 Ohio State	12	187	15.6

TURNOVER MARGIN	G	FR	INT	TOT	FL	INTL	TOT	MAR
1 Clemson	11	13	16	29	2	10	12	1.6
2 Duke	11	12	17	29	4	9	13	1.5
3 Auburn	**11**	**11**	**22**	**33**	**11**	**7**	**18**	**1.4**
4 Mississippi	**11**	**13**	**19**	**32**	**13**	**6**	**19**	**1.2**
4 SMU	11	20	9	29	6	10	16	1.2
4 Kansas State	11	12	12	24	5	6	11	1.2
7 Penn State	11	12	11	23	4	7	11	1.1
8 Utah	11	13	19	32	10	11	21	1.0
8 East Carolina	11	11	22	33	7	15	22	1.0
8 Northern Illinois	11	16	15	31	13	7	20	1.0
8 Mississippi State	**11**	**13**	**22**	**35**	**16**	**8**	**24**	**1.0**
8 Virginia	11	9	27	36	13	12	25	1.0
8 Southern California	11	9	16	25	8	6	14	1.0
8 Southern Miss	11	15	25	40	8	21	29	1.0
8 Air Force	12	11	21	32	16	4	20	1.0

1994

FINAL POLL (JAN. 3)

CNN	AP	SCHOOL	FINAL RECORD
1	1	Nebraska	13-0-0
2	2	Penn State	12-0-0
3	3	Colorado	11-1-0
5	4	Florida State	10-1-1
4	5	**Alabama**	**12-1-0**
6	6	Miami (Fla.)	10-2-0
7	7	Florida	10-2-1
PB	8	Texas A&M	10-0-1
PB	9	**Auburn**	**9-1-1**
8	10	Utah	10-2-0
11	11	Oregon	9-4-0
12	12	Michigan	8-4-0
15	13	Southern California	8-3-1
9	14	Ohio State	9-4-0
13	15	Virginia	9-3-0
14	16	Colorado State	10-2-0
17	17	North Carolina St.	9-3-0
10	18	Brigham Young	10-3-0
16	19	Kansas State	9-3-0
20	20	Arizona	8-4-0
19	21	Washington State	8-4-0
18	22	**Tennessee**	**8-4-0**
22	23	Boston College	7-4-1
25	24	**Mississippi State**	**8-4-0**
23	25	Texas	8-4-0
21		North Carolina	8-4-0

PB: Team on probation

CONSENSUS ALL-AMERICANS

POS	OFFENSE	SCHOOL
QB	Kerry Collins	Penn State
RB	Rashaan Salaam	Colorado
RB	Ki-Jana Carter	Penn State
WR	**Jack Jackson**	**Florida**
WR	Michael Westbrook	Colorado
TE	Pete Mitchell	Boston College
OL	Zach Wiegert	Nebraska
OL	Tony Boselli	Southern California
OL	Korey Stringer	Ohio State
OL	Brenden Stai	Nebraska
C	Cory Raymer	Wisconsin
PK	Steve McLaughlin	Arizona
KR	Leeland McElroy	Texas A&M

OTHERS RECEIVING FIRST-TEAM HONORS

QB	**Eric Zeier**	**Georgia**
WR	Bobby Engram	Penn State
WR	**Frank Sanders**	**Auburn**
WR	Kevin Jordan	UCLA
TE	Kyle Brady	Penn State
TE	Jamie Asher	Louisville
OL	Jeff Hartings	Penn State
OL	Blake Brockermeyer	Texas
OL	Reuben Brown	Pittsburgh
C	Clay Shiver	Florida State
PK	Remy Hamilton	Michigan
KR	**Michael Proctor**	**Alabama**

POS	DEFENSE	SCHOOL
DL	Warren Sapp	Miami (Fla.)
DL	Tedy Bruschi	Arizona
DL	Luther Elliss	Utah
DL	**Kevin Carter**	**Florida**
LB	Dana Howard	Illinois
LB	Ed Stewart	Nebraska
LB	Derrick Brooks	Florida State
DB	Clifton Abraham	Florida State
DB	Bobby Taylor	Notre Dame
DB	Chris Hudson	Colorado
DB	**Brian Robinson**	**Auburn**
DB	Tony Bouie	Arizona
P	Todd Sauerbrun	West Virginia

OTHERS RECEIVING FIRST-TEAM HONORS

DL	Derrick Alexander	Florida State
DL	Simeon Rice	Illinois
DL	DeWayne Patterson	Washington State
LB	Zach Thomas	Texas Tech
LB	Antonio Armstrong	Texas A&M
DB	Ty Law	Michigan
DB	Greg Myers	Colorado State
DB	Herman O'Berry	Oregon
DB	**Chris Shelling**	**Auburn**
DB	Orlando Thomas	Southwestern Louisiana
DB	C.J. Richardson	Miami (Fla.)

HEISMAN TROPHY VOTING

	PLAYER	POS	SCHOOL	TOTAL
1	Rashaan Salaam	RB	Colorado	1743
2	Ki-Jana Carter	RB	Penn State	901
3	Steve McNair	QB	Alcorn State	655
4	Kerry Collins	QB	Penn State	639
5	Jay Barker	QB	Alabama	295
6	Warren Sapp	DT	Miami (Fla.)	192
7	Eric Zeier	QB	Georgia	83
8	Lawrence Phillips	RB	Nebraska	40
9	Napolean Kaufman	RB	Washington	27
10	Zach Wiegert	OT	Nebraska	27

AWARD WINNERS

PLAYER	AWARD
Kerry Collins, QB, Penn State	Maxwell
Zach Wiegert, OT, Nebraska	Outland
Rashaan Salaam, RB, Colorado	Camp
Warren Sapp, DT, Miami (Fla.)	Lombardi
Kerry Collins, QB, Penn State	O'Brien
Dana Howard, LB, Illinois	Butkus
Chris Hudson, DB, Colorado	Thorpe
Jay Barker, QB, Alabama	**Unitas**
Rashaan Salaam, RB, Colorado	Walker
Steve McLaughlin, K, Arizona	Groza
Warren Sapp, DT, Miami (Fla.)	Nagurski
Bobby Engram, WR, Penn State	Biletnikoff

BOWL GAMES

DATE	GAME	SCORE
D15	Las Vegas	UNLV 52, Central Michigan 24
D25	Aloha	Boston College 12, Kansas State 7
D27	Freedom	Utah 16, Arizona 13
D28	Independence	Virginia 20, TCU 10
D29	Copper	Brigham Young 31, Oklahoma 6
D30	Holiday	Michigan 24, Colorado State 14
D30	**Gator**	**Tennessee 45, Virginia Tech 23**
D30	Sun	Texas 35, North Carolina 31
D31	Liberty	Illinois 30, East Carolina 0
D31	Alamo	Washington State 10, Baylor 3
J1	Orange	Nebraska 24, Miami (Fla.) 17
J1	**Peach**	**North Carolina St. 28, Mississippi St. 24**
J2	**Citrus**	**Alabama 24, Ohio State 17**
J2	Fiesta	Colorado 41, Notre Dame 24
J2	Rose	Penn State 38, Oregon 20
J2	**Carquest**	**South Carolina 24, West Virginia 21**
J2	Cotton	Southern California 55, Texas Tech 14
J2	Hall of Fame	Wisconsin 34, Duke 20
J2	**Sugar**	**Florida State 23, Florida 17**

SEC STANDINGS

	CONFERENCE			OVERALL		
	W	L	T	W	L	T
EAST						
Florida	7	1	0	10	2	1
Tennessee	5	3	0	8	4	0
South Carolina	4	4	0	7	5	0
Georgia	3	4	1	6	4	1
Vanderbilt	2	6	0	5	6	0
Kentucky	0	8	0	1	10	0
WEST						
Alabama	8	0	0	12	1	0
Auburn	6	1	1	9	1	1
Mississippi State	5	3	0	8	4	0
LSU	3	5	0	4	7	0
Arkansas	2	6	0	4	7	0
Mississippi	2	6	0	4	7	0

ALL-SEC TEAM

POS	OFFENSE	SCHOOL
QB	Jay Barker	Alabama
RB	Sherman Williams	Alabama
RB	Stephen Davis	Auburn
WR	Jack Jackson	Florida
WR	Frank Sanders	Auburn
C	Shannon Roubique	Auburn
OL	Jason Udom	Florida
OL	Kevin Mays	Tennessee
OL	Jesse James	Mississippi State
OL	Jon Stevenson	Alabama
OL	Willie Anderson	Auburn
TE	David LaFleur	LSU
PK	Michael Proctor	Alabama

POS	DEFENSE	SCHOOL
L	Kevin Carter	Florida
L	Mike Pelton	Auburn
L	Ellis Johnson	Florida
LB	Abdul Jackson	Mississippi
LB	Dwayne Curry	Mississippi State
LB	Ben Hanks	Florida
LB	Gabe Northern	LSU
DB	Larry Kennedy	Florida
DB	Brian Robinson	Auburn
DB	Walt Harris	Mississippi State
DB	Willie Gaston	Alabama
DB	Alundis Brice	Mississippi
P	Terry Daniel	Auburn

SEC CHAMPIONSHIP GAME

DECEMBER 3 | ATLANTA
FLORIDA 24, ALABAMA 23

	1ST	2ND	3RD	4TH	FINAL
ALA	7	3	6	7	23
FLA	7	10	0	7	24

SCORING SUMMARY

ALA	Brown 70 pass from Barker (Proctor kick)
FLA	Anthony 26 pass from Wuerffel (Davis kick)
ALA	FG Proctor 22
FLA	FG Davis 42
FLA	Wuerffel 1 run (Davis kick)
ALA	FG Proctor 42
ALA	FG Proctor 48
ALA	Rudd 27 interception return (Proctor kick)
FLA	Doering 2 pass from Wuerffel (Davis kick)

ALABAMA	TEAM STATISTICS	FLORIDA
16	First Downs	14
116	Rushing Yards	44
10-19-2	Passing	25-43-2
181	Passing Yards	272
297	Total Yards	316
2-45	Punt Returns - Yards	1-1
2-43	Kickoff Returns - Yards	3-58
6-34.3	Punts - Average	6-41.3
1-0	Fumbles - Lost	0-0
6-30	Penalties - Yards	2-10

INDIVIDUAL LEADERS

RUSHING
ALA: Williams 29-99.
FLA: Taylor 14-40.

PASSING
ALA: Barker 10-19-2, 181 yards, TD.
FLA: Wuerffel 23-41-2, 227 yards, 2 TD.

RECEIVING
ALA: Brown 3-119, TD; Lynch 3-28.
FLA: Anthony 8-105, TD; Taylor 7-62.

1995 NCAA Major College Statistical Leaders

Individual Leaders

PASSING	CL	G	ATT	COM	PCT	INT	I%	YDS	YPA	TD	TD%	RATING
1 Danny Wuerffel, Florida	**JR**	**11**	**325**	**210**	**64.6**	**10**	**3.1**	**3266**	**10.1**	**35**	**10.8**	**178.4**
2 Bobby Hoying, Ohio State	SR	12	303	192	63.4	11	3.6	3023	10.0	28	9.2	170.4
3 Donovan McNabb, Syracuse	FR	11	207	128	61.8	6	2.9	1991	9.6	16	7.7	162.3
4 Mike Maxwell, Nevada	SR	9	409	277	67.7	17	4.2	3611	8.8	33	8.1	160.2
5 Matt Miller, Kansas State	SR	11	240	154	64.2	11	4.6	2059	8.6	22	9.2	157.3
6 Steve Taneyhill, South Carolina	**SR**	**11**	**389**	**261**	**67.1**	**9**	**2.3**	**3094**	**8.0**	**29**	**7.5**	**153.9**
7 Jim Arellanes, Fresno State	JR	9	172	102	59.3	6	3.5	1539	9.0	13	7.6	152.4
8 Donald Sellers, New Mexico	JR	10	195	121	62.1	3	1.5	1693	8.7	11	5.6	150.5
9 Steve Sarkisian, Brigham Young	JR	11	385	250	64.9	14	3.6	3437	8.9	20	5.2	149.8
10 Josh Wallwork, Wyoming	JR	10	271	163	60.2	13	4.8	2363	8.7	21	7.8	149.4

ALL-PURPOSE	CL	G	RUSH	REC	PR	KR	YDS	YPG
1 Troy Davis, Iowa State	SO	11	2010	159	0	297	2466	224.2
2 Alex Van Dyke, Nevada	SR	11	6	1854	0	583	2443	222.1
3 Wasean Tait, Toledo	JR	11	1905	183	0	0	2088	189.8
4 Eddie George, Ohio State	SR	12	1826	399	0	0	2225	185.4
5 Abu Wilson, Utah State	SR	11	1476	375	0	153	2004	182.2
6 Winslow Oliver, New Mexico	SR	11	915	228	101	666	1910	173.6
7 Corey Walker, Arkansas St.	JR	11	1013	411	0	459	1883	171.2
8 Leeland McElroy, Texas A&M	JR	10	1122	379	0	208	1709	170.9
9 Darnell Autry, Northwestern	SO	11	1675	130	0	45	1850	168.2
10 Byron Hanspard, Texas Tech	SO	11	1374	474	0	0	1848	168.0

RUSHING/Yards Per Game	CL	G	ATT	YDS	TD	AVG	YPG
1 Troy Davis, Iowa State	SO	11	345	2010	15	5.8	182.7
2 Wasean Tait, Toledo	JR	11	357	1905	20	5.3	173.2
3 George Jones, San Diego State	JR	12	305	1842	23	6.0	153.5
4 Darnell Autry, Northwestern	SO	11	355	1675	14	4.7	152.3
5 Eddie George, Ohio State	SR	12	303	1826	23	6.0	152.2
6 Deland McCullough, Miami (Ohio)	SR	11	321	1627	14	5.1	147.9
7 Moe Williams, Kentucky	**JR**	**11**	**294**	**1600**	**17**	**5.4**	**145.5**
8 Tim Biakabutuka, Michigan	JR	12	279	1724	12	6.2	143.7
9 Karim Abdul-Jabbar, UCLA	JR	10	270	1419	11	5.3	141.9
10 Charles Talley, Northern Illinois	JR	11	285	1540	7	5.4	140.0

RUSHING/Yards Per Carry	CL	G	ATT	YDS	YPC
1 Warrick Dunn, Florida State	JR	11	166	1242	7.5
2 Denvis Manns, New Mexico State	FR	11	157	1120	7.1
3 Tim Biakabutuka, Michigan	JR	12	279	1724	6.2
4 Jerald Moore, Oklahoma	JR	10	165	1001	6.1
5 George Jones, San Diego State	JR	12	305	1842	6.0
6 Eddie George, Ohio State	SR	12	303	1826	6.0
7 Mike Alstott, Purdue	SR	11	243	1436	5.9
8 David Thompson, Oklahoma State	JR	12	256	1509	5.9
9 Troy Davis, Iowa State	SO	11	345	2010	5.8
10 Raymond Priester, Clemson	SO	11	223	1286	5.8

Based on top 30 rushers

RECEIVING	CL	G	REC	YDS	TD	RPG	YPR	YPG
1 Alex Van Dyke, Nevada	SR	11	129	1854	16	11.7	14.4	168.6
2 Marcus Harris, Wyoming	JR	11	78	1423	14	7.1	18.2	129.4
3 Kevin Alexander, Utah State	SR	11	92	1400	6	8.4	15.2	127.3
4 Terry Glenn, Ohio State	JR	11	57	1316	17	5.2	23.1	119.6
5 Chad Mackey, Louisiana Tech	JR	11	90	1255	9	8.2	13.9	114.1
6 Keyshawn Johnson, Southern Cal	SR	11	90	1218	6	8.2	13.5	110.7
7 Will Blackwell, San Diego State	SO	11	86	1207	8	7.8	14.0	109.7
8 Marvin Harrison, Syracuse	SR	11	56	1131	8	5.1	20.2	102.8
9 Brandon Stokley, La.-Lafayette	FR	11	75	1121	9	6.8	14.9	101.9
10 Bobby Engram, Penn State	SR	11	63	1084	11	5.7	17.2	98.6

PUNTING	CL	PUNT	YDS	AVG
1 Brad Maynard, Ball State	JR	66	3071	46.5
2 Brian Gragert, Wyoming	SR	40	1808	45.2
3 Greg Ivy, Oklahoma State	SR	66	2947	44.7
4 Chad Kessler, LSU	SO	47	2072	44.1
5 Sean Liss, Florida State	JR	49	2153	43.9
6 Darrin Simmons, Kansas	SR	51	2233	43.8
7 Tucker Phillips, Rice	JR	57	2487	43.6
8 John Stonehouse, Southern California	SR	44	1918	43.6
9 Sean Terry, Texas A&M	SR	60	2598	43.3
10 Steve Carr, Air Force	SR	45	1946	43.2

PUNT RETURNS	CL	PR	YDS	TD	AVG
1 James Dye, Brigham Young	JR	20	438	2	21.9
2 Brian Roberson, Fresno State	JR	19	346	1	18.2
3 Marvin Harrison, Syracuse	SR	22	369	2	16.8
4 Greg Myers, Colorado State	SR	35	555	3	15.9
5 Paul Guidry, UCLA	JR	24	370	1	15.4
6 Ray Peterson, San Diego State	SR	22	320	0	14.6
7 Kenyatta Watson, Boston College	JR	17	245	2	14.4
8 Dane Johnson, Texas Tech	SO	15	214	0	14.3
9 Brian Musso, Northwestern	JR	28	393	1	14.0
10 Mike Fullman, Nebraska	JR	21	285	1	13.6

KICKOFF RETURNS	CL	KR	YDS	TD	AVG
1 Robert Tate, Cincinnati	JR	15	515	1	34.3
2 Winslow Oliver, New Mexico	SR	21	666	1	31.7
3 Damon Dunn, Stanford	SO	19	539	1	28.4
4 Steve Clay, Eastern Michigan	SR	14	395	1	28.2
5 Emmett Mosley, Notre Dame	JR	15	419	0	27.9
6 Marlon Evans, Stanford	SR	16	446	1	27.9
7 Silas Massey, Central Michigan	FR	16	434	0	27.1
8 Chris Buckhalter, Southern Miss	SR	14	377	0	26.9
9 Vertis McKinney, North Texas	SR	14	373	0	26.6
10 Derrick Mason, Michigan State	JR	31	815	1	26.3

SCORING	CL	TDS	XP	FG	PTS	PTPG
1 Eddie George, Ohio State	SR	24	0	0	144	12.0
2 George Jones, San Diego State	JR	23	0	0	138	11.5
3 Wasean Tait, Toledo	JR	20	0	0	120	10.9
4 Scott Greene, Michigan State	SR	17	2	0	104	10.4
5 Byron Hanspard, Texas Tech	SO	18	0	0	108	9.8
6 Leeland McElroy, Texas A&M	JR	16	0	0	96	9.6
7 Beau Morgan, Air Force	JR	19	0	0	114	9.5
8 Terry Glenn, Ohio State	JR	17	2	0	104	9.5
9 Stephen Davis, Auburn	**SR**	**17**	**0**	**0**	**102**	**9.3**
9 Moe Williams, Kentucky	**JR**	**17**	**0**	**0**	**102**	**9.3**

FIELD GOALS	CL	FGA	FGM	PCT	FGG
1 Michael Reeder, TCU	SO	25	23	0.92	2.09
2 Rafael Garcia, Virginia	JR	27	20	0.74	1.67
3 Dan Pulsipher, Utah	JR	22	17	0.77	1.55
4 Eric Abrams, Stanford	SR	18	16	0.89	1.45
4 Brett Conway, Penn State	JR	24	16	0.67	1.45
4 Eric Richards, Cincinnati	SO	24	16	0.67	1.45
4 Jeff Hall, Tennessee	**FR**	**25**	**16**	**0.64**	**1.45**
8 Remy Hamilton, Michigan	JR	25	17	0.68	1.42
9 Josh Smith, Oregon	FR	21	14	0.67	1.40
10 Jeff Sauve, Clemson	SR	20	15	0.75	1.36

INTERCEPTIONS	CL	INT	YDS	TD	INT/GM
1 Willie Smith, Louisiana Tech	JR	8	65	0	0.80
2 Chris Canty, Kansas State	SO	8	117	2	0.73
2 Sean Andrews, Navy	SO	8	30	0	0.73
4 Sam Madison, Louisville	JR	7	136	0	0.64
5 Plez Atkins, Iowa	SO	6	97	2	0.60
5 Harold Lusk, Utah	JR	6	40	0	0.60
5 Kevin Abrams, Syracuse	JR	6	13	0	0.60
8 Emmanuel McDaniel, East Carolina *	SR	6	111	1	0.55
8 Sam Garnes, Cincinnati *	JR	6	101	0	0.55
8 Jeremy Bunch, Tulsa *	JR	6	76	1	0.55

*Nine tied with 0.55; these had the most yards

Team Leaders

RUSHING OFFENSE	G	ATT	YDS	AVG	TD	YPG
1 Nebraska	11	627	4398	7.0	51	399.8
2 Air Force	12	672	3989	5.9	36	332.4
3 Army	11	699	3632	5.2	36	330.2
4 Clemson	11	611	2855	4.7	24	259.5
5 Toledo	11	564	2690	4.8	32	244.5
6 Notre Dame	11	562	2572	4.6	29	233.8
7 Navy	11	574	2570	4.5	21	233.6
8 Purdue	11	522	2567	4.9	25	233.4
9 Iowa State	11	506	2513	5.0	23	228.5
10 Northern Illinois	11	546	2497	4.6	18	227.0

PASSING OFFENSE	G	ATT	COM	INT	PCT	YDS	YPA	TD	I%	YPC	YPG
1 Nevada	11	509	337	22	66.2	4579	9.0	39	4.3	13.6	416.3
2 Florida	**12**	**457**	**287**	**12**	**62.8**	**4330**	**9.5**	**48**	**2.6**	**15.1**	**360.8**
3 Florida State	11	465	297	14	63.9	3616	7.8	36	3.0	12.2	328.7
4 New Mexico State	11	454	260	20	57.3	3540	7.8	30	4.4	13.6	321.8
5 Brigham Young	11	388	252	14	64.9	3469	8.9	20	3.6	13.8	315.4
6 South Carolina	**11**	**420**	**282**	**10**	**67.1**	**3373**	**8.0**	**32**	**2.4**	**12.0**	**306.6**
7 Eastern Michigan	11	441	254	19	57.6	3323	7.5	23	4.3	13.1	302.1
8 Colorado	11	366	222	11	60.7	3269	8.9	28	3.0	14.7	297.2
9 Fresno State	12	432	247	17	57.2	3483	8.1	25	3.9	14.1	290.3
10 Wake Forest	11	483	289	18	59.8	3073	6.4	19	3.7	10.6	279.4

TOTAL OFFENSE	G	P	YDS	AVG	TD	YPG
1 Nevada	11	917	6263	6.8	63	569.4
2 Nebraska	11	855	6119	7.2	69	556.3
3 Florida State	11	885	6067	6.9	71	551.6
4 Florida	**12**	**867**	**6413**	**7.4**	**72**	**534.4**
5 Ohio State	12	865	5887	6.8	60	490.6
6 Colorado	11	809	5353	6.6	48	486.6
7 San Diego State	12	883	5785	6.6	51	482.1
8 New Mexico State	11	811	5248	6.5	46	477.1
9 Auburn	**11**	**788**	**5049**	**6.4**	**54**	**459.0**
10 Fresno State	12	899	5479	6.1	47	456.6

RUSHING DEFENSE	G	ATT	YDS	AVG	TD	YPG
1 Virginia Tech	11	429	851	2.0	7	77.4
2 Nebraska	11	341	862	2.5	6	78.4
3 Michigan	12	419	1081	2.6	12	90.1
4 Georgia Tech	11	372	1003	2.7	17	91.2
5 Arkansas	**12**	**424**	**1251**	**3.0**	**15**	**104.3**
6 Alabama	**11**	**380**	**1158**	**3.0**	**9**	**105.3**
7 Oregon	11	416	1163	2.8	15	105.7
8 Texas A&M	11	444	1164	2.6	8	105.8
9 Oklahoma	11	424	1200	2.8	11	109.1
10 Virginia	12	424	1310	3.1	15	109.2

PASSING DEFENSE	G	ATT	COM	PCT	INT	I%	YDS	YPA	TD	TD%	RAT
1 Miami (Ohio)	11	303	137	45.2	22	7.3	1544	5.1	11	3.6	85.5
2 Texas A&M	11	329	150	45.6	13	4.0	1671	5.1	8	2.4	88.4
3 Texas Tech	11	372	153	41.1	15	4.0	2020	5.4	14	3.8	91.1
4 Ball State	11	303	128	42.2	10	3.3	1469	4.9	14	4.6	91.6
5 Baylor	11	310	148	47.7	13	4.2	1661	5.4	7	2.3	91.8
6 LSU	**11**	**343**	**158**	**46.1**	**13**	**3.8**	**1907**	**5.6**	**8**	**2.3**	**92.9**
7 East Carolina	11	332	157	47.3	19	5.7	1988	6.0	7	2.1	93.1
8 Cincinnati	11	347	162	46.7	20	5.8	2011	5.8	11	3.2	94.3
9 Louisville	11	350	175	50.0	24	6.9	2130	6.1	8	2.3	95.0
10 Miami (Fla.)	11	302	145	48.0	12	4.0	1631	5.4	10	3.3	96.4

TOTAL DEFENSE	G	P	YDS	AVG	TD	YPG
1 Kansas State	11	673	2759	4.1	16	250.8
2 Miami (Ohio)	11	738	2764	3.7	15	251.3
3 Texas A&M	11	773	2835	3.7	16	257.7
4 Ball State	11	712	2850	4.0	22	259.1
5 Baylor	11	709	2903	4.1	19	263.9
6 North Carolina	11	729	2940	4.0	25	267.3
7 Arizona	11	739	2976	4.0	19	270.5
8 Western Michigan	11	686	3092	4.5	23	281.1
9 Alabama	**11**	**727**	**3125**	**4.3**	**21**	**284.1**
10 Virginia Tech	11	782	3145	4.0	18	285.9

SCORING OFFENSE	G	PTS	AVG
1 Nebraska	11	576	52.4
2 Florida State	11	532	48.4
3 Florida	**12**	**534**	**44.5**
4 Nevada	11	484	44.0
5 Auburn	**11**	**424**	**38.5**
6 Ohio State	12	461	38.4
7 Tennessee	**11**	**411**	**37.4**
8 Colorado	11	406	36.9
9 Kansas State	11	402	36.5
10 South Carolina	**11**	**401**	**36.5**

SCORING DEFENSE	G	PTS	AVG
1 Northwestern	11	140	12.7
2 Kansas State	11	145	13.2
3 Texas A&M	11	148	13.5
4 Nebraska	11	150	13.6
5 Virginia Tech	11	155	14.1
6 LSU	**11**	**160**	**14.5**
7 Louisville	11	165	15.0
7 Miami (Ohio)	11	165	15.0
9 Baylor	11	166	15.1
10 Clemson	11	178	16.2

TURNOVER MARGIN	G	FR	INT	TOT	FL	INTL	TOT	MAR
1 Toledo	11	16	18	34	6	6	12	2.0
2 Louisville	11	17	24	41	12	8	20	1.9
3 Northwestern	11	16	16	32	6	6	12	1.8
4 Florida State	11	18	16	34	6	14	20	1.3
5 Nebraska	11	8	20	28	9	6	15	1.2
5 Washington	11	12	16	28	9	6	15	1.2
7 Miami (Ohio)	11	9	22	31	8	11	19	1.1
8 Virginia	12	8	25	33	9	11	20	1.1
9 Louisiana Tech	11	19	20	39	14	14	28	1.0
9 Missouri	11	13	16	29	9	9	18	1.0
9 Tennessee	**11**	**7**	**16**	**23**	**8**	**4**	**12**	**1.0**

1995

FINAL POLL (JAN. 3)

CNN	AP	SCHOOL	FINAL RECORD
1	1	Nebraska	12-0-0
3	2	Florida	12-1-0
2	3	Tennessee	11-1-0
5	4	Florida State	10-2-0
4	5	Colorado	10-2-0
8	6	Ohio State	11-2-0
6	7	Kansas State	10-2-0
7	8	Northwestern	10-2-0
10	9	Kansas	10-2-0
9	10	Virginia Tech	10-2-0
13	11	Notre Dame	9-3-0
11	12	Southern California	9-2-1
12	13	Penn State	9-3-0
14	14	Texas	10-2-1
15	15	Texas A&M	9-3-0
17	16	Virginia	9-4-0
19	17	Michigan	9-4-0
18	18	Oregon	9-3-0
16	19	Syracuse	9-3-0
PB	20	Miami (Fla.)	8-3-0
PB	21	Alabama	8-3-0
21	22	Auburn	8-4-0
20	23	Texas Tech	9-3-0
24	24	Toledo	11-0-1
22	25	Iowa	8-4-0
23		East Carolina	9-3-0
25		LSU	7-4-1

PB: Team on probation

HEISMAN TROPHY VOTING

	PLAYER	POS	SCHOOL	TOTAL
1	Eddie George	RB	Ohio State	1460
2	Tommie Frazier	QB	Nebraska	1196
3	Danny Wuerffel	QB	Florida	987
4	Darnell Autry	RB	Northwestern	535
5	Troy Davis	RB	Iowa State	402
6	Peyton Manning	QB	Tennessee	109
7	Keyshawn Johnson	WR	Southern Cal	59
8	Tim Biakabutuka	RB	Michigan	31
9	Warrick Dunn	RB	Florida State	29
10	Bobby Hoying	QB	Ohio State	28

AWARD WINNERS

PLAYER	AWARD
Eddie George, RB, Ohio State	Maxwell
Jonathan Ogden, OT, UCLA	Outland
Eddie George, RB, Ohio State	Camp
Orlando Pace, OT, Ohio State	Lombardi
Danny Wuerffel, QB, Florida	O'Brien
Kevin Hardy, LB, Illinois	Butkus
Greg Myers, DB, Colorado State	Thorpe
Tommie Frazier, QB, Nebraska	Unitas
Eddie George, RB, Ohio State	Walker
Michael Reeder, K, TCU	Groza
Pat Fitzgerald, LB, Northwestern	Nagurski
Terry Glenn, WR, Ohio State	Biletnikoff
Pat Fitzgerald, LB, Northwestern	Bednarik

ALL-SEC TEAM

POS	OFFENSE	SCHOOL
QB	Peyton Manning	Tennessee
RB	Moe Williams	Kentucky
RB	Madre Hill	Arkansas
WR	Chris Doering	Florida
WR	Eric Moulds	Mississippi State
C	Jeff Smith	Tennessee
UL	Jason Odom	Florida
OL	Reggie Green	Florida
OL	Willie Anderson	Auburn
OL	Jason Layman	Tennessee
TE	Andy Fuller	Auburn
PK	Jeff Hall	Tennessee

POS	DEFENSE	SCHOOL
L	Shannon Brown	Alabama
L	Mark Campbell	Florida
L	Steven Conley	Arkansas
LB	Gabe Northern	LSU
LB	Ben Hanks	Florida
LB	Dexter Daniels	Florida
LB	Mark Smith	Arkansas
DB	Anthone Lott	Florida
DB	Lawrence Wright	Florida
DB	Walt Harris	Mississippi State
DB	DeRon Jenkins	Tennessee
P	Chad Kessler	LSU

CONSENSUS ALL-AMERICANS

POS	OFFENSE	SCHOOL
QB	Tommie Frazier	Nebraska
RB	Eddie George	Ohio State
RB	Troy Davis	Iowa State
WR	Terry Glenn	Ohio State
WR	Keyshawn Johnson	Southern California
TE	Marco Battaglia	Rutgers
OL	Jonathan Ogden	UCLA
OL	Jason Odom	Florida
OL	Orlando Pace	Ohio State
OL	Jeff Hartings	Penn State
C	Clay Shiver	Florida State
C	Bryan Stoltenberg	Colorado
PK	Michael Reeder	TCU

OTHERS RECEIVING FIRST-TEAM HONORS

QB	Danny Wuerffel	Florida
RB	Karim Abdul-Jabbar	UCLA
WR	Marcus Harris	Wyoming
OL	Dan Neil	Texas
OL	Aaron Graham	Nebraska
OL	Heath Irwin	Colorado
PK	Sam Valenzisi	Northwestern
KR	Marvin Harrison	Syracuse

POS	DEFENSE	SCHOOL
DL	Tedy Bruschi	Arizona
DL	Cornell Brown	Virginia Tech
DL	Marcus Jones	North Carolina
DL	Tony Brackens	Texas
LB	Zach Thomas	Texas Tech
LB	Kevin Hardy	Illinois
LB	Pat Fitzgerald	Northwestern
DB	Chris Canty	Kansas State
DB	Lawyer Milloy	Washington
DB	Aaron Beasley	West Virginia
DB	Greg Myers	Colorado State
P	Brad Maynard	Ball State

OTHERS RECEIVING FIRST-TEAM HONORS

DL	Tim Colston	Kansas State
DL	Brandon Mitchell	Texas A&M
DL	Cedric Jones	Oklahoma
DL	Jason Horn	Michigan
DL	Jared Tomich	Nebraska
DL	Mike Vrabel	Ohio State
LB	Simeon Rice	Illinois
LB	Ray Lewis	Miami (Fla.)
LB	Duane Clemons	California
DB	Ray Mickens	Texas A&M
DB	Kevin Abrams	Syracuse
DB	Marcus Coleman	Texas Tech
DB	Alex Molden	Oregon
DB	Adrian Robinson	Baylor
DB	Percy Ellsworth	Virginia
P	Will Brice	Virginia

BOWL GAMES

DATE	GAME	SCORE
D14	Las Vegas	Toledo 40, Nevada 37 OT
D25	Aloha	Kansas 51, UCLA 30
D27	Copper	Texas Tech 55, Air Force 41
D28	Alamo	Texas A&M 22, Michigan 20
D29	Sun	Iowa 38, Washington 18
D29	Holiday	Kansas State 54, Colorado State 21
D29	Independence	LSU 45, Michigan State 26
D30	Liberty	East Carolina 19, Stanford 13
D30	Carquest	North Carolina 20, Arkansas 10
D30	Peach	Virginia 34, Georgia 27
D31	Sugar	Virginia Tech 28, Texas 10
J1	Cotton	Colorado 38, Oregon 6
J1	Orange	Florida State 31, Notre Dame 26
J1	Outback	Penn State 43, Auburn 14
J1	Rose	Southern California 41, Northwestern 32
J1	Gator	Syracuse 41, Clemson 0
J1	Citrus	Tennessee 20, Ohio State 14
J2	Fiesta	Nebraska 62, Florida 24

SEC STANDINGS

	CONFERENCE			OVERALL		
	W	L	T	W	L	T
EAST						
Florida	8	0	0	12	1	0
Tennessee	7	1	0	11	1	0
Georgia	3	5	0	6	6	0
South Carolina	2	5	1	4	6	1
Kentucky	2	6	0	4	7	0
Vanderbilt	1	7	0	2	9	0
WEST						
Arkansas	6	2	0	8	5	0
Alabama	5	3	0	8	3	0
Auburn	5	3	0	8	4	0
LSU	4	3	1	7	4	1
Mississippi	3	5	0	6	5	0
Mississippi State	1	7	0	3	8	0

SEC CHAMPIONSHIP GAME

DECEMBER 2 | ATLANTA
FLORIDA 34, ARKANSAS 3

	1ST	2ND	3RD	4TH	FINAL
FLA	14	3	14	3	34
ARK	3	0	0	0	3

SCORING SUMMARY
ARK FG Latourette 36
FLA Doering 22 pass from Wuerffel (Edminston kick)
FLA Wuerffel 1 run (Edminston kick)
FLA FG Edminston 31
FLA Hilliard 29 pass from Wuerffel (Edminston kick)
FLA Hanks 95 fumble recovery (Edminston kick)
FLA FG Edminston 20

FLORIDA	TEAM STATISTICS	ARKANSAS
25	First Downs	21
114	Rushing Yards	129
21-29-0	Passing	17-27-2
282	Passing Yards	170
390	Total Yards	299
0-0	Punt Returns - Yards	0-0
2-44	Kickoff Returns - Yards	5-83
3-43.7	Punts - Average	4-34.3
0-0	Fumbles - Lost	3-2
8-55	Penalties - Yards	9-59

INDIVIDUAL LEADERS
RUSHING
FLA: Jackson 11-62.
ARK: Johnson 20-71.
PASSING
FLA: Wuerffel 20-28-0, 276 yards, 2 TD.
ARK: Lunney 17-27-2, 170 yards.
RECEIVING
FLA: Hilliard 7-125, TD; Anthony 5-47.
ARK: Meadors 7-74; Johnson 4-51.

1996 NCAA Major College Statistical Leaders

Individual Leaders

PASSING	CL	G	ATT	COM	PCT	INT	I%	YDS	YPA	TD	TD%	RATING
1 Steve Sarkisian, Brigham Young	SR	14	404	278	68.8	12	3.0	4027	10.0	33	8.2	173.6
2 Danny Wuerffel, Florida	**SR**	**12**	**360**	**207**	**57.5**	**13**	**3.6**	**3625**	**10.1**	**39**	**10.8**	**170.6**
3 Billy Blanton, San Diego State	SR	11	344	227	66.0	5	1.5	3221	9.4	29	8.4	169.6
4 Josh Wallwork, Wyoming	SR	12	458	286	62.5	15	3.3	4090	8.9	33	7.2	154.7
5 John Dutton, Nevada	SO	11	334	222	66.5	6	1.8	2750	8.2	22	6.6	153.8
6 Pat Barnes, California	SR	11	420	250	59.5	8	1.9	3499	8.3	31	7.4	150.1
7 Peyton Manning, Tennessee	**JR**	**11**	**380**	**243**	**64.0**	**12**	**3.2**	**3287**	**8.7**	**20**	**5.3**	**147.7**
8 Mike Fouts, Utah	SR	11	302	177	58.6	7	2.3	2526	8.4	21	7.0	147.2
9 Ryan Clement, Miami (Fla.)	JR	11	246	148	60.2	6	2.4	1983	8.1	18	7.3	147.1
10 Brent Baldwin, Ball State	SR	11	205	121	59.0	5	2.4	1703	8.3	14	6.8	146.5

ALL-PURPOSE	CL	G	RUSH	REC	PR	KR	YDS	YPG
1 Troy Davis, Iowa State	JR	11	2185	61	0	118	2364	214.9
2 Byron Hanspard, Texas Tech	JR	11	2084	192	0	0	2276	206.9
3 Corey Dillon, Washington	JR	11	1555	273	0	357	2185	198.6
4 Kevin Faulk, LSU	**SO**	**11**	**1282**	**134**	**375**	**313**	**2104**	**191.3**
5 Silas Massey, Central Michigan	SO	10	1544	103	0	159	1806	180.6
6 June Henley, Kansas	SR	10	1349	215	0	209	1773	177.3
7 Scott Harley, East Carolina	SO	11	1745	199	0	0	1944	176.7
8 Tiki Barber, Virginia	SR	11	1360	258	241	0	1859	169.0
9 Leon Johnson, North Carolina	SR	11	913	381	191	347	1832	166.6
10 Ron Dayne, Wisconsin	FR	12	1863	133	0	0	1996	166.3

RUSHING/Yards Per Game	CL	G	ATT	YDS	TD	AVG	YPG
1 Troy Davis, Iowa State	JR	11	402	2185	21	5.4	198.6
2 Byron Hanspard, Texas Tech	JR	11	339	2084	13	6.1	189.5
3 Scott Harley, East Carolina	SO	11	307	1745	14	5.7	158.6
4 Ron Dayne, Wisconsin	FR	12	295	1863	18	6.3	155.3
5 Silas Massey, Central Michigan	SO	10	312	1544	16	4.9	154.4
6 Corey Dillon, Washington	JR	11	271	1555	22	5.7	141.4
7 Darnell Autry, Northwestern	JR	10	263	1386	15	5.3	138.6
8 David Thompson, Oklahoma State	SR	11	293	1524	13	5.2	138.6
9 Beau Morgan, Air Force	SR	11	225	1494	18	6.6	135.8
10 June Henley, Kansas	SR	10	302	1349	17	4.5	134.9

RUSHING/Yards Per Carry	CL	G	ATT	YDS	YPC
1 Carl Sanders, UAB	JR	11	168	1154	6.9
2 Beau Morgan, Air Force	SR	11	225	1494	6.6
3 Damon Washington, Colorado State	SO	10	162	1075	6.6
4 Demond Parker, Oklahoma	FR	11	180	1184	6.6
5 Terry Battle, Arizona State	SR	11	160	1043	6.5
6 Ron Dayne, Wisconsin	FR	12	295	1863	6.3
7 Warrick Dunn, Florida State	SR	11	189	1179	6.2
8 Ricky Williams, Texas	SO	12	205	1272	6.2
9 Byron Hanspard, Texas Tech	JR	11	339	2084	6.1
10 Antowain Smith, Houston	SR	11	202	1239	6.1

Based on top 50 rushers

RECEIVING	CL	G	REC	YDS	TD	RPG	YPR	YPG
1 Marcus Harris, Wyoming	SR	12	109	1650	13	9.1	15.1	137.5
2 Chad Mackey, Louisiana Tech	SR	11	85	1466	10	7.7	17.2	133.3
3 Geoffery Noisy, Nevada	SO	11	98	1435	9	8.9	14.6	130.5
4 Nakia Jenkins, Utah State	JR	11	82	1397	8	7.5	17.0	127.0
5 Reggie Allen, Central Michigan	SO	10	66	1229	9	6.6	18.6	122.9
6 Brian Roberson, Fresno State	SR	11	78	1248	5	7.1	16.0	113.5
7 Will Blackwell, San Diego State	JR	9	60	1000	11	6.7	16.7	111.1
8 Eugene Baker, Kent	SO	11	69	1215	13	6.3	17.6	110.5
9 Antonio Wilson, Idaho	JR	11	65	1203	7	5.9	18.5	109.4
10 Reidel Anthony, Florida	**JR**	**12**	**72**	**1293**	**18**	**6.0**	**18.0**	**107.8**

PUNTING	CL	PUNT	YDS	AVG
1 Bill Marinangel, Vanderbilt	**SR**	**77**	**3586**	**46.6**
2 Noel Prefontaine, San Diego State	SR	48	2234	46.5
3 Andy Russ, Mississippi State	**SR**	**53**	**2466**	**46.5**
4 Ty Atteberry, Baylor	SR	60	2781	46.4
5 Tucker Phillips, Rice	SR	53	2433	45.9
6 Brad Maynard, Ball State	SR	59	2705	45.9
7 Jim Wren, Southern California	JR	66	3006	45.6
8 Marc Harris, Iowa State	SR	51	2312	45.3
9 Ryan Longwell, California	SR	60	2714	45.2
10 John Krueger, Duke	SR	58	2619	45.2

PUNT RETURNS	CL	PR	YDS	TD	AVG
1 Allen Rossum, Notre Dame	JR	15	344	3	22.9
2 Tim Dwight, Iowa	JR	22	417	2	19.0
3 James Dye, Brigham Young	SR	20	352	2	17.6
4 Kevin Faulk, LSU	**SO**	**24**	**375**	**1**	**15.6**
5 Keijuan Douglas, Eastern Michigan	FR	12	183	1	15.3
6 Leandrew Childs, San Diego State	JR	22	332	0	15.1
7 Chad Smith, New Mexico	SO	14	200	1	14.3
8 Terry Fair, Tennessee	**JR**	**29**	**400**	**2**	**13.8**
9 Brian Roberson, Fresno State	SR	24	330	1	13.8
10 Tremayne Banks, Miami (Ohio)	SR	29	395	0	13.6

KICKOFF RETURNS	CL	KR	YDS	TD	AVG
1 Tremain Mack, Miami (Fla.)	JR	13	514	1	39.5
2 Terry Battle, Arizona State	JR	17	528	2	31.1
3 Pat Johnson, Oregon	JR	12	368	1	30.7
4 Eric Booth, Southern Miss	JR	12	352	0	29.3
5 Cedric Johnson, Texas-El Paso	SR	25	729	1	29.2
6 Rodnick Phillips, SMU	FR	22	618	1	28.1
7 John Avery, Mississippi	**JR**	**17**	**473**	**2**	**27.8**
8 Tony Knox, Western Michigan	SR	25	690	1	27.6
9 Jim Turner, Syracuse	JR	23	633	1	27.5
10 Tremayne Banks, Miami (Ohio)	SR	19	518	1	27.3

SCORING	CL	TDS	XP	FG	PTS	PTPG
1 Corey Dillon, Washington	JR	23	0	0	138	12.6
2 Troy Davis, Iowa State	JR	21	0	0	126	11.5
3 Calvin Branch, Colorado State	SR	22	0	0	132	11.0
4 Terry Battle, Arizona State	JR	20	0	0	120	10.9
4 Skip Hicks, UCLA	JR	20	0	0	120	10.9
6 June Henley, Kansas	SR	18	0	0	108	10.8
7 Damon Shea, Nevada	SO	0	55	20	115	10.5
8 Beau Morgan, Air Force	SR	18	0	0	108	9.8
8 Sedrick Irvin, Michigan State	FR	18	0	0	108	9.8
10 Silas Massey, Central Michigan	SO	16	2	0	98	9.8

FIELD GOALS	CL	FGA	FGM	PCT	FGG
1 Rafael Garcia, Virginia	SR	27	21	0.78	1.91
2 Marc Primanti, North Carolina St.	SR	20	20	1.00	1.82
2 Damon Shea, Nevada	SO	22	20	0.91	1.82
2 James Anderson, Tulsa	JR	28	20	0.71	1.82
5 Cory Wedel, Wyoming	JR	27	20	0.74	1.67
6 J. Parker, Army	SR	21	18	0.86	1.64
7 John Matich, Boston College	FR	23	16	0.70	1.60
8 Phil Dawson, Texas	JR	24	19	0.79	1.58
9 Chris Gardner, Michigan State	JR	22	17	0.77	1.55
10 Kyle Bryant, Texas A&M	JR	23	18	0.78	1.50
10 Brett Conway, Penn State	SR	24	18	0.75	1.50

INTERCEPTIONS	CL	INT	YDS	TD	INT/GM
1 Dre' Bly, North Carolina	FR	11	141	1	1.00
2 Brian Lee, Wyoming	JR	8	68	0	0.67
3 Kim Herring, Penn State	SR	7	64	0	0.58
3 Kevin Jackson, Alabama	**SR**	**7**	**44**	**1**	**0.58**
5 Chris McAlister, Arizona	JR	6	103	1	0.55
5 Damien Robinson, Iowa	SR	6	99	0	0.55
5 Delmonico Montgomery, Houston	SR	6	87	0	0.55
5 Harold Lusk, Utah	SR	6	86	0	0.55
5 Ramos McDonald, New Mexico	JR	6	78	1	0.55
5 Patrick Surtain, Southern Miss	JR	6	77	0	0.55
5 Sam Madison, Louisville	SR	6	50	1	0.55
5 Darnell Hasson, Nevada	SR	6	25	1	0.55

Team Leaders

RUSHING OFFENSE	G	ATT	YDS	AVG	TD	YPG
1 Army	11	740	3812	5.2	33	346.5
2 Air Force	11	618	3618	5.9	37	328.9
3 Rice	11	637	3360	5.3	34	305.5
4 Nebraska	12	691	3503	5.1	45	291.9
5 Navy	11	628	3120	5.0	31	283.6
6 Ohio U.	12	685	3286	4.8	29	273.8
7 Texas Tech	11	573	3008	5.2	27	273.5
8 Notre Dame	11	567	2965	5.2	34	269.5
9 Missouri	11	553	2758	5.0	24	250.7
10 Arizona State	11	538	2734	5.1	30	248.5

PASSING OFFENSE	G	ATT	COM	INT	PCT	YDS	YPA	TD	I%	YPC	YPG
1 Wyoming	12	486	299	17	61.5	4310	8.9	35	3.5	14.4	359.2
2 Nevada	11	480	307	11	64.0	3907	8.1	34	2.3	12.7	355.2
3 Louisiana Tech	11	475	279	17	58.7	3778	8.0	35	3.6	13.5	343.5
4 Idaho	11	460	270	12	58.7	3772	8.2	29	2.6	14.0	342.9
5 Florida	**12**	**412**	**234**	**16**	**56.8**	**4007**	**9.7**	**42**	**3.9**	**17.1**	**333.9**
6 California	11	427	253	8	59.3	3536	8.3	32	1.9	14.0	321.5
7 Utah State	11	422	233	23	55.2	3493	8.3	15	5.5	15.0	317.5
8 Tennessee	**11**	**399**	**255**	**12**	**63.9**	**3396**	**8.5**	**20**	**3.0**	**13.3**	**308.7**
9 Nevada-Las Vegas	12	530	287	17	54.2	3685	7.0	26	3.2	12.8	307.1
10 Colorado	11	390	221	14	56.7	3338	8.6	22	3.6	15.1	303.5

TOTAL OFFENSE	G	P	YDS	AVG	TD	YPG
1 Nevada	11	915	5800	6.3	57	527.3
2 Florida	**12**	**854**	**6047**	**7.1**	**67**	**503.9**
3 Wyoming	12	905	5987	6.6	54	498.9
4 Arizona State	11	874	5417	6.2	54	492.5
5 Idaho	11	848	5294	6.2	48	481.3
6 Brigham Young	14	1004	6692	6.7	67	478.0
7 Central Michigan	11	871	5252	6.0	45	477.5
8 San Diego State	11	803	5241	6.5	51	476.5
9 Utah State	11	835	5110	6.1	43	464.6
10 Notre Dame	11	817	5096	6.2	49	463.3

RUSHING DEFENSE	G	ATT	YDS	AVG	TD	YPG
1 Florida State	11	418	649	1.6	5	59.0
2 West Virginia	11	364	677	1.9	5	61.5
3 North Carolina	11	334	813	2.4	5	73.9
4 Louisville	11	437	892	2.0	9	81.1
5 Nebraska	12	447	1006	2.3	7	83.8
6 Army	11	325	979	3.0	12	89.0
7 Alabama	**12**	**392**	**1110**	**2.8**	**9**	**92.5**
8 Southern Miss	11	384	1069	2.8	12	97.2
9 Ohio State	11	398	1074	2.7	7	97.6
10 Arizona State	11	407	1078	2.6	10	98.0

PASSING DEFENSE	G	ATT	COM	PCT	INT	I%	YDS	YPA	TD	TD%	RAT
1 Ohio State	11	309	140	45.3	20	6.5	1602	5.2	5	1.6	81.3
2 Miami (Ohio)	11	260	104	40.0	11	4.2	1323	5.1	6	2.3	81.9
3 North Carolina	11	326	148	45.4	20	6.1	1669	5.1	7	2.2	83.2
4 Kansas State	11	299	126	42.1	13	4.4	1509	5.1	9	3.0	85.8
5 West Virginia	11	348	157	45.1	16	4.6	1715	4.9	10	2.9	86.8
6 Florida State	11	358	162	45.3	11	3.1	1875	5.2	9	2.5	91.4
7 Nebraska	12	329	149	45.3	23	7.0	2059	6.3	8	2.4	91.9
8 Tennessee	**11**	**285**	**134**	**47.0**	**14**	**4.9**	**1434**	**5.0**	**12**	**4.2**	**93.4**
9 Alabama	**12**	**319**	**132**	**41.4**	**17**	**5.3**	**1957**	**6.1**	**11**	**3.5**	**93.6**
10 Notre Dame	11	292	131	44.9	13	4.5	1656	5.7	9	3.1	93.8

TOTAL DEFENSE	G	P	YDS	AVG	TD	YPG
1 West Virginia	11	712	2392	3.4	15	217.5
2 North Carolina	11	660	2482	3.8	12	225.6
3 Florida State	11	776	2524	3.3	14	229.5
4 Louisville	11	765	2594	3.4	20	235.8
5 Tennessee	**11**	**708**	**2602**	**3.7**	**16**	**236.5**
6 Ohio State	11	707	2676	3.8	12	243.3
7 Nebraska	12	776	3065	3.9	15	255.4
8 Alabama	**12**	**711**	**3067**	**4.3**	**20**	**255.6**
9 Army	11	626	2819	4.5	23	256.3
10 Syracuse	11	725	2875	4.0	17	261.4

SCORING OFFENSE	G	PTS	AVG
1 Florida	**12**	**559**	**46.6**
2 Nevada	11	497	45.2
3 Arizona State	11	471	42.8
4 Nebraska	12	512	42.7
5 Brigham Young	14	571	40.8
6 Ohio State	11	435	39.5
7 San Diego State	11	428	38.9
8 Florida State	11	426	38.7
9 Wyoming	12	464	38.7
10 Syracuse	11	407	37.0
10 Notre Dame	11	407	37.0

SCORING DEFENSE	G	PTS	AVG
1 North Carolina	11	110	10.0
2 Ohio State	11	114	10.4
3 Florida State	11	122	11.1
4 West Virginia	11	136	12.4
5 Nebraska	12	153	12.8
6 Tennessee	**11**	**157**	**14.3**
7 Alabama	**12**	**181**	**15.1**
8 Michigan	11	167	15.2
9 Virginia Tech	11	168	15.3
9 Miami (Ohio)	11	168	15.3

TURNOVER MARGIN	G	FR	INT	TOT	FL	INTL	TOT	MAR
1 North Carolina	11	14	20	34	6	6	12	2.0
2 Auburn	**11**	**14**	**22**	**36**	**9**	**13**	**22**	**1.3**
2 Southern Miss	11	16	18	34	5	15	20	1.3
2 West Virginia	11	8	16	24	4	6	10	1.3
2 East Carolina	11	23	13	36	6	16	22	1.3
2 Ohio State	11	10	20	30	7	9	16	1.3
7 Arizona	11	13	16	29	9	7	16	1.2
8 Navy	11	15	13	28	10	6	16	1.1
9 Kansas	11	11	12	23	4	8	12	1.0
9 Bowling Green	11	13	13	26	1	14	15	1.0
9 Arizona State	11	15	11	26	5	10	15	1.0

1996

FINAL POLL (JAN. 3)

CNN	AP	SCHOOL	FINAL RECORD
1	1	Florida	12-1
2	2	Ohio State	11-1
3	3	Florida State	11-1
4	4	Arizona State	11-1
5	5	Brigham Young	14-1
6	6	Nebraska	11-2
7	7	Penn State	11-2
8	8	Colorado	10-2
9	9	Tennessee	10-2
10	10	North Carolina	10-2
11	11	Alabama	10-3
13	12	LSU	10-2
12	13	Virginia Tech	10-2
14	14	Miami (Fla.)	9-3
16	15	Northwestern	9-3
15	16	Washington	9-3
17	17	Kansas State	9-3
18	18	Iowa	9-3
21	19	Notre Dame	8-3
20	20	Michigan	8-4
19	21	Syracuse	9-3
22	22	Wyoming	10-2
23	23	Texas	8-5
24	24	Auburn	8-4
25	25	Army	10-2

CONSENSUS ALL-AMERICANS

POS	OFFENSE	CL	SCHOOL
QB	Danny Wuerffel	Sr.	Florida
RB	Byron Hanspard	Jr.	Texas Tech
RB	Troy Davis	Jr.	Iowa State
WR	Marcus Harris	Sr.	Wyoming
WR	Ike Hilliard	Jr.	Florida
WR	Reidel Anthony	Jr.	Florida
TE	Tony Gonzalez	Jr.	California
OL	Orlando Pace	Jr.	Ohio State
OL	Juan Roque	Sr.	Arizona State
OL	Chris Naeole	Sr.	Colorado
OL	Dan Neil	Sr.	Texas
OL	Benji Olson	So.	Washington
C	Aaron Taylor	Jr.	Nebraska
PK	Marc Primanti	Sr.	North Carolina St.

OTHERS RECEIVING FIRST-TEAM HONORS

QB	Jake Plummer		Arizona State
RB	Warrick Dunn		Florida State
RB	Darnell Autry		Northwestern
WR	Rae Carruth		Colorado
TE	David LaFleur		LSU
TE	Itula Mili		Brigham Young
TE	Pat Fitzgerald		Texas
OL	Steve Scifres		Wyoming
OL	Scott Sanderson		Washington State
OL	Billy Conaty		Virginia Tech
C	Rod Payne		Michigan
C	K.C. Jones		Miami (Fla.)
PK	Cory Wedel		Wyoming
KR	Tim Dwight		Iowa
AP	Kevin Faulk		LSU

POS	DEFENSE	CL	SCHOOL
DL	Grant Wistrom	Jr.	Nebraska
DL	Peter Boulware	Jr.	Florida State
DL	Reinard Wilson	Sr.	Florida State
DL	Derrick Rodgers	Jr.	Arizona State
DL	Mike Vrabel	Sr.	Ohio State
LB	Canute Curtis	Sr.	West Virginia
LB	Pat Fitzgerald	Sr.	Northwestern
LB	Matt Russell	Sr.	Colorado
LB	Jarrett Irons	Sr.	Michigan
DB	Chris Canty	Jr.	Kansas State
DB	Kevin Jackson	Sr.	Alabama
DB	Dre' Bly	Fr.	North Carolina
DB	Shawn Springs	Jr.	Ohio State
P	Brad Maynard	Sr.	Ball State

OTHERS RECEIVING FIRST-TEAM HONORS

DL	Cornell Brown		Virginia Tech
DL	Jared Tornich		Nebraska
DL	Tarek Saleh		Wisconsin
DL	Michael Myers		Alabama
LB	Dwayne Rudd		Alabama
LB	Jason Chorak		Washington
LB	Keith Mitchell		Texas A&M
LB	Anthony Simmons		Clemson
DB	Charles Woodson		Michigan
DB	Kevin Abrams		Syracuse
DB	Sam Madison		Louisville
DB	Kim Herring		Penn State
P	Noel Prefontaine		San Diego State

HEISMAN TROPHY VOTING

	PLAYER	POS	SCHOOL	TOTAL
1	Danny Wuerffel	QB	Florida	1363
2	Troy Davis	RB	Iowa State	1174
3	Jake Plummer	QB	Arizona State	685
4	Orlando Pace	OT	Ohio State	599
5	Warrick Dunn	RB	Florida State	341
6	Byron Hanspard	RB	Texas Tech	251
7	Darnell Autry	RB	Northwestern	85
8	Peyton Manning	QB	Tennessee	81
9	Marcus Harris	WR	Wyoming	53
10	Beau Morgan	QB	Air Force	26

AWARD WINNERS

PLAYER	AWARD
Danny Wuerffel, QB, Florida	Maxwell
Orlando Pace OT, Ohio State	Outland
Danny Wuerffel, QB, Florida	Camp
Orlando Pace OT, Ohio State	Lombardi
Danny Wuerffel, QB, Florida	O'Brien
Matt Russell LB, Colorado	Butkus
Lawrence Wright, DB, Florida	Thorpe
Danny Wuerffel, QB, Florida	Unitas
Byron Hanspard, RB, Texas Tech	Walker
Marc Primanti, K, North Carolina St.	Groza
Pat Fitzgerald, LB, Northwestern	Nagurski
Pat Fitzgerald, LB, Northwestern	Bednarik
Marcus Harris, WR, Wyoming	Biletnikoff

BOWL GAMES

DATE	GAME	SCORE
D19	Las Vegas	Nevada 18, Ball State 15
D25	Aloha	Navy 42, California 38
D27	Carquest	Miami (Fla.) 31, Virginia 21
D27	Liberty	Syracuse 30, Houston 17
D27	Copper	Wisconsin 38, Utah 10
D28	Peach	LSU 10, Clemson 7
D29	Alamo	Iowa 27, Texas Tech 0
D30	Holiday	Colorado 33, Washington 21
D31	Independence	Auburn 32, Army 29
D31	Orange	Nebraska 41, Virginia Tech 21
D31	Sun	Stanford 38, Michigan State 0
J1	Outback	Alabama 17, Michigan 14
J1	Cotton	Brigham Young 19, Kansas State 15
J1	Gator	North Carolina 20, West Virginia 13
J1	Rose	Ohio State 20, Arizona State 17
J1	Fiesta	Penn State 38, Texas 15
J1	Florida Citrus	Tennessee 48, Northwestern 28
J2	Sugar	Florida 52, Florida State 20

SEC STANDINGS

	CONFERENCE			OVERALL		
	W	L	T	W	L	T
EAST						
Florida	8	0	0	12	1	0
Tennessee	7	1	0	10	2	0
South Carolina	4	4	0	6	5	0
Georgia	3	5	0	5	6	0
Kentucky	3	5	0	4	7	0
Vanderbilt	0	8	0	2	9	0
WEST						
Alabama	6	2	0	10	3	0
LSU	6	2	0	10	2	0
Auburn	4	4	0	8	4	0
Mississippi State	3	5	0	5	6	0
Mississippi	2	6	0	5	6	0
Arkansas	2	6	0	4	7	0

ALL-SEC TEAM

POS	OFFENSE	SCHOOL
QB	Danny Wuerffel	Florida
RB	Duce Staley	South Carolina
RB	Kevin Faulk	LSU
WR	Joey Kent	Tennessee
WR	Ike Hilliard	Florida
WR	Reidel Anthony	Florida
C	Jeff Mitchell	Florida
OL	Donnie Young	Florida
OL	Adam Meadows	Georgia
OL	Brent Smith	Mississippi State
TE	David LaFleur	LSU
PK	Jeff Hall	Tennessee
PK	Jaret Holmes	Auburn

POS	DEFENSE	SCHOOL
L	Leonard Little	Tennessee
L	Michael Myers	Alabama
L	Ed Chester	Florida
LB	Dwayne Rudd	Alabama
LB	Ralph Staten	Alabama
LB	Jamie Duncan	Vanderbilt
LB	James Bates	Florida
LB	Takeo Spikes	Auburn
DB	Kevin Jackson	Alabama
DB	Lawrence Wright	Florida
DB	Fred Weary	Florida
DB	Anthone Lott	Florida
DB	Terry Fair	Tennessee
P	Bill Marinangel	Vanderbilt

SEC CHAMPIONSHIP GAME

DECEMBER 7 | ATLANTA
FLORIDA 45, ALABAMA 30

	1ST	2ND	3RD	4TH	FINAL
ALA	7	7	14	2	30
FLA	6	18	14	7	45

SCORING SUMMARY

ALA — Riddle 36 pass from Kitchens (Brock kick)
FLA — Hillard 46 pass from Wuerffel (Cooper kick blocked)
FLA — Anthony 21 pass from Wuerffel (Wuerffel pass to Anthony)
FLA — Williams 45 pass from Wuerffel (Cooper kick)
FLA — FG Cooper 35
ALA — Vaughn 8 pass from Kitchens (Brock kick)
ALA — Riddle 5 run (Brock kick)
FLA — Anthony 13 pass from Wuerffel (Cooper kick)
ALA — Vaughn 94 pass from Kitchens (Brock kick)
FLA — Green 85 pass from Wuerffel (Cooper kick)
FLA — Anthony 21 pass from Wuerffel (Cooper kick)
ALA — Team safety

ALABAMA	TEAM STATISTICS	FLORIDA
13	First Downs	22
27	Rushing Yards	69
20-46-1	Passing	20-35-2
269	Passing Yards	401
296	Total Yards	470
0-0	Punt Returns - Yards	2-12
5-85	Kickoff Returns - Yards	4-83
8-40.8	Punts - Average	4-37.0
1-0	Fumbles - Lost	4-1
7-45	Penalties - Yards	14-95

INDIVIDUAL LEADERS

RUSHING
ALA : Riddle 17-42, TD.
FLA: Taylor 13-83.

PASSING
ALA : Kitchens 19-45-1, 264 yards, 3 TD.
FLA: Wuerffel 20-35-2, 401 yards, 6 TD.

RECEIVING
ALA : Riddle 6-81, TD; Vaughn 5-142, 2 TD.
FLA: Anthony 11-171, 3 TD; Green 3-106, TD.

1997 NCAA Major College Statistical Leaders

Individual Leaders

PASSING	CL	G	ATT	COM	PCT	INT	I%	YDS	YPA	TD	TD%	RATING
1 Cade McNown, UCLA	JR	11	283	173	61.1	5	1.8	2877	10.2	22	7.8	168.6
2 Ryan Leaf, Washington State	JR	11	375	210	56.0	10	2.7	3637	9.7	33	8.8	161.2
3 Joe Germaine, Ohio State	SR	12	184	119	64.7	7	3.8	1674	9.1	15	8.2	160.4
4 John Dutton, Nevada	SR	11	367	225	61.3	6	1.6	3526	9.6	20	5.5	156.7
5 Brock Huard, Washington	SO	10	244	146	59.8	10	4.1	2140	8.8	23	9.4	156.4
6 Mike Bobo, Georgia	**SR**	**11**	**306**	**199**	**65.0**	**8**	**2.6**	**2751**	**9.0**	**19**	**6.2**	**155.8**
7 Donovan McNabb, Syracuse	JR	12	265	145	54.7	6	2.3	2488	9.4	20	7.6	154.0
8 Graham Leigh, New Mexico	JR	12	276	166	60.1	8	2.9	2318	8.4	24	8.7	153.6
9 Moses Moreno, Colorado State	SR	12	257	157	61.1	9	3.5	2257	8.8	20	7.8	153.5
10 Chad Pennington, Marshall	SO	12	428	253	59.1	12	2.8	3480	8.1	39	9.1	151.9

ALL-PURPOSE	CL	G	RUSH	REC	PR	KR	YDS	YPG
1 Troy Edwards, Louisiana Tech	JR	11	190	1707	6	241	2144	194.9
2 Ricky Williams, Texas	JR	11	1893	150	0	0	2043	185.7
3 Kevin Faulk, LSU	**JR**	**9**	**1144**	**93**	**192**	**217**	**1646**	**182.9**
4 Randy Moss, Marshall	SO	12	2	1647	266	263	2178	181.5
5 Michael Perry, Rice	JR	10	1034	44	26	680	1784	178.4
6 Tutu Atwell, Minnesota	SR	12	77	924	296	776	2073	172.8
7 Jerome Pathon, Washington	SR	11	0	1245	209	386	1840	167.3
8 Tavian Banks, Iowa	SR	11	1639	200	0	0	1839	167.2
9 Ahman Green, Nebraska	JR	12	1877	105	0	0	1982	165.2
10 Sedrick Irvin, Michigan State	SO	11	1211	339	263	0	1813	164.8

RUSHING/Yards Per Game	CL	G	ATT	YDS	TD	AVG	YPG
1 Ricky Williams, Texas	JR	11	279	1893	25	6.8	172.1
2 Ahman Green, Nebraska	JR	12	278	1877	22	6.8	156.4
3 Amos Zereoue, West Virginia	SO	10	264	1505	16	5.7	150.5
4 Tavian Banks, Iowa	SR	11	246	1639	17	6.7	149.0
5 Ron Dayne, Wisconsin	SO	10	249	1421	15	5.7	142.1
6 Travis Prentice, Miami (Ohio)	SO	11	296	1549	25	5.2	140.8
7 Dwayne Harris, Toledo	JR	10	254	1278	10	5.0	127.8
8 Kevin Faulk, LSU	**JR**	**9**	**205**	**1144**	**15**	**5.6**	**127.1**
9 Demond Parker, Oklahoma	SO	9	194	1143	6	5.9	127.0
10 Chris McCoy, Navy	SR	11	246	1370	20	5.6	124.6

RUSHING/Yards Per Carry	CL	G	ATT	YDS	YPC
1 Kevin McDougal, Colorado State	SO	12	150	1111	7.4
2 Ricky Williams, Texas	JR	11	279	1893	6.8
3 Ahman Green, Nebraska	JR	12	278	1877	6.8
4 Tavian Banks, Iowa	SR	11	246	1639	6.7
5 Mike Cloud, Boston College	JR	10	137	886	6.5
6 Michael Perry, Rice	JR	10	162	1034	6.4
7 Scott Frost, Nebraska	SR	12	176	1095	6.2
8 Damon Washington, Colorado State	JR	12	180	1112	6.2
9 J.R. Redmond, Arizona State	SO	10	142	865	6.1
10 Fred Taylor, Florida	**SR**	**11**	**214**	**1292**	**6.0**

Based on top 50 rushers

RECEIVING	CL	G	REC	YDS	TD	RPG	YPR	YPG
1 Troy Edwards, Louisiana Tech	JR	11	102	1707	13	9.3	16.7	155.2
2 Eugene Baker, Kent State	JR	11	103	1549	18	9.4	15.0	140.8
3 Randy Moss, Marshall	SO	12	90	1647	25	7.5	18.3	137.3
4 Jerome Pathon, Washington	SR	11	69	1245	8	6.3	18.0	113.2
5 Troy Walters, Stanford	JR	11	86	1206	8	7.8	14.0	109.6
6 Geoff Noisy, Nevada	JR	11	86	1184	5	7.8	13.8	107.6
7 Brian Alford, Purdue	SR	11	59	1167	9	5.4	19.8	106.1
8 Trevor Insley, Nevada	SO	11	59	1151	6	5.4	19.5	104.6
9 Pascal Volz, New Mexico	SR	12	69	1229	13	5.8	17.8	102.4
10 Siaha Burley, Central Florida	JR	11	77	1106	7	7.0	14.4	100.6

PUNTING	CL	PUNT	YDS	AVG
1 Chad Kessler, LSU	**SR**	**39**	**1961**	**50.3**
2 John Baker, North Texas	SO	62	2925	47.2
3 Shane Lechler, Texas A&M	SO	56	2631	47.0
4 Brad Hill, Tulane	SR	42	1940	46.2
5 Chad Shrout, Hawaii	SO	68	3133	46.1
6 Rodney Williams, Georgia Tech	JR	47	2145	45.6
7 Jeff Walker, Mississippi State	**SO**	**45**	**2049**	**45.5**
8 Aron Langley, Wyoming	JR	79	3568	45.2
9 Brent Bartholomew, Ohio State	JR	65	2934	45.1
10 Jimmy Kibble, Virginia Tech	SO	50	2255	45.1

PUNT RETURNS	CL	PR	YDS	TD	AVG
1 Tim Dwight, Iowa	SR	19	367	3	19.3
2 R.W. McQuarters, Oklahoma State	JR	32	521	1	16.3
3 Steve Smith, Utah State	SR	22	344	2	15.6
4 Nod Washington, Miami (Ohio)	JR	12	185	0	15.4
5 Geoff Turner, Colorado State	SR	20	304	1	15.2
6 Dee Feaster, Florida State	JR	14	210	0	15.0
7 Quinton Spotwood, Syracuse	SO	31	463	4	14.9
8 Tinker Keck, Cincinnati	JR	39	575	4	14.7
9 Steve Neal, Western Michigan	SO	14	204	1	14.6
10 Jacquez Green, Florida	**JR**	**27**	**392**	**2**	**14.5**

KICKOFF RETURNS	CL	KR	YDS	TD	AVG
1 Eric Booth, Southern Miss	SR	22	766	2	34.8
2 Ben Kelly, Colorado	FR	25	777	1	31.1
3 Pat McGrew, Navy	SR	15	441	0	29.4
4 Boo Williams, South Carolina	**SO**	**18**	**527**	**2**	**29.3**
5 Pat Johnson, Oregon	SR	16	462	0	28.9
6 Allen Rossum, Notre Dame	SR	20	570	2	28.5
7 Ketrick Sanford, Houston	SO	19	530	0	27.9
8 Tony Horne, Clemson	SR	18	491	0	27.3
9 Damon Dunn, Stanford	SR	21	566	0	27.0
10 Tyrone Carter, Minnesota	SO	17	455	0	26.8

SCORING	CL	TDS	XP	FG	PTS	PTPG
1 Ricky Williams, Texas	JR	25	2	0	152	13.8
2 Skip Hicks, UCLA	SR	25	0	0	150	13.6
2 Travis Prentice, Miami (Ohio)	SO	25	0	0	150	13.6
4 Randy Moss, Marshall	SO	25	2	0	152	12.7
5 Curtis Enis, Penn State	JR	20	2	0	122	11.1
6 Ahman Green, Nebraska	JR	22	0	0	132	11.0
7 Chris McCoy, Navy	SR	20	0	0	120	10.9
8 Tavian Banks, Iowa	SR	19	0	0	114	10.4
8 Chris Lemon, Nevada	SO	19	0	0	114	10.4
10 Eugene Baker, Kent State	JR	18	2	0	110	10.0
10 Kevin Faulk, LSU	**JR**	**15**	**0**	**0**	**90**	**10.0**

FIELD GOALS	CL	FGA	FGM	PCT	FGG
1 Brad Palazzo, Tulane	JR	28	23	0.82	2.09
2 Colby Cason New Mexico	SR	30	21	0.70	1.75
3 Martin Gramatica, Kansas State	JR	20	19	0.95	1.73
3 Shayne Graham, Virginia Tech	SO	23	19	0.83	1.73
3 Chris Sailer, UCLA	JR	24	19	0.79	1.73
6 Brian Gowins, Northwestern	SR	27	20	0.74	1.67
7 Kris Brown, Nebraska	JR	21	18	0.86	1.50
7 Kyle Bryant, Texas A&M	SR	22	18	0.82	1.50
9 Sims Lenhardt, Duke	SO	20	16	0.80	1.45
9 Sebastian Janikowski, Florida State	FR	21	16	0.76	1.45
9 Sebastian Villarreal, Houston	SR	21	16	0.76	1.45
9 Robert Nycz, Arizona State	SR	23	16	0.70	1.45
9 Brian Hazelwood, Mississippi State	**JR**	**26**	**16**	**0.62**	**1.45**

INTERCEPTIONS	CL	INT	YDS	TD	INT/GM
1 Brian Lee, Wyoming	SR	8	103	1	0.73
2 Cedric Donaldson, LSU	**SR**	**7**	**192**	**2**	**0.64**
2 John Noel, Louisiana Tech	SR	7	93	0	0.64
2 Omarr Smith, San Jose State	JR	7	80	0	0.64
2 Tevell Jones, Ohio U.	SR	7	36	0	0.64
2 Samari Rolle, Florida State	SR	7	32	0	0.64
2 Charles Woodson, Michigan	JR	7	7	0	0.64
8 Donovin Darius, Syracuse	SR	7	56	0	0.58
9 Paul Jackson, Maryland	JR	5	14	0	0.56
10 Patrick Surtain, Southern Miss *	SR	6	127	0	0.55
10 Efrain Guizar, Fresno State *	JR	6	114	2	0.55
10 Fred Weary, Florida *	SR	6	113	0	0.55
10 Kevin Williams, Oklahoma State *	SR	6	107	1	0.55
10 Arturo Freeman, South Carolina *	**JR**	**6**	**95**	**1**	**0.55**

*10 tied with 0.55; these had the most yards

Team Leaders

RUSHING OFFENSE	G	ATT	YDS	AVG	TD	YPG
1 Nebraska	12	755	4711	6.2	66	392.6
2 Rice	11	690	3660	5.3	38	332.7
3 Navy	11	618	3370	5.5	36	306.4
4 Ohio U.	11	649	3321	5.1	32	301.9
5 Army	11	670	3247	4.8	24	295.2
6 Missouri	11	592	2899	4.9	35	263.5
7 LSU	**11**	**521**	**2823**	**5.4**	**34**	**256.6**
8 Iowa	11	492	2585	5.3	25	235.0
9 Air Force	12	688	2791	4.1	22	232.6
10 Oklahoma State	11	592	2486	4.2	25	226.0

PASSING OFFENSE	G	ATT	COM	INT	PCT	YDS	YPA	TD	I%	YPC	YPG
1 Nevada	11	443	265	11	59.8	4072	9.2	21	2.5	15.4	370.2
2 Kentucky	**11**	**562**	**374**	**19**	**66.5**	**4019**	**7.2**	**37**	**3.4**	**10.7**	**365.4**
3 Louisiana Tech	11	495	301	11	60.8	3965	8.0	34	2.2	13.2	360.5
4 Washington State	11	400	223	12	55.8	3789	9.5	34	3.0	17.0	344.5
5 Florida State	11	440	262	11	59.5	3740	8.5	30	2.5	14.3	340.0
6 Tennessee	**12**	**492**	**296**	**12**	**60.2**	**3981**	**8.1**	**37**	**2.4**	**13.4**	**331.8**
7 Marshall	12	450	264	13	58.7	3688	8.2	41	2.9	14.0	307.3
8 Eastern Michigan	11	438	250	11	57.1	3314	7.6	23	2.5	13.3	301.3
9 Louisville	11	473	276	14	58.4	3282	6.9	19	3.0	11.9	298.4
10 Kent State	11	451	235	16	52.1	3243	7.2	35	3.6	13.8	294.8

TOTAL OFFENSE	G	P	YDS	AVG	TD	YPG
1 Nebraska	12	937	6164	6.6	71	513.7
2 Washington State	11	808	5524	6.8	60	502.2
3 Louisiana Tech	11	813	5456	6.7	48	496.0
4 Tennessee	**12**	**890**	**5794**	**6.5**	**50**	**482.8**
5 Nevada	11	796	5272	6.6	45	479.3
6 Kentucky	**11**	**876**	**5214**	**6.0**	**45**	**474.0**
7 Purdue	11	794	5056	6.4	42	459.6
8 Florida State	11	784	4973	6.3	49	452.1
9 Utah State	11	835	4933	5.9	45	448.5
10 Marshall	12	832	5339	6.4	58	444.9

RUSHING DEFENSE	G	ATT	YDS	AVG	TD	YPG
1 Florida State	11	379	571	1.5	10	51.9
2 Florida	**11**	**362**	**778**	**2.1**	**12**	**70.7**
3 Nebraska	12	407	881	2.2	12	73.4
4 North Carolina	11	371	857	2.3	5	77.9
5 Cincinnati	11	338	930	2.8	10	84.5
6 Clemson	11	362	971	2.7	10	88.3
7 Michigan	11	368	1001	2.7	6	91.0
8 Tennessee	**12**	**382**	**1119**	**2.9**	**11**	**93.3**
9 Southern California	11	381	1032	2.7	12	93.8
10 Wake Forest	11	364	1057	2.9	11	96.1

PASSING DEFENSE	G	ATT	COM	PCT	INT	I%	YDS	YPA	TD	TD%	RAT
1 Michigan	11	292	145	49.7	22	7.5	1275	4.4	4	1.4	75.8
2 Ohio State	12	360	160	44.4	19	5.3	1724	4.8	6	1.7	79.6
3 North Carolina	11	322	148	46.0	15	4.7	1445	4.5	7	2.2	81.5
4 Iowa	11	325	146	44.9	22	6.8	1766	5.4	12	3.7	89.2
5 Kansas State	11	239	99	41.4	5	2.1	1396	5.8	4	1.7	91.8
6 Wyoming	13	374	169	45.2	24	6.4	2358	6.3	11	2.9	95.0
7 Marshall	12	322	146	45.3	15	4.7	1948	6.1	8	2.5	95.0
8 New Mexico	12	333	153	46.0	16	4.8	1989	6.0	10	3.0	96.4
9 UAB	11	337	159	47.2	17	5.0	1912	5.7	12	3.6	96.5
10 Florida State	11	338	164	48.5	22	6.5	2084	6.2	12	3.6	99.0

TOTAL DEFENSE	G	P	YDS	AVG	TD	YPG
1 Michigan	11	660	2276	3.4	10	206.9
2 North Carolina	11	693	2302	3.3	12	209.3
3 Florida State	11	717	2655	3.7	22	241.4
4 Kansas State	11	702	2825	4.0	17	256.8
5 Nebraska	12	717	3088	4.3	25	257.3
6 Navy	11	642	2863	4.5	24	260.3
7 Iowa	11	733	2927	4.0	18	266.1
8 Ohio State	12	820	3215	3.9	13	267.9
9 Vanderbilt	**11**	**704**	**3026**	**4.3**	**22**	**275.1**
10 Air Force	12	756	3471	4.6	16	289.3

SCORING OFFENSE	G	PTS	AVG
1 Nebraska	12	565	47.1
2 Washington State	11	467	42.5
3 UCLA	11	448	40.7
4 Florida State	11	437	39.7
5 Marshall	12	453	37.8
6 Miami (Ohio)	11	412	37.5
7 Florida	**11**	**409**	**37.2**
8 Colorado State	12	442	36.8
9 Iowa	11	404	36.7
10 Navy	11	398	36.2

SCORING DEFENSE	G	PTS	AVG
1 Michigan	11	98	8.9
2 Ohio State	12	139	11.6
3 Air Force	12	149	12.4
4 Iowa	11	142	12.9
5 North Carolina	11	143	13.0
6 Kansas State	11	159	14.5
7 Colorado State	12	179	14.9
8 Florida State	11	167	15.2
9 Syracuse	12	191	15.9
10 Ohio U.	11	177	16.1

TURNOVER MARGIN	G	FR	INT	TOT	FL	INTL	TOT	MAR
1 Colorado State	12	20	18	38	4	9	13	2.1
2 UCLA	11	18	21	39	14	5	19	1.8
3 Texas A&M	12	22	11	33	1	14	15	1.5
4 Florida State	11	10	22	32	6	11	17	1.4
5 Tulane	11	8	26	34	6	14	20	1.3
6 SMU	11	12	15	27	7	7	14	1.2
6 Oklahoma State	11	14	15	29	8	8	16	1.2
6 Navy	11	13	14	27	6	8	14	1.2
9 Texas Tech	11	13	13	26	8	6	14	1.1
9 Purdue	11	11	20	31	5	14	19	1.1
9 LSU	**11**	**12**	**14**	**26**	**7**	**7**	**14**	**1.1**

1997

FINAL POLL (JAN. 3)

ESPN	AP	SCHOOL	FINAL RECORD
2	1	Michigan	12-0
1	2	Nebraska	13-0
3	3	Florida State	11-1
6	4	Florida	10-2
5	5	UCLA	10-2
4	6	North Carolina	11-1
8	7	Tennessee	11-2
7	8	Kansas State	11-1
9	9	Washington State	10-2
10	10	Georgia	10-2
11	11	Auburn	10-3
12	12	Ohio State	10-3
13	13	LSU	9-3
14	14	Arizona State	9-3
15	15	Purdue	9-3
17	16	Penn State	9-3
16	17	Colorado State	11-2
18	18	Washington	8-4
19	19	Southern Miss	9-3
21	20	Texas A&M	9-4
20	21	Syracuse	9-4
22	22	Mississippi	8-4
23	23	Missouri	7-5
24	24	Oklahoma State	8-4
	25	Georgia Tech	7-5

CONSENSUS ALL-AMERICANS

POS	OFFENSE	CL	SCHOOL
QB	Peyton Manning	Sr.	Tennessee
RB	Ricky Williams	Jr.	Texas
RB	Curtis Enis	Jr.	Penn State
WR	Randy Moss	So.	Marshall
WR	Jacquez Green	Jr.	Florida
TE	Alonzo Mayes	Sr.	Oklahoma State
OL	Aaron Taylor	Sr.	Nebraska
OL	Alan Faneca	Jr.	LSU
OL	Kyle Turley	Sr.	San Diego State
OL	Chad Overhauser	Sr.	UCLA
C	Olin Kreutz	Jr.	Washington
PK	Martin Gramatica	Jr.	Kansas State
KR	Tim Dwight	Sr.	Iowa

OTHERS RECEIVING FIRST-TEAM HONORS

QB	Ryan Leaf		Washington State
RB	Skip Hicks		UCLA
RB	Ron Dayne		Wisconsin
WR	Jerome Pathon		Washington
WR	Brian Alford		Purdue
WR	Bobby Shaw		California
TE	Jerame Tuman		Michigan
OL	Flozell Adams		Michigan State
OL	Benji Olson		Washington
OL	Victor Riley		Auburn
OL	Matt Stinchcomb		Georgia
OL	Rob Murphy		Ohio State
C	Ben Fricke		Houston
C	Kevin Long		Florida State
PK	Chris Sailer		UCLA
P	Chris Sailer		UCLA

POS	DEFENSE	CL	SCHOOL
DL	Grant Wistrom	Sr.	Nebraska
DL	Andre Wadsworth	Sr.	Florida State
DL	Greg Ellis	Sr.	North Carolina
DL	Jason Peter	Sr.	Nebraska
LB	Andy Katzenmoyer	So.	Ohio State
LB	Sam Cowart	Sr.	Florida State
LB	Anthony Simmons	Jr.	Clemson
LB	Brian Simmons	Sr.	North Carolina
DB	Charles Woodson	Jr.	Michigan
DB	Dre' Bly	So.	North Carolina
DB	Fred Weary	Sr.	Florida
DB	Brian Lee	Sr.	Wyoming
P	Chad Kessler	Sr.	LSU

OTHERS RECEIVING FIRST-TEAM HONORS

DL	Lamanzer Williams		Minnesota
DL	Jeremy Staat		Arizona State
DL	Glen Steele		Michigan
DL	Kailee Wong		Stanford
LB	Leonard Little		Tennessee
LB	Jamie Duncan		Vanderbilt
LB	Ron Warner		Kansas
LB	Takeo Spikes		Auburn
LB	Pat Tillman		Arizona State
DB	Anthony Poindexter		Virginia
DB	Antoine Winfield		Ohio State
DB	Donovin Darius		Syracuse

HEISMAN TROPHY VOTING

	PLAYER	POS	SCHOOL	TOTAL
1	Charles Woodson	CB	Michigan	1815
2	Peyton Manning	QB	Tennessee	1543
3	Ryan Leaf	QB	Washington St.	861
4	Randy Moss	WR	Marshall	253
5	Ricky Williams	RB	Texas	135
6	Curtis Enis	RB	Penn State	65
7	Tim Dwight	WR	Iowa	32
8	Cade McNown	QB	UCLA	26
9	Tim Couch	QB	Kentucky	22
10	Amos Zereoue	RB	West Virginia	215

AWARD WINNERS

PLAYER	AWARD
Peyton Manning, QB, Tennessee	Maxwell
Aaron Taylor, OG, Nebraska	Outland
Charles Woodson, DB, Michigan	Camp
Grant Wistrom, DE, Nebraska	Lombardi
Peyton Manning, QB, Tennessee	O'Brien
Andy Katzenmoyer, LB, Ohio State	Butkus
Charles Woodson, DB, Michigan	Thorpe
Peyton Manning, QB, Tennessee	Unitas
Ricky Williams, RB, Texas	Walker
Martin Gramatica, K, Kansas State	Groza
Charles Woodson, DB, Michigan	Nagurski
Charles Woodson, DB, Michigan	Bednarik
Randy Moss, WR, Marshall	Biletnikoff
Brock Olivo, RB, Missouri	Tatupu

BOWL GAMES

DATE	GAME	SCORE
D20	Las Vegas	Oregon 41, Air Force 13
D25	Aloha	Washington 51, Michigan State 23
D26	Motor City	Mississippi 34, Marshall 31
D27	Copper	Arizona 20, New Mexico 14
D28	Independence	LSU 27, Notre Dame 9
D29	Humanitarian	Cincinnati 35, Utah State 19
D29	Holiday	Colorado State 35, Missouri 24
D29	Carquest	Georgia Tech 35, West Virginia 30
D30	Alamo	Purdue 33, Oklahoma State 20
D31	Sun	Arizona State 17, Iowa 7
D31	Fiesta	Kansas State 35, Syracuse 18
D31	Liberty	Southern Miss 41, Pittsburgh 7
J1	Florida Citrus	Florida 21, Penn State 6
J1	Outback	Georgia 33, Wisconsin 6
J1	Rose	Michigan 21, Washington State 16
J1	Gator	North Carolina 42, Virginia Tech 3
J1	Cotton	UCLA 29, Texas A&M 23
J1	Sugar	Florida State 31, Ohio State 14
J2	Peach	Auburn 21, Clemson 17
J2	Orange	Nebraska 42, Tennessee 17

SEC STANDINGS

	CONFERENCE			OVERALL		
	W	L	T	W	L	T
EAST						
Tennessee	7	1	0	11	2	0
Georgia	6	2	0	10	2	0
Florida	6	2	0	10	2	0
South Carolina	3	5	0	5	6	0
Kentucky	2	6	0	5	6	0
Vanderbilt	0	8	0	3	8	0
WEST						
Auburn	6	2	0	10	3	0
LSU	6	2	0	9	3	0
Mississippi	4	4	0	8	4	0
Mississippi State	4	4	0	7	4	0
Alabama	2	6	0	4	7	0
Arkansas	2	6	0	4	7	0

ALL-SEC TEAM

POS	OFFENSE	SCHOOL
QB	Peyton Manning	Tennessee
RB	Fred Taylor	Florida
RB	Kevin Faulk	LSU
WR	Jacquez Green	Florida
WR	Hines Ward	Georgia
C	Todd McClure	LSU
OL	Alan Faneca	LSU
OL	Robert Hicks	Mississippi State
OL	Victor Riley	Auburn
OL	Matt Stinchcomb	Georgia
TE	Rufus French	Mississippi
PK	Jaret Holmes	Auburn

POS	DEFENSE	SCHOOL
L	Chuck Wiley	LSU
L	Mike Moten	Florida
L	Greg Favors	Mississippi State
LB	Jevon Kearse	Florida
LB	Al Wilson	Tennessee
LB	Jamie Duncan	Vanderbilt
LB	Takeo Spikes	Auburn
DB	Fred Weary	Florida
DB	Champ Bailey	Georgia
DB	Cedric Donaldson	LSU
DB	Corey Chavous	Vanderbilt
DB	Terry Fair	Tennessee
P	Chad Kessler	LSU

SEC CHAMPIONSHIP GAME

DECEMBER 6 | ATLANTA
Tennessee 30, Auburn 29

	1ST	2ND	3RD	4TH	FINAL
TENN	7	3	13	7	30
AUB	13	7	9	0	29

SCORING SUMMARY

TENN	Price 40 pass from Manning (Hall kick)
AUB	FG Holmes 30
AUB	Ware 24 fumble recovery (Holmes kick)
AUB	FG Holmes 48
AUB	Goodson 51 pass from Craig (Holmes kick)
TENN	FG Hall 27
TENN	Copeland 5 pass from Manning (Hall kick)
AUB	Beasley 24 pass from Craig (Holmes kick)
TENN	Price 46 pass from Manning (Hall kick blocked)
AUB	Reese PAT return
TENN	Nash 73 pass from Manning (Hall kick)

TENNESSEE	TEAM STATISTICS	AUBURN
22	First Downs	9
129	Rushing Yards	-15
25-43-2	Passing	14-34-0
373	Passing Yards	262
502	Total Yards	247
8-171	Punt Returns - Yards	2-15
1-17	Kickoff Returns - Yards	4-89
5-36.4	Punts - Average	10-43.8
6-4	Fumbles - Lost	5-1
9-49	Penalties - Yards	12-78

INDIVIDUAL LEADERS

RUSHING
TENN: Lewis 31-127.
AUB: Williams 6-8.

PASSING
TENN: Manning 25-43-2, 373 yards, 4 TD.
AUB: Craig 14-34-0, 262 yards, 2 TD.

RECEIVING
TENN: Nash 9-126, TD; Price 8-161 2 TD.
AUB: Poor 3-98; Beasley 3-56 TD.

1998 NCAA Major College Statistical Leaders

Individual Leaders

PASSING	CL	G	ATT	COM	PCT	INT	I%	YDS	YPA	TD	TD%	RATING
1 Shaun King, Tulane	SR	11	328	223	68.0	6	1.8	3232	9.9	36	11.0	183.3
2 Akili Smith, Oregon	SR	11	325	191	58.8	7	2.2	3307	10.2	30	9.2	170.4
3 Daunte Culpepper, Central Florida	SR	11	402	296	73.6	7	1.7	3690	9.2	28	7.0	170.2
4 Tim Rattay, Louisiana Tech	JR	12	559	380	68.0	13	2.3	4943	8.8	46	8.2	164.8
5 David Neill, Nevada	FR	9	344	199	57.9	9	2.6	3249	9.4	29	8.4	159.8
6 Michael Bishop, Kansas State	SR	12	295	164	55.6	4	1.4	2844	9.6	23	7.8	159.6
7 Donovan McNabb, Syracuse	SR	11	251	157	62.6	5	2.0	2134	8.5	22	8.8	158.9
8 Marc Bulger, West Virginia	JR	11	369	240	65.0	8	2.2	3178	8.6	27	7.3	157.2
9 Cade McNown, UCLA	SR	11	323	188	58.2	10	3.1	3130	9.7	23	7.1	156.9
10 Joe Germaine, Ohio State	SR	11	346	209	60.4	7	2.0	3108	9.0	24	6.9	154.7

ALL-PURPOSE	CL	G	RUSH	REC	PR	KR	YDS	YPG
1 Troy Edwards, Louisiana Tech	SR	12	227	1996	235	326	2784	232.0
2 Ricky Williams, Texas	SR	11	2124	262	0	0	2386	216.9
3 Kevin Faulk, LSU	**SR**	**11**	**1279**	**287**	**265**	**278**	**2109**	**191.7**
4 Torry Holt, North Carolina St.	SR	11	102	1604	273	0	1979	179.9
5 Jaime Kimbrough, Fresno State	SR	11	1168	391	0	393	1952	177.5
6 Amos Zereoue, West Virginia	JR	10	1430	175	0	168	1773	177.3
7 Mike Cloud, Boston College	SR	11	1726	198	0	0	1924	174.9
8 Travis Prentice, Miami (Ohio)	JR	11	1787	107	0	0	1894	172.2
9 Craig Yeast, Kentucky	SR	11	87	1311	33	410	1841	167.4
10 Kevin Johnson, Syracuse	SR	11	105	894	145	690	1834	166.7

RUSHING/Yards Per Game	CL	G	ATT	YDS	TD	AVG	YPG
1 Ricky Williams, Texas	SR	11	361	2124	27	5.9	193.1
2 Travis Prentice, Miami (Ohio)	JR	11	365	1787	19	4.9	162.5
3 Mike Cloud, Boston College	SR	11	308	1726	14	5.6	156.9
4 Ricky Williams, Texas Tech	SO	11	306	1582	13	5.2	143.8
5 Devin West, Missouri	SR	11	283	1578	17	5.6	143.5
6 Amos Zereoue, West Virginia	JR	10	261	1430	13	5.5	143.0
7 Denvis Manns, New Mexico State	SR	11	269	1469	6	5.5	133.6
8 Edgerrin James, Miami (Fla.)	JR	11	242	1416	17	5.9	128.7
9 Ron Dayne, Wisconsin	JR	10	268	1279	11	4.8	127.9
10 Steve Hookfin, Ohio U.	SR	11	273	1315	11	4.8	119.6

RUSHING/Yards Per Carry	CL	G	ATT	YDS	YPC
1 Trung Canidate, Arizona	JR	11	166	1225	7.4
2 Basil Mitchell, TCU	SR	11	166	1111	6.7
3 Michael Wiley, Ohio State	JR	11	182	1147	6.3
4 Ricky Williams, Texas	SR	11	361	2124	5.9
5 James Johnson, Mississippi State	**SR**	**12**	**236**	**1383**	**5.9**
6 Edgerrin James, Miami (Fla.)	JR	11	242	1416	5.9
7 Chrys Chukwuma, Arkansas	**JR**	**10**	**149**	**870**	**5.8**
8 Mike Cloud, Boston College	SR	11	308	1726	5.6
9 Kevin Faulk, LSU	**SR**	**11**	**229**	**1279**	**5.6**
10 Devin West, Missouri	SR	11	283	1578	5.6

Based on top 50 rushers

RECEIVING	CL	G	REC	YDS	TD	RPG	YPR	YPG
1 Troy Edwards, Louisiana Tech	SR	12	140	1996	27	11.7	14.3	166.3
2 Torry Holt, North Carolina St.	SR	11	88	1604	11	8.0	18.2	145.8
3 Geoff Noisy, Nevada	SR	11	94	1405	7	8.6	14.9	127.7
4 Travis McGriff, Florida	**SR**	**11**	**70**	**1357**	**10**	**6.4**	**19.4**	**123.4**
5 David Boston, Ohio State	JR	11	74	1330	13	6.8	18.0	120.9
6 Craig Yeast, Kentucky	SR	11	85	1311	14	7.7	15.4	119.2
7 Trevor Insley, Nevada	JR	11	69	1220	11	6.3	17.7	110.9
8 Sherrod Gideon, Southern Miss	JR	11	66	1186	13	6.0	18.0	107.8
9 P.J. Franklin, Tulane	JR	11	74	1174	11	6.7	15.9	106.7
10 Brandon Stokley, La.-Lafayette	SR	11	65	1173	8	5.9	18.0	106.6

PUNTING	CL	PUNT	YDS	AVG
1 Joe Kristosik, Nevada-Las Vegas	SR	76	3509	46.2
2 Josh Bidwell, Oregon	SR	47	2153	45.8
3 Stephen Baker, Arizona State	FR	56	2561	45.7
4 Dave Zastudil, Ohio U.	FR	50	2266	45.3
5 Bill Lafleur, Nebraska	SR	52	2337	44.9
6 Andy Pollock, Bowling Green	SR	50	2243	44.9
7 Deone Horinek, Colorado State	JR	52	2331	44.8
8 Brian Schmitz, North Carolina	JR	75	3357	44.8
9 Graham White, Army	JR	47	2101	44.7
10 Kevin Stemke, Wisconsin	SO	67	2949	44.0

PUNT RETURNS	CL	PR	YDS	TD	AVG
1 David Allen, Kansas State	SO	33	730	4	22.1
2 Damon Gourdine, San Diego State	JR	16	294	2	18.4
3 Nick Davis, Wisconsin	FR	27	424	2	15.7
4 David Boston, Ohio State	JR	18	268	1	14.9
5 Payton Williams, Fresno State	JR	24	343	1	14.3
6 Charlie Rogers, Georgia Tech	SR	30	425	2	14.2
7 Siaha Burley, Central Florida	SR	21	293	1	14.0
8 Peter Warrick, Florida State	JR	15	208	0	13.9
9 Gari Scott, Michigan State	JR	32	440	0	13.8
10 J.R. Redmond, Arizona State	JR	18	246	1	13.7

KICKOFF RETURNS	CL	KR	YDS	TD	AVG
1 Broderick McGrew, North Texas	JR	18	587	1	32.6
2 Dee Moronkola, Washington State	SR	16	504	2	31.5
3 Kevin Johnson, Syracuse	SR	23	690	2	30.0
4 Tim Alexander, Oregon State	SR	27	799	1	29.6
5 Craig Yeast, Kentucky	**SR**	**14**	**410**	**1**	**29.3**
6 Toure Butler, Washington	SO	22	626	1	28.5
7 Deltha O'Neal, California	JR	22	624	0	28.4
8 Sam Simmons, Northwestern	FR	22	607	0	27.6
9 Russell Harvey, Illinois	FR	15	406	0	27.1
10 Antwan Edwards, Clemson	SR	13	350	0	26.9

SCORING	CL	TDS	XP	FG	PTS	PTPG
1 Troy Edwards, Louisiana Tech	SR	31	2	0	188	15.7
2 Ricky Williams, Texas	SR	28	0	0	168	15.3
3 Martin Gramatica, Kansas State	SR	0	69	22	135	11.3
4 Travis Prentice, Miami (Ohio)	JR	20	0	0	120	10.9
5 Leroy Collins, Louisville	JR	19	2	0	116	10.6
6 Edgerrin James, Miami (Fla.)	JR	19	0	0	114	10.4
7 Sebastian Janikowski, Florida State	SO	0	42	27	123	10.3
8 Nathan Villegas, Oregon	JR	0	52	20	112	10.2
9 Devin West, Missouri	SR	18	0	0	108	9.8
10 Shayne Graham, Virginia Tech	JR	0	37	22	103	9.4

FIELD GOALS	CL	FGA	FGM	PCT	FGG
1 Sebastian Janikowski, Florida State	SO	32	27	0.84	2.25
2 Brad Bohn, Utah State	SO	28	24	0.86	2.18
3 Paul Edinger, Michigan State	JR	26	22	0.85	2.00
3 Shayne Graham, Virginia Tech	JR	32	22	0.69	2.00
5 Derek Franz, Colorado State	SR	26	21	0.81	1.91
6 Martin Gramatica, Kansas State	SR	31	22	0.71	1.83
7 Nathan Villegas, Oregon	JR	22	20	0.91	1.82
7 Travis Forney, Penn State	JR	29	20	0.69	1.82
9 Todd Latourette, Arkansas	SR	24	17	0.71	1.70
10 Matt Davenport, Wisconsin	SR	20	18	0.90	1.64
10 Brad Selent, Western Michigan	SO	26	18	0.69	1.64

INTERCEPTIONS	CL	INT	YDS	TD	INT/GM
1 Jamar Fletcher, Wisconsin	FR	6	99	2	0.67
2 Pat Dennis, La.-Monroe	SO	7	196	2	0.64
2 Lloyd Harrison, North Carolina St.	JR	7	51	0	0.64
4 Hank Poteat, Pittsburgh	JR	6	53	0	0.60
5 Wade Perkins, Missouri	SR	6	129	1	0.55
5 David Macklin, Penn State	JR	6	120	1	0.55
5 Tim Smith, Stanford	SR	6	69	0	0.55
8 Chris Claiborne, Southern California	JR	6	159	2	0.50
8 Daninelle Derricott, Marshall	JR	6	118	0	0.50
8 Mario Edwards, Florida State	FR	6	109	0	0.50
8 Chappell Mitchell, Arkansas State	SR	6	41	0	0.50

Team Leaders

RUSHING OFFENSE	G	ATT	YDS	AVG	TD	YPG
1 Army	11	610	3232	5.3	25	293.8
2 Ohio U.	11	680	3044	4.5	27	276.7
3 Air Force	12	648	3201	4.9	39	266.8
4 Navy	11	580	2874	5.0	25	261.3
5 Rice	11	624	2829	4.5	25	257.2
6 Nebraska	12	636	3045	4.8	37	253.8
7 New Mexico State	11	579	2790	4.8	18	253.6
8 TCU	11	542	2630	4.9	21	239.1
9 Missouri	11	546	2552	4.7	28	232.0
10 Syracuse	11	521	2512	4.8	34	228.4

PASSING OFFENSE	G	ATT	COM	INT	PCT	YDS	YPA	TD	I%	YPC	YPG
1 Louisiana Tech	12	600	402	13	67.0	5185	8.6	48	2.2	12.9	432.1
2 Kentucky	**11**	**574**	**414**	**16**	**72.1**	**4534**	**7.9**	**39**	**2.8**	**11.0**	**412.2**
3 Louisville	11	515	338	15	65.6	4498	8.7	33	2.9	13.3	408.9
4 Nevada	11	458	265	18	57.9	3992	8.7	32	3.9	15.1	362.9
5 Florida	**11**	**417**	**238**	**15**	**57.1**	**3807**	**9.1**	**35**	**3.6**	**16.0**	**346.1**
6 Central Florida	11	411	302	7	73.5	3771	9.2	29	1.7	12.5	342.8
7 Purdue	12	541	352	17	65.1	3978	7.4	40	3.1	11.3	331.5
8 Stanford	11	513	263	8	51.3	3516	6.9	22	1.6	13.4	319.6
9 Western Michigan	11	409	238	16	58.2	3414	8.3	24	3.9	14.3	310.4
10 North Carolina St.	11	405	210	11	51.9	3401	8.4	20	2.7	16.2	309.2

TOTAL OFFENSE	G	P	YDS	AVG	TD	YPG
1 Louisville	11	883	6156	7.0	62	559.6
2 Louisiana Tech	12	894	6479	7.2	66	539.9
3 Kentucky	**11**	**911**	**5876**	**6.5**	**50**	**534.2**
4 Tulane	11	816	5578	6.8	64	507.1
5 Nevada	11	869	5577	6.4	49	507.0
6 Ohio State	11	853	5539	6.5	46	503.6
7 Central Florida	11	789	5365	6.8	50	487.7
8 UCLA	11	785	5309	6.8	56	482.6
9 Kansas State	12	887	5742	6.5	65	478.5
10 Oregon	11	785	5260	6.7	49	478.2

RUSHING DEFENSE	G	ATT	YDS	AVG	TD	YPG
1 Ohio State	11	348	741	2.1	5	67.4
2 Florida State	12	412	958	2.3	5	79.8
3 Wisconsin	11	377	986	2.6	4	89.6
4 Florida	**11**	**393**	**998**	**2.5**	**6**	**90.7**
5 Brigham Young	13	444	1186	2.7	12	91.2
6 Tennessee	**12**	**420**	**1127**	**2.7**	**5**	**93.9**
7 Arkansas	**11**	**390**	**1050**	**2.7**	**6**	**95.5**
8 Penn State	11	407	1070	2.6	7	97.3
9 Utah	11	344	1071	3.1	9	97.4
10 Kansas State	12	433	1179	2.7	3	98.3

PASSING DEFENSE	G	ATT	COM	PCT	INT	I%	YDS	YPA	TD	TD%	RAT
1 Florida State	12	335	138	41.2	18	5.4	1620	4.8	9	2.7	79.9
2 Ohio State	11	414	197	47.6	17	4.1	2094	5.1	7	1.7	87.4
3 Southern California	12	455	225	49.5	24	5.3	2248	4.9	14	3.1	90.6
4 Colorado	11	290	138	47.6	11	3.8	1633	5.6	4	1.4	91.9
5 Miami (Ohio)	11	298	142	47.7	13	4.4	1659	5.6	6	2.0	92.3
6 Wisconsin	11	337	182	54.0	18	5.3	1987	5.9	5	1.5	97.8
7 Florida	**11**	**380**	**197**	**51.8**	**13**	**3.4**	**2155**	**5.7**	**9**	**2.4**	**100.5**
8 Penn State	11	362	188	51.9	17	4.7	2170	6.0	9	2.5	101.1
9 Kansas State	12	326	141	43.3	16	4.9	2041	6.3	15	4.6	101.2
10 Michigan State	12	385	188	48.8	13	3.4	2298	6.0	11	2.9	101.6

TOTAL DEFENSE	G	P	YDS	AVG	TD	YPG
1 Florida State	12	747	2578	3.5	14	214.8
2 Ohio State	11	762	2835	3.7	12	257.7
3 Kansas State	12	759	3220	4.2	18	268.3
4 Wisconsin	11	714	2973	4.2	9	270.3
5 Brigham Young	13	830	3561	4.3	29	273.9
6 Oklahoma	11	694	3067	4.4	24	278.8
7 Virginia Tech	11	710	3134	4.4	18	284.9
8 Texas Tech	11	710	3135	4.4	21	285.0
9 Florida	**11**	**773**	**3153**	**4.1**	**15**	**286.6**
10 Texas A&M	13	871	3761	4.3	21	289.3

SCORING OFFENSE	G	PTS	AVG
1 Kansas State	12	576	48.0
2 Tulane	11	499	45.4
3 Syracuse	11	468	42.5
4 Louisiana Tech	12	493	41.1
5 UCLA	11	445	40.5
6 Louisville	11	444	40.4
7 Oregon	11	430	39.1
8 Kentucky	**11**	**417**	**37.9**
9 Ohio State	11	406	36.9
10 Miami (Fla.)	11	402	36.5

SCORING DEFENSE	G	PTS	AVG
1 Wisconsin	11	112	10.2
2 Florida State	12	138	11.5
3 Ohio State	11	130	11.8
4 Miami (Ohio)	11	142	12.9
4 Virginia Tech	11	142	12.9
6 Kansas State	12	160	13.3
6 Air Force	12	160	13.3
8 Florida	**11**	**155**	**14.1**
9 Tennessee	**12**	**173**	**14.4**
10 Texas A&M	13	190	14.6

TURNOVER MARGIN	G	FR	INT	TOT	FL	INTL	TOT	MAR
1 Wisconsin	11	13	18	31	4	5	9	2.00
2 La.-Monroe	11	21	18	39	12	11	23	1.45
2 UCLA	11	21	12	33	6	11	17	1.45
4 Air Force	12	14	16	30	7	6	13	1.42
5 Tulane	11	12	14	26	5	6	11	1.36
6 Tennessee	**12**	**17**	**16**	**33**	**10**	**7**	**17**	**1.33**
7 Texas A&M	13	16	15	31	10	5	15	1.23
8 Syracuse	11	13	11	24	5	6	11	1.18
9 Kansas State	12	17	16	33	14	5	19	1.17
10 Fresno State	11	13	12	25	10	4	14	1.00
10 Arkansas	**11**	**15**	**17**	**32**	**13**	**8**	**21**	**1.00**

1998

FINAL POLL (JAN. 5)

ESPN	AP	SCHOOL	FINAL RECORD
1	1	Tennessee	13-0
2	2	Ohio State	11-1
3	3	Florida State	11-2
4	4	Arizona	12-1
6	5	Florida	10-2
5	6	Wisconsin	11-1
7	7	Tulane	12-0
8	8	UCLA	10-2
11	9	Georgia Tech	10-2
9	10	Kansas State	11-2
13	11	Texas A&M	11-3
12	12	Michigan	10-3
10	13	Air Force	12-1
14	14	Georgia	9-3
16	15	Texas	9-3
17	16	Arkansas	9-3
15	17	Penn State	9-3
18	18	Virginia	9-3
20	19	Nebraska	9-4
21	20	Miami (Fla.)	9-3
25	21	Missouri	8-4
22	22	Notre Dame	9-3
19	23	Virginia Tech	9-3
23	24	Purdue	9-4
24	25	Syracuse	8-4

CONSENSUS ALL-AMERICANS

POS	OFFENSE	CL	SCHOOL
QB	Cade McNown	Sr.	UCLA
QB	Michael Bishop	Sr.	Kansas State
QB	**Tim Couch**	**Jr.**	**Kentucky**
RB	Ricky Williams	Sr.	Texas
RB	Mike Cloud	Sr.	Boston College
WR	Torry Holt	Sr.	North Carolina St.
WR	Peter Warrick	Jr.	Florida State
WR	Troy Edwards	Sr.	Louisiana Tech
TE	**Rufus French**	**Jr.**	**Mississippi**
OL	Kris Farris	Jr.	UCLA
OL	Aaron Gibson	Sr.	Wisconsin
OL	**Matt Stinchcomb**	**Sr.**	**Georgia**
OL	Rob Murphy	Jr.	Ohio State
C	Craig Page	Sr.	Georgia Tech
PK	Sebastian Janikowski	So.	Florida State
KR	David Allen	So.	Kansas State

OTHERS RECEIVING FIRST-TEAM HONORS

RB	Ron Dayne	Wisconsin
RB	Devin West	Missouri
WR	David Boston	Ohio State
OL	Mike Rosenthal	Notre Dame
OL	Ben Adams	Texas
OL	Doug Brzezinski	Boston College
OL	Jay Humphrey	Texas
OL	**Brandon Bulsworth**	**Arkansas**
OL	Jason Whitaker	Florida State
OL	Jon Jansen	Michigan
OL	Anthony Cesario	Colorado State
C	Grey Ruegamer	Arizona State
C	**Todd McClure**	**LSU**
PK	Martin Gramatica	Kansas State
KR	Kevin Johnson	Syracuse

POS	DEFENSE	CL	SCHOOL
DL	Tom Burke	Sr.	Wisconsin
DL	Montae Reagor	Sr.	Texas Tech
DL	Jared DeVries	Sr.	Iowa
LB	Chris Claiborne	Jr.	Southern California
LB	Dat Nguyen	Sr.	Texas A&M
LB	Jeff Kelly	Sr.	Kansas State
LB	**Al Wilson**	**Sr.**	**Tennessee**
DB	Chris McAlister	Sr.	Arizona
DB	Antoine Winfield	Sr.	Ohio State
DB	**Champ Bailey**	**Jr.**	**Georgia**
DB	Anthony Poindexter	Sr.	Virginia
P	Joe Kristosik	Jr.	UNLV

OTHERS RECEIVING FIRST-TEAM HONORS

DL	Robaire Smith	Michigan State
DL	Patrick Kerney	Virginia
DL	Corey Moore	Virginia Tech
DL	Corey Simon	Florida State
DL	**Anthony McFarland**	**LSU**
LB	**Jevon Kearse**	**Florida**
LB	Adalius Thomas	Southern Miss
LB	LaVar Arrington	Penn State
DB	Dre' Bly	North Carolina
DB	Tyrone Carter	Minnesota
DB	Damon Moore	Ohio State

HEISMAN TROPHY VOTING

	PLAYER	POS	SCHOOL	TOTAL
1	Ricky Williams	RB	Texas	2355
2	Michael Bishop	QB	Kansas State	792
3	Cade McNown	QB	UCLA	696
4	Tim Couch	QB	Kentucky	527
5	Donovan McNabb	QB	Syracuse	232
6	Daunte Culpepper	QB	Central Florida	67
7	Champ Bailey	DB	Georgia	55
8	Torry Holt	WR	North Carolina St.	44
9	Joe Germaine	QB	Ohio State	43
10	Shaun King	QB	Tulane	38

AWARD WINNERS

PLAYER	AWARD
Ricky Williams, RB, Texas	Maxwell
Kris Farris, OT, UCLA	Outland
Ricky Williams, RB, Texas	Camp
Dat Nguyen, LB, Texas A&M	Lombardi
Michael Bishop, QB, Kansas State	O'Brien
Chris Claiborne, LB, Southern California	Butkus
Antoine Winfield, DB, Ohio State	Thorpe
Cade McNown, QB, UCLA	Unitas
Ricky Williams, RB, Texas	Walker
Sebastian Janikowski, K, Florida State	Groza
Champ Bailey, DB, Georgia	**Nagurski**
Dat Nguyen, LB, Texas A&M	Bednarik
Troy Edwards, WR, Louisiana Tech	Biletnikoff
Chris McAlister, CB, Arizona	Tatupu

BOWL GAMES

DATE	GAME	SCORE
D19	Las Vegas	North Carolina 20, San Diego State 13
D23	Motor City	Marshall 48, Louisville 29
D25	Oahu	Air Force 45, Washington 25
D25	Aloha	Colorado 51, Oregon 43
D26	Insight.com	Missouri 34, West Virginia 31
D29	Micron PC	Miami (Fla.) 46, North Carolina St. 23
D29	Alamo	Purdue 37, Kansas State 34
D29	**Music City**	**Virginia Tech 38, Alabama 7**
D30	Holiday	Arizona 23, Nebraska 20
D30	Humanitarian	Idaho 42, Southern Miss 35
D31	Peach	Georgia 35, Virginia 33
D31	**Independence**	**Mississippi 35, Texas Tech 18**
D31	Sun	TCU 28, Southern California 19
D31	Liberty	Tulane 41, Brigham Young 27
J1	Gator	Georgia Tech 35, Notre Dame 28
J1	**Florida Citrus**	**Michigan 45, Arkansas 31**
J1	**Outback**	**Penn State 26, Kentucky 14**
J1	**Cotton**	**Texas 38, Mississippi State 11**
J1	Rose	Wisconsin 38, UCLA 31
J1	Sugar	Ohio State 24, Texas A&M 14
J2	**Orange**	**Florida 31, Syracuse 10**
J4	**Fiesta**	**Tennessee 26, Florida State 16**

SEC STANDINGS

	CONFERENCE			OVERALL		
	W	L	T	W	L	T
EAST						
Tennessee	8	0	0	13	0	0
Florida	7	1	0	10	2	0
Georgia	6	2	0	9	3	0
Kentucky	4	4	0	7	5	0
Vanderbilt	1	7	0	2	9	0
South Carolina	0	8	0	1	10	0
WEST						
Mississippi State	6	2	0	8	5	0
Arkansas	6	2	0	9	3	0
Alabama	4	4	0	7	5	0
Mississippi	3	5	0	7	5	0
LSU	2	6	0	4	7	0
Auburn	1	7	0	3	8	0

ALL-SEC TEAM

POS	OFFENSE	SCHOOL
QB	Tim Couch	Kentucky
RB	James Johnson	Mississippi State
RB	Kevin Faulk	LSU
WR	Craig Yeast	Kentucky
WR	Travis McGriff	Florida
C	Todd McClure	LSU
OL	Matt Stinchcomb	Georgia
OL	Brandon Burlsworth	Arkansas
OL	Zach Piller	Florida
OL	Chris Terry	Georgia
TE	Rufus French	Mississippi
PK	Jeff Hall	Tennessee

POS	DEFENSE	SCHOOL
L	Anthony McFarland	LSU
L	Reggie McGrew	Florida
L	Leonardo Carson	Auburn
L	Melvin Bradley	Arkansas
LB	Jevon Kearse	Florida
LB	Raynoch Thompson	Tennessee
LB	Al Wilson	Tennessee
LB	Johnny Rutledge	Florida
DB	Zac Painter	Arkansas
DB	Champ Bailey	Georgia
DB	Teako Brown	Florida
DB	Tony George	Florida
DB	Fernando Bryant	Alabama
P	Daniel Pope	Alabama

SEC CHAMPIONSHIP GAME

DECEMBER 5 | ATLANTA
TENNESSEE 24, MISSISSIPPI STATE 14

	1ST	2ND	3RD	4TH	FINAL
MSU	7	0	0	7	14
TENN	0	10	0	14	24

SCORING SUMMARY

MSU	Bean 70 interception return (Hazelwood kick)
TENN	Stephens 2 run (Hall kick)
TENN	FG Hall 31
MSU	Prentiss 83 punt return (Hazelwood kick)
TENN	Price 41 pass from Martin (Hall kick)
TENN	Wilson 26 pass from Martin (Hall kick)

MISSISSIPPI STATE	TEAM STATISTICS	TENNESSEE
9	First Downs	21
36	Rushing Yards	44
10-25-2	Passing	15-33-1
84	Passing Yards	208
149	Total Yards	359
6-152	Punt Returns - Yards	3-7
4-92	Kickoff Returns - Yards	3-75
10-39.7	Punts - Average	9-35.9
2-1	Fumbles - Lost	2-1
10-100	Penalties - Yards	4-30

INDIVIDUAL LEADERS

RUSHING
MSU: Johnson 14-38.
TENN: Henry 26-120.

PASSING
MSU: Madkin 10-22-2, 84 yards.
TENN: Martin 15-32-1, 208 yards, 2 TD.

RECEIVING
MSU: Cooper 5-44; Prentiss 2-27.
TENN: Price 6-97, TD; Copeland 5-76.

1999 NCAA Major College Statistical Leaders

Individual Leaders

PASSING	CL	G	ATT	COM	PCT	INT	I%	YDS	YPA	TD	TD%	RATING
1 Michael Vick, Virginia Tech	SO	10	152	90	59.2	5	3.3	1840	12.1	12	7.9	180.4
2 Joe Hamilton, Georgia Tech	SR	11	305	203	66.6	11	3.6	3060	10.0	29	9.5	175.0
3 Chad Pennington, Marshall	SR	12	405	275	67.9	11	2.7	3799	9.4	37	9.1	171.4
4 Billy Volek, Fresno State	SR	12	355	235	66.2	3	0.9	2559	7.2	30	8.5	152.9
5 Tim Rattay, Louisiana Tech	SR	10	516	342	66.3	12	2.3	3922	7.6	35	6.8	147.9
6 Jay Stuckey, Texas-El Paso	SR	12	225	145	64.4	13	5.8	1918	8.5	15	6.7	146.5
7 Chris Weinke, Florida State	JR	11	377	232	61.5	14	3.7	3103	8.2	25	6.6	145.1
8 Dan Ellis, Virginia	JR	10	258	156	60.5	10	3.9	2050	8.0	20	7.8	145.0
9 Jeff Kelly, Southern Miss	SO	11	260	153	58.9	11	4.2	2062	7.9	21	8.1	143.7
10 Tim Lester, Western Michigan	SR	12	470	282	60.0	13	2.8	3639	7.7	34	7.2	143.4

ALL-PURPOSE	CL	G	RUSH	REC	PR	KR	YDS	YPG
1 Trevor Insley, Nevada	SR	11	5	2060	111	0	2176	197.8
2 Dennis Northcutt, Arizona	SR	12	200	1422	436	191	2249	187.4
3 Thomas Jones, Virginia	SR	11	1798	239	17	0	2054	186.7
4 LaDainian Tomlinson, TCU	JR	11	1850	55	0	69	1974	179.5
5 Travis Prentice, Miami (Ohio)	SR	11	1659	270	0	0	1929	175.4
6 Troy Walters, Stanford	SR	11	6	1456	131	284	1877	170.6
7 Deuce McAllister, Mississippi	**JR**	**10**	**809**	**201**	**30**	**652**	**1692**	**169.2**
8 Ron Dayne, Wisconsin	SR	11	1834	9	0	0	1843	167.6
9 Lamont Jordan, Maryland	JR	11	1632	208	0	0	1840	167.3
10 Demario Brown, Utah State	SR	11	1536	282	0	0	1818	165.3

RUSHING/Yards Per Game	CL	G	ATT	YDS	TD	AVG	YPG
1 LaDainian Tomlinson, TCU	JR	11	268	1850	18	6.9	168.2
2 Ron Dayne, Wisconsin	SR	11	303	1834	19	6.1	166.7
3 Thomas Jones, Virginia	SR	11	334	1798	16	5.4	163.5
4 Travis Prentice, Miami (Ohio)	SR	11	354	1659	17	4.7	150.8
5 Lamont Jordan, Maryland	JR	11	266	1632	16	6.1	148.4
6 Demario Brown, Utah State	SR	11	279	1536	14	5.5	139.6
7 Trung Canidate, Arizona	SR	12	253	1602	11	6.3	133.5
8 Frank Moreau, Louisville	SR	10	233	1289	17	5.5	128.9
9 Darren Davis, Iowa State	SR	11	287	1388	14	4.8	126.2
10 Shaun Alexander, Alabama	**SR**	**11**	**302**	**1383**	**19**	**4.6**	**125.7**

RUSHING/Yards Per Carry	CL	G	ATT	YDS	YPC
1 LaDainian Tomlinson, TCU	JR	11	268	1850	6.9
2 Chester Taylor, Toledo	JR	11	182	1176	6.5
3 Trung Canidate, Arizona	SR	12	253	1602	6.3
4 Lamont Jordan, Maryland	JR	11	266	1632	6.1
5 Ron Dayne, Wisconsin	SR	11	303	1834	6.1
6 Mike Green, Houston	JR	10	142	838	5.9
7 Clinton Portis, Miami (Fla.)	FR	10	143	838	5.9
8 Kevin McDougal, Colorado State	SR	10	207	1164	5.6
9 Deoncé Whitaker, San Jose State	JR	9	137	769	5.6
10 Jamie Wilson, East Carolina	JR	11	156	865	5.5

Based on top 50 rushers

RECEIVING	CL	G	REC	YDS	TD	RPG	YPR	YPG
1 Trevor Insley, Nevada	SR	11	134	2060	13	12.2	15.4	187.3
2 Troy Walters, Stanford	SR	11	74	1456	10	6.7	19.7	132.4
3 Dennis Northcutt, Arizona	SR	12	88	1422	8	7.3	16.2	118.5
4 Arnold Jackson, Louisville	SR	11	101	1209	9	9.2	12.0	109.9
5 Drew Haddad, Buffalo	SR	11	85	1158	6	7.7	13.6	105.3
6 Jajuan Dawson, Tulane	SR	10	96	1051	8	9.6	10.9	105.1
7 Dwight Carter, Hawaii	SR	12	77	1253	9	6.4	16.3	104.4
8 Peter Warrick, Florida State	SR	9	71	934	8	7.9	13.2	103.8
9 Chris Daniels, Purdue	SR	11	109	1133	5	9.9	10.4	103.0
9 Charles Lee, Central Florida	SR	11	87	1133	5	7.9	13.0	103.0

PUNTING	CL	PUNT	YDS	AVG
1 Andrew Bayes, East Carolina	SR	47	2871	48.1
2 Brian Schmitz, North Carolina	SR	74	3538	47.8
3 Shane Lechler, Texas A&M	SR	60	2787	46.5
4 Ray Cheetany, Nevada-Las Vegas	JR	65	2950	45.4
5 Dan Hadenfeldt, Nebraska	SR	65	2924	45.0
6 Drew Hagan, Indiana	SR	44	1971	44.8
7 Nick Harris, California	JR	85	3795	44.7
8 Ryan Smith, Arkansas State	SR	42	1864	44.4
9 Casey Roussel, Tulane	SO	55	2429	44.2
10 Tim Morgan, San Jose State	SR	57	2510	44.0

PUNT RETURNS	CL	PR	YDS	TD	AVG
1 Dennis Northcutt, Arizona	SR	23	436	2	19.0
2 Bobby Newcombe, Nebraska	JR	16	294	1	18.4
3 Vinny Sutherland, Purdue	JR	17	295	2	17.4
4 Rodregis Brooks, UAB	JR	19	325	0	17.1
5 Stevonne Smith, Utah	JR	29	495	3	17.1
6 Dallas Davis, Colorado State	JR	32	541	2	16.9
7 Hank Poteat, Pittsburgh	SR	19	307	1	16.2
8 Keith Stokes, East Carolina	JR	26	404	1	15.5
9 Emmett White, Utah State	SO	24	361	0	15.0
10 Terance Richardson, Oklahoma State	SR	40	591	1	14.8

KICKOFF RETURNS	CL	KR	YDS	TD	AVG
1 James Williams, Marshall	SR	15	493	1	32.9
2 Brandon Daniels, Oklahoma	SR	16	508	1	31.8
3 John Stone, Wake Forest	SO	13	389	1	29.9
4 Deltha O'Neal, California	SR	19	555	1	29.2
5 Ben Kelly, Colorado	JR	19	547	2	28.8
6 Sonny Cook, Oregon	JR	14	402	0	28.7
7 Deoncé Whitaker, San Jose State	JR	14	396	1	28.3
8 Scottie Montgomery, Duke	SR	21	587	1	28.0
9 Chris Lacy, Idaho	SO	15	419	1	27.9
10 Ryan Wells, Stanford	SO	15	412	0	27.5

SCORING	CL	TDS	XP	FG	PTS	PTPG
1 Shaun Alexander, Alabama	**SR**	**24**	**0**	**0**	**144**	**13.1**
2 Travis Prentice, Miami (Ohio)	SR	21	0	0	126	11.5
3 Sebastian Janikowski, Florida State	JR	0	47	23	116	10.6
4 Ron Dayne, Wisconsin	SR	19	0	0	114	10.4
5 Frank Moreau, Louisville	SR	17	0	0	102	10.2
6 LaDainian Tomlinson, TCU	JR	18	0	0	108	9.8
7 Shayne Graham, Virginia Tech	SR	0	56	17	107	9.7
8 Ken Simonton, Oregon State	SO	17	4	0	106	9.6
9 Travis Zachery, Clemson	SO	16	0	0	96	9.6
10 Jamie Rheem, Kansas State	JR	0	41	18	95	9.5

FIELD GOALS	CL	FGA	FGM	PCT	FGG
1 Sebastian Janikowski, Florida State	JR	30	23	0.77	2.09
2 Neil Rackers, Illinois	SR	25	20	0.80	1.82
3 Jamie Rheem, Kansas State	JR	21	18	0.86	1.80
4 Jeff Chandler, Florida	**JR**	**24**	**21**	**0.88**	**1.75**
4 Travis Forney, Penn State	SR	26	21	0.81	1.75
6 Paul Edinger, Michigan State	SR	22	18	0.82	1.64
6 Scott Westerfield, Mississippi State	**JR**	**24**	**18**	**0.75**	**1.64**
6 Owen Pochman, Brigham Young	JR	25	18	0.72	1.64
6 Todd France, Toledo	SO	26	18	0.69	1.64
6 Travis Dorsch, Purdue	SO	28	18	0.64	1.64

INTERCEPTIONS	CL	INT	YDS	TD	INT/GM
1 Deltha O'Neal, California	SR	9	280	4	0.82
1 Deon Grant, Tennessee	**JR**	**9**	**167**	**1**	**0.82**
1 Rodregis Brooks, UAB	JR	9	152	1	0.82
4 Erik Olson, Colorado State	SR	6	93	1	0.67
5 Jamar Fletcher, Wisconsin	SO	7	135	2	0.64
5 Mike James, Houston	SR	7	57	1	0.64
7 Anthony Vontoure, Washington	SO	6	99	2	0.60
7 Kevin Harvey, Temple	SR	6	55	1	0.60
9 Quincy Lejay, Hawaii	SR	7	151	3	0.58
10 Tim Smith, Stanford *	SR	6	86	0	0.55
10 Robert Carswell, Clemson *	JR	6	72	0	0.55
10 Perlo Bastien, West Virginia *	SR	6	62	0	0.55

*Seven tied with 0.55; these had the most yards

Team Leaders

RUSHING OFFENSE	G	ATT	YDS	AVG	TD	YPG
1 Navy	12	680	3506	5.2	30	292.2
2 Air Force	11	635	3140	4.9	25	285.5
3 Wisconsin	11	583	3075	5.3	34	279.5
4 Nebraska	12	633	3191	5.0	37	265.9
5 Army	11	636	2915	4.6	24	265.0
6 Ohio U.	11	624	2883	4.6	26	262.1
7 Rice	11	655	2835	4.3	22	257.7
8 Virginia Tech	11	559	2793	5.0	35	253.9
9 TCU	11	518	2640	5.1	26	240.0
10 Toledo	11	492	2631	5.3	21	239.2

PASSING OFFENSE	G	ATT	COM	INT	PCT	YDS	YPA	TD	I%	YPC	YPG
1 Louisiana Tech	11	566	372	12	65.7	4434	7.8	38	2.1	11.9	403.1
2 Louisville	11	501	322	13	64.3	3687	7.4	29	2.6	11.5	335.2
3 Hawaii	12	577	297	19	51.5	3944	6.8	28	3.3	13.3	328.7
4 Purdue	11	508	306	12	60.2	3608	7.1	23	2.4	11.8	328.0
5 Tulane	11	556	326	25	58.6	3600	6.5	25	4.5	11.0	327.3
6 Nevada	11	457	263	9	57.5	3590	7.9	20	2.0	13.7	326.4
7 Marshall	12	427	286	11	67.0	3901	9.1	37	2.6	13.6	325.1
8 Brigham Young	11	458	280	16	61.1	3567	7.8	25	3.5	12.7	324.3
9 Oklahoma	11	512	319	15	62.3	3539	6.9	31	2.9	11.1	321.7
10 Stanford	11	385	219	12	56.9	3448	9.0	25	3.1	15.7	313.5

TOTAL OFFENSE	G	P	YDS	AVG	TD	YPG
1 Georgia Tech	11	822	5599	6.8	58	509.0
2 Nevada	11	843	5192	6.2	39	472.0
3 Arizona	12	870	5663	6.5	42	471.9
4 Louisiana Tech	11	822	5181	6.3	50	471.0
5 Stanford	11	793	5138	6.5	47	467.1
6 Louisville	11	851	5136	6.0	48	466.9
7 Marshall	12	841	5584	6.6	57	465.3
8 Purdue	11	859	5016	5.8	38	456.0
9 Virginia Tech	11	758	4970	6.6	49	451.8
10 Oregon State	11	857	4774	5.6	41	434.0

RUSHING DEFENSE	G	ATT	YDS	AVG	TD	YPG
1 Mississippi State	**11**	**403**	**736**	**1.8**	**7**	**66.9**
2 Alabama	**12**	**335**	**904**	**2.7**	**6**	**75.3**
3 Virginia Tech	11	388	835	2.2	5	75.9
4 Mississippi	**11**	**369**	**846**	**2.3**	**10**	**76.9**
5 Michigan State	11	376	847	2.3	7	77.0
6 Nebraska	12	427	928	2.2	6	77.3
7 Tennessee	**11**	**364**	**986**	**2.7**	**3**	**89.6**
8 Southern Miss	11	403	1006	2.5	6	91.5
9 Florida	**12**	**416**	**1099**	**2.6**	**15**	**91.6**
10 Florida State	11	387	1087	2.8	6	98.8

PASSING DEFENSE	G	ATT	COM	PCT	INT	I%	YDS	YPA	TD	TD%	RAT
1 Kansas State	11	315	118	37.5	21	6.7	1364	4.3	5	1.6	65.7
2 Nebraska	12	388	165	42.5	18	4.6	2094	5.4	11	2.8	87.9
3 Marshall	12	432	226	52.3	24	5.6	2308	5.3	8	1.9	92.2
4 Mississippi State	**11**	**331**	**172**	**52.0**	**15**	**4.5**	**1712**	**5.2**	**7**	**2.1**	**93.3**
5 Wisconsin	11	351	176	50.1	16	4.6	1994	5.7	8	2.3	96.3
6 Utah	11	359	179	49.9	16	4.5	2113	5.9	7	2.0	96.8
7 Virginia Tech	11	344	166	48.3	10	2.9	1885	5.5	10	2.9	98.1
8 Minnesota	11	340	159	46.8	8	2.4	1921	5.7	9	2.7	98.3
9 Oregon State	11	355	174	49.0	13	3.7	2104	5.9	8	2.3	98.9
10 East Carolina	11	389	200	51.4	17	4.4	2305	5.9	10	2.6	100.9

TOTAL DEFENSE	G	P	YDS	AVG	TD	YPG
1 Mississippi State	**11**	**734**	**2448**	**3.3**	**14**	**222.5**
2 Kansas State	11	693	2585	3.7	18	235.0
3 Virginia Tech	11	732	2720	3.7	15	247.3
4 Nebraska	12	815	3022	3.7	17	251.8
5 TCU	11	729	3129	4.3	24	284.5
6 Texas	13	876	3727	4.3	28	286.7
7 Marshall	12	882	3516	4.0	11	293.0
8 Southern Miss	11	754	3235	4.3	14	294.1
9 Alabama	**12**	**749**	**3568**	**4.8**	**26**	**297.3**
10 Oklahoma State	11	683	3273	4.8	30	297.5

SCORING OFFENSE	G	PTS	AVG
1 Virginia Tech	11	455	41.4
2 Georgia Tech	11	448	40.7
3 Kansas State	11	433	39.4
4 Louisville	11	412	37.5
4 Florida State	11	412	37.5
6 Stanford	11	409	37.2
7 Marshall	12	442	36.8
8 Oklahoma	11	405	36.8
9 Wisconsin	11	392	35.6
10 Louisiana Tech	11	389	35.4

SCORING DEFENSE	G	PTS	AVG
1 Virginia Tech	11	116	10.5
2 Marshall	12	134	11.2
3 Nebraska	12	150	12.5
4 Kansas State	11	144	13.1
5 Wisconsin	11	145	13.2
6 Mississippi State	**11**	**149**	**13.5**
7 Tennessee	**11**	**163**	**14.8**
8 Southern Miss	11	172	15.6
8 Minnesota	11	172	15.6
10 Florida State	11	174	15.8

TURNOVER MARGIN	G	FR	INT	TOT	FL	INTL	TOT	MAR
1 Kansas State	11	17	21	38	12	9	21	1.6
2 Illinois	11	11	14	25	7	5	12	1.2
3 Southern California	12	18	21	39	11	14	25	1.2
4 Marshall	12	6	24	30	6	11	17	1.1
5 Wisconsin	11	6	16	22	8	3	11	1.0
6 Stanford	11	13	17	30	8	12	20	0.9
6 Southern Miss	11	15	15	30	6	14	20	0.9
6 Michigan	11	12	10	22	4	8	12	0.9
9 Texas	13	23	10	33	12	10	22	0.9
10 Boise State	12	15	14	29	5	14	19	0.8

1999

FINAL POLL (JAN. 5)

ESPN	AP	SCHOOL	FINAL RECORD
1	1	Florida State	12-0
3	2	Virginia Tech	11-1
2	3	Nebraska	12-1
4	4	Wisconsin	10-2
5	5	Michigan	10-2
6	6	Kansas State	11-1
7	7	Michigan State	10-2
8	8	Alabama	10-3
9	9	Tennessee	9-3
10	10	Marshall	13-0
11	11	Penn State	10-3
14	12	Florida	9-4
12	13	Mississippi State	10-2
13	14	Southern Miss	9-3
15	15	Miami (Fla.)	9-4
16	16	Georgia	8-4
19	17	Arkansas	8-4
17	18	Minnesota	8-4
18	19	Oregon	9-3
21	20	Georgia Tech	8-4
23	21	Texas	9-5
22	22	Mississippi	8-4
20	23	Texas A&M	8-4
25	24	Illinois	8-4
	25	Purdue	7-5
24		Stanford	8-4

CONSENSUS ALL-AMERICANS

POS	OFFENSE	CL	SCHOOL
QB	Joe Hamilton	Sr.	Georgia Tech
RB	Ron Dayne	Sr.	Wisconsin
RB	Thomas Jones	Sr.	Virginia
WR	Troy Walters	Sr.	Stanford
WR	Peter Warrick	Sr.	Florida State
TE	James Whalen	Sr.	Kentucky
OL	Chris McIntosh	Sr.	Wisconsin
OL	Chris Samuels	Sr.	Alabama
OL	Cosey Coleman	Jr.	Tennessee
OL	Jason Whitaker	Sr.	Florida State
C	Ben Hamilton	Jr.	Minnesota
C	Rob Riti	Sr.	Missouri
PK	Sebastian Janikowski	Jr.	Florida State
AP	Dennis Northcutt	Sr.	Arizona

OTHERS RECEIVING FIRST-TEAM HONORS

QB	Michael Vick		Virginia Tech
RB	Shaun Alexander		Alabama
TE	Ibn Green		Louisville
TE	Bubba Franks		Miami (Fla.)
OL	Brad Bedell		Colorado
OL	Mike Malano		San Diego State
OL	Marvel Smith		Arizona State
OL	Richard Mercier		Miami (Fla.)
OL	Noel LaMontagne		Virginia
AP	David Allen		Kansas State

POS	DEFENSE	CL	SCHOOL
DL	Courtney Brown	Sr.	Penn State
DL	Corey Moore	Sr.	Virginia Tech
DL	Corey Simon	Sr.	Florida State
LB	LaVar Arrington	Jr.	Penn State
LB	Mark Simoneau	Sr.	Kansas State
LB	Brandon Short	Sr.	Penn State
DB	Tyrone Carter	Sr.	Minnesota
DB	Brian Urlacher	Sr.	New Mexico
DB	Ralph Brown	Sr.	Nebraska
DB	Deon Grant	Sr.	Tennessee
DB	Deltha O'Neal	Sr.	California
P	Andrew Bayes	Sr.	East Carolina

OTHERS RECEIVING FIRST-TEAM HONORS

DL	Alex Brown	Florida
DL	Casey Hampton	Texas
DL	Chris Hovan	Boston College
DL	Rob Renes	Michigan
LB	Raynoch Thompson	Tennessee
LB	Keith Adams	Clemson
LB	Julian Peterson	Michigan State
LB	Na'il Diggs	Ohio State
LB	Barrin Simpson	Mississippi State
DB	Mike Brown	Nebraska
DB	Jamar Fletcher	Wisconsin
DB	Ben Kelly	Colorado
P	Shane Lechler	Texas A&M

HEISMAN TROPHY VOTING

	PLAYER	POS	SCHOOL	TOTAL
1	Ron Dayne	RB	Wisconsin	2042
2	Joe Hamilton	QB	Georgia Tech	994
3	Michael Vick	QB	Virginia Tech	319
4	Drew Brees	QB	Purdue	308
5	Chad Pennington	QB	Marshall	247
6	Peter Warrick	WR	Florida State	203
7	Shaun Alexander	RB	Alabama	171
8	Thomas Jones	RB	Virginia	140
9	LaVar Arrington	LB	Penn State	54
10	Tim Rattay	QB	Louisiana Tech	29

AWARD WINNERS

PLAYER	AWARD
Ron Dayne, RB, Wisconsin	Maxwell
Chris Samuels, OT, Alabama	Outland
Ron Dayne, RB, Wisconsin	Camp
Corey Moore, DE, Virginia Tech	Lombardi
Joe Hamilton, QB, Georgia Tech	O'Brien
LaVar Arrington, LB, Penn State	Butkus
Tyrone Carter, DB, Minnesota	Thorpe
Chris Redman, QB, Louisville	Unitas
Ron Dayne, RB, Wisconsin	Walker
Sebastian Janikowski, K, Florida State	Groza
Corey Moore, DE, Virginia Tech	Nagurski
LaVar Arrington, LB, Penn State	Bednarik
Troy Walters, WR, Stanford	Biletnikoff
Deltha O'Neal, CB, California	Tatupu

BOWL GAMES

DATE	GAME	SCORE
D18	Las Vegas	Utah 17, Fresno State 16
D22	GMAC	TCU 28, East Carolina 14
D25	Oahu	Hawaii 23, Oregon State 17
D25	Aloha	Wake Forest 23, Arizona State 3
D27	Motor City	Marshall 21, Brigham Young 3
D28	Alamo	Penn State 24, Texas A&M 0
D29	Holiday	Kansas State 24, Washington 20
D29	Music City	Syracuse 20, Kentucky 13
D30	Humanitarian	Boise State 34, Louisville 31
D30	Micron PC	Illinois 63, Virginia 21
D30	Peach	Mississippi State 17, Clemson 7
D31	Insight.com	Colorado 62, Boston College 28
D31	Independence	Mississippi 27, Oklahoma 25
D31	Sun	Oregon 24, Minnesota 20
D31	Liberty	Southern Miss 23, Colorado State 17
J1	Cotton	Arkansas 27, Texas 6
J1	Outback	Georgia 28, Purdue 25 OT
J1	Gator	Miami (Fla.) 28, Georgia Tech 13
J1	Orange	Michigan 35, Alabama 34 OT
J1	Florida Citrus	Michigan State 37, Florida 34
J1	Rose	Wisconsin 17, Stanford 9
J2	Fiesta	Nebraska 31, Tennessee 21
J4	Sugar	Florida State 46, Virginia Tech 29

SEC STANDINGS

	CONFERENCE			OVERALL		
	W	L	T	W	L	T
EAST						
Florida	7	1	0	9	4	0
Tennessee	6	2	0	9	3	0
Georgia	5	3	0	8	4	0
Kentucky	4	4	0	6	6	0
Vanderbilt	2	6	0	5	6	0
South Carolina	0	8	0	0	11	0
WEST						
Alabama	7	1	0	10	3	0
Mississippi State	6	2	0	10	2	0
Arkansas	4	4	0	8	4	0
Mississippi	4	4	0	8	4	0
Auburn	2	6	0	5	6	0
LSU	1	7	0	3	8	0

ALL-SEC TEAM

POS	OFFENSE	SCHOOL
QB	Tee Martin	Tennessee
RB	Shaun Alexander	Alabama
RB	Deuce McAllister	Mississippi
WR	Freddie Milons	Alabama
WR	Darrell Jackson	Florida
C	Paul Hogan	Alabama
OL	Chris Samuels	Alabama
OL	Cooper Carlisle	Florida
OL	Todd Wade	Mississippi
OL	Cosey Coleman	Tennessee
TE	James Whalen	Kentucky
PK	Jeff Chandler	Florida

POS	DEFENSE	SCHOOL
L	Alex Brown	Florida
L	Shaun Ellis	Tennessee
L	Darwin Walker	Tennessee
LB	Jeff Snedegar	Kentucky
LB	Raynoch Thompson	Tennessee
LB	Barrin Simpson	Mississippi State
LB	Jamie Winborn	Vanderbilt
DB	Kenoy Kennedy	Arkansas
DB	Ashley Cooper	Mississippi State
DB	Deon Grant	Tennessee
DB	Dwayne Goodrich	Tennessee
P	Andy Smith	Kentucky

SEC CHAMPIONSHIP GAME

DECEMBER 4 | ATLANTA
ALABAMA 34, FLORIDA 7

	1ST	2ND	3RD	4TH	FINAL
FLA	7	0	0	0	7
ALA	0	12	3	19	34

SCORING SUMMARY

FLA	Kinney 3 pass from Graham (Chandler kick)
ALA	FG Pflugner 29
ALA	FG Pflugner 48
ALA	McAddley 27 pass from Zow (Zow pass failed)
ALA	FG Pflugner 49
ALA	Milons 77 run (Pflugner kick)
ALA	Grimes 38 interception return (Pflugner kick)
ALA	Alexander 7 run (Pflugner kick)

FLORIDA	TEAM STATISTICS	ALABAMA
6	First Downs	22
31	Rushing Yards	300
8-24-4	Passing	14-25-1
83	Passing Yards	162
114	Total Yards	462
0-0	Punt Returns - Yards	0-0
7-116	Kickoff Returns - Yards	2-28
8-40.5	Punts - Average	3-40
2-0	Fumbles - Lost	1-0
4-30	Penalties - Yards	12-99

INDIVIDUAL LEADERS

RUSHING
FLA: Graham 9-27.
ALA: Milons 6-116, TD.
PASSING
FLA: Palmers 7-20-3, 80 yards.
ALA: Zow 10-17-0, 134 yards, TD.
RECEIVING
FLA: Jackson 3-49; Taylor 2-22.
ALA: Carter 5-71; McAddley 4-46, TD.

2000 NCAA Major College Statistical Leaders

Individual Leaders

PASSING	POS	CL	G	ATT	COM	PCT	INT	I%	YDS	YPA	TD	TD%	RATING
1 Bart Hendricks, Boise State	QB	SR	11	347	210	60.5	8	2.3	3364	9.7	35	10.1	170.6
2 Chris Weinke, Florida State	QB	SR	12	431	266	61.7	11	2.6	4167	9.7	33	7.7	163.1
3 Rex Grossman, Florida	**QB**	**FR**	**11**	**212**	**131**	**61.8**	**7**	**3.3**	**1866**	**8.8**	**21**	**9.9**	**161.8**
4 Casey Printers, TCU	QB	SO	11	176	102	58.0	6	3.4	1584	9.0	16	9.1	156.7
5 Ken Dorsey, Miami (Fla.)	QB	SO	11	322	188	58.4	5	1.6	2737	8.5	25	7.8	152.3
6 George Godsey, Georgia Tech	QB	JR	11	349	222	63.6	6	1.7	2906	8.3	23	6.6	151.9
7 John Turman, Pittsburgh	QB	SR	11	233	128	54.9	7	3.0	2135	9.2	18	7.7	151.4
8 Rocky Perez, Texas-El Paso	QB	SR	11	338	200	59.2	6	1.8	2661	7.9	26	7.7	147.1
9 Mike Thiessen, Air Force	QB	SR	11	195	112	57.4	5	2.6	1687	8.7	13	6.7	147.0
10 Ryan Schneider, Central Florida	QB	FR	9	286	177	61.9	11	3.9	2334	8.2	21	7.3	147.0

ALL-PURPOSE	POS	CL	G	RUSH	REC	PR	KR	YDS	YPG
1 Emmett White, Utah State	HB	JR	11	1322	592	183	531	2628	238.9
2 LaDainian Tomlinson, TCU	TB	SR	11	2158	40	0	0	2198	199.8
3 Robert Kilow, Arkansas State	WR	SR	10	42	1002	133	724	1901	190.1
4 Damien Anderson, Northwestern	RB	SR	11	1914	120	0	0	2034	184.9
5 Justin McCareins, No. Illinois	FL	SR	11	73	1168	362	411	2014	183.1
6 Brock Forsey, Boise State	RB	SO	10	914	399	0	517	1830	183.0
7 Deoncé Whitaker, San Jose State	TB	SR	10	1577	37	0	151	1765	176.5
8 Hodges Mitchell, Texas	RB	SR	11	1118	386	427	0	1931	175.6
9 Michael Bennett, Wisconsin	TB	JR	10	1598	23	0	94	1715	171.5
10 Koren Robinson, North Carolina St.	WR	SO	11	95	1061	218	506	1880	170.9

RUSHING/Yards Per Game	POS	CL	G	ATT	YDS	TD	AVG	YPG
1 LaDainian Tomlinson, TCU	TB	SR	11	369	2158	22	5.9	196.2
2 Damien Anderson, Northwestern	RB	SR	11	293	1914	22	6.5	174.0
3 Michael Bennett, Wisconsin	TB	JR	10	294	1598	10	5.4	159.8
4 Deoncé Whitaker, San Jose State	TB	SR	10	224	1577	15	7.0	157.7
5 Anthony Thomas, Michigan	HB	SR	11	287	1551	16	5.4	141.0
6 Ken Simonton, Oregon State	TB	JR	11	266	1474	18	5.5	134.0
7 Chester Taylor, Toledo	TB	SR	11	250	1470	18	5.9	133.6
8 Robert Sanford, Western Mich.	TB	SR	12	293	1571	18	5.4	130.9
9 Rudi Johnson, Auburn	**TB**	**JR**	**12**	**324**	**1567**	**13**	**4.8**	**130.6**
10 Ennis Haywood, Iowa State	RB	JR	10	230	1237	8	5.4	123.7

RUSHING/Yards Per Carry	POS	CL	G	ATT	YDS	YPC
1 Keith Kenton, New Mexico State	RB	JR	11	109	849	7.8
2 Levron Williams, Indiana	RB	SR	10	116	821	7.1
3 Correll Buckhalter, Nebraska	IB	SR	11	106	750	7.1
4 Deoncé Whitaker, San Jose State	TB	SR	10	224	1577	7.0
5 James Mungro, Syracuse	RB	JR	10	115	797	6.9
6 Dwone Hicks, Middle Tennessee	TB	SO	11	186	1277	6.9
7 Chris Barnes, New Mexico State	RB	SR	11	171	1131	6.6
8 Damien Anderson, Northwestern	RB	SR	11	293	1914	6.5
9 Dan Alexander, Nebraska	IB	SR	11	182	1154	6.3
10 Dicenzo Miller, Mississippi State	**TB**	**JR**	**11**	**160**	**1005**	**6.3**

Based on top 50 rushers

RECEIVING	POS	CL	G	REC	YDS	TD	RPG	YPR	YPG
1 Antonio Bryant, Pittsburgh	WR	SO	10	68	1302	11	6.8	19.2	130.2
2 Freddie Mitchell, UCLA	FL	JR	11	68	1314	8	6.2	19.3	119.5
3 Marvin Minnis, Florida State	FL	SR	12	63	1340	11	5.3	21.3	111.7
4 Justin McCareins, No. Illinois	FL	SR	11	66	1168	10	6.0	17.7	106.2
5 Aaron Jones, Utah State	WR	SR	11	63	1159	11	5.7	18.4	105.4
6 Josh Reed, LSU	**SE**	**SO**	**11**	**65**	**1127**	**10**	**5.9**	**17.3**	**102.5**
7 Robert Kilow, Arkansas State	WR	SR	10	72	1002	3	7.2	13.9	100.2
8 Lee Mays, Texas-El Paso	WR	JR	11	70	1098	15	6.4	15.7	99.8
9 Don Shoals, Tulsa	WR	JR	12	80	1195	5	6.7	14.9	99.6
10 Tyson Hinshaw, Central Florida	WR	SR	11	89	1089	13	8.1	12.2	99.0

PUNTING	POS	CL	PUNT	YDS	AVG
1 Preston Gruening, Minnesota	P	SO	46	2080	45.2
2 Brian Morton, Duke	P	SR	77	3478	45.2
3 Kevin Stemke, Wisconsin	P	SR	65	2915	44.9
4 Brooks Barnard, Maryland	P	SO	49	2191	44.7
5 Dave Zastudil, Ohio U.	P	JR	47	2084	44.3
6 Casey Roussel, Tulane	P	JR	59	2609	44.2
7 Jeff Ferguson, Oklahoma	K	JR	48	2108	43.9
8 Dan Hadenfeldt, Nebraska	P	SR	39	1708	43.8
9 Alan Rhine, Florida	**P**	**SR**	**47**	**2035**	**43.3**
10 Aaron Edmonds, Brigham Young	K	JR	67	2898	43.3

PUNT RETURNS	POS	CL	PR	YDS	TD	AVG
1 Aaron Lockett, Kansas State	WR	JR	22	501	3	22.8
2 Andre Davis, Virginia Tech	WR	JR	18	396	3	22.0
3 Justin McCareins, No. Illinois	FL	SR	19	362	1	19.1
4 Santana Moss, Miami (Fla.)	WR	SR	36	655	4	18.2
5 Jemeel Powell, California	DB	SO	12	218	1	18.2
6 Pete Rebstock, Colorado State	WR	JR	28	469	1	16.8
7 Troy Mason, Nevada-Las Vegas	WR	SO	23	378	1	16.4
8 Joey Getherall, Notre Dame	FL	SR	24	392	2	16.3
9 J.T. Thatcher, Oklahoma	DB	SR	38	599	2	15.8
10 Don Shoals, Tulsa	WR	JR	17	266	2	15.7

KICKOFF RETURNS	POS	CL	KR	YDS	TD	AVG
1 LaTarence Dunbar, TCU	WR	SO	15	506	2	33.7
2 Zek Parker, Louisville	WR	SR	26	752	0	28.9
3 David Mikell, Boise State	RB	FR	16	459	1	28.7
4 Julius Jones, Notre Dame	TB	SO	15	427	1	28.5
5 Ken-Yon Rambo, Ohio State	FL	SR	17	478	0	28.1
6 Kahlil Hill, Iowa	WR	JR	25	680	1	27.2
7 Robert Kilow, Arkansas State	WR	SR	27	724	0	26.8
8 Shawn Terry, West Virginia	WR	JR	27	720	2	26.7
9 Kyle Moore, Duke	WR	JR	13	335	0	25.8
10 James Hickenbocham, Arkansas State	WR	SO	17	435	1	25.6

SCORING	POS	CL	TDS	XP	FG	PTS	PTPG
1 Lee Suggs, Virginia Tech	RB	SO	28	0	0	168	15.3
2 LaDainian Tomlinson, TCU	TB	SR	22	0	0	132	12.0
2 Damien Anderson, Northwestern	RB	SR	22	0	0	132	12.0
4 Dwone Hicks, Middle Tennessee	TB	SO	21	0	0	126	11.5
5 Eric Crouch, Nebraska	QB	JR	20	0	0	120	10.9
6 Thomas Hammock, No. Illinois	TB	SO	16	0	0	96	10.7
7 Chester Taylor, Toledo	TB	SR	19	0	0	114	10.4
8 Ken Simonton, Oregon State	TB	JR	18	0	0	110	10.0
9 Deoncé Whitaker, San Jose State	TB	SR	16	0	0	98	9.8
10 Kris Stockton, Texas	K	SR	0	41	22	107	9.7

FIELD GOALS	POS	CL	FGA	FGM	PCT	FGG
1 Jonathan Ruffin, Cincinnati	K	SO	29	26	0.90	2.36
2 Dan Nystrom, Minnesota	K	SO	34	22	0.65	2.00
2 Kris Stockton, Texas	K	SR	26	22	0.85	2.00
4 Rhett Gallego, UAB	K	SO	24	19	0.79	1.73
4 Dave Adams, Air Force	K	SR	24	19	0.79	1.73
4 Dan Stultz, Ohio State	K	SR	23	19	0.83	1.73
7 Alex Walls, Tennessee	**K**	**SO**	**20**	**18**	**0.90**	**1.64**
8 Owen Pochman, Brigham Young	K	SR	24	19	0.79	1.58
9 Steve Azar, No. Illinois	K	FR	15	14	0.93	1.56
10 Jeff Reed, North Carolina	K	SR	20	16	0.80	1.45
10 Chris Kaylakie, TCU	K	SR	18	16	0.89	1.45
10 Seth Marler, Tulane	K	SO	21	16	0.76	1.45

INTERCEPTIONS	POS	CL	INT	YDS	TD	INT/GM
1 Dwight Smith, Akron	DB	SR	10	208	2	0.91
1 Anthony Floyd, Louisville	DB	SO	10	152	1	0.91
3 Ed Reed, Miami (Fla.)	DB	JR	8	92	2	0.73
4 J.T. Thatcher, Oklahoma	DB	SR	8	162	1	0.67
4 Jamar Fletcher, Wisconsin	DB	JR	6	159	0	0.67
6 Dan Dawson, Rice	LB	JR	7	206	1	0.64
7 Nate Jackson, Hawaii	DB	JR	7	57	0	0.58
8 Tim Wansley, Georgia	**DB**	**JR**	**6**	**148**	**2**	**0.55**
8 Alex Ardley, Clemson	DB	JR	6	61	0	0.55
8 Rashad Holman, Louisville	DB	SR	6	32	0	0.55
8 Lenny Walls, Boston College	DB	JR	6	29	1	0.55
8 Willie Pile, Virginia Tech	DB	SO	6	22	1	0.55
8 Charles Tillman, La.-Lafayette	DB	SO	6	15	0	0.55
8 Todd Howard, Michigan	DB	JR	6	1	0	0.55
8 Shawn Robinson, Pittsburgh	DB	SO	6	-6	0	0.55

Team Leaders

RUSHING OFFENSE	G	ATT	YDS	AVG	TD	YPG
1 Nebraska	11	636	3842	6.0	45	349.3
2 Ohio U.	11	646	3553	5.5	32	323.0
3 Air Force	11	647	3244	5.0	33	294.9
4 TCU	11	588	3032	5.2	33	275.6
5 Virginia Tech	11	570	2975	5.2	46	270.5
6 New Mexico State	11	535	2972	5.6	16	270.2
7 Indiana	11	505	2930	5.8	34	266.4
8 Northwestern	11	565	2830	5.0	36	257.3
9 Toledo	11	514	2792	5.4	29	253.8
10 Clemson	11	557	2600	4.7	33	236.4

PASSING OFFENSE	G	ATT	COM	INT	PCT	YDS	YPA	TD	I%	YPC	YPG
1 Florida State	12	469	290	14	61.8	4608	9.8	36	3.0	15.9	384.0
2 Kentucky	**11**	**564**	**322**	**21**	**57.1**	**3689**	**6.5**	**19**	**3.7**	**11.5**	**335.4**
3 Tulane	11	506	288	16	56.9	3569	7.1	28	3.2	12.4	324.5
4 Hawaii	12	609	309	23	50.7	3875	6.4	25	3.8	12.5	322.9
5 Boise State	11	372	225	8	60.5	3537	9.5	37	2.2	15.7	321.5
6 Purdue	11	489	292	12	59.7	3438	7.0	26	2.5	11.8	312.5
7 Louisiana Tech	12	546	357	28	65.4	3715	6.8	30	5.1	10.4	309.6
8 Florida	**12**	**466**	**265**	**12**	**56.9**	**3698**	**7.9**	**34**	**2.6**	**14.0**	**308.2**
9 Idaho	11	428	265	19	61.9	3357	7.8	24	4.4	12.7	305.2
10 Marshall	12	483	293	10	60.7	3584	7.4	24	2.1	12.2	298.7

TOTAL OFFENSE	G	P	YDS	AVG	TD	YPG
1 Florida State	12	924	6588	7.1	67	549.0
2 Boise State	11	812	5459	6.7	64	496.3
3 Northwestern	11	911	5232	5.7	56	475.6
4 Purdue	11	904	5183	5.7	47	471.2
5 Miami (Fla.)	11	774	5069	6.6	63	460.8
6 Nebraska	11	808	5059	6.3	63	459.9
7 Tulane	11	897	4989	5.6	40	453.6
8 Idaho	11	846	4985	5.9	42	453.2
9 Air Force	11	852	4971	5.8	47	451.9
10 Clemson	11	853	4911	5.8	53	446.5

RUSHING DEFENSE	G	ATT	YDS	AVG	TD	YPG
1 Memphis	11	346	800	2.3	6	72.7
2 Florida State	12	387	887	2.3	6	73.9
3 Tennessee	**11**	**338**	**817**	**2.4**	**7**	**74.3**
4 Louisville	11	395	879	2.2	12	79.9
5 Toledo	11	365	897	2.5	10	81.5
6 UAB	11	386	919	2.4	9	83.5
7 TCU	11	395	928	2.4	3	84.4
8 Arizona	11	393	973	2.5	12	88.5
9 Ohio State	11	396	1008	2.6	10	91.6
10 Oregon State	11	385	1024	2.7	9	93.1

PASSING DEFENSE	G	ATT	COM	PCT	INT	I%	YDS	YPA	TD	TD%	RAT
1 Texas	11	379	171	45.1	17	4.5	2027	5.4	8	2.1	88.0
2 Oklahoma	12	397	196	49.4	22	5.5	2049	5.2	9	2.3	89.2
3 TCU	11	323	143	44.3	15	4.6	1767	5.5	10	3.1	91.2
4 Southern Miss	11	370	186	50.3	14	3.8	1788	4.8	9	2.4	91.4
5 Florida State	12	447	220	49.2	19	4.3	2437	5.5	7	1.6	91.7
6 Kansas State	13	399	204	51.1	20	5.0	2241	5.6	8	2.0	94.9
7 Nebraska	11	393	179	45.6	14	3.6	2291	5.8	10	2.5	95.7
8 Miami (Fla.)	11	428	216	50.5	23	5.4	2427	5.7	11	2.6	95.9
9 Mississippi	**11**	**341**	**160**	**46.9**	**18**	**5.3**	**2064**	**6.1**	**9**	**2.6**	**95.9**
10 Texas Tech	12	343	177	51.6	15	4.4	1969	5.7	7	2.0	97.8

TOTAL DEFENSE	G	P	YDS	AVG	TD	YPG
1 TCU	11	718	2695	3.8	13	245.0
2 Southern Miss	11	784	2950	3.8	21	268.2
3 Toledo	11	703	2959	4.2	16	269.0
4 Kansas State	13	872	3517	4.0	29	270.5
5 Memphis	11	755	3028	4.0	20	275.3
6 Florida State	12	834	3324	4.0	15	277.0
7 Texas	11	766	3061	4.0	26	278.3
8 Oklahoma	12	809	3347	4.1	25	278.9
9 Western Michigan	12	803	3399	4.2	16	283.3
10 Utah	11	735	3171	4.3	24	288.3

SCORING OFFENSE	G	PTS	AVG
1 Boise State	11	494	44.9
2 Miami (Fla.)	11	469	42.6
3 Florida State	12	509	42.4
4 Nebraska	11	456	41.5
5 Virginia Tech	11	443	40.3
6 Kansas State	13	514	39.5
7 Oklahoma	12	468	39.0
8 Texas	11	425	38.6
9 Northwestern	11	424	38.6
10 Florida	**12**	**448**	**37.3**

SCORING DEFENSE	G	PTS	AVG
1 TCU	11	106	9.6
2 Florida State	12	123	10.3
3 Toledo	11	125	11.4
4 Western Michigan	12	139	11.6
5 Miami (Fla.)	11	170	15.5
6 South Carolina	**11**	**174**	**15.8**
7 Oklahoma	12	192	16.0
8 Southern Miss	11	182	16.5
9 UAB	11	192	17.5
10 Texas A&M	11	196	17.8

TURNOVER MARGIN	G	FR	INT	TOT	FL	INTL	TOT	MAR
1 Toledo	11	16	15	31	5	4	9	2.00
2 Georgia Tech	11	15	15	30	6	6	12	1.64
3 Florida	**12**	**16**	**24**	**40**	**9**	**12**	**21**	**1.58**
4 Oregon State	11	10	22	32	9	7	16	1.45
5 Notre Dame	11	9	13	22	4	4	8	1.27
6 Cincinnati	11	15	19	34	9	13	22	1.09
6 Miami (Fla.)	11	10	23	33	16	5	21	1.09
6 Northwestern	11	13	12	25	6	7	13	1.09
6 Louisville	11	11	27	38	14	12	26	1.09
10 Arizona State	11	23	13	36	13	12	25	1.00
10 Michigan	11	12	14	26	10	5	15	1.00
10 Boston College	11	10	16	26	3	12	15	1.00

ANNUAL REVIEW

2000

FINAL POLL (JAN. 6)

ESPN	AP	SCHOOL	FINAL RECORD
1	1	Oklahoma	13-0
2	2	Miami (Fla.)	11-1
3	3	Washington	11-1
5	4	Oregon State	11-1
4	5	Florida State	11-2
6	6	Virginia Tech	11-1
9	7	Oregon	10-2
7	8	Nebraska	10-2
8	9	Kansas State	11-3
11	10	Florida	10-3
10	11	Michigan	9-3
12	12	Texas	9-3
13	13	Purdue	8-4
15	14	Colorado State	10-2
16	15	Notre Dame	9-3
14	16	Clemson	9-3
19	17	Georgia Tech	9-3
20	18	Auburn	9-4
21	19	South Carolina	8-4
17	20	Georgia	8-4
18	21	TCU	10-2
	22	LSU	8-4
24	23	Wisconsin	9-4
22	24	Mississippi State	8-4
23	25	Iowa State	9-3
25		Tennessee	8-4

CONSENSUS ALL-AMERICANS

POS	OFFENSE	CL	SCHOOL
QB	Josh Heupel	Sr.	Oklahoma
RB	LaDainian Tomlinson	Sr.	TCU
RB	Damien Anderson	Jr.	Northwestern
WR	Marvin Minnis	Sr.	Florida State
WR	Antonio Bryant	So.	Pittsburgh
WR	Fred Mitchell	Jr.	UCLA
TE	Brian Natkin	Sr.	Texas-El Paso
OL	Steve Hutchinson	Sr.	Michigan
OL	Ben Hamilton	Sr.	Minnesota
OL	Chris Brown	Sr.	Georgia Tech
OL	Leonard Davis	Sr.	Texas
C	Dominic Raiola	Jr.	Nebraska
PK	Jonathan Ruffin	So.	Cincinnati
AP	Santana Moss	Sr.	Miami (Fla.)

OTHERS RECEIVING FIRST-TEAM HONORS

QB	Chris Weinke	Florida State
RB	Ken Simonton	Oregon State
OL	Tarlos Thomas	Florida State
OL	Joaquin Gonzalez	Miami (Fla.)
OL	Paul Zukauskas	Boston College
OL	Chad Ward	Washington
OL	Russ Hochstein	Nebraska
PK	Jamie Rheem	Kansas State
AP	Andre Davis	Virginia Tech

POS	DEFENSE	CL	SCHOOL
DL	Jamal Reynolds	Sr.	Florida State
DL	Andre Carter	Sr.	California
DL	Casey Hampton	Sr.	Texas
DL	John Henderson	Jr.	Tennessee
LB	Dan Morgan	Sr.	Miami (Fla.)
LB	Rocky Calmus	Jr.	Oklahoma
LB	Keith Adams	Jr.	Clemson
DB	Dwight Smith	Sr.	Akron
DB	Jamar Fletcher	Jr.	Wisconsin
DB	Fred Smoot	Sr.	Mississippi State
DB	Tay Cody	Sr.	Florida State
DB	Edward Reed	Jr.	Miami (Fla.)
DB	J.T. Thatcher	Sr.	Oklahoma
P	Nick Harris	Sr.	California

OTHERS RECEIVING FIRST-TEAM HONORS

DL	Richard Seymour	Georgia
DL	Justin Smith	Missouri
DL	Mario Fatafeni	Kansas State
LB	Levar Fisher	North Carolina St.
LB	Carlos Polk	Nebraska
DB	Anthony Floyd	Louisville
DB	Lito Sheppard	Florida
DB	Sheldon Brown	South Carolina
DB	Mike Doss	Ohio State
P	Brian Morton	Duke

HEISMAN TROPHY VOTING

	PLAYER	POS	SCHOOL	TOTAL
1	Chris Weinke	QB	Florida State	1628
2	Josh Heupel	QB	Oklahoma	1552
3	Drew Brees	QB	Purdue	619
4	LaDainian Tomlinson	RB	TCU	566
5	Damien Anderson	RB	Northwestern	101
6	Michael Vick	QB	Virginia Tech	83
7	Santana Moss	WR	Miami (Fla.)	55
8	Marques Tuiasosopo	QB	Washington	41
9	Ken Simonton	RB	Oregon State	25
10	Rudi Johnson	RB	Auburn	20

AWARD WINNERS

PLAYER	AWARD
Drew Brees, QB, Purdue	Maxwell
John Henderson, DL, Tennessee	Outland
Josh Heupel, QB, Oklahoma	Camp
Jamal Reynolds, DE, Florida State	Lombardi
Chris Weinke, QB, Florida State	O'Brien
Dan Morgan, LB, Miami (Fla.)	Butkus
Jamar Fletcher, DB, Wisconsin	Thorpe
Chris Weinke, QB, Florida State	Unitas
LaDainian Tomlinson, RB, TCU	Walker
Jonathan Ruffin, K, Cincinnati	Groza
Dan Morgan, LB, Miami (Fla.)	Nagurski
Dan Morgan, LB, Miami (Fla.)	Bednarik
Antonio Bryant, WR, Pittsburgh	Biletnikoff
J.T. Thatcher, FS, Oklahoma	Tatupu
Kevin Stemke, P, Wisconsin	Guy
Tim Stratton, TE, Purdue	Mackey
Dominic Raiola, C, Nebraska	Rimington

BOWL GAMES

DATE	GAME	SCORE
D20	GMAC	Southern Miss 28, TCU 21
D21	Las Vegas	Nevada-Las Vegas 31, Arkansas 14
D24	Oahu	Georgia 37, Virginia 14
D25	Aloha	Boston College 31, Arizona St. 17
D27	Galleryfurniture.com	East Carolina 40, Texas Tech 27
D27	Motor City	Marshall 25, Cincinnati 14
D28	Humanitarian	Boise State 38, Texas-El Paso 23
D28	Insight.com	Iowa State 37, Pittsburgh 29
D28	Micron PC	North Carolina St. 38, Minnesota 30
D28	Music City	West Virginia 49, Mississippi 38
D29	Liberty	Colorado State 22, Louisville 17
D29	Peach	LSU 28, Georgia Tech 14
D29	Holiday	Oregon 35, Texas 30
D29	Sun	Wisconsin 21, UCLA 20
D30	Alamo	Nebraska 66, Northwestern 17
D31	Silicon Valley	Air Force 37, Fresno State 34
D31	Independence	Mississippi St. 43, Texas A&M 41 OT
J1	Cotton	Kansas State 35, Tennessee 21
J1	Florida Citrus	Michigan 31, Auburn 28
J1	Fiesta	Oregon State 41, Notre Dame 9
J1	Outback	South Carolina 24, Ohio State 7
J1	Gator	Virginia Tech 41, Clemson 20
J1	Rose	Washington 34, Purdue 24
J2	Sugar	Miami (Fla.) 37, Florida 20
J3	Orange	Oklahoma 13, Florida State 2

SEC STANDINGS

	CONFERENCE			OVERALL		
	W	L	T	W	L	T
EAST						
Florida	7	1	0	10	3	0
Tennessee	5	3	0	8	4	0
South Carolina	5	3	0	8	4	0
Georgia	5	3	0	8	4	0
Vanderbilt	1	7	0	3	8	0
Kentucky	0	8	0	2	9	0
WEST						
Auburn	6	2	0	9	4	0
LSU	5	3	0	8	4	0
Mississippi State	4	4	0	8	4	0
Mississippi	4	4	0	7	5	0
Arkansas	3	5	0	6	6	0
Alabama	3	5	0	3	8	0

ALL-SEC TEAM

POS	OFFENSE	SCHOOL
QB	Josh Booty	LSU
RB	Rudi Johnson	Auburn
RB	Travis Henry	Tennessee
WR	Jabar Gaffney	Florida
WR	Josh Reed	LSU
C	Paul Hogan	Alabama
OL	Kenyatta Walker	Florida
OL	Terrence Metcalf	Mississippi
OL	Mike Pearson	Florida
OL	Kendall Simmons	Auburn
OL	Jonas Jennings	Georgia
OL	Pork Chop Womack	Mississippi State
TE	Derek Smith	Kentucky
TE	Robert Royal	LSU
K	Alex Walls	Tennessee

POS	DEFENSE	SCHOOL
L	Alex Brown	Florida
L	John Henderson	Tennessee
L	Richard Seymour	Georgia
LB	Kalimba Edwards	South Carolina
LB	Eric Westmoreland	Tennessee
LB	Quinton Caver	Arkansas
LB	Jamie Winborn	Vanderbilt
DB	Lito Sheppard	Florida
DB	Fred Smoot	Mississippi State
DB	Tim Wansley	Georgia
DB	Rodney Crayton	Auburn
DB	Ken Lucas	Mississippi
P	Damon Duval	Auburn

SEC CHAMPIONSHIP GAME

DECEMBER 2 | ATLANTA

FLORIDA 28, AUBURN 6

	1ST	2ND	3RD	4TH	FINAL
FLA	14	7	7	0	28
AUB	0	3	3	0	6

SCORING SUMMARY

FLA	Caldwell 10 pass from Grossman (Chandler kick)
FLA	Caldwell 66 pass from Grossman (Chandler kick)
FLA	Gaffney 27 pass from Grossman (Chandler kick)
AUB	FG Duval 44
AUB	FG Duval 21
FLA	Haugabrook 12 pass from Grossman (Chandler kick)

FLORIDA	TEAM STATISTICS	AUBURN
20	First Downs	19
191	Rushing Yards	120
17-26-1	Passing	23-43-2
238	Passing Yards	208
429	Total Yards	328
2-30	Punt Returns - Yards	1-13
2-44	Kickoff Returns - Yards	2-34
4-44.5	Punts - Average	5-41.2
4-2	Fumbles - Lost	3-2
8-61	Penalties - Yards	5-19

INDIVIDUAL LEADERS

RUSHING
FLA: Graham 19-169.
AUB: Evans 8-69.

PASSING
FLA: Grossman 17-26-1, 238 yards, 4 TD.
AUB: Leard 17-30-1, 158 yards.

RECEIVING
FLA: Caldwell 3-91, 2 TD; Gaffney 5-84, TD.
AUB: Evans 4-45; Diamond 4-42.

2001 NCAA Major College Statistical Leaders

Individual Leaders

Passing

		POS	CL	G	ATT	COM	PCT	INT	I%	YDS	YPA	TD	TD%	RATING
1	**Rex Grossman, Florida**	**QB**	**SO**	**11**	**395**	**259**	**65.6**	**12**	**3.0**	**3896**	**9.86**	**34**	**8.6**	**170.8**
2	David Carr, Fresno State	QB	SR	13	476	308	64.7	7	1.5	4299	9.03	42	8.8	166.7
3	Wes Counts, Middle Tennessee	QB	SR	11	259	188	72.6	4	1.5	2327	8.98	17	6.6	166.6
4	Ryan Dinwiddie, Boise State	QB	SO	11	322	201	62.4	11	3.4	3043	9.45	29	9.0	164.7
5	Byron Leftwich, Marshall	QB	JR	12	470	315	67.0	7	1.5	4132	8.79	38	8.1	164.6
6	Jeff Smoker, Michigan State	QB	SO	10	230	144	62.6	7	3.0	2203	9.58	18	7.8	162.8
7	Brandon Doman, Brigham Young	QB	SR	13	408	261	64.0	8	2.0	3542	8.68	33	8.1	159.7
8	Chris Rix, Florida State	QB	FR	11	286	165	57.7	13	4.6	2734	9.56	24	8.4	156.6
9	Jeff Krohn, Arizona State	QB	SO	10	213	115	54.0	7	3.3	1942	9.12	19	8.9	153.4
10	Nick Rolovich, Hawaii	QB	SR	10	405	233	57.5	9	2.2	3361	8.30	34	8.4	150.5

All-Purpose

		POS	CL	G	RUSH	REC	PR	KR	YDS	YPG
1	Levron Williams, Indiana	RB	SR	11	1401	289	0	511	2201	200.1
2	Bernard Berrian, Fresno State	WR	JR	13	101	1270	552	668	2591	199.3
3	Mewelde Moore, Tulane	RB	SO	12	1421	756	0	82	2259	188.3
4	Luke Staley, Brigham Young	RB	JR	11	1582	334	0	102	2018	183.5
5	Emmett White, Utah State	RB	SR	11	1361	408	125	120	2014	183.1
6	William Green, Boston College	RB	JR	10	1559	260	0	0	1819	181.9
7	Chris Douglas, Duke	TB	SO	11	841	233	0	775	1849	168.1
8	Chance Kretschmer, Nevada	RB	FR	11	1732	55	0	0	1787	162.5
9	Brock Forsey, Boise State	RB	JR	12	1207	369	0	362	1938	161.5
10	Bruce Perry, Maryland	TB	SO	11	1242	359	0	117	1718	156.2

Rushing/Yards Per Game

		POS	CL	G	ATT	YDS	TD	AVG	YPG
1	Chance Kretschmer, Nevada	RB	FR	11	302	1732	15	5.7	157.5
2	William Green, Boston College	RB	JR	10	265	1559	15	5.9	155.9
3	Luke Staley, Brigham Young	RB	JR	11	196	1582	24	8.1	143.8
4	Larry Ned, San Diego State	RB	SR	11	311	1549	15	5.0	140.8
5	Anthony Davis, Wisconsin	RB	FR	11	291	1466	11	5.0	133.3
6	Leonard Henry, East Carolina	RB	SR	11	184	1432	16	7.8	130.2
7	Chester Taylor, Toledo	TB	JR	11	268	1430	20	5.3	130.0
8	Levron Williams, Indiana	RB	SR	11	212	1401	17	6.6	127.4
9	Dameon Hunter, Utah	RB	SR	11	257	1396	9	5.4	126.9
10	Marcus Merriweather, Ball State	TB	SR	10	268	1244	12	4.6	124.4

Rushing/Yards Per Carry

		POS	CL	G	ATT	YDS	YPC
1	**Santonio Beard, Alabama**	**TB**	**JR**	**9**	**77**	**633**	**8.2**
2	Luke Staley, Brigham Young	RB	JR	11	196	1582	8.1
3	Leonard Henry, East Carolina	RB	SR	11	184	1432	7.8
4	Reshard Lee, Middle Tennessee	RB	SO	11	108	790	7.3
5	Levron Williams, Indiana	RB	SR	11	212	1401	6.6
6	ShanDerrick Charles, SMU	RB	FR	11	134	860	6.4
7	Marion Barber, Minnesota	RB	FR	11	118	742	6.3
8	Onterrio Smith, Oregon	TB	SO	11	161	1007	6.3
9	Joshua Cribbs, Kent State	QB	FR	11	164	1019	6.2
10	Dwone Hicks, Middle Tennessee	TB	JR	11	191	1144	6.0

Receiving

		POS	CL	G	REC	YDS	TD	RPG	YPR	YPG
1	**Josh Reed, LSU**	**SE**	**JR**	**12**	**94**	**1740**	**7**	**7.8**	**18.5**	**145.0**
2	Ashley Lelie, Hawaii	WR	JR	12	84	1713	19	7.0	20.4	142.8
3	Kevin Curtis, Utah State	WR	JR	11	100	1531	10	9.1	15.3	139.2
4	Lee Evans, Wisconsin	WR	JR	12	75	1545	9	6.3	20.6	128.8
5	Edell Shepherd, San Jose State	WR	SR	12	83	1500	14	6.9	18.1	125.0
6	Darius Watts, Marshall	WR	SO	12	91	1417	18	7.6	15.6	118.1
7	Charles Rogers, Michigan State	WR	SO	11	57	1200	12	5.2	21.1	109.1
8	**Jabar Gaffney, Florida**	**WR**	**SO**	**11**	**67**	**1191**	**13**	**6.1**	**17.8**	**108.3**
9	Rodney Wright, Fresno State	WR	SR	13	91	1331	10	7.0	14.6	102.4
10	Shaun McDonald, Arizona State	WR	SO	11	47	1104	10	4.3	23.5	100.4

Punting

		POS	CL	PUNT	YDS	AVG
1	Travis Dorsch, Purdue	K	SR	49	2370	48.4
2	Dave Zastudil, Ohio U.	P	SR	50	2280	45.6
3	Andy Groom, Ohio State	DT	SR	44	1981	45.0
4	Steve Mullins, Utah State	P	JR	50	2241	44.8
5	John Skaggs, Navy	P	SO	48	2151	44.8
6	Glenn Pakulak, Kentucky	P	JR	56	2492	44.5
7	Brooks Barnard, Maryland	P	JR	54	2401	44.5
8	Dan MacElroy, Army	P	SR	51	2264	44.4
9	Curtis Head, Marshall	P	JR	45	1996	44.4
10	Nate Fikse, UCLA	P	JR	53	2342	44.2

Punt Returns

		POS	CL	PR	YDS	TD	AVG
1	Roman Hollowell, Colorado	WR	SR	29	522	2	18.0
2	Luke Powell, Stanford	FL	JR	19	304	0	16.0
3	DeAndrew Rubin, South Florida	WR	JR	26	406	1	15.6
4	Ronnie Hamilton, Duke	CB	SR	20	311	1	15.6
5	Dexter Wynn, Colorado State	DB	SO	14	214	0	15.3
6	Nathan Vasher, Texas	DB	SO	37	554	1	15.0
7	Phillip Buchanon, Miami (Fla.)	DB	JR	31	464	2	15.0
8	Keenan Howry, Oregon	WR	JR	32	465	2	14.5
9	DeJuan Groce, Nebraska	DB	JR	33	469	1	14.2
10	Bernard Berrian, Fresno State	WR	JR	39	552	1	14.2

Kickoff Returns

		POS	CL	KR	YDS	TD	AVG
1	Chris Massey, Oklahoma State	DB	JR	15	522	1	34.8
2	Chad Owens, Hawaii	WR	FR	24	807	2	33.6
3	Derrick Hamilton, Clemson	WR	FR	15	476	1	31.7
4	Tom Pace, Arizona State	TB	SR	17	537	1	31.6
5	Corey Parchman, Ball State	WR	SR	15	465	2	31.0
6	Roc Alexander, Washington	CB	SO	19	555	1	29.2
7	David Mikell, Boise State	RB	SO	25	709	1	28.4
8	Aaron Lockett, Kansas State	WR	SR	14	397	1	28.4
9	Herb Haygood, Michigan State	WR	SR	19	524	2	27.6
9	**Jason Armstead, Mississippi**	**WR**	**JR**	**19**	**524**	**1**	**27.6**

Scoring

		POS	CL	TDS	XP	FG	PTS	PTPG
1	Luke Staley, Brigham Young	RB	JR	28	0	0	170	15.5
2	Dwone Hicks, Middle Tennessee	TB	JR	24	0	0	148	13.5
3	Chester Taylor, Toledo	TB	JR	23	0	0	138	12.6
4	Todd Sievers, Miami (Fla.)	K	JR	0	56	21	119	10.8
5	Levron Williams, Indiana	RB	SR	19	0	0	114	10.4
6	**Jeff Chandler, Florida**	**PK**	**SR**	**0**	**46**	**19**	**103**	**10.3**
7	William Green, Boston College	RB	JR	17	0	0	102	10.2
8	Leonard Henry, East Carolina	RB	SR	18	0	0	108	9.8
8	Ricky Williams, Texas Tech	TB	SR	18	0	0	108	9.8
10	Eric Crouch, Nebraska	QB	SR	19	0	0	116	9.7

Field Goals

		POS	CL	FGA	FGM	PCT	FGG
1	Todd Sievers, Miami (Fla.)	K	JR	26	21	0.81	1.91
2	**Jeff Chandler, Florida**	**PK**	**SR**	**22**	**19**	**0.86**	**1.90**
3	Travis Dorsch, Purdue	K	SR	25	20	0.80	1.82
3	Jarvis Wallum, Wyoming	K	JR	23	20	0.87	1.82
3	Steve Azar, Northern Illinois	K	SO	26	20	0.77	1.82
6	Asen Asparuhov, Fresno State	K	JR	30	23	0.77	1.77
7	Tim Duncan, Oklahoma	PK	SR	28	20	0.71	1.67
8	Josh Scobee, Louisiana Tech	K	SO	22	18	0.82	1.64
8	Jeremy Flores, Colorado	K	SR	24	18	0.75	1.64
10	Luke Manget, Georgia Tech	K	JR	28	19	0.68	1.58
10	Justin Ayat, Hawaii	K	FR	29	19	0.66	1.58

Interceptions

		POS	CL	INT	YDS	TD	INT/GM
1	Ed Reed, Miami (Fla.)	DB	SR	9	206	2	0.82
2	Lamont Thompson, Washington State	FS	SR	8	96	1	0.73
3	Derek Ross, Ohio State	DB	SR	7	194	1	0.64
3	Kevin Thomas, Nevada-Las Vegas	DB	SR	7	213	3	0.64
5	Nathan Vasher, Texas	DB	SO	7	17	0	0.58
6	Jonas Buckles, North Texas	DB	SO	5	9	0	0.56
7	Stuart Schweigert, Purdue	DB	SO	6	110	0	0.55
7	Steve Smith, Oregon	DB	SR	6	104	1	0.55
7	Glenn Sumter, Memphis	DB	JR	6	61	0	0.55
7	Stephen Persley, New Mexico	DB	SR	6	36	1	0.55
7	Eugene Wilson, Illinois	CB	JR	6	29	0	0.55
7	Tony Jackson, Maryland	SS	SR	6	6	0	0.55

Team Leaders

Rushing Offense

		G	ATT	YDS	AVG	TD	YPG
1	Nebraska	12	672	3776	5.6	47	314.7
2	Rice	12	751	3378	4.5	30	281.5
3	Air Force	12	677	3279	4.8	36	273.3
4	Indiana	11	541	2964	5.5	33	269.5
5	Kansas State	11	606	2835	4.7	34	257.7
6	Ohio U.	11	567	2641	4.7	20	240.1
7	Middle Tennessee	11	471	2615	5.6	32	237.7
8	Colorado	12	575	2742	4.8	27	228.5
9	**Alabama**	**11**	**472**	**2490**	**5.3**	**19**	**226.4**
10	Wake Forest	11	609	2438	4.0	27	221.6

Passing Offense

		G	ATT	COM	INT	PCT	YDS	YPA	TD	I%	YPC	YPG
1	**Florida**	**11**	**464**	**299**	**13**	**64.4**	**4457**	**9.6**	**43**	**3.0**	**14.9**	**405.2**
2	Hawaii	12	570	327	16	57.4	4576	8.0	41	3.7	14.0	381.3
3	Marshall	12	477	319	7	66.9	4201	8.8	40	3.2	13.2	350.1
4	Idaho	11	497	309	15	62.2	3826	7.7	28	3.8	12.4	347.8
5	Texas Tech	11	569	390	11	68.5	3710	6.5	27	2.2	9.5	337.3
6	Fresno State	13	483	311	8	64.4	4336	9.0	42	2.5	13.9	333.5
7	Brigham Young	13	486	315	9	64.8	4225	8.7	39	5.1	13.4	325.0
8	Louisiana Tech	11	482	283	14	58.7	3443	7.1	30	2.6	12.2	313.0
9	Central Florida	11	407	230	12	56.5	3391	8.3	21	4.4	14.7	308.3
10	Washington State	11	393	214	12	54.5	3310	8.4	30	2.1	15.5	300.9

Total Offense

		G	P	YDS	AVG	TD	YPG
1	Brigham Young	13	991	7057	7.1	82	542.9
2	**Florida**	**11**	**788**	**5803**	**7.4**	**61**	**527.6**
3	Marshall	12	880	6060	6.9	61	505.0
4	Fresno State	13	983	6464	6.6	65	497.2
5	Middle Tennessee	11	781	5296	6.9	56	481.5
6	Idaho	11	872	5113	5.9	42	464.8
7	Hawaii	12	855	5552	6.5	61	462.7
8	Miami (Fla.)	11	762	5003	6.6	59	454.8
9	Nevada	11	871	4993	5.7	35	453.9
10	Stanford	11	840	4967	5.9	54	451.6

Rushing Defense

		G	ATT	YDS	AVG	TD	YPG
1	UAB	11	333	630	1.9	6	57.3
2	Virginia Tech	11	371	788	2.1	7	71.6
3	**Tennessee**	**12**	**384**	**1024**	**2.7**	**8**	**85.3**
4	Bowling Green	11	372	949	2.6	5	86.3
5	New Mexico	11	383	961	2.5	9	87.4
6	Texas	12	385	1074	2.8	13	89.5
7	Oklahoma	12	430	1079	2.5	5	89.9
8	Michigan	11	391	996	2.6	9	90.5
9	Maryland	11	387	997	2.6	5	90.6
10	TCU	11	376	1032	2.7	12	93.8

Passing Defense

		G	ATT	COM	PCT	INT	I%	YDS	YPA	TD	TD%	RAT
1	Miami (Fla.)	11	290	129	44.5	27	9.3	1520	5.2	5	1.7	75.6
2	Nebraska	12	395	171	43.3	19	4.8	2043	5.2	8	2.0	83.8
3	Virginia Tech	11	354	161	45.5	19	5.4	1829	5.2	8	2.3	85.6
4	Texas	12	369	187	50.7	15	4.0	1760	4.8	6	1.6	88.0
5	Oklahoma	12	383	177	46.2	20	5.2	2075	5.4	9	2.4	89.0
6	Kansas State	11	320	152	47.5	18	5.6	1825	5.7	11	3.4	95.5
7	North Carolina	12	403	203	50.4	8	2.0	2166	5.4	9	2.2	99.0
8	West Virginia	11	251	122	48.6	11	4.4	1504	6.0	7	2.8	99.4
9	Texas A&M	11	369	206	55.8	14	3.8	1987	5.4	7	1.9	99.7
10	Boston College	11	313	154	49.2	18	5.8	1911	6.1	11	3.5	100.6

Total Defense

		G	P	YDS	AVG	TD	YPG
1	Texas	12	754	2834	3.76	22	236.2
2	Virginia Tech	11	725	2617	3.61	17	237.9
3	Kansas State	11	684	2886	4.22	21	262.4
4	Oklahoma	12	813	3154	3.88	18	262.8
5	UAB	11	719	2925	4.07	24	265.9
6	Miami (Fla.)	11	758	2980	3.93	14	270.9
7	Pittsburgh	11	786	3131	3.98	29	284.6
8	Nebraska	12	813	3446	4.24	24	287.2
9	**Florida**	**11**	**712**	**3192**	**4.48**	**19**	**290.2**
10	Texas A&M	11	798	3234	4.05	24	294.0

Scoring Offense

		G	PTS	AVG
1	Brigham Young	13	608	46.8
2	**Florida**	**11**	**482**	**43.8**
3	Miami (Fla.)	11	475	43.2
4	Fresno State	13	525	40.4
5	Hawaii	12	483	40.3
6	Texas	12	470	39.2
7	Nebraska	12	449	37.4
8	Marshall	12	448	37.3
9	Middle Tennessee	11	408	37.1
9	Stanford	11	408	37.1

Scoring Defense

		G	PTS	AVG
1	Miami (Fla.)	11	103	9.4
2	Virginia Tech	11	147	13.4
3	Texas	12	164	13.7
4	Oklahoma	12	166	13.8
5	**Florida**	**11**	**155**	**14.1**
6	Nebraska	12	189	15.8
7	Kansas State	11	179	16.3
8	Southern Miss	11	186	16.9
9	Michigan	11	192	17.5
10	Louisville	12	213	17.8

Turnover Margin

		G	FR	INT	TOT	FL	INTL	TOT	MAR
1	Miami (Fla.)	11	18	27	45	10	9	19	2.4
2	Fresno State	13	13	23	36	5	8	13	1.8
3	Bowling Green	11	17	18	35	5	13	18	1.6
4	Maryland	11	10	24	34	9	9	18	1.5
5	Oregon	11	7	18	25	6	5	11	1.3
5	Southern California	11	14	19	33	7	12	19	1.3
7	Syracuse	12	17	13	30	7	8	15	1.3
8	Iowa State	11	8	18	26	2	12	14	1.1
8	Purdue	11	18	18	36	11	13	24	1.1
10	Ohio State	11	10	19	29	8	10	18	1.0
10	Washington State	11	13	22	35	12	12	24	1.0

2001

FINAL POLL (JAN. 4)

ESPN	AP	SCHOOL	FINAL RECORD
1	1	Miami (Fla.)	12-0
2	2	Oregon	11-1
3	3	Florida	10-2
4	4	Tennessee	11-2
5	5	Texas	11-2
6	6	Oklahoma	11-2
8	7	LSU	10-3
7	8	Nebraska	11-2
9	9	Colorado	10-3
11	10	Washington State	10-2
10	11	Maryland	10-2
12	12	Illinois	10-2
13	13	South Carolina	9-3
14	14	Syracuse	10-3
15	15	Florida State	8-4
17	16	Stanford	9-3
16	17	Louisville	11-2
18	18	Virginia Tech	8-4
19	19	Washington	8-4
20	20	Michigan	8-4
23	21	Boston College	8-4
25	22	Georgia	8-4
22	23	Toledo	10-2
	24	Georgia Tech	8-5
24	25	Brigham Young	12-2
21		Marshall	11-2

CONSENSUS ALL-AMERICANS

POS	OFFENSE	CL	SCHOOL
QB	Rex Grossman	So.	Florida
RB	Luke Staley	So.	Brigham Young
RB	William Green	Jr.	Boston College
WR	Jabar Gaffney	So.	Florida
WR	Josh Reed	Jr.	LSU
TE	Dan Graham	Sr.	Colorado
OL	Bryant McKinnie	Sr.	Miami (Fla.)
OL	Toniu Fonoti	Jr.	Nebraska
OL	Andre Gurode	Sr.	Colorado
OL	Mike Williams	Sr.	Texas
OL	Mike Pearson	Jr.	Florida
OL	Terrence Metcalf	Sr.	Mississippi
C	LeCharles Bentley	Sr.	Ohio State
PK	Damon Duval	Jr.	Auburn

OTHERS RECEIVING FIRST-TEAM HONORS

QB	Antwaan Randle El	Indiana
QB	Eric Crouch	Nebraska
RB	Travis Stephens	Tennessee
RB	Bruce Perry	Maryland
WR	Marquise Walker	Michigan
WR	Lee Evans	Wisconsin
WR	Kevin Curtis	Utah State
TE	Jeremy Shockey	Miami (Fla.)
OL	Joaquin Gonzalez	Miami (Fla.)
OL	Eric Heitmann	Stanford
OL	Frank Romero	Oklahoma
OL	Melvin Fowler	Maryland
PK	Seth Marler	Tulane
PK	Todd Sievers	Miami (Fla.)
KR	Herb Haygood	Michigan State
KR	Luke Powell	Stanford
KR	Bernard Berrian	Fresno State
PR	Roman Hollowell	Colorado

POS	DEFENSE	CL	SCHOOL
DL	Alex Brown	Sr.	Florida
DL	Dwight Freeney	Sr.	Syracuse
DL	John Henderson	Sr.	Tennessee
DL	Julius Peppers	Jr.	North Carolina
LB	Rocky Calmus	Sr.	Oklahoma
LB	Robert Thomas	Sr.	UCLA
LB	E.J. Henderson	Jr.	Maryland
DB	Quentin Jammer	Sr.	Texas
DB	Edward Reed	Sr.	Miami (Fla.)
DB	Roy Williams	Jr.	Oklahoma
P	Travis Dorsch	Jr.	Purdue

OTHERS RECEIVING FIRST-TEAM HONORS

DL	Wendell Bryant	Wisconsin
DL	Kenyon Coleman	UCLA
DL	Terrell Suggs	Arizona State
LB	Jermaine Petty	Arkansas
LB	Levar Fisher	North Carolina St.
LB	Larry Foote	Michigan
LB	Lawrence Flugence	Texas Tech
LB	Andra Davis	Florida
DB	Mike Doss	Ohio State
DB	Troy Polamalu	Southern California
DB	Tank Williams	Stanford
DB	Lamont Thompson	Washington State
DB	Keyou Craver	Nebraska
P	Dave Zastudil	Ohio U.

HEISMAN TROPHY VOTING

	PLAYER	POS	SCHOOL	TOTAL
1	Eric Crouch	QB	Nebraska	770
2	Rex Grossman	QB	Florida	708
3	Ken Dorsey	QB	Miami (Fla.)	638
4	Joey Harrington	QB	Oregon	364
5	David Carr	QB	Fresno State	280
6	Antwaan Randel El	QB	Indiana	267
7	Roy Williams	DB	Oklahoma	146
8	Bryant McKinnie	OL	Miami (Fla.)	116
9	Dwight Freeney	DL	Syracuse	42
10	Julius Peppers	DL	North Carolina	41

AWARD WINNERS

PLAYER	AWARD
Ken Dorsey, QB, Miami (Fla.)	Maxwell
Bryant McKinnie, OT, Miami (Fla.)	Outland
Eric Crouch, QB, Nebraska	Camp
Julius Peppers, DE, North Carolina	Lombardi
Eric Crouch, QB, Nebraska	O'Brien
Rocky Calmus, LB, Oklahoma	Butkus
Roy Williams, DB, Oklahoma	Thorpe
David Carr, QB, Fresno State	Unitas
Luke Staley, RB, Brigham Young	Walker
Seth Marler, K, Tulane	Groza
Roy Williams, DB, Oklahoma	Nagurski
Julius Peppers, DE, North Carolina	Bednarik
Josh Reed, WR, LSU	Biletnikoff
Kahlil Hill, WR, Iowa	Tatupu
Travis Dorsch, P, Purdue	Guy
Dan Graham, TE, Colorado	Mackey
LeCharles Bentley, C, Ohio State	Rimington

BOWL GAMES

DATE	GAME	SCORE
D18	New Orleans	Colorado State 45, North Texas 20
D19	GMAC	Marshall 64, East Carolina 61, 2 OT
D20	Tangerine	Pittsburgh 34, North Carolina St. 19
D25	Las Vegas	Utah 10, Southern California 6
D27	Seattle	Georgia Tech 24, Stanford 14
D27	Independence	Alabama 14, Iowa State 13
D28	Galleryfurniture.com	Texas A&M 28, TCU 9
D28	Music City	Boston College 20, Georgia 16
D28	Holiday	Texas 47, Washington 43
D29	Motor City	Toledo 23, Cincinnati 16
D29	Alamo	Iowa 19, Texas Tech 16
D29	Insight.com	Syracuse 26, Kansas State 3
D31	Humanitarian	Clemson 49, Louisiana Tech 24
D31	Sun	Washington St. 33, Purdue 27
D31	Silicon Valley Classic	Michigan St. 44, Fresno St. 35
D31	Liberty	Louisville 28, Brigham Young 10
D31	Peach	North Carolina 16, Auburn 10
J1	Cotton	Oklahoma 10, Arkansas 3
J1	Outback	South Carolina 31, Ohio State 28
J1	Gator	Florida State 30, Virginia Tech 17
J1	Florida Citrus	Tennessee 45, Michigan 17
J1	Fiesta	Oregon 38, Colorado 16
J1	Sugar	LSU 47, Illinois 34
J2	Orange	Florida 56, Maryland 23
J3	Rose	Miami (Fla.) 37, Nebraska 14

SEC STANDINGS

	CONFERENCE			OVERALL		
	W	L	T	W	L	T
EAST						
Tennessee	6	2	0	11	2	0
Florida	6	2	0	10	2	0
South Carolina	5	3	0	9	3	0
Georgia	5	3	0	8	4	0
Kentucky	1	7	0	2	9	0
Vanderbilt	0	8	0	2	9	0
WEST						
LSU	5	3	0	10	3	0
Auburn	5	3	0	7	5	0
Mississippi	4	4	0	7	4	0
Arkansas	4	4	0	7	5	0
Alabama	4	4	0	7	5	0
Mississippi State	2	6	0	3	8	0

ALL-SEC TEAM

POS	OFFENSE	SCHOOL
QB	Rex Grossman	Florida
RB	Travis Stephens	Tennessee
RB	LaBrandon Toefield	LSU
WR	Jabar Gaffney	Florida
WR	Josh Reed	LSU
C	Zac Zedalis	Florida
OL	Terrence Metcalf	Mississippi
OL	Fred Weary	Tennessee
OL	Mike Pearson	Florida
OL	Kendall Simmons	Auburn
TE	Randy McMichael	Georgia
K	Damon Duval	Auburn

POS	DEFENSE	SCHOOL
L	Alex Brown	Florida
L	John Henderson	Tennessee
L	Will Overstreet	Tennessee
LB	Kalimba Edwards	South Carolina
LB	Bradie James	LSU
LB	Trev Faulk	LSU
LB	Saleem Rasheed	Alabama
DB	Lito Sheppard	Florida
DB	Syniker Taylor	Mississippi
DB	Tim Wansley	Georgia
DB	Andre Lott	Tennessee
DB	Sheldon Brown	South Carolina
P	Damon Duval	Auburn

SEC CHAMPIONSHIP GAME

DECEMBER 8 | ATLANTA
LSU 31, TENNESSEE 20

	1ST	2ND	3RD	4TH	FINAL
TENN	0	17	0	3	20
LSU	7	3	6	15	31

SCORING SUMMARY

LSU	Mauck 4 run (Corbello kick)
TENN	Washington 31 pass from Clausen (Walls kick)
TENN	Flemming 3 pass from Clausen (Walls kick)
TENN	FG Walls 51
LSU	FG Corbello 45
LSU	FG Corbello 47
LSU	FG Corbello 45
LSU	Mauck 13 run (Reed pass)
TENN	FG Walls 21
LSU	Davis 1 run (Corbello kick)

TENNESSEE	TEAM STATISTICS	LSU
17	First Downs	20
50	Rushing Yards	134
27-43-0	Passing	14-35-0
332	Passing Yards	151
382	Total Yards	285
2-17	Punt Returns - Yards	2-29
6-99	Kickoff Returns - Yards	3-42
4-39.2	Punts - Average	4-45.2
2-2	Fumbles - Lost	0-0
10-78	Penalties - Yards	5-32

INDIVIDUAL LEADERS

RUSHING
TENN: Stephens 14-37.
LSU: Davis 16-78, TD.

PASSING
TENN: Clausen 27-43-0, 332 yards, 2 TD.
LSU: Davey 9-20-0, 84 yards.

RECEIVING
TENN: Washington 9-140, TD; Stallworth 7-96.
LSU: Reed 4-60; Clayton 4-54.

2002 NCAA Major College Statistical Leaders

Individual Leaders

PASSING	POS	CL	G	ATT	COM	PCT	INT	I%	YDS	YPA	TD	TD%	RATING
1 Brad Banks, Iowa	QB	SR	13	294	170	57.8	5	1.7	2573	8.8	26	8.8	157.1
2 Byron Leftwich, Marshall	QB	SR	12	491	331	67.4	10	2.0	4268	8.7	30	6.1	156.5
3 Brian Jones, Toledo	QB	SR	14	423	297	70.2	9	2.1	3446	8.2	23	5.4	152.3
4 Ryan Schneider, Central Florida	QB	JR	12	430	265	61.6	16	3.7	3770	8.8	31	7.2	151.6
5 Carson Palmer, Southern California	QB	SR	13	489	309	63.2	10	2.0	3942	8.1	33	6.8	149.1
6 Matt Schaub, Virginia	QB	JR	14	418	288	68.9	7	1.7	2976	7.1	28	6.7	147.5
7 Jason Gesser, Washington State	QB	SR	13	402	236	58.7	13	3.2	3408	8.5	28	7.0	146.4
8 Ken Dorsey, Miami (Fla.)	QB	SR	13	393	222	56.5	12	3.1	3369	8.6	28	7.1	145.9
9 Kliff Kingsbury, Texas Tech	QB	SR	14	712	479	67.3	13	1.8	5017	7.1	45	6.3	143.7
10 Bryan Randall, Virginia Tech	QB	SO	14	248	158	63.7	11	4.4	2134	8.6	12	4.8	143.1

ALL-PURPOSE	POS	CL	G	RUSH	REC	PR	KR	YDS	YPG
1 Larry Johnson, Penn State	TB	SR	13	2087	349	0	219	2655	204.2
2 Michael Turner, No. Illinois	RB	JR	12	1915	100	0	269	2284	190.3
3 Robbie Mixon, Central Michigan	RB	SR	12	1361	253	0	524	2138	178.2
4 Jason Wright, Northwestern	WR	JR	12	1234	266	0	513	2013	167.8
5 Brock Forsey, Boise State	RB	SR	13	1611	282	0	234	2127	163.6
6 Domanick Davis, LSU	**RB**	**SR**	**13**	**931**	**130**	**499**	**560**	**2120**	**163.1**
7 Bobby Wade, Arizona	WR	SR	12	4	1389	224	332	1949	162.4
8 Willis McGahee, Miami (Fla.)	RB	SO	13	1753	355	0	0	2108	162.2
9 Charley Pauley, San Jose State	WR	SR	13	67	804	237	978	2086	160.5
10 Derek Abney, Kentucky	**WR**	**JR**	**12**	**5**	**569**	**544**	**804**	**1922**	**160.2**

RUSHING/Yards Per Game	POS	CL	G	ATT	YDS	TD	AVG	YPG
1 Larry Johnson, Penn State	TB	SR	13	271	2087	20	7.7	160.5
2 Michael Turner, No. Illinois	RB	JR	12	338	1915	19	5.7	159.6
3 Chris Brown, Colorado	RB	JR	12	303	1841	19	6.1	153.4
4 Willis McGahee, Miami (Fla.)	RB	SO	13	282	1753	28	6.2	134.9
5 Marcus Merriweather, Ball State	RB	SR	12	332	1618	12	4.9	134.8
6 Quentin Griffin, Oklahoma	RB	SR	14	287	1884	15	6.6	134.6
7 Avon Cobourne, West Virginia	RB	SR	13	335	1710	17	5.1	131.5
8 Steven Jackson, Oregon State	RB	SO	13	319	1690	15	5.3	130.0
9 Joffrey Reynolds, Houston	RB	SR	12	316	1545	11	4.9	128.8
10 Terry Caulley, Connecticut	RB	FR	10	220	1247	15	5.7	124.7

RUSHING/Yards Per Carry	POS	CL	G	ATT	YDS	YPC
1 Joshua Cribbs, Kent State	QB	SO	10	137	1057	7.7
2 Larry Johnson, Penn State	TB	SR	13	271	2087	7.7
3 Shaud Williams, Alabama	**RB**	**JR**	**13**	**130**	**921**	**7.1**
4 DeWhitt Betterson, Troy State	RB	SO	11	101	711	7.0
5 DeAngelo Williams, Memphis	RB	FR	11	103	684	6.6
6 Joe Alls, Bowling Green	RB	SR	10	122	801	6.6
7 Quentin Griffin, Oklahoma	RB	SR	14	287	1884	6.6
8 Quincy Wilson, West Virginia	RB	JR	13	140	901	6.4
9 Tatum Bell, Oklahoma State	RB	JR	11	175	1096	6.3
10 Walter Reyes, Syracuse	RB	SO	12	182	1135	6.2

RECEIVING	POS	CL	G	REC	YDS	TD	RPG	YPR	YPG
1 J.R. Tolver, San Diego State	WR	SR	13	128	1785	13	9.9	14.0	137.3
2 Nate Burleson, Nevada	WR	SR	12	138	1629	12	11.5	11.8	135.8
3 Rashaun Woods, Oklahoma State	WR	JR	13	107	1695	17	8.2	15.8	130.4
4 Kassim Osgood, San Diego State	WR	SR	13	108	1552	8	8.3	14.4	119.4
5 Bobby Wade, Arizona	WR	SR	12	93	1389	8	7.8	14.9	115.8
6 Kevin Curtis, Utah State	WR	SR	11	74	1258	9	6.7	17.0	114.4
7 Kevin Walter, Eastern Michigan	WR	SR	12	93	1368	9	7.8	14.7	114.0
8 Charles Rogers, Michigan State	WR	JR	12	68	1351	13	5.7	19.9	112.6
9 Reggie Williams, Washington	WR	SO	13	94	1454	11	7.2	15.5	111.9
10 Doug Gabriel, Central Florida	WR	SR	12	75	1237	11	6.3	16.5	103.1

PUNTING	POS	CL	PUNT	YDS	AVG
1 Matt Payne, Brigham Young	K	SO	51	2427	47.6
2 Mark Mariscal, Colorado	K	SR	67	3186	47.6
3 Glenn Pakulak, Kentucky	**P**	**SR**	**66**	**3008**	**45.6**
4 Andy Groom, Ohio State	P	SR	60	2697	45.0
5 Donnie Jones, LSU	**P**	**JR**	**64**	**2813**	**44.0**
6 Greg Johnson, Vanderbilt	**P**	**FR**	**66**	**2892**	**43.8**
7 Cody Scates, Texas A&M	P	JR	67	2931	43.8
8 Dustin Colquitt, Tennessee	**P**	**SO**	**65**	**2833**	**43.6**
9 Jarad Preston, East Carolina	P	SR	73	3170	43.4
10 Damon Duval, Auburn	**P**	**SR**	**54**	**2344**	**43.4**

PUNT RETURNS	POS	CL	PR	YDS	TD	AVG
1 Dan Sheldon, No. Illinois	WR	SO	21	477	3	22.7
2 Aris Comeaux, Army	WR	SR	12	233	2	19.4
3 Cody Cardwell, SMU	WR	SR	27	467	1	17.3
4 DeJuan Groce, Nebraska	DB	SR	43	732	4	17.0
5 Lynaris Elpheage, Tulane	DB	JR	28	463	1	16.5
6 Dexter Wynn, Colorado State	DB	JR	35	567	1	16.2
7 DeAngelo Hall, Virginia Tech	DB	SO	22	352	2	16.0
7 Craig Bragg, UCLA	WR	SO	16	256	1	16.0
9 Damien Dorsey, Louisville	WR	SR	33	508	1	15.4
10 Kendrick Mosley, Western Michigan	WR	SR	29	440	2	15.2

KICKOFF RETURNS	POS	CL	KR	YDS	TD	AVG
1 Charles Pauley, San Jose State	WR	SR	31	978	2	31.6
2 Broderick Clark, Louisville	WR	FR	31	897	2	28.9
3 LaShaun Ward, California	WR	SR	28	809	1	28.9
4 Jason Wright, Northwestern	WR	JR	18	513	1	28.5
5 Nathan Jones, Rutgers	DB	JR	26	736	2	28.3
6 LaTarence Dunbar, TCU	WR	SR	18	501	1	27.8
7 Jerome Dennis, Utah State	DB	SO	14	388	0	27.7
8 Vontez Duff, Notre Dame	DB	JR	19	526	1	27.7
9 Makonnen Fenton, Temple	RB	JR	14	380	1	27.1
10 Derek Abney, Kentucky	**WR**	**JR**	**30**	**804**	**2**	**26.8**
10 DeAndrew Rubin, South Florida	WR	SR	15	402	1	26.8

SCORING	POS	CL	TDS	XP	FG	PTS	PTPG
1 Brock Forsey, Boise State	RB	SR	32	0	0	192	14.8
2 Willis McGahee, Miami (Fla.)	RB	SO	28	0	0	168	12.9
3 Josh Harris, Bowling Green	QB	JR	22	0	0	134	11.2
4 Larry Johnson, Penn State	TB	SR	23	0	0	140	10.8
5 Lee Suggs, Virginia Tech	RB	SR	24	0	0	144	10.3
6 Art Brown, East Carolina	RB	JR	17	0	0	102	10.2
7 Chance Harridge, Air Force	QB	JR	22	0	0	132	10.2
8 Michael Turner, No. Illinois	RB	JR	20	0	0	120	10.0
9 Maurice Clarett, Ohio State	RB	FR	18	0	0	108	9.8
10 Terry Caulley, Connecticut	RB	FR	16	0	0	96	9.6
10 Nick Calaycay, Boise State	K	SR	0	63	11	96	9.6

FIELD GOALS	POS	CL	FGA	FGM	PCT	FGG
1 Nick Browne, TCU	K	JR	30	23	0.77	1.92
2 Billy Bennett, Georgia	**K**	**JR**	**33**	**26**	**0.79**	**1.86**
3 Mike Nugent, Ohio State	K	SO	28	25	0.89	1.79
4 Sandro Sciortino, Boston College	K	JR	32	23	0.72	1.77
5 Nick Novak, Maryland	K	SO	28	24	0.86	1.71
5 Jeff Babcock, Colorado State	K	SO	32	24	0.76	1.71
7 John Anderson, Washington	K	SR	34	22	0.65	1.69
7 Drew Dunning, Washington State	K	JR	33	22	0.67	1.69
9 Mike Barth, Arizona State	K	SR	33	23	0.70	1.64
9 Asen Asparuhov, Fresno State	K	SR	30	23	0.77	1.64

INTERCEPTIONS	POS	CL	INT	YDS	TD	INT/GM
1 Jim Leonhard, Wisconsin	DB	SO	11	115	0	0.79
2 Jason David, Washington State	DB	JR	7	101	0	0.70
3 Gerald Jones, San Jose State	DB	JR	8	116	1	0.67
3 Jason Goss, TCU	DB	SR	8	27	0	0.67
5 Gabe Franklin, Boise State	DB	SO	8	70	0	0.62
5 Lynaris Elpheage, Tulane	DB	JR	8	133	1	0.62
5 Justin Miller, Clemson	DB	FR	8	70	0	0.62
8 Randee Drew, No. Illinois	DB	JR	7	103	0	0.58
9 Vince Thompson, No. Illinois	DB	SR	5	4	0	0.56
10 Bop White, Ohio U.	DB	SR	6	52	0	0.55
10 Bobby Walker, Kansas State	DB	SR	6	177	3	0.55
10 J.R. Reed, South Florida	DB	JR	6	34	1	0.55

Team Leaders

RUSHING OFFENSE	G	ATT	YDS	AVG	TD	YPG
1 Air Force	13	786	4001	5.1	41	307.8
2 West Virginia	13	714	3687	5.2	39	283.6
3 Navy	12	652	3249	5.0	34	270.8
4 Nebraska	14	724	3762	5.2	29	268.7
5 Kansas State	13	655	3433	5.2	53	264.1
6 Rice	11	606	2725	4.5	24	247.7
7 Wake Forest	13	718	3135	4.4	33	241.2
8 Ohio U.	12	649	2878	4.4	30	239.8
9 Colorado	14	652	3259	5.0	28	232.8
10 Penn State	13	526	2972	5.7	36	228.6

PASSING OFFENSE	G	ATT	COM	INT	PCT	YDS	YPA	TD	I%	YPC	YPG
1 Texas Tech	14	770	515	15	66.9	5444	7.1	50	2.0	10.6	388.9
2 Hawaii	14	731	407	26	55.7	5406	7.4	35	3.6	13.3	386.1
3 Marshall	13	575	383	15	66.6	4804	8.4	35	2.6	12.5	369.5
4 Washington	13	621	372	14	59.9	4501	7.3	28	2.3	12.1	346.2
5 San Diego State	13	584	352	10	60.3	4302	7.4	24	1.7	12.2	330.9
6 Central Florida	12	442	270	17	61.1	3837	8.7	31	3.9	14.2	319.8
7 Utah State	11	487	258	16	53.0	3388	7.0	21	3.3	13.1	308.0
8 Southern California	13	494	313	10	63.4	3988	8.1	33	2.0	12.7	306.8
9 Arizona State	14	558	306	16	54.8	4254	7.6	31	2.9	13.9	303.9
10 Louisiana Tech	12	527	305	19	57.9	3633	6.9	19	3.6	11.9	302.8

TOTAL OFFENSE	G	P	YDS	AVG	TD	YPG
1 Boise State	13	950	6519	6.9	79	501.5
2 Hawaii	14	1039	6939	6.7	66	495.6
3 Marshall	13	991	6439	6.5	59	495.3
4 Texas Tech	14	1155	6835	5.9	71	488.2
5 Toledo	14	1033	6611	6.4	66	472.2
6 Miami (Fla.)	13	887	6056	6.8	70	465.9
7 Purdue	13	1034	5879	5.7	51	452.2
8 Southern California	13	1009	5840	5.8	60	449.2
9 Bowling Green	12	898	5387	6.0	65	448.9
10 Illinois	12	915	5356	5.9	43	446.3

RUSHING DEFENSE	G	ATT	YDS	AVG	TD	YPG
1 TCU	12	393	778	2.0	9	64.8
2 Kansas State	13	446	904	2.0	7	69.5
3 Ohio State	14	418	1088	2.6	5	77.7
4 Alabama	**13**	**390**	**1042**	**2.7**	**10**	**80.2**
5 Iowa	13	416	1065	2.6	17	81.9
6 Southern California	13	388	1081	2.8	9	83.2
7 South Florida	11	420	959	2.3	8	87.2
8 Washington State	13	453	1134	2.5	11	87.2
9 Oregon State	13	479	1225	2.6	13	94.2
10 Notre Dame	13	439	1238	2.8	11	95.2

PASSING DEFENSE	G	ATT	COM	PCT	INT	I%	YDS	YPA	TD	TD%	RAT
1 Miami (Fla.)	13	353	163	46.2	12	3.4	1556	4.4	8	2.3	83.9
2 TCU	12	406	158	38.9	22	5.4	2105	5.2	16	3.9	84.6
3 Kansas State	13	418	191	45.7	20	4.8	2333	5.6	11	2.6	91.7
4 Southern Miss	13	379	177	46.7	16	4.2	2195	5.8	6	1.6	92.1
5 LSU	**13**	**361**	**163**	**45.2**	**17**	**4.7**	**1985**	**5.5**	**13**	**3.6**	**93.9**
6 Oregon State	13	456	222	48.7	20	4.4	2591	5.7	10	2.2	94.9
7 Texas	13	400	192	48.0	22	5.5	2147	5.4	17	4.3	96.1
8 Marshall	13	366	175	47.8	15	4.1	2099	5.7	10	2.7	96.8
9 Oklahoma	14	432	206	47.7	24	5.6	2594	6.0	13	3.0	97.0
10 Notre Dame	13	452	223	49.3	21	4.7	2662	5.9	12	2.7	98.2

TOTAL DEFENSE	G	P	YDS	AVG	TD	YPG
1 TCU	12	799	2883	3.6	27	240.3
2 Kansas State	13	864	3237	3.8	19	249.0
3 Alabama	13	764	3345	4.4	24	257.3
4 Troy State	12	784	3322	4.2	31	276.8
5 Tennessee	**13**	**840**	**3703**	**4.4**	**24**	**284.9**
6 Southern California	13	842	3704	4.4	27	284.9
7 Miami (Fla.)	13	935	3705	4.0	31	285.0
8 LSU	**13**	**825**	**3728**	**4.5**	**30**	**286.8**
9 North Texas	13	870	3778	4.3	23	290.6
10 Oklahoma	14	928	4104	4.4	27	293.1

SCORING OFFENSE	G	PTS	AVG
1 Boise State	13	593	45.6
2 Kansas State	13	582	44.8
3 Bowling Green	12	490	40.8
4 Miami (Fla.)	13	527	40.5
5 Oklahoma	14	541	38.6
6 Texas Tech	14	537	38.4
7 Iowa	13	484	37.2
8 Hawaii	14	502	35.9
9 Southern California	13	465	35.8
10 California	12	427	35.6

SCORING DEFENSE	G	PTS	AVG
1 Kansas State	13	154	11.8
2 Ohio State	14	183	13.1
3 North Texas	13	192	14.8
4 Georgia	**14**	**212**	**15.1**
5 Alabama	**13**	**200**	**15.4**
6 Oklahoma	14	216	15.4
7 Maryland	14	228	16.3
8 Texas	13	212	16.3
9 Notre Dame	13	217	16.7
10 North Carolina St.	14	238	17.0

TURNOVER MARGIN	G	FR	INT	TOT	FL	INTL	TOT	MAR
1 South Florida	11	14	22	36	10	5	15	1.9
2 Tulane	13	21	22	43	11	10	21	1.7
3 California	12	21	15	36	8	10	18	1.5
4 West Virginia	13	15	19	34	6	9	15	1.5
5 Southern California	13	19	17	36	8	10	18	1.4
5 Wake Forest	13	21	13	34	10	6	16	1.4
7 Oklahoma	14	12	24	36	6	11	17	1.4
8 Texas	13	13	22	35	6	12	18	1.3
9 Wisconsin	14	13	22	35	9	8	17	1.3
10 TCU	12	20	22	42	14	13	27	1.3

2002

FINAL POLL (JAN. 4)

ESPN	AP	SCHOOL	FINAL RECORD
1	1	Ohio State	14-0
2	2	Miami (Fla.)	12-1
3	3	Georgia	13-1
4	4	Southern California	11-2
5	5	Oklahoma	12-2
7	6	Texas	11-2
6	7	Kansas State	11-2
8	8	Iowa	11-2
9	9	Michigan	10-3
10	10	Washington State	10-3
PB	11	Alabama	10-3
11	12	North Carolina St.	11-3
13	13	Maryland	11-3
16	14	Auburn	9-4
12	15	Boise State	12-1
15	16	Penn State	9-4
17	17	Notre Dame	10-3
14	18	Virginia Tech	10-4
18	19	Pittsburgh	9-4
21	20	Colorado	9-5
23	21	Florida State	9-5
25	22	Virginia	9-5
22	23	TCU	10-2
19	24	Marshall	11-2
20	25	West Virginia	9-4
24		Florida	8-4

PB: Team on probation

CONSENSUS ALL-AMERICANS

POS	OFFENSE	CL	SCHOOL
QB	Carson Palmer	Sr.	Southern California
RB	Larry Johnson	Sr.	Penn State
RB	Willis McGahee	So.	Miami (Fla.)
WR	Charles Rogers	Jr.	Michigan State
WR	Reggie Williams	So.	Washington
WR	Rashaun Woods	Jr.	Oklahoma State
TE	Dallas Clark	Jr.	Iowa
OL	Shawn Andrews	So.	Arkansas
OL	Eric Steinbach	Sr.	Iowa
OL	Derrick Dockery	Sr.	Texas
OL	Jordan Gross	Sr.	Utah
C	Brett Romberg	Sr.	Miami (Fla.)
PK	Mike Nugent	So.	Ohio State
AP	Derek Abney	Jr.	Kentucky

OTHERS RECEIVING FIRST-TEAM HONORS

QB	Ken Dorsey		Miami (Fla.)
QB	Brad Banks		Iowa
RB	Chris Brown		Colorado
WR	Nate Burleson		Nevada
OL	Bruce Nelson		Iowa
OL	Jon Stinchcomb		Georgia
OL	Brett Williams		Florida State
OL	Wayne Lucier		Colorado
OL	Jeff Faine		Notre Dame
OL	Derrick Roche		Washington State
PK	Nate Kaeding		Iowa
AP	DeJuan Groce		Nebraska

POS	DEFENSE	CL	SCHOOL
DL	Terrell Suggs	Jr.	Arizona State
DL	David Pollack	So.	Georgia
DL	Rien Long	Jr.	Washington State
DL	Tommie Harris	So.	Oklahoma
LB	E.J. Henderson	Sr.	Maryland
LB	Teddy Lehman	Jr.	Oklahoma
LB	Matt Wilhelm	Sr.	Ohio State
DB	Mike Doss	Sr.	Ohio State
DB	Terence Newman	Sr.	Kansas State
DB	Shane Walton	Sr.	Notre Dame
DB	Troy Polamalu	Sr.	Southern California
P	Mark Mariscal	Sr.	Colorado

OTHERS RECEIVING FIRST-TEAM HONORS

DL	Michael Haynes		Penn State
DL	Jimmy Kennedy		Penn State
DL	Cory Redding		Texas
DL	Jerome McDougle		Miami (Fla.)
DL	Calvin Pace		Wake Forest
LB	Boss Bailey		Georgia
LB	Bradie James		LSU
DB	Terrence Holt		North Carolina St.
DB	Brandon Everage		Oklahoma
P	Andy Groom		Ohio State

HEISMAN TROPHY VOTING

	PLAYER	POS	SCHOOL	TOTAL
1	Carson Palmer	QB	Southern Cal	1328
2	Brad Banks	QB	Iowa	1095
3	Larry Johnson	RB	Penn	726
4	Willis McGahee	RB	Miami (Fla.)	660
5	Ken Dorsey	QB	Miami (Fla.)	643
6	Byron Leftwich	QB	Marshall	152
7	Jason Gesser	QB	Washington State	74
8	Chris Brown	RB	Colorado	48
9	Kliff Klingsbury	QB	Texas Tech	33
10	Quentin Griffin	RB	Oklahoma	28

AWARD WINNERS

PLAYER	AWARD
Larry Johnson, RB, Penn State	Maxwell
Rien Long, DT, Washington State	Outland
Larry Johnson, RB, Penn State	Camp
Terrell Suggs, DE, Arizona State	Lombardi
Brad Banks, QB, Iowa	O'Brien
E.J. Henderson, LB, Maryland	Butkus
Terence Newman, DB, Kansas State	Thorpe
Carson Palmer, QB, Southern California	Unitas
Larry Johnson, RB, Penn State	Walker
Nate Kaeding, K, Iowa	Groza
Terrell Suggs, DE, Arizona State	Nagurski
E.J. Henderson, LB, Maryland	Bednarik
Charles Rogers, WR, Michigan State	Biletnikoff
Glenn Pakulak, P, Kentucky	Tatupu
Mark Mariscal, P, Colorado	Guy
Dallas Clark, TE, Iowa	Mackey
Brett Romberg, C, Miami (Fla.)	Rimington
Terrell Suggs, DE, Arizona State	Hendricks

BOWL GAMES

DATE	GAME	SCORE
D17	New Orleans	North Texas 24 Cincinnati 19
D18	GMAC	Marshall 38, Louisville 15
D23	Tangerine	Texas Tech 55, Clemson 15
D25	Las Vegas	UCLA 27, New Mexico 13
D25	Hawaii	Tulane 36, Hawaii 28
D26	Motor City	Boston College 51, Toledo 25
D26	Insight	Pittsburgh 38, Oregon State 13
D27	Houston	Oklahoma St. 33, Southern Miss 23
D27	Independence	Mississippi 27, Nebraska 23
D27	Holiday	Kansas State 34, Arizona State 27
D28	Continental Tire	Virginia 48, West Virginia 22
D28	Alamo	Wisconsin 31, Colorado 28 OT
D30	Music City	Minnesota 29, Arkansas 14
D30	Seattle	Wake Forest 38, Oregon 17
D31	Humanitarian	Boise State 34, Iowa State 16
D31	Sun	Purdue 34, Washington 24
D31	Liberty	TCU 17, Colorado State 3
D31	Silicon Valley Classic	Fresno St. 30, Georgia Tech 21
D31	Peach	Maryland 30, Tennessee 3
D31	San Francisco	Virginia Tech 20, Air Force 13
J1	Outback	Michigan 38, Florida 30
J1	Cotton	Texas 35, LSU 20
J1	Gator	North Carolina St. 28, Notre Dame 6
J1	Capital One	Auburn 13, Penn State 9
J1	Rose	Oklahoma 34, Washington State 14
J1	Sugar	Georgia 26, Florida State 13
J2	Orange	Southern California 38, Iowa 17
J3	Fiesta	Ohio State 31, Miami (Fla.) 24 2OT

SEC STANDINGS

	CONFERENCE			OVERALL		
	W	L	T	W	L	T
EAST						
Georgia	7	1	0	13	1	0
Florida	6	2	0	8	5	0
Tennessee	5	3	0	8	5	0
Kentucky	3	5	0	7	5	0
South Carolina	3	5	0	5	7	0
Vanderbilt	0	8	0	2	10	0
WEST						
Alabama*	6	2	0	10	3	0
Arkansas	5	3	0	9	5	0
Auburn	5	3	0	9	4	0
LSU	5	3	0	8	5	0
Mississippi	3	5	0	7	6	0
Mississippi State	0	8	0	3	9	0

* Not eligible for conference title

ALL-SEC TEAM

POS	OFFENSE	SCHOOL
QB	Davd Greene	Georgia
RB	Artose Pinner	Kentucky
RB	Fred Talley	Arkansas
WR	Taylor Jacobs	Florida
WR	Terrence Edwards	Georgia
C	Ben Nowland	Auburn
OL	Shawn Andrews	Arkansas
OL	Jon Stinchcomb	Georgia
OL	Antonio Hall	Kentucky
OL	Stephen Peterman	LSU
OL	Marico Portis	Alabama
OL	Wesley Britt	Alabama
TE	Jason Witten	Tennessee
K	Billy Bennett	Georgia
RS	Derek Abney	Kentucky

POS	DEFENSE	SCHOOL
L	David Pollack	Georgia
L	Kindal Moorehead	Alabama
L	Kenny King	Alabama
LB	Boss Bailey	Georgia
LB	Karlos Dansby	Auburn
LB	Bradie James	LSU
LB	Eddie Strong	Mississippi
LB	Hunter Hillenmeyer	Vanderbilt
DB	Ken Hamlin	Arkansas
DB	Corey Webster	LSU
DB	Travaris Robinson	Auburn
DB	Matt Grier	Mississippi
DB	Julian Battle	Tennessee
DB	Rashad Baker	Tennessee
P	Glenn Pakulak	Kentucky

SEC CHAMPIONSHIP GAME

DECEMBER 2 | ATLANTA

GEORGIA 30, ARKANSAS 3

	1ST	2ND	3RD	4TH	FINAL
ARK	0	0	3	0	3
UGA	17	6	0	7	30

SCORING SUMMARY

UGA	Smith 2 run (Bennett kick)
UGA	Smith 17 run (Bennett kick)
UGA	FG Bennett 29
UGA	FG Bennett 42
UGA	FG Bennett 39
ARK	FG Carlton 27
UGA	Watson 20 pass from Greene (Bennett kick)

ARKANSAS	TEAM STATISTICS	GEORGIA
12	First Downs	25
65	Rushing Yards	124
10-21-0	Passing	19-33-0
74	Passing Yards	257
139	Total Yards	381
1-10	Punt Returns - Yards	6-36
5-98	Kickoff Returns - Yards	2-46
9-33.2	Punts - Average	3-45.7
0-0	Fumbles - Lost	0-0
10-95	Penalties - Yards	12-115

INDIVIDUAL LEADERS

RUSHING
ARK: Talley 17-51.
UGA: Smith 19-106, 2 TD.

PASSING
ARK: Jones 9-17-0, 60 yards.
UGA: Greene 17-29-0, 237 yards, TD.

RECEIVING
ARK: Smith 5-36; Birmingham 2-12.
UGA: Edwards 7-92, Gibson 5-93.

2003 NCAA Major College Statistical Leaders

Individual Leaders

PASSING	POS	CL	G	ATT	COM	PCT	INT	I%	YDS	YPA	TD	TD%	RATING
1 Philip Rivers, North Carolina St.	QB	SR	13	483	348	72.1	7	1.5	4491	9.3	34	7.0	170.5
2 Ben Roethlisberger, Miami (Ohio)	QB	JR	14	495	342	69.1	10	2.0	4486	9.1	37	7.5	165.8
3 Matt Leinart, Southern California	QB	SO	13	402	255	63.4	9	2.2	3556	8.9	38	9.5	164.5
4 Ryan Dinwiddie, Boise State	QB	SR	14	446	276	61.9	7	1.6	4356	9.8	31	7.0	163.7
5 Asad Abdul-Khaliq, Minnesota	QB	SR	13	250	158	63.2	5	2.0	2401	9.6	17	6.8	162.3
6 Bruce Gradkowski, Toledo	QB	SO	12	389	277	71.2	7	1.8	3210	8.3	29	7.5	161.5
7 Jason White, Oklahoma	QB	SR	14	451	278	61.6	10	2.2	3846	8.5	40	8.9	158.1
8 Rod Rutherford, Pittsburgh	QB	SR	13	413	247	59.8	14	3.4	3679	8.9	37	9.0	157.4
9 Bill Whittemore, Kansas	QB	SR	10	263	159	60.5	6	2.3	2385	9.1	18	6.8	154.7
10 Kevin Kolb, Houston	QB	FR	13	360	220	61.1	6	1.7	3131	8.7	25	6.9	153.8

ALL-PURPOSE	POS	CL	G	RUSH	REC	PR	KR	YDS	YPG
1 DeAngelo Williams, Memphis	RB	SO	11	1430	384	0	299	2113	192.1
2 Darren Sproles, Kansas State	RB	JR	15	1986	287	190	272	2735	182.3
3 Jerry Seymour, Central Michigan	RB	FR	9	1117	103	0	330	1550	172.2
4 Howard Jackson, Texas-El Paso	RB	JR	13	1146	391	0	609	2146	165.1
5 Michael Turner, Northern Ilinois	RB	SR	12	1648	230	0	58	1936	161.3
6 Patrick Cobbs, North Texas	RB	JR	11	1680	43	8	40	1771	161.0
7 Lance Moore, Toledo	WR	JR	12	26	1194	219	456	1895	157.9
8 Chris Perry, Michigan	RB	SR	13	1674	367	0	0	2041	157.0
9 Steven Jackson, Oregon State	RB	JR	13	1545	470	0	0	2015	155.0
10 Anthony Sherrell, Eastern Michigan	RB	JR	12	1531	304	0	0	1835	152.9

RUSHING/Yards Per Game	POS	CL	G	ATT	YDS	TD	AVG	YPG
1 Patrick Cobbs, North Texas	RB	JR	11	307	1680	19	5.5	152.7
2 Michael Turner, Northern Illinois	RB	SR	12	310	1648	14	5.3	137.3
3 Darren Sproles, Kansas State	RB	JR	15	306	1986	16	6.5	132.4
4 Derrick Knight, Boston College	RB	SR	13	321	1721	11	5.4	132.4
5 DeAngelo Williams, Memphis	RB	SO	11	243	1430	10	5.9	130.0
6 Chris Perry, Michigan	RB	SR	13	338	1674	18	5.0	128.8
7 Anthony Sherrell, Eastern Michigan	RB	JR	12	338	1531	12	4.5	127.6
8 Kevin Jones, Virginia Tech	RB	JR	13	281	1647	21	5.9	126.7
9 Jerry Seymour, Central Michigan	RB	FR	9	205	1117	8	5.5	124.1
10 Steven Jackson, Oregon State	RB	JR	13	350	1545	19	4.4	118.9

RUSHING/Yards Per Carry	POS	CL	G	ATT	YDS	YPC
1 Vince Young, Texas	QB	FR	12	135	998	7.4
2 Thomas Lott, Rice	RB	SO	11	98	714	7.3
3 Laurence Maroney, Minnesota	RB	FR	13	162	1121	6.9
4 Vernand Morency, Oklahoma State	RB	FR	13	135	918	6.8
5 Brad Smith, Missouri	QB	SO	13	212	1406	6.6
6 Ryan Moats, Louisiana Tech	RB	SO	12	199	1300	6.5
7 Justin Vincent, LSU	**RB**	**FR**	**14**	**154**	**1001**	**6.5**
8 Darren Sproles, Kansas State	RB	JR	15	306	1986	6.5
9 Tatum Bell, Oklahoma State	RB	SR	11	213	1286	6.0
10 DeAngelo Williams, Memphis	RB	SO	11	243	1430	5.9

RECEIVING	POS	CL	G	REC	YDS	TD	RPG	YPR	YPG
1 Larry Fitzgerald, Pittsburgh	WR	SO	13	92	1672	22	7.1	18.2	128.6
2 Geoff McArthur, California	WR	JR	13	85	1504	10	6.5	17.7	115.7
3 James Newson, Oregon State	WR	SR	12	81	1306	3	6.8	16.1	108.8
4 Martin Nance, Miami (Ohio)	WR	JR	14	90	1498	11	6.4	16.6	107.0
5 Kerry Wright, Middle Tennessee	WR	JR	12	73	1280	9	6.1	17.5	106.7
6 Jerricho Cotchery, NC State	WR	SR	13	86	1369	10	6.6	15.9	105.3
7 Rashaun Woods, Oklahoma State	WR	SR	13	77	1367	15	5.9	17.8	105.2
8 Chad Owens, Hawaii	WR	JR	11	85	1134	9	7.7	13.3	103.1
9 Mark Clayton, Oklahoma	WR	JR	14	83	1425	15	5.9	17.2	101.8
10 Mike Williams, Southern Cal	WR	SO	13	95	1314	16	7.3	13.8	101.1

PUNTING	POS	CL	PUNT	YDS	AVG
1 Matt Prater, Central Florida	K	SO	58	2781	48.0
2 Brandon Fields, Michigan State	P	SO	62	2878	46.4
3 Joel Stelly, La.-Monroe	K	SO	67	3099	46.3
4 Jared Scruggs, Rice	P	FR	51	2341	45.9
5 Ryan Plackemeier, Wake Forest	K	SO	57	2600	45.6
6 Dustin Colquitt, Tennessee	P	JR	68	3081	45.3
7 Kyle Larson, Nebraska	P	SR	66	2978	45.1
8 Eric Wilbur, Florida	**P**	**FR**	**66**	**2954**	**44.8**
9 Ryan Dougherty, East Carolina	P	FR	64	2846	44.5
10 Steve Weatherford, Illinois	P	SO	46	2045	44.5

PUNT RETURNS	POS	CL	PR	YDS	TD	AVG
1 Skyler Green, LSU	**WR**	**SO**	**25**	**462**	**2**	**18.5**
2 Ryne Robinson, Miami (Ohio)	WR	FR	38	654	3	17.2
3 Mark Jones, Tennessee	**WR**	**SR**	**20**	**303**	**1**	**15.2**
4 Gabe Lindsay, Oklahoma State	WR	SR	26	393	1	15.1
5 DeAngelo Hall, Virginia Tech	DB	JR	33	487	3	14.8
6 Marcus James, Missouri	WR	SR	26	377	0	14.5
7 Marion Barber III, Minnesota	RB	SO	28	405	0	14.5
8 Jim Leonhard, Wisconsin	DB	JR	34	470	2	13.8
9 Steve Breaston, Michigan	WR	SO	45	619	2	13.8
10 Marvin Young, Southern Miss	WR	JR	33	450	1	13.6

KICKOFF RETURNS	POS	CL	KR	YDS	TD	AVG
1 Michael Waddell, North Carolina	CB	SR	15	475	1	31.7
1 J.R. Reed, South Florida	DB	SR	18	570	1	31.7
3 Mike Imoh, Virginia Tech	RB	SO	18	549	1	30.5
4 John Eubanks, Southern Miss	DB	SO	17	499	1	29.4
5 Dexter Wynn, Colorado State	DB	SR	27	782	0	29.0
6 Devin Hester, Miami (Fla.)	WR	FR	18	517	1	28.7
7 Senterrio Landrum, Duke	WR	JR	25	709	0	28.4
8 Kendrick Starling, San Jose State	WR	SR	20	562	0	28.1
9 Charles Estes, La.-Monroe	WR	JR	36	988	1	27.4
10 Reggie Bush, Southern California	RB	FR	18	492	1	27.3

SCORING	POS	CL	TDS	XP	FG	PTS	PTPG
1 Patrick Cobbs, North Texas	RB	JR	21	0	0	126	11.5
2 Cedric Benson, Texas	RB	JR	22	0	0	134	11.2
3 Walter Reyes, Syracuse	RB	JR	21	0	0	128	10.7
4 Larry Fitzgerald, Pittsburgh	WR	SO	22	0	0	132	10.2
4 Steven Jackson, Oregon State	RB	JR	22	0	0	132	10.2
6 Jason Wright, Northwestern	RB	SR	21	0	0	126	9.7
6 Kevin Jones, Virginia Tech	RB	JR	21	0	0	126	9.7
6 DonTrell Moore, New Mexico	RB	SO	21	0	0	126	9.7
9 Nick Browne, TCU	K	SR	0	38	28	124	9.5
9 Jonathan Nichols, Mississippi	**K**	**JR**	**0**	**49**	**25**	**124**	**9.5**

FIELD GOALS	POS	CL	FGA	FGM	PCT	FGG
1 Billy Bennett, Georgia	**K**	**SR**	**38**	**31**	**0.82**	**2.21**
2 Nick Browne, TCU	K	SR	33	28	0.85	2.15
3 Drew Dunning, Washington State	K	SR	31	27	0.87	2.08
4 Ben Jones, Purdue	K	SO	30	25	0.83	1.92
4 Jonathan Nichols, Mississippi	**K**	**JR**	**29**	**25**	**0.86**	**1.92**
6 Nick Novak, Maryland	K	JR	32	24	0.75	1.85
7 Connor Hughes, Virginia	OL	SO	25	23	0.92	1.77
8 Steve Azar, Northern Illinois	K	SR	26	21	0.81	1.75
8 Josh Scobee, Louisiana Tech	K	SR	31	21	0.68	1.75
10 Jon Peattie, Miami (Fla.)	P	FR	28	22	0.79	1.69
10 David Rayner, Michigan State	K	JR	29	22	0.76	1.69

INTERCEPTIONS	POS	CL	INT	YDS	TD	INT/GM
1 Sean Taylor, Miami (Fla.)	DB	JR	10	184	3	0.83
2 Josh Bullocks, Nebraska	DB	SO	10	154	0	0.77
3 Jonathan Burke, Arkansas State	DB	SR	9	120	0	0.75
3 Derrick Ansley, Troy State	DB	JR	9	74	1	0.75
5 Keiwan Ratliff, Florida	**DB**	**SR**	**9**	**182**	**2**	**0.69**
6 J.R. Reed, South Florida	DB	SR	7	45	0	0.64
7 Gerald Jones, San Jose State	DB	SR	6	178	2	0.55
8 Jim Leonhard, Wisconsin	DB	JR	7	98	0	0.54
8 Will Poole, Southern California	DB	SO	7	70	1	0.54
8 Erik Coleman, Washington State	DB	SR	7	22	0	0.54

Team Leaders

RUSHING OFFENSE	G	ATT	YDS	AVG	TD	YPG
1 Navy	13	760	4202	5.5	44	323.2
2 Rice	12	687	3800	5.5	35	316.7
3 Minnesota	13	683	3759	5.5	46	289.2
4 Air Force	12	716	3367	4.7	31	280.6
5 Arkansas	**13**	**626**	**3145**	**5.0**	**34**	**241.9**
6 Missouri	13	551	3087	5.6	38	237.5
7 Nebraska	13	716	3063	4.3	28	235.6
8 Texas	13	587	3023	5.2	41	232.5
9 Kansas State	15	688	3429	5.0	42	228.6
10 Louisville	13	518	2966	5.7	35	228.2

PASSING OFFENSE	G	ATT	COM	INT	PCT	YDS	YPA	TD	I%	YPC	YPG
1 Texas Tech	13	780	506	23	64.9	6179	7.9	53	3.0	12.2	475.3
2 Hawaii	14	754	444	27	58.9	5382	7.1	42	3.6	12.1	384.4
3 North Carolina St.	13	496	357	7	72.0	4580	9.2	35	1.4	12.8	352.3
4 Miami (Ohio)	14	535	363	11	67.9	4772	8.9	38	2.1	13.2	340.9
5 Boise State	14	489	295	9	60.3	4708	9.6	33	1.8	16.0	336.3
6 Oregon State	13	534	274	25	51.3	4265	8.0	25	4.7	15.6	328.1
7 Akron	12	449	287	10	63.9	3736	8.3	22	2.2	13.0	311.3
8 Western Michigan	12	450	272	20	60.4	3701	8.2	31	4.4	13.6	308.4
9 Bowling Green	14	528	345	13	65.3	4206	8.0	32	2.5	12.2	300.4
10 Connecticut	12	483	283	14	58.6	3575	7.4	33	2.9	12.6	297.9

TOTAL OFFENSE	G	P	YDS	AVG	TD	YPG
1 Texas Tech	13	1088	7576	7.0	76	582.8
2 Miami (Ohio)	14	1053	7016	6.7	82	501.1
3 Bowling Green	14	1111	6954	6.3	61	496.7
4 Minnesota	13	970	6430	6.6	66	494.6
5 Louisville	13	913	6355	7.0	58	488.9
6 Hawaii	14	1072	6834	6.4	63	488.1
7 Boise State	14	1061	6809	6.4	77	486.4
8 Connecticut	12	946	5730	6.1	54	477.5
9 Akron	12	923	5643	6.1	55	470.3
10 Oregon State	13	1060	6019	5.7	53	463.0

RUSHING DEFENSE	G	ATT	YDS	AVG	TD	YPG
1 Southern California	13	425	782	1.8	9	60.2
2 Ohio State	13	415	810	2.0	12	62.3
3 LSU	**14**	**400**	**938**	**2.4**	**5**	**67.0**
4 Oregon State	13	447	1097	2.5	11	84.4
5 New Mexico	13	428	1119	2.6	11	86.1
6 Washington State	13	441	1181	2.7	8	90.8
7 Auburn	**13**	**440**	**1204**	**2.7**	**8**	**92.6**
8 Iowa	13	480	1205	2.5	10	92.7
9 TCU	13	443	1218	2.8	13	93.7
10 Purdue	13	467	1260	2.7	9	96.9

PASSING DEFENSE	G	ATT	COM	PCT	INT	I%	YDS	YPA	TD	TD%	RAT
1 Nebraska	13	430	218	50.7	32	7.4	2312	5.38	10	2.3	88.7
2 LSU	**14**	**477**	**213**	**44.7**	**21**	**4.4**	**2590**	**5.43**	**12**	**2.5**	**89.8**
3 Oklahoma	14	419	218	52.0	22	5.3	2050	4.89	11	2.6	91.3
4 Miami (Fla.)	13	328	167	50.9	19	5.8	1866	5.69	9	2.7	96.2
5 Washington State	13	547	263	48.1	24	4.4	2960	5.41	19	3.5	96.2
6 Oregon State	13	467	206	44.1	20	4.3	2656	5.69	22	4.7	98.9
7 Boise State	14	614	302	49.2	21	3.4	3470	5.65	17	2.8	99.0
8 South Florida	11	352	173	49.2	13	3.7	1979	5.62	14	4.0	102.1
9 Michigan	13	411	221	53.8	14	3.4	2347	5.71	9	2.2	102.2
10 San Diego State	12	345	176	51.0	12	3.5	1923	5.57	12	3.5	102.3

TOTAL DEFENSE	G	P	YDS	AVG	TD	YPG
1 LSU	**14**	**877**	**3528**	**4.0**	**19**	**252.0**
2 Miami (Fla.)	13	786	3348	4.3	23	257.5
3 Oklahoma	14	881	3635	4.1	27	259.6
4 Georgia	**14**	**880**	**3876**	**4.4**	**23**	**276.9**
5 Auburn	**13**	**802**	**3661**	**4.6**	**25**	**281.6**
6 Kansas State	15	996	4246	4.3	31	283.1
7 Oregon State	13	914	3753	4.1	38	288.7
8 San Diego State	12	813	3477	4.3	22	289.8
9 Memphis	13	879	3845	4.4	32	295.8
10 Ohio State	13	930	3859	4.2	28	296.9

SCORING OFFENSE	G	PTS	AVG
1 Boise State	14	602	43.0
1 Miami (Ohio)	14	602	43.0
3 Oklahoma	14	601	42.9
4 Texas Tech	13	552	42.5
5 Southern California	13	534	41.1
6 Texas	13	533	41.0
7 Minnesota	13	503	38.7
8 North Carolina St.	13	489	37.6
9 Kansas State	15	549	36.6
10 Akron	12	435	36.3

SCORING DEFENSE	G	PTS	AVG
1 LSU	**14**	**154**	**11.0**
2 Nebraska	13	188	14.5
3 Georgia	**14**	**203**	**14.5**
4 Miami (Fla.)	13	196	15.1
5 Oklahoma	14	214	15.3
6 Maryland	13	206	15.8
7 Iowa	13	210	16.2
8 Kansas State	15	244	16.3
9 Auburn	**13**	**212**	**16.3**
10 Florida State	13	217	16.7

TURNOVER MARGIN	G	FR	INT	TOT	FL	INTL	TOT	MAR
1 Nebraska	13	15	32	47	14	10	24	1.8
2 Southern California	13	20	22	42	13	9	22	1.5
3 Miami (Ohio)	14	18	21	39	8	11	19	1.4
4 West Virginia	13	15	21	36	12	8	20	1.2
5 Oklahoma	14	12	22	34	6	11	17	1.2
6 Northern Illinois	12	8	23	31	7	10	17	1.2
7 UNLV	12	19	16	35	12	11	23	1.0
8 Purdue	13	14	14	28	9	7	16	0.9
9 Toledo	12	10	15	25	6	8	14	0.9
10 Arkansas	**13**	**16**	**17**	**33**	**13**	**9**	**22**	**0.9**
10 Missouri	13	15	9	24	5	8	13	0.9
10 North Texas	13	15	18	33	13	9	22	0.9
10 Michigan State	13	14	15	29	3	15	18	0.9

2003

FINAL POLL (JAN. 5)

ESPN	AP	SCHOOL	FINAL RECORD
2	1	Southern California	12-1
1	2	LSU	13-1
3	3	Oklahoma	12-2
4	4	Ohio State	11-2
5	5	Miami (Fla.)	11-2
7	6	Michigan	10-3
6	7	Georgia	11-3
8	8	Iowa	10-3
9	9	Washington State	10-3
12	10	Miami (Ohio)	13-1
10	11	Florida State	10-3
11	12	Texas	10-3
14	13	Mississippi	10-3
13	14	Kansas State	11-4
16	15	Tennessee	10-3
15	16	Boise State	13-1
20	17	Maryland	10-3
19	18	Purdue	9-4
18	19	Nebraska	10-3
17	20	Minnesota	10-3
21	21	Utah	10-2
22	22	Clemson	9-4
23	23	Bowling Green	11-3
25	24	Florida	8-5
24	25	TCU	11-2

CONSENSUS ALL-AMERICANS

POS	OFFENSE	CL	SCHOOL
QB	Jason White	Jr.	Oklahoma
RB	Chris Perry	Jr.	Michigan
RB	Kevin Jones	Sr.	Virginia Tech
WR	Larry Fitzgerald	So.	Pittsburgh
WR	Mike Williams	So.	Southern California
TE	Kellen Winslow	Jr.	Miami (Fla.)
OL	**Shawn Andrews**	**Jr.**	**Arkansas**
OL	Robert Gallery	Sr.	Iowa
OL	Jacob Rogers	Sr.	Southern California
OL	Alex Barron	Jr.	Florida State
C	Jake Grove	Sr.	Virginia Tech
PK	Nate Kaeding	Sr.	Iowa
PK	Nick Browne	Sr.	TCU
AP	Antonio Perkins	Jr.	Oklahoma

OTHERS RECEIVING FIRST-TEAM HONORS

RB	Darren Sproles		Kansas State
WR	Rashaun Woods		Oklahoma State
WR	Mark Clayton		Oklahoma
OL	Jammal Brown		Oklahoma
OL	**Stephen Peterman**		**LSU**
OL	**Shannon Snell**		**Florida**
PK	Drew Dunning		Washington State

POS	DEFENSE	CL	SCHOOL
DL	Dave Ball	Sr.	UCLA
DL	Tommie Harris	Jr.	Oklahoma
DL	**Chad Lavalais**	**Sr.**	**LSU**
DL	Kenechi Udeze	Jr.	Southern California
LB	Teddy Lehman	Sr.	Oklahoma
LB	Derrick Johnson	Jr.	Texas
LB	Grant Wiley	Sr.	West Virginia
DB	Derrick Strait	Sr.	Oklahoma
DB	Sean Taylor	Jr.	Miami (Fla.)
DB	**Keiwan Ratliff**	**Sr.**	**Florida**
DB	Will Allen	Sr.	Ohio State
P	**Dustin Colquitt**	**Jr.**	**Tennessee**

OTHERS RECEIVING FIRST-TEAM HONORS

DL	**David Pollack**		**Georgia**
DL	Will Smith		Ohio State
LB	Jonathan Vilma		Miami (Fla.)
LB	**Karlos Dansby**		**Auburn**
LB	Josh Buhl		Kansas State
DB	**Corey Webster**		**LSU**
DB	**Sean Jones**		**Georgia**
DB	Josh Bullocks		Nebraska
P	Kyle Larson		Nebraska

HEISMAN TROPHY VOTING

	PLAYER	POS	SCHOOL	TOTAL
1	Jason White	QB	Oklahoma	1481
2	Larry Fitzgerald	WR	Pittsburgh	1353
3	**Eli Manning**	**QB**	**Mississippi**	**710**
4	Chris Perry	RB	Michigan	341
5	Darren Sproles	RB	Kansas State	134
6	Matt Leinart	QB	Southern Cal	127
7	Philip Rivers	QB	NC State	118
8	Mike Williams	WR	Southern Cal	78
9	Ben Roethlisberger	QB	Miami (Ohio)	47
10	B.J. Symons	QB	Texas Tech	38

AWARD WINNERS

PLAYER	AWARD
Eli Manning, QB, Mississippi	**Maxwell**
Robert Gallery, OL, Iowa	Outland
Larry Fitzgerald, WR, Pittsburgh	Camp
Tommie Harris, DT, Oklahoma	Lombardi
Jason White, QB, Oklahoma	O'Brien
Teddy Lehman, LB, Oklahoma	Butkus
Derrick Strait, DB, Oklahoma	Thorpe
Eli Manning, QB, Mississippi	**Unitas**
Chris Perry, RB, Michigan	Walker
Jonathan Nichols, K, Mississippi	**Groza**
Derrick Strait, DB, Oklahoma	Nagurski
Teddy Lehman, LB, Oklahoma	Bednarik
Larry Fitzgerald, WR, Pittsburgh	Biletnikoff
Wes Welker, KR, Texas Tech	Tatupu
B.J. Sander, P, Ohio State	Guy
Kellen Winslow II, TE, Miami (Fla.)	Mackey
Jake Grove, C, Virginia Tech	Rimington
David Pollack, DE, Georgia	**Hendricks**

BOWL GAMES

DATE	GAME	SCORE
D16	New Orleans	Memphis 27, North Texas 17
D18	GMAC	Miami (Ohio) 49, Louisville 28
D22	Tangerine	North Carolina St. 56, Kansas 26
D23	Fort Worth	Boise State 34, TCU 31
D24	Las Vegas	Oregon State 55, New Mexico 14
D25	Hawaii	Hawaii 54, Houston 48, 3 OT
D26	Motor City	Bowling Green 28, Northwestern 24
D26	Insight	California 52, Virginia Tech 49
D27	Continental Tire	Virginia 23, Pittsburgh 16
D29	Alamo	Nebraska 17, Michigan State 3
D30	Houston	Texas Tech 38, Navy 14
D30	Holiday	Washington State 28, Texas 20
D30	Silicon Valley Classic	Fresno State 17, UCLA 9
D31	**Music City**	**Auburn 28, Wisconsin 14**
D31	Sun	Minnesota 31, Oregon 30
D31	Liberty	Utah 17, Southern Miss 0
D31	**Independence**	**Arkansas 27, Missouri 14**
D31	San Francisco	Boston College 35, Colorado State 21
J1	**Outback**	**Iowa 37, Florida 17**
J1	Gator	Maryland 41, West Virginia 7
J1	**Capital One**	**Georgia 34, Purdue 27 OT**
J1	Rose	Southern California 28, Michigan 14
J1	Orange	Miami 16, Florida State 14
J2	Fiesta	Ohio State 35, Kansas State 28
J2	**Cotton**	**Mississippi 31, Oklahoma State 28**
J2	**Peach**	**Clemson 27, Tennessee 14**
J3	Humanitarian	Georgia Tech 52, Tulsa 10
J4	**Sugar**	**LSU 21, Oklahoma 14**

SEC STANDINGS

	CONFERENCE			OVERALL		
	W	L	T	W	L	T
EAST						
Georgia	6	2	0	11	3	0
Tennessee	6	2	0	10	3	0
Florida	6	2	0	8	5	0
South Carolina	2	6	0	5	7	0
Kentucky	1	7	0	4	8	0
Vanderbilt	1	7	0	2	10	0
WEST						
LSU	7	1	0	13	1	0
Mississippi	7	1	0	10	3	0
Auburn	5	3	0	8	5	0
Arkansas	4	4	0	9	4	0
Alabama	2	6	0	4	9	0
Mississippi State	1	7	0	2	10	0

ALL-SEC TEAM

POS	OFFENSE	SCHOOL
QB	Eli Manning	Mississippi
RB	Carnell Williams	Auburn
RB	Cedric Cobbs	Arkansas
WR	Michael Clayton	LSU
WR	Chris Collins	Mississippi
C	Scott Wells	Tennessee
OL	Shawn Andrews	Arkansas
OL	Max Starks	Florida
OL	Antonio Hall	Kentucky
OL	Wesley Britt	Alabama
TE	Ben Troupe	Florida
K	Jonathan Nichols	Mississippi
RS	Derek Abney	Kentucky

POS	DEFENSE	SCHOOL
L	David Pollack	Georgia
L	Chad Lavalais	LSU
L	Antwan Odom	Alabama
LB	Karlos Dansby	Auburn
LB	Derrick Pope	Alabama
LB	Dontarrious Thomas	Auburn
LB	Odell Thurman	Georgia
DB	Keiwan Ratliff	Florida
DB	Corey Webster	LSU
DB	Ahmad Carroll	Arkansas
DB	Tony Bua	Arkansas
DB	Sean Jones	Georgia
P	Dustin Colquitt	Tennessee

SEC CHAMPIONSHIP GAME

DECEMBER 6 | ATLANTA
LSU 34, GEORGIA 13

	1ST	2ND	3RD	4TH	FINAL
UGA	0	3	10	0	13
LSU	8	9	7	10	34

SCORING SUMMARY
LSU   Vincent 87 run (Jackson kick failed)
LSU   Team safety
LSU   Clayton 43 pass from Mauck (Jackson kick blocked)
LSU   FG Gaudet 35
UGA   FG Bennett 51
UGA   FG Bennett 49
LSU   Turner 18 interception return (Gaudet kick)
UGA   Watson 18 pass from Greene (Bennett kick)
LSU   Vincent 3 run (Gaudet kick)
LSU   FG Gaudet 22

GEORGIA	TEAM STATISTICS	LSU
14	First Downs	17
50	Rushing Yards	293
17-41-3	Passing	14-22-1
199	Passing Yards	151
249	Total Yards	444
3-(-1)	Punt Returns - Yards	3-33
5-59	Kickoff Returns - Yards	3-55
6-38.7	Punts - Average	6-42.7
0-0	Fumbles - Lost	1-0
3-24	Penalties - Yards	5-45

INDIVIDUAL LEADERS
RUSHING
UGA: Lumpkin 7-54.
LSU: Vincent 18-201, 2 TD.
PASSING
UGA: Greene 17-41-3, 199 yards, TD.
LSU: Mauck 14-22-1, 151 yards, TD.
RECEIVING
UGA: Watson 4-86, TD; Gibson 3-19.
LSU: Clayton 5-81, TD; Henderson 4-47.

2004 NCAA Major College Statistical Leaders

Individual Leaders

PASSING	POS	CL	G	ATT	COM	PCT	INT	I%	YDS	YPA	TD	TD%	RATING
1 Stefan Lefors, Louisville	QB	SR	12	257	189	73.5	3	1.2	2596	10.1	20	7.9	181.7
2 Alex Smith, Utah	QB	JR	12	317	214	67.5	4	1.3	2952	9.3	32	10.1	176.5
3 Jason Campbell, Auburn	**QB**	**SR**	**13**	**270**	**188**	**69.6**	**7**	**2.6**	**2700**	**10.0**	**20**	**7.4**	**172.9**
4 Omar Jacobs, Bowling Green	QB	SO	12	462	309	66.9	4	0.9	4002	8.7	41	8.9	167.2
5 Bruce Gradkowski, Toledo	QB	JR	13	399	280	70.2	8	2.0	3518	8.8	27	6.8	162.6
6 Jason White, Oklahoma	QB	SR	13	390	255	65.4	9	2.3	3205	8.2	35	9.0	159.4
7 Matt Leinart, Southern California	QB	JR	13	412	269	65.3	6	1.5	3322	8.1	33	8.0	156.5
8 Aaron Rodgers, California	QB	JR	12	316	209	66.1	8	2.5	2566	8.1	24	7.6	154.3
9 Lester Ricard, Tulane	QB	SO	9	231	143	61.9	9	3.9	1881	8.1	21	9.1	152.5
10 Kyle Orton, Purdue	QB	SR	11	389	236	60.7	5	1.3	3090	7.9	31	8.0	151.1

ALL-PURPOSE	POS	CL	G	RUSH	REC	PR	KR	YDS	YPG
1 Darren Sproles, Kansas State	RB	SR	11	1318	223	34	492	2067	187.9
2 DeAngelo Williams, Memphis	RB	JR	12	1948	210	0	72	2230	185.8
3 Garrett Wolfe, Northern Illinois	RB	SO	11	1656	117	0	231	2004	182.2
4 Jamario Thomas, North Texas	RB	FR	10	1801	14	0	0	1815	181.5
5 Reggie Bush, Southern California	RB	SO	13	908	509	376	537	2330	179.2
6 J.J. Arrington, California	RB	SR	12	2018	121	0	0	2139	178.3
7 Cedric Benson, Texas	RB	SR	12	1834	179	0	0	2013	167.8
8 Andre Hall, South Florida	RB	JR	11	1357	149	0	332	1838	167.1
9 Jerry Seymour, Central Michigan	RB	SO	11	1284	413	0	105	1802	163.8
10 Cory Rodgers, TCU	WR	SO	11	35	836	183	723	1777	161.6

RUSHING/YARDS PER GAME	POS	CL	G	ATT	YDS	TD	AVG	YPG
1 Jamario Thomas, North Texas	RB	FR	10	285	1801	17	6.3	180.1
2 J.J. Arrington, California	RB	SR	12	289	2018	15	7.0	168.2
3 DeAngelo Williams, Memphis	RB	JR	12	313	1948	22	6.2	162.3
4 Cedric Benson, Texas	RB	SR	12	326	1834	19	5.6	152.8
5 Garrett Wolfe, Northern Illinois	RB	SO	11	256	1656	18	6.5	150.6
6 Adrian Peterson, Oklahoma	RB	FR	13	339	1925	15	5.7	148.1
7 Ryan Moats, Louisiana Tech	RB	JR	12	288	1774	18	6.2	147.8
8 Vernand Morency, Oklahoma State	RB	JR	11	258	1474	12	5.7	134.0
9 Andre Hall, South Florida	RB	JR	11	210	1357	11	6.5	123.4
10 Michael Hart, Michigan	RB	FR	12	282	1455	9	5.2	121.3

RUSHING/YARDS PER CARRY	POS	CL	G	ATT	YDS	YPC
1 Drew Stanton, Michigan State	QB	JR	10	96	687	7.2
2 J.J. Arrington, California	RB	SR	12	289	2018	7.0
3 Leon Washington, Florida State	RB	JR	10	138	951	6.9
4 Wendell Mathis, Fresno State	RB	JR	11	146	995	6.8
5 Garrett Wolfe, Northern Illinois	RB	SO	11	256	1656	6.5
5 Andre Hall, South Florida	RB	JR	11	210	1357	6.5
5 Vince Young, Texas	QB	SO	12	167	1079	6.5
8 Eric Shelton, Louisville	RB	JR	12	146	938	6.4
8 Reggie Bush, Southern California	RB	SO	13	143	908	6.4
10 Jamario Thomas, North Texas	RB	FR	10	285	1801	6.3

RECEIVING	POS	CL	G	REC	YDS	TD	RPG	YPG	YPG
1 Dante Ridgeway, Ball State	WR	JR	11	105	1399	8	9.6	13.3	127.2
2 Roddy White, UAB	WR	SR	12	71	1452	14	5.9	20.5	121.0
3 Mike Hass, Oregon State	WR	JR	12	86	1379	7	7.2	16.0	114.9
4 Eric Deslauriers, Eastern Michigan	WR	JR	11	84	1257	13	7.6	15.0	114.3
5 Braylon Edwards, Michigan	WR	SR	12	97	1330	15	8.1	13.7	110.8
6 Greg Lee, Pittsburgh	WR	SO	12	68	1297	10	5.7	19.1	108.1
7 Derek Hagan, Arizona State	WR	JR	12	83	1248	10	6.9	15.0	104.0
8 Greg Jennings, Western Michigan	WR	SR	11	74	1092	11	6.7	14.8	99.3
9 Chad Owens, Hawaii	WR	SR	13	102	1290	17	7.9	12.7	99.2
10 Jarrett Hicks, Texas Tech	WR	SO	12	76	1177	13	6.3	15.5	98.1

PUNTING	POS	CL	PUNT	YDS	AVG
1 Brandon Fields, Michigan State	P	JR	50	2394	47.9
2 John Torp, Colorado	P	JR	72	3351	46.5
3 Daniel Sepulveda, Baylor	P	SO	62	2850	46.0
4 Steve Weatherford, Illinois	P	JR	57	2589	45.4
5 Matt Payne, Brigham Young	K	SR	62	2808	45.3
6 Joel Stelly, La.-Monroe	P	JR	62	2796	45.1
7 Bryce Benekos, Texas-El Paso	P	SR	62	2732	44.1
8 Ryan Plackemeier, Wake Forest	K	JR	64	2809	43.9
9 Tom Malone, Southern California	P	JR	49	2144	43.8
10 Adam Podlesh, Maryland	P	SO	63	2756	43.8

PUNT RETURNS	POS	CL	PR	YDS	TD	AVG
1 Ted Ginn Jr., Ohio State	DB	FR	15	384	4	25.6
2 Kevin Robinson, Utah State	WR	FR	17	382	2	22.5
3 Darrell Blackmon, North Carolina St.	RB	FR	12	214	1	17.8
4 Travis Williams, East Carolina	CB	FR	20	354	1	17.7
5 Domenik Hixon, Akron	WR	JR	16	275	1	17.2
6 Devin Hester, Miami (Fla.)	WR	SO	19	326	3	17.2
7 Dan Sheldon, Northern Illinois	WR	SR	24	394	1	16.4
8 Roscoe Parrish, Miami (Fla.)	WR	JR	20	324	2	16.2
9 Reggie Bush, Southern California	RB	SO	24	376	2	15.7
10 Jahmal Fenner, Texas-El Paso	DB	SR	21	324	1	15.4

KICKOFF RETURNS	POS	CL	KR	YDS	TD	AVG
1 Justin Miller, Clemson	DB	JR	20	661	2	33.1
2 Larry Taylor, Connecticut	RB	FR	12	376	1	31.3
3 Ashlan Davis, Tulsa	WR	JR	37	1131	5	30.6
4 Lance Bennett, Indiana	RB	SO	20	599	1	30.0
5 John Eubanks, Southern Miss	DB	JR	21	618	1	29.4
6 T.J. Rushing, Stanford	DB	JR	23	653	1	28.4
7 Asante White, Central Michigan	WR	FR	12	336	0	28.0
8 Will Blackmon, Boston College	DB	JR	28	762	1	27.2
9 Diamond Ferri, Syracuse	DB	SR	24	653	0	27.2
10 Pierre Thomas, Illinois	RB	SO	25	677	1	27.1

SCORING	POS	CL	TDS	XP	FG	PTS	PTPG
1 Tyler Jones, Boise State	K	SR	0	69	24	141	11.8
2 DeAngelo Williams, Memphis	RB	JR	23	0	0	138	11.5
3 Garrett Wolfe, Northern Illinois	RB	SO	21	0	0	126	11.5
4 P.J. Pope, Bowling Green	RB	JR	21	0	0	126	10.5
5 Jamario Thomas, North Texas	RB	FR	17	0	0	102	10.2
6 Chad Owens, Hawaii	WR	SR	22	0	0	132	10.2
7 Eric Shelton, Louisville	RB	JR	20	0	0	120	10.0
7 Cedric Benson, Texas	RB	SR	20	0	0	120	10.0
9 Ryan Moats, Louisiana Tech	RB	JR	19	0	0	114	9.5
10 Carlton Jones, Army	RB	JR	17	0	0	104	9.5

FIELD GOALS	POS	CL	FGA	FGM	PCT	FGG
1 Mike Nugent, Ohio State	K	SR	27	24	0.89	2.00
1 Tyler Jones, Boise State	K	SR	27	24	0.89	2.00
3 Andrew Wellock, Eastern Michigan	K	SO	23	21	0.91	1.91
4 David Rayner, Michigan State	K	SR	31	22	0.71	1.83
5 Jonathan Nichols, Mississippi	**K**	**SR**	**27**	**20**	**0.74**	**1.82**
6 Mason Crosby, Colorado	K	SO	29	23	0.79	1.77
7 Kyle Schlicher, Iowa	K	SO	26	21	0.81	1.75
8 Stephen Gostkowski, Memphis	K	JR	24	20	0.83	1.67
8 Matt Nuzie, Connecticut	K	JR	28	20	0.71	1.67
10 Brandon Pace, Virginia Tech	K	SO	27	21	0.78	1.62

INTERCEPTIONS	POS	CL	INT	YDS	TD	INT/GM
1 Charles Gordon, Kansas	CB	SO	7	52	0	0.64
1 Chris Harris, La.-Monroe	DB	SR	7	11	0	0.64
3 Ko Simpson, South Carolina	**DB**	**FR**	**6**	**94**	**1**	**0.55**
4 Keon Newson, Bowling Green	DB	SR	6	107	2	0.50
4 Chris Royal, Marshall	DB	JR	6	103	1	0.50
4 Morgan Scalley, Utah	DB	SR	6	79	0	0.50
4 Brandon Payne, New Mexico	DB	SR	6	69	0	0.50
4 Kerry Rhodes, Louisville	DB	SR	6	56	1	0.50
4 Ray Henderson, Boston College	LB	JR	6	52	0	0.50
4 Mitch Meeuwsen, Oregon St.	DB	SR	6	12	0	0.50

Team Leaders

RUSHING OFFENSE	G	ATT	YDS	AVG	TD	YPG
1 Rice	11	688	3372	4.9	30	306.6
2 Texas	12	615	3590	5.8	41	299.2
3 Navy	12	689	3474	5.0	36	289.5
4 Air Force	11	648	3051	4.7	32	277.4
5 Minnesota	12	572	3082	5.4	29	256.8
6 California	12	509	3081	6.1	30	256.8
7 West Virginia	12	590	3034	5.1	23	252.8
8 Louisville	12	534	3005	5.6	47	250.4
9 Virginia	12	550	2914	5.3	34	242.8
10 Michigan State	12	500	2862	5.7	22	238.5

PASSING OFFENSE	G	ATT	COM	INT	PCT	YDS	YPA	TD	I%	YPC	YPG
1 Texas Tech	12	651	426	18	65.4	4796	7.4	34	2.8	11.3	399.7
2 Hawaii	13	636	370	18	58.2	4402	6.9	38	2.8	11.9	338.6
3 Bowling Green	12	472	313	4	66.3	4057	8.6	41	0.9	13.0	338.1
4 Purdue	12	486	297	8	61.1	3854	7.9	38	1.7	13.0	321.1
5 Arizona State	12	502	289	10	57.6	3808	7.6	35	2.0	13.2	317.3
6 Rutgers	11	473	303	20	64.1	3416	7.2	19	4.2	11.3	310.5
7 Oregon State	12	532	287	17	54.0	3706	7.0	29	3.2	12.9	308.8
8 Toledo	13	449	308	10	68.6	3879	8.6	28	2.2	12.6	298.4
9 Louisville	12	359	256	5	71.3	3463	9.7	27	1.4	13.5	288.6
10 Connecticut	12	464	292	15	62.9	3376	7.3	23	3.2	11.6	281.3

TOTAL OFFENSE	G	P	YDS	AVG	TD	YPG
1 Louisville	12	893	6468	7.2	80	539.0
2 Bowling Green	12	904	6076	6.7	69	506.3
3 Utah	12	869	5997	6.9	75	499.8
4 Boise State	12	951	5912	6.2	74	492.7
5 California	12	840	5909	7.0	59	492.4
6 Texas Tech	12	944	5900	6.3	59	491.7
7 Texas	12	890	5573	6.3	55	464.4
8 Oklahoma	13	971	6007	6.2	61	462.1
9 Memphis	12	903	5524	6.1	53	460.3
10 Michigan State	12	899	5520	6.1	41	460.0

RUSHING DEFENSE	G	ATT	YDS	AVG	TD	YPG
1 Southern California	13	394	1032	2.6	5	79.4
2 California	12	368	990	2.7	7	82.5
3 Florida State	12	418	997	2.4	5	83.1
4 Notre Dame	12	399	1058	2.7	6	88.2
5 Iowa	12	392	1110	2.8	8	92.5
6 Oklahoma	13	402	1230	3.1	10	94.6
7 LSU	**12**	**410**	**1197**	**2.9**	**7**	**99.8**
8 Troy	12	444	1211	2.7	12	100.9
9 North Carolina St.	11	429	1126	2.6	6	102.4
10 Boise State	12	373	1247	3.3	17	103.9

PASSING DEFENSE	G	ATT	COM	PCT	INT	I%	YDS	YPA	TD	TD%	RAT
1 North Carolina St.	11	272	118	43.4	9	3.3	1309	4.8	12	4.4	91.8
2 Alabama	**12**	**242**	**105**	**43.4**	**12**	**5.0**	**1357**	**5.6**	**9**	**3.7**	**92.9**
3 Fresno State	12	362	185	51.1	16	4.4	2097	5.8	9	2.5	99.1
4 Penn State	11	310	175	56.5	16	5.2	1785	5.8	5	1.6	99.9
5 Wisconsin	12	369	180	48.8	11	3.0	2007	5.4	13	3.5	100.2
6 Troy	12	406	217	53.5	25	6.2	2521	6.2	9	2.2	100.6
7 Virginia Tech	13	332	180	54.2	19	5.7	1986	6.0	8	2.4	101.0
8 Oregon State	12	424	186	43.9	19	4.5	2352	5.6	25	5.9	101.0
9 Southern California	13	457	246	53.8	22	4.8	2599	5.7	13	2.8	101.3
10 LSU	**12**	**333**	**160**	**48.1**	**14**	**4.2**	**1886**	**5.7**	**16**	**4.8**	**103.0**

TOTAL DEFENSE	G	P	YDS	AVG	TD	YPG
1 North Carolina St.	11	701	2435	3.5	23	221.4
2 Alabama	**12**	**726**	**2946**	**4.1**	**23**	**245.5**
3 LSU	**12**	**743**	**3083**	**4.2**	**25**	**256.9**
4 Virginia Tech	13	794	3484	4.4	18	268.0
5 Auburn	**13**	**780**	**3609**	**4.6**	**19**	**277.6**
6 Southern California	13	851	3631	4.3	20	279.3
7 Florida State	12	798	3406	4.3	18	283.8
8 Georgia	**12**	**747**	**3467**	**4.6**	**23**	**288.9**
9 Wisconsin	12	756	3495	4.6	22	291.3
10 Penn State	11	753	3207	4.3	18	291.6

SCORING OFFENSE	G	PTS	AVG
1 Louisville	12	597	49.8
2 Boise State	12	587	48.9
3 Utah	12	544	45.3
4 Bowling Green	12	532	44.3
5 Fresno State	12	482	40.2
6 Southern California	13	496	38.2
7 California	12	441	36.8
8 Texas Tech	12	434	36.2
9 Hawaii	13	467	35.9
10 Memphis	12	430	35.8

SCORING DEFENSE	G	PTS	AVG
1 Auburn	**13**	**147**	**11.3**
2 Virginia Tech	13	167	12.8
3 Southern California	13	169	13.0
4 Florida State	12	169	14.1
5 Penn State	11	168	15.3
6 Wisconsin	12	185	15.4
7 Alabama	**12**	**189**	**15.8**
8 California	12	192	16.0
9 Georgia	**12**	**198**	**16.5**
10 Troy	12	200	16.7

TURNOVER MARGIN	G	FR	INT	TOT	FL	INTL	TOT	MAR
1 Southern California	13	16	22	38	12	7	19	1.5
2 Oklahoma State	12	15	11	26	4	5	9	1.4
3 Utah	12	13	16	29	9	5	14	1.3
3 Bowling Green	12	11	14	25	6	4	10	1.3
5 Miami (Fla.)	12	14	13	27	7	6	13	1.2
6 Iowa	12	15	17	32	5	14	19	1.1
6 Pittsburgh	12	9	17	26	6	7	13	1.1
6 North Texas	12	12	14	26	9	4	13	1.1
9 Virginia Tech	13	13	19	32	10	9	19	1.0
10 Louisville	12	10	17	27	11	5	16	0.9
10 Troy	12	7	25	32	10	11	21	0.9

2004

FINAL POLL (JAN. 5)

ESPN	AP	SCHOOL	FINAL RECORD
1	1	Southern California	13-0
2	2	Auburn	13-0
3	3	Oklahoma	12-1
5	4	Utah	12-0
4	5	Texas	11-1
7	6	Louisville	11-1
6	7	Georgia	10-2
8	8	Iowa	10-2
9	9	California	10-2
10	10	Virginia Tech	10-3
11	11	Miami (Fla.)	9-3
13	12	Boise State	11-1
15	13	Tennessee	10-3
12	14	Michigan	9-3
14	15	Florida State	9-3
16	16	LSU	9-3
18	17	Wisconsin	9-3
17	18	Texas Tech	8-4
20	19	Arizona State	9-3
19	20	Ohio State	8-4
21	21	Boston College	9-3
22	22	Fresno State	9-3
23	23	Virginia	8-4
24	24	Navy	10-2
	25	Pittsburgh	8-4
25		Florida	7-5

CONSENSUS ALL-AMERICANS

POS	OFFENSE	CL	SCHOOL
QB	Matt Leinart	Jr.	Southern California
RB	Adrian Peterson	Fr.	Oklahoma
RB	J.J. Arrington	Sr.	California
WR	Braylon Edwards	Sr.	Michigan
WR	Taylor Stubblefield	Sr.	Purdue
TE	Heath Miller	Jr.	Virginia
OL	Jammal Brown	Sr.	Oklahoma
OL	Elton Brown	Sr.	Virginia
OL	David Baas	Sr.	Michigan
OL	Alex Barron	Sr.	Florida State
OL	Michael Munoz	Sr.	Tennessee
OL	Ben Wilkerson	Sr.	LSU
PK	Mike Nugent	Sr.	Ohio State
AP	Reggie Bush	So.	Southern California

OTHERS RECEIVING FIRST-TEAM HONORS

QB	Alex Smith		Utah
RB	Carnell Williams		Auburn
RB	Cedric Benson		Texas
WR	Mark Clayton		Oklahoma
OL	Sam Mayes		Oklahoma State
OL	Chris Kemoeatu		Utah
OL	Greg Eslinger		Minnesota
OL	Vince Carter		Oklahoma
KR	Devin Hester		Miami (Fla.)

POS	DEFENSE	CL	SCHOOL
DL	David Pollack	Sr.	Georgia
DL	Erasmus James	Sr.	Wisconsin
DL	Shaun Cody	Sr.	Southern California
DL	Marcus Spears	Sr.	LSU
LB	Matt Grootegoed	Sr.	Southern California
LB	Derrick Johnson	Sr.	Texas
LB	A.J. Hawk	Jr.	Ohio State
DB	Antrel Rolle	Sr.	Miami (Fla.)
DB	Marlin Jackson	Sr.	Michigan
DB	Carlos Rogers	Sr.	Auburn
DB	Ernest Shazor	Sr.	Michigan
DB	Thomas Davis	Jr.	Georgia
P	Brandon Fields	So.	Michigan State

OTHERS RECEIVING FIRST-TEAM HONORS

DL	Ryan Riddle		California
DL	Mathias Kiwanuka		Boston College
DL	Mike Patterson		Southern California
DL	Jesse Mahelona		Tennessee
DL	Dan Cody		Oklahoma
DL	Jonathan Goddard		Marshall
LB	Ahmad Brooks		Virginia
LB	Kevin Burnett		Tennessee
LB	Michael Boley		Southern Mississippi
DB	Corey Webster		LSU
P	Matt Payne		Brigham Young

HEISMAN TROPHY VOTING

	PLAYER	POS	SCHOOL	TOTAL
1	Matt Leinart	QB	Southern Cal	325
2	Adrian Peterson	RB	Oklahoma	997
3	Jason White	QB	Oklahoma	957
4	Alex Smith	QB	Utah	635
5	Reggie Bush	TB	Southern Cal	597
6	Cedric Benson	RB	Texas	187
7	Jason Campbell	QB	Auburn	162
8	J.J. Arrington	RB	California	115
9	Aaron Rodgers	QB	California	67
10	Braylon Edwards	WR	Michigan	62

AWARD WINNERS

PLAYER	AWARD
Jason White, QB, Oklahoma	Maxwell
Jammal Brown, OL, Oklahoma	Outland
Matt Leinart, QB, Southern California	Camp
David Pollack, DE, Georgia	Lombardi
Jason White, QB, Oklahoma	O'Brien
Derrick Johnson, LB, Texas	Butkus
Carlos Rogers, DB, Auburn	Thorpe
Jason White, QB, Oklahoma	Unitas
Cedric Benson, RB, Texas	Walker
Mike Nugent, K, Ohio State	Groza
Derrick Johnson, LB, Texas	Nagurski
David Pollack, DE, Georgia	Bednarik
Braylon Edwards, WR, Michigan	Biletnikoff
Chad Owens, AP, Hawaii	Tatupu
Daniel Sepulveda, P, Baylor	Guy
Heath Miller, TE, Virginia	Mackey
David Baas, OL, Michigan	Rimington
Ben Wilkerson, C, LSU	Rimington
David Pollack, DE, Georgia	Hendricks

BOWL GAMES

DATE	GAME	SCORE
D14	New Orleans	Southern Miss 31, North Texas 10
D21	Champs Sports	Georgia Tech 51, Syracuse 14
D22	GMAC	Bowling Green 52, Memphis 35
D23	Fort Worth	Cincinnati 32, Marshall 14
D23	Las Vegas	Wyoming 24, UCLA 21
D24	Hawaii	Hawaii 59, UAB 40
D27	Motor City	Connecticut 39, Toledo 10
D27	MPC Computers	Fresno State 37, Virginia 34
D28	Independence	Iowa State 17, Miami (Ohio) 13
D28	Insight	Oregon State 38, Notre Dame 21
D29	Alamo	Ohio State 33, Oklahoma State 7
D29	Houston	Colorado 33, UTEP 28
D30	Continental Tire	Boston Coll. 37, North Carolina 24
D30	Emerald	Navy 34, New Mexico 19
D30	Holiday	Texas Tech 45, California 31
D30	Silicon Valley Classic	Northern Illinois 34, Troy 21
D31	Sun	Arizona State 27, Purdue 23
D31	Liberty	Louisville 44, Boise State 40
D31	Music City	Minnesota 20, Alabama 16
D31	Peach	Miami (Fla.) 27, Florida 10
J1	Outback	Georgia 24, Wisconsin 21
J1	Cotton	Tennessee 38, Texas A&M 7
J1	Gator	Florida State 30, West Virginia 18
J1	Capital One	Iowa 30, LSU 25
J1	Rose	Texas 38, Michigan 37
J1	Fiesta	Utah 35, Pittsburgh 7
J3	Sugar	Auburn 16, Virginia Tech 13
J4	Orange	Southern California 55, Oklahoma 19

SEC STANDINGS

	CONFERENCE		OVERALL	
	W	L	W	L
EAST				
Tennessee	7	1	10	3
Georgia	6	2	10	2
Florida	4	4	7	5
South Carolina	4	4	6	5
Kentucky	1	7	2	9
Vanderbilt	1	7	2	9
WEST				
Auburn	8	0	13	0
LSU	6	2	9	3
Arkansas	3	5	5	6
Alabama	3	5	6	6
Mississippi	3	5	4	7
Mississippi State	2	6	3	8

ALL-SEC TEAM

POS	OFFENSE	SCHOOL
QB	Jason Campbell	Auburn
RB	Carnell Williams	Auburn
RB	Ronnie Brown	Auburn
WR	Fred Gibson	Georgia
WR	Reggie Brown	Georgia
C	Ben Wilkerson	LSU
OL	Wooley Britt	Alabama
OL	Marcus McNeil	Auburn
OL	Max Jean-Gilles	Georgia
OL	Mo Mitchell	Florida
OL	Andrew Whitworth	LSU
TE	Leonard Pope	Florida
K	Brian Bostick	Alabama
RS	Carnell Williams	Auburn

POS	DEFENSE	SCHOOL
L	Marcus Spears	LSU
L	David Pollack	Georgia
L	Jeb Huckeba	Arkansas
LB	Kevin Burnett	Tennessee
LB	Travis Williams	Auburn
LB	Cornelius Wortham	Alabama
LB	Channing Crowder	Florida
LB	Moses Osemwegie	Vanderbilt
LB	Odell Thurman	Georgia
LB	Lionel Turner	LSU
DB	Jason Allen	Tennessee
DB	Thomas Davis	Georgia
DB	Carlos Rogers	Auburn
DB	Junior Rosegreen	Auburn
P	Jared Cook	Mississippi State

SEC CHAMPIONSHIP GAME

DECEMBER 4 | ATLANTA
AUBURN 38, TENNESSEE 28

	1ST	2ND	3RD	4TH	FINAL
AUB	14	7	7	10	38
TENN	7	0	14	7	28

SCORING SUMMARY
AUB Bennett 0 fumble recovery (Vaughn kick)
AUB Williams 5 run (Vaughn kick)
TENN Houston 2 run (Wilhoit kick)
AUB Taylor 4 pass from Campbell (Vaughn kick)
TENN Meachem 17 pass from Clausen (Wilhoit kick)
TENN Riggs 80 run (Wilhoit kick)
AUB Aromashodu 53 pass from Campbell (Vaughn kick)
AUB FG Vaughn 22
TENN Riggs 9 run (Wilhoit kick)
AUB Obomanu 43 pass Campbell (Vaughn kick)

AUBURN	TEAM STATISTICS	TENNESSEE
31	First Downs	9
185	Rushing Yards	228
27-36-1	Passing	8-20-0
374	Passing Yards	69
559	Total Yards	297
2-4	Punt Returns - Yards	0-0
3-42	Kickoff Returns - Yards	1-23
2-29.5	Punts - Average	6-40.5
3-1	Fumbles - Lost	0-0
4-20	Penalties - Yards	12-95

INDIVIDUAL LEADERS
RUSHING
AUB: Williams 19-100, TD.
TENN: Riggs 11-182, 2 TD.
PASSING
AUB: Campbell 27-35-1, 374 yards, 3 TD.
TENN: Clausen 8-20-0, 69 yards, TD.
RECEIVING
AUB: Taylor 6-111, TD; Obomansu 6-93, TD.
TENN: Brown 3-28; Anderson 2-11.

2005 NCAA Major College Statistical Leaders

Individual Leaders

PASSING	POS	CL	G	ATT	COM	PCT	INT	I%	YDS	YPA	TD	TD%	RATING
1 Rudy Carpenter, Arizona State	QB	FR	9	228	156	68.4	2	.9	2273	10.0	17	7.5	175.0
2 Brian Brohm, Louisville	QB	SO	10	301	207	68.8	5	1.7	2883	9.6	19	6.3	166.7
3 Vince Young, Texas	QB	JR	13	325	212	65.2	10	3.1	3036	9.3	26	8.0	163.9
4 Troy Smith, Ohio State	QB	SR	11	237	149	62.9	4	1.7	2282	9.6	16	6.8	162.7
5 Drew Olson, UCLA	QB	SR	12	378	242	64.0	6	1.6	3198	8.5	34	9.0	161.6
6 Phil Horvath, Northern Illinois	QB	JR	9	238	168	70.6	8	3.4	2001	8.4	18	7.6	159.4
7 Brady Quinn, Notre Dame	QB	JR	12	450	292	64.9	7	1.6	3919	8.7	32	7.1	158.4
8 Matt Leinart, Southern California	QB	SR	13	431	283	65.7	8	1.9	3815	8.9	28	6.5	157.7
9 Colt Brennan, Hawaii	QB	SO	12	515	350	68.0	13	2.5	4301	8.4	35	6.8	155.5
10 Drew Stanton, Michigan State	QB	JR	11	354	236	66.7	12	3.4	3077	8.7	22	6.2	153.4

ALL-PURPOSE	POS	CL	G	RUSH	REC	PR	KR	YDS	YPG
1 Reggie Bush, Southern California	RB	JR	13	1740	478	179	493	2890	222.3
2 Garrett Wolfe, Northern Illinois	RB	JR	9	1580	222	0	0	1802	200.2
3 Jerome Harrison, Washington State	RB	SR	11	1900	206	0	7	2113	192.1
4 DeAngelo Williams, Memphis	RB	SR	11	1964	78	0	33	2075	188.6
5 Rafael Little, Kentucky	**RB**	**SO**	**11**	**1045**	**449**	**355**	**133**	**1982**	**180.2**
6 Brian Calhoun, Wisconsin	RB	JR	13	1636	571	0	0	2207	169.8
7 Domenik Hixon, Akron	WR	SR	13	24	1210	200	705	2139	164.5
8 Brandon Williams, Wisconsin	WR	SR	13	47	1095	380	616	2138	164.5
9 Marshawn Lynch, California	RB	SO	10	1246	125	0	271	1642	164.2
10 Jovon Bouknight, Wyoming	WR	SR	11	94	1116	0	555	1765	160.5

RUSHING/Yards Per Game	POS	CL	G	ATT	YDS	TD	AVG	YPG
1 DeAngelo Williams, Memphis	RB	SR	11	310	1964	18	6.3	178.6
2 Garrett Wolfe, Northern Illinois	RB	JR	9	242	1580	16	6.5	175.6
3 Jerome Harrison, Wash. State	RB	SR	11	308	1900	16	6.2	172.7
4 Reggie Bush, Southern California	RB	JR	13	200	1740	16	8.7	133.9
5 Laurence Maroney, Minnesota	RB	JR	11	281	1464	10	5.2	133.1
6 Brian Calhoun, Wisconsin	RB	JR	13	348	1636	22	4.7	125.9
7 Marshawn Lynch, California	RB	SO	10	196	1246	10	6.4	124.6
8 Tyrell Sutton, Northwestern	RB	FR	12	250	1474	16	5.9	122.8
9 Yvenson Bernard, Oregon State	RB	SO	11	299	1321	13	4.4	120.1
10 DonTrell Moore, New Mexico	RB	SR	11	275	1298	14	4.7	118.0

RUSHING/Yards Per Carry	POS	CL	G	ATT	YDS	YPC
1 Reggie Bush, Southern California	RB	JR	13	200	1740	8.7
2 Justin Forsett, California	RB	SO	12	132	999	7.6
3 Jamaal Charles, Texas	RB	FR	13	119	878	7.4
4 Pat White, West Virginia	QB	FR	12	131	952	7.3
5 Reggie McNeal, Texas A&M	QB	SR	10	96	664	6.9
6 Vince Young, Texas	QB	JR	13	155	1050	6.8
7 Yonus Davis, San Jose State	RB	SO	10	95	638	6.7
8 Javon Ringer, Michigan State	RB	FR	11	122	817	6.7
9 Courtney Lewis, Texas A&M	RB	JR	9	109	723	6.6
10 LenDale White, Southern California	RB	JR	13	197	1302	6.6

RECEIVING	POS	CL	G	REC	YDS	TD	RPG	YPG
1 Mike Hass, Oregon State	WR	SR	11	90	1532	6	8.2	139.3
2 Greg Jennings, Western Mich.	WR	SR	11	98	1259	14	8.9	114.5
3 Jason Hill, Washington State	WR	JR	10	62	1097	13	6.2	109.7
4 Jeff Samardzija, Notre Dame	WR	JR	12	77	1249	15	6.4	104.1
5 Sidney Rice, South Carolina	**WR**	**FR**	**11**	**70**	**1143**	**13**	**6.4**	**103.9**
6 Ryan Grice-Mullen, Hawaii	WR	FR	12	85	1228	12	7.1	102.3
7 David Anderson, Colorado State	WR	SR	12	86	1221	8	7.2	101.8
8 Ryan Robinson, Miami (Ohio)	WR	JR	11	75	1119	8	6.8	101.7
9 Jovon Bouknight, Wyoming	WR	SR	11	77	1116	12	7.0	101.5
10 Derek Hagan, Arizona State	WR	SR	12	77	1210	8	6.4	100.8

PUNTING	POS	CL	PUNT	YDS	AVG
1 Ryan Plackemeier, Wake Forest	P	SR	67	3165	47.2
2 Sam Koch, Nebraska	K	SR	71	3302	46.5
3 Daniel Sepulveda, Baylor	P	JR	62	2863	46.2
4 Jim Kaylor, Colorado State	P	SO	53	2400	45.3
5 John Torp, Colorado	P	SR	80	3613	45.2
6 Kody Bliss, Auburn	**P**	**JR**	**44**	**1975**	**44.9**
7 Luke Johnson, Southern Miss	P	SR	53	2378	44.9
8 Kenneth DeBauche, Wisconsin	P	SO	57	2555	44.8
9 Michael Hughes, San Diego State	K	SO	67	3003	44.8
10 Joel Stelly, La.-Monroe	P	SR	59	2634	44.6

PUNT RETURNS	POS	CL	PR	YDS	TD	AVG
1 Maurice Drew, UCLA	RB	JR	15	427	3	28.5
2 Quinton Jones, Boise State	DB	JR	22	459	3	20.9
3 Terrence Nunn, Nebraska	WR	SO	16	293	0	18.3
4 Willie Reid, Florida State	WR	SR	31	541	3	17.5
5 Rafael Little, Kentucky	**RB**	**SO**	**21**	**355**	**0**	**16.9**
6 Joe Burnett, Central Florida	DB	FR	28	463	2	16.5
7 Terry Richardson, Arizona State	WR	JR	22	337	2	15.3
8 Cory Rodgers, TCU	WR	JR	19	290	0	15.3
9 Tim Mixon, California	DB	JR	24	357	1	14.9
10 Aaron Ross, Texas	DB	JR	34	500	2	14.7

KICKOFF RETURNS	POS	CL	KR	YDS	TD	AVG
1 Jonathan Stewart, Oregon	RB	FR	12	404	2	33.7
2 Felix Jones, Arkansas	**TB**	**FR**	**17**	**543**	**1**	**31.9**
3 Cory Rodgers, TCU	WR	JR	17	515	2	30.3
4 Ted Ginn Jr., Ohio State	WR	SO	18	532	1	29.6
5 Tony Pennyman, Utah State	WR	JR	23	675	2	29.4
6 Darrell Blackman, North Carolina St.	RB	SO	20	582	0	29.1
7 Adam Jennings, Fresno State	DB	SR	20	580	0	29.0
8 Steve Breaston, Michigan	WR	SR	23	646	1	28.1
9 Brandon Williams, Wisconsin	WR	SR	22	616	0	28.0
10 Lee Marks, Boise State	RB	SR	17	474	1	27.9

SCORING	POS	CL	TDS	XP	FG	PTS	PTPG
1 Michael Bush, Louisville	RB	JR	24	0	0	144	14.4
2 LenDale White, Southern California	RB	JR	26	0	0	156	12.0
3 Steve Slaton, West Virginia	RB	FR	19	0	0	114	11.4
4 Garrett Wolfe, Northern Illinois	RB	JR	17	0	0	102	11.3
5 Brian Calhoun, Wisconsin	RB	JR	24	0	0	144	11.1
6 Taurean Henderson, Texas Tech	RB	SR	22	0	0	132	11.0
7 DeAngelo Williams, Memphis	RB	SR	19	0	0	114	10.4
8 Maurice Drew, UCLA	RB	JR	20	0	0	120	10.0
9 Gary Russell, Minnesota	RB	SO	19	0	0	116	9.7
10 Dontrell Moore, New Mexico	RB	SR	17	0	0	104	9.5

FIELD GOALS	POS	CL	FGA	FGM	PCT	FGG
1 Paul Martinez, Oregon	K	JR	24	19	0.79	2.11
2 Alexis Serna, Oregon State	K	SO	28	23	0.82	2.09
3 Jad Dean, Clemson	K	JR	31	24	0.77	2.00
4 Darren McCaleb, Southern Miss	K	JR	28	23	0.82	1.92
5 Josh Huston, Ohio State	K	SR	28	22	0.79	1.83
6 Stephen Gostkowski, Memphis	K	SR	25	22	0.88	1.83
7 Brandon Coutu, Georgia	**K**	**SO**	**29**	**23**	**0.79**	**1.77**
8 Connor Hughes, Virginia	K	SR	24	21	0.88	1.75
9 Sam Swank, Wake Forest	K	FR	24	19	0.79	1.73
9 Todd Soderquist, Miami (Ohio)	K	SR	27	19	0.70	1.73

INTERCEPTIONS	POS	CL	INT	YDS	TD	INT/GM
1 Aaron Gipson, Oregon	DB	SR	7	117	1	.58
2 Anthony Smith, Syracuse	DB	SR	6	73	0	.55
2 Dion Bynum, Ohio U.	DB	SR	6	153	2	.55
2 Jelani Jordan, Bowling Green	DB	SR	6	66	0	.55
5 Chaz Williams, La.-Monroe	DB	SO	5	138	1	.50
5 Alan Zemaitis, Penn State	CB	SR	6	35	0	.50
5 Marcus Hamilton, Virginia	CB	JR	6	28	0	.50
8 Nick Graham, Tulsa	DB	JR	6	66	0	.46

Team Leaders

RUSHING OFFENSE	G	ATT	YDS	AVG	TD	YPG
1 Navy	12	671	3824	5.7	45	318.7
2 Texas	13	605	3574	5.9	55	274.9
3 Minnesota	12	610	3277	5.4	34	273.1
4 West Virginia	12	625	3269	5.2	34	272.4
5 Memphis	12	597	3215	5.4	28	267.9
6 Southern California	13	525	3380	6.4	51	260.0
7 La.-Lafayette	11	531	2797	5.3	34	254.3
8 Air Force	11	588	2712	4.6	28	246.6
9 California	12	483	2823	5.8	27	235.3
10 Texas A&M	11	452	2584	5.7	24	234.9

PASSING OFFENSE	G	ATT	COM	INT	PCT	YDS	YPA	TD	I%	YPC	YPG
1 Texas Tech	12	588	391	12	66.5	4666	7.9	34	2.0	11.9	388.8
2 Hawaii	12	578	379	15	65.6	4611	8.0	37	2.6	12.2	384.3
3 Arizona State	12	493	312	11	63.3	4481	9.1	38	2.2	14.4	373.4
4 Notre Dame	12	454	294	8	64.8	3963	8.7	32	1.8	13.5	330.3
5 Southern California	13	481	312	10	64.9	4157	8.6	32	2.1	13.3	319.8
6 BYU	12	516	332	13	64.3	3721	7.2	27	2.5	11.2	310.1
7 Northwestern	12	512	320	9	62.5	3681	7.2	22	1.8	11.5	306.8
8 Oregon	11	482	303	10	62.9	3654	7.6	28	2.1	12.1	304.5
9 UTEP	12	458	268	20	58.5	3607	7.9	29	4.4	13.5	300.6
10 Oregon State	11	459	267	23	58.2	3261	7.1	13	5.0	12.2	296.5

TOTAL OFFENSE	G	P	YDS	AVG	TD	YPG
1 Southern California	13	1006	7537	7.5	87	579.8
2 Arizona State	12	940	6229	6.6	59	519.1
3 Texas	13	941	6657	7.1	88	512.1
4 Northwestern	12	974	6004	6.2	51	500.3
5 Michigan State	11	834	5470	6.6	50	497.3
6 Texas Tech	12	896	5950	6.6	62	495.8
7 Minnesota	12	933	5937	6.4	56	494.8
8 Washington State	11	821	5382	6.6	47	489.3
9 Louisville	12	848	5785	6.8	69	482.1
10 Notre Dame	12	945	5728	6.1	58	477.3

RUSHING DEFENSE	G	ATT	YDS	AVG	TD	YPG
1 Ohio State	12	375	881	2.4	12	73.4
2 Tennessee	**11**	**356**	**907**	**2.6**	**8**	**82.5**
3 Kansas	12	414	999	2.4	8	83.3
4 Oklahoma	12	392	1087	2.8	11	90.6
5 Boston College	12	420	1090	2.6	6	90.8
6 LSU	**13**	**402**	**1190**	**3.0**	**8**	**91.5**
7 Penn State	12	442	1116	2.5	12	93.0
8 Virginia Tech	13	402	1214	3.0	6	93.4
9 Alabama	**12**	**361**	**1132**	**3.1**	**5**	**94.3**
10 Florida	**12**	**373**	**1139**	**3.0**	**14**	**94.9**

PASSING DEFENSE	G	ATT	COM	PCT	INT	I%	YDS	YPA	TD	TD%	RAT
1 Miami (Fla.)	12	354	165	46.6	14	4.0	1826	5.2	8	2.3	89.5
2 Virginia Tech	13	387	192	49.6	19	4.9	2005	5.2	11	2.8	92.7
3 LSU	**13**	**431**	**204**	**47.3**	**10**	**2.3**	**2279**	**5.3**	**12**	**2.8**	**96.3**
4 Texas	13	436	223	51.2	11	2.5	2236	5.1	10	2.3	96.7
5 Alabama	**12**	**352**	**175**	**49.7**	**11**	**3.1**	**1929**	**5.5**	**9**	**2.6**	**97.9**
6 Pittsburgh	11	295	147	49.8	14	4.8	1681	5.7	10	3.4	99.4
7 Connecticut	11	284	132	46.5	14	4.9	1743	6.1	10	3.5	99.8
8 North Carolina St.	12	380	185	48.7	13	3.4	2298	6.1	10	2.6	101.3
9 TCU	12	425	222	52.2	26	6.1	2654	6.2	14	3.3	103.3
10 Nebraska	12	415	212	51.1	13	3.1	2495	6.0	13	3.1	105.7

TOTAL DEFENSE	G	P	YDS	AVG	TD	YPG
1 Virginia Tech	13	789	3219	4.1	19	247.6
2 Alabama	**12**	**713**	**3061**	**4.3**	**15**	**255.1**
3 LSU	**13**	**833**	**3469**	**4.2**	**21**	**266.9**
4 Miami (Fla.)	12	828	3241	3.9	19	270.1
5 Ohio State	12	780	3376	4.3	21	281.3
6 Connecticut	11	732	3269	4.5	28	297.2
7 Tennessee	**11**	**720**	**3280**	**4.6**	**21**	**298.2**
8 North Carolina St.	12	841	3584	4.3	25	298.7
9 Florida	**12**	**748**	**3598**	**4.8**	**30**	**299.8**
10 Texas	13	897	3938	4.4	25	302.9

SCORING OFFENSE	G	PTS	AVG
1 Texas	13	652	50.2
2 Southern California	13	638	49.1
3 Louisville	12	521	43.4
4 Texas Tech	12	473	39.4
5 UCLA	12	469	39.1
6 Fresno State	13	491	37.8
7 Arizona State	12	442	36.8
8 Notre Dame	12	440	36.7
9 Boise State	13	469	36.1
10 Minnesota	12	429	35.8
10 Toledo	12	429	35.8

SCORING DEFENSE	G	PTS	AVG
1 Alabama	**12**	**128**	**10.7**
2 Virginia Tech	13	168	12.9
3 LSU	**13**	**185**	**14.2**
4 Miami (Fla.)	12	171	14.3
5 Ohio State	12	183	15.3
6 Auburn	**12**	**186**	**15.5**
7 Boston College	12	191	15.9
8 Georgia	**13**	**213**	**16.4**
8 Texas	13	213	16.4
10 Penn State	12	204	17.0

TURNOVER MARGIN	G	FR	INT	TOT	FL	INTL	TOT	MAR
1 TCU	12	14	26	40	8	11	19	1.8
2 Southern California	13	16	22	38	7	10	17	1.6
3 Florida	**12**	**15**	**16**	**31**	**6**	**7**	**13**	**1.5**
4 Tulsa	13	14	22	36	10	8	18	1.4
5 Louisiana Tech	11	15	16	31	8	10	18	1.2
5 Miami (Ohio)	11	15	20	35	8	14	22	1.2
7 Iowa State	12	13	22	35	11	10	21	1.2
7 Southern Miss	12	19	15	34	7	13	20	1.2
7 West Virginia	12	14	17	31	10	7	17	1.2
10 Oregon	11	9	23	32	9	10	19	1.1

2005

Final Poll (Jan. 5)

USA	AP	SCHOOL	FINAL RECORD
1	1	Texas	13-0
2	2	Southern California	12-1
3	3	Penn State	11-1
4	4	Ohio State	10-2
6	5	West Virginia	11-1
5	6	LSU	11-2
7	7	Virginia Tech	11-2
8	8	Alabama	10-2
11	9	Notre Dame	9-3
10	10	Georgia	10-3
9	11	TCU	11-1
16	12	Florida	9-3
12	13	Oregon	10-2
14	14	Auburn	9-3
15	15	Wisconsin	10-3
13	16	UCLA	10-2
18	17	Miami (Fla.)	9-3
17	18	Boston College	9-3
20	19	Louisville	9-3
19	20	Texas Tech	9-3
21	21	Clemson	8-4
22	22	Oklahoma	8-4
23	23	Florida State	8-5
24	24	Nebraska	8-4
25	25	California	8-4

Consensus All-Americans

POS	OFFENSE	CL	SCHOOL
QB	Vince Young	Jr.	Texas
RB	Reggie Bush	Jr.	Southern California
RB	Jerome Harrison	Sr.	Washington State
WR	Dwayne Jarrett	So.	Southern California
WR	Jeff Samardzija	Jr.	Notre Dame
TE	Marcedes Lewis	Sr.	UCLA
OL	Jonathan Scott	Sr.	Texas
OL	Marcus McNeill	Sr.	Auburn
OL	Max Jean-Gilles	Sr.	Georgia
OL	Taitusi Lutui	Sr.	Southern California
OL	Greg Eslinger	Sr.	Minnesota
PK	Mason Crosby	Jr.	Colorado
AP/KR	Maurice Drew	Jr.	UCLA

Others receiving first-team honors

QB	Matt Leinart	Southern California
RB	DeAngelo Williams	Memphis
WR	Mike Haas	Oregon State
WR	Calvin Johnson	Georgia Tech
TE	Vernon Davis	Maryland
OL	D'Brickashaw Ferguson	Virginia
OL	Eric Winston	Miami (Fla.)
PK	Alexis Serna	Oregon State
OL	Zach Strief	Northwestern

POS	DEFENSE	CL	SCHOOL
DL	Tamba Hali	Sr.	Penn State
DL	Elvis Dumervil	Sr.	Louisville
DL	Haloti Ngata	Jr.	Oregon
DL	Rodrique Wright	Sr.	Texas
LB	Paul Posluszny	Jr.	Penn State
LB	DeMeco Ryans	Sr.	Alabama
LB	A.J. Hawk	Sr.	Ohio State
DB	Tye Hill	Sr.	Clemson
DB	Greg Blue	Sr.	Georgia
DB	Jimmy Williams	Sr.	Virginia Tech
DB	Michael Huff	Sr.	Texas
P	Ryan Plackemeier	Sr.	Wake Forest

Others receiving first-team honors

DB	Darnell Bing	Southern California
DB	Dion Bynum	Ohio U.
DB	Brandon Meriweather	Miami (Fla.)
DB	Ko Simpson	South Carolina
LB	D'Qwell Jackson	Maryland
DL	Mathias Kiwanuka	Boston College
DL	Darryl Tapp	Virginia Tech
DL	Brodrick Bunkley	Florida State

Heisman Trophy Voting

	PLAYER	POS	SCHOOL	TOTAL
1	Reggie Bush	RB	Southern Cal	2,541
2	Vince Young	QB	Texas	1,608
3	Matt Leinart	QB	Southern Cal	797
4	Brady Quinn	QB	Notre Dame	191
5	Michael Robinson	QB	Penn State	49
6	A.J. Hawk	LB	Ohio State	29
7	DeAngelo Williams	RB	Memphis	26
8	Drew Olson	QB	UCLA	21
9	Jerome Harrison	RB	Washington St.	20
10	Elvis Dumervil	DE	Louisville	9

Award Winners

PLAYER	AWARD
Vince Young, QB, Texas	Maxwell
Greg Eslinger, C, Minnesota	Outland
Reggie Bush, RB, Southern California	Camp
A.J. Hawk, LB, Ohio State	Lombardi
Vince Young, QB, Texas	O'Brien
Paul Posluszny, LB, Penn State	Butkus
Michael Huff, DB, Texas	Thorpe
Matt Leinart, QB, Southern California	Unitas
Reggie Bush, RB, Southern California	Walker
Alexis Serna, K, Oregon State	Groza
Elvis Dumervil, DE, Louisville	Nagurski
Paul Posluszny, LB, Penn State	Bednarik
Mike Hass, WR, Oregon State	Biletnikoff
Ryan Hoffman, P, Illinois State	Tatupu
Ryan Plackemeier, P, Wake Forest	Guy
Marcedes Lewis, TE, UCLA	Mackey
Greg Eslinger, C, Minnesota	Rimington
Elvis Dumervil, DE, Louisville	Hendricks
DeMeco Ryans, LB, Alabama	Lott

Bowl Games

DATE	GAME	SCORE
D20	New Orleans	Southern Miss 31, Arkansas St. 19
D21	GMAC	Toledo 45, UTEP 13
D22	Las Vegas	California 35, Brigham Young 28
D22	Poinsettia	Navy 51, Colorado State 30
D23	Fort Worth	Kansas 42, Houston 13
D24	Hawaii	Nevada 49, UCF 48 OT
D26	Motor City	Memphis 38, Akron 31
D27	Champs Sports	Clemson 19, Colorado 10
D27	Insight	Arizona State 45, Rutgers 40
D28	MPC Computers	Boston College 27, Boise St. 21
D28	Alamo	Nebraska 32, Michigan 28
D29	Emerald	Utah 38, Georgia Tech 10
D29	Holiday	Oklahoma 17, Oregon 14
D30	Music City	Virginia 34, Minnesota 31
D30	Sun	UCLA 50, Northwestern 38
D30	Independence	Missouri 38, South Carolina 31
D30	Peach	LSU 40, Miami (Fla.) 3
D31	Meineke Car Care	NC State 14, South Florida 0
D31	Liberty	Tulsa 31, Fresno State 24
D31	Houston	TCU 27, Iowa State 24
J2	Cotton	Alabama 13, Texas Tech 10
J2	Outback	Florida 31, Iowa 24
J2	Gator	Virginia Tech 35, Louisville 24
J2	Capital One	Wisconsin 24, Auburn 10
J2	Fiesta	Ohio State 34, Notre Dame 20
J2	Sugar	West Virginia 38, Georgia 35
J3	Orange	Penn State 26, Florida State 23 3OT
J4	Rose	Texas 41, Southern California 38

SEC Standings

	CONFERENCE		OVERALL	
	W	L	W	L
EAST				
Georgia	6	2	10	3
Florida	5	3	9	3
South Carolina	5	3	7	5
Tennessee	3	5	5	6
Vanderbilt	3	5	5	6
Kentucky	2	6	3	8
WEST				
LSU	7	1	11	2
Auburn	7	1	9	3
Alabama	6	2	10	2
Arkansas	2	6	4	7
Mississippi	1	7	3	8
Mississippi State	1	7	3	8

All-SEC Team

POS	OFFENSE	SCHOOL
QB	Jay Cutler	Vanderbilt
RB	Kenny Irons	Auburn
RB	Kenneth Darby	Alabama
RB	Darren McFadden	Arkansas
WR	Sidney Rice	South Carolina
WR	Earl Bennett	Vanderbilt
C	Mike Degory	Florida
OL	Tre' Stallings	Mississippi
OL	Marcus McNeill	Auburn
OL	Max Jean-Gilles	Georgia
OL	Arron Sears	Tennessee
OL	Andrew Whitworth	LSU
TE	Leonard Pope	Georgia
K	Brandon Coutu	Georgia

POS	DEFENSE	SCHOOL
DL	Willie Evans	Mississippi State
DL	Quentin Hoses	Georgia
DL	Claude Wroten	LSU
LB	DeMeco Ryans	Alabama
LB	Patrick Willis	Mississippi
LB	Sam Olajubutu	Arkansas
LB	Moses Osemwegie	Vanderbilt
DB	Greg Blue	Georgia
DB	Roman Harper	Alabama
DB	LaRon Landry	LSU
DB	Ko Simpson	South Carolina
P	Kody Bliss	Auburn
RS	Skyler Green	LSU

SEC Championship Game

December 2 | Atlanta
Georgia 34, LSU 14

	1ST	2ND	3RD	4TH	FINAL
UGA	14	7	3	10	34
LSU	0	7	0	7	14

Scoring Summary

UGA — Bailey 45 pass from Shockley (Coutu kick)
UGA — Bailey 29 pass from Shockley (Coutu kick)
LSU — Russell 1 run (David kick)
UGA — Shockley 7 run (Coutu kick)
UGA — FG Coutu 22
UGA — FG Coutu 51
UGA — Jennings 15 interception return (Coutu kick)
LSU — Bowe 19 pass from Flynn (David kick)

GEORGIA	TEAM STATISTICS	LSU
16	First Downs	18
138	Rushing Yards	74
6-12-0	Passing	14-30-2
112	Passing Yards	156
250	Total Yards	230
2-20	Punt Returns - Yards	0-0
2-43	Kickoff Returns - Yards	4-43
4-45.8	Punts - Average	6-33.5
1-0	Fumbles - Lost	0-0
2-15	Penalties - Yards	9-78

Individual Leaders

RUSHING
UGA: Brown 14-62.
LSU: Carey 10-43.

PASSING
UGA: Shockley 6-12-0, 112 yards, 2 TD.
LSU: Russell 11-19-1, 120 yards.

RECEIVING
UGA: Bailey 7-74, 2 TD; Massaquoi 2-15.
LSU: Bowe 5-74, TD; Jones 2-28.

2006 NCAA Major College Statistical Leaders

Individual Leaders

PASSING	POS	CL	G	ATT	COM	PCT	INT	I%	YDS	YPA	TD	TD%	RATING
1 Colt Brennan, Hawaii	QB	JR	14	559	406	72.6	12	2.2	5549	9.9	58	10.4	186.0
2 John Beck, BYU	QB	SR	12	417	289	69.3	8	1.9	3885	9.3	32	7.7	169.1
3 JaMarcus Russell, LSU	**QB**	**JR**	**13**	**342**	**232**	**67.8**	**8**	**2.3**	**3129**	**9.2**	**28**	**8.2**	**167.0**
4 Tyler Palko, Pittsburgh	QB	SR	12	322	220	68.3	9	2.8	2871	8.9	25	7.8	163.2
5 Kevin Kolb, Houston	QB	SR	14	432	292	67.6	4	0.9	3809	8.8	30	6.9	162.7
6 Jared Zabransky, Boise State	QB	SR	13	288	191	66.3	8	2.8	2587	9.0	23	8.0	162.6
7 Troy Smith, Ohio State	QB	SR	13	311	203	65.3	6	1.9	2542	8.2	30	9.7	161.9
8 Colt McCoy, Texas	QB	FR	13	318	217	68.2	7	2.2	2570	8.1	29	9.1	161.8
9 Brian Brohm, Louisville	QB	JR	11	313	199	63.6	5	1.6	3049	9.7	16	5.1	159.1
10 Justin Willis, SMU	QB	FR	11	270	182	67.4	6	2.2	2047	7.6	26	9.6	158.4

ALL-PURPOSE	POS	CL	G	RUSH	REC	PR	KR	YDS	YPG
1 Garrett Wolfe, Northern Illinois	RB	SR	13	1928	249	0	0	2177	167.5
2 Steve Slaton, West Virginia	RB	SO	13	1744	360	0	0	2104	161.9
3 Johnnie Lee Higgins Jr., UTEP	WR	SR	12	-2	1319	281	275	1873	156.1
4 Chris Williams, New Mexico St.	WR	SO	12	53	1415	92	301	1861	155.1
5 Ian Johnson, Boise St.	RB	SO	12	1714	55	0	0	1769	147.4
6 Darren McFadden, Arkansas	**RB**	**SO**	**14**	**1647**	**149**	**0**	**262**	**2058**	**147.0**
7 Patrick Jackson, Louisiana Tech	RB	SO	12	854	181	0	702	1737	144.8
8 Curtis Brown, BYU	RB	SR	13	1010	566	0	288	1864	143.4
9 Keenan Burton, Kentucky	**WR**	**JR**	**13**	**-7**	**1036**	**51**	**765**	**1845**	**141.9**
10 Nate Ilaoa, Hawaii	RB	SR	13	990	837	0	0	1827	140.5

RUSHING/Yards Per Game	POS	CL	G	ATT	YDS	TD	AVG	YPG
1 Garrett Wolfe, Northern Illinois	RB	SR	13	309	1928	18	6.2	148.3
2 Ian Johnson, Boise State	RB	SO	12	276	1714	25	6.2	142.8
3 Ray Rice, Rutgers	RB	SO	13	335	1794	20	5.4	138.0
4 Steve Slaton, West Virginia	RB	SO	13	248	1744	16	7.0	134.2
5 Ahmad Bradshaw, Marshall	RB	JR	12	249	1523	19	6.1	126.9
6 Dwayne Wright, Fresno State	RB	JR	12	261	1462	11	5.6	121.8
7 Jon Cornish, Kansas	RB	SR	12	250	1457	8	5.8	121.4
8 P.J. Hill, Wisconsin	RB	FR	13	311	1569	15	5.1	120.7
9 Michael Hart, Michigan	RB	JR	13	318	1562	14	4.9	120.2
10 Darren McFadden, Arkansas	**RB**	**SO**	**14**	**284**	**1647**	**14**	**5.8**	**117.6**

RUSHING/Yards Per Carry	POS	CL	G	ATT	YDS	YPC
1 Anthony Aldridge, Houston	RB	JR	14	95	959	10.1
2 Felix Jones, Arkansas	**RB**	**SO**	**14**	**154**	**1168**	**7.6**
3 Nate Ilaoa, Hawaii	RB	SR	13	131	990	7.6
4 Patrick White, West Virginia	QB	SO	12	165	1219	7.4
5 C.J. Spiller, Clemson	RB	FR	13	129	938	7.3
6 Steve Slaton, West Virginia	RB	SO	13	248	1744	7.0
7 Mike Goodson, Texas A&M	RB	FR	13	127	847	6.7
8 Dantrell Savage, Oklahoma St.	RB	JR	11	126	820	6.5
9 LaMarcus Coker, Tennessee	**RB**	**FR**	**11**	**108**	**696**	**6.4**
10 Garrett Wolfe, Northern Illinois	RB	SR	13	309	1928	6.2

RECEIVING	POS	CL	G	REC	YDS	TD	RPG	YPG
1 Chris Williams, New Mexico St.	WR	SO	12	92	1415	12	7.7	117.9
2 Johnnie Lee Higgins Jr., UTEP	WR	SR	12	82	1319	13	6.8	109.9
3 Joel Filani, Texas Tech	WR	SR	13	91	1300	13	7.0	100.0
4 Robert Meachem, Tennessee	**WR**	**JR**	**13**	**71**	**1298**	**11**	**5.5**	**99.9**
5 Sammie Stroughter, Oregon St.	WR	JR	14	74	1293	5	5.3	92.4
6 Harry Douglas, Louisville	WR	JR	13	70	1265	6	5.4	97.3
7 Jarett Dillard, Rice	WR	SO	13	91	1247	21	7.0	95.9
8 Davone Bess, Hawaii	WR	SO	14	96	1220	15	6.9	87.1
9 Calvin Johnson, Georgia Tech	WR	JR	14	76	1202	15	5.4	85.9
10 Adarius Bowman, Oklahoma St.	WR	JR	13	60	1181	12	4.6	90.9

PUNTING	POS	CL	PUNT	YDS	AVG
1 Daniel Sepulveda, Baylor	P	SR	66	3068	46.5
2 Chris Miller, Ball State	P	JR	57	2637	46.3
3 Kody Bliss, Auburn	**P**	**SR**	**47**	**2149**	**45.7**
4 Durant Brooks, Georgia Tech	P	JR	79	3596	45.5
5 Geoffrey Price, Notre Dame	P	SR	50	2272	45.4
6 Kip Facer, UNLV	P	SR	46	2078	45.2
7 Britton Colquitt, Tennessee	**P**	**SO**	**46**	**2066**	**44.9**
8 Matt Fodge, Oklahoma St.	P	SO	50	2244	44.9
9 Kyle Stringer, Boise State	P	SR	47	2097	44.6
10 Justin Brantly, Texas A&M	P	SO	50	2215	44.3

PUNT RETURNS	POS	CL	PR	YDS	TD	AVG
1 DeSean Jackson, California	WR	SO	25	455	4	18.2
2 Jeremy Trimble, Army	WR	JR	18	325	2	18.1
3 Sammie Stroughter, Oregon St.	WR	JR	30	470	3	15.7
4 Ean Randolph, South Florida	WR	SR	25	370	1	14.8
5 Yamon Figurs, Kansas State	WR	SR	22	323	2	14.7
6 Mikey Henderson, Georgia	**WR**	**JR**	**25**	**367**	**2**	**14.7**
7 Chris Garrett, Ohio U.	WR	FR	26	378	1	14.5
8 Joe Chapple, Western Michigan	WR	SR	16	230	0	14.4
9 DeAngelo Wilson, Nevada	DB	SO	16	228	0	14.3
10 Derek Pegues, Mississippi St.	**DB**	**SO**	**25**	**350**	**1**	**14.0**

KICKOFF RETURNS	POS	CL	KR	YDS	TD	AVG
1 Marcus Thigpen, Indiana	RB	SO	24	723	3	30.1
2 David Harvey, Akron	WR	FR	17	510	0	30.0
3 Lionell Singleton, Florida Int'l	DB	JR	12	354	1	29.5
4 Darrell Blackman, North Carolina St.	WR	JR	19	549	1	28.9
5 Damon Nickson, Middle Tenn. State	DB	JR	21	605	2	28.8
6 Jonathan Stewart, Oregon	RB	SO	23	646	0	28.1
7 Jeff Smith, Boston College	RB	FR	23	645	1	28.0
8 Brandon West, Western Michigan	RB	FR	22	615	1	28.0
9 Lowell Robinson, Pittsburgh	WR	JR	26	725	1	27.9
10 Kerry Franks, Texas A&M	WR	JR	16	443	1	27.7

SCORING	POS	CL	TDS	XP	FG	PTS	PTPG
1 Ian Johnson, Boise State	RB	SO	25	0	0	152	12.7
2 Ahmad Bradshaw, Marshall	RB	JR	21	0	0	126	10.5
3 Jarett Dillard, Rice	WR	SO	21	0	0	126	9.7
4 Arthur Carmody, Louisville	K	JR	0	60	21	123	9.5
5 Ray Rice, Rutgers	RB	SO	20	0	0	120	9.2
6 Patrick White, West Virginia	QB	SO	18	0	0	108	9.0
7 Garrett Wolfe, Northern Illinois	RB	SR	19	0	0	116	8.9
8 Jorvorskie Lane, Texas A&M	RB	SO	19	0	0	114	8.8
9 Pat McAfee, West Virginia	K	SO	0	62	17	113	8.7
9 Justin Medlock, UCLA	K	SR	0	29	28	113	8.7

FIELD GOALS	POS	CL	FGA	FGM	PCT	FGG
1 Justin Medlock, UCLA	K	SR	32	28	0.88	2.15
2 Jeremy Ito, Rutgers	K	JR	29	22	0.76	1.69
2 Kevin Kelly, Penn State	K	SO	34	22	0.65	1.69
4 Sam Swank, Wake Forest	K	SO	31	23	0.74	1.64
5 Arthur Carmody, Louisville	K	JR	25	21	0.84	1.62
6 Mason Crosby, Colorado	K	SR	28	19	0.68	1.58
7 Alexis Serna, Oregon State	K	JR	29	22	0.76	1.57
8 Michael Torres, Central Florida	K	JR	24	17	0.71	1.55
9 Dan Ennis, Maryland	K	SR	25	20	0.80	1.54
9 Chris Nendick, Northern Illinois	K	JR	27	20	0.74	1.54
9 John Vaughn, Auburn	**K**	**SR**	**24**	**20**	**0.83**	**1.54**

INTERCEPTIONS	POS	CL	INT	YDS	TD	INT/GM
1 Stanley Franks, Idaho	DB	JR	9	220	1	0.75
2 Dwight Lowery, San Jose St.	DB	JR	9	111	0	0.69
3 Daymeion Hughes, California	DB	SR	8	113	2	0.62
4 Agib Talib, Kansas	DB	SO	6	82	0	0.60
5 John Talley, Duke	DB	SR	7	150	1	0.58
5 Quintin Demps, UTEP	DB	JR	7	61	0	0.58
7 Ryan Smith, Florida	**DB**	**JR**	**8**	**44**	**0**	**0.57**
8 DeJuan Tribble, Boston College	DB	JR	7	108	3	0.54
8 Eric Weddle, Utah	DB	SR	7	80	2	0.54
8 Tony Taylor, Georgia	**LB**	**SR**	**7**	**97**	**1**	**0.54**
8 Trae Williams, South Florida	DB	JR	7	8	0	0.54

Team Leaders

RUSHING OFFENSE	G	ATT	YDS	AVG	TD	YPG
1 Navy	13	764	4251	5.6	39	327.0
2 West Virginia	13	590	3939	6.7	48	303.0
3 Air Force	12	660	2753	4.2	22	229.4
4 Arkansas	**14**	**539**	**3199**	**5.9**	**26**	**228.5**
5 Clemson	13	495	2832	5.7	31	217.9
6 Boise State	13	551	2784	5.1	39	214.2
7 Oklahoma State	13	522	2704	5.2	28	208.0
8 Texas A&M	13	540	2689	5.0	32	206.9
9 TCU	13	557	2530	4.5	28	194.6
10 Illinois	12	434	2266	5.2	15	188.8

PASSING OFFENSE	G	ATT	COM	INT	PCT	YDS	YPA	TD	I%	YPC	YPG
1 Hawaii	14	615	444	12	72.2	6178	10.1	62	2.0	13.9	441.3
2 New Mexico State	12	607	421	12	69.4	4792	7.9	34	2.0	11.4	399.3
3 Texas Tech	13	655	438	11	66.9	4803	7.3	39	1.7	11.0	369.5
4 Brigham Young	13	452	311	9	68.8	4206	9.3	33	2.0	13.5	323.5
5 UTEP	12	447	290	17	64.9	3754	8.4	29	3.8	12.9	312.8
6 Purdue	14	541	322	20	59.5	4082	7.6	24	3.7	12.7	291.6
7 Louisville	13	384	245	7	63.8	3770	9.8	22	1.8	15.4	290.0
8 Houston	14	445	300	5	67.4	3889	8.7	30	1.1	13.0	277.8
9 Kentucky	**13**	**436**	**273**	**7**	**62.6**	**3597**	**8.3**	**31**	**1.6**	**13.2**	**276.7**
10 Missouri	13	465	291	11	62.6	3590	7.7	29	2.4	12.3	276.2

TOTAL OFFENSE	G	P	YDS	AVG	TD	YPG
1 Hawaii	14	913	7829	8.6	89	559.2
2 Louisville	13	867	6179	7.1	61	475.3
3 New Mexico State	12	930	5702	6.1	53	475.2
4 BYU	13	889	6051	6.8	63	465.5
5 West Virginia	13	823	5998	7.3	65	461.4
6 Texas Tech	13	875	5822	6.7	54	447.9
7 Houston	14	935	6245	6.7	60	446.1
8 Missouri	13	922	5533	6.0	48	425.6
9 Oregon	13	958	5497	5.7	48	422.9
10 Boise State	13	857	5468	6.4	68	420.6

RUSHING DEFENSE	G	ATT	YDS	AVG	TD	YPG
1 Michigan	13	301	564	1.9	5	43.4
2 TCU	13	367	791	2.2	8	60.8
3 Texas	13	345	795	2.3	8	61.2
4 Miami (Fla.)	13	391	882	2.3	12	67.8
5 Florida	**14**	**370**	**1015**	**2.7**	**8**	**72.5**
6 Western Michigan	13	380	989	2.6	11	76.1
7 Penn State	13	400	1137	2.8	8	87.5
8 Boise State	13	361	1158	3.2	7	89.1
9 UCLA	13	419	1184	2.8	9	91.1
9 Southern California	13	399	1184	3.0	6	91.1

PASSING DEFENSE	G	ATT	COM	PCT	INT	I%	YDS	YPA	TD	TD%	RAT
1 Wisconsin	13	387	185	47.8	15	3.9	1798	4.7	6	1.6	84.2
2 Virginia Tech	13	314	161	51.3	17	5.4	1667	5.3	6	1.9	91.4
3 LSU	**13**	**364**	**172**	**47.3**	**16**	**4.4**	**1894**	**5.2**	**11**	**3.0**	**92.2**
4 Florida	**14**	**458**	**244**	**53.3**	**21**	**4.6**	**2561**	**5.6**	**10**	**2.2**	**98.3**
5 Kent State	12	326	171	52.5	16	4.9	1907	5.9	8	2.5	99.9
6 Georgia	**13**	**342**	**182**	**53.2**	**19**	**5.6**	**1950**	**5.7**	**11**	**3.2**	**100.6**
7 TCU	13	386	207	53.6	16	4.2	2263	5.9	9	2.3	102.3
8 Rutgers	13	312	162	51.9	15	4.8	1966	6.3	8	2.6	103.7
9 Georgia Tech	14	461	238	51.6	13	2.8	2741	6.0	11	2.4	103.8
10 Ohio State	13	415	242	58.3	21	5.1	2368	5.7	10	2.4	104.1

TOTAL DEFENSE	G	P	YDS	AVG	TD	YPG
1 Virginia Tech	13	743	2853	3.8	14	219.5
2 TCU	13	753	3054	4.1	19	234.9
3 LSU	**13**	**764**	**3156**	**4.1**	**20**	**242.8**
4 Rutgers	13	759	3279	4.3	22	252.2
5 Wisconsin	13	775	3290	4.3	18	253.1
6 Florida	**14**	**828**	**3576**	**4.3**	**23**	**255.4**
7 Miami (Fla.)	13	753	3322	4.4	22	255.5
8 Georgia	**13**	**775**	**3357**	**4.3**	**28**	**258.2**
9 Wyoming	12	723	3155	4.4	32	262.9
10 Michigan	13	789	3488	4.4	25	268.3

SCORING OFFENSE	G	PTS	AVG
1 Hawaii	14	656	46.9
2 Boise State	13	516	39.7
3 West Virginia	13	505	38.9
4 Louisville	13	491	37.8
5 BYU	13	478	36.8
6 Texas	13	467	35.9
7 Oklahoma State	13	458	35.2
8 Ohio State	13	450	34.6
9 LSU	**13**	**438**	**33.7**
10 Houston	14	462	33.0

SCORING DEFENSE	G	PTS	AVG
1 Virginia Tech	13	143	11.0
2 Wisconsin	13	157	12.1
3 TCU	13	160	12.3
4 LSU	**13**	**164**	**12.6**
5 Ohio State	13	166	12.8
6 Florida	**14**	**189**	**13.5**
7 Auburn	**13**	**181**	**13.9**
8 Rutgers	13	186	14.3
8 Penn State	13	187	14.4
10 BYU	13	191	14.7

TURNOVER MARGIN	G	FR	INT	TOT	FL	INTL	TOT	MAR
1 Minnesota	13	15	17	32	3	11	14	1.38
2 Boston College	13	16	21	37	11	11	22	1.15
2 Kentucky	**13**	**18**	**14**	**32**	**10**	**7**	**17**	**1.15**
4 BYU	13	9	18	27	4	9	13	1.08
4 Michigan	13	14	12	26	4	8	12	1.08
6 Wake Forest	14	9	22	31	12	6	18	0.93
7 Nevada	13	17	20	37	13	12	25	0.92
7 Western Michigan	13	10	24	34	9	13	22	0.92
9 Syracuse	12	11	17	28	12	5	17	0.92
10 Boise State	13	11	20	31	11	9	20	0.85
10 Rutgers	13	16	15	31	7	13	20	0.85

2006

FINAL POLL (JAN. 9)

USA	AP	SCHOOL	FINAL RECORD
1	1	**Florida**	**13-1**
2	2	Ohio State	12-1
3	3	**LSU**	**11-2**
4	4	Southern California	11-2
6	5	Boise State	3-0
7	6	Louisville	12-1
5	7	Wisconsin	12-1
9	8	Michigan	11-2
8	9	**Auburn**	**11-2**
10	10	West Virginia	11-2
11	11	Oklahoma	11-3
12	12	Rutgers	11-2
13	13	Texas	10-3
14	14	California	10-3
16	15	**Arkansas**	**10-4**
15	16	BYU	11-2
19	17	Notre Dame	10-3
17	18	Wake Forest	11-3
18	19	Virginia Tech	10-3
20	20	Boston College	10-3
22	21	Oregon State	10-4
21	22	TCU	11-2
	23	**Georgia**	**9-4**
25	24	Penn State	9-4
23	25	**Tennessee**	**9-4**
24		Hawaii	11-3

CONSENSUS ALL-AMERICANS

POS	OFFENSE	CL	SCHOOL
QB	Troy Smith	Sr.	Ohio State
RB	**Darren McFadden**	**So.**	**Arkansas**
RB	Steve Slaton	So.	West Virginia
WR	Dwayne Jarrett	Jr.	Southern California
WR	Calvin Johnson	Jr.	Georgia Tech
TE	Zach Miller	Jr.	Arizona State
OL	Jake Long	Sr.	Michigan
OL	Joe Thomas	Sr.	Wisconsin
OL	Justin Blalock	Sr.	Texas
OL	Sam Baker	Jr.	Southern California
OL	Dan Mozes	Sr.	West Virginia
PK	Justin Medlock	Sr.	UCLA
AP/KR	DeSean Jackson	So.	California

OTHERS RECEIVING FIRST-TEAM HONORS

RB	Marshawn Lynch		California
TE	Jonny Harline		BYU
WR	Jeff Samardzija		Notre Dame
WR	**Robert Meachem**		**Tennessee**
WR	Johnnie Lee Higgins		UTEP
TE	Matt Spaeth		Minnesota
OL	Josh Beekman		Boston College
OL	Steve Vallos		Wake Forest
OL	**Arron Sears**		**Tennessee**
PK	Mason Crosby		Colorado
KR	Marcus Thigpen		Indiana

POS	DEFENSE	CL	SCHOOL
DL	LaMarr Woodley	Sr.	Michigan
DL	Gaines Adams	Sr.	Clemson
DL	**Glenn Dorsey**	**Jr.**	**LSU**
DL	Quinn Pitcock	Sr.	Ohio State
LB	Paul Posluszny	Sr.	Penn State
LB	**Patrick Willis**	**Sr.**	**Mississippi**
LB	James Laurinaitis	So.	Ohio State
DB	Leon Hall	Sr.	Michigan
DB	Daymeion Hughes	Sr.	California
DB	**LaRon Landry**	**Sr.**	**LSU**
DB	**Reggie Nelson**	**Jr.**	**Florida**
P	Daniel Sepulveda	Sr.	Baylor

OTHERS RECEIVING FIRST-TEAM HONORS

DB	Aaron Ross		Texas
DB	Dwight Lowery		San Jose State
DB	Eric Weddle		Utah
DB	John Talley		Duke
LB	H.B. Blades		Pittsburgh
LB	Dan Connor		Penn State
LB	Rufus Alexander		Oklahoma
LB	Buster Davis		Florida State
DL	Eric Foster		Rutgers
DL	Justin Hickman		UCLA

HEISMAN TROPHY VOTING

	PLAYER	POS	SCHOOL	TOTAL
1	Troy Smith	QB	Ohio State	2,540
2	**Darren McFadden**	**RB**	**Arkansas**	**878**
3	Brady Quinn	QB	Notre Dame	782
4	Steve Slaton	RB	West Virginia	214
5	Mike Hart	RB	Michigan	210
6	Colt Brennan	QB	Hawaii	202
7	Ray Rice	RB	Rutgers	79
8	Ian Johnson	RB	Boise State	73
9	Dwayne Jarrett	WR	Southern Cal	47
10	Calvin Johnson	WR	Georgia Tech	43

AWARD WINNERS

PLAYER	AWARD
Brady Quinn, QB, Notre Dame	Maxwell
Joe Thomas, OL, Wisconsin	Outland
Troy Smith, QB, Ohio State	Camp
LaMarr Woodley, LB, Michigan	Lombardi
Troy Smith, QB, Ohio State	O'Brien
Patrick Willis, LB, Mississippi	**Butkus**
Aaron Ross, DB, Texas	Thorpe
Brady Quinn, QB, Notre Dame	Unitas
Darren McFadden, RB, Arkansas	**Walker**
Art Carmody, K, Louisville	Groza
James Laurinaitis, LB, Ohio State	Nagurski
Paul Posluszny, LB, Penn State	Bednarik
Calvin Johnson, WR, Georgia Tech	Biletnikoff
A.J. Trapasso, P, Ohio State	Tatupu
Daniel Sepulveda, P, Baylor	Guy
Matt Spaeth, TE, Minnesota	Mackey
Dan Mozes, C, West Virginia	Rimington
LaMarr Woodley, LB, Michigan	Hendricks
Daymeion Hughes, CB, California	Lott

BOWL GAMES

DATE	GAME	SCORE
D19	Poinsettia	TCU 37, No. Illinois 7
D21	Las Vegas	BYU 38, Oregon 8
D22	New Orleans	Troy 41, Rice 17
D23	PapaJohns.com	So. Florida 24, E. Carolina 7
D23	New Mexico	San Jose St. 20, New Mexico 12
D23	Armed Forces	Utah 25, Tulsa 13
D24	Hawaii	Hawaii 41, Arizona State 24
D26	Motor City	C. Michigan 31, Mid. Tennessee 14
D27	Emerald	Florida State 44, UCLA 27
D28	**Independence**	**Oklahoma State 34, Alabama 31**
D28	Texas	Rutgers 37, Kansas State 10
D28	Holiday	California 45, Texas A&M 10
D29	Champs Sports	Maryland 24, Purdue 7
D29	Insight	Texas Tech 44, Minnesota 41 OT
D29	**Liberty**	**South Carolina 44, Houston 36**
D29	**Music City**	**Kentucky 28, Clemson 20**
D29	Sun	Oregon State 39, Missouri 38
D30	Meineke Car Care	Boston College 25, Navy 24
D30	**Chick-fil-A**	**Georgia 31, Virginia Tech 24**
D30	Alamo	Texas 26, Iowa 24
D31	MPC Computers	Miami (Fla.) 21, Nevada 20
J1	Cotton	Auburn 17, Nebraska 14
J1	**Outback**	**Penn State 20, Tennessee 10**
J1	Gator	West Virginia 38, Georgia Tech 35
J1	**Capital One**	**Wisconsin 17, Arkansas 14**
J1	Fiesta	Boise State 43, Oklahoma 42 OT
J1	Rose	Southern California 32, Michigan 18
J2	Orange	Louisville 24, Wake Forest 13
J3	**Sugar**	**LSU 41, Notre Dame 14**
J6	International	Cincinnati 27, Western Michigan 24
J7	GMAC	Southern Miss 28, Ohio U. 7
J8	**BCS Championship**	**Florida 41, Ohio State 14**

SEC STANDINGS

SEC	CONFERENCE		OVERALL	
	W	L	W	L
EAST				
Florida	7	1	13	1
Tennessee	5	3	9	4
Georgia	4	4	9	4
Kentucky	4	4	8	5
South Carolina	3	5	8	5
Vanderbilt	1	7	4	8
WEST				
Arkansas	7	1	10	4
LSU	6	2	11	2
Auburn	6	2	11	2
Alabama	2	6	6	7
Mississippi	2	6	4	8
Mississippi State	1	7	3	9

ALL-SEC TEAM

POS	OFFENSE	SCHOOL
QB	JaMarcus Russell	LSU
RB	Darren McFadden	Arkansas
RB	Kenny Irons	Auburn
WR	Robert Meachem	Tennessee
WR	Dwayne Bowe	LSU
WR	Dallas Baker	Florida
C	Jonathan Luigs	Arkansas
C	Steve Rissler	Florida
OL	Arron Sears	Tennessee
OL	Zac Tubbs	Arkansas
OL	Tim Duckworth	Auburn
OL	Tony Ugoh	Arkansas
TE	Martrez Milner	Georgia
TE	Jacob Tamme	Kentucky
K	John Vaughn	Auburn
K	James Wilhoit	Tennessee

POS	DEFENSE	SCHOOL
DL	Glenn Dorsey	LSU
DL	Quentin Groves	Auburn
DL	Jamaal Anderson	Arkansas
DL	Ray McDonald	Florida
LB	Patrick Willis	Mississippi
LB	Quinton Culberson	Mississippi State
LB	Sam Olajubutu	Arkansas
LB	Earl Everett	Florida
LB	Wesley Woodyard	Kentucky
DB	Reggie Nelson	Florida
DB	Tra Battle	Georgia
DB	Simeon Castille	Alabama
DB	LaRon Landry	LSU
P	Britton Colquitt	Tennessee
RS	Mikey Henderson	Georgia

SEC CHAMPIONSHIP GAME

DECEMBER 2 | ATLANTA
FLORIDA 38, ARKANSAS 28

	1ST	2ND	3RD	4TH	FINAL
ARK	0	7	14	7	28
FLA	3	14	7	14	38

SCORING SUMMARY

FLA	FG Hetland 33
FLA	Leak 9 run (Hetland kick)
FLA	Harvin 37 pass from Leak (Hetland kick)
ARK	Monk 48 pass from Dick (Davis kick)
ARK	Jones 2 pass from McFadden (Davis kick)
ARK	Robinson 40 interception return (Davis kick)
FLA	Pierre-Louis 0 fumble recovery (Hetland kick)
FLA	Harvin 67 run (Hetland kick)
ARK	Jones 29 pass from Washington (Davis kick)
FLA	Casey 5 pass from Caldwell (Hetland kick)

ARKANSAS	TEAM STATISTICS	FLORIDA
18	First Downs	17
132	Rushing Yards	202
12-26-3	Passing	17-31-2
179	Passing Yards	194
311	Total Yards	396
2-(-4)	Punt Returns - Yards	5-29
4-68	Kickoff Returns - Yards	3-23
5-48.6	Punts - Average	7-55.1
1-1	Fumbles - Lost	3-0
5-25	Penalties - Yards	8-67

INDIVIDUAL LEADERS

RUSHING
ARK: McFadden 21-73.
FLA: Harvin 6-105, TD.

PASSING
ARK: Dick 10-22-2, 148 yards, TD.
FLA: Leak 16-30-2, 189 yards, TD.

RECEIVING
ARK: Monk 3-69, Jones 2-31.
FLA: Ingram 6-71, Harvin 5-62.

2007 NCAA Major College Statistical Leaders

Individual Leaders

PASSING	POS	CL	G	ATT	COM	PCT	INT	I%	YDS	YPA	TD	TD%	RATING
1 Sam Bradford, Oklahoma	QB	FR	14	341	237	69.5	8	2.4	3121	9.2	36	10.6	176.5
2 Tim Tebow, Florida	**QB**	**SO**	**13**	**350**	**234**	**66.9**	**6**	**1.7**	**3286**	**9.4**	**32**	**9.1**	**172.5**
3 Dennis Dixon, Oregon	QB	SR	10	254	172	67.7	4	1.6	2136	8.4	20	7.9	161.2
4 Paul Smith, Tulsa	QB	SR	14	544	327	60.1	19	3.5	5065	9.3	47	8.6	159.8
5 Colt Brennan, Hawaii	QB	SR	12	510	359	70.4	17	3.3	4343	8.5	38	7.5	159.8
6 Graham Harrell, Texas Tech	QB	JR	13	713	512	71.8	14	2.0	5705	8.0	48	6.7	157.3
7 Taylor Tharp, Boise State	QB	SR	13	423	289	68.3	11	2.6	3340	7.9	30	7.1	152.9
8 Brian Brohm, Louisville	QB	SR	12	473	308	65.1	12	2.5	4024	8.5	30	6.3	152.4
9 Patrick White, West Virginia	QB	JR	13	216	144	66.7	4	1.9	1724	8.0	14	6.5	151.4
10 Colin Kaepernick, Nevada	QB	FR	11	247	133	53.9	3	1.2	2175	8.8	19	7.7	150.8

ALL-PURPOSE	POS	CL	G	RUSH	REC	PR	KR	YDS	YPG
1 Chris Johnson, East Carolina	RB	SR	13	1423	528	0	1009	2960	227.7
2 Dante Love, Ball State	WR	JR	13	192	1398	0	1100	2690	206.9
3 Chad Hall, Air Force	WR	SR	13	1478	524	176	505	2683	206.4
4 Matt Forte, Tulane	RB	SR	12	2127	282	0	11	2420	201.7
5 Kevin Smith, Central Florida	RB	JR	14	2567	242	0	0	2809	200.6
6 Devin Thomas, Michigan State	WR	JR	13	177	1260	18	1135	2590	199.2
7 Jeremy Maclin, Missouri	WR	FR	14	375	1055	307	1039	2776	198.3
8 Kevin Robinson, Utah State	WR	SR	12	39	640	378	1260	2317	193.1
9 Jonathan Stewart, Oregon	RB	JR	13	1722	145	0	614	2481	190.9
10 Jalen Parmele, Toledo	RB	SR	12	1511	157	0	560	2228	185.7

RUSHING/Yards Per Game	POS	CL	G	ATT	YDS	TD	AVG	YPG
1 Kevin Smith, Central Florida	RB	JR	14	450	2567	29	5.7	183.4
2 Matt Forte, Tulane	RB	SR	12	361	2127	23	5.9	177.3
3 Ray Rice, Rutgers	RB	JR	13	380	2012	24	5.3	154.8
4 Darren McFadden, Arkansas	**RB**	**JR**	**13**	**325**	**1830**	**16**	**5.6**	**140.8**
5 Eugene Jarvis, Kent State	RB	SO	12	279	1669	10	6.0	139.0
6 Michael Hart, Michigan	RB	SR	10	265	1361	14	5.1	136.1
7 Jonathan Stewart, Oregon	RB	JR	13	280	1722	11	6.2	132.5
8 Rashard Mendenhall, Illinois	RB	JR	13	262	1681	17	6.4	129.3
9 Jalen Parmele, Toledo	RB	SR	12	276	1511	14	5.5	125.9
10 Jamaal Charles, Texas	RB	JR	13	258	1619	18	6.3	124.5

RUSHING/Yards Per Carry	POS	CL	G	ATT	YDS	YPC
1 Percy Harvin, Houston	WR	SO	11	83	764	9.2
2 Felix Jones, Arkansas	**RB**	**JR**	**13**	**133**	**1162**	**8.7**
3 Stafon Johnson, Southern Cal	RB	SO	11	98	673	6.9
4 Patrick White, West Virginia	QB	JR	13	197	1335	6.8
5 Reggie Arnold, Arkansas St.	RB	SO	12	163	1060	6.5
6 Chad Hall, Air Force	RB	SR	13	230	1478	6.4
6 Jim Ollis, Air Force	RB	SR	11	106	682	6.4
8 Rashard Mendenhall, Illinois	RB	JR	13	262	1681	6.4
9 James Johnson, Kansas St.	RB	SR	12	174	1106	6.4
10 Jamaal Charles, Texas	RB	JR	13	258	1619	6.3

RECEIVING	POS	CL	G	REC	YDS	TD	RPG	YPG
1 Michael Crabtree, Texas Tech	WR	FR	13	134	1962	22	10.3	150.9
2 Jordy Nelson, Kansas St.	WR	SR	12	122	1606	11	10.2	133.8
3 Harry Douglas, Louisville	WR	SR	10	71	1159	7	7.1	115.9
4 Donnie Avery, Houston	WR	SR	13	91	1456	7	7.0	112.0
5 Casey Fitzgerald, North Texas	WR	JR	12	111	1322	12	9.3	110.2
6 Dante Love, Ball State	WR	JR	13	100	1398	10	7.7	107.5
7 Brandon Gibson, Wash. St.	WR	JR	11	67	1180	9	6.1	107.3
8 Ryan Grice-Mullen, Hawaii	WR	JR	13	106	1372	13	8.2	105.5
9 Kevin Jurovich, San Jose St.	WR	JR	12	85	1183	9	7.1	98.6
10 Mario Manningham, Michigan	WR	JR	12	72	1174	12	6.0	97.8
10 Jason Rivers, Hawaii	WR	SR	12	92	1174	13	7.7	97.8

PUNTING	POS	CL	PUNT	YDS	AVG
1 Kevin Huber, Cincinnati	P	JR	57	2672	46.9
2 Brett Kern, Toledo	P	SR	52	2399	46.1
3 Chris Miller, Ball State	P	SR	61	2772	45.4
4 Ryan Weigand, Virginia	P	SR	52	2352	45.2
5 Durant Brooks, Georgia Tech	P	SR	65	2929	45.1
6 Jacob Richardson, Miami (Ohio)	P	JR	68	3063	45.0
7 Owen Tolson, Army	P	SR	73	3283	45.0
8 Thomas Morstead, SMU	P	JR	57	2545	44.7
9 Tim Reyer, Kansas State	P	SR	58	2583	44.5
10 Patrick Fisher, LSU	**P**	**SR**	**59**	**2627**	**44.5**

PUNT RETURNS	POS	CL	PR	YDS	TD	AVG
1 Kevin Robinson, Utah State	WR	SR	20	378	1	18.9
2 Brandon James, Florida	**RB**	**SO**	**14**	**254**	**1**	**18.1**
3 Deon Murphy, Kansas State	WR	JR	26	454	1	17.5
4 Leodis McKelvin, Troy	DB	SR	25	436	3	17.4
5 Philip Beck, Louisiana Tech	WR	JR	18	313	0	17.4
6 Shiloh Keo, Idaho	DB	SO	19	319	1	16.8
7 Javier Arenas, Alabama	**DB**	**SO**	**21**	**323**	**1**	**15.4**
8 Jeremy Trimble, Army	WR	SR	19	280	1	14.7
9 Derrick Richards, Utah	WR	SR	29	426	1	14.7
10 Eddie Royal, Virginia Tech	WR	SR	31	455	2	14.7

KICKOFF RETURNS	POS	CL	KR	YDS	TD	AVG
1 A.J. Jefferson, Fresno State	DB	SO	26	930	2	35.8
2 Bryan Williams, Akron	RB	JR	21	670	1	31.9
3 Kevin Marion, Wake Forest	WR	SR	28	876	1	31.3
4 Felix Jones, Arkansas	**RB**	**JR**	**22**	**652**	**2**	**29.6**
5 Ryan Mouton, Hawaii	DB	JR	14	414	1	29.6
6 Kevin Robinson, Utah State	WR	SR	43	1260	3	29.3
7 DeMarco Murray, Oklahoma	RB	FR	15	439	2	29.3
8 Darius Marshall, Marshall	RB	FR	19	556	1	29.2
9 Curtis Francis, Central Florida	RB	SR	22	643	1	29.2
10 Malcolm Lane, Hawaii	WR	SO	25	730	2	29.2

SCORING	POS	CL	TDS	XP	FG	PTS	PTPG
1 Kevin Smith, Central Florida	RB	JR	30	0	0	180	12.9
2 Matt Forte, Tulane	RB	SR	23	0	0	140	11.7
3 Ray Rice, Rutgers	RB	JR	25	0	0	150	11.5
4 Chris Johnson, East Carolina	RB	SR	24	0	0	144	11.1
5 Tim Tebow, Florida	**QB**	**SO**	**23**	**0**	**0**	**138**	**10.6**
6 Colt David, LSU	**K**	**JR**	**1**	**63**	**26**	**147**	**10.5**
7 Michael Crabtree, Texas Tech	WR	FR	22	0	0	132	10.2
8 Kalvin McRae, Ohio U.	RB	SR	20	0	0	120	10.0
9 Marcus Thomas, UTEP	RB	SR.	18	0	0	108	9.8
10 John Sullivan, New Mexico	K	SR	0	30	29	117	9.8

FIELD GOALS	POS	CL	FGA	FGM	PCT	FGG
1 John Sullivan, New Mexico	K	SR	35	29	0.83	2.42
2 Gary Cismesia, Florida State	K	SR	34	27	0.79	2.08
3 Leigh Tiffin, Alabama	**K**	**SO**	**34**	**25**	**0.74**	**1.92**
3 Kai Forbath, UCLA	K	FR	30	25	0.83	1.92
5 Colt David, LSU	**K**	**JR**	**33**	**26**	**0.79**	**1.86**
6 Thomas Weber, Arizona St.	K	FR	25	24	0.96	1.85
7 Brooks Rossman, Kansas St.	K	JR	28	22	0.79	1.83
7 Swayze Waters, UAB	K	JR	28	22	0.79	1.83
9 Jeremy Ito, Rutgers	K	SR	31	23	0.74	1.77
9 Travis Bell, Georgia Tech	K	SR	28	23	0.82	1.77

INTERCEPTIONS	POS	CL	INT	YDS	TD	INT/GM
1 Elbert Mack, Troy	DB	SR	8	48	1	0.67
2 DeAngelo Smith, Cincinnati	DB	JR	8	82	1	0.62
2 Alphonso Smith, Wake Forest	DB	JR	8	166	3	0.62
4 Robert Vaughn, Connecticut	DB	SO	7	112	0	0.58
4 P.J. Mahone, Bowling Green	DB	SO	7	220	1	0.58
4 Reggie Corner, Akron	DB	SR	7	142	1	0.58
7 William Moore, Missouri	DB	JR	8	61	1	0.57
7 Jamie Silva, Boston College	DB	SR	8	147	1	0.57
9 Tavious Polo, Fla. Atlantic	DB	FR	7	17	0	0.54
9 Jairus Byrd, Oregon	DB	SO	7	31	0	0.54
9 Shane Carter, Wisconsin	DB	SO	7	92	0	0.54

Team Leaders

RUSHING OFFENSE	G	ATT	YDS	AVG	TD	YPG
1 Navy	13	804	4534	5.6	53	348.8
2 Air Force	13	721	3894	5.4	36	299.5
3 West Virginia	13	628	3864	6.2	49	297.2
4 Arkansas	**13**	**625**	**3725**	**6.0**	**33**	**286.5**
5 Illinois	13	595	3338	5.6	28	256.8
6 Oregon	13	615	3272	5.3	32	251.7
7 La.-Lafayette	12	542	3019	5.6	23	251.6
8 Oklahoma State	13	592	3161	5.3	30	243.2
9 Central Florida	14	670	3287	4.9	41	234.8
10 Houston	13	599	2911	4.9	32	223.9

PASSING OFFENSE	G	ATT	COM	INT	PCT	YDS	YPA	TD	I%	YPC	YPG
1 Texas Tech	13	763	544	15	71.3	6114	8.0	51	2.0	11.2	470.3
2 Hawaii	13	663	459	23	69.2	5713	8.6	51	3.5	12.5	439.5
3 Tulsa	14	564	336	19	59.6	5194	9.2	49	3.4	15.5	371.0
4 Louisville	12	491	316	14	64.4	4103	8.4	30	2.9	13.0	341.9
5 New Mexico State	13	623	429	22	68.9	4315	6.9	28	3.5	10.1	331.9
6 Boston College	14	659	390	19	59.2	4535	6.9	31	2.9	11.6	323.9
7 Nebraska	12	481	296	17	61.5	3886	8.1	31	3.5	13.1	323.8
8 Washington State	12	524	308	18	58.9	3835	7.3	26	3.4	12.5	319.6
9 Missouri	14	582	394	13	67.7	4397	7.6	34	2.2	11.2	314.1
10 Arizona	12	531	332	12	62.5	3702	7.0	28	2.3	11.2	308.5

TOTAL OFFENSE	G	P	YDS	AVG	TD	YPG
1 Tulsa	14	1126	7615	6.8	79	543.9
2 Texas Tech	13	1009	6885	6.8	70	529.6
3 Hawaii	13	942	6657	7.1	76	512.1
4 Houston	13	1036	6525	6.3	59	501.9
5 Missouri	14	1112	6864	6.2	70	490.3
6 Louisville	12	909	5856	6.4	55	488.0
7 Oklahoma State	13	978	6322	6.5	60	486.3
8 Kansas	13	988	6237	6.3	72	479.8
9 Nebraska	12	898	5619	6.3	53	468.3
10 Oregon	13	1028	6078	5.9	62	467.5

RUSHING DEFENSE	G	ATT	YDS	AVG	TD	YPG
1 Oregon State	13	447	918	2.1	12	70.6
2 Boston College	14	436	1057	2.4	8	75.5
3 Ohio State	13	426	1077	2.5	3	82.8
4 Southern California	13	431	1094	2.5	13	84.2
5 Virginia Tech	14	442	1213	2.7	14	86.6
6 Texas	13	425	1214	2.9	12	93.4
7 Penn State	13	449	1219	2.7	9	93.8
8 Kansas	13	401	1232	3.1	8	94.8
9 BYU	13	429	1267	23.0	12	97.5
10 Florida	**13**	**442**	**1343**	**3.0**	**18**	**103.3**

PASSING DEFENSE	G	ATT	COM	PCT	INT	I%	YDS	YPA	TD	TD%	RAT
1 Utah	13	428	216	50.5	17	4.0	2395	5.6	9	2.1	96.5
2 Arkansas	**13**	**485**	**220**	**45.4**	**20**	**4.1**	**2670**	**5.5**	**21**	**4.3**	**97.7**
3 LSU	**14**	**451**	**212**	**47.0**	**23**	**5.1**	**2558**	**5.7**	**19**	**4.2**	**98.4**
4 Ohio State	13	406	216	53.2	11	2.7	1952	4.8	13	3.2	98.7
5 Virginia Tech	14	518	277	53.5	22	4.3	2944	5.7	10	1.9	99.1
6 Southern California	13	444	241	54.3	12	2.7	2457	5.5	9	2.0	102.1
7 Auburn	**13**	**403**	**223**	**55.3**	**14**	**3.5**	**2252**	**5.6**	**11**	**2.7**	**104.3**
8 South Florida	13	474	244	51.5	23	4.9	2757	5.8	21	4.4	105.3
9 Kansas	13	528	303	57.4	23	4.4	2893	5.5	17	3.2	105.3
10 Connecticut	13	430	255	59.3	23	5.4	2522	5.9	12	2.8	107.1

TOTAL DEFENSE	G	P	YDS	AVG	TD	YPG
1 Ohio State	13	832	3029	3.6	20	233.0
2 Southern California	13	875	3551	4.1	25	273.2
3 LSU	**14**	**915**	**4043**	**4.4**	**35**	**288.8**
4 Virginia Tech	14	960	4157	4.3	27	296.9
5 Pittsburgh	12	808	3572	4.4	35	297.7
6 Auburn	**13**	**855**	**3873**	**4.5**	**25**	**297.9**
7 West Virginia	13	871	3922	4.5	29	301.7
8 Oregon State	13	891	3980	4.5	35	306.2
9 Clemson	13	877	3988	4.6	29	306.8
10 BYU	13	877	4002	4.6	27	307.9

SCORING OFFENSE	G	PTS	AVG
1 Hawaii	13	564	43.4
2 Kansas	13	556	42.8
3 Florida	**13**	**552**	**42.5**
4 Boise State	13	551	42.4
5 Oklahoma	14	592	42.3
6 Tulsa	14	576	41.1
7 Texas Tech	13	532	40.9
8 Missouri	14	558	39.9
9 West Virginia	13	515	39.6
10 Navy	13	511	39.3

SCORING DEFENSE	G	PTS	AVG
1 Ohio State	13	166	12.8
2 Southern California	13	208	16.0
3 Virginia Tech	14	225	16.1
4 Kansas	13	213	16.4
5 Utah	13	219	16.8
6 Auburn	**13**	**220**	**16.9**
7 Penn State	13	228	17.5
8 West Virginia	13	235	18.1
9 BYU	13	241	18.5
10 TCU	13	243	18.7
10 Clemson	13	243	18.7

TURNOVER MARGIN	G	FR	INT	TOT	FL	INTL	TOT	MAR
1 Kansas	13	12	23	35	7	7	14	1.62
2 LSU	**14**	**13**	**23**	**36**	**3**	**13**	**16**	**1.43**
2 Florida Atlantic	13	14	19	33	4	11	15	1.38
4 Ball State	13	9	19	28	5	6	11	1.31
4 East Carolina	13	14	17	31	5	9	14	1.31
6 Cincinnati	13	16	26	42	14	12	26	1.23
7 San Jose State	12	7	20	27	3	11	14	1.08
8 Connecticut	13	6	23	29	9	6	15	1.08
9 Clemson	13	9	16	25	6	6	12	1.00
9 West Virginia	13	18	16	34	15	6	21	1.00

2007

FINAL POLL (JAN. 8)

USA	AP	SCHOOL	FINAL RECORD
1	1	LSU	12-2
3	2	Georgia	11-2
2	3	Southern California	11-2
5	4	Missouri	12-2
4	5	Ohio State	11-2
6	6	West Virginia	11-2
7	7	Kansas	12-1
8	8	Oklahoma	11-3
9	9	Virginia Tech	11-3
10	10	Texas	10-3
11	10	Boston College	11-3
12	12	Tennessee	10-4
16	13	Florida	9-4
14	14	BYU	11-2
14	15	Auburn	9-4
13	16	Arizona State	10-3
20	17	Cincinnati	10-3
19	18	Michigan	9-4
17	19	Hawaii	12-1
18	20	Illinois	9-4
22	21	Clemson	9-4
23	22	Texas Tech	9-4
24	23	Oregon	9-4
21	24	Wisconsin	9-4
	25	Oregon State	9-4
25		Penn State	9-4

CONSENSUS ALL-AMERICANS

POS	OFFENSE	CL	SCHOOL
QB	Tim Tebow	So.	Florida
RB	Darren McFadden	Jr.	Arkansas
RB	Kevin Smith	Jr.	Central Florida
WR	Michael Crabtree	Fr.	Texas Tech
WR	Jordy Nelson	Sr.	Kansas State
TE	Martin Rucker	Sr.	Missouri
OL	Ryan Clady	Jr.	Boise State
OL	Jake Long	Sr.	Michigan
OL	Steve Justice	Sr.	Wake Forest
OL	Jonathan Luigs	Jr.	Arkansas
OL	Duke Robinson	Jr.	Oklahoma
PK	John Sullivan	Sr.	New Mexico
KR	Jeremy Maclin	Fr.	Missouri

OTHERS RECEIVING FIRST-TEAM HONORS

QB	Matt Ryan	Boston College
RB	Jonathan Stewart	Oregon
WR	Percy Harvin	Florida
TE	Travis Beckham	Wisconsin
TE	Fred Davis	Southern California
OL	Sam Baker	Southern California
OL	Tony Hill	Texas
OL	Martin O'Donnell	Illinois
OL	Kirk Barton	Ohio State
OL	Alex Mack	California
OL	Hercules Satele	Hawaii
OL	Ryan Stanchek	West Virginia
PK	Thomas Weber	Arizona
PK	Daniel Lincoln	Tennessee
PK	Taylor Mehlhaff	Wisconsin
KR	Felix Jones	Arkansas
AP/KR	DeSean Jackson	California

POS	DEFENSE	CL	SCHOOL
DL	Glenn Dorsey	Sr.	LSU
DL	Sedrick Ellis	Sr.	Southern California
DL	Chris Long	Sr.	Virginia
DL	George Selvie	So.	South Florida
LB	Dan Conner	Sr.	Penn State
LB	Jordan Dizon	Sr.	Colorado
LB	James Laurinaitis	Jr.	Ohio State
DB	Aqib Talib	Jr.	Kansas
DB	Craig Steltz	Sr.	LSU
DB	Antoine Cason	Sr.	Arizona
DB	Jamie Silva	Sr.	Boston College
P	Kevin Huber	Jr.	Cincinnati

OTHERS RECEIVING FIRST-TEAM HONORS

DL	Greg Middleton	Indiana
LB	Xavier Adibi	Virginia Tech
LB	J Leman	Illinois
LB	Curtis Lofton	Oklahoma
DB	Brandon Flowers	Virginia Tech
DB	Mike Jenkins	South Florida
DB	Dwight Lowery	San Jose State
DB	Taylor Mays	Southern California
DB	Chris Horton	UCLA
DB	Mike Mickens	Cincinnati
P	Louie Sakoda	Utah

HEISMAN TROPHY VOTING

	PLAYER	POS	SCHOOL	TOTAL
1	Tim Tebow	QB	Florida	1,957
2	Darren McFadden	RB	Arkansas	1,703
3	Colt Brennan	QB	Hawaii	632
4	Chase Daniel	QB	Missouri	425
5	Dennis Dixon	QB	Oregon	178
6	Pat White	QB	West Virginia	150
7	Matt Ryan	QB	Boston College	63
8	Kevin Smith	RB	Central Florida	55
9	Glenn Dorsey	DT	LSU	30
10	Chris Long	DE	Virginia	17

AWARD WINNERS

PLAYER	AWARD
Tim Tebow, QB, Florida	Maxwell
Glenn Dorsey, DT, LSU	Outland
Darren McFadden, RB, Arkansas	Camp
Glenn Dorsey, DT, LSU	Lombardi
Tim Tebow, QB, Florida	O'Brien
James Laurinaitis, LB, Ohio State	Butkus
Antoine Cason, DB, Arizona	Thorpe
Matt Ryan, QB, Boston College	Unitas
Darren McFadden, RB, Arkansas	Walker
Thomas Weber, K, Arizona State	Groza
Glenn Dorsey, DT, LSU	Nagurski
Dan Conner, LB, Penn State	Bednarik
Michael Crabtree, WR, Texas Tech	Biletnikoff
Durant Brooks, P, Georgia Tech	Guy
Fred Davis, TE, Southern California	Mackey
Jonathan Luigs, C, Arkansas	Rimington
Chris Long, DE, Virginia	Hendricks
Glenn Dorsey, DT, LSU	Lott
Matt Ryan, QB, Boston College	Manning

BOWL GAMES

DATE	GAME	SCORE
D20	Poinsettia	Utah 35, Navy 32
D21	New Orleans	Florida Atlantic 44, Memphis 27
D22	PapaJohns.com	Cincinnati 31, Southern Miss 21
D22	New Mexico	New Mexico 23, Nevada 0
D22	Las Vegas	BYU 17, UCLA 16
D23	Hawaii	E. Carolina 41, Boise State 38
D26	Motor City	Purdue 51, C. Michigan 48
D27	Holiday	Texas 52, Arizona State 34
D28	Champs Sports	Boston College 24, Michigan St. 21
D28	Texas	TCU 20, Houston 13
D28	Emerald	Oregon State 21, Maryland 14
D29	Meineke Car Care	Wake Forest 24, Connecticut 10
D29	Liberty	Mississippi St. 10, Cent. Florida 3
D29	Alamo	Penn State 24, Texas A&M 17
D30	Independence	Alabama 30, Colorado 24
D31	Armed Forces	California 42, Air Force 36
D31	Humanitarian	Fresno State 40, Georgia Tech 28
D31	Sun	Oregon 56, South Florida 21
D31	Music City	Kentucky 35, Florida State 28
D31	Insight	Oklahoma State 49, Indiana 33
D31	Chick-fil-A	Auburn 23, Clemson 20 OT
J1	Outback	Tennessee 21, Wisconsin 17
J1	Cotton	Missouri 38, Arkansas 7
J1	Gator	Texas Tech 31, Virginia 28
J1	Capital One	Michigan 41, Florida 35
J1	Sugar	Georgia 41, Hawaii 10
J1	Rose	Southern California 49, Illinois 17
J2	Fiesta	West Virginia 48, Oklahoma 28
J3	Orange	Kansas 24, Virginia Tech 21
J5	International	Rutgers 52, Ball State 30
J6	GMAC	Tulsa 63, Bowling Green 7
J7	BCS Championship	LSU 38, Ohio State 24

SEC STANDINGS

	CONFERENCE		OVERALL	
	W	L	W	L
EAST				
Georgia	6	2	11	2
Tennessee	6	2	10	4
Florida	5	3	9	4
Kentucky	3	5	8	5
South Carolina	3	5	6	6
Vanderbilt	2	6	5	7
WEST				
LSU	6	2	12	2
Auburn	5	3	9	4
Arkansas	4	4	8	5
Mississippi State	4	4	8	5
Alabama	4	4	7	6
Mississippi	0	8	3	9

ALL-SEC TEAM

POS	OFFENSE	SCHOOL
QB	Tim Tebow	Florida
RB	Darren McFadden	Arkansas
RB	Knowshon Moreno	Georgia
WR	Kenny McKinley	South Carolina
WR	Earl Bennett	Vanderbilt
C	Jonathan Luigs	Arkansas
OL	Robert Felton	Arkansas
OL	Andre Smith	Alabama
OL	Anthony Parker	Tennessee
OL	Herman Johnson	LSU
OL	Michael Oher	Mississippi
OL	Chris Williams	Vanderbilt
TE	Jacob Tamme	Kentucky
K	Colt David	LSU

POS	DEFENSE	SCHOOL
DL	Glenn Dorsey	LSU
DL	Wallace Gilberry	Alabama
DL	Quentin Groves	Auburn
DL	Greg Hardy	Mississippi
DL	Eric Norwood	South Carolina
LB	Ali Highsmith	LSU
LB	Wesley Woodyard	Kentucky
LB	Jerod Mayo	Tennessee
LB	Brandon Spikes	Florida
DB	Craig Steltz	LSU
DB	Chevis Jackson	LSU
DB	Simeon Castille	Alabama
DB	Rashad Johnson	Alabama
DB	Jonathan Hefney	Tennessee
DB	Captain Munnerlyn	South Carolina
P	Patrick Fisher	LSU
RS	Felix Jones	Arkansas

SEC CHAMPIONSHIP GAME

DECEMBER 1 | ATLANTA

LSU 21, Tennessee 14

	1ST	2ND	3RD	4TH	FINAL
TENN	7	0	7	0	14
LSU	6	0	7	8	21

SCORING SUMMARY

TENN — Brown 11 pass from Ainge (Lincoln Kick)
LSU — FG David 30
LSU — FG David 30
LSU — Byrd 27 pass from Perrilloux (David kick)
TENN — Briscoe 6 pass from Ainge (Lincoln kick)
LSU — Zenon 18 interception return (Perrilloux rush)

TENNESSEE	TEAM STATISTICS	LSU
17	First Downs	21
94	Rushing Yards	212
20-40-2	Passing	21-33-1
249	Passing Yards	252
343	Total Yards	464
2-11	Punt Returns - Yards	1-1
4-99	Kickoff Returns - Yards	3-64
5-36.0	Punts - Average	4-45.0
0-0	Fumbles - Lost	3-1
0-0	Penalties - Yards	9-44

INDIVIDUAL LEADERS

RUSHING
TENN: Foster 21-55.
LSU: Hester 23-120.

PASSING
TENN: Ainge 20-40-2, 249 yards, 2 TD.
LSU: Perrilloux 20-30-1, 243 yards, TD.

RECEIVING
TENN: Briscoe 8-79, TD; Foster 2-40.
LSU: Doucet 5-29; Byrd 4-72, TD.

2008 NCAA Major College Statistical Leaders

Individual Leaders

PASSING	POS	CL	G	ATT	COM	PCT	INT	I%	YDS	YPA	TD	TD%	RATING
1 Sam Bradford, Oklahoma	QB	SO	14	483	328	67.9	8	1.6	4720	9.7	50	10.3	180.8
2 David Johnson, Tulsa	QB	SR	14	400	258	64.5	18	4.5	4059	10.1	46	11.5	178.7
3 Colt McCoy, Texas	QB	JR	13	433	332	76.6	8	1.8	3859	8.9	34	7.8	173.8
4 Tim Tebow, Florida	**QB**	**JR**	**14**	**298**	**192**	**64.4**	**4**	**1.3**	**2746**	**9.2**	**30**	**10.0**	**172.4**
5 Zac Robinson, Oklahoma St.	QB	JR	13	314	204	64.9	10	3.1	3064	9.7	25	7.9	166.8
6 Mark Sanchez, Southern California	QB	JR	13	366	241	65.8	10	2.7	3207	8.7	34	9.2	164.6
7 Chase Clement, Rice	QB	SR	13	490	326	66.5	7	1.4	4119	8.4	44	8.9	163.9
8 Graham Harrell, Texas Tech	QB	SR	13	626	442	70.6	9	1.4	5111	8.1	45	7.1	160.0
9 Case Keenum, Houston	QB	SO	13	589	397	67.4	11	1.8	5020	8.5	44	7.4	159.9
10 Chase Daniel, Missouri	QB	SR	14	528	385	72.9	18	3.4	4335	8.2	39	7.3	159.4

ALL-PURPOSE	POS	CL	G	RUSH	REC	PR	KR	YDS	YPG
1 Jeremy Maclin, Missouri	WR	SO	14	293	1260	270	1010	2833	202.3
2 Jahvid Best, California	RB	SO	12	1580	246	0	421	2247	187.2
3 T.Y. Hilton, Florida International	WR	FR	12	43	1013	266	841	2163	180.2
4 Antonio Brown, Central Michigan	WR	SO	13	116	998	410	791	2315	178.0
5 Damaris Johnson, Tulsa	WR	FR	14	327	743	23	1382	2475	176.7
6 Donald Brown, Connecticut	RB	JR	13	2083	125	0	0	2208	169.8
7 Devin Moore, Wyoming	RB	SR	12	1301	40	0	667	2008	167.3
8 DeMarco Murray, Oklahoma	RB	SO	13	1002	395	0	774	2171	167.0
9 Darius Marshall, Marshall	RB	SO	12	1099	98	0	790	1987	165.5
9 Josh Smith, Colorado	WR	SO	12	32	387	292	1276	1987	165.5

RUSHING/YARDS PER GAME	POS	CL	G	ATT	YDS	TD	AVG	YPG
1 Donald Brown, Connecticut	RB	JR	13	367	2083	18	5.6	160.2
2 Shonn Greene, Iowa	RB	JR	13	307	1850	20	6.0	142.3
3 Jahvid Best, California	RB	SO	12	194	1580	15	8.1	131.6
4 Javon Ringer, Michigan State	RB	SR	13	390	1637	22	4.2	125.9
5 MiQuale Lewis, Ball State	RB	JR	14	322	1736	22	5.3	124.0
6 Chris Wells, Ohio State	RB	JR	10	207	1197	8	5.7	119.7
7 Kendall Hunter, Oklahoma State	RB	SO	13	241	1555	16	6.4	119.6
8 Vai Taua, Nevada	RB	SO	13	236	1521	15	6.4	117.0
9 Tyrell Fenroy, La.-Lafayette	RB	SR	12	226	1375	19	6.0	114.5
10 LeSean McCoy, Pittsburgh	RB	SO	13	308	1488	21	4.8	114.4

RUSHING/YARDS PER CARRY	POS	CL	G	ATT	YDS	YPC
1 Percy Harvin, Florida	**WR**	**JR**	**12**	**70**	**660**	**9.4**
2 Shun White, Navy	RB	SR	13	132	1092	8.2
3 Jahvid Best, California	RB	SO	12	194	1580	8.1
4 Joe McKnight, Southern California	RB	SO	11	89	659	7.4
5 LeGarrette Blount, Oregon	RB	JR	13	137	1002	7.3
6 Michael Desormeaux, La.-Lafayette	QB	SR	11	144	1035	7.1
6 Derek Lawson, Arkansas St.	RB	FR	12	97	695	7.1
8 Jeremiah Johnson, Oregon	RB	SR	13	168	1201	7.1
9 Colin Kaepernick, Nevada	QB	SO	13	161	1130	7.0
10 Jonathan Dwyer, Georgia Tech	RB	SO	13	200	1395	6.9

RECEIVING	POS	CL	G	REC	YDS	TD	RPG	YPG
1 Austin Collie, BYU	WR	JR	13	106	1538	15	8.1	118.3
2 Kenny Britt, Rutgers	WR	JR	12	87	1371	7	7.2	114.2
3 Dez Bryant, Oklahoma St.	WR	SO	13	87	1480	19	6.6	113.8
4 Dezmon Briscoe, Kansas	WR	SO	13	92	1407	15	7.0	108.2
5 Chris Williams, New Mexico St.	WR	SR	12	86	1271	9	7.1	105.9
6 Aldrick Robinson, SMU	WR	SO	10	59	1047	11	5.9	104.7
7 James Casey, Rice	TE	SO	13	111	1329	13	8.5	102.2
8 Jarett Dillard, Rice	WR	SR	13	87	1310	20	6.6	100.7
9 Naaman Roosevelt, Buffalo	WR	JR	14	104	1402	13	7.4	100.1
10 Jamarko Simmons, W. Michigan	WR	SR	13	104	1276	7	8.0	98.1

PUNTING	POS	CL	PUNT	YDS	AVG
1 T.J. Conley, Idaho	P	SR	58	2751	47.4
2 Ross Thevenot, Tulane	P	JR	45	2061	45.8
3 Justin Brantly, Texas A&M	P	SR	51	2331	45.7
4 Jacob Richardson, Miami (Ohio)	P	SR	52	2360	45.3
5 Tim Masthay, Kentucky	**P**	**SR**	**53**	**2397**	**45.2**
6 Aaron Perez, UCLA	P	SR	79	3571	45.2
7 Kevin Huber, Cincinnati	P	SR	60	2697	44.9
8 Pat McAfee, West Virginia	P	SR	62	2772	44.7
9 Derek Epperson, Baylor	P	SO	49	2169	44.2
10 Anthony Hartz, Colorado St.	P	JR	44	1940	44.0

PUNT RETURNS	POS	CL	PR	YDS	TD	AVG
1 Antonio Brown, Central Michigan	WR	SO	20	410	1	20.5
2 Ian Clark, New Mexico	DB	JR	12	236	0	19.6
3 Dez Bryant, Oklahoma St.	WR	SO	17	305	2	17.9
4 Kyle Williams, Arizona St.	WR	JR	14	238	0	17.0
5 Robert Dunn, Auburn	**WR**	**SR**	**15**	**240**	**1**	**16.0**
6 Javier Arenas, Alabama	**DB**	**JR**	**41**	**650**	**3**	**15.8**
7 Phillip Livas, Louisiana Tech	WR	SO	16	245	2	15.3
8 Ray Small, Ohio State	WR	JR	24	364	1	15.1
9 T.Y. Hilton, Florida Int'l	WR	FR	18	266	1	14.7
10 Joe Burnett, Central Florida	DB	SR	26	378	0	14.5

KICKOFF RETURNS	POS	CL	KR	YDS	TD	AVG
1 Travis Shelton, Temple	WR	SR	23	720	1	31.3
2 Michael Ray Garvin, Florida State	DB	SR	22	662	1	30.0
3 Perrish Cox, Oklahoma State	DB	JR	30	895	2	29.8
4 A.J. Jefferson, Fresno State	DB	JR	31	908	1	29.2
5 Aaron Brown, TCU	RB	SR	18	526	1	29.2
6 Bryan Williams, Akron	DB	SR	21	609	0	29.0
7 Joe Burnett, Central Florida	DB	SR	26	745	2	28.6
8 L.J. Flintall, Ohio U.	RB	JR	13	368	1	28.3
9 Brandon Banks, Kansas State	WR	JR	18	498	1	27.6
10 DeMarco Murray, Oklahoma	RB	SO	28	774	0	27.6

SCORING	POS	CL	TDS	XP	FG	PTS	PTPG
1 Javon Ringer, Michigan State	RB	SR	22	0	0	132	10.1
2 LeSean McCoy, Pittsburgh	RB	SO	21	0	0	126	9.6
2 Dez Bryant, Oklahoma State	WR	SO	21	0	0	126	9.6
4 Graham Gano, Florida State	PK	SR	0	33	24	105	9.5
5 Tyrell Fenroy, La.-Lafayette	RB	SR	19	0	0	114	9.5
5 Jeff Wolfert, Missouri	K	SR	0	73	20	133	9.5
7 MiQuale Lewis, Ball State	RB	JR	22	0	0	132	9.4
8 Louie Sakoda, Utah	K	SR	0	56	22	122	9.3
9 Jarett Dillard, Rice	WR	SR.	20	0	0	120	9.2
9 Kevin Kelly, Penn State	K	SR	0	60	20	120	9.2

FIELD GOALS	POS	CL	FGA	FGM	PCT	FGG
1 Graham Gano, Florida State	PK	SR	26	24	0.92	2.1
2 Ben Hartman, East Carolina	K	JR	31	21	0.67	1.9
3 Ryan Harrison, Air Force	K	SR	29	24	0.82	1.8
4 Louie Sakoda, Utah	K	SR	24	22	0.91	1.6
4 Brett Swenson, Michigan State	K	JR	28	22	0.78	1.6
6 Nathan Parseghian, Miami (Ohio)	K	SR	23	20	0.87	1.6
6 Jose Martinez, UTEP	K	SR	27	20	0.74	1.6
8 Dustin Keys, Virginia Tech	K	SR	29	23	0.79	1.6
9 Kai Forbath, UCLA	K	SO	22	19	0.86	1.5
9 Swayze Waters, UAB	K	SR	24	19	0.79	1.5
9 Thomas Weber, Arizona State	K	SO	25	19	0.76	1.5

INTERCEPTIONS	POS	CL	INT	YDS	TD	INT/GM
1 Eric Berry, Tennessee	**DB**	**SO**	**7**	**265**	**2**	**0.58**
1 Kevin Sanders, UAB	DB	SR	7	55	0	0.58
3 Trimane Goddard, North Carolina	DB	SR	7	156	1	0.54
3 Darcel McBath, Texas Tech	DB	SR	7	97	2	0.54
3 Morgan Burnett, Georgia Tech	DB	SO	7	95	1	0.54
3 Alphonso Smith, Wake Forest	DB	SR	7	33	0	0.54
7 Ahmad Black, Florida	**DB**	**SO**	**7**	**191**	**2**	**0.50**
7 Joe Pawelek, Baylor	LB	JR	6	56	0	0.50
7 Brian Lainhart, Kent State	DB	SO	6	42	0	0.50
7 Woodny Turenne, Louisville	CB	SR	5	3	0	0.50

Team Leaders

RUSHING OFFENSE	G	ATT	YDS	AVG	TD	YPG
1 Navy	13	715	3801	5.3	32	292.3
2 Oregon	13	585	3641	6.2	47	280.0
3 Nevada	13	593	3611	6.0	39	277.7
4 Georgia Tech	13	640	3552	5.5	32	273.2
5 Tulsa	14	674	3752	5.5	40	268.0
6 Air Force	13	777	3470	4.4	27	266.9
7 La.-Lafayette	12	533	3164	5.9	32	263.6
8 Oklahoma State	13	582	3191	5.4	38	245.4
9 Army	12	635	2897	4.5	17	241.4
10 Florida	**14**	**545**	**3236**	**5.9**	**42**	**231.1**

PASSING OFFENSE	G	ATT	COM	INT	PCT	YDS	YPA	TD	I%	YPC	YPG
1 Texas Tech	13	662	465	10	70.2	5371	8.1	47	1.5	11.5	413.2
2 Houston	13	610	411	11	67.3	5221	8.5	45	1.8	12.7	401.6
3 Oklahoma	14	517	350	9	67.7	4891	9.4	51	1.7	13.9	349.4
4 Missouri	14	565	404	18	71.5	4625	8.1	41	3.1	11.4	330.4
5 Rice	13	516	339	7	65.7	4254	8.2	48	1.3	12.5	327.2
6 BYU	13	493	338	14	68.5	4035	8.1	35	2.8	11.9	310.4
7 Texas	13	447	343	8	76.7	4008	8.9	36	1.7	11.6	308.3
8 Kansas	13	500	333	13	66.6	3973	7.9	33	2.6	11.9	305.6
9 Tulsa	14	423	270	21	63.8	4226	9.9	47	4.9	15.6	301.9
10 New Mexico St.	12	492	330	16	67.0	3616	7.3	25	3.2	10.9	301.3

TOTAL OFFENSE	G	P	YDS	AVG	TD	YPG
1 Tulsa	14	1097	7978	7.2	90	569.8
2 Houston	13	1016	7316	7.2	71	562.7
3 Oklahoma	14	1106	7670	6.9	99	547.8
4 Texas Tech	13	979	6903	7.0	79	531.0
5 Nevada	13	1011	6611	6.5	64	508.5
6 Oklahoma State	13	908	6340	6.9	69	487.6
7 Oregon	13	959	6306	6.5	71	484.8
8 Missouri	14	982	6778	6.9	76	484.1
9 Texas	13	955	6185	6.4	74	475.7
10 Rice	13	965	6122	6.3	74	470.9

RUSHING DEFENSE	G	ATT	YDS	AVG	TD	YPG
1 TCU	13	355	612	1.7	9	47.1
2 Alabama	**14**	**391**	**1038**	**2.6**	**5**	**74.1**
3 Texas	13	356	1086	3.0	8	83.5
4 Mississippi	**13**	**411**	**1112**	**2.7**	**9**	**85.5**
5 Southern California	13	416	1136	2.7	8	87.4
6 Nevada	13	377	1152	3.0	17	88.6
7 Boston College	14	454	1277	2.8	14	91.2
8 Penn State	13	430	1212	2.8	12	93.2
9 Iowa	13	397	1222	3.0	7	94.0
10 South Florida	13	436	1238	2.8	12	95.2

PASSING DEFENSE	G	ATT	COM	PCT	INT	I%	YDS	YPA	TD	TD%	RAT
1 Southern California	13	382	199	52.0	19	4.9	1747	4.5	6	1.5	85.7
2 Boise State	13	449	234	52.1	22	4.9	2472	5.5	8	1.7	94.4
3 Florida	**14**	**456**	**242**	**53.0**	**26**	**5.7**	**2518**	**5.5**	**12**	**2.6**	**96.7**
4 TCU	13	384	193	50.2	15	3.9	2219	5.7	8	2.0	97.9
5 Iowa	13	463	256	55.2	23	4.9	2565	5.5	9	1.9	98.3
6 California	13	432	223	51.6	24	5.5	2509	5.8	12	2.7	98.4
7 Boston College	14	435	244	56.0	26	5.9	2477	5.6	9	2.0	98.8
8 San Jose State	12	356	187	52.5	16	4.4	2043	5.7	9	2.5	100.0
9 Connecticut	13	368	196	53.2	18	4.8	2187	5.9	9	2.4	101.5
10 Clemson	13	428	239	55.8	19	4.4	2243	5.2	14	3.2	101.7

TOTAL DEFENSE	G	P	YDS	AVG	TD	YPG
1 TCU	13	739	2831	3.8	18	217.7
2 Southern California	13	798	2883	3.6	14	221.7
3 Alabama	**14**	**858**	**3689**	**4.3**	**25**	**263.5**
3 Tennessee	**12**	**776**	**3162**	**4.0**	**20**	**263.5**
5 Boston College	14	889	3754	4.2	31	268.1
6 Connecticut	13	791	3614	4.5	30	278.0
7 Virginia Tech	14	794	3912	4.9	27	279.4
8 Penn State	13	829	3614	4.3	22	280.0
9 Florida	**14**	**896**	**3994**	**4.4**	**21**	**285.2**
10 South Florida	13	814	3739	4.5	31	287.6

SCORING OFFENSE	G	PTS	AVG
1 Oklahoma	14	716	51.1
2 Tulsa	14	661	47.2
3 Texas Tech	13	569	43.7
4 Florida	**14**	**611**	**43.6**
5 Texas	13	551	42.3
6 Missouri	14	591	42.2
7 Oregon	13	545	41.9
8 Rice	13	537	41.3
9 Oklahoma State	13	530	40.7
10 Houston	13	528	40.6

SCORING DEFENSE	G	PTS	AVG
1 Southern California	13	117	9.0
2 TCU	13	147	11.3
3 Boise State	13	164	12.6
4 Florida	**14**	**181**	**12.9**
5 Iowa	13	169	13.0
6 Ohio State	13	181	13.9
7 Alabama	**14**	**200**	**14.3**
8 Penn State	13	187	14.4
9 Virginia Tech	14	234	16.7
10 Tennessee	**12**	**201**	**16.8**

TURNOVER MARGIN	G	FR	INT	TOT	FL	INTL	TOT	MAR
1 Oklahoma	14	15	19	34	2	9	11	1.64
2 Florida	**14**	**9**	**26**	**35**	**8**	**5**	**13**	**1.57**
3 Buffalo	14	25	8	33	8	6	14	1.36
4 Baylor	12	11	16	27	6	5	11	1.33
5 Wake Forest	13	19	18	37	13	7	20	1.31
6 Ohio State	13	14	15	29	7	6	13	1.23
7 Navy	13	14	16	30	10	5	15	1.15
7 California	13	10	24	34	9	10	19	1.15
7 Rice	13	15	16	31	9	7	16	1.15
10 Air Force	13	18	12	30	11	6	17	1.00
10 Utah	13	12	19	31	9	9	18	1.00
10 Virginia Tech	14	14	20	34	8	12	20	1.00
10 TCU	13	13	15	28	7	8	15	1.00
10 Southern Miss	13	12	17	29	7	9	16	1.00
10 UTEP	12	13	14	27	6	9	15	1.00

2008

FINAL POLL (JAN. 8)

USA	AP	SCHOOL	FINAL RECORD
1	1	Florida	13-1
4	2	Utah	13-0
2	3	Southern California	12-1
3	4	Texas	12-1
5	5	Oklahoma	12-2
6	6	Alabama	12-1
7	7	TCU	11-2
8	8	Penn State	11-2
11	9	Ohio State	10-3
9	10	Oregon	10-3
13	11	Boise State	12-1
12	12	Texas Tech	11-2
10	13	Georgia	10-3
15	14	Mississippi	9-4
14	15	Virginia Tech	10-4
18	16	Oklahoma State	9-4
17	17	Cincinnati	11-3
19	18	Oregon State	9-4
16	19	Missouri	10-4
20	20	Iowa	9-4
23	21	Florida State	9-4
22	22	Georgia Tech	9-4
	23	West Virginia	9-4
24	24	Michigan State	9-4
21	25	BYU	10-3
25		California	9-4

CONSENSUS ALL-AMERICANS

POS	OFFENSE	CL	SCHOOL
QB	Sam Bradford	So.	Oklahoma
QB	Colt McCoy	Jr.	Texas
RB	Shonn Greene	Jr.	Iowa
RB	Javon Ringer	Sr.	Michigan St.
WR	Michael Crabtree	So.	Texas Tech
WR	Dez Bryant	So.	Oklahoma St.
TE	Chase Coffman	Sr.	Missouri
OL	Michael Oher	Sr.	Mississppi
OL	Andre Smith	Jr.	Alabama
OL	Brandon Carter	Jr.	Texas Tech
OL	Duke Robinson	Sr.	Oklahoma
C	Antoine Caldwell	Sr.	Alabama
PK	Louie Sakoda	Sr.	Utah
K/P	Jeremy Maclin	So.	Missouri
K/P	Brandon James	Jr.	Florida

OTHERS RECEIVING FIRST-TEAM HONORS

QB	Graham Harrell		Texas Tech
RB	Knowshon Moreno		Georgia
RB	Donald Brown		Connecticut
RB	Kendall Hunter		Oklahoma St.
WR	Jarett Dillard		Rice
TE	Jermaine Gresham		Oklahoma
OL	Andy Levitre		Oregon St.
OL	Jason Smith		Baylor
C	A.Q. Shipley		Penn State
KR	Michael Ray Garvin		Florida State

POS	DEFENSE	CL	SCHOOL
DL	Brian Orakpo	Sr.	Texas
DL	Terrence Cody	Jr.	Alabama
DL	Jerry Hughes	Jr.	TCU
DL	Aaron Maybin	So.	Penn State
LB	Brandon Spikes	Jr.	Florida
LB	Rey Maualuga	Sr.	Southern California
LB	James Laurinaitis	Sr.	Ohio State
DB	Eric Berry	So.	Tennessee
DB	Taylor Mays	Jr.	Southern California
DB	Alphonso Smith	Sr.	Wake Forest
DB	Malcolm Jenkins	Sr.	Ohio State
P	Kevin Huber	Sr.	Cincinnati

OTHERS RECEIVING FIRST-TEAM HONORS

DL	Nick Reed		Oregon
DL	George Selvie		South Florida
DL	Michael Johnson		Georgia Tech
DB	Rashad Johnson		Alabama
DT	Gerald McCoy		Oklahoma
CB	D.J. Moore		Vanderbilt
CB	Victor Harris		Virginia Tech
LB	Scott McKillop		Pittsburgh
P	T.J. Conley		Idaho

HEISMAN TROPHY VOTING

	PLAYER	POS	SCHOOL	TOTAL
1	Sam Bradford	QB	Oklahoma	1,726
2	Colt McCoy	QB	Texas	1,640
3	Tim Tebow	QB	Florida	1,575
4	Graham Harrell	QB	Texas Tech	213
5	Michael Crabtree	WR	Texas Tech	116
6	Shonn Greene	RB	Iowa	65
7	Pat White	QB	West Virginia	19
8	Nate Davis	QB	Ball State	10
9	Rey Maualuga	LB	Southern Cal	9
10	Javon Ringer	RB	Michigan St.	8

AWARD WINNERS

PLAYER	AWARD
Tim Tebow, QB, Florida	Maxwell
Andre Smith, OT, Alabama	Outland
Colt McCoy, QB, Texas	Camp
Brian Orakpo, DE, Texas	Lombardi
Sam Bradford, QB, Oklahoma	O'Brien
Aaron Curry, LB, Wake Forest	Butkus
Malcolm Jenkins, DB, Ohio State	Thorpe
Graham Harrell, QB, Texas Tech	Unitas
Shonn Greene, RB, Iowa	Walker
Graham Gano, K, Florida State	Groza
Brian Orakpo, DE, Texas	Nagurski
Rey Maualuga, LB, Southern California	Bednarik
Michael Crabtree, WR, Texas Tech	Biletnikoff
Matt Fodge, P, Oklahoma St.	Guy
Chase Coffman, TE, Missouri	Mackey
A.Q. Shipley, C, Penn State	Rimington
Brian Orakpo, DE, Texas	Hendricks
James Laurinaitis, LB, Ohio State	Lott
Tim Tebow, QB, Florida	Manning

BOWL GAMES

DATE	GAME	SCORE
D20	New Mexico	Colorado St. 40, Fresno St. 35
D20	Las Vegas	Arizona 31, BYU 21
D21	New Orleans	Southern Miss 30, Troy 27
D23	Poinsettia	TCU 17, Boise State 16
D24	Hawaii	Notre Dame 49, Hawaii 21
D26	Motor City	Fla. Atlantic 24, C. Michigan 21
D27	Meineke Car Care	West Virginia 31, UNC 30
D27	Champs Sports	Florida St. 42, Wisconsin 13
D27	Emerald	California 24, Miami (Fla.)17
D28	Independence	Louisiana Tech 17, Northern Ill. 10
D29	Alamo	Missouri 30, Northwestern 23
D29	PapaJohns.com	Rutgers 29, North Carolina St. 23
D30	Holiday	Oregon 42, Oklahoma St. 31
D30	Texas	Rice 38, Western Michigan 14
D30	Humanitarian	Maryland 42, Nevada 35
D31	Armed Forces	Houston 34, Air Force 28
D31	Sun	Oregon St. 3, Pittsburgh 0
D31	Music City	Vanderbilt 16, Boston College 14
D31	Insight	Kansas 42, Minnesota 21
D31	Chick-fil-A	LSU 38, Georgia Tech 3
J1	Outback	Iowa 31, South Carolina 10
J1	Orange	Virginia Tech 20, Cincinnati 7
J1	Gator	Nebraska 26, Clemson 21
J1	Capital One	Georgia 24, Michigan St. 12
J1	Rose	Southern California 38, Penn State 24
J2	Sugar	Utah 31, Alabama 17
J2	Liberty	Kentucky 25, East Carolina 19
J2	Cotton	Mississippi 47, Texas Tech 34
J3	International	Connecticut 38, Buffalo 20
J5	Fiesta	Texas 24, Ohio State 21
J6	GMAC	Tulsa 45, Ball State 13
J7	BCS Championship	Florida 24, Oklahoma 14

SEC STANDINGS

	CONFERENCE		OVERALL	
	W	L	W	L
EAST				
Florida	7	1	13	1
Georgia	6	2	10	3
Vanderbilt	4	4	7	6
South Carolina	4	4	7	6
Tennessee	3	5	5	7
Kentucky	2	6	7	6
WEST				
Alabama	8	0	12	2
Mississippi	5	3	9	4
LSU	3	5	8	5
Auburn	2	6	5	7
Arkansas	2	6	5	7
Mississippi State	2	6	4	8

ALL-SEC TEAM

POS	OFFENSE	SCHOOL
TE	Jared Cook	South Carolina
OL	Andre Smith	Alabama
OL	Michael Oher	Mississippi
OL	Phil Trautwein	Florida
OL	Herman Johnson	LSU
C	Antoine Caldwell	Alabama
WR	Percy Harvin	Florida
WR	Mohamed Massaquoi	Georgia
QB	Tim Tebow	Florida
RB	Knowshon Moreno	Georgia
RB	Charles Scott	LSU
PK	Colt David	LSU
RS	Brandon James	Florida

POS	DEFENSE	SCHOOL
E	Rahim Alem	LSU
T	Peria Jerry	Mississippi
T	Terrence Cody	Alabama
E	Antonio Coleman	Auburn
LB	Brandon Spikes	Florida
LB	Eric Norwood	South Carolina
LB	Rolando McClain	Alabama
S	Eric Berry	Tennessee
CB	D.J. Moore	Vanderbilt
CB	Trevard Lindley	Kentucky
S	Rashad Johnson	Alabama
P	Tim Masthay	Kentucky

SEC CHAMPIONSHIP GAME

DECEMBER 6 | ATLANTA
FLORIDA 31, ALABAMA 20

	1ST	2ND	3RD	4TH	FINAL
ALA	10	0	10	0	20
FLA	7	10	0	14	31

SCORING SUMMARY
FLA	Moore 3 pass from Tebow (Phillips kick)
ALA	Coffee 18 run (Tiffin kick)
ALA	FG Tiffin 30
FLA	FG Phillips 19
FLA	Nelson 5 pass from Tebow (Phillips kick)
ALA	Ingram 2 run (Tiffin kick)
ALA	FG Tiffin 27
FLA	Demps 1 run (Phillips kick)
FLA	Cooper 5 pass from Tebow (Phillips kick)

ALABAMA	TEAM STATISTICS	FLORIDA
18	First Downs	19
136	Rushing Yards	142
12-25-1	Passing	14-22-0
187	Passing Yards	216
323	Total Yards	358
2-20	Punt Returns - Yards	3-25
4-95	Kickoff Returns - Yards	5-121
4-41.0	Punts - Average	3-47.7
0-0	Fumbles - Lost	0-0
2-31	Penalties - Yards	6-45

INDIVIDUAL LEADERS

RUSHING
ALA: Coffee 21-112, TD.
FLA: Tebow 17-57.

PASSING
ALA: Wilson 12-25-1, 187 yards.
FLA: Tebow 14-22-0, 216 yards, 3 TD.

RECEIVING
ALA: Jones 5-124; Walker 3-37.
FLA: Murphy 4-86; Hernandez 3-43.

Acknowledgments

For the *ESPN Southeastern Conference Football Encyclopedia*, I had the privilege of working with an All-American team of skilled writers, editors, designers, proofreaders and fact-checkers.

There is something to be said for book production in the era of the global village, and this is the fourth book I've edited for ESPN from my home in St. Louis. In truth, though, the entire process only works smoothly when you have in New York a smart, committed point person like the indefatigable project coordinator, Bill Vourvoulias, who supervised the book's editorial production flow and the hundreds of accompanying details. Bill is tireless, vigilant, thoughtful and fussy—in short, someone you want on your side when producing anything with *Encyclopedia* in the title.

At a time when everyone was killing stories and cutting back and cowering in the face of the economic downturn, Steve Wulf—the editor-in-chief of ESPN Books—boldly came up with the inspired idea of commissioning a series of new essays on the heritage and traditions of each school, then helped recruit a group of exemplary writers to contribute. This is a much better book because of his vision and direction. Before leaving for other pursuits, Chris Raymond, Steve's predecessor, fought to make this book happen. Key organizational and logistical support were provided by Kathleen A. Fieffe and Bo Wulf.

You can take the fanatic away from King Football, but you can't take King Football away from the fanatic. This was once again proved by Chuck Culpepper, who seems to spend most of his time in exotic continental locales yet still has written the keynote essay for each book in the *College Football Encyclopedia* series. Ivan Maisel returned, as well, to deliver a terrific essay on the all-time SEC team. It was a pleasure teaming up again with Bill Curry, Glen Waggoner, Wright Thompson, Furman Bisher and Gene Wojciechowski, as well as getting to work with Winston Groom, John Ed Bradley, E. Lynn Harris, Tim Dorsey, Tom Farrey, Billy Reed, Buster Olney, Rich Cohen, Kyle Veazey and Lou Holtz (with an assist from Jan Partain).

Geoffrey Norman updated his histories of the 12 teams of the SEC and also did additional reporting for the histories of former SEC schools Georgia Tech and Tulane, all while recovering from a bout of the shingles—observing the old football adage that sometimes you gotta play hurt.

Thanks also to Kevin Gleason and Bob Harig who contributed, respectively, the original Tulane and Georgia Tech essays. Thanks again to Richard Billingsley for his all-time scores database—newly updated—and to Pat Porter, who returned to help us update the winning percentage charts and team records. Gabriel Ruegg was responsible for the design of the charts. Checking and coordinating this latest torrent of information were Craig Winston, chief of research for *ESPN The Magazine*, his deputy, Roger Jackson, as well as LaRue Cook, Doug Mittler, Doug McIntyre, Bill Weisbrod and Tom Biersdorfer.

The operational headaches of getting a 432-page book to press on time were borne by production manager John W. Glenn, who in addition to overseeing our hectic close, tamed some unruly Quark files, supervised many in-house design and production issues, and may also have served as Bill Vourvoulias' cut man in the later rounds.

Copyediting duties were handled by the superb Beth Adelman, with a proofreading assist by Lauren Spencer. Al Wickenheiser, Clement Arhana and all the folks at Manipal Digital Systems handled the page production work. Paul Perlow came on to incorporate some attractive new elements into the design while remaining true to the clean, crisp look of the *ESPN College Football Encyclopedia*. Henry Lee produced the handsome cover.

We want to thank the sports information staffs at the Southeastern Conference member schools for their assistance in the earliest stages of this project.

Each of the books in the growing *ESPN College Football Encyclopedia* series owes a lasting debt of gratitude to patron saints John Walsh and John Skipper.

Finally, I am grateful for the support, guidance and sustenance provided to me along the way by Sloan Harris, Rick Pappas, Trey Gratwick, Kevin Lyttle, Rob Minter; my mother, Lois MacCambridge; my children, Miles and Ella MacCambridge; and my girlfriend, Ivy Tominack. They have come to understand that football season never truly ends.

MJM
St. Louis, May 2009

CONTRIBUTORS

Historian, freelance writer and Bowl Championship Series pollster **Richard Billingsley** has been ranking college football teams for more almost 40 years. Since being selected by the BCS in 1999, Billingsley has been instrumental in shaping the formula used to determine the national championship. Currently he serves as the designated representative of the computer group to the BCS.

Chuck Culpepper has led a misspent and misguided existence following college football since age 9, when he attended a ghastly 6-0 game between Virginia Tech and Virginia yet somehow did not find the experience to be a deterrent. He has covered college football for *Newsday*, relished it while writing sports columns for *The Lexington Herald-Leader* in Kentucky and *The Oregonian* in Portland, marveled at it while attending 11 different bowl games at least once, and found its essence by seeing games at all 12 current Southeastern Conference stadiums. He has lived in London since 2006, during which time he wrote a book

about a different kind of football (*Bloody Confused! A Clueless American Sportswriter Seeks Solace in English Soccer*) and became one of very few, very ill Londoners to spend autumn Saturday nights following college football updates on the Internet until 2 or 3 in the morning.

Ivan Maisel is a senior writer at ESPN.com and has been covering college football on a national basis since 1987. He has written two books about the sport. He is a native of Mobile, Ala., where as a child he was taught that Bear Bryant could walk on water. He awaits proof that Bryant couldn't.

Geoffrey Norman is the author of *Alabama Showdown*, an account of the football rivalry between Alabama and Auburn, and several other books, including *Bouncing Back*, a narrative of the POW experience in Vietnam, and *Two for the Summit*, a record of his mountain climbing experiences with his daughter. His most recent book is *Inch by Inch*, a novel.

ABOUT THE EDITOR

In addition to being the editor of the critically-acclaimed *ESPN College Football Encyclopedia*, **Michael MacCambridge** is the author of *America's Game: The Epic Story of How Pro Football Captured a Nation* and *The Franchise: A History of Sports Illustrated Magazine.* He also edited *The New York Times* bestseller *ESPN SportsCentury* and co-wrote *More Than a Game: The Glorious Present and Uncertain Future of the NFL* with Brian Billick. He was a longtime columnist and critic at the *Austin American-Statesman*, where he wrote about movies, music and popular culture. The father of two children, Miles and Ella, he lives in St. Louis.